June 23–26, 2015
Shanghai, China

Association for
Computing Machinery

Advancing Computing as a Science & Profession

ICMR'15

Proceedings of the 2015 ACM
International Conference on Multimedia Retrieval

Sponsored by:

ACM SIGMM

Supported by:

Samsung, Fudan University, Tencent, Google, Visenze, and SIGMM-China

Association for
Computing Machinery

Advancing Computing as a Science & Profession

The Association for Computing Machinery
2 Penn Plaza, Suite 701
New York, New York 10121-0701

ISBN: 978-1-4503-3274-3

Additional copies may be ordered prepaid from:

ACM Order Department
PO Box 30777
New York, NY 10087-0777, USA

Phone: 1-800-342-6626 (USA and Canada)
+1-212-626-0500 (Global)
Fax: +1-212-944-1318
E-mail: acmhelp@acm.org
Hours of Operation: 8:30 am – 4:30 pm ET

Printed in the USA

Chairs' Welcome

Welcome to the 5th ACM International Conference on Multimedia Retrieval, ICMR 2015. ICMR is a premier conference in the area of multimedia retrieval, offering great opportunities for exchanging leading-edge multimedia retrieval ideas among researchers, practitioners and other potential users of multimedia retrieval systems. Multimedia computing, indexing and retrieval continues to be one of the most exciting and fastest-growing research areas in the field of multimedia technology. However, opportunities for the exchange of ideas among different groups of researchers, and between researchers and potential users of multimedia retrieval systems, are still limited. The conference, which puts together the long-lasting experience of former ACM CIVR and ACM MIR series, was initialized in 2011 to illuminate the state of the art in multimedia retrieval.

This year we received a record-high number of 244 submissions to the main conference from 35 countries. After a rigorous review process by the program committee members, 113 papers from 23 countries were accepted for presentation. Conflict-of-interest papers authored by the program chairs were handled separately by the general chairs, and those from the general chairs were handled by the program chairs.

Details are as follows:

Track	*#Submissions*	*#Accepted*	*Acceptance Rate*
Full Papers	127	48	37.8%
• Oral		• 25	• 19.7%
• Poster		• 23	• 18.1%
Short Papers	84	34	40.5%
Special Session Papers	18	10	55.6%
Demonstrations	12	9	75%

In addition, 12 borderline full papers were recommended to be downgraded to short papers, so the total number of accepted short papers is 46. We also moved 3 accepted special session papers to the regular sessions due to the cancellation of two planned special sessions, leading to a total number of 51 full papers in the regular program. The remaining 7 special session papers are presented in one special oral session and one special poster session.

The program also includes two tutorials and one workshop:

- *Tutorial on "Social Multimedia Computing."*
- *Tutorial on "Multimedia Quality Modeling: Theories and Applications."*
- *Workshop on "Environmental Multimedia Retrieval."*

Putting together the program of ICMR 2015 was a team effort. We first thank the authors for submitting to ICMR. We are very grateful to the program committee members, who worked very hard in reviewing the papers and providing quality feedbacks to the authors. Finally, we thank the members of the organizing committee, ACM SIGMM, and our generous corporate sponsors, Tencent, Samsung, Google and ViSENZE.

General Chairs: Alex Hauptmann *(Carnegie Mellon University, USA)*
Chong-Wah Ngo *(City University of Hong Kong, China)*
Xiangyang Xue *(Fudan University, China)*

Program Chairs: Yu-Gang Jiang *(Fudan University, China)*
Cees Snoek *(University of Amsterdam and Qualcomm Research Netherlands)*
Nuno Vasconcelos *(University of California, San Diego, USA)*

Table of Contents

Oral Session 3: Concepts

Oral Session 4: Analytical Methods for Multimedia Retrieval

Oral Session 5: Photo Applications

Special Oral Session: Weakly Supervised Learning for Big Multimedia Data Analysis

Full Paper Posters Session

Short Paper Posters Session

Special Poster Session: Person Search and Verification from Rich Media Data

Demonstrations

ICMR 2015 Organization

Honorary Chair: Wen Gao *(Peking University, China)*

General Chairs: Alex Hauptmann *(Carnegie Mellon University, USA)*
Chong-Wah Ngo *(City University of Hong Kong, China)*
Xiangyang Xue *(Fudan University, China)*

Technical Program Chairs: Yu-Gang Jiang *(Fudan University, China)*
Cees Snoek *(University of Amsterdam and Qualcomm Research Netherlands)*
Nuno Vasconcelos *(University of California, San Diego, USA)*

Brave New Idea Chairs: Jiebo Luo *(University of Rochester, USA)*
Marcel Worring *(University of Amsterdam, The Netherlands)*

Practitioner Chairs: Yiannis Kompatsiaris *(CERTH/ITI, Greece)*
R. Manmatha *(A9.com, USA)*
Dong Wang *(Aviation Industry Corporation of China)*

Special Session Chairs: Winston Hsu *(National Taiwan University)*
Nicu Sebe *(University of Trento, Italy)*
Jinhui Tang *(Nanjing University of Science and Technology, China)*

Workshop Chairs: Shin'ichi Satoh *(National Institute of Informatics, Japan)*
Qi Tian *(University of Texas at San Antonio, USA)*

Panel Chairs: Tat-Seng Chua *(National University of Singapore, Singapore)*
Lexing Xie *(Australian National University, Australia)*

Doctoral Symposium Chairs: Subhabrata Bhattacharya *(Siemens Corporate Research, USA)*
Xiao-Yong Wei *(Sichuan University, China)*

Tutorial Chairs: Marco Bertini *(University of Florence, Italy)*
Junsong Yuan *(Nanyang Technological University, Singapore)*

Demo Chairs: Benoit Huet *(Eurecom, France)*
Yantao Zheng *(Google, USA)*

Publicity Chairs: Ling Guan *(Ryerson University, Canada)*
Richang Hong *(Hefei University of Technology, China)*
Vasileios Mezaris *(Center for Research and Technology Hellas, Greece)*

Sponsorship Chairs: Peng Cui *(Tsinghua University, China)*
Xiao Wu *(Southwest Jiaotong University, China)*

Student Grant Chair: Meng Wang *(Hefei University of Technology, China)*

Publication Chairs: Xirong Li *(Renmin University, China)*
Xiangdong Zhou *(Fudan University, China)*

Finance Chair: Hong Lu *(Fudan University, China)*

Local Chairs: Feng Wang *(East China Normal University, China)*
Hanli Wang *(Tongji University, China)*
Cheng Jin *(Fudan University, China)*

Web Chair: Xi Wang *(Fudan University, China)*

Program Committee: Laurent Amsaleg *(CNRS-IRISA, France)*
Werner Bailer *(Joanneum Research, Austria)*
Lamberto Ballan *(Stanford University, USA)*
Marco Bertini *(Universita' degli Studi di Firenze, Italy)*
Susanne Boll *(Universität Oldenburg, Germany)*
Damian Borth *(ICSI, USA)*
Carlos Busso *(The University of Texas at Dallas, USA)*
Zhaowei Cai *(University of California, San Diego, USA)*
Vincent Charvillat *(IRIT-ENSEEIHT, France)*
Si Chen *(University of California, San Diego, USA)*
Wen-Huang Cheng *(Academia Sinica, Taiwan)*
Wei-Ta Chu *(National Chung Cheng University, Chiayi, Taiwan)*
Tat-Seng Chua *(National University of Singapore)*
Yung-Yu Chuang *(National Taiwan University)*
John Collomosse *(University of Surrey, UK)*
Matthew Cooper *(FX Palo Alto Lab, Inc., USA)*
Jose Costa-Pereira *(University of California, San Diego, USA)*
Hamdi Dibeklioğlu *(Delft University of Technology, The Netherlands)*
Guiguang Ding *(Tsinghua University, China)*
Mandar Dixit *(University of California, San Diego, USA)*
Mario Doeller *(FH Kufstein Tirol, Austria)*
Lingyu Duan *(Peking University, China)*
Wolfgang Effelsberg *(University of Mannheim, Germany)*
Dan Ellis *(Columbia University, USA)*
Ralph Ewerth *(Jena University of Applied Sciences, Germany)*
Jianping Fan *(UNCC, USA)*
Jiashi Feng *(National University of Singapore)*
Efstratios Gavves *(KU Leuven, Belgium)*
Bernard Ghanem *(King Abdullah University of Science and Technology, Saudi Arabia)*

Program Committee (*continued*): Nikolaos Gkalelis *(CERTH - ITI, Greece)*
William Grosky *(University of Michigan, USA)*
Cathal Gurrin *(Dublin City University, Ireland)*
Martin Halvey *(University of Strathclyde, UK)*
Mei Han *(Google, USA)*
Allan Hanbury *(Vienna University of Technology, Austria)*
Richard Harvey *(University of East Anglia, UK)*
Andreas Henrich *(University of Bamberg, Germany)*
Richang Hong *(Hefei University of Technology, China)*
Frank Hopfgartner *(Technische Universität Berlin, Germany)*
Xian-Sheng Hua *(Microsoft Research)*
Qingming Huang *(Chinese Academy of Sciences, China)*
Tiejun Huang *(Peking University, China)*
Ichiro Ide *(Nagoya University, Japan)*
Bogdan Ionescu *(University Politehnica of Bucharest, Romania)*
Mihir Jain *(University of Amsterdam, The Netherlands)*
Alexis Joly *(INRIA, France)*
Mohan Kankanhalli *(National University of Singapore)*
John Kender *(Columbia University, USA)*
Lyndon Kennedy *(Yahoo! Research, USA)*
Yiannis Kompatsiaris *(CERTH - ITI, Greece)*
Paul Lewis *(University of Southampton, UK)*
Weixin Li *(University of California, San Diego, USA)*
Xirong Li *(Renmin University of China)*
Xuelong Li *(Chinese Academy of Sciences, China)*
Mark Liao *(Academia Sinica, Taiwan)*
Rainer Lienhart *(Universität Augsburg, Germany)*
Suzanne Little *(Dublin City University, Ireland)*
Dong Liu *(Columbia University, USA)*
Haiming Liu *(University of Bedfordshire, UK)*
Xiaoqiang Lu *(Dalian University of Technology, China)*
Zhigang Ma *(Carnegie Mellon University, USA)*
Joao Magalhaes *(Universidade Nova de Lisboa, Portugal)*
Yasushi Makihara *(Osaka University, Japan)*
Tao Mei *(Microsoft Research, USA)*
Thomas Mensink *(University of Amsterdam, The Netherlands)*
Bernard Merialdo *(EURECOM, France)*
Michele Merler *(IBM T. J. Watson Research Center, USA)*
Vasileios Mezaris *(CERTH - ITI, Greece)*
Jayanta Mukherjee *(Indian Institute of Technology Kharagpur, India)*

Program Committee (continued):

Venkatesh N. Murthy *(University of Massachusetts, USA)*
Claudia Niederée *(L3S Research Center, Germany)*
Naoko Nitta *(Osaka University, Japan)*
Pietro Pala *(University of Firenze, Italy)*
Yiannis Patras *(Queen Mary University of London, UK)*
Renaud Peteri *(University of la Rochelle, France)*
Balakrishnan Prabhakaran *(University of Texas at Dallas, USA)*
Guo-Jun Qi *(University of Illinois at Urbana-Champaign, USA)*
Georges Quénot *(Laboratoire d'Informatique de Grenoble, CNRS, France)*
Miriam Redi *(Yahoo, USA)*
Stevan Rudinac *(University of Amsterdam, The Netherlands)*
Stefan Rueger *(Knowledge Media Institute, UK)*
Mohammed Abdel-Mgeed M. Salem *(Ain Shams University, Egypt)*
Maria Luisa Sapino *(Universita' di Torino, Italy)*
Shin'Ichi Satoh *(National Institute of Informatics, Japan)*
Klaus Schöffmann *(University of Klagenfurt, Austria)*
Nicu Sebe *(University of Trento, Italy)*
Heng Tao Shen *(University of Queensland, Australia)*
Weiwei Shen *(GE Global Research, USA)*
Koichi Shinoda *(Tokyo Institute of Technology, Japan)*
Carlos N. Silla Jr. *(Federal University of Technology of Parana, Brazil)*
Pinaki Sinha *(University of California, Irvine, USA)*
Alan Smeaton *(Dublin City University, Ireland)*
John Smith *(IBM T.J. Watson Research Center, USA)*
Thomas Steiner *(Google, USA)*
Hung Khoon Tan *(Universiti Tunku Abdul Rahman, Malaysia)*
Sheng Tang *(Chinese Academy of Sciences, China)*
Bart Thomee *(Yahoo! Research, USA)*
Yonghong Tian *(Peking University, China)*
Christian Timmerer *(Klagenfurt University, Austria)*
Theodora Tsikrika *(CERTH - ITI, Greece)*
Jan van Gemert *(University of Amsterdam, The Netherlands)*
Stefanos Vrochidis *(CERTH - ITI, Greece)*
Changhu Wang *(Microsoft Research Asia, China)*
Jiajun Wang *(Fudan University, China)*
Jian Wang *(LinkedIn Corporation, USA)*
Jinqiao Wang *(Chinese Academy of Sciences, China)*
Meng Wang *(Hefei University of Technology, China)*
Qi Wang *(Chinese Academy of Sciences, China)*
Xiangyu Wang *(National University of Singapore)*

Program Committee
***(continued)*:**

Yan Wang *(Columbia University, USA)*
Xiao-Yong Wei *(Sichuan University, China)*
Marcel Worring *(University of Amsterdam, The Netherlands)*
Fei Wu *(Zhejiang University, China)*
Xiao Wu *(Southwest Jiaotong University, China)*
Zuxuan Wu *(Fudan University, China)*
Can Xu *(University of California, San Diego, USA)*
Shuicheng Yan *(National University of Singapore)*
Keiji Yanai *(Univ. of Electro-Communications, Japan)*
Yi Yang *(Carnegie Mellon University, USA)*
Ting Yao *(City University of Hong Kong)*
Guangnan Ye *(Columbia University, USA)*
Jun Yu *(Xiamen University, China)*
Zheng-Jun Zha *(National University of Singapore)*
Wei Zhang *(City University of Hong Kong)*
Shiai Zhu *(University of Ottawa, USA)*

ICMR 2015 Sponsor & Supporters

Sponsor:

Supporters:

Dense Models from Videos: Can YouTube be the Font of All Knowledge Bases?

Michael Witbrock
Vice President of Research at Cycorp
Austin, USA / witbrock@cyc.com

ABSTRACT

Many recent advances in computer science have been driven by the convergent availability of large numbers of data and of fast machines on which to analyze them. This availability has enabled us to acquire implicit partial models of the underlying generators for the data and apply those models to tasks such as translation, transcription, and image captioning. To date, though, few if any of these models have been dense, in the sense of thoroughly modelling some aspect of the world in way that can facilitate any relevant task. Dense models should support:

a) Prediction: What might happen next in this situation, or what might be true in the vicinity?
b) Interpolation: What may have happened between these situations? What might be located between these things?
c) Causal reasoning: Why did this happen?
d) Purpose reasoning: What is this configuration of things for? For what purpose is that happening?
e) Task performance: The model should be able to aid (e.g.) a robot performing a domain task.
f) Explanation: The model should be at a level that supports communication.

In short, a dense model is the sort of model — including both implicit and explicit components — humans form about aspects of their worlds: aspects like meetings, plants, lawnmowers, rivers and kitchens. These models support pretty-much any kind of relevant reasoning.

These are also the sorts of models that builders of large-scale "commonsense" knowledge bases have been working to construct. But, to date, although some such knowledge bases support particular instances of each kind of reasoning task, they do not approach doing so comprehensively, even within quite narrow domains. Although some work is being done on automating KB construction, this generally aims at breadth, rather than density.

Similarly, although machine vision and NLP researchers have long discussed the potential use of background knowledge in scene and text understanding, demonstrating that utility in any general way has been hampered by the vast incompleteness of available KBs.

The time is ripe for a 5-10 year AI challenge problem in production of dense models directly from data. As a particular example, kitchens are somewhat limited in complexity, from a human point of view, and are densely modelled by most humans; we are not frequently surprised by what we find in a kitchen, or by what happens there. And we are not lacking for data; there are more than 6 million YouTube hits for "kitchen", around 5 million for cooking. If each was a mere 1 minute long, this represents 22 years of kitchen video. Dull perhaps, but also, presumably, enough grist for building a very dense model.

The proposed challenge is this: to have computers automatically build, from just the vast amount of video found on the web, a sufficiently dense local world model to enable that video to be thoroughly understood for prediction, interpolation, explanation and other tasks.

Categories and Subject Descriptors
I.2.6 Learning, I.2.10 Vision and Scene Understanding
Keywords
Online Video; Machine Vision; Model Induction; Knowledge Bases

BIO

Michael Witbrock has a PhD in Computer Science from Carnegie Mellon University and a BSc Hons in Psychology from Otago University. He currently is Vice President for Research at Cycorp. Before joining Cycorp, in 2001, to direct its knowledge formation and dialogue processing efforts, he had been Principal Scientist at Terra Lycos, working on integrating statistical and knowledge based approaches to understanding web user behavior, a research scientist at Just Systems Pittsburgh Research Center, working on statistical summarization, and a systems scientist at Carnegie Mellon on the Informedia visual and spoken document information retrieval project. His current research focuses on automated reading to inferentially-productive representations, application of background knowledge to video retrieval and to reasoning about the molecular biology literature, and automatic and semi-automatic knowledge capture and use, more broadly. He is author of numerous publications in areas ranging across computational linguistics, speech modelling and recognition, neural networks, automated inference, automated reading and multimedia information retrieval, and has dabbled in web browser design, genetic design and parallel computer architecture. As well as his technical work, Dr. Witbrock is very interested in entrepreneurship around AI and for social good, and in the social and economic outcomes of advances in AI. He is pursuing that latter interest, inter alia, via AI4Good.org

ICMR'15, June 23–26, 2015, Shanghai, China.
ACM 978-1-4503-3274-3/15/06.
http://dx.doi.org/10.1145/2671188.2749414

Image Classification and Retrieval are ONE

Lingxi Xie[1], Richang Hong[2], Bo Zhang[3], and Qi Tian[4]
[1,3]LITS, TNLIST, Dept. of Computer Sci&Tech, Tsinghua University, Beijing 100084, China
[2]School of Computer and Information, Hefei University of Technology, Hefei 230009, China
[4]Department of Computer Science, University of Texas at San Antonio, TX 78249, USA
[1]198808xc@gmail.com,[2]hongrc@hfut.edu.cn,
[3]dcszb@mail.tsinghua.edu.cn,[4]qitian@cs.utsa.edu

ABSTRACT

In this paper, we demonstrate that the essentials of image classification and retrieval are the same, since both tasks could be tackled by measuring the similarity between images. To this end, we propose ONE (Online Nearest-neighbor Estimation), a unified algorithm for both image classification and retrieval. ONE is surprisingly simple, which only involves manual object definition, regional description and nearest-neighbor search. We take advantage of PCA and PQ approximation and GPU parallelization to scale our algorithm up to large-scale image search. Experimental results verify that ONE achieves state-of-the-art accuracy in a wide range of image classification and retrieval benchmarks.

Categories and Subject Descriptors

I.4.10 [**Image Processing and Computer Vision**]: Image Representation—*Statistical*; I.4.7 [**Image Processing and Computer Vision**]: Feature Measurement—*Feature representation*

General Terms

Algorithms, Experiments, Performance

Keywords

Image Classification; Image Retrieval; ONE; CNN

1. INTRODUCTION

Past decades have witnessed an impressive bloom of multimedia applications based on image understanding. For example, the number of categories in image classification has grown from a few to tens of thousands [13], and deep Convolutional Neural Networks (CNN) have been verified efficient in large-scale learning [25]. Meanwhile, image retrieval has been transplanted from toy programs to commercial search engines indexing billions of images, and new user intentions such as fine-grained concept search [62] are realized and proposed in this research field.

ICMR'15, June 23–26, 2015, Shanghai, China.

http://dx.doi.org/10.1145/2671188.2749289.

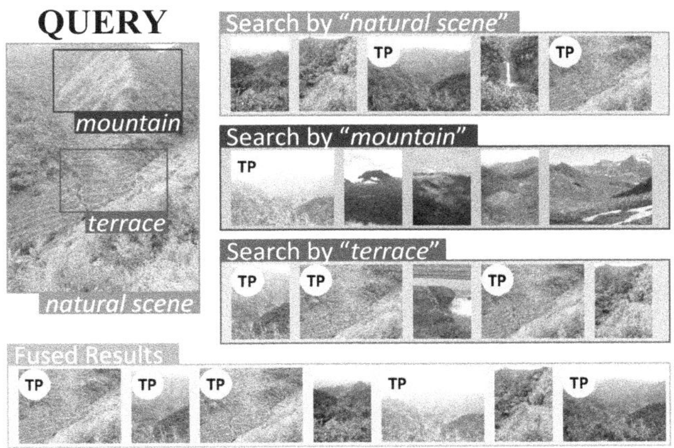

Figure 1: An image retrieval example illustrating the intuition of ONE (best viewed in color PDF). On a query image, it is possible to find a number of semantic objects. Searching for nearest neighbors with one object might not capture the exact query intention, but fusing yields satisfying results. A yellow circle with the word **TP** indicates a true-positive image. Images are collected from the **Holiday** dataset [20].

Both image classification and retrieval receive a **query** image at a time. Classification tasks aim at determining the class or category of the query, for which a number of training samples are provided and an extra training process is often required. For retrieval, the goal is to rank a large number of candidates according to their relevance to the query, and candidates are considered as independent units, *i.e.*, without explicit relationship between them. Both image classification and retrieval tasks could be tackled by the Bag-of-Visual-Words (BoVW) model. However, the ways of performing classification [10][26] and retrieval [46][38] are, most often, very different. Although all the above algorithms start from extracting patch or regional descriptors, the subsequent modules, including feature encoding, indexing/training and online querying, are almost distinct.

In this paper, we suggest using only ONE (Online Nearest-neighbor Estimation) algorithm for both image classification and retrieval. This is achieved by computing similarity between the query and each category or image candidate. Inspired by [4], we detect multiple **object proposals** on the query and each indexed image, and extract high-quality features on each object to provide better image description.

On the online querying stage, the query's relevance to a category or candidate image is estimated by the averaged nearest distance from querying objects to the objects in that category or candidate image. As shown in Figure 1, extracting more objects helps to find various visual clues and obtain better results. To improve efficiency, we leverage the idea of approximate nearest-neighbor search, and take advantage of GPU parallelization for fast computation. Experiments are performed on a wide range of image classification/retrieval datasets. Our algorithm achieves state-of-the-art accuracy with reasonable computational overheads.

The major contribution of this paper is summarized in three aspects. First, we reveal the possibility of unifying image classification and retrieval systems into ONE. Second, ONE achieves the state-of-the-art accuracy on a wide range of image classification and retrieval tasks, defending both training-free models for image recognition and regional features for near-duplicate object retrieval. Finally, we make full use of GPU parallelization to alleviate heavy online computational overheads, which might inspire various multimedia applications and research efforts in the future.

The remainder for this paper is organized as follows. Section 2 briefly introduces related works. Section 3 illustrates the ONE algorithm and key acceleration techniques. After showing experiments in Section 4, we conclude in Section 5.

2. RELATED WORKS

2.1 Image Classification

Image classification is a fundamental task which is aimed at categorizing images according to their semantic contents. Recent years, researchers propose to extend conventional tasks [26][16] in two aspects, *i.e.*, from coarse-grained to fine-grained [33][49][36], and from small-scale to large-scale [13].

The Bag-of-Visual-Words (BoVW) model is widely adopted to represent images with high-dimensional vectors. It often consists of three stages, *i.e.*, descriptor extraction, feature encoding and feature summarization. Due to the limited descriptive power of raw pixels, local descriptors such as SIFT [28][54] and HOG [11] are extracted. A visual vocabulary or codebook is then built to capture data distribution in the feature space. Descriptors are thereafter quantized onto the codebook as compact feature vectors [63][51][37][55], and summarized as an image-level representation [26][17][57][59]. These feature vectors are normalized [56], and fed into generalized machine learning algorithms [15][41] for training and testing. Besides, there are also efforts on designing training-free classification systems [4].

2.2 Image Retrieval

Image retrieval is closely related to a number of real-world multimedia applications. Given an image database and a query, it requires finding relative candidates to the query in a short time. As the rapid growth of the Internet [40], large-scale image search attracts more and more attentions in both academic and industrial fields [62].

The BoVW model is also widely adopted for image retrieval [34]. Handcrafted descriptors such as SIFT [28][58] and SURF [3] are extracted on the detected regions-of-interest (ROI) of an image [29][30]. A codebook, often with a large size, is trained in an approximate manner [38] to capture data distribution. Descriptors are quantized onto the codebook in an either hard [38] or soft manner [39]. Codebook training-free methods [73] are also suggested for feature encoding. Then the flowchart differs from classification in the way of organizing a huge number of features. An inverted index [46] is constructed to store the relationship between images and features. When a query image comes, descriptors are extracted and quantized accordingly to look up the inverted index. When the initial search results are available, they are often sent into a post-processing stage for higher precision and recall. Popular post-processing approaches include geometric verification [8], query expansion [9] and diffusion-based algorithms [23][60].

2.3 Convolutional Neural Networks

Convolutional Neural Networks (CNN) are based on the theory that a multi-layer network is able to fit any complicated functions. In the early years, neural networks are verified efficient on simple recognition tasks [27]. Recent years, the available of large-scale training data (*e.g.*, ImageNet [13]) and powerful GPUs make it possible to train deep CNNs which significantly outperform the BoVW models [25].

A CNN is often composed of a number of layers. In each layer, responses from the previous layer are convoluted and activated by a differentiable function. Thus, the network could be formulated as a composed function, and the error signals produced by the difference between supervised and predicted labels could be back-propagated. Some recently proposed tricks are also crucial to help CNNs converge faster and prevent over-fitting, such as the ReLU activation function and the dropout technique [25]. It is suggested that deeper networks produce better recognition results [45][47], and intermediate responses of CNNs could also be transplanted onto other image applications [14][43]. The discussion of different configurations in CNNs is available in [6][65].

2.4 Approximate Nearest-neighbor Search

It is a common demand that finding the nearest neighbor of a D-dimensional query vector in a large database of N candidates. Since an exhaustive search algorithm requires as many as $O(ND)$ computations which is often intractable, approximate algorithms are adopted to accelerate this process with reasonable accuracy loss.

One family of solutions involve constructing a data structure for efficient lookup. Based on the k-d tree [18] or other similar structures [50], efficient Approximate Nearest Neighbor (ANN) search algorithm is proposed [31], and further applied on other applications such as large-scale vector clustering [38]. A notable drawback of such methods is the unavailability of distance between the query and each candidate, which makes it impossible to provide a ranklist for retrieval and related tasks.

There are also research efforts on encoding high-dimensional data into distance-preserving compact codes. A typical example is quantization, in which the distance between two vectors is estimated by the distance between codewords. Product Quantization (PQ) [21] trains a large codebook with the Cartesian product of small sub-codebooks. PQ then traverses each candidate and computes its distance to the query quickly with a fast pre-computation on codewords. Improvements of PQ include Cartesian K-Means [35] and Composite Quantization [69]. Another efficient approach, Locality Sensitive Hashing (LSH) [19], measures the distance by the Hamming distance and could be embedded to improve image search performance [70].

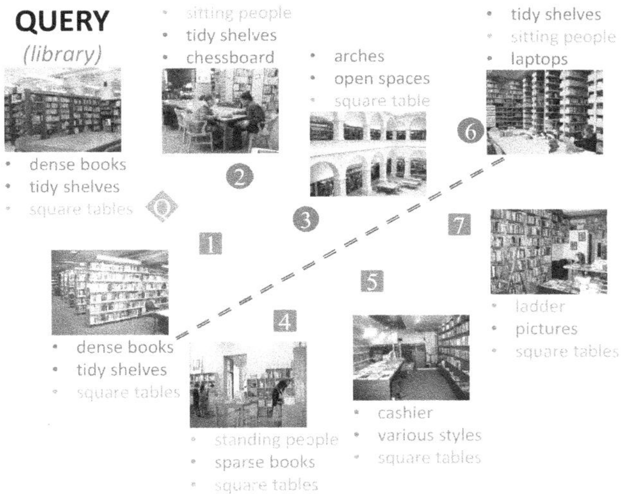

Figure 2: The difference between image classification and retrieval with the same query (green diamond). Red squares and blue circles indicate samples of the *bookstore* and *library* classes, respectively. For each image, three most significant visual attributes are listed, with the colors indicating their bias in visual concepts (red for *bookstore*, blue for *library*, and green for neutral). Candidates are ranked according to their relevance (distance) to the query. The dashed line illustrates the optimal linear classifier between two categories.

3. ALGORITHM

3.1 A Unified Framework

Since we aim at designing a unified framework for image classification and retrieval, we first make a brief discussion on the essential difference between these two tasks.

Both classification and retrieval involve measuring the similarity between the query and training or candidate images. The only difference lies in that a class label is provided for each training sample in classification. Therefore, we are actually computing the similarity between the query and a category, *i.e.*, a set of images. As observed in [4], image-to-class distance is much more stable than image-to-image distance. On the other hand, candidates in retrieval are often considered independently, *i.e.*, without explicit relationship between them. An intuitive example is shown in Figure 2. The query (a *library* image) is closest to a *bookstore* image in the feature space, and the outlier (#1) significantly harms the retrieval performance. However, when more labeled training samples are available, we obtain the optimal linear classifier between *library* and *bookstore* which predicts the correct label of the query.

In summary, classification tasks benefit from the class labels of images, but such information is not available in retrieval datasets. A direct solution is to augment the database by extracting multiple **object proposals** for each image, and consider each object as an individual image sample (with a "class label"). After each object is equipped with a high-quality regional descriptor, it is possible to deal with both image classification and retrieval problems by computing image-to-class distance [4].

3.2 Online Nearest-neighbor Estimation

This part formulates the previous ideas as the ONE (Online Nearest-neighbor Estimation) algorithm. We start from an image classification/retrieval dataset of N images,

$$\mathcal{I} = \{(\mathbf{I}_1, y_1), (\mathbf{I}_2, y_2), \ldots, (\mathbf{I}_N, y_N)\} \tag{1}$$

In which, $\mathbf{I}_n$ and y_n are the image data and label of the n-th image, respectively. For image classification, $y_n \in \{1, 2, \ldots, C\}$ is pre-defined by the dataset, while for image retrieval we simply set $C = N$ and $y_n = n$, indicating that each instance belongs to an independent "category".

For each image $\mathbf{I}_n$, a set of object proposals $\mathcal{P}_n$ is constructed,

$$\mathcal{P}_n = \{\mathbf{p}_{n,1}, \mathbf{p}_{n,2}, \ldots, \mathbf{p}_{n,K_n}\} \tag{2}$$

Here, $\mathbf{p}_{n,k} = (x_{n,k}^{\min}, y_{n,k}^{\min}, W_{n,k}, H_{n,k}, \theta_{n,k})$ is the k-th object of the n-th image, denoted by the coordinate of its upper-left corner, its width and height, and $\theta_{n,k} \in [0^\circ, 360^\circ)$ indicating the angle by which the image is rotated before feature extraction. The designation of $\mathcal{P}_n$ will be discussed in detail later. Cropping and rotating $\mathbf{I}_n$ according to $\mathbf{p}_{n,k}$ yields a subimage $\mathbf{I}_{n,k}$, on which we compute a regional vector representation $\mathbf{f}_{n,k}$. Specifically, we extract 4096-D deep conv-net features which are the intermediate responses of a CNN [45]. Although other features such as VLAD [22] could also be adopted, we choose deep conv-net features because the excellent descriptive ability. According to a simple experiment based on NN feature search on the **Holiday** dataset [20], VLAD obtains a mAP score of 0.526 [20] while deep conv-net features get 0.642 [43].

Next we follow [4] to perform a Naive-Bayes Nearest-Neighbor (NBNN) search. We first define the feature set $\mathcal{F}_c$, $c = 1, 2, \ldots, C$, which is composed of all the features extracted from the objects that belong to the c-th category,

$$\mathcal{F}_c = \{\mathbf{f}_{n,k} \mid y_n = c \wedge 1 \leqslant k \leqslant K_n\} \tag{3}$$

For a query image $\mathbf{I}_0$, we compute its distance to each category $c \in \{1, 2, \ldots, C\}$, which is the averaged distance between each object of $\mathbf{I}_n$ and its nearest neighbor in $\mathcal{F}_c$,

$$\begin{aligned} \mathrm{dist}(\mathbf{I}_0, c) &\doteq \mathrm{dist}(\mathbf{I}_0, \mathcal{F}_c) & (4)\\ &= \frac{1}{K_0}\sum_{k=1}^{K_0}\mathrm{dist}(\mathbf{f}_{0,k}, \mathcal{F}_c) & (5)\\ &= \frac{1}{K_0}\sum_{k=1}^{K_0}\min_{\mathbf{f}\in\mathcal{F}_c}\|\mathbf{f}_{0,k} - \mathbf{f}\|_2^2 & (6) \end{aligned}$$

When all the image-to-category distances are available, it is convenient to analyze them for specified purposes, such as finding the minimum one for category prediction, or sorting them for a ranklist of candidates.

3.3 Object Proposals

It remains to construct an object proposal set $\mathcal{P}_n$ for each image $\mathbf{I}_n$. For this purpose, we might refer to unsupervised object detectors, including Objectness [1], Selective Search [48] and Binarized Normed Gradients (BING) [7]. These algorithms often provide a number of bounding boxes which are the possible locations of objects. By sorting the confidence scores of the boxes, it is possible to obtain an arbitrary number K_D of top-ranked object proposals[1].

[1]Due to the limited space, please refer to the publications above for examples of object detection.

In comparison, we also adopt an alternative approach which extracts manually defined objects on an image. For this, we first define the number of object proposal layers L_{O}, and then enforce that objects within one layer have the same size meanwhile are distributed as dispersive as possible. Denote the width and height of image $\mathbf{I}_n$ as W_n and H_n. In the l-th layer, there are $r_l \times r_l$ objects with a fixed size $\frac{W_n}{s_l} \times \frac{H_n}{s_l}$, where r_l and s_l are the object density and scale parameters which will be discussed later. The upper-left corner of the (a,b)-th box, $0 \leqslant a,b < r_l$, is located at $\left(a \cdot \left(W_n - \frac{W_n}{s_l}\right) / (r_l - 1), b \cdot \left(H_n - \frac{H_n}{s_l}\right) / (r_l - 1)\right)$. An L_{O}-layer model has $K_{L_{\mathrm{O}}} = \sum_{l=1}^{L_{\mathrm{O}}} r_l^2$ object proposals.

Either a detected or manually defined object might be rotated. Here we consider 4 simplest rotations, *i.e.*, $\theta_{n,k} \in \{0°, 90°, 180°, 270°\}$. As an increasing number of objects might result in heavier computational overheads, we might only rotate the top-K_{R} detected regions ($K_{\mathrm{R}} \leqslant K_{\mathrm{D}}$), or regions on the first L_{R} ($L_{\mathrm{R}} \leqslant L_{\mathrm{O}}$) layers. Such a strategy produces $K_{\mathrm{D}} + 3K_{\mathrm{R}}$ or $K_{L_{\mathrm{O}}} + 3K_{L_{\mathrm{R}}}$ object proposals.

The comparison between automatically detected and manually defined object proposals is similar to that between detected and densely sampled descriptors which is well discussed in the conventional Bag-of-Visual-Words (BoVW) models. We will show in Section 4.2 that both strategies obtain satisfying classification and retrieval results.

3.4 Approximate Nearest-neighbor Search

Since ONE requires a huge number of NN queries, linear exhaustive NN search might be computationally expensive. We adopt both Principal Component Analysis (PCA) and Product Quantization (PQ) [21] to reduce time complexity. Deep conv-net features [14] (4096 dimensions) of each region are first reduced to D dimensions by PCA. Then it is partitioned by PQ into M segments and each subvector is quantized onto one of T codewords.

It is worth noting that vector dimensions after PCA reduction are ranked by decreasing energy, whereas PQ works better in the case that each segment contains vectors with approximately equal information. Therefore, we perform dimension rearrangement to make PCA and PQ cooperate better, in which the m-th PQ segment is composed of the $(m, M+m, 2M+m, \ldots, D-M+m)$-th PCA-reduced dimensions. In practise, this strategy consistently boosts the classification/retrieval accuracy by about 2%. It is also instructive to whiten PCA features for similar effects.

Assume there are N training/candidate images in a classification/retrieval task. For each image, K object windows are proposed, on each of which we extract a 4096-dimensional feature. Therefore for each query, we need to process K queries in a database of KN vectors. An exhaustive NN search takes $O(4096K^2N)$ time and $O(4096KN)$ memory. In an approximate NN search, features are PCA-reduced to D dimensions, and quantized with a PQ of M segments and T codewords for each segment. According to PQ [21], the time complexity is $O(K^2NM + KDT)$, meanwhile storing quantized vectors and a codebook requires $KNM \log_2 T$ bits and DT floating numbers in total. Since $M \ll D \ll 4096$ and $T \ll N$, both time and memory costs are greatly reduced. When the parameters are fixed, the computational complexity grows linearly with the dataset size N, which guarantees that our algorithm scales up well. Section 4.4 provides time/memory costs in experiments.

3.5 GPU Acceleration

Despite the approximation by PCA and PQ, the computational cost on the online querying stage is still very high, *e.g.*, about 5×10^{11} floating operations to search one query among one million candidates (see Section 4.4). Fortunately, most of the heavy computation comes from the linear search stage of PQ. We can take advantage of GPU parallelization for efficient acceleration.

Graphics Processing Unit (GPU) is a specialized electronic device designed to rapidly manipulate and alter memory to accelerate image processing in a frame buffer intended for output to a display. It often contains a large number of stream processors in which large data blocks are processed in parallel. The highly parallel structure of GPUs makes them more effective than CPUs for large-scale simple-arithmetic operations. Recent years, GPUs have been widely adopted for accelerating deep CNN training [25].

It is worth noting that the storage of a GPU is often limited, *e.g.*, an NVIDIA GeForce GTX Titan has only 6GB memory. We shall carefully design the parameters discussed above, so that quantized vectors could be stored in a GPU. An extensive study on the proper parameters are provided in Section 4.2.

4. EXPERIMENTS

4.1 Datasets and Implementation Details

For image classification, we use the **LandUse-21** dataset [64], the **Indoor-67** dataset [42] and the **SUN-397** dataset [53] for scene classification. 80, 80 and 50 images per category are randomly selected for training. We also use the Oxford **Pet-37** dataset [36], the Oxford **Flower-102** dataset [33] and the Caltech-UCSD **Bird-200**-2011 dataset [49] for fine-grained object recognition. 100, 20 and 30 images per category are randomly selected for training. The **SUN-397** dataset [53] is one of the largest available datasets for scene understanding, which provides an evidence that our algorithm scales up well. For each dataset, the random training/testing splits are repeated for 10 rounds and averaged classification accuracy is reported.

For image retrieval, we use the **UKBench** dataset [34] and the **Holiday** dataset [20]. They are both near-duplicate instance search datasets. The **UKBench** dataset consists of 2550 objects and 4 photos are taken for each of them (10200 images in total). The **Holiday** dataset is composed of 500 groups of objects or scenes with a handful of instances in each of them. The standard evaluation uses the N-S score (the average number of true-positive images in top-4 results) for **UKBench**, and the mAP (mean average precision) score for **Holiday**. To test the scalability of our model, we also mix the **Holiday** dataset with one million irrelevant images crawled from the Web.

For manually defined objects, we use $L_{\mathrm{O}} = 5$ layers, with fixed parameters $(s_1, s_2, s_3, s_4, s_5) = (1.0, 1.2, 1.5, 2.0, 2.5)$ and $(r_1, r_2, r_3, r_4, r_5) = (1, 2, 3, 4, 5)$, respectively. For automatic object detection, we use Selective Search [48] and choose top-ranked objects according to the confidence scores. For object representation, we compute a pre-trained 19-layer **VGG-Net** [45], and extract the 4096-D responses of the second-to-last fully connected layers, without applying ReLU activation. Feature vectors are square-root normalized and then ℓ_2-normalized after PCA reduction.

Objects	$L_O = 1$	$L_O = 2$	$L_O = 3$	$L_O = 4$	$L_O = 5$
$L_R = 0$	67.18	73.41	77.63	82.18	85.71
$L_R = 1$	67.40	73.69	77.95	82.42	86.11
$L_R = 2$	–	73.78	78.01	82.47	86.14
$L_R = 3$	–	–	78.03	82.51	86.18
$L_R = 4$	–	–	–	82.53	86.22
$L_R = 5$	–	–	–	–	**86.24**

(a) Classification Accuracy (%) on **Flower-102**

Objects	$L_O = 1$	$L_O = 2$	$L_O = 3$	$L_O = 4$	$L_O = 5$
$L_R = 0$	0.751	0.772	0.796	0.826	0.847
$L_R = 1$	0.816	0.832	0.837	0.854	0.871
$L_R = 2$	–	0.838	0.848	0.858	0.874
$L_R = 3$	–	–	0.861	0.868	0.880
$L_R = 4$	–	–	–	0.882	0.883
$L_R = 5$	–	–	–	–	**0.887**

(b) Retrieval Accuracy (mAP) on **Holiday**

Table 1: Classification and retrieval accuracy with respect to the complexity of manually defined objects.

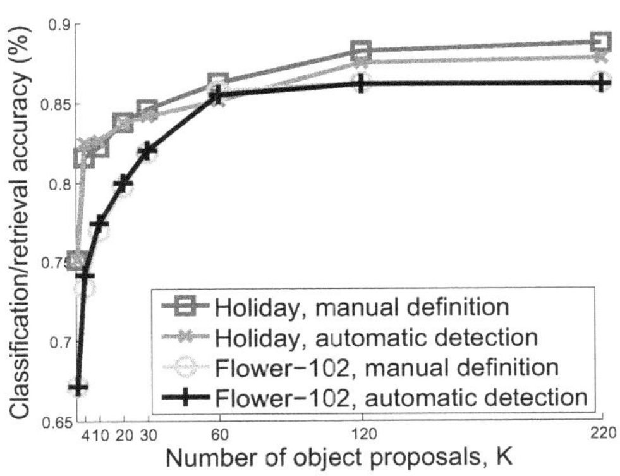

Figure 3: Classification/retrieval accuracy with respect to the way of defining objects and the number of proposals. We first construct $K = 220$ objects ($L_O = L_R = 5$ for manual definition and $K_D = K_R = 55$ for automatic detection), and randomly select a subset of them for evaluation.

4.2 Model and Parameters

We discuss the parameters of the ONE algorithm, *i.e.*, the object proposal set $\mathcal{P}$, the PCA-reduced dimension D, and the number of segments M and codewords T for PQ. For quick evaluations, we evaluate the classification and retrieval accuracy on two relatively smaller datasets, namely the **Flower-102** dataset and the **Holiday** dataset.

We first use accurate NN search to evaluate classification and retrieval accuracy with respect to the object proposals. Results are summarized in Table 1 (the number of layers of manually defined object proposals) and Figure 3 (automatic detection vs. manual definition with random selection), respectively. One can observe that a larger number of object proposals often produce better accuracy. Meanwhile, manually defined and automatically detected objects produce comparable results, suggesting that it is the number of object proposals that makes the major contribution to boosting accuracy. When the number of object proposals is sufficiently large (*e.g.*, $K \geqslant 60$), manually defined objects work even slightly better (86.24% vs. 86.16% on **Flower-102** and 0.887 vs. 0.878 on **Holiday**). Therefore, we only use manually defined objects in later experiments.

	LandUse-21	**Indoor-67**	**SUN-397**
[24]	92.8	63.4	46.1
[61]	–	63.48	45.91
[14]	–	–	40.94
[43]	–	69.0	–
SVM	**94.52**	68.46	53.00
ONE	93.98	**69.61**	**54.47**
ONE+SVM	**94.71**	**70.13**	**54.87**

(a) Scene Recognition Accuracy (%)

	Pet-37	**Flower-102**	**Bird-200**
[2]	54.30	80.66	–
[52]	59.29	75.26	–
[32]	56.8	84.6	33.3
[14]	–	–	58.75
[43]	–	86.8	61.8
SVM	88.05	85.49	59.66
ONE	**89.50**	**86.24**	**61.54**
ONE+SVM	**90.03**	**86.82**	**62.02**

(b) Fine-Grained Recognition Accuracy (%)

Table 2: Classification accuracy on different datasets. In each subtable, the first and second parts contain algorithms without and with using deep conv-net features, respectively.

For large-scale image search, we consider both PCA and PQ for acceleration (see Section 3.4). The impact of parameters, *i.e.*, PCA dimension D, PQ segments M and codewords T, are summarized in Figure 4, 5 and 6, respectively. We use $K = 220$ object proposals ($L_O = L_R = 5$) in these experiments. Empirically, a proper set of parameters achieve a good tradeoff between accuracy and computational overheads. For example, partitioning a vector into 128 segments produces nearly the same accuracy compared to 64 segments, but requires almost doubled time and memory consumption on the online querying stage. We choose parameters $D = 512$, $M = 32$ and $T = 4096$ as an accuracy-complexity tradeoff. For small-scale experiments, *i.e.*, the number of training or candidate images is not greater than 10^4, we use PCA but do not use PQ for higher classification and retrieval accuracy.

Moreover, we need to constraint the number of object proposals K to fit the limited GPU memory. Recall from Section 3.4 that PQ stores $KNM\log_2 T$ bits and DT floating numbers, *i.e*, $\frac{1}{8}KNM\log_2 T + 4DT$ bytes, which should be less than 6GB (the memory of a Titan GPU). When we are dealing with one million images ($N \approx 10^6$) in large-scale experiments, K shall be no larger than 120. We use $L_O = L_R = 4$ ($K = 120$) in practise. Of course the tradeoff between more objects and more rotations could be determined according to detailed conditions. For example, in the **Oxford Buildings** dataset [38] (less image rotation), it might be better to use $L_O = 6$ and $L_R = 2$ ($K = 106$).

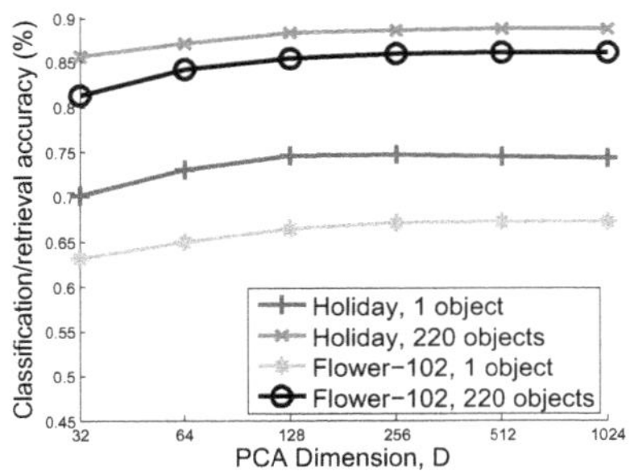

Figure 4: Accuracy w.r.t. PCA dimension D. PQ is not used here.

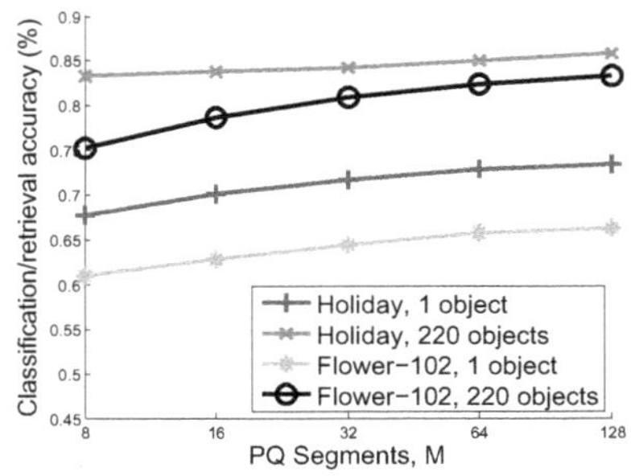

Figure 5: Accuracy w.r.t. PQ segments M, with $D = 1024$ and $T = 4096$.

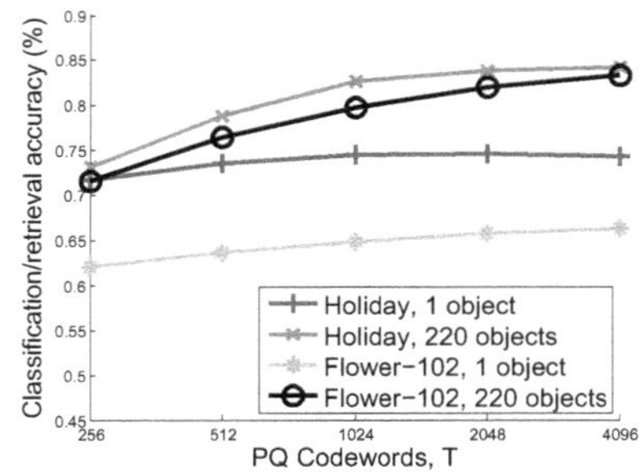

Figure 6: Accuracy w.r.t. PQ codewords T, with $D = 1024$ and $M = 32$.

	BoVW+ONE	ONE	BoVW	[70]	[43]	[71]	[12]	[67]	[68]
Holiday	**0.899**	**0.887**	0.518	0.881	0.843	0.858	0.847	0.846	0.809
UKBench	**3.887**	**3.873**	3.134	3.873	–	3.85	3.75	3.77	3.60

Table 3: Comparison of retrieval accuracy with the state-of-the-arts. Among the competitors, [70] and [43] also use deep conv-net features extracted on the **Alex-Net** [25]). While [70], [12] and [67] adopt post-processing, ONE does not.

4.3 Comparison to the State-of-the-Arts

We compare ONE with the state-of-the-art algorithms.

Image classification results are summarized in Table 2. One could observe that our algorithm achieves competitive accuracy in both scene recognition and fine-grained recognition tasks. For fine-grained recognition, we do not use any part detectors but simply extract regular object proposals, leading to inferior classification accuracy compared to those using complicated part detectors, such as [66] (73.89%) and [5] (85.4%) on the **Bird-200** dataset. Our algorithm could also cooperate with specialized part detectors.

Since a training process provides much benefit for image classification, we also compare our model with conventional machine learning approaches. We adopt LibLINEAR [15], a scalable SVM implementation with a tradeoff parameter $C = 10$. In most cases, ONE outperforms SVM, defending the ability of a training-free algorithm for classification. The fusion of ONE and SVM results, obtained by adding the confidence scores directly and re-ranking, also shows superior performance over both models, suggesting that complementary information is captured by different approaches.

Next we report image retrieval accuracy in Table 3. One could observe that our algorithm, without post-processing, outperforms all the competitors. Similar to image classification, we also compare ONE with the conventional BoVW model. Our model is implemented with SIFT extraction, large codebook training and hard quantization [38], an inverted index structure and ℓ_p-norm weighting [72]. Although ONE outperforms BoVW significantly, we notice that BoVW works better to capture local clues that help retrieval. When we fuse the results generated by both models, they complement each other and produce even higher accuracy. To the best of our knowledge, the 0.899 mAP score on **Holiday** and the 3.887 N-S score on **UKBench** rank among the highest scores ever reported on these two datasets. When **Holiday** is mixed with one million distractors, we get a 0.758 mAP score with PCA and PQ approximation, which outperforms 0.724 reported in [70] and 0.633 in [68].

The excellent classification and retrieval performance comes from a perfect cooperation of object detection and description, *i.e.*, efficient image representation by conv-net features and powerful retrieval process by ONE. Either applying NN search on global image features (see Table 1) or replacing deep conv-net features with BoVW-based features would case dramatic accuracy drop.

4.4 Time and Memory Costs

This part provides an experimental study on the computational overheads of ONE. A theoretical analysis could be found in Section 3.4. Parameters, *i.e.*, $D = 512$, $M = 32$ and $C = 4096$, are inherited from Section 4.2. Time and memory costs of different models are summarized in Table 4.

For image classification, we take **SUN-397** [53], the largest dataset in our experiments, as the example. Following the same setting provided by the authors, the numbers of training and testing images in one split are both $N = 397 \times 50 \approx$ 20K. $K = 220$ ($L_{\mathrm{O}} = L_{\mathrm{R}} = 5$) object proposals are extracted on each image. According to the analysis in Section 3.4, classifying a single image requires approximately 4.5×10^8 floating multiplications and 3.2×10^9 floating summations, which takes less than 0.1s on a Titan GPU, *i.e.*, about 1800s (0.5h) on the whole testing set. The memory storage on GPU is about 200MB in this case. Compared with conventional SVM classification which requires 8h and 2560MB for one training and testing, our method is significantly faster in time and cheaper in memory.

For image retrieval, we evaluate our algorithm on the **Holiday** dataset [20] with one million distractors. With $N \approx$ 1M and $K = 120$ ($L_{\mathrm{O}} = L_{\mathrm{R}} = 4$), we need approximately 2.4×10^8 floating multiplications and 4.5×10^{11} floating summations for each query, which require about 1.2s on a Titan GPU, which is comparable with conventional systems performed on CPU. The storage of about 45G bits and 2M floating numbers fits well in the 6GB GPU memory. Both time and memory costs are comparable to the state-of-the-art approaches with deep conv-net features [70].

	Classification with **ONE**	Classification with BoVW	Retrieval with **ONE**	Retrieval with BoVW
Descriptor Extraction Time (s, per image)	1.81 (CNN)	1.36 (SIFT)	1.75 (CNN)	0.83 (SIFT)
Codebook Training Time (h)	0.39 (PQ)	2.41 (GMM)	0.39 (PQ)	6.18 (AKM)
Codebook Training Memory (GB)	0.63	2.50	0.63	8.31
Feature Quantization Time (s, per image)	0.17 (PQ)	0.23 (FV)	0.17 (PQ)	0.10 (VQ)
Offline Training Time (h)	–	7.71 (SVM)	–	2.85 (IND)
Offline Training Memory (GB)	–	2.50 (SVM)	–	4.19 (IND)
Online Querying Time (s, per query)	0.08	< 0.01	1.17	0.56
Online Querying Memory (GB)	0.21 (PQ)	0.05	5.65 (PQ)	4.19 (IND)

Table 4: Comparison of computational costs between ONE and BoVW. Results are reported on **SUN-397** (about 100K images) for classification, and **Holiday** with 1M distractors for retrieval. For abbreviations: **GMM** – Gaussian Mixture Model, **AKM** – Approximate K-Means [38], **FV** – Fisher Vectors [44], **VQ** – Vector Quantization, **IND** – inverted index.

It is worth noting that the actual computational costs in ONE are much more expensive than conventional algorithms. For example, ONE requires nearly 5×10^{11} floating operations for searching one query among one million candidates, while a simple BoVW-based approach often needs no more than 10^9 [34][73]. GPU is the key to make ONE produce results in a reasonable time (*e.g.* around one second). Conventional algorithms often contain complicated modules (*e.g.*, inverted index, spatial verification, *etc.*) with asynchronous memory access and/or a large number of serial operations, making them difficult to be transplanted to GPU for acceleration. As the rapid development of multi-GPU, our algorithm might attract more attentions in the future.

5. CONCLUSIONS

This paper proposes to unify image classification and retrieval algorithms into ONE (Online Nearest-neighbor Estimation). We demonstrate that, with the help of high-quality regional features, both classification and retrieval tasks could be accomplished with a simple NBNN search [4]. We take advantage of PCA and PQ approximation as well as GPU parallelization to alleviate heavy computational costs. Despite the simplicity, our algorithm achieves state-of-the-art image classification and retrieval performance.

The success of our algorithm inspires future research in three aspects. First, the essence of image classification and retrieval are the same, both of them could be tackled by measuring image similarity. Second, extracting more objects often leads to higher classification/retrieval accuracy, enlightening that image description, even with deep conv-net features, is far from complete. Third, GPU is the future of high performance computing, therefore designing a GPU-friendly algorithm is necessary and beneficial.

6. ACKNOWLEDGMENTS

This work was supported by the 973 Program of China (Grant Nos. 2013CB329403 and 2012CB316301), the NNSF of China (Grant Nos. 61332007, 61273023 and 61429201), and the Tsinghua University Initiative Scientific Research Program (Grant No. 20121088071). This work was also supported in part to Dr. Hong by State High-Tech Development Plan 2014AA015104, and the Program for New Century Excellent Talents in University under grant NCET-13-0764; and in part to Dr. Tian by ARO grant W911NF-12-1-0057, and Faculty Research Awards by NEC Labs of America.

7. REFERENCES

[1] B. Alexe, T. Deselaers, and V. Ferrari. Measuring the Objectness of Image Windows. *TPAMI*, 2012.
[2] A. Angelova and S. Zhu. Efficient Object Detection and Segmentation for Fine-Grained Recognition. *CVPR*, 2013.
[3] H. Bay, T. Tuytelaars, and L. Van Gool. SURF: Speeded Up Robust Features. *ECCV*, 2006.
[4] O. Boiman, E. Shechtman, and M. Irani. In Defense of Nearest-Neighbor Based Image Classification. *CVPR*, 2008.
[5] S. Branson, G. Van Horn, S. Belongie, and P. Perona. Bird Species Categorization Using Pose Normalized Deep Convolutional Nets. *arXiv preprint arXiv:1406.2952*, 2014.
[6] K. Chatfield, K. Simonyan, A. Vedaldi, and A. Zisserman. Return of the Devil in the Details: Delving Deep into Convolutional Nets. *BMVC*, 2014.
[7] M. Cheng, Z. Zhang, W. Lin, and P. Torr. BING: Binarized Normed Gradients for Objectness Estimation at 300fps. *CVPR*, 2014.
[8] O. Chum, M. Perdoch, and J. Matas. Geometric Min-Hashing: Finding a (Thick) Needle in a Haystack. *CVPR*, 2009.
[9] O. Chum, J. Philbin, J. Sivic, M. Isard, and A. Zisserman. Total Recall: Automatic Query Expansion with a Generative Feature Model for Object Retrieval. *ICCV*, 2007.
[10] G. Csurka, C. Dance, L. Fan, J. Willamowski, and C. Bray. Visual Categorization with Bags of Keypoints. *ECCV*, 2004.
[11] N. Dalal and B. Triggs. Histograms of Oriented Gradients for Human Detection. *CVPR*, 2005.
[12] C. Deng, R. Ji, W. Liu, D. Tao, and X. Gao. Visual Reranking through Weakly Supervised Multi-Graph Learning. *ICCV*, 2013.
[13] J. Deng, W. Dong, R. Socher, L. Li, K. Li, and L. Fei-Fei. Imagenet: A Large-scale Hierarchical Image Database. *CVPR*, 2009.
[14] J. Donahue, Y. Jia, O. Vinyals, J. Hoffman, N. Zhang, E. Tzeng, and T. Darrell. DeCAF: A Deep Convolutional Activation Feature for Generic Visual Recognition. *ICML*, 2014.
[15] R. Fan, K. Chang, C. Hsieh, X. Wang, and C. Lin. LIBLINEAR: A Library for Large Linear Classification. *JMLR*, 2008.
[16] L. Fei-Fei, R. Fergus, and P. Perona. Learning Generative Visual Models from Few Training Examples: An Incremental Bayesian Approach Tested on 101 Object Categories. *CVIU*, 2007.
[17] J. Feng, B. Ni, Q. Tian, and S. Yan. Geometric Lp-norm Feature Pooling for Image Classification. *CVPR*, 2011.
[18] J. Friedman, J. Bentley, and R. Finkel. An Algorithm for Finding Best Matches in Logarithmic Expected Time. *ACM ToMS*, 1977.

[19] A. Gionis, P. Indyk, and R. Motwani. Similarity Search in High Dimensions via Hashing. *VLDB*, 1999.

[20] H. Jegou, M. Douze, and C. Schmid. Hamming Embedding and Weak Geometric Consistency for Large Scale Image Search. *ECCV*, 2008.

[21] H. Jegou, M. Douze, and C. Schmid. Product Quantization for Nearest Neighbor Search. *TPAMI*, 2011.

[22] H. Jegou, M. Douze, C. Schmid, and P. Perez. Aggregating Local Descriptors into a Compact Image Representation. *CVPR*, 2010.

[23] Y. Jing and S. Baluja. VisualRank: Applying PageRank to Large-Scale Image Search. *TPAMI*, 2008.

[24] T. Kobayashi. Dirichlet-based Histogram Feature Transform for Image Classification. *CVPR*, 2014.

[25] A. Krizhevsky, I. Sutskever, and G. Hinton. ImageNet Classification with Deep Convolutional Neural Networks. *NIPS*, 2012.

[26] S. Lazebnik, C. Schmid, and J. Ponce. Beyond Bags of Features: Spatial Pyramid Matching for Recognizing Natural Scene Categories. *CVPR*, 2006.

[27] B. LeCun, J. Denker, D. Henderson, R. Howard, W. Hubbard, and L. Jackel. Handwritten Digit Recognition with a Back-Propagation Network. *NIPS*, 1990.

[28] D. G. Lowe. Distinctive Image Features from Scale-Invariant Keypoints. *IJCV*, 2004.

[29] J. Matas, O. Chum, M. Urban, and T. Pajdla. Robust Wide-Baseline Stereo from Maximally Stable Extremal Regions. *Image and Vision Computing*, 2004.

[30] K. Mikolajczyk and C. Schmid. Scale & Affine Invariant Interest Point Detectors. *IJCV*, 2004.

[31] M. Muja and D. Lowe. Fast Approximate Nearest Neighbors with Automatic Algorithm Configuration. *VISIGRAPP*, 2009.

[32] N. Murray and F. Perronnin. Generalized Max Pooling. *CVPR*, 2014.

[33] M. Nilsback and A. Zisserman. Automated Flower Classification over a Large Number of Classes. *Indian Conference on Computer Vision, Graphics & Image Processing*, 2008.

[34] D. Nister and H. Stewenius. Scalable Recognition with a Vocabulary Tree. *CVPR*, 2006.

[35] M. Norouzi and D. Fleet. Cartesian K-Means. *CVPR*, 2013.

[36] O. Parkhi, A. Vedaldi, A. Zisserman, and C. Jawahar. Cats and Dogs. *CVPR*, 2012.

[37] F. Perronnin, J. Sánchez, and T. Mensink. Improving the Fisher Kernel for Large-scale Image Classification. *ECCV*, 2010.

[38] J. Philbin, O. Chum, M. Isard, J. Sivic, and A. Zisserman. Object Retrieval with Large Vocabularies and Fast Spatial Matching. *CVPR*, 2007.

[39] J. Philbin, O. Chum, M. Isard, J. Sivic, and A. Zisserman. Lost in Quantization: Improving Particular Object Retrieval in Large Scale Image Databases. *CVPR*, 2008.

[40] G. Qi, C. Aggarwal, Q. Tian, H. Ji, and T. Huang. Exploring Context and Content Links in Social Media: A Latent Space Method. *TPAMI*, 2012.

[41] G. Qi, X. Hua, Y. Rui, J. Tang, and H. Zhang. Two-Dimensional Multi-Label Active Learning with an Efficient Online Adaptation Model for Image Classification. *TPAMI*, 2009.

[42] A. Quattoni and A. Torralba. Recognizing Indoor Scenes. *CVPR*, 2009.

[43] A. Razavian, H. Azizpour, J. Sullivan, and S. Carlsson. CNN Features off-the-shelf: an Astounding Baseline for Recognition. *CVPR*, 2014.

[44] J. Sanchez, F. Perronnin, T. Mensink, and J. Verbeek. Image Classification with the Fisher Vector: Theory and Practice. *IJCV*, 2013.

[45] K. Simonyan and A. Zisserman. Very Deep Convolutional Networks for Large-Scale Image Recognition. *arXiv preprint arXiv:1409.1556*, 2014.

[46] J. Sivic and A. Zisserman. Video Google: A Text Retrieval Approach to Object Matching in Videos. *ICCV*, 2003.

[47] C. Szegedy, W. Liu, Y. Jia, P. Sermanet, S. Reed, D. Anguelov, D. Erhan, V. Vanhoucke, and A. Rabinovich. Going Deeper with Convolutions. *NIPS*, 2014.

[48] J. Uijlings, K. van de Sande, T. Gevers, and A. Smeulders. Selective Search for Object Recognition. *IJCV*, 2013.

[49] C. Wah, S. Branson, P. Welinder, P. Perona, and S. Belongie. The Caltech-UCSD Birds-200-2011 Dataset. *Technical Report*, 2011.

[50] J. Wang, N. Wang, Y. Jia, J. Li, G. Zeng, H. Zha, and X. Hua. Trinary-Projection Trees for Approximate Nearest Neighbor Search. *TPAMI*, 2013.

[51] J. Wang, J. Yang, K. Yu, F. Lv, T. Huang, and Y. Gong. Locality-Constrained Linear Coding for Image Classification. *CVPR*, 2010.

[52] Z. Wang, J. Feng, and S. Yan. Collaborative Linear Coding for Robust Image Classification. *IJCV*, 2014.

[53] J. Xiao, J. Hays, K. Ehinger, A. Oliva, and A. Torralba. Sun Database: Large-scale Scene Recognition from Abbey to Zoo. *CVPR*, 2010.

[54] L. Xie, Q. Tian, J. Wang, and B. Zhang. Image Classification with Max-SIFT Descriptors. *ICASSP*, 2015.

[55] L. Xie, Q. Tian, M. Wang, and B. Zhang. Spatial Pooling of Heterogeneous Features for Image Classification. *TIP*, 2014.

[56] L. Xie, Q. Tian, and B. Zhang. Feature Normalization for Part-based Image Classification. *ICIP*, 2013.

[57] L. Xie, Q. Tian, and B. Zhang. Hierarchical Part Matching for Fine-Grained Visual Categorization. *ICCV*, 2013.

[58] L. Xie, Q. Tian, and B. Zhang. Max-SIFT: Flipping Invariant Descriptors for Web Logo Search. *ICIP*, 2014.

[59] L. Xie, Q. Tian, and B. Zhang. Generalized Regular Spatial Pooling for Image Classification. *ICASSP*, 2015.

[60] L. Xie, Q. Tian, W. Zhou, and B. Zhang. Fast and Accurate Near-Duplicate Scale Web Image Search via Graph Propagation and Search Process Tradeoff. *CVIU*, 2014.

[61] L. Xie, J. Wang, B. Guo, B. Zhang, and Q. Tian. Orientational Pyramid Matching for Recognizing Indoor Scenes. *CVPR*, 2014.

[62] L. Xie, J. Wang, B. Zhang, and Q. Tian. Fine-Grained Image Search. *TMM*, 2015.

[63] J. Yang, K. Yu, Y. Gong, and T. Huang. Linear Spatial Pyramid Matching Using Sparse Coding for Image Classification. *CVPR*, 2009.

[64] Y. Yang and S. Newsam. Bag-of-Visual-Words and Spatial Extensions for Land-Use Classification. *ICAGIS*, 2010.

[65] M. Zeiler and R. Fergus. Visualizing and Understanding Convolutional Networks. *ECCV*, 2014.

[66] N. Zhang, J. Donahue, R. Girshick, and T. Darrell. Part-Based R-CNNs for Fine-Grained Category Detection. *ECCV*, 2014.

[67] S. Zhang, M. Yang, T. Cour, K. Yu, and D. Metaxas. Query Specific Fusion for Image Retrieval. *ECCV*, 2012.

[68] S. Zhang, M. Yang, X. Wang, Y. Lin, and Q. Tian. Semantic-aware Co-indexing for Image Retrieval. *ICCV*, 2013.

[69] T. Zhang, C. Du, and J. Wang. Composite Quantization for Approximate Nearest Neighbor Search. *ICML*, 2014.

[70] L. Zheng, S. Wang, F. He, and Q. Tian. Seeing the Big Picture: Deep Embedding with Contextual Evidences. *arXiv preprint arXiv:1406.0132*, 2014.

[71] L. Zheng, S. Wang, Z. Liu, and Q. Tian. Packing and Padding: Coupled Multi-Index for Accurate Image Retrieval. *CVPR*, 2014.

[72] L. Zheng, S. Wang, and Q. Tian. Lp-Norm IDF for Scalable Image Retrieval. *TIP*, 2014.

[73] W. Zhou, Y. Lu, H. Li, and Q. Tian. Scalar Quantization for Large Scale Image Search. *ACM Multimedia*, 2012.

Social Event Mining in Large Photo Collections

Maia Zaharieva[1,2] Matthias Zeppelzauer[3] Manfred Del Fabro[4] Daniel Schopfhauser[1]

[1]Multimedia Information Systems, University of Vienna, Austria
[2]Interactive Media Systems, Vienna University of Technology, Austria
[3]Creative Media Technologies, St. Pölten Univ. of Applied Sciences, Austria
[4]Distributed Multimedia Systems, Klagenfurt University, Austria

ABSTRACT

A significant part of publicly available photos on the Internet depicts a variety of different social events. In order to organize this steadily growing media content and to make it easily accessible, novel indexing methods are required. Essential research questions in this context concern the efficient detection (clustering), classification, and retrieval of social events in large media collections. In this paper we explore two aspects of social events mining. First, the initial clustering of a given photo collection into single events and, second, the retrieval of relevant social events based on user queries. For both aspects we employ commonly available metadata information, such as user, time, GPS data, and user-generated textual descriptions. Performed evaluations in the context of social event detection demonstrate the strong generalization ability of our approach and the potential of contextual data such as time, user, and location. Experiments with social event retrieval clearly indicate the open challenge of mapping between previously detected event clusters and heterogeneous user queries.

Categories and Subject Descriptors

H.3.1 [**Information Storage and Retrieval**]: Content Analysis and Indexing; H.3.3 [**Information Storage and Retrieval**]: Information Search and Retrieval

General Terms

Algorithms, Experimentation, Performance

Keywords

Event detection; event retrieval; event clustering; MediaEval Benchmark; Flickr

1. INTRODUCTION

A social event is defined as "an event that is organized and attended by people and illustrated by social media content created by people" [21]. Events are strongly varying in type (e.g. concert, exhibition, sport), duration (from less than an hour to several days), and spatial coverage (from a small stage to large festival areas). Since social events are an integral part of everyone's life, with growing simplicity of capturing and sharing media online, a large part of publicly available images, e.g. on Flickr[1] and Instagram[2], depicts such events. This increasing amount of shared media requires for efficient methods for the organization and retrieval of media related to particular social events. As a result, a lot of recent research focuses primarily on the detection and clustering of event-related data. The resulting event clusters provide the foundations for higher-level event analysis such as event retrieval. The retrieval of events from user-specified queries is a complex task, due to the enormous variety of possible social events and search queries. The major challenge is the design of generic and efficient indexing and analysis methods that are not tailored to the characteristics of a specific dataset or user query.

The term event detection is often interchangeably used for two different research tasks: event identification and (more commonly) event clustering. While *event identification* refers to the process of distinguishing between event-related and event-unrelated data, *event clustering* involves the detection of single events in a set of event-related data. In the remaining sections of this paper, by social event detection we refer to social event clustering.

In this paper we address two tasks: the detection (clustering) and the retrieval of social events. For social event detection, we employ commonly available metadata only including user information, capture time, potentially existing GPS data, and user-provided textual descriptions. We consider the task of clustering event-related data as unsupervised data mining problem and propose a multi-stage approach that begins with the most reliable information in the first stages (user, time, and GPS data) and inlcudes less reliable data in subsequent stages (textual descriptions). Additionally, we explore the performance of the employed metadata individually and in combination in order to determine the most reliable and efficient approach for social event detection. In a next step, we employ detected event clusters for social event retrieval. We design a generic approach that is not tailored to the characteristics of a specific user query and that considers all available metadata for retrieval. Additionally, we investigate the potential of supervised learning for event retrieval and apply geo-tagging and query expansion. Performed experiments on different

[1]http://www.flickr.com
[2]http://instagram.com

ICMR'15, June 23–26, 2015, Shanghai, China.

http://dx.doi.org/10.1145/2671188.2749313.

datasets demonstrate the outstanding performance of the proposed approaches and outline open research questions for future work in the context of social event mining.

This paper is organized as follows. Section 2 outlines recent research in social event detection and retrieval. Section 3 presents the proposed approach in detail. Section 5 discusses the performed experiments and achieved results. Eventually, Section 6 concludes the paper and provides an outlook on future work.

2. RELATED WORK

In general, *social event detection* is a data mining task aiming at the identification of all social events in a media collection without any prior knowledge about their amount, type, and characteristics. Existing approaches in the context of social event detection can be divided into supervised and unsupervised methods [17].

Unsupervised approaches usually apply combined similarity measures or a fusion of similarity matrices to cluster media into social events based on user, spatio-temporal information, and keywords [9][11][14][24][28][30]. For example, [9] employ a sequence of agglomerative hierarchical clustering operations to identify groups of images depicting the same social event. Existing approaches differ mainly in the ordering they process each modality and in the employed clustering approach. Some works additionally consider external sources to improve the understanding of user-provided textual descriptions. For example, [10] propose a semantic similarity measure based on WordNet concepts.

Supervised methods for social event detection typically employ machine learning algorithms to learn the properties of a retrieval model for the identification of unknown events using a training set with existing, known social event data [2][13][19][20][29]. For example, [2] cluster Flickr photos using text-, time-, and location-based similarity features. The authors employ ensemble and classification-based similarity learning techniques in combination with an incremental clustering algorithm to predict whether a pair of images belongs to the same event cluster. A crucial limitation of supervised methods concerns the dependence on the training dataset.

Only few approaches additionally explore the visual information to identify content captured at the same venue, e.g. [5][7][13][31]. This is mainly due to the fact, that visual information can be misleading as different events at the same location may have highly similar visual appearance, i.e. *high inter-class visual similarity*, and, at the same time, images captured at the same event may show very different aspects and points-of-view resulting in *high intra-class visual dissimilarity* [31]. Experiments on event clustering have shown that visual information has only limited value on the overall performance and that contextual information is most important for this task.

Social event retrieval is a retrieval task concerning the identification of specific events in a pre-clustered set of events using a user-defined query such as "Find all music events that took place in Amsterdam in 2014". Early approaches for social event retrieval were highly tailored to the characteristics of a specific query and, thus, not applicable in a general context. For example, in [6] queries were manually extended by synonyms. Additionally, the authors employed external services that were manually selected depending on the requested event type in the user-provided query. In [4] the authors incorporate query-specific data sources to extract specific days of a concert tour for music-related queries and stadium names for soccer-related queries. Similarly, [1] determine exact dates and times of soccer matches before processing a soccer-related query. Such tailored systems lack in overall applicability and are not useful for general user-defined queries.

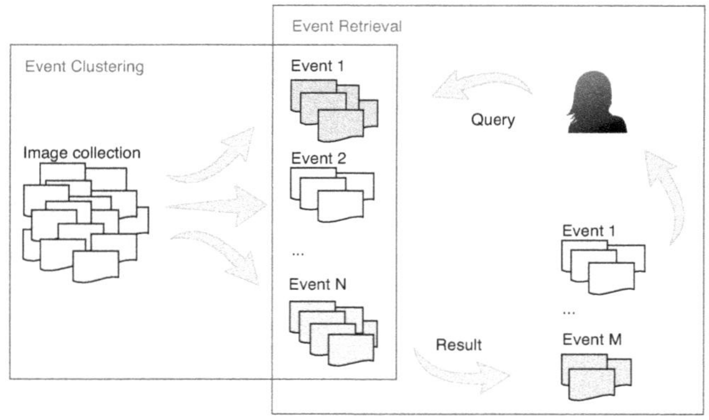

Figure 1: Social event detection (clustering) vs. social event retrieval.

A more general approach for event retrieval is introduced in [31]. The authors propose a step-wise matching approach that subsequently filters and refines the result set for each query by a comprehensive analysis of the available metadata (capture time information, location data, and textual descriptions). The method does not make any assumptions about the dataset and the underlying event types. Since no external data is employed for retrieval, the performance is weaker than that of highly tailored approaches. A general approach that additionally takes external information into account is proposed in [23] and [25]. The authors retrieve Flickr images to build unigram language models of the requested event types and locations in order to enable a more robust matching with the user-provided query. The authors report that the selection of a suitable threshold, which provides the minimum matching score an event has to gain to be retrieved for the given query, is a sensitive part of the algorithm. In contrast to the approach proposed in [25], we build event models from the available data. Additionally, we propose an adaptive threshold for the selection of the result set for each query.

3. APPROACH

We consider event clustering and event retrieval as two independent components that share a common interface in a global social event mining system (see Figure 1). *Social event clustering* aims at the organization of an unorganized media collection into clusters that represent unique social events. Based on this clustering, *social event retrieval* aims at the identification of event clusters relevant to a (user-) provided query.

3.1 Social Event Clustering

We propose an unsupervised, three-stage approach for the clustering of photos into social events using commonly available metadata only. Initially, we assign each image to a sin-

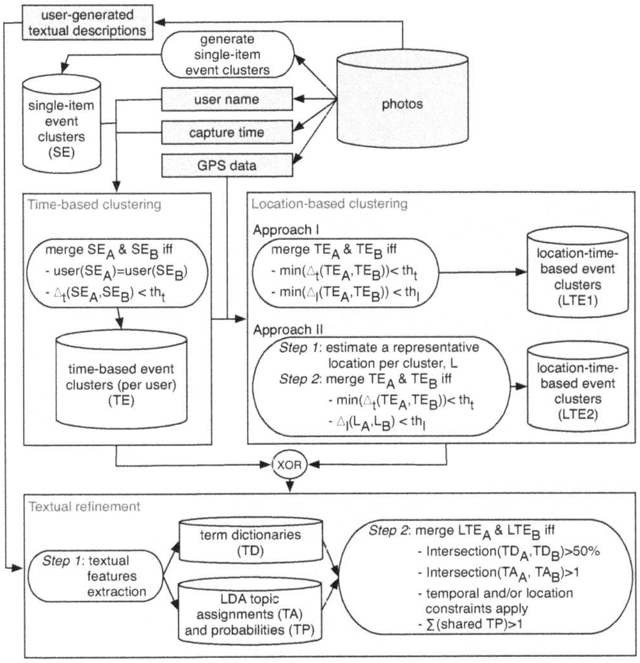

Figure 2: Social event clustering workflow.

gle item event cluster. At each stage we perform merging of previously detected events by considering different aspects of the available image metadata. First, we start with user information and capture time. Next, we additionally account for potentially available location data. Eventually, we integrate user-provided textual descriptions. Figure 2 shows an overview of the proposed social event clustering approach.

In the first stage, *time-based clustering*, we employ an adaptive approach to merge clusters from the initial set of single items clusters. Since a user can only be present at a single event within a given time span, we explore the difference between consecutive images captured by the same user. If the time difference does not exceed a predefined threshold, th_t, the corresponding images (singe item clusters) are merged. This step is repeated iteratively to successively grow clusters until no additional merges are possible.

In the next stage, we consider the same adaptive approach for *location-based clustering* (Approach I in Figure 2), i.e. if the temporal and spatial distances between two clusters are within the predefined thresholds, th_t and th_l respectively, they are merged. Thus, our approach allows detected social events to vary strongly in both their temporal duration and spatial coverage. For example, a music festival may span several days and comprise multiple spatially distributed stages whereas a sport event may last for less than an hour and take place in a well-defined location. We measure the distance between two event clusters by means of the minimum Harvesine distance [27].

An alternative approach for location-based clustering (Approach II) considers a predefined radius for the merging of event clusters. First, we determine a representative location for each time-based event cluster by calculating the sum of distances for each item to all other items in the same cluster. The distance calculation is based on the spherical law of cosines. Items without location information are omitted. The location of the item having the minimum distance to all other items using the spherical law of cosines is selected as representative location. Next, the DBSCAN algorithm [8] is employed to merge clusters that have representative locations within the predefined radius th_l. Clusters that contain items without location information only and, thus, have no representative location, are not merged with other clusters in this stage.

The final stage of the proposed social event clustering employs *textual refinement*. Textual descriptions provide useful clues for the association of items that belong to the same event, especially in the case of missing information about location and capture time. The input to the textual refinement step is a time- or location-based clustering which usually represents an over-segmentation. During the textual refinement clusters with similar textual descriptions or topics are merged. We compute a term dictionary for each cluster from the textual descriptions of its members. The term dictionary contains all terms that appear at least 2 times in the textual descriptions. Term dictionaries of different clusters are compared by a variant of the Jaccard index. The similarity sim_{TD} between two dictionaries X and Y is computed as:

$$sim_{TD} = \frac{1}{2}\left(\frac{|X \cap Y|}{|X|} + \frac{|X \cap Y|}{|Y|}\right),$$

which better estimates the similarity than the Jaccard index when the amount of textual information for two clusters (and, thus, the sizes of the dictionaries) strongly differs, i.e. similarity scores for items with few textual descriptions are promoted.

As a complementary feature to the term dictionaries, we extract global topics from all photos in the employed data set using Latent Dirichlet Allocation (LDA) [3] and generate a list of topics (together with their probabilities) for each cluster. Topics which are associated with too many different clusters are removed. Therefore, we compute the distribution d of the topic occurrences over all clusters and remove topics with occurrence frequency above $\mu(d)+2\sigma(d)$. For the similarity comparisons between two clusters we compute the number of intersecting topics and the sum of probabilities of all shared topic.

Textual refinement is an iterative process. We start with a randomly chosen cluster and compare it to all other clusters that fulfill the temporal and (if available) spatial constraints of the previous processing steps. The current cluster is merged with all candidate clusters that fulfill one of the following constraints: (i) the intersection of the term dictionaries sim_{TD} exceeds 50%, (ii) the two clusters share more than one topic, or (iii) the sum of shared topic probabilities is larger than one. When two clusters are merged we also merge their textual features as well as their temporal and spatial information. This iterative merging and updating scheme assures that clusters can grow successively. The refinement terminates when each cluster has been considered once for merging.

3.2 Social Event Retrieval

Figure 3 shows an overview of the proposed method for social event retrieval. The input to the system is a set of photos, which is already clustered into social events, and a textual query that provides thematic constraints and option-

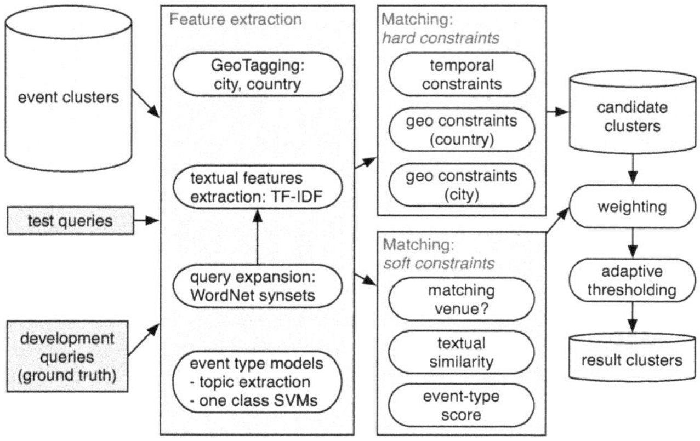

Figure 3: Social event retrieval workflow.

Table 1: Datasets characteristics.

	SED2013		SED2014	
	Train	Test	Train	Test
# photos	306,159	131.211	362,578	110,541
# unique users	4,107	2,581	4,345	2,310
Events:				
# events	14,882	6,287	17,834	6,635
% events with GPS	48.09%	47.77%	41.30%	37.35%
# photos per event:				
μ	20.57	20.87	20.33	16.66
σ	45.51	50.59	45.73	36.54
Employed metadata:				
username	100.00%	100.00%	100.00%	100.00%
capture time	100.00%	100.00%	100.00%	100.00%
GPS data	45.88%	46.07%	20.12%	21.69%
title	97.48%	97.91%	97.58%	97.30%
description	37.48%	38.49%	38.95%	59.74%
tags	94.94%	96.05%	95.09%	95.91%

ally temporal and geographical restrictions. For each event cluster we apply geo-tagging to identify the city and the country of the underlying event. For this purpose we employ the GPS coordinates provided with the event's photos and GeoNames[3] to determine the city and its country. For events with non-geotagged photos, we try to infer city and country from the user-provided textual descriptions. For each event we apply majority voting in order to determine the most probable city and country.

We build a TF-IDF representation for each event cluster from the textual descriptions of its member photos. TF-IDF vectors represent the thematic context of an event. Additionally, we train models for different event types (e.g. music events) using the ground truth provided with the development queries. We extract LDA topics for all photos and generate topic affiliation vectors for each photo. Following, one-class support vector machines (SVMs) [26] are trained for the event types represented by the development queries.

The matching of event clusters is performed in two steps. First, we apply hard constraints and filter the set of all events by the city (if available) and the country provided in the query. Next, from the remaining events we remove those that do not fulfill the temporal constraints that may optionally be provided in the query. This is straight forward as each photo of an event has an associated capture time.

For the remaining candidate events, a weighting based on soft constraints is applied which results in a score for each candidate. The score is a weighted combination of four components: First, the query itself is mapped to a TF-IDF vector. Prior to the mapping we optionally extend the query by Wordnet synsets[4]. We compare the query's TF-IDF representation to those of the candidate events using cosine similarity. The result is a similarity score sim_{TFIDF}. Second, the similarity for each candidate event to the query's event type is determined (if a trained one-class SVM model for the event type exists) resulting in a second score sim_{type}. Third, if the query contains an explicit venue name, we search for the venue in the user-provided textual description for each photo of all events. If the venue can be found, we provide a reward w_{venue} for this event. Fourth, if the query contains a named entity (e.g. a band name or the name of a person) we provide an additional reward w_{entity} if the entity is found in an event's metadata. The final score s for an event is obtained by a linear combination of all scores and weights:

$$s = A \cdot sim_{TFIDF} + B \cdot sim_{type} + w_{venue} + w_{entity},$$

where A and B determine the influence of the scores for the TF-IDF vectors and the event models. If there is no pre-trained model for an event type, B equals 0.

The number of relevant events for different queries may vary considerably. In order to avoid a constant threshold we define the threshold implicitly as a percentage of the highest score obtained for a given query, i.e. the threshold is a fixed percentage of the maximum score. This results in an adaptive threshold for each query. We finally return all candidate events with an overall score above the adaptive threshold.

4. DATASETS

For our experiments we employ publicly available data from the Social Event Detection (SED) task of the MediaEval Benchmark Initiative[5] from 2013 [21][22] and 2014 [15]. The datasets are divided into training and test subsets. Although our approach for social event detection does not require for any training we report results on each subset separately in order to allow for comparison with related works in this context. Both datasets contain images collected from Flickr and the corresponding metadata such as user information, capture and upload times, GPS data, and user-provided textual descriptions (title, description, tags). Overall, the datasets show similar characteristics except for the availability of GPS data (46% in SED2013 vs. 20% in SED2014, see Table 1 for some details). A crucial aspect of the datasets are the underlying events which are highly heterogeneous with respect to the event type, the corresponding temporal duration and spatial coverage, and the number of available images per event. For example the "Exit" music festival spans several stages and lasts for several days and is captured by over 1000 images. On the opposite, several small concerts have a limited duration of a few hours and were captured (and shared) by single users only.

[3] http://www.geonames.org/
[4] http://wordnet.princeton.edu
[5] http://www.multimediaeval.org

Table 2: **Evaluation results for event clustering using user and capture time information.**

	SED2013				SED2014			
	Train		Test		Train		Test	
th_t	F1	NMI	F1	NMI	F1	NMI	F1	NMI
3	85.60	97.00	84.50	96.30	85.29	96.99	90.27	97.81
6	86.28	97.20	85.39	96.61	86.08	97.23	90.82	97.98
12	87.54	97.48	87.03	97.02	88.34	97.69	91.64	98.19
24	**90.77**	**98.14**	90.97	97.94	**90.98**	**98.22**	**93.86**	**98.66**
48	90.33	98.05	**91.11**	**97.97**	90.16	98.04	92.56	98.38

While both datasets, SED2013 and SED2014, allow for the evaluation and comparison of approaches for social event clustering, event retrieval is evaluated using the SED 2014 training subset only. For this subset the organizers provide ground truth information for 8 development and 10 test queries [16]. Each user query may provide information about the location of the event (city, country, venue), its type (e.g. sport event or concert), and potential entities involved (e.g. a music band). The queries vary strongly in the precision and ambiguity of their specification, e.g. *Find all music events with the band Metallica* vs. *Find all community events that took place in London.*

5. EVALUATION RESULTS

In this section we present the results of the performed evaluation on event clustering and event retrieval. Results on social event clustering are reported in terms of F1-score ($F1$) representing the harmonic mean between recall and precision and normalized mutual information (NMI) measuring the goodness of clustering of retrieved events. Results on social event retrieval are detailed by means of (averaged) recall, precision, and F1-scores for the development and test queries. For the test queries we additionally report aggregated measures for queries with and without location constraints.

5.1 Social Event Clustering

In our first experiment we investigate the potential of employing user and capture time information only. We explore different settings for the temporal threshold, $th_t = \{3h, 6h, 12h, 24h, 48h\}$, describing the temporal distance between two consecutive photos captured by the same user. Results show that the proposed approach generalizes well since there are only minor differences in the performances of the employed datasets (see Table 2). Additionally, achieved results are highly competitive given the fact that in this experiment we only rely on user and capture time information. Overall, best performances (F1-scores of ~91% and ~94% for the SED2013 and for the SED2014 respectively) are achieved for $th_t = 24$ hours implying that users tend to visit a single social event within a day.

Since the results of the time-based clustering are pure (i.e. of high precision) but potentially highly oversegmented event clusters, in a next step we explore the potential of considering available location information. We evaluate the top three temporal thresholds, $th_t = \{12h, 24h, 48h\}$, in a combination with three spatial thresholds, $th_l = \{500m, 1km, 5km\}$. Both proposed approaches slightly improve the results achieved by the time-based clustering (see Table 3 and Table 4). The effect of spatial refinement depends on

Table 3: **Evaluation results for event clustering using user, capture time, and location information (Approach I).**

		SED2013				SED2014			
		Train		Test		Train		Test	
th_t	th_l	F1	NMI	F1	NMI	F1	NMI	F1	NMI
12	500	88.65	97.73	88.27	97.38	89.21	97.89	91.88	98.24
	1000	88.75	97.75	88.30	97.39	89.27	97.91	91.89	98.24
	5000	88.67	97.74	88.33	97.40	89.20	97.89	91.88	98.24
24	500	91.76	98.35	92.17	98.26	91.78	98.40	94.05	98.71
	1000	**91.78**	**98.35**	92.17	98.26	**91.78**	**98.40**	**94.07**	**98.72**
	5000	91.51	98.28	92.20	98.27	91.47	98.32	93.96	98.69
48	500	91.24	98.24	**92.25**	**98.28**	90.88	98.21	92.61	98.39
	1000	91.22	98.24	92.24	98.28	90.85	98.20	92.63	98.40
	5000	90.69	98.10	92.13	98.25	90.24	98.05	92.44	98.35

Table 4: **Evaluation results for event clustering using user, capture time, and location information (Approach II).**

		SED2013				SED2014			
		Train		Test		Train		Test	
th_t	th_l	F1	NMI	F1	NMI	F1	NMI	F1	NMI
12	500	88.19	97.64	87.91	97.28	88.85	97.81	91.83	98.23
	1000	88.16	97.64	87.97	97.30	88.81	97.81	91.83	98.23
	5000	88.11	97.62	87.90	97.28	88.74	97,79	91.80	98.22
24	500	**91.49**	**98.30**	91.94	98.19	**91.59**	**98.36**	**94.04**	**98.71**
	1000	91.44	98.28	91.98	98.21	91.51	98.34	94.01	98.70
	5000	91.36	98.26	91.91	98.19	91.32	98.30	93.92	98.68
48	500	91.07	98.21	92.19	98.26	90.77	98.19	92.70	98.42
	1000	90.89	98.17	**92.22**	**98.27**	90.57	98.14	92.66	98.41
	5000	90.63	98.10	92.00	98.22	90.20	98.05	92.55	98.39

the availability of location information (GPS data). The SED2013 dataset contains more geo-tagged content than the SED2014 dataset (46% vs. 20%). Our experiments reflect this observation. For the SED2013 dataset both location-based clustering approaches improve the performance metrics slightly more (F1 of +1.07% in average) than for the SED2014 dataset (F1 of +0.5% in average). In all experiments the location-based clustering shows low dependency on the employed spatial threshold. We assume that this is due to the fact that, usually, large social events are spatially well-separated from each other in order to prevent any potential disturbance between them. For example, two music concerts do not take place next door to each other as this may result in mutual sound interaction. This might not be the case for smaller events such as art exhibitions or show acts. Nevertheless, the results indicate that within the employed datasets, the underlying events are well-separated (distance between the concurrent events is larger than $1km$ as identified by Approach I) and well-localized (event radius of $500m$ as identified by Approach II). Overall, the two investigated location-based clustering approaches do not show any significant differences in the achieved results. Hence, we employ only Approach I in the following experiments focusing on the potentials of textual refinement.

The results achieved by the proposed textual refinement step are presented in Table 5. We evaluate the three top performing temporal thresholds, $th_t = \{12h, 24h, 48h\}$, at a spatial threshold of $th_l = 500m$. We compare the performances for two input clusterings: (i) the initial clustering based on time and user information only (T) and (ii) the spatially refined clustering (TL) generated by Approach I. For all experiments a number of 3000 latent topics is used as

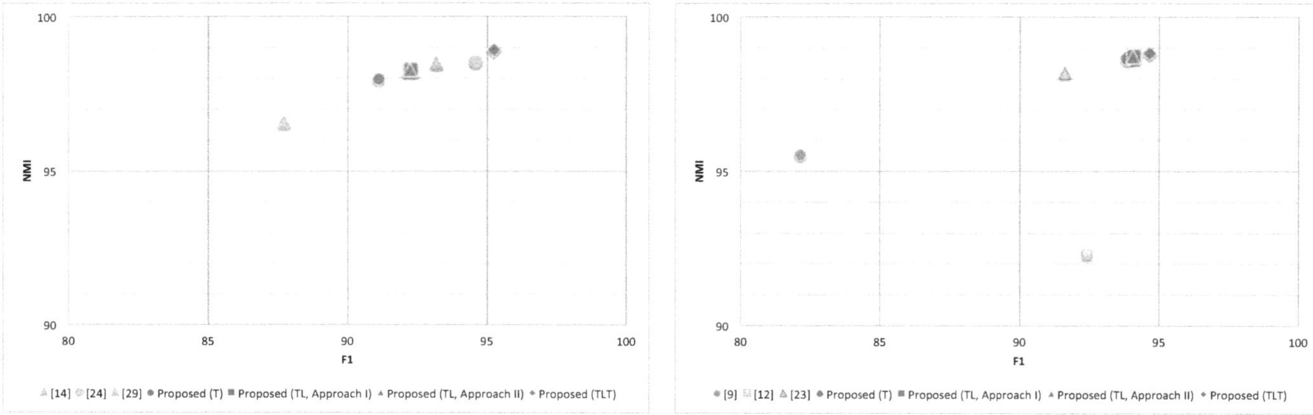

(a) SED2013 Test

(b) SED2014 Test

Figure 4: Comparison with the best results achieved on the employed datasets by competing methods. ***T*** **indicates the proposed time-based clustering,** ***TL*** **the corresponding (time-)location-based clustering approaches, and** ***TLT*** **the best performing textual refinement employing both time- and location-based clustering.**

Table 5: Evaluation results for event clustering using user, capture time, location, and textual information. Input to the textual refinement is either time-based clustering "T" or time and location-based clustering (Approach I) "TL".

		SED2013				SED2014			
		Train		Test		Train		Test	
th_t	Input	F1	NMI	F1	NMI	F1	NMI	F1	NMI
12	T	88.71	97.76	89.74	97.76	90.56	98.18	92.10	98.30
24	T	92.07	98.41	94.67	98.81	93.51	98.72	94.47	98.80
48	T	92.74	98.55	94.91	98.87	92.24	98.48	93.14	98.52
12	TL	89.31	97.89	90.82	98.00	91.01	98.27	92.27	98.33
24	TL	92.51	98.50	95.11	98.91	**93.56**	**98.73**	**94.65**	**98.84**
48	TL	**92.85**	**98.57**	**95.23**	**98.93**	92.06	98.44	93.07	98.50

a basis for the computation of topic affiliation vectors and topic probabilities.

The textual refinement improves the clustering in terms of F1-score and NMI for all experiments we performed. The strongest improvement is obtained for the SED2013 test set (+4.12% in terms of F1 in comparison to the time-based clustering) and (+2.98% in terms of F1 in comparison to the location-based clustering). The overall best clustering performance obtained is an F1 of 95.23% and 94.65% for the SED2013 and SED2014 test datasets, respectively. NMI values are improved as well but only slightly as they are already very high after the initial clustering.

Eventually, there is a small portion of clusters, which cannot be merged or are merged incorrectly. A closer investigation of these cases reveals that, usually, incorrect merging during textual refinement occurs due to missing or ambiguous descriptions in the user-provided metadata. In particular event clusters with only little textual description (e.g. only one or two words) are merged incorrectly, especially when the words are rather general, such as "concert" and "live". Nevertheless, the rate of correctly merged clusters in our textual refinement step lies between 70% and 80%.

Figure 4 puts the achieved performance in relation to the best results reported by competing approaches on the employed datasets. For the SED2013 we achieve highly competitive results. Our complete social event detection system considering all employed metadata (user and capture time information, sparsely available GPS data, and user-provided textual descriptions) outperforms all available top results on this dataset [14][24][29]. In this context, it must be noted that [29] is a supervised approach, which employs the training dataset to learn tuning parameters. Hence, this approach has probably lower general applicability for different datasets. For the SED2014 test dataset any single stage of our social event detection approach (time-, location-, and text-based clustering) clearly outperforms reported top results [9][12][23]. The achieved results demonstrate the generalization ability of the approach and the strong potential of basic metadata such as location and capture time. The consideration of user-provided textual descriptions gains in importance in the presence of incomplete location information.

5.2 Social Event Retrieval

In order to provide a baseline for the comparison of different methods, we first evaluate a completely unsupervised variant of our approach for social event retrieval. Table 6 summarizes the achieved results in the first row. We observe that the performance measures are lower than those of social event detection in the previous section, which is due to the higher complexity of the event retrieval task. Our baseline method achieves an F1 of 23.72% on the development queries. For the test queries, the averaged F1 over all queries increases to 33.75%. The higher performance on the test set shows that our method has no bias towards the development queries and generalizes well to the test queries.

Next, we additionally consider the optional query expansion step to enrich the provided queries by Wordnet synsets. Surprisingly, this yields a drop in the performance in comparison to the baseline (see the second row in Table 6). A closer look at the derived synsets shows that aside from useful synonyms, misleading terms are contained as well. For the query type "conference", for example, the synset con-

Table 6: Event retrieval results for development queries (DQs) and test queries (TQs). Results for text queries are split into location-based and location-invariant queries. We evaluate unsupervised vs. supervised retrieval, as well as query expansion (QExp).

	Dev. Queries (DQs)			Test Queries (TQs)			Location-based TQs			Location-invariant TQs		
Approach	R	P	F1	R	P	F1	R	P	F1	R	P	F1
No QExp. + unsupervised	17.90	52.85	23.72	37.76	51.86	33.75	33.02	43.99	30.70	**51.98**	**75.47**	**42.91**
With QExp. + unsupervised	30.62	27.84	17.02	33.12	24.94	22.63	42.84	33.16	30.00	3.9	2.8	5.1
No QExp. + supervised	**36.14**	**65.53**	**41.52**	**37.92**	**59.10**	**35.22**	**33.23**	**53.98**	**32.92**	**51.98**	74.49	42.14

tains among others "session" and "seminar" but also "football" and "basketball" is returned by Wordnet. As a result, the misleading terms lead to wrong matches. This influences in particular the location-invariant queries, which are more challenging to process as the possible search space is the entire dataset due to the missing location constraints.

As a second extension of our approach we employ event type models learned from the dataset. We model each event type present in the development queries by a one-class SVM, which is trained from the available ground truth of the development queries. For those test queries for which an event type model exists, we apply the matching score with the respective model as an additional weight. Results are summarized in the last row in Table 6. For the supervised approach only the results of the test queries are representative. The usage of event type models increases the overall performance to an F1 of 35.22%. The event type models improve in particular the precision (from 51.86% to 59.10% in comparison to the baseline). Recall remains approximately at the same level. These results show that event type models are a useful extension for social events retrieval.

Finally, we investigate the weighting factors that balance the score function introduced in Section 3.2. The most important parameter is A, which weights the similarity score of the TF-IDF vectors. We observe that a larger score tends to improve the achieved results (values from 1 to 4 have been investigated). For event type models a weighting factor between 0.5 and 1 has shown to provide best results. The rewards for venue w_{venue} and entity w_{entity} were fixed at 0.5. We varied the percentage N for the adaptive threshold from 0.3 to 0.95. The threshold trades off recall vs. precision and, thus, it is an important design parameter. With an increasing threshold, the precision increases at the cost of recall. The best results in terms of F1 score were obtained with $N = 0.50$.

There is currently only one related approach which allows for an objective comparison with our work. In contrast to our approach, which trains its models only from data available in the dataset, the authors of [23] make an extensive use of external data from Flickr to build models for particular event types and apply a location model for geotagging [18]. The authors obtain an overall F1 of 46.04% on the test queries, which shows that the incorporation of external data is of high relevance for the task of event retrieval. The approach of [23] provides a baseline for event retrieval using external models. In contrast, our method provides a first baseline for event retrieval without the use of external models.

6. CONCLUSION AND DISCUSSION

The mining of social event data gains in importance with the increasing amount of publicly available data depicting social events. In general, social event mining passes three well-defined stages. The first stage, *the identification of social events*, considers the differentiation between event-related and event-unrelated data. This area is still an open research issue as the public information on social events is sparse and highly distributed over different online platforms.

The second stage, *social event detection*, addresses the organization of event-related data into distinct groups according to the event they represent. This research area has been subject to very active research in recent years investigating the performance of supervised vs. unsupervised approaches, the potentials of available metadata, the combination of visual and textual information, and the employment of external sources. Achieved results of our approach show that for data originating from the same source (e.g. Flickr) the performance based on available metadata is outstanding. Our experiments additionally show that the proposed approach considering user, capture time, and location information achieves already strongly competitive results and generalize well for different datasets. Since GPS information is not always available, text-based refinement can further improve the overall performance. In our experiments the textually improved clustering outperforms all competing approaches. While social event detection in the context of a single data provider yields high performance and achieves results that can be reliably employed for further analysis, social event detection across different sharing platforms and heterogeneous media is still barely explored and will be subject to further research.

The final stage, *social event retrieval*, aims at the identification of previously identified event clusters that match an arbitrary user-provided textual query. As a result, the complexity and variety of possible user queries must be considered in addition to the complexity and variety of social data. Current top results achieved in this context (F1 scores between 40% and 45%) indicate the challenge of this task. Performed experiments and analyses show that the performance that can be obtained from available metadata alone is limited. The incorporation of external data is, thus, of high relevance to improve the understanding of user-provided queries. In all three stages, it is crucial for the research community to have publicly available, real-world, benchmark datasets that facilitate the development of new approaches and the objective comparison with existing methods.

Acknowledgments

This work has been partly funded by the Vienna Science and Technology Fund (WWTF) through project ICT12-010 and the Carinthian Economic Promotion Fund (KWF) under grant KWF-20214/22573/33955.

7. REFERENCES

[1] B.-K. Bao, W. Min, K. Lu, and C. Xu. Social event detection with robust high-order co-clustering. In *ACM Int. Conf. on Multimedia Retrieval*, pages 135–142, 2013.

[2] H. Becker, M. Naaman, and L. Gravano. Learning similarity metrics for event identification in social media. In *ACM Int. Conf. on Web Search and Data Mining*, pages 291–300, 2010.

[3] D. M. Blei, A. Y. Ng, and M. I. Jordan. Latent dirichlet allocation. *Journal of Machine Learning Research*, 3:993–1022, 2003.

[4] M. Brenner and E. Izquierdo. Social event detection and retrieval in collaborative photo collections. In *ACM Int. Conf. on Multimedia Retrieval*, 2012.

[5] M. Brenner and E. Izquierdo. Multimodal detection, retrieval and classification of social events in web photo collections. In *ICMR Workshop on Social Events in Web Multimedia*, pages 5–10, 2014.

[6] M.-S. Dao, G. Boato, F. G. De Natale, and T.-V. Nguyen. Jointly exploiting visual and non-visual information for event-related social media retrieval. In *ACM Int. Conf. on Multimedia Retrieval*, pages 159–166, 2013.

[7] S. Denman, D. Dean, C. Fookes, and S. Sridharan. SAIVT-ADMRG @ MediaEval 2014 Social Event Detection. In *MediaEval Multimedia Benchmark Workshop*. CEUR-WS.org, 2014.

[8] M. Ester, H. P. Kriegel, J. Sander, and X. Xu. A Density-Based Algorithm for Discovering Clusters in Large Spatial Databases with Noise. In *Int. Conf. on Knowledge Discovery and Data Mining*, pages 226–231, 1996.

[9] C. Guinaudeau, A. Laurent, and H. Bredin. LIMSI @ mediaeval SED 2014. In *MediaEval Multimedia Benchmark Workshop*, 2014.

[10] I. Gupta, K. Gautam, and K. Chandramouli. Vit@mediaeval 2013 social event detection task: Semantic structuring of complementary information for clustering events. In *MediaEval Multimedia Benchmark Workshop*, 2013.

[11] D. Manchon-Vizuete, I. Gris-Sarabia, and X. Giro-i Nieto. Photo clustering of social events by extending phototoc to a rich context. In *ICMR Workshop on Social Events in Web Multimedia*, pages 11–18, 2014.

[12] D. Manchon-Vizuete, I. Gris-Sarabia, and X. Giró-i Nieto. UPC at MediaEval 2014 Social Event Detection Task. In *MediaEval Benchmark Workshop*, 2014.

[13] T.-V. Nguyen, M.-S. Dao, R. Mattivi, and F. De Natale. Event detection from social media: User-centric parallel split-n-merge and composite kernel. In *ICMR Workshop on Social Events in Web Multimedia*, pages 19–26, 2014.

[14] T.-V. Nguyen, M.-S. Dao, R. Mattivi, E. Sansone, F. G. De Natale, and G. Boato. Event clustering and classification from social media: Watershed-based and kernel methods. In *MediaEval Multimedia Benchmark Workshop*, 2013.

[15] G. Petkos, S. Papadopoulos, V. Mezaris, and Y. Kompatsiaris. Social event detection at MediaEval 2014: Challenges, datasets, and evaluation. In *MediaEval Multimedia Benchmark Workshop*, 2014.

[16] G. Petkos, S. Papadopoulos, V. Mezaris, and Y. Kompatsiaris. Social event detection at MediaEval 2014: Challenges, datasets, and evaluation. In *MediaEval Multimedia Benchmark Workshop*, 2014.

[17] G. Petkos, S. Papadopoulos, V. Mezaris, R. Troncy, P. Cimiano, T. Reuter, and Y. Kompatsiaris. Social event detection at MediaEval: a three-year retrospect of tasks and results. In *ICMR Workshop on Social Events in Web Multimedia*, pages 27–34, 2014.

[18] A. Popescu. CEA LIST's participation at MediaEval 2013 Placing Task. In *MediaEval Multimedia Benchmark Workshop*, 2013.

[19] F. Psallidas, H. Becker, M. Naaman, and L. Gravano. Effective event identification in social media. *IEEE Data Engineering Bulletin Issues*, 36(3):42–50, 2013.

[20] T. Reuter and P. Cimiano. Event-based classification of social media streams. In *ACM Int. Conf. on Multimedia Retrieval*, pages 22:1–22:8, 2012.

[21] T. Reuter, S. Papadopoulos, V. Mezaris, and P. Cimiano. ReSEED: Social Event dEtection Dataset. In *ACM Multimedia Systems Conf.*, pages 35–40, 2014.

[22] T. Reuter, S. Papadopoulos, G. Petkos, V. Mezaris, Y. Kompatsiaris, P. Cimiano, C. de Vries, and S. Geva. Social event detection at MediaEval 2013: Challenges, datasets, and evaluation. In *MediaEval Multimedia Benchmark Workshop*, 2013.

[23] M. Riga, G. Petkos, S. Papadopoulos, E. Schinas, and Y. Kompatsiaris. CERTH @ MediaEval 2014 Social Event Detection Task. In *MediaEval Multimedia Benchmark Workshop*, 2014.

[24] S. Samangooei, J. Hare, D. Dupplaw, M. Niranjan, N. Gibbins, P. H. Lewis, J. Davies, N. Jain, and J. Preston. Social event detection via sparse multi-modal feature selection and incremental density based clustering. In *MediaEval Multimedia Benchmark Workshop*, 2013.

[25] E. Schinas, G. Petkos, S. Papadopoulos, and Y. Kompatsiaris. CERTH @ MediaEval 2012 Social Event Detection Task. In *MediaEval Multimedia Benchmark Workshop*, 2012.

[26] B. Schölkopf, R. C. Williamson, A. J. Smola, J. Shawe-Taylor, and J. C. Platt. Support vector method for novelty detection. *Neural Information Processing Systems*, 12:582–588, 1999.

[27] R. W. Sinnott. Virtues of the haversine. *Sky and Telescope*, 68(2):159, 1984.

[28] T. Sutanto and R. Nayak. The ranking based constrained document clustering method and its application to social event detection. In *Database Systems for Advanced Applications*, pages 47–60, 2014.

[29] M. Wistuba and L. Schmidt-Thieme. Supervised clustering of social media streams. In *MediaEval Multimedia Benchmark Workshop*, 2013.

[30] M. Zaharieva, D. Schopfhauser, M. Del Fabro, and M. Zeppelzauer. Clustering and retrieval of social events in flickr. In *MediaEval Multimedia Benchmark Workshop*, 2014.

[31] M. Zaharieva, M. Zeppelzauer, and C. Breiteneder. Automated social event detection in large photo collections. In *ACM Int. Conf. on Multimedia Retrieval*, pages 167–174, 2013.

Unified YouTube Video Recommendation via Cross-network Collaboration

Ming Yan[1,2], Jitao Sang[1,2], Changsheng Xu[1,2]
[1]National Lab of Pattern Recognition, Institute of Automation, CAS, Beijing 100190, China
[2]China-Singapore Institute of Digital Media, Singapore, 117867, Singapore
{ming.yan, jtsang, csxu}@nlpr.ia.ac.cn

ABSTRACT

The ever growing number of videos on YouTube makes recommendation an important way to help users explore interesting videos. Similar to general recommender systems, YouTube video recommendation suffers from typical problems like new user, cold-start, data sparsity, etc. In this paper, we propose a unified YouTube video recommendation solution via cross-network collaboration: users' auxiliary information on Twitter are exploited to address the typical problems in single network-based recommendation solutions. The proposed two-stage solution first transfers user preferences from auxiliary network by learning cross-network behavior correlations, and then integrates the transferred preferences with the observed behaviors on target network in an adaptive fashion. Experimental results show that the proposed cross-network collaborative solution achieves superior performance not only in term of accuracy, but also in improving the diversity and novelty of the recommended videos.

Categories and Subject Descriptors

H.3.5 [**Online Information Services**]: Web-based services

General Terms

Theory

Keywords

YouTube video recommendation; cross-network collaboration; user modeling

1. INTRODUCTION

With the emergence and popularity of social media, people now usually engage in disparate Online Social Networks (OSNs) simultaneously for different purposes [1]. For example, the same individual may communicate with his/her friends on Facebook, follow real-time hot events on Twitter, subscribe and watch videos on YouTube, share and discuss favorite restaurants on Yelp, etc. These *cross-network* activities together record people's integral online footprints and reflect their demographics as well as interests from different perspectives.

Typical social media services, however, are usually conducted on one OSN. For example, the video recommendation service on YouTube, has been one of the most important ways to lead users to their interested videos from the huge repository [2]. The limitation of single network-based solutions is that, the available user data on one OSN are usually not sufficient to understand user interests and capture the ever-changing user preferences. The notorious cold-start and sparsity issues have significantly hindered accurate user modeling and practical personalized social media services [3]. Therefore, our work is motivated to exploit the scattered user data in multiple OSNs towards improved personalized services on the target OSN. In this paper, we aim to leverage users' rich cross-network activity data to help estimate their video preferences on YouTube, and design a unified video recommendation solution.

The unified YouTube video recommendation solution is expected to address the following three problems: (1) *New user.* When a user newly registers to YouTube and starts using the recommender, the system has no knowledge of the user's interactions on the videos. In literatures, new users are either modeled using the limited registration information [4] or treated as the average users with recommendation of the most popular items [5]. (2) *Cold-start.* This is related to situations in which the recommender is unable to provide accurate recommendations due to an initial lack of user preferences. We refer to the users with few historical behavior records as *light user* [1]. Current solutions to facilitate the light users include relying on their content information (e.g., demographics and tagging) and resorting to a content-based recommendation solution [6, 7], or exploiting the available social relations as regularization to predict user preferences and warm up the recommender [8]. (3) *Sparsity.* In typical recommender systems, most users have no chance to browse or rate most items and hence the user-item interaction matrix is very sparse. This is especially the case in systems with a very high item-to-user ratio, e.g., YouTube, which has hosted over 2 billion videos. Efforts have been taken to alleviate the sparsity problem by filling the missing user-item entries with default values [9], utilizing latent factor models and projecting the users and items to a low-dimension space to capture the salient structure [10],

[1] Conversely, the users with a lot of behavior records are referred to as *heavy user*.

ICMR'15, June 23–26, 2015, Shanghai, China.

http://dx.doi.org/10.1145/2671188.2749344.

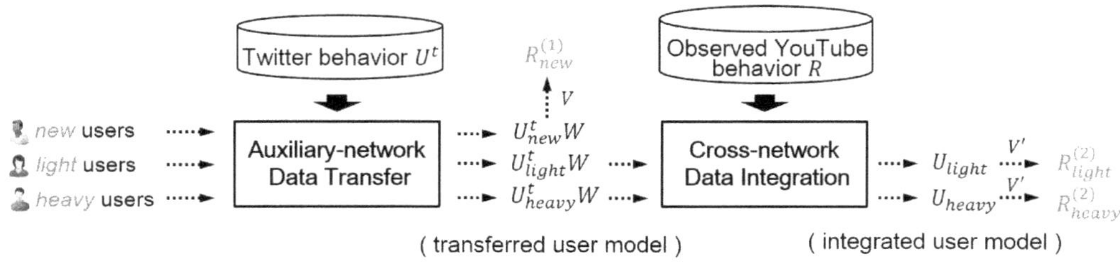

Figure 1: The proposed solution framework.

or discovering the high-order correlations between users by means of spread or iterative models [11].

New user, *cold-start*, and *sparsity* have been the most challenging problems in the field of recommender systems. Although received extensive attentions in the past decades, these problems still remain open. While the existing work propose to deal with one or two of the problems, a unified solution framework addressing all the three problems is unexplored. Moreover, most of the current efforts are devoted to designing advanced models to better exploit the limited and possibly unpromising data within the target OSN [2], but largely ignore the abundant user data available outside on the auxiliary OSNs. Recent practices on big data [12] have also suggested that "more data beats complex models". Therefore, in this work, we attempt to leverage more user data from Twitter, introduce a simple solution framework to simultaneously address all the mentioned problems, and benefit three types of typical YouTube users. Specifically, for *new users*, we estimate their video preferences on YouTube by analyzing the tweeting activities collected on Twitter, based on which an initial recommendation list is generated; for *light users*, we bootstrap the recommender by integrating the auxiliary information transferred from Twitter and the available information on YouTube; for *heavy users*, their recommendation is benefitted as a result of the reduced sparsity. The auxiliary information contributes to the correlation calculation between users.

The challenge lies in two-fold. (1) User data on different OSNs are heterogenous. There exist no explicit correlations between these cross-network user data. We cannot directly utilize the user tweeting data collected from Twitter to estimate the YouTube video preference. (2) For light and heavy users, the estimated preferences from Twitter and the observed behaviors on YouTube may contradict each other. It is critical to align the two potentially contradictory user models, and balance the contribution of either model in the final recommendation. To address the above challenges, as illustrated in Fig. 1, the proposed solution framework consists of two stages, i.e., auxiliary-network data transfer, and cross-network data integration. At the first stage, the correlations between the auxiliary-network and target-network behaviors are embedded in a transfer matrix, by which the users' tweeting activities on Twitter can be mapped to a latent user space on YouTube. With the derived transfer matrix, we can estimate a user's video preferences given his/her tweeting history. For new users, the recommender is ready to exploit the transferred video preferences to generate recommendations. At the second stage, viewing the transferred preference as a priori, we introduce a regularization-based formulation to integrate the two sources of user data. Moreover, a weighting matrix is added to adapt their contributions according to the amount of available YouTube data. In this way, the obtained user models for the light and heavy users consider both the Twitter tweeting activities and historical interactions with YouTube videos. A straightforward recommender can be designed to utilize the user model for recommendation.

We summarize the contributions of this work as follows:

1. We introduce a novel personalized recommendation solution by leveraging cross-network data. This is consistent with users' multi-OSN engagement phenomenon and entails user modeling from versatile aspects.
2. A unified video recommendation framework is presented, with goals to simultaneously address three long-standing problems in recommender system, i.e., new user, cold-start and sparsity.
3. Experimental results on the collected YouTube-Twitter dataset validate the effectiveness of the proposed solution on three kinds of typical users, in term of not only accuracy, but also diversity and novelty.

2. RELATED WORK

Cross-network collaborative applications have recently attracted attentions. One line is on cross-network user modeling, which focuses on integrating various social media activities. In [13], the authors introduced a cold-start recommendation solution by aggregating user profiles in Flickr, Twitter and Delicious. Deng et al. proposed a personalized YouTube video recommendation solution by incorporating user information from Google+ [14]. Another line is devoted to taking advantage of different OSNs' characteristics. Suman et al. exploited the real-time and socialized characteristics of the Twitter tweets to facilitate video applications in YouTube [15]. In [16], Twitter event detection is conducted by employing Wikipedia pages as the authoritative references. Qi et al. proposed a cross-network link prediction approach by borrowing links from another more densely linked network [17]. Our work belongs to the first line, where users' auxiliary behaviors on Twitter are transferred to facilitate user modeling on YouTube, and a unified solution is designed to address three problems of new user, cold-start and data sparsity.

To conduct cross-network collaborative applications, one important issue is the acquisition of cross-network user accounts corresponding to the same individual. Currently

[2] Due to the privacy concerns, the user demographic information obtained from registration is very sparse and sometimes not accurate, which may negatively affect the quality of a content-based recommender. Also, in many cases, the tagging behaviors are not adequate to reflect the user's preferences or customized needs. Using complex algorithms to complement these limitations in data doesnot always pay off.

Table 1: **Statistics of users who share accounts in other OSNs within the 137,317 Google+ users.**

	YouTube	Twitter	Facebook	Flickr
#account	52,390	43,772	31,020	12,242
proportion	0.3815	0.3188	0.2259	0.0892

Table 2: % user overlap between four OSNs.

	YouTube	Twitter	Facebook	Flickr
YouTube	1	0.4253	0.3109	0.1294
Twitter	0.5090	1	0.5376	0.2223
Facebook	0.5251	0.7586	1	0.2207
Flickr	0.5537	0.7948	0.5591	1

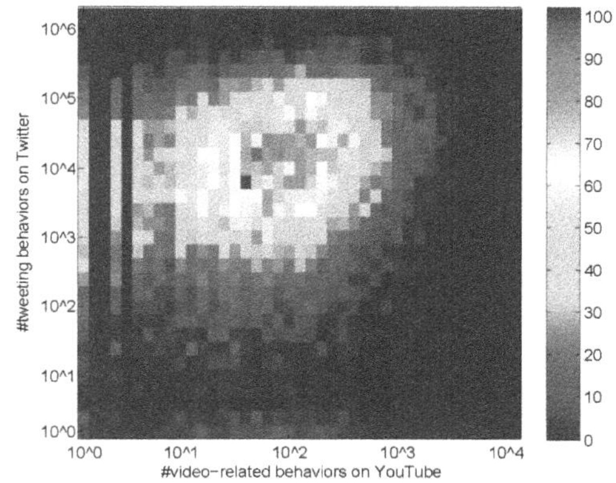

Figure 2: The heatmap of user behavior counts on YouTube and Twitter. (best viewed in color)

there are three ways. (1) Increasing people are voluntary to disclose their user accounts online, by filling in SNS registration information (such as Facebook, Google+) or maintaining an aggregated profiles on services like About.me and Friendfeed. (2) Many IT giants share identical account among their different OSNs, or allow third-party services to access their user base, such as Google account for YouTube and Google+, and Facebook's open platform. (3) With the trend that netizens are using a multitude of OSNs, many researchers are devoted to the field of user account linkage identification, which have achieved satisfied accuracies [18, 19]. In this work, we adopt the first way to construct our cross-network dataset, which will be detailed in the next section.

3. PROBLEM JUSTIFICATION

3.1 Data Set

Google+ encourages users to share their user accounts on other OSNs in the Google profile. We collected Google profiles of 137,317 Google+ users, and obtained 22,279 users who provide their user accounts on both YouTube and Twitter. We further examined these users on YouTube and Twitter via the respective APIs, and crawled data of 17,617 users who are publicly accessible and have behaviors on the both OSNs. These 17,617 users are recorded as the *overlapped users* in the rest of this paper. Specifically, on YouTube, for each of the overlapped users, we downloaded his/her uploaded videos, favorite videos and video playlists. For each video, the video tags, titles and descriptions are also collected. On Twitter, for each user we downloaded his/her recent 1,000 tweets and the user profile. As a result, the collected YouTube-Twitter dataset consists of 1,097,982 video-related behaviors and 9,253,729 tweet-related behaviors.

3.2 Data Analysis

To justify our motivation and the practical feasibility of cross-network collaborative solution, we conducted preliminary data analysis to answer two questions: (1) Is it easy to obtain the user accounts across different OSNs? (2) Are user's Twitter tweeting behaviors adequate to make up the video-related data shortage on YouTube?

For the first question, within the total 137,317 Google+ users, we examined the number of available user accounts on four popular OSNs: YouTube, Twitter, Facebook, and Flickr. The results are shown in Table 1. We can see that a noticeable portion of Google+ users disclose their user accounts on other OSNs, especially on YouTube and Twitter (more than 30%). In Table 2, we also examined the user overlap among the four OSNs. The user overlap proportion between OSN A and B is calculated as $overlap(A, B) = \frac{|A \cap B|}{|A|}$, where $|A|$ indicates the number of available user accounts on OSN A. We can see that the user overlaps between different OSNs are significant, which is consistent with a Pew Internet study conducted over a global sample of online adults [20]. This validates the fact that users are voluntary to disclose their multiple-OSN accounts, and opens up opportunities for large-scale cross-network collaboration practices.

For the second question, for each user, we counted the number of his/her video-related behaviors on YouTube and tweeting behaviors on Twitter. In Fig. 2, x-axis and y-axis indicate the number of video-related and tweeting behaviors in log scale, respectively. We marked each user on the coordinate system and obtained a heatmap over all the 17,617 overlapped users. The depth of the red color is proportional to the number of users having the corresponding behavior count combination at this point. Two observations are made. (1) The red-color points locate largely in the upper left of the diagonal line. This indicates that most users have more tweeting behaviors on Twitter than video-related behaviors on YouTube. (2) For users who have sparse video-related behaviors, e.g., 10^0-10^1 along x-axis, the number of their available tweeting behaviors has a wide range from 10^2-10^5. This validates our motivation to address the cold-start and sparsity problems on YouTube by leveraging the auxiliary user data on Twitter.

4. A UNIFIED VIDEO RECOMMENDATION FRAMEWORK

This section introduces the proposed video recommendation solution via cross-network collaboration. We first provide some key notations to formulate the problem.

Given a set of overlapped users $\mathcal{U}$, each user $u \in \mathcal{U}$ corresponds to a two-dimensional tuple $[\mathcal{T}_u, \mathcal{V}_u]$, where $\mathcal{T}_u$ indicates his/her tweet collection on Twitter and $\mathcal{V}_u$ indicates the videos he/she has interacted with on YouTube. Each $v \in \mathcal{V}_u$ is represented by its contained textual words and visual keyframes $[\mathbf{w}_v, \mathbf{f}_v]$. We use R to denote the observed user-video interaction matrix on YouTube, where the row

$R_{i,\cdot}$ indicates the ith user u_i's observed video interaction. The goal is to make use of the users' tweeting activity $\mathcal{T}_u$, and the video-related behaviors R, to design a unified video recommendation solution that facilitates three kinds of users whose $R_{i,\cdot}$ is empty, sparse or dense.

4.1 Preliminaries

Our proposed solution is based on regularized matrix factorization. In this subsection, we provide the necessary formulation of standard regularized matrix factorization (MF) model and introduce the preprocessing utilized in our work.

In recommender systems, MF model maps both users and videos to a latent factor space, where user-video interactions are modeled as the inner products. To avoid overfitting, state-of-the-art MF models suggest discovering the latent structure based only on the observed interactions [21, 10]. The standard formulation is as follows:

$$\min_{U,V} ||Y \odot (R - UV^{\mathrm{T}})||_F^2 + \lambda(||U||_F^2 + ||V||_F^2) \quad (1)$$

where $U = \{\mathbf{u}_1; \cdots; \mathbf{u}_M\} \in \mathbb{R}^{M\times K}$, $V = \{\mathbf{v}_1; \cdots; \mathbf{v}_N\} \in \mathbb{R}^{N\times K}$ are the user and video representations in the K-dimension latent space, and $Y \in \mathbb{R}^{M\times N}$ is a binary mask matrix recording the observed user-video entries. Given the obtained latent factor representations U, V, we can directly estimate the user u_i's preference on video v_j as: $r_{ij} = \mathbf{u}_i \cdot \mathbf{v}_j^{\mathrm{T}}$.

In the context of our problem, we construct the user-video interaction matrix $R \in \mathbb{R}^{M\times N}$ by aggregating user's three kinds of video-related behaviors, i.e., upload, favorite and adding to playlists. Therefore, each entry $r_{ij} \in \{0, 1, 2, 3\}$.

To reduce the influence of sparsity, many existing recommendation solutions also incorporate the content information for regularization [22, 6]. The basic assumption is: the videos with similar content should have close representations in the derived latent factor space. Realizing this assumption, the objective function in Eq. (1) is further regularized with a Laplacian term and can be written as follows:

$$\min_{U,V} ||Y \odot (R - UV^{\mathrm{T}})||_F^2 + \theta Tr(V^{\mathrm{T}}LV) + \lambda(||U||_F^2 + ||V||_F^2) \quad (2)$$

where $Tr(\cdot)$ is the matrix trace, L is a Laplacian matrix defined as $L = D - S$, θ is the weighting parameter controlling the importance of the Laplacian regularization. Here $S \in \mathbb{R}^{N\times N}$ is the similarity matrix between videos and $D \in \mathbb{R}^{N\times N}$ is a diagonal matrix with $D_{ii} = \sum_j s_{ij}$.

In our work, a topic-based method is utilized to calculate the video similarity matrix S. Specifically, for YouTube video v : $[\mathbf{w}_v, \mathbf{f}_v]$, $\mathbf{f}_v = \{f_1, \cdots, f_N\}$ is a collection of N visual feature vectors associated with v's keyframes, and $\mathbf{w}_v = \{w_1, \cdots, w_M\}$ is the collection of v's M caption and tag words. Viewing each video as one document, we modify a multi-modal topic model [23] to discover the YouTube video topics. After topic modeling, each video v can be represented as a topical distribution $\hat{\mathbf{v}} \in \mathbb{R}^{1\times K^v}$, where K^v is the dimension of the derived topic space. The similarity between the ith and j^{th} video is then calculated as the histogram intersection of their topic distributions:

$$s_{ij} = \sum_{k=1}^{K^v} \min(\hat{v}_i^k, \hat{v}_j^k)$$

where $\hat{v}_i^k$ is the ith video's distribution on the kth topic.

4.2 Auxiliary-network Data Transfer

The goal at the first stage of our solution is to estimate the user's preference on YouTube videos given his/her tweeting activities on Twitter. Although user data on different OSNs are heterogeneous which prevents from direct aggregation, for the same overlapped user, the behaviors on different OSNs can be viewed as the reflections of his/her unique attributes. For example, the preference on advertising videos on YouTube and the interest to tweet news about the release of new products on Twitter are both related to the occupation as a market strategist. Therefore, it is reasonable to assume that the overlapped users' cross-network behaviors have some general association patterns.

We discover the association patterns by examining how the overlapped users' auxiliary data on Twitter can be transferred to their preferences on YouTube videos. Users' preferences on YouTube videos are readily embedded in the user-video interaction matrix R as mentioned above. To represent users' tweeting activities on Twitter, viewing each user's tweeting history as one document, we apply the standard LDA to the corpus constituted by all the Twitter users. As a result, each user can be represented as a topical distribution $\mathbf{u}^t \in \mathbb{R}^{1\times K^t}$, where K^t is the number of topics in the derived Twitter topic space.

For each overlapped user $u \in \mathcal{U}$, we assume that there exists a transfer matrix $W \in \mathbb{R}^{K^t\times K}$ entailing the map from his/her Twitter topical distribution $\mathbf{u}^t$ to his/her user representation $\mathbf{u}$ in the YouTube latent space extracted from R. This assumption is formulated as: $\mathbf{u} = \mathbf{u}^t \cdot W$. Therefore, the task of transferring auxiliary-network data changes to learn the transfer matrix W with observations of the overlapped users' Twitter and YouTube behaviors. We replace the user latent factor matrix U in Eq. (2) to incorporate W, and obtain the following objective function [3]:

$$\min_{W,V} ||Y \odot (R - U^t W V^{\mathrm{T}})||_F^2 + \theta Tr(V^{\mathrm{T}}LV) + \lambda(||W||_F^2 + ||V||_F^2) \quad (3)$$

In the new formulation, instead of directly finding the optimal user representations, we change to optimize for the transfer matrix, which captures the association between users' behaviors on the auxiliary and target networks.

Since we are only interested to reconstruct the observed user-video entries in R, we define Ω as the collection of all the observed user-video pairs, i.e., $\forall (i, j) \in \Omega, Y_{ij} = 1$. Eq. (3) can be rewritten as:

$$\begin{aligned}\min_{\mathbf{v}_j, W} & \sum_{(i,j)\in\Omega} (r_{ij} - \mathbf{u}_i^t W \mathbf{v}_j^{\mathrm{T}})^2 + \theta \sum_j F(\mathbf{v}_j) \\ & + \lambda(||W||_F^2 + \sum_j ||\mathbf{v}_j||_F^2)\end{aligned} \quad (4)$$

$$F(\mathbf{v}_j) \triangleq \mathbf{v}_j(V^{\mathrm{T}}L_j) + (V^{\mathrm{T}}L_j)^{\mathrm{T}}\mathbf{v}_j^{\mathrm{T}} - \mathbf{v}_j L_{jj} \mathbf{v}_j^{\mathrm{T}}.$$

where $\mathbf{v}_j$ is the jth row of V, L_j is the jth column of L, L_{jj} is the entry located in the jth column and j^{th} row of L.

We can see that Eq. (4) is convex to $\mathbf{v}_j$ and W respectively with the other variables fixed. Therefore, we adopt stochastic gradient descent for solution and alternatively loop

[3] Since the goal is to learn the transfer matrix, at this stage, we only keep the users who have sufficient behaviors on both YouTube and Twitter as the training samples. A relative dense R and accurate $\mathbf{u}^t$ contribute to an improved inference of W.

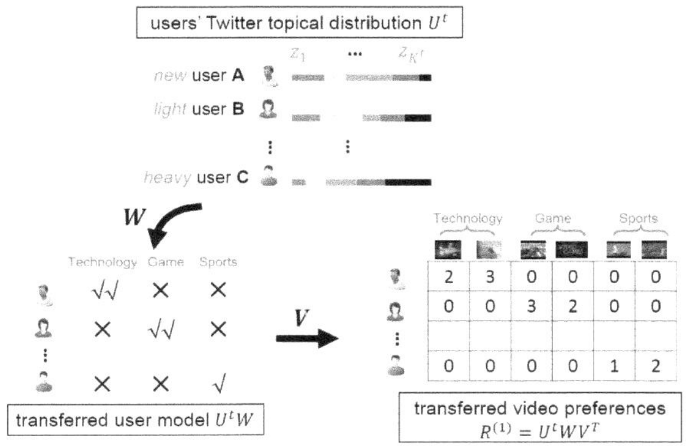

Figure 3: Toy example illustrating the first stage.

through all the observed user-video pairs in Ω [4]. Specifically, for $(i, j) \in \Omega$, let the prediction error $e_{ij} = r_{ij} - \mathbf{u}_i^t W \mathbf{v}_j^{\mathrm{T}}$, then the partial derivatives of the objective function can be derived as:

$$\frac{d}{d\mathbf{v}_j} = -2e_{ij}\mathbf{u}_i^t W + 2\theta(L_j^{\mathrm{T}} V - L_{jj}\mathbf{v}_j) + 2\lambda\mathbf{v}_j$$
$$\frac{d}{dW} = -2e_{ij}\mathbf{u}_i^{t\mathrm{T}}\mathbf{v}_j + 2\lambda W$$

Based on this, we update $\mathbf{v}_j$ and W iteratively until convergence or maximum iteration. The update rules are:

$$\mathbf{v}_j \leftarrow \mathbf{v}_j - \gamma\frac{d}{d\mathbf{v}_j}$$
$$W \leftarrow W - \gamma\frac{d}{dW}$$

where γ denotes the learning rate.

With the derived transfer matrix W and video latent factor representations V, given a test user u_i with his/her tweeting activity and Twitter topical distribution $\mathbf{u}_i^t$, we can estimate u_i's preferences on YouTube videos as:

$$R_{i,\cdot}^{(1)} = \mathbf{u}_i^t W V^{\mathrm{T}} \tag{5}$$

In Fig. 3, we show a toy example by simulating three typical YouTube users. Transferred by W, we estimate the users' interests on latent YouTube video topics indicating *Technology*, *Game*, and *Sports* (×, ✓, ✓✓denote "not like", "like", and "very like", respectively). Further multiplied by V, we can discover their preferences on specific videos. Therefore, even no behavior records are available on the target network, we can still build an initial user model by transferring the data from auxiliary networks. This has actually addressed the first scenario in our unified recommendation solution: *new user*.

4.3 Cross-network Data Integration

For the light and heavy users, they already have some observed behaviors on the target network. It is not practical to directly aggregate the observed behaviors with the estimated preference $R_{i,\cdot}^{(1)}$ as they may contradict each other. Therefore, at the second stage of our solution, we introduce another formulation to update the user latent representation U for light and heavy users, by considering both the observed YouTube user-video matrix R and the transferred user model U^tW.

In the new formulation, we view the transferred user model U^tW as a prior to the integrated user model U. This can be interpreted in two-fold: (1) For users with few observed behaviors on the target network, the transferred user model serves as good indication of the integrated user model, i.e., U should resemble U^tW. This actually corresponds to the cold-start problem. (2) The obtained transfer matrix W defines a latent space where the users are located. This helps to measure the correlation between users, and can be employed to alleviate the sparsity problem in the target user-video matrix R. Based on these two interpretations, we introduce the formulation for cross-network data integration as follows [5]:

$$\min_{U,V'} ||Y \odot (R - UV'^{\mathrm{T}})||_F^2 + \alpha||P(U - U^tW)||_F^2 + \beta||V' - V||_F^2 + \lambda(||U||_F^2 + ||V'||_F^2) \tag{6}$$

Two notations for the above objective function: (1) V is known quantity as the output from the first stage. The reason we also update the learnt video latent representations V' is to better couple with the update of U in fitting the observed user-video matrix R. (2) $P = diag(p_1, \cdots, p_{|\mathcal{U}|})$ is a diagonal matrix to control the contribution of the transferred information. Different from the weighting parameters α, β, and λ which apply on all users, P works on micro-level and defines adaptive weights for different users. To define the user-specific weight p_i, we expect that the user having dense behaviors on YouTube deserves a small p_i, which indicates that more emphasis should be given on modeling of his/her observed video interactions on YouTube to estimate the integrated user model. Specifically, we employ the relative amount of behaviors each user has on YouTube to that on Twitter to define p_i, and the definition is:

$$p_i = \left(1 + e^{\frac{|\mathcal{V}_{u_i}|}{avg.(|\mathcal{V}_u|)} - \frac{|\mathcal{T}_{u_i}|}{avg.(|\mathcal{T}_u|)}}\right)^{-1} \tag{7}$$

where $|\mathcal{T}_{u_i}|$, $|\mathcal{V}_{u_i}|$ indicate the numbers of available tweets and interacted videos of user u_i, $avg.(|\mathcal{T}_u|)$, $avg.(|\mathcal{V}_u|)$ are the corresponding numbers averaged over all the examined users.

Similar to the manipulation of Eq. (3), we rewrite Eq. (6) as follows:

$$\min_{\mathbf{u}_i,\mathbf{v}_j'} \sum_{(i,j)\in\Omega} \left(r_{ij} - \mathbf{u}_i\mathbf{v}_j'^{\mathrm{T}}\right)^2 + \alpha\sum_i ||p_i(\mathbf{u}_i - \mathbf{u}_i^t W)||_F^2 + \beta\sum_j ||\mathbf{v}_j' - \mathbf{v}_j||_F^2 + \lambda(\sum_i ||\mathbf{u}_i||_F^2 + \sum_j ||\mathbf{v}_j'||_F^2) \tag{8}$$

The stochastic gradient descent is again adopted to learn the model parameters. For each observed user-video pair $(i, j) \in \Omega$, we can update the parameters with learning rate γ as:

$$\mathbf{u}_i \leftarrow \mathbf{u}_i + \gamma(e_{ij}\mathbf{v}_j' - \alpha p_i^2(\mathbf{u}_i - \mathbf{u}_i^t W) - \lambda\mathbf{u}_i)$$
$$\mathbf{v}_j' \leftarrow \mathbf{v}_j' + \gamma(e_{ij}\mathbf{u}_i - \beta(\mathbf{v}_j' - \mathbf{v}_j) - \lambda\mathbf{v}_j') \tag{9}$$

[4]The fact that each video latent representation vector $\mathbf{v}_j$ can be updated independently of other vectors provides opportunities for parallel implementation. Distributed storing also allows for processing large matrices with huge number of videos.

[5]Note that different from the training samples used at the first stage (Eq. (3)), R and Y in this equation correspond to the test light and heavy users.

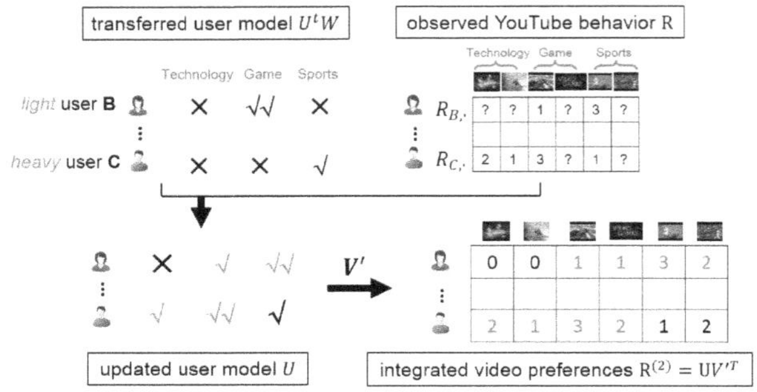

Figure 4: Toy example illustrating the second stage.

In this way, the user latent representation $\mathbf{u}_i$ and video latent representation $\mathbf{v}_j{}'$ are updated. For each test light or heavy user u_i, his/her preferences on YouTube videos can be calculated as:

$$R_{i,\cdot}^{(2)} = \mathbf{u}_i V'^{\mathrm{T}} \tag{10}$$

In Fig. 4, continuing the toy example in Fig. 3, we show how the user models of light and heavy users are updated at the second stage. It is shown that the transferred user model and video representations are revised according to the observed behaviors on YouTube (revised entries are highlighted with red color). The obtained final video preferences consider both the auxiliary information and well fit the observed target-network information.

5. EXPERIMENT

5.1 Experimental Settings

5.1.1 Dataset Partition

To construct a dataset with adequate user behaviors for model learning and performance evaluation, we filtered the raw overlapped user set by keeping the ones who interacted with over 10 YouTube videos and posted over 10 tweets on Twitter. The YouTube videos interacted by less than three users are also filtered out. This results in a dataset of 2,560 users and 4,414 YouTube videos. The resultant user-video matrix has a sparsity score of 99.45%.

Within the experimental dataset, we first randomly selected 1,060 active users who have more than 30 video-related interactions and posted more than 200 tweets, to construct the training dataset used at the first stage to learn the transfer matrix W. Since the proposed solution is expected to be evaluated on three kinds of users, we evenly separated the remaining 1,500 users into three subsets according to the number of their video-related interactions in ascending order, which are denoted as $\mathcal{U}^{new}$, $\mathcal{U}^{light}$, and $\mathcal{U}^{heavy}$. For user $u \in \mathcal{U}^{new}$, all the observed video-related interactions are hidden in the training stage and taken as ground truth for evaluation. For user $u \in \mathcal{U}^{light}$, 30% of the video-related interactions are used to update the user model $\mathbf{u}$, with the rest 70% for evaluation. For user $u \in \mathcal{U}^{heavy}$, 80% of the video-related interactions are used as training data, with the rest 20% for evaluation. We can see that the training partitions from $\mathcal{U}^{light}$ and $\mathcal{U}^{heavy}$ actually constitute the dataset used in in Eq. (6) at the second stage. The statistics of the three user sets is summarized in Table 3.

Table 3: Statistics (per user) of video-related interactions for three kinds of user sets.

Dataset	Statistics	$\mathcal{U}^{new}$	$\mathcal{U}^{light}$	$\mathcal{U}^{heavy}$
Train	*min.*	0	6	24
	avg.	0	7.3	43.3
	max.	0	9	172
Test	*min.*	10	10	11
	avg.	10.8	12.1	19.2
	max.	12	15	74

5.1.2 Parameter Settings

In preprocessing, the topical distributions of YouTube videos and Twitter users are derived from topic modeling. We resorted to the standard perplexity measure [24] and selected the topic number that leads to small perplexity and fast convergence. As a result, the topic number is set as: $K^v = 70$ and $K^t = 60$. The hyperparameters are fixed as $\alpha_{LDA} = 0.8$ and $\beta_{LDA} = 0.1$ according to the empirical expectation for the output distribution.

In the proposed video recommendation solution, six parameters are involved: the dimension of latent factor space K, regularization coefficient λ, learning rate γ, and weighting parameters θ, α, β. Considering the settings without video Laplacian regularization, i.e., set $\theta = 0$, we firstly jointly select K and λ in Eq. (3) by grid search and 2-fold cross validation. As a result, we set $K = 40$ and $\lambda = 0.1$. The learning rate γ is fixed as a small value 0.005 to ensure the convergence to the local minimum. With K, λ and γ fixed, we finally select θ, α, β by the same grid search strategy respectively, and set the parameters leading to the best results, i.e., $\theta = 0.45, \alpha = 20, \beta = 1$.

5.2 Experimental Results and Analysis

To evaluate the effectiveness of the proposed two-stage solution on addressing the mentioned three problems, we implemented four single-network baselines and two different settings of our solution. The six examined methods are listed as follows:

- *Popularity*: recommending popular videos with the most view count, which serves as a simple baseline to address the new user problem;
- *KNN*: the typical item-based collaborative filtering recommendation algorithm [25];
- *LFM*: state-of-the-art Latent Factor Model [10], which is mainly designed to address the sparsity problem;
- *rPMF*: probabilistic Matrix Factorization method incorporating video content Laplacian regularization [6], as shown in Eq. (2);
- *auxTransfer*: the proposed solution that only considers auxiliary-network data transfer, shown in Eq. (3);
- *crossIntegration*: the proposed solution considering both auxiliary-network data transfer and cross-network data integration, shown in Eq. (6).

We view personalized video recommendation as a top-k recommendation task and adopt *top-k precision*, *recall* and *F-score* as the evaluation metrics [26]. For each test user u_i, we recommend the top k YouTube videos with the highest entry score ($r_{ij}^{(1)}$ for new users, $r_{ij}^{(2)}$ for light and heavy users). The evaluation metrics are calculated by examining whether the recommended videos are included in u_i's interested video set $\mathcal{V}_{u_i}$. The final results are averaged over all the test users.

Table 4: Top-10 precision, recall and F-score for the examined methods on three test user sets.

Test set	Metrics	Popularity	KNN	LFM	rPMF	auxTransfer	crossIntegration
new users	*precision*	0.0108	-	-	-	**0.0246**	**0.0246**
	recall	0.0101	-	-	-	**0.0229**	**0.0229**
	F-score	0.0105	-	-	-	**0.0237**	**0.0237**
light users	*precision*	0.0126	0.0160	0.0060	0.0190	0.0242	**0.0274**
	recall	0.0105	0.0083	0.0050	0.0159	0.0201	**0.0227**
	F-score	0.0115	0.0109	0.0055	0.0173	0.0220	**0.0248**
heavy users	*precision*	0.0076	0.0286	0.0088	0.0300	0.0330	**0.0436**
	recall	0.0047	0.0181	0.0045	0.0157	0.0170	**0.0222**
	F-score	0.0058	0.0221	0.0060	0.0206	0.0224	**0.0294**

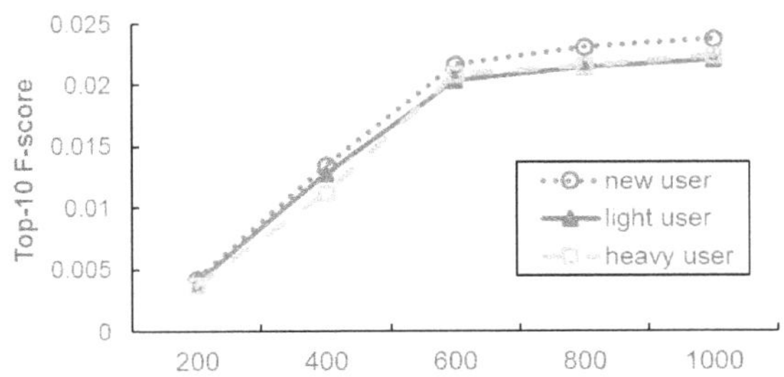

Figure 5: Top-10 F-score as the number of overlapped users at the first stage changes.

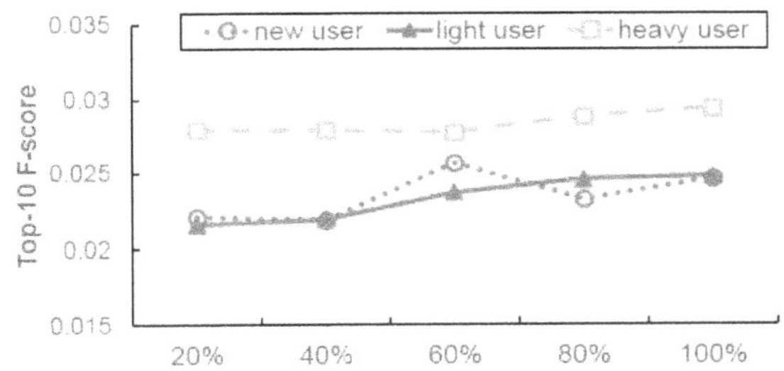

Figure 6: Top-10 F-score as the ratio of Twitter user activities changes.

The evaluation results of the examined methods are shown in Table 4. It is easy to find that the two settings of our solution well address different kinds of users and obtain the best performances. Other observations include: (1) Among the four compared baselines, only *Popularity* can address all three kinds of users. However, recommending the global popular videos fails to capture users' personalized needs and thus achieves inferior performances (heavy users with even lower F-score). (2) For light users, the fact that *auxTransfer* outperforms the four single-network baselines validates our motivation of exploiting auxiliary-network information. *crossIntegration* performs slightly better than *auxTransfer* by further incorporating the limited target-network information. (3) For heavy users, single-network baselines (*KNN*, *rPMF*) achieve comparable results. The improvement of *crossIntegration* ascribes to the prior from auxiliary user model, where user-user correlations are pre-defined to help alleviate the sparsity.

Influence of #overlapped users. We further examined how the number of overlapped users influence the inference of transfer matrix and thus contributes to the final recommendation performance. Different numbers of users are randomly sampled to construct the training set in Eq. (3). We utilize the obtained respective W and evaluate the performance on the *auxTransfer* setting. The top-10 F-score for the three test user sets is shown in Fig. 5, showing a gradual improvement as the number of overlapped users increases. This leads to a coarse conclusion that, more users for training leads to more accurate estimation of W and thus positively affect the recommendation performance.

Sensitivity to #auxiliary-network data. We also investigated whether the performance is sensitive to the number of available auxiliary activities at the cross-network data integration stage. In Fig. 6 we show the top-10 F-score on *crossIntegration* setting by varying the test users' ratio of Twitter activities (i.e., 20%, 40%, 60%, 80%, 100%). It is observed that the performance is not a monotonically increasing function of the Twitter activities. We can understand this result by looking into Eq. (6), that it is the Twitter topical distribution $\mathbf{u}^t$ that directly relates to the update of user model. As long as the scale of Twitter activities is adequate to obtain an accurate topical distribution, more activities will not much influence the final performance.

5.3 Discussion

The goal of cross-network collaboration is to complement the data shortage on target networks. A natural question arises: compared with the case when users have adequate target-network behaviors, will cross-network solution on limited target-network behaviors with auxiliary-network information beat single-network solution on adequate target-network behaviors? will cross-network collaborative recommendation have other advantages except for accuracy?

To investigate into this question, we considered the recommendation to the heavy users $\mathcal{U}^{heavy}$ with two different data settings: (1) using all their training interactions on YouTube videos, and (2) keeping only 20% of the training YouTube interactions with all the available Twitter activities. These data settings simulate the case of adequate target-network behaviors (*adequate*) and limited behaviors with auxiliary-network information (*limited*), respectively. We employ the single-network solutions of *KNN* and *rPMF* on the *adequate* data setting, and the proposed *crossIntegration* on the *limited* data setting. The results of top-10 F-score in Table 5 show that in term of accuracy, cross-network collaborative solution with limited target-network behaviors is not so effective compared with single-network solutions with adequate target-network behaviors.

In practical recommender systems, only considering the accuracy is not sufficient to provide useful recommendation-

Table 5: Performance comparison in term of different evaluation metrics.

Methods/*data setting*	Evaluation metrics		
	F-score	*Similarity*	*Novelty*
KNN/*adequate*	**0.0221**	0.4312	0.0142
rPMF/*adequate*	0.0206	0.3909	0.0139
crossIntegration/*limited*	0.0211	**0.3430**	**0.0159**

s. Therefore, we also investigated into other advantages of cross-network collaborative recommendation, by examining evaluation metrics of *diversity* and *novelty* [6]. From Table 5 we can see that, *crossIntegration* achieves improved diversity and novelty over single-network solutions, even with much fewer target-network behaviors. This shows the advantage of cross-network collaborative recommendation in exploiting users' versatile interests in different domains and the potentials in serendipity recommendation.

6. CONCLUSION AND FUTURE WORK

We have introduced a unified YouTube video recommendation solution to address three typical problems in recommender systems, i.e., new user, cold-start, data sparsity. The evaluation results on different metrics of accuracy, diversity and novelty suggest that, by incorporating auxiliary-network information and employing a cross-network collaborative solution, novel recommenders may lead to a higher satisfaction and utility for users.

To interpret the mechanism of proposed solution, we are conducting some case studies to examine into the obtained transfer matrix. An updated formulation is expected to allow for non-linear cross-network behavior correlation. Moreover, the selection of auxiliary network and auxiliary information is critical to the performance of cross-network collaborative recommendation. Except for the user behavior information, we are also very interested in exploiting the social relation information, e.g., to transfer user preferences from Twitter friend network.

7. ACKNOWLEDGMENT

This work is supported in part by National Basic Research Program of China (No. 2012CB316304), National Natural Science Foundation of China (No. 61225009, 61332016, 61303176, 61432019, U1435211), and Beijing Natural Science Foundation (No. 4131004).

8. REFERENCES

[1] Terence Chen, Mohamed Ali Kaafar, Arik Friedman, and Roksana Boreli. Is more always merrier?: a deep dive into online social footprints. In *Proceedings of the 2012 ACM workshop on Workshop on online social networks*, pages 67–72. ACM, 2012.

[2] James Davidson, Benjamin Liebald, Junning Liu, Palash Nandy, Taylor Van Vleet, Ullas Gargi, Sujoy Gupta, Yu He, Mike Lambert, et al. The youtube video recommendation system. In *Proceedings of the fourth ACM conference on Recommender systems*, pages 293–296. ACM, 2010.

[3] Francesco Ricci, Lior Rokach, and Bracha Shapira. *Recommender Systems Handbook: A Complete Guide for Scientists and Practioners*. Springer, 2011.

[6]While *diversity* measures the average pairwise similarity between all the top recommended videos, *novelty* encourages the recommendation of less popular videos. Due to space limitation, we skip the detailed definition. Please refer to [27] for details.

[4] Marco Degemmis, Pasquale Lops, and Giovanni Semeraro. A content-collaborative recommender that exploits wordnet-based user profiles for neighborhood formation. *User Modeling and User-Adapted Interaction*, 17(3):217–255, 2007.

[5] Dietmar Jannach, Markus Zanker, Alexander Felfernig, and Gerhard Friedrich. *Recommender systems: an introduction*. Cambridge University Press, 2010.

[6] Michael J Pazzani and Daniel Billsus. Content-based recommendation systems. In *The adaptive web*, pages 325–341. Springer, 2007.

[7] Zi-Ke Zhang, Chuang Liu, Yi-Cheng Zhang, and Tao Zhou. Solving the cold-start problem in recommender systems with social tags. *EPL (Europhysics Letters)*, 92(2):28002, 2010.

[8] Hao Ma, Dengyong Zhou, Chao Liu, Michael R Lyu, and Irwin King. Recommender systems with social regularization. In *Proceedings of the fourth ACM international conference on Web search and data mining*, pages 287–296. ACM, 2011.

[9] Mukund Deshpande and George Karypis. Item-based top-n recommendation algorithms. *ACM Transactions on Information Systems (TOIS)*, 22(1):143–177, 2004.

[10] Yehuda Koren. Factorization meets the neighborhood: a multifaceted collaborative filtering model. In *ACM SIGKDD 2008*, pages 426–434. ACM.

[11] Zan Huang, Hsinchun Chen, and Daniel Zeng. Applying associative retrieval techniques to alleviate the sparsity problem in collaborative filtering. *ACM Transactions on Information Systems (TOIS)*, 22(1):116–142, 2004.

[12] Viktor Mayer-Schönberger and Kenneth Cukier. *Big data: A revolution that will transform how we live, work, and think*. Houghton Mifflin Harcourt, 2013.

[13] Fabian Abel, Samur Araújo, Qi Gao, and Geert-Jan Houben. Analyzing cross-system user modeling on the social web. In *Web Engineering*, pages 28–43. Springer, 2011.

[14] Zhengyu Deng, Jitao Sang, and Changsheng Xu. Personalized video recommendation based on cross-platform user modeling. In *ICME 2013*, pages 1–6. IEEE.

[15] Suman Deb Roy, Tao Mei, Wenjun Zeng, and Shipeng Li. Socialtransfer: cross-domain transfer learning from social streams for media applications. In *ACM Multimedia 2012*, pages 649–658. ACM.

[16] Miles Osborne, Saša Petrovic, Richard McCreadie, Craig Macdonald, and Iadh Ounis. Bieber no more: First story detection using twitter and wikipedia. In *TAIA 2012*, volume 12.

[17] Guo-Jun Qi, Charu C Aggarwal, and Thomas Huang. Link prediction across networks by biased cross-network sampling. In *Data Engineering (ICDE), 2013 IEEE 29th International Conference on*, pages 793–804. IEEE, 2013.

[18] Jing Liu, Fan Zhang, Xinying Song, Young-In Song, Chin-Yew Lin, and Hsiao-Wuen Hon. What's in a name?: an unsupervised approach to link users across communities. In *Proceedings of the sixth ACM international conference on Web search and data mining*, pages 495–504. ACM, 2013.

[19] Reza Zafarani and Huan Liu. Connecting users across social media sites: a behavioral-modeling approach. In *ACM SIGKDD 2013*, pages 41–49. ACM.

[20] Maeve Duggan and Aaron Smith. Social media update 2013. *Pew Internet and American Life Project*, 2013.

[21] Andriy Mnih and Ruslan Salakhutdinov. Probabilistic matrix factorization. In *Advances in neural information processing systems*, pages 1257–1264, 2007.

[22] Marko Balabanović and Yoav Shoham. Fab: content-based, collaborative recommendation. *Communications of the ACM*, 40(3):66–72, 1997.

[23] David M Blei and Michael I Jordan. Modeling annotated data. In *SIGIR 2003*, pages 127–134.

[24] David M Blei, Andrew Y Ng, and Michael I Jordan. Latent dirichlet allocation. *the Journal of machine Learning research*, 3:993–1022, 2003.

[25] George Karypis. Evaluation of item-based top-n recommendation algorithms. In *Proceedings of the tenth international conference on Information and knowledge management*, pages 247–254. ACM, 2001.

[26] Jonathan L Herlocker, Joseph A Konstan, Loren G Terveen, and John T Riedl. Evaluating collaborative filtering recommender systems. *ACM Transactions on Information Systems (TOIS)*, 22(1):5–53, 2004.

[27] Guy Shani and Asela Gunawardana. Evaluating recommendation systems. In *Recommender systems handbook*, pages 257–297. Springer, 2011.

Bridging the Ultimate Semantic Gap: A Semantic Search Engine for Internet Videos

Lu Jiang[1], Shoou-I Yu[1], Deyu Meng[2], Teruko Mitamura[1], Alexander G. Hauptmann[1]
[1] School of Computer Science, Carnegie Mellon University
[2] School of Mathematics and Statistics, Xi'an Jiaotong University
{lujiang, iyu, teruko, alex}@cs.cmu.edu, dymeng@mail.xjtu.edu.cn

ABSTRACT

Semantic search in video is a novel and challenging problem in information and multimedia retrieval. Existing solutions are mainly limited to text matching, in which the query words are matched against the textual metadata generated by users. This paper presents a state-of-the-art system for event search without any textual metadata or example videos. The system relies on substantial video content understanding and allows for semantic search over a large collection of videos. The novelty and practicality is demonstrated by the evaluation in NIST TRECVID 2014, where the proposed system achieves the best performance. We share our observations and lessons in building such a state-of-the-art system, which may be instrumental in guiding the design of the future system for semantic search in video.

Categories and Subject Descriptors

H.3.3 [**Information Search and Retrieval**]: Search process; I.2.10 [**Vision and Scene Understanding**]: Video analysis

General Terms

Algorithms, Experimentation, Performance

Keywords

Semantic Search; Video Search; Video Understanding; 0Ex; Content-based Retrieval; Multimedia Event Detection

1. INTRODUCTION

The explosion of multimedia data is creating impacts on many aspects of society. The huge volumes of accumulated video data bring challenges for effective multimedia search. Existing solutions, such as shown in YouTube, are mainly limited to text matching where the query words are matched against the textual metadata generated by the uploader [7]. This solution, though simple, proves to be futile when such metadata are either missing or less relevant to the video content. Content-based search, on the other hand, searches semantic features such as people, scenes, objects and actions that are automatically detected in the video content. A representative content-based retrieval task, initiated by the TRECVID community, is called Multimedia Event Detection (MED) [32]. The task is to detect the occurrence of a main event in a video clip without any textual metadata. The events of interest are mostly daily activities ranging from "birthday party" to "changing a vehicle tire".

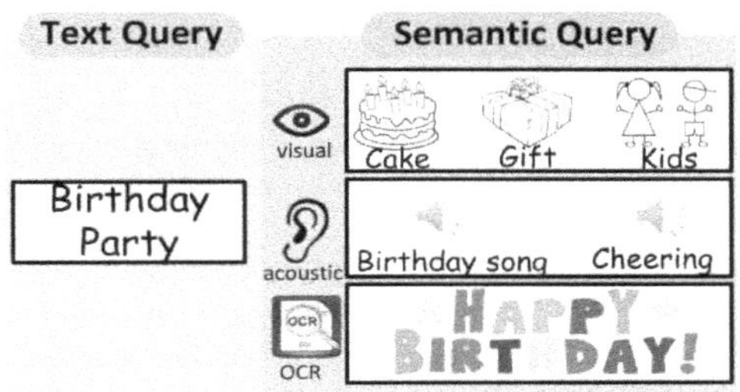

Figure 1: Comparison of text and semantic query for the event "birthday party". Semantic queries contain visual/audio concepts about the video content.

This paper discusses a setting in MED called zero-example search [18], or 0Ex for short, in which no relevant video is given in the query. 0Ex supports semantic search which relies on substantial video content understanding as opposed to shallow text matching in conventional methods. The query words are semantic features that are expected to occur in the relevant videos. For example, as illustrated in Fig. 1, the semantic query for the event "birthday party" might consist of visual concepts "cake", "gift" and "kids", audio concepts "birthday song" and "cheering sound". 0Ex also allows for flexible semantic search such as temporal or Boolean logic search. For example, searching for videos where opening gifts happens before consuming birthday cakes.

This paper details a state-of-the-art 0Ex system called E-Lamp semantic search engine, and according to National Institute of Standards and Technology (NIST), the proposed system achieves the best performance in TRECVID 2014 on a large collection of 200,000 Internet videos [32]. Our performance is about three times of the second best system. The outstanding performance is attributed to our rational pipeline as well as its effective components. We share our observations and lessons in building such a state-of-the-art system. The lessons are valuable because of not only the effort in designing and conducting numerous experiments but also the considerable computational resource to make the experiments possible. For example, building the semantic detectors costs us more than 1.2 million CPU core hours, which is equivalent to 140 years if it is running on a single core. We believe the shared lessons may significantly

ICMR'15, June 23–26, 2015, Shanghai, China.

http://http://dx.doi.org/10.1145/2671188.2749399.

save the time and computational cycles for others who are interested in this problem.

The outstanding performance evaluated by NIST is a convincing demonstration of the novelty and practicality of the proposed system. Specifically, the novelty of this paper includes the solutions in system design and the insight on a number of empirical studies on semantic video search. The discussed techniques may also benefit other related tasks such as video summarization and recommendation. In summary, the contribution of this paper is twofold:

- We share our observations and lessons in building a state-of-the-art 0Ex event search system.
- Our pilot studies provide compelling insights on the comparison of modality contributions, semantic mapping methods and retrieval models for event search.

2. RELATED WORK

Multimedia event detection is an interesting problem. A number of studies have been proposed to tackle this problem on using several training examples (typically 10 or 100 examples) [14, 9, 38, 11, 31, 19, 34, 3, 36]. Generally, in a state-of-the-art system, the event classifiers are trained by low-level and high-level features, and the final decision is derived from the fusion of the individual classification results. For example, Habibian et al. [11] found several interesting observations about training classifiers only by semantic concept features. Gkalelis et al. [9] learned a representation for linear SVMs by subclass discriminant analysis, which yields 1-2 orders of magnitude speed-up. Wang et al. [38] discussed a notable system in TRECVID 2012 that is characterized by applying feature selection over so-called motion relativity features. Oh et al. [31] presented a latent SVM event detector that enables for temporal evidence localization. Jiang et al. [19] presented an efficient method to learn "optimal" spatial event representations from data.

Event detection with zero training examples is called 0Ex. It mostly resembles a real-world video search scenario, where users usually start the search without any example video. 0Ex is an understudied problem, and only few studies have been proposed very recently [6, 10, 26, 40, 18, 23]. Dalton et al. [6] discussed a query expansion approach for concept and text retrieval. Habibian et al. [10] proposed to index videos by composite concepts that are trained by combining the labeled data of individual concepts. Wu et al. [40] introduced a multimodal fusion method for semantic concepts and text features. Given a set of tagged videos, Mazloom et al. [26] discussed a retrieval approach to propagate the tags to unlabeled videos for event detection. Jiang et al. [18, 15] studied pseudo relevance feedback approaches which manage to significantly improve the original retrieval results. Existing related works inspire our system. However, to the best of our knowledge, there have been no studies on the 0Ex system architecture nor the analysis of each component.

3. FRAMEWORK

Semantic search in video can be modeled as a typical retrieval problem in which given a user query, we are interested in returning a ranked list of relevant videos. The proposed system comprises four major components, namely Video Semantic INdexing (VSIN), Semantic Query Generation (SQG), Multimodal Search, and Pseudo-Relevance Feedback (PRF)/Fusion, where VSIN is an offline indexing component, and the rest are the online search modules.

The VSIN component extracts semantic features from input videos, and indexes them for efficient online search. Typically, a video clip is first represented by low-level features such as dense trajectory features [39] for visual modality or deep learning features [27, 28] for audio modality. The low-level features are then input into the off-the-shelf detectors to extract the high-level features. Each dimension of the high-level feature corresponds to a confidence score of detecting a semantic concept in the video [14, 13]. Compared with low-level features, high-level features have a much lower dimension, which makes them economic for both storage and computation. The visual/audio concepts, Automatic Speech Recognition (ASR) [27] and Optical Character Recognition (OCR) are four types of high-level features in the system, in which ASR and OCR are textual features. ASR provides complementary information for events that are characterized by acoustic evidence. It especially benefits close-to-camera and narrative events such as "town hall meeting" and "asking for directions". OCR captures the characters in videos with low recall but high precision. The recognized characters are often not meaningful words but sometimes can be a clue for fine-grained detection, e.g. distinguishing "baby shower" and "wedding shower". The union of the dictionary vocabulary of high-level features constitutes the *system vocabulary*.

Users can express a query in various forms, such as a few concept names, a sentence or a structured description. NIST provides a query in the form of event-kit descriptions, which includes a name, definition, explication and visual/acoustic evidences (see the left corner of Fig. 2). The SQG component translates a user query into a multimodal *system query*, all words of which exist in the *system vocabulary*. Since the vocabulary is usually limited, addressing the out-of-vocabulary issue is a major challenge for SQG. The mapping between the user and system query is usually achieved with the aid of an ontology such as WordNet and Wikipedia. For example, a user query "golden retriever" may be translated to its most relevant alternative "large-sized dog", as the original concept may not exist in the system vocabulary.

Given a system query, the multimodal search component aims at retrieving a ranked list for each modality. As a pilot study, we are interested in leveraging the well-studied text retrieval models for video retrieval. To adapt the difference between semantic features and text features, we empirically study a number of classical retrieval models on various types of semantic features. We then apply the model to its most appropriate modalities. One notably benefit of doing so is that it can easily leverage the existing infrastructures and algorithms originally designed for text retrieval.

PRF (also known as reranking) refines a ranked list by reranking its videos. A generic PRF method first selects a few feedback videos, and assign assumed positive or negative labels to them. Since no ground-truth label is used, the assumed labels are called pseudo labels. The pseudo samples are then used to build a reranking model to improve the original ranked lists. A recent study shows that reranking can be modeled as a self-paced learning process [15], where the reranking model is built iteratively from easy to more complex samples. The easy samples are the videos ranked at the top, which are generally more relevant than those ranked lower. In addition to PRF, the standard late fusion is applied in our system.

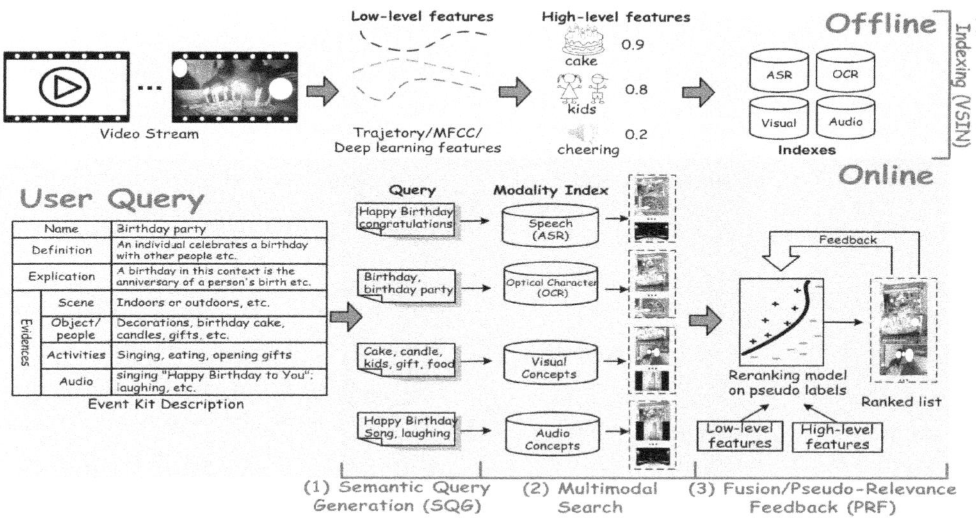

Figure 2: Overview of the E-Lamp video search system.

4. SYSTEM IMPLEMENTATIONS

The devil is in the detail. Careful implementations often turn out to be the cornerstone in many systems. To this end, this section discusses each component in more detail.

4.1 Large-scale Semantic Indexing

Concept detectors can be trained on still images or videos. The latter is more desirable due to the minimal domain difference and the capability for action and audio detection. A visual/audio concept in our system is represented as a multimodal document which includes a name, description, category, reliability (accuracy) and examples of the top detected video snippet. This definition provides a more tangible understanding about the concept for users.

The quantity (relevance) and quality of the semantic detectors are two crucial factors in affecting performance. The relevance is measured by the coverage of the concept vocabulary to the query, and thus is query-dependent. For convenience, we name it quantity as a larger vocabulary tends to increase the coverage. Quality is evaluated by the accuracy of the detector. Given limited resources, there exists a tradeoff between quality and quantity, i.e. building many unreliable detectors versus building a few reliable detectors. This tradeoff has been studied when there are several training examples [12, 11]. This paper presents a novel understanding about the tradeoff when there is no training example. The observations suggest that training more reasonably accurate detectors tends to be a sensible strategy.

Training detectors on large-scale video datasets increases both quantity and quality. But it turns out to be quite challenging. We approach this challenging problem with effort in two aspects. In theoretical aspect, a novel and effective method named self-paced curriculum learning [17] is explored. The idea is that, as opposed to training a detector using all samples at a time, we train increasingly complex detectors iteratively on balanced data subsets. The scheme of selecting samples to be trained in each iteration is controlled by a regularizer [22, 16, 17], and can be conveniently replaced to fit various problems. As for practical aspect, the module is optimized by storing kernel matrices in large shared-memory machines. This strategy yields 8 times speedup in training, enabling us training 3 thousand detectors over around 2 million videos (and video segments). In practice, in order to index huge volume of video data, the detectors need to be linear models (linear SVM or logistic regression), and nonlinear models have to be first transformed to the linear models (e.g. by explicit feature mapping [37]).

The ASR module is built on Kaldi [33] by training the HMM/GMM acoustic model with speaker adaptive training [27, 29] on videos. The trigram language model is pruned aggressively to speed up decoding. OCR is extracted by a commercial toolkit. The high-level features are indexed. The confidence scores for ASR and OCR are discarded, and the words are indexed by the standard inverted index. The visual/audio concepts are indexed by dense matrices to preserve their detection scores.

4.2 Semantic Query Generation

SQG translates a user query into a multimodal *system query* which only contains words in the system vocabulary. The first step in SQG is to parse negations in the query to recognize counter-examples. The recognized examples can be either discarded or to be associated with a "NOT" operator in the system query. Given TRECVID provides user queries in the form of event-kit description (see the left corner of Fig. 2), an event can be represented by the event name (1-3 words) or the frequent words in the event-kit description (after removing the template and stop words). These representations can be directly used as system queries for ASR/OCR as their vocabularies are sufficiently large to cover most words. For visual/audio concepts, the representations are used to map the out-of-vocabulary query words to their most relevant concepts in the system vocabulary. This mapping in SQG is challenging because of the complex relation between concepts. The relation between concepts includes mutual exclusion, subsumption, and frequent co-occurrence. For example, "cloud" and "sky" are frequently co-occurring concepts; "dog" subsumes "terrier"; and "blank frame" excludes "dog". Our system includes the following mapping algorithms to map a word in the user query to the concept in the system vocabulary:

Exact word matching: A straightforward mapping is matching the exact query word (usually after stemming) against the concept name or description. Generally, for unambiguous words, it has high precision but low recall.

WordNet mapping: This mapping calculates the similarity between two words in terms of their distance in the

WordNet taxonomy. The distance can be defined in various ways such as structural depths in the hierarchy [41] or shared overlaps between synonymous words [1]. WordNet mapping is good at capturing synonyms and subsumption relations between two nouns.

PMI mapping: The mapping calculates the Point-wise Mutual Information (PMI) [5] between two words. Suppose q_i and q_j are two words in a user query, we have:

$$\text{pmi}(q_i; q_j) = \log \frac{P(q_i, q_j|C_{ont})}{P(q_i|C_{ont})P(q_j|C_{ont})}, \quad (1)$$

where $P(q_i|C_{ont}), P(q_j|C_{ont})$ represent the probability of observing q_i and q_j in the ontology C_{ont} (e.g. a collection of Wikipedia articles), which is calculated by the fraction of the document containing the word. $P(q_i, q_j|C_{ont})$ is the probability of observing the document in which q_i and q_j both occur. PMI mapping assumes that similar words tend to cooccur more frequently, and is good at capturing frequently co-occurring concepts (both nouns and verbs).

Word embedding mapping: This mapping learns a word embedding that helps predict the surrounding words in a sentence [30, 24]. The learned embedding, usually by neural network models, is in a lower-dimensional vector space, and the cosine coefficient between two words is often used to measure their distance. It is fast and also able to capture the frequent co-occurred words in similar contexts.

4.3 Multimodal Search

Given a system query, the multimodal search component aims at retrieving a ranked list for each modality. We are interested in leveraging the well-studied text retrieval models for video retrieval. There is no single retrieval model that can work the best for all modalities. As a result, our system incorporates several classical retrieval models and applies them to their most appropriate modalities. Let $Q = q_1, \ldots, q_n$ denote a system query. A retrieval model ranks videos by the score $s(d|Q)$, where d is a video in the video collection C. Our system includes the following retrieval models:

Vector Space Model (VSM): This model represents both a video and a query as a vector of the words in the system vocabulary. The common vector representation includes generic term frequency (tf) and term frequency-inverse document frequency (tf-idf) [42]. $s(d|Q)$ derives from either the product or the cosine coefficient between the video and the query vector.

Okapi BM25: This model extends tf-idf representation:

$$s(d|Q)=\sum_{i=1}^{n}\log\frac{|C|-df(q_i)+\frac{1}{2}}{df(q_i)+\frac{1}{2}}\frac{tf(q_i,d)(k_1+1)}{tf(q_i,d)+k_1(1-b+b\frac{len(d)}{\overline{len}})}, \quad (2)$$

where $|C|$ is the total number of videos. $df(\cdot)$ returns the document frequency for a given word in the collection; $tf(q_i, d)$ returns the raw term frequency for the word q_i in the video d. $len(d)$ calculates the sum of concept or word detection scores in the video d, and $\overline{len}$ is the average video length in the collection. k_1 and b are two parameters to tune [25]. In the experiments, we set $b = 0.75$, and tune k_1 in [1.2, 2.0].

Language Model-JM Smoothing (LM-JM): The score is considered to be generated by a unigram language model [45]:

$$s(d|Q) = \log P(d|Q) \propto \log P(d) + \sum_{i=1}^{n} \log P(q_i|d), \quad (3)$$

where $P(d)$ is usually assumed to be following the uniform distribution, i.e. the same for every video. $P(q_i|d)$ equals:

$$P(q_i|d) = \lambda \frac{tf(q_i, d)}{\sum_w tf(w, d)} + (1-\lambda)P(q_i|C), \quad (4)$$

where w enumerates all words or concepts in a given video, and $P(q_i|C)$ is called a smoother that can be calculated by $df(q_i)/|C|$. Eq. (4) linearly interpolates the maximum likelihood estimation (first term) with the collection model (second term) by a coefficient λ. The parameter is usually tuned in the range of [0.7, 0.9]. This model is good for retrieving long text queries, e.g. the frequent words in the event kit description.

Language Model-Dirichlet Smoothing (LM-DL): This model adds a conjugate prior to the language model:

$$P(q_i|d) = \frac{tf(q_i, d) + \mu P(q_i|C)}{\sum_w tf(w, d) + \mu}, \quad (5)$$

where μ is the coefficient balancing the likelihood model and the conjugate prior, and is usually tuned in [0, 2000] [45]. This model is good for short text queries, e.g. the event name representation.

4.4 Pseudo Relevance Feedback

PRF (or reranking) is a cost-effective method in improving performance. Studies have shown that it might hurt a few queries but generally improves the overall performance across all queries. We incorporate a general multimodal PRF method called SPaR [15] in our system.

Self-Paced Reranking (SPaR): This method is inspired by the cognitive and learning process of humans and animals that gradually learning from easy to more complex samples [2, 22, 17, 46]. The easy samples in this problem are the videos ranked at the top, which are generally more relevant than those ranked lower. SPaR can take the input of either a single fused ranked list or a number of ranked lists from each of the modalities.[1] For convenience of notation, we mainly discuss the case of a single ranked list. Let Θ denote the reranking model. $\mathbf{x}_i$ denotes the feature of the ith video and y_i for the ith pseudo label. Note that x_i could be both high-level and low-level features [18]. We have:

$$\min_{\Theta,\mathbf{y},\mathbf{v}} \sum_{i=1}^{n} v_i L(\mathbf{x}_i, y_i; \Theta) + f(\mathbf{v}; \lambda) \quad (6)$$
$$\text{s.t. Constraints on } \Theta, \mathbf{y} \in \{-1,+1\}^n, \mathbf{v} \in [0,1]^n,$$

where $\mathbf{v} = [v_1, \ldots, v_n]$ are latent weight variables for each sample; L is the loss function in Θ; f is self-paced function which determines the learning scheme, i.e. how to select and weight samples. λ is a parameter controlling the model age. When λ is small, a few easy samples with smaller loss will be considered. As λ grows, more samples with larger loss will be gradually appended to train a mature model.

To run PRF in practice, we first need to pick a reranking model Θ (e.g. SVM or regression model), a self-paced function (e.g. binary, linear or mixture weighting) [15, 17], and reasonable starting values for the pseudo labels. The starting values can be initialized either by top ranked videos in the retrieved ranked lists or by other PRF methods. After the initialization, we iterate the following three steps:

[1]When different retrieval models are used for different features, and their ranked lists have very different score distributions, we may need to solve a linear programming problem to determine the starting pseudo positives [18].

1) training a model based on the selected pseudo samples and their weights (fixing $\mathbf{v}, \mathbf{y}$, optimize Θ); 2) calculating pseudo positive samples and their weights by the self-paced function f, and selecting some pseudo negative samples randomly (fixing Θ, optimize $\mathbf{v}, \mathbf{y}$)[2]; the weights of pseudo positive samples may be directly calculated by the closed-form solutions of f [15]; 3) increasing the model age to include more positive samples in the next iteration (increase λ). The value of λ is increased not by the absolute value but by the number of positive samples to be included. For example, if 5 samples need to be included, we can set λ by the $6th$ smallest loss so that the samples whose loss are greater than λ will have 0 weight. In our system, MMPRF [18] and SPaR [15] are incorporated, in which MMPRF is used to assign the starting values, and SPaR is used as the core algorithm. Average fusion of the PRF result with and original ranked list is used to obtain better results.

PRF is a cost-effective method in improving the performance of event search. We observed that the precision of the pseudo positives determines the performance of PRF (see Fig.5 in [18]). Therefore, high precision features such as OCR and ASR often turns out to be very useful. In addition, soft weighting self-paced functions that discriminate samples at different ranked positions tend to be better than binary weighting functions [15]. In this case, the model should support sample weighting (e.g. Libsvm tools-weights [4]). We observed two scenarios where the discussed reranking method could fail. First, SPaR may not help when the accuracy of the starting pseudo positive samples is below some threshold (e.g. the precision of pseudo positive is less than 0.1). This may be due to less relevant queries or poor quality of the high-level features. In this case, SPaR may not be useful. Second, SPaR may not help when the features used in PRF are not discriminative.

5. EXPERIMENTS

5.1 Setups

Dataset and evaluation: The experiments are conducted on the TRECVID Multimedia Event Detection (MED) MED13Test and MED14Test, evaluated by the official metric Mean Average Precision (MAP). Each set includes 20 events and 25,000 testing videos. The official test split released by NIST is used, and the reported MAP is comparable with others on the same split. The experiments are conducted without using any examples. We also evaluate each experiment on 10 randomly generated splits to reduce the bias brought by the split partition. The mean and 90% confidence interval are reported. Besides, the official results on MED14Eval evaluated by NIST TRECVID is also reported in the performance overview.

Features and queries: High-level features are Automatic Speech Recognition (ASR), Optical Character Recognition (OCR), and visual semantic concepts. ImageNet features are trained on still images by deep convolution neural networks [21]. The rest are directly trained on videos by the SVM-based self-paced learning pipeline [16, 17]. The video datasets include: Sports [20], Yahoo Flickr Creative Common (YFCC) [35], Internet Archive Creative Common (IACC) [32] and Do it Yourself (DIY) [43]. The details of these datasets can be found in Table 1. In total, 3,043 video-based concept detectors are trained using the improved dense trajectory features [39], which costs more than 1.2 million CPU core hours (1,024 cores for about 2 months) in Pittsburgh Super-computing Center. Once trained, the detection (semantic indexing) for test videos is very fast. Two types of low-level features are used: dense trajectories [39] and MFCC [44] in the PRF model. The detailed configuration about PRF is available in the supplementary materials[3]. The input user query is the event-kit description. The system query is obtained by a two-step procedure: a preliminary mapping is automatically generated by the discussed mapping algorithms. The results are then examined by human experts to figure out the final system query. See supplementary materials for the example of user and system queries. For ASR/OCR, the automatically generated event name and description representation are used as the system query. Note that manual query examination is allowed in TRECVID and is used by many teams [32]. The automatically generated queries will be discussed in Section 5.5.

5.2 Performance Overview

We first examine the overall MAP ($\times 100$) of the full system. Table 2 lists the MAP and the runtime (ms/query)[4] across six datasets. The average MAP and the 90% confidence interval on the 10-splits are reported on MED13Test and MED14Test. The ground-truth data on MED14Eval has never been released, and thus the MAP evaluated by NIST TRECVID is only available on the single split. We observed that the results on a single split can be deceiving as no training data makes the result prone to overfitting. Therefore, we evaluate the MAP also on the ten splits. We observed that an improvement is statistically significant if it can be observed in the both cases.

Our system achieves the best performance across all of the datasets. According to [32], for example, Fig. 3 illustrates the comparison on the largest set of around 200,000 Internet videos, where the x-axis lists the system of each team, and the y-axis denotes the MAP evaluated by NIST TRECVID. The red bars represent our system with and without PRF. As we see, our system achieves the best performance which is about three times of the second best system. The improvement of PRF is evident as it is the only difference between the two red bars in Fig. 3. It is worth noting that the evaluation is very rigid because each system can only submit a single run within 60 minutes after getting the query, and the ground-truth data is not released even after the submission. In addition, for the ad-hoc events (see Fig. 3(b)) the query are generated online and unknown to the system beforehand. Since blind queries are more challenging, all systems perform worse on ad-hoc events. Nevertheless, our system still achieves an outstanding MAP.

5.3 Modality/Feature Contribution

Table 3 compares the modality contribution, where each run represents a system with a certain configuration. The MAP is evaluated on MED14Test and MED13Test, where the ground-truth data is available. As we see, visual modality is the most contributing modality, which by itself can recover about 85% MAP of the full system. ASR and OCR

[2] The reason we can randomly select pseudo negative samples is that they have negligible impacts on performance [18].

[3] http://www.cs.cmu.edu/~lujiang/0Ex/icmr15.html

[4] The time is the search time evaluated on an Intel Xeon 2.53GHz CPU. It does not include the PRF time, which is about 238ms over 200K videos.

Table 1: Summary of the datasets for training semantic visual concepts. ImageNet features are trained on still images, and the rest are trained on videos.

Dataset	#Samples	#Classes	Category	Example Concepts
DIY [43, 44]	72,000	1,601	Instructional videos	Yoga, Juggling, Cooking
IACC [32]	600,000	346	Internet archive videos	Baby, Outdoor, Sitting down
YFCC [35]	800,000	609	Amateur videos on Flickr	Beach, Snow, Dancing
ImageNet [8]	1,000,000	1000	Still images	Bee, Corkscrew, Cloak
Sports [20]	1,100,000	487	Sports videos on YouTube	Bullfighting, Cycling, Skiing

Table 2: Overview of the system performance.

Dataset	#Videos	MAP (×100)		time
		1-split	10-splits	(ms)
MED13Test	25K	20.75	19.47±1.19	80
MED14Test	25K	20.60	17.27±1.82	112
MED14EvalSub-PS	32K	24.1	-	192
MED14EvalSub-AH	32K	22.1	-	200
MED14Eval-PS	200K	18.1	-	1120
MED14Eval-AH	200K	12.2	-	880

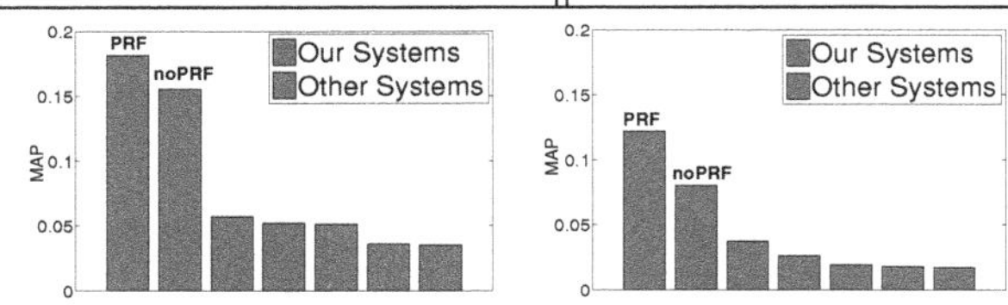

(a) Pre-Specified (PS) (b) Ad-Hoc (AH)

Figure 3: The official results released by NIST TRECVID 2014 on MED14Eval (200, 000 videos).

provide contribution to the full system but prove to be much worse than the visual features. PRF is beneficial in improving the performance of the full system.

To understand the feature contribution, we conduct leave-one-feature-out experiments. The performance drop, after removing the feature, can be used to estimate its contribution to the full system. As we see in Table 4, the results show that every feature provides some contribution. As the feature contribution is mainly dominated by a number of discriminative events, the comparison is more meaningful at the event-level (see supplementary materials[3]), where one can tell that, for example, the contribution of ImageNet mainly comes from three events E031, E015 and E037. Though the MAP drop varies on different events and datasets, the average drop on the two datasets follows: Sports > ImageNet > ASR > IACC > YFCC > DIY > OCR. The biggest contributor Sports is also the most computationally expensive feature. In fact, the above order of semantic concepts highly correlates to #samples in their datasets, which suggests the rationale of training concepts over big data sets.

Table 3: Comparison of modality contribution.

Run	MED13Test		MED14Test	
	1-split	10-splits	1-split	10-splits
FullSys+PRF	22.12	-	22.05	-
FullSys	20.75	19.47±1.19	20.60	18.77±2.16
VisualSys	18.31	18.30±1.11	17.58	17.27±1.82
ASRSys	6.53	6.90±0.74	5.79	4.26±1.19
OCRSys	2.04	4.14±0.07	1.47	2.20±0.73

5.4 Quantity (Relevance) & Quality Tradeoff

To study the concept quantity (relevance) and quality trade-off, we conduct the following experiments where the IACC and ImageNet concepts are gradually added to the query, one at a time, according to their relevance. The relevance judgment is manually annotated by a group of assessors on 20 events. Fig. 4 illustrates the results on a representative event, where the x-axis denotes the number of concepts included, and the y-axis is the average precision. Each curve represents a trial of only selecting concepts of certain quality. The quality is manually evaluated by the precision of the top 10 detected examples on a third dataset. For example, the red curve indicates selecting only the relevant concepts whose precision of the top 10 detected examples is greater than 0.5. The blue curve marked by circles ($p@10 > 0$) is a trial of the largest vocabulary but on average the least accurate concepts. In contrast, the dashed curve is of the smallest vocabulary but the most accurate concepts, and thus for a query, there are fewer relevant concepts to choose from. As we see, neither of the settings is optimal. Selecting concepts with a reasonable precision, between 0.2 and 0.5 in this case, seems to be a better choice. The results suggest that incorporating more relevant concepts with reasonable quality is a sensible strategy. We also observed that merely increasing the number of low-quality concepts may not be helpful.

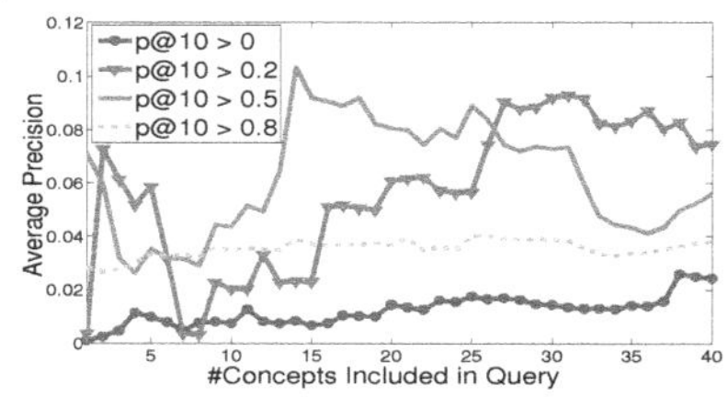

Figure 4: Adding relevant concepts in "E037 Parking a vehicle" using concepts of different precisions.

5.5 Semantic Matching in SQG

We apply the SQG algorithms to map the user query to the concept in the vocabulary. We use two metrics to compare these mapping algorithms. One is the precision of the 5 most relevant concepts returned by each algorithm. We manually assess the relevance for 10 events (E031-E040) on 4 concept features (i.e. 200 pairs for each mapping algorithm). The other is the MAP obtained by the 3 most relevant concepts. Table 5 lists the results, where the last column lists the runtime of calculating the mapping between 1,000 pairs of words. The second last row (Fusion) indicates the average fusion of the results of all mapping algorithms. As we see, in terms of P@5, PMI is slightly better than others, but it is also the slowest because its calculation involves looking up a index of 6 million articles in Wikipedia. Fusion of all mapping results yields a better P@5.

We then combine the automatically mapped semantic concepts with the automatically generated ASR and OCR query to test the MAP. Here we assume users have specified which feature to use for each query, and SQG is used to automatically find relevant concepts or words in the specified features. Our result can be understood as an overestimate of a fully-automatic SQG system, in which users do not even need to specify the feature. As we see in Table 5, PMI performs the best on MED13Test whereas on MED14Test it is Exact Word Matching. The fusion of all mapping results (the

Table 4: Comparison of feature contribution.

SysID	Visual Concepts					ASR	OCR	MAP		MAP Drop(%)
	IACC	Sports	YFCC	DIY	ImageNet			1-split	10-splits	
MED13/IACC		✓	✓	✓	✓	✓	✓	18.93	18.61±1.13	9%
MED13/Sports	✓		✓	✓	✓	✓	✓	15.67	14.68±0.92	25%
MED13/YFCC	✓	✓		✓	✓	✓	✓	18.14	18.47±1.21	13%
MED13/DIY	✓	✓	✓		✓	✓	✓	19.95	18.70±1.19	4%
MED13/ImageNet	✓	✓	✓	✓		✓	✓	18.18	16.58±1.18	12%
MED13/ASR	✓	✓	✓	✓	✓		✓	18.48	18.78±1.10	11%
MED13/OCR	✓	✓	✓	✓	✓	✓		20.59	19.12±1.20	1%
MED14/IACC		✓	✓	✓	✓	✓	✓	18.34	17.79±1.95	11%
MED14/Sports	✓		✓	✓	✓	✓	✓	13.93	12.47±1.93	32%
MED14/YFCC	✓	✓		✓	✓	✓	✓	20.05	18.55±2.13	3%
MED14/DIY	✓	✓	✓		✓	✓	✓	20.40	18.42±2.22	1%
MED14/ImageNet	✓	✓	✓	✓		✓	✓	16.37	15.21±1.91	20%
MED14/ASR	✓	✓	✓	✓	✓		✓	18.36	17.62±1.84	11%
MED14/OCR	✓	✓	✓	✓	✓	✓		20.43	18.86±2.20	1%

second last row) improves the MAP on both the datasets. We then fine-tune the parameters of the mapping fusion and build our AutoSQG system (the last row). As we see, AutoSQG only achieves about 55% of the full system's MAP. Several reasons account for the performance drop: 1) the concept name does not accurately describe what is being detected; 2) the quality of mapping is limited (P@5=0.42); 3) relevant concepts may not necessarily be discriminative. For example, "animal" and "throwing ball" appear to be relevant to the query "playing a fetch", but the former is too general and the latter is about throwing a baseball which is visually different; "dog" is much less discriminative than "group of dogs" for the query "dog show". The results suggest that the automatic SQG is not well-understood. The proposed automatic mappings are still very preliminary, and could be further refined by manual inspection. We found it is beneficial to represent a concept as a multimodal document that includes a name, description, category, reliability (accuracy) and examples of the top detected video snippet.

Table 5: Comparison of SQG mapping algorithms.

Mapping Method	P@5	MAP		Time (s)
		13Test	14Test	
Exact Word Matching	0.340	9.66	7.22	0.10
WordNet	0.330	7.86	6.68	1.22
PMI	0.355	9.84	6.95	22.20
Word Embedding	0.335	8.79	6.21	0.48
Mapping Fusion	0.420	10.22	9.38	-
AutoSQGSys	-	12.00	11.45	-

5.6 Comparison of Retrieval Methods

Table 6 compares the retrieval models on MED14Test using four features: ASR, OCR and two types of visual concepts. As we see, there is no single retrieval model that works the best for all features. For ASR and OCR words, BM25 and Language Model with JM smoothing (LM-JM) yield the best MAPs. An interesting observation is that VSM can only achieve 50% MAP of LM-JM on ASR (2.94 versus 5.79). This observation suggests that the role of retrieval models in video search is substantial. For semantic concepts, VSM performs no worse than other models. We hypothesize that it is because the concept representation is dense, i.e. every dimension has a nonzero value, and thus is quite different from sparse text features. To verify this hypothesis, we sparsify the Sports representation using a basic approach, where we only preserve the top m dimensions in a video, and m is set proportional to the concept vocabulary size. As we see, the sparse feature with 1% nonzero elements can recover 85% of its dense representation. Besides, BM25 and LM exhibit better MAPs in the sparse representation. Since the dense representation is difficult to index and search, the results suggest a promising direction for large-scale search using the sparse semantic feature.

Table 6: Comparison of retrieval models on MED14Test using ASR, OCR, Sports and IACC.

Feat.	Split	VSM-tf	VSM-tfidf	BM25	LM-JM	LM-DP
ASR	1	2.94	1.26	3.43	**5.79**	1.45
	10	2.67	1.49	3.03	**4.26**	1.14
OCR	1	0.56	0.47	**1.47**	1.02	1.22
	10	2.50	2.38	**4.52**	3.80	4.07
Sports	1	**9.21**	8.97	8.83	8.75	7.57
	10	**10.61**	10.58	10.13	10.25	9.04
IACC	1	3.49	**3.52**	2.44	2.96	2.06
	10	**2.88**	2.77	2.05	2.45	2.08

Table 7: Study of retrieval performance using sparse concept features (Sports) on MED14Test.

Density	VSM-tf	BM25	LM-JM	LM-DP
1%	9.06	**9.58**	9.09	9.38
2%	9.93	10.12	**10.14**	10.07
4%	10.34	10.36	10.26	**10.38**
16%	**10.60**	10.45	10.03	9.89
100%	**10.61**	10.13	10.25	9.04

6. CONCLUSIONS AND FUTURE WORK

We proposed a state-of-the-art semantic video search engine called E-Lamp. The proposed system goes beyond conventional text matching approaches, and allows for semantic search without any textual metadata or example videos. We shared our lessons on system design and compelling insights on a number of empirical studies. From the experimental results, we arrive at the following recommendations.

- **Recommendation 1**: Training concept detectors on big data sets is ideal. However, given limited resources, building more detectors of reasonable accuracy seems to be a sensible strategy. Merely increasing the number of low-quality concepts may not improve performance.
- **Recommendation 2**: PRF (or reranking) is an effective approach to improve the search result.
- **Recommendation 3**: Retrieval models may have substantial impacts to the search result. A reasonable strategy is to incorporate multiple models and apply them to their appropriate features/modalities.
- **Recommendation 4**: Automatic query generation for queries in the form of event-kit descriptions is still very challenging. Combining mapping results from various mapping algorithms and applying manual examination afterward is the best strategy known so far.

This paper is merely a first effort towards semantic search in Internet videos. The proposed system can be improved in various ways, e.g. by incorporating more accurate visual and audio concept detectors, by studying more appropriate retrieval models, by exploring search interfaces or interactive search schemes. As shown in our experiments, the automatic semantic query generation is not well understood. Closing the gap between the manual and automatic query may point to a promising direction.

Acknowledgments

The authors would like to thank Yajie Miao, Chuang Gan, Shicheng Xu, and Susanne Burger for meaningful discussions and kind support.

This work was partially supported by the Intelligence Advanced Research Projects Activity (IARPA) via Department of Interior National Business Center contract number D11PC20068. Deyu Meng was partially supported by the China NSFC project under contract 61373114. The U.S. Government is authorized to reproduce and distribute reprints for Governmental purposes notwithstanding any copyright annotation thereon. Disclaimer: The views and conclusions contained herein are those of the authors and should not be interpreted as necessarily representing the official policies or endorsements, either expressed or implied, of IARPA, DoI/NBC, or the U.S. Government. This work used the Extreme Science and Engineering Discovery Environment (XSEDE), which is supported by National Science Foundation grant number OCI-1053575. It used the Blacklight system at the Pittsburgh Supercomputing Center (PSC).

7. REFERENCES

[1] S. Banerjee and T. Pedersen. An adapted lesk algorithm for word sense disambiguation using wordnet. In *CICLing*, 2002.

[2] Y. Bengio, J. Louradour, R. Collobert, and J. Weston. Curriculum learning. In *ICML*, 2009.

[3] S. Bhattacharya, F. X. Yu, and S.-F. Chang. Minimally needed evidence for complex event recognition in unconstrained videos. In *ICMR*, 2014.

[4] C.-C. Chang and C.-J. Lin. LIBSVM: A library for support vector machines. *ACM TIST*, 2:27:1–27:27, 2011.

[5] K. W. Church and P. Hanks. Word association norms, mutual information, and lexicography. *Computational linguistics*, 16(1):22–29, 1990.

[6] J. Dalton, J. Allan, and P. Mirajkar. Zero-shot video retrieval using content and concepts. In *CIKM*, 2013.

[7] J. Davidson, B. Liebald, J. Liu, et al. The youtube video recommendation system. In *RecSys*, 2010.

[8] J. Deng, W. Dong, R. Socher, L.-J. Li, K. Li, and L. Fei-Fei. Imagenet: A large-scale hierarchical image database. In *CVPR*, 2009.

[9] N. Gkalelis and V. Mezaris. Video event detection using generalized subclass discriminant analysis and linear support vector machines. In *ICMR*, 2014.

[10] A. Habibian, T. Mensink, and C. G. Snoek. Composite concept discovery for zero-shot video event detection. In *ICMR*, 2014.

[11] A. Habibian, K. E. van de Sande, and C. G. Snoek. Recommendations for video event recognition using concept vocabularies. In *ICMR*, 2013.

[12] A. Hauptmann, R. Yan, W.-H. Lin, M. Christel, and H. Wactlar. Can high-level concepts fill the semantic gap in video retrieval? a case study with broadcast news. *TMM*, 9(5):958–966, 2007.

[13] N. Inoue and K. Shinoda. n-gram models for video semantic indexing. In *MM*, 2014.

[14] L. Jiang, A. Hauptmann, and G. Xiang. Leveraging high-level and low-level features for multimedia event detection. In *MM*, 2012.

[15] L. Jiang, D. Meng, T. Mitamura, and A. G. Hauptmann. Easy samples first: Self-paced reranking for zero-example multimedia search. In *MM*, 2014.

[16] L. Jiang, D. Meng, S.-I. Yu, Z. Lan, S. Shan, and A. G. Hauptmann. Self-paced learning with diversity. In *NIPS*, 2014.

[17] L. Jiang, D. Meng, Q. Zhao, S. Shan, and A. G. Hauptmann. Self-paced curriculum learning. In *AAAI*, 2015.

[18] L. Jiang, T. Mitamura, S.-I. Yu, and A. G. Hauptmann. Zero-example event search using multimodal pseudo relevance feedback. In *ICMR*, 2014.

[19] L. Jiang, W. Tong, D. Meng, and A. G. Hauptmann. Towards efficient learning of optimal spatial bag-of-words representations. In *ICMR*, 2014.

[20] A. Karpathy, G. Toderici, S. Shetty, T. Leung, R. Sukthankar, and L. Fei-Fei. Large-scale video classification with convolutional neural networks. In *CVPR*, 2014.

[21] A. Krizhevsky, I. Sutskever, and G. E. Hinton. Imagenet classification with deep convolutional neural networks. In *Advances in neural information processing systems*, pages 1097–1105, 2012.

[22] M. Kumar, B. Packer, and D. Koller. Self-paced learning for latent variable models. In *NIPS*, 2010.

[23] H. Lee. Analyzing complex events and human actions in" in-the-wild" videos. In *UMD Ph.D Theses and Dissertations*, 2014.

[24] O. Levy and Y. Goldberg. Dependency-based word embeddings. In *ACL*, 2014.

[25] C. D. Manning, P. Raghavan, and H. Schütze. *Introduction to information retrieval*, volume 1. Cambridge university press Cambridge, 2008.

[26] M. Mazloom, X. Li, and C. G. Snoek. Few-example video event retrieval using tag propagation. In *ICMR*, 2014.

[27] Y. Miao, L. Jiang, H. Zhang, and F. Metze. Improvements to speaker adaptive training of deep neural networks. In *SLT*, 2014.

[28] Y. Miao and F. Metze. Improving low-resource cd-dnn-hmm using dropout and multilingual dnn training. In *INTERSPEECH*, 2013.

[29] Y. Miao, F. Metze, and S. Rawat. Deep maxout networks for low-resource speech recognition. In *ASRU*, 2013.

[30] T. Mikolov, I. Sutskever, K. Chen, G. S. Corrado, and J. Dean. Distributed representations of words and phrases and their compositionality. In *NIPS*, 2013.

[31] S. Oh, S. McCloskey, I. Kim, A. Vahdat, K. J. Cannons, H. Hajimirsadeghi, G. Mori, A. A. Perera, M. Pandey, and J. J. Corso. Multimedia event detection with multimodal feature fusion and temporal concept localization. *Machine vision and applications*, 25(1):49–69, 2014.

[32] P. Over, G. Awad, M. Michel, J. Fiscus, G. Sanders, W. Kraaij, A. F. Smeaton, and G. Quéenot. TRECVID 2014 – an overview of the goals, tasks, data, evaluation mechanisms and metrics. In *TRECVID*, 2014.

[33] D. Povey, A. Ghoshal, G. Boulianne, et al. The kaldi speech recognition toolkit. In *ASRU*, 2011.

[34] B. Safadi, M. Sahuguet, and B. Huet. When textual and visual information join forces for multimedia retrieval. In *ICMR*, 2014.

[35] B. Thomee, D. A. Shamma, G. Friedland, B. Elizalde, K. Ni, D. Poland, D. Borth, and L.-J. Li. The new data and new challenges in multimedia research. *arXiv preprint arXiv:1503.01817*, 2015.

[36] W. Tong, Y. Yang, L. Jiang, et al. E-lamp: integration of innovative ideas for multimedia event detection. *Machine Vision and Applications*, 25(1):5–15, 2014.

[37] A. Vedaldi and A. Zisserman. Efficient additive kernels via explicit feature maps. *PAMI*, 34(3):480–492, 2012.

[38] F. Wang, Z. Sun, Y. Jiang, and C. Ngo. Video event detection using motion relativity and feature selection. In *TMM*, 2013.

[39] H. Wang and C. Schmid. Action recognition with improved trajectories. In *ICCV*, 2013.

[40] S. Wu, S. Bondugula, F. Luisier, X. Zhuang, and P. Natarajan. Zero-shot event detection using multi-modal fusion of weakly supervised concepts. In *CVPR*, 2014.

[41] Z. Wu and M. Palmer. Verbs semantics and lexical selection. In *ACL*, 1994.

[42] E. Younessian, T. Mitamura, and A. Hauptmann. Multimodal knowledge-based analysis in multimedia event detection. In *ICMR*, 2012.

[43] S.-I. Yu, L. Jiang, and A. Hauptmann. Instructional videos for unsupervised harvesting and learning of action examples. In *MM*, 2014.

[44] S.-I. Yu, L. Jiang, Z. Xu, et al. Cmu-informedia@trecvid 2014. In *TRECVID*, 2014.

[45] C. Zhai and J. Lafferty. A study of smoothing methods for language models applied to information retrieval. *TOIS*, 22(2), 2004.

[46] Q. Zhao, D. Meng, L. Jiang, Q. Xie, Z. Xu, and A. G. Hauptmann. Self-paced learning for matrix factorization. In *AAAI*, 2015.

Fast Democratic Aggregation and Query Fusion for Image Search

Zhanning Gao[‡] gaozn1990@stu.xjtu.edu.cn
Jianru Xue[‡] jrxue@mail.xjtu.edu.cn
Wengang Zhou[§] zhwg@ustc.edu.cn
Shanmin Pang[‡] pangshanminn@sina.com
Qi Tian[¶] qitian@cs.utsa.edu

[‡]Institute of Artificial Intelligence and Robotics, Xi'an Jiaotong University
[§]Department of EEIS, University of Science and Technology of China
[¶]Department of Computer Science, University of Texas at San Antonio

ABSTRACT

In image search using local features, to avoid indexing each feature individually, encoding methods are popularly adopted to embed and aggregate local features of an image into a compact vector. Democratic aggregation with triangulation embedding (T-embedding) exhibits significant retrieval accuracy improvement over previous works. However, it suffers high computational complexity. To address this problem and consistently improve the retrieval performance, we propose a new democratic method to accelerate aggregating step without accuracy lost. We also embed weak spatial context in the kernel construction to depress co-occurrence caused by local feature detector. Furthermore, we enhance the retrieval performance with an efficient query fusion strategy. The evaluation on public datasets shows that our democratic aggregation is an order of magnitude faster than the original democratic aggregation with comparable retrieval accuracy, and the query fusion achieves a significant accuracy improvement over previous works.

Categories and Subject Descriptors

I.4.10 [**Image Representation**]: Multidimensional, Statistical; H.3.3 [**Information Search and Retrieval**]: Relevance feedback

General Terms

Algorithms, Experimentation, Verification

Keywords

Democratic aggregation; Query fusion; Image retrieval

ICMR'15, June 23–26, 2015, Shanghai, China.

ACM 978-1-4503-3274-3/15/06 ...$15.00.
http://dx.doi.org/10.1145/2671188.2749293.

1. INTRODUCTION

Large-scale content-based image retrieval (CBIR) has attracted a sustained attention over the last decade. Most state-of-the-art CBIR techniques are based on the bag-of-visual-word (BOW) representation introduced in [26]. However, search time and memory footprint are nontrivial issues for BOW based approaches [12, 23, 30, 31, 32] when considering more than 10 million images [14].

Recently, several encoding methods that aggregate local descriptors into a compact vector have been proposed, such as VLAD [14], Fisher vector [22], Sparse-coded feature [8] and T-embedding with democratic aggregation [15]. Being equipped with dimensionality reduction and approximate nearest neighbor search algorithms, *e.g.*, product quantization [13] and Inverted Multi-Index [3], these methods make the goal of Web-scale image search feasible.

Existing encoding methods usually involve two steps: embedding/coding step and aggregating/pooling step [8, 14, 15]. The embedding step maps each local descriptor into a high-dimensional vector, and the aggregating step aggregates all the mapped vectors into a single vector. Perronnin *et al.* [22] use Gaussian Mixture Model (GMM) as the generative model, and aggregate normalized gradient vectors into a fixed-size Fisher vector. As a simplification of Fisher vector, VLAD [14] aggregates the concatenated residual vectors, which are mapped by a small codebook, to a single vector. Ge *et al.* [8] apply sparse coding to map local feature descriptors and max-pooling them into a single vector. Different from VLAD [14], T-embedding [15] calculates the residual vectors with each visual word instead of the nearest one and localizes the residual vectors in feature space with triangulation strategy. The evaluation on public datasets [15] shows that T-embedding based encoding methods outperform previous works by a large margin. Benefiting from the construction of a "democratic" kernel, democratic aggregation strategy [15] for T-embedding vectors can consistently improve the retrieval performance.

However, the democratic aggregation is extremely time consuming because of the coupling between T-embedding and calculation of the kernel matrix which contains all pairwise similarities derived from T-embedding vectors of an image (see details in Section 2). Moreover, the objective of democratic aggregation is to remove the interference between the embedded vectors of an image. However, it ignores the influence of co-occurrences [4].

We address the above problems by proposing a new way to construct the kernel matrix embedded with weak spatial context efficiently. This new matrix combines both local SIFT descriptors [18] and their weak spatial context in an image. First, to avoid extra whitening operation caused by the coupling between T-embedding and the calculation of kernel matrix, we adopt the original SIFT descriptors instead of embedded vectors to calculate the kernel matrix. Second, we take into account the spatial context of SIFT descriptors in an image to limit the dependence caused by artificial visual co-occurrences [9], *e.g.*, an image patch can be described multiple times for different orientations, producing several different yet co-occurring descriptors. The evaluation shows that our *fast democratic aggregation* is an order of magnitude faster than the original democratic aggregation with comparable retrieval accuracy.

To consistently improve the retrieval performance, inspired by query expansion [5] and the property of T-embedding vectors, we further propose a post-processing method, *query fusion*, for our compact image representation. Query expansion [5] significantly improves the retrieval accuracy of BOW based image search techniques [4, 12, 21, 24] at the expense of efficiency. Due to its sensitivity to false positives, spatial verification must be adopted before expanding features in the result image to the new query. For the short or mid-size vector representation, the original local descriptors and their geometric information are dropped after the embedding and aggregating steps. Therefore, the query expansion cannot be applied to our new image representation. However, considering the property of T-embedding, *i.e.*, the inner product between two unrelated vectors is close to zero with high probability [15], we can simply average query vector and the vectors of retrieval results to form a new refined query while escaping from the false positives issue. Experimental results show that our *query fusion* yields a significant improvement over previous works.

This paper is organized as follows. Section 2 reviews the background of T-embedding and presents the complexity analysis of the original democratic aggregation with T-embedding. After that, we introduce our *fast democratic aggregation* and *query fusion* schemes in Section 3 and Section 4, respectively. Experimental results are, then, presented in Section 5. Finally, we conclude the paper in Section 6.

2. MOTIVATION

In this section, in order to analyze the computational complexity of the original democratic aggregation, we first briefly introduce the original democratic aggregation with T-embedding, and then discuss the key steps that consume the majority time.

2.1 Triangulation Embedding

Let $\mathcal{X} = \{\mathbf{x}_1, ..., \mathbf{x}_n\}_i, \mathbf{x}_i \in \mathbb{R}^d, \|\mathbf{x}_i\| = 1$, be a set of local descriptors from an image. Triangulation embedding (T-embedding) maps each local descriptor into a high dimensional vector $\phi_\triangle(\mathbf{x}_i)$.

First, a set $\mathcal{C} = \{\mathbf{c}_1, ..., \mathbf{c}_{|\mathcal{C}|}\}_j, \mathbf{c}_j \in \mathbb{R}^d$, is learned by k-means from an independent training vectors set [15], which is similar to visual vocabularies learned in VLAD [14]. Then the residual vectors $r_j(\mathbf{x}_i) = \mathbf{x}_i - \mathbf{c}_j$[1] of $\mathbf{x}_i$ is calculated with each visual word $\mathbf{c}_j$ instead of using the nearest one. All the residual vectors are normalized by

$$\bar{r}_j(\mathbf{x}_i) = \{r_j(\mathbf{x}_i)/\|r_j(\mathbf{x}_i)\|\} \quad \text{for } j = 1, ..., |\mathcal{C}| \tag{1}$$

to discard the magnitude information. Accordingly, only directional information is preserved to localize local features in feature space with the triangulation strategy. After that, an intermediate vector $\mathbf{R}(\mathbf{x}_i) = [\bar{r}_1(\mathbf{x}_i)^\top, ..., \bar{r}_{|\mathcal{C}|}(\mathbf{x}_i)^\top]^\top$ is obtained by concatenating normalized residual vectors $\bar{r}_j$. Since $\mathbf{R}(\mathbf{x}_i)$ is redundant and gives too much weight to the dominant directions [15], a whitening operation [9, 17] is performed at last. T-embedding function can be derived as

$$\phi_\triangle(\mathbf{x}_i) = \Sigma^{-1/2}(\mathbf{R}(\mathbf{x}_i) - \mathbf{R}_0), \tag{2}$$

where $\mathbf{R}_0 = \mathbb{E}_\mathcal{Z}[\mathbf{R}(\mathcal{Z})]$ and $\Sigma^{-1/2}$ are learned from an independent training set $\mathcal{Z} = \{\mathbf{z}_1, ..., \mathbf{z}_h\}_i, \mathbf{z}_i \in \mathbb{R}^d, \|\mathbf{z}_i\| = 1$.

$$\Sigma^{-1/2} = \text{diag}(\sqrt{\gamma_1}, ..., \sqrt{\gamma_{|\mathcal{C}|\times d}})\mathbf{P}^\top, \tag{3}$$

where $\mathbf{P}$ is formed by the eigenvectors of the covariance matrix, which is estimated by the centered training set $\mathbf{R}(\mathcal{Z}) - \mathbf{R}_0$. γ_i is the eigenvalue associated with the ith eigenvector. To reduce the variance of the cosine similarity between unrelated T-embedding vectors, the first d components of $\phi_\triangle(\mathbf{x}_i)$ associated with the largest eigenvalues are discarded.

The final T-embedding vector is l_2-normalized and the dimensionality of $\phi_\triangle(\mathbf{x}_i)$ is $\text{D} = (|\mathcal{C}| - 1) \times d$. It should be noted that a key property of T-embedding vector [15] is that the inner product between two unrelated vectors is close to zero with high probability. This property is an important precondition to our *query fusion* strategy, which will be discussed in Section 4. The evaluation on public datasets [15] shows that T-embedding based encoding methods outperform previous works by a large margin. Therefore, we select T-embedding in our embedding step.

2.2 Original Democratic Aggregation

Let $\mathcal{X} = \{\mathbf{x}_1, ..., \mathbf{x}_n\}$ and $\mathcal{Y} = \{\mathbf{y}_1, ..., \mathbf{y}_m\}$ be two sets of local descriptors from two images. After T-embedding step, these two images can be compared with a match kernel $\mathcal{K}$ of the form

$$\mathcal{K}(\mathcal{X}, \mathcal{Y}) = \sum_{\mathbf{x}\in\mathcal{X}} \sum_{\mathbf{y}\in\mathcal{Y}} \phi_\triangle(\mathbf{x})^\top \phi_\triangle(\mathbf{y}). \tag{4}$$

The match kernel in matrix form is written as

$$\mathcal{K}(\mathcal{X}, \mathcal{Y}) = \mathbf{1}_n^\top \mathbf{K}(\mathcal{X}, \mathcal{Y})\mathbf{1}_m, \tag{5}$$

where $\mathbf{1}_m = \underbrace{[1, ..., 1]}_{m}$ and $\mathbf{K}(\mathcal{X}, \mathcal{Y})$ is calculated by T-embedding vectors as $\mathbf{K}(\mathcal{X}, \mathcal{Y}) =$

$$\begin{bmatrix} \phi_\triangle(\mathbf{x}_1)^\top \phi_\triangle(\mathbf{y}_1) & \cdots & \phi_\triangle(\mathbf{x}_1)^\top \phi_\triangle(\mathbf{y}_m) \\ \vdots & \ddots & \vdots \\ \phi_\triangle(\mathbf{x}_n)^\top \phi_\triangle(\mathbf{y}_1) & \cdots & \phi_\triangle(\mathbf{x}_n)^\top \phi_\triangle(\mathbf{y}_m) \end{bmatrix}. \tag{6}$$

In the aggregating step, a single D-dimensional vector is derived from the set $\{\phi_\triangle(\mathbf{x}_1), ..., \phi_\triangle(\mathbf{x}_n)\}$ by a function ψ, *e.g.*, a simple summation or sum-aggregation ψ_s, used in VLAD and Fisher vector [8]:

$$\psi_s(\mathcal{X}) = \sum_{\mathbf{x}\in\mathcal{X}} \phi_\triangle(\mathbf{x}). \tag{7}$$

[1] $\mathbf{x}_i \neq \mathbf{c}_j$ because $\|\mathbf{x}_i\| = 1$ and $\mathbf{c}_j$ are obtained by k-means

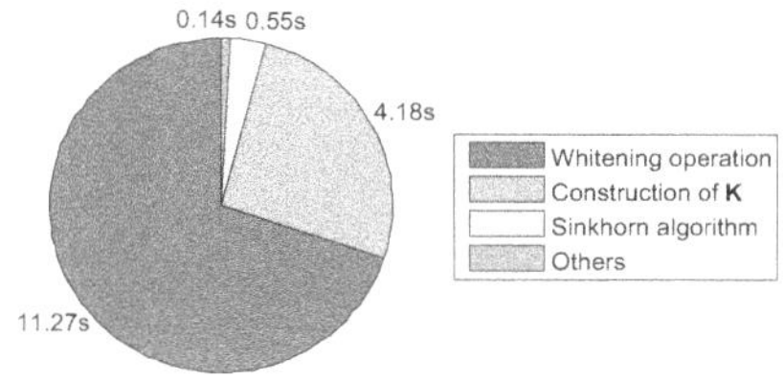

Figure 1: CPU timings of each stage in original democratic aggregation (DA). $|\mathcal{C}| = 64$, $\mathrm{D} = (|\mathcal{C}| - 1) \times d = 8064$.

Thus, the match kernel can be computed with a simple inner product as

$$\mathcal{K}(\mathcal{X}, \mathcal{Y}) = \sum_{\mathbf{x} \in \mathcal{X}} \sum_{\mathbf{y} \in \mathcal{Y}} \phi_{\triangle}(\mathbf{x})^{\top} \phi_{\triangle}(\mathbf{y}) = \psi_s(\mathcal{X})^{\top} \psi_s(\mathcal{Y}). \quad (8)$$

Instead of using a simple summation of the $\phi_{\triangle}(\mathbf{x})$, Jégou [15] propose a democratic aggregation method, which weights the summation:

$$\psi_d(\mathcal{X}) = \sum_{\mathbf{x}_i \in \mathcal{X}} \lambda_{\mathbf{x}_i} \phi_{\triangle}(\mathbf{x}_i). \quad (9)$$

The set of weighting coefficients $\{\lambda_{\mathbf{x}_1}, ..., \lambda_{\mathbf{x}_n}\}$ is used to modify the original match kernel $\mathcal{K}$ to a *democratic* kernel, which is defined as, for a set $\mathcal{X}$, if and only if the kernel matrix $\mathbf{K}$ satisfies

$$\mathbf{K}(\mathcal{X}, \mathcal{X})\mathbf{1}_n = c \cdot \mathbf{1}_n, \quad (10)$$

where c is a constant. Suppose the democratic kernel matrix of set $\mathcal{X}$ is $\mathbf{K}_d$, *i.e.*, $\mathbf{K}_d = c \cdot \mathbf{1}_n$, then

$$\mathbf{K}_d(\mathcal{X}, \mathcal{X}) = \mathbf{\Lambda} \mathbf{K}(\mathcal{X}, \mathcal{X}) \mathbf{\Lambda}, \quad (11)$$

where $\mathbf{\Lambda} = \mathrm{diag}(\lambda_{\mathbf{x}_1}, ..., \lambda_{\mathbf{x}_n})$ is a matrix whose diagonal is positive and $\mathbf{K}(\mathcal{X}, \mathcal{X})$ is derived from equation (6). Therefore, the set $\{\lambda_{\mathbf{x}_1}, ..., \lambda_{\mathbf{x}_n}\}$ is determined by solving the following equation

$$\mathbf{\Lambda} \mathbf{K}(\mathcal{X}, \mathcal{X}) \mathbf{\Lambda} \mathbf{1}_n = c \cdot \mathbf{1}_n. \quad (12)$$

After setting all negative elements of $\mathbf{K}$ to 0 and $c = 1$, equation (12) can be solved by a symmetic variant of the Sinkhorn scaling algorithm [16].

2.3 Complexity Analysis

Figure 1 shows the timings of each stage in democratic aggregation. The results are obtained from the 1491 images of **INRIA Holidays** [10]. We present the CPU time which accumulates all active threads with the MATLAB code released by Jégou [15]. It shows that the whitening operation and calculation of the matrix $\mathbf{K}$ are bottlenecks of democratic aggregation, especially the whitening step of projecting each residual vector separately with the matrix $\Sigma^{-1/2}$. The democratic aggregation with T-embedding vectors can be derived by equations (2) and (9) as

$$\psi_d(\mathcal{X}) = \sum_{\mathbf{x}_i \in \mathcal{X}} \lambda_{\mathbf{x}_i} \Sigma^{-1/2} \left(\mathrm{R}(\mathbf{x}_i) - \mathrm{R}_0 \right). \quad (13)$$

$\{\lambda_{\mathbf{x}_1}, ..., \lambda_{\mathbf{x}_n}\}$ relies on the matrix $\mathbf{K}$ which is calculated with equation (6). Unlike sum-aggregation which could be computed efficiently as

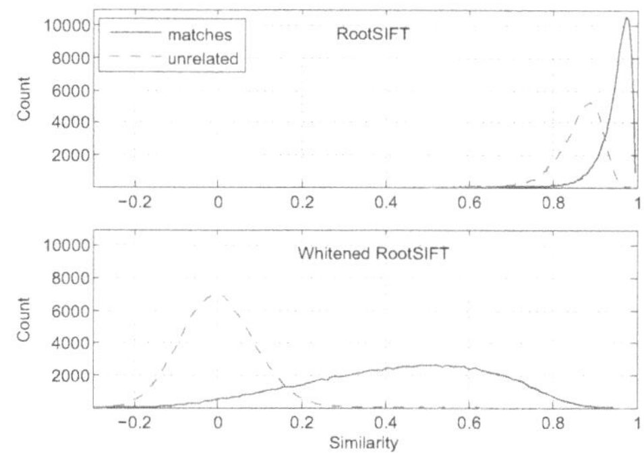

Figure 2: Histogram of the cosine similarity between related and unrelated image patches described by RootSIFT (first row) and Whitened RootSIFT(second row).

$$\psi_s(\mathcal{X}) = \Sigma^{-1/2} \sum_{\mathbf{x}_i \in \mathcal{X}} \left(\mathrm{R}(\mathbf{x}_i) - \mathrm{R}_0 \right), \quad (14)$$

equation (13) cannot be optimized due to the coupling between T-embedding and calculation of the matrix $\mathbf{K}$. Moreover, Construction of $\mathbf{K}$ is also time consuming due to the high dimensionality of T-embedding vector $\phi_{\triangle}(\mathbf{x})$.

3. FAST DEMOCRATIC AGGREGATION

We present our fast democratic aggregation method based on T-embedding vectors in this section. Other than using the original democratic aggregation, which uses T-embedding vectors to calculate the kernel matrix, we propose a simpler yet more effective strategy to obtain the kernel matrix, and develop a new democratic aggregation method.

The T-embedding vectors have two important properties. First, due to its high dimensionality, T-embedding reduces the loss of local features' distinctiveness in the aggregation step. Second, as mentioned in Section 2, the inner product between two unrelated vectors is close to zero with high probability, yet the inner product between two related T-embedding vectors, which are obtained from two matched descriptors, is often much greater than zero, *i.e.*, a better similarity metric. The kernel matrix $\mathbf{K}$ reflects the similarity between each pair of local descriptors of an image, which is similar to the affinity matrix [20] constructed in spectral clustering algorithm. Although the second property is important to obtain the similarity matrix, mapping local descriptors to high dimensionality vectors (T-embedding vectors) is unnecessary. First, the similarity between each pair of descriptors is calculated individually without aggregation. Second, mapping original descriptors to T-embedding vectors cannot enhance the distinctiveness of local descriptors. In other words, we may use the original descriptors to calculate the matrix $\mathbf{K}$ directly. However, as evaluated in [15] and illustrated in Figure 2, the inner product between two unrelated original descriptors (RootSIFT [1]) is also much larger than zero. Thus, if we can map the original descriptors to satisfy the second property without embedding step which increases the dimensionality, we can obtain the kernel matrix $\mathbf{K}$ efficiently before the aggregating step.

Figure 3: Examples of co-occurrences caused by the feature detector. Local features are extracted with Hessian-affine detector. Green ellipses denote the scale of local features. Red lines denote the main orientation of local features. Different orientations (red lines) also produce different descriptors. However, these descriptors sharing similar spatial location are extracted at the same time.

Whitened RootSIFT. Inspired by the whitening operation [9, 17] in the T-embedding step (see equation (2) and (3)), we propose to map the original RootSIFT $\mathbf{x}_i$ to whitened RootSIFT $\mathbf{d}_i$,

$$\mathbf{d}_i = \mathrm{diag}(\sqrt{\gamma_1}, ..., \sqrt{\gamma_d})\mathbf{Q}^\top(\mathbf{x}_i - \mathbf{z}_0), \tag{15}$$

where $\mathbf{z}_0 = \mathbb{E}_Z[\mathcal{Z}]$, and $\mathbf{Q}$ is formed by the eigenvectors of the covariance matrix, which is estimated by the centered training set $\mathcal{Z}$. γ_i is the eigenvalue associated with the ith eigenvector. After that, $\mathbf{d}_i$ is l_2-normalized. In the following we prove that similarity metric between whitened RootSIFT satisfies the second property.

To evaluate the similarity metric between whitened RootSIFT, we use the datasets *Liberty harris* and *Notredame harris* [2] [28] to compare the statistics of the cosine similarity for related and unrelated patches. About 110k pairs of matched image patches and the same number of pairs of unrelated patches are employed from *Notredame harris* to calculate the cosine similarity between the original RootSIFT descriptors and the whitened RootSIFT descriptors, respectively. The training stage of whitening operation is performed on *Liberty harris*. Figure 2 illustrates the different distribution of cosine similarity between RootSIFT and whitened RootSIFT. It shows that whitening operation increases the contrast between related and unrelated descriptors. In addition, the whitened RootSIFT descriptors satisfy the second property proposed above, *i.e.*, the cosine similarity between two unrelated descriptors is close to zero yet much larger than zero for related descriptors.

[2]http://www.cs.ubc.ca/~mbrown/patchdata/patchdata.html

Therefore, we can use the whitened RootSIFT to construct a new kernel matrix,

$$\mathbf{K}_{\mathrm{SIFT}} = \begin{bmatrix} \mathrm{sim}(\mathbf{d}_1, \mathbf{d}_1) & \cdots & \mathrm{sim}(\mathbf{d}_1, \mathbf{d}_n) \\ \vdots & \ddots & \vdots \\ \mathrm{sim}(\mathbf{d}_n, \mathbf{d}_1) & \cdots & \mathrm{sim}(\mathbf{d}_n, \mathbf{d}_n) \end{bmatrix}, \tag{16}$$

where

$$\mathrm{sim}(\mathbf{d}_i, \mathbf{d}_j) = \begin{cases} \langle \mathbf{d}_i | \mathbf{d}_j \rangle & \text{if } \langle \mathbf{d}_i | \mathbf{d}_j \rangle > t \\ 0 & \text{if } \langle \mathbf{d}_i | \mathbf{d}_j \rangle \le t. \end{cases} \tag{17}$$

Due to low dimensionality of the whitened RootSIFT, we can calculate the kernel matrix more efficiently compared with equation (6). Furthermore, the weighting coefficients for democratic aggregation can be pre-computed once the local features are extracted. Thus, like sum-aggregation (See equation (14)), we can achieve democratic aggregation efficiently with

$$\psi_{Fd}(\mathcal{X}) = \Sigma^{-1/2} \sum_{\mathbf{x}_i \in \mathcal{X}} \lambda'_{\mathbf{x}_i} (\mathrm{R}(\mathbf{x}_i) - \mathrm{R}_0), \tag{18}$$

and the set of weighting coefficients $\{\lambda'_{\mathbf{x}_1}, ..., \lambda'_{\mathbf{x}_n}\}$ is determined by solving the equation

$$\mathbf{\Lambda}'\mathbf{K}_{\mathrm{SIFT}}\mathbf{\Lambda}'\mathbf{1}_n = \mathbf{1}_n, \tag{19}$$

where $\mathbf{\Lambda}' = \mathrm{diag}(\lambda'_{\mathbf{x}_1}, ..., \lambda'_{\mathbf{x}_n})$.

Spatial Context. To further limit the dependence caused by co-occurrence, especially the artificial co-occurrences [9], we take into account the spatial context between local features in an image. Either the whitened RootSIFT descriptors or T-embedding vectors can only measure the similarity between local features. However, the co-occurrences [4, 9] of different local features in an image is also an important factor to evaluate the dependence between local features. Besides some visual patterns, such as water surface, lawn and brick wall, which introduce co-occurrences between different images, the feature detector may also introduce some artificial co-occurrences [9]. Figure 3 shows examples of co-occurrences caused by the feature detector. Chum [4] uses 10^6 visual words to capture the co-occurrences based on BOW framework. Although [15] employs RN (Rotation and Normalization) to addresses the co-occurrences issue, considering the small visual vocabulary, it is difficult to capture all of the co-occurrences only based on the covariance matrix [9]. As a supplement of RN, we introduce the spatial context of local features to capture the artificial co-occurrences in aggregating step.

The dependence matrix based on spatial context between local features is calculated by

$$\mathbf{K}_{\mathrm{SP}} = \begin{bmatrix} \mathrm{dep}(\mathbf{l}_1, \mathbf{l}_1) & \cdots & \mathrm{dep}(\mathbf{l}_1, \mathbf{l}_n) \\ \vdots & \ddots & \vdots \\ \mathrm{dep}(\mathbf{l}_n, \mathbf{l}_1) & \cdots & \mathrm{dep}(\mathbf{l}_n, \mathbf{l}_n) \end{bmatrix}, \tag{20}$$

where

$$\mathrm{dep}(\mathbf{l}_i, \mathbf{l}_j) = \begin{cases} 1 - \frac{1}{\beta}\sqrt{||\mathbf{l}_i - \mathbf{l}_j||} & \text{if } \sqrt{||\mathbf{l}_i - \mathbf{l}_j||} < \beta \\ 0 & \text{if } \sqrt{||\mathbf{l}_i - \mathbf{l}_j||} \ge \beta, \end{cases} \tag{21}$$

and $\mathbf{l}_i$ denote the location of each local feature on the image. Thus, we can combine spatial context to $\mathbf{K}_{\mathrm{SIFT}}$ by

$$\mathbf{K}_{\mathrm{new}} = (1 - \rho) \cdot \mathbf{K}_{\mathrm{SIFT}} + \rho \cdot \mathbf{K}_{\mathrm{SP}}, \tag{22}$$

Table 1: Complexity comparison with multiplications times. DA – Original democratic aggregation, FDA – Fast democratic aggregation. $card(\mathcal{X}) = n$, $\mathrm{D} = (|\mathcal{C}| - 1) \times d$.

method	Calculation of $\psi(\mathcal{X})$	Calculation of $\mathbf{K}/\mathbf{K}_{\text{new}}$
DA	$O(n\mathrm{D}^2)$	$O(n^2\mathrm{D})$
FDA	$O(\mathrm{D}^2)$	$O(n^2 d)$

and the weighting coefficients are computed by

$$\mathbf{\Lambda}'\mathbf{K}_{\text{new}}\mathbf{\Lambda}'\mathbf{1}_n = \mathbf{1}_n. \tag{23}$$

Experimental results show that, with the increase of $|\mathcal{C}|$, the capability of RN to improve retrieval performance is declining. However, benefiting from weak spatial constraint of local features, our new democratic aggregation consistently improves the retrieval performance.

In our experiments, we set $\beta = 5$ to get a sparse matrix. Note most of the cosine similarity $\langle \mathbf{d}_i | \mathbf{d}_j \rangle$ between unrelated descriptors, see Figure 2, is less than 0.2. Thus, we set $t = 0.2$. Table 1 shows the computational complexity comparing original and our fast democratic aggregation.

4. QUERY FUSION

In this section, we introduce our query retrieval strategy – *query fusion*. Query expansion [5] has significantly improved the retrieval accuracy of BOW based image search techniques [4, 12, 21, 24] at the expense of efficiency. However, due to its sensitivity to false positives, spatial verification, which works like a feature filter, shall be adopted before expanding the feature in the resulting image to the new query. The baseline of query expansion [5] that simply averages the BOW vectors computed from resulting image and the query without spatial verification obtains even worse retrieval result than that not using query expansion. In other word, the spatial verification is vital for query expansion.

Since no geometric information of local features is preserved after embedding and aggregating steps, the query expansion is not consistent with our new image representation. However, as mentioned in Section 2, the T-embedding vectors demonstrate a important property, that the cosine similarity between two unrelated T-embedding vectors is close to zero yet much larger than zero for related vectors. The similarity metric between T-embedding vectors is much robust for false positivity. This good property has similar effect as spatial verification. Thus, we can simply average query vector and resulting vectors to form a new refined query. We name this simple yet effective retrieval strategy as *query fusion*. An outline of our strategy is as follows:

1. Given a query and the number of iterations M, search the dataset vectors, and select the first N ranked vectors as fusion vector.
2. Average current query vector with N fusion vectors to form a new query.
3. Re-query the dataset with the new query, and get better retrieval results.
4. Repeat step 1-3 M times.

The influence of N and M will be discussed in next section. Experimental results show that our *query fusion* gives a significant improvement over previous works.

5. EXPERIMENTS

In this section, we present experimental results about our fast democratic aggregation and query fusion. We adopt T-embedding method in embedding step. The original democratic aggregation method [15] is employed as baseline to evaluated our fast democratic aggregation.

5.1 Datasets and Evaluation Protocol

To compare with the original democratic aggregation, we evaluate our method on two public datasets, **INRIA Holidays** [10] and **Oxford5k** [23]. We also report the performance on **Oxford105k**, which is a combination of Oxford5k with 100k distractor images, to evaluate the search quality on a larger scale.

INRIA Holidays contains 1491 images of different locations and objects. 500 images are selected as queries for each of the 500 partitioning groups on the image set. The retrieval performance is measured by mean average precision (mAP) with the query removed from the ranked list. All training stages are performed on the independent dataset **Flickr60k** provided with Holidays.

Oxford5k contains 5062 images of Oxford famous buildings. There are 55 query images corresponding to 11 distinct buildings. A bounding box is provided for each query to define the area of the query image depicting a landmark building. We only use the local descriptors inside the bounding box to construct the query vector similar as [15]. The retrieval performance is also measured by mean average precision (mAP) with the *junk* images removed from the ranked list. For the experiments on Oxford5k, all the training stages are performed on the **Paris6k** [24].

5.2 Implementation Details

Local descriptors. We use Hessian-Affine detector [19] to extract the regions of interest which are described by SIFT descriptors [18] post-processed with RootSIFT [1], *i.e.*, the same descriptors provided in previous works [2, 15].

Post-processing. We employ the same post-processing method as [15]. The final vector is power-law normalized [14, 22]. This process improves the performance by efficiently suppressing the visual bursts [11]. The power-law exponent α is set to 0.5 standardly as same as previous work to obtain the best or close-to-best performance. The resulting vector is l_2-normalized. As mentioned in Section 3, RN (Rotation and Normalization) operation is employed to address the co-occurrences issue. It is conducted with a second power-law normalization ($\alpha = 0.5$) after rotating the aggregated vectors with a PCA rotation matrix [25].

Dimensionality reduction. We keep only the first D' components of the aggregated vectors after RN operation to evaluate the performance of short vector representation.

Query fusion is compatible with power-law normalization and the RN operation. Therefore, the query fusion is performed after all these post-processing methods.

5.3 Fast Democratic Aggregation Evaluation

5.3.1 Impact of parameters

Compared with original aggregation method, our fast democratic aggregation introduces mixing coefficient ρ, threshold t and β, in addition to the vocabulary size $|\mathcal{C}|$, respectively. We empirically set $\beta = 5$ and $t = 0.2$ to obtain a sparse and positive kernel matrix $\mathbf{K}_{\text{new}}$.

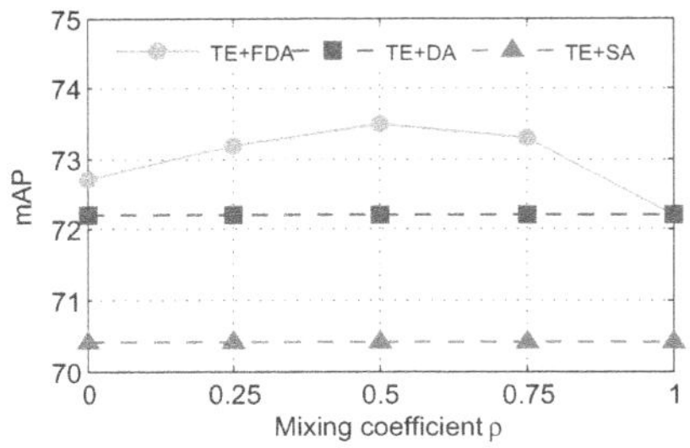

Figure 4: Influence of ρ on the Holidays dataset. TE – T-embedding, DA – Original democratic aggregation, FDA – Fast democratic aggregation, SA – Sum-aggregation.

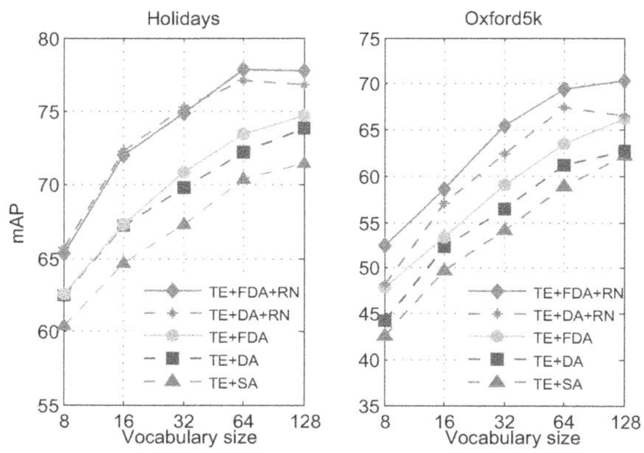

Figure 5: Retrieval performance with different vocabulary size on two datasets. RN – Rotation and normalization.

Influence of mixing coefficient. $\rho = 0$ means that the spatial context is ignored in aggregating step, while $\rho = 1$ means only spatial context is taken into account without the whitened RootSIFT descriptors. To evaluate the influence of ρ, we employ different ρ in democratic aggregating step with $|\mathcal{C}| = 64$ on Holidays dataset. Figure 4 illustrates the results. It shows that either whitened RootSIFT descriptors or spatial context can improve the performance compared with sum-aggregation (TE+SA). In addition, combining two of them achieves better democratic aggregation vectors. Therefore, in the following experiments, we set $\rho = 0.5$.

Vocabulary size $|\mathcal{C}|$. As Figure 5 shown, for different vocabulary size, our fast democratic aggregation obtains comparable or even better retrieval accuracy compared with original democratic aggregation. With the increase of vocabulary size, the capability of RN to improve retrieval performance is declining. However, duo to spatial context of local features, our new democratic aggregation combined with RN consistently improves the retrieval performance for larger vocabulary size.

5.3.2 Comparison with Original Aggregation

Timings. Figure 6 reports the timings for fast democratic aggregation and the original democratic aggregation. The evaluations are carried out on a Xeon E5-2680v2/2.8GHz (10cores) with the INRIA Holidays dataset. Both original and our aggregation methods are implemented with MATLAB code. Note, the CPU time is larger than elapsed time because it accumulates all active threads. Figure 6 shows that our fast democratic aggregation is an order of magnitude faster than the original democratic aggregation when $|\mathcal{C}| = 64$. The reason is that, first, the kernel matrix is calculated efficiently. Second, the weighting coefficients for democratic aggregation can be pre-computed without embedded vectors. Thus, like sum-aggregation, The final compact vector can be computed efficiently with equation (18).

Table 2: Performance comparison between original aggregation (DA) and our proposed fast democratic aggregation (FDA). We also present the results after dimensionality reduction to short vectors. TE – T-embedding, SA – Sum-aggregation, RN – Rotation and normalization.

		mAP		
Method	dim.	Holidays	Oxford5k	Ox105k
TE+SA		70.4	58.9	52.3
TE+DA		72.2	62.0	54.1
TE+FDA	8064	73.5	63.5	60.7
TE+DA+RN		77.1	67.6	61.1
TE+FDA+RN		**78.0**	**69.5**	**62.5**
TE+DA+RN	↓	72.0	56.2	49.2
TE+FDA+RN	1024	72.3	58.3	50.1
TE+DA+RN	↓	70.0	52.8	45.1
TE+FDA+RN	512	70.2	53.4	45.4

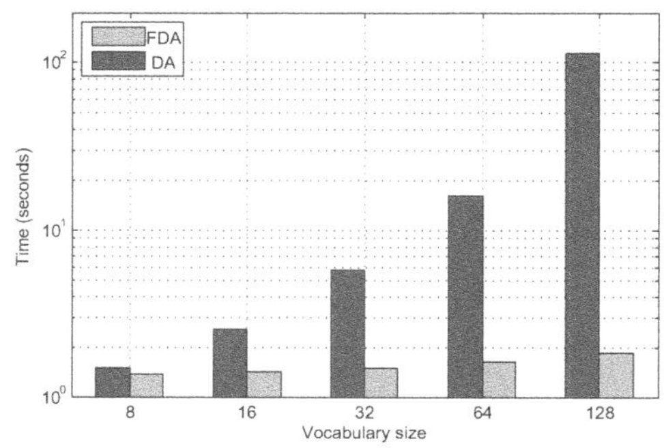

Figure 6: The average CPU timings for fast democratic aggregation (FDA) and the original democratic aggregation (DA) on Holidays. The vertical axis is shown in log-scale.

Performance. As Table 2 shown, besides efficient computation, our fast aggregation still achieves better retrieval accuracy than original aggregation methods. The performance after dimensionality reduction is also presented in Table 2. It shows that our method works well with RN operation and dimensionality reduction.

5.4 Query Fusion Evaluation

Impact of parameters. We first evaluate the influence of iteration number M and fused result vector number N for retrieval performance. Figure 7 illustrates the performance of query fusion with different M and N. It shows that no further improvement is obtained for larger M. The number

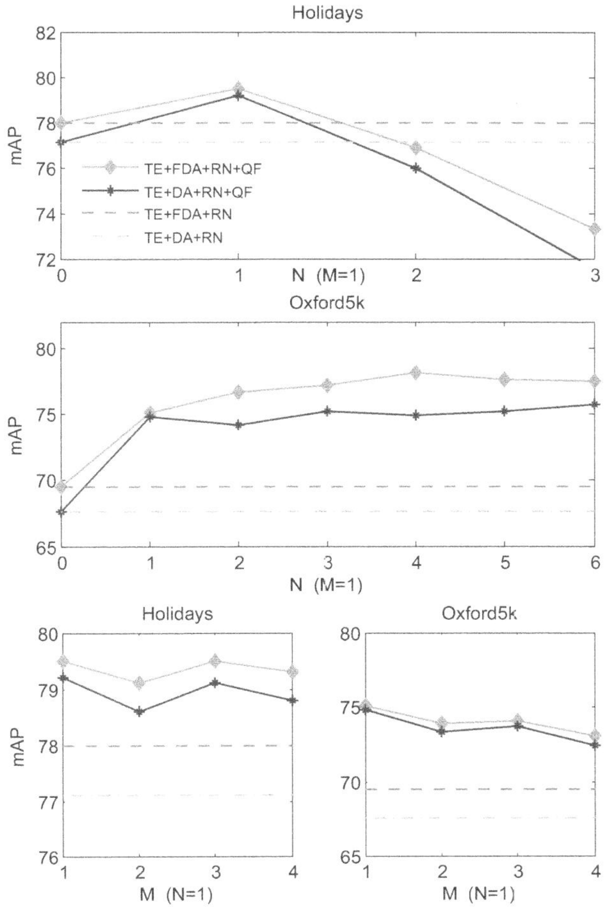

Figure 7: The performance of query fusion with different M and N. Note, we fix $M = 1$(or $N = 1$) to evaluate the influence of N(or M). $|\mathcal{C}| = 64$. QF – Query fusion.

of fusion vectors N has different influence on Holidays and Oxford5k. This is expected, since Holidays dataset contains only a few images of the same object. Therefore, previous works about query expansion [4, 5, 12, 21, 24] evaluate the performance of query expansion only with Oxford5k and Paris6k, which have quite a few related images for each query image. Our query fusion improves the retrieval accuracy on both Holiday and Oxfor5k with $N = 1$. On Oxford5k, the best result mAP = **78.1%** is obtained with $N = 4$ and $M = 1$. To obtain a trade off between accuracy and efficiency, $N = 1$ and $M = 1$ are our recommend parameters setting. Thus, query fusion needs search the dataset twice.

Performance. Table 3 presents the improvement obtained by query fusion. The short vectors after dimensionality reduction are also compatible with query fusion. Comparing the results on two different datasets, our query fusion strategy is more suitable for Oxford5k-like dataset, *i.e.*, the dataset that contains plenty related images for a query. Figure 8 shows some examples of image retrieval results on Oxford5k employed the query fusion strategy.

Table 3: Performance comparison between exhausted search and exhausted search combined with query fusion (QF). We also present the results after dimensionality reduction to short vectors. TE – T-embedding, DA – Original democratic aggregation, FDA – Fast democratic aggregation, RN – Rotation and normalization.

Method	dim.	mAP Hol.	mAP Ox5k	mAP Ox105k
TE+DA+RN		77.1	67.6	61.1
TE+DA+RN+QF	8064	79.2	74.8	69.0
TE+FDA+RN		78.0	69.5	62.5
TE+FDA+RN+QF		**79.5**	**75.1**	**71.8**
TE+DA+RN		72.0	56.2	49.2
TE+DA+RN+QF	↓	**74.5**	62.0	54.8
TE+FDA+RN	1024	72.3	58.3	50.1
TE+FDA+RN+QF		73.5	**67.3**	**58.5**
TE+DA+RN		70.0	52.8	45.1
TE+DA+RN+QF	↓	70.8	58.7	52.0
TE+FDA+RN	512	70.2	53.4	45.4
TE+FDA+RN+QF		**71.4**	**61.0**	**55.2**

Table 4: Performance comparison with other encoding methods. Results are compared with full vector representation.

Method	dim.	mAP Hol.	mAP Ox5k	mAP Ox105k
VLAD[14]	4096	55.6	37.8	–
Fisher[14]	4096	59.5	41.8	–
VLAD-intra[2]	32536	65.3	55.8	–
VLAD+[6]	8192	65.8	51.7	45.6
CVLAD[29]	32768	68.8	42.7	–
FV+Attr.[7]	6755	69.9	–	–
SC[8]	11024	76.7	–	–
TE+DA+RN[15]	8064	77.1	**67.6**	**61.1**
Fisher⊗[27]	17920	**81.2**	60.7	52.2
TE+FDA+RN	8064	78.0	69.5	62.5
TE+FDA+RN+QF	8064	**79.5**	**75.1**	**71.8**

5.5 Comparison with Other Methods

Table 4 shows that our method outperforms most of existing encoding methods. We find that Fisher⊗ [27] achieves better mAP on Holidays dataset than ours. However, The orientation covariant aggregation [27] leads to higher dimensionality of vector representation and sensitivity to the orientation of image. To obtained rotation invariance, multiple queries are computed for several hypothesis of angle rotation. Therefore, searching with Fisher⊗ is more expensive in computation than our mid-size vector representation. In fact, our fast democratic aggregation is compatible with orientation covariant aggregation and can be enhanced with it if necessary. Note, our method outperforms all of previous methods on Oxford5k.

6. CONCLUSION

In this paper, we concentrate on the construction of a short or mid-size vector representation for an image and its retrieval strategy. We first proposed a fast democratic aggregation method embedded with weak spatial context.

Figure 8: Example results on Oxford5k. The first row of each query shows retrieval results with query fusion, and the second row shows results without query fusion. False positives are marked with a red box, and *junk* [23] image is marked with blue box.

our method is an order of magnitude faster than the original democratic aggregation with comparable or even better retrieval accuracy. Then, based on the good property of T-embedding, we further propose a simple yet effective retrieval strategy, query fusion, to improve the retrieval accuracy. Experimental results show that this strategy achieves significant gain (**+8.1%** on Oxford5K) on retrieval performance.

It should be noted that other geometric information besides spatial context could be taken into account in future work to address the co-occurrences issue in aggregating step. Additionally, our query fusion is verified based on exhausted search which needs to keep all original vectors in memory. For large scale image search equipped with approximate nearest neighbor search algorithms, query fusion should be modified since original vectors are discarded.

7. ACKNOWLEDGMENTS

This work was supported by National Basic Research Program of China (973 Program) project 2012CB316400, and the National Natural Science Foundation of China (NSFC) projects 61429201 and 61472378. This work was also supported in part to Dr. Qi Tian by ARO grant W911NF-12-1-0057 and Faculty Research Award by NEC Laboratories of America, Inc. This work was also supported by the Fundamental Research Funds for the Central Universities.

8. REFERENCES

[1] R. Arandjelovic and A. Zisserman. Three things everyone should know to improve object retrieval. In *CVPR*, 2012.

[2] R. Arandjelovic and A. Zisserman. All about VLAD. In *CVPR*, 2013.

[3] A. Babenko and V. Lempitsky. The inverted multi-index. In *CVPR*, 2012.

[4] O. Chum and J. Matas. Unsupervised discovery of co-occurrence in sparse high dimensional data. In *CVPR*, 2010.

[5] O. Chum, J. Philbin, J. Sivic, M. Isard, and A. Zisserman. Total recall: Automatic query expansion with a generative feature model for object retrieval. In *ICCV*, 2007.

[6] J. Delhumeau, P.-H. Gosselin, H. Jégou, and P. Pérez. Revisiting the VLAD image representation. In *ACM MM*, 2013.

[7] M. Douze, A. Ramisa, and C. Schmid. Combining attributes and fisher vectors for efficient image retrieval. In *CVPR*, 2011.

[8] T. Ge, Q. Ke, and J. Sun. Sparse-coded features for image retrieval. In *BMVC*, 2013.

[9] H. Jégou and O. Chum. Negative evidences and co-occurences in image retrieval: The benefit of PCA and whitening. In *ECCV*. 2012.

[10] H. Jégou, M. Douze, and C. Schmid. Hamming embedding and weak geometric consistency for large scale image search. In *ECCV*. 2008.

[11] H. Jégou, M. Douze, and C. Schmid. On the burstiness of visual elements. In *CVPR*, 2009.

[12] H. Jégou, M. Douze, and C. Schmid. Improving bag-of-features for large scale image search. *IJCV*, 87(3):316–336, 2010.

[13] H. Jégou, M. Douze, and C. Schmid. Product quantization for nearest neighbor search. *TPAMI*, 33(1):117–128, 2011.

[14] H. Jégou, F. Perronnin, M. Douze, J. Sánchez, P. Pérez, and C. Schmid. Aggregating local image descriptors into compact codes. *TPAMI*, 34(9):1704–1716, 2012.

[15] H. Jégou and A. Zisserman. Triangulation embedding and democratic aggregation for image search. In *CVPR*, 2014.

[16] P. A. Knight. The sinkhorn-knopp algorithm: convergence and applications. *SIAM Journal on Matrix Analysis and Applications*, 30(1):261–275, 2008.

[17] W. Liu, J. Wang, S. Kumar, and S.-F. Chang. Hashing with graphs. In *ICML*, 2011.

[18] D. G. Lowe. Distinctive image features from scale-invariant keypoints. *IJCV*, 60(2):91–110, 2004.

[19] K. Mikolajczyk and C. Schmid. Scale and affine invariant interest point detectors. *IJCV*, 60(1):63–86, 2004.

[20] A. Y. Ng, M. I. Jordan, and Y. Weiss. On spectral clustering: Analysis and an algorithm. In *NIPS*, 2002.

[21] M. Perd'och, O. Chum, and J. Matas. Efficient representation of local geometry for large scale object retrieval. In *CVPR*, 2009.

[22] F. Perronnin, Y. Liu, J. Sánchez, and H. Poirier. Large-scale image retrieval with compressed fisher vectors. In *CVPR*, 2010.

[23] J. Philbin, O. Chum, M. Isard, J. Sivic, and A. Zisserman. Object retrieval with large vocabularies and fast spatial matching. In *CVPR*, 2007.

[24] J. Philbin, O. Chum, M. Isard, J. Sivic, and A. Zisserman. Lost in quantization: Improving particular object retrieval in large scale image databases. In *CVPR*, 2008.

[25] B. Safadi and G. Quénot. Descriptor optimization for multimedia indexing and retrieval. In *Workshop on CBMI*, 2013.

[26] J. Sivic and A. Zisserman. Video Google: A text retrieval approach to object matching in videos. In *ICCV*, 2003.

[27] G. Tolias, T. Furon, and H. Jégou. Orientation covariant aggregation of local descriptors with embeddings. In *ECCV*. 2014.

[28] S. A. Winder and M. Brown. Learning local image descriptors. In *CVPR*, 2007.

[29] W. Zhao, H. Jégou, and G. Gravier. Oriented pooling for dense and non-dense rotation-invariant features. In *BMVC*, 2013.

[30] W. Zhou, H. Li, R. Hong, Y. Lu, and Q. Tian. BSIFT: towards data-independent codebook for large scale image search. *TIP*, 24(3):967–979, 2015.

[31] W. Zhou, Y. Lu, H. Li, Y. Song, and Q. Tian. Spatial coding for large scale partial-duplicate web image search. In *ACM MM*, 2010.

[32] W. Zhou, M. Yang, H. Li, X. Wang, Y. Lin, and Q. Tian. Towards codebook-free: Scalable cascaded hashing for mobile image search. *TMM*, 16(3):601–611, 2014.

DeepIndex for Accurate and Efficient Image Retrieval

Yu Liu, Yanming Guo, Song Wu, Michael S. Lew
LIACS Media Lab, Leiden University
Niels Bohrweg 1, 2333 CA Leiden, The Netherlands
{y.liu, y.guo, s.wu, m.s.lew}@liacs.leidenuniv.nl

ABSTRACT

In the well-known Bag-of-Words model, local features, such as the SIFT descriptor, are extracted and quantized into visual words. Then, an index is created to reduce computational burden. However, local clues serve as low-level representations that can not represent high-level semantic concepts. Recently, the success of deep features extracted from convolutional neural networks(CNN) has shown promising results toward bridging the semantic gap. Inspired by this, we attempt to introduce deep features into inverted index based image retrieval and thus propose the DeepIndex framework. Moreover, considering the compensation of different deep features, we incorporate multiple deep features from different fully connected layers, resulting in the multiple DeepIndex. We find the optimal integration of one mid-level deep feature and one high-level deep feature, from two different CNN architectures separately. This can be treated as an attempt to further reduce the semantic gap. Extensive experiments on three benchmark datasets demonstrate that, the proposed DeepIndex method is competitive with the state-of-the-art on Holidays(85.65% mAP), Paris(81.24% mAP), and UKB(3.76 score). In addition, our method is efficient in terms of both memory and time cost.

Categories and Subject Descriptors

H.3.1 [**Information Storage and Retrieval**]: Content Analysis and Indexing; I.4.7 [**Image Processing and Computer Vision**]: Feature Measurement

General Terms

Algorithm, Experimentation, Performance

Keywords

Image Retrieval, Convolutional Neural Networks, Bag of Deep Features, DeepIndex

ICMR'15, June 23–26, 2015, Shanghai, China.

http://dx.doi.org/10.1145/2671188.2749300.

1. INTRODUCTION

Image retrieval is one of the most significant and popular research tasks in the multimedia community[18, 22], and aims to quickly search for the similar images through their visual features. Bag-of-Words(BoW) is the most efficient model in existing state-of-the-art image retrieval systems, in which local features, such as the SIFT[19], and the color clues[32], are extracted and quantized to visual words with a pretrained codebook. Then, similar to document retrieval[27, 22], an inverted index is built to reduce computational costs and memory requirements for scalable image search. Recently, Zheng,*et al.*,[35] performed low-level feature fusion with the SIFT and color features using a coupled inverted index level. However, image retrieval remains one of the most challenging problems, which is mainly due to the well-known "semantic gap" challenge that exists between low-level image representations and high-level semantic concepts perceived by human.

Machine learning is treated as one promising technique that attempts to address this grand challenge. Recently, one important technique, called deep learning, has shown significant promise in computer vision and speech recognition. In deep learning, there are a family of machine learning algorithms that extract high-level abstractions in data by employing deep architectures composed of multiple neural layers[5]. An important model in deep learning is convolutional neural networks(CNN)[7], which has achieved top rankings in many international benchmarks for computer vision applications, such as image classification[16, 29] and object detection[9]. Also, many works[31, 4, 24, 6] have started to employ this kind of deep features for image retrieval and aim to evaluate how much retrieval improvement can be achieved by developing the deep learning techniques, and whether deep features are a desirable key to bridge the semantic gap in the long term[31].

Inspired by these successes and attempts, we propose a novel DeepIndex framework that explores deep features for accurate and efficient image retrieval based on the BoW model and inverted index. Firstly, we use the Bag-of-Deep-Features(BDF) model that clusters visual words directly with deep features. The spatial pyramid method is used to partition the image into many patches. Then every patch is equally input to extract activations from the fully connected(fc) layers in one pretrained CNN model, denoted as deep features. All the feature patches of the image dataset are clustered for the 'deep' codebook. In this work, we extract deep features with two widely-used pretrained CNN models that are Alexnet[16] and VGGnet[26]. Based on the different number of neural layers, we categorize them as 'low' CNN and 'high' CNN, respectively. Secondly, different from other works based on CNN that use resource-consuming image matching and nearest neighbor search for retrieving images, our work, called DeepIndex(DPI), introduces an efficient inverted index as a search strategy for deep features, which can achieve promising performance while significantly reducing the computational cost and memory space. Thirdly, we use multiple deep features to narrow the semantic gap between mid-level and high-level features. Here, we integrate multiple fc layers, and then build a multiple DeepIndex(multi-DPI) structure. Specifically, The 2-D DeepIndex is performed in this paper consisting of two kinds of variants: intra-CNN and inter-CNN. The former one uses two fc layers from the same CNN architecture, such as Alexnet. In contrast, the latter one selects two fc layers from two different CNN architectures, such as Alexnet and VGGnet. It is found that the performance of inter-CNN is better than that of intra-CNN. There are two reasons to explain it. First, it is due to the close relationship of two fc layers from the same CNN model that can not fully develop the advantage of the 2-D inverted index. The second reason is that, for inter-CNN, we select one fc layer in Alexnet, and one fc layer in VGGnet. Alexnet is a kind of 'low' CNN(eight layers), so its fc feature can be treated as some kind of mid-level representation. However, VGGnet belongs to a kind of 'high' CNN with nineteen layers, and thus its fc feature corresponds closer to a high-level representation. Owing to the mutual compensation of mid-level and high-level features in inter-CNN, it obtains better results and bridges the semantic gap with feature fusion at the 2-D inverted index level. However, it is noteworthy that intra-CNN is simpler and faster than inter-CNN. Finally, a special signature for the global image, called global image signature(GIS), is integrated into DPI which enhances the matching precision.

Finally, experimental results demonstrate the advantages of DeepIndex, and the necessity and efficiency of multiple DeepIndex. In several well known, public datasets, our comparisons with the state-of-the-art clearly validate these advantages. The contributions of this paper can be summarized as follows:

- We introduce the DeepIndex framework that uses the inverted index scheme for deep features(this is the first to the best of our knowledge).
- We propose to use multiple deep features with the multiple DeepIndex which improves retrieval accuracy. It consists of two variants: intra-CNN and inter-CNN.
- We further employ the deep feature of the whole image as a signature for improving matching accuracy, which is called the global image signature.

The rest of this paper is organized as follows. Related works are briefly introduced in Section 2. Section 3 describes the bag-of-deep-features scheme. The DeepIndex framework is introduced in Section 4. The experimental results are summarized in Section 5. Finally, Section 6 summarizes the conclusions.

2. RELATED WORK

In this section, we will briefly discuss related works as well as emphasize our differences with them.

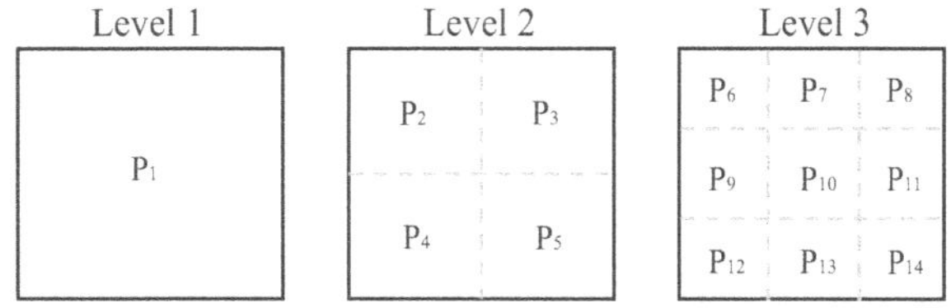

Figure 1: Spatial pyramid with three levels, and there are 14 different patches P_i in total, where $i = 1, \ldots, 14$.

In Gong,*et al.*[10], they proposed to extract patches at multiple scales, and then aggregated local patch responses at the finer scales via VLAD[14] encoding. In Razavian,*et al.*[24], their system first augmented the training set by adding cropped and rotated samples. Then for each image, it used crude search to extract multiple sub-patches of different sizes at different locations. Each sub-patch was computed for its CNN representation. The work of Wan, *et al.*[31] revealed that a deep CNN model pre-trained on a large dataset can be directly used for feature extraction in new CBIR tasks. When being applied for feature representation in new domain, it is found that similarity learning can further boost the retrieval performance. Another work by Sun, *et al.*[28] extracted object-like image patches with a general object detector. Then one CNN feature is extracted in each object patch. Without sliding windows or multiple-scales patches in Babenko,*et al.*[4], they focused on holistic descriptors where the whole image is mapped to a single feature vector. Recently, in Zhang,*et al.*[34], they proposed deep embedding that used deep feature as global and regional signatures instead of a Hamming embedding[11]. In fact, it belongs to an incorporation of the SIFT descriptor and CNN feature, and achieves desirable results. All these works only choose one fully connected feature, either the first or the second one. In Agrawal, *et al.*[1], they analyzed and compared the differences and discriminative abilities of different layers.

In contrast to the prior works, our work focuses on both search strategy and feature fusion at the indexing level. We directly cluster visual words with deep features and then introduce the DeepIndex scheme as the search strategy. Furthermore, we propose building the multiple DeepIndex to utilize multiple deep features which can compensate each other mutually toward improving the retrieval precision.

3. BAG OF DEEP FEATURES

Many state-of-the-arts image retrieval methods employ the low-level features, such as SIFT and color descriptors, and rely on the Bag-of-Features(BoF) or Bag-of-Words(BoW) model. However, few works have shown the usage of deep features into BoF. In this section, we use the Bag-of-Deep-Features(BDF) model, in which visual deep-words are clustered directly on CNN features.

3.1 Spatial Patches

Generally, extracting the only feature vector from the whole image is not discriminative enough for image retrieval tasks, and loses relatively useful information, such as contextual and spatial information. Thus it is quite important and necessary to consider features within finer scales. Generally,

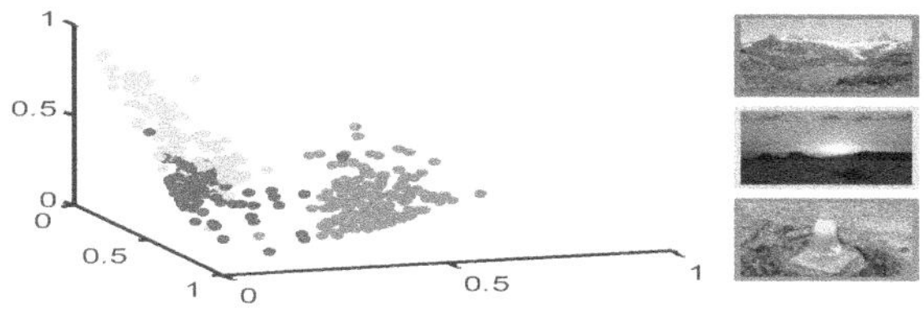

Figure 2: Visualizing the deep features for three groups of images from Holidays. One image from each group is shown in the right side, and the color of outer frame corresponds to the color of points in the 3D space. Best viewed in color.

there are many kinds of methods enlarging the number of features in one image, including "sliding windows", "region proposals", and "spatial pyramid".

Firstly, sliding windows is a quite common approach in object recognition and object detection that scans an image using windows of different scales, locations, and aspect ratios. For example, Gong, *et al.*[10], scanned the whole image with two levels of overlapping windows that generates numerous local patches. Secondly, the region proposals method is proposed to detect the objects of interest in images using fewer candidates than sliding windows. For object detection, RCNN[9] adopts this kind of selective search into CNN replacing sliding windows. In Sun, *et al.*[28], they also extract CNN features only on object-like image patches with a region proposal detector. Thirdly, in contrast to the above two methods, the spatial pyramid model[17] is an efficient way to preserve the spatial information. In Razavian, *et al.*[24], they first augment the datasets by cropping and rotating images in several directions, and then use spatial search to divide the whole image into different levels of patches whose union covers the whole image.

Comparison with three methods mentioned above, we employ the spatial pyramid to refine the image representation because of its simplicity and efficiency. As seen in Fig. 1 , we partition one image into three levels: Level 1 only contains a patch P_1 that is the whole image; Level 2 separates the image into four patches(P_1, P_2, P_3, P_4)whose union covers the whole image; Level 3 consists of nine non-overlapping patches, from P_5 to P_{14}. In total, there are 14 patches for one image, and their features are computed independently. In contrast to methods[24] which uses larger levels for training images than query images, we apply the same spatial levels for all images. Furthermore, we do not perform prior data augmentation, such as crops and rotations.

3.2 Feature Extraction and Quantization

The success of convolutional neural networks used in image classification[16] has shown the strong efficiency and discrimination of learning features by layer-wise architecture. Also, several works[9, 31] suggest that the features located in the upper layers of CNN can serve as good descriptors for various image applications.

It is common to prefer to use the fully connected layers for feature representations[8, 24], because of their closer to class posteriors, but there are also differences about which fc layer is favorable[1].

Different from these works using either the first or the second fully connected activations, we focus on how to incorporate multiple fully connected features. In this work, we employ two commonly CNN architectures pretrained on ILSVRC[25] as feature extractors. The one is proposed by Krizhevsky[16] in 2012 and implemented by the Caffe framework[15]. The other one is from Simonyan[26] in 2014 and released in the MatConvNet[26] framework. We refer to them as Alexnet and VGGnet respectively. In Alexnet, there are eight ordered layers(5 convolutional layers, 3 fully connected layers), thus we name the first and second fc layers as fc6 and fc7. Note that VGGnet has various configurations, and we choose to use the one with nineteen weight layers (16 convolutional layers, 3 fully connected layers), and the first and second fc layers are codenamed as fc17 and fc18.

To visually demonstrate the discrimination of deep features, we select three groups of images from the Holidays dataset[11]. The fc18 features for patches of these images are computed and mapped into a 3D space by classical Multi-Dimensional Scaling[1]. As seen in Fig. 2, the degrees of separations of data points from three groups are promising.

The feature extraction and quantization is conducted as in Fig. 3. Given an image I, x_i represents the feature vector of the ith patch, where $i = 1, \ldots, 14$. After extracting features of all image patches, we perform feature quantization to map deep features into visual deep-words. With the codebook clustered on the training dataset using the k-means algorithm, the quantization function $q(\cdot)$ maps a patch feature x_i to its nearest centroid v_k in the codebook, with $q(x_i) \mapsto v_k$, where v_k is the kth visual word. Note that codebooks for different fc features, including fc6, fc7, fc17, fc18, are trained independently. Typically, the dimension of the fc feature is usually 4096, and L_2 normalization is used for these features.

4. DEEPINDEX

To reduce the computational time and memory, we propose the DeepIndex(DPI) framework in which the inverted index is created based on visual deep-words. Afterwards, we integrate multiple deep features with the multiple DeepIndex. Finally, the global image signature is utilized to elevate the matching accuracy.

4.1 Single DeepIndex

Although several works have exploited deep features for image retrieval tasks, they typically focus on the usage of deep features themselves and the retrieving algorithm they use is simply nearest neighbor search performed by computing matching similarity among image(or patches). Our work also improves the search strategy by using inverted index for deep features.

We create an inverted index structure in which each entry corresponds to a visual deep-word defined in the pre-computed codebook. Assume that there are a total of N images in an image database, denoted as $\{I_i\}_{i=1}^{N}$. Each image I_i has a set of patches features $\{x_j\}_{j=1}^{d_j}$, where d_j is the number of patches. Given a codebook $\{v_i\}_{i=1}^{K}$ of size K, we represent the inverted index as $\mathcal{W} = \{W_1, W_2, \ldots, W_K\}$. In $\mathcal{W}$, each entry W_i consists of a list of indexed items, such as image ID, term-frequency(TF) score and other metadata[22, 13, 35].

Given a query deep feature, its corresponding entry W_i is identified by feature quantization mapping. The indexed

[1]Here, we use the Matlab function 'cmdscale'.

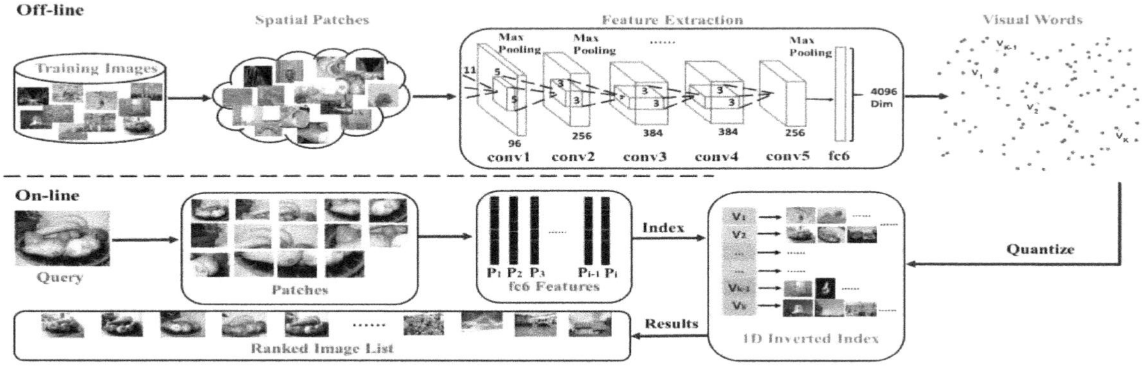

Figure 3: The flowchart of Single DeepIndex framework, including off-line and on-line stages. For example, The pretrained Alexnet serves as the feature extractor and fc6 activations are obtained for features. Image patches in different levels are shown in the same size.

items following entry W_i are counted as the candidate nearest features of the query feature. Therefore, the matching function $h_q(\cdot)$ of two deep features x and y with mapping function $q(\cdot)$ is computed as

$$h_q(x, y) = \delta_{q(x),q(y)}, \quad (1)$$

where δ is the Kronecker delta response. The voting score is accelerated by all $h_q(x, y)$ values.

At this point, the matching function do not consider the $tf-idf$ scheme[27], which weights the visual words according to their frequency. Generally, rare visual words are assumed to be more discriminative and should be assigned higher weights. In this case, the matching function can be updated as

$$h(x, y) = \delta_{q(x),q(y)} \cdot idf(q(y))^2, \quad (2)$$

where $idf(i) = N/n_i$, n_i is the number of images containing the visual word v_i.

We call the proposed indexing scheme as single DeepIndex (1-D DPI) because of using one kind of deep features. This work consists of four kinds of 1-D DPI, which are presented as DPI_6,DPI_7,DPI_{17}, and DPI_{18}. The whole procedure of image search with BDF and 1-D DPI is illustrated in Fig. 3. This figure takes the DPI_6 method for example, and it is also suitable for other deep features. There are two stages: off-line stage and on-line stage. The former one mainly cluster codebook with training patches, and generate the DeepIndex structure. The latter stage is to query one image by searching the inverted index and to return similar images.

4.2 Multiple DeepIndex

Currently, most works mainly focus on comparing performance of different fully connected layers, and only choose the favorable one. However, different neural layers implying different levels of abstracts for the input image demonstrate distinct aspects. It is not preferable to take one layer as the only representation for feature matching. Thus we utilize different layers to compensate each other and to improve the matching accuracy. Based on this idea, we propose to integrate multiple fully connected layers with the multiple DeepIndex(multi-DPI).

The structure of the multi-index was first proposed in Babenko, *et al.*[3]. It decomposes the SIFT descriptor into several blocks by product quantization. The multi-index is thus organized around the codebooks of corresponding blocks. Recently, Zheng, *et al.*[35], built the coupled multi-index with traditional SIFT features and additional discriminative color names. Their results demonstrate that the feature fusion at indexing level is better than the single indexing. Motivated by these works, we aim to exploit incorporation of deep features by multi-DPI structure. In this paper, we take the two dimensional DeepIndex(2-D DPI) as an example.

Considering the 2-D DeepIndex, we denote $\mathcal{X} = [x^r, x^c]$ as a coupled deep features for a patch P_i in Image I, where x^r is extracted from one fully connected layer as row indexing, and x^c comes from another fc layer as column indexing. Then, the row and column codebooks are generated with training images separately, noted by $\mathcal{U} = u_1, u_2, \ldots, u_M$ and $\mathcal{V} = v_1, v_2, \ldots, v_N$, where M and N are codebook sizes. As a result, this 2-D DPI structure contains $M \times N$ entries, as $\mathcal{W} = W_{11}, W_{12}, \ldots, W_{ij}, \ldots, W_{MN}, i = 1, 2, \ldots, M, j = 1, 2, \ldots, N$.

After building the 2-D DPI, all feature tuples like $\mathcal{X} = [x^r, x^c]$ are quantized into visual word pairs (u_i, v_j) using codebooks $\mathcal{U}$ and $\mathcal{V}$, where u_i and v_j are the nearest centroids to features x^r and x^c, respectively. Then other useful clues(e.g. image ID, and other metadata) related to the current feature tuple $\mathcal{X}$ are saved in the corresponding entry W_{ij}, similar to the 1-D DeepIndex.

Now, assume two feature tuples $\mathcal{X} = [x^r, x^c]$ and $\mathcal{Y} = [y^r, y^c]$, the matching function considering 2-D indexing is rewritten as

$$h(\mathcal{X}, \mathcal{Y}) = \delta_{q^r(x^r),q^r(y^r)} \cdot \delta_{q^c(x^c),q^c(y^c)} \cdot idf^2, \quad (3)$$

where $q^r(\cdot)$ and $q^c(\cdot)$ present quantization functions for two different features in row and column spaces, and idf is the 2D extension of the 1D one in Eq.(2). Here, a right match is valid only when the two features tuples are similar in both two indexes. Thus, the 2-D DeepIndex enhances matching strength and improve retrieval precision. Moreover, we define two models about how to select fc features, named intra-CNN and inter-CNN.

Intra-CNN model uses two fc layers from the same CNN architecture. As the two black solid lines seen in Fig. 4, fc6 activation is taken as column indexing, and the fc7 activation

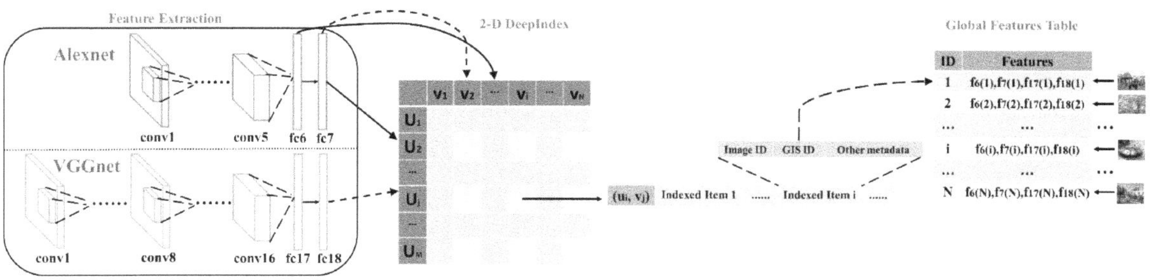

Figure 4: The framework of 2-D DeepIndex for deep features, including intra-CNN and inter-CNN. For intra-CNN, it uses the fc6 and fc7 jointly. For inter-CNN, the fc7 and fc18 are incorporated for indexing. Besides, global image signature serves as additional clue in indexed items, stored in a table.

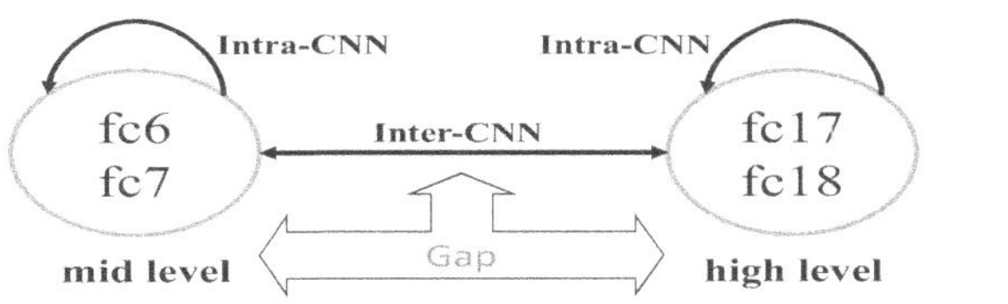

Figure 5: Comparison between the Intra-CNN and the Inter-CNN.

serves as row indexing. In this work, there are two kinds of Intra-CNN members, called $DPI_{6,7}$ and $DPI_{17,18}$.

Inter-CNN model chooses two fc layers coming from two different CNN architectures. For example the two black dot lines in Fig. 4, fc7 from Alexnet('low' CNN) and fc18 from VGGnet('high' CNN) represent column and row indexing, respectively. In total, there are four Inter-CNN members, including $DPI_{7,17}$,$DPI_{6,17}$,$DPI_{7,18}$, and $DPI_{6,18}$.

We draw one more example for Intra-CNN and Inter-CNN in Fig. 5. We categorize the fc6 and fc7 as mid-level features, and fc17, fc18 as high-level features. The Intra-CNN is relatively simple, but the importance and necessity of Inter-CNN is its ability to bridge the gap between mid-level and high-level features to some extent. More comparison and analysis about the performance of intra-CNN and inter-CNN is followed in the experiment of Sec. 5.3.

4.3 Global Image Signature

To further improve the matching accuracy in the inverted index structure, we employ additional discriminative feature to constrain the matching condition and to filter out false matches, which is called the 'signature'. The most popular one is the hamming embedding signature[11] that uses a 64-D binary signature for each SIFT descriptor, and stores it in the metadata of the inverted items. In zheng,*et al.*[35], they use the hamming embedding for SIFT features and generates another signature for color names.

Recently, the global discrimination of deep feature has been demonstrated in many works[24, 31, 1], in which only one fully connected feature vector(4096-D) extracted from the whole image can achieve desirable results. In this paper, we propose to use the deep feature for the whole images as an additional signature for DeepIndex, called global image signature(GIS). Although the spatial patches in Sec. 3.1 already consist of the global feature at Level1, the purpose of spatial patches is to rich the representations of images and exploit more features at object-level. Also, all the patches features are clustered into visual words and quantized to another space that are different from the original feature space. Thus, it is not a repeated process to use the global feature again. Moreover, GIS is quite efficient, because all the patches in one image share the same GIS. We store all GIS features in a pre-computed table searched by the indexed items, as seen in Fig. 4.

We compute the similarity of two GIS with the root feature process. Similar to prior work[2, 28], we obtain the root feature by first L_1 normalizing the feature vector and then computing the square root per dimension. The distance is computed with the Hellinger kernel $S(x,y) = \sum_{i=1}^{m} \sqrt[2]{x_i y_i}$. The distance is counted as:

$$d(x,y) = 2 - 2 \cdot S(x,y),$$

Then we take GIS into DeepIndex, and add this distance to update the matching score in Eq.(2). For 1-D DeepIndex, given two patches features x and y, the final matching function becomes:

$$h(x,y) = \delta_{q(x),q(y)} \cdot idf^2 \cdot c(x,y), \quad (4)$$

where $c(x,y) = exp(\alpha \cdot d(gis(x), gis(y)))$, $gis(\cdot)$ returns the corresponding global image feature of the current patch, and α measures the GIS matching strength. For 2-D DeepIndex, there are two feature tuples $\mathcal{X} = [x^r, x^c]$ and $\mathcal{Y} = [y^r, y^c]$. Finally, the 2-D matching function is rewritten as:

$$h(\mathcal{X},\mathcal{Y}) = \delta_{q^r(x^r),q^r(y^r)} \cdot \delta_{q^c(x^c),q^c(y^c)} \cdot idf^2 \cdot c(\mathcal{X},\mathcal{Y}), \quad (5)$$

where $c(\mathcal{X},\mathcal{Y}) = c(gis(x^r), gis(y^r)) \cdot c(gis(x^c), gis(y^c))$. when selecting different fc layers, $gis(\cdot)$ returns the corresponding global deep feature for one image.

In this case, two patches are really matched only when their visual deep-words are identical and their GIS features are similar. Indeed, GIS is a kind of global constraint and compensation for patches matching. A recent and similar work[34] extracts features from the whole image and different levels of images patches as signatures, named deep embedding, which becomes a strong constraint for inverted index built on the SIFT features. Moreover, they try to convert the feature into binary signatures. Different from them, we directly build the visual words and DeepIndex based on deep features and without using SIFT features, and we further exploit multiple DeepIndex to enhance matching accuracy. In addition, we use less image patches(14) than that of 81 patches in[34].

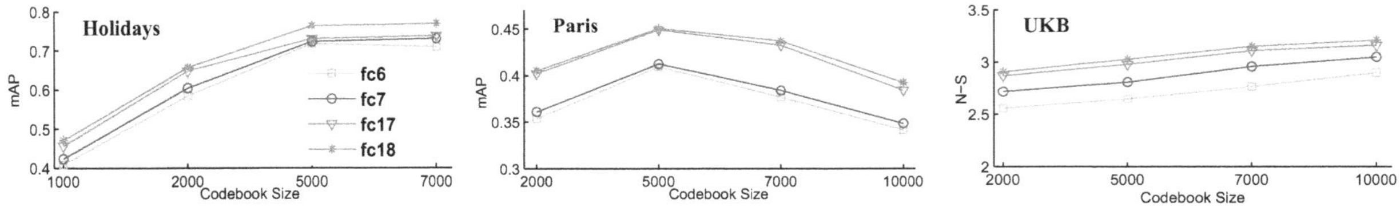

(a) (b) (c)

Figure 6: Codebook sizes on three dataset. The selected sizes are 5000, 5000, 10000 on Holidays, Paris, UKB.

Table 1: Ratio between training features and codebook size. Assume that each image has 500 SIFT keypoints.

Dataset	Training features	Codebook size	Ratio
Holidays	991×14	5000	2.8
Paris	6337×14	5000	17.7
UKB	10200×14	10000	14.3
[35] for SIFT	$60K \times 500$	20K	1500
[35] for color	$60K \times 500$	200	150K

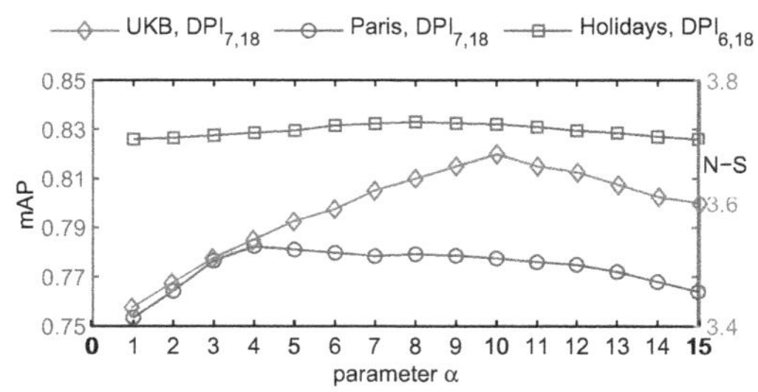

Figure 7: Influence of parameter α.

5. EXPERIMENTS

In this section,we evaluate the proposed method on three public datasets: Holidays , Paris and UKB.

5.1 Datasets

Holidays[11] contains 1491 vacation photographs corresponding to 500 groups. There are 500 queries, most of which have 1-2 ground truth images which have been rectified to a natural orientation. The performance is measured by mean average precision(mAP)[22] over the provided queries.

Paris[23] has 6412 images obtained from Flickr. 55 images serve as queries. For each image and landmark, one of four possible labels is generated: good, ok, bad, and junk. The mAP is again used as the accuracy measurement.

UKB[21] includes 10200 indoor photos of 2550 objects(4 images per object). Each image is used to query the rest of the dataset in turn. The performance is reported by the average recall of the top four results, referred to as N-S score that is a number between 0 and 4. But some works still measure this dataset with mAP.

5.2 Codebook Generation

In this paper, the visual words are clustered with the training images from every dataset itself. To elevate the efficiency of k-means, we use the algorithm from Fast Library for Approximate Nearest Neighbors(FLANN)[20]. We perform four kinds of 1-D DeepIndex(fc6,fc7,fc17,fc18) to find desirable codebook sizes. The results are drawn in Fig. 6. Considering the accuracy and efficiency, we set codebook sizes $K = 5000, 5000, 10000$ for Holidays, Paris, and UKB.

It is noteworthy that the codebook sizes of deep features are smaller than traditional BoW with SIFT features. Also, the ratios between training deep-features and codebook sizes are relatively smaller. More details in Table 1, the ratios in this paper is under 20, but the ratios in[35] that uses coupled multi-index of SIFT and color features are quite large with about 1500 and 150K. This demonstrates that patches features has desirable discrimination, though there are relatively less training descriptors and smaller clusters.

Table 3: Results with PCA Compression

Datasets	Holidays	Paris	UKB
Dim=4096	0.833	0.7824	3.68
Dim=2048	0.8411	0.7945	3.72
Dim=1024	0.8463	0.8065	3.74
Dim=512	**0.8565**	**0.8124**	**3.76**
Dim=256	0.8367	0.7875	3.71
Dim=128	0.8272	0.7724	3.65

5.3 Evaluation

In this experiment, we compare the performance of 1-D DPI and 2-D DPI in Table 2. It is shown that the 2-D method is not better than the 1-D method using the single multiple assignment(MA=1), due to the low recall. To further improve the recall, we use the multiple assignment(MA) method[13], which improves the 2-D DPI performance.

Furthermore, the inter-CNN methods are better than intra-CNN ones. The reason is that deep features in intra-CNN are from the same CNN architecture, such as fc6 and fc7, so they have close relationship(fc6 is the input of fc7) restraining the ability of 2-D inverted index. Here we call the fc6 and fc7 feature as 'mid-level' descriptions and the fc17 and fc18 features as 'high-level' descriptions because of their deeper network. The result shows that the integration of 'mid-level' and 'high-level' features plays a role in improving the overall representation which results in significant improvement compared with 1-D DPI. Finally, $DPI_{6,18}$ obtains 82.38% mAP on Holidays; $DPI_{7,18}$ has 75.35% mAP on Paris; $DPI_{7,18}$ achieves 3.37 N-S score. In Fig. 8, we show two queries from Holidays and UKB. It can be seen that the 2-D DPI method returns more relevant images than 1-D DPI.

Next, we consider to evaluate the influence of global image signature for 2-D DPI. We choose to test the superiority results on each dataset, as listed in Table 2. The parameter α in GIS ranges from 1 to 15 and the results are shown in Fig. 7. For Holidays, the GIS increases $DPI_{6,18}$ to 83.3% mAP

Table 2: Results with 1-D DeepIndex and 2-D DeepIndex

Dataset	Holidays Dataset			Paris Dataset			UKB Dataset		
Methods	MA=1	MA=3	MA=5	MA=1	MA=5	MA=10	MA=1	MA=5	MA=10
DPI_6	0.7173	0.7354	0.7201	0.4094	0.5689	0.6521	2.90	3.03	3.02
DPI_7	0.7234	0.7490	0.7358	0.4124	0.5745	0.6578	3.05	3.12	3.04
DPI_{17}	0.7302	0.7322	0.7262	0.4487	0.6101	0.7024	3.16	3.19	3.15
DPI_{18}	0.7631	0.7672	0.7563	0.4503	0.6123	0.7133	3.21	3.25	3.19
DPI_{6+7}	0.7200	0.7888	0.7717	0.2935	0.6289	0.7120	3.02	3.13	3.05
DPI_{17+18}	0.7575	0.7996	0.7934	0.3228	0.6329	0.7169	3.16	3.25	3.26
DPI_{7+17}	0.7401	0.8053	0.8020	0.3345	0.6412	0.7324	3.21	3.25	3.19
DPI_{6+17}	0.7332	0.8162	0.8115	0.3395	0.6508	0.7435	3.22	3.26	3.22
DPI_{7+18}	0.7466	0.8123	0.8174	0.3656	0.6618	**0.7535**	3.26	**3.37**	3.32
DPI_{6+18}	0.7382	0.8164	**0.8238**	0.3412	0.6540	0.7452	3.19	3.23	3.29

when α is 8. Similarly, the result of $DPI_{7,18}$ for Paris arrives at 78.24% mAP with $\alpha = 4$. Also, The $DPI_{7,18}$ method gets 3.68 N-S score on UKB with $\alpha = 10$. All these results valid the necessity of GIS that provides a global constraint to enhance the matching strength. Thus, all the following results contain the GIS process.

5.4 Dimensionality reduction

To evaluate the influence of feature compression for deep feature, we conduct PCA compression for the 4096-D deep feature with different dimensions (The GIS is also compressed by PCA). In Table 3, when the dimension is 512, the results obtain most improvement on Holidays(+2.35% mAP), Paris(+3% mAP), UKB(+0.08 score). Although the dimension is down to 128, it can even obtain desirable results compared with many of SIFT-based methods. This implies that PCA affects the performance of deep features less than the ones of SIFT-like methods.

5.5 Comparison with the state-of-the-art

We compare our results with the state-of-the-art methods that are simply divided into three groups: CNN methods, Non-CNN methods and SIFT-CNN methods. Note that we do not consider and perform various post-processing algorithms, such as query expansion, spatial verification, and graph fusion. For CNN methods, we also do not conduct fine-tuning for specific tasks in this work. Thus we compare the results in other methods that exclude the post-processing and fine-tuning stages.

The whole comparison is listed in Table 4. For Holidays, the proposed method(85.56%) exceeds other CNN-based methods, and is competitive to the best results[30] and[34]. In the work by Tolias, *et al.*[30], their representation would take about millions of features per image which is not scalable to large datasets. In Zhang,*et al.*[34], they use both SIFT and CNN features to improve matching precision. For Paris, our result(81.24%) outperforms most other methods, except the recent work that introduces the similarity learning algorithm into deep learning[31]. In UKB, the proposed method(score 3.76) is better than the coupled multiindex method[35], and is competitive to the state-of-the-art approaches[34].

5.6 Complexity analysis

To quantize the efficiency, we compare the computing complexity of the DeepIndex with the state-of-the-art[34] on Holidays, as listed in Table 5. Our experimental environment is CPU i7 at 2.67Ghz with 12GB RAM and NVIDIA Titan Black with 6GB GRAM. Assume that every images has 500 SIFT keypoints. Considering the memory cost per image, both 1-D DPI(2.06KB) and 2-D DPI(4.06KB) are lower than [34], which needs to spend extra memory for numerous SIFT features. In addition, due to the smaller codebook size, the average query time of our approach is shorter with less than 0.5 seconds [2]. This shows the efficiency and feasibility of our method.

Table 4: Comparison results with the state-of-the-art on three datasets. * means the improved results in the papers.

Groups	Methods	Holidays	Paris	UKB
CNN	[4]	74.70	-	3.43
CNN	[28]	79.00	-	3.61
CNN	[10]	80.20	-	-
CNN	[24]	84.30	79.50	-(91.1)
CNN	[31]	-	**86.83**	-
CNN	Ours	85.65	81.24	3.76
Non-CNN	[32]	78.90	-	3.50
Non-CNN	[33]	80.86	-	3.60
Non-CNN	[13]	81.30	-	3.42(87.8)
Non-CNN	[30]	82.20	78.20	-
Non-CNN	[12]	83.90	-	3.54(90.7)
Non-CNN	[35]	84.02	-	3.71(94.7)
Non-CNN	[30]*	88.00	80.50	-
SIFT-CNN	[34]	85.30	-	3.79
SIFT-CNN	[34]*	**88.08**	-	**3.85**

Table 5: Memory cost (bytes) and query time (seconds) for one image on Holidays dataset

Methods	[34]	1-D DPI	2-D DPI
ImageID	4×500	4×14	4×14
Signature	10.18KB	512×4	$512 \times 4 \times 2$
Total Memory	12.13KB	2.06KB	4.06KB
Query Time	2.32	0.25	0.45

6. CONCLUSIONS AND FUTURE WORK

In this paper, we proposed the DeepIndex framework for accurate and efficient image retrieval that introduced the inverted index into deep features. Moreover, we integrated multiple deep features with the multiple DeepIndex which attempted to bridge the gap between mid-level and high-level representations. Experimental results showed that our method achieved competitive performance in the well-known and frequently benchmarked Holidays, Paris, UKB datasets.

[2]Our query time does not include the feature extraction.

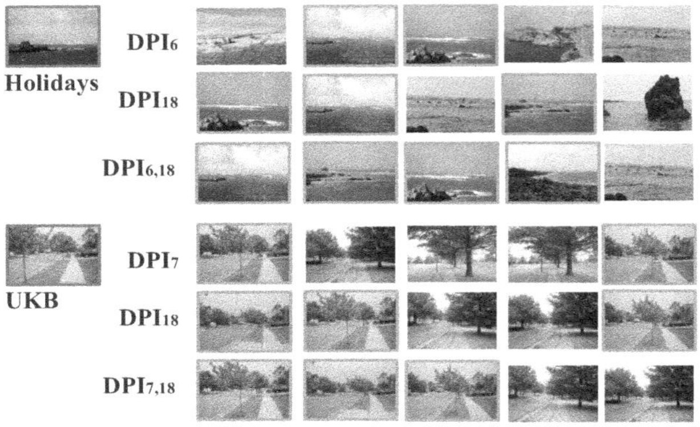

Figure 8: Retrieval results in Holidays and UKB datasets. The left image with blue frame is query one, and the images with green frame are right results. Best viewed in color.

In the future, we think it is promising to investigate the possibilities of using posting-processing or finetuning stage within the DeepIndex approach. Codes and pre-computed data are released on our website[3].

7. ACKNOWLEDGMENTS

This work was supported by the LIACS Media Lab at Leiden University and the China Scholarship Council(CSC).

8. REFERENCES

[1] P. Agrawal, R. Girshick, and J. Malik. Analyzing the performance of multilayer neural networks for object recognition. In *ECCV*, 2014.

[2] R. Arandjelović and A. Zisserman. Three things everyone should know to improve object retrieval. In *CVPR*, 2012.

[3] A. Babenko and V. S. Lempitsky. The inverted multi-index. In *CVPR*, 2012.

[4] A. Babenko, A. Slesarev, A. Chigorin, and V. S. Lempitsky. Neural codes for image retrieval. In *ECCV*, 2014.

[5] Y. Bengio, A. C. Courville, and P. Vincent. Unsupervised Feature Learning and Deep Learning: A Review and New Perspectives. *CoRR*, abs/1206.5538, 2012.

[6] K. Chatfield, R. Arandjelović, O. M. Parkhi, and A. Zisserman. On-the-fly learning for visual search of large-scale image and video datasets. *IJMIR*, 4(2), 2015.

[7] L. Cun, B. Boser, J. S. Denker, D. Henderson, R. E. Howard, W. Hubbard, and L. D. Jackel. Handwritten digit recognition with a back-propagation network. In *NIPS*, 1990.

[8] J. Donahue, Y. Jia, O. Vinyals, J. Hoffman, N. Zhang, E. Tzeng, and T. Darrell. Decaf: A deep convolutional activation feature for generic visual recognition. In *ICML*, 2014.

[9] R. Girshick, J. Donahue, T. Darrell, and J. Malik. Rich feature hierarchies for accurate object detection and semantic segmentation. In *CVPR*, 2014.

[10] Y. Gong, L. Wang, R. Guo, and S. Lazebnik. Multi-scale orderless pooling of deep convolutional activation features. In *ECCV*, 2014.

[11] H. Jegou, M. Douze, and C. Schmid. Hamming embedding and weak geometric consistency for large scale image search. In *ECCV*, 2008.

[12] H. Jégou, M. Douze, and C. Schmid. On the burstiness of visual elements. In *CVPR*, 2009.

[13] H. Jégou, M. Douze, and C. Schmid. Improving bag-of-features for large scale image search. *IJCV*, 87(3):316–336, 2010.

[14] H. Jégou, M. Douze, C. Schmid, and P. Pérez. Aggregating local descriptors into a compact image representation. In *CVPR*, 2010.

[15] Y. Jia, E. Shelhamer, J. Donahue, S. Karayev, J. Long, R. Girshick, S. Guadarrama, and T. Darrell. Caffe: Convolutional Architecture for Fast Feature Embedding. In *ACM Multimedia*, 2014.

[16] A. Krizhevsky, I. Sutskever, and G. E. Hinton. Imagenet classification with deep convolutional neural networks. In *NIPS*, 2012.

[17] S. Lazebnik, C. Schmid, and J. Ponce. Beyond bags of features: Spatial pyramid matching for recognizing natural scene categories. In *CVPR*, 2006.

[18] M. S. Lew, N. Sebe, C. Djeraba, and R. Jain. Content-based multimedia information retrieval: State of the art and challenges. *TOMCCAP*, 2(1):1–19, 2006.

[19] D. G. Lowe. Distinctive image features from scale-invariant keypoints. *IJCV*, 60(2):91–110, 2004.

[20] M. Muja and D. G. Lowe. Fast approximate nearest neighbors with automatic algorithm configuration. In *International Conference on Computer Vision Theory and Application*, 2009.

[21] D. Nister and H. Stewenius. Scalable recognition with a vocabulary tree. In *CVPR*, 2006.

[22] J. Philbin, O. Chum, M. Isard, J. Sivic, and A. Zisserman. Object retrieval with large vocabularies and fast spatial matching. In *CVPR*, 2007.

[23] J. Philbin, O. Chum, M. Isard, J. Sivic, and A. Zisserman. Lost in quantization: Improving particular object retrieval in large scale image databases. In *CVPR*, 2008.

[24] A. S. Razavian, H. Azizpour, J. Sullivan, and S. Carlsson. CNN features off-the-shelf: an astounding baseline for recognition. In *CVPR, DeepVision workshop*, 2014.

[25] O. Russakovsky, J. Deng, H. Su, J. Krause, S. Satheesh, S. Ma, Z. Huang, A. Karpathy, A. Khosla, M. Bernstein, A. C. Berg, and L. Fei-Fei. ImageNet Large Scale Visual Recognition Challenge. *arXiv:1409.0575*, 2014.

[26] K. Simonyan and A. Zisserman. Very deep convolutional networks for large-scale image recognition. *CoRR*, abs/1409.1556, 2014.

[27] J. Sivic and A. Zisserman. Video Google: A text retrieval approach to object matching in videos. In *ICCV*, 2003.

[28] S. Sun, W. Zhou, H. Li, and Q. Tian. Search by detection: Object-level feature for image retrieval. In *ICIMCS*, 2014.

[29] C. Szegedy, W. Liu, Y. Jia, P. Sermanet, S. Reed, D. Anguelov, D. Erhan, V. Vanhoucke, and A. Rabinovich. Going deeper with convolutions. *CoRR*, abs/1409.4842, 2014.

[30] G. Tolias, Y. Avrithis, and H. Jégou. To aggregate or not to aggregate: selective match kernels for image search. In *ICCV*, 2013.

[31] J. Wan, D. Wang, S. C. H. Hoi, P. Wu, J. Zhu, Y. Zhang, and J. Li. Deep learning for content-based image retrieval: A comprehensive study. In *ACM Multimedia*, 2014.

[32] C. Wengert, M. Douze, and H. Jégou. Bag-of-colors for improved image search. In *ACM Multimedia*, 2011.

[33] M. Yang, X. Wang, Y. Lin, and Q. Tian. Semantic-aware co-indexing for near-duplicate image retrieval. In *ICCV*, 2014.

[34] L. Zheng, S. Wang, F. He, and Q. Tian. Seeing the big picture: Deep embedding with contextual evidences. *CoRR*, abs/1406.0132, 2014.

[35] L. Zheng, S. Wang, Z. Liu, and Q. Tian. Packing and padding: Coupled multi-index for accurate image retrieval. In *CVPR*, 2014.

[3] press.liacs.nl/lml/deepindex.

Effective, Efficient, and Scalable Unsupervised Distance Learning in Image Retrieval Tasks

Lucas Pascotti Valem[1], Daniel Carlos Guimarães Pedronette[1],
Ricardo da S. Torres[2], Edson Borin[2], Jurandy Almeida[3]
[1]Dept. of Statistic, Applied Math. and Computing, Universidade Estadual Paulista (UNESP), Rio Claro, Brazil
[2]Institute of Computing, University of Campinas (UNICAMP), Campinas, Brazil
[3]Institute of Science and Technology, Federal University of São Paulo (UNIFESP), São José dos Campos, Brazil

ABSTRACT

Various unsupervised learning methods have been proposed with significant improvements in the effectiveness of image search systems. However, despite the relevant effectiveness gains, these approaches commonly require high computation efforts, not addressing properly efficiency and scalability requirements. In this paper, we present a novel unsupervised learning approach for improving the effectiveness of image retrieval tasks. The proposed method is also scalable and efficient as it exploits parallel and heterogeneous computing on CPU and GPU devices. Extensive experiments were conducted considering five different public image collections and several descriptors. This rigorous experimental protocol evaluates the effectiveness, efficiency, and scalability of the proposed approach, and compares it with previous methods. Experimental results demonstrate that high effectiveness gains (up to +29%) can be obtained requiring small run times.

Categories and Subject Descriptors

H.3.3 [**Information Search and Retrieval**]: Search process

General Terms

Experimentation, Performance

Keywords

content-based image retrieval; unsupervised learning; effectiveness; efficiency; scalability

1. INTRODUCTION

Advances in image acquisition technologies coupled with sharing and storage facilities have triggered a huge growth of image collections. Given the increasing amount of available digital images, the development of effective and efficient systems for indexing and organizing this visual content is mandatory. In this scenario, the use of Content-Based Image Retrieval (CBIR) systems for dealing with this challenge constitutes one of the most promising approaches.

The general goal of CBIR systems consists in retrieving a collection of relevant images according to their visual similarity to query patterns defined by users. A common retrieval task, for example, consists in retrieving similar images to a given query image by considering visual properties such as shape, texture, and color. In general, CBIR approaches extract low-level features of images generating a feature vector which represents them. The similarity between images is computed according to the distance between their correspondent feature vectors, using a distance measure (e.g., the Euclidean distance).

The creation of novel visual features and distance measures has supported the development of CBIR approaches for decades. This development, however, has not been addressing properly the *semantic gap* problem, which consists in the difficulties in mapping low-level features to high-level concepts. More recently, aiming at dealing with the semantic gap and improving the search effectiveness performance, other stages of the retrieval pipeline not directly related to low-level feature extraction have been considered [21].

In this scenario, unsupervised post-processing methods capable of computing a more effective distance measure among images have been proposed [16, 38]. The general objective of these methods consists in replacing pairwise similarities by more global affinity measures [39]. Several methods have been employed with this purpose, such as diffusion process [38, 39], graph-based learning methods [37], and iterative re-ranking approaches [28, 29]. Other methods improve the distance measures by capturing and exploiting the intrinsic manifold structure of the datasets [2, 15].

In fact, different approaches have demonstrated the capability of producing relevant gains in terms of quality of image searches. Nevertheless, most of the proposed approaches are evaluated considering only effectiveness aspects, ignoring efficiency and scalability properties. Focusing on real-word applications, however, the three aspects should be considered at the same time. In addition to the quality of the retrieval process, the time spent to obtain the results and the capability of handling growing image collections are also indispensable.

This paper presents a novel unsupervised distance learning method that considers these three relevant aspects. The proposed RL-Recommendation algorithm exploits the information encoded in the ranked lists through unsupervised recommendations among images. While the effectiveness

ICMR'15, June 23–26, 2015, Shanghai, China.

DOI: http://dx.doi.org/10.1145/2671188.2749336.

gains are comparable with other similar approaches, the algorithm requires very low computation efforts as it uses only a portion of the ranked lists. The use of only top positions of ranked lists allows for taking advantage of existing indexing schemes, making it suitable for large image collections. In addition, we also designed and implemented a parallel solution of the algorithm that considers heterogeneous computing using CPUs and GPUs.

An extensive set of experiments was conducted, considering five public datasets of different sizes and several image descriptors. Different experiments were conducted aiming at assessing the effectiveness, efficiency, and scalability of the proposed approach. The experimental evaluation demonstrates that the proposed method can achieve significant effectiveness improvements in several image retrieval tasks. Experimental results also show that the gains can be obtained for various size of image collections with very small run times. The proposed RL-Recommendation algorithm is also evaluated in comparison with other recently proposed methods and several state-of-the-art approaches considering a shape dataset commonly used for benchmarking.

The paper is organized as follows: Section 2 introduces the problem definition; Section 3 presents the proposed unsupervised learning algorithm; Section 4 shows the experimental results; finally, Section 5 discusses the conclusions and presents possible future work.

2. PROBLEM FORMULATION

This section aims at providing a formal definition of image retrieval model and the unsupervised distance learning problem considered. Let $\mathcal{C}$=$\{img_1, img_2, \ldots, img_n\}$ be an image collection, where n is the size of the collection $\mathcal{C}$.

Let $\mathcal{D}$ be an image descriptor that can be defined [9] as a tuple (ϵ, ρ), where ϵ: $\hat{I} \rightarrow \mathbb{R}^m$ is a function, which extracts a feature vector $v_{\hat{I}}$ from an image in $\hat{I}$; and ρ: $\mathbb{R}^m \times \mathbb{R}^m \rightarrow \mathbb{R}$ is a distance function that computes the distance between two images according to the distance between their corresponding feature vectors. The value of $\rho(\epsilon(img_i), \epsilon(img_j))$ defines the distance between two images img_i and img_j. The notation $\rho(i,j)$ is used for denoting this distance along the paper for simplicity and readability purposes.

The distance $\rho(i,j)$ among all images img_i, $img_j \in \mathcal{C}$ can be computed to obtain a squared $n \times n$ distance matrix A, such that $A_{ij} = \rho(i,j)$. The distance matrix A is used as the input for various unsupervised learning algorithms, but often cause scalability difficulties for large image collections, leading to storage and time complexity of at least $O(n^2)$.

An alternative representation of retrieval results is based on ranked lists. Based on the distance function ρ, a ranked list τ_q can be computed in response to a query image img_q. The ranked lists can contain information from the entire collection, and especially their top positions are expected to contain the most relevant images related to the query image. Therefore, one suitable strategy for speeding up the searching process consists in considering a subset of the L most similar images, where $L \ll n$ is the number of images at top positions of the ranked list. This is a useful strategy specially for large collections, where n is very large, and therefore τ_q is very expensive to compute.

The ranked list τ_q=$(img_1, img_2, \ldots, img_L)$ can be defined as a permutation of the image collection $\mathcal{C}_s \subset \mathcal{C}$, which contains the most similar images to query image img_q, such that and $|\mathcal{C}_s| = L$. A permutation τ_q is a bijection from the set $\mathcal{C}_s$ onto the set $[L] = \{1, 2, \ldots, L\}$. For a permutation τ_q, we interpret $\tau_q(i)$ as the position (or rank) of image img_i in the ranked list τ_q. We can say that, if img_i is ranked before img_j in the ranked list of img_q, that is, $\tau_q(i) < \tau_q(j)$, then $\rho(q,i) \leq \rho(q,j)$.

Taking every image $img_i \in \mathcal{C}$ as a query image img_q, we can obtain a set $\mathcal{R} = \{\tau_1, \tau_2, \ldots, \tau_n\}$ of ranked lists for each image of the collection $\mathcal{C}$. The objective of this work consists in proposing an algorithm for redefining the set of ranked lists $\mathcal{R}$ producing a more effective set $\mathcal{R}_e$. Therefore, the unsupervised distance learning algorithm can be defined as a function f_u, such that:

$$\mathcal{R}_e = f_u(\mathcal{R}). \tag{1}$$

The objective of function f_u is to exploit the set $\mathcal{R}$ by performing unsupervised recommendations based on information encoded in the top positions of ranked lists.

3. RL-RECOMMENDATION ALGORITHM

The proposed RL-Recommendation (*Ranked Lists-Recommendation*) algorithm is mainly based on the concept of supporting unsupervised recommendations among images. Recommendation approaches, originally created for automatically selecting items that match personal preferences, are simulated by the proposed algorithm in an unsupervised way. The recommendations are performed based on information encoded in ranked lists, in which images at top positions are recommended to each other. In this scenario, the recommendation means that the distance between two images should be decreased, and therefore, they should be moved up in the ranked lists of each other.

The presented method is closely related to the recently proposed Pairwise Recommendation [28] algorithm. However, our approach differs in important aspects. While the Pairwise Recommendation [28] requires the distance among all images in a dataset as data entry, our method requires only the top positions of ranked lists, which can be obtained taking advantage of indexing strategies. In addition, the proposed RL-Recommendation algorithm dispenses the use of clustering steps and requires a low number of iterations for convergence. As a result, the algorithm requires much less computing power being designed for parallel computation and becoming suitable for ever-growing real-world datasets.

The RL-Recommendation algorithm can be broadly described considering four main steps:

1. **Computing the Sparse Distance Matrix:** the expected input of the algorithm consists of the set ranked lists $\mathcal{R}$, which ensures scalability properties of the algorithm. However, since the unsupervised recommendations require distance scores, they are computed based on ranked lists. Only the distances among images at top positions of ranked lists are considered, leading to a sparse distance matrix A.
2. **Computing the Cohesion Measure:** the cohesion [28] measure provides an unsupervised estimation of effectiveness of ranked lists. The motivation is based on the conjecture that effective ranked lists have more authority for making recommendations. The cohesion measure is also used as a convergence criterion: the recommendations are performed while the cohesion of ranked lists are increasing.

3. **Performing Unsupervised Recommendations:** the top positions of ranked lists represent the information with the higher accuracy provided by image descriptors. This information, exploited for creating a top-k *image profile*, supports the unsupervised recommendations. If two images are contained in this profile, it constitutes an indication of similarity, producing a recommendation which reduces the distance between them.
4. **Sorting Ranked Lists:** the recommendations change the distances among images. Therefore, ranked lists must be updated to reflect the new ranking. A sorting procedure is performed aiming at updating the ranked lists according to the new computed distances.

Steps 2-4 are repeated while the average cohesion of ranked lists continues increasing above a given threshold. The parameter k, which defines the top-k positions used for cohesion and recommendations, is incremented at each iteration. Next sections describe in details each step and present the parallel solution proposed.

3.1 Computing the Sparse Distance Matrix

The expected input of the algorithm (as discussed in Section 2) consists of the set of ranked lists. In fact, since the unsupervised recommendations require distance scores, we propose to estimate distances based on the information given by the ranked lists. We consider only the distances among images at top-L positions of ranked lists, leading to a very sparse distance matrix A (with approximately $n \times L$ values used). The objective is to ensure the scalability of the algorithm.

The distance between two images is computed based on the sum of the reciprocal references at their ranked lists. Formally, given two images img_q and img_i, their distance $\rho(q,i)$ is defined as $\rho(q,i) = \tau_q(i) + \tau_i(q)$. According to this formulation, the distance matrix A (such that $A_{qi} = \rho(q,i)$) can be easily computed processing all ranked lists by summing up the reciprocal positions. However, the references are not symmetric and the ranked lists do not contain all images (only top L positions). Therefore, we can observe situations where img_i is in the ranked lists of img_q but the inverse is not true ($img_i \in \tau_q$ but $img_q \notin \tau_i$).

An alternative solution is proposed in Algorithm 1. In the first part (Lines 1-6), the ranked lists are processed and all pairs of images, which present references, have their distances set to $2 \times L$ (even if the references are not reciprocal). In the second part (Lines 7-11), each ranked list reference produces a decrement of L and an increment of the reference position ($\tau_q(i)$). In this way, for pairs of images which refer to each other at top L positions, the initial values are replaced by their respective positions. For pairs in which only one image refers the other, one of the two position remains L. The algorithm has the complexity of $O(n \times L)$.

Algorithm 1 Sparse Distance Matrix Computing.

Require: Blank matrix A and set of ranked lists $\mathcal{R}$
Ensure: Processed sparse distance matrix A
//Sparse Distance Matrix Computing - Part I
1: **for all** $img_q \in \mathcal{C}$ **do**
2: **for all** $img_i \in \tau_q$ **do**
3: $A_{qi} \leftarrow 2 \times L$
4: $A_{iq} \leftarrow 2 \times L$
5: **end for**
6: **end for**
//Sparse Distance Matrix Computing - Part II
7: **for all** $img_q \in \mathcal{C}$ **do**
8: **for all** $img_i \in \tau_q$ **do**
9: $A_{qi} \leftarrow A_{qi} + \tau_q(i) - L$
10: **end for**
11: **end for**

3.2 Cohesion Measure

A cohesion measure [28] is used to provide an unsupervised estimation of the effectiveness of ranked lists. High cohesion scores indicate that ranked lists have more authority to recommend than others. The cohesion measure aims at assessing the quality of ranked lists by analyzing how images refer to each other in their ranked lists. The objective consists in evaluating the density of references among images at top positions of a given ranked list. For highly-effective ranked lists, the images at top positions are expected to refer to each other at the top positions of their ranked lists.

Let $k(\tau_i)$ be a subset of a ranked list τ_i with its top-k positions (or k-Nearest Neighbors). Let $img_j \in k(\tau_i)$ be an image of this subset, and let $k(\tau_j)$ be a subset of the ranked list of image img_j. Finally, let $img_p \in k(\tau_j)$ be an image at position $\tau_j(p)$ of the ranked list τ_j. The cohesion $c(\tau_i, k)$ of a ranked list τ_i can be defined as follows:

$$c(\tau_i, k) = \frac{\sum_{img_j \in k(\tau_i)} \sum_{img_p \in k(\tau_j)} w(\tau_j(p)) \times s(k(\tau_i), img_p)}{\sum_{img_j \in k(\tau_i)} \sum_{img_p \in k(\tau_j)} w(\tau_j(p))} \tag{2}$$

where function s determines if the image img_p (that belongs to subset $k(\tau_i)$) also belongs to subset $k(\tau_k)$ and is defined as follows:

$$s(k(\tau_i), img_p) = \begin{cases} 1, & \text{if } img_p \in k(\tau_i) \\ 0, & \text{otherwise.} \end{cases} \tag{3}$$

The function w takes as input the position of an image in a ranked list and gives high weights to images at the first positions ($w(p) = 1/p$). Notice that, if all referenced images are in the subset $k(\tau_i)$, we have a perfect cohesion. In this situation, the function s assumes the value 1 for all images and therefore cohesion is set to 1.

The cohesion measure is used not only for estimating the authority of ranked lists in making recommendations, but also for defining the convergence criterion and the stop condition of the algorithm. Regarding the convergence criterion, the average cohesion of all ranked lists is computed for each iteration. The algorithm is iteratively executed until the variation of cohesion is smaller than a threshold ϵ. Let $\bar{c}$ denotes the average cohesion of all ranked lists and let the superscript $^{(t)}$ denotes the current iteration, the algorithm is executed while the follow criterion is met:

$$(\bar{c}^{\,(t)} - \bar{c}^{\,(t-1)}) \geq (\bar{c}^{\,(t)} \times \epsilon). \tag{4}$$

3.3 Unsupervised Recommendations

The unsupervised recommendations [28] are associated with decreases of the distances among images and are defined based on information encoded in the ranked lists. The main idea behind the unsupervised recommendation given by a ranked list τ_i is: *"the image img_y is recommended to image img_x, if both img_x and img_y are in the top-k positions of the ranked list of τ_i."*

Each recommendation is associated with a different weight, which defines how much the distance should be de-

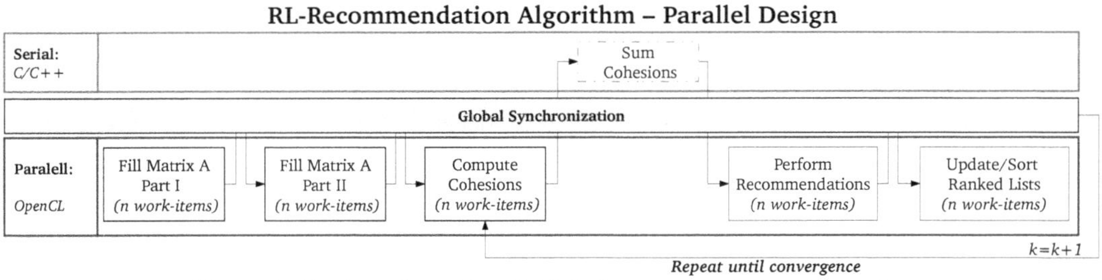

Figure 1: Design of the Parallel RL-Recommendation Algorithm.

creased. The recommendation weight considers the position of images in ranked lists and the authority estimation of the ranked lists, given by the cohesion measure. Algorithm 2 presents the unsupervised recommendation approach for a given ranked list τ_i.

Algorithm 2 Unsupervised Recommendations.

Require: Distance matrix A, ranked list τ_i and cohesion c_i
Ensure: Updated matrix A
1: **for all** $img_x \in k(\tau_i)$ **do**
2: $\quad w_x \leftarrow 1 - (\tau_i(x)/k)$
3: $\quad$ **for all** $img_y \in k(\tau_i)$ **do**
4: $\quad\quad w_y \leftarrow 1 - (\tau_i(y)/k)$
5: $\quad\quad w \leftarrow c_i \times w_x \times w_y$
6: $\quad\quad \lambda \leftarrow 1 - min(1, \alpha \times w)$
7: $\quad\quad A_{xy} \leftarrow min(\lambda A_{xy}, A_{yx})$
8: $\quad$ **end for**
9: **end for**

Values w_x and w_y (Lines 2 and 4) represent the weight assigned to images img_x and img_y in the recommendation. The weights are computed based on the position of images in the ranked lists: for images at top positions of the ranked list a higher weight is assigned. The weights associated with the first positions indicate where it is more likely to find the most similar images, that is, positions that represent more reliable recommendations. In Line 5, the weight w of a recommendation is computed. That represents the *reputation* of the recommendation. For computing w, we consider w_x, w_y and the cohesion c_i computed for the ranked list τ_i.

The λ coefficient combines information of positions and cohesion of the ranked list and is used for determining how the distances between img_x and img_y should be decreased. The constant α aims at adjusting the impact of recommendations. By increasing the value of α, the distances among images will decrease faster. A *min* function (Line 7) avoids negative values limiting the coefficient λ to 0.

3.4 Parallel Design

This section discusses the parallel design of the RL-Recommendation algorithm. We adopted the OpenCL standard, which is an open cross-platform, low-level API for parallel heterogeneous computing. The OpenCL code is executed on a computational *device*, which can be a CPU, GPU, or other accelerator. OpenCL supports both *data-parallel* and *task-parallel* programming models, as well as hybrid models.

Parallel pieces of code are defined in a *kernel*, which is a function declared in an OpenCL Programming Language (a subset of C language, with some restrictions and special keywords). The kernels are executed on an OpenCL *device* and each instance of a kernel running on a compute unit is called a *work-item*. The same code is executed in parallel by different *work-items*, and each *work-item* executes the code with different data.

Figure 1 illustrates the design of the Parallel RL-Recommendation Algorithm using six distinct kernels. Different kernels in OpenCL ensure global synchronization among all work-items, i.e., all work-items of a given kernel should finish so that the next can be started.

The first two kernels compute the distance matrix, as discussed in Section 3.1. Two kernels are used since all work-items of "*Part I*" should finish before the start of "*Part II*." The third kernel computes the cohesion measure for all ranked lists. Each work-item computes the cohesion for a given ranked list. The cohesion of ranked lists are serially summed up for computing the average cohesion used for checking the convergence criterion.

The unsupervised recommendations are computed by the fourth kernel. We also have n work-items, each one processing a ranked list. Although the recommendations processing are independent, different ranked lists can update concurrent positions of the Distance Matrix A causing the lost of some updates. A possible solution is to ensure exclusive access, but the overhead associated with fine grained synchronization in OpenCL is significant. Therefore, as suggested by other works [30], we allow direct updates to matrix A because the loss of some updates has a very low impact on the effectiveness of the algorithm (as demonstrated by confidence intervals of Section 4.4).

The last kernel executes a sorting procedure for updating the ranked lists. Since most of changes occur only in the beginning of the ranked lists [30], we use the insertion sort algorithm, whose complexity tends to be linear when the input is almost sorted.

Regarding memory transfers, the algorithm's data should be available in the device memory before the execution of kernels starts. The input and output data are composed of the set of ranked lists, which should be transferred before the beginning of the execution and copied back after its conclusion. In this work, we consider two memory transfer models defined by the OpenCL standard: write buffer and map buffer. For the write buffer model, the main memory transfer should be explicitly transferred to the device memory. On the other hand, the map buffer model consists in copying only memory pointers. Both strategies are evaluated in our experiments (Section 4.4).

4. EXPERIMENTAL EVALUATION

A large experimental evaluation was conducted for assessing the effectiveness, efficiency, and scalability properties of the proposed method. Section 4.1 describes datasets and image descriptors considered. Section 4.2 discusses the impact of parameters. Section 4.3 presents the results of the effectiveness evaluation, while Section 4.4 presents the efficiency evaluation. Section 4.5 discusses scalability aspects.

Table 1: Datasets and images descriptors used in the experimental evaluation.

Dataset	Size	Type	General Description	Descriptors	Effectiv. Measure
Soccer [36]	280	Color Scenes	Dataset composed of images from 7 soccer teams, containing 40 images per class	Border/Interior Pixel Classification (BIC) [32], Auto Color Correlograms (ACC) [14], and Global Color Histogram (GCH) [33]	MAP (%)
MPEG-7 [18]	1,400	Shape	A well-known dataset composed of 1400 shapes divided in 70 classes. Commonly used for evaluation of unsupervised distance learning approaches.	Segment Saliences (SS) [10], Beam Angle Statistics (BAS) [3], Inner Distance Shape Context (IDSC) [19], Contour Features Descriptor (CFD) [27], Aspect Shape Context (ASC) [20], and Articulation-Invariant Representation (AIR) [12]	MAP (%), Recall@40
Brodatz [6]	1,776	Texture	A popular dataset for texture descriptors evaluation composed of 111 different textures divided into 16 blocks	Local Binary Patterns (LBP) [25], Color Co-Occurrence Matrix (CCOM) [17], Local Activity Spectrum (LAS) [34]	MAP (%)
N-S [24]	10,200	Objects/ Scenes	Composed of 2,550 objects or scenes. Each object/scene is captured 4 times from different viewpoints, distances, and illumination conditions	ACC [14], BIC [32], Color and Edge Directivity Descriptor (CEED) [7], Fuzzy Color and Texture Histogram (FCTH) [8], Joint Composite Descriptor (JCD) [40], Scale-Invariant Feature Transform (SIFT) [22]	N-S score
ALOI [11]	72,000	Objects	Images from 1,000 classes of objects, with different viewpoint, occlusion, and illumination conditions.	ACC [14], BIC [32], GCH [33], Color Coherence Vectors (CCV) [26], Local Color Histograms (LCH) [23]	MAP (%)

4.1 Datasets, Descriptors, and Experimental Setup

The experimental evaluation was conducted on five different datasets with diverse characteristics and size ranging from 280 to 72,000 images. The evaluation also used 18 different local and global descriptors, considering shape, color, and texture properties. Table 1 summarizes information about datasets and descriptors.

All images of each dataset are considered as query images in the effectiveness evaluation. The Mean Average Precision (MAP) was used as effectiveness measure for most of datasets, except for the N-S collection [24]. For the MPEG-7 [18] dataset, the Recall@40 is also considered in addition to MAP. For the ALOI dataset, we used the BP-Tree [1] indexing structure for the computation of the ranked lists.

The efficiency evaluation experiments considered the average run time of 10 executions and 95% confidence intervals. The hardware environment is composed of a CPU Intel Xeon CPU E3-1240 and a GPU AMD Radeon HD 7900 Series. The software environment is given by the operating system Linux 3.11.0-15 - Ubuntu 12.04 and OpenCL 1.2 AMD-APP.

4.2 Impact of Parameters

The RL-Recommendation algorithm considers three parameters: *(i)* k: number of initial neighbors; *(ii)* α: a constant that defines the weight of recommendations; and *(iii)* ϵ: the threshold parameter used for the convergence criterion. A set of experiments were conducted for evaluating the influence of different parameter settings on the retrieval scores for defining the best parameters values.

The first experiment aims at analyzing the impact of parameters k and ϵ. We computed the MAP scores ranging the parameter k in the interval $[0, 20]$ and the parameter ϵ from 0.005 to 0.02. The MPEG-7 [18] dataset and the CFD [27] shape descriptor were used in the experiment. The analysis of the variation of the MAP according to k and ϵ is shown in the surface illustrated in Figure 2. We can observe small variations on MAP scores, from 90% to 92%, which demonstrates the robustness of the proposed method for different parameters settings. The best effectiveness results were obtained for $k = 8$ and $\epsilon = 0.0125$. We used $\alpha = 2$, as suggested in [28]. These values were used in most of the experiments. Only the N-S [24] and ALOI [11] datasets used $k = 4$ and $k = 40$, respectively. Both datasets have very small and large number of images per class.

The second experiment analyzes the constant L, which

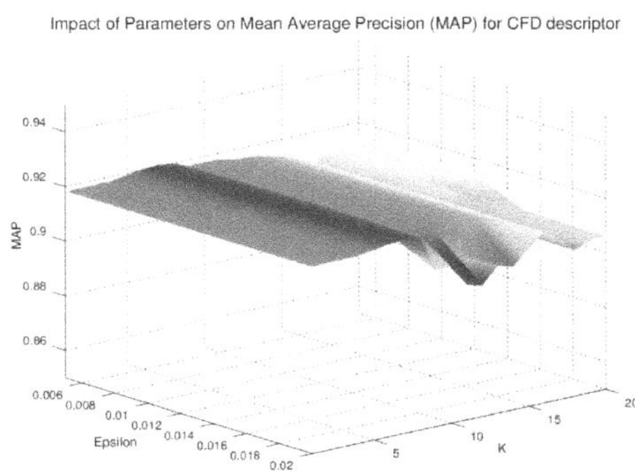

Figure 2: Impact of parameters k and ϵ on effectiveness.

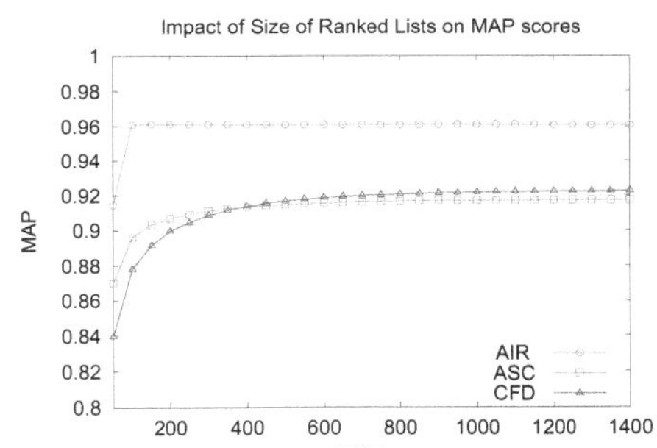

Figure 3: Impact of size of ranked lists L on effectiveness.

defines the size of ranked list used as input. As previously discussed, the RL-Recommendation algorithm does not require the use of the entire ranked list. An experiment was conducted using the MPEG-7 [18] dataset for verifying the impact of the size of ranked lists on the effectiveness results. We computed the MAP scores ranging L in the interval $[50, 1400]$. The results for three different descriptors are shown in Figure 3.

The curve behavior reveals that a small subset of the dataset (low L values) is enough for producing good effectiveness results. In addition, for values of L greater than 400, the MAP scores stop increasing expressively for all the descriptors. We used the value of $L = 400$ for most of experiments.[1]

[1]The value of L used for the Soccer [36] dataset is limited by the dataset size ($L = 280$). For the ALOI [11] and N-S datasets we used $L = 7200$ and $L = 200$, respectively.

Table 2: Effectiveness evaluation of the proposed RL-Recommendation algorithm considering various datasets and descriptors (MAP as score).

Descriptor	Dataset	Original MAP	Pairwise Recom. [28]	RL-Recom. Serial	RL-Recom. Parallel GPU	Gain
SS [10]	MPEG-7	37.67%	39.90%	48.68%	48.64% ± 0.0062	+29.22%
BAS [3]	MPEG-7	71.52%	77.65%	79.58%	79.57% ± 0.0047	+11.27%
IDSC [19]	MPEG-7	81.70%	86.83%	88.80%	88.78% ± 0.0067	+11.86%
CFD [27]	MPEG-7	80.71%	91.38%	91.39%	91.37% ± 0.0055	+13.23%
ASC [20]	MPEG-7	85.28%	91.80%	91.34%	91.32% ± 0.0050	+7.11%
AIR [12]	MPEG-7	89.39%	95.50%	96.12%	96.12% ± 0.0071	+7.53%
GCH [33]	Soccer	32.24%	32.35%	34.38%	34.44% ± 0.0340	+6.64%
ACC [14]	Soccer	37.23%	40.31%	41.23%	41.20% ± 0.0239	+10.74%
BIC [32]	Soccer	39.26%	42.64%	45.15%	45.17% ± 0.0693	+15.00%
LBP [25]	Brodatz	48.40%	51.92%	51.26%	51.24% ± 0.0047	+5.91%
CCOM [17]	Brodatz	57.57%	66.46%	64.34%	64.32% ± 0.0059	+11.76%
LAS [34]	Brodatz	75.15%	80.73%	79.71%	79.71% ± 0.0031	+6.07%

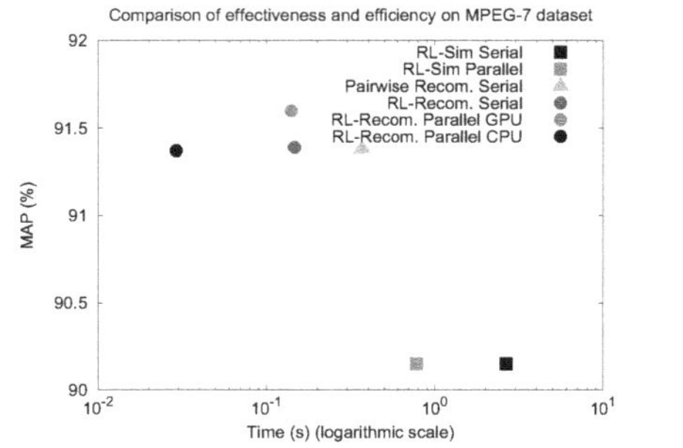

Figure 4: Effectiveness and efficiency analysis on the MPEG-7 [18] dataset.

Table 3: Effectiveness evaluation on the N-S [24] dataset, considering the N-S score.

Descriptor	Type	Original Score	RL-Recom.	Gain
ACC [14]	Color	3.36	3.53	+5.06%
BIC [32]	Color	3.04	3.15	+3.62%
CEED [7]	Color/Text.	2.61	2.72	+4.21%
FCTH [8]	Color/Text.	2.73	2.80	+2.56%
JCD [40]	Color/Text.	2.79	2.88	+3.23%
SIFT [22]	Local	2.54	2.88	+13.39%

Table 4: Effectiveness evaluation on the ALOI dataset [11], considering MAP as score.

Descriptor	Original MAP	Baseline: RL-Sim [13]	RL-Recom.	Gain
ACC [14]	44.15%	46.12%	50.11%	+13.50%
BIC [32]	71.95%	78.84%	80.35%	+11.67%
CCV [26]	47.77%	50.96%	53.52%	+12.04%
GCH [33]	50.87%	53.14%	55.81%	+9.71%
LCH [23]	58.85%	66.03%	72.63%	+23.42%

4.3 Effectiveness Evaluation

This sections aims at assessing the effectiveness of the proposed algorithm. A large set of experiments was conducted, considering various datasets and several descriptors.

Table 2 presents the MAP results for three datasets, considering shape, color, and texture features. We report the MAP scores for both serial and parallel GPU implementation of the RL-Recommendation algorithm. For the parallel GPU execution, the result is an average of 10 executions with the respectively 95% confidence interval. Notice that the confidence intervals are very small, indicating a low variation among different executions. The relative gain is computed based on serial execution. Very significant gains are observed for most of descriptors, ranging from +5.92% to +29.22%. For comparison purposes, we also reported the MAP scores of the Pairwise Recommendation [28] algorithm. The effectiveness results of the RL-Recommendation are significantly superior for most of the descriptors.

The effectiveness results considering the N-S [24] dataset are presented in Table 3. For this dataset, the N-S retrieval score between 1 and 4 is computed. This score corresponds to the number of relevant images among the first four image returned (the highest achievable score is 4). The N-S [24] is a very challenging dataset for unsupervised learning algorithms due to the small number of images per class (only 4). Despite this characteristic of the dataset, the RL-Recommendation achieved gains ranging from +2.56% to +13.39%.

Table 4 presents the MAP scores considering the ALOI [11] dataset. The ALOI [11] dataset is the biggest considered in the experiments and used indexing structures of the ranked lists computation. The gains obtained by the RL-Recommendation are also very significant for this dataset ranging from +9.71% to 23.42%. We also report the MAP scores for a recent baseline, the RL-Sim [13] algorithm. Notice that the RL-Recommendation effectiveness results are superior for all the descriptors.

A joined effectiveness and efficiency analysis conducted on the MPEG-7 [18] dataset is presented in Figure 4. The Pairwise Recommendation [28] and the RL-Sim algorithms [29, 31] are considered as baselines. The position of algorithms in the graph is given by the MAP score and the run time. Therefore, an ideal algorithm, with high effectiveness and low run time, is positioned at the top-left corner of the graph. Notice that the RL-Recommendation Algorithm (serial and parallel) occupies the best positions.

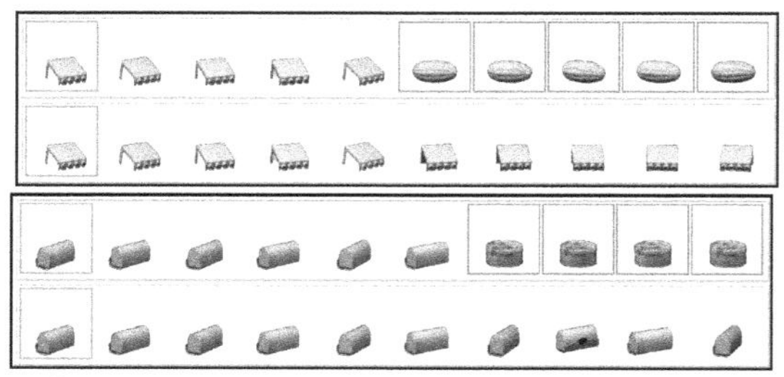

Figure 5: Impact of the RL-Recommendation on the ALOI [11] dataset: two ranked lists before and after the algorithm (query images with green borders and wrong results with red borders).

Two visual examples of the impact of the RL-Recommendation algorithm on ranked lists are illustrated in Figure 5. The query images are presented in green borders and wrong results in red borders. The first line represents the original retrieval results and the second line, the results after the algorithm execution.

Finally, we also evaluate our method in comparison with several other state-of-the-art unsupervised learning methods. We use the MPEG-7 [18] and the Bull's Eye Score (Recall@40), commonly used for evaluation and comparison of post-processing methods. Table 6 presents the results. We can observe that the RL-Recommendation achieved comparable effectiveness results, despite of the low computational efforts required.

4.4 Efficiency Evaluation

We conducted a set of experiments aiming at evaluating the efficiency of the proposed RL-Recommendation algorithm. Several aspects were evaluated, considering various datasets, the serial and OpenCL parallel implementations,

Table 5: Efficiency evaluation: runtime (in seconds) of the RL-Recommendation for different devices and datasets.

Algorithm	Exec.	Device	Soccer [36]	MPEG-7 [18]	Brodatz [6]	N-S Dataset [24]
Pairwise Recom. [28]	Serial	CPU	0.1149 ± 0.00018	0.3663 ± 0.00094	0.6672 ± 0.00140	14.802 ± 0.11059
RL-Recommendation	Serial	CPU	0.0607 ± 0.00000	0.1462 ± 0.00021	0.1108 ± 0.00102	0.1868 ± 0.00018
RL-Recommendation	Parallel	GPU[1]	0.1380 ± 0.00642	0.1401 ± 0.00250	0.1004 ± 0.00412	**0.0582 ± 0.00633**
RL-Recommendation	Parallel	GPU[2]	0.1538 ± 0.01056	0.2438 ± 0.00371	0.2376 ± 0.00326	0.3754 ± 0.00604
RL-Recommendation	Parallel	CPU[1]	0.0131 ± 0.00100	0.0319 ± 0.00043	0.0299 ± 0.00129	0.1166 ± 0.00085
RL-Recommendation	Parallel	CPU[2]	**0.0128 ± 0.00104**	**0.0290 ± 0.00075**	**0.0284 ± 0.00114**	0.1149 ± 0.00055

Memory Transfer Model: [1]Write Buffer; [2]Map Buffer.

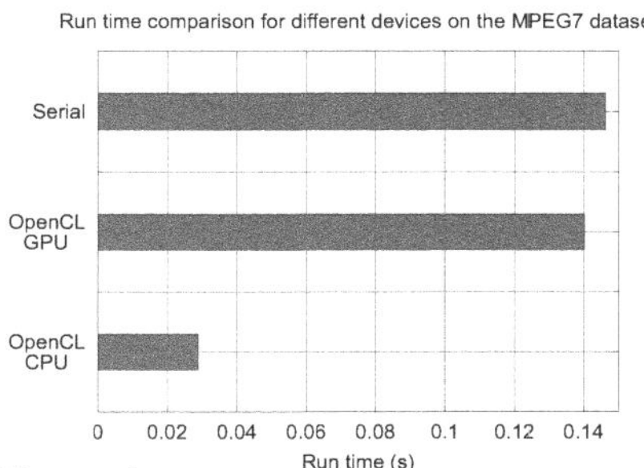

Figure 6: Runtime comparison on the MPEG-7 [18] dataset.

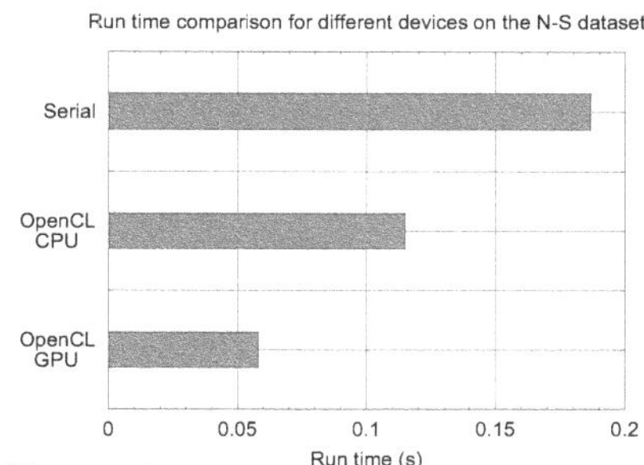

Figure 7: Runtime comparison on the N-S [24] dataset.

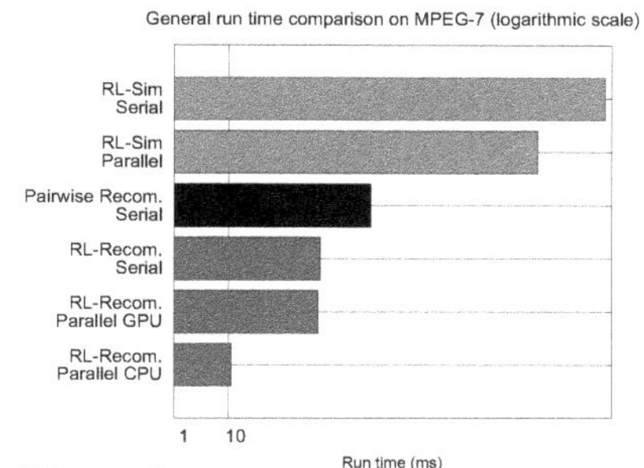

Figure 8: General runtime comparison on the MPEG-7 [18] dataset.

Table 6: Comparison of post-processing methods on the MPEG-7 [18] dataset - Bull's Eye Score (Recall@40).

Shape Descriptors		
DDGM [35]	-	80.03%
CFD [27]	-	84.43%
IDSC [19]	-	85.40%
SC [5]	-	86.80%
ASC [20]	-	88.39%
AIR [12]	-	93.67%
Post-Processing Methods		
Algorithm	**Descriptor(s)**	**Score**
Locally C. Diffusion Process [38]	IDSC	93.32%
Shortest Path Propagation [37]	IDSC	93.35%
Mutual kNN Graph [16]	IDSC	93.40%
RL-Sim [29]	CFD	94.13%
RL-Recommendation	**CFD**	**94.38%**
RL-Recommendation	**ASC**	**94.40%**
Locally C. Diffusion Process [38]	ASC	95.96%
Self-Smoothing Operator [15]	SC+IDSC	97.64%
Co-Transduction [4]	SC+IDSC	97.72%
Self-Smoothing Operator [15]	SC+IDSC+DDGM	99.20%
Pairwise Recommendation [28]	CFD+IDSC	99.52%
RL-Recommendation	**AIR**	**99.78%**
Tensor Product Graph [39]	AIR	99.99%

different devices (CPU, GPU), and memory transfer models. The reported results do not consider the OpenCL build and environment time, since the build can be executed once off-line and the environment time is constant independently of dataset sizes. We also present a comparison with other two unsupervised learning algorithms: the Pairwise Recommendation [28] and the RL-Sim algorithms [29, 31].

Table 5 presents the average run time and confidence intervals for the RL-Recommendation algorithm considering different criteria. For comparison, the run time for the Pairwise Recommendation [28] algorithm is also reported. The best performance for each dataset is highlighted in boldface. As we can observe, the performance results of the RL-Recommendation are very superior to the Pairwise Recommendation [28] algorithm. Considering only the serial executions, the RL-Recommendation is up to 79.3× faster, for the N-S [24] dataset. Considering the parallel implementations, the results are still more significant. The speedup obtained over the serial implementation ranges from 3.2× (N-S [24] dataset) to 5× (MPEG-7 [18] dataset). We can also observe that the performance of Parallel GPU in comparison with Parallel CPU increases according to size of the dataset, indicating that GPU devices can be better exploited for large amounts of computation. The overall run time for the whole N-S [24] dataset (with 10,200 images) is only $0.0582s$ for the Parallel GPU execution.

Figures 6 and 7 illustrate a comparison between the serial and parallel implementations for the N-S [24] and MPEG-7 [18] datasets, respectively. For the parallel implementations, different devices (CPU, GPU) are considered. Significant performance were obtained by the parallel implementation. Figure 8 presents a more general comparison of the RL-Recommendation (both serial and parallel) with baselines. The run time of Pairwise Recommendation [28] (serial) and the RL-Sim [29, 31] (serial and parallel) are reported. The MPEG-7 [18] dataset was considered for the experiment. Notice that, even using a logarithmic scale, the run time of the proposed RL-Recommendation (in blue) algorithm is significant smaller than other considered approaches.

4.5 Scalability Evaluation

This section evaluates the scalability of the proposed algorithm. We conducted an experiment varying the size of the ranked lists used as input and analyzing the behavior of the algorithm. The size of the ranked lists is defined by the constant L. Therefore, this constant defines an important trade-off control between effectiveness and efficiency. The ALOI [11] dataset and the LCH [23] descriptor were considered. We ranged the value of L from 70 to 7000, reporting for the average time of the unsupervised distance learning per ranked list. We also reported the same results for the RL-Sim [13] algorithm, as a baseline.

Figure 9 shows the results. We can observe very small average times for growing values of L for the RL-Recommendation Algorithm. This behavior enables the use of the algorithm in different datasets of any sizes, demonstrating its scalability characteristics. Even larger values of L were not considered because the effectiveness gains stabilizes after certain values of L (discussion in Section 4.2).

5. CONCLUSIONS

In this paper, we have presented a novel unsupervised

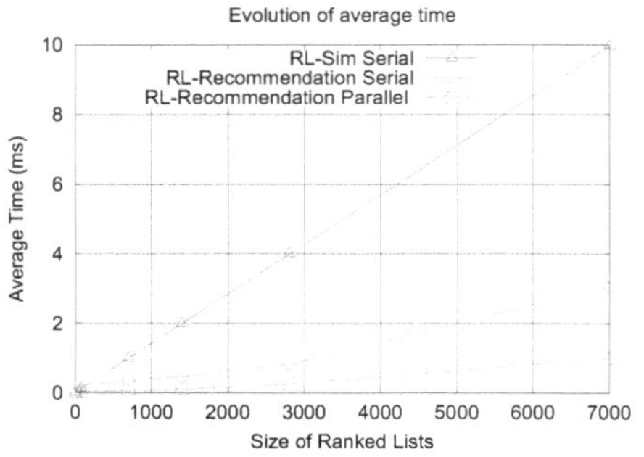

Figure 9: Scalability analysis: impact of size of ranked lists on average time for the ALOI dataset [11].

learning algorithm for image retrieval tasks. The main motivation consists in exploiting information of ranked lists for improving the effectiveness of CBIR tasks. The proposed approach differs from previous works, as it considers at the same time effectiveness, efficiency, and scalability issues. In addition to the significant effectiveness gains, the algorithm requires low computation efforts, presenting very positive efficiency and scalability properties. We have also exploited parallel computing for heterogeneous environments. We have conducted a large set of experiments on various public datasets and several descriptors. The results and comparisons with other recent state-of-the-art approaches demonstrate the effectiveness and efficiency of the proposed method. Future work includes the use of the proposed method for combining different descriptors and different modalities (e.g., visual and textual descriptors).

6. ACKNOWLEDGMENTS

The authors are grateful to São Paulo Research Foundation - FAPESP (grants 2013/08645-0, 2014/04220-8, and 2013/50169-1), CNPq (grants 306580/2012-8 and 484254/2012-0), CAPES, AMD, and Microsoft Research.

7. REFERENCES

[1] J. Almeida, R. da S. Torres, and N. J. Leite. BP-tree: An efficient index for similarity search in high-dimensional metric spaces. In *CIKM*, pages 1365–1368, 2010.

[2] J. Almeida, D. C. G. Pedronette, and O. A. B. Penatti. Unsupervised manifold learning for video genre retrieval. In *CIARP*, pages 604–612, 2014.

[3] N. Arica and F. T. Y. Vural. BAS: a perceptual shape descriptor based on the beam angle statistics. *Pattern Recognition Letters*, 24(9-10):1627–1639, 2003.

[4] X. Bai, B. Wang, X. Wang, W. Liu, and Z. Tu. Co-transduction for shape retrieval. In *ECCV*, volume 3, pages 328–341, 2010.

[5] S. Belongie, J. Malik, and J. Puzicha. Shape matching and object recognition using shape contexts. *PAMI*, 24(4):509–522, 2002.

[6] P. Brodatz. *Textures: A Photographic Album for Artists and Designers*. Dover, 1966.

[7] S. A. Chatzichristofis and Y. S. Boutalis. Cedd: color and edge directivity descriptor: a compact descriptor for image indexing and retrieval. In *ICVS*, pages 312–322, 2008.

[8] S. A. Chatzichristofis and Y. S. Boutalis. Fcth: Fuzzy color and texture histogram - a low level feature for accurate image retrieval. In *WIAMIS*, pages 191–196, 2008.

[9] R. da S. Torres and A. X. Falcão. Content-Based Image Retrieval: Theory and Applications. *Revista de Informática Teórica e Aplicada*, 13(2):161–185, 2006.

[10] R. da S. Torres and A. X. Falcão. Contour Salience Descriptors for Effective Image Retrieval and Analysis. *Image and Vision Computing*, 25(1):3–13, 2007.

[11] J.-M. Geusebroek, G. J. Burghouts, and A. W. M. Smeulders. The amsterdam library of object images. *International Journal of Computer Vision*, 61(1):103–112, 2005.

[12] R. Gopalan, P. Turaga, and R. Chellappa. Articulation-invariant representation of non-planar shapes. In *ECCV*, volume 3, pages 286–299, 2010.

[13] D. C. Guimarães Pedronette, J. Almeida, and R. Da S. Torres. A scalable re-ranking method for content-based image retrieval. *Information Sciences*, 265:91–104, May 2014.

[14] J. Huang, S. R. Kumar, M. Mitra, W.-J. Zhu, and R. Zabih. Image indexing using color correlograms. In *CVPR*, pages 762–768, 1997.

[15] J. Jiang, B. Wang, and Z. Tu. Unsupervised metric learning by self-smoothing operator. In *ICCV*, pages 794–801, 2011.

[16] P. Kontschieder, M. Donoser, and H. Bischof. Beyond pairwise shape similarity analysis. In *ACCV*, pages 655–666, 2009.

[17] V. Kovalev and S. Volmer. Color co-occurence descriptors for querying-by-example. In *ICMM*, page 32, 1998.

[18] L. J. Latecki, R. Lakmper, and U. Eckhardt. Shape descriptors for non-rigid shapes with a single closed contour. In *CVPR*, pages 424–429, 2000.

[19] H. Ling and D. W. Jacobs. Shape classification using the inner-distance. *PAMI*, 29(2):286–299, 2007.

[20] H. Ling, X. Yang, and L. J. Latecki. Balancing deformability and discriminability for shape matching. In *ECCV*, volume 3, pages 411–424, 2010.

[21] Y. Liu, D. Zhang, G. Lu, and W.-Y. Ma. A survey of content-based image retrieval with high-level semantics. *Pattern Recognition*, 40(1):262 – 282, 2007.

[22] D. Lowe. Object recognition from local scale-invariant features. In *ICCV*, pages 1150–1157, 1999.

[23] H. Lu, B. Ooi, and K. Tan. Efficient image retrieval by color contents. In *ADB*, pages 95–108, 1994.

[24] D. Nistér and H. Stewénius. Scalable recognition with a vocabulary tree. In *CVPR*, volume 2, pages 2161–2168, 2006.

[25] T. Ojala, M. Pietikäinen, and T. Mäenpää. Multiresolution gray-scale and rotation invariant texture classification with local binary patterns. *PAMI*, 24(7):971–987, 2002.

[26] G. Pass, R. Zabih, and J. Miller. Comparing images using color coherence vectors. In *ACM-MM*, pages 65–73, 1996.

[27] D. C. G. Pedronette and R. da S. Torres. Shape retrieval using contour features and distance optmization. In *VISAPP*, volume 1, pages 197 – 202, 2010.

[28] D. C. G. Pedronette and R. da S. Torres. Exploiting pairwise recommendation and clustering strategies for image re-ranking. *Information Sciences*, 207:19–34, 2012.

[29] D. C. G. Pedronette and R. da S. Torres. Image re-ranking and rank aggregation based on similarity of ranked lists. *Pattern Recognition*, 46(8):2350–2360, 2013.

[30] D. C. G. Pedronette, R. da S. Torres, E. Borin, and M. Breternitz. Efficient image re-ranking computation on GPUs. In *ISPA*, 2012.

[31] D. C. G. Pedronette, R. da S. Torres, E. Borin, and M. Breternitz. Rl-sim algorithm acceleration on GPUs. In *SBAC*, 2013.

[32] R. O. Stehling, M. A. Nascimento, and A. X. Falcão. A compact and efficient image retrieval approach based on border/interior pixel classification. In *CIKM*, pages 102–109, 2002.

[33] M. J. Swain and D. H. Ballard. Color indexing. *International Journal on Computer Vision*, 7(1):11–32, 1991.

[34] B. Tao and B. W. Dickinson. Texture recognition and image retrieval using gradient indexing. *JVCIR*, 11(3):327–342, 2000.

[35] Z. Tu and A. L. Yuille. Shape matching and recognition - using generative models and informative features. In *ECCV*, pages 195–209, 2004.

[36] J. van de Weijer and C. Schmid. Coloring local feature extraction. In *ECCV*.

[37] J. Wang, Y. Li, X. Bai, Y. Zhang, C. Wang, and N. Tang. Learning context-sensitive similarity by shortest path propagation. *Pattern Recognition*, 44(10-11):2367–2374, 2011.

[38] X. Yang, S. Koknar-Tezel, and L. J. Latecki. Locally constrained diffusion process on locally densified distance spaces with applications to shape retrieval. In *CVPR*, pages 357–364, 2009.

[39] X. Yang, L. Prasad, and L. Latecki. Affinity learning with diffusion on tensor product graph. *PAMI*, PP(99):1, 2012.

[40] K. Zagoris, S. Chatzichristofis, N. Papamarkos, and Y. Boutalis. Automatic image annotation and retrieval using the joint composite descriptor. In *PCI*, pages 143–147, 2010.

Twin Feature and Similarity Maximal Matching for Image Retrieval

Lei Wang Hanli Wang* Fengkuangtian Zhu

Department of Computer Science and Technology, Tongji University, Shanghai, China
Key Laboratory of Embedded System and Service Computing, Ministry of Education,
Tongji University, Shanghai, China
{110_wangleixx,hanliwang,2zhufengkuangtian}@tongji.edu.cn

ABSTRACT

In recent years, most advanced image retrieval algorithms are built upon local features, and various up-to-date match kernels are developed to boost image retrieval performances. However, most of these image retrieval algorithms need to face up two challenging issues: (1) the locality property of local features as well as quantization noise and (2) the phenomenon of burstiness, which significantly affect image retrieval performances. In this paper, two novel techniques including Twin Feature (TF) and Similarity Maximal Matching (SMM) are proposed for image retrieval performance improvement, which can be employed with non-aggregated kernel models, for example, the Selective Match Kernel (SMK). The proposed TF employs extra information from neighboring image patches to refine visual matching. As far as SMM is concerned, it tries to control burstiness by dynamically searching the match-pair combinations to maximize the global similarity score and thus removes multiple matches. Experimental results on two benchmark image datasets including Oxford5k and Paris6k demonstrate that the new techniques SMK_{tf} (SMK with TF) and SMK_{smm} (SMK with SMM) can greatly enhance image retrieval accuracy performances as compared to SMK, and their combination, *i.e.*, SMK_{tf+smm}, is able to achieve better image retrieval accuracies than a number of state-of-the-art approaches.

*H. Wang is the corresponding author.

This work was supported in part by the National Natural Science Foundation of China under Grant 61472281, the "Shu Guang" project of Shanghai Municipal Education Commission and Shanghai Education Development Foundation under Grant 12SG23, and the Fundamental Research Funds for the Central Universities under Grant 0800219270.

ICMR'15, June 23-26, 2015, Shanghai, China.

http://dx.doi.org/10.1145/2671188.2749345.

Categories and Subject Descriptors

H.3.3 [**Information Search and Retrieval**]: Relevance feedback; I.4.7 [**Feature Measurement**]: Feature representation

Keywords

Non-aggregated kernel, local feature, visual matching, image retrieval, burstiness

1. INTRODUCTION

Image retrieval is a fundamental but challenging task that has always been concerned in computer vision realm. Recently, the image retrieval approaches based on local features have experienced a rapid growth [31]. Among all, local feature based models have been widely used in many state-of-the-art image retrieval systems, with the Bag-of-Words (BoW) [25] model as the representative due to its effectiveness and efficiency. In the BoW model, local interest points are firstly detected from images with effective detectors such as the Hessian-Affine [18] detector and then described using feature descriptors, *e.g.*, the Scale Invariant Feature Transform (SIFT) [17] descriptor. Then, each descriptor is assigned to the nearest visual word(s) in a visual dictionary pre-trained before. Finally, all the information is integrated into an inverted index [24] to reduce memory requirements and accelerate online retrieval.

A number of researches have been proposed to improve image retrieval performances. On the one hand, in order to reduce the quantization errors when assigning and matching feature descriptors, multiple descriptor assignment [11, 13] and soft quantization [29] which assign the feature descriptors to more than one visual word are proposed. Moreover, Hamming Embedding (HE) is another typical powerful approach proposed in [9, 11] to refine the matching process. By calculating the hamming distance between two binary signatures, the discriminative power of features can be dramatically improved. On the other hand, several research efforts are focused on post-processing techniques such as spatial reranking [22, 4, 3] and query expansion [5, 6, 27]. These post-processing techniques improve the image retrieval performance by executing extra calculations on the initial retrieval result list. In this work, we mainly concentrate on improving the initial retrieval result set and do not employ these post-processing techniques.

Recently, in order to handle larger size of data, several advanced image retrieval approaches have been designed.

For instance, hashing based method like [15] encodes high-dimensional features into hamming space to support effective and efficient search. Moreover, the technique of Vector of Locally Aggregated Descriptors (VLAD) [12, 7] is proposed and has also made a great progress in image retrieval [1, 14]. It considers feature descriptors in a joint manner so that the elements belonging to the same visual word can be encoded together. In this way, images can be represented by a few bytes and thus be able to scale to large databases. Moreover, Tolias *et al.* [26] make an in-depth investigation of these effective models such as BoW, HE and VLAD, and introduce the non-aggregated kernel and aggregated kernel. Non-aggregated kernels individually match all the elements belonging to the same visual word while aggregated kernels pre-combine all the elements on one visual word and match them as an entirety. Then, the selectivity of both of the non-aggregated and aggregated kernels are studied. Moreover, the Selective Match Kernel (SMK) and Aggregated Selective Match Kernel (ASMK) are proposed in [26], which combine the matching-based approaches like HE and aggregated representation models such as VLAD to achieve better image retrieval performances.

In this work, we propose two novel techniques to further improve image retrieval performances based on Selective Match Kernel (SMK) [26]. First, we construct a new feature by utilizing the full attributes of original local features (including location, scale and orientation) and local image patches nearby to improve the robustness of matches during retrieval. We call it Twin Feature (TF) because it follows the original local feature tightly and they share most attributes just like the twin of the original feature. The basic idea of TF is that true positive matches have a high probability that their neighboring patches are also similar to each other. Second, a new strategy named as Similarity Maximal Matching (SMM) is designed to handle the multiple matching problem. Different from existing methods, SMM tries to find the best matching combination and thus to maximize the similarities of matches belonging to the same visual word. Besides the above two contributions, we further refine the SMK by improving the quality of matches. The experimental results demonstrate that better image retrieval performances in terms of mean Average Precision (mAP) can be achieved by employing the proposed TF and SMM on the two benchmark image retrieval datasets Oxford5k [21] and Paris6k [23] as compared with some other state-of-the-art approaches, all of which do not additionally employ post-processing techniques such as spatial re-ranking and query expansion.

The rest of this paper is organized as follows. Section 2 gives an overview of the framework of image retrieval based on SMK. The details of the proposed TF and SMM are described in Section 3. The experimental results are presented in Section 4 and finally Section 5 concludes this paper.

2. NON-AGGREGATED KERNEL

In this section, we make a brief introduction to image retrieval based on non-aggregated match kernels.

2.1 Common Model

Suppose that an image is described with a set of n d-dimensional features $X = \{x_1, ..., x_n\}$, and all the features are quantized by a K-Means quantizer as

$$\begin{aligned} q : \mathbb{R}^d &\rightarrow \mathcal{C} \subset \mathbb{R}^d, \\ x &\mapsto q(x), \end{aligned} \tag{1}$$

where $\mathcal{C} = \{c_1, ..., c_K\}$ denotes the visual vocabulary of K words. $X_c = \{x \in X : q(x) = c\}$ is defined as the subset of features of X that are mapped to the visual word c. In a similar fashion, Y and Y_c represent the corresponding sets of another image. In general, we simply assume that $\#X_c = m$ and $\#Y_c = n$, where $\#$ stands for the cardinality of a set.

As the name implies, non-aggregated kernels [26] match all of the elements belonging to the same visual word independently, and the kernel $\mathcal{K}$ can be written as

$$\mathcal{K}(X_c, Y_c) = \sum_{i=1}^{m}\sum_{j=1}^{n} \sigma(\phi(x_i)^{\mathrm{T}}\phi(y_j)), \tag{2}$$

where $\phi(z)$ is a scalar or vector related to the descriptor z, and $\sigma(\cdot)$ is a scalar selectivity function.

2.2 Selective Match Kernel

Actually, there is a number of candidates for choosing the kernel $\mathcal{K}$ in Eq. (2). In this work, we mainly discuss SMK for non-aggregated matching and all of the following improvements are based on this kernel.

As learned from [26], in SMK, $\sigma(\cdot)$ is set to be $\sigma_\alpha(\cdot) : \mathbb{R} \rightarrow \mathbb{R}^+$, where

$$\sigma_\alpha(u) = \begin{cases} \mathrm{sign}(u)|u|^\alpha, & \text{if} \quad u > \tau \\ 0, & \text{otherwise} \end{cases}, \tag{3}$$

where α balances strong and weak matches and τ is a threshold to filter out weak matches.

Regarding $\phi(\cdot)$, a l_2-normalized residual $\hat{r}(\cdot)$ which is a little different from VLAD [12] is employed as

$$\hat{r}(z) = \frac{z - q(z)}{\|z - q(z)\|}, \tag{4}$$

and by setting $\phi(z) = \hat{r}(z)$, SMK is finally formed as

$$\mathrm{SMK}(X_c, Y_c) = \sum_{i=1}^{m}\sum_{j=1}^{n} \sigma_\alpha(\hat{r}(x_i)^{\mathrm{T}}\hat{r}(y_j)). \tag{5}$$

3. PROPOSED TWIN FEATURE AND SIMILARITY MAXIMAL MATCHING

In this section, we introduce the proposed TF and SMM techniques as well as their combination with SMK to improve image retrieval performances.

3.1 Twin Feature

The proposed twin feature takes the advantage of neighboring patches of local image features to assist in visual matching. It should be noted that in the rest of the paper, *feature* refers to the original local image features detected by existing techniques, and *twin* refers to the proposed twin features.

3.1.1 Motivation

As aforementioned, there are two challenging issues for local feature based image retrieval systems. One is the feature locality as well as quantization noise. Regarding the locality of local features, false positive matches appear inevitably even though advanced techniques are applied, since feature vectors of local descriptors are generated within limited local patches. Therefore, more information is desired to make local descriptors more discriminative.

Typically, the original local image features are restricted to the image patches around their centers. Two matched features within two image patches may be totally different in semantics. These kinds of mismatches are hard to be filtered out since the numerical distance between those features are extremely small.

To tackle this problem, we tend to add extra information into the matching process and propose the twins of local features with the following two reasons. First, objects in images are usually composed of several image patches, which means that more than one features can be detected inside an object. Second, similar features detected from similar objects have a fair chance of sharing similar neighboring patches, while dissimilar features can hardly own similar neighboring patches. In other words, if the twins of two local features can be matched accurately as the original ones, the confidence of this match should be high, and vice versa.

3.1.2 Twin Construction

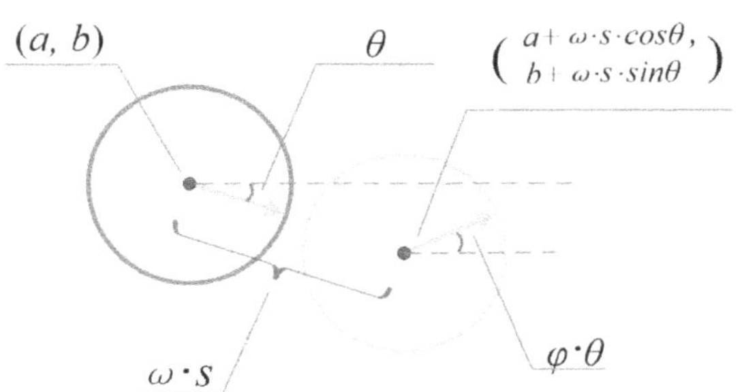

Figure 1: A toy example of constructing twin. The different colors denote different type of features, with the red corresponding to the original local feature, the yellow in dashed corresponding to the potential twin features and the yellow in solid corresponding to the finally selected twin feature.

In order to assist in visual matching, we propose to design a new feature from the original feature and most particular attributes of the original local features should be utilized, including location, scale and orientation. Let (a, b) be the center of an original feature f, with its dominant orientation θ and scale s. In a similar fashion, (a_{tf}, b_{tf}), θ_{tf} and s_{tf} represent the corresponding twin's center, orientation and scale, respectively. In a way, twin can be considered as a copy of the original feature, and they should be similar in location, consistent in orientation and exactly the same in scale and patch size. Therefore, it is assumed that $s_{tf} = s$.

More specifically, the center of the twin is of crucial importance. If the twin is too close to the original feature,

(a) Standard BoW based matching without twin.

(b) BoW based matching with twin enabled.

Figure 2: Effects of visual matching using twin.

only a little extra information would be obtained since they share most of the same image patch. Otherwise, if the twin is far from the original feature, too much noise would be brought in and tremendously affect the results. Moreover, there would be innumerable potential twins around one feature when the distance is determined, as shown in Fig. 1. It would be improper if the corresponding twins of two matched features are selected randomly. To address this issue, the orientation of the original feature is utilized. As illustrated in Fig. 1, the twin which directly faces the orientation of the original feature is finally selected, as the original feature is invariant to rotation changes, so the same as the twin.

To summarize, the center of twin is determined as

$$\begin{aligned} a_{tf} &= a + \omega \cdot s \cdot \cos\theta \\ b_{tf} &= b + \omega \cdot s \cdot \sin\theta\text{'} \end{aligned} \tag{6}$$

where three factors affect the twin's center location, including θ, s and a control parameter ω. The details about the impact of ω on image retrieval performance will be analyzed in Section 4.2.1.

After determining the center and image patch of twin, the SIFT descriptor is employed for twin description due to the following two reasons. First, SIFT descriptors perform well in most image related tasks and are regarded as discriminative and robust. Second, SIFT descriptors are able to be integrated into existing systems or frameworks more easily.

In order to calculate the twin descriptor, the dominant orientation is a crucial parameter that affects the description performance. In fact, there are two ways to determine the dominant orientation of twin: (1) manual appointment according to the original feature or (2) self-calculation within the patches of twin. The second way is inferior, since the neighboring patches usually bring in noise, while the first method could reduce the impact of noise to some extent. Based on the above analysis, the dominant orientation of twin is calculated as

$$\theta_{tf} = \theta + \varphi \cdot \pi. \tag{7}$$

Typically, different values of φ will cause different results when employing SIFT descriptions. However, there would be little difference on the final retrieval performance as long as all twins follow the same rule of construction. For simplicity, we set the control parameter $\varphi = 0$.

Moreover, to further verify the effects of TF in visual matching, we apply it to the standard BoW model with a representative example illustrated in Fig. 2. As shown in Fig. 2(a), due to the quantization errors and locality of features, more than half of the matches are false positive when TF is not employed. When TF is enabled, most of the mismatches can be eliminated as revealed in Fig. 2(b).

3.2 Similarity Maximal Matching

The proposed SMM technique is detailed herein, which can be applied to deal with the burstiness problem.

3.2.1 Motivation

As we know, local feature based image retrieval systems encounter the phenomenon of burstiness [10]. Due to the properties of local feature and retrieval model, a visual element may appear more times in an image than a statistically independent model would predict. The similarity scores gained by multiple matches would affect the final retrieval accuracy to different degrees and should be penalized to some extent.

In fact, there are several methods designed to reduce the impact of burstiness via various normalization functions such as the intra-image burstiness normalization and Multiple Match Removal (MMR) [10]. Intra-image burstiness normalization reduces the impact of burstiness by penalizing the matching scores, and MMR removes multiple matches by matching only once for each query point (*i.e.*, only the best match is kept). The proposed SMM follows the design concept of MMR but removes multiple matches from the perspective of global optimum, while MMR only considers a local maximal similarity of single match.

3.2.2 SMM Calculation

Assume there are two candidate lists $X = \{x_1, \cdots, x_m\}$ and $Y = \{y_1, \cdots, y_n\}$ with their cardinalities $\#X = m$ and $\#Y = n$, respectively. For the convenience of discussion, we suppose that $m \geq n$, and add $m - n$ elements of 0 to Y so that these two lists have equal number of elements.

Since the matching problem is closely connected with the problem of permutation, we introduce a list P as

$$P = \{p_1, \cdots, p_k, \cdots, p_{m!}\}, \tag{8}$$

which is composed of all possible permutations of m positive integers, with its element $p_k = (a_1^k, ..., a_j^k, ..., a_m^k)$, in which

$$a_j^k \in \{a_j \in \mathbb{Z}^+ \mid 1 \leq a_j \leq m\}. \tag{9}$$

Therefore, one particular permutation of all elements in X can be written with the form of

$$X_{p_k} = \{x_{a_1^k}, ..., x_{a_m^k}\}. \tag{10}$$

Simply, we rewrite Eq. (10) as

$$X_{p_k} = \{x_1^k, ..., x_m^k\}. \tag{11}$$

Suppose $\xi(x_i, y_i)$ defines a sort of matching operation between the elements in X and Y. Then, the similarity between the two lists of X_{p_k} and Y can be calculated as

$$S_k = \sum_{i=1}^{m} \xi(x_i^k, y_i). \tag{12}$$

Therefore, the similarity kernel for global maximization is finally defined as

$$\begin{aligned} \text{SMM} &= \max_{1 \leq k \leq m!} (S_k) \\ &= \max_{1 \leq k \leq m!} \sum_{i=1}^{m} \xi(x_i^k, y_i). \end{aligned} \tag{13}$$

As a matter of fact, it is time consuming to directly compute the global similarity score in Eq. (13), especially when m is large. To tackle this problem, the Hungarian algorithm [16] is employed, which is a combinatorial optimization algorithm to solve the assignment problem in polynomial time.

3.3 Proposed Match Kernels

After introducing the proposed TF and SMM methods, three novel match kernels are designed based on the powerful SMK for image retrieval performance improvement, including SMK with TF (SMK_{tf}), SMK with SMM (SMK_{smm}) as well as the combination of SMK with TF and SMM ($\text{SMK}_{\text{tf+smm}}$).

3.3.1 SMK with Twin Feature

Thanks to the same properties between original and twin features, the twin feature can be easily combined with SMK. As derived from Eq. (5), the twin version of the kernel can be written as

$$\text{SMK}_{\text{tf}}(X_c, Y_c) = \sum_{i=1}^{m} \sum_{j=1}^{n} \sigma_\alpha(u_{ij}) \cdot \delta_\beta(u_{ij}, v_{ij}), \tag{14}$$

where $\delta_\beta(u_{ij}, v_{ij})$ is a weighting function which represents the confidence of matching between two elements assigning to the same visual word. Consistently, $u_{ij} = \hat{r}(x_i)^{\mathrm{T}} \hat{r}(y_j)$ and $v_{ij} = \hat{r}_{tf}(x_i)^{\mathrm{T}} \hat{r}_{tf}(y_j)$. Unlike $\hat{r}(z)$ given in Eq. (4), the definition of $\hat{r}_{tf}(z)$ is

$$\hat{r}_{tf}(z) = \frac{z_{tf}}{\|z_{tf}\|}, \tag{15}$$

which is a l_2-normalized twin vector instead of a residual vector, since there is no relevance between the twin and the corresponding visual word of original feature. And the general weighting function δ_β is given by

$$\delta_\beta(u, v) = (u + \text{sign}(v) \cdot v^2)^\beta, \tag{16}$$

where β is a control parameter and typically $\beta \geq 0$. The impact of β will be analyzed later in Section 4.2.2. Specially, we use the square of v in Eq. (16) which is not in an homogeneous manner with u to balance the impact between twin features and original features. In fact, v is consistently positive in these kernels, since the SIFT descriptors are positive. Therefore, we can simplify Eq. (16) as

$$\delta_\beta(u, v) = (u + v^2)^\beta. \tag{17}$$

3.3.2 *SMK with Similarity Maximal Matching*

For consistency, let X_c and Y_c be the set X and Y defined in Section 3.2. Then, Equation (13) can be rewritten as

$$\text{SMK}_{\text{smm}} = \max_{1 \le k \le m!} \sum_{i=1}^{m} \sigma_\alpha(\phi(x_i^k)^{\mathrm{T}} \phi(y_i)), \tag{18}$$

where $\phi(x_i^k)$ denotes a scalar or vector representing the descriptor under the k-th permutation of X_c. To conclude, the proposed kernel for SMK_{smm} becomes

$$\text{SMK}_{\text{smm}} = \max_{1 \le k \le m!} \sum_{i=1}^{m} \sigma_\alpha(\hat{r}(x_i^k)^{\mathrm{T}} \hat{r}(y_i)). \tag{19}$$

In a similar manner, the kernel of $\text{SMK}_{\text{tf+smm}}$ is a direct combination of SMK_{tf} and SMK_{smm}, which inherits the advantages of both of these two kernels and is expected to be more discriminative. After mathematical manipulations, the kernel of $\text{SMK}_{\text{tf+smm}}$ can be formulated as

$$\text{SMK}_{\text{tf+smm}} = \max_{1 \le k \le m!} \sum_{i=1}^{m} (\sigma_\alpha(\hat{r}(x_i^k)^{\mathrm{T}} \hat{r}(y_i)) \cdot (\hat{r}(x_i^k)^{\mathrm{T}} \hat{r}(y_i) + (\hat{r}_{tf}(x_i^k)^{\mathrm{T}} \hat{r}_{tf}(y_i))^2)^\beta). \tag{20}$$

4. EXPERIMENTAL RESULTS

4.1 Experimental Setup

In order to evaluate the proposed SMK_{tf}, SMK_{smm} and $\text{SMK}_{\text{tf+smm}}$, two benchmark datasets including Oxford5k [21] and Paris6k [23] are employed for experiments. The mean Average Precision (mAP) is used as the evaluation criterion of image retrieval accuracy. Moreover, in order to make a fair comparison with up-to-date techniques, we follow the experimental implementations of [26]. In particular, the implementation details are listed as follows.

- The modified Hessian-Affine detector [20] and the SIFT descriptor are employed for local feature detection and description. It should be noted that most of the following evaluations are based on the default detector threshold value (also called small set [26]). The large sets of features are also used by lowering the detector threshold. Additionally, we follow [26] to post-process the SIFT descriptors.
- The flat K-Means algorithm is utilized to generate visual vocabularies. As same as [26], the vocabularies used for Oxford5k are trained on Paris6k, and vice versa.
- The query-side Multiple Assignment (MA) [11, 13] is applied to further reduce the impact of quantization error. In order to perform MA, each descriptor is assigned to 5 nearest visual words. Note that most of our experiments are executed with MA, except for those settings indicated with the Single Assignment (SA).
- For the parameters in Eq. (3) to calculate SMK, we set $\alpha = 3$ and $\tau = 0$, which are configured as the same as that in [26].
- In order to make a fair comparison, both of the spatial re-ranking and query expansion techniques are not implemented by all the comparative approaches for performing experiments.

4.2 Parameter Analysis

In the following, we study the effects of different parameters involved by the proposed methods, including SMK_{tf}, SMK_{smm} and $\text{SMK}_{\text{tf+smm}}$, on image retrieval performances.

4.2.1 *ω for Twin Feature*

As mentioned before, the parameter ω in Eq. (6) is a key factor to determine the center of the twin feature. Therefore, experiments are firstly performed to investigate the impact of ω. Figure 3 shows the results of using different ω values with a 16k-size visual dictionary, combined with different kernels for image retrieval on the two benchmark datasets Oxford5k and Paris6k, as compared with the baseline SMK.

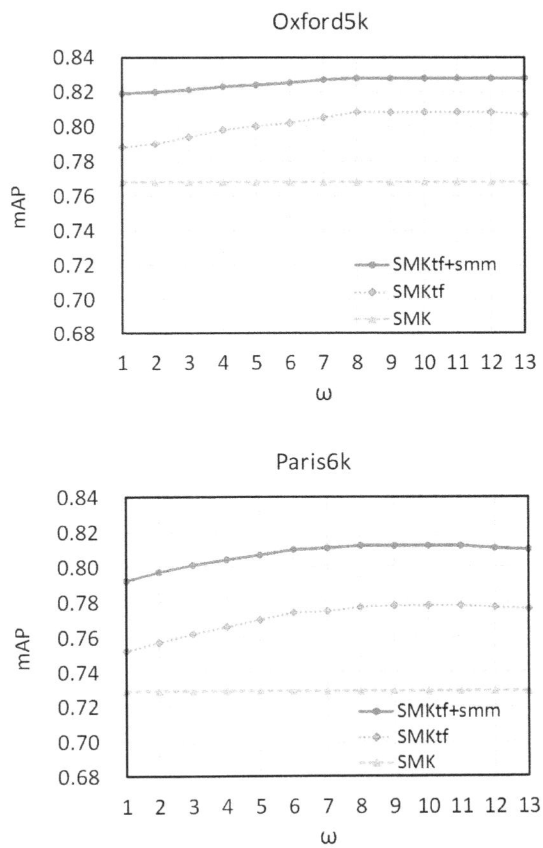

Figure 3: Impact of parameter ω for SMK_{tf} and $\text{SMK}_{\text{tf+smm}}$. In these experiments, the vocabulary size is 16k and $\beta = 4$ in Eq. (16), respectively.

From the results, it can be observed that the proposed SMK_{tf} technique outperforms the baseline SMK in all the cases. Particularly, the best performances are obtained consistently when $\omega = 10$ with all kernels and on both of the two datasets. This also demonstrates that a suitable distance between the original feature and its twin is required, since two close image patches are lack of diversity while large distance inevitably leads to noise. Therefore, ω is set to 10 in all the following experiments.

4.2.2 Choice of β

We evaluate the image retrieval performance of different values of β as required in Eq. (16) on Oxford5k and Paris6k with two kernels SMK_{tf} and SMK_{tf+smm}. As mentioned in Section 3.3.1, β controls the impact of twin on original similarity. Different β values may magnify or reduce the matching score at different levels.

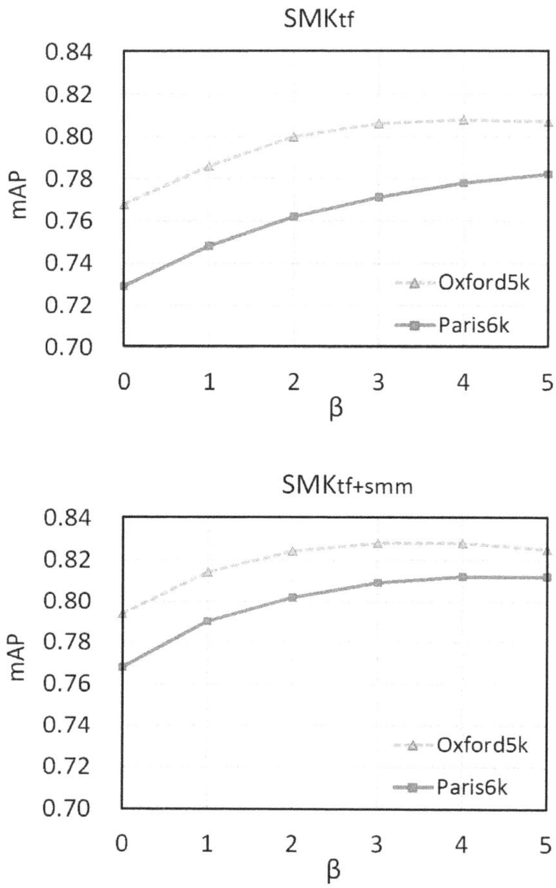

Figure 4: Impact of parameter β on Oxford5k and Paris6k with 16k-size visual dictionary for SMK_{tf} and SMK_{tf+smm} kernels.

The investigation of the impacts caused by β is illustrated in Fig. 4, where it can be seen that a suitable value for β is of great importance and significantly affects the retrieval performance. Particularly, the mAP of Oxford5k achieved by SMK_{tf+smm} reaches 0.828, which is about +6.0% improvement as compared with the baseline SMK. The same trend can also be observed on Paris6k. When $\beta = 4$, the proposed SMK_{tf+smm} is able to achieve the highest mAP performance, therefore we choose this setting in all of the following experiments.

4.2.3 Vocabulary Size

A plenty of experiments have been conducted to evaluate the impact of vocabulary size on our proposed kernels as shown in Fig. 5.

From the results, we have the following observations. The proposed SMK_{tf+smm} obtains better performances than SMK and Aggregated Selective Match Kernel (ASMK) [26] in all cases. The superiority of the proposed SMK_{tf+smm} over SMK and ASMK is even obvious when the vocabulary size is small. Particularly, by employing SMK_{tf+smm}, the improvements of +9.6% and +4.7% have been achieved as compared with SMK and ASMK on Paris6k when the vocabulary size is 8k. Similar results can also be observed on Oxford5k. Moreover, the best retrieval performances are achieved with 16k vocabularies, and the mAP are 0.828 and 0.812 on Oxford5k and Paris6k, respectively. It is interesting but reasonable that the proposed SMK_{tf+smm} is more suitable for smaller visual dictionaries, since smaller dictionaries own higher recall when assigning descriptors to visual words, which provides more chances for calculating twin features and thus dramatically increases the matching accuracy. Moreover, the multiple matching problem on smaller dictionaries is more general and serious, and the effect of SMM would decrease with the growth of vocabulary size, since multiple matches are significantly reduced.

We further conduct several experiments with extremely small vocabularies such as 64. Just as expected, the retrieval performance is still satisfactory, which achieves a comparable mAP of 0.715 on Paris6k, which verify our conclusions.

4.2.4 Detector Threshold

As mentioned in [26], when a larger set of features are applied, superior performances can be achieved, which can be implemented by lowering the detector threshold. Table 1 shows the retrieval results for two different feature sets. From the results, it can be observed that the mAP performances achieved on large feature sets are higher than that on small feature sets. Additionally, the proposed SMK_{tf+smm} further amplifies the impact of the number of features as compared with SMK and ASMK, since more multiple matching pairs are handled by SMM.

	Oxford5k					
	Small			Large		
	SMK	ASMK	Ours	SMK	ASMK	Ours
SA	0.756	0.782	**0.793**	0.758	0.787	**0.803**
MA	0.768	0.800	**0.828**	0.770	0.809	**0.835**
	Paris6k					
	Small			Large		
	SMK	ASMK	Ours	SMK	ASMK	Ours
SA	0.721	0.768	**0.782**	0.734	0.783	**0.811**
MA	0.729	0.778	**0.812**	0.733	0.792	**0.829**

Table 1: Retrieval results on different feature sets. Small means feature sets detected by default threshold 16, and large means feature sets detected by a lower threshold of 5, as same as [26]. The vocabulary size is 16k and different kernels with or without MA are presented ('Ours' stands for SMK_{tf+smm}).

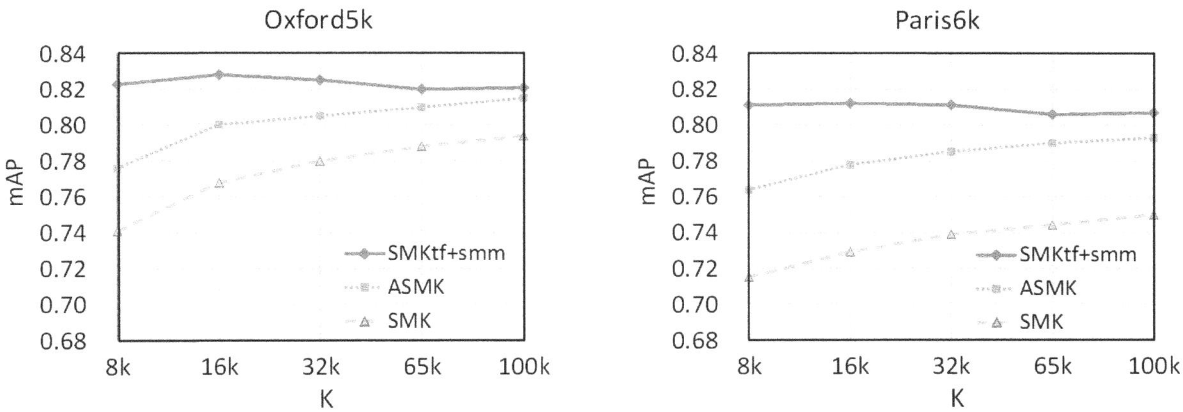

Figure 5: Impact of vocabulary size K with different kernels on Oxford5k and Pairs6k. The other key parameters are set as MA=5, $\omega = 10$, $\beta = 4$ and with default detector threshold.

4.2.5 *Matching Kernel*

In addition, the image retrieval performances achieved by different kernel methods are studied as shown in Table 2. It is remarkable that the proposed TF and SMM are both effective and can dramatically improve the retrieval performances. Specifically, MA and TF are two complementary techniques that mutually reinforce, since MA enhances the recall of visual matching while TF improves the precision.

Kernel	Method			Dataset	
	MA	TF	SMM	Oxford5k	Paris6k
SMK				0.756	0.721
SMK	×			0.768	0.729
SMK		×		0.778	0.756
SMK	×	×		0.808	0.778
SMK			×	0.782	0.763
SMK	×		×	0.794	0.768
SMK		×	×	0.793	0.782
SMK	×	×	×	**0.828**	**0.812**
ASMK				0.782	0.768
ASMK	×			0.800	0.778

Table 2: Comparison of retrieval performances with various kernel methods.

4.3 Comparison to State-of-The-Art

We compare the proposed $\text{SMK}_{\text{tf+smm}}$ with a number of state-of-the-art methods in Table 3. Note that these results are all obtained without post-processing techniques such as spatial re-ranking and query expansion. From the results in Table 3, it can be observed that the proposed $\text{SMK}_{\text{tf+smm}}$ outperforms almost all the other comparative methods except the ASMK approach with large feature set on the Oxford5k dataset. In this case, the ASMK approach achieves an mAP of 0.838 when a 65k-size visual dictionary is employed, which is a little bit higher than ours (*i.e.*, 0.835 achieved by $\text{SMK}_{\text{tf+smm}}$ (large)). More importantly, the vocabulary size of 16k that we use in this experiment is much smaller than that employed by all the other methods. Inevitably, twin feature and similarity maximal matching require more computational resources when compared with SMK and ASMK. Fortunately, it can be improved by some techniques like binarization or hardware acceleration.

As a matter of fact, better mAP performances may be achieved when spatial re-ranking and query expansion are further combined. However, our current work is only focused on improving initial rank lists, and the combination of those post-processing techniques will be one of our future research efforts.

5. CONCLUSION AND FUTURE WORK

In this paper, we propose two effective methods to improve image retrieval accuracy based on non-aggregated kernels. The first is twin feature, which is considered as a fruitful attempt to enhance visual matching accuracy by applying neighboring image information. The second is called similarity maximal matching, which is able to effectively remove multiple matches from the perspective of global similarity optimization and reduce the impact of burstiness. These two methods are integrated with the selective match kernel favorably and satisfactory performances on Oxford5k and Paris6k are achieved by our proposed methods.

In the future, more research efforts will be made to the application of the proposed methods integrated with other matching kernels such as the aggregated kernel like ASMK to make the retrieval process more efficient. As aforementioned, it is also worth investigating the combination with the post-processing techniques of spatial re-ranking and query expansion.

6. REFERENCES

[1] R. Arandjelovic and A. Zisserman. All about VLAD. In *Proc. CVPR'13*, pages 1578–1585, Jun. 2013.

[2] Y. Avrithis. Quantize and conquer: A dimensionality-recursive solution to clustering, vector quantization, and image retrieval. In *Proc. ICCV'13*, pages 3024–3031, Dec. 2013.

Methods	MA	K	Oxford5k	Paris6k
HE+WGC [11]		200k	0.545	-
HE+WGC [11]	×	200k	0.615	-
HE-BURST [10]		20k	0.596	-
HE-BURST [10]	×	20k	0.647	-
AHE-BURST [8]		20k	0.660	-
AHE-BURST [8]	×	20k	0.704	-
Rep.Struc. [28]	×	100k	0.656	-
Nested-SIFT [30]		1M	0.720	-
Dim.Recursive [2]		$4k^4$	0.703	0.696
Fine Voc. [19]		16M	0.742	0.749
ASMK (small) [26]		65k	0.781	0.760
ASMK (small) [26]	×	65k	0.817	0.782
ASMK (large) [26]		65k	0.820	0.787
ASMK (large) [26]	×	65k	**0.838**	0.805
SMK_{tf+smm} (small)		16k	0.793	0.782
SMK_{tf+smm} (small)	×	16k	**0.828**	**0.812**
SMK_{tf+smm} (large)		16k	0.803	0.811
SMK_{tf+smm} (large)	×	16k	0.835	**0.829**

Table 3: Performance comparison with state-of-the-art methods without spatial re-ranking or query expansion. The results of SMK_{tf+smm} are achieved with $\omega = 10$, $\beta = 4$ and $K = 16k$. 'small' and 'large' indicate small feature set and large feature set.

[3] Y. Avrithis and G. Tolias. Hough pyramid matching: Speeded-up geometry re-ranking for large scale image retrieval. *IJCV*, 107(1):1–19, Oct. 2013.

[4] Y. Chen, X. L, A. Dick, and R. Hill. Ranking consistency for image matching and object retrieval. *Pattern Recognition*, 47(10):3466–3476, Oct. 2014.

[5] O. Chum, A. Mikulik, M. Perdoch, and J. Matas. Total recall II: Query expansion revisited. In *Proc. CVPR'11*, pages 889–896, Jun. 2011.

[6] O. Chum, J. Philbin, J. Sivic, M. Isard, and A. Zisserman. Total recall: Automatic query expansion with a generative feature model for object retrieval. In *Proc. ICCV'07*, pages 1–8, Oct. 2007.

[7] J. Delhumeau, P.-H. Gosselin, H. Jégou, and P. Pérez. Revisiting the VLAD image representation. In *Proc. ACM MM'13*, pages 653–656, Oct. 2013.

[8] M. Jain, H. Jégou, and P. Gros. Asymmetric hamming embedding: Taking the best of our bits for large scale image search. In *Proc. ACM MM'11*, pages 1441–1444, Nov.-Dec. 2011.

[9] H. Jégou, M. Douze, and C. Schmid. Hamming embedding and weak geometric consistency for large scale image search. In *Proc. ECCV'08*, pages 304–317, Oct. 2008.

[10] H. Jégou, M. Douze, and C. Schmid. On the burstiness of visual elements. In *Proc. CVPR'09*, pages 1169–1176, Jun. 2009.

[11] H. Jégou, M. Douze, and C. Schmid. Improving bag-of-features for large scale image search. *IJCV*, 87(3):316–336, May 2010.

[12] H. Jégou, M. Douze, C. Schmid, and P. Pérez. Aggregating local descriptors into a compact image representation. In *Proc. CVPR'10*, pages 3304–3311, Jun. 2010.

[13] H. Jégou, H. Harzallah, and C. Schmid. A contextual dissimilarity measure for accurate and efficient image search. In *Proc. CVPR'07*, pages 1–8, Jun. 2007.

[14] H. Jégou and A. Zisserman. Triangulation embedding and democratic aggregation for image search. In *Proc. CVPR'14*, pages 3310–3317, Jun. 2014.

[15] Y.-G. Jiang, J. Wang, X. Xue, and S.-F. Chang. Query-adaptive image search with hash codes. *TMM*, 15(2):442–453, Feb. 2013.

[16] H. W. Kuhn and B. Yaw. The hungarian method for the assignment problem. *Naval Res. Logist. Quart*, pages 83–97, 1955.

[17] D. Lowe. Distinctive image features from scale-invariant keypoints. *IJCV*, 60(2):91–110, Nov. 2004.

[18] K. Mikolajczyk and C. Schmid. Scale and affine invariant interest point detectors. *IJCV*, 60(1):63–86, Oct. 2004.

[19] A. Mikulik, M. Perdoch, O. Chum, and J. Matas. Learning vocabularies over a fine quantization. *IJCV*, 103(1):163–175, May 2013.

[20] M. Perdoch, O. Chum, and J. Matas. Efficient representation of local geometry for large scale object retrieval. In *Proc. CVPR'09*, pages 9–16, Jun. 2009.

[21] J. Philbin, R. Arandjelovic, and A. Zisserman. Oxford5k image dataset. http://www.robots.ox.ac.uk/~vgg/data/oxbuildings/.

[22] J. Philbin, O. Chum, M. Isard, J. Sivic, and A. Zisserman. Object retrieval with large vocabularies and fast spatial matching. In *Proc. CVPR'07*, pages 1–8, Jun. 2007.

[23] J. Philbin and A. Zisserman. Paris6k image dataset. http://www.robots.ox.ac.uk/~vgg/data/parisbuildings/.

[24] G. Salton and C. Buckley. Term-weighting approaches in automatic text retrieval. *Info. Processing & Management*, 24(5):513–523, Aug. 1988.

[25] J. Sivic and A. Zisserman. Video google: A text retrieval approach to object matching in videos. In *Proc. ICCV'03*, pages 1470–1477, Oct. 2003.

[26] G. Tolias, Y. Avrithis, and H. Jégou. To aggregate or not to aggregate: Selective match kernels for image search. In *Proc. ICCV'13*, pages 1401–1408, Dec. 2013.

[27] G. Tolias and H. Jégou. Visual query expansion with or without geometry: Refining local descriptors by feature aggregation. *Pattern Recognition*, 47(10):3466–3476, Oct. 2014.

[28] A. Torii, J. Sivic, T. Pajdla, and M. Okutomi. Visual place recognition with repetitive structures. In *Proc. CVPR'13*, pages 883–890, Jun. 2013.

[29] J. van Gemert, C. Veenman, A. Smeulders, and J.-M. Geusebroek. Visual word ambiguity. *TPAMI*, 32(7):1271–1283, Jun. 2010.

[30] P. Xu, L. Zhang, K. Yang, and H. Yao. Nested-SIFT for efficient image matching and retrieval. *MultiMedia*, 20(3):34–46, 2013.

[31] Y. Yang, F. Nie, D. Xu, J. Luo, and Y. Pan. A multimedia retrieval framework based on semi-supervised ranking and relevance feedback. *TPAMI*, 34(4):723–742, Aug. 2012.

Fusing Pointwise and Pairwise Labels for Supporting User-adaptive Image Retrieval

Lin Chen
Computer Sicence, Arizona State University
lin.chen.6@asu.edu

Peng Zhang*
Alibaba Group
minghua.zp@alibaba-inc.com

Baoxin Li
Computer Sicence, Arizona State University
baoxin.li@asu.edu

ABSTRACT

User-adaptive image retrieval/recommendation has drawn a lot of research interests in recent years, owing to fast development of various Web applications where retrieving images is a key enabling task. Existing challenges include the lack of user-adaptive training data, the ambiguity of user query and the real-time interactivity of a system. This paper proposes a hybrid learning strategy that fuses knowledge from both pointwise and pairwise training data into one framework for attribute-based, user-adaptive image retrieval. Under this framework, we develop an online learning algorithm for updating the ranking performance based on user feedback. Furthermore, we derive the framework into a kernel form, allowing easy application of kernel techniques. The proposed approach is evaluated on two image datasets and experimental results show that it achieves obvious performance gains over ranking and zero-shot learning from either type of training data independently. In addition, the online learning algorithm is able to deliver much better performance than batch learning, given the same elapsed running time, or can achieve better performance in much less time.

Categories and Subject Descriptors

H.3.3 [**Information Storage and Retrieval**]: [Miscellaneous]; I.4.8 [**Image Processing and Computer Vision**]: [Scene Analysis]

General Terms

Algorithms, Design, Experiment

Keywords

Adaptive Image Retrieval, Attribute Learning, Learning to Rank

*Effort performed while being a research fellow at ASU.

ICMR'15, June 23–26, 2015, Shanghai, China.

ACM 978-1-4503-3274-3/15/06 ...$15.00.
DOI: http://dx.doi.org/10.1145/2671188.2749358.

(a) **unstylish** (b) **stylish?** (c) **stylish**

(d) **more stylish?** (e) **more stylish?**

Figure 1: stylish and unstylish cars. Considering pointwise label, to most people (a) would be unstylish and (c) would be considered stylish. However, it is ambiguous to classify (b) to be stylish or unstylish. Considering pairwise label, people may have different preference to compare whether (d) or (e) is more stylish.

1. INTRODUCTION

The social media era has witnessed phenomenal growth of user-generated images on the Internet. The ever-growing number of images has brought about new challenges for efficient image retrieval, and in turn, for applications that rely on image retrieval. Conventional content-based image retrieval approaches learn some general ranking models purely based on the underlying images. In recent years, adaptive image retrieval [5][10][20] has emerged as a new trend, which intends to satisfy a user's specific requirements or preference. For example, in search of art images, some people like realism paintings while some may prefer abstract art. A retrieval engine being able to support such personalization would have the best potential to deliver what a user is really looking for. In practice, it is still difficult to learn a well generalized model due to the lack of user-adaptive training data. For example, in applications like on-line shopping, it is unreasonable to assume a user's personal preference data have been made available *a priori* for training the system. Often, desired is an on-line learning approach that accumulates such information over time interactively. Our approach adopts a model adaptation strategy and proposes a new ranking model and an online learning algorithm. Such a method is especially proper for applications that utilize interactive input/feedback of a user in achieving adaptive image retrieval/recommendation.

Beneath the above challenge of personalization lie the fundamental problems of **semantic gap** and **intent gap** in general image retrieval. The semantic gap refers to the discrepancy between extractable low-level image features and high-level semantic concepts of images, while the intent gap refers to inadequacy of the representation of a query in expressing a user's true intent. In recent years, towards bridging the semantic gap, methods exploiting semantic attributes of visual objects have attracted significant attention in applications including object recognition [26][14][6], face verification [13] and image search [25][12][18]. Instead of using low-level features, these approaches describe images by high-level, human-nameable visual attributes, such as keep hair color, presence of beard or mustache, presence of eyeglasses, etc., to describe human faces.

In the meantime, towards bridging the intent gap, learning-to-rank approaches have been proposed. Recent literature on this regard includes three types of approaches distinguished by how the training data are used: pointwise, pairwise and listwise approaches. The first two types of approaches have been adopted in image ranking problems. Pointwise approaches [15][23] adopt category labels in the training samples to learn a ranking function. For example, to describe the car images in Fig. 1, the car in Fig. 1(c) is categorized as a "stylish" car and the one in Fig. 1(a) is labelled "unstylish". In a different way, pairwise approaches [2][24][7][8][3] learn a ranking function by taking comparative sample pairs for training. For example, most people would agree that the car in Fig. 1(c) looks more "stylish" than the one in Fig. 1(a). Such pair of samples with relative labels can be used to learn ranking functions for processing new images.

Pointwise data and pairwise data have different advantages and limitations in terms of data availability, labelling complexity and representational capability, as elaborated below.

Data availability In practical applications pointwise and pairwise labels are not always available for every data sample, especially considering the subjectivity of the labels. For example, in pointwise labelling, most people would agree that Fig. 1(c) is a "stylish" car and Fig. 1(a) is an "unstylish" car, but it would be difficult to tell whether Fig. 1(b) is a "stylish" car. Some people may think it is "stylish" because of the design of the headlights, while some others may deem the body design unattractive. Similarly, ambiguity also exists in pairwise data labelling. For example, comparing Fig. 1(d) and 1(e), people may have different opinions on which car is more "stylish" because of subjective preference. When ambiguity exists, it is better not to allow the data to be labeled so as not to produce noisy labels.

Labelling complexity In general, pairwise data may be more expensive to label. For example, given 10 images, we only need to label 10 samples to assign each image into one category. Also, category labels can be acquired from other sources such as image tags. On the other hand, to assign pairwise labels for all 10 images, we would need to compare 45 pairs to completely capture the ranking information. (Although the relative relation is transferable such as $(A \succ B) \& (B \succ C) \Rightarrow A \succ C$, it is difficult to discover those "key pairs" since we usually have to randomly pick pairs without any prior knowledge.) We note, however, that sometimes it is easier for a user to assign pairwise labels through comparison than having to give a pointwise label for a given image.

Representational capability Pairwise data tend to have stronger representational capability than pointwise data in ranking problems, as pointwise label only implies the relative order of data samples from different categories but not those from the same category. In contrast, pairwise labels already give the relative order of every training pairs, and thus contain more knowledge to learn a better ranking model.

As pointwise and pairwise labels encapsulate information of different types/amounts and may have different availability, we set out to develop a new framework for fusing both types of training data for improved ranking performance. Most of current fusion approaches [16][19] only use pointwise labels and the fusion only appears in the cost function. To our best knowledge, the only work considering fusing pointwise and pairwise data is presented by Sculley [21] whose object function is simply a linear combination of loss functions from regression and ranking.

In this paper, towards supporting adaptive image retrieval, we propose a new ranking-based framework. Our approach uses visual attributes to describe images, which helps to partially overcome the semantic gap problem. To alleviate the problem of lacking adaptive training samples, our approach attempt to maximize the utilization of all available training data by fusing both pointwise and pairwise labelled data in training. Compared to [21], our approach is formulated as a soft margined SVM which is able to achieve better generalization performance. Furthermore, to support interactivity, which is one natural way of gathering adaptive training data on the fly, we derive an online learning algorithm which can incrementally acquire a user's online feedback to improve the performance of the model incrementally with additional amount of data. As will be demonstrated by experiments, the proposed framework is able to take advantage of both types of data and deliver better performance than the baseline approaches that use only one type of data for learning.

There are three key **contributions** of our work. (1) We propose a new ranking framework termed "hybrid ranking" which takes both pointwise and pairwise labelled data for learning. (2) We propose an online learning algorithm for our proposed hybrid ranking framework, which can better support applications like adaptive image ranking. (3) We derive our hybrid ranking framework into a kernel form so that different kernel functions (depending on the application) may be applied for better performance.

In the remaining of the paper, we first give a formal problem definition in Section 2. The proposed approach is presented in Section 3. Experiments and results are demonstrated in Section 4. We conclude the paper in Section 5.

2. PROBLEM DEFINITION

Adaptive Image Retrieval We consider the following adaptive image retrieval procedure illustrated in Fig. 2: Given a training dataset including both the attribute existence labels of images (pointwise) and the relative attribute strength labels of image pairs (pairwise), we first train a general image ranking functions (the "Offline trained model" in the figure). This is used to retrieve images for a user based on his/her query. Looking at the initial retrieval results, the user may interactively provide feedback,

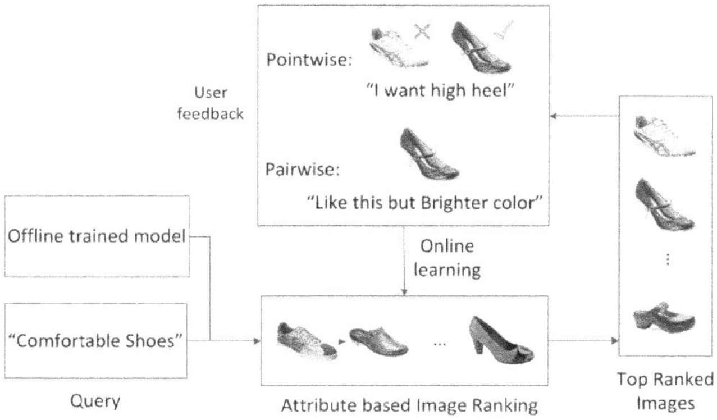

Figure 2: Adaptive image retrieval via on-line feedback.

in forms of newly labelled attribute existence labels and/or relative attribute strength labels. Such feedback is used as new training samples by an on-line-learning algorithm for updating the ranking function. As the feedback is specific to a user, the updated ranking function (and thus the retrieval engine) is presumably adapted to a user's preferences and hence achieving some level of personalization.

Hybrid Ranking To solve the above adaptive image retrieval task, we propose a hybrid ranking SVM framework. Given (1) the pointwise dataset $\mathcal{P}$ where each data sample $\boldsymbol{x}_i \in \mathcal{P}$ is assigned a category label and (2) the pairwise datasets including both the ordered pair set $\mathcal{O}$ and the unordered pair set $\mathcal{S}$ where for any pair $(\boldsymbol{x}_i, \boldsymbol{x}_j) \in \mathcal{O}$, $\boldsymbol{x}_i \succ \boldsymbol{x}_j$ (e.g., $\boldsymbol{x}_i$ has a stronger attribute than $\boldsymbol{x}_j$), and for any pair $(\boldsymbol{x}_i, \boldsymbol{x}_j) \in \mathcal{S}$, $\boldsymbol{x}_i \sim \boldsymbol{x}_j$ (e.g., $\boldsymbol{x}_i$ has a similar attribute value to $\boldsymbol{x}_j$), we attempt to learn a ranking model taking both the pointwise and pairwise data into consideration. This hybrid ranking approach aims to capture as much information as possible from all available data so as to achieve better ranking performance especially when labelled data are scarce.

Notations In this paper, we represent scalars as lower case letters (e.g., x), vectors as bold face lower case letters (e.g., $\boldsymbol{x}$), matrices as capital letters (e.g., X) and sets as calligraphic capital letters (e.g., $\mathcal{X}$). The standard inner product between the vectors $\boldsymbol{u} \in \mathcal{R}^n$ and $\boldsymbol{v} \in \mathcal{R}^n$ is denoted as $\langle \boldsymbol{u}, \boldsymbol{v} \rangle = \sum_{i=1}^{n} u_i v_i$ with u_i/v_i the i-th element of $\boldsymbol{u}/\boldsymbol{v}$.

3. PROPOSED APPROACH

In this section we propose a general hybrid ranking SVM framework and an online algorithm to solve this problem.

3.1 Hybrid Ranking SVM

To make the best use of the available knowledge, we propose a hybrid ranking SVM which takes both pointwise and pairwise labelled data samples for learning.

The approach presented in [23] for ordinal regression learns a number of parallel hyperplanes by the large margin principle as a ranking model. One implementation of the approach tries to maximize a fixed margin for all the adjacent classes. Relative attributes [18] applies pairwise learning-to-rank approach on image attributes for image ranking. This approach learns a ranking function for each human-nameable attribute of an image. The relative "strength" of an attribute is measured by some distance metrics learned through SVM-like optimization using (relatively) labeled pairs. Both of these two SVM models aim to optimize a project direction $\boldsymbol{w}$, such that $\langle \boldsymbol{w}, \boldsymbol{w} \rangle$ (i.e., the inverse of the margin) is minimized subject to the separability constraints (modulo margin errors in the non-separable case).

In the situation that the training data are very limited, learning $\boldsymbol{w}$ based on both pointwise and pairwise datasets jointly would become a necessity in order to achieve reasonable performance. To fuse information from both types of data, the margins assigned to them should be different. To this end, we introduce a new superparameter ρ representing the margin corresponding to the pairwise data. We propose the hybrid ranking approach as follows:

$$
\begin{aligned}
\min_{\boldsymbol{w}, \boldsymbol{b}, \boldsymbol{\xi}, \boldsymbol{\zeta}, \boldsymbol{\eta}} \; & \frac{1}{2}\|\boldsymbol{w}\|^2 + c_1\tau_1 \sum_i \sum_j (\xi_i^j + \xi_i^{*j+1}) \\
& + c_2\tau_2 \sum \zeta_{ij} + c_2\tau_3 \sum \eta_{ij} \\
s.t. \; & \boldsymbol{w} \cdot \boldsymbol{x}_i^j - b_j \leq -1 + \xi_i^j, \\
& \boldsymbol{w} \cdot \boldsymbol{x}_i^{j+1} - b_j \geq 1 - \xi_i^{*j+1}, \\
& \boldsymbol{w} \cdot (\boldsymbol{x}_i - \boldsymbol{x}_j) \geq \rho - \zeta_{ij}, \forall (i,j) \in \mathcal{O}, \\
& |\boldsymbol{w} \cdot (\boldsymbol{x}_i - \boldsymbol{x}_j)| \leq \eta_{ij}, \forall (i,j) \in \mathcal{S}, \\
& \xi_i^j \geq 0, \xi_i^{*j} \geq 0, \zeta_{ij} \geq 0; \eta_{ij} \geq 0
\end{aligned}
$$

where $\boldsymbol{x}_i^j \in \mathcal{R}^n$ is an object (feature vector) with $j = 1, ..., k-1$ denoting the class number, $i = 1, ..., i_j$ is the index within class j, and k is the total number of classes. $(\boldsymbol{x}_i, \boldsymbol{x}_j)$ is sample pairs, ξ_i^j and ξ_i^{*j} are non-negative slack variables measuring the degree of misclassified data, ζ_{ij} and η_{ij} are soft margin slack variables for pairwise ranking, c_1 and c_2 are super parameters controlling the weight for the pointwise and pairwise data, τ_i is the weight function penalizing different training datasets according to the data size. Specifically, let n_1, n_2 and n_3 denote the data sizes of the pointwise, ordered and unordered pairwise datasets respectively, then $\tau_i = \frac{n_i}{\sum_{j=1}^{3} n_j}, i = 1, 2, 3$. Note that if only pointwise data are provided then the framework is equivalent to regression, and if only pairwise data are provided the framework becomes pairwise ranking.

In the following discussion, we focus on the image retrieval task which can be simplified as a hybrid ranking model with "binary type " of pointwise label (i.e., existence/non-existence of certain attribute). For clarity, in the following, we use $\boldsymbol{x}_i^{\mathcal{P}}$ to denote the i-th pointwise training sample $x_i \in \mathcal{P}$, and $\boldsymbol{x}_i^{\mathcal{O}}(\boldsymbol{x}_i^{\mathcal{S}})$ denotes the difference of the i-th ordered(unordered) pairwise training sample as $x_p - x_q$ for any $(x_p, x_q) \in \mathcal{O}(\mathcal{S})$. Then the ranking model can be formulated as the following primal form of the hybrid learning problem:

$$
\begin{aligned}
\min_{\boldsymbol{w}, \boldsymbol{b}, \boldsymbol{\xi}, \boldsymbol{\zeta}, \boldsymbol{\eta}} \; & \frac{1}{2}\|\boldsymbol{w}\|^2 + c_1\tau_1 \sum_i \xi_i \\
& + c_2\tau_2 \sum \zeta_i + c_2\tau_3 \sum \eta_i \\
s.t. \; & y_i \cdot (\boldsymbol{w} \cdot \boldsymbol{x}_i^{\mathcal{P}} + b) \geq 1 - \xi_i, \\
& \boldsymbol{w} \cdot \boldsymbol{x}_i^{\mathcal{O}} \geq \rho - \zeta_i, \\
& \left| \boldsymbol{w} \cdot \boldsymbol{x}_i^{\mathcal{S}} \right| \leq \eta_i, \\
& \xi_i \geq 0, \zeta_i \geq 0; \eta_i \geq 0.
\end{aligned}
\tag{1}
$$

This formulation can be solved by quadratic programming.

Algorithm 1 The Mini-Batch Online Learning Algorithm

Input:

1. Training set $\mathcal{A}$ with data type flags;
2. Parameters ρ, c_1, c_2, $\tilde{t}$, k;

Output: $\boldsymbol{w}_{\tilde{t}}$;

```
Set w_0 = 0;
for t = 1, 2, ..., t̃ do
    Choose A_t ⊆ A where |A_t| = k uniformly at random;
    Set A_t^P = {i ∈ A_t : (x_i, y_i) ∈ P ∧ y_i⟨x_i, w_t⟩ < 1}, n_1 = |A_t^P|;
    Set A_t^O = {i ∈ A_t : (x_i, y_i) ∈ O ∧ ⟨x_i, w_t⟩ < ρ}, n_2 = |A_t^O|;
    Set A_t^S = {i ∈ A_t : (x_i, y_i) ∈ S, n_3 = |A_t^S|;
    Set η_t = 1/((n_1+n_2+n_3)t);
    Set τ_1 = n_1/Σ_{j=1}^3 n_j, τ_2 = n_2/Σ_{j=1}^3 n_j, τ_3 = n_3/Σ_{j=1}^3 n_j;
    Set w_t ← (1 − η_t)w_{t−1} + η_t(c_1τ_1 Σ_{i∈A_t^P} y_i x_i + c_2τ_2 Σ_{i∈A_t^O} x_i) + c_2τ_3 Σ_{i∈A_t^S} sgn⟨x_i, w_t⟩x_i);
end for
return w_t;
```

Step formulas in LaTeX:

$\mathcal{A}_t^{\mathcal{P}} = \{i \in \mathcal{A}_t : (x_i, y_i) \in \mathcal{P} \wedge y_i\langle \boldsymbol{x}_i, \boldsymbol{w}_t\rangle < 1\}$, $n_1 = |\mathcal{A}_t^{\mathcal{P}}|$; $\mathcal{A}_t^{\mathcal{O}} = \{i \in \mathcal{A}_t : (x_i, y_i) \in \mathcal{O} \wedge \langle \boldsymbol{x}_i, \boldsymbol{w}_t\rangle < \rho\}$, $n_2 = |\mathcal{A}_t^{\mathcal{O}}|$; $\mathcal{A}_t^{\mathcal{S}} = \{i \in \mathcal{A}_t : (x_i, y_i) \in \mathcal{S}, n_3 = |\mathcal{A}_t^{\mathcal{S}}|$; $\eta_t = \frac{1}{(n_1+n_2+n_3)t}$; $\tau_1 = \frac{n_1}{\sum_{j=1}^{3} n_j}$, $\tau_2 = \frac{n_2}{\sum_{j=1}^{3} n_j}$, $\tau_3 = \frac{n_3}{\sum_{j=1}^{3} n_j}$; $\boldsymbol{w}_t \leftarrow (1 - \eta_t)\boldsymbol{w}_{t-1} + \eta_t(c_1\tau_1 \sum_{i\in\mathcal{A}_t^{\mathcal{P}}} y_i\boldsymbol{x}_i + c_2\tau_2 \sum_{i\in\mathcal{A}_t^{\mathcal{O}}} \boldsymbol{x}_i) + c_2\tau_3 \sum_{i\in\mathcal{A}_t^{\mathcal{S}}} \text{sgn}\,\langle \boldsymbol{x}_i, \boldsymbol{w}_t\rangle\boldsymbol{x}_i)$;

3.2 Mini-Batch Online Learning Algorithm

We now propose an online learning algorithm for the hybrid ranking SVM for adaptive image retrieval. In the retrieval application, we first train a general ranking function for the user. Based on the retrieval results, the user may provide feedback (new category and relative labels) according to their preferences. Then our online learning approach will update the ranking function based on the newly labelled data to make the ranking results better fit to the user's personal needs.

The constrained quadratic programming problem of Eq. (1) can be cast as an unconstraint empirical loss minimization with a penalty term for the norm of the classifier that can be learned in the following form:

$$\begin{aligned}\min_{\boldsymbol{w}} \frac{1}{2}\|\boldsymbol{w}\|^2 &+ c_1\tau_1 \sum_{i\in\mathcal{P}} \ell_1(\boldsymbol{w}; (\boldsymbol{x}_i^{\mathcal{P}}, y_i^{\mathcal{P}})) \\ &+ c_2\tau_2 \sum_{i\in\mathcal{O}} \ell_2(\boldsymbol{w}; \boldsymbol{x}_i^{\mathcal{O}}) + c_2\tau_3 \sum_{i\in\mathcal{S}} \ell_3(\boldsymbol{w}; \boldsymbol{x}_i^{\mathcal{S}})\end{aligned} \tag{2}$$

where

$$\begin{aligned}\ell_1(\boldsymbol{w}; (\boldsymbol{x}_i^{\mathcal{P}}, y_i^{\mathcal{P}})) &= \max\{0, 1 - y_i^{\mathcal{P}}\langle \boldsymbol{x}_i^{\mathcal{P}}, \boldsymbol{w}\rangle\}, \\ \ell_2(\boldsymbol{w}; \boldsymbol{x}_i^{\mathcal{O}}) &= \max\{0, \rho - \langle \boldsymbol{x}_i^{\mathcal{O}}, \boldsymbol{w}\rangle\}, \\ \ell_3(\boldsymbol{w}; \boldsymbol{x}_i^{\mathcal{S}}) &= \left|\langle \boldsymbol{x}_i^{\mathcal{S}}, \boldsymbol{w}\rangle\right|.\end{aligned}$$

Inspired by the Pegasos algorithm [22], we also considered the mini-batch algorithm which utilize k ($1 \leq k \leq m$) examples at each iteration. We initiate the model by setting $\boldsymbol{w}_0$ to the zero vector. In iteration t of the algorithm, given a training set $\mathcal{A}$ with m samples of both pointwise and pairwise data (a flag bit is used to identify the type of the data), we choose a subset $\mathcal{A}_t \subseteq \mathcal{A}$ with k examples uniformly at random among the training subset. Thus we will optimize the following approximate objective function:

$$\begin{aligned}f(\boldsymbol{w}; \mathcal{A}_t) =& \frac{1}{2}\|\boldsymbol{w}\|^2 + c_1\tau_1 \sum_{i\in\mathcal{A}_t} \ell_1(\boldsymbol{w}; (\boldsymbol{x}_i^{\mathcal{P}}, y_i^{\mathcal{P}})) \\ &+ c_2\tau_2 \sum_{i\in\mathcal{A}_t} \ell_2(\boldsymbol{w}; \boldsymbol{x}_i^{\mathcal{O}}) + c_2\tau_3 \sum_{i\in\mathcal{A}_t} \ell_3(\boldsymbol{w}; \boldsymbol{x}_i^{\mathcal{S}})\end{aligned} \tag{3}$$

We employ the stochastic gradient methods in our algorithm. The sub-gradient of Eq. (3) at iteration t is given by

$$\begin{aligned}\nabla_t =& \boldsymbol{w}_t - c_1\tau_1 \sum_{i\in\mathcal{A}_t} \chi_{\Re^+}(1 - y_i^{\mathcal{P}}\langle \boldsymbol{x}_i^{\mathcal{P}}, \boldsymbol{w}_t\rangle)y_i^{\mathcal{P}}\boldsymbol{x}_i^{\mathcal{P}} \\ &- c_2\tau_2 \sum_{i\in\mathcal{A}_t} \chi_{\Re^+}(\rho - \langle \boldsymbol{x}_i^{\mathcal{O}}, \boldsymbol{w}_t\rangle)\boldsymbol{x}_i^{\mathcal{O}} \\ &- c_2\tau_3 \sum_{i\in\mathcal{A}_t} \text{sgn}\,\langle \boldsymbol{x}_i^{\mathcal{S}}, \boldsymbol{w}_t\rangle\boldsymbol{x}_i^{\mathcal{S}}\end{aligned} \tag{4}$$

where $\chi_A(x)$ is the eigenfunction and $\text{sgn}(x)$ the symbolic function. Then the weight vector can be updated by

$$\boldsymbol{w}_{t+1} = \boldsymbol{w}_t - \eta_t\nabla_t$$

with the step size $\eta_t = \frac{1}{(n_1+n_2+n_3)t}$. After a predetermined number $\tilde{t}$ of iterations, we output the final $\boldsymbol{w}_{\tilde{t}}$ as the learned projection model. The pseudocode of our algorithm is given in Algorithm (1). It can be shown that our proposed framework have the same convergence property with [22] and thus we can terminate the procedure at a random stopping time and in at least half of the cases the last hypothesis is an accurate solution.

3.3 Kernelization

We further derive the framework into the kernel form which strengthens our approach to learn non-linear model. Note that although the derivation is based on the online learning form, it can be generalized to batch learning since we are considering mini-batch learning in this paper.

Instead of considering predictors which are linear functions of the training instances $\boldsymbol{x}$ themselves, we consider predictors which are linear functions of some implicit mapping $\phi(\boldsymbol{x})$ of the instances. Then the original optimization problem can be redefined as:

$$\begin{aligned}\min_{\boldsymbol{w}} \frac{1}{2}\|\boldsymbol{w}\|^2 &+ c_1\tau_1 \sum_{i\in\mathcal{P}} \ell_1(\boldsymbol{w}; (\phi(\boldsymbol{x_i}^{\mathcal{P}}), y_i^{\mathcal{P}})) \\ &+ c_2\tau_2 \sum_{i\in\mathcal{O}} \ell_2(\boldsymbol{w}; \phi(\boldsymbol{x}_i^{\mathcal{O}})) + c_2\tau_3 \sum_{i\in\mathcal{S}} \ell_3(\boldsymbol{w}; \phi(\boldsymbol{x}_i^{\mathcal{S}}))\end{aligned} \tag{5}$$

where

$$\begin{aligned}\ell_1(\boldsymbol{w}; (\phi(\boldsymbol{x}_i^{\mathcal{P}}), y_i^{\mathcal{P}})) &= \max\{0, 1 - y_i^{\mathcal{P}}\langle \phi(\boldsymbol{x}_i^{\mathcal{P}}), \boldsymbol{w}\rangle\}, \\ \ell_2(\boldsymbol{w}; \phi(\boldsymbol{x}_i^{\mathcal{O}})) &= \max\{0, \rho - \langle \phi(\boldsymbol{x}_i^{\mathcal{O}}), \boldsymbol{w}\rangle\}, \\ \ell_3(\boldsymbol{w}; \phi(\boldsymbol{x}_i^{\mathcal{S}})) &= |\langle \phi(\boldsymbol{x}_i^{\mathcal{S}}), \boldsymbol{w}\rangle|.\end{aligned} \tag{6}$$

Next we will directly derive the primal problem into the kernel form. For each t, let x_j represents the data sample, and let

$$\begin{aligned}\alpha_t[j] &= |\{t' \leq t : i_{t'} = j \wedge y_j^{\mathcal{P}}\langle \boldsymbol{w}_{t'}, \phi(\boldsymbol{x}_j^{\mathcal{P}})\rangle < 1\}|, \\ \beta_t[j] &= |\{t' \leq t : i_{t'} = j \wedge \langle \boldsymbol{w}_{t'}, \phi(\boldsymbol{x}_j^{\mathcal{O}})\rangle < \rho\}|, \\ \gamma_t[j] &= \sum_j \text{sgn}\,\langle \phi(\boldsymbol{x}_j^{\mathcal{S}}), \boldsymbol{w}_{t'}\rangle, \forall j \in \{t' \leq t : i_{t'} = j\},\end{aligned}$$

then Eq. (5) and (6) can be rewritten as

$$\boldsymbol{w}_{t+1} = \frac{1}{\lambda t}(c_1\tau_1 \sum_{j=1}^{n_1} \alpha_{t+1}[j] y_j^{\mathcal{P}} \phi(\boldsymbol{x}_j^{\mathcal{P}}) + c_2\tau_2 \sum_{j=1}^{n_2} \beta_{t+1}[j]\phi(\boldsymbol{x}_j^{\mathcal{O}}) + c_3\tau_3 \sum_{j=1}^{n_3} \gamma_{t+1}[j]\phi(\boldsymbol{x}_j^{\mathcal{S}})).$$

According to the Representer Theorem [9], the optimal solution to Eq. (2) can be expressed as a linear combination of the training instances, thus we can rewrite $\boldsymbol{w}$ as:

$$\boldsymbol{w} = \sum_{j=1}^{n_1} \alpha[j]\phi(\boldsymbol{x}_j^{\mathcal{P}}) + \sum_{j=1}^{n_2} \beta[j]\phi(\boldsymbol{x}_j^{\mathcal{O}}) + \sum_{j=1}^{n_3} \gamma[j]\phi(\boldsymbol{x}_j^{\mathcal{S}}),$$

Let $\boldsymbol{\vartheta}$ be the whole parameter vector and $\mathcal{D}$ be the whole training dataset include all three types of labeled data

$$\boldsymbol{\vartheta} = [\alpha[1\cdots n_1], \beta[1\cdots n_2], \gamma[1\cdots n_3]],$$
$$\mathcal{D} = [\phi(\boldsymbol{x}^{\mathcal{P}}_{[1\cdots n_1]})^T, \phi(\boldsymbol{x}^{\mathcal{O}}_{[1\cdots n_2]})^T, \phi(\boldsymbol{x}^{\mathcal{S}}_{[1\cdots n_3]})^T]^T,$$

and $\boldsymbol{d}_i$ is the i-th in $\mathcal{D}$, $n = n_1 + n_2 + n_3$, then the objective function can be written in the following kernel form through a kernel operator $K(\boldsymbol{x}, \boldsymbol{x}') = \langle\phi(\boldsymbol{x}), \phi(\boldsymbol{x}')\rangle$, yielding the inner products after the mapping $\phi(\cdot)$:

$$\min_{\boldsymbol{\vartheta}} \frac{1}{2} \sum_{i,j=1}^{n} \boldsymbol{\vartheta}[i]\boldsymbol{\vartheta}[j]K(\boldsymbol{d}_i, \boldsymbol{d}_j) + c_1\tau_1 \sum_{i=1}^{n_1} \max\{0, 1 - y_i^{\mathcal{P}} \sum_{j=1}^{n} \boldsymbol{\vartheta}[j]K(\boldsymbol{x}_i^{\mathcal{P}}, \boldsymbol{d}_j)\} + c_2\tau_2 \sum_{i=1}^{n_2} \max\{0, \rho - \sum_{j=1}^{n} \boldsymbol{\vartheta}[j]K(\boldsymbol{x}_i^{\mathcal{O}}, \boldsymbol{d}_j)\} + c_2\tau_3 \sum_{i=1}^{n_3} |\sum_{j=1}^{m} \boldsymbol{\vartheta}[j]K(\boldsymbol{x}_i^{\mathcal{S}}, \boldsymbol{d}_j)|$$

4. EXPERIMENTS

We evaluate our approach on two datasets with augmented relative attribute labels: (1) the **Outdoor Scene Recognition(OSR)** dataset [17][18] with 2688 images and 7 attributes, and the **Shoes** dataset [1][11] with 14568 images and 10 attributes. We directly use the features provided with the dataset of 512-dimensional gist descriptor for the **OSR** and 960-dimensional gist descriptor plus 20-dimensional color histogram for the **Shoes**.

4.1 Accuracy of Hybrid Ranking

We first demonstrate that the proposed approach is capable of utilizing information from both type of labeled data with the comparison of three baseline approaches: Relative Attributes [18], pointwise SVM for ordinal regression [23] and CRR [21] which optimizes regression and ranking simultaneously. We compute the average ranking accuracy with standard deviation by running 10 rounds of each implemented approach. The average ranking accuracy is evaluated by the frequency of correctly ranked pairs. The parameters are selected by cross validation of 5 randomly selected small subsets per dataset.

Tables 1 and 2 demonstrate the average ranking accuracy with standard deviation of each attribute per dataset. Pointwise and pairwise training samples are randomly selected as 100 for **OSR** and 200 for **Shoes** with the rest of

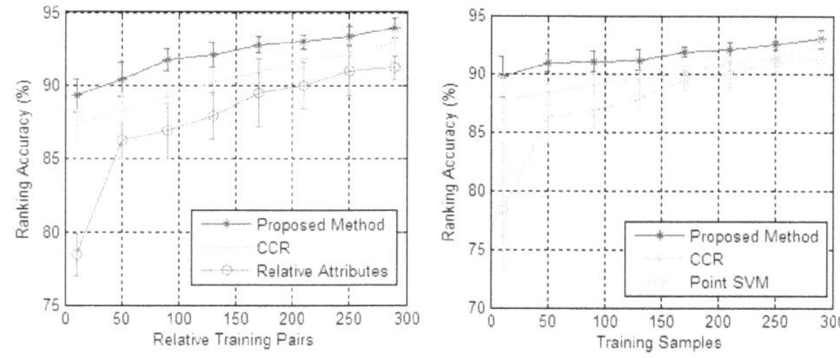

(a) OSR

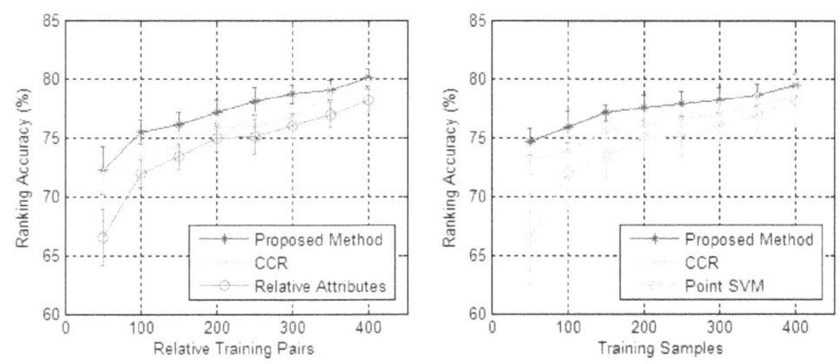

(b) Shoes

Figure 3: Learning curve of average ranking accuracy and corresponding standard deviation with regard to different number of pairwise or pointwise training samples on both dataset.

OSR and 6000 samples (due to memory limitation) from **Shoes** for test. The result shows that our approach apparently outperforms all baseline approaches in average ranking accuracies while generating lower standard deviations.

Fig. 3 illustrates how the ranking accuracy changes with different size of training samples on the attribute "Natural" of **OSR** and "Open" of **Shoes**. Specifically, the result in Fig. 3 Left is achieved by keeping the pointwise data size fixed at 100 and increasing the size of pairwise data. The blue curve shows the average ranking accuracy and standard deviation of our approach and the red and cyan curves shows the result of baseline approaches. In Fig. 3 Right, results of our approach (blue curve) compared with baseline approaches are shown where the size of training pairs is fixed at 100 and the size of training samples increases gradually. The results show that, in both configurations, our approach achieves obvious higher ranking accuracy and lower standard deviation than all baseline approaches. Besides, the result implies that, when fewer training samples were used, a higher performance gain was observed. For example, the best performance gain is 11% compared with Relative Attributes and 14% compared with pointwise SVM in "natural", when only 10 training samples or pairs are fed.

Fig. 4 shows some examples of ranked image pairs. In each column, the top image is more "natural" than the bottom image according to the ranking groundtruth. Fig. 4(a) is the comparison of our hybrid approach with Relative Attributes. The first three pairs (columns) are correctly ranked by our approach but incorrectly ranked by Relative Attributes, e.g., coast is more natural than highway, forest is more natural than inside city, mountain is more natural than buildings. The last three pairs are incorrectly ranked by our

Attribute Name	Hybrid Ranking(%)	CCR(%)	Relative Attribute(%)	Pointwise SVM(%)
Natural	**91.56±0.89**	88.75±0.90	87.09±2.08	88.86±2.24
Open	**88.50±0.62**	87.25±0.82	86.83±1.76	85.72±1.26
Perspective	**83.40±0.78**	82.23±0.81	80.20±1.69	80.56±1.73
Size-large	**72.93±1.04**	70.62±1.21	67.89±1.55	65.17±3.53
Diagonal-plane	**80.35±1.15**	78.42±1.08	76.25±1.76	76.61±2.73
Depth-cloth	**87.06±0.87**	85.24±0.95	84.27±1.66	82.32±1.51
Average	**83.97±0.80**	82.08±0.96	80.42 ±1.75	79.87±1.78

Table 1: Ranking accuracies and standard deviation of 6 attributes on the OSR dataset when the number of training samples and pairs are 100 for each attribute.

Attribute Name	Proposed Method(%)	CRR(%)	Relative Attribute(%)	Pointwise SVM(%)
Point at the front	**82.25±0.79**	81.42±0.82	80.61±1.08	79.13±1.53
Open	**76.02±0.83**	74.24±0.80	71.72±0.88	69.10±1.78
Bright in color	**64.40±0.76**	62.43±0.75	59.38±1.86	58.63±0.76
Covered with ornaments	**71.19±0.58**	70.02±0.61	68.88±0.72	59.10±3.87
Shiny	**79.60±0.52**	78.28±0.68	76.94±0.66	74.12±1.30
High at the heel	**80.71±0.75**	78.93±0.77	77.43±0.99	76.59±1.60
Long on the leg	**75.19±0.92**	73.32±0.82	72.44±1.07	69.08±2.19
Formal	**75.78±0.90**	74.45±0.91	72.37±1.10	70.76±1.57
Sporty	**80.24±0.90**	78.25±0.95	77.39±0.90	68.98±1.70
Feminine	**83.37±0.68**	82.42±0.70	81.38±0.71	81.86±1.50
Average	**76.88±0.76**	75.38±0.78	73.85±1.00	70.74±1.78

Table 2: Ranking accuracies and standard deviation of 10 attributes on the Shoes dataset when the number of training samples and pairs are 200 for each attribute.

approach but correctly ranked by Relative Attributes. The reason for the incorrect classification may be that our approach assigned a wrong category label to the scene. For instance, our approach also classified the bottom image of the fifth column as forest because of a tree appears in the scene. Fig. 4(b) illustrates the comparison of our approach with pointwise SVM. The first three pairs are correctly ranked by our approach but incorrectly ranked by pointwise SVM, e.g., coast is more natural than street, mountain is more natural than open county and forest is more natural than inside city. The last three pairs are incorrectly ranked by our approach but correctly ranked by pointwise SVM.

Based on these experiments, the potential performance gains of our approach appear to come from the extra information captured from different types of labels. In particular, the smaller standard deviation may result from the joint use of both information sources that help to denoise the training process.

(a) Hybrid v.s. Relative Attribute

(b) Hybrid v.s. Pointwise SVM

Figure 4: Samples illustrating the ranking results. In groundtruth the top image is more "natrual" than the bottom image. The left three column is correctly ranked by the proposed approach while incorrectly ranked by the baseline. The right three is inverse.

4.2 Zero-Shot Learning

To further evaluate the proposed approach, we now consider the popular application of zero-shot learning. Given some training samples from some "seen" categories and some "unseen" categories without any training samples, zero-shot learning would predict the category labels of new samples. We compare our approach with the baseline approach Relative Attributes since [18] has shown that this approach outperforms most of the state of the art approaches on this regard. We followed the same parameter prediction rules of unseen categories as [4]. We adopted the same super parameters in Sect. 4.1 for model training. The average ranking accuracies with corresponding standard deviations are re-

Accuracy	70%	72.5%	75%	77.5%	80%	82.5%	85%
Online Learning	0.003 s	0.004 s	0.006 s	0.009 s	0.042 s	0.105 s	0.156 s
Batch Learning	0.006 s	0.098 s	0.104 s	0.231 s	0.451 s	1.558 s	6.308 s

Table 3: Elapsed times in order to achieve the same ranking accuracy (the less the better). The first row shows given ranking accuracies, and the second/third row shows the times needed for online/batch learning respectively to achieve the corresponding accuracy.

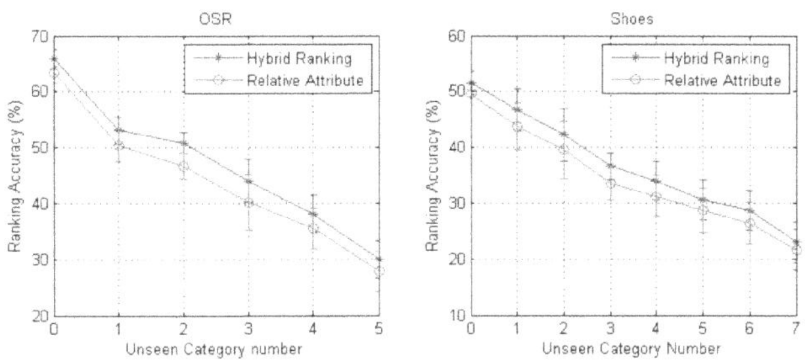

(a) Different unseen categories

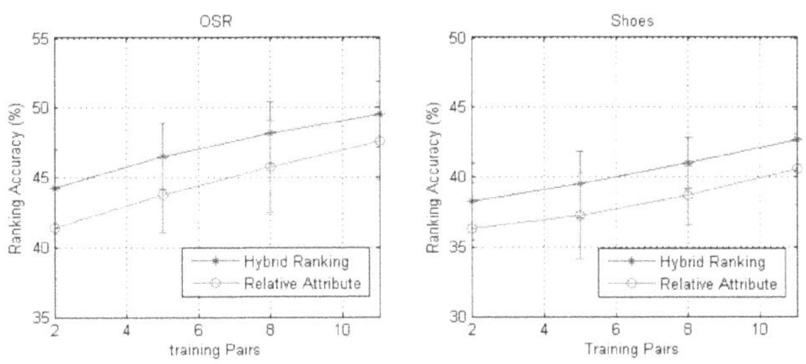

(b) Different training pairs

Figure 5: Learning curve of zero-shot learning accuracy with regard to different unseen category numbers and training sample size on both dataset.

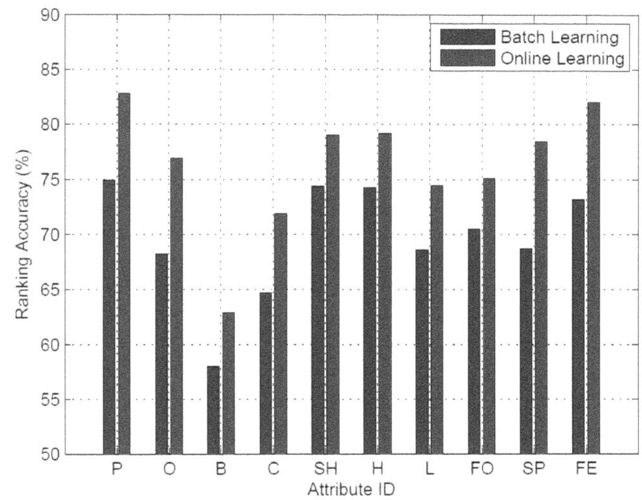

Figure 6: Average ranking accuracy of 10 attributes on the Shoes dataset by running the algorithms for 0.1 seconds. In each group the first bar is the result of batch learning and the second bar is the result of online learning.

ported by running each experiment 10 rounds. Assuming the data follows a Gaussian distribution, we estimated the mean and the covariance matrix of each (seen and unseen) category and assigned the category label of the new sample through maximum likelihood.

Fig. 5(a) shows the accuracy as a function of the number of unseen categories. For each seen category 30 images are left out for category parameter prediction, and 10 pointwise and 10 pairwise labelled samples are randomly picked for training. Results show that the ranking accuracy decreases as the number of unseen category increases. Our approach outperforms the baseline approach by around 3%.

Fig. 5(b) shows how the accuracy changes with the number of training pairs. In each run, 2 unseen categories and 30 images from the other seen categories are left out. 10 pointwise labelled samples are randomly picked for hybrid approach. Results show that ranking accuracies of both approaches increase with the increase of training pairs. Our approach yields performance gains by around 3% compared with the baseline approach.

4.3 Online Learning Evaluation

In this subsection, we compare the performance of the proposed online learning algorithm with the batch learning algorithm on the shoes dataset. For the online learning algorithm, the super parameters are set as $c_1 = 0.2$, $c_2 = 3$, $\rho = 0.1$. In training, we first construct a data pool mixed with both pointwise and pairwise data, and then randomly pick one data sample without considering the specific label type from the data pool for training. For batch learning, we construct the training dataset as half pointwise and half pairwise samples.

Fig. 6 illustrates the average ranking accuracy of 10 attributes by running both implemented approaches 10 rounds for a small time interval T (T=0.1 second in this experiment), simulating very limited training data availability. In each group, the first bar (blue) shows the result of batch learning and the second bar (red) shows the result of online learning. The results shows that in the same elapsed time of 0.1 second, the online learning algorithm clearly outperforms batch learning. The highest performance gain is obtained on the attribute "Sporty" by 9.69% and the lowest performance gain is for the attribute "Formal" by 4.63%.

Table 3 collects the elapsed time after both approaches achieved the same ranking performance from 70% to 85%. The results show that the batch learning approach takes longer time than online learning to achieve the same accuracy. With the ranking accuracy increased, the time difference become much more obvious. For example, batch learning takes double time (0.006s vs 0.003s) than online learning to achieve the accuracy of 70%, and takes 40 times (6.308s vs 0.156s) more time to achieve the accuracy of 85%.

5. CONCLUSIONS

We proposed a hybrid ranking framework for supporting adaptive, attribute-based image retrieval. We evaluated the proposed approach on two image datasets. The results show that through capturing the information from both relative attribute strength (pairwise) and absolute attribute scale (pointwise), our method is able to achieve better ranking performance than Relative Attribute and pointwise SVM, which are current leading approaches that learn the ranking function purely based on either pairwise or pointwise data. We also proposed an online learning algorithm for the proposed framework and derived the formulation into the kernel form. The experiments of online learning and batch learning show that our online learning algorithm can achieve much better ranking performance than batch learning given the same running time or can achieve better performance in much less time. The results also suggest that the less training data are available, the more relative performance gains can be obtained by our approach than independent learning.

6. ACKNOWLEDGMENTS

The work was supported in part by a grant from National Science Foundation and a grant from Army Research Office. Any opinions and conclusions expressed in this material are those of the author(s) and do not necessarily reflect the view of sponsors.

7. REFERENCES

[1] T. L. Berg, A. C. Berg, and J. Shih. Automatic attribute discovery and characterization from noisy web data. In *Proc. of ECCV'10*, pages 663–676, Berlin, Heidelberg, 2010. Springer-Verlag.

[2] C. Burges, T. Shaked, E. Renshaw, A. Lazier, M. Deeds, N. Hamilton, and G. Hullender. Learning to rank using gradient descent. In *Proc. of ICML '05*, pages 89–96. ACM, 2005.

[3] Y. Cao, J. Xu, T.-Y. Liu, H. Li, Y. Huang, and H.-W. Hon. Adapting ranking svm to document retrieval. In *Proc. of SIGIR '06*, pages 186–193. ACM, 2006.

[4] L. Chen, Q. Zhang, and B. Li. Predicting multiple attributes via relative multi-task learning. In *Proc. of CVPR '14*, pages 1027–1034, July 2014.

[5] N. Elahi, R. Karlsen, and E. J. Holsbø. Personalized photo recommendation by leveraging user modeling on social network. In *Proc. of IIWAS '13*, pages 68:68–68:71. ACM, 2013.

[6] A. Farhadi, I. Endres, D. Hoiem, and D. Forsyth. Describing objects by their attributes. In *Proc. of CVPR '09*, pages 1778–1785, June 2009.

[7] Y. Freund, R. Iyer, R. E. Schapire, and Y. Singer. An efficient boosting algorithm for combining preferences. *J. Mach. Learn. Res.*, 4:933–969, Dec. 2003.

[8] T. Joachims. Optimizing search engines using clickthrough data. In *Proc. of KDD '02*, pages 133–142. ACM, 2002.

[9] G. Kimeldorf and G. Wahba. Some results on tchebycheffian spline functions. *Journal of Mathematical Analysis and Applications*, 33(1):82 – 95, 1971.

[10] A. Kovashka and K. Grauman. Attribute adaptation for personalized image search. In *Proc. of ICCV '13*, pages 3432–3439, Dec 2013.

[11] A. Kovashka, D. Parikh, and K. Grauman. Whittlesearch: Image search with relative attribute feedback. In *Proc. of CVPR'12*, pages 2973–2980, June 2012.

[12] N. Kumar, P. Belhumeur, and S. Nayar. Facetracer: A search engine for large collections of images with faces. In *Proc. of ECCV '08*, pages 340–353. Springer-Verlag, 2008.

[13] N. Kumar, A. Berg, P. Belhumeur, and S. Nayar. Attribute and simile classifiers for face verification. In *Proc. of CVPR '09*, pages 365–372, Sept 2009.

[14] C. Lampert, H. Nickisch, and S. Harmeling. Learning to detect unseen object classes by between-class attribute transfer. In *Proc. of CVPR '09*, pages 951–958, June 2009.

[15] P. Li, Q. Wu, and C. J. Burges. Mcrank: Learning to rank using multiple classification and gradient boosting. In *Proc. of NIPS '08*, pages 897–904. Curran Associates, Inc., 2008.

[16] T. Moon, A. Smola, Y. Chang, and Z. Zheng. Intervalrank: Isotonic regression with listwise and pairwise constraints. In *WSDM*, 2010.

[17] A. Oliva and A. Torralba. Modeling the shape of the scene: A holistic representation of the spatial envelope. *Int. J. Comput. Vision*, 42(3):145–175, May 2001.

[18] D. Parikh and K. Grauman. Relative attributes. In *Proc. of ICCV '11*, pages 503–510, Nov 2011.

[19] C. Renjifo and C. Carmen. The discounted cumulative margin penalty: Rank-learning with a list-wise loss and pair-wise margins. In *MLSP*, Sept 2012.

[20] J. Sang, C. Xu, and D. Lu. Learn to personalized image search from the photo sharing websites. *Multimedia, IEEE Transactions on*, 14(4):963–974, Aug 2012.

[21] D. Sculley. Combined regression and ranking. In *Proc. of SIGKDD'10*, pages 979–988, New York, NY, USA, 2010. ACM.

[22] S. Shalev-Shwartz, Y. Singer, and N. Srebro. Pegasos: Primal estimated sub-gradient solver for svm. In *Proc. of ICML '07*, pages 807–814. ACM, 2007.

[23] A. Shashua and A. Levin. Ranking with large margin principle: Two approaches. In *Proc. of NIPS '03*, pages 961–968. MIT Press, 2003.

[24] M.-F. Tsai, T.-Y. Liu, T. Qin, H.-H. Chen, and W.-Y. Ma. Frank: A ranking method with fidelity loss. In *Proc. of SIGIR '07*, pages 383–390. ACM, 2007.

[25] D. Vaquero, R. Feris, D. Tran, L. Brown, A. Hampapur, and M. Turk. Attribute-based people search in surveillance environments. In *Proc. of WACV'09*, December 2009.

[26] Y. Wang and G. Mori. A discriminative latent model of object classes and attributes. In *Proc. of ECCV'10*, pages 155–168. Springer-Verlag, 2010.

Facial Action Unit Classification with Hidden Knowledge under Incomplete Annotation

Jun Wang
University of Science and Technology of China
Hefei, Anhui
P.R.China, 230027
junwong@mail.ustc.edu.cn

Shangfei Wang*
University of Science and Technology of China
Hefei, Anhui
P.R.China, 230027
sfwang@ustc.edu.cn

Qiang Ji
Rensselaer Polytechnic Institute
Troy, NY
USA, 12180
qji@ecse.rpi.edu

ABSTRACT

Facial action unit (AU) recognition is an important task for facial expression analysis. Traditional AU recognition methods typically include a supervised training, where the AU annotated training images are needed. AU annotation is a time consuming, expensive, and error prone process. While AU is hard to annotate, facial expression is relatively easy to label. To take advantage of this, we introduce a new learning method that trains an AU classifier using images with incomplete AU annotation but with complete expression labels. The goal is to use expression labels as hidden knowledge to complement the missing AU labels. Towards this goal, we propose to construct a Bayesian Network (BN) to capture the relationships between facial expression and AUs. Structural Expectation Maximum is used to learn the structure and parameters of the BN when the AU labels are missing. Given the learned BNs and measurements of AUs and expression, we can then perform AU recognition within the BN through a probabilistic inference. Experimental results on the CK+ and ISL databases demonstrate the effectiveness of our method.

Categories and Subject Descriptors

I.5.1 [**Pattern Recognition**]: Models—*Statistical*

General Terms

Theory

Keywords

facial action unit recognition, Bayesian Network, multi-label recognition, incomplete labels, structural expectation maximum

*This is the corresponding author (Telephone: +86-551-3602824).

ICMR'15, June 23–26, 2015, Shanghai, China.

DOI: http://dx.doi.org/10.1145/2671188.2749311.

1. INTRODUCTION

Facial expression recognition has attracted increasing attention due to its wide applications in human-computer interaction [21]. There are two kinds of descriptors of expressions: expression category and Facial Action Units (AUs) [3]. The former describes facial behavior globally, and the latter represents facial muscle actions locally. To recognize AUs and expressions, a large number of annotated training images are required. The AUs should be labeled by qualified FACS experts. Thus, AU annotation is expensive. Furthermore, current research [9, 13, 20, 24] reveals that some AUs are obvious and easy to be annotated, while others are subtle and hard to annotate. This phenomenon not only increases the difficulty of AU annotation, but also makes the AU labels error prone. Compared with AU annotation, expression is much easier to annotate, and can be labeled with great accuracy.

In this work, we try to design an AU recognition method with the help of expression labels as hidden knowledge under the incomplete AU labeling. Specifically, during training, instead of trying to label every AU in each image as being done by the existing AU recognition methods, we only label AUs that can be labeled confidently and leave those difficult and subtle AUs unlabeled. In addition, we provide expression label for each image. Using such annotated images, we then train an AU recognition algorithm by leveraging on the relationships among AUs and the knowledge of the expressions. We refer to expression labels as the hidden knowledge since they are only available and used during training, and they will not be available during testing. To take advantage of the available expression labels during training, we propose to construct a BN to systematically capture the dependencies among AUs and expressions. The nodes of the BN represent the AUs and expressions. The links and their parameters capture the probabilistic relations among AUs and expressions. Since some AU labels are missing for some training images, Structural Expectation Maximisation (SEM) is adopted to learn the structure and parameters of the BN. Given the learned BN, we can infer the AUs by combining the AU/Expression relationships encoded in the BN and the AU image measurements. The experimental results on CK+ database show that, with complete annotation, our method outperforms state of the art model-based and image-driven AU recognition methods; with incomplete annotation, our method performs much better than state of the art AU recognition methods. Furthermore, we train our model using the CK+ database and test it on the IS-

L database, and the experimental results demonstrate the cross-database generalization ability of our method.

2. RELATED WORK

Usually, several AUs can be present at the same image or image sequence. Thus, AU recognition can be formulated as a multi-label classification problem. Due to the large number of possible label sets, multi-label classification is rather challenging. Successfully exploiting the dependencies inherent in multiple labels is the key to facilitate the learning process. Accounting for dependencies among AUs, present AU recognition research can be divided into three groups.

The first group recognizes each AU individually [18, 19] directly from images or sequences. They are referred to as image-driven AU recognition methods. Valstar and Pantic [18] proposed an automatic method to detect 22 AUs. They first detected and tracked 20 facial points, and then used a combination of gentleBoost, support vector machines, and hidden Markov models as a classifier. Laurens van der Maaten et al. [19] adopted Active Appearance Model features and linear chain conditional random field to detect the presence of AUs. These works treat each AU recognition individually as one-vs.-all scheme, ignoring the dependencies among AUs. However, multiple AUs can appear together, and there exist dependencies, and such AU relationships may help AU recognition.

The second group recognizes AU combinations. Bartlett et al. [8] analyzed the AU combinations of 1+2,2+4,1+4,and 1+2+4 using a linear SVM with Gabor features. Lucey et al. [10] used SVM and Nearest Neighbor to detect a few combinations of AUs (i.e. 1,1+2,4,5) with AAM features. Although the co-existent relations among AUs in an AU combination have been exploited by the used features and classifier in these works, the combinations are manually determined and fixed. Each combination is regarded as a new AU. Thus, it is only feasible for a few combinations, and hard to detect thousands of possible combinations.

The third group explicitly exploits the co-existent and mutual exclusive relations among AUs from target labels. They are referred to as model-based AU recognition methods. Tong et al. [15, 16] used Gabor features and SVM to recognize each AU first, then they model the relations among AU labels by Dynamic Bayesian Network(DBN). Their work assumes complete AU labeling and only involves AUs without using expressions. All the model-based AU recognition methods require completely annotated images.

To the best of our knowledge, there is so far no reported work that recognizes AUs assisted by expressions, although there exist a few works considering the relations between expressions and AUs to help expression recognition, or to jointly recognize AUs and expressions [7]. For example, Pantic and Rothkrantz [11] summarized the production rules of expressions from AUs using the AUs-coded descriptions of the six basic emotional expressions given by Ekman [3]. Velusamy et al. regarded AU to expression mapping as a problem of approximate string matching, and adopted a learned statistical relationship between AUs and expressions to build template strings of AUs for six basic expressions [20]. Zhang et al. proposed dynamic Bayesian networks to model the probabilistic relations of facial expressions to the complex combination of facial AUs, and temporal behaviors of facial expressions [24]. Li et al. [7] introduced a dynamic model to capture the relationships among AUs, expressions, and facial feature points, and use the model to perform simultaneous AU and expression recognition, and facial feature tracking.

Current AU recognition methods require complete AU label assignments. However, AU recognition with incomplete AU label assignments is frequently encountered in realistic scenarios, due to the large number of AUs and difficulty in manual AU annotations. Till now, little research has addressed the challenge of AU recognition with incomplete AU labels. While AUs are hard to annotate, facial expression is relatively easy to label. The available expression labels during training and the dependencies among expression and AUs may be useful for AU recognition. Thus, in the paper, we construct AU classifiers with the ability of learning and inferring from incomplete AU annotations with the help of expression knowledge that is available during training only.

Compared with related work, we propose to model both the dependencies between expression and AUs, and the dependencies among AUs to help AU recognition. We further explore the relations between expression and AUs to infer AUs with incomplete label assignments.

3. METHODS

Assuming $D = \{X_i, (\lambda_{1i}, ..., \lambda_{ni}, \lambda_{n+1i})\}_{i=1}^{m}$ is the training data, where m is the number of training samples, n is the number of AU labels. For the ith training image, we denote X_i as the image feature vector, and $\lambda_{1i}, ..., \lambda_{ni}$ as the n AU labels, and λ_{n+1i} as the expression label respectively. All the other data are complete, except for the AU label data, which may be missing due to the hard annotations. The expression label λ_{n+1i}, while available during training, is unavailable during testing. The goal of this work is to construct an AU classifier with the abilities of learning and inferring from incomplete AU data with the help of expression knowledge that is available during training. As shown in Fig. 1, our approach consists of two modules: AU and expression measurement extraction, and AUs and expression' relations modeling by BN. The training phase of our approach includes training the traditional image-driven classifier for AU measurement extraction and training the BN to capture the semantic relationships among AUs and expressions. For measurement extraction, a current image-driven algorithm is used. Given the measurements, we infer the final labels of samples through the most probable explanation (MPE) inference with the BN model. The details are provided as follows.

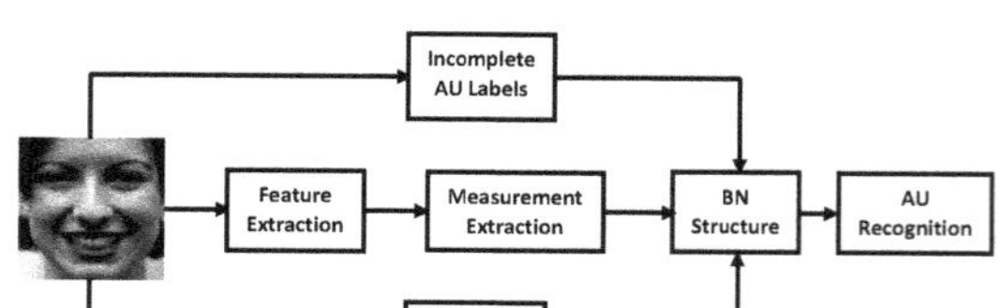

Figure 1: The framework of our method.

3.1 Measurement extraction

The measurements $m\lambda$ are the preliminary estimations of the AU and expression labels using an existing image-driven recognition method based on training data. In this work, the movements of the x and y coordinates of the feature points between the apex and neutral images are used as the image features, and Support Vector Machines (SVMs) are used as the classifiers to obtain the initial AU measurements. To be specific, for each label, we adopt leave-one-subject-out strategy to get the recognition results as measurements. During training, the measurements of training samples are input to the BN model (i.e. the shaded nodes showed in Fig. 2) to get the parameters of the BN, and during testing, the measurements of testing samples are input to the BN model(as well as the shaded nodes showed in Fig. 2) to infer the true labels of testing samples.

3.2 AUs and expressions dependencies modeling by Bayesian Network

In order to model the semantic relationships among AUs and expressions, a BN model is utilized in this work. As a probabilistic graphical model, BN can effectively capture the dependencies among variables in data. In our work, each node of the BN is an AU or expression label, and the links and their conditional probabilities capture the probabilistic dependencies among AUs and Expressions, and each node in BN is linked with an extra node called measurement whose available values are same as the white source node, as shown in Fig. 2.

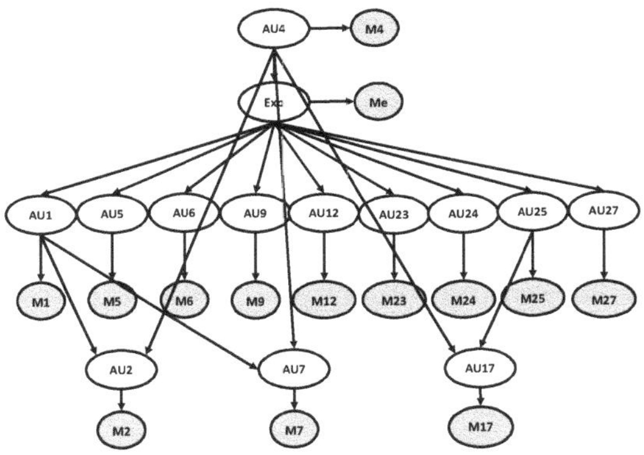

Figure 2: The BN model learned by our method. (The unshaded nodes are the hidden nodes we want to infer and the shaded nodes are the corresponding measurement nodes)

BN structure and parameters learning for incomplete AUs' label. A BN is a directed acyclic graph (DAG) $G = (\Lambda, E)$, where $\Lambda = \{\lambda_i\}_{i=1}^{n+1}$ represents a collection of $n+1$ nodes and E denotes a collection of arcs.

Given the dataset of multiple target labels $TD = \{\lambda_{ij}\}$, where $i = 1, 2, ..., n, n+1$ is an index to the number of nodes, and $j = 1, 2, ..., m$ is index to the number of samples. The structure and parameter learning is to find a structure G that maximizes a score function. In this work, we employ the Bayesian Information Criterion (BIC) score function which is defined as Eq. 2. Since AU labels are incomplete, the structural EM algorithm is adopted to address incomplete labels. In structural EM, we iterate over a pair of steps. In the E-step, we use the current model to generate a completed data set, based on which we compute expected sufficient statistics. In the M-step, we use these expected sufficient statistics to improve our model, including both parameters and structure. The detailed learning algorithm is summarized in Algorithm 1.

Algorithm 1 Structural EM algorithm for structure and parameter learning of the BN model

1. Initialize the structure G^0 and the parameter set $\theta^0 = \{P(pa(\lambda_i)|\lambda_i), P(\lambda_i)\}$, ($pa(\lambda_i)$ is the parent of λ_i) based on algorithm proposed in [2] for the BN model based on the training data, where the incomplete AU annotation samples are ignored.

repeat

2. E-step
Use the new BN structure and parameters to infer the missing labels of the incomplete samples and update the training set D.

3. M-step

$$\{G^t, \theta^t\} = argmax_{G,\theta} Q(G, \theta : G^{t-1}, \theta^{t-1}) \quad (1)$$

In which, $Q(G, \theta : G^\star, \theta^\star)$ is the expectation of the Bayesian Information Criterion (BIC) score of any Bayesian network $\{G, \theta\}$ calculated using a distribution of the data $P(D|G^\star, \theta^\star)$, which is defined as following:

$$\begin{aligned} &Q^{BIC}(G, \theta : G^*, \theta^*) = \\ &E_{G^*, \theta^*}[logP(D|G, \theta)] - \frac{Dim(G)}{2} \log m \end{aligned} \quad (2)$$

where the first term is the log-likelihood function of structure G with respect to data D, representing how well G fits the data. The second term is a penalty term relating to the complexity of the network, where Dim_G is the number of independent parameters and m is the number of samples.

until converges

BN inference. During the BN inference, the posterior probability of categories can be estimated by combining the likelihood from measurement with the prior model. Let λ_i and $m\lambda_i$, $i \in \{1, ..., n, n+1\}$, respectively denote the label variable and the corresponding measurement obtained by a traditional image-driven method. Then, most probable explanation (MPE) [12] inference is used to estimate the joint probability.

$$\begin{aligned} Y^\star &= \arg\max_{\lambda_1,...,\lambda_n} P(\lambda_1, ..., \lambda_n \mid m\lambda_1, ..., m\lambda_n, m\lambda_{n+1}) \\ &= \arg\max_{\lambda_1,...,\lambda_n} \sum_{\lambda_{n+1}} (\prod_{i=1}^{n+1} P(m\lambda_i \mid \lambda_i) \prod_{i=1}^{n+1} P(\lambda_i \mid pa(\lambda_i))) \end{aligned} \quad (3)$$

The condition probabilities in the equation are learned from training set. In the work, the inferred results are the labels ($\lambda_1, ..., \lambda_n$, a binary vector) with the highest probability given $m\lambda_1, ..., m\lambda_n, m\lambda_{n+1}$.

4. EXPERIMENTS

4.1 Experimental conditions

The Extended Cohn-Kanade Dataset (CK+) [9], in which 7 expression categories (i.e. Anger, Contempt, Disgust, Fear,

Happy, Sadness and Surprise) and 30 AU labels are provided for parts of the samples, is used to validate our method. The CK+ database provides 68 facial feature points for each image as well. Finally, 327 samples with both expression category and FACS labels are selected, and 13 AUs whose frequencies of all the selected samples are more than 10% are considered, which are: $AU1$, $AU2$, $AU4$, $AU5$, $AU6$, $AU7$, $AU9$, $AU12$, $AU17$, $AU23$, $AU24$, $AU25$, and $AU27$.

To validate the supplementary role of expression in assisting AU recognition, three experiments are conducted: the image-driven AU recognition, the model-based method that models only AU relations and our model that considers both the relations among AUs, and the relations between AUs and expressions. The image-driven AU recognition is the same as the initial AU measurement estimation discussed in section 3.1.

To illuminate the effectiveness of our constructed AU classifier under incomplete AU annotation, we randomly miss each AU label at certain probabilities, i.e. 5%, 10%, 15%, 20%, 25%, 30%, 35%, 40%, 45% and 50%. We compare our proposed method with image-driven method, and the model based method that models only AU relations. Both of our proposed method and model-based method considering only AU relations handle incomplete labels by structural EM, while the image-driven method are trained with only the complete portion of the data. Leave-one-subject-out cross-validation is adopted.

Furthermore, in order to evaluate the generalization ability of the proposed method, the cross-database AU recognition experiments are conducted. We train the BN models using the AU and expression labels from the CK+ database, and then combine the learned BN model and the obtained measurements from ISL database [5]. The ISL database is collected under real-world conditions with uncontrolled illumination and background, as well as moderate head motion. The 19 frontal view video clips for 7 subjects displaying facial expressions are adopted in this work, and we manually label facial feature points on the images.

AU recognition is a multi-label classification problem, whose evaluation metric is different from that of single label classification, since for each instance there are multiple labels which may be classified partly correctly or partly incorrectly. Thus, there are two kinds of commonly used metrics, example-based and label-based measures [14], evaluating the multi-label classification performance from the view of instances and labels respectively. We adopt both measures in this work. Let Y_i denotes the true labels for instance i, which is a binary vector, and Z_i is the predicted labels for instances i, m represents the number of the instances and n is the number of labels.

The example-based measures: Hamming Loss, and the label-based measures: averaged MacroF_1 score, are defined in Eq. 4 and Eq. 5 respectively.

$$HammimgLoss = \frac{\sum_{i=1}^{m} xor(Y_i, Z_i)}{m \times n} \tag{4}$$

$$F_1 = \frac{1}{n}\sum_{j=1}^{n} \frac{2\sum_{i=1}^{m} Y_i^j Z_i^j}{\sum_{i=1}^{m} Y_i^j + \sum_{i=1}^{m} Z_i^j} \tag{5}$$

4.2 Experimental results with complete AU annotation on CK+ database

Results and analysis of AUs and expressions dependencies modeling by BN. We quantify the dependence between different AUs and the dependence between AUs and expressions via the whole database using a conditional probability of $P(\lambda_j|\lambda_i)$, as shown in Table 1, which measures the probability of label λ_j happens, given label λ_i happens. From Table 1, we can find that there exist two kinds of relationships between AUs, and between AUs and expressions: co-occurrence and mutual exclusion. For example, $P(AU1|AU2)$ is 1.00, which shows $AU1$ is always coexistent with $AU2$. $P(AU25|surprise)$ is 0.988, indicating that $AU25$ is an important AU to express surprise. $P(AU1|AU9)$ and $P(AU4|happy)$ are 0.00, which means $AU1$ never coexists with AU9, and $AU4$ is rarely active when users express happiness. Both of the proportions of the co-occurrence and mutual exclusion relations between AUs and expressions are larger than those between AUs. Specifically, 39.6% of the conditional probabilities between AU and expression are extremely mutually exclusive, since they are equal to 0.00 and 22.0% of them are extremely coexistent since they are larger than 0.70. While among the condition probabilities between AUs, only 14.7% of them are extremely mutual exclusion or coexistent. It indicates that the relations between AUs and expressions may be stronger that those between AUs.

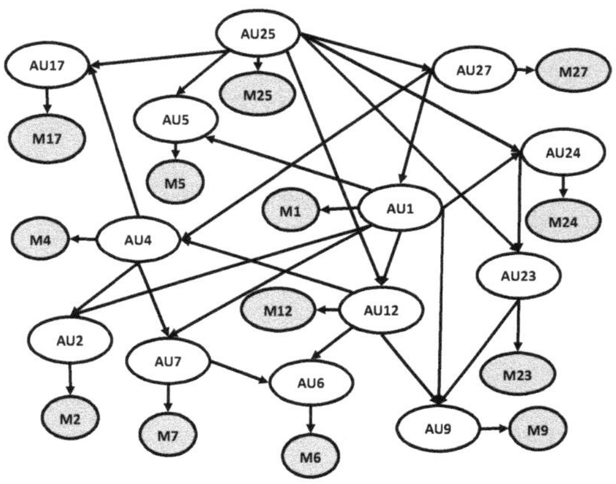

Figure 3: The BN model learned by model-based method. (The unshaded nodes are the hidden nodes we want to infer and the shaded nodes are the corresponding measurement nodes.)

To systematically capture relationships between AUs, and relations between AUs and expressions, we learned two BNs, shown in Fig. 3 and Fig. 2 respectively. The links in the structure represent the dependencies among labels. Comparing two learned BNs with the dependency tables, we find that the label pairs whose conditional probabilities are top ranked or bottom ranked are linked in the BNs in most cases. It demonstrates the effectiveness of the BN structure learning method capturing the mutual exclusive and co-existent relationships among multiple labels. Comparing Fig. 2 with Fig. 3, we find that by adding the expression node which takes 7 discrete values representing 7 different expressions, many links between AUs are removed. Specifically, in Fig. 3, each AU node is connected with at least two other AU nodes,

Table 1: **Dependencies between labels (each entry a_{ij} represents $P(\lambda_j = 1|\lambda_i = 1)$)**

λ_i \ λ_j	AU1	AU2	AU4	AU5	AU6	AU7	AU9	AU12	AU17	AU23	AU24	AU25	AU27
AU1	1.000	0.762	0.315	0.646	0.023	0.038	0.000	0.038	0.223	0.038	0.008	0.777	0.546
AU2	1.000	1.000	0.121	0.788	0.000	0.000	0.000	0.040	0.101	0.030	0.010	0.909	0.717
AU4	0.336	0.098	1.000	0.156	0.180	0.508	0.311	0.025	0.754	0.287	0.254	0.213	0.008
AU5	0.913	0.848	0.207	1.000	0.033	0.043	0.011	0.043	0.098	0.076	0.000	0.924	0.652
AU6	0.032	0.000	0.232	0.032	1.000	0.347	0.189	0.705	0.211	0.074	0.032	0.737	0.000
AU7	0.063	0.000	0.785	0.051	0.418	1.000	0.443	0.076	0.696	0.329	0.329	0.228	0.000
AU9	0.000	0.000	0.623	0.016	0.295	0.574	1.000	0.033	0.705	0.082	0.148	0.148	0.000
AU12	0.063	0.050	0.038	0.050	0.838	0.075	0.025	1.000	0.025	0.000	0.025	0.900	0.038
AU17	0.252	0.087	0.800	0.078	0.174	0.478	0.374	0.017	1.000	0.304	0.278	0.052	0.000
AU23	0.116	0.070	0.814	0.163	0.163	0.605	0.116	0.000	0.814	1.000	0.581	0.023	0.023
AU24	0.023	0.023	0.721	0.000	0.070	0.605	0.209	0.047	0.744	0.581	1.000	0.000	0.000
AU25	0.558	0.497	0.144	0.470	0.387	0.099	0.050	0.398	0.033	0.006	0.000	1.000	0.398
AU27	0.986	0.986	0.014	0.833	0.000	0.000	0.000	0.042	0.000	0.014	0.000	1.000	1.000
anger	0.000	0.000	0.889	0.133	0.178	0.711	0.067	0.022	0.867	0.800	0.733	0.000	0.000
contempt	0.056	0.056	0.056	0.000	0.000	0.000	0.000	0.278	0.278	0.056	0.111	0.000	0.000
disgust	0.000	0.000	0.610	0.000	0.305	0.559	0.983	0.034	0.695	0.034	0.119	0.153	0.000
fear	0.880	0.400	0.840	0.640	0.120	0.240	0.000	0.080	0.120	0.000	0.000	0.920	0.000
happy	0.000	0.000	0.000	0.000	0.957	0.101	0.000	0.971	0.000	0.000	0.000	0.971	0.000
sad	0.929	0.250	0.821	0.000	0.000	0.036	0.000	0.000	0.964	0.107	0.036	0.000	0.000
surprise	0.976	0.976	0.012	0.843	0.000	0.000	0.000	0.036	0.000	0.012	0.000	0.988	0.867

while in Fig. 2, all of the 13 AUs nodes are connected with the expression node directly or indirectly. It further confirms that the relations between AUs and expressions are stronger than those between AUs. It also says that AU relations are mostly expression dependent or AUs are more likely to relate to each other via the expression. Specifically, AU dependencies can be classified into two types: expression-dependent and expression-independent. By introducing the expression node, many direct links among AUs disappear. This means that AUs are mostly dependent on each other through the facial expression, i.e. most of the AU relationships are expression dependent. The remaining direct links among AUs in Fig. 2 capture the expression-independent AU dependencies, i.e., AU dependencies as a result of the underlying facial anatomy. Therefore, the AU recognition performance may be better improved by considering both the relations among AUs, and AUs and expressions.

Results and analysis of AU recognition. The experimental results of AU recognition with complete AU annotations on the CK+ database are shown in the left part named "CK+" of Table 2. From the table, we can obtain the following observations:

1. The image-driven method performs worst among the three methods, since its hamming loss is the highest, and the averaged label-based MacroF_1 score is the lowest. The image-driven method predicts each AU independently from the image features only. However, the AUs are not totally independent. There exist co-occurrent and mutually exclusive relations among AUs, and the relations among AUs and expressions are even much stronger as discussed above. The two learned BNs systematically capture these relations. Our method capturing expression-dependent AU relations and combining it with AU measurements improve the performance.

2. Our AU recognition method considering both AUs' relations and AU-expression relations not only performs better than the image-driven method but also the model-based method only considering AUs relations, with lower Hamming loss and higher label-based MacroF_1 score. It suggests that the stronger relations among AUs and expressions can facilitate AU recognition better than using the AUs' relations only, although the expression labels are available during training and unavailable during testing.

Table 2: Experimental results of CK+ database and cross database with complete AU annotations

	CK+		cross database	
method	Hamming	F_1 score	Hamming	F_1 score
Image-driven	0.106	0.738	0.105	0.834
Model-based	0.100	0.793	0.101	0.844
Our's	**0.096**	**0.800**	**0.097**	**0.846**

4.3 Experimental results with incomplete AU annotation on CK+ database

To investigate robustness of the proposed method with respect to missing AUs, we conducted leave-one-subject-out validation with missing each AU annotation by special ratios. We totally perform 13(AUs)$*$10(missing ratios) groups of experiments, in the $i * j^{th}$ group of experiment, we randomly select $j * 5\%$ of all the samples, set the ith AU of these samples as missing and then perform AU recognition experiments. The results are summarized in Fig. 4, and each subfigure shows the hamming loss or Macro F_1 score of the three method of one AU under 10 different missing ratios. From Fig. 4, we can conclude:

1. The image-driven method performs worst among the three methods. Since the label-based MacroF_1 score under all the missing ratios of all the 13 AUs with image-driven method are all much lower than those of model-based method and our method, and the hamming loss under all of the missing ratios of 8 AUs (including $AU4$, $AU5$, $AU6$, $AU7$, $AU12$, $AU24$, $AU25$ and $AU27$) with image-driven method are all much higher than those of model-based method and our method, while on the other 5 AUs, in most missing ratios, image-driven method performs worse than the other two methods. The reason may lie in two aspects, first, the image-driven method is trained on part of the training data where the samples with complete AU annotations are used, while ignoring the other samples with in-

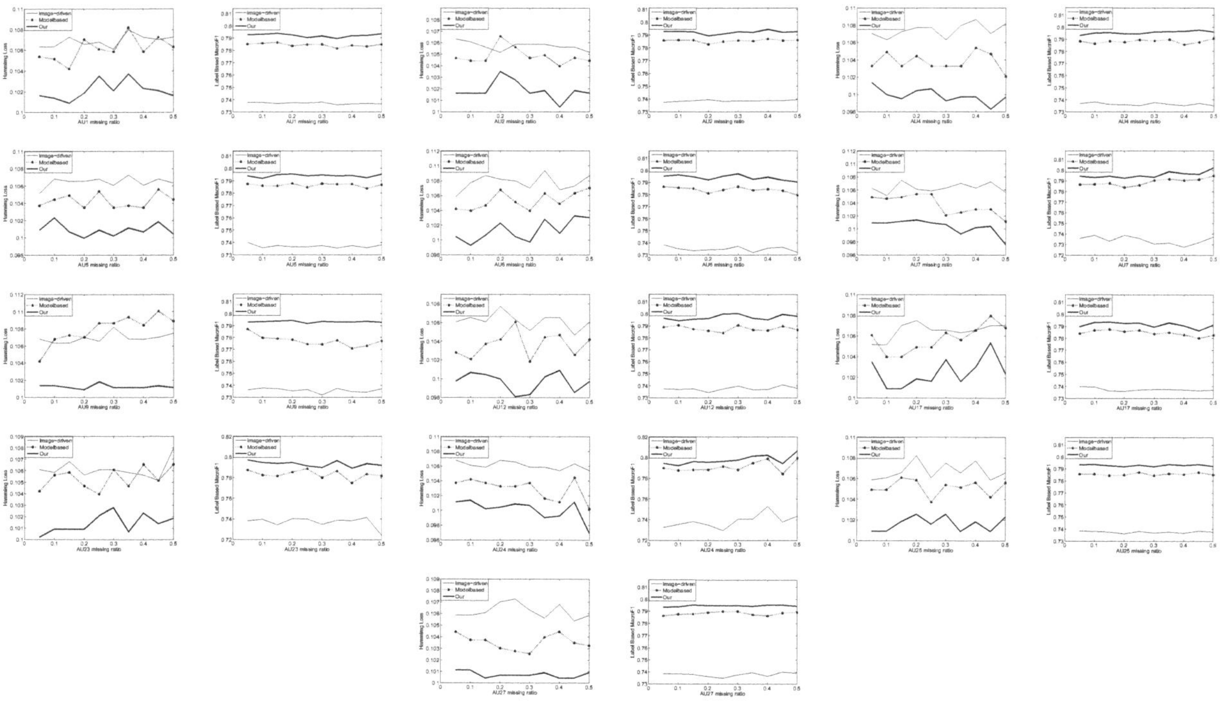

Figure 4: AU recognition results on CK+ database under 10 different missing proportions .

complete AU annotations, and second, image-driven method predicts each label independently, leaving the relations among labels out of account. Therefore, the results of image-driven method are obviously worse than the other two methods.

2. Our method considering both AUs' relations and AU-expression relations performs best of the three methods. Since for all of the missing ratios of all the 13 AUs, both the hamming loss and the label-based MacroF_1 score are better than those of image-driven method and model-based method. And the model-based method also outperforms the image-driven method significantly in most cases. It verifies that both the relations among the AUs and the relations between each AU and expression can apparently improve the multi-label recognition. In addition, we can obtain the conclusion that expressions can better help AU recognition with incomplete AU annotation than that considering the relations among AUs only, due to the higher performance of our method than the model-based method.

3. Although in most cases, both of our method and the model-based method clearly outperforms the image-driven method, our method performs totally better than the image-driven method, while in some cases, the model-based method performs worse than the image-driven method, especially considering the hamming loss of AU9(i.e., the 13rd subfigure in Fig. 4). Therefore, we can conclude that our method is more stable than the model-based method for different missing ratios and different AUs.

4.4 Comparison with related work

Although many studies have been done on AU recognition, and achieved good performance, only a few works exploit the dependencies among AUs. One representative work is Tong et al. [17], who propose to use a dynamic Bayesian network (DBN) to model the relationships among different AUs and their temporal evolutions for AU recognition and conduct the experiments on the CK database. Since they do not report the experimental results on CK+ database and their method utilize dynamic sequence, we can not compare with their work directly. However, the AU recognition considering AU relations only (i.e., the model-based method) is similar to Tong et al. [17]'s work, as shown in Fig. 3, so we use the model-based method as a reference of the method proposed by Tong et al.. From section 4.2, we can find that our proposed method using expression to assist AU recognition performs better than Tong et al. [17]'s work, when the AU annotation is complete.

There exists lots of AU recognition works that evaluate on CK+ databases. We report the comparison of the proposed method with six current works, which also use F_1 score as the evaluation metric, in Table 3. From the table, we can conclude: 1, for four AUs, including $AU1$, $AU2$, $AU9$ and $AU25$, the performance of our method is the best among the seven works; 2, our averaged F_1 score of all the AUs are not the best among the seven works, the reason is that different works perform experiments on different AUs and the recognition results of some AUs are too worse than the other, such as $AU24$. Therefore, we compare our method with others in another way, i.e., we compute the averaged F_1 score in terms of the AUs used in the other works. Considering the AUs of [7], our averaged F_1 score is 81.8, considering the AUs of [1] and [4], our averaged F_1 score is 82.1, considering the AUs of [23] and [22], our averaged F_1 score is 86.8, considering the AUs of [6], our averaged F_1 score is 83.8. From this

Table 3: Comparison with current image-driven works in terms of F_1 score

AUs	Ours	[7]	[1]	[4]	[23]	[22]	[6]
1	**94.5**	77.9	62.2	76.2	85.0	88.0	82.0
2	**93.5**	80.1	76.2	76.3	87.0	92.0	87.0
4	78.5	77.5	69.1	78.5	82.0	**89.0**	81.0
5	79.8	63.6					**81.0**
6	77.6	77.1	79.6	70.3	89.0	**93.0**	70.0
7	60.1	62.4	**79.1**	63.4			67.0
9	**91.1**	78.8					91.0
12	84.7	**90.0**	77.2	86.8	84.0	**90.0**	88.0
17	83.7	81.1	84.8	**85.9**	72.0	76.0	82.0
23	68.9						**76.0**
24	44.7	**60.1**					
25	**95.2**	88.2			75.0	73.0	90.0
27	97.7	**99.5**					94.0
avg	80.8	78.0	75.5	76.8	82.0	**85.9**	82.4

point of view, our method outperforms all these six works. It demonstrates that for complete AU annotation, our method outperforms the current AU recognition method.

For comparison with related works under incomplete AU annotation, we mainly compare with Tong's work. Since their method cannot handle incomplete multi-label recognition, so we extend Tong's model to handle incomplete data using EM algorithm as shown in Algorithm 1, where we also give detailed results in Fig. 4. Table 4 (where "Model" is short for "Model-based") shows the averaged recognition results of all the 13 AUs under 10 missing ratios on the CK+ database. From the results we can conclude that our model outperforms Tong's model, since under all of the 10 missing ratios, the averaged hamming loss value is lower than that of the model-based method and the averaged MacroF_1 score value is higher than that of the model-based method, and all of the standard deviation of our method are either equal to or less than those of the model-based method. It demonstrates once again that adding the expression label can improve AU recognition even under insufficient fully labeled AU data. Thus, our method outperforms the current model-based AU recognition for both complete and incomplete AU annotations.

4.5 Cross-database experiments

The right part named "cross database" in Table 2 and Table 5(where "Model" is short for "Model-based") show the cross-database AU recognition results under complete and incomplete AU annotations respectively, where the model is trained on the CK+ database and tested on the ISL database. From the two tables, we can obtain that the performance of the proposed method is better than that of the model-based method considering AU relations only for both complete and incomplete AU annotations, with lower hamming distance and higher MacroF_1 score. Our method performs more stably than the model-based method considering AU relations only, since our method has the lower standard deviation of the two parameters. Therefore, the cross-database experiments demonstrate the generalization ability and the robust of our method.

5. CONCLUSIONS

Current AU recognition requires complete AU annotations for training. However, the efforts for training human experts and manually scoring the AUs are expensive and time consuming. Furthermore, the reliability of manually AU annotation is inherently attenuated by the subjectivity of human coder, especially for the AUs that are difficult to label. In contrast, expressions are much easier to annotate with great accuracy. Therefore, we design an AU recognition method with the help of expression labels as hidden knowledge under incomplete AU labeling. We propose to construct a BN model to capture the dependencies not only among AUs but also between AUs and expressions. During training, the image features and expression labels are complete, while the AU labels may be missing. Structural EM is adopted to learn the structure and parameters of the BN. The traditional image-driven method is adopted to obtain the expression and AU measurements. During testing, the AUs are inferred by combining the measurements and the AU relations in the BN model. Both within database and cross-database experiments are conducted to compare our method with image-driven method and model-based method. The experimental results of within database show that our method outperforms state of art model-based AU recognition methods for both complete and incomplete AU annotations; The AU recognition assisted by expression performs better than the current image-driven method for complete AU annotations. The cross-database experimental results demonstrate that our method has better generalization ability and is more robust compared with current model-based and image-driven methods.

6. ACKNOWLEDGMENTS

This paper is supported by the NSFC (61175037, 61228304, 61473270).

7. REFERENCES

[1] W.-S. Chu, F. D. L. Torre, and J. F. Cohn. Selective transfer machine for personalized facial action unit detection. In *Computer Vision and Pattern Recognition (CVPR), 2013 IEEE Conference on*, pages 3515–3522. IEEE, 2013.

[2] C. P. de Campos and Q. Ji. Efficient structure learning of bayesian networks using constraints. *Journal of Machine Learning Research*, 12(3):663–689, 2011.

[3] P. Ekman and W. V. Friesen. Facial action coding system: A technique for the measurement of facial movement. palo alto. *CA: Consulting Psychologists Press. Ellsworth, PC, & Smith, CA (1988). From appraisal to emotion: Differences among unpleasant feelings. Motivation and Emotion*, 12:271–302, 1978.

[4] X. D. W.-S. C. Fernando, F. De la Torre2 Jeffery, and Q. Wang. Facial action unit detection by cascade of tasks.

[5] Q. Ji. Rpi intelligent systems lab (isl) image databases. `http://www.ecse.rpi.edu/homepages/cvrl/database/database.html`.

[6] M. Khademi and L.-P. Morency. Relative facial action unit detection. In *Applications of Computer Vision (WACV), 2014 IEEE Winter Conference on*, pages 1090–1095. IEEE, 2014.

[7] Y. Li, S. Wang, Y. Zhao, and Q. Ji. Simultaneous facial feature tracking and facial expression recognition. *Image Processing, IEEE Transactions on*, 22(7):2559–2573, 2013.

Table 4: Averaged recognition results on the CK+ database under 10 missing ratios

Missing ratio		5%	10%	15%	20%	25%	30%	35%	40%	45%	50%
Hamming	Model	0.1044 (0.001)	0.1045 (0.001)	0.1047 (0.001)	0.1051 (0.001)	0.1050 (0.002)	0.1045 (0.002)	0.1049 (0.002)	0.1050 (0.002)	0.1054 (0.002)	0.1047 (0.003)
	Ours	**0.1012** (0.001)	**0.1010** (0.001)	**0.1008** (0.001)	**0.1013** (0.001)	**0.1012 (0.001)**	**0.1010** (0.002)	**0.1010 (0.001)**	**0.1010 (0.001)**	**0.1013** (0.002)	**0.1007 (0.002)**
F_1	Model	0.7868 (0.002)	0.7859 (0.003)	0.7858 (0.003)	0.7849 (0.003)	0.7858 (0.004)	0.7858 (0.005)	0.7859 (0.005)	0.7849 (0.006)	0.7845 (0.005)	0.7863 (0.007)
	Ours	**0.7938** (0.002)	**0.7936 (0.001)**	**0.7943 (0.001)**	**0.7936 (0.002)**	**0.7938 (0.003)**	**0.7941 (0.003)**	**0.7948 (0.003)**	**0.7944 (0.003)**	**0.7937 (0.003)**	**0.7952 (0.005)**

Table 5: Averaged cross database recognition results on ISL database under 10 missing ratios

Missing ratio		5%	10%	15%	20%	25%	30%	35%	40%	45%	50%
Hamming	Model	0.1004 (0.003)	0.0995 (0.006)	0.0997 (0.005)	0.1000 (0.006)	0.1022 (0.004)	0.1011 (0.004)	0.1019 (0.006)	0.0997 (0.008)	0.1032 (0.005)	0.1022 (0.005)
	Ours	**0.0975 (0.001)**	**0.0984 (0.002)**	**0.0978 (0.002)**	**0.0985 (0.004)**	**0.0988** (0.004)	**0.0976 (0.002)**	**0.0995 (0.005)**	**0.0980 (0.003)**	**0.0975 (0.004)**	**0.0979 (0.003)**
F_1	Model	0.8434 (0.004)	0.8427 (0.011)	0.8404 (0.010)	0.8404 (0.007)	0.8360 (0.009)	0.8375 (0.008)	0.8342 (0.013)	0.8386 (0.009)	0.8330 (0.009)	0.8340 (0.010)
	Ours	**0.8453 (0.002)**	**0.8437 (0.004)**	**0.8448 (0.004)**	**0.8439 (0.006)**	**0.8416 (0.008)**	**0.8439 (0.004)**	**0.8410 (0.008)**	**0.8444 (0.006)**	**0.8431 (0.008)**	**0.8434 (0.005)**

[8] G. Littlewort, J. Whitehill, T. Wu, I. Fasel, M. Frank, J. Movellan, and M. Bartlett. The computer expression recognition toolbox (cert). In *Automatic Face & Gesture Recognition and Workshops (FG 2011), 2011 IEEE International Conference on*, pages 298–305. IEEE, 2011.

[9] P. Lucey, J. F. Cohn, T. Kanade, J. Saragih, Z. Ambadar, and I. Matthews. The extended cohn-kanade dataset (ck+): A complete dataset for action unit and emotion-specified expression. In *Computer Vision and Pattern Recognition Workshops (CVPRW), 2010 IEEE Computer Society Conference on*, pages 94–101. IEEE, 2010.

[10] S. Lucey, A. B. Ashraf, and J. Cohn. Investigating spontaneous facial action recognition through aam representations of the face. *Face recognition*, pages 275–286, 2007.

[11] M. Pantic and L. J. Rothkrantz. Expert system for automatic analysis of facial expressions. *Image and Vision Computing*, 18(11):881–905, 2000.

[12] J. Pearl. *Probabilistic reasoning in intelligent systems: networks of plausible inference.* Morgan Kaufmann, 1988.

[13] A. M. Rahman, M. I. Tanveer, and M. Yeasin. A spatio-temporal probabilistic framework for dividing and predicting facial action units. In *Affective Computing and Intelligent Interaction*, pages 598–607. Springer, 2011.

[14] M. S. Sorower. A literature survey on algorithms for multi-label learning. Technical report, Technical report, Oregon State University, Corvallis, OR, USA (December 2010), 2010.

[15] Y. Tong, J. Chen, and Q. Ji. A unified probabilistic framework for spontaneous facial action modeling and understanding. *Pattern Analysis and Machine Intelligence, IEEE Transactions on*, 32(2):258–273, 2010.

[16] Y. Tong, W. Liao, and Q. Ji. Inferring facial action units with causal relations. In *Computer Vision and Pattern Recognition, 2006 IEEE Computer Society Conference on*, volume 2, pages 1623–1630. IEEE, 2006.

[17] Y. Tong, W. Liao, and Q. Ji. Facial action unit recognition by exploiting their dynamic and semantic relationships. *Pattern Analysis and Machine Intelligence, IEEE Transactions on*, 29(10):1683–1699, 2007.

[18] M. F. Valstar and M. Pantic. Fully automatic recognition of the temporal phases of facial actions. *Systems, Man, and Cybernetics, Part B: Cybernetics, IEEE Transactions on*, 42(1):28–43, 2012.

[19] L. van der Maaten and E. Hendriks. Action unit classification using active appearance models and conditional random fields. *Cognitive processing*, 13(2):507–518, 2012.

[20] S. Velusamy, H. Kannan, B. Anand, A. Sharma, and B. Navathe. A method to infer emotions from facial action units. In *Acoustics, Speech and Signal Processing (ICASSP), 2011 IEEE International Conference on*, pages 2028–2031. IEEE, 2011.

[21] Z. Zeng, M. Pantic, G. I. Roisman, and T. S. Huang. A survey of affect recognition methods: Audio, visual, and spontaneous expressions. *Pattern Analysis and Machine Intelligence, IEEE Transactions on*, 31(1):39–58, 2009.

[22] X. Zhang, M. H. Mahoor, S. M. Mavadati, and J. F. Cohn. A l p-norm mtmkl framework for simultaneous detection of multiple facial action units. In *Applications of Computer Vision (WACV), 2014 IEEE Winter Conference on*, pages 1104–1111. IEEE, 2014.

[23] X. Zhang, M. H. Mahoor, and R. D. Nielsen. On multi-task learning for facial action unit detection. In *Image and Vision Computing, 2013 28th International Conference on*, pages 202–207. IEEE, 2013.

[24] Y. Zhang and Q. Ji. Active and dynamic information fusion for facial expression understanding from image sequences. *Pattern Analysis and Machine Intelligence, IEEE Transactions on*, 27(5):699–714, 2005.

Extracting 3D Trajectories of Objects from 2D Videos using Particle Filter

Zeyd Boukhers, Kimiaki Shirahama, Frédéric Li, and Marcin Grzegorzek
Research Group for Pattern Recognition, University of Siegen
Hoelderlinstr. 3, D-57076, Siegen, Germany
{zeyd.boukhers,kimiaki.shirahama,marcin.grzegorzek}@uni-siegen.de
frederic.li@ensta-paristech.fr

ABSTRACT

Depth estimation is a method to estimate the depth information in a 2D image/video, where the original 3D space is projected onto an image plane. This paper introduces a novel extension of depth estimation in the video domain, where we extract *3D trajectories* which individually represent the transition of an object in the 3D space. Such 3D trajectories are useful for appropriately characterising spatio-temporal object relations for video event detection. While we extract 3D trajectories by combining depth estimation and object detection results, the major problem is the inconsistency between these results. For example, significantly different depths may be estimated for the region of the same object, and an object region that is appropriately shaped by estimated depths may be missed. To overcome this, we first initialise the 3D position of an object using the frame with the highest consistency between the depth estimation and object detection results. Then, we track the object in the 3D space using *particle filter*, where a 3D position of the object is modelled as a hidden state to generate its 2D visual appearance. Experimental results demonstrate the effectiveness of our method.

Categories and Subject Descriptors

I.2.10 [**Vision and Scene Understanding**]: Video analysis; I.4.8 [**Computing Methodologies**]: Scene Analysis

General Terms

Algorithms, Performance, Experimentation

Keywords

3D trajectory extraction; Depth estimation; Object detection; Particle filter; Event detection

1. INTRODUCTION

ICMR '15, June 23 - 26, 2015, Shanghai, China
Copyright 2015 ACM 978-1-4503-3274-3/15/06 ...$15.00
http://dx.doi.org/10.1145/2671188.2749331 .

The most fundamental issue in video retrieval is to detect various semantic meanings in videos. Recently, accurate detection of certain objects has been made possible by building detectors with a large amount of training videos. In particular, some prominent worldwide competitions on object detection like ILSVRC [26] and TRECVID [35] are promoting the performance improvement. Thanks to the progress on object detection, the video retrieval community has started to explore ways of how to extract high-level *events* from detectable objects [13, 35]. An event is derived from the interaction of multiple objects at a specific place and time. The detection of such events requires to capture the spatio-temporal relation among objects in a video.

However, a video only displays the 2D information and does not hold the depth information in the original 3D space. For example, a 2D video (or frame) just shows that regions of a person and a table are overlapping even though the former stands in front of the latter. Additionally, a ball kicked hard and far by a football player may still overlap with the player's 2D region. Despite the facts described above, existing event detection methods [13, 20, 24] analyse spatio-temporal relations among objects in 2D videos.

In contrast, humans can easily recognise the depth information in a video. This inspires researchers to develop *depth estimation* methods which estimate depths in 2D videos (or images) [11, 14, 15, 30, 31]. These methods estimate depths in an unseen video by referring to depths in visually similar training videos, where the depth of each pixel is annotated (recorded) with a depth sensor like Kinect. This paper introduces a novel extension of depth estimation, where it is combined with object detection in order to extract *3D trajectories* of objects from 2D videos. Each trajectory represents the transition of an object's positions in the 3D space. We believe that 3D trajectories extracted by our method offer a new means to overcome the long-standing 'semantic gap' problem between physical video representations and semantic events [36].

Fig. 1 illustrates our 3D trajectory extraction. The images at the left show object detection results where detected regions are depicted by coloured rectangles. The images at the centre present depth estimation results where pixels are coloured depending on the estimated depths. The major challenge is the way of how to combine 'inconsistent' object detection and depth estimation results, in order to extract a 3D trajectory which represents the 'consistent' transition of an object's 3D positions. The comparison between object detection and depth estimation results in Fig. 1 reveals that detected regions of persons contain significantly differ-

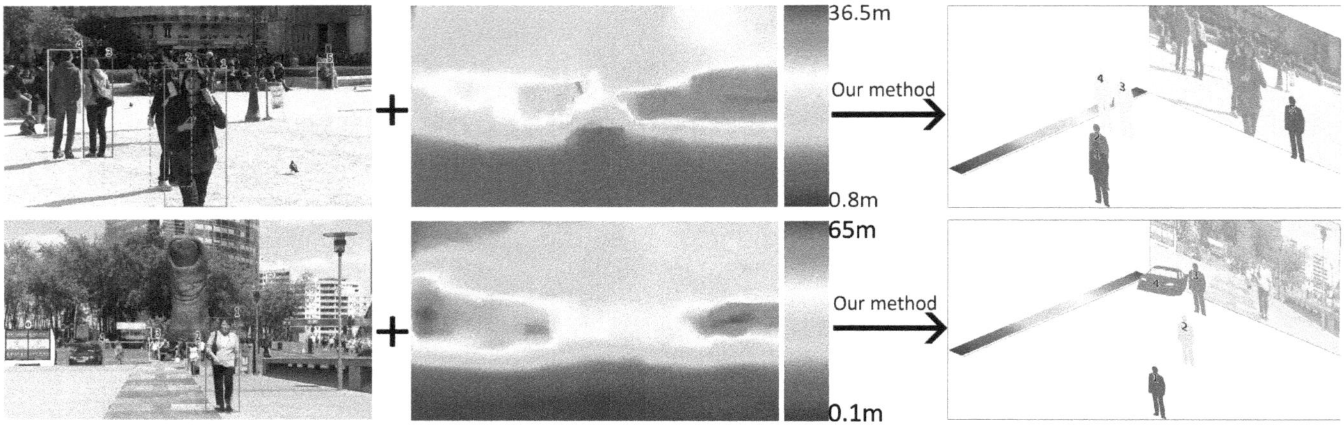

Figure 1: An illustration of our 3D trajectory extraction based on the combination of object detection and depth estimation.

ent depths, although the region of the same object should have similar depths. In addition, the region of an object may be missing even though estimated depths have appropriately characterised that region. Moreover, results of object detection or depth estimation may be temporally inconsistent if it is applied to each frame independently.

To appropriately extract 3D trajectories, we first select the frame with the highest consistency between the object detection and depth estimation results. Then, we use these results to initialise the 3D position of each object, and track that object in the 3D space. Fig. 2 shows an overview of our 3D trajectory extraction method. It begins with performing object detection and depth estimation on each frame in a video. The method subsequently selects the frame with the highest consistency between the object detection and depth estimation results, by assuming that depths should be similar within the region of each object, and their transition should occur on boundaries between object regions. For each object detected in the selected frame, we define its 3D position in the 'temporal' coordinates where the horizontal and vertical positions are based on the image coordinates, and the depth represents the distance between the object and the camera in the camera coordinates.

After that, we track each object in the 3D space using *particle filter*, which is a time-series modelling approach by approximating the probability distribution of a hidden state with random samples (particles) [1]. The main idea is to represent the object's 3D position for each frame as the hidden state. Particle filter enables us to flexibly approximate the non-linear probability distribution of the hidden state based only on minimal assumptions. For each frame, we regard the object's 3D position as the one which is the most likely to be observed based on the approximated probability distribution. Finally, we form the 3D trajectory of the object by transforming estimated 3D positions in the temporal coordinates into the ones in the camera coordinates.

2. RELATED WORK

We describe the novelties of our method by reviewing existing methods in the four related categories:

1. 3D video analysis: Methods in this category exploit 3D (RGB-D) videos captured by depth sensors or multi-view cameras, in order to enhance the detection of semantic meanings. Han *et al.* review the recent developments of Kinect technologies showing the utility in object track-

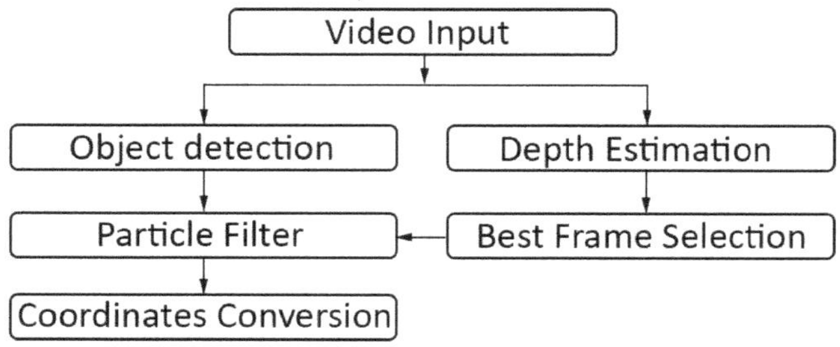

Figure 2: An overview of our 3D trajectory extraction method.

ing and recognition, human activity analysis, hand gesture recognition and indoor 3D mapping [9]. Hadfield *et al.* extend spatio-temporal local feature extraction (including region detection and description) to encode the depth information in commercial 3D movies [8]. Wei *et al.* propose a method which jointly performs object and event detection for RGB-D videos captured by Kinect [38]. The method is based on a 4D human-object interaction model consisting of the 3D spatial and the 1D temporal domains.

The major disadvantage of the above mentioned methods is the assumption of the availability of 3D videos, because usual videos do not involve the depth information. In contrast, our method can extract 3D trajectories directly from 2D videos. Also, Kinect has several restrictions, such as that it can only be used indoors and the maximum measurable depth is five meters. Compared to this, depth estimation discussed below uses training 3D videos captured by a high-performance 3D scanner, which can be used in both indoor and outdoor situations and measure depths up to 81 meters [14, 30]. This allows us to extract 3D trajectories with a wide range of depths, irrespective of whether videos are taken indoors or outdoors.

2. Depth estimation: Several methods have been developed to estimate depths from 2D images/videos. Saxena *et al.* propose a method which estimates depths in an image using Markov random field, where the depth of a small patch is estimated by considering its feature and relative depths of nearby patches [30, 31]. Karsch *et al.* develop a method which first selects visually similar training images to an input image (or frame) [14, 15]. Then, depths in each of these training images are transferred to the input image by extracting corresponding points between these images. Additionally, depth estimation for videos is improved by using optical flows and discriminating between moving and static objects. Hoiem *et al.* propose a method which estimates depths in an image based on hierarchical image segmentation [11]. As regions are merged into more coherent ones, each region is associated with a more accurate depth based on regions corresponding to the ground and the occlusion relation among regions.

So far, depth estimation has been applied for the creation of a 3D model from a single image [30, 31], the conversion of 2D videos into 3D [14, 15], and the detection of the occlusion relation among objects [11]. This paper is the first to apply depth estimation for the extraction of 3D trajectories. Especially, depth estimation is not stable from one frame to another and from one object to another. We overcome this by firstly selecting the frame with the highest consistency between object detection and depth estimation, and then tracking objects in this frame with particle filter.

3. 3D trajectory extraction: Existing methods for extracting 3D trajectories from videos can be classified into three types, 'multi-cue', 'knowledge-based', and 'mapping-based'. Multi-cue methods localise an object in the 3D space by fusing different views of the scene from multiple cameras [7, 27] or additionally using a depth sensor [33]. Knowledge-based methods use laws of physics [29] or kinematics [3] as constraints for appropriate 3D localisation of objects. Mapping-based methods assume that some camera parameters (e.g., focal length and projection matrix) are known, based on which the position of an object is transformed from 2D to 3D [25, 40].

Compared to multi-cue methods, our method extracts 3D trajectories from videos without any special device. Knowledge-based methods lack the generality because the tracking mechanism needs to be tuned for each object. In contrast, our method is general in the sense that it can adopt any object detection method. In other words, with no modification, 3D trajectories for various objects can be extracted by adopting large-scale object detection methods, which are developed and being improved on annual worldwide competitions [26, 35]. Finally, mapping-based methods can be used only for limited number of videos because of the assumption of camera parameters. As far as we know, object detection in mapping-based methods [25, 40] is based on background subtraction, which further limits the practical utility. Compared to these methods, our method can extract 3D trajectories from a much larger variety of videos because depth estimation bypasses the assumption of camera parameters, and we use robust object detectors built with a large amount of training data.

4. Particle filter: In the computer vision field, particle filter has been extensively explored because of its simplicity, flexibility and extensibility to approximate non-linear probability distributions of hidden states. From the methodological point of view, particle filter is extended to approximate a mixture of probability distributions of hidden states [37], to use a discriminative classifier for modelling state transitions [23], to incorporate a Markov random field prior into state transitions [17], to approximate the probability distribution of a hidden state based on the cascade of off-line and on-line trained classifiers [21], and to optimise filter parameters using training samples [10]. From the perspective of applications, particle filter is mainly used for object tracking in 2D videos [10, 17, 21, 23, 37] and 3D (RGB-D) videos [4, 7, 28]. Other applications in computer vision are image segmentation [5], image denoising [2], video decoding [19] and shape correspondence extraction [18].

This paper introduces the first application of particle filter to 3D trajectory extraction. In particular, we demonstrate that 3D trajectories can be appropriately extracted even with a basic particle filter approach [1]. The improvement of our method is possible by adopting methodologically more sophisticated particle filter approaches described above.

3. 3D TRAJECTORY EXTRACTION

In this section, we explain our 3D trajectory extraction method consisting of five steps shown in Fig. 2.

3.1 Object Detection and Depth Estimation

We first estimate depths in all frames of a video then we detect objects only in the best frame selected in Section 3.2. For depth estimation, we use the method developed in [14] according to the reported performance comparison[1] and our actual preliminary experiment. Given a frame, this method transfers depths in visually similar training images based on corresponding points between the frame and these training images. The output is the 'depth map' which represents the estimated depth of each pixel in the frame. In the subsequent steps, we use detected regions of objects and depth maps. For object detection, we use the method proposed in [6] because of its generality and effectiveness proven in many existing works. Given a frame, the method detects a region of an object by considering positions and deformations of parts, where each part is defined as a filter to capture its shape. As a result, one or more rectangular regions (bounding boxes) in which the object is regarded as present, are located in the frame. Besides such regions representing the whole object, the method outputs smaller regions which represent the locations of parts (we use these part regions only for small tuning of our 3D trajectory extraction method).

3.2 Best Frame Selection

For a frame where the object detection and depth estimation results are highly consistent, we assume that the depth map has a smooth continuity of depths in regions defined by edges, and a large difference of depths between regions separated by edges. Based on this, we compute the *Depth Consistency Score* (DCS) of the tth frame f_t in a video. Let A_t and C_t be the depth map and the edge map for f_t, respectively. Here, C_t is obtained by applying Canny edge detector to f_t. We compute f_t's DCS, $S(f_t)$, by considering the spatial continuity of depths in A_t, with the exception that depths are discontinuous on edges in C_t. This is formulated as follows:

$$S(f_t) = \frac{S_1(f_t)}{\sum_{l=1}^{L} S_1(f_l)} + \frac{\sum_{l=1}^{L} S_2(f_l)}{S_2(f_t)}, \qquad (1)$$

where L is the number of frames in the video. For the first term, $S_1(f_t)$ considers the spatial continuity of depths in non-edge regions. It is computed as follows:

$$S_1(f_t) = \frac{1}{\sum_{i=1}^{W} \sum_{j=1}^{H} C_t(i,j)} \sum_{i=1}^{W} \sum_{j=1}^{H} C_t(i,j) V_t(i,j), \qquad (2)$$

[1] http://make3d.cs.cornell.edu/results_stateoftheart.html

where $C_t(i,j)$ is 1 if the pixel at the position (i,j) is regarded as non-edge, otherwise $C_t(i,j) = 0$. W and H represent the width and height of f_t, respectively. $V_t(i,j)$ represents the continuity of depths at (i,j) using the following difference:

$$V_t(i,j) = \max_{\substack{i-1 \leqslant m,m' \leqslant i+1 \\ j-1 \leqslant n,n' \leqslant j+1}} |A_t(m,n) - A_t(m',n')|, \quad (3)$$

where we calculate the maximum depth difference within the 3-by-3 region centred at (i,j). That is, $S_1(f_t)$ represents the mean of $V_t(i,j)$ in non-edge pixels. Similarly, to consider the discontinuity of depths, $S_2(\lambda_t)$ representing the mean of $V_t(i,j)$ in edge pixels is computed on C'_t. It is the inverse of C_t where $C'_t(i,j) = 1$ if the pixel at (i,j) is regarded as edge, otherwise $C'_t(i,j) = 0$.

$$S_2(f_t) = \frac{1}{\sum_{i=1}^{W}\sum_{j=1}^{H} C'_t(i,j)} \sum_{i=1}^{W}\sum_{j=1}^{H} C'_t(i,j) V_t(i,j). \quad (4)$$

Finally, we select the best frame with the highest $S(f_t)$ among all frames in the video. Then, we calculate the depth of each detected object in the best frame as the mean of depths in its parts. In this way, we can obtain the 3D position of the object in the best frame.

3.3 Particle Filter

For an object detected in the best frame f_0 in a video, let $\mathbf{q}_0 = (x_0, y_0, \alpha_0, \beta_0, z_0)$ be its 3D position in the 'temporal' coordinates. Here, (x_0, y_0) represent the top-left position of the object's region with the width α_0 and the height β_0 in the image coordinates. z_0 indicates the depth representing the distance between the object and the camera in the camera coordinates. We denote by $f_0(\mathbf{q}_0)$ the visual appearance of the object's region in f_0 (z_0 is not related to $f_0(\mathbf{q}_0)$). Starting with $\mathbf{q}_0$, we estimate the object's 3D position $\mathbf{q}_t = (x_t, y_t, \alpha_t, \beta_t, z_t)$ in the tth frame.

Given a sequence of observations, particle filter approximates the posterior probability distribution of a hidden state using a set of *particles*, which are weighted random samples of the hidden state. We consider $\mathbf{q}_t$ as a hidden state and $f_t(\mathbf{q}_t)_{0:t} = (f_0(\mathbf{q}_0), \cdots, f_t(\mathbf{q}_t))$ as the sequence of observed visual appearances of the object's region from the best to the tth frames. Using particle filter, we approximate the following posterior probability distribution:

$$p(\mathbf{q}_t | f_t(\mathbf{q}_t)_{0:t}) \approx \sum_{i=1}^{N} w_t^i \, \delta(\mathbf{q}_t - \mathbf{q}_t^i), \quad (5)$$

where N is the number of particles and $\delta(.)$ is the Dirac delta function. The ith particle is represented by the pair $\{\mathbf{q}_t^i, w_t^i\}$ where $\mathbf{q}_t^i$ is the ith random sample for $\mathbf{q}_t$, and w_t^i is the weight representing the probability of $\mathbf{q}_t^i$ ($\sum_{i=1}^{N} w_t^i = 1$). In other words, $p(\mathbf{q}_t | f_t(\mathbf{q}_t)_{0:t})$ is approximated by N (discrete) grids corresponding to $\mathbf{q}_t^i$s. We regard $\mathbf{q}_t^i$ with the highest probability as the estimation of the object's 3D position for the tth frame, and use it as $\mathbf{q}_t$ in the subsequent process.

According to the framework of particle filter [1], we approximate $p(\mathbf{q}_t | f_t(\mathbf{q}_t)_{0:t})$ for all frames in the video by iterating the following three processes:

1. Prediction: Given $\mathbf{q}_{t-1}$ estimated for the $(t-1)$th frame, we draw $\mathbf{q}_t^i$ for the tth frame from the transition (prior) distribution $p(\mathbf{q}_t | \mathbf{q}_{t-1})$. In Section 3.3.1, we model this based on the velocity of the object's 3D position.

2. Update: This process determines the weight w_t^i for $\mathbf{q}_t^i$ by computing the probability $p(f_t(\mathbf{q}_t^i) | \mathbf{q}_t^i)$ which represents the suitability of $f_t(\mathbf{q}_t^i)$ as the object's region. As a result, the ith particle $\{\mathbf{q}_t^i, w_t^i\}$ is formed and the posterior distribution in Equation (5) is updated. In Section 3.3.2, we assume that $f_0(\mathbf{q}_0)$ correctly represents the object's region, and compute $p(f_t(\mathbf{q}_t^i) | \mathbf{q}_t^i)$ by extracting the correspondence points between $f_t(\mathbf{q}_t^i)$ and $f_0(\mathbf{q}_0)$.

3. Resampling: To avoid the degeneracy problem that all but one particle get negligible weights, this process samples N particles based on the distribution obtained in the update process, where each particle is tuned so as to have the same weight $1/N$ [1]. Considering our preliminary experimental result and the computational efficiency, we only sample the particle with the highest weight, and regard the corresponding $\mathbf{q}_t^i$ as the estimated object's 3D position $\mathbf{q}_t$. In the prediction process for the $(t+1)$th frame, N particles are drawn from the transition distribution created based on $\mathbf{q}_t$.

3.3.1 *Modelling a Transition Distribution*

We model the transition distribution $p(\mathbf{q}_t | \mathbf{q}_{t-1})$ based on the first-order AutoRegressive (AR) process. Let v_t^x, v_t^y and v_t^z be the displacements of an object between the $(t-1)$th and tth frames on the x, y and z axes, receptively. At the beginning, we initialise $v_0^x = W/6$, $v_0^y = H/6$, and $v_0^z = 2 \times 10^2$mm for slow objects like persons, and $v_0^z = 2 \times 10^4$mm for fast objects like cars. For the tth frame, we select N samples ($\{\mathbf{q}_t^i\}_{i=1}^N$) from $p(\mathbf{q}_t | \mathbf{q}_{t-1})$, created based on the object's 3D position $(x_{t-1}, y_{t-1}, z_{t-1})$ and displacements $(v_{t-1}^x, v_{t-1}^y, v_{t-1}^z)$ for the $(t-1)$th frame. For accurate tracking, N samples need to adequately cover the whole of $p(\mathbf{q}_t | \mathbf{q}_{t-1})$ (i.e., all possible regions which may contain the object). However, this requires a large number of samples and thus a high computational cost. Hence, we strategically collect a small number of samples which capture the overall characteristic of $p(\mathbf{q}_t | \mathbf{q}_{t-1})$.

We respectively divide the x, y and z axes into a_x, a_y and a_z discrete values, so that $N = a^x \cdot a^y \cdot a^z + r$ where $|v^x/a^x| \approx |v^y/a^y| \approx |v^z/10a^z|$. Intuitively, the number of discrete values on each axis is proportional to the displacement, and N samples are formed as combinations of discrete values for all axes. By assuming that the object maintains its velocity, for each axis, we densely locate discrete values around two positions, which are determined as the previous position plus/minus the displacement (e.g., $x_{t-1} \pm |v_{t-1}^x|$ for the x axis). This is a simple approximation of the mixture of two Gaussian distributions (see Fig. 3). In addition to the above mentioned $a^x \cdot a^y \cdot a^z$ samples, we randomly select the remaining r samples. Fig. 3 illustrates a 2D view of N selected samples where blue points represent samples that are systematically sampled by combining a^x, a^y and a^z discrete values, contrary to red points that are random samples. Finally, we now have x_t^i, y_t^i and z_t^i of each sample $\mathbf{q}_t^i$. We determine α_t^i and β_t^i of $\mathbf{q}_t^i$ by linearly scaling α_0 and β_0 of $\mathbf{q}_0$ based on the inverse ratio of z_t^i to z_0 (i.e., $\alpha_t^i = \alpha_0 \cdot z_0 / z_t^i$ and $\beta_t^i = \beta_0 \cdot z_0 / z_t^i$).

3.3.2 *Weight computation*

To form the particle $\{\mathbf{q}_t^i, w_t^i\}$, we calculate the weight w_t^i as the similarity between the visual appearance of $\mathbf{q}_t^i$ ($f_t(\mathbf{q}_t^i)$) and that of the reference region $\mathbf{q}_0$ ($f_0(\mathbf{q}_0)$). An object can have visually different appearances depending on its direction, shape deformation, illumination change etc., and its rectangular region often includes the background. To ro-

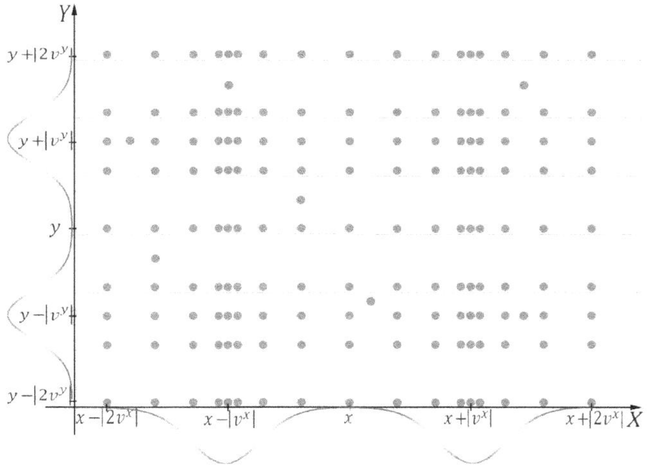

Figure 3: A 2D view of N selected samples.

bustly align such regions in the whole video sequence, we use *SIFT flow* which produces the dense, pixel-to-pixel correspondence between $f_t(\mathbf{q}_t^i)$ and $f_0(\mathbf{q}_0)$ [22]. Based on the computational framework of optical flow, SIFT flow matches SIFT descriptors instead of raw pixels. The idea is to extract the SIFT descriptor at each pixel to characterise the local image structure and encode the contextual information. Then, the discrete discontinuity preserving flow estimation algorithm is used to match SIFT descriptors between $f_t(\mathbf{q}_t^i)$ and $f_0(\mathbf{q}_0)$.

Fig. 4 illustrates the process of matching $f_t(\mathbf{q}_t^i)$ with $f_0(\mathbf{q}_0)$ using SIFT flow. Because of the movement of the object in the z axis, its region becomes larger or smaller. Thus, as shown in Fig. 4, we first resize the region defined by $\mathbf{q}_t^i$ to the same size as the one defined by $\mathbf{q}_0$. Then, as the result of matching $f_t(\mathbf{q}_t^i)$ with $f_0(\mathbf{q}_0)$, we obtain the energy $E(f_t(\mathbf{q}_t^i), f_0(\mathbf{q}_0))$ which represents a pixel displacement field. Fig. 4 shows that pixels ($\circ$) in $f_0(\mathbf{q}_0)$ are regarded as corresponding to pixels ($+$) in $f_t(\mathbf{q}_t^i)$. Here, $f_t(\mathbf{q}_t^3)$ is judged as the most similar to $f_0(\mathbf{q}_0)$ because of the smallest energy, which is based on the sum of line lengths between $\circ$s and $+$s with the same colours. Using such an energy, we measure the similarity between $f_t(\mathbf{q}_t^i)$ and $f_0(\mathbf{q}_0)$ as $1/E(f_t(\mathbf{q}_t^i), f_0(\mathbf{q}_0))$, and use it as the particle's weight w_t^i.

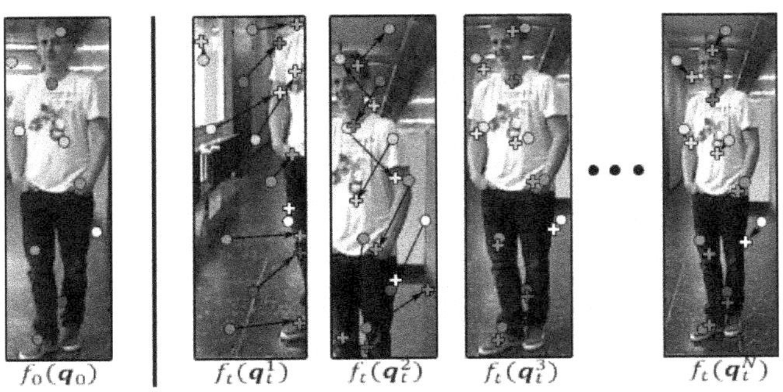

Figure 4: An illustration of the SIFT flow matching.

Let w_t be the maximum weight among those of N particles. The corresponding $\mathbf{q}_t^i$ is used as the object's 3D position $\mathbf{q}_t$ for the tth frame. Because the appearance of the object may significantly change according to the development of the video, we update $f_0(\mathbf{q}_0)$ to adaptively follow the latest appearance of the object. For this, we calculate $\psi_t = w_t / \max\{w_l\}_{l=1}^{t}$ where the denominator is used to normalise w_t using the maximum weight among all weights computed before. We update $f_0(\mathbf{q}_0)$ with $f_t(\mathbf{q}_t)$ if ψ_t is more than the threshold (0.8 in our experiments). This is because the high similarity between $f_0(\mathbf{q}_0)$ and $f_t(\mathbf{q}_t)$ expresses that $\mathbf{q}_t$ reliably shows the object. Conversely, the low similarity between $f_0(\mathbf{q}_0)$ and $f_t(\mathbf{q}_t)$ indicates that the estimated $\mathbf{q}_t$ is not so reliable. Hence, we check whether ψ is smaller than another threshold (0.3 in our experiments). If this is the case, we consider $\mathbf{q}_t$ as unreliable and set the displacement (v_t^x, v_t^y, v_t^z) to $(2v_{t-1}^x, 2v_{t-1}^y, 2v_{t-1}^z)$. This means not only that we do not use the unreliable $\mathbf{q}_t$ to compute the displacement, but also that the 3D position for the $(t+1)$th is searched in a larger region.

3.4 Coordinate conversion

For each object, we now have its 3D positions estimated for all frames in the video. However, each of these positions (x, y, z) is in the temporal coordinates where x and y are defined in the image coordinates shown in the left side of Fig. 5, and z is the distance between the camera and the object depicted in the right side. According to geometrical optic rules [16], we convert (x, y, z) into (x', y', z') in the camera coordinates where the origin is at the centre of the camera, as shown in Fig. 5.

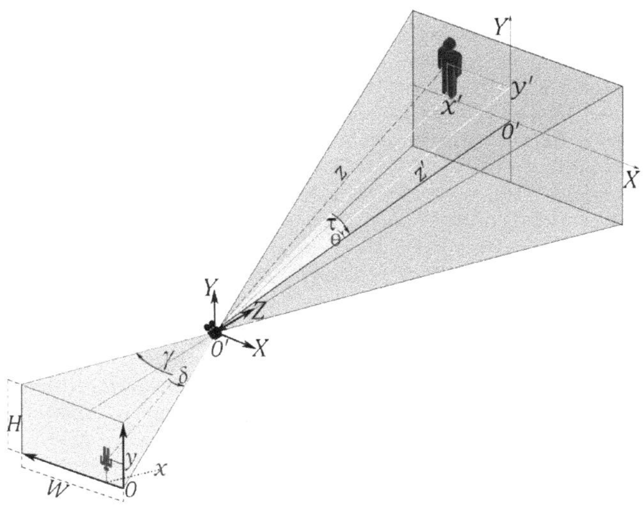

Figure 5: A standard optical geometry system.

Since cameras provide images with different aspect ratios, we calculate the horizontal and vertical angle of view γ and δ based on the default angles of view $\gamma' = 60°$ and $\delta' = 45°$ with the aspect ratio (3:4) as follow:

$$\begin{cases} \gamma = \gamma', \delta = \delta' & \text{if } \frac{W}{H} \simeq 1.333 \\ \gamma = \gamma', \delta = 2\arctan\left(\frac{1.333h\tan(\frac{\delta'}{2})}{W}\right) & \text{if } \frac{W}{H} > 1.333 \\ \gamma = 2\arctan\left(\frac{W\tan(\frac{\gamma'}{2})}{1.333H}\right), \delta = \delta' & \text{if } \frac{W}{H} < 1.333 \end{cases} \quad (6)$$

where we consider that the maximum horizontal and vertical angles of view for a normal camera do not exceed γ' and δ' respectively, and they vary according to the aspect ratio. Given γ and δ, we calculate the angles τ and θ which are formed by the axis OZ and the vector Ox', and OZ and

Oy', respectively (see Fig. 5):

$$\begin{cases} \tau = \arctan(\frac{2(x-\frac{W}{2})\tan(\frac{\gamma}{2})}{W}). \\ \theta = \arctan(\frac{2(y-\frac{H}{2})\tan(\frac{\delta}{2})}{H}). \end{cases} \quad (7)$$

Then, the object's 3D position (x, y, z) in the camera coordinates can be calculated as $x' = \sin(\tau)z$, $y' = \sin(\theta)z$ and $z' = \cos(\tau)\cos(\theta)z$.

4. EXPERIMENTAL RESULTS

In this section, we evaluate our 3D trajectory extraction method from different perspectives.

4.1 Evaluation in terms of Depth Estimation

This experiment aims to evaluate whether 3D trajectories extracted with our method represent temporally consistent depths. We use the dataset *LIRIS* which contains 180 videos taken by Kinect placed at different positions in a building to capture people's movements [39]. All videos are down-sampled to 1 fps. Using *LIRIS* allows us to define depths obtained by Kinect as the ground truth. For comparative evaluation, we compare our method to the one which independently estimates depths of each frame using the technique in [14]. We call the former and the latter *Ours* and *D-Independent*, respectively. *Ours* extracts 3D trajectories using 700 particles. On the other hand, 3D trajectories cannot be extracted only with *D-Independent* because it does not yield the depth of an object region, but just delivers the depth map for a frame. Regarding this, for *D-Independent*, we form a 3D trajectory using depths of object regions detected by *Ours*. That is, both methods provide sequences of depths for the same object regions. Similarly, we define the ground truth by referring to Kinect depths for object regions by *Ours*. Also, we select 80 videos from *LIRIS* because the rest of videos only display static objects.

Table 1 presents the performance comparison between *Ours* and *D-Independent*. *d1* represents the difference between a depth in a 3D trajectory obtained by *Ours* (or *D-Independent*) and the corresponding ground truth depth. Since *d1* only considers 'absolute' differences of depths, it may be undesirably large for 3D trajectories which have similar trends to the ground truth, but start with significantly different depths. Thus, we compute *d2* as *d1* after moving 3D trajectories so as to start with the same depth to the ground truth. Furthermore, we evaluate depth changes in 3D trajectories. For each 3D trajectory, we first compute 'derivatives' using depths for two consecutive frames. Then, *d3* is computed as the difference between a derivative in a 3D trajectory and the one in the ground truth. In Table 1, *d1*, *d2* and *d3* are averaged over all frames involved in 3D trajectories. This table shows that *Ours* significantly outperforms *D-Independent* for all of *d1*, *d2* and *d3*. Especially, the very small *d3* (only 21 cm) of *Ours* indicates that the transition of depths in each 3D trajectory is very similar to the one in the ground truth. We think that 3D trajectories with such properties are useful for video event detection, because the interaction of objects is defined as the relation among their relative positions, rather than absolute ones.

Fig. 6 shows depths of 3D trajectories obtained by *Ours*, *D-Independent* and the ground truth for three different videos. Each graph corresponds to one video where the horizontal and vertical axes represent frames and estimated (or ground truth) depths, respectively. Depths are plotted by different

	d1 (mm)	*d2* (mm)	*d3* (mm)
D-Independent	7227.09	10524.68	3641.75
Ours	1058.62	982.61	212.75

Table 1: Performance comparison between *Ours* and *D-Independent* on *LIRIS* (the unit is millimetre (mm)).

colours depending on methods. As seen from Fig. 6, *Ours* successfully estimates depths very similar to those of the ground truth, while depths estimated by *D-Independent* are very unstable. This result is attributed to our best frame selection. In Fig. 6, we circle depths for the selected best frames, from which particle filter starts tracking of 3D positions. Hence, we can extract 3D trajectories with temporally consistent, accurate depths. Finally, Fig. 7 (a) and (b) depict two 3D trajectories extracted by *Ours* (red) and the corresponding ground truth (blue). This figure also exemplifies the successful 3D trajectory extraction. The above mentioned results validate the effectiveness of our method based on the best frame selection and particle filter.

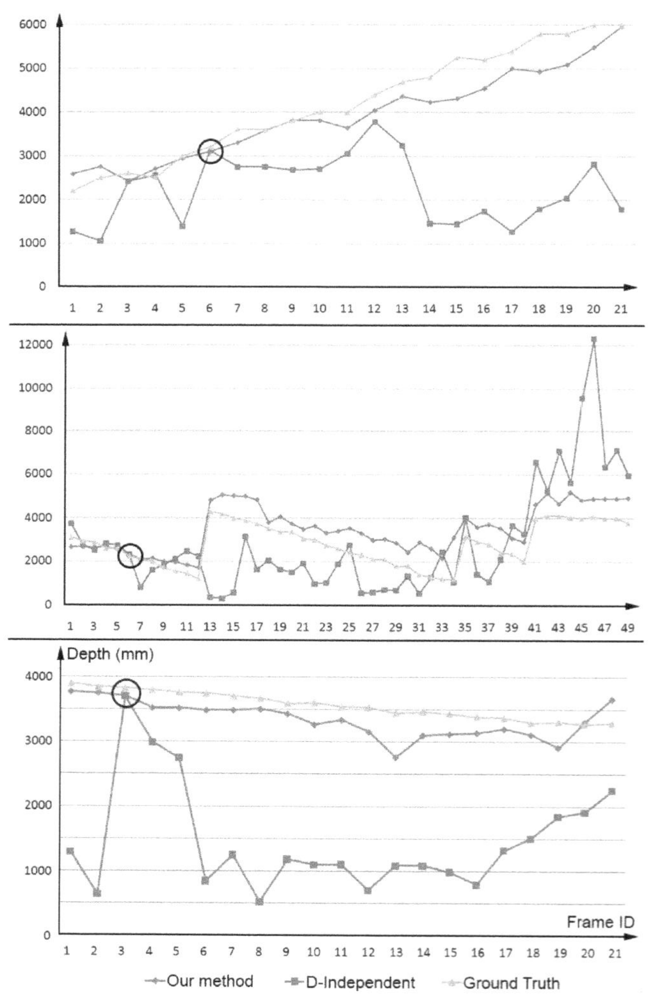

Figure 6: Examples of depths of 3D trajectories obtained by *Ours*, *D-Independent* and the ground truth.

4.2 Evaluation in terms of Object Detection

We evaluate how effective our method is for achieving temporally consistent object detection. We adopt 3D trajecto-

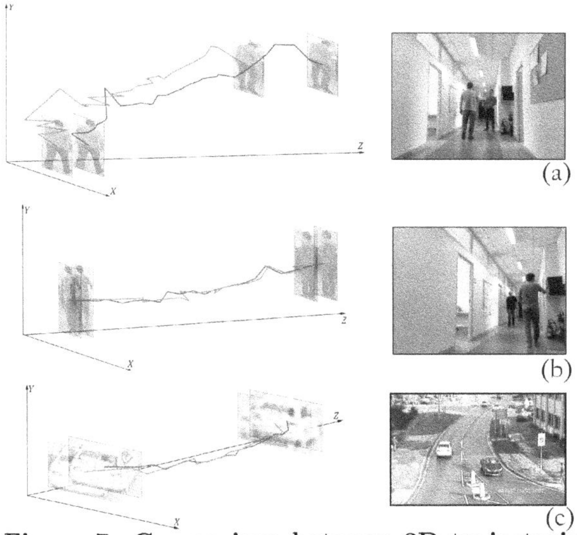

Figure 7: Comparison between 3D trajectories extracted by *Ours* (red) and the ground truth (blue).

ries extracted from 30 videos in *LIRIS* using *Ours* in the previous section, and assess the accuracy of object regions represented by those trajectories. Moreover, we compare this accuracy to the one obtained by *O-Independent* where the object detection technique in [6] is independently applied to each frame. Table 2 shows the comparison between *Ours* and *O-Independent*. The second row represents the percentage of correctly detected regions, where we regard a detected region as correct if more than 50% of it overlaps the manually provided ground truth region. The third row presents the percentage of incorrectly detected regions, whose overlapping ratios with ground truth regions are less than 50%. The bottom row indicates the percentage of ground truth regions that are missed by *Ours* or *O-Independent*. Note that there is another important evaluation measure representing the percentage of 'false positive regions', which do not overlap ground truth ones. However, avoiding false positive regions is not a task of our trajectory extraction method, but a task of an object detection method, so we do not consider false positive regions.

	Ours	*O-Independent*
Correct regions	85.61 %	69.17 %
Incorrect regions	14.38 %	19.17 %
Missed regions	0 %	11.64 %

Table 2: Comparison between *Ours* and *O-Independent* on 30 videos in *LIRIS* in terms of object detection.

As shown in Table 2, 3D trajectories extracted by *Ours* characterise object regions much more accurately than *O-Independent*. This validates the contribution of our method to temporally consistent object detection. Also, although this experiment is very small-scale, *Ours* involves no missed region. One main reason is the best frame selection step which selects frames with clear edges.

4.3 Evaluation for Long Shots

Particle filter tracks 3D positions of an object by matching its regions with SIFT flow. However, this matching may not work well if the object's regions are small. Thus, we need to test the capability of our method in dealing with videos (long shots), where objects are distant from the camera and thus their regions are small. For this, *LIRIS* is based on Kinect which cannot provide larger depths than 5 metres. Hence, we use the dataset *i-Lids* which contains 80 surveillance videos taken in different streets and train stations (we have obtained these videos by splitting originally provided long videos) [12]. We choose 75 videos from *i-Lids* and down-sample them to 1 fps. Since depth data are unavailable for *i-Lids*, we manually annotate each object in every frame with an approximate depth.

Table 3 shows the performance comparison between *Ours* (with 400 particles) and *D-Independent* on *i-Lids* in terms of *d1*, *d2* and *d3* described in Section 4.1. We can see that *Ours* works much better than *D-Independent* even for long shots. In particular, all of *d1*, *d2* and *d3* in Table. 1 are similar to those in Table. 3. This indicates the robustness of our method to long shots. We actually observed that our method can appropriately estimate depths for cars and persons which move in the ranges of 0.5 $\sim$ 45 and 0.5 $\sim$ 15 metres, respectively. Fig. 7 (c) shows the 3D trajectory extracted for a car in a long shot.

	d1 (mm)	*d2* (mm)	*d3* (mm)
D-Independent	8937.36	5808.9	1910.88
Ours	1462.85	1091.6	256.42

Table 3: Performance comparison between *Ours* and *D-Independent* on *i-Lids* (the unit is millimetre (mm)).

5. CONCLUSION AND FUTURE WORK

In this paper, we introduced a novel method which can extract 3D trajectories of objects from 2D videos. Experimental results validated the effectiveness of our method using the best frame selection and particle filter. To enhance our method, we will explore the following four issues in the future: First, the object detection performance and the number of detectable objects are key for our method to accurately extract 3D trajectories of various objects. We plan to adopt the top-ranked method at the latest worldwide competition on large-scale object detection (e.g., [34]). Second, our current method cannot extract 3D trajectories from videos taken by moving cameras. We will resolve this by discriminating between camera-induced and object-induced motions in a video [32]. Third, we will parallelise our method on GPUs to reduce the computational time. Last, we will extend experiments by using more and larger-scale datasets relative to those used in this paper. We will also analyse the sensitivity of object detection to false positive regions.

6. REFERENCES

[1] M. S. Arulampalam, S. Maskell, N. Gordon, and T. Clapp. A tutorial on particle filters for online nonlinear/non-gaussian bayesian tracking. *IEEE Trans. Signal Process.*, 50(2):174–188, 2002.

[2] N. Azzabou, N. Paragios, and F. Guichard. Image reconstruction using particle filters and multiple hypotheses testing. *IEEE Trans. Image Process.*, 19(5):1181–1190, 2010.

[3] M. A. Brubaker, L. Sigal, and D. J. Fleet. Estimating contact dynamics. In *Proc. of ICCV 2009*, pages 2389–2396, 2009.

[4] G. Catalin and S. Nedevschi. Oject tracking from stereo sequences using particle filter. In *Proc. of ICCP 2008*, pages 279–282, 2008.
[5] M. de Bruijne and M. Nielsen. Image segmentation by shape particle filtering. In *Proc. of ICPR 2004*, pages 722–725, 2004.
[6] P. F. Felzenszwalb, R. B. Girshick, D. McAllester, and D. Ramanan. Object detection with discriminatively trained part-based models. *IEEE Trans. Pattern Anal. Mach. Intell.*, 32(9):1627–1645, 2010.
[7] J. Garcia, A. Gardel, I. Bravo, J. Lazaro, and M. Martinez. Tracking people motion based on extended condensation algorithm. *IEEE Trans. Syst. Man Cybern. Syst.*, 43(3):606–618, 2013.
[8] S. Hadfield and R. Bowden. Hollywood 3d: Recognizing actions in 3d natural scenes. In *Proc. of CVPR 2013*, pages 3398–3405, 2013.
[9] J. Han, L. Shao, D. Xu, and J. Shotton. Enhanced computer vision with microsoft kinect sensor: A review. *IEEE Trans. Cybern.*, 43(5):1318–1334, 2013.
[10] R. Hess and A. Fern. Discriminatively trained particle filters for complex multi-object tracking. In *Proc. of CVPR 2009*, pages 240–247, 2009.
[11] D. Hoiem, A. A. Efros, and M. Hebert. Recovering occlusion boundaries from an image. *Int. J. Comput. Vis.*, 91(3):328–346, 2011.
[12] i Lids. i-lids AVSS 2007 dataset. `http://www.eecs.qmul.ac.uk/~andrea/avss2007_d.html`.
[13] Y.-G. Jiang, S. Bhattacharya, S.-F. Chang, and M. Shah. High-level event recognition in unconstrained videos. *Int. J. Multimed. Inf. Retr.*, 2(2):73–101, 2013.
[14] K. Karsch, C. Liu, and S. B. Kang. Depth extraction from video using non-parametric sampling. In *Proc. of ECCV 2012*, pages 775–788, 2012.
[15] K. Karsch, C. Liu, and S. B. Kang. Depth transfer: Depth extraction from video using non-parametric sampling. *IEEE Trans. Pattern Anal. Mach. Intell.*, 36(11):2144–2158, 2014.
[16] M. Katz. *Introduction to Geometrical Optics*. 2002.
[17] Z. Khan, T. Balch, and F. Dellaert. MCMC-based particle filtering for tracking a variable number of interacting targets. *IEEE Trans. Pattern Anal. Mach. Intell.*, 27(11):1805–1819, 2005.
[18] R. Lakaemper and M. Sobel. Using the particle filter approach to building partial correspondences between shapes. *Int. J. Comput. Vis.*, 88(1):1–23, 2010.
[19] J.-B. Lee, M.-J. Kim, S. Yoon, and E.-Y. Chung. Application-support particle filter for dynamic voltage scaling of multimedia applications. *IEEE Trans. Comput.*, 61(9):1256–1269, 2012.
[20] K. Li and Y. Fu. Prediction of human activity by discovering temporal sequence patterns. *IEEE Trans. Pattern Anal. Mach. Intell.*, 36(8):1644–1657, 2014.
[21] Y. Li, H. Ai, T. Yamashita, S. Lao, and M. Kawade. Tracking in low frame rate video: A cascade particle filter with discriminative observers of different life spans. *IEEE Trans. Pattern Anal. Mach. Intell.*, 30(10):1728–1740, 2008.
[22] C. Liu, J. Yuen, and A. Torralba. Sift flow: Dense correspondence across scenes and its applications. *IEEE Trans. Pattern Anal. Mach. Intell.*, 33(5):978–994, 2011.
[23] K. Okuma, A. Taleghani, N. de Freitas, J. J. Little, and D. G. Lowe. A boosted particle filter: Multitarget detection and tracking. In *Proc. of ECCV 2004*, pages 28–39, 2004.
[24] A. Prest, V. Ferrari, and C. Schmid. Explicit modeling of human-object interactions in realistic videos. *IEEE Trans. Pattern Anal. Mach. Intell.*, 35(4):835–848, 2013.
[25] R. Rosales and S. Sclaroff. 3d trajectory recovery for tracking multiple objects and trajectory guided recognition of actions. In *Proc. of CVPR 1999*, pages 117–123, 1999.
[26] O. Russakovsky *et al.* Imagenet large scale visual recognition challenge, 2014.
[27] P. Saisan, S. Medasani, and Y. Owechko. Multi-view classifier swarms for pedestrian detection and tracking. In *Proc. of OTCBVS 2005*, pages 18–18, 2005.
[28] Y. Salih and A. S. Malik. Comparison of stochastic filtering methods for 3d tracking. *Pattern Recognit.*, 44(10-11):2711–2737, 2011.
[29] M. Salzmann and R. Urtasun. Physically-based motion models for 3d tracking: A convex formulation. In *Proc. of CVPR 2011*, pages 2064–2071, 2011.
[30] A. Saxena, S. Chung, and A. Ng. 3-d depth reconstruction from a single still image. *Int. J. Comput. Vis.*, 76(1):53–69, 2008.
[31] A. Saxena, M. Sun, and A. Ng. Make3d: Learning 3d scene structure from a single still image. *IEEE Trans. Pattern Anal. Mach. Intell.*, 31(5):824–840, 2009.
[32] W. Shandong, O. Oreifej, and M. Shah. Action recognition in videos acquired by a moving camera using motion decomposition of lagrangian particle trajectories. In *Proc. of ICCV 2011*, pages 1419–1426, 2011.
[33] J. Shotton *et al.* Real-time human pose recognition in parts from single depth images. *Commun. ACM*, 56(1):116–124, 2013.
[34] K. Simonyan and A. Zisserman. Very deep convolutional networks for large-scale image recognition. *CoRR*, abs/1409.1556, 2014.
[35] A. F. Smeaton, P. Over, and W. Kraaij. Evaluation campaigns and TRECVid. In *Proc. of MIR 2006*, pages 321–330, 2006.
[36] A. W. M. Smeulders, M. Worring, S. Santini, A. Gupta, and R. Jain. Content-based image retrieval at the end of the early years. *IEEE Trans. Pattern Anal. Mach. Intell.*, 22(12):1349–1380, 2000.
[37] J. Vermaak, A. Doucet, and P. Perez. Maintaining multimodality through mixture tracking. In *Proc. of ICCV 2003*, pages 1110–1116, 2003.
[38] P. Wei, Y. Zhao, N. Zheng, and S.-C. Zhu. Modeling 4d human-object interactions for event and object recognition. In *Proc. of ICCV 2013*, pages 3272–3279, 2013.
[39] C. Wolf *et al.* Evaluation of video activity localizations integrating quality and quantity measurements. *Comput. Vis. Image Underst.*, 127:14–30, 2014.
[40] T. Zhao and R. Nevatia. Tracking multiple humans in complex situations. *IEEE Trans. Pattern Anal. Mach. Intell.*, 26(9):1208–1221, 2004.

Space-time Histograms And Their Application To Person Re-identification In TV Shows

Rémi Auguste, Jean Martinet, and Pierre Tirilly
CRIStAL (UMR CNRS 9189) – Lille 1 University – Villeneuve d'Ascq, France
remi.auguste@univ-lille1.fr, jean.martinet@univ-lille1.fr, pierre.tirilly@univ-lille1.fr

ABSTRACT

The annotation of video streams by automatic content analysis is a growing field of research. The possibility of recognising persons appearing in TV shows allows to automatically structure ever-growing video archives. We propose a new descriptor to re-identify persons featured in videos, that is to say, to spot all occurrences of persons throughout a video. Our approach is dynamic as it benefits from motion information contained in videos, whereas the static approaches are solely based on still images. We extract persontracks from videos and match them using a new descriptor and its associated similarity measure: the space-time histogram. The originality of our approach is the integration of temporal data into the descriptor. Experiments show that it provides a better estimation of the similarity between persontracks. Our contribution has been evaluated using a corpus of real life french TV shows broadcasted on BFMTV and LCP TV channels and on some annotated episodes from "Buffy: the Vampire Slayer". Experimental results show that our approach significantly improves the precision of the re-identification process thanks to the use of the temporal dimension.

Categories and Subject Descriptors

I.4.8 [**Image processing and computer vision**]: Scene Analysis—*Tracking*; D.2.8 [**Software Engineering**]: Metrics—*Performance measures; Complexity measures*

Keywords

person re-identification; video; spatial-temporal descriptor

1. INTRODUCTION

When automatically annotating a large video database, the computational cost and the precision are the main concerns in choosing the most suited algorithm. Usually, one has to find a trade-off between these two constraints depending on one's needs and available resources. One of the main aspects of the video to be annotated is the persons featured in it. We therefore propose a new descriptor to discriminate among the persons in videos, using color, space and time information: space-time histograms. Our approach is lightweight, comparable to color histograms, and yet conveys better re-identification rate.

ICMR'15, June 23–26, 2015, Shanghai, China.

ACM 978-1-4503-3274-3/15/06$15.00.
http://dx.doi.org/10.1145/2671188.2749332.

The goal of re-identification is to assign a unique label to persons' occurrences from a video. It is not to find the name of a person since no identity is involved.

First, we formally define the various notions used in our work. We define a video V_i, part of a corpus of videos V, as a set of ordered shots s_j^i:

$$(V_i, \leq) = \{s_0^i, s_1^i, \ldots, s_{|V_i|-1}^i\} \tag{1}$$

A shot s_j^i of a video V_i is defined as an ordered set of contiguous frames recorded by a single camera:

$$(s_j^i, \leq) = \{f_t, f_{t+1}, \ldots, f_{t+|s_j^i|-1}\} \tag{2}$$

where t is the temporal index of the first frame of the shot of the video. This index induces an ordering relationship ($\leq$) between the frames of a shot. The shot ends when the camera changes or when a cut is encountered. Those two notions can be found in most of the video-based person recognition systems [28].

The region of pixels that compose a person in a frame forms a blob. The sequence of sucessive blobs of a single person in a shot form a persontrack [7]. In order to extract persontracks from a video shot, the consecutive detections are merged using a tracking algorithm. We define the unordered set of persontracks $\mathbb{O}_i$ from a video V_i as:

$$\mathbb{O}_i = \{o_0, o_1, \ldots, o_{|\mathbb{O}_i|-1}\} \tag{3}$$

We define the set of identities featured in all videos as:

$$\mathbb{I} = \{\iota_0, \iota_1, \ldots, \iota_{|\mathbb{I}|-1}\} \tag{4}$$

and the ground truth function id that associates a persontrack o to its identity ι:

$$\begin{aligned} id: \ \mathbb{O} &\rightarrow \mathbb{I} \\ o &\rightarrow \iota \end{aligned} \tag{5}$$

The objective of person re-identification is to label the persontracks using a unique label $\Omega_{\iota,i}^*$ for each identity. The result is a set of labeled persontracks:

$$\Omega_{\iota,i}^* = \{o \in \mathbb{O}_i | id(o) = \iota\} \tag{6}$$

Our objective is to propose a discriminative signature for persontracks. This signature is used to select a label for each track. The proposed signature is dynamic as it uses temporal features of the videos. Most approaches of the state of the art do not consider time in their description of a persontrack [3]; they only provide a representation based on the static visual aspect of the persons.

2. RELATED WORK

A typical re-identification approach is global, as it is based on the overall appearance of the persons (e.g. the upper-body, the complete body, the silhouette, etc.) to compute a signature. Local approaches use interest points to compute the signatures. Those approaches require for that a higher image quality and pose numerous constraints concerning the pose or illumination of the persons. Furthermore, local approaches usually require a classification algorithm to re-identify the persons. The classification is trained on annotated data; this goes against the fully unsupervised aspect of re-identification. For these reasons, local approaches are seldom used in the context of person re-identification [3].

Several methods for person re-identification can be found in the litterature. Bird et al.[5] presented a multi-camera re-identification system where pedestrians are detected and annotated. They are re-identified based on the color of their clothes and the way these colored region are correlated. A Linear Discriminant Analysis (LDA) is applied to accentuate the difference between the individuals in the feature space. It simplifies the matching of a person going from one camera to another. In a multi-camera person re-identification context, Fu et al. [10] proposed an image-based approach robust to some degrees of corruption. This is done by dividing each image of a person into color stripes. The different views of the person are used to detect corrupted area of a view and estimating the missing or corrupted data from other views. Their approach require training data for each person in order to re-identify them. The approach of Ngo et al.[18] is based on tracking interest points found on faces using the algorithm of Shi et al.[22]. In order to track such interest points, the authors apply an optical flow algorithm and count the number of points shared by both faces. Above a given threshold, the faces are labeled as belonging to the same person. In a similar way, Hamdoun et al.[14] use interest points obtained by a method inspired by SURF[2]. In their work, the signature is built from the interest points of a persontrack. The authors calculate the sum of absolute differences (SAD) between the set of points of the known persontrack and the set of the query persontrack for matching purposes. Zheng et al.[29] formulated person re-identification as a distance learning problem. The aim is to learn an optimal distance that maximises the matching accuracy regardless of the choice of representation. They introduced a probabilistic model that learns this distance from correct and incorrect examples. Recently, Gandhi and Ronfard[12] re-identified the characters from Alfred Hitchcock's movie "Rope" (1948) by using an appearance model based on colored ellipses. This approach does not use a person detector; instead, a sliding window moves across each frame and generates an appearance model. If the model matches one of the characters, the position of the person is saved. This approach allows person re-identification in many cases, with fair robustness to occlusions. The main drawback is that the method generates many false detections. In a similar way, Zeng et al.[27] proposed to model the persons by a color topology. This representation takes into account how color regions are connected one to another. Their approach gives good results for pedestrian re-identification. The main issue of this approach is that the person have to be featured in the same way each time in order to be re-identified correctly.

Several approaches are based on histograms to re-identify the persons[24, 21, 15]. In the work by Truong Cong et al.[24], passengers of a moving train are re-identified across two cameras positioned in a single coach. For each person, a color histogram, a spatiogram and a color-path are built separatly and avaluated. The spatiograms were defined by Elmongui et al.[8], who proposed to use them for classification and search in numerical databases. The performances of the various approaches were evaluated and the color histograms did not obtain good re-identification scores. Spatiograms obtained the best results, which were slightly better than those of color-path. In the work of Schwartz et al.[21] et Hirzer et al.[15] color histograms obtained good re-identification results for face identification against Local Binary Patterns (LBP) and Histograms of Oriented Gradients (HOG).

3. SPACE-TIME HISTOGRAMS

To benefit from color, geometry and motion information from videos and to distinguish persons better, we extended the spatiogram to the temporal aspect and applied them to videos. The proposed space-time histograms are lightweight, and are easy to compute and to compare.

3.1 Definition

Space-time histograms are an extension of the spatiograms proposed in [4], which are themselves an extension of the classic color histograms. The data structure of the space-time histogram sth_o built on a persontrack o is defined as:

$$\mathrm{sth}_o(b) = < n_b, \mu_b, \Sigma_b >, \quad b = 1, \dots, B \tag{7}$$

where n_b is the number of pixels in bin b and B is the total number of bins. The average position in space and time, μ_b, is defined as:

$$\mu_b = (\bar{x}_b, \bar{y}_b, \bar{t}_b) \tag{8}$$

where $\bar{x}_b$, $\bar{y}_b$ and $\bar{t}_b$ are the average normalized positions of the pixels in space and time. Σ_b is the covariance matrix of the space-time positions:

$$\Sigma_b = \begin{pmatrix} cov(x_b, x_b) & cov(x_b, y_b) & cov(x_b, t_b) \\ cov(y_b, x_b) & cov(y_b, y_b) & cov(y_b, t_b) \\ cov(t_b, x_b) & cov(t_b, y_b) & cov(t_b, t_b) \end{pmatrix} \tag{9}$$

This covariance matrix is symetric since $cov(a, b) = cov(b, a)$. Space-time histograms, as defined in Equation 7, contain spatiograms, in the same way, spatiograms contain the color histograms. In the terminology of [4], space-time histograms could be called third order spatio-tempo-gram. The complexity of space-time histograms is comparable to that of other approaches that consider the temporal data of videos like cumulative color histograms or cumulative spatiograms.

3.2 Time complexity

The calculatory cost $T_{\text{cumul}}(p, f, B)$ of the construction of space-time histograms, cumulative spatiograms and color histograms can be estimated by the following formula:

$$T_{\text{cumul}}(f, p, B) = O(f \times p + B) \tag{10}$$

where p is the number of pixels per frame, f the number of frames and B the number of bins of the considered histogram.

Another approach, where each frame from a video sequence could be represented independently by several spatiograms or several color histograms is possible. In this case, the calculatory cost of the construction is higher since each frame is associated to a descriptor. The final step has to be applied to each descriptor. The construction cost $T_{\text{ind}}(p, f, B)$ in such case is estimated by the formula:

$$T_{\text{ind}}(p, f, B) = O(f \times (p + B)) \tag{11}$$

This calculatory cost does not take into account the cost of allocating a new descriptor containing B bins; however, it is necessary to allocate as many descriptors as there are frames in the video. When the video duration is more than a few seconds, the allocation cost becomes non-negligible over the total cost of the construction.

3.3 Space complexity

Let d be the position number of dimensions of the position of the pixels considered. Color histograms do not take into account any position, thus $d = 0$ in this case. Spatiograms take only into account spatial data so $d = 2$ in this case. Finally, space-time histograms consider the space-time position of the pixels, $d = 3$ in this case. This allows us to express the memory cost $M_{\text{cumul}}(B, d)$ of space-time histograms, cumulative spatiograms and cumulative histograms as a function of d:

$$\begin{aligned} M_{\text{cumul}}(B, d) &= O(c \times B), c = 1 + d + \frac{d(d+1)}{2} \\ &= O(d^2 \times B) \end{aligned} \quad (12)$$

where B is the number of bins and c the amount of data stored by the model. For example, in the case of space-time histograms, $c = 10$ because: the pixel count has a cost of 1, the average position $\bar{x_b}, \bar{y_b}, \bar{t_b}$ has a cost of 3 and the covariance matrix has a cost of 6. The covariance matrix is of dimension 3×3, but because of its symmetry, only 6 elements need to be memorised.

In the case where the descriptor is built independently for each frame, the memory cost $M_{\text{ind}}(B, d, f)$ is again much higher than the one cumulating over the frames:

$$\begin{aligned} M_{\text{ind}}(B, d, f) &= O(f \times c \times B) \\ &= O(f \times d^2 \times B) \end{aligned} \quad (13)$$

3.4 Similarity measure

In order to compare space-time histograms, we propose a similarity measure inspired from the measure used for spatiograms [24]. A temporal dimension was added to it. Space-time histograms combine the frequencies of colors with space-time distributions of pixels.

To measure whether two histograms come from the same statistical distribution, the Mahalanobis distance is used. Let ψ_b be the measure based on the Mahalanobis distance, measuring the similarity of the bins of index b coming from two space-time histograms.

$$\psi_b = 1 - \sqrt{(\mu_b - \mu_b')^t \hat{\Sigma}_b^{-1} (\mu_b - \mu_b')} \quad (14)$$

In Equation 14, the covariance matrix is estimated using the following formula:

$$\hat{\Sigma}_b^{-1} = (\Sigma_b^{-1} + (\Sigma_b')^{-1}) \quad (15)$$

The χ^2 distance has the property of measuring the dissimilarity between two bins that is proportionnate to their size. This property is interesting in that a large bin with a small difference between two space-time histograms will not influence the measure too much.

We have defined χ_b^2 as similarity measure between two bins of index b as:

$$\chi_b^2(n_b, n_b') = 1 - \frac{(n_b - n_b')^2}{n_b + n_b'} \quad (16)$$

The combination of this measure with Mahalanobis' measure allows us to take into account the various aspects of the space-time histograms. This similarity measured between two space-time histograms sth_o and $sth_{o'}$ of identical size is defined as:

$$s(sth_o, sth_{o'}) = \sum_{b=1}^{B} \psi_b \times \chi_b^2(n_b, n_b') \quad (17)$$

3.5 Comparison complexity

The calculatory cost of space-time histogram comparison $T_{\text{sim\_cumul}}(B, d)$ is:

$$T_{\text{sim\_cumul}}(B, d) = O(B \times d^3) \quad (18)$$

This cost is similar for spatiograms and color histograms built cumulatively.

The descriptor built for individual frames cannot be compared using a similar algorithm like cumulatively built descriptors. This is due to the possible length difference between the video sequences. Dynamic Time Warping can solve this issue of *n-by-m* comparison between two timely ordered sequences of descriptors (or observations). This algorithm usually has a complexity of $O(f^2)$, that can be improved in numerous ways [26]. The total comparison cost $T_{\text{sim\_ind}}(f, B, d)$ is:

$$T_{\text{sim\_ind}}(f, B, d) = O(f^2 \times B \times d^3) \quad (19)$$

The descriptors built cumulatively upon every frames of the video have much lower time and complexities, than those considering independently every frame.

4. PERSON RE-IDENTIFICATION

The proposed similarity measure between two space-time histograms can be used on video-based persontracks to re-identify persons. Our hypothesis is that the similarity $s(\text{sth}_o, \text{sth}_{o'})$ is high (close to 1) when $id(o) = id(o')$, in other words, when two persontracks contain the same person. On the contrary, this similarity is low (close to 0) when $id(o) \neq id(o')$. This hypothesis requires that the compared persontracks are taken from the same video V_i, so that the global appearance of the persons shows minor variations.

Once the persontracks have been described as space-time histograms, they can be compared by measuring their similarity. A similarity matrix M is generated to keep the comparison results. This matrix will be used to measure the precision of our approach. Because our similarity measure is symmetric, the matrix is also symmetric.

The first step of our approach is to build a space-time histogram for each persontrack and then calculate the similarity matrix.

This matrix can be seen as a set of lines:

$$M = \left[M_1, \ldots, M_{|M|}\right]^T \quad (20)$$

where each row M_i of the matrix M gives the similarity measure between a space-time histogram sth_{o_i} and every space-time histograms.

Using the lines of the similarity matrix M, we sort each one in descending order of similarity. We define a matrix R containing, in each row, the sorted similarities of each persontrack taken from matrix M:

$$R = \{r_{ij} = o_k | \operatorname{rank}(o_k, M_i) = j\} \quad (21)$$

where $\operatorname{rank}(o_k, M_i)$ is the rank of the value of the similarity S_{ik} of the persontrack o_k in the line M_i. When we consider this rank in descending order of similarity: rank 1 for the highest similarity, rank 2 for the second higher, etc. The first value is a self-match: the similarity measure between the space-time histogram representing the persontrack and itself (value 1).

4.1 Evaluation Metric

For each line M_i, we want to measure the matching's precision between o_i and the other persontracks in the video bearing the same identity as o_i. The problem of the classic precision measure is that the number of persontrack per identity may vary. The identities with a few number of persontracks would contribute too much to the average without this. We used the *precision at n (P@N)* [19]. It is the precision measured by considering the n first elements, where n is the number of correct answers. In our approach, for the persontrack o_i, n_i is the number of persontracks of a video V_v bearing the same identity as o_i:

$$n_i = |id^{-1}(id(o_i))|, \forall o_i \in \mathbb{O}_v \tag{22}$$

This precision at n_i for o_i is given by P_i:

$$P_i = \frac{|\{r_{ij} \in R | j \leq n_i\} \cap id^{-1}(id(o_i))|}{n_i} \tag{23}$$

We then calculate the weighted average $\bar{P}$ of the precisions values:

$$\bar{P} = \frac{\sum_{i=1}^{|M|} P_i n_i}{\sum_{i=1}^{|M|} n_i} \tag{24}$$

This average is weighted by the number of persontracks by identity. It avoids the introduction of a bias in the final metric.

4.2 Data

The data we use was distributed in the context of the ANR[1] REPERE challenge[2] [11]. It contains several hours of annotated french TV shows from LCP and BFMTV channels. Several shows from these channel are included in this dataset, with large variation in length and settings. Some shows contain outdoor scenes. For our experiments, we manually inspected and filtered the original dataset to remove any ambiguity and to provide a sound groundtruth for video-based person re-idenfication. Our dataset called FoxPersonTracks is available[3] and thoroughly described in [1].

In total, the subset we considered for our experiments consists of 303 different persons whose names are given in the annotations. Each person appears in average in 15 different shows. The anchors have a larger number of persontracks as they are visible more frequently than the other persons. They can appear more thant 50 times per show where some persons can only appear once.

4.3 Data filtering

The persontracks are extracted from 141 videos. We used the annotations to make sure that each persontrack contains only one person. Some faces in the REPERE dataset are not annotated because of size or semantic criteria. Furthermore, the faces position are annotated on the keyframes but the annotated parts do not take into account the shot boundaries. We used the Viola and Jones face detection algorithm[25] to detect the presence of more than one face in a persontrack. Then, we manually filtered each persontrack to ensure the quality of our dataset. This avoids any confusion between the persons during the evaluation.

At the end of the filtering we have 5279 video persontracks of 303 different persons. Each person appears in average in 5 videos. The anchors are more represented than the other persons.

4.4 Persontrack extraction

The persontracks are extracted from the video by first detecting the person in each frame using Viola and Jones face detector[25] (see Figure 2a). The detection is optimised to maximise the proportion of skin color in the detection (see Figure 1). This is done to eliminate most of the background from the detection when the person is not perfectly facing the camera. The calculated face's position and size is used to initialise a set of masks provided to Grabcut algorithm[20] in order to separate the person from the background (see Figure 2c). The masks are initialized from ellipses calculated from the detected face (see Figure 2b). The extracted person's image is then resized to a fixed size. This size was empirically deduced from our experimentations, we noticed that using 50% of the original frame size was good to fit most of the occurrences without resizing them. This is done so the person's position are centered and the number of pixels in each frame is normalized. The illumination is not normalised in our approach as the illumination is stable enough throughout a TV show. This step should otherwise be done.

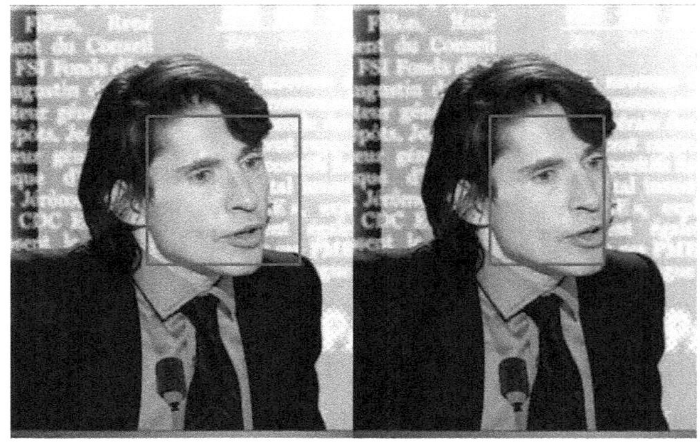

Figure 1: Example of face detection before and after our optimisation based on the skin color proportion.

After the persontrack extraction, we obtain short videos, each centered on one person in front of a zero value pixel background. Our approach is therefore robust to camera zooming or panning. The persontrack can then be viewed as a normalised volume as shown in Figure 3, composed of the extracted person stacked through time. The depth of the volume is the temporal dimension. Space-time histograms, spatiograms and color histograms are built upon those extracted persontracks. During the construction, the background pixels are ignored.

5. EXPERIMENTS

We will now evalutate the space-time histograms and compare its precision to other approaches.

5.1 Precision

We compare the evolution of the precision of different approaches where the number of bins vary. This way, we can study their behavior and compare their precision.

We observe in Figure 4 that the precision of each approach evolves parallelly. The precision of each approach increases rapidly for a low number of bins (between 10 and 1,000). The precision reaches a maximum and starts decreasing at around 5,000 bins. Our approach based on space-time histograms (sth) obtained a better precision than color histograms (h) or spatiograms (sp). This improvement in precision is very significant as the p-value of the student-test is very low (close to zero). This confirms our hypothesis that space-time information is important to re-identify the persons in persontracks.

[1]Agence Nationale de la Recherche
[2]REPERE Evaluation Package,
ELRA catalog (http://catalog.elra.info),
ISLRN: 360-758-359-485-0, ELRA ID: ELRA-E0044
[3]FoxPersonTracks dataset,
ELRA catalog (http://catalog.elra.info),
ISLRN: 168-132-570-218-1, ELRA ID: ELRA-S0374

(a) Original frame with the detected face. (b) Mask calculated from the detected face. (c) Result of the Grabcut algorithm applied on the original image using the mask.

Figure 2: Example of our person extraction process on a single frame and a single person.

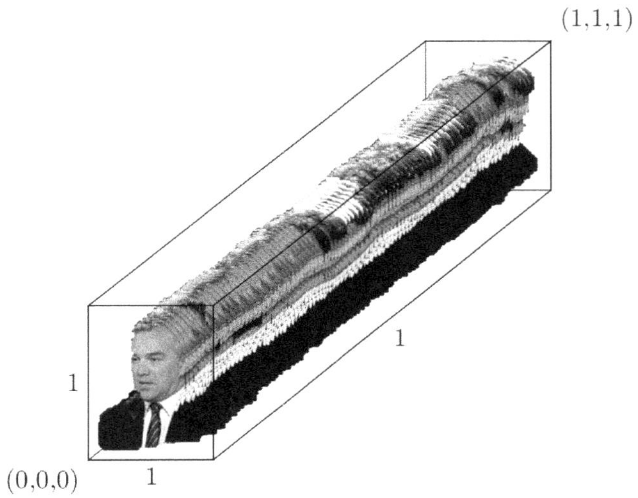

Figure 3: Example of extracted persontrack from a BFMTV TV show.

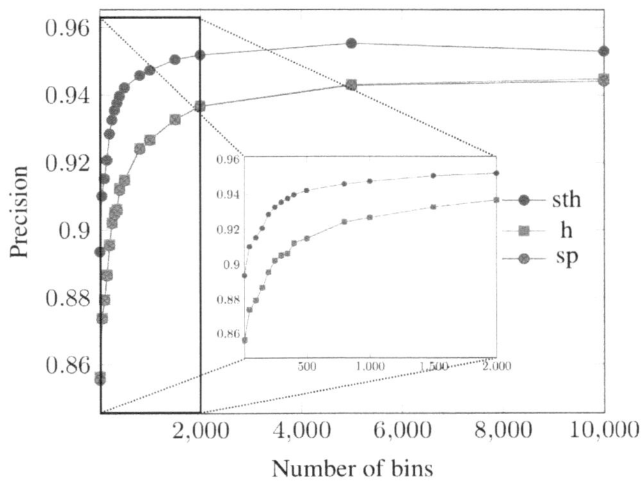

Figure 4: Evolution of the precision as the number of bins in the descriptors increases, from 10 to 10,000 bins. The curves of color histograms and spatiograms are overlaping.

It is interesting to observe that the precision of spatiograms is almost identical to that of color histograms. This indicates that space information along with color is not better at distinguishing between the persons featured in the persontracks than color alone.

5.2 Complexity

In this experiment, we only compare their memory cost. Color histograms has a memory cost of 1 by bin (the data count). Spatiograms have a memory cost of 6 and space-times histograms have a memory cost of 9 (cf. Section 3).

Figure 5 shows the precision of the different approaches with their relative (to color histograms) memory cost relative. We observe that for a memory cost lower than 4,500, color histograms yield the best precision. For a memory cost of 4,500, space-time histograms and the color histograms have a similar precision. This means that a 500 bins space-time histogram is equivalent in precision to a 4,500 bins color histogram. With a memory cost higher than 4,500, space-time histograms give the highest precision that is even increasing, whereas the precision of color histograms decreases slowly. Thus, a color histogram cannot reach the precision of a space-time histogram using more than 500 bins.

Spatiograms give a much lower precision, relative to their memory cost, than the other approaches. It is only with a memory cost of over 30,000 than the precision of the spatiograms reaches and overtakes that of the color histograms. Therefore a 5,000 bins spatiogram is equivalent in precision to a 30,000 bins color histogram. The precisions of spatiograms and space-time histograms seem to evolve parallel one to another. Thus, the precision of spatiograms cannot match the one of space-time histograms.

In conclusion, the space-time histograms yield a higher precision, for an equivalent memory cost, than color histograms and spatiograms. This result clearly shows the contribution of temporal and spatial information to re-identify the persons featured in the persontracks.

In order to compare our approach to other approaches, we evaluated it to the "Buffy" dataset [ ]. We used the detections provided in the dataset along with the identities as groundtruth. In order to extract the persontracks, we applied the process presented in Sec-

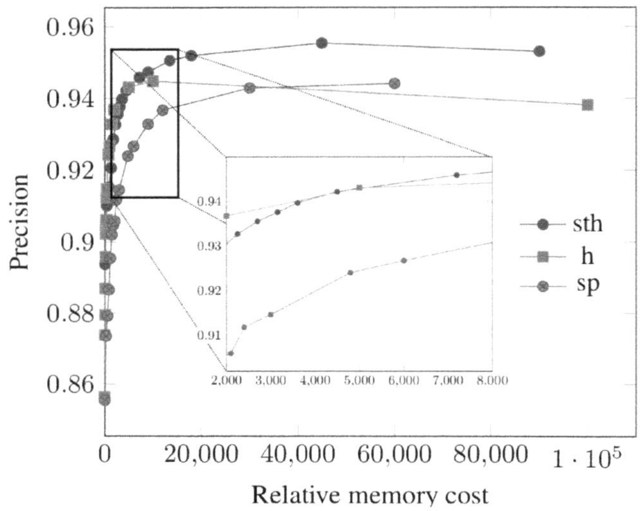

Figure 5: Evolution of the precision as the memory cost increases for each approach.

	Episode 05-02		Episode 05-05	
Approach	$\bar{P}$	# of tracks	$\bar{P}$	# of tracks
STH (All)	0.455	876	0.373	663
STH (Mixed)	0.414	677	0.498	544
STH (Frontal)	0.463	337	0.492	324
Sp (All)	0.333	876	0.370	663
Sp (Mixed)	0.376	677	0.458	544
Sp (Frontal)	0.428	337	0.457	324
H (All)	0.285	876	0.368	663
H (Mixed)	0.328	677	0.409	544
H (Frontal)	0.380	337	0.408	324
[9]	0.682	516	0.692	477
[17]	0.312	491		

Table 1: $\bar{P}$ measure of our approach against other on episode 2 and 5 of the fifth season of "Buffy: the Vampire Slayer".

tion 4.4. During the extraction the persontracks annotated as false detections were ignored.

The precision $\bar{P}$ was measured on the entire dataset and on two subsets modeled by space-time histograms (1500 bins, RGB). One subsets includes the persontracks containing at least one frontal face. The other is composed of persontracks containing only frontal faces. The results, given in Table 1, show that our approach performs better with frontal faces. This is due to the fact that the persontrack extraction process is not designed for non-frontal facing persons: it tends to incorporate a lot of background pixels, thus adding noise to the signature. The medium re-identification rate can be explained by the fact that the characters featured in the show change clothes several time during an episode. However, these results show that our approach performs better on this dataset than [17]. Our precision is lower than the one obtained by [9] for a recall of 100%. We also observe that spatiograms and color histograms, yield lower results than space-time histograms.

In order to automatically group the persontracks according to their identity, we applied an agglomerative hierarchical clustering on our similarity matrix (see Table 2). We observe that the purity and the fragmentation both improve when using only frontal facing persontracks. Those results are consistent with those (reported in [16]) obtained by [16], [6] and [13] on the other "Buffy" dataset[13]. Unfortunately the dataset [13] and [9] are using different episodes of "Buffy: the Vampire Slayer", so we cannot compare to them. We do observe that the space-time histograms tend to create less and purer clusters.

6. CONCLUSION AND FUTURE WORK

We introduced a new descriptor to re-identify persons featured in videos called space-time histogram. It takes into account color, spatial and temporal data contained in a persontrack to generate a discriminative signature. This signature is used to re-identify each person in a video. The originality of our approach is the integration of temporal data into the descriptor. Experiments show that it provides a better estimation of the similarity between persontracks. Our descriptor is evaluated using the REPERE dataset [11], featuring real life TV shows broadcasted from BFMTV and LCP TV channels, and the well known "Buffy" dataset [23]. Experimental results show that our approach significantly improves the precision as compared to color histograms and spatiograms for a person re-identification task, thanks to the use of the temporal dimension. Compared to state-of-the-art approaches, our results are lower while having a much lower complexity.

In our future research, we want to improve the persontracks' extraction to obtain higher quality persontracks while taking less time. Our experiments show that the direction the persons are facing has a very high impact on the results.

7. REFERENCES

[1] R. Auguste, J. Martinet, and P. Tirilly. Introducing FoxPersonTracks: a benchmark for person re-identification from tv broadcast shows. *Proceedings of the 13th International Workshop on Content-Based Multimedia Indexing (CBMI)*, 2015.

[2] H. Bay, T. Tuytelaars, and L. Van Gool. Surf: Speeded up robust features. In *European Conference on Computer Vision (ECCV)*, pages 404–417. Springer, 2006.

[3] A. Bedagkar-Gala and S. K. Shah. A survey of approaches and trends in person re-identification. *Image and Vision Computing*, 32(4):270–286, 2014.

[4] S. T. Birchfield and S. Rangarajan. Spatiograms versus histograms for region-based tracking. In *Computer Vision and Pattern Recognition (CVPR)*, volume 2, pages 1158 – 1163. IEEE, june 2005.

[5] N. D. Bird, O. Masoud, N. P. Papanikolopoulos, and A. Isaacs. Detection of loitering individuals in public transportation areas. *IEEE Transactions on Intelligent Transportation Systems*, 6(2):167–177, June 2005.

[6] R. G. Cinbis, J. Verbeek, and C. Schmid. Unsupervised metric learning for face identification in tv video. In *IEEE International Conference on Computer Vision (ICCV)*, pages 1559–1566, 2011.

[7] X. W. Duy-Dinh Le and S. Satoh. *Encyclopedia of multimedia*, chapter Face Detection, tracking, and recognition for broadcast video, pages 228–238. Springer-Verlag New York Inc, 2008.

[8] H. G. Elmongui, M. F. Mokbel, and W. G. Aref. Spatio-temporal histograms. *Advances in Spatial and Temporal Databases*, pages 19–36, 2005.

[9] M. Everingham, J. Sivic, and A. Zisserman. "Hello! My name is... Buffy" – automatic naming of characters in TV

	Episode 05-02			Episode 05-05		
Approach	Purity	Fragmentation	# of clusters	Purity	Fragmentation	# of clusters
STH (All)	0.349	23.26	189	0.409	19.23	149
STH (Mixed)	0.378	17.24	140	0.424	14.93	119
STH (Frontal)	0.428	9.90	83	0.416	11.11	81
Sp (All)	0.332	24.45	213	0.382	21.01	174
Sp (Mixed)	0.398	17.63	159	0.423	17.15	146
Sp (Frontal)	0.425	10.01	93	0.406	11.83	91
H (All)	0.323	24.44	215	0.389	20.69	175
H (Mixed)	0.364	17.60	159	0.416	17.01	148
H (Frontal)	0.423	10.00	92	0.404	11.42	89

Table 2: Clustering analysis of our approach on episode 2 and 5 of the fifth season of "Buffy: the Vampire Slayer".

video. In *Proceedings of the British Machine Vision Conference*, 2006.

[10] M.-H. Fu, Y.-C. Wang, and C.-S. Chen. Exploiting low-rank structures from cross-camera images for robust person re-identification. *IEEE International Conference on Image Processing (ICIP)*, pages 2427–2431, 2014.

[11] O. Galibert and J. Kahn. The first official repere evaluation. *First Workshop on Speech, Language and Audio for Multimedia (SLAM 2013)*, 2013.

[12] V. Gandhi and R. Ronfard. Detecting and naming actors in movies using generative appearance models. In *IEEE Conference on Computer Vision and Pattern Recognition (CVPR)*, pages 3706–3713, 2013.

[13] M. Guillaumin, J. Verbeek, and C. Schmid. Is that you? metric learning approaches for face identification. In *IEEE International Conference on Computer Vision (ICCV)*, pages 498–505, 2009.

[14] O. Hamdoun, F. Moutarde, B. Stanciulescu, and B. Steux. Person re-identification in multi-camera system by signature based on interest point descriptors collected on short video sequences. In *Second ACM/IEEE International Conference on Distributed Smart Cameras (ICDSC)*, pages 1–6, 2008.

[15] M. Hirzer, C. Beleznai, P. Roth, and H. Bischof. Person re-identification by descriptive and discriminative classification. In A. Heyden and F. Kahl, editors, *Image Analysis*, volume 6688 of *Lecture Notes in Computer Science*, pages 91–102. Springer Berlin Heidelberg, 2011.

[16] E. Khoury, P. Gay, and J.-M. Odobez. Fusing matching and biometric similarity measures for face diarization in video. In *Proceedings of the 3rd ACM conference on International conference on multimedia retrieval*, pages 97–104, 2013.

[17] M. Kostinger, P. Wohlhart, P. M. Roth, and H. Bischof. Learning to recognize faces from videos and weakly related information cues. In *IEEE Conference on Advanced Video and Signal-Based Surveillance (AVSS)*, pages 23–28, 2011.

[18] T. D. Ngo, D.-D. Le, S. Satoh, and D. A. Duong. Robust face track finding in video using tracked points. *IEEE International Conference on Signal Image Technology and Internet Based Systems (SITIS)*, pages 59–64, 2008.

[19] V. Raghavan, P. Bollmann, and G. S. Jung. A critical investigation of recall and precision as measures of retrieval system performance. *ACM Transactions on Information Systems (TOIS)*, 7(3):205–229, 1989.

[20] C. Rother, V. Kolmogorov, and A. Blake. Grabcut: Interactive foreground extraction using iterated graph cuts. In *ACM Transactions on Graphics (TOG)*, volume 23, pages 309–314, 2004.

[21] W. Schwartz, H. Guo, and L. Davis. A robust and scalable approach to face identification. In K. Daniilidis, P. Maragos, and N. Paragios, editors, *European Conference on Computer Vision (ECCV)*, volume 6316 of *Lecture Notes in Computer Science*, pages 476–489. Springer Berlin / Heidelberg, 2010.

[22] J. Shi and C. Tomasi. Good features to track. In *IEEE Conference on Computer Vision and Pattern Recognition (CVPR)*, pages 593–600, 1994.

[23] J. Sivic, M. Everingham, and A. Zisserman. "Who are you?" – learning person specific classifiers from video. In *IEEE Conference on Computer Vision and Pattern Recognition (CVPR)*, pages 1145–1152, 2009.

[24] D. Truong Cong, C. Achard, L. Khoudour, and L. Douadi. Video sequences association for people re-identification across multiple non-overlapping cameras. In P. Foggia, C. Sansone, and M. Vento, editors, *Image Analysis and Processing (ICIAP)*, volume 5716 of *Lecture Notes in Computer Science*, pages 179–189. Springer Berlin / Heidelberg, 2009.

[25] P. Viola and M. Jones. Robust real-time object detection. *International Journal of Computer Vision (IJCV)*, 57(2):137–154, 2002.

[26] X. Wang, A. Mueen, H. Ding, G. Trajcevski, P. Scheuermann, and E. Keogh. Experimental comparison of representation methods and distance measures for time series data. *Data Mining and Knowledge Discovery*, 26(2):275–309, 2013.

[27] G. Zeng, H.-M. Hu, Y. Geng, and C. Zhang. A person re-identification algorithm based on color topology. *IEEE International Conference on Image Processing (ICIP)*, pages 2447–2451, 2014.

[28] W. Zhao, R. Chellappa, P. J. Phillips, and A. Rosenfeld. Face recognition: A literature survey. *ACM Computing Surveys (CSUR)*, 35(4):399–458, 2003.

[29] W.-S. Zheng, S. Gong, and T. Xiang. Person re-identification by probabilistic relative distance comparison. In *IEEE Conference on Computer Vision and Pattern Recognition (CVPR)*, pages 649–656, June 2011.

Temporal Order-Preserving Dynamic Quantization for Human Action Recognition from Multimodal Sensor Streams

Jun Ye
University of Central Florida
jye@cs.ucf.edu

Kai Li
University of Central Florida
kaili@eecs.ucf.edu

Guo-Jun Qi
University of Central Florida
guojun.qi@ucf.edu

Kien A. Hua
University of Central Florida
kienhua@eecs.ucf.edu

ABSTRACT

Recent commodity depth cameras have been widely used in the applications of video games, business, surveillance and have dramatically changed the way of human-computer interaction. They provide rich multimodal information that can be used to interpret the human-centric environment. However, it is still of great challenge to model the temporal dynamics of the human actions and great potential can be exploited to further enhance the retrieval accuracy by adequately modeling the patterns of these actions. To address this challenge, we propose a temporal order-preserving dynamic quantization method to extract the most discriminative patterns of the action sequence. We further present a multimodal feature fusion method that can be derived in this dynamic quantization framework to exploit different discriminative capability of features from multiple modalities. Experiments based on three public human action datasets show that the proposed technique has achieved state-of-the-art performance.

Categories and Subject Descriptors

I.2.10 [**ARTIFICIAL INTELLIGENCE**]: Vision and Scene Understanding—*3D/stereo scene analysis*

Keywords

Human Action Recognition; Temporal Order; Temporal Dynamic Quantization; Multimodal Feature Fusion

1. INTRODUCTION

Recent commodity depth sensors (e.g. Kinect) provide us high-quality data that was expensive to obtain in the past. With the access to the multimodal data including RGB, depth and skeleton stream, the field of human-computer interaction has been dramatically changed in the last few years. The natural user interface (NUI) in terms of gesture recognition and speech recognition has now been applied in the field of video games, education, business and health care. Among all these applications, human action recognition plays a key role and directly determines the quality of those products and services.

Although intensive research efforts have been made to this area, human action recognition is still a very challenging problem due to the complexity of the spatio-temporal patterns of the human actions. Other factors including the noise of the sensing data and the variations of size and execution rate of individual human subjects also make the problem challenging [20].

The temporal modeling is one of the most challenging problems in human action recognition. There are many visual words and histogram based methods [5, 16, 21, 19] which can effectively discriminate human actions composed of distinct postures. However, the lack of interpretation on the temporal layout of the actions makes these methods confused by actions of similar postures but different temporal order, for example, "sitting down" and "standing up". Other methods such as graph model-based methods [6, 2] and motion template-based methods [7, 20, 10] emphasize on the modeling of the temporal dynamics. But they frequently suffer from the temporal misalignment due to the temporal translation and execution rate variation. The temporal pyramid [14, 9] was proposed to interpret the temporal order of a video, but the uniform partition of the temporal sequence cannot handle the variation of execution rate either.

To address the issues of the temporal misalignment and the execution rate, we formulate the temporal modeling problem from a new perspective which aims at finding an optimal quantization of the temporal sequence. We also give a solution to the optimization problem by proposing the temporal order-preserving dynamic quantizing algorithm. The general framework of the proposed approach is illustrated in Figure 1. The video sequence is dynamically partitioned by the temporal quantization and an aggregation procedure is performed to produce a quantized vector from each partition. This partition-aggregation process is recursively performed on the sequence of frames in a hierarchical way and finally produces a quantized representation of fixed size for the original video sequence. The above process is applied to

ICMR'15, June 23–26, 2015, Shanghai, China.

DOI: http://dx.doi.org/10.1145/2671188.2749340.

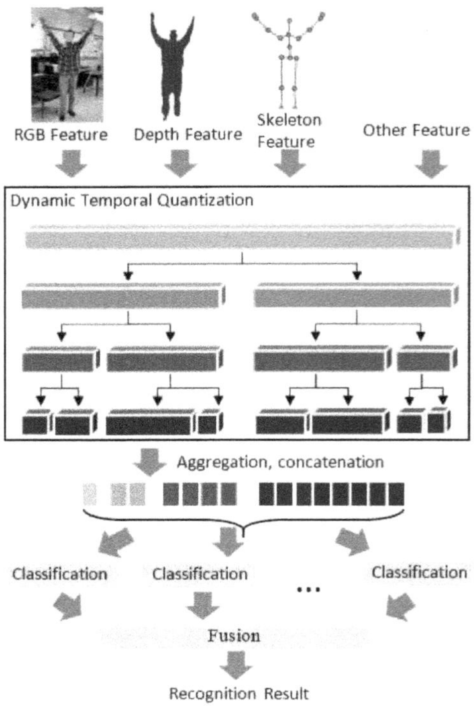

Figure 1: The general framework of the proposed approach.

multimodal features and generates their own feature-based quantization of the sequence. Supervised learning is then employed to learn the temporal model of the actions and predict the label of the new sequence upon the obtaining of the dynamic quantization vectors. The recognition rate can be further enhanced by leveraging the fusion of multimodal features in the same quantization frame.

The main contributions of the paper are:

1. We provide a quantization-based perspective for the problem of temporal modeling of human action sequences and propose a novel temporal order-preserving dynamic quantization algorithm as the solution.
2. We present a multimodal feature fusion approach which exploits the discriminative capability of features from different data modalities; and
3. We demonstrate the performance of the proposed approach by evaluating it on three public human action datasets. Experimental results show the proposed approach has achieved state-of-the-art performance.

The remainder of the paper is organized as follows. We provide a brief review of the related work in Section 2. The dynamic quantization algorithm is presented in Section 3. Multimodal feature fusion is discussed in Section 4. Experiments and performance evaluations are presented in Section 5. Finally, we conclude the paper in Section 6.

2. RELATED WORK

Many of the existing approaches for human action recognition focus on the spatio-temporal feature and local motions and do not explicitly model the temporal patterns of the action sequence. Most of these works are histogram-based. Space-time interest point (STIP) [3] and its extension [8] were introduced to describe the local spatial-temporal features. Normally, a bag-of-word representation was then used to discriminate different types of human actions. Xia and Aggarwal [15] extended the 3D cuboid and described the local depth cuboid by measuring the depth cuboid similarity. In [5], the bag-of-3D-points from the depth maps was sampled and clustered to model the dynamics of human actions. Similar ideas were proposed in [19], where the histogram of oriented gradient (HoG) was computed from the depth motion maps to classify human actions. Oreifej and Liu [9] proposed the 4D normals from the surface of the 3D point cloud and introduced the histogram of oriented 4D normals (HON4D) to achieve higher discriminative capability.

With the success of skeleton joints estimation from the depth images [11], joint-based features [12, 16, 21] are widely exploited in the human action recognition. Joint features were further quantized into code words and histogram of 3D joints (HOJ3D) [16] and histogram of visual words [21] were employed to describe the action sequences. The above methods all adopt the histogram-based representations of features. Although the distribution of the spatial-temporal feature has good discriminative capability in its feature space, it doesn't preserve the temporal layout of the individual primitive postures of the action. The missing of a holistic representation in the temporal dimension may lead to the poor performance in actions with similar postures but different temporal order.

Different from the above histogram-based approaches, there are many methods focusing on the temporal order of the sequence and modeling the temporal dynamics in a holistic way. Motion template-based approaches [7, 20] introduced another way of modeling the temporal characteristics of human actions. In these methods, a number of motion templates indicating different action classes were trained. Dynamic Time Warping (DTW) was employed to warp the sequences of variant length and execution rate. The labels of the unknown action sequences were then determined by measuring the similarity between the unknown sequences and the motion templates.

Temporal Pyramid [14, 9] was developed to capture the temporal structure of the sequence by uniformly subdividing the sequence into partitions. Spatio-temporal feature descriptors were then applied to each partition. Since the uniform partition along the temporal axis is employed, the temporal pyramid is less flexible to handle the execution rate variation. Adaptive temporal pyramid [18] was proposed to overcome the above disadvantage by subdividing the temporal sequence according to the motion energy. A Super Normal Vector is generated from the space-time partition and served as the comprehensive representation of the sequence. However, this method relies on sophisticated features such as 3D surface normals and polynormals which are inapplicable to more general problems.

Vemulapalli [13] proposed a body-part representation of the skeleton and modeled the geometric transformation between different body parts in the 3D space. The temporal dynamics in terms of the 3D transformation were captured and projected as a curved manifold in the Lie group. Classifications on the curves eventually determined the labels of the action.

3. TEMPORAL ORDER-PRESERVING DYNAMIC QUANTIZATION

The modeling of the temporal dynamics of action sequences is one of the most challenging problems in human action recognition. Many temporal modeling methods [7, 20, 14] suffer from the temporal misalignment problem due to the variations in the execution rate. A more sophisticated modeling method which considers the dynamics quantization of the sequence is desired.

3.1 Dynamic Temporal Quantization

In order to address the misalignment caused by the variations of the execution rate, the action sequences must be dynamically quantized. Ideally, the quantization needs to be in accordance with the transition between sub-actions of the sequences. Two requirements must be satisfied to achieve such quantization, 1) frames with similar human postures are clustered together, 2) the temporal order of the sequence must be preserved.

The problem can then be formulated as follows. Denote $S = \{s_1, s_2, \cdots, s_n\}$ as an action sequence with n frames. Each frame s_i is represented by a k-dimensional feature vector $\mathbf{x_i} = (x_{i1}, x_{i2}, \cdots, x_{ik})$. The length n of each sequence can vary across different videos, so we wish to dynamically quantize each video into a new sequence $V = \{\mathbf{v}_1, \mathbf{v}_2, \cdots, \mathbf{v}_m\}$ of fixed size m. Each element of feature vector $\mathbf{v}_j$ in this new sequence represents an unknown hidden stage of a category of human action, whose temporal order is preserved. Mathematically, we use $a_i \in \{1, 2, \cdots, m\}$ to denote a frame s_i in the original sequence S is assigned to the quantized vector $\mathbf{v}_{a_i}$ in V. Obviously, for any two consecutive frames s_i and s_{i+1} in original sequences, in order to preserve their temporal order in the quantized sequence, their assignments a_i and a_{i+1} should satisfy $a_i \leq a_{i+1}$.

Then, a natural way to jointly optimize the assignment $\mathbf{a} = \{a_1, a_2, \cdots, a_n\}$ and the quantized sequence V can be obtained by jointly minimizing

$$\min_{\mathbf{a},V} \sum_{i=1}^{n} \|\mathbf{v}_{a_i} - \mathbf{x}_i\|^2, \tag{1}$$

$$s.t.\ \forall i \in [1, n-1],\ \ a_i \leq a_{i+1}, a_i \in [1, m]$$

where $\|\cdot\|$ can be any distance measurement. For convenience and efficiency consideration, we use Euclidean distance in the proposed algorithm.

It is nontrivial to jointly solve the optimal assignment $\mathbf{a}$ that satisfies the constraint of preserving the temporal order in each video, along with the optimal quantized sequence V. Our idea is to break down this optimization problem iteratively in a coordinate descent fashion.

Aggregation step: given the assignment $\mathbf{a}$ is fixed and Euclidean distance is adopted, it is not difficult to show that each element $\mathbf{v}_j$ of the optimal quantized sequence is the mean vector of all the elements $\mathbf{x}_i$ assigned to v_j. In other worlds, we have

$$\mathbf{v}_i = \frac{1}{|\{a_i = j\}|} \sum_{a_i = j} \mathbf{x}_i \tag{2}$$

where $|\cdot|$ is the set cardinality and $\{a_i = j\}$ is the set of elements in $\mathbf{a}$ whose value is j.

Assignment step: when V is fixed, the assignment $\mathbf{a}$ can be updated to minimize the above distance to these quantized vectors in V subject to the temporal order-preserving constraint. We are inspired to develop a dynamic programming approach by dynamic time warping (DTW) to solve this subproblem. Specifically, the minimal distance $D_{l+1,k+1}$ given by the best assignment from $S_{1:l+1}$ to $V_{1,k+1}$ can be induced by the following iterative equation

$$D_{l+1,k+1} = \min\{D_{l+1,k}, D_{l,k}, D_{l,k+1}\} + \|\mathbf{x}_{l+1}, \mathbf{v}_{k+1}\|^2, \tag{3}$$

where $\|\mathbf{x}_{l+1}, \mathbf{v}_{k+1}\|$ is the distance between the current video frame $\mathbf{x}_{l+1}$ and the current quantized frame $\mathbf{v}_{k+1}$. Then by starting with $D_{1,k} = \min_k \|\mathbf{x}_1 - \mathbf{v}_k\|^2$ and $D_{l,1} = \min_l \|\mathbf{x}_l - \mathbf{v}_1\|^2$, the best assignment can be found iteratively according to the above equation. The resulting assignment has the same characteristics of DTW [7]. It always measures the closest frame when choosing the next warping step, and the warping path is guaranteed to be non-decreasing in the temporal order.

The assignment $\mathbf{a}$ of the video frames and the update of V proceed iteratively until convergence. The above process can produce an optimal dynamic quantization of video frames.

Algorithm 1 Iterated Dynamic Quantizing Algorithm

```
Input  length of quantized sequence m,  feature sequence X = (x_1, x_2, ..., x_n),
Output a = {a_1, a_2, ..., a_n}, V = {v_1, ..., v_m}
procedure IDQA(X, m)
    Initialize assignment a by the uniform partition.
    repeat
        V = Aggregation(X, V)
        a = DynamicAssignment(X, V)
    until Convergence
    return a, V
end procedure
```

The pseudo code of the proposed Iterated Dynamic Quantizing Algorithm is presented in Algorithm 1. In the initialization, S is evenly split into m partitions, each of which is assigned to an element $\mathbf{v}_j$ of V. An *Aggregation* subprocedure is exploited to update the quantized sequence V according to the frame assignment results. Then, a *DynamicAssignment* subprocedure is used to warp the original feature X to the quantized sequence V. We propose a modified DTW algorithm for the warping process. The assignment $\mathbf{a}$ can be determined from the warping path. The above two steps iterate until V converges or the maximum iteration times is reached. The output is the converged quantization sequence V and the final frame assignment to it. The above iteration algorithm modifies the initial quantization result step by step by the warping and aggregation and eventually generates a result that not only considers the similarity of human postures but also preserves frame order.

The **Aggregation** subprocedure summarizes the original feature of the partition into a quantized vector. This vector must provide a highly discriminative representation of the partition. Several aggregation methods can be applied such as mean, sum, max and min. Different aggregation methods have different advantages. As an example, the mean method (Eq(2)) is robust to noise and is theoretically optimal under Euclidean distance. However, some salient human postures may be mitigated by the averaging process especially when the action sequence contains many neutral postures. The salient postures normally have higher discriminative capability than the neutral postures for the action recognition.

Considering these factors, we also test the max-pooling as the aggregation method in our proposed algorithm. It also provides a form of temporal translation invariance by taking the maximum values of the corresponding elements from the feature of the partition.

The **DynamicAssignment** subprocedure contains two parts. The first part computes the matrix $D_{m,n}$ storing the minimal distance between any pair of subsequences of X and V starting from the beginning. This part can be solved using Eq(3). The second part computes the warping path based on the obtained optimal D. Considering that the original feature sequence X is warped to a much shorter quantized sequence V, the step size of the warping path is restricted to $(1,0)$ and $(1,1)$, which is different from the classic DTW method that also allows $(0,1)$. In other words, the iteration Eq(3) changes to a more restricted form of $D_{l+1,k+1} = \min\{D_{l,k+1}, D_{l,k}\} + \|\mathbf{x}_{l+1}, \mathbf{v}_{k+1}\|^2$. This is to prevent the warping path from going too fast on the direction of the quantized sequence resulting in the effect that most of the frames are assigned to the last portion of V. It also avoids the scenario of one frame assigned to multiple quantized vectors at the same time.

3.2 Hierarchical Representation

Inspired by the Spatial Pyramid [4] and the Temporal Pyramid [14], we further extend the Dynamic Temporal Quantization by incorporating the hierarchical structure. Figure 2 illustrates the hierarchical architecture of the proposed dynamic quantization. The original sequence is recursively partitioned by the Iterated Dynamic Quantizing Algorithm and forms a pyramid structure. The i_{th} level has $2^i - 1$ partitions. As a result of the dynamic quantization, the length of each partition varies. A quantized vector is then aggregated from each partition and eventually the final feature vector is generated by concatenating the quantization vector of all layers. Figure 2 shows a pyramid structure with 4 levels. The proposed technique may benefit from a structure with higher levels. Nevertheless, a large number of quantizations may over-segment the action sequence and compromise the generalization capability. We study the relationship between the height of the pyramid and the performance in the experiments.

The proposed dynamic quantization approach has several benefits. First, by exploiting the dynamic temporal quantizing of the sequence, it can address the challenge of execution rate variation by achieving a dynamic temporal quantization. Second, feature vectors with highly discriminative capability can be extracted by the aggregation procedure of the quantization. Third, the hierarchical description in terms of the multi-layer pyramid achieves a comprehensive representation of the temporal dynamics of the action by capturing both the global and local temporal patterns of the action.

4. MULTIMODAL FEATURE FUSION

Multimodal sensors such as Kinect can provide data from different modalities including depth image, RGB image and skeleton map. In this approach, we extract features from all three data modalities and adopt supervised learning for the classification. The final recognition result is computed by the fusion of the classification results of each individual feature.

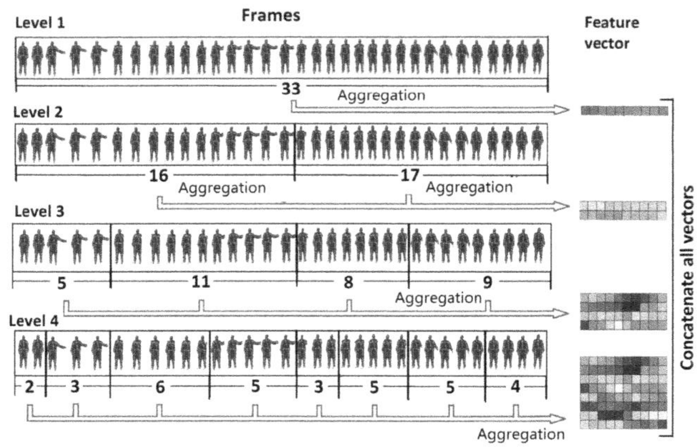

Figure 2: Illustration of the Dynamic Temporal Quantization and its hierarchical representation.

4.1 View-invariant Features

To leverage the discriminative capability from different data modalities, we use the following features in the proposed approach.

1. **Position:** 3D coordinates of the 20 joints of the skeleton.
2. **Angle:** normalized pairwise-angle feature.
3. **Offset:** offset of the 3D joint positions between the current and the previous frame [21].
4. **Velocity:** histogram of the velocity components of the point cloud.

The position feature is computed from the skeleton map by concatenating the x, y and z coordinates of all joints. It holds the raw information of the skeleton map and no special feature extraction is needed. In the angle feature, body segments are first computed by connecting each pair of adjacent joints. The normalized cosine value of each pair of the body segments are then computed and concatenated as the angle feature.

To better leverage the multimodal data, we propose the velocity feature of the point cloud. Generally speaking, the velocity feature describes the distribution of the movement of the point cloud at the neighborhood of each joint in the 3D space. Specifically, the 3D point cloud can be constructed from the depth image. In order to track the movement of the point cloud, optical flow is first extracted on the RGB image to compute the displacement of pixels between two consecutive frames. By leveraging the pixel-to-pixel correspondence between the depth image and the RGB image, the displacement of each pixel of the point cloud can be obtained and is used to compute the 3D velocity. To maintain the spatial information, the point cloud is split into clusters according to the joints. A square window with the joint at the center is applied to sample the region in the 3D neighborhood of each joint. The velocity of each 3D point is further decomposed into x, y and z components which are further quantized into three bins indicating the positive, zero and negative values, respectively. Finally, a 9-bin histogram is generated for each joint and a 180D velocity feature is produced by concatenating all the 20 joints. Different from the above features levering only the joint information, the velocity feature is extracted from the cloud point which gives more details about the micro temporal dynamics of the human actions.

Among the above four features, the angle feature are view-independent by nature. To handle the viewpoint variation for the other features, the 3D point cloud are transformed from the world coordinate system to a human-centric coordinate system by placing the "hip-center" at the origin and aligning the "spine" with the y-axis. The PCA (Principle Component Analysis) is adopt to the above features for the dimension reduction and noise reduction purposes. The above four features cover all three modalities of the sensing data from the Kinect and provide a rich representation of the human actions.

4.2 Frame Assignment Sharing

In the previous section, the Dynamic Temporal Quantizing Algorithm is computed based on the original feature of the action sequence. All of the above four features can be used to compute their own temporal quantization of the video frames. Should the frame assignment of the quantization be computed by one feature and shared by all other features or should it be done independently? Intuitively, the independent quantization strategy may produce the best classification result with respect to individual feature that has been used. Nevertheless, it may encounter the overfitting problem and compromise the generalization capability when multimodal features are fused. Therefore, we compute the frame assignment of the quantization based on the feature with the highest discriminative capability. This assignment is applied to all the other three features to compute their own quantization results. We performed experimental study to justify the benefit of the sharing strategy and will discuss the result in the experiment section.

4.3 Classification and Fusion

We employ the supervised learning to learn the temporal dynamics of different actions from the quantized sequence discussed in the last section. A multi-class model is learned from the training samples for each feature. The trained model is then used to predict the type of the unknown actions based on this feature. The final recognition result is the fusion of the predictions of all individual features.

To be more specific, the SVM (Support Vector Machine) [1] is employed as the classifier in our method. A multi-class SVM is trained for each feature independently. In the predicting phase, each SVM estimates the label of an action with a probability. The final classification result is then fused from the estimation of the multi-class SVM of each feature.

5. EXPERIMENTS

We evaluate the performance of the proposed method on three public datasets: UTKinect-Action [17], MSR-Action3D [5] and MSR-ActionPairs [9]. We choose these datasets because they provide data from at least two modalities and satisfy our multimodal feature fusion framework. In our experiment, the levels of hierarchical quantization structure is set to 4 and $2^4 - 1 = 15$ partitions are generated to represent the entire action sequence. The PCA dimension reduction is set to preserve 99.5% of the energy of the raw feature. The window size for the velocity feature is set to 51×51. These parameters are tuned according to the performances in the training set. We use the LibSVM [1] with the RBF kernel as the classifier in our experiments. The fusion process computes the mean probability of the prediction from each individual feature and decides the final label of the action by the highest mean probability.

Levels	5	4	3	2	1	0
Accuracy (%)	77.39	81.61	71.26	67.82	66.28	73.56

Table 1: Experiment on different levels of quantization pyramid on the MSR-Action3D dataset.

5.1 MSR-Action3D Dataset

The MSR-Action3D dataset [5] contains 20 action classes and 10 subjects. Each subject performs each action two or three times. The 20 action types are chosen in the context of gaming. They cover a variety of movements related to arms, legs, torso, etc. The noise of the joint locations in the skeleton as well as the high intra-class variations and the inter-class similarities make the dataset very challenging. As an example, the action "Draw x" is easily confused with the action "Draw tick". We followed exactly the same experiment settings of [14], that all 20 action classes are tested in one group. Half of the subjects are used for training and the rest are for testing. We note there is another experiment setting used in the literature which splits the 20 action types into three subsets and only performs the evaluation within each subset [5]. The experiment setting we followed is more challenging than the subset one because all actions are evaluated together and the chance of confusion is much higher.

To evaluate how the height of the quantization pyramid can affect the recognition accuracy, we perform experiments on different levels of pyramid on the position feature and test their performances. Results are summarized in Table 1. In this experiment, zero to five levels of pyramid are evaluated. Zero means no hierarchical structure is employed, the entire sequence is quantized into 8 partitions by the proposed Iterated Dynamic Quantizing Algorithm. It can be regarded as the leaf-nodes of the 4-level pyramid. Two observations can be found from the results. First, as the increase of the height of the pyramid, the recognition accuracy is also increasing. However the performance begins to drop when the height reaches five. This can be explained that the higher levels of the pyramid, the deeper hierarchical structure can be captured to describe the temporal dynamics. That's why the classification rate keeps increasing. Nevertheless, when the sequence is over quantized with too many small partitions, the method becomes less generalized and the turning point occurs. Second, the accuracy of the 4-level pyramid (81.61%) is higher than that of using only the leaf-nodes (0-level, 73.56%). This has demonstrated that the hierarchical structure has contributed to the dynamic quantization of the sequence. The inclusion of the upper layers has enhanced the generalization capability of the modeling method.

To also evaluate the effects of the Iterated Dynamic Quantizing Algorithm, we compare it against a deterministic quantizing method that always evenly splits the sequence. This

Feature	Accuracy		
	Proposed	Deterministic quantization	w/o assignment sharing
position	81.61%	76.24%	81.23%
angle	73.95%	71.65%	72.41%
offset	73.95%	68.20%	64.75%
velocity	80.84%	72.80%	80.08%
fused result	90.42%	83.15%	88.51%

Table 2: Experiments on the effects of the dynamic temporal quantization and the frame assignment sharing strategy on the MSR-Action3D dataset.

Method	Accuracy
Actionlet Ensemble [14]	88.2%
HON4D [9]	88.89%
DCSF [15]	89.3%
Lie Group [13]	89.48%
Super Normal Vector [18]	93.09%
Proposed approach	90.42%

Table 3: Comparison with state-of-the-art results.

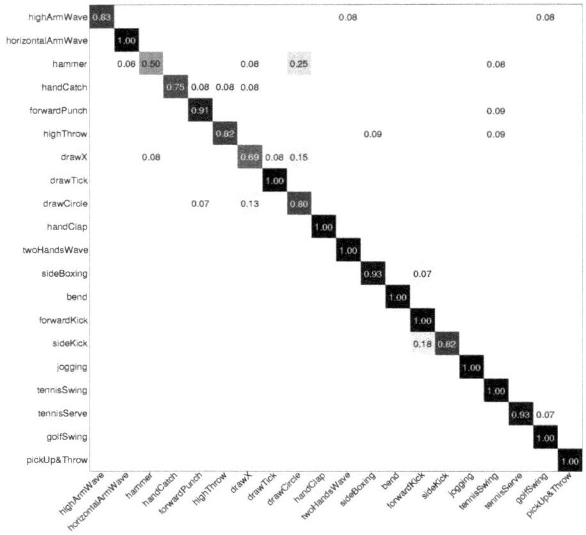

Figure 3: Confusion Matrix on the MSR-Action3D dataset.

is the same method used in the Fourier Temporal Pyramid [14]. Experiments results are summarized in Table 2. The second column and the third column show, the proposed algorithm with the dynamic quantization has a higher accuracy than the deterministic quantization method on all individual features as well as the fused result. Such performance increase demonstrates the advantage of the dynamic temporal quantization over the deterministic quantization method.

We also evaluate the performance of the frame assignment sharing strategy and compare it against the independent strategy. In the proposed method, the frame assignment of the quantization is computed with the position feature. The fourth column of Table 2 shows the performances of the strategy without the frame assignment sharing. We can see that the performance of the independent strategy is lower than the proposed method with the sharing. Other features which are less discriminative than the position feature benefit from the assignment computed based on the position feature. This has demonstrated the advantage of the frame assignment sharing strategy.

Last but not least, the fused result is significantly higher than the recognition rates of all individual features in all three columns in Table 2. One possible explanation is the multimodal features have complimentary discriminative capabilities which can be leveraged by the fusion and therefore yield superior performance over individual features alone. As an example, the position feature, in terms of joint coordinates, is good at describing the human pose from the global point of view. Meanwhile, the velocity feature based on the 3D point cloud is good at capturing the micro movements of the body parts. Therefore these two features from different modalities are complimentary to each other and can generate enhanced performance when fused.

We list state-of-the-art approaches in the recent years in Table 3 for comparison. As can be seen, the proposed method achieves a higher recognition rate than most of state-of-the-art results. The only method achieves a higher accuracy than ours is the super normal vector method [18].

Figure 3 shows the confusion matrix on the MSRAction-3D dataset. Most of the confusions between similar actions have been correctly addressed. The remaining confusions are between actions containing very similar primitive postures such as "Side kick" and "Forward kick" and "Draw x" and "Draw circle".

5.2 UTKinect-Action Dataset

The UTKinect-Action dataset [17] consists of 199 action sequences in total. These sequences have 10 action types performed by 10 subjects. All subjects perform each action two times. Different from the previous dataset, subjects perform actions at varied locations in the scene. The huge viewpoint variation and intra-class variance make the dataset very challenging. We follow the same cross-subject test setting as in [13]. Half of the subjects are used for training and the rest are for testing.

We follow the same strategy in the MSR-Action3D dataset that the frame assignment of the quantization is computed based on the position feature and is applied to all other features. The performances of individual features and the fused result are summarized in Table 4. Similar results can be found that the proposed dynamic quantization algorithm achieved higher performance than the deterministic quantization on most of the features as well as the fused result. This has again demonstrated the advantage of the dynamic temporal quantizing algorithm. To our surprise, the fused result achieved the 100% accuracy. All samples in the testing set are correctly classified, which strongly demonstrates the performance of the proposed approach.

Table 5 shows the comparison of the classification accuracy between the proposed algorithm and state-of-the-art methods. Although the Lie Group [13] method achieves very good performance on this dataset (97.08%), the pro-

Feature	Accuracy		
	Proposed	Deterministic quantization	w/o assign-ment sharing
position	94.95%	88.89%	94.95%
angle	91.92%	87.88%	94.95%
offset	80.81%	74.75%	74.75%
velocity	79.80%	81.82%	78.79%
fused result	100%	96.97%	97.98%

Table 4: Experiments on the effects of the dynamic temporal quantization and the frame assignment sharing on the UTKinect-Action dataset.

Method	Accuracy
Histogram of 3D joints [17]	90.92%
Combined features with random forest [21]	91.9%
Lie Group [13]	97.08%
Proposed approach	100%

Table 5: Comparison with state-of-the-art results on the UTKinect-Action dataset.

posed algorithm still outperformed state-of-the-art results by achieving the 100% accuracy.

5.3 MSR-ActionPairs Dataset

The MSR-ActionPairs dataset [9] is composed of 12 actions performed by 10 subjects. Each subject performs all actions three times. Therefore, the dataset contains 360 action sequences in total. Different from the other two datasets, this dataset contains 6 pairs of actions. Each pair of actions have exactly the same primitive postures but the reversed temporal order. As an example, "Pick up" and "Put down", "Put on a hat" and "Take off a hat". This dataset is collected to investigate the effects of temporal order on the recognition of the actions. The huge within-pair similarity makes the dataset very challenging. Therefore, histogram-based temporal modeling methods relying on the bag-of-words or visual codes may perform poorly on this dataset if the dynamic patterns are not properly interpreted. We follow the same test setting of [9] that the first 5 subjects are used for testing and the last 5 subjects are used for training. Experimental results are summarized in Table 6.

Similar to the results from the other two datasets, the position feature and the velocity feature show higher dis-

Feature	Accuracy		
	Proposed	Deterministic quantization	w/o assign-ment sharing
position	86.28%	86.85%	86.28%
angle	82.86%	82.86%	82.86%
offset	81.71%	81.14%	70.86%
velocity	89.71%	88.57%	90.28%
fused result	93.71%	91.43%	93.14%

Table 6: Experiments on the effects of the dynamic temporal quantization and the frame assignment sharing strategy on the MSR-ActionPairs dataset.

Method	Accuracy
Skeleton + LOP + Pyramid [14]	82.22%
HON4D [9]	93.33%
HON4D + D_{disc} [9]	96.67%
Super Normal Vector [18]	98.89%
Proposed approach	93.71%

Table 7: Comparison with state-of-the-art results on the MSR-ActionPairs dataset.

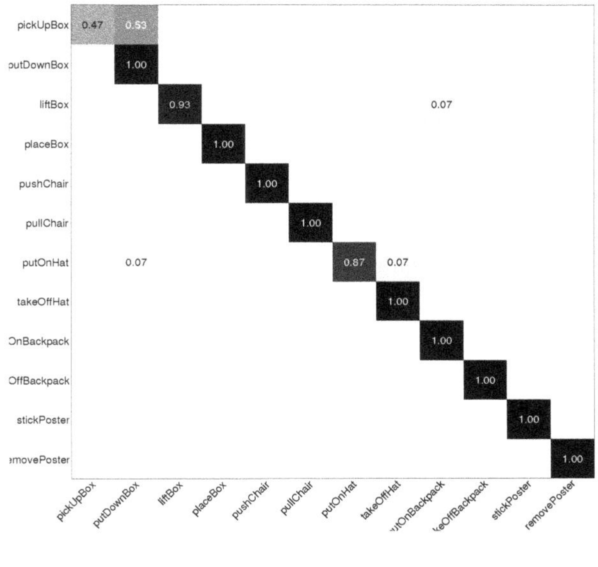

Figure 4: Confusion Matrix on the MSR-ActionPairs dataset.

criminative capability than the other features in all three columns of Table 6. The fused results, by leveraging the fusion of multimodal data, all achieve higher performance than any individual feature alone. One interesting result is, the strategy without the assignment sharing has equal or higher accuracy than the proposed method on all feature except the offset feature. However, fused result is still lower than that of the proposed method enabled with the sharing strategy. Such results justify our hypothesis that the dynamic quantization may get overfitted on some individual features and the overall generalization is compromised when multimodal results are fused.

We further compare the accuracy of the proposed method with state-of-the-art methods and report the results in Table 7. It can be seen that the proposed method achieves a comparable accuracy to the methods listed. The only methods having a higher classification rate than ours are the histogram of 4D normals with discriminative projection [9] and the super normal vector [18]. These two methods rely on sophisticated features such as 4D surface normals and polynormals which are inapplicable to more general problems. Nevertheless, the proposed method provides a generic solution to the optimal temporal quantization problem and is independent from any features which makes the direct comparison unfair.

Figure 4 shows the confusion matrix of the dataset. Although the actions within each pair are highly confusing, the proposed method still achieves very good performance by discriminating the actions in each pair. It can be seen that the within-pair confusion only occurs between "Pick up box" and "Put down box". Most of the actions with similar postures and temporal variations are correctly distinguished by the proposed method. Such performance has demonstrated the advantages of the proposed Dynamic Temporal Quantization method.

6. CONCLUSIONS

In this paper, we address the challenge of temporal modeling for human action recognition in multimodal streams. We study the problem of optimal temporal quantization of the video sequences and provide a solution of dynamic temporal quantizing. We further present a fusion method under this quantization framework to leverage the complementary discriminative capability of multimodal features. Experimental results on three public action datasets show the proposed approach has achieved state-of-the-art performance.

7. ACKNOWLEDGMENTS

This material is partially supported by NASA under Grant Number NNX14AQ29A. Any opinions, findings, and conclusions or recommendations expressed in this materials are those of the authors and do not necessarily reflect the views of NASA.

8. REFERENCES

[1] C.-C. Chang and C.-J. Lin. LIBSVM: A library for support vector machines. *ACM Transactions on Intelligent Systems and Technology*, 2, 2011.

[2] L. Han, X. Wu, W. Liang, G. Hou, and Y. Jia. Discriminative human action recognition in the learned hierarchical manifold space. *Image and Vision Computing*, 28(5):836–849, 2010.

[3] I. Laptev. On space-time interest points. *International Journal of Computer Vision*, 64(2-3):107–123, 2005.

[4] S. Lazebnik, C. Schmid, and J. Ponce. Beyond bags of features: Spatial pyramid matching for recognizing natural scene categories. In *Computer Vision and Pattern Recognition, IEEE Computer Society Conference on*, volume 2, pages 2169–2178, 2006.

[5] W. Li, Z. Zhang, and Z. Liu. Action recognition based on a bag of 3d points. In *Computer Vision and Pattern Recognition Workshops, 2010 IEEE Computer Society Conference on*, pages 9–14.

[6] F. Lv and R. Nevatia. Recognition and segmentation of 3-d human action using hmm and multi-class adaboost. In *Computer Vision–ECCV 2006*, pages 359–372.

[7] M. Müller and T. Röder. Motion templates for automatic classification and retrieval of motion capture data. In *Proceedings of the 2006 ACM SIGGRAPH*, pages 137–146.

[8] B. Ni, G. Wang, and P. Moulin. Rgbd-hudaact: A color-depth video database for human daily activity recognition. In *Consumer Depth Cameras for Computer Vision*, pages 193–208. Springer, 2013.

[9] O. Oreifej and Z. Liu. Hon4d: Histogram of oriented 4d normals for activity recognition from depth sequences. In *Computer Vision and Pattern Recognition, 2013 IEEE Conference on*, pages 716–723.

[10] G.-J. Qi, X.-S. Hua, Y. Rui, J. Tang, T. Mei, M. Wang, and H.-J. Zhang. Correlative multilabel video annotation with temporal kernels. *ACM Transactions on Multimedia Computing, Communications, and Applications (TOMM)*, 5(1):3, 2008.

[11] J. Shotton, T. Sharp, A. Kipman, A. Fitzgibbon, M. Finocchio, A. Blake, M. Cook, and R. Moore. Real-time human pose recognition in parts from single depth images. *Communications of the ACM*, 56(1):116–124, 2013.

[12] L. Sun and K. Aizawa. Action recognition using invariant features under unexampled viewing conditions. In *Proceedings of the 21st ACM international conference on Multimedia*, pages 389–392, 2013.

[13] R. Vemulapalli, F. Arrate, and R. Chellappa. Human action recognition by representing 3d skeletons as points in a lie group. In *Computer Vision and Pattern Recognition, IEEE Conference on*, 2014.

[14] J. Wang, Z. Liu, Y. Wu, and J. Yuan. Mining actionlet ensemble for action recognition with depth cameras. In *Computer Vision and Pattern Recognition, 2012 IEEE Conference on*, pages 1290–1297.

[15] L. Xia and J. Aggarwal. Spatio-temporal depth cuboid similarity feature for activity recognition using depth camera. In *Computer Vision and Pattern Recognition, 2013 IEEE Conference on*, pages 2834–2841.

[16] L. Xia, C.-C. Chen, and J. Aggarwal. View invariant human action recognition using histograms of 3d joints. In *Computer Vision and Pattern Recognition Workshops, 2012 IEEE Computer Society Conference on*, pages 20–27.

[17] L. Xia, C.-C. Chen, and J. Aggarwal. View invariant human action recognition using histograms of 3d joints. In *Computer Vision and Pattern Recognition Workshops, 2012 IEEE Computer Society Conference on*, pages 20–27.

[18] X. Yang and Y. Tian. Super normal vector for activity recognition using depth sequences. In *Computer Vision and Pattern Recognition, IEEE Conference on*, 2014.

[19] X. Yang, C. Zhang, and Y. Tian. Recognizing actions using depth motion maps-based histograms of oriented gradients. In *Proceedings of the 20th ACM international conference on Multimedia*, pages 1057–1060, 2012.

[20] X. Zhao, X. Li, C. Pang, X. Zhu, and Q. Z. Sheng. Online human gesture recognition from motion data streams. In *Proceedings of the 21st ACM international conference on Multimedia*, pages 23–32, 2013.

[21] Y. Zhu, W. Chen, and G. Guo. Fusing spatiotemporal features and joints for 3d action recognition. In *Computer Vision and Pattern Recognition workshops, 2013 IEEE Conference on*.

Fine-Grained Image Categorization by Localizing Tiny Object Parts from Unannotated Images

Luming Zhang[†], Yi Yang[‡], and Roger Zimmermann[†]
†School of Computing, National University of Singapore, Singapore
‡Centre for Quantum Computation & Intelligent Systems
the University of Technology, Sydney

ABSTRACT

This paper proposes a novel fine-grained image categorization model where no object annotation is required in the training/testing stage. The key technique is a dense graph mining algorithm that localizes multiscale discriminative object parts in each image. In particular, to mimick human hierarchical perception mechanism, a superpixel pyramid is generated for each image, based on which graphlets from each layer are constructed to seamlessly describe object parts. We observe that graphlets representative to each category are densely distributed in the feature space. Therefore a dense graph mining algorithm is developed to discover graphlets representative to each sub-/super-category. Finally, the discovered graphlets from pairwise images are encoded into an image kernel for fine-grained recognition. Experiments on the UCB-200 [32] shown that our method performs competitively to many models relying on the annotated bird parts.

Categories and Subject Descriptors

H.3.4 [**Information Storage and Retrieval**]: Systems and Software

Keywords

Fine-grained; graph mining; hierarchical; perception; image kernel

1. INTRODUCTION

A large number of object recognition models have been developed in multimedia retrieval and analysis. Many of them focus on discriminatively learning to distinguish objects belonging to different basic-level categories. Inspired by applications in areas such as agriculture, medicine, and forestry, fine-grained domain recognition has become a hot research topic recently. For example, some Apps have been developed to recognize different species of pests, based on which suitable chemicals can be employed to eliminate them. Intuitively, successfully recognizing objects from multiple sub-categories is a difficult task. Even a knowledgeable person might be confused to distinguish poisonous/non-poisonous mushrooms. In summary, existing approaches suffer from the following challenges:

ICMR'15, June 23–26 2015, Shanghai, China.

DOI: http://dx.doi.org/10.1145/2671188.2749299.

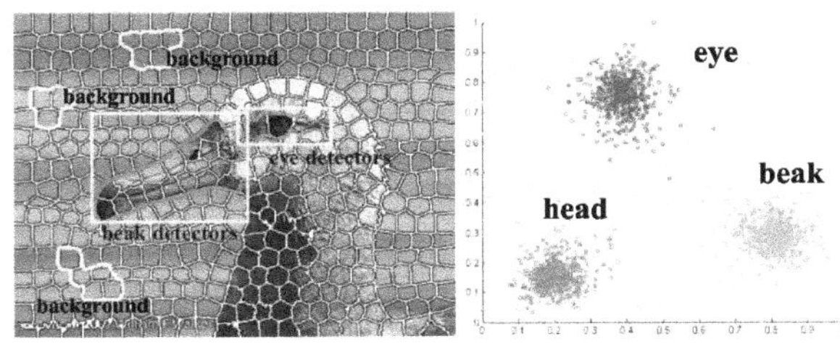

Figure 1: Left: bird beak/eye detectors built upon graphlets (red) and rectangular window (yellow) respectively; Right: distribution of graphlets from the sub-category "black foot albatross" (the yellow points denote the non-discriminative bird parts).

- Many fine-grained recognition models are part-based models, where object parts are either manually annotated or discovered by a set of object detectors. For the former, the annotation quality is good but the annotation process is labor-intensive. For the latter, a set of object component detectors are pre-defined for a specific data set, making the model difficult to be transferred from one data set to another.

- Fine-grained recognition discriminates similar objects with subtle differences. It requires the recognition model can discover the discriminative object details. Typically, a scanning window is used for part detection. However, the rectangular scanning window cannot well capture those arbitrarily shaped object components, such as the bird beak in Figure 1.

To solve the above problems, this paper presents hierarchical graphlet matching (HGM) for fine-grained image categorization. The key advantage is that discriminative object parts with different scales can be localized automatically from unannotated images. As shown in Figure 2, to mimick the coarse-to-fine visual perception of humans, a KL-divergence-based clustering is employed to construct the hierarchy of the super-/sub-categories. To seamlessly describe an object in each hierarchy layer, we construct a superpixel pyramid and further propose graphlets by connecting spatially connected superpixels from each pyramid layer. As the number of graphlets is huge, only those discriminative for fine-grained categorization should be preserved. As shown on the right of Figure 1, **highly discriminative graphlets to each super-/sub-category are densely distributed in the feature space, as these graphlets are similar**

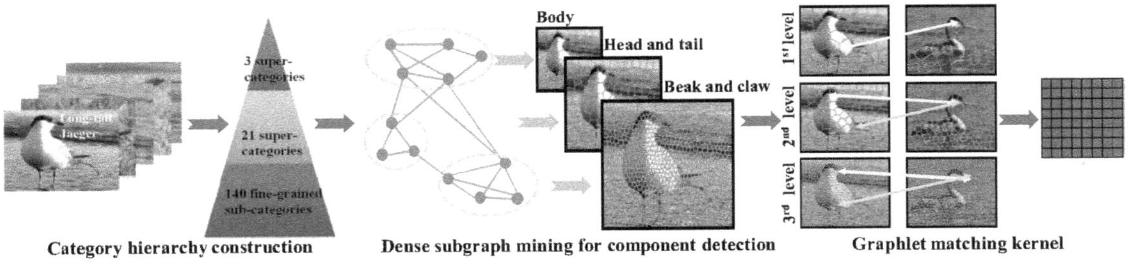

Figure 2: The pipeline of the proposed fine-grained image categorization model

in appearance. Therefore, an affinity graph is constructed to describe the similarity of graphlets to each super-/sub-category, based on which dense subgraphs containing the discriminative graphlets are selected. Finally, an image kernel is calculated by matching the selected graphlets from pairwise images hierarchically.

The contributions of this paper are two-fold: 1) the first fine-grained recognition model discovering multiscale discriminative object parts from unannotated training and testing images; and 2) a graphlet matching kernel that stimulates human hierarchial visual perception.

2. RELATED WORK

Our work is closely related to the graph-based image modeling in multimedia retrieval [38, 39, 40, 41]. As a natural binary relationship descriptor, graphical models are frequently used to exploit the geometric property of different regions in an image. In [5], Harchaoui *et al.* proposed walk-/tree-kernel that capture the walk/tree structures among local image regions using a finite sequence of neighboring regions. In [6], Duchenne *et al.* proposed a graph matching kernel for object categorization. That is, the graph vertices correspond to a set of image grids, and the edges reflect the grid structure, functioning as springs preserving the geometry of neighboring grids. Lin *et al.* [7] introduced an object categorization framework based on sketch graphs, *i.e.*, a learnable And-Or graph model. Further, in [8], Zhang *et al.* proposed to measure the similarity between aerial images by selectively matching their respective graphlets. Note that all these graphical models exploit geometric descriptors for basic-level categories, which fail to capture the detailed visual cues discriminative to sub-categories. Besides, many of them rely on the prior knowledge of a specific data set, limiting the application across different data sets.

Recently, many fine-grained categorization models have been developed. Most of them focus on learning part detectors from training annotated images [10, 11, 12, 14, 45, 34, 35, 36, 37], or localizing distinctive object details by human interaction [15, 17]. A few approaches are reviewed as follows. Yao *et al.* [12] represented an image by pooling template matching responses. The templates are sampled from 1.5× the size of the object bounding box. In [14], Berg *et al.* proposed a grid-level saliency model for describing fine-grained image categories. Annotated object parts are aligned and cropped to indicate the discriminative parts. Deng *et al.* [15] designed a human interactive crowdsourcing system allowing users to localize discriminative object parts. Angelova *et al.* [18] "zoom in" the foreground objects segmented from an image for fine-grained recognition. Compared to the previous fine-grained models, our approach is free from annotated object parts in both the training and the testing stages. Zhang *et al.* [44] proposed a one-vs-all mid-level features for fine-grained recognition. The method is dimension friendly since the dimension of learned mid-level features is only related with the number of classes and far less than that of the low level ones.

3. CATEGORY HIERARCHY CONSTRUCTION

3.1 Topological Object Descriptors

As aforementioned, besides the large object components reflecting the basic-level category, fine-grained recognition depends on an accurate description of the tiny object parts. In our work, both the large objects and their tiny parts are constructed from superpixels, which align neatly with object boundaries. More specifically, objects and their parts are described by graphlets:

$$\mathcal{G} = (\mathcal{V}, \mathcal{E}), \tag{1}$$

where $\mathcal{V}$ is a set of vertices, each representing a superpixel; $\mathcal{E}$ is a set of edges, each connecting pairwise spatially adjacent superpixels. The number of constituent superpixels of a graphlet is called the graphlet size. As shown in Figure 3, graphlets well capture different object parts, which are descriptive to each sub-category.

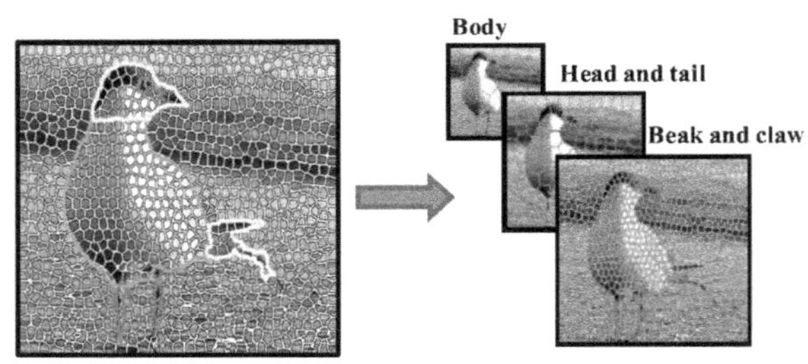

Figure 3: Left: A single superpixel mosaic describing a bird and its parts; Right: A superpixel pyramid where differently sized object parts are described in different layers.

3.2 KL-divergence-based Category Hierarchy

To mimick the hierarchical perception of humans, we cluster the sub-categories into super-categories. We first measure the similarity between images from two sub-categories. Unfortunately, global feature-based distance or unselectively local feature matching is not suitable here. We want to compare the object parts that are representative to each sub-category. For pairwise images, we first establish the matchings between their SIFT descriptors. Among all the SIFT descriptor matchings, some are between patches from the foreground objects, while the rest are between patches from the backgrounds. As shown in Figure 4, if we model the distribution of all the pairwise matched SIFT descriptors from a sub-category, those from the foreground objects will closely distributed since they have similar appearance. While SIFT descriptors from the background will distribute dispersedly, since the patches can have arbitrary appearances. This reveals that the divergence between SIFT distribution from two sub-categories can well distinguish two sub-categories. In this work, the distribution of the matched SIFT descriptors from a sub-category is modeled by a GMM $\mathcal{N}$. Then, the similarity between sub-categories can be described by the KL-divergence between their SIFT distributions. Due to the non-symmetry of KL-divergence, it is difficult to integrate it into a semi-definite matrix for clustering. Instead, we use the square root of Jensen-Shannon divergence [22], a symmetric metric derived from KL-divergence.

Based on the Jensen-Shannon divergence, we encode it into

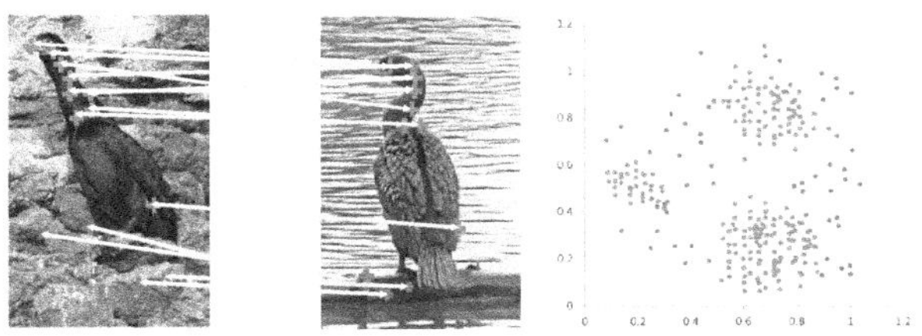

Figure 4: Left: SIFT descriptor matching between images; Right: distribution of matched SIFT descriptors (red: objects, blue: background).

spectral clustering for building the category hierarchy. More specifically, we construct an affinity matrix $\mathbf{W}$ wherein the ij-th element is computed as:

$$\mathbf{W}_{ij} = \exp\left(-\frac{D_{JS}(\mathcal{N}_i||\mathcal{N}_j)}{2\psi^2}\right), \quad (2)$$

where $\mathcal{N}_i$ and $\mathcal{N}_j$ denote the SIFT distributions of i-th and the j-th sub-categories respectively, and D_{JS} is the Jensen-Shannon divergence. Then, we calculate the Laplacian matrix accordingly and group the sub-categories into H parent-categories[1]. We empirically observe that a three layer hierarchy achieves a good performance. And the number of categories from the i-th layer is fixed to 1/7 to that from the $(i+1)$-th layer $(i = 1, 2)$.

4. DISCRIMINATIVE OBJECT PARTS DISCOVERY

Obviously, discriminative object parts from each sub-category (*e.g.*, the bird beaks) distribute densely in the feature space (can be quantified into an affinity graph). In contrast, non-discriminative object components distribute dispersedly. Thus, a dense graph mining framework is proposed to discover graphlets representative to different sub-/super-categories, as the pipeline shown in Figure 5.

4.1 Affinity Graph Construction

To construct an affinity graph that describes the similarity between graphlets, a similarity measure is required. In the color channel, the appearance similarity between graphlets can be measured by a Gaussian kernel, *i.e.*, $\mathbf{S}^c_{i,j} \propto \exp\left(-||x^c_i - x^c_j||^2/\sigma^2\right)$, where x^c_i describes the color channel graphlets by a 9-dimensional color moment (CM) [25], and σ^2 is the empirical variance.

[1]In this work, parent-categories are super-categories one layer higher than the those in the current layer.

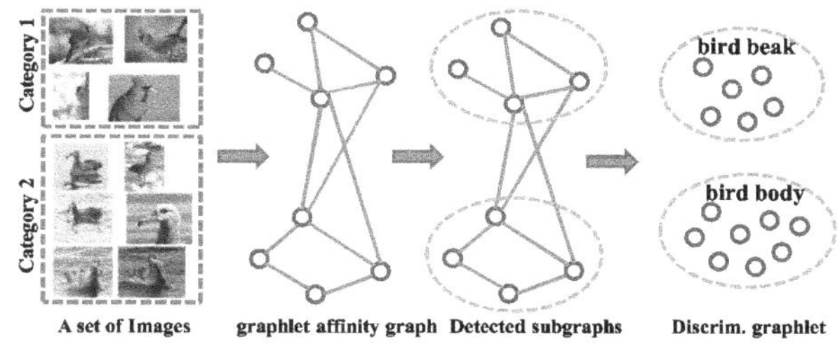

Figure 5: Detecting discriminative object parts using the dense graph mining technique. Each purple vertex denotes a graphlet and each edge connects pairwise similar graphlets.

Though it is common to use color channel as the similarity metric for object classification. It is not sufficiently descriptive for our object parts detection. HOG [24] based sliding window is standard for object detection. Thus, the similarity between graphlets is calculated by combining both the CM and the HOG descriptors:

$$\mathbf{S}_{i,j} = \mathbf{S}^c_{i,j} \cdot \mathbf{S}^t_{i,j}, \quad (3)$$

where $\mathbf{S}^t_{i,j}$ denotes the similarity in the textural channel, which is computed similarly to $\mathbf{S}^c_{i,j}$.

4.2 Mining Dense Subgraphs by Graph Shift

To effectively discover dense subgraphs from an affinity graph, two conditions are required. First, *compatibility with graph representation*: many similarity metrics are defined based on binary relation, such as our color+texture-based similarity. Only graph-based clustering can utilize this pairwise relation directly. Second, *robustness to outliers*: many graphlets, such as those from the background and highly occluded, may not belong to any sub-category. Methods insisting on partitioning all input data into coherent groups without explicit outliers may fail to preserve the structure of sub-categories. Conventional clustering algorithms, *e.g.*, k-means, are not suitable here as they insist on partitioning all the input data. Comparatively, graph shift [26], which is efficient and robust for graph mode seeking, is particularly suitable for the discriminative graphlet mining. It directly works on graph, supports an arbitrary number of clusters, and leaves the outlier points ungrouped.

Formally, we define an individual graph $\mathbf{G} = (\mathbf{V}, \mathbf{A})$ for each category, $\mathbf{V} = \{v_1, v_2, \cdots, v_{N_i}\}$ is a set of vertices denoting the graphlets extracted from images in category i. $\mathbf{A}$ is a symmetric matrix with non-negative elements. The diagonal elements of $\mathbf{A}$ are one while the non-diagonal element measures the similarity between graphelts, as detailed in (3). The modes of a graph $\mathbf{G}$ are defined as local maximizers of graph density function $g(y) = y^T\mathbf{A}y$, $y \in \Delta^{N_i}$, where $\Delta^{N_i} = \{y \in \mathbb{R}^{N_i} : y \geq 0 \text{ and } ||y||_{l_1} = 1\}$. More specifically, the similarity between graphlets is expressed as the edge weights of graph $\mathbf{G}$. The vertices represent the graphlets corresponding to a category. Therefore, discriminative object parts correspond to vertices of those strongly connected subgraphs. It is worth emphasizing that those strongly connected subgraphs correspond to large local maxima of $g(y)$ over simplex, which is an approximation of the average affinity score of these subgraphs.

The target patterns are the local maximizers of $g(y)$, which are detected by solving the quadratic optimization problem as follows:

$$\max_y g(y) = y^T\mathbf{A}y, \;\; s.t. \;\; y \in \Delta^n, \quad (4)$$

Obtaining an analytic solution of (4) is difficult. Therefore, we employ replicator dynamics to find the local maxima of (4). Given an initialization $y(0)$, the corresponding local solution y^* can be iteratively computed by the discrete-time version of the first-order replicator equation:

$$y_i(t+1) = y_i(t)\frac{(\mathbf{A}y(t))_i}{y(t)^T\mathbf{A}y(t)}. \quad (5)$$

5. HIERARCHICAL GRAPHLET MATCHING KERNEL

After discovering the discriminative graphlets for each sub-/super-category, each image can be represented by a collection of planar visual features in $\mathbb{R}^2$. Unfortunately, conventional classifiers such as SVM can only handle 1-D vector form features. Moreover, the number of discovered graphlets from each image varies. Thus, it would be impractical for a conventional classifier such as SVM to carry out classification directly. To tackle this problem, a hierarchical graphlet kernel is calculated by quantizing the extracted graphlets from an image into a 1-D vector.

The proposed quantization method is built upon the Euclidean

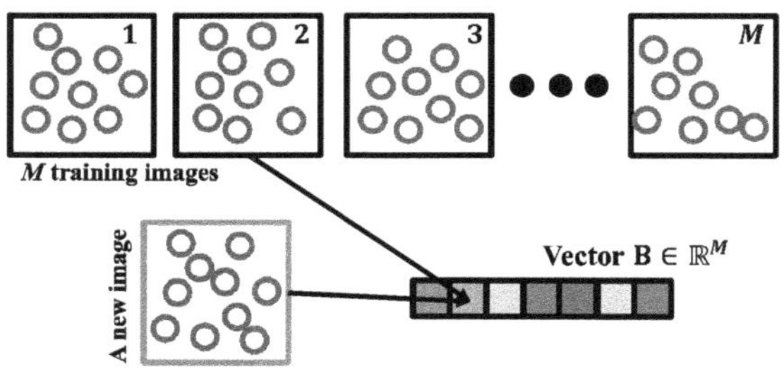

Figure 6: Hierarchical graphlet matching kernel calculation.

distance between images, which is computed based on the extracted graphlets. As shown in Figure 6, given an image, discriminative graphlets corresponding to sub- and super-categories are extracted. The extracted graphlets are then converted into a vector $\mathbf{B} = [\beta_1, \beta_2, \cdots, \beta_M]$, where each element of $\mathbf{B}$ is computed as:

$$\beta_i \propto \exp\left(-\frac{1}{T \cdot T'}\sum_{i=1}^{3}\sum_{G\in\mathcal{H}_i, G'\in\mathcal{H}_i'} d_E(f(G), f(G'))\right), \quad (6)$$

where $d_E(\cdot,\cdot)$ is the Euclidean distance; M is the number of training images; T and T' denote the number of discovered graphlets in image I and I'; $\mathcal{H}_i$ and $\mathcal{H}_i'$ contains the discovered graphlets in the i-th level category, from image I and I' respectively; $f(G)$ and $f(G')$ are the combined color and texture descriptors of graphlet G and G'.

Based on the feature vector $\mathbf{B}$, a multi-class SVM is trained for fine-grained label prediciton. For the training images from the p-th and the q-th sub-categories, we construct a binary SVM classifier as:

$$\max_{\alpha\in\mathbb{R}^{M_{pq}}} W(\alpha) = \sum_{i=1}^{M_{pq}} \alpha_i - \frac{1}{2}\sum_{i=1}^{M_{pq}} \alpha_i\alpha_j l_i l_j k(\mathbf{B}_i, \mathbf{B}_j)$$

$$s.t. \quad 0 \le \alpha_i \le C, \quad \sum_{i=1}^{M_{pq}} \alpha_i l_i = 0, \quad (7)$$

where $\mathbf{B}_i \in \mathbb{R}^M$ is the quantized vector from the i-th training image; l_i is the category label (+1 for the p-th sub-category and -1 for the q-th sub-category) to the i-th training image; α determines the hyper-plane that separates images in the p-th sub-category from those in the q-th sub-category; $C > 0$ trades the complexity of the machine off the number of nonseparable images; and M_{pq} is the number of training images either from the p-th or from the q-th sub-category.

We summarize the procedure of our fine-grained image categorization framework in Algorithm 1.

Algorithm 1 Fine-grained Image Categorization based on Dense Subgraph Mining

//**Training stage**:
Input: Training images $\{I_1, I_2, \cdots, I_M\}$ and their sub-category labels;
Output:Discovered object parts, and the trained SVM classifier.
1) Extract graphlets from the M training images, and build a category hierarchy based on KL-divergence;
2) Construct an affinity graph to model the similarity between graphlets, based on (3). Then apply dense graph mining technique to discover discriminative graphlets to each sub-/super-category;
3) Calculate an image kernel using the discovered graphlets from the training data using (6); learn a multi-class SVM.
//**Testing stage**:
Input: A test image I_{test}; **Output**: the sub-category label of I_{test};
1) Extract graphlets from the image I_{test}, discover the discriminative object parts by dense graph mining;
2) Compute the vector representation of I_{test} based on (6), and use the trained SVM to predicted its sub-category label.

6. EXPERIMENTS

In this section, we evaluate our fine-grained recognition model based on four experiments. The first experiment compares our approach with some previous categorization models. Then, we testify the important components in our model. Third, we evaluate the influence of different parameter settings. Finally, we visualize the detected discriminative graphlets, which can explain the impressive performance of our approach.

We experiment on four popular fine-grained data sets: the CUB-200 [32], the Standford dogs [20], the Oxford flowers [21], and the Leeds butterflies [33]. Different from the other fine-grained categorization models we compared, our approach **does not** require the object or object part annotations in the four data sets.

6.1 A Comparative Study

This section compares our method with 1) a series of SPM-based generic classification models, and 2) several well-known fine-grained recognition models.

We first compare our method with SPM [27] and its two variants: SC-SPM [28] and LLC-SPM [29]. The parameter settings are as follows. For SPM, SC-SPM, and LLC-SPM, we construct a three layer spatial pyramid. Then we extract nearly one million SIFT descriptors from 16×16 patches computed over a grid with spacing of eight pixels for all the training images. Finally, a codebook with size 256 is generated by k-means clustering on the one million SIFT descriptors. For our method, a three layer superpixel pyramid is constructed. Each image is represented by nearly 150 (*i.e.*, 110 (the 3rd layer)+ 30 (the 2nd layer)+10 (the 1st layer)) graphlets mined from the superpixel hierarchy. For each of the three data sets, 30% and 50% images are used for training respectively, while the rest are for testing. We report the categorization accuracy in Table 1. As can be seen, the proposed method outperforms SPM and its two variants. This is because the discovered graphlets from multiple pyramid layers are more descriptive to object parts than the grids in the SPM. Further, our algorithm performs better than Russakovsky *et al.* [4]. This reflects the advantage of mining object-shape parts for fine-grained categorization.

Besides, we compare our method with five recent fine-grained categorization models that are proposed by Yao *et al.* [12], Berg *et al.* [14], Duan *et al.* [17], Angelova *et al.* [18], and Zhang *et al.* [31], respectively. The parameters are the same as in the publication.

Table 1: Comparison of of our approach with SPM-based models

	Method	CUB-200	Leeds	SF dogs	OF flowers
30% train	SPM	35.4%	31.6%	17.65%	62.23%
	SC-SPM	38.9%	32.4%	18.23%	63.35%
	LLC-SPM	38.7%	31.9%	18.01%	64.11%
	Russakovsky	41.9%	36.4%	19.26%	65.58%
	Our	**44.1%**	**39.6%**	**20.6%**	**68.87%**
50% train	SPM	40.1%	36.4%	17.65%	63.2%
	SC-SPM	44.3%	39.1%	18.42%	70.34%
	LLC-SPM	44.1%	37.7%	19.68%	72.13%
	Russakovsky	47.8%	74.32%	41.3%	19.38%
	Our	**49.1%**	**47.7%**	**25.78%**	**76.47%**

Different proportion of training images are adopted by selecting 30%, 50%, and 70% training images respectively. As shown in Figure 7, our approach outperforms its competitors. Noticeably, the first three approaches depend on the bird parts annotation during training. However, our method can detect tiny object parts from unannotated images automatically.

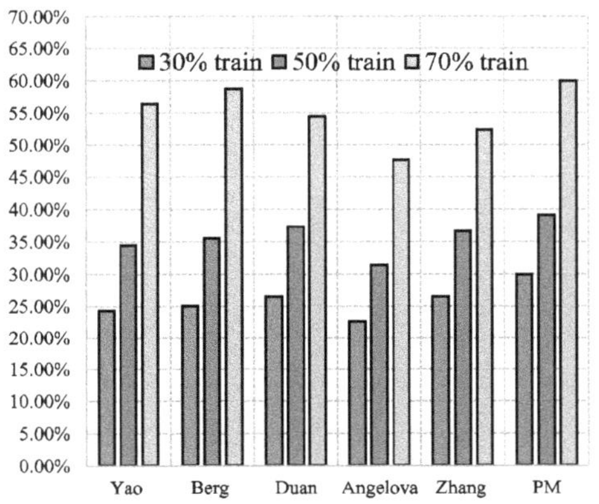

Figure 7: Comparison of the five state-of-the-art fine-grained categorization models on the CUB-200

6.2 Important Components Evaluation

In this experiment, we evaluate the two key components in our method: 1) the KL-divergence-based category hierarchy, and 2) the dense-graph-mining-based discriminative graphlets discovery.

Component 1 We calculate the distribution of the matched SIFT descriptors from images in each sub-category. For the testing images in the CUB-200, we manually annotate the distinctive object parts, *i.e.*, bird beak, head, body, tail and claw. Then, graphlets corresponding to the five parts are represented as differently colored points in the scatter plots. As shown in the first two rows of Figure 8, we select 10 scatter plots from the 200 bird sub-categories. As can be seen, in each sub-category, SIFT descriptors from discriminative object parts are densely distributed. And the SIFT distribution of each sub-category is unique. Therefore, the KL-divergence between SIFT distribution of two sub-categories can quantify their similarity. In addition, we visualize SIFT distribution by combining sub-categories randomly. As shown in the last row of Figure 8, SIFT descriptors from discriminative bird parts are dispersedly scattered, since the appearance of the discriminative bird parts are different across sub-categories.

Component 2 To evaluate the second component, we compare the affinity graph constructed based on different local descriptors in each image: $10 \times 10/20 \times 20$ grids respectively, and 100/400 superpixels respectively. As the scatter plots shown in Figure 9, different discriminative object parts are densely distributed in the constructed affinity graph. These discriminative object patterns can be easily discovered by graph shift [26]. Comparatively, affinity graphs generated using the above four schemes are sub-optimal, as different object parts are mixed. Besides the qualitative results, we further calculate the ratio of accumulated distance within and between sub-categories as in LDA [19]. As shown in Table 2, the lowest ratio is achieved by our graphlet-based affinity graph.

6.3 Parameters and Time Consumption

This subsection evaluates the performance of our approach under different parameter settings: 1) the structure of the category hierarchy; and 2) the number of outliers (*i.e.*, non-discriminative graphlets) in graph shift [26].

First, we evaluate our approach under different ratios between

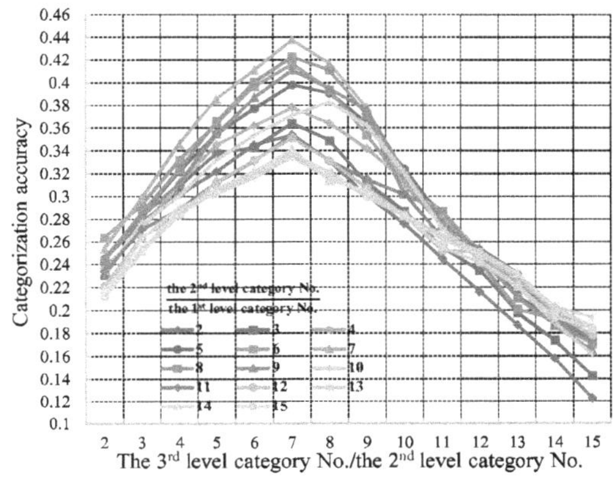

Figure 10: Influence of fine-grained categorization under the influence of the structure of the three layer category hierarchy.

the number of categories from the $(i+1)$-th layer and that from the i-th layer ($i = 1, 2$). As shown in Figure 10, when the ratio between the third and the second layer is tuned from 2 to 15, the categorization accuracy increases and peaks when the ratio is seven or eight. Then, the category accuracy decreases to a low level. Further, we notice that the best performance is achieved when the ratio between the second and the first layer is seven. Based on this, we set the ratio between the $(i+1)$-th layer and that from the i-th layer to seven in our experiment.

Second, we evaluate our approach when different numbers of outliers are adopted in the graph shifting [26] algorithm. As shown in Figure 11, when a small or a moderate number of outliers are used, our graph-shifting mining outperforms the conventional clustering algorithms such as k-means [23] and spectral clustering [30]. This is consistent with the theoretical analysis in Sec 4.2. When a large number of outliers are used, some discriminative graphlets are abandoned in the fine-grained categorization, which hampers the fine-grained categorization.

The time consumption analysis of the proposed method is as follows. All experiments are carried out on a computer equipped with an Intel Xeon X5482 CPU and 8GB RAM. All the comparative algorithms are implemented on the Matlab 2011 platform. Take the CUB-200 [32] for example, there are about 12,000 images in total. We use a half images for training. For each image, it takes about 0.12 seconds to extract all the graphlets (1330 graphlets in each image on average) based on the depth-first-search [43]. Then, it takes

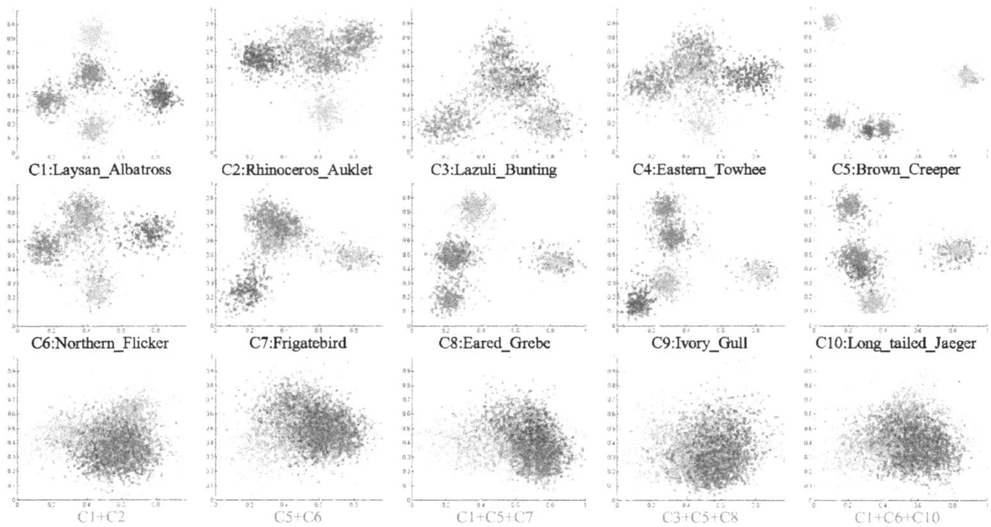

Figure 8: The first two rows: Distribution of SIFT descriptors from images belonging to the same sub-category. The last row: Distribution of SIFT descriptors from images from two and three sub-category (red points: beak, pink points: head, blue points: body, green points: tail, and cyan points: claw).

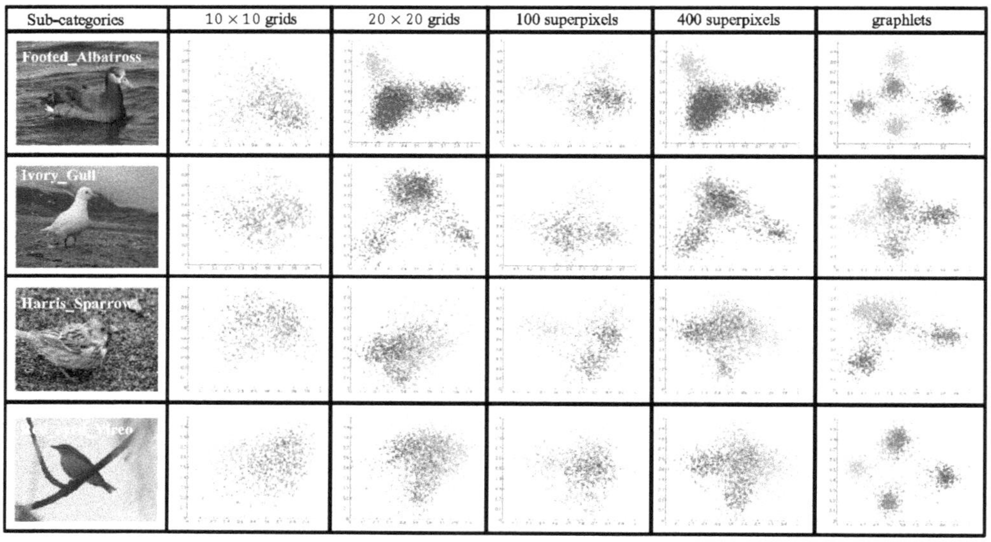

Figure 9: Affinity graphs generated using different schemes.

Table 2: The ratio $\phi = S_w/S_b$ of affinity graphs generated using different schemes

Data set	10 × 10 grids	20 × 20 grids	100 superpixels	400 superpixels	graphlets
CUB-200	0.0121	0.0171	0.008	0.0076	**0.0042**

Table 3: Comparison of Time Consumption of Different Categorization Models

Model	SPM	SC-SPM	LLC-SPM	Yao *et al.*	Berg *et al.*	Duan *et al.*
Time	0.76 seconds	1.12 seconds	0.87 seconds	2.34 seconds	1.05 seconds	1.37 seconds
Model	Algelova *et al.*	Zhang *et al.* [31]	Walk kernel	Tree kernel	PM	
Time	2.13 seconds	1.34 seconds	2.87 seconds	3.34 seconds	**0.51 seconds**	

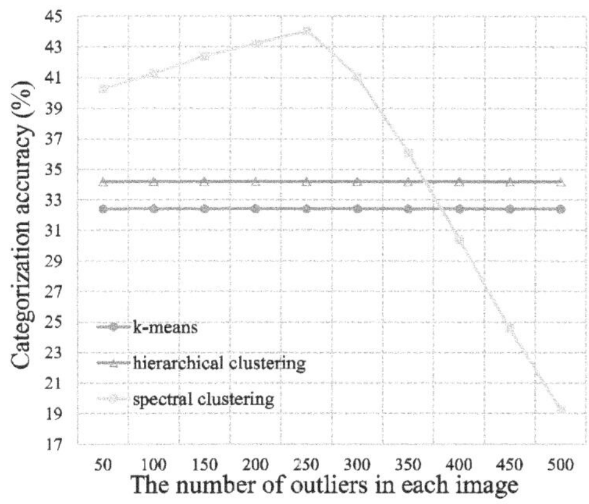

Figure 11: Performance under different number of outliers in the graph-shift-based discriminative graphlet discovery.

about 0.16 seconds to construct the KL-divergence-based category hierarchy. The dense graph mining for all training graphlets takes 5.23 minutes. Finally, the graphlet-based kernel construction and SVM learning take 1.21 minutes. Therefore, our training stage consumes about 20 minutes. Comparatively, the test stage is carried out rapidly. Given a test image, it takes 0.12 seconds to extract the graphlets and 0.31 seconds to detect the discriminative graphlets. Then, it consumes 0.06 seconds to calculate the feature vector as shown in Figure 6. Finally, the SVM classification takes 0.02 seconds. In total, it takes 0.51 seconds to predict the category label of a test image. In Table 3, we present the average time consumption of categorizing an image using different models. Our model requires the lowest time to predict the fine-grained category label for an image.

6.4 Visualization of the Discovered Graphlets

This subsection visualizes the discovered discriminative object parts from the CUB-200 [32]. As shown in Figure 12, by utilizing the dense graph mining technique, our approach seamlessly constructs the discriminative/salient objects in each image. Discriminative object parts with multiple sizes are captured by superpixel hierarchy from multiple layers. Our approach can accurately localize tiny object parts and then seamlessly capture them by graphlets. This is the underlying reason why the fine-grained categorization accuracy can be greatly improved by our approach.

7. CONCLUSIONS

This paper presents a novel fine-grained image categorization algorithm. The key is a graph mining algorithm that detects discriminative object parts with multiple scales. By extracting graphlets from the training images, an affinity graph was constructed to describe their similarity. Since discriminative object parts are densely distributed in each sub-category, we used graph shift [26] to mine them efficiently. Finally, these discovered object parts were encoded into an image kernel for categorization.

8. APPENDIX

Theoretically, our hierarchical graphlet-based image kernel is an extension of many existing image kernels. This can uncover the good performance of our method.

The proposed image kernel is closely related to several graph-based image kernels: walk-/path-/tree-kernels [5] and the two graphlet kernels [8, 42]. As elaborated in Figure 13, graphlet can generalize topologies like path, walk, and tree. Each of the three topologies have certain constraints (*e.g.*, the hierarchical structure of the tree). In addition, in Zhang *et al.* [42]'s model, all the graphlets from an image are integrated into the kernel. Some graphlets might be non-discriminative or even noisy. Moreover, Zhang *et al.* [8] selects graphlets in the topology level. This scheme is less effective as graphlets with the same topology may have different discrimination. In summary, the graphlet kernel in our work either generalizes or improves the previous graph-based image kernels.

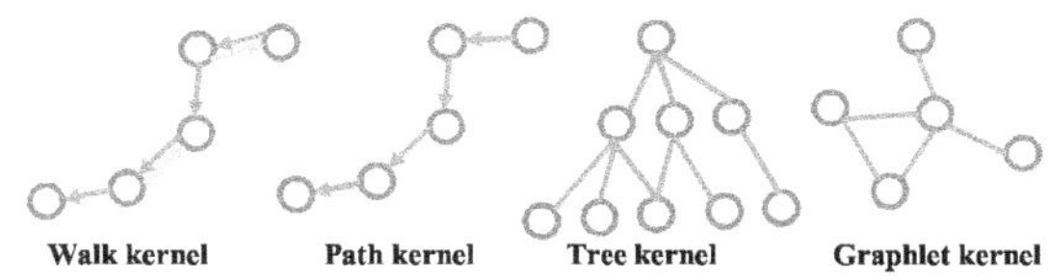

Figure 13: Topologies in different image kernels (The yellow arrows in the walk kernel indicate that each vertex can be revisited.)

9. ACKNOWLEDGMENTS

This research has been supported by the Singapore National Research Foundation under its International Research Centre@ Singapore Funding Initiative and administered by the IDM Programme Office through the Centre of Social Media Innovations for Communities (COSMIC).

10. REFERENCES

[1] Jinjun Wang, Jianchao Yang, Kai Yu, Fengjun Lv, Thomas Huang, Yihong Gong, Locality-constrained Linear Coding for Image Classification, *CVPR*, 2010.

[2] Li-Jia Li, Hao Su, Eric P. Xing, Li Fei-Fei, Object Bank: A High-Level Image Representation for Scene Classification and Semantic Feature Sparsification, *NIPS*, 2010.

[3] Yangqing Jia, Chang Huang, Trevor Darrell, Beyond Spatial Pyramids: Receptive Field Learning for Pooled Image Features, *CVPR*, 2012.

[4] Olga Russakovsky, Yuanqing Lin, Kai Yu, Li Fei-Fei, Object-Centric Spatial Pooling for Image Classification, *ECCV*, 2012.

[5] Zaïd Harchaoui, Francis Bach, Image Classification with Segmentation Graph Kernels, *CVPR*, 2007.

[6] Olivier Duchenne, Armand Joulin, Jean Ponce, A Graph-Matching Kernel for Object Categorization, *ICCV*, 2011.

[7] Liang Lin, Xiaobai Liu, Shaowu Peng, Hongyang Chaoa, Yongtian Wang, Bo Jiang, Object Categorization with Sketch Representation and Generalized Samples, *PR*, 45(10): 3648–3660, 2012.

[8] Luming Zhang, Yahong Han, Yi Yang, Mingli Song, Shuicheng Yan, Qi Tian, Discovering Discriminative Graphlets for Aerial Image Categories Recognition, *IEEE T-IP*, 22(12): 5071–5084, 2013.

[9] Honglak Lee, Alexis Battle, Rajat Raina, Andrew Y. Ng, Efficient Sparse Coding Algorithms, *NIPS*, 2006.

[10] Ryan Farrell, Om Ozal, Ning Zhang, Vlad I. Morariu, Trevor Darrell, Larry S. Davis, Birdlets: Subordinate Categorization Using Volumetric Primitives and Pose-Normalized Appearance, *ICCV*, 2011.

[11] Ning Zhang, Ryan Farrell, Trever Darrell, Pose Pooling Kernels for Sub-category Recognition, *CVPR*, 2012.

[12] Bangpeng Yao, Gary Bradski, Li Fei-Fei, A Codebook-Free and Annotation-Free Approach for Fine-Grained Image Categorization, *CVPR*, 2012.

[13] Asma Rejeb Sfar, Nozha Boujemaa, Donald Geman, Vantage Feature Frames For Fine-Grained Categorization, *CVPR*, 2013.

[14] Thomas Berg, Peter N. Belhumeur, POOF: Part-Based One-vs.-One Features for Fine-Grained Categorization, Face Verification, and Attribute Estimation, *CVPR*, 2013.

[15] Jia Deng, Jonathan Krause, Li Fei-Fei, Fine-Grained Crowdsourcing for Fine-Grained Recognition, *CVPR*, 2013.

[16] Jiefeng Cheng, Jeffrey Xu Yu, Philip S. Yu, Graph Pattern Matching: A Join/Semijoin Approach, *IEEE T-KDE*, 2(7): 1006–1021, 2011.

[17] Kun Duan, Devi Parikh, David Crandall, Kristen Grauman, Discovering Localized Attributes for Fine-grained Recognition, *CVPR*, 2013.

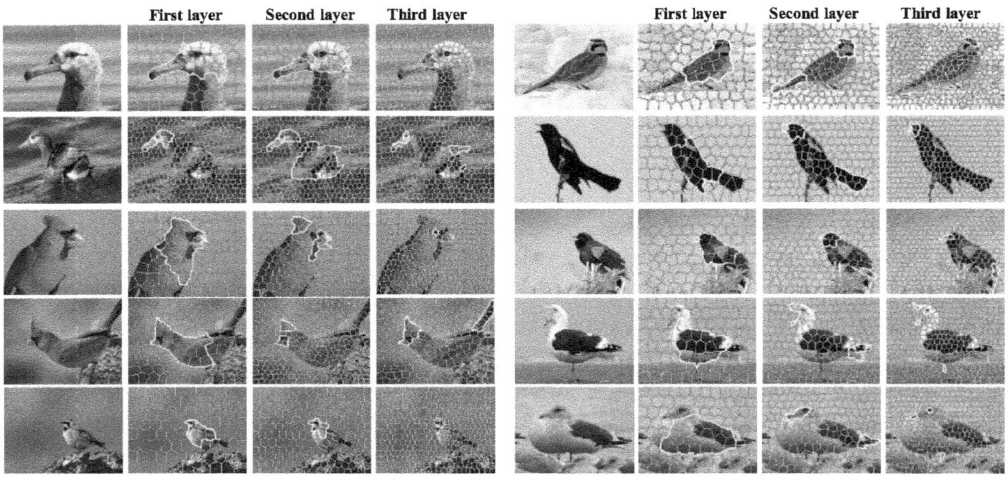

Figure 12: An example of the detected discriminative object parts from the CUB-200

[18] Anelia Angelova, Shenghuo Zhu, Efficient Object Detection and Segmentation for Fine-grained Recognition, *CVPR*, 2013.

[19] Dacheng Tao, Xuelong Li, Xindong Wu, Stephen J Maybank, Geometric mean for subspace selection, *IEEE T-PAMI*, 31(2): 260–274, 2009.

[20] Aditya Khosla, Nityananda Jayadevaprakash, Bangpeng Yao, Li Fei-Fei, Novel dataset for Fine-Grained Image Categorization, *CVPR Workshop*, 2011.

[21] Maria-Elena Nilsback, Andrew Zisserman, A Visual Vocabulary for Flower Classification, *CVPR*, 2006.

[22] Ferdinand Ôsterreicher, Igor Vajda, A New Class of Metric Divergences on Probability Spaces and its Statistical Applications, *Annals of the Institute of Statistical Mathematics*, 55(3): 639–653, 2003.

[23] Inderjit Dhillon, Yuqiang Guan, Brian Kulis, A Unified View of Kernel K-means, Spectral Clustering and Graph Cuts, *UTCS Technical Report*, 2005.

[24] N. Dalal, B.Triggs. Histograms of Oriented Gradients for Human Detection, *CVPR*, 2005.

[25] Markus Stricker, Markus Orengo. Similarity of Color Images, *Storage and Retrieval of Image and Video Databases*, 1995.

[26] Hairong Liu, Shuicheng Yan, Robust Graph Mode Seeking by Graph Shift, *ICML*, 2010.

[27] Svetlana Lazebnik, Cordelia Schmid, Jean Ponce, Beyond Bags of Features: Spatial Pyramid Matching for Recognizing Natural Scene Categories, *CVPR*, 2006.

[28] Jianchao Yang, Kai Yu, Yihong Gong, Thomas Huang, Linear Spatial Pyramid Matching using Sparse Coding for Image Classification. *CVPR*, 2009.

[29] Jinjun Wang, Jianchao Yang, Kai Yu, Fengjun Lv, Thomas Huang, Yihong Gong, Locality-constrained Linear Coding for Image Classification, *CVPR*, 2010.

[30] Yang Yang, Yi Yang, Heng Tao Shen, Yanchun Zhang, Xiaoyong Du, Xiaofang Zhou, Discriminative Nonnegative Spectral Clustering with Out-of-Sample Extension, *IEEE T-KDE*, 25(8): 1760–1771, 2013.

[31] Luming Zhang, Yi Yang, Roger Zimmermann, Discriminative Cellets Discovery for Fine-Grained Image Categories Retrieval, *ICMR*, 2014.

[32] Peter Welinder, Steve Branson, Takeshi Mita, Catherine Wah, Florian Schroff, Caltech-UCSD Birds 200, *California Institute of Technology*, CNS-TR-2010-001, 2010.

[33] Josiah Wang, Katja Markert, Mark Everingham, Object-Centric Spatial Pooling for Image Classification, *BMVC*, 2009.

[34] Luming Zhang, Yue Gao, Yingjie Xia, Qionghai Dai, Xuelong Li, A Fine-Grained Image Categorization System by Cellet-Encoded Spatial Pyramid Modeling, *IEEE Transcations on Industrial Electronics* (T-IE), 62(1), pages: 564-571, 2015

[35] Luming Zhang, Yue Gao, Chaoqun Hong, Yinfu Feng, Jianke Zhu, Deng Cai, Feature Correlation Hypergraph: Exploiting High-order Potentials for Multimodal Recognition, *IEEE Transcations on Cybernetics* (T-CYB),), 44(8), pages: 1408-1419, 2013.

[36] Luming Zhang, Yue Gao, Rongrong Ji, Lv Ke, Jiale Shen, Representative Discovery of Structure Cues for Weakly-Supervised Image Segmentation, *IEEE Transcations on Multimedia* (T-MM), 16(2): 470–479, 2014.

[37] Luming Zhang, Mingli Song, Yi Yang, Qi Zhao, Zhao Chen, Nicu Sebe, , Weakly Supervised Photo Cropping, *IEEE Transcations on Multimedia* (T-MM), 16(1): 94–107, 2014.

[38] Luming Zhang, Mingli Song, Zicheng Liu, Xiao Liu, Jiajun Bu, Chun Chen, Probabilistic Graphlet Cut: Exploring Spatial Structure Cue for Weakly Supervised Image Segmentation, *IEEE Computer Vision and Pattern Recognition* (CVPR), pages: 1908–1915, 2013.

[39] Luming Zhang, Yue Gao, Rongrong Ji, Qionghai Dai, Xuelong Li, Actively Learning Human Gaze Shifting Paths for Photo Cropping, *IEEE Transcations on Image Processing* (T-IP), 23(5), pages: 2235–2245, 2014.

[40] Luming Zhang, Yue Gao, Roger Zimmermann, Qi Tian, Xuelong Li, Fusion of Multi-Channel Local and Global Structural Cues for Photo Aesthetics Evaluation, *IEEE Transcations on Image Processing* (T-IP), 23(3): 1419–1429, 2014.

[41] Luming Zhang, Yi Yang, Yue Gao, Changbo Wang, Yi Yu, Xuelong Li, A Probabilistic Associative Model for Segmenting Weakly- Supervised Images, *IEEE Transcations on Image Processing* (T-IP), 23(9), pages: 4150-4159, 2014.

[42] Luming Zhang, Mingli Song, Li Sun, Xiao Liu, Yinting Wang, Dacheng Tao, Jiajun Bu, Chun Chen, Spatial Graphlet Matching Kernel for Recognizing Aerial Image Categories, *ICPR*, 2012.

[43] Thomas H. Cormen, Charles E. Leiserson, Ronald L. Rivest, Clifford Stein, Introduction to Algorithms, *MIT Press and McGraw-Hill*, pages: 540-549,2001.

[44] Xiaopeng Zhang, Hongkai Xiong, Wengang Zhou, Qi Tian, Fused One-vs-All Mid-Level Features for Fine-Grained Visual Categorization, *ACM Multimedia*, 2014.

[45] Hanwang Zhang, Zheng-Jun Zha, Yang Yang, Shuicheng Yan, Yue Gao and Tat-Seng Chua, Attributes-augmented Semantic Hierarchy for Image Retrieval, *ACM Multimedia*, 2013.

Robust and Discriminative Concept Factorization for Image Representation

Yuchen Guo
Tsinghua Univeristy
Beijing, China
yuchen.w.guo@gmail.com

Guiguang Ding
Tsinghua Univeristy
Beijing, China
dinggg@tsinghua.edu.cn

Jile Zhou
Sohu Inc.
Beijing, China
jile.zip@gmail.com

Qiang Liu
Tsinghua Univeristy
Beijing, China
liuqiang@tsinghua.edu.cn

ABSTRACT

Concept Factorization (CF), as a variant of Nonnegative Matrix Factorization (NMF), has been widely used for learning compact representation for images because of its psychological and physiological interpretation of naturally occurring data. And graph regularization has been incorporated into the objective function of CF to exploit the intrinsic low-dimensional manifold structure, leading to better performance. But some shortcomings are shared by existing CF methods. 1) The squared loss used to measure the data reconstruction quality is sensitive to noise in image data. 2) The graph regularization may lead to trivial solution and scale transfer problems for CF such that the learned representation is meaningless. 3) Existing methods mostly ignore the discriminative information in image data. In this paper, we propose a novel method, called **R**obust and **D**iscriminative **C**oncept **F**actorization (RDCF) for image representation. Specifically, RDCF explicitly considers the influence of noise by imposing a sparse error matrix, and exploits the discriminative information by approximate orthogonal constraints which can also lead to nontrivial solution. We propose an iterative multiplicative updating rule for the optimization of RDCF and prove the convergence. Experiments on 5 benchmark image datasets show that RDCF can significantly outperform several state-of-the-art related methods, which validates the effectiveness of RDCF.

General Terms

Algorithms, Performance, Experimentation

Keywords

Concept Factorization, Graph Regularization, Discriminability, Noise, Image Representation

ICMR '15 June 23 - 26, 2015, Shanghai, China

http://dx.doi.org/10.1145/2671188.2749317.

1. INTRODUCTION

Because of the *curse of dimensionality*, applying statistic techniques to image data which is always represented by high-dimensional vector becomes infeasible [8]. Thus learning low-dimensional compact representation lays the fundamental for many real-world applications, like pattern recognition, computer vision and image processing, etc [7, 9, 12, 13, 21]. Among different methods, Nonnegative Matrix Factorization (NMF) [16, 17] which aims to find two *nonnegative* matrices as the basis and the corresponding coefficients whose product can well approximate the original data, has attracted considerable attention because it can learn *parts-based* representation for images which has psychological and physiological interpretation of naturally occurring data [19, 22]. And as a variant of NMF, Concept Factorization (CF) [23], which aims to represent basis by the linear combination of original data, has also shown promising performance for data representation. In addition, previous works on *manifold learning* [1] have been incorporated into CF as the *graph regularization* to exploit the intrinsic low-dimensional manifold structure embedding the high-dimensional data, which leads to better visual analysis performance. One representative and effective work is Locality Consistent Concept Factorization (LCCF) [2], which incorporates graph regularization to the objective function of conventional CF to learn locality consistent data feature.

In spite of its state-of-the-art performance, LCCF can be further improved because it still suffers from the following three shortcomings. First, because of the squared loss adopted in LCCF to measure the quality of data reconstruction, it's very unstable and sensitive to noise in data. Thus the factorization may be dominated by the noise which can degrade the quality of learned representation. Second, the graph regularization may lead to trivial solution and scale transfer problems because it's actually not well-defined and the objective function is not lower-bounded [10]. These problems may result in meaningless representation for image data. Thirdly, though it fully considers the local information of data, it ignores the discriminative information of original data, which is also important for visual analysis tasks like clustering. Furthermore, some recent works claim that guaranteeing sparseness of representation for NMF and CF can produce much better performance [5, 14, 18]. But LCCF always results in dense representation for image data.

Table 1: **Comparison between Some Related Works**

	CF	LNMF	LCF	LCCF	RDCF
Feature Learning	√	√	√	√	√
Locality			√	√	√
Discriminability					√
Robustness		√			√
Trivial Solution	√	√	√		√
Sparseness	?		√		√

To address theses issues, in this paper we propose a novel method, referred to as Robust and Discriminative Concept Factorization (RDCF) for image representation. We establish our method based on LCCF such that RDCF has the advantages of CF and can preserve locality naturally. We utilize a *sparse error matrix* to explicitly capture noise which has significant influence upon the data reconstruction. Thus the factorization can capture more intrinsic information from the cleaned data. And we propose to add *approximate orthogonal constraints* to the objective function. With the constraints, RDCF can 1) exploit the discriminative information of data which leads to better representation; 2) avoid trivial solution and scale transfer problems even with strong graph regularization; 3) learn relatively sparse representation for image. Our RDCF is strongly related to but different from several previous works. In table 1, we compare RDCF to several related methods, CF[23] (NMF [16]), LNMF [15], LCCF [2] (GNMF [3]), LCF [18] (NLCF [5]), and NSDR [24]. RDCF can simultaneously perform feature learning, dimension reduction, locality preserving, and discriminative information exploiting. And It's robust to data noise and can avoid trivial solution and scale transfer problems even with graph regularization. The properties mentioned above are all important to achieve superior performance, but previous works always ignores some of them. Furthermore, RCDF can result in sparse representation, which is also very meaningful for image representation. In summary, this paper makes contributions as below,

- We propose a novel method RDCF for image representation. RDCF is robust to data noise, can avoid trivial solution and scale transfer problem and exploit the discriminative information of data, which are the major problems LCCF suffers from. Actually, RDCF satisfies several important properties for image feature learning while previous methods ignore some of them.
- We propose an effective and efficient iterative strategy with multiplicative updating rules for the optimization for RDCF, and we theoretically prove the convergence.
- We carried out extensive experiments on five public image datasets. The experimental results show that RDCF can significantly outperform several state-of-the-art methods, validating the effectiveness of RDCF.

The rest of this paper is organized as follows. Some related works are briefly reviewed in Section 2. We will introduce the proposed RDCF in detail in Section 3 and the corresponding theoretical analysis is given in Section 4. The experimental results on benchmark datasets are presented in Section 5. In the end, conclusions are made in Section 6.

2. RELATED WORK

Given a set of nonnegative image data represented as $\mathbf{X} = [\mathbf{x}_1, ..., \mathbf{x}_n] \in \mathbb{R}^{d \times n}$, where n is the number of samples and d is the number of feature dimension. CF aims to find two nonnegative matrices $\mathbf{W} \in \mathbb{R}^{n \times k}$ and $\mathbf{V} \in \mathbb{R}^{n \times k}$ where k is the dimension of the new representation, such that the original data can be well approximate. The objective function of the conventional CF can be written as

Table 2: Notations and descriptions in this paper

Notation	Description	Notation	Description
$\mathbf{X}$	input data matrix	n	#images
$\mathbf{W}$	basis coefficients	d	#dimension
$\mathbf{V}$	new representation	k	#basis vectors
$\mathbf{L}$	graph Lap. matrix	p	#NN
$\mathbf{S}$	sparse error matrix	λ	sparse para.
$\mathbf{K}, \hat{\mathbf{K}}$	kernel matrix	α	graph para.
$\mathbf{F}$	scaled indi. matrix	β	orth. para.

$$\mathcal{O}_{\text{CF}} = \|\mathbf{X} - \mathbf{X}\mathbf{W}\mathbf{V}^T\|_F^2 \quad \text{s.t. } \mathbf{W}, \mathbf{V} \geq 0 \tag{1}$$

where $\|\cdot\|_F$ is the *Frobenius norm* of matrix. Generally, Eq. (1) can be optimized by an iterative strategy with multiplicative updating rules for $\mathbf{W}$ and $\mathbf{V}$ as suggested in [23],

$$w_{jl} \leftarrow w_{jl}\frac{(\mathbf{K}\mathbf{V})_{jl}}{(\mathbf{K}\mathbf{W}\mathbf{V}^T\mathbf{V})_{jl}}, v_{jl} \leftarrow v_{jl}\frac{(\mathbf{K}\mathbf{W})_{jl}}{(\mathbf{V}\mathbf{W}^T\mathbf{K}\mathbf{W})_{jl}} \tag{2}$$

where $\mathbf{K} = \mathbf{X}^T\mathbf{X}$ is the kernel matrix. We can first define a p-nearest neighbor matrix $\mathbf{G}$ whose elements are as follows

$$G_{ij} = \begin{cases} 1, & \text{if } \mathbf{x}_i \in \mathcal{N}(\mathbf{x}_j) \text{ or } \mathbf{x}_j \in \mathcal{N}(\mathbf{x}_i) \\ 0, & \text{otherwise} \end{cases} \tag{3}$$

where $\mathcal{N}(\mathbf{x}_i)$ denotes the p-nearest neighbor of $\mathbf{x}_i$. Now we can further define the graph Laplacian $\mathbf{L} = \mathbf{D} - \mathbf{G}$, where $\mathbf{D}$ is the diagonal degree matrix whose diagonal element $D_{ii} = \sum_{j=1}^{n} G_{ij}$. By incorporating this graph regularization, we can obtain the objective function of LCCF as below

$$\begin{gathered}\mathcal{O}_{\text{LCCF}} = \|\mathbf{X} - \mathbf{X}\mathbf{W}\mathbf{V}^T\|_F^2 + \alpha tr(\mathbf{V}^T\mathbf{L}\mathbf{V}) \\ \text{s.t. } \mathbf{W}, \mathbf{V} \geq 0\end{gathered} \tag{4}$$

where α is the graph regularization parameter. The local information can't be fully exploited with a small value for α. However, if α is too large, the graph regularization may dominate the objective function and Eq. (4) reduces to

$$\mathcal{O}'_{\text{LCCF}} = tr(\mathbf{V}^T\mathbf{L}\mathbf{V}) = \sum_{i=1}^{k} \mathbf{v}_{*i}^T\mathbf{L}\mathbf{v}_{*i} \tag{5}$$

where $\mathbf{v}_{*i}$ is the i-th column of $\mathbf{V}$. Actually Eq. (5) can be optimized as k independent subproblems $\mathcal{O}_i = \mathbf{v}_{*i}^T\mathbf{L}\mathbf{v}_{*i}$, leading to the same solutions up to a scale, i.e., $\mathbf{v}_{*1} \propto \mathbf{v}_{*2} \propto ... \propto \mathbf{v}_{*k}$. In fact, the learned representations are meaningless, e.g., the cosine similarity between any images is 1. And this is the so-called *trivial solution* problem in [10].

Furthermore, because the graph regularization isn't well-defined and lower-bounded, suppose we obtain any solution $(\mathbf{W}^*, \mathbf{V}^*)$ to Eq. (4). Given $\forall \gamma > 1$, it's easy to verify that $(\gamma\mathbf{W}^*, \frac{1}{\gamma}\mathbf{V}^*)$ can lead to smaller objective function value. Consequently the ultimate solution will be $\mathbf{W}^* \to \infty$ and $\mathbf{V}^* \to 0$, which is referred to as the *scale transfer* problem.

2.1 Other Work

Recent years, some works have made some effort to address some problems mentioned in Section 1. Though they are actually for NMF, we find they can be applied to CF too. In LNMF [15], $\ell_{2,1}$ norm is utilized to measure the quality of reconstruction, which is more robust than squared loss.

In DRCC [11], they use ℓ_2 normalization in each optimization iteration. In NSDR [24], discriminative information is exploited in the clustering. Here we need to point out that NSDR is a spectral clustering method, but not a feature learning method as others. Hence its applications are limited. In LCF [18], they require the basis to be close to original data points such that $\mathbf{V}$ can be sparse, which is motivated by Local Coordinate Coding [27]. Though the trivial solution and scale transfer problems are avoided in LCF and the locality is preserved, LCF still suffers from the other two main shortcomings of LCCF such thut its best performance is just comparable to LCCF's. In summary, these methods focus on some perspectives for designing effective NMF or CF, but they ignore some others. Motivated by them, we propose a unified method taking all the perspectives into consideration, which will lead to much better performance.

3. THE PROPOSED METHOD

3.1 Objective Function

In spite of the trivial solution and scale transfer problem, graph regularization is still a powerful and effective tool to preserve the locality of image data. Thus we establish our RDCF upon LCCF. Actually, in RDCF, the trivial solution and the scale transfer problems can be effectively addressed.

The first step is to address the problem that squared loss widely utilized in CF is sensitive to noise in data. Two alternatives are available. Using other loss function instead of squared loss as in LNMF, or remove noise from data. In this paper, we choose the latter. Motivated by Robust PCA [4], a data matrix can be $\mathbf{M}$ can be decomposed as the sum of a low-rank component $\mathbf{L}$ and a sparse component $\mathbf{S}$, i.e., $\mathbf{M} = \mathbf{L} + \mathbf{S}$. Actually, we can observe that the term $\mathbf{XWV}^T$ is essentially low-rank. But in CF and LCCF, the sparse component that is always noise is ignored but it indeed has considerable effect. In fact, the sparse component, i.e., noise, often dominates the factorization leading to unsatisfactory representation for data. Thus, we can impose a sparse component into the factorization to capture the noise such that the factorization can capture more intrinsic information from the cleaned data. By incorporating this idea into LCCF, we can obtain the objective function as follows,

$$\begin{aligned}\mathcal{O}_1 =&\|\mathbf{X} - \mathbf{S} - \mathbf{XWV}^T\|_F^2 + \lambda\|\mathbf{S}\|_1 \\ &+ \alpha tr(\mathbf{V}^T\mathbf{LV}) \quad \text{s.t. } \mathbf{W}, \mathbf{V} \geq 0\end{aligned} \tag{6}$$

where $\|\mathbf{S}\|_1 = \sum_{ij} |S_{ij}|$ is the ℓ_1 norm of matrix, which can guarantee the sparseness of the matrix. By imposing this sparse error matrix, the influence of noise is removed and a cleaned data matrix $\mathbf{X} - \mathbf{S}$ can be constructed thus the reconstruction can capture more intrinsic information. Consequently our model is robust to the noise in image data.

Then we need to make the learned representation $\mathbf{V}$ discriminative, i.e., capture some discriminative information of data. Here we follow the works in [25] and [26]. First we introduce a group indicator matrix $\mathbf{Y} = \{0,1\}^{n\times k}$ where $Y_{ij} = 1$ if the i-th image belongs to the j-th group. The scaled indicator matrix with respect to $\mathbf{Y}$ is defined as below

$$\mathbf{F} = \mathbf{Y}(\mathbf{Y}^T\mathbf{Y})^{-\frac{1}{2}} \tag{7}$$

where each column in $\mathbf{F}$, i.e., each image group, is given by

$$\mathbf{F}_{*j} = [0, ..., 0, \underbrace{1, ..., 1}_{n_j}, 0, ...0]^T/\sqrt{n_j} \tag{8}$$

where n_j is the number of samples in the j-th group. We want the learned representation $\mathbf{V}$ to characterize the discriminative structure in $\mathbf{F}$. Intuitively, we just need to force them to be close to each other, i.e., $\|\mathbf{V} - \mathbf{F}\|_F^2 \leq \epsilon$, where ϵ is a small constant. Now we can incorporate this constraint on $\mathbf{V}$ to the objective function defined in Eq. (6) as follows

$$\begin{aligned}\mathcal{O}_2 =& \|\mathbf{X} - \mathbf{S} - \mathbf{XWV}^T\|_F^2 + \lambda\|\mathbf{S}\|_1 \\ &+ \alpha tr(\mathbf{V}^T\mathbf{LV}) \text{ s.t. } \mathbf{W}, \mathbf{V} \geq 0,\ \|\mathbf{V} - \mathbf{F}\|_F^2 \leq \epsilon\end{aligned} \tag{9}$$

Unfortunately, it's impossible to know $\mathbf{F}$ in prior because we have no label information under unsupervised scenario. But in Eq. (7), we can observe that $\mathbf{F}$ is strictly orthogonal

$$\mathbf{F}^T\mathbf{F} = (\mathbf{Y}^T\mathbf{Y})^{-\frac{1}{2}}\mathbf{Y}^T\mathbf{Y}(\mathbf{Y}^T\mathbf{Y})^{-\frac{1}{2}} = \mathbf{I}_k \tag{10}$$

where $\mathbf{I}_k$ is a $k \times k$ identity matrix. Look back to Eq. (9), if we set $\epsilon = 0$, then $\mathbf{V}$ is strictly equal to $\mathbf{F}$. Consequently $\mathbf{V}$ should be orthogonal too. However, this constraints may be too heave. Actually, given a small ϵ, the learned $\mathbf{V}$ is close but not totally equal to $\mathbf{F}$. Thus $\mathbf{V}$ isn't strictly but approximately orthogonal, which can be formulated as $\|\mathbf{V}^T\mathbf{V} - \mathbf{I}_k\|_F^2 \leq \epsilon$. By substituting the term containing $\mathbf{F}$ in Eq. (9) with the approximate orthogonal constraints as above, now we can obtain the objective function as follows,

$$\begin{aligned}\mathcal{O}_3 =& \|\mathbf{X} - \mathbf{S} - \mathbf{XWV}^T\|_F^2 + \alpha tr(\mathbf{V}^T\mathbf{LV}) \\ &+ \lambda\|\mathbf{S}\|_1 \quad \text{s.t. } \mathbf{W}, \mathbf{V} \geq 0,\ \|\mathbf{V}^T\mathbf{V} - \mathbf{I}_k\|_F^2 \leq \epsilon\end{aligned} \tag{11}$$

Further we can rewrite Eq. (11) for optimization issues, and obtain the overall objective function of our RDCF as below,

$$\begin{aligned}\mathcal{O} =&\|\mathbf{X} - \mathbf{S} - \mathbf{XWV}^T\|_F^2 + \alpha tr(\mathbf{V}^T\mathbf{LV}) \\ &+ \lambda\|\mathbf{S}\|_1 + \beta\|\mathbf{V}^T\mathbf{V} - \mathbf{I}_k\|_F^2 \quad \text{s.t. } \mathbf{W}, \mathbf{V} \geq 0\end{aligned} \tag{12}$$

where β is the regularization parameter for *approximate orthogonal constraints*. In fact, given any ϵ, a large enough β can make RDCF satisfy the constraint $\|\mathbf{V}^T\mathbf{V} - \mathbf{I}_k\|_F^2 \leq \epsilon$.

Besides capture the discriminative information in data, the approximate orthogonal constraints can also address the trivial solution and scale transfer problems. In fact, given a large β, i.e., $\beta = 10000$, only few elements in each row of $\mathbf{V}$ may have significantly large value because $\mathbf{V}$ is nonnegative and approximately orthogonal, and each column of $\mathbf{V}$ tends to be as different as possible to each other. Thus, even with heavy graph regularization, the solution to Eq. (12) can be nontrivial. Furthermore, if we substitute $\mathbf{V}^*$ by $\frac{1}{\gamma}\mathbf{V}^*$ ($\gamma > 1$), the term $\beta\|\mathbf{V}^T\mathbf{V} - \mathbf{I}_k\|_F^2$ may have larger value leading to larger objective function value with a large β. Consequently the scale transfer problem can be avoided. In addition, a proper β also results in sparse $\mathbf{V}$ for images. As mentioned in [5, 14, 18], the sparse representations can lead to better performance for visual analysis as clustering.

3.2 Optimization Algorithm

The objective function in Eq. (12) is non-convex with $\mathbf{W}, \mathbf{V}$ and $\mathbf{S}$ together. But fortunately, it's convex with respect to any one of them while fixing the others. So we can adopt an iterative strategy for optimizing Eq. (12).

3.2.1 Update U and V

For the convenience for derivation, firstly we can make the following denotations, $\hat{\mathbf{X}} = \mathbf{X} - \mathbf{S}$, $\mathbf{K} = \mathbf{X}^T\mathbf{X}$, and $\hat{\mathbf{K}} = \hat{\mathbf{X}}^T\mathbf{X}$. By applying the properties of matrix norm $\|\mathbf{A}\|_F^2 = tr(\mathbf{A}^T\mathbf{A})$, $tr(\mathbf{AB}) = tr(\mathbf{BA})$ and $tr(\mathbf{A}) = tr(\mathbf{A}^T)$, we can obtain the objective function from Eq. (12) as follows,

$$\begin{aligned}\mathcal{O} &= tr(\mathbf{V}\mathbf{W}^T\mathbf{K}\mathbf{W}\mathbf{V}^T) - 2tr(\hat{\mathbf{K}}\mathbf{W}\mathbf{V}^T) + \lambda\|\mathbf{S}\|_1 \\ &+ \alpha tr(\mathbf{V}^T\mathbf{L}\mathbf{V}) + \beta tr(\mathbf{V}^T\mathbf{V}\mathbf{V}^T\mathbf{V}) \\ &- 2\beta tr(\mathbf{V}^T\mathbf{V}) + \beta + tr(\hat{\mathbf{X}}^T\hat{\mathbf{X}}) \quad \text{s.t. } \mathbf{W}, \mathbf{V} \geq 0\end{aligned} \tag{13}$$

Now let ψ_{jl} and ϕ_{jl} be the Lagrange multiplier for constraints $w_{jl} \geq 0$ and $v_{jl} \geq 0$ respectively, and denote $\mathbf{\Psi} = [\psi_{jl}]$ and $\mathbf{\Phi} = [\phi_{jl}]$. Then we can write the Lagrange

$$\mathcal{L} = \mathcal{O} + tr(\mathbf{\Psi}\mathbf{W}^T) + tr(\mathbf{\Phi}\mathbf{V}^T) \tag{14}$$

The partial derivatives of $\mathcal{L}$ with respect to $\mathbf{W}$ and $\mathbf{V}$ are as

$$\frac{\partial \mathcal{L}}{\partial \mathbf{W}} = 2\mathbf{K}\mathbf{W}\mathbf{V}^T\mathbf{V} - 2\hat{\mathbf{K}}\mathbf{V} + \mathbf{\Psi} \tag{15}$$

$$\begin{aligned}\frac{\partial \mathcal{L}}{\partial \mathbf{V}} =& 2\mathbf{V}\mathbf{W}^T\mathbf{K}\mathbf{W} - 2\hat{\mathbf{K}}\mathbf{W} + 2\alpha\mathbf{L}\mathbf{V} \\ &+ 4\beta\mathbf{V}\mathbf{V}^T\mathbf{V} - 4\beta\mathbf{V} + \mathbf{\Phi}\end{aligned} \tag{16}$$

By using the Karush-Kuhn-Tucker conditions, i.e., $\psi_{jl}w_{jl} = 0$ and $\phi_{jl}v_{jl} = 0$, we get the following equations,

$$(\mathbf{K}\mathbf{W}\mathbf{V}^T\mathbf{V})_{jl}w_{jl} - (\hat{\mathbf{K}}\mathbf{V})_{jl}w_{jl} = 0 \tag{17}$$

$$\begin{aligned}&(\mathbf{V}\mathbf{W}^T\mathbf{K}\mathbf{W})_{jl}v_{jl} - (\hat{\mathbf{K}}\mathbf{W})_{jl}v_{jl} + \alpha(\mathbf{L}\mathbf{V})_{jl}v_{jl} \\ &+ 2\beta(\mathbf{V}\mathbf{V}^T\mathbf{V})_{jl}v_{jl} - 2\beta(\mathbf{V})_{jl}v_{jl} = 0\end{aligned} \tag{18}$$

Then we obtain the following multiplicative updating rules:

$$w_{jl} \leftarrow w_{jl}\frac{(\hat{\mathbf{K}}\mathbf{V})_{jl}}{(\mathbf{K}\mathbf{W}\mathbf{V}^T\mathbf{V})_{jl}} \tag{19}$$

$$v_{jl} \leftarrow v_{jl}\frac{(\hat{\mathbf{K}}\mathbf{W} + \alpha\mathbf{G}\mathbf{V} + 2\beta\mathbf{V})_{jl}}{(\mathbf{V}\mathbf{W}^T\mathbf{K}\mathbf{W} + \alpha\mathbf{D}\mathbf{V} + 2\beta\mathbf{V}\mathbf{V}^T\mathbf{V})_{jl}} \tag{20}$$

3.2.2 Update S

We can observe that the optimization problem with respect to $\mathbf{S}$ is element-wise decoupled, i.e., we can optimize every element independently. Denote $\mathbf{E} = \mathbf{X} - \mathbf{X}\mathbf{W}\mathbf{V}^T = [e_{ij}]$. Then each subproblem with respect to s_{ij} can be written as,

$$\mathcal{O}_{ij} = (e_{ij} - s_{ij})^2 + \lambda|s_{ij}| \tag{21}$$

After some simple derivation, we could obtain the solution to Eq. (21) as follows, which is also the updating rule for $\mathbf{S}$

$$s_{ij} = \begin{cases} 0, & \text{if } |e_{ij}| \leq \frac{\lambda}{2} \\ e_{ij} - \frac{\lambda}{2}\text{sign}(e_{ij}), & \text{otherwise} \end{cases} \tag{22}$$

In addition, by substituting Eq. (22) into Eq. (21), we have

$$\mathcal{O}_{ij} = \begin{cases} e_{ij}^2, & \text{if } |e_{ij}| \leq \frac{\lambda}{2} \\ \lambda|e_{ij}| - (\frac{\lambda}{2})^2, & \text{otherwise} \end{cases} \tag{23}$$

This is an interesting and important result. Intuitively, the large reconstruction error is often caused by data noise. If ℓ_2 norm (squared loss) is applied to all entries, the factorization will be dominated by the large-error entries, i.e., noise data. But from Eq. (23), we can observe that the factorization is self-adaptive to the reconstruction error. With the presence of $\mathbf{S}$, the factorization uses ℓ_1 norm as measure for large-error entries to alleviate the influence of noise, while ℓ_2 norm is applied to small error entries for more accurate factorization to capture the intrinsic information. Thus the factorization in RDCF can be robust to noise in image data.

4. THEORETICAL ANALYSIS

4.1 Proof of Convergence

We can use Eq. (19), Eq. (20) and Eq. (22) iteratively to update $\mathbf{W}$, $\mathbf{V}$ and $\mathbf{S}$ respectively, and the value of objective function in Eq. (12) will finally converge to a local minimum, which is theoretically guaranteed by Theorem 1.

THEOREM 1. *Objective function $\mathcal{O}$ in Eq. (12) is nonincreasing under rules in Eq. (19), Eq. (20) and Eq. (22).*

In fact, it's obvious that $\mathcal{O}_{ij}$ reaches the minimum when s_{ij} is computed as Eq. (22). Thus $\mathcal{O}$ is definitely nonincreasing under the updating rule for $\mathbf{S}$ in Eq. (22). Now we need to prove that $\mathcal{O}$ is nonincreasing under Eq. (19) and Eq. (20). Because of the limitation of space, we just show the the proof with respect to Eq. (20). Actually, the proof with respect to Eq. (19) is analogous. Our proof takes advantage of the *auxiliary function* [6] which can be defined as follows

DEFINITION 1. $G(v, v')$ is an *auxiliary function* for $F(v)$ if

$$G(v, v') \geq F(v), \quad G(v, v) = F(v) \tag{24}$$

are satisfied.

Then we need to make use of an important lemma as below,

LEMMA 1. If $G(v, v')$ is an auxiliary function of $F(v)$, then $F(v)$ is nonincreasing under the following updating rule

$$v^{(t+1)} = \arg\min_v G(v, v^{(t)}) \tag{25}$$

PROOF (PROOF OF LEMMA 1).

$$F(v^{(t+1)}) \leq G(v^{(t+1)}, v^{(t)}) \leq G(v^{(t)}, v^{(t)}) = F(v^{(t)})$$

□

Now we need to show the updating rule for $\mathbf{V}$ in Eq. (20) is exactly the update in Eq. (25) with a proper auxiliary function. Let F_{ab} denote the the part of $\mathcal{O}$ that is only relevant to v_{ab}. The second-order partial derivative of F_{ab} is as follows

$$\begin{aligned}F_{ab}^{''} =& 2(\mathbf{W}^T\mathbf{K}\mathbf{W})_{bb} + 2\alpha\mathbf{L}_{aa} - 4\beta\mathbf{I}_{ab}^{ab} \\ &+ 4\beta(\mathbf{I}^{ab}\mathbf{V}^T\mathbf{V} + \mathbf{V}\mathbf{I}^{ab^T}\mathbf{V} + \mathbf{V}\mathbf{V}^T\mathbf{I}^{ab})_{ab}\end{aligned} \tag{26}$$

where $\mathbf{I}^{ab}$ is a $n \times k$ matrix with 1 at (a, b) and 0 at all others. It's easy to validate the following three inequalities,

$$(\mathbf{V}\mathbf{W}^T\mathbf{K}\mathbf{W})_{ab} \geq v_{ab}^{(t)}(\mathbf{W}^T\mathbf{K}\mathbf{W})_{bb} \tag{27}$$

$$(\mathbf{D}\mathbf{V})_{ab} = \sum_{i=1}^{n} D_{aj}v_{jb}^{(t)} \geq (\mathbf{D} - \mathbf{W})_{aa}v_{ab}^{(t)} \tag{28}$$

$$\begin{aligned}(\mathbf{V}\mathbf{V}^T\mathbf{V})_{ab} &= \sum_{j=1}^{n}\sum_{i=1}^{k} v_{ai}v_{ji}v_{jb} \\ &\geq (\mathbf{I}^{ab}\mathbf{V}^T\mathbf{V} + \mathbf{V}\mathbf{I}^{ab^T}\mathbf{V} + \mathbf{V}\mathbf{V}^T\mathbf{I}^{ab} - 1)_{ab}v_{ab}\end{aligned} \tag{29}$$

Table 3: Description of benchmark datasets

Dataset	#Example	#Features	#Classes
ORL	400	1024	40
YALE	165	1024	15
UMIST	398	644	20
MNIST	1000	784	10
Semeion	1593	256	10

Here we need to point out that the inequality in (29) does not mathematically and strictly hold. In fact, during the derivation of it, we need to prove that $\sum_{j\neq a}^{n}\sum_{i\neq b}^{k} v_{ai}v_{ji}v_{jb} \geq 2v_{ab}^3 - v_{ab}$. In fact, just by setting $\mathbf{V} = \mathbf{I}^{ab}$, this inequality is wrong. However, in real application, this inequality is always true because of the following two reasons. First, if the right part of the equality is nonpositive, e.g., $v_{ab} \in [0, \frac{1}{\sqrt{2}}]$, the left part which is nonnegative is definitely greater than the nonpositive right part. In fact, if $\mathbf{V}$ can capture the structure of $\mathbf{F}$, the largest element in $\mathbf{V}$ is close to $\frac{1}{\sqrt{n_j}}$ where $n_j \gg 2$ in real world. Thus the right part is always nonpositive. And this can be guaranteed by setting a large value for β. Second, even though the right part is positive, we can observe that the left part contains $(n-1)(k-1)$ terms, whose sum is always very large. Thus we can expect the sum of these terms could generate a larger value than the right part.

LEMMA 2. The function

$$\begin{aligned}G(v, v_{ab}^{(t)}) &= F_{ab}(v_{ab}^{(t)}) + F_{ab}^{'}(v_{ab}^{(t)})(v - v_{ab}^{(t)}) \\ &+ \frac{(\mathbf{V}\mathbf{W}^T\mathbf{K}\mathbf{W} + \alpha\mathbf{D}\mathbf{V} + 2\beta\mathbf{V}\mathbf{V}^T\mathbf{V})_{ab}}{v_{ab}^{(t)}}(v - v_{ab}^{(t)})^2\end{aligned} \tag{30}$$

is an auxiliary function for $F_{ab}(v)$.

PROOF (PROOF TO LEMMA 2). It's obvious that $G(v, v) = F_{ab}(v)$. Now we need to show $G(v, v_{ab}^{(t)}) \geq F_{ab}(v)$. Here we compare the Taylor series expansion of $F_{ab}(v)$ at $v_{ab}^{(t)}$ as

$$\begin{aligned}F_{ab}(v) =& F_{ab}(v_{ab}^{(t)}) + F_{ab}^{'}(v_{ab}^{(t)})(v - v_{ab}^{(t)}) \\ &+ \frac{1}{2}F_{ab}^{''}(v_{ab}^{(t)})(v - v_{ab}^{(t)})^2\end{aligned} \tag{31}$$

Based on the definition in Eq. (26) and Eq. (30), and three important inequalities mentioned in Eq. (27), Eq. (28) and Eq. (29), it's very easy to validate that $G(v, v_{ab}^{(t)}) \geq F_{ab}(v)$. □

PROOF (PROOF OF THEOREM 1). We can replace $G(v, v_{ab}^{(t)})$ in Eq. (25) by Eq. (30), which result in the following rule,

$$\begin{aligned}v_{ab}^{(t+1)} =& v_{ab}^{(t)} - v_{ab}^{(t)} \frac{F_{ab}^{'}(v_{ab}^{(t)})}{2(\mathbf{V}\mathbf{W}^T\mathbf{K}\mathbf{W} + \alpha\mathbf{D}\mathbf{V} + 2\beta\mathbf{V}\mathbf{V}^T\mathbf{V})_{ab}} \\ =& v_{ab}^{(t)} \frac{(\hat{\mathbf{K}}\mathbf{W} + \alpha\mathbf{G}\mathbf{V} + 2\beta\mathbf{V})_{ab}}{(\mathbf{V}\mathbf{W}^T\mathbf{K}\mathbf{W} + \alpha\mathbf{D}\mathbf{V} + 2\beta\mathbf{V}\mathbf{V}^T\mathbf{V})_{ab}}\end{aligned} \tag{32}$$

which is identical to Eq. (20). Because $G(v, v_{ab}^{(t)})$ is an auxiliary function of F_{ab}, F_{ab} is nonincreasing under this updating rule. Therefore $\mathcal{O}$ is nonincreasing under Eq. (20). □

4.2 Complexity Analysis

The time complexity for p-nearest graph construction is $\mathcal{O}(n^2d)$. In each iteration, the complexity for updating is $\mathcal{O}(n^2d + n^2k)$. Suppose the optimization terminate at iteration t, thus the overall complexity is $\mathcal{O}(n^2((t+1)d + tk))$, which is linear to n^2. Consequently RDCF, LCCF and LCF will have similar computational complexity with a large n.

5. EXPERIMENT AND DISCUSSION

5.1 Datasets, Metrics and Baseline Methods

To demonstrate the effectiveness of RDCF for image representation, we carried out extensive experiment on five public image dataset, ORL[1], YALE[2], UMIST[3], MNIST[4] and Semeion[5]. The details of them are presented in Table 3.

Following previous works [3, 5, 18], we utilize clustering performance to evaluate the effectiveness of image representation. And Clustering Accuracy (ACC) and Normalized Mutual Information (NMI) are adopted as the evaluation metrics for clustering, whose definitions are as follows

$$\text{ACC} = \frac{\sum_{i=1}^{n}\delta(s_i, map(r_i))}{n} \tag{33}$$

$$\text{NMI}(C, C') = \frac{\text{MI}(C, C')}{\sqrt{H(C)H(C')}} \tag{34}$$

$\delta(x, y)$ is the indicator function that equals one if $x = y$ and zero otherwise. $map(r_i)$ is the permutation mapping function that maps each cluster label r_i to the equivalent label from the data corpus. And the best mapping can be found by the Kuhn-Munkres algorithm [20]. $H(C)$ and $H(C')$ are the entropies of C and C' respectively. And $\text{MI}(C, C')$ is the mutual information between C and C' defined as below

$$\text{MI}(C, C') = \sum_{c_i \in C, c_j^{'} \in C'} p(c_i, c_j^{'}) \cdot \log_2 \frac{p(c_i, c_j^{'})}{p(c_i) \cdot p(c_j^{'})} \tag{35}$$

where $p(c_i)$ and $p(c_j^{'})$ represents the probabilities that an image arbitrarily selected from the data corpus belongs to clusters c_i and $c_j^{'}$ respectively. Analogously, $p(c_i, c_j^{'})$ stands for the joint probability that the any arbitrarily selected image belongs to the clusters c_i and $c_j^{'}$ at the same time.

We compare RDCF to the following NMF and CF methods. Kmeans is chosen as the base algorithm. Then are NMF [16], CF [23] and LNMF [15]. Graph regularized methods, GNMF [3] and LCCF [2]. NLCF [5] and LCF [18] based on Local Coordinate Coding. We also compare RDCF to NSDR [24] which is a spectral clustering method taking discriminative information into consideration. For all baseline methods above except NSDR, the cluster label can be generated from $\mathbf{V}$ in two ways. One is applying Kmeans to the learned representation and the other is setting the cluster label of image i as $c = \text{argmax}_j \mathbf{v}_{ij}$. Both ways are applied and the best performance of each baseline method is presented. And RDCF just utilizes the latter one.

5.2 Implementation Details

There are several important tunable parameters for baseline methods. For meaningful comparison, we perform grid

[1]http://www.cl.cam.ac.uk/research/dtg/attarchive
[2]http://cvc.yale.edu/projects/yalefaces/yalefaces.html
[3]http://www.sheffield.ac.uk/eee/research/iel/research/face
[4]http://yann.lecun.com/exdb/mnist/
[5]https://archive.ics.uci.edu/ml/datasets

Table 4: Clustering Accuracy (%)

Dataset	Kmeans	NMF	LNMF	GNMF	NLCF	NSDR	CF	LCF	LCCF	RDCF
ORL	41.00	52.75	52.50	54.50	53.75	57.75	53.25	54.00	53.50	**63.00**
YALE	32.73	35.15	36.15	39.39	41.21	39.39	36.00	40.14	39.15	**47.23**
UMIST	46.48	46.23	47.34	56.28	53.37	64.08	47.11	54.13	56.28	**68.59**
MNIST	47.50	47.90	47.10	50.70	48.70	55.80	47.40	51.00	52.00	**63.50**
Semeion	55.56	45.49	46.42	58.43	56.41	63.34	45.21	57.21	55.49	**73.57**
Average	44.65	45.50	45.90	51.86	50.69	56.07	45.79	51.30	51.29	**63.19**

Table 5: Normalized Mutual Information (%)

Dataset	Kmeans	NMF	LNMF	GNMF	NLCF	NSDR	CF	LCF	LCCF	RDCF
ORL	67.01	74.76	73.85	75.81	74.90	75.78	75.04	75.22	76.36	**80.67**
YALE	40.32	44.97	44.84	46.37	48.80	48.29	44.82	47.17	46.58	**53.43**
UMIST	63.81	64.74	65.16	75.85	72.13	76.03	65.02	74.31	76.18	**82.37**
MNIST	47.16	44.93	44.84	48.19	50.09	58.11	44.61	51.05	54.02	**65.17**
Semeion	50.94	41.04	42.27	55.88	54.21	61.90	41.84	53.57	51.60	**65.87**
Average	53.85	54.09	54.19	60.42	60.03	64.02	54.27	60.26	60.95	**69.50**

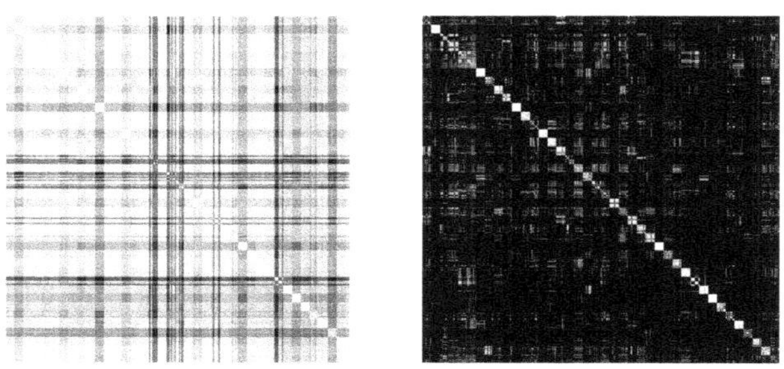

(a) Similarity of LCCF (b) Similarity of RDCF

Figure 1: Similarity between Images

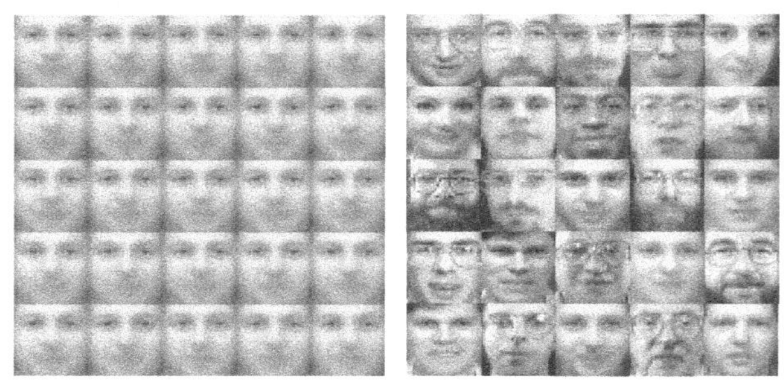

(a) LCCF (b) RDCF

Figure 2: Basis Images

search in the parameter space for each method and the best results are reported. Specifically, we search p, the number of nearest neighbors for constructing NN-graph, in $\{1, 2, ..., 9\}$. And the graph regularization parameter α for GNMF and LCCF is chosen from $\{0.1, 0.5, 1, 5, ..., 10^5\}$. The regularization parameter for NLCF and LCF is selected from $\{10^{-2}, ..., 10^4\}$. And for all factorization-based methods including RDCF, we set k, the dimension of latent space, to the number of true classes of dataset, as in [3, 18].

There are also some important parameters for RDCF, i.e., p for constructing nearest neighbor graph, λ for noise regularization, α for graph regularization and β for approximate orthogonal constraints. Specifically, We can set λ empirically according to the properties of the specific dataset. Therefore λ can be adaptive to the dataset. And we set $p = 5$ for MNIST and $p = 3$ for the others. We set $\alpha = 1,000$ for UMIST and Semeion and $\alpha = 500$ for the others. And we set $\beta = 1,000$ for all datasets. Actually, compared to LCCF and LCF, RDCF is more robust to parameter change. In the coming section, we conduct empirical analysis on parameter sensitivity, and the results show that RDCF can achieve superior and stable performance under a wide range of value for both α and β.

5.3 Clustering Performance

The clustering results of all methods on five datasets measured by ACC and NMI are shown in Table 4 and Table 5 respectively. We can observe that RDCF can significantly outperform all baseline methods regardless of datasets because RDCF are robust to data noise and can preserve locality and exploit discriminative information simultaneously. Besides validating the effectiveness and superiority of RDCF, the experiment also reveals some important points.

First, NMF and CF can outperform Kmeans though slightly. This phenomenon verifies the effectiveness of NMF and CF as feature learning methods, as discussed in [2, 3].

Second, we can observe that methods considering the local geometry structure of data, such as GNMF, LCCF, LCF and RDCF, significantly outperform NMF and CF, which also validates the importance of preserving locality of data.

Third, among all methods, NSDR and RDCF are the only two methods which explicitly exploit the discriminative information of data. And they are also the best two methods highlighting the power of discriminative information. But NSDR is affected by the noise and outlier in data, thus significantly degrading the performance compared with RDCF.

At last, RDCF is the only method satisfying all the following properties, i.e., being robust to data noise, preserving locality, exploiting discriminative information. Therefore it can achieve the best performance. Actually, satisfying any one of these properties can lead to better performance, and combining them all can fully exploit their power and they can as well promote each other for superior result.

Now we directly compare RDCF to LCCF on ORL dataset. The cosine similarity between images represented by the learned features (i.e., $\mathbf{V}$) is shown in Figure 1, where brighter color indicates larger similarity. We can observe RDCF achieves large inter-class similarity and small inter-class similarity, which is an ideal result, while LCCF achieves large

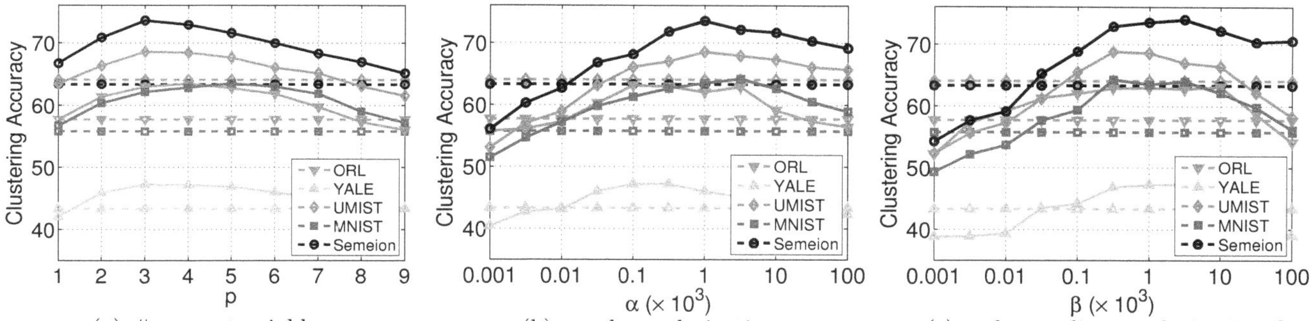

(a) # nearest neighbor p (b) graph regularization α (c) orthogonality regularization β

Figure 3: Parameter Sensitivity Analysis

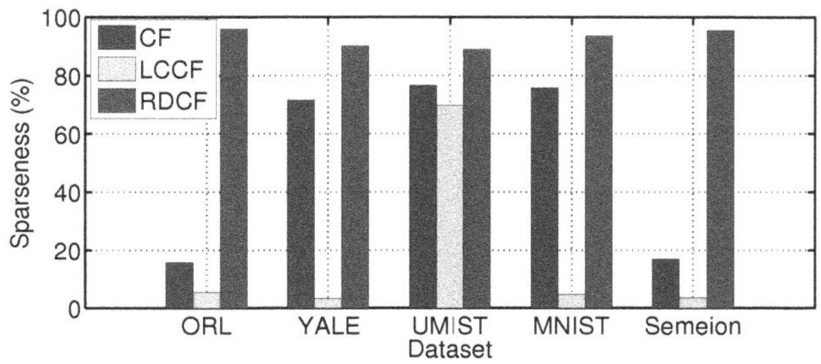

Figure 4: Sparseness Comparison.

inter and intra class similarity simultaneously. In addition, we show 25 basis images learned by LCCF and RDCF in Figure 2. Obviously, RDCF can capture more intrinsically discriminative information in images, while the basis learned by LCCF are almost indistinguishable. Although the representation learned by LCCF may achieve state-of-the-art performance for image clustering, this representation can't capture the discriminative information in image data, and is actually meaningless to some extent. But our RDCF is able to overcome the shortcomings of LCCF. RDCF can not only achieve much better clustering performance than state-of-the-art methods, but also learn discriminative and meaningful representation for images. Hence RDCF is more practical in real-world scenarios than LCCF.

5.4 Parameter Sensitivity Analysis

We further conduct empirical analysis on parameter sensitivity on all datasets. The results are shown in Figure 3. The dashed lines are the best results of all baseline methods.

The performance of RDCF with respect to p is shown in Figure 3(a). p controls the complexity of the graph. If it's too small, the graph may be too simple to fully exploit the local information. If it's too large, two images with different label may be connected such that decrease the quality of graph. Both will degrade the performance of graph-regularized methods, like GNMF, LCCF and RDCF. RDCF outperforms best baselines on each dataset when $p \in [2, 7]$.

The influence of α is shown in Figure 3(b). α controls the weight of graph regularization. A small α will lead to weak regularization thus it can't affect the objective function such that the locality can't be preserved. While a too large α may cause trivial solution problem to graph-regularized methods, like GNMF and LCCF. Though RDCF has graph regularization, we also incorporate approximate orthogonal constraints such that the trivial solution problem can be effectively avoided. Thus RDCF can achieve superior performance even with a large α. In fact, GNMF and LCCF are sensitive to α to some extent. But RDCF can achieve superior and stable performance under a very wide range of parameter value, i.e., $\alpha \in [10, 10^5]$ and it markedly outperforms all baselines on all datasets when $\alpha \in [10^2, 5 \times 10^4]$.

We plot the performance of RDCF with respect to different values of β in Figure 3(c). The parameter β controls the orthogonality of learned representations. Theoretically, if β is too small, the orthogonal constraint will be too weak and RDCF will be ill-defined and prone to trivial solution like GNMF and LCCF. On the contrary, if β is too large, the constraint may dominate the objective function of RDCF and it's so heave that the learned representation can be extremely sparse (under the ultimate situation, i.e., $\beta = \infty$, there is only one non-zero element in each row of $\mathbf{V}$) which is also unexpected in real-world scenarios. Fortunately, we can observe from the results that RDCF consistently outperforms best baseline methods on five datasets when $\beta \in [10^2, 10^4]$.

5.5 Other Issues

Previous works [5, 14, 18] mentioned that sparseness is also an important property of good image representation. Here we compare the sparseness of $\mathbf{V}$ learned by CF, LCCF and RDCF. As in [5], the sparseness is measured as follows,

$$\mathrm{SP}(\mathbf{V}) = \frac{1}{n}\sum_{i=1}^{n} \frac{\sqrt{k} - (\sum_{j=1}^{k} |v_{ij}| / \sqrt{\sum_{j=1}^{k} v_{ij}^2})}{\sqrt{k} - 1} \tag{36}$$

where $\mathrm{SP} \in [0, 1]$ and larger value indicates more sparse representation. The sparseness of them on five datasets are shown in Figure 4. We can observe that RDCF can indeed learn sparse representation while LCCF always learns dense one, and the sparseness of CF depends on datasets. Actually, larger β can result in more sparse representation. But this is unexpected in real world. With a proper β, the sparseness is about 90%, which leads to effective image representation.

It has been proven theoretically in Section 4 that the objective function will converge under the proposed multiplicative updating rules. Now we want to show how fast it can converge. The objective function value (averaged by the number of samples) with respect to the number of iterations is shown in Figure 5(b). We can observe that the objective function value is decreasing steadily with more iterations and can converge very fast, usually within 100 iterations. In addition, we compare the convergency property of RDCF to conventional CF whose result is shown in Figure 5(a). We can see RDCF can converge faster and more stablely than CF which requires more than 200 iterations to convergency.

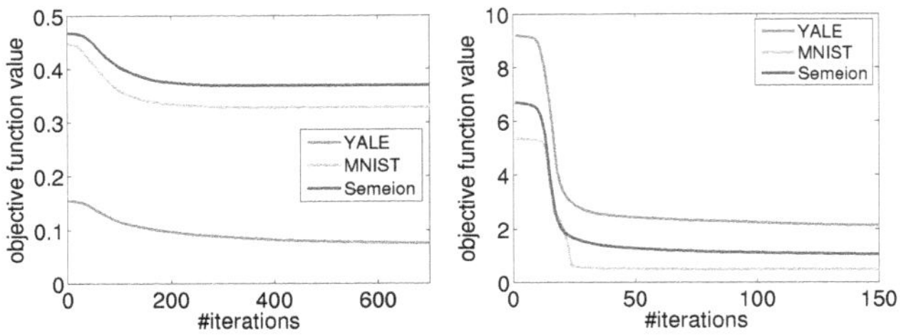

(a) CF (b) RDCF

Figure 5: Convergency Study

6. CONCLUSION

In this paper, we propose a novel method called RDCF, which can simultaneously preserve local geometry structure and exploit discriminative information. It's also robust to data noise while previous works with squared loss can't address this problem. Furthermore, RDCF can avoid trivial solution and scale transfer problems even with graph regularization. All properties above make RDCF an effective method for image representation. We also propose an iterative strategy with multiplicative updating rules for the optimization of RDCF and prove the convergence theoretically. Extensive experiments on five public image datasets are carried out and the results demonstrate that RDCF can significantly outperform several state-of-the-art related methods. Analysis about parameter sensitivity validates that RDCF can achieve superior and stable performance under wide range of parameter values, even if it's regularized by graph.

7. ACKNOWLEDGEMENT

This research was supported the National Natural Science Foundation of China (Grant No. 61271394), and the National HeGaoJi Key Project (No. 2013ZX01039-002-002). And the authors would like to thank the anonymous reviewers for their valuable comments.

8. REFERENCES

[1] M. Belkin, P. Niyogi, and V. Sindhwani. Manifold regularization: A geometric framework for learning from labeled and unlabeled examples. *JMLR*, 2006.

[2] D. Cai, X. He, and J. Han. Locally consistent concept factorization for document clustering. *IEEE Transactions on Knowledge and Data Engineering*, 2011.

[3] D. Cai, X. He, J. Han, and T. S. Huang. Graph regularized nonnegative matrix factorization for data representation. *IEEE Transaction Pattern Anal. Mach. Intell.*, 2011.

[4] E. Cands, X. Li, Y. Ma, and J. Wright. Robust principal component analysis? *JACM*, 2011.

[5] Y. Chen, J. Zhang, D. Cai, W. Liu, and X. He. Nonnegative local coordinate factorization for image representation. *IEEE Transactions on Image Processing*, 2013.

[6] A. P. Dempster, N. M. Laird, , and D. B. Rubin. Maximum likelihood from incomplete data via the em algorithm. *Journal of the Royal Statistical Society. Series B (Methodological)*, 39(1):1–38, 1977.

[7] G. Ding, Y. Guo, and J. Zhou. collective matrix factorization hashing for multimodal data. In *IEEE Conference on Computer Vision and Pattern Recognition, CVPR*, 2014.

[8] R. O. Duda, P. Hart, and D. Stork. Pattern classification. In *Wiley-Interscience, Hoboken, NJ, 2nd edition*, 2000.

[9] J. Fan, Y. Gao, and H. Luo. Integrating concept ontology and multitask learning to achieve more effective classifier training for multilevel image annotation. *TIP*, 2008.

[10] Q. Gu, C. Ding, and J. Han. On trivial solution and scale transfer problems in graph regularized nmf. In *Proc. of 22nd International Joint Conference on Artificial Intelligence*, 2011.

[11] Q. Gu and J. Zhou. Co-clustering on manifolds. In *Proc. of ACM SIGKDD*, 2009.

[12] Y. Guo, G. Ding, X. Jin, and J. Wang. Learning predictable and discriminative attributes for visual recognition. In *AAAI Conference on Artificial Intelligence*, 2015.

[13] X. He. Laplacian regularized d-optimal design for active learning and its application to image retrieval. *TIP*, 2010.

[14] P. O. Hoyer. Non-negative matrix factorization with sparseness constraints. *Journal of Machine Learning Research*, 5:1457–1469, 2004.

[15] D. Kong, C. Ding, and H. Huang. Robust nonnegative matrix factorization using l21-norm. In *CIKM*, 2011.

[16] D. D. Lee and H. S. Seung. Learning the parts of objects by nonnegative matrix factorization. In *Nature*, 1999.

[17] D. D. Lee and H. S. Seung. Learning the parts of objects by nonnegative matrix factorization. In *Advances in Neural Information Processing Systems*, 2001.

[18] H. Liu, Z. Yang, J. Yang, Z. Wu, and X. Li. Local coordinate concept factorization for image representation. *IEEE Trans. Neural Netw. Learning Syst.*, 2014.

[19] N. K. Logothetis and D. L. Sheinberg. Visual object recognition. *Annual Review of Neuroscience*, 19, 1996.

[20] L. Lovasz and M. Plummer. *Matching Theory*, 1986.

[21] D. Tao, X. Li, X. Wu, and S. J. Maybank. Geometric mean for subspace selection. *TPAMI*, 2009.

[22] M. W. O. E. Wachsmuth and D. I. Perrett. Recognition of objects and their component parts: Responses of single units in the temporal cortex of the macaque. *Cerebral Cortex*, 4(5):509–522, 1994.

[23] W. Xu and Y. Gong. Document clustering by concept factorization. In *Proc. of ACM RDIR*, 2004.

[24] Y. Yang, H. Shen, F. Nie, R. Ji, and X. Zhou. Nonnegative spectral clustering with discriminative regularization. In *Proc. of 25th AAAI*, 2011.

[25] Y. Yang, D. Xu, F. Nie, S. Yan, , and Y. Zhuang. Image clustering using local discriminant models and global integration. *IEEE Transactions on Image Processing*, 2010.

[26] J. Ye, Z. Zhao, and M. Wu. Discriminative k-means for clustering. In *Advances in Neural Information Processing Systems*, 2007.

[27] K. Yu, T. Zhang, and Y. Gong. Nonlinear learning using local coordinate coding. In *NIPS*, 2009.

Encoding Concept Prototypes for Video Event Detection and Summarization

Masoud Mazloom†, Amirhossein Habibian†, Dong Liu⋆, Cees G.M. Snoek†‡, Shih-Fu Chang⋆
†University of Amsterdam ‡Qualcomm Research Netherlands ⋆Columbia University

ABSTRACT

This paper proposes a new semantic video representation for few and zero example event detection and unsupervised video event summarization. Different from existing works, which obtain a semantic representation by training concepts over images or entire video clips, we propose an algorithm that learns a set of relevant frames as the concept prototypes from web video examples, without the need for frame-level annotations, and use them for representing an event video. We formulate the problem of learning the concept prototypes as seeking the frames closest to the densest region in the feature space of video frames from both positive and negative training videos of a target concept. We study the behavior of our video event representation based on concept prototypes by performing three experiments on challenging web videos from the TRECVID 2013 multimedia event detection task and the MED-summaries dataset. Our experiments establish that i) Event detection accuracy increases when mapping each video into concept prototype space. ii) Zero-example event detection increases by analyzing each frame of a video individually in concept prototype space, rather than considering the holistic videos. iii) Unsupervised video event summarization using concept prototypes is more accurate than using video-level concept detectors.

Categories and Subject Descriptors

1.2.10 [**Artificial Intelligence**]: Vision and Scene Understanding—*Video Analysis*

Keywords

concept prototype, video event detection and summarization

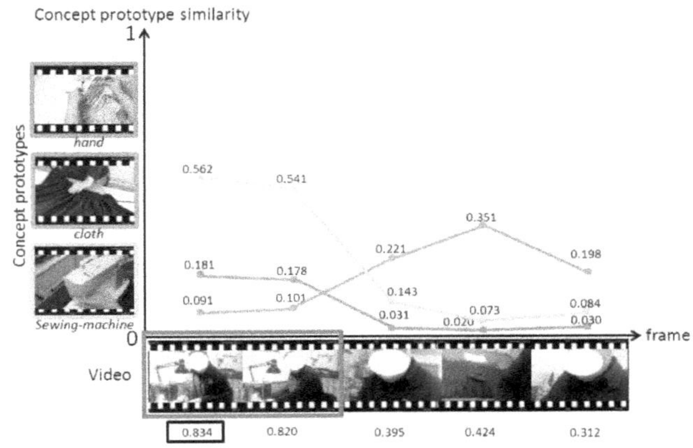

Figure 1: We propose an algorithm that learns from web data a set of relevant frames to the concept, which we call concept prototypes (y-axis). We encode videos as concept prototypes (x-axis) and show that for unseen videos it is able to detect events from few or zero examples. In addition, we demonstrate how the new representation can be exploited for unsupervised video event summarization (red border).

1. INTRODUCTION

The goal of this paper is to detect an event from very few examples and to summarize a video containing the event in its most descriptive frames. The common tactic for few- and zero-example event detection is to rely on a video representation consisting of concept detector scores indicating presence of concepts like *cake, rock* or *tire* in the video [4, 5, 7, 10, 11, 17, 19, 22, 25]. Such a representation is known to outperform the traditional low-level representation when examples are scarce [3, 9, 18, 23]. In [4, 8, 12, 24], it is further shown that semantic representations are capable of event detection without examples, from just a textual description of an event (and the corresponding event-to-concept mapping). We observe that concept detectors are included in the representation whenever they are available and are learned from either image- or video-level annotations. In this paper we propose a new video representation for few- and zero-example event detection, which also uses concept detectors, but we place special emphasis on what concepts to include and from what video-frames they are learned.

In [25] Merler *et al.* used a mixture of 280 relevant and irrelevant concepts to the events which are trained from thousands of labeled web images. In [10] Habibian *et al.* used a collection of concepts consisting of 1,346 relevant and irrelevant concepts to the event trained from ImageNet [1] and TRECVID [27]. In [22] Mazloom *et al.* proposed a learn-

ICMR'15, June 23–26, 2015, Shanghai, China.
Copyright © 2015 ACM 978-1-4503-3274-3/15/06 ...$15.00
http://dx.doi.org/10.1145/2671188.2749402.

ing algorithm to find conceptlets, a set of concept detectors deemed relevant to an event, from the same 1,346 concepts used in [10]. In [4] Chen *et al.* use a collection of 2,000 concepts trained on Flickr images, deemed relevant to an event from analyzing the textual description. We note that in all these works [4,10,22,25] concept detectors are trained from a collection of images, which have the appealing ability that they can be applied on each frame of a video. However the source of training data used in these methods is images from Flickr and ImageNet, applying them on frames extracted from web video results in an unreliable video representation due to the domain mismatch between images and videos. To counter the domain mismatch, recently several works propose to use web video for training concept detectors [2,8,9,19,31], which is not only much more efficient, but also suffers less from the domain mismatch problem. However, the drawback of these works is that they operate on a video-level, although concepts and events may be visible in a part of the video only. Hence, they include many irrelevant frames in their pooled representation leading to a sub-optimal representation.

In [14–16] methods are proposed that find relevant video parts by formulating the problem of video event detection as multiple instance learning. These works show the efficiency of training an event model only on relevant parts of video. Inspired by [14–16], in this paper we attempt to find an informative representation per concept by considering only the frames from web-video that are relevant to the concept, without using frame-level annotations. We call the informative subset of frames per concept the concept prototypes and use them to represent video for few- and zero-example event detection.

In [6], Ding *et al.* propose a method to generate a text which summarizes the important information in a video of an event. The algorithm selects relevant concepts to the event using lots of video examples. We also aim for video event summarization, but we use concept prototypes by selecting the relevant frames of a video to the event without relying on any video examples. In [28], Potapov *et al.* proposed video event summarization by learning from lots of positive and negative video examples. Each event model is applied on various segments of a video, the segments with the highest scores are returned as summary. Since they train a model over the video-level representation of videos in the training set, including all irrelevant parts, applying their model on small video segments are unlikely to reflect an accurate score. Since our prototypes are a frame-level representation of concepts deemed relevant to the event, we have the ability of applying them on each video frame and computing a reliable score per frame without the need for any event model. We simply consider the highest scoring frames as the video summary, see Figure 1. To the best of our knowledge no method currently exists in the literature for summarizing a video event using only a textual event definition.

We make the following contributions:

- We model selecting the concept prototypes out of a large set of frames of positive videos per concept, as seeking the frames closest to the densest region in the feature space of positive and negative videos.
- We introduce concept prototypes as a new semantic video representation for few example event detection.
- We show the effectiveness of the video representation by concept prototypes in few- and zero-example event detection as well as unsupervised event summarization.

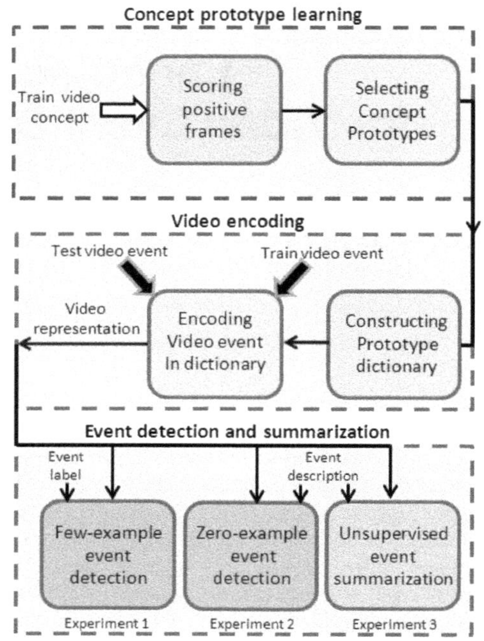

Figure 2: The flow chart for our proposal which consist of three modules. At first, we propose an algorithm which learns from a video dataset and corresponding captions a set of prototypes per concept. Secondly, we construct a prototype dictionary by collecting concept prototypes of all concepts and encode the video event in the dictionary. At the end we show the ability of our video representation for few- and zero-example event detection and unsupervised event summarization.

We organize the remainder of this paper as follows. We present our encoding using concept prototypes in Section 2. We introduce the experimental setup on the challenging TRECVID 2013 Multimedia Event Detection [26] and MED-summaries datasets [28] in Section 3. Results are presented in Section 4. We conclude in Section 5.

2. ENCODING CONCEPT PROTOTYPES

In this paper we aim to arrive at a semantic space with the ability for video event detection and summarization. We propose concept prototypes and leverage it for a new video representation. In this work, we define concept prototypes as a set of diversified video frames with variant visual appearance depicting the same concept in videos. For example, one can reasonably expect that for the concept *car*, prototypes are those frames related to various types and models of cars such as frames containing *city cars, sport car, truck,*. Because of their diversity, prototypes are beneficial over using a set of frames which describe only a specific type of car, e.g. *sport car*, or a set of frames which includes irrelevant frames to the concept *car*. In other words, concept prototypes for an arbitrary concept are those frames which appear in the most informative parts of the positive videos and not in the negative videos of the concept.

Since the concept prototypes are frame-level detectors, we have the ability of applying them in each frame of a video, which has several benefits. Firstly, by representing each frame of a video by concept prototypes, we can analyze each frame of the video individually. It gives us the opportunity of proposing a powerful video representation by aggregating all frames of a video in concept prototype space. Secondly, it allows us to do zero-example video event detection by considering the score of the frames in a video to each concept prototypes, and therefore help localize the key information in the video for zero shot event detection. It also offers us to to do unsupervised video event summarization by selecting the relevant frames of video to the event.

Our framework contains three parts, schematically illustrated in Figure 2. At first, we learn from a video dataset harvested from the web a set of concept prototypes per concept. Secondly, we construct a prototype dictionary by collecting concept prototypes of all concepts and encode each video from a train and test video event set in the prototype dictionary. At the end we show the ability of the concept prototype encoding for event video detection and summarization. Each part is detailed next.

2.1 Concept prototype learning

Our algorithm for learning concept prototypes of an arbitrary concept consists of two steps. i) Scoring positive frames which aims to compute a score for each frame of a positive videos containing the concept. ii) Selecting a subset of positive frames and consider them as concept prototypes.

Scoring positive frames: Suppose D is a dataset of web videos which are annotated for d concepts in a collection $C = \{c_1, c_2, ..., c_d\}$. Let consider $X_c \subset D$ is a set of n video/label pairs for arbitrary concept $c \in C$. We denote positive videos as V_i^+ which consist of n_i^+ frames v_{ij}^+, $j = 1, ..., n_i^+$. l^+ shown the number of positive videos in X_c, $X_c = \{\{V_i^+\}_{i=1}^{l^+}, \{V_i^-\}_{i=1}^{l^-}\}$. Similarly, V_i^-, n_i^-, v_{ij}^-, and l^- represent negative videos, the number of frames in the video, the jth frames in the video, and number of negative video in X_c respectively. We suppose all frames v_{ij} belong to the feature space $\mathbb{R}^m$. We collect all frames of positive videos V_i^+ of concept c in P_c , $P_c = \{v_{ij}\}(i = 1, \dots, l^+, j = 1, \dots, n_i^+)$.

To compute a score per frame $v \in P_c$ we need a function to precisely return a value for v indicating its confidence of being applied as a prototype of the concept. It has to describe how relevant the frame v is w.r.t. concept c in the positive videos, V_i^+, and while departing away from the negative videos, V_i^-. We use a diverse density function which is well known and frequently used in machine learning [20,21]. The Diverse Density function (DD) at frame $v \in P_c$ returns a real value which expresses the probability that frame v agrees with the densest regions within the frames of both positive and negative videos. It reflects the coherence with the visual appearance of the concept and is defined as:

$$DD(v) = Pr(v|V_1^+, ..., V_l^+, V_1^-, ..., V_l^-) \tag{1}$$

where $Pr()$ represents the probability function. By applying Bayes'rule to Eq. 1 and assuming that all videos are conditionally independent given v, we write Eq. 1 as:

$$DD(v) = \prod_{i=1}^{l^+} Pr(v|V_i^+) \prod_{i=1}^{l^-} Pr(v|V_i^-) \tag{2}$$

To estimate $Pr(v|V_i^+)$ and $\Pr(v|V_i^-)$ we use the proposed way in [20]:

$$Pr(v|V_i^+) = \max_j \quad exp\left(-\|v_{ij}^+ - v\|\right) \tag{3}$$

$$Pr(v|V_i^-) = 1 - \max_j \quad exp\left(-\|v_{ij}^+ - v\|\right) \tag{4}$$

Eq.(3) uses the maximum similarity between all frames in a positive video and the given frame as the probability of choosing v as a prototype of video V_i^+. On the contrary, Eq.(4) measures how dissimilar a negative video should depart from the candidate prototype frame. After considering Eq.(3) and Eq.(4) in Eq.(2) the DD function computes a real value between 0 and 1 for frame v. A larger value of DD at frame v indicates a higher probability that the frame v fits better with the frames from all positive videos than with those from all negative videos, and therefore have higher chance to be chosen as a concept prototype.

Selecting concept prototypes: After computing a score per each frame of P_c, we select the concept prototypes for concept c by considering two constraints: i) They need to be distinctive from each other so that the prototype collection has no redundancy. ii) They need to have large DD values. Applying the first constraint, we remove some of the frames that are similar to each other. In our algorithm we control the repetition of frames by considering coefficient α. It is a parameter which defines the degree of closeness of frames to concept prototypes. Its value is between 0 and 1. Closer to 1 causes our algorithm generate small number of prototypes per concept. The second constraint limits concept prototypes to those that are most informative in terms of co-occurrence in different positive videos. In our algorithm, we consider it by picking frames with DD value greater than a threshold T.

Our learning algorithm for obtaining concept prototypes for concept category c is summarized in Table 1. The inputs are a set of positive and negative videos for concept c, threshold T and coefficient α which are parameters to define

Table 1: Pseudocode of learning concept prototypes for concept category c.

INPUT: Positive videos for concept c (V_i^+),
Negative videos for concept c (V_i^-),
Threshold (T), and coefficient α
OUTPUT: Concept prototypes for concept c (CP_c)
1. Set P_c be the set of all frames of videos in V_i^+
2. $H = []$ an array for keeping DD values
3. $M = length(P_c)$
4. for $q = 1, \dots, M$
5. $H(q) =$ compute $DD(P_c(q))$ using Eq. 2
6. *end*
7. $i = 1$
8. Repeat
9. Select concept prototype, a frame of P_c corespond to maximum value of DD
$CP_c(i) = P_c(find(H = max(H)))$
10. Remove from H all elements a satisfying
$\|CP_c(i) - P_c(a)\| < \alpha\|CP_c(i)\|$ OR $H(a) < T$
11. i = i + 1
12. While $(P_c \neg = [])$
13. Output: CP_c, concept prototypes for concept c

Figure 3: Learned prototypes for five arbitrary concepts. Prototypes ordered from left (best) to right.

the number of concept prototypes for concept c. The pseudo code learns a set of concept prototypes for concept c which is represented by CP_c. In the pseudo code in Table 1, lines 1-6 compute the value of the DD function for all frames of positive videos in P_c. Line 7-12 describe an iterative process to select a collection of distinct concept prototypes. In each iteration, a frame of P_c with the maximum value of DD function is selected as a concept prototype (line 9). The frames of P_c that are close to the selected concept prototype or that have DD values lower than a threshold are removed from P_c (line 10). A new iteration starts when there is no any frame in P_c. In Figure 3 we visualize several concept prototypes.

2.2 Video encoding

In this section we first describe the process of constructing a prototype dictionary using concept prototypes, then we explain how to encode video events of train and test set into the prototype dictionary.

Constructing prototype dictionary: To make a prototype dictionary we first learn m concept prototypes for each of d concept $c_i \in C$ using the method which we explained in section 2.1. We consider $CP_{c_i} = \{cp_{i1}, cp_{i2}, ..., cp_{im}\}$ as concept prototypes for concept c_i. Then we construct a prototype dictionary PD by collecting all concept prototypes of concepts in $C, PD = \{CP_{c_1}, CP_{c_2}, ..., CP_{c_d}\}$ which element cp_{jk} is k^{th} concept prototype of jth concept.

Encoding video in prototype dictionary: We consider each element cp_{jk} as a feature in new feature space $\mathbb{F}_{PD}$. We define a function $g_{jk}(:)$ to compute the value of the feature cp_{jk} on video event V, which consist of n frames $V = \{v_1, v_2, ..., v_n\}$ as:

$$g_{jk}(V) = Pr(cp_{jk}|V) = \max_{i=1,...,n} similarity(cp_{jk}, v_i). \quad (5)$$

We can interpret $g_{jk}(V)$ as a measure of similarity between the concept prototype cp_{jk} and the video event V. It is determined by the value of similarity between concept prototype cp_{jk} and the closest frame in the video V.

As a result, each video event V can be encoded in $\mathbb{F}_{PD}$ using all concept prototypes in PD. It can be defined as a point ,$\varphi(V)$, in feature space $\mathbb{F}_{PD}$ which define as:

$$\varphi(V) = [g_{11}(V), g_{12}(V), ..., g_{jk}(V), ..., g_{dm}(V)]^T \quad (6)$$

where each element of $\varphi(V)$ is defined by one concept prototype and one frame from the video event V, the frame that is *closest* to the concept prototype. Also it can be viewed as a measure of the degree that a concept prototype is visible in the video event V.

2.3 Event detection and summarization

After representing video events in concept prototypes space, we use it for the problem of few- and zero-example event detection, and unsupervised video event summarization.

Few-example event detection: Suppose $TR = \{V_1^+, ..., V_{n^+}^+, V_1^-, ..., V_{n^-}^-\}$ is a train set consist of n^+ positive videos and n^- negative videos, and $TE = \{W_1, ..., W_n\}$ is a test sets for an event category e. By mapping each video of train and test set to concept prototype space using Eq. 6 we define TR and TE as two matrix representation of all videos in $\mathbb{F}_{PD}$:

$$TR = [\varphi(V_1^+), ..., \varphi(V_{n^+}^+), \varphi(V_1^-), ..., \varphi(V_{n^-}^-)]^T \quad (7)$$

$$TE = [\varphi(W_1), ..., \varphi(W_n)]^T \quad (8)$$

Each row of TR and TE represents a video, k^{th} column of TR and TE represent k^{th} feature in $\mathbb{F}_{PD}$. We train a model on TR and report the result of event detection accuracy on TE.

Zero-example event detection: In this scenario there is only a textual query explaining the event. Suppose T is an explanation for event e which consist of n words, $T = \{w_1, w_2, ..., w_n\}$, $C = \{c_1, c_2, ..., c_d\}$ is a set of concepts, and PD is a prototype dictionary which consists of $m{\cdot}d$ elements (m concept prototypes for each of d concept in C). Let's consider $W_i = \{w_{i1}, w_{i2}, ..., w_{il}\}$, which consist of l frames, be a video of event e in test set TE. We use following steps for computing a score per each video W_i in TE. i) At first we define a binary representation for event e as a query, $\mathbf{Q} = [\mathbf{a_1}, \mathbf{a_2}, ..., \mathbf{a_d}] \in \mathbb{F}_{PD}$, by comparing the concepts in C with the words in T. The value of a_i computes as:

$$a_i = \begin{cases} \vec{1} \in \mathbb{N}^m & \text{if } c_i \in T \\ \vec{0} \in \mathbb{N}^m & \text{if } c_i \notin T \end{cases}$$

ii) We map each frame of W_i to prototype dictionary PD by computing similarity between each frame of W_i and each of concept prototypes in PD. As a result, each frame of W_i is represented as a vector of concept prototype score, $W_i = \{x_{i1}, x_{i2}, ..., x_{il}\}, x_{ij} \in \mathbb{F}_{PD}$. iii) We compute a score per each frame of W_i by multiplying query Q with $x_{ij}, j = 1, ..., l$ and define vector $Y = [Q \cdot x_{i1}, Q \cdot x_{i2}, ..., Q \cdot x_{il}]$. The value of jth element of Y describe how much the content of the jth frame of W_i matches to event e. At the end iv) We score video W_i with maximum value of vector Y, $S(W_i) = max(Y)$.

After computing a score S per each video $W_i, i = 1, ..., n$ of TE, we sort the videos with their scores and compute the accuracy of zero-example event detection for event e.

Unsupervised video event summarization: We demonstrate the feasibility of using our concept prototypes, for summarizing the content of a video event by selecting relevant frames to an event category. Suppose W_i is a positive video of event category e consist of l frame, $W_i = \{w_{i1}, w_{i2}, ..., w_{il}\}$. We follow the first three steps of zero-example event detection, to compute vector Y which the value of jth element of Y show how much the content of the jth frame of W_i is match to event e. We sort the vector Y

from the best frame, that completely matches the content of the event, to the worst frame. We select the best frames based on how many percent of frames of video W_i we want to report as summarization of W_i.

3. EXPERIMENTAL SETUP

3.1 Datasets

In our experiments we report on two large corpora of challenging real-world web video: the TRECVID 2013 Multimedia Event Detection dataset [26], and MED-summaries provided by Potapov *et al.* [28].

Event detection: TRECVID 2013 MED [26]. This corpus contains 56k user-generated web videos with a large variation in quality, length and content of 20 real-world events. This corpus consists of several partitions, we consider the Event Kit training, Background training, and MED test set, containing about 200, 5K, and 27K, videos. We follow the *10Ex evaluation procedure* outlined by the NIST TRECVID event detection task [27]. It means that for each event the training data consist of 10 positive videos from the Event Kit training data along with about 5K negative videos from the Background training data. We also consider the *0Ex evaluation procedure* as specified by NIST, where we don't have any positive video example available. We rely only on a provided brief textual definition of the event containing some evidences of concepts which can be expected to be visible in positive video examples of a particular event.

Event summary: MED-summaries [28]. This set consist of 160 videos selected from the TRECVID 2011 Multimedia Event Detection task: the validation set consist of 60 videos and the test set consist of 100 videos. Every segment of all these 160 videos is annotated with a category-specific importance value (0, 0.333, 0.666, and 1). All segments of all videos are annotated by different users to obtain the ground truth video summary for evaluation. High scores indicate the human annotators consider the segment is close to the event of interest. We report all results on the test set containing 10 videos for a total of 10 events. We adapt the provided annotation format from segment level to frame level by simply propagating the segment annotation to each of its frames.

3.2 Implementation details

Concept prototypes training data. To train our concept prototypes, we use a video dataset that is disjunct from both the TRECVID 2013 MED and MED summaries collections. We adapt the VideoStory46K from Habibian *et al.* [9] which contains a collection of 46k video from YouTube. Every video has a short title caption provided by the user who uploaded the video. From these captions we generate individual terms which serves as positive concept labels for the corresponding video. In total there are 19,159 unique terms in the captions. We filter the terms by: removing stop words, noisy terms, terms which are not visually detectable such as *God* (we used the visualness filter from [9]), terms with frequency less than 100, and keep those terms which match with the words in the definition text of the events. After this step we reach to a list of 479 different concept labels.

Features. For representing the frames in all of our datasets we use deep learning features. At first we extract the frames of videos uniformly every 2 seconds. Then, similar to [13], we use a pre-trained convolutional neural network for mapping every frame of videos to a 4,096-dimensional feature vector which is the output of the second fully connected layer of the convolutional neural network. The network is pre-trained on all the 15,0254 categories in the ImageNet dataset, for which at least 50 positive examples are available.

Concept prototypes learning. For learning concept prototypes for each of the 479 concepts we repeat the following steps. i) We construct a set of videos for each concept label by considering all its positive videos and supplement it with negatives up to ten times the number of positives by random sampling from other concept labels. ii) We apply our concept prototypes learning algorithm (Section 2.1). We set parameter T as the average of the maximum and minimum of the DD function in H (Table 1), and we empirically found 0.05 to be a good value for α. We map the videos from TRECVID 2013 MED and MED-summaries to concept prototypes space using cosine similarity.

Event detection. We train for each event a one-versus-all linear support vector machine [29] and fix the value of its regularization parameter C to 1.

3.3 Experiments

In order to establish the effectiveness of our concept prototypes for event detection and summarization we perform three experiments.

Experiment 1: ***Few-example event detection*** In this experiment we compare the event detection accuracy of our proposed concept prototype encoding versus five baselines. *Baseline 1:* DeepNet. Video representation using deep learning features. *Baseline 2:* 15k-Concepts. A video event representation consisting of 15k concept detectors trained on ImageNet (inspired by [10]). *Baseline 3:* Conceptlets [22]. Video representation consisting of the most informative ImageNet 15K concepts per event. *Baseline 4:* 479-Concepts. Video representation using 479 video-level concept detectors trained on VideoStory46k (inspired by [11]). *Baseline 5:* VideoStory [9]. Video event representation which strives to encode the caption of a video rather than a single word. All six methods are evaluated by their event detection performance on the TRECVID 2013 MED test set.

Experiment 2: ***Zero-example event detection*** We compare the accuracy of our concept prototypes for zero-example event detection versus four baselines. *Baseline 1:* Flickr concepts. As a first baseline we report the result in [4] which used 2,000 relevant concepts per event as trained from flickr images. *Baseline 2:* 15k-Concepts. Same as above. *Baseline 3:* Composite concepts [8]. Video representation using 138 video-level concept detectors which are the result of combining several concepts using logical connectors. *Baseline 4:* 479-Concepts. Video representation using 479 video-level concept detectors trained on VideoStory46k. For all methods we build a query Q per event as a binary vector indicating presence or absence of the concept in the event description, as detailed in Section 2.3. We compute a score for a video in the test set by multiplying Q with a histogram containing the scores of concept detectors when applied on the video. From the resulting ranking, we compute the zero-example accuracy. We again evaluate the accuracy of all methods on the TRECVID 2013 MED test set.

Experiment 3: ***Unsupervised event summarization*** We compare the accuracy of our concept prototypes in video event summarization versus three baselines. *Baseline 1:*

Table 2: **Experiment 1: Few-example event detection on TRECVID 2013 MED test set. Best AP result per event in bold.**

Event	DeepNet	15k-Concepts [10]	Conceptlet [22]	479-Concepts [11]	VideoStory [9]	This paper
Birthday party	0.137	0.114	0.145	0.146	0.118	**0.188**
Changing a vehicle tire	0.391	0.388	0.401	0.444	0.103	**0.464**
Flash mob gathering	0.405	0.347	0.377	0.425	**0.535**	0.439
Getting a vehicle unstuck	0.334	0.323	0.390	0.377	0.319	**0.418**
Grooming an animal	0.084	0.108	0.110	0.126	0.151	**0.154**
Making a sandwich	0.031	0.074	0.075	0.100	0.074	**0.131**
Parade	0.171	0.109	0.145	0.246	**0.452**	0.303
Parkour	0.320	0.309	0.319	0.317	**0.721**	0.326
Repairing an appliance	0.169	0.127	0.133	**0.320**	0.184	0.244
Working on a sewing project	0.058	0.071	0.103	0.072	**0.151**	0.109
Attempting a bike trick	0.054	0.030	0.047	0.106	0.061	**0.144**
Cleaning an appliance	0.021	0.019	0.020	0.031	**0.078**	0.055
Dog show	0.232	0.134	0.165	**0.379**	0.354	0.313
Giving directions to a location	0.012	0.005	0.008	0.020	0.004	**0.022**
Marriage proposal	0.002	0.002	0.003	**0.004**	**0.004**	**0.004**
Renovating a home	0.019	0.024	0.032	**0.056**	0.051	0.033
Rock climbing	0.070	0.063	0.083	0.080	0.100	**0.110**
Town hall meeting	0.268	0.201	0.229	0.158	0.118	**0.290**
Winning a race without a vehicle	0.150	0.126	0.164	0.116	**0.217**	0.182
Working on a metal crafts project	0.054	0.068	0.078	0.116	0.118	**0.144**
MAP	0.150	0.135	0.156	0.181	0.196	**0.202**

Random. Video event summarization with relevant frames selected randomly. To cancel out the accidental effects of randomness, we repeat the random frame selection 10 times and report the mean. *Baseline 2:* 15k-Concepts. A video event summarization with relevant frames selected using 15k ImageNet concepts. *Baseline 3:* 479-Concepts. A video event summarization with relevant frames selected using concept detectors. *Oracle* Video event summarization using the ground truth user annotation value from [28], to create an upper bound for video event summarization. In *Baseline 2* and *3*, similar to our method in section 2.3, we make a vector Y with the value of each of its elements being the result of multiplying Q, a binary representation of event, and a histogram of applying concept detectors on each frame of video. Then we follow the steps which we explained in Section 2.3 for summarizing the video. We evaluated the accuracy of all methods in video event summarization on the MED-summaries dataset [28] by keeping 10, 20, 30, ..., 100 percent of the frames per video. For those videos annotated by more than one user, we report the mean accuracy. At the end we report the mean accuracy for all 10 videos of each of the 10 events.

Evaluation criteria For event detection performance we consider the average precision (AP) [30]. We also report the average performance over all events as the mean average precision (MAP). Similar to [28], for evaluating event summarization performance we propose a new metric, importance ratio. We defined information ratio (IR) as average of user annotation value of selected p frames of the video. The value of IR shows the quality of the video event summarization. We consider the average of the p highest user annotation value as a ground truth. The closeness of the value of IR to ground truth value shows the better summarization.

4. RESULTS

4.1 Few-example event detection

We show the result of experiment 1 in Table 2. Results demonstrate that the video event representation based on our concept prototypes performs better than all baselines. Our concept prototypes reach 0.202 MAP in event detection, where using DeepNet feature, 15k-Concepts, Conceptlet, 479-Concepts, and VideoStory results in 0.150, 0.135, 0.156, 0.181, and 0.196 respectively.

We explain the good results of our concept prototypes from several observations. First, most of the concepts in 15k-concepts are irrelevant to the event categories. Moreover, as these detectors originate from ImageNet, they are trained on images and not on video leading to a domain-mismatch. Using Conceptlets [22] to find the most informative concepts, out of the 15k, per event improves the event detection accuracy, but it cannot compensate for the domain mismatch. Interestingly, learning the events directly from DeepNet features is advantageous over using 15k-concepts. However, when we learn the detectors from video annotations, as suggested in [11], result improve considerably (from 0.150 to 0.181). VideoStory further improves upon this result, but our concept prototypes are more accurate. There are two reasons. First, VideoStory trains detectors using all frames from both positive and negative training videos. By adding lots of irrelevant frames it leads to a noisy video concept representations. In contrast, our concept prototypes identify the relevant frames of video only, making the representation more clean. Secondly, since the concept detectors from VideoStory are trained over a video-level representation, they have to apply on a video-level representation for event detection as well. Since most of the events happen in a part of the video only, aggregating all frames is sub-optimal. In contrast, our concept prototypes have the ability to apply the concepts on individual frames, which decreases the effect of irrelevant frames.

The results of experiment 1 confirm that few-example event detection accuracy profits from using concepts that are relevant to the event and which are learned from a video, rather than the image dataset. Moreover, it is beneficial to represent video using concept prototypes as the influence of irrelevant frames is reduced.

4.2 Zero-example event detection

The results of this experiment are shown in Table 3. It indicates our concept prototypes outperform all four baselines in zero-example event detection. We reach to 0.119 MAP where the alternatives reach to 0.024, 0.032, 0.063, and 0.100 MAP. Since our concept prototypes are frame-

Table 3: **Experiment 2: Zero-example event detection on TRECVID 2013 MED test set. Best AP result per event in bold.**

Event	Flickr concepts [4]	15k-Concepts [10]	Composite Concepts [8]	479-Concepts [11]	This paper
Birthday party	0.032	0.022	0.076	0.096	**0.154**
Changing a vehicle tire	0.038	0.099	0.018	0.238	**0.320**
Flash mob gathering	0.058	0.104	**0.319**	0.266	0.271
Getting a vehicle unstuck	0.010	0.107	0.055	0.356	**0.406**
Grooming an animal	0.011	0.019	0.009	0.079	**0.095**
Making a sandwich	0.028	0.021	0.079	0.082	**0.164**
Parade	0.130	0.094	0.223	0.221	**0.240**
Parkour	0.027	0.020	0.021	0.077	**0.112**
Repairing an appliance	0.048	0.078	0.025	**0.221**	0.213
Working on a sewing project	0.012	0.016	0.014	0.087	**0.089**
Attempting a bike trick	0.003	0.017	0.021	0.056	**0.061**
Cleaning an appliance	0.013	0.006	0.006	0.022	**0.026**
Dog show	0.003	0.003	0.001	**0.011**	**0.011**
Giving directions to a location	0.002	0.004	**0.025**	0.004	0.008
Marriage proposal	0.009	0.004	0.002	0.003	**0.005**
Renovating a home	0.002	0.017	0.023	**0.029**	0.026
Rock climbing	0.014	0.003	**0.146**	0.015	0.036
Town hall meeting	0.020	0.008	0.014	0.023	**0.035**
Winning a race without a vehicle	0.028	0.012	**0.110**	0.095	0.101
Working on a metal crafts project	0.002	0.002	0.006	0.010	**0.014**
MAP	0.024	0.032	0.063	0.100	**0.119**

based we have the ability to apply them on each frame. As a result we describe how well the frame is related to an event. Irrelevant frames are simply ignored.

Flickr concepts are relevant to the event but they are trained on images of Flickr leading to a domain mismatch. The same holds for the 15k-Concepts trained on ImageNet. Moreover, most of its concepts are irrelevant to the event of interest. Both the composite concepts and 479-Concepts are trained on video-level labels. It means they suffer less from the domain mismatch leading to improved zero-example event detection results. However, both of these methods suffer from the fact that they treat all frames equally, which adds lots of irrelevant frames to the representation. Our concept prototypes contain concepts that are relevant to the event, are trained on video, and consider only the most relevant frames.

4.3 Unsupervised event summarization

We show the result of experiment 3 on MED-summaries [28] in Figure 4. The result demonstrates the effectiveness of our concept prototypes for unsupervised video event summarization against random frame selection, 15k-Concepts, and 479-Concepts for all summarization settings. When we request a summary containing 30% of the video we reach to 0.600 accuracy in IR, where random frame selection,15k-Concepts, and 479-Concepts reach to 0.221, 0.274, and 0.384 accuracy in IR. The accuracy of the oracle upper bond is 0.923 IR. Since our concept prototypes are frame-based, we can apply them on each frame of a video and reach to an accurate video representation. Where the others are video-level by nature which makes them less suited for frame-level classification, resulting in a less reliable summary.

We visualize the result of video event summarization for two videos of the events *birthday party* and *Changing a vehicle tire* using our concept prototypes and the 479-concept detectors, as the best baseline, in Figure 5. In both examples we see the effectiveness of using our concept prototypes against concept detectors in video event summarization.

5. CONCLUSIONS

In this paper we propose *concept prototypes* a new semantic video representation for few and zero example event detection and unsupervised video summarization. Different from existing works, which obtain a semantic representation by training concepts over images or an entire video, we propose an algorithm that learns a set of relevant frames as the concept prototypes from web video examples, without the need for frame-level annotations.

We formulate the problem of learning the concept prototypes as seeking the frames closest to the densest region in the feature space of video frames containing both positive and negative training videos. The prototypes represent a class of frames that are more likely to appear in positive videos than in negative videos. Since the concept prototypes are a frame-level representation of concepts, we have the ability of mapping each frame of a video in concept prototype space which has several benefits. First, few-example event detection accuracy increases when using relevant concept prototypes. Second, the accuracy of zero-example event detection increases by analyzing each frame of a video individually in concept prototype space. Finally, unsupervised video event summarization using concept prototypes is more accurate than recent alternatives.

We conclude that selective use of relevant frames of a video to the concept, by means of concept prototypes, is beneficial for detecting and summarizing video events.

Acknowledgments This research is supported by the STW STORY project, the Dutch national program COMMIT, and by the Intelligence Advanced Research Projects Activity (IARPA) via Department of Interior National Business Center contract number D11PC20067. The U.S. Government is authorized to reproduce and distribute reprints for Governmental purposes notwithstanding any copyright annotation thereon. Disclaimer: The views and conclusions contained herein are those of the authors and should not be interpreted as necessarily representing the official policies or endorsements, either expressed or implied, of IARPA, DoI/NBC, or the U.S. Government.

6. REFERENCES

[1] A. Berg, J. Deng, S. Satheesh, H. Su, and F.-F. Li. ImageNet large scale visual recognition challenge 2011. http://www.image-net.org/challenges/LSVRC/2011.

[2] S. Bhattacharya, M. Kalayeh, R. Sukthankar, and M. Shah.

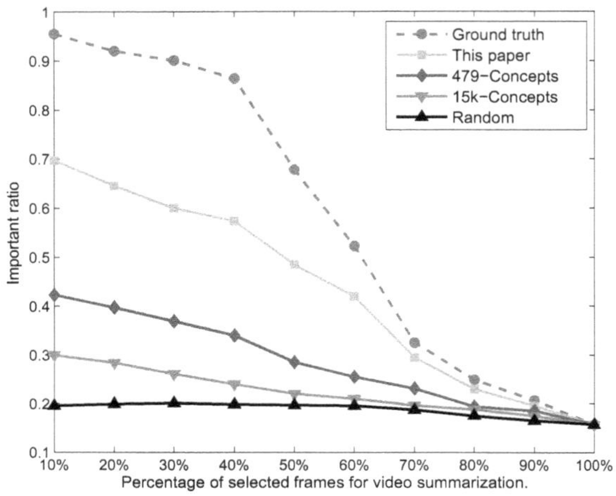

Figure 4: Experiment 3. Video event summarization on MED-summaries dataset. The result shows the effectiveness of our concept prototypes.

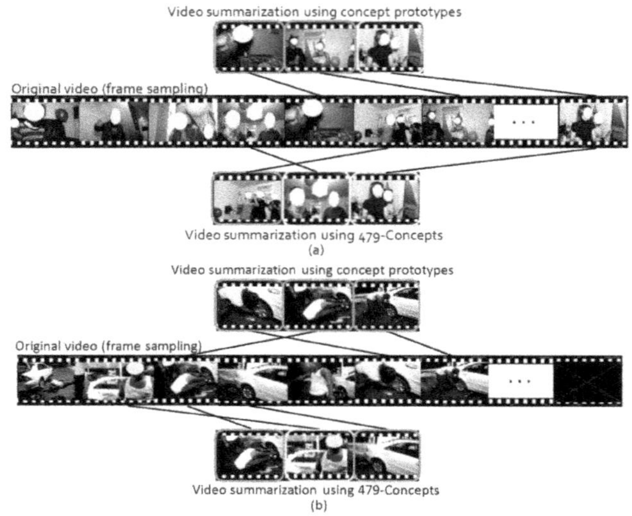

Figure 5: Experiment 3. Two examples of video event summarization using concept prototypes and 479-Concepts. We denote the ground truth annotation value of each frame with four colors. Green indicates 1, yellow 0.666, orange 0.333, and red 0 (higher is better). The color coding shows the effectiveness of concept prototypes.

Recognition of complex events exploiting temporal dynamics between underlying concepts. In *CVPR*, 2014.

[3] E. F. Can and R. Manmatha. Modeling concept dependencies for event detection. In *ICMR*, 2014.

[4] J. Chen, Y. Cui, G. Ye, D. Liu, and S.-F. Chang. Event-driven semantic concept discovery by exploiting weakly tagged internet images. In *ICMR*, 2014.

[5] Y. Cui, D. Liu, J. Chen, and S.-F. Chang. Building a large concept bank for representing events in video. *arXiv preprint arXiv:1403.7591*, 2014.

[6] D. Ding et al. Beyond audio and video retrieval: Towards multimedia summarization. In *ICMR*, 2012.

[7] N. Gkalelis, V. Mezaris, and I. Kompatsiaris. High-level event detection in video exploiting discriminant concepts. In *CBMI*, 2011.

[8] A. Habibian, T. Mensink, and C. G. M. Snoek. Composite concept discovery for zero-shot video event detection. In *ICMR*, 2014.

[9] A. Habibian, T. Mensink, and C. G. M. Snoek. Videostory: A new multimedia embedding for few-example recognition and translation of events. In *MM*, 2014.

[10] A. Habibian and C. G. M. Snoek. Recommendations for recognizing video events by concept vocabularies. *CVIU*, 124:110–122, 2014.

[11] H. Izadinia and M. Shah. Recognizing complex events using large margin joint low-level event model. In *ECCV*, 2012.

[12] L. Jiang, T. Mitamura, S.-I. Yu, and A. G. Hauptmann. Zero-example event search using multimodal pseudo relevance feedback. In *ICMR*, 2014.

[13] A. Krizhevsky, I. Sutskever, and G. E. Hinton. Imagenet classification with deep convolutional neural networks. In *NIPS*, 2012.

[14] K.-T. Lai, D. Liu, M.-S. Chen, and S.-F. Chang. Recognizing complex events in videos by learning key static-dynamic evidences. In *ECCV*, 2014.

[15] K.-T. Lai, F. Yu, M.-S. Chen, and S.-F. Chang. Video event detection by inferring temporal instance labels. In *CVPR*, 2014.

[16] W. Li, Q. Yu, A. Divakaran, and N. Vasconcelos. Dynamic pooling for complex event recognition. In *ICCV*, 2013.

[17] J. Liu, Q. Yu, O. Javed, S. Ali, A. Tamrakar, A. Divakaran, H. Cheng, and H. S. Sawhney. Video event recognition using concept attributes. In *WACV*, 2013.

[18] Z. Ma, Y. Yang, Z. Xu, N. Sebe, and A. G. Hauptmann. We are not equally negative: fine-grained labeling for multimedia event detection. In *MM*, 2013.

[19] Z. Ma, Y. Yang, Z. Xu, N. Sebe, S. Yan, and A. Hauptmann. Complex event detection via multi-source video attributes. In *CVPR*, 2013.

[20] O. Maron. *Learning from Ambiguity*. PhD thesis, 1998.

[21] O. Maron and T. Lozano-Pérez. A framework for multiple instance learning. In *NIPS*, 1998.

[22] M. Mazloom, E. Gavves, and C. G. M. Snoek. Conceptlets: Selective semantics for classifying video events. *TMM*, 16(8):2214–2228, 2014.

[23] M. Mazloom, A. Habibian, and C. G. M. Snoek. Querying for video events by semantic signatures from few examples. In *MM*, 2013.

[24] M. Mazloom, X. Li, and C. G. M. Snoek. Few-example video event retrieval using tag propagation. In *ICMR*, 2014.

[25] M. Merler, B. Huang, L. Xie, G. Hua, and A. Natsev. Semantic model vectors for complex video event recognition. *TMM*, 14(1), 2012.

[26] NIST TRECVID Multimedia Event Detection (MED) Evaluation Track. `http://www.nist.gov/itl/iad/mig/med.cfm`.

[27] P. Over et al. Trecvid 2013 – an overview of the goals, tasks, data, evaluation mechanisms and metrics. In *TRECVID*, 2013.

[28] D. Potapov, M. Douze, Z. Harchaoui, and C. Schmid. Category-specific video summarization. In *ECCV*, 2014.

[29] S. Shalev-Shwartz, Y. Singer, N. Srebro, and A. Cotter. Pegasos: primal estimated sub-gradient solver for svm. *Math. Program.*, 127(1), 2011.

[30] A. F. Smeaton, P. Over, and W. Kraaij. Evaluation campaigns and TRECVid. In *MIR*, 2006.

[31] C. Sun and R. Nevatia. Discover: Discovering important segments for classification of video events and recounting. In *CVPR*, 2014.

Discovering Semantic Vocabularies for Cross-Media Retrieval

Amirhossein Habibian[†], Thomas Mensink[†], Cees G. M. Snoek[†‡]
[†]University of Amsterdam ‡Qualcomm Research Netherlands

ABSTRACT

This paper proposes a data-driven approach for cross-media retrieval by automatically learning its underlying semantic vocabulary. Different from the existing semantic vocabularies, which are manually pre-defined and annotated, we automatically discover the vocabulary concepts and their annotations from multimedia collections. To this end, we apply a probabilistic topic model on the text available in the collection to extract its semantic structure. Moreover, we propose a learning to rank framework, to effectively learn the concept classifiers from the extracted annotations. We evaluate the discovered semantic vocabulary for cross-media retrieval on three datasets of image/text and video/text pairs. Our experiments demonstrate that the discovered vocabulary does not require *any* manual labeling to outperform three recent alternatives for cross-media retrieval.

1. INTRODUCTION

We consider the problem of cross-media retrieval, where for an image query we search for the relevant text or vice versa. Initially, cross-media retrieval emphasized on simple queries made of few keywords or tags [6, 11], but recently they have addressed more complex retrieval problems like searching for an image based on a long article [22, 27, 7, 3, 9], or automatically finding the best sentences as the caption to describe a video [12].

The major challenge in cross-media retrieval is that the query and the retrieval set instances belong to different domains, so they are not directly comparable. In other words, the images are represented by visual feature vectors which have a different intrinsic dimensionality, meaning, and distribution than the textual feature vectors used for the sentences. As a solution, many works aim to *align* the two feature spaces so they become comparable. We discuss below related work based on the level of alignment of feature spaces used, as also illustrated in Figure 1.

Low-level Alignment Works based on low-level alignment aim to align the images and texts directly from the low-level feature spaces, *i.e.*, the low-level visual descriptors and the individual words. Cross-media hashing [25, 28], canonical correlation analysis (CCA) [13] and its variants, such as cross-modal factor analysis [17] and Kernel-CCA [2, 7], are the main techniques for learning the low-level alignments. In a nutshell, these techniques extract the highly correlated features in the two feature spaces and use them to make a correlated representation of images and text. While encouraging results for cross-media retrieval using the low-level alignments have been reported, they suffer from two limitations. First, a low-level feature space is not the most effective place to find correlations, as the semantic gap is maximized. Second, the learned alignments are difficult to interpret, making it hard for a user to explain why a certain result was retrieved.

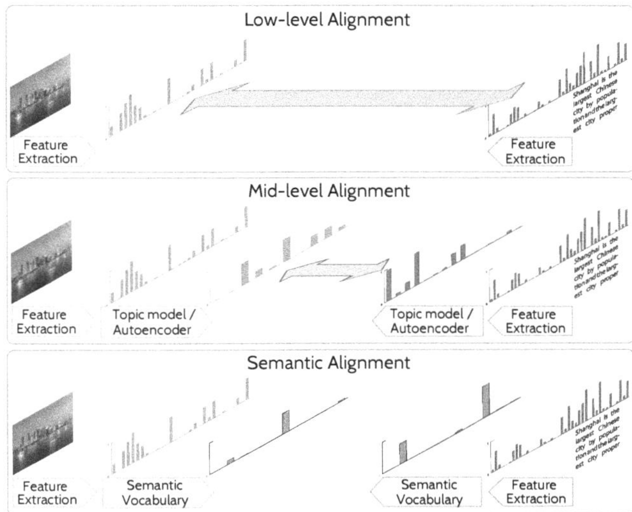

Figure 1: Level of alignments (gray) for cross-media retrieval using visual (orange) and textual (blue) features. This paper contributes to semantic alignment.

Mid-level Alignment Works based on mid-level alignment first extract mid-level features from each modality. Then the alignment is learned between the two mid-level feature spaces. Multi-modal topic models [6, 26] and multimodal autoencoders [9, 19, 21] are the two major trends for learning the mid-level alignments

Blei and Jordan [6] were the first to extend the latent Dirichlet allocation (LDA) to align text and images at the

ICMR'15, June 23-26, 2015, Shanghai, China.

http://dx.doi.org/10.1145/2671188.2749403.

topic level. Despite their effectiveness in aligning the discrete visual features, such as the traditional bag-of-visual-words, applying the multi-modal topic models on modern visual features, such as Fisher vectors [23] or deep learned visual features [20], is not straightforward. Since probabilistic topic models rely on assumptions about the prior distribution of features, which are not well known for state-of-the-art visual descriptors, the multi-modal topic models cannot benefit from them.

Recently, there has been a trend of developing multi-modal autoencoders with deep architectures for learning the mid-level alignments [9, 19, 24]. These works learn the mid-level representation of images and texts by training autoencoders. Then they align the learned representation by CCA [19] or regression [24]. Recently, Feng *et al.* [9] propose to learn the alignments jointly with the autoencoders. These techniques are shown to be effective for learning the mid-level alignments from large training collections. However, when there is not enough training data available, the deep autoencoders might be overfitted due to their large number of parameters. Moreover, similar to the low-level alignments, the mid-level alignments are incapable of recounting why an image and text are similar.

Semantic Alignment Instead of explicitly learning the correspondences between the images and texts, either at low-level or mid-level features, Rasiswasia *et al.* [22, 7] propose to embed the images and texts into a mutual *semantic space*. In the semantic space, each image or text is represented in terms of the probabilities of being relevant to a pre-defined *vocabulary* of semantic concepts. By representing the images and texts as their concept probabilities, they have aligned representations which are directly comparable.

The semantic representations are obtained by following three consecutive steps: First, the vocabulary is defined by specifying its concepts. The vocabulary concepts should be diverse and comprehensive enough to provide a descriptive representation of images and texts. As the second step, a train set of image/text pairs are labeled as relevant or irrelevant to each vocabulary concept. Finally using the labeled train data, a set of visual and textual concept classifiers are trained to predict the vocabulary concepts on images and texts. Each visual concept classifier is trained on the image parts and the concept labels as a binary classifier *i.e.,* binary SVM or logistic regression. The textual concept classifiers are trained in a similar way, but on the textual data of the train set. After training the concept classifiers, each image or text is embedded into the semantic space by simply applying the visual and textual concept classifiers.

In [22, 7], Rasiswasia *et al.* rely on manual annotations for learning the vocabulary concept classifiers. More specifically, they manually specify the vocabulary concepts and also manually annotate each image/text pair as positive or negative with respect to each vocabulary concept. This requires a substantial amount of annotation effort, which is restrictive in creating descriptive vocabularies with a comprehensive set of concepts. Moreover, for each new dataset a new vocabulary, which is relevant and descriptive to the data at hand need to be defined manually. To overcome these problems, we propose a data-driven approach to automatically discover the vocabulary concepts and their annotations from the textual data, which are available in the dataset.

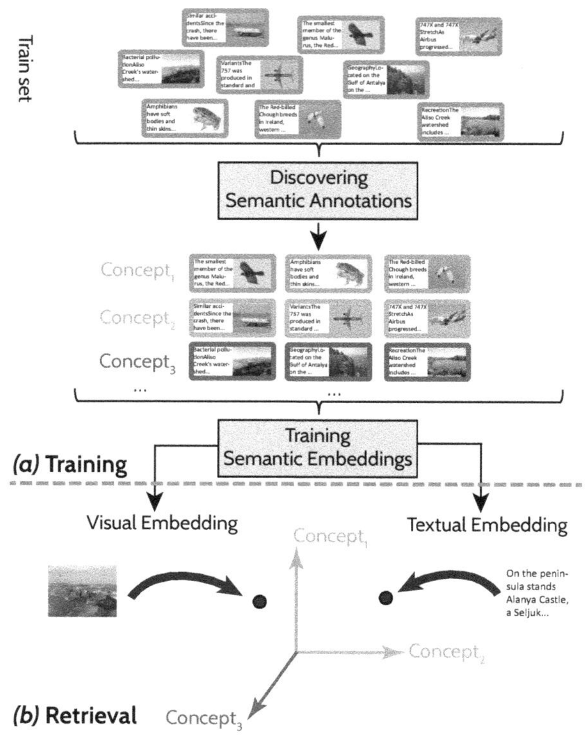

Figure 2: The overall pipeline, which we follow for cross-media retrieval. The "discovering semantic annotations" and "training semantic embeddings", as our main contributions, are detailed in Section 2.1 and Section 2.2

Semantic alignment is related to an attribute-based representation, commonly used for image and video classification from few training examples [8, 3, 11, 10]. In these works, the images or videos are represented as the outputs of attribute classifiers. However, the attribute classifier are applied with the purpose of enriching the image representations by transferring the knowledge from the attributes' training source. This is different from the intention behind the semantic alignment, where the concept classifiers are applied to align the textual and visual instances.

Contributions We propose a data-driven approach to cross-media retrieval using semantic alignment that automatically discovers the vocabulary concepts and their annotations from multimedia collections. Different from [22, 7], we do not pre-define the vocabulary and we do not require *any* human annotation effort to learn the concept classifiers. Moreover, we propose a learning framework for training the vocabulary concept classifiers from the discovered annotations. We experimentally show that our discovered vocabulary outperforms the state-of-the-art low-level, mid-level, and semantic alignments in three datasets of image/text and video/text pairs.

2. OUR PROPOSAL

The overall pipeline, which we follow for cross-media retrieval is shown in Figure 2. In the training phase, we learn two sets of visual and textual embeddings to map each visual or textual instance into a mutual semantic space. We learn the embeddings from a training collection of multimedia in-

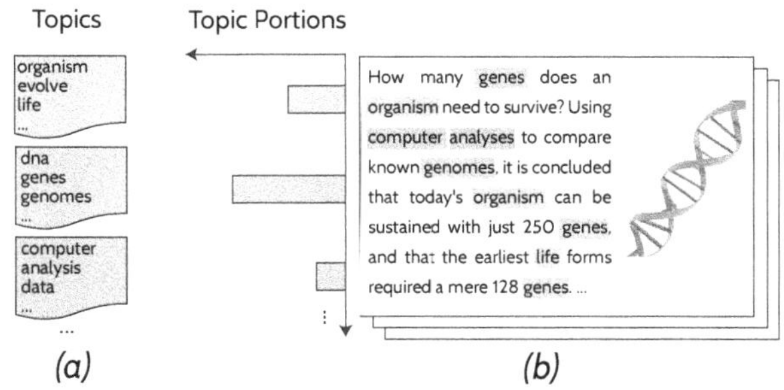

Figure 3: Illustration of topics and topic portions. (a) Three examples of topics extracted from a text collection. (b) Topic portions estimated by LDA for a multimedia instance. Figure inspired from [5].

stances including images or videos and their corresponding textual descriptions. Wikipedia articles, which are made of textual articles and their illustrative images, and captioned videos, which are made of videos and their textual captions, are examples of the multimedia instances used in this paper.

As the first step for learning the embeddings, we automatically specify the vocabulary concepts by discovering a set of concepts, which can effectively describe the training collection. Moreover, we automatically annotate each multimedia instance in the train set as relevant or irrelevant with respect to the vocabulary concepts. Our method for automatically discovering the semantic annotations is detailed in Section 2.1. After extracting the semantic annotations we use them for training visual and textual embeddings, as detailed in Section 2.2.

In the retrieval phase (Figure 2-b), we use the learned visual and textual embeddings to embed the query and the test set instances into the semantic space. Then the cross-media retrieval is cast into a single media retrieval problem, where the traditional similarity measurements, such as cosine similarity, are applicable for the retrieval.

2.1 Discovering Semantic Annotations

Instead of manually specifying the vocabulary concepts and their annotations we propose to automatically discover them by applying a probabilistic topic model.

Probabilistic topic models are statistical models for discovering the hidden semantic structure in a collection of text [1]. They automatically discover sets of interrelated terms, as *topics*, based on co-occurrences of terms in the collection. Figure 3-a illustrates three examples topics extracted from a collection of text.

In addition to discovering the topics, probabilistic topic models also extract *topic portions* for each textual instance in the collection. For each text, the topic portions determine the relevance of the text to each topic, as a probability value between 0 and 1. In the example in Figure 3-b, the text includes the terms from all three topics but with different portions. The more terms from a topic occur in a text, the higher the topic portion value assigned to the topic.

We observe that topics and topic portions are suitable to serve as the vocabulary concepts and their annotations. The topics provide a comprehensive summary of the collection, so a vocabulary composed of topics has a high descriptiveness. Moreover, as experimentally validated in Section 4.1, combining the interrelated concepts into a more abstract concept, as performed by topic modeling, generally improves learning the concept classifiers. More specifically, the abstract concepts, such as "animal", are in general more accurately predicted in images/videos than the specific concepts, such as "goat", "elephant", and "tiger", partly due to the amount of train data available per concept. Hence, a vocabulary composed of discovered topics serves as good concepts for the semantic representation.

To summarize, we apply the latent Dirichlet allocation (LDA) [1], as a widely used probabilistic topic model, on the textual instances in the train set. The number of topics is a parameter which is determined by cross-validation, as is detailed in Section 4.1. Then the discovered topics are considered as the vocabulary concepts. Moreover, the discovered topic portions are considered as the concept annotations and are used for training the visual and textual embeddings.

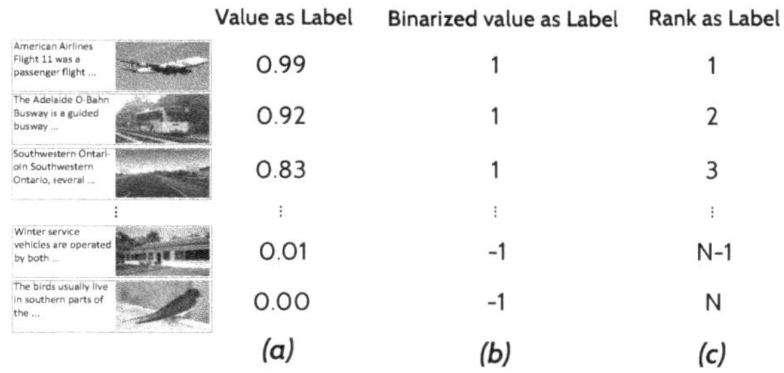

Figure 4: Strategies for extracting concept labels from estimated topic portions.

2.2 Training Semantic Embeddings

The semantic embeddings are defined as projections from visual or textual feature spaces into a mutual semantic space, by predicting the relevance of each instance to the vocabulary concepts. We train the visual and textual embeddings in a similar way. Hence, we first explain our learning algorithm for the visual embedding. Then we explain how the proposed algorithm can be applied for training the textual embedding.

Training Visual Embedding. We denote the visual embedding by $\Phi_{\boldsymbol{W}}(\boldsymbol{x}) : \mathbb{R}^{D_v} \rightarrow \mathbb{R}^k$ as the projection of each visual instance $\boldsymbol{x} \in \mathbb{R}^{D_v}$ into its k-dimensional representation in the semantic space. The visual embedding is defined as:

$$\Phi_{\boldsymbol{W}}(\boldsymbol{x}) = \boldsymbol{W}^\top \boldsymbol{x},$$

where $\boldsymbol{W} \in \mathbb{R}^{D_v \times k}$ is the visual prediction matrix stacking the weight vectors corresponding to each vocabulary concept classifier denoted as $\boldsymbol{w}_c \in \mathbb{R}^{D_v}$.

Each vocabulary concept classifier $\boldsymbol{w}_c$ is trained on its train set $\mathcal{D}_c = \{(\boldsymbol{x}_i, y_i), i = 1 \dots N\}$, where $\boldsymbol{x}_i \in \mathbb{R}^{D_v}$ denotes the visual instances in the train set. For example, in a train set of Wikipedia articles, $\boldsymbol{x}_i$ refer to the visual features extracted from the article's image. Moreover, y_i is the concept label denoting the relevance of the visual instance $\boldsymbol{x}_i$ to the concept c.

As proposed in Section 2.1, instead of manually annotating the concept labels, we automatically extract them from the topic portions estimated by LDA. More specifically, for each visual instance x_i we use the estimated topic portion of its corresponding text to extract the concept label y_i. However, the topic portions are estimated as continuous probability values between 0 and 1, so using them as labels for training the classifiers is not trivial. We consider three possible strategies for defining the concept labels based on the topic portions and discuss their applicability as follows:

- *Topic portion values as labels*, where the topic portion values are directly used as the concept labels (Figure 4-a). In this case, the concept labels are continuous, so the concept classifier is trained as a regressor. In other words, the $\boldsymbol{w}_c$ is trained to predict the exact value of the topic portions from the visual instances.
- *Binarized topic portion values as labels*, where the topic portion values are first quantized into binary labels, based on a threshold parameter. More specifically, the binary label is equal to 1, if the topic portion is higher than the threshold, otherwise the binary label is set to -1 (Figure 4-b). Then, the concept classifier $\boldsymbol{w}_c$ can be trained as a binary classifier using the binarized labels.
- *Topic portion ranks as labels*, where the visual instances are ordered based on their topic portion values and their rank is considered as the label, (Figure 4-c). In this case, the concept classifier is trained as a ranking function. In other words, the $\boldsymbol{w}_c$ is trained to rank the visual instances by predicting their relative concept relevancies.

Neither continuous values nor binarized labels are appropriate for training the concept classifiers from the estimated topic portions. Predicting the continuous label values from the images is difficult and ineffective, as we will show in the experiments. Although predicting binary labels is in general more simple than predicting continuous labels, a substantial amount of information in the topic portions can be lost by the binarization. Hence, we speculate that defining the topic portion ranks as labels and learning the concept classifiers as a learning to rank problem is the most effective solution for training the concept classifiers from the automatically discovered topic portions.

More formally, we first define each concept label $y_i \in \mathcal{D}_c$ by measuring its topic portion rank as follows:

$$y_i = \sum_{j=1}^{N} \mathbb{1}(\theta_i^c < \theta_j^c), \tag{1}$$

where $\mathbb{1}(.)$ is the indicator function. Moreover, θ_i^c is the estimated topic portion value for instance i for topic c. After determining the labels, the concept classifier $\boldsymbol{w}_c$ can be learned by any learning to rank method. In this paper, we follow the rankSVM formulation [15], which learns the ranking function by minimizing the following objective function:

$$\frac{\lambda}{2}\|\boldsymbol{w}_c\|^2 + \frac{1}{N}\sum_{i=1}^{N}\sum_{j=1, y_i<y_j}^{N} \max(0, 1 - \boldsymbol{w}_c^\top(\boldsymbol{x}_j - \boldsymbol{x}_i)), \tag{2}$$

where λ is the regularizer penalty parameter. By minimizing this objective we learn to predict a higher value for the jth visual instance than the ith visual instance, if its label has a higher rank. We minimize the Eq. (2) for each concept c independently using stochastic gradient descent [1], note that the ranking of the documents will be different for each topic.

Training Textual Embedding. While we could have used the LDA model directly as the textual embedding, we propose to yield a textual embedding which is more aligned with the visual embedding. The textual embedding are trained in a similar fashion as the visual embeddings, however instead of using the visual features the concept classifiers are now trained on the textual features.

For each vocabulary concept c, the train set $\mathcal{D}_c = \{(\boldsymbol{x}_i, y_i), i = 1 \dots N\}$ is defined, where $\boldsymbol{x}_i \in \mathbb{R}^{D_t}$ denotes the textual instances in the train set. For example, in a train set of Wikipedia articles, $\boldsymbol{x}_i$ refer to the textual features extracted from the article's text. Moreover, y_i are the concept labels, which are defined as the topic portion ranks as determined by Eq. (1). Note, that for each concept c the labels y_i are identical for both the visual embedding and the textual embedding, yielding a desired alignment between the two embeddings. Based on the train set $\mathcal{D}_c$, the textual classifier of the concept $\boldsymbol{w}_c \in \mathbb{R}^{D_t}$ is trained by minimizing the objective function of Eq. (2).

Figure 5: Two examples of the videos and their captions from the Captioned Videos dataset [21].

3. EXPERIMENTAL SETUP

3.1 Datasets

We use three multimedia datasets in our experiments, as summarized in Table 1. The first two datasets are made of image/text pairs, while the third set includes video/text pairs.

1. Wikipedia [22]. This dataset is provided by Rasiswasia *et al.* [22] and includes 2,866 Wikipedia articles from 10 categories. Each article is made of few paragraphs in text explaining the article, as well as an illustrative image. We adopt the protocol in [9] and use 2,173 articles as train set, 231 articles as validation set, and the remaining 462 articles as test set.

2. Wikipedia++. We expand the Wikipedia dataset [22] by collecting more articles from more categories. Our dataset, which we name as Wikipedia++, is collected by exactly following the same procedure as used for creating the Wikipedia dataset [22]. More specifically, we collected the articles from the Wikipedia "featured articles". Each featured article is categorized by Wikipedia into one of 30 categories. Excluding scarce categories, with less than 50 articles, we end up with the 20 article categories listed in Table 1. We split each article into sections, based on its section headings, and assign each image in the article to the section in which it was placed. This leads to a set of short and focused articles, containing a single image. Then the dataset is pruned by excluding the sections without any image. The final corpus contains 12,617 articles. We randomly split the articles into three partitions: 50% of the articles as train set, 25% as validation set, and 25% as test set. We make our collected

Table 1: **Statistics of the Wikipedia++ and the Captioned Videos datasets used in our experiments. The statistics of the Wikipedia dataset are available in [22]. Our created Wikipedia++ dataset is publicly available at** `http://www.mediamill.nl`.

Wikipedia++		Captioned Videos [21]	
Category	Size	Category	Size
Animal	1,454	Attempting board trick	160
Art & architecture & archaeology	695	Feeding animal	161
Biology	477	Landing fish	119
Business & economics & finance	234	Wedding ceremony	123
Culture & society	326	Working wood working project	141
Education	271	Birthday party	343
Engineering & technology	231	Changing vehicle tire	221
Geography & places	1,758	Flash mob gathering	303
History	793	Getting vehicle unstuck	211
Literature & theatre	453	Grooming animal	218
Media	566	Making sandwich	255
Meteorology	345	Parade	322
Music	400	Parkour	213
Physics & astronomy	573	Repairing appliance	196
Religion & mysticism & mythology	212	Working sewing project	196
Royalty & nobility & heraldry	583	Attempting bike trick	130
Sport & recreation	700	Cleaning appliance	130
Transport	638	Dog show	130
Video gaming	401	Giving directions location	130
Warfare	1,507	Marriage proposal	129
		Renovating home	130
		Rock climbing	130
		Town hall meeting	130
		Winning race without vehicle	130
		Working metal crafts project	130
Total	12,617		4,481

Wikipedia++, which is four times larger than the Wikipedia dataset [22], publicly available.

3. Captioned Videos [21]. This dataset is part of the TRECVID Multimedia Event Detection corpus [21]. It consists of user-generated videos accompanied with human provided textual captions. The dataset contains videos depicting 25 complex events, including life events, instructional events, and sport events. The textual caption of each video summarizes what happens in the content, as shown in Figure 5. We use the videos, which are assigned to one of the 25 event categories. It leads to 4,481 videos and their captions, where 50% of them are used as train set, 25% as validation set and the remaining 25% as test set.

3.2 Evaluation Protocol

We perform our cross-media retrieval experiments by exactly following [22, 9]. The multimedia instances in the train set and validation set are used for learning the visual and textual embeddings. The test set instances are used to perform two cross-media retrieval experiments: *i) Visual Query* experiments, where each image or video in the test set is considered as a query, for which we rank the textual instances in the test set by measuring their similarities. *ii) Textual Query* experiments, where each textual instance in the test set is considered as a query, for which we rank the images or videos in the test set by measuring their similarities. The similarities are measured by first projecting the instances into the semantic space, by the trained visual and textual embeddings, then we use the normalized correlation as the similarity metric [22].

The retrieval performance is evaluated using the mean average precision (mAP) metric, as in [22, 9]. More specifically, for each query and its R top retrieved instances, the

(a) (b)

Figure 7: Eight examples of the topics extracted from the Wikipedia++ dataset. Each topic is represented by its five most relevant terms in the same color. The topics in (a) and (b) are more specific than the predefined concepts "sport & recreating" and "warfare", respectively.

AP is measured as:

$$\frac{1}{M}\sum_{r=1}^{R} p(r).rel(r),$$

where M is the total number of relevant instances in the retrieved set, $p(r)$ is the precision at r, and $rel(r)$ is a binary value determining the relevance of the rth ranked instance. If the retrieved instance and the query has the same category label the $rel(.)$ is one, otherwise it is zero. Finally, mAP is obtained by averaging the measured AP values over all the queries. Similar to [9] we report the mAP@50 (R = 50) in all the experiments.

3.3 Implementation Details

Features. We use the deep learned visual descriptors [20] as ***image features***. Each image is fed into a pre-trained convolutional neural network and the output of the second fully connected layer is considered as a 4,096 dimensional feature vector. The convolutional neural network has an AlexNet architecture [16]. It is pre-trained on all the 15,293 categories in ImageNet dataset, for which there are at least 50 positive examples available. The ***video features*** are obtained by first extracting the video frames by uniformly sampling the frames every two seconds. Then each video frame is represented by deep learning features, which are extracted in the same way as the image features. Afterward, each video is represented by the average pooling of its frames as a 4,096 dimensional feature vector. As the ***text features*** we use the term histograms. More specifically, a dictionary of 3,000 high-frequency terms are extracted per dataset. Then each textual instance is represented as the histogram of its terms with respect to the dictionary [9].

Learning parameters. We learn all the vocabulary concept classifiers by the stochastic gradient descent solver [1]. The learning rate parameter η, the regularization penalty parameter λ, and the number of epochs are empirically set to 0.01, 0.001, and 100, respectively.

Topic model parameters. We extract the topics by MALLET implementation of LDA [18]. The Dirichlet prior parameters α and β are empirically set to 1 and 0.1. Moreover, the optimal number of topics for each dataset is obtained by cross-validation over 5, 10, 20, 50, 100, 500, and 1000 topics.

3.4 Experiments

1. Discovering Semantic Vocabulary. We evaluate the effectiveness of our automatically discovered concept labels, as proposed in Section 2.1, for training semantic vocab-

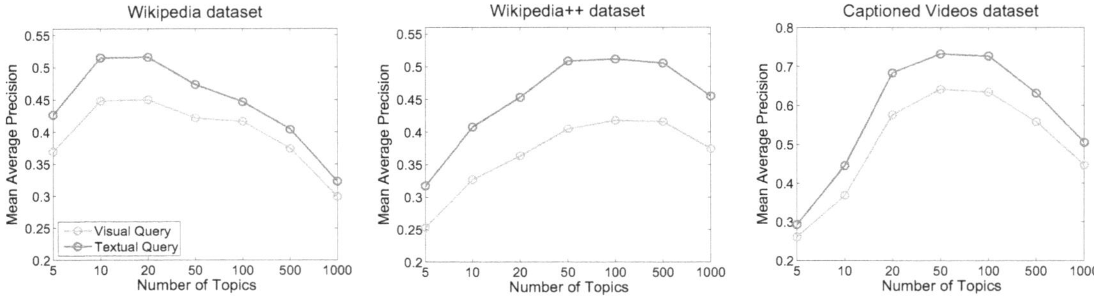

Figure 6: Effect of increasing the number of vocabulary concepts by extracting more topics from text. Extracting more topics generally improves the vocabulary by making it more descriptive. However, extracting too many topics is prone to overfitting, which degrades the effectiveness of the trained vocabulary .

ularies. We compare two concept vocabularies: First, our proposed ***discovered vocabulary***, which is trained on the automatically extracted concept labels, as detailed in Section 2. Second, the ***pre-defined vocabulary*** baseline [7], which is trained on manually provided concept labels. In this baseline, each category in the train set is considered as a vocabulary concept, and the concept labels come from the category labels, which are manually provided per instance. Please note that our proposed discovered vocabulary does not need *any* manual category labels in the train set, so we ignore all of them when training the discovered vocabulary. Each vocabulary is evaluated by its cross-media retrieval accuracy.

2. Training Semantic Embeddings. We evaluate our proposed strategy for training the semantic embeddings from the discovered vocabulary labels, as detailed in Section 2.2, by comparing three concept vocabularies: First, our proposed vocabulary of ***concept rankers***, where the concept classifiers are trained as rankers on the topic portion ranks as labels. The rankers are trained based on the rankSVM formulation [15]. Second, a baseline vocabulary of ***concept binary classifiers***, where the concept classifiers are trained as binary classifiers on the binarized topic portion as labels. The binary classifiers are trained based on the binary SVM formulation. Third, a baseline vocabulary of ***concept regressors***, where the concept classifiers are trained as regressors on the topic portion values as labels. The regressors are trained based on the ridge regression formulation. To be consistent, we use the stochastic gradient descent solver for training all the rankers, binary classifiers, and regressors with the same parameter settings as detailed in Section 3.3.

3. Comparison to Others Alignments. We investigate the effectiveness of our discovered vocabulary for cross-media retrieval by comparing it with three state-of-the-art baselines: ***i) CCA*** [22], as a low-level alignment, which uses CCA to align the two modalities. ***ii) Correspondence AE*** [9], as a recent mid-level alignment, which uses correspondence autoencoders with deep architectures to align the textual and visual features. ***iii) pre-defined vocabulary*** [7], as a semantic alignment, which uses a pre-defined vocabulary of concept classifiers to embed the textual and visual instances in the mutual semantic space. For the CCA and pre-defined vocabulary baselines, we run the author's implementation on our features. For the correspondence AE baseline the numbers are exactly reported from [9].

Table 2: Experiment 1. Evaluating the discovered vocabulary. The discovered vocabulary is more effective and does not require manual supervision during training of concept classifiers.

	Visual Query		*Textual Query*	
Dataset	Pre-defined [7]	Discovered	Pre-defined [7]	Discovered
Wikipedia	0.431	**0.450**	0.491	**0.516**
Wikipedia++	0.377	**0.418**	0.493	**0.511**
Captioned Videos	0.528	**0.642**	0.627	**0.732**

4. RESULTS

4.1 Discovering Semantic Vocabulary

The results are shown in Table 2. The proposed discovered vocabulary outperforms the pre-defined vocabulary consistently for both cross-media retrieval tasks on all the three datasets. It demonstrates that the vocabulary concept labels can be effectively extracted from the textual instances in the train set without any manual supervision.

We provide two reasons to explain the better performance of the discovered vocabularies over the predefined vocabularies: First, many of the manually defined vocabulary concepts are very general, *i.e.,* the concepts "warfare" and "sport & recreation" in the *Wikipedia++*. These general concepts have a large diversity in their training examples, which undermines the accuracy of their concept classifiers. In contrast, the discovered vocabulary defines the vocabulary concepts by topic modeling, so is able to define more specific concepts by extracting an appropriate number of topics. Figure 7 shows some examples of the specific concepts, which are discovered by topic modeling.

As the seconds reason, the pre-defined vocabularies include a limited number of concepts, which are not enough to effectively represent all of the instances. More specifically, for the *Wikipedia*, *Wikipedia++*, and *Captioned Videos* datasets, the pre-defined vocabulary includes 10, 20, and 25 concepts as pre-defined in the dataset. In contrast, our discovered vocabulary is able to discover higher number of vocabulary concepts by extracting more topics from the textual instances. We further investigate the impact of increasing the number of vocabulary concepts by extracting more topics in Figure 6. It demonstrates that extracting more topics generally leads to more comprehensive and descriptive concept vocabulary, which is more effective for cross-media retrieval. However, after a certain vocabulary size,

Figure 8: Top three retrievals for a caption query (left) and a video query (right) in the Captioned Videos dataset. The semantic representations are shown in the gray box. The common concepts between the query and the retrieved instances, as highlighted by colors, explain why the query and the retrieved instances are similar. Each highlighted concept is represented by its three most relevant terms in the bottom.

Table 3: Experiment 2. Evaluation of the three strategies for training vocabulary classifiers from the discovered concept labels. The most effective vocabulary is obtained by training ranking functions on topic portion ranks as labels.

	Visual Query			*Textual Query*		
Dataset	Concept Binary Classifiers	Concept Regressors	Concept Rankers	Concept Binary Classifiers	Concept Regressors	Concept Rankers
Wikipedia	0.416	0.412	**0.450**	0.497	0.487	**0.516**
Wikipedia++	0.342	0.401	**0.418**	0.406	0.495	**0.511**
Captioned Videos	0.453	0.594	**0.642**	0.522	0.706	**0.732**

extracting more topics has a negative effect on the vocabulary. We explain it by the fact that when we extract too many topics from a small collection of texts, the extracted topics might be overfitted to the random co-occurrences of terms. It is also observable in Figure 6, where there is a relation between the dataset size and the optimal number of topics. The optimal number of topics for *Wikipedia++*, as the largest dataset in our experiments, is 100 that is higher than for the other two datasets.

As the conclusion, the results demonstrate that by discovering the concept labels from the textual instances, we not only alleviate the manual labeling but also train a more effective vocabulary of concepts for cross-media retrieval.

4.2 Training Semantic Embeddings

The results are shown in Table 3. The vocabulary of concept rankers consistently outperforms the vocabularies of concept binary classifiers and concepts regressors for the both cross-media retrieval tasks on all the three datasets. It demonstrates that defining the concept labels as the topic portion ranks and training ranking functions on them is the most effective strategy for learning from the automatically discovered concept labels.

The lowest performing vocabulary is obtained with the concept binary classifiers, which are trained as binary SVMs on the binarized topic portions as labels. We explain it by the fact that lots of information in the topic portions are lost by binarization. More specifically, all the instances above the binarization threshold are equally considered as positive examples without consideration of their relevancy degrees encoded in topic portions. The low performance of the concept binary classifiers implies the importance of the relevancy degrees for training the vocabulary.

The concept regressors vocabulary performs better than the binary classifiers vocabulary, but it is still outperformed by the vocabulary of concept rankers. As an explanation, we speculate that the concept regressors does not binarize the topic portions, so are not suffered by the information lost as in the binary classifiers. However, predicting the exact value of the topic portions from the visual features, as targeted by the concept regressors, is generally very hard. Hence the trained concept regressors might be inaccurate. This drawback is relaxed by the concept rankers by predicting the relative orders between the topic portions instead of their exact values. As a conclusion, training the concept rankers is the most effective strategy, compared to the alternatives, for training concept classifiers from the automatically discovered labels.

4.3 Comparison to Other Alignments

The results are shown in Table 4. Our discovered vocabulary consistently outperforms the state-of-the-art alternatives for the both cross-media retrieval tasks on all the three datasets. It demonstrates the effectiveness of our proposed vocabulary for cross-media retrieval.

Furthermore, the results demonstrate that the both predefined and discovered vocabularies substantially outperform the CCA and correspondence autoencoders baselines. We explain the relatively low performance of the correspondence autoencoders by the fact that this baseline uses a deep

Table 4: Experiment 3. Comparison of our discovered vocabulary with three state-of-the-art alignments. The discovered vocabulary consistently outperforms the alternatives.

	Visual Query				*Textual Query*			
Dataset	CCA [22]	Correspondence AE [9]	Pre-defined [7]	Discovered	CCA [22]	Correspondence AE [9]	Pre-defined [7]	Discovered
Wikipedia	0.348	0.335	0.431	**0.450**	0.359	0.368	0.491	**0.516**
Wikipedia++	0.352	N.A.	0.377	**0.418**	0.412	N.A.	0.493	**0.511**
Captioned Videos	0.475	N.A.	0.528	**0.642**	0.545	N.A.	0.627	**0.732**

architecture, which generally requires large amount of training data to be effectively learnt. However, the largest train set in our experiments includes 6K examples, which seems to be not large enough. Moreover, the low performance of CCA baseline, as a low-level alignment, validates that learning the correspondences between the two modalities directly from the low-level features is not effective, since the semantic gap is maximized.

Besides their higher retrieval accuracies, the semantic vocabularies provide interpretable representation of instances, which make it possible to explain why two visual and textual instances are similar, as shown in Figure 8. In summary, the discovered vocabulary is not only effective for cross-media retrieval, but also recounts why the instances are retrieved.

5. CONCLUSION

We propose a data-driven approach for cross-media retrieval by automatically learning its underlying semantic vocabulary, rather than specifying and annotating the vocabulary as commonly done. We demonstrate that the textual instances in cross-media collections are a rich source of semantics, which can be utilized to (weakly) supervise the concept classifier training. More specifically, we demonstrate that probabilistic topic models are effective tools to extract the underlying semantic structures from a collection of text. Moreover, we experimentally show that learning to rank is an effective strategy for learning the classifiers from the text-driven annotations. Our experiments show that the discovered vocabulary outperform the state-of-the-art alternatives for cross-media retrieval. These conclusions may generalize for any other problem, where the textual descriptions are served as labels for concept classifier training.

Acknowledgments This research is supported by the STW STORY project and the Dutch national program COMMIT.

6. REFERENCES

[1] Z. Akata, F. Perronnin, Z. Harchaoui, and C. Schmid. Good practice in large-scale learning for image classification. *IEEE TPAMI*, 36:507–520, 2014.

[2] L. Ballan, T. Uricchio, L. Seidenari, and A. Del Bimbo. A cross-media model for automatic image annotation. In *ICMR*, 2014.

[3] T. L. Berg, A. C. Berg, and J. Shih. Automatic attribute discovery and characterization from noisy web data. In *ECCV*, 2010.

[4] D. Blei, A. Ng, and M. Jordan. Latent dirichlet allocation. *JMLR*, 3:993–1022, 2003.

[5] D. M. Blei. Probabilistic topic models. *Communications of the ACM*, 55:77–84, 2012.

[6] D. M. Blei and M. I. Jordan. Modeling annotated data. In *ACM SIGIR*, 2003.

[7] J. Costa Pereira, E. Coviello, G. Doyle, N. Rasiwasia, G. Lanckriet, R. Levy, and N. Vasconcelos. On the role of correlation and abstraction in cross-modal multimedia retrieval. *IEEE TPAMI*, 36:521–535, 2014.

[8] A. Farhadi, I. Endres, D. Hoiem, and D. Forsyth. Describing objects by their attributes. In *CVPR*, 2009.

[9] F. Feng, X. Wang, and R. Li. Cross-modal retrieval with correspondence autoencoder. In *ACM MM*, 2014.

[10] A. Habibian, T. Mensink, and C. G. Snoek. Videostory: A new multimedia embedding for few-example recognition and translation of events. In *ACM MM*, 2014.

[11] A. Habibian and C. Snoek. Recommendations for recognizing video events by concept vocabularies. *CVIU*, 124, 2014.

[12] A. Habibian and C. G. Snoek. Video2sentence and vice versa. In *ACM MM*, 2013.

[13] D. Hardoon, S. Szedmak, and J. Shawe-Taylor. Canonical correlation analysis: An overview with application to learning methods. *Neural computation*, 16:2639–2664, 2004.

[14] J. Jeon, V. Lavrenko, and R. Manmatha. Automatic image annotation and retrieval using cross-media relevance models. In *ACM SIGIR*, 2003.

[15] T. Joachims. Optimizing search engines using clickthrough data. In *ACM SIGKDD*, 2002.

[16] A. Krizhevsky, I. Sutskever, and G. E. Hinton. Imagenet classification with deep convolutional neural networks. In *NIPS*, 2012.

[17] D. Li, N. Dimitrova, M. Li, and I. K. Sethi. Multimedia content processing through cross-modal association. In *ACM MM*, 2003.

[18] A. K. McCallum. Mallet: A machine learning for language toolkit. http://mallet.cs.umass.edu, 2002.

[19] J. Ngiam, A. Khosla, M. Kim, J. Nam, H. Lee, and A. Y. Ng. Multimodal deep learning. In *ICML*, 2011.

[20] M. Oquab, L. Bottou, I. Laptev, and J. Sivic. Learning and transferring mid-level image representations using convolutional neural networks. In *CVPR*, 2014.

[21] P. Over, J. Fiscus, G. Sanders, et al. TRECVID 2013-an overview of the goals, tasks, data, evaluation mechanisms and metrics. In *TRECVID*, 2013.

[22] N. Rasiwasia, J. Costa Pereira, E. Coviello, G. Doyle, G. Lanckriet, R. Levy, and N. Vasconcelos. A new approach to cross-modal multimedia retrieval. In *ACM MM*, 2010.

[23] J. Sánchez, F. Perronnin, T. Mensink, and J. Verbeek. Image classification with the fisher vector: Theory and practice. *IJCV*, 105, 2013.

[24] R. Socher, M. Ganjoo, C. D. Manning, and A. Ng. Zero-shot learning through cross-modal transfer. In *NIPS*, 2013.

[25] J. Song, Y. Yang, Y. Yang, Z. Huang, and H. T. Shen. Inter-media hashing for large-scale retrieval from heterogeneous data sources. In *ACM SIGMOD*, 2013.

[26] Y. Wang, F. Wu, J. Song, X. Li, and Y. Zhuang. Multi-modal mutual topic reinforce modeling for cross-media retrieval. In *ACM MM*, 2014.

[27] F. Wu, X. Lu, Z. Zhang, S. Yan, Y. Rui, and Y. Zhuang. Cross-media semantic representation via bi-directional learning to rank. In *ACM MM*. ACM, 2013.

[28] J. Zhou, G. Ding, and Y. Guo. Latent semantic sparse hashing for cross-modal similarity search. In *ACM SIGIR*, 2014.

Semi-Supervised Image Classification by Nonnegative Sparse Neighborhood Propagation

Zhao Zhang, Li Zhang
School of Computer Science and Technology, Soochow University
Suzhou 215006, P. R. China
cszzhang@gmail.com,
zhangliml@suda.edu.cn

Mingbo Zhao
Electronic Engineering Department
City University of Hong Kong
Tat Chee Avenue, Kowloon
Hong Kong
mzhao4@cityu.edu.hk

Weiming Jiang, Yuchen Liang, Fanzhang Li
School of Computer Science and Technology, Soochow University
Suzhou 215006, P. R. China
lfzh@suda.edu.cn

ABSTRACT
This paper proposes an enhanced semi-supervised classification approach termed *Nonnegative Sparse Neighborhood Propagation* (SparseNP) that is an improvement to the existing neighborhood propagation due to the fact that the outputted soft labels of points cannot be ensured to be sufficiently sparse, discriminative, robust to noise and be probabilistic values. Note that the sparse property and strong discriminating ability of predicted labels is important, since ideally the soft label of each sample should have only one or few positive elements (i.e., less unfavorable mixed signs are included) deciding its class assignment. To reduce the negative effects of unfavorable mixed signs on the learning performance, we regularize the $l_{2,1}$-norm on the soft labels during optimization for enhancing the prediction results. The non-negativity and sum-to-one constraints are also included to ensure the outputted labels are probabilistic values. The proposed framework is solved in an alternative manner for delivering a more reliable solution so that the accuracy can be improved. Simulations show that satisfactory results can be obtained by the proposed SparseNP compared with other related approaches.

Categories and Subject Descriptors
I.2.6[Artificial Intelligence]: *Learning*, I.5.2[Pattern Recognition]: *Design Methodology - Classifier design and evaluation*

General Terms
Algorithms, Performance, Design, Experimentation

Keywords
Semi-supervised learning; label propagation; image classification; $l_{2,1}$-norm regularization; sum-to-one constraint

1. INTRODUCTION
Graph driven semi-supervised classification has been attracting considerable interests and is an important research topic in the fields of data mining, computer vision and image recognition [1] [2][25]. This is mainly because most multimedia data (such as images, videos and documents) from the practical applications in the real world are usually unlabeled without any supervised prior knowledge that can be used to recognize or distinguish them. The main advantage of semi-supervised learning for classification is that they can use both supervised information of small number of labeled points and large number of unlabeled data for enhancing performance [3][4][5][6][7][11][12].

Recently, label propagation for semi-supervised learning and classification has been arousing more attention by the researchers due to its efficiency and effectiveness. Different settings of label propagation (LP) schemes and effective extensions [4][5][6][7] [11] that can propagate label information of labeled points to the unlabeled data according to the distributions between them have been proposed for predicting or estimating image label. Typical LP methods include the *Gaussian Fields and Harmonic Function* (GFHF)[4], *Learning with Local and Global Consistency* (LLGC) [3], *Linear Neighborhood Propagation* (LNP) [5], and *Special Label Propagation* (SLP) [7]. As clearly described in [11], both LNP and SLP can not only well detect outliers in data, but also output the estimated soft labels of samples as probabilistic values. Note that one core step of LP methods is about how to construct a faithful and informative weighted graph based on the well-known clustering and manifold assumptions [3][28] to measure pairwise relationships of labeled and unlabeled points. Two most popular weight assignment approaches are Gaussian function[3][4][7] and Locally Linear Embedding (LLE)-style reconstruction weights [5] [21]. Compared with LLE-style weights, Gaussian function has to estimate width σ, which is never easy in practice.

It is worth noting that virtually all existing LP studies expect to enhance the label prediction capability by defining a faithful and reliable graph to measure pairwise similarities of vertices in graph more accurately. In other words, the current main direction for label propagation research is to improve weight construction for enhancing accuracy. But note that existing methods have one obvious shortcoming. That is, the outputted soft labels cannot be guaranteed to be sufficiently sparse, discriminative and robust to noise, which is very important for accurate label estimation and image classification, because ideally the predicted soft label vector of each point should have only one or few positive entries determining its class assignment. The sparse and discriminating properties of the soft labels mainly correspond to the commonly included unfavorable mixed signs that may directly and greatly affect the label prediction power in previous works.

ICMR'15, June 23–26, 2015, Shanghai, China.

http://dx.doi.org/10.1145/2671188.2749292

To address the above issue, we in this paper propose a new label propagation framework dedicated to making the soft labels of samples sufficiently sparse, discriminative and robust to noise, so that the label prediction performance can be improved. The proposed framework is inspired by the successful applications of sparse representation for image representation and classification [14][16][18][19][22][24]. The contributions of this paper can be described as follows. First, a *Nonnegative Sparse Neighborhood Propagation* or simply called *SparseNP*, is technically proposed for enhancing semi-supervised learning and label prediction. To make the predicted results sufficiently sparse, discriminative and robust against outliers and noise, the $l_{2,1}$-norm is regularized on the soft label matrix during the iterative optimization to form a new joint framework. It is noted that the prediction results are no longer probabilistic values (i.e., any one soft label vector satisfies the properties of non-negativity and sum of the entries equaling to one) because of the $l_{2,1}$-norm regularization on the soft label matrix during the optimization. To this end, we also propose to impose both the non-negativity and sum-to-one constraints on the soft labels during optimization so that the outputted results are always probabilistic values in any cases. As a result, our method can integrate the merits of both label propagation, non-negativity constraint and the $l_{2,1}$-norm regularization, compared with the regular LP criteria. Second, the proposed approach of $l_{2,1}$-norm regularization on the soft labels can be applied to any other label propagation algorithm for enhancing performance. To the best of our knowledge, no prior study has been done to improve the label propagation power by regularizing the $l_{2,1}$-norm and sum-to-one constraints on the label matrix to deliver a more reliable solution so that the performance can be enhanced.

The paper is outlined as follows. Section 2 reviews the related LP methods. Section 3 proposes SparseNP. Section 4 shows the settings and results. Finally, Section 5 concludes the paper.

2. PRELIMINARIES

2.1 Label Propagation by Neighborhood

One representative label propagation algorithm by neighborhood is LNP [5]. For a given a collection of N sample points in $X=[X_L, X_U]\in\mathbb{R}^{n\times(l+u)}$, where n is the original dimension of data, $l+u=N$ is the number of samples, $X_L=[x_1,x_2,\dots,x_l]\in\mathbb{R}^{n\times l}$ is a labeled set, $X_U=[x_{l+1},x_{l+2},\dots,x_{l+u}]\in\mathbb{R}^{n\times u}$ is an unlabeled set and each column vector $x_i\in\mathbb{R}^{n\times 1}$ represents a sample in an n-dimensional input space. We assume that there are c classes in X_L, all classes are present in X_L and each sample in X_L has a unique label $l(x_i)$ belonging to $\{1,2,\dots,c\}$.

Then similar to SLP, LNP can propagate label information of labeled samples in X_L to the unlabeled points in X_U according their relationships based on the constructed weighted similarity graph [5]. To predict label formation of the samples, LNP uses neighborhood information of each point to construct *G=(X, E)* by assuming that each point x_i can be optimally reconstructed with the linear combination of its neighbors [5], formulated as

$$\underset{w_i}{Min}\sum_i\left\|x_i-\sum_{j:x_j\in\mathbb{N}(x_i)}\tilde{w}_{i,j}x_j\right\|_2^2,\ \text{Subj}\sum_{j:x_j\in\mathbb{N}(x_i)}\tilde{w}_{i,j}=1,\tilde{w}_{i,j}\geq 0,\quad(1)$$

where $\mathbb{N}(x_i)$ is the K-neighbor set of x_i, $\|\bullet\|_2$ is l_2-norm, and $\tilde{w}_{i,j}$ measures the contribution of x_j for reconstructing x_i. By repeating the above steps for each vertex v_i over G, a similarity matrix $\tilde{W}=[\tilde{w}_{i,j}]\in\mathbb{R}^{N\times N}$ can be formed. Clearly, the more similar x_i and x_j, the larger $\tilde{w}_{i,j}$ will be. That is, $\tilde{w}_{i,j}$ can characterize how similar x_j to x_i [5]. Let $Y=[y_1,y_2,\dots,y_{l+u}]\in\mathbb{R}^{c\times(l+u)}$ be initial labels of all the points, where $y_{i,j}=1$ if x_j is labeled as i ($1\leq i\leq c$) and $y_{i,j}=0$ otherwise. Then the result of LNP can be approximated by the solution of the following problem [5]:

$$J(F)=\arg\min_F Tr\left(F\left(I^N-\tilde{W}\right)F^{\mathrm{T}}\right)+\mu\sum_{i=1}^{l+u}\|f_i-y_i\|_2^2,\quad(2)$$

where μ is a positive weighting parameter for trade-offing the terms, I^N denotes an identity matrix in $\mathbb{R}^N$, and $I^N-\tilde{W}$ can be considered as the graph Laplacian of a graph [5]. Let $\alpha=1/(\mu+1)$, the solution of LNP can be obtained as

$$F^*=(1-\alpha)\left(I^N-\alpha\tilde{W}\right)^{-1}Y.\quad(3)$$

Then, the label of each x_j can be assigned as $\arg\max_{i\leq c}F^*_{i,j}$. Another one similar label propagation algorithm by neighborhood is *Label Propagation through Sparse Neighborhood* (LPSN) [10]. Resembling LNP, LPSN assumes that each point x_i has the same class label as its sparse neighborhood computed by sparse coding (SC) [14], and the label of each x_i can be linearly reconstructed by the labels of its sparse neighbors. Note that LPSN proceeds label prediction in three steps. First, LPSN solves a standard SC problem to define the sparse neighborhood $SN(x_i)$ of each x_i by involving a threshold ε, which is challenging. Then LPSN seeks the weights $\tilde{w}_{i,j}$ by solving another SC problem with the sparse neighbors $SN(x_i)$ as dictionary and compute sparse codes of x_i. Finally, the labels of all points can be estimated as

$$F=\arg\min_F\sum_{i=1}^{l+u}\left\|f_j-\sum_{j:x_j\in SN(x_i)}\tilde{w}_{i,j}f_j\right\|_2^2=tr\left(FQF^{\mathrm{T}}\right),\quad(4)$$

where f_i denotes the predicted soft label for each data point x_i, $tr(\bullet)$ is a trace operator, $Q=\left(I^N-\tilde{W}\right)^{\mathrm{T}}\left(I^N-\tilde{W}\right)$ is the propagation matrix. After the optimal solution F^* is obtained, the unlabeled samples can be effectively classified.

2.2 Remarks

The predicted labels decide the class assignment of points, and the entries of F are the probabilities of data points belonging to different classes, so the entries in F should be nonnegative by definition. But not all the existing LP algorithms can ensure the solution always satisfies this property, such as GFHF and LLFC, etc. In addition, the formulation in Eq.4 also cannot guarantee the non-negativity property of estimated soft labels of samples if the constructed weight matrix $\tilde{W}$ has negative entries. Besides, the solution of existing methods cannot ensure the soft labels are sufficiently sparse, discriminant and robust to noise, leaning to enhanced image classification and representation performance, since the solution F usually contains unfavorable mixed signs that increased the difficulty in achieving accurate hard labels of data. Ideally, the predicted label of each point should have only one positive entry deciding its class assignment and all others are zeros. In such cases, the soft label matrix F can be used to assign the class labels of samples accurately.

To make the prediction results sufficiently sparse, discriminant and robust to noise, we propose to regularize the $l_{2,1}$-norm on the soft label matrix during the iterative optimization. To ensure the solution is always probabilistic values, we also incorporate both the non-negativity and sum-to-one constraints explicitly on the soft label matrix. That is one of the major differences between our model and almost all other existing LP methods, because we propose a new strategy (i.e., $l_{2,1}$-norm, non-negativity and sum-to-one constraints on soft label matrix) to enhance performance rather than improving the weighted graph construction as other existing schemes. In addition, although we regularize the sparse $l_{2,1}$-norm, our formulation is intrinsically different from existing LP methods by neighborhood (e.g.[10][13]) that involves sparse coding to gain adaptive neighborhoods for weight construction.

To illustrate the advantages of regularizing the $l_{2,1}$-norm on the soft labels, we take an example. The public face set available at *http://www.zjucadcg.cn/dengcai/Data/FaceData.html/Pose27 (lights-change)* is tested. In this set, the pose and expressions are fixed, and there are 21 images per individual of 68 persons (1428 images) under different lighting conditions. We select 8 images from each person as labeled and the remaining as unlabeled. For comparison, we visualize the predicted soft labels of both labeled and unlabeled images in Fig.1. It can be observed that the result of our SparseNP includes less unfavorable mixed signs.

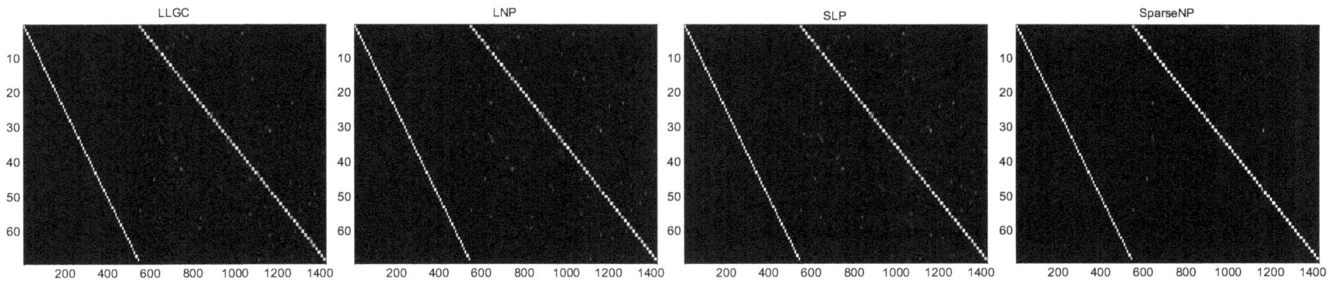

Figure 1. Comparison of the estimated soft labels of LLGC, SLP, LNP and our SparseNP on CMU PIE Pose (lights change).

3. NONNEGATIVE SPARSE NEIGHBORHOOD PROPAGATION (SPARSENP)

3.1 Proposed Formulation

Our nonnegative sparse neighborhood propagation (SparseNP) method assumes the label space and the original data space share the same local reconstruction relationships, resembling [5][10]. Specifically, we hope the label of each sample is partly received from its neighbors by linear reconstruction and the rest from its initial label. Firstly, we can similarly construct the initial label matrix $Y=\left[y_1,y_2,...,y_{l+u}\right]\in\mathbb{R}^{c\times(l+u)}$ that consists of the initial labels of all points, and denote the predicted soft label matrix F as $F=\left[f_1,f_2,...,f_{l+u}\right]\in\mathbb{R}^{c\times(l+u)}$, where f_j is a column vector and the maximal entry $f_{i,j}$ in f_j decides the class assignment of x_j.

Note that we expect to obtain a more reliable solution that has an enhanced discriminating power, i.e., $f_{i,j}$ is uniquely equal to one or few entries $f_{i,j}$ are positive if x_j is classified to class i; otherwise, all $f_{i,j}=0$ or almost all other entries $f_{i,j}$ are zeros. That is, less number of unfavorable mixed signs is included. To make the prediction results sufficiently sparse, discriminant and robust to noise, we propose to regularize the $l_{2,1}$-norm on the soft label matrix during the iterative optimization. Then, the resulted label neighborhood propagation problem can be defined as

$$F=\arg\min_F \Re(F)=\sum_{i=1}^{l+u}\left\|f_i-\sum\nolimits_{j:x_j\in\mathbb{N}(x_i)}W_{i,j}f_j\right\|_2^2 + \sum_{i=1}^{l+u}\mu_i D_{ii}\left\|f_i-y_i\right\|_2^2+\psi\sum_{i=1}^{l+u}\left\|\hat{f}^i\right\|_2, \quad (5)$$

$$\text{Subj } f_i\geq 0, e^{\mathrm{T}}f_i=1 \ for \ i=1,2,...,l+u$$

where W is a normalized symmetric similarity matrix, that is, we first symmetrize $\widetilde{W}=\left[\tilde{w}_{i,j}\right]$ as $\widetilde{W}\leftarrow\left(\widetilde{W}+\widetilde{W}_i^{\mathrm{T}}\right)/2$ and then normalize it as $W=\widetilde{D}^{-1/2}\widetilde{W}\widetilde{D}^{-1/2}$, $\widetilde{D}_{ii}=\sum_j\widetilde{W}_{i,j}$, $\hat{f}^i$ is the i-th row vector of $\hat{F}=F^{\mathrm{T}}$, e is a column vector of all ones, D is a diagonal matrix with the entries being $D_{ii}=\sum_j W_{i,j}$, μ_i and ψ are parameters. Since the prediction results cannot be ensured to be probabilistic values due to the $l_{2,1}$-norm regularization, the non-negativity constraint $f_i\geq 0$ and sum-to-one constraint $e^{\mathrm{T}}f_i=1$, $i=1,2,...,l+u$ are also included to ensure the outputted results are always probabilistic values in any cases.

Since $\sum_{i=1}^{l+u}\left\|f_i-\sum_{j:x_j\in\mathbb{N}(x_i)}W_{i,j}f_j\right\|_2^2=\left\|F-FW^{\mathrm{T}}\right\|_F^2$ [23], by using the matrix expressions, the above formulation can be rewritten as

$$F=\arg\min_F \Re(F)=tr\left(\left(F-FW^{\mathrm{T}}\right)\left(F-FW^{\mathrm{T}}\right)^{\mathrm{T}}\right) + tr\left(\left(F-Y\right)UD\left(F-Y\right)^{\mathrm{T}}\right)+\psi\left\|F^{\mathrm{T}}\right\|_{2,1}, \quad (6)$$

subject to $F\geq 0$ and $e^{\mathrm{T}}F=e^{\mathrm{T}}$, where $\left(F-FW^{\mathrm{T}}\right)\left(F-FW^{\mathrm{T}}\right)^{\mathrm{T}}=F\left(I^N-W\right)^{\mathrm{T}}\left(I^N-W\right)F^{\mathrm{T}}$. Note that $\partial\left\|F^{\mathrm{T}}\right\|_{2,1}/\partial F=\partial\left(FVF^{\mathrm{T}}\right)/\partial F$ holds for $f_i\neq 0$, $i=1,2,\ldots,N$, and $\sum_{i=1}^{N}\left\|\hat{f}^i\right\|_2=\left\|F\right\|_{2,1}$, where $V\in\mathbb{R}^{N\times N}$ is a diagonal matrix with the i-th entry v_{ii} being

$$v_{ii}=1/2\left\|\hat{f}^i\right\|_2, i=1,2,...,N\cdot \quad (7)$$

Then, the proposed formulation associated with variables F and V for our SparseNP can be rewritten as

$$\underset{F,V}{Min}\,\widetilde{\Re}(F,V)=tr\left(F\left(\Omega+\psi V\right)F^{\mathrm{T}}\right)+tr\left(\left(F-Y\right)^{\mathrm{T}}\left(F-Y\right)UD\right), \quad (8)$$

where $\Omega=\left(I^N-W^{\mathrm{T}}\right)\left(I^N-W\right)=I^N-W^{\mathrm{T}}-W+W^{\mathrm{T}}W$. Clearly, $l_{2,1}$-norm is regularized on F, so many entries of the soft label matrix to the above problem will shrink to zeros [17][22]. Note that the proposed formulation "seems" questionable, since it was pointed out that the regularized $l_{2,1}$-norm on F^{T} tend to make rows of optimal F^{T} be close to zeros [22]. But it is worth noting that there are three terms associated with F in our criterion, and parameters μ_i and ψ trade-off the contributions of terms during iterative optimization. Specifically, the first two terms indicate that label information of each sample is partly received from its neighbors and the rest from its initial label. It should be noticed that most entries in each row of F should have been zeros and usually only the positions in rows of F^{T} corresponding to the sample classes are non-zeros (ideally, all ones). Thus, by trading-off the terms, the delivered solution F is still promising for image classification, as can be observed from the simulations. Note that the process of minimizing $tr\left(FVF^{\mathrm{T}}\right)$ adds the explicit sparsity constraint on F [17], i.e., the matrix F holds the sparsity property, which is vital for accurate label estimation due to the robustness improvement.

As $\hat{f}^i \neq 0$, i =1, 2,..., N, by taking the derivative of $\tilde{\Re}(F,V)$ *w.r.t* the variable F and setting it to zero, we have

$$\partial\tilde{\Re}(F,V)/\partial F = F(\Omega+\psi V+UD)-YUD=0. \quad (9)$$

Next, we show how to gain the nonnegative sparse soft labels.

3.2 Optimization for Label Estimation

Note that the two variables (F and V) in SparseNP depends on each other, so they cannot be solved independently. This paper solves the variables alternately. We first fix V and update F. By splitting the graph Laplacian Ω after the l-th row and l-th column at the $(k+1)$-th iteration, similarly as [4], we can obtain

$$\Omega=\begin{bmatrix}\Omega_{ll} & \Omega_{lu}\\ \Omega_{ul} & \Omega_{uu}\end{bmatrix}\in\mathbb{R}^{N\times N}. \quad (10)$$

Similarly, by splitting the soft label matrix F at the $(k+1)$-th iteration, the initial label matrix Y, and the diagonal matrix V at the k-th iteration into blocks respectively as

$$F^{k+1}=\left[F_l^{k+1},F_u^{k+1}\right], Y=\left[Y_l,Y_u\right], V^k=\left[V_l^k,0;0,V_u^k\right], \quad (11)$$

where $F_l^{k+1},Y_l\in\mathbb{R}^{c\times l}, F_u^{k+1},Y_u\in\mathbb{R}^{c\times u}, V_l^k\in\mathbb{R}^{l\times l}, V_u^k\in\mathbb{R}^{u\times u}$. F_l^{k+1} and Y_l are the predicted and initial label submatrices of labeled data, F_u^{k+1} and Y_u are the predicted and initial label submatrix for unlabeled samples. Then we can re-formulate Eq.9 as

$$\begin{aligned}&\left[F_l^{k+1},F_u^{k+1}\right]\begin{bmatrix}\Omega_{ll}+\psi V_l^k+U_lD_l & \Omega_{lu}\\ \Omega_{ul} & \Omega_{uu}+\psi V_u^k+U_uD_u\end{bmatrix}\\ &-\left[Y_l,Y_u\right]\begin{bmatrix}U_lD_l & 0\\ 0 & U_uD_u\end{bmatrix}=0\end{aligned}, \quad (12)$$

where the matrices $D=\left[D_l,0;0,D_u\right]$ and U are also split into blocks according to labeled and unlabeled data. Then, the above criteria are equivalent to twol sub-problems:

$$\begin{cases}F_u^{k+1}\left(\Omega_{uu}+\psi V_u^k+U_uD_u\right)+F_l^{k+1}\Omega_{lu}-Y_uU_uD_u=0\\ F_l^{k+1}\left(\Omega_{ll}+\psi V_l^k+U_lD_l\right)+F_u^{k+1}\Omega_{ul}-Y_lU_lD_l=0\end{cases}, \quad (13)$$

from which we can easily achieve the soft labels for both labeled and unlabeled data at the $(k+1)$-th iteration as

$$\begin{cases}F_u^{k+1}=\left(Y_uU_uD_u-F_l^{k+1}\Omega_{lu}\right)\left(\Omega_{uu}+\psi V_u^k+U_uD_u\right)^{-1}\\ F_l^{k+1}=\left(Y_lU_lD_l-F_u^{k+1}\Omega_{ul}\right)\left(\Omega_{ll}+\psi V_l^k+U_lD_l\right)^{-1}\end{cases}. \quad (14)$$

Since the above two problems contain two variables (F_l^{k+1} and F_u^{k+1}) to compute, we can obtain a unique pair of solution. Note that we aim at updating both F_l^{k+1} and F_u^{k+1}. After both F_u^{k+1} and F_l^{k+1} are achieved, we can update V for labeled and unlabeled samples similarly via the equation in Eq.7, namely,

$$\begin{cases}v_l^{k+1}(i,i)=1/2\left\|\left(\hat{f}_l^i\right)^{k+1}\right\|_2, & i=1,2,\ldots,l\\ v_u^{k+1}(i,i)=1/2\left\|\left(\hat{f}_u^i\right)^{k+1}\right\|_2, & i=l+1,l+2,\ldots,l+u\end{cases}, \quad (15)$$

where $\left(\hat{f}_l^i\right)^{k+1}$ is the i-th row of $\left(F_l^{k+1}\right)^{\mathrm{T}}$ for the labeled points, $\left(\hat{f}_u^i\right)^{k+1}$ is the i-th row of $\left(F_u^{k+1}\right)^{\mathrm{T}}$ for unlabeled data, $v_l^{k+1}(i,i)$ is the i-th diagonal entry of V_l^{k+1} at the $(k+1)$-th iteration, and $v_u^{k+1}(i,i)$ is the i-th diagonal entry of V_u^{k+1}. Based on the above optimization, when the proposed method converges, the final soft label matrix is obtained as $F^*=\left[F_l^{k+1},F_u^{k+1}\right]\in\mathbb{R}^{c\times(l+u)}$.

3.3 Discussion: *Simplified Optimization*

We show an approach to simplify the computation for optimizing F_l^{k+1} and F_u^{k+1}, that is, we simply set $F_l^{k+1}=Y_l$ at each iteration, similarly as [7]. That is, the resulted label information of labeled points will not change from initial label, so F_u^{k+1} can be simply estimated as $F_u^{k+1}=\left(Y_uU_uD_u-Y_l\Omega_{ul}\right)\left(\Omega_{uu}+\psi V_u^k+U_uD_u\right)^{-1}$. Note that we can split the matrices I_α and I_β into four blocks as

$$I_\alpha=\begin{bmatrix}I_\alpha^l & 0\\ 0 & I_\alpha^u\end{bmatrix}\in\mathbb{R}^{N\times N}, I_\beta=\begin{bmatrix}I_\beta^l & 0\\ 0 & I_\beta^u\end{bmatrix}\in\mathbb{R}^{N\times N}, \quad (16)$$

where I_α^l and I_β^l are diagonal matrices with elements being α_l and $1-\alpha_l$ for labeled points respectively, and I_α^u and I_β^u are diagonal matrices with the entries being α_u and $1-\alpha_u$ for the unlabeled samples respectively. Then, the solution F_u^{k+1} at the $(k+1)$-th iteration can be formulated as

$$\begin{aligned}F_u^{k+1}&=\left(Y_uU_uD_u-Y_l\Omega_{lu}\right)\left(\Omega_{uu}+\psi V_u^k+U_uD_u\right)^{-1}\\ &=Y_uU_u\left(I^u+U_u\right)^{-1}\left(I^u+U_u\right)\left(\Omega_{uu}D_u^{-1}+U_u+\psi V_u^kD_u^{-1}\right)^{-1}\\ &\quad-Y_l\Omega_{lu}D_u^{-1}\left(I^u+U_u\right)^{-1}\left(I^u+U_u\right)\left(\Omega_{uu}D_u^{-1}+U_u+\psi V_u^kD_u^{-1}\right)^{-1}\\ &=\left(Y_uI_\beta^u-Y_l\Omega_{lu}D_u^{-1}I_\alpha^u\right)\left(\Omega_{uu}D_u^{-1}I_\alpha^u+I_\beta^u+V_u^kD_u^{-1}I_\omega^u\right)^{-1}\end{aligned}, \quad (17)$$

$F_u^{k+1}=\max\left(F_u^{k+1},0\right)$ and $e^{\mathrm{T}}F^{k+1}=e^{\mathrm{T}}$, where $I_\omega^u=\psi I_\alpha^u$, I^u is an identity matrix in $\mathbb{R}^u$, and $F^{k+1}=[Y_l,F_u^{k+1}]$. After the solution F_u^{k+1} is gained, we only need to update V_u for unlabeled data.

Note that this scheme that fixes $F_l^{k+1}=Y_l$ and updates F_u^{k+1} at each iteration is slightly different from the one shown in the last subsection that updates both F_l^{k+1} and F_u^{k+1} at each iteration at the same time. According to [7], when $\alpha_l=0$ or $F_l^{k+1}=Y_l$, the noisy labels cannot be detected, i.e., one implicitly considers that label information of labeled samples are convincible and correct. In contrast, if label information is not reliable or includes noisy labels, we can update both F_l^{k+1} and F_u^{k+1} at each iteration.

3.4 Convergence Analysis

The proposed SparseNP algorithm optimizes the two variables (F and V) in an alternative manner, thus it is important to analyze its convergence behavior. First, a lemma in [24] is reviewed.

Lemma 1. For any pair of non-zero vectors $p,q\in\mathbb{R}^m$, we have the following inequality held:

$$\|p\|_2-\|p\|_2^2/2\|q\|_2\le\|q\|_2-\|q\|_2^2/2\|q\|_2. \quad (18)$$

Then, the convergence behavior of our SparseNP approach can be described as the following theorem, similarly as [17][22].

Proposition 1. The objective function of our SparseNP method, that is, $Min_F\ tr\left(F\Omega F^{\mathrm{T}}\right)+tr\left((F-Y)UD(F-Y)^{\mathrm{T}}\right)+\psi\left\|F^{\mathrm{T}}\right\|_{2,1}$, is non-increasing at each iteration of the optimizations.

Proof. Note that we fix V^k and update the label matrix F^{k+1} at the $(k+1)$-th iteration, that is,

$$\underset{F}{Min}\ tr\left(F^{\mathrm{T}}F\Omega\right)+\psi tr\left(F^{\mathrm{T}}FV^k\right)+tr\left((F-Y)^{\mathrm{T}}(F-Y)UD\right). \quad (19)$$

Therefore, we can have the following inequality held:

$$\begin{aligned}&tr\left(F^{k+1}\left(\Omega+\psi V^k\right)\left(F^{k+1}\right)^{\mathrm{T}}\right)+tr\left(\left(F^{k+1}-Y\right)UD\left(F^{k+1}-Y\right)^{\mathrm{T}}\right)\\ &\le tr\left(F^k\left(\Omega+\psi V^k\right)\left(F^k\right)^{\mathrm{T}}\right)+tr\left(\left(F^k-Y\right)UD\left(F^k-Y\right)^{\mathrm{T}}\right)\end{aligned}. \quad (20)$$

Denote $\mho^k = tr\left(F^k \Omega F^{kT}\right) + tr\left(\left(F^k - Y\right)UD\left(F^k - Y\right)^{\mathrm{T}}\right)$. Since we have $\left\|\left(F^k\right)^{\mathrm{T}}\right\|_{2,1} = \sum_{i=1}^{l+u}\left\|\left(\hat{f}^i\right)^k\right\|_2$ and $v_{ii}^k = 1/2\left\|\left(\hat{f}^i\right)^k\right\|_2$, the above inequality can be reformulated as

$$\mho^{k+1} + \psi\left\|\left(F^{k+1}\right)^{\mathrm{T}}\right\|_{2,1} - \psi\left[\sum_i\left\|\left(\hat{f}^i\right)^{k+1}\right\|_2 - \sum_i\frac{\left\|\left(\hat{f}^i\right)^{k+1}\right\|_2^2}{2\left\|\left(\hat{f}^i\right)^k\right\|_2}\right] \le \mho^k + \psi\left\|\left(F^k\right)^{\mathrm{T}}\right\|_{2,1} - \psi\left[\sum_i\left\|\left(\hat{f}^i\right)^k\right\|_2 - \sum_i\frac{\left\|\left(\hat{f}^i\right)^k\right\|_2^2}{2\left\|\left(\hat{f}^i\right)^k\right\|_2}\right]. \quad (21)$$

Note that f_i^k at the k-th iteration is the soft label of x_i, so f_i^k is a non-zero vector. According to Lemma 1, we have

$$-\psi\left[\sum_i\left\|\left(\hat{f}^i\right)^{k+1}\right\|_2 - \sum_i\frac{\left\|\left(\hat{f}^i\right)^{k+1}\right\|_2^2}{2\left\|\left(\hat{f}^i\right)^k\right\|_2}\right] \ge -\psi\left[\sum_i\left\|\left(\hat{f}^i\right)^k\right\|_2 - \sum_i\frac{\left\|\left(\hat{f}^i\right)^k\right\|_2^2}{2\left\|\left(\hat{f}^i\right)^k\right\|_2}\right]. \quad (22)$$

By combing the above two inequalities, we can easily obtain $\mho^{k+1} + \psi\sum_i\left\|\left(\hat{f}^i\right)^{k+1}\right\|_2 \le \mho^k + \psi\sum_i\left\|\left(\hat{f}^i\right)^k\right\|_2$, which is equivalent to

$$tr\left(F^{k+1}\Omega\left(F^{k+1}\right)^{\mathrm{T}}\right) + tr\left(\left(F^{k+1} - Y\right)UD\left(F^{k+1} - Y\right)^{\mathrm{T}}\right) + \psi\left\|\left(F^{k+1}\right)^{\mathrm{T}}\right\|_{2,1} \le tr\left(F^k\Omega\left(F^k\right)^{\mathrm{T}}\right) + tr\left(\left(F^k - Y\right)UD\left(F^k - Y\right)^{\mathrm{T}}\right) + \psi\left\|\left(F^k\right)^{\mathrm{T}}\right\|_{2,1}, \quad (23)$$

which explicitly indicates that the objective function value of our SparseNP is decreasing monotonically in iterative optimizations. Note that the above theorem indicates that the objective function is non-increasing, but it is also vital to show F also converges. Since the label matrix F is the major variable to optimize and the optimization of V relies on F, the convergence condition (where ε is a small positive parameter set to 10^{-5}) is simply defined as

$$\nabla = \left\|F^{k+1} - F^k\right\|_F = \sqrt{\sum_{j=1}^{l+u}\sum_{i=1}^{c}\left|F_{i,j}^{k+1} - F_{i,j}^k\right|^2} \le \varepsilon, \quad (24)$$

which measures the variance between two sequential predicted soft label matrix and can ensure the predicted soft labels will not change drastically, which will be verified by simulations, where $\|\bullet\|_F$ is the Frobenius norm of a matrix.

4. SIMULATION RESULTS AND ANALYSIS

We mainly evaluate our SparseNP for classification and describe the comparison results with GFHF, LLGC, SLP and LNP.

4.1 Settings and Data Preparation

The LLE-reconstruction weights [21][23] computed from Eq.1 is used in each method for efficiency and fair comparison. Since the LLE-weight matrix is asymmetric, we similarly preprocess it by symmetrizing $\tilde{W}$ as $W = \left(\tilde{W} + \tilde{W}^{\mathrm{T}}\right)/2$ for GFHF, LLGC and SLP. The diagonal entries of W are also set as zeros for LLGC [3]. GFHF, LLGC, SLP, LNP and our SparseNP have a common parameter (i.e., K) to estimate. For fair comparison, its number is chosen from {3, 5, ..., 15}. We determine parameters ψ and K empirically using grid search, where ψ is selected from {10^{-8}, 10^{-6},...,10^{6},10^{8}}, resembling [17]. The regularization parameters α_l and α_u are simply set to 0 and 0.999999 respectively for our SparseNP, and the other methods use their respective parameters. We perform all simulations on a PC with Intel (R) Core (TM) i7-3770 CPU @ 3.4 GHz 3.4GHz 4G.

In this study, two toy datasets and several real image datasets are involved. For classification, we randomly split each dataset into labeled and unlabeled sets. Then, we estimate the labels of unlabeled data by GFHF, LLGC, LNP, SLP and our SparseNP. Finally, the accuracy is obtained by comparing the predicted hard labels with the ground-truth hard labels that are provided by the original data corpus. Prior to label prediction, all the datasets are preliminarily processed by using *Principal Component Analysis* (PCA) [9] to eliminate the null space [8].

4.2 Transductive Learning on Toy Data

Toy Problem One. We first compare our SparseNP with SLP for propagating the labels on toy. We prepare two toy examples to show the advantages of our model. Note that the standard SLP used the Gaussian function to assign weights. Hence in the first example, we mainly compare the propagation performance of our SparseNP in terms of robustness to the parameters on a two-cycle set of two classes, where each class follows a cycle distribution. In each class, two points are chosen to form the labeled set and the remaining as unlabeled set. The results are shown in Figure 2, where Figures 2(a-c) are the results of SLP and Figures 2(d-f) correspond to our SparseNP. We can see that the performance of SLP is very sensitive to the width σ in Gaussian function, since a relatively small variation of σ results in dramatically different results. In contrast, our SparseNP avoids estimating an optimal σ. Moreover, we observe that our SparseNP performs well in a wide range of α_u, indicating that our method is robust to α_u.

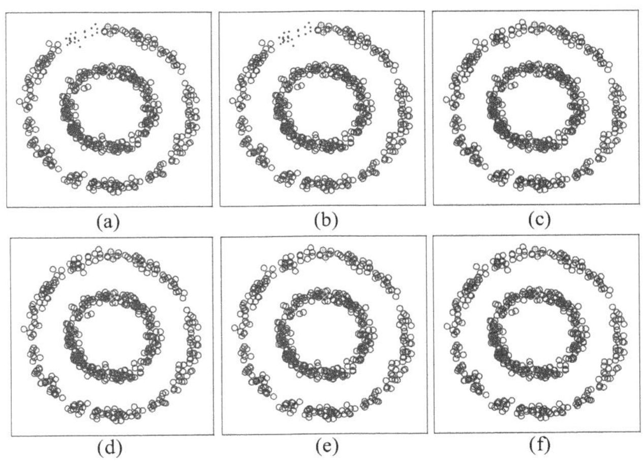

Figure 2. Results of SLP and SparseNP on toy. First row: the results of SLP under different Gaussian variance. (a) $\sigma = \tilde{\sigma}/0.1$, **(b)** $\sigma = \tilde{\sigma}$, **(c)** $\sigma = \tilde{\sigma}/10$, **where** $\tilde{\sigma}$ **is the half of the average distance of all pair-wise neighbor points. Second row: the performance of our SparseNP under different** μ_u. **(d)** $\mu_u = 0.999$, **(e)** $\mu_u = 0.999999$, **(f)** $\mu_u = 0.999999999$.

Toy Problem Two. We address another toy case to show our SparseNP can automatically detect and erase the noisy labels in data, which may exist in real applications due to the careless of annotator. In this study, we still generate a two-class two-circle dataset with several wrongly labeled points in each class. Figure 3 illustrates the results of our SparseNP with different numbers of iterations on noisy case. Note that SparseNP handles the noisy labels by alternately updating F_l^{k+1} and F_u^{k+1} at each iteration. We can see clearly that SparseNP can effectively detect the noisy labels and correct them accurately when we increase the times of iteration to 15. But note that the results are also acceptable using very less number of iterations in our SparseNP.

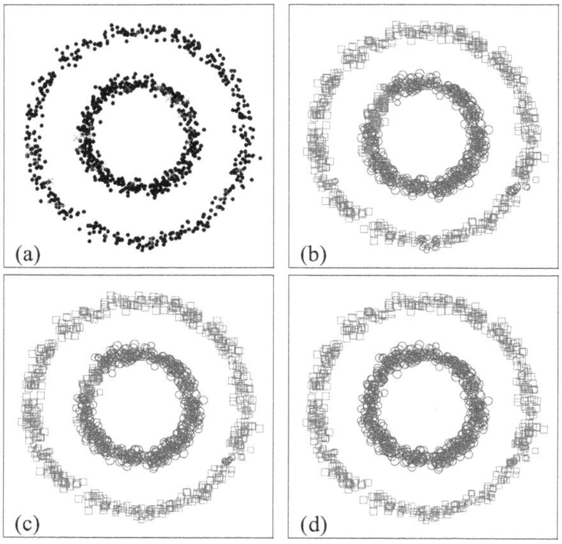

Figure 3. Results of SparseNP with noisy labels on toy: (a) Original partition, (b) 3 times iterations, (c) 9 times iterations, and (d) 15 times iterations.

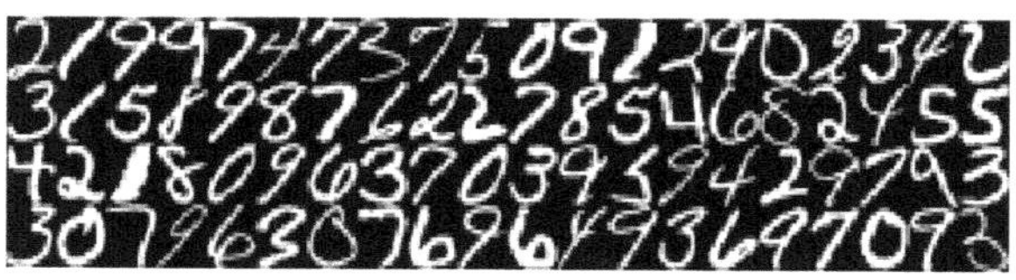

(a) USPS

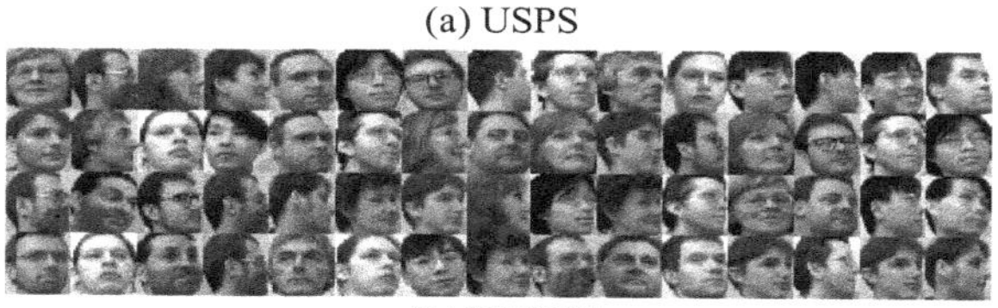

(b) UMIST

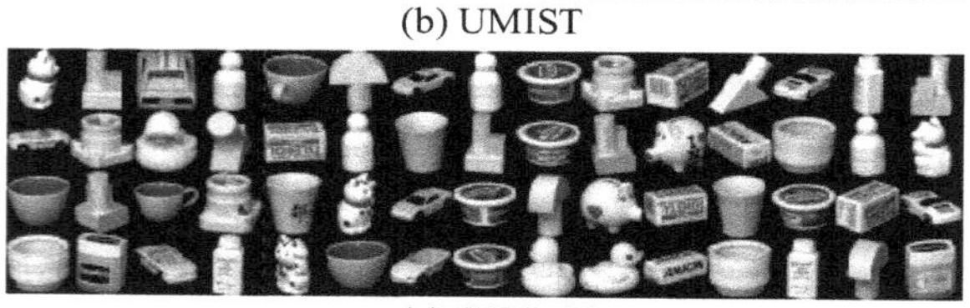

(c) COIL-20

Figure 4. Sample images of the used real-world databases.

4.3 Image Classification on Real Datasets

In this study, we examine our SparseNP for image classification. Three image databases, including a face image database (UMIST [20]), a handwriting digit database (USPS) available from *http://www.cs.nyu.edu/~roweis/data.html*, and an object image database (COIL-20 [29]), are tested. We choose 1500 handwriting digital images (i.e., 150 per digit) from USPS for simulations due to the consideration of computational efficiency. As is common practice, all the images of UMIST and COIL-20 databases are resized into 32×32 pixels, so each image corresponds to a sample point in a 1024-dimensional space. The data partitioning for each dataset is given in Table I, where "Labeled Ratios" represents the ratios of randomly labeled number of data to the total number of samples in each class (that is, all data in given datasets are used as inputs for propagable learning of labels), and 'balance' term represents the ratio of the number of data in the smallest class to the sample number in the largest class. From the balance term, we can find that UMIST has imbalanced data distributions in classes. Since we use the labeled ratios to denote the labeled number of data in each class, the effects of imbalanced data distributions on the performance can be greatly reduced. We also show some samples of each database in Figure 4. In this experiment, we extract the Histograms of Oriented Gradients (HOG) [27] features of images for classification. The number of orientation histogram bins is set to 9, the cell size is set as 16×16, and the block size is 2×2.

4.4 Convergence Results

We then provide some results to show the convergence behavior of our SparseNP. The three image databases, i.e., UMIST, USPS and COIL-20, are used. We simply fix K=7 and $\psi = 10^{-6}$, since similar results can be gained with other parameter configurations. For each dataset, all data points are employed as inputs and the labeled ratio is simply fixed to 0.1 to show the convergence behavior between two consecutive soft label matrices. In Figure 5, we describe the results with 15 numbers of iterations, where the horizontal-axis is the number of iterations and the vertical-axis is the divergence between two consecutive F. We see clearly that the divergence between two consecutive F converges to zero, i.e., the final labels will not be changed drastically. More importantly, we observe the convergence speed is very fast and the number of iteration (t) is usually less than 8 in most cases.

Table 1. List of used datasets and dataset description.

Dataset	n	N	c	Balance	Labeled Ratios
UMIST	102	575	2	0.3958	0.05, 0.1, …, 0.5
USPS	256	1500	1	1	0.02, 0.04,…, 0.2
COIL-20	102	1440	2	1	0.03, 0.06,…, 0.3

4.5 Parameter Sensitivity Analysis

We also analyze the effects of model parameters (K and ψ) on the performance of our SparseNP. Due to the page limitation, we only show the results on UMIST and USPS databases in Figure 6. Specifically, we report two kinds of results for each database. The first one is to test the effects of K and ψ on performance by using grid search, and the other one is to fix ψ and evaluate K to explore the effects of K. The classification is repeated for 100 times over different splits. The following observations can be found. (1) From the results on the first evaluation, our SparseNP can perform effectively for a wide range of ψ for each K. More importantly, we see that SparseNP delivers promising and stable results as ψ is less than 1 for each image database. Thus, ψ can be simply set to 10^{-6} for simulation. (2) For the second evaluation on K, we also illustrate the results of the other related methods for comparison. We observe that the increasing number of K may decreased the performance of each method. Also, the performance of SparseNP is superior to other approaches.

4.6 Classification Results

In this subsection, we evaluate our SparseNP for classification. We prepare the classification simulation by changing the labeled ratios in each class. For each labeled ratio, we report averaged accuracy based on 30 times randomly labeled images. Since the neighborhood size (i.e., *K*) depends on datasets to some extent, we fix *K* to 15 for each method for fair comparison. The averaged accuracies are plotted in Figure 7. We find that the performance of each method can be significantly improved by increasing the labeled ratios in each class. Besides, our SparseNP outperforms other methods by gaining higher accuracies in most cases. More importantly, it achieves promising results using small number of labeled points, which is desired in semi-supervised classification. The obtained results of LNP and SLP are comparable in most cases, and both are superior to GFHF and LLGC in most cases.

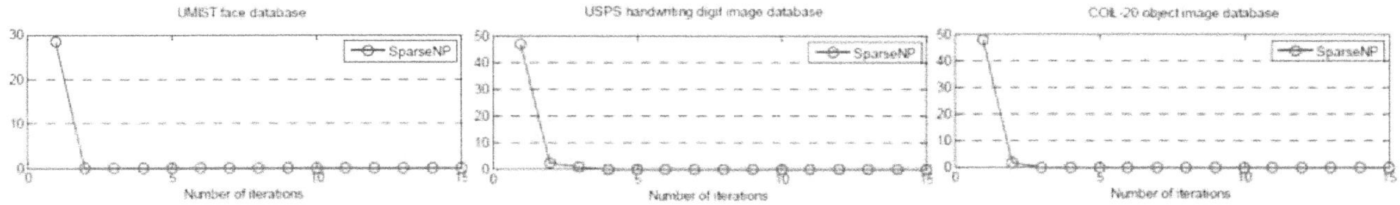

Figure 5. Convergence behavior of our SparseNP on the real-world image databases.

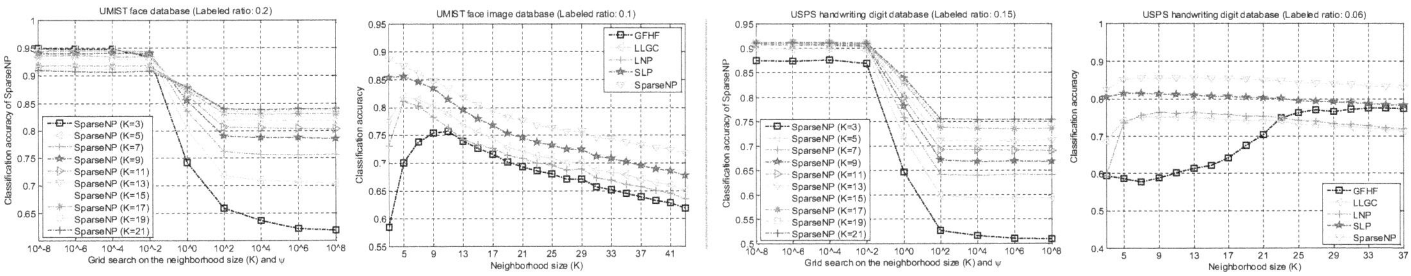

Figure 6. Classification performance of the algorithms vs. different parameter configurations on UMIST (left) and USPS (right) .

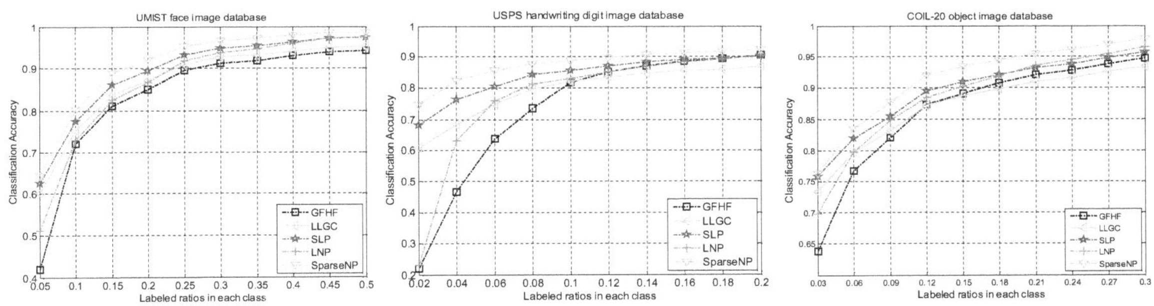

Figure 7. Accuracy of each algorithm vs. labeled ratios on the real-world image databases.

5. CONCLUDING REMARKS

We mainly investigate the problem of nonnegative sparse label prediction. A new *Sparse Neighborhood Propagation* (SparseNP) framework is proposed to enhance semi-supervised classification. To improve existing linear neighborhood propagation by ensuring the outputted labels are sufficiently sparse, discriminative, robust to noise and are probabilistic values, the $l_{2,1}$-norm is regularized on soft labels for optimization to enhance the prediction results by weakening the negative effects of unfavorable mixed signs. The proposed framework is solved in an alternative manner so that a more reliable solution can be achieved to boost accuracy.

We mainly evaluated SparseNP for transductive learning and classification on toy and real image databases. Results show that our SparseNP delivers comparable or even higher accuracies than other related label propagation techniques. In future, proposing effective out-of-sample extensions for our SparseNP is important. Investigate how to use SparseNP to handle images directly rather than using the vector patterns [26] also needs further exploration, since images in the real-world are intrinsically matrices.

6. ACKNOWLEDGMENTS

This work is partially supported by the National Natural Science Foundation of China (Nos.61402310 and 61373093), the Major Program of National Natural Science Foundation of China (Grant No.61033013), and the Natural Science Foundation of Jiangsu Province of China (Grant No. BK20140008).

7. REFERENCES

[1] O. Chapelle, B. Scholkopf, and A. Zien, "Semi-Supervised Learning," *Cambridge: MIT Press*, 2006.

[2] X. Zhu, "Semi-supervised learning literature survey," *Technical Report 1530*, Univ. Wisconsin-Madison. 2005.

[3] D. Zhou, O. Bousquet, T. N. Lal, J. Weston, B. S cholkopf, "Learning with local and global consistency," In: *Proc. Advances in Neural Information Processing Systems*, 2004.

[4] X. Zhu, Z. Ghahramani, and J. D. Lafferty, "Semi-supervised learning using Gaussian fields and harmonic functions. In: *Proceedings of the International Conference on Machine Learning*, 2003.

[5] F. Wang, and C. S. Zhang, "Label propagation through linear Neighborhoods," *IEEE Trans. on Knowledge and Data Engineering*, vol.20, no.1, pp.55-67, 2008.

[6] Z. Zhang, M. B. Zhao, and T. W. S. Chow, "Graph based Constrained Semi-Supervised Learning Framework via Label Propagation over Adaptive Neighborhood," *IEEE Trans. on Knowledge and Data Engineering*, Dec 2013. DOI: 10.1109/ TKDE.2013.182.

[7] F. P. Nie, S. M. Xiang, Y. Liu, and C. S. Zhang, "A general graph-based semi-supervised learning with novel class discovery," *Neural Computing Applications*, vol. 19, no.4, pp. 549-555, 2010.

[8] J. Yang, A. F. Frangi, J.Y. Yang, D. Zhang, and J. Zhong, "KPCA plus LDA: a Complete Kernel Fisher Discriminant Framework for Feature Extraction and Recognition," *IEEE Trans. on Pattern analysis and machine intelligence*, vol.27, no.2, pp.230-244, 2005.

[9] M. Turk, A. Pentland, "Face recognition using eigenfaces," In: *Proceedings of the IEEE International Conference on Computer Vision and Pattern Recognition*, 1991.

[10] F. Zang, and J. S. Zhang, "Label propagation through sparse neighborhood and its applications, "*Neurocomputing*, vol.97, pp.267-277, 2012.

[11] Y. Liu, F.P. Nie, J.G. Wu, and L.H. Chen, "Semi-supervised feature selection based on label propagation and subset selection," In: *Proceedings of the International Conference on Computer and Information Application*, 2010.

[12] Z. Zhang, T. Chow, M. Zhao, "Trace Ratio Optimization based Semi-Supervised Nonlinear Dimensionality Reduction for Marginal Manifold Visualization," *IEEE Transactions on Knowledge and Data Engineering*, vol.25, iss.5, pp.1148-1161, 2013.

[13] H. Cheng, Z. Liu, and J. Yang, "Sparsity induced similarity measure for label propagation," In: *Proceedings of the IEEE International Conference on Computer Vision*, pp.317-324, 2009.

[14] J. Wright, Y. Ma, J. Mairal, G. Sapiro, T. Huang, S.C Yan, "Sparse Representation for Computer Vision and Pattern Recognition," *Proceedings of the IEEE*, vol.98, no.6, pp.1031 -1044, 2010.

[15] T. Sim, S. Baker, M. Bsat, "The CMU pose, illuminlation, and expression database," *IEEE Transactions on Pattern Analysis and Machine Intelligence*, vol.25, no.12, pp.1615-1618, 2003.

[16] Z. Zhang, M. B. Zhao, and T. W. S. Chow, "Binary- and Multi-Class Group Sparse Canonical Correlation Analysis for Feature Extraction and Classification," *IEEE Transactions on Knowledge and Data Engineering*, vol.25, no.10, pp. 2192-2205, October 2013.

[17] C. P. Hou, F. P. Nie, D.Y. Yi, Yi Wu, "Feature Selection via Joint Embedding Learning and Sparse Regression," In: *Proceedings of the International Joint Conferences on Artificial Intelligence*, pp.1324-1329, 2011.

[18] L. S. Qiao, S. C. Chen, and X. Y. Tan, "Sparsity Preserving Projections with Applications to Face Recognition," *Pattern Recognition*, vol.43, no.1, pp.331-341, 2010.

[19] Z. Zhang, S. C. Yan, and M. B. Zhao, "Pairwise Sparsity Preserving Embedding for Unsupervised Subspace Learning and Classification," *IEEE Transactions on Image Processing*, vol.22, iss.12, pp.4640-4651, 2013.

[20] D. B. Graham, and N. M. allinson, "Characterizing virtual eigensignatures for general 870 purpose face recognition in face recognition: from theory to application," *NATO ASI Series F, Computer and Systems Sciences,* Vol. 163; H. Wechsler, P. J. Phillips, V. Bruce, F. Fogelman-Soulie and T. S. Huang (eds), pp.446-456, 1998.

[21] S. Roweis and L. Saul, "Nonlinear dimensionality reduction by locally linear embedding," *Science*, vol.290, no.5500, pp.2323-2326, 2000.

[22] Y. Yang, H. T. Shen, Z. G. Ma, Z. Huang, and X. F. Zhou, "$L_{2,1}$-Norm Regularized Discriminative Feature Selection for Unsupervised Learning," In: *Proceeding of the International Joint Conferences on Artificial Intelligence*, 2011.

[23] E. Kokiopoulou, J. Chen, and Y. Saad, "Trace optimization and eigenproblems in dimension reduction methods," *Numerical Linear Algebra with Applications*, vol.18, no.3, pp.565-602, 2011.

[24] F. Nie, H. Huang, X. Cai, and C. Ding, "Efficient and robust feature selection via joint $l_{2,1}$-norms minimization," In: *Proceeding of the Neural Information Processing Systems* (NIPS), 2010.

[25] M. Culp, and G. Michailidis, "Graph-based semi-supervised learning," *IEEE Transactions on Pattern Analysis and Machine Intelligence*, vol.30, no.1, pp.174-179, 2008.

[26] Z. Zhang, T. W. S. Chow, "Maximum Margin Multisurface Support Tensor Machines with Application to Image Classification and Segmentation," *Expert Systems with Applications*, vol.39, iss.1, pp. 850-861, 2012.

[27] N. Dalal, and B. Triggs, "Histograms of Oriented Gradients for Human Detection," *Proceedings of the IEEE International Conference on Computer Vision and Pattern Recognition*, pp.886-893, 2005.

[28] M. Belkin, and P. Niyogi, "Laplacian Eigenmaps for Dimensionality Reduction and Data Representation," *Neural Computation*, vol.15, no.6, pp.1373-1396, 2003.

[29] S. A. Nene, S. K. Nayar, and H. Murase, "Columbia Object Image Library (COIL-20)," *Technical Report CUCS-005-96*, 1996.

Hierarchical Encoding of Binary Descriptors for Image Matching

Zhendong Mao
[1]Institute of Information Engineering,Chinese Academy Of Sciences
maozhendong@iie.ac.cn

Lingling Tong*
National Computer network Emergency Response technical Team/Coordination Center of China

Hongtao Xie
Institute of Information Engineering,Chinese Academy Of Sciences
xiehongtao@iie.ac.cn

Qi Tian
University of Texas at San Antonio
qitian@cs.utsa.edu

ABSTRACT

Binary descriptors are increasingly popular such as BRIEF, ORB, and BRISK. Typically, binary descriptors are computed by comparing pairs of image pixel intensities over a sampling pattern. To improve matching performance, lots of progresses have been made on the selection of pixel pairs, yet the discriminative power of pixel pairs is not fully studied.

In this paper,we hierarchically encode the intensity differences between pixel pairs to build our discriminative binary feature. To avoid efficiency loss, a stepwise distance metric is proposed for directly matching these descriptors without decoding. Extensive experiments on benchmark database demonstrate that we outperform the state-of-the-art binary descriptors in image matching performance. In addition, we show that our encoded descriptor is as efficient as the state-of-the-art binary descriptors in both computing and matching.

Categories and Subject Descriptors

I.2.10 [**Vision and Scene Understanding**]: VISION; I.4.7 [**Feature Measurement**]: Feature representation

General Terms

Algorithms, Measurement, Experimentation, Performance, Theory.

Keywords

local feature, binary feature

*Corresponding author. Email: tonglingling@cert.org.cn

ICMR '15, June 23 - 26, 2015, Shanghai, China

ISBN 978-1-4503-3274-3/15/06 ...$15.00
DOI: http://dx.doi.org/10.1145/2671188.2749304

1. INTRODUCTION

Local image features have been vastly used in a wide range of image matching applications, including image retrieval, object recognition and stereo matching. Many such applications are constrained by the computational power of their platforms, which demand higher requirements for local descriptors: faster to compute, easier to compare. To best address the above requirements, various binary descriptors have been recently proposed in the literature, including BRIEF [4], ORB [23], BRISK [11], FREAK [2] and USB [27]. However, these new descriptors tend to be less robust and discriminative than slower approaches such as SIFT [13] and SURF [3]. A clear advantage of binary descriptors is that the Hamming distance, which is very fast to compute, can be used instead of Euclidean distance [16]. The Hamming distance between two binary features can be computed by performing a bitwise XOR operation followed by non-zero bit count on the result. This involves only bit manipulation operations and therefore is much faster than Euclidean distance. With Hamming distance metric, we can efficiently identify approximate nearest neighbors of binary features [28, 26, 9].

The aforementioned binary descriptors are computed by comparing pairs of image pixel intensities over a sampling pattern. Lots of progresses have been made on the selection of pixel pairs to improve image matching performance, yet the discriminative power of such pairs is not fully studied. The inherent difficulty in utilizing the difference lies in balancing two competing goals: high quality description and low computational requirements. For example, directly using the intensity difference between pixel pairs instead of 0-1 in each dimension results in two problems. First, the new descriptor will be very sensitive to noise. Second, Euclidean distance should be used for this descriptor rather than Hamming distance, causing the same matching cost as SIFT and SURF.

In this paper, a hierarchically encoded binary descriptor is proposed to maximize the discriminative power of selected pixel pairs and a stepwise distance metric is proposed aiming at keeping efficiency. The intensity differences between pixel pairs are hierarchically encoded based on their distribution and a stepwise distance metric can be directly applied to the encoded descriptor. Experiments on benchmark database demonstrate that the encoding strategy together with the stepwise distance metric promotes a substantial performance increase, while the time efficiency remains almost unchanged.

The rest of our paper is organized as follows. In Section 2, we discuss the related work. In Section 3, we investigate the sampling pair difference of prevalent binary descriptors and propose a general encoding strategy to build discriminative descriptor. The detail of stepwise distance metric for encoded descriptors is presented in Section 4. In Section 5, we compare our hierarchically encoded binary descriptor with BRIEF, ORB and BRISK. The computation time of description and matching are also compared in this section. Conclusions are presented in Section 6.

2. RELATED WORK

Since local feature is the basis of vast applications including image retrieval, object recognition and so on, research on it continues to be a very active area of computer vision. Obtaining features that exhibit high robustness and distinctiveness against common image transformations (e.g. blurring, viewpoint, noise, etc.), and during the same time cost low storage and computation time, is of extreme importance in practical applications. In the context of matching and recognition, several comprehensive evaluation of local features are presented in [25] and [5]. In general, local features consist of two parts: feature detector and feature descriptor. In this section, we briefly review the common detectors and mainly focus on descriptors.

2.1 Feature Detectors

Feature detectors, or in other words, key point detectors, are used as the first step of many vision tasks and can be traced a long way back in the literature. Many different techniques for detecting local key points have been developed.

The commonly used detectors can be divided into gradient based approaches (such as Harris Corners [6], difference-of-Gaussian [13] and so on), Hessian-based approaches (such as Hessian affine [19], Fast Hessian [3] and so on), region-based approaches (such as maximally stable extremal regions (MSER) [17] and so on) and learning-based approaches (such as features from accelerated segment test (FAST) [22], AGAST based on FAST [14] and so on). The most important characteristic of detectors is repeatability, that is: given two images of the same or very similar scene, taken under different viewing conditions, a high percentage of the key point detected on the scene part visible in both images should be found in both images [25].

2.2 Feature Descriptors

Feature descriptor is used as the next step of feature detector. The characteristics of what makes a good representation of key points are depended on the applications. In various use cases of copy detection it is, for example, reasonable to expect that the copy can be detected no matter what transformations are applied to. Traditional descriptors such as SIFT [13] facilitate this by using a floating points vector representation. The SIFT descriptor is highly discriminative and robustness, to be specifical, it is invariant to image scaling and rotation, and partially invariant to illumination and viewpoint changes. Therefore, SIFT is applied in many fields [7, 12] and a number of its variants and extensions have been developed [10, 1]. Other examples include SURF [3] proposed by Bay, gradient location and orientation histogram (GLOH) by Mikolajczyk and Schmid [18] and so on.

However, an important shortcoming of above traditional descriptors is that they impose large burdens on computation and matching, making them unsuitable for mobile or real-time applications. Binary descriptors of key points are increasingly popular recently given that they enable fast computing and can be fast matched with Hamming distance. A prime example is BRIEF (Binary Robust Independent Elementary Features), proposed by Calonder *et al.* in [4]. The BRIEF vector is directly computed on image patches by comparing the intensity of 128 random pixel pairs from an isotropic Gaussian distribution centered at the feature location. BRIEF is very simple, and has low compute and storage requirements, but is very sensitive to in-plane rotation. In view of this, ORB (Oriented FAST and Rotated BRIEF) was proposed by Rublee *et al.* in [23] to overcome the lack of rotation invariance of BRIEF. The local orientation of each key point is computed by considering the weighted average of pixel intensities. Compared to BRIEF, ORB is much robust to image rotation. To improve discriminative power, Leutenegger *et al.* propose BRISK (Binary Robust Invariant Scalable Keypoints) in [11]. BRISK turns away from the random patterns of BRIEF and ORB, and instead makes a judicious selection of pairs. It uses a circular pattern similar to the DAISY descriptor [24], where points are equally spaced on circles concentric. Alahi *et al.* [2] propose FREAK (Fast Retina Keypoint) on the basis of BRISK. They believe that patterns similar to retina would bring more discriminative power. The sampling pattern of FREAK is nearly the same as BRISK but having higher density of points near the center. With the aim of achieving more discriminative power, Mao *et al.* propose COGE (Combinatorial Comparison of Gradient Element based descriptor) in [15]. COGE replaces the simple intensity test with two novel gradient tests, namely intra-cell comparison and inter-cell comparison, which exploit the anisotropy and the non-uniformity of the underlying gradient distributions. A comprehensive evaluation of binary descriptor is referred to [8]. The efficiency of binary descriptors comes at a price of lower recognition performances.

3. HIERARCHICAL ENCODING OF BINARY DESCRIPTORS

3.1 Difference between Selected Pixel Pairs

BRIEF, ORB, BRISK and FREAK are recent binary feature descriptors that are designed for fast description and matching. For these descriptors, a N-dimensional binary descriptor A is formed by a binary string of length N.

$$A = \sum_{i=1}^{N} 2^{i-1} f(d_i) \tag{1}$$

d_i is the intensity difference of a pre-selected pixel pair, and:

$$f(d_i) = \begin{cases} 0 & if \quad d_i < 0 \\ 1 & otherwise \end{cases} \tag{2}$$

Despite of the simplicity and efficiency of above binary descriptors, it is necessary to improve the matching performance under a variety of image transformations. To obtain more discriminative power, lots of efforts have been made on the selection of pixel pairs. BRIEF and ORB use random pairs, BRISK and FREAK uses a circular pattern similar to DAISY [5]. The selection strategies in these works are illustrated in Figure 1.

Different from above mentioned methods which concentrate on developing better selection strategies, we focus on maximizing the discriminative power of intensity difference (denoted by d) between selected pairs. The distribution of d is given in Figure 2.

As seen from Figure 2, d has a wide distribution, which means the 0-1 quantization may be too coarse to describe d . More effective utilization of d should be explored. For example, we can extend the possible value of $f(d)$ from $\{0, 1\}$ to $\{0, 1, .., m\}$, resulting in an increase in storage. However, storage is not a bottle-neck for

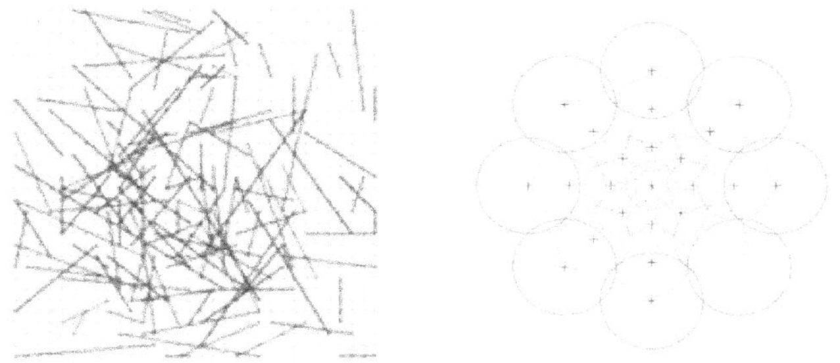

(a) Selected pixels of BRIEF and ORB

(b) Selected pixels of BRISK and FREAK

Figure 1: Different approaches to select the test pixels. The points at the ends of lines in (a) denote the selected pixels of BRIEF and ORB. The "+" sign in (b) represents the selected pixels of BRISK and FREAK. (a) select pixels randomly and (b) select pixels using a circular pattern.

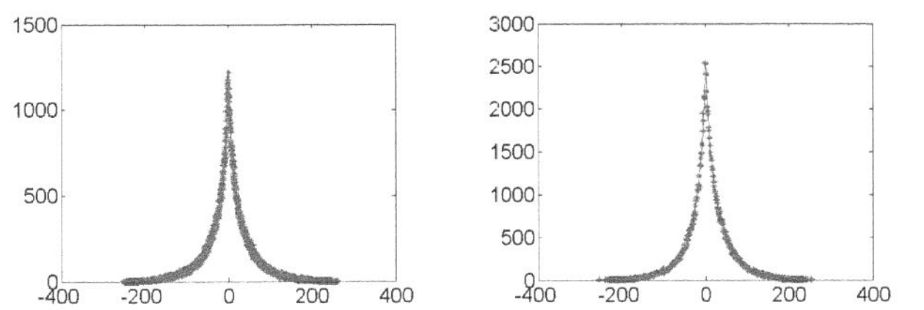

(a) Pair Difference Distribution of BRISK

(b) Pair Difference Distribution of ORB

Figure 2: The distribution of pair difference of BRISK and ORB is showed in (a) and (b), respectively. The horizontal axis is the intensity differences of selected pixel pairs. The vertical axis is the number of selected pixel pairs.

binary descriptors in many applications. The challenge lies on two requirements: improvement on discriminative power and no loss of computing/matching speed.

3.2 Hierarchical Encoding of Binary Descriptors

In this section, we propose a hierarchical encoding strategy to build binary descriptors aiming at improving their discriminative power without loss of computing and matching speed. The intrinsic mechanism to formulate the proposed descriptor is still based on the differences between pre-selected pairs. Any strategy of selecting pixel pairs can be directly used in our framework and progresses in pixel pairs selection would benefit our binary descriptors. After pixel pairs selection, the hierarchical encoding is applied to build the descriptors.

The hierarchical encoding consists of two parts: quantization and encoding. The intensity differences between all pre-selected pairs are quantized and then encoded to form the descriptor. Each dimension in the proposed descriptor is a codeword. We find that uniform quantization with coding in sequence leads to the requirement of Euclidean distance metric, which increases much computation cost. Therefore, we propose a distribution based quantization and a hierarchical encoding strategy to build descriptor. The quantization and encoding parts are described as follows (See Figure 3):

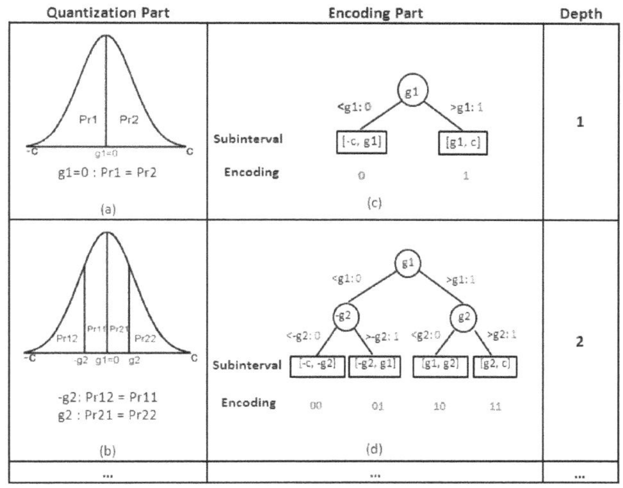

Figure 3: Illustration of hierarchical encoding. (a) and (b) show quantization part, (c) and (d) show encoding part. Pr represents the probability.

- **Quantization part:**

  Suppose d is distributed on an interval $[a, b]$:$d \in [a, b]$. We propose to recursively segment this interval and the segmentation can be formulated as:

$$[a_i, b_i] = [a_i, g(a_i, b_i)] + [g(a_i, b_i), b_i] \quad (3)$$

  where $[a_i, b_i]$ is a subinterval, and $g(a_i, b_i)$ is the median of the probability distribution of d on $[a_i, b_i]$. To be more specifical:

$$Pr(d \in [a_i, g(a_i, b_i)]) = Pr(d \in [g(a_i, b_i), b_i]) \quad (4)$$

  Iteratively, we get a set G of median points:

$$G = \{g_k\}, k = 1, 2, ..., g_k \in [a, b] \quad (5)$$

  g_1 represents the median of $[a, b]$, g_2 represents the median point of $[a, g_1]$, g_3 represents the median of $[g_1, b]$, and so on.

  Furthermore, we verify that the distribution of d is symmetric, regardless of sampling pattern (See Figure 2). Then the interval $[a, b]$ turns to be $[-c, c]$, and median points set G can be written as:

$$G = \{\pm g_k\}, k = 1, 2, ..., g_k \geq 0, g_1 = 0 \quad (6)$$

- **Encoding part:**
  The set G can be used to construct a full binary tree with arbitrary depth. In case that depth = 1, the root is the median point $g_1 = 0$, the left and right leafs representing two subintervals are: $[-c, g_1]$ and $[g_1, c]$, respecitively (see Figure 3(c)). In case that depth = 2, the root of left subtree is $-g_2$

, and the root of right subtree is g_2. Then the leafs representing four subintervals are:$[-c, -g_2], [-g_2, -g_1], [g_1, g_2], [g_2, c]$ (see Figure 3(d)).

The binary tree is used as the coding tree. Given a value of d, we can find which subinterval it belongs to, then the path from the root to the leaf is used as its codeword (see Figure 3(d)). The depth of the coding tree is the number of bits required for representing a single dimension.

The quantization part depends only on the distribution of d. Therefore, this part can be pre-computed by obtaining median points set G from a training set. The encoding part relies on several comparisons. This can be done by using simple if-else operations. Compared with some time-consuming parts in generating descriptors (*e.g.* smoothing), the computation cost of hierarchical encoding is negligibly small.

4. STEPWISE DISTANCE METRIC

In this section, we present a stepwise distance metric in details. First, the similarity between hierarchically encoded descriptors can be correctly measured by their stepwise distance. Second, the computation of stepwise distance is as fast as Hamming distance.

Note that for a hierarchically encoded descriptor it has multiple dimensions and for each dimension it has multiple bits. Assuming there are two hierarchically encoded descriptors X, Y :

$$X = [x_1, x_2, ...x_N] \quad x_i = [x_{i1}, x_{i2}, ...x_{im}]^T \tag{7}$$

$$Y = [y_1, y_2, ...y_N] \quad y_i = [y_{i1}, y_{i2}, ...y_{im}]^T \tag{8}$$

N denotes the number of dimensions and m denotes the number of bits in each dimension. Then descriptors X and Y are formulated as two $m \times N$ dimensional matrix.

The stepwise distance between descriptors X and Y is the sum of distances between corresponding dimensions:

$$S(X, Y) = \sum_{k=1}^{N} S(x_k, y_k) \tag{9}$$

In Section 4.1, we give the definition of $S(x_k, y_k)$, which is the stepwise distance of a single dimension. In Section 4.2, we show how to efficiently calculate $S(X, Y)$, which is the stepwise distance of between two descriptors.

4.1 Stepwise Distance of a Single Dimension

In this section,we use a single dimension instead of the whole descriptor for stepwise distance metric discussion (See figure 4). For the sake of simplicity, take x as the kth dimension of the descriptor X, and a_i as the ith bit of x. Likewise, take y as the kth dimension of Y, and b_i as the ith bit of y. Then we can get

$$\begin{aligned} x = [a_1, a_2, ...a_m]^T (a_i = 0, 1, x \equiv x_k, a_i \equiv x_{ki}) \\ y = [b_1, b_2, ...b_m]^T (b_i = 0, 1, y \equiv y_k, b_i \equiv y_{ki}) \end{aligned} \tag{10}$$

The Hamming distance between x and y is the bits difference:

$$H(x, y) = \sum_{i=1}^{m} d(a_i, b_i) \tag{11}$$

where

$$d(a_i, b_i) = a_i \wedge b_i \tag{12}$$

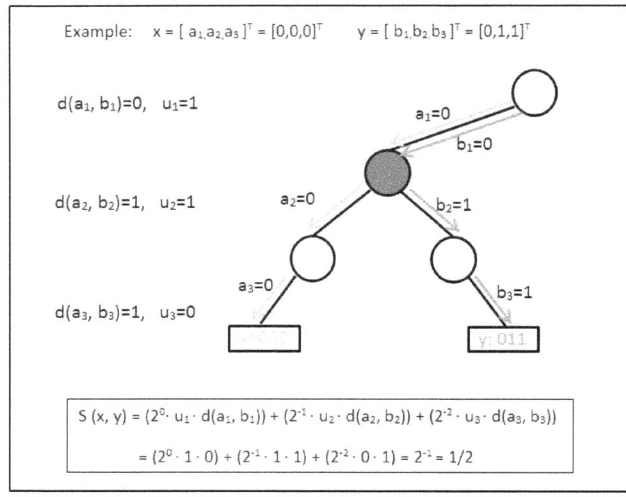

Figure 4: Example of stepping distance of a single dimension.

$\wedge$ represents a bitwise XOR. However, according to Section 3.2, x and y represent two paths respectively, and thus the Hamming distance $H(x, y)$ is not appropriate since a_i, b_i can only be compared on condition that $a_j = b_j, j = 1, ..., i-1$. We develop $H'(x, y)$ as:

$$H'(x, y) = \sum_{i=1}^{m} u_i \cdot d(a_i, b_i) \tag{13}$$

where

$$u_i = \begin{cases} 1 & if \quad \sum_{j=1}^{i-1} d(a_j, b_j) = 0 \\ 0 & otherwise \end{cases} \tag{14}$$

It is worth noting that the calculation of $H'(x, y)$ is in sequence. The calculation will stop at first $a_i \neq b_i, i \in [1, m]$, which means $H'(x, y)$ always equals to 1. Note that it is not the value of $H'(x, y)$, but the index i of the first difference is important: $\{i | a_i \neq b_i, a_k = b_k, k = 1, 2, ..., i-1\}$. The bigger the index i, the smaller the distance between x and y.

We then give our stepwise distance metric:

$$S(x, y) = \sum_{i=1}^{m} 2^{1-i} \cdot u_i \cdot d(a_i, b_i) \tag{15}$$

The weight 2^{1-i} is given considering two factors: First, the distance denoted by index i should be larger than the sum of distances denoted by index $i+1, i+2, ..., m$, respectively. Second, in encoding part, the index i represents a subinterval which is twice the size of that represented by index $i+1$. An example of $S(x, y)$ is shown in Figure 4.

4.2 Stepwise Distance between Descriptors

In order to quickly compute the stepwise distance between encoded descriptors, we form encoded descriptors in this order : the first bit of all dimension, then the second bit of all dimension, and so on. It can be formulated as:

$$X = [Bx_1, Bx_2, ..., Bx_m]^T, Bx_i = [x_{1i}, ..., x_{Ni}]$$
$$Y = [By_1, By_2, ..., By_m]^T, By_i = [y_{1i}, ..., y_{Ni}] \quad (16)$$

N denotes the number of dimensions and m denotes the number of bits in each dimension. Then the stepwise distance between descriptors can be seen as a linear combination of substring's Hamming distance:

$$S(X,Y) = \sum_{i=1}^{m} 2^{1-i} \cdot H(v_i|Bx_i, v_i|By_i) \quad (17)$$

where | denotes a bitwise OR and

$$v_1 = 0, v_i = v_{i-1}|((v_{i-1}|Bx_{i-1}) \wedge (v_{i-1}|By_{i-1})) \quad (18)$$

Note that $(v_{i-1}|Bx_{i-1}) \wedge (v_{i-1}|By_{i-1})$ is a byproduct of computing $H(v_{i-1}|Bx_{i-1}, v_{i-1}|By_{i-1})$. If the calculation of $S(X,Y)$ is sequential, computing v_i needs only one extra bitwise OR operation. Therefore, compared with Hamming distance calculation, the additional operations of stepwise distance are $3(m-1)-1$ times of bitwise OR ($v_0 = 0$ reduces one operation). Since $m << N$(m is less than 5 in common case), the additional computation cost is almost insignificant.

5. EXPERIMENTS

5.1 Experimental setup

In this section, we present experimental results obtained on benchmark dataset for evaluating the proposed method. Several state-of-the-art binary features are used in our experiment, aiming at validating the generality of our method.

- **Data set**: The testing environment is the benchmark image set proposed by Mikolajczyk and Schmid[19] [18]. The image dataset consists of 8 categories: Graffiti, Wall, Boat, Bikes, Trees, Leuven, Ubc and Bark. Each category contains a sequence of six images exhibiting an increasing amount of transformation (rotation, zoom + rotation, viewpoint change, image blur, JPEG compression, and light change).

- **Binary features**: The state-of-the-art binary features are used in our experiment. They are BRIEF [4], ORB [23] and BRISK [11]. BRIEF is 256-dimensional, ORB is 256-dimensional and BRISK is 512-dimensional. The key points are detected by Fast detector [2], and we detect 2000 key points in each image. All features are implemented by using public OpenCV source code with default parameters.

- **Correct matches identification**: The matching strategy is nearest neighbor matching: a database is searched for the match with the lowest descriptor distance. Same as ASIFT [21], correct matches are identified by the Moisan-Stival ORSA (Optimized Random Sampling Algorithm) algorithm [20]. The implementation of ORSA is author's source code.

5.2 Performance Evaluation

We compared BRIEF, ORB, and BRISK with 2-bits hierarchically encoded descriptors based on them, namely hierarchically encoded BRIEF(HE-BRIEF), hierarchically encoded ORB(HE-ORB) and hierarchically encoded BRISK(HE-BRISK). BRIEF, ORB and BRISK are using Hamming distance, while HE-BRIEF, HE-ORB and HE-BRISK are using stepwise distance. In order to quantify the discriminative power of pixel pairs, we evaluate descriptors with increasing pixel pairs. For each descriptor, pixel pairs from 32 to 128 are used (pixel pairs are selected in dimension sequence: m selected pairs are those pixel pairs determining the first m dimension).

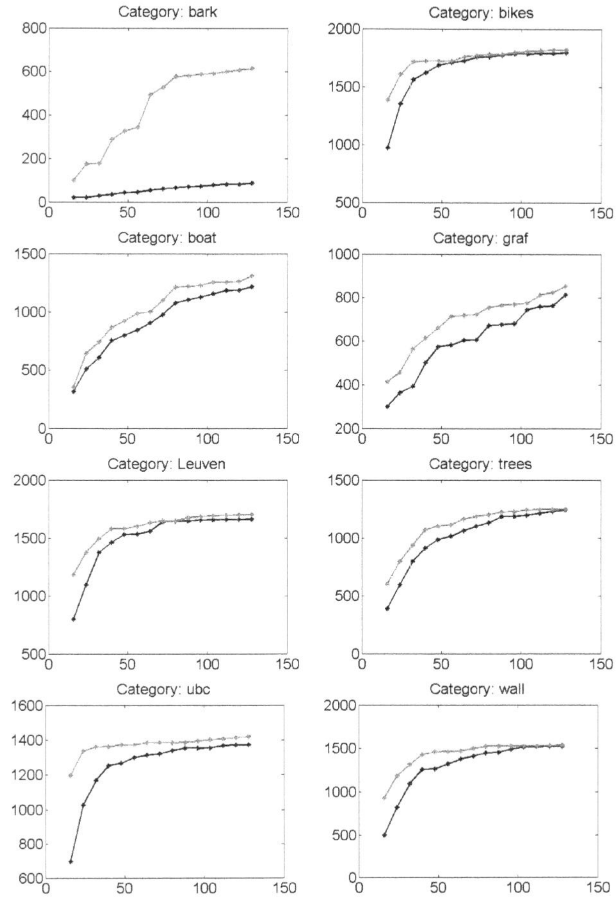

Figure 5: Comparison of BRIEF (black line) and HE-BRIEF (red line) on eight categories. The horizontal axis is the number of sampling pairs. The vertical axis is the number of correct matches. It can be seen that our method HE-BRIEF performs better on all categories.

Figures 5 to 7 present the quantitative results of comparisons. The numbers of correct matches are recorded on the vertical scale, and the horizontal axis represents the number of pixel pairs. We can see that for all binary descriptors, the encoded descriptors show a substantial performance increase. When the number of sampling pairs drops to 16, the hierarchically encoded descriptors achieve more than twice higher precision. It means we double the discriminative power of each single pair. As the number of sampling pairs increases, the number of correct matches finally comes up to a limit. As a result, the performance of binary descriptors and hierarchically encoded descriptors gets close as the number of sampling pairs increases.

- **BRIEF**
  Figure 5 presents the results of BRIEF and HE-BRIEF. We can see that HE-BRIEF outperforms BRIEF on all categories.

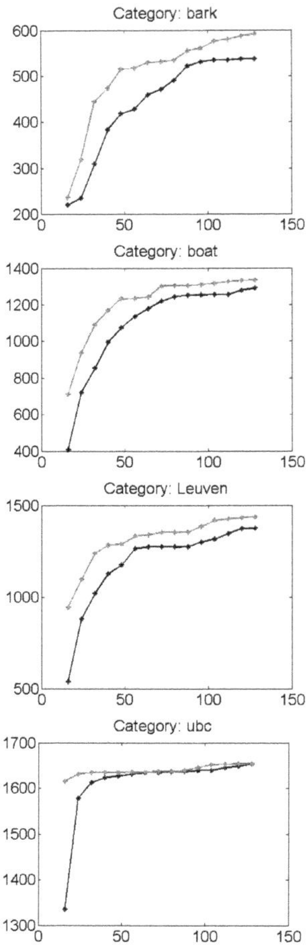

Figure 6: Comparison of ORB (black line) and HE-ORB (red line) on eight categories. The horizontal axis is the number of sampling pairs. The vertical axis is the number of correct matches. It can be seen that our method HE-ORB performs better on all categories.

The performance gap between them are relatively higher on category Graf and Bark than on others. It indicates that the robustness to viewpoint change is improved most by extend BRIEF to HE-BRIEF.

- **ORB**
Figure 6 presents the results of ORB and HE-ORB. As illustrated in figure 6, the performance improvement of HE-ORB is substantial and stable on all categories. In our experiment, the precision and recall of HE-ORB are highest among all descriptors. One possible reason is that we used the detector introduced by ORB.

- **Brisk**
Figure 7 shows that BRISK with 16 sampling pairs fail to generate any correct matching on 6 categories while HE-BRISK with 16 sampling pairs only fail on one. We further experiment to reduce the number of key points from 2000 to 1000, then BRISK with 16 sampling pairs fail only on 4 subsets and HE-BRISK with 16 sampling pairs find correct matches on all categories successfully.

Note that hierarchical encoding cannot achieve better performance than 0-1 encoding if the pixel pairs are sufficient for the database.

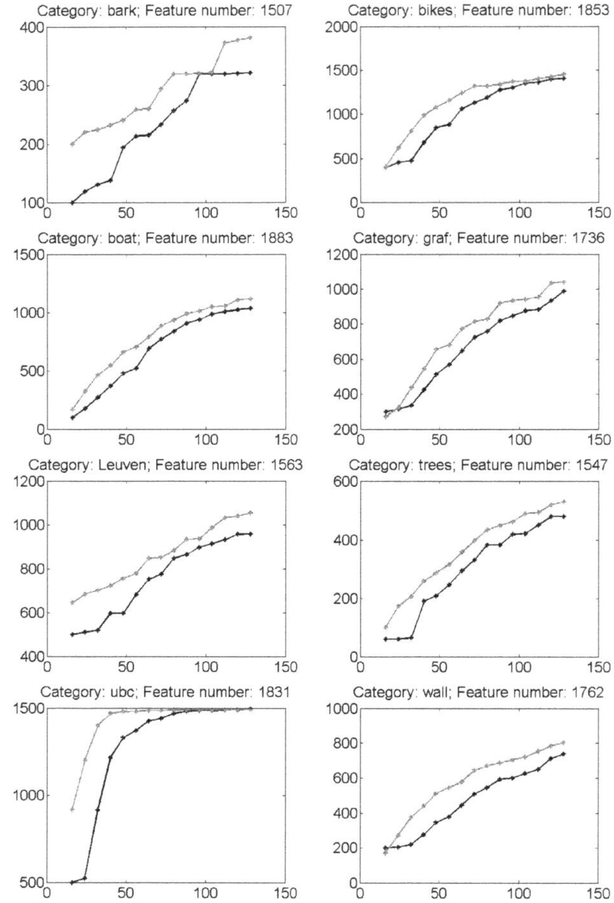

Figure 7: Comparison of BRISK (black line) and HE-BRISK (red line) on eight categories. The horizontal axis is the number of sampling pairs. The vertical axis is the number of correct matches. It can be seen that our method HE-BRISK performs better on all categories.

For example, 64 pixel pairs with 0-1 encoding is quite enough for finding matches in a database with fewer than 100 points. In this case, neither increasing pixel pairs nor hierarchically extending each dimension can improve matching precision. As could be expected, a stable increase of performance would be achieved in larger database by either increasing pixel pairs or hierarchically extending each dimension. Since the quantity of comparable pixel pairs has a limit, hierarchical encoding is an effective way of further improving discriminative power of binary descriptors for large database. Furthermore, any progresses made on pixel pairs selection would benefit our binary descriptors.

5.3 Time Cost

All algorithms are are running on an Intel quad-core of 2.83 GHZ using a single core. The descriptors have a length of default (BRIEF and ORB:256 bit, BRISK and FREAK:512bits). There are 2000 key points to describe and to match in two corresponding images, respectively. For the sake of fairness, we sampled all binary descriptor into 128 bits before matching.

Table 1 presents time costs of encoded descriptors and original descriptors. As seen from Table 1, the time cost of generating encoded descriptor is exactly the same as original descriptor. The

(a) Matching result of ORB

(b) Matching result of HE-ORB

	Number of correct matches	Increase based on ORB
ORB	384	-
HE-ORB	716	86.5%

(c) The number of correct matches of ORB and HE-ORB in this image

Figure 8: Illustration of matching results of ORB and HE-ORB based on 16 pixel pairs. Our method HE-ORB achieves 86% more correct matches.

time cost of computing stepwise distance is also very close to that of computing Hamming distance. As a conclusion, the time cost (generation + matching) of encoded descriptor is nearly the same as original descriptor.

5.4 An Matching Example

A explicit example of matching is provide in Figure 8 as the complementary to the extensive evaluation. Figure 8a is the matching result of ORB with 16 pixel pairs and Figure 8b is the matching result of HE-ORB with 16 pixel pairs. ORB has 384 correct matches and HE-ORB has 716 correct matches. As a result, HE-ORB gets 86.5% performance increase compared with ORB on this benchmark image. The quantitative results are given in the Table(c) of Figure 8.

6. CONCLUSION

In this paper, we propose a binary descriptor aiming at obtaining highly discriminative power and extremely low computation cost. The proposed binary descriptor is built by hierarchically encoding the intensity difference between pre-selected pixel pairs. To efficiently match the encoded descriptor, a stepwise distance metric is also proposed.

We evaluate our binary descriptor with stepwise distance metric on benchmark image dataset, the results show that the proposed descriptor outperforms state-of-the-art binary descriptors in matching performance. The efficiency of the proposed descriptor and distance metric is also validated with the experiment results.

7. ACKNOWLEDGMENTS

This work was supported by the Strategic Priority Research Program of the Chinese Academy of Sciences, No. XDA06030200; the National Key Technology R&D Program, No. 2012BAH46B03. This work was supported in part to Dr. Qi Tian by ARO grant W911NF-12-1-0057 and Faculty Research Award by NEC Labora-

Table 1: Time cost of state-of-the-art methods and our methods. Our methods achieve comparable time performance.

Picture1 vs. Pcture2 (2000 point)	BRIEF	HE-BRIEF	ORB	HE-ORB	BRISK	HE-BRISK
Total Description time (ms)	1092	1092	296	296	125	125
Time per Description (ms)	0.273	0.273	0.074	0.074	0.031	0.031
Total Matching time(ms)	1107	1125	905	940	712	762
Time per Comparison (ns)	276	281	226	235	178	190

tories of America, Inc. This work was supported in part by National Science Foundation of China (NSFC) 61429201,61303171.

8. REFERENCES

[1] A. E. Abdel-Hakim and A. A. Farag. Csift: A sift descriptor with color invariant characteristics. In *Computer Vision and Pattern Recognition, 2006 IEEE Computer Society Conference on*, volume 2, pages 1978–1983. IEEE, 2006.

[2] A. Alahi, R. Ortiz, and P. Vandergheynst. Freak: Fast retina keypoint. In *Computer Vision and Pattern Recognition (CVPR), 2012 IEEE Conference on*, pages 510–517. IEEE, 2012.

[3] H. Bay, T. Tuytelaars, and L. Van Gool. Surf: Speeded up robust features. *Computer Vision–ECCV 2006*, pages 404–417, 2006.

[4] M. Calonder, V. Lepetit, C. Strecha, and P. Fua. Brief: Binary robust independent elementary features. *Computer Vision–ECCV 2010*, pages 778–792, 2010.

[5] S. Gauglitz, T. Höllerer, and M. Turk. Evaluation of interest point detectors and feature descriptors for visual tracking. *International journal of computer vision*, 94(3):335–360, 2011.

[6] C. Harris and M. Stephens. A combined corner and edge detector. In *Alvey vision conference*, volume 15, page 50. Manchester, 1988.

[7] T. Hassner, V. Mayzels, and L. Zelnik-Manor. On sifts and their scales. In *Computer Vision and Pattern Recognition (CVPR)*, pages 1522–1528. IEEE, 2012.

[8] J. Heinly, E. Dunn, and J.-M. Frahm. Comparative evaluation of binary features. In *Computer Vision–ECCV 2012*, pages 759–773. Springer, 2012.

[9] Y.-G. Jiang, J. Wang, X. Xue, and S.-F. Chang. Query-adaptive image search with hash codes. *Multimedia, IEEE Transactions on*, 2013.

[10] Y. Ke and R. Sukthankar. Pca-sift: A more distinctive representation for local image descriptors. In *Computer Vision and Pattern Recognition (CVPR), 2004 IEEE Conference on*. IEEE, 2004.

[11] S. Leutenegger, M. Chli, and R. Siegwart. Brisk: Binary robust invariant scalable keypoints. In *Computer Vision (ICCV), 2011 IEEE International Conference on*, pages 2548–2555. IEEE, 2011.

[12] C. Liu, J. Yuen, A. Torralba, J. Sivic, and W. Freeman. Sift flow: Dense correspondence across different scenes. *Computer Vision–ECCV 2008*, pages 28–42, 2008.

[13] D. Lowe. Distinctive image features from scale-invariant keypoints. *International Journal of Computer Vision*, 60(2):91–110, 2004.

[14] E. Mair, G. Hager, D. Burschka, M. Suppa, and G. Hirzinger. Adaptive and generic corner detection based on the accelerated segment test. *Computer Vision–ECCV 2010*, pages 183–196, 2010.

[15] Z. Mao, Y. Zhang, and Q. Tian. Coge: A novel binary feature descriptor exploring anisotropy and non-uniformity. In *Advances in Multimedia Information Processing–PCM 2013*, pages 359–371. Springer, 2013.

[16] Z. Mao, Y. Zhang, and Q. Tian. What are the distance metrics for local features? In *Proceedings of the 21st ACM international conference on Multimedia*. ACM, 2013.

[17] J. Matas, O. Chum, M. Urban, and T. Pajdla. Robust wide-baseline stereo from maximally stable extremal regions. *Image and Vision Computing*, 22(10):761–767, 2004.

[18] K. Mikolajczyk and C. Schmid. A performance evaluation of local descriptors. *Pattern Analysis and Machine Intelligence, IEEE Transactions on*, 27(10):1615–1630, 2005.

[19] K. Mikolajczyk, T. Tuytelaars, C. Schmid, A. Zisserman, J. Matas, F. Schaffalitzky, T. Kadir, and L. Gool. A comparison of affine region detectors. *International Journal of Computer Vision*, 65(1):43–72, 2005.

[20] L. Moisan and B. Stival. A probabilistic criterion to detect rigid point matches between two images and estimate the fundamental matrix. *International Journal of Computer Vision*, 57(3):201–218, 2004.

[21] J. Morel and G. Yu. Asift: A new framework for fully affine invariant image comparison. *SIAM Journal on Imaging Sciences*, 2(2):438–469, 2009.

[22] E. Rosten and T. Drummond. Machine learning for high-speed corner detection. *Computer Vision–ECCV 2006*, pages 430–443, 2006.

[23] E. Rublee, V. Rabaud, K. Konolige, and G. Bradski. Orb: an efficient alternative to sift or surf. In *Computer Vision (ICCV), 2011 IEEE International Conference on*, pages 2564–2571. IEEE, 2011.

[24] E. Tola, V. Lepetit, and P. Fua. Daisy: An efficient dense descriptor applied to wide-baseline stereo. *Pattern Analysis and Machine Intelligence, IEEE Transactions on*, 32(5):815–830, 2010.

[25] T. Tuytelaars and K. Mikolajczyk. Local invariant feature detectors: a survey. *Foundations and Trends® in Computer Graphics and Vision*, 3(3):177–280, 2008.

[26] L. Zhang, Y. Zhang, J. Tang, X. Gu, J. Li, and Q. Tian. Topology preserving hashing for similarity search. In *Proceedings of the 21st ACM international conference on Multimedia*. ACM, 2013.

[27] S. Zhang, Q. Tian, Q. Huang, W. Gao, and Y. Rui. Usb: Ultra short binary descriptor for fast visual matching and retrieval. *IEEE Transactions on Image Processing (TIP)*, 2014.

[28] Y. Zhang, L. Zhang, and Q. Tian. A prior-free weighting scheme for binary code ranking. *IEEE transactions on multimedia*, 2014.

Kernelizing Spatially Consistent Visual Matches for Fine-Grained Classification

Valentin Leveau
INA / INRIA Zenith, France
valentin.leveau@ina.fr

Alexis Joly
INRIA Zenith, France
alexis.joly@inria.fr

Olivier Buisson
INA, France
olivier.buisson@ina.fr

Patrick Valduriez
INRIA Zenith, France
patrick.valduriez@inria.fr

ABSTRACT

This paper introduces a new image representation relying on the spatial pooling of geometrically consistent visual matches. We therefore introduce a new match kernel based on the inverse rank of the shared nearest neighbors combined with local geometric constraints. To avoid overfitting and reduce processing costs, the dimensionality of the resulting over-complete representation is further reduced by hierarchically pooling the raw consistent matches according to their spatial position in the training images. The final image representation is obtained by concatenating the resulting feature vectors at several resolutions. Learning from these representations using a logistic regression classifier is shown to provide excellent fine-grained classification performances outperforming the results reported in the literature on several classification tasks.

1. INTRODUCTION

For a few years, one can observe an increasing interest of the computer vision community towards specialized image classification tasks such as recognizing a specific model of car or a specific species of animals [3, 7]. As powerful and impressive as generalist classification methods are, they are actually useless for lots of practical usage requiring a finer knowledge, notably in professional contexts. The most popular generalist challenge ImageNet [1] is for instance highly heterogeneous in terms of annotations quality, image quality and degree of coverage of a specific topic. So that the overall scores measured on it as well as the resulting classifiers are of little interest for many real-world domains such as e-commerce, medicine, life sciences, media archiving, marketing, etc. On the other side, so called *fine-grained* classification challenges which are based on more accurate and more complete training data of a specific domain, open the door to powerful new usages of computer vision technologies.

[1]http://www.image-net.org/

ICMR'15, June 23–26, 2015, Shanghai, China.

DOI:http://dx.doi.org/10.1145/2671188.2749328 .

Generalist and specialized image classification tasks are in essence not that different. Given an input image I_q, the aim is to find to which category it belongs to, providing a training set Z of images of the targeted categories. As pointed in [3], the problem is however slightly different in that fine-grained challenges usually involve more cluttered backgrounds and a lower intra-class variability. Beyond this, any specialized classification task actually comes with its own specific constraints. Plants are for instance much more deformable objects than cars and might reach a high intra-class variability in terms of color and structure. Logos in natural scenes are very rigid objects but might involve extremely cluttered and changing background. Interesting patterns in medical images usually rely on subtle localized details in a rather fixed but cluttered background. Yet, the real challenge lies in the ambition to develop generic but adaptive classification methods as a foundation of a wide range of specialized applications involving complex and heterogeneous objects. In this paper, our main contribution is on embedding the parametric geometry consistency of small visual patterns into a high-dimensional image representation to be used in efficient linear classifiers. We actually show that several fine-grained classification tasks of the literature can highly benefit from such localized spatial consistency, in particular when the objects are not too much deformable.

2. RELATED WORKS

Pooling-based image representations Our work is primarily related to image classification. Most popular methods for this problem are typically based on pooling local visual features into global image representations and on the use of powerful classifiers in the resulting high-dimensional embedded space such as linear support vector machines [21, 28]. The Bag-of-Word representation (BoW) notably remains a key concept although the raw initial scheme of [32] is now outperformed by several alternative new schemes [21, 14, 27, 34, 13]. Its principle is to first train a so called visual vocabulary thanks to an unsupervised clustering algorithm computed on a given training set of local features. The produced partition is then used to quantize the visual features of a given new image into *visual words* that are aggregated within a single high-dimensional histogram. Partial geometry can be embedded in the image representation by using the Spatial Pyramid Matching scheme of [21]. As it relies on vector quantization, the BoW representation is however affected by quantization errors. Very similar visual

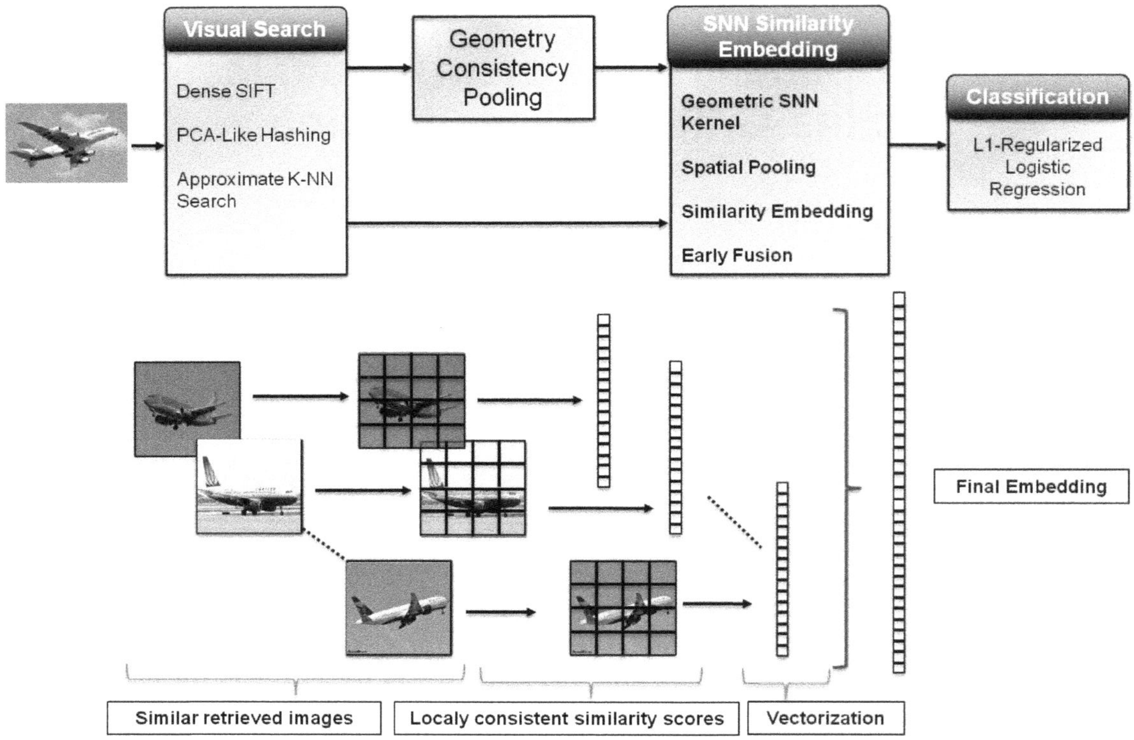

Figure 1: Overview of the proposed classification scheme. For each image, local features are densely extracted and indexed via a data-dependent hashing scheme. For each training image, similar images are searched thanks to a fast approximate k nearest neighbor algorithm. Retrieved images are uniformly subdivided forming a spatial grid of a given resolution. The similarity between the query image and the sub-regions of the similar retrieved images are evaluated and aggregated into a global vector that can be fed to a linear regression classification algorithm. In order to allow the system to learn spatially consistent visual patterns, we perform local geometry consistency analysis in a RANSAC fashion to refine the similarity score of the retrieved sub-regions. In top of that, we make use of an early fusion scheme to allow combination of geometric and non geometric local information letting the system deciding what should be learnt.

features might be split across distinct clusters whereas more dissimilar ones might be affected to the same visual word. This results in both mismatches and potentially irrelevant matches. To alleviate this problem, several improvements have been proposed in the literature. The first one consists in expanding the assignment of a given local feature to its nearest visual words [14, 29, 34, 18]. This allows reducing the number of mismatches without degrading much the encoding time. Other researchers have investigated alternative ways to avoid the vector quantization step, using sparse coding [37] or locality-constrained linear coding [36]. Such methods optimize the affectation of a given local feature to a few number of visual words thanks to sparsity or locality constraints on the global representation. Another alternative is to use aggregation-based models such as the improved Fisher Vector of [27] or the VLAD encoding scheme [13]. Such methods do not only encode the number of occurrences of each visual word but also encode additional information about the distribution of the descriptors by aggregating the component-wise differences. When used with discriminative linear classifiers, such high-dimensional representations benefit of both generative and discrimination approaches leading to state-of-the-art classification performances on fine-grained classification benchmarks [7].

Instance-based image retrieval and classification Another family of techniques related to our work is *image retrieval* techniques [22, 12, 1, 30, 16, 22]. These techniques are primarily aimed at retrieving instances of a given query object in an unsupervised way but any of them can be used for classification purposes when the search is performed on a labelled set of pictures (typically by voting on the top-K retrieved images or through any other instance-based classifier). They usually rely on local descriptors quantization methods (such as hamming embedding [11], data-dependent hashing [17] or product quantizer [12]) and scalable indexing structures (such as inverted lists or hash tables). This allows matching all local descriptors one by one in the full index and favors a more precise matching of small objects in highly cluttered pictures. Using geometry in addition to this raw scheme has been proved to achieve further performance gains, either by the inclusion of weak geometry constraints in the matching phase [11] or by post-checking the geometry consistency of the matches, typically by using a RANSAC algorithm [16]. The method proposed in [22] improves such techniques in order to construct precise class-specific saliency maps and build a strong image classifier highly robust to noise and clutter.

Kernelized and similarity-based representations Another line of research related to our work consists in building *match kernels*, i.e. kernels based on the aggregation of the individual matches between any two images. One of the pioneering work in this way is the normalized sum match kernel of [25] which simply consists in summing the pair-wise distances between all the features of an image I_x and the one of an image I_y. Another seminal work was the Pyramid Match Kernel of [8] which uses hash-based partitions to efficiently aggregate the matches in the visual space. Interestingly, the linear product between the BoW representation [32] of two images is a specific case of match kernel consisting in pooling the matches in the k-means clusters. More recently, several new match kernels have been proposed such as the NBNN kernel [33] which is a kernelized version of the naive Bayes nearest neighbor classifier or the graph-matching kernel of [4] which models the images as graphs whose nodes correspond to a dense set of regions, and edges reflect the underlying grid structure of the image. Other kernels rather make use of the Hamming Embedding principle to build efficient match kernels usable in the large scale [35, 9]. Note that some methods such as [2, 9, 33] makes use of an indirect matching between the features by using some intermediate training data. In that case we sometimes rather speak about *similarity-based representations* rather than match kernels. Our method belongs to this family of technique as discussed in our more details later in the paper.

Deep Convolutional Neural Networks An radically different approach to image classification is the use *deep convolutional neural networks*. Rather than extracting the features according to hand-tuned or psycho-vision oriented filters, such methods directly work on the image signal. The weights learned by the first convolutional layers allow to automatically build relevant image filters whereas the intermediate layers are in charge of pooling these raw responses into high-level visual patterns. The last fully connected layers work more traditionally as any discriminative classifier on the image representation resulting from the previous layers. Deep convolutional neural networks have been recently proved to achieve better results on large-scale image classification datasets such as ImageNet [20] and do attract more and more interest in the computer and multimedia vision communities. A known drawback of Deep Convolutional Neural Networks is however that they require a lot of training data mainly because of the huge number of parameters to be learned. Their performances on fine-grained classification are consequently more controversial and they are still often outperformed by local features based approaches, as shown in our experiments. Besides, it is important to notice that they inspire the investigation of new deep learning models making use of more traditional visual features embedding methods (e.g. [31]).

Our approach : Our approach was primarily inspired by instance-based image retrieval methods. It makes use of efficient indexing and approximate k-nearest neighbors search techniques to match individual local features (such as in [12, 15]) and it uses a parametric spatial consistency checking such as in [24, 22]. Our main contribution is that we do kernelize such methods to build high-dimensional image representations suitable for advanced machine learning algorithms, rather than simply relying on an instance-based classification scheme such as in [22]. Our experiments show that doing so allows very strong performance gains. Our method also has some strong connexions with kernelized and similarity-based representations. Kernelized representations notably offer us a nice formalization framework from which we can derive an explicit image representation space tractable by linear classifiers. Our two main contributions over existing methods in this research line are (i) the use of a rank-based activation function of the shared neighbors in the training set to compare pairs of features, and (ii) the embedding of the local geometric consistency in the kernel. Finally our method shares some common issues with soft assignment and sparse coding methods used to improve BoW representations. Our approximate k-nn search method, based on probabilistic multi-probe accesses in hash tables, can actually be considered as a soft assignment over a huge vocabulary composed of all the features in the dataset. Its main advantage is that it offers a high quality control thanks to a trained probabilistic search model allowing to select the most probable regions of the feature space for each local feature.

3. GEOMETRICALLY CONSISTENT MATCH KERNEL

This section describes our new *geometrically consistent match kernel* as well as the *geometrically consistent image representation* we derive from it to train linear classifiers. Let us first introduce some notations and concepts.

3.1 Shared Nearest Neighbors Match Kernel

We consider two images I_x and I_y represented by sets of local features $X = \{\mathbf{x}\}$ and $Y = \{\mathbf{y}\}$ where $\mathbf{x}$ and $\mathbf{y}$ are d-dimensional feature vectors (SIFT features [23] in our experiments). We then build on the *normalized sum match kernel* proposed by [25] to compare feature sets:

$$K(X,Y) = \Phi(X)^T\Phi(Y) = \frac{1}{|X|\,|Y|}\sum_{\mathbf{x},\mathbf{y}} k(\mathbf{x},\mathbf{y}) \qquad (1)$$

where $k()$ is itself a Mercer kernel allowing to compare two individual local features $\mathbf{x}$ and $\mathbf{y}$. In our case, $k()$ is however not defined as a direct matching between $\mathbf{x}$ and $\mathbf{y}$ but rather as the degree of correlation of their matches in a large training set. Let denote as $\mathcal{Z}$ such a training set composed of N d-dimensional feature vectors $\mathbf{z}$. We introduce the following *shared nearest neighbors (SNN) match kernel* :

$$K_S(X,Y) = \frac{1}{|X|\,|Y|}\sum_{\mathbf{x},\mathbf{y}}\sum_{\mathbf{z}} \varphi(r_{\mathbf{x}}(\mathbf{z})).\varphi(r_{\mathbf{y}}(\mathbf{z})) \qquad (2)$$

with $\varphi(.)$ a rank-based activation function given by :

$$\varphi(r_{\mathbf{x}}(\mathbf{z})) = \begin{cases} \frac{K-r_{\mathbf{x}}(\mathbf{z})}{K} & r_{\mathbf{x}}(\mathbf{z}) \leq K \\ 0 & else \end{cases} \qquad (3)$$

where $r_{\mathbf{x}}(\mathbf{z}) : \mathcal{Z} \to \mathbb{R}^+$ is a ranking function returning the rank of an item $\mathbf{z} \in \mathcal{Z}$ according to its distance to $\mathbf{x}$ and K is the number of nearest neighbors we decide to return for each point. The distance itself could be a L_2 metric in the original feature space but, as we will see in section 4, we

use in practice a more efficient Hamming embedding scheme. Whatever the distance used, the intuition of the *SNN match kernel* is that it counts the number of common neighbors in the neighborhood of $\mathbf{x}$ and in the one of $\mathbf{y}$. The product $k_{\mathbf{z}}(\mathbf{x},\mathbf{y}) = \varphi(r_{\mathbf{x}}(\mathbf{z})).\varphi(r_{\mathbf{y}}(\mathbf{z}))$ is actually equal to one if $\mathbf{z}$ is the nearest neighbor of both $\mathbf{x}$ and $\mathbf{y}$ and close to zero if $\mathbf{z}$ is not in the top neighbors of either $\mathbf{x}$ or $\mathbf{y}$.
Using this *shared nearest neighbors kernel* instead of a more classical distance in the feature space has several justifications and advantages. First, shared-neighbors techniques are known to overcome several shortcomings of traditional metrics. They are notably less sensitive to the dimensionality curse, more robust to noisy data and more stable over unusual features distribution [5, 10] . Measuring the similarity between features by the degree to which their neighbourhoods in the training set resemble one another is actually a form of generative metric learning. Features belonging to dense clu sters are actually more likely to share neighbors than uniformly distributed and isolated features. So that their contribution in the global kernel will be enhanced. Secondly, using an indirect matching rather than a direct one allows to have en explicit formulation of the embedded space $\Phi(X)$. By factorizing equation 3, it is actually easy to show that $K_S(X,Y) = \Phi_S(X)^T \Phi_S(Y)$ with:

$$\Phi_S(X) = \sum_{i=1}^{N} \frac{1}{|X|} \sum_{\mathbf{x}} \varphi(r_{\mathbf{x}}(\mathbf{z}_i)).\vec{e_i} \quad (4)$$

So that, the explicit N-dimensional feature vector $\Phi(X)$ representing each image in the training set can be computed before training a simple linear classifier on top of them. This principle of this approach was already introduced in the *intermediate matching kernel* of [2] and further re-used in many methods including the NBNN kernel of [33]. Such methods did however rely on the distance between the features of the candidate image X and the ones of the training set $\mathcal{Z}$ so that they did not benefit from the nice properties of the SNN-kernel. Last but not least, one of the main advantage of the *SNN match kernel* is that is that it can be easily converted to a sparse representation as the ratio of the number of values equal to zeros is very high. Only the features $\mathbf{z}$ lying in the top neighbors of both $\mathbf{x}$ and $\mathbf{y}$ lead to consistent component values. In practice, it is therefore sufficient to consider only the top-m neighbors of each feature $\mathbf{x}$ and $\mathbf{y}$ to get a good approximation of $K(X,Y)$. This allows using efficient nearest neighbors search techniques to construct the explicit representations $\Phi(X)$ and to use an efficient sparse encoding when training linear classifiers on top of them.

3.2 Geometrically Consistent SNN match Kernel

The problem of the classical match kernels defined in the literature is that they do not integrate the information of the relative position of the local features in the images. We therefore propose to extend our SNN match kernel so as to include geometrical constraints on the considered matches. In this case, we consider that each local feature $\mathbf{z}$ in the training set $\mathcal{Z}$ was extracted from an image $I(z)$ at a given spatial position $\mathbf{P}_{\mathbf{z}}$. A first geometrically consistent SNN kernel could then be simply constructed by adding geometrical consistency indicators in equation 3 such as:

$$K(X,Y) = \frac{1}{|X||Y|} \sum_{\mathbf{x},\mathbf{y}} \sum_{\mathbf{z}} \delta_{\mathbf{x}}(\mathbf{z}).\delta_{\mathbf{y}}(\mathbf{z}).\varphi(r_{\mathbf{x}}(\mathbf{z})).\varphi(r_{\mathbf{y}}(\mathbf{z})) \quad (5)$$

where $\delta_{\mathbf{x}}(\mathbf{z})$ would be equal to one if $\mathbf{z}$ is an inlier of a RANSAC-like algorithm estimating the best affine transformation between I_x and I_z (and zero otherwise). Estimating a global affine transformation between the images might however lead to a high number of mismatches as the targeted visual patterns in fine-grained classification are typically small and the background very cluttered. It is therefore preferable to focus on more localized geometric transformations. We therefore estimate an affine transformation for each local feature $\mathbf{x}$ (respectively $\mathbf{y}$) based on the set $\mathcal{N}_p(\mathbf{x})$ of its p spatial neighbors in I_x and their matches in I_z. The estimation of the best transformation for a given central feature $\mathbf{x}$ is performed by exhaustively probing all possible pairs of the form $(\mathbf{x},\mathbf{x}')$ with $\mathbf{x}' = \mathcal{N}_p(\mathbf{x})$ and keeping only their best matches in the training image I_z. As our affine model is restricted to rotation and scaling transformations, each pair of matches generates a single candidate transformation parameterized by a projection matrix $\mathbf{A}_{\mathbf{x},\mathbf{x}'}(I_z)$ and a translation parameter $\mathbf{B}_{\mathbf{x},\mathbf{x}'}(I_z)$. The best transformation $(\mathbf{A}_{\mathbf{x}}(I_z), \mathbf{B}_{\mathbf{x}}(I_z))$ among the set of candidate ones is then selected as the one maximizing the number of inliers in the set $\mathcal{N}_p(\mathbf{x})$ of neighboring matches, using a threshold θ on the projected spatial positions. We finally count the number of inliers of that best transformation by weighting the contribution of each inlier match according to its rank-based activation function:

$$g_{\mathbf{x}}(I_z) = \sum_{x' \in \mathcal{N}_p(\mathbf{x})} \varphi(r_{\mathbf{x}}(\mathbf{z}')).\delta(\|(\mathbf{A}_{\mathbf{x}}\mathbf{P}_{\mathbf{x}'} + \mathbf{B}_{\mathbf{x}}) - \mathbf{P}_{\mathbf{z}'}\| < \theta) \quad (6)$$

where $\mathbf{z}'$ is the best match of $\mathbf{x}'$ in I_z.
We can now define the following geometrically consistent match kernel:

$$K_G(X,Y) = \sum_{\mathbf{x},\mathbf{y}} \sum_{\mathbf{z}} \delta_{\mathbf{x}}(\mathbf{z}).\delta_{\mathbf{y}}(\mathbf{z}).g_{\mathbf{x}}(I_z).g_{\mathbf{y}}(I_z).\varphi(r_{\mathbf{x}}(\mathbf{z})).\varphi(r_{\mathbf{y}}(\mathbf{z})) \quad (7)$$

Note that in this case, the indicator function $\delta_{\mathbf{x}}(\mathbf{z})$ is equal to one only if $\mathbf{z}$ is an inlier of the local transformation $(\mathbf{A}_{\mathbf{x}}(I_z), \mathbf{B}_{\mathbf{x}}(I_z))$ optimized on the neighborhood $\mathcal{N}_p(\mathbf{x})$. The introduction of the scores $g_{\mathbf{x}}(I_z)$ allow to give more importance to the highly consistent patches with high numbers of inliers. This embedding of the geometry of course use an extra computation time for the construction of the explicit representation of each image (about 3 seconds).
As an improvement of $K_G(X,Y)$, we define an alternative version based on the max pooling over the features of I_x and I_y rather than the normalized sum:

$$K_G(X,Y) = \max_{\mathbf{x},\mathbf{y}} . \sum_{\mathbf{z}} \delta_{\mathbf{x}}(\mathbf{z}).\delta_{\mathbf{y}}(\mathbf{z}).g_{\mathbf{x}}(I_z).g_{\mathbf{y}}(I_z).\varphi(r_{\mathbf{x}}(\mathbf{z})).\varphi(r_{\mathbf{y}}(\mathbf{z})) \quad (8)$$

We did show in our experiments that it can lead to better performances than $K_G(X,Y)$. Note that this new formulation can still be factorized as $K'_G(X,Y) = \Phi'_G(X)^T \Phi'_G(Y)$ with the following explicit image representation:

$$\Phi'_G(X) = \sum_{i=1}^{N} \max_{\mathbf{x}} \delta_{\mathbf{x}}(\mathbf{z}_i).g_{\mathbf{x}}(I_{z_i}).\varphi(r_{\mathbf{x}}(\mathbf{z}_i)).\vec{e_i} \quad (9)$$

3.3 Spatial Pooling of the raw SNN-based image representations

As elegant as the explicit image representations $\Phi'_S(X)$ and $\Phi'_G(X)$ are, they do not conduct to good classification results in practice. Their very high dimensionality, equals to the number of local features in the training set (often tens of millions), actually leads to strong overfitting even when using $L2$ regularizers with high values of the regularization control parameter λ. As an illustration, the classification mAP obtained by training a logistic regression classifier from the raw feature vectors $\Phi'_G(X)$ on the Vehicle dataset introduced in [19] ranges from 0.283 (for $\lambda = 1$) to 0.286 (for $\lambda = 100$). It is therefore required to group the individual matches of the SNN kernels before deriving an effective explicit image representation. In this paper, we do focus on the *spatial* pooling of the raw matches rather than aggregating them in the feature space as done in many kernels in particular in the popular image representations such as BoW, Fisher Vectors or VLAD. We consequently loose some generalization capacity in the visual space compared to these methods but on the other side we strongly boost the locality, the interpretability and the discrimination of the trained visual patterns (particularly when using the geometrically consistent SNN kernel). Our spatial pooling strategy is very close to the one proposed in [?]. We subdivide the images I_z of the training set using spatial grids of different sizes and we aggregate the matches falling in the same cell. The main difference of our method over the one of [?] relies on the computation of the raw matching scores. Whereas they use a simple Hamming distance on the hash codes derived from the original features, our method relies on the rank-based activation function of the approximate nearest neighbors (with a quality control) combined with our geometrically consistency filtering and weighting. As discussed in [?], this spatial pooling strategy is also much more powerful than the popular Spatial Pyramid Matching of Lazebnik et al. [21] although it is somehow similar. Spatially pooling the matches in the training set rather than pooling the features in the image actually provides much more invariance to translation and rotation while providing similar benefits in terms of partial geometry.

More formally, we can reformulate our raw SNN match kernel as:

$$K_S^R(X,Y) = \frac{1}{|X|\,|Y|}\sum_{\mathbf{x},\mathbf{y}}\sum_{j=1}^{N_R}\sum_{\mathbf{z}\in Z_j}\varphi(r_{\mathbf{x}}(\mathbf{z})).\varphi(r_{\mathbf{y}}(\mathbf{z})) \tag{10}$$

where Z_j is the j-th image region of the whole training set containing in total N_R regions (e.g. for a regular grid subdividing each image of the training set in 4 cells, N_R is equal to the number of training images multiplied by 4). This reformulation allows to derive an alternative explicit image representation at the region level rather than at the feature level:

$$\Phi_S^R(X,Y) = \sum_{\mathrm{j}=1}^{N_R}\frac{1}{|X|}\sum_{\mathbf{z}\in Z_j}\sum_{\mathbf{x}}\varphi(r_{\mathbf{x}}(\mathbf{z}_i)).\vec{e_j} \tag{11}$$

So that training a linear classifier on such representation will affect weights to the regions in the training set rather than to the local features themselves.

Similar image representations can be derived from the geometrically consistent kernels but we rather use a max pooling strategy to aggregate the raw matches falling in the same cell as we discovered that this was more beneficial in that case. The explicit image representation derived from the SNN kernel $K'_G(X,Y)$ mapped onto an image grid R is then:

$$\Phi_G^R(X) = \sum_{\mathrm{j}=1}^{N_R}\max_{\mathbf{z}\in Z_j}\max_{\mathbf{x}}\delta_{\mathbf{x}}(\mathbf{z}_i).g_{\mathbf{x}}(I_{z_i}).\varphi(r_{\mathbf{x}}(\mathbf{z}_i)).\vec{e_j} \tag{12}$$

In our experiments we used a simple pyramidal partition of the images recursively subdividing the image in 4 regular cells, up to a depth d_p. The image representations of each level of the pyramid are simply concatenated before being passed to the linear classifier. We denote the resulting representation as $\Phi_G^{0,1,2,\ldots,d_p}(X)$. Note that $\Phi_G^0(X)$ is the representation at the image level, without any subdivision of the image. In that case the dimensionality of the representation is equal to the number of images in the training set and the classifier learns contributive weights of the images for each class.

3.4 Early fusion and power normalization

In many classification problems, it is difficult to predict whether the rigid local geometry will help or not. For some of our experiments (detailed in section 5), we therefore combine the geometry-free and the geometrically consistent match kernels by simply concatenating their representations Φ_S^R and Φ_G^R. Each image region of the training set is then represented by two complementary scores (with or without geometry) and it is to the charge of the linear classifier to learn which one contributes the most to the recognition.

As suggested in [19], we also study in our cross-validation experiments the impact of a power-law normalization of our representations, which is a popular post-processing stage applied after coding schemes such as bag-of-words or Fisher vectors [28]. This normalization is parameterized by a single power parameter γ applied to all components. It usually ensures that infrequent (yet potentially highly informative patches) are not overpowered by frequent (yet not necessarily informative patches) such as uniform background patches.

4. APPROXIMATE K-NN SEARCH SCHEME

In practice, to speed up the computation of our SNN-based image representations, the ranking function $r_{\mathbf{x}}(\mathbf{z}) : \mathcal{Z} \rightarrow \mathbb{R}^+$ is implemented as an approximate nearest neighbors search algorithm based on hashing and probabilistic accesses in the hash table. It takes as input each query feature $\mathbf{x}$ of the image I_x to be described and returns a set of m approximated neighbors in $\mathcal{Z}$ with an approximated rank $r_{\mathbf{x}}^m(\mathbf{z})$. The exact ranking function $r_{\mathbf{x}}^m(\mathbf{z})$ is simply replaced by this approximated ranking function in all equations above. Note that the features $\mathbf{z} \in \mathcal{Z}$ that are not returned in the top-m approximated nearest neighbors are simply *removed* from the SNN match kernels equations conducting to a considerable reduction of the computation time as they have a rank-based activation function $\varphi(r_{\mathbf{x}}(\mathbf{z}))$ equal to zero.

Let us now describe more precisely our approximate nearest neighbors indexing and search method. It first compresses the original feature vectors $\mathbf{z} \in \mathcal{Z}$ into compact binary hash codes $\mathbf{h}(\mathbf{z})$ of length b. This is done by first computing a principal component analysis in the original space followed by a binary quantization of the b components with the higher eigenvalues. The binary quantization of each component is computed as:

$$h_j(\mathbf{z}) = sgn(a_j^T \mathbf{z} - \mu_j)$$

where

$$\mu_j = \frac{1}{N} \sum_{\mathbf{z}} a_j^T \mathbf{z}$$

is the mean of all the projected values. The distance between any two features $\mathbf{x}$ and $\mathbf{z}$ can then be efficiently approximated by the Hamming distance between $\mathbf{h}(\mathbf{z})$ and $\mathbf{h}(\mathbf{x})$. According to our experiments, this hashing method provides in our context better performances than several other tested methods, including random projections or hamming embedding [11] (orthogonal random projections). In all our experiments we used $b = 128$ bits.
To avoid scanning the whole dataset, the hash codes $\mathbf{h}(\mathbf{z})$ derived from the local features of the training set $\mathcal{Z}$ are then indexed in a hash table whose keys are the t-length prefix of the hash codes $\mathbf{h}(\mathbf{z})$. At search time, the hash code $\mathbf{h}(\mathbf{x})$ of a query feature $\mathbf{x}$ is computed as well as its t-length prefix. We then use a probabilistic multi-probe search algorithm inspired by the one of [15] to select the buckets of the hash table that are the most likely to contain exact nearest neighbors. This is done by using a probabilistic search model that is trained offline on the exact m-nearest neighbors of M sampled features $\mathbf{z} \in \mathcal{Z}$. We however use a simpler search model than the one of [15]. We actually use a normal distribution with independent components parameterized by a single vector σ that is trained over the exact nearest neighbors of the training samples. At search time, we also use a slightly different probabilistic multi-probe algorithm trading stability for time. Instead of probing the buckets by decreasing probabilities, we rather use a greedy algorithm that computes the probability of neighboring buckets and select only the ones having a probability greater than a threshold ζ that is fixed over all queries. The value of ζ is trained offline on M training samples and their exact nearest neighbors so as to reach on average cumulative probability α over the visited buckets. In our experiments, we always used $\alpha = 0.80$ meaning that on average we retrieve 80% of the exact nearest neighbors in the original feature space. Once the most probable buckets have been selected, the refinement step computes the Hamming distance between $\mathbf{h}(\mathbf{x})$ and the $\mathbf{h}(\mathbf{z})$'s belonging to the selected buckets and keep only the top-m matches thanks to a max heap.

5. EXPERIMENTS

5.1 Experimental setup

Datasets We experimented our method on the following datasets mixing instance classification tasks with fine-grained classification tasks:
FlickrLogos32 [30] - 8,240 images composed of 2,240 images labelled with 32 logo classes and 6000 distractors considered as a no-logo class. Evaluation protocol is the same than [19].
Vehicles29 [19] - 10,622 images labelled with 29 car models of 7 brands (divided into 5,266 training and 5,356 test images). Evaluation protocol is the same than [19].
FGVC-Aircraft - This dataset is composed of 10,000 photographs of aircrafts labeled with 100 models that are very specific such as $A340-200$, $A340-600$ or $Boeing-737-400$. The dataset is split into $3,333$ images for the test set and $6,667$ images for the training set.

Local Features For the *FlickrLogos32* and *Vehicles29* datasets we used the same features extraction procedure as the one used in [19] for the same datasets. SIFT descriptors [23] are extracted from points detected by the rotation-invariant Harris-Hessian-Laplace interest point detector [26]. Following prior works [1], the descriptors are L_2-normalized to the unit ball and square-rooted. For the *FGVC-Aircraft* dataset we rather used the features extraction procedure used in [7] for the same datasets. The main difference is that SIFT descriptors are extracted on a dense dense multi-resolution grid instead of Harris-Hessian-Laplace interest points. The number of resolution and step size on the x- and y-axis are respectively set to 5, 3 and 3.

Linear classifier All our classification experiments are performed using the logistic regression classifier of the LibLinear library [6].

Parameters values We did not spend a lot of time in tuning the parameters of our method by cross-validation mainly because of lacking time. Most of them are therefore fixed arbitrary or based on previous works. This includes the number p of spatial neighbors used in the geometrically consistent kernel (fixed to 20% of the total number of features in the image), the number of neighbors m returned by the approximate knn search method (fixed to 100), the quality control parameter of the approximate search (fixed to $\alpha = 0.8$), the length b of the hash codes (fixed to 128 bits), the length t of the hash code prefix used to construct the hash table (fixed to $t = log_2 N + 2$).

5.2 Comparison to state-of-the-art on instance classification tasks

In this section we compare our method to the instance classification results reported in [19] and [22], which are the baseline methods for the *FlickrLogos32* and *Vehicles29* datasets. For our own method, we only used the geometrically consistent SNN kernel as it already gave excellent performances alone. We did use a spatial pyramid of depth $d_p = 2$ without any power-law normalization on the resulting image representations ($\Phi_G^{0,1,2}(X)$). We used the logistic regression classifier of LibLinear with a L_1 regularization parameterized by the default contribution factor value $\lambda = 1$. The used evaluation metric is the IC-mAP as in [19] and [22].

Method	FlickrL32	Vehicles29
Fisher Vector 128x4,096 [19]	0.866	0.497
Prototype voting [19]	0.914	0.557
S-Ransac [22]	0.928	0.597
Our method	**0.981**	**0.79**

Table 1: Classification performances on the *FlickrLogos32* and *Vehicles29* datasets measured by IC-mAP.

Results are reported in table 2. They show that our method definitely outperform the previous baseline of [22] as well as the fisher vector representation evaluated in [19] or the new prototype voting scheme they introduced. We achieve a near perfect classification score of **0.981** on *FlickrLogos32* whereas we did not tune any parameter by cross-validation. Note that for some test queries, the background is highly cluttered and the objects of interest rather small and slightly deformed [22]. As they also use some local geometry in their matching scheme, the gap is rather due to the kernerlization principle of our approach. It actually allows us to train a powerful discriminant classifier rather than using less effective instance-based classification scheme as they do.

5.3 Comparison to state-of-the-art on fine-grained classification tasks

In this section we compare our method to the fine-grained classification results reported in [7] on the *OFGVC-Aircraft* dataset. As the authors of that study spent a lot of efforts to cross-validate their parameters, we also performed some cross-validation tuning as discussed in 5.3.1. The final results obtained on the official test sets are then presented in 5.3.2. The evaluation metric for all experiments is the mean accuracy and we focused on the track 1 challenge, i.e. with the bounding boxes available for both test and training data.

5.3.1 *Cross-validation experiments*

To tune some of the parameters of our method, we used a 2-fold cross-validation scheme on the training data of each dataset (using the logistic regression classifier of LibLinear with a L1 regularizer). We particularly studied the impact of using geometry or not in our SNN match kernels. the impact of the power-law normalization factor γ, the impact of the $L1$ regularizer factor λ, and, last but not least, the impact of the pyramid depth d_p. Default values of the parameters when studying the others were $\gamma = 1$, $\lambda = 1$, $d_p = 0$, $kerneltype = geom$. Table 2 and Figure 2 display the results obtained on the *FGVC-Aircraft* dataset.

Kernel type	without geom	with geom	early fusion
Accuracy	68.7	72.2	**74.5**

Table 2: Cross-validation performances on the kernel type for the *FGVC-Aircraft* dataset.

We then took the best parameters to perform the final run reported in the next subsection (e.g. early fusion of geom + non geom, $\gamma = 0.6$, $\lambda = 4$, $d_p = 2$).

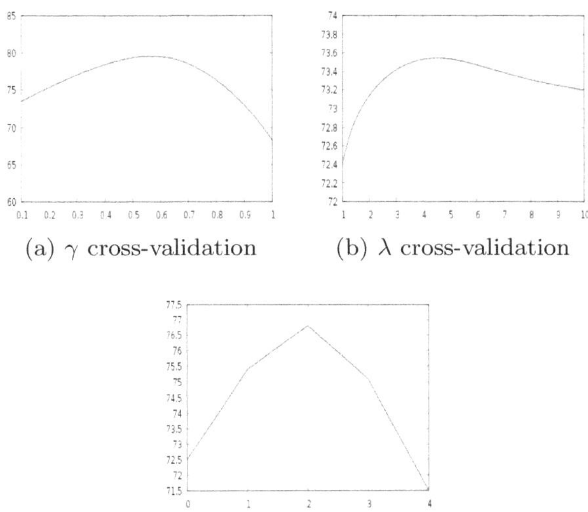

(a) γ cross-validation (b) λ cross-validation

(c) d_p cross-validation

Figure 2: Cross-validation experiments for the *FGVC-Aircraft* dataset.

5.3.2 *Final experiments*

In table 3, we report our final results compared to the best three runs reported in [7] on the *FGVC-Aircraft* dataset. It shows that our method outperforms the heavily tuned fisher vectors configurations of [7] as well as the of the deep convolutional neural network of [20] used in the CafeNet run. From table 3, we see that, for the *FGVC-Aircraft* dataset, the use of the geometric kernel gives better results than the use of the non-geometric kernel. This is mainly because aircrafts correspond to rigid objects involving rigid patterns to visually describe them. However, it is interesting to look at the result obtained by the non-geometric kernel that is not so bad compared to the geometric one while being less heavy in terms of computation time. This means that raw visual matches still bring quite enough information to solve fine-grained classification problems. Actually, this is also the case for aggregation-based method such as Fisher Vectors that also performs a sum-pooling scheme on soft-assignment of local features to the elements of a visual vocabulary. The result obtained by the early fusion scheme between non-geometric and geometric kernel clearly shows that geometric and non-geometric information are complementary and then combination of this two kinds of information leads to better classification performances. Please notice that only the fisher vector configuration S_B uses the same visual features as ours whereas the configuration S_A (and consequently $S_A + S_B$) uses some color features additionally. The real comparison of our method to the fisher vector encoding scheme should therefore rather be restricted to S_B. It is also important to note that the CafeNet run extensively made use of external training data to pre-train the deep convolutional neural network (i.e. ImageNet data).

Method	*FGVC-Aircraft*
CafeNet	78.85
Fisher Vectors S_A	75.88
Fisher Vectors S_B	80.59
Fisher Vectors $S_A + S_B$	81.46
Our method with non-geometric Kernel	**76.5**
Our method with geometric Kernel	**79.7**
Our method with early fusion	**82.8**

Table 3: Classification performances on the *FGVC-Aircraft* dataset measured by Mean Accuracy.

5.3.3 *Discussion on the computation time and complexity*

The respective complexity for the knn search procedure is $O(N^{1+\rho})$ (with $\rho < 1$) and the complexity of the construction of the explicit representation computation is $O(N * k)$ because we iterate over the k nearest neighbors of each points. The total complexity of the algorithm for the training phase is then $O(N * k + N^{1+\rho})$ and $O(N_{test} * k + N^{1+\rho})$ for the testing phase (with N and N_{test} the respective number of local features in the training and testing dataset) leading to a practical computation time of about 9 seconds per image (on a Bi-Xeon(R) E5-2650 CPU 2.00GHz) to compute its SNN-based explicit representation without the geometry embedding and 15 seconds with it for datasets like *FGVC-Aircraft*. It is important to note that this method can be considered as scalable when we look at the number of descriptors to be searched as nearest neighbors for each point of each image (about 122, 000, 000 descriptors for the *FGVC-Aircraft* training dataset).

6. CONCLUSION AND PERSPECTIVES

This paper introduced a new match kernel based on shared-nearest neighbors information and local geometric constraints. We did show that it allows to achieve high performance gains on instance based classification tasks involving pretty rigid objects and slightly better performances than state-of-the-art on two fine-grained classification challenges. The main perspective of this work is to complete the spatial pooling strategy used to aggregate the raw matches with a generative step aggregating the features in the visual space. Another perspective is to study more in details the trained visual patterns as we believe they might be highly interpretable thanks to the use of the geometry.

7. REFERENCES

[1] R. Arandjelovic and A. Zisserman. Three things everyone should know to improve object retrieval. In *Computer Vision and Pattern Recognition (CVPR), 2012 IEEE Conference on*, pages 2911–2918. IEEE, 2012.

[2] S. Boughorbel, J. P. Tarel, and N. Boujemaa. The intermediate matching kernel for image local features. In *Neural Networks, 2005. IJCNN'05. Proceedings. 2005 IEEE International Joint Conference on*, volume 2, pages 889–894. IEEE, 2005.

[3] Y. Chai, V. Lempitsky, and A. Zisserman. Symbiotic segmentation and part localization for fine-grained categorization. In *Computer Vision (ICCV), 2013 IEEE International Conference on*, pages 321–328. IEEE, 2013.

[4] O. Duchenne, A. Joulin, and J. Ponce. A graph-matching kernel for object categorization. In *Computer Vision*

(ICCV), 2011 IEEE International Conference on, pages 1792–1799. IEEE, 2011.

[5] L. Ertoz, M. Steinbach, and V. Kumar. A new shared nearest neighbor clustering algorithm and its applications. In *Workshop on Clustering High Dimensional Data and its Applications at 2nd SIAM International Conference on Data Mining*, pages 105–115, 2002.

[6] R.-E. Fan, K.-W. Chang, C.-J. Hsieh, X.-R. Wang, and C.-J. Lin. Liblinear: A library for large linear classification. *The Journal of Machine Learning Research*, 9:1871–1874, 2008.

[7] P.-H. Gosselin, N. Murray, H. Jégou, and F. Perronnin. Revisiting the Fisher vector for fine-grained classification. *Pattern Recognition Letters*, 49:92–98, Nov. 2014.

[8] K. Grauman and T. Darrell. The pyramid match kernel: Discriminative classification with sets of image features. In *Proceedings of the 10th International Conference on Computer Vision,ICCV*, volume 2, pages 1458–1465. IEEE Computer Society, 10 2005.

[9] M. Jain, R. Benmokhtar, H. Jégou, and P. Gros. Hamming embedding similarity-based image classification. In *Proceedings of the 2nd ACM International Conference on Multimedia Retrieval*, page 19. ACM, 2012.

[10] R. A. Jarvis and E. A. Patrick. Clustering using a similarity measure based on shared near neighbors. *Computers, IEEE Transactions on*, 100(11):1025–1034, 1973.

[11] H. Jegou, M. Douze, and C. Schmid. Hamming embedding and weak geometric consistency for large scale image search. In *ECCV*, 2008.

[12] H. Jegou, M. Douze, and C. Schmid. Product quantization for nearest neighbor search. *PAMI*, 2011.

[13] H. Jégou, F. Perronnin, M. Douze, C. Schmid, et al. Aggregating local image descriptors into compact codes. *Pattern Analysis and Machine Intelligence, IEEE Transactions on*, 34(9):1704–1716, 2012.

[14] Y.-G. Jiang, C.-W. Ngo, and J. Yang. Towards optimal bag-of-features for object categorization and semantic video retrieval. In *Proceedings of the 6th ACM international conference on Image and video retrieval*, pages 494–501. ACM, 2007.

[15] A. Joly and O. Buisson. A posteriori multi-probe locality sensitive hashing. In *Proceedings of the 16th ACM international conference on Multimedia*, pages 209–218. ACM, 2008.

[16] A. Joly and O. Buisson. Logo retrieval with a contrario visual query expansion. In *ACM MM*, 2009.

[17] A. Joly and O. Buisson. Random maximum margin hashing. In *CVPR*, 2011.

[18] H. JÃl'gou, M. Douze, and C. Schmid. Improving bag-of-features for large scale image search. *International Journal of Computer Vision*, 87:316–336, 2010.

[19] J. Krapac, F. Perronnin, T. Furon, and H. Jégou. Instance classification with prototype selection. In *ICMR*, 2014.

[20] A. Krizhevsky, I. Sutskever, and G. E. Hinton. Imagenet classification with deep convolutional neural networks. In *NIPS*, volume 1, page 4, 2012.

[21] S. Lazebnik, C. Schmid, and J. Ponce. Beyond bags of features: Spatial pyramid matching for recognizing natural scene categories. In *Computer Vision and Pattern Recognition, 2006 IEEE Computer Society Conference on*, volume 2, pages 2169–2178. IEEE, 2006.

[22] V. Leveau, A. Joly, O. Buisson, P. Letessier, and P. Valduriez. Recognizing Thousands of Legal Entities through Instance-based Visual Classification. In *ACM MM 14*, Orlando, FL, USA, Apr. 2014.

[23] D. Lowe. Object recognition from local scale-invariant features. In *ICCV*, 1999.

[24] Q. Lv, W. Josephson, Z. Wang, M. Charikar, and K. Li. Multi-probe lsh: efficient indexing for high-dimensional similarity search. In *Proceedings of the 33rd international conference on Very large data bases*, VLDB '07, pages 950–961. VLDB Endowment, 2007.

[25] S. Lyu. Mercer kernels for object recognition with local features. In *Computer Vision and Pattern Recognition, 2005. CVPR 2005. IEEE Computer Society Conference on*, volume 2, pages 223–229. IEEE, 2005.

[26] K. Mikolajczyk, T. Tuytelaars, C. Schmid, A. Zisserman, J. Matas, F. Schaffalitzky, T. Kadir, and L. Van Gool. A comparison of affine region detectors. *International journal of computer vision*, 65(1-2):43–72, 2005.

[27] F. Perronnin and C. Dance. Fisher kernels on visual vocabularies for image categorization. In *CVPR*, 2007.

[28] F. Perronnin, J. Sánchez, and T. Mensik. Improving the fisher kernel for large-scale image classification. In *ECCV*, 2010.

[29] J. Philbin, O. Chum, M. Isard, J. Sivic, and A. Zisserman. Lost in quantization: Improving particular object retrieval in large scale image databases. In *CVPR*, 2008.

[30] S. Romberg, L. G. Pueyo, R. Lienhart, and R. van Zwol. Scalable logo recognition in real-world images. In *ICMR*, 2011.

[31] K. Simonyan, A. Vedaldi, and A. Zisserman. Deep Fisher networks for large-scale image classification. In *Advances in Neural Information Processing Systems*, 2013.

[32] J. Sivic and A. Zisserman. Video google: A text retrieval approach to object matching in videos. In *CVPR*, 2003.

[33] T. Tuytelaars, M. Fritz, K. Saenko, and T. Darrell. The nbnn kernel. In *Computer Vision (ICCV), 2011 IEEE International Conference on*, pages 1824–1831. IEEE, 2011.

[34] J. van Gemert, C. Veenman, A. Smeulders, and J. Geusebroek. Visual word ambiguity. *Pattern Analysis and Machine Intelligence, IEEE Transactions on*, 32(7):1271–1283, 2010.

[35] F. Wang, W.-L. Zhao, C.-W. Ngo, and B. Merialdo. A hamming embedding kernel with informative bag-of-visual words for video semantic indexing. *ACM Transactions on Multimedia Computing, Communications, and Applications (TOMCCAP)*, 10(3):26, 2014.

[36] J. Wang, J. Yang, K. Yu, F. Lv, T. Huang, and Y. Gong. Locality-constrained linear coding for image classification. In *Computer Vision and Pattern Recognition (CVPR), 2010 IEEE Conference on*, pages 3360–3367. IEEE, 2010.

[37] J. Yang, K. Yu, Y. Gong, and T. Huang. Linear spatial pyramid matching using sparse coding for image classification. In *Computer Vision and Pattern Recognition, 2009. CVPR 2009. IEEE Conference on*, pages 1794–1801. IEEE, 2009.

High-Dimensional Indexing by Sparse Approximation

Pedro Borges, André Mourão and João Magalhães
Dept. Computer Science
Universidade Nova Lisboa
Campus de Caparica
{p.borges,a.mourao}@campus.fct.unl.pt, jm.magalhaes@fct.unl.pt

ABSTRACT

In this paper we propose a high-dimensional indexing technique, based on sparse approximation techniques to speed up the search and retrieval of similar images given a query image feature vector. Feature vectors are stored on an inverted indexed based on a sparsifying dictionary for l_0 regression, optimized to reduce the data dimensionality. It concentrates the energy of the original vector on a few coefficients of a higher dimensional representation. The index explores the coefficient locality of the sparse representations, to guide the search through the inverted index. Evaluation on three large-scale datasets showed that our method compares favorably to the state-of-the-art. On a 1 million dataset of SIFT vectors, our method achieved 60.8% precision at 50 by inspecting only 5% of the full dataset, and by using only 1/4 of the time a linear search takes.

Categories and Subject Descriptors

H.3.3 [**Information Search and Retrieval**]

Keywords

High-dimensional indexing; image indexing; Approximate nearest neighbor search; Sparse coding; l_0 penalty

1. INTRODUCTION

New approaches to the problem of nearest neighbor search shows that it is possible to achieve good scalability as the number of dimensions increase by trading precision over speed. That is, by giving only a probabilistic guarantee that the top k most similar documents are retrieved.

In a metric space S, multimedia information is represented as feature vectors $x = (x_1, \ldots, x_n)$, where $x_i \in \mathbb{R}$ and n is the dimensionality of the space. Let $S \subseteq Fv$ be a set of document feature vectors, were Fv is the set of all possible feature vectors, and $d : Fv \times Fv \to \mathbb{R}_0^+$ a metric. Formally, the k-Nearest Neighbors Query is defined as follows: given a pair (q, k) with $q \in Fv$ and $k \in \mathbb{N}^+$, retrieve from S the k most similar vectors to q. Formally, we wish to retrieve a set of vectors $Y = \{y_1, y_2, \ldots, y_k\}$ such that, $\forall y_i \in Y$, $\forall x_i \in S - Y$, $d(q, y_i) \leq d(q, x_i)$.

A linear scan on the metric space S, is not feasible when the cardinality of S grows rapidly. Recent approaches have relaxed the search process by either (i) hashing the vectors into a Hamming embedding [2,5,6,19] where the metric function as a very low computational cost, or (ii) leveraging the probabilistic density of data to reduce the search space complexity [11,12,14,23,25]. As we shall see in the related work section, there are several recent data structures that can answer approximate nearest-neighbor searches more efficiently by avoiding scanning the entire set of feature vectors.

The hypothesis we address in this paper is that retrieval efficiency can be improved by designing a dictionary for mapping the feature vectors onto sparse feature vectors embedded in a higher dimensional space. This space preserves locality structure on the non-zero coefficients of the sparse representation. That is, similar feature vectors in the original feature space should yield similar feature vectors in the target vector space. The left side of Figure 1 depicts an ideal case where two similar feature vectors, represented by similar blue colors are transformed into sparse feature vectors matching many of their non-zero coefficients. Conversely, dissimilar feature vectors in the original space would be mapped to vectors with different non-zero coefficients, right side of Figure 1.

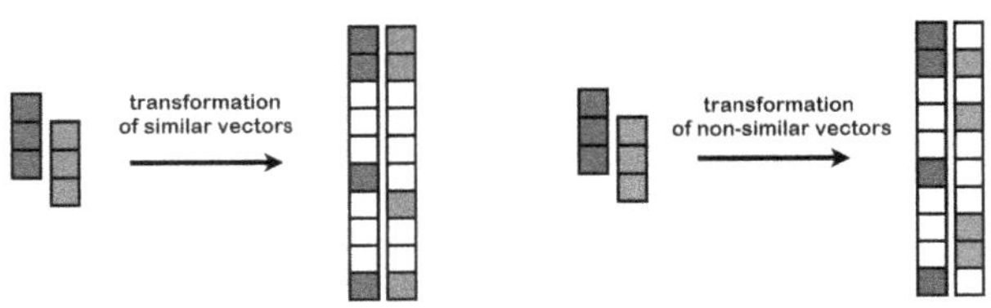

Figure 1: Insertion in the index. The colored positions on each vector are the non-null coefficients.

Our contributions are two-fold: we describe a sparsifying dictionary design process based on l_0 regression and an adapted K-SVD algorithm that explores feature vector locality and an indexing and retrieval system, optimized for the high-dimensional sparse space.

This paper is organized as follows: first we review approximate nearest neighbor techniques; in section 3 we formalize our indexing by sparse approximation method; section 4 describes the sparse regression algorithms; section 5 details the sparsifying dictionary and section 6 details the evaluation.

ICMR '15 June 23 - 26, 2015, Shanghai, China
Copyright 2015 ACM ISBN 978-1-4503-3274-3/15/06 ...$15.00.
DOI: http://dx.doi.org/10.1145/2671188.2749371.

2. RELATED WORK

Indexes that use space partitioning to improve the performance of exact similarity search were refined over the years so they could index bigger multimedia repositories and generate better space partitions. However, this improvements become more and more marginal as the dimensionality of the indexed features increases, [24]. The effectiveness of the index can degrade so much that a linear scan over all features might be faster than using the index. This fundamental difficulty lead researchers to investigate new kinds of similarity queries that drop the exactness requirement and do not use the dissimilarity function to partition the search space in order to improve the search performance.

Algorithms for approximate similarity search tackle the complexity of searching high-dimensional spaces by trading precision over performance. Some approximate methods rely on the trees, combined with a dimensionality reduction approach (e.g. PCA). A second family of techniques which have received much attention recently, are hash-based techniques. These techniques transform the original feature space into a Hamming embedding, where each sample is represented as a binary code. Similar feature vectors are converted to the same binary code (bucket), causing a collision. Thus, nearby buckets are within a short Hamming distance.

The Locality Sensitive Hashing (LSH), [2], is an indexing algorithm that can answer both randomized c-approximate R-near neighbor queries and randomized R-near neighbor queries. LSH hashes similar features to the same bins with more probability than dissimilar features. The algorithm is applicable when the features are real or boolean vectors and an appropriate family of hash functions exists for the employed similarity metric. These approaches, rely in hash functions that are either random [5, 8, 19], or deterministic because they follow a given structure, e.g., a grid [24] or a distribution [6].

More recent approaches to multimedia indexing [10, 12, 14, 23, 25] try to leverage the latent relationships in the data to guide the construction of representations and data-structures to accelerate similarity queries. Using machine learning techniques to learn these relationships it is possible to beat the search speed and accuracy of the LSH algorithm. Spherical hashing [9] is a data depended variant of LSH that partitions the high-dimensional query space in hyperspheres instead of hyperplanes. Torralba et al. [23] propose a method to learn small binary feature vectors from real valued vector features using Boosting. Hinton et al. [10] generate compact hash representations using an autoencoder based on Restricted Boltzmann machines. Spectral Hashing [25] binary codes are calculated by thresholding a subset of eigenvectors of the Laplacian of the similarity graph.

Approaches based in binary codes and Hamming distances make it possible to search millions of multimedia documents in less than a second. However, it still requires a linear search to be performed over the entire dataset. Other approaches, explore a divide-and-conquer strategy to tackle the large-scale scalability problem. Li et al. [14] proposed learning a data structure that balances between precision and computational cost. Based in boosted search forests, it can naturally be integrated in a search index. Jegou et al. [12, 13] proposed a series of methods that rely on an inverted index to organize the data into manageable parts. The inverted index [12] is constructed with a balanced K-means that quantizes the feature space into codewords with similar priors [20]. The sparse hashing method proposed by Zhu et al. [26], departs from the dense codes and designs large but sparse binary codes. MSIDX [21] is a novel technique that explores the divide-and-conquer strategy. It is based on the theory that descriptors' dimensions with higher cardinality have higher discriminative power. The algorithm multi-sorts the indexed descriptors according to their value cardinalities. Indexed descriptors are re-ordered with descriptors higher values on the most discriminative dimensions being most important. The querying algorithm follows the same principle: the closest match to the query is found using the sort algorithm.

3. EFFICIENT SIMILARITY MATCHING WITH SPARSE REPRESENTATIONS

The careful transformation of data into a high-dimensional, but sparse approximations can achieve a high degree of compression. This new space preserves locality structure on the non-zero coefficients of the sparse representation. That is, similar feature vectors in the original feature space should yield similar feature vectors in the the target vector space. Conversely, dissimilar feature vectors in the original space would be mapped to a vectors with different non-zero coefficients. With such locality preserving transformation, finding similar feature vectors in higher dimensional space would be as simple as checking which other sparse representations had non-zero coefficients in the same coefficients as the query, and rank those candidates with the original metric. A setup like this has three major advantages:

- traversing the data structure does not depend on the metric function, which allow us to avoid the previously discussed limitations of the tree indexes and other indexes based on space partitioning;
- sparse representations can be encoded efficiently in terms of space which should make it possible to build an index for a dataset with low storage overhead;
- it is more efficient than searching the entire search space, since the representations are sparse only a small number of coefficients would have to be searched for similar vectors. Hence, using this mechanism enables search space pruning.

Mathematically, these goals can be expressed as an optimization problem:

$$\begin{gathered} \operatorname{argmin}_{A,X} \|B - AX\|_F^2 \\ \text{subject to} \\ \|X_i\|_0 \leq k \\ \text{for } i = 0, 1, \cdots, n \end{gathered} \tag{1}$$

where A is the dictionary, B is a matrix where each column is a measurement vector, X is the matrix where each column X_i is the sparse signal recovered for the measurement vector B_i, k is the sparsity threshold for each signal and n is the number of columns of X. Solving this problem for A and X simultaneously is computational hard due to the presence of the l_0 norm and the non-convexity of the problem in both A and X. In this process there are two main components: the sparse approximation procedure to solve Eq. (1), section

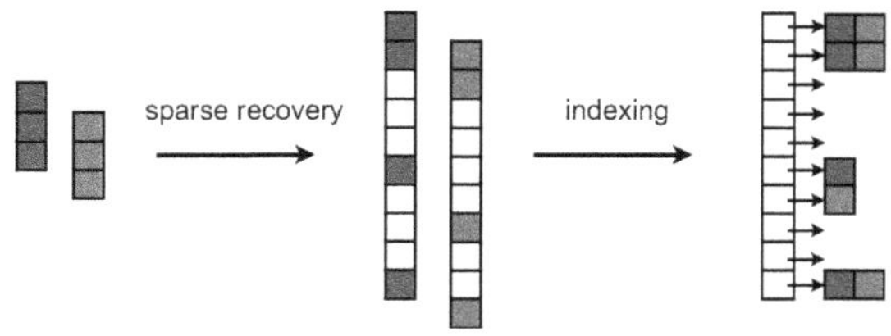

Figure 2: Collision of similar descriptors.

4 and the sparsifying dictionary A that preserves locality information in high-dimensional spaces, section 5.

3.1 Inverted indexes

The construction of the inverted index for sparse representations is illustrated by Figure 2. It shows the indexing of two descriptors using their sparse representations. Algorithm 1 describes the indexing construction process. Given a set of descriptors B, we can recover their sparse solutions X with a dictionary A (line 3) (section 5). This sparse representation can be interpreted as determining the atoms of the dictionary whose coefficient are non-zero. The goal is to build an index to efficiently retrieve feature vectors whose sparse representation contains the same atoms as the query feature vectors, line 6. The final step is to sort each bucket, by placing the descriptors with higher coefficients at the beginning, line 8. This final sort is necessary so that, at query time, the most representative descriptors of each bucket are examined first.

If the sparse recovery of the descriptors preserves similarity in the sparse domain, the inverted index can be used to retrieve similar descriptors for a given query, by inspecting the lists corresponding to its non-zero coefficients in the sparse domain. The ideal situation is depicted in Figure 2 were two similar descriptors are indexed in many common positions.

Algorithm 1 Indexing algorithm

Input: a sparsifying dictionary A, a set of vectors to index B.
Output: Inverted index I with $cols(A)$ buckets

1: $I \leftarrow []$
2: **for** b_i in B **do**
3: $\quad x_i \leftarrow sparseApproximation(A, b_i)$
4: $\quad$ **for** j in $1, ..., dim(x_i)$ **do**
5: $\quad\quad$ **if** $x_{ij} \neq 0$ **then**
6: $\quad\quad\quad I_j \leftarrow I_j \cup \{x_{ij}, b_i\}$
7: **for** I_j in I **do**
8: $\quad I_j \leftarrow sortByCoef(I_j)$ $\quad\triangleright$ sort vectors by $coef_j$
9: **return** I

The per document memory overhead of the indexing structure is $O(2L)$, where L is the number of non-zero coefficients (set to be at most 10), and 2 represents bucket metadata: document id and bucket coefficient value.

3.2 Retrieval

The task of the retrieval algorithm is to search for descriptors that have a collision in the buckets where the non-zero coefficients of the sparse representation of the query are located. The search procedure gives priority to the buckets where the coefficients are larger. Intuitively, this tries to exploit the fact that sparse regression greedy algorithms for sparse regression, select the most correlated atom of the dictionary first.

Algorithm 2 describes the retrieval process, given the previously computed index I. When the user submits a query q, its sparse representation is recovered, line 2. Then, the coefficients $x_{0,\dots,i}$ (that correspond to the buckets) of the sparse representation are extracted and sorted in descending order according to their absolute values, line 3. Buckets with higher coefficient values are visited first. The search algorithm visits each bucket adding each feature vector found in a temporary candidates (*cand*) list, line 10. This process continues until the procedure visits every entry of the index or the limit for the visited feature vectors is reached, lines 6 and 9. After the search stops, the descriptors in the temporary list are sorted by their distance to the query, line 16 and the k closest descriptors returned, line 17.

Algorithm 2 Retrieval procedure

Input: a sparsifying dictionary A, an inverted index I, a set of indexed vectors B, a query vector q, the number of neighbors to retrieve k and a percentage of the index to examine w.
Output: a list of k (nearest) neighbors R.

1: $limit \leftarrow w \times len(b)$
2: $X \leftarrow sparseApproximation(A, q)$
3: $O \leftarrow sortCoefs(X)$ $\quad\triangleright$ get sorted coefficients
4: $cand \leftarrow \emptyset$
5: $i \leftarrow 0$
6: **while** $len(cand) < limit \cap i < len(O)$ **do**
7: $\quad bucket \leftarrow O_i$
8: $\quad j \leftarrow 0$
9: $\quad$ **while** $len(cand) < limit \cap j < len(I_{bucket})$ **do**
10: $\quad\quad cand \leftarrow cand \cup I_{bucket,j}$
11: $\quad\quad j \leftarrow j + 1$
12: $\quad i \leftarrow i + 1$
13: $R \leftarrow []$
14: **for** c in $cands$ **do**
15: $\quad R \leftarrow R \cup \{\|q, c\|_2, c\}$
16: $R \leftarrow sortByNorm(R)$ $\quad\triangleright$ Perform final l_2 re-ranking
17: **return** $R_{1,\dots,k}$

4. SPARSE APPROXIMATIONS

The proposed inverted indexed is based on the l_0 or l_1 regression for obtaining the high-dimensional sparse representations. This algorithm is fundamental in reducing the data dimensionality, by concentrating the energy of the original vector on a few coefficients of a higher dimensional space. The sparse reconstruction algorithm should answer two requirements: (1) be sufficiently fast to be run in query time, (2) compute highly sparse representations while preserving maximum locality. In this section we compare four candidate algorithms for our sparse reconstruction step.

4.1 l_0 approximations

The sparse approximation can be viewed as the recovery of a k-sparse signal from its measurement vector given a dictionary. A possible way is to solve the constrained l_0

minimization problem,

$$\min_{x} \|Ax - b\|_2 \quad \text{subject to} \quad \|x\|_0 \leq k, \tag{2}$$

where $A \in \mathbb{R}^{m \times n}$ is the dictionary, $b \in \mathbb{R}^m$ the measurement vector, and k is the sparsity factor that we wish to obtain. By solving the relaxed problem we allow the recovery of sparser solutions even though these solutions violate the equality constrains by a small margin. Next, we describe two greedy algorithms that selects the atoms at each iteration that have the best fit according to a rule to integrate the solution.

Orthogonal Matching Pursuit. The basic idea behind the OMP algorithm, [18], is to, at each iteration, choose the atom of the dictionary that best correlates with the residual, a vector holding the recovery error using the currently selected atoms. Initially, the residual vector, r, is set to the measurement vector and the solution vector x is set to a zero vector, since no atom of the dictionary was selected. In the iterative procedure, each iteration computes the correlation between each atom of the dictionary and the residual. With the correlations computed the atom with the maximum correlation is considered to integrate the solution.

Thresholding. The thresholding algorithm can be seen as a simplification of the OMP algorithm described before. Instead of taking multiple steps and making a greedy decision, thresholding uses just one step where it picks the most correlated atoms with the measurements to take part in the solution.

4.2 l_1 approximations

The sparse recovery problem has an inherently combinatorial nature due to the usage of the l_0 norm. An alternative research direction to the greedy algorithms presented in the previous subsection has been the reformulation of the sparse recovery into a problem that exhibits properties that allow the usage of efficient optimization algorithms and, under certain conditions, can still recover the original sparse solution.

One of the possible modifications to the optimization problem is to replace the l_0 norm with another function f. Results by Tao and Candés [4] and Donoho and Elad [7] demonstrate conditions under which the minimization of the l_1 norm leads to the same solution as the l_0 norm. Thus, in this section we describe algorithms to solve the sparse recovery problem using the l_1 norm:

$$\min_{x \in \mathbb{R}^n} \|x\|_1 \quad \text{subject to} \quad Ax = b \tag{3}$$

Fast Iterative Shrinkage Thresholding Algorithm. FISTA, [3], is an algorithm that solves problem 3 by taking an unconstrained approximation of the original problem. FISTA has its roots in the iterative soft thresholding algorithm (ISTA). ISTA iterates by solving the unconstrained problem at a given point using a thresholding function and then taking a gradient step from the local optimal point. FISTA improves the ISTA algorithm by using an improved method to determine the next point at which the minimization step is evaluated that guarantees faster convergence.

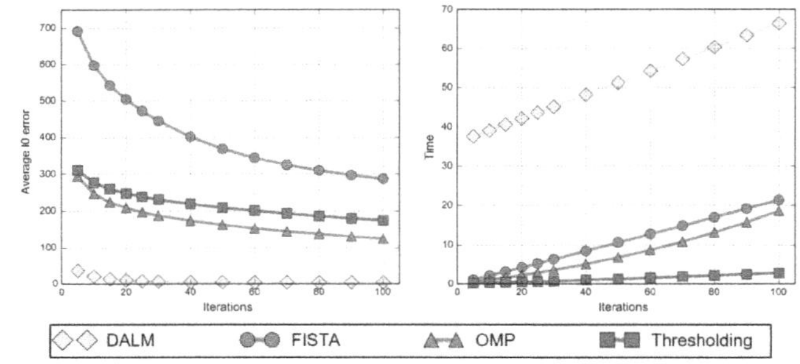

Figure 3: Average recovery error (a) and time (b) over 100 iteration on a 504 dimensional space; (c) DALM recovery after 100 iterations using 30 dimensions zoomed.

Augmented Lagrangian Methods. Augmented Lagrangian Methods extend the unconstrained problem with quadratic penalization, by adding a Lagrangian term to the objective function. The addition of this term improves the conditioning of the problem and guarantees the convergence under more general assumptions, [16]. A lower bound for the solution of the problem can be obtained by solving the dual problem of the augmented objective function which is more efficient than solving the original problem.

4.3 Experimental comparison of reconstruction time, sparsity and error

Figure 3 illustrates the recovery time and error for the implemented algorithms. DALM exhibits an interesting behavior with an almost constant and low recovery error. A more careful look into the coefficients computed by DALM showed that the solutions have a very large number of near-zero coefficients, which defeats our sparse index goal. In terms of recovery time the OMP and the Thresholding methods were the best. We chose OMP, as it delivers the lowest recovery error with a sparse solution and its the second fastest method.

5. SPARSIFYING DICTIONARY

Our inverted index structure is designed to use a dictionary created to yield sparse representations that approximate the original feature vectors. In this section we describe the dictionary construction algorithm, a modified K-SVD [1] algorithm, to explicitly take into account the proximity between the descriptors used in its training. The idea is to add a penalty term to the dictionary learning problem that promotes similar descriptors to have similar sparse representations. Ideally, this penalty would take into account all pair-wise distances between the descriptors of the training dataset. In practice that approach is infeasible for learning dictionaries from large datasets of examples because the size of the problem would scale at least quadratically with the number of training examples. To simplify the optimization problem we group the training descriptors in clusters according to their similarity and penalize the differences in the sparse representations within the cluster at once.

Instead of computing a new dictionary all at once, K-SVD iteratively optimizes each atom and their corresponding coefficients in the sparse representations. For the dictionary update step the alternate optimization scheme is achieved by splitting the contributions of each atom and the respective coefficients for the value of the objective function, f:

$$\begin{aligned} f &= \|AX - B\|_F^2 \\ f &= \|A_i X_{\text{row}(i)} + \textstyle\sum_{j \neq i} A_j X_{\text{row}(j)} - B\|_F^2 \\ f &= \|A_i c_i + \textstyle\sum_{j \neq i} A_j c_j - B\|_F^2, \end{aligned} \tag{4}$$

here c_i is the row of the matrix X holding the coefficients for the atom A_i of the dictionary. The last expression in 4 immediately suggests the alternative optimization used by K-SVD. For each atom of the dictionary, the algorithm fixes the other atoms and the respective coefficients and iteratively solves problems of the form:

$$\underset{A_i, c_i}{\text{argmin}} \|A_i c_i + E_i\|_F^2 \tag{5}$$

where $E_i = (\sum_{j \neq i} A_j c_j - B)$ and A_i and c_i are the new atom and its new coefficients respectively. Since A_i is a column vector and c_i is a row vector their product results in a matrix with rank-1, so the problem 5 is equivalent to finding the rank-1 matrix approximation of E_i and then factoring this matrix into the vector A_i and c_i. The SVD factorization that gives name to the algorithm provides a convenient way to determine the approximation matrix and a suitable factorization at once. Given the matrix $E_i \in \mathbb{R}^{m \times n}$ its SVD factorization is given by:

$$E_i = G \Sigma V^T.$$

Assuming that the singular vectors in the matrix Σ are sorted in decreasing order through its diagonal, the best rank-1 approximation matrix for the matrix E_i is:

$$approx(E_i) = G \Sigma^1 V^T$$

where Σ^1 is the matrix Σ where every entry but $\Sigma_{0,0}$, the entry corresponding to the largest singular value, are null. The factorization into the new A_i and c_i can be done by taking $A_i = G_0$ and $c_i = \Sigma^1_{0,0} V_{\text{row}(0)}$, this makes the product equivalent to the factorization 5 since the null entries of Σ_1 cancel every other column of G and row of V^T.

The optimization procedure described previously reduces the recovery error of the system but has the undesirable effect of producing coefficient vectors c_i less sparse than the originals since the sparsity is not enforced anywhere during the decomposition. To overcome this problem, only the subset of signals with non zero coefficients in the dictionary atom under consideration take part in the optimization. Assuming I is the set including the index of all signals with non-zero coefficients in A_i atom the update step is:

$$\underset{A_i, (c_i)_I}{\text{argmin}} \|A_i (c_i)_I + (E_i)_I\|_F^2.$$

6. EXPERIMENTS

In this section we present the initial experiments to determine the number of iterations of the dictionary training algorithm and other parameters. A thorough set of experiments were then run over 3 large-scale datasets where we compared our method to other methods (which include state-of-the-art solutions). All experiments were run on a machine with an i7-3930K processor and 64GB of RAM. All descriptors, indexes and other structures were placed in the main memory. The code for the Sparse Approximation (SA) indexer is available online [1].

6.1 Datasets

We tested 3 datasets for the large-scale indexing experiments: the Tiny Images dataset, [22] and the Billion vectors dataset (2 feature types) [12]. These datasets were used to train the indexing dictionaries, to build the indexes and provide query examples. These datasets were also previously used in the literature in the same settings [25].

The Tiny Images dataset [22], contains over 80 million images and the corresponding GIST descriptors [17] with 384 dimensions. This makes the dataset particularly adequate to simulate the conditions of a large-scale high-dimensional search. All descriptors are stored in a single contiguous binary file of floating point numbers.

The Billion vectors dataset [12], contains over 1 billion feature vectors. It was designed to evaluate the quality of nearest neighbors search algorithm with different descriptors and database sizes. A subset of 1 million images [12] and their GIST and SIFT descriptors (960 and 128 dimensions, respectively), are divided into training, indexing and testing subsets.

6.2 Experiment Design

6.2.1 Data Setup

The datasets were split into a training, validation and test subsets (see Table 6.2.1). For BV1 and BV2, we used the splits provided by the authors[2] for comparison. As the provided splits don't provide validation vectors, we selected the validation set randomly from the training set. For the TI, we used 3 disjoint data setups extracted from the original dataset. The results are the average of all data setup results.

6.2.2 Methods

We tested our Sparse Approximation (*SA*) method against a set of widely known indexing algorithms:

- **Trees:** [15] provides a k-means tree (*kMeansTree*), a randomized kd-tree (*kdTree*) and an exhaustive linear search (*Linear*) implementations[3]; We varied the number of trees in the kd-tree algorithm and the branching factor in the k-means algorithm;
- **LSH:** we tested the implementation[4] described in [9], with multiple hash code sizes;
- **Spherical Hashing:** The tested implementation is described in [9], and based on exhaustive search in the index of training hashes with the Hamming (*SH*) and Spherical Hamming (*SH_shd*) distance. We tested multiple hash code sizes;
- **MSIDX:** The tested implementation[5] is from the original authors [21]. We varied the percentage of database to examine {0.5%, 1%, 2.5%, 5%, 10%, 15%, 20%, 25%, 30%, 40%, 50%};

[1] `https://novasearch.org/software/`
[2] `http://corpus-texmex.irisa.fr/`
[3] `http://www.cs.ubc.ca/research/flann/`
[4] `http://sglab.kaist.ac.kr/Spherical_Hashing/`
[5] `http://vcl.iti.gr/msidx/`

Table 1: Data types and setup. The last four columns contain the number of vectors used for training, validation index, validation queries, test index and test queries. Sets marked with an asterisk represent vectors extracted from the provided training set.

Name	Dataset	Features	Dims	Train vectors	Val. index	Val. queries	Test index	Test queries
TI	Tiny Image	GIST	384	100,000	100,000	1,000	1,000,000	1,000
BV1	Billion vectors	GIST	960	100,000*	100,000*	1,000*	1,000,000	1,000
BV2	Billion vectors	SIFT	128	49,000*	50,000*	1,000*	1,000,000	1,000

6.2.3 *Protocol*

We wanted to assess the efficiency and quality of the retrieval results of the proposed method, and compare it to other state-of-the-art methods. We opted for following metrics, widely used in the multimedia retrieval literature [9,21, 23]: **average precision @50 and @1000** vs. **query time** and vs. **inspected percentage of the dataset.**

For each query, we measure the retrieval efficiency of each method and compare the retrieval precision to the linear search output. Hence, the top k nearest neighbors correspond to the relevant items.

6.3 Parameters learning

The validation set was used to assess the combination of relevant parameters that yield the best results. The two main parameters that have a direct influence in the retrieval performance are the:

- **Bucket size:** as the number of buckets of the index increases the number of descriptor indexed per entry will decrease. In practice, this should lead to more discrimination in how close the other descriptors must be to be indexed in the same dimensions;
- **Number of indexed positions:** using more iterations of the OMP algorithm will result in the recovery of denser representations which means each vector is indexed in more buckets. In this case, the probability of collision between two descriptors increases. The goal is to find the best collision parameter for the index.

Figure 4 (a) shows the average percentage of the 50 nearest neighbors retrieved from indexes with 1024, 2048, 4096 and 8192 buckets, constrained to inspect just a fraction of the index descriptors. Due to space constrains, we will only display the results for the TI dataset with multiple bucket counts. The same behavior was observed on the other dataset. As a baseline, the blue dashed line represents a random limited linear search on an uniformly distributed dataset (examining 10% of the dataset returns 10% of relevant query results). This figure indicates a rapid increase in the number of neighbors found on average as the percentage of allowed descriptor inspections increases from 0 to 10% of the database.

Figure 4 (b) details the results in terms of query time versus retrieval precision. When examining this figure, we observe that a higher bucket size decreased the retrieval performance and increased query time. We reckon that this is due to the greedy nature of the indexing and querying algorithms.

Following this analysis, we set the bucket size to 1024, as we were able to achieve higher precision while reducing the query time when examining more than 3% of the dataset.

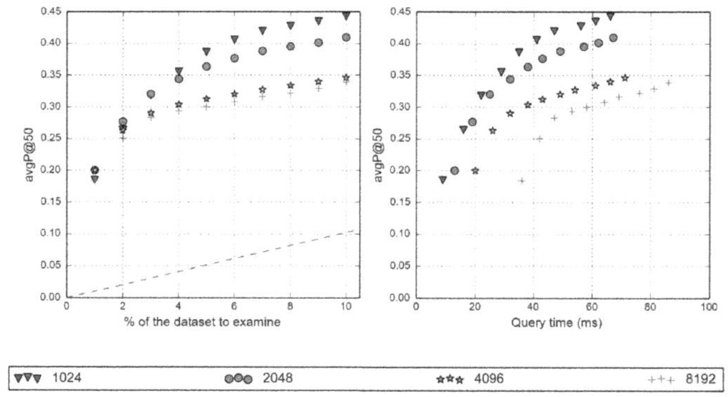

Figure 4: Average precision of the 50 nearest neighbors retrieved with limited number of index inspections for multiple bucket count. The dashed line represents a random linear search on a uniformly distributed dataset.

6.4 Results and discussion

In this section, we discuss the comparative performance (percentage of relevant documents retrieved vs. query time) of our method versus other state-of-the-art methods. The hashing based methods (LSH, SH and SH-shd) were tested with {64, 128, 256, 512} bit codes. The number of trees in the k-d-tree was set to {4, 8, 16, 32, 64, 128}. The kMeansTree branching factor was set to {16, 32, 64}. Both our method and MSIDX were set to inspect a fixed percentage of the index {1% ,2% ,3%, 4%, ... ,10% ,20% ,30% ,40% ... ,100%}. For each one of these methods/settings we measured retrieval time and precision.

6.4.1 *Robustness analysis*

To examine the global behavior in terms of robustness and stability of the tested methods, we compared the retrieval results for a long rank of documents ($k = 1000$) in all three datasets. Observing the first row of Figure 5, two major trends stand-out. The first trend occurs in the initial part of the curve where precision grows very rapidly as query time increases. In the second trend precision grows linearly towards the maximum possible precision. These two trends are more noticeable in the MSIDX method and the Sparse Approximation method. The different slopes indicate that both methods are optimized for efficiently retrieving the top nearest neighbors. As a consequence, after a given point, the curve slope is not as steep showing a loss in performance, as a side-effect of the top-results optimization. The same conclusions can be drawn from all datasets. Other hash-based methods do not exhibit these two trends.

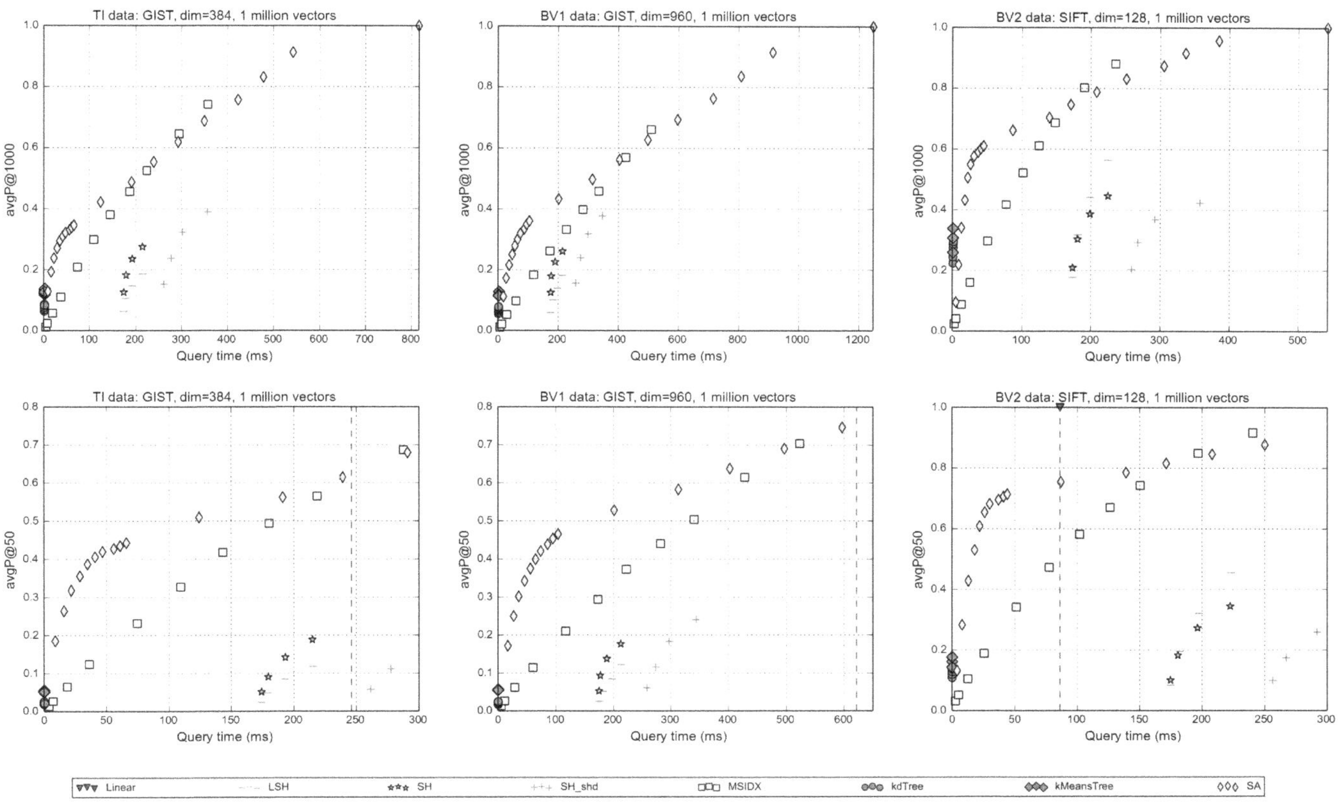

Figure 5: Average % of 1000 and 50 nearest neighbors retrieved vs. time per retrieved neighbor Comparative results for all datasets and algorithms.

6.4.2 *Top-precision analysis*

To assess the proposed algorithm on the top-retrieved results, we evaluated its performance on the top $k = 50$ results. Figure 5 shows the comparative results for $k = 50$. The vertical dashed line marks the linear search time (i.e., 100% precision).

All methods show a behavior similar to the 1000 nearest neighbor experiment. Both MSIDX and SA methods show the two trends but in a more pronounced way: there are two clearly different trends. In this experiment, the first trend is steeper which evidences how effective is the proposed sparse optimization framework at achieving a high precision on the top results.

On the second trend, which the SA optimization did not consider during the training phase, our method examines a larger percentage of the dataset (therefore examining more buckets), causing the performance to degrade, becoming sub-optimal.

In general, the SA results compare favorably to the other tested methods. The MSIDX algorithm scales linearly with the percentage of the dataset examined on all examined datasets. When examining a larger set of the dataset, MSIDX is able to be faster than our approach, but with a query time similar or slower than a linear search. LSH and variants (SH) achieve slower results: the algorithms' performance improve with the size of the binary codes, but they are still slower than the proposed method. The tested LSH-based algorithms also suffer a linear search in the Hamming space.

In the bottom row of Figure 5, we can carefully analyse the performance of the faster algorithms (faster than 100 ms). When looking closer at these results, we observe the full advantage of the proposed method: in the Tiny Images dataset, we achieved 38% precision by inspecting 5% of data and in less than 15% of the linear search time (5% of inspected data corresponds to the fifth point in the SA curve). When using SIFT features (BV2 dataset) we obtained 60.8% precision at 50, after inspecting only 5% of data in 25% of time a linear search takes.

In our experiments, tree-based algorithms were very fast, but at the cost of very low precisions. These methods were not able to retrieve more than a few of the nearest neighbors. The hashing based approaches were slower and can even be slower than linear searches.

7. CONCLUSION

In this paper we introduced a high-dimensional indexing structure and a matching retrieval algorithm by sparse approximation. We also refined the optimization of the dictionary used to index and retrieve descriptors to explicitly take into account the locality of their sparse representations. The described algorithms were analyzed in terms of retrieval quality, computational time and compared against existing state-of-the-art methods and other well-known indexing trees for a comprehensive evaluation.

The proposed indexing data structure compared favorably with the other state-of-the-art methods, achieving a precision of 60.8% by inspecting only 5% of the full dataset, and by using only 1/4 of the time a linear search takes in the same conditions.

We are currently researching how to improve the learned dictionary for indexing. More specifically we are researching the use of label information to adjust the dictionaries to non-linearities in the feature space.

Acknowledgements. This work has been partially funded by the projects PTDC/EIA-EIA/111518/2009 and UTA-Est/MAI/0010/2009 funded by the Portuguese National Foundation for Science and Technology (FCT).

8. REFERENCES

[1] M. Aharon, M. Elad, and A. Bruckstein. K-SVD: An Algorithm for Designing Overcomplete Dictionaries for Sparse Representation. *IEEE Trans. on Sig. Proc.*, 54(11):4311–4322, Nov. 2006.

[2] A. Andoni and P. Indyk. Near-optimal hashing algorithms for approximate nearest neighbor in high dimensions. *ACM Commun.*, 51(1):117–122, Jan. 2008.

[3] A. Beck and M. Teboulle. A fast iterative shrinkage-thresholding algorithm for linear inverse problems. *SIAM J. Img. Sci.*, 2(1):183–202, Mar. 2009.

[4] E. J. Candes and T. Tao. Decoding by Linear Programming. *IEEE Transactions on Information Theory*, 51(12):4203–4215, Dec. 2005.

[5] O. Chum, J. Philbin, and A. Zisserman. Near duplicate image detection: min-hash and tf-idf weighting. In *BMVC'08*, 2008.

[6] M. Datar, N. Immorlica, P. Indyk, and V. S. Mirrokni. Locality-sensitive hashing scheme based on p-stable distributions. In *SCG'04*, pages 253–262, New York, NY, USA, 2004. ACM.

[7] D. L. Donoho and M. Elad. Optimally sparse representation in general (non-orthogonal) dictionaries via l1 minimization. In *Proc. Natl Acad. Sci.*, 2002.

[8] A. Gionis, P. Indyk, and R. Motwani. Similarity search in high dimensions via hashing. In *VLDB'99*, VLDB '99, pages 518–529, San Francisco, CA, USA, 1999. Morgan Kaufmann Publishers Inc.

[9] J.-P. Heo, Y. Lee, J. He, S.-F. Chang, and S.-E. Yoon. Spherical hashing. In *CVPR'12*, pages 2957–2964, June 2012.

[10] G. E. Hinton and R. R. Salakhutdinov. Reducing the dimensionality of data with neural networks. *Science*, 313(5786):504–507, 2006.

[11] H. Jégou, M. Douze, and C. Schmid. Hamming embedding and weak geometric consistency for large scale image search. In *ECCV'08*, ECCV '08, pages 304–317, Berlin, Heidelberg, 2008.

[12] H. Jégou, M. Douze, and C. Schmid. Product quantization for nearest neighbor search. *Pattern Analysis and Machine Intelligence, IEEE Transactions on*, 33(1):117–128, 2011.

[13] H. Jégou, T. Furon, and J.-J. Fuchs. Anti-sparse coding for approximate nearest neighbor search. In *ICASSP'12*, pages 2029–2032, 2012.

[14] Z. Li, H. Ning, L. Cao, T. Zhan, Y. Gong, and T. S. Huang. Learning to search efficiently in high dimensions. In *NIPS'11*, 2011.

[15] M. Muja and D. G. Lowe. Fast approximate nearest neighbors with automatic algorithm configuration. In *International Conference on Computer Vision Theory and Application VISSAPP'09)*, pages 331–340. INSTICC Press, 2009.

[16] J. Nocedal and S. J. Wright. *Numerical Optimization.* Springer, Aug. 2000.

[17] A. Oliva and A. Torralba. Modeling the shape of the scene: A holistic representation of the spatial envelope. *Int. J. Comput. Vision*, 42:145–175, May 2001.

[18] Y. Pati, R. Rezaiifar, and P. Krishnaprasad. Orthogonal Matching Pursuit : recursive function approximation with application to wavelet decomposition. In *Asilomar Conf. on Signals, Systems and Computer*, 1993.

[19] M. Raginsky and S. Lazebnik. Locality-sensitive binary codes from shift-invariant kernels. In *NIPS*, pages 1509–1517, 2009.

[20] R. Tavenard, H. Jégou, and L. Amsaleg. Balancing clusters to reduce response time variability in large scale image search. In *CBMI'11*, Madrid, Spain, June 2011.

[21] E. Tiakas, D. Rafailidis, A. Dimou, and P. Daras. Msidx: Multi-sort indexing for efficient content-based image search and retrieval. *Multimedia, IEEE Transactions on*, 15(6):1415–1430, Oct 2013.

[22] A. Torralba, R. Fergus, and W. Freeman. 80 million tiny images: A large data set for nonparametric object and scene recognition. *IEEE Trans on PAMI'08*, 30(11):1958–1970, Nov 2008.

[23] A. Torralba, R. Fergus, and Y. Weiss. Small codes and large image databases for recognition. In *Computer Vision and Pattern Recognition, 2008. CVPR 2008. IEEE Conference on*, pages 1–8, June 2008.

[24] R. Weber, H.-J. Schek, and S. Blott. A quantitative analysis and performance study for similarity-search methods in high-dimensional spaces. In *VLDB'98*, pages 194–205, San Francisco, CA, USA, 1998. Morgan Kaufmann Publishers Inc.

[25] Y. Weiss, A. Torralba, and R. Fergus. Spectral hashing. *NIPS*, 9(1):6, 2008.

[26] X. Zhu, Z. Huang, H. Cheng, J. Cui, and H. T. Shen. Sparse hashing for fast multimedia search. *ACM Trans. Inf. Syst.*, 31(2):9:1–9:24, May 2013.

Diffusion-on-Manifold Aggregation of Local Features for Shape-based 3D Model Retrieval

Takahiko Furuya
University of Yamanashi
4-3-11 Takeda, Kofu-shi
Yamanashi-ken, 400-8511, Japan
+81-55-220-8570
g13dm003AT yamanashi.ac.jp

Ryutarou Ohbuchi
University of Yamanashi
4-3-11 Takeda, Kofu-shi
Yamanashi-ken, 400-8511, Japan
+81-55-220-8570
ohbuchiAT yamanashi.ac.jp

ABSTRACT

Aggregating a set of local features has become one of the most common approaches for representing a multi-media data such as 2D image and 3D model. The success of Bag-of-Features (BF) aggregation [2] prompted several extensions to BF, that are, VLAD [12], Fisher Vector (FV) coding [22] and Super Vector (SV) coding [34]. They all learn small number of codewords, or representative local features, by clustering a set of large number of local features. The set of local features extracted from a media data (e.g., an image) is encoded by considering distribution of features around the codewords; BF uses frequency, VLAD and FV uses displacement vector, and SV uses a combination of both. In doing so, these encoding algorithms assume linearity of feature space about a codeword. Consequently, even if the set of features form a non-linear manifold, its non-linearity would be ignored, potentially degrading quality of aggregated features. In this paper, we propose a novel feature aggregation algorithm called *Diffusion-on-Manifold (DM)* that tries to take into account, via diffusion distance, structure of non-linear manifold formed by the set of local features. In view of 3D shape retrieval, we also propose a local 3D shape feature defined for oriented point set. Experiments using shape-based 3D model retrieval scenario show that the DM aggregation results in better retrieval accuracy than the existing aggregation algorithms we've compared against, that are, VLAD, FV, and SV, etc.

Categories and Subject Descriptors

H.3.3 [**Information Search and Retrieval**]: Information filtering. I.2.10 [**Vision and Scene Understanding**]: 3D/stereo scene analysis.

General Terms

Algorithms, Experimentation.

Keywords

Feature aggregation, content-based retrieval, manifold learning, manifold ranking, diffusion distance, local feature, bag-of-features, sparse coding, fisher vector, super vector, 3D shape, 3D oriented point set.

ICMR '15, June 23 - 26, 2015, Shanghai, China
Copyright 2015 ACM 978-1-4503-3274-3/15/06…$15.00
http://dx.doi.org/10.1145/2671188.2749380

1. INTRODUCTION

Majority of state-of-the-art shape-based 3D model retrieval (3DMR) algorithms represent a 3D model as a set of local features extracted from its 3D geometry or 2D appearances [4, 5, 6, 14, 15, 17, 19, 20]. Using a set of local features with an appropriate aggregation algorithm yields a 3D shape descriptor robust against articulation or global deformation of 3D models. Aggregation of local feature also make comparison among a pair of 3D models much more efficient than comparing local features individually.

Bag-of-Features (BF) [2] (Figure 1a) is first-of-a-kind local feature aggregation algorithm and is widely used to realize classification, segmentation, annotation, or *retrieval* of 2D images or 3D models. BF first learns a set of codewords by clustering the set of local features extracted from all the 3D models in a training set database. Each of a set of local features extracted from a 3D model is vector-quantized into its nearest codeword, and the codewords are accumulated into a histogram to become an aggregated feature vector for the 3D model. The vector quantization (VQ) process of the BF throws away a lot of information, e.g., relative positions or global arrangement of the set of local features. Consequently, the quality of aggregated feature suffers.

Several refinements to BF aggregation have been proposed [12, 16, 22, 23, 29, 30, 31, 34] to remedy this issue. They use either sparse coding (SC) or higher-order statistics (HS) to reduce information loss due to VQ. Both SC-based and HS-based algorithms use a number of codewords much smaller than the one for BF, and complement VQ with additional information. The Local Coordinate (LC) coding [31], Locality-constrained Linear (LL) coding [29], and localized soft-assigment coding [16] sparsely encode each local feature as weighted linear sum of neighboring codewords (Figure 1b). The Vector of Locally Aggregated Descriptor (VLAD) [12], Fisher Vector (FV) coding [22], and Super Vector (SV) coding [34] all try to encode local features by using higher-order statistics around the codewords (Figure 1c). The FV aggregates the set of local features by using displacement of mean and variance between the local features and the codewords, each of which is defined as a multivariate normal distribution derived by GMM clustering. The VLAD, which can be considered as an approximation of the FV, uses displacement of mean only.

These SC-based and HS-based algorithms aggregate a set of local features more accurately than a VQ-based approach, i.e., BF. However, most of them still can't handle non-linear distribution of local features in feature space. Small number of codewords essentially ignores local geometry of feature distribution. Extensions employed by the SC-based and HS-based algorithms listed above won't be able to completely capture non-linear nature of distribution of a set of local features in its feature space.

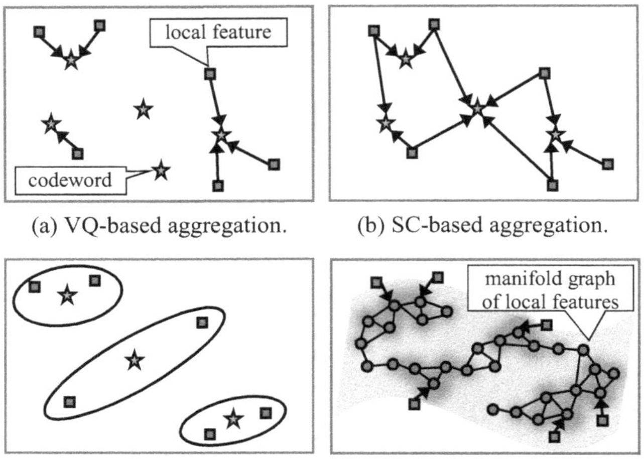

(a) VQ-based aggregation. (b) SC-based aggregation. (c) HS-based aggregation. (d) Proposed DM aggregation.

Figure 1. The proposed Diffusion-on-Manifold (DM) algorithm (d) aggregates a set of local features by relevance diffusion on the manifold graph of local features to generate more accurate aggregated features than VQ-based (a), SC-based (b), and HS-based (c) approaches.

In this paper, we propose a novel local feature aggregation algorithm called *Diffusion-on-Manifold* (*DM*) that exploits structure of potentially non-linear manifold of local features. Figure 1 illustrates the proposed algorithm along with the existing algorithms for feature aggregation. Previous aggregation algorithms learn a set of cluster centers, that are, codewords, from a large number (e.g., 250k) of local features in a training set. During training stage, our algorithm generates a graph representing potentially non-linear manifold of all the training set features. Given a query, e.g., a 3D model, unseen local features extracted from it are vector quantized to their respective nearest neighbors in the manifold graph. Then, using these local features of the query as sources, relevance values are diffused over the manifold graph. After diffusion, relevance values from *all* the features on the manifold graph are aggregated into a feature vector for the query. The proposed DM aggregation algorithm may be regarded as an extension of LL coding [29] to non-linear manifold.

In view of 3DMR, in addition to the feature aggregation algorithm, the choice of low-level local shape feature to be aggregated is equally important. Local features for 3D models can be classified into two groups; local 3D geometric feature [8, 13, 17, 20, 24, 27] and local 2D visual feature [4, 5, 6, 19]. At this point, the latter has an advantage in retrieval accuracy. Many state-of-the-art 3DMR algorithms employ local 2D visual features extracted densely from images rendered from multiple viewpoints of 3D model. For example, top two finishers in the SHape REtrieval Contest (SHREC) 2014 Large-scale Comprehensive 3D shape retrieval (SH14LC) track used aggregation of local 2D visual features [15]. Despite their success, a 2D visual feature has its drawback; it is incapable of describing internal structures of 3D models. To capture internal structure of 3D models represented as surfaces, voxels, or point set, an accurate and efficient local 3D geometrical feature is desired.

We thus propose a local 3D geometric feature called *Position and Orientation Distribution* (*POD*) for 3D oriented point set. To accurately describe a geometry represented by distribution of a set of oriented points enclosed in a local region of a 3D model, POD encodes the oriented point sets by using SV coding.

An experimental evaluation of proposed DM aggregation using multiple local features and multiple benchmark databases shows that it significantly outperforms existing SC-based and HS-based aggregation methods. Furthermore, POD features aggregated by using DM yields retrieval accuracy comparable to state-of-the-art 3DMR algorithms using local 2D visual features.

Contributions of this paper can be summarized as follows.

- Proposition of Diffusion-on-Manifold (DM) aggregation of local features. DM exploits non-linear manifold structure of local features for more accurate aggregation.
- Proposition of a local 3D geometric feature for oriented point set. POD feature performs comparably in retrieval accuracy to state-of-the-art local 2D visual features for 3DMR.

The rest of this paper is structured as follows. We will describe related work in the next section. The proposed algorithms are described in Section 3. Empirical evaluation of the proposed algorithms will be presented in Section 4, followed by conclusion and future work in Section 5.

2. RELATED WORK

2.1 Aggregation of Local Features

The BF [2] is first-of-a-kind feature aggregation algorithm and was first introduced to 3DMR by Liu et al. [17]. The BF counts the number of vector-quantized local features to generate frequency histogram of codewords. Retrieval accuracy of BF-aggregated features are insufficient since positional information of local features in their feature space is lost due to VQ.

To more accurately aggregate the set of local features, several SC-based aggregation algorithms and HS-based aggregation algorithms have been proposed. The ScSPM [30], LC coding [31], LL coding [29], and localized soft-assignment coding [16] are grouped in SC-based approach. They sparsely encode each local feature as weighted linear sum of neighboring codewords. The VLAD [12], VLAT [23], FV [22], and SV [34] are grouped in HS-based approach. They all try to encode local features by using higher-order statistics around the codewords. They compute displacement vector between the mean of local features and the codeword, possibly with some additional information. In addition to displacement vector of mean, FV accumulates displacement vector with respect to variance of local features and SV accumulates frequency of codewords as with the BF. VLAT encodes local features around the codeword by using their covariance in addition to displacement vector of mean.

These SC-based approaches and HS-based approaches produce higher accuracy than BF in 2D image classification [1] or 3DMR [5]. However, accuracy of these methods may be still insufficient since they ignore structure of non-linear manifold of local features. The FV can essentially capture non-linearity of features due to its use of multivariate Gaussian distributions as codewords. But, in practice, it is difficult to approximate the structure of feature manifold by using small number (e.g., tens to hundreds) of multivariate Gaussians.

2.2 Manifold Learning

Manifold learning is used in many applications such as information retrieval, classification, clustering, or segmentation, to improve their accuracies. It learns better distance metric in the feature space by analyzing the structure of non-linear distribution of features, i.e., manifold. Typically, the manifold is represented as a graph where each node corresponds to a feature of a multi-media data (e.g., 3D model), and each edge indicates similarity between two features.

For information retrieval, several diffusion distance-based ranking algorithms have been proposed [3] to improve retrieval accuracy. One of the representative algorithms is the Manifold Ranking (MR) by Zhou et al. [33]. The MR diffuses relevance from source node(s), which correspond to given query(s), over the manifold graph. Retrieval ranking is generated base on relevance values diffused on the manifold.

While most of studies using manifold learning apply it on the feature space of multi-media data such as 3D model, only a few studies apply it on the local feature space. Tao et al. [26] computed the MR on the manifold of local 3D geometric features extracted from a 3D model for mesh saliency detection. Torki et al. [28] and Zhu et al. [35] reduced dimensionality of local features by eigen-analyzing the manifold graph of local 2D visual features for accurate feature matching. In this paper, we utilize the manifold of local features for feature aggregation.

2.3 3D Local Feature for Oriented Point Set

Recently, 3D oriented point set has been becoming one of the most used 3D shape representation due to proliferation of inexpensive 3D range scanners. To compare or recognize 3D models represented as oriented point set, many local 3D geometric features for oriented point set have been proposed [8, 13, 20, 24, 27].

Given an oriented point set of a 3D model, a set of *Sphere-Of-Interest* (*SOI*), in which a local feature is computed, is densely sampled. SPFH [24] describes the SOI by angular statistics of pairs of oriented points to form a 125-dim. feature vector. LSF [20] uses distances among the oriented points within the SOI in addition to angular statistics to generate 625-dim. feature vector. Spin Image (SI) [13] projects a set of oriented points in the SOI into a cylindrical coordinate and counts frequency of points for each region of the coordinate. SI feature is a 153-dim. vector. SPFH, LSF, and SI are invariant against 3D rotation of SOIs. RoPS [8] describes density of the point set within the SOI. It first normalizes 3D rotation of the SOI by using PCA. The rotation-normalized SOI is then rendered from multiple viewpoints to generate a set of 2D images. For each rendered image, RoPS computes first- and second-order moments to generate 135-dim. feature vector.

3. PROPOSED ALGORITHM

3.1 Overview of the Algorithm

For accurate 3DMR, we propose a novel feature aggregation algorithm called *Diffusion on Manifold* (*DM*) and a novel local 3D geometric feature *Position and Orientation Distribution* (*POD*).

The DM algorithm aggregates a set of local features extracted from a 3D model into a feature vector by using relevance diffusion on a manifold graph of local features (Figure 1d). As a pre-processing for DM aggregation, the manifold graph is generated from a set of large number of training local features. However, the manifold graph may suffer from *burstiness* of local features [11], which is a phenomenon where certain types of local features appear more frequently due to repetitive structures in 3D models or small-scale features that capture too primitive shapes such as flat surfaces. These "bursty" local features are thought to form dense clusters on the manifold. In such a case, relevance from bursty local features would diffuse only within the dense clusters. As a result, the aggregated features would become inaccurate since they are dominated by relevance values diffused within the bursty clusters.

To alleviate this burstiness problem, we perform weighting of nodes on the manifold graph. We use L_p-norm IDF weighting algorithm by Zheng et al. [32] to assign smaller weights to bursty nodes and to assign larger weights to non-bursty nodes. These node weights are used in relevance diffusion on the manifold graph for more accurate aggregation.

The POD feature describes distribution of oriented points within a SOI by using SV coding. The SOI is divided into multiple cells by using a regular grid. For each cell, positions of the oriented points within the cell are encoded by using SV, and normals of the oriented points are described by their covariance. A set of POD features is densely extracted from a 3D model, and is aggregated by the DM algorithm for accurate 3D model comparison.

3.2 Diffusion-on-Manifold Aggregation

3.2.1 *Aggregating Local Features*

Given a set of local features extracted from a 3D model, DM algorithm aggregates the set of local features into a feature vector per 3D model by relevance diffusion on the manifold graph of local features. The manifold graph is represented as a sparse matrix **P**, whose construction process will be described in Section 3.2.2.1. The matrix **P** has a size $N_t \times N_t$ where N_t is the number of nodes, i.e., training local features, on the manifold graph (e.g., N_t=250K).

The DM algorithm first generates an N_t-dim. source vector **y** for relevance diffusion. For each local feature **x** of a 3D model, **x** is vector-quantized into its nearest node (i.e., nearest training local feature) and the nearest node is set as a source for relevance diffusion. We use a *k*d-forest having 20 *k*d-trees to efficiently and accurately search nearest nodes. The source value y_n for the node n in the source vector **y** is computed by using the following equation;

$$y_n = w_n N_n \quad (1)$$

where N_n is the number of local features vector-quantized into the node n, and w_n is the weight for the node n. An algorithm for computing w_n will be described in Section 3.2.2.2.

We then compute relevance diffusion on the manifold graph to generate the aggregated feature vector for the 3D model. Relevance is diffused from the multiple sources defined by the source vector **y** over the manifold graph **P**. We use the following iterative form of relevance diffusion used in the Manifold Ranking algorithm [33].

$$\mathbf{f}(t+1) = \alpha \mathbf{f}(t)\mathbf{P} + (1-\alpha)\mathbf{y} \quad (2)$$

The N_t-dim. vector **f** is initialized by the source vector, i.e., **f**(0)=**y**. The number of iteration T determines range of relevance diffusion on the manifold. As we will show in the experiments, small T (e.g., T=5) is sufficient to obtain high retrieval accuracy. α=[0, 1) is a regularization parameter for relevance diffusion. Since the matrix **P** is sparse, computing Equation (2) is quite efficient.

After relevance diffusion, the N_t-dim. vector **f**(T) is normalized by using the similar method to the existing feature aggregation methods such as FV or VLAD. **f**(T) is power-normalized by taking square-root of each element of **f**(T). Then, the power-normalized **f**(T) is normalized by its L2-norm to generate the aggregated feature vector for the 3D model. Similarity between a pair of two DM-aggregated features is computed by using Cosine similarity.

3.2.2 *Pre-processing for DM Aggregation*

3.2.2.1 *Constructing a Manifold Graph*

In this section, we describe the method for constructing the manifold graph **P** used for DM aggregation. We first randomly sub-sample the set of N_t (e.g., N_t=250K) training local features from the set of local features extracted from all the 3D models in the database. A sparse affinity matrix **W** having size $N_t \times N_t$ is generated by connecting the training local features which are close to each other in the local feature space. The element $W(i,j)$ of **W**, which indicates the similarity between the local feature i and the local feature j, is computed by using the following equation;

$$W(i,j)=\begin{cases}\exp\left(-d(i,j)/\sigma\right) & \text{if } i\neq j \text{ and } j\in kNN(i)\\ 0 & \text{otherwise}\end{cases} \quad (3)$$

where $kNN(i)$ is a set of k nearest neighbor local features of a local feature i. Using smaller k (e.g., k=5) makes the affinity matrix **W** sparser, resulting in faster aggregation. $d(i,j)$ is L1 distance, whose range is normalized in [0,1], between a pair of two local features. σ is a scaling parameter for distance. We fix σ to 0.5 in this paper.

The affinity matrix **W** is then normalized to generate the probability transition matrix **P** as $\mathbf{P}=\mathbf{D}^{-1}\mathbf{W}$ where **D** is a diagonal matrix whose i-th diagonal element is $D(i,i)=\sum_{j=1}^{N_t} W(i,j)$. The element $P(i,j)$ in **P** indicates the transition probability of relevance from the local feature i to the local feature j. **P** represents the manifold graph of training local features and is used for DM aggregation.

3.2.2.2 *Weighting Nodes on a Manifold Graph*

To alleviate the burstiness problem of local features, we compute a weight for each of N_t nodes on the manifold graph **P**. We use L_p-norm IDF weighting algorithm [32]. It assigns smaller weights to bursty nodes and assigns larger weights to non-bursty nodes.

We perform clustering on the set of N_t training local features. For efficiency, we use the Extremely Randomized Clustering Tree (ERC-Tree) algorithm [7]. The ERC-Tree algorithm recursively splits the local feature space until the number of training local features within the cluster becomes less than S_{min}. We use S_{min}=40 in this paper. The weight w_c for the cluster c is computed by using the following equation;

$$w_c=\log\left(1+N_M\Big/\sum_{m\in M_c} f_{m,c}^{\,p}\right) \quad (4)$$

where N_M is the number of 3D models in the database, M_c is a set of 3D models containing local features that belong to the cluster c, and $f_{m,c}$ denotes the frequency of local features of the 3D model m within the cluster c. p is a parameter. The weight w_c is assigned to all the training local features within the cluster c.

Since the ERC-Tree is a randomized clustering algorithm, accuracy of node weights due to a single tree would be insufficient. To obtain reliable node weights, we perform ERC-Tree clustering for N_{tree} times and take an average of N_{tree} weights produced by N_{tree} trees to generate final weight w_n for the node n. We use N_{tree}=200 trees in this paper. The set of N_t weights for all the N_t nodes is used for generating the source vector **y** (Equation 1) for DM aggregation.

3.2.3 *Reducing Dimensions of Aggregated Features*

Since DM aggregation tends to produce high-dimensional (e.g., N_t=250K dim.) vector, comparing DM-aggregated features is costly. To accelerate feature comparison, we reduce the dimensionality of DM-aggregated feature vectors by using Kernel PCA (KPCA) with dot kernel as with [5]. To train the KPCA, we use a set of DM-aggregated features extracted from 5,000 randomly selected 3D models in the database. The number of reduced dimensions N_d is less than 100 for most cases, which is much smaller than the dimensionality of the DM-aggregated feature vectors. Comparison among dimension-reduced features is done by Cosine similarity.

3.3 POD Feature for 3D Oriented Point Set

3.3.1 *Generating Oriented Point Set*

The POD feature extraction algorithm expects 3D model defined as oriented point set. For a 3D model defined as polygonal mesh, we first convert it into oriented point set by sampling its surfaces. We use the algorithm by Osada et al. [21] for converting a polygonal model into an oriented point set. The algorithm randomly and uniformly samples points on the surfaces of the 3D polygonal model. Each point is associated with the normal vector of the triangle on which the point is sampled. In this paper, we sample N_p=3,000 oriented points per 3D model. Oriented point set of the 3D model is scaled to fit a sphere having diameter 1.

3.3.2 *Extracting Local Features*

Given an oriented point set of the 3D model, we densely extract a set of POD features from the oriented point set (Figure 2). For each oriented point, we define a *Sphere-Of-Interest* (*SOI*) whose radius is R. For robustness against scale change of the local 3D shapes, we use multi-scale SOIs. For each SOI, R is selected randomly from a range [r-v, r+v]. For example, if we use r=0.5 and v=0.2, R is randomly selected from a range [0.3, 0.7].

To achieve invariance against 3D rotation of local 3D shapes, we normalize orientation of the SOIs. For each SOI, we perform PCA on coordinates of oriented points within the ROI to obtain principle axes in the rotated coordinate system. We then disambiguate the directions, or signs, of the principle axes by using the method similar to SHOT [27] or RoPS [8]. That is, the sign s_1 for the first principal axis $\mathbf{e}_1$ is computed as $s_1=sign\left(\sum_{i=1}^{n_p}(\mathbf{p}_i-\mathbf{p})\cdot\mathbf{e}_1\right)$ where n_p is the number of oriented points within the SOI, $\mathbf{p}_i$ is the position of i-th oriented point, and **p** is the center of the SOI. The sign s_3 for the third principal axis $\mathbf{e}_3$ is computed in the same manner as s_1. The second principal axis $\mathbf{e}_2$ is computed as $\mathbf{e}_2=s_3\mathbf{e}_3\times s_1\mathbf{e}_1$ where × denotes cross product of two vectors.

After orientation normalization, we extract a POD feature from the rotated SOI. We first compute a bounding box of the SOI, which may be a cuboid. And we normalize the cuboid bounding box by transforming it into a cube. We then split the normalized bounding box into $N_1\times N_2\times N_3$ cuboid cells by using a regular grid. N_1 (N_2, N_3) is the number of cells along the first (second, third) principal axis. In this paper, we set $N_1>N_2>N_3$ to make the POD feature compact. That is, we put finer grids along the principal axis having larger variance of oriented point distribution. We use $N_1\times N_2\times N_3$=4×2×1.

For each cell c, we describe the distribution of oriented points. The position of oriented points within the cell is described by using SV coding [34]. We count the number of oriented points n_c within the cell c and pool displacements of the n_c oriented points from the center of the cell c. The normals of oriented points within the cell is described by their 3×3 covariance matrix **C**. These statistics are concatenated to form a 10-dimensional feature vector for the cell c; $\mathbf{f}_c=\left[\beta\cdot\sqrt{n_c},\ \left(1/\sqrt{n_c}\right)\mathbf{d}_c,\ \mathbf{v}_c\right]$ where $\mathbf{d}_c$ is the 3-dim. displacement vector pooled within the cell c, and $\mathbf{v}_c$ is the 6-dim. vector whose elements are upper triangle elements of the covariance matrix **C**.

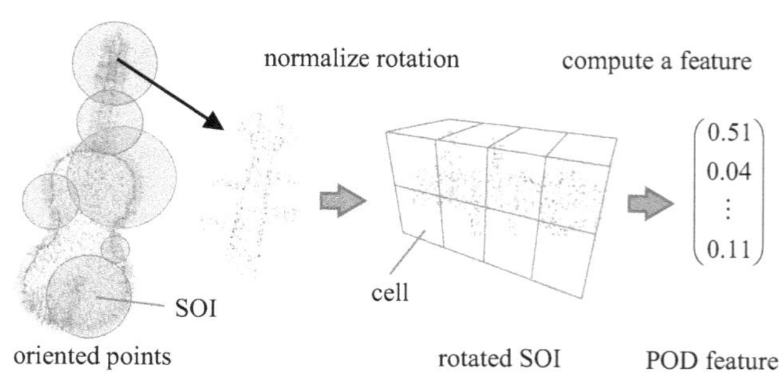

Figure 2. Extracting POD features from an oriented point set.

β is a balancing parameter between the frequency and the two vectors $\mathbf{d}_c$ and $\mathbf{v}_c$. We set β=0.001 in this paper.

The set of 10-dimensional vectors $\mathbf{f}_c$ computed for all the $N_1 \times N_2 \times N_3$ cells is concatenated to form a POD feature vector for the SOI. If we use $N_1 \times N_2 \times N_3$=4×2×1, the POD feature has 80 dim., which is more compact than other existing local 3D geometric features such as SI (153 dim.), LSF (625 dim.), FPFH (125 dim.), RoPS (135 dim.), and SHOT (320 dim.).

4. EXPERIMENTS AND RESULTS

4.1 Experimental Setup

4.1.1 Benchmark Databases

To evaluate accuracy and efficiency of the proposed algorithms, we use four benchmark databases; the Princeton Shape Benchmark (PSB) [25], the Engineering Shape Benchmark (ESB) [10], the SHREC 2011 Non-Rigid watertight meshes dataset (SH11NR) [14], and the SHREC 2014 Large-scale Comprehensive 3D shape retrieval dataset (SH14LC) [15]. Figure 3 shows examples of 3D models as well as the number of 3D models and the number of categories contained in the datasets. The PSB and SH14LC contain generic, rigid 3D shapes. The ESB consists of mechanical CAD models. The SH11NR has articulated, non-rigid 3D shapes.

For all the benchmarks, a 3D model in the database is used as a query and remaining 3D models are used as retrieval targets. We use Mean Average Precision (MAP) [%] as an index of retrieval accuracy. For the SH11NR, to make local feature more robust against articulation, 3D models are deformed to their canonical forms by using a method by Jain et al. [9] prior to feature extraction.

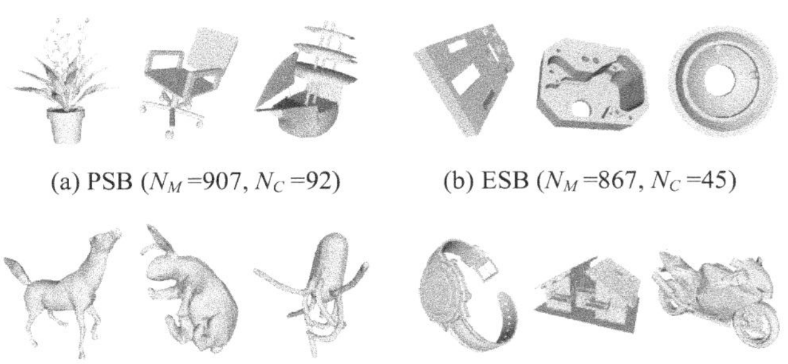

(a) PSB (N_M=907, N_C=92) (b) ESB (N_M=867, N_C=45)

(c) SH11NR (N_M=600, N_C=30) (d) SH14LC (N_M=8,987, N_C=171)

Figure 3. Benchmark databases used in the experiments (N_M : number of 3D models, N_C : number of categories).

4.1.2 Feature Aggregation

We compare the DM aggregation algorithm against five existing feature aggregation methods; BF [2], LL [29], FV [22], VLAD (VL) [12], and SV [34]. For SV, we use two variants of SV; one is *k*SV which learns codewords by using *k*-means clustering, and another is gSV [5] which learns codewords by GMM clustering and assigns each local feature to multiple codewords according to posterior probabilities that the local features belong to the codewords.

For BF, we use ERC-Tree clustering to generate about 30K codewords. For LL, we use *k*-means to learn 8K codewords. The number of codewords for FV, VL, *k*SV, and gSV are determined so that dimensionality of aggregated feature vector becomes about 300K. For DM, we use N_t=250K training local features. The aggregated vectors are power-normalized and are then L2-normalized. We use Cosine similarity to generate ranking results.

4.1.3 Local Features

We compare the POD against five local features; SI [13], LSF [20], and RoPS [8] as local 3D geometric feature, and DSIFT [4, 5] and MO1SIFT [5] as local 2D visual feature. Table 1 summarizes parameters for DM aggregation used for PSB.

Table 1. Parameters used for DM aggregation (PSB).

	POD	DSIFT	MO1SIFT	LSF	SI	RoPS
k	5	5	10	5	5	5
α	0.1	0.01	0.5	0.1	0.1	0.1
p	1.5	1.5	2.5	1.5	2.0	1.5

For local 3D geometric features, i.e., POD, SI, LSF, and RoPS, we sample N_p=3,000 oriented points from surfaces of a 3D model. The parameters for radius of SOIs are set to r=0.5, v=0.4 for PSB, ESB, and SH14LC and r=0.1, v=0.1 for SH11NR.

For local 2D visual features, i.e., DSIFT and MO1SIFT, a 3D model is rendered from 42 viewpoints spaced uniformly in solid angle. For DSIFT, We densely and randomly extract a set of 300 SIFT [18] features from a rendered image, resulting in about 13,000 SIFT features per 3D model. To reduce bursty SIFT features, we use scale-weighted sampling of DSIFT [19]. Specifically, for PSB, ESB, and SH14LC, we set the scale-weighting parameter W [19] to 0.25, which means more SIFT features are sampled at larger scales on the image. On the other hand, for SH11NR, we use W=4.0 meaning that more SIFT features are extracted from smaller scales. MO1SIFT rotates the rendered image to 16 different orientations and describes each rotated image by a global SIFT feature. Since we use 42 views for rendering, 42×16=672 MO1SIFT features are extracted per 3D model.

4.2 Experimental Results

4.2.1 Effectiveness of DM Aggregation

Figure 4 compares retrieval accuracies of the feature aggregation algorithms for the PSB. We use POD as a local feature. In Figure 4, we plot MAP scores by varying the number of training local features N_t for DM aggregation or the number of codewords for other aggregation algorithms. The DM aggregation significantly outperforms other feature aggregation algorithms. Aggregating local features considering the non-linear manifold structure of local features is effective for higher retrieval accuracy.

Table 2, 3, 4, and 5 summarizes retrieval accuracies of feature aggregation algorithms for the PSB, ESB, SH11NR and SH14LC, respectively. For benchmarks containing rigid shapes, i.e., PSB, ESB, SH14LC, the DM aggregation performs the best among the seven feature aggregation algorithms for most local features. DM aggregation is effective for both local 3D geometric features and local 2D visual features.

On the other hand, for SH11NR having non-rigid shapes, the DM aggregation and its competitors produce similar MAP scores for most cases. We speculate that a key factor behind high accuracy of DM aggregation is "smoothness" of the manifold graph of local features. That is, if local features extracted from 3D models distribute smoothly or continuously in the local feature space, relevance would diffuses appropriately on the manifold graph of local features. For PSB, ESB, and SH14LC, SOIs are highly overlapped each other since we used SOIs having large radius. In such a case, local features, whose sampled positions on 3D model surfaces are near each other, can also located near in the local feature space with high possibility. Therefore, the manifold graph of the large-scale local features becomes smooth and DM aggregation works well for PSB, ESB, and SH14LC. On the other hand, the manifold graph for SH11NR might not be smooth since SOIs with small radius don't overlap each other. Consequently, improvement of accuracy due to DM aggregation would be limited for the SH11NR.

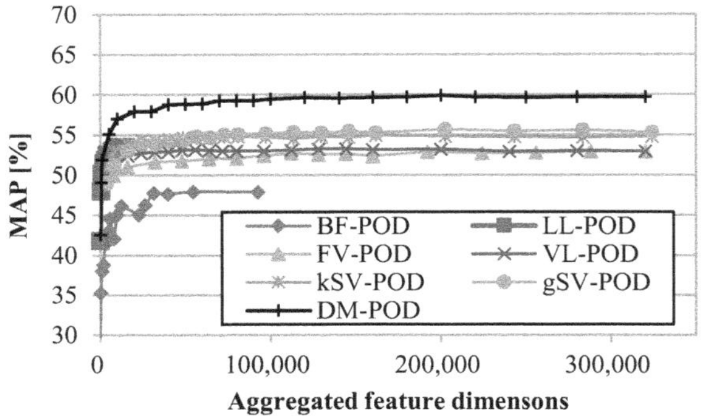

Figure 4. Comparison of feature aggregation methods (PSB).

Table 2. MAP [%] of feature aggregation (PSB).

	POD	DSIFT	MO1SIFT	LSF	SI	RoPS
BF	47.8	54.0	51.9	33.0	38.1	40.5
LL	53.1	57.6	56.5	33.8	41.0	46.4
FV	52.9	61.7	54.2	36.7	44.9	46.3
VL	52.9	60.9	50.6	38.3	45.5	42.7
*k*SV	54.8	61.3	49.6	40.1	47.8	46.8
gSV	55.3	63.8	53.2	40.2	**49.6**	48.4
DM	**60.1**	**64.7**	**61.1**	**41.4**	47.3	**50.4**

Table 3. MAP [%] of feature aggregation (ESB).

	POD	DSIFT	MO1SIFT	LSF	SI	RoPS
BF	52.1	53.6	49.1	47.1	48.3	47.2
LL	53.0	56.0	53.8	50.7	50.9	49.1
FV	54.4	57.8	52.2	52.8	51.7	48.3
VL	49.8	57.5	47.3	49.7	46.5	44.0
*k*SV	52.4	58.7	47.6	51.8	47.1	49.9
gSV	54.0	**59.2**	47.9	52.6	50.9	49.8
DM	**57.2**	59.0	**57.4**	**54.3**	**54.1**	**51.1**

Table 4. MAP [%] of feature aggregation (SH11NR).

	POD	DSIFT	MO1SIFT	LSF	SI	RoPS
BF	87.3	94.3	75.7	87.5	85.8	89.0
LL	94.7	97.0	82.4	93.8	94.2	94.2
FV	**96.7**	95.6	74.7	93.0	95.2	94.9
VL	95.9	96.8	73.1	95.9	95.8	95.2
*k*SV	96.1	**97.2**	74.5	96.0	95.9	**95.6**
gSV	96.5	97.0	75.5	**96.2**	95.4	93.3
DM	95.8	96.8	**89.2**	95.7	**96.9**	93.8

Table 5. MAP [%] of feature aggregation (SH14LC).

	POD	DSIFT	MO1SIFT	LSF	SI	RoPS
BF	39.6	38.5	36.5	30.9	32.7	35.8
LL	44.7	41.7	39.4	31.4	34.6	39.2
FV	44.8	44.1	36.6	35.7	38.6	38.6
VL	44.0	43.4	34.9	34.5	37.1	35.5
*k*SV	45.2	44.1	35.5	36.2	38.9	38.2
gSV	45.3	**45.5**	36.3	37.1	**40.2**	40.1
DM	**50.7**	44.9	**45.5**	**38.5**	39.3	**42.4**

Table 6 shows effectiveness of node weighting on manifold graph for the PSB. In Table 6, "without weighting" indicates accuracies of DM aggregation without node weighting, that is, node weights w_n in Equation 1 is fixed to 1, and "with weighting" shows accuracies of DM aggregation with node weighting. We can observe that node weighting improves retrieval accuracy. Decreasing weights for densely distributed nodes on manifold graph alleviates the problem of local feature burstiness to generate more accurate aggregated feature vectors.

Table 6. Effectiveness of node weighting (MAP [%] for PSB).

	DM-POD	DM-DSIFT	DM-MO1SIFT
without weighting	57.8	61.4	60.8
with weighting	60.1	64.7	61.1

Figure 5 plots retrieval accuracies against the number of iterations *T* for relevance diffusion on the manifold graph. Interestingly, for DM-POD and DM-DSIFT, accuracies saturate at T=1. While DM-MO1SIFT has a slight peak at around T=5. For larger *T*, retrieval accuracies are almost unchanged. This is because, presumably, we use small number of neighbors *k* for constructing manifold graphs (k=5 for POD and DSIFT, k=10 for MO1SIFT as shown in Table 1) to make feature aggregation efficient. In such a case, the manifold graph would consist of multiple sub-manifolds which have almost no connections among them. Relevance diffuses only within a sub-manifold and thus retrieval accuracy remains unchanged if we use larger *T*.

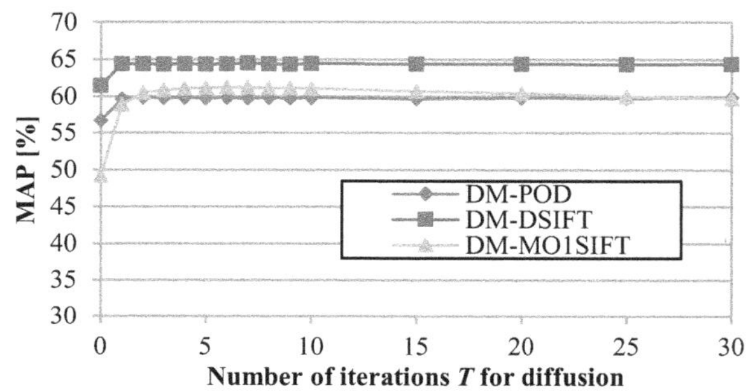

Figure 5. Number of iterations for relevance diffusion and retrieval accuracy (PSB).

Figure 6 plots retrieval accuracies against dimensionality of KPCA-processed feature for the PSB. For all the three features, i.e., DM-POD, DM-DSIFT, and DM-MO1SIFT, MAP score has a peak at around 100 dimensions. As the dimensionality of DM-aggregated feature is 250K, dimension reduction by KPCA down to about 100 dimensions significantly improve computational efficiency of feature comparison among 3D models.

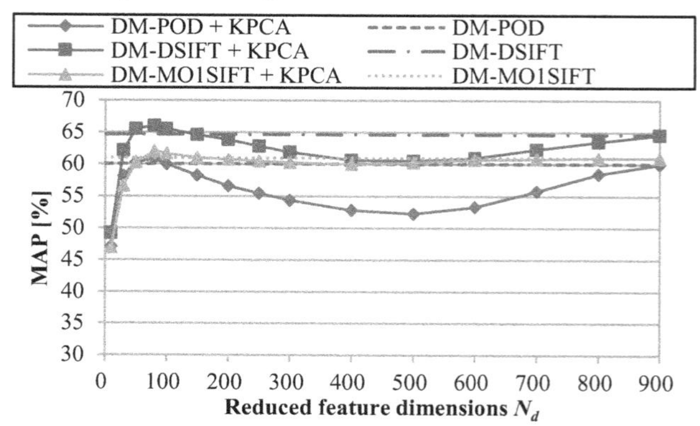

Figure 6. Reduced dimensions and retrieval accuracy (PSB).

4.2.2 *Effectiveness of POD Feature*

Figure 7 compares retrieval accuracy of POD feature against other existing local 3D geometric features, i.e., SI, LSF, and RoPS, for the PSB. We use DM algorithm to aggregate a set of local features. In Figure 7, the POD performs the best among the four local features. Describing distribution of oriented points within SOI by using SV coding works well for 3DMR.

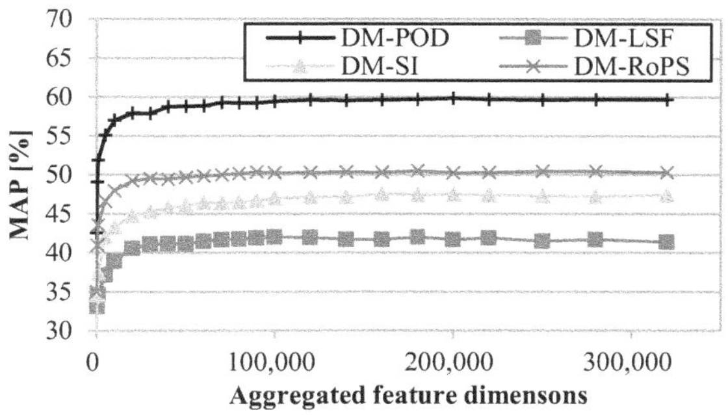

Figure 7. Retrieval accuracies for 3D local features (PSB).

Next, we evaluate impact of radius for SOIs on retrieval accuracy. Figure 8 plots MAP scores, for the PSB, against the parameter r of SOIs. For single scale POD, we fix another parameter v for SOI radius to 0. For multi-scale POD, we set v to values described in Section 4.1.3. We use the DM for aggregating the set of POD features. For the PSB, accuracies have peaks at around r=0.3 to 0.5 and multi-scale POD shows higher MAP than single-scale POD. For SH11NR, on the other hand, the peaks exist at r=0.1 and single-scale POD and multi-scale POD performs comparably well. The articulated models in SH11NR prefer local features extracted from smaller radius for robustness against articulation. On the other hand, the rigid models in the PSB prefers SOIs having more global and more diverse radius.

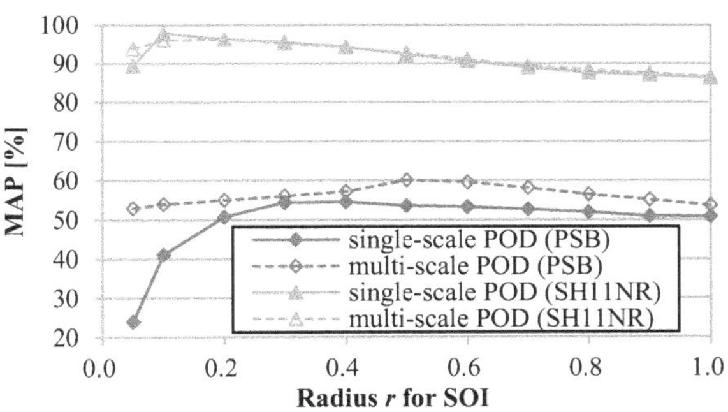

Figure 8. Feature scale and retrieval accuracy (PSB).

4.2.3 *Efficiency*

In this section, we evaluate efficiency of DM aggregation and POD feature. We use a PC having two *Intel Xeon E5-2650V2* CPUs and 256GB DRAM. All the programs run on a single thread.

Table 7 compares computation times for DM, gSV, and VL with respect to their pre-processing time and feature aggregation time. We sample N_p=3,000 POD features per 3D model. For VL and gSV, pre-processing means learning 3,000 codewords. For DM, pre-processing includes manifold graph construction and node weighting on the manifold graph. The DM aggregation shows the shortest pre-processing time as it doesn't require costly clustering such as k-means or GMM clustering of local features. On the other hand, the DM is slightly slower than the gSV for aggregating N_p=3,000 POD features per 3D model. However, 0.66 [s] for aggregating the set of local features of the 3D model is still acceptable for efficient 3DMR.

Table 7. Computation time [s] of feature aggregation.

algorithm	pre-processing	feature aggregation / model
VL	213.4	0.09
gSV	2876.2	0.50
DM	167.2	0.66

Table 8 shows computation time per query for the SH14LC. In table 8, column "Feat." is a time for extracting a set of N_p=3,000 POD features from a query 3D model, "Agg." is a time for aggregating the set of POD features of the query by using DM, "KPCA" is a time for reducing dimensionality of DM-aggregated feature of the query from N_f=250K dimensions down to N_d=50 dimensions, and "Sim." is a time for computing similarities among the query and 8,987 3D models in the database. The proposed DM-POD takes only about 1.5 [s] to query the SH14LC, which is one of the largest dataset for 3DMR.

Table 8. Computation time [s] per query for the SH14LC.

algorithm	Feat.	Agg.	KPCA	Sim.	total
DM-POD	0.75	0.66	0.03	0.01	1.45

4.2.4 *Comparison with Other Retrieval Algorithms*

Table 9 compares retrieval accuracy of the proposed DM-POD algorithm with five state-of-the-art 3DMR algorithms; SV-DSIFT [5], LL-MO1SIFT [5], ZFDR [15] and DBSVC [15]. Of the five algorithms, ZFDR combines both 2D visual feature and 3D geometric feature, and others extract 2D visual feature. We also evaluate effectiveness of distance metric learning using Manifold Ranking (MR) [33]. In table 9, "without MR" indicates accuracy without MR, that is, feature vectors for 3D models are directly compared using fixed similarity metric such as Cosine similarity to generate ranking results. And "with MR" shows accuracy using MR algorithm, that is, ranking results are generated by relevance diffusion on the manifold graph of 3D model features.

The proposed DM-POD shows the highest accuracy when MR isn't used. The new local 3D geometric feature combined with the DM aggregation significantly outperforms other 2D view-based retrieval algorithms. On the other hand, when MR is applied, DM-POD shows MAP comparable to that of the DBSVC, which is the best performing algorithm among the SH14LC track entries [15].

Table 9. MAP [%] for the SH14LC.

algorithm	without MR	with MR
SV-DSIFT [5]	46.4	53.1
LL-MO1SIFT [5]	39.9	46.5
ZFDR [15]	38.7	
DBSVC [15]	44.6	54.1
DM-POD (proposed)	**49.5**	**54.3**

5. CONCLUSION AND FUTURE WORK

In this paper, we proposed *Diffusion-on-Manifold* (*DM*), a novel aggregation algorithm for local features, and evaluated it in a shape-based 3D model retrieval (3DMR) setting. The DM exploits, via manifold graph of features and diffusion distance, non-linear manifold structure of local features for more accurate aggregation. Existing feature aggregation algorithms such as Bag-of-Features [2], VLAD [12], Fisher Vector coding [22], Super Vector (SV) coding [34], on the other hand, often fail to capture non-linearity in feature space due to their use of small number of codewords.

We also proposed *Position and Orientation Distribution* (*POD*), a local 3D geometrical feature for 3D oriented point set. It describes distribution of oriented points by using SV coding to generate compact yet accurate local feature.

In experiments, the DM aggregation showed higher accuracy than the existing aggregation. The POD feature also outperformed existing local 3D geometric features for oriented point. As a future work, we will evaluate effectiveness of the DM aggregation on 2D image retrieval setting.

6. ACKNOWLEDGMENTS

This research is supported by *JSPS Grant-in-Aid for Scientific Research on Innovative Areas* #26120517 and *JSPS Grants-in-Aid for Scientific Research* (*C*) #26330133.

7. REFERENCES

[1] Chatfield, K., Lempitsky, V., Vedaldi, A., Zisserman, A. 2011. The devil is in the details: an evaluation of recent feature encoding methods, *British Machine Vision Conference* (*BMVC*) 2011.

[2] Csurka, G., Dance, C.R., Fan, L., Willamowski, J., Bray, C. 2004. Visual Categorization with Bags of Keypoints, *Proc. ECCV 2004 workshop on Statistical Learning in Computer Vision*, 59–74.

[3] Donoser, M., Bischof, H. 2013. Diffusion Processes for Retrieval Revisited, *Proc. CVPR 2013*, 1320–1327.

[4] Furuya T., Ohbuchi. R. 2009, Dense sampling and fast encoding for 3D model retrieval using bag-of-visual features, *Proc. ACM CIVR* 2009, Article No. 26.

[5] Furuya, T., Ohbuchi, R. 2014. Fusing Multiple Features for Shape-based 3D Model Retrieval, *Proc. British Machine Vision Conference* (BMVC) *2014*.

[6] Gao, Y., Dai, Q. 2014. View-Based 3D Object Retrieval: Challenges and Approaches, *IEEE MultiMedia*, **21**(3), 52–57.

[7] Geurts, P., Ernst, D., Wehenkel, L. 2006. Extremely randomized trees, *Machine Learning*, **63**(1), 3–42.

[8] Guo, Y., Sohel, F., Bennamoun, M., Lu, M., Wan, J. 2013. Rotational Projection Statistics for 3D Local Surface Description and Object Recognition, *IJCV*, **105**(1), 63–86.

[9] Jain V., Zhang, H. 2006. Robust 3D Shape Correspondence in the Spectral Domain, *Proc. SMI 2006*.

[10] Jayanti, S., Kalyanaraman, Y., Iyer, N., Ramani, K. 2006. Developing an engineering shape benchmark for CAD models, *Proc CAD*, **38**(9), 939–953.

[11] Jégou, H., Douze, M., Schmid, C. 2009. On the burstiness of visual elements, *Proc. CVPR 2009*, 1169–1176.

[12] Jégou, H., Douze, M., Schmid, C., P. Perez. 2010. Aggregating local descriptors into a compact image representation, *Proc. CVPR 2010*, 3304–3311.

[13] Johnson, A.E., Hebert, M. 1999. Using spin images for efficient object recognition in cluttered 3D scenes, *Pattern Analysis and Machine Intelligence*, **21**(5), 433–449.

[14] Lian, Z., Godil, A., Bustos, B., Daoudi, M., Hermans, J., Kawamura, S., Kurita, Y., Lavoué, G., Nguyen, H.V., Ohbuchi, R., Ohkita, Y., Ohishi, Y., Porikli, F., Reuter, M., Sipiran, I., Smeets, D., Suetens, P., Tabia, H., Vandermeulen, D. 2011. SHREC'11 Track: Shape Retrieval on Non-rigid 3D Watertight Meshes, *Proc. EG 3DOR 2011*, 79–88.

[15] Li, B., Lu, Y., Li, C., Godil, A., Schreck, T., Aono, M., Chen, Q., Chowdhury, N. K., Fang, B., Furuya, T., Johan, H., Kosaka, R., Koyanagi, H., Ohbuchi, R., Tatsuma, A. 2014. Large Scale Comprehensive 3D Shape Retrieval, *Proc. EG 3DOR 2014*, 131–140.

[16] Liu, L., Wang, L., Liu, X. 2011. In defense of soft-assignment coding, *Proc. ICCV 2011*, 2486–2493.

[17] Liu, Y., Zha, H., Qin, H. 2006. Shape Topics: A Compact Representation and New Algorithms for 3D Partial Shape Retrieval, *Proc. CVPR 2006*, 2025–2032.

[18] Lowe, D. G. 2004. Distinctive Image Features from Scale-Invariant Keypoints, *IJCV*, **60**(2), 91–110.

[19] Ohbuchi, R., Furuya, T. 2009. Scale-Weighted Dense Bag of Visual Features for 3D Model Retrieval from a Partial View 3D Model, *Proc. ICCV 2009 workshop on Search in 3D and Video* (*S3DV*), 63–70.

[20] Ohkita, Y., Ohishi, Y., Furuya, T., Ohbuchi, R. 2012. Non-rigid 3D Model Retrieval Using Set of Local Statistical Features, *Proc. ICME 2012 Workshop on Hot Topics in 3D Multimedia*, 593–598.

[21] Osada, R., Funkhouser, T., Chazelle, B., Dobkin, D. 2002. Shape Distributions. *ACM Trans. on Graphics*, **21**(4), 807–832.

[22] Perronnin, F., Sánchez, J., Mensink, T. 2010. Improving the fisher kernel for large-scale image classification, *Proc. ECCV 2010*, Part IV, 143–156.

[23] Picard, D., Gosselin, P.-H. 2011, Improving Image Similarity with Vectors of Locally Aggregated Tensors, *Proc. ICIP 2011*, 669–672.

[24] Rusu, R. B., Blodow, N., Beetz, M. 2009. Fast Point Feature Histograms (FPFH) for 3D registration, *Proc. ICRA 2009*, 3212–3217.

[25] Shilane, P., Min, P., Kazhdan, M., Funkhouser, T. 2004. The Princeton Shape Benchmark, *Proc. SMI 2004*, 167–178.

[26] Tao, P., Cao, J., Li, S., Liu, X., Liu, L. 2015. Mesh saliency via ranking unsalient patches in a descriptor space, *Computers & Graphics*, Volume 46, 264–274.

[27] Tombari, F., Salti, S., Stefano, L. D. 2010. Unique signatures of histograms for local surface description, *Proc. ECCV 2010*, 356–369.

[28] Torki, M., Elgammal, A. 2010. Putting Local Features on a Manifold, *Proc. CVPR 2010*, 1743-1750.

[29] Wang, J., Yang, J., Yu, K., Lv, F., Huang, T., Gong. Y. 2010, Locality-constrained Linear Coding for Image Classification, *Proc. CVPR 2010*, 3360–3367.

[30] Yang, J., Yu, K., Gong, Y., Huang, T. 2009, Linear spatial pyramid matching using sparse coding for image classification, *Proc. CVPR 2009*, 794–1801.

[31] Yu, K., Zhang, T., Gong, Y. 2009. Nonlinear Learning using Local Coordinate Coding, *Proc. NIPS 2009*.

[32] Zheng, L., Wang, S., Liu, Z., Tian, Q. 2013. Lp-norm IDF for Large Scale Image Search, *CVPR 2013*, 1626–1633.

[33] Zhou, D., Weston, J., Gretton, A., Bousquet, O., Schölkopf, B. 2004. Ranking on Data Manifolds, *Proc. NIPS 2004*.

[34] Zhou, X., Yu, K., Zhang, T., Huang, T.S. 2010. Image Classification using Super-Vector Coding of Local Image Descriptors, *Proc. ECCV* 2010, 141–154.

[35] Zhu, G., Wang, Q., Yuan, Y., Yan, P. 2013. SIFT on manifold: An intrinsic description, *Neurocomputing*, **113**(30), 227–233.

Bundling Centre for Landmark Image Discovery

Qian Zhang
School of Computer Science
University of Nottingham
Nottingham, UK
psxqz1@nottingham.ac.uk

Guoping Qiu
School of Computer Science
University of Nottingham, Nottingham, UK
and International Doctoral Innovation Centre
University of Nottingham, Ningbo, China
Guoping.Qiu@nottingham.ac.uk

ABSTRACT

This paper introduces a novel method to efficiently discover/cluster landmark images in large image collection. We consider each cluster as a combination of several sub-clusters, which is composed of images taken from different view points of the identical landmark. For each sub-cluster, we find its local centre represented by a group of similar images, and define it as the bundling centre (BC). We therefore start the image discovery/clustering by identifying the BCs and accomplish the task by efficiently growing and merging those sub-clusters represented by different BCs. In our proposed method, we use min-hash based method to build a sparse graph so as to avoid the time-consuming full-scale exhaustive pairwise image matching. Based on the information provided by the sparse graph, BCs are identified as local dense neighbors sharing high intra-similarity. We have also proposed a weighted voting method to efficiently grow these BCs with high accuracy. More importantly, the fixed local centres can ensure each sub-cluster contains identical landmark and generate result with high precision. In addition, compared to a single representative(iconic) image, the group of similar images obtained by each BC can provide more comprehensive cluster information and, thus, overcome the problem of low recall caused by information lost during visual word quantization. We present experimental results on two landmark datasets and show that, without query expansion, our method can boost landmark image discovery/clustering performances of state of the art techniques.

Categories and Subject Descriptors

H.3.3 [**Information Storage and Retrieval**]: Clustering; H.2.8 [**Database Applications**]: Image databases

General Terms

Algorithms, Experimentation

Keywords

Landmark image discovery, min-Hash, sparse matching graph

ICMR'15, June 23–26, 2015, Shanghai, China.
Copyright 2015 ACM 978-1-4503-3274-3/15/06 ...$15.00
DOI: http://dx.doi.org/10.1145/2671188.2749295.

Figure 1: Examples of images from the Oxford building and Paris datasets

1. INTRODUCTION

With the rapid development of the Internet and online sharing social networks such as Flickr, Instagram and Facebook, sharing photos has increasingly become part of our daily life. Consequently, because of the easy accessibility of the Internet and the widespread use of digital cameras, tremendous numbers of high-quality image collections now exist all over the Internet. Tourist landmark images in particular contribute to many of these image collections. There is a need to group and mine these image collections efficiently so that further functions can be performed, such as identifying popular (frequently appearing) landmark images to provide proper tourist advice, grouping the images so that image retrieval can be performed on a much smaller image collections; and structuring the image collection for efficient browsing or image annotation [9].

The mining of image collections has been treated as an image discovery and clustering problem in recent researches [2, 7, 10, 14, 17, 20]. The objective of image discovery is to find all groups of images containing the same object. Different from clustering, the technique of image discovery required to be more sensitive to outliers, which means that images in the same cluster must be similar to each other while dissimilar to images from other clusters and outliers. This is challenging as the similarity and size of each cluster can vary greatly, and a large number of outliers may exist that do not belong to any of the clusters. Simultaneously, images containing the same objects (landmarks) may vary a lot from each other due to the difference in capturing conditions, such as illumination, scale, clutter, occlusion and affine transformation.

Some of the existing literature attempted to find each cluster an iconic view [18], which can act as the centre to represent the whole cluster/category, so as to grow clusters through image retrieval techniques. Similar to [7], we consider that the image collection of one identical landmark cannot be adequately represented by only one iconic view. Instead, each cluster should consist of several local iconic views that represent the image sub-collection/cluster taken from different view points, and each iconic view should consist of several images to represent the iconic view more comprehensively. The centre of cluster is considered as the object/objects that close to all the other objects from the same cluster, we can therefore define the local centres as the groups of images that share high visual similarity with others. Thus, in this paper, we propose a new image discovery method that starts from finding these local centres (groups of images) of image sub-clusters. The local centres are referred to as "bundling centres" in the rest of this paper.

Our proposed bundling centre image discovery method introduces a very efficient method to represent the visual similarity relationships contained in the image collection. We first build a sparse affinity matrix by filtering out most of the unrelated image pairs (outliers) using a modified tree partitioning min-Hash (TmH) [19]. The sparse affinity matrix can provide us with a sparse graph that contains the dataset's structure and density information over the metric space. Based on the matrix, dense neighbours of each image from the sparse graph are generated, and bundling centres are identified as local dense neighbour clusters with high average similarity score. Image discovery is then accomplished by growing and merging those bundling centres through exploring the connectivity provided by the sparse graph.

In detail, our method enjoys the following advantages. (1) By exploiting the min-Hash based method, we can efficiently detect the unrelated image pairs so as to avoid building the full-scale affinity matrix (dissimilarity matrix) that is required in [7, 14, 17, 20]. Since reliable image based pairwise feature matching appears to be the most expensive step, we can improve the discovery/clustering efficiency by an order of magnitude. (2) In contrast to [2, 10, 18] which adopt the min-Hash collisions as seeds to query the whole dataset, we directly use these collisions to build a sparse graph, and detect the bundling centres based on the density information provided by the sparse affinity matrix. The experimental results shows that we can correctly identify those local centres without query expansion and redundant spatial verification. (3) Instead of a single seed image, we choose a group of similar images to perform as the local centre of a sub-collection, and then grow the centre by locally exploring the connectivity between each BC with a weighted voting method. The BCs allow us to comprehensively catch the information of each image sub-collection. In addition, without recursively adjusting the centre, constant BCs can guarantee each sub-collection consist of images that containing the identical landmark. The experimental results show that, without costly query expansion [5], our method obtains similar precision and recall results compared to state-of-the-art method [4].

2. RELATED WORK

Many of the state-of-the-art image matching, retrieval, discovery and clustering systems use the popular bag of visual words (BoW)[16] feature to represent images. Because of its efficiency and ease of application, the min-Hash based method has drawn a lot of attention for use in the first step of image discovery/clustering [2, 4, 10, 18]. Meanwhile, some researches have tried to use other types of features to partition large-scaled image collections roughly into smaller sub-collections, such as the global GIST feature [7, 15, 17] and geotagging [14, 20]. They all have the same objective, which is to reduce the dataset's size so as to increase efficiency and make the algorithm scalable to even larger image collections. The difference is that the min-Hash method targets finding similar image pairs, while the pre-partition method simply reduces the collection size to deal with each time. However, the min-Hash method can hardly handle the partial duplicate image pairs, while similar image pairs may be possibly neglected due to random selecting. Thus, by itself, min-Hash can not guarantee a acceptable recall while hashing the dataset. On the other hand, precise and reliable geotagging and meta-data of images/photos is hard to obtain in the real world, and coarse-to-fine(partitioning) model approaches cannot guarantee good precision and recall, either.

To generate more comprehensive and structured image clusters, much research effort has been put into image discovery/clustering techniques. They can be briefly divided into two types: hierarchial clustering and centre-based growing clustering. Authors of [7, 14, 17, 20] performed image clustering in a widely used hierarchical agglomerative fashion, where a full dissimilarity matrix is calculated with pairwise feature vector matching (Euclidean distance/histogram intersection/cosine similarity); RANSAC[3] was used to estimate the number of inlier SURF/SIFT features so that false positive matches were removed, clusters were then found by recursively merging two similar images/clusters into coarser partitions. Conversely, based on the full dissimilarity matrix, authors of [6, 10] extract the cluster in a top-down hierarchical manner with spectral clustering techniques, which is computationally expensive and it is hard to decide the number of clusters. Both types of hierarchical technique are insensitive to outliers, and highly dependent on the pre-computed full-scale dissimilarity matrix. On the other hand, in [2, 4], image collisions found by min-Hash are used as seeds (centroid) to transfer the discovery/clustering into an image retrieval problem. Query expansion [5] is used to find partially overlapping images and the task is accomplished by iteratively querying all the image seeds. However, the query expansion is very time consuming, and the result clusters may contain a lot of images containing other objects or building caused by transitive closures. To handle this problem, the authors of [18] replace query expansion with iconoid shift, and perform a medoid shift on homography overlap metric to find the centre of cluster (iconic view) recursively. However, it targets finding the centre of the main cluster, and as a result of unreliable BoW feature, its transitive overlap matching manner may cause false matching.

3. BUNDLING CENTRE IMAGE DISCOVERY

To give a clear view of our proposed method, we first give the overall structure of bundling centre image discovery and then provide details of each step.

As shown in Figure. 2, our proposed method is comprised of three main steps. In the first step, similar image pairs (image seeds) are identified by min-Hash based techniques. A sparse affinity graph is built on these identified similar image pairs. In the second step, which is derived from [8], dense neighbours of each image from the sparse affinity graph are located. Local dense neighbour clusters with high intra-similarity are then identified as **Bundling Centres (BC)**. In the last step, different BCs linked by simultaneously appeared images are added together into super bundling centres; weighted voting and spatial verification methods are used to ensure precision of clustered images. Clusters of identical landmark images are finally formed by growing and merging similar super BCs.

3.1 Filtering with min-Hash and building a sparse graph

In the first step, our objective is to use a min-Hash based method to filter the whole image set, so as to narrow down the range of costly image pairwise comparisons and build a sparse affinity matching graph. Different from [2, 4, 10, 18], who use min-Hash collisions as seeds to iteratively query and grow a cluster, our method uses the min-Hash based method to describe the dataset's overall dense structure over the metric space, so that centres of image subcollection can be found efficiently and correctly in the following steps. Therefore, the min-Hash method is required in our method to find many more similar image pairs (collisions), rather than one pair for each cluster as declared in [2, 4, 10, 18].

Standard min-Hash Suppose we have two images, I_1 and I_2, which can be represented as sets of BoW [16] visual words, A_1 and A_2. Min-hash is the hashing technique that generates the similarity of two visual word sets by repeatedly applying the hash function:

$$mHf = f(A_i, f_j) = argmin_{w \in A_i} f_j(w) \tag{1}$$

where f_j is the independent random hash function that randomly assigns a real number to each visual word, and the min-Hash value w is the smallest element of set A_i in the permutation introduced by hash function f_j. The more frequently the two sets share identical visual words, the more likely it is that two images contain duplicate regions. To improve efficiency, the min-Hash value can be firstly grouped into s-tuples called **sketches** $sk(A_i) = (mHf(A_i, f_1), mHf(A_i, f_2), ..., mHf(A_i, f_s))$, where s is the number of min-Hash functions in each sketch. For instance,in the case of $s = 2$, we say two images have identical sketches if and only if $mHf(A_1, f_1) = mHf(A_2, f_1)$ and $mHf(A_1, f_2) = mHf(A_2, f_2)$. Images are potentially matched when they share at least α identical sketches (out of n total sketches).

Modified Tree Partitioning min-Hash The standard min-Hash algorithm appears to be very efficient at identifying near duplicate image pairs in large image collections. However, as the number of overlapping visual words decreases, partially matched images have a lower chance of being identified, which leads to relatively low recall. As mentioned earlier, we need to further discover similar image pairs (including partial duplicate ones) to ensure a clearer dense structure and higher recall. Thus, we choose the alternative mode of tree partitioning min-Hash [19] to hash the whole dataset.

For each image in the dataset, we first divide its visual word set into several small subsets with a partitioning tree. While growing the tree, we alternately apply rp-tree and kd-tree partitioning techniques [19] in each level. Then, instead of hashing the whole image's visual word set A_i, we perform hashing on much smaller visual word subset $P_{t,i}$ each time, where $P_{1,i} \bigcup P_{2,i} \bigcup ... \bigcup P_{t,i} = A_i$ and t is the total number of partitions generated by each image. The tree partitioning min-Hash is then accomplished by counting the number of collisions N_{TmH} with a given number of hash functions:

$$N_{TmH}(A_1, A_2, N) = \sum_{sk_i} \delta(sk_i, \sum_{P_{m,1} \in A_1} P_{m,1}, \sum_{P_{n,2} \in A_2} P_{n,2}) \tag{2}$$

where $\delta(sk_i, \sum_{P_{m,1} \in A_1} P_{m,1}, \sum_{P_{n,2} \in A_2} P_{n,2})$ is the step function that returns 1 if any of pair subset $P_{m,1}$ and $P_{n,2}$ have identical sketch sk_i, and otherwise, it returns 0. N is the total number of sketches. We say two images are potentially matched if their N_{TmH} is larger than threshold value α.

In such a way, each image will be hashed t times when generated by a single hash function. Thus, the same amount of calculation can increase the chance of collision by a factor of t. Additionally, the kd-tree divides the visual word set into subsets with their visual words spatially close to each other, and the rp-tree generates subsets whose visual words are near each other in the feature space. By combining the properties of both partitioning trees, for each pair of visual word subsets, we can decrease their disjoint set as well as increase the intersect set at the same time. As a result, we can increase the overlap between similar image patches to further increase the chance of collision.

Constructing the sparse graph After performing the tree partitioning min-Hash, as shown in the first step of Figure. 2, we have a sparse affinity matrix with each marked item in the matrix denoting the dataset's two potentially matched images. Conversely, the empty entries express that the corresponding pairs of images are not similar to each other, and will not be considered in the later matching steps. To better capture the image similarity, we use the cosine similarity between word weighted term frequency histogram vectors to estimate the edge weight:

$$sim_w(A_1, A_2) = \frac{\sum_i^v h_{1i} \cdot h_{2i} \cdot d_i}{\|h_1\| \cdot \|h_2\|} \tag{3}$$

where h_1 is the normalised frequency histogram of A_1 with vocabulary size v, and each component h_{1i} of h_1 represents the term frequency of visual word w_i in the image visual word list A_1. The term d_i is the inverse document frequency (*idf*) that measures the discriminative power of visual word w_i.

Combining equations (2) and (3), we can obtain the complete sparse affinity matrix:

$$A_{sparse}(i,j) = \begin{cases} 0 & if \ N_{TmH}(i,j) \leqq \alpha \vee i = j \\ sim_w(i,j) & N_{TmH}(i,j) > \alpha \wedge i \neq j \end{cases} \tag{4}$$

Based on the sparse affinity matrix, we can further build an undirected weighted graph, in which vertices set $| V |= D$ are the images that contain at least one potentially matched image from the dataset, and the edges $| E |$ are the pairwise similarity sim_w between two linked vertices calculated by equation (3).

3.2 Identifying local bundling centres

Unlike other centre-based image discovery/clustering methods, which iteratively adjust the centre to minimise the total distances between the centre and a cluster's remaining images, we believe each cluster may have more than one centre that is not centralised in the middle but distributed across the cluster as several local centres. As mentioned earlier, we use groups of similar images to comprehensively represent such local centres and identify them as bundling centres(BCs). By increasing the number of images used to represent each local centre, we can increase the connectivity of each BC to other similar images, so as to capture undetected similar image pairs. The objective of this method is to identify local cluster BCs based on the cluster structure provided by the sparse affinity matrix.

Each image in the graph, as shown in step 2 of Figure.2, can possibly come from one of the BCs. The most straightforward way to find the centre of the cluster is first to find the k-nearest neighbours (kNN) of each image, merge the similar (connected) images, and then calculate the centre of the cluster in the feature space. However, pairwise affinities are computed independently and BoW based matching is sometimes unreliable. To ensure the BCs contain the images having the highest feature-based similarity in their neighbourhood, we need to identify the images that are similar to all of their neighbours while also being similar to each other. Thus, we use the *dense neighbours* proposed in [8] to preserve the structure underlying the data and thus making it possible to identify the clusters' local BCs. Dense neighbours are defined as the elements that are locally similar to all of the other elements inside the neighbourhood instead of close to a single element.

As stated in [8], the problem is formulated to find maximal cliques

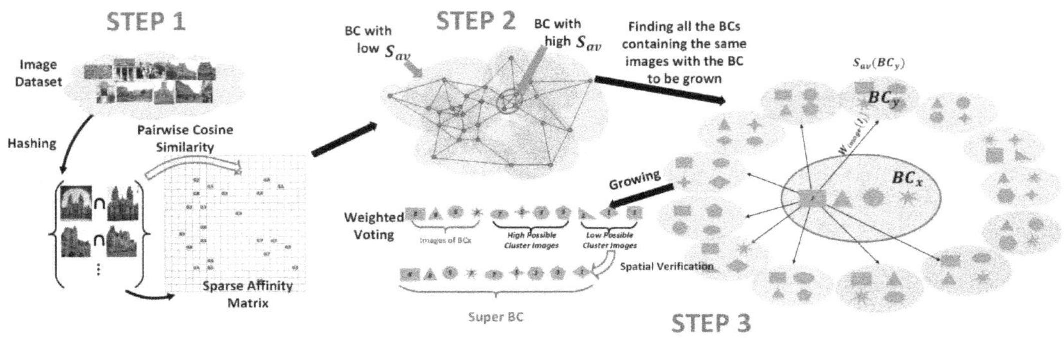

Figure 2: The pipeline of the bundling centre image discovery. In the first step, similar image pairs are identified with hashing and a sparse affinity matrix is built using cosine similarity image measures. In the second step, Bundling Centres (BCs) are identified as the local dense neighbour clusters, BCs with low S_{av} are coloured blue and BCs with high S_{av} are coloured yellow. In the third step, for each BC with high S_{av} (BC_x in the graph), a super bundling centre is formed by adding together different BCs containing the same images (detailed in Algorithm 1). Weighted voting and spatial verification methods are used to ensure the super BC consists of images having an identical landmark.

U that have a high average intra-cluster affinity score calculated by:

$$S_{av} = \frac{1}{k^2} \sum_{i \in U, j \in U} A_{sparse}(i,j) = y(U)^T A_{sparse} y(U) \quad (5)$$

where a clique U is defined as a subset of the whole set V , and $y(U)$ is the indicator function that $y_i(U) = 1$ if the ith component(image) of V belongs to clique U and 0 otherwise. If we define k as the number of dense neighbours in clique (subset) U, this means there are k elements equal to 1 in the indicator function $y(U)$ for each clique U. Given $x = \frac{y}{k}$, then the maximal cliques can be found by solving the quadratic function:

$$\begin{cases} \text{maximise} & f(x) = x^T A_{sparse} x \\ \text{subject to} & x \in \Delta \end{cases} \quad (6)$$

where Δ is the solution space defined as $\{x | \Sigma_i^n x_i = 1, x_i \in \{0, \frac{1}{k}\}, x_0 = 1\}$.

Each maximal clique U corresponds to a local solution of equation (6), a large maxima with a high average affinity score S_{av} indicates a strong possibility of a cluster while a small one corresponds to a meaningless subset. We followed the algorithm proposed in [8] to find all the cliques.

In other words, for each local image I_a in graph V, we obtain $(k-1)$ dense neighbours and its corresponding average affinity score S_{av}. Thus, we have a total $|V|$ number of k-sized small dense neighbour clusters. We define the **Bundling Centre (BC)** as the $k-$sized dense neighbour clusters whose images share high visual similarity. As shown in step 2 of Figure. 2, the yellow eclipses represent BCs with high S_{av} and the blue ones are BCs with low S_{av}. Note, the same image may appear in different BCs corresponding to a different local image I_a. Clearly, the higher the S_{av}, the more likely it is that the BC is the centre of the cluster. On the contrary, the BC with low S_{av} may appear to be an outlier or the centre of a cluster that obtains insignificant amounts of duplicate image content.

3.3 Grow and Merge Bundling Centres

After identifying those local BCs, edges are added between each pair of images within the same BC and BCs are connected by images that simultaneously appear in different BCs. The objective of the following step is to add links (edges) to similar image pairs that belong to different BCs but are visually similar to each other (contain the identical landmark in our case). It can be achieved by two steps, which are growing the BCs to super BCs and then merging these super BCs. Note, as mentioned previously, BCs with low S_{av} may appear to be outliers or the centre of a cluster that obtains insignificantly small parts of duplicate image content. Thus, for the purpose of efficiency, we only grow the BCs that obtain high S_{av}. In addition, for the purpose of precision, we also perform spatial verification on BCs that are chosen to be grown.

3.3.1 Grow Bundling Centres

We grow the bundling centres into super bundling centres by adding together different clusters containing the same images. For example, if image I_a exists in both bundling centres, BC_1 and BC_2, and both similarity scores S_{av1} and S_{av2} are large enough, we could say images from BC_1 have a high probability of being similar to images from BC_2. In this way, we can retrieve the related images through all the clusters connected by the same images used to grow each bundling centre.

As shown in the step 3 of Figure. 2, starting from the highest S_{av}, we treat each bundling centre BC_x as the centre of the image cluster. For each image I_j from BC_i we find all of the bundling centres $\{BC\}$ that contain this image. We define all the BCs containing at least one identical image with the centre BC_x as centre BC_x's link BCs (shown as the BCs surrounding BC_x in Figure. 2), and all the images contained in these linked BCs form a linked image list. We then assign all the linked images to a temporary image cluster c_{tmp}, which holds all of the images that potentially belong to the same cluster as BC_x. Clearly, most of the images may appear more than one time in c_{tmp}. We believe that the more times an image appears in the linked BCs, and the larger these BCs' s_{av} are, the more likely that it is a true matched image. Thus, we assign each image I_a from c_{tmp} a weight w_{td} measuring its likelihood of true matching. We then divide these linked images according to their corresponding w_{td} by a certain value $wRate$ (which is discussed in Section. 4.3) into a high possibility image subset c_{HIGH} and a low possibility image subset c_{LOW} as shown in the last step in Figure.2.

For the low possibility image subset c_{LOW} , we select the true matching images with a spatial verification technique, and then add the matched images together with the high possibility image subset c_{HIGH} to the bundling centre BC_x, so as to form a much bigger **super bundling centre**(Super BC) with images that contain the same object taken from similar viewpoints.

Details of the algorithm are shown in Algorithm 1 and the matching likelihood weight are given by:

$$w_{td}(I_a) = \sum_{j=1}^{k+1} w_{image}(I_j) \cdot \sum_{y=1}^{s} s_{av}(c_y) \quad (7)$$

where the $w_{image}(I_j)$ defines the importance of the simultaneously appearing image I_j in the bundling centre BC_x, which can be calculated by

$$w_{image}(I_j) = \frac{\sum_{I_i \in c_i} A_{sparse}(I_j, I_i)}{\sum_{I_l \in V} A_{sparse}(I_j, I_l)} \quad (8)$$

V is the whole set of images in the affinity matrix and $s_{av}(c_y)$ defines the average similarity score of linked BCs; there are a total of s different c_{BC} linked by image I_j which contains image I_a.

Algorithm 1 Grow BC into super BC

Input: bundling centres $\{BC\}$, average affinity score list S_{av} and weight information rate $wRate$
Output: Super bundling centres $\{SBC\}$

sort $\{BC\}$ in descending order according to its S_{av} value;
set $M = \emptyset$;
for every BC_i in $\{BC\}$ **do**
  set $c_{tmp} = \emptyset$
  for every image I_j in BC_i **do**
    if $I_j \notin M$ **then**
      find all the linked bundling centres in $\{BC\}$ containing image I_j and add all the linked images to c_{tmp};
      for every image I_a in cluster c_{tmp} **do**
        calculate weight $w_{td}(I_a)$;
        $w_{tmp_a} \leftarrow w_{td}(I_a))$
      end for
    end if
  end for
  $[c_{HIGH_i}, c_{LOW_i}] \leftarrow WeightCut(c_{tmp}, w_{tmp}, wRate)$;
  $c_{MATCH} \leftarrow spatialVerification(c_{LOW_i})$
  $SBC_i \leftarrow CB_i \bigcup c_{HIGH_i} \bigcup c_{MATCH}$
  $M \leftarrow M \bigcup SBC_i$
end for

3.3.2 *Merge Super Bundling Centres*

As shown in Algorithm 1, we have set M to record images that already existed in other super BCs, and skip growing the BC when encountering images already appearing in M. It helps us to avoid redundant calculation and ensures that the grown super BCs do not have overlapping images. At this stage, images of the same object that were taken from different viewpoints may spread across several super bundling centres. Our aim is now to identify and merge these clusters.

For each super bundling centre, SBC_i, we generate its representative vector h_{avg} with:

$$h_{avg} = \frac{1}{p} \sum_{a=1}^{p} h_a \quad (9)$$

where h_a is a normalised visual word histogram of image I_a in cluster c_i, and p is the number of images in cluster c_i. We use the histogram intersection to measure the distance between a pair of super centre bundles, which is given by:

$$d_{SBC}(SBCi, SBCj) = \frac{\sum_w min(h^w_{avg_i}, h^w_{avg_j})}{\sum_w max(h^w_{avg_i}, h^w_{avg_j})} \quad (10)$$

Similar super BCs with small distance d_{SBC} are merged into large clusters and spatial verification [3] is used to make sure the merged super centre bundles contain the same object. Alternatively, the gLDA proposed in [13] and 3D reconstruction in [7] can also be used to decide whether to merge two super BCs. Some of the true matching images are still uncovered at this stage, hence we could accomplish the discovery/clustering by querying all the merged cluster images with an efficient inverted file based voting scheme as introduced in [12].

4. EXPERIMENT AND EVALUATION

Datasets: The experiments are conducted on two publicly available datasets, which are the Oxford Paris dataset used in [11] and the Oxford building dataset [2, 4, 16]. The Oxford building dataset consists of 5062 images collected from Flickr by searching for famous landmarks. It provides 55 queries coming from 11 different landmarks. This dataset mainly contains building images taken from different viewpoints, and ground truth images from the same group containing identical buildings. The Paris dataset contains 6392 photos depicting 11 different landmark in Paris, such as 'Eiffel Tower'or 'Louvre Paris'. Similar to the Oxford building dataset, each landmark obtains a collections of photos taken from different viewpoints. The difference is that, in the Paris dataset, not all of the landmark images contain identical buildings (some image collections may consist of similar scenes); and the size of each cluster is much bigger than the Oxford building dataset, with cluster size ranges $200 \sim 500$ instead of $10 \sim 200$. Different from image retrieval techniques, our proposed method focused on unsupervised image discovery/clustering and we don't use any of the ground truth related to query and interest region in the following experiment.

Setting: To ensure a fairer comparison, we use the BoW visual word and $SIFT$ feature downloaded from the Website of the 5k Oxford building dataset and extract the features using open source library(VLFeat) for Paris dataset. In detail, we use the Hessian-Affine detector to extract the $SIFT$ feature and use the eight randomised kd-trees to obtain a $1M$-codebook from the 16M $SIFT$ features provided by the 5k Oxford building dataset. The BoW feature of the dataset is then extracted using an AKM [12] quantisation technique with the same 1M codebook.

4.1 Performance on Landmark Datasets

Ideally, the objective of unsupervised landmark image discovery is to detect the image clusters and automatically locate all the images in each cluster. We assume that images from different view points of the same landmark, or images of nearby land marks that share the same context should all belong to the same cluster. We use the mean average precision (mAP, precision-recall curve) score to measure the accuracy of the discovery/clustering result. For each cluster, recall is given by the percentage of discovered true images out of the total number of true images, precision can be calculated as the number of true discovered images divided by the total number of images in the cluster. To make the mAP result comparable to other results, we directly use the ground truth downloaded from the Oxford building dataset. We also noticed that some of the images are classified as false, even though they contains one of the 11 landmarks (or are spatially connected to them) as shown in the first two rows of Figure.1. To provide a more comprehensive result, we also measured the recall and provide the number of visually unrelated images by visual inspection.

Oxford dataset: We test our proposed method with the sparse affinity graph generated by both standard min-Hash (SmH) and tree partitioning min-Hash (TmH). The average precision (ap) score, cluster recall and false positive (fp) numbers are shown in Table.

	GT	LDA	gLDA	SC	Our (SmH)	Our (TmH)	SR		GmH		Our (SmH)		Our (TmH)	
	No.	ap	ap	ap	ap	ap	recall	fp	recall	fp	recall	fp	recall	fp
All Souls	78	0.90	0.95	0.93	0.93	0.95	0.97	0	0.987	0	0.94	1	0.97	1
Ashmolean	25	0.49	0.59	0.62	0.62	0.71	0.68	0	0.76	0	0.64	0	0.80	0
Balliol	12	0.23	0.23	0.33	0.5	0.83	0.33	0	0.92	0	0.5	0	0.83	0
Bodleian	24	0.51	0.64	0.61	0.75	0.75	0.96	1	1.00	1	1.00	0	1.00	0
Christ Church	78	0.45	0.60	0.67	0.81	0.85	0.90	0	0.97	0	0.90	0	0.92	0
Cornmarket	9	0.41	0.41	0.65	0.33	0.78	0.67	0	0.78	0	0.33	0	0.78	0
Hertford	54	0.64	0.65	0.70	0.85	0.88	0.96	1	1.00	1	0.89	1	0.96	0
Keble	7	0.57	0.57	0.93	0.75	0.82	0.86	0	1.00	0	0.86	0	1.00	0
Magdalen	54	0.20	0.20	0.20	0.15	0.39	0.06	0	0.39	0	0.15	0	0.41	1
Pitt Rivers	6	1.00	1.00	1.00	1.00	1.00	1.00	0	1.00	0	1.00	0	1.00	0
Radcliffe Carmera	221	0.82	0.97	0.97	0.98	0.98	0.99	0	0.996	0	0.98	0	0.99	1
mAP		0.56	0.61	0.69	0.70	0.81								

Table 1: Accuracy performance comparison with other state of the art discovery/clustering techniques (LDA (gLDA)[13] spectral cut (SC) [10] Spatial Related image discovery (SR) [2] and GmH [4])

1. Compared to other state-of-the-art image discovery/clustering techniques, our method obtained a better mAP score and similar ground truth cluster recall/fp. We also noticed that the recall result is only a little lower than GmH[4]; this is only because we have not included the query expansion process [5], which could dramatically increase recall, while the recursively transitive expansion operation is considered to be quite time consuming.

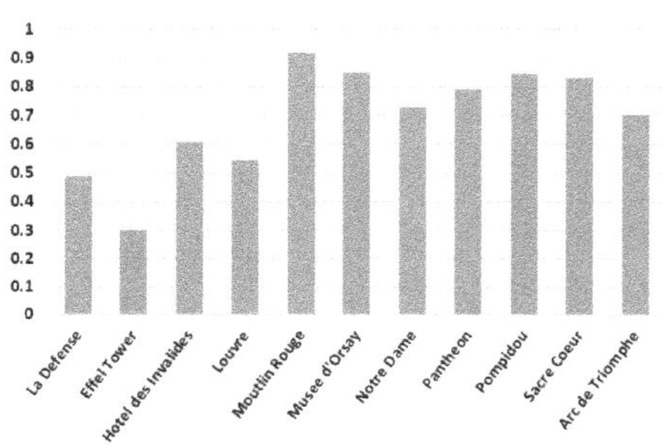

Figure 3: mAP score of each cluster in Paris dataset.

Paris Dataset: We only implement TmH for this dataset. With hard-assigned vocabularies and no query expansion, we obtained an average AP score of **0.708** (reported as 0.632 in [1] and 0.654 in [11]). As shown in Figure. 3, the results of the 'La Defense', 'Eiffel Tower'and 'Louvre'are not as good as others. By visual inspection, it is evident that these collections contain landmarks that are composed of simple-shaped (rectangle, tower shaped or triangle, as shown in the third rows of Figure. 1) and repeated visual content. In comparison, the landmarks showing good results obtained quite complex and structured visual content (as shown in the last row of Figure. 1), which makes the local feature ($SIFT$-based feature) more distinguishable and simpler to identify by the min-Hah based method. Thus, in this case of landmark with simple shaped outline and visual content, an alternative image feature should be considered in future work.

4.2 Evaluation of sparse graph and bundling centres

In the following section, we evaluate our proposed method in detail. The evaluation below is performed using the 5k Oxford building dataset.

To begin with, we first evaluate the sparse graph generated by step 1, which uses min-Hash to filter unrelated image pairs. In our experiment, we performed both standard min-Hash (SmH) and 5-level tree partitioning min-Hash (TmH) with each obtaining $N = 1000$ min-Hash sketches with sketch size $s = 2$. For both of the min-Hash techniques (SmH and TmH) results generated a sparse affinity graph using the method described in Section 3.1, where $\alpha_{SmH} = 0$ and $\alpha_{TmH} = 0.02$. The total number of edges $Nedge$ in two sparse affinity graphs are $Nedge_{SmH} = 98956$ and $Nedge_{TmH} = 267904$ for the 5k Oxford building dataset, and $Nedge_{TmH} = 2384682$ for the the Paris dataset, which are respectively 0.39%, 1.04% and 5.95% of the full sized graph. Note, the cluster size in Paris dataset is much bigger than the Oxford building dataset, thus, the percentage of similar pairs detected by the min-Hash based step is different between the two datasets.

To give some insight into the procedure of our proposed method, in Figure. 4, we have also shown the qualitative analysis of the sparse graph on the ground truth images of the Oxford building dataset. The first column is the ground truth ((a)), the second column ((b) and (e)) is the affinity graphs generated by min-Hash based functions, the third column ((c) and (f)) describes the image pair relations of the cluster bundle and the last column ((d) and (g))shows the final results of bundling centre image discovery. As shown in the ground truth figure, the 11 clusters have different sizes, with four relatively small clusters and one extremely large cluster (221 images). The black pixels describe a connection between pairs of images, and the white otherwise. Images from the same cluster should be connected to each other, and those between clusters should not. Obviously, the denser it is inside the ground truth region and the sparser outside of it, the better the result. From the second column we can see that both of the two min-Hash based functions have dense connections inside the ground truth cluster region, and similar sparse connections outside it. In the spares graph of TmH (Figure. 4(b)) there is an approximate boundary for each cluster, even for Magdalen, the hardest ninth landmark cluster. Conversely, in the affinity graph generated by standard min-Hash (Figure. 4(e)), we can only identify the boundaries of seven clusters.

In the third column of Figure. 4((c) and (f)), we show the sparse graphs generated by the BCs with a bundle size $k = 5$ as described in 3.2. This means that, in each BC, an image is connected with four other dense neighbour images. Since images could appear in multiple BCs, we can see from the figure that the connections are

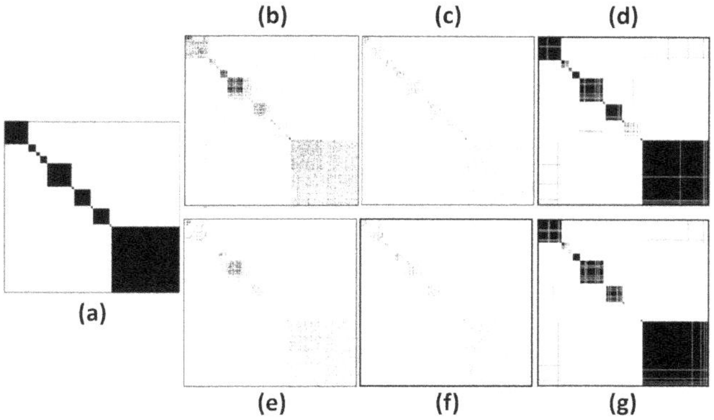

Figure 4: Qualitative comparisons of affinity graphs in each step on the ground truth images, with an upper row generated by TmH and lower row corresponded to the result of standard min-Hash(SmH).

evenly distributed within each cluster, and the connections across images from different clusters are automatically removed. Clearly, this step helps us remove outliers as well as redundant connections.

The last column gives us an intuitive view of discovery/clustering performance comparisons between our proposed method based on SmH (Figure. 4(g)) and TmH (Figure. 4(d)). Apart for the hardest 'Magdalen' cluster, the other 10 clusters appear to be quite complete in the TmH evaluation. On the other hand, the standard min-Hash based result performs well in large clusters but performs poorly when the cluster size is small or the duplicate image part is small. In both results, there are very few overlapping images between the first and the last cluster, which is caused by images containing both landmarks. One of the examples is shown as the third image in the second row of Figure. 1.

In conclusion, Figure. 4 has intuitively illustrated the objective of each step: in step 1, min-Hash based method is used to detect similar image pairs, and modified TmH is chosen to increase the number of true collisions while maintain similar number of random collision; in step 2, false connections are removed from the graph and similar image pairs within a cluster are distributed more evenly; in step 3, edges within each cluster are added and clustering is finally accomplished.

4.3 Evaluation of growing bundling centres with different size k

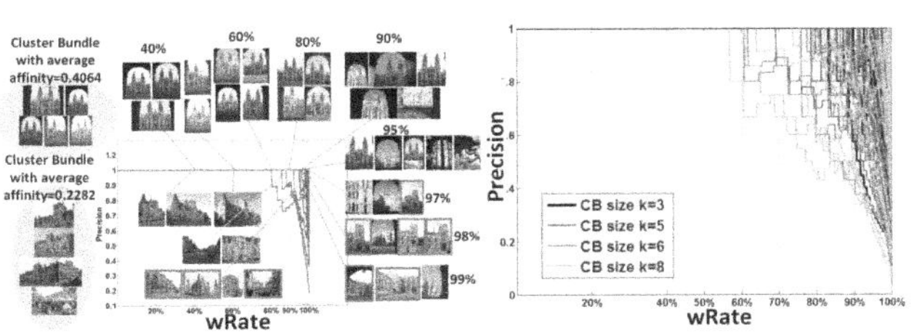

Figure 5: The supper bundling centre precision with different cut value $wRate$ and bundle size k

Cut Value: After finding all the BCs, we further grow them by exploring the connectivity between different BCs with Algorithm 1 as shown in step 3 of Figure.2. During growing, potentially matched unseen images are found by the connections, and the likelihood of matching is measured and ranked by the value w_{td}. The linked image list is then cut into the higher possible and lower possible image sets with cut value $wRate$. In detail, the weight information $wRate$ is calculated by the percentage of cumulative summation of weight w_{td}.

We have shown the detail of tests on different $wRate$ on the ground truth images. As shown on the left-hand side of Figure.5, two $k = 5$ BCs examples are drawn, the BC of 'All Souls'with an average affinity score of 0.4064 and the BC of 'Balliol'with an average affinity score of 0.2282. The graph, surrounded by example images, describes the ground truth precision of the linked images cut by different rate $wRate$. We can observe from the figure, that as the $wRate$ continues to increase, the precision decreases. The first false positive image appeared at $wRate = 97\%$ when growing the 'All Souls'BC, and the first false positive appeared at $wRate = 95\%$ in the 'Balliol'case.

We have also shown ground truth precision and $wRate$ corresponding to different bundle sizes $k = 3, 5, 6, 8$ on the right-hand side of Figure. 5. It is quite obvious that the $wRate$ corresponding to the appearance of the first false positive image decreases when there is an increase in the bundle size. Even though a couple of the curves appeared in the range $55\% - 75\%$, most are located in the region after 80% and the last 10% decrease very sharply. This is because in the linked image list, most of the true matched images are located at the top of the list with the likelihood of a much larger weight w_{td} (defined in equation 7) than the false matched images at the bottom of the list. This property allows us to avoid pairwise spatial verification on the top part of the image list while still maintaining a high level of accuracy.

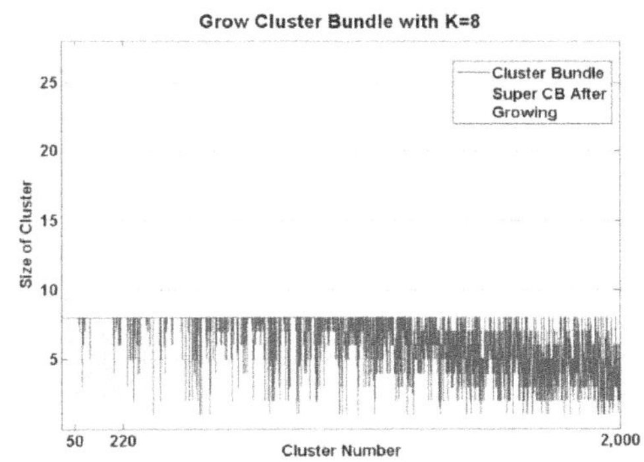

Figure 6: Cluster size before and after growing top 2000 BCs with bundle size $k = 8$

Bundle size k: In Figure. 6, we show the number and size of clusters before and after growing the top 2000 BCs with bundle size $k = 8$. The yellow curve measures the size of the super BC after performing a BC growing process. Because of the connective and repetitive nature of BCs, there are only around 220 super BCs left, which is a relatively small number of clusters to be merged in the final step.

Meanwhile, since enlarging the cluster size will increase the connectivity of the whole graph, the number of potentially matched images that are linked to each BC will be increased by an order of magnitude. In Table. 2, we show the cluster number and cluster growing size with different bundle sizes k. In the first row, we counted the number of clusters that consist of ground truth images, and show there is a significant decrease when enlarging the bundle size. For each bundle size, to measure the growing rate with precision, we stop growing the BC with the $wRate$ that encounters the first false positive image. We give the average growing number (C_{gt}) a different bundle size in the second rows of Table. 2 and the average of total linked image numbers (I_{link}) is shown in the last row of the table. From this table we can see that, although enlarging the bundle size will increase the connectivity and therefore centralise the cluster, it will also result in a lot of unnecessary pairwise spatial verification. Meanwhile, the average number of grown true positives (I_{tp}) appears to be similar among sizes ranging from 5 to 10. We can conclude that the size of a cluster bundle has little impact on the accuracy performance of discovery.

k	3	5	6	8	10
# C_{gt}	92	50	41	40	27
Average # I_{tp}	2.96	5.34	4.17	5.28	6.04
Average # I_{link}	9.88	30.4	46.4	103.8	210.2

Table 2: Cluster growing size comparison.

4.4 Efficacy

According to the image discovery/clustering literature, both affinity matrix building and image pairwise spatial verification (RANSAC) are considered to be the most time consuming process. Compared to other hierarchical agglomerative or graph-based discovery/clustering techniques, our method only obtains a sparse affinity matrix instead of a full matrix, with 0.39%(SmH) and 1.04%(TmH) of pairwise image matching for the Oxford building dataset.

In other min-Hash based discovery/clustering literature[2, 4, 10], the task is accomplished by querying spatially verified seed with transitive query expansion (which also requires spatial verification). Its time complexity of spatial verification is $O(DV)$ [2], where D is the size of the database and V is the number of images in all clusters. In our case, since each Super BC represents the local centre of one image sub-collection (usually containing images of a landmark taken from a similar view point), we only need to perform spatial verification between the target image and one or two images from the Super BC. This singals the time complexity of this step as $O(DN_{SBC})$. In addition to the spatial verification performed within each BC with $O(Dk)$, we have total time complexity required for spatial verification as $O(D(N_{SBC} + k))$, where k is the size of BC and N_{SBC} is the number of Super BCs. As mentioned earlier, both super BC size and BC size are relatively small ($N_{SBC} = 220$ in the Oxford 5k building dataset with bundle size $k = 8$). Since $O(D(N_{SBC}+k)) < O(DV)$, we can conclude that the time complexity over spatial verification of our method is smaller than other min-Hash based unsupervised image discovery/clustering methods.

5. CONCLUSION

In conclusion, our proposed method takes a compromise between traditional hierarchical agglomerative clustering [14] and centre based image discovery [2, 10]. Using a dense neighbour detection method [8], our method is robust to outliers and is able to obtain image cluster with flexible sizes and similarities compared to other hierarchical agglomerative clustering methods. Meanwhile, by utilising the efficiency provided by the min-Hash based function in the first step, our approach performs a local exploration without iteratively adjusting the centre (required in other centre based image discovery approaches). Furthermore, since both the min-Hash based methods and fixed bundling centre local exploration can be applied in parallel, our proposed method has the ability to be adopted in large-scale image collections. Our experimental results show that, without full-scale pairwise image matching graph, redundant spatial verification and query expansion, our method can generate discovery/clustering results with a high level of recall and state-of-the-art precision capabilities.

6. ACKNOWLEDGMENTS

This work is partially supported by Ningbo Science and Technology Bureau (Project No 2012B10055 and 2013D10008) and by the International Doctoral Innovation Centre (IDIC) at the University of Nottingham Ningbo China.

References

[1] Y. Cao, C. Wang, Z. Li, L. Zhang, and L. Zhang. Spatial-bag-of-features. *2010 IEEE Computer Society Conference on Computer Vision and Pattern Recognition*, pages 3352–3359, June 2010.

[2] O. Chum and J. Matas. Large-scale discovery of spatially related images. *IEEE transactions on pattern analysis and machine intelligence*, 32(2):371–7, Feb. 2010.

[3] O. Chum, J. Matas, and J. Kittler. Locally optimized RANSAC. *Pattern Recognition*, 2003.

[4] O. Chum, M. Perdoch, and J. Matas. Geometric min-Hashing : Finding a (Thick) Needle in a Haystack. In *CVPR*, 2009.

[5] O. Chum, J. Philbin, J. Sivic, M. Isard, and A. Zisserman. Total Recall: Automatic Query Expansion with a Generative Feature Model for Object Retrieval. *2007 IEEE 11th International Conference on Computer Vision*, pages 1–8, 2007.

[6] D. Crandall, L. Backstrom, D. Huttenlocher, and J. Kleinberg. Mapping the world's photos. In *18th International Conference on World Wide Web*, pages 761–770, 2009.

[7] X. Li, C. Wu, C. Zach, S. Lazebnik, and J. Frahm. Modeling and recognition of landmark image collections using iconic scene graphs. In *ECCV Proceedings of the 10th European Conference on Computer Vision*, pages 427–440, 2008.

[8] H. Liu, L. Latecki, and S. Yan. Robust clustering as ensembles of affinity relations. In *NIPS*, pages 1–9, 2010.

[9] S. Papadopoulos, C. Zigkolis, and Y. Kowmpatsiaris. Cluster Based landmark and Event Detection Collections for tagged photo coleection. *IEEE Multimedia*, 18(1):52–63, 2011.

[10] J. Philbin. Object Mining using a Matching Graph on Very Large Image Collections. In *Indian Conference on Computer Vision, Graphics & Image Processing*, 2008.

[11] J. Philbin, O. Chum, M. Isard, J. Sivic, and A. Zisserman. Lost in quantization: Improving particular object retrieval in large scale image databases. *2008 IEEE Conference on Computer Vision and Pattern Recognition*, pages 1–8, June 2008.

[12] J. Philbin, M. Isard, J. Sivic, and A. Zisserman. Object retrieval with large vocabularies and fast spatial matching. *CVPR*, 2007.

[13] J. Philbin, J. Sivic, and A. Zisserman. Geometric Latent Dirichlet Allocation on a Matching Graph for Large scale Image Datasets. *International Journal of Computer Vision*, 95(2):138–153, June 2010.

[14] T. Quack, B. Leibe, and L. Van Gool. World-scale mining of objects and events from community photo collections. *Proceedings of the 2008 international conference on Content-based image and video retrieval - CIVR '08*, page 47, 2008.

[15] M. Rubinstein, C. Liu, and W. Freeman. Annotation propagation in large image databases via dense image correspondence. *Computer Vision-ECCV*, 2012.

[16] J. Sivic and A. Zisserman. Video Google: a text retrieval approach to object matching in videos. *Proceedings Ninth IEEE International Conference on Computer Vision*, (Iccv):1470—-1477 vol.2, 2003.

[17] X.-J. Wang, L. Zhang, and C. Liu. Duplicate Discovery on 2 Billion Internet Images. *2013 IEEE Conference on Computer Vision and Pattern Recognition Workshops*, pages 429–436, June 2013.

[18] T. Weyand and B. Leibe. Discovering favorite views of popular places with iconoid shift. *2011 International Conference on Computer Vision*, pages 1132–1139, Nov. 2011.

[19] Q. Zhang, H. Fu, and G. Qiu. Tree partition voting min-hash for partial duplicate image discovery. In *IEEE International conference on Multimedia and Expo(ICME)*, pages 1–6, 2013.

[20] Y.-t. Zheng, M. Zhao, Y. Song, H. Adam, U. Buddermeier, A. Bissacco, F. Brucher, T.-S. Chua, and H. Neven. Tour the world: Building a web-scale landmark recognition engine. In *CVPR*, pages 1085–1092. Ieee, June 2009.

To Keep or not to Keep: An Expectation–oriented Photo Selection Method for Personal Photo Collections

Andrea Ceroni
L3S Research Center
Leibniz Universität Hannover
ceroni@L3S.de

Vassilios Solachidis
Information Technologies
Institute / CERTH
vsol@iti.gr

Claudia Niederée
L3S Research Center
Leibniz Universität Hannover
niederee@L3S.de

Olga Papadopoulou
Information Technologies
Institute / CERTH
olgapapa@iti.gr

Nattiya Kanhabua
L3S Research Center
Leibniz Universität Hannover
kanhabua@L3S.de

Vasileios Mezaris
Information Technologies
Institute / CERTH
bmezaris@iti.gr

ABSTRACT

When selecting important photos from a personal photo collection – e.g. for creating an enjoyable sub-collection for revisiting or preservation – photos are not considered in isolation. Therefore, collection-level criteria are also taken into account by automated photo selection methods. However, the typical two-step process of first clustering and subsequently picking from the clusters seems to overstress coverage as a criterion when applied to the task of selecting the photos most important to a user. We, therefore, propose a novel expectation-oriented photo selection method, which combines a variety of collection-level and image-level selection criteria in a flexible way. In our evaluation, which is based on large real-world personal photo collections with overall more than 18,000 images, we show that our method outperforms state-of-the-art photo selection methods. In addition, the proposed method does not rely on any manual annotations, making it applicable in realistic settings of personal photo collections.

Categories and Subject Descriptors

H.3.3 [**Information Search and Retrieval**]: Selection Process

Keywords

Photo Selection; User Expectations; Clustering; Coverage

1. INTRODUCTION

With digital photography and the many possible devices, photo taking is effortless and tolerated nearly everywhere. This makes us easily ending up with hundreds of photos, for example, when returning from a holiday trip. Furthermore, photos are also taken of more mundane motives, such as food or everyday scenarios, further increasing the number of photos to be dealt with. So, what to best do with all of these photos? With the decreased storage prices it is not a problem to store the photos somewhere. However, this often ends up as a kind of "dark archive" of photo collections, which are rarely accessed (and enjoyed) again. The mere size of the collection makes going through them as well as manual annotation and sorting of photos tedious tasks.

Furthermore, there is the risk of losing photos by a random form of "digital forgetting" [8]: over decades storage devices break down, and formats and storage media become obsolete, making random parts of photo collections inaccessible. Just consider, how difficult it would be today to access photos stored years ago in .mos format in a floppy disk.

Both the risk of dark archives and of digital forgetting suggest to select, supported by automated methods, the most important photos and to invest some effort into keeping them enjoyable and accessible. However, to *foster adoption*, such automated selection methods have to keep the level of user investment low. We do not rely on any additional user investment such as photo annotation with text [14, 17, 18] or eye tracking information [21], because we believe it is exactly the reluctance of further investment that lets large photo collections unattended on our hard disks.

When developing methods for semi-automatic photo selection, it is important to consider human expectations and practices. An important observation is that photo selection is a complex, partially subjective process, which does not consider images in isolation. Selection decisions also take the context of the other photos in the collection and of the photos already selected into account. Therefore, the aspect of coverage is used in a variety of photo selection methods [3, 10, 14]. In more detail, photo selection is modeled as a two-step process of first clustering the photo collection (for reflecting sub-events in the collection) and subsequently picking the most representative photos from the clusters. While coverage surely plays an important role for many photo selection tasks (see e.g. [21]), we believe that the complex decision making in selecting important and personal photos can be better modeled by avoiding the strict splitting into a two step process, which overstresses the role of coverage. We suggest to model a multifaceted notion of image importance driven by user expectations, which represents what photos users perceive as important and would have selected.

In this paper, we present an expectation-oriented method for photo selection, which relies on such a model of image

ICMR '15, June 23-26, 2015, Shanghai, China.
Copyright 2015 ACM 978-1-4503-3274-3/15/06 ...$15.00
http://dx.doi.org/10.1145/2671188.2749372.

importance. We aim at modeling user expectations considering information at both image- and collection-level, and we learn their different impact through a single model to predict importance. This information consists in (a) advanced concept detection (to capture the semantic content of images beyond aesthetic and quality indicators), (b) face detection (reflecting the importance of the presence of people in photos), (c) near-duplicate detection (to take the redundancy of many pictures of the same scene as a signal of importance, and to eliminate very similar images), (d) quality assessment (good quality photos might be preferred in case of comparable photos). This is complemented by (e) temporal event clustering and, more generally, collection-level information, to reflect the role of coverage in photo selection.

In summary, in this paper we make the following contributions: (i) we present a novel, effective, low-investment method for selecting important photos from personal photo collections, which is driven by user expectations; (ii) as a first work, we study the role of coverage in a systematic way by combining our expectation-oriented photo selection method with an explicit modeling of coverage in different ways, showing that comparable results to our method can be achieved only when coverage is not considered as a primary selection aspect; (iii) in our evaluation with real-world personal collections, we show that our method outperforms state-of-the-art methods to photo selection that rely on explicit modeling of coverage, when considering human selections as evaluation criterion.

2. RELATED WORK

Automated photo selection has already been studied in various other contexts, such as, photo summarization [10, 17, 18], identification of appealing photos based on quality and aesthetics [9, 23], selection of representative photos [3, 21], and the creation of photo books from social media content [14]. We consider the task of selecting important photos from personal collections (e.g. for revisiting or preservation), which meet user expectations. Among the works mentioned above, image importance has been considered only in [9, 23], nevertheless based on quality and aesthetic criteria.

Different photo selection and summarization works consider coverage by identifying clusters of images based on time and visual content [3, 10, 14]. Differently, our approach does not impose such a strict notion of coverage but rather considers clusters and other global information together with image-level information, learning their different impact in a single model. The works in [17, 18] are closer to ours, as they consider coverage in a relaxed way as part of a multi-goal optimization, but they still consider coverage as a key component and do not use user assessments in their evaluation. Moreover, they make partial use of manually created text to associate semantic descriptors to images, while our concept detection does not require any manual input, once the model has been learned.

Finally, Walber et al. [21] also use human judgments to evaluate selections, but the users have to wear eye trackers when using the system to make automatic selections.

Considering image processing, in our work we perform concept detection, temporal clustering, near–duplicate detection, face-detection, and quality assessment. Recent methods for concept detection (i) select specific locations on the image grid where features should be computed and extract at these locations local descriptors such as SIFT, SURF, and others [19], (ii) build a global image representation from the local features using BoW, VLAD, Fisher vectors [2], (iii) use such representations of ground-truth-annotated training corpora to train concept detectors that rely on machine learning techniques. Many approaches have been proposed for near-duplicate detection, such as employing multi-resolution histograms [22] or aggregating local descriptors into global representations [7]. Since time is the dominant data dimension for sub-event clustering, several time-based image clustering methods have been presented in the literature [4, 6]. They can incorporate other data dimensions, e.g. geolocation information (if any) and visual information. For face detection, one of the most successfully approaches is the Haar-like-feature-based detector introduced in [20], whose modifications and extensions have been presented in [15]. Concerning Image Quality Assessment, a variety of no–reference techniques have been proposed for detecting quality degradations such as image blur, e.g. in [12].

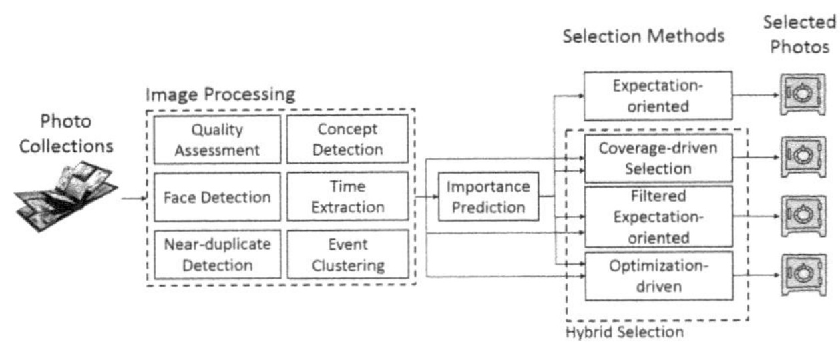

Figure 1: Approach overview of automatic photo selection.

3. PROBLEM DEFINITION

Definition 1. *Let the photo collection P be a set of N photos, where $P = \{p_1, p_2, \ldots, p_N\}$. The photo selection problem is to select a subset S of size θ ($S \subset P$ and $|S| = \theta$), which is as close as possible to the subset S^* that the user would select as the photos most important to her, i.e. S meets user expectations.*

In our model, we represent each photo collection as a set $C = \{P, CL, ND\}$, where P is the set of original photos, and CL and ND are sets of clusters and near-duplicate photos identified in the collection, respectively. A cluster $cl \in CL$ contains a set of photos P_{cl} grouped together with respect to a *defined* notion of similarity, whereas a near-duplicate set $nd \in ND$ is a set of highly similar photos P_{nd}.

Each photo $p \in P$ is modeled as a set of features $p = \{\boldsymbol{q}, \boldsymbol{c}, F, t\}$, where $\boldsymbol{q} \in \mathbb{R}^{n_q}$ is the quality vector of the photo, $\boldsymbol{c} \in \mathbb{R}^{n_c}$ is the concept vector of the photo, F is the set of faces f appearing in the photo, t is its timestamp. Each face $f = \{f_l, f_s\}$ is described by its location f_l and relative size f_s in the photo. For each photo p, we will estimate the importance value I using the extracted features.

3.1 Approach Overview

The overview of our approach to photo selection is presented in Figure 1. Given a photo collection, we apply different image processing techniques (Section 4) in order to extract information used by our computational methods for automatic photo selection. Our main approach is the Expectation-oriented selection (Section 5), which learns to generate selections by taking into account user selection patterns. In this approach, Importance Prediction is the core idea and it will be presented in Section 5.2. Furthermore, we present three different Hybrid Selection methods (Coverage-driven, Filtered Expectation-oriented, Optimization-driven), with the goal of investigating whether our method can be improved by combining it with state-of-the-art methods that explicitly consider coverage. The Hybrid Selection methods will be discussed in detail in Section 6.

4. IMAGE PROCESSING

The image processing techniques that we employ are concept detection, near–duplicate detection, image quality assessment, image clustering, and face detection.

Concept Detection. Concept Detection involves analyzing the visual content of an image and automatically assigning concept labels to it. This moves the description of an image to a semantic level, where it is possible to identify abstract concepts like *joy*, *cheering*, *entertainment*, as well as more concrete ones like *crowd*, *girl*, *stadium*. We trained 346 concept detectors for the 346 concepts defined as part of the TRECVID 2013 benchmarking activity [13]. As training corpus, the TRECVID 2013 dataset comprising 800 hours of video was used. We used SIFT, SURF, and ORB local descriptors and their color variants [11] for visual feature extraction. Then, PCA was applied on each descriptor for reducing their dimensionality to 80 and VLAD encoding [2] was applied to calculate the final image representation. The methodology that we followed has been introduced in [11].

Near-Duplicate Detection. Photographers can shoot a scene multiple times, which results in creating near–duplicate images that can be evidence of the importance of the scene. We used the method described in [1] to detect near-duplicates. This method detects at most 500 keypoints using the SIFT detector (Harris-Laplace) and extracts their corresponding descriptors using the SIFT extractor. It then forms a vocabulary by applying k-means on SIFT features using 192 cluster centers, and then encodes the image using VLAD encoding. The images with very similar VLAD vectors are efficiently retrieved using a KD forest index (using 5 KD–trees). Finally, Geometric Coding [24] is used to check geometric consistency of image's keypoints and to accept or reject the hypothesis that they are near-duplicates.

Image Quality Assessment. We computed four quality measures, namely blur, contrast, darkness, and noise, along with their aggregated value (weighted pooling using Minkowski metric), following the procedure presented in [12].

Temporal Event Clustering. In a photo collection captured by a single camera, time is a dominant dimension to reveal the sub-events that are represented in the collection. Thus, we apply time-based clustering in order to cluster collections into sub-events. Our method follows the approach presented in [4]. Images are sorted according to the time information extracted from them, and a similarity matrix of the ordered images is constructed using the time information and a sensitivity parameter. Then, for different values of the sensitivity parameter, the novelty scores and then their first derivatives are calculated. First derivatives which are greater than a threshold based on the maximum peak (at least 0.5 times greater than the maximum peak) are selected. The procedure results is a set of boundary lists (one list per sensitivity parameter). Finally, the confidence measure for each boundary list is calculated and the list that corresponds to the largest confidence measure is selected.

	TP	Tot	Precision
front_face_alt	467	576	81.08
front_face_alt_tree	449	544	82.54
front_face_alt2	482	627	76.87
front_face_def	486	733	66.30
merged	495	763	65.74
SCT	442	486	90.95
FE	471	653	72.13
all	439	490	89.59
SCT **and** *FE*	424	457	92.78
SCT **or** *all*	487	576	84.55
(*SCT* **and** *FE*) **or** *all*	484	564	85.82

Table 1: Performances of different face detectors.

Face Detection. We introduce a face detection approach which combines several face detectors to maximize the number of detected faces. We apply the approach in [20] using four pre-trained Haar Cascades detectors (frontalface_alt, frontalface_alt_tree, frontalface_alt2, frontalface_default) publicly provided by OpenCV[1]. In order to reduce the amount of false positive detections, we consider the detected faces as potential facial regions and, in every region, (i) we try to detect other facial characteristics (eyes, nose, and mouth) and (ii) we calculate the percentage of skin-like pixels. If facial characteristics are detected and are located in a valid location (e.g. eyes are centered and on the upper half for facial region) and the skin-like pixels percentage is above a threshold (set to 0.3 after experiments), then the detected region is classified as face. Furthermore, a facial region is accepted as a face if it has been detected by all face detectors (regardless of the existence of facial features or the ratio of skin-color pixels). This last case is effective in dark images where facial characteristics can not be detected and face color is too dark to be considered as skin-like.

This method was tested on a set of 484 images before applying it to the photos considered in this paper, and the results are listed in Table 1. As expected, if we merge the output of the four previously mentioned detectors (*merged*), the number of true positives increases but precision decreases. We experiment various constraints to decrease false detections: if the number of skin-color pixels are above a threshold (*SCT*), if at least one facial element (mouth, eyes, or nose) has been detected (*FE*), if the face has been detected by all detectors (*all*), and combinations of them (last three rows). Given these results, we chose the detector in the last row since it represents a good compromise between absolute number of true positives and precision.

5. EXPECTATION-ORIENTED SELECTION

The photo selection model presented in this section aims at meeting human expectations when selecting photos that are most important to the user from a collection, for instance for revisiting or preservation purposes. This is different from current approaches to photo selection for summarization, which aim at creating summaries that resemble the original collection as much as possible, either based on clustering [3, 10, 14] or explicitly considering coverage [17, 18].

We claim that selecting photos that are important to a user from personal collections is a different task than generating comprehensive summaries: the set of images impor-

[1]https://github.com/Itseez/opencv/tree/master/data/haarcascades

tant to the user might not be a proportioned subsample of the original collection. For instance, considering photos taken during a vacation, a user might ignore photos depicting joyless or boring moments. For this reason, we do not impose a strict notion of coverage but rather consider clusters and other global information as a set of features, along with photo-level features, learning their different impact in a single selection model. We then explicitly learn selection behaviors and preferences from real user data through a wide set of features. A characteristic of our features is that they do not require any manual annotation or external knowledge, differently from other works [14, 17, 18] that make partial use of manually created text associated to photos.

The features are combined via machine learning, providing a model that predicts the probability of a photo to be selected, i.e. its importance. The selected sub-collection is created by ranking photos in the collection based on their predicted importance and by taking the top-k of them, where k can assume any value lower than the collection size.

5.1 Features

Four groups of features have been designed to be used in the photo selection task, based on the information extracted from images as presented in Section 4.

Quality-based features. They consist of the 5 quality measures described before: blur, contrast, darkness, noise, and their fused value. The assumption is that users might tend to select good quality photos.

Face-based features. The presence and position of faces might be an indicator of importance and might influence the selection. We capture this by considering, for each photo, the number of faces within it as well as their positions and relative sizes. In more detail, we divided each photo in nine quadrants, and computed the number of faces and their size in each quadrant. This results in 19 features: two for number and size of faces in each quadrant, plus an aggregated one representing the total number of faces in the photo.

Concept-based features. The semantic content of photos, which we model in terms of concepts appearing in them, is expected to be a better indicator than low-level image features, because it is closer to what a picture encapsulates. We associate to each photo a vector of 346 elements, one for each concept, where the i-th value represents the probability for the i-th concept to appear in the photo.

Collection-based features. When users have to identify a subset of important photos, instead of just making decisions for each photo separately, the characteristics of the collection a photo belongs to might influence the overall selection of the subset. For the same reasons, but moving to a finer granularity, it might be worth considering information about the cluster a photo belongs to. For each photo, we consider the following collection-base features to describe the collection and cluster the photo belongs to: size of the collection, number of the clusters in the collection, number of near–duplicate sets in the collection, size of the near–duplicate sets (avg, std, max, min), quality of the collection (avg, std), faces in the collection (avg, std, max, min), size of the cluster (avg, std, max, min), quality of the cluster (avg, std, max, min), faces in the cluster (avg). Since the redundancy introduced by taking many pictures of the same scene can be evidence of its importance for the user, we also consider whether photos have near-duplicates or not, as well as how big is the near-duplicate set the photo belongs to.

5.2 Importance Prediction and Ranking

Once photos have been described in terms of the features presented above, a prediction model represented by a Support Vector Machine (SVM) [5] is learned to predict the selection probabilities of new unseen photos. Given a training set made of photos p_i, their corresponding feature vectors $\boldsymbol{f}_{p_i}$, and their selection labels l_{p_i} (i.e. *selected* or *not selected*), an SVM is trained and the learned model M is used to predict the importance of a new unseen photo p_{new}

$$I = M\left(\boldsymbol{f}_{p_{new}}\right) \quad (1)$$

i.e. its probability to be selected by the user. To avoid overfitting, the model was trained and evaluated via 10-fold cross validation over the collections and the generated output probabilities were considered in our evaluation.

Ranking. Once the importance of each photo is predicted, photos in the same collection are ranked based on this value and the top-k is finally selected. The parameter k represents the requested size of the selection and has to be specified in advance. It will be discussed during our evaluation (Section 7.1).

6. HYBRID SELECTION

As the evaluation will show (Section 7.3), our expectation-oriented selection clearly outperforms state-of-the-art methods for photo selection based on explicit modeling of coverage. However, we want to better understand the role of coverage in photo selection, in order to see if and in which way our method can be improved by combining it with explicit consideration of coverage. Therefore, we propose and investigate three ways of combining our importance prediction model with coverage-oriented photo selection methods, denoted *hybrid selection* methods and described hereafter.

6.1 Coverage–driven Selection

The coverage-driven selection is based on a two-step process of first clustering and subsequently picking photos from the clusters, which has been already used in other works. First, for a given collection C, a set of clusters CL_C is computed as described in Section 4 and the importance $I(p)$ of each photo $p \in P_C$ is given by our importance prediction model (Equation 1). Given the clusters CL_C, we use the importance $I(p)$ for each photo $p \in P_C$ to pick an equal number of top-ranked photos from each cluster in order to produce the selection S of required size k.

Cluster Visiting. One first issue to resolve in such approach is how to iterate over clusters when picking photos until the requested size of the selection is reached. After experimenting a number of alternatives, we identified a round-robin strategy with a greedy selection at each round as the best performing one. The pseudocode is listed in Algorithm 1. Given an initial set of candidate clusters CL_{cand}, the greedy strategy in each step selects the cluster cl^* containing the photo p^* with the highest importance, according to the prediction model M. The photo p^* is added to the selection S and removed from its cluster cl^*. The cluster cl^* is then removed from the set of candidate clusters for this iteration, and the greedy strategy is repeated until the candidate set is empty. Once it is, all the not empty clusters are considered available again and a new iteration of the cluster visiting starts. This procedure continues until the requested selection size k is reached.

Algorithm 1: Coverage–driven Selection (Greedy)

```
Input  : clusters CL, size k, prediction model M
Output: selection S
Set S = ∅
while |S| < k do
    Set CL_cand = CL
    while |CL_cand| > 0 do
        {cl*, p*} = get_most_important_cluster
        (CL_cand, M)
        S = S ∪ {p*}
        P_cl* = P_cl* − {p*}
        CL_cand = CL_cand − {cl*}
        if |cl*| = 0 then
            CL = CL − {cl*}
        end
    end
end
return S
```

Cluster Filtering. Intuitively, not all the clusters are equally important for the user. We tackle this issue by proposing a cluster filtering method to automatically predict the clusters that are not important for the user, in order to ignore them when picking photos from each cluster. We train a classifier (SVM) to detect and filter out clusters which are not important to the user. First, each cluster is described with the following features: size, quality vector (avg, std), average concept vector, number of faces (avg, std, min, max), number of near-duplicate sets and near-duplicate photos in it, near-duplicate sets size (avg, std, min, max), photo time (avg, std, min, max), photo importance (avg, std, min, max). The label associated to a cluster is *good* if it contains at least one selected photo, *bad* otherwise. Given a training set made of clusters c_i, their corresponding feature vectors $\boldsymbol{f}_{c_i}$, and their classes l_{c_i}, an SVM is trained and the learned model N is used to predict the class $L = N\left(\boldsymbol{f}_{c_{new}}\right)$ of new unseen clusters c_{new}. The model was trained via 10-fold cross validation over the collections.

6.2 Filtered Expectation-oriented Selection

The coverage-driven selection, coherently with all the selection methods based on clustering, is characterized by two steps: first clusters are identified and handled by possibly filtering and sorting them, and then photos in each cluster are ranked based on their predicted importance. Within the *filtered expectation-oriented selection*, we give priority to importance prediction by first ranking photos in a collection based on the predicted importance and then performing cluster filtering. The result is a ranked list of photos, where those belonging to clusters classified as *bad* have been removed. Note that the second phase of this paradigm, which contains cluster filtering in our case, can incorporate any other computation that exploits cluster information.

After the filtering, the selection S of size k is created by choosing the top–k photos in the list, as done in Section 5.2.

6.3 Optimization–driven Selection

Another more flexible way of explicitly incorporating coverage into a photo selection process is to consider it as part of a multi-goal optimization problem. This is done in [18] to generate representative summaries from personal photo collections. In more detail, in this work *quality*, *coverage*, and *diversity* of the summary are jointly optimized and the optimal summary S^* of a requested size k is defined as:

$$S^* = \underset{S \subset P_C}{\arg\max}\, F\left(Qual\left(S\right), Div\left(S\right), Cov\left(S, P_C\right)\right) \qquad (2)$$

where $Qual\left(S\right)$ determines the interestingness of the summary S and it aggregates the *interest* values of the individual photos in the summary, $Div\left(S\right)$ is an aggregated measure of the diversity of the summary measured as $Div\left(S\right) = \min_{p_i, p_j \in S, i \neq j} Dist\left(p_i, p_j\right)$, and $Cov\left(S, P_C\right)$ denotes the number of photos in the original collection C that are represented by the photos in the summary S in a concept space.

We incorporate our expectation-oriented selection within this framework, creating the *optimization–driven selection*, by computing the $Qual\left(\cdot\right)$ function in Equation 2 based on the importance prediction model (Equation 1), that is:

$$Qual\left(S\right) = \sum_{p \in S} M\left(p\right) \qquad (3)$$

Since part of the concepts in [18] are discrete categorical attributes, associated to photos using textual information and external knowledge bases not available in our task, we binarized the elements of our automatically detected concept vector (which includes the probability that a given concept appears in the photo) by using a threshold τ. The threshold has been empirically identified as $\tau = 0.4$ as the value that led to the most meaningful binary results. The rest of the computation of the $Div\left(\cdot\right)$ and $Cov\left(\cdot\right)$ functions in Equation 2 is performed as in the original work.

Regarding the resolution of Equation 2, we experimented the different approaches presented in [18] and we will report the best performing ones in the experimental analysis.

7. EXPERIMENTS AND RESULTS

In this section we evaluate the approaches presented in Sections 5 and 6, and we discuss their performances.

7.1 Experimental Setup

Dataset. For our experiments we use personal photo collections with importance judgments given by the owners of the collections as dataset. We decided to focus on personal collections because we wanted to observe the personal photo selection decisions in a setting that is as realistic as possible. This gives us a ground truth for assessing user expectations.

Given the unavailability of such a dataset, we performed a user study where participants were asked to provide their personal photo collections and to select the 20% that they perceive as the most important for revisiting or preservation purposes. The selection percentage (20%) has been empirically identified as a reasonable amount of representative photos, after a discussion with a subset of users before the study. We obtained 91 collections from 42 users, resulting in 18,147 photos. The collection sizes range between 100 and 625 photos, with an average of 199.4 (SD = 101.03).

Near-duplicates have been detected and filtered by considering the centroid of each set as representative photo, as done in [3]. Similarly to [16], each representative is marked as selected if at least one photo in its set has been marked as selected, and marked as not selected otherwise.

Evaluation Metrics. The selection methods presented in this paper can generate a selection S of size k from the original collection, where k can assume different values. We evaluate the different methods considering the precision P@k of the selection S of size k that they produce, computed as the ratio between number of photos in S that were originally selected by the user and the size of S. Since the collections in our dataset have high size variability, absolute values of k, although traditionally used in IR tasks, would result in selecting very different relative portions of the collections depending on their sizes. This makes the impact of the selection different between collections. We, therefore, decided to express k as a percentage of the collection size, instead of an absolute value. In particular, we compute the precision for $k = 5\%, 10\%, 15\%, 20\%$, which are indicated as P@5%, P@10%, P@15%, P@20%, respectively. We concentrate the discussion on P@20%, because our ground truth was gathered by asking users to select the 20% of their collections.

Statistical significance was performed using a two-tailed paired t-test and is marked as $^\blacktriangle$ and $^\vartriangle$ for a significant improvement (with $p < 0.01$ and $p < 0.05$, respectively), and significant decrease with $^\blacktriangledown$ and $^\triangledown$ (for $p < 0.01$ and $p < 0.05$, respectively) with respect to the baselines. If not stated otherwise, the significance outcome reported in the tables always refers to the comparisons with both the baselines.

Parameter Settings. The classifiers employed in this paper for importance prediction and cluster filtering, built using the Support Vector Machine implementation of LibSVM[2], have Gaussian Kernels and have been trained via 10-fold cross validation. The open parameters were tuned via grid search to $C = 1.0$, $\gamma = 1.0$. The evaluation has been done using the predictions generated during the 10-fold cross validation, in order to separate training and test data.

7.2 Baselines

Two baselines are considered in our evaluation, one based on clustering and one representing the optimization framework presented in [18].

Clustering. Similarly to what was described at the beginning of Section 6.1, for a given collection C, a set of clusters CL_C is computed. The selection is built by iterating the clusters, temporally sorted, in a round-robin fashion and picking at each round the most important photo from the current cluster (until the requested selection size is reached). The importance of each photo $p \in P_C$ is modeled as $I(p) = \alpha \cdot \|\boldsymbol{q}_p\| + (1 - \alpha) \cdot \dim(F_p)$, which is a weighted sum of the quality vector of the photo and the number of faces in it. This notion of photo importance covers different state-of-the-art works, such as [10, 14]. We experimented with different values of the parameter α, identifying the best value as $\alpha = 0.3$, which gives more importance to the number of faces in the photos. We report the performances obtained with this parameter value in our evaluation.

Summary Optimization. We implemented the approach presented in [18] as another baseline, where summaries are generated by optimizing *quality*, *coverage*, and *diversity* as in Equation 2. The *quality* of summaries is computed by summing the *interest* of photos in it, defined as a measure depending on photo quality and presence of portraits, groups, and panoramas. We computed the interest of photos as in the original work, using the concepts *face*, *3 or more people*, and *landscape* available in our concept set to represent portraits, groups, and panoramas respectively. Also *diversity* and *coverage* of summaries are computed coherently with their original computation, as already described in 6.3. We experimented the different approaches presented in [18] for the optimization of the cost functional (Equation 2), and the greedy optimization with equal weights for *quality*, *diversity*, and *coverage* was the one that achieved the best performances. Thus we will report the performances for this setup in the following evaluation, denoting it *SummOpt*.

[2]http://www.csie.ntu.edu.tw/~cjlin/libsvm/

7.3 Results

The discussion of the results is organized as follows. First, we show the performances of our expectation-oriented selection with respect to the baselines (Section 7.3.1). Second, we present the results of the hybrid selection methods and we compare them both with the baselines (Section 7.3.2) and with the expectation-oriented selection (Section 7.3.3).

7.3.1 Expectation-oriented Selection

This section presents the evaluation of our expectation-oriented selection with respect to the two baselines. Different importance prediction models have been trained by using the subsets of the features described in Section 5.1, so that the impact of different groups of features on the precision can be analyzed. The results for different selection sizes (k) are listed in Table 2. The two baselines exhibit comparable performances, with *SummOpt* performing slightly better for all considered values of k (5%, 10%, 15%, 20%).

Regarding our model, *quality* features are the ones that perform weakest individually, which has already been observed for other photo selection tasks [21]. *Faces* features alone already show better performances than the baselines: the presence, number, and position of people in photos, largely used as one selection criterion in other works, is indeed a meaningful indicator of importance. The performance achieved when only using *concepts* features is better than the ones of *quality* and *faces*: they are able to capture the semantic content of the photos, going beyond their superficial aesthetic and quality. Examples of concepts with a high importance in the model are *person*, *joy*, *cheering*, *entertainment*, and *crowd*. The model trained with the combination of all aforementioned features, denoted *photo-level* because the features are extracted from photo level, slightly improves the performance of using concept features alone.

If we include global features for each photo representing information about the collection, the cluster, and the near-duplicate set the photo belongs to, we get a comprehensive set of features, which we call *all*. The precision of the selection for this global model further increases for every selection size: this reveals that decisions for single photos are also driven by considering general characteristics of the collection the photo belongs to: e.g. number of photos, clusters, average quality of photos in the collection and in the same cluster, how many duplicates for the photo there are. This is a point of distinction with respect to state-of-the-art methods (represented by the two baselines), because our selection approach does not strictly handle collection-level information by imposing clustering (*Clustering*) or optimizing measures like coverage and diversity along with photo importance only based on quality and presence of people (*SummOpt*). It rather takes this global information in consideration in a flexible way through a set of features, whose impact to the selection is learned from user selections and expectations. The expectation-oriented model using all the available features (named *Expo* in the rest of the evaluation) leads to an improvement of 38.5% and 33.75% over *Clus-*

	P@5%	P@10%	P@15%	P@20%
Baselines				
Clustering	0.3741	0.3600	0.3436	0.3358
SummOpt	0.3858	0.3843	0.3687	0.3478
Expectation-oriented Selection				
quality	0.3431	0.3261	0.3204	0.3168
faces	0.4506▲	0.3968▲	0.3836△	0.3747△
concepts	0.5464▲	0.4599▲	0.4257▲	0.4117▲
photo-level	0.5482▲	0.4760▲	0.4434▲	0.4266▲
all (Expo)	0.7124▲	0.5500▲	0.4895▲	0.4652▲

Table 2: Precision of the expectation-oriented selection, distinguishing different sets of features.

tering and *SummOpt* respectively, considering P@20%, and even higher improvements when considering smaller values of k (90.4% and 84.6% for P@5%).

Considering the trend of precision performances over different values of k, all the models reach higher precision values for smaller selection sizes. This can be due to the presence of a limited number of selected photos that are relatively easy to identify for the methods, which give them highest selection probability. Another reason is that there might be *noisy* selections originally done by the user, due to the fixed amount of photos required to select: if the user had selected less photos than requested, the selection done to reach the requested selection size might not really reflect her preferences and expectations.

Summarizing, modeling different promising aspects in terms of features and flexibly combining them through machine learning leads (except when using quality information alone) to consistent and statistically significant improvements over state-of-the-art summarization and selection methods.

7.3.2 Hybrid Selection

This section discusses the precision of the hybrid selection methods presented in Section 6 with respect to the baselines, along with a comparative analysis to assess the benefit of using cluster filtering and a greedy visiting strategy.

The results are listed in Table 3, where they have been split based on the three different classes of hybrid selection described in Section 6. For coverage-driven selection, we report results of different combinations: *basic* refers to the coverage–driven selection which only uses our importance prediction model defined in Section 5.2 as photo importance measure, picking photos in a round-robin fashion from clusters temporally ordered; the term *filtered* means the use of cluster filtering, while the presence of the term *greedy* indicates the use of the greedy visiting strategy. The filtered expectation-oriented selection is denoted *F-Expo*.

For the optimization-driven method, we experimented the different optimization methods described in [18] after introducing our importance prediction model in place of the original importance measure used in that work ($Qual(\cdot)$). We found out that the best performing method was still the greedy approach but with a parameter combination that gives more importance to the *quality* of the photos (0.6 *Qual*, 0.3 *Cov*, 0.1 *Div*), and we consider the results of this setup in the evaluation. This difference in weights with respect to the *SummOpt* baseline already anticipates that our expectation-based measure of importance has a bigger impact in the performances than the native quality measure defined in [18]. The method will be referred to as *SummOpt++*.

	P@5%	P@10%	P@15%	P@20%
Baselines				
Clustering	0.3741	0.3600	0.3436	0.3358
SummOpt	0.3858	0.3843	0.3687	0.3478
Coverage-driven Selection				
basic	0.4732▲	0.4113▲	0.3902△	0.3809△
filtered	0.5351▲	0.4617▲	0.4325▲	0.4170▲
filtered+greedy	0.6271▲	0.4835▲	0.4391▲	0.4262▲
F-Expo	0.7065▲	0.5502▲	0.4863▲	0.4600▲
SummOpt++	0.7115▲	0.5533▲	0.4937▲	0.4708▲
Expo	0.7124▲	0.5500▲	0.4895▲	0.4652▲
Filtering with Oracle				
greedy+oracle	0.6499▲	0.5107▲	0.4665▲	0.4484▲
F-Expo+oracle	0.7150▲	0.5606▲	0.4982▲	0.4753▲

Table 3: Precision of the hybrid selection methods.

The results in Table 3 show that all hybrid methods outperform the baselines, with statistical significance, revealing that the inclusion of the importance prediction model to assess photo importance has a strong impact compared to the baselines methods, which model photo importance with simple functions of quality and people occurrence. Similarly to the performances of the expectation-oriented models, both the absolute precision values and the improvements with respect to the baselines increase for decreasing k.

The results in Table 3 also show that cluster filtering increments the precision of the *basic* approach of an amount between 9.48% (P@20%) and 13.1% (P@10%). The greedy visiting strategy leads to improvements as well. Statistical significance tests revealed that the improvements introduced by *filtered* and *filtered+greedy* are statistically significant.

A comparative analysis between the hybrid selection methods shows that *F-Expo* and *SummOpt++* achieve better precision performances than the coverage-driven methods, and a t-test confirms that these improvements are statistically significant. This shows that the measure of photo importance modeled by our importance prediction has a bigger impact in the precision of the selection than coverage, and those methods that strictly model it through clustering (*coverage-driven selection*) get a smaller benefit when incorporating the expectation-oriented model. On the other side, methods that either give priority to expectations (*F-Expo*) or consider expectations, coverage, and global information in a flexible way via optimization (*SummOpt++*) can better exploit the expectation-oriented model.

7.3.3 Expectation vs. Hybrid Analysis

In this section we make a comparative analysis between the expectation-oriented selection model exploiting all the available features (*Expo*), and the hybrid selection models. Considering Table 3, we can observe that the performances of *Expo* are better or comparable with the ones of the hybrid-selection models. In particular, the improvements of *Expo* with respect to the *coverage-driven* methods are statistically significant. The only improvements over *Expo* (which anyway are not statistically significant) are obtained when considering methods that prioritize expectations (*F-Expo*) or possess a relaxed consideration of coverage and global information in general (*SummOpt++*). These results further support our assumption that for the photo selection task, which we consider, a strong consideration of coverage overstresses this aspect as a selection criterion. Only for the methods with a more flexible consideration of coverage the performances are similar to the pure expectation-oriented method.

Cluster filtering is an attempt to eliminate clusters uninteresting to the user, and in order to further alleviate this aspect we conducted experiments considering only important clusters, i.e. those ones containing at least one selected photo. This is done by assuming to have a perfect classifier, i.e. an *oracle*, to filter out not important clusters and to focus the hybrid selection strategies only on the important ones. Although getting improvements compared to *filtered+greedy* and *F-Expo*, the performances when using such oracle, reported in the bottom part of Table 3, did not lead to consistent and statistically significant improvements with respect to *Expo*. *Greedy+oracle* does not beat *Expo*, while *F-Expo+oracle* only introduces a limited and not statistically significant improvement. These results show that the aspect that mostly drives user selections and expectations is the personal perception of importance, although this can produce unbalanced selections which are not representative of the original collection. Another problem related to clustering, even considering the important ones, might be the decision of how many photos to pick from each of them.

We also conducted experiments based on recall, which were in line with what was observed regarding the precision: both the expectation-oriented model and the hybrid selection methods outperformed the baselines, and the former was overall better than or comparable to the latter class.

8. CONCLUSION

In this paper, we presented an expectation-oriented method exploiting image as well as collection level features for helping the user in selecting the most important photos for creating an enjoyable sub-collection of a personal photo collection for preservation and revisiting. Our experiments with real world photo collections showed that our method outperforms state-of-the-art works in photo selection, which stress coverage as a selection criterion. Therefore, we investigated the role of coverage for our photo selection task in more detail, showing that coverage plays only a secondary role here.

Future works consist in incorporating more discriminative features to better predict user expectations, and designing models that optimize recall when generating selections.

Acknowledgments This work was partially funded by the European Commission in the context of the FP7 ICT project ForgetIT (under grant no: 600826).

9. REFERENCES

[1] K. Apostolidis, C. Papagiannopoulou, and V. Mezaris. CERTH at MediaEval 2014 synchronization of multi-user event media task. In *Proc. of MediaEval 2014 Workshop*, 2014.

[2] R. Arandjelovic and A. Zisserman. All about vlad. In *Proc. of CVPR '13*, 2013.

[3] W.-T. Chu and C.-H. Lin. Automatic selection of representative photo and smart thumbnailing using near-duplicate detection. In *Proc. of MM '08*, 2008.

[4] M. Cooper, J. Foote, A. Girgensohn, and L. Wilcox. Temporal event clustering for digital photo collections. *In ACM TOMCCAP*, 2005.

[5] C. Cortes and V. Vapnik. Support-vector networks. *Mach. Learn.*, 20(3):273–297, 1995.

[6] M.-S. Dao, A.-D. Duong, and F. G. De Natale. Unsupervised social media events clustering using user-centric parallel split-n-merge algorithms. In *Proc. of ICASSP '14*, 2014.

[7] H. Jégou, F. Perronnin, M. Douze, J. Sánchez, P. Pérez, and C. Schmid. Aggregating local image descriptors into compact codes. *Pattern Analysis and Machine Intelligence, IEEE Transactions on*, 2012.

[8] N. Kanhabua, C. Niederée, and W. Siberski. Towards concise preservation by managed forgetting: Research issues and case study. In *Proc. of iPres '13*, 2013.

[9] C. Li, A. C. Loui, and T. Chen. Towards aesthetics: A photo quality assessment and photo selection system. In *Proc. of MM '10*, 2010.

[10] J. Li, J. H. Lim, and Q. Tian. Automatic summarization for personal digital photos. In *Proc. of ICICS-PCM '03*, 2003.

[11] F. Markatopoulou, N. Pittaras, O. Papadopoulou, V. Mezaris, and I. Patras. A study on the use of a binary local descriptor and color extensions of local descriptors for video concept detection. In *MultiMedia Modeling*, 2015.

[12] E. Mavridaki and V. Mezaris. No-reference blur assessment in natural images using fourier transform and spatial pyramids. In *Proc. of ICIP '14*, 2014.

[13] P. Over, G. Awad, M. Michel, J. Fiscus, G. Sanders, W. Kraaij, A. F. Smeaton, and G. Quéenot. Trecvid 2013 – an overview of the goals, tasks, data, evaluation mechanisms and metrics. In *TRECVID 2013*, 2013.

[14] M. Rabbath, P. Sandhaus, and S. Boll. Automatic creation of photo books from stories in social media. *ACM TOMM*, 2011.

[15] S. Roy and S. K. Bandyophadyay. Face detection using a hybrid approach that combines hsv and rgb. *IJCSMC*, 2013.

[16] A. E. Savakis, S. P. Etz, and A. C. P. Loui. Evaluation of image appeal in consumer photography. 2000.

[17] B.-S. Seah, S. S. Bhowmick, and A. Sun. Prism: Concept-preserving social image search results summarization. In *Proc. of SIGIR '14*, 2014.

[18] P. Sinha, S. Mehrotra, and R. Jain. Summarization of personal photologs using multidimensional content and context. In *Proc. of ICMR '11*, 2011.

[19] K. E. Van De Sande, T. Gevers, and C. G. Snoek. Evaluating color descriptors for object and scene recognition. *IEEE TPAMI*, 2010.

[20] P. Viola and M. J. Jones. Robust real-time face detection. *Proc. of IJCV*, 2004.

[21] T. Walber, A. Scherp, and S. Staab. Smart photo selection: Interpret gaze as personal interest. In *Proc. of CHI '14*, 2014.

[22] M.-N. Wu, C.-C. Lin, and C.-C. Chang. Novel image copy detection with rotating tolerance. *Journal of Systems and Software*, 80, 2007.

[23] C.-H. Yeh, Y.-C. Ho, B. A. Barsky, and M. Ouhyoung. Personalized photograph ranking and selection system. In *Proc. of MM '10*, 2010.

[24] W. Zhou, H. Li, Y. Lu, and Q. Tian. Large scale image search with geometric coding. In *MM '11*, 2011.

Latent Factors of Visual Popularity Prediction

Spencer Cappallo† Thomas Mensink† Cees G. M. Snoek†‡
†University of Amsterdam ‡Qualcomm Research Netherlands
{cappallo, tmensink, cgmsnoek}@uva.nl

ABSTRACT

Predicting the popularity of an image on social networks based solely on its visual content is a difficult problem. One image may become widely distributed and repeatedly shared, while another similar image may be totally overlooked. We aim to gain insight into how visual content affects image popularity. We propose a latent ranking approach that takes into account not only the distinctive visual cues in popular images, but also those in unpopular images. This method is evaluated on two existing datasets collected from photo-sharing websites, as well as a new proposed dataset of images from the microblogging website Twitter. Our experiments investigate factors of the ranking model, the level of user engagement in scoring popularity, and whether the discovered senses are meaningful. The proposed approach yields state of the art results, and allows for insight into the semantics of image popularity on social networks.

Categories and Subject Descriptors

I.4.9 [**Image Processing and Computer Vision**]: Applications

Keywords

latent model; visual popularity; twitter

1. INTRODUCTION

Popularity is a difficult quantity to measure, predict, or even define. It is the result of many sundry factors and lies mercy to the whim of the zeitgeist. Still, we observe that humans exhibit some capability to predict what others will enjoy. For example, one expects that a photo of a cute kitten will yield a more positive response than a blurry photo of the ground. This fact suggests that there is an objective commonality to the appeal of certain images. The topic of this paper is the prediction of the popularity of images on social networks, such as photo-sharing websites and microblogging services, with the aim to gain insight into what qualities make a particular image popular.

Popularity prediction has been explored in the textual domain, *e.g.* [19, 18], but limited work has been done on the challenging problem of predicting popularity of images based on image content. Prior work has investigated the relative effectiveness of various features, both social and visual, for predicting the popularity of images on social networks [9, 3, 15]. These works demonstrate that visual features can be used to predict popularity of images. We build upon this foundation to explore the visual cues that determine popularity, identifying latently both the visual themes associated with popularity as well as those bound to unpopular images.

Previous work on image popularity has viewed the problem through the lenses of several different paradigms. Both [3] and [9] address popularity prediction as a regression problem, using support vector regression and random forests respectively. Meanwhile, McParlane et al.[15] cast the problem as one of binary classification, and utilize an SVM with a nonlinear kernel to make predictions. The method proposed in this paper instead views popularity prediction as

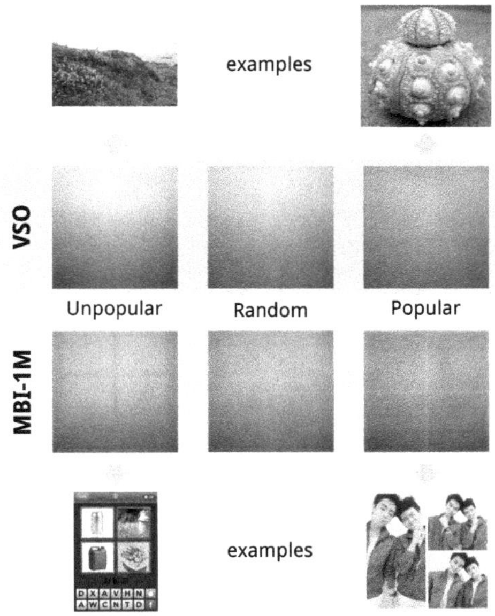

Figure 1: The average of 10,000 popular, unpopular, and random images for two datasets. Note the suggestion of a horizon line in the unpopular images of the Visual Sentiment Ontology dataset [2], while the popular images appear to have a more central composition. Meanwhile, our proposed dataset of 1M Micro-Blog Images from Twitter appear less organic, with highly defined structures indicative of many near-identical images. There is also horizontal striation suggestive of text. We report our visual popularity prediction experiments in the context of both photo sharing websites and microblogging.

ICMR'15, June 23–26, 2015, Shanghai, China.
Copyright © 2015 ACM 978-1-4503-3274-3/15/06 ...$15.00.
http://dx.doi.org/10.1145/2671188.2749405.

Figure 2: Thumbnails of a random selection of photos from two datasets. Note the larger emphasis on natural images in the Flickr-based dataset on the left, versus the large number of graphics in the proposed Micro-Blog Images dataset on the right.

essentially a retrieval problem, and introduces a novel application of latent weights to improve performance and gain insight on visual popularity. Furthermore, previous papers have focused on a comparison and combination of visual and other features, while we seek to understand more about the nature of visual popularity itself.

There is a fundamental question as to whether popularity can be measured objectively. Following previously published work [18, 3, 9] we assume that recorded metrics like view count, comment count, and "likes" are indicative of overall popularity. However, there is no unified evaluation metric in the literature, which is in part due to the difference between viewing the problem of popularity prediction as either binary classification or regression. McParlane et al. [15] report the mean class accuracy, choosing a binarization of the annotations where the 20% most popular images belong to the positive class, and the remaining 80% belong to the negative class. Alternatively, Can et al.[3] report the root-mean-square error in the log domain, as they have approached the popularity prediction as a regression problem. Finally, Khosla et al.[9] address the problem as a ranking problem and report results in Spearman's correlation coefficient, a measure of the similarity between two rankings. Since our methods also consider popularity prediction as a ranking problem, we follow [9] and use Spearman's correlation coefficient for evaluation.

Both [9, 15] use large-scale datasets from the photo-sharing website Flickr. Khosla et al.[9] use the Visual Sentiment Ontology dataset [2], while McParlane et al.[15] use the MIR-1M dataset [13]. Despite using a large dataset, [15] experiments only on a small subset of the MIR-1M dataset of 1000 images. Flickr is a photo-sharing website, and thus the nature of its images may differ greatly from the nature of visual popularity on a microblogging website, like Twitter or Weibo. While Can et al.[3] investigate popularity prediction on the microblogging service Twitter, and present results on the improvement of adding visual features to social features, none of these previous works investigate how visual popularity changes between different types of social media-sharing networks.

In this paper we investigate what factors contribute to visual popularity prediction. We formalize the prediction as a ranking problem with a latent-SVM objective for both positive and negative senses of popularity. In an effort to draw conclusions which generalize beyond popularity on photo sharing websites, we propose a new dataset using images from the microblogging website Twitter (Figures 1 and 2). Our experiments on three datasets investigate factors of the ranking model, the level of user engagement in scoring popularity, and whether the discovered senses are meaningful. Before detailing our experiments, we first introduce our ranking model.

2. RANKING (UN)POPULAR IMAGES

2.1 Popular latent senses

We view image popularity prediction as a retrieval problem: Given a large set of images, we wish to rank the images in order of likely popularity. For this reason, we follow a ranking SVM [8] approach. We assume a set of n training examples $\{x_i, y_i\}_{i=1}^{n}$, where $x_i \in \mathbb{R}^{1\times d}$ denotes the d-dimensional visual features of image i, which is based on deep convolutional networks [10] in our case, and where y_i denotes the popularity of an image, which is defined as $y_i = log(c_i + 1)$ where c_i is a measure of popularity, such as view count or number of comments.[1] The ranking SVM framework then minimizes the following objective function:

$$L_{\text{rnk}} = \sum_i \sum_j |1 - f(x_i) + f(x_j)|_+ \qquad (1)$$
$$\forall i, j \text{ s.t. } y_i > y_j$$

where $f(x) = w^\top x$ is the prediction function, and $w \in \mathbb{R}^{1\times d}$ is the weight vector to learn. Due to the size of our training sets, we train all our models using stochastic gradient descent [1] with mini-batches of around 100 images where all viable pairs are incorporated into the computed gradient.

Visual popularity is a challenging problem, and the visual clues which determine popularity may cover a wide range of image types. As an example, consider photos of celebrities and photos of beautiful landscapes. Both types of photo are more likely to be popular on social media than photos of spatulas, but they have two distinct sets of visual cues associated with them. The problem becomes needlessly difficult if approached with a model that is not sufficiently complex to exploit the very different properties of landscapes and celebrity portraits.

Therefore we turn to the idea of learning latent popularity senses, where each image is ranked according to the highest scoring latent sense, leading to a latent-SVM objective.

[1] Note that the log transform does not influence the standard ranking SVM objective, but later on we redefine the margins based on the values of y_i.

The latent-SVM objective is probably best known for object detection, where it is used in the seminal Deformable Parts Model [6] to find the location of the part filters. In our paper, we do not aim to find the best location of a part, but instead to find a visual popularity sense to which the image belongs. This is conceptually similar to latently learning multiple models for image classification [16] and for query-based image retrieval [12]. For the latter, a latent ranking algorithm is introduced for binary classification which uses latent weights to capture the distinct visual senses of a label. For example, 'jaguar' may correctly refer to either the animal or the automobile, which have very different visual appearances which would be challenging to fully capture in a single representation without latent senses. We draw inspiration from these approaches and adapt them to the problem of popularity prediction, with the intent to both improve prediction performance and gain additional insight into the visual themes of popular images.

Following this rationale, we alter the ranking SVM objective in the following manner:

$$L_{\text{lat}} = \sum_i \sum_j |1 - f_s(x_i) + f_s(x_j)|_+ \quad (2)$$
$$\forall i, j \text{ s.t. } y_i > y_j$$

where $f_s(x) = \max_{s \in S} w_s^\top x$, corresponding to selecting the score of latent sense with the maximum response to x, and S is the set of all latent weights.

The method selects pairs of images with different popularity annotations and identifies the latent weights which respond most strongly to each image. It then updates the weights accordingly, by punishing the latent sense that responds strongly to the less popular image, while encouraging the latent sense that responds most strongly to the more popular image.

Due to the fickle nature of popularity, it is unclear whether it is wise to learn as large a separation between two images with similar popularity value as between two images with extremely different popularity scores. For this reason, we replace the fixed margin with a soft-margin that is dependent on the difference in popularity:

$$L_{\text{sft}} = \sum_i \sum_j |\Delta(y_i, y_j) - f_s(x_i) + f_s(x_j)|_+ \quad (3)$$
$$\forall i, j \text{ s.t. } y_i > y_j$$

where $\Delta(a, b)$ defines the margin between between a and b, which is similar to the margin rescaling formulation used in structural SVMs [20], and $f_s(x) = \max_{s \in S} w_s^\top x$, as before.

Several approaches for selecting Δ are possible, including:

$$\Delta(i, j) = y_i - y_j$$

where in our case y corresponds to the log of the popularity annotation. However, especially in the log domain, the separation between y_i and y_j can be very small. To encourage greater separation between examples, we also propose the following alternative:

$$\Delta(i, j) = \max(\alpha, y_i - y_j)$$

where α is a predefined constant minimum margin between examples. In preliminary experiments, we found that maintaining a constant minimum margin yielded the best results, and we use $\alpha = 1.0$ in all our experiments.

2.2 Unpopular latent senses

The proposed latent model discovers categories of images which are informative for ranking visual popularity. It focuses on amplifying those visual cues which correspond positively to popularity. However, it is reasonable to assume that there are also visual cues which suggest an image is unpopular. To draw from the earlier example, photographs of spatulas might be plentiful, yet consistently unpopular on social media. If the model focuses solely on optimizing for popular cues, it may underutilize this informative data. Furthermore, on a qualitative side, identifying common visual aspects to what makes an image *unpopular* is equally as interesting as identifying what makes an image *popular.*

For these reasons, we introduce latent senses for identifying unpopular images which are learned in parallel to those optimizing for popularity. To do this, the latent senses learned by the model are split into two halves. The weights of the first half are learned in the manner described in the previous section, while the weights of the second half are learned in a contrary manner to encourage the discovery of visual cues that correspond inversely to popularity. These two sets of weights are modified accordingly:

$$L_{\text{p\&n}} = \sum_i \sum_j \Big[|\Delta(y_i, y_j) - f_{s_+}(x_i) + f_{s_+}(x_j)|_+ +$$
$$|\Delta(y_i, y_j) - f_{s_-}(x_j) + f_{s_-}(x_i)|_+ \Big] \quad (4)$$
$$\forall i, j \text{ s.t. } y_i > y_j$$

At test time, the popular and unpopular senses are combined to form a single score:

$$f_{\text{p\&n}}(x) = \max_{p \in S_+} w_p^\top x - \max_{n \in S_-} w_n^\top x \quad (5)$$

where S_+ and S_- are the sets of senses focusing on popular and unpopular images, respectively.

3. EXPERIMENTAL SETUP

3.1 Datasets

We explore two domains for popularity prediction in our experiments, micro-blogging and photo-sharing, for which we make use of three large scale image datasets. Descriptions of the datasets follow. See Tables 1 and 2 for an overview of basic statistics.

MBI-1M We introduce a new and challenging dataset for the task of popularity prediction, the 1M Micro-Blog Images (MBI-1M). This new dataset consists of over 1M images taken from Twitter. The images selected are taken from a subset of the 240 million tweets collected for the TREC 2013 microblog track [11] and these datasets can thus be used in conjunction. Users on Twitter are able to share images through Twitter's image hosting service, and 1 million tweets from February and March 2013 which contained such images were selected. The images were collected through the Twitter API, and up-to-date retweet and favorite counts (our measures of popularity on Twitter) were collected for the 1 million selected Tweets. MBI-1M has been released.[2]

VSO The Visual Sentiment Ontology (VSO) dataset [2] consists of 930k images from Flickr, which were collected based on a search through the Flickr API for 3,244 adjective-noun pairs. Two examples of these adjective noun pairs are "beautiful girl" and "little house". This dataset was used in

	MBI-1M
Images	1,007,197
Average Favorites	0.866
Average Re-tweets	1.133
Average Re-tweets + Favorites	1.998

Table 1: Statistics of the proposed MBI-1M dataset

	VSO	MIR-1M
Images	891,297	865,833
Average Views	422.2	904.2
Average Comments	4.6	12.5
Average Views + Comments	426.8	912.5

Table 2: Statistics of the photo-sharing datasets

[9], and thus serves a fair comparison point to establish state of the art. It further serves as a testbed for making comparisons regarding the nature of visual popularity on different social networks. We choose the total number of views and total number of comments as our measures of popularity on Flickr. However, since these have not been made available for this dataset, we collected our own data through the Flickr API, which we have released.[2] Due to deleted photos and other changes, the meta data was available for 891,297 of the images. This subset is used in our experiments.

MIR-1M We also provide some results on the MIR-1M [13] dataset, a dataset of 1M images from Flickr with a creative commons license. The images are selected based on their Flickr interestingness scores. The MIR-1M dataset was introduced for benchmarking image retrieval, however McParlane et al. [15] has made available popularity data for 865,833 images. For this dataset we use the total number of views as our measure of popularity.

Visual features For all experiments, we use features from a ConvNet structured after AlexNet [10] and trained to identify 15k ImageNet classes [4]. The features used are 4096-dimensional features from the last fully connected layer of the network, and have proven to work well as general and state-of-the-art features for many computer vision tasks [7, 14], including view count prediction [9].

Data Splits For all three datasets, we randomly allocate the data into training, validation, and test sets, consisting of 70%, 10%, and 20% of the images respectively.

The nature of the images on Flickr and Twitter are very different. As can be seen in Figure 2, Flickr has a greater focus on photography, while Twitter contains a large number of graphics and images of text. This is further illustrated in Figure 1, where the mean of popular, random, and unpopular images is displayed. For the Flickr-based VSO dataset, gradients suggestive of landscape photos appear unpopular, while the most popular images appear to have some central subject like a face. Meanwhile, a lot of structure is evident in both the most and least popular Twitter images, suggesting a repetition of certain types of graphics.

[2] Released datasets can be found at:
`http://staff.fnwi.uva.nl/s.h.cappallo/data.html`

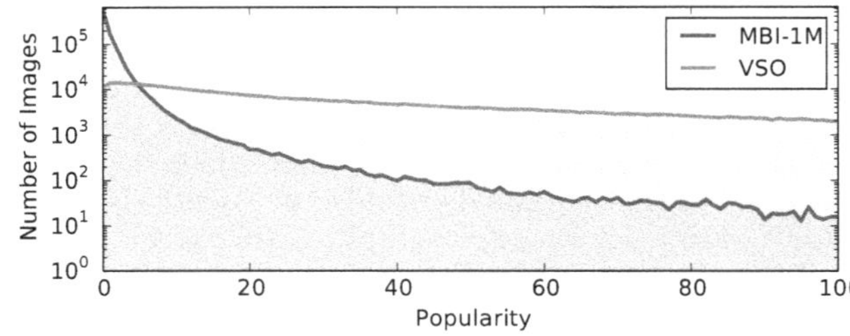

Figure 3: Distribution of view count for VSO dataset and the sum of retweets and favourites for the proposed MBI-1M dataset, plotted with a logarithmic y-axis. The Twitter-based MBI-1M dataset is dominated by images with low or zero popularity counts, while Flickr-based VSO exhibits a broader distribution.

3.2 Evaluation criteria

As stated previously, we see popularity prediction primarily as a ranking problem. Therefore the results are evaluated with Spearman's rank correlation coefficient, ρ. Spearman's correlation coefficient is a measure of the dependence between two rankings [17]. We use it to correlate the predicted ranking $\hat{R}$ with the ground-truth ranking R, as follows:

$$\rho = 1 - \frac{6\sum_i^n(\hat{r}_i - r_i)^2}{n(n^2-1)} \tag{6}$$

where n is the number of datapoints, $\hat{r} \in \hat{R}$, $r \in R$, and the sum term measures the square difference between the predicted rank and ground-truth rank for all examples. The value ρ therefore measures how closely the predicted rank aligns with the ground truth ranking. In the case of a perfect, monotonic relationship, $\rho = 1.0$, and in the case of a random relationship it receives a value of $\rho = 0$.

3.3 Experiments

We evaluate the effect of incorporating latent senses with and without a fixed margin term, including latent senses focusing on unpopular images. We investigate the difference in predictive ability of Flickr views and comments, as well as Twitter retweets and favorites. Finally, we also explore the semantics of the latently learned senses. We structure our experiments by four questions.

Do latent senses improve popularity prediction? This experiment explores whether adding latent senses to the proposed model improves performance. For these experiments, the model attempts to enforce a fixed margin of 1.0 between example pairs during training. We test this approach with no latent senses, and with varying numbers of latent senses.

Few images become massively popular, which results in popularity distributions with very long tails (Figure 3). The difference in popularity between the most and least popular images may be very large, while the difference in popularity among the bulk of the images remains small. It is perhaps advantageous, therefore, to exploit the long-tail nature of the popularity distribution during learning. For this reason, we also investigate the effect of enforcing a large separation between very popular and unpopular images, while reducing the penalty for examples that have similar popularity scores. To this end, a "soft" margin is introduced, which varies in

Latent Senses	MBI-1M Fixed Margin	MBI-1M Soft Margin	VSO Fixed Margin	VSO Soft Margin	MIR-1M Soft Margin
None	0.161	0.160	0.330	0.331	0.330
5	0.166	**0.165**	0.333	0.334	0.346
10	0.165	0.165	0.335	**0.337**	0.346
20	**0.167**	0.165	**0.336**	0.335	**0.346**

Table 3: The effect of adding latent senses to the ranking SVM with both a fixed margin of 1.0 and a soft margin. All values reported as Spearman's ρ. Note a unilateral improvement with adding latent senses, along with diminishing returns with increased number of senses. Due to similarity between VSO and MIR-1M datasets, only soft margin experiments are reported for the latter.

width according to the delta between popularity values, and serves to enforce a more dynamic separation between images.

Does engagement level affect predictability? Popularity is a multi-faceted and highly abstract concept, which is impossible to quantify directly. Instead, highly correlated values like view count or re-tweets are employed as proxy measures. No single metric among these has an absolute correspondence to popularity.

The common thread among different popularity metrics is that they all represent some countable interaction between a broadcaster and recipients. We put forth the notion that all these measures lay along a spectrum of engagement, defined by the level of interaction required by the recipients. The popularity measures discussed can be lumped into two broad categories along this spectrum: "High Engagement" measures, where recipients have a high degree of interaction with or investment in the image that is broadcast, and "Low Engagement" measures, where recipients have a small or passive level of interaction or investment. For the purposes of the datasets and popularity measurements discussed within this paper, the act of commenting on or re-broadcasting an image is seen as high engagement, while merely viewing or "liking" an image are labelled low engagement.

To explore the effect of these alternate measures on the predictability of visual popularity, we test our model on low and high engagement metrics, as well as the sum of both types of metric. Results are presented for both the Flickr-based VSO dataset and the proposed MBI-1M dataset.

How do unpopular latent senses alter prediction? Beyond the existence of popular imagery, it is likely that there also exists consistently unpopular imagery. For this reason, a modification to our approach is tested wherein the existing latent senses are split into two distinct sets: senses attempting to maximize visual popularity, and senses attempting to maximize consistently unpopular imagery.

Can semantics be extracted from latent senses? In the process of training, the proposed model attempts to learn latent visual senses which are informative for predicting popularity. Such senses can be viewed as categories describing the common visual themes of popularity. The question arises, then, as to whether anything meaningful can be said about or extracted from the photos contained within these latent categories.

The visual cohesiveness of such latent categories is difficult to evaluate empirically. To that end, we explore whether any semantics can be attached to these categories. The VSO dataset contains adjective-noun pair ground truth annotation for its images. We evaluate whether there are any dominant adjectives or nouns within a visual category, which would be suggestive of cohesive visual semantics.

For MBI-1M, there is no ground truth annotation to evaluate latent category semantics, but each image has accompanying text from the original tweet. To test whether we can pull any descriptive semantics from this text, we perform *tf-idf* on the nouns of the top most highly ranked tweets per category. The combined text from these tweets in each latent category is treated as a document for the purposes of *tf-idf*, and the words with the highest *tf-idf* values per sense are viewed as the most descriptive.

Finally, the proposed method is also compared against previously published results.

4. RESULTS

4.1 Latent senses

As seen in Table 3, the inclusion of latent senses within the ranking SVM model improves performance, but there are limited or diminishing returns after only a few senses have been added. It is important to note that this is merely a reflection of the overall ranking performance of the model, and does not necessarily say anything about whether additional senses may improve the semantic interpretability of popularity. Whether these latent senses have any semantic cohesiveness will be investigated in a later section.

Also visible in Table 3, introducing a more dynamic margin has a small effect on the performance of the model. For the MBI-1M, we see broadly similar, though slightly smaller ρ values. Only 35% of the tweets in the dataset have received any re-tweets or favourites whatsoever, and of those, over half have received only one re-tweet or favourite. This means that only 18% of all examples have a popularity value other than 0 or 1. It is posited, therefore, that the benefits of a dynamic margin are largely irrelevant when the variability of popularity values is so limited. The results on the VSO dataset lend weight to this argument, as a small improvement over the fixed margin is observed. The VSO dataset has a distribution with a much wider spread across popularity scores, and therefore the incorporation of this information within the model is expected to be more useful than in the case of MBI-1M.

During learning, a gradient is only calculated for those latent senses which exhibit the maximum response to the example images. This raises a concern that a random initialization of the weights could result in overly dominant senses being subject to the majority of the learning. Latent senses with less fortuitous initializations might then languish, being rarely or never selected during training. To help ensure

⇐ *Predicted more popular*

Figure 4: An example of three latent senses learned on the VSO dataset, showing the test images each sense predicts as most popular. Note that, while the model learns latent visual categories, there is no guarantee of semantic similarity. In particular, the top row exhibits a visual cohesion but a semantic diversity.

that all latent senses have a chance to learn, we use the centroids of a k-means clustering on the top 1000 most popular images to initialize our latent weights. We observe an improvement from $\rho = 0.162$ to $\rho = 0.165$ on MBI-1M when latent weights are initialized with k-means rather than being randomly initialized.

Adding latent senses improves popularity prediction. However, there is little difference in the overall predictive capability as the total number of latent senses moves beyond only a handful. The use of a soft margin has a only small impact on popularity prediction, and whether that impact is positive or not appears to depend on the properties of the distribution of the annotations.

4.2 Engagement level

Interestingly, as seen in Table 4, low engagement popularity metrics are more predictable across both datasets than high engagement popularity. Especially marked is the large difference between view counts and comment counts for predictability on the VSO dataset. It appears that the factors which determine total comment count are further removed from the visual features of the image than those of view count. This is perhaps indicative of the influence of an image's larger context on a user's decision to comment on a photo. For example, an embarrassing photo of a political leader may engender lengthy discussion in its comments, but be visually indistinct from any number of other portraits. In contrast, a photo of a beautiful sunset may be more universally appealing in content, but lacks the grander context that would drive users to comment.

It also seems likely that a similar effect may occur in the microblog popularity data. For example, though our model can identify the general visual properties of images of text, it does not incorporate the content of that text, which may play a large role in whether or not a user will re-broadcast a particular image. Meanwhile, a photograph of a broadcaster's family member may warrant a *favorite* from a recipient, but is unlikely to be re-broadcasted by that recipient unless it also holds special relevance for them. Notably, the combination of high and low engagement measures outperforms either alone on MBI-1M, which suggests that *retweets* and *favorites* may be more closely linked than *views* and *comments*.

Engagement	MBI-1M (ρ)	VSO (ρ)
Low	0.151	**0.337**
High	0.130	0.110
Combined	**0.165**	0.328

Table 4: The relative predictive capability of high and low engagement measures of popularity. Low engagement measures outperform high engagement measures on both datasets, perhaps indicative of the wider context of an image playing a larger role in high engagement measures. There is a larger discrepancy for Flickr-based dataset VSO, compared with Twitter-based MIB-1M, indicative of the differences between social networks and their popularity measures.

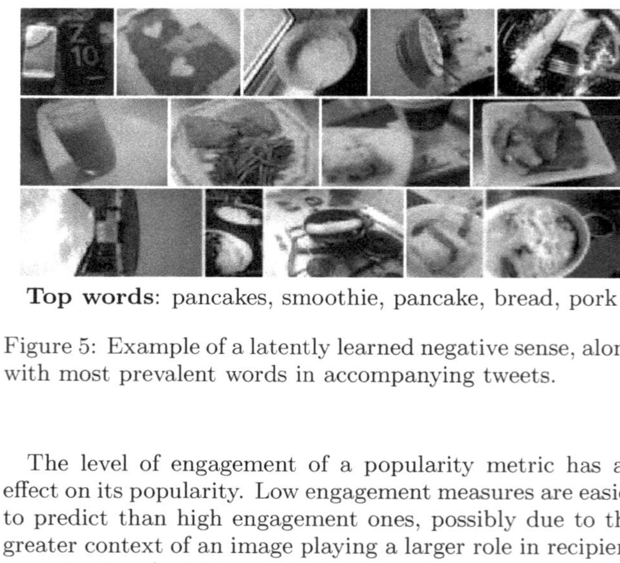

Top words: pancakes, smoothie, pancake, bread, pork

Figure 5: Example of a latently learned negative sense, along with most prevalent words in accompanying tweets.

The level of engagement of a popularity metric has an effect on its popularity. Low engagement measures are easier to predict than high engagement ones, possibly due to the greater context of an image playing a larger role in recipient participation for high engagement metrics.

4.3 Unpopular latent senses

As shown in Table 5, there is an improvement when including latent senses identifying unpopular imagery over focusing solely on popular imagery. When learning only popular latent senses, the focus is on those visual cues which signify a popular image. Visual cues which are uniformly

Latent Senses	MBI-1M ρ	VSO ρ	MIR-1M ρ
Popular	0.165	0.337	0.346
Popular and Unpopular	**0.172**	**0.345**	**0.365**

Table 5: The effect on popularity prediction of adding latent senses focusing on unpopular images. Values reported here for models with 10 latent senses, either entirely popular or split into 5 popular and 5 unpopular. Learning to identify unpopular images in parallel to popular ones yields improvement across all three datasets.

indicative of unpopular images are learned only to the extent that no popular senses should respond strongly to them; once the responses for those images are pushed down sufficiently far, learning halts. This has perhaps little effect on the top ranked results, but has an effect on the overall ranking. Overlooking these visual cues that suggest an image is unpopular means that the tail end of the ranking is not optimized.

Incorporating latent senses to detect the visual cues of unpopular imagery is important for the overall performance of a ranking approach. The learned senses are informative for identifying those images that are categorically unpopular. Furthermore, as seen in Figure 5, these unpopular senses can be interesting in their own right, telling us something about the types of images which are commonly posted and routinely ignored.

4.4 Semantics from latent senses?

In Figure 6a, the top predicted test images for two latent senses are displayed alongside the adjectives and nouns that most frequently appear within the top 500 predicted images of the senses. Note that while both latent categories appear to have cohesive visual styles, the most common words are only descriptive for one of them. This suggests that the adjectives and nouns within the VSO annotations happen to capture the visual semantics of one of the categories, but not the other.

On the other hand, in Figure 6b are the top ranked test images of latently learned categories from MBI-1M alongside the most common nouns from the accompanying tweets of the top 10,000 predicted test images. As the words are not restricted to the small set of VSO annotations, we observe that the top words for a category of text and graphics is representative of its content.

The model proposed within this paper seeks to group visually similar images together which aid in predicting popularity. For this reason, it differs from a straightforward clustering approach which seeks merely to group visually similar images. This means that the latent categories are likely to have broader content variety than you might see with clustering, especially with a low number of latent senses. In the earlier section, it was shown that increasing the total number of latent senses learned did not have a significant impact on overall performance. However, it is important to note that such a change does have an impact on the visual diversity of each latently learned category.

The categories which are latently learned appear to have largely cohesive visual semantics. Through utilizing accompanying text, we are able to automatically extract some

Nouns: dog, animals, cat, face, eyes, puppy, animal
Adjectives: wild, happy, funny, little, cute, great, dirty

Nouns: girls, smile, eyes, face, lady, hair, dress
Adjectives: young, sexy, little, beautiful, hot, happy

(a) *VSO*

Top words: dress, shoes, fashion, wear, bacon, corn

Top words: followers, conversation, text, quote, stupid

(b) *MBI-1M*

Figure 6: Top-ranked images for two latent senses of the VSO dataset (*a*) and two from the MBI-1M dataset (*b*), along with the most common words from the ground truth annotation and text of the tweets, respectively. Note that the VSO ground truth does not have sufficient semantic overlap with the bottom category, but performs well for the top category. In contrast, because the text of tweets is less semantically restricted, the top words of both categories for MBI-1M relate to their visual themes.

Method	VSO (ρ)
Khosla et al. [9]	0.315
This paper	**0.345**

Table 6: Comparison of our proposed method to the regression model of Khosla et al.[9] using our features.

descriptive text for these semantics. The ability to assign words to these latent categories allows insight into the visual themes that determine whether an image is popular or unpopular.

4.5 Comparison to others

First we compare our proposed latent ranking method to the approach of Khosla et al. [9] in Table 6 on the VSO dataset. Following [9], we use Decaf image features [5] with a linear support-vector regression model to obtain a ρ of 0.28. Our deep-learning ConvNet features, trained on 15K instead of 1K classes, using the same linear support-vector regression model obtains a larger ρ of 0.315. However, using our latent ranking method we obtain a ρ of 0.345, an improvement over the current state-of-the-art, which is not explainable merely through the use of improved features, but by using a more complex popularity prediction model.

We also compare the proposed latent ranking against the results published in McParlane et al.[15] on the MIR-1M dataset. In an attempt to make our comparison as fair as possible, we evaluate our trained ranking models on a binarized testset. McParlane et al. binarized their data in such a way that the top 20% most popular images were assigned to the positive, "popular" class, and the remainder were assigned to the "unpopular" class. They report 53% accuracy on a test set of 1,000 images comprised of 50 % popular and 50% unpopular images, and 59% accuracy using a combination of visual, social and textual features. To approximate their testing environment, we calculate accuracy on a subset of our test images, which is comprised of the 20% most popular images, and an equal number of random images from the remaining 80%, resulting in over 60K test images. To binarize the prediction of our ranking model, we use $l_i = [\![\hat{y}_i > \text{thr}]\!]$, where $\hat{y}_i$ is the predicted popularity, we find the optimal threshold value based on the performance on the training data. Our model performs with 64% accuracy, which compares favourably to the published results of McParlane et al.

5. CONCLUSIONS

We have explored various factors of image popularity on social media: popular and unpopular visual senses, low and high engagement popularity measurements, and different sources of social media. Our proposed ranking model outperforms the current state-of-the-art in predicting popularity, yet the community has a long way to go before image popularity prediction is fully understood. By making available the MBI-1M dataset and our full evaluation protocol, we hope to engage other researchers into the challenging quest of image popularity prediction as well.

Acknowledgments This research is supported by the STW STORY project and the Dutch national program COMMIT.

6. REFERENCES

[1] Z. Akata, F. Perronnin, Z. Harchaoui, and C. Schmid. Good practice in large-scale learning for image classification. *IEEE Trans. PAMI*, 36(3):507–520, 2014.

[2] D. Borth, R. Ji, T. Chen, T. Breuel, and S.-F. Chang. Large-scale visual sentiment ontology and detectors using adjective noun pairs. In *MM*, 2013.

[3] E. F. Can, H. Oktay, and R. Manmatha. Predicting retweet count using visual cues. In *CIKM*, 2013.

[4] J. Deng, W. Dong, R. Socher, L.-J. Li, K. Li, and L. Fei-Fei. Imagenet: A large-scale hierarchical image database. In *CVPR*, 2009.

[5] J. Donahue, Y. Jia, O. Vinyals, J. Hoffman, N. Zhang, E. Tzeng, and T. Darrell. Decaf: A deep convolutional activation feature for generic visual recognition. Technical report, arXiv preprint 1310.1531, 2013.

[6] P. Felzenszwalb, R. Girshick, D. McAllester, and D. Ramanan. Object detection with discriminatively trained part based models. *IEEE Trans. PAMI*, 32(9):1627–1645, 2010.

[7] D. Fleet, T. Pajdla, B. Schiele, and T. Tuytelaars, editors. *Proceedings of the European Conference on Computer Vision*. Springer, 2014.

[8] T. Joachims. Optimizing search engines using clickthrough data. In *SIGKDD*, 2002.

[9] A. Khosla, A. Das Sarma, and R. Hamid. What makes an image popular? In *WWW*, 2014.

[10] A. Krizhevsky, I. Sutskever, and G. E. Hinton. Imagenet classification with deep convolutional neural networks. In *NIPS*, 2012.

[11] J. Lin and M. Efron. Overview of the trec2013 microblog track. In *TREC*, 2013.

[12] A. Lucchi and J. Weston. Joint image and word sense discrimination for image retrieval. In *ECCV*, 2012.

[13] B. T. Mark J. Huiskes and M. S. Lew. New trends and ideas in visual concept detection: The mir flickr retrieval evaluation initiative. In *ICMR*, 2010.

[14] A. Martinez, R. Basri, R. Vidal, and C. Fermuller, editors. *Proceedings of the Conference on Computer Vision and Pattern Recognition*. IEEE, 2014.

[15] P. J. McParlane, Y. Moshfeghi, and J. M. Jose. Nobody comes here anymore, it's too crowded; predicting image popularity on flickr. In *ICMR*, 2014.

[16] T. Mensink, J. Verbeek, F. Perronnin, and G. Csurka. Distance-based image classification: Generalizing to new classes at near-zero cost. *IEEE Trans. PAMI*, 2013.

[17] C. Spearman. The proof and measurement of association between two things. *The American Journal of Psychology*, 15(1):72–101, 1904.

[18] G. Szabo and B. A. Huberman. Predicting the popularity of online content. *Comm. ACM*, 53(8):80–88, 2010.

[19] M. Tsagkias, W. Weerkamp, and M. De Rijke. Predicting the volume of comments on online news stories. In *CIKM*, 2009.

[20] I. Tsochantaridis, T. Joachims, T. Hofmann, and Y. Altun. Large margin methods for structured and interdependent output variables. *Journal of Machine Learning Research*, 6:1453–1484, 2005.

Visual Event Summarization on Social Media using Topic Modelling and Graph-based Ranking Algorithms

Manos Schinas
Information Technologies Institute, CERTH
57001, Thessaloniki, Greece
manosetro@iti.gr

Symeon Papadopoulos
Information Technologies Institute, CERTH
57001, Thessaloniki, Greece
papadop@iti.gr

Yiannis Kompatsiaris
Information Technologies Institute, CERTH
57001, Thessaloniki, Greece
ikom@iti.gr

Pericles A. Mitkas
ECE Department
Aristotle University of Thessaloniki, Greece
mitkas@eng.auth.gr

ABSTRACT

Due to the increasing popularity of microblogging platforms, the amount of messages (posts) related to public events, especially posts encompassing multimedia content, is steadily increasing. The inclusion of images can convey much more information about the event, compared to their text, which is typically very short (e.g., tweets). Although such messages can be quite informative regarding different aspects of the event, there is a lot of spam and redundancy making it challenging to extract pertinent insights. In this work, we describe a summarization framework that, given a set of social media messages about an event, aims to select a subset of images derived from them, that, at the same time, maximizes the relevance of the selected images and minimizes their redundancy. To this end, we propose a topic modelling technique to capture the relevance of messages to event topics and a graph-based algorithm to produce a diverse ranking of the selected high-relevance images. A user-centred evaluation on a large Twitter dataset around several real-world events demonstrates that the proposed method considerably outperforms a number of state-of-the-art summarization algorithms in terms of result relevance, while at the same time it is also highly competitive in terms of diversity. Namely, we get an improvement of 25% in terms of precision compared to the second best result, and 7% in terms of diversity.

Categories and Subject Descriptors

H.3 [**Information Search and Retrieval**]: Information Storage and Retrieval

Keywords

event summarization, social media, multimedia ranking

ICMR'15, June 23–26, 2015, Shanghai, China.

ACM 978-1-4503-3274-3/15/06 ...$15.00.
http://dx.doi.org/10.1145/2671188.2749407.

1. INTRODUCTION

Due to their increasing popularity, microblogging platforms, and especially Twitter, have evolved into a powerful means for getting connected with large scale public events. In such events, ranging from sports, such as football matches, to political events and festivals, users typically use social media to share their experiences and engage in discussions. Thus, not surprisingly, the amount of event-related messages has reached impressive levels [1]. Also for such type of events, a growing number of microblogging messages carry multimedia content that provides additional insights into the event. Without doubt, the existence of an image in a micro-post can convey a much better impression for the specific moment of the ongoing event compared to the limited textual content of the micro-post.

However, a significant percentage of microblogging messages can be considered as non-informative. This fact combined with the huge number of messages, makes it very challenging for interested users to monitor the evolution of the event and understand its important moments. In case we consider messages with visual content, this becomes even more difficult due to the existence of images that carry little information about the event, e.g., Internet memes and screenshots. In addition, the sharing mechanisms provided by social media, result in considerable amounts of duplication in terms of textual and visual content. In other words, an event-related stream of messages with images is quite diverse and noisy, with different associated topics and conversations among users, and a high degree of redundancy. Thus, there is a profound need for event-based summarization methods that can produce concise visual summaries, covering its main aspects.

To this end, we propose MGraph, a framework that aims to create visual summaries of real-world events by post-hoc analysis of the stream of event-related messages that leverages multiple modalities and signals of the messages. First, we calculate the significance of each message, based on the social attention it receives (i.e. the number of reposts). Then, we apply topic modelling to discover the underlying aspects of the event and assign messages to the detected topics. Next, we calculate the relevance of the message to the topic it belongs to. Finally, we use DivRank, a graph-based ranking algorithm, to obtain a set of relevant and significant messages that at the same time maximize the coverage of the event by selecting the maximum possible number of topics and minimize redundancy across selected messages.

The proposed approach captures multiple aspects of the summarization problem in a single framework. Through the multi-graph representation, it captures different notions of similarity (textual, visual, temporal, social), while the use of sophisticated graph-based methods, Clique Percolation for near-duplicate removal [17], SCAN [22] for topic detection, and DivRank [15] for diversity-oriented ranking, enables the extraction of high-quality visual summaries of events. To demonstrate the effectiveness of the proposed approach, we present a comprehensive evaluation on a reference dataset [13] and demonstrate that it leads to superior summarization performance in terms of precision and diversity compared to a number of state-of-the-art methods.

2. RELATED WORK

2.1 Text-based Event Summarization

A substantial body of work exists in literature on the problem of textual summarization of microblogs, which is a special case of the multi-document summarization (MDS) problem. One of the first MDS approaches relies on the computation of centroids, based on textual content. Namely, the summary of a set of documents, represented by $tf \cdot idf$ vectors, consists of those documents that are closest to the centroid of the set [18]. Graph-based approaches have also been proposed to detect salient sentences from multiple documents, with LexRank [8] being the most notable among them. First, a graph of sentences is constructed, with the textual similarity between two sentences serving as the connection between them. Then, the saliency of each sentence is calculated using some centrality measure, such as the Eigenvector Centrality or the PageRank algorithm.

However, the text brevity, the existence of noisy documents, and the diversity of the underlying topics in a set of microblog documents make the summarization problem much more challenging compared to the traditional MDS. In addition, the temporal dimension, that arises from the timestamped micro-posts and the social interaction between users in these platforms, are totally ignored by the aforementioned methods. To this end, a lot of methods have been proposed in the literature, that incorporate not only the textual information of the documents, but also their temporal dimension and their social features. The core idea of the majority of previous works is the segmentation of documents set into coherent topics or sub-events and the selection of the most "representative" documents in each segment.

Nichols et al. [16] describe an algorithm that generates a summary of sports events. They use a peak detection algorithm to detect important moments in the timeline of tweets and then apply a graph-based method to extract sentences from the tweets around these moments. In [6], the authors propose a probabilistic model for topic detection in Twitter that handles the short length of tweets and considers time as well. Instead of relying only on the co-occurrences of words (as the majority of traditional probabilistic text models do), the proposed model uses the temporal correlation of Twitter content to make denser the co-occurrences of terms. For each detected topic, a set of tweets with the highest correlation with respect to the topic word distribution is considered as representative. Shen et al. [20] present a participant-based approach for event summarization. First, the participants of the event are detected and then a mixture model is applied to detect sub-events at participant level. Finally, the $tf \cdot idf$ centroid approach is used to select a tweet for each detected sub-event. Similarly, Chakrabarti and Punera [4] propose the use of a Hidden Markov Model to obtain a time-based segmentation of the stream that captures the underlying sub-events.

Recent works have focused on the creation of visualizations that summarize the key concepts of events, as presented through social media. TwitInfo ([12]) is a system for summarizing events on Twitter by using a timeline-based display that highlights peaks of high activity. Alonso and Shiells [2] create timelines for football games, annotated with the key aspects of the event, in the form of popular tags and keywords. Dork et al. [7] propose an interface for large events that employs several visualizations, e.g., image and tag clouds, for interactive presentation of the event. However, these methods use only textual and social features to create visualizations and ignore the visual content of the embedded multimedia items.

2.2 Multimedia Event Summarization

Taking into account the increasing use of multimedia content in microblog platforms, there have been many studies that consider visual information along with the textual content of microblog messages. Bian et al. [3] proposed a multimodal extension of LDA that detects topics by capturing the correlations between textual and visual features of microblogs with embedded images. The output of this method is a set of representative images that describe, in a visual way, the underlying event. A slightly different problem is tackled by Lin et al. [10]. Unlike other methods that generate summaries as sets of messages or images, that method aims to create a storyline from a set of event-related multimedia objects. A multi-view graph of objects is constructed, where two types of edges capture the content similarity, visual and textual, along with the temporal proximity among objects. Then a time-ordered sequence of important objects is obtained via graph optimization.

The authors of [14] propose a method to select and rank a diverse set of images with high degree of relevance to the event. An interesting part of their work, is the use of external websites as sources of multimedia content, when the amount of embedded images is insufficient for the creation of a meaningful visual summary. They use visual features first to discard irrelevant images and images of low quality, and then to detect near duplicates among them to increase diversity. Then, they apply several ranking methods to select a small number of images that describe the event.

To our knowledge, there is a lot of space for improvements on the problem of multimedia summarization, as most of the related methods are mainly based in the textual and temporal information and ignore the richness of visual and social signals in social media. To this end, our proposed framework incorporates textual, visual, temporal and social features to support the generation of visual summaries from event-focused social media content. The proposed framework extends our previous work, namely the StreamGrid framework [19], improving it in a number of ways: a) not requiring explicit temporal intervals to be defined, b) more careful handling of visual duplicates, c) using SCAN [22] instead of LDA for topic detection, d) incorporating social interactions (mentions) in the message graph construction, e) using a more effective significance score, f) using DivRank [15] for diversity-oriented ranking.

3. APPROACH DESCRIPTION

3.1 Overview

Our intention is to use an event-related set of social media items, to create a visual summary that describes the main moments of the event. As visual summary we define a set of images that are highly relevant to the event and contain visually, the key aspects of the event. As a first step we apply a set of filters in the social media items to keep only the informative ones among them. Then, we create a multi-graph that captures the similarity of items across different modalities. Using this graph, we first detect and remove visual duplicates and we then apply topic modelling to detect the main topics of the events. Based on the detected topic models, we calculate a selection score for each message that captures the social attention that a message receives over time and the coverage of the corresponding topic. Finally, we use a graph-based ranking algorithm to diversify the top ranked social media items. An overview of the proposed method is depicted in Figure 3. Note that, although the goal is to select a subset of images to form a visual summary, the proposed framework makes use of all the available social media items, even those that do not have any associated multimedia content.

3.2 Representation of Social Media Items

We represent each message m as a tuple $\{id, t_s, C, E, u, p\}$, where id is a unique identifier of the message, t_s its publication time, C the content, E is the set of detected named entities and mentions contained in this message, u an identifier of the posting user, and p the number of times that this message has been reposted. Content C consists of two parts: textual and visual. The textual part of the content (C_{text}) is represented as a $tf \cdot idf$ vector v_m, where the tf part is the frequency of a term in the message normalized by the maximum frequency in the message. Due to the short length of the documents in microblogging platforms, this component often equals to one. The inverse document frequency (idf) of each term is calculated over the whole set of messages. Note that we extend $tf \cdot idf$ by using a constant boosting factor b to give more weight to terms that are expected to be particularly relevant for the sub-event, i.e. named entities and mentions. In other words, if a term w is a recognized named entity, its weight is given by $b \cdot tf_w \cdot idf_w$. The intuition is that two messages that share the same set of named entities or mention the same user, have a higher probability of belonging to the same topic. The visual part (C_{visual}) is optional, as not all items are associated with multimedia. In case they are, we represent them using the combination of Speeded Up Robust Features (SURF) with the VLAD scheme as implemented in [21].

3.3 Aggressive filtering

Content quality plays a key role in the generation of informative, but concise summaries. To this end, we first apply a set of heuristic rules to discard a significant amount of the initial set of event-related messages that are considered noisy and of low quality. More specifically, we apply two types of filters on the messages. The first is based on the textual content and is applied on items that do not contain any embedded image. The second one, is based on visual features and is applied only to messages with embedded images.

Regarding text-based filtering, we discard a message if it has very short text (e.g., less than six terms) and mentions more than three users, or contains more than three URLs or hashtags. The core idea behind the aforementioned filtering rules is that messages of that type do not carry enough textual content to be usable in a summary. Also the co-existence of a URL with many popular hashtags or mentions, is a strong indication that the corresponding message is spam that aims to redirect the user to the website pointed by the URL. Also, in order to discard messages that have an incorrect or incomplete syntactic structure, we apply Part-Of-Speech tagging and keep only messages that match the regular expression of Equation 1. Namely, we keep only items that contain at least one sentence that consists of at least one noun followed by one verb. Determiners and adjectives are optional. Finally we keep only original messages and discard all the reposts. However, for each original message we keep the number of times it has been reposted by other users, and we use it as a signal of the social attention it receives over time.

$$\texttt{regex} = (\texttt{determiner?}\ \texttt{adjective*}\ \texttt{noun+}\ \texttt{verb})+ \quad (1)$$

Regarding visual filtering, first we discard small images, i.e. images having width or height less than 200px. To discard memes, screenshots and images having heavy text we use the semi-supervised method presented in [11] to build a model that detects these types. Typically, using a set of labelled and unlabelled images, represented as normalized VLAD vectors, we consider a similarity graph and we construct the Approximate Laplacian Eigenmaps (ALE) of this graph. More precisely, each ALE vector is a low dimensional representation of an image that captures in a compact way the position of the image in the manifold of the similarity graph. Intuitively, images of the same type will share the same neighbours and subsequently will have similar ALE representations. Finally, we use the set of labelled images and their ALEs to train an SVM classifier that classifies images into four types: memes, screenshots, images with overlay text, and real photos.

3.4 Multigraph generation

Given a set of message $M = \{m_1, m_2, ..., m_n\}$ we construct a multi-graph $\mathcal{G}_M = \{\mathcal{V}, \mathcal{E}_{textual}, \mathcal{E}_{visual}, \mathcal{E}_{social}, \mathcal{E}_{time}\}$, where vertex $v_i \in \mathcal{V}$ corresponds to message m_i. $\mathcal{E}_{textual}$ is a set of undirected edges expressing the textual similarity between nodes. For textual similarity we used the well known cosine similarity between the corresponding $tf \cdot idf$ vectors. $\mathcal{E}_{visual}$ is a set of undirected edges that represent the visual similarity between messages with images. Visual similarity is based on the L_2 distance between the corresponding SURF+VLAD vectors. Note that we add an edge in $\mathcal{E}_{textual}$ or $\mathcal{E}_{visual}$, only if the textual or visual similarity between the corresponding nodes is higher than $th_{textual}$ or th_{visual} respectively. Introduction of textual and visual thresholds at this step aims to prune the graph, make it more sparse, and avoid the addition of "noisy" associations between nodes. The directed unweighted edges of $\mathcal{E}_{social}$ are based on the social interactions between users: we connect two messages m_i and m_j, with a directed edge from m_j to m_i, if message m_j is a direct reply to m_i. Finally, the

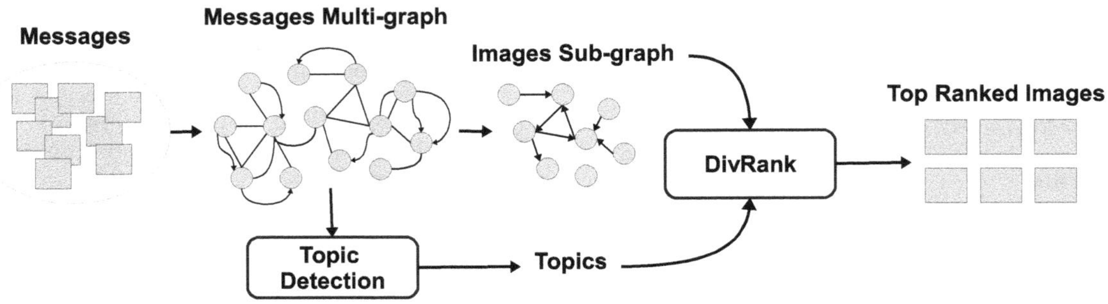

Figure 1: Overview of the proposed approach.

directed edges $\mathcal{E}_{time}$ are based on the temporal proximity between messages. Temporal proximity (TS) between two messages m_i, m_j, published with difference $\Delta t = |t_i - t_j|$, is modelled by using the Gaussian kernel function of Equation 2. Parameter σ controls the spread of the sub-events within the main event. In general, the optimal value of σ depends on the type of the event, because sub-events are wider in events of certain types, thus requiring a higher value for σ and vice versa. The direction of an edge is from m_j to m_i, meaning that message m_j is posted after m_i.

$$TS(\Delta t) = \exp(\frac{-\Delta t^2}{2\sigma^2}) \tag{2}$$

The multi-graph generation step requires the calculation of visual, textual and temporal similarity between all pairs of messages. The complexity of this step is $O(n^2)$, which would make it inapplicable to very big events. To reduce the complexity, for each message we efficiently retrieve its k nearest messages in terms of time, textual and visual content and calculate contextual similarities only to the union of these three sets. Temporal similarity retrieval is speeded up using range queries on a B-Tree index. For text, we used an efficient retrieval scheme based on Locality Sensitive Hashing [5]. For visual-based retrieval we used Product Quantization, an indexing scheme for visual features described in [9].

3.5 Visual deduplication

As mentioned before, we handle de-duplication of messages by keeping only original messages and discarding explicit reposts. However, there are duplicates for which there is no explicit connection. This is more obvious in case of visual content, as users can post the same image or near duplicates found in different sources, e.g., different news websites. To handle this high degree of visual redundancy we use the Clique Percolation Method, presented in [17], to find sets of messages that are visual duplicates. In particular, we use CPM on sub-graph $\mathcal{G}_{visual} = \{\mathcal{V}, \mathcal{E}_{visual}, \}$ to generate cliques of visual duplicates. We represent message cliques in a similar manner as single messages. More specifically, message clique mc is a tuple $\{id, M_{mc}, t_s, C, E, p\}$, where id is a unique identifier of the clique, M_{mc} is the messages of the clique, t_s is the mean value of publication time of the messages in M_{mc}, and p is the aggregated value of reposts of each message. Regarding the textual part of the content we use a merged $tf \cdot idf$ vector V_{mc} (Equation 3).

$$V_{mc} = \sum_{m \in M_{mc}} v_m \tag{3}$$

To create a single visual representation for clique mc, we use the SURF descriptors of all images in the clique and aggregate them in a single VLAD vector. In this way, we take into account small variations between images (e.g., cropping, rotation, brightness adjustment, etc.). After the detection of message cliques, we replace clustered messages in $\mathcal{G}_M$ with cliques and re-calculate the corresponding edges of $\mathcal{E}_{textual}$, $\mathcal{E}_{visual}$, $\mathcal{E}_{social}$ and $\mathcal{E}_{time}$.

3.6 Topic Detection

To detect the topics on a main event we opted for a graph clustering algorithm, namely the Structural Clustering Algorithm for Networks (SCAN) [22]. SCAN is applied on a graph $G = \{\mathcal{V}, \mathcal{E}\}$, where nodes correspond to the filtered set of event-related messages and message cliques and edges $\mathcal{E}$ represent the content-based similarities between adjacent nodes. Apart from content similarity, we also use social interactions to add edges that enhance the density of inter-topic links. Namely, we connect two messages if the one is a reply to the other, as the probability that these messages belong to the same topic is very high. We apply SCAN on the message graph, to identify dense sub-graphs of messages. These sub-graphs represent the topics that exist in the stream of messages. Hence, each topic is represented as a set of highly connected messages in the graph. Once topics T are detected, we use the messages M_i associated with each $topic_i \in T$ to calculate a merged $tf \cdot idf$ vector V_i that describe its content, in a similar manner to how we calculate merged vectors for cliques.

However, a substantial amount of messages is kept outside of the detected clusters. These messages are divided into two categories, hubs and outliers. Hubs are bridges to more than one clusters, while outliers are messages that are not related to any of the clusters. Some of these messages can be considered as non-informative messages that cannot contribute valuable information to the summary. However this is not the case for all of them, as some messages, despite not belonging to any cluster, may include valuable information that attracts a lot of social attention. This is more obvious in case of messages with images. Such messages could have little textual information, therefore very low textual similarity to the other messages. Moreover, visual content could be different, even between messages of the same topic. Therefore, it is likely that important images could be left unclustered. To this end, we do not discard the unassigned messages, but we form single item clusters and use them in the ranking process, as will be described in the next section.

3.7 Message Selection and Ranking

Our goal is to calculate an overall importance score for each of the messages or message cliques of the filtered set, and rank them according to it. The importance score of a message m or clique mc is a combination of two factors: a) the social attention it receives over time, and b) the significance of the topic it may belong to.

Social Attention. The popularity of a message or clique, i.e. the number of the reposts is receives over time, can be considered as a measure of the social attention it receives. A high value of social attention, indicates implicitly an important and hence representative message regarding the event. We measure social attention using Equation 4, where p is the number of reposts and λ a smoothing parameter. We opted for the use of a logarithmic function due to the fact that the number of reposts in social media follows a power law distribution.

$$S_{att}(m) = \log_2(p + \lambda) \tag{4}$$

Topic Coverage. The association of a message with a detected topic is a strong indication of its importance. Namely, a message that is part of a topic contributes valuable information about an aspect of the event and should get a high importance score. However some messages of a topic are more representative than others. Also some topics are more significant than others, hence messages from these topics should receive higher scores. To this end, we quantify the topic coverage of a message using Equation 6. Its first part captures the relevance to the topic and is calculated as the textual similarity of m to the topic centroid V_i. Its second part captures the significance S of the underlying topic, so that messages from largest clusters get higher scores.

$$S(topic_i) = \exp\left(\frac{|M_i|}{\max\limits_{k \in T} |M_k|}\right) \tag{5}$$

$$S_{cov}(m) = \cos(u_m, V_i) \cdot S(topic_i) \tag{6}$$

The overall significance score of a message or clique is the product between its social attention and the respective topic relevance (Equation 7).

$$S_{sig}(m) = S_{att}(m) * S_{cov}(m) \tag{7}$$

3.8 Image Ranking and Diversification

The motivation behind computing the importance score of Equation 7 is to generate a diverse set of images in the top ranked positions of the summary. However, there are images that are considered relevant to an event and extremely popular, but they are not specific to the event of interest. For example, an image depicting the flag of Ukraine could be considered to be relevant for an event about the Ukraine crisis, but it does not provide important information about the event. To tackle this, we introduce a specificity factor that penalizes such images. Image specificity is a measure of how much information a specific message provides for a specific event. In other words, whether the message is common or rare across all topics of the event. In a similar manner as [14], we use the deduplication technique presented in section 3.6 to measure the number of topics $|T_I|$ that contain an image I. Then we calculate an *idf*-like score for each image using Equation 8.

$$S_{spec}(I) = \log\left(\frac{|T|}{|T_I|}\right), \tag{8}$$

where $|T|$ is the number of topics in the event and $|T_I|$ is the number of topics containing image I. Finally, the image selection score $S(I)$ of image I is the product of the importance score (Equation 7) and the image specificity score.

To incorporate diversity into the score calculation, we employ DivRank [15], a variant of PageRank that aims at diversity. We use the multi-graph $\mathcal{G}_M$ that was created initially, to get a directed sub-graph $\mathcal{G}_V = \{\mathcal{V}_V, \mathcal{E}_V\}$. Vertices $\mathcal{V}_V \subset \mathcal{V}$ are the subset of messages that contain an embedded image and will be used in the generation of a visual summary. For the creation of the set $\mathcal{E}_V$, we combine the two sets $\mathcal{E}_{visual}$ and $\mathcal{E}_{time}$. In particular, for each pair of vertices $v_i, v_j \in \mathcal{V}_V$, we create a weighted directed edge $e \in \mathcal{E}_V$ with the same direction as the corresponding edge in $\mathcal{E}_{time}$. The weight of this edges is the product of visual similarity and time proximity between the adjacent vertices. To ensure convergence of DivRank, we normalize the weights of the edges, such that the sum of the adjacent out-edges of each message equals to one.

To calculate the new selection score, we apply DivRank using the iterative scheme of Equations 9 and 10.

$$\mathbf{r} = dW^{-1}\mathbf{r} + (1 - d)\mathbf{h} \tag{9}$$

$$W = dW\mathbf{r} + (1 - d)\mathbf{h} \tag{10}$$

Vector $\mathbf{r}$ holds the DivRank scores and d is a dumping factor that controls the impact of the initial score to the re-ranking procedure. The initial value of matrix W is the adjacency matrix derived from the directed graph $\mathcal{G}_V$. Also, instead of using a uniform value for priors $\mathbf{h}$, we use the value of the calculated score of each image in the graph. Specifically, the prior $\mathbf{h}[i]$ of the ith node in the graph that corresponds to image I_i is $\mathbf{h}[i] = S(I_i)$.

4. EXPERIMENTS AND RESULTS

4.1 Dataset and experimental setting

To evaluate the proposed framework, we conducted a set of experiments in the dataset of McMinn et al. [13] that contains more than 500 events of different domains. We used the 50 largest events in terms of tweets, as in the work of McParlane et al. [14]. These events range from sports events, e.g., the Sochi winter Olympics, to political events such as the Ukraine crisis and Venezuelan protests. The dataset contains 364,005 tweets in total, while each event is associated with 4730 tweets on average. However, due to suspended accounts and deleted messages we managed to get only 296,160 of these tweets. About 3,51% of these, i.e. 12,772 tweets, contain an embedded image.

In [14], the authors used CrowdFlower[1] to create relevance judgements for the top five images selected for summarization for each of the 50 events. This resulted in the generation of judgements for a very small percentage of the images in the dataset. To this end, we follow the same approach as [14] to create relevance judgements for the union

[1]`http://www.crowdflower.com/`

of images selected as summaries by all the methods used in the evaluation. In order to have a better insight into the performance of the methods we selected 20 images for each event. We asked from a group of human annotators to evaluate how relevant and representative are the selected images to the corresponding event. We ensured that each pair received three judgements at least, from different users. The group of annotators comprised 20 persons 24-32 years old, educated in the field of computer science, having some experience in the use of Twitter and social media. The task given to annotators was the following:

Task Description

You are presented with an image and an event title (describing a "trending" topic in Twitter). For each image and event title, you are asked to answer the following question:

Question: Is this image relevant to the event?

Possible Answers:

1. *The image is clearly not relevant to the event.*
2. *The image is probably not relevant to the event, but I am not entirely sure.*
3. *The image is somewhat relevant to the event, but I have my doubts on whether I would like to see it in a photo coverage of the event.*
4. *The image is clearly relevant to the event, and I would like to see it in a photo coverage of the event.*

For the text representation, we used several open source projects to analyse the text of the tweets. For tokenization we opted for the `StandardAnalyser` provided by Lucene, which performs well in English text. For named entity detection we used the Stanford NER library with the default 3-class model. For part of speech tagging we used the Stanford POS Tagger, but we opted for the Twitter-specific POS model from the ARK research group[2]. For visual features, we extracted Speeded Up Robust Features (SURF) from each image of the dataset. Then we used four codebooks of 128 visual words (in total 512) to quantize each descriptor and used the VLAD scheme to aggregate the descriptors of each image into a single vector of $64 \cdot 512 = 32,768$ dimensions. Finally, we used PCA to create a 1024-dimensional $L2$-normalized reduced vector that represents the visual content of the image.

For the generation of multi-graph $\mathcal{G}_M$, we retrieve the $k = 500$ nearest neighbours of each message in terms of textual, visual and temporal similarity. The visual and textual similarity thresholds were empirically set to 0.5 and 0.6 respectively. Parameter σ^2 of the temporal kernel was empirically set to 24 hours as most of the important sub-events in the dataset last less than a day. In other words, the temporal proximity between tweets in the same day is more than 0.6. In the topic detection step, we set the parameters of SCAN to $\mu = 2$ and $\epsilon = 0.65$. Finally, in the ranking step with DivRank we set $d = 0.75$ to the most of the experiments. However, we also conducted an experiment to investigate the effect of this factor in the results.

[2]`http://www.ark.cs.cmu.edu/TweetNLP`

4.2 Evaluation metrics and baselines

We applied the proposed method (denoted as **MGraph**) to the dataset tweets to generate a representative summary for each of the contained events. In particular, we ranked the images according to their DivRank score and kept the top N as the summary. We evaluated the average performance of our method in a similar manner as [14] by calculating the following metrics:

- **Precision (P@N)**: The percentage of images among the top N that are relevant to the corresponding event, averaged among all events. We calculate precision for N equal to 1, 5, and 10.
- **Success (S@N)**: The percentage of events, where there exist at least one relevant image amongst the top N returned, for N=10.
- **Mean Reciprocal Rank (MRR)**: Computed as $1/r$, where r is the rank of the first relevant image returned, averaged over all events.
- **α-normalized Discounted Cumulative Gain**: α-nDCG@N measures the usefulness, or gain, of the returned images based on their position in the summary (N=10).
- **Average Visual Similarity**: AVS@N measures the average visual similarity among all pairs of images in the top N selected images, averaged over all events. Lower AVS values are preferable since they imply higher diversity in terms of visual content.

We compare the proposed **MGraph** scheme with several methods for image ranking. Note that we applied the same filtering and deduplication steps to all methods. More specifically, we evaluated the following summarization methods:

- **Random:** randomly selects N images from the (filtered) set of images as the summary set.
- **MostPopular:** picks up the most popular images in terms of reposts. This corresponds with ranking based on the score of Equation 4.
- **LexRank:** uses the graph $G = \{\mathcal{V}, \mathcal{E}\}$ of Section 3.6 and ranks the nodes using the LexRank algorithm [8]. Then, it selects the top N nodes that contain images.
- **TopicBased:** selects the most relevant messages from the most significant topics according to the score of Equation 6.
- **P-TWR:** ranks images in descending order using the weighting scheme described in [14].
- **S-TWR:** groups the tweets of each event into subclusters and select the highest ranked tweet of each cluster using the weighting scheme of [14].

4.3 Results

Table 1 contains several precision-oriented metrics for both `MGraph` and the competing methods. Not surprisingly, the worst results for all the metrics are those of `Random` selection. Regarding P@N the best results were achieved from `MGraph`. For P@1, popularity-based methods, such as `Most-Popular` and `P-TWR`, achieved very good results as would

Table 1: Comparison of summarization methods in terms of precision. Bold values indicate the highest performing method for the given metric.

Method	P@1	P@5	P@10	S@10	MRR
Random	0.391	0.400	0.405	0.800	0.562
MostPop	0.522	0.469	0.446	0.848	0.669
LexRank	0.456	0.452	0.420	0.847	0.611
TopicBased	0.457	0.473	0.469	0.847	0.620
P-TWR	0.521	0.486	0.437	0.826	0.673
S-TWR	0.478	0.452	0.435	0.869	0.661
MGraph	**0.587**	**0.518**	**0.544**	**0.913**	**0.728**

be expected. This means that the image having the highest value of popularity, has a higher possibility of being relevant to the event. However, the performance of these two methods drops significantly for P@5 and P@10. This is explained by the fact that although some image might be considered as irrelevant or marginally relevant, it could still attract the attention of OSN users for a number of other reasons (e.g., it could be funny), and would therefore be highly ranked by popularity-based methods. Success for the top 10 retrieved images is high for all methods, even for the `Random` one. However, even in this case our method achieves a better value of S@10. The average mean reciprocal rank (MRR) is also higher for our method, with the popularity-based method achieving the next best results. Note that the average performance for this metric for the popularity based methods is benefiting from the cases that the most popular image is relevant. This mainly occurs when the number of reposts of an image gets extremely high values, e.g., hundreds or thousands of reposts. However, in events that there are no such images the performance drops significantly. In contrast our method handles successfully such cases, as it does not solely rely on the popularity of images, but also considers their association with the underlying topics.

Table 2 presents a comparison among methods in terms of their diversity performance. According to it, `MGraph` achieves the best value of α-nDCG@10, with `S-TWR` having the second best performance. This indicates that the use of the DivRank algorithm resulted in a more diverse set of relevant images compared to the other methods. Compared to the `S-TWR` method that aims to achieve diversity by using clustering of images, our method achieves an α-nDCG score that is improved by a factor of 7%. It is noteworthy that this improvement is achieved without sacrificing precision, as P@10 compared to `S-TWR` is also improved by 25%. In case of average visual similarity between images the best result is obtained by `S-TWR`. Our method has somewhat worse performance in terms of AVS@5, where it is ranked second, while for AVS@10, it is ranked third. The worst results in terms of AVS are obtained using `LexRank`. This is reasonable as `LexRank` is based on the PageRank algorithm, and hence it favours images that are highly connected, i.e. images that are highly similar in terms of visual content. One should be cautious regarding the interpretation of AVS: although it is a reasonable measure of diversity, it is solely based on the use of visual features, hence it might not be able to capture the users' perception. In addition, it is expected that the inclusion of irrelevant images in the set of selected, would result in lower values for AVS, but this is obviously not desirable.

Table 2: Comparison of summarization methods in terms of diversity. Bold values indicate the highest performing method for the given metric.

Method	α-nDCG@10	AVS@5	AVS@10
Random	0.657	0.024	0.019
MostPop	0.717	0.022	0.018
LexRank	0.685	0.081	0.056
TopicBased	0.689	0.035	0.027
P-TWR	0.717	0.020	0.016
S-TWR	0.722	**0.011**	**0.010**
MGraph	**0.774**	0.018	0.021

Table 3: Performance of MGraph across different event categories.

Category	P@10	α-nDCG	AVS@10
Law & Politics	0.536	0.729	0.047
Arts & Entertainment	0.700	0.721	0.048
Science & Technology	0.800	0.896	0.059
Disasters & Accidents	0.450	0.492	0.013
Sports	0.500	0.624	0.025
Miscellaneous	0.368	0.606	0.053

The events in the test dataset belong to six categories, as shown in Table 3. Each of these categories has different characteristics, thus the performance of our method differs among them. For example, the Arts & Entertainments category is more prone to duplicate messages and images, e.g., tweets with images of celebrities shared by users. The best P@10 measure is obtained for events about Science & Technology, but this should be taken with caution, as this category contains very few events. The second best P@10 is obtained for events about Arts & Entertainment. This can be explained by the fact that these events refer mostly to celebrities and the corresponding images usually depict them in a manner that is relevant to the event. Regarding average visual similarity, the best value is achieved for events about disasters & accidents. This is easily explained, taking into account that images of this type, e.g., earthquakes, can be very different in terms of their visual information even in cases they refer to the same event.

Finally, we study how parameter d of DivRank affects the precision and diversity of MGraph, using different values of d, from 0 to 1, and calculating P@10, S@5, MRR and α-nDCG@10 for each of them. The results are depicted in Figure 2. The worst results for all metrics are obtained for $d = 0$. Essentially, in this marginal case, the re-ranking procedure of DivRank is not performed as the first part of Equations 9 and 10 is equal to zero. The best results are achieved for $0.7 \leq d \leq 0.8$, but even for $d > 0.8$ the performance remains almost steady for most of the metrics. The slight decrease for $d > 0.8$ can be explained by the fact that for such extreme values of d, DivRank attempts to create a more diverse set of images, thus it is more likely to introduce some irrelevant images in the top ranks of the result set.

5. CONCLUSIONS AND FUTURE WORK

We presented MGraph, a framework for the generation of visual summaries for real world events using messages from social media. To achieve this goal we proposed a method that assigns a significance score on each image of the event-

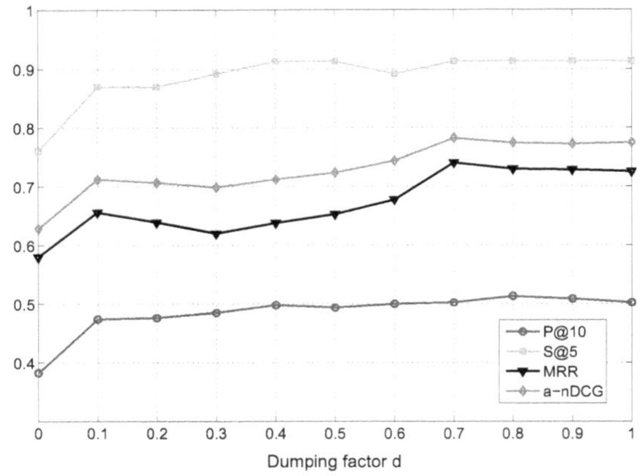

Figure 2: Effect of the dumping factor d on P@10, S@5, MRR and α-nDCG@10.

related set of messages, that maximizes the coverage of the underlying topics and the diversity at the same time.

In future work, we plan to extend the proposed method by using more advanced topic modelling techniques that identify not only topics but also hierarchies and relations between them. Regarding ranking we plan to investigate the use of co-ranking algorithms to rank mutually text and image nodes in a more principled way. Finally, we intend to integrate additional features such as users' popularity, influence and trustworthiness, as recent research indicates that these could improve the results, and especially the quality of the selected images.

6. ACKNOWLEDGMENTS

This work was supported by the SocialSensor and REVEAL projects, partially funded by the European Commission under contract numbers 287975 and 610928.

7. REFERENCES

[1] Celebrating #SB48 on Twitter. `https://blog.twitter.com/2014/celebrating-sb48-on-twitter`, 2014. [Online; accessed 27-Feb-2014].

[2] O. Alonso and K. Shiells. Timelines as summaries of popular scheduled events. In *Proceedings of the 22nd International Conference on World Wide Web (WWW) companion*, pages 1037–1044. International World Wide Web Conferences Steering Committee, 2013.

[3] J. Bian, Y. Yang, and T.-S. Chua. Multimedia summarization for trending topics in microblogs. In *Proceedings of the 22nd ACM International Conference on Information and Knowledge Management*, CIKM '13, pages 1807–1812, New York, NY, USA, 2013. ACM.

[4] D. Chakrabarti and K. Punera. Event summarization using tweets. In *Proceedings of 6th AAAI International Conference on Weblogs and Social Media (ICWSM)*, 2011.

[5] M. S. Charikar. Similarity estimation techniques from rounding algorithms. In *Proceedings of the 34th Annual ACM Symposium on Theory of Computing*, STOC '02, pages 380–388, New York, NY, USA, 2002. ACM.

[6] F. C. T. Chua and S. Asur. Automatic summarization of events from social media. In *Proceedings of 8th AAAI International Conference on Weblogs and Social Media (ICWSM)*, 2013.

[7] M. Dork, D. Gruen, C. Williamson, and S. Carpendale. A visual backchannel for large-scale events. *IEEE Transactions on Visualization and Computer Graphics*, 16(6):1129–1138, 2010.

[8] G. Erkan and D. R. Radev. Lexrank: Graph-based lexical centrality as salience in text summarization. *Journal of Artificial Intelligence Research*, 22(1):457–479, Dec. 2004.

[9] H. Jegou, M. Douze, and C. Schmid. Product quantization for nearest neighbor search. *IEEE Transactions on Pattern Analysis and Machine Intelligence*, 33(1):117–128, 2011.

[10] C. Lin, C. Lin, J. Li, D. Wang, Y. Chen, and T. Li. Generating event storylines from microblogs. In *Proceedings of the 21st ACM International Conference on Information and Knowledge Management*, CIKM '12, pages 175–184, New York, NY, USA, 2012. ACM.

[11] E. Mantziou, S. Papadopoulos, and Y. Kompatsiaris. Large-scale semi-supervised learning by Approximate Laplacian Eigenmaps, VLAD and pyramids. In *14th Int. Workshop on Image Analysis for Multimedia Interactive Services (WIAMIS)*, pages 1–4, 2013.

[12] A. Marcus, M. S. Bernstein, O. Badar, D. R. Karger, S. Madden, and R. C. Miller. Twitinfo: Aggregating and visualizing microblogs for event exploration. In *Proceedings of the SIGCHI Conference on Human Factors in Computing Systems*, CHI '11, pages 227–236, New York, NY, USA, 2011. ACM.

[13] A. J. McMinn, Y. Moshfeghi, and J. M. Jose. Building a large-scale corpus for evaluating event detection on twitter. In *Proceedings of the 22nd ACM International Conference on Information and Knowledge management*, pages 409–418. ACM, 2013.

[14] P. J. McParlane, A. J. McMinn, and J. M. Jose. Picture the scene...: Visually summarising social media events. In *Proceedings of the 23rd ACM International Conference on Information and Knowledge Management*, pages 1459–1468. ACM, 2014.

[15] Q. Mei, J. Guo, and D. Radev. Divrank: The interplay of prestige and diversity in information networks. In *Proceedings of the 16th ACM SIGKDD International Conference on Knowledge Discovery and Data Mining*, KDD '10, pages 1009–1018, New York, NY, USA, 2010. ACM.

[16] J. Nichols, J. Mahmud, and C. Drews. Summarizing sporting events using twitter. In *Proceedings of the 2012 ACM International Conference on Intelligent User Interfaces*, IUI '12, pages 189–198, New York, NY, USA, 2012. ACM.

[17] G. Palla, I. Derényi, I. Farkas, and T. Vicsek. Uncovering the overlapping community structure of complex networks in nature and society. *Nature*, 435(7043):814–818, 2005.

[18] D. R. Radev, H. Jing, M. Styś, and D. Tam. Centroid-based summarization of multiple documents. *Information Processing and Management*, 40(6):919–938, Nov. 2004.

[19] M. Schinas, S. Papadopoulos, Y. Kompatsiaris, and P. Mitkas. StreamGrid: Summarization of large scale events using topic modelling and temporal analysis. In *Proceedings of the 1st International ICMR Workshop on Social Multimedia and Storytelling, Glasgow, UK*, 2014.

[20] C. Shen, F. Liu, F. Weng, and T. Li. A participant-based approach for event summarization using twitter streams. In *Proceedings of NAACL-HLT*, pages 1152–1162, 2013.

[21] E. Spyromitros-Xioufis, S. Papadopoulos, K. I., G. Tsoumakas, and I. Vlahavas. A comprehensive study over vlad and product quantization in large-scale image retrieval. *IEEE Transactions on Multimedia*, 16(6):1713–1728, 2014.

[22] X. Xu, N. Yuruk, Z. Feng, and T. A. J. Schweiger. Scan: A structural clustering algorithm for networks. In *Proceedings of the 13th ACM SIGKDD International Conference on Knowledge Discovery and Data Mining*, KDD '07, pages 824–833, New York, NY, USA, 2007. ACM.

Attribute-Guided Dictionary Learning

Wei Wang
DISI, University of Trento
wei.wang@unitn.it

Yan Yan
DISI, University of Trento
yan@disi.unitn.it

Nicu Sebe
DISI, University of Trento
sebe@disi.unitn.it

ABSTRACT

Attributes have shown great potential in visual recognition recently since they, as mid-level features, can be shared across different categories. However, existing attribute learning methods are prone to learning the correlated attributes which results in the difficulties of selecting attribute specific features. In this paper, we propose an attribute specific dictionary learning approach to address this issue. Category information is incorporated into our framework while learning the over-complete dictionary, which encourages the samples from the same category to have similar distributions over the dictionary bases. A novel scheme is developed to select the attribute specific dictionaries. The attribute specific dictionary consists of the bases which are only shared among the positive samples or the negative samples. The experiments on the Animals with Attributes (AwA) dataset show the effectiveness of our proposed method.

Categories and Subject Descriptors

H.3 [INFORMATION STORAGE AND RETRIEVAL]: Content Analysis and Indexing

General Terms

Algorithms, Experimentation

Keywords

Attribute Learning, Dictionary Learning, Dictionary Bases

1. INTRODUCTION

In the real world, there exist numerous object categories. The performance of current machine learning approaches heavily relies on the sufficiency of training examples. However, the labeled data are often difficult and expensive to obtain. How to annotate images [29] and videos [28] is still an open problem. In order to leverage the knowledge of annotated categories to classify novel objects without training examples, visual attributes were proposed [5]. Visual attributes are the middle-level descriptors which bridge the low-level features and high-level concepts such as object categories.

The most important property of the attributes, such as color and shape, is that they can be transferred among different object categories. Zero-shot learning [13] is proposed as an attribute-based classification method based on this property. First, attribute classifiers are pre-learned independently from related objects. Then the target object can be recognized based on its attribute representation, which requires no training examples.

Jayaraman *et al.* [11] pointed out that the performance of attribute classifiers could be improved through feature selection because of the intrinsic relations between attributes and features. For example, color attributes (*red, green, yellow, etc.*) can be better trained on the dimensions corresponding to color histogram bins, wheres texture attributes (*furry, silky, etc.*) prefer texture features. Current attribute learning methods usually map the low-level features directly to the attributes. However, the dimension of low-level feature vectors is usually very high because of the concatenation of various features, such as SIFT, Color SIFT and HOG.

Conventional methods perform feature selection by incorporating both l_1-norm & l_2-norm or $l_{2,1}$-norm regularizer, which encourage sparsity selection of features and incorporate the attributes' correlation at the same time [8, 9, 11]. For instance, l_1-norm encourages feature competition among groups, l_2-norm encourages feature sharing among groups, and $l_{2,1}$-norm encourages intra-group feature sharing and inter-group competition. Regardless of regularizer types, the underlying intuition remains the same, i.e., encourage the semantically close attributes to share similar feature dimensions. The semantic correlation is either measured according to the semantic distance mined from the web, e.g., using WordNet [7], or from attributes' co-occurrence probability as proposed by Han *et al.* [9]. However, it is usually hard to judge to what extent the semantic closeness can reflect the visual appearance similarity, and there is no guarantee that the semantically close attributes are visually similar. For example, the similarity between *cat* and *man* is 0.14 and 0.11 between *cat* and *dolphin*, based on the Leacock-Chodorow similarity measurement from WordNet [7]. However, we could not say that the appearance of *man* is more similar to *cat* compared with *dolphin*. Moreover, feature selection over the low-level features discards the structure information as each feature dimension is treated independently.

ICMR'15, June 23–26, 2015, Shanghai, China.

http://dx.doi.org/10.1145/2671188.2749337.

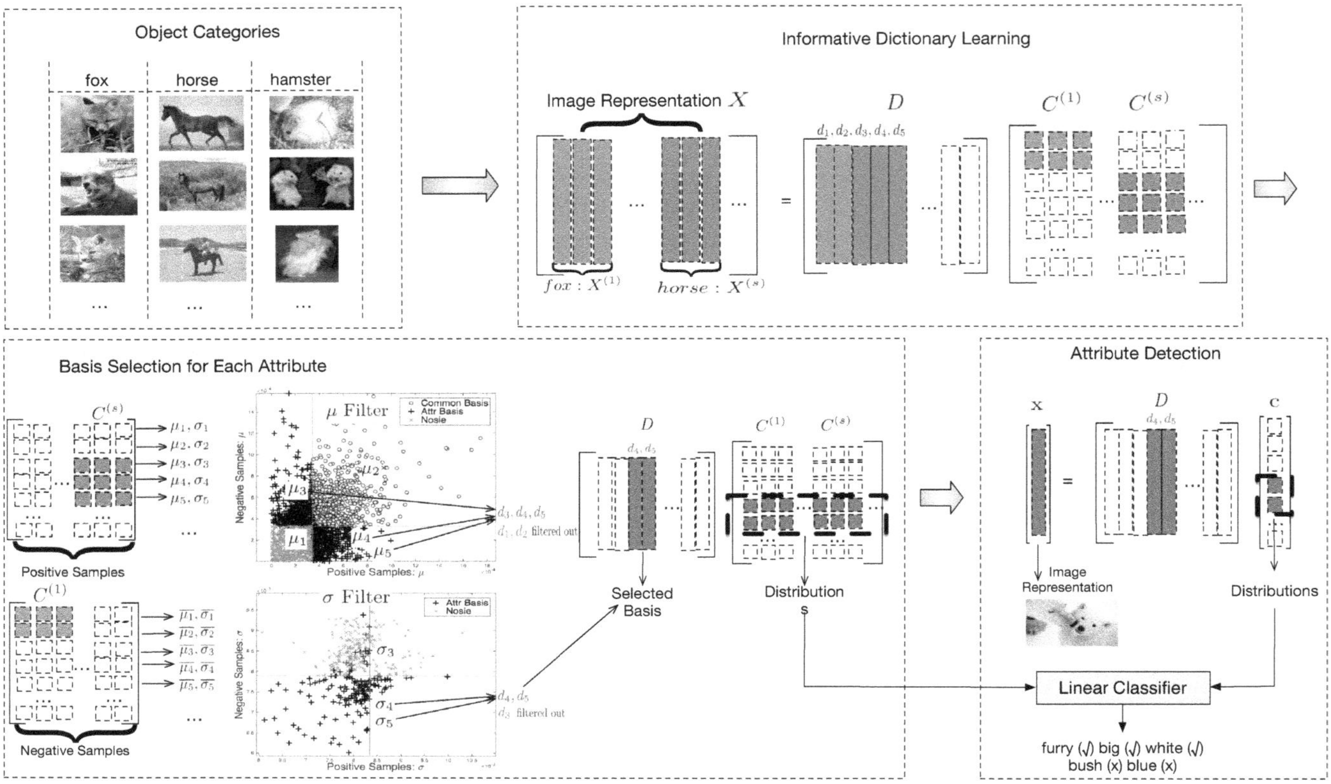

Figure 1: Overview of Proposed Framework. (top) An informative dictionary is learned by incorporating category labels. A novel multi-vector FISTA algorithm is designed to learn the new dictionary. (bottom left) two filters: μ-Filter & σ-Filter are used to select a set of robust and representative attribute specific bases to reconstruct each attribute. (bottom right) Final attributes are predicted by linear SVM classifiers using their distributions over the attribute specific bases.

To address this issue, in this paper, we propose a novel attribute specific dictionary learning approach. Fig.1 shows the overview of our proposed framework. Unlike the conventional methods which map the low-level features directly to the attribute, we adopt feature selection over dictionary, as a dictionary is expected to capture higher-level structure of images [15]. First, an informative dictionary is constructed by incorporating the label information of training data. Second, we perform basis selection according to distribution statistics for each attribute. Attribute specific bases are selected if only the positive or only the negative examples have large and stable distribution over the bases. The larger the distribution is, the more representative the bases will be. Another important factor which needs to be considered is that the robustness of a basis can be quantified by standard deviation. The smaller the standard deviation is, the more robust the basis will be. Therefore, in our proposed method, two filters are designed to select the attribute specific bases, namely, μ-Filter and σ-Filter. The μ-Filter will select the representative bases first. Then the σ-Filter will measure the robustness of the bases and judge whether they are qualified to be selected as attribute specific bases. Common bases are marked if both the positive and negative examples have large distribution over them. The common bases are only used for the reconstruction while the attribute specific bases are used both for reconstruction and attribute classifier training. Finally, the attributes are predicted by a linear SVM classifier using the distribution over the attribute specific bases. To sum up, this paper makes the following contributions:

- A novel informative dictionary learning method is proposed by incorporating label information from the data. The training data with the same labels are encouraged to have similar distributions. A novel multi-vector FISTA algorithm is designed to solve the problem.
- A new dictionary basis selection method is proposed to perform feature selection. Two filters, namely μ-Filter and σ-Filter are designed to select the robust and representative bases for each attribute.

This paper is organized as follows. Section 2 reviews related work. Section 3 introduces our proposed method. Experiments are described in Section 4, while Section 5 concludes this paper.

2. RELATED WORK

In this section, we review the related work on attribute learning, feature selection for attributes and dictionary learning for attributes.

2.1 Attribute Learning

Attributes usually provide more details about an image. In some situations, people may want to know not only the object categories (*e.g., cat, dog, bike*), but also the attributes (*e.g., is silky, has legs, is cute*) in an image. As a type of mid-level features, attributes have shown great potential in object recognition tasks [4, 5]. Lampert *et al.* [13] proposed zero-shot learning to predict unseen objects based on attribute learning. Farhadi *et al.* [6] proposed describing an image based on the generated structured semantic triples <*object, action, scene*>. Han *et al.* [10] proposed a hierarchical tree-structured semantic unit to describe an image at different semantic levels (*attribute level, category level, etc*). Since attribute learning is widely used, the performance of an attribute classifier is essential to its success.

2.2 Feature Selection for Attributes

The conventional methods learn the attribute classifier by mapping the low-level image features directly to semantic attributes, in which regularization plays an important role. The most important function of the regularizer is to perform feature selection in order to prevent over-fitting.

There exist many different attribute groups, such as person-related attributes (*e.g., is male, has hat, has glasses*), scene attributes (*e.g., trees, clouds, leaves*) and animal attributes. In animal attributes group, there are also subgroups, such as textures (*e.g., stripes, furry, spots*), part-of-body (*horns, claws, tusks*) and colors (*black, white, blue*). Jayaraman *et al.* [11] pointed out that the attribute classifiers would have different performances when different features were used because of the intrinsic relations between attributes and features. For example, color attributes can be better trained on the dimensions corresponding to color histogram bins, whereas texture attributes prefer texture features.

Thus, feature selection is an important process to improve attribute classifiers' performance. Many works imposed feature selection directly on the low-level features by using regularizers, such as l_1-norm combined with l_2-norm, $l_{2,1}$-norm [11, 19], or $l_{2,p}$-norm [26, 25] as well as different loss functions, such as *linear regression* or *logistic regression*. Most current works showed that attribute classifiers' performance can be further improved by incorporating correlation between attributes into the regularizer. To capture the correlation between attributes, various methods are proposed. Han *et al.* [9] constructed a connected graph to represent the correlation between each pair of attributes and incorporated the relation into l_1-norm regularizer. Chang *et al.* [3, 2] proposed mining the correlation between semantic labels from the shared common structures of the training data in a low-dimensional subspace. Song *et al.* [17, 18] proposed hashing methods for large-scale image and video retrieval by imposing semantic attribute information. Jayaraman *et al.* [11] proposed using $l_{2,1}$-norm regularizer which encouraged intra-group feature sharing by l_2-norm and discouraged inter-group feature sharing by l_1-norm. Regardless of the regularizer types, all these methods depend on the regularizer for doing feature selection.

2.3 Dictionary Learning for Attributes

Dictionary learning has been successfully applied into supervised learning tasks. This approach significantly improves classification performance as shown in Raina *et al.* [15]. More recently, dictionary learning has been applied into event detection problems [27]. It can also be used for image clustering tasks. Ramirez *et al.* [16] proposed building a dictionary for each individual cluster. The new data are assigned to the cluster whose corresponding dictionary can reconstruct the data with the minimum reconstruction error. However, the dictionaries of different clusters have intersections and their associated reconstruction coefficients are usually large. The discriminative power can be enhanced by neglecting the coefficients of the shared bases.

Some work tried to bridge attribute and dictionary learning. Feng *et al.* [8] proposed an adaptive dictionary learning method for object recognition. Each image is reconstructed by a linear binary combination of dictionary bases, and each basis is regarded as an attribute. Attributes can also be also applied into action recognition. Instead of employing 3D models [20] or body segmentation method [21], Qiu *et al.* [14] proposed learning a compact dictionary for action recognition, in which every basis is regarded as an action attribute. However, all these attributes have no semantic meanings, and thus can hardly be generalized to a novel action. Besides, the dictionary is usually trained by using unlabeled data [16, 15]. When labeled data are available, a more informative dictionary can be learned, which is expected to encourage the data with the same label to have similar distributions. In our work, this is implemented by a special regularizer and a novel multi-vector FISTA is adopted to solve the problem.

3. ATTRIBUTE GUIDED DICTIONARY LEARNING

Inspired by [14], we propose selecting attribute specific bases for each attribute. First, an informative dictionary is learned by incorporating label information of training data. Then the attribute specific bases are selected. It is worth noticing that two types of attribute specific basis are considered: the basis that is only shared among the positive examples, and the one that is only shared among the negative examples. These two basis types are named as *positive stimulus basis* which reflects what the attribute *has* and *negative stimulus basis* which reflects what the attribute does *not have*.

3.1 Informative Dictionary Learning

The classical dictionary learning model only considers reconstruction error and sparsity of distribution. The model is defined as follows:

$$\min_{\mathbf{D},\mathbf{C}} \|\mathbf{X} - \mathbf{DC}\|_F^2 + \lambda \sum_{i=1}^{N} \|\mathbf{c_i}\|_1$$

where $\mathbf{X} \in \mathbb{R}^{M \times N}$, M is the dimension of training data, N is the number of data, $\mathbf{D} \in \mathbb{R}^{M \times L}$ is the dictionary, L is the number of bases, $\mathbf{C} \in \mathbb{R}^{L \times N}$ is the distribution matrix of training data, and $\mathbf{c_i}$ is the i-th column of $\mathbf{C}$, l_1-norm is the lasso constraint which encourages sparsity, and λ balances the trade-off between the reconstruction error and the sparsity.

Ramirez *et al.* [16] proposed learning multiple dictionaries for multiple categories to better embed the class information. Instead of learning multiple dictionaries, we only learn one informative dictionary for all categories which encourages the data with same labels to have similar distributions. We propose solving the following novel optimization problem:

$$\min_{\mathbf{D},\mathbf{C}} \|\mathbf{X} - \mathbf{DC}\|_F^2 + \alpha \sum_{i=1}^{N} \|\mathbf{c_i}\|_1 + \beta \sum_{s=1}^{K} \|\mathbf{C^{(s)}} - \overline{\mathbf{C^{(s)}}}\mathbf{E_s}\|_F^2 \quad (1)$$

The third term $\sum_{s=1}^{K} \|\mathbf{C^{(s)}} - \overline{\mathbf{C^{(s)}}}\mathbf{E_s}\|_F^2$ helps minimizing the distribution variances within each category. K is the number of categories. $\mathbf{C^{(s)}} = [\mathbf{c_1^{(s)}}, \mathbf{c_2^{(s)}}, ..., \mathbf{c_k^{(s)}}]$ denotes the distribution of data from category s. $\overline{\mathbf{C^{(s)}}}$ is the mean of $\mathbf{C^{(s)}}$. $\mathbf{E_s} = [1, 1, ...]_{1\times s_k}$, where s_k is the number of data from category s. α balances the reconstruction error against sparsity while β provides the trade-off between the measurements and variance penalty. By encouraging the data from the same category to have similar sparse representations, the model will focus on learning the shared attributes among the instances in the same category. In addition, learning all the bases in the same dictionary, instead of multiple dictionaries, allows bases sharing across different categories. Thus, the attribute bases can be isolated by searching the shared bases across different categories whom containing the same specific attribute.

3.1.1 Optimization

To solve the proposed optimization problem, we decompose the objective into sub-objectives and then optimize the sub-objectives alternatively. We adopt a novel multi-vector FISTA algorithm to solve the sub-objectives. The details are shown in Algorithm 1.

Algorithm 1 Solution Structure

```
Initialization: D ← D0 , C ← C0
repeat
    fix D, update C:
    for C^(s) ∈ C do
        ratio ← 1
        while ratio > threshold do
            run Multi-Vector FISTA
            update ratio
        end while
    end for
    fix C, update D
until converges
```

(1) Fix C, Optimize D: By setting the derivative of Eqn.(1) with respect to $\mathbf{D}$ equal to $\mathbf{0}$, we obtain,

$$(\mathbf{DC} - \mathbf{X})\mathbf{C^T} = \mathbf{0} \Rightarrow \mathbf{D} = \mathbf{XC^T}(\mathbf{CC^T})^{-1}$$

In case $\mathbf{CC^T}$ is singular, we use the following equation to update $\mathbf{D}$.

$$\mathbf{D} = \mathbf{XC^T}(\mathbf{CC^T} + \lambda\mathbf{I})^{-1}$$

λ is a small number and it guarantees that the matrix $\mathbf{CC^T} + \lambda\mathbf{I}$ is invertible when $\mathbf{CC^T}$ is singular.

(2) Fix D, Optimize C: To update $\mathbf{C}$, we decompose the objective into a group of sub-objectives. Each sub-objective corresponds to one category. The following are important steps of decomposition. The first term in Eqn.(1) can be re-organized as:

$$\begin{aligned}\|\mathbf{X} - \mathbf{DC}\|^2 &= \sum_{i=1}^{N} \|\mathbf{Dc_i} - \mathbf{x_i}\|^2 \\ &= \sum_{s=1}^{K} \|\mathbf{DC^{(s)}} - \mathbf{X^{(s)}}\|^2\end{aligned} \tag{2}$$

For the second term, we have:

$$\sum_{i=1}^{N} \|\mathbf{c_i}\|_1 = \sum_{s=1}^{K} \|\mathbf{C^{(s)}}\|_1 \tag{3}$$

By putting Eqn.(2) and Eqn.(3) back into the objective function of Eqn.(1), we can obtain the new form of the objective function:

$$\min_{\mathbf{D},\mathbf{C}} \sum_{s=1}^{K} L(\mathbf{D}; \mathbf{C^{(s)}}; \mathbf{X^{(s)}})$$

where

$$L(\mathbf{D}; \mathbf{C^{(s)}}; \mathbf{X^{(s)}}) = \|\mathbf{DC^{(s)}} - \mathbf{X^{(s)}}\|_F^2 + \alpha\|\mathbf{C^{(s)}}\|_1 + \beta\|\mathbf{C_{(s)}} - \overline{\mathbf{C^{(s)}}}\mathbf{E_s})\|^2$$

Note that when $\mathbf{D}$ is fixed, $L(\mathbf{D}; \mathbf{C^{(s)}}; \mathbf{X^{(S)}})$ is independent from each other with respect to s. Then the objective can be written as:

$$\min_{\mathbf{C}} \sum_{s=1}^{K} L(\mathbf{D}; \mathbf{C^{(s)}}; \mathbf{X^{(s)}}) = \sum_{s=1}^{K} \min_{\mathbf{C^{(s)}}} L(\mathbf{D}; \mathbf{C^{(s)}}; \mathbf{X^{(s)}})$$

Thus the original objective function can be decomposed into a group of sub-objective functions with respect to each category. Beck *et al.* [1] proposed using the Fast Iterative Soft-Thresholding Algorithm (FISTA) algorithm to solve the classical dictionary learning problem, which is proved to converge very fast. As introduced by Beck *et al.* [1], a soft-threshold step is incorporated into FISTA to guarantee the sparseness of the solution. FISTA converges in function values as $O(1/k^2)$, in which k denotes the iteration times, while for the traditional ISTA method, the complexity is $O(1/k)$.

However, the original FISTA can not be applied to our model because of the third term in Eqn.(1). The third term makes the $\mathbf{c_i}$ and $\mathbf{c_j}$ within the same category become dependent on each other. Thus, $\mathbf{c_i}$ and $\mathbf{c_j}$ must be updated simultaneously in order to make the whole system converge. We propose a novel multi-vector FISTA algorithm to tackle the problem.

3.1.2 Multiple-Vector FISTA

Our objective function is quite different from the classical dictionary learning objective. In the classical model, the distributions of different data are independent from each other. Thus when the overall objective is decomposed into sub-objectives, each sub-objective can be optimized independently. However, in our model, we require the training data $\mathbf{x}$ which belong to the same group $\mathbf{X^{(s)}}$ to have similar distributions. Thus, the new sub-objectives are not independent. The sub-objective with respect to each training data is as follows,

$$\|\mathbf{Dc} - \mathbf{x}\|^2 + \alpha\|\mathbf{c}\|_1$$

The new sub-objective in our model is as follows,

$$\sum_{c\in C^{(s)}} \|\mathbf{Dc} - \mathbf{x}\|^2 + \alpha\|\mathbf{c}\|_1 + \beta\|\mathbf{c} - \frac{1}{N}\sum_{c_k\in C^{(s)}} \mathbf{c_k}\|^2$$

From the equation above, we can find that, for training data $\mathbf{x} \in \mathbf{X^s}$, its distribution $\mathbf{c}$ ($\mathbf{c} \in \mathbf{C^s}$) depends on other $\mathbf{c_k}$ ($\mathbf{c_k} \in \mathbf{C^s}$). Thus, the sub-objectives cannot be optimized independently. Based on FISTA, we propose a multi-vector FISTA to optimize the sub-objectives from the same group simultaneously. The sub-objectives are grouped together if the training data belong to the same group.

The gradient of $\mathbf{c}$, $\frac{\partial \mathbf{F}}{\partial \mathbf{c}} = 2\mathbf{D^T}(\mathbf{Dc} - \mathbf{x})$, is replaced by

$$\frac{\partial \mathbf{F}}{\partial \mathbf{C^{(s)}}} = \begin{cases} \dots \\ \frac{\partial \mathbf{F}}{\partial \mathbf{c_j}} = 2\mathbf{D^T}(\mathbf{Dc_j} - \mathbf{x}) + 2\beta(\mathbf{c_j} - \frac{1}{N}\sum_{c_k \in C^{(s)}} \mathbf{c_k}) \\ \dots \end{cases} \tag{4}$$

Then when updating $\mathbf{C^{(s)}}$, all $\mathbf{c_j} \in \mathbf{C^{(s)}}$ are updated simultaneously for $j = 1, ..., i_k$.

$$\mathbf{c_j} := \mathbf{c_j} - \gamma \frac{\partial \mathbf{F}}{\partial \mathbf{c_j}}$$

This updating procedure of $\mathbf{C^{(s)}}$ continues until it converges. To judge whether all the $\mathbf{c_j}$ in the same category converge or not, we refer to the metric *ratio*, which is defined as:

$$ratio = \min_{\mathbf{c_j} \in \mathbf{C^{(s)}}} \|\mathbf{c_j} - \widehat{\mathbf{c}}_\mathbf{j}\|^2 / \|\widehat{\mathbf{c}}_\mathbf{j}\|^2$$

in which $\widehat{\mathbf{c}}_\mathbf{j}$ denotes the updated value of $\mathbf{c_j}$.

If *ratio* < *threshold*, the update procedure for the category will be terminated. For each of the categories, we run the same procedure. In Algorithm 1, line 4 to line 10 represent the pseudo-code to update $\mathbf{C}$.

3.2 Basis Selection

To judge whether a basis belongs to **common bases** or to **attribute specific bases**, we rely on the statistics of distribution $\mathbf{C}$. *Common Bases* are the bases on which both the positive and negative examples have large distributions. *Attribute Specific Bases* are the bases on which only the positive or only the negative examples have large and stable distributions. Two metrics, the mean μ and the standard deviation σ, are used to describe the distribution of samples over the bases. Thus, we design two filters for basis selection: μ-Filter and σ-Filter.

For attribute specific bases, two types of attribute specific bases are considered, the positive stimulus bases, which are only shared among the positive examples, and negative stimulus bases, which are only shared among the negative examples. *Positive stimulus basis* represents what the attribute *has* while *negative stimulus basis* represents what the attribute does *not have.*

Let $c_{i,j}$ denotes the j-th sample's value over i-th basis. The mean of positive samples over the i-th basis is $\mu_i = \frac{1}{|P|}\sum_{j \in P} c_{i,j}$. P is the set of positive samples and $| P |$ is the cardinality of the set. Similarly, we have $\overline{\mu_i} = \frac{1}{|N|}\sum_{j \in N} c_{i,j}$ for the negative set N. Then the criteria for basis selection is shown in Fig.2. μ_P, $\overline{\mu_N}$, σ_P and $\overline{\sigma_N}$ are threshold values that control the amount of selected bases for each type.

μ-Filter The candidates of positive stimulus bases are the ones which are located in **region 2** in the μ-Filter section of Fig.2. The candidates of negative stimulus are located in **region 4** in the μ-Filter. The common bases are located in **region 1**. Among those candidates, only the robust candidates will finally be selected as attribute specific bases.

σ-Filter σ-Filter is the second layer filter. Given a candidate of positive stimulus basis, it will be selected as a positive stimulus if the standard deviation of positive examples over the basis is small, as shown in **region 4**

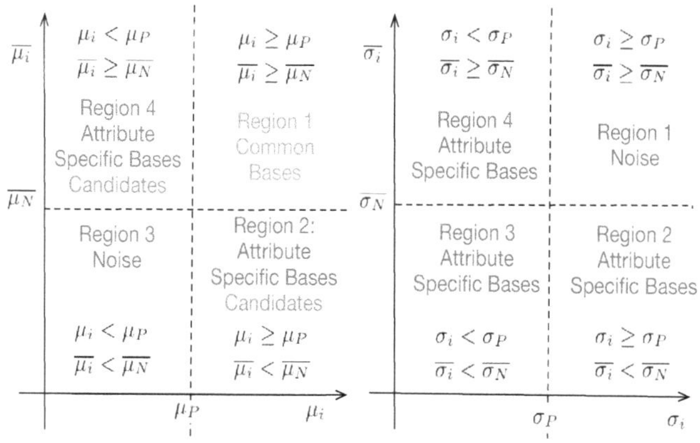

Figure 2: μ-Filter & σ-Filter

& **region 3** in the σ-Filter section of Fig.2. The robust negative stimulus bases are selected in the same way, located in **region 2** & **region 3**.

3.3 Attribute Classifier

After the attribute specific basis selection, we adopt linear SVM as attribute classifiers. The distributions over the attribute specific bases are selected as the training data for the classifiers. To detect whether an image contains a certain attribute, the image is first reconstructed by all the bases. Then its distribution over the attribute specific bases will be used to perform attribute detection.

To evaluate the performance of our method, we use F_1 score, which is the harmonic mean of precision and recall:

$$F_1 = 2\frac{precision \cdot recall}{precision + recall}$$

After obtaining the F_1 scores of multiple attributes, their average value is used as the evaluation metric.

4. EXPERIMENTS

In this section, we conduct extensive experiments to evaluate our proposed method.

4.1 Dataset

'Animal with Attributes' (AwA) dataset [12] is used in our experiment. This dataset contains 50 animal categories, which are separated into 2 parts: 40 seen animal categories and 10 unseen animal categories. The attribute classifiers are trained by the data instances from the seen categories and are tested on the data instances from the unseen categories. 85 semantic attributes are defined in the dataset, which are grouped into 9 groups (*color, texture, shape, etc.*). The attributes are mapped to the categories according to the attribute-category matrix. Fig.3 shows some examples from the AwA dataset. We evaluate our method with different types of features.

4.2 Parameter Settings

In the category dictionary learning phase, α and β are tuned from $[10^{-3}, 10^{-2}, ..., 10^3]$. Dictionary size is tuned from $[1, 1.5, ..., 3] \times 10^3$. In the basis selection phase, the threshold values μ_P, $\overline{\mu_N}$, σ_P, $\overline{\sigma_N}$ control the ratio of bases that are selected for each attribute. The ratio is tuned

Figure 3: Examples from the AwA dataset

from [10%, 20%, ..., 100%]. In the attribute classifier training phase, the penalty parameter C in the SVM classifier is tuned from [10^{-3}, 10^{-2}, ..., 10^{3}].

4.3 Results

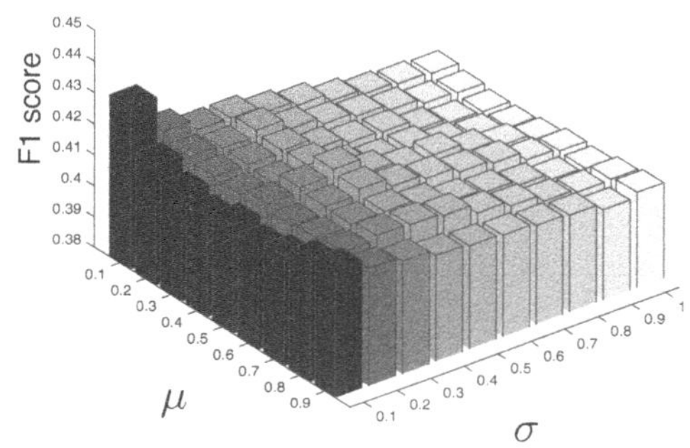

Figure 4: F_1 Score over μ & σ

Fig.4 shows the grid plot of F_1 score with respect to different filter parameters when the dictionary size is set to be 2000. μ-Filter and σ-Filter control the amount of selected bases. The ratio of the selected bases is coarsely grained, ranging from 10% to 100%. The performance is measured on the unseen object categories. The value of the bar is the mean F_1 score of all the 85 attributes. From Fig.4, we observe that when more bases are selected either by the μ-Filter or by the σ-Filter, the mean F_1 score tends to decrease, even though it does not decrease monotonically. The maximum F_1 score is obtained when both the μ-Filter and the σ-Filter only select 10% bases. From this observation, we can conclude that, the basis selection improves the performance of attribute detectors, and the best ratio of the basis selection lies between 0% to 20% which could be mined out by doing a fine-grained search of the ratio.

Fig.5 shows the scatter plot of basis selection with the μ-Filter. The two decision boundaries control the ratio of the selected candidates of the attribute specific bases. Then

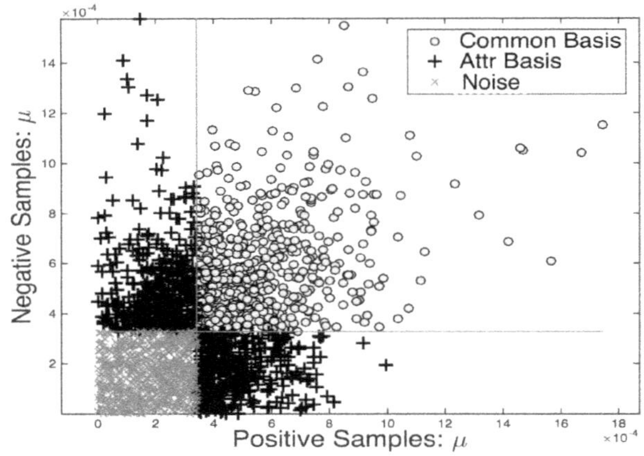

Figure 5: Scatter Plot of bases in μ-Filter

the selected bases are filtered again with the σ-Filter, as shown in Fig.6. Thus, the robust and representative bases are obtained. The decision boundaries in the μ-Filter are determined by two threshold values, μ_P, $\overline{\mu_N}$ which correspond to the mean of the distribution of the positive samples, and to the mean of the distribution of the negative samples respectively. The two boundaries divide the bases into four regions. However, only the bases in the upper-left region and the lower-right region are selected as representative bases. The bases in the upper-left region represent what the attribute does *not have*. The bases in the lower-right region represent what the attribute *has*. The bases in lower-left region are regarded as noises as both positive and negative samples have small distributions over them. By setting the boundaries to different values, different amount of bases can be selected.

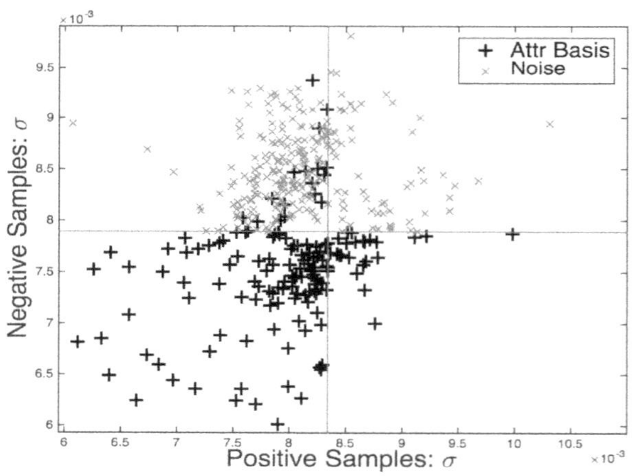

Figure 6: Scatter Plot of bases in σ-Filter

Fig.6 illustrates the second layer filter, namely, the σ-Filter. The σ-Filter is applied to judge whether the representative bases are robust and thus can be selected as attribute specific bases. The decision boundaries in the σ-Filter are determined by two threshold values, σ and $\overline{\sigma_N}$ which correspond to the standard deviation of positive samples, and the

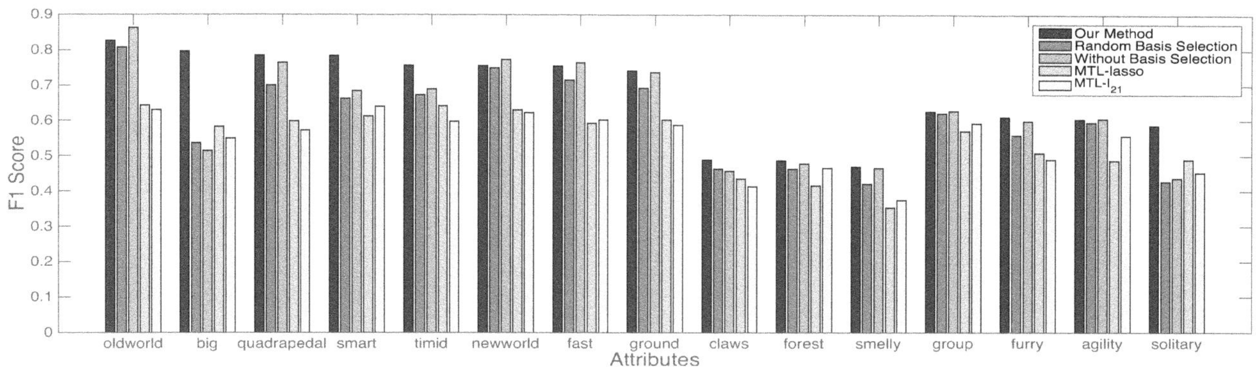

Figure 7: F_1 Score of Attribute Detection on Unseen Animal Categories

Table 1: Performance Comparison with Baselines Based on Different Features

Methods	**Features**							
	SIFT		Color-SIFT		Pyramid-HOG		DeCaf	
	F_1 score	Precision	F_1 score	Precision	F_1 score	Precision	F_1 score	Precision
Without Basis Selection	0.4011	0.4165	0.3981	0.4064	0.4270	0.4193	0.4163	0.4346
Random Basis Selection	0.4122	0.4140	0.4070	0.4071	0.4273	0.4233	0.4159	0.4179
MTL *lasso*	0.4088	0.4077	0.4401	0.4187	0.4311	0.3843	0.4177	0.3797
MTL $l_{2,1}$-norm	0.4107	0.4097	0.4167	0.4112	0.4166	0.3860	0.4432	0.4386
Our method	**0.4789**	**0.4493**	**0.4465**	**0.4348**	**0.4815**	**0.4328**	**0.4752**	**0.4568**

standard deviation of negative samples respectively. If either the positive samples or the negative samples have large mean and small standard deviations over the representative bases, the bases will be selected as attribute specific bases. Otherwise, they will be filtered out.

After performing basis selection for the 85 attributes, the next step is to train the attribute classifiers and apply these classifiers to unseen categories. Three baselines are used to compare with our method. The first is the one without basis selection. The second is the one which performs feature selection randomly. We also use multi-task learning (MTL) methods [24, 22, 23] with lasso regularizer and $l_{2,1}$-norm regularizer as baselines.

Fig.7 shows the F_1 score for some attributes using SIFT feature. It shows that our method outperforms the other methods in 64 out of 85 attributes. Table 1 shows the comparison with other baselines on attribute detection using different features. We measure the performance of an attribute detector by averaging the F_1 score of all the 85 attributes, as well as the precision. We can see from Table 1 that the performance of our method is better than the others.

We also study the convergence of our algorithm. Fig.8(a) shows the convergence curve of the overall function. Fig.8 (b) is the log plot of the loss when updating $C^{(s)}$ for five categories. It shows that all the five sub-objectives converge very fast.

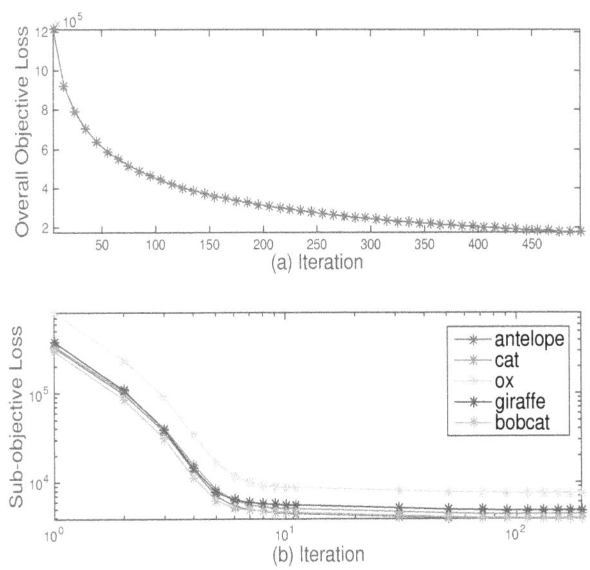

Figure 8: Convergence curve of the overall function

5. CONCLUSIONS

In this paper, we propose a novel attribute guided dictionary learning method to improve the performance of attribute detectors. First, an informative dictionary is learned utilizing the label information. Then we design a multi-vector FISTA algorithm to solve the problem. Specifically, we propose μ-Filter and σ-Filter to select a group of robust and representative attribute specific bases for each attribute. The extensive experimental results show that our proposed method outperforms other important baselines.

Acknowledgment: This research is partially supported by the xLiMe EU project.

6. REFERENCES

[1] A. Beck and M. Teboulle. A fast iterative shrinkage-thresholding algorithm for linear inverse problems. *SIAM Journal on Imaging Sciences*, 2(1):183–202, 2009.

[2] X. Chang, F. Nie, Y. Yang, and H. Huang. A convex formulation for semi-supervised multi-label feature selection. In *AAAI*, 2014.

[3] X. Chang, H. Shen, S. Wang, J. Liu, and X. Li. Semi-supervised feature analysis for multimedia annotation by mining label correlation. In *PAKDD*. 2014.

[4] A. Farhadi, I. Endres, and D. Hoiem. Attribute-centric recognition for cross-category generalization. CVPR, 2010.

[5] A. Farhadi, I. Endres, D. Hoiem, and D. Forsyth. Describing objects by their attributes. CVPR, 2009.

[6] A. Farhadi, M. Hejrati, M. A. Sadeghi, P. Young, C. Rashtchian, J. Hockenmaier, and D. Forsyth. Every picture tells a story: Generating sentences from images. ECCV, 2010.

[7] I. Feinerer and K. Hornik. *WordNet: WordNet Interface*, 2014. R package version 0.1-10.

[8] J. Feng, S. Jegelka, S. Yan, and T. Darrell. Learning scalable discriminative dictionary with sample relatedness. CVPR, 2014.

[9] Y. Han, F. Wu, X. Lu, Q. Tian, Y. Zhuang, and J. Luo. Correlated attribute transfer with multi-task graph-guided fusion. ACM Multimedia, 2012.

[10] Y. Han, Y. Yang, Z. Ma, H. Shen, N. Sebe, and X. Zhou. Image attribute adaptation. *IEEE Trans. Multimed*, 16(4):1115–1126, 2014.

[11] D. Jayaraman, F. Sha, and K. Grauman. Decorrelating semantic visual attributes by resisting the urge to share. In *CVPR*, 2014.

[12] C. H. Lampert, H. Nickisch, and S. Harmeling. Learning to detect unseen object classes by between-class attribute transfer. CVPR, 2009.

[13] C. H. Lampert, H. Nickisch, and S. Harmeling. Attribute-based classification for zero-shot visual object categorization. *IEEE Transactions on Pattern Analysis and Machine Intelligence*, 36(3):453–465, 2014.

[14] Q. Qiu, Z. Jiang, and R. Chellappa. Sparse dictionary-based representation and recognition of action attributes. ICCV, 2011.

[15] R. Raina, A. Battle, H. Lee, B. Packer, and A. Y. Ng. Self-taught learning: transfer learning from unlabeled data. ICML, 2007.

[16] I. Ramirez, P. Sprechmann, and G. Sapiro. Classification and clustering via dictionary learning with structured incoherence and shared features. CVPR, 2010.

[17] J. Song, Y. Yang, Z. Huang, H. T. Shen, and R. Hong. Multiple feature hashing for real-time large scale near-duplicate video retrieval. In *ACM MM*, 2011.

[18] J. Song, Y. Yang, Y. Yang, Z. Huang, and H. T. Shen. Inter-media hashing for large-scale retrieval from heterogeneous data sources. In *ACM SIGMOD*, 2013.

[19] S. Wang, X. Chang, X. Li, Q. Z. Sheng, and W. Chen. Multi-task support vector machines for feature selection with shared knowledge discovery. *in press, 2015*.

[20] D. Xu, Y.-L. Chen, C. Lin, X. Kong, and X. Wu. Real-time dynamic gesture recognition system based on depth perception for robot navigation. In *IEEE Int Conf on Robotics*, 2012.

[21] D. Xu, Y.-L. Chen, X. Wu, Y. Ou, and Y. Xu. Integrated approach of skin-color detection and depth information for hand and face localization. In *IEEE Int Conf on Robotics*, 2011.

[22] Y. Yan, G. Liu, E. Ricci, and N. Sebe. Multi-task linear discriminant analysis for multi-view action recognition. In *ICIP*, 2013.

[23] Y. Yan, E. Ricci, G. Liu, and N. Sebe. Recognizing daily activities from first-person videos with multi-task clustering. In *ACCV*, 2014.

[24] Y. Yan, E. Ricci, R. Subramanian, O. Lanz, and N. Sebe. No matter where you are: Flexible graph-guided multi-task learning for multi-view head pose classification under target motion. In *ICCV*, 2013.

[25] Y. Yan, H. Shen, G. Liu, Z. Ma, C. Gao, and N. Sebe. Glocal tells you more: Coupling glocal structural for feature selection with sparsity for image and video classification. *CVIU*, 2014.

[26] Y. Yan, Z. Xu, G. Liu, Z. Ma, and N. Sebe. Glocal structural feature selection with sparsity for multimedia data understanding. In *ACM MM*, 2013.

[27] Y. Yan, Y. Yang, H. Shen, D. Meng, G. Liu, A. Hauptmann, and N. Sebe. Complex event detection via event oriented dictionary learning. In *AAAI*, 2015.

[28] Y. Yang, Z. Ma, Z. Xu, S. Yan, and A. G. Hauptmann. How related exemplars help complex event detection in web videos? In *ICCV*, 2013.

[29] Y. Yang, F. Wu, F. Nie, H. T. Shen, Y. Zhuang, and A. G. Hauptmann. Web and personal image annotation by mining label correlation with relaxed visual graph embedding. *IEEE Transactions on Image Processing*, 21(3):1339–1351, 2012.

Online Multimodal Co-indexing and Retrieval of Weakly Labeled Web Image Collections

Lei Meng[1], Ah-Hwee Tan[2], Cyril Leung[1,3], Liqiang Nie[4], Tat-Seng Chua[4], Chunyan Miao[1,2,*]

[1]Joint NTU-UBC Research Centre of Excellence in Active Living for the Elderly (LILY), Nanyang Technological University, Singapore

[2]School of Computer Engineering, Nanyang Technological University, Singapore

[3]Department of Electrical and Computer Engineering, The University of British Columbia, Canada

[4]School of Computing, National University of Singapore, Singapore

{lmeng,asahtan,ascymiao,cleung}@ntu.edu.sg, nieliqiang@gmail.com, dcscts@nus.edu.sg

ABSTRACT

Weak supervisory information of web images, such as captions, tags, and descriptions, make it possible to better understand images at the semantic level. In this paper, we propose a novel online multimodal co-indexing algorithm based on Adaptive Resonance Theory, named OMC-ART, for the automatic co-indexing and retrieval of images using their multimodal information. Compared with existing studies, OMC-ART has several distinct characteristics. First, OMC-ART is able to perform online learning of sequential data. Second, OMC-ART builds a two-layer indexing structure, in which the first layer co-indexes the images by the key visual and textual features based on the generalized distributions of clusters they belong to; while in the second layer, images are co-indexed by their own feature distributions. Third, OMC-ART enables flexible multimodal search by using either visual features, keywords, or a combination of both. Fourth, OMC-ART employs a ranking algorithm that does not need to go through the whole indexing system when only a limited number of images need to be retrieved. Experiments on two published data sets demonstrate the efficiency and effectiveness of our proposed approach.

Categories and Subject Descriptors

H.3.1 [**Content nalysis and Indexing**]: Indexing methods; H.3.3 [**Information Search and etrieval**]: Clustering, Information filtering.

General Terms

Algorithms, Theory, Experimentations

*Corresponding author.

ICMR'15, June 23–26, 2015, Shanghai, China.

 ISBN 978-1-4503-3274-3/15/06 ...$15.00

DOI: http://dx.doi.org/10.1145/2671188.2749362.

Keywords

Hierarchical image co-indexing; multimodal search; online learning; clustering; weakly supervised learning

1. INTRODUCTION

Automatic indexing and retrieval of images based on visual features has been a widely studied problem. However, due to the diverse visual content of images, the low-level visual features are typically not consistent in modeling the characteristics of images belonging to the same class, a problem known as the semantic gap [19, 2]. Recently, a number of studies make use of the surrounding text of images, such as captions, tags, and descriptions, as additional features for better understanding and representation of images [21, 15, 22, 7, 11, 20, 10, 18, 17]. The surrounding text of images, also referred to as weak supervision [8], side information [16], and meta-information [15], typically involves high-level semantics that describe the background, objects, and even events about the images. On one hand, using multimodal information helps to improve the indexing and retrieval performance of images. On the other hand, multimodal indexing facilitates multimodal image search based on visual content, keywords, or their combination [9, 1].

Existing studies on multimodal image indexing and retrieval typically focus on techniques that can either identify a latent feature space for the image representations by fusing the multimodal feature representations, such as the Latent Semantic Indexing (LSI) [2, 3], probabilistic Latent Semantic Analysis (pLSA) [10, 3], and Non-negative Matrix Factorization (NMF) [1], or infer the associations among the multimodal features in order to generate a new representation for each image [7, 20, 9]. However, several limitations of such approaches have been identified. First, these approaches cannot perform online learning. Therefore, they cannot handle the large live streams of images that require frequent updates. Second, the surrounding text of images typically has several descriptive keywords together with a relatively large number of words that are not descriptive to the image content [15]. Such noisy information may result in spurious relation between images and have side-effect on the distribution of images in the derived feature space. Third, some of the existing approaches support only one type of queries while those supporting multiple types of queries typically require the generation of multiple transformation matrices, which limits their flexibility for multimodal search. Lastly, all existing approaches return the search result to the query by directly ranking the images of the whole data set. This results in a slow response time for a given query when the data set is large.

To address the aforementioned issues, we propose an online unsupervised learning algorithm, named Online Multimodal Co-indexing Adaptive Resonance Theory (OMC-ART), for the automatic multimodal co-indexing and retrieval of weakly labeled web image collections. In contrast to existing approaches, OMC-ART performs online learning, which allows the adaptation of the learnt indexing system, rather than a re-indexing of the whole data set that will incur heavy computation. To alleviate the side-effect of noisy information and reduce computation complexity, OMC-ART formulates the indexing process as that of simultaneously identifying the clusters of similar images and the key features from their generalized feature distributions, in terms of visual and textual features. As such, OMC-ART generates a two-layer indexing structure, wherein images are co-indexed by the key visual and textual features based on the generalized distributions of the clusters in the cluster-level layer, named the abstraction layer; and their own feature distribution in the image-level layer, named the object layer. Moreover, OMC-ART enables multimodal search by using either visual features, keywords, or a combination of both; and employs a ranking algorithm that iteratively selects the most similar cluster in the abstraction layer and subsequently sorts the images therein in a ranked list. This ranking algorithm may reduce the computational cost because of the pre-ranking of clusters, and will be more efficient when only a limited number of images need to be retrieved.

We evaluate the performance of OMC-ART using two published web image datasets, namely, the NUS-WIDE and Corel5k data sets. In the experiments, we report our studies on parameter selection, retrieval performance comparison, and efficiency analysis. The experimental results show that OMC-ART has a much better performance in terms of the mean Average Precision, Precision, and Recall, and has a much faster response time.

The remainder of this paper is organized as follows. Section 2 summarizes existing studies on multimodal image indexing and retrieval. Section 3 presents the problem formulation. The technical details and experimental evaluation of OMC-ART are described in Section 4 and Section 5, respectively. Section 6 summarizes the main findings of the study and suggests several extensions.

2. RELATED WORK

Multimodal image indexing and retrieval typically follow two main approaches. The first approach is to extend existing algorithms for image indexing with single type of features for integrating multiple types of features. Examples include Latent Semantic Indexing (LSI) [2, 3], probabilistic Latent Semantic Analysis (pLSA) [10, 3], and Non-negative Matrix Factorization (NMF) [1]. Caicedo et al. [2] proposed a Latent Semantic Kernel (LSK), based on LSI, which adopts kernel methods to compute the similarity between the query and the indexed images. Multimodal LSI (MMLSI) [3] utilizes tensors for multimodal image representation and employs Higher Order Singular Value Decomposition (HOSVD) [5] for obtaining the feature representation of images. Chandrika et al. [3] extended pLSA by jointly considering visual and textual features in a probabilistic model, and employed EM algorithm to obtain the derived representation of the images. The Multilayer Multimodal probabilistic Latent Semantic Analysis (MM-pLSA) [10] handles the visual and textual information of images by a multi-layer model, which consists of two leaf pLSA models for learning the visual and textual representation of images respectively, and a node pLSA for obtaining a unified representation. Caicedo et al. [1] proposed two methods based on Non-negative Matrix Factorization (NMF), of which the first method concatenates the matrices for visual and textual features in order to enable search by both visual and textual features, while the second method aims to successively optimize the transformation matrices of textual and visual features, which enables search by using either visual features or keywords.

The second approach is to construct a new representation by exploring the association among multimodal features. Li et al. [9] proposed four methods to infer the similarity matrices for the visual and textual features. The learned similarities are utilized for tackling image retrieval based on visual or textual features. Escalante et al. [7] proposed two methods for image indexing based on the occurrences and co-occurrences information of terms in the surrounding text and the object labels associated to images. The hybrid framework [20], named iSMIER, performs image retrieval by predicting the captions and annotations for the query image, and indexing it by its visual fuzzy membership of clusters.

3. PROBLEM FORMULATION

Given a weakly labeled image collection $\mathcal{D} = \{d_1, ..., d_N\}$ with their associated visual features $\mathcal{V} = \{\mathcal{V}_1, ..., \mathcal{V}_M\}$ and textual features $\mathcal{T} = \{\mathcal{T}_1, ..., \mathcal{T}_H\}$, the nth image is represented by the visual feature vector $\mathbf{v}_n = [v_{n,1}, ..., v_{n,M}]$, and the textual feature vector $\mathbf{t}_n = [t_{n,1}, ..., t_{n,H}]$ $(n = 1, ..., N)$.

The multimodal co-indexing and retrieval problem of weakly labeled images is defined as the process of simultaneously identifying a set of clusters of similar images $\mathcal{C} = \{c_1, ..., c_J\}$ and their generalized visual and textual feature representations as weight vectors $\mathbf{w}_j^v = [w_{j,1}^v, ..., w_{j,M}^v]$ and $\mathbf{w}_j^t = [w_{j,1}^t, ..., w_{j,H}^t]$ $(j = 1, ..., J)$. In this way, the key visual and textual features of each cluster c_j $(j = 1, ..., J)$ can be identified according to the cluster weight vectors $\mathbf{w}_j^v$ and $\mathbf{w}_j^t$, denoted as $\mathcal{K}_j^v = \{v_m | v_m \in key\, features\, of\, c_j\}$ and $\mathcal{K}_j^t = \{t_m | t_m \in key\, features\, of\, c_j\}$, respectively. As such, images in the indexing system, e.g. the nth image $d_n \in c_j$, will be co-indexed by the identified key visual features $\mathcal{K}_n^v = \{v_{n,m} | v_m \in \mathcal{K}_j^v\}$ and textual features $\mathcal{K}_n^t = \{t_{n,h} | t_h \in \mathcal{K}_j^t\}$.

The subsequent retrieval problem is defined as a ranking process. Specifically, a query q can either be an image, or several keywords, or a combination of both. When q is presented to OMC-ART, the corresponding visual and textual feature vectors $\mathbf{v}_q$ and $\mathbf{t}_q$ will be constructed based on $\mathcal{V}$ and $\mathcal{T}$. By calculating the similarities between the query and images in the indexing system $S(q, d_n)$, a list of most similar images $\mathcal{L}$ is returned as the retrieval result.

4. ONLINE MULTIMODAL CO-INDEXING ADAPTIVE RESONANCE THEORY

Online Multimodal Co-indexing Adaptive Resonance Theory (OMC-ART) comprises three steps. First, OMC-ART employs an adaptation method to extend the heterogeneous

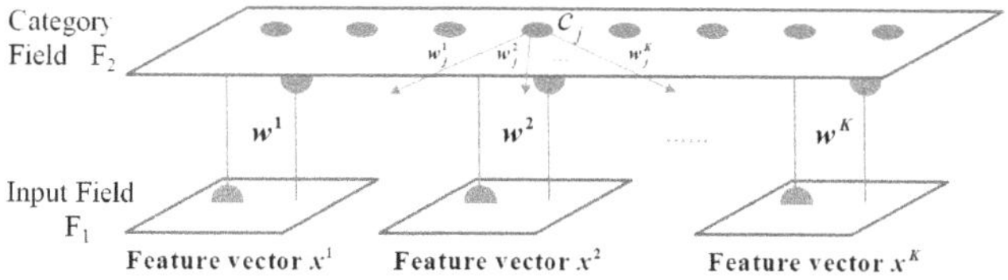

Figure 1: The architecture of GHF-ART for integrating K types of feature vectors.

data co-clustering algorithm, named Generalized Heterogeneous Fusion Adaptive Resonance Theory (GHF-ART) [15], to perform online learning and generate the clusters of similar images with the respective generalized visual and textual feature distributions. Second, making use of the learnt weight vectors of the discovered image clusters, OMC-ART dynamically selects the key features of each cluster in order to co-index the images in the clusters using a two-layer hierarchical indexing structure. Third, OMC-ART incorporates a ranking algorithm that allows multiple types of queries for retrieving images in the indexing system.

4.1 GHF-ART

4.1.1 Heterogeneous Feature Representation

GHF-ART [15], as shown in Figure 1, consists of K independent feature channels in the input field, each of which handles one feature modality $\mathbf{x}^k$ of the input data object, and a category field consisting of clusters that are represented by weight vectors $\mathbf{w}^k$ $(k = 1, ..., K)$. It allows for different representation and learning methods for different feature modalities. Regarding the weakly labeled image collection, given an image d_n, GHF-ART may receive any type of visual features in the form of a vector $\mathbf{v}_n = [v_{n,1}, ..., v_{n,M}]$, which should be further normalized by the *min-max normalization* that guarantees the input values are in the interval $[0, 1]$. The corresponding textual feature vector $\mathbf{t}_n = [t_{n,1}, ..., t_{n,H}]$ is represented by the presence of words in d_n, defined by

$$t_{n,h} = \begin{cases} 1, & if\ t_h \in d_n \\ 0, & otherwise \end{cases}. \tag{1}$$

4.1.2 Clustering Procedures of GHF-ART

GHF-ART performs clustering of composite data objects in an incremental manner. Given an input data object d_n represented by K types of features $\mathcal{I}_n = \{\mathbf{x}_n^k|_{k=1}^K\}$, the clustering process of GHF-ART has three steps:

1) Category Choice: When the input vectors $\mathcal{I}_n$ of the data object d_n is presented, a choice function is firstly employed to evaluate the overall similarity between d_n and each cluster c_j in the category field, which is defined by

$$T(d_n, c_j) = \sum_{k=1}^{K} \gamma^k \frac{|\mathbf{x}_n^k \wedge \mathbf{w}_j^k|}{\alpha + |\mathbf{w}_j^k|}, \tag{2}$$

where $\mathbf{w}_j^k$ denotes the weight vector of the jth cluster for the kth feature modality, the contribution parameter $\gamma^k \in [0, 1]$ is the weight for the kth feature modality, the choice parameter $\alpha \approx 0$ is a positive real value to balance the denominator, the operation $\wedge$ is defined by $(\mathbf{x}_n^k \wedge \mathbf{w}_j^k)_i \equiv \min(x_{n,i}^k, w_{j,i}^k)$, and $|.|$ is the ℓ_1 norm.

2) Template Matching: After identifying the winner cluster c_{j^*}, a match function is used to evaluate if c_{j^*} matches d_n in terms of each feature modality. For the kth feature modality, the match function is defined by

$$M(\mathbf{x}_n^k, \mathbf{w}_{j^*}^k) = \frac{|\mathbf{x}_n^k \wedge \mathbf{w}_{j^*}^k|}{|\mathbf{x}_n^k|}. \tag{3}$$

3) New Cluster Creation or esonance: Given the vigilance parameter $\rho^k \in [0, 1]$ for the kth feature modality, if the vigilance criteria $M(\mathbf{x}_n^k, \mathbf{w}_{j^*}^k) > \rho^k$ for $k = 1, ...K$ are not satisfied, a reset occurs so that a new winner is selected. If all clusters in the category field do not meet the vigilance criteria, a new cluster, denoted as c_{new}, will be created to encode d_n such that $\mathbf{w}_{c_{new}}^k = \mathbf{x}_n^k$ for $k = 1, ..., K$. Otherwise, a resonance occurs so that the weight vectors $\{\mathbf{w}_{j^*}^k|_{k=1}^K\}$ of c_{j^*} are updated in terms of different modalities. Assuming that $\mathbf{w}_{j^*}^k$ contains the features extracted from images, the corresponding update equation is defined by

$$\hat{\mathbf{w}}_{j^*}^k = \beta(\mathbf{x}_n^k \wedge \mathbf{w}_{j^*}^k) + (1 - \beta)\mathbf{w}_{j^*}^k, \tag{4}$$

where $\beta \in [0, 1]$ is the learning parameter. In contrast, assuming that $\mathbf{w}_{j^*}^k$ contains the features extracted from the surrounding text of images, the update equation is defined by

$$\hat{w}_{j^*,h}^k = \begin{cases} \eta w_{j^*,h}^k & if\ x_{n,h}^k = 0 \\ \eta(w_{j^*,h}^k + \frac{1}{L}) & otherwise \end{cases}, \tag{5}$$

where $w_{j^*,h}^k$ is the hth feature of $\mathbf{w}_{j^*}^k$, $x_{n,h}^k$ is the hth feature of $\mathbf{x}_n^k$, L is the number of data objects in c_{j^*}, and $\eta = \frac{L}{L+1}$.

4.1.3 Adaptive Weighting for Heterogeneous Features

GHF-ART adaptively tunes the weights γ^k $(k = 1, ...K)$ for different feature modalities as used in Equation (2) through the *Robustness Measure*, which evaluates the importance of different feature modalities in recognizing similar data objects. Considering a cluster c_j with L data objects, each of which is denoted by $\mathcal{I}_l = \{\mathbf{x}_l^1, \ldots, \mathbf{x}_l^K\}$ for $l = 1, \ldots, L$, and the corresponding weight vectors for the K feature modalities are denoted by $\mathcal{W}_j = \{\mathbf{w}_j^1, \ldots, \mathbf{w}_j^K\}$, the *Difference* for the kth feature modality of c_j is measured by

$$D_j^k = \frac{\frac{1}{L}\sum_l |\mathbf{w}_j^k - \mathbf{x}_l^k|}{|\mathbf{w}_j^k|}. \tag{6}$$

Considering all the J clusters, the *Robustness* of the kth feature modality can be measured by

$$R^k = \exp(-\frac{1}{J}\sum_j D_j^k). \tag{7}$$

Finally, the contribution parameter for the kth feature channel γ^k is defined by

$$\gamma^k = \frac{R^k}{\sum_{k=1}^K R^k}. \tag{8}$$

For efficiency purpose, the respective incremental update equations for γ^k $(k = 1, ...K)$ are further derived:

- **esonance in existing cluster**: Assuming the input data object d_{L+1} with feature vectors $\mathcal{I}_{L+1} = \{\mathbf{x}_{L+1}^1, \ldots, \mathbf{x}_{L+1}^K\}$ is assigned to the cluster c_j. For the kth feature modality, the update equations for the features extracted from images and surrounding text are defined by equations (9) and (10) respectively:

$$\hat{D}_j^k = \begin{cases} \frac{\eta}{|\hat{\mathbf{w}}_j^k|}(|\mathbf{w}_j^k|D_j^k + |\mathbf{w}_j^k - \hat{\mathbf{w}}_j^k| + \frac{1}{L}|\hat{\mathbf{w}}_j^k - \mathbf{x}_{L+1}^k|), & (9) \\ \frac{\eta}{|\hat{\mathbf{w}}_j^k|}(|\mathbf{w}_j^k|D_j^k - |\hat{\mathbf{w}}_j^k - \eta\mathbf{w}_j^k| + \frac{1}{L}|\hat{\mathbf{w}}_j^k - \mathbf{x}_{L+1}^k|) & (10) \end{cases}$$

After the update for all feature modalities, the updated contribution parameter can then be obtained using Equations (7) and (8).

- **Generation of new cluster**: When generating a new cluster, the differences of other clusters remain unchanged. Therefore, it just introduces a proportional change in *Difference*. Considering the *robustness* R^k ($k = 1, ..., K$) for all feature modalities, the update contribution parameter for the kth feature modality is defined by:

$$\hat{\gamma}^k = \frac{(R^k)^{\frac{J}{J+1}}}{\sum_{k=1}^{K}(R^k)^{\frac{J}{J+1}}}. \quad (11)$$

4.2 Online Adaptation of Normalized Feature Distributions

GHF-ART may not be directly applicable to online learning, because the *min-max normalization* requires the maximum and minimum values of each feature for normalizing the features extracted from document content. To address this issue, OMC-ART employs an adaptation method that updates the normalized feature vectors of data objects and cluster weights to what they should be when an input data object incurs a change in such values, as defined by Equations (12) and (13) below,

$$x^{(new)} = \frac{x_{max}^{(old)} - x_{min}^{(old)}}{x_{max}^{(new)} - x_{min}^{(new)}} x^{(old)} + \frac{x_{min}^{(old)} - x_{min}^{(new)}}{x_{max}^{(new)} - x_{min}^{(new)}}, \quad (12)$$

$$w^{(new)} = \frac{x_{max}^{(old)} - x_{min}^{(old)}}{x_{max}^{(new)} - x_{min}^{(new)}} w^{(old)} + \frac{x_{min}^{(old)} - x_{min}^{(new)}}{x_{max}^{(new)} - x_{min}^{(new)}}, \quad (13)$$

where x denotes a feature extracted from document content, $x^{(old)}$ is the value of x calculated based on the old maximum value $x_{max}^{(old)}$ and minimum value $x_{min}^{(old)}$, and $x^{(new)}$ is the updated value calculated based on the new maximum value $x_{max}^{(new)}$ and minimum value $x_{min}^{(new)}$.

As an online algorithm, the initial maximum and minimum values $x_{max}^{(1)}$ and $x_{min}^{(1)}$ should be carefully considered. Without the loss of generalization, we set $x_{max}^{(1)} = x^{(0)}$ and $x_{min}^{(1)} = x^{(0)} - 1$, where $x^{(0)}$ is the original value of x without normalization.

THEOREM 1. *Considering a feature x that will be continuously normalized by N set of maximum and minimum values $\{x_{max}^{(n)}, x_{min}^{(n)}\}_{n=1}^N$, the value of x with n round of normalization $x^{(n)}$ can be inferred directly by that of $x^{(n-1)}$ by Equation (12).*

PROOF. Given $x_{max}^{(n)}$ and $x_{min}^{(n)}$, we have

$$x^{(n)} = \frac{x^{(0)} - x_{min}^{(n)}}{x_{max}^{(n)} - x_{min}^{(n)}}, \quad (14)$$

$$x^{(n-1)} = \frac{x^{(0)} - x_{min}^{(n-1)}}{x_{max}^{(n-1)} - x_{min}^{(n-1)}}. \quad (15)$$

By substituting $x^{(0)}$ in Equation (14) using the expression of $x^{(0)}$ derived from Equation (15), we have

$$x^{(n)} = \frac{x_{max}^{(n-1)} - x_{min}^{(n-1)}}{x_{max}^{(n)} - x_{min}^{(n)}} x^{(n-1)} + \frac{x_{min}^{(n-1)} - x_{min}^{(n)}}{x_{max}^{(n)} - x_{min}^{(n)}}. \quad (16)$$

□

THEOREM 2. *Considering the value of weight w, denoted by $w^{(N)}$, which learns from the features $\{x_n^{(N)}\}_{n=1}^N$ of N data objects, and is normalized by $\{x_{max}^{(N)}, x_{min}^{(N)}\}$. If a new input data object d_{N+1} introduces $x_{max}^{(N+1)}$ and $x_{min}^{(N+1)}$, the adapted weight value $w^{(N+1)}$ can be derived by Equation (13).*

PROOF. Section 4.1.2 indicates that $w^{(1)} = x_1^{(N)}$, and the value of w is updated by learning from input data objects following Equation (4). Therefore, we have

$$w^{(n)} = \begin{cases} w^{(n-1)} & if\ x_{n-1}^{(N)} \geq w^{(n-1)} \\ (1-\beta)w^{(n-1)} + \beta x_n^{(N)} & otherwise \end{cases}. \quad (17)$$

Based on Equation (17), we may infer that $w^{(N)} = c_1 x_1^{(N)} + ... + c_N x_N^{(N)}$ and $c_1 + ... + c_N = 1$. Therefore, when $x_{max}^{(N+1)}$ and $x_{min}^{(N+1)}$ are introduced, we obtain $w^{(N+1)} = c_1 x_1^{(N+1)} + ... + c_N x_N^{(N+1)}$. By denoting Equation (16) by $x^{(n)} = a^{(n)} x^{(n-1)} + b^{(n)}$, we have

$$\begin{aligned} w^{(N+1)} &= a^{(N+1)}(c_1 x_1^{(N)} + ... + c_N x_N^{(N)}) + (c_1 + ... + c_N) b^{(N+1)} \\ &= a^{(N+1)} w^{(N)} + b^{(N+1)}. \end{aligned} \quad (18)$$

□

4.3 Dynamic Selection of Key Features and Hierarchical Co-Indexing of Images

The learning functions of GHF-ART for document content and surrounding text, as discussed in Section 4.1.2, essentially aim to discover the key features by preserving or increasing the values of key features while decreasing those of noisy features. Therefore, the representative visual and textual features $\mathcal{V}$ and $\mathcal{T}$ can be obtained from the corresponding cluster weight vectors $\{\mathbf{w}_j^k\}_{j=1}^J$ ($k = \{v, t\}$) of the clusters $\{c_j\}_{j=1}^J$. The key visual and textual features $\mathcal{K}_j^v$ and $\mathcal{K}_j^v$ of c_j are selected based on the following criteria,

$$\mathcal{K}_j^v = \{v_m | w_{j,m}^v > \frac{1}{M}\sum_{i=1}^{M} w_{j,i}^v\}, \quad (19)$$

$$\mathcal{K}_j^t = \{t_h | w_{j,h}^t > \frac{1}{H}\sum_{i=1}^{H} w_{j,i}^t\}. \quad (20)$$

The proposed criteria select the features of values above average as key features. They are based on the idea that the high dimensional features are usually sparse and noisy, especially for the surrounding text of images. Therefore, the proposed method may filter the features providing little information while keeping those that are useful for indicating the difference between clusters.

In this way, each image $d_n \in c_j$ in the indexing system of OMC-ART is hierarchically indexed by the key weight values, $\mathcal{KW}_j^v = \{w_{j,m}^v | v_m \in \mathcal{K}_j^v\}$ and $\mathcal{KW}_j^t = \{w_{j,h}^t | t_h \in \mathcal{K}_j^t\}$, in the abstraction layer and the corresponding feature values, $\mathcal{K}_n^v = \{v_{n,m} | v_m \in \mathcal{K}_j^v\}$ and $\mathcal{K}_n^t = \{t_{n,h} | t_h \in \mathcal{K}_j^t\}$, in the object layer.

4.4 Ranking for Multimodal Queries

OMC-ART enables multimodal search by using either visual features, keywords, or combination of both. Given a query q, the visual and/or textual feature vectors, $\mathbf{v}_q$ and $\mathbf{t}_q$, for the provided query image and/or keywords will be constructed based on $\mathcal{V}$ and $\mathcal{T}$. Taking advantage of the two-layer indexing structure, we employ a ranking algorithm based on binary insertion sort. In the first step, the similarity between the query q and the clusters c_j for $j = 1, ..., J$ in the abstraction layer will be computed. We first define the dissimilarity between two feature values as

$$DIS(a_i, b_i) = \frac{\max(a_i, b_i) - \min(a_i, b_i)}{\alpha + a_i}. \quad (21)$$

The dissimilarity evaluates the degree of the difference between a_i and b_i to a_i, and α is defined in Equation (2). Subsequently, the similarity between q and c_j is defined as

$$\begin{aligned} S_a(q, c_j) = \gamma^v & \sum_{w^v_{j,i} \in \mathcal{KW}^v_j} \max(0, 1 - DIS(v_{q,i}, w^v_{j,i})) \\ +\gamma^t & \sum_{w^t_{j,i} \in \mathcal{KW}^t_j} \max(0, 1 - DIS(t_{q,i}, w^t_{j,i})), \end{aligned} \quad (22)$$

where γ^v and γ^t are the weights learnt by Equation (8) during clustering, which assign higher weights to the more important feature modality. For queries using either image or keywords, the corresponding part in Equation (22) will not be considered. Here, the max(.) function is utilized to avoid the case that the selected key features of clusters are not the key features of the query.

Given the cluster $c_j \in \mathcal{L}_c$ that is most similar to query q, each $d_n \in c_j$ is inserted to the ranking list $\mathcal{L}$ according to the binary insertion sort. Considering an image $d_n \in c_j$, the similarity between the query q and d_n is defined as

$$\begin{aligned} S_o(q, d_n) = \gamma^v & \sum_{v_{n,i} \in \mathcal{K}^v_n} w^v_{j,i} \max(0, 1 - DIS(v_{q,i}, v_{n,i})) \\ +\gamma^t & \sum_{t_{n,i} \in \mathcal{K}^t_n} w^t_{j,i} \max(0, 1 - DIS(t_{q,i}, t_{n,i})). \end{aligned} \quad (23)$$

Note that the weights for similarities are introduced here to enhance the impact of key features. In addition, with a predefined length u of $\mathcal{L}$, the ranking algorithm may stop without traversing the entire indexing system if the ranking list keeps unchanged for a certain period of time, in view that the images most similar to the query are presented prior to those of lower similarity.

4.5 Computational Complexity Analysis

OMC-ART includes a co-indexing module and a retrieval module. Regarding the co-indexing module, for each data object, OMC-ART first normalizes the features, which requires a time complexity of $O(n_i n_f)$, where n_i denotes the number of images and n_f denotes the total number of features. A change in the bound values of features x_{max} and x_{min} will incur a computation cost of $O(n_i n_f)$ in the worst case. Second, the clustering process of OMC-ART, as demonstrated in [15], has an overall time complexity of $O(n_i n_c n_f)$, where n_c is the number of clusters. Finally, the hierarchical co-indexing process has a time complexity of $O((n_i + n_c) n_f)$. Therefore, the co-indexing module of OMC-ART has a total time complexity of $O(n_i n_c n_f)$.

The retrieval module of OMC-ART includes the construction of features, the similarity evaluation between the query and the indexed images, and the ranking algorithm. The feature construction for the query occurs in real-time. If the ranking list $\mathcal{L}$ includes all images in the data set, the overall time complexity for the similarity measure and ranking is of $O(n_i n_{kf} + n_i log n_i)$, where $n_{kf} < n_f$ is the total number of key features. In our experiment on the NUS-WIDE data set, we have $n_f = 2000$ while n_{kf} of a cluster is typically less than 30. In contrast, if $\mathcal{L}$ has a limited length u, the overall time complexity is $O(n_u n_{kf} + n_u log n_u)$, where $n_u < n_i$ is the number of images used to achieve a stable $\mathcal{L}$.

---

lgorithm 1 OMC-ART - Co-Indexing

Input: Images $\{d_n\}_{n=1}^N$ with the corresponding visual and textual features $\{\mathbf{v}_n\}_{n=1}^N$ and $\{\mathbf{t}_n\}_{n=1}^N$, and parameters $\alpha = 0.001$, $\beta = 0.6$, ρ^v and ρ^t.

Present d_1 with $\mathbf{v}_1$ and $\mathbf{t}_1$ to the input field.
Initialize x_{max} and x_{min} for each feature x of $\mathbf{v}_1$, and perform min-max normalization on $\mathbf{v}_1$.
Set $J = 1$. Create cluster c_J with $\mathbf{w}^v_J = \mathbf{v}_1$ and $\mathbf{w}^t_J = \mathbf{t}_1$.
Set $n = 2$.
repeat
  Present d_n to the input field.
  If x_{max} and x_{min} are changed, update normalized features according to Equations (12) and (13). Normalize $\mathbf{v}_n$ with x_{max} and x_{min}.
  For $\forall c_j$ $(j = 1, ..., J)$, calculate the choice value $T(d_n, c_j)$ according to Equation (2).
  repeat
    Identify a winner cluster c_{j^*} so that $j^* = \arg\max_{j: c_j \in F_2} T(d_n, c_j)$.
    Calculate the match values $M(\mathbf{v}_n, \mathbf{w}^v_{j^*})$ and $M(\mathbf{t}_n, \mathbf{w}^t_{j^*})$ according to Equation (3).
    If $M(\mathbf{v}_n, \mathbf{w}^k_{j^*}) < \rho^k (k = \{v, t\})$, set $T(d_n, c_{j^*}) = -1$.
  until Identify c_{j^*} such that $M(\mathbf{v}_n, \mathbf{w}^k_{j^*}) > \rho^k$ for $k = \{v, t\}$, or $T(d_n, c_{j^*}) = -1$.
  If $T(d_n, c_{j^*}) \neq -1$, set $d_n \in c_{j^*}$, update $\mathbf{w}^k_{j^*}$ for $k = \{v, t\}$ according to Equations (4) and (5) respectively, and update γ^v and γ^t according to Equations (7)-(10).
  If $T(d_n, c_{j^*}) = -1$, set $J = J + 1$, create a new node c_J such that $\mathbf{w}^v_J = \mathbf{v}_n$ and $\mathbf{w}^t_J = \mathbf{t}_n$, and update γ^v and γ^t according to Equation (11).
  Set $n = n + 1$.
until All images are presented.
Identify key features of clusters according to Equations (19) and (20), and obtain the indexes $\mathcal{KW}^v_j$ and $\mathcal{KW}^t_j$ of clusters $\{c_j\}_{j=1}^J$ and the indexes $\mathcal{K}^v_n$ and $\mathcal{K}^t_n$ of images $\{d_n\}_{n=1}^N$ as discussed in Section 4.3.

Output: Clusters $\{c_j\}_{j=1}^J$, cluster assignment of images $\{A_n\}_{n=1}^N$, and indexes $\mathcal{KW}^k_j$ and $\mathcal{K}^k_n$ for $k = \{v, t\}$.

---

5. EXPERIMENTS

5.1 Data Sets

We conducted experiments on two data sets. The first is the NUS-WIDE data set [4], consisting of 269,648 images with surrounding text and their ground-truth labels of 81 concepts. We used 16,000 images belonging to 10 classes, including dog, birds, flower, lake, sunset, beach, bridge,

lgorithm 2 OMC-ART - Retrieval

Input: Query q (image, keywords, or combination of both).

Construct the visual feature vector $\mathbf{v}_q$ and/or textual feature vector $\mathbf{t}_q$, and present them to the input field.
Perform min-max normalization on $\mathbf{v}_q$ based on the current x_{max} and x_{min}. If $\exists i$ such that $v_{q,i} > x_{max}$ or $v_{q,i} < x_{min}$, set $v_{q,i} = 1$ or 0, respectively.
Calculate $S_a(q, c_j)$ for $j = 1, ...J$ according to Equation (22), and obtain the ranking list $\mathcal{L}_c = \{c_i\}_{i=1}^{J}$.
Set $i = 1$.
repeat
  Select cluster $c_i \in \mathcal{L}_c$.
  repeat
    Select an image $d_n \in c_i$, and calculate $S_o(q, d_n)$ according to Equation (23).
    Find its ranking in the retrieval list $\mathcal{L}$ using the binary search algorithm.
  until all images $d_n \in c_i$ are presented to $\mathcal{L}$, or $\mathcal{L}$ of length u remains unchanged for a period of time.
  Set $i = i + 1$.
until All images are presented, or $\mathcal{L}$ of length u remains unchanged for a period of time.

Output: The list $\mathcal{L}$ of ranked images to the query q.

cars, coral, and garden, each of which includes 1,600 images. We used a concatenation of Grid Color Moment (255 features), Edge Direction Histogram (73 features) and Wavelet Texture (128 features) as visual features. For the textual features, we filtered the surrounding text of images and considered all distinctive and high frequency tags. In total, we selected 2,000 tags and ensured that each selected image is associated with at least five tags. For the retrieval performance evaluation, we used 1,500 images of each class, i.e. 15,000 images, for building the indexing system and the remaining 1,000 images for queries.

The second data set used is the Corel5k data set, which is originally used in [6] for visual object recognition. This data set consists of 5,000 images from 50 Corel Stock Photo CDs, each of which contains 100 images of the same class. Each image is typically manually annotated by 3-4 tags from a dictionary of 374 words. However, our obtained data set contains only 4,999 images with one missing. Similar to the NUS-WIDE data set, we utilized the same visual features and 374 words to build the visual and textual feature vectors. We treated images in the same folder as belonging to the same class, and 10 images of each class were selected as queries while the remaining 4,499 images were used to build the indexing system.

5.2 Evaluation Measures

We evaluated the retrieval performance of OMC-ART using four measures, including the mean Average Precision@k ($mAP@K$), Precision@K, Recall@K, and the response time. Given the number of queries, N, the number of relevant images in the indexing system, M_n, to the nth query, and the number of retrieved images K, $mAP@K$ is defined as

$$mAP@K = \frac{1}{N} \sum_{n=1}^{N} AP_n@K, \tag{24}$$

$$AP_n@K = \frac{1}{\min(M_n, K)} \sum_{k=1}^{K} r_{n,k} \sum_{i=1}^{k} \frac{r_{n,i}}{k}. \tag{25}$$

Note that $AP_n@K$ is the Average Precision (AP) obtained by the nth query, $r_{n,k} = 1$ if the kth retrieved image is relevant to the nth query, and $r_{n,k} = 0$ otherwise. $AP_n@K$ considers positions of the relevant images in the ranking list, and the top ranked relevant images will result in a high performance. It essentially calculates the weighted sum of $Precision_n@k$ for $k = 1, ..., K$ when $K < M_n$, and calculates the weighted sum of $Recall_n@k$ when $K > M_n$. In addition, $Precision_n@K = \sum_{i=1}^{K} \frac{r_{n,i}}{K}$, and $Recall_n@K = \sum_{i=1}^{K} \frac{r_{n,i}}{M_n}$. $Precision@K$ and $Recall@K$ are the respective mean values over N queries.

5.3 Parameter Selection

OMC-ART requires three parameters for GHF-ART in order to build the co-indexing module, namely, the choice parameter α, the learning rate β and the vigilance parameters ρ^v and ρ^t. As demonstrated in several studies [12, 13, 14], the performance of GHF-ART is generally robust to the values of α and β, and $\alpha = 0.01$ and $\beta = 0.6$ are commonly used. Therefore, we consistently used $\alpha = 0.01$ and $\beta = 0.6$ across our experiments on the two data sets.

The vigilance parameter ρ essentially constrains the minimum intra-cluster similarity. As specified in [13], a suitable value of ρ typically results in the generation of a few small clusters, typically 10% of the total number of the generated clusters. Besides, a small cluster typically contains several or tens of data objects. Therefore, the moderate values of ρ^v and ρ^t can be obtained based on the clustering results produced by the respective visual and textual features. Note that ρ^v and ρ^t affect the retrieval performance of OMC-ART in terms of the selection of key features and the accuracy of grouping similar data objects. Therefore, relatively higher values of ρ^v and ρ^t are preferred in order to enhance the accuracy of co-indexing with some increase in the computational cost for building the indexing system. In our experiments, we consistently used $\rho^v = 0.8$ and $\rho^t = 0.3$.

5.4 Performance Comparison

The performance of OMC-ART is compared with four state-of-the-art multimodal images indexing and retrieval algorithms, namely (1) the Latent Semantic Kernels (LSK) [2] which supports query by image, keywords and combination of both; (2) Content-based Image Retrieval ($CBIR$) and Text-based Image Retrieval ($TBIR$) [9] which support query by image and keywords respectively; (3) Multimodal Probabilistic Latent Semantic Analysis ($MMpLSA$) [3] which supports query by combination of image and keywords; and (4) the algorithms based on Non-negative Matrix Factorization (NMF) [1] which support query by image, keywords, and combination of both, denoted as NMF_v, NMF_t, and NMF_{both}, respectively.

For a fair comparison, we normalized the visual features so that they fit the input of all algorithms. Regarding the algorithm implementations that are not mentioned or have alternatives in the respective papers, for LSK, we used the cosine kernels for feature similarity measure and the linear kernel for combining visual and textual similarities; For CBIR and TBIR, the cosine similarity was used for similarity measure. Because the ranking algorithms of all four algorithms were not mentioned in the respective papers, we used

Table 1: The retrieval performance of OMC-ART and the baselines on the NUS-WIDE and Corel5k data sets.

mAP / dataset	uery by mage				uery by eywords				uery by oth			
	S	C	NMF_v	C-A T	S	T	NMF_t	C-A T	S	p SA	NMF_{both}	C-A T
NUS-W DE	0.1382	0.1763	0.2287	**0.2729**	0.2794	0.3345	0.2936	**0.3804**	0.3474	0.3948	0.3469	**0.4974**
Corel5k	0.1418	0.1976	0.1712	**0.2877**	0.3391	0.3412	0.3682	**0.4865**	0.3552	0.3991	0.3875	**0.5283**

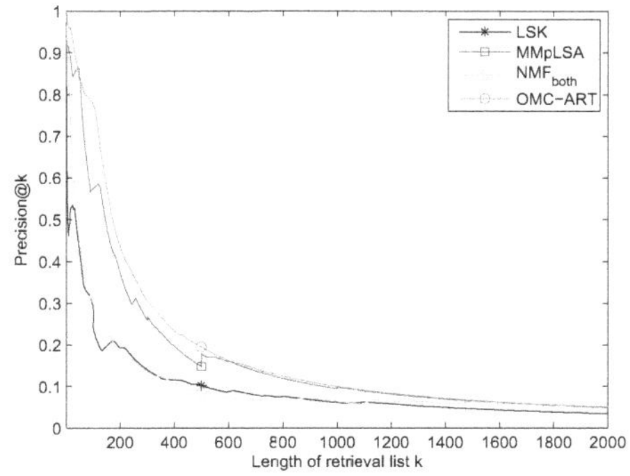

(a)

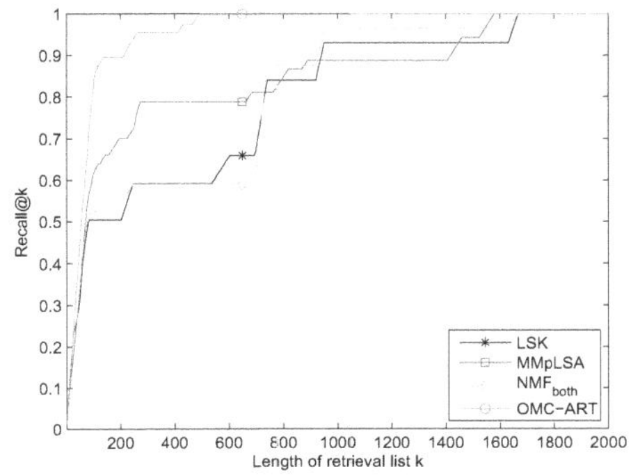

(b)

Figure 2: The retrieval performance of OMC-ART and the compared algorithms on Corel5k data set with queries of both image and keywords, in terms of (a) Precision@k and (b) Recall@k.

the binary insertion sort as used in OMC-ART. Regarding the parameters such as the weights of features, the number of iterations, and the number of clusters/dimensionality of latent space, we first followed the suggestions in the respective papers, and then empirically tuned them so that each algorithm achieved roughly the best retrieval performance.

Table 1 summarizes the retrieval performances of OMC-ART and the compared algorithms on the NUS-WIDE and Corel5k data sets, evaluated by mAP. We observed that OMC-ART consistently achieved the best performance in terms of all types of queries and data sets, which was usually over 10% higher than that achieved by the compared algorithms. Besides, we found that, when querying with combined image and keywords, the performance of OMC-ART was significantly better than that of querying by using either image or keywords. The above findings demonstrated the effectiveness of the proposed co-indexing method, which indexes the images using the discovered key features of each modality to enhance the accuracy of similarity measure.

In addition, we evaluated the retrieval performance of OMC-ART and the compared algorithms using query by combination of both image and keywords on the Corel5k data set. The performance was measured by Precision@k and Recall@k with respect to the increase in the length of

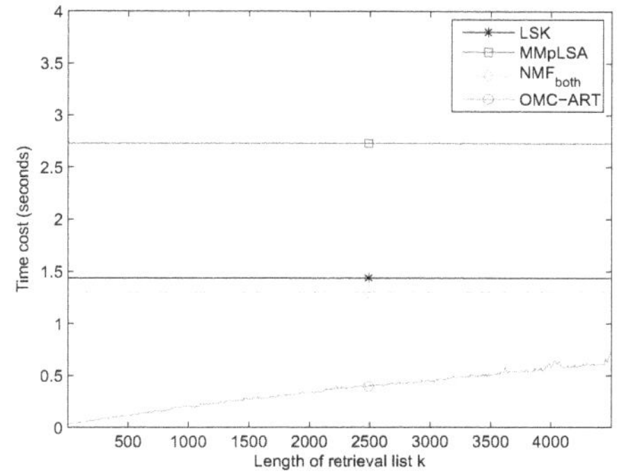

Figure 3: The time cost of OMC-ART and the compared algorithms on Corel5k data set with respect to the increase in the length of retrieval list k.

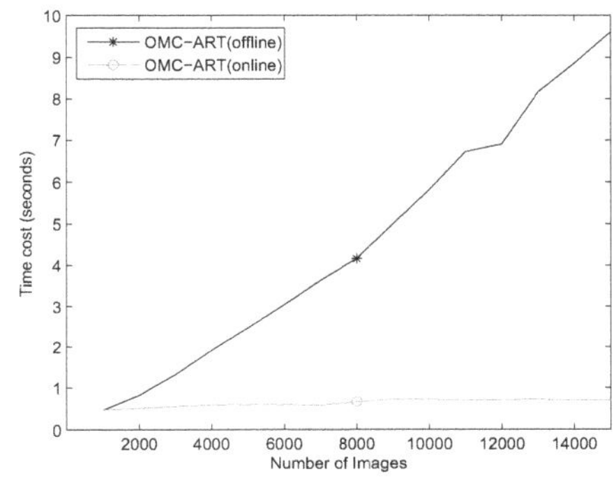

Figure 4: The time cost of OMC-ART with online learning (OMC-ART(online)) and offline learning (OMC-ART(offline)) to build the indexing system with live streams of images from NUS-WIDE data set.

the retrieval list k, as shown in Figure 2. In Figure 2(a), we observed that OMC-ART always obtained the best results of precision with different numbers of k, and the performance decreased slower than other algorithms along with the increase in k. Regarding the recall shown in Figure 2(b), we observed that OMC-ART had a much better recall than other algorithms, and typically identified all images similar to a given query at $k \geq 500$.

5.5 Efficiency Analysis

To demonstrate the efficiency of OMC-ART, we first evaluated the response time of OMC-ART and the compared algorithms on the Corel5k data set using both image and keywords as queries, with respect to the length of the retrieval list k. To make a fair comparison, we empirically tuned the dimensionality of latent space of LSK, $MMpLSA$ and NMF_{both} to be the same under their respective best settings as used in Section 5.4. As illustrated in Figure 3, OMC-ART requires the least time cost among all algorithms, which can be shorter with respect to the decrease in k. This benefits from the fact that OMC-ART uses key features to index images so that its computational cost during retrieval is low. Moreover, the hierarchical indexing structure of OMC-ART essentially provides a batch-mode pre-ranking of the indexed images. Therefore, the groups of images similar to the query are likely to be selected for ranking prior to those of dissimilar images. This allows OMC-ART to stop the ranking process when the retrieval list is full and remains unchanged for a certain period of time.

To demonstrate the effective of the online indexing property of OMC-ART, we simulated the scenario of processing live streams of images and evaluated the processing times required by OMC-ART with online and offline learning to index the data set. Specifically, we separated the 15,000 images of NUS-WIDE data set into 15 groups of equal size and presented them sequentially to OMC-ART to build the indexing system. As shown in Figure 4, we observed that, with offline learning, the time cost of OMC-ART(offline) required to indexing the data set linearly increases with respect to the increase in the size of the data set. In contrast, that of OMC-ART(online) roughly remains the same as only the new data are handled.

6. CONCLUSIONS

This paper presented a novel idea for the automatic multimodal indexing and retrieval of weakly labeled image collections, wherein each image is associated with a textual description. In contrast to most existing approaches that aim to create a new feature space utilizing multimodal information for indexing images, the proposed OMC-ART aims to identify the representative features of each modality for groups of similar images and indexes the images using these key features. This idea is achieved by producing a two-layer hierarchical indexing structure for the images based on the heterogeneous data co-clustering algorithm, named GHF-ART. In addition, by extending GHF-ART with an adaptation method, OMC-ART is able to perform online learning, which favors web image collections requiring frequent update. With the proposed co-indexing method, OMC-ART allows flexible multimodal search by using either images, keywords, or a combination of both. Moreover, OMC-ART employs a ranking algorithm, using which enables images more similar to the query to be more likely to be selected for ranking prior to those dissimilar ones. It also enables OMC-ART to stop the ranking process when the retrieval list remains unchanged for a certain period of time.

In this paper, we have demonstrated the feasibility of the proposed co-indexing approach and the ranking algorithm. However, there remains places that require further exploration. First, OMC-ART requires the tuning of the vigilance parameters ρ for each modality to control the intra-cluster similarities. Currently they are manually tuned as discussed in Section 5.3, further efforts are required to make them self-adapted. Second, more effective methods for the key feature selection can be incorporated to enhance the indexing accuracy. Third, parallel implementation of OMC-ART can be studied in order to improve the efficiency of indexing very large data.

Acknowledgments

This research is supported by the National Research Foundation, Prime Minister's Office, Singapore under its IDM Futures Funding Initiative and administered by the Interactive and Digital Media Programme Office.

7. REFERENCES

[1] J. C. Caicedo, J. BenAbdallah, F. A. González, and O. Nasraoui. Multimodal representation, indexing, automated annotation and retrieval of image collections via non-negative matrix factorization. *Neurocomputing*, 76(1):50–60, 2012.

[2] J. C. Caicedo, J. G. Moreno, E. A. Niño, and F. A. González. Combining visual features and text data for medical image retrieval using latent semantic kernels. *In Proceedings of the international conference on Multimedia information retrieval*, pages 359–366, 2010.

[3] P. Chandrika and C. V. Jawahar. Multi modal semantic indexing for image retrieval. *In CIVR*, pages 342–349, 2010.

[4] T.-S. Chua, J. Tang, R. Hong, H. Li, Z. Luo, and Y. Zheng. NUS-WIDE: a real-world web image database from national university of singapore. *In CIVR*, 2009.

[5] L. De Lathauwer, B. De Moor, and J. Vandewalle. A multilinear singular value decomposition. *SIAM journal on Matrix Analysis and Applications*, 21(4):1253–1278, 2000.

[6] P. Duygulu, K. Barnard, J. F. de Freitas, and D. A. Forsyth. Object recognition as machine translation: Learning a lexicon for a fixed image vocabulary. *In ECCV*, pages 97–112, 2002.

[7] H. J. Escalante, M. Montes, and E. Sucar. Multimodal indexing based on semantic cohesion for image retrieval. *Information Retrieval*, 15(1):1–32, 2012.

[8] Y. Gong, L. Wang, M. Hodosh, J. Hockenmaier, and S. Lazebnik. Improving image-sentence embeddings using large weakly annotated photo collections. *In Proceedings of the European Conference on Computer Vision (ECCV)*, pages 529–545, 2014.

[9] M. Li, X.-B. Xue, and Z.-H. Zhou. Exploiting multi-modal interactions: A unified framework. pages 1120–1125, 2009.

[10] R. Lienhart, S. Romberg, and E. Hörster. Multilayer pLSA for multimodal image retrieval. *In Proceedings of the ACM International Conference on Image and Video Retrieval*, 2009.

[11] T. Mei, Y. Rui, S. Li, and Q. Tian. Multimedia search reranking: A literature survey. *ACM Computing Surveys (CSUR)*, 46(3):38, 2014.

[12] L. Meng and A.-H. Tan. Semi-supervised hierarchical clustering for personalized web image organization. *In Proceedings of International Joint Conference on Neural Networks (IJCNN)*, pages 1–8, 2012.

[13] L. Meng and A.-H. Tan. Community discovery in social networks via heterogeneous link association and fusion. *In Proceedings of the SIAM International Conference on Data Mining (SDM)*, pages 803–811, 2014.

[14] L. Meng, A.-H. Tan, and D. C. Wunsch. Vigilance adaptation in adaptive resonance theory. *In Proceedings of International Joint Conference on Neural Networks (IJCNN)*, pages 1–7, 2013.

[15] L. Meng, A.-H. Tan, and D. Xu. Semi-supervised heterogeneous fusion for multimedia data co-clustering. *IEEE Transactions on Knowledge and Data Engineering*, 26(9):2293–2306, 2014.

[16] Y. Mu, J. Shen, and S. Yan. Weakly-supervised hashing in kernel space. *In Proceedings of the IEEE Conference on Computer Vision and Pattern Recognition (CVPR)*, pages 3344–3351, 2010.

[17] L. Nie, M. Wang, Y. Gao, Z.-J. Zha, and T.-S. Chua. Beyond text QA: Multimedia answer generation by harvesting web information. *IEEE Transactions on Multimedia*, 15(2):426–441, 2013.

[18] L. Nie, M. Wang, Z.-J. Zha, G. Li, and T.-S. Chua. Multimedia answering: Enriching text QA with media information. *In SIGIR*, pages 695–704, 2011.

[19] A. W. Smeulders, M. Worring, S. Santini, A. Gupta, and R. Jain. Content-based image retrieval at the end of the early years. *IEEE Transactions on Pattern Analysis and Machine Intelligence*, 22(12):1349–1380, 2000.

[20] J.-H. Su, B.-W. Wang, T.-Y. Hsu, C.-L. Chou, and V. S. Tseng. Multi-modal image retrieval by integrating web image annotation, concept matching and fuzzy ranking techniques. *International Journal of Fuzzy Systems*, 12(2):136–149, 2010.

[21] F. X. Yu, R. Ji, M.-H. Tsai, G. Ye, and S.-F. Chang. Weak attributes for large-scale image retrieval. *In Proceedings of the IEEE Conference on Computer Vision and Pattern Recognition (CVPR)*, pages 2949–2956, 2012.

[22] S. Zhang, M. Yang, X. Wang, Y. Lin, and Q. Tian. Semantic-aware co-indexing for image retrieval. *In Proceedings of the IEEE International Conference on Computer Vision (ICCV)*, pages 1673–1680, 2013.

Weakly Supervised Random Forest for Multi-Label Image Clustering and Segmentation

Yingjie Xia
College of Computer Science, Zhejiang University
No.38, Zheda Road
Hangzhou, P.R. China
xiayingjie@zju.edu.cn

Qianqian Zhu
Institute of Service Engineering, Hangzhou Normal University
No.58, Haishu Road
Hangzhou, P.R. China
zhuqianqian@hznu.edu.cn

Wei Wei
School of Information Systems, Singapore Management University
No.80 Stamford Road
Singapore 178902
weiwei8329@gmail.com

ABSTRACT

Clustering is a useful statistical tool in data mining and computer vision. Supervised information is introduced to improve the clustering performance. However, labeling each piece of data accurately is extremely expensive when the amount of data is huge. Existing supervised clustering methods handle the huge workload of labeling large amount of data by transferring the bag-level labels into the instance-level descriptors. However, each bag has only one label limits the application scope seriously. In this paper, we propose weakly supervised multi-label clustering, which allows to label a bag of data multiple labels. The key technique is a weakly supervised random forest which can calculate the model parameters with a deterministic annealing strategy to optimize the non-convex objective function. The proposed algorithm is applied to two typical applications, image clustering and segmentation problems. Impressive efficiency in both training and testing stages on the state-of-the-art image data sets is achieved in our experiments.

Categories and Subject Descriptors

I.4 [**Computing Methodologies**]: Image Processing and Computer Vision; I.5.2 [**Pattern Recognition**]: Design Methodology—*Classifier design and evaluation*

Keywords

Weakly supervised, Multi-label, Clustering, Semantic, Annealing

1. INTRODUCTION

Clustering is a useful technique in computer vision [10, 14] and multimedia systems [4, 29]. It is widely used to better organize, represent and browse images as well as to improve the performance of the related applications [8]. For example, many image categorization models [1, 9] cluster local descriptors into codebooks. Thereby, a complex concept can be represented by a bag of local image descriptors efficiently. Kmeans [17] is the most common clustering algorithm, while mean-shift [5], and hierarchical k-means [24] are also popular choices. Some recent approaches [18, 11] have shown that the supervised clustering methods outperform the conventional unsupervised ones due to their discrimination. However, a fully supervised clustering method requires to assign instance-level labels to the individual objects in an image, which is highly time-consuming. Even worse, the local descriptors such as SIFT [16] are usually online extracted. Thus, it may be infeasible to label the descriptors offline due to the lack of position information.

To successfully avoid instance-level labeling burden, bag-level labeling has been proposed [18]. It assumes a bag of descriptors share one and only one label. Thus, labels are provided for bags instead of the individual instance-level descriptors. Therefore, labeling a feature bag is much convenient than labeling the individual descriptors. However, this method is still limited by the assumption that each bag has a single label, while it is not practical for many applications.

To address the above problems, this paper proposes a weakly supervised clustering algorithm [36, 37] that supports multiple labels of each bag. The descriptors are clustered by preserving the locality and discrimination under the bag-level semantic constraints. In particular, the clustering is firstly formulated into a constrained objective function minimization problem such that the most discriminative codebook can be calculated under the bag-level constraints. Then, a Weakly Supervised Random Forest (WSRF) is derived to model it into a constrained margin maximization problem and an efficient deterministic annealing algorithm is used to optimize the corresponding non-convex objective function. Finally, the instance level descriptors are clustered under the guidance of the given bag-level labels. To the best of our knowledge, this is the first attempt of weakly supervised clustering using a random forest architecture [30]. To evaluate the effectiveness of the proposed algorithm, we apply it to image clustering and image segmentation [38, 35].

The key contributions of this work can be summarized as: 1) A weakly supervised clustering framework and its applications in the well-known image clustering and segmentation task; 2) the weakly supervised random forest (WSRF) that effectively learns the model parameters of the proposed weakly supervised clustering; 3) an efficient WSRF construction scheme using deterministic annealing optimization.

ICMR 2015 June 23-26, Shanghai, China
Copyright 2015 ACM 978-1-4503-3274-3/15/06 $15.00
http://dx.doi.org/10.1145/2671188.2749377.

The rest of this paper is organized as follows. In Sec II we introduce the proposed weakly supervised clustering framework. Sec III to Sec IV formulate weakly supervised clustering into a random forest architecture, where the model parameters are learned efficiently using the deterministic annealing optimization. Experimental results in Sec V thoroughly demonstrate the effectiveness of the proposed method. Sec VI draws conclusion and gives some future work.

2. WEAKLY SUPERVISED CLUSTERING

Let $\mathcal{Y} = \{1, \cdots, K\}$ denote the label set and $\mathcal{B} = \{B_i\}_{i=1,\cdots,n}$ denote the training bags. Each bag B_i contains multiple descriptor instances $B_i = \{x_{ij}\}_{j=1\cdots n_i}$. Each bag B_i is associated with multiple human specified bag-level labels $Y_i = \{y_i^k\}_{k=1,\cdots,K}$ where y_i^k is either 0 or 1. We call a label valued one as *legal label* and *illegal label* if the label is not one. We denote the set of all the instances as $\mathcal{X} = \{x_{ij}\}_{i=1,\cdots,n,j=1,\cdots,n_i}$. Note that the instance level labels $\{y_{ij}\}$ are unavailable at the training stage.

In order to cluster the instances into discriminative codebooks without violating the bag-level constraints, we learn the clustering function $\mathcal{C}(\cdot)$. The function can determine the cluster which an instance belongs to. The data locality is preserved by that if two instances belong to the same cluster they should be placed as neighbors in a certain metric.

Based on $\mathcal{C}(\cdot)$, the following two functions are defined. First, a matching function $\mathcal{F}(x_O, k)$ between an instance and a class is defined to return the probability showing that the instance x_O matches the kth class.

$$\mathcal{F}(x_O, k) = \frac{\sum_{x_{ij} \in \mathcal{C}(x_O)} [y_{ij} = k]}{|\mathcal{C}(x_O)|}. \quad (1)$$

Second, based on $\mathcal{F}(\cdot)$, we define $\mathcal{L}(\cdot)$ as the discrimination that predicts the label of an instance

$$\mathcal{L}(x_O, y_O) = \mathcal{F}(x_O, y_O) - \underset{k \in \mathcal{Y}, k \neq y_O}{\arg\max} \mathcal{F}(x_O, k). \quad (2)$$

In weakly supervised clustering, the ground-truth instance-level labels are unknown. Thus, the following objective functions are required to be achieved in the clustering procedure

$$\begin{aligned} \{y_{ij}^*, \mathcal{C}(\cdot)^*\} &= \underset{y_{ij}, \mathcal{C}(\cdot)}{\arg\min} \sum_{i=1}^{n} \sum_{j=1}^{n_i} -\mathcal{L}(x_{ij}, y_{ij}), \\ s.t. \forall y_i^j &= 1, \sum_{j=1}^{n_i} [y_{ij} = k] > 0, \quad (3) \\ \forall y_i^j &= 0, \sum_{j=1}^{n_i} [y_{ij} = k] = 0. \end{aligned}$$

The optimization procedure of Eq.(3) aims to minimize the global loss $\{y_{ij}^*, \mathcal{C}(\cdot)^*\}$ in discrimination by considering the weakly supervised constraints $s.t. \forall y_i^j$ and $\forall y_i^j$. The optimization extends the multiple instance constraints in two aspects. 1) Multiple labels are associate with a bag, not just single label; and 2) positive and negative constraints are considered, not just positive constraint. Thus, for each bag, all the legal bag-level labels should be assigned to one or more instances.

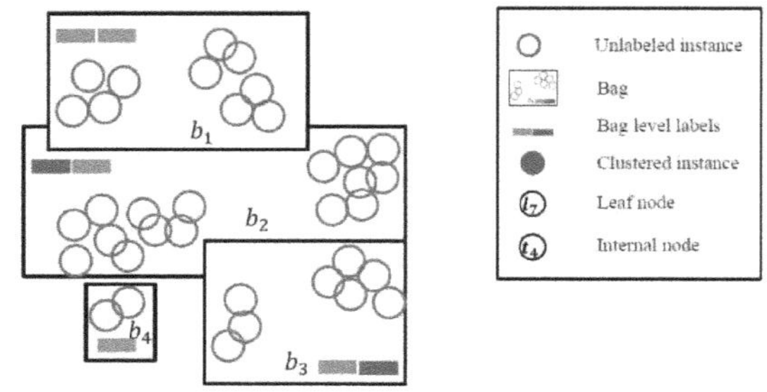

(a)

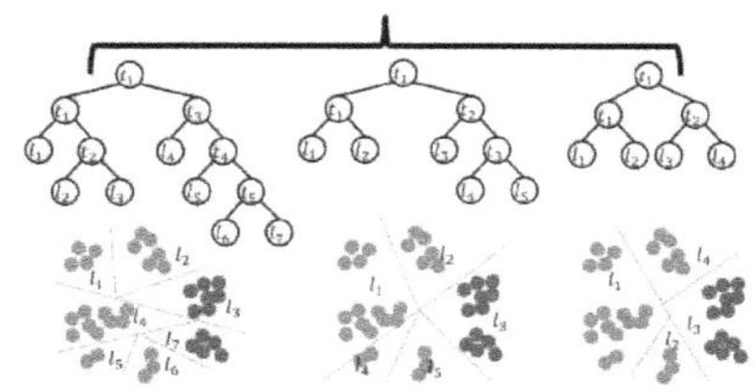

(b)

Figure 1: WSRF-based weakly supervised clustering.

3. WEAKLY SUPERVISED CLUSTERING BASED ON RANDOM FOREST

The solution to the aforementioned weakly supervised clustering problem is based on an extension of Random Forest (RF). The original RF can only be used for instance level clustering. To overcome this limitation, we introduce weakly supervised constraints that support multiple bag-level labels, named WSRF-based weakly supervised clustering. The WSRF-based weakly supervised clustering can minimize the objective function of Eq.(3) by constructing a weakly supervised random forest. The missing labels are treated as the additional optimization variables. Therefore, the WSRF can be formulated into the following objective function

$$\begin{aligned} \{y_{ij}*, \mathcal{G}(\cdot)*\} &= \underset{y_{ij}, \mathcal{G}(\cdot)}{\arg\min} \sum_{i=1}^{n} \sum_{j=1}^{n_i} -\mathcal{M}_{\mathcal{G}}(x_{ij}, y_{ij}), \\ s.t. \forall y_i^j &= 1, \sum_{j=1}^{n_i} [y_{ij} = k] > 0, \quad (4) \\ \forall y_i^j &= 0, \sum_{j=1}^{n_i} [y_{ij} = k] = 0. \end{aligned}$$

According to Eq. (4), the WSRF is trained using unlabeled instances under the weakly supervised constraints. Figure 1 shows the WSRF-based weakly supervised clustering. Unlabeled instances and their bag level labels are shown in Figure 1 (a), and WSRF for weakly supervised clustering is shown in Figure 1 (b). The unlabeled instance level descriptors are clustered with the guidance of the given bag level labels.

4. LEARNING FOR WEAKLY SUPERVISED RANDOM FOREST

The WSRF learning can be considered as the the optimization problem defined in Eq. (4). Given the labels of all the instances, the conventional RF can minimize multi-class classification-margin in an empirical sense. However, due to the lack of instance level labels, WSRF learning is a non-convex problem. Actually, it is an integer programming problem. It is computationally intractable to obtain an close-form solution. In this work, a deterministic annealing algorithm [21] is employed to obtain an approximate solution to this problem.

Deterministic annealing (DA) is deemed as a special case of the homotopy method. Instead of solving the above non-convex integer programming problem directly, DA treats it as a continuous optimization by replacing the discrete variables with random continuous variables, over which a space of probability distributions is defined. In this way, the goal of the optimization switches to calculating a distribution in the defined space that minimizes the expected value of the objective function. An entropy term is further added to make the problem convex. More specifically, the WSRF learning can be formulated into a minimization problem as

$$p^* = \arg\min_{p \in P} E_p(\mathcal{J}(y)) - T \cdot \mathcal{H}(p), \quad (5)$$

where y denotes the unknown variables, $\mathcal{J}(y)$ is the objective function defined by Eq. (4), p is the distribution of y, E_p is the expectation with distribution p, $\mathcal{H}$ is the distribution entropy, and T is a cooling parameter called temperature. When the temperature is large, the entropy is the dominant term and the model is uncertain. When the system cools down by setting T to zero, the optimization gradually focus on the original form. Therefore, given a temperature, the WSRF learning can be re-formulated as minimizing the following function

$$\begin{aligned} \mathcal{Q}(\mathcal{G}, p) &= E_p(\mathcal{J}(y)) - T \cdot \mathcal{H}(p) \\ &= T \sum_{i=1}^{n} \sum_{j=1}^{n_i} \sum_{k=1}^{K} p(k|x_{x_{ij}}) \log(p(k|x_{ij})) \\ &- \sum_{i=1}^{n} \sum_{j=1}^{n_i} \sum_{k=1}^{K} p(k|x_{x_{ij}}) \mathcal{M}_{\mathcal{G}}(x_{ij}, k), \end{aligned} \quad (6)$$

in which the weakly supervised constraints, *i.e.* the last two terms in Eq. (3), are also held. To minimize $\mathcal{Q}(\mathcal{G}, p)$, we conduct the following two iterative steps in details.

4.1 Instances Level Labels Generation under Weakly Supervised Constraints

Given the fixed distributions $p(k|x_{ij})$ of the instances, generate the instance level labels $Y_i = \{y_i^k\}_{k=1\cdots K}$ according to fixed distribution p and the weakly supervised constraints. In this step, the optimization can be formulated as

$$\max_{y_{ij} \in \mathcal{Y}} \sum_{i=1}^{n} \sum_{j=1}^{n_i} \sum_{k=1}^{K} p(y_{ij}|x_{ij}), \quad (7)$$

According to the weakly supervised constraints, for each bag the labels are generated from the list of legal bag-level labels. We also check each of the legal bag level-labels to ensure that there is at least one instance associated with it. The following Algorithm 1 shows the details of generating instance-level labels under weakly supervised constraints.

Algorithm 1 Generating instance-level labels under weakly supervised constraints

Input: The distribution $p(k|x_{ij})$; the bag level labels $Y_i = \{y_i^k\}_{k=1\ldots K}$. **Output:** The instance level labels y_{ij}.

1) For each bag B_i
   for each instance x_{ij}
   Re-arrange the distribution such that only legal labels are considered
   $$\hat{p}(k|x_{ij}) = \begin{cases} \frac{p(k|x_{ij})}{\Psi(i,j)} & y_i^k = 1 \\ 0 & y_i^k = 0 \end{cases},$$
   where $\Psi(i,j) = \sum_{k=1}^{K} p(k|x_{ij})$ is the normalization factor. Generate y_{ij} from $\hat{p}(k|x_{ij})$.
2) For each legal label $y_i^k = 1$ in B_i
   if $\nexists y_{ij} = k$
   Set $y_{ij}^* = k$, where $j^* = \arg\max_j p(k|x_{ij})$.
   end if;

4.2 Margin Maximization and Distribution Adjustment

Given the instance level labels, maximize the margin $\mathcal{M}_{\mathcal{G}}$ by constructing an RF with fixed instance level labels, and adjust the label distribution p according to Eq. (5). As an RF can be constructed to facilitate maximizing the margin, in this step the optimization function is formulated as follows.

$$\begin{aligned} \min_P \mathcal{D}(P) &= T \sum_{i=1}^{n} \sum_{j=1}^{n_i} \sum_{k=1}^{K} p(k|x_{x_{ij}}) \log(p(k|x_{ij})) \\ &- \sum_{i=1}^{n} \sum_{j=1}^{n_i} \sum_{k=1}^{K} p(k|x_{ij}) \mathcal{M}_{\mathcal{G}}(x_{ij}, k). \end{aligned} \quad (8)$$

There are no global constraints for the distribution. Thus, the label distribution p_{ij} can be adjusted independently. Denoting $p_{ijk} = p(k|x_{ij})$ and taking the derivative of $\mathcal{D}(p)$, we can obtain

$$\frac{\partial \mathcal{D}}{\partial p_{ijk}} = T(1 + \log(p_{ijk})) - \mathcal{M}_{\mathcal{G}}(x_{ij}, k). \quad (9)$$

By taking the derivative to zero, we get an optimal choice of p_{ijk}, *i.e.*,

$$p_{ijk}^* = \frac{\exp((\mathcal{M}_{\mathcal{G}}(x_{ij}, k) - T)/T)}{\Phi(i,j)}, \quad (10)$$

where

$$\Phi(i,j) = \sum_{k=1}^{K} p_{ijk}* \quad (11)$$

is a normalization factor.

By summarizing the above two iterative steps, the Algorithm 2 of the deterministic annealing optimization for WSRF learning is shown as follows. The deterministic annealing method is employed to optimize the MIL-Forest [13] in which the multiple instance label generation can be seen as a special case of WSRF.

5. EXPERIMENTAL RESULTS AND ANALYSIS

This section evaluates the effectiveness of the proposed weakly supervised clustering. We first evaluate our algorith-

Algorithm 2 Deterministic annealing optimization for WS-RF

Input: Training bags B; bag level labels Y; and the cooling function $c(t)$. **Output:** A clustering forest.

1) Set the iteration $t = 0$;
2) Initialize the distribution to each instance level label;
3) Generate the instance level labels;
4) Train a RF:
   repeat until enough iterations are reached
      $t = t + 1$;
      Get the current temperature $T = c(t)$;
      Adjust the distributions;
      Generate the instance level labels;
      Re-Train the forest;
   Output the trained forest.

m on a toy data set. Then, we apply the proposed algorithm on the image clustering and image segmentation tasks.

5.1 Experiment Data Set

Our experiment is conducted on the Satimage and Pendigits data sets from the LibSVM [26] repository. The Satimage data set has 4435 training samples and 2000 testing samples, and the Pendigits data set has 7494 training samples and 3498 testing samples. The random forest algorithm implemented is Breiman's Random Forests [2] which includes four different splitting criteria, *i.e.*, information gain, normalized information gain, Gini index, and Bayesian classification error. The proposed weakly supervised clustering was applied to the four criteria. For each data set, we randomly chose a part of the training data as the labeled data and left the remainder as unlabeled data. The weights of the labeled samples were set at 1.0 while the weights of the unlabeled samples were set through cross-validation. We built the RF with 100 trees, and 100 hyperplanes were randomly generated as candidates in the internal node of RF. The experiments are executed ten times to get the average accuracy results. In Figure 2, the classification accuracy of RF with traditional splitting criteria was shown in dashed lines and the proposed weakly supervised splitting was shown in solid lines. It is clear that performance improvement is obviously achieved as results of using the weakly supervised methods.

5.2 Image Clustering Tasks

In this experiment, over 20,000 images from five data sets are used to evaluate the image clustering. The USPS contains 9,298 gray-scale handwritten digit images scanned from envelopes by the U.S. Postal Service. The image size is 16×16. The MNIST [12] has a training set of 6,000 examples, and a test set of 1,000 examples with an image size of 28×28 and two sub data sets are chosen from the MNIST data set. Following [32], we use the first part of the test set of the MNIST database (referred to as MNIST-T) which is cleaner than the second part [12]. MNIST-T consists of 5,000 images of handwritten numbers with each digital number having 500 images. In the second subdatabase (referred to as MNIST-S), for each class we randomly sample one handwritten digit image per ten images. Thus, we totally have 6996 hand-written images in MNIST-S. The USF HumanID constructed by Sarkar et al. [22] consists of people walking in elliptical path in front of the camera. We resize each average silhouette image to 32×32 and then represent

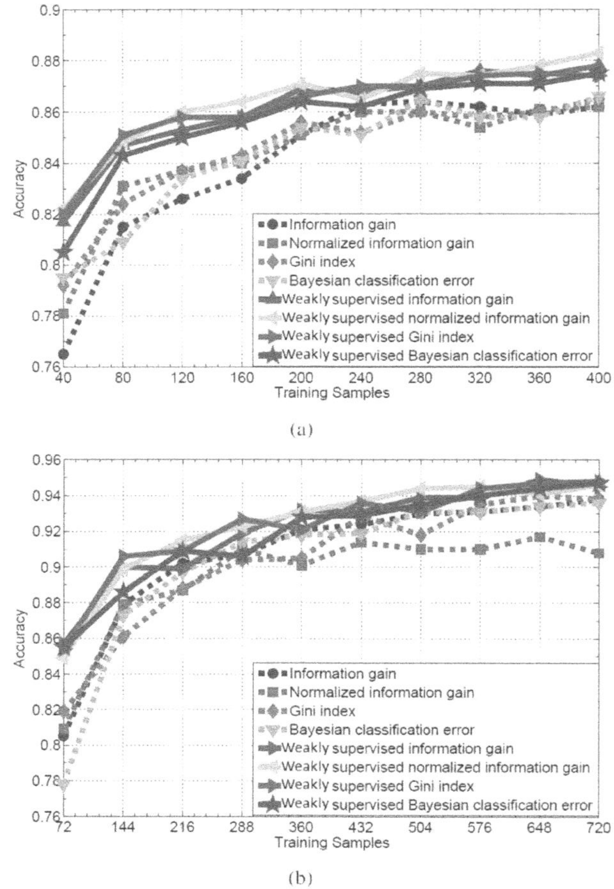

Figure 2: The classification accuracy comparison between traditional splitting criteria and the proposed weakly supervised splitting on the Satimage data set (a) and the Pendigits data set (b).

it as a 704-dimensional feature vector. 2,190 sampled images are used. The YALE-B contains 2,414 near frontal images from 38 persons under different illuminations. Each image is resized to 32×32. The statistics of the five data sets are presented in Table 1. We notice that the weak supervision of the five data sets are unavailable. Thus, we use k-means to cluster the fine-grained image labels into coarser ones (weak labels in Table 1), which are used as weak supervision to evaluate our algorithm.

We use clustering accuracy (ACC) and normalized mutual information (NMI) for performance evaluation in this work.

Clustering Accuracy (ACC): For the ith image, let us denote q_i as the clustering result from the clustering algorithm and p_i as the ground-truth label. Then the ACC is defined as

$$ACC = \frac{\sum_{i=1}^{n} \sigma(p_i, map(q_i))}{n}, \tag{12}$$

where n is the total number of images, $\sigma(x, y) = 1$ if $x = y$ ($\sigma(x, y) = 0$ otherwise), and $map(q_i)$ is the optimal mapping function that permutes clustering labels to match the ground-truth labels. The optimal mapping can be obtained using the Kuhn-Munkres algorithm [20]. A larger ACC indicates a better performance of a clustering algorithm.

Table 1: Data Set Description

Data set	Sample Size	Feature Dimension	Class Number	Weak Labels Number
USPS	9298	256	10	2
MINST-T	5000	784	10	2
MINST-S	6996	784	10	2
USF HumanID	2190	704	122	9
YALE-B	2414	1024	38	5

Normalized Mutual Information (NMI): NMI is another widely used measure for evaluating the clustering results. For two variables P and Q, their NMI is defined as

$$NMI(P,Q) = \frac{I(P,Q)}{\sqrt{H(P)H(Q)}}, \tag{13}$$

where $I(P,Q)$ is the mutual information between P and Q; $H(P)$ and $H(Q)$ denote the entropies of P and Q respectively. It is obvious that $NMI(P,Q)$ equals 1 if P is identical with Q, and it becomes 0 if P is independent from Q. Let t_l be the number of samples in the cluster $C_l (1 \leq l \leq c)$ obtained using a clustering algorithm and $\tilde{t}_h$ the number of samples in the hth ground-truth class $(1 \leq h \leq c)$. The overall NMI is calculated as

$$NMI = \frac{\sum_{l=1}^{c}\sum_{h=1}^{c}\log(\frac{n \cdot t_{l,h}}{t_l \tilde{t}_h})}{\sqrt{(\sum_{l=1}^{c} t_l \log \frac{t_l}{n})(\sum_{l=1}^{c} \tilde{t}_l \log \frac{\tilde{t}_l}{n})}}, \tag{14}$$

where $t_{l,h}$ is the number of samples intersected between the cluster C_l and the hth ground truth class. Again, a larger NMI indicates a better clustering result.

We compare the proposed clustering algorithm with K-means, DisKmeans [33] and two spectral clustering algorithms NCut [23] and LLC [27]. For our clustering algorithm, NCut, and LLC, spectral rotation [34] is used to obtain the clustering results. For LLC, both a Gaussian kernel (denoted as LLC-G) and a linear kernel (denoted as LLC-L) are used as the kernel function. Several parameters need to be set beforehand for these clustering techniques. The total number of clusters is provided for each of five data sets. For NCut and LLC, we have to determine the parameter k that specifies the number of nearest neighbors. Generally, k should be small in order to preserve the local manifold structure. To fairly compare the performance of NCut and LLC with our approach, we fix k to five. For the rest parameters, they are tuned carefully using cross validation. As shown in Table 2, 3, and 4, all the three evaluation metrics: ACC, NMI, and mean ACC with standard derivation, demonstrate the effectiveness of the proposed weakly supervised clustering.

5.3 Image Segmentation

Image annotation is to assign keywords to images, which is a good application to validate the proposed weakly supervised clustering since assigning different keywords to images can be seen as associating multiple labels to a bag.

The MSRC [6] and the LabelMe (LMO) data sets [15] are two representative benchmarks for image annotation. The MSRC contains 240 images from nine categories of semantic concepts. The LMO has 2,688 images from 33 categories of semantic concepts. Each image is associated with multiple categories. To describe the images, local descriptors are firstly extracted as instances at the local extreme difference-of-Gaussian corners following the method of [16], in which we use 9-bins color moment [25], 48-bins histogram of RGB, 59-bins histogram of LBP [19] and 128-bins SIFT feature [16] to describe an instance. Each image is a bag of instances and its bag level labels are given by the data set.

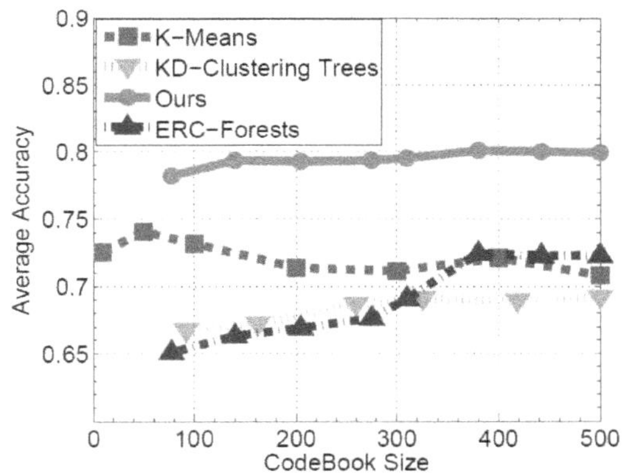

(a)

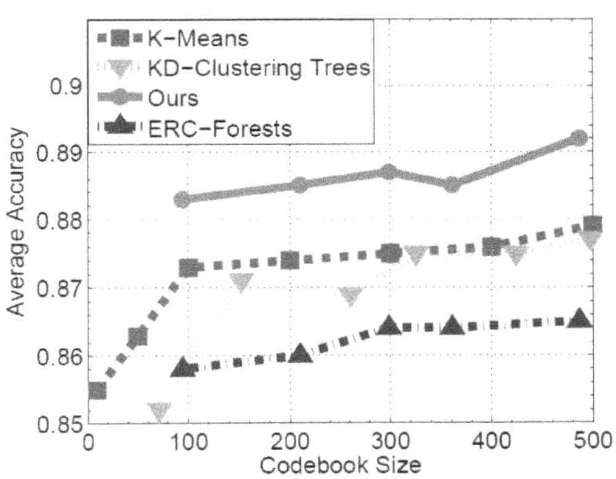

(b)

Figure 3: The average classification accuracy of K-means, KD-Clustering Trees, ERC-Forest, and our weakly supervised clustering on MSRC (a) and LMO (b).

In our experiment, four different clustering methods: K-means [17], KD-clustering Trees [7] ERC-Forest [18] and the proposed weakly supervised clustering, are compared. In particular, since ERC-Forest cannot handle the situation where a bag has multiple labels directly, we make the following modifications on the training data. For each bag with k labels, we make k copies of the bag where each copy is

Table 2: Performance comparison (ACC%) of K-Means, DisKmeans, NCut, LLC (LLC-L and LLC-G), and our proposed weakly supervised clustering.

	K-means	DisKmeans	NCut	LLC-L	LLC-G	Ours
USPS	67.9	71.5	78.7	70.1	71.6	**78.3**
MINIST-T	56.5	50.4	68.2	66.1	68.5	**70.2**
MINIST-S	53.2	51.8	66.2	71.0	71.2	**74.3**
USF Hu.	36.9	40.8	42.9	42.6	40.3	**42.3**
YALE-B	12.3	43.9	47.7	48.9	49.0	**53.2**

Table 3: Performance comparison (NMI%) of K-Means, DisKmeans, NCut, LLC (LLC-L and LLC-G), and our proposed weakly supervised clustering.

	K-means	DisKmeans	NCut	LLC-L	LLC-G	Ours
USPS	61.2	68.4	83.6	77.6	78.2	**78.9**
MINIST-T	50.3	48.4	68.4	61.3	64.2	**69.6**
MINIST-S	49.5	46.8	67.3	68.6	66.8	**72.1**
USF Hu.	68.9	72.6	75.2	74.8	72.6	**76.1**
YALE-B	18.3	55.2	67.1	65.1	64.9	**70.2**

Table 4: Performance comparison (Mean ACC± standard deviation%) of K-Means, DisKmeans, NCut, LLC (LLC-L and LLC-G), and our proposed weakly supervised clustering.

	K-means	DisKmeans	NCut	LLC-L	LLC-G	Ours
USPS	64.9±3.6	69.4±3.7	73.4±6.3	66.6±3.1	70.1±3.9	**80.5**±5.6
MINIST-T	55.3±2.6	48.8±3.4	66.2±3.4	66.1±2.3	64.7±3.6	**70.8**±3.8
MINIST-S	53.0±4.1	48.6±5.6	64.5±2.0	66.7±3.4	68.2±4.5	**74.7**±3.7
USF HumanID	35.9±1.0	39.7±1.1	42.6±0.4	42.3±0.3	40.1±0.4	**43.5**±2.1
YALE-B	11.3±0.7	41.1±3.1	46.2±1.5	48.5±0.6	46.7±0.6	**55.0**±1.2

associated with a single label. In this way, we create a new training data set where each bag has a single label. Then, we construct the ERC-Forest using the new training data set and the resulting ERC-forest served as a codebook.

In the testing phase, a binary SVM [3] is trained for each semantic category, using the global histogram of visual words. The average accuracy over all the classes is reported as the final classification accuracy, as shown in Figure 3. 120 images are chosen in random as the training set and the remainder as the testing set for MSRC. 2488 images are chose as training set and 200 images as the testing set for LMO. We repeat the training and testing procedure of the proposed WSRF for weakly supervised clustering for ten times. The variance of average accuracy is no more than two percent. The comparison clearly shows the superiority of our method.

6. CONCLUSION AND FUTURE WORK

Clustering is an important component in data mining and computer vision. In this paper, we propose a weakly supervised random forest for multi-label clustering and its applications in image clustering and segmentation. The weakly supervised clustering is firstly formulated into a constrained objective function minimization problem. Then, a WSRF is proposed to formulate the weakly supervised clustering into a constrained margin maximization problem by construction a random forest structure. For solving the margin maximization problem, a deterministic annealing algorithm is employed and conducted in two iterative steps. Finally, the instance-level clustering is achieved with guidance of the given bag-level labels. The experimental results demonstrate that our clustering algorithm can improve the performance of two real-world applications in image clustering and image segmentation.

In the future, we will further conduct research on evaluating the accuracy of clustering by trade-off between bag-level labeling and instance-level labeling. Furthermore, we will explore to apply our algorithm to more practical applications in data mining and computer vision [31, 28].

7. ACKNOWLEDGEMENTS

This research is supported in part by the following funds: National Natural Science Foundation of China under grant number 61472113 and 61304188, and Zhejiang Provincial Natural Science Foundation of China under grant number LZ13F020004 and LR14F020003.

8. REFERENCES

[1] D. M. Blei, A. Y. Ng, and M. I. Jordan. Latent dirichlet allocation. *Journal of Machine Learning Research*, 3:993–1022, 2003.

[2] L. Breiman. Random forests. *Machine learning*, 45(1):5–32, 2001.

[3] C.-C. Chang and C.-J. Lin. Libsvm: a library for support vector machines. *ACM Transactions on Intelligent Systems and Technology*, 3(2):2:27:1–27:27, 2011.

[4] L. Chen, D. Xu, I. W.-H. Tsang, and X. Li. Spectral embedded hashing for scalable image retrieval. *IEEE Transactions on Cybernetics*, 44(7):1180–1190, 2014.

[5] Y. Cheng. Mean shift, mode seeking, and clustering. *IEEE Transactions on Pattern Analysis and Machine Intelligence*, 17(8):790–799, 1995.

[6] A. Criminisi. *Microsoft research cambridge object recognition image data set.* 2004.

[7] S. Dasgupta and Y. Freund. Random projection trees and low dimensional manifolds. In *Proceedings of ACM symposium on Theory of computing*, pages 537–546, 2008.

[8] R. Datta, D. Joshi, J. Li, and J. Z. Wang. Image retrieval: Ideas, influences, and trends of the new age. *ACM Computing Surveys*, 5:1–60, 2008.

[9] L. Fei-Fei and P. Perona. A bayesian hierarchical model for learning natural scene categories. In *Proceedings of IEEE Conference on Computer Vision and Pattern Recognition*, pages 524–531, 2005.

[10] C. Hou, F. Nie, X. Li, D. Yi, and Y. Wu. Joint embedding learning and sparse regression: A framework for unsupervised feature selection. *IEEE Transactions on Cybernetics*, 44(6):793–804, 2014.

[11] B. Kulis, S. Basu, I. Dhillon, and R. Mooney. Semi-supervised graph clustering: a kernel approach. *Machine Learning*, 74(1):1–22, 2009.

[12] Y. Lecun, L. Bottou, Y. Bengio, and P. Haffner. Gradient-based learning applied to document recognition. In *Proceedings of IEEE*, pages 2278–2324, 1998.

[13] C. Leistner, A. Saffari, and H. Bischof. Miforests: Multiple-instance learning with randomized trees. In *Proceedings of European Conference on Computer Vision*, pages 29–42, 2010.

[14] J. Li, Y. Xia, Z. Shan, and Y. Liu. Scalable constrained spectral clustering. *IEEE Transactions on Knowledge and Data Engineering*, 27(2):589–593, 2015.

[15] C. Liu, J. Yuen, and A. Torralba. Nonparametric scene parsing via label transfer. *IEEE Transactions on Pattern Analysis and Machine Intelligence*, 12(33):2368–2382, 2011.

[16] D. G. Lowe. Distinctive image features from scale-invariant keypoints. *International Journal of Computer Vision*, 2(60):91–110, 2004.

[17] J. MacQueen. Some methods for classification and analysis of multivariate observations. In *Proceedings of the Fifth Berkeley Symposium on Mathematical Statistics and Probability*, pages 281–297, 1967.

[18] F. Moosmann, B. Triggs, and F. Jurie. Fast discriminative visual codebooks using randomized clustering forests. In *Proceedings of Annual Conference on Neural Information Processing Systems*, pages 985–992, 2007.

[19] T. Ojala, M. Pietikainen, and T. Maenpaa. Multiresolution gray-scale and rotation invariant texture classification with local binary patterns. *IEEE Transactions on Pattern Analysis and Machine Intelligence*, 7(24):971–987, 2002.

[20] C. H. Papadimitriou and K. Steiglitz. *Combinatorial Optimization: Algorithms and Complexity (Dover Books on Computer Science)*. Dover Publications, 1998.

[21] K. Rose. Deterministic annealing, constrained clustering, and optimization. In *Proceedings of International Joint Conference on Neural Networks*, pages 2515–2520, 1991.

[22] S. Sarkar, P. J. Phillips, Z. Liu, I. Robledo, Vega, P. Grother, and K. W. Bowyer. The humanid gait challenge problem: Data sets, performance, and analysis. *IEEE Transactions on Pattern Analysis and Machine Intelligence*, 27(2):162–177, November 2005.

[23] J. Shi and J. Malik. Normalized cuts and image segmentation. *IEEE Transactions on Pattern Analysis and Machine Intelligence*, 22(8):888–905, 2000.

[24] J. Sivic and A. Zisserman. Video google: A text retrieval approach to object matching in videos. In *Proceedings of IEEE Conference on Computer Vision and Pattern Recognition*, pages 1470–1477, 2003.

[25] M. A. Stricker and M. Orengo. Similarity of color images. In *IS&T/SPIE's Symposium on Electronic Imaging: Science & Technology*, pages 381–392, 1995.

[26] S. Wei, D. Xu, X. Li, and Y. Zhao. Joint optimization toward effective and efficient image search. *IEEE Transactions on Cybernetics*, 43(6):2216–2227, 2013.

[27] M. Wu and B. Schölkopf. Normalized cuts and image segmentation. In *Proceedings of Annual Conference on Neural Information Processing Systems*, pages 1529–1536, 2006.

[28] Y. Xia, X. Li, and Z. Shan. Parallelized fusion on multisensor transportation data: A case study in cyberits. *International Journal of Intelligent Systems*, 28(6):540–564, 2013.

[29] Y. Xia, C. Wang, X. Shi, and L. Zhang. Vehicles overtaking detection using rgb-d data. *Signal Processing*, 112:98–109, 2015.

[30] Y. Xia, W. Xu, L. Zhang, X. Shi, and K. Mao. Integrating 3d structure into traffic scene understanding with rgb-d data. *Neurocomputing*, 151:700–709, 2015.

[31] Y. Xia, T. Zhang, and S. Wang. A generic methodological framework for cyber-its: Using cyber-infrastructure in its data analysis cases. *Fundamenta Informaticae*, 133(1):35–53, 2014.

[32] D. Xu, S. Yan, L. Zhang, S. Lin, H.-J. Zhang, and T. S. Huang. Reconstruction and recognition of tensor-based objects with concurrent subspaces analysis. *IEEE Transactions on Circuits Systems for Video Technology*, 18(1):36–47, 2008.

[33] J. Ye. Discriminative k-means for clustering. In *Proceedings of Annual Conference on Neural Information Processing Systems*, pages 1649–1656, 2008.

[34] S. X. Yu and J. Shi. Multiclass spectral clustering. In *Proceedings of IEEE Conference on Computer Vision and Pattern Recognition*, pages 313–319, 2003.

[35] L. Zhang, Y. Gao, C. Hong, Y. Feng, J. Zhu, and D. Cai. Feature correlation hypergraph: Exploiting high-order potentials for multimodal recognition. *IEEE Transactions on Cybernetics*, 44(8):1408–1419, 2014.

[36] L. Zhang, X. Li, L. Nie, Y. Yang, and Y. Xia. Weakly supervised human fixation prediction. *IEEE Transactions on Cybernetics*, 2015.

[37] L. Zhang, M. Song, Y. Yang, Q. Zhao, Z. Chen, and N. Sebe. Weakly supervised photo cropping. *IEEE Transactions on Multimedia*, 16(1):94–107, 2014.

[38] L. Zhang, Y. Yang, Y. Gao, C. Wang, Y. Yu, and X. Li. A probabilistic associative model for segmenting weakly-supervised images. *IEEE Transactions on Image Processing*, 23(9):4150–4159, 2014.

Harvesting Multiple Sources for User Profile Learning: a Big Data Study

Aleksandr Farseev, Liqiang Nie, Mohammad Akbari and Tat-Seng Chua
farseev@u.nus.edu; nieliqiang@gmail.com; {akbari, chuats}@nus.edu.sg
School of Computing, National University of Singapore

ABSTRACT

User profile learning, such as mobility and demographic profile learning, is of great importance to various applications. Meanwhile, the rapid growth of multiple social platforms makes it possible to perform a comprehensive user profile learning from different views. However, the research efforts on user profile learning from multiple data sources are still relatively sparse, and there is no large-scale dataset released towards user profile learning. In our study, we contribute such benchmark and perform an initial study on user mobility and demographic profile learning. First, we constructed and released a large-scale multi-source multi-modal dataset from three geographical areas. We then applied our proposed ensemble model on this dataset to learn user profile. Based on our experimental results, we observed that multiple data sources mutually complement each other and their appropriate fusion boosts the user profiling performance.

Categories and Subject Descriptors

H.3.1 [**Information Storage and Retrieval**]: Content Analysis and Indexing

General Terms

Algorithms, Experimentation, Performance

Keywords

Multiple Source Integration; User Profile Learning; Mobility Profile; Demographic Profile

1. INTRODUCTION

Regarded initially as a hub for teenagers and college students, social media in recent years has increased its impact on the way people live and communicate all around the world. Moreover, some popular social networks like Facebook and Twitter are constantly growing by involving more and more people of different genders, ages and lifestyles [6]. The rapid growth and interconnections between online social services are somehow related to the popularity of smartphones, which enable users to communicate while on the move. Furthermore, it is well known that more than half of online adults use more than one social network in their daily life[1]. These social services are often connected to each other by deploying the so-called cross-linking functionality [4]. With multi-source and mobility-related data, understanding user behaviours via user profile learning is promising and possible [13][15][17][25][26].

In this work, we define user profile as comprising of user mobility profile and user demographic profile, as shown in Figure 1. *Mobility* is a contemporary paradigm, which involves various types of people movement. It can be a physical movement in space, the movement from one social group to another or even a virtual movement between web pages while surfing the Internet [22]. The user mobility profile describes users' behavioural habits and interests. It is useful in many application scenarios, such as transport routes planning [11][20] or the control of spread of diseases [19]. On the other hand, the user *demographic profile*[2] typically includes age, gender and social class. These demographic attributes were also studied in a popular evaluations named PAN [18][21]. In general, the demographic profile is often used in marketing to describe a demographic grouping or a market segment. By considering users' demographic aspects, we are able to gain deep insights into users' behaviour and interests understanding. For example, in advertisement domain, age and gender significantly affect the list of potential products that can be routed to a given consumer: cars may be advertised mostly to adult males; while toys to kids and their parents. At the same time, it can also be used to support recommendation [13] and personalized question answering [12]. The combination of mobility and demographic profile opens the possibility of urban facility planning according to demographic properties of city areas: government organizations may consider building more kindergartens and schools in areas with high concentration of young families; while more food courts near professionals' work places.

User profile learning by jointly considering multiple sources is, however, non-trivial, due to following reasons:

- *Multiple data sources:* Users frequently enroll in multiple on-line social forums, which captures the

[1] www.pewinternet.org

[2] en.wikipedia.org/wiki/Demographic_profile

ICMR '15 Jun 23 - 26 2015, Shanghai, China

ACM ACM 978-1-4503-3274-3/15/06 ...$15.00.
DOI: http://dx.doi.org/10.1145/2671188.2749381

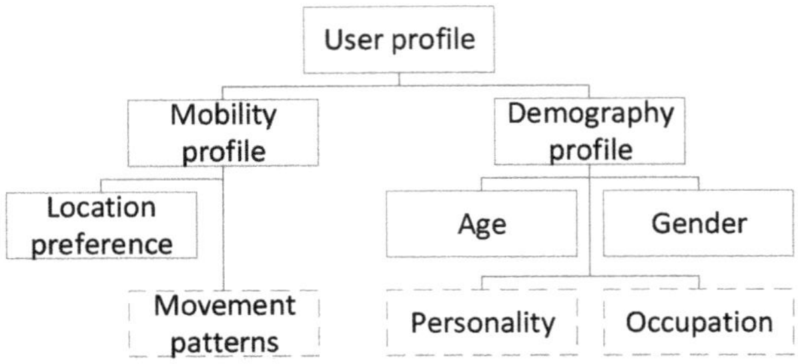

Figure 1: User profile and its compositions.

same users from different views. For example, Linkedin conveys users' formal career path; while Twitter casually uncovers users' daily activities. Effective integration of multi-view data from different sources is a tough challenge.

- *Multi-modal data:* Beyond texts, other modalities often appear in users' messages. Users may take and share pictures in photo-sharing services like Instagram, upload videos to Youtube and perform Foursquare/Swarm (Foursquare) check-ins. Users' messages on social media platform such as Twitter also include more multimedia. User profile learning on these heterogeneous information requires new theories that can seamlessly integrate such heterogeneous data in a complementary way.
- *Benchmark Dataset:* As far as we know, there is no a publicly accepted benchmark dataset towards user profile learning with multi-source multi-modal data. Due to the sensitivity of privacy, only a limited amount of data can be collected for internet active users. Even worse, after the collection of necessary data, it is a big challenge to align various social network accounts to the same user. Another problem is the lack of ground truth, which greatly hinders the development of learning algorithms.

To facilitate user profile learning via multi-source multi-modal data, we build a representative data collection from three prevailing social resources, namely, Twitter, Foursquare and Instagram. The ground truth is obtained by crawling publicly available information from users' Facebook pages. Based upon the constructed dataset, we conduct the preliminary study of profile learning. In particular, user mobility is modelled as a location-topic distribution and reflects user's location category preferences. We also perform first-order data analysis by calculating mobility-related statistics that describe users' activities for different social sources. In addition, we infer some attributes of the demographic profile, such as the age and gender. We regard the demographic profile learning as an ensemble learning task by fusing multiple and heterogeneous information cues. We claim and verify that multi-source multi-modal data fusion is able to boost the results of the demographic profile learning, as compared to the use of a mono source.

Several prior research efforts have already been dedicated to user profile learning. Some prior works were devoted to urban user mobility analysis [8][13][14]; while others focused mostly on location-based user community detection and profiling [27] or market trade area analysis [17]. The user demographic profiling task gained popularity following the works in [18][21], where participants were asked to build a model to predict user's age and gender based on users' textual posts. Users' occupation prediction from a large Twitter text corpora was also explored in [1]. However, most of these works are either based on a single-source or a single-modality dataset. Few of them explored and leveraged multi-source multi-modal data.

In this work, we constructed and released [7] a multi-source dataset, provided users demographics and mobility ground truth, and performed preliminary studies in these two directions.

2. MULTI-SOURCE BIG DATA

This section details the dataset construction. In order to cover the most popular modalities (visual, textual and location data), we incorporate following social media sources:

- Foursquare as a location data source;
- Twitter as a textual data source;
- Instagram as a visual data source;
- Facebook as a demographics-related ground truth source.

The data was obtained from three geographical regions with high Foursquare user activity, namely: Singapore London and New York. It can be used for research on *user profile learning* and other contemporary problems such as *venue recommendation* [27], *user identification* across multiple social networks [23], and *cross-region user community detection* [28]. Considering the sensitivity of users' private information, we release the extracted features instead of the original data.

We first collected a set of active users, who have recently posted tweets through the cross-linking functionality of Instagram or Swarm mobile apps. We utilized Twitter REST API[3] to perform the location-dependent tweets search in Singapore, London and New York regions. This crawling method offers the possibility to map Twitter user IDs to Foursquare and Instagram user IDs, which allows us to overcome the multi-source user identification problem [23]. Based upon the active user list, we crawled user generated contents for those users, who posted their activities on Twitter. Tweet streams can be monitored with the key words specified as "swarmapp.com" and "instagram.com" to receive tweets posted from Swarm and Instagram mobile applications, respectively. For example, each sampled check-in message contains a short link to the original check-in page, where the check-in details are available. By following this, we performed check-ins and media crawling for previously identified active users. Noticeably, this crawling strategy can be applied to crawl other social networks as well.

2.1 Statistics of the Dataset

The dataset crawling process started on 10 July 2014 in Singapore, London and New York regions, and ended on 20 Dec 2014. The number of data records for each city is summarized in Table 1. In our current work, we perform data analysis and user profile learning for users from Singapore region only. It means that all our following statements refer only to users in Singapore, while cross-region profile learning could be addressed in future work.

Figure 2(a) presents the percentage of users with respect to the number of posts. It can be seen that the users'

[3]`dev.twitter.com/rest/public`

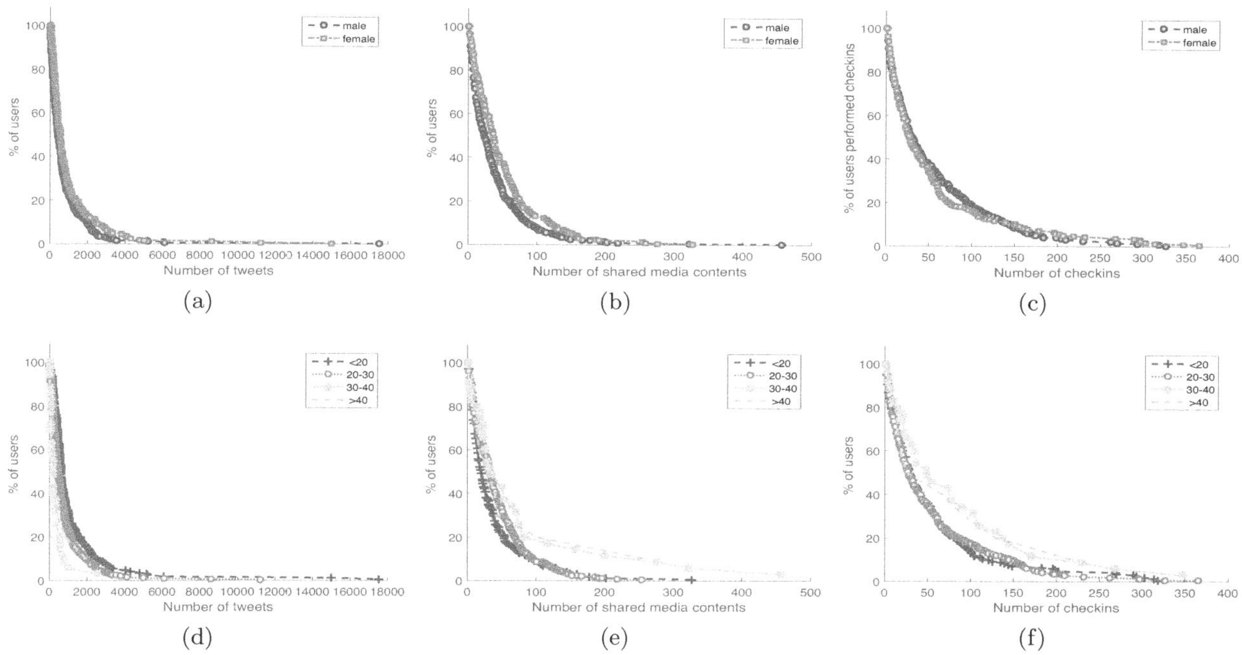

Figure 2: **The statistics of Singapore dataset: (a) illustrates the percentage of users with respect to the number of posted tweets based on gender; (b) and (c) respectively show users posted multimedia on Instagram and checkins in Foursquare. (d) illustrates the percentage of users with respect to the number of posted tweets based on their age group; (e) and (f) respectively show users posted multimedia on Instagram and checkins in Foursquare.**

Table 1: Number of data records in our constructed dataset from Singapore, London and New York.

City	#users	#tweets	#ch-ins	#images
Singapore	7,023	11,732,489	366,268	263,530
London	5,503	2,973,162	127,276	65,088
NY	7,957	5,263,630	304,493	230,752

microblog activity is not very correlated to their gender. Figure 2(b) shows the percentage of users with respect to the amount of multimedia contents which they shared through Twitter. It shows that female users in general share more media content than male users. Figure 2(c) shows the analysis results of user check-in behaviors. It can be seen that males tent to perform more check-ins than females.

We also analyzed users' posting behavior with respect to users' age. Figure 2(d), 2(e) and 2(f) respectively show user behavior distributions in terms of writing microblog messages, sharing media contents, and posting check-ins. It is interesting but surprising to notice that, users from 30 - 40 age group are less active in microblog than younger users (< 20 y.o; 20 - 30 y.o); while in image and location sharing services, older users in average (30 - 40 y.o; >40 y.o) more active.

In order to visualize the semantic component of data, we plot the distributions of users among popular Foursquare venue categories and Instagram image concepts for users of different age and gender. Figure 3(a) shows the most popular venue categories in our dataset with respect to users' gender. As it can be seen, there is a meaningful difference in venue preference between male and female users. In particular, men are more interested to visit night clubs and food courts, while female users often perform check-ins from home or cafe. Figure 3(c), in contrast, visualizes user mobility with respect to age. It shows that adult users (older than 20 y.o) often perform check - ins in malls, while children and teenagers (<20 y.o.) often stay at home.

Besides, we analyzed users' media sharing behaviours on Instagram. Figures 3(b) and 3(d) demonstrate the distribution of the extracted image concepts for users' gender and age groups, respectively. From Figure 3(b), we can see that images posted by woman often include hairs and dresses, which are represented by "Wig" and "Pajama" concepts, while men mostly shared images with cloth-related ("Ski mask", "Bulletproof vest") and daily life ("Comic book", "Chocolate sauce") concepts. Figure 3(d) explicitly reflects that distinct age groups are interested in different concepts. For example, food-related concepts such as "Plate", "Pot-pie", and "Burrito" are frequently shared by senior age group, while "Comic book" and "Toy shop" are often shared by users of between 30-40 years old[4].

2.2 Ground Truth

The ground truth was crawled from the publicly available Facebook pages. The Facebook-Foursquare-Twitter account ID mapping was obtained via Foursquare REST API[5]. The significant part of users in Singapore (3,849 records) have mentioned their gender, while only a few have provided their actual age (305 records). In order to complement age-related ground truth, we estimated the missing age from their education path. To encourage other broad research, we have also released [7] ground truth records about user's Education, Employment, Demography, Location and Family.

[4]Image concepts were extracted from ImageNet [5].

[5]`developer.foursquare.com`

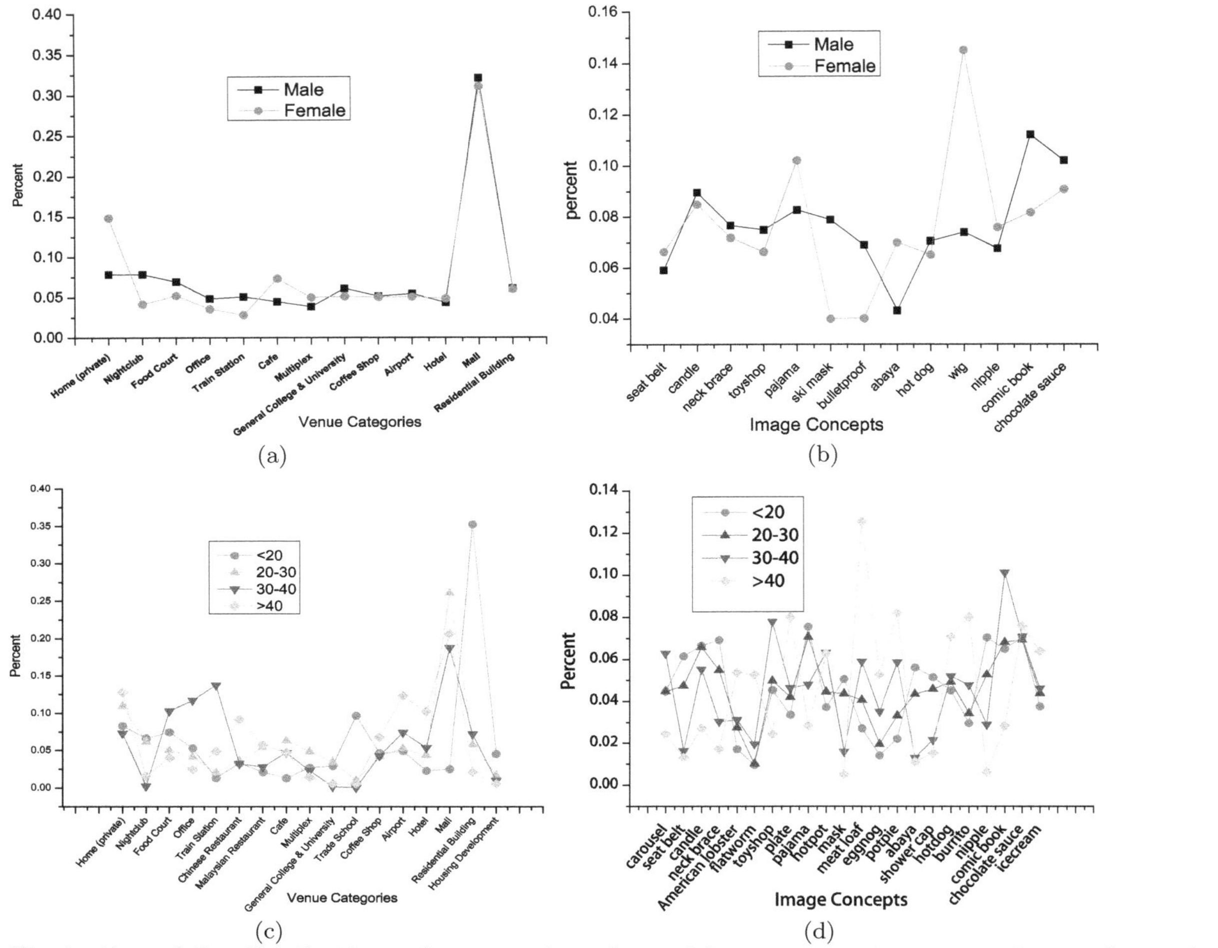

Figure 3: Illustration of the distributions of venue categories and image concepts over genders and ages for the Singapore dataset. (a) and (b) respectively illustrate the distribution of categories and image concepts for different genders; while (c) and (d) illustrate the distribution of categories and image concepts for different age groups, respectively.

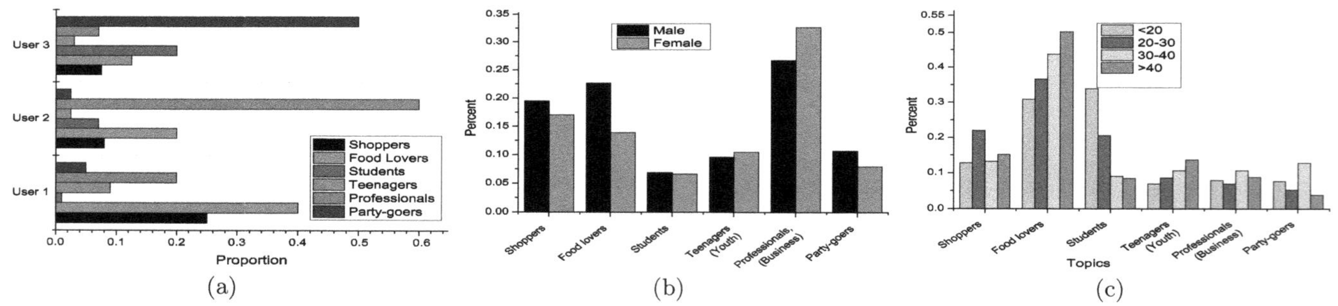

Figure 4: The personal mobility statistics for the Singapore dataset: (a) shows a category-based user mobility profiles for three users; (b) and (c) show the distribution of users among mobility categories based on gender and age respectively

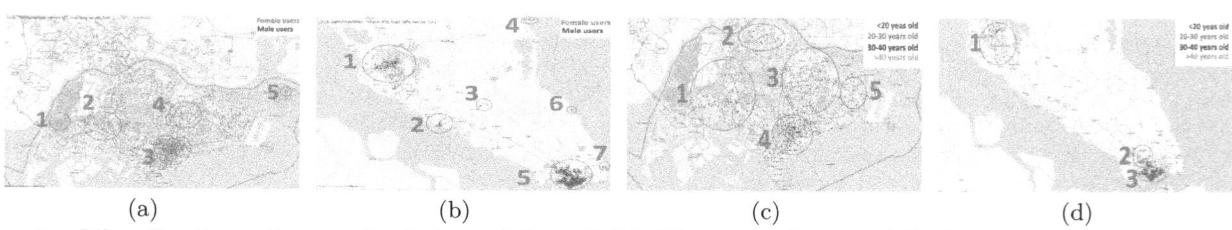

Figure 5: Visualization of user check-ins. (a) and (b) illustrate the spatial distribution of check-ins for different gender on Singapore and regional map respectively; (c) and (d) illustrate the spatial distribution of check-ins for different age groups on Singapore and regional map respectively.

3. USER PROFILE LEARNING

3.1 User Mobility Profiling

3.1.1 Individual User Mobility

One way to create category-based user mobility profile is by counting the check-ins frequency for each venue category. As can be seen from previous sections, most of the time users preferred to visit venues that belong to popular categories such as "Mall", "Home", or "Nightclub". However, the dimension of such user profile would be the same as the number of categories in Foursquare category hierarchy (i.e. 592 in Singapore), and thus cannot be easily interpreted or visualized. Moreover, it is more useful to extract individual users' interests that are represented by the tail of user-category distribution.

To address these problems, we apply LDA [2] on venue category and their descriptions, which has been found to be a good approach for location-based user profiling [17]. In LDA terminology, each user is modelled as a LDA document, while each venue category is considered as a LDA word. We empirically found the number of LDA topics equals to 6, since it gives more human-interpretable category-topic distribution results. The venue category distribution for different LDA topics is presented in Table 2.

We label each topic by considering the corresponding top 5 most popular venue categories. As a result, we can clearly define 6 interest groups, namely, "Food Lovers", "Travellers (Business)", "Party Goers", "Family Guys", "Students" and "Teenagers (Youth)". It is worth noting that in most of the obtained mobility groups (LDA topics), users are represented by the popular categories that obviously reflect *personal* user mobility profile. Such user mobility profiling tackles the human interpretability and visualization problems as well. Each user profile can be visualized based on the mobility groups learned such as that based on 3 users described in Figure 4(a), where "User 1" often performed business trips, while "User 2" and "User 3" are Student and Teenager respectively. Next, we compare the obtained users' profiles for different demographic categories. Specifically, we draw the distribution of users among mobility "topics" based on users' gender (Figure 4(b)) and age group (Figure 4(c))). From Figure 4(b), it can be seen that males often manifest their professional side, while female users often demonstrate student's lifestyle. Regarding the age differences, most of the "Party-goers" belong to 10-20 age group, while people > 40 tend to make business trips and spend time with family. Therefore, the obtained mobility patterns clearly separate users from different age groups and gender, and can thus be considered as a powerful approach for *individual* user mobility profiling.

3.1.2 Group Mobility

To make deeper insights into user group mobility, we visualize users' check - ins on Singapore map for different age groups and genders. We also provide smaller scaled map to visualize inter - city user mobility. From Figure 5(a), it can be seen that the city population is concentrated in several dense regions, which represent peoples' housing (Regions 2 and 3) and working (Region 3) areas. Generally, male and female users are evenly distributed in these areas. However, there are some regions where male (Blue markers) user check-in density is much higher than that of female (Pink markers). It can be explained by the special purposes of the land usage, which includes military objects and army polygons (Regions 1 and 5). From the inter-city perspective (Figure 5(b)), it can be seen that both female and male users often perform trips to nearby cities for shopping and leisure purposes (Regions 1, 2, 4, 5). However, there are some geographical areas that are popular only by female users (Regions 2, 3). It can be explained by attractiveness of these regions to users who travel with family. For example, Region 2 is the city of "Malacca" which is famous by it's resorts, while Region 3, the "Segamat Distinct", is the leisure area with natural waterfall and national park, which could be popular among family groups. From the user age distribution map (Figure 5(c)), we can see that people of different ages perform check-ins in different city areas, i.e. teenagers and children (Brown markers) mostly perform check-ins in housing city areas and around schools (Regions 1,2,3,5), while students (Green markers) and working professionals (Blue and Red markers) are concentrated in city center (Region 4). this clearly shows the places where these users spend most of their time; for example, young people spend most of their time studying in school or at home with their parents, while students and working professionals tend to make longer trips from home to office or university. From the small scale map (Figure 5(d)), it can be seen that young users (brown circles) are rarely travel to nearby cities due to their age (Region 3), while young adults (green circles) often make such trips (Regions 1 and 2). These users may be students or young professionals who visit their families during weekends. The temporal aspect of user movement is not considered in our work. However, it is an important factor for user mobility study, thus need to be analyzed in future. In summary, user behaviour patterns are tightly knit to users' demographic profiles, such as gender and age.

3.2 User Demographic Profiling

This section describes the feature extraction from multi-source multi-modal data, and the ensemble learning model we proposed for demographic profiling.

3.2.1 Location Features

We obtained 592 venue categories from Foursquare[6]. Take a user as an example. The user has performed three check-ins in two restaurants and airport, but did not perform any check-in in other venues; then the user's venue category feature vector will consist of 592 real values with c_r (the feature representing restaurant) equals to 2/3 and another c_a (the feature representing airport) equals to 1/3. All the other values of feature vector will be equal to 0.

3.2.2 Text Features

We extracted the following textual features:

- *LDA-based Features.* We merged all the tweets of each user into a document. All documents were projected into a latent topic space using Latent Dirichlet Allocation (LDA) [2]. All users' tweets can be represented as a mixture of different topics. We empirically set $\alpha = 0.5$, $\beta = 0.1$ and utilized KNIME[7] to train the topic model with $T = 50$ topics for $1,000$

[6] developer.foursquare.com/categorytree
[7] www.knime.org

Table 2: Category distribution among LDA topics

ID	Categories	LDA Topics
T1	Malay Res-t, Mall, University, Indian Res-t, Aisian Res-t	Food Lovers
T2	Cafe, Airport, Hotel, Coffee Shop, Chinese Res-t	Travelers (Business)
T3	Nightclub, Mall, Food Court, Trade School, Res-t, Coffee Shop	Party Goers
T4	Home, Office, Build., Neighbor-d, Gov. Build., Factory	Family Guys (Youth)
T5	University (Collage), Gym, Airport, Hotel, Fitness Club	Students
T6	Train St., Apartment, Mall, High School, Bus St.	Teenagers (Youth)

iterations. We ultimately built the topic-based user feature vectors.

- *Linguistic Features.* We extracted LIWC linguistic features [16], which were founded to be a powerful mechanism for age and gender prediction purposes [21]. For each user tweet list, we extracted 71 LIWC features.
- *Heuristically-inferred Features.* We extracted some heuristically inferred features. First, we counted the *number of URLs*, *number of hash tags* and *number of user mentions*, since these features are correlated with user's social network activity level and can, thus, indicate user's age. Second, we counted the *number slang words*, *number of emotion words*[8], *number of emoticons* and computed *an average sentiment score.* These features can be good signals of user personality traits, which in turn are gender and age dependent [21]. Third, we computed the linguistic style features: "Number of repeated characters" in words, "number of misspellings", and "number of unknown to the spell checker words", which are often reflected by user's age.

3.2.3 Visual Features

We mapped each Instagram photo to the pre-defined image concept dictionary. The concept dictionary, comprising of 1000 daily life concepts (such as ball, flower, and chair), is constructed from ImageNet. We trained the concept classifiers based on the concatenation of "Bag-of-visual-words", "Local Binary Patterns"(LBP) and "64-D Color Histogram"(CH) features [5]. For the bag-of-visual-words, we used the difference of Gaussians to detect keypoints in each image and extracted their SIFT descriptors. By building a visual codebook of size 1000 based on K-means, we obtained a 1000-dimensional bag-of-visual-words histogram for each image. We then applied Principal Component Analysis (PCA) to reduce the dimension of image feature space [10] to 50 condensed features.

3.2.4 Age and Gender Prediction

Two most popular approaches for multi-source fusion are early and late fusion. In early fusion strategy, features are concentrated in one long feature vector to feed into the classifier, while late fusion incorporates the independently learned results from each modality [24]. In our work, we have evaluated both approaches. First, we performed an early fusion and trained a Random forest classifier with 145 random trees (the number of random trees was

[8]sentiwordnet.isti.cnr.it

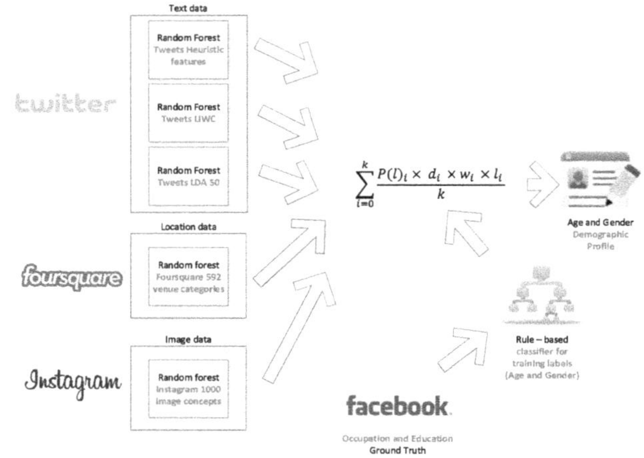

Figure 6: Demographic profiling ensemble.

estimated empirically). However, as it can be seen from the experimental results (Table 3), most of the introduced approaches outperform the early fusion models. Inspired by the previously reported results [1, 18] and considering the comparably high performance of single source features (See Table 3), we employed the late fusion approach to train models from different combinations of feature sets. The structure of the demographic profiling framework is presented in Figure 6. It can be seen that our framework consists of multi-label Random Forest classifiers trained on five feature types described earlier. The Random Forest classification model was selected due to its well-known ability to perform classification on high dimensional space by randomized feature selection approach. Moreover it was noticed [21] that the Random Forest classifier often outperforms other machine learning approaches, like SVM or Naive Bayes for Age and Gender prediction tasks. The optimal number of random trees for each classifier is found by 10-fold cross-validation. The number of random trees for "Location", "LIWC", "Heuristic", "LDA 50", and "Image concepts" features are set to 140, 120, 75, 70, 130 respectively. To obtain balanced label distribution in the training set, we performed the "SMOTE" data oversampling technique [3].

The five Random Forest classifiers were integrated into the ensemble learning model; with the final classification score for each label computed as:

$$Score(l) = \sum_{i=0}^{k} \frac{P(l)_i \times d_i \times w_i \times l_i}{k},$$

where $P(l)_i$ is a positive prediction confidence for label l of the i-th classification model, d_i is the number of data records that were collected from current user to train the i-th classification model, divided by average number of data records of given type collected for all users, w_i is the accuracy of the i-th classification model, and l_i is the "strength" of the i-th classification model. In our experiments, we set w_i to be equal to the macro accuracy level of the corresponding i classifier, which is estimated after performing 10-fold cross validation on each individual features set. We jointly learned the l_i coefficient for each modality by performing the "Stochastic Hill climbing with Random Restart (SHCR)" optimization[9], which is able to

[9]en.wikipedia.org/wiki/Hill_climbing

obtain local optimum for non-convex problems and, can, thus, produce reasonable ensemble weighting.

We present an example on how ensemble model works for different data sources. Suppose users u_x and u_y have 100 and 300 tweets respectively and we have already obtained the classification accuracy for some Twitter features set as 0.321. Then the score of classifier trained on these features $P(l)_{i_k}$ will be multiplied by: $w_{u_x} = 0.321$, $d_{u_x} = 100/200 = 0.5$ and $w_{u_y} = 0.321$, $d_{u_y} = 300/200 = 1.5$ for u_x and u_y respectively. These score will also be multiplied by the current iteration assignment of l_{i_k}. After all the five classifiers are weighted as described above, the output scores will be averaged and the result will represent the classification ensemble score assigned to label l on the current iteration k. The above procedure will be repeated until the SHCR coveraged, by varying the l_{i_k} parameters on each iteration aiming to maximize the overall accuracy.

3.2.5 Experimental results

As we mention before, the number of male and female users in our dataset is similar while the users' age is mainly in the range of between 10 and 40 years old. The similar age distribution was also observed in related works [21][18]. Due to the uneven users' age distribution, we have divided users' on age groups as follows: "< 20", "20-30", "30-40", "> 40".

We evaluated the performance of our approach in terms of *macro accuracy*, which is the average accuracy between all classification labels. The evaluation metric was selected due to its capability of equally treating all data labels in unbalanced datasets, so that the overall performance will not be overpriced. The evaluation of gender and age prediction was based on 222 users who have reported their exact age and perform activity in all three data sources, and can thus be considered as reliable ground truth. The age group prediction model was trained based on other users whose age group was estimated from their education-related information by performing rule-based classification (548 users). According to our experiment, the bias of estimated ages does not exceed ± 2.31 years. It is thus reasonable to use the estimated age for training the age group prediction classifier. The gender prediction model was trained based on $3,544$ users who have reported their gender and are not in evaluation set. The age and gender prediction results are presented in Table 3.

From Table 3, it can be seen that different data sources perform differently in predicting different demographic attributes. For example, in gender prediction task, the LDA features play a crucial role and perform the best among other single sources. The reason is that there exists high difference in interests between male and female users. For example, female users may discuss family and children, while male users tent to tweet about cars and finance. By integrating all text-based features together with visual features, it introduces the best combination for age and gender prediction among all bi-source ensembles, while the location plays a minor role. The possible reason is that there are distinct differences in picture taking preferences and writing style among different users' age groups and genders. For example, older people may take pictures of food and scenery, while younger users could be more emotional in their tweets.

However, the best results for both gender and age group prediction are obtained by late fusion of all features using the

Table 3: Performance of demographic profiling in terms of Macro Accuracy. RF - Random Forest; NB - Naive Bayes; SVM - Support Vector Machine

Method	Gender	Age
State-of-the-arts techniques		
SVM Location Cat. (Foursquare)	0.581	0.251
SVM LWIC Text(Twitter)	0.590	0.254
SVM Heuristic Text(Twitter)	0.589	0.290
SVM LDA 50 Text(Twitter)	0.595	0.260
SVM Image Concepts(Instagram)	0.581	0.254
NB Location Cat. (Foursquare)	0.575	0.185
NB LWIC Text(Twitter)	0.640	0.392
NB Heuristic Text(Twitter)	0.599	**0.394**
NB LDA 50 Text(Twitter)	**0.653**	0.343
NB Image Concepts(Instagram)	0.631	0.233
Single-Source		
RF Location Cat. (Foursquare)	0.649	0.306
RF LWIC Text(Twitter)	0.716	0.407
RF Heuristic Text(Twitter)	0.685	**0.463**
RF LDA 50 Text(Twitter)	**0.788**	0.357
RF Image Concepts(Instagram)	0.784	0.366
Multi-Source combinations		
RF LDA + LIWC(Late Fusion)	0.784	0.426
RF LDA + Heuristic(Late Fusion)	0.815	0.480
RF Heuristic + LIWC (Late Fusion)	0.730	0.421
RF All Text (Late Fusion)	0.815	0.425
RF Media + Location (Late Fusion)	0.802	0.352
RF Text + Media (Late Fusion)	**0.824**	**0.483**
RF Text + Location (Late Fusion)	0.743	0.401
All sources together		
RF Early fusion for all features	0.707	0.370
RF Multi-source (Late Fusion)	**0.878**	**0.509**

Random Forests ensemble. It outperforms all single source models, different combinations of classifiers in ensemble models, state-of-the-arts techniques, and model trained on early fused sources.

4. RELATED WORK

User profile learning via multi-sources is a comparably new topic in social media research, and there are little work devoted to it. The emergence of new cross-linking functionality in modern social Web platforms is related to our work. For instance, the work conducted by Wang et al. [25] performed high level comparison between Facebook, Twitter and Foursquare profiles for randomly sampled Foursquare users; they performed both content level and network level analysis. From the network point of view, it was noted that "67 percent of friend pairs on Foursquare are also friends on Facebook, and 43 percent of friend pairs on Foursquare follow each other on Twitter" [25]. The authors observed that active Foursquare users are usually active in Twitter as well, which is consistent with the observations derived from our dataset. In other study, Chen et al. [4] tried to discover cross-site linking regularities in large-scale online social networks dataset. By gathering almost all Foursquare user network graph and applying first order statistical analysis, the authors [4] were able to extract comprehensive knowledge about the Foursquare network structure and users cross social network behaviour. At the same time, Zhong et al. [29] attempted to discover network evolution relations across various social forums datasets (Tencent, Epinion, Facebook, Xiaonei, Twitter, Sina Weibo, Github, StackOverflow). As a result, the proposed by authors statistical approach outperformed the baselines in link prediction task. Finally, Ottoni et al. [15] discovered user generated data relations across Pinterest and Twitter social services; however, the work focused mostly on data description, but not model for profile learning.

5. CONCLUSIONS AND FUTURE WORK

This work presented an initial study of user profile learning via integration of multiple data sources. We constructed a dataset by crawling information from Twitter, Foursquare and Instagram. To facilitate research by other researchers, we have released this dataset [7]. Based upon this dataset, we conducted first-order and higher-order learning for user mobility and demographic profiling in Singapore region. User mobility was modelled as a location-topic distribution, while demographic profile was represented by age and gender attributes. From our experimental outputs, we can draw the conclusions that: multi-source data of the same users mutually complements each other and their appropriate fusion boosts the user profiling performance.

We list some potential research topics that can be conducted on our released dataset:

- *Complete demographic profiling.* Researchers are encouraged to learn other demographics attributes, such as occupation, personality and social status [1].
- *Extended mobility profiling.* In current study, we focused on category-specific user mobility profiling; while it would be useful to incorporate spatio-temporal factors of users' movement [17].
- *Causality pattern extraction.* It is important to discover potential causal relationships between events from multiple data sources [9]. For example, the "flower" image concept could be temporally related with flower shop check-ins or tweets about flowers.
- *Cross-source user identification.* The alignment of user accounts across multiple social resources [23] can benefit from user profile compilation [25].
- *Cross-region user profiling and community matching.* This direction [28] may offer insight on differences and similarities between users' preferences.

6. ACKNOWLEDGMENTS

This research is supported by the Singapore National Research Foundation under its International Research Centre @ Singapore Funding Initiative and administered by the IDM Programme Office.

The Microsoft Windows Azure Cloud and Microsoft MSDN subscription were provided by "MB-Guide"[10] project and as part of Microsoft BizSpark program.

7. REFERENCES

[1] E. Amigó, J. Carrillo-de Albornoz, I. Chugur, A. Corujo, J. Gonzalo, E. Meij, M. de Rijke, and D. Spina. Overview of replab 2014: author profiling and reputation dimensions for online reputation management. In *Information Access Evaluation. Multilinguality, and Interaction.* 2014.

[2] D. M. Blei, A. Y. Ng, and M. I. Jordan. Latent dirichlet allocation. *Journal of Machine Learning Research*, 2003.

[3] N. V. Chawla, K. W. Bowyer, L. O. Hall, and W. P. Kegelmeyer. Smote: synthetic minority over-sampling technique. *Journal of artificial intelligence research*, 2002.

[4] Y. Chen, C. Zhuang, Q. Cao, and P. Hui. Understanding cross-site linking in online social networks. In *Proceedings of the Workshop on Social Network Mining and Analysis*, 2014.

[5] J. Deng, W. Dong, R. Socher, L.-J. Li, K. Li, and L. Fei-Fei. Imagenet: A large-scale hierarchical image database. In *IEEE Conference on Computer Vision and Pattern Recognition.*

[10] mb-guide.com

[6] M. Duggan and J. Brenner. *The demographics of social media users.* 2013.

[7] A. Farseev and T.-S. Chua. NUS-MSS: A Multi-Source Social Dataset from National University of Singapore. `http://lms.comp.nus.edu.sg/research/NUS-MULTISOURCE.htm`, 2015.

[8] M. C. Gonzalez, C. A. Hidalgo, and A.-L. Barabasi. Understanding individual human mobility patterns. *Nature*, 2008.

[9] R. Jain and L. Jalali. Objective self. *MultiMedia, IEEE*, 2014.

[10] I. Jolliffe. *Principal component analysis.* Wiley Online Library, 2002.

[11] P. Kasemsuppakorn and H. A. Karimi. Pedestrian network data collection through location-based social networks. In *IEEE International Conference on Collaborative Computing: Networking, Applications and Worksharing*, 2009.

[12] L. Nie, M. Wang, Z.-J. Zha, G. Li, and T.-S. Chua. Multimedia answering: Enriching text qa with media information. In *Proceedings of the International ACM SIGIR Conference*, 2011.

[13] A. Noulas, S. Scellato, N. Lathia, and C. Mascolo. A random walk around the city: New venue recommendation in location-based social networks. In *Privacy, Security, Risk and Trust, International Conference on Social Computing*, 2012.

[14] A. Noulas, S. Scellato, C. Mascolo, and M. Pontil. An empirical study of geographic user activity patterns in foursquare. *The International Conference on Weblogs and Social Media*, 2011.

[15] R. Ottoni, D. Las Casas, J. P. Pesce, W. Meira Jr, C. Wilson, A. Mislove, and V. Almeida. Of pins and tweets: Investigating how users behave across image-and text-based social networks. 2014.

[16] J. W. Pennebaker, M. E. Francis, and R. J. Booth. Linguistic inquiry and word count: Liwc 2001. *Mahway: Lawrence Erlbaum Associates*, 2001.

[17] Y. Qu and J. Zhang. Trade area analysis using user generated mobile location data. In *Proceedings of the International Conference on World Wide Web*, 2013.

[18] F. Rangel, P. Rosso, M. Koppel, E. Stamatatos, and G. Inches. Overview of the author profiling task at pan 2013. *Notebook Papers of CLEF*, 2013.

[19] A. Sadilek, H. A. Kautz, and V. Silenzio. Predicting disease transmission from geo-tagged micro-blog data. In *Association for the Advancement of Artificial Intelligence*, 2012.

[20] S. Shang, D. Guo, J. Liu, and K. Liu. Human mobility prediction and unobstructed route planning in public transport networks. In *IEEE International Conferebce on Mobile Data Management*, 2014.

[21] E. Stamatatos, W. Daelemans, B. Verhoeven, M. Potthast, B. Stein, P. Juola, M. A. Sanchez-Perez, and A. Barrón-Cedeño. Overview of the author identification task at pan 2014. *Analysis*, 2014.

[22] C. Von Der Weth, V. Hegde, and M. Hauswirth. Virtual location-based services: Merging the physical and virtual world. *IEEE International Conference on Web Services*, 2013.

[23] J. Vosecky, D. Hong, and V. Y. Shen. User identification across multiple social networks. In *Networked Digital Tech.*, 2009.

[24] M. Wang, H. Li, D. Tao, K. Lu, and X. Wu. Multimodal graph-based reranking for web image search. *IEEE Transactions on Image Processing*, 2012.

[25] P. Wang, W. He, and J. Zhao. A tale of three social networks: User activity comparisons among facebook, twitter, and foursquare. 2014.

[26] X. Wang, Y.-L. Zhao, L. Nie, Y. Gao, W. Nie, Z.-J. Zha, and T.-S. Chua. Semantic-based location recommendation with multimodal venue semantics. *IEEE Transactions on Multimedia*, 2015.

[27] Y.-L. Zhao, Q. Chen, S. Yan, T.-S. Chua, and D. Zhang. Detecting profilable and overlapping communities with user-generated multimedia contents in lbsns. *ACM Transactions on Multimedia Computing, Communications, and Applications*, 2013.

[28] Y.-L. Zhao, L. Nie, X. Wang, and T.-S. Chua. Personalized recommendations of locally interesting venues to tourists via cross-region community matching. *ACM Transactions on Intelligent Systems and Technology*, 2014.

[29] E. Zhong, W. Fan, Y. Zhu, and Q. Yang. Modeling the dynamics of composite social networks. In *Proceedings of the ACM International KDD Conference*, 2013.

A Privacy-Preserving Bipartite Graph Matching Framework for Multimedia Analysis and Retrieval

Wei-Ta Chu
National Chung Cheng University
Chiayi, Taiwan
wtchu@ccu.edu.tw

Feng-Chi Chang
National Chung Cheng University
Chiayi, Taiwan
winderif@gmail.com

ABSTRACT

The emergence of cloud computing provides an unlimited computation/storage for users, and yields new opportunities for multimedia analysis and retrieval research. However, privacy of users, e.g., search intention, may be leaked to the server and maliciously utilized by companies or individuals with animus. This paper presents a privacy-preserving multimedia analysis framework based on a widely-adopted structure, i.e., bipartite graph, so that multimedia analysis and retrieval in the encrypted domain is enabled. This work aims to keep the server unaware of what the user wants to retrieve, and at the same time take advantage of the server's computation power. Homomorphic encryption schemes and communication protocols in the encrypted domain are integrated to facilitate bipartite graph construction and implement the Hungarian algorithm to find the best matching. Two applications, video tag suggestion and video copy detection, are developed on top of the privacy-preserving framework, and the evaluation results demonstrate that performance obtained in the encrypted domain is comparable with that obtained in the plain text domain.

Categories and Subject Descriptors

H.2.0 [**Database Management**]: General – Security, integrity, and protection. H.3.3 [**Information Storage and Retrieval**]: Information Search and Retrieval – *retrieval models, search process, selection process.*

Keywords

Bipartite graph matching; privacy preserving; Paillier cryptosystem; DGK cryptosystem; garbled circuit; Hungarian algorithm

1. INTRODUCTION

With the advancement of network throughput, distributed storage, and flourishing of social media platforms, the web has become the largest database that conveys almost unlimited amount of information. Technologies of parallel processing, efficient indexing, and multiple cores, further facilitate the development of a cloud computing environment, so that the web can be viewed as a powerful storage and computation platform. This trend has especially urged multimedia retrieval research due to its demand for large storage and immense computation. It can be envisioned that more multimedia data would be uploaded to the cloud environment, not only for storage or sharing, but also for retrieval or analysis purposes.

ICMR'15, June 23–26, 2015, Shanghai, China.

http://dx.doi.org/10.1145/2671188.2749286

Despite popularity and powerful computation of a cloud environment, storing personal data or uploading image queries in an open environment give rise to severe privacy issues. Recently, although researchers have studied privacy-preserving methodologies in many fields, such as privacy-preserving data mining [8] and text document search in the encrypted domain [9], relatively fewer studies have been conducted for privacy-preserving multimedia retrieval. In a client-server content-based image retrieval architecture, users upload their query images to the server, and request the server's database and computation power to conduct large-scale image retrieval. These query images may contain users' personal information, or from multiple queries the server may collect statistics that may leak users' private matters. Privacy-preserving multimedia retrieval, therefore, gives rise to an exacting technical challenge: After receiving the data sent from users, the server should not be able to infer what have been uploaded, but it should be able to find from its database the ones similar to the uploaded data. For the server side, the server may just answer YES or NO to users about whether it holds data similar to queries, without revealing what exactly it has in the database. Depending on application fields, sometimes data available on the server are collected with huge efforts and are very valuable, such as medical images that are highly privacy sensitive and big multimedia that embed implicit correlation between heterogeneous media. Therefore, in this work we focus on a combination of multimedia analysis and privacy-preserving protocols to build a two-way privacy system, i.e., protecting both the client's and the server's privacy.

Figure 1(a) shows a general multimedia retrieval framework. Alice uploads a query in the representation of feature vectors to Bob, who then calculates similarity between the query and data from his database. Bob sends Alice the data with largest similarity to the query or just an answer of YES or NO. For the server side, Bob needs to calculate similarity and performs sorting to find best results to be sent back to the client. Figure 1(b) shows a general privacy-preserving multimedia retrieval framework, where operations in the shaded area are in the encrypted domain. Alice sends encrypted feature vectors to Bob. Bob then operates similarity calculation and sorting in the encrypted domain, and sends encrypted retrieval results to Alice, who later decrypts the returned results to get the plain text results. In this paper, we propose a bipartite graph framework in the encrypted domain and adopt private value comparison protocols to implement the shaded area.

Contributions of this paper are twofold. First, with encryption techniques we design a privacy-preserving multimedia analysis framework on top of bipartite graph matching. Cryptosystems with homomorphic encryption operations and communication protocols for comparing private numbers are introduced to enable privacy

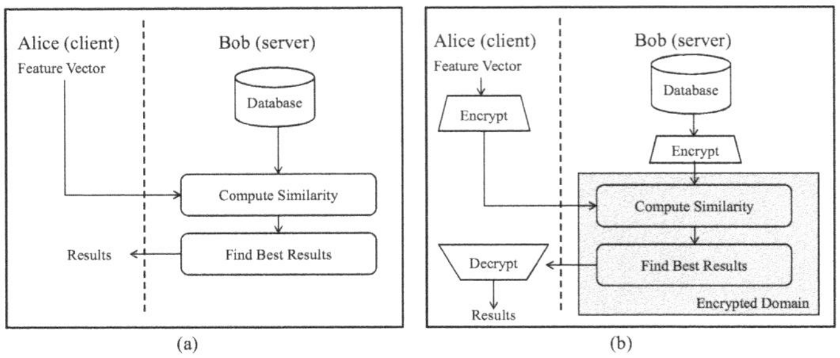

Figure 1. General multimedia retrieval frameworks in the (a) plain text domain and in the (b) encrypted domain

protection. Second, based on the general framework, two applications of video tag suggestion and video copy detection are developed to validate the proposed framework and embody privacy-preserving multimedia analysis that has not widely studied before.

The rest of this paper is organized as follows. Section 2 presents related works. Section 3 first introduces the basics of bipartite graph matching, and then describes details of graph construction. Section 4 provides the details of privacy-preserving bipartite graph matching. With the proposed framework, two applications are described in Section 5. Section 6 presents evaluation results to validate the proposed framework, followed by concluding remarks in Section 7.

2. RELATED WORKS

2.1 Privacy-Preserving Multimedia Retrieval

Shashank et al. [24] proposed one of the first privacy-preserving image retrieval systems, which was originally designed for private information retrieval with index structures like hierarchical structure and hash. With cryptographic techniques, including order preserving encryption and randomized hash functions, Lu et al. [11] developed secure and efficient image retrieval system where query images, data images, and the corresponding index structures, are processed in the encrypted domain. For secure image feature extraction, Hsu et al. [12] proposed privacy-preserving SIFT (Scale-Invariant Feature Transform) extraction. Not specifically for multimedia retrieval, privacy-preserving face recognition is a highly related topic and was first proposed by Erkin et al. [4]. They introduced cryptographic tools to project face images into eigenfaces and measure face similarity. Sadeghi et al. [7] modified the encryption schemes mentioned in [4] with garbled circuits, and made privacy-preserving face recognition more efficient. Generally, although cryptographic techniques may be ready for data analysis and manipulation in the encrypted domain, potential and embodiment of privacy-preserving multimedia retrieval systems are still not well investigated.

2.2 Bipartite Graph Matching for MM Retrieval

The processing pipeline of a multimedia retrieval system mainly includes feature extraction, indexing, similarity measurement, and result ranking. Existing works [11][12][24] primarily concentrate on either secure index structure or feature extraction. In this paper, we investigate similarity measurement between images in the encrypted domain. Although selection of similarity measurement is application-dependent, we notice that bipartite graph matching has been widely adopted in many video analysis researches. In such works, videos are first divided into shots, and shots respectively from two videos are viewed as two disjoint sets in a bipartite graph. Similarity between two videos is then measured by finding the minimum cost (or maximum weight) bipartite graph matching. Conceptually, the minimum cost (maximum weight) matching denotes the minimum distance (maximum similarity) we can obtain among all possible matchings between two sets of video shots.

More specifically, the work in [13] constructed a bipartite graph between a query video clip and a targeted video, and by finding the maximum cardinality matching, in the targeted video the clip similar to the query clip is located. The same research group also adopted this idea to detect gradual transition in videos [14], where parts of pixels were sampled from two frames and were viewed as disjoint node sets to construct a bipartite graph, followed by similarity measured by finding the maximum cardinality matching. Xu et al. [15] constructed a bipartite graph to describe similarity between keyframes of two videos. They slightly modified the standard matching algorithm to achieve fast near-duplicate video detection. Kim et al. [16] determined the maximum cardinality matching based on a bipartite graph describing keyframe similarity, and demonstrated robust performance on video copy detection. Based on a similar idea, Bai et al. [17] conducted rush video summarization after measuring similarity between video shots. Images can be described by local patches, which can be treated as nodes in the bipartite graph, and thus image similarity can be measured by the matching situation [18]. 3D models can be represented by sets of 2D views. A bipartite graph can be constructed based on sets of views, and the same idea is used to measure similarity between 3D models [19]. Chu et al. [20] described video keyframes and text-based tags as bags of visual words, which were then treated as nodes to construct a bipartite graph linking two modalities. The maximum weight matching was then determined to facilitate tag suggestion and localization.

We clearly see the importance of bipartite graph matching on multimedia analysis and retrieval. Our work investigates using encryption techniques to construct bipartite graphs and enabling the well-known Hungarian algorithm [1] in the encrypted domain to find the best matching. The reasons to develop the framework based on bipartite graphs are twofold. First, bipartite graphs are widely adopted in various multimedia analysis researches, and generality and effectiveness have been extensively demonstrated. Second, processes for graph construction and graph matching are mostly linear operations, which can be effectively implemented in the encrypted domain by cryptosystems and communication protocols.

Specifically, the Paillier cryptosystem [2] is utilized to construct homomorphic operations for evaluating distances between nodes, and weighted bipartite graphs can be constructed. Homomorphic operations associated with a comparison protocol, which compares encrypted values through communication between user and server, are then employed to implement the Hungarian algorithm. Computation intensive jobs (in the encrypted domain) are taken by the server, such as graph construction and graph matching. The meaning of encrypted matching results can be realized only when they are decrypted by the user. This is why user's privacy is protected, and computation power of the server is well adopted in the meantime.

3. PRIVACY-PRESERVING BIPARTITE GRAPH CONSTRUCTION

3.1 Basics of Bipartite Graph Matching

Formulation of Bipartite Graph Matching. Consider two sets $\mathcal{A}$ and $\mathcal{B}$ that both consist of n elements (nodes). Let $c_{i,j}$ denote the cost of the assignment $i \rightarrow j$, $i \in \mathcal{A}$, $j \in \mathcal{B}$. Let the binary variable $x_{i,j}$ denote an assignment:

$$x_{i,j} = \begin{cases} 1 & \text{if the element } j \in \mathcal{B} \text{ is assigned to the element } i \in \mathcal{A}, \\ 0 & \text{otherwise.} \end{cases}$$

The problem of minimum cost bipartite graph matching is defined as

$$minimize \sum_{i=1}^{n} \sum_{j=1}^{n} c_{i,j} x_{i,j}$$

$$\text{subject to } \sum_{i=1}^{n} x_{i,j} = 1, \forall j = 1, 2, ..., n \text{ and } \sum_{j=1}^{n} x_{i,j} = 1, \forall i = 1, 2, ..., n.$$

To simplify the discussion, we assume that the cardinalities of $\mathcal{A}$ and $\mathcal{B}$ are the same. In the real case, we can always make this assumption true. If $|\mathcal{A}| = m$, $|\mathcal{B}| = n$, and $m < n$, we set $c_{k,j} = 0$ for $k = m+1, ..., n$. It can be easily seen that, because $\sum_{k=m+1}^{n} \sum_{j=1}^{n} c_{k,j} x_{k,j} = 0$, the minimum cost found based on the newly derived $n \times n$ matrix is the same as that based on the original $m \times n$ matrix.

In real applications, each node of $\mathcal{A}$ and $\mathcal{B}$ is represented by a feature vector, and the cost $c_{i,j}$ of an assignment is usually measured by the Euclidean distance between two vectors. Generally, a high cost $c_{i,j}$ means that features of the ith node of $\mathcal{A}$ and the jth node of $\mathcal{B}$ are very dissimilar.

The Hungarian Algorithm. The minimum cost bipartite graph matching problem can be solved by the Hungarian algorithm originally proposed by Kuhn and Munkres [1]. A variation of this algorithm facilitating fast implementation is described as follows.

Let C be the cost matrix whose elements are $c_{i,j}$, $1 \le i \le n$, $1 \le j \le n$. The Hungarian algorithm proceeds as:

➢ Step 1: For each row in C, find the smallest entry of the row, and subtract it from all entries of the row. This yields that at least one entry in each row is zero. An entry $c_{i,j}$ equal to zero after subtraction means that assigning the ith node of $\mathcal{A}$ to the jth node of $\mathcal{B}$ yields the least cost.

➢ Step 2: For each column in C, find the smallest entry of the column, and subtract it from all entries of the column.

➢ Step 3: Chose the row or column with the minimum positive number of zeros (if there are more than one with this minimum number of zeros, choose arbitrarily). If a row was selected, trace a vertical line through one of the zeros of the selected row. If a column was selected, trace a horizontal line through one of the zeros of the selected column. Trace lines until each zero has at least one line through it. Denote the number of lines k.
  - If $k < n$, find the minimum uncovered number (no line through it), denoted as ν. Subtract ν from every uncovered number. Add ν to every number covered by two lines. Go back to the start of Step 3.
  - If $k = n$, go to Step 4.

➢ Step 4: Start with the top row, and work downwards to make assignments. An assignment is uniquely made when there is exactly one zero in the row. Once an assignment is made, delete the row and the column containing this zero.
  - If fewer than n assignments can be made, and all the remaining rows contain more than one zero, switch to columns. Start with the leftmost column, and work rightwards to make assignments.
  - Iterate between row assignments and column assignments until as many unique assignments as possible. If n assignments are still not achieved, i.e., no unique assignment can be made either with rows or columns, make one arbitrarily by selecting an entry with a zero.

Privacy-preserving graph construction and matching. To ensure privacy protection, operations of graph construction and the Hungarian algorithm should be conducted in the encrypted domain.

- Graph construction: The most critical operation at this stage is calculating the assignment cost between nodes, which is often measured by the Euclidean distance. We need encrypted subtraction and multiplication operators.
- Steps 1 and 2 of the Hungarian algorithm: The smallest entry should be found first, and thus an encrypted comparison scheme is urgently needed. An encrypted subtraction is then needed.
- Step 3 of the Hungarian algorithm: The encrypted comparison scheme is again applied, and encrypted subtraction and addition are needed.
- Step 4 of the Hungarian algorithm: This step consists of only condition matching. Because feature vectors are encrypted before graph construction, the server just conducts condition matching, and knows nothing about the meaning of an assignment. The number n is known to the server, but this would not reveal the result of graph matching.

In the following, we briefly describe the application scenario of privacy-preserving multimedia retrieval based on the bipartite graph matching framework. Assume that an element of $\mathcal{A}$ is represented by a vector $\boldsymbol{a}_i = (a_1, a_2, ..., a_m)$, $i = 1, ..., n$, and an element of $\mathcal{B}$ is represented by a vector $\boldsymbol{b}_j = (b_1, b_2, ..., b_m)$, $j = 1, ..., n$, and two parties, Alice and Bob, jointly participate in this process. The set $\mathcal{A}$ is uploaded by Alice, who would like to know whether there is a set $\mathcal{B}$ in Bob's database that is identical or similar to the uploaded set. Alice wants to take advantage of Bob's computation power to calculate data similarity, but meanwhile she is not willing to leak anything about the uploaded data to Bob.

Figure 2 shows the framework for privacy-preserving bipartite graph matching. Alice sends encrypted feature vectors to Bob. Bob encrypts his database, constructs the bipartite graph, and finds the minimum cost bipartite graph matching by the Hungarian algorithm in the encrypted domain. The matching results are sent back to Alice, who decrypts and postprocesses them to interpret matching results, e.g., the degree of similarity between nodes or node assignment situations.

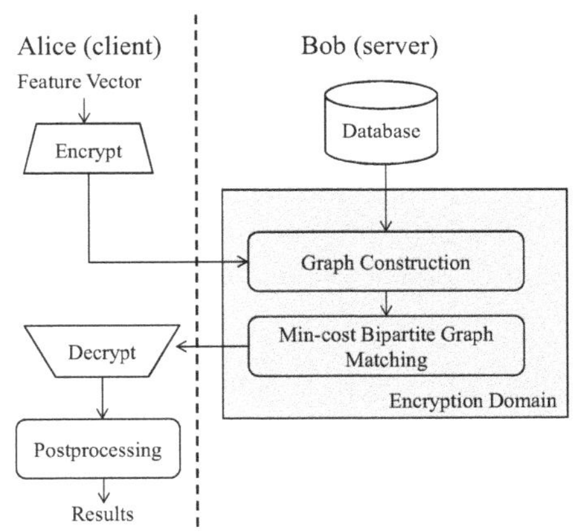

Figure 2. The privacy-preserving bipartite graph matching framework

3.2 Graph Construction

The central step to construct a bipartite graph is calculating the cost linking any two nodes in two different sets. In the plain text domain, the cost between $\boldsymbol{a}_i = (a_1, a_2, ..., a_m)$ and $\boldsymbol{b}_j = (b_1, b_2, ..., b_m)$ is usually measured by the squared Euclidean distance:

$$c_{i,j} = (b_1 - a_1)^2 + (b_2 - a_2)^2 + \cdots + (b_m - a_m)^2$$
$$= \underbrace{\sum_{k=1}^{m} b_k^2}_{T_1} + \underbrace{\sum_{k=1}^{m} (-2a_k b_k)}_{T_2} + \underbrace{\sum_{k=1}^{m} a_k^2}_{T_3}, \quad (1)$$

In the following, we use the notation $[s]$ to denote the ciphertext generated by the Paillier cryptosystem [2] based on s. With the homomorphic property, to compute $[c_{ij}]$, it suffices to compute encrypted T_1, T_2, and T_3, and then

$$[c_{i,j}] = [T_1] \cdot [T_2] \cdot [T_3]. \quad (2)$$

In real applications, Alice sends $[a_1], [a_2], ..., [a_m]$ to Bob, and Bob knows the plain text $b_1, b_2, ..., b_m$ from his database. Therefore, for the first term T_1, Bob can directly compute $\sum_{k=1}^{m} b_k^2$ and encrypt it to obtain $[T_1]$. For the second term T_2, the value $[-2a_k b_k]$ can be calculated by $[a_k]^{(-2b_k)}$, where $(-2b_k)$ is directly computed by Bob, and $[a_k]$ is received from Alice. Bob finally computes $[T_2] = \prod_{k=1}^{m}[-2a_k b_k]$. The third term T_3 is constituted by the sum of squared a_k's. However, Bob only knows $[a_k]$, and $[a_k]^2 \neq [a_k^2]$. Therefore, Bob blindly adds an uniformly random element r_k to a_k to obtain $[x_k] = [a_k + r_k] = [a_k] \cdot [r_k]$. Note that for different a_k's, the random elements r_k's are different. Bob sends $[x_k]$ to Alice for decryption. Alice thus obtains x_k and is able to compute x_k^2 as well as $T_3' = \sum_{k=1}^{m} x_k^2$. She encrypts T_3' and sends $[T_3']$ to Bob, who then computes

$$[T_3] = [T_3'] \cdot \prod_{k=1}^{m}([a_k]^{(-2r_k)} \cdot [-r_k^2]), \quad (3)$$

because

$$[x_k^2] \cdot [a_k]^{(-2r_k)} \cdot [-r_k^2] = [(a_k + r_k)^2 - 2r_k a_k - r_k^2] = [a_k^2]. \quad (4)$$

After all three terms are obtained, the encrypted squared Euclidean distance between two vectors can be computed by Bob. After evaluating all distances between elements of $\mathcal{A}$ and $\mathcal{B}$, a weighted bipartite graph is constructed.

In multimedia applications where high-dimensional feature vectors may be extracted, the computation and communication costs of the protocol would be high. An improved protocol called *packing* was thus proposed in [7] to reduce the complexity.

Packing. In order to fully take advantage of capacity of one ciphertext, assume that any a_k can be compactly represented by ℓ bits, and a ciphertext is represented by K bits according to the setting of the encryption algorithm. The random value r_k added to form x_k is selected to be represented by $\ell + \sigma$ bits, and thus x_k is represented by $\ell + \sigma$ bits. Therefore, the number of encrypted x_k that can be packed into a single ciphertext is $K' = \left\lfloor \frac{K}{\ell+\sigma} \right\rfloor$. For $k = 1, ..., K'$, encrypted a_k's with random perturbation r_k's in a pack is

$$\begin{aligned}[x] &= \left[\sum_{k=1}^{K'} 2^{(\ell+\sigma)(k-1)}(a_k + r_k)\right] \\ &= \left[\sum_{k=1}^{K'} 2^{(\ell+\sigma)(k-1)} r_k\right] \prod_{k=1}^{K'} \left[a_k\right]^{2^{(\ell+\sigma)(k-1)}}. \end{aligned} \quad (5)$$

Bob sends $[x]$ to Alice, who decrypts it to obtain $x = (x_{K'} ... x_1)$ with $x \in \{0,1\}^{\ell+\sigma}$. By accumulating all necessary x's, she can compute $T_3' = \sum_{k=1}^{m} x_k^2$ and sends the encrypted $[T_3']$ to Bob.

The packing scheme reduces the number of communication from m to $\lceil \frac{m}{K'} \rceil$. In our implementation, a ciphertext obtained by the Paillier cryptosystem is represented by 1024 bits ($K = 1024$), the a_k's are represented by at most 15 bits ($\ell = 15$), and the random value r_k is selected to be represented by 95 bits $(\ell + \sigma) = (15 + 80) = 95$. Therefore, at most $K' = \left\lfloor \frac{K}{\ell+\sigma} \right\rfloor = \left\lfloor \frac{1024}{95} \right\rfloor = 10$ ciphertexts are packed together.

Pre-computation. Alternatively, an assumption can be reasonably made to alleviate the communication cost without leaking client's privacy. Assume that Alice knows that Bob needs the encrypted squared norm of $\boldsymbol{a}_i = (a_1, a_2, ..., a_m)$ in advance, and thus she can calculate $\sum_{k=1}^{m} a_k^2$ and encrypt it as $[T_3] = \left[\sum_{k=1}^{m} a_k^2\right]$ before sending to Bob.

4. PRIVACY-PRESERVING BIPARTITE GRAPH MATCHING

After graph construction, the Hungarian algorithm operated in the encrypted domain is designed to find the minimum cost matching. Assume that the cost matrix in ciphertext is $[C] = [c_{i,j}]$, $1 \leq i, j \leq n$. At Step 1 (Step 2) of the Hungarian algorithm, the smallest entry in each row (column) should be found first. Consider the first row $[c_{1,j}]$, $1 \leq j \leq n$, for example, we compare encrypted costs $[c_{1,2j+1}]$ and $[c_{1,2j+2}]$, for $1 \leq j \leq \lfloor \frac{n}{2} \rfloor - 1$, by using a comparison protocol that will be described later. After processing all entries, the $\lfloor \frac{n}{2} \rfloor$ smaller entries are then compared by the same procedure again, and so forth. After $\lceil \log_2 n \rceil$ iterations, the minimum entry $[c_{1,j^*}]$ can be found. The minimum value is subtracted from each entry in the row, i.e., $[c_{1,j} - c_{1,j^*}] = [c_{1,j}] \cdot [c_{1,j^*}]^{(-1)}$.

At Step 3 of the Hungarian algorithm, the matrix entries with values equal to encrypted zeros are first found, and then we use as few lines as possible to pass through them. To determine whether a ciphertext is equal to an encrypted zero, a zero checking process is adopted. If the number of lines k is less than the dimension of the cost matrix, we find the minimum uncovered number by the comparison protocol, and then subtract the value from every uncovered number in the encrypted domain, and add the value to every number covered by two lines in the encrypted domain also. If the number of lines k is equal to the dimension of the cost matrix, the Step 4 of the Hungarian algorithm proceeds, where no special encryption operations are required. After Step 4, the minimum cost matching is found, and the matching results are sent to Alice. Alice then decrypts to interpret the meaning of matching, and conducts postprocesses if needed.

In the following, we design the core components of the privacy-preserving Hungarian algorithm. Readers may need to refer details of the cryptosystems in reference.

4.1 Comparison Protocol

Assume that two ciphertext values $[a]$ and $[b]$ known to Bob are ℓ-bit. Bob first computes

$$[z] = [2^\ell + a - b] = [2^\ell] \cdot [a] \cdot [b]^{-1}, \quad (6)$$

where z is a positive $(\ell + 1)$-bit value because $0 \leq a, b < 2^\ell$. If $a < b$, the most significant bit of z, denoted by z_ℓ, is 0. Therefore, by checking z_ℓ, whether $[a]$ is larger than $[b]$ can be immediately determined. The value of z_ℓ can be computed by

$$z_\ell = 2^{-\ell} \cdot (z - (z \mod 2^\ell)). \quad (7)$$

This equation only consists of linear combination (one multiplication and one subtraction) in the encrypted domain, and can be easily conducted by Bob. As Bob knows $[a]$ and $[b]$ and can easily compute $[z]$, now the problem is the computation of $[z \mod 2^\ell]$.

Finding $[\mathbf{z} \mod \mathbf{2}^\ell]$. Erkin et al. [4] design a comparison protocol where Bob seeks help from Alice. First, Bob generates a uniformly random $(\kappa + \ell + 1)$-bit value r. The value κ is a security parameter, and $\kappa + \ell + 1 \ll \log_2 N$, where N is the multiplication result of two prime numbers. Similar to calculation of the third term of eqn. (1), Bob blindly adds the number r to z by doing encrypted domain multiplication:

$$[d] = [z + r] = [z] \cdot [r]. \quad (8)$$

The value $[d]$ is sent to Alice, who decrypts it and reduces d modulo 2^ℓ. The obtained value is then encrypted and returned to Bob.

From the design of eqn. (6), we have $d = z + r \mod 2^\ell$ and

$$(z \mod 2^\ell) = ((d \mod 2^\ell) - (r \mod 2^\ell)) \mod 2^\ell. \quad (9)$$

Alice has sent $[d \mod 2^\ell]$ and Bob knows r. Bob thus can compute

$$\begin{aligned}[\tilde{z}] &= [(d \mod 2^\ell) - (r \mod 2^\ell)] \\ &= [(d \mod 2^\ell)] \cdot [(r \mod 2^\ell)]^{-1}. \end{aligned} \quad (10)$$

If $d \mod 2^\ell \geq r \mod 2^\ell$, it is safe to take modulo 2^ℓ for $[\tilde{z}]$, and $[\tilde{z}]$ is the right result equal to $[z \mod 2^\ell]$. If $r \mod 2^\ell \geq d \mod 2^\ell$, an underflow will occur when taking modulo 2^ℓ, and thus adding 2^ℓ to $[\tilde{z}]$ would give the right result. So far, Bob could correctly obtain $[z \mod 2^\ell]$ if he could compare two private inputs: $\hat{d} = d \mod 2^\ell$ held by Alice and $\hat{r} = r \mod 2^\ell$ held by Bob.

Comparing private values. To compare private values, the DGK homomorphic encryption scheme is utilized. As mentioned in [5] and [6], comparing with the Paillier system, the DGK scheme provides more efficient encryption as it works in very small plaintext space. This characteristic is especially good for us to compare $\hat{d}$ and $\hat{r}$, which are much smaller than the message needed to be encrypted in the Paillier system. We use $\langle\cdot\rangle$ to denote DGK encryption.

Assume that Alice has run the DGK key generation algorithm and has sent the public key to Bob. Alice takes the bit representation of $\hat{d} = \hat{d}_{\ell-1}\hat{d}_{\ell-2}...\hat{d}_0$, encrypts each bit to obtain $\langle\hat{d}_{\ell-1}\rangle, ..., \langle\hat{d}_0\rangle$, and sends them to Bob. Bob then chooses $t \in \{1, -1\}$ and computes

$$\begin{aligned}\langle o_i\rangle &= \langle \hat{d}_i - \hat{r}_i + t + 3\textstyle\sum_{j=i+1}^{\ell-1} w_j\rangle \\ &= \langle\hat{d}_i\rangle \cdot \langle -\hat{r}_i\rangle \cdot \langle t\rangle \cdot \left(\textstyle\prod_{j=i+1}^{\ell-1}\langle w_j\rangle\right)^3, \end{aligned} \quad (11)$$

where $\langle w_j\rangle = \langle \hat{d}_j \oplus \hat{r}_j\rangle$, which can be used because Bob knows $\hat{r}_j$. Specifically, this value can be computed by

$$\langle w_j\rangle = \langle \hat{d}_j \oplus \hat{r}_j\rangle = \langle \hat{d}_j + \hat{r}_j - 2\hat{d}_j\hat{r}_j\rangle = \langle\hat{d}_j\rangle \cdot \langle\hat{r}_j\rangle \cdot \langle\hat{d}_j\rangle^{-2\hat{r}_j}. \quad (12)$$

To avoid $\hat{d} = \hat{r}$, differing bits are appended to both $\hat{d}$ and $\hat{r}$ so that actually $2\hat{d} + 1$ and $2\hat{r}$ are compared.

In the case of $t = 1$, if $\hat{d}$ is larger than $\hat{r}$, all o_i are nonzero. If $\hat{r}$ is larger than $\hat{d}$, then exactly one o_i is equal to zero, which is at the position of the most significant differing bit. When t is selected as -1, the same situation occurs, except that the zero occurs if $\hat{d}$ is larger.

To avoid leaking any statistics of private values in Bob's side, Bob now masks $\langle o_i\rangle$ with a uniformly random number $r_i \in Z_u^*$, where u is the small prime defined in the DGK system, by

$$\langle e_i\rangle = \langle o_i \cdot r_i\rangle = \langle o_i\rangle^{r_i}, \quad (13)$$

and sends them to Alice. Alice decrypts all e_i and checks whether one of them is zero. She encrypts a bit λ, which indicates whether the condition is satisfied, by the Paillier encryption, i.e., $[\lambda]$, and sends it to Bob. There are totally four cases about the selection of t (two choices) and the result $[\lambda]$ (two possibilities). As Bob knows the selection of t, he can derive the correspondence between $[\lambda]$ and the condition after a few communications.

Finally, Bob knows whether $\hat{d}$ is larger than $\hat{r}$, with which he can compute $[z \mod 2^\ell]$, and thus can determine the larger one of two ciphertext values $[a]$ and $[b]$. By embedding this comparison protocol into the Hungarian algorithm, the minimum-cost bipartite graph matching can be determined in the encrypted domain.

Note that the comparison protocol mainly works based on the DGK scheme, and graph construction mentioned in Sec. 3.2 mainly works based on the Paillier scheme. The reason for this difference is that only small plaintext space can be adopted in the DGK cryptosystem, and the dynamic ranges of feature vectors for constructing a graph are too large to be affordable. On the other hand, the encrypted numbers to be compared at the graph matching stage are much smaller, and can be processed by the more efficient DGK cryptosystem.

4.2 Checking Zero

At Step 3 of the Hungarian algorithm, we need to determine which entry is zero in the encrypted domain, which can be done by the comparison protocol. We know $z_\ell = 0 \Leftrightarrow p < q$ in the comparison protocol, where z_ℓ is the most significant bit of z and $z = 2^\ell + p - q$. Assume that we let $p = 0$ and $q = x$, and then we know $z_\ell = 0 \Leftrightarrow 0 < x$. In other words, the value x is not equal to zero. On the other hand, $z_\ell = 1 \Leftrightarrow 0 \geq x$. But x is certainly not negative number, and thus we know $z_\ell = 1 \Leftrightarrow 0 = x$. With this protocol, we are able to compare a private number $[x]$ with $[0]$.

4.3 Garbled Circuit for Minimum Search

Comparing two encrypted numbers in the encrypted domain mentioned above relies on homomorphic operations and the comparison protocol. The computation of exponents and frequent interaction between server and client give rise to high costs. In order to reduce computation and communication, the garbled circuit can be used to improve the efficiency of minimum search, in which operations are based on Boolean circuits [22][23].

The garbled circuit for minimum search is described in the following. Bob wants to find the minimum of encrypted numbers. Note that the garbled circuit works only for plain text, and thus Bob cannot directly employ it to find the minimum. He needs to send encrypted numbers and the setting of the garbled circuit to Alice, and then Alice can evaluate the minimum value using the garbled circuit, encrypt it, and send it back to Bob.

Figure 3 shows the protocol for minimum search with a garbled circuit. Assume that Bob wants to find the minimum of two encrypted numbers $[p]$ and $[q]$, he chooses two random values r_p and r_q, adds these to $[p]$ and $[q]$, and obtains the encrypted values $[y_p]$ and $[y_q]$. Next, Bob sends $[y_p]$ and $[y_q]$ to Alice, and then she can decrypt them to obtain y_p and y_q. With y_i and r_i, the minimum value of encrypted numbers can be determined by using the garbled circuit. Figure 4 shows the garbled circuit for minimum search, including two SUBTRACTION gates, one MINIMUM gate, and one ADDITION gate. In the garbled circuit, p and q are first recovered from y_i and r_i, i.e., $p = y_p - r_p$, and then Alice can obtain the minimum value x_{min}. To protect Bob's information, the garbled circuit runs the blinding protocol using a random number r_{min} provided by Bob. After evaluation of the garbled circuit, Alice obtains the output y_{min} without learning anything about x_{min}. Alice encrypts y_{min} and sends $[y_{min}]$ to Bob. Finally, Bob can use the chosen random number r_{min} to get the encrypted minimum value $[x_{min}] = [y_{min} - r_{min}]$, which is the minimum of $[p]$ and $[q]$.

5. APPLICATIONS

The proposed framework is employed to build two applications: video tag suggestion and localization, and video copy detection.

5.1 Privacy-Preserving Video Tag Suggestion

We slightly modify the framework proposed in [20] to enable privacy-preserving video tag suggestion. This framework simultaneously accomplishes tag suggestion and location, as illustrated in Figure 5. A user uploads his personal video and roughly provides some tags, e.g., the tag t_0 in Figure 5, to describe this video.

The goal of this work is to localize user-provided tags into appropriate video shots, and suggest new tags, which are retrieved from the web, to each video shot. Relationships between video keyframes and tags retrieved from the web are described by a bipartite graph, and the best matching is determined to suggest tags best fit the keyframes.

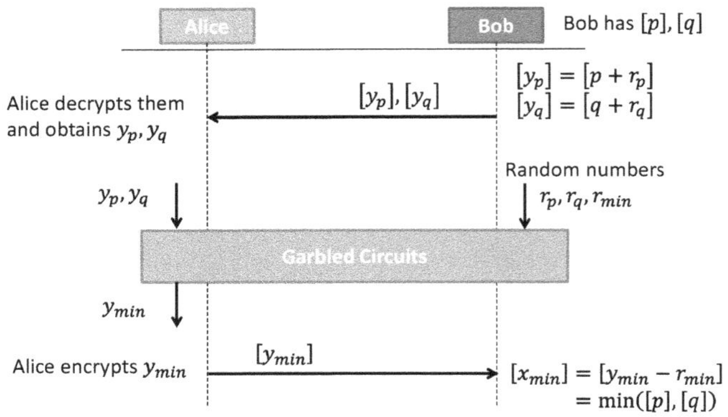

Figure 3. The protocol for minimum search with garbled circuit

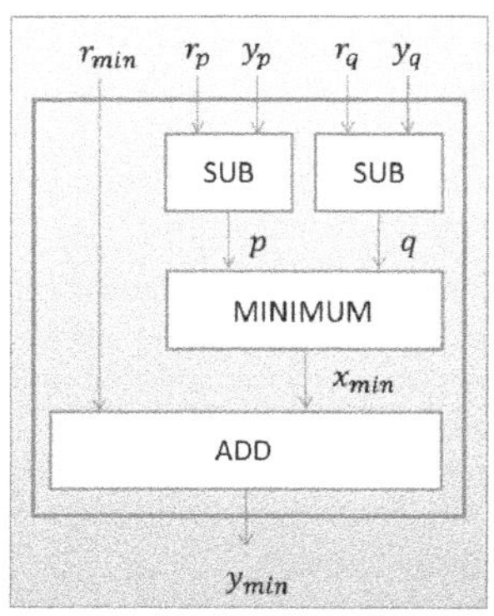

Figure 4. The garbled circuit for minimum search

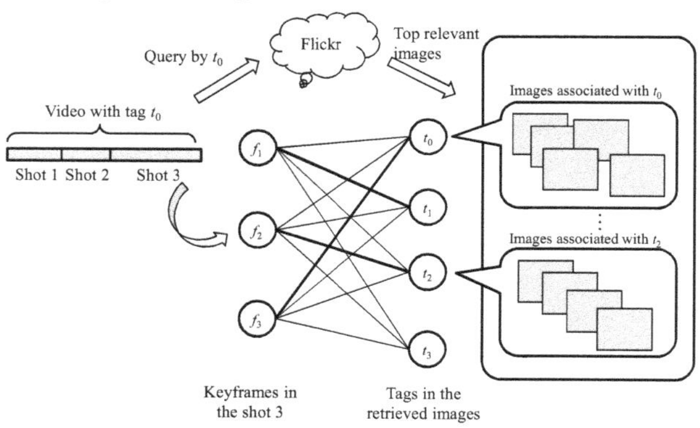

Figure 5. Video tag suggestion and localization based on bipartite graph matching

At the client side, shot boundaries in the test video are first detected, and keyframes for each video shot are extracted by the global K means algorithm [3]. Keyframes of the video, denoted by $\mathcal{A} = \{\boldsymbol{a}_1, \boldsymbol{a}_2, ..., \boldsymbol{a}_M\}$, are then represented by visual word histograms, which are built on top of the TOP-SURF toolkit [21]. At the server side, the server retrieves the top N images related to each commonly used tag from Flickr by tag search. Each retrieved image may be associated with multiple tags, and these tags provide extensive knowledge to facilitate tag expansion and localization. Images associated with the same tag are then clustered together. That is, if there are T different tags in the retrieved images, T image clusters would be formed. Let $\mathcal{B}_i = \{\boldsymbol{b}_{i,1}, \boldsymbol{b}_{i,2}, ..., \boldsymbol{b}_{i,L}\}$ denote the retrieved images associated with the tag t_i. The tag t_i is represented by the average visual word histogram of $\mathcal{B}_i$. With this design, tags are represented as the same way as keyframes. Note that these processes are separately conducted in the client side and the server side, in the plain text domain.

The client encrypts the visual word histograms $\{\boldsymbol{a}_i\}$ and sends to the server, and in the server a bipartite graph is constructed in the encrypted domain. Two disjoint sets of nodes in this graph respectively denote keyframes and tags, and each edge is given a weight calculated based on the *encrypted squared Euclidean distances* $[D(\boldsymbol{a}_i, t_j)]$ defined in eqn. (1) between keyframes and tags. That is,

$$[D(\boldsymbol{a}_i, t_j)] = \left[\sum_{k=1}^{K} (h_i^a(k) - h_j^t(k))^2\right] = [H_1] \cdot [H_2] \cdot [H_3], \quad (14)$$

where $h_i^a(k)$ and $h_j^t(k)$ respectively denote the kth histogram values of the keyframe $\boldsymbol{a}_i$ and the tag t_j, $[H_1]$ is the encrypted value of $\sum(h_j^t(k))^2$, $[H_2]$ is the encrypted value of $\sum(-2h_i^a(k)h_j^t(k))$, and $[H_3]$ is the encrypted value of $\sum(h_i^a(k))^2$ calculated based on the communication protocol mentioned previously. After graph construction, the minimum cost bipartite matching is then found by the Hungarian algorithm implemented in the encrypted domain. After decrypting matching results, the keyframe-tag correspondence is found. Tags associated with keyframes in the same shot are collected to annotate each video shot. Taking Figure 5 as an example, the third video shot has three keyframes, which are best matched (shown in bold edges) with t_0, t_1, and t_2, respectively. Therefore, the original tag t_0 is localized into the third video shot, and new tags t_1 and t_2 are suggested to tag this shot as well.

5.2 Privacy-Preserving Video Copy Detection

The Video Linkage system [16] is respectively implemented in the plain text and encrypted domains, and performance obtained from two domains will be compared. First, keyframes are extracted from video shots and are represented by HSV color histograms, YCbCr color layouts, and motion vector histograms. The distance between two keyframes f_i and f_j is calculated by linearly combining the squared Euclidean distances $d_{ij}^{(k)}$, $k = 1, 2, 3$, derived from three features, as illustrated in Figure 6. That is,

$$D(f_i, f_j) = \sum_{k=1}^{3} w_k d_{ij}^{(k)}. \quad (15)$$

Three weights are $w_1 = w_2 = w_3 = 1/3$.

A video can be viewed as a collection of keyframes. Taking keyframes of two videos as two disjoint sets of nodes, denoted by $g_1 = \{f_{11}, f_{12}, ..., f_{1m_1}\}$ and $g_2 = \{f_{21}, f_{22}, ..., f_{2m_2}\}$, a bipartite graph is constructed by evaluating the distance $D(f_i, f_j)$ between any two frames f_i and f_j. Based on this graph, the minimum cost bipartite graph matching M is found by the Hungarian algorithm. The matching result is sent from the server to the client, and the client determines whether two videos are copies by calculating the similarity measure:

$$VL(g_1, g_2) = \frac{\sum_{f_{1i}, f_{2j} \in M} (1 - D(f_i, f_j))}{m_1 + m_2 - |M|}, \quad (16)$$

where $|M|$ denotes the number of edges in the match M . If $VL(g_1, g_2)$ is larger than an empirical threshold, these two videos are said to be video copies. The equation (15) is written in the plain text domain, but in the privacy-preserving framework it is implemented by encryption-based operations. That is,

$$[D(f_i, f_j)] = \left[\sum_{k=1}^{3} w_k d_{ij}^{(k)}\right] = \prod_{k=1}^{3} \left[d_{ij}^{(k)}\right]^{w_k}, \quad (17)$$

where $[d_{ij}^{(k)}]$ is calculated by eqn. (1) and three weights are $w_1 = w_2 = w_3 = 1/3$.

Note that in [16] other measurement variants based on graph matching are proposed. Performance based on these measurements is similar, but some variants are more efficient to be calculated. In this work we only implement one of the basic measurements for copy detection to demonstrate that the proposed encryption framework is adaptable for video copy detection.

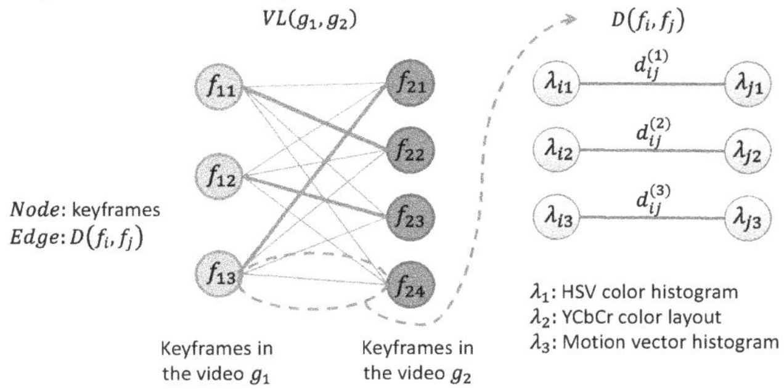

Figure 6. Video copy detection using bipartite graph matching

6. EVALUATION

Two applications were implemented in Java and executed in a PC with Intel Core 2 Quad 2.40GHz, 4GB RAM. Client and server were implemented as different programs passing messages to each other. The secure parameter for both Paillier and DGK cryptosystems is set as 1024 bits, and the secure parameter κ for uniform random numbers is set as 80 bits. Settings of the packing method described in Sec. 3.2 are $\ell = 50$, $K' = 10$, and $\sigma = 80$. The input length of the comparison protocol described in Sec. 4.1 is set as 30 bits.

6.1 Privacy-Preserving Tag Suggestion

The video tag suggestion application is evaluated based on the Youtube videos provided in [20], in which top three rated videos from 15 categories in Youtube were downloaded, consisting of 1368 shots and 3176 keyframes. There are averagely 11.67 tags for each video after filtering out stop words. Through Flickr API, images with associated tags relevant to a query were retrieved.

We use the visual dictionary consisting of 10,000 visual words, which is provided by the TOP-SURF toolkit [21]. With the bag of visual words representation, similarity between keyframes and tags can be measured to construct a bipartite graph.

We respectively implement this process in the plain text domain and in the encrypted domain, and show the average tag suggestion accuracy for each category of Youtube in Table 1. The tag suggestion accuracy of a video is calculated as the ratio of the number of correct tags (manually judged) to the number of all suggested tags. From Table 1, the overall performance obtained in the encrypted domain is comparable with that obtained in the plain text domain, although tagging accuracy is content dependent as we expected. Performance difference between two domains comes that in the encrypted domain all values are quantized into integers and the rounding errors yield slight difference in similarity calculation as well as the results of graph construction.

Table 2 shows the average time for calculating the squared norm of the query vector, i.e., $[T_3]$ defined in eqn. (3). As we expect, the basic operation involves frequent communication between Alice and Bob, and thus requires more execution time. By the packing method reducing the number of communication, and the pre-computation scheme further eliminating two-way communication, execution time can be significantly reduced.

Table 3 shows execution time of minimum search for different number of private values. If the number of private values is larger, the ratio of time needed by homomorphic operations to that needed by the garbled circuit would be larger. The results reveal that the garbled circuit is efficient in graph matching if the server has a large number of collected tags. Note that we emphasize relative execution time rather than absolute execution time in Table 2 and Table 3, because we only implemented this system on a single PC rather than a real cloud environment having extremely powerful computation.

Figure 7 shows sample results of tag suggestion. The suggested tags for each video shot are displayed as subtitles. In the first three examples, the suggested tags appropriately describe the corresponding visual content; in the last example, the "image" tag is too general and the "century" tag is inappropriate to describe the baby laughing shot.

Table 1. Tag suggestion accuracy in the plain text domain and in the encrypted domain

Categories	Plain text domain	Encrypted domain
Autos & Vehicles	0.63	0.62
Comedy	0.48	0.47
Education	0.36	0.39
Entertainment	0.63	0.62
Film & Animation	0.35	0.35
Gaming	0.31	0.27
Howto & Style	0.55	0.52
Music	0.66	0.65
News_Politics	0.78	0.77
Nonprofits & Activism	0.63	0.61
People & Blogs	0.46	0.47
Pets & Animals	0.61	0.61
Science & Technology	0.76	0.78
Sports	0.71	0.67
Travel & Events	0.65	0.65
Average	0.57	0.56

Table 2. Average time to calculate $[T_3]$ defined in eqn. (3)

	Basic	Packing	Pre-computation
Average Time (sec.)	16.83	2.19	0.08

Table 3. The execution time (sec.) of minimum search for different number of elements (N)

N	Garbled circuit	Homomorphic operations	Time ratio
100	36.5	101.2	2.77
200	61.9	203.3	3.29
500	137.8	509.1	3.69
1000	265.5	1020.6	3.84
2000	519.2	2051.7	3.95

6.2 Privacy-Preserving Video Copy Detection

Following the experimental setting of [16], the MUSCLE-VCD-2007 dataset [10] is used to evaluate the privacy-preserving video copy detection. The source dataset includes 101 videos with a total length of 80 hours, consisting of 49,751 shots and 204,510 keyframes. There are two sets of query videos, and we only use the first query set consisting of 15 query videos, with total 2,983 shots and 10,702 keyframes. A query video may be generated from a clip from a source video with various transformations, such as color adjustment and blur.

With the combination of HSV color histogram, YCbCr color layout, and motion vector histogram, squared Euclidean distances between query video keyframes and source video keyframes can be measured to construct a bipartite graph, and the best matching between them is determined by the Hungarian algorithm. We respectively implement this process in the plain text domain and in the encrypted domain, and found that, in both domains, correct video copies can be detected.

Figure 7. Sample results of video tag suggestion and localization. The first three samples shows correct suggestion results, while the fourth sample shows incorrect suggestion results (tags shown in red).

for 13 of 15 queries. This again verifies the encrypted-domain process achieves the same performance as in the plain text domain.

7. CONCLUSION

We have proposed adopting homomorphic cryptosystems and secure comparison protocols to build a privacy-preserving bipartite matching framework that can be utilized in a wide range of multimedia analysis researches. With the proposed framework, the user can take advantage of server's computation power to accomplish multimedia analysis, while the server keeps unaware of the user' data so that user's privacy is protected.

Two stages are involved in the bipartite graph matching framework: graph construction and graph matching. At the graph construction stage, the Paillier cryptosystem is used to implement homomorphic encryption, and a communication protocol is utilized to facilitate calculating edge weights. At the matching stage, the encrypted-domain Hungarian algorithm is developed based on the DGK homomorphic encryption scheme and a private number comparison protocol. The garbled circuit is further adopted to reduce computation cost. Two applications of video tag suggestion and video copy detection are built to verify correctness of the proposed framework. The privacy preserving framework achieves performance comparable to the plaintext version, even though the bipartite graph is constructed and analyzed in the encrypted domain.

Acknowledgements

The work was partially supported by the Ministry of Science and Technology in Taiwan under the grant MOST103-2221-E-194-027-MY3.

8. REFERENCES

[1] R. Diestel. Graph Theory. Heidelberg, Springer, 2005.

[2] P. Paillier. Public-key cryptosystems based on composite degree residuosity classes. Proceedings of the International Conference on Theory and Application of Cryptographic Techniques, pp. 223-238, 1999.

[3] A. Likas, N. Vlassis, N., and J.J. Verbeek, The global k-means clustering algorithm. Pattern Recognition, vol. 36, pp. 451-461, 2003.

[4] Z. Erkin, M. Franz, and J. Guajardo. Privacy-preserving face recognition, Proceedings of International Symposium on Privacy Enhancing Technologies, pp. 235-253, 2009.

[5] I. Damgard, M. Geisler, M. Kroigaard. Efficient and secure comparison for online auctions. Proceedings of the Australasian Conference on Information Security and Privacy, pp. 416-430, 2007.

[6] I. Damgard, M. Geisler, M. Kroigaard. A correction to efficient and secure comparison for online auctions. International Journal of Applied Cryptography, vol. 1, no. 4, 2009.

[7] A.-R. Sadeghi, T. Schneider, and I. Wehrenberg. Efficient privacy-preserving face recognition. Proceedings of International Conference on Information Security and Cryptology, pp. 229-244, 2009.

[8] R. Agrawal and R. Srikant. Privacy-preserving data mining. Proceedings of ACM SIGMOD International Conference on Management of Data, pp. 439-450, 2000.

[9] A. Swaminathan, Y. Mao, G.-M. Su, H. Gou, A. Varna, S. He, M. Wu, and D. Oard. Confidentiality-preserving rank-ordered search. Proceedings of ACM Workshop on Storage Security and Survivability, pp. 7-12, 2007.

[10] J. Law-To, A. Joly, and N. Boujemaa. Muscle-VCD-2007: a live benchmark for video copy detection, 2007. http://www-rocq.inria.fr/imedia/civr-bench/.

[11] W. Lu, A. Swaminathan, A.L. Varna, and M. Wu. Enabling search over encrypted multimedia databases. Proceedings of SPIE Conference on Media Forensics and Security, 2009.

[12] C.-Y. Hsu, C.-S. Lu, and S.-C. Pei. Image feature extraction in encrypted domain with privacy-preserving SIFT. IEEE Transactions on Image Processing, vol. 21, no. 11, pp. 4593-4607, 2012.

[13] Z.K.G. do Patrocinio, S.J.F. Guimaraes, and H.B. de Paula. Bipartite graph matching for video clip localization. Proceedings of Brazilian Symposium on Computer Graphics and Image Processing, pp. 129-138, 2007.

[14] S.J.F. Guimaraes, Z.K.G. do Patrocinio, K.J.F. Souza, and H.B. de Paula. Gradual transition detection based on bipartite graph matching. Proceedings of IEEE International Workshop on Multimedia Signal Processing, 2009.

[15] H. Xu, L. Liu, L.-F. Sun, and S.-Q. Yang. Fast and robust detection of near-duplicates in web video database. Proceedings of IEEE International Conference on Multimedia & Expo, pp. 293-296, 2008.

[16] H.-S. Kim, J. Lee, H. Liu, and D. Lee. Video linkage: group based copied video detection. Proceedings of International Conference on Content-Based Image and Video Retrieval, pp. 397-406, 2008.

[17] L. Bai, Y. Hu, S. Lao, A.F. Smeaton, and N.E. O'Connor. Automatic summarization of rushes video using bipartite graphs. Multimedia Tools and Applications, vol. 49, no. 1, pp. 63-80, 2010.

[18] Z. Zhang, Z.-N. Li, and M.S. Drew. Learning image similarities via probabilistic feature matching. Proceedings of IEEE International Conference on Image Processing, pp. 1857-1860, 2010.

[19] Y. Gao, Q. Dai, M. Wang, and N. Zhang. 3D model retrieval using weighted bipartite graph matching. Signal Processing: Image Communication, vol. 26, pp. 39-47, 2011.

[20] W.-T. Chu, C.-J. Li, and Y.-K. Chou, Tag suggestion and localization for web videos by bipartite graph matching. Proceeding of International ACM Workshop on Social Media, pp. 35-40, 2011.

[21] B. Thomee, E.M. Bakker, and M.S. Lew. TOP-SURF: a visual words toolkit. Proceedings of ACM Multimedia Conference, pp. 1473-1476, 2010.

[22] V. Kolesnikov, A.-R. Sadeghi, and T. Schneider. Improved garbled circuit building blocks and applications to auctions and computing minima. Proceedings of International Conference on Cryptology and Network Security. vol. 5888, pp. 1-20, 2009.

[23] R. Lagendijk, Z. Erkin, and M. Barni, Encrypted signal processing for privacy protection, IEEE Signal Processing Magazine, vol. 30, no. 1, pp. 82-105, 2013.

[24] J. Shashank, P. Kowshik, K. Srinathan, and C. Jawahar, Private content based image retrieval, Proceedings of IEEE Conference on Computer Vision and Pattern Recognition, 2008.

Describing Images with Hierarchical Concepts and Object Class Localization

Yahong Han
School of Computer Science and Technology
Tianjin key Lab. of Cognitive Computing & Application
Tianjin University, Tianjin, China
yahong@tju.edu.cn

Guang Li
School of Computer Science and Technology
Tianjin University, Tianjin, China
lguang@live.cn

ABSTRACT

Current research into automatic generation of semantic descriptions centers mainly on improving the annotation accuracy for individual tag or attributes. In this paper, we focus on the generation of more informative descriptions for images. We proposes to generate layered, semantically meaningful descriptions and create summaries of key aspects of the data from the component detectors. In particular, the output descriptions include superclass, class, attributes, and the location of the area of the object which may interest users. We propose to integrate ROI (Region of Interest) identification and hierarchical semantic elements detection into a joint framework. The joint optimization of the ROI localizer and the hierarchical concept detection make them mutually beneficial and reciprocal. In this way, we create a discriminative image description generation framework based on a tightly coupled multi-layer optimization. The output descriptions contain richer information of the image content with layered contextual information, thereby enabling better management and usage of image data. Experiments on two public open benchmark datasets demonstrate that the proposed method obtains state of the art performance.

Categories and Subject Descriptors

H.3 [**INFORMATION STORAGE AND RETRIEVAL**]: Content Analysis and Indexing

General Terms

Algorithms, Experimentation

Keywords

Image Descriptions, Multi-layer Semantic Elements, ROI Identification, Visual Attributes

1. INTRODUCTION

Most of the existing efforts toward automatically generating semantic descriptions to images mainly focus on the automatic image annotation [20] and describing images with attributes [5] [16]. To be more descriptive, some works even try to generate sentences [6] or some structural semantic triples [9] [11] to images. Recently, the task of multimedia event recounting has been proposed by the TREC Video Retrieval Evaluation of NIST to produce a textual description that summarizes the key evidence of the event [19]. These informative descriptions have been shown to be helpful to multimedia retrieval [10] [19].

Though the above works are more than just "labels" and "tags", some detailed semantic and context information are not well explored. As a further step beyond the existing research, we focus in this paper on generating more detailed image descriptions with semantic context. Firstly, no works have been done to identify the location of the object which may interest users when generating image descriptions. It will be more helpful to assign the concepts like "tree" to specific regions of images when describing imagres. While object detection was performed in [11], they prposed to construct conditional random field for textual analysis and the output is still the textual descriptions at image level. Recent studies in tag localization have shown that, if the correspondence between image regions and semantic tags is obtained, we can expect the better understanding of image content and reliable content-based image retrieval.

Secondly, though better results are obtained, the methods in [6] [11] require additional associated texts and related natural language processing techniques. Thus, for the sake of better performance in image retrieval, not only collecting associated texts and processing of these texts are time consuming, but the sentences and semantic triples are not easy to be indexed for retrieval. Another way to describe an image is by using an ontology. Ontology deals with questions concerning what entities exist or can be expected to exist, and how such entities can be grouped, related within a hierarchy, and subdivided according to similarities and differences. For example, a visual counterpart of the online word ontology of WordNet, ImageNet organizes images by 12 root categories, which constitute 12 subtrees of sub-categories. Each image in ImageNet is indexed according to the concepts in its path of the hierarchy, which has been demonstrated to be effective in image retrieval [12] [8]. We propose a new form of image content description, which contains hierarchically organized semantic concepts as the multi-layer semantic elements, the goal of which is to describe the image at different semantic levels. As "classes (or concepts)" and "relations" are two modeling primitives of ontology, we firstly choose one of the 12 root categories as *superclass* to describe the

ICMR'15, June 23–26, 2015, Shanghai, China.

http://dx.doi.org/10.1145/2671188.2749290.

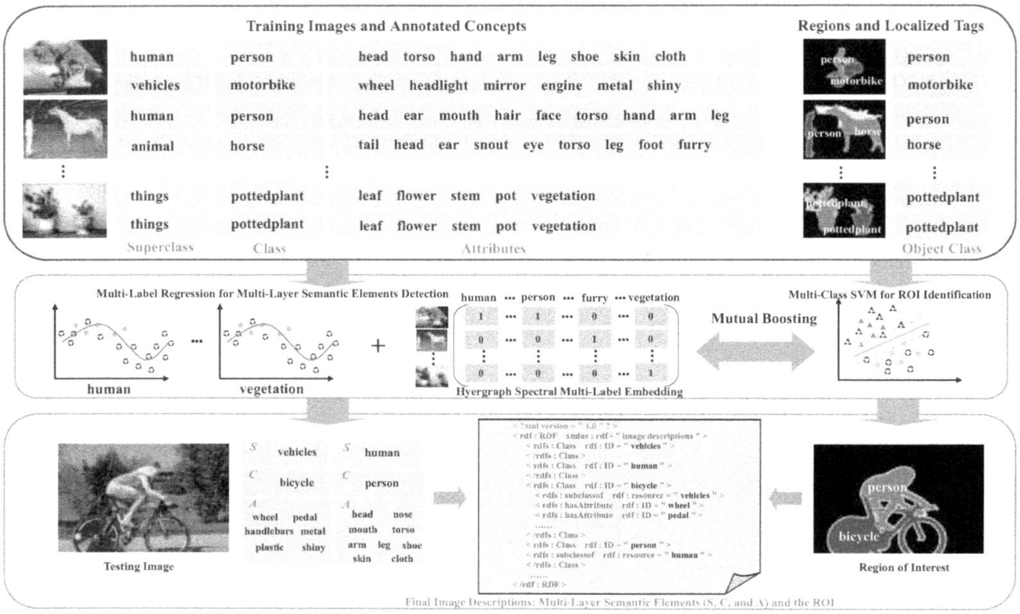

Figure 1: Illustration of our framework. In the training process, multi-label regression for multi-layer semantic elements detection and multi-class SVM for ROI identification are integrated for the mutual boosting of the performance. The final output descriptions are a tetrad of (S, C, A) and the ROI.

abstract semantics of one object or region within one image. Then the object class name along the indexed path of 12 subtrees of sub-categories is considered as *class* to tag the corresponding region or object. The relations between *class* and *superclass* is "Subclass-of". As a middle-level semantic cue, *attributes* are used to describe the object *class* and the relations between *class* and *attributes* is "has-Attributes".

Based on the above discussions, we define the output descriptions to be a tetrad of <Superclass, Class, Attributes, and the ROI>, in which the first three elements are organized into a multi-layer semantic structure and the last one pointing to the most salient area. We illustrate the proposed framework in Fig. 1. Taking the second image in Fig. 1 as an example, intuitively, if we know there is a horse in the center of an image, this is strong prior knowledge that "furry" will be probably detected and such information can be used as context for each of the sub-tasks to improve the accuracy. We propose to formulate the contextual information from superclass, class, and attribute detectors at different levels so as to leverage such information for a more reliable output. In order to utilize the contextual information, we incorporate a hypergraph spectral multi-label embedding into the detectors of multiple concepts. As a further step beyond the detection of the multi-layer semantic elements, our system aims to generate more detailed descriptions of images. Specifically, we train a multi-class SVM for the ROI (Region of Interest) identification. Then the joint optimization of the ROI localizer and the multi-layer semantic elements make them mutually beneficial and reciprocal. The ROI dependent multi-layer semantic elements detection not only accurately reflects the target concept in ROI, but also improves the accuracy of the specific concept classifiers for the semantic elements. In this way, we creat a discriminative image description generation framework based on a tightly coupled multi-layer optimization. The multi-layer semantic elements can be easily described using the RDF (Resource Description Framework). Organizing the semantic elements in RDF will enable flexible multi-layer semantic indexing and facilitate the retrieval of images by the query of certain semantic elements, e.g., using the SQL-like query language for RDF. The main contributions of our work are summarized as below:

(1) A novel form of image descriptions, i.e., a tetrad of <Superclass, Class, Attributes, and the ROI> is defined. This well-structured semantic descriptions of the image can feed into a statistical generative language model (e.g., simplified head-driven phrase structure grammar (HPSG) [17] or even simply language template [4]) to summarize the detected concepts and other evidence in the data so that a human readable semantically meaningful description of the image can be automatically generated.

(2) We integrate the ROI identification and multi-layer semantic elements detection into a joint framework, which makes each of the sub-tasks mutually beneficial.

The rest of this paper is organized as follows. In Section 2, we present the framework and the solution. The experimental analysis is given in Section 3. Conclusions are drawn in Section 4.

2. THE PROPOSED FRAMEWORK

In this section, we present the framework of generating image descriptions by the integration of multi-layer semantic elements detection and ROI identification.

2.1 The Joint Framework of Hierarchical Concept Detection and ROI Identification

2.1.1 Terms and Notations

Denote $\mathcal{X} = \{\mathbf{x}_1, \mathbf{x}_2, \ldots, \mathbf{x}_{n_1}\}$ as the training set of images, where $\mathbf{x}_i \in \mathbb{R}^d (i = 1, \ldots, n_1)$ is the i-th image and n_1

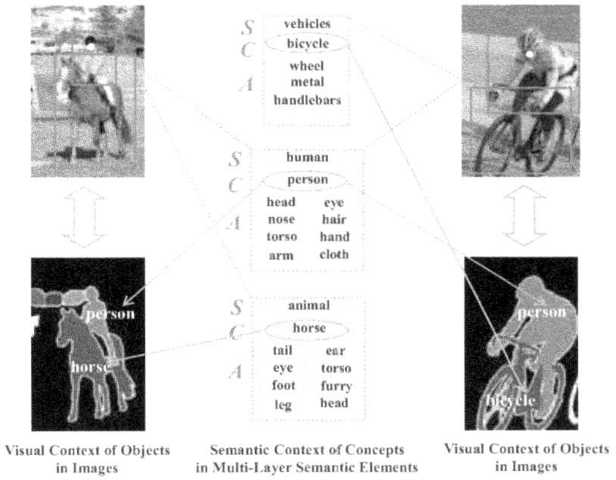

Figure 2: Illustration of the mutual boosting for hierarchical concept detection and ROI identification. Structure concepts of superclass (S), class (C), and attributes (a) define the semantic context of each concept. Co-occurrence of objects in images provides the visual context of the ROI.

is the total number of training images. Suppose the n_1 training images $\mathbf{x}_1, \mathbf{x}_2, \ldots, \mathbf{x}_{n_1}$ are sampled from m_s superclasses, m_c classes, and are associated with m_a attributes, we define $\mathbf{y}_i^s \in \{0,1\}^{m_s \times 1}$, $\mathbf{y}_i^c \in \{0,1\}^{m_c \times 1}$, and $\mathbf{y}_i^a \in \{0,1\}^{m_a \times 1}$ $(i = 1, \ldots, n_1)$ as the label vectors of superclass, class, and attributes, respectively, for image $\mathbf{x}_i$. The j-th element of $\mathbf{y}_i^s$ (or $\mathbf{y}_i^c$ and $\mathbf{y}_i^a$) is 1 if image $\mathbf{x}_i$ is labeled by the j-th concepts of superclass (or class and attributes), and 0 otherwise. $X_1 = [\mathbf{x}_1, \mathbf{x}_2, \ldots, \mathbf{x}_{n_1}] \in \mathbb{R}^{d \times n_1}$ is the data matrix of training images. $Y^s = [\mathbf{y}_1^s, \mathbf{y}_2^s, \ldots, \mathbf{y}_n^s] \in \{0,1\}^{m_s \times n_1}$, $Y^c = [\mathbf{y}_1^c, \mathbf{y}_2^c, \ldots, \mathbf{y}_{n_1}^c] \in \{0,1\}^{m_c \times n_1}$, and $Y^a = [\mathbf{y}_1^a, \mathbf{y}_2^a, \ldots, \mathbf{y}_{n_1}^a] \in \{0,1\}^{m_a \times n_1}$ are the label matrix for superclass, class, and attributes, respectively. We let $Y_1 = [Y^s; Y^c; Y^a] \in \{0,1\}^{m \times n_1}$ denote the label matrix of all the concepts of superclass, class, and attributes, where $m = m_s + m_c + m_a$ is the number of all the concepts in superclass, class, and attributes.

Suppose N_i regions have been detected from the ith image $\mathbf{x}_i \in \mathcal{X}$ $(i = 1, \ldots, n_1)$, such that $\mathbf{x}_i = [x_{i1}, \ldots, x_{iN_i}] \in \mathbb{R}^{d \times N_i}$. $X_2 = [x_{11}, \ldots, x_{1N_1}, \ldots, x_{n_1 N_{n_1}}] \in \mathbb{R}^{d \times n_2}$ is the data matrix of training regions, where $n_2 = \sum_{i=1}^{n_1} N_i$. As each of the n_2 regions belongs to one of the m_c object classes, we let $Y_2 \in \{0,1\}^{m_c \times n_2}$ denote the label matrix of training regions.

In this paper, I is the identity matrix. For a constant k, $\mathbf{1}_k \in \mathbb{R}^k$ is a column vector with all of its elements being 1 and $H_k = I - \frac{1}{k}\mathbf{1}_k \mathbf{1}_k^T \in \mathbb{R}^{k \times k}$ is the centering matrix. For an arbitrary matrix $A \in \mathbb{R}^{r \times p}$, its $\ell_{2,1}$-norm is defined as $||A||_{2,1} = \sum_{i=1}^{r} \sqrt{\sum_{j=1}^{p} A_{ij}^2}$. $Tr(\cdot)$ represents the trace operator.

2.1.2 The Mutual Boosting Method

As illustrated in Fig. 2, the combination of the hierarchical concept detection and ROI identification provides more context information for each of these two tasks and therefore the performance of the two tasks will be improved. Firstly, if we can precisely identify the region of interest, e.g., "horse", in the image, the correspondence between the target concept and specific visual content is obtained. This correspondence will help improve the specific concept classifiers for the semantic elements. Secondly, the multi-layer semantic elements define the semantic context for the target concept in ROI. This contextual information will help improve the performance of ROI identification. For example, similar concepts of attributes like "head" and "hand" will help identify the target tag of "horse" and "person" in ROI. Thus, the joint optimization of the ROI localizer and the multi-layer semantic elements detection makes them mutually beneficial.

As discussed above, in order to perform the detection of multi-layer semantic elements for testing images, we define and label each training image $\mathbf{x}_i \in \mathcal{X}$ $(i = 1, \ldots, n_1)$ with the structured concepts of superclass, class, and attributes. We assume there are transformation matrices $W_1 \in \mathbb{R}^{d \times m}$ and $W_2 \in \mathbb{R}^{d \times m_c}$ which respectively map each d dimensional image and region onto a lower-dimensional subspace. In practice, the number of concepts to be labeled is smaller than the dimensionality of image features. Thus we have $m < d$ and $m_c < d$. We formulate the training process of generating the structured descriptions as to solve the following optimization problem.

$$\begin{aligned}\min_W \Big(&||W_1^T X_1 + b\mathbf{1}_{n_1}^T - Y_1||_F^2 + \lambda_1 Tr(W_1^T X_1 L X_1^T W_1) \\ &+ \lambda_2 ||W_1||_{2,1} + \sum_{i=1}^{n_2} \big(1 - \mathbf{w}_{\mathbf{y}_i}^T x_i^{(2)} + \max_{t \neq \mathbf{y}_i} \mathbf{w}_t^T x_i^{(2)}\big)_+ \\ &+ \lambda_3 ||W_2||_{2,1}\Big) + \alpha ||W||_{2,1}, \end{aligned} \tag{1}$$

where $\lambda_1, \lambda_2, \lambda_3, \alpha > 0$ are the regularization parameters and $b \in \mathbb{R}^{m \times 1}$ is the bias term for the regression. $W_2 = [\mathbf{w}_1, \ldots, \mathbf{w}_{m_c}]$ and $X_2 = [x_1^{(2)}, \ldots, x_{n_2}^{(2)}]$. The index $\mathbf{y}_i \in \{1, \ldots, m_c\}$ and $\mathbf{y}_i = j$ if $Y_2(j, i) = 1$. Functions $||W_1^T X_1 + b\mathbf{1}_{n_1}^T - Y_1||_F^2$ and $\sum_{i=1}^{n_2} \big(1 - \mathbf{w}_{\mathbf{y}_i}^T x_i^{(2)} + \max_{t \neq \mathbf{y}_i} \mathbf{w}_t^T x_i^{(2)}\big)_+$ are the loss functions of least square regression and multi-class SVM, respectively. We explain the objective function in Eq. (1) as follows.

The first three terms in Eq. (1) define a multi-label regression for hierarchical concept detection. As the structured concepts of superclass, class, and attributes are associated with each image, the correlations among these visual concepts should be well exploited. We add a regularization term $Tr(W_1^T X_1 L X_1^T W_1)$ to incorporate the correlations among these structured concepts into the training process. We take the label matrix $Y_1 \in \{0,1\}^{n_1 \times m}$ as a hypergraph, where n_1 denotes the number of vertices and each concept corresponds to a hyperedge. Then the matrix $L \in \mathbb{R}^{n_1 \times n_1}$ is a hypergraph Laplacian defined on Y_1 [21]. Following from the spectral graph embedding theory, the transformation matrix W_1 will be learned to preserve the inherent relationship among data points captured by L, such that the images sharing many common semantic elements tend to be close to each other in the embedded subspace.

Because m_c target tags need to be identified in ROI in the images, the training process for ROI identification of testing images is a multi-class classification problem. The forth term of the objective function in Eq. (1) is a hinge loss of multi-class SVM [3].

As the minimization of a co-regularization term has been shown to be an effective way to reduce disagreement of different classifiers [1], we propose to integrate the training processes of hierarchical concept detection and ROI identification by adding a co-regularization term $||W||_{2,1}$, where

$W = [W1, W2]$. The co-regularization function $||W||_{2,1}$ lets the model of these two related tasks to be mutual regularized and therefore the performance will be mutually boosted. Furthermore, the $\ell_{2,1}$-norm of W will uncover the common irrelevant or noisy components in W_1 and W_2 and therefore led to a better performance of classification.

In the objective function of Eq. (1), there are two unknown variables W_1 and W_2 to be estimated. Though the objective function in Eq. (1) is not jointly convex w.r.t. W_1 and W_2, it is convex w.r.t. one variable when we fix the other variables. In the following section, we present an alternating optimization algorithm to solve the optimization problem in Eq. (1).

Algorithm 1 Joint Optimization of Hierarchical Concept Detection and ROI Identification

Input: Data matrix $X_1 \in \mathbb{R}^{d \times n_1}$ of training images and their label matrix $Y_1 = [Y^s; Y^c; Y^a] \in \{0,1\}^{m \times n_1}$, where Y^s, Y^c, and Y^a denote the label matrix of superclass, class, and attributes, respectively. Data matrix $X_1 \in \mathbb{R}^{d \times n_2}$ of training regions and their label matrix $Y_2 \in \{0,1\}^{m_c \times n_2}$. Regularized parameters λ_1, λ_2, and α.

Output: Matrix W.

1: Set $r = 0$ and initialize $W_1 \in \mathbb{R}^{d \times m}$ and $W_2 \in \mathbb{R}^{d \times m_c}$ randomly;
2: $W = [W_1, W_2]$;
3: **repeat**
4: Compute the diagonal matrix D_1^r, D_2^r, and D^r;
5: Update W_1 by $W_1^{r+1} = (X_1 H_{n_1} H_{n_1}^T X_1^T + \lambda_1 D_2 + \alpha D)^{-1} X_1 H_{n_1} Y_1^T$ using Eq. (5);
6: Update W_2 by solving Eq. (6);
7: Update $W^{r+1} = [W_1, W_2]$;
8: $r = r + 1$;
9: **until** Convergence
10: Return W.

2.2 Solution and Algorithm

In this section, we introduce the optimization of the objective function in Eq. (1). In the following, we denote $W_1 = [w_1^1, \ldots, w_1^d]$, $W_2 = [w_2^1, \ldots, w_2^d]$, and $W = [w^1, \ldots, w^d]$, where d is the number of features. Firstly, we fix W_2 and the optimization problem in Eq. (1) becomes:

$$\min_{W_1} ||W_1^T X_1 + b\mathbf{1}_{n_1}^T - Y_1||_F^2 + \lambda_1 Tr(W_1^T X_1 L X_1^T W_1)$$
$$+\lambda_2 Tr(W_1^T D_1 W_1) + \alpha Tr(W_1^T D W_1), \quad (2)$$

where D_1 and D are diagonal matrices with each element on the diagonal, i.e., d_{ii}^1 and d_{ii} $(i = 1, \ldots, d)$, are respectively defined as $d_{ii}^1 = \frac{1}{2||w_1^i||_2}$ and $d_{ii} = \frac{1}{2||w^i||_2}$.

By setting the derivative of Eq. (2) w.r.t. b to 0, we have $b = \frac{1}{n_1} Y \mathbf{1}_{n_1} - \frac{1}{n_1} W_1^T X_1 \mathbf{1}_{n_1}$.

Then we obtain

$$\min_{W_1} \left\| W_1^T X_1 + (\frac{1}{n_1} Y_1 \mathbf{1}_{n_1} - \frac{1}{n_1} W_1^T X_1 \mathbf{1}_{n_1}) \mathbf{1}_{n_1}^T - Y_1 \right\|_F^2$$
$$+\lambda_1 Tr(W_1^T X_1 L X_1^T W_1) + \lambda_2 Tr(W_1^T D_1 W_1)$$
$$+\alpha Tr(W_1^T D W_1)$$
$$\Rightarrow \min_{W_1} \left\| W_1^T X_1 H_{n_1} - Y_1 H_{n_1} \right\|_F^2 + \lambda_1 Tr(W_1^T X_1 L X_1^T W_1)$$
$$+\lambda_2 Tr(W_1^T D_1 W_1) + \alpha Tr(W_1^T D W_1). \quad (3)$$

By setting the derivative of Eq. (3) w.r.t. W_1 to 0, we have

$$(X_1 H_{n_1} H_{n_1}^T X_1^T + \lambda_1 X_1 L X_1^T + \lambda_2 D_1 + \alpha D) W_1 = X_1 H_{n_1} Y_1^T. \quad (4)$$

Therefore, we have

$$W_1 = (X_1 H_{n_1} H_{n_1}^T X_1^T + \lambda_1 X_1 L X_1^T + \lambda_2 D_1 + \alpha D)^{-1} X_1 H_{n_1} Y_1^T. \quad (5)$$

Then we fix W_1, the objective function in Eq. (1) becomes

$$\min_{W_2} \sum_{i=1}^{n_2} (1 - \mathbf{w}_{\mathbf{y}_i}^T x_i^{(2)} + \max_{t \neq \mathbf{y}_i} \mathbf{w}_t^T x_i^{(2)})_+ + \lambda_3 ||W_2||_{2,1} + \alpha ||W||_{2,1}. \quad (6)$$

The objective function in Eq. (6) is the objective function of multi-class $\ell_{2,1}$-norm SVM, which can be efficiently solved by the algorithm in [2]. Alternately updating W_1 and W_2 using Eq. (5) and Eq. (6) until convergency, we can obtain an optimal W for classification. We propose an alternating algorithm to optimize the objective function in Eq. (1) and summarize it in Algorithm 1. In step 5 of Algorithm 1, the update rule of W_1 using Eq. (5) is the solution to optimize the objective function of the $\ell_{2,1}$-norm regularized least square regression [15] and its convergence has been proved in [15]. The convergence of solving Eq. (6) has been proved in [2]. Thus, in each iteration of Algorithm 1, the updated values of W_1 and W_2 make the value of the objective function in Eq. (1) decrease and Algorithm 1 is guaranteed to coverage. Once the optimal W is obtained, we sort the d features of images and regions according to the value of $||w^i||_F$ $(i = 1, \ldots, d)$ in descending order and select the top ranked ones for classification.

3. EXPERIMENTS

3.1 Experimental Configuration

3.1.1 *Dataset and Groundtruth*

We choose two datasets aPascal [5] and aYahoo [5], which provide the groundtruth of target tags in ROI, and attribute annotation to describing the objects. As introduced in the introduction, we augment the image descriptions according to the concepts in the path of the concept hierarchy indexed in ImageNet.

Images in aPascal are selected from the Pascal VOC 2008 dataset, which contains 20 object class names. For images in aYahoo, additional 12 object classes are collected from Yahoo image search. These object classes are considered as the "class" in the multi-layer semantic elements and also as the target tags for each ROI of aPascal and aYahoo, as these two datasets provide the groundtruth of target tags in ROI. For each class name in aPascal and aYahoo, we retrieve it from the path of the concept hierarchy indexed in ImageNet and select the top-level concept as the "superclass" of the class. For example, the class name "birdąř is indexed along the path "animal-chordate-craniate-bird" in ImageNet. Thus, we choose the concept "animal" as the "superclass" of "bird" to describe the image that the object belongs to. In this way, four concepts of superclass, i.e., "human", "animal", "vehicle", and "thing", are used to describe the images in aPascal and aYahoo. For the detected ROI in aPascal and aYahoo, attribute annotations are collected from Amazon's Mechanical Turk and a list of 64 attributes are used to describe the objects. In this experiment, these 64 attributes are used to describe the corresponding images that

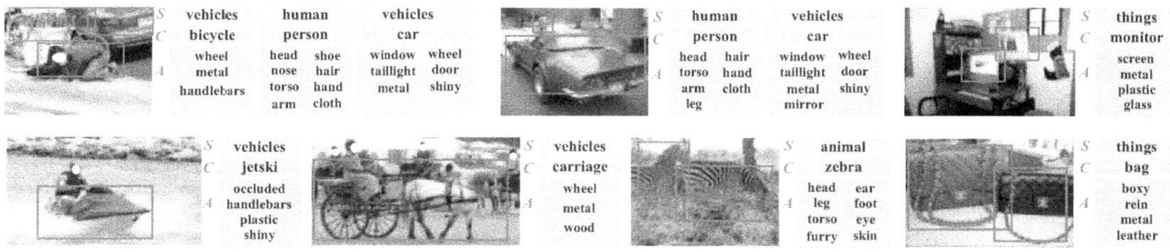

Figure 3: Example images from aPascal (top row) and aYahoo (bottom row). Each image is associated with structured concepts of superclass (S), class (C), and attributes (A). Target class concepts are localized to the ROI, which are pointed out by the red rectangular.

the annotated object belongs to. For aPascal, the number of concepts for superclass, class, and attributes are respectively $m_s = 4$, $m_c = 20$, and $m_a = 64$. For aYahoo, the number of concepts for superclass, class, and attributes are respectively $m_s = 4$, $m_c = 12$, and $m_a = 64$. Thus, the number of the target tags in ROI (concept of object classes) are $m_c = 20$ and $m_c = 12$ for aPascal and aYahoo, respectively. In Fig. 3, we show some example images and associated concepts from aPascal and aYahoo.

3.1.2 Visual Features and the Partition of Training Samples

Because the keypoint based local features are more robust in object recognition, we use bag-of-visual-words (BoW) to represent each image and region. The randomly selected subset of SIFT points are clustered and generated the 1,000 centers as the visual dictionary. Note that, we generate dictionaries for images and regions in aPascal and aYahoo, respectively. As there are regions in which no SIFT points are detected. We omit these regions in this experiment. Finally, there are 12,640 regions and 4,340 images in aPascal. For aYahoo, there are 2,642 regions and 2,374 images.

For the partition of training regions, we set the number of the labeled data per object class to {50, 60, 70, 80, 90, 100} and randomly sample these labeled objects to form the training regions in X_2. In each sampling process, corresponding images that the sampled regions belong to are selected to form the training images in X_1. As the numbers of object classes in aPascal and aYahoo are $m_c = 20$ and $m_c = 12$ respectively, the size of training regions is set to {100, 1200, 1400, 1600, 1800, 2000} for aPascal and {600, 720, 840, 960, 1080, 1200} for aYahoo. We repeat the sampling for 10 times and report the average results.

3.1.3 Evaluation Metrics

The area under the receive operating characteristic curve (AUC) [7] and F1 score [7] are used to measure the performance of both multi-layer semantic elements detection and ROI identification. Because of the multiple concepts in the final descriptions, to measure the global performance across multiple concepts, we use the microaveraging methods, by which the AUC and F1 score are respectively calculated by constructing a global contingency table and then calculating the measure using these sums.

3.1.4 Comparison Methods and Parameter Setting

In this experiment, we use the kNN ($k = 1$) classifier to conduct classification on the selected visual features for the detection of concepts and identification of ROI. To show the better performance of the proposed joint optimization framework proposed in Algorithm 1, we compare our method with one baseline and three state-of-the-arts algorithms:

- kNN ($k = 1$) Classifier which adopts all the 1,000 original visual features for classification. It predicts each concept of multi-layer semantic elements and target tags in ROI, respectively.
- Structural Adaptive Regression (SAR) [14]. SAR integrates two robust regression processes into a joint optimization framework by a co-regularization $\ell_{2,p}$-normčň which can be used to better compare the performance with that of our proposed algorithm.
- Sub-Feature Uncovering with Sparsity (SFUS) [13]. S-FUS leverages the joint feature selection with sparsity and considers the correlation between different concept labels, which is similar in spirit as the hyperspectral multi-label embedding incorporated in our framework.
- Multi-Label Sparse Coding (MLSC) [18], which has been used to automatic image annotation. We use MLSC to perform sparse reconstruction on both image features and multiple concepts. In ROI identification, we only use MLSC to perform sparse reconstruction on region features.

Furthermore, to show the mutual boosting effect and the advantages of simultaneously performing the two tasks of multi-layer semantic elements detection and ROI identification, we compare our algorithm with the components combined in our joint optimization framework. The two combined components are as follows.

- Multi-label Regression with Feature Selection (MLRF-S). This is the first classifier integrated into the mutual boosting method (see Eq. (1)).
- Multi-class Support Vector Machine with Feature Selection (SVMFS) which is an $\ell_{2,1}$-norm regularized SVM. This is the second classifier integrated into the mutual boosting method (see Eq. (1)).

In this experiment, we set λ_1, λ_2, and λ_3 in Eq. (1) to be the same value. Thus, there are two parameters λ (denotes the same value of λ_1, λ_2, and λ_3) and α to be tuned. For the comparison methods of SAR, SFUS, MLSC, MLRFS, and SVMFS, regularization parameters also need to be tuned. To fairly compare these methods, we tune all the parameters by a grid search strategy from $\{10^{-6}, 10^{-3},$

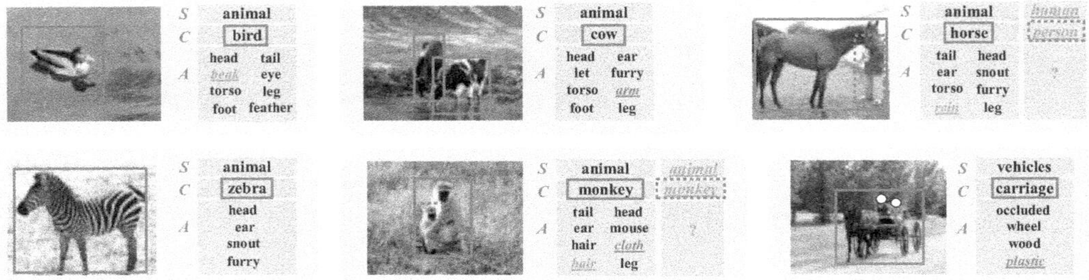

Figure 4: Output descriptions of six tetrad of <S, C, A, and the ROI> for test images of aPascal (top row) and aYaoo (bottom row). Red rectangular denotes the target tags in ROI. Red texts denote the false positive concepts. Green texts denote the true positive concepts that are not detected. Dashed red rectangular denote the ROI not identified.

Table 1: Comparison results of multi-layer semantic elements detection and ROI identification on aPascal and aYahoo datasets. The number of the labeled objects per class is 50.

Datasets	aPascal			
Tasks	Concept Detection		ROI Identification	
Criterion	AUC	F1	AUC	F1
Our Method	**0.7105**	**0.4694**	**0.5266**	**0.1133**
kNN Classifier	0.6956	0.4429	0.5117	0.0835
SAR	0.6991	0.4521	0.5233	0.1007
SFUS	0.6981	0.4480	0.5152	0.1095
MLSC	0.6688	0.3733	0.5134	0.1056
Datasets	aYahoo			
Tasks	Concept Detection		ROI Identification	
Criterion	AUC	F1	AUC	F1
Our Method	**0.7125**	**0.4705**	**0.6867**	**0.3800**
kNN Classifier	0.6897	0.4010	0.6575	0.3222
SAR	0.6960	0.4417	0.6738	0.3643
SFUS	0.6927	0.4336	0.6668	0.3560
MLSC	0.6940	0.4469	0.6643	0.3523

Table 2: Comparison results of multi-layer semantic elements detection and ROI identification on aPascal and aYahoo datasets. The number of the labeled objects per class is 100.

Datasets	aPascal			
Tasks	Concept Detection		ROI Identification	
Criterion	AUC	F1	AUC	F1
Our Method	**0.7279**	**0.4912**	**0.5632**	**0.1586**
kNN Classifier	0.7117	0.4612	0.5409	0.1230
SAR	0.7181	0.4798	0.5483	0.1382
SFUS	0.7170	0.4745	0.5317	0.1216
MLSC	0.7054	0.4277	0.5374	0.1332
Datasets	aYahoo			
Tasks	Concept Detection		ROI Identification	
Criterion	AUC	F1	AUC	F1
Our Method	**0.7455**	**0.5208**	**0.7460**	**0.4634**
kNN Classifier	0.7206	0.4656	0.7044	0.3763
SAR	0.7325	0.4920	0.7328	0.4373
SFUS	0.7250	0.4869	0.7247	0.4489
MLSC	0.7305	0.5023	0.7268	0.4291

Table 3: Comparison results when the number of the labeled objects per class is 50.

Datasets	aPascal			
Tasks	Concept Detection		ROI Identification	
Criterion	AUC	F1	AUC	F1
Our Method	**0.7105**	**0.4694**	**0.5266**	**0.1133**
MLRFS	0.6969	0.4471	0.5160	0.0896
SVMFS	0.6947	0.4451	0.5202	0.0959
Datasets	aYahoo			
Tasks	Concept Detection		ROI Identification	
Criterion	AUC	F1	AUC	F1
Our Method	**0.7125**	**0.4705**	**0.6867**	**0.3800**
MLRFS	0.6896	0.4244	0.6610	0.3266
SVMFS	0.6906	0.4235	0.6727	0.3443

10^{-1}, 1, 10, 10^3, 10^6}. We set the number of selected features to $\{100, 200, \ldots, 900\}$. For all the methods, we report the best results from different parameters.

3.2 Experimental Results

3.2.1 Performance Comparison

As introduced in Section 3.1.4, the main difference between our method and SAR is that, we incorporate two different representative classifiers, i.e., least square regression and SVM, into our framework, which can leverage the strength of different classifiers for better performance of hierarchical concept detection and ROI identification, simultaneously. The correlations between our method and the comparison methods are that, to utilize the correlations among the structured concepts of superclass, class, and attributes, we incorporate a hypergraph spectral multi-label embedding into the least square regression for a better performance of hierarchical concept detection, which is similar in spirit of the multi-label strategy used in SFUS and MLSC.

In Table 1 and Table 2, we report the comparison results when the number of the labeled objects per class is set to 50 and 100, respectively. From the results we observe that: (1) Our method obtains the better performance of the hierarchical concept detection and ROI identification than that of kNN classifier on full features, SAR, SFUS, and MLSC, in terms of both the AUC and F1 score. For example, considering the performance of concept detection in Table 1, our method gains performance improvement about 3.8% (in

Table 4: Comparison results when the number of the labeled objects per class is 100.

Datasets	aPascal			
Tasks	Concept Detection		ROI Identification	
Criterion	AUC	F1	AUC	F1
Our Method	**0.7279**	**0.4912**	**0.5632**	**0.1586**
MLRFS	0.7106	0.4649	0.5415	0.1239
SVMFS	0.7083	0.4666	0.5477	0.1326
Datasets	aYahoo			
Tasks	Concept Detection		ROI Identification	
Criterion	AUC	F1	AUC	F1
Our Method	**0.7455**	**0.5208**	**0.7460**	**0.4634**
MLRFS	0.7283	0.5059	0.7175	0.4205
SVMFS	0.7168	0.4697	0.7198	0.4011

terms of F1 score) compared to the SAR on the aPascal dataset, and about 6.5% (in terms of F1 score) on the aYahoo dataset. Considering the performance of ROI identification in Table 1, our method gains performance improvement about 12.5% (in terms of F1 score) compared to the SAR on the aPascal dataset, and 4.3% (in terms of F1 score) on the aYahoo dataset. (2) Comparing the results in Table 1 and Table 2 we can see that, when the number of the labeled training objects per class increase from 50 to 100, the performance of all the comparison methods increase. Our method also obtains the better performance than that of the comparison methods. For example, considering the performance of concept detection in Table 2, our method gains performance improvement about 2.4% (in terms of F1 score) compared to the SAR on the aPascal dataset, and about 5.8% (in terms of F1 score) on the aYahoo dataset. Considering the performance of ROI identification in Table 2, our method gains performance improvement about 14.7% (in terms of F1 score) compared to the SAR on the aPascal dataset, and 5.9% (in terms of F1 score) on the aYahoo dataset. (3) From the comparison results in Table 1 and 2 we can see, though our method is effective, the performance of ROI identification is low on the aPascal dataset. The reason may be that, in the experimental settings of this experiment, the number of the labeled training objects is very small (e.g., 50 per class) compared to the total number of objects (about 12,640) in the dataset.

In Fig. 4, we show examples of the final image descriptions output by our system. As can be seen, in most cases, our system outputs the detailed descriptions of the superclass, class, attributes, and the ROI. Because the attributes, such as "arm" and "cloth", transcend specific semantic categories and are correlated with each other, some false positive concepts are produced. Some attributes describing specific object class, such as "beak" and "rein", are not correctly produced. Because of the occlusion and small size of the regions, some ROIs are not identified. Although there is room for improving, our algorithm provides a human semantically meaningful and well-structured image description.

3.2.2 Effectiveness of the Mutual Boosting

In this section, we investigate the effectiveness of the proposed mutual boosting framework. As we simultaneously perform hierarchical concept detection and ROI identification, we will show the advantages of our method by comparing the performance of these two tasks with that of the combined components, i.e., MLRFS and SVMFS, respectively. In Table 3 and Table 4, we report the comparison results when the number of the labeled objects per class is set to 50 and 100, respectively. From the results we observe that: (1) Our mutual boosting method obtains the best performance of the hierarchical concept detection and ROI identification in terms of both the AUC and F1 score. For example, considering the performance of concept detection in Table 3, our method gains performance improvement about 2.3% (for AUC score) and 5.4% (for F1 score) compared to SVMFS on the aPascal dataset, and about about 3.2% (for AUC score) and 11.1% (for F1 score) on the aYahoo dataset. Considering the performance of ROI identification in Table 3, our method gains performance improvement about 1.2% (for AUC score) and 18.1% (for F1 score) compared to SVMFS on the aPascal dataset, and about 2.1% (for AUC score) and 10.4% (for F1 score) on the aYahoo dataset. (2) Owing to the strength of the co-regularization term in our mutual boosting method, the tightly related tasks of hierarchical concept detection and ROI identification are mutual regularized. As discussed in Section 2.1.2, because we define use the $\ell_{2,1}$-norm of the combined transformation matrices, the common irrelevant or noisy components in W_1 and W_2 are uncovered and therefore led to a better performance of classification. In Table 3 and 4, as the results of our method are obviously better than that of MLRFS and SVMFS, the proposed mutual boosting strategy is effective.

To further show the performance improvement when the number of the labeled objects per class varies, we report the results of hierarchical concept detection and ROI identification of our method, SVMFS, and MLRFS on aPascal and aYahoo in Fig. 5 and Fig. 6, respectively. From the results we observe that: (1) As the number of labeled objects per class increases, the performance of increases, especially for the performance in terms of the F1 score. (2) For all the settings of the labeled objects per class, the performance of our method is better than that of the SVMFS and MLRFS.

4. CONCLUSIONS

In this paper, we propose a joint framework of describing image by the context, which integrates the multi-layer semantic elements detection and ROI (Region of Interest) identification into one optimization process. A multi-label regression for hierarchical concept detection and and a multi-class SVM for ROI identification are combined to better describe the testing images. In the experiments, training images are associated with multi-layer concepts of superclass, class, and attributes. Our goal is to make the joint optimization mutually beneficial and reciprocal. Experimental results demonstrate the effectiveness of our mutual boosting framework. The output descriptions in form of a tetrad of superclass, class, attributes, and the ROI help improve the performance of image retrieval in the future, as these descriptions contains richer information of the image content with layered contextual information, thereby enabling better management and usage of image data.

5. ACKNOWLEDGMENTS

This work was supported by the NSFC (Grant 61202166, 61472276), the Major Project of National Social Science Fund(Grant 14ZDB153) and Doctoral Fund of Ministry of Education of China (Grant 20120032120042).

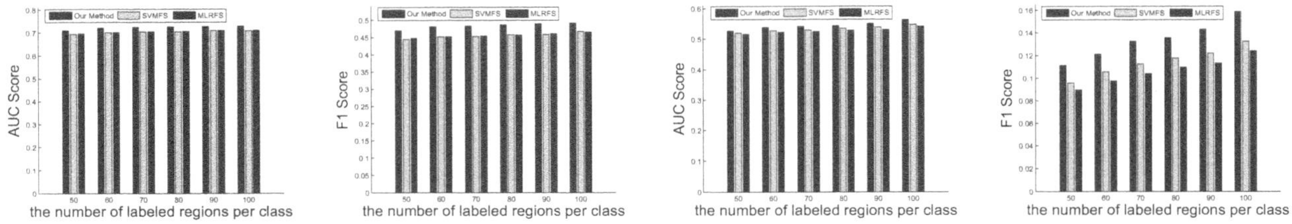

(a) aPascal: Hierarchical Concept Detection (b) aPascal: Hierarchical Concept Detection (c) aPascal: ROI Identification (d) aPascal: ROI Identification

Figure 5: Comparison results of multi-layer semantic elements detection and ROI identification on the aPascal dataset. The number of the labeled objects per class is set to {50, 60, 70, 80, 90, 100}.

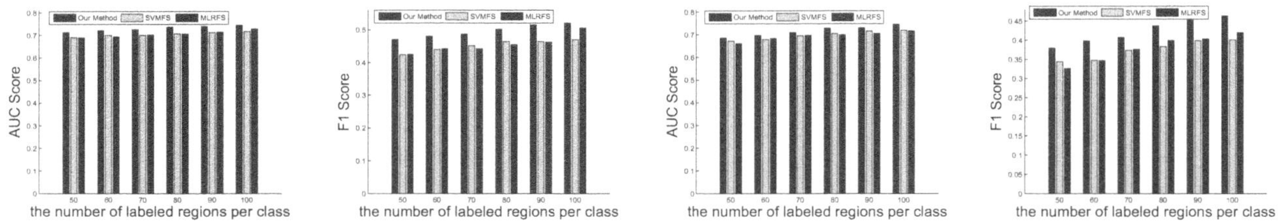

(a) aPascal: Hierarchical Concept Detection (b) aYahoo: Hierarchical Concept Detection (c) aYahoo: ROI Identification (d) aYahoo: ROI Identification

Figure 6: Comparison results of multi-layer semantic elements detection and ROI identification on the aYahoo dataset. The number of the labeled objects per class is set to {50, 60, 70, 80, 90, 100}.

6. REFERENCES

[1] U. Brefeld, T. Gärtner, T. Scheffer, and S. Wrobel. Efficient co-regularised least squares regression. In *NIPS*, pages 137–144, 2006.

[2] X. Cai, F. Nie, H. Huang, and C. H. Ding. Multi-class $\ell_{2,1}$-norm support vector machine. In *IEEE International Conference on Data Mining*, pages 91–100, 2011.

[3] K. Crammer and Y. Singer. On the algorithmic implementation of multiclass kernel-based vector machines. *The Journal of Machine Learning Research*, 2:265–292, 2002.

[4] D. Ding, F. Metze, S. Rawat, P. F. Schulam, S. Burger, E. Younessian, L. Bao, M. G. Christel, and A. Hauptmann. Beyond audio and video retrieval: towards multimedia summarization. In *Proceedings of the 2012 ACM International Conference on Multimedia Retrieval*, 2012.

[5] A. Farhadi, I. Endres, D. Hoiem, and D. Forsyth. Describing objects by their attributes. In *CVPR*, pages 1778–1785, 2009.

[6] A. Farhadi, M. Hejrati, M. Sadeghi, P. Young, C. Rashtchian, J. Hockenmaier, and D. Forsyth. Every picture tells a story: Generating sentences from images. *ECCV*, pages 15–29, 2010.

[7] T. Fawcett. An introduction to roc analysis. *Pattern recognition letters*, 27(8):861–874, 2006.

[8] Y. Gong, S. Lazebnik, A. Gordo, and F. Perronnin. Iterative quantization: A procrustean approach to learning binary codes for large-scale image retrieval. *IEEE Transactions on Pattern Analysis and Machine Intelligence*, 2012.

[9] S. Guadarrama, N. Krishnamoorthy, G. Malkarnenkar, S. Venugopalan, R. Mooney, T. Darrell, and K. Saenko. Youtube2text: Recognizing and describing arbitrary activities using semantic hierarchies and zero-shot recognition. In *ICCV*, pages 2712–2719. IEEE, 2013.

[10] A. Hauptmann, R. Yan, W.-H. Lin, M. Christel, and H. Wactlar. Can high-level concepts fill the semantic gap in video retrieval? a case study with broadcast news. *IEEE Transactions on Multimedia*, 9(5):958–966, 2007.

[11] G. Kulkarni, V. Premraj, S. Dhar, S. Li, Y. Choi, A. C. Berg, and T. L. Berg. Baby talk: Understanding and generating simple image descriptions. In *CVPR*, pages 1601–1608, 2011.

[12] X. Liu, Y. Mu, B. Lang, and S.-F. Chang. Compact hashing for mixed image-keyword query over multi-label images. In *ACM Multimedia*, page 18, 2012.

[13] Z. Ma, F. Nie, Y. Yang, J. R. Uijlings, and N. Sebe. Web image annotation via subspace-sparsity collaborated feature selection. *IEEE Transactions on Multimedia*, 14(4):1021–1030, 2012.

[14] Z. Ma, Y. Yang, Y. Cai, N. Sebe, and A. G. Hauptmann. Knowledge adaptation for ad hoc multimedia event detection with few exemplars. In *ACM Multimedia*, pages 469–478, 2012.

[15] F. Nie, H. Huang, X. Cai, and C. H. Ding. Efficient and robust feature selection via joint $\ell_{2,1}$-norms minimization. *NIPS*, 23:1813–1821, 2010.

[16] D. Parikh and K. Grauman. Relative attributes. In *ICCV*, pages 503–510, 2011.

[17] C. Pollard and I. A. Sag. *Head-driven phrase structure grammar*. University of Chicago Press, 1994.

[18] C. Wang, S. Yan, L. Zhang, and H.-J. Zhang. Multi-label sparse coding for automatic image annotation. In *CVPR*, pages 1643–1650, 2009.

[19] S.-I. Yu, Z. Xu, D. Ding, W. Sze, F. Vicente, Z. Lan, Y. Cai, S. Rawat, P. Schulam, S. Bahmani, et al. Informedia e-lamp@ trecvid 2012 multimedia event detection and recounting (med and mer). 2012.

[20] D. Zhang, M. M. Islam, and G. Lu. A review on automatic image annotation techniques. *Pattern Recognition*, 45(1):346–362, 2012.

[21] D. Zhou, J. Huang, and B. Scholkopf. Learning with hypergraphs: Clustering, classification, and embedding. *NIPS*, 19:1601, 2007.

Supervised Multi-scale Locality Sensitive Hashing

Li Weng *
LinkMedia group
Inria Rennes - Bretagne Atlantique
35042 Rennes, France

I-Hong Jhuo †
Institute of Information Science
Academia Sinica
11529 Taipei, Taiwan

Miaojing Shi
Key Laboratory of Machine Perception
Peking University
100871 Beijing, China

Meng Sun ‡
IIP Lab, PLA University of Science and Technology
210007 Nanjing, China

Wen-Huang Cheng
MCLab, CITI
Academia Sinica
11529 Taipei, Taiwan

Laurent Amsaleg
IRISA Lab
CNRS Rennes
35042 Rennes, France

ABSTRACT

LSH is a popular framework to generate compact representations of multimedia data, which can be used for content based search. However, the performance of LSH is limited by its unsupervised nature and the underlying feature scale. In this work, we propose to improve LSH by incorporating two elements – supervised hash bit selection and multi-scale feature representation. First, a feature vector is represented by multiple scales. At each scale, the feature vector is divided into segments. The size of a segment is decreased gradually to make the representation correspond to a coarse-to-fine view of the feature. Then each segment is hashed to generate more bits than the target hash length. Finally the best ones are selected from the hash bit pool according to the notion of bit reliability, which is estimated by bit-level hypothesis testing.

Extensive experiments have been performed to validate the proposal in two applications: near-duplicate image detection and approximate feature distance estimation. We first demonstrate that the feature scale can influence performance, which is often a neglected factor. Then we show that the proposed supervision method is effective. In particular, the performance increases with the size of the hash bit pool. Finally, the two elements are put together. The integrated scheme exhibits further improved performance.

*L. Weng was supported by the French project Secular under grant ANR-12-CORD-0014.

†I-H. Jhuo is a co-first author. He and W.-H. Cheng were supported by the Ministry of Science and Technology of Taiwan under grant MOST-103-2911-I-001-531.

‡M. Sun was supported by the National Natural Science Foundation of China under grant 61402519 and the Natural Science Foundation of Jiangsu Province under grant BK20140071.

ICMR'15, June 23–26, 2015, Shanghai, China.

http://dx.doi.org/10.1145/2671188.2749291.

Categories and Subject Descriptors

H.3.3 [**Information Systems**]: Information Search and Retrieval; I.4.7 [**Computing Methodologies**]: Image Processing and Computer Vision—*feature representation*

General Terms

Algorithms, Design

Keywords

perceptual image hash, locality sensitive hashing, robust representation, multiple scale, supervised feature selection

1. INTRODUCTION

Hash algorithms for multimedia data have recently received much attention, because the compactness of hash values is the key for indexing and search in large-scale database systems. A hash value is typically a short binary string, whose length varies from tens to thousands of bits. It is a compact digest of the input data to a hash algorithm. In order to support content-based similarity search, multimedia hash algorithms emerged in recent years. They are typically designed to be *robust*, i.e., the hash value is independent of the binary representation of a multimedia object. On the other hand, they are also *discriminative*, i.e., different content should have different hash values.

In general, hashing techniques for multimedia data can divide into two categories – perceptual hashing and semantic hashing. They cover three applications – content classification, content identification, and content authentication. Existing algorithms generally differ in two aspects: 1) whether particular features are required; 2) whether training is required. Perceptual hashing [9] mainly deals with the latter two applications. Corresponding algorithms are typically feature-dependent, and do not require training. Semantic hashing [15], on the other hand, mainly addresses content classification. Corresponding algorithms are typically feature-independent and require training.

In this work, we focus on a class of feature-independent hash algorithms, called locality-sensitive hashing (LSH) [1]. LSH is a generic framework originally used for approximate nearest neighbor (ANN) search. An LSH scheme is a distribution on a family F of hash functions operating on a collection of objects, such that for two objects x, y,

$$\Pr_{h \in F}[h(x) = h(y)] = sim(x, y), \quad (1)$$

where $sim(x, y) \in [0, 1]$ is some similarity function defined on the collection of objects, and Pr means probability. A popular implementation of LSH is based on scalar quantization [17]:

$$h_{r,b}(v) = \left\lfloor \frac{r \cdot v + b}{w} \right\rfloor, \quad (2)$$

where $\lfloor \cdot \rfloor$ is the floor operation, v is a feature vector, r is a random Gaussian vector, w is a quantization step, and b is a random variable uniformly distributed between 0 and w. In this work, our implementation of LSH is based on Charikar's work [3]:

$$h_r(v) = \begin{cases} 1 & \text{if } v \cdot r \geq 0 \\ 0 & \text{if } v \cdot r < 0 \end{cases} \quad (3)$$

This implementation actually measures the angular similarity between two feature vectors:

$$\Pr[h_r(u) = h_r(v)] = 1 - \frac{\theta(u, v)}{\pi}, \quad (4)$$

where $\theta(u, v) = \cos^{-1} \frac{u \cdot v}{||u|| \cdot ||v||}$ is the angle between u and v. This representation is the foundation of random projection based hash algorithms. In order to approximately quantize a feature vector, hyperplanes are randomly generated. The encoding depends on the relationship between the hyperplanes and the feature vector. The essential difference between LSH and later approaches lies in the way that hyperplanes are generated. Instead of using random hyperplanes, supervised algorithms try to search for hyperplanes that are more suitable for the problem at hand.

1.1 Contribution

In this paper, we propose an extension of LSH, which we call Supervised Multi-scale LSH (SMLSH). Two approaches are explored – supervised hash bit selection and multi-scale feature representation. Specifically, a feature vector is first represented by multiple scales; then each scale is hashed to generate more bits than the target hash length; finally, the best hash bits are selected from the candidate bit pool. This extension can effectively improve the performance of LSH in various applications with the following desirable properties:

- Compatibility to existing LSH schemes;
- Asymptotically guaranteed effectiveness;
- Scalability to large hash lengths.

The main advantage of the proposal is its versatility and thus the potential to be applied to other feature-independent hash algorithms. As an extension framework, we do not significantly modify an existing LSH scheme, so that conventional systems can be easily upgraded.

The scalability in hash lengths is very important for large-scale systems. According to the birthday paradox [18], one may find a pair of multimedia objects with the same n-bit hash value (a collision) among $2^{n/2}$ pairs. In practice, the collision rate can be higher for multimedia hashing due to the robustness requirement. Short hash lengths such as 32, 64 are more likely to cause false positives. In order to manage millions or billions of multimedia objects, a sufficient hash length is critical in a system design. A large hash length is also desirable for ANN applications where the conventional recall@R setting is used.

Existing supervised hash algorithms typically use various optimization techniques to compute hash bits. Due to the curse of dimensionality, this approach is intrinsically difficult when the hash length exceeds a certain level. SMLSH takes a different approach. It inherits the virtues of both supervised and randomized algorithms. As a randomized algorithm, SMLSH can easily extend to arbitrary hash lengths. As a *weakly* supervised approach, SMLSH does not greedily search for the best hyperplanes in order to be efficient and avoid over-fitting. Consequently, it improves performance with affordable complexity.

Multi-scale feature representation, to the best of our knowledge, is an unexplored approach in multimedia hashing. Existing algorithms typically assume a certain feature scale, which potentially limits performance. SMLSH unlocks this limit by considering multiple scales simultaneously.

1.2 Related work

Perceptual hashing started from the late 90's. Typical work includes Schneider and Chang's framework [16] and Fridrich's algorithm [5]. The latter is essentially a block-based LSH variant. Afterwards various algorithms based on different features are proposed, such as RASH [11] based on the Radon transform, Philips' audio hashing algorithm [7] based on the Mel-frequency cepstrum, the robust and secure hash based on the Fourier-Mellin transform [20]. Other features include higher-order statistics [25, 27], shapes [26], DFT phases [28], DCT or DWT signs [23, 24, 22], etc.

Feature-independent hashing or semantic hashing started from LSH. Typical work includes Charikar's LSH [3] for cosine similarity and Datar *et al.*'s LSH [4] for L_p distance. Later, various approaches are proposed to adapt the algorithm to the data and accommodate more semantics and modalities. For example, unsupervised training is used in spectral hashing [21], which is based on spectral clustering. The kernel trick is used in the Kernelized LSH [10]. Recently, supervised training is more widely used to overcome the semantic gap, such as [15, 6, 12].

2. SUPERVISED MULTI-SCALE LSH

Our goal is to improve LSH. Without loss of generality, the problem is defined as follows:

- Given an LSH algorithm with n-bit output, build a new algorithm with the same output length but improved performance.

In order to be versatile, we do not modify the internal realization of LSH. Since LSH can support arbitrary hash lengths, our solution to the above problem is the following:

- Given an LSH algorithm, generate n_o-bit output ($n_o \geq n$), form a hash value with improved performance by selecting n bits out of n_o bits.

The question is then how to select the bits. The key idea of SMLSH is that the choice of projections and features should both adapt to the problem. Thus SMLSH consists of two parts: multi-scale feature representation and hypothesis-testing-driven bit selection. A schematic diagram is shown in Fig. 1. The basic work-flow is the following:

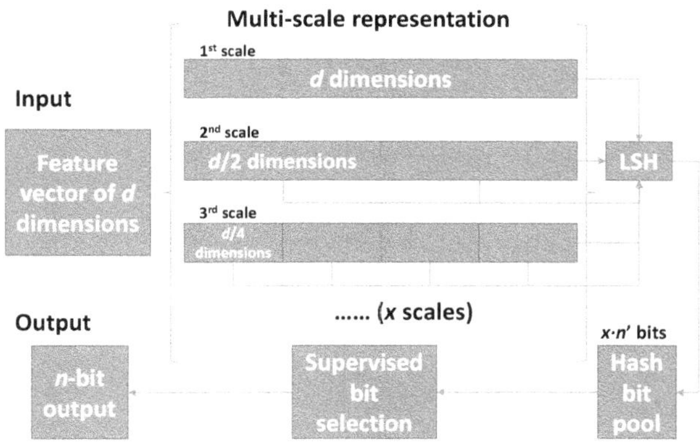

Figure 1: Schematic diagram of SMLSH.

1. The input feature vector is represented by x scales;
2. At each scale, the feature vector is fed into an LSH algorithm to obtain n' ($n' \geq n$) bits;
3. The best n bits are selected from all scales among the $n_o = x \cdot n'$ candidates.

In the following, the hash bit selection strategy and the multi-scale feature representation are described in detail.

2.1 Hash bit selection

Intuitively, we need to select the "best" n bits from the n_o-bit output. We realize it according to the criterion of *bit reliability*, a metric to measure the quality of each bit. It can be obtained through a training procedure. Once the bit reliability information is obtained, bit selection is just a sorting procedure:

1. Estimate the reliability of all n_o bits;
2. Sort the reliability of all n_o bits;
3. Output the most reliable n bits.

The above description gives an overview of the proposed scheme. Next, we define the bit reliability.

We consider an n-bit hash value as n binary classifiers, each represented by a single bit. The bit reliability can be evaluated by hypothesis testing. Denote the difference between two hash values at position i as $d_i \in \{0, 1\}$ ($i = 0, \cdots, n-1$). A decision is made from two hypotheses:

- $\mathbb{H}_0$ – the images correspond to irrelevant content;
- $\mathbb{H}_1$ – the images correspond to relevant content.

If $d_i = 0$, we choose $\mathbb{H}_1$; otherwise we choose $\mathbb{H}_0$.

The reliability of a hash bit can be characterized by the false positive rate p_{fp} and the false negative rate p_{fn}:

- p_{fp} = Probability $\{d_i = 0|\mathbb{H}_0\}$;
- p_{fn} = Probability $\{d_i = 1|\mathbb{H}_1\}$.

Overall, we define the bit reliability as

$$r_b = C_{fp} \cdot p_{fp} + C_{fn} \cdot p_{fn} , \tag{5}$$

where C_{fp} and C_{fn} are weight factors representing the cost for different mistakes. A smaller r_b corresponds to better reliability. This formulation is not biased by class skewness. It has some similarity to the objective function in LDA-Hash [19]. In the rest of the paper, we assume the weights are equal to 1/2.

If we obtain some ground truth labels for training, the bit reliability can be estimated. Thus we can improve an existing LSH scheme without modifying its internal realization.

2.2 Multi-scale feature representation

In practice, given a d-dimensional feature vector, an $\{l, k\}$ LSH scheme generates l sub-hash values, each with k bits. The two parameters l and k are important - the former typically corresponds to the number of hash tables; the latter is the size of a sub-hash value. The overall hash value consists of $l \times k$ bits. An interesting property of LSH is that it supports arbitrary hash lengths by varying l and k.

An often neglected factor in feature-independent hash algorithms is the *scale* of the feature vector. In order to hash (project) a feature vector, there are at least two ways: we could either compute $l \times k$ bits from the whole feature vector, or divide it into l parts and compute k hash bits from each part. Which approach is better?

This is similar to the question – whether we should use global or local features? In general, global features have good robustness but relatively weak discrimination, and local features show the opposite. For a certain problem, *one cannot decide in advance which scale is the best.* Therefore, we propose to test features of different scales and select the suitable ones.

Assume we consider x scales (Fig. 1). For each scale index $s_i = s_0 + i$ ($i = 0, 1, \cdots, x-1$), we evenly divide the feature vector into $l = 2^{s_i}$ parts and compute k_o ($k_o \geq k$) hash bits from each part, so that $n' = l \cdot k_o$. The parameter s_0 (set to 0 by default) decides the starting scale. The parameter x is determined in such a way that the minimum feature length $d/2^{s_0+x-1}$ is not too small. There are certainly other ways to construct feature vectors of different scales. We adopt our approach mainly because of the implementation simplicity.

3. PERFORMANCE AND COMPLEXITY

When the Hamming distance is used for hash comparison, two hash values are judged as relevant if their distance d is less than t. The performance of a hash algorithm can be characterized by the true positive rate P_{tp} and the false positive rate P_{fp}:

- P_{tp} = Probability $\{d < t|\mathbb{H}_1\}$;
- P_{fp} = Probability $\{d < t|\mathbb{H}_0\}$.

Assuming the n bits are independent and have average performance $\{p_{tp}, p_{fp}\}$, the performance of the overall scheme can be formulated as:

$$P_{tp} = f(p_{tp}) \tag{6}$$
$$P_{fp} = f(p_{fp}), \tag{7}$$

where $p_{tp} = 1 - p_{fn}$ and

$$f(p) = \sum_{k=n-t}^{n} \binom{n}{k} \cdot p^k \cdot (1-p)^{n-k}. \tag{8}$$

The above equation was used in Condorcet's jury theorem to show that a decision is more likely to be correct with more juries. In our proposal, the bit selection procedure essentially increases p_{tp} and decreases p_{fp} by replacing the original n bits with better candidates, i.e., we improve the quality of juries. Given a pool of n_o hyperplanes, the probability that our scheme fails is equal to the probability that the original n bits are the best among the n_o choices, which is $1/\binom{n_o}{n}$. This probability can be made arbitrarily small by increasing n_o. In practice, this property asymptotically guarantees that our scheme is always effective. For example, $\binom{256}{128}$ is larger than 10^{15}.

Assuming each coefficient of a hyperplane is represented by b bit precision, for a feature vector segment of length d/l, there are totally $2^{d/l \cdot b}$ hyperplanes. That implies searching for a hyperplane in a high-dimensional space is computationally difficult. The training cost of greedy algorithms becomes prohibitively high for large hash lengths.

The computational cost of SMLSH consists of training cost and running cost. The training cost can be manually controlled. When there are N samples (e.g. images) available, there are maximum $\binom{N}{2}$ hash comparisons. We can have enough ground truths even when the training set is small. For example, $\binom{1000}{2}$ is approximately half a million.

The running cost depends on the implementation. In the worst case, when all the candidate hyperplanes are generated online by a pseudo-random number generator and are all used for projection (despite that not all results are used), the cost is about $x \cdot \frac{k_0}{k}$ times the cost of the original LSH. In practice, the computation can be reduced by pre-computing the selected hyperplanes offline.

4. EXPERIMENT

Since LSH is a general technique in content based search, we evaluate SMLSH in two different applications:

- Case 1: Near duplicate image detection;
- Case 2: Approximate feature distance estimation.

The former is related to content and copyright management; the latter is related to nearest neighbor search. The first application is a typical example with semantic gaps, i.e., relevant items do not necessarily result in small distances. The second application is an example of more ideal situations.

In the first application, SMLSH is used for identifying near-duplicate images. A near-duplicate is defined as a quasi-copy of an original multimedia object, typically resulted by incidental noise. We use 100 images to generate the training set and another 100 images to generate the testing set. They are randomly selected from the validation set of ILSVRC'2012.[1] Each set consists of 10,600 images, including the 100 original ones and 10,500 near-duplicates. The near-duplicates are created by applying a series of distortion to each of the 100 images. The list of distortion (15 categories, 7 levels each) is shown in Table 1. The relationship between the original images and their near-duplicates are used as the ground truth. GIST [14] feature vectors are extracted from all these images.

In the second application, SMLSH is used for estimating the similarity between SIFT vectors [13]. A dataset of ten thousand SIFT vectors is used [8].[2] Half of it is used for training and the other half is used for testing. The ground truth is set as follows: two SIFT vectors are determined as relevant if their cosine similarity is larger than 0.8.

Both datasets have been transformed by PCA in order to remove the correlation between feature dimensions. In particular, the GIST feature vectors are reduced to 256 dimensions. The SIFT vectors still keep 128 dimensions.

[1] http://www.image-net.org/challenges/LSVRC/2012/
[2] http://corpus-texmex.irisa.fr

Table 1: Distortions for near-duplicate generation.

Distortion name	Parameter range, step
1. Rotation	Angle: $1° - 7°$, $1°$
2. Central cropping	Percentage: $1\% - 7\%$, 1%
3. Row removal	Percentage: $1\% - 7\%$, 1%
4. Asymmetric cropping	Percentage: $1\% - 7\%$, 1%
5. Circular shifting	Percentage: $1\% - 7\%$, 1%
6. Down-scaling	Ratio: $0.7 - 0.1$, 0.1
7. Shearing	Percentage: $1\% - 7\%$, 1%
8. JPEG compression	Quality factor: $70 - 10$, 10
9. Median filter	Window size: $7 - 19$, 2
10. Gaussian filter	Window size: $7 - 19$, 2
11. Sharpening	Strength: $0.7 - 0.1$, 0.1[1]
12. Gaussian noise	PSNR: $45 - 15$ dB, 5 dB
13. Salt & pepper	Noise density: $0.01 - 0.07$, 0.01[2]
14. Gamma correction	Gamma: $0.5 - 1.7$, 0.2
15. Block tampering	Block number: $1 - 7$, 1[3]

[1] Parameters for the MATLAB function *fspecial('unsharp')*.
[2] Parameters for the MATLAB function *imnoise()*.
[3] The size of a block is 1/64 of an image.

Table 2: Notations of SMLSH.

Notation	Definition
n	Hash length (bits)
x	Number of scales
s_i	Scale index ($i = 0, \cdots x-1$)
k	Initial sub-hash size (for s_0)
l	Initial number of feature segments (for s_0)

4.1 Baselines and experiment setting

We mainly use the basic LSH algorithm defined in (3) as the baseline. Specifically, the first scale is used without supervision ($l = 1, k_o = k$). Another algorithm for performance comparison is the recently proposed qoLSH [2] in symmetric mode. It is only used in Fig. 3b and Fig. 5c for Case 2 to generate 256-bit hash values, because it requires the hash length to be larger than the number of feature dimensions while we have only tested hash lengths of 64, 128, and 256 so far. The experiments investigate the relationship between the performance and typically the following factors:

- The hash size (64, 128, 256);
- The size of the bit selection pool (200%, 400%);
- The number of available feature scales (1–3);

Hypothesis testing is used for evaluating SMLSH in both scenarios. The receiver operating characteristic (ROC) curves are used for representing the performance. The two cases take $\binom{10600}{2} = 56,174,700$ and $\binom{5000}{2} = 12,497,500$ pairwise comparisons respectively. We do not use a retrieval setting because we focus on the hash performance only.

In the following, we first evaluate the effects of single scales and supervision separately, then put them together. The notations used in this work are summarized in Table 2.

4.2 Effect of single feature scales

Recall that different feature scales may have different impacts on the performance. We consider the parameter settings listed in Table 3. For the same hash length n, different $\{k, l\}$ combinations are considered. In general, longer feature vectors are likely to enable more combinations.

The ROC curves are shown in Fig. 2 for the two scenarios. Results indicate that the feature scale indeed matters. In Case 1, when the false positive rate is small, the scale can make a big difference. In Case 2, the scale effect is not as

Table 3: Parameters for different feature scales.

n	64		128			256			
k	64	32	128	64	32	256	128	64	32
l	1	2	1	2	4	1	2	4	8
x	1								

Table 4: Parameters for different hash pool sizes.

n	64			128			256		
k	64	128	256	128	256	512	256	512	1024
l	1								

obvious as in Case 1 – the performance is not very different for the same hash length, but still there is always a small difference. In Case 1, the scale effect becomes more obvious with larger hash sizes, where a smaller scale is possible. On the other hand, a fine scale is not always better than a coarse scale. For example, the performance of the first two scales is not significantly different. That implies the scale effect is more important for larger hash sizes and thus for high dimensional feature vectors.

4.3 Effect of supervised bit selection

Next, we consider the effect of supervised bit selection. For the same hash length, different hash bit pool sizes are used. Only the first scale is used. The parameters are listed in Table 4.

The ROC curves are shown in Fig. 3 for the two scenarios. The results confirm that our proposed supervision approach is effective. The performance gain is significant for both cases, and increases with the hash bit pool size. This is consistent with intuition, because a larger bit pool is likely to provide better hyperplanes. For example, with proper supervision, 128 bits can even outperform 256 bits. In addition, Fig. 3b shows that qoLSH outperforms LSH at 256 bits, but supervised LSH performs even better.

4.4 Put things together

Previously, we have observed that the performance increases with the size of the hash bit pool. In this section, we put together our two leverages, i.e., supervision based on multiple scales. The main parameters are listed in Table 5.

Figure 4 demonstrates the selection of 256 bits from four scales according to the bit reliability. The figure shows that each scale contributes a significant amount of bits. The ROC curves are shown in Fig. 5 for the two scenarios. The results show that supervision based on multiple scales can achieve even better performance. For example, "64/256,3" outperforms "64/256,1". In general, the performance increases with the number of scales, especially when there are more than two scales. It is clear for Case 2 (Fig. 5c-d), while Case 1 is worth more analysis. In Fig. 5a-b, when the number of scales increases from one to two, the ROC curves typically intersect at a certain middle point: on the left the performance is decreased and on the right the performance is increased. In other words, the true positive rate rises for high false positive rates and drops for low false positive rates. We call this phenomenon the "s-shape effect". Since the x-axis is in log-scale, although it is not very obvious in the figures, the overall performance is still increased. For the same scale number, the intersection point moves towards the right side (higher true positive rate) as we increase the hash length. When the scale number is further increased, the performance on the left region rises again and the intersection disappears.

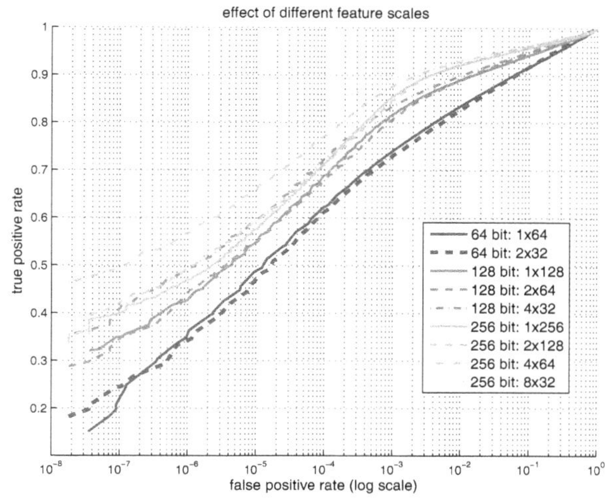

(a) Case 1, GIST

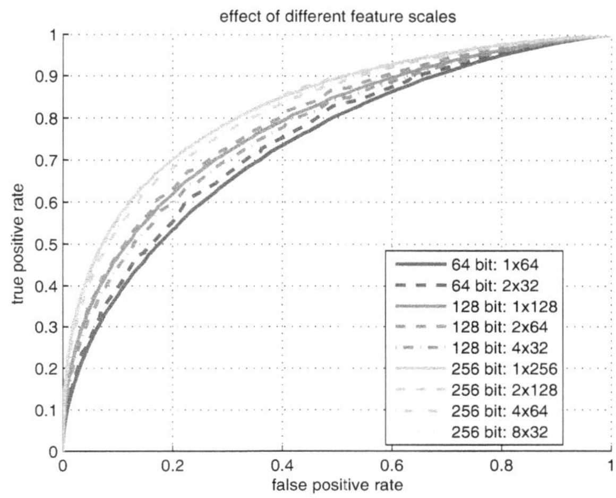

(b) Case 2, SIFT

Figure 2: The effect of different scales. "n bit: $l \times k$": feature vector divided into l parts, k bits each. Different scales influence the performance.

Note that there are also some intersections at the left ends of the curves, but we are not really interested in that region due to lack of sufficient statistics. Additionally, Fig. 4c confirms again that SMLSH outperforms qoLSH at 256 bits.

Figure 6 shows how the performance evolves with different configurations for 64 bits. It is interesting that for the same hash length the performance could vary so much. Therefore the effectiveness of SMLSH is verified.

5. DISCUSSION

Compared with other multimedia hash algorithms, the advantage of our proposal is that it improves performance through supervision, yet it is still a randomized algorithm. The complexity of the algorithm increases linearly with the hash length, which is a desirable property for large-scale multimedia data applications. The proposed concept of supervision based on multiple scales is not limited to LSH. In fact it applies to any hash algorithm that is able to generate sufficiently many bits, i.e., hyperplanes. In particular,

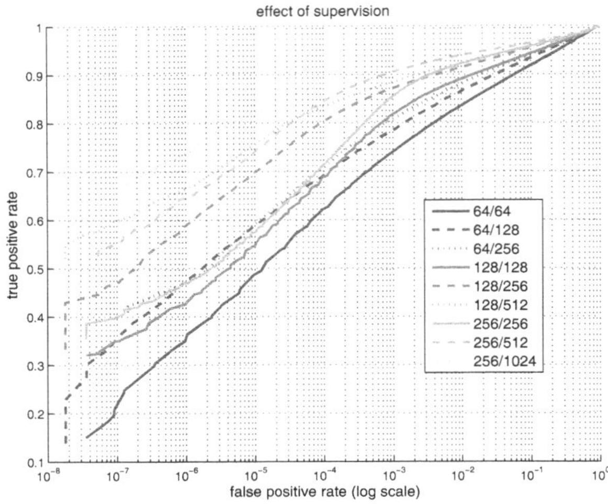

(a) Case 1, GIST

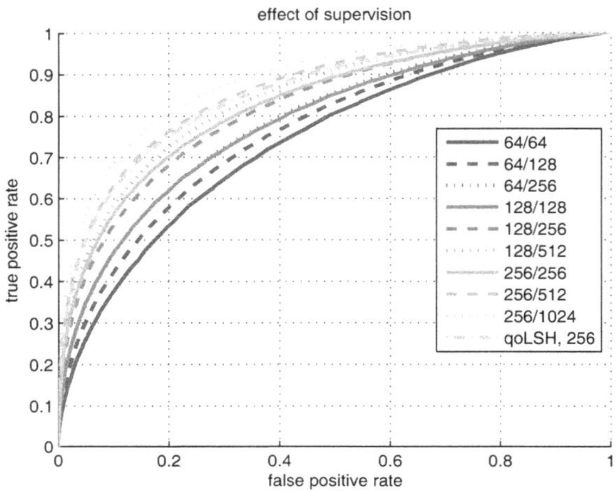

(b) Case 2, SIFT

Figure 3: The effect of supervision. "n/n_o": n bits selected from n_o bits. The performance increases with the hash bit pool size n_o. qoLSH 256 outperforms LSH 256 in (b).

SMLSH is not explicitly limited by feature dimensions, unlike e.g. qoLSH which is only effective when the hash length is larger than the number of feature dimensions.

An interesting question is what is the best number of scales for a particular application. Our experiment results show that generally it is better to have more than two scales. On the other hand, the number of scales cannot increase arbitrarily, because after a certain scale the feature is no longer meaningful and become unstable. In our near-duplicate detection example, we have observed the s-shape effect. This is essentially due to the semantic gap. Note that increasing the hash length on the same scale cannot avoid this effect, but increasing the number of scales can. From this point of view, SMLSH provides more flexible trade-offs between robustness and discrimination.

Analogous to approaches in chemistry and physics, the proposed method actually introduces a way to observe features in a *microscopic* way. We no longer look at features as a whole, no matter global or local. Instead we turn features into bits: those from large scales are like molecules, and those from small scales are like atoms; each of them carry different information, and can be utilized separately.

Table 5: Parameters for multi-scale supervision.

n	64			128			256		
k	128,256			256,512			512,1024		
l	1								
x	1	2	3	1	2	3	1	2	3

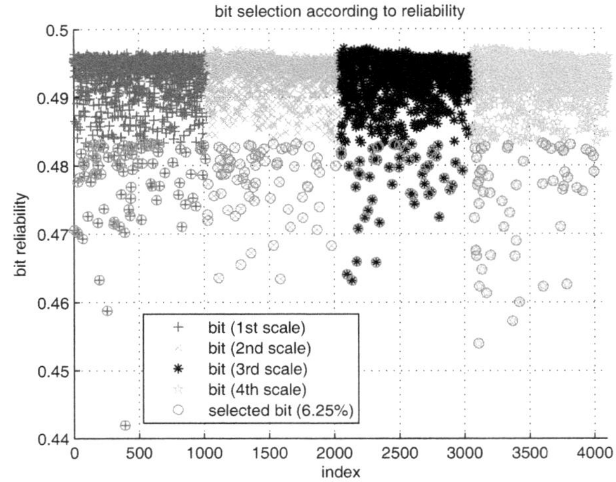

Figure 4: Bit selection from four scales. A small value means better reliability. Each scale contributes significantly.

Our method of constructing a multi-scale representation is quite simple. There are certainly other ways. For example, if some prior information about the feature is available, such as inherent structures, we may derive a better multi-scale representation. In our experiment, the GIST and SIFT features are relatively short compared with current high dimensional descriptors. With thousands of or even more feature dimensions, we conjecture that the scale effect can make significant influence on the performance.

6. CONCLUSION

In this work, we improve the classic LSH framework by incorporating two novel elements: supervised hash bit selection and multi-scale feature representation. The basic idea is to generate more bits than the target hash length, and select the best ones out of the hash bit pool. Each bit is considered as a weak binary classifier. The notion of bit reliability is used for estimating the quality of each bit, which is defined as a weighted average of the false positive rate and the false negative rate in a hypothesis test during the training stage. In addition, a feature vector is represented by multiple scales. At each scale, the feature vector is divided into segments, and each segment is independently hashed. The size of the segment is decreased gradually so that the hash bit pool corresponds to a coarse-to-fine view of the feature.

Extensive experiments have been performed based on hypothesis testing. Two applications are simulated: near-duplicate image detection and approximate feature distance estimation. We first demonstrate that the choice of feature scale indeed can make a difference in performance, which is an often neglected factor in content-based applications utilizing various sorts of features. Then we show that the proposed supervision method is effective. In particular, the performance increases with the size of the hash bit pool. This is an intuitive result because our supervision approach is asymptotically guaranteed to be effective. Finally, the two elements are combined to obtain better performance. In addition, initial results imply that SMLSH outperforms the recently proposed qoLSH in a symmetric setting.

7. REFERENCES

[1] A. Andoni and P. Indyk. Near-optimal hashing algorithms for approximate nearest neighbor in high dimensions. In *Proc. of 47th IEEE Symposium on Foundations of Computer Science (FOCS)*, pages 459–468, 2006.

[2] R. Balu, T. Furon, and H. Jégou. Beyond "project and sign" for cosine estimation with binary codes. In *Proc. of International Conference on Acoustics, Speech, and Signal Processing (ICASSP)*, pages 6884–6888, May 2014.

[3] M. S. Charikar. Similarity estimation techniques from rounding algorithms. In *Proc. of 34th ACM Symposium on Theory of Computing (STOC)*, pages 380–388, 2002.

[4] M. Datar, N. Immorlica, P. Indyk, and V. S. Mirrokni. Locality-sensitive hashing scheme based on p-stable distributions. In *Proc. of 20th Symposium on Computational Geometry (SCG)*, pages 253–262, 2004.

[5] J. Fridrich. Robust bit extraction from images. In *Proc. of IEEE International Conference on Multimedia Computing and Systems*, volume 2, pages 536–540, 1999.

[6] Y. Gong and S. Lazebnik. Iterative quantization: A procrustean approach to learning binary codes. In *Proc. of IEEE Conference on Computer Vision and Pattern Recognition (CVPR)*, pages 817–824, June 2011.

[7] J. Haitsma and T. Kalker. A highly robust audio fingerprinting system. In *Proc. of 3rd International Conference on Music Information Retrieval*, pages 107–115, October 2002.

[8] H. Jégou, M. Douze, and C. Schmid. Product quantization for nearest neighbor search. *IEEE Transactions on Pattern Analysis and Machine Intelligence*, 33(1):117–128, 2011.

[9] F. Khelifi and J. Jiang. Perceptual image hashing based on virtual watermark detection. *IEEE Transactions on Image Processing*, 19(4):981–994, April 2010.

[10] B. Kulis and K. Grauman. Kernelized locality-sensitive hashing. *IEEE Transactions on Pattern Analysis and Machine Intelligence*, 34(6):1092–1104, June 2012.

[11] F. Lefèbvre, B. Macq, and J.-D. Legat. RASH: RAdon Soft Hash algorithm. In *Proc. of 11th European Signal Processing Conference*, volume 1, pages 299–302, Toulouse, France, Sep. 2002.

[12] W. Liu, J. Wang, R. Ji, Y.-G. Jiang, and S.-F. Chang. Supervised hashing with kernels. In *Proc. of IEEE Conference on Computer Vision and Pattern Recognition (CVPR)*, pages 2074–2081, 2012.

[13] D. G. Lowe. Distinctive image features from scale-invariant keypoints. *International Journal of Computer Vision*, 60(2):91–110, Nov. 2004.

[14] A. Oliva and A. Torralba. Modeling the shape of the scene: A holistic representation of the spatial envelope. *International Journal of Computer Vision*, 42(3):145–175, May 2001.

[15] R. Salakhutdinov and G. E. Hinton. Learning a nonlinear embedding by preserving class neighbourhood structure. In *Proc. of International Conference on Artificial Intelligence and Statistics*, volume 11, pages 412–419, 2007.

[16] M. Schneider and S.-F. Chang. A robust content based digital signature for image authentication. In *Proc. of International Conference on Image Processing (ICIP)*, volume 3, pages 227–230, 1996.

[17] M. Slaney and M. Casey. Locality-sensitive hashing for finding nearest neighbors [lecture notes]. *Signal Processing Magazine, IEEE*, 25(2):128–131, 2008.

[18] W. Stallings. *Cryptography and Network Security*. Prentice Hall, 4th edition, 2005.

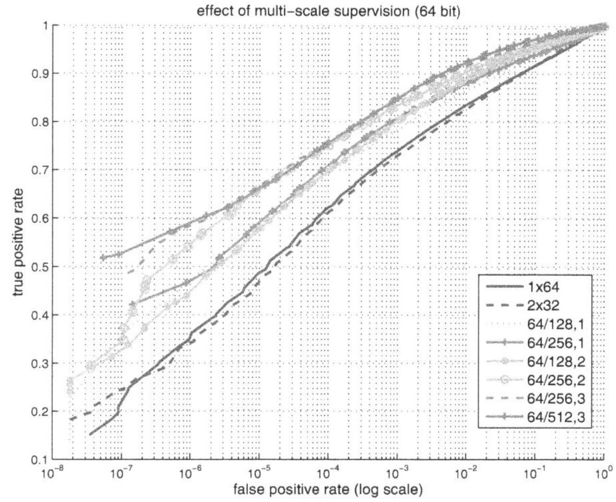

(a) Case 1, GIST

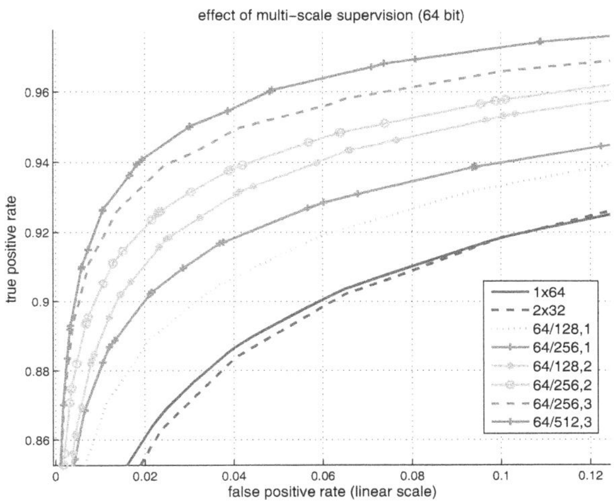

(b) Case 1, GIST, close-up

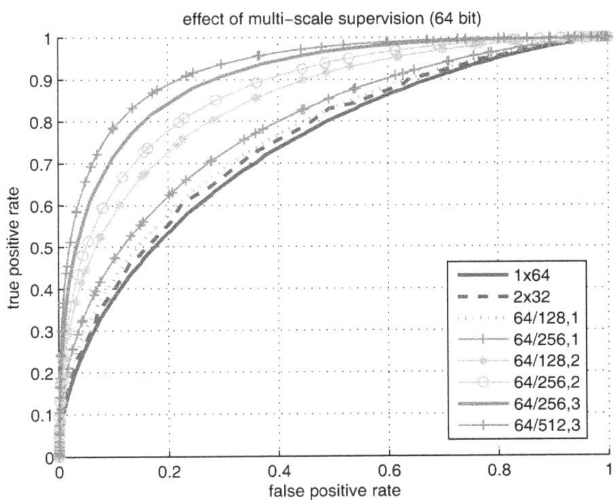

(c) Case 2, SIFT

Figure 6: Different ways to generate the same hash length (64 bits) lead to different performance. "$n/n', x$": n bits selected from $n' \cdot x$ bits in x scales.

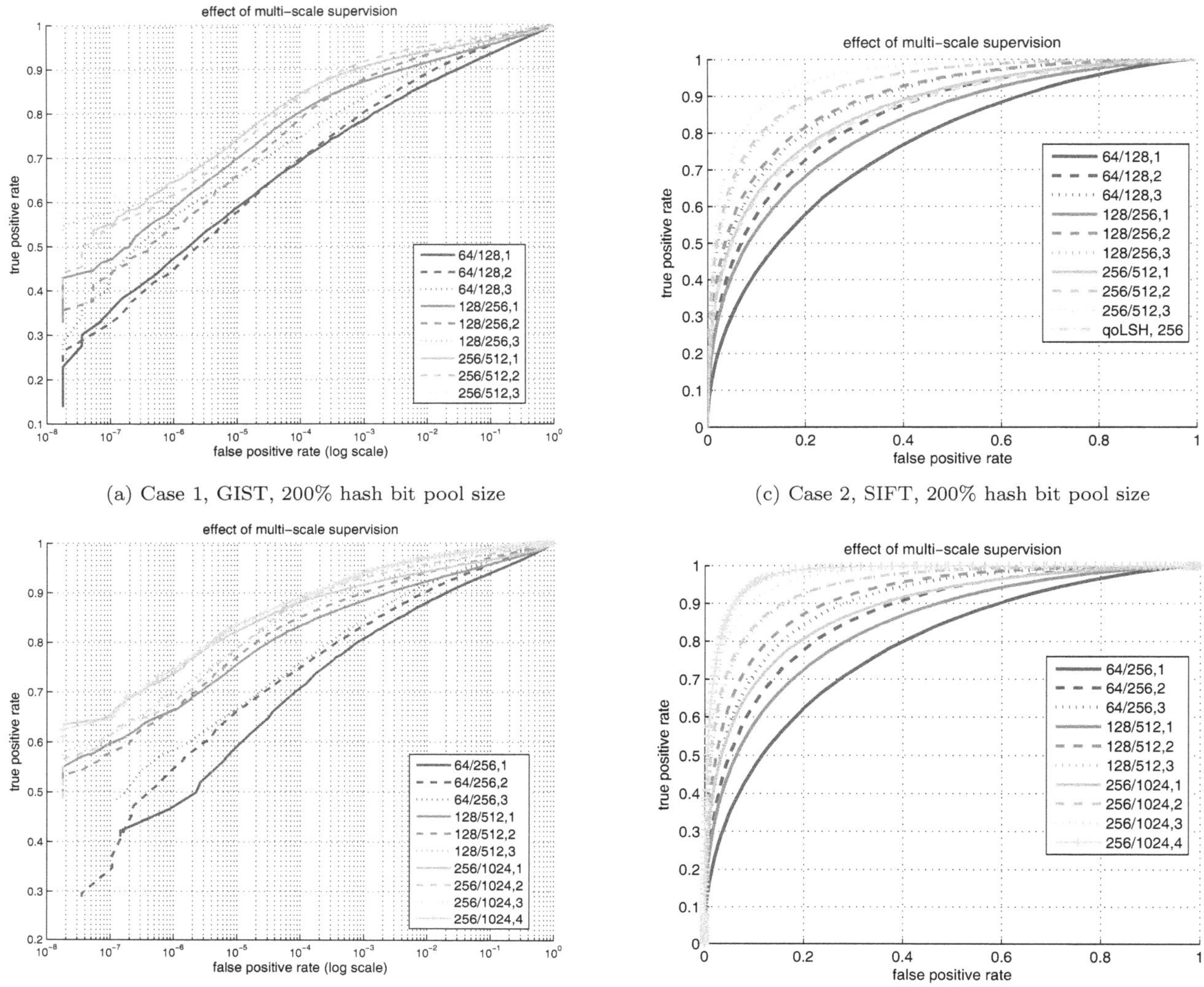

(a) Case 1, GIST, 200% hash bit pool size

(c) Case 2, SIFT, 200% hash bit pool size

(b) Case 1, GIST, 400% hash bit pool size

(d) Case 2, SIFT, 400% hash bit pool size

Figure 5: The effect of multi-scale supervision. "$n/n', x$": n bits selected from $n' \cdot x$ bits in x scales. The combined scheme can further improve the performance. SMLSH 256/512,1 outperforms qoLSH 256 in (c).

[19] C. Strecha, A. M. Bronstein, M. M. Bronstein, and P. Fua. LDAHash: Improved matching with smaller descriptors. *IEEE Transactions on Pattern Analysis and Machine Intelligence*, 34(1):66–78, 2012.

[20] A. Swaminathan, Y. Mao, and M. Wu. Robust and secure image hashing. *IEEE Transactions on Information Forensics and Security*, 1(2):215–230, June 2006.

[21] Y. Weiss, A. Torralba, and R. Fergus. Spectral hashing. In *NIPS*, pages 1753–1760, 2008.

[22] L. Weng, L. Amsaleg, A. Morton, and S. Marchand-Maillet. A privacy-preserving framework for large-scale content-based information retrieval. *IEEE Transactions on Information Forensics and Security*, 10(1):152–167, Jan. 2015.

[23] L. Weng, G. Braeckman, A. Dooms, and B. Preneel. Robust image content authentication with tamper location. In *Proc. of IEEE International Conference on Multimedia and Expo*, pages 380–385, 2012.

[24] L. Weng, R. Darazi, B. Preneel, B. Macq, and A. Dooms. Robust image content authentication using perceptual hashing and watermarking. In *Proc. of 13th Pacific-Rim Conference on Multimedia (PCM)*, volume 7674 of *LNCS*, pages 315–326, 2012.

[25] L. Weng and B. Preneel. On secure image hashing by higher-order statistics. In *Proc. of IEEE International Conference on Signal Processing and Communications*, pages 1063–1066, 2007.

[26] L. Weng and B. Preneel. Shape-based features for image hashing. In *Proc. of IEEE International Conference on Multimedia and Expo (ICME)*, pages 1074–1077, 2009.

[27] L. Weng and B. Preneel. A novel video hash algorithm. In *Proc. of ACM International Conference on Multimedia*, pages 739–742, October 2010.

[28] L. Weng and B. Preneel. A secure perceptual hash algorithm for image content authentication. In *Proc. of International Conference on Communications and Multimedia Security*, volume 7025 of *LNCS*, pages 108–121, 2011.

A Novel Visual-Region-Descriptor-based Approach to Sketch-based Image Retrieval

Cheng Jin, Zheming Wang, Tianhao Zhang, Qinen Zhu, Yuejie Zhang
School of Computer Science, Shanghai Key Laboratory, of Intelligent Information Processing
Fudan University, Shanghai 200433, China
{jc, 13210240035, 14210240058, 13210240131, yjzhang}@fudan.edu.cn

ABSTRACT

A novel *Visual-Region-Descriptor-based* approach is developed in this paper to facilitate more effective Sketch-based Image Retrieval (SBIR), which can be treated as a problem of bilateral visual mapping and modeled as an inter-related correlation distribution over visual semantic representations of sketches and images. For crossing the matching barrier between binary query sketches and full color natural images, we focus on constructing a visual pre-analysis via the sketch-like representation transformation to improve the general sketch-image resemblance, creating a special visual region descriptor to obtain better visual feature generation for sketches and images, and a dynamic sketch-image matching scheme to achieve more precise characterization of the correlations between sketches and images. Such a visual-region-descriptor-based SBIR pattern can not only enable users to present whatever they imagine in their mind on the sketch query panel but also return the most similar images to the picture in users' mind. Very positive results were obtained in our experiments using a large quantity of public data.

Categories and Subject Descriptors

H.3.3 [**Information Storage and Retrieval**]: Information Search and Retrieval – *Search Process.*

Keywords

Sketch-based image retrieval; visual region descriptor; sketch-like representation; feature generation; matching; dynamic gridding

1. INTRODUCTION

With the explosive growth of images available both online and offline, how to achieve more effective image retrieval has become an important research focus [1, 2]. However, an image user's query intention is always a little complicated, which cannot be easily formulated as an exact keyword text query or similar image query that could meet his/her real needs. In specific scenarios searching images by text or image query will return frustrating and dubious results [3, 4]. Thus a natural solution of Sketch-based Image Retrieval (SBIR) emerged as a more accurate and convenient way than the traditional text/content-based manners, which enables users to flexibly express what they want with hand-drawn strokes of imaginary pictures.

Although SBIR has been extensively studied since recent years, it still remains the necessity of optimal solutions and three inter-related issues should be addressed simultaneously: 1) in-depth visual analysis to improve the resemblance between hand-drawn sketches and natural images; 2) intermediate descriptor generation to bridge the representational gap between sketches and images; and 3) pairwise sketch-image matching optimization to identify better correspondences between sketches and images. To address the first issue, it's very important to establish a robust visual pre-analysis mechanism that can transform a natural image into a sketch-like representation more reasonably. To address the second issue, it's critical to explore an optimal descriptor that can achieve more precise and comprehensive visual feature expression for both sketches and images. To address the third issue, it's significant to develop an appropriate matching scheme with high accuracy but low cost, which can efficiently exploit correlations among visual attributes of sketches and images.

Based on these observations, a novel *Visual-Region-Descriptor-based* approach is developed in this paper to facilitate more effective SBIR. Our scheme significantly differs from other earlier work in: a) The visual pre-analysis via the sketch-like representation transformation for images is constructed based on the globalPb contour detector and edge pixel screening, in which the edge points that humans find important on the natural images are preserved to greatly improve the general sketch-image resemblance. b) The visual region descriptor is created for encoding both the local and global features in sketches and images to obtain better visual feature generation for both, in which an adaptive weighting quantization is especially proposed to quantify local features as discrete types and the global spatial location is encoded from a series of sub-regions based on a novel dynamic grid algorithm. c) A dynamic sketch-image matching scheme is designed to achieve more precise characterization of the correlations between binary query sketches and full color images, in which each sketch or image is partitioned into a series of non-equal-sized rectangular regions and a global matching kernel is particularly constructed as a weighted sum of the separate region kernels. d) A new real-time SBIR framework is built by fusing the above pre-analysis, representation and matching patterns, which not only enables users to present on the sketch query panel whatever they imagine in their mind, but also returns the most similar images to the picture in users' mind. Such a visual-region-descriptor-based SBIR pattern can be modeled as an inter-related correlation distribution over visual semantic representations of sketches and images, in which the most important is to create more effective visual feature association and measure what degree they are related. Our experiments on a large number of public data have obtained very positive results.

2. RELATED WORK

SBIR has first received attention from 1990 and arguably began to gain momentum in the mid-nineties, but little progress has been made in the past decade [5, 6]. Earlier research is typically driven by queries comprising blobs of color or predefined texture, and later augmented with shape and spectral descriptors [7, 8]. To achieve the interactive response, it is impossible to compare the

ICMR '15, June 23 - 26, 2015, Shanghai, China
 ISBN 978-1-4503-3274-3/15/06…$15.00
DOI: http://dx.doi.org/10.1145/2671188.2749302

sketch to all images in the database directly, and the irrelevant results may be produced by utilizing the simple sketch-image matching [9, 10]. Thus the increasing research interests focus on satisfying more rigid requirements on the precision and efficiency of pre-analysis, representation and matching schemes.

In recent years, the Bag-of-Visual-Word (BoVW) SBIR approach is becoming more popular than traditional content-based ones [11, 12, 13]. Referred to the Bag-of-Word (BoW) model in text retrieval, the general BoVW approach in SBIR attempts to describe an image as a set of visual words and then create a codebook of visual words [14, 15]. Cao *et al.* proposed the contour-based EdgelIndex method, in which the matching process seemed similar to the BoVW model and the matching cost between a sketch and an image was defined by the number of edge points fallen into each point's surrounding region [16]. Eitz *et al.* developed new descriptors based on the bag-of-feature approach for large-scale SBIR systems, which explored the standard HOG within a BoVW framework and computed HOG at random points in the image [17]. Hu *et al.* also described Gradient Field HOG (GF-HOG), an adapted form of the HOG descriptor suitable for SBIR, incorporated GF-HOG into a BoVW retrieval framework, and demonstrated this combination may be harnessed both for robust SBIR and localizing sketched objects within an image [18]. However, tailoring BoVW to SBIR is challenging in two aspects: a) due to having little or no color and texture information, the visual information contained in a sketch is much sparser than that in an image; and b) a sketch is usually defined by the relative spatial positions of their constituent strokes. In the general BoVW-based SBIR framework, the missing of such important visual and spatial information for sketch description may result in the huge uncertainty on the correspondence relations between binary sketches and natural images, and the performance of retrieval accuracy, efficiency and effectiveness for such methods is not very ideal. Therefore, there has been increasing research interests in gridding the image and concatenating the descriptors from each cell to form a novel descriptor with strong descriptive ability, so as to fully exploit the visual and spatial information implied in sketches and images to support more precise SBIR.

While existing descriptors in Content-based Image Retrieval (CBIR) like Color Histogram, Edge Histogram Descriptor (EHD), Histograms of Oriented Gradients (HOG), Scale-invariant Feature Transform (SIFT), and others can also be used in SBIR, there exists a huge amount of research work on finding different ways to reduce the gap between sketch and image through the chosen effective descriptors [19, 20, 21]. Manjunath *et al.* has adapted the Edge Histogram Descriptor (EHD) for SBIR, which has been proposed in the MPEG-7 standard for texture image characterization [19]. The Histograms of Oriented Gradients (HOG) descriptor for SBIR can be seen as an improved variant of the edge EHD, which collects information about the gradients in each image of the database, and is specifically designed to be independent of the sign of gradients. Chalechale *et al.* proposed a descriptor of Angular Radial Partitioning (ARP) explicitly developed for SBIR that is robust against small offsets in location and scale and designed to be rotation invariant [20]. Eitz *et al.* developed a new Tensor descriptor that is based on structure tensors to elegantly address the asymmetry between the binary user sketch on the one hand and the full color image on the other hand [17]. The descriptors like above from each cell of an image are concatenated to form a global image feature, which is effective for SBIR but involves a computationally expensive scaling optimization with the dataset size [21, 22, 23]. This implies that the advantages in speed conferred by the simplicity of image division based on such descriptors may be diluted by the limited affine invariance to changes in position, scale or orientation. Therefore, the visual-descriptor-based approaches have been adopted to alleviate the above problems, which have been proved to be successful for SBIR in more recent works.

Unfortunately, all these existing approaches have not yet provided good solutions for the following crucial issues, which are tightly coupled with each other.

(1) Improving the Sketch-Image Resemblance – Most existing methods regard an image's edge map obtained through a simple edge detection as an identical object of sketch and do not consider the obvious differences between the edge maps and hand-drawn sketches. We consider that a sketch depicts the most important part of an object from the view of humans' perception, that is, the best exhibition of object boundary. However, the general simple edge detection algorithm cannot preserve the important structural properties in an image and reduce the noisy boundary information. Meanwhile, the visual information contained in a sketch is also much sparser than that in many edge maps. This will result in a serious asymmetric between sketches and images that makes it very difficult to achieve more accurate sketch-image matching.

(2) Discovering Enough Information for Visual Feature Generation – Most existing methods focus on exploiting the regular feature description of visual exhibition in sketches/images, and do not consider the obvious differences among the features in different regions (e.g., marginal and central regions) of the same sketch/image. This will result in a serious information loss problem for local adjacent neighborhood or global spatial position, and forms the insufficient feature descriptions for sketches/images. With the deep exploration of visual appearances for sketches/images, it appears that such a discovery mechanism can mitigate the lack of local and global feature information. According to our best knowledge, no existing research has made full use of such both local and global information to achieve more accurate visual feature generation for sketches/images.

(3) Analysis and Measurement for Precise Matching in Deep Level – Most existing work concerns finding the best matches between query sketch and images underlying such a precondition that the feature quantization only need to consider the single feature itself through the simple distance computation, and the effect of surrounding neighborhood features can be ignored. Therefore, the quantized feature cannot well represent the global feature of local region that a feature is located. Meanwhile, finding the best matches is very difficult and complex, and may become a *NP*-hard problem. The simplified similarity measurement based on pure histogram distance can be used for computing the matching likelihood, but have the serious problem of missing the important spatial position information and getting stuck in a lower retrieval precision. It's a very significant way to fuse local and global feature information, set a global quantization weighting function, and form an optimal global matching scheme.

3. SKETCH-LIKE REPRESENTATION

In order to make more reasonable comparison between sketches and images, it's necessary to address the problem of the asymmetry between the hand-drawn sketch with a set of binary outlines and the natural images with color and texture information. Thus first we have to create a novel visual pre-analysis pattern to improve the sketch-image resemblance, which aims at transforming the images into the sketch-like representations through the edge map generation and edge pixel screening.

3.1 Edge Map Construction

A simple way to carry out the sketch-like representation for images is to use the edge detection. A classic *Canny* edge detector can be utilized to produce the chaotic edge image [24]. However, in the *Canny* algorithm, many edge pixels cannot provide the relevant structural information, which may introduce more noises. Thus we prefer utilizing the globalPb contour detector to detect the edge pixels in an image, because it can capture the important boundary information and combine multiple local cues into a globalization framework based on the spectral clustering [22].

First the globalized probability is calculated for each pixel in an image by the globalPb contour detector. The higher probability indicates that the pixel has the higher possibility to be a boundary point which appears in the relevant sketch. Such a globalized probability of boundary can be defined as a weighted sum of local and spectral signals, as shown in Formula (1)

$$gPb(x,y,\theta)=\sum\sum \beta_{i,s}G_{\sigma(i,s)}(x,y,\theta)+\gamma.sPb(x,y,\theta) \quad (1)$$

where s is the index scale, i denotes the index feature channel (i.e., brightness, color a, color b and texture), and $G_{i,\sigma(i,s)}(x, y, \theta)$ measures the histogram difference in the channel i between two halves of a disc with the radius $\sigma(i, s)$ centered at (x, y) and divided by a diameter at the angle θ, $sPb(x, y, \theta)$ provides the spectral component of the globalPb contour detector, $\beta_{i,s}$ and γ are two weights learned by the gradient ascent on the training images.

3.2 Edge Pixel Screening

After the above edge detection, only the important edge pixels are preserved for each image and the edge map for an image becomes more similar to its relevant sketches. However, in many cases the number of pixels in an edge map may be still more than those in the relevant sketch. To improve the general resemblance of the hand-drawn sketches and the resulting edge maps, we especially add a "*screening*" processing for the edge maps with much more pixels than their relevant sketches. Thus the pixel with the smaller probability will be discarded, as a smaller value indicates the lower possibility for the pixel to be an edge point in the relevant sketch. When some pixels have the same lower probability values, we randomly select the pixels from them to discard.

Given an edge map E and sketch S, N_E denotes the number of edge pixels in E, N_S denotes the number of none-zero pixels in S. When N_E is 20% larger than N_S, the edge map will go through the screening to reduce the pixels. The screening rules is defined as:

Rule 1: *Sort the edge pixels in descending order according to the globalized probability values.*

Rule 2: *Discard the edge pixels with the smaller values until* N_E *is no more than* 20% *of* N_S.

After that, the sketch-image resemblance can be greatly improved, which is very beneficial to the further extraction of visual features.

4. FEATURE GENERATION VIA VISUAL REGION DESCRIPTOR

Sketches are usually defined by the relative spatial positions of strokes with few or no textures, thus we need an effective feature descriptor to represent this specific visual characteristic. Existing feature descriptors for SBIR can be roughly classified as local and global descriptors. The local descriptors can be utilized to generate features using the local neighborhood information of interest points, in which the relative spatial positions between descriptors are abstracted away. The global descriptors can encode features that suffice to carry more local details surrounding an interest point. Thus a novel combined descriptor called *Visual Region Descriptor*, which integrates the advantages of local and global descriptors, is constructed to encode both the local and global feature information in sketches/images.

4.1 Encoding Local Feature

The local feature for an interest point is generated by a *local visual region descriptor*, that is, an optimized form of the HOG descriptor with the adaptive weighting quantization, in which the neighborhood information (i.e., a region with the size $r\times r$ centered at the point) is integrated to quantify features as discrete types.

All the sketches and images are pre-scaled to the same size (i.e., 256×256 in our experiment). Our interest point selection is local to the pixels comprising strokes for sketches and edge maps for images. Each image is first converted into a sketch-like representation, and then a set of HOG descriptors can be computed to represent the interest points. The HOG descriptor is computed with the size of 8×8 for a HOG cell, 2×2 cells for a block, and 9 orientation histogram bins. Such a setting is reasonable to find a balance between capturing both the large-scale spatial and small-scale detail information for SBIR. A codebook is then created by applying the k-means clustering algorithm on the HOG descriptors. Subsequently, the HOG descriptors are quantified as M discrete types based on our Adaptive Weighting Quantization (AWQ). Compared to the general quantization based on the interest point's feature itself, our AWQ is designed to quantize features by fusing the surrounding neighborhood information into the distance calculation between the feature and codeword, in which the local feature surrounding the interest point can be represented accurately and the noise interference can be minimized as possible.

Considering an interest point $IP_i(j, k)$ in the image img_i, the codebook V consists of k codewords, that is, $V=[v_1,\ldots,v_k]$, the distance between $IP_i(j, k)$ and each v_k can be computed as:

$$Dist'(IP_i(j,k),v_k)=\sum_{(j',k')\in\varphi(IP_i(j,k))}\omega(IP_i(j,k),IP_i(j',k'))*Dist(IP_i(j',k'),v_k) \quad (2)$$

where $\omega(IP_i(j, k), IP_i(j', k'))$ is a weighting function for the Euclidean distance measurement $Dist(IP_i(j', k'), v_k)$; $\phi(IP_i(j, k))$ represents a square window of size $r\times r$ centered at $IP_i(j, k)$.

An intuitive definition for $\omega(IP_i(j, k), IP_i(j', k'))$ is to set it as $1/|\phi(IP_i(j, k))|$, that is, the average distance between all the interest points in the region of square window. Although it seems an easy way to evaluate the distance, the poor distance measurement results may be acquired and affect the matching cost evaluation. The main reason is because that such an average weighted manner completely ignores the relationships between an interest point and its surrounding interest points, and not all the surrounding points have the same contributions for the distance measurement.

To formulate a more reasonable weighting function for better sketch-image matching, we make two assumptions:

Assumption 1: *The surrounding interest points with the closer distance to the central interest point should have the higher weight.*

Assumption 2: *The surrounding interest points with more similar edge gradient orientation to the central interest point should have the higher weight.*

As shown in Figure 1, the red one is the central interest point r that needs the quantization, the green part represents the region of square window $\phi(r)$, the black line denotes the image boundary, and the yellow and blue ones are the surrounding interest points y and b. It can be observed that in 1(a) both y and b are closer to the adjacent r, but y has more similar edge gradient orientation to r than b, thus y will be given the higher weight than b; in 1(b), the orientations of y and b are both similar to that of r, but b is closer to r than y, thus b will get the higher weight than y; in 1(c), b will have the higher weight than y due to its closer distance and more similar orientation to r; and in 1(d), y and b will get the almost same weights due to their nearly same distances and similar orientations to r. To simultaneously satisfy these assumptions, our adaptive weighting function is defined as:

$$\omega(IP_i(j,k),IP_i(j',k')) = \frac{1}{\rho(j,k)}\exp\left(-\frac{(IP_i(j,k)-IP_i(j',k'))}{\sigma_S^2}\right)\exp\left(-\frac{(\theta(IP_i(j,k))-\theta(IP_i(j',k')))}{\sigma_{GO}^2}\right) \quad (3)$$

where $\rho(j, k)$ is a normalization coefficient to guarantee $\sum_{IPi(j,k)\in\phi(IPi(j,k))}\omega(IP_i(j,k), IP_i(j',k'))=1$; σ_S and σ_{GO} are two preset coefficients for adjusting the difference of spatial attribute and orientation between the central point $IP_i(j, k)$ and the surrounding point $IP_i(j', k')$; and $\theta(IP_i(j, k))$ and $\theta(IP_i(j', k'))$ represent the orientations for $IP_i(j, k)$ and $IP_i(j', k')$.

(a) (b) (c) (d)

Figure 1. An instantiation of two assumptions for weighting function.

It's worth noting that with the spatial position and gradient orientation changing, the weight for the related interest point can be adjusted dynamically by fusing such significant information. Thus our mathematical model for the adaptive weighting quantization can be formalized as Formula (4), in which the local distance between each interest point and its final associated codeword can reach the minimum value.

$$\arg\min_{vw_l\in VV(j,k)} Dist'(IP(j,k),vw_l) = \arg\min_{vw_l\in VV(j,k)} \sum_{(j',k')\in\varphi(IPi(j,k))}\omega(IP_i(j,k),IP_i(j',k'))*Dist(IP_i(j',k'),vw_l) \quad (4)$$

4.2 Encoding Global Feature

The spatial location information is very important for sketches and images, especially for the sketches that are generally defined by the relative spatial positions of their constituent strokes. To effectively capture such global spatial information, the global visual region descriptor is applied to encode the global feature.

Given a certain region R with N interest points in a sketch/image, the average distance d_{mean} from each interest point p to all the other points in R is first calculated, as shown in Formula (5).

$$d_{mean} = \frac{1}{N}\sum_{i=1}^{N} dist(p,p_i),\ dist(p,p_i) = \|p-p_i\|^2 \quad (5)$$

where $\|\cdot\|$ denotes the $L2$-norm of vectors.

Secondly, each interest point q in R can be classified into a group according to the distance $dist(p, q)$, as shown in Formula (6).

$$q \in \begin{cases} group_1, & dist(p,q) \le d_{mean}/8 \\ group_2, & d_{mean}/8 < dist(p,q) \le d_{mean}/4 \\ group_3, & d_{mean}/4 < dist(p,q) \le d_{mean}/2 \\ group_4, & d_{mean}/2 < dist(p,q) \le d_{mean} \\ group_5, & d_{mean} < dist(p,q) \le 2d_{mean} \\ group_6, & 2d_{mean} < dist(p,q) \end{cases} \quad (6)$$

The above six groups reflect the distribution of relative position for the other interest points to the current interest point p. As shown in Figure 2, the red point represents the point p and the green points represent the other interest points in R.

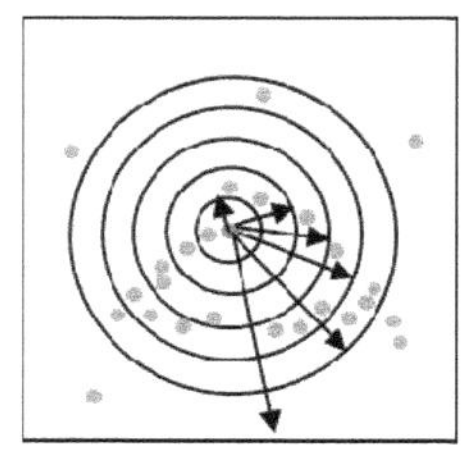

Figure 2. An instantiation of the interest point distribution in *R*.

After such a grouping mechanism, the total number N_i of interest points in each group can be calculated. The normalization is then performed through dividing each N_i by the total point number N in R. The generation proportion f_i for each group can be defined as:

$$f_i = N_i/N,\ i = 1, 2, 3, 4, 5, 6 \quad (7)$$

A binarization threshold θ, which is chosen empirically, is set to generate the following binary value feature f_i'.

$$f_i' = \begin{cases} 0, & f_i < \theta \\ 1, & f_i \ge \theta \end{cases} \quad (8)$$

Thus a compact binary string G can be acquired as follows:

$$G = "f_1, f_2, f_3, f_4, f_5, f_6" \quad (9)$$

The value of G can vary from "000000" to "111111". The binary strings are converted into the decimal numbers that vary from 0 to 63, and finally taken as the global features.

It's worth noting that the global feature with our global visual region descriptor is created in a relatively relaxed way. We do not encode the spatial layout information for all the features strictly, on the contrary, we use the proportion of interest points in a certain annulus to represent the feature spatial layout. Our strategy is established based on the fact that most people are not faithful artists, and they use shared and iconic representations of objects or make dramatic simplifications or exaggerations. This often results in sketches departing from their target object and exhibiting the variation in rotation, scale and translation within the scene. Our global visual region descriptor can be invariant to the absolute position of the sketch and tolerant against the local and global deformations, even if the users' sketches cannot exactly depict the outlines and proportions of image objects.

5. SKETCH-IMAGE MATCHING VIA DYNAMIC GRIDDING

The core part for the sketch-image matching in SBIR is the evaluation and optimization of all the possible sketch-image similarity relations. Most matching models usually remove the important information about the spatial layout of visual features and cannot capture the shape or segment an object from its background, which increases the invariance to scale, translation and deformation but severely limits the feature description ability. Thus a novel matching scheme via "*dynamic gridding*" is established to implement the optimal similarity measurement with the spatial layout information, in which the sketch/image can be dynamically gridded into a series of non-equal-sized rectangular sub-regions based on the distribution of interest points.

5.1 Dynamic Gridding

The main problem of general gridding methods is the generation of regions as there is no formal definition for an object or image and the best number of regions required for each image is not known. When the region size is too large, the discriminative power is lower. When the region size is too small, many objects may cross region boundaries and it's limited for the affine invariance to changes in the position, scale or orientation. Therefore, we develop a dynamic gridding algorithm, in which the selection of region number is generated and a sketch/image is gridded into a series of non-equal-sized rectangular sub-regions.

Assume a certain region R need to be partitioned in such cases:

Case 1: *The number of interest points in R occupies a large proportion of this region*;

Case 2: *The number of interest points in R occupies a large proportion of the total number of interest points in its parent-region.*

The following three partition rules are particularly defined to grid R into a series of sub-regions:

Rule 1: *Each sketch/image carries out the partition at least once.*

Rule 2: *Assume the depth of the sketch/image is* 0, *if we get R after the partition for k times, we define R's depth as k, in which a maximum depth d_{max} is specified for all the regions.*

Rule 3: *If R satisfies the partition condition $f(\alpha, \beta)$, R is partitioned into* 4 *sub-regions in* 2 *rows and* 2 *columns*, thus R is *called as the parent-region to its sub-regions.*

Let R^{d+1} be a sub-region of R^d (i.e., the region R with the depth d), the total number of interest points in R^d and R^{d+1} are n_1 and n_2 respectively, and the size of R^{d+1} is $m*m$, $f(\alpha, \beta)$ can be defined as:

$$f(\alpha,\beta)=\begin{cases}1, & \alpha \geq \gamma \text{ or } \beta \geq \sigma \\ 0, & others\end{cases}, \quad \alpha=\frac{n_2}{n_1}, \beta=\frac{n_2}{m \times m} \quad (10)$$

where γ and σ are two threshold parameters. If $f(\alpha, \beta)$=1, R^{d+1} is partitioned into 4 sub-regions in 2 rows and 2 columns, else R^{d+1} is not partitioned. The partition process will finish until no R^{d+1} satisfies the partition condition or the depth exceeds d_{max}. Figure 3 is an instantiation of the partition for the sample sketch/image.

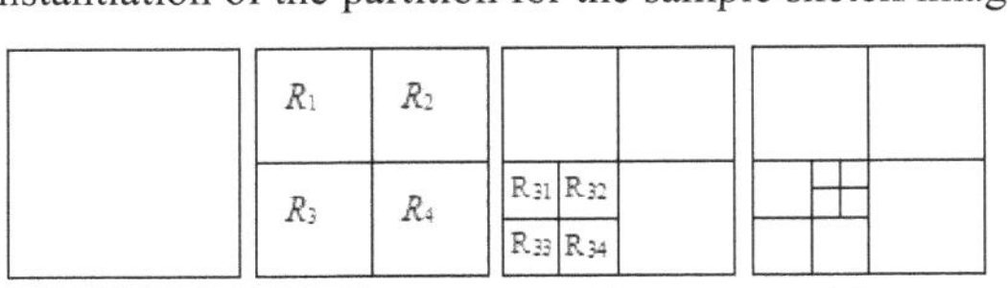

(a) (b) (c) (d)

Figure 3. An instantiation of partition.

In Figure 3, 3(a) represents a sketch/image and is partitioned into 4 regions in 2 rows and 2 columns according to *Rule* 1, i.e., 3(b). The partition condition for each region is calculated, that is, $f_1(\alpha_1, \beta_1)$ for R_1, $f_2(\alpha_2, \beta_2)$ for R_2, $f_3(\alpha_3, \beta_3)$ for R_3 and $f_4(\alpha_4, \beta_4)$ for R_4. Assume $f_3(\alpha_3, \beta_3)$=1, R_3 will be further partitioned into 4 regions according to *Rule* 3, i.e., 3(c). The partition condition for each sub-region is calculated and then the further partition continues.

5.2 Matching Scheme

Given a sketch and an image, their specific representations are first obtained based on the dynamic gridding to measure the sketch-image similarity, in which a particular *two-way-partition* strategy is applied according to the *same partition* principle. This principle can be understood that if the region R in the sketch S is partitioned, the region of the same position in the image I will also be partitioned. For example, after S is partitioned into S_{P1} according to the partition rules for the dynamic gridding, I is partitioned into I_{P1} with the same partition of S_{P1}; and then I is further partitioned into I_{P2} according to the partition rules, after that S is further partitioned into S_{P2} with the same partition of I_{P2}. Thus each sketch-image pair can be represented as S_{P1}, I_{P1}, S_{P2}, I_{P2}.

Based on the sketch/image partition, the Local Feature (LF) and Global Feature (GF) can then be calculated for each interest point in the sketch and image, and the combination (*LF*, *GF*) of such local and global features forms the final feature representation for each point, that is, (*LF*, *GF*) is used to constitute a $L_{dim} \times G_{dim}$ feature histogram H, L_{dim} is the dimension of local feature (i.e., the size of codebook), G_{dim} is the dimension of global feature (i.e., 64), and H is normalized through dividing by the sum of all bins.

Let X and Y be two sets of visual region descriptors from the same region R_i in the sketch S and image I, the depth of R_i is d_i, $H_X(R_i, d_i)$ and $H_Y(R_i, d_i)$ denote the histograms of X and Y. H_X and H_Y are compared by using the *Histogram Intersection* similarity measure to find an approximate correspondence between both. Thus the similarity between R_i in S (R_i-S) and R_i in I (R_i-I) is defined as:

$$Sim(R_i - S, R_i - I) = \sum_{LF=0}^{L\dim} \sum_{GF=0}^{G\dim} \min(H_X(R_i - S, d_i), H_Y(R_i - I, d_i)) \quad (11)$$

where $Sim(R_i\text{-}S, R_i\text{-}I)$ is a real value in the interval [0, 1]. When the same regions of R_i-S and R_i-I are similar, the $Sim(R_i\text{-}S, R_i\text{-}I)$ value will be near 1; otherwise when R_i-S and R_i-I are dissimilar, the $Sim(R_i\text{-}S, R_i\text{-}I)$ value is near 0. The S_{P1}-to-I_{P1} matching kernel can then be defined as a weighted sum of the separate region matching kernels, as show in Formula (12).

$$Sim(S_{P1}, I_{P1}) = \sum_{i=1}^{m} w_i(d_i) Sim(R_i - S, R_i - I) \quad (12)$$

where m is the number of regions in S_{P1} and I_{P1}, and $w_i(d_i)$ denotes the weight for the depth d_i, which can be defined as:

$$w_i(d_i) = 1/2^{d\max - d_i} \quad (13)$$

It can be observed that $w_i(d_i)$ is inversely proportional to the region size. Likewise, the I_{P2}-to-S_{P2} matching kernel is defined as:

$$Sim(I_{P2}, S_{P2}) = \sum_{i=1}^{n} w_i(d_i) Sim(R_i - S, R_i - I) \quad (14)$$

where n is the number of regions of S_{P2}. Thus the sketch-to-image matching kernel can be defined to measure the similarity between the query sketch and each image, and the top k similar images are returned as the final matching result, as shown in Formula (15).

$$Sim(S, I) = Sim(S_{P1}, I_{P1}) + Sim(S_{P2}, I_{P2}) \quad (15)$$

6. EXPERIMENT AND ANALYSIS

6.1 Dataset and Evaluation Metrics

To evaluate the effectiveness of our approach, we use two benchmark datasets from *Flickr*, *Flickr*15*k* created by Hu *et al.* [18] (Dataset *A*, 330 sketch queries and 14,660 images) and the dataset proposed by Eitz *et al.* [17] (Dataset *B*, 31 sketch queries, 1,240 benchmark images and 100,000 distractor images), and another dataset for a specific application scenario (Dataset *C*, 30 sketch queries, 900 target images and 100,000 distractor images).

The official criteria of Mean Average Precision (MAP) and Mean Rank Precision (MRP) are introduced to evaluate the retrieval performance. *MAP* is a benchmark indicator for information retrieval, which is computed for each query first and then averaged over the query set to produce the MAP score from the result rankings. *MRP* aims at measuring the precision of the top *k* returned relevant images, which is defined as:

$$MRP(k)=\sum_{i=1}^{N} p_i(k)/N, \quad p_i(k)=n(T)/k \tag{16}$$

where $n(T)$ is the number of returned relevant images in the top *k* returned images, and *N* is the total number of query sketches.

6.2 Experiment on Parameter Setting

To show the effect of the important parameters on the whole retrieval performance, we compare the performance rising speeds for different settings of four parameters on Dataset *B*: (i) the size of codebook; (ii) two partition threshold values (γ and σ); (iii) the global feature binarization threshold (θ); and (iv) the maximum depth of region (d_{max}), as shown in Figure 4~6 and Table 1.

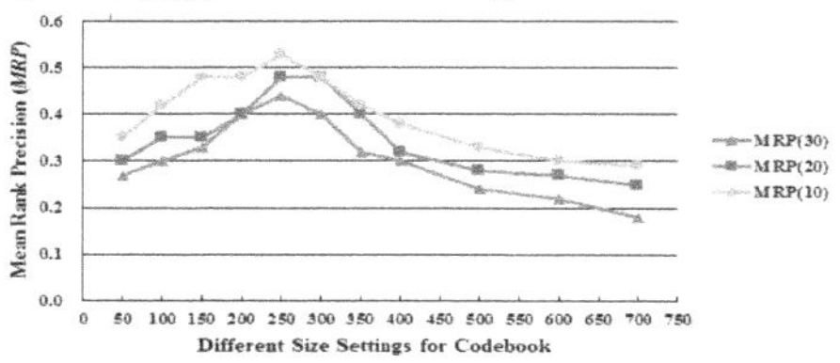

Figure 4. The *MRP* values on different size settings for codebook.

It can be observed from Figure 4 that with the codebook size increasing from 50 to 250, the *MRP*(30), *MRP*(20) and *MRP*(10) values can be improved very fast from about 0.3 to about 0.5 and reaches the highest value with the size of 250. After that, the *MRP* values begin to drop with the growth of size, and then trend to a plateau when the size is larger than 600. It can be concluded that the optimal retrieval performance can be acquired when the codebook size is set in [200, 300], and the size of 250 is the most appropriate for our framework on Dataset *B*. It's worth noting that such a setting is significantly smaller than that typically used in the example-based image retrieval. We attribute this phenomenon to two reasons: 1) the information encoded in the sketch is much sparser than those in the image; 2) we make the simplified assumption that only the features of the same type can be matched each other on sub-regions, and few features can be matched if the local feature are quantified as too many discrete types.

Table 1. The *MRP* (20) values on different settings for partition threshold γ and σ.

σ \ γ	0.1	0.15	0.2	0.25	0.3	0.35
0.1	0.3	0.4	0.4	0.4	0.4	0.3
0.2	0.4	0.4	0.4	0.4	0.4	0.3
0.3	0.3	0.3	0.3	0.2	0.2	0.1
0.4	0.3	0.3	0.2	0.2	0.1	0.1
0.5	0.2	0.2	0.2	0.1	0.1	0.1
0.6	0.2	0.2	0.2	0.1	0.1	0.0

It can be viewed from Table 1 that when σ is fixed, with γ increasing from 0.1 to 0.35, the *MRP*(20) value can be first improved to reach the highest value, and then begins to drop with the growth of γ. When γ is fixed, with σ increasing from 0.1 to 0.6, the *MRP*(20) can also be first improved to reach the highest value, and then begins to drop with the growth of σ. The best *MRP*(20) can be obtained with γ=0.2 and σ=0.2, and the other combinations such as γ=0.2, σ=0.1 and γ=0.25, σ=0.2 can also get the higher *MRP*. It's worth noting that the smaller γ and σ can achieve the better results, due to two aspects: 1) the interest points in a sketch edge map are much fewer than the non-interest points; 2) if the interest points are evenly distributed, the proportion of points in each sub-region is 25% of those in the parent-region, thus it's normal for γ of about 0.25 to achieve the better *MRP*.

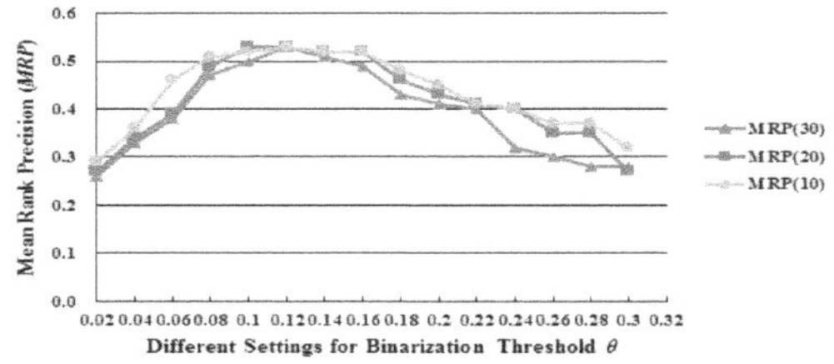

Figure 5. The *MRP* values on different settings for binarization threshold θ.

It can be found from Figure 5 that with the θ value increasing from 0.02 to 0.12, the *MRP*(30), *MRP*(20) and *MRP*(10) values can be improved very fast from below 0.3 to above 0.5 and reaches the highest value with θ=0.12. After that, the *MRP* value begins to drop with the growth of θ, and then trends to a plateau when the threshold θ is larger than 0.28. It can be concluded that the optimal retrieval performance can be acquired when θ is set in [0.1, 0.14], and θ=0.12 is the most appropriate for our framework.

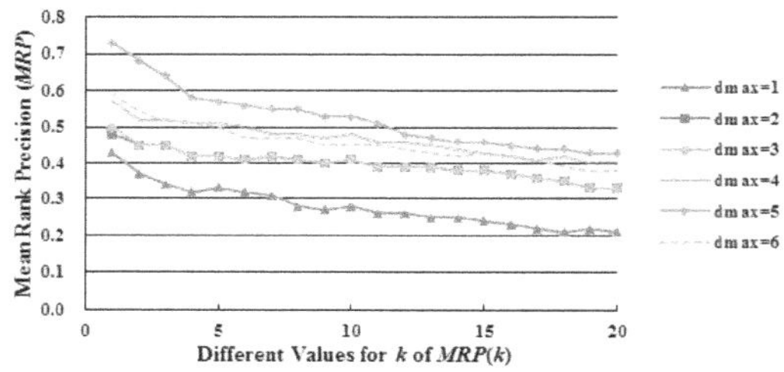

Figure 6. The *MRP* values on different settings for maximum depth d_{max}.

It can be observed from Figure 6 that with d_{max} increasing from 1 to 6, the *MRP* value can be improved very fast and reaches the highest value with the d_{max} of 5. After that, the *MRP* value begins to drop with the growth of region depth. It can be concluded that the maximum depth of 5 is the most appropriate for our framework. It's worth noting that in our experiments all the sketches and images are pre-scaled to the same size of 256×256. When the region depth is larger than 5, the region size is very small and few features can be matched in this region. If the size of sketches/images are much larger than 256×256, the most appropriate maximum depth may be larger than 5.

6.3 Experiment on Sketch-based Image Retrieval

Since there might be large intra-class variations in human drawings, it's significant to find how the sketch quality impacts the whole retrieval performance. The sketch queries are generated based on eight translated and rotated versions of each input sketch. The translated sketches are generated by translating the original sketch in a random direction according to the product of a random shift between [-0.25, 0.25] and the sketch width. The rotated sketches are generated by rotating the sketch to a random degree in the range of [-20, 20]. Thus we get 5,280 affine transformed sketches for Dataset *A*, 496 sketches for Dataset *B*, 480 sketches for Dataset *C*. Figure 7~8 shows the retrieval performance on the original datasets and the datasets with the affine transformation.

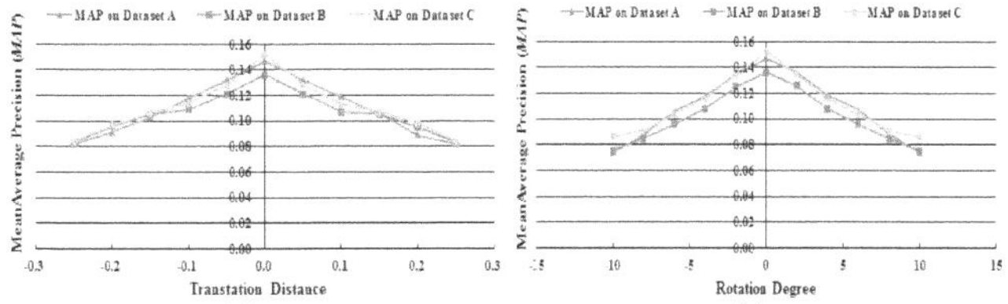

Figure 7. The experimental results on *MAP*.

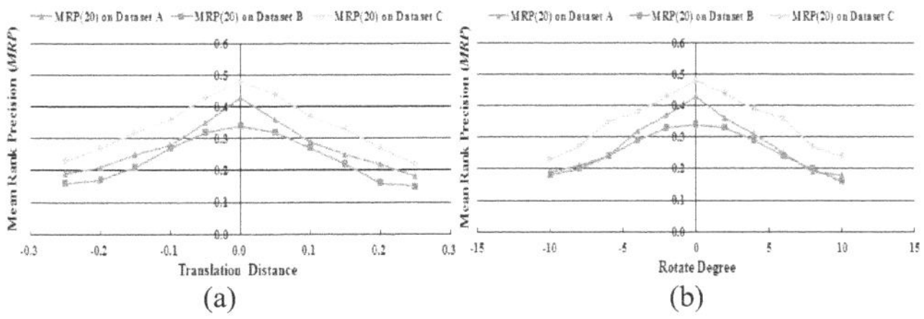

Figure 8. The experimental results on *MRP*.

It can be seen from Figure 7(a) that with the distorted sketches under different translation distance settings, the *MAP* value consistently drops from 0.147 to 0.082 on Dataset *A*, from 0.0136 to 0.083 on Dataset *B*, and from 0.152 to 0.084 on Dataset *C* as the increase of translation distance. From Figure 7(b) we can observe that with the distorted sketches under different rotation degree settings, the *MAP* value consistently drops from 0.147 to 0.074 on Dataset *A*, from 0.136 to 0.075 on Dataset *B*, and from 0.152 to 0.086 on Dataset *C* as the increase of rotation degree. As expected, the greater the affine deviation of the query sketch from the target objects is, the greater the performance degradation for the translation and rotation will be. However, when the translation distance is lower than 0.2 and the rotation degree is lower than 5, the *MAP* value is more than 0.100. Although this value is lower than the best *MAP*, it can also be regarded as the positive performance exhibition. This can be attributed to two aspects: 1) our matching scheme via dynamic gridding, in which an image is not divided into equal-sized rectangular regions; and 2) our visual-region-descriptor-based feature generation, in which the spatial layout information is not encoded for all the features strictly and very benefit for the translation invariance to some extent. From Figure 8, the same conclusions can be drawn from three different testing sets for *MRP*, which shows the obvious consistence of our model for two benchmark performance indicators on different data sources. An instantiation of some query sketches and their relevant images is shown in Figure 9.

Figure 9. An instantiation of query sketches and their relevant images.

6.4 Comparison with Existing Approaches

To give full exhibition to the superiority of our framework, we have performed a comparison between our and the other existing classical approaches in recent years. As BoVW model has been successfully used in image retrieval tasks, we have experimented a variety of local descriptors such as SIFT, HOG and GF-HOG with the BoVW model. For the SIFT and HOG descriptors we compare against a publicly available and third-party authored reference implementation, and for GF-HOG we compare against a publicly available implementation [18]. Our framework is also compared with the non-BoVW approaches that are analogous with ours to some extent, such as EHD [15, 21], Structure Tensor [15, 21], and Angular Partitioning (AP) [20]. We have accomplished all the approaches on the same datasets of Dataset *A*~*C* and the related comparison results are presented in Table 2~3, which reflect the difference of power among our and these approaches.

Table 2. The comparison results on *MAP*.

Approach	*MAP*		
	Dataset	Dataset	Dataset
BoVW-SIFT	0.091	0.096	0.094
BoVW-HOG	0.111	0.105	0.109
BoVW-GFHOG [18]	0.122	0.113	0.116
EHD [15, 21]	0.073	0.087	0.082
Tensor [15, 21]	0.076	0.092	0.086
Angular Partitioning (AP)	0.081	0.071	0.085
Our Approach	**0.147**	**0.136**	**0.152**

It can be found from Table 2 that our proposed framework can obtain the best *MAP* values on all the three datasets, in which our best performer produces the *MAP* value of 0.152 on Dataset *C*. In comparison with the *MAP* values of the other six approaches, ours can achieve the obviously better retrieval performance exhibition, which is 161.54% of BoVW-SIFT, 132.43% of BoVW-HOG, 120.49% of BoVW-GFHOG, 156.32% of EHD, 193.42% of Tensor and 181.48% of AP on Dataset *A*; 161.70% of BoVW-SIFT, 129.52% of BoVW-HOG, 120.35% of BoVW-GFHOG, 147.83% of EHD, 193.42% of Tensor and 191.55% of AP on Dataset *B*; and 161.54% of BoVW-SIFT, 139.45% of BoVW-HOG, 131.03% of BoVW-GFHOG, 185.37% of EHD, 176.74% of Tensor and 178.82% of AP on Dataset *C*. This indicates that by introducing the specific sketch-like representation for images, visual region descriptor for features and dynamic gridding for matching, our approach can improve the correlation judgement between sketches and images to a great degree and then the relatively prominent retrieval performance can be acquired.

Table 3. The comparison results on *MRP*(20).

Approach	*MRP*(20)		
	Dataset	Dataset	Dataset
BoVW-SIFT	0.21	0.18	0.22
BoVW-HOG	0.26	0.24	0.31
BoVW-GFHOG [18]	0.37	0.26	0.39
EHD [15, 21]	0.21	0.16	0.26
Tensor [15, 21]	0.23	0.17	0.31
Angular Partitioning (AP)	0.24	0.17	0.27
Our Approach	**0.43**	**0.34**	**0.48**

It can also be found from Table 3 that our framework can obtain the best *MRP*(20) values on all the three datasets, in which our best performer produces the *MRP*(20) value of 0.48 on Dataset *C*. In comparison with the other six approaches, ours can once more achieve the dramatically better retrieval performance. This does not only verify the prominent roles of our pre-analysis, representation and matching strategies once again, but also confirms that our approach is exactly a better way for determining sketch-image associations and can support SBIR more effectively.

6.5 Analysis and Discussion

Through the analysis for the error or failure in the retrieval results, it can be found that our SBIR quality is highly related to the following aspects. (1) The other edge interest points or codewords that co-occur in sketch-image pairs related to the same sketch query maybe helpful for facilitating this sketch's relevant image finding and judgement. Such a kind of edge interest point or codeword co-occurrence information can be utilized to further improve the retrieval relevance measurement. (2) At present, the social tagged image is becoming a new trend, and almost all the Web images are exhibited with the form of captioned/annotated images. Instead of only concerning the visual appearances for images, it's helpful to exploit the appropriate multimodal information involved in both image and the corresponding caption/annotation text for optimizing the correlation measurement between sketches and images. (3) It is a novel way to implement SBIR from the view of our Visual-Region-Descriptor-based framework. Although our approach has gained more satisfactory performance on large-scale image dataset, making more highly specialized considerations about the pre-analysis, representation and matching for the sketches with more complex contours and lines will be very beneficial to acquiring better solutions and efficiency for various kinds of sketches and images. (4) Some particular sketches or images present an extreme vision of vague contours and cluttered lines. With very limited useful information and too much noises, it's hard for such sketches or images to successfully implement precise SBIR. This may be a more stubborn problem in our approach.

7. CONCLUSIONS

A new framework is introduced in this paper to support more precise SBIR for large-scale images. The sketch-like representation is introduced to achieve an optimal pre-analysis for images. The visual region descriptor is particularly established for characterizing the meaningful visual information in sketches and images more precisely. The dynamic gridding is utilized to make sketch-image matching optimization more accurately and acquire more ideal retrieval effectiveness. Thus a novel model is developed by integrating pre-analysis, feature generation and dynamic matching to effectively exploit correlations between sketches and images. We have made our Visual-Region-Descriptor-based SBIR system online for Dataset *C* (*http://omap.fudan.edu.cn/sketch_based_image_retrieval*), so that more Internet users can benefit from our research. Our future work will focus on setting up a specialized learning mechanism to implement the in-depth analysis and mining for real sketches, except the existing and further efforts for natural images.

8. ACKNOWLEDGMENTS

This work is supported by National Science & Technology Pillar Program of China (2012BAH59F04), National Natural Science Fund of China (61170095), Shanghai Philosophy Social Sciences Planning Project of China (2014BYY009), and Zhuoxue Program of Fudan University. Yuejie Zhang is the corresponding author.

9. REFERENCES

[1] Datta, R., Joshi, D., Li, J., and Wang, J. Z. 2008. Image Retrieval: Ideas, Influences, and Trends of the New Age. *ACM Computing Survey*, 40(2): 5:1-5:60.

[2] Cao, Y., Wang, H., Wang, C. H., Li, Z. W., Zhang, L. Q., and Zhang, L. 2010. MindFinder: Interactive Sketch-based Image Search on Millions of Images. *In Proceedings of MM2010*, 1605-1608.

[3] Furuya, T., and Ohbuchi, R. 2014. Visual Saliency Weighting and Cross-Domain Manifold Ranking for Sketch-based Image Retrieval. In *Proceedings of MMM2014*, 37-49.

[4] Sun, X. H., Wang, C. H., Xu, C., and Zhang, L. 2013. Indexing Billions of Images for Sketch-based Retrieval. In *Proceedings of MM2013*, 233-242.

[5] Lowe, D. G. 1999. Object Recognition from Local Scale-invariant Features. In *Proceedings of ICCV1999*, 1150-1157.

[6] Zhang, J., Marszalek, M., Lazebnik, S., and Schmid, C. 2007. Local Features and Kernels for Classification of Texture and Object Categories: An In-depth Study. International Journal of Computer Vision, 73(2): 213-238.

[7] Belongie, S., Malik, J., and Puzicha, J. 2002. Shape Matching and Object Recognition Using Shape Contexts. *IEEE Transactions on Pattern Analysis and Machine Intelligence*, 24(4): 509-522.

[8] Dalal, N., and Triggs, B. 2005. Histograms of Oriented Gradients for Human Detection. In *Proceedings of CVPR2005*, 886-893.

[9] Namboodiri, A., and Jain, A. 2004. Retrieval of On-line Hand-drawn Sketches. In *Proceedings of ICPR 2004*, 2: 642-645.

[10] Bozas, K., and Izquierdo, E. 2012. Large Scale Sketch based Image Retrieval Using Patch Hashing. In *Proceedings of ISVC2012*, 210-219.

[11] Lazebnik, S., Schmid, C., and Ponce, J. 2006. Beyond Bags of Features: Spatial Pyramid Matching for Recognizing Natural Scene Categories. In *Proceedings of CVPR2006*, 2: 2169-2178.

[12] Springmann, M., and Al Kabary, I., Schuldt, H. 2010. Image Retrieval at Memory's Edge: Known Image Search based on User-Drawn Sketches. In *Proceedings of CIKM2010*, 1465-1468.

[13] Chatbri, H., and Kameyama, K. 2012. Towards Making Thinning Algorithms Robust Against Noise in Sketch Images. In *Proceedings of ICPR2012*, 3030-3033.

[14] Davis, R. 2007. Magic Paper: Sketch-Understanding Research. *IEEE Computer*, 40(9): 34-41.

[15] Eitz, M., Hays, J., and Alexa M. 2012. How Do Humans Sketch Objects. In *Proceedings of SIGGRAPH2012*.

[16] Cao, Y., Wang, C. H., Zhang, L. Q., and Zhang, L. 2011. Edgel Index for Large-Scale Sketch-based Image Search. 2011. In *Proceedings of CVPR2011*, 761-768.

[17] Eitz, M., Hildebrand, K., Boubekeur, T., and Alexa, M. Sketch-based Image Retrieval: Benchmark and Bag-of- Features Descriptors. 2011. *IEEE Transactions on Visualization and Computer Graphics*, 17(11): 1624-1636.

[18] Hu, R., and Collomossea, J. 2013. A Performance Evaluation of Gradient Field HOG Descriptor for Sketch based Image Retrieval. *Computer Vision and Image Understanding*, 117(7): 790-806.

[19] Manjunath, B. S., Ohm J. R., Vasudevan, V. V., and Yamada, A. 2001. Color and Texture Descriptors. *IEEE Transactions on Circuits and Systems for Video Technology*, 11(6): 703-715.

[20] Chalechale, A., Naghdy, G., and Mertins, A. 2005. Sketch-based Image Matching Using Angular Partitioning. *IEEE Transactions on System Man Cybernetics*, Part A, 35(1): 28-41.

[21] Eitz, M., Hildebrand, K., Boubekeur, T., and Alexa, M. 2009. A Descriptor for Large Scale Image Retrieval based on Sketched Feature Lines. In *Proceedings of SBIM2009*, 29-38.

[22] Arbelaez, P., Maire, M., Fowlkes, C., and Malik, J. 2011. Contour Detection and Hierarchical Image Segmentation. *IEEE Pattern Analysis and Machine Intelligence*, 33(5): 898-916.

[23] Jose, M. S., and Benjamin, B. 2013. Sketch-based Image Retrieval Using Keyshapes. *Multimedia Tools and Applications*, 73(3): 2033-2062.

[24] Canny, J. 1986. A Computational Approach to Edge Detection. *IEEE Transaction Pattern Analysis and Machine Intelligence*, 8(6):679-698.

Location Prediction of Social Images via Generative Model

Xiaoming Zhang[1], Zhoujun Li[1], Senzhang Wang[1], Yang Yang[1], Xueqiang Lv[2]
[1]School of Computer Science and Engineering, Beihang University, China
[2]Beijing Key Laboratory of Internet Culture and Digital Dissemination Research, China
{yolixs, lizj, szwang, yangyangfuture }@buaa.edu.cn ; lxq@bistu.edu.cn

ABSTRACT
The vast amount of geo-tagged social images has attracted great attention in research of predicting location using the plentiful content of images, such as visual content and textual description. Most of the existing researches use the text-based or vision-based method to predict location. There still exists a problem: how to effectively exploit the correlation between different types of content as well as their geographical distributions for location prediction. In this paper, we propose to predict image location by learning the latent relation between geographical location and multiple types of image content. In particularly, we propose a geographical topic model GTMI (geographical topic model of social image) to integrate multiple types of image content as well as the geographical distributions, In GTMI, image topic is modeled on both text vocabulary and visual feature. Each region has its own distribution over topics and hence has its own language model and vision pattern. The location of a new image is estimated based on the joint probability of image content and similarity measure on topic distribution between images. Experiment results demonstrate the performance of location prediction based on GTMI.

Categories and Subject Descriptors
H.3.1 [**Information storage and retrieval**]: Content Analysis and Indexing. H.2.8 [**Database management**]: Data mining.

General Terms
Algorithms, Measurement, Experimentation.

Keywords
Image topic; Location prediction; Geographical topic; Topic model

1. INTRODUCTION
With the rapid development of Web 2.0 and GPS-equipped mobile terminals, geo-tagged social media data are tremendously increasing. These location-based social network (LBSN) services, such as Flick and Google Latitude, not only allow users to maintain cyber links with other users, but also enable users to share their activities happening at certain locations in various forms. Usually, users associate their documents in social network with a geographic record which is mainly denoted by a two dimensional vector, i.e., latitude and longitude. Nowadays, Flickr hosts more than 100 million images associated with textual descriptions (e.g., titles, comments, and tags), visual contents, and GPS records. This large amount of geo-tagged social images presents various popularities across different geographical regions. That is, the language models and vision patterns of social images relate to their locations. For example, images about New York City might cover entirely different events compared to those about Beijing. The preference of tag words and visual contents are different for the two cities. On the other side, there are also many social images remained untagged. These characteristics make it possible to learn a reasonable model to identify the relation between location and distribution of image content including textual description and visual content, which is important for predicting the location of a untagged image.

Recently, many approaches have been proposed to estimate the geographic location of social image [1, 2, 4, 6, 22]. These approaches can be categorized into two classes. The first class of approaches is vision-based, which estimates the location of new image based on the locations of visually similar images [1, 11, 22]. However, due to the large variety of visual content and semantic gap problem [23, 24], exploiting visual content only is challenging. Another class of approaches is text-based, which exploits the relation between text description and location to predict where the image was taken [3, 16]. These approaches perform better than vision-based approaches, since the text words are more effective in conveying the location information. Besides, some location-specific tags (e.g., Summer Palace and Forbidden City) are helpful to disambiguate some visually similar images. However, these approaches mainly employ a pure language model, and thus they are ineffective to process social images with rich visual contents. Unlike textual document, geo-tagged social image contains multiple types of contents, i.e., textual description, visual contents, and geographical information. Each location has its own characteristic of both language model and vision pattern, and different types of content are also correlated with each other. These contents should be incorporated simultaneously in a model to identify relations between social image and location. Although there are some works on using different content for landmark prediction and representation, these works unite different types of feature linearly. There still exists an challenge: how to learn the latent correlation between visual content and text content for each location and in turn estimate the location based on the latent correlation.

To address this problem, we propose a geographical topic model of social image (GTMI), by simultaneously incorporating geographical information, textual description and visual contents. To combine the different data modalities of text content and visual content, we propose a common structure shared by both domains, i.e., image topic. Each topic is modeled as a distribution on both text words and visual features. GTMI could identify different

ICMR'15, June 23-26, 2015, Shanghai, China.

http://dx.doi.org/10.1145/2671188.2749308

topic patterns across regions, where the geographical characteristics of languages and visual contents are integrated by topics consistently. That is, each region has its own topic distribution, and hence has its own language models and vision patterns. A generative procedure is employed to model the production of text content and visual content, i.e., image patches that comprise of the pixels that are spatially coherent, based on location information. The location of a new image can be predicted by a two-step method. First, the region which has the greatest joint probabilities of the query image's content is selected. Then, the location is estimated by propagating the locations from the most similar images in this region to the query image, and the influences of these similar images are determined by their weights. Experimental results show that our GTMI outperforms non-trivial baselines on predicting image location. Compared with existing works, our main contributions are as follows:

1. We propose a geographically generative model of image content and locations, which incorporates multiple facets of image environments in an integral fashion. A Gibbs sampling method is employed to infer the model parameters.
2. A two-stage strategy is proposed to predict image location based on GTMI, which exploits the latent topic distribution of region and image.
3. A set of experiments are conducted on a real-world social image dataset, and the experimental result shows that the proposed model outperforms several state-of-the-art models on image location prediction.

The remainder of this paper is organized as follows. In the next section, we introduce related works. We describe our model in Section 3, and location prediction based on GTMI is introduced in Section 4. The experiments are described in section 5. Finally, the paper is concluded in section 6.

2. RELATED WORKS

The study of predicting the location at which an image was taken has drawn much research attention from the computer vision and data mining community. Most of the studies addressing this task fall into two categories: text-based prediction, which predict the location based on the text content associated with social image using language model, and vision based prediction, which propagates the locations from visually similar images to the query image.

User-contributed text tags have been used as a basis of a large range of successful geo-coordinate predication algorithms. These works exploit the geographical characteristic of language model to mine what tags are location-specific. LGTA (Latent Geographical Topic Analysis) [3] combines geographical clustering and topic modeling to identify the geographical topics of social images, as well as estimate the topic distributions in different geographical locations for topic comparison. Another work proposes a language model based on user annotations, to place the annotated Flickr images on the map [6]. The MDP-based geographical topic model (MGTM) captures dependencies between geographical regions to support the detection of text topics with complex, non-Gaussian distributed spatial structures [15]. This model is based on a multi-Dirichlet process (MDP). In [16], a two-step approach is proposed to estimate where a given image or video was taken, using only the tags that a user has assigned to it. In the first step, a language modeling approach is adopted to find the area which most likely contains the geographic location of the image. Then, a precise location is determined within the area that was found to be most plausible. Those works mainly use a pure language model to identify the link between text content and location, which neglect the relation between text content and visual features as well as their distributions over locations.

Another category of approaches are vision-based. These works predict the location of image based on the visual features of image only. The method IM2GPS first retrieves visually similar images and form clusters based on geo-coordinate information [1]. The geo-centroid of the cluster containing the most images is used as the predicted location. GVR [11] searches a set of candidate images that are visual neighbors of the query image and expands each candidate image with a geo-visual expansion set of images that are geographical neighbors of the candidate. The candidate images are ranked according to the visual similarity of their geo-visual expansion sets and the query image. Then, the locations of the top ranked candidates are propagated to the query image. There are also some vision-based approaches for landmark recognition [17] and scenes matching [18]. The performance of most of these approaches falls short of the performance of text-based approaches in the large-scale location prediction.

Besides, there are also some works using both text description and visual content to mine the link between landmark and image. For example, the content analysis (based on text tags and visual features) is combined with structural analysis (based on geospatial data) for landmark recognition [2]. Similarly, multiple types of contents, i.e., locations, tags and visual features, are used to generate diverse and representative images for landmarks in [5]. However, these approaches consider different types of feature independently, which are not effective in learning the latent relation between different types of contents. In this paper, a novel generative model integrating geographical information, textual description and visual contents with their correlation is proposed to mine the distributions of geographical language and vision patterns across different regions, by which new image locations are predicted.

3. GEOGRAPHICAL TOPIC MODEL of SOCIAL IMAGE

Geo-tagged image contains multiple types of content, i.e., visual content, textual description, and geographical information. Usually, the text content and image visual content are highly correlated [19] and they also relate to the location. We propose to identify the language models and vision patterns for each location, based on which location prediction can be developed. However, incorporating those contents simultaneously in the model to identify relations between image content and location is challenging, since the text space and visual content space have inherently different structures. To address this problem, it is necessary to apply a common structure to link them. On the other hand, this structure is also can be used to discover the geographical characteristic of each location. Thus, we propose a geographical image topic model GTMI, in which latent topic is used as the common structure and modeled on both text feature and visual feature. The geographical language models and visual content patterns are reflected by the topic distribution corresponding to the location. We accomplish this thanks to the large amount of social image data and the diversity of language and visual content variations appearing in social images. There are many factors that influence the language and visual content used in a social image taken in a particular location. For example, textual words used in an image depend on the local culture and the visual content of the image, while the visual content depend on the local view of the geographical region, e.g., famous building, nature view, and local sports activity. We will take these factors into the construction of GTMI.

The graphic representation of GTMI is shown in figure.1. In GTMI, geo-coordinates are grouped into regions, and each image belongs to a region which has its own distribution over topics. Each topic is represented by two topic-specific distributions: topic-specific word distribution and topic-specific distribution over visual features. The two topic-specific distributions are correlated with each other. The topic-specific word distribution is modeled as a multinomial distribution, and the topic-specific distribution over visual features is modeled as a normal distribution. Then, the location of a query image is predicted based on the geographical model, i.e., estimating the joint probability of its contents given a region and propagating the location from the most similar images of this region to the query image. The geographical topic model can also be used to other image application, such as image tagging, image retrieval, and image clustering and so on.

3.1 The generative procedure

Compared with the text words, visual features, e.g., color, edge, and texture, are much lower level representation on semantics. We introduce a middle-level feature for image representation. Each image is segmented into multiple patches that comprise of the pixels that are spatially coherent and perceptually similar with respect to certain appearances [20]. Then, each patch is represented by a $|f|$-dimensional visual features, e.g., Bag-of-Words (BOW) features. Therefore, each geo-tagged social image $p=\{w_p, f_p, l_p\}_{p\in \mathbf{P}}$ consists of three atoms: w_p is a vector of words extracted from its textual contents, e.g., tags, titles, comments, $f_p =(f_{p,1}, f_{p,2}, \ldots, f_{p,N_{f_p}})$ is a set of patches segmented from p, and l_p is a real-valued pair $l_p=\{la, lo\}$, representing the latitude and longitude where the image is taken. For simplicity, we assume that all the textual contents in our data are generated by a fixed vocabulary of W words, and the geographical locations are clustered into R latent regions and the topic number is K. Each topic $z\in Z$ is generated from regions instead of documents. The notations are list in Table 1.

Table 1. Notations used in the paper

Notation	Size	Description
μ^l	R^2	Mean location of a latent region
Σ^l	$R^{2\times 2}$	Covariance matrix of a latent region
μ^f	$R^{\|f\|}$	Mean visual feature of a latent topic
Σ^f	$R^{\|f\|\times\|f\|}$	Covariance matrix of a latent topic
ψ	$R\times W$	Region-specific word distribution
β	$K\times W$	Topic-specific word distribution
ξ	$R\times K$	Region-specific topic distribution
τ	$R\times 2$	Region-specific topic type distribution

The geographical distribution of each region is assumed to be normal $N(\mu_r^l, \Sigma_r^l)_{r:1\ldots R}$, where μ_r^l and Σ_r^l are the mean vector and covariance matrix of region r, respectively. Moreover, the topic-specific visual features are also assumed to follow a normal distribution, parameterized as $(\mu^f, \Sigma^f) = \{(\mu_k^f, \Sigma_k^f)\}_{k:1\ldots K}$. The words that are close in space are more likely to belong to the same region, and they are more likely to be generated by the same topics. Similarly, the visual features that are close in space are more likely to appear in the same region, and they are more likely to be clustered into the some topic. Our model GTMI has the following intuitions:

1. Words used in a social image depend on both the location and topic of the image, while the topic generating the words depends on the topic distribution of the location and has influence on the topics of visual contents of this image.
2. Visual features used in a social image depend on the semantic of this image, and therefore the topic of visual feature depend on the topics assigned to the text words corresponding to the image.
3. Topics have different distributions over different regions. Different geographical regions have different language variations and different distributions of visual patterns.

Figure. 1 depicts a graphical representation of GTMI. To generate a geo-tagged image p, the generative procedure of GTMI can be described as following:

1. Sampling a region r from the discrete distribution of region importance ε, $r \sim Discrete(\varepsilon)$.

2. Sample location l_p from normal distribution of $N(\mu_r^l, \Sigma_r^l)$.

3. To generate the visual feature of each patch $f_{p,i}$ in image p

   i: Sample topic: $z_{f_{p,i}}^p \sim Multinomial(\xi)$

   ii: Sample visual features: $f_{p,i} \mid z_{f_{p,i}}^p = k \sim N(\mu_k^f, \Sigma_k^f)$.

4. To generate every word $w_{p,i}$ in image p

   Sample a coin: $x_i \sim Bernoulli(\tau_r)$.

   If $x_i = 0$

   Sample word: $w_{p,i} \sim Multinomial(\psi_r)$.

   If $x_i = 1$

   i: Sample topic: $z_i^p \sim Multinomial(\xi)$ conditioned on image patches.

   ii: Sample word: $w_{p,i} \mid z_i^p = k \sim Multinomial(\beta_k)$.

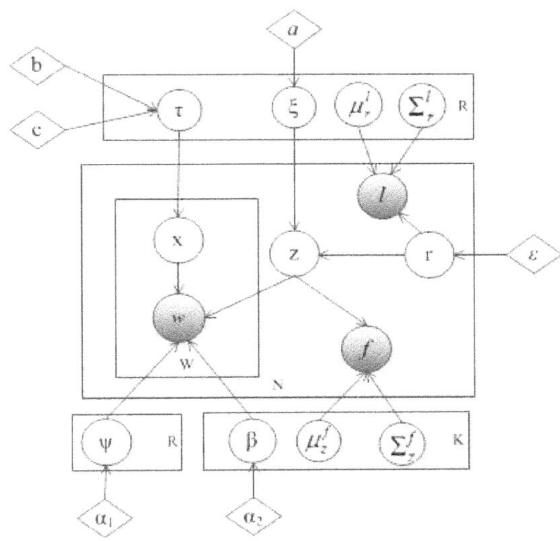

Figure. 1. A graphical representation of GTMI

3.1.1 Generation of Textual Words

Textual word describes the context or the semantic information of image's visual contents, which suggests that each word can be generated by correlating them to the collective set of topic indicators selected from the image generating region. As different regions have their own language characteristics, we adopt an additional machinery to handle special words, which are similar to the subtraction of document-specific words [9]. Beside the standard latent topic produced by standard topic model [12], we introduce a region-specific topic ψ (sampled from Dir(α_l) once for each region) to generate the region-specific words. Thus, the topics in our model consist of two types, i.e., region topic and standard latent topic which is similar to those produced by the LDA topic model [12].

The generative process for textual words now proceeds as follows. For each image p, we associate a Bernoulli distribution τ with prior parameters b and c, which models the distributions of region-specific words, and latent topic words. As shown in step 4 of the generative procedure, to generate a word $w_{p,i}$ of image p, we first sample a random variable x_i from a region-specific Bernoulli distribution τ_r, which in turn has prior parameters b and c. If x=0, the word is sampled from the region-specific topic; if x=1, a standard latent topic indicator, z_i^p, is selected according to topic distributions on the region and visual feature generation. The intuition is that, if a topic has a high co-occurrence with the region from which the image is sampled and has a high productive probability for the corresponding words and image patches, it has a high probability to be chose.

3.1.2 *Generation of Visual Features*

The visual feature of each image patch is modeled as a normal distribution whose mean and variance are topic-specific. Many works embellish the parameters of a normal distribution with an inverse Wishart prior [13], which are computationally expensive. In this paper, we take a simpler approach by placing a non-informative Jeffrey's prior over the values of the mean parameters, i.e. $\mu_z^f \sim Unif$. Meanwhile, an inverse prior over the variance is placed to penalized large variances, i.e. $P(\Sigma_z^f) \propto (\Sigma_z^f)^{-1}$ [13]. It is because that the calculation of image features might introduce noises. With such prior, the estimation of Σ_z^f for a give topic is more robust to outliers. Then, the pdf function for an image, given a topic-specific normal distribution, is revised as a function $t(f;\mu,\Sigma,n)$, which is a student t-distribution with mean μ, variance Σ, and n degree of freedom. Similarly, the pdf function $P(l_p \mid \mu_r^l, \Sigma_r^l)$ for a geographical location, given a region-specific normal distribution, is also revised as a student t-distribution function.

3.2 Inference

Under the generative process, we seek to compute the posterior probability:

$$P(\gamma, \psi_{1:R}, \beta_{1:K}, \xi_{1:R}, \mu_{1:R}^l, \Sigma_{1:R}^l, \mu_{1:K}^f, \Sigma_{1:K}^f \mid a, b, c, \alpha_{0:2}, \mathbf{w}, \mathbf{f}, \mathbf{l}) \quad (1)$$

The above posterior probability can be easily written down from the generative model. However, the posterior is intractable. We approximate it via a collapsed Gibbs Sampling procedure [7, 8], by integrating the hidden variables, e.g., the topic-mixing vectors of each region, the coin base for each region, and the topic distributions over all modalities. Therefore, the state of the sampler at each iteration contains the topic indicators for all regions. We alternate sampling each of these variables conditioned on its Markov blanket until convergence. When it converges, the expected values of all the parameters that were integrated out can be calculated. To simplify the calculation of the Gibbs sampling update equations, we keep a set of sum matrices with the form C_{xy}^{XY} to denote the number of times instance x appeared with instance y. Moreover, the subscript $-i$ is used to denote the same quantity it is added to without the contribution of item i. For example, C_{wk}^{WZ} denotes the number of times word w as sampled from latent topic k, and $C_{wk,-i}^{WZ}$ is the same as C_{wk}^{WZ} without the contribution of word w_i. The sampling procedure can be described as following:

For each image p, a latent region r is firstly drawn from the following distribution, conditioned on the old topic assignments:

$$r \mid p, \Phi \sim P(r_j \mid \varepsilon) P(l_p \mid \mu_{r_j}^l, \Sigma_{r_j}^l) P(w_p \mid r_j) P(f_p \mid r_j) \quad (2)$$

where $P(l_p \mid \mu_{r_j}^l, \Sigma_{r_j}^l)$ is the pdf function for a multivariate normal distribution corresponding to region r_j. $P(r_j \mid \varepsilon)$, μ_r and Σ_r are estimated as following:

$$\mu_{r_j}^l = \frac{1}{Num(p, r_j)} \sum_{p \in \mathbf{P}} g(r(p) = r_j) l_p \quad (3)$$

$$\Sigma_{r_j}^l = \frac{\sum_{p \in \mathbf{P}} g(r(p) = r_j)(l_p - \mu_{r_j}^l)^T (l_p - \mu_{r_j}^l)}{Num(p, r_j) - 1} \quad (4)$$

$$P(r_j \mid \varepsilon) = \frac{\sum_{p \in \mathbf{P}} g(r(p) = r_j) + \varepsilon}{|\mathbf{P}| + \varepsilon |\mathbf{R}|} \quad (5)$$

where $Num(p, r_j)$ is the number of images assigned to region r_j, and $g(r(p) = r_j)$ is a indicator function which is 1 if and only if the image p is assigned to region r_j. The component $P(w_p \mid r_j)$ is estimated as following:

$$P(w_p \mid r_j) = \prod_{w_{p,i}} P(w_{p,i} \mid r_j) = \prod_{w_{p,i}} (P(x_i = 0 \mid r_j) P(w_{p,i} \mid \psi_j) + P(x_i = 1 \mid r_j) \sum_{z \in Z} P(w_{p,i} \mid z) P(z \mid r_j)) \quad (6)$$

$$P(x = s \mid r_j) = \frac{C_{rs}^{RX} + \lambda_s(b, c)}{\sum_{x'} C_{rx'}^{RX} + b + c} \quad (7)$$

$$P(w_{p,i} \mid \psi_j) = \frac{C_{ir}^{WR} + \alpha_1}{\sum_{w'} C_{w'r}^{WR} + W\alpha_1} \quad (8)$$

$$P(w_{p,i} \mid z = k) = \frac{C_{ik}^{WZ} + \alpha_2}{\sum_{w'} C_{w'k}^{WZ} + W\alpha_2} \quad (9)$$

$$P(z = k \mid r_j) = \frac{C_{rk}^{RZ} + a}{\sum_{k'} (C_{rk'}^{RZ} + a)} \quad (10)$$

where C_{rk}^{RZ} denotes the times that topic k is assigned to the word tokens in region r, $\lambda_s(b, c)$ =b and c for s= 0 and 1 respectively, and the variable x_i act as a switch: if x_i=1, the word is generated by the standard topic production mechanism, whereas if x_i=0 the word is sampled from a region-specific multinomial. C_{rs}^{RX} counts the number of words in region r is assigned the region-specific topic (s=0), and the number of words in region r is assigned a standard latent topic (s=2) . $P(f_p \mid r_j)$is estimated as following:

$$P(f_p \mid r_j) = \prod_{f_{p,i}} \sum_{k=1}^{K} P(f_{p,i} \mid z = k) P(z{=}k \mid r_j) \tag{11}$$

where $P(f_{p,i} \mid z = k){=}P(f_{p,i} \mid \mu_k^f, \Sigma_k^f)$ is the productive probability of the visual features, the pdf of a multivariate normal distribution, μ_k^f is the sample mean of the values of image feature that are assigned to topic k, and Σ_k^f is defined similarly.

Then, we update the topic assignments for the textual words and visual features of image p conditioned on the region assignment as following:

Sample a topic for every patch $f_{p,i}$:

$$P(z = k \mid f_{p,i}, w_p) \propto \frac{C_{rk}^{RZ} + a}{\sum_{k'} (C_{rk'}^{RZ} + a)} \cdot P(f_{p,i} \mid z_{f_{p,i}} = k) \tag{12}$$

where the first part measures the comparability of joining a topic, given the region. As described above, the pdf function for a patch, given a topic-specific normal distribution, can be revised as a function $t(f; \mu, \Sigma, n)$ of a student t-distribution. Thus, the second part is calculated by:

$$P(f_{p,i} \mid z = k) \propto t(f; \hat{\mu}_k^f, \hat{\Sigma}_k^f, C_{fk,-i}^{FZ} - 1) \tag{13}$$

where $\hat{\mu}_k^f$ is the sample mean of the values of image features assigned to topic k, $\hat{\Sigma}_k^f$ is defined similarly, and C_{fk}^{FZ} is the number of times that image patches are sampled from topic k. Additionally, the pdf function $P(l_p \mid \mu_{r_j}^l, \Sigma_{r_j}^l)$ in Eq. (2) can also be calculated similarly.

Sample a topic for every word token $w_{p,i}$ in p:

$$P(x_i = 0 \mid \boldsymbol{w}, x_{-i}, z_{-i}, \alpha_1, b, c) \propto \frac{C_{r0,-i}^{RX} + b}{\sum_{x'} C_{rx',-i}^{RX} + b + c} \cdot \frac{C_{wr,-i}^{WR} + \alpha_1}{\sum_{w'} C_{w'r,-i}^{WR} + W\alpha_1} \tag{14}$$

$$P(x_i = 1, z = k \mid \boldsymbol{w}, x_{-i}, z_{-i}, a, \alpha_2, b, c) \propto \frac{C_{r2,-i}^{RX} + c}{\sum_{x'} C_{rx',-i}^{XR} + b + c} \cdot (C_{rk,-i}^{RZ} + a) \cdot Multi(f_p \mid z_i = k) \cdot \frac{C_{wk,-i}^{WZ} + \alpha_2}{\sum_{w'} C_{w'k,-i}^{WZ} + W\alpha_2} \tag{15}$$

Since the generation of visual feature is affected by text words, the topic assignment of word should consider the topic assignment of image patches. In Eq. (15), *Multi*(.) denotes how likely the topic assignment of $w_{p,i}$ matches the topic assignment of image patches, calculated as following:

$$Multi(f_p \mid z_i = k) = \prod_{j=1}^{N_{f_p}} \frac{C_{rz_i,-i}^{RZ} + a + g(z_{f_{p,j}} = k)}{\sum_{k'} C_{rk',-i}^{RZ} + a + g(z_{f_{p,j}} = k)} \tag{16}$$

where $g(z_{f_{p,j}} = k)$ is an indicator function, equal to 1 if and only if the express inside is evaluated to be true. Equation (15) indicates that the topic assignment for a word is affected by the region preference of the topic and the topic assignments of the patches of the corresponding image.

4. LOCATION PREDICTION

To predict the location for a query image, we first find the region that has the greatest joint probability of image content. In reality, a uploaded image may contains only visual content or contains both of visual content and text description. For a query image q with only visual content f_q, we selected the target region $\hat{r}$ which has the greatest joint probability as following:

$$\hat{r} = \max_r P(r \mid \varepsilon) P(f_q \mid r) = \max_r P(r \mid \varepsilon) \sum_z P(f_q \mid z) P(z \mid r) \tag{17}$$

For a query image q with both text content w_q and visual content f_q, the joint probability is revised as following:

$$\hat{r} = \max_r P(r \mid \varepsilon) P(f_q \mid r) P(w_q \mid r) \tag{18}$$

where $P(w_q \mid r)$ can be estimated with a similar formulation as (6). Then, the location of the query image can be estimated based on the locations of the images located in this region. There are two method to propagate the locations of the images in the target region to the query image. The first method uses the mean location of the selected region as the predicted location directly. This method may be sensitive to outliers. Instead of the mean location, we use the weighted locations of the most similar images in the selected region as the predicted location in the second method. That is, the location of a query image q is estimated as following:

$$l_q = \frac{\sum_{g \in N_n(q)} wei(g) \cdot l_g}{\sum_{g \in N_n(q)} wei(g)} \tag{19}$$

where $N_n(q)$ denotes the n most similar images selected from region $\hat{r}$, and $wei(g)$ is a weight which determines how strongly the result is influenced by image g. The similarity between two images is estimated by using JSD (*Jensen-Shannon-Divergence*) to measure the similarity between their two probability distributions over topics which can be obtained from the topic count matrices, i.e., $sim(q,g) = \exp(-D_{js}(P(\mathbf{z} \mid q), P(\mathbf{z} \mid g)))$. The weight is determined by the coherence of image g_i with other images. Since the n images are selected based on their similarity with the query image rather than randomly selected, many of these images should cover the same semantic with the query image and they are more coherent with each other. However, the noisy ones of the top-n images are relatively different from other images, and it is less coherent with other images. Based on this intuition, we estimate $wei(g_i)$ as following:

$$wei(g) = \frac{\sum_{y \in N_n(q)/g} sim(g, y)}{n-1} \quad (20)$$

Equation (20) indicates that, if a image is more similar to other ones of the top-n images, it is more important in determining the location of the query image.

5. EXPERIMENTS

In this section, we study the effectiveness of our approach on a real-world dataset.

5.1 Dataset

The evaluation dataset is a set of images released by the MediaEval2012 Placing Task [21]. MediaEval2012 contains geo-tagged Flickr (http://www.flickr.com/) images randomly sampled with a method that attempts to maintain coverage of the globe. Since this released dataset includes only the metadata and not the images themselves, we download the raw images using the links in the metadata. Because some images were removed after the dataset was collected, we download one million of images to evaluate the performance. We divided the dataset into 90% for training and 10% for testing. We resize all the images to the resolution of 320*240 pixels and set the maximal patch size M_l =300 [20]. For each image, we obtain about 40 to 50 patches. The SIFT feature [14] is used to represent the visual content of each patch. Specifically, we sample a number of keypoints per image, and all the SIFT features of these keypoints are clustered to create a "visual vocabulary". We set the number of clusters to be 1000, and each patch is represented by a 1000-dimensional vector. Textual words are extracted from image's tags, title, and description after filtering the stop words. Some tags contain more than one word. To avoid destroying the semantic information of these tags, we take the whole tag as a single word token.

5.2 Baselines and evaluation measure

Here, we are to study the performance of GTMI on image location prediction. Other four approaches are used as baselines in this set of experiments.

The first two approaches are text-based ones, i.e., LGTA [3] and LMSS (language model and similarity search) [16]. We realize LGTA by two steps. First, the region index which maximizes the query image likelihood is selected. Then, the mean location of the region is used as the predicted location. As for LMSS, we use the hybrid method proposed in [16].

The other two approaches are vision-based ones, i.e., IM2GPS [1] and GVR [11]. IM2GPS uses the visual feature distance to find the 130 nearest neighbors and derive the location from these geo-tagged neighbors. To estimate the location of the query image, mean-shift [10] (scale=0.00001) is used to cluster the neighbors based on the location information. Then, the mean location of the cluster which has the highest cardinality is used as the location of the query image. GVR first retrieves a set of top-K visual-neighbors as candidates. Then the candidate whose geographical neighbors that are also in the candidates set and is visually similar to the query image is selected as the target, and the location of the target image is used as the location of the query image.

In practice, image might be uploaded with or without text description. Therefore, we test the performance of location prediction for both types of query image, i.e., query image containing text content and query image without text content, respectively. The two implementations are named GTMI-TV and GTMI-V respectively. For performance evaluation, we calculate the Euclidean distance between the predicted location and real location, using the metric of average distance error (ADE) calculated as following:

$$ADE = \frac{1}{N}\sum_{i=1}^{N} dis(\hat{l}_i, l_i) \quad (21)$$

where N is the total number of query images, and $dis(\hat{l}_i, l_i)$ is the Euclidean distance between the predicted location and the true location. Moreover, the percentages of distances within different ranges are also taken for performance evaluation.

5.3 Experimental results

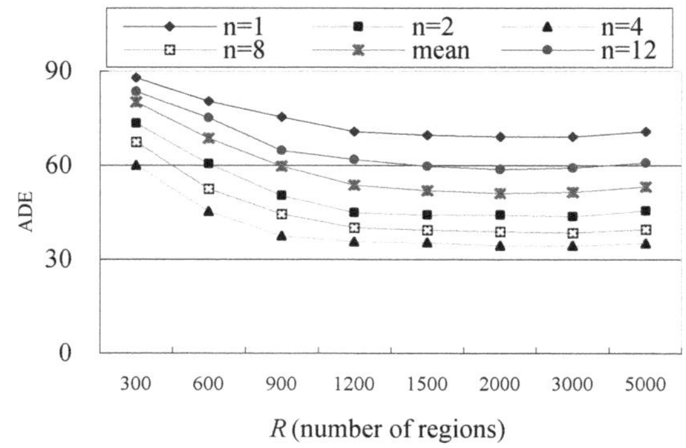

Figure 2. ADE of the query image containing both text content and visual content with different setting of *n* and *R*

There are several parameters in our approach, i.e., R-the number of regions used to cluster the training images, and K-the number of latent topics in GTMI, n-the number of most similar images selected from the target region. First, we fix the topic number to be 100 and evaluate the performance of our approach with different values of n and R. Fig. 2 and Fig. 3 show the average distance errors that are obtained for a variety of cluster sizes and number of similar images to consider, where the *mean* line denotes the performance of setting the location of the query image with the mean location of the target region. In Fig. 2, we show the performance of GTMI-TV that predict the location using both of the visual content and text content of the query image, In Fig. 3, we evaluate the performance of another implementation of our approach, i.e., GTMI-V that uses only the visual content of query image to predict its location. From these figures, we find that the performance is not always proportionate to the number of similar images to be selected. The optimal choice of n is 4 for the query image containing both visual content and text content, and 8 for the query image containing only visual content. Setting with the mean location is worse than the method propagating location from similar images to the query image except n=1. This is because that the mean location of a region is effect by the outliers. All of the performances are affected by the number of regions that are clustered. If the number is too small, the region will be too coarse, and each region will cover a great number of geo-tagged images many of that may be noisy images. These noisy images may be selected to estimate the location of the query image, and thus the performance decreases. If the number is too large, the chance of selecting a wrong region which has the greatest joint probability of the query image increases, and the time complexity also increases. Therefore, there is trade-off found in figure 2 and figure 3. It can also be concluded that combining different types of content to predict location has a better performance than using only the visual content to predict location, which is because that image text words are related to the geographical location of image greatly. Then, we conduct experiments to analyze how the performance is affected by the parameter of topic number. As LGTA is also based on a topic model, we compare GTMI-TV against LGTA with different numbers of topics and a fixed region number of 1500. As shown in Fig. 4, the average distance error does not change greatly as the number of topics varies. It might because that LGTA predict the location based on the mean vectors of latent regions. Fixing the number of regions is approximate to fixing the range of regions. Thus, a fixed number of regions would bound the prediction performance to some range. Our approach also has a dependence on the result regions. Second, it is clear that GTMI significantly outperforms LGTA. It is because that GTMI learns special words for different regions, which are helpful to discriminate different regions. Moreover, the visual features as well as their relations with textual contents are exploited in GTMI, which is complementary to geographical language model mining. As different region has its own vision patterns and great vision variety, the language model is inadequate to discriminate the geographical characteristic of different regions, which might explain why LGTA performs worse.

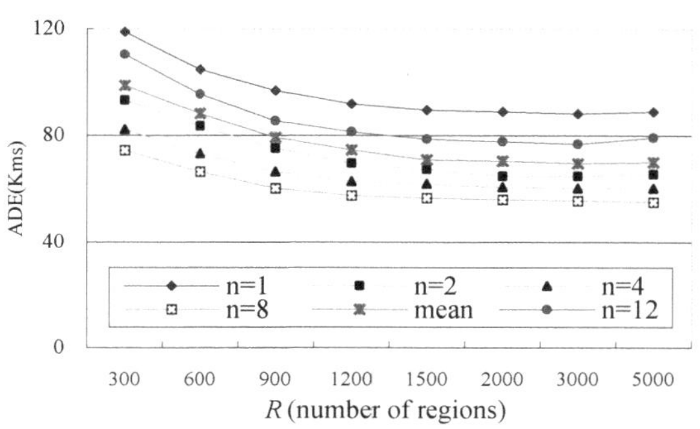

Figure 3. ADE of the query image containing only visual content with different setting of *n* and *R*

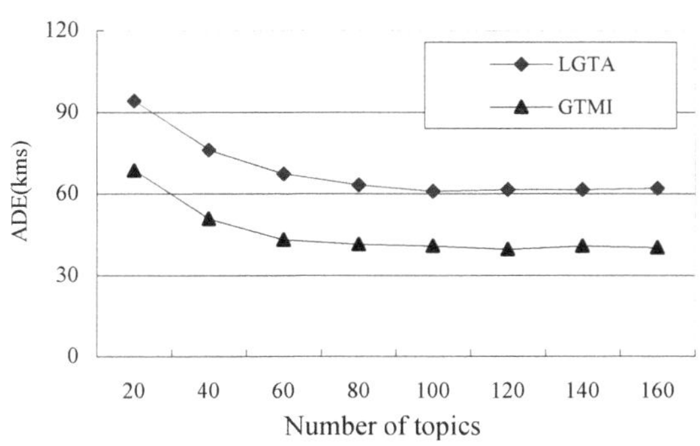

Figure. 4. Performance comparison with different number of topics

Previous experiments are used to evaluate how the performance is effected by the parameters setting. In this set of experiments, we compare our approach with other approaches by fixing n=4 (n=8 for GTMI-V), K=100, and R=1500. Fig. 5 shows the average distance error of different approaches, with the training data used in these approaches varied from 20% to 100%. It can be concluded that all the performances are affected by the volume of training data. This is might because that when the training dataset is too small, the distributions of images in many locations are very sparse, especially in the locations that are less frequently photographed. Therefore, the prediction of these locations is less effective. It is interesting to find that the text-based approaches perform better than the vision-based approaches. This is because that text content is more effective in conveying the semantic information than the visual content. The result shows that our approach GTMI-TV consistently outperforms other approaches, and GTMI-V perform better than other vision-based approaches. The performances of both IM2GPS and GVR have a high dependency on the selection of visually similar images. However, the visually similar images might be semantically dissimilar images due to the "semantic gap" problem. Thus, visually similar images could be far away from each other. Our approach GTMI-V can discover the geographical discrimination of visual feature based on its correlation with text content and geographical information in the training process. Thus, GTMI-V perform better than these visual similarity based methods, and it performs comparably against other text-based approaches LGTA and LMSS. LGTA and LMSS use the pure text model to discover the geographical language characteristic of each region based on the text content of geo-tagged images, which ignore the large variety of visual content in each geographical location. Therefore their performance is affected. Our approach GTMI-TV integrates different types of contents, using their correlations to identify the latent relation between locations and image's textual content and visual content, which is more effective in location prediction.

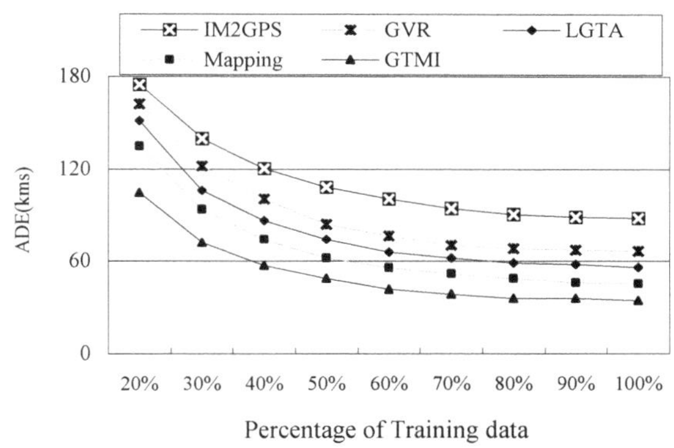

Figure. 5. Performance comparison with different percentage of training data

In fig. 6, the percentage of distance errors belonging to different ranges is used as the evaluation measure. It shows the comparison of our approaches against other approaches, with the distance error range varied from 10 Kms to 150 Kms, which indicates that GTMI-TV has the greatest percentages in the former distance ranges compared with other approaches, e.g., 1-10(Kms), 10-30(Kms). Therefore, more number of the query images are predicted by GTMI-TV more accurately, which denotes that GTMI-TV has the lowest ADE. As for GTMI-V, its percentages corresponding to the former distance ranges are greater than other vision-based approaches, and is similar to the text-based approaches. This figure also indicates that the text-based approaches are more effective than the vision-based approaches, since the text content usually is more effective in conveying the semantic information.

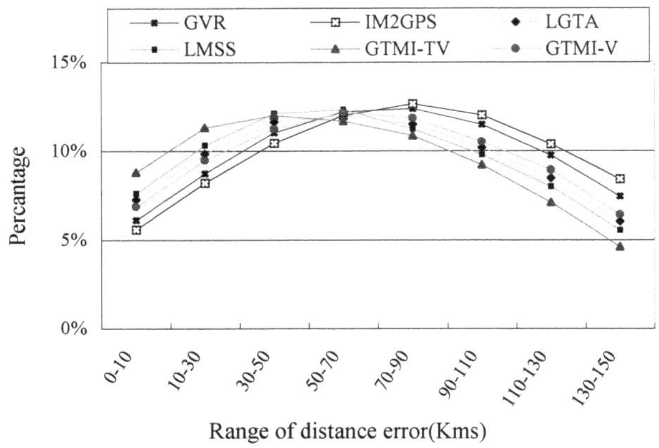

Figure. 6. Model comparison with different ranges of error

6. CONCLUSION

The emerging trend of geo-tagged social image stimulates a wide variety of novel researches and applications. In this paper, we address the problem of image location prediction by introducing a geographical topic model of social image (GTMI), which simultaneously incorporates multiple types of image contents, i.e., textual description, visual contents, and location information. GTMI introduces the topic structure to combine both text features and visual features, and the latent relation between image content and geo-location is captured by the coherence of topic distributions between image content and regions. A real-life datasets and several baselines are used for comparative studies. Experimental results show that GTMI is effective in location prediction, for new images. Specifically, GTMI is more effective in predicting location for the query image with only visual content than other vision-based approaches, and it is more effective than other text-based approaches in predicting location for the query image with both text content and visual content.

7. ACKNOWLEDGMENTS

This work was supported by the National Natural Science Foundation of China (No. 61202239, No. 61170189, and No. 60973105), the Fundamental Research Funds for the Central Universities (No. YWF-14-JSJXY-16), the Opening Project of Beijing Key Laboratory of Internet Culture and Digital Dissemination Research (NO. ICDD201403), and the Fund of the State Key Laboratory of Software Development Environment (No. SKLSDE-2015ZX-11)

8. REFERENCES

[1] J. Hays, and A. Efros. im2gps: estimating geographic information from a single image. In *CVPR*, pp. 1-8., 2008.

[2] D. Crandall, L. Backstrom, D. Huttenlocher, and J. Kleinberg. Mapping the world's photos. In *WWW*, 2009.

[3] Z. Yin, L. Cao, J. Han, C. Zhai, and T. Huang. Geographical topic discovery and comparison. In *WWW*, 2011.

[4] C. Hauff and G. Houben. Placing images on the world map: a microblog-based enrichment approach. In *SIGIR*, 2012.

[5] L. S. Kennedy, and M. Naaman. Generating diverse and representative image search results for landmarks. In *WWW*, 2008.

[6] P. Serdyukov, V. Murdock, and R. V. Zwol. Placing Flickr Photos on a Map. In *SIGIR*, 2009.

[7] H. M. Wallach. Topic modeling: beyond bag-of-words. In *ICML*, 2006.

[8] T. L. Griffiths, and M. Steyvers. Finding scientific topics. In *National Academy of Sciences of the United States of America*. pp. 5228-5235, 2004.

[9] C. Chemudugunta, P. Smyth, and M. Steyvers. Modeling general and specific aspects of documents with a probabilistic topic model. In *NIPS*, 006.

[10] D. Comaniciu, and P. Meer. Mean shift: A robust approach toward feature space analysis. In *IEEE Transactions on Pattern Analysis and Machine Intelligence*, 24(5):603–619, 2002.

[11] X.C. Li, M. Larson, and A. Hanjalic. Geo-visual ranking for location prediction of social images. In *ICMR*, 2013.

[12] D. M. Blei, A. Y. Ng, and M. I. Jordan. Latent Dirichlet allocation, *Journal of Machine Learning*, Research 3: 993-1022 (2003).

[13] A. Gelman, J. Carlin, H. Stern, and D. Rubin. Bayesian Data Analysis 2nd edition. Chapman-Hall, 2003.

[14] D. Lowe. Distinctive image features from scale-invariant keypoints, *Int. J. Computer Vision*, 60(2), 2004.

[15] C. C. Kling, J. Kunegis, S. Sizov, S. Staab. Detecting Non-Gaussian Geographical Topics in Tagged Photo Collections. In *WSDM*, 2014.

[16] O. Van Laere, S. Schockaert, and B. Dhoedt. Finding locations of Flickr resources using language models and similarity search. In *ICMR*, 2011.

[17] Y. Li, D. Crandall, and D. Huttenlocher. Landmark classification in large-scale image collections. In *ICCV*, 2009.

[18] K. Yannis et al. VIRaL: Visual image retrieval and localization. *Multimedia Tools and Applications*, 51:555-592, 2011.

[19] G.-J. Qi, C. Aggarwal, and T. Huang. Towards semantic knowledge propagation from text corpus to web images. In *WWW*, 2011.

[20] P. Felzenszwalb and D. Huttenlocher. Efficient graph-based image segmentation. *International Journal of Computer Vision*, 59(2):167–181, 2004.

[21] A. Rae and P. Kelm. Working notes for the Placing Task at MediaEval 2012. In *MediaEval 2012 Workshop*, 2012.

[22] L. Zhu, J. Shen, H. Jin, R. Zheng, L. Xie. Content-Based Visual Landmark Search via Multimodal Hypergraph Learning. To appear in *IEEE Transactions on Cybernetics*, 10.1109/TCYB.2014.2383389 , 2015.

[23] J. Shen, D. Tao, X. Li. Modality Mixture Projections for Semantic Video Event Detection. *IEEE Transactions on Circuits and Systems for Video Technology*, 18(11), 2008.

[24] A. W. M. Smeulders , M. Worring, S. Santini, A. Gupta, R. Jain, Content-Based Image Retrieval at the End of the Early Years, *IEEE Transactions on Pattern Analysis and Machine Intelligence*, 22(12), 2000.

Scalable Multimodal Search with Distributed Indexing by Sparse Hashing

André Mourão and João Magalhães
NOVA LINCS
Departamento de Informática
Faculdade de Ciências e Tecnologia
Universidade Nova de Lisboa
a.mourao@campus.fct.unl.pt, jm.magalhaes@fct.unl.pt

ABSTRACT

Multimedia search systems must deal with an increasingly large and heterogeneous amount of data. Several challenges exist when deploying real-world search engines for such data. Existing literature does not properly tackle the many efficiency issues that such task requires. In this paper, we address several of the key efficiency aspects required to deploy a distributed search engine, capable of handling several millions of multimedia documents. The search engine builds on a framework designed to: first, ease the distribution of documents and queries across cluster-nodes, second, index media efficiently for fast similarity search and third aggregate ranked results from several heterogeneous sources. Moreover, the proposed framework is flexible enough to support several state-of-the-art indexing and aggregation techniques.

At the heart of the indexing architecture lies an inverse index structure optimized for sparse hashes, that speeds up the retrieval of similar descriptors. To leverage the distributed nature of the search framework, the proposed aggregation technique offers a low temporal complexity overhead and it is agnostic to the index type (a key aspect to support simultaneous modalities). A comprehensive evaluation with both general IR metrics and efficiency metrics, provides a unique assessment of the several efficiency bottlenecks faced by a search engine. In addition, we test the scalability of the search framework to multiple index sizes, i.e., up to 5 million documents per cluster-node.

Categories and Subject Descriptors

H.3.3 [**Information Search and Retrieval**]

Keywords

Distributed search, Rank fusion, Scalable search, Sparse hashing

1. INTRODUCTION

Multimedia documents are taking an ever growing share of the web – 100 hours of video are uploaded to YouTube every minute. In addition to keyword-based search, some systems are beginning to allow novel types of queries on these large scale datasets. Google Images and TinEye allow for content-based images search on a large subset of web images. On some expert domains, such as the biomedical domain[1], search engines allow seamless multimodal (text and images) queries that leverage on multiple types of image features and state-of-the-art text retrieval indexes. Thus, multimodal search engines must support heterogeneous sources and types of documents, and provide a fast and meaningful rank aggregation to produce the final search results.

Research works that address scalability and efficiency challenges of large-scale retrieval, are largely focused in the crawling and indexing processes of the textual component of documents. Detailed information about efficiency and architectural aspects of scalable search engines supporting several types of media, is quite scarce in the literature. Thus, this paper revolves around a key question: *how to characterize scalability and efficiency aspects of a multimodal search engine capable of addressing large-scale heterogeneous documents in real-time?*

Research in large-scale text indexing and retrieval [3,6], contrasts with multimedia indexing and retrieval, mainly focused in the benchmarking algorithms individually and in single machine [14,32]. Current approaches for multimedia search have shown that it is possible to achieve good scalability as the number of dimensions increase by trading precision over speed. Hash-based techniques like LSH [4] create efficient lower dimensional representations of the original data, but require expensive searches over the hash space. We evaluate a hybrid hashing approach, based in the transformation of feature vectors onto sparse hashes embedded in a higher dimensional space but with few non-null entries. Efficient retrieval is guaranteed by the usage of a locality-aware sparse coding dictionary: at retrieval time, only the entries with common non-null values on the hash space are inspected. Thus, the search space is drastically reduced during retrieval time.

A common task across all retrieval systems supporting heterogeneous data types, is to merge several sorted lists of documents (ranks). After searching multiple indexes (one for each feature space), each returning a rank, one needs to merge the individual ranks into a single final rank. Rank aggregation techniques have been applied to solve multiple problems: combining results from multiple textual retrieval functions [10], combining the results of multimodal multifeature queries [24], federated search and expert search [20]. Our proposal is to use rank-based aggregation of multimodal ranks, as they have a low computational complexity. Also, since score normalization across modalities [23] is an unsolved challenging task, we opted for a rank-based aggregation, independent of the rank-scores.

ICMR '15 June 23 - 26, 2015, Shanghai, China
Copyright 2015 ACM ISBN 978-1-4503-3274-3/15/06 ...$15.00.
DOI: http://dx.doi.org/10.1145/2671188.2749310.

[1] http://shangrila.khresmoi.eu/

In summary, the contributions of this paper are twofold. First, we describe and evaluate all stages of a scalable distributed architecture capable of handling heterogeneous large-scale search, with minimal partitioning and aggregation overhead. Second, we compare our Sparse Approximation (SA) algorithm with other state-of-the art solutions on a large scale evaluation using datasets with millions of media documents.

2. BACKGROUND AND RELATED WORK

Distributed media search. Large-scale media search is an open research problem that has been studied from many different angles. Batko et al. [7] describe a large scale (50 million images from Flickr) distributed content-based image retrieval (CBIR) system capable of sub-second querying time. Their system includes distributed crawling, feature extraction and retrieval. Local node indexing is based on an enhanced M-tree [29] and data distribution between nodes is based on an M-Chord [26] peer-to-peer search network. Their distribution architecture is intertwined with the intra-node indexing algorithm, making it hard to generalize for alternative indexers.

The MapReduce model [11] is widely deployed to process large amounts of data on a machine cluster. It is divided into a Map procedure, the processing function to apply to data and a Reduce procedure that aggregates the results from the Map procedure. Parallel data processing is achieved by running Map and Reduce on multiple machines in parallel with disjoint data partitions. Data distribution and communication are managed by the MapReduce framework like Apache Hadoop[2]. Moise et al. [22] tested a single feature high-dimensional indexing algorithm based on Hadoop and MapReduce [11]. Mohamed et Marchand-Maillet [21] implemented a MapReduce adaptation for media retrieval. Muja and Lowe [25] recently tested several approximated nearest neighbour search algorithms (e.g. kd-tree) on a distributed setting. Their approach is based on disjoint data partitioning and a map-reduce operation where all indexes are searched and their results combined by a master server. These papers reached similar conclusion: although MapReduce can reduce the programing effort for large-scale data distribution and increase performance, there were some issues with non-trivial parameter tuning and bad data distribution temporal performance (on some experiments, slower than retrieval).

Document distribution strategies. Multimodal multifeature indexes pose a challenge to document allocation policies: *how to distribute features across cluster-nodes and how to aggregate and sort the final rank?* There are two main techniques to partition documents across cluster-nodes [9]: (i) divide documents over multiple machines (horizontal partition or sharding) or (ii) divide features over multiple machines (vertical partition). In sharding, there are two main approaches to distribute documents and queries across shards: Two-tier search process - searching a small index with a subset documents from all shards and select shards with the most results on the subset [6]; select shards probabilistically by comparing individual shard document statistics with the query statistics [3]. Vertical partitioning offers some advantages over sharding when dealing with multimodal data: support for multimodal queries requires handling vastly heterogeneous data requiring a specific index for each modality. As vertical partition always queries all cluster-nodes, it does not suffer from "vocabulary drift"; on horizontally partitioned indexes, dynamically indexed documents may become different (drift) from the ones used to create the distribution index or vocabulary, leading to sub-optimal document (or query) distribution. Performance analysis on retrieval tasks [5] argues that feature partition outperforms sharding, due to the better paralelization potential and resilience to cluster-node failure (a single document is scattered across different nodes).

High-dimensional media indexing. Scanning individual indexes is the most time consuming task on large-scale distributed retrieval systems. On individual nodes, a linear scan on a high-dimensional metric space S is not feasible, when the cardinality of S grows rapidly (*curse of dimensionality*). Recent approaches have relaxed the search process by either (i) hashing the vectors into a Hamming embedding where the metric function has very low cost, or (ii) leveraging the probabilistic density of data to reduce the search space complexity [14, 32, 33].

Locality Sensitive Hashing (LSH) [4] and other hashing functions transform the original feature space into a Hamming embedding, where each sample is represented as a binary code. Similar feature vectors are converted to the same binary code (bucket), causing a collision. Thus, nearby buckets are within a short Hamming distance. Nearest neighbour search is performed by examining similar binary codes using an hash table to find document sets with a high probability of similarity. More recent approaches [32, 33] try to leverage the latent relationships in the data to guide the construction of lower dimensional representations and data-structures to accelerate similarity queries. Techniques line Spherical Hashing [13] or Spectral Hashing [33] deliver compact (lower dimensional) representations of multimedia data and compare favorably in terms of query time with previous approaches, making linear searches over millions of documents slow but feasible.

Search space pruning techniques can also be used to improve temporal performance by searching only on the more promising subsections of the index. On [15], the inverted index is constructed with a balanced K-means that quantizes the feature space into codewords with similar priors. An alternative search space pruning technique is found on MSIDX [30]. It is based on the idea that descriptors' dimensions with higher cardinality have higher discriminative power. The algorithm multi-sorts the indexed descriptors according to their value cardinalities and, at query time, prunes the search space to descriptors with close values on the most discriminative feature values. A less researched approach for multimedia retrieval is learning sparse hash representations of the original documents. A recent work by Zhu et al. [35] departs from the dense codes and designs sparse low-dimensional (about 64 bits) binary codes for hashing. Sparse coding techniques based on overcomplete dictionaries [34] are mainly explored for image classification. Dictionaries designed in this domain [2] do not usually take into account descriptor locality nor reconstruction time constraints.

Aggregating node results. Aggregating ranks is the final step on multifeature late-fusion retrieval systems. Late-fusion methods can be divided into score-based, rank-based and voting algorithms. Fox and Shaw [28] introduced score based fusion techniques (CombSUM, CombMAX, CombMNZ and other variants), based on applying an aggregation function (e.g. average, minimum, maximum) on the scores of the individual ranks. These techniques have some shortcomings: score distribution is usually different across different indexes in the search engine and their normalization is hindered by document insertions and updates [23]. Reciprocal Rank and Reciprocal Rank Fusion [10] are the most widely known rank-fusion approaches. These techniques consider the inverse of the rank of each document in each one of the individual lists as the score. These techniques do not require normalization and are more stable to differences between heterogeneous systems. On existing studies, rank based approaches outperform score based [10] and learning to rank methods [20].

[2]http://hadoop.apache.org/

3. SPARSE HASHING

The proposed framework must be prepared to handle large scale data on each individual node. We designed an efficient search algorithm for high-dimensional data at a large scale, leveraging on the locality preserving properties of our adapted K-SVD algorithm and on sparse reconstruction algorithms. The algorithm is described in detail in [8]. In this paper, we give an overview of its design and focus its integration into the distributed retrieval framework.

Lewicki et Sejnowski [19] demonstrate that transformation of data into a sparse high-dimensional representation can achieve a high degree of compression preserving locality structure on the non-null coefficients of the sparse representation.

The transformation onto a higher dimensional space is shown on Figure 1: three feature vectors are transformed into a higher dimensional sparse document hashes using the projection dictionary. The gray elements on the hash represent the non-null reconstruction coefficients. Finding similar feature vectors in this higher dimensional space is as simple as checking which other hash share the same non-zero coefficients as the query, and rank those candidates according the original metric.

Such setup offers efficient data distribution, enabling search space pruning by inspecting only index entries (buckets) where the hash has non-null coefficients. This approach can also be easily extended to perform data distribution across multiple machines.

Mathematically, our dictionary design goals can be expressed as a sparse coding problem, as described by Lee et al. [18], using the l_0 norm:

$$\begin{aligned} &\text{argmin}_{A,X} \|B - AX\|_F^2 \\ &\text{subject to} \\ &\|X_i\|_0 \leq k \\ &\text{for } i = 0, 1, \cdots, n \end{aligned} \tag{1}$$

where A is the dictionary, B is a matrix where each column is a measurement vector, X a matrix where each column X_i is the sparse signal recovered for the measurement vector B_i, k is the sparsity threshold for each signal and n is the number of columns of X. Solving this problem for A and X simultaneously is computational hard due to the presence of the l_0 norm and the non-convexity of the problem in both A and X. In this process there are two main components: the sparsifying dictionary A that preserves locality information in high-dimensional spaces, and the sparse approximation procedure to solve Eq. 1.

3.1 Sparse Approximations

l_0 regression is fundamental for reducing dimensionality, by concentrating the energy of the original vector on a few coefficients of a higher dimensional space. The sparse reconstruction algorithm should answer two requirements: (1) be sufficiently fast to be run in query time, (2) compute highly sparse representations while preserving maximum locality. In this section we compare four candidate algorithms for our sparse reconstruction step.

The sparse approximation can be viewed as the recovery of a k-sparse signal from its measurement vector given a dictionary. A possible method is to solve the constrained l_0 minimization:

$$\begin{aligned} &\min_X \|AX - B\|_2 \\ &\text{subject to} \\ &\|X\|_0 \leq k, \end{aligned} \tag{2}$$

where $A \in \mathbb{R}^{m \times n}$ is the dictionary, $B \in \mathbb{R}^m$ the measurement

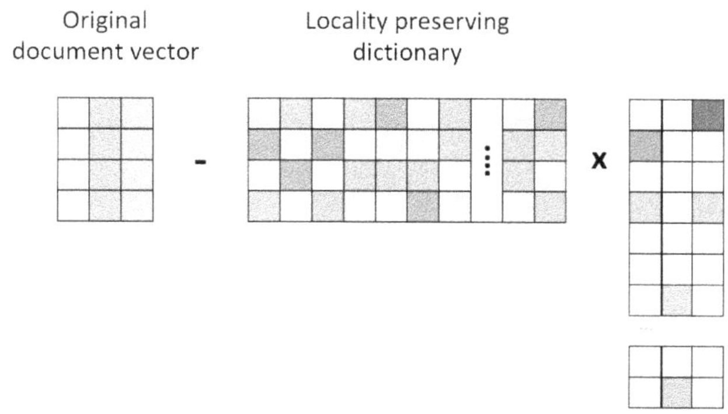

Figure 1: Sparse reconstruction process.

vector, X is the sparse hash produced and k is the sparsity factor that we wish to obtain.

To solve this problem, we tested Orthogonal Matching Pursuit (OMP) [27]. In our experiments [8], it offered the best trade-off between time, sparsity and reconstruction error, when compared with with OMP, Thresholding and l_1 regression techniques (DALM and FISTA).

3.2 Locality Preserving Dictionary

Our sparse-hashing indexing structure relies on the created dictionary to yield sparse representations that approximate the original feature vectors, as the dictionary training algorithm does not enforce constraints on the locality of the sparse coefficients. We adapted K-SVD [2] to explicitly take into account the proximity between the descriptors used to build the dictionary. The idea is to add a penalty term to the dictionary learning problem 1 that promotes similar descriptors to have similar sparse representations. The details are available at [8].

4. DISTRIBUTED INDEXING AND RETRIEVAL

4.1 Architecture Design

Our cluster architecture is based on two types of nodes: the processor and the aggregator nodes. Processor nodes index and process queries for a document's single feature space; aggregator nodes serve as the framework's entry and exit points: it routes queries to the processor nodes and aggregates results from the these nodes. Each processor node processes one type of media and it is up to the aggregator to distribute the query across nodes. Figure 2 shows the full search process. Documents are parsed by the aggregator node and split by media type (e.g. text or images). For each media type, the aggregator node makes a request to each relevant processor node and collects results. All communication between nodes is made through REST requests using an optimized format, containing a list of sorted document ids. The code for the aggregator node server and SA indexer is available online [3].

4.2 Document-to-node allocation

An important challenge for web scale search systems concerns the distribution of documents across nodes for indexing. Existing frameworks like MapReduce are optimized for horizontal partitioning, as they apply the same function to all data subsets. In multimodal search systems, this is a challenge. Different types of media (e.g.

[3]https://novasearch.org/software/

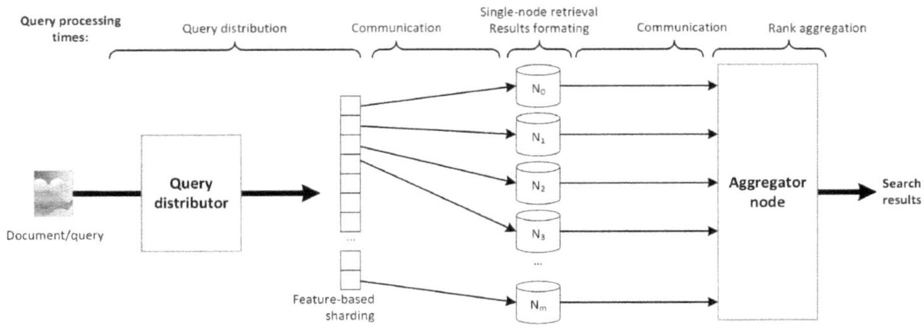

Figure 2: Architecture design.

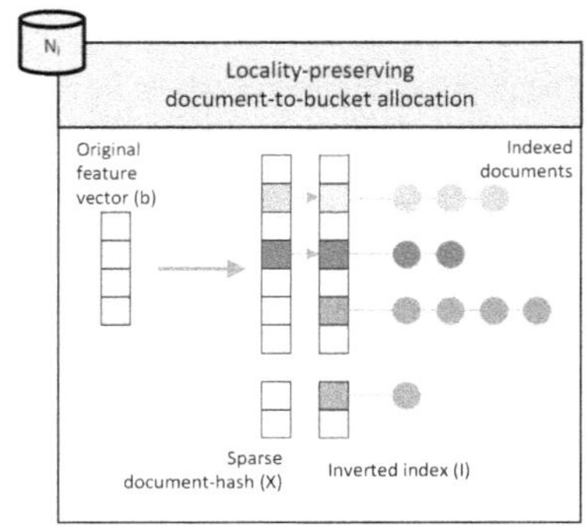

Figure 3: Single-node indexing.

text document only vs. text + images + video) require different types of processing and indexing. Another key observation is that document descriptors are independent and can be indexed separately from each other.

Our document-to-node allocation is flat by media type: each media type on each documents is processed by relevant nodes. This process is managed by the aggregator node: at indexing and query time, it partitions the query by type into subqueries and queries relevant nodes.

The full process is described in Section 4.5. This system works seamlessly on multifeature image retrieval systems, heterogeneous systems (e.g. textual retrieval + image retrieval) and multimodal retrieval systems (e.g. video retrieval system with audio, image and textual features). Such system can also deal with self-managed distributed systems running on multiple machines [17], if the single feature index does not fit into a single machine. Another key advantage of the proposed architecture is its resilience to nodes failure. In multimodal data each document is represented by many different descriptors: image search engines can easily have more that 10 descriptors [1] per image corresponding to 10 independent indexes in at least 10 processor nodes. Thus, if a node fails to respond to requests, it's results are simply ignored and the system returns the result from the remaining nodes.

4.3 Single-node indexing

Some state-of-art CBIR methods focused on how to transform descriptors into a set of codewords. Jégou et al. [14] train a K-means quantizer to transform descriptors into codewords; Ji et al. [17] use a model based on Vocabulary Trees to learn a vocabulary for distribution. Using sparse approximation techniques, one can also create a dictionary and a sparse representation that represents the importance of each dictionary word for the original descriptor. If the sparse recovery of the descriptors preserves similarity in the sparse domain, the inverted index can be used to retrieve similar descriptors for a given query, by inspecting the lists corresponding to its non-null coefficients in the sparse domain.

The construction of the Sparse Approximation inverted index is illustrated by Figure3. The indexing construction process is the following: given a set of descriptors b, we can recover their sparse solutions X with a dictionary A. This sparse representation set A determines the non-null coefficients to match descriptors to buckets of the index I. The final step is to sort each bucket by placing the descriptors with higher coefficients at the beginning. This final sort guarantees that, at query time, the most representative descriptors of each bucket are examined first.

4.4 Single-node retrieval

The framework's support for heterogeneous indexes gives individual indexes freedom to define the better individual intra-node retrieval process.

Algorithm 1 Single-node retrieval procedure

Input: a sparsifying dictionary A, an inverted index I, a set of indexed vectors B, a query vector q, the number of neighbors to retrieve k and a percentage of the index to examine w.

Output: a list of k (nearest) neighbors R.

```
limit ← w × len(b)
get sparse approximation X for query q using A
get bucket indexes O from X by descending coef.
cand ← ∅
for b in O do
    for v in b do
        add v to cand list
        if len(cand) > limit then
            break
return cand list sorted by l2 to the query
```

The SA retrieval algorithm's goal is to provide fast limited search by examining descriptors that have a collision in the buckets where the non-null coefficients of the sparse representations. It is described in Algorithm 1. When the aggregator node submits a query q, the indexer extracts the sparse representation and inspects the buckets of the index, in descending coefficient order. The search algorithm adds feature vectors to a temporary candidates on selected bucket until it reaches the desired limit. After the search stops, the descriptors in the temporary list are sorted by their distance to the query and the k closest descriptors returned to the user. It exploits the fact that the tested sparse coding algorithms (e.g. OMP) are greedy and select the most correlated atom of the dictionary first.

4.5 Distributed retrieval and aggregation

Algorithm 2 lists the full retrieval procedure: For each media type in the query, line 2, the aggregator node simultaneously queries each relevant processor node and collects the results. Each processor node extracts features (if not previously extracted), queries the index, line 5 and returns the sorted rank. In our experiments, we relied on previously extracted features, as our objective is to test indexing and retrieval, and extracting features introduces additional temporal variability across nodes. The aggregator node collects the results and aggregates individual ranks into a single final rank (line 7).

Algorithm 2 Distributed retrieval algorithm

Input: query Q, num. neighbors to retrieve k, S set of indexes grouped by type
Output: a list of k (nearest) neighbors R.

```
Rcand ← ∅
for each data type q in Q do
    for each search engine s in S with type q do        ▷ concurrent
        extract features f for q on s                    ▷ optional
        r_s ← search f on s
        add r_s to Rcand
aggregate ranks in Rcand into R
return R_{1,...,k}
```

The aggregation algorithm can be generalized as a function T that takes a set of ranks and returns a combined rank. These techniques can be either unsupervised or augmented by determining the relevance or weight of each index to a dataset using learning-to-rank approaches.

In this paper, we focus on unsupervised late-fusion techniques, as they do not require explicit relevance judgements or score normalization. We tested inverse rank approaches e.g. RRF,

$$\mathrm{RRF}(i) = \sum_{k=1}^{N(i)} \frac{1}{R_k(i) + 60} \tag{3}$$

where $R_k(i)$ is the rank of document i on the kth rank. Inverse Square Rank (ISR) [24] combines the inverse rank approach of RR and RRF with document frequency weighing:

$$\mathrm{ISR}(i) = N(i) \times \sum_{k=1}^{N(i)} \frac{1}{R_k(i)^2} \tag{4}$$

$$\mathrm{logN\_ISR}(i) = log(N(i) + \sigma) \times \sum_{k=1}^{N(i)} \frac{1}{R_k(i)^2}. \tag{5}$$

where $N(i)$ is document frequency (number of times it appears on a rank) and $\sigma \in [0, 1]$ is a variable for smoothing of documents that appear on few ranks. In this paper, it was set to 0.01 through experimental evaluation.

5. EXPERIMENTS

We run a through set of experiments on 4 large-scale datasets to test and compare our framework methods to alternative state-of-the-art solutions:

- Single node retrieval: we evaluated the retrieval performance on an individual node (Section 5.2);
- Distributed multi-feature retrieval: we evaluated the retrieval performance using multiple feature types on a distributed setting (Section 5.3);
- Multimodal image and text retrieval: we evaluated aggregation efficiency on a multimodal task, using multimodal (textual and image) documents (Section 5.4).

The datasets tested were:

- **Billion Vectors** [14,16]: contains over 1 million descriptors from two feature types: GIST (960 dimensions) and SIFT features (128 dimensions), subsequently named as BV1 and BV2 respectively. The datasets were split into a training, validation and test subsets [4]. We extracted 1000 queries per feature type from the test set.
- **Tiny Images** (TI) [31]: contains 80 million GIST descriptors (384 dimensions). We extracted multiple random subsets from the full dataset for the scalability experiment. We also extracted 1000 non-overlapping documents to use as queries.
- **ImageCLEF Medical** [12]: contains 75,000 journal articles with 300,000 images. It also includes a total of 36 (judged) queries, containing a textual case description and 2 to 6 case images each. We used all queries for evaluation.

Experiments were run on a set of five machines, all running Ubuntu 14.04: four processor nodes with an i7-3930K processor and 64GB of RAM and one aggregator node with i7-920 with 12GB of RAM. All descriptors, indexes and other structures were placed in the main memory. The indexer algorithm implementation on the processor nodes was written in C++ and the aggregator algorithm was written in Python.

5.1 Parameter tuning

The validation set of the BV1 dataset was used to assess the combination of relevant parameters that yield the best results. The first relevant parameter to be set is the number of iterations for the K-SVD dictionary learning: we chose to limit the dictionary training iterations to 25 since from this point onward the average recovery error did not vary significantly ($< 1\%$). We tested multiple bucket counts (1024, 2048, 4096 and 8192 buckets), constrained to inspect variable fractions of the index and set the bucket size to 1024, as we were able to achieve higher precision while reducing the query time. All results reported in this section used 10 OMP iterations. For larger numbers of OMP iterations, we observed residual gains. The number of KSVD learning iterations was set to 25.

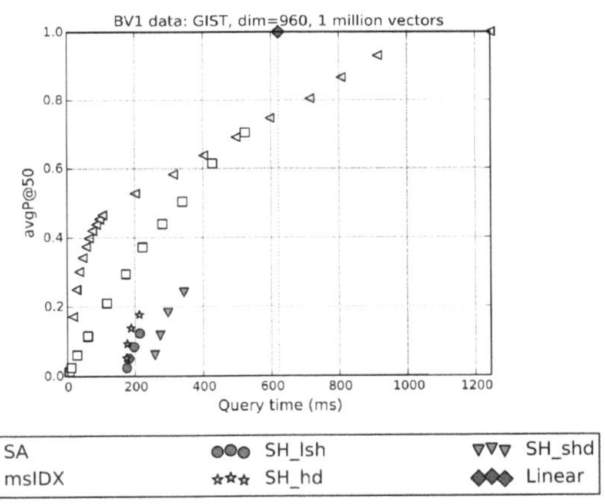

Figure 4: Parameter tuning on the BV1 dataset. Avg. P@50 vs. query time. Vertical line marks the time for linear index

We tested our Sparse Approximation (*SA*) method against a set of widely known indexing algorithms: the LSH implementation[5] described in [13], with multiple code sizes {64, 128, 256, 512} bits, Spherical Hashing [13] (with multiple code sizes {64, 128, 256, 512 code sizes) and the MSIDX method [30] [6]. We varied the

[4] `http://corpus-texmex.irisa.fr/`
[5] `http://sglab.kaist.ac.kr/Spherical_Hashing/`
[6] `http://vcl.iti.gr/msidx/`

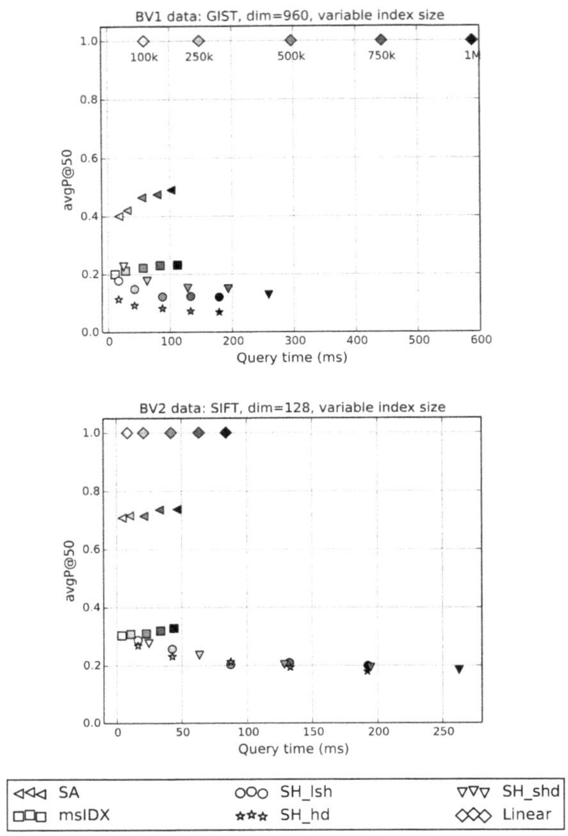

Figure 5: Avg. P@50 vs. query time. BV1 and BV2 datasets. Index size: from lightest to darkest: 100k, 250k, 500k, 750k and 1M.

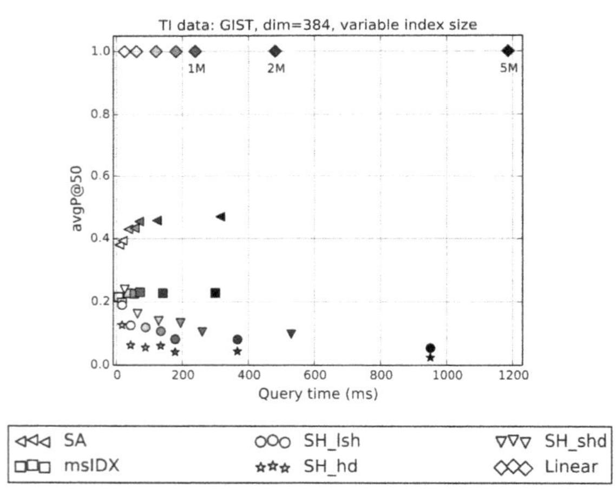

Figure 6: Avg. P@50 vs. query time. TI dataset. Index size: from lightest to darkest: 100k, 250k, 500k, 750k, 1M, 2M and 5M.

maximum percentage of database to examine {0.5%, 1%, 2.5%, 5%, 10%, 15%, 20%, 25%, 30%, 40%, 50%}. For the SA algorithm, we varied the maximum percentage of the index to examine {1% ,2% ,3%, 4%, ... ,10% ,20% ,30% ,40% ... ,100%}. To assess the efficiency and quality of the proposed method we opted to use the same setup as [13, 30, 32]: average of the percentage of the 50 nearest neighbors retrieved while inspecting a given percentage of the dataset and **avgP50** average of the percentage of the 50 nearest neighbors retrieved vs. **query time**. For each query, we measure the retrieval efficiency of each method and compare the retrieval precision to the linear search output. Hence, the top k nearest neighbours correspond to the relevant items.

We tested all indexes on the BV1 to assess the precision of our proposal versus time and other state-of-art algorithms and to determine the best parameter combination for each algorithm. Observing Figure 4, two major trends stand-out. The first trend occurs in the initial part of the curve, where precision grows very rapidly as query time increases; in the second trend, precision grows linearly towards the maximum precision. These two trends are clearly visible in the MSIDX method and the SA method. The different slopes indicate that both methods are optimized for efficiently retrieving the top nearest neighbors. As a consequence, after a given point, the curve slope is not as steep, showing a loss in performance as a side-effect of the top-results optimization.

Our proposal achieved 49% precision by inspecting 10% of data and in less than 20% of the linear search time (10% of inspected data corresponds to the tenth point in the SA curve). The same results were observed on experiments with $k = 1000$.

5.2 Single-node retrieval efficiency

For the scalability experiments, we fixed the parameters for the algorithms according to their performance on the previous experiment: SA and MSIDX: 10% index search limit, SH_hd, SH_shd, SH_lsh: 128 bit codes. Figure 5 lists the comparative performance when using indexes with variable size and with different dimensionalities. The precision differences between indexing algorithms does not change with index size. All algorithms appear to scale linearly with index size, but, for SA and to a lesser effect, MSIDX, avgP50 increases until the index contains 1M documents and then it stabilizes. This effect is opposite on hash based algorithms, where precision drops with index size. We reckon that the small hashes become less discriminative as the index size grows and that the sparse hashes remain discriminative for all tested index sizes.

The performance differences between features is also clear: the benefits are more clear on the (high dimensional) GIST features: speedup of SA and MSIDX vs. linear is about 5.2×. All indexers get better precision on the lower dimensional (128) SIFT features, but speedup vs. linear on the faster indexes (SA and MSIDX) is not as high, about 2×. SA stands out for both features: it is the faster or one of the fastest index on all experiments and achieved the highest precision (73% on SIFT and 43% on GIST).

Figure 6 lists the performance on the larger TI dataset (up to 5 millions), with GIST features with 384 dimensions. Index performance is close to BV1 experiments: SA is the fastest and achieves higher precision. Experiments on the larger 2M and 5M descriptor indexes follow the expected trends: SA and MSIDX precision is mostly stable while other hash based approaches perform worse as the index size increases. In general, the SA results compare favorably to the other tested methods. MSIDX offers lower precision on the desired time frame (sub 100 ms.). LSH and variants (SH) achieve the slowest results: the retrieval performance improves with the size of the binary codes, but they are still slower than the proposed method.

5.3 Distributed retrieval efficiency

To study the performance of our framework in a distributed setting across multiple index sizes and features, we tested the SIFT and GIST (BV1 and BV2) indexes on a distributed setting (aggregator makes the query and aggregates the results from the processor nodes searches). Figure 7 contains the detailed account of the time taken by the individual framework components, for the SA indexer with 1M vectors. The times for query distribution, communication, formatting and aggregation processes are average times, determined using a set of 5000 queries and 3 individual indexes with $k = 1000$. These times correspond to the process described in the architecture framework diagram, Figure 2 The total overhead of the framework is about 20 ms., meaning that the total query time will be the retrieval time of the slowest index plus 20 ms. This overhead is small when compared to individual index retrieval time, lowering the cost of using multiple features.

Table 1 contains the precision and temporal values for the full framework experiments. The n column contains index size, the Time SIFT and Time GIST column corresponds to processor node times on Figure 5 and Total Time column correspond to the total query time at the aggregator for the multifeature querying process. These results follow the same pattern as the scalability results on the previous section. The SA index continues to offer the best balance between temporal and retrieval performance for all index sizes. Note that it is not possible to measure the combined rank retrieval efficiency, as the Billion Vector dataset does not offer relevance judgements.

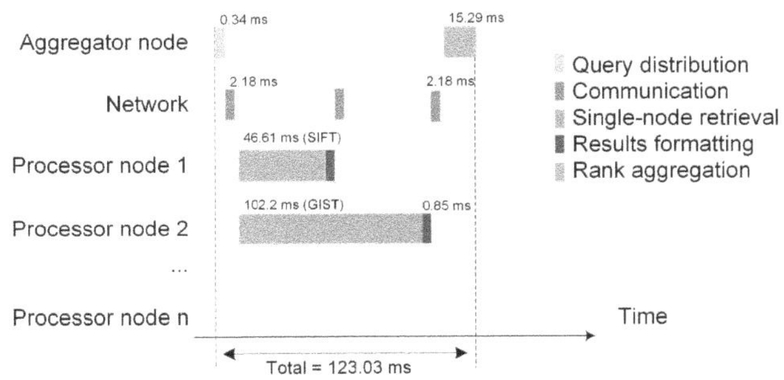

Figure 7: Querying process benchmarking for the 1M distributed experiment.

5.4 Retrieval precision

In the previous sections, we thoroughly assessed search efficiency and single-modality retrieval precision. While in the previous datasets we only had a single feature-space, in this section we consider an evaluation scenario where we have the ground-truth to evaluate multimodal retrieval precision – the ImageCLEF dataset. The indexes tested on this experiment were: 3 SA indexes with GIST (960 dimensions), CEDD (144 dimensions) and HSV histograms (216 dimensions) limited to 10% inspection and a textual index based on Apache Lucene[7] and with domain-specific features (query expansion and pseudo-relevance feedback).

Table 2 contains standard IR metrics for the multimodal aggregation experiment. ISR attains the best result of all metrics, closely followed by RRF. logN_ISR is the worse performer, as it is optimized for the aggregation of more than 4 ranks. From a distributed point of view, these functions are a good approximation of the temporal overhead added by the aggregation process. From a retrieval point of view, these results may improve by leveraging on learning-to-rank techniques, on datasets with judged training data.

[7]https://lucene.apache.org

Table 1: Retrieval times on SIFT and GIST Billion vector dataset with variable index size

Name	n	SIFT Time	AP@50	GIST Time	AP@50	Total Time
Linear	100k	8.52	1	59.38	1	80.22
	250k	21.14	1	148.28	1	169.12
	500k	42.08	1	297.20	1	318.04
	750k	63.36	1	442.32	1	463.16
	1M	84.03	1	588.17	1	609.01
SA	100k	4.43	0.71	17.32	0.40	38.16
	250k	10.34	0.72	31.35	0.42	52.19
	500k	21.29	0.72	55.18	0.47	76.02
	750k	33.27	0.74	79.80	0.48	100.64
	1M	46.61	0.74	102.20	0.49	123.04
MSIDX	100k	3.84	0.30	10.86	0.20	31.70
	250k	10.84	0.31	27.75	0.21	48.59
	500k	22.77	0.31	56.84	0.22	77.68
	750k	33.72	0.32	84.05	0.23	104.89
	1M	43.85	0.33	111.98	0.23	132.82
SH_lsh	100k	16.41	0.29	16.54	0.18	37.38
	250k	42.57	0.26	42.73	0.15	63.57
	500k	87.22	0.20	87.53	0.12	108.37
	750k	132.59	0.21	132.91	0.12	153.75
	1M	192.56	0.20	178.54	0.12	199.38
SH_hd	100k	16.41	0.27	16.55	0.11	37.39
	250k	42.62	0.23	42.67	0.09	63.51
	500k	87.24	0.21	87.59	0.08	108.43
	750k	133.12	0.19	132.81	0.07	153.65
	1M	192.09	0.18	178.77	0.07	199.61
SH_shd	100k	24.79	0.28	24.70	0.23	45.54
	250k	63.32	0.24	63.02	0.18	83.86
	500k	128.66	0.20	128.33	0.15	149.17
	750k	194.62	0.19	193.29	0.15	214.13
	1M	262.56	0.18	258.98	0.13	279.82

Table 2: ImageCLEF dataset aggregation results

Function	MAP	bpref	P@10	P@30	nDCG
ISR	0.1532	0.1887	0.1743	0.1229	0.4386
RRF	0.1335	0.1477	0.1600	0.1171	0.4227
logN_ISR	0.1200	0.1358	0.1514	0.1105	0.4119

6. CONCLUSION

In this paper, we described the challenges behind a framework for large-scale heterogeneous search engine. The proposed architecture is generic, scalable and adds little overhead to the single node retrieval process. To the best of our knowledge, there aren't any other articles that focus on heterogeneous systems of such scale. Our aggregation approach achieves good retrieval performance and is agnostic to the chosen features. The Sparse Approximation algorithm is capable of sub 100 ms retrieval, scalable to millions of documents per index, while offering the best precision results across the tested approaches.

Acknowledgements. This work has been partially funded by projects PTDC/EIA-EIA/111518/2009, UTA-Est/MAI/0010/2009, funded by the Portuguese Foundation for Science and Technology (FCT) and FCT/MEC NOVA LINCS PEst UID/CEC/04516/2013, funded by national funds through FCT/MEC (PIDDAC).

7. REFERENCES

[1] M. Abedini, L. Cao, N. Codella, J. H. Connell, A. Garnavi, Rahiland Geva, M. Merler, Q.-B. Nguyen, J. U. Pankanti, Sharathchandraand R. Smith, and A. Sun, Xingzhiand Tzadok. Ibm research at imageclef 2013 medical tasks. In *WN of CLEF'13*, 2013.

[2] M. Aharon, M. Elad, and A. Bruckstein. K-SVD: An Algorithm for Designing Overcomplete Dictionaries for Sparse Representation. *IEEE Trans. on Signal Processing*, 54(11):4311–4322, 2006.

[3] R. Aly, D. Hiemstra, and T. Demeester. Taily: Shard selection using the tail of score distributions. In *SIGIR'13*, pages 673–682, 2013.

[4] A. Andoni and P. Indyk. Near-optimal hashing algorithms for approximate nearest neighbor in high dimensions. *Commun. ACM*, 51(1):117–122, 2008.

[5] C. Badue, R. Baeza-Yates, B. Ribeiro-neto, and N. Ziviani. Distributed query processing using partitioned inverted files. In *SPIRE'01*, pages 10–20. IEEE CS Press, 2001.

[6] R. Baeza-Yates, V. Murdock, and C. Hauff. Efficiency trade-offs in two-tier web search systems. In *SIGIR'09*, pages 163–170, 2009.

[7] M. Batko, F. Falchi, C. Lucchese, D. Novak, R. Perego, F. Rabitti, J. Sedmidubsky, and P. Zezula. Building a web-scale image similarity search system. *Multimedia Tools and Applications*, 47(3):599–629, 2010.

[8] P. Borges, A. Mourão, and J. Magalhães. High-dimensional indexing by sparse approximation. In *ICMR'15*. ACM, 2015.

[9] S. Büttcher, C. L. Clarke, and G. V. Cormack. *Information retrieval: Implementing and evaluating search engines*. Mit Press, 2010.

[10] G. V. Cormack, C. L. A. Clarke, and S. Buettcher. Reciprocal rank fusion outperforms condorcet and individual rank learning methods. In *Proc of. SIGIR '09*, pages 758–759, 2009.

[11] J. Dean and S. Ghemawat. Mapreduce: Simplified data processing on large clusters. *Commun. ACM*, 51(1):107–113, 2008.

[12] A. Garcia Seco de Herrera, J. Kalpathy-Cramer, D. Demner Fushman, S. Antani, and H. Müller. Overview of the imageclef 2013 medical tasks. In *WN on CLEF'13*, 2013.

[13] J.-P. Heo, Y. Lee, J. He, S.-F. Chang, and S.-E. Yoon. Spherical hashing. In *CVPR'12*, pages 2957–2964, 2012.

[14] H. Jégou, M. Douze, and C. Schmid. Product quantization for nearest neighbor search. *IEEE Trans. on PAMI*, 33(1):117–128, 2011.

[15] H. Jégou, T. Furon, and J.-J. Fuchs. Anti-sparse coding for approximate nearest neighbor search. In *Proc. on ICASSP'98*, pages 2029–2032, 2012.

[16] H. Jégou, R. Tavenard, M. Douze, and L. Amsaleg. Searching in one billion vectors: re-rank with source coding. *ArXiv e-prints*, 2011.

[17] R. Ji, L.-Y. Duan, J. Chen, L. Xie, H. Yao, and W. Gao. Learning to distribute vocabulary indexing for scalable visual search. *IEEE Trans. on Multimedia*, 15(1):153–166, 2013.

[18] H. Lee, A. Battle, R. Raina, and A. Ng. Efficient sparse coding algorithms. *NIPS'06*, pages 801–808, 2006.

[19] M. S. Lewicki and T. J. Sejnowski. Learning overcomplete representations. *Neural Comput.*, 12(2):337–365, 2000.

[20] C. Macdonald and I. Ounis. Voting for candidates: adapting data fusion techniques for an expert search task. In *CIKM'06*, 2006.

[21] H. Mohamed and S. Marchand-Maillet. Distributed media indexing based on mpi and mapreduce. *Multimedia Tools and Applications*, 69(2):513–537, 2014.

[22] D. Moise, D. Shestakov, G. Gudmundsson, and L. Amsaleg. Indexing and searching 100m images with map-reduce. In *ICMR'13*, pages 17–24, 2013.

[23] M. Montague and J. A. Aslam. Relevance score normalization for metasearch. In *CIKM'01*, pages 427–433, 2001.

[24] A. Mourão, F. Martins, and J. Magalhães. Inverse square rank fusion for multimodal search. In *CBMI'14*, pages 1–6. IEEE, 2014.

[25] M. Muja and D. G. Lowe. Scalable nearest neighbor algorithms for high dimensional data. *IEEE Trans. on PAMI*, 36, 2014.

[26] D. Novak and P. Zezula. M-chord: A scalable distributed similarity search structure. In *InfoScale'06*, 2006.

[27] Y. Pati, R. Rezaiifar, and P. Krishnaprasad. Orthogonal Matching Pursuit: recursive function approximation with application to wavelet decomposition. In *ASILOMAR*, pages 40–44, 1993.

[28] J. A. Shaw and E. A. Fox. Combination of multiple searches. In *TREC'94*, pages 243–252, 1994.

[29] T. Skopal, J. Pokorný, and V. Snasel. Pm-tree: Pivoting metric tree for similarity search in multimedia databases. In *ADBIS'04*, 2004.

[30] E. Tiakas, D. Rafailidis, A. Dimou, and P. Daras. Msidx: Multi-sort indexing for efficient content-based image search and retrieval. *Trans. on Multimedia*, 15(6):1415–1430, 2013.

[31] A. Torralba, R. Fergus, and W. Freeman. 80 million tiny images: A large data set for nonparametric object and scene recognition. *Trans. on PAMI*, 30(11):1958–1970, 2008.

[32] A. Torralba, R. Fergus, and Y. Weiss. Small codes and large image databases for recognition. In *CVPR'08*, pages 1–8, 2008.

[33] Y. Weiss, A. Torralba, and R. Fergus. Spectral hashing. *NIPS'08*, 9(1):1–8, 2008.

[34] A. Y. Yang, A. Ganesh, Z. Zhou, S. Sastry, and Y. Ma. A review of fast l1-minimization algorithms for robust face recognition. *Arxiv CoRR*, abs/1007.3753, 2010.

[35] X. Zhu, Z. Huang, H. Cheng, J. Cui, and H. T. Shen. Sparse hashing for fast multimedia search. *ACM Trans. Inf. Syst.*, 31(2):1–9, 2013.

Insight in Image Collections by Multimedia Pivot Tables

Marcel Worring
Informatics Institute, University of Amsterdam
P.O. Box 94323, 1098 XH Amsterdam
The Netherlands
m.worring@uva.nl

Dennis Koelma
Informatics Institute, University of Amsterdam
P.O. Box 94323, 1098 XH Amsterdam
The Netherlands
d.c.koelma@uva.nl

ABSTRACT

We propose a multimedia analytics solution for getting insight in image collections by extending the powerful method of pivot tables, found in the ubiquitous spreadsheets, to multimedia. Our proposed solution is designed by considering the characteristics of multimedia data as well as insight and provides integral access to visual content through concept detection results, tags, geolocation, and other metadata. We present a set of scenarios of using the pivot tables for a collection of images, tags, and metadata from Flickr. User experiments have been instrumental in realizing the final design presented in this paper. The accompanying video shows the solution in action.

Categories and Subject Descriptors

H.3 [**Information storage and retrieval**]: Information Search and Retrieval

General Terms

Search Process

Keywords

Exploration; Visual Analytics; Information Visualization

1. INTRODUCTION

Visual collections contain a wealth of information for scientific or investigative purposes. For social scientists and marketing managers alike social media is a crucial resource in which visual data plays an ever increasing role. In biology, astrophysics, or medicine, images are a valuable source of scientific knowledge. Visual information is also becoming a prime carrier of evidence and clues in forensics and security. In all these application domains the deluge of visual collections holds tremendous value, but how do we gain insight in such a collection?

The insight might pertain to a lot of different elements of the dataset. It might e.g. be found in the content of the images in relation to the tags and their geographic distribution. Or it requires to study what scenes are depicted on images for different quality ratings by clients and their dependence on the age of the client making the judgment. When analyzing data using queries the result is a set of images each of which has corresponding metadata. We can either go through the set of images, typically visualized in a 2D-grid, and study the statistics of the metadata, or start from the metadata and decompose the set using subqueries to study the different values. In both cases it is hard to relate the results of different queries, constraining the user's expresiveness and explorative possibilities.

An approach in which the user interactively builds up the results and assesses them throught different visualizations is more appropriate. And indeed for factual and geographic data this approach is for example successfully employed in the commercial Tableau system building upon the query paradigm in [24]. Doing similar things for image collections needs to take into account the specific nature of images. A brief look at a small number of images is sufficient to reveal their meaning and relations. Based on this we immediately trigger knowledge we have about these objects [27]. For a human it requires, however, seeing each image at sufficient resolution. For a computer interpreting visual data is a challenging task, hampered by the semantic gap, but clearly can work on much larger collections. A solution in which both the machine and the machine play a role in understanding the visual collection is the best path to success.

Interactive methods for gaining insight are precisely the target of Visual analytics methods [16]. Yet multimedia analytics, the combination of multimedia analysis and visual analytics [3] is just starting as a field and its potential still needs to be unlocked. One reason is the research emphasis in the underlying communities. The multimedia community has a strong emphasis on benchmark driven data analysis [29] assuming a simple query to result list based user interaction paradigm. In contrast, the visual analytics community has advanced visualizations and interaction paradigms, but rarely delves into the content of the visual material, relying instead on metadata and text analysis. In addition they argue that benchmarks are not suited as mechanisms to evaluate and design insight gaining processes [20]. Moving forward in multimedia analytics requires a true integration of methods for analyzing the visual data and associated descriptions on the one hand and visual analytics solutions on the other.

Analytics tools are many and each of them has the potential to be combined with multimedia analysis. Due to

ICMR'15 June 23–26, 2015, Shanghai, China

DOI: http://dx.doi.org/10.1145/2671188.2749312 ...$15.00.

their ubiquitous presence and their proven power in a broad range of applications, we propose to consider spreadsheets as candidate analytic tools to extend to multimedia. Some interesting approaches in this direction have been proposed [2][15]. These methods solely rely on the metadata for querying and visualizing the image collection. The MediaTable [5] uses automatic concept detection to analyze the content and organizes the results in a tabular form.

Arguably one of the most powerful features of spreadsheets for understanding complex data are pivot tables. These tables let the user interactively create summaries of the data in the spreadsheet in various ways. In this manner the user gets different views of the data, aggregated along different dimensions, and hence can see patterns and trends. But pivot tables are primarily based on nominal, ordinal, and numeric variables. How to create and use pivot tables for image collections is an open question, which we aim to address here.

In this paper we make the following contributions:

- Formally define the concept of multimedia pivot tables extending its informal design in our earlier 2-page paper [28].
- Intricately link multimedia analytics with multimedia pivot tables to the characteristics of insight.
- Develop design rules for multimedia pivot tables based on the characteristics of the data and insight.
- Show scenarios of use and provide a user study.

2. RELATED WORK

We consider related work along three lines. First we consider methods which are also addressing large image collections ranging from visualization only to multimedia analytics following various paradigms. We then consider methods aiming at aggregating and visualizing metadata along various dimensions using metaphors other than a spreadsheet. Finally, we review methods which are following the spreadsheet paradigm.

2.1 Multimedia Visualization and Analytics

As search engines are still the primary way to access image collections visualizing a set of ranked images in a 2D grid, implicitly using reading order, is still dominant. Such a grid doesn't reflect the score of each image. In [26] they therefore organize the query result as a spiral starting in the center with size reflecting score. For longer lists [32] proposes to decompose the list into several linked grids, each organized to reflect similarity instead of ranking. Photoland [21] combines grids with groupings based on temporal and spatial information. The grid based methods make optimal use of available screen estate, yet for relations they can only show crude approximations.

Similarity based methods start from the relations among all images instead of a ranking. Such methods project the data from the high dimensional space induced by all (visual) similarities among images into the two dimensional screen space. The main goal of the projection techniques is to best preserve in the visualization the relations among the images in the high dimensional space. This leads to many overlapped images, [19] therefore adds overview and visibility as criteria to optimize. To allow for local interaction [14] provides efficient local projections. MediaGlow [9] combines similarity based visualization with additional metadata based visualizations. The difference in metadata values can also be used as a similarity function so the projection methods might create groups of images sharing similar metadata. The method in [30] combines an MDS based 2D similarity based visualization with a rank based visualization based on query by example. Finally, [22] considers color similarity in a 3D image browser. These similarity based visualizations are good for showing relations among the images while showing relations between the images and the metadata is missing or difficult.

Methods combining multimedia analysis of images and metadata with visual analytics [3] are still limited. One of the first systems is the Informedia system which employs speech and video analysis in conjunction with effective user interfaces [4]. A system targeting computer vision algorithm developers is presented in [12] allowing the user to gain insight in features and how to use these features in surveillance. Canopy [1] is an advanced system combining text analysis, various visualizations and visual similarity based matching to explore visual collections. Hierarchical visualizations for understanding news data, based on analysis of closed-captions, are presented in [17] using hyperbolic trees as visualization to explore the hierarchical structure of the data. Concept detectors are used in both [30] and [5]. Where [30] uses grids and similarity based displays, [5] uses a heatmap like visualization simultaneously showing a large set of ranked lists. The above methods are all interesting and have their own merits, yet they have only started to unlock the potential that multimedia analytics methods can bring.

2.2 Visualizing and summarizing metadata

Text is important in many applications and interactive visualizations to access them are widespread. We consider some advanced examples here. The event based system in [6] summarizes information on people in a spiral visualization, topics over time as themestreams, and the images associated with the text as an imagecloud. For metadata structured in facets PivotPaths [7] provide an advanced visualization and exploration method. The majority of visualizations for tags, so common in image collection applications, are based on a variant of a tagcloud.

For heterogeneous collections, visualization mosaics [18] provide a very flexible way of creating a summary putting the control fully in the hand of the user. This allows for easy personalization and targeted presentations for different audiences. Such full flexibility also limits explicit structure or constraints on the final result which makes it more difficult to interactively build up insight. Mosaics are therefore very well suited as summaries for presentation, they have less utility in analytics.

2.3 Spreadsheets and their extensions

Spreadsheets are the best known analytic tools and their origins go back a long time. The tabular visualization which forms the basis for any spreadsheet is simple yet effective. In information visualization early systems already employed the important mechanism of being able to coordinate sorting of one column with all others. Through the visualizations in the different columns correlations become evident. The

LineUp [10] takes the coordination a step further and also visualizes the relations among the different columns. No other spreadsheet functionality is added though.

Modern spreadsheets allow for the integration of visual data into the spreadsheet [8] and connecting it to web resources. They do not make images a true part of the analytics process. Integrating the spreadsheet paradigm with images is proposed in [2] to visualize the effect of different parameter settings in an experimental setting. The Photospread [15] system extends the spreadsheet to image collections by allowing groups of images in the individual cells with formula like definitions to fill the cells with the user desired selection. Using formulas in grid cells is a first step towards multimedia analytics using the capabilities of spreadsheets. The above methods are, however, all based on the standard table based spreadsheet.

The Datacube [11] has introduced a powerful mechanism for organizing data, steering the development of the pivot table summaries in spreadsheets. The flexible and powerful mechanism which underly the well known Tableau system rely on a language which is very similar to the Datacube mechanism integrating it with constraints on the possible visualizations [24]. The way users interact with the system bears great similarities with pivot tables. Pivot tables for image collections do not exist yet although the PhotoCube system [25] makes a step in the direction. They rely, however, on a 3D space rather than a 2D pivot table. We believe that pivot tables for image collections in 2D would provide a very powerful mechanism in an analytics context.

3. METHODS

To arrive at a multimedia analytics solution based on pivot tables, we first have to consider the characteristics of the data in multimedia collections and how this affects their use in an analytics context. Multimedia collections contain many different variables. For this paper we distinguish four different types. Core to the approach are the *images* themselves. For automatic analysis of the images automatic visual concepts descriptors, even if limited to a couple of hundred, form a solid base for multimedia analytics. In our case, the images are analyzed using visual detectors from a given vocabulary following the analysis pipeline in [23]. For each visual concept it yields a *concept score* between 0 and 1 as indication of concept presence. Each of these images might have a set of *tags*, taken from an unconstrained vocabulary, which could range from describing specific aspects of the content to personalized interpretations or contexts of the images. In addition to those we have any *metadata* composed of numeric, categorical, or geolocation attributes of each image.

In the following, we will first consider the characteristics of insight and then use them to develop our multimedia pivot tables. The corresponding multimedia analytics process is illustrated in figure 1.

3.1 Multimedia insights

The goal of any analytics system is to gain valuable insight in the data. Insight is hard to define in a precise way, [20] however, identifies five major characteristics of insight:

- *Complex:* Insight is complex, involving all or large amounts of the given data in a synergistic way, not simply individual data values.

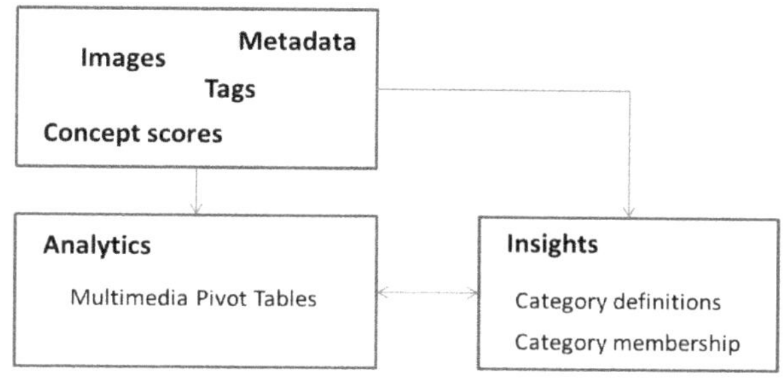

Figure 1: The multimedia analytics process.

- *Deep:* Insight builds up over time, accumulating and building on itself to create depth often generating further questions and, hence, further insight.
- *Qualitative:* Insight is not exact, can be uncertain and subjective, and can have multiple levels of resolution.
- *Unexpected:* Insight is often unpredictable, serendipitous, and creative.
- *Relevant:* Insight is deeply embedded in the data domain, connecting the data to existing domain knowledge and giving it relevant meaning going beyond dry data analysis, to relevant domain impact.

So how to support the extraction of insight from an image collection? Clearly mere statistics on the metadata are not sufficient to grab the essence of the collection. Statistics on features are only relevant when the features themselves like use of color are the object of study. For the more complex statistics, based on the visual concent represented in concept scores in relation to all other variables, understanding is far more complex. To that end, we consider the essence of the visual content to be captured by the description of the individual images and the similarities among the images along any of the dimensions. Various groupings of the data based on the similarities poses structure on the collection. In [31] we argue, based on an extensive literature review, that these groupings or categories are an essential ingredient in insight gaining processes. To be precise, when category definition is in the hand of the interacting expert the labels given by the user to categories, being it derived in a unsupervised or supervised way, provide the current view of the expert on the domain dependent relevant terms in relation to the collection. But the label alone is not enough to capture insight, we need to take into account any connotations the expert has with the data and which elements in the dataset comprise the different categories. Accordingly we define the insight C_I to be defined by its N categories:

- *Insight* : $C_I = \{\text{label}_i, \text{members}_i, \text{connotations}_i\}_{i=1,..N}$

It should be noted that in the course of a session with the system the labels in C_I don't have to be fixed. Although current systems typically work with a fixed set of categories, humans dynamically refine their understanding of the collection, an instantiation of the pragmatic gap [31]. Hence, while interacting with the system the expert should be given the tools to manipulate any of the elements comprising the insight.

To bootstrap the analytic process the user has to define an initial set of categories in which images can be placed. To emphasize the action of adding elements to categories we denote the categories as buckets [5], a metaphor for a place where elements can be put. Each bucket has a color used throughout the system. Every bucket also has a corresponding bucket note with which the user can define a label/name for the bucket and put any free text capturing reflections on the content of the bucket. When a user is interacting with the collection new insights arise and categories might also be put into new and dynamically changing context. Therefore, in the course of the interactive process, the bucket names can be refined or changed.

Through keyboard shortcuts selections of images are placed in a user-selected bucket. Such bucket membership can change dynamically by moving images between different buckets. Images can also be put in several buckets at the same time as their semantics is much richer than one category. This non-exlusiveness of buckets gives the analyst full conceptual freedom in attaining insight. Although simple, the above techniques allow for a rich way of interacting with the buckets and their content.

The final result of the interactive process is the set of buckets, the images put into each bucket, the corresponding categories, and all reflections the user has made while interacting, a direct correspondence to insight C_I as defined above.

3.2 Pivot based Multimedia analytics

As indicated, we propose to use multimedia pivot tables as a mechanism for multimedia analytics. To that end, we first give a quick review of the general concept of pivot tables and from there look at the specifics of multimedia variables to come to our proposed solution.

Pivot tables are a way of summarizing data in a spreadsheet which can be interactively defined by a user. At its core the pivot table is a matrix of cells which can contain values. The power of pivot tables comes from the flexibility in assigning different roles for the variables in the dataset [13]. A pivot table is created by assigning variables to be used as *filter* to select the part of the dataset to work on, a variable to define the *rows* of the table, and one to define the *columns* of the table. The set of elements for each cell is now restricted to those having the corresponding row and column nominal label. The final variable determines the *value* to be used for the cell, which are integrated over the set of elements by applying a user selected *aggregation operator* such as mean, mode, or maximum value. In addition to these aggregations, a pivot table also aggregates all values for respectively one column or row. So how do we achieve this for images, concept scores, tags, and metadata?

The first role of a variable we consider is when it is used as a filter. As multimedia collections are large and composed of various types of information, a facet based model in which every facet adds an additional constraint to limit the result and where the results are combined using an AND function is most appropriate. Thus we have:

- *Filter variable:* in this role the variables define a faceted combination of nominal labels, numeric range, concept score range, tags, and buckets to give the active image dataset $I = \{I_1, ..., I_N\}$.

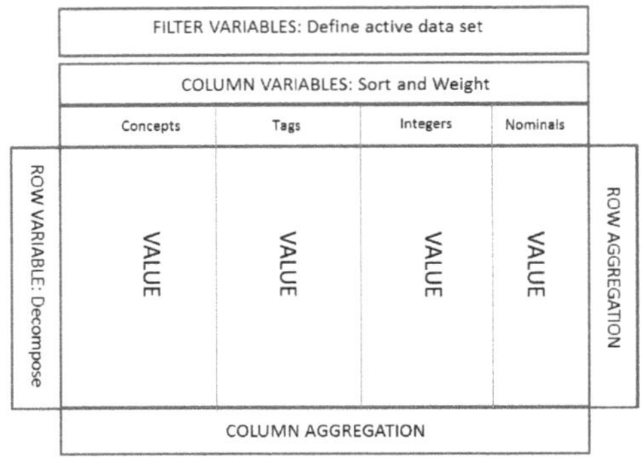

Figure 2: Schematic view of multimedia pivot tables.

For filtering it is important to find a natural way to specify the IDs of the individual images of interest based on the variable. For nominal variables this is simply by filtering based on one or more specific labels. The same holds for keeping only the elements in a specific bucket. Both numeric metadata and concept scores can be filtered by using a range on the values. For concepts it should be noted that the cut-off point is often not clear. Hence, when using the ranking for filtering out images not containing the concept, thresholding the list should be done with care. We therefore support the selection by a simple interactive histogram based visualization. Tags or other textual descriptions can be selected through regular expressions. Specifying geolocation by ranges is cumbersome so we provide a map visualization in which users can select elements by dragging a (rectangular) region. Selecting images through other means than concepts or metadata can only be done via visual inspection. We do so by letting the user interactively select them in any of the visualizations. The user can then put the selection in a bucket for filtering, or any other future reference.

To decide what elements can be row or column variables, we make two observations. First there can be thousands of individual images and a magnitude more of tags. Second numeric values and thus also concepts can not be enumerated, they do induce an ordering though. Enumerating individual images or tags in both colums and rows would yield an explosion of cells. Therefore, we put such enumeration only as rows. This leaves the role for the column variable free and therefore we use variables put there to sort and possibly weight the data. Decomposition into the elements to use and the way of sorting defines which variables can be placed where. Location data cannot be enumerated nor can they be used for sorting or weighting. So they can not be placed as row and neither as column variable. Nominal data can only be used as rows. Finally, numeric data and concepts can be used to sort and weight and hence are suited as column variable. Numeric data and concepts can be used as rows only after decomposing them into ranges. We do so by using 7-points summaries based on percentiles.

How to create a 7-point summary depends on the shape of the distribution. For the highly skewed concept score distribution they are based on fixed percentiles denoted by p^{th}, where for numeric metadata exhibiting a more or less normal distribution we also provide the choice to having it based on the Interquartile range $Q = 75^{\text{th}} - 25^{\text{th}}$ to define

Type	Filter	Column	Row	Value	Visualization
Images	Selection to bucket	x	Individual images	Sorted list of images	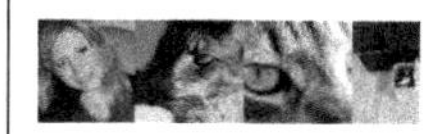
Concepts	Range selection	Concept scores as weights	7-point summary (fixed)	Distribution	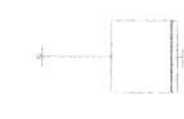
Tags	Tag selection	BM25 / Frequency weights	Individual tags	Sorted and weighted tag histogram	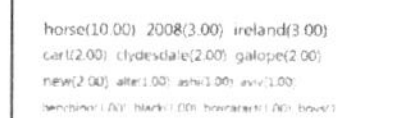
Nominal	Label selection	x	Individual labels	Sorted and weighted text histogram	
Geo	Selection to bucket	x	x	Map with weighted elements	
Numeric	Range selection	Value as weights	7-point summary (fixed/derived)	Sum, max, avg, distribution	 *24.5*
Buckets	Bucket selection	x	Individual buckets	Weighted histogram	

Table 1: Design rules for the different roles of variables and their visualization in multimedia pivot tables.

the normal range $[Q^-, Q^+]$ given by $[25^{\text{th}} - 1.5Q, 75^{\text{th}} + 1.5Q]$. Any data outside this range are considered statistical outliers. The two types of summaries are thus given as:

- *Fixed-7:* $(\text{min}, 5^{\text{th}}, 25^{\text{th}}, \text{median}, 75^{\text{th}}, 95^{\text{th}}, \text{max})$
- *Derived-7:* $(\text{min}, Q^-, 0.25^{\text{th}}, \text{median}, 75^{\text{th}}, Q^+, \text{max})$

So the row and column variables are defined as:

- *Row variable*: in this role the range of nominal values, tags, images, and ranges of numeric or concept scores define the different rows of the matrix decomposing I into not necessarily disjunct subsets $\{S_1, ..., S_M\}$.
- *Column variable*: in this role the numeric values, concept scores, or tag frequencies define a weight w_{ji} corresponding to each $I_{ji} \in S_j$ and maps it to an ordered sequence $\mathbf{S_j}$ with corresponding weight vector $\mathbf{w_j}$.

Determining the weights is most difficult for tags. So let us consider that class of variables explicitly here. Let T_j denote the enumeration of all tags corresponding to the images in row S_j, let $t_{jk} \in T_j$ be the k_{th} unique tag and $f(t_{jk})$ the count of the tag in T_j. For a *frequency* weight we simply normalize $f(t_{jk})$ by $\#(T_j)$ the total number of tags. It is more interesting to highlight the set of tags in a cell which are typical for subset S_j with tags which are very common receiving less emphasis. The Okapi BM25 measure in information retrieval is precisely doing that for computing the relevance of keywords in text documents with respect to a query. Here we consider each tag as a query and consider the contribution of each tag t_{jk} within subset S_j. With $n(t_{jk})$ being the number of rows in which the tag occurs we can compute *BM25 weights* of tag importance. To that end let us first define the inverse term frequency measure IDF:

$$\text{IDF}(t_{jk}) = \log \frac{M - n(t_{jk}) + 0.5}{n(t_{jk}) + 0.5} \quad (1)$$

Using this term we can define the weight as follows, with $\kappa = 1.6$ and $\beta = 0.75$ set to the recommended values:

$$w_{jk} = \text{IDF}(t_{jk}).\frac{f(t_{jk})(\kappa + 1)}{f(t_{jk}) + \kappa\left(1 - \beta + \beta\frac{\#(T_j)}{1/M\sum_j \#(T_j)}\right)} \quad (2)$$

We have finally arrived at assignment of variables to the value part of the pivot table. To allow to work with the diverse variables we are considering, we assign a variable to a column rather than to the whole table. In fact, we let users interactively define the variable to use in the value field and which variable to use as variable to sort and weight this particular column. So for each cell in the table we have a row variable defining which set of images to use for this particular cell, where each of them is giving a weight which also is providing the basis for sorting. When no column variable is used, we simply have a set of elements without a weighting function. All variables can be used for the value fields, the difference lies in how to aggregate the data and especially how to visualize the result.

- *Value variable*: in this role the variable defines the set of attribute values $\mathbf{V_j}$ corresponding to the images in the ordered sequence $\mathbf{S_j}$ and the appropriate aggregation and visualization operators acting on $\mathbf{V_j}$ and weight vector $\mathbf{w_j}$.

So how to aggregate and visualize the weighted set of images or their metadata in each cell? In all cases every cell will contain some value or a simple visualization. The latter makes use of the principle of small multiples, a powerful mechanism for quick comparisons of subsets of the data. For images, we only use weights for creating a ranked list visualized by the actual sorted images. For numeric variables, we can either take standard aggregations like max, sum, or average, or we visualize the 7-point summary as a boxplot. For concepts, we want to show the whole distribution so we only show a boxplot. Combining this with weights would yield a rather complicated visualization which might be difficult to comprehend by the user. So when a concept is chosen as value we automatically use the same concept as column variable. Geolocations are shown on a map where weights are mapped to the size of the various elements.

To visualize tags and nominal variables, we use a simple tagcloud mechanism. As for both geo and tags the weight might vary considerably, and can be very different for each individual cell, we employ a 7-point summary to map the values to 7 different radii or font sizes. Finally, buckets are visualized as a bar chart where the weights are accumulated per bucket. In fact we visualize two things at the same time. The weighted values are shown as a normalized barchart in the vertical direction and a stacked bar chart in the horizontal dimension shows the normalized number of elements in each bucket.

All columns perform *column aggregation* to have their totals over all elements visualized in the same manner as the individual cells to allow for assessments of an individual cell with respect to the whole. *Row aggregation* is performed to show the value and name of the maximal scoring concept over all concepts per row to define the dominant concept for each subset of the data.

The whole set of possible assignments to variables for filtering, rows, columns, and values and their associated visualizations are summarized in table 1.

4. USE CASES AND EVALUATION

The multimedia pivot table provides a number of different ways to look at the data, many of which would be difficult to achieve by iteratively posing queries. We will first describe two use case scenarios and then report on a user evaluation which led to design improvements, and paved the way for future expert testing of the system.

4.1 Use case scenarios

The first scenario is a **developer of new detectors** for visual data (see Figure 3). A promising way of doing this is by leveraging data from photo sharing sites where the data is tagged by users. The developer is aiming to extend an existing building detector with a substantially larger set of positive examples to improve the quality of the detector. Initially building is the only category. She starts with a large set of images taken from Flickr and filters it by the tag building. She puts the concept building as row variable so yielding six rows according to the 7-point summary. She puts two columns with building as column variable and respectively geo-location and a sorted image list as value. Finally she adds a tag column with tags also as values (with BM25 weighting). In the maps she observes that the building dataset is mostly from big cities in North-America and Europe, so one way of finding better samples is using major city names, she also decides to introduce a subcategory for skyscrapers. The tags reveal that the tag architecture is often associated with building and the images reveal that these are more varied, so she decides to look for tags associated with architecture.

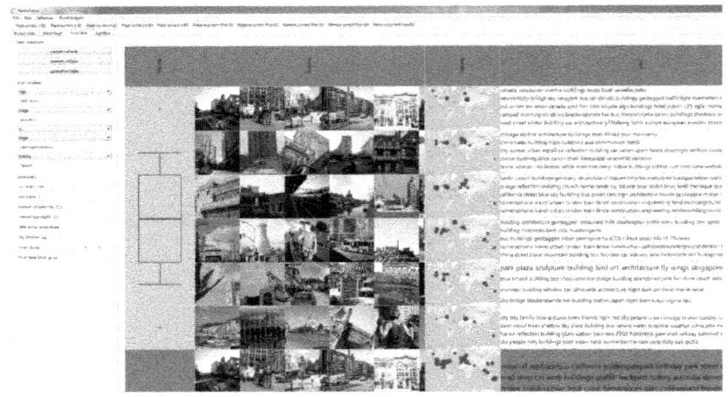

Figure 3: Scenario in which a building detector is optimized.

The second scenario is for a **marketing manager** at a car company who wants to know how a certain type of image influences popularity. He therefore considers a set of images from Flickr with their tags and metadata. The initial insight categories are popular and non-popular. He filters the set by thresholding the concept score for car to throw out most of the non-car images. He uses tags as row variables and adds images as values sorted by the concept car. Looking at the rows he selects the car brands BMW, Mercedes, Ferrari, and Chevrolet as targets. He creates separate buckets for each of those and uses the buckets as row variable. He creates two sorted image sets as values for the concepts indoor and car racing respectively. He creates a column for number of views as a measure of popularity (taking the average number of views as aggregation). As additional information he also adds a geo-location column, weighted by the number of views. This leads to the insight that Mercedes is much more prevalent in South America than the other brands. He uses this insight to further study whether tags associated with Mercedes in South America have a positive nature or not.

Figure 4: A scenario in marketing research.

4.2 Evaluation setup

The collection of images we worked on for these experiments is a set of 17.000 images publicly available from Flickr using a set of 20 query terms for specific types of objects and scenes. The process was done such that in the result all images are having geo coordinates. In addition to the images, we collected metadata such as number of views, title, ownername, tags, camera used, and camera parameters. In principle any detector set yielding a score between 0 and 1 can be used. We apply a set of 150 concept detectors using the techniques in [23] which are trained on data outside of the current dataset. This set is a good comprise between providing sufficient accurary while providing sufficient choice to select a small set of detectors relevant to the given task and query.

Participants of the experiment were a group of 34 master students in information sciences and artificial intelligence as well as 7 PhD students in various tehnical disciplines. Each student worked between 2 and 3 hours in total on the task. Part of this time was devoted to an intro by the instructor and some free exploration of the tool before notes had to be written down.

Working towards an insight based system, we designed the experiment to a large extent following the guidelines in [20]. In particular, the participants were not given a particular task, they were rather freely exploring the dataset for insights of interest. The participants were given a form in which they indicated what categories/buckets they used at the start and which new categories they found. The new categories were seen as insights and they also filled in whether the insight was based on one cell, a single column, a single row, distributions of elements in one column, distribution of elements in one row, multiple row observations, or multiple column observations. After the experiments they could comment on the weak and strong points of the tool and make suggestions for further improvement.

4.3 Results and discussion

Each of the participants came to between two and eight observations of interest. Many of them were related to the performance of detectors, where they worked and where they didn't. We analyzed all observations the participants wrote down and the different ways in which they reached these insights. Within the relatively short time given to work with the tool, most students were finding some simpler forms of insight. A few students were able to indeed find observations requiring complex relations between different columns and or rows.

The results and comments led to a number of rounds of improvements of the tool. E.g. the filter function now indicates a count of the number of elements passing the filter. Category names can now interactively be indicated and bucket notes were added as a mechanism to collect intermediate insights. Maps were added as a new variable to use as value. A more significant improvement to the system was the move from a situation where column and value variable were always the same where now the value can be chosen indepedently from the column or row variable, much more in line with the standard pivot paradigm. Many comments were related to the use of the concepts. The students had no prior experience in using concepts and didn't have sufficient feeling with the limits on accuracy that the detectors sometimes have. Therefore, next to a sorted list of images you can now view the distribution of the corresponding concept as a boxplot. This distribution might reveal that for the current row the concept scores are not relevant as they represent elements at the bottom of the initial ranked list.

The evaluations have been a highly valuable tool in developing the system. They revealed both the strenghts and weaknesses of the initial design. Next step in the evaluation would be taking the tool to expert users bringing in domain knowledge on the topics present in their image collections. This brings a direct match between category definition and insight gained.

5. CONCLUSION

Multimedia analytics is urgently needed in a world in which multimedia data is so pervasive. The nature of multimedia, especially the difference between how we perceive data and how computers understand data, makes this a challenging task. We have proposed a new approach which takes the pivot tables so common in spreadsheets as basis and brings it into the realm of multimedia. We have identified that column variables should be used for sort and weight, while row variables should yield the decomposition of the set. The value variables determine what is visualized (Figure 2). This way of handling the variables yield a rule set for putting variables in the table and their subsequent visualization. These rules are summarized in table 1. The result is a framework supporting the process of gaining insight following the characteristics identified in section 3:

- *Complex:* Multimedia pivot tables allow interactive assignment of variables of different types to each of the pivot variable roles constraint only by the possibility to either being able to sort (column) or decompose (row) (table 1).
- *Deep:* Building up insights over time is facilitated by the ability to define new categories and dynamically change category membership and as buckets can be used as variables in the pivot table evolving insight can be reflected upon immediately.
- *Qualitative:* Categories are qualitative by definition and can be dynamically annotated with free text descriptions through the bucket notes.
- *Unexpected:* The highly flexible variable assignments lead to easy generation of user defined summaries integrating various dimensions allowing to see complex relations and patterns not revealed by simple query based results.
- *Relevant:* The category definition is in the hand of the expert, directly reflecting domain dependent terms and although the automatic concept vocabulary is domain independent, new categories can be learned on the fly when the elements share consistent visual appearance.

The ultimate goal of multimedia analytics is insight in large multimedia collections. The use case scenarios we have indicated reveal the rich functionality of multimedia pivot tables. User experiments have led to various improvements of the system. The resulting tool yields a highly interactive and rich way of doing multimedia analytics. But insight is hard to define and can only be captured in its characteristics. True insight delivering multimedia analytics will be a challenge for many years to come. Our multimedia pivot tables have made a contribution by not addressing one of the insight characteristics, but making a step towards the integral support of the different characteristics.

6. REFERENCES

[1] R. Burtner, S. Bohn, and D. Payne. Interactive visual comparison of multimedia data through type-specific views. In *SPIE, Visualization and data analysis*, 2013.

[2] E. Chi, J. Riedl, P. Barry, and J. Konstan. Principles for information visualization spreadsheets. *Computer Graphics and Applications*, July/August 1998.

[3] N. Chinchor, J. Thomas, P. C. Wong, M. Christel, and W. Ribarsky. Multimedia analysis + visual analytics = multimedia analytics. *Computer Graphics and Applications, IEEE*, 30(5):52–60, 2010.

[4] M. Christel. *Automated Metadata in Multimedia Information Systems: Creation, Refinement, Use in Surrogates, and Evaluation.* Morgan and Claypool Publishers, 2009.

[5] O. de Rooij, M. Worring, and J. J. van Wijk. Mediatable: Interactive categorization of multimedia collections. *IEEE Computer Graphics and Applications*, 30(5):42–51, 2010.

[6] M. Dörk, D. Gruen, C. Williamson, and S. Carpendale. A visual backchannel for large-scale events. *IEEE Trans. on Visualization and Computer Graphics*, 16(6):1129–1138, 2010.

[7] M. Dörk, H. Riche, R. Gonzalo, and S. Dumais. Pivotpaths: strolling through faceted information spaces. *IEEE Transactions on Visualization and Computer Graphics*, 2012.

[8] D. Fisher, S. Drucker, R. Fernandez, and S. Ruble. Visualizations everywhere: A multiplatform infrastructure for linked visualizations. *IEEE Transactions on Visualization and Computer Graphics*, 16(6), 2010.

[9] A. Girgensohn, F. Shipman, T. Turner, and L. Wilcox. Flexible access to photo libraries via time, place, tags, and visual features. In *Proceedings of JCDL*, 2010.

[10] S. Gratzl, A. Lex, N. Gehlenborg, H. Pfister, and M. Streit. Lineup: Visual analysis of multi-attribute rankings. *IEEE Trans. Vis. Comput. Graph.*, 19(12):2277–2286, 2013.

[11] J. Gray, S. Chaudhuri, A. Bosworth, A. Layman, D. Reichart, and M. Venkatrao. Data cube: a relational aggregation operator generalizing group-by, cross-tab, and sub-totals. In *Data Mining and Knowledge Discovery*, 1997.

[12] B. Höferlin, R. Netzel, M. Höferlin, D. Weiskopf, and G. Heidemann. Inter-active learning of ad-hoc classifiers for video visual analytics. In *IEEE Conference on Visual Analytics Science and Technology (VAST), 2012*, pages 23–32, 2012.

[13] B. Jelen and M. Alexander. *Pivot Table Data Chrunching.* Que Publishing, 2005.

[14] P. Joia, F. Paulovich, J. C. D. Coimbra, and L. Nonato. Local affine multidimensional projection. *IEEE Transactions on Visualization and Computer Graphics*, 17(12), 2011.

[15] S. Kandel, E. Abelson, H. Garcia-Molina, A. Paepcke, and M. Theobald. Photospread: A spreadsheet for managing photos. In *Proceedings of SIGCHI*, 2008.

[16] D. Keim, G. Andrienko, J.-D. Fekete, C. Gorg, J. Kohlhammer, and G. Melancon. Visual analytics : Definition, process, and challenges. In *Information Visualization, LNCS 4960*, 2008.

[17] H. Luo, J. Fan, S. Satoh, J. Yang, and W. Ribarsky. Integrating multi-modal content analysis and hyperbolic visualization for large-scale news video retrieval and exploration. *Signal Processing: Image Communication*, 23(7), 2008.

[18] S. MacNeil and N. Elmqvist. Visualization mosaics for multivariate visual exploration. *Computer Graphics Forum*, 2013.

[19] G. P. Nguyen and M. Worring. Interactive access to large image collections using similarity-based visualization. *Journal of Visual Languages and Computing*, 19(2):203–224, 2008.

[20] C. North. Toward measuring visualization insight. *IEEE Comput. Graph. Appl.*, 26(3):6–9, 2006.

[21] D.-S. Ryu, W.-K. Chung, and H.-G. Cho. Photoland: a new image layout system using spatio-temporal information in digital photos. In *Proceedings of the 2010 ACM Symposium on Applied Computing*, SAC '10, pages 1884–1891, 2010.

[22] K. Schoeffmann, D. Ahlström, and L. Böszörmenyi. 3D storyboards for interactive visual search. In *ICME*, 2012.

[23] C. G. M. Snoek and et.al. Mediamill at TRECVID 2013: Searching concepts, objects, instances and events in video. In *Proceedings of TRECVID Workshop, Gaithersburg, USA*, 2013.

[24] C. Stolte, D. Tang, and P. Hanrahan. Polaris: a system for query, analysis, and visualization of multidimensional relations databases. *IEEE Transactions on Visualization and Computer Graphics*, 8(1), 2002.

[25] G. Tómasson, H. Sigurthórsson, B. Jónsson, and L. Amsaleg. Photocube: effective and efficient multi-dimensional browsing of personal photo collections. In *Proceedings of the ICMR*, 2011.

[26] C. Wang, J. Reese, H. Zhang, J. Tao, Y. Gu, J. Ma, and R. Nemiroff. Similarity-based visualization of large image collections. *Information Visualization*, 6, 2013.

[27] C. Ware. *Visual Thinking for Design.* Morgan Kaufmann, 2008.

[28] M. Worring and D. C. Koelma. Multimedia pivot tables. In *Proceedings of Visual Analytics Science and Technology (VAST)*, 2013.

[29] M. Worring, P. Sajda, S. Santini, D. A. Shamma, A. F. Smeaton, and Q. Yang. Where is the user in multimedia retrieval? *IEEE Multimedia*, 19:6–10, 2012.

[30] J. Yang, J. Fan, D. Hubball, Y. Gao, H. Luo, W. Ribarsky, and W. M. Semantic image browser: Bridging information visualization with automated intelligent image analysis. In *IEEE Symposium on Visual Analytics Science and Technology*, 2006.

[31] J. Zahalka and M. Worring. Towards interactive, intelligent, and integrated multimedia analytics. In *IEEE Conference on Visual Analytics Science and Technology*, 2014.

[32] E. Zavesky, S.-F. Chang, and C.-C. Yang. Visual islands: Intuitive browsing of visual search results. In *Proceedings of the 2008 International Conference on Content-based Image and Video Retrieval*, pages 617–626, 2008.

Distribution Regularized Nonnegative Matrix Factorization for Transfer Visual Feature Learning

Yuchen Guo
Tsinghua Univeristy
Beijing, China
yuchen.w.guo@gmail.com

Guiguang Ding
Tsinghua Univeristy
Beijing, China
dinggg@tsinghua.edu.cn

Qiang Liu
Tsinghua Univeristy
Beijing, China
liuqiang@tsinghua.edu.cn

ABSTRACT

Transfer visual feature learning (TVFL), which learns compact representations for images such that we can build accurate classifier for target domain by leveraging rich labeled data in the source domain, has attracted increasingly attention recently. Previous methods mainly focus on reducing the distribution difference between domains but ignore the intrinsic hidden semantics in data. In this paper, we put forward a novel method for TVFL, called **D**istribution **R**egularized **N**onnegative **M**atrix **F**actorization (DRNMF). Specifically, we employ Nonnegative Matrix Factorization (NMF) to uncover the intrinsic information in visual data, and regularize it with geometrical distribution, marginal probability distribution and conditional probability distribution. Thus, DRNMF can discover the intrinsic information, preserve the manifold structure and reducing both marginal and conditional probability distribution difference simultaneously, which all perspectives above are important for TVFL. We also propose an effective and efficient algorithm for the optimization of DRNMF and theoretically prove the convergence. Extensive experiments on three types of cross-domain image classification tasks in comparison with several state-of-the-art methods demonstrate the superiority of our DRNMF, which validates its effectiveness.

General Terms

Algorithms, Performance, Experimentation

Keywords

Nonnegative Matrix Factorization, Transfer Learning, Geometrical Distribution, Probability Distribution

1. INTRODUCTION

Given a new target domain for classification, it's sometimes burdensome and difficult, even if not impossible, to obtain sufficient labeled data to train accurate classifiers [23, 26]. Fortunately, there are always related source domains where labeled data is abundant and we can use the knowledge in source domains to help build accurate classifiers for target domain, which is termed in literatures as *transfer learning* [24] who has shown promising results in image classification [14, 29], object recognition [1, 11], feature learning [13, 15] and retrieval [7]. Because of the probability distribution difference between domains, previous works on transfer learning mainly focus on learning *transfer features* such that the inter-domain probability difference can be reduced by preserving statistical properties [13, 25], geometric structure [8, 27] shared by different domains, or explicitly minimizing the pre-defined distance measures [21, 22, 23, 28, 30]. Though the learned transfer features can alleviate the probability distribution difference between domains such that we can train standard classifiers like Logistic Regression and SVM on them, they can't capture the intrinsic hidden semantics of image data which is also a very important perspective for building effective classifiers.

Actually, one may always hope to construct compact low-dimensional representations which can also uncover the intrinsic hidden semantics of image data. Several feature learning techniques have been proposed for image data to achieve this goal. Among them, Nonnegative Matrix Factorization (NMF) [16, 17] has recently attracted increasingly attention because the nonnegative constraints can lead to *parts-based* representation for images because only additive, not subtractive, combinations of basis vectors are allowed. And there is psychological and physiological evidence for parts-based representations in human brain [19]. NMF has been proved to be an effective tool to extract intrinsic hidden semantics and applied to several tasks like face recognition [18] and image clustering [3, 5]. But when the labeled and unlabeled images are drawn from different probability distributions, NMF will be greatly challenged because it may generate quite different representations for images drawn from different probability distributions even if they share the same semantic label, e.g., images of one object but collected from different illumination conditions. Fortunately, compared to other feature learning techniques like Sparse Coding which always leads to high-dimensional representation with over-complete basis, it's more natural to incorporate transfer learning to NMF since NMF leads to features with low dimensionality which is more favored than the high one in transfer learning who always looks for low-dimensional shared subspace for domains [21, 23, 28].

Motivated by recent works in transfer learning and NMF, in this paper we propose a novel method for transfer visual feature learning, called Distribution Regularized Non-

ICMR '15 June 23 - 26, 2015, Shanghai, China

http://dx.doi.org/10.1145/2671188.2749316.

negative Matrix Factorization (DRNMF). Specifically, it's build on NMF, and regularized by geometrical distribution, marginal probability distribution and conditional probability distribution. Thus it can simultaneously uncover the intrinsic hidden semantics, preserve local geometric structure, reduce difference of both marginal and conditional probability distributions. By utilizing the power of NMF, DRNMF can learn more effective visual features to build accurate cross-domain classifiers. Meanwhile, DRNMF can also be regarded as an enhanced and extended version of NMF such that NMF can handle the probability distribution difference between datasets, which is also very common in real world. In summary, this paper makes some contributions as below.

- We propose a novel DRNMF for transfer visual feature learning. It can learn more effective compact features for cross-domain image classification task by simultaneously extracting intrinsic hidden semantics, preserving geometric structure, and reducing marginal as well as conditional distribution difference among domains.
- Conventional NMF is extended by DRNMF such that it can handle the probability distribution difference in data while previous works on NMF almost ignore this.
- We put forward an effective and efficient iterative algorithm with multiplication updating rules for the optimization problem of DRNMF, and give the theoretical analysis on the convergency property of this algorithm.
- We conduct extensive experiments on three types of cross-domain image classification problems. The experiment results demonstrate that DRNMF can significantly outperform several state-of-the-art related methods, validating the effectiveness of our DRNMF.

The rest of this paper is organized as follows. In Section 2, some important related works are reviewed. The the proposed DRNMF is introduced in detail in Section 3. The theoretical analysis is shown in Section 4. Then we present experiment in Section 5 and draw conclusion in Section 6.

2. RELATED WORK

Maximum Mean Discrepancy (MMD)[9] is widely used as an nonparametric distance measure between probability distributions. It will asymptotically approach to zero if and only if the two distributions are identical. By minimizing MMD of features, the probability distribution difference of original features in different domains can be alleviated. Specifically, Transfer Component Analysis (TCA) [23] aims to minimize the MMD of marginal probability distribution between domains and the reconstruction error of data simultaneously based on PCA. And Joint Distribution Adaptation (JDA) [21] extends TCA by further minimizing the MMD of conditional probability distribution between domains. Though the probability distribution difference between domains can be reduced, these methods can't discover the intrinsic hidden semantics, as mentioned above, which is also a key difference between their methods and DRNMF who focuses on learning effective image representations by building an adaptive model based on NMF.

We also noticed that some efforts have been made to incorporate effective feature learning methods into transfer learning such that the learned transfer visual features can reduce the probability distribution difference while discover intrinsic hidden semantics [20, 26]. These methods adopt Sparse Coding (SC) for feature learning. But SC always requires over-complete basis such that it's difficult to directly apply SC to high-dimensional image data and the learned features are not compact and low-dimensional. And they need to solve an ℓ_1-regularized least square problem which is highly inefficient compared to NMF. Furthermore, kernel density estimation technique is adopted in [26] which is more restricted than DRNMF and is prone to be over-fitting, while conditional probability distribution is ignored in [20].

Table 1: Notations and descriptions in this paper

Notation	Description	Notation	Description
$\mathcal{D}_s$	source domain	$\mathcal{D}_t$	target domain
n_s	#source images	n_t	#target iamges
m	#original features	C	#classes
k	#basis vectors	p	#NN
α	graph para.	β	MMD para.
$\mathbf{X}$	input matrix	$\mathbf{U}$	basis matrix
$\mathbf{V}$	transfer features	$\mathbf{W}$	NN matrix
$\mathbf{L}$	graph Lap. matrix	$\mathbf{M}_c$	MMD matrix

3. THE PROPOSED METHOD

3.1 Problem Definition

Following the conventional definition for transfer feature learning, such as in [21], our problem is defined as follows,

PROBLEM 1. *Given a labeled dataset in source domain* $\mathcal{D}_s = \{(\mathbf{x}_1, y_1), ..., (\mathbf{x}_{n_s}, y_{n_s})\}$*, and an unlabeled dataset in target domain* $\mathcal{D}_t = \{\mathbf{x}_{n_s+1}, ..., \mathbf{x}_{n_s+n_t}\}$*, where the marginal and conditional probability distributions are both different, i.e.,* $P_s(\mathbf{x}_s) \neq P_t(\mathbf{x}_t)$ *and* $P_s(y_s|\mathbf{x}_s) \neq P_t(y_t|\mathbf{x}_t)$*, our goal is to learn a new representation such that classifiers trained on labeled dataset can work robustly on unlabeled dataset.*

where n_s and n_t are the number of images in source and target domain respectively. Totally, we can first define $\mathbf{X} = [x_1, ..., x_{n_s+n_t}] \in \mathbb{R}^{m\times(n_s+n_t)}$ as the nonnegative data matrix where each data is represented by an m-dimensional vector. Our goal is to learn a basis matrix $\mathbf{U} \in \mathbb{R}^{m\times k}$ and corresponding k-dimensional nonnegative transfer features $\mathbf{V} = [\mathbf{v}_1, ..., \mathbf{v}_{n_s+n_t}] \in \mathbb{R}^{k\times(n_s+n_t)}$. Now we can train any supervised classifiers on $\{(\mathbf{v}_1, y_1), ..., (\mathbf{v}_{n_s}, y_{n_s})\}$, and then classify $\{\mathbf{v}_{n_s+1}, ..., \mathbf{v}_{n_s+n_t}\}$ with obtained classifiers.

3.2 Objective Function

3.2.1 Nonnegative Matrix Factorization

Given a nonnegative data matrix $\mathbf{X}$, NMF aims to find two nonnegative matrices $\mathbf{U}$ as basis of latent space and the corresponding coordinates $\mathbf{V}$ which can well approximate the original data matrix $\mathbf{X}$. And the quality of approximation is always measured by the squared loss function. Therefore the objective function of NMF can be written as below [16],

$$\mathcal{O}_{\text{NMF}} = \|\mathbf{X} - \mathbf{U}\mathbf{V}\|_F^2 \quad \text{s.t.} \quad \mathbf{U}, \mathbf{V} \geq 0 \qquad (1)$$

where $\|\cdot\|_F$ is the Frobenius norm of matrix. NMF has been proved to be a powerful tool to learn compact low-dimensional representations and uncover the intrinsic hidden semantics of image data because the nonnegative constraints may lead to parts-based representations for image data which has psychological and physiological evidence in human brain [19]. Generally, minimizing Eq. (1) can be effectively and efficiently achieved by utilizing an iterative strategy with the following multiplicative updating rules [17]

$$u_{il} \leftarrow u_{il}\frac{(\mathbf{X}\mathbf{V}^T)_{il}}{(\mathbf{U}\mathbf{V}\mathbf{V}^T)_{il}}, \quad v_{lj} \leftarrow v_{lj}\frac{(\mathbf{U}^T\mathbf{X})_{lj}}{(\mathbf{U}^T\mathbf{U}\mathbf{V})_{lj}} \tag{2}$$

3.2.2 Geometrical Distribution Regularization

In real world, natural data always lies on a low-dimensional manifold embedded in high-dimensional ambient space. However, conventional NMF ignores this *geometrical distribution* underlying the image data. In [3], an extension of NMF called Graph Regularized NMF (GNMF) is proposed to further explore the geometrical distribution of data. Specifically, the geometrical distribution is exploited by preserving the locality of data based on the locality invariant idea [12], i.e., the nearby points in original space should be close to each other in low-dimensional latent space. Firstly we can construct a p (such as 5) nearest neighbor matrix as

$$W_{ij} = \begin{cases} 1, & \text{if } \mathbf{x}_i \in \mathcal{N}(\mathbf{x}_j) \text{ or } \mathbf{x}_j \in \mathcal{N}(\mathbf{x}_i) \\ 0, & \text{otherwise} \end{cases} \tag{3}$$

where $\mathcal{N}(\mathbf{x}_i)$ denotes the p nearest neighbor of $\mathbf{x}_i$. Then we can define a diagonal degree matrix with diagonal element $D_{ii} = \sum_{j=1}^{n} W_{ij}$ and the graph Laplacian matrix $\mathbf{L} = \mathbf{D} - \mathbf{W}$. So the locality invariant idea can be formulate as minimizing $\frac{1}{2}\sum_{i,j=1}^{n} W_{ij}\|\mathbf{v}_i - \mathbf{v}_j\|_F^2 = tr(\mathbf{V}\mathbf{L}\mathbf{V}^T)$. By incorporating this geometrical distribution regularization (or termed as graph regularization in [3]) into NMF, we have the objective function of GNMF written as below,

$$\mathcal{O}_{\text{GNMF}} = \|\mathbf{X} - \mathbf{U}\mathbf{V}\|_F^2 + \alpha tr(\mathbf{V}\mathbf{L}\mathbf{V}^T) \text{ s.t. } \mathbf{U}, \mathbf{V} \geq 0 \tag{4}$$

where α is the regularization parameter to control the weight of the regularization. Actually, GNMF has shown promising result on single-domain problems because it's able to uncover the intrinsic hidden semantics and preserve the geometrical distribution of data. However, when applying it directly to cross-domain problems, the performance of GNMF may degrade severely because it ignores the probability distribution difference between domains. But it lays the foundation of our DRNMF as a feature learning method.

3.2.3 Probability Distribution Regularization

In the k-dimensional representation learned by GNMF, the distribution difference between domains is still significantly large. Thus we need to reduce the distribution difference by explicitly minimize some predefined distance measure during the feature learning procedure. In this paper we follow [9, 22, 23] and utilize a nonparametric distance measure, Maximum Mean Discrepancy (MMD), to compare different distributions, which is defined as the distance between the sample means of source and target domains as

$$\|\frac{1}{n_s}\sum_{i=1}^{n_s}\mathbf{v}_i - \frac{1}{n_t}\sum_{j=n_s+1}^{n_s+n_t}\mathbf{v}_j\|_F^2 = tr(\mathbf{V}\mathbf{M}_0\mathbf{V}^T) \tag{5}$$

where $\mathbf{M}_0$ is the MMD matrix which is defined as follows,

$$(M_0)_{ij} = \begin{cases} \frac{1}{n_s n_s}, & \text{if } \mathbf{x}_i, \mathbf{x}_j \in \mathcal{D}_s \\ \frac{1}{n_t n_t}, & \text{if } \mathbf{x}_i, \mathbf{x}_j \in \mathcal{D}_t \\ \frac{-1}{n_s n_t}, & \text{otherwise} \end{cases} \tag{6}$$

By minimizing Eq. (5), we can reduce the **marginal** probability distribution difference between domains in learned representations like in TCA, i.e., we have $P_s(\mathbf{v}_s) \approx P_t(\mathbf{v}_t)$.

Furthermore, the conditional probability distribution is also important for transfer feature learning, especially when the learned features are utilized in classification task. Some works have been proposed to match the conditional probability distributions [2, 4, 26, 30]. But they all require some labeled data in target domain. Thus they can't be applied to our problem. Instead, we follow the idea in [21] where *pseudo* labels of target domain data predicted by base classifier which is trained on the labeled source domain data are exploited to match the conditional probability distributions.

Actually, directly matching the sample-conditional probability distribution $P(y|\mathbf{v})$ is infeasible because this posterior probability is very difficult to estimate. Instead, we can match the class-conditional probability distribution $P(\mathbf{v}|y)$, i.e., we hope the learned representations can satisfy $P_s(\mathbf{v}_s|y = c) \approx P_t(\mathbf{v}_t|y = c)$ for $\forall c \in \{1, ..., C\}$, where C is the number of class. Besides the difficulty to estimate sample-conditional probability distribution, here is another reason why we can utilize class-conditional probability distribution. If Eq. (5) is effectively minimized, we can obtain $P_s(\mathbf{v}_s) \approx P_t(\mathbf{v}_t)$. Under the ultimate situation, we have $P_s(\mathbf{v}_s) = P_t(\mathbf{v}_t)$. Then by assuming $P(y)$ is consistent in both domains, i.e., $P_s(y) = P_t(y)$, we can get $P_s(y|\mathbf{v}_s) - P_t(y|\mathbf{v}_t) \propto P_s(\mathbf{v}_s|y) - P_t(\mathbf{v}_t|y)$ based on Bayesian formula $P(y|\mathbf{v}) = P(\mathbf{v}|y)P(y)/P(\mathbf{v})$. Therefore matching the class-conditional probability distribution $P(\mathbf{v}|y)$ is equivalent to matching the sample-conditional probability distribution $P(y|\mathbf{v})$. Thus, given the true labels of labeled source domain data and pseudo labels of unlabeled target domain data, we can match the class-conditional probability distributions of different domains by minimizing the MMD for images in each class c as follows,

$$\|\frac{1}{n_s^c}\sum_{\mathbf{x}_i \in \mathcal{D}_s^c}\mathbf{v}_i - \frac{1}{n_t^c}\sum_{\mathbf{x}_j \in \mathcal{D}_t^c}\mathbf{v}_j\|_F^2 = tr(\mathbf{V}\mathbf{M}_c\mathbf{V}^T) \tag{7}$$

where $\mathcal{D}_s^c$ is the subset of $\mathcal{D}_s$ in which the **true** labels of images are c and $n_s^c = |\mathcal{D}_s^c|$. And $\mathcal{D}_t^c$ is the subset of $\mathcal{D}_t$ in which the **pseudo** labels of images are c and $n_t^c = |\mathcal{D}_t^c|$. And the MMD matrix $\mathbf{M}_c$ for class c is defined as follows,

$$(M_c)_{ij} = \begin{cases} \frac{1}{n_s^c n_s^c}, & \text{if } \mathbf{x}_i, \mathbf{x}_j \in \mathcal{D}_s^c \\ \frac{1}{n_t^c n_t^c}, & \text{if } \mathbf{x}_i, \mathbf{x}_j \in \mathcal{D}_t^c \\ \frac{-1}{n_s n_t}, & \text{if } \mathbf{x}_i(\mathbf{x}_j) \in \mathcal{D}_s^c, \mathbf{x}_j(\mathbf{x}_i) \in \mathcal{D}_t^c \\ 0, & \text{otherwise} \end{cases} \tag{8}$$

Then by minimizing Eq. (7), the conditional probability distribution difference between domains for each class can be effectively reduced in the learned feature representations.

Here, the pseudo labels for target domain can be generated by applying a classifier trained on the labeled source domain to the target domain. Generally, 1 nearest neighbor (1NN) classifier can lead to satisfactory result. However, many of initial pseudo labels are incorrect because the conditional probability distributions aren't correctly matched at first. To address this issue, we can conduct the feature learning step and pseudo label generating step iteratively thus we can expect to obtain more correct pseudo labels with more iterations, leading to better matched conditional probability distributions and vice versa. In our experiment, we find out that satisfactory result can be achieved in 5 to 10 iterations.

3.2.4 Overall Objective Function

We first define the overall MMD matrix as $\mathbf{M} = \sum_{c=0}^{C}\mathbf{M}_c$.

Algorithm 1 Learning Transfer Features by DRNMF

Input:

Image data $\mathbf{X} = [\mathbf{X}_s, \mathbf{X}_t]$, true labels $\mathbf{Y}_s$, #basis vectors k, graph Lap. $\mathbf{L}$, regul. para. α, β, #iteration T

Output:

The learned basis $\mathbf{U}$ and transfer features $\mathbf{V}$.

1: Construct $\mathbf{M}_0$ by Eq. (6), and $\mathbf{M}_c = \mathbf{0}$, $c = 1, ..., C$
2: **for** $t = 1 : T$ **do**
3: Construct $\mathbf{R} = \alpha\mathbf{L} + \beta\sum_{c=0}^{C}\mathbf{M}_c$.
4: Initialize $\mathbf{U}$ and $\mathbf{V}$ by randomization.
5: **repeat**
6: Update $\mathbf{U}$ by Eq. (16).
7: Update $\mathbf{V}$ by Eq. (17).
8: **until** Convergence
9: Update pseudo labels $\hat{\mathbf{Y}}_t$ by 1NN classifier.
10: Construct $\mathbf{M}_c$ by Eq. (8), $c = 1, ..., C$.
11: **end for**
12: Return basis $\mathbf{U}$ and transfer features $\mathbf{V}$.

Then by combining Eq. (4), Eq. (5) and Eq. (7), we can obtain the overall objective function of DRNMF as follows,

$$\mathcal{O} = \|\mathbf{X} - \mathbf{U}\mathbf{V}\|_F^2 + tr(\mathbf{V}\mathbf{R}\mathbf{V}^T) \text{ s.t. } \mathbf{U}, \mathbf{V} \geq 0 \quad (9)$$

where $\mathbf{R} = \alpha\mathbf{L}+\beta\mathbf{M}$ is the overall distribution regularization matrix which combines the geometric distribution regularization, marginal probability distribution regularization and conditional probability distribution regularization. $\alpha > 0$ and $\beta > 0$ are the regularization parameters which trade off the weight of geometrical distribution regularization and probability distribution regularization respectively.

Actually, every term in Eq. (9) is indispensable for transfer feature learning. NMF uncovers the intrinsic hidden semantics of data leading to more meaningful representation, which is an important difference and improvement compared to several transfer **feature** learning methods like TCA and JDA. The geometrical distribution regularization explores the low-dimensional geometric structure underlying the data, which can promote the effectiveness of the learned representations. The probability regularization can reduce both the marginal and conditional probability distribution difference between domains such that we can build accurate classifiers on the learned representations, which is also a basic requirement for a **transfer** feature learning method.

3.3 Optimization Algorithm

The optimization problem of minimizing Eq. (9) is not convex with $\mathbf{U}$ and $\mathbf{V}$ together. Fortunately, it's convex with respect to any one while fixing the other. Therefore we can utilize the following iterative strategy by updating one while fixing the other which will achieve the local minima.

Based on the following matrix properties, $\|\mathbf{A}\|_F^2 = tr(\mathbf{A}\mathbf{A}^T)$, $tr(\mathbf{A}\mathbf{B}) = tr(\mathbf{B}\mathbf{A})$ and $tr(\mathbf{A}) = tr(\mathbf{A}^T)$, the objective function of DRNMF in Eq. (9) can be rewritten as follows,

$$\begin{aligned}\mathcal{O}_1 =& tr(\mathbf{X}\mathbf{X}^T) - 2tr(\mathbf{X}\mathbf{V}^T\mathbf{U}^T) + tr(\mathbf{V}\mathbf{R}\mathbf{V}^T)\\ &+ tr(\mathbf{U}\mathbf{V}\mathbf{V}^T\mathbf{U}^T), \text{ s.t. } \mathbf{U}, \mathbf{V} \geq 0\end{aligned} \quad (10)$$

Now denote ψ_{il} and ϕ_{lj} as the Lagrange multiplier for constraint $u_{il} \geq 0$ and $v_{lj} \geq 0$ respectively, and $\mathbf{\Psi} = [\psi_{il}]$ and $\mathbf{\Phi} = [\phi_{lj}]$. Then we can rewrite the Lagrange $\mathcal{L}$ as follows,

$$\mathcal{L} = \mathcal{O}_1 + tr(\mathbf{\Psi}\mathbf{U}^T) + tr(\mathbf{\Phi}\mathbf{V}^T) \quad (11)$$

The partial derivatives of $\mathcal{L}$ with respect to $\mathbf{U}$ and $\mathbf{V}$ are

$$\frac{\partial\mathcal{L}}{\partial\mathbf{U}} = -2\mathbf{X}\mathbf{V}^T + 2\mathbf{U}\mathbf{V}\mathbf{V}^T + \mathbf{\Psi} \quad (12)$$

$$\frac{\partial\mathcal{L}}{\partial\mathbf{V}} = -2\mathbf{U}^T\mathbf{X} + 2\mathbf{U}^T\mathbf{U}\mathbf{V} + 2\mathbf{V}\mathbf{R} + \mathbf{\Phi} \quad (13)$$

Then by using the Karush-Kuhn-Tucker conditions, that is, $\psi_{il}u_{il} = 0$ and $\phi_{lj}v_{lj} = 0$, we get the following equations,

$$-(\mathbf{X}\mathbf{V}^T)_{il}u_{il} + (\mathbf{U}\mathbf{V}\mathbf{V}^T)_{il}u_{il} = 0 \quad (14)$$

$$-(\mathbf{U}^T\mathbf{X})_{lj}v_{lj} + (\mathbf{U}^T\mathbf{U}\mathbf{V})_{jl}v_{jl} + (\mathbf{V}\mathbf{R})_{jl}v_{jl} = 0 \quad (15)$$

Then we obtain the following multiplicative updating rules:

$$u_{il} \leftarrow u_{il}\frac{(\mathbf{X}\mathbf{V}^T)il}{(\mathbf{U}\mathbf{V}\mathbf{V}^T)_{il}} \quad (16)$$

$$v_{lj} \leftarrow v_{lj}\frac{(\mathbf{U}^T\mathbf{X} + \mathbf{V}\mathbf{R}^-)_{lj}}{(\mathbf{U}^T\mathbf{U}\mathbf{V} + \mathbf{V}\mathbf{R}^+)_{lj}} \quad (17)$$

where $\mathbf{R}^+ = \frac{1}{2}(|\mathbf{R}| + \mathbf{R})$ is the positive part of $\mathbf{R}$ and $\mathbf{R}^- = \frac{1}{2}(|\mathbf{R}| - \mathbf{R})$ is the negative part of $\mathbf{R}$. Applying Eq. (16) and Eq. (17) iteratively, $\mathcal{O}$ in Eq. (9) can reach local minima. Then based on the learned transfer representation $\mathbf{V}$, we can update the pseudo labels of target domain data by a new 1NN classifier trained on source domain data. We can repeat these two steps for T times for the final representation. Generally, setting $T = 10$ can result in satisfactory performance and guarantee efficiency. We summarize the overall optimization algorithm for DRNMF in Algorithm 1.

4. THEORETICAL ANALYSIS

4.1 Proof of Convergence

Actually, it's important to note that there is no theoretical evidence that the outer iteration can converge because we have no labeled data and prior knowledge in target domain. And because of the random initialization and the local minima, we may obtain different pseudo labels even with the same $\mathbf{L}$ and $\mathbf{M}$. But fortunately, we find out in our experiment that we can usually obtain more correct pseudo labels in each iteration because the conditional probability distribution is indeed better matched. And it will finally achieve a relatively stable performance, generally within about 10 iterations. Thus this EM-like iterative strategy is always effective in reality, which is also validated in our experiment.

But we need to guarantee the convergence of the inner iteration, i.e., the feature learning step (line 5 to 8). Otherwise we can't obtain effective and meaningful representations. The convergence is guaranteed by Theorem 1 below.

THEOREM 1. *The objective function $\mathcal{O}$ in Eq. (9) is nonincreasing under updating rules in Eq. (16) and Eq. (17).*

The objective function is obviously lower-bounded by zero. Thus $\mathcal{O}$ will certainly converge if it's nonincreasing. To prove Theorem 1, we need to show $\mathcal{O}$ is nonincreasing under Eq. (16) and Eq. (17). Actually, The part of $\mathcal{O}$ which is only relevant to $\mathbf{U}$ is the same as NMF and the updating rule in Eq. (16) is also exactly the same as in original NMF. Therefore $\mathcal{O}$ is nonincreasing under Eq. (16), whose detailed proof can be found in [17]. Now we need to show $\mathcal{O}$ is nonincreasing under Eq. (17). Following the proof in [6], firstly we introduce the definition of *auxiliary function*

Definition 1. $A(v, v')$ is an *auxiliary function* for $B(v)$ if

$$A(v, v') \geq B(v), \quad A(v, v) = B(v) \tag{18}$$

are satisfied.

Then we need to introduce the following important lemma,

Lemma 1. If $A(v, v')$ is an auxiliary function of $B(v)$, then $B(v)$ will be nonincreasing under the following update

$$v^{(t+1)} = \arg\min_{v} A(v, v^{(t)}) \tag{19}$$

Proof proof of Lemma 1.

$$B(v^{(t+1)}) \leq A(v^{(t+1)}, v^{(t)}) \leq A(v^{(t)}, v^{(t)}) = B(v^{(t)})$$

□

Now we need to show the updating rule for $\mathbf{V}$ in Eq. (17) is exactly the update in Eq. (19) with a proper auxiliary function. Let B_{ab} denote the the part of $\mathcal{O}$ that is only relevant to v_{ab}. Then the second-order partial derivative of B_{ab} is as

$$B_{ab}^{''} = 2(\mathbf{U}^T\mathbf{U})_{aa} + 2\mathbf{R}_{bb} \tag{20}$$

And it is quite easy to verify the following two inequalities,

$$(\mathbf{U}^T\mathbf{U}\mathbf{V})_{ab} = \sum_{i=1}^{k} (\mathbf{U}^T\mathbf{U})_{ak} v_{kb}^{(t)} \geq (\mathbf{U}^T\mathbf{U})_{aa} v_{ab}^{(t)} \tag{21}$$

$$(\mathbf{V}\mathbf{R}^+)_{ab} = \sum_{j=1}^{n} v_{aj}^{(t)} \mathbf{R}_{jb}^+ \geq v_{ab}^{(t)} \mathbf{R}_{bb}^+ \geq v_{ab}^{(t)} \mathbf{R}_{bb} \tag{22}$$

Lemma 2. The function

$$\begin{aligned} A(v, v_{ab}^{(t)}) =& B_{ab}(v_{ab}^{(t)}) + B_{ab}^{'}(v_{ab}^{(t)})(v - v_{ab}^{(t)}) \\ &+ \frac{(\mathbf{U}^T\mathbf{U}\mathbf{V} + \mathbf{V}\mathbf{R}^+)_{ab}}{v_{ab}^{(t)}}(v - v_{ab}^{(t)})^2 \end{aligned} \tag{23}$$

is an auxiliary function for $B_{ab}(v)$.

Proof proof to Lemma 2. It's obvious that $A(v, v) = B_{ab}(v)$. Now we need to show $A(v, v_{ab}^{(t)}) \geq B_{ab}(v)$. Here we compare the Taylor series expansion of $B_{ab}(v)$ at $v_{ab}^{(t)}$ as

$$\begin{aligned} B_{ab}(v) =& B_{ab}(v_{ab}^{(t)}) + B_{ab}^{'}(v_{ab}^{(t)})(v - v_{ab}^{(t)}) \\ &+ \frac{1}{2} B_{ab}^{''}(v_{ab}^{(t)})(v - v_{ab}^{(t)})^2 \end{aligned} \tag{24}$$

Based on the definition in Eq. (20) and Eq. (23), and two important inequalities presented in Eq. (21) and Eq. (22), it's quite straightforward to verify that $A(v, v_{ab}^{(t)}) \geq B_{ab}(v)$. □

Proof proof of Theorem 1. We can replace $A(v, v_{ab}^{(t)})$ in Eq. (19) by Eq. (23), which result in the following rule,

$$\begin{aligned} v_{ab}^{(t+1)} &= v_{ab}^{(t)} - v_{ab}^{(t)} \frac{B_{ab}^{'}(v_{ab}^{(t)})}{2(\mathbf{U}^T\mathbf{U}\mathbf{V} + \mathbf{V}\mathbf{R}^+)_{ab}} \\ &= v_{ab}^{(t)} \frac{(\mathbf{U}^T\mathbf{X} + \mathbf{V}\mathbf{R}^-)_{ab}}{(\mathbf{U}^T\mathbf{U}\mathbf{V} + \mathbf{V}\mathbf{R}^+)_{ab}} \end{aligned} \tag{25}$$

which is identical to Eq. (17). Because $A(v, v_{ab}^{(t)})$ is an auxiliary function of B_{ab}, B_{ab} is nonincreasing under this updating rule. Therefore $\mathcal{O}$ is nonincreasing under Eq. (17). □

Table 2: Statistics of benchmark datasets

Dataset	Type	#Img	#Fea	#Class
MNIST	Digit	1,000	256	10
USPS	Digit	1,000	256	10
Semeion	Digit	1,000	256	10
COIL1,2	Object	720	1024	20
PIE1,...,5	Face	1,360	1024	68

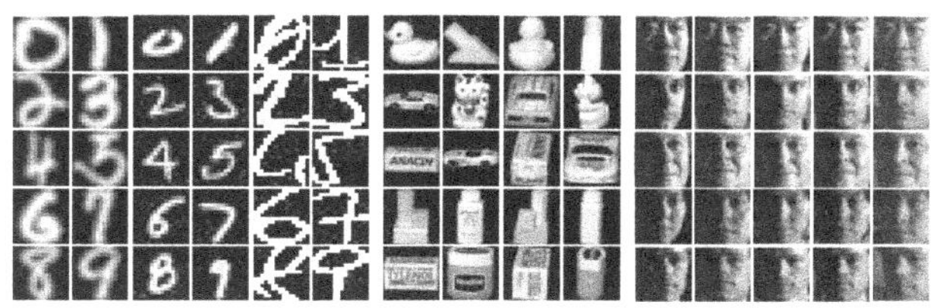

Figure 1: USPS, MNIST, Semeion, COIL, and PIE

4.2 Complexity Analysis

Suppose we have T outer iterations and t inner iterations, then the overall time complexity for Algorithm 1 is $\mathcal{O}(Tt(mnk+(m+n)(k^2+k)+n^2k))$. We can observe that the complexity is linear to the feature dimension m. Therefore the optimization algorithm is efficient for high-dimensional feature which is very common for images data.

5. EXPERIMENT AND DISCUSSION

5.1 Experiment Setting

5.1.1 Benchmark Datasets

We conduct extensive experiment on three types of benchmark datasets for cross-domain image classification task, MNIST[1]+USPS[2] +Semeion[3], COIL[4] and PIE[5]. We construct several subsets from them for implementation efficiency. The statistics of these datasets are summarized in Table 2. We also present several sample images in Figure 1.

USPS, MNIST and Semeion are three widely used handwritten digit datasets. To speed up experiments, we select $1,000$ images from each dataset, which consists of 10 classes and 100 images per class. We rescale all images to size 16×16 and represent each image by a vector encoding the gray-scale pixel values. From Figure 1, we can observe that these three datasets follow quite different distributions. Thus we can construct 6 cross-domain classification tasks, e.g., *USPS vs MNIST* in which we use USPS as the labeled source domain and MNIST as the unlabeled target domain.

COIL contains 1,440 images of 20 objects taken from different degrees. We split it into two subsets, COIL1 containing images taken in directions of $[0°, 85°] \cup [180°, 265°]$ and COIL2 in directions of $[90°, 175°] \cup [270°, 355°]$. Both contain 20 classes and 36 images per class. Thus COIL1 and COIL2 follow different distributions. Each image is represented by a 1,024-dimension vector encoding the gray-scale

[1]http://yann.lecun.com/exdb/mnist/
[2]1http://www-i6.informatik.rwth-aachen.de
[3]https://archive.ics.uci.edu/ml/datasets
[4]http://www.cs.columbia.edu/CAVE/software/softlib/coil-20.php
[5]https://www.ri.cmu.edu/research-project-detail.html

Table 3: Cross-domain Image Classification Accuracy (%)

Dataset	LR	PCA	NMF	GNMF	TCA	TSL	GFK	TSC	JDA	Ours
MNIST vs USPS	41.30	41.40	47.08	50.36	50.20	66.40	64.28	67.84	71.30	**88.83**
USPS vs MNIST	34.30	34.30	36.64	39.71	40.00	46.10	38.91	46.85	53.30	**56.07**
MNIST vs Semeion	7.50	6.30	10.19	10.41	7.10	16.20	11.37	17.85	19.10	**30.63**
Semeion vs MNIST	10.40	10.50	8.14	11.74	7.90	17.80	13.80	20.57	28.20	**29.49**
USPS vs Semeion	38.90	38.40	34.31	36.69	41.60	48.00	39.71	41.32	55.30	**58.11**
Semeion vs USPS	42.30	42.00	36.97	41.72	55.30	58.90	52.17	65.41	69.10	**76.13**
COIL1 vs COIL2	76.11	75.56	74.33	77.31	78.47	82.84	76.31	85.12	88.75	**94.31**
COIL2 vs COIL1	74.03	73.75	73.56	75.06	78.61	80.61	77.84	84.33	86.67	**95.00**
PIE1 vs PIE5	21.03	20.15	30.15	30.64	36.25	38.75	32.26	40.31	42.87	**52.13**
PIE2 vs PIE4	64.56	62.35	55.88	59.37	68.75	73.28	63.41	71.85	76.18	**80.02**
PIE3 vs PIE1	29.49	29.19	35.66	38.18	46.83	44.84	40.08	46.84	49.56	**61.10**
PIE4 vs PIE3	67.21	64.48	68.68	70.59	72.21	75.85	70.26	76.21	80.22	**86.69**
PIE5 vs PIE2	31.39	29.63	30.81	32.62	37.57	38.17	39.78	36.04	42.79	**44.12**
Average	40.86	39.65	41.77	43.94	49.38	53.53	47.54	54.13	58.17	**64.93**

pixel values. And we can construct two cross-domain classification tasks, *COIL1 vs COIL2* and *COIL2 vs COIL1*.

PIE face dataset contains images of 68 individuals under different poses, illuminations and expressions. For thoroughly comparison, we construct 5 subsets with each corresponding to a different poses, i.e., PIE1 (left), PIE2 (upward), PIE3 (downward), PIE4 (frontal) and PIE5 (right). Each subset contains 68 classes (individuals) with 20 images per class where each image is represented by a 1,024-dimension feature. So we can construct 20 cross-domain classification tasks, i.e., *PIEi vs PIEj* $(i, j = 1, ..., 5, i \neq j)$.

5.1.2 Baseline Methods

The proposed DRNMF is compared to several state-of-the-art related feature learning methods for cross-domain image classification task, including both standard feature learning and transfer feature learning methods below.

- Logistic Regression (LR)
- Principle Component Analysis (PCA) + LR
- Nonnegative Matrix Factorization (NMF) [16] + LR
- Graph Regularized NMF (GNMF) [3] + LR
- Transfer Component Analysis (TCA) [23] + LR
- Transfer Subspace Learning (TSL) [28] + LR
- Geodestic Flow Kernel (GFK) [8] + LR
- Transfer Sparse Coding (TSC) [20] + LR
- Joint Distribution Adaptation (JDA) [21] + LR

We choose LR as the base classifier following the setting in [20]. PCA, NMF and GNMF are standard learning methods that NMF can uncover the intrinsic hidden semantics and GNMF has geometrical distribution regularization. TCA, TSL, GFK, TSC and JDA are transfer learning methods. TCA and TSL only consider the marginal probability distribution while JDA considers both marginal and conditional distributions. They can't uncover the hidden semantics of data and ignore local geometric structure. TSC uncovers the hidden semantics by Sparse Coding while it fails to reduce the conditional probability distribution difference.

5.1.3 Implementation Details

For fair comparison, we fix some unimportant parameters for all experiments as follows. The regularization parameter for LR, i.e., c, is consistently set to 1. And for all feature learning methods, we set k, the dimension of the new representation, to 100. And p for constructing p-NN matrix, is set as 5 for GNMF, TSC and DRNMF.

There are some important model parameters for different baseline methods which may have significant effect on the performance of these methods. For meaningful comparison, we empirically search the parameter space for each baseline methods and the *best* result for each baseline method in each experiment is reported. Specifically, the graph regularization parameter in GNMF and TSC, is chosen from $\{0.001, 0.005, 0.01, 0.05, ..., 100\}$. The adaptation regularization parameter for TSL, TCA and JDA is empirically searched in $\{0.01, 0.1, 1, 10, 100\}$. And the MMD regularization and the sparsity regularization parameters in TSC are selected from $\{10^0, ..., 10^6\}$ and $\{0.001, 0.005, ..., 10\}$ respectively.

There are two important parameters for DRNMF, i.e., the geometrical distribution regularization parameter α and the probability distribution regularization parameter β. In the coming section, we conduct empirical analysis on parameter sensitivity which demonstrates that DRNMF can achieve superior and stable performance under a wide range of parameter values for α and β. When comparing with baseline methods, we set 1) $\alpha = 0.1$ and $\beta = 100$ for digit and object datasets, and 2) $\alpha = 0.01$ and $\beta = 10$ for face datasets. And we further set the number of outer iterations, T, to 10.

The classification *Accuracy* on the target domain data is adopted as the evaluation metric, which is widely utilized in related literatures [21, 23, 28]. And it is defined as follows,

$$Accuracy = \frac{|\mathbf{x} : \mathbf{x} \in \mathcal{D}_t \wedge \hat{y}(\mathbf{x}) = y(\mathbf{x})|}{|\mathbf{x} : \mathbf{x} \in \mathcal{D}_t|} \qquad (26)$$

where $\mathcal{D}_t$ is the target domain, $\hat{y}(\mathbf{x})$ is the predicted label by LR and $y(\mathbf{x})$ is the true label of $\mathbf{x}$. To remove randomness caused by random initialization, like in NMF and DRNMF, all results reported are the average over 10 runs.

5.2 Experiment Result

5.2.1 Cross-domain Classification Result

The classification results of DRNMF and other 9 baseline methods on all 28 cross-domain datasets are shown in Table 3 and Figure 2. Because of the limit of space, we just list 5 datasets of PIE in Table 3, and all 20 results of PIE are shown in Figure 2. We can observe that DRNMF can consistently and significantly outperform all baseline methods on all three types of tasks, i.e., digit, object and face. The average accuracy of DRNMF on all 28 datasets is **64.93**%, and the improvement compared to best baseline methods, i.e.,

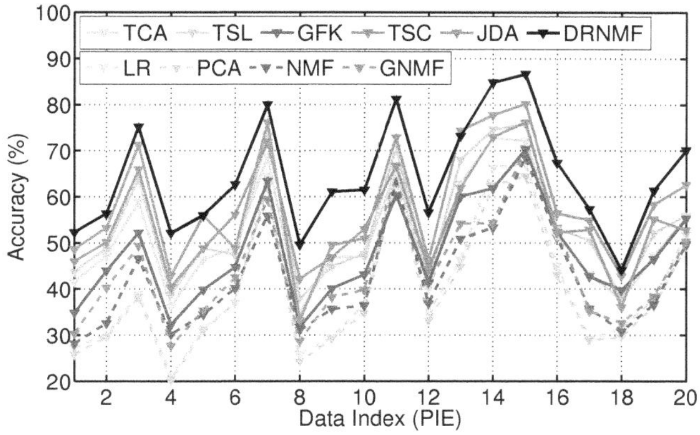

Figure 2: All Results on PIE

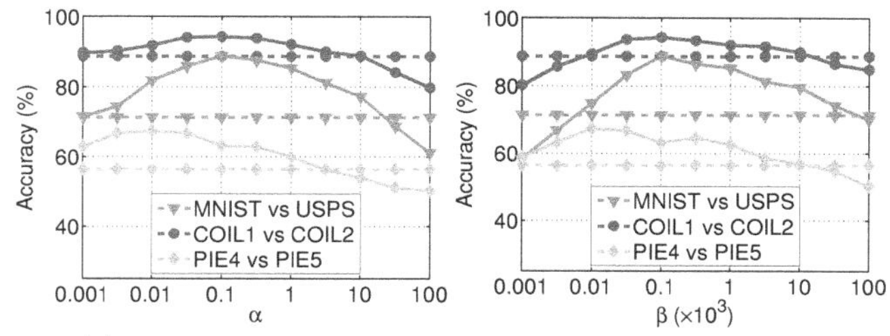

(a) Accuracy w.r.t. α (b) Accuracy w.r.t. β

Figure 3: Parameter sensitivity analysis

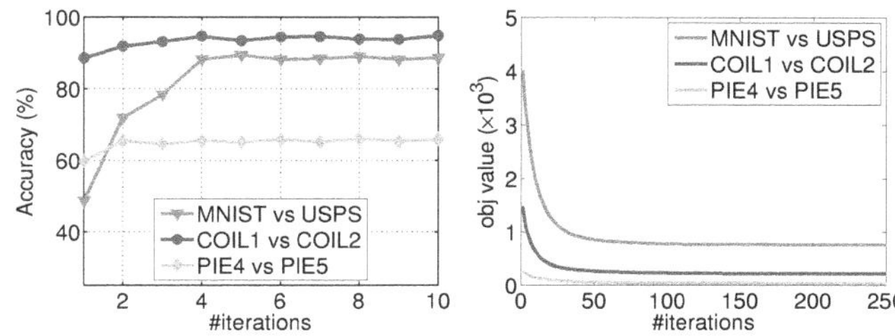

(a) Acc. w.r.t. #iteration (b) Obj. w.r.t. #iteration

Figure 4: Other issues

JDA, is **6.76%**, implying DRNMF can significantly reduce the classification error by **16.16%**. The results verify the effectiveness and superiority of DRNMF for learning robust visual features for transfer feature learning. In addition, the results also reveal some important points as below.

First, comparing PCA, TCA and JDA to GNMF, TSC and DRNMF respectively, we can observe that GNMF, TSC and DRNMF achieve much better performance. This phenomenon implies that discovering intrinsic hidden semantics (by NMF or SC) of data and considering the geometrical distribution can indeed result in more effective features, and only considering probability distribution is not enough. This is an important reason for the superiority of DRNMF compared to other transfer learning methods which only focus on reducing the distribution difference, which is as well a main motivation for combining NMF to transfer learning.

Second, transfer feature learning methods can markedly outperform standard feature learning methods, since distribution difference is a crucial issue under cross-domain settings which is ignored by standard feature learning methods.

Third, DRNMF and JDA, who take the conditional probability distribution into consideration, outperforms TSC and TCA who ignore it, which validates the importance of conditional probability distribution for transfer feature learning.

Last, DRNMF, which takes all perspectives above, i.e., discovering intrinsic hidden semantics, geometrical distribution, marginal and conditional probability distributions, into consideration, achieves best performance. Combining three points above, we can see that all these perspectives are important and indispensable for learning effective and robust visual features for cross-domain image classification.

5.2.2 *Parameter Sensitivity Analysis*

We conduct extensive analysis to validate that DRNMF can achieve stable and superior performance under a wide range of parameter values for α and β, as shown in Figure 3(a) and 3(b) respectively. Because of the limit of space, we just report the results on *MNIST vs USPS*, *COIL1 vs COIL2* and *PIE4 vs PIE5*. Actually, results on other datasets have similar trends. The dashed lines stand for the best baseline results. When we analyze one parameter, we fix the other one to the parameter setting we mentioned in Section 5.1.3.

The parameter α controls the weight of geometrical regularization. If it's too small (e.g., $\alpha < 0.001$), the geometrical distribution can't be preserved in the learned representations which may lower the performance as in [3]. On the other hand, if it's too large (e.g., $\alpha > 100$), this term may dominate the objective function in Eq. (9) such that the others can't work. And a too large α may also lead to the trivial solution and scale transfer problem [10] as GNMF. We can observe from Figure 3(a) that DRNMF can consistently outperform the best result of baseline methods when $\alpha \in [0.001, 1]$, which is a quite wide range for parameter α.

The weight of probability distribution regularization is controlled by parameter β. If it's too small (e.g., $\beta < 10$), the distribution difference can't be reduced, which may markedly degrade the performance of classifiers under cross-domain setting. On the contrary, if it's too large (e.g., $\beta > 10^5$), only the probability distributions of different domains are matched while the NMF and the geometrical distribution are discarded. As we have proved previously, it's not enough if only the probability distribution is taken into consideration. The result proves again that the intrinsic hidden semantics, geometrical distribution, marginal and conditional probability distributions are all important and indispensable perspectives for TVFL. Fortunately, it's not difficult to choose a proper value for β from $[10, 10^4]$, where DRNMF consistently outperforms the best baseline.

5.2.3 *Other Issues*

Though there is no theoretical evidence that Algorithm 1 can converge w.r.t. outer iteration, the experimental results validates that DRNMF has better performance with more iterations, implying more correct pseudo labels are obtained and conditional probability distributions between domains are better matched indeed with more iterations, which also demonstrates the effectiveness of our EM-like iterative strategy. And superior and stable performance can be reached within 10 outer iterations, as shown in Figure 4(a).

The optimization algorithm in inner iterations (for minimizing Eq. (9)) is theoretically guaranteed to converge as proved in Section 4, but we also care about how fast it can converge. In Figure 4(b), we plot the objective function value (averaged by the number of images) w.r.t. the number of iterations. We can observe that the objective function value decreases steadily and converges very fast, generally within 100 iterations, which validates the effectiveness of the multiplication updating rules in Eq. (16) and Eq. (17).

6. CONCLUSION

In this paper, we propose a novel method DRNMF for TVFL, who simultaneously uncovers the intrinsic hidden semantics of data, preserves geometrical distribution, and reduces both marginal and conditional probability distribution difference between domains, which are all indispensable and important for TVFL. We carried out extensive experiments on three types of cross-domain image classification tasks, and the results demonstrate that DRNMF can significantly outperform several state-of-the-art related methods, verifying the superiority and effectiveness of DRNMF.

7. ACKNOWLEDGEMENT

This research was supported the National Natural Science Foundation of China (Grant No. 61271394), and the National HeGaoJi Key Project (No. 2013ZX01039-002-002). And the authors would like to thank the anonymous reviewers for their valuable comments.

8. REFERENCES

[1] Y. Aytar and A. Zisserman. Tabula rasa: Model transfer for object category detection. In *International Conference on Computer Vision*, 2011.

[2] L. Bruzzone and M. Marconcini. Domain adaptation problems: A dasvm classification technique and a circular validation strategy. *IEEE TPAMI*, 2010.

[3] D. Cai, X. He, J. Han, and T. S. Huang. Graph regularized nonnegative matrix factorization for data representation. *IEEE TPAMI*, 2011.

[4] M. Chen, K. Q. Weinberger, and J. C. Blitzer. Co-training for domain adaptation. In *Advances in neural information processing systems*, 2011.

[5] Y. Chen, J. Zhang, D. Cai, W. Liu, and X. He. Nonnegative local coordinate factorization for image representation. *IEEE TIP*, 2013.

[6] A. P. Dempster, N. M. Laird, , and D. B. Rubin. Maximum likelihood from incomplete data via the em algorithm. *JRSS*, 39(1):1–38, 1977.

[7] G. Ding, Y. Guo, and J. Zhou. collective matrix factorization hashing for multimodal data. In *IEEE Conference on Computer Vision and Pattern Recognition, CVPR*, 2014.

[8] B. Gong, Y. Shi, F. Sha, and K. Grauman. Geodesic flow kernel for unsupervised domain adaptation. In *IEEE Conference on Computer Vision and Pattern Recognition, CVPR*, 2012.

[9] A. Gretton, K. M. Borgwardt, M. J. Rasch, B. Scholkopf, and A. J. Smola. A kernel method for the two-sample problem. In *Advances in neural information processing systems*, 2006.

[10] Q. Gu, C. Ding, and J. Han. On trivial solution and scale transfer problems in graph regularized nmf. In *International Joint Conference on Artificial Intelligence*, 2011.

[11] M. Guillaumin and V. Ferrari. Large-scale knowledge transfer for object localization in imagenet. In *IEEE Conference on Computer Vision and Pattern Recognition, CVPR*, 2012.

[12] R. Hadsell, S. Chopra, and Y. LeCun. Dimensionality reduction by learning an invariant mapping. In *IEEE Conference on Computer Vision and Pattern Recognition, CVPR*, 2006.

[13] I. H. Jhuo, D. Liu, D. T. Lee, and S. Chang. Robust visual domain adaptation with low-rank reconstruction. In *IEEE Conference on Computer Vision and Pattern Recognition, CVPR*, 2012.

[14] L. Jie, T. Tommasi, and B. Caputo. Multiclass transfer learning from unconstrained priors. In *International Conference on Computer Vision*, 2011.

[15] C. H. Lampert and O. Krąğomer. Weakly-paired maximum covariance analysis for multimodal dimensionality reduction and transfer learning. In *European Conference on Computer Vision (ECCV)10.*

[16] D. D. Lee and H. S. Seung. Learning the parts of objects by nonnegative matrix factorization. In *Nature*, 1999.

[17] D. D. Lee and H. S. Seung. Learning the parts of objects by nonnegative matrix factorization. In *Advances in neural information processing systems*, 2001.

[18] S. Z. Li, X. Hou, H. Zhang, and Q. Cheng. Learning spatially localized, parts-based representation. In *IEEE Conference on Computer Vision and Pattern Recognition, CVPR*, 2001.

[19] N. K. Logothetis and D. L. Sheinberg. Visual object recognition. *Annual Review of Neuroscience*, 1996.

[20] M. Long, G. Ding, J. Wang, J. Sun, Y. Guo, and P. S. Yu. Transfer sparse coding for robust image representation. In *CVPR*, 2013.

[21] M. Long, J. Wang, G. Ding, J. Sun, and P. S. Yu. Transfer feature learning with joint distribution adaptation. In *ICCV*, 2013.

[22] S. J. Pan, I. Tsang, J. T. Kwok, and Q. Yang. Transfer learning via dimensionality reduction. In *AAAI*, 2008.

[23] S. J. Pan, I. Tsang, J. T. Kwok, and Q. Yang. Domain adaptation via transfer component analysis. *IEEE TNN*, 2011.

[24] S. J. Pan and Q. Yang. A survey on transfer learning. *IEEE TKDE*, 2010.

[25] Q. Qiu, V. M. Patel, P. Turaga, and R. Chellappa. Domain adaptive dictionary learning. In *ECCV*, 2012.

[26] B. Quanz, J. Huan, and M. Mishra. Knowledge transfer with low-quality data: A feature extraction issue. *IEEE TKDE*, 2012.

[27] S. D. Roy, T. Mei, W. Zeng, and S. L. Socialtransfer. Cross-domain transfer learning from social streams for media applications. In *ACM MM*, 2012.

[28] S. Si, D. Tao, and B. Geng. Bregman divergence-based regularization for transfer subspace learning. *IEEE TKDE*, 2010.

[29] H. Wang, F. Nie, H. Huang, and C. Ding. Dyadic transfer learning for cross-domain image classification. In *ICCV*, 2011.

[30] E. Zhong, W. Fan, J. Peng, K. Zhang, J. Ren, D. Turaga, and O. Verscheure. Cross domain distribution adaptation via kernel mapping. In *KDD*, 2009.

Heterogeneous Semantic Level Features Fusion for Action Recognition

Junjie Cai†,* Michele Merler‡, Sharath Pankanti‡ and Qi Tian†
†Department of Computer Science, University of Texas at San Antonio
‡IBM Thomas J. Watson Research
caijunjieustc@gmail.com,{mimerler,sharat}@us.ibm.com,qitian@cs.utsa.edu

ABSTRACT

Action recognition is an important problem in computer vision and has received substantial attention in recent years. However, it remains very challenging due to the complex interaction of static and dynamic information, as well as the high computational cost of processing video data. This paper aims to apply the success of static image semantic recognition to the video domain, by leveraging both static and motion based descriptors in different stages of the semantic ladder. We examine the effects of three types of features: low-level dynamic descriptors, intermediate-level static deep architecture outputs, and static high-level semantics. In order to combine such heterogeneous sources of information, we employ a scalable method to fuse these features. Through extensive experimental evaluations, we demonstrate that the proposed framework significantly improves action classification performance. We have obtained an accuracy of 89.59% and 62.88% on the well-known UCF-101 and HMDB-51 benchmarks, respectively, which compare favorably with the state-of-the-art.

1. INTRODUCTION

Human action recognition has been one of the challenging problems explored by the computer vision community. An action comprises a combination of semantic visual elements (people, objects, scenes) and motions, which are related to individual element movements or their interactions with each other. Therefore both the static visual information and the dynamics of the scene constitute necessary and complementary information to recognize an action. A myriad of works have been proposed to improve action recognition and classification performance [11, 21, 22], with efforts driven by the release of increasingly larger and more challenging datasets [12, 13, 36].

Out of all the proposed approaches, dense trajectories based methods with GMM codebook generation and Fisher Vector encoding have achieved competitive performances and have shown their effectiveness on this problem [11]. The motion trajectory is capable of describing subtle movements and is suitable for representing both the dynamics and appearance of a scene on a *local* level.

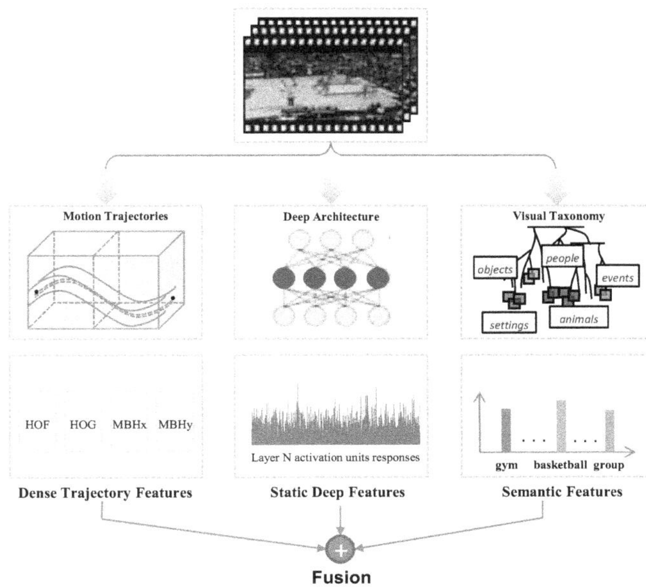

Figure 1: Overview of the proposed action recognition framework combining heterogeneous semantic level features. The semantic level of the extracted decriptors ranges from low to high as we move from left (low-level descriptors) to right (high-level semantics).

However, using only low level descriptors can not always be sufficient for action recognition purposes. This is due mostly to the gap with the semantics of an action at a global scale. Consider the example in Figure 2 showing two clips from the UCF101 dataset: for some reason the HOF descriptor of the two video clips is very similar, but on a semantic level it is quite clear that the instrument being played is completely different. Such limitation can be alleviated by the use of a set of static **Semantic** classifiers, especially in the case where some relevant concepts are part of the pool (in the example, *Grand Piano* and *Flute*).

*This work was done when Junjie Cai was an intern at IBM T.J Watson Research Center.

ICMR'15, June 23–26, 2015, Shanghai, China.

http://dx.doi.org/10.1145/2671188.2749320.

Besides providing complementary information to low level dynamic descriptors, using sets of Semantic models constitutes also a way to transfer the knowledge accumulated from the large scale annotated training data on top of which such models were learned.

In this work, we propose to use descriptors at Higher Semantic levels in combination with the low-level dynamic ones. Figure 1 gives a conceptual view of the feature extraction process. First, we extract visual features at different semantic levels: *low-level* dynamic trajectory features (e.g., histogram of oriented gradients (HOG) [15], histogram of optical flow (HOF) [15] and motion boundary histogram (MBH) [11]), *intermediate-level* static deep features extracted from one of the intermediate layers of a Deep convolutional network trained on ImageNet, and *high-level* semantic features in the form of concatenated predictions of two sets of static visual classifiers trained from web images. The first set contains 1,000 classes from the same Deep convolutional network as the intermediate level features, the other has 1,414 classes trained as ensemble SVMs from web images.

In order to mine and fully exploit the complementary information among heterogeneous features, we explore the features relationship via a selection of fusion strategies, of which SVM based fusion proved to be the best performing.

While the use of deep features for action recognition in videos has been introduced before [3, 8], the semantic analysis to the output of the final layer of the neural network has not been yet fully explored.

The main contributions of this paper can be summarized as follows:

- We propose to use high-level static semantic classifiers to perform action recognition in videos.
- We propose a framework that jointly combines dynamic trajectory features, static deep features and high level semantic predictors for improving action classification performance.
- Extensive empirical evaluations are provided to corroborate the effectiveness of the proposed framework in detail, which achieved an accuracy of 89.59% and 62.88% on the well-known UCF-101 and HMDB51 benchmarks, respectively, which compare favorably to the state-of-the-art.

The remainder of this paper is organized as follows. After an overview of related work in Section 2, we describe the proposed action recognition framework in Section 3. In Section 4, the experimental results are presented and discussed. Finally, we conclude in Section 5.

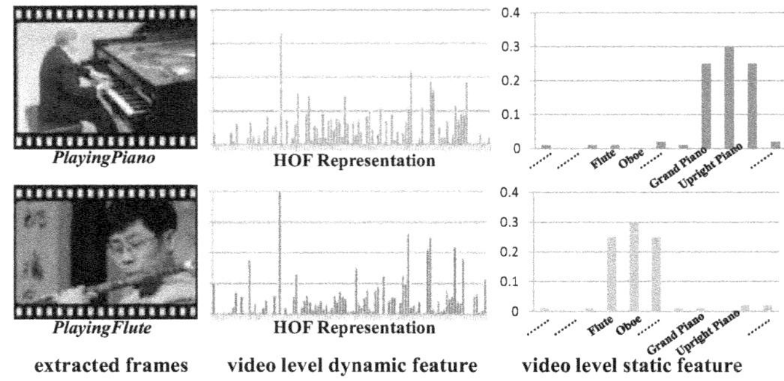

Figure 2: Comparison between a "PlayingPiano" clip and "PlayingFlute" video based on Fisher Vector HOF representation and static semantic features. In this example, the two low-level trajectory features are considered as a good match both by FV equality and Euclidean distance consistency. However, they differ significatly in static semantic space. Our proposed approach can distinguish between the two since it can overcome the shortcomings of one descriptor.

2. RELATED WORK

The complete literature on action recognition is quite extensive and beyond the scope of this paper. In this Section, we focus on works closely related to our approach, mainly covering systems which employ features of low, intermediate, and high semantic level.

Low-level Features unlike static images, video data exhibits different views of visual patterns, such as appearance changes and motions with different boundaries, all of which play an important role in action recognition. Therefore multiple descriptors are usually extracted directly from video and each descriptor corresponds to one specific aspect of visual data. Researchers in action recognition widely made use of low-level features with BoW model. Typical low-level features employed to recognize actions in videos include histogram of oriented gradients (HOG) [15], histogram of optical flow (HOF) [15] and motion boundary histogram (MBH) [11], which are computed in local cuboids obtained around detected spatial-temporal interest points or with dense sampling schemes [16]. A combination of several features is shown to further boost recognition accuracy by leveraging fisher vector encoding. For instance, participants in THUMOS challenge [36] are encouraged to employ various kinds of dynamic features to develop novel approaches for action recognition to operate in realistic conditions [11, 34].

Moreover, a couple of works explored the integration of multiple low level descriptors to generate semantics for action recognition. Wang et al. [6] correlate interest points together and construct an action unit set to represent all actions classes with semantics. Liu et al. [22] use diffusion maps to automatically learn a semantic visual vocabulary from low-level features. In the above model, low-level trajectory features are extracted and clustered into the codebook via a generative process (e.g. GMMs), and then each feature is quantized and encoded into a high dimensional vector (e.g. Fisher Vector). However, such representation suffers from two major limitations, which are interconnected. On one hand, similarly to all other low-level descriptors, the semantic gap between the Dense Trajectories features and the nameable semantics of an action at a global scale results in a lack of interpretability of the results. This also limits the generalization power of such descriptor to other domains, which is lost in its intrinsic need to learn a codebook and Fisher vector encoding parameters for each dataset in order to obtain competitive performance. Hence, the vocabularies or units above are not discriminative and representative enough in larger video datasets, which limits their applicability in different domains.

Intermediate-Level Features Besides low-level features, recent efforts for action and event recognition in video have been devoted to mining intermediate-level semantic representations. A number of researchers have been building a variety of semantic concept detectors, such as those related to people (face, anchor), acoustics (speech, music), genre (weather, financial, sports), scene, etc. [6, 20, 33, 37]. Liu et al. [24] proposed to leverage attribute-based features for action recognition. Yao et al. [24] jointly modeled the attributes (i.e. actions) and parts (i.e., objects or poselets related actions) by learning a set of sparse bases that are shown to carry much meaning. Chen et al. [31] proposed a concept discovery approach by investigating the event textual descriptions. However, most of such approaches require copious labeled data to train specifically targeted intermediate concept or attribute classifiers, which involves a costly annotation process.

Deep Neural Network There have also been some attempts to leverage a deep neural architecture for visual recognition. Deep features are generally extracted from intermediate layers of convolutional neural networks. They have been shown to set the state-of-the-art in many applications such as OCR [26], speech recognition [25] and object detection [27]. Moreover, for action recognition, Karpathy et al. [5] used raw video data as inputs instead of the hand-crafted features and compared several ConvNets architectures. Interestingly, their results indicated that the spatial temporal features learnt from 1.1M YouTube videos could not capture motion characteristics well enough to successfully generalize to other datasets. The performance turned out to be less competitive than hand-crafted trajectory-based representations. Simonyan et al. [8] further explored how to capture the complementary information from static extracted frames and motion (optical flow) via deep ConvNets.

From a semantic standpoint, the output of the hidden layer in a pre-trained neural network can be utilized to convey discriminative semantic information with respect to the data from which it was trained. One popular example in this space is the task of large scale image classification ImageNet task [9].

Our work departs from the ones reported above in two aspects. First, the dynamic trajectory features are widely used in action recognition and remain the central components of video analytical systems that generated state-of-the-art results. We aim to efficiently combine the advantages of off-the-shelf low-level dynamic trajectory features to improve the recognition performance, without discarding them completely for an independently trained deep architecture. Second, we investigate the use of semantics generated by static deep and shallow visual classifiers which provide a complementary cue to further enhance the discriminative power of action classifiers.

3. PROPOSED APPROACH

In this Section we provide a formal description of the proposed framework, starting from the details of the heterogeneous semantic level features employed and then discussing the different fusion strategies adopted to combine them.

3.1 Feature Extraction

Dynamic Dense Trajectory Features: Dynamic information is an important cue for human action understanding from video. Therefore we extract the state of the art improved dense trajectories features from input videos. To describe motion, different types of motion feature descriptors are computed in a spatial-temporal volume (i.e., spatial size of 2×2 with temporal length of 15) around the $3D$ neighborhood of the tracked points along the trajectory. Following [11], each trajectory is described by a concatenation of HOG, HOF, and MBH(along x and y directions) descriptors, forming a 396-dimensional vector (96+108+96+96).

Fisher Vector (FV) coding, derived from Fisher Kernel, was originally proposed for large scale image classification. Compared with other coding methods such as vector quantization and sparse coding, FV coding can easily obtain high-dimensional feature codes starting from a small codebook size, which has been shown to provide considerable performance improvements when utilizing linear classifiers.

Following best practices reported in the literature [7], we process the descriptors independently. For each of them, we first reduce the dimensionality by performing PCA with a ratio of 0.5. We then randomly sample 0.3 million features to learn a codebook of Gaussian Mixture Models (GMM) for each descriptor. We apply the Fisher Vector high-dimensional encoding scheme to each descriptor and the resulting super vectors are normalized by intra power normalization [35]. The normalization strategy is carried out in a block-by-block manner and each block represents the vector related to one codeword. We use $\mathbf{p^k}$ to denote a vector related to k-th Gaussian and $\|.\|$ stands for ℓ_2-norm. The normalization could be represented as $\mathbf{p}^k / \left\|\mathbf{p}^k\right\|$, where $k \in [1, K]$. Finally the normalized super vectors are concatenated to represent the motion information for a given video clip.

Static Deep Features: We leverage an existing deep learning framework as a feature extractor for video frames. Each video clip is uniformly sampled at a rate of two frames per second, and deep learning features are extracted from each frame. In order to produce a whole video clip level feature representation, we adopt a simple max pooling scheme on the individual frame descriptors over the duration of each video. We utilize the open source CAFFE [2] implementation, which is based on the deep convolutional neural network architecture by Krizhevsky et al. [4]. Since the frames in the action videos we investigate are independent from the ImageNet dataset on which the CAFFE architecture was trained, we are basically using the ImageNet model trained for previous ILSVRC image classification tasks [9] as an analog to using the prior knowledge a human obtained from previous visual experiences to learn new tasks more efficiently (in our case, action recognition).

The activations of the neurons in the intermediate hidden layers could be used as strong features for a variety of video recognition tasks because they contain much richer and more complex representations than any earlier convolutional layer in the network. In this work, we leverage as deep feature the output of the intermediate layer named with fc_6 in the CAFFE implementation. We set the network input to the raw RGB values of the frames, resized to 256*256 pixels, and the values are forward propagated through 5 convolutional layers (i.e., pooling and ReLU non-linearities) and 3 fully-connected layers (i.e., to determine its final neuron activities). We obtain the 4096-dimension vector from the intermediate fc_6 hidden layer.

The deep feature produced by this architecture has a large variation in its value distribution (i.e., [-72.8,24.8]), which is potentially problematic due to sensibility to outliers in one of its dimensions. This problem could be severe if we consider the fact that the negative values are produced by suppressed neurons, and convey less useful cues compared with the positive ones. To address this problem, and thus produce more uniformly distributed values, we normalize each dimension using the following function:

$$f(x) = sign(x)|x|^{\alpha} \quad (1)$$

where $sign(\cdot)$ denotes the signum function and $\alpha \in [0, 1]$ is the exponent parameter. Here we empirically set α as 0.5. Finally, the feature vector is ℓ_2-normalized.

In the field of action recognition, the effectiveness of deep features has not been yet extensively studied, especially in a complementary way with dynamic trajectory features and higher level semantics. In this work, we make initial attempts on this issue, and provide feasible ways of integrating static deep features into the classification pipeline.

High Level Semantic Concepts Features: In order to richly represent the visual semantic concept space, we employ two diverse sets of static semantic classifiers which were trained on different datasets using different learning techniques.

- CAFFE1K : the set of 1,000 classifiers originating from the output of the last layer of the Deep convolutional network described in the previous Section. Each of those outputs carries one specific semantic information associated with a visual concept from the ImageNet taxonomy.

- ConceptsWeb : a set of 1,418 models trained from a set of half a million images downloaded from the web and manually annotated and organized in a hierarchical faceted taxonomy [ ]. This taxonomy includes concepts related to "objects","scenes", "people", "activities" and "events". Each model SC_i is an ensemble of SVMs with linearly approximated χ^2 kernel, learned on top of bags of examples randomly sampled from the set of thousands of manually labeled web images. Each individual SVM uses one of 13 different global visual descriptors including color histogram, color correlogram, color moment, wavelet texture, edge histogram, etc., extracted at multiple different regions of the image, in a similar fashion to the spatial pyramid framework.

  The score for a Semantic Concept i on in a new image x is then

$$SC_i(x) = \sum_{k=1}^{N_i} w_k b_k(x) \quad (2)$$

  $SC_i(x)$ is the weighted sum of the scores on x of the individual SVMs, which we define base models b_k in the ensemble. The weights w_k are learned via cross-validation during training.

  For each video frame x, we concatenate all the models scores into a N-dimensional Semantic Model Vector, that is, a vector in which each dimension has a semantic meaning

$$SMV(x) = [SC_1(x), ..., SC_i(x), ..., SC_N(x)] \quad (3)$$

  We then use this concatenated vector as a regular feature for action modeling.

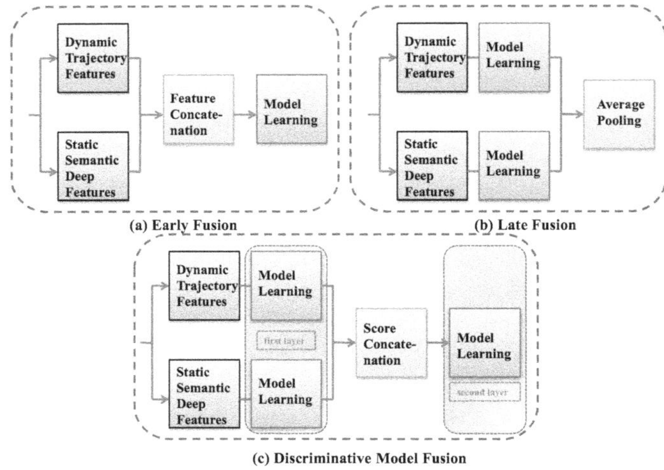

Figure 3: Illustration of heterogeneous feature fusion strategies.

In our experiments we built one separate vector for each of the two sets of classifiers.

3.2 Heterogeneous Information Fusion Strategies

Given the intuitive complementary nature of the different levels of semantic information we extract, it is natural to combine them into an integrated prediction system. There are many possible methods for combining heterogeneous information. As presented in Figure 3 we explored two standard ones (early fusion and average score based late fusion) and a discriminative one inspired by stacked SVMs approaches.

Early Fusion (EF): Early fusion strategy concatenates all the features into a single vector representation. The concatenated heterogeneous features are then directly fed into the multiclass SVM to train model for action categories.

Late Fusion (LF): In contrast to early fusion, where features are then combined into a universal representation, approaches for late fusion train models directly from each individual feature. The prediction scores from each model are then normalized to a common range and linearly combined in a late fusion step. In our experiments, we adopted the arithmetical mean as late fusion strategy.

Discriminative Model Fusion (DMF): we investigated the fusion performance following a two-layer model-learning strategy, instead of the one-layer model adopted in standard early and late fusion. In the first layer, as in the previous late fusion approach, models are trained individually on top of each descriptor. The predictions from the different models are then concatenated into a vector that is passed as input to the second layer, where an SVM with RBF kernel is learned on top of it. We did not tune any SVM parameter.

Discussion: Complementary information among heterogenous features mentioned above may be of vital importance. Video-level feature description could be largely complementary to low-level dynamic visual features. For example, although two low-level features (HOF) quantized to the same fisher vector representation, videos may convey different semantics and false match could occur frequently (see Figure 2 for an illustration). Notwithstanding a significant difference in visual appearance, the FV representation in the "PlayingPiano" clip closely resembles that of actions in "PlayingFlute".

4. EXPERIMENTS

In this section, we first describe our implementation details used in the experiments. Then we present recognition results on two popular datasets to examine the performance of the proposed approach. A comparison to the state-of-the-art methods is given at the end of this section.

4.1 Experimental Setting

We conduct experiments on two popular action datasets, namely HMDB51 [13] and UCF101 [12]. We summarize them and the experimental protocols as follows. The HMDB51 dataset consists 51 actions with 6,766 manually annotated clips which are extracted from a variety of sources ranging from digitized movies to Youtube. We follow the experimental settings in [13] and report the mean average accuracy over all classes. The UCF101 dataset [12] has been the largest action recognition dataset so far, and exhibits the highest diversity in terms of actions, with the presence of large variations in camera motion, object appearance and pose, object scale, viewpoint, cluttered background, illumination conditions and so on. It contains 13,320 videos collected from YouTube and includes total number of 101 action classes. We perform evaluation on three train/test splits[1] and report the mean average accuracy over all classes.

Dense trajectories were extracted using the code provided by Wang et al.[11].

The extraction of deep features and CAFFE1K are conducted on a single Nvidia Telas K10 GPU with python interface, which speeds up by about 10 times than a decent Intel CPU with 8 cores.

The ConceptsWeb semantics were extracted using a CPU cluster running the LibSVM library [2].

In our experiments, we choose linear SVM as our classifier with the implementation of LIBLINEAR [5]. Then for multiclass classification, we use one-vs-all approach to perform action recognition and select the class with the highest score.

4.2 Results and Discussion

4.2.1 Comparison with feature fusion

We compute the performance of the different components of our system . To combine the representative capabilities, we investigate the performance of the fusion of dynamic trajectory features, static deep features as well as global taxonomy features. The combined features are used to train SVM model for each concept. There are three different fusion strategies–early fusion, late fusion and discriminative model fusion.

From Table 1 and Table 2, we could see that combining multiple types of dynamic trajectory descriptors can significantly improve recognition performance. Comparing across the alternative approaches, early fusion tends to generate better results with clear gains than late fusion. The reasons are two-folds. First, this should be partially ascribed to high-dimensional representations in early fusion we used. Second, the strategy of late fusion result in the heterogeneity among the confidence scores provided by different models. Such heterogeneity results from the variation of the discriminative capability of each model in a certain feature space, producing incomparable confidence scores at different numeric scales.

We also compare the performance of CAFFE features of the two fully-connected layers (fc_6 and fc_7), denoted as CAFFE-1K and CAFFE-4K. We observe from Table 2 that features from the six-layer are superior to those from the seventh layer. We speculate that the fully connected layer exert some negative effect on the features. Specifically, features extracted using "fc_6" (CAFFE-4K) obtains an mAP of 65.88% on UCF101 and 37.63% on HMDB51 dataset.

Then we augment the sematic features to the motion features. By including the static deep features, we can clearly see that for all methods, *i.e.*, "Dynamic + CAFFE4K", "Dynamic + CAFFE1K", the performance boost of feature fusion in both HMDB51 and UCF101 database is consistent and obvious, as compared and illustrated in Table 2. These results strongly prove that the contextual cues of static deep features are perfectly complementary to the low-level trajectory features. Besides, an intuitive analysis could also be easily provided. For instance, the action of "Basketball Dunk", we can know which object is contained (semantic static feature) and how is the object being played (motion feature). Notice that there are 37 classes out of 101 categories which are recognized with 100% accuracy. The full list UCF101 classes is reported in Table 4, where the categories for which we achieve perfect classification highlighted in blue.

Moreover, we also found that semantic ConceptsWeb features have less positive impact than static deep features on both evaluation datasets. For instance, on the UCF101 dataset, it yields 86.10% and 89.00% in mean average accuracy for ConceptsWeb and CAFFE1K features, respectively. It demonstrates that static deep features is more powerful in mitigating the semantic gap in comparison with intermediate-level semantic representation.

In Figure 4 we visualize the semantic meanings provided explicitly by the high level semantics features. For six actions, we sorted the weighs of the linear SVM trained on top of the CAFFE1K descriptor and picked the top three. Since each dimension (which is associated to a weight) in the CAFFE1K feature corresponds to one of the 1000 ImageNet categories, in this way we could extract the top 3 most discriminative concepts for each action. We then report the four keyframes from the entire dataset for which the concepts classifiers scored the highest. In this way we can qualitatively evaluate at the same time the correlation between action classes static concepts, and the quality of the indivisual concepts on the given dataset (which is not guaranteed since they were trained on different data). We can see that the most discriminative concepts for each action tend to make sense. For example "Biking" is mostly distinguished by *bicycle*, *mountain bike* and *moped*. It is interesting to notice that even in the cases in which the semantic meaning of a distinguishing concept does not appear to be correct (for example *abacus* for "Typing"), the classifier is actually recognizing useful information which is correlated to the action class (one or two hands on a device).

4.2.2 Comparison with the state of the art

We also compare our results with state-of-the-art methods on each dataset. Table 3 displays our best results and several recently published results in the literature. These method-

[1] http://crcv.ucf.edu/ICCV13-Action-Workshop/
[2] http://www.csie.ntu.edu.tw/ cjlin/libsvm

Methods	Dynamic Trajectory Features HOF	HOG	MBHx	MBHy	Static Deep Features CAFFE-4K	High Level Semantics CAFFE-1K	ConceptsWeb
UCF101	78.37%	73.65%	75.93%	77.91%	63.83%	65.88%	57.10%
HMDB51	49.19%	42.37%	41.11%	48.28%	37.63%	33.05%	25.23%

Table 1: Classification Performance comparison of individual descriptors: low-level dynamic dense trajectory features, intermediate-level static deep features and high-level semantic features.

Approaches	UCF101 EF	UCF101 LF	UCF101 DMF	HMDB51 EF	HMDB51 LF	HMDB51 DMF
HOF + HOG + MBHx + MBHy	87.37%	86.00%	88.00%	59.24%	58.06%	59.26%
CAFFE4K + CAFFE1K + ConceptsWeb	69.27%	68.27%	70.58%	40.24%	39.56%	41.27%
HOF + HOG + MBHx + MBHy + CAFFE4K	89.22%	88.48%	89.52%	62.68%	61.74%	62.81%
HOF + HOG + MBHx + MBHy + CAFFE1K	89.00%	88.80%	89.32%	61.00%	60.23%	61.74%
HOF + HOG + MBHx + MBHy + ConceptsWeb	86.10%	85.80%	86.20%	59.20%	58.23%	60.56%
HOF + HOG + MBHx + MBHy + Static	89.57%	89.53%	89.59%	62.71%	62.31%	62.88%

Table 2: Performance comparison of multiple fusion strategies with heterogeneous features.

s (e.g., mid-level parts [14]and deep architecture [10]) that utilize the responses of discriminative action parts combined with low-level features perform inferior to our approach with a certain margin consistently. For UCF-101 dataset, we achieve the best average accuracy 89.59%, which exceeds all the recent results reported in [3, 7, 8]. All these works are based on either low level trajectory features or ConvNets approach regardless of contextual semantic information. Note that extracting features in [3, 8] using neural networks needs more layers of neurons that incur significant number of additional parameters to be tuned, requiring much more training data and several weeks to train. While in many video classification tasks, the amount of available training data is far less from sufficient for training a neural network with too many layers. Moreover, since these adopted datasets are very challenging and have been widely used, it is interesting and competitive to obtain an absolute performance gain of 1.6% in comparison with [8].

For HMDB51 dataset, our result (62.88%) also outperforms the state-of-the-art approaches [7, 8]. To further prove the effectiveness of our approach on action recognition, we present the confusion matrix for HMDB51 dataset in Figure 5. By comparison, we observe that static deep features provide explicit enhancement to the low-level trajectory features. For instance, it could be easily found that the performance improvement on action of "kickball" is benefited from semantic description on objects such as "soccer", "soccer ball".

4.2.3 *Comparison with low-level and intermediate-level features*

We provide further a detail of the classification performance of state of the art static features (SIFT encoded with Fisher Vectors) and mid-level semantics such as Classemes and its derivatives PiCodes and MetaClasses.

The static information of Deep features and Semantics achieved good recognition performances and provided complementary information with respect to Dynamic descriptors. Therefore we analyzed alternative static descriptors, both *low-level* (i.e., SIFT [29]) and *intermediate-level* (i.e. semantic attributes [28]) on the UCF-101 dataset.

For low-level visual features, we extract SIFT and leverage the GMM model followed by Fisher Vector over the features extracted from all the frames in a video produce the whole clip-level representation. Specifically, we first densely extract local SIFT descriptors with a spatial stride of 4 pixels at 9 scales and the width of SIFT spatial bins is fixed as 8 pixels, which are the default settings in the VLFeat toolbox [30]. We learn a GMM dictionary sampled from a subset of 0.3 million SIFT descriptors. All descriptors are whitened after PCA processing to 64-dimension with a ratio of 0.5. We then conduct FV encoding and apply intra power normalization to the resulting super vectors. This state of the art *static* low-level feature obtains an average classification accuracy of 25.24% on the UCF-101 dataset, which as expected is significantly inferior to the performance of the *dynamic* low-level descriptors (Dense Trajectories). More interestingly, SIFT with FV encoding achieve recognition rates significantly lower than other static descriptors both at mid and high semantic levels.

Feature	Max	Average	Min
Classemes	53.16%	49.62%	-
Picodes	33.97%	52.39%	33.97%
Meta-Classes [28]	61.55%	45.76%	-
SIFT [29]+FV		25.24%	

Table 5: Performance comparison of multiple pooling strategies with intermediate-level semantic features. State of the art static descriptors (SIFT with Fisher Vectors encoding) provide a significantly worse performance.

Additionally, we compared the experimental performance of popular intermediate-level features (akin to semantic attributes) which were recently introduced by Bergamo et al. [28]: Classemes and its derivatives Picodes and Meta-Classes. Since each of those descriptors are extracted from individual frames, we tested several basic pooling approaches (Max, Average, Min) in order to produce a video-level feature representation which aggregates the frames responses. As reported in Table 5, we observe that such intermediate-level features achieved less competitive performance (best average accuracy of 61.55% over all feature types and aggregation strategies) than their Deep counterparts at the same semantic level (Deep features, 63.83%).

5. CONCLUSION

We proposed a novel unified framework that jointly combines dynamic trajectory features and exploits the class re-

Methods	Ours	[17]	[8]	[11]	[3]	[12]	[7]	[18]	[10]	[14]	[19]	[22]	[21]
UCF101	**89.6%**	84.2%	88.0%	85.9%	65.4%	43.9%	87.9%	83.5%	87.7%	-	73.1%	-	-
HMDB51	**62.9%**	56.3%	59.4%	57.2%	-	-	61.1%	55.9%	59.8%	37.2%	49.9%	48.7%	66.8%

Table 3: Performance comparison with state-of-the-art methods.

YoYo	Archery	JumpRope	Basketball	HeadMassage	FrisbeeCatch	ApplyLipstick	BoxingSpeedBag	*BoxingPunchingBag*
Punch	Bowling	Kayaking	*BenchPress*	*HorseRiding*	JavelinThrow	BaseballPitch	CricketBowling	*TrampolineJumping*
Swing	*Fencing*	*Knitting*	*FrontCrawl*	*JumpingJack*	MoppingFloor	BrushingTeeth	MilitaryParade	*VolleyballSpiking*
Biking	Haircut	LongJump	IceDancing	PlayingDhol	*ParallelBars*	JugglingBalls	SoccerJuggling	FieldHockeyPenalty
Diving	PullUps	*Billiards*	PlayingDaf	*PommelHorse*	PizzaTossing	PlayingGuitar	WalkingWithDog	*RockClimbingIndoor*
Lunges	PushUps	GolfSwing	*StillRings*	TennisSwing	*PlayingCello*	PlayingViolin	*WritingOnBoard*	
Mixing	Rafting	Hammering	UnevenBars	ThrowDiscus	PlayingFlute	SkateBoarding	*FloorGymnastics*	
Rowing	Shotput	*HorseRace*	BalanceBeam	WallPushups	*PlayingPiano*	*SoccerPenalty*	TableTennisShot	
Skiing	Surfing	Nunchucks	BlowDryHair	BabyCrawling	*PlayingSitar*	SumoWrestling	*BodyWeightSquats*	
Skijet	Drumming	*PoleVault*	CliffDiving	BandMarching	*PlayingTabla*	ApplyEyeMakeup	CuttingInKitchen	
TaiChi	HighJump	*SalsaSpin*	CricketShot	*BreastStroke*	RopeClimbing	BasketballDunk	*HandstandPushups*	
Typing	HulaHoop	SkyDiving	*HammerThrow*	*CleanAndJerk*	ShavingBeard	*BlowingCandles*	HandstandWalking	

Table 4: Illustration of 37 categories (in Blue) which obtained 100% accuracy in UCF101 dataset.

lationship via static deep features and high-level semantic descriptors for improving action classification performance. This unique capacity distinguishes the proposed method from most of the existing works that often adopted low-level dense features without considering the inter-class semantic correlations. Our investigation also implies that static deep and semantic features are largely complementary to low-level dynamic trajectory features. The SVM based fusion approach provided the best framework to combine the information coming from the heterogeneous static and dynamic features at different semantic levels. Extensive empirical evaluations proved the effectiveness of the proposed framework, which achieves an accuracy of 89.59% and 62.88% on the well-known UCF-101 and HMDB51 benchmarks, respectively, which compare favorably with the state-of-the-arts.

We plan to explore multiple classification kernels with heterogenous types of features. We also plan on learning the temporal evolution of semantic descriptors representing more complex activities.

6. ACKNOWLEDGEMENTS

We would like to thank Liangliang Cao, Noel Codella, John Smith, Quoc-Bao Nguyen and Quanfu Fan for fruitful discussions. This work was supported in part to Dr. Qi Tian by ARO grant W911NF-12-1-0057 and Faculty Research Award by NEC Laboratories of America, Inc. This work was supported in part by National Science Foundation of China (NSFC) 61429201.

7. REFERENCES

[1] M. Merler, B. Huang, L. Xie, G. Hua and A. Natsev. Semantic model vectors for complex video event recognition. In *IEEE Transactions on Multimedia*, 2013.

[2] Y. Jia. Caffe: An Open Source Convolutional Architecture for Fast Feature Embedding. http://caffe.berkeleyvision.org/, 2013.

[3] A. Karpathy, G. Toderici, S. Shetty, T. Leung, R. Sukthankar and L. Fei-Fei. Large-scale video classification with convolutional neural networks. In *Proceedings of the IEEE conference on Computer Vision and Pattern Recognition*, 2014.

[4] A. Krizhevsky, I. Sutskever and G.E. Hinton. ImageNet classification with deep convolutional neural networks. In *Proceedings of Advanced in Neural Inforamtion Processing System*, 2012.

[5] R. Fan, K. Chang, C. Hsieh, X. Wang and C. Lin. LIBLINEAR: a library for large linear classification. In *Journal of Machine Learning Research*, 2008.

[6] H. Wang, C. Yuan, W. Hu, H. Hu and C. Sun. Action recognition using nonnegative action component representation and sparse basis selection. In *Transaction on Image Processing*, 2014.

[7] X. Peng, L. Wang, X. Wang and Y. Qiao. Bag of Visual Words and Fusion Methods for Action Recognition: Comprehensive Study and Good Practice. In *arXiv*, 2014.

[8] K. Simonyan and A. Zisserman. Two-stream convolutional networks for action recognition in videos. In *Proceedings of Advanced in Neural Inforamtion Processing System*, 2014.

[9] Large scale visual recogntion challenge. http://www.image-net.org/challenges/LSVRC/2012/, 2012.

[10] X. Peng, L. Wang, Y. Qiao and Q. Peng. Boosting VLAD with Supervised Dictionary Learning and Higher-Order Statics. In *Proceedings of the European Conference on Computer Vision*, 2014.

[11] H. Wang and C. Schmid. Action recogntion with improved trajectories. In *Proceedings of the IEEE International Conference on Computer Vision*, 2013.

[12] K. Soomro, A. R. Zamir, and M. Shah. UCF101: A dataset of 101 human actions classes from videos in the wild. In *arXiv:1212.0402*, 2012.

[13] H. Kuehne, H. Jhuang, E. Garrote, T. Poggio, and T. Serre. HMDB: A Large Video Database for Human Motion Recognition. In *Proceedings of the IEEE International Conference on Computer Vision*, 2011.

[14] M. Sapienza, F. Cuzzolin and P. S. Torr. Learning discriminative space-time action parts from weakly labelled videos. In *International Journal of Computer Vision*, 2014.

[15] I. Laptev, M. Marszalek, C. Schmid and B. Rozenfeld. Learning realistic human actions from movies. In *Proceedings of the IEEE conference on Computer Vision and Pattern Recognition*, 2008.

[16] I. Laptev. On space-time interest points. In *International Journal of Computer Vision*, 2005.

[17] J. Wu, Y. Zhang, W. Lin. Towards good practice for action video encoding. In *Proceedings of the IEEE conference on Computer Vision and Pattern Recognition*, 2014.

[18] Z. Cai, L. Wang, X. Peng, Y. Qiao. Multi-view super vector for action recogntion. In *Proceedings of the IEEE conference on Computer Vision and Pattern Recognition*, 2014.

[19] O. V. R. Murthy and R. Goecke. Ordered Trajectories for Large Scale Human Action Recognition. In *Proceedings of the IEEE conference on Computer Vision and Pattern Recognition*, 2013.

[20] Z. Ma, Y. Yang, N. Sebe, K. Zheng and A. G. Hauptman. Multimedia event detection using a classifier-specific intermediate representation. In *IEEE Transactions on Multimedia*, 2013.

[21] X. Peng, C. Zhou, Y. Qiao and Q. Peng. Action recognition with stacked fisher vectors. In *Proceedings of the European Conference on Computer Vision*, 2014.

[22] J. Liu, Y. Yang and M. Shah. Learning semantic visual vocabularies using diffusion distance. In *Proceedings of the IEEE conference on Computer Vision and Pattern Recognition*, 2009.

[23] J. Liu, B. Kuipers and S. Savarese. Recognizing Human Actions by Attributes. In *Proceedings of the IEEE conference on Computer Vision and Pattern Recognition*, 2011.

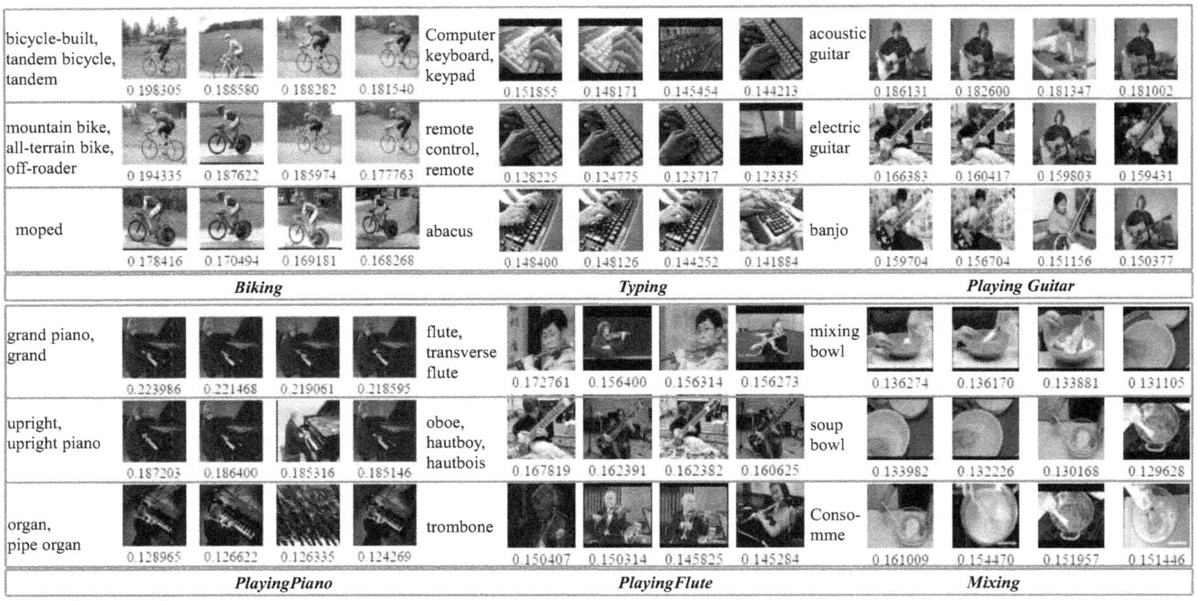

Figure 4: Top three discriminative concepts (out of 1,000 ImageNet categories) for six action classes.

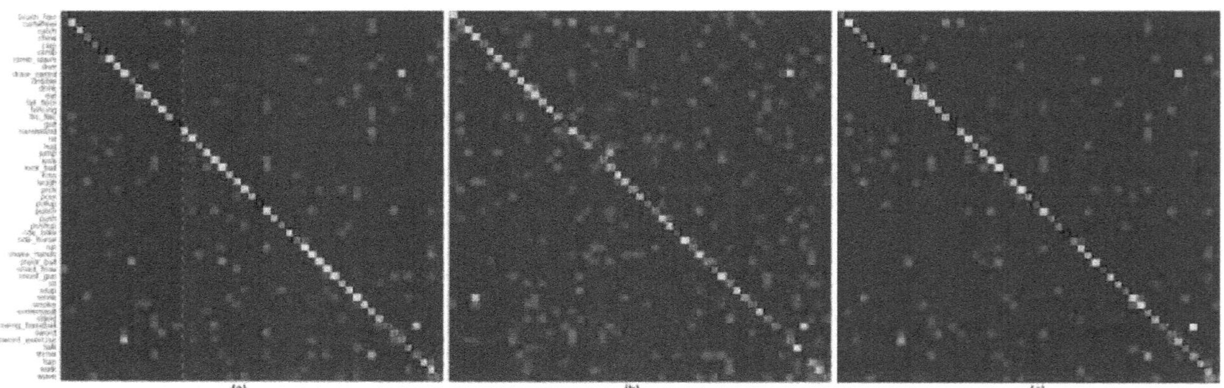

Figure 5: Performance comparison in terms of confusion matrix on the HMDB-51 dataset. (a) Dynamic Trajectory Feature. (b) Combination of Static Deep and Semantic Features. (c) Fusion of Dynamic and Static Feature

[24] B. Yao, X. Jiang, A. Khosla and L. Feifei. Human action recogntion by learning bases of acion attributes and parts. In *Proceedings of the IEEE International Conference on Computer Vision*, 2011.

[25] G. Hinton, L. Deng, D. Yu, G. Dahl, A. Mohamed and N. Jaitly. Deep neural networks for acoustic modeling in speech recognition: The shared views of four research groups. In *IEEE Signal Processing Magazine*, 2012.

[26] Y. Lecun, K. Kavukcuoglu and C. Farabet. Convolutional networks and applications in vision. In *Proceedings of IEEE International Symposium on Circuits and Systems*, 2010.

[27] O. Russakovsky, J. Deng, H. Su and A. Berg. ImageNet large scale visual recogntion challenge. In *arXiv*, 2014.

[28] A. Bergamo and L. Torresani. Classemes and Other Classifier-based Features for Efficient Object Categorization. In *IEEE Transaction on Pattern Analysis and Machine Intelligence*, 2013.

[29] D. G. Lowe. Distinctive image features from scale-invariant keypoints. In *International Journal of Computer Vision*, 2004.

[30] A. Vedaldi and B. Fulkeson. VLFeat: An open and portable library of computer vision algorithms. 2008.

[31] J. Chen, Y. Cui, G. Ye, D. Liu and S.-F. Chang. Event-Driven semantic concept discovery by exploiting weakly tagged internet images. In *Proceedings of the IEEE Conference on Multimedia and Retrieval*, 2014.

[32] Z.-Z. Lan, L. Bao, S. Yu. Multimedia classification and event detection using double fusion. In *Multimedia Tools and Applications*, 2014.

[33] S. Sadanand and J. Corso. Action bank: a high-level representation of activity in video. In *CVPR*, 2012.

[34] D. Oneata, J. Verbeek and C. Schmid. The Lear submission at Thumos 2014. In *THUMOS Workshop*, 2014.

[35] R. Arandjelovic and A. Zisserman. All about VLAD. In *In Proceedings of the IEEE conference on Computer Vision and Pattern Recognition*, 2013.

[36] Y.-G. Jiang, J. Liu and A. Zamir, G. Toderici,I. Laptev, M. Shah and B. Sukthankar. THUMOS Challenge: Action Recognition with a Large Number of Classes. http://crcv.ucf.edu/THUMOS14/, 2014.

[37] J. Cai, Z. Zha, M. Wang, S. Zhang and Q. Tian An Attribute-assisted Reranking Model for Web Image Retrieval. In *Transaction on Image Processing*, 2014.

Social Friend Recommendation Based on Network Correlation and Feature Co-Clustering

Shangrong Huang
Advanced Analytics Inst.
Uni. of Tech. Sydney
shangrong11@hotmail.com

Jian Zhang
Advanced Analytics Inst.
Uni. of Tech. Sydney
Jian.Zhang@uts.edu.au

Shiyang Lu
CSIRO
shiyang@gmail.com

Xian-Sheng Hua
Microsoft Research Redmond
xsha@microsoft.com

ABSTRACT

Friend recommendation is an important recommender application in social media. Major social websites such as Twitter and Facebook are all capable of recommending friends to individuals. However, friend recommendation is a difficult task and most social websites use simple friend recommendation algorithms such as similarity and popularity, whose level of accuracy does do not satisfy the majority of users. In this paper we propose a two-stage procedure for more accurate friend recommendation: In the first stage, based on the relationship of different social networks, the Flickr tag network and contact network are aligned to generate a "possible friend list"; In the second stage, making the assumption that "a friend's friends also tend to be friends", co-clustering is applied to the tag and image information of the list to refine the recommendation result in the first stage. Experimental results show that the proposed method achieves good performance and every stage contributes to the recommendation.

Categories and Subject Descriptors

H.4 [**Information Systems Applications**]: Miscellaneous

General Terms

Algorithms, Recommendation System

Keywords

Friend Recommendation, Social Network, Co-clustering

1. INTRODUCTION

Social media have experienced explosive growth in the last decade. Social websites such as Twitter, YouTube and Flickr have billions of users who share opinions, photos and videos every day. Users make on-line friends through these social media platforms. One challenging issue is how to help these users to efficiently find new social friends. On-line social friend recommendation has therefore become a new research topic and several methods have been proposed[1][2].

Content similarity (such as text or image visual similarity) has been a primary aid for friend recommendation[1]. However, we argue that many other social aspects need to be explored to systematically build high-performance social friend recommendations, rather than basing recommendation purely on content similarity matching. People usually make friends based on their social environment(where they live and work[3]), social behaviours and actions(their working performance, shopping habits, hobbies, and, importantly, interactions with one another[4]), and social status(gender, age, position, etc.[5]). These different social roles can be perceived in the wide range of social networks, such as a basketball-fan network, football-fan network, etc.

These networks have the same set of nodes(each node represents one individual) but have different edge connections between nodes, because meanings of the edges are different. Although each network represents one kind of relationship, its topology is not independent of other networks. This is because an individual's various social roles are related to each other — a person's hobbies are usually related to gender and age, while their friend circle is related to hobbies/positions, and so on. We can also observe individual's social roles on the web. For example, an individual who uses the big image sharing website Flickr[1] has different on-line social roles, such as a photo provider who shares his photos, as well as tags about his/her feelings about the photos, a photo connoisseur, or simply one who wants to find friends who have photos in which they have an interest. These individuals' on-line social roles form different networks and these networks are related to each other. According to the relationship of different networks, we can find approximate isomorphisms between these similar networks[6] and find the "possible friend list" for each user. In other words, we can make friend recommendations by aligning other networks to the friend network.

To model the network correlations, in this paper, we propose to align tag and contact networks through important tag feature selection. The reason we select important tag features is that a person usually presents different social signals in different social networks, which may have different degrees of importance in mining the network correlations. To give a specific example, a photographer uploads images to Flickr tags such as "natural animals", "historical buildings", "street views" and "people". We view these tags as different tag features. In the Flickr network, the photographer

[1]http://www.flickr.com/

ICMR'15, June 23–26, 2015, Shanghai, China.
Copyright © 2015 ACM 978-1-4503-3274-3/15/06 ...$15.00.
http://dx.doi.org/10.1145/2671188.2749325.

may find that most of his friends contact him because of the photos tagged "natural animals" and "historical buildings", rather than "street views" and "people". This indicates that the first two feature words are more important than the last two for friend recommendation. On the other hand, those "unimportant features" may illustrate certain aspects of a person's personality, which we will discuss later.

By alignment we obtain a "possible friend list". However, an on-line social network is usually a very complex and sparse network that contains much noise, and the result of one-stage friend recommendation is usually not satisfactory. For example, both the recent work [2] and our experiment in 6.1.4 show that by applying one stage recommendation can only achieve a recommendation precision of less than 20%, which has little significance in practice. On the other hand, in addition to the tag information we considered in the previous alignment step, there is plenty of helpful information in the photos people have uploaded. The appearances of these photos are definitely very important for individual's decisions about making on-line friends. In this paper, we design a refining step to further raise friend recommendation accuracy. The intuition of our second stage is based on the following assumption: the friends of user A's friends are also likely to be user A's friends. This is a common phenomenon in human society and many on-line society has applied the idea for friend recommendation. We extend it to refine the recommendation result.

Based on the possible friend list of user A, generated by the first step, we first enlarge the list by adding the friends of those on this list, and choose the friends for the final recommendation from this list. In addition to the tag information in the previous step, we also apply the image features in our algorithm and we co-cluster three sets: one user's possible friend list, all the tag features related to this list, and all the image features related to this list. After co-clustering, the entire possible friend list is divided into several clusters. This enables us to view each cluster as a group that interests user A. In the last step, we choose representative users in each cluster as user A's friends.

A number of technologies other than co-clustering such as topic model[7] may also find social groups. In this paper, we apply the co-clustering method because it is more direct and the structure of clusters is more similar to the communities found in on-line society. It is also a good method for simultaneously clustering heterogeneous yet correlated modalities, as in our case. The whole system is illustrated in figure 1:

In summary, this paper makes the following contributions:

1. We propose to align different social networks to select features for friend recommendation.

2. A co-clustering procedure of user, tag and image feature is applied to refine the result of friend recommendation.

3. We have conducted comprehensive experiments to show that the proposed method significantly improves the accuracy of friend-recommendation.

The rest of the paper is organized as follows. Section 2 outlines related work. Section 3 introduces our framework and system model. Sections 4 and 5 give the details for network alignment and co-clustering. Section 6 shows the performance of our method and analysis is made according to the result. Lastly, Section 7 concludes our work.

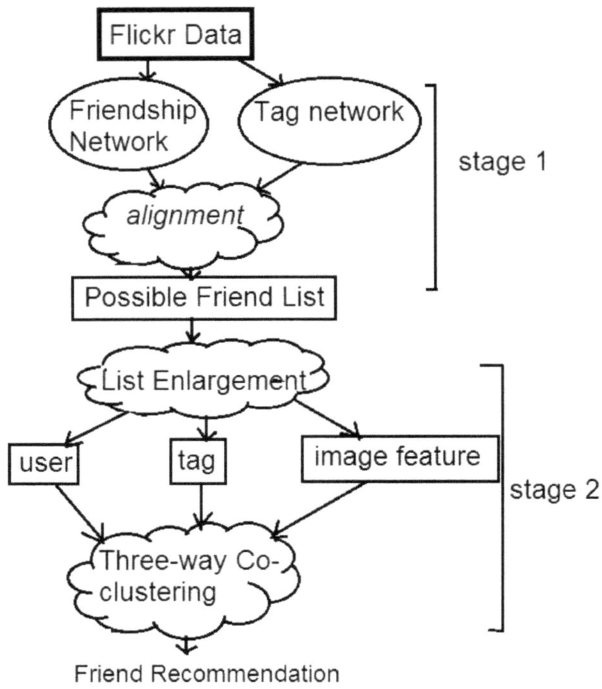

Figure 1: System Illustration

2. RELATED WORKS

In this section we introduce several research fields that directly relate to our work.

2.1 Friend Recommendation in Social Network

Recommendation systems have been widely used for different purposes such as item[8], media recommendation[9] and friend recommendation[10][11][12]. For friend recommendation, different methods and applications have been published: [10] considers user generated content on Twitter and develops a fast algorithm for real-time user-to-user similarity for follower/followee recommendation. It is developed only for text similarity. [11] concentrates on mobile applications and makes friend recommendations by considering the influence of various social aspects such as locations and common interesting words. It defines a transition probability for friendship recommendation based on location neighbourhood and interesting word co-occurrence.

[12] also combines social information from different layers. It takes both context and content information and associates them with domain knowledge. It takes the implicit feedback of users to combine different kinds of information. In addition to these works that synthesize different features such as location, time, and text for similarity calculation, we first mine the network structure and select important features via network alignment. We then apply the co-clustering method for a more accurate result.

2.2 Network Alignment

To find the correlations between different social networks, we propose to use network alignment methods. A number of researches have considered the combination of different social networks for user behaviour prediction. [13]

considers different behaviours such as music listening and book reading for a composite behaviour prediction. It uses a graphical model to build the relationships between various networks. [14] utilizes the application installation information from mobile devices. In both these researches, it would be an improvement to utilize the ample network topological information to achieve a better result. In [15], different networks for image, tag and contact are combined using a Borda Count voting method.

In this paper, we address the problem by considering the social roles of individuals and utilizing the topological information of networks by alignment. The concept of network alignment is applied in fields that study the relationship of big networks. In addition to the fields of bio-informatics and image processing problems[16][17], it has also been applied to fields that deal with large networks problems such as internet network management[18]. In [18], alignment is used to find the co-occurrence of elements of several networks to reduce the traffic of internet data. In this work, we extend the network alignment concept to social networks, by considering the variety of social roles of individuals to achieve better recommendation.

2.3 Co-clustering

Co-clustering is the process of clustering instances and their features at the same time. Early works such as [19] deal with bipartite graph between documents and words which can be relaxed to a spectral clustering problem. Later researches have extended the data to be high-order rather than bipartite graphs: [20] uses a star-structured K-partite graph to illustrate multi-modality data that has relationships in different domains, and co-clusters these data by reducing the mutual information. [21] introduces tensor decomposition for co-clustering multi-modal internet data.

None of the work cited above has taken sparsity into account, yet social media data is usually sparse. [22] provides a good solution for co-clustering sparse data that decomposes three- or higher-way data into sparse indicator vectors. In this paper we extend the idea to deal with image and text data in the field of multimedia.

3. SYSTEM MODEL

In this section we present our framework in two stages. The details of each stage are given in Section 4 and 5.

3.1 Problem Statement and System Description

As shown in Figure 1, our system has two main stages: network alignment and co-clustering. These two stages ensure that we obtain a more accurate recommendation.

3.1.1 Network Alignment

There are two stages in our work on making accurate friend recommendation on Flickr. In the first stage, we align the contact network $\mathcal{C}$ and tag similarity network $\mathcal{T}$ to extract important tag features and generate the "possible friend list" for each user. The nodes in the contact network $\mathcal{C}$ stand for users and the edges stand for if there are friend relationship between each of two users. The nodes in the tag network $\mathcal{T}$ also stand for users, while the edges stand for tag similarity between each of two users. $\mathcal{C}$ and $\mathcal{T}$ have exactly the same nodes but different topologies. As mentioned in the Introduction, the social roles of individuals are related to one another. $\mathcal{T}$ shows an individual's interests and $\mathcal{C}$ shows the friendship, so it is reasonable to assume that the topologies of tag and contact networks are correlated.

When a new node comes into network $\mathcal{T}$, we know its links with other nodes in $\mathcal{T}$, but we do not know its links in network $\mathcal{C}$. Our research seeks to predict its links in $\mathcal{C}$. A real world example for this scenario is that when a new user comes into a social network, he/she may provide interesting keywords. The system should then make relevent friend recommendations for the new user. In our approach, the alignment between different social role networks is considered and important tag features are chosen. New friends are recommended based on these features.

3.1.2 Co-Clustering

There are two problems for the "possible friend list" following the network alignment. First, the ample image features, which may carry much important information about personal tastes, are not utilized in the system. Second, all users use the same set of important features. As a result, it may fail to take individual's personality into account, which is actually very important in a social network. We therefore design a co-clustering process as our second stage.

To address the first problem mentioned above, the image feature set is marked as $\mathcal{I}$. As mentioned in 1, we enlarge the "possible friend list" of user A by adding the friends of the users in the list. To consider the personality of each user, we also add other users who are more similar to user A on those "unimportant features". Then we crawl the photos of all users in the list, as well as the tags. Now we have three sets: the user set, the tag set, and the image feature set. The three sets have links with each other; if a photo uploaded by user B contains one tag $\mathbf{t}_1$ and one image feature $\mathbf{i}_1$, then the node B, $\mathbf{t}_1$, and $\mathbf{i}_1$ in three different sets have links with each other. The relationship of these three datasets can be expressed as a three-way matrix $\underline{\mathbf{X}}$. As an example, if user A uploads an image, this image has an image feature i, and this image contains a tag t, then $\underline{\mathbf{X}}_{Ait}$ should be 1, otherwise 0.

We can carry out co-clustering with these links between sets. Details are given in Section 5. Following the co-clustering, we obtain clusters in the user set, and we are able to choose representatives from each cluster as user A's friends.

4. NETWORK ALIGNMENT

In this section, we give the details of the network alignment considering the correlation of two networks.

4.1 Approach Overview

In this paper, we align two networks by selecting important features that capture the similarity of those networks. Taking the tag and contact networks as an example, we usually judge a person who is a potential friend by only few words. For example, when we find a friend on Twitter, we rarely read all posts of a person, which is too time consuming. Instead, we only read the titles of several of their posts to obtain a rough but to some extent accurate understanding of that person's tastes. Inspired by this phenomenon, we assume that an individual's friend-making decisions are determined by a small number of features from a large feature set. The whole feature set may contain tags, photos, comments, geo information, etc., and according to the previous discussion, we assume that various networks should be well-aligned based on a relatively small number of features. In this paper, we choose tag features for correlation with contact information, and this idea can be extended to different kinds of network.

We choose features from two aspects. In the first aspect, features are chosen that correlate well between two networks. In this paper, we fix one network $\mathcal{C}$ and align the topologies of the other network such as $\mathcal{T}$ in a subspace. Details for network correlation are given in 4.2.

In the second aspect, we choose features that preserve the original structure of the modified network $\mathcal{C}$ in addition to network alignment. In other words, nodes that are close to each other in the original network should also be close in the modified network. Thus the network alignment does not change the pairwise similarity between nodes. The effectiveness of pairwise similarity preservation has been shown in [23]. In this way, we are able to predict links for new nodes for network $\mathcal{C}$ according to the existing links in the modified network $\mathcal{T}$.

4.2 Network Alignment

As mentioned in 4.1, we first consider minimizing the gap between graph $\mathcal{C}$ and $\mathcal{T}$ by selecting important features. Assume we have a feature selection matrix $\mathbf{W}$, to make the user-user similarity between $\mathcal{C}$ and $\mathcal{T}$ as close as possible, we have the following formulation:

$$\min_{\mathbf{W}} \| \mathbf{S}\mathbf{W}\mathbf{W}^T\mathbf{S}^T - \mathbf{K} \|_F^2 \quad (1)$$

$$\text{subject to} : \mathbf{W} \in \{0,1\}^{F\times r}$$

$$\mathbf{W}^T \mathbf{1}_{F\times r} = \mathbf{1}_{r\times 1}$$

where $\mathbf{K}$ is the similarity matrix of $\mathcal{C}$ defined in 3.1. $\mathbf{K}_{ij} = 0$ means that user i and j are not friends, and $\mathbf{K}_{ij} = 1$ means that i and j are friends. $\mathbf{S}^{N\times F}$ is the feature matrix that $\mathbf{S}_{ij} \in \{0,1\}$ illustrates if the photos that user i uploads contain feature j. $\mathbf{W} \in \{0,1\}^{F\times r}$ means that $\mathbf{W}$ can only be chosen from $\{0,1\}$ and $\mathbf{W}^T\mathbf{1}_{F\times r} = \mathbf{1}_{r\times 1}$ means that the sum of each row in $\mathbf{W}$ is exactly 1. These two constraints ensure that each feature can only be chosen once to avoid a linear combination of features. This is a discrete problem and is difficult to solve. The user similarity in (1) measured by the inner product also makes the dimension too high for optimization. In [23], the problem is approximated by the following:

$$\min_{\mathbf{W}} \| \mathbf{S}\mathbf{W} - \mathbf{V} \|_F^2 \quad (2)$$

where $\mathbf{V} \in R^{N\times r}$ stands for the r eigenvectors corresponding to the largest eigenvalues of $\mathbf{K}$. r also stands for the dimension of the subspace into which the data is projected. [23] shows that the upper bound of the solutions between eq.(2) and eq.(1) is small. By adding a regularization term we have the following optimization problem:

$$\min_{\mathbf{W}} \| \mathbf{S}\mathbf{W} - \mathbf{V} \|_F^2 + \lambda \| \mathbf{W} \|_{2,1} \quad (3)$$

The regularization term $\| \mathbf{W} \|_{2,1}$ forces $\mathbf{W}$ to be sparse. Considering only the gap minimization between two networks might lead to a problem that the structure of the modified network might change greatly. [23] have shown in experiments that the clustering and classification performance is improved by preserving the pairwise similarity of the original data structure, compared to pure gap minimization. [23] studies the problem in image and biological data. We extend the idea of pairwise similarity relationship to the social network field. The equation is given as follows:

$$\min_{\mathbf{W}} \|\mathbf{S}\mathbf{W} - \mathbf{V}\|_F^2 + \mu \text{tr}(\mathbf{W}^T\mathbf{S}^T\mathbf{L}\mathbf{S}\mathbf{W}) + \lambda \|\mathbf{W}\|_{2,1} \quad (4)$$

where λ and μ are regularization parameters. $\mathbf{L}$ is the similarity matrix of tag vectors and can be calculated from $\mathbf{S}$. This is a convex problem and $\mathbf{W}$ can efficiently be solved iteratively.[23].

With $\mathbf{W}$ we can determine the important features by ranking the norm of rows in $\mathbf{W}$, this is because each row of $\mathbf{W}$ represents one feature, and the norm illustrate their importance. Then we generate a "possible friend list" for the new arriving user A according to the similarity on the important features.

5. CO-CLUSTERING AND FRIEND RECOMMENDATION

5.1 Friend Circle Enlargement

Following network alignment, we have a "possible friend list" for new user A, and we now want to extend it for more accurate recommendation. According to the assumption that "a friend's friends also tend to be friends", we add possible friends to the list. For example, as shown in Figure 2, in Stage One we get 20 "possible friends" of user A. By adding the friends of these 20 "possible friends" into the list we have about 1000 friends in total, To consider the personality of user A, we also add 500 similar users of A based on the "unimportant features", as described in 3.1.2. We then crawled all the images uploaded by these 1500 users.

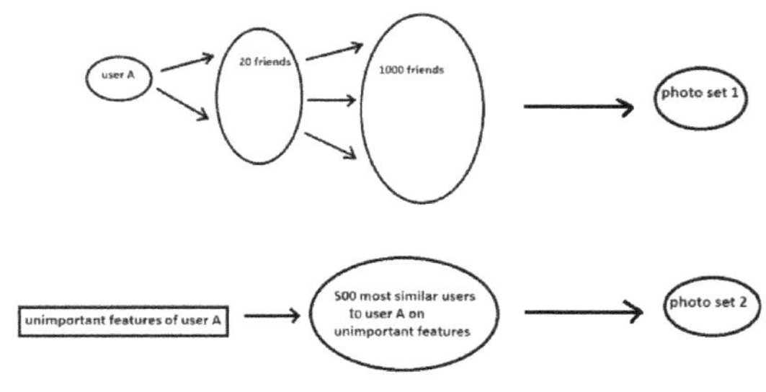

Figure 2: Friend List Extension

5.2 Three-Way Co-clustering

After obtaining all the photos and tags of the users on the list, we can conduct the three-way clustering to obtain topics that might interest user A. Because the number of image features is very large, (the number of photos for 1500 users can be hundreds of thousands, and the number of image features such as SIFT can be tens of millions), we first cluster the image features and then build a structure such as inverted index table for fast search.

5.2.1 Feature Clustering and Inverted Index Table

We give only a brief summary of the feature clustering and inverted index table, as this is not the main contribution of our paper. We use the K-means method to form approximately 20,000 feature cluster centres. These cluster centres are saved in an inverted index table. When a new feature arrives, we can find which feature centre the new coming feature belongs to with the help of the inverted index table. Each feature is represented by its feature centre, and a single image is recorded by hundreds of feature centres. The illustration of the feature clustering process is given in Figure 3. In which the upper part shows how to build the inverted index table and the lower part shows how to quickly find the cluster to which the feature of a new photo belongs when it arrives. In Table 1, the structure of an inverted index table is given.

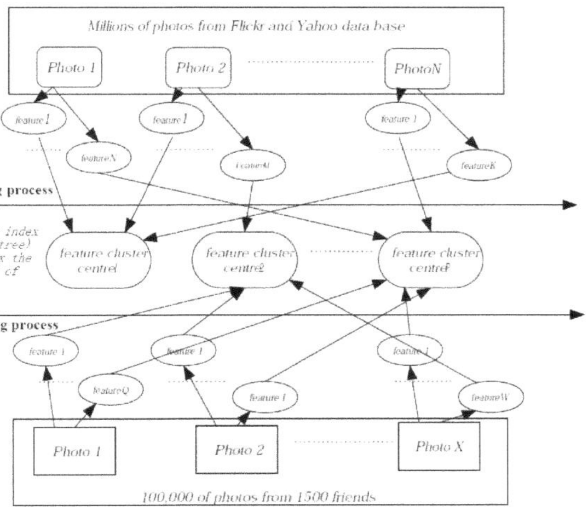

Figure 3: Feature Clustering

Table 1: Inverted Index Table

image 1	feature cluster centre 1, 3, 5,...
image 2	feature cluster centre 1, 5, 6,...
...	...
image 100,000	feature cluster centre 2, 6, 9,...

5.2.2 *Three-way Co-Clustering*

Now we have three datasets from different domains: the user set, the tag set, and the image feature set. The nodes in each dataset have links with the nodes in the other datasets. We co-cluster the data from the three datasets to find the groups that user A may be interested in.

According to [22], a three-way array $\underline{\mathbf{X}}$ has a low rank approximation as the sum of the product of three vectors as follows:

$$\underline{\mathbf{X}} \cong \sum_{k=1}^{K} \mathbf{a}_k \circ \mathbf{b}_k \circ \mathbf{c}_k \tag{5}$$

where $\mathbf{a} \circ \mathbf{b} \circ \mathbf{c}$ is a rank-one three-way array with (i,j,n)-th element of $\mathbf{a}_i \mathbf{b}_j \mathbf{c}_n$. Let $\mathbf{A} = [\mathbf{a}_1, ..., \mathbf{a}_K]$, $\mathbf{B} = [\mathbf{b}_1, ..., \mathbf{b}_K]$, $\mathbf{C} = [\mathbf{c}_1, ..., \mathbf{c}_K]$, and we express the three-dimensional $I \times J \times N$ array $\underline{\mathbf{X}}$ with three two-dimensional matrix as:

$$\mathbf{X}_{(1)} = \begin{bmatrix} \underline{\mathbf{X}}(:,1,:)^T \\ \vdots \\ \underline{\mathbf{X}}(:,J,:)^T \end{bmatrix}, \mathbf{X}_{(2)} = \begin{bmatrix} \underline{\mathbf{X}}(:,:,1)^T \\ \vdots \\ \underline{\mathbf{X}}(:,:,N)^T \end{bmatrix}, \mathbf{X}_{(3)} = \begin{bmatrix} \underline{\mathbf{X}}(1,:,:)^T \\ \vdots \\ \underline{\mathbf{X}}(I,:,:)^T \end{bmatrix} \tag{6}$$

and $\mathbf{X}_i$ can be expressed as:

$$\mathbf{X}_{(1)} = (\mathbf{B} \odot \mathbf{C})\mathbf{A}^T, \mathbf{X}_{(2)} = (\mathbf{C} \odot \mathbf{A})\mathbf{B}^T, \mathbf{X}_{(3)} = (\mathbf{A} \odot \mathbf{B})\mathbf{C}^T \tag{7}$$

where $\odot$ stands for the Khatri-Rao product. To co-cluster $\underline{\mathbf{X}}$ into K clusters, we can make $\mathbf{A}$, $\mathbf{B}$ and $\mathbf{C}$ as indicator matrix as follows:

$$\min_{\{\mathbf{a}_k,\mathbf{b}_k,\mathbf{c}_k\}_{k=1}^K} \|\underline{\mathbf{X}} - \sum_{k=1}^{K} \mathbf{a}_k \circ \mathbf{b}_k \circ \mathbf{c}_k\|^2 \tag{8a}$$

$$\mathbf{a}_k, \mathbf{b}_k, \mathbf{c}_k \in \{0,1\} \tag{8b}$$

$$\sum_{k=1}^{K} \mathbf{A}(l,k) = 1, \sum_{k=1}^{K} \mathbf{B}(l,k) = 1, \sum_{k=1}^{K} \mathbf{C}(l,k) = 1 \tag{8c}$$

(8b) and (8c) make the constraints that each node belongs to one and only one cluster. For computational efficiency (8b) and (8c) are often replaced by the sparsity constraints [24] as follows:

$$\min_{\{\mathbf{a}_k,\mathbf{b}_k,\mathbf{c}_k\}_{k=1}^K} \|\underline{\mathbf{X}} - \sum_{k=1}^{K} \mathbf{a}_k \circ \mathbf{b}_k \circ \mathbf{c}_k\|^2 + \lambda_a \sum_k \|\mathbf{a}_k\|_1 + \lambda_b \sum_k \|\mathbf{b}_k\|_1 + \lambda_c \sum_k \|\mathbf{c}_k\|_1 \tag{9}$$

where $\lambda_{a,b,c}$ in (9) control the sparsity of each indicator vector. Following [22], this provides a computationally efficient algorithm for solving (9).

5.3 Friend Recommendation

Following three-way co-clustering, we simultaneously obtain three kinds of clusters of users, their uploaded tags and their image features. We can interpret each cluster of users as one group that might interest user A. User A's friends should come from these groups. There are different strategies for choosing friends from each of the groups. We list several below and will give the experimental results later to see which strategies work better:

1.(S1)Choose users that are near the centre of each cluster.

2.(S2)Choose users that are most active in each cluster. A user's "activeness" is measured by the following aspects: his/her communication with others, the number of photos uploaded, and the popularity of his/her photos.

3.(S3)Combine the above two criteria by averaging their ranks.

When new users come they will first upload a number of tags and photos. With these tags and the image features of photos, we can make accurate friend recommendations.

A potential problem for our algorithm is that it takes time to extract the image features for a new user and do the co-clustering, thus it is not appropriate for on-line recommendation. However, with some modifications we can make it operable in real-time. We can build up a large dataset and co-cluster its users,tags,images, and then build a large inverted index table as mentioned in 5.2.1 to quickly find those clusters to which the user belongs.

The whole algorithm is given in Algorithm 1.

6. EXPERIMENTS

In this section, we conduct extensive experiments to show the effectiveness of our proposed method, and also illustrate several interesting properties. First, we briefly introduce of our social media dataset, and then we discuss our algorithm from different aspects.

Algorithm 1 Proposed Algorithm

Input:
tag feature matrix **S**, contact matrix **K**, image feature matrix **I**, tag feature vector **f** and image feature matrix **i** of the new user, number of recommending friends T

Output:
Friend recommendation list

Stage One
1: Calculate the tag relationship matrix **L** from **S**
2: Determine λ, μ via cross validation on training set
3: Calculate **V** by eigen-decomposition of Laplacian of **K**
4: Iteratively get **W** according to [23].
5: Choose tag features by ranking the norm of rows of **W**.
6: Choose "possible friend list" on important features.

Stage Two
7: Enlarge "possible friend list" according to 5.1.
8: Extract image features of users in the list.
9: Co-cluster user, tag, and image feature set[22].
10: Recommending friends by choosing users from each cluster.

6.1 Experimental Settings

6.1.1 Dataset

We crawled a social network from the big image sharing site Flickr. As the data set is quite large, a relatively unbiased dataset was obtained. In total we crawled the data of 10000 users, and for each user, we crawled all their photos, and tags of each photo. The SIFT features for all photos were extracted. In this paper we do not concentrate on what kind of image features are more indicative for matching images, so we choose the popular SIFT feature that has been widely in image retrieval problems. In future works, we may also study the properties of different features for more precise result. We then crawled the user contact information to form the contact network. Contact information in Flickr is acquired by when a user adds another user to his/her friend list, or vice versa. We crawled all the contacts between any two users in our dataset. A short summary of our dataset is given in Table 2 :

Table 2: Dataset Statistics

Users	10000
Photos	543,754 photos from 10000 users
Image Features	46,443,754 SIFT features
Contact	145,684 friend links among users
Tags	35,574 words after filtering

6.1.2 Settings and Metrics

Our task is to make precise contact information prediction,so that way when a new user enters into the social network, we recommend new friends according to key words and photos that represent the user's interests..

In friend recommendation, assume we recommend T friends to each user. We use the existing contact information as the ground truth for training and testing. In the first stage, the parameters of eq. (4) λ, μ are determined on the training set by a fourfold cross validation to find the best. The ranges for these parameters are: $\lambda \in 10^{[-2:1:3]}$, $\mu \in 10^{[-2:1:3]}$, and $p \in [1, 1.5, 2, 2.5, 3]$.

We use the method summarized in 5.3 to recommend friends to new users. We use the recommendation precision metrics to show the effectiveness of the proposed algorithm. In our experiment, precision is defined as the number of correctly recommended friends divided by all the recommended users.

6.1.3 Reference Methods

We use several reference methods to show the advantage of our proposed algorithm in friend recommendation for our first stage. These are: 1). pure tag similarity. 2). online collaborative filtering(OLCF), and 3) Relational Domain Recommendation(RDR)[25].

The first is the simple tag similarity comparison. We recommend the friends of each user purely on the tag and image feature similarity.

The second method is OLCF. The collaborative filtering method is widely used in recommender systems. It fills the blank entries of the user-item matrix. In our experiment, we use a model-based collaborative filtering method[8] to determine the votes of each user on each feature of the whole feature space, and then calculate the cosine similarity between users. We recommend friends by ranking these similarities. The feature space here contains the tag features and image SIFT feature clusters, as mentioned in 5.2.1

Lastly, we consider a multi-network based algorithm for comparison. Transition probability propagation is a method that is frequently used to consider social multiple network problems[25][26]. We choose [25] as a reference method for the following reasons: 1) It considers the relationships of different networks, which is similar to our idea, though in [25], different networks have different nodes, and 2) It uses the information of other networks for recommendation, which again has some similarities with ours. [25] enhances the links in one network and among different networks using a random walk propagation method. In our experiment, it has three networks: user, tag, and image feature networks.

6.1.4 Stage One: Network Alignment

First we study the performance of Stage one with varying numbers of tag features. We change the selected number of features from 300 to 10800, each time increase 1500. Then we test the recommendation precision on selected number of features. We recommend the first 20 most similar users as friends. The result of precision@20 is shown in Figure 4:

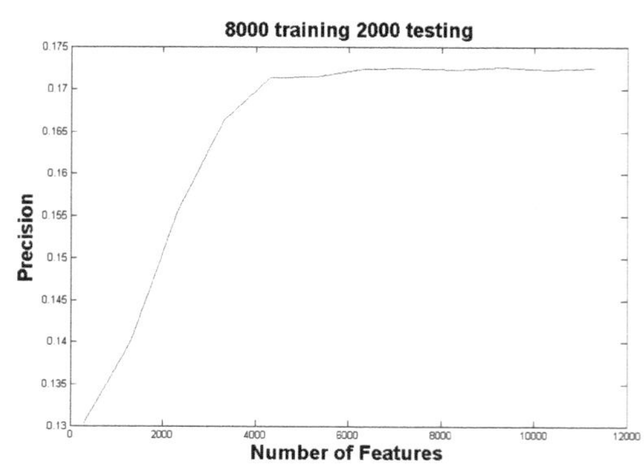

Figure 4: Stage one: Precision@20 with the Increase in the Number of Features

From Figure 4 we see that the performance of the algorithm quickly increases when the number of features is relatively small. There is a turning point when we select around 4000 features. When the number of features exceeds 4500, the increase in performance is marginal. This means that when a user looks for friends, he/she only concentrates on some characteristics of others, not all aspects.

6.1.5 *Stage Two: Co-clustering*

With the "possible friend list" generated in Stage One, we can start the co-clustering process for Stage Two. This is a refinement process which selects three criteria for friend recommendation as stated in 5.3. Figure 5 illustrates one cluster from the co-clustering result. For convenience, we use a simple voting strategy in this illustration to determine which cluster an image should belongs to, instead of using SIFT features. We can see that most of the conceptually similar tags and images are clustered together.

Figure 5: Result of Co-clustering

Most Flickr users are unlikely to upload photos that illustrate too many aspects of their interest, therefore the number of clusters in Stage Two should not be too large. We set K in 5.2.2 to be 5,10, and 20, and choose 4, 2, 1 users as the final recommended friends from each cluster. We take 1000 users in total and make recommendations for them. The tag feature number of the first stage is fixed at 4500. The results of the three criteria are shown in Figure 6.

From Figure 6, we see that the combination of near-centre users and most active users have slightly better performance. We achieve the best performance when we choose 10 as the number of clusters, but the difference is not great. Stage Two increases recommendation precision by about 8%, compared with Stage One. This illustrates the effectiveness of our assumption that "a friend's friends also tend to be friends". Figure 7 shows the improvement of Stage Two compared with Stage One with the change of tag features in Stage One.

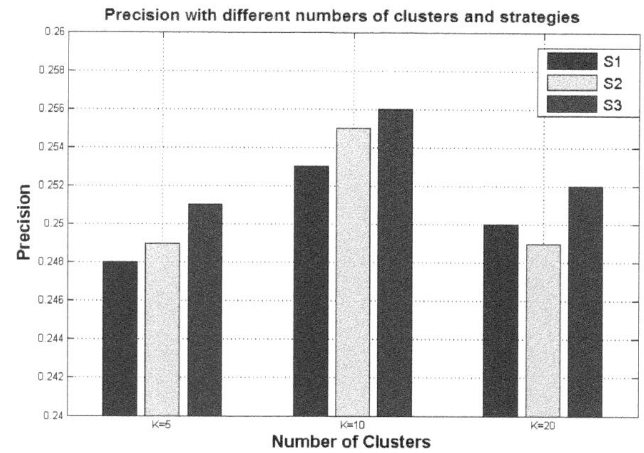

Figure 6: Stage Two: Precision@20 with different numbers of clusters and different strategies

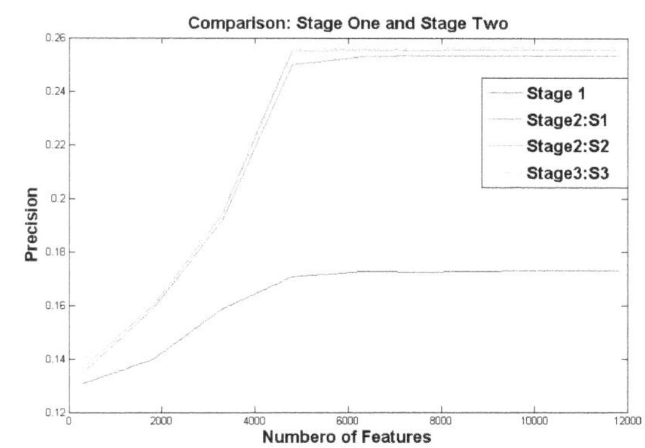

Figure 7: Comparison of Stage One and Two: Precision@20 with Increase in the Number of Features

6.1.6 *Comparison with Reference Methods*

Next we compare our proposed methods with the reference methods. For the proposed method, we use the strategy of combining the near-centre and most active users. For $P@5$,$P@10$, $P@15$ and $P@20$, we choose the co-clustering parameter of $K = 5, 10, 15, 20$ in Stage Two, and choose one friend from each cluster. The result is shown in Figure 8.

Figure 8 shows that the proposed algorithm outperforms all the reference methods in the recommendation precision by at least 15%.

7. CONCLUSION AND FUTURE WORK

In this paper, we develop a two-stage friend recommendation scenario utilizing multimedia information. In the first stage, tag information is utilized to build a tag network and is aligned to a contact network by a number of important features, to generate a "possible friend list". In the second stage, a co-clustering procedure is proposed to co-cluster user, tag, and image features to form groups and make more precise recommendations.

Experimental results show that the proposed method outperforms other methods in friend recommendation, with our method achieving the highest precision in friend prediction. The network alignment of Stage One is effective and proves

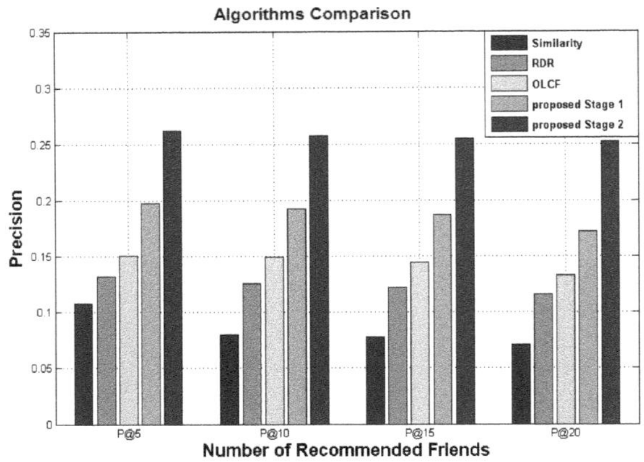

Figure 8: Stage Two: Precision@20 of different methods

that a small number of features is sufficient for friend recommendation. Co-clustering in Stage Two shows that conceptually similar tags and images can be successfully clustered, improving the recommendation result has been improved by about 8%.

In the future, we will further develop our algorithm in the following aspects. 1) We will extend our ideas to further applications such as product recommendation, media retrieval, etc., and 2) We will develop other algorithms in each of our two stages to achieve better, more acceptable recommendations.

8. REFERENCES

[1] J. Chen, W. Geyer, C. Dugan, M. Muller, and I. Guy. Make new friends, but keep the old: Recommending people on social networking sites. In *CHI'09*, New York, NY, April 2009.

[2] S. Wan, Y. Lan, J. Guo, C. Fan, and X. Cheng. Informational friendship recommendation in social media. In *SIGIR'13*, pages 1045–1048, Dublin, Ireland, July 2013.

[3] E. Barnett and M. Casper. A defination of 'social environment'. *American Journal of Public Health*, 91 (3), March 2001.

[4] R. J. Rummel. *The Conflict Helix:Principles and Practices of Interpersonal, Social, and International Conflict and Cooperation.* New Brunswick, N.J, 1991.

[5] R. Brym. *Sociology: Your Compass for a New World, Brief Edition.* Cengage Learning, 2009.

[6] M. Bayati, M. Gerritsen, D. Gleich, A. Saberi, and Y. Wang. Algorithms for large, sparse network alignment problems. In *ICDM'09*, pages 705–710, Miami, FL, Dec 2009.

[7] D. M. Blei, A. Y. Ng, and M. I. Jordan. Latent dirichlet allocation. In *Journal of Machine Learning Research*, Jan 2003.

[8] H. Ma, H. Yang, M. R. Lyu, and I. King. Sorec: social recommendation using probabilistic matrix factorization. In *CIKM'08*, pages 931–940, Napa Valley, CA, November 2008.

[9] S. D. Roy, T. Mei, W. Zeng, and S. Li. Socialtransfer: Cross-domain transfer learning from social streams for media applications. In *MM'12*, Nara, Japan, Oct 2012.

[10] J. Hannon, M. Bennett, and B. Smyth. Recommending twitter users to follow using content and collaborative filtering approaches. In *RecSys'10*, pages 199–206, Barcelona, Spain, September 2010.

[11] N. Li and G. Chen. Multi-layered friendship modeling for location-based mobile social networks. In *MobiQuitous'09*, pages 1–10, Toronto, Canada, July 2009.

[12] X. Xie. Potential friend recommendation in online social networking. In *CPSCom'10*, pages 831–835, Hangzhou, China, December 2010.

[13] E. Zhong, W. Fan, and Q. Yang. User behavior learning and transfer in composite social networks. *ACM Trans. on Knowledge Discovery from Data*, 8, February 2014.

[14] W. Pan, N. Aharony, and A. S. Pentland. Composite social network for predicting mobile apps installation. In *AAAI'11*, San Francisco, CA, August 2011.

[15] A. Rae, B. Sigurbjoernsson, and R. v. Zwol. Improving tag recommendation using social networks. In *RIAO'10*, Paris, France, 2010.

[16] G. Klau. A new graph-based method for pairwise global network alignment. *BMC Bioinformatics*, 10 (S1):S59, January 2009.

[17] D. Conte, P. P. Foggia, C. Sansone, and M. Vento. Thirty years of graph matching in pattern recognition. *Intl. J. of Pattern Recognition and Artificial Intelligence*, 18(3):265–298, May 2004.

[18] C. Kreibirch and J. Crowcroft. Efficient sequence alignment of network traffic. In *IMC'06*, pages 307–312, Rio de Janeiro, Brazil, October 2006.

[19] I. Dhillon, S. Mallela, and D. Nodha. Information-theoretic co-clustering. In *SIGKDD'01*, New York, NY, 2003.

[20] B. Bao, W. Min, K. Lu, and C. Xu. Social event detection with robust high-order co-clustering. In *ICMR'13*, pages 135–142, New York, NY, 2013.

[21] Q. Zhou, G. Xu, and Y. Zong. Web co-clustering of usage network using tensor decomposition. In *IEEE Trans. on Signal Processing*, pages 493–506, Oct 2012.

[22] E. E. Parpalexakis, N. D. Sidiropoulous, and R. Bro. From k-means to higher-way co-clustering: Multilinear decomposition with sparse latent factors. In *WI-IAT'09*, pages 311–314, Milan, Italy, 2009.

[23] X. Liu, L. Wang, J. Zhang, J. Yin, and H. Liu. Global and local structure preservation for feature selection. *IEEE Trans. on Neural networks and learning systems*, pages 1083–1095, November 2014.

[24] R. Tibshirani. Regression shrinkage and selection via the lasso. In *Journal of the Royal Statistical Society, Series B*, pages 267–288, 1994.

[25] M. Jiang, P. Cui, F. Wang, Q. Yang, W. Zhu, and S. Yang. Social recommendation across multiple relational domains. In *CIKM'12*, Maui, HI, Oct 2012.

[26] D. Liu, G. Ye, C. Chen, S. Yan, and S. Chang. Hybrid social media network. In *MM'12*, pages 659–668, Nara,Japan, October 2012.

Improving Diversity in Image Search via Supervised Relevance Scoring

Eleftherios Spyromitros-Xioufis
CERTH-ITI / AUTH, Greece
espyromi@iti.gr

Symeon Papadopoulos
CERTH-ITI, Greece
papadop@iti.gr

Alexandru Lucian Ginsca
CEA, LIST, France
alexandru.ginsca@cea.fr

Adrian Popescu
CEA, LIST, France
adrian.popescu@cea.fr

Yiannis Kompatsiaris
CERTH-ITI, Greece
ikom@iti.gr

Ioannis Vlahavas
AUTH, Greece
vlahavas@csd.auth.gr

ABSTRACT

Results returned by commercial image search engines should include relevant and diversified depictions of queries in order to ensure good coverage of users' information needs. While relevance has drastically improved in recent years, diversity is still an open problem. In this paper we propose a reranking method that could be implemented on top of such engines in order to provide a better balance between relevance and diversity. Our method formulates the reranking problem as an optimization of a utility function that jointly considers relevance and diversity. Our main contribution is the replacement of the unsupervised definition of relevance that is commonly used in this formulation with a supervised classification model that strives to capture a query and application-specific notion of relevance. This model provides more accurate relevance scores that lead to significantly improved diversification performance. Furthermore, we propose a stacking-type ensemble learning approach that allows combining multiple features in a principled way when computing the relevance of an image. An empirical evaluation carried out on the datasets of the MediaEval 2013 and 2014 "Retrieving Diverse Social Images" (RDSI) benchmarks confirms the superior performance of the proposed method compared to other participating systems as well as a state-of-the-art, unsupervised reranking method.

Categories and Subject Descriptors

H.3.3 [**Information Storage and Retrieval**]: Information Search and Retrieval—*relevance feedback*

Keywords

image retrieval, diversity, relevance feedback, image classification, image reranking

ICMR'15, June 23–26, 2015, Shanghai, China.

ACM 978-1-4503-3274-3/15/06 ...$15.00.
http://dx.doi.org/10.1145/2671188.2749334.

1. INTRODUCTION

The importance of presenting a set of results that are at the same time relevant to the query but also exhibit diversity has been pointed out long ago in the Information Retrieval (IR) community [3]. Diversity in top results provides a more comprehensive and concise answer to the query which in turn enables faster access to the desired information and ultimately results in increased user satisfaction. Despite this fact, existing image search engines (either operating on web scale, e.g., Google Images, or within media sharing platforms, e.g., Flickr) still focus primarily on relevance. As a consequence, top results usually contain many similar images and the user has to go deeper down the list of results in order to discover diverse views of the query. In addition, the deeper one goes down the list, the higher the probability to encounter irrelevant results becomes, thus impeding the discovery of diverse views. This focus on relevance is perhaps due to the limitations imposed by relying mostly on the textual modality of the images [15] (e.g., surrounding web page text in the case of Google Images, tags and textual descriptions in the case of Flickr). Obviously, ignoring the visual content of the images limits the ability of a search engine to provide either relevant or diverse results. Figure 1 shows the first 10 results returned by Flickr (top) and Google images (middle) in response to a query about "La Madeleine" church in Paris. Both result sets are not optimal in the sense that they contain irrelevant and/or similar images.

In this paper, we propose a method that aims at refining the initial ranking of existing image search engines so that both the relevance and the diversity of the top results are improved, as shown on Figure 1 (bottom). Our method builds upon a diversification method [7] that casts the above problem into the optimization of a utility function that jointly considers relevance and diversity. In contrast to [7] that used a generic, unsupervised definition for relevance, we propose a query and application-specific definition that is directly learned from user feedback. This supervised definition alleviates several shortcomings of the unsupervised counterpart and manages to provide a significantly more accurate relevance scoring which, as we show, has a direct positive impact on the overall diversification performance of the algorithm. Although our method assumes the existence of relevance annotations, we explain that such annotations do not necessarily need to be given by experts but can also be acquired via implicit user feedback. Another important property of the proposed diversification approach is that it allows the com-

Figure 1: The first 10 results returned by Flickr (top) and Google (middle) in response to a query about "La Madeleine" church in Paris. The bottom row corresponds to an optimal result set where each image captures a different aspect of the query. t_i denotes the topic that an image belongs to.

bination of multiple types of features in a principled and effective way when computing the relevance of an image.

Our approach can be applied to different retrieval scenarios. However, in this paper we focus on landmark retrieval mainly due to the fact that a social image retrieval benchmark is available for this scenario (RDSI benchmark of MediaEval 2013 [9] and 2014 [10]). Specifically, we consider the case of a tourist who wants to plan a trip to an unfamiliar location. Knowing only the name of the landmark, the person uses it to learn more about it by visiting the corresponding Wikipedia article where he/she can get a textual description and some example photos. Before deciding whether this landmark is worth visiting, the tourist wants to get an informative visual summary of it. A query using existing search engines tends to return many similar images or holiday photos that prominently feature people as the main subject. Other results may include low quality images or images of completely different locations. Ideally, the person would like to receive photos capturing different visual characteristics of the target location, e.g., different viewpoints, architectural details, creative views, etc., so that most of the perceived visual information is different from one photo to another as in Figure 1 (bottom).

Using an early version of our method (briefly described in [5] and [14]), we achieved top results in the RDSI benchmarks of MediaEval 2013 and 2014. In this paper, we develop the method further and provide an extensive analysis of its performance. In particular, this paper makes the following contributions:

- We highlight the connection between the accuracy of the relevance scoring component of the diversification method of [7] and its diversification performance.
- We show that relevance scoring accuracy can be significantly improved by exploiting relevance annotations and performing the scoring in a supervised manner.
- We evaluate supervised relevance scoring models built from training sets of various compositions and show that a small number of query-specific positive annotations combined with application-specific positive and negative annotations yield very good results.
- We develop a novel ensemble learning algorithm that combines multi-dimensional and one-dimensional features in a principled and effective way.

As a result, our method achieves significantly better diversification performance than a state-of-the-art reranking method that uses an unsupervised definition of relevance and outperforms the best performing systems of the 2013 and 2014 RDSI benchmarks by 7.5% and 5.7% respectively.

2. RELATED WORK

One of the first and seminal works on diversity in information retrieval is the work of Carbonell and Goldstain [3]. Recognizing that in the context of text retrieval and summarization, pure relevance ranking is not sufficient, they proposed Maximal Marginal Relevance (MMR). MMR is a reranking method that linearly combines independent measurements of relevance and diversity (their relative weight is a user-tunable parameter) into a single metric that is maximized in a greedy, iterative fashion. In [17], MMR was combined with a language modelling framework to solve the problem of subtopic retrieval where the task is to find documents that cover as many different subtopics of a query topic as possible. In [4], a greedy algorithm is developed for maximizing the probability of finding at least one relevant document in top n. This algorithm is similar to MMR and is also shown to be a greedy maximizer of the instance or cluster recall metric, i.e. the number of different subtopics covered by a given set of results. More recently, a similar formulation of the diversification problem was given by Deselaers et al. [7] and was found to outperform a common clustering-based diversification approach, in the context of diverse image retrieval. As in MMR, diversification is achieved via the optimization of a criterion that linearly combines relevance and diversity. However, [7] gives a more general formulation and uses dynamic programming algorithms to perform the optimization in addition to the greedy, iterative algorithm presented in [3]. In our work, we adopt the formulation of [7] but combine it with a supervised definition of relevance that leads to significantly better performance. Also, compared to [7], where different modalities were combined in an ad-hoc way, the use of learning allows us to develop a more principled and effective way of combining multiple features.

Diversity in social image retrieval was the focus of the MediaEval 2013 and 2014 RDSI benchmarks that attracted the interest of many groups working in this area. Most participants developed diversification approaches that combined clustering with a strategy to select and return representative images from each cluster. Our MMR-based approach has the advantage of targeting the diversification problem in a more straightforward way compared to clustering-based approaches which first try to solve a different and presumably more difficult problem (i.e. finding groups of similar images). Also, despite the fact that most systems involved a mechanism to improve relevance before enforcing diversity, the majority did not exploit relevance annotations. Instead, top-performing solutions ([11], [6]) used specialized filters (e.g., face and blur detectors) and hand-coded rules (distant images are irrelevant) in order to discard irrelevant images according to the verbal definitions of relevance and irrelevance given by the task organizers. By learning the concept of relevance through the use of query and application-specific relevance annotations, our method can adapt automatically to different queries and retrieval scenarios and thus represents a more general solution.

3. METHOD

3.1 Problem Definition

Let q be a query[1] and $I = \{im_1, \dots, im_N\}$ be a ranked list of images that have been retrieved by an existing search engine in response to q. Although the quality of the results depends on the specific query and search engine, we expect that for values of N up to a few hundreds, I will typically comprise both relevant and irrelevant images and that some of the relevant images might contain duplicate information[2] (see Figure 1). The goal of a diversification method, is to refine the initial ranking of the images in I so that relevant images are ranked higher than irrelevant and top positions contain as little duplicate images as possible. Since users usually inspect only the top few results, reranking the whole list is not needed and we instead request a K-sized subset of images from I that are as relevant (to the query) and as diverse (with each other) as possible. Among the many measures that have been proposed in order to quantify the above qualitative goal of a diversification method is, for instance, the subtopic or cluster recall at K (CR@K) [17] that measures the percentage of different topics/aspects retrieved in the first K results. Note that a perfect CR@K requires all K results to be relevant. A typical cut-off is $K = 20$ (adopted in MediaEval 2014 [10] and ImageCLEF 2008 [1]), as most search engines present around 20 results on their first page.

3.2 Maximal Marginal Relevance

MMR formulates the goal of a diversification method as an optimization problem where one tries to maximize a linear combination of relevance and diversity, the so called "marginal relevance". According to the formulation given in [7], the objective is to find the K-sized set $S \subset I$ that maximizes the following utility function:

$$\arg\max_{S \subset I, |S|=K} U(S|q) = w * R(S|q) + (1-w) * D(S), \quad (1)$$

where $R(S|q)$ is a measure of the relevance of S to the query, $D(S)$ is a measure of the diversity in S, and w is a parameter that controls the relative importance of relevance and diversity. w can be either adjusted by the user or tuned (on a diversity annotated validation set) to optimize a particular quantitative measure (e.g., CR@20). Note that as implied by Equation 1, diversity is independent of the query.

[1]Note that q can be expressed as a textual, visual or mixed query without loss of generality.

[2]These assumptions are shown to hold (Subsection 4.1) when Flickr is used as search engine for landmark queries.

Figure 2: Wikipedia image of "Angkor Wat" (left), a relevant inside view (center) and an irrelevant image with a person in front of the monument (right).

3.3 Relevance

3.3.1 *Unsupervised Relevance*

The relevance of a set of images S was defined in [7] as

$$R(S|q) = \sum_{im_i \in S} R(im_i|q) = \sum_{im_i \in S} s(im_i, im_q), \quad (2)$$

where $R(im_i|q)$ denotes the relevance of each individual image to the query and $s(im_i, im_q)$ is a normalized similarity measure between im_i and im_q. Depending on the type of representation chosen for the query and the database images, several different similarity functions may be used. For instance, when both the query and the database images are represented as text, $s(im_i, im_q)$ could be the cosine similarity between bag of word vectors, while in cases where the query is expressed via an example image, $s(im_i, im_q)$ could be the (normalized) inverse of the Euclidean distance between the respective visual feature representations.

A limitation of the unsupervised definition of relevance described above is that similarity, as quantified by common textual or visual representation-measure combinations, does not attempt to capture the concept of relevance as conceived by users. In addition, similarity does not imply relevance and vice versa. Consider, for instance, the landmark retrieval use case described in Section 1. As exemplified in Figure 1 the optimal set of results might contain images that are dissimilar to a reference, visual representation of the query (e.g., the Wikipedia image) but are still considered relevant to it e.g., inside views, architectural details, etc. On the other hand, images that are visually similar to the query might be considered irrelevant due to people being the main focus of the image (Figure 2). The situation is even more problematic when a textual representation is used because textual similarity is often a poor proxy for visual similarity (noisy or missing tags/descriptions). Although the use of multiple modalities is expected to improve the accuracy of relevance scoring, their combination is usually performed with arbitrarily chosen weights [7].

3.3.2 *Learning Relevance from User Feedback*

Motivated by the shortcomings of unsupervised relevance scoring described above and by the fact that improving the relevance scoring quality within the MMR framework has a direct positive impact on common diversification performance measures (Subsection 5.1), we propose a supervised relevance scoring method that exploits relevance annotations in order to induce a more accurate definition of relevance.

More specifically, for each query q, we build a probabilistic model $h_q : X \rightarrow [0, 1]$ that takes a n-dimensional representation of the image $X = R^n$ as input and outputs the probability that the image is relevant to the query given the input. These probabilistic outputs $(h_q(im_i))$ replace the unsupervised similarity measurements $(s(im_i, im_q))$ in Equation 2. In order to train this model, we assume the existence of a set $D_q = \{(x_1, y_1), \ldots, (x_m, y_m)\}$ of m training examples where $x_i \in X$ is the input vector and $y_i \in Y = \{0, 1\}$ is the class value with $y_i = 1/0$ denoting a relevant/irrelevant example.

Ideally, D_q will be composed of examples that have explicitly been annotated as relevant/irrelevant to q by the user and will therefore constitute an accurate representation of what the user considers relevant. This, however, requires considerable effort from the user. A more realistic scenario is the collection of relevance annotations by exploiting implicit relevance feedback given by multiple users for the same query q. A search engine can count the number of times that each image $im_i \in I$ is clicked (viewed) by users when returned in response to a query q. Then, we can reasonably assume that images with high click counts are relevant to the query and images with lower click counts are irrelevant. In fact, even a single click (or few to exclude noise) will be sufficient to claim relevance of an image. On the other hand, multiple feedback signals will be required to confidently claim irrelevance of an image due to the implicit and partial nature of the feedback: a) an image might be relevant but contain duplicate information with another image and therefore not clicked or b) an image far down the list might have not been inspected at all. Therefore, exploiting implicit user feedback as described above could result in a set of query-specific positive (relevant) examples and, in case of popular queries, negative (irrelevant) examples.

In this paper, we focus on infrequent queries for which negative (irrelevant) examples are unavailable. To train h_q in this case, we combine few query-specific positive examples with positive and negative examples from other (popular) queries of similar type (e.g., landmark queries). Despite being a seemingly counter-intuitive choice, the inclusion of positive and negative examples from other queries of the same type, increases the generalization ability of the classifier (Subsection 5.2) because it helps capture an application specific notion of relevance/irrelevance (e.g., out-of-focus or human-in-focus images are irrelevant and drawings are relevant in the RDSI task scenario).

3.3.3 A Multimodal Ensemble Classifier

When relevance annotations are used, a further advantage over unsupervised approaches is that the combination of multiple features can be incorporated into the learning process. Here, we present Multimodal Stacking (MMS), an ensemble classification scheme that learns how to combine the outputs of multiple, independently trained classifiers (each one using a different type of features) in order to make a better relevance prediction. The algorithm is inspired from stacked generalization [16], a method for the fusion of heterogeneous classifiers, widely known as stacking. The training of MMS consists of the following steps: Initially, k independent probabilistic classifiers $h_{q_i} : X_i \rightarrow [0, 1], i = \{1, \ldots, k\}$ are built, one for each multi-dimensional feature representation $X_i \in R^{n_i}, n_i > 1$. Each of these single-modality classifiers is then used to predict the classes of all training examples and their predictions are gathered to form a meta training set $D'_q = \{(x'_1, y_1), \ldots, (x'_m, y_m)\}$, where the input vectors $x'_i = [h_{q_1}(x_1), \ldots, h_{q_k}(x_k)]$ consist of the outputs of the single-modality classifiers. This meta training set is used to train a meta classifier $h'_q : X' \rightarrow [0, 1]$, where $X' \in R^k$ is the meta input space and its output is the probability that the image is relevant. At prediction time, the single-modality classifiers are first applied to classify the unknown instance and their outputs are used to form a meta instance that is fed to the meta classifier which makes the final prediction. Compared to early fusion approaches, MMS has the advantage that features of different dimensionalities can be easily combined since all models contribute one-dimensional features to the meta classifier. Furthermore, additional features can be easily incorporated into the final model by directly augmenting the input space of the meta classifier.

3.4 Diversity

Assuming a ranking $im_{r1}, \ldots, im_{rK}$ of the images in S, Deselaers et al. [7] define diversity as

$$D(S) = \sum_{i=1}^{K} \frac{1}{i} \sum_{j=1}^{i} d(im_{ri}, im_{rj}), \quad (3)$$

where $d(im_{ri}, im_{rj})$ is the dissimilarity between the images ranked at positions i and j. Thus, high diversity scores are given to image sets with a high average dissimilarity. We notice that with this definition of diversity, an image set that contains pairs of highly similar (and therefore not diverse) images is allowed to receive a high diversity score if the average dissimilarity is high. This results in a direct negative impact on diversification measures such as CR@K. Therefore, we adopt the following stricter definition:

$$D(S) = \min_{im_i, im_j \in S, i \neq j} d(im_i, im_j), \quad (4)$$

where the diversity of a set S is defined as the dissimilarity between the most similar pair of images in S.

3.5 Optimization

An exhaustive optimization of U has high complexity as it would require computing the utility of all $\frac{N!}{K!(N-K)!}$ K-subsets of I. The computational cost becomes prohibitive even if N is small (e.g., $N \approx 300$) and one is interested in identifying $K = 20$-sized MMR-optimal subsets. Therefore, we apply a greedy, iterative optimization algorithm that was also used in [3], with appropriate changes to reflect our new definitions for relevance and diversity. This algorithm starts with an empty set S and sequentially expands it by adding at each step $J = 1, \ldots, K$ the image im^* that scores highest (among the unselected images), to the following incremental utility function:

$$U(im^*|q) = w \cdot h_q(im^*) + (1-w) \cdot \min_{im_j \in S^{J-1}} d(im^*, im_j), \quad (5)$$

where S^{J-1} represents S at step $J - 1$. In the first step, the diversity term of Equation 5 is undefined (S is empty) and thus the image with the highest relevance score is selected.

4. EXPERIMENTAL SETUP

4.1 Retrieving Diverse Social Images Task

During the task, participants were provided with a reference annotated development set of 30 queries - to build

Table 1: Dataset statistics: number of queries (#q), avg. number of relevant/irrelevant images (#r/#i), avg. number of clusters (#c), F1@20 of Flickr ranking (#fp).

Set	#q	#r	#i	#c	#fp
Dev	30	208.5	88.8	23.2	0.477
Test	123	199.9	96.4	22.6	0.470

their approaches - as well as a test set of 123 queries - upon which they were evaluated - of which the ground truth was disclosed only after the end of the task. Ground truth consisted of relevance and diversity annotations provided by experts for all images of each POI. Specifically, each image was first labelled as either relevant or irrelevant and then visually similar relevant images were grouped together into clusters. Performance on each query was assessed using the F1@20 metric that is equal to the harmonic mean of CR@20 and P@20 (the percentage of relevant images in the top 20). Table 4.1 provides some key statistics of the RDSI 2014 dataset. In Section 5.4 we also apply our method on the RDSI 2013 task that is structured similarly to RDSI 2014. The main difference is that RDSI 2013 uses CR@10 as the main evaluation metric. Further details about RDSI 2013 can be found at the corresponding overview paper [9].

A note on ground truth: Although the relevance annotations provided in the RDSI task come from expert annotators, the same type of ground truth could be acquired (for popular queries) from implicit user feedback as described in Subsection 3.3.2. Also, note that relevance annotated images from only 30 queries are used when building the model that estimates the relevance of the images of each test query. In addition to these images, we use the reference Wikipedia page and images provided for each POI as query-specific positive examples. As we explained in Subsection 3.3.2, positive examples can be easily acquired even for rare queries.

4.2 Features

The different features used to represent the dataset are grouped in three categories: a) visual - computed directly from the image content, b) textual - computed from textual annotations, and c) meta - computed from the metadata associated with the images. For all types of multi-dimensional features unit length normalization is applied and cosine similarity/distance is used for relevance/diversity computations.

Visual: After initial experiments with the features made available by the task organizers [9], we extracted the following state-of-the-art features that lead to significantly better performance:

VLAD: $d = 24,576$-dimensional VLAD+CSURF vectors [13] are computed using a 128-dimensional visual vocabulary and then projected to d' dimensions with PCA and whitening. Using $d' = 128$ leads to near-optimal results for both relevance and diversity.

CNN: Convolutional neural network features adapted for the landmark retrieval domain. These features were computed using the Caffe framework [12], with the reference model architecture but using images of 1,000 landmarks instead of ImageNet classes. We collected approximately 1,200 images for each landmark and fed them directly to Caffe for training after preliminary experiments that validated the resilience of the CNN architecture to noisy images. This change of training classes was inspired by recent domain adaptation work presented in [2] that demonstrated higher effectiveness in feature transfer when the training classes are conceptually close to the datasets used in experiments. The outputs of the *fc7* layer, which includes 4,096 dimensions, constitute the initial features. Similarly to *VLAD*, the dimensionality of *CNN* was reduced to $d' = 128$ with PCA, a value which gives near-optimal results.

Textual: To generate textual features we first transformed each query and each Flickr image into a text document. For queries, we used a parsed version of the corresponding Wikipedia page and for Flickr images we used a concatenation of the words in their titles, descriptions and tags. Bag-of-words features (*BOW*) were then computed for each document using the 10K most frequent terms of the collection as the dictionary and term frequencies as term weights. We found that by repeating the terms in the image titles and descriptions two and three times respectively to increase their contribution in the similarity compared to the terms in the tags that are usually more noisy, lead to increased performance.

Meta: The following one-dimensional features were computed from the textual metadata and used as additional features in the meta input space of the MMS algorithm: distance from the POI, Flickr rank, number of views.

5. EXPERIMENTS

5.1 Relevance Scoring Impact on Quality

In this experiment we want to study the relationship between the quality of the scores provided by the relevance scoring component and the diversification performance as measured by F1@20. A natural way to characterize the quality of relevance scoring is to measure the ability of the scoring function (either supervised or unsupervised) to assign higher relevance scores to relevant images than irrelevant ones. A suitable measure that is commonly used to asses the performance of probabilistic classifiers (as well as scoring functions that assign higher scores to instances that are considered more representative of the class) is the area under ROC curve (AUC). AUC is equal to the probability that a classifier will rank a randomly chosen positive instance higher than a randomly chosen negative. Thus, an AUC score of 0.5 corresponds to a random classifier and an AUC score equal to 1 corresponds to a perfect classifier that ranks all positives examples higher than negative.

Classifiers of various AUC scores are generated as follows: A positive $r_p = [p_{low}, 1], p_{low} \geq 0$ and a negative $r_n = [0, n_{high}], n_{high} \leq 1$ relevance score range are defined and each positive/negative example is assigned a random score, drawn uniformly from the corresponding range. When $p_{low} > n_{high}$ we have a perfect class separation and AUC equals to 1, while for $p_{low} \leq n_{high}$ classifiers of lower AUC scores can be generated. Using the above process we generated classifiers with average (across all test queries) AUC scores of $\{0.5, 0.6, \ldots, 1.0\}$. Figure 3 shows the average (across all test queries) F1@20 performance when each of the above classifiers is plugged into the MMR algorithm in combination with VLAD (red line), CNN (blue line) and BOW (green line) features for diversity computation. In all cases, we fix $w = 0.5$. We observe that with all types of diversification features, F1@20 shows a strong positive correlation with AUC, suggesting that improving the relevance scoring quality is important for good diversification.

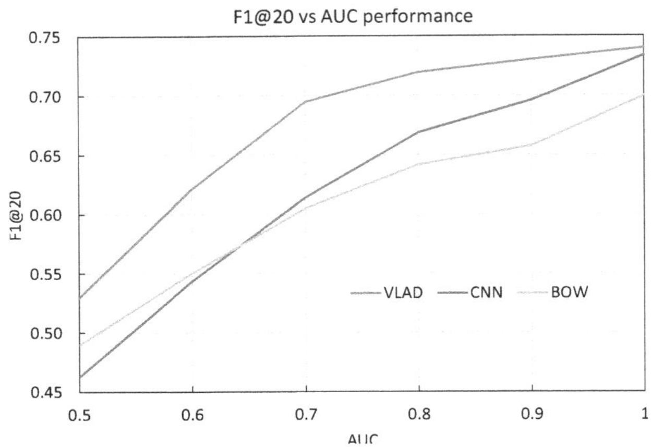

Figure 3: F1@20 vs AUC.

5.2 Unsupervised vs Supervised Relevance

In this section we compare the unsupervised variant of the MMR method [7] (*uMMR*), with the proposed supervised variant, named *sMMR*. In both cases, we use the definition of diversity presented in Equation 4 as it systematically led to better results. We show experiments when either a visual (VLAD)[3] or a textual (BOW) representation is used for both relevance and diversity to highlight potential differences between visual and textual features.

When a visual representation is used, the unsupervised definition of relevance needs to be adapted because the RDSI benchmark provides up to five (instead of 1) example images per query. Rather than arbitrarily choosing one of the available images, we use two alternative definitions of relevance that lead to better results. Given a composite query $q = \{im_{q1}, \ldots, im_{qm}\}$, uMMR$_{avg}$ defines the relevance of each image im_i as the average similarity $R(im_i|q) = \frac{1}{m}\sum_{im_{qi}\in q} s(im_i, im_{qi})$ and uMMR$_{max}$ defines relevance as the maximum similarity $R(im_i|q) = \max_{im_{qi}\in q} s(im_i, im_{qi})$. The two variants coincide when $m = 1$. sMMR can be instantiated with any classification algorithm. We choose L2-regularized Logistic Regression (the LibLinear implementation of [8]) as it provided a good trade-off between efficiency and accuracy compared to other state-of-the-art classifiers in preliminary experiments. To select the regularization parameter c, we perform leave-one(-query)-out cross-validation on the development set and choose the value $c \in \{10^{-2}, 10^{-1}, \ldots, 10^{2}\}$ that gives the best average AUC. Depending on how the training set is composed for each query, three different variants of the sMMR method are created:

sMMR$_q$: The training set contains only the Wikipedia images or the textual representation of the Wikipedia page. Since these are positive examples, we add few randomly chosen Flickr images from other queries as negative examples. sMMR$_q$ represents the case where only few query-specific positive examples are available and attempts to capture the query-specific notion of relevance.

sMMR$_a$: The training set is composed of Flickr images from other queries as positive and negative examples. This variant represents the case where query-specific training examples are unavailable and we can only use positive and negative training examples from other queries, for which sufficient user feedback is available. sMMR$_a$ attempts to capture the application-specific notion of relevance.

sMMR$_{aq}$: The training set is composed of Flickr images from other queries as positive and negative examples as well as the Wikipedia page/images as positive examples. This variant represents the case where few query-specific positive examples are combined with positive and negative examples from other queries for which an adequate amount of user feedback is available. We found that simply combining the few query-specific positive examples with a significantly larger number of application-specific positive examples generates very similar models with the sMMR$_a$ variant. Therefore, we experimented with assigning higher weights to the query-specific positive examples in order to increase their contribution to the formation of the classification boundary. sMMR$_{aq}$ attempts to capture both the query and the application-specific notion of relevance.

[3]Similar results were obtained with CNN features.

Table 2: AUC and F1@20 performance (averaged over test set queries) of the uMMR and sMMR variants using visual and textual features.

	VLAD		BOW	
Method	AUC	F1@20	AUC	F1@20
uMMR$_{avg}$	0.622	0.536	0.660	0.503
uMMR$_{max}$	0.613	0.528	0.660	0.503
sMMR$_q$	0.624	0.535	0.666	0.553
sMMR$_a$	0.664	0.536	0.571	0.481
sMMR$_{aq\times1}$	0.665	0.536	0.575	0.487
sMMR$_{aq\times10}$	0.669	0.532	0.589	0.514
sMMR$_{aq\times100}$	0.690	0.545	0.640	0.541
sMMR$_{aq\times1000}$	**0.693**	**0.561**	**0.670**	**0.555**

Table 2 presents the test set AUC and F1@20 scores of the variants of uMMR and sMMR presented above. AUC is calculated on the relevance rankings produced by each variant (without diversification). The reported F1@20 scores correspond to using a value for $w \in \{0.0, 0.1, \ldots, 1.0\}$ that was tuned to optimize F1@20 on the development set.

When VLAD features are used, we observe that all sMMR variants outperform the uMMR variants in terms of AUC. Among the uMMR variants uMMR$_{avg}$ obtains better AUC than uMMR$_{max}$. Interestingly, despite the absence of any query-specific relevance information, the sMMR$_a$ variant obtains a significantly better AUC than both uMMR$_{avg}$ and sMMR$_q$, suggesting that capturing an application-specific notion of relevance is important in relevance scoring using visual features. As expected, when the query and application-specific relevance information are combined in the sMMR$_{aq}$ variant, AUC performance improves even further, especially when a large weight is assigned to query-specific examples. AUC performance increases from 0.665 when equal weight is given to the query-specific examples (sMMR$_{aq\times1}$) to 0.693 when a 1000 times higher weight is given (sMMR$_{aq\times1000}$). With respect to F1@20, although a strong correlation with AUC is still observed, there are cases where a better AUC does not necessarily lead to better F1@20. This is attributed to a poor tuning of the w parameter as a result of using a small amount of training queries. Nevertheless, we notice that sMMR$_{aq\times1000}$, the best performing variant in terms of AUC, also obtains the best F1@20 score (0.561) that is about 5% better than the 0.536 score obtained by uMMR$_{avg}$.

When textual features are used, the uMMR method (the two variants coincide in this case) is only slightly outperformed by $sMMR_q$ and $sMMR_{aq \times 1000}$ in terms of AUC. Contrarily to when visual features are used, $sMMR_a$ obtains a significantly lower AUC compared to both uMMR and the sMMR variants that use query-specific information. This suggests that application-specific information is not sufficient to produce a good relevance scoring when this scoring is based only on the textual modality. Nevertheless, the relevance scoring produced by $sMMR_a$ is better than random scoring (AUC=0.5) and the $sMMR_{aq \times 1000}$ variant that combines query and application-specific information is again the best performer. With respect to F1@20, we observe that, with the exception of the $sMMR_a$ and $sMMR_{aq \times 1}$ variants, all other variants produce better F1@20 scores than uMMR. When $sMMR_{aq \times 1000}$ is used, F1@20 increases from 0.503 to 0.555, a 10% improvement.

To test whether there is statistical significance in the observed differences in F1@20 between uMMR and sMMR we performed the Wilcoxon signed-ranks test between their best performing variants separately for each feature. The null hypothesis is rejected in all cases (VLAD, CNN and BOW) with a $p \leq 0.01$ confirming the superiority of sMMR.

5.3 Multimodal Fusion

So far, we compared instantiations of the uMMR and sMMR methods that used only a single type of features for relevance scoring. In this section, we want to evaluate the performance of the two methods when more features are combined to assign relevance scores.

In particular, to create a multi-feature instantiation of the uMMR method given k types of features, we compute the relevance of each image to the query as $R(im|q) = \frac{1}{k}\sum_{i=1}^{k} R_i(im|q)$, where $R_i(im|q)$ is computed according to equation 2. That is, unsupervised relevance scores are computed independently for each feature and then averaged to produce an overall relevance score. In the case of composite queries, the $uMMR_{avg}$ variant is used as it gave slightly better results than $uMMR_{max}$ in Subsection 5.2. The resulting method is called *uMMR-M*.

To combine multiple features in sMMR, we use the MMS method presented in Subsection 3.3.3. More precisely, the $sMMR_{aq \times 1000}$ configuration is used for the single-modality models since it was found superior to other configurations in Subsection 5.2. L2-regularized Logistic Regression is used as classification algorithm for both the single-modality models and the meta model and the regularization parameter is tuned as described in Subsection 5.2 but searching in a wider range of values ($c \in \{10^{-4}, 10^{-3}, \ldots, 10^{-4}\}$) for the meta model. The resulting method is called *sMMR-MMS*.

Table 3 presents the AUC and F1@20 scores obtained with uMMR-M and sMMR-MMS using pairs of the three multi-dimensional features presented in Subsection 4.2 (rows 4-6). We also present results for sMMR-MMS when the three one-dimensional features (meta) presented in Subsection 4.2 are used within the MMS algorithm as described in Subsection 3.3.3 (rows 7-9). Results using each of the three features alone for both relevance and diversity are also reported to facilitate comparison (rows 1-3). AUC scores are calculated on the relevance rankings produced by each variant and the reported F1@20 scores correspond to using a value for $w \in \{0.0, 0.1, \ldots, 1.0\}$ that was tuned to optimize F1@20 on the development set. In all multi-feature instantiations,

Table 3: AUC and F1@20 performance (averaged over test set queries) of uMMR-M and sMMR-MMS using various combinations of features.

Feature(s)	AUC	F1@20	AUC	F1@20
	$uMMR_{avg}$		$sMMR_{aq \times 1000}$	
VLAD	0.622	0.536	*0.693*	*0.561*
CNN	0.733	0.530	***0.808***	***0.572***
BOW	0.660	0.503	*0.670*	*0.555*
	uMMR-M		sMMR-MMS	
VLAD+CNN	0.729	0.580	*0.806*	*0.594*
VLAD+BOW	0.697	*0.586*	*0.727*	0.578
CNN+BOW	0.765	0.588	***0.814***	***0.608***
VLAD+CNN+meta	N/A	N/A	**0.828**	0.619
VLAD+BOW+meta	N/A	N/A	0.740	0.590
CNN+BOW+meta	N/A	N/A	0.827	**0.631**

VLAD features were used for diversification as they gave the best F1@20 scores when tested with artificial classifiers of various AUC performances in Subsection 5.1.

Looking at the results obtained with single-modality instantiations we observe that the AUC performance obtained with CNN features is significantly better compared to VLAD and BOW when either $uMMR_{avg}$ or $sMMR_{aq \times 1000}$ is used for relevance scoring. This superiority of CNN for relevance scoring explains also the better F1@20 performance obtained with CNN features despite the fact that VLAD were found better for diversity scoring in Section 5.1.

With respect to two-feature instantiations we observe that sMMR-MMS obtains better AUC scores than uMMR-M in all cases. The situation is similar with respect to F1@20 where uMMR-M obtains better F1@20 only in one case (VLAD+BOW). We also observe that with either uMMR-M or sMMR-MMS, both AUC and F1@20 are always better than using any of the two features alone with the exception of the VLAD+CNN combination where slightly worse performance is obtained in terms of AUC compared to using the CNN features alone. This can be attributed to the facts that a) CNN and VLAD are both visual representations and thus have a small degree of complementarity and b) CNN significantly outperforms VLAD in terms of AUC. Using the CNN+BOW feature combination and the sMMR-MMS method, a 0.631 F1@20 score is obtained that is about 6% better than the F1@20 obtained by the best single-modality instantiation. To test whether there is statistical significance in the observed differences in F1@20 between uMMR-M and sMMR-MMS we performed the Wilcoxon signed rank test between their best two-feature instantiations (CNN+BOW). The null hypothesis is rejected with a $p \leq 0.01$.

Finally, we see that when the meta features are used, both AUC and F1@20 improve further. In particular, the CNN+BOW+meta combination obtains the highest F1@20 followed by VLAD+CNN+meta and VLAD+BOW+meta.

Time efficiency: Compared to uMMR, sMMR has the additional computational cost of training the relevance detection models. However, these models will typically be trained offline. During the online reranking phase, uMMR has to compute similarity scores between the query image and the top-N results of a search engine while sMMR has to classify each of the top-N images. When a linear model is used (as done here), the computational cost is similar.

Table 4: Comparison to best RDSI task results.

Method	2013 (CR@10)	2014 (F1@20)
Best in RDSI	0.440 [11]	0.597 [6]
This paper	**0.473** +7.5%	**0.631** + 5.7%

Using one core of an i5 2.4 GHz processor, the training of a $\text{sMMR}_{aq\times1000}$ model on 8919 images took ~0.5 sec with VLAD and CNN and ~9 sec with BOW features while using such a model to predict the relevance score of a single image took ~0.01 ms and ~0.3 ms respectively. A sMMR-MMS model combining the predictions of any two such models took an additional time of 200 ms to train and ~0.007 ms to make a prediction. Reranking 300 images to select a 20-sized subset with the greedy algorithm of Subsection 3.5 using VLAD features for diversity took ~50 ms.

5.4 Comparison to Best RDSI Results

Table 4 compares the test performance of our best diversification method, sMMR-MMS, with that of the best performing systems of the MediaEval 2013 and 2014 RDSI tasks. As in previous experiments, the c parameter of the logistic regression models used in the MMS algorithm was tuned to optimize AUC on the development set. Using this procedure, we built MMS relevance scoring models with the feature combinations presented above and then applied diversification using VLAD. For each sMMR-MMS instantiation, we evaluated its performance on the development set using values for $w \in \{0.0, 0.05, \dots, 1.0\}$ and selected the instantiation that obtained the maximum F1@20 score and the corresponding w value, and applied it on the test set. For the RDSI 2013 task, CR@10 was used instead of F1@20 for model selection since it was the primary evaluation measure of this benchmark. In both cases, the best results were obtained using the CNN+BOW+meta combination. As shown in Table 4, our method outperforms the best systems of RDSI 2013 and 2014 by 7.5% and 5.7% respectively.

6. CONCLUSIONS - FUTURE WORK

We introduced a supervised version of the popular MMR diversification algorithm and showed that using few query-specific, positive relevance annotations combined with extra-query but application-specific, positive and negative relevance annotations leads to significant performance improvements of relevance scoring in terms of AUC. Furthermore, we captured the strong relationship between the AUC score and a common diversification measure (F1@K) within the MMR framework and showed that improved relevance results in better diversification. Finally, we presented a novel multi-modal ensemble classifier (MMS) and showed that it effectively combines different types of multi- and one-dimensional features. The resulting diversification method significantly outperformed competing methods in two benchmarks.

Despite its computational efficiency, the greedy maximization algorithm that we used might fail to find the global optimum of the utility function in Equation 1. To deal with this problem, [7] developed dynamic programming algorithms that consider many alternative paths simultaneously, thus increasing the chance of finding an optimal solution. Although these variants were not considered here, they are directly applicable to our method and could further improve its performance. In this paper, we focused on the relevance scoring component of the MMR method, however, the quality of diversity scoring plays an equally important role. In the future, we want to investigate supervised techniques for improving the quality of diversity scoring and a principled way of combining multiple features to compute diversity scores. Application-wise, we would like to evaluate our method in a privacy-aware retrieval setting.

7. ACKNOWLEDGMENTS

This work is supported by the USEMP FP7 project, partially funded by the EC under contract number 611596.

8. REFERENCES

[1] T. Arni, P. Clough, M. Sanderson, and M. Grubinger. Overview of the imageclefphoto 2008 photographic retrieval task. In *Evaluating Systems for Multilingual and Multimodal Information Access*, pages 500–511. 2009.

[2] A. Babenko, A. Slesarev, A. Chigorin, and V. Lempitsky. Neural codes for image retrieval. In *ECCV*, 2014.

[3] J. Carbonell and J. Goldstein. The use of mmr, diversity-based reranking for reordering documents and producing summaries. In *SIGIR*, pages 335–336, 1998.

[4] H. Chen and D. R. Karger. Less is more: probabilistic models for retrieving fewer relevant documents. In *SIGIR*, pages 429–436, 2006.

[5] D. Corney, C. Martin, A. Göker, E. Spyromitros-Xioufis, S. Papadopoulos, Y. Kompatsiaris, L. Aiello, and B. Thomee. Socialsensor: Finding diverse images at mediaeval 2013. In *MediaEval*, 2013.

[6] D.-T. Dang-Nguyen, L. Piras, G. Giacinto, G. Boato, and F. De Natale. Retrieval of diverse images by pre-filtering and hierarchical clustering. In *MediaEval*, 2014.

[7] T. Deselaers, T. Gass, P. Dreuw, and H. Ney. Jointly optimising relevance and diversity in image retrieval. In *ACM CIVR '09*, New York, USA, 2009.

[8] R.-E. Fan, K.-W. Chang, C.-J. Hsieh, X.-R. Wang, and C.-J. Lin. LIBLINEAR: A library for large linear classification. *Journal of Machine Learning Research*, 9:1871–1874, 2008.

[9] B. Ionescu, M. Menéndez, H. Müller, and A. Popescu. Retrieving diverse social images at MediaEval 2013: Objectives, dataset and evaluation. In *MediaEval*, 2013.

[10] B. Ionescu, A. Popescu, M. Lupu, A. Gînsca, and H. Müller. Retrieving diverse social images at MediaEval 2014: Challenge, dataset and evaluation. In *MediaEval*, 2014.

[11] N. Jain, J. Hare, S. Samangooei, J. Preston, J. Davies, D. Dupplaw, and P. H. Lewis. Experiments in diversifying flickr result sets. In *MediaEval*, 2013.

[12] Y. Jia, E. Shelhamer, J. Donahue, S. Karayev, J. Long, R. Girshick, S. Guadarrama, and T. Darrell. Caffe: Convolutional architecture for fast feature embedding. *arXiv preprint arXiv:1408.5093*, 2014.

[13] E. Spyromitros-Xioufis, S. Papadopoulos, I. Kompatsiaris, G. Tsoumakas, and I. Vlahavas. A comprehensive study over vlad and product quantization in large-scale image retrieval. *IEEE Transactions on Multimedia*, 2014.

[14] E. Spyromitros-Xioufis, S. Papadopoulos, Y. Kompatsiaris, and I. Vlahavas. Socialsensor: Finding diverse images at mediaeval 2014. In *MediaEval*, 2014.

[15] R. H. van Leuken, L. Garcia, X. Olivares, and R. van Zwol. Visual diversification of image search results. In *WWW*, pages 341–350, 2009.

[16] D. H. Wolpert. Stacked generalization. *Neural networks*, 5(2):241–259, 1992.

[17] C. X. Zhai, W. W. Cohen, and J. Lafferty. Beyond independent relevance: methods and evaluation metrics for subtopic retrieval. In *SIGIR*, pages 10–17, 2003.

Unsupervised Distance Learning by Rank Correlation Measures for Image Retrieval

César Yugo Okada[1], Daniel Carlos Guimarães Pedronette[1], Ricardo da S. Torres[2]
[1]Dept. of Statistic, Applied Math. and Computing, Universidade Estadual Paulista (UNESP), Rio Claro, Brazil
[2]RECOD Lab, Institute of Computing, University of Campinas (UNICAMP), Campinas, Brazil
okada@rc.unesp.br, daniel@rc.unesp.br, rtorres@ic.unicamp.br

ABSTRACT

Ranking accurately collection images is the main objective of Content-based Image Retrieval (CBIR) systems. In fact, the set of images ranked at the first positions generally defines the effectiveness of provided search services, i.e., they are used for assessing automatically the quality of search systems as this set usually contains the collection images that are of interest. Recently, the use of ranking information (e.g., rank correlation) has been used in different research initiatives with the objective of improving the effectiveness of image retrieval tasks. This paper presents a broad rank correlation analysis for unsupervised distance learning on image retrieval tasks. Various well-known rank correlation measures are considered and two new measures are proposed. Several experiments were conducted considering various image datasets involving shape, color, and texture descriptors. Experimental results demonstrate that ranking information can be exploited for distance learning tasks successfully. Evaluated approaches yield better results in terms of effectiveness than various state-of-the-art algorithms.

Categories and Subject Descriptors

H.3.3 [**Information Search and Retrieval**]: Search process

General Terms

Experimentation, Performance

Keywords

content-based image retrieval; rank correlation; measures

1. INTRODUCTION

The increasing availability of large image collections has demanded the development of novel search and indexing methods. In this scenario, Content-Based Image Retrieval (CBIR) systems have emerged as promising approaches, as they are able of considering the image visual content.

ICMR'15, June 23–26, 2015, Shanghai, China.

DOI: http://dx.doi.org/10.1145/2671188.2749335.

Typically, the implementation of a content-based image retrieval system relies on the definition of three important concepts in the retrieval pipeline [7]: (*i*) image representation, (*ii*) image similarity measure, and (*iii*) result refinement by post-processing methods. The first two steps were exploited for decades and several visual features and distance measures have been proposed for image retrieval tasks (based on shape, color, and texture properties).

Recently, post-processing methods have attracted a lot of attention, mainly due to the significant effectiveness gains obtained [27, 32, 35]. Different approaches have been employed, as diffusion process [35], graphs [32], and clustering [26]. More recently, ranking approaches have been proposed, presenting important advantages, such as simplicity, low-computational efforts, and total independence of distance measures [27]. Ranking scores and ranking correlation measures have been used as the basis of various of these methods.

This paper discusses methods for improving the effectiveness of image retrieval results based on rank correlation measures. Two novel rank correlation measures are proposed for unsupervised distance learning procedures on image retrieval tasks. The paper also presents an extended version of the recently proposed RL-Sim (*Ranked Lists Similarities*) algorithm [27] that exploits the proposed measures. In summary, the contributions of this paper are threefold: (*i*) presentation of the RL-Sim* Algorithm, which uses information from both rank correlation measures and top-k lists overlap for improving the effectiveness of distance measures; (*ii*) the evaluation of six different rank correlation measures for the proposed algorithm; and (*iii*) the proposal of two novel rank correlation measures for unsupervised distance learning.

A large experimental evaluation was conducted, considering different datasets and image descriptors. Experiments were conducted on four image datasets considering 16 different visual descriptors (shape, color, texture, and local descriptors). Other aspects of the proposed approach were also considered, such as the analysis of the impact of parameters and the relationship among the considered rank correlation measures.

The experimental evaluation demonstrates that the effectiveness performance of the proposed RL-Sim* Algorithm is superior to the original algorithm. Experimental results also show that the proposed rank correlation measures achieved significant effectiveness gains in several image retrieval tasks. The proposed RL-Sim* Algorithm is also evaluated in comparison with several state-of-the-art approaches considering a shape dataset commonly used as benchmarking. The proposed unsupervised learning approach yields better results in terms of effectiveness performance than various methods recently proposed in the literature.

The paper is organized as follows: Section 2 discusses related work and Section 3 presents the problem formulation. Section 4 briefly describes the original RL-Sim Algorithm, while Section 5 presents the proposed RL-Sim* Algorithm. In Section 6, we describe the evaluated rank correlation measures and present two novel measures. Section 6 discusses our approach for measure combination. Section 7 presents and discusses conducted experiments and, finally, Section 8 discusses conclusions and presents future work.

2. RELATED WORK

Rank correlation measures have been used in information retrieval applications with the aim of computing similarities or distances between rankings produced by different systems. Generally, these measures are based on simple ranking functions, and provide information about the similarity among different systems used to compute the rankings. Many measures used to compare rankings are based on statistical associations of objects in different ranked lists, such as Kendall τ and Spearman's Footrule [10].

Although various measures have been used along decades, the research field remains active and, even recently, novel measures continue being proposed. The developing of new measures is mainly based on statistical or probabilistic models. The Rank Biased Overlap [33] (RBO) measure, for example, was recently proposed based on a model which compares the overlap of two ranked lists at different increasing depths. The RBO [33] measure consists in a measure adapted to information retrieval, assigning to the top-k objects high weights. In a different venue, some studies are proposing new measures that use classical methods as part of the process, as SKT [14] measure that uses Kendall τ.

More recently, rank correlation measures have been used [7, 27] to compare ranked results, aiming at increasing the effectiveness of CBIR systems. Although several approaches were employed in post-processing methods (e.g., graph transduction [34], diffusion process [35], affinity learning [36]), the use of ranking information presents significant advantages and have attracted a lot of research interest.

A ranking consistency model is proposed in [7], using a result refinement procedure that re-ranks images based on an improved image similarity measure. Basically, the rank-consistency information indicates that query images are likely to contain similar content. Rank correlation analysis is also employed for metric learning in content-based medical image retrieval applications [14].

The RL-Sim Algorithm [27] is an unsupervised distance learning method recently proposed that considers the similarity between ranked lists for computing a more effective distance measure. Its main motivation relies on the conjecture that ranked lists encode contextual information in CBIR systems, providing not only a pairwise relation as traditional distance measures, but a more global contextual measure. In addition, the method presents important features such as scalability, and low-computational complexity [24].

This paper presents the RL-Sim* Algorithm, a new post-processing method, which extends the original algorithm by exploiting more contextual information. The proposed method is based on information regarding the overlap between ranked lists combined with rank correlation measures. In addition, two novel rank correlation measures are proposed aiming at characterizing distance learning procedures on image retrieval tasks.

3. PROBLEM DEFINITION

A formal definition of the image retrieval model considered is presented in this section. Let $\mathcal{C}=\{img_1, img_2, \ldots, img_n\}$ be an image collection. Let $n = |\mathcal{C}|$ be the size of the collection $\mathcal{C}$. Let $\mathcal{D}$ be an image descriptor, which can be defined [8] as a tuple (ϵ, ρ), where ϵ: $\hat{I} \rightarrow \mathbb{R}^n$ is a function, which extracts a feature vector $v_{\hat{I}}$ from an image $\hat{I}$; and ρ: $\mathbb{R}^n \times \mathbb{R}^n \rightarrow \mathbb{R}$ is a distance function that computes the distance between two images according to the distance between their corresponding feature vectors, i.e., the distance distance between two images img_i and img_j is given by the value of $\rho(\epsilon(img_i), \epsilon(img_j))$. The notation $\rho(i,j)$ is used along the paper for readability purposes.

The distance $\rho(i,j)$ among all images img_i, $img_j \in \mathcal{C}$ can be computed to obtain a squared $n \times n$ distance matrix A, such that $A_{ij} = \rho(i,j)$. Also based on the distance function ρ, a ranked list τ_q can be computed in response to a query image img_q. The ranked list τ_q=(img_1, img_2, ..., img_n) can be defined as a permutation of the collection $\mathcal{C}$. A permutation τ_q is a bijection from the set $\mathcal{C}$ onto the set $[N] = \{1, 2, \ldots, n\}$. For a permutation τ_q, we interpret $\tau_q(i)$ as the position (or rank) of image img_i in the ranked list τ_q. We can say that, if img_i is ranked before img_j in the ranked list of img_q, that is, $\tau_q(i) < \tau_q(j)$, then $\rho(q,i) \leq \rho(q,j)$. We also can take every image $img_i \in \mathcal{C}$ as a query image img_q, in order to obtain a set $\mathcal{R} = \{\tau_1, \tau_2, \ldots, \tau_n\}$ of ranked lists for each image of the collection $\mathcal{C}$.

The objective of the unsupervised learning algorithm consists in redefining the initial distance ρ by computing a more effective distance function. The general objective is to improve the effectiveness of distances among images by using the contextual information encoded in the ranked lists defined by the set $\mathcal{R}$. More formally, we can define the algorithm as a function f_r:

$$\hat{A} = f_r(\mathcal{R}, A). \tag{1}$$

A new distance matrix $\hat{A}$ can be computed by the function f_r, which takes as input the set of ranked lists $\mathcal{R}$.

4. RL-SIM ALGORITHM

The RL-Sim Algorithm [27] is a recently proposed unsupervised distance learning method that improves the effectiveness of image retrieval tasks though an iterative re-ranking scheme. The RL-Sim Algorithm [27] exploits contextual information encoded in the similarity between ranked lists with the objective of improving the effectiveness of CBIR descriptors. Ranked lists represent a relevant source of information, since ranked lists establish a relationship among a set a images contained in ranked lists, instead of only between pairs of images.

In general, if two images are similar, their ranked lists should be similar as well. Therefore, the main objective of the algorithm is to improve the effectiveness of distance measures by computing the similarity between the ranked lists. The modeling of contextual information considering only the similarity between ranked lists represents an advantage of this approach strategy. Instead of using the distance information, the algorithm requires only the ranking information.

Given an initial set of ranked lists, an iterative approach is used. Let the superscript $^{(t)}$ denote the current iteration, a new and more effective set of ranked lists $\mathcal{R}^{(t+1)}$ is computed by taking into account distances among ranked lists. Next, $\mathcal{R}^{(t+1)}$ is used for the next execution of our re-ranking algorithm and so on. These steps are repeated along iterations aiming to improve the effectiveness incrementally. After a number T of iterations a definitive re-ranking is performed. In the following, this procedure is detailed.

Ranking Contextual Distance Measure

In this section, we briefly describe the RL-Sim Algorithm [27] by using a ranking contextual distance measure based on similarity/dissimilarity of ranked lists. The ranking contextual distance measure is based on the conjecture that top-ranked images are similar to each other and their ranked lists contain many images in common [27]. In this scenario, one straightforward strategy for computing the similarity between images relies on the use of rank correlation measures.

A ranking contextual distance measure is iteratively learned in a unsupervised setting, by incorporating the contextual information provided by rank correlation measures. Let us consider the neighborhood set $\mathcal{N}(i,k)$ of an image img_i, which contains the k most similar images to img_i, according to a given distance (say ρ defined by the image descriptor). The set $\mathcal{N}(i,k)$ can be obtained by the well-known k-Nearest Neighbor approach, where the cardinality of the set is denoted by $\mid \mathcal{N}(i,k) \mid = k$.

Let $d(\tau_i, \tau_j, k)$ denote a rank correlation measure between ranked lists τ_i and τ_j, considering their top-k positions given by the sets $\mathcal{N}(i)$ and $\mathcal{N}(j)$ and defined in the interval $[0,1]$. A non-iterative contextual distance measure $\rho_c(img_i, img_j)$ based on the comparison of ranked lists τ_i, τ_j can be defined as follows:

$$\rho_c(img_i, img_j) = d(\tau_i, \tau_j, k) \tag{2}$$

Based on the conjecture that the contextual distance measure ρ_c represents a more effective distance between images [27], the distance among all images in a collection can be recomputed based on this measure. Therefore, a new set of ranked lists can be obtained, such that the contextual distance can also be recomputed and the process can be repeated in an iterative way. Let $^{(t)}$ denote the current iteration and let $\tau_i^{(t)}$ denote the ranked list at iteration t. Let $\rho_c^{(0)}$ be the contextual distance at first iteration, which is equal to the distance defined by the image descriptor, such that $\rho_c^{(0)}(img_i, img_j) = \rho(img_i, img_j)$ for all images $img_i, img_j \in \mathcal{C}$. The iterative contextual measure is defined as:

$$\rho_c^{(t+1)}(img_i, img_j) = d(\tau_i^{(t)}, \tau_j^{(t)}, k) \tag{3}$$

It is expected that the effectiveness of the distance measure improves along iterations, so non-relevant images are moved out from the first positions of the ranked lists. In this way, the size of the neighborhooed k can be increased for considering more images along iterations. Therefore the contextual measure can be redefined as:

$$\rho_c^{(t+1)}(img_i, img_j) = d(\tau_i^{(t)}, \tau_j^{(t)}, k+t) \tag{4}$$

After a given number of T iterations, a new distance $\hat{\rho}$ is computed based on contextual distance measure ρ_c:

$$\hat{\rho}(img_i, img_j) = \rho_c^{(T)}(img_i, img_j) \tag{5}$$

Finally, using the distance $\hat{\rho}$ a new distance matrix can be computed such $\hat{A}_{ij} = \hat{\rho}(img_i, img_j)$. Based on $\hat{A}$, a new set of ranked lists $\hat{\mathcal{R}}$ can be also computed.

5. RL-SIM* ALGORITHM

The RL-Sim Algorithm [27] computes a new distance between images img_i, img_j by analyzing the similarity between their respectively ranked lists τ_i, τ_j considering the top-k positions defined by the sets $\mathcal{N}(i,k)$ and $\mathcal{N}(j,k)$.

The effectiveness gain, however, is obtained by redefining the distances among the query image and images at initial positions of ranked lists. It occurs since is very unlikely to found similar images at the end of ranked lists. Therefore, the distances are redefined considering the rank correlation measure $d(\tau_i, \tau_j, k)$ for the first positions of the each ranked list, such that $L \in \mathbb{N}$ and $k \leq L \ll N$. For images in the remaining positions of the ranked lists, the new distance is redefined based on the current distances (or rank positions) and the function $d(\tau_i, \tau_j, k)$ does not need to be computed. As a result, this step of the algorithm depends only on a constant L, and not on the collection size N.

Although this approach allows decreasing the demanded computational costs, it still presents a limitation. Since the rank correlation measures are computed considering the top-k positions defined in terms of the neighborhood set $\mathcal{N}(i,k)$, their accuracy tends to be low when there is no overlap between the ranked lists being compared at top positions. For measures based on intersection analysis, it is still more critical, producing the same distance values for all pairs of images without overlap at top-k positions. In theses situations, the effectiveness of distance can be worsened.

Based on this observation, we propose the extended *RL-Sim* Algorithm* which aims at computing a different distance when there is no overlap between the ranked lists being compared. In this way, considering a query image img_i we propose to divide the ranked list τ_i in three segments. Each segment defines a subset of the ranked list, which is processed differently:

(i) First Segment (top-L positions, with overlap): this segment contains an image img_j at top-L positions if the neighborhood sets of img_i, img_j present other images in common. Formally, if $(\tau_i(j) < L) \wedge (\mathcal{N}(i,k) \cap \mathcal{N}(j,k) \neq \emptyset)$. For these cases, the new distance between img_i and img_j is computed by the rank correlation measure (defined in the $[0,1]$ interval).

(ii) Second Segment (top-L positions, no overlap): if the img_j appears at top-L positions of τ_i, but there is no overlap between top-k positions $(\mathcal{N}(i,k) \cap \mathcal{N}(j,k) = \emptyset)$, the rank correlation measures have no enough information for improving the distance measure. In this situations, the current distance is only incremented by 1, such $A_{ij}^{(t+1)} = A_{ij}^{(t)} + 1$. Notice that images with no overlap always will be ranked after that with overlap.

(iii) Remaining Images: the remaining images, i.e., images after top-L positions have their distances incremented by 2, such that $A_{ij}^{(t+1)} = A_{ij}^{(t)} + 2$. This procedure keeps these images at the end of ranked lists, ensuring that they are not mixed with images at top-L positions.

Notice that the simple addition of constants (1 and 2)

are enough to differentiate images at different positions of ranked lists. Algorithm 1 outlines the proposed RL-Sim* Algorithm. We can observe that the conditional structure at Line 8 defines the first (Line 9) and second segments (Line 12). The remaining images are processed at Lines 17-19.

Algorithm 1 RL-Sim* Algorithm

Require: Distance matrix A, Set of ranked lists $\mathcal{R}$ and parameters k, T, L
Ensure: Processed set of ranked lists $\hat{\mathcal{R}}$
1: $t \leftarrow 0$
2: $k \leftarrow k_s$
3: $\mathcal{R}^{(t)} \leftarrow \mathcal{R}$
4: $A^{(t)} \leftarrow A$
5: **while** $t < T$ **do**
6:   **for all** $\tau_i \in \mathcal{R}^{(t)}$ **do**
7:     **for all** $\{img_j \in \mathcal{C} \mid \tau_i(j) \leq L\}$ **do**
8:       **if** $\mathcal{N}(i,k) \cap \mathcal{N}(j,k) \neq \emptyset$ **then**
9:         //First Segment - With Overlap
10:         $A^{(t+1)}[i,j] \leftarrow d(\tau_i, \tau_j, k)$
11:       **else**
12:         //Second Segment - No Overlap
13:         $A_{ij}^{(t+1)} \leftarrow A_{ij}^{(t)} + 1$
14:       **end if**
15:     **end for**
16:     //Remaining Images - After top-L positions
17:     **for all** $\{img_j \in \mathcal{C} \mid \tau_i(j) > L\}$ **do**
18:       $A_{ij}^{(t+1)} \leftarrow A_{ij}^{(t)} + 2$
19:     **end for**
20:   **end for**
21:   $\mathcal{R}^{(t+1)} \leftarrow sortRankedLists(A^{(t+1)})$
22:   $k \leftarrow k + 1$
23:   $t \leftarrow t + 1$
24: **end while**
25: $\hat{\mathcal{R}} \leftarrow \mathcal{R}^{(T)}$

6. RANK CORRELATION MEASURES

The RL-Sim* (Algorithm 1) is not dependent on the rank correlation measure used, so we can define $d(\tau_i, \tau_j, k)$ using various approaches. However, only two measures were evaluated for the original RL-Sim Algorithm [27].

In fact, the effectiveness gains are directly associated with the measure used. Therefore, for obtaining high effectiveness gains it is required the definition of appropriate measures. In this paper, we perform a comparative study of eight correlation measures: six measures of the literature (Intersection, Kendall τ, Spearman, Goodman, Jaccard, and RBO); and two novel measures, named Jaccard$_l$ and Kendall τ_w. These measures are described in the following.

6.1 Intersection Measure

An approach to define the distance between two top-k lists τ_i and τ_i proposed in [10] is to capture the extent of overlap between τ_i and τ_i. This idea of overlap can be extended by considering not only the overlap at depth k, but also the cumulative overlap at increasing depth. For each depth $d \in \{1 \ldots k\}$, it is computed the overlap at d, and then those overlaps are averaged to derive a similarity measure. The measure assigns higher weights to the first positions of top k lists, which are considered many times. Equation 6 formally defines the intersection similarity measure ψ.

$$\psi(\tau_i, \tau_j, k) = \frac{\sum_{d=1}^{k} \mid \mathcal{N}(i,d) \cap \mathcal{N}(j,d) \mid}{k} \quad (6)$$

Note that if two ranked lists present the same images at the first positions, the size of the intersection set is larger, and therefore the value of ψ is higher as well. Since we are interested in a distance measure, we define d_I as follows:

$$d_I(\tau_i, \tau_j, k) = \frac{1}{1 + \psi(\tau_i, \tau_j, k)} \quad (7)$$

6.1.1 Kendall τ

The Kendall's τ is a traditional distance measure between permutations, used to measure rank correlation. Its value turns out to be equal to the number of exchanges needed in a bubble sort to convert one permutation to the other [10]. The normalized Kendall's tau measure is defined as follows:

$$d_\tau(\tau_i, \tau_j, k) = \frac{\sum_{x,y \in \mathcal{N}(i,k) \cup \mathcal{N}(j,k)} \bar{K}_{x,y}(\tau_i, \tau_j)}{k \times (k-1)}, \quad (8)$$

where $\bar{K}_{x,y}(\tau_i, \tau_j)$ is a function that determines if images img_x and img_y are in the same order in compared ranked lists τ_i and τ_j. This function can be defined as follows:

$$\bar{K}_{x,y}(\tau_i, \tau_j) = \begin{cases} 0 & \text{if } (\tau_i(x) \leqslant \tau_i(y) \wedge \tau_j(x) \leqslant \tau_j(y)), \\ 0 & \text{if } (\tau_i(x) \geqslant \tau_i(y) \wedge \tau_j(x) \geqslant \tau_j(y)), \\ 1 & \text{otherwise.} \end{cases}$$

The maximum value of defined Kendall's tau meausure is given by $k \times (k-1)$, which occurs when $\mathcal{N}(i,k) \cap \mathcal{N}(j,k) = \emptyset$ and τ_i is the reverse of τ_j.

6.1.2 Spearman

The Spearman's metric, commonly denoted by the letter ρ, can be seen as the L1 distance between two permutations [10]. The metric can also be defined as a non-parametric measure, which evaluates the relationship between two variables. Equation 9 formally defines the measure.

$$d_\rho(\tau_i, \tau_j, k) = \frac{\sum_{x,y \in \mathcal{N}(i,k) \cup \mathcal{N}(j,k)} |\tau_i(j) - \tau_j(i))|}{2 \times k \times n}, \quad (9)$$

6.1.3 Goodman

The Goodman and Kruskal's measure [11], commonly denoted by letter γ, is a measure of rank correlation based on pairwise analysis. The measure considers the relationship between the number of discordant (N_d) and concordant pairs (N_s), in a given set. The number of discordant pairs N_d can be defined based on the function $\bar{K}_{x,y}$ (Equation 6.1.1), as follows:

$$N_d(\tau_i, \tau_j, k) = \sum_{x,y \in \mathcal{N}(i,k) \cup \mathcal{N}(j,k)} \bar{K}_{x,y}(\tau_i, \tau_j) \quad (10)$$

We can also define the number of concordant pairs N_s as the inverse of N_d, such $N_s(\tau_i, \tau_j, k) = |\mathcal{N}(i,k) \cup \mathcal{N}(j,k)| - N_d$. Finally, the distance d_γ is formally defined by Equation 11.

$$d_\gamma(\tau_i, \tau_j, k) = \frac{N_s(\tau_i, \tau_j, k) - N_d(\tau_i, \tau_j, k)}{N_s(\tau_i, \tau_j, k) + N_d(\tau_i, \tau_j, k)}. \quad (11)$$

6.1.4 Jaccard

The Jaccard coefficient is a well-known distance between sets. Given two non-empty sets, it measures the probability that an element of at least one of two sets is an element of both, and thus is a reasonable measure of similarity or overlap between the two [18]. The Jaccard Coefficient is defined as follows:

$$J(\tau_i, \tau_j, k) = \frac{|\mathcal{N}(i,k) \cap \mathcal{N}(j,k)|}{|\mathcal{N}(i,k) \cup \mathcal{N}(j,k)|}, \quad (12)$$

As the coefficient $J(\tau_i, \tau_j, k)$ computes a similarity score, the distance measure is defined as:

$$d_J(\tau_i, \tau_j, k) = \frac{1}{1 + J(\tau_i, \tau_j, k)}. \quad (13)$$

6.1.5 Rank Overlap Biased (RBO)

The Rank-Biased Overlap (RBO) is a recently proposed measure [33] that compares the overlap of the two rankings at incrementally increasing depths. The measure takes a parameter that specifies the probability of considering the overlap at the next level. The weight of the overlap measured at each depth is computed based on these probabilities. The RBO measure is defined by Equation 14:

$$RBO(\tau_i, \tau_j, k, p) = (1-p)\sum_{d=1}^{k} p^{d-1} \times \frac{|\mathcal{N}(i,k) \cap \mathcal{N}(j,k)|}{d}, \quad (14)$$

where p is a constant. The distance measure can be computed as the inverse of RBO function, as follows.

$$d_R(\tau_i, \tau_j, k) = \frac{1}{1 + RBO(\tau_i, \tau_j, k)}. \quad (15)$$

6.1.6 Kendall τ_w

The original Kendall τ measure is a non-weighted measure. Pairs of images in a discordant order but with a small difference between their positions have the same weight of pairs very distant in the ranking. In this way, we propose a Kendall τ_w measure, which aims at giving higher weights to distant pairs. The measure is defined as follows:

$$d_{\tau_w}(\tau_i, \tau_j, k) = \frac{\sum_{x,y \in \mathcal{N}(i,k) \cup \mathcal{N}(j,k)} \bar{W}_{x,y}(\tau_i, \tau_j)}{n^2 \times k^2 \times (k-1)}. \quad (16)$$

The measure is very similar to the original Kendall measure, except by the function $\bar{W}_{x,y}$ that computes the weight of each pair. The function $\bar{W}_{x,y}$ is defined as follows:

$$\bar{W}_{x,y}(\tau_i, \tau_j) = \begin{cases} 0 \text{ if } (\tau_i(x) \leqslant \tau_i(y) \wedge \tau_j(x) \leqslant \tau_j(y)), \\ 0 \text{ if } (\tau_i(x) \geqslant \tau_i(y) \wedge \tau_j(x) \geqslant \tau_j(y)), \\ f \times (k - min(\tau_i(y), \tau_j(x), \tau_i(y), \tau_j(x)) \text{ otherwise}, \end{cases}$$

where f is a factor that aims at penalizing discordant pairs which are distant in the ranked lists. The pairs are considered distant when the difference between their positions are greater than k. Therefore, the value $f = 2$ is assigned when $(|\tau_i(x) - \tau_i(y)| + |\tau_j(x) - \tau_j(y)|) > (2 \times k)$, and $f = 1$, otherwise.

6.1.7 Jaccard$_l$

The traditional Jaccard coefficient establishes a relationship between the size of the union and the intersection sets, at a certain depth in the ranked list defined by k. However, in information retrieval tasks this approach ignores the information provided by top positions, smaller than k. In this way, we proposed to compute a accumulated Jaccard score considering different depths, as Intersection and RBO measures. Equation 17 formally defines the proposed approach:

$$J_l(\tau_i, \tau_j, k) = \frac{\sum_{d=1}^{k} J(\tau_i, \tau_j, k)}{k} \quad (17)$$

As the accumulated score gives a similarity score, the respectively distance is defined as follows:

$$d_{J_l}(\tau_i, \tau_j, k) = \frac{1}{1 + J_l(\tau_i, \tau_j, k)}. \quad (18)$$

7. EXPERIMENTAL EVALUATION

A large experimental evaluation was conducted aiming at assessing the effectiveness of the presented approach. Section 7.1 describes the image descriptors and datasets considered. Section 7.2 discusses the impact of parameters. Sections 7.3 and 7.4 present the experimental results for the original and the proposed algorithm considering all discussed rank correlation measures. Various shape, color, and texture descriptors were considered. Section 7.5 presents a comparison with other state-of-the-art approaches and Section 7.6 discusses the correlation among different measures.

7.1 Datasets and Image Descriptors

The experimental evaluation was conducted considering four different datasets with diverse characteristics and size ranging from 280 to 10,200 images. Various local and global descriptors were used, considering shape, color, and texture properties. Table 1 summarizes information about datasets and descriptors. All images of each dataset are considered as query images for effectiveness evaluation purposes. The Mean Average Precision (MAP) was used as effectiveness measure for most of datasets. For the N-S [22] dataset, the N-S retrieval score is used and for the MPEG-7 [17] dataset, the Recall@40 is considered in addition to MAP.

7.2 Analysis of Parameters

The computation of RL-Sim* Algorithm considers three parameters: *(i)* k: the size of the neighborhood set; *(ii)* T: the number of iterations; and *(iii)* L: the position at which the ranked lists are considered in the distance learning procedure. To evaluate the impact of different parameter settings on the effectiveness of the method and for determining the best parameters values, we conducted various experiments considering the MPEG-7 [17] dataset.

The first experiment aims at analyzing the impact of parameters k and T on the effectiveness of the proposed method. We set $L = 700$ and varied the values of parameter k and T in the intervals $[5, 20]$ and $[1, 5]$, respectively. We considered the RBO [33] measure and the CFD [25] descriptor. The MAP was used as effectiveness measure. Figure 1 illustrates the obtained results. A large red region can be observed around $k = 15$, indicating high effectiveness scores and robustness of the method regardless the parameter value variations. We used $L = 700$ and $k = 15$ for all experiments. The only exception is the N-S [22] dataset, which has a very small number of relevant images per class. In this case, we used $k = 5$ and $L = 200$.

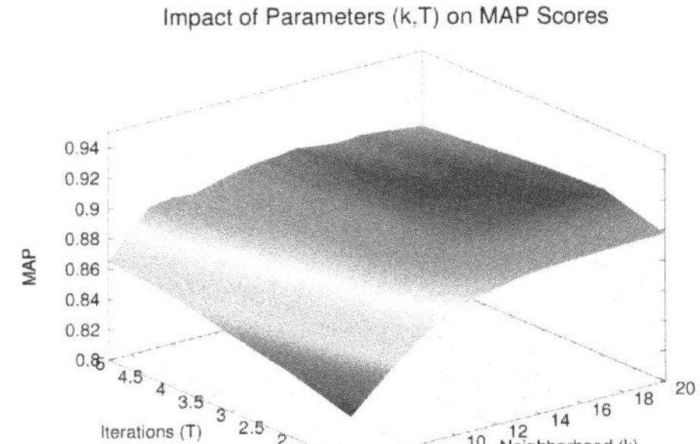

Figure 1: Impact of parameters k, T on MAP scores - CFD [25] descriptor and RBO [33] measure.

The number of iterations is more dependent on the rank correlation measure than the size of neighborhood. There-

Table 1: **Datasets and images descriptors used in the experimental evaluation.**

Dataset	Size	Type	General Description	Descriptors	Effectiv. Measure
Soccer [31]	280	Color Scenes	Dataset composed of images from 7 soccer teams, containing 40 images per class	Border/Interior Pixel Classification (BIC) [28], Auto Color Correlograms (ACC) [13], and Global Color Histogram (GCH) [29]	MAP (%)
MPEG-7 [17]	1,400	Shape	A well-known dataset composed of 1400 shapes divided in 70 classes. Commonly used for evaluation of unsupervised distance learning approaches.	Segment Saliences (SS) [9], Beam Angle Statistics (BAS) [1], Inner Distance Shape Context (IDSC) [19], Contour Features Descriptor (CFD) [25], Aspect Shape Context (ASC) [20], and Articulation-Invariant Representation (AIR) [12]	MAP (%), Recall@40
Brodatz [4]	1,776	Texture	A popular dataset for texture descriptors evaluation composed of 111 different textures divided into 16 blocks	Local Binary Patterns (LBP) [23], Color Co-Occurrence Matrix (CCOM) [16], Local Activity Spectrum (LAS) [30]	MAP (%)
N-S [22]	10,200	Objects/ Scenes	Composed of 2,550 objects or scenes. Each object/scene is captured 4 times from different viewpoints, distances and illumination conditions	ACC [13], BIC [28], Color and Edge Directivity Descriptor (CEED) [5], Fuzzy Color and Texture Histogram (FCTH) [6], Joint Composite Descriptor (JCD) [37], Scale-Invariant Feature Transform (SIFT) [21]	N-S score

Table 2: Effectiveness of the RL-Sim [27] Algorithm for various rank correlation measures. MAP scores (%) for shape, color, and texture descriptors considering different datasets. Best score for each descriptor in bold.

Descriptor	Type	Initial MAP	Intersection	Kendallτ	Spearman	Goodman	Jaccard	RBO	Jaccard$_l$	Kendallτ_w
SS [9]	Shape	37.67	43.06	44.24	44.53	40.95	45.18	43.34	46.11	**46.60**
BAS [1]	Shape	71.52	74.57	73.25	75.78	61.66	73.79	76.39	**76.58**	76.01
IDSC [19]	Shape	81.70	86.75	86.93	84.26	69.79	86.09	**87.76**	87.25	86.67
CFD [25]	Shape	80.71	88.97	88.40	85.32	72.43	88.72	**90.64**	90.51	89.13
ASC [20]	Shape	85.28	88.81	88.10	87.11	70.26	88.46	89.70	**89.75**	89.39
AIR [12]	Shape	89.39	93.54	96.27	**97.86**	84.84	96.68	94.84	96.43	96.44
GCH [29]	Color	32.24	33.66	32.96	**34.66**	32.16	32.65	33.13	33.23	33.60
ACC [13]	Color	37.23	43.54	44.29	**45.23**	39.49	44.81	41.83	43.33	43.59
BIC [28]	Color	39.26	43.45	43.76	**46.28**	39.31	43.19	42.58	43.86	42.23
LBP [23]	Texture	48.40	47.77	45.20	47.07	44.80	45.55	**50.22**	49.28	48.53
CCOM [16]	Texture	57.57	62.01	60.30	58.52	56.68	60.72	**63.62**	63.49	61.67
LAS [30]	Texture	75.15	77.81	75.62	75.13	69.29	76.04	**79.31**	79.00	78.30
Average	-	61.34	65.33	64.86	65.14	56.80	60.61	66.11	**66.57**	66.01

fore, we conducted an experiment for evaluating the impact of T considering different measures in order to defining the best values for this parameter. Figure 2 shows the results. The CFD [25] descriptor and the MPEG-7 [17] dataset were used, but other experiments were conducted considering other descriptors and datasets with similar results. The value of T was defined as 3, 2, 1, 1, 2, 3, 2, and 2 for the measures Intersection, Kendall τ, Spearman, Goodman, Jaccard, and RBO, Jaccard$_l$, and Kendall τ_w, respectively. We used $p = 0.9$ as suggested by [33] for RBO measure.

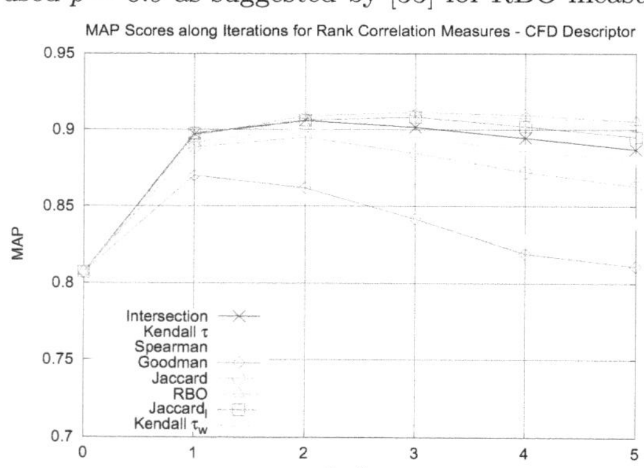

Figure 2: Evolution of MAP scores along Iterations for various Rank Correlation Measures.

7.3 Rank Correlation Measures for RL-Sim Algorithm

This section presents the evaluation of the two rank correlation measures proposed and the other six measures discussed in Section 6 for the original RL-Sim [27] Algorithm. Table 2 presents the results considering MAP scores for twelve descriptors and three datasets.

We can note that, considering shape descriptors, there is not a clear best measure, although RBO, Jaccard$_l$, and Kendallτ_w measures have reached higher scores. The Spearman measure obtained the best MAP scores for color descriptors, while RBO measure obtained the best results considering texture descriptors. In a more general analysis, considering the average of all descriptors, Jaccard$_l$, RBO, and Kendallτ_w obtained the best scores.

7.4 Rank Correlation Measures for RL-Sim* Algorithm

We conducted a set experiments aiming at evaluating the proposed RL-Sim* Algorithm, considering different rank correlation measures and comparing the results with the original RL-Sim [27] Algorithm.

Table 3 presents the experimental results considering MAP scores for shape, color, and texture descriptors. We can observe a significant increase in the best value observed for each descriptor in most cases, when compared with Table 2. The Kendallτ_w and RBO measures obtained the best scores for most descriptors. The Jaccard$_l$ and Kendallτ_w proposed measures reached the best average scores. We can also observe an increase of the average values for all measures evaluated in comparison with Table 2, demonstrating the effectiveness of proposed of RL-Sim* Algorithm.

We also considered the Bull's Eye Score , commonly used in the literature for the MPEG-7 [17] dataset. This score counts all matching objects within the 40 most similar candidates. Since each class consists of 20 objects, the retrieved score is normalized with the highest possible number of hits and is equivalent to Recall@40. Table 4 presents the obtained results.

Table 5 presents the experimental results for the N-S [22]

Table 3: Effectiveness of the RL-Sim* Algorithm for various rank correlation measures. MAP scores (%) for shape, color, and texture descriptors considering different datasets. Best score for each descriptor in bold.

Descriptor	Type	Initial MAP	Intersection	Kendallτ	Spearman	Goodman	Jaccard	RBO	Jaccard$_l$	Kendallτ_w
SS [9]	Shape	37.67	44.10	46.54	44.70	44.11	45.49	44.23	46.60	**47.87**
BAS [1]	Shape	71.52	76.05	76.12	75.94	72.61	74.87	77.34	77.51	**77.75**
IDSC [19]	Shape	81.70	87.38	87.59	85.03	83.50	87.03	**88.26**	88.08	88.02
CFD [25]	Shape	80.71	90.15	90.07	86.57	86.19	89.51	**91.13**	90.91	90.81
ASC [20]	Shape	85.28	89.96	90.14	88.03	85.75	89.54	90.57	90.77	**90.84**
AIR [12]	Shape	89.39	96.17	95.94	**97.86**	96.08	97.72	96.08	96.78	97.23
GCH [29]	Color	32.24	33.99	33.93	34.29	33.38	33.43	33.99	34.04	**34.39**
ACC [13]	Color	37.23	45.19	**45.94**	44.91	42.77	45.63	44.03	44.60	45.75
BIC [28]	Color	39.26	45.42	45.10	45.40	43.05	44.56	45.10	45.47	**45.50**
LBP [23]	Texture	48.40	48.83	48.94	47.32	49.06	46.53	**51.00**	50.10	49.92
CCOM [16]	Texture	57.57	62.89	62.44	59.02	61.19	61.37	**64.23**	64.06	63.53
LAS [30]	Texture	75.15	78.58	78.49	75.74	75.76	76.76	**79.80**	79.57	79.34
Average	-	61.34	66.56	66.77	65.4	59.93	66.04	67.15	67.37	**67.59**

Table 4: RL-Sim* Algorithm: Rank Correlation Measures on the MPEG-7 [17] dataset - Recall@40 (%).

Descriptor	Original	Intersection	Kendallτ	Spearman	Goodman	Jaccard	RBO	Jaccard$_l$	Kendallτ_w
SS [9]	43.99	52.92	53.96	51.97	51.5	53.76	51.61	53.92	**54.92**
BAS [1]	75.20	82.94	82.25	80.91	81.93	81.32	**83.45**	83.23	82.86
IDSC [19]	85.40	92.20	91.73	88.68	90.79	91.18	**92.73**	92.15	91.70
CFD [25]	84.43	94.16	93.77	89.64	92.32	93.20	**94.67**	94.43	94.24
ASC [20]	88.39	94.66	94.06	91.35	92.85	93.74	**94.67**	94.39	94.11
AIR [12]	93.67	99.90	98.27	**100**	99.79	99.95	99.87	99.91	99.92
Average	78.51	88.13	85.67	83.76	84.87	85.52	86.17	**86.34**	86.29

Table 5: Rank Correlation Measures for the RL-Sim* Algorithm on the N-S Dataset [22].

Descriptor	Initial Score	Intersection	Kendallτ	Spearman	Goodman	Jaccard	RBO	Jaccard$_l$	Kendallτ_w
ACC [13]	3.36	3.54	3.51	3.45	1.06	3.47	3.54	**3.55**	3.52
BIC [28]	3.04	3.20	3.17	3.02	1.05	3.13	3.19	**3.21**	3.19
CEED [5]	2.61	2.75	2.71	2.56	1.04	2.68	2.75	**2.76**	2.74
FCTH [6]	2.73	2.84	2.79	2.63	1.04	2.77	2.84	**2.85**	2.81
JCD [37]	2.79	2.92	2.88	2.72	2.87	2.85	2.92	**2.93**	2.9
SIFT [21]	2.54	2.81	2.82	**2.86**	1.03	2.77	2.79	2.80	2.80
Average	2.84	3.01	2.98	2.87	1.35	2.94	3.01	**3.02**	2.99

dataset.[1] Each image is used as query and the N-S retrieval score [22] between 1 and 4 is computed. The score corresponds to the number of relevant images among the first four image returned (the highest achievable score is 4). The propose Jaccard$_l$ measure obtained the best scores for this dataset.

A summary of the best MAP results is presented in Table 6, considering the twelve descriptors and three datasets. The table also presents the relative effectiveness gains obtained for each descriptor. We can observe very significant gains ranging from +5.37% to +27.08%.

Table 6: Summary of best MAP Scores (%).

Descriptor	Initial MAP	Rank Measure	RL-Sim* MAP	Relative Gain (%)
SS [9]	37.67	Kendall τ_w	47.87	+27.08
BAS [1]	71.52	Kendall τ_w	77.75	+8.71
IDSC [19]	81.70	RBO	88.26	+8.03
CFD [25]	80.71	RBO	91.13	+12.91
ASC [20]	85.28	Kendall τ_w	90.84	+6.52
AIR [12]	89.39	Spearman	97.86	+9.48
GCH [29]	32.24	Kendall τ_w	34.39	+6.67
ACC [13]	37.23	Kendall τ	45.94	+23.40
BIC [28]	39.26	Kendall τ_w	45.50	+15.89
LBP [23]	48.40	RBO	51.00	+5.37
CCOM [16]	57.57	RBO	64.23	+11.57
LAS [30]	75.15	RBO	79.80	+6.19

7.5 Comparison with Other Approaches

We also evaluated the proposed approach in comparison with state-of-the-art post-processing methods. We considered the MPEG-7 [17] dataset and the Bull's Eye Score, commonly used for post-processing methods evaluation and comparison. Table 7 presents the comparison, with two selected best results of our approach. We can observe that high scores were obtained by the proposed approach, comparable or superior to various recently proposed methods.

7.6 Correlation Among Measures

Finally, we also conducted an experiment aiming at evaluating the correlation among measures. The hypothesis is that non-correlated measures encode diverse information, what justifies the evaluation of different measures and enables the investigation of approaches for combining them. The Pearson Correlation Coefficient was computed between each pair of measures, based on distances given by each measure for top images at ranked lists. We considered top 200 images, $k = 15$ and $T = 1$. Table 8 presents the results, with hot colors indicating low correlation scores. As we can observe, various measures present low correlation. That opens a novel research venue related to the investigation of approaches for combining the information provided by ranked lists obtained considering the use of different correlation measures.

8. CONCLUSIONS

In this paper, we have presented an unsupervised distance learning approach based on rank correlation measures. We propose the RL-Sim* Algorithm, which considers the rank correlation measures and the overlap between the neighborhood sets aiming at computing a more effective distance measure. Six traditional measures were evaluated and two novel rank correlation measures were proposed specially for the unsupervised distance learning problem on image retrieval tasks.

[1]For the N-S [22] dataset we used $T = 1$ for all measures.

Table 7: Post-processing methods comparison on the MPEG-7 [17] dataset - Bull's Eye Score (Recall@40).

Shape Descriptors		
CFD [25]	-	84.43%
IDSC [19]	-	85.40%
SC [3]	-	86.80%
ASC [20]	-	88.39%
AIR [12]	-	93.67%
Post-Processing Methods		
Algorithm	**Descriptor(s)**	**Score**
Graph Transduction [34]	IDSC	91.00%
Locally C. Diffusion Process [35]	IDSC	93.32%
Shortest Path Propagation [32]	IDSC	93.35%
Locally C. Diffusion Process [35]	ASC	95.96%
Pairwise Recommendation [26]	CFD	96.15%
Tensor Product Graph [36]	ASC	96.47%
Self-Smoothing Operator [15]	SC+IDSC	97.64%
Co-Transduction [2]	SC+IDSC	97.72%
Pairwise Recommendation [26]	CFD+IDSC	99.52%
RL-Sim* with Jaccard	**AIR**	**99.95%**
Tensor Product Graph [36]	AIR	99.99%
RL-Sim* with Spearman	**AIR**	**100%**

Table 8: Correlation Among Measures.

Rank Measures	(I)	(K)	(S)	(G)	(J)	(R)	(J_l)	(K_w)
(I) Intersection	1	0.23	0.31	0.74	0.77	0.65	0.65	0.31
(K) Kendallτ	0.23	1	0.75	0.22	0.55	0.61	0.63	0.98
(S) Spearman	0.31	0.75	1	0.19	0.52	0.47	0.65	0.76
(G) Goodman	0.74	0.22	0.19	1	0.82	0.86	0.86	0.28
(J) Jaccard	0.77	0.55	0.52	0.82	1	0.86	0.91	0.55
(R) RBO	0.65	0.61	0.47	0.86	0.86	1	0.99	0.65
(J_l) Jaccard$_l$	0.65	0.63	0.49	0.86	0.91	0.99	1	0.66
(K_w) Kendallτ_w	0.31	0.98	0.76	0.28	0.55	0.65	0.66	1

We conducted a large set of experiments for assessing the effectiveness of the proposed approach, considering different descriptors, datasets and rank correlation measures. Experimental results demonstrated that high effectiveness results were obtained by the proposed approach when compared with recent related work [27] and other state-of-the-art methods. Future work focuses on the investigation of: (i) novel rank correlation measures; and (ii) approaches for combining different rank correlation measures.

9. ACKNOWLEDGMENTS

The authors are grateful to PROPe/UNESP, São Paulo Research Foundation - FAPESP (grants 2013/08645-0 and 2013/50169-1), CNPq (grants 306580/2012-8 and 484254/2012-0), CAPES, AMD, and Microsoft Research.

10. REFERENCES

[1] N. Arica and F. T. Y. Vural. BAS: a perceptual shape descriptor based on the beam angle statistics. *Pattern Recognition Letters*, 24(9-10):1627–1639, 2003.

[2] X. Bai, B. Wang, X. Wang, W. Liu, and Z. Tu. Co-transduction for shape retrieval. In *ECCV*, volume 3, pages 328–341, 2010.

[3] S. Belongie, J. Malik, and J. Puzicha. Shape matching and object recognition using shape contexts. *PAMI*, 24(4):509–522, 2002.

[4] P. Brodatz. *Textures: A Photographic Album for Artists and Designers*. Dover, 1966.

[5] S. A. Chatzichristofis and Y. S. Boutalis. Cedd: color and edge directivity descriptor: a compact descriptor for image indexing and retrieval. In *ICVS'08*.

[6] S. A. Chatzichristofis and Y. S. Boutalis. Fcth: Fuzzy color and texture histogram - a low level feature for accurate image retrieval. In *WIAMIS '08*, pages 191–196, 2008.

[7] Y. Chen, X. Li, A. Dick, and R. Hill. Ranking consistency for image matching and object retrieval. *Pattern Recognition*, 47(3):1349 – 1360, 2014.

[8] R. da S. Torres and A. X. Falcão. Content-Based Image Retrieval: Theory and Applications. *Revista de Informática Teórica e Aplicada*, 13(2):161–185, 2006.

[9] R. da S. Torres and A. X. Falcão. Contour Salience Descriptors for Effective Image Retrieval and Analysis. *Image and Vision Computing*, 25(1):3–13, 2007.

[10] R. Fagin, R. Kumar, and D. Sivakumar. Comparing top k lists. In *SODA'03*, pages 28–36, 2003.

[11] L. A. Goodman and W. H. Kruskal. Measures of association for cross classifications. *Journal of the American Statistical Association*, 49(268):pp. 732–764, 1954.

[12] R. Gopalan, P. Turaga, and R. Chellappa. Articulation-invariant representation of non-planar shapes. In *ECCV'2010*, volume 3, pages 286–299, 2010.

[13] J. Huang, S. R. Kumar, M. Mitra, W.-J. Zhu, and R. Zabih. Image indexing using color correlograms. In *CVPR*, pages 762–768, 1997.

[14] W. Huang, K. Chan, H. Li, J. Lim, J. Liu, and T. Wong. Content-based medical image retrieval with metric learning via rank correlation. In *MLMI*, pages 18–25, 2010.

[15] J. Jiang, B. Wang, and Z. Tu. Unsupervised metric learning by self-smoothing operator. In *ICCV*, pages 794–801, 2011.

[16] V. Kovalev and S. Volmer. Color co-occurence descriptors for querying-by-example.

[17] L. J. Latecki, R. Lakmper, and U. Eckhardt. Shape descriptors for non-rigid shapes with a single closed contour. In *CVPR*, pages 424–429, 2000.

[18] M. Levandowsky and D. Winter. Distance between sets. *Nature*, 243:34 – 35, 1971.

[19] H. Ling and D. W. Jacobs. Shape classification using the inner-distance. *PAMI*, 29(2):286–299, 2007.

[20] H. Ling, X. Yang, and L. J. Latecki. Balancing deformability and discriminability for shape matching. In *ECCV*, volume 3, pages 411–424, 2010.

[21] D. Lowe. Object recognition from local scale-invariant features. In *ICCV*, pages 1150–1157, 1999.

[22] D. Nistér and H. Stewénius. Scalable recognition with a vocabulary tree. In *CVPR*, volume 2, pages 2161–2168, 2006.

[23] T. Ojala, M. Pietikäinen, and T. Mäenpää. Multiresolution gray-scale and rotation invariant texture classification with local binary patterns. *PAMI*, 24(7):971–987, 2002.

[24] D. C. G. Pedronette, J. Almeida, and R. da S. Torres. A scalable re-ranking method for content-based image retrieval. *Information Sciences*, 265(0):91 – 104, 2014.

[25] D. C. G. Pedronette and R. da S. Torres. Shape retrieval using contour features and distance optmization. In *VISAPP*, volume 1, pages 197 – 202, 2010.

[26] D. C. G. Pedronette and R. da S. Torres. Exploiting pairwise recommendation and clustering strategies for image re-ranking. *Information Sciences*, 207:19–34, 2012.

[27] D. C. G. Pedronette and R. da S. Torres. Image re-ranking and rank aggregation based on similarity of ranked lists. *Pattern Recognition*, 46(8):2350–2360, 2013.

[28] R. O. Stehling, M. A. Nascimento, and A. X. Falcão. A compact and efficient image retrieval approach based on border/interior pixel classification. In *CIKM*, pages 102–109, 2002.

[29] M. J. Swain and D. H. Ballard. Color indexing. *International Journal on Computer Vision*, 7(1):11–32, 1991.

[30] B. Tao and B. W. Dickinson. Texture recognition and image retrieval using gradient indexing. *JVCIR*, 11(3):327–342, 2000.

[31] J. van de Weijer and C. Schmid. Coloring local feature extraction. In *ECCV*, pages 334–348, 2006.

[32] J. Wang, Y. Li, X. Bai, Y. Zhang, C. Wang, and N. Tang. Learning context-sensitive similarity by shortest path propagation. *Pattern Recognition*, 44(10-11):2367–2374, 2011.

[33] W. Webber, A. Moffat, and J. Zobel. A similarity measure for indefinite rankings. *ACM Transactions on Information Systems*, 28(4):20:1–20:38, 2010.

[34] X. Yang, X. Bai, L. J. Latecki, and Z. Tu. Improving shape retrieval by learning graph transduction. In *ECCV*, volume 4, pages 788–801, 2008.

[35] X. Yang, S. Koknar-Tezel, and L. J. Latecki. Locally constrained diffusion process on locally densified distance spaces with applications to shape retrieval. In *CVPR*, pages 357–364, 2009.

[36] X. Yang, L. Prasad, and L. Latecki. Affinity learning with diffusion on tensor product graph. *PAMI*, 35(1):28–38, 2013.

[37] K. Zagoris, S. Chatzichristofis, N. Papamarkos, and Y. Boutalis. Automatic image annotation and retrieval using the joint composite descriptor. In *14th PCI*, pages 143–147, 2010.

Exploring Pooling Strategies based on Idiosyncrasies of Spatio-Temporal Interest Points

Yuancheng Ye, Xiaodong Yang, and Yingli Tian
The Graduate Center and The City College
City University of New York
yye@gradcenter.cuny.edu, {xyang02, ytian}@ccny.cuny.edu

ABSTRACT

Recent studies have demonstrated that the implementation of local space-time interest points has good competence and robustness in the area of human action recognition, which has become one of the challenging problems in multimedia analysis. While most research focuses on the techniques of detecting feature points or capturing spatial and temporal information around those points, there has been very limited research on delving into the pooling strategies which are also important components of action recognition algorithms. In this paper, we propose a novel pooling framework by categorizing the interest points with respect to their idiosyncrasies. Specifically, we discuss three pooling strategies based on the optical flow orientation, foreground weight and spatio-temporal locations respectively and further investigate the fusion of different pooling strategies. For the encoding process, instead of the popular bag-of-visual words (BoV) method, we adopt the improved Fisher Vector (FV) approach. Our proposed methods are evaluated on a benchmark dataset with controlled settings (KTH), and two more challenging datasets with realistic background (HMDB51 and UCF101). The experimental results demonstrate that pooling strategies based on the appropriate idiosyncrasies of individual interest points can improve the performance of action classification.

Keywords

Action recognition, local interest points, pooling strategy, spatio-temporal pyramid, optical flow, foreground weight

1. INTRODUCTION

Recent years, action recognition has drawn more and more attentions in the area of multimedia analysis. Among many approaches developed to solve this challenging problem, local space-time features have demonstrated good robustness and competence since they can describe relatively independent representation of actions with respect to their spatio-temporal shifts. These features are usually detected directly from videos and therefore without pre-processing procedures such as motion segmentation and tracking [30].

ICMR '15, June 23 - 26, 2015, Shanghai, China
 ISBN 978-1-4503-3274-3/15/06 ...$15.00
DOI: http://dx.doi.org/10.1145/2671188.2749339.

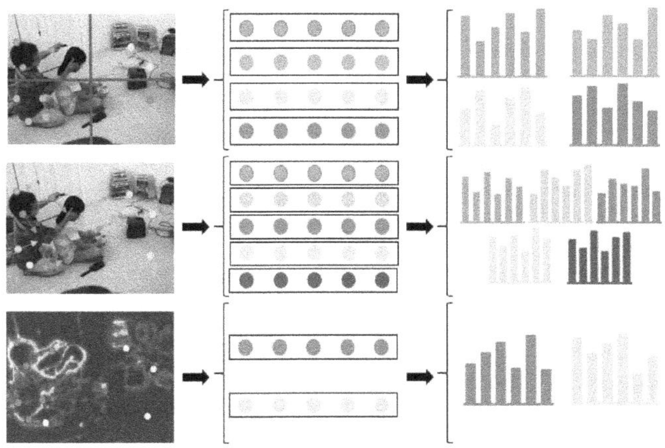

Figure 1: An illustration of three pooling strategies we evaluate in this paper: spatio-temporal pyramid pooling strategy (top row), the optical flow orientation-based pooling strategy (middle row) and foreground weight-based pooling strategy (bottom row). In the first column, the circles in the figure represent different detected interest points, and different colors represent the distinct properties associated with them. Second column shows the procedure of the interest points categorized according to their idiosyncrasies. Third column illustrates the vectors of different channels after sum pooling and normalization procedures respectively.

1.1 Related Work

Various local feature detectors have been proposed in the past years. These detectors are usually obtained by maximizing a certain saliency function with respect to given spatio-temporal scales.

By extending the Harris corner detector to the 3D domain, Laptev and Lindeberg first proposed the STIPs for action recognition [14] by extracting sparse interest points in the space-time domain. Cuboid detector [6] and 3D-Hessain detector [31] were proposed by Dollár *et al.* and Willems *et al.* respectively. Chakraborty *et al.* proposed selective spatio-temporal interest points [5]. By employing state-of-art optical flow fields, Wang *et al.* [28, 29] introduced dense

Figure 2: A traditional pipeline of action recognition algorithms instead of what this paper presents.

trajectories.

To capture the unique appearance and motion information around interest points, a number of descriptors have been proposed [21]. Schüldt *et al.* [23] tried to tackle action recognition problems by applying high-order derivatives to compute local N-jets descriptors. Laptev [15] introduced HOG/HOF based on the distribution of image gradients and optical flow around the neighborhood of interest points. Dollár and his colleagues proposed cuboid descriptor along with the cuboid feature detector [6]. 3D-SIFT [24] and HOG3D [12] descriptors both were introduced by extending successful 2D image descriptors into 3D domain. In particular, the paper [30] conducted exhaustive experiments to evaluate the performance of different feature detectors and feature descriptors.

In the literatures of human action recognition, bag-of-visual words (BOV) method is a common encoding strategy to compute the representation of action videos. It entails codebook vocabularies usually computed by the K-means algorithm. The number of clusters is set empirically to obtain the best results. Additionally, to achieve a good classification performance, a non-linear support vector machine (SVM) is usually necessary. However as underlined in the work of Boiman *et al.*, the descriptor quantization is a lossy process which is one of the main shortcomings of the BOV representation [2]. Recent research has demonstrated that the improved Fisher Vector (FV) encoding approach consistently outperforms the traditional BOV method [22] by implementing the ℓ_2 normalization and power normalization [11]. The FV representation works well with linear SVM which makes the action recognition tasks possible for large-scale datasets while achieving comparable or even better results than the BOV encoding approach with non-linear SVM.

Pooling process often follows the encoding procedure in action recognition algorithms [17]. Two aggregating strategies are commonly used: sum pooling and max pooling. The paper [3] conducted an extensive theoretical analysis of feature pooling strategies, and as it pointed out that sparse features prefer max pooling approach [20]. These two pooling strategies are performed on a global scale, therefore may neglect the discriminative properties of intra-descriptors in the same video. In our paper, instead of pooling all descriptors without prejudice, we prove that pooling strategies based on the idiosyncrasies of local interest points can improve the discriminative ability of video representations.

1.2 Our Proposed Framework

As discussed above, a classical action recognition algorithm usually comprises of four main components: feature extraction, feature encoding, pooling and normalization, and classification as shown in Figure 2. Although many studies have been done on feature extraction and feature encoding, there is limited research delving into the pooling strategies based on the idiosyncrasies of individual interest points.

Most action recognition algorithms employ sum pooling or max pooling strategy depending on the encoding process implemented. Specifically, sparse coding employs max pooling while traditional BoV encoding algorithm uses sum pooling. These two standard pooling strategies are based on the elements of descriptors and they are more likely regarded as the integrating procedures. However, as demonstrated by our experiments, the discernability provided by appropriate properties-based pooling strategies can have positive influence on the classification performance. As one of the most commonly implemented pooling strategies based on the properties of interest points, spatio-temporal pyramid pooling method [16], which can be shown to be a special pooling case in our framework, categorizes detected feature points by their space-time positions in video clips. Many previous studies have demonstrated that this approach conspicuously improves recognition results. Most literature regards the spatio-temporal pyramid pooling strategy merely as a special implementation of pyramid match kernel [7]. However we argue that it can also be regarded as a specific pooling strategy based on the positions of interest points.

Inspired by the spatio-temporal pyramid pooling strategy, which capitalizes the location information of individual interest points, we propose two other idiosyncrasies-based pooling strategies to improve the discernability of video representations: the optical flow orientation-based and foreground weight-based pooling strategies. The purpose of the first pooling strategy is to utilize the optical flow orientation information, while the second is to decide whether the point belonging to the foreground scenes. Figure 1 illustrates the three pooling strategies we discussed in this paper. As with the location information, we argue that optical flow orientation and foreground weight information of interest points are also informative properties that could be applied to pooling procedures.

In addition to the specific pooling strategies we evaluate in this paper, we generalize a new pooling framework based on the idiosyncrasies of individual interest points. In our new framework, interest points are pooled according to their distinct properties. As demonstrated by our experiments, more discriminative power can be rendered to the representation by implementing our pooling framework.

1.3 Contributions and Paper Organization

In this paper, we propose a novel pooling framework by exploring the idiosyncrasies of individual interest points. Specifically, we study two novel pooling strategies based on the interest points properties of optical flow orientation and foreground weight respectively and further integrate these two new pooling methods with the popular spatio-temporal pyramid strategy to achieve better recognition results on different datasets of human action recognition. As presented in Figure 3, we first conduct three pooling strategies respectively, and then to integrate the performance of these pooling strategies, we employ a decision-level fusion to further improve the results. Our experiments demonstrate that pooling strategies based on categorizing interest points with respect to their appropriate and reasonable properties can improve the action recognition performance.

The rest of the paper is organized as follows. Section 2 discusses the general idiosyncrasies-based pooling framework and two novel pooling strategies: the optical flow orientation-

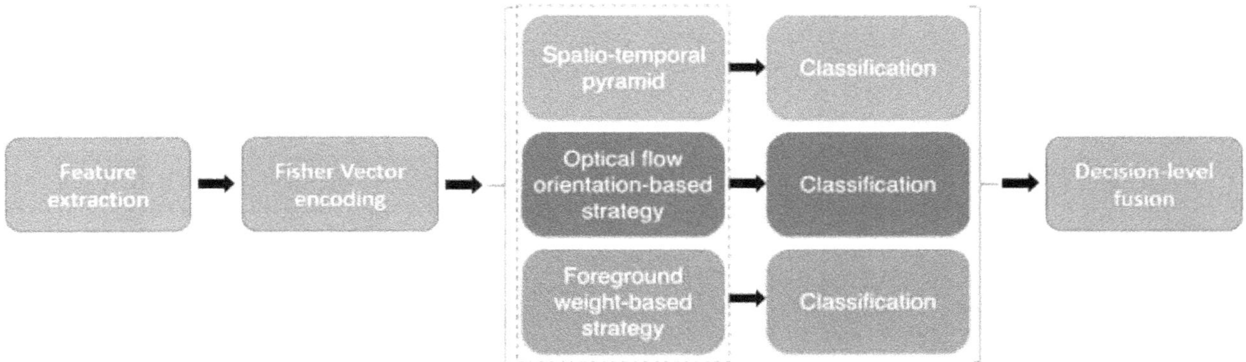

Figure 3: The pipeline of our proposed methods. The main contribution of this paper is denoted by the dashed box which represents our proposed idiosyncrasies of interest points-based pooling framework. Spatio-temporal pyramid, optical flow orientation-based strategy and foreground weight-based strategy are all the specific examples of our new pooling framework.

based and foreground weight-based methods. Spatio-temporal pyramid pooling strategy is also briefly discussed from a different point of view. Section 3 presents the experimental setup details and results on different datasets. We conclude the paper in Section 4.

2. IDIOSYNCRASIES OF INTEREST POINTS-BASED POOLING STRATEGIES

Two popular encoding frameworks are commonly employed in action recognition algorithms: BOV words and Fisher Vector (FV) [32]. Recent research has demonstrated that the Fisher Vector encoding procedure consistently achieves more accurate results with appropriate setups. In order to clearly present our proposed pooling framework, we firstly simply introduce the FV encoding process.

Let $\chi = \{x_1, x_2, \ldots, x_T\}$ be the descriptors in an action video, assuming our GMMs have the form:

$$u_\lambda(x_t) = \sum_{j=1}^{K} \omega_j u_j(x_t), \qquad t = 1, 2, \ldots, T, \tag{1}$$

in which $\lambda = \{\omega_i, \mu_i, \Sigma_i, i = 1 \ldots K\}$, and ω_i, μ_i and Σ_i are the mixture weight, mean vector and covariance matrix of Gaussian u_i respectively. Here K is the number of the GMMs components. We also assume that the covariance matrices are diagonal and then denote the variance vector by σ_i^2. $\gamma_t(i)$ is the soft assignment of descriptor x_t to Gaussian component i:

$$\gamma_t(i) = \frac{\omega_i u_i(x_t)}{\sum_{j=1}^{K} \omega_j u_j(x_t)}. \tag{2}$$

Encoded vector of x_t is then given by the concatenation of vectors $\Theta_{\mu,i}^t$ and $\Theta_{\sigma,i}^t$, which are defined as follows:

$$\Theta_{\mu,i}^t = \frac{1}{\sqrt{\omega_i}} \gamma_t(i) \left(\frac{x_t - \mu_i}{\sigma_i} \right), \tag{3}$$

$$\Theta_{\sigma,i}^t = \frac{1}{\sqrt{2\omega_i}} \gamma_t(i) \left(\frac{(x_t - \mu_i)^2}{\sigma_i^2} - 1 \right). \tag{4}$$

The concatenation process can then be expressed as:

$$\rho(x_t) = [\Theta_{\mu,1}^t, \Theta_{\sigma,1}^t, \ldots, \Theta_{\mu,K}^t, \Theta_{\sigma,K}^t]. \tag{5}$$

Suppose the dimension of the descriptor x_i is D, then the encoded descriptor $\rho(x_t)$ has the size $2DK$.

After the encoding procedure, an appropriate pooling strategy should be applied. The standard pooling approach is the sum pooling procedure. Then the power normalization and ℓ_2-normalization are performed to obtain the final representation. Since sum pooling strategy is based on the elements of vectors respectively on a global scale, it does not discriminate descriptors in the same video. Therefore it may neglect some discernabilities intrinsic among descriptors. To underline the different properties of interest points, spatio-pyramid pooling strategy is usually applied before standard sum pooling process.

Grauman *et al.* first introduced pyramid kernel to classify different features [7]. Inspired by this work, Lazebnik *et al.* [16] proposed a simple but effective spatial pyramid technique of pooling feature points into different bins based on their positions in an image. By extending this pooling strategy into 3D domain, the spatio-temporal pyramid pooling strategy was employed in the paper [27]. This approach consistently improves recognition performance on different datasets.

Inspired by the success of spatio-pyramid pooling strategy, we propose a general pooling framework in this paper which projects interest points based on their distinct properties. Let $\eta = \{y_1, y_2, \ldots, y_T\}$ be the set of locations of detected interest points. Assuming the projection procedure is denoted as φ, the mathematical expression of our idiosyncrasies-based pooling process is defined as:

$$C_n = \varphi(\{y_t\}), \tag{6}$$

where C_n is an element of the pooling set $\{C_1, C_2, \ldots, C_N\}$ whose components are the feature indices. The aggregated vector h_n belonging to the pooling component C_n then can be expressed as:

$$h_n = \frac{1}{|C_n|} \sum_{x_t \in C_n} \rho(x_t). \tag{7}$$

Finally, the normalized aggregated vectors are concatenated to form the video representation:

$$z = [h_1', h_2', \ldots, h_N']^T. \tag{8}$$

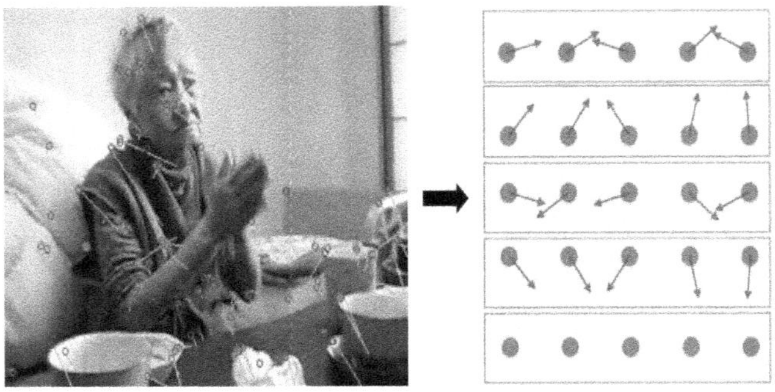

Figure 4: An intuitive illustration of optical flow orientation-based pooling strategy. According to their optical flow orientation information, interest points are projected into five categories: $-90^o \sim -45^o, -45^o \sim 0^o, 0^o \sim 45^o, 45^o \sim 90^o$ and *static*.

where $h'_n, n = 1, 2, \ldots, N$, denotes the normalized and transposed form of the aggregated vector h_n.

One main contribution of this paper is to evaluate the effectiveness of the discernability of video representation by carefully applying reasonable pooling procedure φ. In our proposed framework, interest points are categorized according to their properties, and then encoded descriptors are computed respectively. After that standard pooling and normalization procedures are operated on each category. Finally a representation is formed by concatenating vectors of different categories.

Like the spatio-temporal pyramid pooling strategy, the pooling procedure φ groups interest points into different categories and therefore increases the discriminative power of final representation. As implementations of our proposed pooling framework based on the idiosyncrasies of interest points, two novel pooling strategies are presented in our paper: optical flow orientation-based and foreground weight-based pooling strategies.

2.1 Optical Flow Orientation-based Pooling Strategy

Optical flow is commonly used for tracking, motion estimation, etc. The paper [1] discussed several most commonly used optical flow algorithms. Since optical flow encodes the motion information of points in a frame relative to the next frames, it is an intuitive source to describe action motion. We incorporate the optical flow orientation information in the pooling process φ to project interest points into different categories.

As illustrated in Figure 4, the detected interest points are associated with different optical flow angles. These optical flow angles indicate the orientations where those interest points will be in the next frame. Interest points with different optical flow angles contain different information. By pooling interest points according to optical flow orientations, more discriminative information is represented for video actions.

At first, by discarding the interest points without optical flow value, we compute the optical flow angles by the *arctan* function of the projections of amplitudes on X-coordinate and Y-coordinate, and divide the angles into four categories: $-90^o \sim -45^o, -45^o \sim 0^o, 0^o \sim 45^o, 45^o \sim 90^o$. The categorization process is the implementation of the pooling procedure φ in Eq.(6). However, results on action recognition are even worse than the baseline. The main reason is that, as shown in Figure 4, there are many interest points associated with relatively small or even zero amplitudes of optical flow. A straightforward intuition is that these interest points are on the background settings and should be eliminated for further action recognition. However the experiment results do not support this conjecture.

Actually there are many existing literatures discussing the discernability of background scenes. Furthermore, those static interest points may also be generated by temporary action pause which still provide rich information about action movement. Neglecting these points will inevitably deteriorate the performance. Therefore, we add a *static* category to accommodate for this situation, which helps to improve the performance. This phenomenon of many detected interest points falling in the static background settings inspires us to separate the feature points into foreground and background bins, which will be discussed in next Section.

2.2 Foreground Weight-based Pooling Strategy

Recently, an interesting experiment discussing the background discriminativity demonstrated that comparable recognition results can be achieved by dealing with the features points extracted only on the background regions [26]. Inspired by this work, we employ the value of foreground weight to measure the confidence of how likely a point belongs to the foreground scenes based on the information of optical flow gradients, color gradients, and visual saliency.

The optical flow gradients-based foreground confidence, f_m, can be calculated as follows:

$$f_m(x, y) = \sqrt{\mu_x^2 + \mu_y^2 + v_x^2 + v_y^2} * g, \quad (9)$$

where μ_x and v_x are the gradients of the projection of optical flow magnitude on the X-coordinate, and correspondingly μ_y and v_y are the gradients on the Y-coordinate. g represents the 2D Gausian filter with a fixated variance and the symbol $*$ denotes the convolution process. A visualization of the confidence map computed by optical flow gradients is shown in Figure 5(a).

The Frobenius form of the color gradients, f_c, is:

$$f_c(x, y) = \sqrt{L_x^2 + L_y^2 + a_x^2 + a_y^2 + b_x^2 + b_y^2} * g, \quad (10)$$

where (L_x, a_x, b_x) and (L_y, a_y, b_y) are the horizontal and vertical color gradients of the pixel at the position (x, y). Figure 5(b) presents the heatmap of the foreground confidence map calculated by color gradients.

For the visual saliency, we implement the graph-based visual saliency (GBVS) algorithm, which was originally proposed by Harel [8].

Assuming that the dissimilarity of two points $M(i, j)$ and $M(p, q)$ is defined as:

$$d((i, j) \parallel (p, q)) = \left| log \frac{M(i, j)}{M(p, q)} \right|. \quad (11)$$

Considering all pixels in a frame as connecting nodes in a graph, the GBVS algorithm attempts to assign a weight to every directed edge from the node (i, j) to the node (p, q):

$$w((i, j) \parallel (p, q)) = d((i, j) \parallel (p, q)) \cdot F(i - p, j - q). \quad (12)$$

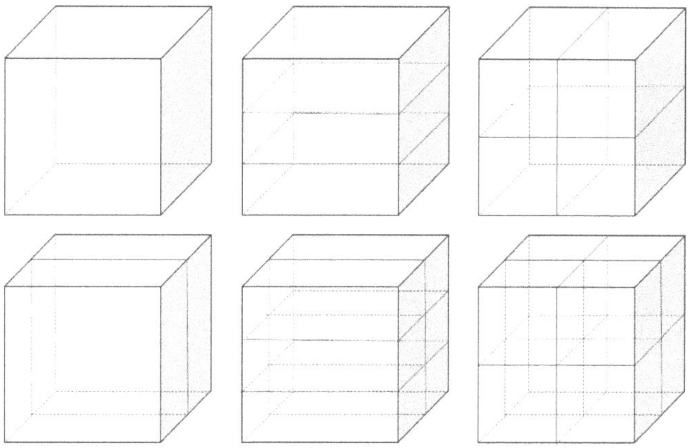

Figure 6: An illustration of spatio-temporal grids distributions in our experiments. Top row: $1 \times 1 \times 1$, $1 \times 3 \times 1$, $2 \times 2 \times 1$. Bottom row: $1 \times 1 \times 2$, $1 \times 3 \times 2$ and $2 \times 2 \times 2$. Total of 24 grids are used.

The function $F(a, b)$ is defined as below:

$$F(a, b) = exp\left(-\frac{a^2 + b^2}{2\sigma^2}\right), \quad (13)$$

where σ is a user defined parameter, usually in the domain of one tenth to one fifth of the video width.

After assigning every edge a saliency weight, the outbound edges are then normalized and the graph is treated as a Markov chain. The equilibrium distribution of this chain can be computed as the saliency measure, $f_s(x, y)$, of each pixel. A visualization of visual saliency heatmap is demonstrated by Figure 5(c).

By incorporating all of three confidence weights, the final foreground confidence map can be obtained:

$$f_{conf} = log(f_m(f_c + f_s) + 1). \quad (14)$$

Figure 5(d) shows the heatmap of final foreground confidence map.

The foreground weight-based pooling strategy is an implementation of our pooling framework φ. It takes into account the discernability of background and foreground by deciding whether an interest point belonging to the foreground scenes to improve the discriminative power of video representations.

2.3 Spatio-Temporal Pyramid-based Pooling Strategy

As a successful pooling strategy, spatio-temporal pyramid has been used in many existing action recognition algorithms. It groups interest points according to their positions in action videos belonging into corresponding geometric grids and calculate their descriptors respectively. Aggregated vectors are obtained after conducting pooling and normalization process on each category. The concatenation of these vectors is presented as the final representation. Although spatio-pyramid approach is evolved from pyramid classification kernel, it can be regarded as a specific example of the idiosyncrasies-based pooling strategies which categorizes interest points with respect to their geometric information. Therefore by applying other reasonable properties of interest points, recognition performance can also be improved due to more discriminative power of representations.

In our paper, we also evaluate how the other two properties, i.e., optical flow orientation and foreground weight, can be applied to our proposed pooling framework to improve the action recognition results. In addition to be an integrating process, the pooling procedure φ, can also improve the discernability of representations by applying appropriate properties.

Methods	baseline	4-bins	5-bins
Lucas–Kanade	92.7	91.3	92.2
Horn–Schunck	92.7	92.4	93.2

Table 1: Average accuracies (%) of optical flow orientation-based pooling strategies on the KTH dataset. Baseline column represents the results with standard Fisher Vector method.The 5-bins column presents the results of our final approach which projects STIPs into four angle bins and one *static* bin, while the column of 4-bins lists the outcomes only with four angle bins.

3. EXPERIMENTS

3.1 Experimental Setup

Our experiments focus on the pooling strategies based on the distinct properties of individual detected interest points. In our implementation, we employ the STIPs developed by Laptev *et al.* as the interest points and the popular HOG/HOF as the descriptors.

HOG/HOF descriptor divides the neighborhood of each interest point into 18 grids and for each grid 4-bin histograms of gradient orientations (HOG) and 5-bin histograms of optical flow (HOF) are computed. Therefore for each interest point, the dimension of the descriptor is 162. After that, a principal component analysis (PCA) procedure is performed for the purpose of decorrelation. The dimension of PCA matrix is set to reserve 98% energy of the original descriptor, which reduces primitive vector size of HOG/HOF from 162 to 126 for all the datasets. Our Gaussian Mixture Models (GMMs) are trained using the VLFeat library and the number of components K is set to 256. Therefore for each interest point, a Fisher Vector is formed with dimension $2 \times 256 \times 126 = 64512$.

3.1.1 Datasets

Experiments have been conducted on the following datasets:

KTH dataset [23] consists of six action classes: walking, jogging, running, boxing, waving and clapping. There are total of 2391 videos under controlled background settings. Following the original experimental setup of the authors, video samples are divided into training set and test set according to different subjects.

HMDB51 dataset [13] is collected from various sources. It consists of 51 action categories and 6766 video sequences. We follow the original protocol using three train-test splits. For each action class, there are 70 video samples for training and 30 video samples for testing. This dataset provides both original and stabilized videos, our results are based on the original videos.

UCF101 dataset [25] is the newest and largest dataset

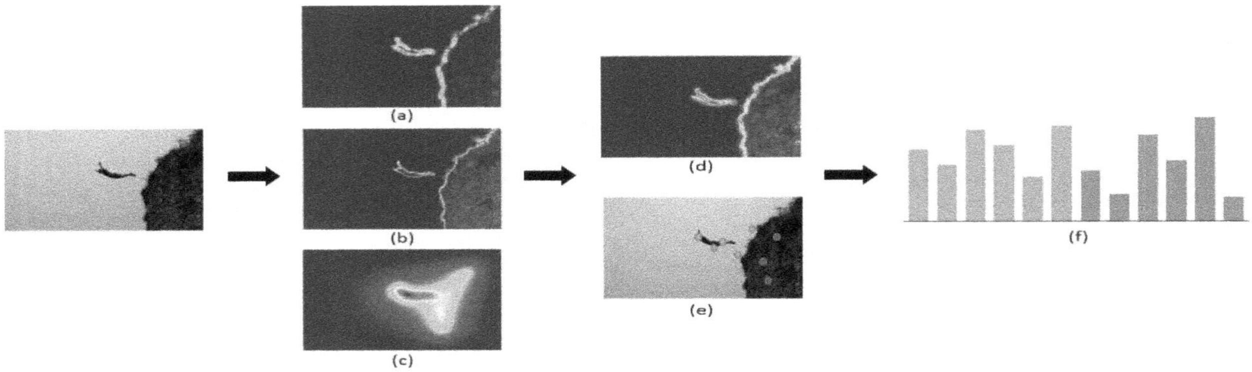

Figure 5: The illustrative pipeline of foreground weight-based pooling strategy. (a) The confidence heatmap computed by optical flow gradients, while (b) and (c) are computed from color gradients and visual saliency respectively. (d) The final foreground confidence map. (e) An illustration of detected interest points in the foreground (blue points) and background (brown points) scenes. (f) The concatenation of encoded vectors of interest points pooling into the foreground and background bins respectively.

which is the extension of the UCF50 dataset. It contains 101 action classes that can be divided into five types: human-object interaction, body-motion, human-human interaction, playing musical instruments, and sports. There are total of 13320 video clips, with fixed frame rate of 25 FPS and resolution of 320×240. Our algorithm is evaluated based on the three train/test splits provided by the authors.

3.1.2 Optical Flow Orientation-based Pooling Strategy

For the optical flow orientation-based method, we compare two optical flow algorithms on the KTH dataset: 1) Horn–Schunck [9] and 2) Lucas–Kanade [19]. As observed in Table 1, the outcomes with Horn–Schunck algorithm outperform that with Lucas–Kanade method. The reason may be that Lucas–Kanade method is a local approach, the optical flow computed for each interest point can differ very much from others. In contrast, the Horn–Schunck optical flow algorithm is a global approach and the optical flow information of each interest point is relatively continuous with each other. Because STIPs extracted by feature detectors are sparsely scattered in the whole video, the global Horn–Schunck optical flow algorithm is more suitable for our algorithm.

At first we divide the optical flow angles into four bins and categorize detected STIPs accordingly. However the performance decreases. As discussed in the Section 2.1, the static STIPs also provide discernable information. By only using four bins, many STIPs with relative small or even zero optical flow magnitudes are very likely ignored. Discarding this information inevitably results in inferior outcomes.

To accommodate for those static STIPs, we categorize the interest points into five bins by adding a *static* category: $-90^o \sim -45^o, -45^o \sim 0^o, 0^o \sim 45^o, 45^o \sim 90^o$ and *static*. Fisher Vectors are computed for each interest points and then standard sum pooling is performed on each bin. After that power normalization and ℓ_2 normalization are conducted to these five vectors respectively. Finally they are concatenated into one representation with a dimension of 322560. Linear SVMs are used as the classifiers. Our experiments demonstrate that by categorizing the STIPs according to the angles of optical flow, the recognition performance can be improved, which confirms our primitive conjecture about pooling strategies.

3.1.3 Foreground Weight-based Pooling Strategy

In addition to the optical flow orientation-based pooling strategy, we also propose a foreground weight-based pooling strategy inspired by [26]. According to Cao *et al.* [4], there are only 18% of all the STIPs detected by Laptev's detector corresponding to the actions performed in the MSR I dataset, while the rest of the STIPs belong to the background. However, based on the discussion in [26], the information of STIPs associated with the background can also benefit action classification. For example the action of riding a bike, the background of a road is most likely associated with the action. Indeed, the background discriminativity can achieve comparable performance as well, which inspires us to categorize the STIPs into foreground and background bins respectively.

We compute the foreground weight by taking into account of motion gradients, color gradients and visual saliency. To cancel out the effect of camera motion, instead of directly using optical flow magnitudes, we compute the derivatives of the horizontal and vertical amplitudes of optical flow respectively, and then the Frobenius form of these gradients. Color information is also an important cue for the foreground. In this paper, we employ the LAB color space to compute the color gradients of each pixel. Then visual saliency is conducted to compute the areas capturing most human attentions. All these three kinds of information are integrated to obtain the final foreground confidence map f_{conf}.

Unlike the approach employed by [26], which applied max-normalization directly to the confidence map f_{conf}, we perform power normalization prior to the max-normalization. This technique is also employed in [22] to reduce the peak phenomenon and improve the performance of Fisher Kernel. Figure 5 illustrates the foreground weight-based pooling strategy and presents visualizations of the confidence maps computed from optical flow gradients (f_m), color gradients (f_c) and visual saliency (f_s). We can observe that optical flow and color gradients are computed with respect

Methods	KTH	HMDB51	UCF101
BoV	91.8	24.5	43.9
FV	92.7	36.2	64.3
OFA	93.2	37.8	66.4
ForeW	92.5	38.0	65.8
Pyramid	93.0	40.2	69.2
Fusion	**93.6 (+0.9)**	**41.5 (+5.3)**	**71.8 (+7.5)**

Table 2: Average accuracies (%) of optical flow orientation-based (OFA) and foreground weight-based (ForeW) pooling strategies compared with BoV, FV, and spatio-temporal pyramid (Pyramid) method on the KTH, HMDB51, and UCF101 datasets. The average accuracies of decision-level fusion of OFA, ForeW and Pyramid are also presented. Improvements compared with the FV method are shown in the parentheses.

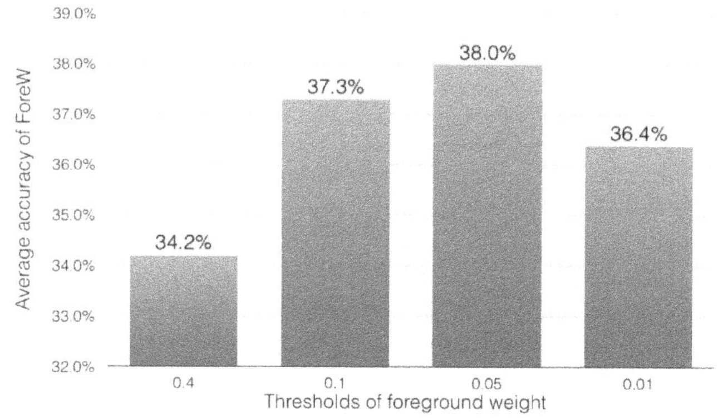

Figure 7: The average accuracies of foreground weight-based pooling strategy on the HMDB51 dataset according to different foreground thresholds.

to motion and spatial edges, while visual saliency providing complementary information about the areas capturing main focus of human attention. The outlines of the heatmap f_{conf} are thicker than that of optical flow gradients and color gradients heatmaps. Therefore, more STIPs are incorporated in the foreground to improve the robustness of our algorithm.

We project the STIPs into two different bins according to a threshold of foreground weight. Fisher Vectors are computed for these interest points respectively. And then same pooling and normalization procedures are conducted as the optical flow orientation-based approach. These two bins are concatenated to form the final representation with a dimension of 129024.

3.1.4 Spatio-Temporal Pyramid-based Pooling Strategy

We also implement spatio-temporal pyramid approach with Fisher Vector encoding procedure on all of three datasets. Six spatio-temporal grids distributions are employed: $1 \times 1 \times 1$, $1 \times 3 \times 1$, $2 \times 2 \times 1$, $1 \times 1 \times 2$, $1 \times 3 \times 2$ and $2 \times 2 \times 2$.

A visualization of our spatio-pyramid approach is presented in Figure 6. How to divide grids distributions to achieve best results is an engineering trick depending on different datasets. Since our paper focuses on a generalized pooling approach, we apply the same parameters of pooling strategies to all the datasets.

By decision-level fusion of spatio-temporal pyramid, optical flow orientation-based and foreground weight-based pooling methods, an improved performance is achieved compared with the baseline.

3.2 Experimental Results and Analysis

As shown in Table 2, the Fisher Vector encoding procedure outperforms BOV words approach on all datasets. The reason is that Fisher Vector is based on a generative model which encodes more higher order information, while BOV words method is based on hard assignments to generated codewords [18]. In following analysis, we choose the results of Fisher Vector encoding procedure with standard sum pooling strategy as the baseline.

The performance of the foreground weight-based pooling strategy is slightly lower than the baseline on the KTH dataset, since the background is relatively clean for the KTH dataset while the majority of the STIPs lay on the foreground scenes, which makes the *static* bin relatively redundant. For the other two datasets, both optical flow orientation-based and foreground weight-based methods have positive influence on the recognition performance. Specifically, for the HMDB51 dataset, OFA method improves performance from 36.2% to 37.8% and ForeW method improves to 38.0%. For the dataset UCF101, OFA achieves an improvement of 2.1% compared with the baseline outcome 64.3% and ForeW method has 1.5% increase.

However, except for the KTH dataset, the spatio-temporal pyramid approach consistently outperforms other methods. It improves 4.0% and 4.9% respectively for the HMDB51 dataset and the UCF101 dataset. Since the dimension of the representation of spatio-temporal pyramid approach is $24 \times 64512 = 1548288$, it is an unwise idea to fuse spatio-temporal method with the other two in the descriptor level or representation level [10]. Decision-level fusion approach is applied to produce a better recognition performance. In our experiments, we apply a geometric mean approach to the KTH and UCF101 datasets and an arithmetical mean method to the HMDB51 dataset to achieve a better performance.

As shown in the last row of Table 2, for the KTH dataset there is 0.9% boost after fusion compared with the baseline results. As for the HMDB51 and UCF101 datasets, the improvements are 5.3% and 7.5% respectively.

We also explore the influence of the selection of threshold of foreground weight on the HMDB51 dataset. As shown in Figure 7, the best result is achieved with 0.05 threshold among four thresholds: 0.4, 0.1, 0.05, 0.01. All the results of ForeW method presented in the Table 2 are obtained with the threshold 0.05.

4. CONCLUSION

In this paper, we have explored the importance of pooling strategies based on the idiosyncrasies of individual STIPs. Specifically three pooling approaches are discussed: spatio-temporal pyramid, optical flow orientation-based and foreground weight-based methods.

Unlike the commonly used sum pooling and max pooling strategies which are performed on the elements of vectors respectively in the global domain and may neglect the discriminative power of different descriptors of STIPs, our proposed pooling framework emphasizes the distinct properties of individual STIPs and therefore renders more discernability to video representations. For the local space-temporal interest points-based action recognition algorithms, the appropriate pooling strategies based on the peculiar idiosyncrasies of individual interest points can provide important complementary information to improve the final performance.

5. ACKNOWLEDGEMENT

This work was supported in part by NSF Grants IIS-1400802 and EFRI-1137172.

6. REFERENCES

[1] S. Baker, D. Scharstein, J. Lewis, S. Roth, M. J. Black, and R. Szeliski. A database and evaluation methodology for optical flow. *International Journal of Computer Vision*, 2011.

[2] O. Boiman, E. Shechtman, and M. Irani. In defense of nearest-neighbor based image classification. In *Computer Vision and Pattern Recognition*, 2008.

[3] Y.-L. Boureau, J. Ponce, and Y. LeCun. A theoretical analysis of feature pooling in visual recognition. In *International Conference on Machine Learning*, 2010.

[4] L. Cao, Z. Liu, and T. S. Huang. Cross-dataset action detection. In *Computer Vision and Pattern Recognition*, 2010.

[5] B. Chakraborty, M. B. Holte, T. B. Moeslund, and J. Gonzàlez. Selective spatio-temporal interest points. *Computer Vision and Image Understanding*, 2012.

[6] P. Dollár, V. Rabaud, G. Cottrell, and S. Belongie. Behavior recognition via sparse spatio-temporal features. In *Visual Surveillance and Performance Evaluation of Tracking and Surveillance*, 2005.

[7] K. Grauman and T. Darrell. The pyramid match kernel: Discriminative classification with sets of image features. In *International Conference on Computer Vision*, 2005.

[8] J. Harel, C. Koch, and P. Perona. Graph-based visual saliency. In *Advances in neural information processing systems*, 2006.

[9] B. K. Horn and B. G. Schunck. Determining optical flow. In *Technical Symposium East*, 1981.

[10] N. Ikizler-Cinbis and S. Sclaroff. Object, scene and actions: Combining multiple features for human action recognition. In *European Conference on Computer Vision*. 2010.

[11] T. Jaakkola, D. Haussler, et al. Exploiting generative models in discriminative classifiers. *Advances in neural information processing systems*, 1999.

[12] A. Kläser and M. Marszalek. A spatio-temporal descriptor based on 3d-gradients. 2008.

[13] H. Kuehne, H. Jhuang, E. Garrote, T. Poggio, and T. Serre. Hmdb: a large video database for human motion recognition. In *International Conference on Computer Vision*, 2011.

[14] I. Laptev and T. Lindeberg. Space-time interest points. In *International Conference on Computer Vision*, 2003.

[15] I. Laptev, M. Marszalek, C. Schmid, and B. Rozenfeld. Learning realistic human actions from movies. In *Computer Vision and Pattern Recognition*, 2008.

[16] S. Lazebnik, C. Schmid, and J. Ponce. Beyond bags of features: Spatial pyramid matching for recognizing natural scene categories. In *Computer Vision and Pattern Recognition*, 2006.

[17] D. Lin, C. Lu, R. Liao, and J. Jia. Learning important spatial pooling regions for scene classification. In *Computer Vision and Pattern Recognition*, 2014.

[18] L. Liu, L. Wang, and X. Liu. In defense of soft-assignment coding. In *International Conference on Computer Vision*, 2011.

[19] B. D. Lucas, T. Kanade, et al. An iterative image registration technique with an application to stereo vision. In *International Joint Conferences on Artificial Intelligence*, 1981.

[20] J. Mairal, F. Bach, J. Ponce, and G. Sapiro. Online dictionary learning for sparse coding. In *Proceedings of the 26th Annual International Conference on Machine Learning*, 2009.

[21] X. Peng, Y. Qiao, Q. Peng, and X. Qi. Exploring motion boundary based sampling and spatial-temporal context descriptors for action recognition. In *British Machine Vision Conference*, 2013.

[22] F. Perronnin, J. Sánchez, and T. Mensink. Improving the fisher kernel for large-scale image classification. In *European Conference on Computer Vision*. 2010.

[23] C. Schuldt, I. Laptev, and B. Caputo. Recognizing human actions: a local svm approach. In *International Conference on Pattern Recognition*, 2004.

[24] P. Scovanner, S. Ali, and M. Shah. A 3-dimensional sift descriptor and its application to action recognition. In *Proceedings of the 15th international conference on Multimedia*, 2007.

[25] K. Soomro, A. R. Zamir, and M. Shah. Ucf101: A dataset of 101 human actions classes from videos in the wild. *arXiv preprint arXiv:1212.0402*, 2012.

[26] W. Sultani and I. Saleemi. Human action recognition across datasets by foreground-weighted histogram. In *Computer Vision and Pattern Recognition*, 2014.

[27] J. Sun, X. Wu, S. Yan, L.-F. Cheong, T.-S. Chua, and J. Li. Hierarchical spatio-temporal context modeling for action recognition. In *Computer Vision and Pattern Recognition*, 2009.

[28] H. Wang, A. Klaser, C. Schmid, and C.-L. Liu. Action recognition by dense trajectories. In *Computer Vision and Pattern Recognition*, 2011.

[29] H. Wang and C. Schmid. Action recognition with improved trajectories. In *International Conference on Computer Vision*, 2013.

[30] H. Wang, M. M. Ullah, A. Klaser, I. Laptev, C. Schmid, et al. Evaluation of local spatio-temporal features for action recognition. In *British Machine Vision Conference*, 2009.

[31] G. Willems, T. Tuytelaars, and L. Van Gool. An efficient dense and scale-invariant spatio-temporal interest point detector. In *European Conference on Computer Vision*. 2008.

[32] X. Yang and Y. Tian. Action recognition using super sparse coding vector with spatio-temporal awareness. In *European Conference on Computer Vision*. 2014.

Image-Text Cross-Modal Retrieval via Modality-Specific Feature Learning

Jian Wang, Yonghao He, Cuicui Kang, Shiming Xiang, Chunhong Pan
{jian.wang, yhhe, cckang, smxiang, chpan}@nlpr.ia.ac.cn

ABSTRACT

Cross-modal retrieval extends the ability of search engines to deal with the massive cross-modal data. The goal of image-text cross-modal retrieval is to search images (texts) by using text (image) queries by computing the similarities of images and texts directly. Many existing methods rely on low-level visual features and textual features for cross-modal retrieval, ignoring the characteristics existing in the raw data of different modalities. In this paper, a novel model based on modality-specific feature learning is proposed. Considering the characteristics of different modalities, the model uses two types of convolutional neural networks to map the raw data to the latent space representations for images and texts, respectively. Particularly, the convolution based network used for texts involves word embedding learning, which has been proved effective to extract meaningful textual features for text classification. In the latent space, the mapped features of images and texts form relevant and irrelevant image-text pairs, which are used by the one-vs-more learning scheme. This learning scheme can achieve ranking functionality by allowing for one relevant and more irrelevant pairs. The standard backpropagation technique is employed to update the parameters of two convolutional networks. Extensive cross-modal retrieval experiments are carried out on three challenging datasets that consist of image-document pairs or image-query clickthrough data from a search engine, and the results firmly demonstrate that the proposed model is much more effective.

Keywords

Cross-modal Retrieval; Convolutional Neural Network; Feature Learning; Deep Neural Network

1. INTRODUCTION

Cross-modal retrieval can extend the services of traditional search engines. Text-to-document search and keyword-to-image search are two major applications provided by search engines. Text-to-document search is a task of single modality. Keyword-to-image search is a pseudo "cross-modal" issue, because the query keywords are matched with tags annotated to the images, not the images themselves. The goal of image-text cross-modal retrieval is to search images (texts) by using text (image) queries without any auxiliary information. The main challenges is how to correlate data from different modalities while capturing their respective inner properties.

There are some approaches proposed for cross-modal retrieval [25, 37, 32, 20, 35, 34, 36, 6, 33]. However, most methods do not pay attention to learning modality-specific features. Instead, they directly use hand-crafted visual features, such as SIFT [19] based bag of words feature, Gist [24] feature, MPEG-7 [21] descriptors and color histograms, and popular textural features, such as latent dirichlet allocation (LDA) [2] feature, replicated softmax model (RSM) [10], one-hot feature and word frequency feature. However, these features have some weaknesses, since the artificial features may not contain enough information that are useful for the different modalities. For example, visual features always reflect one aspect property of image contents, and one-hot feature ignores the orders of words. In [6] and [33], auto-encoders are used to relearn the hand-crafted features. The structure of auto-encoders is not delicate enough to grasp the inner properties of different modalities, which prevents these methods from further improvements.

Conventionally, there are some typical image-text cross-modal datasets employed for evaluation. For example, the Wikipedia dataset [25] is widely used for cross-modal retrieval. It contains 2866 image-text pairs from "Wikipedia featured articles", falling into 10 semantic categories. The texts alongside each image are long descriptions, always resulting in paragraphs. This type of "text" is constructed via words, which has strong sequential and structural information. Another well known dataset NUS-WIDE [4] is also used for cross-modal retrieval task. There are 269,648 images collected from Flickr in this dataset. Different from Wikipedia, each image associates with some tags, rather than textual descriptions. These tags have no sequential and structural information. Additionally, the prior knowledge, namely the class labels for image-text pairs, is provided by above two datasets. In our view, such prior information is not easy to obtain in practice. On the Internet, massive web data contains multimedia components, such as texts, images, audio signals and videos, whereas they are seldom classified. Based on these discussions, we focus on using the datasets that have the following properties:

ICMR '15, June 23 - 26, 2015, Shanghai, China
Copyright 2015 ACM 978-1-4503-3274-3/15/06 ...$15.00
http://dx.doi.org/10.1145/2671188.2749341.

- The data form is image-text pair, and the text part should be sentences or paragraphs.
- The prior knowledge is not provided.

To satisfy above properties, we use three datasets for the experiments: IAPRTC-12 [7], Attribute Discovery [1] and MSR Bing challenge dataset [12].

In this paper, we propose a novel cross-modal retrieval model based on modality-specific feature learning for images and texts. Two types of convolution based networks are employed. Specifically, conventional convolutional neural network (CNN) [18] is used to model the image modality. CNN has greatly boosted the performance of image classification due to its power of image feature learning [17]. We leverage the benefits of CNN to build up the proposed model. As for the text modeling, we also use a convolution based network (WCNN) [15] which has achieved state-of-the-art performance on text classification. WCNN takes sentences in forms of word embeddings as inputs, and performs convolution operations with different filter widths sequentially to the word embeddings. Finally, max-pooling operations are applied to the outputs of the convolution. It should be noted that WCNN can handle sentences with different lengths and outcome feature vectors with the identical dimension.

By using CNN and WCNN, the proposed model can transform the raw image and text data into a latent space while maintaining the data characteristics. To accomplish the retrieval task, we use cosine similarity to calculate the relevance scores between images and texts in the latent space. The relevant and irrelevant image-text pairs are gathered to form the one-vs-more learning scheme: one relevant and more irrelevant image-text pairs are put to the objective of maximizing posterior likelihood of the relevant pairs. By doing this, the objective function can rank relevant pairs ahead of irrelevant ones. Comprehensively, the proposed model associates the modality-specific feature learning with the goal of cross-modal retrieval. Extensive experiments are conducted on three datasets: IAPRTC-12 [7], Attribute Discovery [1] and MSR Bing challenge dataset [12]. The results consistently demonstrate the effectiveness of the proposed model compared with the existing methods.

2. RELATED WORK

The issue of cross-modal retrieval has attracted much attention from researchers. In the past few years, many methods are proposed. Some of them [25, 32, 35, 36] take advantages of prior knowledge (namely label information) while establishing their models, and some of them [20, 34] leverage ranking information. Since the experiments are conducted on datasets in the form of image-text pairs without any additional information, these methods are hardly applied to such data. Thus, we do not make further discussions of these methods.

Generally, methods that can project heterogeneous data into a latent space are potential to do cross-modal retrieval, since the similarity of heterogeneous data can be computed in the latent space. Canonical correlation analysis (CCA) [8] is one of the candidate algorithms. The method in [25] is developed based on CCA. The key idea of CCA is to learn a common latent space in which the correlations between projected features of two modalities are maximized. Once the heterogeneous data is projected to the latent space, some popular similarities, such as ℓ_2 distance and cosine distance, are used to generate search results. Another method is the partial least squares (PLS) [27], which has been used for heterogeneous face recognition [29]. PLS is a regression model to project data of one modality to another through a latent space. Specifically, two data types are first projected to the latent space instead of a direct mapping. Although CCA and PLS are not designed for cross-modal retrieval, they can project heterogeneous data to a common latent space, which is a key step to address cross-modal retrieval.

Recently, some methods based on deep learning are also proposed for cross-modal tasks. In [30] and [23], deep boltzmann machines [28] and deep auto-encoders [9] are employed to model cross-modal data. They result in generative models and learn unified representations for both modalities, but not aim at retrieval task. Kiros *et al.* [16] proposed to use log-bilinear language model [22] to predict word sequences combined with image information. This model can jointly learn text and image features by using CNN. In recent works [6] and [33], the deep auto-encoders are used to do feature learning with the objective of cross-modal retrieval. In fact, the method in [6] is an extension of [23], in which auto-encoders reconstruct both modalities while integrating the objective of retrieval. Similarly, Wang *et al.* [33] utilized single-modality auto-encoders to separately handle different modalities. Both of them use outputs of middle layers of auto-encoders to represent data of different modalities. And their final objective functions are also similar: minimize the ℓ_2 distance of paired cross-modal data and the reconstruction error, simultaneously. Auto-encoder based methods successfully combine feature learning with the goal of cross-modal retrieval and achieve promising results. However, feature learning in auto-encoders is the relearning of hand-crafted features, which is not able to reflect the inner properties of each modality. On the contrast, in the proposed model, two convolutional networks are used to extract modality-specific features, which is verified to be more effective than auto-encoders.

3. THE PROPOSED MODEL

3.1 Notation

Some important notations are first defined. In this paper, we focus on image-text cross-modal retrieval. Suppose the training set consists of image-text pairs $\{(I_i, T_i)\}_{i=1}^{N}$, N is the number of pairs, I_i and T_i are raw image and text data respectively. Let $\mathbf{x}_i$ and $\mathbf{y}_i$ be the hand-crafted features for images and texts. Additionally, T_i is composed of words from the vocabulary $\mathcal{V}$, and the size of $\mathcal{V}$ is M. Embedding vectors $\{\mathbf{w}_j\}_{j=1}^{M}$ are created for each word. The dimension of $\mathbf{w}_j$ is set manually.

3.2 Feature Learning for Image Modality

Convolutional neural network (CNN) [18] is chosen to handle image modality. In recent years, CNN has demonstrated its outstanding capability in several vision tasks, such as image classification [17], face keypoints detection [31]. A typical CNN structure is shown in Fig. 1. Spatial convolution and pooling operations can preserve inner properties of images. In the proposed model, raw images with RGB channels are taken as inputs of CNN, and the outputs of full connection layer are representations for images:

$$\tilde{\mathbf{x}}_i = CNN(I_i), \tag{1}$$

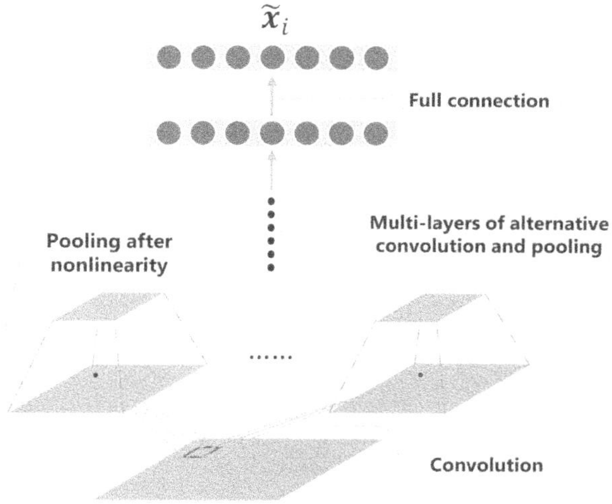

Figure 1: Structure of CNN containing alternative convolution and pooling layers, and full connection layers as well.

where $\tilde{\mathbf{x}}_i$ are image features in the latent space. The details of our CNN structure can be found in Section 4.2.

3.3 Feature Learning for Text Modality

In most previous work, latent dirichlet allocation (LDA) [2] based feature, one-hot feature and word frequency feature are ordinary choices for texts. However, these features have some limitations. LDA relies on corpus to generate topic probabilities. This process needs prior knowledge from corpus and can be influenced by the quality of corpus. As for one-hot feature and word frequency feature, they ignore word sequences and semantic correlations. For example, two words "car" and "vehicle" are semantically similar, and they may be represented as $[\cdots, 1, 0, \cdots]$ and $[\cdots, 0, 1, \cdots]$ in one-hot form. With such one-hot features, the cosine similarity between these two words is zero, which is not rational in practice. What's more, the dimensions of one-hot feature and word frequency feature will linearly increase along with the size of vocabulary. Once the number of unique words is massive, such kinds of features become intractable.

In natural language processing, recent works [15],[3] and [11] propose to model sentences using convolution based structures. The method in [15] achieve state-of-the-art performance on sentence classification with only one convolution layer and one max-pooling layer. We adopt this method (WCNN) to extract text features in the proposed model.

An illustration of WCNN is shown in Fig. 2. The input sentence is represented as a matrix of word embeddings. The word embeddings are aligned to have the same sequence as the words in the sentence. In the phase of convolution, a large number of convolutional filters are applied to the embedding matrix. Filters may have different widths (in Fig. 2, filters in orange and blue have the width of 2, while the width of filter in purple is 3), but they have the same length as the word embedding. It is noticed that the convolution is performed within adjacent word embeddings, which can extract local semantics. The convolutional stride is 1 for

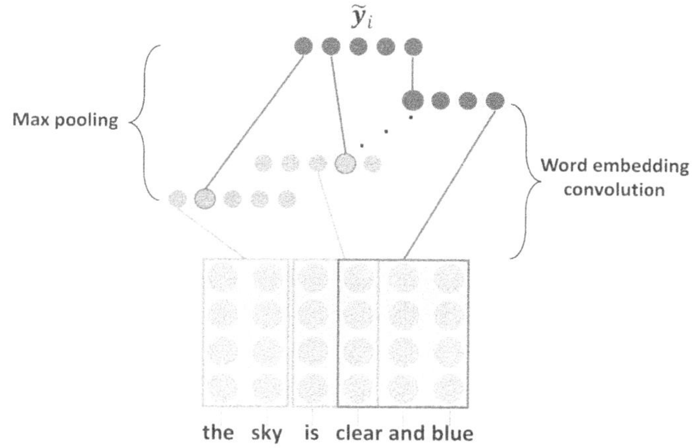

Figure 2: Structure of WCNN containing only one convolutional layer and one max-pooling layer.

all filters, and the outputs of the convolution operation are vectors with different lengths after nonlinearity. Afterwards, each vector is max-pooled to form the final representation of the sentence as illustrated in Fig. 2. The dimension of output feature is equal to the number of filters. This process is notated as:

$$\tilde{\mathbf{y}}_i = WCNN(T_i), \tag{2}$$

where $\tilde{\mathbf{y}}_i$ are text features in the latent space. The detailed calculation of WCNN can be referred in [15].

There are some advantages of WCNN. First, WCNN can naturally handle sentences with variable lengths. The dimension of output features depends on the number of filters, not the length of sentences. Second, the sequential and structural information of sentences can be maintained by convolution and max-pooling operations, which is neglected by one-hot feature and word frequency feature. Third, WCNN is easy to deal with large vocabulary size. The lengths of inputs are related to the lengths of sentences, not the size of the vocabulary.

3.4 Modality-Specific Deep Structure

The structure of the proposed model is illustrated in Fig. 3. The proposed model, named as **M**odality-**S**pecific **D**eep **S**tructure (**MSDS**), is motivated by [13]. Next, we discuss the model in detail.

The one-vs-more learning scheme is adopted here. The model focuses on text modality as queries[1]. For each text query, the text and its matched image form the relevant pair, and the irrelevant pairs are constructed by the text and a few unmatched images. Specifically, the relevant pair is (T_i, I_i). For irrelevant pairs, c random unmatched images are selected $\{(T_i, I_{ij}^-)\}_{j=1}^c$ (c is set to 4 in the experiments). Notice that, in the training process, unmatched images selected for the text T_i are different in each iteration. The input text and images are transformed to the latent space

[1] Actually, the goal of the model is to score the image-text pairs. No matter what the query modality is, the model can be sufficiently learned and then used to do cross-modal retrieval. Here, we use the text modality as queries.

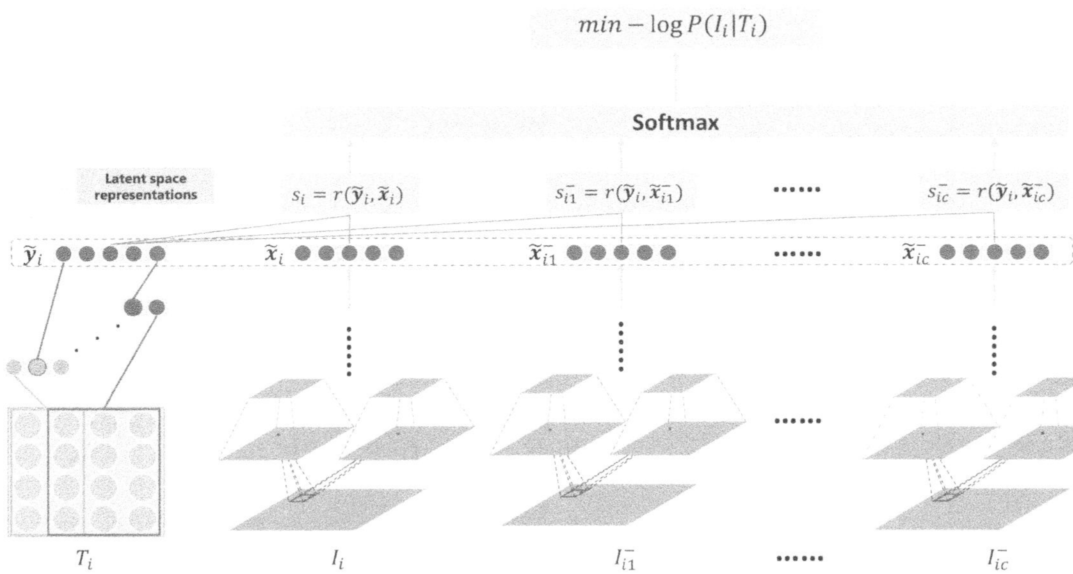

Figure 3: Structure of the proposed model. The one-vs-more scheme can involve one relevant and multiple irrelevant image-text pairs. Image modality and text modality are processed by CNN and WCNN, respectively. The relevance scores of image-text pairs are calculated using cosine similarity. The posterior probability of relevant image given the text query is estimated by softmax function. Finally, a maximum likelihood framework is adopted to optimize the model parameters.

using WCNN and CNNs. In the latent space, the relevance scores of image-text pairs are estimated by cosine similarity:

$$s_i = r(\tilde{\mathbf{y}}_i, \tilde{\mathbf{x}}_i) = \frac{\tilde{\mathbf{y}}_i^T \tilde{\mathbf{x}}_i}{\|\tilde{\mathbf{y}}_i\| \|\tilde{\mathbf{x}}_i\|}. \quad (3)$$

Our objective is to enlarge the relevance scores of relevant pairs while suppressing the relevance scores of irrelevant pairs. To achieve this goal, a maximum likelihood framework is employed. First, the relevance scores of the relevant and irrelevant pairs are gathered to compute the posterior probability of the relevant image given the text query via the softmax function:

$$P(I_i|T_i) = \frac{exp(s_i)}{exp(s_i) + \sum_{j=1}^{c} exp(s_{ij}^{-})}. \quad (4)$$

Next, minimizing the negative logarithmic likelihood of the posterior probability of the relevant images over the training set is formulated as:

$$\min_{\boldsymbol{\theta}} -\log\{\prod_{i=1}^{N} P(I_i|T_i)\}, \quad (5)$$

where $\boldsymbol{\theta}$ is the model parameter, including WCNN parameters and CNN parameters (each CNN substructure in Fig. 3 share the same parameters).

From the description above, the architecture in the proposed model can engage both relevant and irrelevant pairs. This design can make the model sufficiently explore the interactions between relevant and irrelevant pairs, which is not considered in [6, 33].

In test phase, the features for images and texts are first extracted by trained CNN and WCNN. Next, the relevance scores of image-text pairs are computed using Eq. 3. Finally, images (texts) are ordered into the ranking lists according to their relevance scores.

3.5 Variations of the Proposed Structure

Furthermore, two trivial variations of the original structure are studied. The first variation (**MSDS-v1**) takes the hand-crafted features as inputs. WCNN and CNN are replaced by deep forward neural networks (DNN). DNNs are ordinary methods of feature learning without considering the characteristics of a specific modality. This process of feature learning is formulated as:

$$\tilde{\mathbf{x}}_i = DNN_I(\mathbf{x}_i), \quad (6)$$
$$\tilde{\mathbf{y}}_i = DNN_T(\mathbf{y}_i), \quad (7)$$

where $DNN_I(\cdot)$ and $DNN_T(\cdot)$ are DNNs for images and texts, respectively. The comparison between **MSDS** and **MSDS-v1** will provide insights of the power of modality-specific feature learning. The second variation (**MSDS-v2**) only replaces CNNs with DNNs, preserving WCNN. This modification is to prove that features extracted by WCNN are more effective than hand-crafted features, such as LDA based feature and word frequency feature.

The model and its variations can be optimized using standard stochastic gradient descend (SGD) and backpropagation algorithm.

4. EXPERIMENT

In this section, the proposed model is compared with some representative methods on three datasets. The datasets are first introduced in subsection 4.1. Then, the implementation details of the proposed model are described. Next, compared methods and evaluation metric are briefly introduced. Subsequently, the experimental results are shown and discussed.

4.1 Datasets

IAPRTC-12. This dataset is initially released by Grubinger *et al.* [7] for cross-lingual retrieval. There are 19,627 images and each image is attached with several descriptive sentences. The vocabulary size is 4,576. The dataset is split into two subsets: 17,627 images-text pairs for training and 2000 pairs for test. The texts in this dataset are grammatical with little noise. The language in the sentences is well organized and the content of the sentences is closely related to images. As for the hand-crafted features, we use word frequency feature for text modality (the feature dimension is equal to the size of vocabulary) and CNN feature[2] for image modality (the feature dimension is 4096). The same hand-crafted features are extracted for other two datasets.

Attribute Discovery. This dataset is created for visual attribute discovering from noisy text descriptions by Berg *et al.* [1], which consists of 37,794 images. Dissimilar to IAPRTC-12, the texts in Attribute Discovery are in form of sentences but less informative to images with much noisy. The vocabulary size is 27,570. 32,794 image-text pairs are used for training and 5,000 pairs for test. Notably, the content of images is very simple, since each image only depicts one product without background clutter.

MSR-Bing Challenge Dataset. This dataset is originally used for image retrieval challenge [12]. The data is collected from a practical search engine—Bing[3], with the form of triplets: <query, image, click count>. The meaning of a triplet is that an image is clicked several times by users under a text query. In this dataset, there are 23M triplets including 1M images and 11.7M queries, and the click count varies from zero to thousands. In the experiments, image-query pairs with large click counts are selected, since they are highly correlated. The final dataset results in 40,000 image-query pairs for training and 5,000 pairs for test. The vocabulary size is 24078. A difference between this dataset and other datasets is that user queries are short and arbitrary. We notice that the queries suffer typos, near-duplications and reversed order. Additionally, user queries are less structural than sentences, which make it a big challenge.

4.2 Implement Details

In this section, we describe the settings of the proposed structure including WCNN, CNN and DNN in detail.

WCNN. The structure of WCNN is determined by three factors: the embedding size, the number of filters and filter widths. For IAPRTC-12 and Attribute Discovery, the embedding size is set to 25, filter widths are $\{3, 4, 5, 6, 7, 8\}$ and 50 filters are created for each width. For MSR-Bing Dataset, the embedding size is also set to 25, filter widths are $\{1, 2, 3, 4, 5\}$ and there are 60 filters for each width. Thus, for all datasets, the output dimension of WCNN is 300. Additionally, all word embeddings and filters are initialized with random variables. These WCNN settings are applied to MSDS and MSDS-v2.

CNN. The CNN used in the proposed model has the same structure as that in Caffe (details can be found in http://caffe.berkeleyvision.org/). Furthermore, we use the trained model on Imagenet to initialize our model, which is known as supervised pre-training [26]. The output dimension of CNN is 4096 that is not equal to the output dimension of WCNN, thus two extra fully connected layers with sizes of 1024 and 300 are sequently added to the output layer of CNN. The parameters of these additional layers are randomly initialized. This CNN setting is applied in three datasets for MSDS.

DNN. Image DNN and text DNN are used in MSDS-v1 and MSDS-v2. The input dimension of text DNN depends on the vocabulary size, since word frequency feature is used. For IAPRTC-12 and Attribute Discovery, text DNN has two hidden layers (vocabulary_size-512-512), and image DNN also has two hidden layers (4096-1024-512). For MSR-Bing Dataset, text DNN has the structure of vocabulary_size-1024-512, and image DNN is the same as the other two datasets. All parameters for DNNs are initialized with random variables.

Input images for CNN are centered and input features for DNNs are processed to have zero mean and unit variance. The learning rates for WCNN, CNN and DNN are 0.01, 0.001 and 0.001, respectively. Some other techniques, such as ℓ_2 decay and momentum, are also utilized. Actually, the one-vs-more scheme can naturally generate much more data. For example, if there are 100 matched image-text pairs, the number of inputs can reach to $C^1_{100} \times C^4_{99}$. This may partially overcome the overfitting.

4.3 Compared Methods and Evaluation Metric

Some comparative methods are listed below:

- **CCA**. CCA takes the CNN feature and the word frequency feature as inputs to calculate the projection matrices. In the latent space, we use ℓ_2 distance to measure the similarity between two modalities.
- **PLS**. Similar with CCA, PLS also project the hand-crafted features of both modalities to the latent space in which the similarity between two modalities is measured by ℓ_2 distance.
- **corr-AE**. This method is proposed in [6]. Two auto-encoders are used to reconstruct the input hand-crafted features. Each auto-encoder in this method is for single modality, namely the input modality is consistent with the output modality. Particularly, the input layer of text auto-encoder is modeled using replicated softmax [10]. The middle layer is used for features in latent space, and the modality similarity is measured by ℓ_2 distance.
- **cross-corr-AE**. This method is also proposed in [6]. Different from corr-AE, cross-corr-AE uses cross-modal auto-encoders that take one modality as input to reconstruct another modality.

The cross-modal retrieval has two tasks: search images by text queries and search texts by image queries. In previous works [25, 37, 32, 20, 35, 34, 36, 6, 33], the evaluation metric widely used is the mean average precision (MAP). However, in practice, users always care the top ranked results. Thus, we suggest to use top@k precision instead of MAP.

[2]CNN features are extracted using the tool of Caffe [14]. This CNN model is trained based on Imagenet dataset [5]. The output of the *6th* layer is used for features.

[3]www.bing.com

Table 1: Cross-modal retrieval results on three datasets. Two tasks, searching images by text queries and searching texts by image queries, are evaluated.

(a)IAPRTC-12 (search images by text queries)

Method	top@1	top@2	top@4	top@10	top@20	top@40	top@100	top@200	top@500	top@1000
Random	0.0005	0.0010	0.0020	0.0050	0.0100	0.0200	0.0500	0.1000	0.2500	0.5000
CCA	0.0724	0.0943	0.1254	0.1692	0.2171	0.2691	0.3502	0.4511	0.6157	0.8119
PLS	0.1677	0.2569	0.3435	0.5051	0.6152	0.7222	0.8287	0.8899	0.9506	0.9806
corr-AE	0.0285	0.0510	0.0765	0.1412	0.2136	0.3038	0.4730	0.6203	0.8344	0.9429
cross-corr-AE	0.0958	0.1463	0.2171	0.3333	0.4475	0.5647	0.7105	0.8211	0.9363	0.9913
MSDS-v1	0.1750	0.2700	0.3800	0.5590	0.6970	0.8120	0.9170	0.9590	**0.9920**	0.9980
MSDS-v2	0.1860	0.2800	0.3920	0.5680	0.6990	0.8230	**0.9250**	**0.9660**	**0.9920**	**0.9990**
MSDS	**0.2560**	**0.3640**	**0.4710**	**0.6260**	**0.7400**	**0.8360**	0.9210	0.9600	0.9900	0.9970

(b)IAPRTC-12 (search texts by image queries)

Method	top@1	top@2	top@4	top@10	top@20	top@40	top@100	top@200	top@500	top@1000
Random	0.0005	0.0010	0.0020	0.0050	0.0100	0.0200	0.0500	0.1000	0.2500	0.5000
CCA	0.0938	0.1407	0.1942	0.2773	0.3440	0.4225	0.5082	0.5780	0.6779	0.7895
PLS	0.1035	0.1529	0.2095	0.2992	0.3710	0.4383	0.5423	0.6147	0.7263	0.8405
corr-AE	0.1570	0.2385	0.3502	0.5117	0.6284	0.7554	0.8879	0.9439	0.9913	0.9985
cross-corr-AE	0.1009	0.1483	0.2171	0.3491	0.4664	0.5928	0.7416	0.8405	0.9414	0.9837
MSDS-v1	0.1620	0.2600	0.3810	0.5530	0.6870	0.8120	0.9150	0.9620	0.9800	0.9990
MSDS-v2	0.1680	0.2530	0.3710	0.5300	0.6710	0.7950	0.9160	**0.9640**	**0.9920**	**1.0000**
MSDS	**0.2550**	**0.3620**	**0.4790**	**0.6330**	**0.7420**	**0.8320**	**0.9190**	0.9610	0.9880	0.9970

(c)Attribute Discovery (search images by text queries)

Method	top@1	top@5	top@10	top@25	top@50	top@100	top@500	top@1000	top@2000	top@3000
Random	0.0002	0.0010	0.0020	0.0050	0.0100	0.0200	0.1000	0.2000	0.4000	0.6000
CCA	**0.3454**	0.4608	0.4958	0.5362	0.5608	0.5782	0.6112	0.6260	0.6502	0.6832
PLS	0.2044	0.3636	0.4320	0.5250	0.6070	0.6792	0.8392	0.8990	0.9444	0.9638
corr-AE	0.0284	0.1036	0.1592	0.2498	0.3422	0.4478	0.7446	0.8528	0.9274	0.9642
cross-corr-AE	0.1066	0.2514	0.3360	0.4686	0.5818	0.6960	0.9168	0.9706	0.9948	**0.9978**
MSDS-v1	0.1114	0.3100	0.4272	0.5948	0.7208	0.8376	**0.9750**	**0.9896**	**0.9954**	0.9976
MSDS-v2	0.2688	0.5152	0.6184	0.7388	0.8092	0.8696	0.9606	0.9794	0.9920	0.9960
MSDS	0.3298	**0.5748**	**0.6760**	**0.7904**	**0.8536**	**0.9024**	0.9618	0.9828	0.9934	0.9968

(d)Attribute Discovery (search texts by image queries)

Method	top@1	top@5	top@10	top@25	top@50	top@100	top@500	top@1000	top@2000	top@3000
Random	0.0002	0.0010	0.0020	0.0050	0.0100	0.0200	0.1000	0.2000	0.4000	0.6000
CCA	**0.3286**	**0.4376**	0.4746	0.5172	0.5562	0.5874	0.6750	0.7266	0.8060	0.8748
PLS	0.0982	0.1988	0.2530	0.3368	0.4008	0.4810	0.6648	0.7466	0.8468	0.9112
corr-AE	0.0886	0.2464	0.3456	0.4892	0.6038	0.7170	0.9384	0.9810	**0.9964**	0.9986
cross-corr-AE	0.0560	0.1790	0.2674	0.4120	0.5418	0.6724	0.9308	0.9758	0.9952	0.9978
MSDS-v1	0.1122	0.2978	0.4154	0.5816	0.7124	0.8286	**0.9736**	**0.9908**	0.9962	**0.9988**
MSDS-v2	0.1988	0.4358	**0.5528**	**0.6928**	**0.7886**	**0.8560**	0.9582	0.9810	0.9928	0.9968
MSDS	0.2986	0.4134	0.5138	0.6548	0.7502	0.8244	0.8968	0.9330	0.9632	0.9802

(e)MSR-Bing Dataset (search images by text queries)

Method	top@1	top@5	top@10	top@25	top@50	top@100	top@500	top@1000	top@2000	top@3000
Random	0.0002	0.0010	0.0020	0.0050	0.0100	0.0200	0.1000	0.2000	0.4000	0.6000
CCA	0.0060	0.0126	0.0188	0.0312	0.0484	0.0730	0.1986	0.3200	0.5154	0.7014
PLS	**0.0240**	**0.0650**	0.0954	0.1518	0.2072	0.2776	0.5000	0.6226	0.7598	0.8558
corr-AE	0.0010	0.0038	0.0072	0.0154	0.0256	0.0486	0.1638	0.2826	0.4792	0.6674
cross-corr-AE	0.0008	0.0026	0.0060	0.0126	0.0204	0.0420	0.1620	0.2892	0.4958	0.6832
MSDS-v1	0.0106	0.0322	0.0528	0.0966	0.1652	0.2566	0.5332	0.6720	0.8144	0.9090
MSDS-v2	0.0094	0.0326	0.0564	0.1112	0.1776	0.2666	0.5410	0.6870	0.8420	0.9230
MSDS	0.0198	0.0618	**0.1002**	**0.1778**	**0.2602**	**0.3634**	**0.6208**	**0.7488**	**0.8748**	**0.9386**

(f)MSR-Bing Dataset (search texts by image queries)

Method	top@1	top@5	top@10	top@25	top@50	top@100	top@500	top@1000	top@2000	top@3000
Random	0.0002	0.0010	0.0020	0.0050	0.0100	0.0200	0.1000	0.2000	0.4000	0.6000
CCA	0.0086	0.0236	0.0346	0.0598	0.0834	0.1070	0.2154	0.3266	0.5068	0.6626
PLS	0.0162	0.0494	0.0726	0.1128	0.1494	0.1922	0.3174	0.4586	0.6364	0.7834
corr-AE	0.0042	0.0196	0.0370	0.0774	0.1234	0.1858	0.4166	0.5654	0.7528	0.8816
cross-corr-AE	0.0030	0.0086	0.0128	0.0238	0.0352	0.0564	0.1822	0.3110	0.5094	0.6916
MSDS-v1	0.0104	0.0330	0.0676	0.1404	0.2190	0.2568	0.5169	0.6883	0.8536	0.9230
MSDS-v2	0.0100	0.0346	0.0586	0.1170	0.1780	0.2636	0.5272	0.6772	0.8336	0.9162
MSDS	**0.0222**	**0.0712**	**0.1072**	**0.1798**	**0.2614**	**0.3634**	**0.6176**	**0.7418**	**0.8734**	**0.9378**

4.4 Results and Discussions

We present the results of cross-modal retrieval in Table 1. For each dataset, searching images by text queries (the first task) and searching texts by image queries (the second task) are performed. Notice that, there is only one matched image (text) for each text (image). The evaluation metric top@k covers a wide range of k values. In practice, users only concentrate on top ranked items. So the discussions are mainly for top 10% (IAPRTC-12: ≤top@200, Attribute Discovery and MSR-Bing Dataset: ≤top@500).

4.4.1 On IAPRTC-12 (Table 1(a)-(b))

On IAPRTC-12, MSDS significantly outperforms other methods including its two variations in both tasks. Particularly, top@1 performance of MSDS is 25.6% which is much larger than the second 18.6% obtained by MSDS-v2. MSDS-v2 is slightly better than MSDS-v1, which indicates that WCNN offers limited promotion compared with word frequency feature in the scenario of "clean" texts and small vocabulary size. PLS performs surprisingly well. As for the auto-encoder based methods, they achieve unsatisfactory results on the first task (namely searching images by text queries), particularly when k is small. But they perform better on the second task. IAPRTC-12 is the ideal one among three datasets. The good performance of MSDS relies on the modality-specific feature learning that extract good representations for input modalities.

4.4.2 On Attribute Discovery (Table 1(c)-(d))

On Attribute Discovery, the CCA achieves the best performance for top@1 on both tasks. Recall that the images in this dataset are very simple, this may lead to easy correspondences between images and texts, which is considered by CCA. PLS can only obtain good performance on the first task. Although the proposed method MSDS and MSDS-v2 are marginally lower than CCA at top@1 and top@5, they consistently perform well when $k \leq 100$. MSDS-v1 can not get a good performance when $k \leq 10$. This is due to the poor feature learning ability of DNN for text modality. Text descriptions in this dataset are noisy and less informative, and the vocabulary size is larger than that in IAPRTC-12. Thus word frequency feature is less functional. Noticeably, MSDS-v2 can perform much better than MSDS-v1 with WCNN for text feature learning. Auto-encoder based methods do not perform well when k is small, but when $k \geq 500$, their performances are beyond CCA and PLS except corr-AE on the first task.

4.4.3 On MSR-Bing Dataset (Table 1(e)-(f))

As aforementioned, MSR-Bing Dataset comes from a real-world search engine, making it a big challenge. Overall, the average performances of all methods are relatively lower than those in the other two datasets. PLS achieves satisfactory results on both tasks. MSDS still obtains the best performances in most cases. Whereas, MSDS-v1 and MSDS-v2 do not obtain the expected performances. Furthermore, MSDS-v2 dose not get performance gain compared with MSDS-v1 due to the short and noisy user queries, since WCNN is suitable for sequential and structural sentences. In this dataset, auto-encoder based methods are failed to give ordinary performances.

In summary, MSDS is constantly superior than other methods, and its two variations are proved to be effective as well. The good performances of MSDS and its variations firmly demonstrate the effectiveness of modality-specific feature learning and the one-vs-more learning scheme. Although CCA and PLS show their potential to do cross-modal retrieval, they need in-memory computation, which limits them to scale to large datasets. Whereas, the proposed model uses minibatch based stochastic gradient descend optimization that is easy to be applied to large datasets. As for auto-encoder based methods, they do not exhibit the good potential for cross-modal retrieval.

5. CONCLUSIONS

In this paper, a novel model based on modality-specific feature learning is proposed. We adopted two convolution based neural networks, namely CNN and WCNN, to fulfill feature learning for image and text modalities, respectively. CNN and WCNN take the modality-specific characteristics into consideration, and thus they can extract better features from raw data. As a result, data from two modalities are transformed to a latent space where the inter-modality similarity is calculated via cosine distance. Subsequently, the one-vs-more learning scheme with maximum posterior likelihood objective function is used to optimize the model parameters. In summary, we combine the modality-specific feature learning with the goal of cross-modal retrieval. Extensive experiments are carried out on three datasets with different properties, and the results firmly demonstrate the effectiveness of the proposed model compared with state-of-the-art methods.

6. ACKNOWLEDGMENTS

This work was supported in part by the National Basic Research Program of China under Grant 2012CB316304, and the National Natural Science Foundation of China under Grants 91338202, 61203277 and 91438105.

7. REFERENCES

[1] T. Berg, A. Berg, and J. Shih. Automatic attribute discovery and characterization from noisy web data. In *Proceddings of European Conference on Computer Vision*, pages 663–676. 2010.

[2] D. Blei, A. Ng, and M. Jordan. Latent dirichlet allocation. *Journal of Machine Learning Research*, 3:993–1022, 2003.

[3] P. Blunsom, E. Grefenstette, and N. Kalchbrenner. A convolutional neural network for modelling sentences. In *Proceedings of the Annual Meeting of the Association for Computational Linguistics*, 2014.

[4] T. Chua, J. Tang, R. Hong, H. Li, Z. Luo, and Y. Zheng. Nus-wide: a real-world web image database from national university of singapore. In *ACM International Conference on Image and Video Retrieval*, page 48, 2009.

[5] J. Deng, W. Dong, R. Socher, L. Li, K. Li, and L. Fei-Fei. Imagenet: a large-scale hierarchical image database. In *IEEE International Conference on Computer Vision and Pattern Recognition*, pages 248–255, 2009.

[6] F. Feng, X. Wang, and R. Li. Cross-modal retrieval with correspondence autoencoder. In *ACM International Conference on Multimedia*, pages 7–16, 2014.

[7] M. Grubinger, P. Clough, H. Muller, and T. Deselaers. The iapr tc-12 benchmark: a new evaluation resource for visual information systems. In *International Workshop OntoImage*, pages 13–23, 2006.

[8] D. Hardoon, S. Szedmak, and J. Shawe-Taylor. Canonical correlation analysis: an overview with application to learning methods. *Neural Computation*, 16(12):2639–2664, 2004.

[9] G. Hinton and R. Salakhutdinov. Reducing the dimensionality of data with neural networks. *Science*, 313(5786):504–507, 2006.

[10] G. Hinton and R. Salakhutdinov. Replicated softmax: an undirected topic model. In *Advances in Neural Information Processing Systems*, pages 1607–1614, 2009.

[11] B. Hu, Z. Lu, H. Li, and Q. Chen. Convolutional neural network architectures for matching natural language sentences. In *Advances in Neural Information Processing Systems*, pages 2042–2050, 2014.

[12] X. Hua, L. Yang, J. Wang, J. Wang, M. Ye, K. Wang, Y. Rui, and J. Li. Clickage: towards bridging semantic and intent gaps via mining click logs of search engines. In *ACM International Conference on Multimedia*, pages 243–252, 2013.

[13] P. Huang, X. He, J. Gao, L. Deng, A. Acero, and L. Heck. Learning deep structured semantic models for web search using clickthrough data. In *International Conference on Information and Knowledge Management*, pages 2333–2338, 2013.

[14] Y. Jia, E. Shelhamer, J. Donahue, S. Karayev, J. Long, R. Girshick, S. Guadarrama, and T. Darrell. Caffe: Convolutional architecture for fast feature embedding. In *ACM International Conference on Multimedia*, pages 675–678, 2014.

[15] Y. Kim. Convolutional neural networks for sentence slassification. In *Proceedings of the Conference on Empirical Methods in Natural Language Processing*, pages 1746–1751, 2014.

[16] R. Kiros, R. Salakhutdinov, and R. Zemel. Multimodal neural language models. In *International Conference on Machine Learning*, 2014.

[17] A. Krizhevsky, I. Sutskever, and G. Hinton. Imagenet classification with deep convolutional neural networks. In *Advances in Neural Information Processing Systems*, pages 1097–1105, 2012.

[18] Y. LeCun, L. Bottou, Y. Bengio, and P. Haffner. Gradient-based learning applied to document recognition. *Proceedings of the IEEE*, 86(11):2278–2324, 1998.

[19] D. Lowe. Distinctive image features from scale-invariant keypoints. *International Journal of Computer Vision*, 60(2):91–110, 2004.

[20] X. Lu, F. Wu, S. Tang, Z. Zhang, X. He, and Y. Zhuang. A low rank structural large margin method for cross-modal ranking. In *ACM SIGIR International Conference on Research and Development in Information Retrieval*, pages 433–442, 2013.

[21] B. Manjunath, J. Ohm, V. Vasudevan, and A. Yamada. Color and texture descriptors. *IEEE Transactions on Circuits and Systems for Video Technology*, 11(6):703–715, 2001.

[22] A. Mnih and G. Hinton. Three new graphical models for statistical language modelling. In *International Conference on Machine Learning*, pages 641–648, 2007.

[23] J. Ngiam, A. Khosla, M. Kim, J. Nam, H. Lee, and A. Ng. Multimodal deep learning. In *International Conference on Machine Learning*, pages 689–696, 2011.

[24] A. Oliva and A. Torralba. Modeling the shape of the scene: a holistic representation of the spatial envelope. *International Journal of Computer Vision*, 42(3):145–175, 2001.

[25] N. Rasiwasia, J. Costa Pereira, E. Coviello, G. Doyle, G. Lanckriet, R. Levy, and N. Vasconcelos. A new approach to cross-modal multimedia retrieval. In *ACM International Conference on Multimedia*, pages 251–260, 2010.

[26] A. Razavian, H. Azizpour, J. Sullivan, and S. Carlsson. Cnn features off-the-shelf: an astounding baseline for recognition. *arXiv preprint arXiv:1403.6382*, 2014.

[27] R. Rosipal and N. Krämer. Overview and recent advances in partial least squares. In *Subspace, Latent Structure and Feature Selection*, pages 34–51. 2006.

[28] R. Salakhutdinov and G. Hinton. Deep boltzmann machines. In *International Conference on Artificial Intelligence and Statistics*, pages 448–455, 2009.

[29] A. Sharma and D. Jacobs. Bypassing synthesis: Pls for face recognition with pose, low-resolution and sketch. In *IEEE International Conference on Computer Vision and Pattern Recognition*, pages 593–600, 2011.

[30] N. Srivastava and R. Salakhutdinov. Multimodal learning with deep boltzmann machines. In *Advances in Neural Information Processing Systems*, pages 2222–2230, 2012.

[31] Y. Sun, X. Wang, and X. Tang. Deep convolutional network cascade for facial point detection. In *IEEE International Conference on Computer Vision and Pattern Recognition*, pages 3476–3483, 2013.

[32] K. Wang, R. He, W. Wang, L. Wang, and T. Tan. Learning coupled feature spaces for cross-modal matching. In *IEEE International Conference on Computer Vision*, pages 2088–2095, 2013.

[33] W. Wang, B. Ooi, X. Yang, D. Zhang, and Y. Zhuang. Effective multi-modal retrieval based on stacked auto-encoders. *Proceedings of the VLDB Endowment*, 7(8), 2014.

[34] F. Wu, X. Lu, Z. Zhang, S. Yan, Y. Rui, and Y. Zhuang. Cross-media semantic representation via bi-directional learning to rank. In *ACM International Conference on Multimedia*, pages 877–886, 2013.

[35] L. Xie, P. Pan, and Y. Lu. A semantic model for cross-modal and multi-modal retrieval. In *ACM International Conference on Multimedia Retrieval*, pages 175–182, 2013.

[36] X. Zhai, Y. Peng, and J. Xiao. Effective heterogeneous similarity measure with nearest neighbors for cross-media retrieval. In *Proceedings of Advances in Multimedia Modeling*, pages 312–322, 2012.

[37] Y. Zhuang, Y. Yang, and F. Wu. Mining semantic correlation of heterogeneous multimedia data for cross-media retrieval. *IEEE Transactions on Multimedia*, 10(2):221–229, 2008.

Location-Based Parallel Tag Completion for Geo-tagged Social Image Retrieval

Jiaming Zhang[†], Shuhui Wang[†], Qingming Huang[⋆†]
[†]Institute of Computing Technology, Chinese Academy of Sciences, Beijing, 100190, China
[⋆]University of Chinese Academy of Sciences, Beijing, 100049, China
jiaming.zhang@vipl.ict.ac.cn wangshuhui@ict.ac.cn qmhuang@ucas.ac.cn

ABSTRACT

Benefit from tremendous growth of user-generated content, social annotated tags get higher importance in organization and retrieval of large scale image database on Online Sharing Websites (OSW). To obtain high-quality tags from existing community contributed tags with missing information and noise, tag-based annotation or recommendation methods have been proposed for performance promotion of tag prediction. While images from OSW contain rich social attributes, existing studies only utilize the relations between visual content and tags to construct global information completion models. In this paper, beyond the image-tag relation, we take full advantage of the ubiquitous GPS locations and image-user relationship, to enhance the accuracy of tag prediction and improve the computational efficiency. For GPS locations, we define the popular geo-locations where people tend to take more images as Points of Interests (POI), which are discovered by mean shift approach. For image-user relationship, we integrate a localized prior constraint, expecting the completed tag sub-matrix in each POI to maintain consistency with users' tagging behaviors. Based on these two key issues, we propose a unified tag matrix completion framework which learns the image-tag relation within each POI. To solve the proposed model, an efficient proximal sub-gradient descent algorithm is designed. The model optimization can be easily parallelized and distributed to learn the tag sub-matrix for each POI. Extensive experimental results reveal that the learned tag sub-matrix of each POI reflects the major trend of users' tagging results with respect to different POIs and users, and the parallel learning process provides strong support for processing large scale online image database.

Categories and Subject Descriptors

H.3.1 [**Information Storage and Retrieval**]: Content Analysis and Indexing

ICMR'15, June 23–26, 2015, Shanghai, China.

DOI: http://dx.doi.org/10.1145/2671188.2749353.

General Terms

Algorithms, Experimentation, Performance

Keywords

tag matrix completion, geo-location information, social image retrieval

1. INTRODUCTION

The Online Sharing Websites(OSW), such as Flickr[1] and Panoramio[2], have experienced vigorous evolution in Web 2.0 era. Benefit from tremendous growth of user-generated content (UGC) on OSW, the massive number of social tags provide rich information in understanding the content of online images. Therefore, it has become more and more important to discover the true semantic information from the social tags towards the need of efficient large scale online image retrieval.

However, according to the principle of least effort [10, 13], the majority of users usually prefer to choose abstract and fuzzy phrases as tags for the images uploaded by themselves in order to save time on tedious tagging jobs. This phenomenon leads to certain level of incompleteness and noise existing in the manually annotated tags of the ever-growing images on OSW. Therefore, it gives rise to a challenging research problem that how to achieve a sufficient number of high-quality tags for social images based on existing user-generated tags with massive absence and noise.

There are two possible paradigms to solve this problem. One feasible way is classifier-based models [7, 1, 12], which formulate the problem with a standard multi-class classification [2] or multi-label classification [11, 29], and the missing tags are obtained via image annotation process [31, 2]. However, classifier-based methods are highly dependent on the quantity and quality of manual tags annotated by OSW users. Moreover, the rich information in the social attributes (e.g., location, time, user, group) of images from OSW may not be easily incorporated by classifier-based models.

Another way to solve this problem is tag refinement and completion, which aims at alleviating the number of noisy tags [28, 32, 21, 15] and enhancing the number of informative tags [4, 25] by modeling the relation between visual content and tags. Generally, the tag refinement and completion can be achieved by information averaging [14, 4] and latent factor learning [25]. For example, neighborhoods [14] and

[1] www.flickr.com
[2] www.panoramio.com

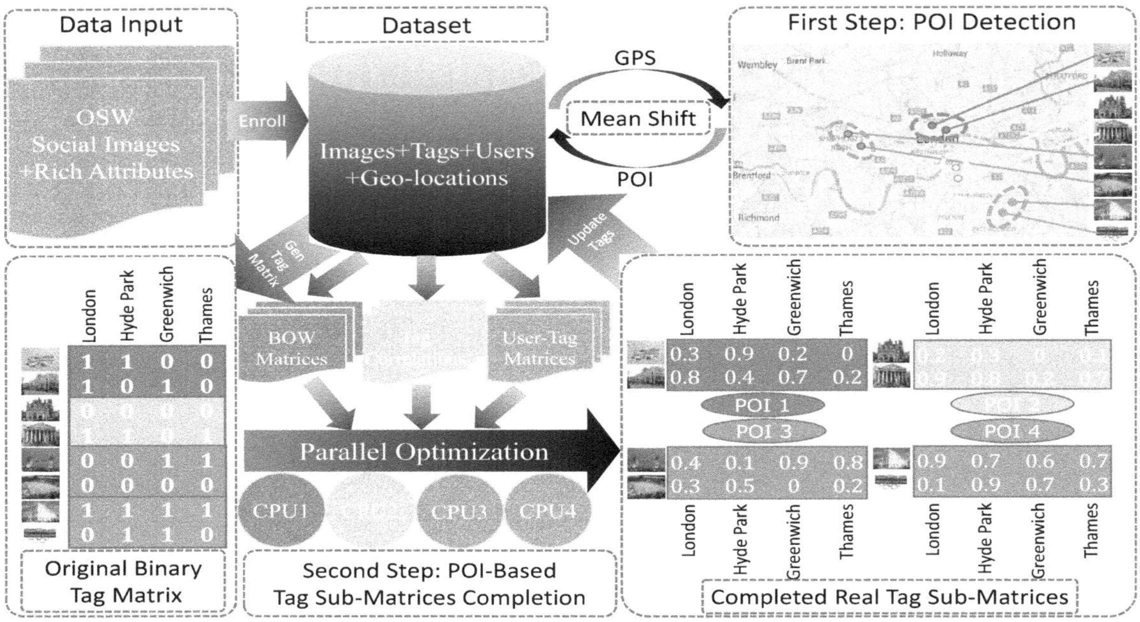

Figure 1: Framework of Location-Based Parallel Tag Completion

graphs are usually exploited, and the tagging information from visually similar social images is borrowed to construct probabilistic description on the uncertainty of the social tags. Wu et al. [25] propose an *image-tag matrix* completion framework based on matrix factorization method, and automatically fill in the missing tags and correct noisy tags for given images. However, existing works have not taken full advantage of rich social attributes and auxiliary information associated with social images.

In general, we consider three key issues to address the tag completion problem. First, the similarities calculated independently on tag space and visual space are different. Such difference should be minimized in order to achieve more semantically consistent representation on both spaces. Second, the correlation among individual tags reflects the tag co-occurrence in real world, and thus provides important hints on the true semantics of visual content. Last but not the least, the social attributes from OSW provide rich information in deriving the true semantics of the images. For example, the location of the image may be strongly correlated with the tags with geographical information. The diversified backgrounds and preference styles of online users also lead to complementary expressions in social tags to the visual content. Therefore, by jointly considering the contents, tags and social attributes (e.g., locations and users), a better social tag learning model can be achieved towards the real world applications.

In this paper, beyond the image-tag relation, we take advantage of rich social attributes of images available on OSW, especially the ubiquitous GPS locations and image-user relationship, to enhance the accuracy of tag completion and improve the computational efficiency. For geo-locations, we define the popular places where people tend to take images as Points of Interests(POI). We discover the POIs by mean shift approach to obtain the geographical clustering result on OSW image collections. We then propose a POI-based tag matrix completion framework which processes the images within each POI in parallel. For image-user relationship, we integrate a localized prior constraint into our proposed model, expecting the completed tag sub-matrices to maintain consistency with users' tagging behaviors in single POI. We formulate the tag matrix completion problem with a unified matrix factorization framework which combines both serial modeling and parallel learning steps. To solve the proposed model, an efficient proximal sub-gradient descent algorithm is designed. The model optimization can be easily parallelized and distributed to learn the tag sub-matrix for each POI. The POI-based parallel tag matrix completion method is formulated into a unified model computation framework as illustrated in Figure 1. The contributions of this paper are summarized as below:

- We propose a unified framework which considers information in visual content, tags and other ubiquitous social attributes such as the location information and the associated user behaviors for learning social tags.
- We decompose the overall tag completion problem into a set of sub-problems with the help of location information. By localizing in geographical coordinate space and matrix partition with respect to the POI, the computational process of the tag matrix completion can be largely accelerated.
- We introduce a user-related prior constraint term into the formulation of our framework. It improves the quality of completed tag matrix, which is validated by performance promotion in automatic image annotation.
- Experimental results demonstrate that our approach achieves higher performance in social tag completion on real world social media images.

The rest of this paper is structured as follows. We overview the related work on several research aspects in Section 2. Section 3 gives notations and definitions of the tag completion problem, and provides a description in detail for our proposed framework and algorithm. We summarize the experiment results on automatic image annotation and tag-based image retrieval in Section 4. Section 5 concludes this study with some suggestions for future work.

2. RELATED WORK

Many algorithms for automatic image annotation have been proposed in the past decades. Both global [7] and local visual features [1, 12] are taken into account for feasible solutions of image annotation. Moreover, several recent works [26, 20] focus on spatial structure of visual content for performance promotion. Most content-based algorithms for automatic image annotation require fully annotated image samples for training confidential models. Despite the developments made by these algorithms, the room for performance improvement of existing automatic image annotation techniques is restricted by this limitation.

Besides general content-based image annotation techniques, many recent works exploit multilabel learning techniques to deal with image annotation as multilabel classification problem. Desai et al. [6] introduce a discriminative model in multilabel learning. Hariharan et al. [11] combine Support Vector Machine with multilabel learning to manage large scale data collection. Zha et al. [29] propose a graph-based multilabel learning approach for image annotation. These multilabel learning approaches usually need complete and well class assignments in the period of model training. However, manually annotated tags on OSW contain many incorrect and noisy ones, which does not match the requirement of multilabel learning approaches.

Meanwhile, several researchers choose other tag-based approaches to solve image annotation problem, such as image retagging, tag recommendation, tag propagation, etc. Li et al. [14] propose a neighbor voting method for social tagging. Guillaumin et al. [9] propose a tag propagation (TagProp) method to transfer tags through a weighted nearest neighbor graph. Chen et al. [4] propose an image retagging approach processing in batch-mode. Liu et al. [16] propose a graph-based algorithm including both tag-specific visual similarity graphs and tag semantic similarity graph to handle image retagging problem. However high-quality annotated tags are also essential for these approaches mentioned above. Therefore, they do not match the reality of manual tags on the OSW.

In recent years, matrix completion techniques are also introduced to address poor initial image annotation problem, getting brilliant experiment results. Goldberg et al. [8] propose a matrix completion for transductive classification. Wu et al. [25] build a concise tag matrix completion computational framework. They not only strengthen the consistency between the similarity of tag semantic and visual content, but also restrict the tag correlation consistency between completed and observed tag matrix.

Besides numerous research works on image annotation, there are many research works focusing on combining geographical attributes and visual content [19, 5, 18, 17, 30]. Moxley et al. [19] adopt geographical based search strategy to provide candidate tags and images which are similar in visual content. To analyze large scale online image collections with both geographical and visual content information, Crandall et al. [5] formularize the image location estimation as a classification problem by classifying images into POI categories. Liu et al. [17] propose a unified framework using subspace learning in personalized and geo-specific tag recommendation for images on OSW.

Algorithm 1 POI-based Tag Matrix Completion Algorithm

Input:
Original Tag Sub-Matrices: $\widehat{T}_k, k \in \{1, \ldots, p\}$
Image-User Sub-Matrices: $\widehat{U}_k, k \in \{1, \ldots, p\}$
Visual Feature Sub-Matrices: $V_k, k \in \{1, \ldots, p\}$
Parameters: $\alpha, \beta, \gamma, \eta, \lambda, \epsilon$
Output:
Completed Tag Sub-Matrices: $T_k, k \in \{1, \ldots, p\}$;
Initialization: $W_1 = I_{d \times m}, T_k^1 = \widehat{T}_k^1, t = 1$;
while $\|\mathcal{L}^{t+1} - \mathcal{L}^t\| \le \epsilon \mathcal{L}^t$ **do**
  Step size $\delta_t = \delta_0 / t$;
  {The loop below is executed in parallel}
  for $k = 1$ to p **do**
    Calculate $\overline{T}_k^{t+1}$: Equation 13
    Update T_k^{t+1}: Equation 17
    t = t + 1;
  end for
  Calculate $\overline{W}^{t+1}$: Equation 14
  Update W^{t+1}: Equation 18
end while
return $T_k^t, k \in \{1, \ldots, p\}$;

3. APPROACH

Our POI-based parallel tag matrix completion framework consists of two steps. The first step is the POI detection step dealing with GPS locations of images by mean shift procedure, which aims at matrix partition preprocessing. The second step is the proposed POI-based tag matrix completion model. Detail information is provided as follows.

3.1 Notations and Problem Definitions

The problem that we try to solve is that given a large scale image collection with abundant annotated tags, how to automatically complement the missing tags and filter noisy tags for tag-related applications. First we denote n as the number of images uploaded by l users in the dataset and m as the number of unique tags. To address this problem, our goal is to automatically complete a real tag matrix $T \in \mathbb{R}^{n \times m}$ based on an observed binary tag matrix $\widehat{T} \in \{0,1\}^{n \times m}$, where T_{ij} indicates the probability of assigning tag j to image i. Each element $\widehat{T}_{ij}$ of $\widehat{T}$ is set to 1 if tag j is assigned to image i and otherwise 0. The i-th row of $\widehat{T}$ can be regarded as a term frequency (TF) vector of all tags for image i. Similarly, we can define the corresponding observed user-tag matrix $\widehat{U} \in \mathbb{R}^{l \times m}$, where $\widehat{U}_{rj} = \sum_i \widehat{T}_{ij}$ if image i belongs to user r. The r-th row of $\widehat{U}$ can be considered as a histogram of tags for user r.

Besides tag matrices, the visual content is also involved in our proposed method. We represent the visual content of images by $V \in \mathbb{R}^{n \times d}$ where i-th row corresponds to a d dimension visual feature of image i. Furthermore, to take the relationship between different tags into account, we define the tag correlation matrix $R \in \mathbb{R}^{m \times m}$. We use cosine distance to measure the correlation score between two tags as follows:

$$R_{ij} = \widehat{T}_{\cdot i}^{\top} \cdot \widehat{T}_{\cdot j} \quad (1)$$

where $\widehat{T}_{\cdot i}$ is the i-th column vector of $\widehat{T}$, as in [17].

3.2 Finding POIs using Mean Shift

In general, large value of n makes the original tag matrix T very large. Therefore, the computational burden for di-

Table 1: Statistics of the Datasets Used in the Experiments

Dataset	Image		User		Tag				
						#Tag per Image		#Image per Tag	
	#Total	#GPS	#User	#Image per User	#Tag	mean	max	mean	max
YFCC100M	99,206,564	48,469,829	581,099	170.72	N/A	N/A	N/A	N/A	N/A
London	1,338,388	771099	16225	47.52	1000	5.2	63	4016.4	481957
New York	1,210,094	732555	15344	47.74	1000	5.5	71	4031.5	299867

rectly handling such large matrices is costly and prohibitive. As discussed in previous section, geographically adjacent images may have similar visual content or semantic information with higher probability. Therefore, we utilize the geolocations as the auxiliary information to partition the whole image collection into isolated blocks for improving the computation efficiency.

We observe from OSM data that there are lots of images uploaded around certain places. That is to say, the areas with massive uploaded images with similar GPS information are potential Point of Interests (POI). Therefore, we apply mean shift approach to detect POIs from the GPS location information (latitudes and longitudes) of social images. With the POI detection results, we can partition all relative matrices into a set of sub-matrices according to POIs. The key step of mean shift procedure is calculated as:

$$m(\mathbf{x}) = \frac{\sum_{i=1}^{n} \mathbf{x}_i g\left(\|\mathbf{x}-\mathbf{x}_i\|^2/h\right)}{\sum_{i=1}^{n} g\left(\|\mathbf{x}-\mathbf{x}_i\|^2/h\right)} - \mathbf{x} \tag{2}$$

where $\mathbf{x} = \langle lat, lon \rangle$ and $\mathbf{x}_i = \langle lat_i, lon_i \rangle$ denote the latitude and longitude of POI center and the i-th image, respectively. The kernel function g is used for density estimation with bandwidth parameter h. The mean shift algorithm is performed in an iterative process, where the update rule is:

$$\mathbf{x}^{(l+1)} = \mathbf{x}^{(l)} + m\left(\mathbf{x}^{(l)}\right) \tag{3}$$

The GPS locations clustering results are gained until the mean shift procedure converges. After that, we achieve our goal for finding POIs. Then we obtain partitioned sub-matrices of each detected POI for our proposed framework.

3.3 POI-Based Tag Completion Algorithm

Without loss of generality, we take POI k as an example for clearer presentation of the formulation of our proposed algorithm. Correspondingly, the notations with subscript k refer to the k POI. For better description, we permutate images in each sub-matrix of $\widehat{T}$ grouping by the users' order in each sub-matrix $\widehat{U}_k \in \mathbb{R}^{l_k \times n_k}$ of $\widehat{U}$ and denote the new one as $\widehat{T}_k \in \mathbb{R}^{n_k \times m}$ $(k \in \{1, 2, \cdots, p\}, \sum_{k=1}^{p} n_k = n)$. For example, image 1, 2 belong to user I, image 3, 4, 5 belong to user II and so on. To build the unified framework of POI-based tag matrix completion, we consider three types of significant constraint terms.

The first type is image-wise constraint terms. To address the coherence in visual content and tags, we penalize the difference of similarities in visual feature space and tag space with a Frobenius norm $\|T_k T_k^\top - V_k V_k^\top\|_F^2$ corresponding to POI k. However, low level visual features are less capable compared to tags for semantic representation of image. To reduce this semantic gap, we introduce a feature mapping matrix $W \in \mathbb{R}^{d \times m}$, which can directly map the visual feature into textual semantic space. Then the visual constraint term is defined as $\|F_k\|_F^2$, where

$$F_k = T_k T_k^\top - V_k W W^\top V_k^\top. \tag{4}$$

Besides the visual constraint term, we also introduce a user-related prior constraint term according to the least effort principle. For all of the images uploaded by the same user belonging to the same POI, the user's tagging behavior tend to have no difference among these images. Without loss of generality, suppose user r has r_u image in POI k. Then we build an auxiliary matrix $A_k \in \mathbb{R}^{l_k \times n_k}$ defined as follows:

$$A_k = \begin{bmatrix} C_{(l_k - r_k)\times(n_k - r_k)} & 0 \\ 0 & I_{r_k} \end{bmatrix} \tag{5}$$

where $C_{ri} = \frac{1}{r_u}$ if image i belongs to user r, and $C_{ri} = 0$ otherwise. The identity matrix $I_{r_k} \in \mathbb{R}^{r_k \times r_k}$ is attached to the rest r_k images lack of user information in POI k by assigning an anonymous user to each image.

Similar as the i-th row of T_k depicting the actual tag distribution of image i, the i-th row in the product $A_k \widehat{U}_k$ reveals the average tag distribution for all the images related to user r. So $A_k \widehat{U}_k$ can be regarded as a refined prior estimation for T_k using the group of images for each user. With the assistance of $A_k \widehat{U}_k$, we define the POI-based user-related prior constraint term by calculating the difference of similarities between $A_k \widehat{U}_k$ and T_k in a Frobenius norm. The user-related prior constraint term is denoted as $\|G_k\|_F^2$, where G_k is denoted as follows:

$$G_k = T_k T_k^\top - A_k \widehat{U}_k \widehat{U}_k^\top A_k^\top. \tag{6}$$

Both visual and user-related prior constraint term compare similarities differences among different images.

The second type is tag-wise constraint terms. Tag co-occurrence is proved to be effective in image tagging [24]. Its key idea is that the more common tags two images share, the higher semantic similarity they have beyond the tags. To maintain the tag co-occurrence consistency of T_k before and after the optimization, we expect a minor difference between the completed and the original tag correlation matrix. The tag correlation constraint term is denoted as $\|H_k\|_F^2$, where $H_k = T_k^\top T_k - R_k$.

Since we reconstruct the completed tag matrix T_k based on an observation version $\widehat{T}_k$, the completed one should be similar to the observed one. That is, we prefer the solution of T_k with small value of a tag consistency constraint term denoted as $\|K_k\|_F^2$, where $K_k = T_k - \widehat{T}_k$. These two tag-wise constraint terms focus on the preservation of consistency between the completed and the observed tag sub-matrix.

The last but not least type is regularization terms. To avoid dense solution of T_k, we require that only a small number of entries of T_k are nonzero, i.e. several unique tags are attached to each image. As studied in many sparse coding literatures, we consider to introduce an ℓ_1-norm regularization term $\|T_k\|_1$ for a sparse solution of T_k. For the shared

Table 2: Performance comparison about MAP for Automatic Image Annotation

London	MAP@5			MAP@10			MAP@15			MAP@20		
	TMC	PTC-U	PTC	TMC	PTC-U	PTC	TMC	PTC-U	PTC	TMC	PTC-U	PTC
r=1	82.37	83.15	85.68	73.42	74.32	78.12	70.45	71.27	73.98	66.87	67.55	71.18
r=2	82.49	83.78	87.50	73.61	75.74	79.70	71.74	71.89	75.22	67.93	68.86	72.47
r=3	82.79	84.03	88.17	73.57	76.57	80.28	69.60	72.43	75.75	67.61	69.46	73.04
r=4	82.87	84.36	88.64	73.65	76.28	80.67	69.62	72.39	76.12	67.75	69.53	73.38
r=5	83.61	85.67	**89.01**	74.60	77.71	**81.75**	71.53	73.96	**77.54**	68.49	70.68	**74.78**
New York	MAP@5			MAP@10			MAP@15			MAP@20		
	TMC	PTC-U	PTC	TMC	PTC-U	PTC	TMC	PTC-U	PTC	TMC	PTC-U	PTC
r=1	77.13	78.06	83.39	68.70	71.79	77.21	65.07	67.62	73.56	62.48	64.30	70.36
r=2	77.41	78.38	85.58	68.90	71.99	77.57	65.09	68.01	72.81	62.81	64.34	69.97
r=3	77.68	78.66	87.33	68.85	71.74	78.52	65.07	67.94	73.90	62.92	64.39	**70.92**
r=4	77.60	78.70	86.84	68.38	71.72	78.84	65.15	67.77	**74.07**	63.00	64.21	70.90
r=5	78.24	79.35	**87.50**	68.90	71.78	**79.17**	65.11	67.73	73.52	62.98	64.27	70.46

mapping matrix W, we also add an ℓ_1-norm regularization term $\|W\|_1$ for sparsity.

Finally, with respect to all of these criteria, we formulate our POI-based tag matrix completion framework as follows:

$$\min_{T_{1,2\ldots,p},W} \sum_{k=1}^{p} \mathcal{L}_k + \eta\|W\|_1 \quad (7)$$

$$\mathcal{L}_k = \|F_k\|_F^2 + \alpha\|G_k\|_F^2 + \beta\|H_k\|_F^2 + \gamma\|K_k\|_F^2 + \lambda\|T_k\|_1 \quad (8)$$

where $\alpha, \beta, \gamma, \lambda, \eta > 0$ are parameters whose values are fixed in cross-validation procedure.

3.4 Optimization in Parallel

As we can see from the formulation above, the ℓ_1-norm regularization terms $\|T_k\|_1$ and $\|W\|_1$ make the whole objective function non-convex. While subgradient descent approach is one of the commonly used iterative methods dealing with non-convex optimization problems. Its remarkable less calculation time per iteration makes it more practical in processing large scale image datasets. So we adopt subgradient descent approach to solve the non-convex optimization problem that we proposed above.

However, we may get dense immediate solutions $T_k^t, k \in \{1, \ldots, p\}$ if we directly use subgradient descent approach to solve the original optimization problem. It will significantly increase the calculation time per iteration. To avoid this potential difficulty, we split the objective function into two parts according to the composite function optimization method [3]. In particular, we construct an auxiliary function as follows:

$$A_k = \|F_k\|_F^2 + \alpha\|G_k\|_F^2 + \beta\|H_k\|_F^2 + \gamma\|K_k\|_F^2 \quad (9)$$

Then the original loss function in equation 7 (denoted as $\mathcal{L}$) can be rewritten as:

$$\mathcal{L} = \sum_{k=1}^{p}(A_k + \lambda\|T_k\|_1) + \eta\|W\|_1 \quad (10)$$

We divide the optimization procedure into two steps for each iteration t.

At the first step we calculate the subgradients of the auxiliary function subject to both T_k^t and W^t as follows:

$$\nabla_{T_k^t} A_k = 2F_k T_k^t + 2\alpha G_k T_k^t + 2\beta T_k^t H_k + \gamma K_k \quad (11)$$

$$\nabla_{W^t} A_k = 2(\sum_{k=1}^{p} V_k^\top F_k V_k) W^t \quad (12)$$

Then we update the immediate solutions $\overline{T}_k^{t+1}, \overline{W}^{t+1}$ of auxiliary function by:

$$\overline{T}_k^{t+1} = T_k^t - \delta_t \nabla_{T_k^t} A_k \quad (13)$$

$$\overline{W}^{t+1} = W^t - \delta_t \nabla_{W^t} A_k \quad (14)$$

while δ_t is the step size.

At the second step, we are going to solve another optimization problem:

$$T_k^{t+1} = \arg\min_{T_k} \frac{1}{2}\|T_k - \overline{T}_k^{t+1}\|_F^2 + \lambda\delta_t\|T_k\|_1 \quad (15)$$

$$W^{t+1} = \arg\min_{W} \frac{1}{2}\|W - \overline{W}^{t+1}\|_F^2 + \eta\delta_t\|W\|_1 \quad (16)$$

Combined with the immediate solutions, we obtain the solution as follows:

$$T_k^{t+1} = \max(\mathbf{0}, \overline{T}_k^{t+1} - \lambda\delta_t \mathbf{1}_n \mathbf{1}_m) \quad (17)$$

$$W^{t+1} = \max(\mathbf{0}, \overline{W}^{t+1} - \eta\delta_t \mathbf{1}_d \mathbf{1}_m) \quad (18)$$

where $\mathbf{1}_d$ is a vector with all ones of the d dimensions.

Parallel processing within POIs. After the introduction of our proposed POI-based tag matrix completion algorithm in single POI above, we discuss the whole optimization procedure in all of the POIs. Since the matrices T, V and U are divided into different POIs in the clustering step 3.2, we conduct the optimization procedure in parallel on different POI-specific sub-matrices.

For the tag sub-matrix T_k of POI k, its calculation progress is independent from sub-matrices in other POIs. But for the feature mapping matrix W, it will lead to abnormal synchronization if each W_k differs from one another among POIs in parallel processing environment. So we make W shared by all of the sub-matrices V_k in parallel computation. Algorithm 1 illustrates the main steps in our solution for the optimization problem.

4. EXPERIMENTS

We evaluate the performance of our proposed POI-based tag completion (PTC) approach on two application tasks: automatic image annotation and tag-based image retrieval.

4.1 Dataset and Experiment Settings

According to our application scenario, we use a large scale social image database published by Yahoo Web Lab[3] called YFCC100M to conduct the experiments. The first row in Table 1 shows some statistical information about this dataset.

[3] http://webscope.sandbox.yahoo.com/

Photos	Ground Truth	TMC	PTC-U	PTC
	london united kingdom westminster big ben parliament palace	london united kingdom biorhythms big ben palace silhouette	united kingdom westminster big ben southbank parliament palace	london united kingdom westminster big ben parliament palace
	london england united kingdom great britain greater london trafalgar square	london england united kingdom great britain greater london city of westminster	london england great britain greater london city of westminster feggy	london england great britain greater london city of westminster rebel
	london england united kingdom great britain greater london river thames	london england united kingdom great britain greater london lambeth	london united kingdom great britain live river thames lambeth	london united kingdom great britain river thames comedian lambeth
	london england united kingdom olympics stratford athletics	london england united kingdom olympics lifelog athletics	london england united kingdom stratford construction athletics	london england united kingdom olympics stratford athletics
	london england big ben architecture night westminster	england big ben architecture lifelog night trafalgar square	london big ben architecture westminster trafalgar square one	london england big ben architecture westminster trafalgar square
	london olympics stadium london 2012 stratford olympic park	london england uk united kingdom 2012 lifelog	london 2012 park olympics olympic park stadium	london 2012 park olympics olympic park stadium

Figure 2: Examples of image annotation results by different methods

Users' tagging behavior in specific POI may become uncertain as the geographical scope goes larger. According to *'landmark-scale'* POI defined in [5], we fix the bandwidth parameter h as 0.005 in the Mean Shift procedure for POI detection. This bandwidth parameter is in correspondence with 500 meters as maximum geographical radius for the POIs detected in our experiments. On the basis of POI setting, we extract two city subset from this large dataset by geographical restriction. We choose two famous international metropolises, *London* and *New York* (also used as the name of the subset), for the reason that there are more images in them than other cities.

For each city subset, we first choose a maximum bounding rectangle on the world map, and then select images whose latitude and longitude fall in the region. Then we totally obtain 1,026,345 and 924,707 images for *London* and *New York*, respectively. As studied in [27], the tag distribution among images is extremely unbalanced and the majority of tags belong to a few images. Then we rank the tags according to its number of annotated images and select the top 1000 to serve as the vocabulary in experiment. After this operation, the size of *London* shrinkages to 771,099, and *New York* to 732,555 respectively. The second and third row in Table 1 show some statistical information about *London* and *New York*.

For both *London* and *New York*, we extract dense SIFT [22] descriptor as local visual feature. Then we cluster randomly chosen 1,000,000 descriptor samples into 1000 visual words. Each local feature descriptor is quantized to one of these 1,000 visual words for Bag-Of-Words representation. After cross-validation procedure, we determine that $\alpha = 100, \beta = 10, \gamma = 1, \lambda = 1, \eta = 1$. For the TMC method, we adopt the parameter settings reported in their paper.

Figure 3: Illustration of some examples in TBIR with single tag queries

The initial step size δ_0 is set as 10^{-6} according to experience.

4.2 Comparison Methods

We compare the proposed method and its weakening variant with a baseline state-of-the-art approach as follows:

- **Tag Matrix Completion (TMC)** [25], which directly completes the tag matrix by exploiting the tag correlation and image examples similarity to ensure the consistency between the observed tag matrix and the completed tag matrix.
- **PTC**, our method containing both user-related prior constraint term in loss function and POI-based matrix partition strategy for parallel processing.
- **PTC-U**, our proposed method without user-related prior constraint term, corresponding to the case of $\alpha = 0$ in Eq. 8.

4.3 Automatic Image Annotation

Given a query image q in automatic image annotation task, we simply rank all the tags in descending order of their probability scores attached to image q, corresponding to the q-th row in T. In particular, to test the robustness of our proposed method to the number of initial tags, we vary the number of initial training tags (denoted as e) for each training image from $\{1, 2, 3, 4, 5\}$. Without loss of generality, suppose image i has m_i manually annotated tags, corresponding to m_i non-zero entries in the i-th row of the observed tag matrix in training set. If $e \leq m_i$, we randomly select e tags as partial annotation for image i. Otherwise if $e > m_i$, we drop out image i from the training set. We use the Mean Average Precision (MAP) at top s ($s \in \{5, 10, 15, 20\}$) of completed tags to measure the performance of different algorithms.

As shown in Table 2, the annotation accuracy goes up along with the increase of the number of initial tags for all

Table 3: Performance of Tag-Based Image Retrieval with Single-Tag Queries

London	MAP@5			MAP@10			MAP@15			MAP@20		
	TMC	PTC-U	PTC	TMC	PTC-U	PTC	TMC	PTC-U	PTC	TMC	PTC-U	PTC
r=1	64.03	64.03	64.03	63.89	64.02	64.03	63.54	63.84	64.00	63.42	63.77	63.88
r=2	72.92	72.93	72.94	72.84	72.93	72.94	72.63	72.74	72.87	72.62	72.68	72.78
r=3	80.86	80.86	80.86	80.77	80.82	80.86	80.49	80.65	80.79	80.39	80.61	80.78
r=4	87.75	87.79	87.79	87.60	87.71	87.79	87.36	87.64	87.75	87.12	87.59	87.75
r=5	90.21	90.24	90.26	90.08	90.17	90.25	89.80	90.11	90.23	89.61	90.03	90.20
New York	MAP@5			MAP@10			MAP@15			MAP@20		
	TMC	PTC-U	PTC	TMC	PTC-U	PTC	TMC	PTC-U	PTC	TMC	PTC-U	PTC
r=1	88.58	88.58	88.58	88.50	88.58	88.58	88.46	88.57	88.57	88.42	88.56	88.56
r=2	93.49	93.49	93.49	93.48	93.49	93.49	93.47	93.46	93.46	93.44	93.46	93.46
r=3	95.43	95.43	95.43	95.43	95.43	95.43	95.43	95.43	95.43	95.43	95.43	95.43
r=4	97.14	97.15	97.15	97.13	97.15	97.14	97.13	97.13	97.13	97.13	97.13	97.13
r=5	98.74	98.74	98.74	98.74	98.74	98.74	98.74	98.74	98.74	98.74	98.73	98.73

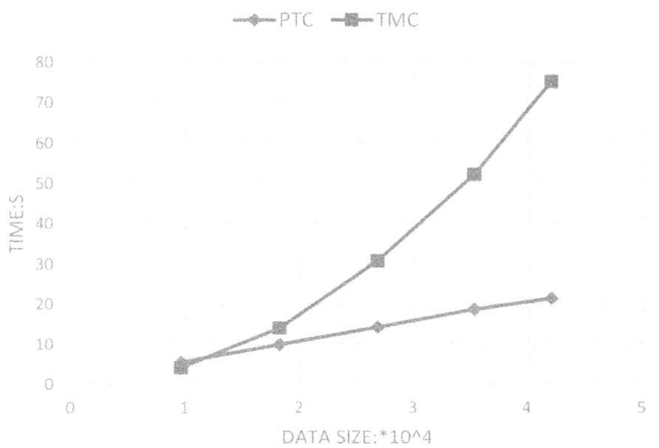

Figure 4: CPU Execution Time of different methods

methods in vertical comparison. It is in line with our expectation because more initial tags for each image means lower systemic risk. In horizontal comparison, we observe that the proposed PTC approach outperforms its weakening variant PTC-U method and PTC-U method outperforms the TMC method. This experimental phenomenon demonstrates that both our matrix partition strategy and user-related prior constraint term make contributions to the performance promotion. The matrix partition strategy makes locality consistency more compact in tag space. And the user-related prior constraint term makes coincidence with common sense. Figure 2 shows several annotation results selected from *London* in condition of $e = 5$.

4.4 Tag-Based Image Retrieval

In tag-based image retrieval task, we consider a simple scenario that the query is a single tag. We rank all of the gallery images according to their relevance scores to the given query tag in descending order as the retrieval results. The relevance score of each image to the given query tag is represented by the corresponding column in the completed tag matrix T. Since every tag can be used as a query, we exploit all of the 1,000 tags in the vocabulary as queries. We keep the same setting of initial training tags as in automatic image annotation task. However we do not distinguish training or testing images. Instead we gather all the images in each dataset to serve as gallery images for retrieval. The rule of the relevance between image and query tag [23] [27] we adopt in the experiment is that: an image is relevant if its annotation contains the query.

Table 3 shows the MAP at top s ($s \in \{5, 10, 15, 20\}$) results of tag-based image retrieval using single tag queries for *London* and *New York*. We can see that there is almost no significant difference in performance between all of the three methods. It means that our method has little promotion compared with the TMC method. We attribute this phenomenon to poor original annotation which we used as ground truth.

However, we observe that the MAP value of our PTC method decreases more slowly than the TMC method as the number of recall results goes up. It reveals that our proposed method is more robust than the TMC method to a certain extent. Figure 3 illustrates some examples of single tag queries and the images returned by different methods in *New York*. Each word on the left side is the tag query. Besides each query, images displayed in three rows are the retrieval results corresponding to our proposed PTC method, the PTC-U method, and the TMC method from top to bottom, respectively.

4.5 Computational Efficiency Analysis

We evaluate the computational efficiency of our proposed PTC method and the TMC method. To make fair environment for comparison, we use the same hardware and software platform to calculate the running time in each iteration. Both of the two algorithms are implemented on MATLAB R2014a, and run on the Intel (R) Core (TM) i7-4770K CPU @3.50 GHz and 32 GB RAM PC. Figure 4 reveals the running time per iteration of both PTC and TMC method. The shape of the curves demonstrates that our proposed PTC method has much less computational time cost than the TMC method as the increase of scalability. There is no surprising that our parallel computational framework conducted by matrix partition strategy is the key point of efficiency improvement.

5. CONCLUSIONS AND FUTURE WORK

In this paper, we propose an efficient POI-based parallel tag matrix completion method for social image tagging and retrieval. By using geo-location information, we exploit clustering results as auxiliary clustering labels to make the framework easily processed in parallel. Then by using image-user relationship, we introduce a localized prior constraint term to improve the performance for tag prediction. In order to evaluate our method, we conduct experiments on two applications: automatic image annotation and tag-based image retrieval. Extensive experiments on two subsets of a new large scale social image dataset illustrate that the proposed method not only achieves better accuracy for automatic image annotation than the state-of-the-art method, but also enhances the computational efficiency. In future work, we combine our method with stream clustering techniques to handle streaming social images according to reality scenario. And we would like to improve our method to handle variant tag vocabulary.

6. ACKNOWLEDGMENTS

This work was supported in part by National Basic Research Program of China (973 Program) : 2012CB316400 and 2015CB351802, National Natural Science Foundation of China : 61025011, 61332016, 61390511 and 61303160, 863 program of China : 2014AA015202, Postdoctoral Science Foundation of China : 2014T70126, and Basic Research Program of Shenzhen: JCYJ20140610152828686.

7. REFERENCES

[1] K. Barnard, P. Duygulu, D. Forsyth, N. De Freitas, D. M. Blei, and M. I. Jordan. Matching words and pictures. *Journal of Machine Learning Research*, 3:1107–1135, 2003.

[2] G. Carneiro, A. B. Chan, P. J. Moreno, and N. Vasconcelos. Supervised learning of semantic classes for image annotation and retrieval. *Pattern Analysis and Machine Intelligence, IEEE Transactions on*, 29(3):394–410, 2007.

[3] C. Cartis, N. I. Gould, and P. L. Toint. On the evaluation complexity of composite function minimization with applications to nonconvex nonlinear programming. *SIAM Journal on Optimization*, 21(4):1721–1739, 2011.

[4] L. Chen, D. Xu, I. W. Tsang, and J. Luo. Tag-based web photo retrieval improved by batch mode re-tagging. In *Computer Vision and Pattern Recognition (CVPR), 2010 IEEE Conference on*, pages 3440–3446. IEEE, 2010.

[5] D. J. Crandall, L. Backstrom, D. Huttenlocher, and J. Kleinberg. Mapping the world's photos. In *WWW'09*, pages 761–770. ACM, 2009.

[6] C. Desai, D. Ramanan, and C. C. Fowlkes. Discriminative models for multi-class object layout. *International Journal of Computer Vision*, 95(1):1–12, 2011.

[7] K.-S. Goh, E. Y. Chang, and B. Li. Using one-class and two-class svms for multiclass image annotation. *Knowledge and Data Engineering, IEEE Transactions on*, 17(10):1333–1346, 2005.

[8] A. Goldberg, B. Recht, J. Xu, R. Nowak, and X. Zhu. Transduction with matrix completion: Three birds with one stone. In *Advances in neural information processing systems*, pages 757–765, 2010.

[9] M. Guillaumin, T. Mensink, J. Verbeek, and C. Schmid. Tagprop: Discriminative metric learning in nearest neighbor models for image auto-annotation. In *Computer Vision, 2009 IEEE 12th International Conference on*, pages 309–316. IEEE, 2009.

[10] H. Halpin, V. Robu, and H. Shepherd. The complex dynamics of collaborative tagging. In *Proceedings of the 16th international conference on World Wide Web*, pages 211–220. ACM, 2007.

[11] B. Hariharan, L. Zelnik-Manor, M. Varma, and S. Vishwanathan. Large scale max-margin multi-label classification with priors. In *Proceedings of the 27th International Conference on Machine Learning (ICML-10)*, pages 423–430, 2010.

[12] Y.-G. Jiang, C.-W. Ngo, and J. Yang. Towards optimal bag-of-features for object categorization and semantic video retrieval. In *Proceedings of the 6th ACM international conference on Image and video retrieval*, pages 494–501. ACM, 2007.

[13] M. E. Kipp and D. G. Campbell. Patterns and inconsistencies in collaborative tagging systems: An examination of tagging practices. *Proceedings of the American Society for Information Science and Technology*, 43(1):1–18, 2006.

[14] X. Li, C. G. Snoek, and M. Worring. Learning social tag relevance by neighbor voting. *Multimedia, IEEE Transactions on*, 11(7):1310–1322, 2009.

[15] X. Li, T. Uricchio, L. Ballan, M. Bertini, C. G. Snoek, and A. Del Bimbo. Socializing the semantic gap: A comparative survey on image tag assignment, refinement and retrieval. *arXiv preprint arXiv:1503.08248*, 2015.

[16] D. Liu, S. Yan, X.-S. Hua, and H.-J. Zhang. Image retagging using collaborative tag propagation. *Multimedia, IEEE Transactions on*, 13(4):702–712, 2011.

[17] J. Liu, Z. Li, J. Tang, Y. Jiang, and H. Lu. Personalized geo-specific tag recommendation for photos on social websites. *IEEE Transactions on Multimedia*, 16(3):588–600, 2014.

[18] S. Liu, Y. Liu, L. M. Ni, J. Fan, and M. Li. Towards mobility-based clustering. In *Proceedings of the 16th ACM SIGKDD international conference on Knowledge discovery and data mining*, pages 919–928. ACM, 2010.

[19] E. Moxley, J. Kleban, and B. Manjunath. Spirittagger: a geo-aware tag suggestion tool mined from flickr. In *ACM MIR*, pages 24–30. ACM, 2008.

[20] B. C. Russell, A. Torralba, K. P. Murphy, and W. T. Freeman. Labelme: a database and web-based tool for image annotation. *International journal of computer vision*, 77(1-3):157–173, 2008.

[21] J. Sang, C. Xu, and J. Liu. User-aware image tag refinement via ternary semantic analysis. *Multimedia, IEEE Transactions on*, 14(3):883–895, 2012.

[22] A. Vedaldi and B. Fulkerson. Vlfeat: An open and portable library of computer vision algorithms. In *ACM Multimedia*, pages 1469–1472. ACM, 2010.

[23] L. Wu, S. C. Hoi, R. Jin, J. Zhu, and N. Yu. Distance metric learning from uncertain side information with application to automated photo tagging. In *ACM Multimedia*, pages 135–144. ACM, 2009.

[24] L. Wu, X.-S. Hua, N. Yu, W.-Y. Ma, and S. Li. Flickr distance. In *ACM Multimedia'08*, pages 31–40. ACM, 2008.

[25] L. Wu, R. Jin, and A. K. Jain. Tag completion for image retrieval. *Pattern Analysis and Machine Intelligence, IEEE Transactions on*, 35(3):716–727, 2013.

[26] L. Wu, M. Li, Z. Li, W.-Y. Ma, and N. Yu. Visual language modeling for image classification. In *Proceedings of the International Workshop on MIR*, pages 115–124. ACM, 2007.

[27] L. Wu, L. Yang, N. Yu, and X.-S. Hua. Learning to tag. In *WWW'09*, pages 361–370. ACM, 2009.

[28] H. Xu, J. Wang, X.-S. Hua, and S. Li. Tag refinement by regularized lda. In *Proceedings of the 17th ACM international conference on Multimedia*, pages 573–576. ACM, 2009.

[29] Z.-J. Zha, T. Mei, J. Wang, Z. Wang, and X.-S. Hua. Graph-based semi-supervised learning with multiple labels. *Journal of Visual Communication and Image Representation*, 20(2):97–103, 2009.

[30] J. Zheng, S. Liu, and L. M. Ni. User characterization from geographic topic analysis in online social media. In *Advances in Social Networks Analysis and Mining (ASONAM), 2014 IEEE/ACM International Conference on*, pages 464–471. IEEE, 2014.

[31] N. Zhou, W. K. Cheung, G. Qiu, and X. Xue. A hybrid probabilistic model for unified collaborative and content-based image tagging. *Pattern Analysis and Machine Intelligence, IEEE Transactions on*, 33(7):1281–1294, 2011.

[32] G. Zhu, S. Yan, and Y. Ma. Image tag refinement towards low-rank, content-tag prior and error sparsity. In *Proceedings of the international conference on Multimedia*, pages 461–470. ACM, 2010.

Exploiting Spatial Relationship between Scenes for Hierarchical Video Geotagging

Yifang Yin, Luming Zhang, Roger Zimmermann
School of Computing, National University of Singapore, Singapore 117417
{yifang,zglumg,rogerz}@comp.nus.edu.sg

ABSTRACT

Predicting the location of a video based on its content is a very meaningful, yet very challenging problem. Most existing work has focused on developing representative visual features and then searching for visually nearest neighbors in the development set to achieve a prediction. Interestingly, the relationship between scenes has been overlooked in prior work. Two scenes that are visually different, but frequently co-occur in same location, should naturally be considered similar for the geotagging problem. To build upon the above ideas, we propose to model the geo-spatial distributions of scenes by Gaussian Mixture Models (GMMs) and measure the distribution similarity by the Jensen-Shannon divergence (JSD). Subsequently, we present the Spatial Relationship Model (SRM) for geotagging which integrates the geo-spatial relationship of scenes into a hierarchical framework. We segment the Earth's surface into multiple levels of grids and measure the likelihood of input videos with an adaptation to region granularities. We have evaluated our approach using the YFCC100M dataset in the context of the MediaEval 2014 placing task. The total set of 35,000 geotagged videos is further divided into a training set of 25,000 videos and a test set of 10,000 videos. Our experimental results demonstrate the effectiveness of our proposed framework, as our solution achieves good accuracy and outperforms existing visual approaches for video geotagging.

Categories and Subject Descriptors

H.3.3 [**Information Storage and Retrieval**]: Information Search and Retrieval

General Terms

Algorithm, Experimentation

Keywords

Video geotagging, visual approach, scene distribution modeling, spatial relationship analysis

ICMR '15, June 23 - 26, 2015, Shanghai, China.

http://dx.doi.org/10.1145/2671188.2749354.

1. INTRODUCTION

Nowadays, video recording and sharing have become popular activities in people's lives. Due to the increasing number of sensor-equipped cameras and smartphones, geo-metadata can be automatically recorded together with multimedia content. The geo-context is of great importance, as it facilitates many location-based applications such as annotation [19, 25] and retrieval [24]. However, the number of geotagged videos is still very limited on content sharing platforms. According to Song *et al.* [21], only 2.5% of the most-viewed videos on YouTube are geotagged. Therefore, predicting the geographic location of where a video was captured has become an urgent yet challenging task in recent years. In the MediaEval benchmarking initiative, the Placing Task is held every year to capture the challenge of estimating the geo-locations of multimedia items. Since the geo-coordinates associated with multimedia items, which are used as the ground truth, do not always mark the precise locations, the methods are usually evaluated at different geographical margins of error of 0.1 km, 1 km, 10 km, 100 km, 1,000 km, and 10,000 km [11]. The process of estimating a capture location is often known as geotagging in the multimedia field [15].

Estimating the geo-location of a video can be achieved based on visual features [17, 14], textual information [18], social context [21], and their combinations [12, 23, 20]. Considering that some textual and social metadata used in multimodal frameworks are not always available in real life, visual approaches for video geocoding are important because they infer the geo-coordinates of a video using the visual content only. Based on the idea that videos located adjacently share similar visual content, efforts have been made to develop compact and high-level video representations to improve geocoding accuracy [9, 17]. In the most recent geotagging approaches, spatial segmentation is usually adopted [10, 18]. This method maps the original task into a classification problem. Considering the difference in granularity between spatial cells and input videos, new challenges have been revealed in feature pooling and matching techniques.

In the most recent visual approaches for video geocoding, the Bag-of-Scenes (BoS) model has been shown to be simple and effective [17, 12]. This approach first generates a dictionary of scenes, each of which represents a specific semantic concept. Next, it assigns frames to one or more visual scenes, followed by a pooling step to generate the final representation. However, one limitation is that such methods assume the scenes in the dictionary to be independent. More emphasis should be placed on modeling the relationship among scenes to achieve better performance. In this study, we analyze the geo-distributions of scenes in different spatial segments. The raw geo-coordinates of frames are replaced and smoothed with Gaussian distributions. The reason for substituting the geo-coordinates with continuous kernel functions is to reduce the sensitivity to noise in the data. Subsequently, we measure the spatial similarity of scenes based on their distributions using the Jensen-Shannon divergence (JSD), and discuss its use in geotagging problems. The contributions of this paper are twofold: (1) we model the connections between scenes by comparing their geo-spatial distributions, and (2) we integrate the spatial relationship of scenes into a hierarchical geotagging framework that can achieve better accuracies. The basic idea is that *scenes that show similar geo-spatial patterns are more likely to be captured in the same video.* As shown in Figure 1, our proposed geotagging system hierarchically segments the Earth's surface into grids with different granularities. We not only pool the visual features, but also measure the spatial similarity of scenes in each of the cells in the hierarchy. Given a test video, we extract the same visual features, and estimate the posterior probability based on both the visual similarity and the spatial consistency. Using a dataset of 35,000 Flickr videos, we show that our method outperforms existing visual approaches by exploiting the spatial patterns of scenes.

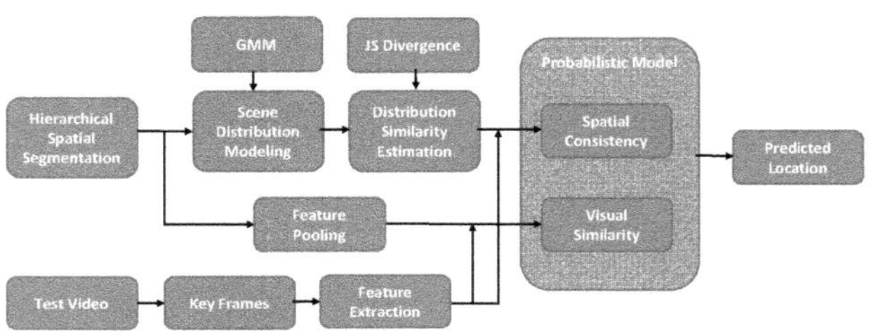

Figure 1: The proposed hierarchical framework for video geotagging.

The rest of this paper is organized as follows. We first report on the important related work in Section 2. Next, we discuss the limitations of existing approaches and present our solution in Section 3. We introduce the distribution modeling and similarity estimation of scenes in Section 4. The proposed hierarchical framework is introduced in Section 5. The thorough experimental results of Section 6 validate the effectiveness of our system. Section 7 concludes and suggests future work.

2. RELATED WORK

Video geotagging has become a popular topic in recent years. Started from 2010, MediaEval has offered a placing task as an annual competition of web video geocoding [11]. Leveraging the textual annotations and visual features, approaches have been proposed to map the original placing task into a classification problem. Serdyukov *et al.* [18] segmented the Earth's surface into an $m \times n$ grid, and then estimated a language model from the textual annotations in each cell. After applying smoothing techniques to the spatial ambiguity, they were able to classify a test video into the cell with the highest probability. Kelm *et al.* [10] proposed a hierarchical spatial segmentation framework for video geotagging. Not only textual information but also visual features were pooled for each spatial segment at different hierarchy levels. Hays and Efros [7] proposed a purely visual approach that estimates image locations as a probability distribution over the globe. Penatti *et al.* [17] followed this line of thought and proposed an approach called Bag-of-Scenes for video location prediction. Song *et al.* [21] proposed to utilize the social relationship between web videos to propagate the geotags. They established this relationship graph by considering semantically related and same-author videos. Multimodel geocoding frameworks [12, 23, 6, 20] have also been proposed that process multiple sources of information for effective location estimation. Trevisio *et al.* [23] presented a divide & conquer strategy to better exploit the tags associated with videos. A multimodal approach was adopted which processes the information sources by decreasing order of expected informativeness: tags, user's upload history and social graph, user's personal information (home town) and visual content. Hare *et al.* [6] estimated a continuous probability density function (PDF) over the surface of the Earth from multiple features including location prior, tags, and a number of visual features. By simultaneously taking the social, visual, and textual relationships into consideration, Song *et al.* [20] modeled the geotagging problem as a propagation of the geography information among the web video social networks.

The task of predicting a video location by exclusively using the visual content has drawn much research attention in the computer vision community. However, according to Kelm *et al.* [10], visual features alone show low correlation with locations and a purely visual approach achieves limited precision. Traditionally videos can be represented by global features such as color, texture, and edge descriptors [10], local features such as SIFT and SURF [14], or motion features such as HMP [2]. To reduce the high dimensionality of visual features, methods have been developed to aggregate image descriptors into compact codes while preserving accuracy [9, 23]. As Penatti *et al.* [17] pointed out, scenes are elements with more semantic information in videos. Therefore, they presented a high-level video representation based on a dictionary of scenes. The distance between videos can be calculated by the Euclidean norm. Since videos located adjacently usually share similar content, most visual approaches estimate the location of a test video based on its most visually similar neighbors in the development set. We can either use the geo-coordinate of the first nearest neighbor as the prediction [7, 12, 17], or interpret it as a voting result of the top k nearest neighbors [7, 23]. For the prediction of image locations, Li *et al.* [14] modeled a location as an area and ranked images by comparing among their geo-visual neighbors as well. Thus, they were able to enrich the visual aspects of a location and therefore achieved better performance.

3. VIDEO LOCATION MODELING

The problem of estimating the geotag associated with a video can be seen as determining the location g with the highest probability where the video v was recorded,

$$\underset{g}{\text{argmax}}\ P(g|v) \tag{1}$$

By applying Bayes' law, the posterior probability $P(g|v)$ can be formulated as Eq. 2 if we assume that the video prior $P(v)$ is uniformly distributed.

$$P(g|v) \propto P(v|g)P(g) \tag{2}$$

Here $P(v|g)$ denotes the likelihood of video v given location g, and $P(g)$ represents the prior probability of location g where a video was captured.

Researchers have attempted to find a good estimation of $P(v|g)$ based on various assumptions. Next, we will briefly introduce the previous visual approaches, most of which have only considered the visual similarity between video v and location g when estimating $P(v|g)$. Subsequently, we will discuss existing issues and then illustrate our proposed solution.

3.1 Visual Similarity

Traditionally, a location has been modeled by a single photo [7]. The visual similarity between a test video v and a training video with a geotag of g was used as an estimate for $P(v|g)$. In image geotagging, Li *et al.* [14] argued that one photo only covers limited visual aspects of a location, and therefore they modeled a location as an area with the set of images in it. A similar idea has also been applied in video geotagging. Kelm *et al.* [10] proposed to hierarchically segment the Earth's surface and pool visual features for each spatial segment using the mean value. Thereafter, regions and videos can be directly compared and the most visually similar spatial segment is determined iteratively by calculating the Euclidean norm. Although promising results were reported, one major issue with this approach is that it ignores the granularity difference between regions and videos. This simplification hinders achieving a better accuracy.

To illustrate this problem, let us adopt the BoS [17] model for the high-level visual descriptors of videos. Given a dictionary of scenes $S = \{s_1, s_2, \ldots, s_n\}$, a video can be represented by a vector whose length equals the dictionary size, $X_v = \{x_1^v, x_2^v, \ldots, x_n^v\}$. Each element x_i^v can be interpreted as the saliency score of its corresponding scene s_i based on its appearance in the video. Similarly, the BoS descriptor can also be generated for a region by coding and pooling all the frames in it. However, the salient scenes that appear frequently in a region are not guaranteed to have any overlaps due to the coarse granularity. As illustrated in Figure 2, the peaks represent the distributions of two scenes in a cell. For two scenes that have no overlaps at all in geo-distributions (see Figure 2a), they can rarely be captured in a same video. Therefore, given a test video which contains both of the scenes, it is more likely taken in a cell as shown in Figure 2b. However, the existing approaches have taken little consideration of scene distributions while comparing a test video to spatial segments.

3.2 Spatial Consistency

In our approach we also model a location as an area. To solve the issues discussed above, we propose the Spatial Relationship Model (SRM) which combines spatial consistency with visual similarity when estimating $P(v|g)$ in Eq. 2 as follows

$$P(v|g) = SpatialCon_{v,g} \cdot VisualSim_{v,g} \tag{3}$$

where $VisualSim_{v,g}$ denotes the visual similarity between video v and region g, and $SpatialCon_{v,g}$ represents the spatial consistency of the scenes captured by video v in region g. Here we model $SpatialCon_{v,g}$ by

(a) Without overlap. (b) With overlap.

Figure 2: Illustration of the relations between distributions of scenes.

$$SpatialCon_{v,g} = X_v M^g X_v^\intercal \tag{4}$$

where $X_v = \{x_1^v, x_2^v, \ldots, x_n^v\}$ denotes the video's BoS representation, and M^g is an $n \times n$ matrix whose element m_{ij}^g represents the geo-spatial similarity between the two scenes s_i and s_j in region g. A larger m_{ij}^g means the two scenes are more likely to be captured at the same locations in region g. Thus, we are able to promote the spatial segments as illustrated in Figure 2b while depressing the ones as shown in Figure 2a. Next, we will first discuss how to compute the matrix M^g in Section 4, and then introduce a hierarchical framework for geotagging in Section 5.

4. DISTRIBUTION OF SCENES

The location of a video is closely related to the visual scenes of its content. However, most of the existing work has only focused on developing representative visual features, and has searched for nearest neighbors with little consideration for the relationship between scenes. To compute the geo-spatial similarity matrix M^g, we first model the scene distribution using GMMs, and then estimate the pairwise geo-spatial similarity scores using JSD.

4.1 Modeling Scene Distribution

We adopt the BoS [17] model as the high-level video representation. Given a dictionary of scenes, we quantize every video frame to its visually nearest scene through hard coding. Thereafter, each scene (cluster) is formed by a set of frames whose geo-coordinates are likely to be uneven distributed. As the geotags associated with frames are discrete and noisy, we smooth the raw locations in each of the clusters to create continuous distributions by the Gaussian Mixture Models as follows

$$p(\mathbf{x}|\lambda) = \sum_{i=1}^{n} \omega_i g(\mathbf{x}|\mu_\mathbf{i}, \mathbf{\Sigma_i}) \tag{5}$$

where $\mathbf{x} = (lat, lon)^\intercal$ is a two dimensional vector representing the geo-coordinates of a frame, ω denotes the mixture weights *s.t.* $\sum_{i=1}^{n} \omega_i = 1$, and $g(\mathbf{x}|\mu_i, \Sigma_i)$ represents a 2D Gaussian distribution

$$g(\mathbf{x}|\mu_\mathbf{i}, \mathbf{\Sigma_i}) = \frac{1}{2\pi|\mathbf{\Sigma_i}|^{\frac{1}{2}}} e^{-\frac{1}{2}(\mathbf{x}-\mu_\mathbf{i})^\intercal \mathbf{\Sigma_i}^{-1}(\mathbf{x}-\mu_\mathbf{i})} \tag{6}$$

To estimate the parameters λ of the GMMs, we derive the likelihood function as

$$L(\lambda|\mathbf{X}) = p(\mathbf{X}|\lambda) = \prod_{j=1}^{m} p(\mathbf{x_j}|\lambda) \tag{7}$$

or the more convenient log-likelihood function as

$$l(\lambda|\mathbf{X}) = \log L(\lambda|\mathbf{X}) = \sum_{j=1}^{m} \log p(\mathbf{x_j}|\lambda) \quad (8)$$

where $\mathbf{X}$ represents the geo-coordinates of the frames quantized to a cluster, and $m = |X|$ is the cardinality of set $\mathbf{X}$. The target is to find the parameters that can best match the distribution of the training samples, that is,

$$\underset{\lambda}{\operatorname{argmax}}\ l(\lambda|\mathbf{X}) \quad (9)$$

This problem can be solved by applying the off-the-shelf expectation maximization (EM) algorithm [5]. The EM algorithm is an iterative method: it alternates between performing an expectation (E) step, which creates a function for the expectation of the log-likelihood evaluated using the current estimate for the parameters, and a maximization (M) step, which computes parameters maximizing the expected log-likelihood found in the E step. The number of confederate Gaussian distributions n can be automatically decided by recruiting a v-fold cross-validation [1].

By replacing the geo-coordinates with continuous kernel functions such as Gaussian probability distributions, we are able to create summary statistics that are less sensitive to high-frequency noise in the data. Such techniques have been widely used in geographical information systems [3].

4.2 Estimating Geo-spatial Similarity

In different areas, the spatial relationship of scenes is also divergent accordingly. Therefore, our next task is to calculate a good estimate of M^g in each spatial segment of the Earth's surface. As the geographic distributions of scenes have already been modeled by GMMs, the Jensen-Shannon divergence can be a good choice for estimating the geo-spatial similarity between scenes. JSD is a widely used approach to measure the similarity between two probability distributions. As shown in Eq. 10, it is a symmetrized and smoothed version of the Kullback-Leibler divergence (KLD).

$$D_{JS}(P \parallel Q) = \frac{1}{2} D_{KL}(P \parallel M) + \frac{1}{2} D_{KL}(Q \parallel M) \quad (10)$$

Here $M = \frac{1}{2}(P+Q)$. For distributions P and Q of a continuous random variable, the KLD is defined to be the integral

$$D_{KL}(P \parallel Q) = \int_{-\infty}^{\infty} \ln\left(\frac{p(x)}{q(x)}\right) p(x)\, \mathrm{d}x \quad (11)$$

where $p(x)$ and $q(x)$ represent the densities of the distributions P and Q. The KLD between two Gaussian mixture models can be estimated by the Monte-Carlo algorithm [8]. In our system, we utilized the Java library *jMEF*[1] which can create and manage mixtures of exponential families.

Recall that a location is modeled as an area in our approach. To compute the matrix M^g in region g, let $P^g = \{P_1^g, P_2^g, \ldots, P_n^g\}$ denote the distributions of scenes estimated as introduced in Section 4.1. The elements m_{ij}^g in matrix M^g are computed as

$$m_{ij}^g = D_{JS}\left(P_i^g \parallel P_j^g\right) \quad (12)$$

which is the spatial similarity between the corresponding scenes s_i and s_j, measured by the Jensen-Shannon divergence.

[1]http://vincentfpgarcia.github.io/jMEF/

5. HIERARCHICAL FRAMEWORK

In the following, we will introduce our proposed automatic video geotagging framework. Technical details of spatial segmentation, visual feature pooling, probability score estimation and integration will be presented.

5.1 Hierarchical Spatial Segmentation

Similar to the work by Kelm *et al.* [10], we segment the Earth's surface into regions of different granularities. As shown in Figure 3, *Level 1* represents the largest grid with coarse granularity. In this study, we adopt a hierarchy of three levels. The lowest hierarchy level uses a large grid of 36×18 segments in which the size of the cells is 10×10 , followed by a small grid of 360×180 segments. Considering that one video can only cover limited aspects of a location, we decide to use small patches of 0.02×0.02 at the highest hierarchy level instead of directly matching to individual videos.

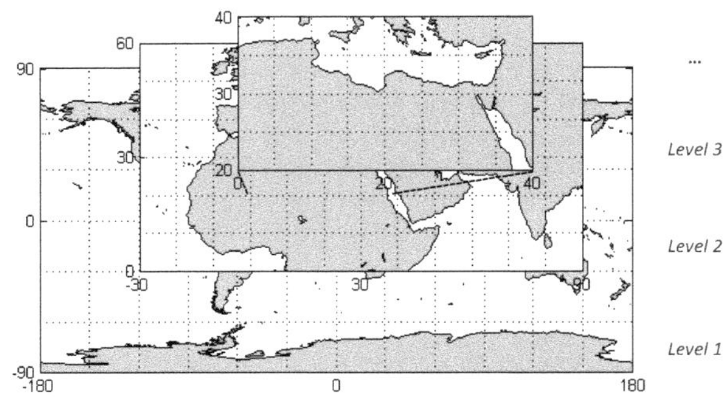

Figure 3: The hierarchical spatial segmentation of the Earth's surface.

5.2 Visual Feature Pooling

Recall that in the feature extraction for videos, we quantized each frame to its most visually nearest scene in the dictionary. This process is referred to as hard coding. Let $\tilde{X_v} = \{\tilde{x_1^v}, \tilde{x_2^v}, \ldots, \tilde{x_n^v}\}$, where $\tilde{x_i^v}$ is the number of frames in video v that have been quantized to scene s_i. The final visual representation of the video is achieved by normalizing $\tilde{X_v}$ by its Manhattan norm.

Similarly, the visual features of a region g can be computed by pooling all the frames in it. Let $\tilde{Y_g} = \{\tilde{y_1^g}, \tilde{y_2^g}, \ldots, \tilde{y_n^g}\}$, then $\tilde{Y_v}$ can be computed as $\tilde{y_i^g} = \sum_{\{v\ in\ g\}} \tilde{x_i^v}$ where $\{v\ in\ g\}$ represents all the videos located in region g. However, to avoid placing too much emphasis on individual videos, we propose to pool the visual features as

$$\tilde{y_i^g} = \sum_{v\ in\ g} \min\{\tilde{x_i^v}, Scene_{max}\} \quad (13)$$

where $Scene_{max}$ is a threshold that limits the influence of individual videos. Note that it may not be a good idea to assign high weights to the scenes that only frequently appear in a limited number of videos, because they are not likely to carry much valuable information of the location. Later we will see in the experiments that the geotagging accuracy can be improved by using a small value of $Scene_{max}$. Finally, we normalize $\tilde{Y_g}$ by its Manhattan norm.

5.3 Score Estimation and Integration

So far we have presented the spatial segmentation and visual feature pooling techniques of our proposed framework. Next we will introduce the computation of the probability scores of spatial segments at different hierarchical levels with respect to a given test video. The geotagging process is illustrated in Algorithm 1. Recall that $P(g|v) \propto P(v|g)P(g)$. The location prior $P(g)$ models the distribution of where in the world videos are likely to have been taken [6]. In our approach, we compute $P(v|g)$ and $P(g)$ with adaptation to region granularities. At *Levels 1* and *2* (36×18 and 360×180 cells) in the hierarchy, $P(g)$ is estimated as the number of training videos located in a spatial segment divided by the total number of videos in the training set. $P(v|g)$ is computed using Eq. 3, namely $P(v|g) = SpatialCon_{v,g} \cdot VisualSim_{v,g}$. At *Level 3*, $P(g)$ is set to be a small constant and the calculation of $P(v|g)$ is simplified as $P(v|g) = VisualSim_{v,g}$ because the uncertainty of spatial consistency is reduced when using a fine-grained segmentation. Thereafter, $VisualSim_{v,g}$ is computed as the cosine similarity between the BoS visual features of video v and spatial segment g. $SpatialCon_{v,g}$ is estimated using Eq. 4, i.e., $SpatialCon_{v,g} = X_v M^g X_v^\intercal$.

In the existing approaches, the geo-coordinates of training videos are usually considered as the candidates for geotags. Then the best location candidate for a video is selected by iteratively determining the most similar spatial segment at each level. In our proposed framework, two key modifications have been made as follows. First, let G_i denote the spatial grid of *Level i* and G represent the geotag candidate set. We generalize the approach by combining the probability scores of cells at different hierarchical levels

$$\underset{\hat{g}\in G}{\operatorname{argmax}} \sum_{i=1}^{n} \sum_{g\in G_i} {}_{\{g \text{ } contains \text{ } \hat{g}\}} \cdot \mu^{(n-i)} P(v|g)P(g) \quad (14)$$

where n represents the total number of levels, i denotes the current level, and μ is a balancing factor. ${}_{\{g \text{ } contains \text{ } \hat{g}\}}$ is an indicator function that only selects cells g containing location $\hat{g}$. When $\mu \to 0$, this can be interpreted as the process that iteratively determines the most similar spatial segment from the lowest to the highest level. When μ becomes larger, the influence of the cells from higher levels becomes bigger on the final geotagging results.

Secondly, as mentioned earlier, we use small patches of 0.02×0.02 at the highest hierarchy level instead of matching to individual videos. The location candidates are chosen with adaptation to test videos instead of simply using the centers of patches. For the scenes that appear in a test video, we first find the geo-coordinates of all the relevant frames in the training set. Then, we weigh the geo-coordinates by the saliency score of its corresponding scene with reference to the test video. Thereafter, the weighted geo-coordinates are smoothed by a Gaussian kernel in each patch. Finally, the location candidates for geotagging are formed by the peaks of the Gaussian kernels.

Algorithm 1 A hierarchical framework for video geotagging

X_v represents the visual feature of a test video v
Y_g represents the visual feature of cell g
G_i is the spatial grid of *Level i*
G is the candidate set of geotags
N_g = number of training videos located in cell g
N = total number of training videos
μ is a balancing factor for score fusion
for $i = 1$ to 3 **do**
  for every cell g in G_i **do**
    $VisualSim_{v,g} = \frac{X_v \cdot Y_g}{\|X_v\| \|Y_g\|}$
    $SpatialCon_{v,g} = X_v M^g X_v^\intercal$
    if $i == 1$ or $i == 2$ **then**
      $P(v|g) = SpatialCon_{v,g} \cdot VisualSim_{v,g}$
      $P(g) = \frac{N_g}{N}$
    else
      $P(v|g) = VisualSim_{v,g}$
      $P(g)$ is set to be a small constant
    end if
  end for
end for
return $\underset{\hat{g}\in G}{\operatorname{argmax}} \sum_{i=1}^{3} \sum_{g\in G_i} {}_{\{g \text{ } contains \text{ } \hat{g}\}} \mu^{(3-i)} P(v|g)P(g)$

6. EXPERIMENTS

We implemented the hierarchical geotagging framework and evaluated its effectiveness. First, we introduce the dataset and the features we used in the experiments. Next, we analyze the proposed approach based on different model settings. Finally, we compare our proposed model with the existing visual approaches and demonstrate its advantages over its competitors.

6.1 Dataset and Experimental Setup

We evaluated the effectiveness of our approach with the YFCC100M dataset [22], which has also been used in the MediaEval 2014 placing task. The set contains 35,000 geotagged videos in total which have been divided into a training set of 25,000 videos and a test set of 10,000 videos. The training and the test set are mutually exclusive with respect to the users who contributed the media. The geo-coordinates associated with the videos were used as the ground truth. Since the raw geo-coordinates do not always serve as the precise location of a video, we evaluated our method at different accuracy levels of 0.1 km, 1 km, 10 km, 100 km, 1,000 km, and 10,000 km.

Keyframes were extracted at every second of a video. The visual feature we used is GIST [16]. It describes an image based on its spatial envelope, which is a set of perceptual dimensions (naturalness, openness, roughness, ruggedness and expansion) that are related to the shape of space. In the multidimensional space it generates, scenes that share membership in semantic categories (*e.g.*, streets, highways, coasts) are able to be projected closed together.

In our experiments, the vocabulary size is set to 500. Traditionally, k-means clustering is usually applied for dictionary generation. Here we use a simple random selection of scenes due to its high efficiency and similar effectiveness [17]. Thereafter, the keyframes are assigned to the nearest visual scene. Note that here we use hard assignments because it results in a sparse representation. This property greatly accelerates the process of scene distribution modeling. Soft assignments can also be used, but it would take much more time for model building. As we can observe in the experiments, promising results can be achieved by using sparse representation. The evaluation on soft assignment is left as part of the future work.

6.2 Model Analysis

As we mentioned before, our approach segments the globe into grids and models the distribution of scenes in each cell. In our first experiment, we tested two grids that differ in size: a coarse one that segments the Earth's surface into 36×18 cells and a fine one that consists of 360×180 cells. Visual features were pooled for each cell as introduced in Section 5.2. A test video was iteratively classified to the spatial segment with the highest similarity score. We varied the threshold $Scene_{max}$ for feature pooling and reported the classification results in Table 1. We not only showed the classification accuracy, but also computed the geo-location entropy of the correctly classified videos. We first built a histogram, $D = \{d_1, d_2, \ldots, d_n\}$, regarding the location distribution of the correctly classified videos over the cells. Then we calculated the geo-location entropy, $Entropy_{geo}(D)$, using the following equation

$$Entropy_{geo}(D) = -\sum_{i=1}^{n} d_i \log d_i$$

The video location was interpreted as the same as its most visually similar video in the selected cell. We calculated the average distance error over all the test videos and reported it in the last column.

Table 1: Classification results over different geo-spatial segments.

(a) Spatial grid: 36×18 over the globe.

$Scene_{max}$	Accuracy	Entropy	Avg. Error (km)
1	10.07%	0.71	5201.60
5	10.12%	0.73	5194.59
10	9.99%	0.74	5207.87
Infinity	9.52%	0.92	5267.19
Prior	7.59%	0	5047.52

(b) Spatial grid: 360×180 over the globe.

$Scene_{max}$	Accuracy	Entropy	Avg. Error (km)
1	3.71%	0.61	5934.90
5	3.66%	0.65	5949.81
10	3.59%	0.66	5936.82
Infinity	3.45%	0.74	5887.86
Prior	3.39%	0	6013.72

As shown, when the value of $Scene_{max}$ is increased, the classification accuracy drops and the geo-location entropy increases. One possible reason is that we place too much stress on individual videos if we use a large $Scene_{max}$. A scene that only frequently appears in one or two videos may not carry much valuable information for geotagging. Therefore, a small value of $Scene_{max}$ should be adopted in our framework. Note that the last row in the table shows the results computed using only the location priors. All test videos were assigned to the spatial segment with the highest prior, so the geo-location entropy was naturally zero. The classification accuracy and average distance error served as a baseline for comparison.

Next, we fused the probability scores of cells in different hierarchical levels by a parameter μ as shown in Eq. 14. In this experiment, $n = 2$ and the location candidates are formed by the geo-coordinates of the most visually similar video in every cell of the small grid. Next, we varied the value of μ and reported the results in Table 2. The second column shows the classification accuracy over the small grid (360×180). The third column reports the average distance error over all the videos in the test set. The last column depicts the ratio of the previous two, which serves as an evaluation metric. A larger ratio indicates a more effective performance, because high precision and low average error are always preferred.

Table 2: Score fusion over different geo-spatial hierarchical levels.

μ	Acc. (%)	Err. (10^3 km)	Acc./Err.
$\to 0$	3.71	5.935	0.625
0.1	3.68	5.860	0.628
0.2	3.63	5.761	0.630
0.3	3.47	5.659	0.613
0.4	3.36	5.570	0.603
0.5	3.40	5.534	0.614
0.6	3.37	5.486	0.614
0.7	3.29	5.458	0.603
0.8	3.25	5.425	0.599
0.9	3.19	5.398	0.591
1.0	3.25	5.375	0.605

As illustrated, both the classification accuracy and the average distance error decrease when μ grows bigger. Generally speaking, by combining the scores we were able to decrease the average distance error. However, it was difficult to maintain the precision at a given small geographical margin of error at the same time. Table 2 gives us some hints on how to choose a good value for μ to balance the scores. The ratio of precision and average error remained high when $\mu \leq 0.2$, but decreased afterwards. Therefore, we set $\mu = 0.2$ in the following experiments. Compared with $\mu \to 0$, the tradeoff is a 2.93% decrease in the average distance error and a 2.16% decrease in the classification accuracy.

To evaluate the effectiveness of scene distribution modeling in video geotagging, we compared our proposed Spatial Relationship Model (SRM) with VRM which computes the score only as the product of the location prior and the cosine similarity between their visual features. Moreover, instead of matching to individual videos in the last step, we used small patches as introduced in Section 5.1. The patch size was set to 0.02×0.02 . The results are shown in Table 3. As in the previous experiments, we also calculated the classification accuracy and the geo-location entropy of the correctly classified videos over the small grid (360×180) and reported the statistics in the last two columns.

We can see from Table 3 that SRM achieved a relatively low average distance error, high accuracy, and high entropy. This indicates the effectiveness of the utilization of scene geo-spatial relationships in geotagging. Moreover, the precision of geotagging at a small margin of error ($Radius < 100$ km) was greatly improved by using patches instead of individual videos in the last matching step. One possible reason is that the geo-metadata associated with images is usually automatically recorded by GPS, which contains varied errors. Additionally, only one video is unlikely to cover the

Table 3: Evaluation on the utilization of scene distribution modeling in the hierarchical geotagging framework.

Method	Precision at Radius (km)						Avg. Error (km)	Accuracy	Entropy
	0.1	1	10	100	1000	10000			
VRM_{video}	0.01%	0.13%	1.38%	5.21%	14.81%	83.21%	5812.95	3.57%	0.83
VRM_{patch}	0.02%	0.48%	2.15%	5.35%	14.82%	83.17%	5811.72	3.57%	0.83
SRM_{video}	0.01%	0.12%	1.42%	5.14%	15.25%	83.67%	5761.00	3.63%	0.89
SRM_{patch}	0.03%	0.51%	2.24%	5.24%	15.25%	83.64%	5760.33	3.63%	0.89

whole nearby region. Therefore, it would provide a better visual summary of a location when we use small patches rather than videos.

6.3 Comparative Study

To demonstrate the effectiveness of our proposed method, we compared it with the following visual approaches and report the results:

- **Random**: Use the location of a randomly selected video from the development set. It serves as the baseline method and reflects the characteristics of the dataset.
- **ICSI**: A video is represented by the temporal middle keyframe. It searches keyframes in the development set and uses the location of the most visually similar keyframe as the prediction [4].
- **BoS**: Keyframe visual features are pooled into a BoS video representation. The location of the most visually similar video in the development set is used [17].
- **TUB**: The Earth's surface is hierarchically segmented into cells. Video representations are pooled for each spatial segment using the mean value. A test video is iteratively classified to its nearest neighbor at each level [10].

To provide a fair comparison, we used GIST, as one of the most geographically discriminative features according to Hays and Efros [7], in all methods. The performance can be improved by using more features, but that is not the focus of this study. Kelm *et al.* [10] detected the national borders using textual information at the first hierarchy level of spatial segments. However, as we purely rely on visual features in this experiment, the national border detection module in TUB was skipped. The similarity score between a cell and a video was calculated as the product of the location prior and the cosine similarity between the visual features. Table 4 reports the geotagging results achieved by different methods. TUB_{large} signifies a large grid of 360×180 segments of the Earth's surface, while TUB_{small} denotes that the large grid is further halved in each dimension. We also plotted the precision against the geographical margin of error in Figure 4.

The ideas behind ICSI and BoS are the same. Both methods try to estimate the video location as a probability distribution over the globe by matching it to training videos. ICSI chooses to use the visual feature of the middle keyframe as it is likely to be a good representative for the video. BoS has developed a more compact and high-level video representation to improve the geocoding accuracy. However, it still performed relatively poorly for exact location prediction if we directly compare a test video to the ones in the development set. This is likely to be caused by errors in GPS readings and lack of information in individual videos.

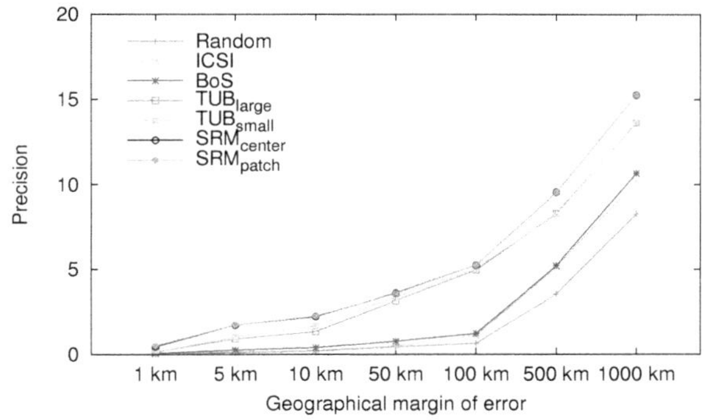

Figure 4: Graph of the precision versus the geographical margin of error for different techniques.

To solve this issue, TUB uses a hierarchical framework and iteratively classifies a test video to its nearest neighbor at each level. As we can see, our proposed approach SRM outperforms all the other methods and achieves the best results overall. SRM_{center} interpreted the location as the center of the patch, while SRM_{patch} modeled the distribution of relevant scenes in the patch and interpreted the location as the center of the Gaussian kernel. These results show that the modeling of the scene distribution really helps to improve the effectiveness of geotagging. By considering the probability of scene co-occurrences in different areas, we were able to improve the accuracy of classification to the correct cell, and thus outperform the existing approaches.

Finally, we compared our method with the visual approach of RECOD [13], proposed for the Placing Task of MediaEval 2014, in Table 5. Most of this year's participants of the placing task focused more on image geotagging, and did not present any results on the test video dataset. As reported in the working note [13], the RECOD team evaluated their visual approach on the 10,000 test videos with different configurations. $RECOD_5$ used only one single visual feature HMP, while $RECOD_2$ applied re-ranking to combine multiple visual and audio features including HMP, GIST and MFCC. As can be observed, our method achieves a better precision at all different accuracy levels, except 0.1 km. Since we currently only use the GIST descriptor, we expect that our method can be further improved by applying a multi-feature fusion approach.

7. CONCLUSIONS

This paper presented a hierarchical visual approach for the automatic prediction of video geotags. First, we discussed the drawbacks of existing methods, and then noted the importance of exploiting the connections between scenes. We modeled the geographic distribution of scenes by GMMs and estimated their spatial similarity by JSD. We implemented a

Table 4: Geotagging results comparison of the proposed and the existing visual approaches.

Radius (km)	Random	ICSI	BoS	TUB_{large}	TUB_{small}	SRM_{center}	SRM_{patch}
0.1	0	2	0	3	3	0	3
1	1	6	5	15	17	46	51
10	19	24	39	134	166	223	224
100	65	108	123	496	506	524	524
1000	828	1022	1068	1364	1367	1525	1525
10000	7404	7596	7785	8272	8270	8364	8364
Avg. Error	6944.52	6680.65	6511.84	5918.26	5916.83	5760.46	5760.33

Table 5: Precision comparison with those reported by participants of the MediaEval 2014 Placing Task.

Method	0.1 km	1 km	10 km	100 km	1,000 km
$RECOD_2$	0.04%	0.18%	1.28%	2.49%	10.38%
$RECOD_5$	0.03%	0.14%	1.33%	3.10%	13.93%
SRM_{patch}	0.03%	0.51%	2.24%	5.24%	15.25%

hierarchical framework and showed that the geotagging accuracy can be improved by utilizing the geo-spatial relationship between scenes. We carried out experiments using the YFCC100M dataset in the context of the MediaEval 2014 placing task. The experimental results clearly demonstrate the effectiveness of our proposed approach.

In our future work, we will investigate the use of geo-spatial relationships of scenes in dictionary creation. Visual features other than GIST should be fused. To benefit from the large amount of geotagged images on the web, we also plan to include images in the development set for scene distribution modeling and visual feature pooling.

Acknowledgements

This research has been supported by the Singapore National Research Foundation under its International Research Centre @ Singapore Funding Initiative and administered by the IDM Programme Office through the Centre of Social Media Innovations for Communities (COSMIC).

8. REFERENCES

[1] *Electronic Statistics Textbook.* StatSoft, Inc, 2011.

[2] J. Almeida, N. Leite, and R. Torres. Comparison of Video Sequences with Histograms of Motion Patterns. In *Image Processing*, 2011.

[3] C. Brunsdon, A. Fotheringham, and M. Charlton. Geographically Weighted Summary Statistics – A Framework for Localised Exploratory Data Analysis. *Computers, Environment and Urban Systems*, 2002.

[4] J. Choi, H. Lei, and G. Friedland. The 2011 ICSI Video Location Estimation System. In *Working Notes Proc. MediaEval Workshop*, 2011.

[5] A. P. Dempster, N. M. Laird, and D. B. Rubin. Maximum Likelihood from Incomplete Data via the EM Algorithm. *Journal of the Royal Statistical Society*, 1977.

[6] J. Hare, J. Davies, S. Samangooei, and P. Lewis. Placing Photos with a Multimodal Probability Density Function. In *ACM ICMR*, 2014.

[7] J. Hays and A. A. Efros. IM2GPS: Estimating Geographic Information from a Single Image. In *IEEE CVPR*, 2008.

[8] J. R. Hershey and P. A. Olsen. Approximating the Kullback Leibler Divergence between Gaussian Mixture Models. In *IEEE ICASSP*, 2007.

[9] H. Jegou, F. Perronnin, M. Douze, J. Sanchez, P. Perez, and C. Schmid. Aggregating Local Image Descriptors into Compact Codes. *IEEE Transactions on Pattern Analysis and Machine Intelligence*, 2012.

[10] P. Kelm, S. Schmiedeke, and T. Sikora. Multimodal Geo-tagging in Social Media Websites using Hierarchical Spatial Segmentation. In *ACM SIGSPATIAL GIS*, 2012.

[11] M. Larson, M. Soleymani, P. Serdyukov, S. Rudinac, C. Wartena, V. Murdock, G. Friedland, R. Ordelman, and G. J. F. Jones. Automatic Tagging and Geotagging in Video Collections and Communities. In *ACM CIVR*, 2011.

[12] L. T. Li, D. C. G. a. Pedronette, J. Almeida, O. A. B. Penatti, R. T. Calumby, and R. da S. Torres. Multimedia Multimodal Geocoding. In *ACM SIGSPATIAL GIS*, 2012.

[13] L. T. Li, O. A. Penatti, J. Almeida, G. Chiachia, R. T. Calumby, P. R. M. Júnior, D. C. G. Pedronette, and R. d. S. Torres. Multimedia Geocoding: The RECOD 2014 Approach. In *Working Notes Proc. MediaEval Workshop*, 2014.

[14] X. Li, M. Larson, and A. Hanjalic. Geo-visual Ranking for Location Prediction of Social Images. In *ACM ICMR*, 2013.

[15] J. Luo, D. Joshi, J. Yu, and A. Gallagher. Geotagging in Multimedia and Computer Vision-A Survey. *Multimedia Tools and Applications*, 2011.

[16] A. Oliva and A. Torralba. Modeling the Shape of the Scene: A Holistic Representation of the Spatial Envelope. *Int. J. Comput. Vision*, 2001.

[17] O. A. B. Penatti, L. T. Li, J. Almeida, and R. da S. Torres. A Visual Approach for Video Geocoding using Bag-of-scenes. In *ACM ICMR*, 2012.

[18] P. Serdyukov, V. Murdock, and R. van Zwol. Placing Flickr Photos on a Map. In *ACM SIGIR*, 2009.

[19] Z. Shen, S. Arslan Ay, S. H. Kim, and R. Zimmermann. Automatic Tag Generation and Ranking for Sensor-rich Outdoor Videos. In *ACM Multimedia*, 2011.

[20] Y. Song, Y. Zhang, J. Cao, J. Tang, X. Gao, and J. Li. A Unified Geolocation Framework for Web Videos. *ACM Trans. Intell. Syst. Technol.*, 2014.

[21] Y.-C. Song, Y.-D. Zhang, J. Cao, T. Xia, W. Liu, and J.-T. Li. Web Video Geolocation by Geotagged Social Resources. *IEEE Transactions on Multimedia*, 2012.

[22] B. Thomee, D. A. Shamma, G. Friedland, B. Elizalde, K. Ni, D. Poland, D. Borth, and L.-J. Li. The New Data and New Challenges in Multimedia Research. arXiv:1503.01817 [cs.MM], 2015.

[23] M. Trevisiol, H. Jégou, J. Delhumeau, and G. Gravier. Retrieving Geo-location of Videos with a Divide & Conquer Hierarchical Multimodal Approach. In *ACM ICMR*, 2013.

[24] Y. Yin, B. Seo, and R. Zimmermann. Content vs. Context: Visual and Geographic Information Use in Video Landmark Retrieval. *ACM Transactions on Multimedia Computing, Communications and Applications*, 2015.

[25] Y. Yin, Z. Shen, L. Zhang, and R. Zimmermann. Spatial-Temporal Tag Mining for Automatic Geospatial Video Annotation. *ACM Transactions on Multimedia Computing, Communications and Applications*, 2015.

Using Viewer's Facial Expression and Heart Rate for Sports Video Highlights Detection

Prithwi Raj Chakraborty
Queensland University of Technology
p1.chakraborty@qut.edu.au

Dian Tjondronegoro
Queensland University of Technology
dian@qut.edu.au

Ligang Zhang
Xi'an University of Technology
ligzhang@gmail.com

Vinod Chandran
Queensland University of Technology
v.chandran@qut.edu.au

ABSTRACT
Viewer interest, evoked by video content, can potentially identify the highlights of the video. This paper explores the use of facial expressions (*FE*) and heart rate (*HR*) of viewers captured using camera and non-strapped sensor for identifying interesting video segments. The data from ten subjects with three videos showed that these signals are viewer dependent and not synchronized with the video contents. To address this issue, new algorithms are proposed to effectively combine *FE* and *HR* signals for identifying the time when viewer interest is potentially high. The results show that, compared with subjective annotation and match report highlights, 'non-neutral' *FE* and 'relatively higher and faster' *HR* is able to capture 60%-80% of *goal*, *foul*, and *shot-on-goal* soccer video events. *FE* is found to be more indicative than *HR* of viewer interest, but the fusion of these two modalities outperforms each of them.

Categories and Subject Descriptors
H.1.2 [**User/Machine Systems**]: Human information processing.

General Terms
Algorithms, Reliability, Experimentation.

Keywords
Facial expression, Heart rate, Video segmentation, Viewer interest, Sports video highlight.

1. INTRODUCTION
Rapid growth of video data increases the need for indexing interesting video segments for supporting user-centric retrieval. Current content indexing approaches either focus on internal content (e.g., audio-visual features) or viewer's response to automatically detect 'interest evoking' segments. In particular, facial expressions and physiological responses have been found to carry information about viewer's interest in video contents [1]. Physiological signals, such as heart rate, manifest internal responses that can only be measured via biosensors. In contrast, facial expression can be observed externally and only requires a standard video camera, therefore can be more easily deployed in real-life scenarios [2, 3].

ICMR '15, June 23 - 26, 2015, Shanghai, China
© 2015 ACM. ISBN 978-1-4503-3274-3/15/06…$15.00
DOI: http://dx.doi.org/10.1145/2671188.2749361

The main contribution of this paper is to demonstrate the benefits of using sports videos, which have well-established structure (e.g. play-break), for investigating the temporal mapping between events, continuous heart rate, and discrete facial expression. Combination and comparison between heart rate and facial expression signals have been investigated as well. The experimental setting is more practical, compared to most of the current work, as it uses non-strapped sensors. The structure of the paper is as follows. Section 2 discusses the related work. Section 3 describes the experimental protocol, while Section 4 describes the data analysis algorithms. Section 5 and 6 describes the experimentation and analysis of results. Section 7 and 8 outlines the discussions and future work.

2. RELATED WORK
Heart rate reactions alongside valence and arousal have been used for identifying viewer's interest in movie clips [6]. Studies found that correlations between physiological features and self-assessed evaluation scores vary across users. Other physiological signals, such as galvanic skin resistance, electromyogram, and respiration pattern are also sensitive to viewer's response and have been used along with heart rate to measure interests in movie clips, music videos, and static images [7, 8]. However, current sensors for these signals require strapped components, therefore limiting the practicality for use in natural or day-to-day settings.

Facial expression is another important modality for understanding viewers' interest in response to video stimuli. Facial expression and activity features extracted from head and face regions have been used for personal highlights detection from movie, drama and TV commercial clips [9, 10]. Head oriented features (i.e., head roll, head position) can be aggregated with facial features to measure low/high engagement levels [2]. Such systems can be used for home video editing and viewer experience modelling [11, 12]. Crowdsourced facial response (smirk, smile, and valence) to video stimuli on presidential debate can be used to measure voting preference and it has been found that facial response has subjective bias [13].

Current literature has not explored the correlations between facial expression and heart rate in response to sports video, particularly for highlights detection purposes. The main challenge is due to the time delays between an interesting event and the corresponding viewer's response. Moreover, an event may not be interesting for every person (i.e. subjectivity of viewers). This paper represents the first attempt to address all of these challenges.

3. EXPERIMENTAL PROTOCOL
3.1 Video Stimuli and Annotation
The study used three soccer matches from UEFA Euro 2012 (Spain vs Italy), English Premier League 2013-14 (Manchester City vs Tottenham), and Champion's League 2014-15 (Real

Madrid vs Basel). It was ensured that none of the subjects had previously seen these matches based on a questionnaire. These three video clips (i.e., *vid1*, *vid2*, *vid3* with a frame rate of 25 frame-per-second) were trimmed to the first 20 minutes, 15 minutes and 17 minutes but was manually confirmed to contain three types of events, including *goal*, *shot-on-goal*, and *foul*. Full-length matches were not used to maintain subject's concentration and patience.

To develop the ground truth (of interesting events), two methods were adopted. The first method is extracting events based on the match report highlights (*HL*) collected from soccer websites (ESPN.com, UEFA.com, SkySports.com). The second method is identifying specific segments based on subjects' manual annotation (*MA*) during data collection. The scoping of a highlight segment was specified by a sequence of play-break frames [14]. In total, the ground truth contained 30 sets of manually annotated segments from 10 subjects for 3 video clips. To reduce the impact of subjectivity, the final set of *MA* segments were selected from those manually annotated by more than 5, out of 10, subjects (> 50% agreement).

Table 1 summarises the ground truth data. In total, 3 goals, 14 shots-on-goal, and 5 fouls were included in highlight segments (*HL*). Manually annotated segments (*MA*) consisted of 3 goals, 17 shots-on-goal, and no foul.

Table 1. Annotation of each type of ground truth segments (HL, MA) from three video clips. It shows the number of soccer events annotated against each type

Soccer Events	Vid 1		Vid 2		Vid 3	
	HL	MA	HL	MA	HL	MA
Goal	1	1	1	1	1	1
Shot-on-goal	5	8	4	4	5	5
Foul	0	0	4	0	1	0

3.2 Participants and Apparatus

Ten subjects (age: mean = 26.4, standard deviation = 3.2) were recruited through a pre-questionnaire for obtaining information on their support for soccer, favourite soccer team, last seen soccer match. Subjects were in good health and had no visual impairment. All of them were familiar with video watching.

A less-confined environment was established with a closed and quiet room (with no access of other people) involving a 21.5 inches Dell monitor for showing video stimuli, a video camera and strapless heart rate sensor (*Mio Alpha*) for recording facial expression and heart rate, and a comfortable revolving chair (shown in figure 1). Facial recording involved only natural daylight rather than artificial or extra lighting. Distances from subjects to the monitor and the video camera were 80-90 cm and 100-120 cm respectively. The used heart rate sensor is a wrist watch which is very convenient and easier to use than other strapped sensors (e.g., ECG chest strap).

3.3 Recording of Facial Expression (FE) and Heart Rate (HR)

Each subject was put through three separate trials including identical steps, where each trial involves simultaneous recording of facial expression and heart rate data during watching video stimuli. Prior to each trial, a short demonstration and a preliminary training were used to familiarise each subject with the data collection procedure. Consecutive trials had a break for two weeks. The sampling frequencies of facial video and time stamped (in beats-per-minute) heart rate data were 25 frame-per-seconds (fps) and 1/3 Hz. Heart rate data was stored through an iOS application (*Digifit*) which requires 5-8 seconds for calibration. A resting time of 5 minutes was given to each subject before data collection commences, for making his/her heart rate steady. Each trial of data collection involves the following steps.

(1) *Recording*: Subject's facial video and heart rate were recorded simultaneously during watching a soccer clip. Facial video and heart rate recording were triggered using a remote controller and an iPhone.

(2) *Manual Annotation*: Each subject was asked to manually annotate each segment he/she felt interest into from the seen soccer clip, using the 'capture' option of *KMPlayer*. Annotation includes a set of starting and ending frames for each annotated segment.

(3) *Rating*: Each subject was asked to watch and rate the match report highlights in a scale from 0 to 1, where '1' indicates 'interesting' and '0' indicates 'non-interesting' segments.

(4) *Post-questionnaire*: A list of the players was presented so that each subject could tick his/her preferred player(s) and team from the seen clip. This information was obtained through a paper-based questionnaire.

Figure 1. A subject watching soccer stimuli wearing a heart rate sensor on his left hand while his facial expression being recorded by a video camera

Collection of facial expression and heart rate data from 10 subjects in response to 3 video clips produced 30 sets of facial expression data, 30 sets of heart rate data, and 30 sets of subjective manual annotation data. Following section describes the processing techniques of this data.

4. DATA ANALYSIS

An illustration of our system framework is provided in figure 2. Facial expression data are processed with an off-the-shelf system which provides frame-by-frame intensity scores for three emotion categories (i.e., positive, negative, and neutral). Scores of these three categories are processed separately (as functions of time) to identify consecutive frames with relatively high intensity scores, as forms of video segments. A number of temporal features are extracted from the pre-processed heart rate data. We then combine these feature values to obtain a collection of fused feature values as a function of time. Consecutive instances with high fused (feature) values are identified similarly as video segments. A segment-wise fusion method was then applied to combine segments identified from facial expression and heart rate data. More details on data processing are described in following sub-sections.

4.1 Recognition of Viewer Facial Expression

We used the facial expression recognition (FER) system described in [15] for facial expression classification which provides frame-by-frame outputs and is capable of handling facial movement and pose variation. Training data of this FER system includes field-based data from TV, news, and web. This system detects the face region from a facial video with the Viola-Jones face detector and extracts as well as tracks facial landmark points using a multi-view active shape model (ASM) tracker. Scale-invariant feature transform (SIFT) features and distances between the 53 interior facial points are used as texture and geometric features. SIFT features are dimensionally reduced by the minimum redundancy maximum relevance (mRMR) algorithm and fused with geometric features. A support vector machine (SVM) classifier then predicts the fused features into one of three categorical emotion classes (i.e., positive, negative, neutral) with an accuracy between 71.3% - 83%. The output of the classification phase is frame-by-frame probability (i.e., emotion intensity) scores for each of positive (*POS*), negative (*NEG*), and neutral (*NEU*) emotion categories, where each of these scores varies between [0, 1] and the summation of three scores is equal to 1. Frames in video containing face region which the ASM tracker fails to track are usually dropped from the final output.

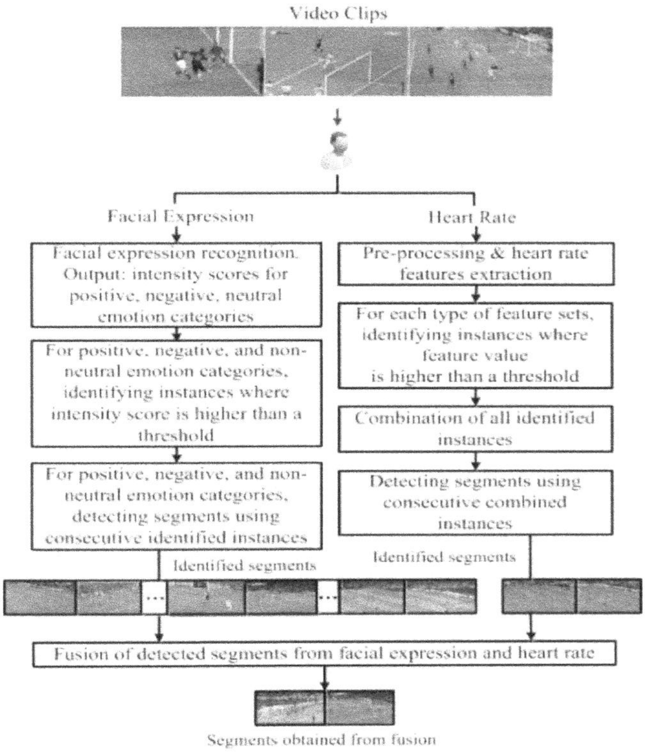

Figure 2. System framework

4.2 Identifying Interesting Video Segments from Viewer FE

This work identifies three types of video segments using intensity scores obtained for three emotion categories from the FER system. The output of the FER system was considered as a signal containing three (i.e., *POS*, *NEG*, *NEU*) channels of continuous frame-based intensity scores (from 0 to 1). For example, intensity scores for i^{th} frame can be represented as $P_i^{\{POS,NEG,NEU\}}$. For any instance, summation of these three scores is equal to 1 and thus, effectively two-dimensional continuous representations (time (in frame number) vs intensity scores) are obtained for facial expression. This was important for obtaining a mapping between facial expressions and watched video clips. In the proposed method, a non-neutral (*NNEU*) score is assigned by using the maximum of positive or negative scores instead of their sum. The following procedure (algorithm 1) describes how video frames with high positive intensity scores are separated using a threshold and used for identifying interesting video segments. We used analogous procedures for identifying interesting video segments using negative and non-neutral intensity scores.

Intensity score of each missing frame (i.e., dropped from FER output) is computed using linear interpolation between the intensity scores of two neighbouring frames. For noise removal, a low-pass-filter with a $\gamma = 5$ seconds window was applied. It was found that any window less than 5 seconds was not suitable to remove the rapid change in frame-by-frame scores. Our goal was to identify segments (collection of frames) with relatively high positive intensity scores. For this purpose, we computed a threshold, $Thres_1$ from mean and standard deviation of the positive intensity scores. For identifying consecutive frames, a frame-by-frame labelling was utilised where each frame was labelled as '1' if corresponding positive score is greater than corresponding negative and neutral scores as well as $Tresh_1$ (labelled as '0' otherwise). Each set of consecutive frames, labelled as '1', was considered as a preliminary interesting video segment. In such way, we identified a set of preliminary interesting video segments $S = \{s_1, s_2,...\}$ where each segment s_i contains a number of frames labelled as '1'. Semantics of soccer match events are unlikely to vary by lesser than one second and based on this assumption any two sequential segments from S were merged together if distance between them (in number of frames) was less than 1 second (i.e., 25 frames). Consider the new segments were $S' = \{s'_1, s'_2, ..\}$. To remove significantly smaller segments, another threshold, $Thres_2$ was computed based on mean and standard deviation of the lengths (in number of frames) of all segments in S' and any segment in S' with length lesser than $Thres_2$ was discarded. The remaining segments were considered as the final interesting video segments, which are $S^{POS} = \{s_1, s_2,....\}$, where s_1 contains the starting and ending frame numbers of first identified video segment as indices.

Algorithm 1. Video segmentation using *POS* intensity scores

Input: FE intensity scores: $P_i^{\{POS,NEG,NEU\}}$ for each of m frames

Output: Identified video segments, $S^{POS} = \{s_1, s_2, ...\}$

1. Compute intensity values for missing frames using linear interpolation;
2. Smooth intensity values using a moving average low-pass-filter with γ seconds window and output is $P_i^{'\{POS,NEG,NEU\}}$;
3. $Thres_1 \leftarrow \mu\,(P^{POS'}) + \sigma\,(P^{POS'})$;
4. Label, $L \leftarrow \emptyset$;
5. For $i = 1$ to m
6.   If ($P_i^{POS'} > P_i^{NEG'}$) & ($P_i^{POS'} > P_i^{NEU'}$) & ($P_i^{POS'} > Thres_1$)
7. $L_i \leftarrow 1$;
8.   Else
9. $L_i \leftarrow 0$;
10. Find consecutive segments, $S = \{s_1, ..., s_p\}$ labelled as '1';
11. Merge any sequential segment with a distance less than 1 second (25 frames) and the output is a new set of segments $S' = \{s'_1, s'_2,...\}$;
12. $Thres_2 \leftarrow \mu$(lengths of all s'_i in S') - σ(lengths of all s'_i in S');
13. Discard any segment s'_i with length < $Thres_2$ and consider the remaining segments as final segments, $S^{POS} = \{s_1, s_2,...\}$;

4.3 Heart Rate Feature Extraction

Heart rate data was obtained with time, T in seconds. Consider, $HRate = \{hr_1, hr_2, \ldots, hr_n\}$ is the heart rate signal for any particular subject which contains n heart rate samples in beats-per-minutes. The following procedure (algorithm 2) describes how features are extracted from *HRate*. Prior work have used derivative of heart rate (rate-of-change) and spectral features such as energy from low frequency band, maximum approximate heart rate to understand cognitive and emotional reaction of human [7, 8, 16, 17]. We used similar features in this study. For removing the rapid fluctuation and smoothing, we used a low-pass-filter over *HRate* data containing a sliding window of $\beta = 9$ seconds (over 4 *HRate* samples). A separate sliding window was used to obtain the temporal features from smoothed *HRate* data, which were rate-of-change, gradient, variance, local maxima, and energy from low frequency band (0.04-0.15 Hz). The length of the sliding window was kept 9 seconds since smaller window (including less than 4 samples) might not capture the subtle changes in temporal features.

We computed rate-of-changes of *HRate* samples using the total absolute difference between neighbouring samples and the difference of time stamped with first and last samples within the sliding window. Standard MATLAB functions were used for computing local maxima, gradient, and variance. Function used for gradient returns a set of directional values for increasing order of the input signal and hence, averages of the absolute directional values were used as gradient features. Because of the resolution of our collected heart rate data, we computed energy feature only from low frequency band using a finite impulse response (FIR) band-pass-filter. Five extracted features were parallel to each other and scaled with time, T, in seconds.

Algorithm 2. Temporal HR feature extraction

Input: HR samples, $HRate = \{hr_1, hr_2, \ldots, hr_n\}$
Output: Temporal feature set: *RateOfChange*, *LocalMaxima*, *Energy*, *Variance*, *Gradient*

1. Smooth *HRate* with a moving average low-pass-filter with β seconds window and output is $HRate' = \{hr'_1, hr'_2, \ldots, hr'_n\}$;
2. For $i = 1$ to n-1
3. | $diff_i \leftarrow | hr'_i - hr'_{i+1}|$;
4. $RateOfChange \leftarrow \emptyset$; $LocalMaxima \leftarrow \emptyset$;
5. $Variance \leftarrow \emptyset$; $Gradient \leftarrow \emptyset$; $Energy \leftarrow \emptyset$;
6. For $i = 1$ to n-4
7. | $LocalMaxima_i = \max\{hr'_i, \ldots, hr'_{i+3}\}$;
8. | $D_t = Time_{i+3} - Time_i$;
9. | $D_x = \sum_{m=i}^{i+3} diff_m$;
10. | $RateOfChange_i = D_x / D_t$;
11. | $Variance_i = \sigma^2\{hr'_i, \ldots, hr'_{i+3}\}$;
12. | $Gradient_i = \mu(|\delta\{hr'_i, \ldots, hr'_{i+3}\}/\delta\{i, \ldots, i+3\}|)$;
13. Design a band-pass-filter, *filter* with pass bands 0.04 Hz and 0.15 Hz;
14. $HRate'' \leftarrow$ filter(*HRate*);
15. For $i = 1$ to n-4
16. | $Energy_i \leftarrow hr''_i * hr''_i$;

4.4 Identifying Segments from Viewer HR

Three from five extracted features (i.e., *RateOfChange*, *LocalMaxima*, and *Energy*) were selected for further processing, since *Variance* and *Gradient* were found to be highly correlated with *RateOfChange* (overall, r = 0.84, 0.96). The following procedure (algorithm 3) describes how interesting video segments are identified from the selected heart rate features. This shows how heart rate samples with higher (than a threshold) are selected and how these consecutive selected samples are converted into segments.

Our goal here was to see whether high changes in heart rate feature signify viewer interest in any manner. We computed separate threshold (i.e., *Thres*) for each selected feature set to separate the consecutive features with values higher than that threshold. As these features are time stamped, time (in seconds) was obtained from T as indices for all separated features and combined (i.e., as *Idx*). Each set of consecutive features was treated as a segment and beginning and ending of that segment was stored as time (in seconds) in S'. We then combined sequential segments with distance less than $\alpha = 3$ (seconds) since it is unusual that two interesting events may occur in soccer match in an interval less than three seconds. Stored time indices were converted to frame number from second.

Algorithm 3. Video segmentation using HR features

Input: $x = \{feat_1, feat_2, \ldots, feat_n\}$, where x is *RateOfChange*, *LocalMaxima*, *Energy*
Output: Identified segments, $S^{HR} = \{s_1, s_2, \ldots, s_n\}$

1. Indices, $Idx \leftarrow \emptyset$;
2. For each of $x = \{$ *RateOfChange*, *LocalMaxima*, *Energy* $\}$
3. | $Thres \leftarrow \mu(x) + \sigma(x)$;
4. | $I \leftarrow \emptyset$;
5. | Store index i of any $feat_i$ in I if $feat_i > Thres$;
6. | $Idx \leftarrow Idx \cup I$;
7. $S' \leftarrow \emptyset$; $j \leftarrow 1$;
8. Starting of first segment, $S'_{1,1} \leftarrow T(Idx_1)$;
9. For each index Idx_i in Idx
10. | If there is a break between indices, $(Idx_{i+1} - Idx_i) > 1$
11. | | Ending of the current segment, $S'_{j,2} \leftarrow T(Idx_i)$;
12. | | Starting of next segment, $S'_{j,1} \leftarrow T(Idx_{i+1})$;
13. Merge consecutive segments with distance less than α, $(S'_{j,2} - S'_{j+1,1} < \alpha)$ and S is the new set of segments;
14. For $m = 1$ to length of S
15. | $S_{m,1} \leftarrow S_{m,1} * frm\_rate$;
16. | $S_{m,2} \leftarrow S_{m,2} * frm\_rate$;
17. $S^{HR} \leftarrow S = \{(S_{1,1}, S_{1,2}), (S_{2,1}, S_{2,2}), \ldots\}$;

4.5 Fusion of Video Segments Identified from FE and HR

We fused the segments identified from non-neutral facial expressions with those identified from heart rate signals. Segments identified from positive and negative facial expression were not used in fusion since non-neutral score had already included both. All the identified segments were scaled with time (in frame number) and hence, we used frame-by-frame set union operation for fusing these two types of segments for all subjects. Intersection was not used since it was expected that facial expression and heart rate complements each other in detecting segments which might be lost if intersection is used (described in section 6.2). Consider, the resultant fused set of segments was S^{FUSED}.

5. EXPERIMENT

From the procedures described in above section, we identified five types of video segments (S^{POS}, S^{NEG}, S^{NNEU}, S^{HR}, S^{FUSED}) from positive, negative, non-neutral facial expression and heart rate data collected from each subject in response to each video clip. We computed four statistical measurements, which are **similarity,**

temporal alignment (synchronicity), detection rate, and accuracy, based on the comparison between identified video segments and the ground truth segments. Ground truth segments for our study were match report highlights and manually annotated segments (*HL*, *MA*) and the statistical measurement were done separately on each of them.

Algorithm 4 includes the steps to compute similarity score, alignment score, and detection rate. We compared each of the ground truth segments against all identified segments and computed a similarity score each time when there is any overlapping. This score was actually a Jaccard index which measures the similarity between two finite set of samples. If two sets of samples are A and B, the Jaccard index is given by equation 1.

$$J(A, B) = (A \cap B) / (A \cup B) \quad (1)$$

According to our methods, each segment was considered as a set of frame numbers and Jaccard index (i.e., *jaccard_idx*) have been calculated between two such sets of frame numbers each time. We tried to find out a particular identified segment which is most similar to a particular highlight or annotated segment. Therefore, maximum of the similarity scores was kept as the final similarity score.

Algorithm 4. Measuring similarity, synchronicity, and detection rate

Input: Identified segment set, $S^x = \{s_1, s_2, \ldots, s_n\}$, ground truth segment set, $Y = \{y_1, y_2, \ldots, y_m\}$, where x is *POS*, *NEG*, *NNEU*, *HR*; Y is *HL*, *MA*; and $y_i = \{f_{start}, f_{end}\}$, $s_j = \{S_{j,1}, S_{j,2}\}$
Output: Jaccard indices, *jaccard_idx*; misalignment, *misalignment*; detection rate, *det_rate*,

$jaccard\_idx \leftarrow \emptyset$; $misalignment \leftarrow \emptyset$; $det\_rate \leftarrow \emptyset$;
For each ground truth segment, y_i in Y
  $jaccard\_idx_i \leftarrow 0$; $alignment \leftarrow \emptyset$;
  $seg\_annotoaed \leftarrow \{f_{start}, f_{start} + 1, \ldots, f_{end}\}$;
  For each identified segment, s_j in S
    $seg\_identified \leftarrow \{S_{j,1}, S_{j,1} + 1, \ldots, S_{j,2}\}$;
    $union \leftarrow seg\_annotaed \cup seg\_identified$;
    $intersect \leftarrow seg\_annotaed \cap seg\_identified$;
    $score \leftarrow |intersect| / |union|$;
    If there is an overlap and current score is higher, $((intersect \neq \emptyset)$ & $(jaccard\_idx_i < score))$
      Jaccard index, $jaccard\_idx_i \leftarrow score$;
    If there is an overlap, $(intersect \neq \emptyset)$
      Detection rate, $det\_rate_i \leftarrow |intersect| * 100 / |y_i|$;
      If s_j completely overlaps y_i or vice versa, $((S_{j,1} > f_{start})$ & $(f_{end} > S_{j,2})$ | $(S_{j,1} < f_{start})$ & $(f_{end} < S_{j,2}))$
        $alignment_j \leftarrow 0$; break;
      If s_j partially overlaps and follows y_i, $((S_{j,2} > f_{start})$ & $(f_{start} - S_{j,1} < alignment_j))$
        $alignment_j \leftarrow (f_{start} - S_{j,1}) / frm\_rate$;
      Else if s_j partially overlaps and precedes y_i, $((f_{end} > S_{j,1})$ & $(S_{j,2} - f_{end} < alignment_j)$
        $alignment_j \leftarrow (S_{j,2} - f_{end}) / frm\_rate$;
    Else If $(S_{j,2} < f_{start})$ & $(f_{start} - S_{j,2} < alignment_j)$
      $alignment_j \leftarrow (f_{start} - S_{j,2}) / frm\_rate$;
    Else If $(f_{end} < S_{j,1})$ & $(S_{j,1} - f_{end} < alignment_j)$
      $alignment_j \leftarrow (S_{j,1} - f_{end}) / frm\_rate$;
  $misalignment_i \leftarrow \min(alignment)$;

To investigate the temporal synchronicity between identified and ground truth segments, we measured the incorrect positioning between these two types of segments as misalignment (i.e., *misalignment*) where smaller misalignment score means higher synchronicity. Misalignment was measured by computing the distance between each ground truth segment and its closest identified segment. An identified segment is considered closest if it is overlapped or contains a minimum distance to a ground truth segment. Distance was measured in term of number of frames and the misalignment score was converted into second. Overlapping was measured using set intersection operation. Value of *frame_rate* was kept same as the frame rate of video which is 25 fps. We computed the percentage of overlapping between each ground truth segment and identified segments, where a ground truth segment is considered as 'detected' if it overlaps any identified segment.

Detection rate, *det_rate* was computed each time when there was an overlap between identified segment and ground truth segment. For each ground truth segment, we want to see how much (in %) of that segment was overlapped with any of the identified segments.

We computed accuracy by measuring precision, recall, and F1 scores between identified segments and ground truth segments, as described in algorithm 5. Each time there is an overlap between each ground truth segment and any identified segment and we incremented two variables, for counting the number of ground truth (i.e., *gt_seg*) and identified segments (i.e., *id_seg*) which were detected (i.e., overlapped). From these two measures we computed number of true positive, *TP*, false positive, *FP* and false negative, *FN*.

Algorithm 5. Measuring accuracy

Input: Identified segment set, $S^x = \{s_1, s_2, \ldots, s_n\}$, ground truth segment set, $Y = \{y_1, y_2, \ldots, y_m\}$, where x is *NNEU*, *HR*, *FUSED*; Y is *HL*, *MA*; and $y_i = \{f_{start}, f_{end}\}$, $s_j = \{S_{j,1}, S_{j,2}\}$
Output: Precision, *precision*; recall, *recall*; F1 score, F

$TP \leftarrow 0$; $FP \leftarrow 0$; $FN \leftarrow 0$; $gt\_seg \leftarrow 0$;
For each ground truth segment, y_i in Y
  $id\_seg \leftarrow 0$;
  For each identified segment, s_j in S
    If there is an overlap between s_j and y_i
      $id\_seg \leftarrow id\_seg + 1$;
      $gt\_seg \leftarrow gt\_seg + 1$;
  If overlapping is found, $(id\_seg > 0)$
  $TP \leftarrow TP + id\_seg$;
$FP \leftarrow n - TP$;
$FN \leftarrow m - gt\_seg$;
$precision \leftarrow TP / (TP + FP)$;
$recall \leftarrow TP / (TP + FN)$;
$F \leftarrow (2 * precision * recall) / (precision + recall)$;

6. ANALYSIS OF RESULTS

This section describes the findings from the results. This includes how subjects with different demography responded differently to the same soccer events. It has also shown that heart rate response can be a complementary to facial expression in measuring viewer interest. Besides, results from similarity and temporal synchronicity have shown that fusion of facial expression and heart rate performs better than each of them. Detection rate and accuracy depicts similar impression.

6.1 Subjective Dependency in Responses

Figure 3(a) illustrates identified segments from positive and negative facial expression (*POS*, *NEG*) in response to the *goal* events from the video clips across ten subjects. Out of ten subjects three (*S1*, *S3*, *S8*) were not soccer fans. It was found that negative emotion was evoked in cases of those subjects in response to *goal* events. For other subjects, the majority of the identified segments were positive emotion evoking. Figure 3(c) illustrates similar identified segments from positive and negative facial expressions in response to *shot-on-goal* events from three video clips for all subjects. It can be seen from figure 3(c) that *shot-on-goal* events evoked both positive and negative facial expression equally where subject dependency is still evident. In the third case, majority of the *foul* events stimulated negative facial expression in all subjects regardless of soccer fans or not, as illustrated in figure 3(b). Figures 3(a) and 3(c) show that segments (marked) of opposite emotions were evoked from subject 2 and 3 in response of *goal* and *shot-on-goal* events, who were supporting opposite teams. Also, subject 7 expressed negative emotion (figure 3(a)) as the *goal* is scored from the opposite team he was supporting.

6.2 Heart Rate as Complementary to Facial Expression

It was found that segments identified from facial expression were not able to detect all of the ground truth segments. Some ground truth segments which were not detected by facial expression were detected by segments identified from heart rate signal. Figure 4 plots the ground truth segments as well as segments identified from facial expression (*NNEU*) and heart rate and it can be seen that these two modalities complements each other in identifying viewer interest. Therefore, fusion based on union of segments identified from facial expression and heart rate was found to have better correspondence with ground truth segments than individual modalities. Following sections will show how performance is enhanced by fusing facial expression and heart rate.

6.3 Overlapping in term of Jaccard Index

Algorithm 4 describes how we computed the similarity score (Jaccard index) for each of the five types of video segments identified from each subject's response to soccer events in ground truth segments. These scores were averaged across all subjects for each type of soccer events and each type of identified segments. Figure 5 illustrates averaged Jaccard index scores for all subjects, between identified segments and events (goal, shot-on-goal, foul) of ground truth segments (i.e., *HL*, *MA*). The Jaccard index varies between 0 to 1, where 1 means 'similarity' and 0 means 'no similarity'.

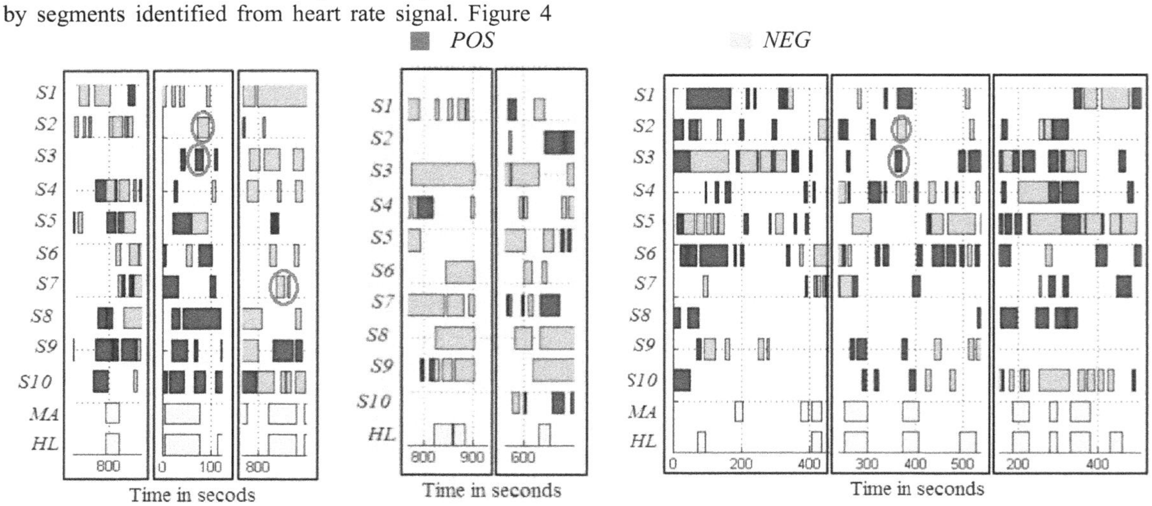

(a) Goal (b) Foul (c) Shot-on-goal

Figure 3. Examples of identified segments from positive (*POS*) and negative (*NEG*) facial expression for all subjects (*S1* to *S10*) in response to goal, foul, and shot-on-goal events in three video clips (note that *Vid 1* and *MA* do not contain any foul event)

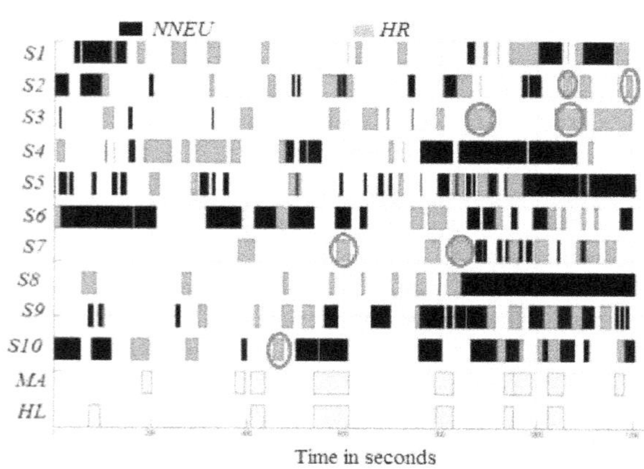

Figure 4. Identified segments from non-neutral facial expression (NNEU) and heart rate (HR) for all subjects (S1 to S10) in response to video clip 1 show the lagging (with ground truth) and complementary nature of NNEU and HR

Results show that the Jaccard index of *POS* segments for *goal* event (0.4) is higher than *NEG* segments (0.2) and is opposite (*POS*: 0.27, *NEG*: 0.61) in case of *foul* events. *NNEU* segments include the best results from both *POS* and *NEG*. Segments identified by heart rate show lesser similarity compared to segments identified from *POS*, *NEG*, and *NNEU* scores. Segments identified from fusion of *NNEU* and *HR* show the highest similarity (Jaccard index: 0.54 and 0.53 for *goal* events) with ground truth segments.

6.4 Temporal Synchronicity

Algorithm 4 describes how distance (in seconds) between each ground truth segment (*HL* and *MA*) and its closest identified segment has been measured as misalignment scores. Table 2 illustrates the averaged score across all subjects for each type of ground truth segments and each type of identified segments. All ground truth segments (both which are detected and not detected) were compared during computing the misalignment scores. Segments identified from *NEG* segments are found to be mostly misaligned. Segments identified from *NNEU* scores have better temporal alignment (lower misalignment score) with both types of ground truth segments.

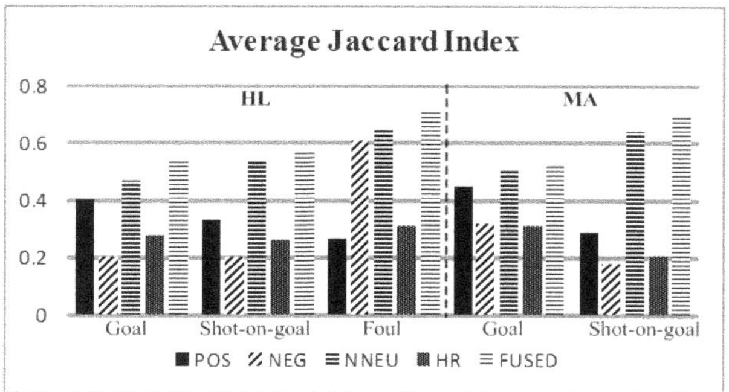

Figure 5. Averaged Jaccard index for different soccer events for video segments identified from positive, negative, non-neutral facial expression, heart rate, and fusion

Subjects' annotated segments have lesser misalignment with segments identified from *HR*. Segments identified from *HR* signals have more consistent alignment in relation to both highlights and subjects' annotated segments. Segments obtained from fusion were found to be mostly synchronous across all events regardless of highlights or subjects' annotated segments. It is visible from figure 4 that segments identified (marked) from heart rate are delayed from the ground truth segments, which means there heart rate response lags stimuli. The misalignment we found can be corrected by adding these computed values as offset with ground truth segments.

Table 2. Average misalignment score for different soccer events across identified segments

Average Misalignment Scores (in seconds)				
Ground truth	**Segment categories**	**Goal**	**Shot-on-goal**	**Foul**
HL	POS	3.3	4.57	12.72
	NEG	13.59	7.89	2.21
	NNEU	4.36	9.35	2.3
	HR	4.11	8.35	7.21
	FUSED	**0.23**	**1.15**	**1.43**
MA	POS	3.18	5.4	-
	NEG	43.56	21.33	-
	NNEU	7.22	10.20	-
	HR	3.39	5.32	-
	FUSED	**0.78**	**2.72**	-

6.5 Event Detection

This section describes the insights of event detection, measured as detection rate (*det_rate*). The algorithm is described in section 5. Mixtures of common soccer events such as *goal*, *shot-on-goal*, and *foul* helped us to investigate both positive and negative evoked emotions. Figure 6 illustrates the average detection rate across all subjects for each type of ground truths and each soccer event. Results show that the majority of 'Goal' events were corresponding to extracted segments from *POS* scores (71.11%, 69.23%) while the least correspondence was found to segments from *NEG* scores (40.12%, 34.12%). A majority of 'Foul' events were corresponding to *NEG* segments (50%, 59.13%). Segments extracted from *NNEU* values outperform *POS* and *NEG* as *NNEU* contains the maximum absolute value of POS and *NEG* (see figure 6). Segments identified from *HR* show most consistent detection for all events. This is because heart rate can be affected regardless of the 'positive' or 'negative' nature of the emotional response. However, it is not accurate in terms of detection rate. Segments found from fusion were found to have higher detection rate (90%-100%) than all.

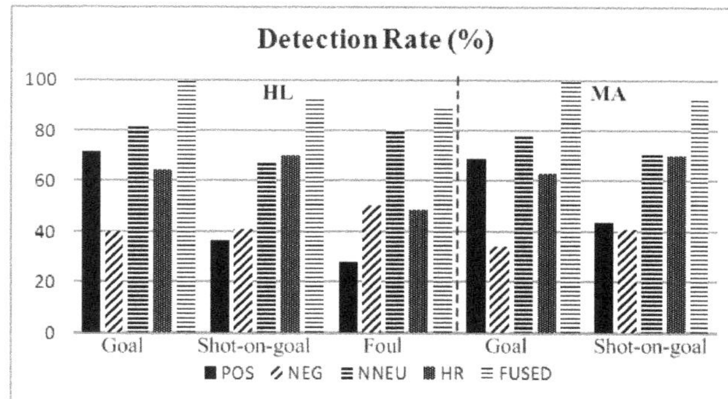

Figure 6. Average detection rate for different soccer events

6.6 Accuracy

We computed precision, recall and F1 scores by comparing identified segments (from each subject's response) with highlight and annotated segments separately and then averaged the scores across all subjects for each type of identified segments (see table 3). Results show that segments obtained through fusion outperform others (F1 scores: 0.71, 0.72). Segments identified from *POS* scores have the least accuracy (F1 score: 0.44). In overall, precision score is higher than recall score which means that number of false positive is fewer than number of false negative.

Table 3. Precision, recall, and F1 scores

Accuracy				
Ground Truth	**Segment categories**	**Precision**	**Recall**	**F1**
HL	POS	0.39	0.49	0.44
	NEG	0.80	0.41	0.54
	NNEU	0.72	0.59	0.65
	HR	0.45	0.53	0.47
	FUSED	**0.86**	**0.61**	**0.71**
MA	POS	0.61	0.53	0.57
	NEG	0.74	0.51	0.61
	NNEU	0.80	0.62	0.70
	HR	0.63	0.48	0.54
	FUSED	**0.82**	**0.64**	**0.72**

7. DISCUSSION AND LIMITATION

The goal of our study was to explore facial expression and non-invasively collected heart rate data of viewer in response to soccer stimuli, for highlight event detection. Therefore, the main contribution of this paper is more focused on data and result analysis instead of technical novelty, though existing methods have been adopted in proposed algorithms. It is a common understanding that heart rate response is more subtle and carries more sophisticated emotion information than facial expression. However, our findings show that facial expression performs better than heart rate in identifying viewer interest. To maintain less constrained and non-invasive setting for data collection, we used a photo diode based heart rate sensor (*Mio Alpha*) instead of strapped ECG sensor and therefore, the heart rate we collected had smaller resolution than standard ECG. According to a recent study, pulse plethysmography (PPG) based Mio Alpha has a mean absolute error of 4.43 bpm and the overall reliability score found was 77.83% against standard ECG for heart rate data collected during physical activity and exercise [18]. But our findings show that low resolution heart rate data is still useful to extract interest information of viewer with a reasonable accuracy (F1 score: 0.47, 0.54). Moreover, compared to strapped ECG sensor, the advantage of strapless heart rate sensor is that it can be easily applicable in real-life scenarios.

Viewer interest information extracted from heart rate was found different and independent of facial expression. Heart rate signals can identify interesting segments which are missed by facial expression and therefore heart rate signals can be used as a complementary to facial expression. Therefore, fusion of these two modalities (*HR* and *FE*) demonstrated better results than each of them individually.

This study used only soccer stimuli to investigate the response collected from ten subjects. The scope of soccer events included in the stimuli was limited to *goal*, *foul*, and *shot-on-goal*. The proposed methods use a few heuristics for defining window span, and post-processing shorter segments, which are adopted for soccer events. The methods are expected to work for other domains but the performance may not be the same as soccer.

8. CONCLUSION AND FUTURE WORK

This study collects facial expression and heart rate data from ten subjects in three different trials using three stimuli. It has been shown that interesting video segments can be identified using facial expression and heart rate which complement each other. Our findings show that a useful temporal mapping can be obtained between viewer response and interesting soccer video events and in our case it was found that viewer response may not necessarily (temporally) synced with different types of key soccer events. The proposed data collection requires users to be video tapped wearing heart rate monitor watch, which is a common constraint in the current studies. The current study can be extended involving more subjects, different stimuli, more accurate sensor, and lesser constrained set-up (e.g., webcam, couch). The collected data can be made available for public upon receiving ethics approval.

9. REFERENCES

[1] Money, A.G. and Agius, H., 2009. Analysing user physiological responses for affective video summarisation. *Displays* 30, 2, 59-70.

[2] Hernandez, J., Liu, Z., Hulten, G., Debarr, D., Krum, K., and Zhang, Z., 2013. Measuring the engagement level of TV viewers. In *10th IEEE International Conference and Workshops on Automatic Face and Gesture Recognition* (April, 2013). FG '13. IEEE, 1-7.

[3] Wang, S., Liu, Z., Zhu, Y., He, M., Chen, X., and Ji, Q., 2014. Implicit video emotion tagging from audiences' facial expression. *Multimedia Tools and Applications*, 1-28.

[4] Arapakis, I., Konstas, I., and Jose, J.M., 2009. Using facial expressions and peripheral physiological signals as implicit indicators of topical relevance. In *17th ACM international conference on Multimedia* (October, 2009). MM '09. ACM, 461-470. DOI= http://doi.acm.org/10.1145/1631272.1631336.

[5] Lang, P.J., Greenwald, M.K., Bradley, M.M., and HAMM, A.O., 1993. Looking at pictures: Affective, facial, visceral, and behavioral reactions. *Psychophysiology* 30, 3, 261-273.

[6] Bos, M.G.N., Jentgens, P., Beckers, T., and Kindt, M., 2013. Psychophysiological Response Patterns to Affective Film Stimuli. *PLoS ONE* 8, 4. DOI= http://dx.doi.org/10.1371/journal.pone.0062661.

[7] Soleymani, M., Chanel, G., Kierkels, J.J., and Pun, T., 2008. Affective ranking of movie scenes using physiological signals and content analysis. In *2nd ACM Workshop on Multimedia Semantics*. MS' 08. ACM, 32-39.

[8] Soleymani, M., Chanel, G., Kierkels, J.J., and Pun, T., 2009. Affective characterization of movie scenes based on content analysis and physiological changes. *International Journal of Semantic Computing* 3, 2, 235-254.

[9] Joho, H., Jose, J.M., Valenti, R., and Sebe, N., 2009. Exploiting facial expressions for affective video summarisation. In *ACM International Conference on Image and Video Retrieval*. ACM, 31.

[10] Joho, H., Staiano, J., Sebe, N., and Jose, J.M., 2011. Looking at the viewer: analysing facial activity to detect personal highlights of multimedia contents. *Multimedia Tools and Applications* 51, 2, 505-523.

[11] Peng, W.-T., Chu, W.-T., Chang, C.-H., Chou, C.-N., Huang, W.-J., Chang, W.-Y., and Hung, Y.-P., 2011. Editing by viewing: automatic home video summarization by viewing behavior analysis. *IEEE Transactions on Multimedia* 13, 3, 539-550.

[12] Peng, W.-T., Huang, W.-J., Chu, W.-T., Chou, C.-N., Chang, W.-Y., Chang, C.-H., and Hung, Y.-P., 2009. A user experience model for home video summarization. In *Advances in Multimedia Modeling Springer*, 484-495.

[13] McDuff, D., El Kaliouby, R., Kodra, E., and Picard, R., 2013. Measuring Voter's Candidate Preference Based on Affective Responses to Election Debates. In *Humaine Association Conference on Affective Computing and Intelligent Interaction*. ACII '13. IEEE, 369-374.

[14] Tjondronegoro, D., Chen, Y.-P.P., and Pham, B., 2004. The power of play-break for automatic detection and browsing of self-consumable sport video highlights. In 6th *ACM SIGMM international workshop on Multimedia information retrieval*. ACM, 267-274.

[15] Zhang, L., Tjondronegoro, D., and Chandran, V., 2014. Facial expression recognition experiments with data from television broadcasts and the World Wide Web. *Image and Vision Computing* 32, 2, 107-119.

[16] Fleureau, J., Guillotel, P., and Huynh-Thu, Q., 2012. Physiological-Based Affect Event Detector for Entertainment Video Applications. *IEEE Transactions on Affective Computing* 3, 3, 379-385.

[17] Soleymani, M., Koelstra, S., Patras, I., and Pun, T., 2011. Continuous emotion detection in response to music videos. In *IEEE International Conference on Automatic Face & Gesture Recognition and Workshops*. FG '11. IEEE, 803-808.

[18] Parak, J. and Korhonen, I., 2014. Evaluation of wearable consumer heart rate monitors based on photopletysmography. In *36th Annual International Conference of the IEEE Engineering in Medicine and Biology Society*. EMBC '14. IEEE, 3670-3673.

A Deep Neural Network for Modeling Music

Pengjing Zhang, Xiaoqing Zheng,* Wenqiang Zhang, Siyan Li,
Sheng Qian, Wenqi He, Shangtong Zhang, Ziyuan Wang
School of Computer Science, Fudan University, Shanghai, China
Shanghai Key Laboratory of Intelligent Information Processing
fduzhpj@gmail.com, zhengxq@fudan.edu.cn, wqzhang@fudan.edu.cn,
leecontrolhot@gmail.com, arielqiancheng@gmail.com, maggiehwq@gmail.com,
zhangshangtong.cpp@gmail.com, ziyuan_wang@hotmail.com

ABSTRACT

We propose a convolutional neural network architecture with k-max pooling layer for semantic modeling of music. The aim of a music model is to analyze and represent the semantic content of music for purposes of classification, discovery, or clustering. The k-max pooling layer is used in the network to make it possible to pool the k most active features, capturing the semantic-rich and time-varying information about music. Our network takes an input music as a sequence of audio words, where each audio word is associated with a distributed feature vector that can be fine-tuned by backpropagating errors during the training. The architecture allows us to take advantage of the better trained audio word embeddings and the deep structures to produce more robust music representations. Experiment results with two different music collections show that our neural networks achieved the best accuracy in music genre classification comparing with three state-of-art systems.

Categories and Subject Descriptors

H.5.5 [**Sound and Music Computing**]: Methodologies and techniques, Modeling, Systems

General Terms

Algorithms, Performance

Keywords

Music classification; feature learning; neural network

1. INTRODUCTION

Over the past decade, large collections of music are increasingly available on various application platforms. Therefore, tasks such as music discovery, navigation, and organization have become progressively harder for humans without the help of automatic systems. Extensive research effort (see [5, 3, 27, 15] for reviews) has been invested in content-based music information retrieval (MIR) at the intersection of signal processing, music modeling, and machine learning. Although designed for different objectives (e.g. tagging, clustering, classification, and ranking), many MIR systems follow the same recipe with minor variations, adopting a three-step strategy: some hand-crafted features are extracted from a single or multiple frames of music audio; then, these short-term features are summarized over the entire audio to generate a music representation (or descriptor); finally, a machine learning model is trained over the summarized representations for the task of interest.

Steady improvements in the performance through perseverance and ingenuity of the MIR community indicate that this three-step recipe is effective and its optimization is not yet over. However, less attention has been paid on modeling the interaction among the segments of music, and inducing low-dimensional music representations capturing their high-level semantic information, particularly characterizing the temporal dynamics. A song normally consists of multiple sections incorporating different instrumental or vocal tones in a structured and continuous manner. The majority of musical experiences in human perception and comprehension do not live in short-term signal, but in acoustic variation over longer durations, and interplay between consecutive sections. Simply aggregating short-term features by computing statistical summaries over time generally does not produce a comprehensive and discriminative music representation because the information about temporal dynamics and order is lost, which has been proved to be very useful for music analysis and retrieval [5, 8, 11, 15, 33].

The overwhelming majority of MIR systems that follow three-step strategy operate in the paradigm of shallow architectures (with one or two levels of feature projections), which might be less efficient at representing functions that can be represented compactly by a deep architecture [1]. The advantage of the deep architectures is that high-level (normally compact) representations can be learned by multiple stacking layers, each of them combining features at lower levels in a hierarchy way. Very recently, some studies on the deep architectures (i.e. neural networks with multiple hidden layers) [10, 11, 7, 28] have shown such advantage over the shallow ones on a variety of MIR benchmarks.

In this paper, we presents a novel convolutional neural network architecture with k-max pooling layer for semantic

*Corresponding author.

ICMR'15, June 23–26, 2015, Shanghai, China.

http://dx.doi.org/10.1145/2671188.2749367.

modeling of music. The aim of a music model is to analyze and represent the semantic content of music for purposes of classification, discovery, or clustering. An input music is transformed into a sequence of "audio words". A codebook of the audio words is constructed by clustering multiple continuous frames extracted from a collection of raw audio signals into K clusters, and each audio word is initialized by one of cluster centers learned by the clustering.

Taking a text-like music representation as input, the neural network produces local features around each audio word of the music thanks to convolutional layers, and combines these features by k-max pooling into a global feature vector or representation which can then be fed to standard affine layers. The k-max pooling operation captures the k most active features produced by the topmost convolutional layer. The pooling result is insensitive to their specific positions, but preserves the order of these features. The desirable properties of the k-max pooling layer make it possible to capture the characteristics of the temporal dynamics in music.

Given a task of interest, a relevant representation of each audio word is given by the corresponding lookup table[1] feature vector, which can be trained by backpropagating errors, starting from an initialization. Our architecture allows us to take advantage of better trained audio word representations, by moving the semantically similar audio words to be closer to each other than to those with dissimilar concepts in the vector space. Experiment results with two different music collections confirm the advantage of the trained audio word representations, which help to produce better song-level representations and improve the classification accuracy.

The remainder of this paper is organized as follows. Section 2 presents a brief overview of related work. In section 3, we introduce our neural network architecture. Experimental results are reported in Section 4. The conclusions are given in Section 5.

2. RELATED WORK

The goal of music modeling is to produce a robust representation from an observed audio signal, hopefully preserving important characteristics while discarding noise, redundancy or irrelevant information, and this problem is at the core of many tasks including classification, annotation, and retrieval. The better a representation is produced to reflect a desired semantic meaning, the simpler it is to assign or infer labels or concepts to it. Music modeling is usually conducted at two levels: *frame−level*, and *song-level* representation generations[2]. The frame-level representations are produced by extracting features from a single or few frames, and the song-level representations are constructed by aggregating the frame-level features by computing statistical summaries over the entire audio.

Most of the frame-level representations are based on traditionally well-known audio features, such as Mel-Frequency Cepstral Coefficients (MFCCs), spectral centroid, spectral flux, linear prediction coefficients, etc., which are mainly adapted from earlier work in speech recognition. Typically, a music signal is broken into small, possibly overlapping frames (e.g. 46 ms) that are processed to feature extraction. Many systems have been proposed by using these low-level acoustic features for music classification [21, 29, 23], although they may differ in the features used or the classification models applied. The features are predominantly hand-crafted, and choosing the right features is crucial for these music classification systems. However, good feature representations are hard to come forth and more difficult to optimize. It has been shown that the features chosen by task-specific engineering can be replaced by the features learned from data in an unsupervised manner [19, 10, 28].

Unsupervised feature learning is usually conducted either by mapping the input signal into a new feature space of given *codebook* or by means of deep learning. A great deal of work has used Vector Quantization (VQ) as a tool for constructing the codebook or dictionary. A codebook is usually formed by the cluster centers of a collection of frame-level feature vectors. For instance, Riley et al compared three clustering algorithms for the codebook construction, and found that the K-means algorithm achieved comparative result with relatively less computational cost [30]. Seyerlehner et al proposed a multi-level clustering architecture to accelerate vector quantization [32]. McFee et al used a soft variant of K-means to cluster a collection of frame-level MFCC vectors [26]. Recently, many researchers have sought to employ sparse coding for the dictionary generation which produces better features than those learned with VQ methods.

Sparse coding (SC) has emerged as a strong alternative to traditional VQ approaches, and has been exploited for MIR applications [16]. Smith and Lewicki found that when the features are optimized for coding acoustic signal with sparse decomposition, they show striking similarities to time-domain cochlear filter estimates, and yield greater coding efficiency than conventional signal representations [34]. Henaff et al achieved state-of-art accuracy in music genre classification at that time by using an efficient approximated sparse coding approach with predictive sparse decomposition [12]. Yeh and Yang showed the superiority of sparsity-enforced codebook learning over traditional VQ-based or exemplar-based methods [43]. Coates and Ng found that it is more important to choose a good encoder than to choose a set of basis functions (i.e. dictionary) by systematically comparing several training and encoding schemes, including sparse coding and VQ methods [6]. They suggested that the dictionary can be generated by using fast VQ algorithms or randomly choosing exemplars from the training set.

There has been a great deal of recent interest in investigating unsupervised feature learning by deep architectures. The first successful instance is that of Convolutional Neural Network (CNN) based onset detection by [17]. Lee et al proposed a Convolutional Deep Belief Network (CDBN) that was applied to the audio spectrogram for music genre and artist classification [19]. Dieleman et al also employed the CDBN but based on engineered features (beat-aligned timbre and chroma) and pre-trained with a large data set for artist, genre, and key recognition tasks [7]. Hamel and Eck showed that the features learned by the Deep Belief Network (DBN) on Discrete Fourier Transforms (DFTs) of audio signal performed better than MFCCs for genre classification [10]. Schlüter and Osendorfer applied the mean-covariance RBM on audio spectrogram excerpts for similarity-based music classification task, and achieved close to state-of-the-art performance [31].

[1] A lookup table maps each of these audio word indices into a feature vector.

[2] MIR literature, such as [12], also mentioned a *segment-level* representation that aggregates the frame-level features by the similar methods, but whose time-scale is smaller than the song-level ones.

The frame-level features need to be summarized over time to generate the song-level representations, which allows us to map a variable-length sequence into a fixed-size feature vector that can be fed to a classifier. The song-level representations could be derived by at least three methods: *pooling*, *voting*, or *bag-of-frames*. The most straightforward way to summarize features is pooling that is to extract simple statistics such as maximum, minimum, mean or variance of the features over an excerpt of a period of time. Both the choice of the pooling operation and the temporal scale at which the pooling is applied have a great impact on the performance [11]. The voting method has been used by [10] as follows: after the classifier yields a prediction for each frame, all predictions for a song are averaged, and the prediction with the highest score is chosen as the winner.

The bag-of-frames (BoF) is another popular way to aggregate the local features for song-level representation [22, 20, 25, 42, 8]. Given a codebook, any frame-level representation can be replaced by the occurrence of codewords, and each music piece is represented as a histogram over the codebook. The BoF model is originated from the bag-of-words model, which was first proposed for document classification. Su et al investigated the influence of different keyword weighting schemes, including many different combinations of term frequency-inverse document frequency (tf-idf) measures [36]. The BoF models features as a probability distribution by simply counting the frequency of occurrence of the codewords, which is unable to characterize the temporal dynamics of high-level concepts like genre or mood, and arguably contribute to the "semantic gap" in music informatics [14].

To the best of our knowledge, the work closest to ours in terms of modeling music for classification are [33] and [43]. Shen et al proposed a Stochastic Music Concept Histogram (SMCH) scheme that represents a piece of music as the probability distribution over a set of predefined concepts [33]. Although both their and our models all take an input music as a sequence of audio words, theirs derive the music representations by estimating probabilistic association between the audio words and music concepts (e.g. genre or mood), while ours generates the compact representations of music by employing multiple network layers to learn several levels of feature extraction from the inputs. Moreover, they convert each short segment of music to a symbolic ID of audio words, whereas we assign each audio word a distributed vector representation that can be tuned during the training. Yeh and Yang investigated how to incorporate labeled data in the codebook learning process by constructing a subcodebook for each class and combing them to encode the input music [43]. In comparison, we leveraged the labeled data to obtain more robust and better music representations for the task of interest.

3. THE NETWORK ARCHITECTURE

A fairly recent trend in machine learning is to use deep architectures to discover multiple levels of features or representations from data. The popularity of deep architectures may be partially attributed to their biological plausibility: humans typically organize their thoughts with different levels of abstractions in hierarchical manner [1]. Although modeling music has been a long-standing topic for the MIR community, it is still a great challenge to discover robust representations that can capture the rich and time-varying information about music whose most expressive qualities probably relate to its structural changes across time [9]. In this paper, we introduce a convolutional neural network architecture with k-max pooling layer (KCNN) to learn music representations by extracting higher level features from acoustic signals, particularly characterizing their temporal dynamics. Before describing its components, we give our learning framework of neural network-based model in Figure 1.

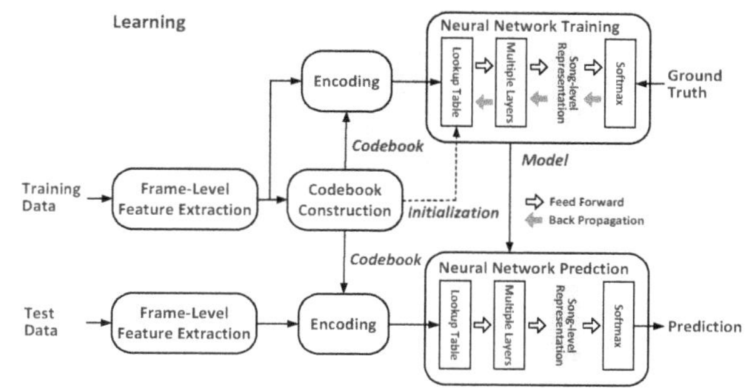

Figure 1: A learning framework of neural network-based model.

The system takes a collection of songs as training data, which are partitioned into several fix-sized frames. Some short-term features are extracted from those frames to produce their representations. The concatenations of multiple consecutive frame representations[3] are used to form segment feature vectors. To construct the codebook, the K-means algorithm is employed to cluster those vectors into groups. The audio words of the constructed codebook are used to define a mapping (an "encoding") of the input music into a new feature space. Taking a sequence of audio words as input, the first layer of our network maps each of these words into a feature vector, by a lookup table operation. A vector representation[4] of each audio word is initialized by one of cluster centers and can be fine-tuned by backpropagation with a collection of songs and their corresponding ground truth labels. The learned codebook is used to compute the encoding (i.e. a sequence of audio words) of a test song, which then is fed into the trained network for classification.

Our network architecture is shown in Figure 2. The first layer of the network extracts the frame-level features from an input music. The next convolutional layer extracts features from a window of frames, which are called "texture windows" by [38], as it corresponds to the minimum time span of music that is necessary to identify a particular music "texture". Convolutional layers are often stacked, interleaved with a non-linearity function, to extract higher level features, but just one convolutional layer is drawn in Figure 2 for clarity. The k-max pooling operation is applied after the topmost convolutional layer to pool the k most active features. It also guarantees that the input to the next layer of the network is independent of the length of the input, which allows us to apply the same subsequent layers. The following layers are standard affine layers, and the last layer is a simple softmax layer that predicts categories for the input music. The network outputs can be interpreted as a conditional probability

[3] Our initial experiments showed that using multiple consecutive frames as an input unit for learning algorithms significantly improves performance over using a single frame.

[4] It is also known as word "embeddings" in the literature of deep learning.

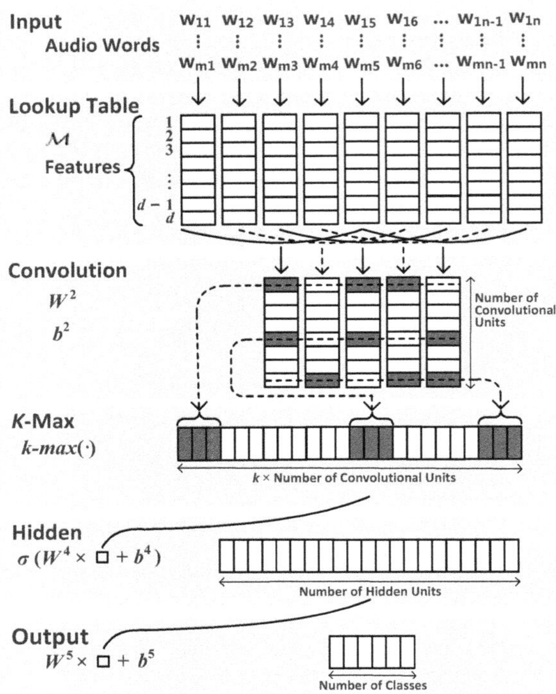

Figure 2: The neural network architecture.

by taking it to the exponential (making the score positive) and normalizing it over all possible categories.

3.1 Mapping Audio Words into Feature Vectors

The audio words are fed into the network as indices that are used by a lookup operation to transform audio words into their feature vectors. We consider a fix-sized codebook $\mathcal{D}$, whose size is equal to the number of clusters (a hyper-parameter). The vector representations are stored in a word embedding matrix $\mathcal{M} \in \mathbb{R}^{d \times |\mathcal{D}|}$, where d is the dimensionality of the vector space and $|\mathcal{D}|$ is the size of the codebook.

Formally, assume we are given a song $s_{[1:n]}$ that is first partitioned into fix-sized segments, and represented as a sequence of n audio words $s_i, 1 \leq i \leq n$. For each word $s_i \in \mathcal{D}$ that has an associated index k_i into the column of the embedding matrix, a d-dimensional feature vector representation is retrieved by the lookup table layer $\mathcal{Z}_{\mathcal{D}}(\cdot) \in \mathbb{R}^d$:

$$\mathcal{Z}_{\mathcal{D}}(s_i) = \mathcal{M} e_{k_i} \tag{1}$$

where we use a binary vector $e_{k_i} \in \mathbb{R}^{|\mathcal{D}| \times 1}$ which is zero in all positions except at the k_i-th index. The lookup table layer can be seen as a simple projection layer. If different types of features are used, we associate a lookup table with each feature, and the feature vector becomes the concatenation of the outputs of all these lookup tables. The feature vector of each word is initialized by one of the cluster centers after the codebook is constructed by vector quantization. The vector representations of audio words can be trained by backpropagation to be relevant to the task of interest. We take the audio words as the "true words" in texts, and want semantically and structurally similar words to be closer to each other than to those with dissimilar concepts in the embedding space.

3.2 Convolutional Layer

The lookup table layer extracts features for each single segment, but they are normally influenced by its surrounding segments. We assume that the features of a particular segment depend mainly on their neighboring segments, and extract these features from a fix-sized window w (a hyper-parameter) of segments. More precisely, given an input song $s_{[1:n]}$, the segment feature window produced by the lookup table layer at position s_i can be written as:

$$f_\theta^1(s_i) = \begin{pmatrix} \mathcal{Z}_{\mathcal{D}}(s_{i-w/2}) \\ \vdots \\ \mathcal{Z}_{\mathcal{D}}(s_i) \\ \vdots \\ \mathcal{Z}_{\mathcal{D}}(s_{i+w/2}) \end{pmatrix} \tag{2}$$

where f_θ^1 is a function with trainable parameters θ. The idea behind the convolution is to perform affine transformations over each segment feature window, siding over the segment $s_{[i:j]}$ from segment s_i to s_j, to obtain a matrix:

$$f_\theta^2(s_{[i:j]}) = (W^2 f_\theta^1(s_i) + b^2, \cdots, W^2 f_\theta^1(s_j) + b^2) \tag{3}$$

where the matrices $W^2 \in \mathbb{R}^{V \times (wd)}$ and $b^2 \in \mathbb{R}^V$ are parameters to be optimized during the training. A hyper-parameter V is called the *number of convolutional units*. The convolutional layer extracts local features around each window of a given segment. Multiple convolutional layers can be stacked to extract higher level features.

3.3 Max Pooling Layer

A k-max pooling operation is applied to the output of the topmost convolutional layer. The size of the outputs of Equation (3) depends on the number of segments in the input music. The local features extracted by the convolutional layers must be further combined to obtain the global feature vector with a fixed size, in order to apply the same subsequent layers independent of the length of the music.

Traditional convolutional networks often apply an average or a max operation over the time dimension of the sequence. In the context of music processing, the time here refers to the segment in a song. The average operations do not make much sense in our case, as in general not all the segments in a piece of music have equivalent influence on the meaning of its expression. In practice, the average values tend to smooth out the most active features. Instead, we use the k-max pooling approach, which forces the network to capture the k most relevant features produced by the convolutional layers. Hamel et al have shown that maximum pooling operation performs best with operations such as mean, variance, minimum, 3rd and 4th centered moments [11].

Given a number k and a sequence $\mathcal{Q} \in \mathbb{R}^p$, k-max pooling operation selects the subsequence $\mathcal{Q}_{max}^k$ of k-highest values in $\mathcal{Q}$. The selected values of $\mathcal{Q}_{max}^k$ preserve their relative order in $\mathcal{Q}$. Given a matrix output f_θ^2 by a convolutional layer, the k-max pooling layer yields a matrix:

$$f_\theta^3(f_\theta^2) = \begin{pmatrix} k\text{-max}([f_\theta^2]_{1,1} \cdots [f_\theta^2]_{1,m}) \\ \vdots \quad \vdots \quad \vdots \\ k\text{-max}([f_\theta^2]_{V,1} \cdots [f_\theta^2]_{V,m}) \end{pmatrix} \tag{4}$$

where $[f_\theta^2]_{i,j}$ is the element in the i-th row and j-th column of matrix f_θ^2, and m is the length of segments.

3.4 Label Prediction and Training

The fix-sized vector produced by concatenating each column vector of f_θ^3 is fed to the standard *Linear Layers* that successively perform affine transformations over the vector, interleaved with some non-linearity function $\sigma(\cdot)$, to extract highly non-linear features. As for a non-linear function, we choose a sigmoidal function:

$$\sigma(x) = 1/(1 + e^{-x}) \tag{5}$$

We add a simple softmax layer to the end of the networks to predict category labels for each input song. The neural networks are trained by minimizing the cross-entropy error of the softmax layer using the gradient descent algorithm. This is equivalent to minimizing the KL-divergence between the prediction distribution y and the target distribution t. We use the 1-of-K coding scheme in which the target distribution t for an instance i belonging to a class k is a binary vector with all elements zero except for the element k. The error as a function of the network parameters $\theta = (\mathcal{M}, \mathbf{W}, \mathbf{b})$ for n training instances is:

$$E(\theta) = -\frac{1}{n}\sum_{i=1}^{n} t_i \log(y_i(\theta)) + \frac{\lambda}{2}||\theta||^2 \tag{6}$$

where the coefficient λ governs the relative importance of the regularization term compared with the error.

4. EXPERIMENTS

We conducted three sets of experiments. The goal of the first one is to test several variants for the KCNN on the development set, to gain some understanding of how the choice of hyperparameters impacts the performance. We ran this set of experiments on the GTZAN[5] dataset. Ninety percent of the samples (900) were randomly chosen for training, and the rest (100) was used as development set. The second is to see how well the k-max pooling operation and the audio word representations fine-tuned by supervised learning work in improving the performance. We turned off the effect of the k-max pooling by setting the value of k to 1. We also ran a set of experiments to see the impacts of the fine-tuned audio word representations on the performance by keeping the lookup tables unchanged at the supervised training stage after they were initialized. In the third set of experiments, we compared the performance of the KCNN with the existing state-of-the-art models on two different music collections by extracting their song-level representations to train and test the SVM-based classifiers.

4.1 Datasets

We used two different datasets to evaluate the performance on music genre classification, one of most well studied problems in MIR [8, 15]. The first dataset GTZAN[6] is composed of 1,000 30-second clips covering ten genres[7], which is a balanced dataset, with 100 clips per genre [39]. The second dataset ISMIR2004Genre[8] consists of 1,458 full-length songs covering six genres[9], which is unbalanced (e.g. 320 examples for classical but 26 for jazz_blues). All songs in the two datasets were converted into a standard mono-channel and 22,050 Hz sampling rate WAV format.

Evaluation on GTZAN is conducted using a 10-fold cross validation, with the class distribution in each fold balanced like [41, 12, 43]. ISMIR2004Genre comes with predefined training and development split, so we used the development set for testing. The standard (average) classification accuracy was used to measure the performance, and all reported results have been averaged over ten runs.

4.2 Short-term audio representations

In this study, we take an input music as a sequence of audio words. To construct the codebook of audio words, raw audio signals are partitioned into fix-sized frames, and some short-term features are extracted from the frames. Many short-term audio features have been proposed in the literature. The spectrogram might be the most fundamental one that is computed by short-term Fourier transform [27]. It describes the time-varying energy across different frequency bands in a linear frequency scale of the signal. Moreover, we also consider two other representations.

- **Mel-spectrogram** that is computed by wrapping the linear-frequency scale into a nonlinear, Mel-frequency scale by triangular filters [27]. The Mel-frequency sacle is designed to approximate the frequency resolution of human ear, which is more sensitive to differences at low frequencies.
- **Spectral flatness measures (SFM) and Spectral crest factors (SCF)** are both related to the noisiness of audio signal [37]. SFM is defined as the ratio between geometric mean and arithmetic mean of the power spectrum, whereas SCF is computed as the ratio between the peak amplitude and the root-mean-square amplitude.

We used the MIR toolbox [18] to compute Mel-spectrogram, and the Marsyas [37] to extract SFM and SCF. The frame size and hop size were set to 1,024 samples and 50% of the frame size, respectively. As previously mentioned, we take multiple frames as an input unit for feature learning, and the segment feature vectors formed by the concatenations of multiple-frame representations. Hamel et al showed that simple Principal Component Analysis (PCA) whitened spectrogram can provide good performance by combining different type of temporal pooling [11], so we applied the PCA-whitening on the segment feature vectors to remove pair-wise correlation in the input data domain and, as a result, to reduce the data dimensionality. The PCA-whitened segment feature representations were used to learn the codebook of audio words by the K-means algorithm.

4.3 Competitors for performance comparison

Unsupervised feature learning typically can be conducted either by mapping the input signal into a new sparse feature

[5]Available at http://opihi.cs.uvic.ca/sound/genres.tar.gz

[6]Although the correctness of the data set has been argued in recent paper [35], it provides a benchmark on which music classification algorithm can be compared.

[7]The genre classes of GTZAN are classical, country, disco, hiphop, jazz, rock, blues, reggae, pop, and metal.

[8]Available at http://ismir2004.ismir.net/genre_contest/

[9]The genre classes of ISMIR2004Genre are classical (320), electronic (115), jazz_blues (26), metal_punk (45), rock_pop (101), and world (122).

space or by means of deep learning. We thus compared the performance of the KCNN against three state-of-art feature learning algorithms: sparse coding, autoencoder, and deep belief network.

- **Sparse coding** represents a given input as a sparse linear combination of elements in a dictionary, which is learned using the L1-penalized sparse coding formulation [24]. SC has been used for many MIR applications, including genre classification [16, 34, 12, 43]. We used the SPAMS[10] to train the dictionary and the L1-encoding to extract features from input data.
- **Autoencoder** is a neural network to learn a compressed, distributed representation for a set of data. It is trained to reconstruct its own inputs, typically for the purpose of dimensionality reduction [2]. A denoising autoencoder has been used for genre classification by [41]. In our experiments, the DeepLearnToolbox[11] was used to learn the codings of input data.
- **Deep belief network** can be viewed as a composition of restricted Boltzmann machines that are learned to probabilistically reconstruct its inputs [13]. Hamel and Eck applied the DBN to perform genre classification [10], and Schlüter and Osendorfer used the mean-covariance RBM for similarity-based music classification [31]. It is worth mentioning that RBMs and basic classical autoencoders are very similar in their functional form, although their interpretation and the procedures used for training them are quite different. We reimplemented the system of [10] by the RBMLIB[12].

To systematically compare with the above feature learning algorithms in a controlled way, all algorithms were applied on the same set of short-term features (see Section 4.2) to learn the frame-level representations. Since the learned feature vectors are generally sparse and high-dimensional, we used the max-pooling to aggregate the frame-level representations over the entire audio to produce the song-level representations. The max-pooling has been widely used [7, 28], and shown to achieve consistently higher performance on benchmark datasets over the min, mean and variance pooling operations [11].

The song-level representations learned by different algorithms were used to train the SVM-based classifiers and evaluated on the test data. We separated out the contributions of classifiers to ensure fairness of comparison. The song-level representations of the KCNN were extracted by collecting the outputs of the topmost hidden layer (see the shaded ellipses in Figure 1). The convolutional neural networks were also used to perform many MIR tasks including onset detection [17] and genre classification [7]. To compare with the classical CNN and its pretrained variant, the KCNN was turned off the effect of k-max pooling and adaptable lookup tables to approximate their results.

4.4 The choice of hyper-parameters

We tuned the hyper-parameters by trying only a few different networks. All the test results were obtained over ten runs with different random initialization for each setting of the network.

[10] Available at http://spams-devel.gforge.inria.fr/
[11] Available at https://github.com/rasmusbergpalm/
[12] Available at https://code.google.com/p/matrbm/

Table 1: Hyper-parameters of the KCNN.

Hyper-parameter	Value
Window size	5
Value k in k-max pooling operation	5
Number of convolutional units	500
Number of hidden units	300
Learning rate	0.02
Regularization parameter λ	0.0001

Generally, the numbers of convolutional and hidden units, provided they are large enough, have a limited impact on the generalization performance. The value k of k-max pooling layer was set to 5, which achieved a good trade-off between training speed and performance. We found that the performance improve marginally when the window size is larger than 5, but the training time increases drastically. Training could be faster with a larger learning rate, but we preferred to stick to a small one which works, rather than finding the optimal one for speed. The hyper-parameters of the network used in all the following experiments are shown in Table 1.

4.5 Results

We report the experimental results for the GTZAN in Table 2, in which our networks are indicated by "KCNN". The "ALL" in the first row indicates that all the three features were used to construct the codebook of audio words. From these numbers, a handful of trends are readily apparent. First, we note that the "full-fledged" KCNN is superior to that whose lookup tables are not modified in the supervised training stage (indicated with "ULT") by a fairly significant margin (7.68% in average). Another striking result of these experiments is the success of the k-max pooling layer, which boosts the classification accuracy about 7.23% in average. In addition, we do get surprised that it is possible to achieve better performance simply by using the nonlinear SVM as classifier instead of the softmax layer.

Table 2: Classification accuracy for the GTZAN.

Algorithms	MEL	SFM	SCF	ALL
Sparse coding + SVM	74.30	59.00	55.60	75.10
Autoencoder + SVM	59.90	48.80	55.70	64.30
DBN + SVM	63.20	45.50	42.30	60.90
KCNN ($k = 5$) ULT	61.80	47.50	39.80	66.30
KCNN ($k = 5$)	75.30	50.90	42.30	77.60
KCNN ($k = 1$) + SVM	72.90	56.50	39.80	74.60
KCNN ($k = 5$) + SVM	80.70	59.60	48.50	83.90

The results reported in Table 2 also show that the KCNN outperforms the other unsupervised feature learning methods for music genre classification problem, highlighting the potential of the proposed network architecture for practical music classification systems. To the best of our knowledge, by far the two best results for GTZAN were achieved by Hamel and Eck [10] (84.30%), and Yeh and Yang [43] (84.70%). Although the proposed KCNN does not outperform these two prior arts, it performs competitively. The main goal of this study is to investigate how well the KCNN can produce the compact song-level representations comparing with the other unsupervised feature learning algorithms. The two best results were achieved by high-dimensional representations (taking the concatenation of the outputs of

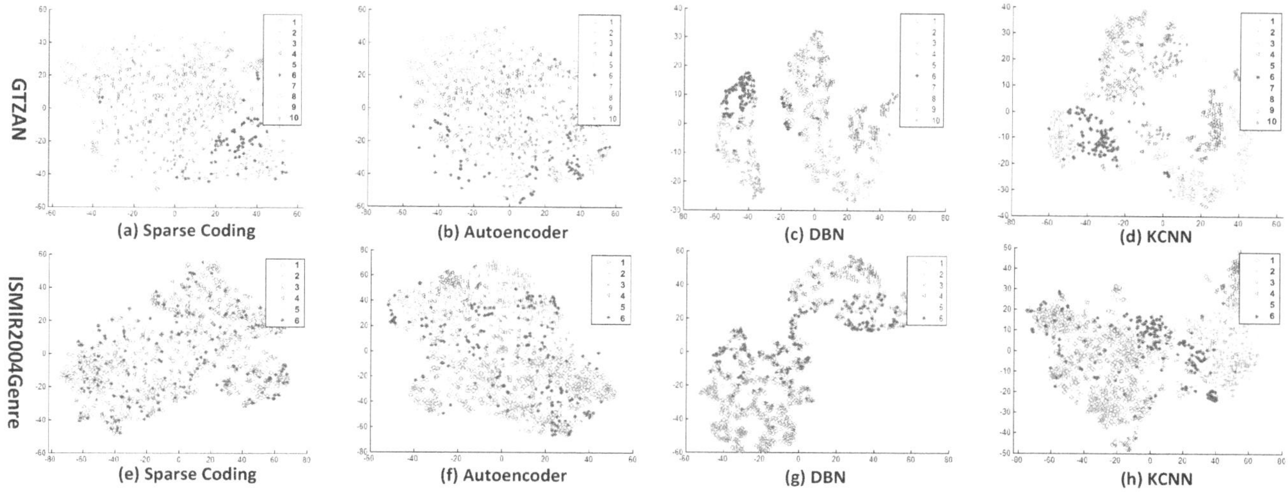

Figure 3: Two-dimensional projections of different representations of the audio with respect to their genres.

all layers as representation [10] or using the codebook with larger size [43]) that might be inappropriate for indexing and similarity-based music recommendation purposes. Furthermore, we tried only a few different network configurations, and there are many ways (such as unsupervised pre-training, and dynamic k-max pooling) that we could improve it further. The results for the ISMIR-2004Genre is reported in Table 3, and we found the similar trends as that for the GTZAN. The results for both benchmark datasets show that the KCNN achieves consistently higher performance over the three competitors.

Table 3: Classification accuracy for the ISMIR2004-Genre.

Algorithms	MEL	SFM	SCF	ALL
Sparse coding + SVM	72.44	62.05	60.80	72.52
Autoencoder + SVM	70.03	69.88	63.55	64.61
DBN + SVM	69.50	68.45	58.30	70.08
KCNN (k = 5) ULT	70.03	53.92	53.57	71.08
KCNN (k = 5)	72.74	63.40	61.60	73.49
KCNN (k = 1) + SVM	69.28	63.70	69.28	71.39
KCNN (k = 5) + SVM	78.29	68.52	69.67	79.68

4.6 Visualization

To illustrate how well the song-level representations were learned by the KCNN, we plotted a two-dimensional projection of the representations produced by the KCNN and the other three competitors in Figure 3. We used the t-SNE algorithm [40] to perform the projection. It is worth noting that the clustering of the song-level representations generated by the KCNN is more definite than those by the sparse coding, autoencoder, and DBN for both GTZAN and ISMIR2004Genre datasets. It gives the evidence that the KCNN can derive better representations, which help to improve the accuracy of the classifiers.

5. CONCLUSION

We have described a novel convolutional neural network architecture with k-max pooling layer for semantic modeling of music. The convolutional nature of the network allows us to model the interaction among the neighboring segments of music, and summarize the features over musically significant timescales. The k-max pooling operation is designed to pool the k most relevant features produced by the topmost convolutional layer, with the order of pooled features preserved, which makes it possible to capture the characteristics of the temporal dynamics in music. More importantly, the representations of audio words initialized by vector quantization can be fine-tuned by backpropagating errors at the supervised training stage, leading to a significant increase in accuracy. Experiment results with two different music datasets show that the KCNN outperformed the three state-of-art unsupervised feature learning methods for music genre classification. For future work, we would like to test the KCNN on the other MIR tasks, such as automatic tagging and artist recognition. It also would be interesting to see how well our network scales to much larger music databases, by applying it to a larger dataset, such as the Million Song dataset [4].

6. ACKNOWLEDGMENTS

The authors would like to thank the anonymous reviewers for their valuable comments. This work was supported by a grant from Shanghai Municipal Natural Science Foundation (No. 13ZR1403800).

7. REFERENCES

[1] Y. Bengio. Learning deep architectures for AI. *Foundations and Trends in Machine Learning*, 2:1–127, 2009.

[2] Y. Bengio and Y. LeCun. *Scaling learning algorithms towards AI. In Large Scale Kernel Machines, L. Bottou, O. Chapelle, D. DeCoste, and J. Weston (eds).* MIT Press, 2007.

[3] T. Bertin-Mahieux, D. Eck, and M. Mandel. *Automatic tagging of audio: The state-of-art. In Machine Audition: Principles, Algorithms and Systems.* IGI Publishing, 2010.

[4] T. Bertin-Mahieux, D. P. W. Ellis, B. Whitman, and P. Lamere. The million song dataset. In *International Society for Music Information Retrieval (ISMIR'11)*, 2011.

[5] M. Casey, R. Veltkamp, M. Goto, M. Leman, C. Rhodes, and M. Slaney. Content-based music information retrieval: Current directions and future challenges. *IEEE*, 96(4):668–696, 2008.

[6] A. Coates and A. Y. Ng. The importance of encoding versus training with sparse coding and vector quantization. In *International Conference on Machine Learning (ICML'11)*, 2011.

[7] S. Dielemann, P. Brakel, and B. Schrauwen. Audio-based music classification with a pretrained convolutional network. In *International Society for Music Information Retrieval (ISMIR'11)*, 2011.

[8] Z. Fu, G. Lu, K. M. Ting, and D. Zhang. A survey of audio-based music classification and annotation. *IEEE Transaction on Multimedia*, 13(99):303–319, 2011.

[9] P. Gomez and B. Danuser. Relations between musical structure and psychophysiological measures of emotion. *Emotion*, 7(2):377–87, 2007.

[10] P. Hamel and D. Eck. Learning features from music audio with deep belief networks. In *International Society for Music Infromation Retrieval (ISMIR'10)*, 2010.

[11] P. Hamel, S. Lemieux, Y. Bengio, and D. Eck. Temporal pooling and multiscale learning for automatic annotation and ranking of music audio. In *International Society for Music Infromation Retrieval (ISMIR'11)*, 2011.

[12] M. Henaff, K. Jarrett, K. Kavukcuoglu, and Y. LeCuu. Unsupervised learning of sparse features for scalable audio classification. In *International Society for Music Information Retrieval (ISMIR'11)*, 2011.

[13] G. E. Hinton, S. Osindero, and Y. W. Teh. A fast learning algorithm for deep belief nets. *Neural Computation*, 18:1527–1554, 2006.

[14] E. J. Humphrey, J. P. Bello, and Y. LeCun. Moving beyond feature design: deep architectures and automatic feature learning in music informatics. In *International Society for Music Information Retrieval (ISMIR'12)*, 2012.

[15] M. Kaminskas and F. Ricci. Contextual music information retrieval and recommendation: State of the art and challenges. *Computer Science Review*, 6:89–119, 2012.

[16] P. D. C. Kereliuk. Sparse atomic modeling of audio: A review. In *International Conference on Digital Audio Effects (DAFx'11)*, 2011.

[17] A. Lacoste and D. Eck. A supervised classification algorithm for note onset detection. *EURASIP Journal on Applied Signal Processing*, (1):1–14, 2007.

[18] O. Lartillot and P. Toiviainen. A matlab toolbox for musical feature extraction from audio. In *International Conference on Digital Audio Effects (DAFx'07)*, 2007.

[19] H. Lee, P. Pham, Y. Largman, and A. Y. Ng. Unsupervised feature learning for audio classification using convolutional deep belief networks. In *Neural Information Processing Systems (NIPS'09)*, 2009.

[20] M. Levy and M. Sandler. Music information retrieval using social tags and audio. *IEEE Transactions on Multimedia*, 11:383–395, 2009.

[21] G. Li and A. A. Khokhar. Content-based indexing and retrieval of audio data using wavelets. In *International Conference on Multimedia and Expo (ICME'00)*, 2000.

[22] L. Lu and A. Hanjalic. Audio keywords discovery for text-like audio content analysis and retrieval. *IEEE Transactions on Multimedia*, 10(1):74–85, 2008.

[23] L. Lu, H. Zhang, and S. Z. Li. Content-based audio classification and segmentation by using support vector machines. *Multimedia Systems*, 8(6):482–492, 2003.

[24] J. Mairal, F. Bach, J. Ponce, and G. Sapiro. Online dictionary learning for sparse coding. In *International Conference on Machine Learning (ICML'09)*, 2009.

[25] M. I. Mandel, D. Eck, and Y. Bengio. Learning tags that vary within a song. In *International Society for Music Information Retrieval (ISMIR'10)*, 2010.

[26] B. McFee, L. Barrington, and G. Lanckriet. Learning content similarity for similarity for music recommendation. *IEEE Transactions on Audio, Speech, and Language Processing*, 20:2207–2218, 2012.

[27] M. Muller, D. P. W. Ellis, A. Klapuri, and G. Richard. Signal processing for music analysis. *IEEE Journal of Selected Topics in Signal Processing*, 5(6):1088–1110, 2011.

[28] J. Nam, J. Herrera, M. Slaney, and J. Smith. Learning sparse feature representations for music annotation and retrieval. In *International Society for Music Information Retrieval (ISMIR'12)*, 2012.

[29] U. Nam and J. Berger. Addressing the same but different—different but similar problem in automatic music classification. In *International Symposium on Music Information Retrieval*, 2001.

[30] M. Riley, E. Heinen, and J. Ghosh. A text retrieval approach to content-based audio retrieval. In *International Society for Music Information Retrieval (ISMIR'08)*, 2008.

[31] J. Schlẗer and C. Osendorfer. Music similarity estimation with the mean-covariance restricted boltzmann machine. In *International Conference on Machine Learning and Applications (ICMLA'11)*, 2011.

[32] K. Seyerlehner, G. Widmer, and P. Knees. Frame level audio similarity: A codebook approach. In *International Conference on Digital Audio Effects (DAFx'08)*, 2008.

[33] J. Shen, H. Pang, M. Wang, and S. Yan. Modeling concept dynamics for large scale music search. In *Special Interest Group on Information Retrieval (SIGIR'12)*, 2012.

[34] E. C. Smith and M. S. Lewicki. Efficient auditory coding. *Nature*, 439(7079):978–982, 2006.

[35] B. L. Sturm. An analysis of the gtzan music genre dataset. In *ACM Workshop Music Information Retrieval with User-Centered and Multimodal Strategies*, 2012.

[36] L. Su, C.-C. M. Yeh, J.-Y. Liu, J.-C. Wang, and Y.-H. Yang. A systematic evaluation of the bag-of-frames representation for music information retrieval. *IEEE Transactions on Multimedia*, 16(5):1188–1200, 2014.

[37] G. Tzanetakis. *Marsyas: a case study in implementing Music Information Retrieval Systems. In Intelligent Music Information Systems: Tools and Methodologies, Shen, Shepherd, Cui, and Liu (eds).* IGI Publishing, 2008.

[38] G. Tzanetakis and P. Cook. Musical genre classification of audio signals. *IEEE Transactions on Speech and Audio Processing*, 10:93–302, 2002.

[39] G. Tzanetakis, G. Essl, and P. Cook. Automatic musical genre classification of audio signals. In *International Society for Music Information Retrieval (ISMIR'01)*, 2001.

[40] L. J. P. van der Maaten and G. E. Hinton. Visualizing high-dimensional data using t-sne. *Journal of Machine Learning Research*, 9:2579–2605, 2008.

[41] P. Vincent, H. Larochelle, I. Lajoie, Y. Bengio, and P.-A. Manzagol. Stacked denoising autoencoders: learning useful representations in a deep network with a local denoising criterion. *Journal of Machine Learning Research*, 11:3371–3408, 2010.

[42] J.-C. Wang, H.-S. Lee, H.-M. Wang, and S.-K. Jeng. Learning the similarity of audio music in bag-of-frames representation from tagged music data. In *International Society for Music Information Retrieval (ISMIR'11)*, 2011.

[43] C.-C. M. Yeh and Y.-H. Yang. Supervised dictionary learning for music genre classification. In *International Conference on Multimedia Retrieval (ICMR'12)*, 2012.

Robust Seed Localization and Growing with Deep Convolutional Features for Scene Text Detection

Hailiang Xu
mf1333052@smail.nju.edu.cn

Feng Su*
suf@nju.edu.cn

State Key Laboratory for Novel Software Technology
Nanjing University
Nanjing 210023, China

ABSTRACT

Text detection in natural scene images is an open and challenging problem due to the significant variations of the appearance of the text itself and its interaction with the context. In this paper, we present a novel text detection method based on robust localization and adaptive growing of seed text components. The method consists of two main ingredients. First, convolutional neural network is exploited to localize seed candidate characters from the maximally stable extremal regions of the image with learned discriminative deep convolutional features. Next, an iterative and adaptive growing algorithm is employed to grow from seed characters to search for other degraded text components in same text line based on their conformity to the seed, and an associative quality is learned to measure the conformity combining both the geometric and appearance constraints between two neighbouring text components. The effectiveness of the proposed method is demonstrated by the state-of-the-art results achieved on the public datasets.

Categories and Subject Descriptors

H.3.1 [**Information Storage and Retrieval**]: Content Analysis and Indexing

General Terms

Algorithms, Experimentation

Keywords

Text detection; convolutional neural network; MSER; natural scene image; SWT

1. INTRODUCTION

With the fast growth of the number of images and videos created by people using digital camera or smartphone and expediently shared through Internet and social networks such as Facebook and Flickr, to effectively extract and make use of the text information present in the image in variant forms has been attracting significant research attentions in computer vision, multimedia retrieval and related fields. As the first step of exploiting such textual data, however, to detect the text in natural scene images is often challenging due to the complexity and variety of text's appearance and its interaction with the scene context.

Since the past decade, various methods have been proposed for the task of detecting text in natural images, which is usually divided into two stages (despite some variants): the character components are first extracted from the image, on which basis the text lines are generated by grouping together character components. Many existing methods are devoted to the first stage, which can be further categorized into two groups: the exhaustive search based methods [1, 10, 16, 18] and the selective search based methods [2, 12, 13, 6, 14, 21, 3, 9]. The former uses a multiple-scale sliding window to extract features such as HOG and LBP, and learns classifiers on these features to discriminate text and non-text. However, the huge search space often results in the significant computational cost. The latter category of method selectively searches for candidate text regions on the basis of connected component analysis, and exploits trained classifiers or heuristic rules on sophisticated (usually hand-engineered) features like stroke width to discriminate text components from non-text components. Compared to sliding window based methods, these methods are convenient in dealing with text of variant scales and orientations.

Despite the progress having been made, to reliably discover character components with high accuracy remains an open and difficult problem. On the other hand, the second stage of text detection - text line aggregation, is also nontrivial, especially when the first stage cannot extract some character components due to degradation of text or complicated scene composition. However, as long as the first stage yields correct detections for some well-conditioned characters (a.k.a. seed characters), we can seek for other missed (usually degraded) text components based on the conformity between text components, instead of the stricter constraints exploited in the first stage for discriminating text/non-text. This provides the possibility for improved detection results on the basis of the former stage.

In this paper, we present a robust scene text detection method, which, on the basis of localizing seed candidate characters with the boosted Convolutional Neural Network (CNN) detector from Maximally Stable Extremal Regions (MSERs), places much of the focus on iterative growing and filtering of text components to acquire as complete and ac-

ICMR'15, June 23–26, 2015, Shanghai, China.

http://dx.doi.org/10.1145/2671188.2749370.

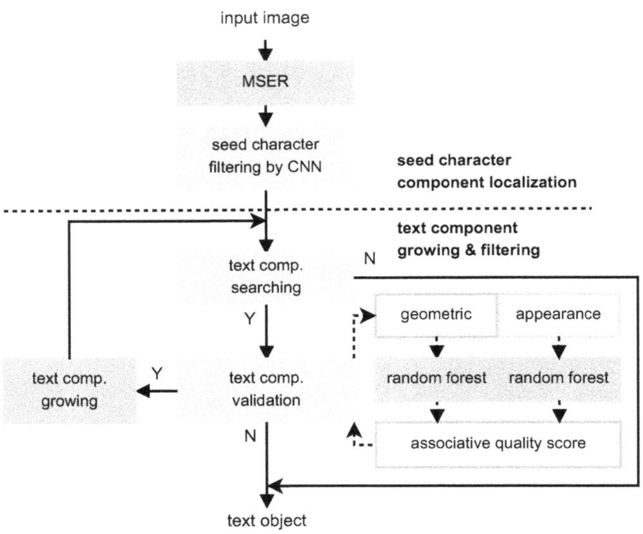

Figure 1: The framework of the proposed method.

curate text objects as possible from the image. The basic idea is, once seed characters are extracted with effective representation of text learned by deep neural network, we can grow from the seeds to discover more text components, exploiting the associative characteristics (both geometric and appearance-based) between them, and at the same time, adaptively filter out non-text components. Correspondingly, the proposed method consists of two main processing stages: 1) seed character component localization and 2) text component growing & validation, as shown in Fig. 1.

The remainder of the paper is organized as follows. Section 2 briefly introduces some related existing work on scene text detection. Section 3 presents the CNN-based localization of seed character components, and Section 4 describes the algorithm for text component growing in detail. In Section 5, we present the experiment results, which demonstrate the effectiveness and state-of-the-art performance of our method.

2. PREVIOUS WORK

The original work by Epstein et al. in [2] proposes a local image operator named Stroke Width Transform (SWT) for scene text detection, which computes per pixel the width of the most likely stroke containing the pixel. The SWT operator is applied on the edge image generated using the Canny detector from the input image, and the stroke width pixels are grouped into character candidates. A heuristic rule-based character filtering is then applied to eliminate false character candidates, and neighbouring characters are finally merged into text lines. Despite being very efficient, the method is sensitive to noisy and blurry images for its dependency on a successful edge detection.

Neumann et al. [13] combines the sliding-window and connected component methods. Stroke is modelled as the responses to oriented filters in the gradient projection scale space, and relative stroke positions are modelled by subsampling the responses into a fixed-size matrix. Regions containing at least one stroke are considered the candidate character regions. Then character candidates are extracted by recognizing a known stroke pattern with a classifier.

The MSER-based text detection methods are very likely the state of the art method recently for their outstanding effectiveness and high efficiency. Yin et al. [20] exploits MSER to extract character candidates and remove the repeating components by several heuristic rules. Then the distance weights and clustering threshold are learned to cluster the character candidates into text candidates. The posterior probabilities of the text candidates corresponding to non-texts are estimated using the character classifier, and text candidates with high non-text probabilities are removed. An AdaBoost classifier is trained to decide whether a text candidate corresponding to the true text or not.

Recently, deep neural networks (especially CNN) have started to be exploited in text detection task on natural images. [18] employs two separate CNNs for text detection and recognition respectively. In detection, specifically, CNN is exploited to determine whether the multiscale sliding window on the scene image contains a centered character, by classifying the window of pixels to either text or non-text. In [3], CNN is used to predict and assign a confident value to each MSER component, which is exploited to both localize text components to be aggregated into text-lines and, with information of MSERs trees, help to identify and split error-connected components. [4] proposes a novel CNN architecture with efficient feature sharing and other technical changes, which is used as the character classifier and extended for character detection and bigram classification.

One main difference of our method to previous CNN-based methods is, CNN is exploited only to detect the relatively well-conditioned seed text component, leaving the localization of text outliers to the adaptive component growing process that makes use of the cues provided by the seeds, to help achieving improved performance.

3. SEED CHARACTER COMPONENT LOCALIZATION

In this first stage of our method, we look for *seed character components (SCCs)*, which are connected components preserving relatively complete appearance characteristics of the character, from all candidate *character components (CCs)* outputted by the MSER algorithm. Fig. 2 shows some examples of SCC, non-seed CC and non-character components. As seed characters constitute the basis for the subsequent processing and have a critical impact on the final detection performance, we need to acquire as precise and complete localization as possible for SCCs.

To discriminate SCCs from non-SCC objects, however, is difficult due to the degradations of text appearance in complicated images, which often result in the large variance of feature distribution of character components. On the other hand, given samples as shown in Fig. 2, a sophisticated representation for SCC could be learned that helps to improve the detection accuracy. Due to the promising potential of deep learning models for generatively discovering effective representations from data, we exploit the convolutional neural network model for SCC localization.

3.1 Component Extraction by MSER

As the very first step of processing, connected components potentially corresponding to candidate characters need to

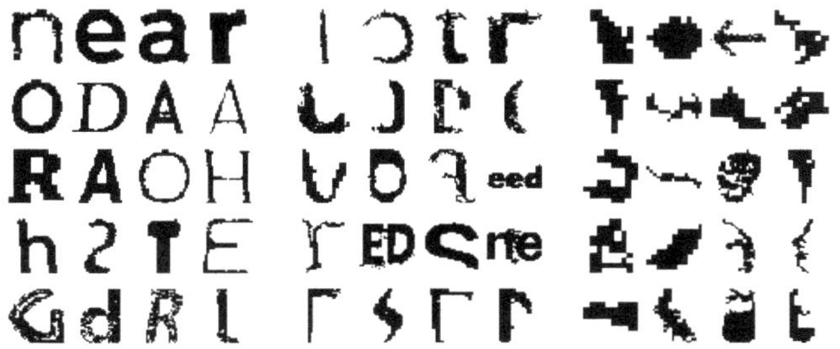

(a) (b) (c)

Figure 2: Illustration of SCCs (a), non-seed CCs (b) and non-character components (c).

be extracted from the input image as complete as possible, which constitute the basis of subsequent processing. Due to the robustness of MSERs to low-contrast, blurring and illumination/color variation of scene text, the MSER algorithm is exploited in this work to reliably generate candidate character components. Specifically, the MSER algorithm is preformed separately on four channels - the HLS channels and the composite gradient channel computed in LAB color space. For each candidate CC, similar to SWT, we match the opposite pixels on the component contour, and compute the statistical median of the distance between the matching pair of pixels and take it as the *stroke width* of the CC. We also compute a *retention value* r as defined by Eq. (1) for each candidate CC.

$$r = \max \delta \quad s.t. \quad |R_{l+\delta}| \leq 3|R_l| \tag{1}$$

where, l and $l + \delta$ are intensity levels, R_l and $R_{l+\delta}$ are the MSER regions corresponding to respective intensity level, thus $R_{l+\delta}$ is parent region of R_l, and $|R|$ denotes the area of region. MSER with a higher retention value has higher contrast to the background.

Besides components corresponding to text, however, the outputs of MSER also comprise quite a large quantity of non-text components, since no text-specific characteristic of connected components is exploited by MSER but the extremal property of the intensity function on the region and outer boundary of component. For better accuracy, such non-text components should be filtered out from subsequent processing while preserving those components belonging to characters.

3.2 Seed Character Component Filtering by CNN

Convolutional neural network is exploited in this work to learn effective representations for reliably discriminating an input component to SCCs or non-SCCs. Being a generative multi-layer deep neural network, each convolutional layer of CNN acts as one non-linear feature extractor by convolving the output of the previous layer with multiple learned filter masks, on which an element-wise non-linear activation function is then applied, and optionally combining the outputs by a pooling operation. The last several layers of CNN are fully connected layers that multiply the input with a matrix of learned parameters followed by a non-linear activation function. The output of the network are scores for each of the learned categories. Fig. 3 shows the structure of the CNN used in this work.

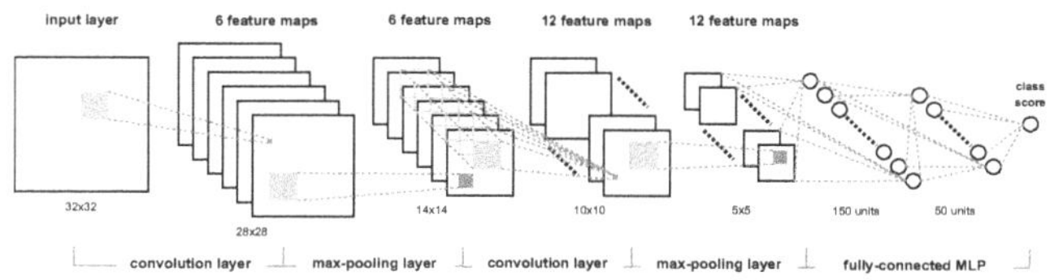

Figure 3: CNN used for seed character component detection.

Table 1: Properties for component filtering. $u(c)$ **and** $s(c)$ **are the mean and standard deviation of stroke width in component** c**.** n_{all} **is the set of pixels on the out-boundary contour of the component, and** n_e **is the set of edge pixels in** n_{all}**.** E_s **is the set of edge pixels whose matching opposite edge pixel can be found in the component, and** E_{all} **is the set of all edge pixels.**

Prop.	Description	Valid Ranges
AR	component aspect ratio	[0.2, 2.0]
SWV	$s(c)/u(c)$	[0, 0.5]
SWR	stroke width divided by component height	[0.1, 0.4]
SCR	stroke count (the number of different SWT rays in component) divided by component height	[0.9, ∞)
$SWTR$	$\|E_s\|/\|E_{all}\|$	[0.9, 1]
SER	$\|n_e\|/\|n_{all}\|$	[0.9, 1]

Given component samples from the training set, CNN is learned by feeding each component (normalized to $32 * 32$ pixels and preserving character aspect) to the input layer of CNN. For an unknown component, it's taken as a SCC only if it achieves a *character score* (the value of the output unit of CNN) higher than the threshold 0.5.

To generate CC-level training set for CNN, we devise an automatic training sample generation scheme on top of the existing datasets such as ICDAR's, which provide only the word-level ground truth (i.e. the bounding box annotations for each word). Specifically, we first perform SWT on training images of ICDAR dataset to generate the SWT response image and extract the connected components from it. Next, the resulting connected components are filtered with the experimentally determined thresholds on 6 features of component - aspect ratio (AR), stroke width variation (SWV), stroke width ratio (SWR), stroke count ratio (SCR), SWT ratio ($SWTR$), surround edge ratio (SER), as shown in Tab. 1. The components, which pass the filtering and fall in the bounding boxes of the ground truth text in ICDAR dataset, are then considered *SWT components*. On the other hand, we perform the MSER algorithm on the same training image to extract *MSER components*. If one MSER component has a high pixel overlapping ratio with one SWT component, it's taken as a true SCC sample. On the other hand, MSER components that have no intersection with the ground truth bounding boxes and whose *stroke_width/component_width* > 0.6 are considered false SCC samples.

To further increase the localization accuracy of SCC, we employ a boosting framework that cascades two CNNs aforementioned together. Accordingly, we divide the training sample set into three subsets $\{D_1, D_2, D_3\}$. D_1 consists of all the true SCC samples. D_2, which has the same size as D_1, is composed of false SCC samples randomly selected from the whole training set. The other false SCC samples constitute D_3. We first use D_1 and D_2 to train the level-1 CNN classifier and use it to classify the D_3. Then, the misclassified samples of D_3 are combined with D_1 to form a new sample set D', and if the misclassified samples of D_3 is less than the samples of D_1, we randomly select some correctly classified samples of D_3 to be added into D' to balance the true and false SCC samples. We then use D' to train the level-2 CNN classifier. More levels of CNNs can be incorporated in the similar manner.

4. TEXT COMPONENT GROWING

In this second stage of our method, given the set of seed character components extracted, we grow from every SCC to search for other (possibly degraded) non-seed character components. Note that, hereafter we use the term *text component* to refer to the set of individual character components detected (either SCC or non-seed CC).

One common scheme [2, 20] for text line aggregation employs a two-stage processing: first generate the candidate text line from character components, then impose certain filtering criteria on the text line to determine either accept or discard it. The duty of filtering or validating of the text line conformity is usually put on the second stage, while the first stage is only required to give coarse results satisfying simple geometric constraints. The main drawback of this scheme is, when one text line outputted by the first stage is composed of several true characters followed by a few false components like noises or non-text objects and therefore fails the checking of the second stage, the whole text line is discarded, although part of it is correct. To overcome this drawback, we propose an iterative and incremental growing algorithm that puts more duty of checking the conformity of components in candidate text line on the growing phase, rather than relying on the post-filtering after formation of text lines. The algorithm performs the filtering of unconformable components at every growing step to timely end the growing and avoid incorporating non-text components, so that as much as possible valid text parts will be preserved.

Another major difference of our method is, besides the geometric and spatial constraints between character components of a text line, which are exploited by most existing methods, our method considers also the appearance constraint in determining whether or not to merge one candidate component into the current set of detected text components of a candidate text line. This contributes to additionally improved accuracy to text component aggregation.

To measure the conformity of an unknown component being considered to be grown into a candidate text line that comprises at least one SCC, we compute an *associative quality* on the geometric and appearance constraints between both objects. The component is merged into the text line only if their associative quality is higher than certain threshold, and once merged, the newly updated text line is used as the basis of searching for other potential text components.

4.1 Associative Quality

To depict and measure the associative quality or strength between two text components during growing, which essentially reflects the conformity of both, we exploit two complementary aspects of component characteristics: the *geometric* and the *appearance* conformity.

4.1.1 Geometric Conformity

Typically the components in the same word or text line share similar geometric properties, e.g. character height and stroke width. We define the geometric-based features in Tab. 2 to measure the conformity between two components. Note we incorporate the average pixel color distance in this description for its computation simplicity, though it's related to the appearance aspect of component. Finally, these features are concatenated into the 6-dim geometric conformity description vector.

4.1.2 Appearance Conformity

Besides the conformity on geometric properties, we propose to consider also the appearance conformity between two text components in growing. However, it's inefficient to measure directly the appearance similarity on pixel level, since two adjacent text components may correspond to different characters. On the other hand, the activations of the units on the intermediate hidden layer of the CNN model aforementioned encode the high order non-linear transformations learned from the input pixel data, and therefore can be exploited here as the essential appearance description.

Specifically, given two components C_i and C_j, we extract the 50-dim appearance description vector of each component from the second fully connected layer of CNN, then compute the difference between the appearance description vectors of C_i and C_j, and use it as the 50-dim appearance conformity description vector for the two components being considered.

4.1.3 Associative Quality Computation by Random Forest

To compute the associative quality for two text components that incorporates both geometric and appearance conformity cues, we first exploit the *random forest* model to learn the mapping from each individual conformity description (either geometric or appearance) to the corresponding associative quality score, and then combine two scores together as the final score used in component growing. Note we directly assign the associative quality of two components to 0 if they are not horizontally aligned.

Random forest is a collection of binary decision tree predictors, in which the binary test at each non-leaf node performs thresholding on one feature channel to determine the branch the input feature goes down, and the choice for feature channel and thresholds are learned in training stage. To train the random forest for associative quality computation, we construct the training samples automatically from ICDAR training dataset. Since the ground truth of ICDAR dataset gives the word-level bounding box, we first collect the component that has over 60% overlapping area with one ground truth bounding box and their height ratio falls in $[0.3, 1.5]$. Next, for any pair of two neighbouring and horizontally aligned components C_i and C_j, if they belong to the same ground truth bounding box and their color distance is smaller than 10.0, we consider them as one positive sample for associative quality learning. Otherwise, if only one component in the pair is in a ground truth bounding box, we consider the pair a negative sample.

Table 2: **Geometric associative feature. C_i and C_j are two components under consideration.**

Feature	Description
Height ratio	The height of C_i divided by the height of C_j.
Horizontal overlap ratio	The overlapping of height between C_i and C_j, divided by the min. height of them.
Pixel count ratio	The pixel count of C_i divided by the pixel count of C_j.
Stroke width ratio	The stroke width of C_i divided by the stroke width of C_j.
Retention ratio	The retention value of C_i divided by the retention value of C_j.
Color distance	The color distance (computed by CIE94 in Lab color space) between C_i and C_j.

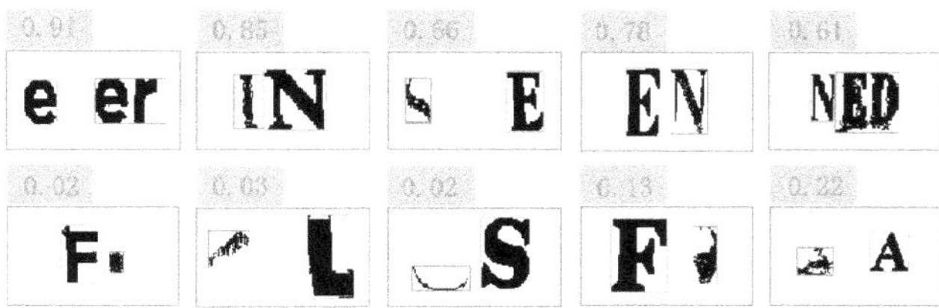

Figure 4: Examples of associative quality of two components.

Once trained, given an input conformity description of two text components, random forest maps it to an output probability, which is used as the associative quality score for two components. The closer the associative quality is to 1.0, the two components are more conformable to be merged. If it's close to 0.0, the two components are unlikely belonging to the same text line.

To combine the two separate associative quality scores Q_a^g and Q_a^p computed as above based on the geometric and appearance conformity description respectively by two dedicated random forests, we use Eq. (2) to compute the holistic associative quality score Q_a for two components:

$$Q_a = \beta Q_a^g + (1 - \beta) Q_a^p \quad (2)$$

where β is the combinatorial weight learned by experiment. Fig. 4 shows some examples of computing associative quality for two components.

4.2 Iterative and Incremental Growing of Text Components

Based on the associative quality computed for any two text components, we propose an incremental growing algorithm that starts from every seed character component extracted in the first stage of the method and iteratively searches for non-seed character components (NSCC) satisfying the associative quality threshold, which determines whether or not the component can be merged into a candidate text line comprising the seed component.

Let $Q_a(C_i, C_j)$ denote the associative quality of two components C_i and C_j, $D_c(C_i, C_j)$ denote the distance between C_i and C_j divided by the width of C_j, the extraction of text lines from all the CCs is divided into two main steps: 1) aggregating SCCs into initial candidate text lines as described by Alg. 1, and 2) growing and validating candidate text lines as described by Alg. 2. Fig. 5 shows the example results of text component growing.

Note that, the *redundant components* to be eliminated in Alg. 1 are those having > 30% of bounding box area overlapped with each other, for which the one with smaller character score will be discarded. Also, as the algorithms show, once an initial candidate text line is generated or a new component is about to be added to one candidate text line, the conformability validation of text line described in Section 4.2.1 is executed to exclude false text lines or timely stop growing to prevent incorporating incompatible components into candidate text line.

Algorithm 1 Aggregate SCCs into initial candidate text line

```
INIT: Create an initially empty set T to store the candidate text lines, which are represented as the subsets of CCs.
for each pair of two seed character components SCC_i and SCC_j do
  if Q_a(SCC_i, SCC_j) > 0.5 and D_c(C_i, C_j) < 3 then
    Create a candidate text line < SCC_i, SCC_j > and add it to T.
  end if
end for
loop
  Find two candidate text lines t_i ∈ T and t_j ∈ T that share at least one same SCC.
  if exists such pair of t_i and t_j then
    Join t_i and t_j to create a new candidate text lines t' = t_i ∪ t_j. Add t' to T, and remove t_i, t_j from T.
  else
    Exit loop.
  end if
end loop
Make SCC ∉ T an individual candidate text line.
Eliminate redundant components.
Assign an initial conformability label l_i to each t_i ∈ T, as described in Section 4.2.1.
```

4.2.1 *Text Line Validation*

To evaluate the holistic conformability of components in one candidate text line, a separate random forest classifier is exploited on the statistical features of the text line. Specifically, to characterize the conformability inside one text line, we reuse the features in Tab. 2, but since here we focus on measuring the consistency of all components in the line instead of comparing two components for growing as in Section 4.1, we compute the coefficient of variation (CV) (instead of the pairwise 'ratio') of each feature in Tab. 2. Moreover, we incorporate the CV and mean of the *component character score* defined in Section 3.2 and the CV of the *distance* between adjacent CCs in text line, and two statistics to discriminate from non-text, the *component count* and the *proportion of SCCs* in all CCs of the text line. We hereby form a 10-dim final feature vector, based on which one candidate

Algorithm 2 Text line growing & validating

Require: $T = \{t_k, l_k\}$ consisting of candidate text lines t_k and their initial labels l_k.

for Each text line (t_k, l_k) in T **do**

  loop

    Suppose t_k consisting of n_k SCCs and m_k NSCCs:

    $t_k = \{SCC_{k,1}, ..SCC_{k,n_k}\} \cup \{NSCC_{k,1}, ..NSCC_{k,m_k}\}$

    Construct the set $S_{NSCC} = \{NSCC_i\}$ composed of all NSCCs not appearing in T and satisfying following two conditions:

    1) $\min_{j=1}^{n_k} D_c(NSCC_i, SCC_{k,j}) < 3$ **or** $\min_{j=1}^{m_k} D_c(NSCC_i, NSCC_{k,j}) < 3$

    2) The average associative quality

    $$\bar{Q}_a(NSCC_i, t_k) = \frac{1}{n_k} \sum_{j=1}^{n_k} Q_a(NSCC_i, SCC_{k,j}) > 0.5$$

    Sort NSCCs in S_{NSCC} in the descending order of $\bar{Q}_a(NSCC_i, t_k)$.

    for each $NSCC_i \in S_{NSCC}$ in order **do**

      Compute the label l'_k for the hypothetical text line $< t_k \cup NSCC_i >$ as described in Section 4.2.1.

      if not (l_k=**true and** l'_k=**false**) **then**

        $t_k = t_k \cup NSCC_i, \quad l_k = l'_k$

      end if

    end for

    if t_k not change in the loop **then**

      Exit loop.

    end if

  end loop

end for

Discard text lines in T with **false** label.

text line will be classified into either True or False for the conformability.

We construct the training set for the random forest based on the ICDAR dataset. For one text line extracted with the aforementioned algorithms from ICDAR training images, if more than 80% of total CCs in the text line fall in the ground truth bounding box provided by the ICDAR dataset, the text line is considered a positive sample, otherwise it's a negative sample. One CC is considered falling in a bounding box if the rectangle of CC has sufficient overlapping ($> 70\%$) with the bounding box and the height of the former exceeds 40% of that of the latter. In this work, a training set of 1,115 true text lines and 868 false ones is constructed on the basis of ICDAR 2011 dataset.

5. EXPERIMENTS

We evaluate and compare our text detection method with some other representative methods reported on ICDAR 2003, 2011 and 2013 datasets. We set $\beta = 0.6$ in Eq. (2) in the experiments unless explicitly stated otherwise. Tab. 3 shows the parameters used for the CNN construction and training.

5.1 Datasets

We evaluated our method on several public datasets, including ICDAR 2003 Text Locating Competition dataset [8],

Figure 5: Illustration of text component growing: (a) input image, (b) result of seed character localization, (c) result of component growing, (d) text line output. Seed characters are marked with green box while non-seed text components grown from seeds are in red box in (b) & (c).

Robust Reading Competition datasets of ICDAR 2011 [15], ICDAR 2013 (Challenge 2: Reading Text in Scene Images) dataset [5] and Street View Text (SVT) [17] dataset. The ICDAR 2003 dataset contains 509 fully annotated text images including 258 images for training and 251 images for testing. The ICDAR 2011 dataset consists of 484 text images with 229 training images and 255 testing images. The ICDAR 2013 dataset contains 562 images including 229 images for training and 233 images for testing. The SVT dataset contains 647 words and 3,796 letters in 249 images harvested from Google Street View. All the images are full-color and vary in size from $307 * 93$ to $3888 * 2592$ pixels. For processing convenience, they are resized so that the maximum of height and width is equal to 1,600 pixels, considering the trade-off of runtime and detection accuracy. The average

Table 3: Parameters of CNN for seed character component localization.

Parameter	Value
input image size	32×32
kernel size	5×5
# of convolution/subsampling layers	2
# of fully-connected layers	2
convolution layer 1	$28 \times 28 \times 6$
subsampling layer 1	$14 \times 14 \times 6$
convolution layer 2	$10 \times 10 \times 12$
subsampling layer 2	$5 \times 5 \times 12$
fully-connected layer 1 units	150
fully-connected layer 2 units	50
output layer units	1
training batch size	100
training iterations	100

processing time for one testing image by our algorithm on ICDAR 2011 dataset is about 6s (without optimization) on a PC platform with one Intel Core i3 CPU at 3.30 GHz.

We adopt the official evaluation protocol of ICDAR for corresponding datasets and the ICDAR 2011's evaluation protocol for SVT dataset, in which, the f measure is the harmonic mean value $\frac{2*p*r}{p+r}$ where p is the precision rate and r is the recall rate. Notice ICDAR 2003's protocol yields lower f measures than that from ICDAR 2011 and 2013 protocols.

5.2 Results

Tab. 4 shows the performance comparisons of our method with some other methods evaluated on the ICDAR 2003 competition dataset. Among all methods, ours and that of Hinnerk Becker are evaluated with the official evaluation protocol of ICDAR 2003, while the other methods use slightly different evaluation protocol that tends to yield higher results than the official one. Our method achieves the overall highest precision, recall rates and f measure (2%, 5% and 4% better than the second best result) among compared methods.

In Tab. 5 and Tab. 6, we compare the performances of our method with some other methods evaluated on the ICDAR 2011 and 2013 datasets, respectively. Our method achieves again the significantly highest recall rate (8% and 10% better than the second best method) and the highest f measure (2% and 5% better), while its precision being slightly lower than the top one but better than most of other methods.

Table 4: Comparison on ICDAR 2003 dataset

Methods	p	r	f
Our method	**0.78**	**0.75**	**0.75**
A. Mosleh [11]	0.76	0.66	0.71
X.B. Wang [19]	0.71	0.70	0.70
H.I. Koo [6]	0.77	0.64	0.70
B. Epshtein [2]	0.73	0.60	0.66
H. Becker [7]	0.62	0.67	0.62

Table 5: Comparison on ICDAR 2011 dataset

Methods	p	r	f
Our method	0.83	**0.79**	**0.80**
W. Huang [3]	**0.88**	0.71	0.78
X.C. Yin [20]	0.86	0.68	0.76
H.I. Koo [6]	0.81	0.68	0.74
L. Neumann [13]	0.79	0.66	0.72
Kim's [15]	0.83	0.63	0.71
X.B. Wang [19]	0.73	0.67	0.70
L. Neumann [12]	0.73	0.65	0.69

Table 6: Comparison on ICDAR 2013 dataset

Methods	p	r	f
Our method	0.85	**0.78**	**0.81**
X.C. Yin [20]	**0.88**	0.66	0.76
Text Spotter [5]	0.88	0.65	0.75
CASIA NLPR [5]	0.79	0.68	0.73
Text Detector CASIA [5]	0.85	0.63	0.72

Table 7: Comparison on SVT dataset

Methods	p	r	f
Our method	**0.31**	**0.58**	**0.40**
L. Neumann [12]	0.19	0.33	0.24

For the SVT dataset, since fewer results have been reported for the text localization task, we choose [12] as the baseline method. Tab. 7 shows the comparison of our method's

Figure 6: Detected texts in some sample images from ICDAR 2003, 2011 and 2013 datasets.

Figure 7: Detected texts in some sample images from SVT dataset.

performance on SVT dataset with the results of [12]. Our method significantly outperforms [12] on all three indices. Note that the significantly lower precision of our method on SVT dataset is mainly due to the incomplete annotation of the ground truth.

The comparison results on all datasets used in the experiment indicate the effectiveness of the proposed method, which consistently outperforms all compared methods on the recall rate and f measure, with precisions comparable to the state-of-the-art methods.

Fig. 6 shows the texts detected by the proposed method from some sample images of the ICDAR datasets, which were interfered by complicated illumination, shadow, low contrast or color variation. Fig. 7 shows the texts detected by the proposed method from some sample images of the SVT dataset, in which the variety of fonts is bigger and the images are noisy. The proposed method exhibits sufficient robustness to these interferences.

Tab. 8 compares the performance of different configurations of the proposed method on ICDAR 2011 dataset, in which, 'MSER with SVM' refers to the baseline method

Table 8: **Performance comparison of different configurations of the proposed method.**

Config.	p	r	f
MSER with SVM	0.70	0.77	0.73
Geometric	0.80	0.76	0.78
Geom. + Appr.	**0.83**	**0.79**	**0.80**

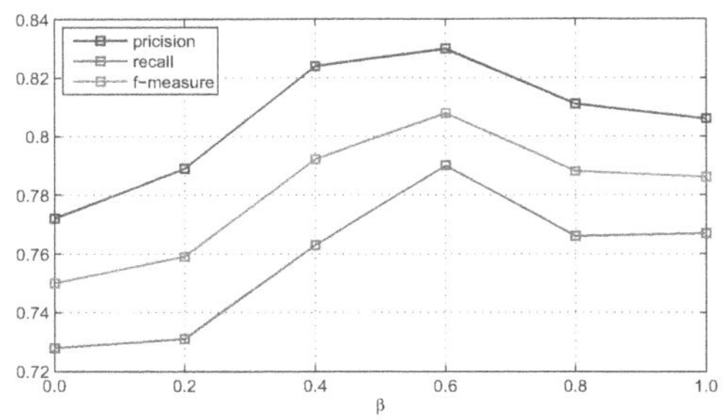

Figure 8: Comparison of performances of the proposed method with different β values in Eq. (2).

by us that applies SVM on hand-crafted features extracted from MSERs, 'Geometric' refers to only the geometric conformity being considered in computing associative quality score, while 'Geom. + Appr.' refers to both geometric and appearance conformity being exploited as proposed. The result shows the effectiveness of the adaptive text component growing algorithm exploiting both appearance and geometric constraints and the CNN-based representation learning for seed character localization.

Fig. 8 compares the performance of the proposed method using different β values in Eq. (2) on ICDAR 2011 dataset, showing the complementarity of the geometric and appearance constraints.

6. CONCLUSIONS

In this paper, we present a robust text detection method for natural scene images, which combines two main ingredients: the boosted CNN-based seed character localization on basis of MSER and learned discriminative deep convolutional features, and the iterative and adaptive growing from seed characters to other (possibly degraded) text components based on an associative quality learned to measure the geometric and appearance conformity of components. The effectiveness of the proposed method is demonstrated by the state-of-the-art results achieved on the public datasets.

Acknowledgments

Research supported by the National Science Foundation of China under Grant Nos. 61003113, 61272218 and 61321491.

7. REFERENCES

[1] X. Chen and A. L. Yuille. Detecting and reading text in natural scenes. In *CVPR*, pages II–366–II–373 Vol.2, 2004.

[2] B. Epshtein, E. Ofek, and Y. Wexler. Detecting text in natural scenes with stroke width transform. In *CVPR*, pages 2963–2970, 2010.

[3] W. Huang, Y. Qiao, and X. Tang. Robust scene text detection with convolution neural network induced mser trees. In *ECCV*, pages 497–511, 2014.

[4] M. Jaderberg, A. Vedaldi, and A. Zisserman. Deep features for text spotting. In *ECCV*, pages 512–528, 2014.

[5] D. Karatzas, F. Shafait, S. Uchida, M. Iwamura, L. G. i Bigorda, S. R. Mestre, J. Mas, D. F. Mota, J. A. Almazan, and L. P. de las Heras. ICDAR 2013 robust reading competition. In *ICDAR*, pages 1484–1493, 2013.

[6] H. I. Koo and D. H. Kim. Scene text detection via connected component clustering and nontext filtering. *IEEE Trans. Image Processing*, 22(6):2296–2305, June 2013.

[7] S. M. Lucas. ICDAR 2005 text locating competition results. In *ICDAR*, pages 80–84 Vol.1, 2005.

[8] S. M. Lucas, A. Panaretos, L. Sosa, A. Tang, S. Wong, and R. Young. ICDAR 2003 robust reading competitions. In *ICDAR*, pages 682–687, 2003.

[9] R. Minetto, N. Thome, M. Cord, J. Stolfi, F. Precioso, J. Guyomard, and N. Leite. Text detection and recognition in urban scenes. In *ICCVW*, pages 227–234, 2011.

[10] A. Mishra, K. Alahari, and C. V. Jawahar. Top-down and bottom-up cues for scene text recognition. In *CVPR*, pages 2687–2694, 2012.

[11] A. Mosleh, N. Bouguila, and A. B. Hamza. Image text detection using a bandlet-based edge detector and stroke width transform. In *BMVC*, pages 63.1–63.12, 2012.

[12] L. Neumann and J. Matas. Real-time scene text localization and recognition. In *CVPR*, pages 3538–3545, 2012.

[13] L. Neumann and J. Matas. Scene text localization and recognition with oriented stroke detection. In *ICCV*, pages 97–104, 2013.

[14] Y.-F. Pan, X. Hou, and C.-L. Liu. A hybrid approach to detect and localize texts in natural scene images. *IEEE Trans. Image Processing*, 20(3):800–813, March 2011.

[15] A. Shahab, F. Shafait, and A. Dengel. ICDAR 2011 robust reading competition challenge 2: Reading text in scene images. In *ICDAR*, pages 1491–1496, 2011.

[16] K. Wang, B. Babenko, and S. Belongie. End-to-end scene text recognition. In *ICCV*, pages 1457–1464, 2011.

[17] K. Wang and S. Belongie. Word spotting in the wild. In *ECCV*, pages 591–604, 2010.

[18] T. Wang, D. J. Wu, A. Coates, and A. Y. Ng. End-to-end text recognition with convolutional neural networks. In *ICPR*, pages 3304–3308, 2012.

[19] X. Wang, Y. Song, and Y. Zhang. Natural scene text detection with multi-channel connected component segmentation. In *ICDAR*, pages 1375–1379, 2013.

[20] X.-C. Yin, X. Yin, K. Huang, and H.-W. Hao. Robust text detection in natural scene images. *IEEE Trans. PAMI*, 36(5):970–983, May 2014.

[21] J. Zhang and R. Kasturi. A novel text detection system based on character and link energies. *IEEE Trans. Image Processing*, 23(9):4187–4198, Sep. 2014.

Swap Retrieval: Retrieving Images of Cats When the Query Shows a Dog

Amir Ghodrati, Xu Jia, Marco Pedersoli, Tinne Tuytelaars
KU Leuven, ESAT - PSI, iMinds
Leuven, Belgium
firstname.lastname@esat.kuleuven.be

ABSTRACT

Query-by-example remains popular in image retrieval because it can exploit contextual information encoded in the image, that is difficult to express in a traditional textual query. Textual queries, on the other hand, give more flexibility in that it's easy to reformulate and refine a text query based on initial results.

In this work we make a first step towards getting the best of both worlds: we use an image to specify the context, but let the user specify a related category as main search criterion. For instance, starting from an image of a dog in a certain situation/context, the goal is to find images of cats with a similar situation/context.

We present an evaluation scheme for this new and challenging task, which we call swap retrieval, and use it to compare various methods. Results show that standard query-by-example techniques do not adapt well to the new task. Instead, techniques based on semantic knowledge extracted from textual descriptions available at training time perform reasonably well, although they are still far from the performance needed for practical use.

Categories and Subject Descriptors

H.3.3 [**Information Storage and Retrieval**]: Information Search and Retrieval—*Retrieval models*; I.2.6 [**Artificial Intelligence**]: Learning—*Concept learning*; I.5.4 [**Pattern Recognition**]: Application—*Computer Vision*

Keywords

Image Retrieval, Attribute (Concept) Discovery, Multimodal Content Analysis

1. INTRODUCTION

Image-based retrieval (aka query-by-example) is an important and well-studied problem in computer vision [30, 3, 10, 20, 9, 6]. However, it is not that flexible, especially when compared with text-based retrieval. When using text-based queries for retrieval, the search for images of a certain topic of interest can be an interactive process, where the user refines the query based on the results given by the retrieval algorithm. When searching based on images, on the other hand, a query cannot be easily refined, as altering an image is not straightforward. Image editing tools (e.g. pasting a cropped part of another image) are cumbersome and typically generate disturbing artefacts that affect the search results.

ICMR'15, June 23–26, 2015, Shanghai, China.

DOI: http://dx.doi.org/10.1145/2671188.2749373.

Figure 1: Category-swap image retrieval. Given the query image of a dog with a hat and the user input "- dog + cat", the goal of this work is to retrieve images of a cat with a hat.

At the same time, text-based retrieval also has its limitations. First, most text-based retrieval schemes rely on associated text (e.g. in the form of filenames, image captions or descriptions). In case that text is not available for candidates, the textual query needs to be "translated" into visual description– typically done using pretrained classifiers for various concepts, a process that, in spite of a lot of progress, is still quite noisy. Second, and this is what we will focus on in this paper, there are aspects that cannot be easily represented with a textual query. For instance, the whole content of an image, such as specific color, spatial layout and composition, or the conditions under which the picture was taken cannot be easily specified by text. However, such information can be easily conveyed by an image. In this respect, letting the method figure out what are the important characteristics of an image and retrieve similar ones can give more satisfactory results than starting from a text-based query.

In this paper, we propose a novel retrieval task where the query is a combination of image and text instead of either image or text alone. It explores the possibility of using a more advanced and human-friendly query for image retrieval, which not only brings more flexibility to the user, but also takes advantage of additional information contained in the query image. Given a query image from one category, a set of images from a different category but semantically as similar as possible to the original image are to be retrieved. The new task can require semantic understanding of visual data, for instance knowing what happens in the scene and which objects participate in an action. We define this task as *category-swap image-based retrieval*, or *swap retrieval* in short. In summary, in this paper we propose, discuss and evaluate a task that extends the standard image-based query towards a more semantic and compositional representation.

We adapt and evaluate several possible solutions using existing methods from the literature. Starting from a feature representation based on DeCAF [5] or Classemes [32], the simplest solution is to directly compare images of two different object categories in the feature space. We also test a domain adaptation based technique [7] where the domains are the two different object categories and a metric learning method [4], where similarity and dissimilarity are computed based on textual descriptions associated to the image. We show that those methods tend to perform poorly and therefore are not suitable for this new task. Thus, we propose an approach based on visual attribute classifiers learned from textual descriptions.

For evaluation we select some pairs of classes from the recently released COCO dataset [19]. In the experiments we mainly focus on the pair dog/cat because it is one of the most interesting and familiar and there are many contexts where both pets can fit but also others that are unique for only one of the two (*e.g.*a dog catching a frisbee). Additionally, we also experiment with cow/sheep and chair/toilet. As the task involves a semantic understanding of the image and may be subjective, for a proper evaluation we resort to two evaluation strategies: the first ranks the images based on text similarity (using the associated textual descriptions provided in the dataset), while the second is based on human evaluation.

The main contributions of this work are: first, we propose swap-retrieval, a new and challenging way of querying data, that provides more flexibility to standard image-based retrieval; Second, two meaningful evaluations of the task are explored, one based on the given image descriptions and the other based on collected human annotations; Third, we explore several possible solutions using existing methods, and further propose a new method which leverages textual descriptions at training time to learn a more semantic representation of the images.

The remainder of the paper is structured as follows: in sec. 2 we present and analyze previous work on similar topics. Sec. 3 introduces swap retrieval in a more formal way, as well as a methodology for its evaluation. Several methods applied to the task are first introduced in sec. 4 and then evaluated in the experimental results in sec. 5. Sec. 6 concludes the paper.

2. RELATED WORK

Image Retrieval. In a traditional query-by-example image retrieval task, the goal is to retrieve relevant images from a dataset given a query image. Relevance in this context implies images with similar visual content. Many works focused on improving the accuracy and efficiency of large-scale image search either for a specific object instance [23, 6, 9, 24] or at category level [1, 34, 28, 8, 12, 33]. Different from the traditional image retrieval task which aims at finding visually similar images, the new task presented in this paper aims at identifying images with similar content but containing an object from a different category. Concept or attribute based representations seem beneficial for this new task. Leveraging attribute representations for image retrieval and related tasks have been investigated in [15, 31]. Kumar *et al.* [15] use describable visual attributes for face verification and image search. Attributes that correspond to hair, eyes and nose are combined to produce semantic descriptions at multiple levels such as categories and object instances. Siddiquie *et al.* [31] propose an approach for image retrieval with multiple attributes as query. The retrieval performance is improved by modeling the correlation between different attributes. For interactive image search, relative attributes [21] provide a powerful tool. Kovashka *et al.* [14, 13] propose a framework for image search with relative attribute feedback, which guides a user through a coarse-to-fine strategy.. The most related work is probably Bi-Concept Search from Li *et al.* [18], where they represent a query with two tags, one for the object and one for the scene. Instead, in our work we express the object with a tag but represent the scene/context with the query image.

Automatic Attribute Discovery. Our work is also related to work on "automatic attribute discovery". Yu *et al.* [36] develop a general framework for attribute-based image retrieval by leveraging a large pool of weak attributes. Weak attributes are defined as a collection of mid-level image representations which are learned in various ways and may not have semantic meanings. Li *et al.* [17] automatically discover and model groups of objects which are composites of objects that have consistent spatial layout and interactions across images. The discovered groups of objects act as distinct visual patterns and help object detection and scene recognition. Yu *et al.* [35] propose an approach to automatically select discriminative "category-level attributes" for visual recognition. These methods automatically discover concept or attribute representations using only image information. In contrast, our attributes are learned leveraging both image and text information, hence having clearer semantic meanings.

Recently, there have been several works which automatically discover attributes or concepts using both image and text information. Quattoni *et al.* [25] propose a framework for classification by training a visual classifier for each word in the corpus of captions associated with images. Instead of directly using the output of the word classifiers as features (as in Classemes [32]), they map the output of the word classifiers into a new space. Berg *et al.* [2] treat strings in descriptions accompanying images as attributes and train a visual classifier for each of them. The discovered attributes are further merged and refined to describe an object's visual appearance. In [16], Layne *et al.* learn semantic attributes by clustering internet photos with tags and use them for re-identification. Similar to such approaches, the proposed method also automatically discovers attributes by mining both image and text data. However, the used attributes are different from the above. We use single (based on one word) and paired (based on the co-occurrence of two words) attributes and find that these two kinds of attributes are complementary and the combination of the two provides an effective tool to describe different aspects of an image. Visual phrases which model the interaction between objects are also explored in [17], [26] and [11]. Our work further supports the effectiveness of such visual phrases models.

3. PROBLEM DEFINITION

In the proposed task, given a query image, we are interested in identifying images with similar context but containing an object from another category. The query image is meant to provide the context where an object (e.g. 'dog') of a given class appears, while a textual query provides the target class (e.g., 'cat') that a user is interested in.

Although at first sight swap retrieval looks similar to standard image-based retrieval, and one would hope that methods for standard retrieval also perform well on this more challenging task, we have experimentally noticed that swapping the class of the query puts forward higher requirements to semantic image understanding. CNN-based features such as DeCAF [5] have been shown to perform well in computer vision tasks including image retrieval [29]. However, as shown in Fig. 2, their performance in standard image retrieval is much better than in swap retrieval (for the evaluation we use the NDCG30@k metric defined in section 3.2). Therefore, in this work, we are interested in two problems: i) is there a good way to perform this task? and ii) which is the best metric to evaluate the performance of the different methods?

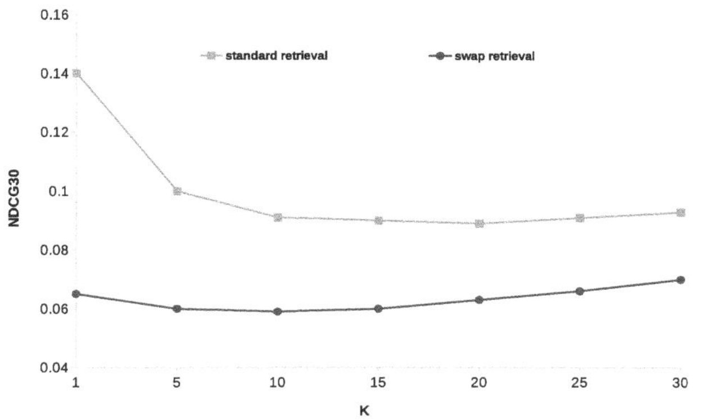

Figure 2: NDCG30@k for standard image retrieval and category-swap retrieval. The swap retrieval is much more difficult than the standard retrieval.

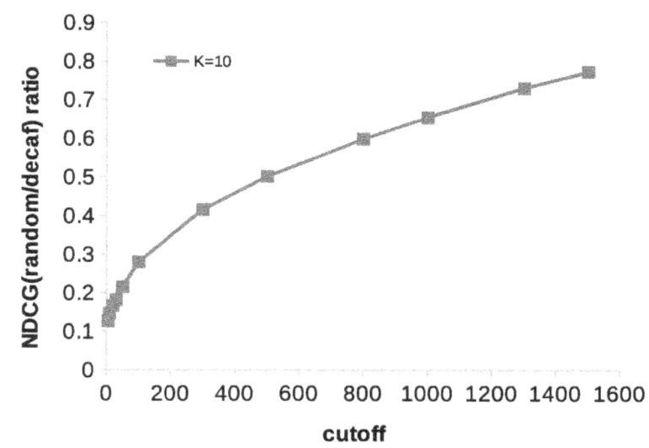

Figure 3: NDCG@k ratio between a random ranking and DeCAF ranking varying the cutoff value. For high values of cutoff, the ratio tends to 1, indicating that the measure loses its meaning.

3.1 Ground truth annotations

For evaluation we resort to two complementary strategies. The first is based on human annotations. This is of course the most reliable, but also expensive to obtain. Thus, from the full set of 1400 cats and dogs queries from the COCO dataset, we have selected a random subset of 50 for which we obtained the lists of the swap-retrieval ranking from 10 human annotators. We refer to the supplementary material for more details on the annotation procedure.

The second evaluation strategy relies on the available image descriptions from COCO dataset. This does not require human judgment and therefore can be applied on a large scale, using all 1400 queries. In particular, we rank images based on their textual distance measured based on the bag-of-words representation of descriptions. In the experimental results we compare this evaluation with the annotations provided by humans and show that the two ranks are quite correlated and therefore using the ranking based on textual distance as reference makes sense.

3.2 Evaluation metrics

A common metric for measuring ranking performance is the Discounted Cumulative Gain at position k, defined as:

$$\mathrm{DCG_k} = \sum_{i=1}^{k} \frac{2^{rel_i} - 1}{\log_2(i+1)}.$$

DCG and NDCG, its normalized version, measure the ranking quality of a retrieved image based on its graded relevance rel_i and position k in the ranking list. For our specific task, there is only a limited number of relevant images. So if we distribute the relevance among all images, the measurement would be mostly noise because the relevance of similar images is close to that of dissimilar images. An alternative metric is the mean average precision (mAP) but we believe this task is by nature a ranking problem and in AP we cannot give a different relevance to differently ranked images.

Thus, to reduce the aforementioned NDCG problem we propose to assign a graded relevance to the first m similar images only and set the relevance for all others to zero. Figure 3 shows the ratio between the NDCG score of random ranking and the NDCG of the rank obtained using DeCAF features (section 4.1), for varying the cutoff value m. When the cutoff increases, the ratio tends to 1 indicating that the measure loses its meaning. Based on this observation, for all experiments we set the cutoff value to 30.

4. METHODS

In this section we explore various possible solutions to address the novel task. We first adapt existing well-known techniques for image based classification and retrieval to swap retrieval. Afterwards, we propose an attribute-based method where attributes are automatically mined from images and texts. In all methods, we assume the labels of query and candidate images are given. So for performing swap retrieval, given the query and its label, we retrieve images from the other category.

4.1 DeCAF

Our strong baseline is based on DeCAF features [5]. It is an image description obtained from the 6th layer of a convolutional neural network (CNN) trained on ImageNet. In contrast to other features, they indirectly exploit the information of the 1000 ImageNet classes used for training the CNN. Hence they are expected to be more semantic than other low level features and therefore better suited for this task. CNN-based features such as DeCAF have obtained state-of-the-art results on many visual tasks, including image retrieval [29].All the other methods presented here, excluding Classemes, use DeCAF as basic feature representation. For our baseline based on DeCAF, we rank the images according to the similarity score computed as the cosine similarity between the query image of a given category and the candidate images from the swapped category.

4.2 Classemes

Classemes [32] are high level features, that are the output of classifiers trained for a large amount of categories. They have been tested in image retrieval with excellent results in [6]. We can consider Classemes as pre-defined attributes and therefore they are considered an interesting baseline for swap retrieval. For ranking the images we use the same procedure as explained in DeCAF, but with the features extracted from Classemes.

4.3 Domain Adaptation

Domain adaptation learns a mapping function which aligns the feature space of the source domain to the target domain in order to account for the shift between these two different but related distributions. We can consider swap retrieval as a special case of domain adaptation, where the domain shift is actually a change in the object category that we are looking for. Pereira and Vasconcelos [22] for instance apply a cross-modal domain adaptation to the task of image retrieval by considering image and text as source and target domains. In our task, we consider the features corresponding to the object category in the query image and the swapped category as source and target domains. Given a query image in the source domain, our goal is finding a similar image in the target domain. We use the method proposed by Fernando *et al.* [7], because of its effectiveness and simplicity. We learn a subspace for each domain and then seek a mapping function that transforms the source subspace into the target subspace. For our task, we learn the subspaces X_S and X_T for each object category using PCA. Hence, the images are ranked based on similarity with the query image in the target subspace, which is defined as: $S(x_q, x_c) = x_q A x_c{}^\top$, where $A = X_S X_S^T X_T X_T{}^\top$.

4.4 Metric Learning

A possible way of performing swap retrieval is to learn a metric that properly ranks the images based on the query. This is similar to the work in [27] which employs metric learning for cross-domain adaptation. Here, similar to [27], we use Information Theoretic Metric Learning (ITML) [4] to learn a metric for our task. ITML employs the information theoretic regularization term and learns the metric by minimizing the LogDet divergence. To generate the similarity and dissimilarity constraints suitable to our task, we learn the distance based on the text description associated to images because as already mentioned in section 3.1, text-based distance is semantically more meaningful. For example, for each cat image we choose as similarity constraints 3 images from the dog category whose textual descriptions are the most similar to the cat image, and also the 3 most dissimilar as dissimilarity constraints. These constraints are then used to learn the metric defined by M. Given the learned distance metric M we compute the similarity between the query x_q and the candidate image x_c as $x_q M x_c^\top$ and use it for ranking the images for swap retrieval.

4.5 Attributes

In this section, our goal is to automatically discover visual attributes from images and associated textual descriptions. Here attributes are defined as semantically meaningful concepts that are able to describe the essence of an image consisting of objects, scenes and actions.

Attribute selection. To build an initial candidate list of attributes, we collect a large set of single words from textual descriptions as potential visual attributes. We define the *discriminativity score* of a word a for a pair of classes c_1 and c_2 as follows:

$$\mathbf{discr}(a) = \left| \frac{1}{|T_{c_1}|} \sum_{t \in T_{c_1}} \mathbf{f}_t(a) - \frac{1}{|T_{c_2}|} \sum_{t \in T_{c_2}} \mathbf{f}_t(a) \right|, \quad (1)$$

where T_{c_i} denotes the set of text descriptions for class i, $|T_{c_i}|$ is its cardinality and $\mathbf{f}_t(a)$ is the frequency of attribute a appearing in the text description t. Since we use a bag-of-words representation to encode the textual description, intuitively, Eq.1 selects words that occur frequently in one class but not in the other. We select the top scoring K words and add those that occur more than 20 times in the training set to the candidate attribute set.

For this set of candidate attributes, we measure the *visual compactness* of each attribute in terms of variance of the images (l_2 norm of the vector composed by the variance of each dimension of the CNN representation) containing that attribute. At this stage, we

Algorithm 1 Attribute selection

Input: Candidate attribute set A, whose elements $a_i, i = 1 \cdots N$ are sorted by compactness score, and two thresholds τ_{min} and τ_{max}
initialize: $A^* \leftarrow a_1$
for $i = 2 \cdots N$ **do**
  $a_j = \text{argmin}_{a_j \in A^*} \mathbf{dist}(a_i, a_j)$
  if $\mathbf{dist}(a_i, a_j) > \tau_{min}$ **then**
    Add a_i to A^*
  else if $\mathbf{dist}(a_i, a_j) < \tau_{max}$ **then**
    Add a_i to $\mathbf{synset}(a_j)$
  end if
end for

select the 60% of the attributes with lower variance (visually more compact). From these attributes, we greedily select those that are far from each other in visual space using algorithm 1. That is, if its distance to the closest attribute in the candidate list A^* is higher than τ_{min} then it is added to candidate list. The distance of two attributes in visual space is defined as:

$$\mathbf{dist}(a_i, a_j) = 1 - \frac{< E(\mathbf{x}_{a_i}), E(\mathbf{x}_{a_j}) >}{|E(\mathbf{x}_{a_i})||E(\mathbf{x}_{a_j})|}, \quad (2)$$

where x_{a_i} denotes the image representation whose textual description contains the attribute a_i and $E(\cdot)$ denotes the mean. The distance here is defined as the negative cosine similarity between images containing the attribute a_i and images contain the attribute a_j.

In addition, in algorithm 1, similar to [2], we collect for each attribute a set of visual synonym words or words that co-occur together and we call this list synsets. The attributes are added in the synsets list if their distance is less than fixed threshold τ_{max}. Some examples of learned synsets are shown in table 1 (left column).

Single and paired attributes. Learning high quality attributes leads to a better representation and therefore better performance. Though single word attributes have good descriptive ability, they cannot capture the relationship between objects. For example one can train "mirror", "car" and "rear" attributes independently using images containing these attributes but they cannot by themselves be representative for "rear mirror of a car". Therefore, similar to "visual phrase" and "bi-concept" in [26] and [11], we also define paired words attributes that aim at representing those more complex concepts that cannot be characterized well by a single word attribute. For simplicity, we abuse the notion and denote the single word attribute as single attribute and paired words attribute as paired attribute. The paired attributes are more suitable for our task since they can capture different relationship between an object and other object/action/scene, hence providing better cues for the swap retrieval.

Learning models for all possible paired-attributes is prohibitive. Also, some pairs are not meaningful and many of them are redundant. Therefore, to extract a set of meaningful paired-attributes we follow the same procedure described above for the single attributes, but this time computing statistics on pairs of words instead of single words. As for single attributes, we also build synsets for paired-attributes as shown in table 1 (right column).

Attributes for swap retrieval For swap retrieval we split the paired-attributes into 2 sets: class-specific paired attributes and common paired attributes. In class-specific paired attributes one of the words in the pair corresponds to the class label. For example $\langle$cat,bed$\rangle$

single synset	paired synset
luggage, suitcase	⟨motorcycle,man⟩, ⟨motorcycle,riding⟩
television, tv	⟨keyboard,sleep⟩, ⟨computing + sleep⟩
bathroom, sink	⟨hat,cat⟩, ⟨hat,head⟩
naps, asleep	⟨food,table⟩, ⟨eat,table⟩
boys, young	⟨people,kite⟩, ⟨people,fly⟩
mothers, baby	⟨boat,cow⟩, ⟨beach,cow⟩
remote, control	⟨camera,close⟩, ⟨close,stare⟩
bicycling, biking	⟨grass,lay⟩, ⟨field,lay⟩

Table 1: Some example sysnets detected by algorithm 1

is class-specific if the swap retrieval is effectuated on cat/dog. Exploiting the text information, for each class-specific paired attribute in one class, we build the corresponding paired-attribute in the second class and vice versa. That is, if there is a paired-attribute ⟨cat,bed⟩ in the attribute set, the pair ⟨dog,bed⟩ is also added to the attribute set. With such symmetry, given a query, the retrieval can resort to the class-specific attribute detectors and simply by swapping the detector scores of the attributes, we retrieve images with same attributes but from the opposite class. In contrast, those attributes that do not contain the class names but occur in both classes like ⟨pillow,bed⟩, are called common paired-attributes. The common paired-attributes can help discover a similar context between images and thereby improve the retrieval performance.

Attribute detector. We learn a linear visual classifier for each visual attribute using images of the synset associated to the attribute. For learning we use a support vector machine with C, the parameter controlling the trade-off between the training error and regularization set to 100 in all experiments. In addition, to cope with unbalanced data during learning, we weigh the classes inversely proportional to the number of samples in the classes. Hence, for each attribute we obtain a vector of parameters w whose dot product with the corresponding image features x gives a score that predicts the presence of the attribute in the image.

Ranking score. Now, for the swap retrieval we describe an image as a vector of scores $\psi_a(\mathbf{x})$, where its elements are the scores of all single and paired attributes. Thus, the similarity between two images is defined as:

$$\begin{aligned} \mathbf{sim_a}(\mathbf{x}_q, \mathbf{x}_c) &= \psi_a(\mathbf{x}_q)^T \psi_a(\mathbf{x}_c) \\ \psi_a(\mathbf{x}) &= [\psi_a^s(\mathbf{x}), \psi_a^p(\mathbf{x})] \\ \psi_a^s(\mathbf{x}) &= [\dots, \mathbf{w}_i^s \mathbf{x}, \dots], \quad \psi_a^p(\mathbf{x}) = [\dots, \mathbf{w}_{ij}^p \mathbf{x}, \dots] \end{aligned} \tag{3}$$

$\mathbf{w}_i^s$ denotes the parameter of an attribute detector for a single attribute a_i and $\mathbf{w}_{ij}^p$ is the one for a paired attribute $\langle a_i, a_j \rangle$. Reformulating Eq.3, we have

$$\begin{aligned} \mathbf{sim_a}(\mathbf{x}_q, \mathbf{x}_c) &= \sum_{i \in A_s} \mathbf{x}_q^T \mathbf{W}_i^s \mathbf{x}_c + \sum_{i,j \in A_p} \mathbf{x}_q^T \mathbf{W}_{ij}^p \mathbf{x}_c \\ \mathbf{W}_i^s &= \mathbf{w}_i^s (\mathbf{w}_i^s)^T, \mathbf{W}_{ij}^p = \mathbf{w}_{ij}^p (\mathbf{w}_{ij}^p)^T \end{aligned} \tag{4}$$

Thus, $\mathbf{W}$ denotes a matrix that computes similarity of two images in the attribute space. Note that $\mathbf{W}$ is not necessarily a valid metric matrix.

5. EXPERIMENTS

In this section we first describe the dataset and the experimental setup that we use. Then we evaluate and compare the methods introduced in section 4 and analyze the results in three different pairs of classes. Finally, we evaluate the paired-attributes in a normal retrieval task.

5.1 Experimental Setup

We evaluate our methods on the Microsoft COCO (Common Objects in Context) dataset [19]. COCO contains 82783 training images and 40504 validation images, where a majority of images are non-iconic. Each image, is associated with around 5 sentences that describe the image. In total, 80 common objects are labeled in their natural context. We selected three pairs of categories that are suitable for the specific task of category-swap image retrieval, namely (cat,dog), (cow,sheep) and (toilet,chair). For each pair, images that contain either the first or the second class (but not both) are selected. We use the training images for learning our models and perform leave-one-query-out on the validation set to evaluate the ranking performance. Specifically, at each round one image from COCO validation set is regarded as query and the remaining validation images are used as candidates for retrieval. For training we use both the images and their textual description. At test time, given only the image query we assume that the class label of the query is given so the task is retrieving similar images from the other class.

For visual features we use DeCAF. For textual features, we first remove the stop words from the corpus and after stemming the words, unique words are used for building a *tf-idf* weighted bag-of-words representation. Both visual and textual features are $L2$ normalized in all experiments.

5.2 Results and discussion

Here we evaluate the proposed methods on the full dataset, using the text similarity as proxy for the ground truth.

Cats and Dogs. We first focus on cast and dogs. In figure 4 (left) we evaluate the ranking in terms of NDCG30@k for several methods. The combination of paired and single attributes is the best performing method. Paired-attributes by itself is better than single attributes and both are better than DeCAF. The performance of the cosine similarity for DeCAF is surprisingly good. Domain adaptation applied on DeCAF features could only slightly improve the ranking for the first top retrieved images. Surprisingly, ITML, a state-of-the-art metric learning approach, degrades the performance of DeCAF, probably because the definition of the metric (i.e. similar/dissimilar pairs) is not straight forward in our case. Classemes, a different attribute-based representation, also could not perform well in this case. These attributes are trained on an external dataset with different feature types, which may explain why they do not reach the performance of our single attributes.

The absolute values of the NDCG30@k metric are small. As explained in section 3.2, this is because we compare the ranking methods with the first 30 ground-truth images only. Increasing the cutoff value leads to higher absolute value of NDCG, however, at the same time, the measure loses its meaning as shown in Fig. 3. Rather than the absolute values, it's the relative performance of different methods that counts. In figure 5, some examples of swap retrieval are shown to assess qualitative performance of attributes versus DeCAF.

Other classes. We also evaluate our methods on two other pairs of classes, namely (cow,sheep) and (toilet,chair). In these experiments we have used the same setting but evaluate it on top performing methods only (i.e. DeCAF and attributes). In (cow,sheep) the difference between DeCAF and attributes is smaller than in (cat,dog). One possible explanation is that the scene plays an important role in (cow,sheep) and DeCAF is a strong baseline for capturing scene elements of a picture like grass and sky. On the other hand, attributes are performing much better than DeCAF in the (toilet,chair) pair. Surprisingly single attributes are stronger here probably because the distance between the two classes is higher in this case, so there

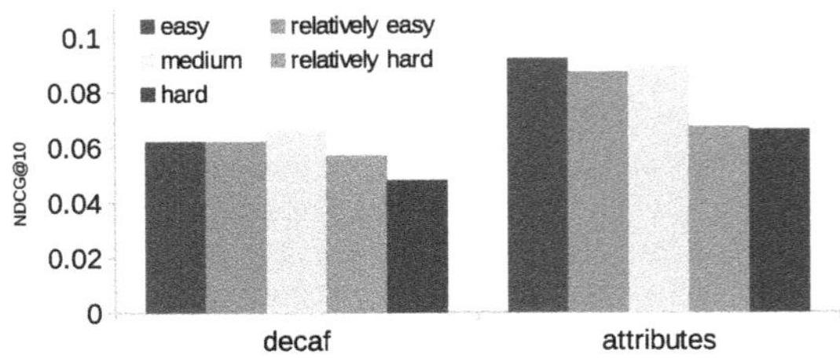

Figure 6: NDCG30@10 for different groups of query for (**left**) DeCAF, (**right**) single+paired attributes

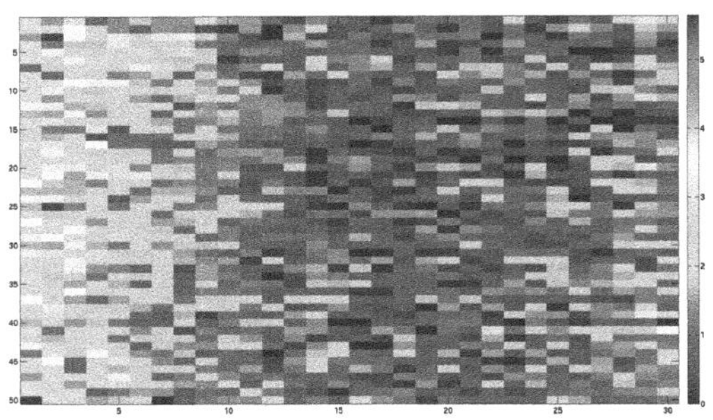

Figure 7: Matrix of agreement between human ranking and text ranking for 50 queries. Each row represents a query. For more details see the text.

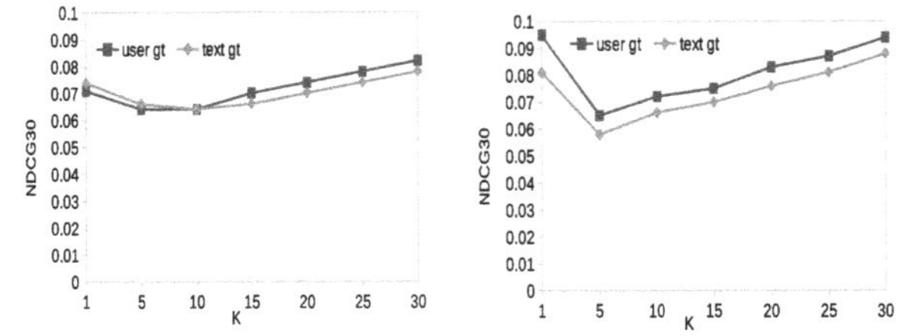

Figure 8: Performance of (**left**) DeCAF, (**right**) single+paired attributes for user ranking vs. text ranking as ground-truth

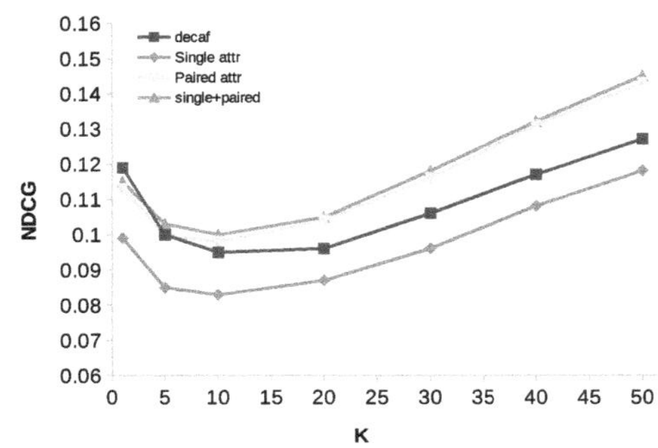

Figure 9: Results of NDCG30@k for standard image retrieval task on COCO dataset.

is not enough class-specific paired-attributes for both classes to train a good paired-attribute detector.

Query difficulty. In general, for some queries, there are no relevant images for the swap retrieval task in the dataset. To take this effect into account, we analyze the results in function of the difficulty of the query. We divide the queries in 5 groups based on their difficulty, where the difficulty is measured based on the average similarity of the top 30 most similar images (based on text similarity). As shown in figure 6, there is a direct relation between the quality of a query and its retrieval performance. This trend is more outspoken for the attributes than for DeCAF.

5.3 User Evaluation

Here, we analyze the data collected from human evaluations, where human input was used to re-rank the first 30 most similar images for 50 selected queries. To this end, we provide the user a pair of images and ask him/her to select the most similar one to the given query. The $O(n^2)$ growth of comparisons between n images prohibits an exhaustive human evaluation. Based on these annotations, we re-rank the images using ranking SVM and use this as ground truth.

Figure 7 shows for each query (row) how often (relatively speaking) a given image (column) was ranked higher than its competitor in the binary comparisons. Images are ranked from left to right based on textual similarity to the query. The agreement between text and human ranking is quite high. Moreover, human ranking loosely agree that the first 10 images are more similar to the query than the next 20 images. This is consistent with our assumption about the cutoff value. In figure 8 we compare the performance of both DeCAF and attributes for the 50 queries for which the human annotation are available. This figure verifies that the experiments of the previous sections with text as ground-truth are a valid evaluation for this task.

5.4 Image Retrieval

Finally, in order to assess the usefulness of our attributes in a normal retrieval task, we set up an experiment by selecting training and validation data from 80 categories of the COCO dataset. The task is to find similar object categories to the query image. Same as above, the validation part of the dataset is used for testing in a leave-one-query-out strategy. We sub-sample 200 images from each of these 80 categories for our experiments. To be consistent with the previous experiments, the **NDCG30** is used for reporting results. For finding single attributes, 10 discriminative words from each pair of classes are selected (Eq. 1) and then aggregated to build one list of candidates for the dataset. We use the same method as explained in section 4.5 for extracting paired-attributes except that in this case we only use common paired-attributes and there is no symmetric class-specific paired-attributes.

As shown in figure 9, the combination of single and paired attributes are outperforming DeCAF in $k > 5$ which suggests the effectiveness of the proposed attributes in a standard retrieval task.

6. CONCLUSION

In this work we have presented swap retrieval, a new and challenging task that combines the semantic of text-based queries and the power of example-based retrieval. Given an image query containing a certain object class, it consists of searching for an image with similar content but swapping the object class with another similar one.

We have adapted a metric used in standard retrieval to the proposed swap retrieval and through a human validation we have shown that the text associated to images can be used for meaningful evaluations. In this sense we have compared standard methods for image retrieval and image classification and have shown that their performance on this task is low. Instead, a better performance is obtained by a set of learned attributes that can better represent the semantics of an image and therefore it is better suited for swap retrieval.

7. ACKNOWLEDGMENT

The work was supported in part by FWO through the project G.0.398.11.N.10 “Multi-camera human behavior monitoring and unusual event detection” and FP7 ERC Grant 240530 COGNIMUND.

8. REFERENCES

[1] A. Andoni and P. Indyk. Near-optimal hashing algorithms for approximate nearest neighbor in high dimensions. *Commun. ACM*, 51(1):117–122, 2008.

[2] T. L. Berg, A. C. Berg, and J. Shih. Automatic attribute discovery and characterization from noisy web data. In *ECCV*, 2010.

[3] R. Datta, D. Joshi, J. Li, and J. Z. Wang. Image retrieval: Ideas, influences, and trends of the new age. *ACM Comput. Surv.*, 40(2), 2008.

[4] J. V. Davis, B. Kulis, P. Jain, S. Sra, and I. S. Dhillon. Information-theoretic metric learning. In *ICML*, 2007.

[5] J. Donahue, Y. Jia, O. Vinyals, J. Hoffman, N. Zhang, E. Tzeng, and T. Darrell. Decaf: A deep convolutional activation feature for generic visual recognition. *arXiv preprint arXiv:1310.1531*, 2013.

[6] M. Douze, A. Ramisa, and C. Schmid. Combining attributes and fisher vectors for efficient image retrieval. In *CVPR*, 2011.

[7] B. Fernando, A. Habrard, M. Sebban, and T. Tuytelaars. Unsupervised visual domain adaptation using subspace alignment. In *ICCV*, 2013.

[8] Y. Gong and S. Lazebnik. Iterative quantization: A procrustean approach to learning binary codes. In *CVPR*, 2011.

[9] A. Gordo, J. A. Rodríguez-Serrano, F. Perronnin, and E. Valveny. Leveraging category-level labels for instance-level image retrieval. In *CVPR*, 2012.

[10] D. Grangier and S. Bengio. A discriminative kernel-based approach to rank images from text queries. *TPAMI*, 30(8):1371–1384, 2008.

[11] A. Habibian, T. Mensink, and C. G. M. Snoek. Composite concept discovery for zero-shot video event detection. In *ICMR*, 2014.

[12] H. Jégou, M. Douze, and C. Schmid. Product quantization for nearest neighbor search. *TPAMI*, 33(1):117–128, 2011.

[13] A. Kovashka and K. Grauman. Attribute pivots for guiding relevance feedback in image search. In *ICCV*, 2013.

[14] A. Kovashka, D. Parikh, and K. Grauman. Whittlesearch: Image search with relative attribute feedback. In *CVPR*, 2012.

[15] N. Kumar, A. C. Berg, P. N. Belhumeur, and S. K. Nayar. Describable visual attributes for face verification and image search. *TPAMI*, 33(10):1962–1977, 2011.

[16] R. Layne, T. M. Hospedales, and S. Gong. Re-id: Hunting attributes in the wild. In *BMVC*, 2014.

[17] C. Li, D. Parikh, and T. Chen. Automatic discovery of groups of objects for scene understanding. In *CVPR*, 2012.

[18] X. Li, C. G. M. Snoek, M. Worring, and A. W. M. Smeulders. Harvesting social images for bi-concept search. *IEEE Transactions on Multimedia*, 14(4):1091–1104, 2012.

[19] T.-Y. Lin, M. Maire, S. Belongie, L. Bourdev, J. Hays, P. Perona, D. Ramanan, P. Dollar, and L. Zitnick. Microsoft coco: Common objects in context. In *ECCV*, 2014.

[20] P. Over, G. Awad, M. Michel, J. G. Fiscus, G. Sanders, B. Shaw, W. Kraaij, A. F. Smeaton, and G. Quénot. TRECVID 2012 - an overview of the goals, tasks, data, evaluation mechanisms and metrics. In *Proceedings of the TRECVID Conference*, 2012.

[21] D. Parikh and K. Grauman. Relative attributes. In *ICCV*, 2011.

[22] J. C. Pereira and N. Vasconcelos. Cross-modal domain adaptation for text-based regularization of image semantics in image retrieval systems. *CVIU*, 124:123–135, 2014.

[23] J. Philbin, O. Chum, M. Isard, J. Sivic, and A. Zisserman. Lost in quantization: Improving particular object retrieval in large scale image databases. In *CVPR*, 2008.

[24] D. Qin, C. Wengert, and L. J. V. Gool. Query adaptive similarity for large scale object retrieval. In *CVPR*, 2013.

[25] A. Quattoni, M. Collins, and T. Darrell. Learning visual representations using images with captions. In *CVPR*, 2007.

[26] M. A. Sadeghi and A. Farhadi. Recognition using visual phrases. In *CVPR*, 2011.

[27] K. Saenko, B. Kulis, M. Fritz, and T. Darrell. Adapting visual category models to new domains. In *ECCV*, 2010.

[28] R. Salakhutdinov and G. E. Hinton. Semantic hashing. *Int. J. Approx. Reasoning*, 50(7):969–978, 2009.

[29] A. Sharif Razavian, H. Azizpour, J. Sullivan, and S. Carlsson. Cnn features off-the-shelf: An astounding baseline for recognition. In *CVPR Workshops*, 2014.

[30] N. V. Shirahatti and K. Barnard. Evaluating image retrieval. In *CVPR (1)*, 2005.

[31] B. Siddiquie, R. S. Feris, and L. S. Davis. Image ranking and retrieval based on multi-attribute queries. In *CVPR*, 2011.

[32] L. Torresani, M. Szummer, and A. W. Fitzgibbon. Efficient object category recognition using classemes. In *ECCV*, pages 776–789, 2010.

[33] J. Wang, S. Kumar, and S. Chang. Semi-supervised hashing for large-scale search. *TPAMI*, 34(12):2393–2406, 2012.

[34] Y. Weiss, A. Torralba, and R. Fergus. Spectral hashing. In *NIPS*, 2008.

[35] F. X. Yu, L. Cao, R. S. Feris, J. R. Smith, and S. Chang. Designing category-level attributes for discriminative visual recognition. In *CVPR*, 2013.

[36] F. X. Yu, R. Ji, M.-H. Tsai, G. Ye, and S.-F. Chang. Weak attributes for large-scale image retrieval. In *CVPR*, 2012.

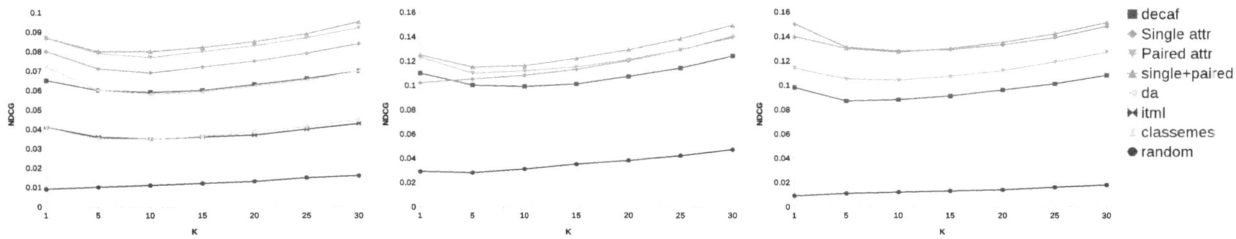

Figure 4: NDCG30@k for different methods using label information for (**left**) cat and dog (**middle**) cow and sheep and (**right**) chair and toilet

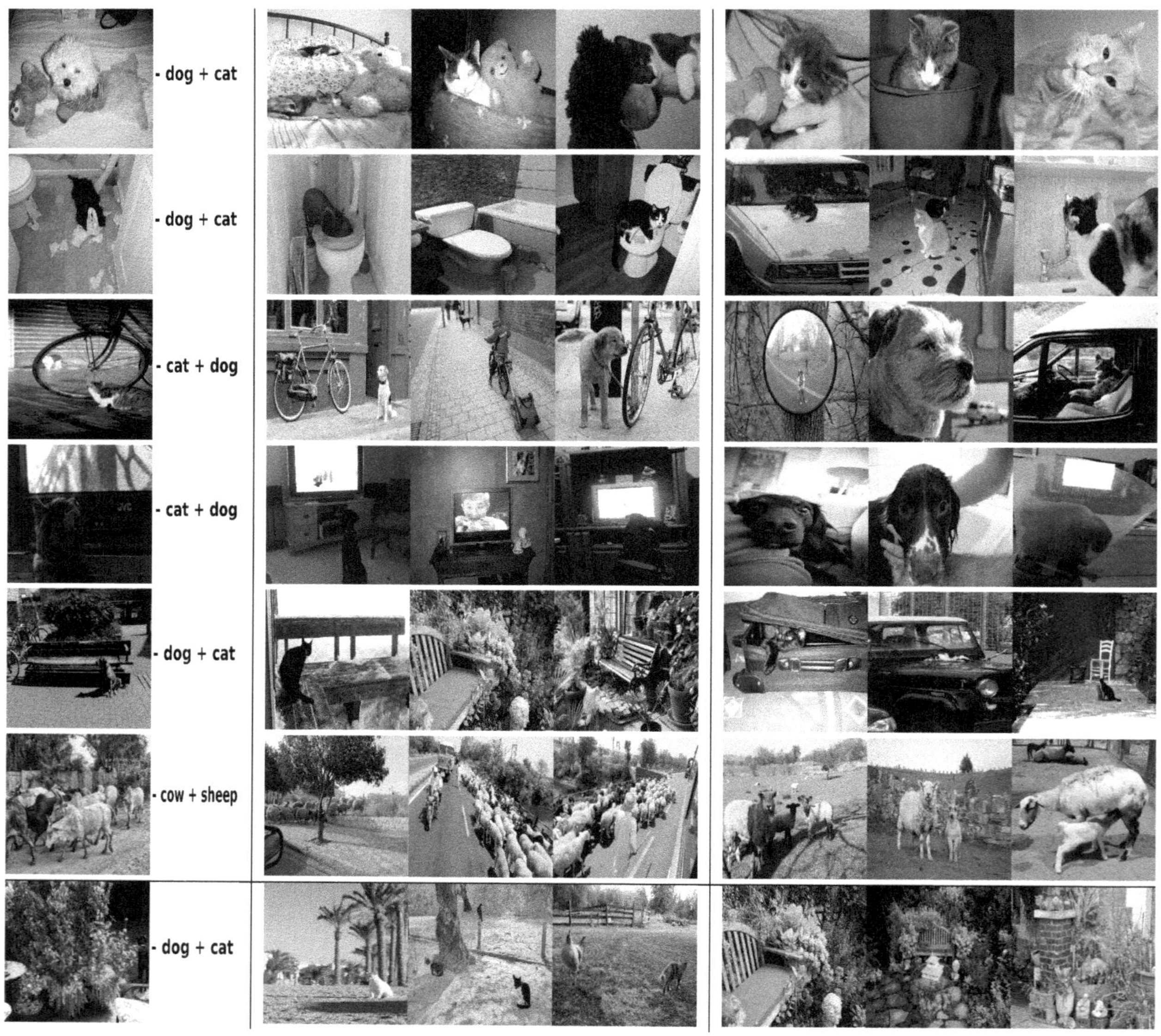

Figure 5: Qualitative examples of swap retrieval. The first column is a query. The next three are the retrieved images using single and paired attributes and next three are the retrieved images using DeCAF. The last row is an example of poor retrieval based on attributes.

Graph Learning on K Nearest Neighbours for Automatic Image Annotation

Feng Su
suf@nju.edu.cn

Like Xue
mg1233042@smail.nju.edu.cn

State Key Laboratory for Novel Software Technology
Nanjing University
Nanjing 210023, China

ABSTRACT

Image annotation is an open and challenging task, especially with large label vocabulary. In this paper, we propose a novel graph learning based method for image annotation, which takes both advantages of the nearest neighbour based and the graph-based methods, by exploiting the graph learning method to propagate the labels on the graph corresponding to the K nearest neighbours of a test image. To acquire more effective graph weights for computing score for each label, besides the similarity of visual features, our method also considers the similarity of two label sets, which is computed based on the label correlation that captures the semantic information between two labels. In addition, we combine the image-to-label distance with the graph learning based score to compute the final decision value for labelling. The proposed method is evaluated on three benchmark datasets for image annotation. The result shows our method substantially outperforms the previous graph learning based methods, and our result matches the current state-of-the-art results in annotation quality.

Categories and Subject Descriptors

H.3.1 [**Information Storage and Retrieval**]: Content Analysis and Indexing; I.2.10 [**Artificial Intelligence**]: Vision and Scene Understanding

General Terms

Algorithms, Experimentation

Keywords

Image annotation; graph learning; label correlation; k nearest neighbours; image-to-label distance

1. INTRODUCTION

The number of images and videos has been growing fast both on-line and off-line over the past decades. People can take photos or videos using digital camera or smartphone at any time of the day easily, and with the growth of media sharing websites such as Flickr and social networks such as Facebook or Weibo, people can share their images or videos with their friends on the Internet expediently. To facilitate the sharing and searching of image, labels are attached to the image, depicting the semantic, appearance, location, purpose and other relevant information of the image. However, manually annotating vast volumes of images is time-consuming and even infeasible, for which automatic image annotation attracts ever increasing research interests and becomes more and more important due to the increasing number of images and their applications.

For a given image, the purpose of automatic image annotation is to automatically assign relevant textual labels to that image which reflect its semantic content. It can be used in many interesting applications such as image retrieval, object recognition, image archive management, etc. More relevant labels assigned to image will help text-based image search engines to achieve improved image retrieval quality.

However, image annotation is still a difficult task because of the well-known semantic gap problem that it is hard to match between the low level image features such as colour, texture and high level semantics. For discriminability, we should choose image features that are capable of distinguishing the similar objects correctly. On the other hand, the chosen features have to be robust to variations of the image such as scale, illumination changes and deformations. Apparently, these two goals are inconsistent and we should take balance between them. Another reason resulting in the difficulty of this task is the lack of correspondence between labels and image regions. For a training image, it is unknown one specific label matches with which region of the image. This brings difficulty to learning classifiers for each label. The class imbalance and weak labelling of image make the task even more difficult.

Recently, various methods have been proposed for the image auto-annotation problem [14, 8, 19, 28, 3, 16, 18, 26, 29, 9, 23, 11, 5, 22]. Despite its difficulty, progress has been made in evaluations on standardized annotated datasets. However, previous work doesn't make full use of the image-to-image, image-to-label and label-to-label similarities altogether. Basically, image labels are semantically related. For example, the labels 'ocean' and 'ship' are likely annotated to the same image, while 'ocean' and 'flowers' are unlikely occurring in the same image. Such correlations of labels could be exploited for predicting labels for an unseen image. Though [4] considers label correlations, it takes the label

ICMR'15, June 23–26, 2015, Shanghai, China.

http://dx.doi.org/10.1145/2671188.2749383.

correlations only as an additional constraint on the graph-based model.

In this paper, we propose a novel graph learning based method for image annotation, which takes both advantages of the nearest neighbour based and the graph-based methods. We exploit the correlations of labels to compute the similarity between two label sets that annotate two images respectively. We incorporate this similarity into the graph-based learning algorithm as part of the graph weights. For better leverage of the image-to-label similarity, we combine the image-to-label distance with the ranking score learned from the graph-based algorithm as the final score, and assign the labels with the highest scores to the input image. In experiments on three standard datasets - Core 5K [7], IAPR TC12 [18] and ESP Game [24], the proposed method achieves the comparable (and better in some aspects) results to the state-of-the-art results.

The rest of this paper is organized as follows. We give a review of some previous representative work in Section 2. In Section 3, we describe in detail the proposed method. Section 4 and 5 present the datasets and experimental results.

2. RELATED WORK

Automatic image annotation has attracted attentions of many researchers, and a large number of methods have been proposed to address the problem, which can be divided into four main groups: generative models, discriminative models, graph-based learning methods and nearest neighbour based methods.

The generative model based methods can be further categorized to mixture models and topic models. Mixture model based methods define a joint distribution over image features and labels [14, 8, 3], and convert the image annotation task to learning the non-parametric density estimators over the co-occurrence of images and labels. Usually, Gaussian density is used for image features and multinomials or separate Bernoullis density is used for the distribution of labels. For a test image, these models compute the conditional probability over each label given the image features based on the joint distribution, and annotate the image with the fixed number of labels with the highest probabilities. For example, SML [3] uses the fixed number of Gaussian mixture components over image features for each label. Other models, such as Continuous Relevance Model (CRM) [14], Multiple Bernoulli Relevance Model (MBRM) [8] and cross-media relevance model (CMRM) [13], treat the training images as components and estimate the mixture model over the features and labels.

The topic model based methods consider the images as samples from a specific mixture of topics, with each topic being a distribution over image features and annotation words. Examples of topic models for image annotation include latent Dirichlet allocation (CorrLDA) [1], hierarchical Dirichlet processes [27], probabilistic latent semantic analysis (pLSA) [20] and machine translation methods [7]. CorrLDA considers the associations between labels and image regions as a mixture of latent topics. [7] uses a statistical machine translation model and translates discrete visual features into the label vocabulary by learning a maximum likelihood association of labels to image regions. However, the topic model suffers many difficulties in image annotation task, for example it is sensitive to the choice of topic model and the segmentation of image.

The above two models aim to maximize the generative data likelihood, which is not optimal for predictive performance. Besides the generative models, some researchers have proposed discriminative models for annotation task. These models learn a specific classifier for each label in the vocabulary. For a test image, each classifier predicts whether it belongs to the positive or the negative class of the label. Examples of this category of methods include support vector machine (SVM), Bayes point machine and multiple-instance learning [6, 10, 12, 23]. For example, recently [23] proposed an SVM based model which modified the SVM hinge loss function to tolerate the issue of confusing labels. However, such models are faced with the problem of the imbalanced training data for the positive and negative label class, and typically the number of negative images is huge. The label interdependency may also influence these models.

Graph-based learning methods [30, 16, 17, 4, 25] have also been used for image annotation. Such techniques perform label propagation on a similarity graph of labelled and unlabelled images. These methods usually work well on a small label vocabulary, but their performances become worse when the vocabulary becomes large, e.g. a few hundreds of labels in the vocabulary, which is due to the class-imbalance problem of the datasets. [4, 25] also use label correlations as an additional constraint on their graph-based models.

Despite their simplicity, nearest neighbour based methods have become more attractive due to their effectiveness on image annotation task [18, 11, 15, 22, 29]. It can be interpreted as similar images sharing common labels. Typically, these methods first select similar images from the training set based on visual features, then annotate the labels based on labels transferred from neighbours. JEC [18] treats the image annotation task as a retrieval problem. For a test image, the nearest neighbours of it are selected according to the average of several distances computed from multiple visual features. It then uses a greedy label transfer algorithm to determine the labels. The method also uses logistic regression with L_1 penalty to learn the weights between feature distances, which, however, did not give better results than using an equally weighted combination of distances. TagProp [11] is a weighted KNN based method that transfers labels by taking a weighted combination of label absence and presence among neighbours. To overcome the class-imbalance problem, the method introduces the label-specific logistic discriminant model, which can boost the probability for rare labels and decrease that for very frequent ones. Recently, 2PKNN [22] gives the state-of-the-art performance on three annotation task datasets. It's a two pass method. In the first pass, it constructs a balanced neighbours for a test image using the visual distances, and then assigns the actual labels with the maximum posterior probability to the test image. The method also exploits the metric learning to learn the weights over multiple features as well as the base distances that maximize the annotation performance.

3. OUR APPROACH

Our approach takes both advantages of the nearest neighbour based and the graph-based methods, by exploiting the graph learning method to propagate the labels on the graph corresponding to the K nearest neighbours of a test image. We also make use of the label correlation information in the label propagation process to calculate the similarity between two label sets, and we incorporate the similarity into the graph-based learning algorithm as part of graph weight. Further more, we compute the image-to-label distance (first used for Naive-Bayes Nearest-Neighbour (NBNN) classifier for image classification [2]), and combine it with the score learned from the graph-based algorithm. We denote our method as GLKNN for brevity hereafter.

3.1 Graph Learning on Semantic Neighbours of Image

Let $X = \{x_1, \cdots, x_n\}$ be a collection of n images and $\mathcal{Y} = \{l_1, \cdots, l_c\}$ be a vocabulary of c labels (tags or words). The training set $\mathcal{T} = \{(x_1, z_1), \cdots, (x_n, z_n)\}$ consists of pairs of the image x_i and its corresponding label set z_i, which is represented by a binary vector $z_i \in \{0,1\}^c$ such that $z_i(k) = 1$ if x_i is annotated with the k-th label, otherwise $z_i(k) = 0$. Thereby, the corresponding label matrix has the form $Z = [z_1, z_2, \cdots, z_n]^T = [z_{(1)}, z_{(2)}, \cdots, z_{(c)}]$. To address the class-imbalance problem, we adopt the method in [22] to choose a set of semantic neighbours for a test image. Denoting $\mathcal{T}_k \subset \mathcal{T}$ be the training image subset that consists of all the images annotated with the label l_k ($k \in [1..c]$), $\mathcal{T}_k$ can be considered a semantic group of images for the images share one common label.

Given a test image I, we select K nearest neighbours from each semantic group $\mathcal{T}_k$ according to the visual distance, resulting c image subsets $\{\mathcal{T}_{I,k}\}_{k\in[1..c]}$. The images in each $\mathcal{T}_{I,k}$ are semantic neighbours of the test image I. Hence, the neighbourhood of image I is given by $N(I) = \bigcup_{k\in[1..c]} \mathcal{T}_{I,k}$. Note that each label corresponds to at least K images in $N(I)$, which solves the class-imbalance problem. For the test image I, we can now use $N(I)$ as its training data.

Denoting the image superset composed of the test image I and its neighbour image set $N(I)$ by $\chi = \{x_1, \cdots, x_m\}$, in which the first $m-1$ images are from $N(I)$ and the m-th image is I itself. We define a $m \times c$ matrix $Y = [y_1, y_2, \cdots, y_m]^T = [y_{(1)}, y_{(2)}, \cdots, y_{(c)}]$ where $Y_{i,k} = 1$ if x_i is annotated with label l_k, otherwise $Y_{i,k} = 0$. Thus, y_i denotes the associated labels of image x_i. Our goal is to predict the annotation label y_m for the test image I. We then represent the image set by graph. Generally, a graph G can be formalized as $G = (V, E, W)$, where, V is the set of vertices in the graph with each representing a data point (i.e. one image in this work), $E \subseteq V \times V$ is the set of edges connecting the related vertices, and $W \in R^{m\times m}$ is a weight matrix, whose element W_{ij} indicates the pairwise weight of the edge connecting vertices i and j. The goal of graph learning is to decide the importance of a vertex in a graph, based on local or global information, by estimating a score function on the graph.

Let $F = [f_1, f_2, \cdots, f_m]^T = [f_{(1)}, f_{(2)}, \cdots, f_{(c)}]$ be a $m\times c$ scoring matrix, which gives an estimation for the annotation of x_i according to the vector f_i. $f_{(l)} : \chi \to R^m$ is a real-valued scoring function on graph G, which returns the predicted decision values. The matrix element $F_{i,k}$ is the confidence that image x_i is annotated with label l_k. Then, label propagation can be defined as estimating F so that the values in F change smoothly on a given graph, provided they are close to the given labels on the labelled examples. Our graph learning method aims to find an optimal $f^*_{(l)}$ for $l = 1, \cdots, c$ by minimizing the following object function [30]:

$$E(F) = \mu E_l(F) + E_r(F) \tag{1}$$

where, $\mu > 0$ is the regularization parameter, $E_l(F)$ is a loss function to penalize the deviation from the given labels, so that to guarantee the predicted labels are close to those given in the labelled examples. $E_r(F)$ is a regularization term to enforce label smoothness on the whole graph, a.k. nearby vertices in the graph having close labels. Specifically, $E_l(F)$ is defined as follows:

$$E_l(F) = \sum_{i=1}^{m} \|f_i - y_i\|^2 \tag{2}$$

and

$$E_r(F) = \frac{1}{2}\sum_{i=1}^{m}\sum_{j=1}^{m} W_{ij}\|f_i/\sqrt{D_{ii}} - f_j/\sqrt{D_{jj}}\|^2 \tag{3}$$

where, D is a diagonal matrix with $D_{ii} = \sum_{j=1}^{m} W_{ij}$.

We can obtain the closed form optimal F that minimizes the cost function $E(F)$ as follows:

$$F^* = (I_n - \alpha L)^{-1} Y \tag{4}$$

where, $\alpha = \frac{1}{1+\mu}$, I_n is a $m \times m$ identity matrix, and $L = D^{-1/2} W D^{-1/2}$ is the symmetrical normalization of W. For large graph, we can employ the iterative method in place of the closed form solution, as defined by Eq. (5), until convergence.

$$F(t+1) = \alpha L F(t) + (1-\alpha) Y \tag{5}$$

where t is the number of iteration. In each iteration, one data point receives information from its neighbours (first term), and combines it with its initial information (second term). Finally, we obtain the decision or ranking scores f_i for each label of the test image, which can be viewed as a metric of the manifold distance measuring the semantic relevance.

Different from the previous work that exploits only the visual feature to compute the weight matrix W of the graph, our method incorporates also the label correlation information in evaluating the similarity between label sets. Formally, the similarity matrix is computed as follows:

$$W = \beta W^V + W^L, \tag{6}$$

where, W^V is the visual similarity matrix computed on the visual feature, W^L is the label similarity matrix computed from the label sets of images, while the parameter β controls the balance of these two similarities. For efficiency of graph learning, we only connect one vertex (i.e. image) x_i of the graph with its K' nearest neighbours according to W, and set its similarities with others to zero.

To compute W_V, the Gaussian kernel function is exploited as:

$$W^V_{ij} = \begin{cases} \exp\left(-\frac{1}{2\sigma_1^2} D_{avg}(x_i, x_j)\right) & i \neq j \\ 0 & i = j \end{cases} \tag{7}$$

where, $D_{avg}(x_i, x_j)$ is the average distance between two images. In our work, each image has t different visual features, and we employ different distance measure for each feature (such as L_1 for color histogram, χ_2 for SIFT and hue feature, etc.), and then combine them together, see details in section 4.2. σ_1 is the scale hyperparameter for average distance. Hence, the small distance between the visual features of two images will result in the large edge weight between their corresponding graph vertices.

The label similarity weight matrix W^L is defined by the following equation:

$$W_{ij}^L = \begin{cases} \exp\left(-\lambda(1 - \delta S(y_i, y_j))\right) & i \neq j \\ 0 & i = j \end{cases} \tag{8}$$

where, λ and δ are hyperparameters, $S(y_i, y_j)$ is the similarity between two label sets y_i and y_j, described later in this section. Note that the label set similarity of two images can be easily computed as the inner product $\langle y_i, y_j \rangle = y_i^T y_j$, which takes the number of overlapping labels of two label sets as the measurement for their similarity. The more overlapping labels, the more similar between two label sets.

However, computing similarity in this manner potentially assumes that all the labels are mutually independent, thus doesn't exploit sufficiently the label correlation information, which is important for the annotation task. Specifically, when there is no overlapping labels between two label sets, the similarity value will become zero, which is inappropriate if the potential label correlation is considered. For example, considering two images with the label sets {'ocean', 'sky'} and {'water', 'ship'} respectively, which have no common label, intuitively they should be similar due to the correlation between label 'ocean' and 'water'. In other words, the first label set should also have included label 'water' since it has been annotated with 'ocean'. It's highly probably due to weak-labelling that it hasn't been labelled with 'water'.

To rationalize the exploitation of label correlations, we define a symmetric label correlation matrix $C \in R^{c \times c}$, which only needs to be computed on the whole training data once. Recall that the n-dim vector $z_{(k)}$ indicates whether or not the training image $i \in [1..n]$ is labelled with l_k by its element $z_{(k)}(i) = 1$ or $z_{(k)}(i) = 0$, respectively. We exploit the cosine similarity to compute the label correlation as follows:

$$C_{ij} = \cos(z_{(i)}, z_{(j)}) = \frac{\langle z_{(i)}, z_{(j)} \rangle}{\|z_{(i)}\| \|z_{(j)}\|} \tag{9}$$

where, C_{ij} is the similarity between label l_i and l_j, and $\langle z_{(i)}, z_{(j)} \rangle$ denotes the inner product of $z_{(i)}$ and $z_{(j)}$, which is the number of training images that are annotated with both labels l_i and l_j. For example, we find the labels 'sky' and 'clouds' have high correlation value on Corel 5K [7] dataset, which agrees with the common sense in real life that clouds appear in the sky. This shows Eq. (9) captures the semantic information of correlated labels as expected.

Now, we can use the matrix C to compute the similarity between two label sets y_i and y_j as follows:

$$S(y_i, y_j) = \frac{y_i^T C y_j}{\|y_i\| \|y_j\|} \tag{10}$$

Note that, even if y_i and y_j share no common label, $S(y_i, y_j)$ will still have big value if y_i and y_j consist of strong correlated labels.

3.1.1 *Initial Labelling of Test Image*

Though our final aim is to compute the annotation labels for the unseen test image, to compute the label sets similarity between the labelled and unlabelled images as aforementioned, however, we need to first assign initial labels to the test image. We can employ any suitable method to predict the initial labels for the test image. In this work, the nearest neighbour method is used for label initialization due to its effectiveness and simplicity. Although the initial labels for the test image may not be completely correct, we can usually assume some of them are correct, and the correct ones will impose a positive effect on the similarity computation between the test image and other (training) images. Note that, other than the simple nearest neighbour method employed, we can also incorporate other existing annotation approaches to obtain more accurate initial labels.

3.2 Image-to-Label Similarity

For its attractive performance comparing with other top learning-based methods, the image-to-label distance, which was first used in Naive-Bayes Nearest Neighbour (NBNN) classifier for image classification by [2], is also exploited in our method. The reason using image-to-label distance here is that, even though a test image had same labels with the labelled image, their distance could be still large due to the possible large variability of images with the same label, the image-to-label distance, however, is usually small.

Denoting the t features of the image I by $\{d_1^I, d_2^I, \cdots, d_t^I\}$ and $N(I,k)$ being the set of images in $N(I)$ that are annotated with label l_k, the image-to-label similarity is defined as follows:

$$D(I,k) = \frac{1}{t} \sum_{i=1}^{t} \log \frac{1}{L} \sum_{J \in N(I,k)} K(d_i^I, d_i^J) \tag{11}$$

where, L is the number of images in $N(I,k)$, and $K()$ is a Gaussian kernel function $K(d_i^I, d_i^J) = \exp(-\frac{1}{2\sigma^2}\|d_i^I - d_i^J\|^2)$.

3.3 Combination of Two Scores

Finally, we combine both the proposed graph learning based score and the image-to-label similarity score as follows, which is used as the final decision value for labelling.

$$P(I,k) = \lambda F_{m,k} + (1-\lambda) D(I,k) \tag{12}$$

where, $F_{m,k}$ is the confidence that the test image is annotated with label l_k as aforementioned, supposing the test image corresponds to the m-th image in F. By this way, we make full use of all the image-to-image, image-to-label and label-to-label similarities altogether.

4. EXPERIMENTS

In this section, we describe the datasets used in the work, and present the features and the evaluation measures for the image annotation task.

4.1 Datasets

Three standard image annotation datasets are used in our experiments, which are identical to those used in the previous work referred such as [18, 11, 22]. Tab. 1 shows the statistics of these datasets in detail.

Corel 5K dataset, which was first used by [7], is the most common dataset for keyword based image retrieval and image annotation. The dataset consists of 4,500 training images and 499 testing images with 260 labels. Each image is manually annotated with 1 to 5 different labels (3.4 labels on average).

IAPR TC12 dataset is a collection of 19,627 images of natural scenes, including different sports, actions, animals and many other aspects of contemporary life. The dataset is divided into 17,665 training images and 1,962 testing images. As used by [18], the vocabulary size is 291 with an average of 5.7 labels per image.

(a) Corel 5K Dataset

(b) IAPR TC12 Dataset

(c) ESP Game Dataset

Figure 1: Examples of annotations by our method on some images from three datasets. The corresponding top 5 labels predicted are shown. Labels in green are same with the ground truth while the red ones do not appear in ground truth.

Table 1: Details of the datasets used in this work. Image and label counts are given in the format mean/maximum.

Dataset	# of img.	Vocab. size	Training img.	Testing img.	Labels per image	Images per label
Corel 5K	4999	260	4500	499	3.4 / 5	58.6 / 1004
IAPR TC12	19627	291	17665	1962	5.7 / 23	347.7 / 4999
ESP Game	20770	268	18689	2081	4.7 / 15	326.7 / 4553

ESP Game dataset contains images annotated through an on-line game, in which two players gain points by predicting the same label for one image without communicating with each other outside the game [24]. Hence the players are encouraged to provide important and meaningful labels to images. The training and testing set of this dataset contain 18,689 and 2,081 images, respectively, and are composed of a wide variety of images including logos, drawings, and personal photos. Each image has 4.7 labels on average from a vocabulary of 268 labels.

4.2 Features

In our work, we used the same features [31] as [25] without modification to ease the comparison of our method with other works. These features consist of 15 global and local features. The global features include GIST, color histograms of RGB, Lab and HSV. The local features include SIFT and robust hue feature, both extracted densely on a multi-scale grid, and Harris-Laplacian interest points. To encode spatial information, color histograms, SIFT and hue features are also computed over three equal horizontal partitions (denoted by V3H1) of each image. All features, except for GIST, are L1-normalized. To compute the distance between two features, we use L_1 measure for color histograms, L_2 for GIST, and χ^2 for SIFT and hue features as in [25].

4.3 Evaluation Measures

Same to the work [25, 22], we annotate a test image with the fixed number of 5 labels with the highest scores in our method. We then compute the annotation recall and precision for each label in the testing set. Suppose a label l_k is annotated for $m1$ images in the ground-truth, and the number of images that are predicted with label l_k during testing is $m2$, in which $m3$ predictions are correct. Then, the precision for label l_k will be $p = \frac{m3}{m2}$, and the recall will be $r = \frac{m3}{m1}$. These values are computed for each testing label and averaged to obtain the average precision P per label and the average recall R per label. In addition, we also compute the N_+ metric as the number of labels that are correctly assigned to at least one test image, so as to measure how well the method deals with the class imbalance and the poor labelling problems.

5. RESULTS

We evaluate the performance of our automatic image annotation method and compare it with several previous representative work. Tab. 2 presents the experimental results of our method on 3 datasets (Corel 5K, IAPR TC12, ESP Game) along with previously reported results. It shows the performance of our method is comparable to the state of the art, such as the recall on IAPR TC12 / ESP Game datasets and the N_+ on the latter dataset, and better in some metrics - our method achieves the highest recall on Corel 5K dataset and the highest N_+ value on IAPR TC12 dataset.

Specifically, we first compare our method with other graph learning based annotation methods. As most of these methods presented mainly the results on small vocabularies rather than the 3 challenging datasets used in our experiments, one specific graph learning based method - TGLM [16], which provided experiment results on Corel 5K dataset, is chosen for comparison with our method. The result shows our method outperforms TGLM substantially on Corel 5K dataset, which should owe to the exploitation of K nearest

Table 3: Influence on performance by different K value.

	K										
	1	2	3	4	5	6	7	8	9	10	15
R	41	43	46	47	48	45	43	43	42	41	38
P	30	33	36	36	35	36	35	36	36	35	33
N	176	180	185	184	183	176	179	177	176	173	161

neighbours in our method to construct the graph, which effectively handles the class imbalance problem, and the modelling of label similarity that helps to obtain more appropriate weights between two images for label propagation.

We also compare our method with the neighbour based methods [18, 11, 22]. As the result shows, our method outperforms JEC [18] on all 3 datasets. Note [11] and [22] proposed both the metric learning and the non-metric learning variants of algorithm. Our method outperforms the non-metric learning variant (Tagprop σSD and 2PKNN in Tab. 2) of these two work on the recall and N_+ on all 3 datasets. Compared to the metric learning variant (Tagprop σML) of [11], our method achieves the better recall and N_+ on all datasets. Compared to the metric learning variant (2PKNN ML) of [22], the recall and N_+ of our method are higher on ESP Game dataset, while being comparable to [22] on the other two datasets. These comparisons indicate the effectiveness of our label propagation method based on graph learning. Despite not exploiting the metric learning mechanism to seek a better distance metric, we still acquire the comparable (and better in some aspects) results to the state of the art. On the other hand, due to its effectiveness to the nearest neighbour and graph learning based methods, incorporating metric learning into our method is supposed to further increase the performance.

Fig. 1 shows some annotation examples by our method on three datasets. True positives, i.e., the labels annotated in ground truth and also predicted by our method, are shown in green, while false positives (i.e. those not appearing in ground truth) are shown in red. Note that each image is forced to be annotated with five labels in the experiment, even if the image has fewer (e.g. Corel 5K) or more (e.g. IAPR TC12 and ESP Game) labels in the ground truth. It shows that, for quite a lot of images, our method yields relevant annotations, though some of them are missing in the ground truth. For example, for the 5th instance in Fig. 1(c), the predicted labels 'purple' and 'singer' are clearly relevant to the image, while they do not appear in the ground truth. As another example, the label 'cloud' for the 8th image in Fig. 1(b) should also be considered a true positive.

In the experiments of Tab. 2, we fix the value of K (the number of nearest neighbours in Section 3.1) to 4 for all three datasets. To show the influence of different choices for K's value, in Tab. 3, we present the precision, recall, and N_+ for different $K \in [1, 10]$ and $K = 15$ on Corel 5K dataset. It shows that the performance of our method is improved with relatively small K and descends when K becomes too large or too small. This may be explained as, when the value of K is too small, there are not sufficient neighbours for graph learning, while the neighbours of a test image will include most of training images when K is too large, leading to the less descriptiveness of the data.

Table 2: Comparison of annotation performance of our method with different previous methods on three image annotation benchmark datasets - Corel 5K, IAPR TC12 and ESP Game. R: Average Recall, P: Average Precision, N_+: Number of labels with non-zero recall value.

Method	Corel 5K			IAPR TC12			ESP Game		
	R	P	N_+	R	P	N_+	R	P	N_+
CRM[14]	19	16	107	-	-	-	-	-	-
MBRM[8]	25	24	122	23	24	223	19	18	209
InfNet[19]	24	17	112	-	-	-	-	-	-
NPDE[28]	21	18	114	-	-	-	-	-	-
SML[3]	29	23	137	-	-	-	-	-	-
TGLM[16]	29	25	131	-	-	-	-	-	-
JEC[18]	32	27	139	29	28	250	25	22	224
MRFA[26]	36	31	172	-	-	-	-	-	-
GS[29]	33	30	146	29	32	252	-	-	-
RF-opt[9]	40	29	157	31	44	253	26	41	235
CCD[21]	41	36	159	29	44	251	24	36	232
Tagprop σSD[11]	35	28	145	30	41	259	24	39	232
Tagprop ML[11]	37	31	146	25	48	227	20	49	213
Tagprop σML[11]	42	33	160	35	46	266	27	39	239
KSVM-VT[23]	42	32	179	29	47	268	32	33	259
FastTag[5]	43	32	166	26	47	280	22	46	247
2PKNN[22]	40	39	177	32	49	274	23	51	245
2PKNN ML[22]	46	44	191	37	54	278	27	53	252
GLKNN(this work)	47	36	184	36	41	282	31	34	255

Different from many existing work that evaluates only the performance of predicting the fixed number (usually 5) of labels, in our experiment, we also investigated the automatic determination of the appropriate number of labels based on one decision threshold, which is defined as $Dv(I) = \theta \max_{k=1}^{c} P(I,k)$. Only the labels, whose decision value computed by Eq. (12) is larger than $Dv(I)$, will be assigned to the image I. Apparently, parameter θ controls the final number of labels, and we present our method's performances on IAPR TC12 dataset with different θ values in Fig. 2. The result shows that, the recall and N_+ decrease when θ becomes large, while the precision increases. The appropriate θ can be chosen according to the practical requirements of applications.

6. CONCLUSIONS

We proposed a novel method that models and exploits the label correlations for automatic annotation of images based on the K nearest neighbours and graph-based learning. The method requires neither any training in the form of global mapping between visual features and labels nor the label specific discriminant models. Besides the similarity of visual features, our method considers the similarity of two label sets, which is computed based on the label correlation that captures the semantic information between two labels. In addition, we combine the image-to-label distance with the graph learning based score to compute the final decision value for labelling. Experimental results on three benchmark datasets show that our method substantially outperforms the previous graph learning based methods, and our result matches the current state-of-the-art results in annotation quality.

Possible extensions of this work include exploiting metric learning to seek better distance metric between two images and incorporating more effective method for label initialization. We can also explore the semantic correlations between annotation labels from the Web information with natural language processing techniques.

Acknowledgments

Research supported by the National Science Foundation of China under Grant Nos. 61003113, 61272218 and 61321491.

7. REFERENCES

[1] K. Barnard, P. Duygulu, D. Forsyth, N. de Freitas, D. M. Blei, and M. I. Jordan. Matching words and pictures. *Journal of Machine Learning Research*, 3:1107–1135, 2003.

[2] O. Boiman, E. Shechtman, and M. Irani. In defense of nearest-neighbor based image classification. In *CVPR 2008*, pages 1–8, 2008.

[3] G. Carneiro, A. B. Chan, P. J. Moreno, and N. Vasconcelos. Supervised learning of semantic classes for image annotation and retrieval. *IEEE TPAMI 2007*, 29(3):394–410, 2007.

[4] G. Chen, Y. Song, F. Wang, and C. Zhang. Semi-supervised multi-label learning by solving a Sylvester equation. In *Proceedings of the 2008 SIAM International Conference on Data Mining*, pages 410–419, 2008.

[5] M. Chen, A. Zheng, and K. Q. Weinberger. Fast image tagging. In *ICML 2013*, pages 1274–1282, 2013.

[6] C. Cusano, G. Ciocca, and R. Schettini. Image annotation using SVM. *Proc. SPIE*, 5304(5):330–338, 2003.

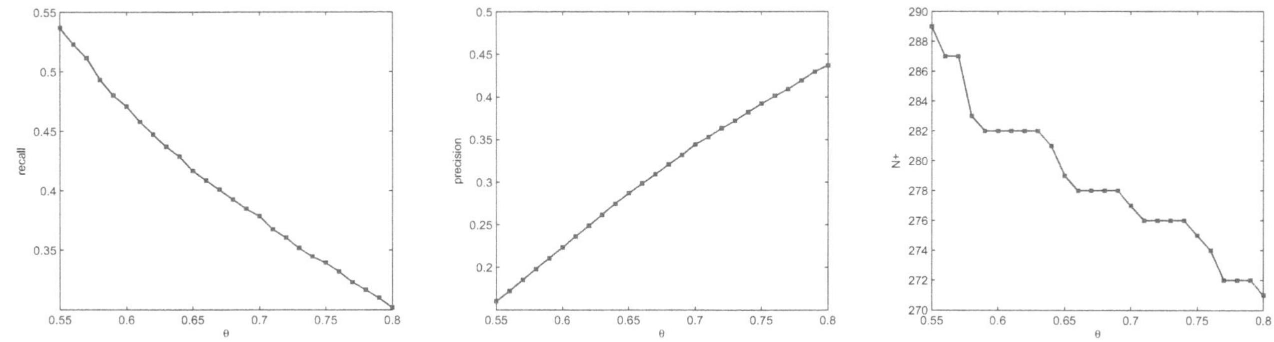

Figure 2: The recall, precision and N_+ of the proposed method on IAPR TC12 dataset with different θ values.

[7] P. Duygulu, K. Barnard, J. de Freitas, and D. Forsyth. Object recognition as machine translation: Learning a lexicon for a fixed image vocabulary. In *ECCV 2002*, pages 97–112. Springer Berlin Heidelberg, 2002.

[8] S. Feng, R. Manmatha, and V. Lavrenko. Multiple Bernoulli relevance models for image and video annotation. In *CVPR 2004*, pages II–1002–II–1009 Vol.2, 2004.

[9] H. Fu, Q. Zhang, and G. Qiu. Random forest for image annotation. In *ECCV 2012*, pages 86–99. TeX Users Group, March 2012.

[10] D. Grangier and S. Bengio. A discriminative kernel-based approach to rank images from text queries. *IEEE TPAMI 2008*, 30(8):1371–1384, 2008.

[11] M. Guillaumin, T. Mensink, J. Verbeek, and C. Schmid. TagProp: Discriminative metric learning in nearest neighbor models for image auto-annotation. In *ICCV 2009*, pages 309–316, 2009.

[12] T. Hertz, A. Bar-Hillel, and D. Weinshall. Learning distance functions for image retrieval. In *CVPR 2004*, pages II–570–II–577 Vol.2, 2004.

[13] J. Jeon, V. Lavrenko, and R. Manmatha. Automatic image annotation and retrieval using cross-media relevance models. In *SIGIR 2003*, pages 119–126, 2003.

[14] V. Lavrenko, R. Manmatha, and J. Jeon. A model for learning the semantics of pictures. In *Advances in Neural Information Processing Systems 16*, pages 553–560, 2004.

[15] X. Li, C. G. M. Snoek, and M. Worring. Learning social tag relevance by neighbor voting. *IEEE TMM 2009*, 11(7):1310–1322, 2009.

[16] J. Liu, M. Li, Q. Liu, H. Lu, and S. Ma. Image annotation via graph learning. *Pattern Recognition*, 42(2):218–228, 2009.

[17] J. Liu, M. Li, W.-Y. Ma, Q. Liu, and H. Lu. An adaptive graph model for automatic image annotation. In *Proceedings of the 8th ACM International Workshop on Multimedia Information Retrieval*, pages 61–70, 2006.

[18] A. Makadia, V. Pavlovic, and S. Kumar. A new baseline for image annotation. In *ECCV 2008*, pages 316–329. Springer Berlin Heidelberg, 2008.

[19] D. Metzler and R. Manmatha. An inference network approach to image retrieval. In *Image and Video Retrieval*, pages 42–50, 2004.

[20] F. Monay and D. Gatica-Perez. PLSA-based image auto-annotation: Constraining the latent space. In *ACM MM 2004*, pages 348–351, 2004.

[21] H. Nakayama. *Linear distance metric learning for large-scale generic image recognition.* PhD thesis, The University of Tokyo, 2011.

[22] Y. Verma and C. Jawahar. Image annotation using metric learning in semantic neighbourhoods. In *ECCV 2012*, pages 836–849. Springer Berlin Heidelberg, 2012.

[23] Y. Verma and C. Jawahar. Exploring SVM for image annotation in presence of confusing labels. In *BMVC 2013*, 2013.

[24] L. von Ahn and L. Dabbish. Labeling images with a computer game. In *Proceedings of the SIGCHI Conference on Human Factors in Computing Systems*, pages 319–326, 2004.

[25] H. Wang, H. Huang, and C. Ding. Image annotation using multi-label correlated Green's function. In *ICCV 2009*, pages 2029–2034, 2009.

[26] Y. Xiang, X. Zhou, T.-S. Chua, and C.-W. Ngo. A revisit of generative model for automatic image annotation using Markov Random Fields. In *CVPR 2009*, pages 1153–1160, 2009.

[27] O. Yakhnenko and V. Honavar. Annotating images and image objects using a hierarchical Dirichlet process model. In *ACM SIGKDD 2008*, MDM '08, pages 1–7, 2008.

[28] A. Yavlinsky, E. Schofield, and S. Ruger. Automated image annotation using global features and robust nonparametric density estimation. In *Image and Video Retrieval*, pages 507–517, 2005.

[29] S. Zhang, J. Huang, Y. Huang, Y. Yu, H. Li, and D. N. Metaxas. Automatic image annotation using group sparsity. In *CVPR 2010*, pages 3312–3319, 2010.

[30] D. Zhou, O. Bousquet, T. N. Lal, J. Weston, and B. Scholkopf. Learning with local and global consistency. *Advances in neural information processing systems*, 16(16):321–328, 2004.

[31] INRIA features for image annotation and classification data sets. http://lear.inrialpes.fr/people/guillaumin/data.php.

Scalable Organization of Collections of Motion Capture Data via Quantitative and Qualitative Analysis

Songle Chen Zhengxing Sun* Yan Zhang

State Key Lab for Novel Software Technology, Nanjing University

*Corresponding Author: szx@nju.edu.cn

ABSTRACT

This paper proposes a scalable method for organizing the collection of motion capture data for overview and exploration, and it mainly addresses three core problems, including data abstraction, neighborhood construction and data visualization. To alleviate the contradiction between limited visual space and the ever-increasing size of real-word datasets, hierarchical affinity propagation (HAP) is adopt to perform data abstraction on low-level pose features to generate multi-layers of data aggregations in consistent with coarse to fine abstraction levels of human cognition. To construct a meaningful neighborhood for user choosing a browsing path and positioning themselves, quartet analysis-based phylogenetic tree is created upon high-level pose features to produce more reliable neighbors for different aggregations of the specific abstraction level. To provide a convenient interactive environment for user navigation, a phylogenetic tree-centric visualization strategy in three-dimensional space is present. Experimental results on HDM05 motion capture dataset verify the effectiveness of the proposed method.

Categories and Subject Descriptors

H.3.1 [**Information Storage and Retrieval**]: Content Analysis and Indexing-*Abstracting methods.*

General Terms

Algorithms, Experiments, Performance.

Keywords

Motion Capture Data, Collections, Organization, Data Abstraction, Neighborhood Construction, Visualization.

1. INTRODUCTION

In recent years, as a new kind of digital media, motion capture data has been widely used in computer animation, virtual reality, film special effects, etc. With the emergence of motion capture data and the presence of large motion capture datasets [1, 2], how to organize such large collections so as to facilitate overview and exploration has become one of the key problems of reusing existing captured data [3, 4]. In general, there are three core components for any such organization: data abstraction, neighborhood construction and data visualization.

ICMR '15, June 23 - 26, 2015, Shanghai, China

©2015 ACM. ISBN 978-1-4503-3274-3/15/06…$15.00

DOI: http://dx.doi.org/10.1145/2671188.2749384

Data abstraction is the process of hiding detail of data while maintaining the essential characteristics of data, and it is an effective tool to alleviate the contradiction between limited visual space and the rapidly increasing size of real-world datasets [5]. Because the sampling frame rate of motion capture data is high and different movements may share the common transitional poses, there are large amount of similar poses in the motion capture dataset. The task of the data abstraction is to utilize the similarity between the data and produce a set of typical exemplars to represent the whole collection. Neighborhood construction casts the collection into a structure that provides a meaningful neighborhood for user choosing a browsing path and positioning themselves in an area of interest [6]. It is the basis for data visualization and directly determines whether the overview and exploration can be conducted effectively. The task of neighborhood construction is to arrange the similar objects to be located adjacent to each other, so the user can analyze and compare the difference among the contiguous objects which will help to understand the main content of the collections or choose the object much closer to the search target. Data visualization maps the needed data to visual space according to the users' interactive navigation, and it is a necessary condition to carry out the effective overview and exploration [7]. Data visualization should support interactive manipulations such as zoom, pan, drill-down and roll-up. Meanwhile, it also should provide as much information as possible to help user more completely understand his or her current environment, such as the layer, count and median of the aggregation etc.

In this paper, we present a novel scalable organization method via quantitative and qualitative analysis to support the overview and exploration for the collections of motion capture data. The main contributions of this paper include:

1) A data abstraction approach via quantitative analysis on low-level pose features is present. It adopts HAP [8] to perform hierarchical aggregation and generate multi-layers of data aggregations, which is more in consistent with coarse to fine abstraction levels of human cognition.

2) A neighborhood construction approach via qualitative analysis on high-level pose features is proposed. It uses quarters representing topological constrains of poses to create the phylogenetic tree [9], which can produce more reliable neighbors for different aggregations of the specific abstraction level.

3) A phylogenetic tree-centric visualization analysis strategy for the collection of motion capture data in three-dimensional space is present. The tree map and degree of separate (DOS) chart with other information visualization widgets provide

a convenient interactive environment to facilitate the user overview and exploration.

2. RELATED WORK

The rapid growth of motion capture data demands effective ways to organize the large collections to meet the requirements of different applications. For instance, to compress the motion capture data, Siddhartha [10] and Liu [11] built body animation parameters index and piecewise-linear modeling index, and the aim of which is to remove the spatial and temporal redundancy of raw data. To speed up the process of motion retrieval, Keogh [12] and Pradhan [13] built R-Tree and DGSOT index, and the aim of which is to divide the given measure space for fast search. To synthesize novel motions based on the existing motion data, Kovar [14] and Min [15] built the motion graph and the enhanced motion graph++, and the aim of which is to extract motion building-blocks from the collection and build the transition relation of these blocks. The work of this paper focuses on how to organize the collections of the motion data for visual analysis-based overview and exploration, and the aim is to provide meaningful neighborhood for the user choosing a browsing path and positioning themselves in the limited visual space.

At present, the research of organization the collections of motion capture data for overview and exploration is still at the outset stage. As far as the authors know, only a little work has been done to specifically tackle this problem. Schroeder et al. [4] presents a method for analyzing motion collections based on trend-centric motion visualization. However, this method is suitable for the collection of motion data the elements of which belong to the same category, while our method have no this restriction and the motions of the collection possess rich variations including different types and different styles. The work of Bernard et al. [3] is very close to this paper. It combines a number of information visualization techniques to support user overview and exploration.

For data abstraction, Bernard et al. [3] applied the divisive hierarchical clustering algorithm [16] (k-means/DBScan) to the low-level pose features (joint position) to create hierarchical aggregations, and the similar organization for overview and exploration also can be found in other multimedia types including image and video and so on [17] [18] [19]. However, pose clustering in this approach is done by interactive clustering and the quality of the data abstraction severely relies on the user being able to find useful cluster parameters and interpret the obtained cluster. Apart from this, too much and clutter hierarchies of the organization also diverge from the conception of abstraction level of human cognition. In this paper, we adopt HAP to perform data abstraction, which optimizes a global objective function and produces multi-layers of data aggregations to reflect different abstraction levels of human cognition.

For neighborhood construction, Bernard et al. [3] first used SOM on joint position features of poses to train a topology-preserving grid of poses, then got the system-global color legend to color each cluster obtained from the data abstraction. However, it has been proved that joint position is the numerical similarity measure and it cannot represent the perceptional pose similarity [20]. Furthermore, SOM is carried out via quantitative analysis relying critically on the distance measure chosen. In this paper, we uses quarters representing topological constrains inferring from multiple high-level pose features to create the phylogenetic tree [9], and it can produce more reliable neighbors for different aggregations of the specific abstraction level.

For data visualization, Bernard et al. [3] use binary tree visualization and node-link diagram to illustrate the pose clusters and motion sequences in 2D visual space. However, the data illustrated by the tree is the pose cluster belonging to different abstraction level, while human usually compare different objects on the same abstraction level. Furthermore, showing poses in 2D space will inevitably lead to the problems such as shelter, the best viewpoint selection and so on. Our method propose a phylogenetic tree-centric visualization analysis strategy in 3D space. The tree map and degree of separate (DOS) chart provides the meaningful neighborhood on the specific abstraction level, while fairly enough interactive manipulations such as zoom, pan, rotate and other visualization widgets provide a convenient environment to facilitate the user overview and exploration.

3. DATA ABSTRACTION VIA QUANTITATIVE ANALYSIS WITH LOW-LEVEL POSE FEATURES

3.1 Low-level features of human poses

In the preprocessing stage, motion capture data in the original format such as C3D file is converted into standard Biovision Hierarchy (BVH) format, in which the body hierarchy is well-defined and the rotation angle (Euler) of each joint is stored frame by frame. In a normalization step, the pelvis of each human pose is shifted to the origin of the coordinate system. To obtain poses that are always viewed "head-on", each pose is normalized by a rotation around the z-axis. To keep most of the original information, we extract 3D position of each joint of the normalized pose as the low-level feature representation for data abstraction. The skeleton model of human body used in our implementation is shown in Fig. 1.

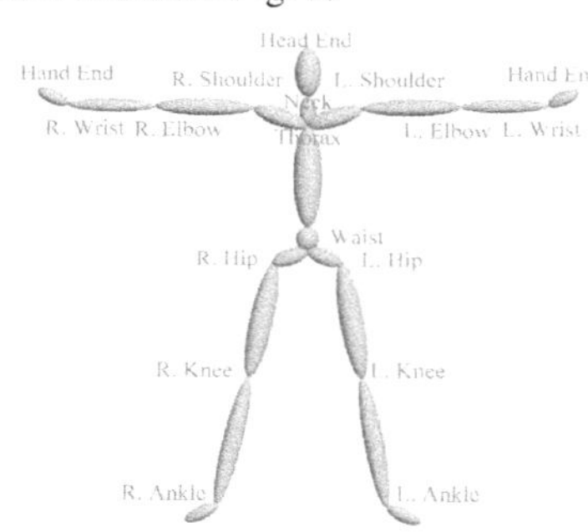

Figure 1. The skeleton model of human body.

3.2 Multi-layered aggregation of human poses

In this paper, HAP is introduced to carry out the data abstraction for the collection of poses. Affinity propagation (AP) [21] is an attractive exemplar-based clustering method and has been applied in many real-world applications. HAP extends AP to allow layered clustering for finding hierarchical structure in data. For N data points, the input of AP is a set of pairwise similarities $\{s_{i,j}\}$, where $s_{i,j}$ is the similarity of point j to point i, and a set of exemplar preferences $\{c_j\}$, where c_j is the preference for choosing pose j as an exemplar. The goal of AP is to select a subset of poses as exemplars and assign every non-exemplar pose to exactly one exemplar, so as to maximize the overall sum of similarities between poses and their exemplars and the exemplar preferences. HAP generalizes the flat AP model to a hierarchical one, and find a set of L consecutive layers of clustering, where the points to be clustered in layer l are constrained to be in the exemplar set of layer $l-1$. Let $\{h^l_{i,j}\}$ is a set of N binary hidden variables where $h^l_{i,j}=1$ indicates that point i has chosen point j as its exemplar at layer l. Furthermore, let $\{e^l_j\}$ be a set of N binary hidden variables, where $e^l_j=1$ indicates point j is chosen as an exemplar at layer l. The objective function of HAP is to max:

$$\sum\nolimits_{i,j,l} S^l_{i,j}(h^l_{i,j}) + \sum\nolimits_{j,l} C^l_j(e^l_j) + \sum\nolimits_i I^1_i(h^1_{i,:}) \\ + \sum\nolimits_{i,l>1} I^l_i(h^l_{i,:}, e^{l-1}_i) + \sum\nolimits_{j,l} E^l_j(h^l_{:,j}, e^l_j) , \qquad (1)$$

where $C^l_j(e^l_j) = c^l_j \cdot e^l_j$, $S^l_{i,j}(h^l_{i,j}) = s^l_{i,j} \cdot h^l_{i,j}$, I and E are two constrains function force each point to be assigned to exactly one exemplar and exemplar consistency, i.e., a point must be an exemplar if other points choose it as an exemplar. Similarly to AP, this objective function is solved by inferring approximate MAP values for the hidden variables using the max-sum algorithm. Compared with the approach of applying AP to the data points by layer and layer, HAP considers the connectivity between layers and a change in the exemplar preference in the top layer affects the number of exemplars found in every layer, so it can obtain the more global optimal results.

With the given collection of motion capture data, we first calculate the Euclidean distance of any two poses by the feature vector of 3D joint position, and obtain the similarity matrix. The similarity between poses is the negative distance between them. Then, we input the similarity matrix, the number of layers L and the preference of poses of each layer $\{c^l_j\}$ into HAP to obtain multi-layered data abstraction. Because 3D pose is the structured but high-dimensional data, it will lead some dissimilar pose are aggregated into the common cluster if L is set to be too large. For HDM05 database which contain about 130 action classes, we found $L=4$ can get the better results. Figure 2 gives an example of multi-layered data abstraction by using HAP.

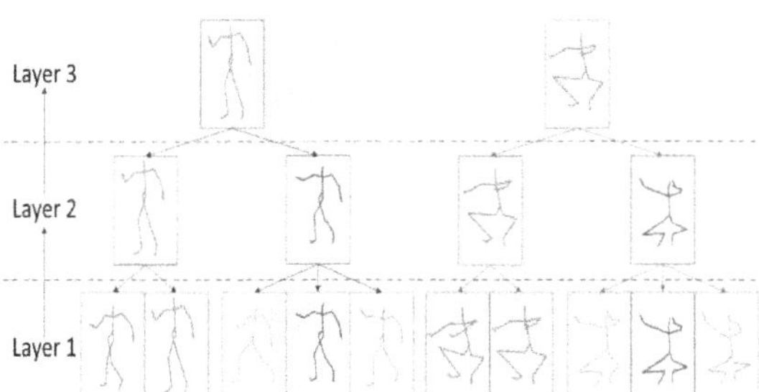

Figure 2. Multi-layered exemplar-based data abstraction.

4. NEIGHBORHOOD CONSTRUCTION VIA QUALITATIVE ANALYSIS WITH HIGH-LEVEL POSE FEATURES

4.1 High-level features of human poses

In the previous section, we use the 3D coordinates of joints to perform data abstraction to eliminate the redundant information. However, it is proven that it is a numerical similarity measure and there is a substantial gap between perceptual pose distance and numerical similarity measures. On the other hand, more and more research results indicate that relative geometry feature (RGF) is an effective representation for perceptional pose similarity measure [22]. In this paper, distance of two joints (J2JD), distance of a joint and a plane (J2PD), angle of two bones (B2BA), angle of a bone and a plane (B2PA) are taken as the high-level feature representation to measure the perceptional similarity between poses. These four types of RGF are shown in Fig. 3, and we also carry out the feature combination experiments in section 5.2.

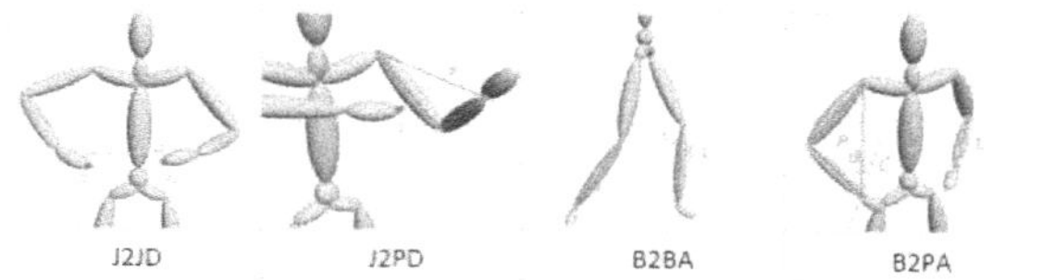

Figure 3. 4 types of RGF.

It is obvious that human does not put equal emphasis on different body parts when understanding poses [22]. In this paper, we suggest using the probability of the joint position to evaluate the weight of each joint, and this strategy is based on two basic points. First, the cognitive bias model indicates that people pay more attention to the unusual or different, so if a joint of pose appear in an unusual position, it should be assigned more weights. Second, the rapidly increasing size of motion capture data makes it possible to obtain the more accurate distribution of the position of each joint. For any given type of RGF, the distance of a pair of pose A and pose B is the average distance of A to B and B to A.

4.2 Defining reliable quarters

After obtaining the distance between two poses on each type of relative geometry feature, we will define a set of reliable quartets for building the phylogenetic tree. A quartet is a minimal tree which defines the topological (qualitative) constraints between four poses, namely, two pairs of poses are close to each other among themselves, but far apart between them. It is obvious that a quarter separates two pairs of poses. Based on a given type of relative geometry feature, the clearer the topological structure of this separation is, the more reliable the quartet is. Fig. 4 illustrates an example of quarter definition. The small collection of 78 poses is listed in Fig. 4(a), while several quarters inferred from the collection using B2BA relative geometry feature are given in Fig. 4(b). It can be seen that the poses in a quarter can satisfy the topological constrains.

Defining reliable quartets is critical to the success of building a phylogenetic tree. The process of acquiring a reliable quarter is shown in Fig. 5. First, select any four poses (A, B, C, D) in the collection and construct a full connected graph including six edges, as shown in Fig. 5(a), where each node represents a pose and the edge is associated with a distance based on the specific type of RGF described in section 4.1. Second, sort the six edges according to their distance magnitudes. If four poses can't remain connected after removing three edges corresponding to the largest distance, this quartet is discarded. Otherwise let the largest edge of the three remaining edges be d3 and the other two edges be d1 and d2. If d3 is not a bridge, that is, if its removal does not separate the four nodes into two pairs, then the quarter is again discarded. The remaining set of quarters have a potential of being a reliable quartet, as shown in Fig. 5(b). Third, examine the ratio between the values of the edges using a threshold R. If

$d3/d1 > R$ and $d3/d2 > R$, then this quartet is defined as a reliable quartet, as shown in Fig. 5(c) and Fig. 5(d). The topological constrains of this quartet is the pair of two poses connected by d1 is far from the pair of two poses connected by d2, while two poses in each pair is close to each other.

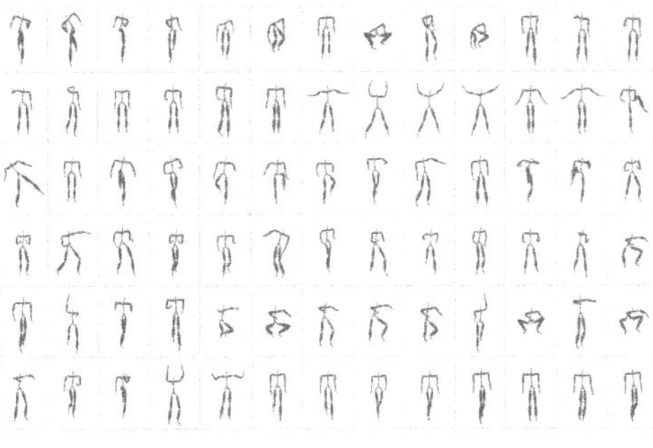

(a) Small collection of 78 poses.

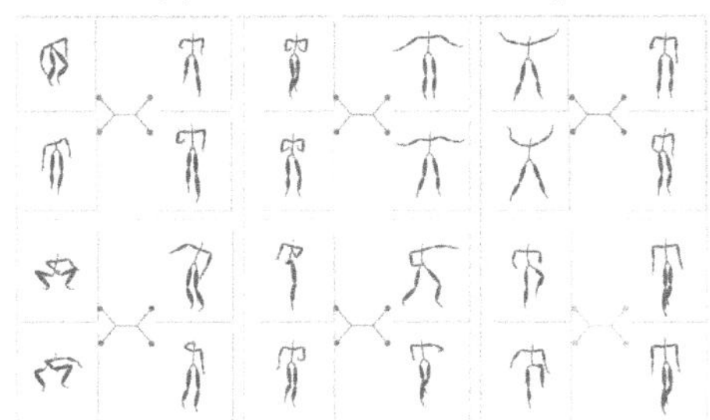

(b) Several quarters defined based on the B2BA relative geometry feature.

Figure 4. An example of quarter definition.

For each combination of four different poses of the collections and for each type of RGF, we first calculate the distances between any two poses according to section 4.1, and then apply the above process to acquire a set of reliable quartets. Threshold R controls the number of quartets. When R is too small the quartets are no longer reliable and the total number is too large. However, when R is too large, the reliable quartets are too conservative resulting in a small number of quartets, which can again reduce accuracy. In our experiment, we have achieved good results by adjusting R to get the minimum number of quarters based on which the phylogenetic tree contains all the poses in the collection.

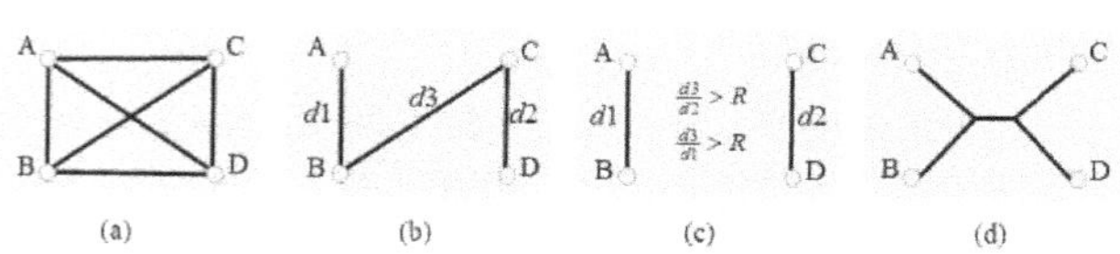

Figure 5. The process of acquiring reliable quarters. (a): Full connected graph constructed by 4 poses; (b): Potential reliable quartet after removing the 3 largest edges; (c): Distance condition of becoming a reliable quarter; (d): Topological constrains defined by a reliable quarter.

4.3 Building phylogenetic tree

The problem of reconstructing a tree from a set of quartets has received a lot of attention in bioinformatics, and it is used as a means to reconstruct phylogenetic trees. After obtaining a set of reliable quartets of poses, we adopt the Quartets MaxCut algorithm (QMC) [23] from this domain to construct a phylogenetic tree. The QMC algorithm works in two stages. In the first stage, it embeds points representing the poses into a metric space based on the topological information of the quartets. In the second stage, it uses the distance metric between points in this space to recursively partition the set of points in a top-down manner, creating a hierarchical tree structure. For a more comprehensive overview of QMC, we refer the readers to [23].

The phylogenetic tree is a no root tree, and it can in maximum preserve the topological constrains of the poses defined by the quartets. Each quartet becomes a sub-tree and each leaf in the phylogenetic tree represents a pose. If two leafs have the same parent node, it indicates these two leafs are very similar with each other. If two non-leaf nodes have the same parent node, it indicates their sub-trees are similar with each other in some degree. The degree of separation of any two poses in the collection can be represented by the number of edge hops between their corresponding leaves in the phylogenetic tree. The phylogenetic tree built from the collections shown in Fig. 4(a) is given in Fig. 6. The quartets colored in red and green in Fig. 4(b) is highlighted in Fig. 6 with the same color. It can be seen that the phylogenetic tree can produce more reliable neighbors for each poses by using the reliable topological constraints.

Figure 6. The phylogenetic tree built from the collections shown in Figure 4(a), where the green and red subtrees embed the relations of the green and red quartet examples shown in Figure 4(b).

5. EXPERIMENTS AND EVALUATION

5.1 Evaluation of the data abstraction

We first directly apply AP to HDM05 human motion database and obtain 1376 clusters. The differences of the poses within each cluster are very small. If we use the whole data set, it will overwhelm the difference of different data abstraction approaches, so this compact collection containing 1376 exemplar poses will be used in the following experiments.

To evaluate the performance of data abstraction of the proposed approach, we compare HAP with multi-layered version of AP (MLAP) and multi-layered version of Kmeans

(MLKMeans). For building a multi-layered organization for the collection of poses, MLAP recursively applies AP to the exemplar set found in the previous layer, while MLKMeans recursively applies the traditional Kmeans algorithm to the poses nearest to the cluster means of the previous layer.

We compared the performance of HAP, MLAP and MLKMeans in terms of the objective function described in formula 1. The number of layers L is set to be 4. For HAP and MMAP, the preference range is generated by using a heuristic approach proposed by AP author and this range was divided in log-linear scale. In our experiment, we obtain a total of 2596 different settings. For MLKMeans, the number of clusters in each layer is determined by each HAP solution with the specific setting. In this way, we were able to compute the net similarity obtained by HAP and HKMC for solutions that had the same number of clusters in corresponding layers. The net similarity of three approaches for each setting are given in Fig. 7.

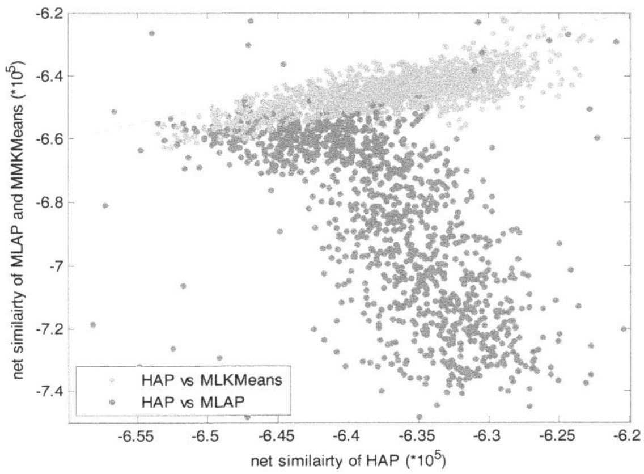

Figure 7. Comparison of the net similarity achieved by HAP vs. MLAP, and HAP vs. MLKMeans for a variety of exemplar preference settings.

From Fig. 7, it can be seen that HAP outperforms MLAP and MLKMeans in almost all experiments. The main reason is MLAP and MLKMeans are greedy methods, and they suffer by making hard decisions in lower layers that turn out to be suboptimal when higher layers are examined, since they don't optimize a global objective function that accounts for all layers simultaneously. Conversely, by using a message passing method, HAP is able to consider all points as potential exemplars at different layers of the hierarchy and send information up and down the hierarchy to identify exemplars at each layer. In this way, HAP is able to outperform MLAP and MLKMeans and can obtain better performance of data abstraction for the collection of motion capture data.

5.2 Evaluation of the neighborhood construction

After performing the data abstraction on HDM05 motion capture database, there are 253 representative poses on the top layer, and 587 representative poses on the secondary top layer. These two collections of poses are labeled to build the ground truth phylogenetic trees for the evaluation of neighborhood construction. The manual organization of the phylogenetic tree is an iterative process with 14 users where each one receives the previous user's tree and can move poses from one leaf to another until the tree converges. Fig. 8 shows an example of the labeled phylogenetic tree corresponding to the collections shown in Fig. 4(a). It should be noted that although the ground truth phylogenetic tree is subjective, but the actions in HDM05 are common motions and the users are very familiar with them, so the neighbors of each pose in the ground truth phylogenetic tree are reliable.

Figure 8. Example of the labeled phylogenetic tree corresponding to the collections shown in Fig. 4(a).

To evaluate the performance of different approaches for neighborhood construction, we also need to define the compatible evaluation criterion. Given a pair of poses p_i and q_i, the distance between them is defined as the number of poses which are nearer to p_i than q_i i.e.,

$$\Delta(p_i, q_i) = count(v_i),\ v_i \text{ s.t. } d(v_i, p_i) < d(q_i, p_i)\,. \tag{2}$$

d is the function getting the quantitative distance of two poses in a given visual representation. For a 2D plane such as produced by PCA, it can be Euclidean distance. For the proposed phylogenetic tree, it is the number of edge hops between two leaves. The average distance of S nearest neighbors between a neighborhood representation R and the ground truth neighborhood representation RT is defined as

$$D(RT,R,S) = \frac{1}{N}\sum_{i=1}^{N}\frac{1}{k}\sum_{k=1}^{K}|\,\Delta(p_i,q_k)_{RT} - \Delta(p_i,q_k)_R\,|, \quad q_k \text{ s.t. } \Delta(p_i,q_k)_{RT} < S\,. \tag{3}$$

where N is the total number of poses in the collection and K is the total number of pairs satisfying $\Delta(p_i,q_k)_{RT} < S$. In the following, this criterion will be used to evaluate the performance of different approaches.

To verity the strength of combining multiple distance measures of the proposed approach, we use four type of RGF described in section 4.1 and compare the quality of the resulting phylogenetic trees when only a subset type of RGF are used. The set of quartets created using only the jth type of RGF is denoted by Q_j ($j = 1,...,4$). I_k ($k = 1,...,4$) is the set of all combined quartet sets by merging k of the Q_j , so there are C_4^1 sets of quartets in I_1, C_4^2 sets of quartets in I_2 and so on. For each I_k, we build the set of phylogenetic trees corresponding to the quartet sets in I_k and calculate the average distance from the ground truth phylogenetic tree. Fig. 9 shows the results of different combinations on the two collections. It can be seen that the performance of using two types of RGF to build the quartet set is clearly better than the performance of using only a single one. Combining three or four types of RGF also increases the accuracy but less significantly. It indicates the final result will be not much affect by adding more types of RGF. In the following experiments, the phylogenetic tree built by the combined quartet set $Q_1 \cup Q_2 \cup Q_3 \cup Q_4$ will be used to compare with other approaches, and the corresponding tree of the pose collection of the top layer is shown in Fig. 12.

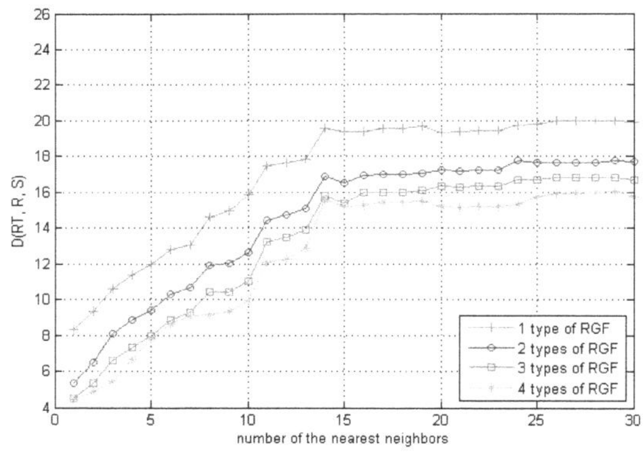

(a) Results on the pose collection of the top layer.

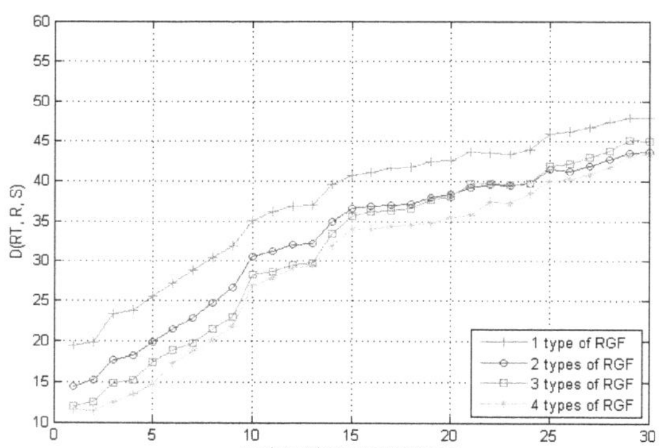

(b) Results on the pose collection of the secondary top layer.

Figure 9. Average distance of the phylogenetic trees from the ground truth merging one to four features to create the quartets.

To evaluate the effectiveness of the proposed approach for neighborhood construction, we compare it with three traditional approaches for visual overview and exploration. They include 2D plane produced by PCA [19], 2D plane produced by SOM [24] and phylogenetic tree produced by Neighbor Joining. For each algorithm, the combinations of the four types of RGF are input to construct the neighborhood and the best performance is compared with the proposed approach. For PCA and SOM, the feature matrix of RGF is input directly. For Neighbor Joining, the pose distance matrix is input. Fig. 10 shows the performance of neighborhood construction of four approaches.

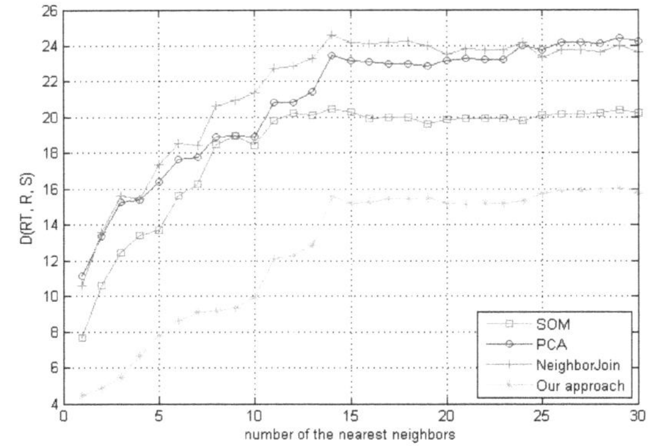

(a) Results on the pose collection of the top layer.

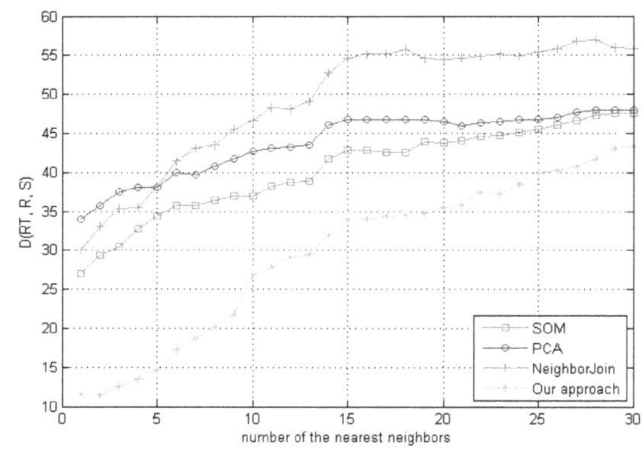

(b) Results on the pose collection of the secondary top layer.

Figure 10. Performance of neighborhood construction of four approaches.

It can be seen that the performance of Neighbor Joining is the worst among all. The main reason is that Neighbor Joining is a greedy but not global optimization algorithm, so it can't achieve the global optimal solution. The performance of PCA is better than Neighbor Joining. However, PCA uses the first two components to project the data into 2D plane, but the high-dimensional feature representation and the wide range of poses lead the first two components can't capture the main content of the collection. The performance of SOM is better than PCA, but the boundaries of different partitions lead to the visual continuous 2D plane is abruptly separated. The proposed approach achieves the best performance. The main reason is the objective of our approach is more global and the optimization accounts for reliable topological constraints rather than directly satisfying the less reliable quantitative distances, while the above three approaches heavily rely on the quantitative distances measures.

5.3 Prototype of our system

We have implemented a prototype system which allows the user carry out the overview and exploration on the collections of motion capture data. The interface of the prototype system is shown in Fig. 11. It supports interactive manipulations such as zoom, pan, drill-down and roll-up. It provides two view mode: tree map view mode (Fig. 11 (a)) and DOS view mode (Fig. 11 (b)). The tree map view mode allows displaying 2D neighbor maps in 3D environment, which facilitate the exploration of the collection. When the user select a pose, he/she can change to the DOS view mode, and the rest of the poses are automatically repositioned to form a DOS chart around the selected one. The

DOS chart is formed in such a way that poses closer to the selected pose will be located at the inner circles of the DOS chart. This organization provides the user with intuitive understanding of how other poses in the collection compare with the currently selected one. When the user select an interesting pose, he/she also can view the short movements including the selected pose or its offspring. According to the response from the user, our prototype system provides a convenient interactive environment to facilitate the user overview and exploration.

(a) Tree map view mode.

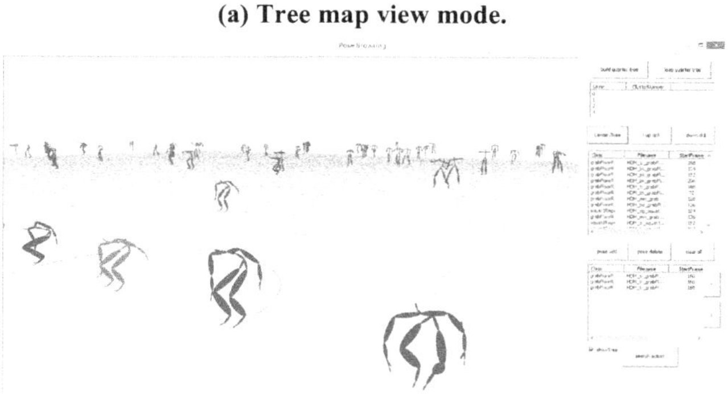

(b) DOS view mode.

Figure 11. A prototype system for overview and exploration on the collections of motion capture data.

6. CONCLUSIONS, LIMITATIONS AND FUTURE WORK

This paper proposes a novel method for organizing the collection of motion capture data for overview and exploration. First, it adopts HAP to perform data abstraction and produces multi-layers of data aggregations, which can be adapted to the expansion of the data scale. Second, for each layer of data abstraction, quartet analysis-based phylogenetic tree is created upon high-level pose features, which can construct a meaningful neighborhood for user choosing a browsing path and positioning themselves. Third, a phylogenetic tree-centric visualization strategy in three-dimensional space is present, which can provide a convenient interactive environment for user navigation. Experimental results on HDM05 motion capture dataset verify the effectiveness of the proposed method.

However, certain limitations still exist. First, similar with the work of [3], the proposed approach concerns mostly on human poses, so the user has to first search the pose included in the target action, and there is still much work to be done to directly support the overview and exploration of movement. Second, at present, the system lists all short movements which contain the selected pose or its offspring. However, it seems that these movements also should be carefully organized.

Organizing the collection of motion capture data for overview and exploration is a new and challenge issue. We have only made a primary attempt in this problem. The limitations and extension possibilities of our work guides the directions of our future work.

7. ACKNOWLEDGEMENTS

This work is supported by National Natural Science Foundation of China (61272219, 61100110 and 61321491), Program for New Century Excellent Talents of Ministry of Education of China (NCET-04-0460), Science and Technology Plan of Jiangsu Province (BE2010072, BE2011058, BY2012190 and BY2013072-04), Innovation Foundation of State Key Lab for Novel Software Technology of China (ZZKT2013A12).

8. REFERENCES

[1] CMU. "Motion Capture Database," http://mocap.cs.cmu.edu/.

[2] H. d. Medien. "HDM Motion Capture Database (HDM05)," http://www.mpi-inf.mpg.de/resources/HDM05/.

[3] J. Bernard, N. Wilhelm, B. Kruger *et al.*, "MotionExplorer: Exploratory Search in Human Motion Capture Data Based on Hierarchical Aggregation," *Visualization and Computer Graphics, IEEE Transactions on,* vol. 19, no. 12, pp. 2257-2266, 2013.

[4] D. Schroeder, F. Korsakov, C. M. P. Knipe *et al.*, "Trend-Centric Motion Visualization: Designing and Applying a New Strategy for Analyzing Scientific Motion Collections," *Visualization and Computer Graphics, IEEE Transactions on,* vol. 20, no. 12, pp. 2644-2653, 2014.

[5] Q. Cui, M. O. Ward, E. A. Rundensteiner *et al.*, "Measuring Data Abstraction Quality in Multiresolution Visualizations," *Visualization and Computer Graphics, IEEE Transactions on,* vol. 12, no. 5, pp. 709-716, 2006.

[6] D. Heesch, "A survey of browsing models for content based image retrieval," *Multimedia Tools and Applications,* vol. 40, no. 2, pp. 261-284, 2008.

[7] N. Elmqvist, and J. Fekete, "Hierarchical Aggregation for Information Visualization: Overview, Techniques, and Design Guidelines," *Visualization and Computer Graphics, IEEE Transactions on,* vol. 16, no. 3, pp. 439-454, 2010.

[8] I. Givoni, C. Chung, and B. J. Frey, "Hierarchical affinity propagation," in Proceedings of the Twenty-Seventh Uncertainty in Artificial Intelligence , 2011, pp. 238–246.

[9] S.-S. Huang, A. Shamir, C.-H. Shen *et al.*, "Qualitative organization of collections of shapes via quartet analysis," *ACM Trans. Graph.,* vol. 32, no. 4, pp. 1-10, 2013.

[10] C. Siddhartha, S. M. Bhandarkar, and L. Kang, "Human Motion Capture Data Compression by Model-Based Indexing: A Power Aware Approach," *Visualization and Computer Graphics, IEEE Transactions on,* vol. 13, no. 1, pp. 5-14, 2007.

[11] G. Liu, J. Zhang, W. Wang *et al.*, "A system for analyzing and indexing human-motion databases," in Proceedings of the 2005 ACM SIGMOD international conference on Management of data, Baltimore, Maryland, 2005, pp. 924-926.

[12] E. Keogh, T. Palpanas, V. B. Zordan *et al.*, "Indexing large human-motion databases," in Proceedings of the Thirtieth

international conference on Very large data bases, Toronto, Canada, 2004, pp. 780-791.

[13] G. N. Pradhan, and B. Prabhakaran, "Indexing 3-D Human Motion Repositories for Content-Based Retrieval," *IEEE Transactions on Information Technology in Biomedicine,* vol. 13, no. 5, pp. 802-809, 2009.

[14] L. Kovar, M. Gleicher, Fr *et al.*, "Motion graphs," in Proceedings of the 29th annual conference on Computer graphics and interactive techniques, San Antonio, Texas, 2002, pp. 473-482.

[15] J. Min, and J. Chai, "Motion graphs++: a compact generative model for semantic motion analysis and synthesis," *ACM Trans. Graph.,* vol. 31, no. 6, pp. 1-12, 2012.

[16] W. Plant, and G. Schaefer, "Visualisation and Browsing of Image Databases," *Multimedia Analysis, Processing and Communications*, Studies in Computational Intelligence W. Lin, D. Tao, J. Kacprzyk *et al.*, eds., pp. 3-57: Springer Berlin Heidelberg, 2011.

[17] S. Krishnamachari, and M. Abdel-Mottaleb, "Image browsing using hierarchical clustering." in Proceedings of IEEE International Symposium on Computers and Communications, 1999, pp. 301-307.

[18] D. Borth, C. Schulze, A. Ulges *et al.*, "Navidgator-Similarity Based Browsing for Image and Video Databases," *KI 2008: Advances in Artificial Intelligence*, Lecture Notes in Computer Science A. Dengel, K. Berns, T. Breuel *et al.*, eds., pp. 22-29: Springer Berlin Heidelberg, 2008.

[19] Z. Pečenovió, M. Do, M. Vetterli *et al.*, "Integrated Browsing and Searching of Large Image Collections," *Advances in Visual Information Systems*, Lecture Notes in Computer Science R. Laurini, eds., pp. 279-289: Springer Berlin Heidelberg, 2000.

[20] C. Chen, Y. Zhuang, J. Xiao *et al.*, "Perceptual 3D pose distance estimation by boosting relational geometric features," *Computer Animation and Virtual Worlds,* vol. 20, no. 2-3, pp. 267-277, 2009.

[21] B. J. Frey, and D. Dueck, "Clustering by passing messages between data points," *Science,* vol. 315, no. 5814, pp. 972-976, 2007.

[22] C. Chen, Y. Zhuang, F. Nie *et al.*, "Learning a 3D Human Pose Distance Metric from Geometric Pose Descriptor," *IEEE Transactions on Visualization and Computer Graphics,* vol. 17, no. 11, pp. 1676-1689, 2011.

[23] S. Snir, and S. Rao, "Quartets MaxCut: A Divide and Conquer Quartets Algorithm," *Computational Biology and Bioinformatics, IEEE/ACM Transactions on,* vol. 7, no. 4, pp. 704-718, 2010.

[24] J. Laaksonen, M. Koskela, and E. Oja, "PicSOM-self-organizing image retrieval with MPEG-7 content descriptors," *Neural Networks, IEEE Transactions on,* vol. 13, no. 4, pp. 841-853, 2002.

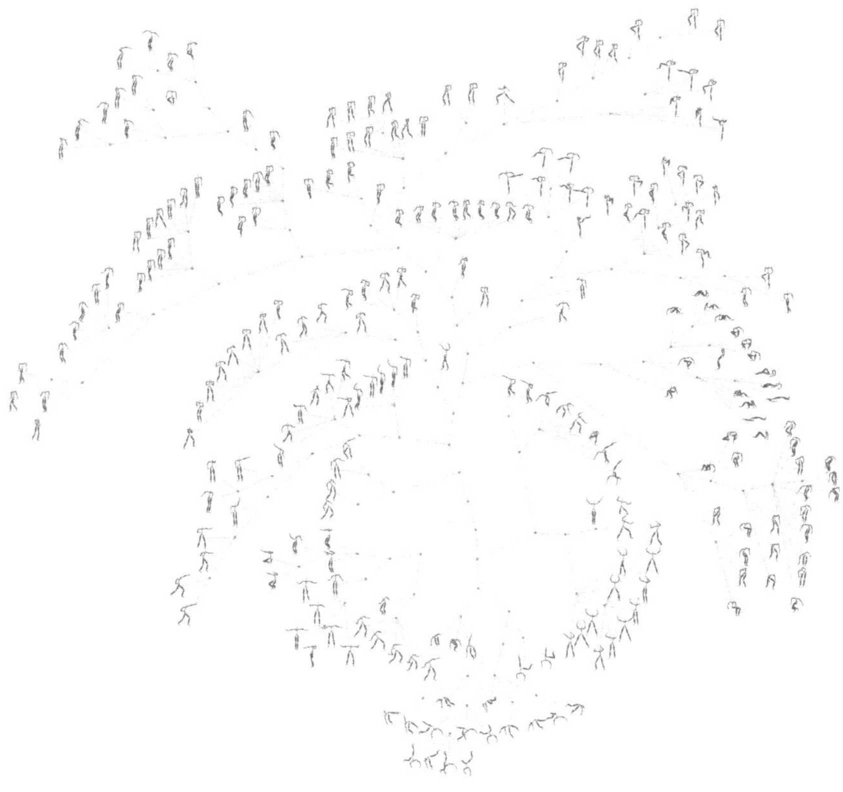

Fig. 12. The phylogenetic tree built by the proposed approach on the pose collection of the top layer.

Content-Based Video Search over 1 Million Videos with 1 Core in 1 Second

Shoou-I Yu[1], Lu Jiang[1], Zhongwen Xu[2], Yi Yang[2], Alexander G. Hauptmann[1]
[1]Language Technologies Institute, Carnegie Mellon University
[2]Centre for Quantum Computation and Intelligent Systems, University of Technology, Sydney
{iyu, lujiang, alex}@cs.cmu.edu, zhongwen.xu@student.uts.edu.au, yi.yang@uts.edu.au

ABSTRACT

Many content-based video search (CBVS) systems have been proposed to analyze the rapidly-increasing amount of user-generated videos on the Internet. Though the accuracy of CBVS systems have drastically improved, these high accuracy systems tend to be too inefficient for interactive search. Therefore, to strive for real-time web-scale CBVS, we perform a comprehensive study on the different components in a CBVS system to understand the trade-offs between accuracy and speed of each component. Directions investigated include exploring different low-level and semantics-based features, testing different compression factors and approximations during video search, and understanding the time v.s. accuracy trade-off of reranking. Extensive experiments on data sets consisting of more than 1,000 hours of video showed that through a combination of effective features, highly compressed representations, and one iteration of reranking, our proposed system can achieve an 10,000-fold speedup while retaining 80% accuracy of a state-of-the-art CBVS system. We further performed search over 1 million videos and demonstrated that our system can complete the search in 0.975 seconds with a single core, which potentially opens the door to interactive web-scale CBVS for the general public.

Categories and Subject Descriptors

H.3.1 [**Information Storage and Retrieval**]: Content Analysis and Indexing; H.4 [**Information Systems Applications**]: Miscellaneous

General Terms

Algorithms, Experimentation, Performance

Keywords

Content-Based Video Search; Multimedia Event Detection; Product Quantization; Reranking; Semantic Concept Detection

1. INTRODUCTION

Large-scale analysis of video data becomes ever more important as we see an unprecedented growth of user-generated videos on the Internet. To perform search, current video search engines mostly rely on user provided text metadata. However, text metadata is not a comprehensive representation of the video as an user cannot possibly annotate all pieces of information in a video. Also, it is often the case that the users do not provide any metadata at all, and these videos can never be retrieved by a metadata-based search engine. Therefore, we turn to content-based video analysis, which leverages the very rich content in the visual and audio channels of a video, for search. In the multimedia community, this task has been studied in the form of Multimedia Event Detection (MED) [20]. The task can be split into two main phases: feature extraction and search. The main goal of feature extraction is to extract discriminative feature representations from the video's raw visual and audio channels. Extracting effective, generalizable and efficient representations is a key challenge of this phase. During the search phase, which we refer to as Content-Based Video Search (CBVS), the queries are a set of example videos, and the CBVS system will utilize the previously extracted features to retrieve relevant videos. As the extracted feature representations are not text-based, traditional text-retrieval techniques are not directly applicable, and new search techniques need to be developed.

Much research have been proposed to improve the accuracy of content-based video analysis systems [19, 28, 30, 10, 25, 8, 23, 29, 2] and optimizing the speed of feature extraction [14, 16], but an important direction which is still under-explored is achieving real-time CBVS. For a CBVS system to be conveniently utilized by an user, the retrieval of large video collections needs to be done in real-time. However, near real-time content-based video search is a challenging task because, unlike text vectors which are high dimensional but very sparse, visual and audio features are all high dimensional dense vectors. Thus many state-of-the-art CBVS systems [30] still require a few minutes to perform retrieval, which is still too slow for interactive use. Though there are some work [17] which have found that compact semantics-based representations potentially achieve better performance than low-level features, these studies did not focus on utilizing such compact representations to optimize the speed of CBVS systems. Therefore, in this paper we focus on performing a comprehensive study on the different directions and methods to optimizing the speed of CBVS systems.

We introduce a number of aspects to optimize existing state-of-the-art CBVS systems, which include the set of features used, the learning algorithm, different compression and approximation configurations, and the number of reranking iterations. Comprehensive experiments to explore the speedup and accuracy trade-offs in each direction were performed, which resulted in a CBVS system that achieves a 10,000-fold speedup while retaining 80% Mean Average Precision[1] (MAP) of a top performing system [30] in the

[1]Official metric of TRECVID MED task 2014

ICMR'15, June 23–26, 2015, Shanghai, China.

http://dx.doi.org/10.1145/2671188.2749398.

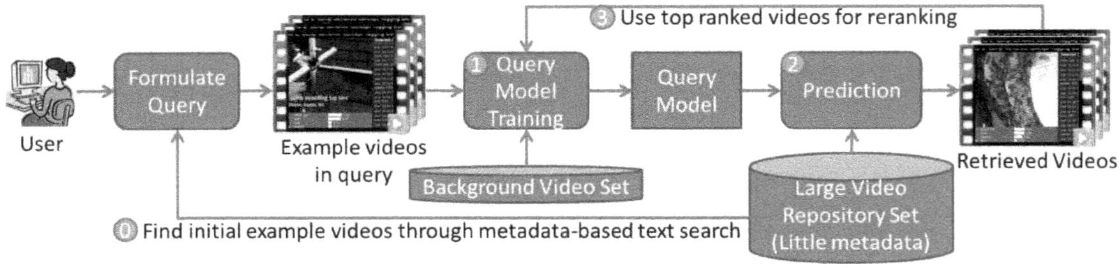

Figure 1: Pipeline of CBVS system.

TRECVID 2014 MED [20] task. In sum, the contributions of our paper are as follows.

1. A CBVS system which can search over 1 million videos with only 1 core in about 1 second is proposed. The proposed CBVS system provides over 10,000-fold speedup while retaining 80% of the MAP of a state-of-the-art system [30]. This potentially opens the door to interactive web-scale CBVS for the general public.
2. We comprehensively explore the speedup and accuracy tradeoffs of many different components in state-of-the-art CBVS systems. These experiments may provide insight to the designing of future CBVS systems.

2. THE CBVS SYSTEM

Assume the following typical usage scenario for CBVS. The user performs an initial metadata-based text search to find a few videos of interest in the video repository. As the user would like to find more relevant videos, the user-selected videos of interest, which we refer to as the "example videos", can be provided to the CBVS system. The system will retrieve, based on video content, more videos related to the query and return them to the user. The videos retrieved by CBVS may or may not have metadata, which is the key advantage of CBVS systems over metadata-based text search.

Our proposed CBVS system, which follows the pipeline of the top-performing TRECVID MED systems [19, 30, 23], has three main components: query model training, prediction and reranking. The query model training step trains query models for each feature representation based on the example videos provided by the user. The prediction step takes the trained query models and performs prediction on an indexed repository set. Weighted fusion is performed to fuse the features from different modalities. Finally, the reranking step will enhance the initial retrieved results. The pipeline of our proposed CBVS system is shown in Figure 1.

To design a fast CBVS system, understanding the details of each component is necessary to find the sweet spot between speed and accuracy. Also, since we are allowed to perform offline preprocessing to index videos, the algorithms should be carefully designed such that most of the time-consuming computation is done in the offline phase, and only the necessary computation is done in the time-critical online phase. In the following sections, the details of each step are described and the implications of each design choice are discussed.

2.1 Fast Query Model Training

Query model training learns a model to discriminate relevant and irrelevant videos to the user query. To train the model, example videos are treated as positive samples and background videos are treated as negative samples. Support Vector Machines (SVM) [3] have been a popular choice for training query models [30, 22]. Furthermore, linear SVMs are very efficient during prediction, because prediction on an unseen instance only involves a single dot-product. In the following paragraphs, we will describe how to efficiently train query models for both linear and non-linear feature representations with linear SVMs.

It has been shown that SVMs with χ^2-kernels are very effective for bag-of-words features [22], which is an effective encoding method for low-level features. However, for SVMs, kernel-based prediction of an input vector is slow because prediction requires a dot product with all support vectors. Therefore, to still utilize kernel-based features but achieve fast prediction, the Explicit Feature Map [26] can effectively convert a kernel-based feature to a linear-based feature [22]. This results in substantial speedup with unsubstantial performance drop.

We now focus on efficient training of linear SVMs, which needs to be fast as the query models are trained on the fly. Linear SVMs can be trained at approximately $\mathcal{O}(nd)$ [13] time by solving the primal, or at approximately $\mathcal{O}(n^2d + n^3)$ [1] time by solving the dual, where n is the number of training vectors and d is the dimensions of a feature representation. There are two terms in the complexity formula of solving the SVM dual: pair-wise dot-product matrix computation time $\mathcal{O}(n^2d)$ and model training time $\mathcal{O}(n^3)$. The primal is in general faster to solve, but when d becomes very large, the dual can be faster to solve if the dot-product matrix can be precomputed offline. The online cost of solving the dual form becomes only $\mathcal{O}(n^3)$, which in practice is very fast. Experiments in Section 3.1 substantiates this claim.

For efficiently solving the dual form of SVMs, the pair-wise dot-product matrix needs to be precomputed offline. If we have n_c videos in the repository set, the entire dot-product matrix is of size $\mathcal{O}(n_c^2)$, which is prohibitively large as the repository set may have up to millions of videos. However, the training of SVMs only require the pair-wise dot-product of all vectors in the training set, which only includes the example videos and the background set, so precomputing the full matrix is not required. Let $C \in \mathbb{R}^{d \times n_c}$ be the feature matrix for all n_c videos in the search repository. Let $E \in \mathbb{R}^{d \times n_e}$ be the feature matrix for n_e example videos, which is a subset of C as the example videos are included in the search repository. Let $B \in \mathbb{R}^{d \times n_b}$ be the feature matrix for n_b background videos. We combine E and B to create the training feature matrix $F = [E, B] \in \mathbb{R}^{d \times (n_e + n_b)}$. Then the pair-wise dot-product matrix is as follows:

$$F^T F = \begin{bmatrix} E^T \\ B^T \end{bmatrix} \begin{bmatrix} E & B \end{bmatrix} = \begin{bmatrix} E^T E & E^T B \\ B^T E & B^T B \end{bmatrix}. \quad (1)$$

Since the background set is fixed and relatively small (several thousand videos), we can precompute $B^T B$ and store it in memory. To quickly acquire $E^T B$, we first precompute $C^T B$ offline, and during the online step only n_e rows need to be read from $C^T B$ to form $E^T B$ because E is a subset of C. $C^T B$ is stored on disk. Finally, the only part remaining is $E^T E$, which can be computed quickly on the fly as there will not be many example videos (tens of videos).

To summarize, the three steps taken to efficiently train a linear SVM is as follows. First, the pair-wise dot-product matrix for the query is assembled on the fly, which is fast because most of the matrix is already precomputed. Second, the SVM is trained by solving the dual, and a set of support vectors and their corresponding weights are acquired. Finally, the dual solution is converted to the primal solution, so that the final linear SVM model is only a d dimensional vector which supports fast prediction. This step consists of a weighted sum of all the support vectors' raw features, i.e. matrices E and B. This can be performed quickly if E and B are pre-loaded in main memory. In our actual implementation, B is pre-loaded, and E is read from disk on the fly, which is still fast since there are only a few example videos.

2.2 Fast Prediction

We describe how one could achieve fast prediction of linear SVM models over testing data. The prediction of a single instance requires a dot product with the model. A simple way to find top-ranked videos in the repository set is to exhaustively compute the dot-product for all videos. However, this is too inefficient as the repository size grows larger. As the dot product is highly related to the Euclidean distance [21], approximate nearest neighbor techniques can be used to save computation time. Many approximate nearest neighbor search methods have been proposed, such as KD-Tree-based Approximate Nearest Neighbors [18] and Locality Sensitive Hashing [5], but these methods tend to be too memory consuming [9]. Also, these methods tend to be not as effective when the number of dimensions of the vector space is significantly higher than the number of instances in the search set. Therefore, we focus on using Product Quantization (PQ) [9], which takes into account efficiency in both computation and memory. Given a d dimensional feature representation, PQ will split the high-dimensional space into s subspaces, where each subspace is of dimension $c = \frac{d}{s}$ assuming d is divisible by s. Then, the vector belonging to each of the subspace are quantized with a short code. The short codes from different subspaces are concatenated to form a compact representation of the original vector. The dot-product between two vectors can be efficiently estimated using this compact representation.

The PQ framework has a codebook learning, quantization, and prediction phase. In the codebook learning phase, a codebook for each small subspace is learned with K-Means clustering where $K = 256$. $K = 256$ is preferable because the cluster ID can be represented by a single byte. We define $D_i \in \mathbb{R}^{c\times 256}$, $1 \leq i \leq s$ as the codebook for the i-th subspace.

In the quantization phase, each input vector is split into s subspaces and quantized according to the corresponding codebooks. Specifically, let $v = [v_1^T, v_2^T, \ldots, v_s^T] \in \mathbb{R}^d$ be an input vector, where $v_i \in \mathbb{R}^c$ falls in subspace i. For each v_i, a nearest neighbor is found in D_i, and v_i is represented by the ID of the nearest neighbor: q_i, which ranges from 0 to 255 and takes up 1 byte. At the end, v is quantized with s bytes, i.e. $q = [q_1, q_2, \ldots, q_s] \in \{0, 1, \ldots, 255\}^s$. This is a compact representation in that we have succeeded in compressing a d dimensional floating point vector, which takes up at least $4d$ bytes assuming single-precision, to only s bytes. Therefore, the effective compression factor is $\frac{4d}{s} = 4c$.

In the prediction phase, given a query vector $w \in \mathbb{R}^d$ (the linear SVM model), we would like to quickly compute the dot-product over all quantized vectors (videos in repository set). The naïve way to compute the dot-product between two vectors requires d multiplications and additions, but PQ exploits the fact that the vectors in the repository set have been quantized to achieve fast dot-product computation. First, the query vector is also split according to the s subspaces, i.e. $w = [w_1^T, w_2^T, \ldots, w_s^T]$, where $w_i \in \mathbb{R}^c$. Then for each subspace, the dot-product between a subspace of the query vector (w_i) and all codewords in the corresponding codebook of the subspace (D_i) is computed and stored in a lookup table (LUT) Specifically, $L = [D_1^T w_1, D_2^T w_2, \ldots, D_s^T w_s] \in \mathbb{R}^{256\times s}$. With the LUT, computing the dot-product between the query vector and a quantized vector consists of 1) for each subspace, look up the dot-product value given q_i (the quantized vector's cluster membership), and 2) sum up the dot-products from each subspace. For example, we would compute the dot-product between q and w as follows. Let $L(k, l)$ denote the element on the k-th row and l-th column of the LUT. Then the dot product is $\sum_{i=1}^{s} L(q_i+1, i)$. $+1$ is required because cluster membership starts from 0. Therefore, with the LUT, the complexity of a dot-product drops from $\mathcal{O}(d)$ to $\mathcal{O}(s)$. We see that not only does PQ compress the feature representation, but also the prediction time is decreased.

In practice, codebook learning and quantization are performed offline, and the prediction step is performed online. To accelerate the prediction step, the codes for the videos in the search repository set are all loaded into memory. This is feasible because PQ significantly compresses the feature representations.

However, when the amount of videos to be searched becomes very big, spending $\mathcal{O}(s)$ per video may still be too long. [9] proposes to build an inverted index to prune out search candidates that are highly unlikely to be nearest neighbors. The codewords in the inverted index are acquired by quantizing with another coarse codebook learned in the d dimensional space. However, in [9], the largest d is only 960. This is very small compared to the dimensions of our video representations, which can go up to 100,000 dimensions. Therefore, this method may not be applicable in our scenario, and we tackle this problem from another direction. Instead of summing the dot-products for all s subspaces, we propose to only sum over a dynamically selected set of subspaces.

High Variance Subspaces First

We propose to speed up the dot-product computation process by only summing the dot-product for selected subspaces. The selected subspaces should be the subspaces which can enable us to quickly discriminate whether a video could be a top-ranked video or not. Motivated by KD-Tree-based Approximate Nearest Neighbors [18], which perform KD-tree splits according to dimensions having larger variance, we only select the subspaces which have high variance in the dot-product values. The intuition is that these subspaces provide more information in separating a relevant video from an irrelevant one. We name this method High Variance Subspaces First (HVSF).

The variance can be efficiently computed on the fly based on the LUT. For the i-th subspace, let $u_i(1), u_i(2), \ldots, u_i(256)$ correspond to the frequency of each codeword occurring in the repository set, which can be computed offline during the quantization step. The sum of all frequencies is n_c, i.e. $\sum_{j=1}^{256} u_i(j) = n_c$. We denote the average dot-product values of the classifier w for subspace i as $\mu_i = \sum_{j=1}^{256}(u_i(j)L(j,i))/n_c$. Then the variance for subspace i is as follows: $\sigma_i^2 = \sum_{j=1}^{256} u_i(j)\left(L(j,i) - \mu_i\right)^2/n_c$.

For the prediction phase of HVSF, there are three main steps. First, high variance subspaces are selected. Second, we perform summation of dot products only over the selected subspaces. Finally, to obtain a more accurate ranked list for the top-ranked videos, the top scoring videos (2500 in our experiments) are selected and their exact dot-product (summation over all subspaces) computed. In the following sections, HVSF hX means that only the top $\frac{100}{h}$% of the subspaces with higher variance were used for the dot-product summation.

Stages	Query Model Training	Prediction	Reranking
Stored in memory (shared by all queries)	1. Background set pair-wise dot-product matrix (B^TB) 2. Background set raw features (B)	1. Quantized features for large video repository set	(All loaded by previous steps)
Read from disk	1. Example video v.s. background set dot-product matrix (E^TB) 2. Example video raw features (E)	(None)	1. Top-ranked video v.s. background set dot-product matrix 2. Top-ranked video raw features
Compute on the fly	1. Compute example video pair-wise dot-product matrix (E^TE) 2. Assemble training set dot-product matrix (F^TF) 3. Train SVM model, convert SVM dual solution to primal solution 4. Quantize SVM model	1. Predict with quantized SVM model 2. Fuse ranked lists from all features	1. Compute top-ranked video pair-wise dot-product matrix 2. Assemble top-ranked video augmented training set dot-product matrix 3. Continue to Query Model Training step 3

Table 1: Overview of memory usage, disk usage and computational tasks of each stage in the online phase of the CBVS system.

2.3 Fast Reranking

Unsupervised reranking of an initial ranked list, which is also known as pseudo-relevance feedback, has shown to be a promising method in improving CBVS results, increasing the MAP by at least 1% absolute in TRECVID MED 2014 [30]. Under the assumption that top-ranked videos in a retrieved ranked list are highly likely to be correct, the reranking algorithm can obtain more training data for the query model by treating the top-k-ranked videos as positive examples. These positive examples are added into the example video set, and a better query model could be trained with the newly added positive examples. However, we are not perfectly sure that the top-k-ranked videos are positives, so they should be treated with more scrutiny than the user-selected example videos. Also, the top k videos with slightly lower rank are less likely to be positives than the higher ranked videos. Therefore, [11] proposed to assign gradually decreasing weights to the loss incurred by the top-k-ranked videos in the SVM loss function. In our work, we simplified the reranking method proposed in [30, 11] and arrive at the following algorithm. Let $\mathcal{T}$ be the set of videos already in the training set, e.g. the background videos and the example videos. Let $\mathcal{U}$ be the set of top-k-ranked videos in the current ranked list. In each iteration, we iterate the following three steps: 1) train a SVM model using the samples in $\mathcal{T} \cup \mathcal{U}$; 2) fix the SVM model, and select some pseudo positive samples, calculate their weights, and put them in $\mathcal{U}$; 3) adjust threshold so that more samples will be added in $\mathcal{U}$ in the next iteration.

When we fix the SVM model, let $\text{rank}(v), v \in \mathcal{U}$ be the rank of testing video v in the ranked list. The weights of a video $v \in \mathcal{U}$ can be calculated by the following closed-form solution:

$$l_v = \begin{cases} 1 & \text{if rank}(v) \leq p \\ \frac{k-\text{rank}(v)+1}{k-p} & \text{otherwise} \end{cases}, \forall v \in \mathcal{U}, \quad (2)$$

where p is the pivot. For videos ranked before rank p, their weight is 1. For videos ranked after the pivot, their weights decrease linearly. The weights of videos in the training set $\mathcal{T}$ are all 1. A similar mixture weighting scheme has been shown to be effective in [11].

When we fix the samples in $\mathcal{U}$, the modified linear SVM loss function, which re-weights the loss incurred by the videos in $\mathcal{U}$, is as follows.

$$\begin{aligned} &\min_{\mathbf{w},b,\boldsymbol{\xi}} \frac{1}{2}\mathbf{w}^T\mathbf{w} + C\sum_{v \in \mathcal{T}} \xi_v + C\sum_{v \in \mathcal{U}} l_v \xi_v \\ &s.t.\ \forall v \in (\mathcal{T} \cup \mathcal{U}),\ y_v(\mathbf{w}^T x_v + b) \geq 1 - \xi_v,\ \xi_v \geq 0, \end{aligned} \quad (3)$$

where $\mathbf{w}$ is the classifier, b is the bias, ξ_v is the slack for video v, C is the cost parameter, and x_v and y_v are the feature representations and label for video v respectively. $y_v = 1$ for all videos in $\mathcal{U}$. Equation 3 can be solved with slight modifications to the SVM solver [11]. Once a model is trained for each feature, we quantize the model with our PQ codebooks and run prediction only on the top 2500 videos to achieve faster reranking.

2.4 Memory and I/O Efficient CBVS System

Careful design is required to implement the aforementioned 3 components in a memory and I/O efficient way. The key to achieve fast speed is try to offload as much computation as possible to the offline phase, and also try to load data that is shared across all queries into memory during the online phase. Our CBVS system takes these offline-computed data as input:

1. Product quantized feature representations: feature extraction and quantization are very time consuming and should definitely be done offline.
2. Background set pair-wise dot-product matrix (B^TB): as the background set is predefined and universal to all queries, the dot-product matrix of the background set itself can be precomputed for each feature representation.
3. Repository set v.s. background set pair-wise dot-product matrix (C^TB): as the background set and the repository set is predefined, the dot-product matrix can also be precomputed. This is for fast distance matrix building in model training and reranking, as the video examples and the videos used for reranking are from the repository set.

Table 1 summarizes the memory, disk access, and required computation of the online phase. The raw features of the videos in the training set are still necessary for model training, but as the raw features of the repository set is too large to fit in memory, the features of the positive examples are read from disk on the fly. However, this process is fast as there will not be many positive examples. On the other hand, the raw features of the background set, which is shared by all queries and only in the order of thousands of videos, are stored in memory. Other data that is shared across all queries, such as the background set distance matrix and quantized features for the prediction set, are all stored in memory. With this method, we are able to design an efficient CBVS system.

3. EXPERIMENTS

We tested the accuracy and efficiency of our CBVS system by following the TRECVID MED data sets and evaluation protocol, which have been widely used to evaluate CBVS systems. Experiments were performed on MEDTEST13 and MEDTEST14, which are two standard data sets defined by the organizers of TRECVID MED. These two data sets contain around 33,000 unconstrained videos (~1200 hours of video). For both data sets, the data can be

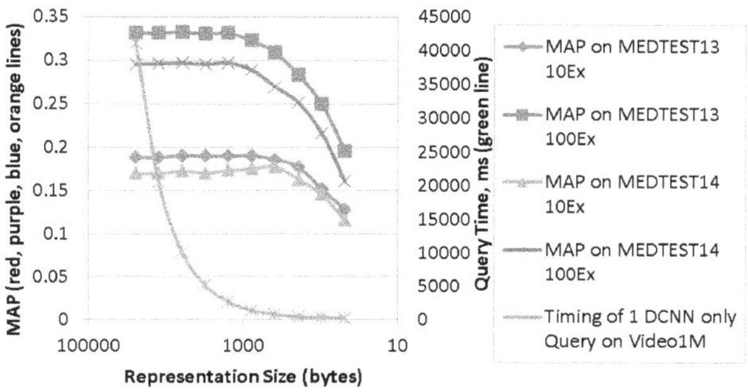

(a) DCNN accuracy and timing with different PQ compressions factors.

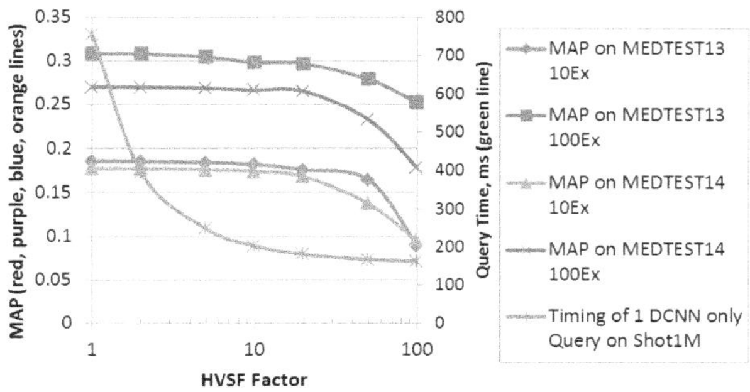

(b) DCNN PQ 384 byte representation: accuracy and timing with varying HVSF factors.

Figure 2: Accuracy and speed trade-off analysis for the DCNN feature. MAP is computed on MEDTEST14 10Ex. Search time is computed on Video1M set. Much of the accuracy can still be retained under aggressive PQ compression and HVSF approximation.

split into 3 sets: the positive examples, the background set and the testing set. The positive examples contain videos corresponding to different events such as Birthday Party, Performing a Bike Trick and Rock-climbing. There are two different query settings defined by the organizers: the 10 exemplar (10Ex) and the 100 exemplar (100Ex) settings. In the 10Ex (100Ex) setting, 10 (100) positive example videos are provided to the system. The background set contains 4992 videos. The positive examples and the background set combined together form the training set. The testing set contains around 24,000 videos. Query models are trained on the training set and predicted on the testing set. There are a total of 20 events/queries each for the two data sets. The evaluation metric used is Mean Average Precision (MAP).

For scalability tests, we also created a Video1M set which contains one million videos. These videos were collected by sampling one million shots from the MEDTEST14 video collection. Shot-level labels were not provided by the organizers, so this set is only used for evaluating the efficiency our CBVS system.

All our experiments were run on a single Intel Xeon E5-2640 @ 2.50GHz core. A SSD RAID is utilized to enable fast accessing of on disk data during the training and reranking steps. We now present experiments on these data sets and explore the trade-off points of each component in our CBVS system.

3.1 Fast Query Model Training

The timing of training a SVM query model is measured. We utilize LIBSVM [3] for solving the dual and LIBLINEAR [7] for solving the primal. The results are shown in Table 2. Though solving primal form SVMs are in general faster, when the dimensions of the features become large, and also when the dot-product matrix can be precomputed, solving the dual form is significantly faster. Once the dual form solution is acquired, we still need to convert the solution to primal form, which is also fast as shown in Table 5.

MEDTEST14 20 Events	Training Time (ms)		Speedup
	SVM Primal	SVM Dual	
10 Ex	11257 ± 615	115 ± 14	98x
100 Ex	11228 ± 716	362 ± 84	31x

Table 2: Training time for one SVM model with varying number of positives by solving either the primal or dual form on the Improved Dense Trajectories Fisher Vector feature (110592 dimensions). The dual form assumes that the dot-product matrix is already computed offline. Both models assume that the required data is loaded into memory. 4992 negatives are used for all models.

	Original Feature Dimensions	Subspace Dimensions	PQ Subspaces (Bytes in Representation)
DCNN	98304	256	384
MFCC	12288	64	192
Sports	512	2	256
YFCC	640	2	320
Total additions per prediction of video			1152
Total additions with 5x HVSF			230

Table 3: PQ parameters for the DMSY CBVS system. The total number of PQ subspaces (s) is the total number of additions required to compute the prediction score for a video.

3.2 Effective Feature Representations and PQ with HVSF

The accuracy and speed of the CBVS system relies heavily not only on the set of features utilized, but also on the compression and approximation of each feature representation. We explore the trade-offs of these design decisions in this section. There are two main kinds of feature representations: low-level features and semantics-based features. Low-level features are extracted directly from the visual or audio channels and do not contain semantic information. Effective low-level visual features include the Improved Dense Trajectories Fisher Vectors (IDT FV, 110592 dimensional) from [27, 4]. Effective low-level audio features include the MFCC (12288 dimensional) [30] features. Semantics-based features are features derived from the prediction of a set of semantic concept detectors. These detectors take low-level features as input and detect whether the semantic concept it was trained for exists or not in the video. Effective semantics-based features include those concept detectors trained on the Yahoo Flickr Creative Commons (YFCC, 640 dimensional) [24, 30] and Google Sports set (Sports, 512 dimensional) [15]. Both YFCC and Sports concept detectors are trained by a SVM-based self-paced learning pipeline [12] using IDT FV. On the other hand, the Deep Convolutional Neural Network (DCNN, 98304 dimensional) features from [30, 28] is actually a hybrid feature, including both low-level neural network features and semantics-based features corresponding to prediction scores of object detectors trained on ImageNet [6]. Explicit Feature Maps were applied to the DCNN and MFCC features. Note that the dimensions of our features have been slightly enlarged (by appending zeros) so that they are divisible by 128 for YFCC and Sports, and divisible by 2048 for IDT FV, DCNN and MFCC. This is done to conveniently perform PQ with high compression factors.

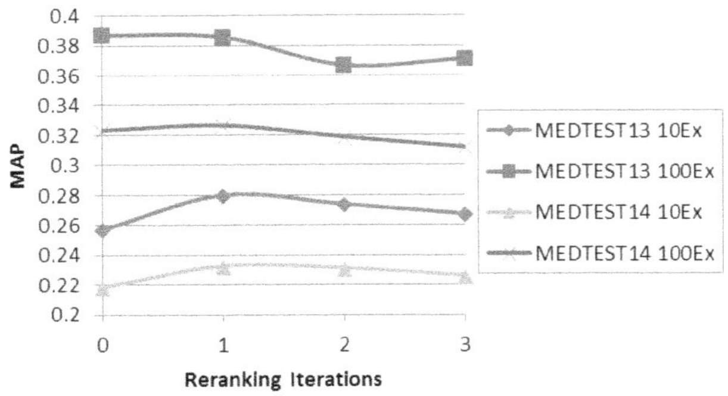

Figure 3: Reranking performance under different amounts of reranking iterations on the DMSY + HVSF 5X system.

MAP per Condition	[30]	DMSY + 5X HVSF + 1R	Performance Difference
MEDTEST13 10Ex	0.313	0.280	89.4%
MEDTEST13 100Ex	0.464	0.386	83.1%
MEDTEST14 10Ex	0.285	0.233	81.6%
MEDTEST14 100Ex	0.419	0.326	77.9%
Time per query (ms)	558400 × 12	507.7	1319834%

Table 4: Performance comparison between our DMSY + 5X HVSF + 1R system and the state-of-the-art MED system [30]. The breakdown of our system's timing is shown in Table 5. 12 is multiplied to the timing of the 10Ex system from [30], because the system was run on a 12 core machine with 4 K-20 GPUs. This is still an underestimate as the GPU timings were not taken into account.

Compact representations for each video enable fast search, which we propose to achieve with PQ compressions and HVSF approximation. Figure 2 shows the accuracy and speed difference under different PQ compression and HVSF factors. Even under aggressive compression, the performance of DCNN only drops slightly, but the speed of search increased by 160x if we compare the search time of the PQ 24576 byte representation with the 384 byte representation + HVSF 5X (only 20% subspaces used). This shows the effectiveness of PQ compressions and HVSF approximation.

A comprehensive study on the affect of PQ compression on different features is performed. Figure 5 shows the MAP of different features under varying compression factors. A clear trend is that the MAP of IDT FV drops as less bytes are used in the feature representation. If around 1000 bytes are used to represent each video, the most effective features are DCNN, Sports and YFCC. This hints at the effectiveness of semantics-based features. Therefore, to strike a balance between accuracy and efficiency, we utilize the feature representations and compression parameters shown in Table 3. All feature representations have been compressed to take up around 300 bytes per video. The total amount of bytes to represent a video is around 1KB. We refer to this combination as the DMSY (DCNN, MFCC, Sports, YFCC) system. As learning fusion weights for each query may be slow, the fusion weights are universal for all queries and set empirically to be 2, 0.5, 1, 1 for the DCNN, MFCC, Sports and YFCC features respectively. This system will be the basis of further experiments. IDT FV has shown to perform poorly under high compression factors, so it was not used.

3.3 Reranking

Reranking experiments based on our DMSY system combined with 5X HVSF (DMSY + HVSF 5X) were performed. Three iterations of reranking were performed, where the top 2, 4, and 6

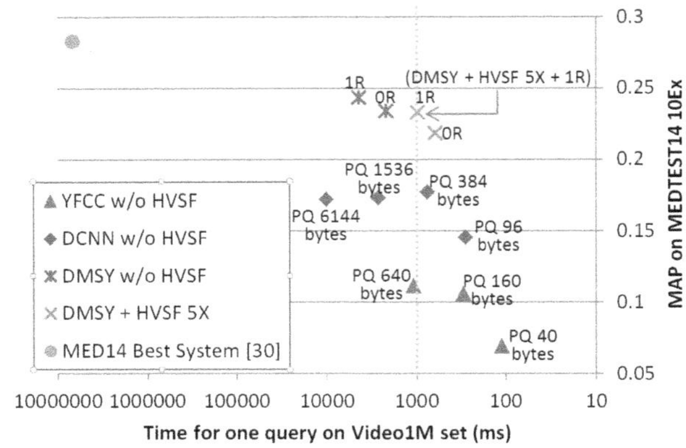

Figure 4: MAP and timing scatter plot of different CBVS systems. MAP was computed under MEDTEST14 10Ex condition. Timings were computed from searching the Video1M set. 0R means no reranking. 1R means one round of reranking.

videos were used for reranking in each iteration respectively. The pivot value was selected by $p = \lfloor \frac{k}{3} \rfloor$, where k is the amount of top-ranked videos used for reranking. The results are shown in Figure 3. Results show that 1 iteration of reranking already provides most of the performance gain. More iterations may cause a performance drop. The main reason is that the MEDTEST13 and MEDTEST14 data sets only have around 20 positives in the testing set. Therefore, when the top 4 or top 6 videos are selected for reranking, the likelihood of selecting negative videos increases significantly. For a larger data set with more positives, this problem can potentially be alleviated.

From our previous experiments, we have found that DMSY + HVSF 5X combined with 1 round of reranking (DMSY + HVSF 5X + 1R for short) achieves high performance. Table 4 compares DMSY + HVSF 5X + 1R with the MAP of a state-of-the-art system [30], which achieved top results in the TRECVID MED 2014 task. Results show that our DMSY + HVSF 5X + 1R system retains 80% of the performance which providing a 13,000 thousand times speedup. This demonstrates the effectiveness of our proposed compression, approximation and reranking schemes.

3.4 Searching 1 Million Videos

Armed with an effective and efficient DMSY + HVSF 5X + 1R system, we tackle the challenge of searching 1 million videos on 1 core in 1 second. Query model training was done under the MEDTEST14 10Ex condition. The search was performed on the Video1M set. Qualitative results are shown in Figure 6, and detailed timing results are shown in Table 5. Our system can complete the search in 0.975 seconds, which is one of the best systems in terms of trade-off between speed and accuracy as shown in Figure 4. Note that when HVSF 5X is combined with 1 iteration of reranking, we are able achieve nearly the same performance as the DMSY system without HVSF, while requiring less time. This indicates that fast reranking could perform error correction and compensate for some of the performance loss caused by approximations. In terms of timing, as shown in Table 5, not surprisingly the prediction phase of our system takes the longest time, but with 1 round of reranking, the query model training phase also takes up a significant portion of the time. In terms of memory usage, the dot-product matrices, raw features, and quantized features for prediction took 0.37GB, 2.09GB and 1.07GB respectively. The memory usage was less than 4GB and could potentially run on a laptop.

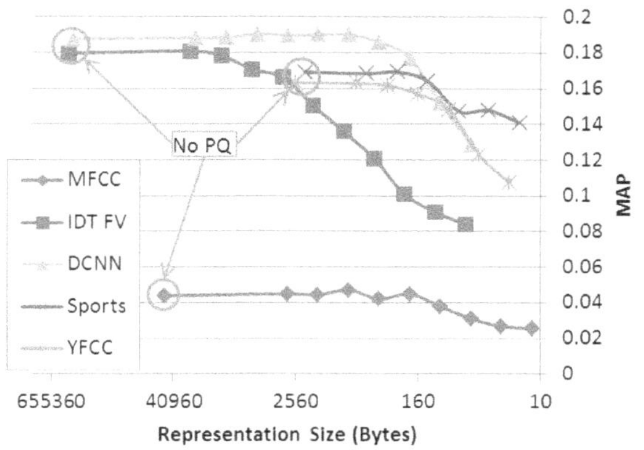

(a) MEDTEST13 10Ex

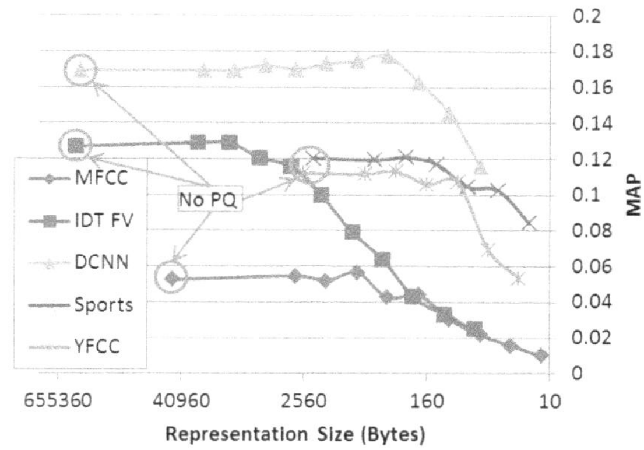

(b) MEDTEST14 10Ex

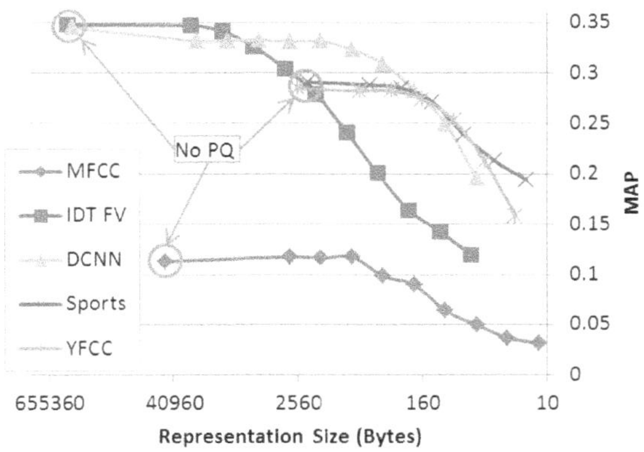

(c) MEDTEST13 100Ex

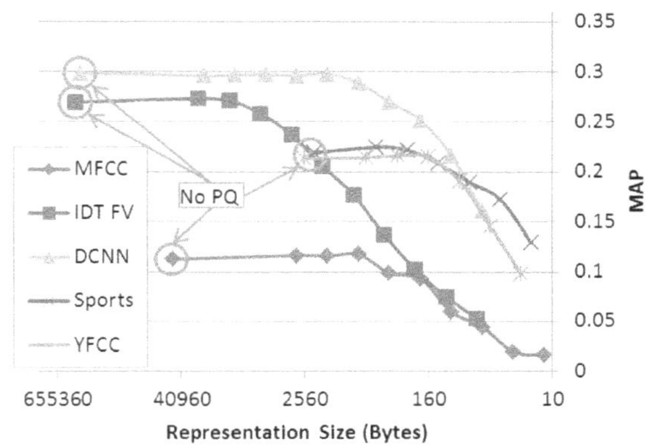

(d) MEDTEST14 100Ex

Figure 5: Performance of different feature representations under different PQ compression factors. The representation size corresponds to the amount of bytes required to encode one video. The performance and representation size of the original features (no PQ) are also shown in the orange circles.

Figure 6: Qualitative results of retrieval by DMSY + HVSF 5X + 1R system on Video1M set. Due to space limitations only selected queries are shown.

Timing (ms)	First Pass			1 Iteration of Reranking				Total
	SVM training	Convert Dual Sol. to Primal	Prediction	Load Top Ranked Video Data	SVM training	Convert Dual Sol. to Primal	Prediction	
MEDTEST14 10Ex	136.1 ± 24.6	87.9 ± 9.1	17.3 ± 1.3	4.9 ± 4.8	136 ± 33.5	87.5 ± 13	10.4 ± 0.7	507.7 ± 73.1
Video1M 10Ex	128.9 ± 21.3	83 ± 5	380.3 ± 5.7	20.6 ± 9.8	127.7 ± 25.3	85.1 ± 5.7	104.9 ± 17.1	975.3 ± 63.4

Table 5: Timing breakdown for DMSY + HVSF 5X + 1R system for one MEDTEST14 10Ex and Video1M 10Ex query.

4. CONCLUSIONS

We have proposed a system which can search 1 million videos with 1 core in less than 1 second while retaining 80% of the performance of a state-of-the-art CBVS system. This potentially opens the door to content-based video search on web-scale video repositories. The speed gains in our system mainly come from three aspects. First, we perform approximations in locations which will not cause significant change in performance, such as increasing the PQ compression factor and only computing the dot-products for PQ subspaces with higher variance. Second, fast reranking can perform some error correction and compensate for some of the performance loss caused by approximations. Finally, our proposed system relies on 3 semantics-based features, which enabled us to significantly lower the amount of bytes required to represent each video. This may suggest that for the next challenge: searching 1 billion videos, even more compact semantics-based representations might be a promising solution.

Acknowledgments

This work was partially supported by the Intelligence Advanced Research Projects Activity (IARPA) via Department of Interior National Business Center contract number D11PC20068. The U.S. Government is authorized to reproduce and distribute reprints for Governmental purposes notwithstanding any copyright annotation thereon. Disclaimer: The views and conclusions contained herein are those of the authors and should not be interpreted as necessarily representing the official policies or endorsements, either expressed or implied, of IARPA, DoI/NBC, or the U.S. Government. This work used the Extreme Science and Engineering Discovery Environment (XSEDE), which is supported by National Science Foundation grant number OCI-1053575. Specifically, it used the Blacklight system at the Pittsburgh Supercomputing Center (PSC).

5. REFERENCES

[1] A. Bordes, S. Ertekin, J. Weston, and L. Bottou. Fast kernel classifiers with online and active learning. In *JMLR*, 2005.

[2] E. F. Can and R. Manmatha. Modeling concept dependencies for event detection. In *ICMR*, 2014.

[3] C.-C. Chang and C.-J. Lin. LIBSVM: A library for support vector machines. In *ACM Transactions on Intelligent Systems and Technology*, 2011.

[4] K. Chatfield, V. Lempitsky, A. Vedaldi, and A. Zisserman. The devil is in the details: an evaluation of recent feature encoding methods. In *BMVC*, 2011.

[5] M. Datar, N. Immorlica, P. Indyk, and V. S. Mirrokni. Locality-sensitive hashing scheme based on p-stable distributions. In *Proceedings of the 20-th annual symposium on Computational geometry*, 2004.

[6] J. Deng, W. Dong, R. Socher, L.-J. Li, K. Li, and L. Fei-Fei. Imagenet: A large-scale hierarchical image database. In *CVPR*, 2009.

[7] R.-E. Fan, K.-W. Chang, C.-J. Hsieh, X.-R. Wang, and C.-J. Lin. Liblinear: A library for large linear classification. In *JMLR*, 2008.

[8] A. Habibian, T. Mensink, and C. G. M. Snoek. Videostory: A new multimedia embedding for few-example recognition and translation of events. In *ACM MM*, 2014.

[9] H. Jegou, M. Douze, and C. Schmid. Product quantization for nearest neighbor search. In *IEEE TPAMI*, 2011.

[10] L. Jiang, A. G. Hauptmann, and G. Xiang. Leveraging high-level and low-level features for multimedia event detection. In *ACM MM*, 2012.

[11] L. Jiang, D. Meng, T. Mitamura, and A. G. Hauptmann. Easy samples first: Self-paced reranking for zero-example multimedia search. In *ACM MM*, 2014.

[12] L. Jiang, D. Meng, S.-I. Yu, Z. Lan, S. Shan, and A. G. Hauptmann. Self-paced learning with diversity. In *NIPS*, 2014.

[13] T. Joachims. Training linear svms in linear time. In *KDD*, 2006.

[14] V. Kantorov and I. Laptev. Efficient feature extraction, encoding and classification for action recognition. In *CVPR*, 2014.

[15] A. Karpathy, G. Toderici, S. Shetty, T. Leung, R. Sukthankar, and L. Fei-Fei. Large-scale video classification with convolutional neural networks. In *CVPR*, 2014.

[16] Z.-Z. Lan, Y. Yang, N. Ballas, S.-I. Yu, and A. Hauptmann. Resource constrained multimedia event detection. In *MultiMedia Modeling*, 2014.

[17] M. Mazloom, E. Gavves, K. van de Sande, and C. Snoek. Searching informative concept banks for video event detection. In *ICMR*, 2013.

[18] M. Muja and D. G. Lowe. Fast approximate nearest neighbors with automatic algorithm configuration. In *Proceedings of the International Conference on Computer Vision Theory and Applications*, 2009.

[19] P. Natarajan, S. Wu, S. Vitaladevuni, X. Zhuang, S. Tsakalidis, U. Park, and R. Prasad. Multimodal feature fusion for robust event detection in web videos. In *CVPR*, 2012.

[20] P. Over, G. Awad, M. Michel, J. Fiscus, G. Sanders, W. Kraaij, A. F. Smeaton, and G. Quénot. TRECVID 2014 – an overview of the goals, tasks, data, evaluation mechanisms and metrics. In *TRECVID*, 2014.

[21] A. Shrivastava and P. Li. Asymmetric lsh (alsh) for sublinear time maximum inner product search (mips). In *NIPS*, 2014.

[22] M. Sjöberg, M. Koskela, S. Ishikawa, and J. Laaksonen. Large-scale visual concept detection with explicit kernel maps and power mean svm. In *ICMR*, 2013.

[23] A. Tamrakar, S. Ali, Q. Yu, J. Liu, O. Javed, A. Divakaran, H. Cheng, and H. Sawhney. Evaluation of low-level features and their combinations for complex event detection in open source videos. In *CVPR*, 2012.

[24] B. Thomee, D. A. Shamma, G. Friedland, B. Elizalde, K. Ni, D. Poland, D. Borth, and L.-J. Li. The new data and new challenges in multimedia research. *arXiv preprint arXiv:1503.01817*, 2015.

[25] W. Tong, Y. Yang, L. Jiang, S.-I. Yu, Z. Lan, Z. Ma, W. Sze, E. Younessian, and A. Hauptmann. E-lamp: integration of innovative ideas for multimedia event detection. In *Machine Vision and Applications*, 2014.

[26] A. Vedaldi and A. Zisserman. Efficient additive kernels via explicit feature maps. In *IEEE TPAMI*, 2012.

[27] H. Wang and C. Schmid. Action recognition with improved trajectories. In *ICCV*, 2013.

[28] Z. Xu, Y. Yang, and A. G. Hauptmann. A discriminative CNN video representation for event detection. In *CVPR*, 2015.

[29] Y. Yang, Z. Ma, Z. Xu, S. Yan, and A. G. Hauptmann. How related exemplars help complex event detection in web videos? In *ICCV*, 2013.

[30] S.-I. Yu, L. Jiang, Z. Xu, Z. Lan, et al. Informedia@ TRECVID 2014 MED and MER. In *TRECVID Video Retrieval Evaluation Workshops*, 2014.

Bag-of-Fragments: Selecting and Encoding Video Fragments for Event Detection and Recounting

Pascal Mettes†, Jan C. van Gemert†, Spencer Cappallo†, Thomas Mensink†, Cees G. M. Snoek†*
†University of Amsterdam *Qualcomm Research Netherlands

ABSTRACT

The goal of this paper is event detection and recounting using a representation of concept detector scores. Different from existing work, which encodes videos by averaging concept scores over all frames, we propose to encode videos using fragments that are discriminatively learned per event. Our *bag-of-fragments* split a video into semantically coherent fragment proposals. From training video proposals we show how to select the most discriminative fragment for an event. An encoding of a video is in turn generated by matching and pooling these discriminative fragments to the fragment proposals of the video. The bag-of-fragments forms an effective encoding for event detection and is able to provide a precise temporally localized event recounting. Furthermore, we show how bag-of-fragments can be extended to deal with irrelevant concepts in the event recounting. Experiments on challenging web videos show that i) our modest number of fragment proposals give a high sub-event recall, ii) bag-of-fragments is complementary to global averaging and provides better event detection, iii) bag-of-fragments with concept filtering yields a desirable event recounting. We conclude that fragments matter for video event detection and recounting.

Categories and Subject Descriptors

I.2.10 [**Vision and Scene Understanding**]: Video analysis

Keywords

Event detection; event recounting; bag-of-fragments; discriminative fragments

1. INTRODUCTION

In this work, we focus on detecting events in videos and recounting why an event is relevant by providing the most relevant semantic concepts. This problem is typically addressed by globally aggregating concept detector scores over the whole video [15, 16, 18]. Global aggregation of detector scores poses two problems to event detection and recounting. First, event videos are a complex interplay of various sub-events with a varying degree of relevance [1] which are blended into a single representation. Second, in a global aggregation, the event recounting is unable to state where in the video relevant concepts occur. Similar to related work, we compute concepts scores for frames in a video as the semantic representation, but we aim to perform event detection and recounting on the level of video fragments.

We propose a pipeline to encode a video using fragments that form discriminative sub-events for a complex event, which we call *bag-of-fragments*. For such an encoding, we first need to generate fragments from a video. As the search space of all possible fragments in a video is vast, we propose a hierarchical clustering algorithm to yield a concise set of semantically coherent fragment proposals. The algorithm, inspired by object proposals in images [10, 24], iteratively merges only the most informative fragments. As a result, fragments are generated across all temporal locations and scales of a video, without exhaustively preserving the full search space of fragments.

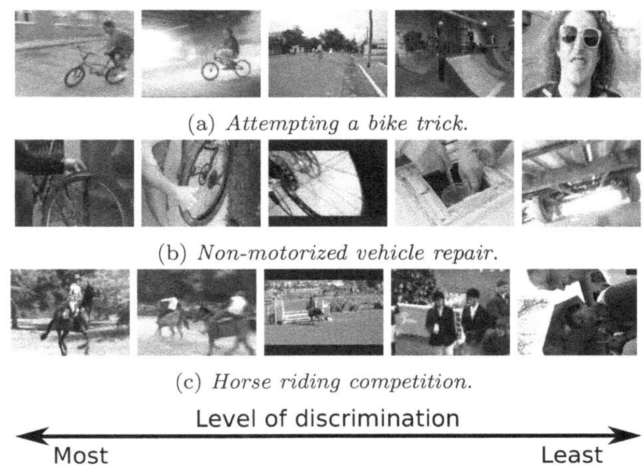

(a) *Attempting a bike trick.*

(b) *Non-motorized vehicle repair.*

(c) *Horse riding competition.*

Figure 1: We propose bag-of-fragments, a video representation that finds and encodes the most discriminative fragments for event detection and recounting. The figure shows the middle frame of five fragments for three events, ordered by level of discrimination. The most discriminative fragments are exemplary for the event and will be included in the bag-of-fragments, while the more ambiguous and less discriminative fragments are ignored.

ICMR'15, June 23–26, 2015, Shanghai, China.

http://dx.doi.org/10.1145/2671188.2749404.

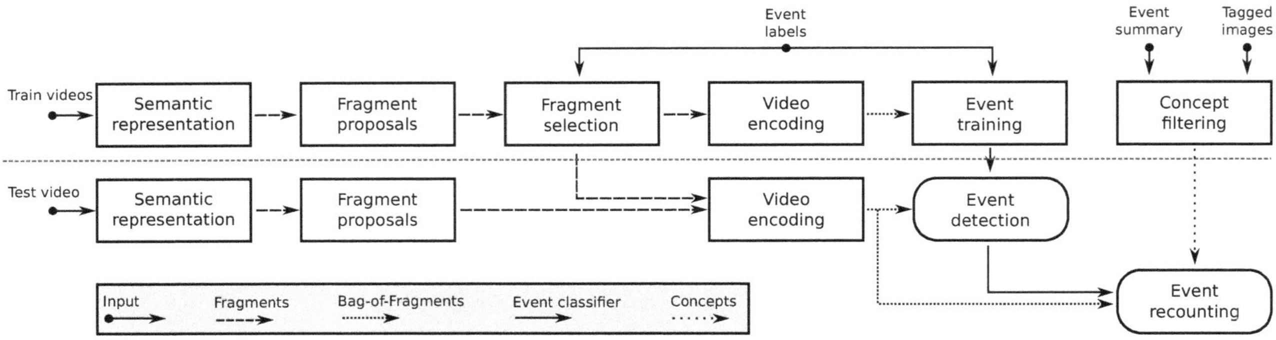

Figure 2: The pipeline of our bag-of-fragments for event detection and recounting.

Based on the fragments proposals of a set of training videos, we select the most discriminative ones of an event. Fig. 1 highlights a number of fragments with various levels of discrimination according to our selection. The selected discriminative fragments form the basis of our bag-of-fragments encoding. The discriminative fragments of an event are matched and pooled over the fragment proposals of a single video, resulting in an effective encoding for event detection. What is more, as the encoding is performed per fragment, information regarding the most informative fragments of a video is retained. Event recounting can therefore be performed by providing the most relevant concepts within the most informative fragments of a video. Lastly, we show how co-occurrence statistics from social tagged images can aid our event recounting by filtering irrelevant concepts.

Experimental evaluation on challenging web videos from the THUMOS [12] and TRECVID benchmarks [20] highlights the effectiveness of our bag-of-fragments for event detection and recounting. First, we show that our fragment proposals are able to retain the most informative fragments at a fraction of full search space of fragments. Second, we show the effectiveness and complementary nature of our bag-of-fragments encoding for event detection compared to a global aggregation of concept scores. Third, we show qualitatively that our bag-of-fragments with concept filtering yields desirable event recounting results.

2. RELATED WORK

Video encodings for event and action detection typically use low-level features that describe the spatio-temporal signal [7, 14, 26]. While these features are well-suited for recognition, they lack any semantic interpretation which complicates recounting why a video is recognized. A solution is offered by Videostory [8], that learns a representation to jointly embeds user tags with video features. The features of a new video can be mapped to this joint feature-tag space and the embedded tags allow recounting the detection evidence. Instead of user tags, which may be noisy, we use high-quality concept classifiers to allow recounting. We will experimentally compare against Videostory [8].

Instead of low-level features, recent video encodings apply a bank of concept classifiers to individual frames and average the frame-based responses for forming a video representation [15, 16, 18]. Such a representation has shown excellent accuracy for event recognition [16, 18] with the added benefit that the concept classification scores provide valuable clues for recounting why the whole video is relevant [8, 15]. Where these works recount a complete video, we instead recount on video fragments, which offer a more precise fine-grained temporal granularity. Rather than averaging concept scores over the whole video, we aggregate scores on coherent video fragments and use them for event detection and recounting.

Although a complex event consists of various sub-events, it can be recognized by a human after seeing only a few well-chosen discriminative video fragments [1]. In automatic event recognition, fragments have been used as latent variables in an SVM optimization [23, 25]. Since latent-SVM is computationally expensive, only a limited number of latent fragments can be used. Instead, our method can exploit a larger set of possible discriminative fragments, which increases the likelihood of finding the most discriminative ones. We draw inspiration from mid-level parts as used in image classification [5, 13]; we automatically discover discriminative video fragments and use them to encode full videos as a bag of their best matching fragments.

To perform a bag-of-fragments encoding of a video, we need to first split a video into coherent fragments that are likely to contain a discriminative sub-event. Instead of a brute-force sliding window [19] or detecting shot boundaries [27] we base our fragments on proposal methods [10, 11, 24]. We propose a fast clustering method to generate a small set of fragment proposals with a high sub-event recall. We will experimentally evaluate our proposals against sliding windows and shot boundary detection.

For event recounting, the highest scoring concept scores in a video are typically used as evidence [4, 15]. Because the highest score is sensitive to noise, Sun et al. [22] propose a manually defined white-list of acceptable concepts per event. We extend this work by replacing the manual white-list with an automatically found list based on co-occurrence statistics using a high-level event description and tagged images, as recently proposed for zero-shot image classification [17]. Automatic white-listing eliminates any manual effort, which is labor intensive and may be prone to errors or subjectivity.

3. BAG-OF-FRAGMENTS

The key contribution of this paper is an encoding of discriminative fragments, which we call bag-of-fragments, for event detection and recounting. The pipeline consists of four major stages. The first stage generates fragment proposals by splitting a video into a set of fragments. The second stage performs fragment selection, by identifying the most discriminative fragment proposals for provided event exam-

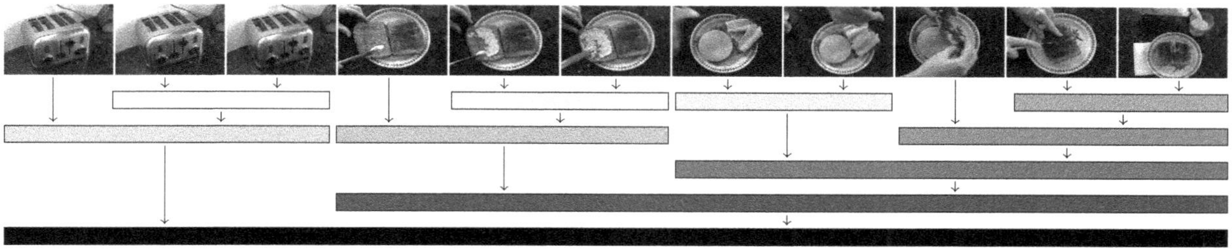

Figure 3: A video of *Making a sandwich*, where the fragment proposals are hierarchically merged using the combined similarity. Note how semantically more correlated proposals of the video are merged earlier (indicated by the colors of the bars).

ples. In the third stage we utilize the discriminative fragments to generate a bag-of-fragments encoding of a video. The encoding forms the basis for both event detection and recounting. The fourth component, concept filtering, is introduced to generate a relevant event recounting. We summarize the pipeline in Fig. 2 and detail the stages next.

3.1 Fragment proposals

To generate a set of fragment proposals for a video, we employ a hierarchical clustering algorithm to cluster fragments into proposals. The main idea behind the hierarchical clustering is to iteratively merge only the most informative fragments, rather than considering all fragment merges. For the clustering, we employ two similarity measures, a semantic and syntactic similarity. The two similarity measures aim to merge the most semantically similar fragments (semantic similarity), while maintaining a balanced cluster tree (syntactic similarity).

Semantic fragment similarity. Let $\mathbf{f}_i \in \mathbb{R}^d$ denote the semantic representation of fragment i containing the scores of d concepts. The semantic similarity between two fragments i and j is then estimated as:

$$S_c(\mathbf{f}_i, \mathbf{f}_j) = \sum_{k=1}^{d} |f_i(k) - f_j(k)|, \tag{1}$$

where $f_i(k)$ denotes the kth concept of $\mathbf{f}_i$. Using this equation as a similarity measure, the two consecutive fragments to be merged at each iteration are the fragments for which Eq. 1 is minimized. Such a clustering algorithm combines the semantically most similar fragments at each iteration, generating semantically coherent fragments. Updating fragments i and j into fragment t can be done efficiently, as we apply average pooling of the concepts within a fragment:

$$\begin{aligned} f_t(k) &= \tfrac{r(\mathbf{f}_i)\cdot f_i(k)+r(\mathbf{f}_j)\cdot f_j(k)}{r(\mathbf{f}_i)+r(\mathbf{f}_j)}, \qquad k = \{1, .., d\}, \\ r(\mathbf{f}_t) &= r(\mathbf{f}_i) + r(\mathbf{f}_j), \end{aligned} \tag{2}$$

where $r(f_i)$ denotes the number of frames in fragment i.

Syntactic fragment similarity. To prevent that a single video fragment gobbles up small fragments one by one, we add another similarity measure that enforces a more balanced cluster tree:

$$S_s(\mathbf{f}_i, \mathbf{f}_j) = r(\mathbf{f}_i) + r(\mathbf{f}_j). \tag{3}$$

The idea behind the similarity measure of Eq. 3 is to penalize large fragments from merging in favor of smaller fragments.

Combined similarity. A combination of semantic and syntactic similarities is given by a linear combination of the terms,

$$S(\mathbf{f}_i, \mathbf{f}_j) = S_c(\mathbf{f}_i, \mathbf{f}_j) + \alpha \cdot S_s(\mathbf{f}_i, \mathbf{f}_j). \tag{4}$$

As the ranges of the two similarity measures are different, the variable α is set to the sum of the concept scores divided by the sum of the sizes for all consecutive fragments at each iteration. This makes both similarity measures of equal importance.

The hierarchical clustering with the combined similarity measure results in a concise set of fragment proposals, ideally retaining those fragment proposals that are semantically coherent. An example of the fragment proposals generated for a video with eleven sampled frames is shown in Fig. 3.

3.2 Fragment selection

From the set of fragment proposals P generated for a set of event training videos, we aim to select the most discriminative ones. We utilize the training videos in two stages. In the first stage, the training videos are used to select which fragment proposals are most discriminative for a given event. In the second stage, a bag-of-fragments encoding is generated for each training and test video based on the discriminative fragments. The encodings are then used to train an event classifier with an off-the-shelf SVM classifier. During training, we are given N training videos $X = [\mathbf{x}_1, .., \mathbf{x}_N]$, where $\mathbf{x}_i \in \mathbb{R}^{s_i \times d}$ denotes the ith training video containing s_i fragment proposals. Furthermore, video labels are provided as $Y = [y_1, .., y_N]$, where $y_i \in \{-1, +1\}$ states whether training video i contains the event. We outline a three step procedure for selecting the discriminative fragments.

1) Generating event fragment classifiers. We first compute an event classifier for each fragment proposal of the positive event training videos. As negative examples we simply use the fragment proposals of negative videos. Rather than explicitly training an SVM classifier for each (positive) proposal separately, we prefer a faster alternative using discriminative decorrelation [9]. We assume that the maximum likelihood estimate of the covariance matrix Σ used in linear discriminant analysis is the sample covariance over all the fragments in the training set X, ignoring class labels. As a result the linear discriminant analysis parameters μ and Σ only need to be computed once over the whole training set. Then, a classifier $\mathbf{w}_{ij}$ for $\mathbf{x}_{ij}$, proposal j of training video i, is efficiently computed as:

$$\mathbf{w}_{ij} = \Sigma^{-1}(\mathbf{x}_{ij} - \mu). \tag{5}$$

Eq. 5 results in a classifier for each fragment proposal, ready to be evaluated on all N training videos.

2) Matching fragment classifiers for video pooling. For each fragment proposal $p \in P$, we perform a matching to all the N training videos by computing the dot-product between the event fragment classifier of p and the fragment proposals of the training video. After the matching we perform a max-pooling operation, which simply retains the maximum dot-product value of the matching for the entire video. The pooling value expresses how much the training video is related to proposal p. By ranking the training videos according to their max-pooled values and comparing the ranking to labels Y, we are able to determine how well the fragment proposal is able to distinguish positive from negative videos containing a specific event. We note that each fragment proposal has a bias in the matching and pooling, namely to the video from which it has originally been retrieved. However, as the bias is equal among all the proposals, it does not lead to overfitting towards specific fragment proposals.

3) Selecting discriminative classifiers. From the set of all fragment proposals P, we aim to select a discriminative subset $F \subset P$. This is performed by selecting the fragment proposals with the best ranking scores. To avoid inclusion of visually similar and therefore redundant proposals, we enforce a constraint on each fragment proposal. The event fragment classifier of each fragment proposal should have a cosine distance of at least 0.5 with respect to the better performing proposals, otherwise, it is removed. Such a constraint results in a diverse set of discriminative fragments [13].

3.3 Video encoding

Now that we have the discriminative fragments for the event, we utilize them to perform a fragment encoding for both the training and test videos. The encoding is performed with the same matching and pooling operation as in step 2 above. Let f denote the number of selected discriminative fragments, i.e. $f = |F|$, then the fragment encoding results in an f-dimensional feature vector for a video. The number of discriminative fragments f is a hyperparameter. In the experiments, we evaluate the influence of the number of selected discriminative fragments per event on the detection performance. The encoding is performed over all training and test videos.

3.4 Concept filtering

Apart from a video representation for event detection, our encoding is also able to perform event recounting. To that end, the fragment proposals of the test video that have resulted in the highest max-pooled values are selected as the most informative fragments. For each of these informative fragments we select the concepts that have contributed most to the corresponding dot-product of the max-pooled value as the informative concepts. For each test video this results in a list of informative fragments and their corresponding concepts.

As indicated by Sun et al. [22], directly selecting the top scoring concepts as the recounting for each selected fragment leads to noisy results, mostly because of concept detector noise. The noise results in incorrect or irrelevant concepts in the recounting, as they were erroneously given a high score. Rather than manually determining which concepts are relevant for an event [22], we propose to automatically filter concepts. More specifically, we use co-occurrence statistics [17] to compare the concepts used in our representation to a textual summary of the event.

As shown in Fig. 2, the concept filtering takes as input a textual summary of the event and a collection of social-tagged images from which we compute the co-occurrence statistics. Each concept in the semantic representation is compared to each concept in the textual event summary using a co-occurrence score. Intuitively, the co-occurrence statistic states that two concepts are related if they occur together relatively often as tags in the same images. As such, concepts with high co-occurrence scores are deemed relevant with respect to the event.

For the social tag dataset, we have retrieved the available subset of 4,770,156 Flickr images in ImageNet [3]. For the set of Flickr images, we have in turn collected the corresponding meta-data, in the form of 14,088,893 unique tags. Roughly 95% of the images contain multiple tags, which make the co-occurrence practical. We have made the meta-data of the Flickr images available online[1].

Let $\mathcal{Z}$ denote the set of concepts from the textual summary of the event. Then for a concept i in the semantic representation, we compute the co-occurrence score to all concepts in $\mathcal{Z}$ using the Dice coefficient [17] and keep the maximum score:

$$C_i = \max_{z \in \mathcal{Z}} \left[2 \frac{c_{iz}}{c_i + c_z} \right], \tag{6}$$

where c_i and denotes the number of images with tag i and c_{iz} the number of images with both tag i and z.

The final score C_i is used here as the relevancy score of concept i with respect to the event. For the concept filtering, we select the concepts with the highest scores according to Eq. 6, where the number of concepts to retain is a parameter. Finally, the event recounting is altered by only recounting the most informative concepts that are also relevant according to the concept filtering. This makes for an event recounting that is less sensitive to the noise in concept detectors and more relevant for the event, as we will show in the experiments.

4. EXPERIMENTAL SETUP

4.1 Experiments

4.1.1 Fragment proposal quality

In the first experiment, we evaluate the fragments generated by our fragment proposal algorithm. This evaluation is performed on the THUMOS'14 temporal localization dataset [12]. The dataset consists of 1010 validation videos, each containing several semantically different action-related events at different time intervals. The annotations of the events and their time intervals are provided.

Evaluation. The quality of the fragment proposals is evaluated by examining the recall ratio. For each video, we compare our fragment proposals to the ground truth fragments using the intersection-over-union [6]. Sufficient overlap is achieved if the maximum intersection-over-union is at least 0.5. The ratio of the annotated fragments with sufficient overlap forms the final score.

Baselines. We compare our fragment proposals to two baseline strategies. The first is a shot boundary detection algorithm, where a video is split into a number of non-overlapping fragments based on detected shots within the

[1] https://staff.fnwi.uva.nl/s.h.cappallo/flickrnet.html

video. More specifically, we employ a graph partition model, as proposed in [27]. Here, opponent color histograms are used to represent frames and the continuity signal is thresholded to get shot detections [27]. The second baseline is a sliding window procedure, where a video is split into a number of fragments by sliding a temporal chunk across a video at all temporal positions and scales.

4.1.2 *Event detection*

In the second experiment, we investigate the potential of the bag-of-fragments in the context of event detection. We rely on the TRECVID MED 2014 dataset [20]. This dataset consists of 20 events, where 100 positive videos are provided per event. A general set of 4991 background videos is provided as negative set.

Evaluation. We focus on two evaluations. First, we examine the effect of the number of selected discriminative fragments in our encoding and compare it to a bag-of-fragment encoding using all fragment proposals, instead of the discriminative fragments. Second, we compare our bag-of-fragments to baseline encodings and we evaluate their fusion. The performance of a single event is measured using the Average Precision (AP). At test time, roughly 24,000 videos are given for an event, where the goal is to rank the videos displaying the actual event higher than the negative videos. The quality measure on the whole dataset is in turn measured by the mean Average Precision (mAP) across all the events.

Methods. For the second evaluation, a total of four different methods are applied to the TRECVID MED 2014 dataset. The first is a global model, where the concept scores of a video are averaged over the frames [15, 16, 18]. The second is the state-of-the-art VideoStory, which uses a global model as the visual representation [8]. In addition to these two baselines we evaluate our bag-of-fragments. Finally, we consider a fusion to show the complementary power of bag-of-fragments. For each of the individual methods, the corresponding representations are ℓ_2 normalized and fed to a linear SVM [2]. The SVM outputs are in turn converted to probability values using Platt scaling [21] and the ranking of the videos is performed on these probability values. The fusion is simply performed by computing the product of the probability values for each video.

4.1.3 *Event recounting*

The third experiment focuses on the recounting using the same dataset as used for event detection. We use the model trained for event detection to recount the semantic evidence of a test video, in combination with our concept filtering. We use the textual summary provided by TRECVID for each event to compute the co-occurrence scores.

Evaluation. The evaluation of the event recounting is completed on a qualitative basis. First, we examine the quality of the co-occurrence method for concept selection for 25 concepts in the semantic representation, compared to all 20 events. Second, we show the event recounting results for three test videos from different events, both with and without concept selection.

4.2 Implementation details

Semantic representation. We apply convolutional neural networks to provide the frame-based semantic representations. More specifically, we employ an in-house implementation of [28] trained on 15,293 ImageNet [3] concepts. The frames in each video are sampled once every second. For each frame, we extract the features from the third fully connected layer, the layer before the soft-max, such that the frame is represented by a 15,293-dimensional semantic vector. The aggregation of the frames in a single fragment is performed by averaging the scores per concept [16, 18].

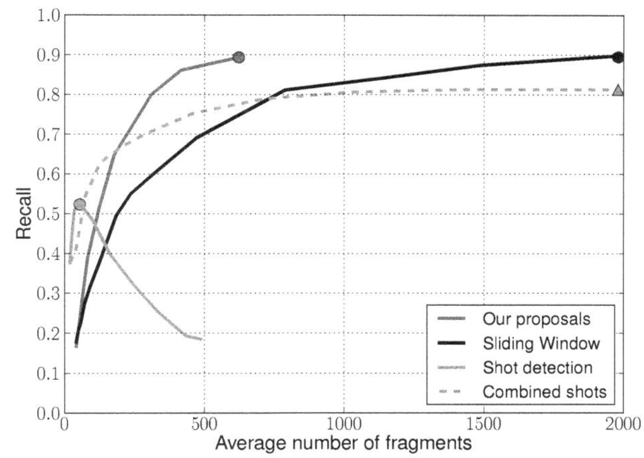

Figure 4: Achieved recall scores as a function of the number of video fragments. Our fragment proposals yield improved recall scores using a fraction of the fragments.

Bag-of-Fragments. For our discriminative fragments, we first extract all the fragment proposals from the positive videos, apply ℓ_2 normalization on each proposal, and compute the efficient event fragment classifier. All the event fragments classifiers are max-pooled over the train videos and the top discriminative fragments are selected. For the discriminative fragment selection, the Average Precision score is used to evaluate the ranking of the max-pooled values per fragment proposal.

5. EXPERIMENTAL RESULTS

5.1 Fragment proposal quality

An overview of the recall as a function of the number of fragments is shown in Fig. 4. For our proposal algorithm and for the sliding window, the number of fragments is varied by varying the size of the initial temporal chunk. For the shot boundary detection, the number of fragments is a function of the shot threshold; the stricter the threshold, the more fragments. We have also added a shot boundary baseline that combines the fragments from multiple thresholds.

As the graph of Fig. 4 shows, our fragment proposal algorithm compares favorably in terms of recall to the two shot detection baselines. Our algorithm yields a peak recall of 0.89, while the shot boundary detection yields a peak recall of 0.52. The limited recall scores of the shot boundary detection are caused by its non-hierarchical nature. By splitting videos solely into non-overlapping fragments, important information is missed. This is further confirmed by the combined shot boundary detection baseline, which yields higher recall scores. The peak recall is however not only 8% lower (at 0.81), but also requires roughly three times as many fragments as our algorithm.

Event	Global		This paper	
	Average [16, 18]	VideoStory [8]	Bag-of-Fragments	Combination
Attempting a bike trick	5.6%	12.0%	10.6%	20.9%
Cleaning an appliance	5.3%	15.6%	13.2%	25.0%
Dog show	56.6%	74.5%	73.8%	76.5%
Giving directions to a location	6.8%	5.6%	2.4%	9.9%
Marriage proposal	0.6%	0.8%	0.9%	1.4%
Renovating a home	4.3%	10.8%	11.5%	16.7%
Rock climbing	7.3%	14.9%	8.6%	19.7%
Town hall meeting	53.8%	42.2%	37.9%	52.8%
Winning a race without a vehicle	19.3%	17.7%	15.2%	30.4%
Working on a metal crafts project	8.1%	9.5%	18.2%	23.0%
Beekeeping	72.1%	70.3%	78.1%	91.7%
Wedding shower	25.1%	20.4%	30.4%	45.6%
Non-motorized vehicle repair	43.0%	42.6%	52.9%	60.9%
Fixing musical instrument	38.3%	44.2%	58.5%	66.0%
Horse riding competition	50.2%	50.1%	45.0%	64.7%
Felling a tree	12.3%	11.4%	22.5%	28.7%
Parking a vehicle	17.8%	24.1%	16.8%	30.4%
Playing fetch	3.2%	8.0%	4.2%	10.9%
Tailgating	29.6%	30.1%	40.7%	54.3%
Tuning a musical instrument	4.8%	12.2%	10.4%	17.4%
mean	23.2%	25.9%	27.6%	37.3%

Table 1: Event detection results on TRECVID MED 2014 for global averaging, VideoStory, and our bag-of-fragments in average precision. We also report the combination between global averaging and bag-of-fragments. Bag-of-fragments is best and highly complementary to existing encodings.

The peak recall of the sliding window baseline is equal to our algorithm, but sliding window requires far more fragments (3.2x). This result highlights the effectiveness of our method. Rather than going through all possible fragment combinations, we only examine the most promising combinations across the hierarchy. This results in less fragment proposals, without sacrificing recall.

5.2 Event detection

For the event detection, we first evaluate the primary bag-of-fragments parameter, namely the number of selected discriminative fragments. Fig. 5 shows the effect of the number of fragments on the mean Average Precision (mAP) score. Using only two discriminative fragments yields a mAP of 6.0%. The performance increases monotonously as the number of discriminative fragments increases, indicating that a rich set of fragments to represent an event is beneficial. At roughly 2000 discriminative fragments, the performance starts saturating, with an mAP of 27.6% and we will use this setting for the rest of the experiments. Furthermore, we have evaluated the performance using all fragment proposals, which resulted in a mAP of 26.6%. This result indicates that only using discriminative fragments not only results in a more compact encoding, but also leads to improved results.

For the comparative evaluation we show an overview of the results for the four different methods for the 20 events Table 1. Compared to the global averaging baseline, our algorithm yields improved Average Precision scores for 15 of the 20 events, with an absolute increase of 4.4% in mean Average Precision, from 23.2% to 27.6%.

Noteworthy is the difference in performance across different events. Our discriminative fragments improves upon the baseline with 20.2%, 17.2%, and 10.2% (absolute difference) for the events *Fixing a musical instrument*, *Dog show*, and *Felling a tree*. The baseline method performs 15.9% and 5.2% better for the events *Town hall meeting* and *Horse riding competition*. This indicates a complementary nature between the two models. Indeed, a fusion between the two

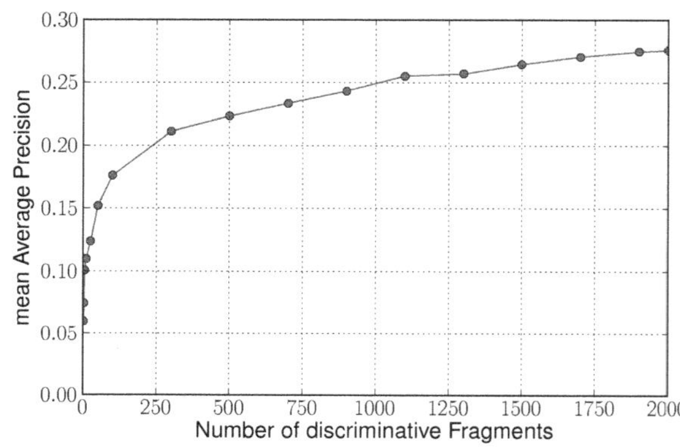

Figure 5: The influence of the number of discriminative fragments for event detection.

improves the performance significantly with a mean Average Precision of 37.3%, an notable absolute improvement of 14.1% over the baseline model. Note that from the fragment point-of-view, the fusion with the global averaging baseline comes computationally for free, as the global average is always the last merge in our hierarchical clustering.

Table 1 also shows the result of VideoStory on the same dataset [8]. Although VideoStory similarly improves upon the global baseline, it does not match the bag-of-fragments result, indicating the effectiveness of the bag-of-fragments.

To further highlight the effectiveness of fragment-based event detection, we show a fragment ranking for three events in Fig. 1. The Figure shows that the most discriminative fragments of an event are exemplary snapshots of the event. Examples of this include a person on a BMX for *Attempting a bike trick*, a bicycle tire for *Non-motorized vehicle repair*, and a person on a horse for *Horse riding competition*. Also, the Figure shows that more ambiguous fragments are deemed less discriminative for the event.

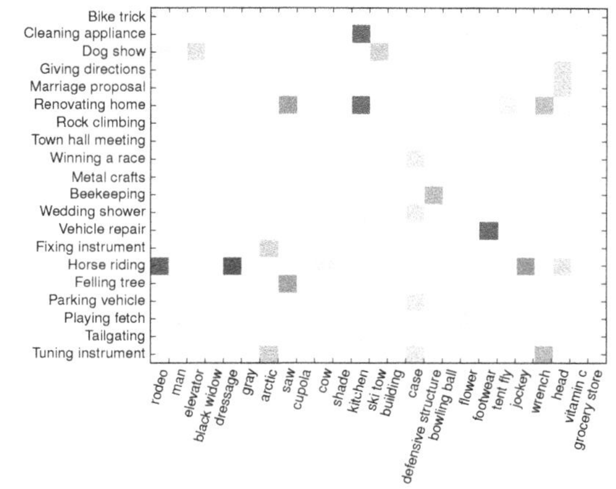

Figure 6: Plot of the maximum co-occurrence value for 25 concepts with respect to the 20 TRECVID MED 2014 events.

5.3 Event recounting

For event recounting, we first highlight the effect of co-occurrence for a number of concepts in the semantic representation. In Fig. 6, the maximum co-occurrence values are shown for 25 concepts with respect to all 20 TRECVID MED 2014 events. For a number of peaks in the plot, the concept-event relation is as expected. Examples include the relationship between rodeo/jockey and *Horse riding competition*, between kitchen and *Cleaning an appliance*, and between saw and *Felling a tree*. These discovered concept-event relationships indicate that visual co-occurrence from social tagged image data may serve as a fruitful proxy for automatic concept selection.

However, Fig. 6 also indicates a limit of our use of co-occurrence. The concept elevator fires on the event *Dog show*, while they are seemingly uncorrelated. However, the textual summary of the event contains the concept lift. In the context of *Dog show*, lift is a verb (to lift; to move upward), but the co-occurrence statistics use the concept as a noun (lift; elevator). As the co-occurrence statistic is oblivious to the ambiguity of concepts, seemingly uncorrelated concepts might yield a high co-occurrence value.

Second, we perform a qualitative evaluation on the effect of concept filtering for event recounting. In Fig. 7, the recounting results of our discriminative fragments are shown for three videos from different events, both with and without concept selection. For each video, the three most informative video fragments are selected and for each selected fragment, the two most informative concepts are shown. The discriminative fragments are able to select the fragments of the test video that are correlated to the event. Without the concept filtering, the recounted concepts are at times incorrect or over-specific. This is exemplified in Fig. 7a and Fig. 7b, with noisy concepts such as millipede and abacus for *Tuning an instrument* and guillotine for *Renovating a home*. These results indicate the negative influence of the noise, as these concepts do not help to convince a user that the corresponding event is in the video.

However, if our concept selection is added to the recounting, the resulting concepts become both more generic and more relevant. This is for example visible in Fig. 7c. Without concept filtering, incorrect concepts such as dulcimer and wildcat are recounted. Upon adding the concept selection, concepts that are more relevant to the event *Beekeeping* are shown, such as honeycomb.

6. CONCLUSIONS

We propose encoding of videos using fragments. We show how to generate a concise set of fragment proposals for a single video. From the set of fragment proposals of the training videos for an event, we select the most discriminative ones. By matching and pooling these discriminative fragments over the fragment proposals of a video, we arrive at our bag-of-fragments encoding. Experimental evaluation shows the effectiveness of the encoding for event detection, as well as its complementary nature to a global aggregation of semantic concepts. Furthermore, we propose an automatic algorithm to filter relevant concepts in the semantic representation with respect to an event by leveraging co-occurrence statistics from a social tag image dataset. Qualitative evaluation highlights the capability of our bag-of-fragments in combination with concept filtering for event recounting.

Acknowledgements

This research is supported by the STW STORY project and the Dutch national program COMMIT.

7. REFERENCES

[1] S. Bhattacharya, F. X. Yu, and S.-F. Chang. Minimally needed evidence for complex event recognition in unconstrained videos. In *ICMR*, 2014.

[2] C. Cortes and V. Vapnik. Support-vector networks. *ML*, 20(3), 1995.

[3] J. Deng, W. Dong, R. Socher, L.-J. Li, K. Li, and L. Fei-Fei. ImageNet: A large-scale hierarchical image database. In *CVPR*, 2009.

[4] D. Ding, F. Metze, S. Rawat, P. F. Schulam, S. Burger, E. Younessian, L. Bao, M. G. Christel, and A. Hauptmann. Beyond audio and video retrieval: towards multimedia summarization. In *ICMR*, 2012.

[5] C. Doersch, A. Gupta, and A. A. Efros. Mid-level visual element discovery as discriminative mode seeking. In *NIPS*, 2013.

[6] M. Everingham, L. Van Gool, C. K. Williams, J. Winn, and A. Zisserman. The pascal visual object classes (voc) challenge. *IJCV*, 88(2), 2010.

[7] I. Everts, J. C. van Gemert, and T. Gevers. Evaluation of color spatio-temporal interest points for human action recognition. *TIP*, 23(4), 2014.

[8] A. Habibian, T. Mensink, and C. G. M. Snoek. Videostory: A new multimedia embedding for few-example recognition and translation of events. In *ACM MM*, 2014.

[9] B. Hariharan, J. Malik, and D. Ramanan. Discriminative decorrelation for clustering and classification. In *ECCV*, 2012.

[10] J. Hosang, R. Benenson, and B. Schiele. How good are detection proposals, really? *BMVC*, 2014.

[11] M. Jain, J. C. Van Gemert, H. Jégou, P. Bouthemy, and C. G. M. Snoek. Action localization with tubelets from motion. In *CVPR*, 2014.

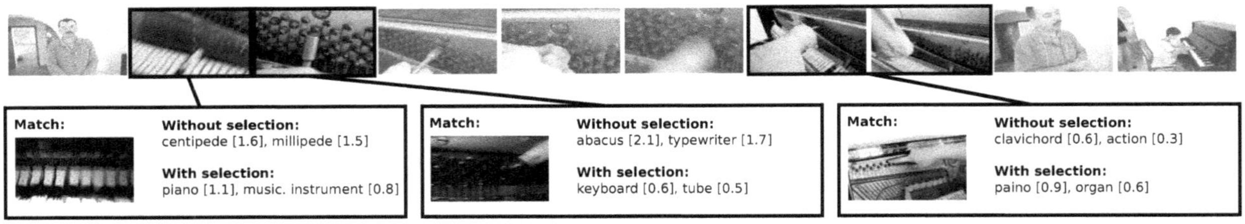

(a) Recounting results for a video of the event *Tuning an instrument.*

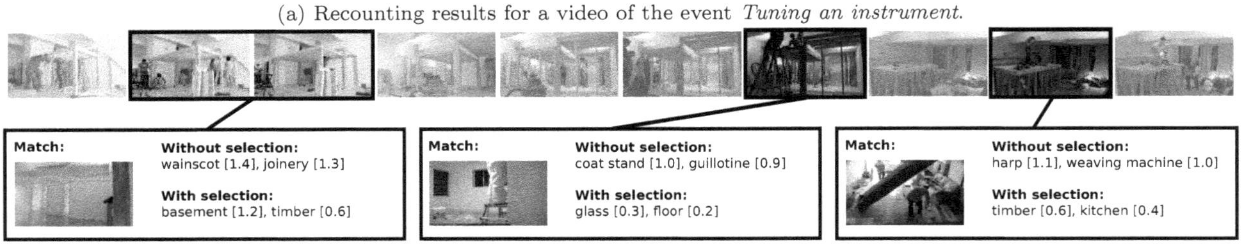

(b) Recounting results for a video of the event *Renovating a home.*

(c) Recounting results for a video of the event *Beekeeping.*

Figure 7: Qualitative event recounting results with and without the concept filtering for three different videos. For each video, the top three fragments are selected and the top two concepts for each selected fragment are shown, along with their fragment-based score. For each recounted fragment, the matching discriminative fragment from the training set is shown.

[12] Y.-G. Jiang, J. Liu, A. Roshan Zamir, G. Toderici, I. Laptev, M. Shah, and R. Sukthankar. THUMOS challenge: Action recognition with a large number of classes. In *ECCV Workshop*, 2014.

[13] M. Juneja, A. Vedaldi, C. V. Jawahar, and A. Zisserman. Blocks that shout: Distinctive parts for scene classification. In *CVPR*, 2013.

[14] I. Laptev, M. Marszalek, C. Schmid, and B. Rozenfeld. Learning realistic human actions from movies. In *CVPR*, 2008.

[15] J. Liu, Q. Yu, O. Javed, S. Ali, A. Tamrakar, A. Divakaran, H. Cheng, and H. Sawhney. Video event recognition using concept attributes. In *WACV*, 2013.

[16] M. Mazloom, A. Habibian, and C. G. M. Snoek. Querying for video events by semantic signatures from few examples. In *ACM MM*, 2013.

[17] T. Mensink, E. Gavves, and C. G. M. Snoek. Costa: Co-occurrence statistics for zero-shot classification. In *CVPR*, 2014.

[18] M. Merler, B. Huang, L. Xie, G. Hua, and A. Natsev. Semantic model vectors for complex video event recognition. *TMM*, 14(1), 2012.

[19] D. Oneata, J. Verbeek, and C. Schmid. The lear submission at thumos 2014. In *ECCV Workshop*, 2014.

[20] P. Over et al. Trecvid 2014 – an overview of the goals, tasks, data, evaluation mechanisms and metrics. In *TRECVID Workshop*, 2014.

[21] J. C. Platt. Probabilistic outputs for support vector machines and comparisons to regularized likelihood methods. In *Advances in large margin classifiers*, 1999.

[22] C. Sun, B. Burns, R. Nevatia, C. G. M. Snoek, B. Bolles, G. Myers, W. Wang, and E. Yeh. Isomer: Informative segment observations for multimedia event recounting. In *ICMR*, 2014.

[23] C. Sun and R. Nevatia. Discover: Discovering important segments for classification of video events and recounting. In *CVPR*, 2014.

[24] J. R. R. Uijlings, K. E. A. van de Sande, T. Gevers, and A. W. M. Smeulders. Selective search for object recognition. *IJCV*, 104(2), 2013.

[25] A. Vahdat, K. Cannons, G. Mori, S. Oh, and I. Kim. Compositional models for video event detection: A multiple kernel learning latent variable approach. In *ICCV*, 2013.

[26] H. Wang and C. Schmid. Action recognition with improved trajectories. In *ICCV*, 2013.

[27] J. Yuan, H. Wang, L. Xiao, W. Zheng, J. Li, F. Lin, and B. Zhang. A formal study of shot boundary detection. *TCSVT*, 17(2), 2007.

[28] M. D. Zeiler and R. Fergus. Visualizing and understanding convolutional networks. In *ECCV*, 2014.

Evaluating Two-Stream CNN for Video Classification

Hao Ye, Zuxuan Wu, Rui-Wei Zhao, Xi Wang, Yu-Gang Jiang*, Xiangyang Xue
School of Computer Science, Shanghai Key Lab of Intelligent Information Processing,
Fudan University, Shanghai, China
{haoye10, zxwu,rwzhao14, xwang10, ygj, xyxue}@fudan.edu.cn

ABSTRACT

Videos contain very rich semantic information. Traditional hand-crafted features are known to be inadequate in analyzing complex video semantics. Inspired by the huge success of the deep learning methods in analyzing image, audio and text data, significant efforts are recently being devoted to the design of deep nets for video analytics. Among the many practical needs, classifying videos (or video clips) based on their major semantic categories (e.g., "skiing") is useful in many applications. In this paper, we conduct an in-depth study to investigate important implementation options that may affect the performance of deep nets on video classification. Our evaluations are conducted on top of a recent two-stream convolutional neural network (CNN) pipeline, which uses both static frames and motion optical flows, and has demonstrated competitive performance against the state-of-the-art methods. In order to gain insights and to arrive at a practical guideline, many important options are studied, including network architectures, model fusion, learning parameters and the final prediction methods. Based on the evaluations, very competitive results are attained on two popular video classification benchmarks. We hope that the discussions and conclusions from this work can help researchers in related fields to quickly set up a good basis for further investigations along this very promising direction.

Categories and Subject Descriptors

I.5.2 [**Pattern Recognition**]: Design Methodology; H.3.1 [**Information Storage and Retrieval**]: Content Analysis and Indexing

General Terms

Algorithms, Measurement, Experimentation.

Keywords

Video Classification, Deep Learning, CNN, Evaluation.

*Corresponding author.

ICMR'15, June 23 - 26, 2015, Shanghai, China
 ISBN 978-1-4503-3274-3/15/06...$15.00
DOI: http://dx.doi.org/10.1145/2671188.2749406.

1. INTRODUCTION

With the popularity of video recording devices and content sharing activities, there is a strong need for techniques that can automatically analyze the huge scale of video data. Video classification serves as a fundamental and essential step in the process of analyzing the video contents. For example, it would be extremely helpful if the massive consumer videos on the Web could be automatically classified into predefined categories. Learning semantics from the complicated video contents is never an easy task, and methods based on traditional hand-crafted features and prediction models are known to be inadequate [1].

In recent years, deep learning based models have been proved to be more competitive than the traditional methods on solving complex learning problems in various domains. For example, the deep neural network (DNN) has been successfully used for acoustic modeling in the large vocabulary speech recognition problems [2]. Moreover, the deep learning based methods have been shown to be extremely powerful in the image domain. In 2012, Krizhevsky *et al.* were the first to use a completely end-to-end deep convolutional neural network (CNN) model to win the famous ImageNet Large Scale Visual Recognition Challenge (ILSVRC), outperforming all the traditional methods by a large margin [13]. In the most recent 2014 edition of the ILSVRC, Szegedy *et al.* developed an improved and deeper version of the CNN, which further reduced the top-5 label error rate to just 6.7% over one thousand categories [30]. In the text domain, deep models have also been successfully used for sentence parsing, sentiment prediction and language translation problems [27, 18, 11, 29].

On video data, however, deep learning often demonstrated worse results than the traditional techniques [8, 12]. This is largely due to the difficulties in modeling the unique characteristics of the videos. On one hand, the spatial-temporal nature demands more complex network structures and maybe also advanced learning methods. One the other hand, so far there is very limited amount of training data with manual annotations in the video domain, which limits the progress of developing new methods as neural networks normally require extensive training. Very recently, Simonyan *et al.* proposed two-stream CNN, an effective approach that trains two CNNs using static frame and temporal motion separately [24]. The temporal motion stream is converted to successive optical flow images so that the conventional CNN designed for images can be directly deployed.

Although promising results were observed in [24], we underline that the performance of deep learning in video classification is subject to many implementation options, and there are no in-depth and systematic investigations on this in the field. In this paper, we conduct extensive experiments on two popular benchmarks to evaluate several important options, including not only network structures and learning parameters, but also model fusion that combines results from different networks and prediction strategies that map network outputs to classification labels. The two-stream CNN approach is adopted as the basic pipeline for the evaluations in this work. By evaluating the implementation options, we intend to answer the question of what network settings and implementation options are likely to produce good video classification results. As implementing a deep learning based system for video classification is a very difficult task, we hope that the discussions and conclusions from this work are helpful for researchers in this field and can stimulate future studies.

The rest of this paper is organized as follows. Section 2 reviews related works. In Section 3, we briefly introduce the two-stream CNN approach. Section 4 discusses the evaluated implementation options and Section 5 reports and analyzes experimental results. Finally, Section 6 summarizes the findings in this work.

2. RELATED WORKS

Extensive studies have been conducted on video classification in the multimedia and computer vision communities. State-of-the-art video classification systems are usually built on top of multiple discriminative feature representations. To achieve better performance, various features have been developed. For instance, Laptev *et al.* extended the traditional SIFT features to obtain the Space-Time Interest Points (STIP) by finding representative tubes in 3D space [15]. Wang *et al.* proposed the dense trajectory features, which densely sample local patches from each frame at different scales and then track them in a dense optical flow field over time [32]. Besides the feature descriptors, one can obtain further improvements by adopting advantageous feature encoding strategies like the Fisher Vector [19] or utilizing fusion techniques [26, 34, 33] to integrate information from different features.

The aforementioned hand-crafted features like the dense trajectories have demonstrated state-of-the-art performance on many video classification tasks. However, these features are still unsatisfying and the room for further improvements may be limited. In contrast to the hand-crafted features, there is a growing trend of learning features directly from raw data using deep learning methods, among which the CNN [16] has attracted wide attentions due to their great success in image classification [13, 30], visual object detection [4], etc.

Compared with the extensive studies on using deep learning for image analysis, only a few works have exploited this approach for video analysis. Ji *et al.* and Karpathy *et al.* extended the CNN into temporal domain by stacking static frames, upon which convolution can be performed with space-temporal filters [8, 12]. However, the learned representations from these methods produced worse results than the state-of-the-art hand-crafted features like the dense trajectories [32]. More recently, Simonyan *et al.* [24] achieved very competitive performance by training two CNNs on spatial (static frames) and temporal (optical flows) streams separately and then fusing the two networks.

Most CNN-based approaches rely on the neural networks to perform the final class label prediction, normally using a softmax layer [12, 24] or a linear layer [8]. Instead of direct prediction by the network, Jain *et al.* conducted action recognition using support vector machines (SVMs) with features extracted from off-the-shelf CNN models [6]. Their impressive results in the THUMOS action recognition challenge [9] indicate that CNN features are very powerful. In addition, a few works attempted to apply the CNN representations with Recurrent Neural Network (RNN) models to capture the temporal information in videos and perform classification within the same network. Donahue *et al.* leveraged the Long-Short Term Memory (LSTM) RNN model for action recognition [3] and Venugopalan *et al.* proposed to translate videos directly to sentences with the LSTM model by transferring knowledge from image description tasks [31]. RNN shares the same motivation with the temporal pathway in the two-stream framework [24].

In this paper, we provide an in-depth study on various implementation choices of deep learning based video classification. On top of the two-stream CNN pipeline [24], we examine the performance of the spatial and temporal streams separately and jointly with different network architectures under various sets of parameters. In addition, we also examine the effect of different prediction options, including directly using a CNN with a softmax layer for end-to-end classification and adopting SVMs on the features learned from the CNNs. The RNN models are not considered since they have not been fully explored and only demonstrated limited performance gain in the context of video classification. This paper fills the gap in the existing works on deep learning for video classification, where most people have focused on designing a new classification pipeline or a deeper network structure without systematically evaluating and discussing the implementation options.

3. TWO-STREAM CNN

According to the findings in neuroscience, human visual system processes what we see through two kinds of streams, namely the ventral pathway and the dorsal pathway respectively. The ventral pathway is responsible for processing the spatial information, such as shape and color, while the dorsal pathway is responsible for processing the motion information [14, 5]. Mimicking the human vision mechanism, the video data, i.e., sequential image frames, can be naturally decomposed into the spatial and temporal components in a similar way. More specifically, image content including scenes and objects belong to the spatial component. The complementary temporal component contains motion information across video frames. As an early attempt, Schindler *et al.* extracted spatial and temporal features on still images and optical flows by using the Gabor filters [22]. With the recent success of the CNN, as briefly mentioned earlier, Simonyan *et al.* promoted this framework by the two-stream CNN structure that models both the spatial and the temporal information [24]. Figure 1 shows the processing pipeline of this approach. One CNN is applied to process the spatial stream of the video data, and the other CNN is used to handle the temporal stream.

The processing data flow of the spatial stream is shown on top of Figure 1. This CNN has the same structure as a general deep CNN for image classification [35, 13, 30]. It directly takes individual video frames as network inputs

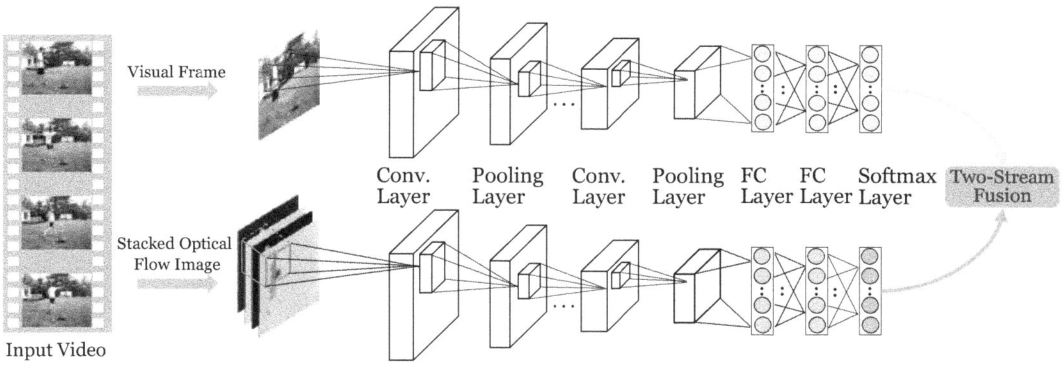

Figure 1: The processing pipeline of the two-stream CNN [24], which has demonstrated competitive video classification performance. "Conv." indicates "Convolution" and "FC" is the abbreviation of "Fully Connected". Our evaluations in this work are conducted on top of this pipeline.

followed by several convolutional layers, pooling layers and fully connected (FC) layers. Finally, after a softmax layer, the network outputs in the range of [0, 1] are taken as the predicted probabilities of the video classes. Multiple frames are sampled from each input video. The network processes one frame each time and the predictions on individual frames are merged simply by average probability fusion.

For the temporal stream, in order to capture the motion information, the temporal CNN takes stacked optical flows as input, rather than the frames in the spatial stream. Specifically, dense optical flow can be seen as a set of displacement vector fields between consecutive frames. For a given pair of consecutive frames, the horizontal and vertical components of the calculated displacement vector fields between them can be used to generate two "optical flow images", respectively. To further consider temporal information, one can stack the optical flow images of each frame at time t and its L subsequent frames into a stacked $2L$-channel optical flow image (in contrast to the traditional 3-channel RGB images). The network architecture and training process of the temporal CNN are basically the same as the spatial counterpart, except that the input images have a different number of channels. There are multiple stacked $2L$-channel optical flow images in a video. The way of fusing predictions on these individual images is also the same as that of the spatial channel.

We now have predictions from the two CNNs, based on the spatial and temporal streams separately. The last step is to combine the two streams to produce the final output. For this, linear fusion with fixed weights was used in [24].

4. IMPLEMENTATION OPTIONS

In this section, we discuss several important implementation options that can affect the performance of deep learning for video classification, including network architectures, fusion strategies, learning parameters and prediction options.

4.1 Network Architectures

Network architecture plays a very important role in the performance of a deep learning model. The current surge of the CNNs in many tasks heavily relies on the use of superior network architectures, such as the AlexNet [13] and the GoogLeNet [30]. Popular CNN architectures usually have alternating convolutional layers and auxiliary layers (e.g., pooling layers), and are toped by a few fully connected (FC) layers. Recent studies demonstrate that better recognition accuracies can be achieved by deepening the CNN architectures [25, 30], which means that deeper architectures can lead to progressively more discriminative features at higher layers. To evaluate the performance of different network architectures, in this work, we adopt and evaluate a *medium* network structure, CNN_M [24], and a very recent *deeper* network architecture, VGG_19 [25]. See Table 1 for the detailed configurations of CNN_M and VGG_19.

CNN_M Network.

CNN_M basically follows the same spirit as the widely adopted AlexNet [13]. It contains five convolutional layers followed by three FC layers and the input image is fixed to the size of 224×224. Compared with AlexNet [13], CNN_M possesses more convolutional filters. On the first convolutional layer, the size and stride are both smaller (7×7 and 2 respectively) than those in AlexNet, while the remaining convolutional layers have the same filter size and stride. By increasing the number of filters and reducing the filter size and the stride step, CNN_M can discover more subtle information from input images, and hence can obtain more robust feature representations and better predictions. Note that CNN_M offers a 13.5% top-5 error on the ILSVRC-2012 validation set [24] (a famous image recognition benchmark), which is generally considered as a good result.

VGG_19 Network.

VGG_19 not only further reduces the size of convolutional filters and the stride, but more importantly, it also extends the depth of the network. More precisely, VGG_19 consists of nineteen layers, including sixteen convolutional layers and three fully connected layers. In addition, the size of all the convolutional filters decreases to 3×3 and the stride reduces to only 1 pixel, which enables the network to explore finer-grained details from the feature maps. With this much deeper architecture, VGG_19 possess strong capabilities of learning more discriminative features and the high-level final predictions. It can produce a 7.1% top-5 error rate on the ILSVRC-2012 validation set [25].

4.2 Fusion Strategies

Fusing multiple clues is a standard technique in video analysis, which can often lead to better performance. We divide this part into model fusion and modality fusion.

	CNN_M	VGG_19
Convolutional Layers	$96 \times 7 \times 7$ (stride: 2, padding: 0) LRN ×2 pooling $256 \times 5 \times 5$ (stride: 2, padding: 1) LRN ×2 pooling $512 \times 3 \times 3$ (stride: 1, padding: 1) $512 \times 3 \times 3$ (stride: 1, padding: 1) $512 \times 3 \times 3$ (stride: 1, padding: 1) ×2 pooling	$64 \times 3 \times 3$ $64 \times 3 \times 3$ ×2 pooling $128 \times 3 \times 3$ $128 \times 3 \times 3$ ×2 pooling $256 \times 3 \times 3$ $256 \times 3 \times 3$ $256 \times 3 \times 3$ $256 \times 3 \times 3$ ×2 pooling $512 \times 3 \times 3$ $512 \times 3 \times 3$ $512 \times 3 \times 3$ $512 \times 3 \times 3$ ×2 pooling $512 \times 3 \times 3$ $512 \times 3 \times 3$ $512 \times 3 \times 3$ $512 \times 3 \times 3$ ×2 pooling
FC Layers	4,096 neurons	4,096 neurons
	2,048 neurons	4,096 neurons
	softmax	softmax

Table 1: Configurations of two networks: CNN_M and VGG_19. The convolutional kernel parameter is denoted in the form "# filters × kernel size x × kernel size y". For both networks, max-pooling with a sampling factor of 2 is used ("×2 pooling"). In VGG_19, both stride and padding are set to 1 for all the convolutional layers. The VGG_19 does not contain the Local Response Normalization (LRN), which requires considerable computation but contributes little to the performance.

4.2.1 Model Fusion

Combining various deep learning models can usually produce better performance than using just a single model, because models using different architectures or trained with different parameters may contain complementary information. For instance, a model trained with larger convolutional filters may focus more on large patterns, while one with smaller filters may be more sensitive to finer-grained details. Since both the two CNN architectures, CNN_M and VGG_19, can be trained with multiple parameters, there are consequently several candidate models that can be exploited in this experiment. We examine different combinations to integrate information from these candidate models.

4.2.2 Modality Fusion

As aforementioned, videos are naturally multimodal, and hence the integration of the spatial and the temporal streams is very important. Simonyan *et al.* [24] adopted a simple linear fusion method and fixed weights without explanations. We will examine the effect of this fusion weight on two very different datasets. Notice that another very important modality, the audio channel, is not considered in this work because we focus on examining options of training models using only the visual data following the two-stream pipeline. However, we strongly believe that better performance can be achieved by further including the audio information, because this has been observed in many recent works [10].

4.3 Learning Parameters

Although deep learning has achieved promising results on many tasks, training and fine-tuning a good model normally require significant efforts as there are several important parameters that need to be evaluated, such as learning rate, dropout ratio and the number of training iterations. These seemingly arbitrarily chosen parameters can influence the performance significantly. For instance, a small learning rate may demand much more iterations to converge, while a large value may accelerate the convergence but can possibly result in oscillation. In addition, a larger dropout ratio may lead to a better model but could probably slow down the convergence. There is no universal rule for parameter selection. With the goal of providing some insights on parameter selection specially for the problem of video classification, we study different sets of parameters using the two aforementioned network architectures and two datasets.

In particular, the dropout ratio and the number of iterations are jointly evaluated and discussed. For learning rate, we set it to 10^{-2} initially, and then decreased to 10^{-3} after 100K iterations, then to 10^{-4} after 200K iterations. In the fine-tuning case, the rate starts from 10^{-3} and decreases to 10^{-4} after 14K iterations, then to 10^{-5} after 20K iterations. This setting is similar to [24], but we start from a smaller rate of 10^{-3} instead of 10^{-2}. Note that other choices on learning rate are not evaluated as we find that the final performance is less sensitive to this parameter as long as it is set following the suggested rules in [23].

4.4 Prediction Options

While neural networks can act as end-to-end classifiers by using a final softmax layer, traditional classifiers like the SVMs can also be deployed on the features extracted by the CNN, which are generally the outputs of the last several fully connected layers. Recently, Razavian *et al.* [21] adopted features extracted from a CNN model pre-trained on ImageNet to perform classification with SVMs. They demonstrated strong performance on image analysis tasks like scene recognition, object detection, etc. In addition, Jain *et al.* [6] leveraged the CNN features using SVMs for action recognition in videos, and achieved superior performance on the THUMOS action recognition benchmark [9]. The results suggest that the CNN features may be used in combination with traditional classifiers for improved performance, but these existing works were performed only on images or the spatial frames. This paper investigates the performance of features extracted from different layers of both the spatial and the temporal CNNs using SVMs for classification. Results are compared with that of the end-to-end neural network based approach.

5. EXPERIMENTS

5.1 Datasets and Evaluation Criteria

UCF-101 [28]. The UCF-101 dataset is a widely adopted benchmark for action recognition in videos, which consists of 13,320 video clips (27 hours in total). There are 101 annotated classes that can be divided into five types: Human-Object Interaction, Body-Motion Only, Human-Human Interaction, Playing Musical Instruments and Sports. We perform evaluation according to the popular 3 train/test splits following [9]. Results are measured by classification accuracy on each split and mean accuracy over the 3 splits. For some evaluations, we only report results on the first split due to computation limitation.

Columbia Consumer Videos (CCV) [10]. The CCV dataset contains 9,317 YouTube videos annotated according to 20 classes, such as "wedding ceremony", "birthday party", "skiing" and "playground". We follow the protocol defined in [10] to use a training set of 4,659 videos and a test set of 4,658 videos. Results are measured by average precision (AP) for each class and mean AP (MAP) across all the classes [10]. Note that, different from the UCF101 actions, most classes in CCV are social events, sports, objects and scenes. In addition, the average duration of this dataset is around 80 seconds, which is over ten times longer than that of the UCF-101. We hope that using the two datasets with different characteristics can help lead to more generalizable conclusions.

For both datasets, we adopt the same data augmentation strategies as [24].

5.2 Network Options

Using what network structure is the first decision we have to make in the implementation of a deep learning based video classification system. There are numerous options. In this work, we evaluate and compare the two popular structures CNN_M and VGG_19.

Results of the spatial stream are summarized in Table 2. As can be seen, VGG_19 produces consistently better results on both datasets, indicating that larger (deeper) networks are generally better. This is consistent with the observations on the large scale image classification tasks. Results of different dropout rates are listed in this table because this can ofter a more complete understanding of the power of the networks under different settings of learning parameters. Detailed discussions on the effect of dropout rates will be given later.

For the temporal stream, we also tried to use the VGG_19 network under a few parameter settings, but observed clearly worse results than the CNN_M. As the gap is clear, we did not proceed to finish all the parameters to fully compare the two networks. The key reason is that the temporal stream has to be trained from scratch, which is different from the spatial stream that can use fine-tuning to adjust the pre-trained network based on millions of images [24]. In this case, learning a smaller temporal network is more feasible with limited training data. We expect that better results can be achieved by VGG_19 for the temporal stream when there is sufficient training data.

5.3 Model and Modality Fusion

Next, we discuss results by fusing models and modalities. For the combination of different models, we use the spatial stream and 10 network models (2 structures each trained with 5 dropout rates). We tried all the possible modal combinations by averaging their prediction scores and identified the top 3 results in order to learn which model is more reliable and what combinations are good. Results are shown in Table 3. We see that VGG_19 models are more "popular" in the top combinations on both datasets, confirming the fact that fusing good models generally offers good results. However, comparing the model fusion results with the individual model results in Table 2, it is clear that fusing models does not improve results significantly. For instance, on the UCF-101, the 2nd best results by fusing five models is actually the same with just using the best single model (VGG_19 dr5). Therefore, one conclusion is that fusing a strong network (VGG_19) with a relatively weaker network (CNN_M) does not help much (if not becoming worse). Notice that average model prediction fusion is adopted here. Using dynamic fusion weights may lead to better results, but the gain is unlikely to be significant.

For modality fusion, we use the best spatial network configurations to fuse with a temporal network trained using the CNN_M architecture. Results of different fusion weights are plotted in Figure 2. Comparing the temporal stream with the spatial counterpart, the latter produces better results on both datasets. The gap is larger on CCV as its categories are easier to be recognized by viewing just one or a few frames, e.g., the sports classes "basketball" and "skiing". Fusing the two modalities is effective, leading to significant improvement on UCF-101 (best fusion: 86.7%; spatial: 80.5%; temporal: 78.3%). The gain on CCV is limited as the result of the temporal stream is not good (best fusion: 75.9%; spatial: 75.3%; temporal: 59.4%), which is generally consistent with the results of the hand-crafted fea-

Models	UCF-101 (split-1)	CCV
CNN_M dr1	71.58%	68.78%
CNN_M dr3	68.65%	68.81%
CNN_M dr5	68.25%	68.64%
CNN_M dr7	68.15%	67.40%
CNN_M dr9	60.85%	51.81%
VGG_19 dr1	75.87%	74.66%
VGG_19 dr3	79.59%	74.47%
VGG_19 dr5	80.41%	75.04%
VGG_19 dr7	76.66%	74.90%
VGG_19 dr9	76.39%	73.09%

Table 2: Spatial stream results of two network architectures on UCF-101 and CCV under different dropout rates ("dr1" indicates the 0.1 dropout rate). See texts for discussions.

Models	UCF-101 (split-1)			CCV		
	1	2	3	1	2	3
CNN_M dr1	✓	✓				✓
CNN_M dr3						
CNN_M dr5						
CNN_M dr7						
CNN_M dr9		✓	✓	✓		
VGG_19 dr1						✓
VGG_19 dr3	✓	✓			✓	✓
VGG_19 dr5	✓	✓	✓	✓	✓	
VGG_19 dr7				✓	✓	✓
VGG_19 dr9	✓	✓				✓
Perf. (%)	80.46	80.41	80.33	75.31	75.31	75.30

Table 3: Top-3 spatial stream model fusion results on both datasets. The "✓" sign indicates the used models in each of the top combinations. A general observation is that fusing good models like the VGG_19 based ones tend to generate good results, but the improvement is fairly limited.

	Feature	Spatial (VGG_19)		Temporal (CNN_M)		Spatial-Temporal Fusion	
		Early Fusion	Late Fusion	Early Fusion	Late Fusion	Early Fusion	Late Fusion
UCF-101 (split-1)	FC1	75.84%	70.71%	78.22%	76.74%	87.55%	82.34%
	FC2	72.75%	64.42%	77.85%	76.24%	85.94%	80.52%
	FC1&FC2	75.73%	70.29%	78.30%	76.63%	87.71%	82.00%
CCV	FC1	70.75%	67.34%	58.04%	54.08%	73.25%	68.87%
	FC2	70.45%	68.85%	55.86%	52.52%	72.76%	70.06%
	FC1&FC2	71.15%	69.25%	58.79%	54.40%	73.27%	69.90%

Table 4: Prediction results of SVMs classifiers on the CNN features. FC1 (FC2) indicates the output feature of the first (second) fully connected layer. "FC1&FC2" is the concatenation of the FC1 and FC2 features.

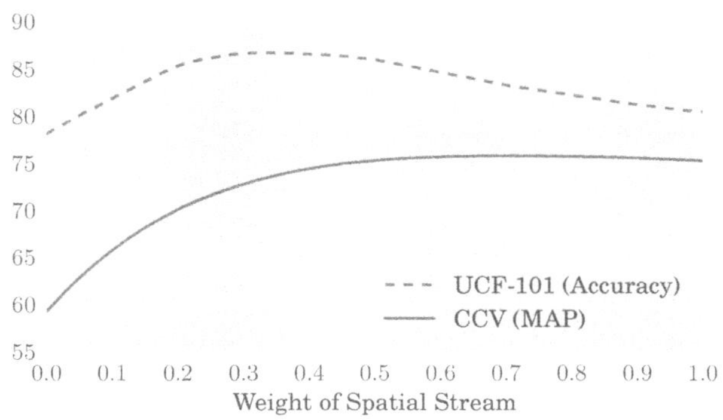

Figure 2: Performance (%) of combining spatial and temporal streams using linear fusion with different weights. Temporal stream weight is set as "1−spatial weight". Thus the left-end points of the curves indicate the performance of using the temporal stream alone, while the right-end is the spatial stream performance.

tures on this dataset [10][1]. As for the suitable fusion weight, the results indicate that similar or higher temporal weight is preferred for classes that can be better recognized by viewing a clip (not just a frame), even when the temporal stream performs worse than the spatial stream.

5.4 Effect of Learning Parameters

We jointly evaluate the effect of two learning parameters: the dropout ratio and the number of training iterations. We first study the spatial stream. Figure 3 and Figure 4 visualize the results on UCF-101 and CCV respectively. Notice that the spatial networks are fine-tuned based on the models pre-trained on the Image-Net (only the last three FC layers are fine-tuned), and therefore they start from a fairly good initialization and become stable quickly after just 10-20 thousands of iterations. With the uniform settings on learning rate (cf. Section 4.3), the number of iterations required to reach convergence is similar across different network architectures and dropout ratios. One interesting observation is that large dropout ratios (e.g., 0.9) are especially unsuited for small networks like the CNN_M. This is probably because a small network can hardly learn anything if as high as 90% of the information are dropped at each iteration, particularly for the case of fine-tuning where only the last three layers are adjusted.

[1] On CCV, it was reported that static frame features are significantly better than spatial-temporal features.

Figure 5 plots the temporal stream results on both datasets, using the CNN_M architecture with various learning parameters. We observe that a large dropout ratio requires more iterations to reach a high level of performance, which is easy to understand. Different from the spatial stream observations on CNN_M, a large dropout ratio can also lead to comparable results. This may be because the temporal stream networks are trained from scratch, and, even using the same architecture, training the entire framework is more complex than fine-tuning (only tuning three FC layers). Furthermore, some researchers expressed the view that dropout can be considered as a form of training set augmentation [23]. Complex networks may be more suitable to learn from highly augmented input data.

5.5 Softmax vs. SVMs

As discussed in Section 4.3, neural networks can be used as an end-to-end classifier or a feature extractor. In this section, we discuss results of using SVMs on the CNN features, and compare with softmax. We train linear SVMs using outputs from the first and the second FC layers. VGG_19 and CNN_M are adopted for the spatial and temporal stream respectively. As each video has multiple spatial frames and stacked optical flow images, there are two ways to train the SVMs classifiers. One is early fusion by averaging features from all the frames first before classifier training and testing. The other is late fusion, which takes all the frames as inputs separately and uses average prediction scores as the final video-level score.

Table 4 summarizes the results of spatial, temporal, and their fusion on both datasets. Compared with the softmax based prediction, SVMs is only slightly better on the UCF-101 under the spatial-temporal modality fusion setting using the early frame fusion method. On CCV, the performance is significantly lower than softmax. Comparing early frame fusion with late fusion, early fusion is consistently good, indicating that averaging frame features before classification may help suppress noises that affect SVMs training. Interestingly, the neural networks take individual frames as inputs like the late fusion based SVMs, but are quite robust.

5.6 Comparison with the State of the Arts

Finally, we compare our results with the state of the arts on both datasets. For UCF-101, we report average accuracies over the three official train-test splits. As shown in Table 5, our results are competitive on both datasets. The performance on CCV is significantly better than the state of the arts, all of which adopted traditional features like the dense trajectories [32]. On UCF-101, our results are comparable to a very recent work [20], which uses an extensive

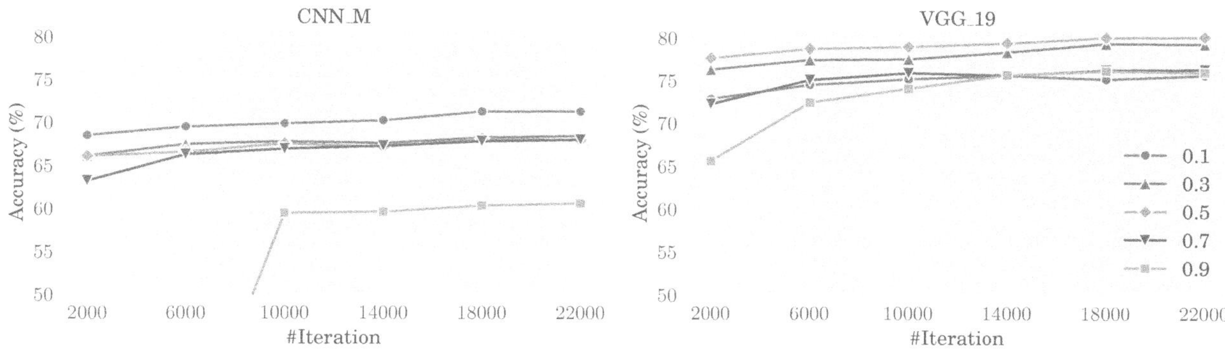

Figure 3: Spatial stream results on UCF-101 (split-1), under different dropout ratios (from 0.1 to 0.9) and iteration numbers.

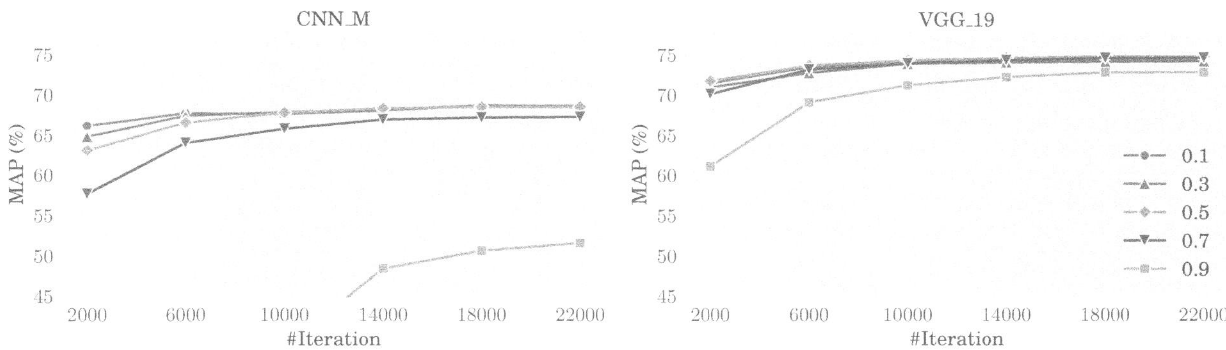

Figure 4: Spatial stream results on CCV, under different dropout ratios and iteration numbers.

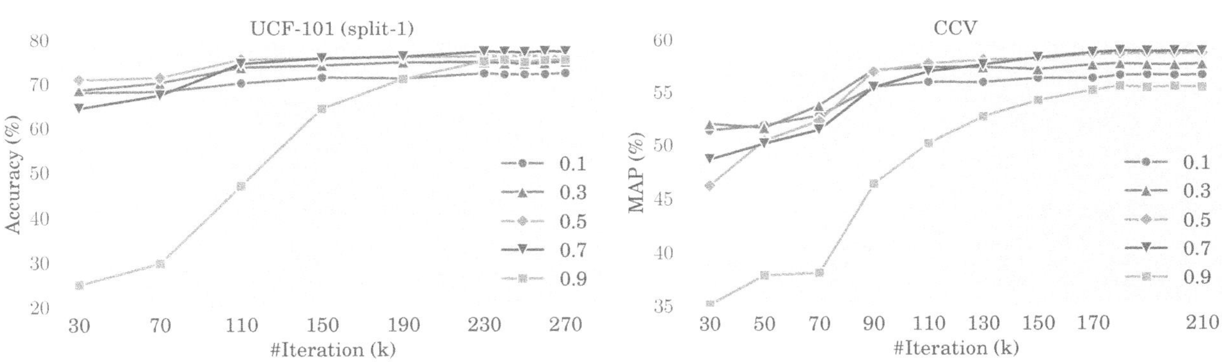

Figure 5: Temporal stream results on both UCF-101 (split-1) and CCV, using CNN_M with different dropout ratios and iteration numbers.

fusion approach on top of state-of-the-art hand-crafted features. Our results are also similar to that of [24]. Note that the 88.0% reported in [24] was attained by using *external training data* from another human action benchmark. If only trained on UCF-101, the performance is lower.

6. SUMMARY AND DISCUSSION

Building a deep learning system for video classification is not an easy task. We have evaluated several important implementation options. The major findings are summarized in the following. Note that knowing what works and what does not work is equally important.

For network architectures, one observation is that deeper networks like the VGG_19 are better, but a sufficient amount of training data is required. This is fine for the spatial stream, as the image annotations like the ImageNet can be used to pre-train the network. For the temporal stream, as we cannot use the image collections for model pre-training, the results of very deep networks are not good. We envision that the they would work well on the temporal stream once we have a large amount of training data in the video domain.

UCF-101		CCV	
Simonyan *et al.* [24]	88.0%	Ye *et al.* [34]	64.0%
Peng *et al.* [20]	87.9%	Jhuo *et al.* [7]	64.0%
Wang *et al.* [32]	85.9%	Liu *et al.* [17]	68.2%
Karpathy *et al.* [12]	65.4%	Wu *et al.* [33]	69.3%
Ours - Softmax	86.7%	Ours - Softmax	75.9%
Ours - SVM	87.7%	Ours - SVM	73.3%

Table 5: Comparison with the state-of-the-art results.

Results indicate that fusing multiple network models is not very helpful, especially when combining a strong network with a weak one. Fusing two networks with a similar performance level but different architectures might help, but this is not verified based on our experiments. In addition, combining predictions from the spatial and the temporal streams is useful. This is important for the classification of long-term procedural actions, which benefits significantly from the temporal clues. The linear weighted spatial-temporal fusion method works well but is not ideal. This aspect deserves more investigations.

We also observe that a moderate dropout ratio (0.5 for spatial fine-tuning and 0.7 for temporal training) is consistently good. Large dropout ratios like 0.9 may be unsuited for small networks with less layers, particularly under the fine-tuning setting that only adjusts the last several layers. Finally, we find that softmax seems a better choice with consistently good results.

Deep learning based approaches are already showing better results than the traditional techniques for video classification. We believe that the room for further improvement is huge. First, the temporal stream results might be significantly boosted if we could have sufficient labeled video data to train a deeper network. Second, although the two-stream framework is adopted in this work, future approaches do not necessarily need to follow this pipeline. After all, it is all about the way of modeling the temporal dimension of the videos, which can be achieved by using alternative solutions like the RNN or devising new network architectures.

Acknowledgments

The project is supported in part by the National 863 Program (#2014AA015101), a grant from NSF China (#61201387), and two grants from the STCSM (#13PJ1400400, #13511504503). We thank Jie Shao and Xiaoteng Zhang for their help.

7. REFERENCES

[1] Y. Bengio, A. Courville, and P. Vincent. Representation learning: A review and new perspectives. *IEEE TPAMI*, 2013.

[2] G. E. Dahl, D. Yu, L. Deng, and A. Acero. Context-Dependent Pre-Trained Deep Neural Networks for Large-Vocabulary Speech Recognition. *IEEE TASLP*, 2012.

[3] J. Donahue, L. A. Hendricks, S. Guadarrama, M. Rohrbach, S. Venugopalan, K. Saenko, and T. Darrell. Long-term recurrent convolutional networks for visual recognition and description. *CoRR*, 2014.

[4] R. Girshick, J. Donahue, T. Darrell, and J. Malik. Rich feature hierarchies for accurate object detection and semantic segmentation. In *CVPR*, 2014.

[5] M. A. Goodale and A. D. Milner. Separate Visual Pathways for Perception and Action. *Trends in neurosciences*, 1992.

[6] M. Jain, J. van Gemert, and C. G. M. Snoek. University of amsterdam at thumos challenge 2014. In *ECCV THUMOS Challenge 2014*, 2014.

[7] I.-H. Jhuo, G. Ye, S. Gao, D. Liu, Y.-G. Jiang, D. T. Lee, and S.-F. Chang. Discovering joint audio-visual codewords for video event detection. *Machine Vision and Applications*, 2014.

[8] S. Ji, W. Xu, M. Yang, and K. Yu. 3d convolutional neural networks for human action recognition. In *ICML*, 2010.

[9] Y.-G. Jiang, J. Liu, A. Roshan Zamir, G. Toderici, I. Laptev, M. Shah, and R. Sukthankar. THUMOS challenge: Action recognition with a large number of classes. `http://crcv.ucf.edu/THUMOS14/`, 2014.

[10] Y.-G. Jiang, G. Ye, S.-F. Chang, D. Ellis, and A. C. Loui. Consumer video understanding: A benchmark database and an evaluation of human and machine performance. In *ACM ICMR*, 2011.

[11] N. Kalchbrenner, E. Grefenstette, and P. Blunsom. A Convolutional Neural Network for Modelling Sentences. *CoRR*, 2014.

[12] A. Karpathy, G. Toderici, S. Shetty, T. Leung, R. Sukthankar, and L. Fei-Fei. Large-scale video classification with convolutional neural networks. In *CVPR*, 2014.

[13] A. Krizhevsky, I. Sutskever, and G. E. Hinton. Imagenet classification with deep convolutional neural networks. In *NIPS*, 2012.

[14] N. Krüger, P. Janssen, S. Kalkan, M. Lappe, A. Leonardis, J. Piater, A. J. Rodríguez-Sánchez, and L. Wiskott. Deep Hierarchies in the Primate Visual Cortex: What Can We Learn for Computer Vision? *IEEE TPAMI*, 2013.

[15] I. Laptev, M. Marszalek, C. Schmid, and B. Rozenfeld. Learning realistic human actions from movies. In *CVPR*, 2008.

[16] Y. LeCun, L. Bottou, Y. Bengio, and P. Haffner. Gradient-based learning applied to document recognition. In *Intelligent Signal Processing*, 2001.

[17] D. Liu, K.-T. Lai, G. Ye, M.-S. Chen, and S.-F. Chang. Sample-specific late fusion for visual category recognition. In *CVPR*, 2013.

[18] T. Mikolov, I. Sutskever, K. Chen, G. S. Corrado, and J. Dean. Distributed Representations of Words and Phrases and Their Compositionality. In *NIPS*, 2013.

[19] D. Oneata, J. Verbeek, C. Schmid, et al. Action and event recognition with fisher vectors on a compact feature set. In *ICCV*, 2013.

[20] X. Peng, L. Wang, X. Wang, and Y. Qiao. Bag of visual words and fusion methods for action recognition: Comprehensive study and good practice. *CoRR*, 2014.

[21] A. S. Razavian, H. Azizpour, J. Sullivan, and S. Carlsson. CNN features off-the-shelf: an astounding baseline for recognition. *CoRR*, 2014.

[22] K. Schindler and L. Van Gool. Action snippets: How many frames does human action recognition require? In *CVPR*, 2008.

[23] J. Schmidhuber. Deep learning in neural networks: An overview. *CoRR*, 2014.

[24] K. Simonyan and A. Zisserman. Two-stream convolutional networks for action recognition in videos. In *NIPS*, 2014.

[25] K. Simonyan and A. Zisserman. Very deep convolutional networks for large-scale image recognition. *CoRR*, 2014.

[26] C. G. Snoek, M. Worring, and A. W. Smeulders. Early versus late fusion in semantic video analysis. In *ACM Multimedia*, 2005.

[27] R. Socher, C. C.-Y. Lin, A. Y. Ng, and C. D. Manning. Parsing Natural Scenes and Natural Language with Recursive Neural Networks. In *ICML*, 2011.

[28] K. Soomro, A. R. Zamir, and M. Shah. UCF101: A dataset of 101 human actions classes from videos in the wild. *CoRR*, 2012.

[29] I. Sutskever, O. Vinyals, and Q. V. Le. Sequence to Sequence Learning with Neural Networks. In *NIPS*, 2014.

[30] C. Szegedy, W. Liu, Y. Jia, P. Sermanet, S. Reed, D. Anguelov, D. Erhan, V. Vanhoucke, and A. Rabinovich. Going Deeper with Convolutions. *CoRR*, 2014.

[31] S. Venugopalan, H. Xu, J. Donahue, M. Rohrbach, R. J. Mooney, and K. Saenko. Translating videos to natural language using deep recurrent neural networks. *CoRR*, 2014.

[32] H. Wang and C. Schmid. Action recognition with improved trajectories. In *ICCV*, 2013.

[33] Z. Wu, Y.-G. Jiang, J. Wang, J. Pu, and X. Xue. Exploring inter-feature and inter-class relationships with deep neural networks for video classification. In *ACM Multimedia*, 2014.

[34] G. Ye, D. Liu, I.-H. Jhuo, and S.-F. Chang. Robust late fusion with rank minimization. In *CVPR*, 2012.

[35] M. D. Zeiler, G. W. Taylor, and R. Fergus. Adaptive Deconvolutional Networks for Mid and High Level Feature Learning. In *ICCV*, 2011.

Content-based Image Retrieval Using Rotation-invariant Histograms of Oriented Gradients

Jinhui Chen[1], Toru Nakashika[1], Tetsuya Takiguchi[2], Yasuo Ariki[2]
[1]Graduate School of System Informatics, Kobe University, Kobe, 657-8501, Japan
[2]Organization of Advanced Science and Technology, Kobe University, Kobe, 657-8501, Japan
{ianchen, nakashika}@me.cs.scitec.kobe-u.ac.jp, {ariki, takigu}@kobe-u.ac.jp

ABSTRACT

Our research focuses on the question of feature descriptors for robust effective computing, proposing a novel feature representation method, namely, rotation-invariant histograms of oriented gradients (Ri-HOG) for image retrieval. Most of the existing HOG techniques are computed on a dense grid of uniformly-spaced cells and use overlapping local contrast of rectangular blocks for normalization. However, we adopt annular spatial bins type cells and apply radial gradient to attain gradient binning invariance for feature extraction. In this way, it significantly enhances HOG in regard to rotation-invariant ability and feature descripting accuracy. In experiments, the proposed method is evaluated on Corel-5k and Corel-10k datasets. The experimental results demonstrate that the proposed method is much more effective than many existing image feature descriptors for content-based image retrieval.

Categories and Subject Descriptors

H.3.1 [**Information Storage and Retrieval**]: Content Analysis and Indexing

General Terms

Algorithms, Experimentation

Keywords

Ri-HOG, image retrieval, content-based image category

1. INTRODUCTION

The image is one type of the most important multimedia data in human communication and it provides a rich amount of visible information for people to understand the world. With the development of Internet and digital image technologies, diverse image data appear everyday. Consequently, it has become a high demand for searching the image information that we need from the large image collections. Generally, there are main 3 types of technologies for image retrieval: the text-based, the content-based and the semantic-based. The text-based image retrieval can be traced back to 1970s. In daily life, people usually search for images mainly via Google, Yahoo, *etc.*, on text keywords, but individual perception, cognition and concept lead to many available results, which are not what they primitively needed. Therefore, in this information explosion age, textual image retrieval becomes impractical and inefficient. About the semantic-based, current image retrieval methods are usually based on low-level features (*e.g*, color, texture, spatial layout), but low-level features often fail to describe high-level concepts, *i.e.*, there is a "semantic gap" between low-level features and high-level concepts. Hence, semantic-based image retrieval is still an open problem [8]. Our research focuses on content-based image retrieval (CBIR). In this paper, we propose an effective method for integrating low-level features of images into individual perception, cognition and concept.

There are many precursors who focus on CBIR based on feature representation methods. In the MPEG-7 standard, color descriptors consist of a number of histogram descriptors, such as the dominant color descriptor, the color layout descriptor, and a scalable color descriptor [6, 5]; In the related works of CBIR, researchers also widely use texture descriptors, which provide the important information of the smoothness, coarseness and regularity of many real-world objects such as fruit, skin, clouds, trees, bricks and fabric, *etc.*, including Gabor filtering [4],local binary pattern (LBP) [7] *etc.* Generally, texture descriptors consist of the homogeneous texture descriptor, the texture browsing descriptor and the edge histogram descriptor. More recently, researchers also combine color descriptor and texture descriptor together, such as, the multi-texton histogram (MTH) [3] and the micro-structure descriptor (MSD) [2]. They use Gabor features to separately compute the color channels, in order that they can combine the color channels with classical texture descriptors to improve the feature describing ability.

In this paper, without any training procedure, clustering implementation or image segmentation, we adopt the distance metric based on a novel feature representation method for the image retrieval. The proposed feature is based on histogram descriptors. It is well known that histogram is a useful tool for image feature representation, but the robustness of many algorithms based on histogram descriptor does not reach maturity. In order to address this problem, this paper presents a new method of feature representation for CBIR, *i.e.* rotation-invariant histograms of oriented gradi-

ICMR'15, June 23–26, 2015, Shanghai, China.

http://dx.doi.org/10.1145/2671188.2749287

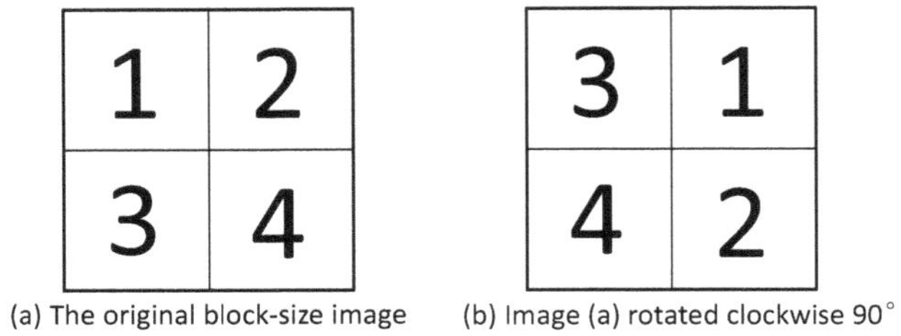

Figure 1: Analyzing the robustness of conventional HOG descriptors in regard to image rotation.

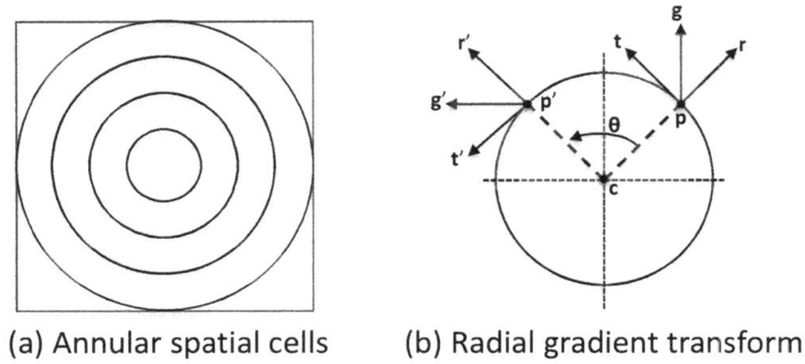

Figure 2: Illustration of rotation-invariant HOG descriptors.

ents (Ri-HOG) for image retrieval. The proposed feature is reminiscent of Dalal *et al.*'s HOG [1], but the proposed feature descriptors noticeably enhance Dalal *et al.*'s version in the rotation-invariant ability and robust representation ability. We subdivide the local patch into annular spatial bins to achieve spatial binning invariance. Besides, inspired by Takacs *et al.*'s approach [9], we apply radial gradient to attain gradient binning invariance. These technical details will be discussed in Sect. 2. They are quite different from previous HOG features in the way that blocks are constructed and cells' gradient is calculated.

In the remainder of this paper, the Ri-HOG for image retrieval is presented in Sect. 2. Sect. 3 gives the detailed stages of the process in experimental evaluation, and conclusions are drawn in Sect. 4.

2. PROPOSED METHOD

2.1 Background and Problems

HOG are feature descriptors, which are computed on a dense grid of uniformly-spaced cells and use overlapping local contrast normalization for improved accuracy. This features set based on *cells* and *blocks* is widely used as object feature descriptors, especially the descriptors in human detection task. The describing ability of HOG features set outperforms many existing features [10]. However, the HOG feature is seldom applied to image retrieval successfully, because any feature descriptor algorithm for image retrieval must be efficient, effective and rotationally invariant. The robustness of HOG against image rotation does not reach maturity: See Fig. 1 for an example. Supposing Fig. 1(a) is a HOG block-size image, there are 4 cells in the block. Fig. 1(b) is an image of Fig. 1(a) after making a quarter turn. HOG features are extracted from the two images individually. If the histogram of oriented gradients obtained from the regions 1, 2, 3, and 4 are respectively denoted as x_1, x_2, x_3, x_4, then, the HOG features extracted from Fig. 1(a) and Fig. 1(b) are (x_1, x_2, x_3, x_4) and (x_3, x_1, x_4, x_2) respectively. This means that the rotation of image accompanies with the change of its HOG descriptors.

But why can HOG features be successfully applied to feature extraction for human detection? Because the people are usually standing, it is not necessary to worry that the orientation of task images is rotated frequently. Moreover, blocks of HOG use overlapping local contrast normalization, to some extent, which can restrain impacts brought by image rotation. Therefore, the conventional HOG just needs to be able to robustly describe the people who appear in some limited orientations and against a wide variety of background image including crowds. The high describing ability of conventional HOG makes it possible to reach this goal. However, differing from human detection situations where the people are usually standing, CBIR has to deal with the problems that the tasks in images are rotated frequently and own variable appearances. Hence, we have to substantially enhance the robustness of HOG descriptors.

2.2 Descriptors Extraction

Our approach: Now, the question is how to significantly improve the robustness of traditional HOG against the sharp orientation rotation of the task regions. In this paper, the answer is rotation-invariant HOG; *i.e.*, we proposed a variant of HOG owning an annular spatial cells type blocks, see Fig. 2(a). This form of blocks is reminiscent of C-HOG [1], but essentially, the approaches of C-HOG feature descriptors are the same as the R-HOG's [1]. Therefore, it cannot make HOG be rotation-invariant. Moreover, its form limits the describing ability of C-HOG. Unlike C-HOG, we use annular spatial cells to replace rectangular cells. Furthermore, these cells are computed on a dense radial gradients as feature descriptors to achieve the goal of making HOG be rotation-invariant.

How to calculate these descriptors? See Fig. 2(b), $\forall$ point p in circle c, the task is to compute the radial gradient magnitude of point p (x, y). Decompose vector g into its local coordinate system as $(g^T r, g^T t)$, by projecting g into the r and t orientations as shown in Fig. 2(b). Because the component vectors of g in r and t orientations can be obtained by $r = \frac{p-c}{\|p-c\|}$ and $t = R_{\frac{\pi}{2}} r$ quickly, and we can obtain the gradient g easily on the gradient filter. In addition, R_θ is the rotation matrix by angle θ.

Now that we have discussed the arrangement of blocks and how to obtain the feature descriptors from cells, we summarize the four steps of rotation-invariant HOG features extraction:

1. Subdivide the local patch into annular spatial cells as shown in Fig. 2(a);
2. Calculate $(g^T r, g^T t)$ of each pixel in the cell;
3. Calculate the radial gradient magnitude (M_{GR}) and its orientation (θ) on location (x, y), using the Eq. 1:

$$M_{GR}(x, y) = \sqrt{(g^T r)^2 + (g^T t)^2}, \qquad \theta(x, y) = \arctan \frac{g^T t}{g^T r}; \tag{1}$$

Table 1: **Average accuracy of annuli spatial cell with different bins on Corel datasets.**

Dataset	Performance	Accuracy of annular spatial cell with different bins												
		1	2	3	4	5	6	7	8	9	10	11	12	13
Corel-5K	Precision (%)	23.06	35.19	36.43	42.08	45.25	53.08	56.83	56.71	56.79	54.33	53.02	52.50	43.51
	Recall (%)	2.76	4.22	4.37	5.05	5.43	6.37	6.82	6.80	6.81	6.52	6.36	6.30	5.22
Corel-10K	Precision (%)	11.96	21.93	25.12	27.70	35.05	36.93	43.52	52.13	52.11	50.56	47.79	42.30	39.82
	Recall (%)	1.43	2.63	3.01	3.32	4.20	4.43	5.22	6.25	6.25	6.08	5.76	5.70	4.83

4. Accumulating the gradient magnitude of radial gradient for each pixel over each annular spatial cells into 8 bins.

Block normalization: We tried all of 4 normalization approaches that have been listed by Dalal *et al.* in [1]. In practice, $L_2 - Hys$, L_2 normalization followed by clipping is shown working best. The feature patch includes 10 cells and each cell contains 8 bins. The feature patch size is 100×100 pixels, which further allows different aspect ratios (the ratio of width and height). In this way, the feature can adapt various scenes and image sizes robustly. The descriptors are extracted according to the order from the inside to the outside of cells. Hence, concatenating features in 10 cells together yield a 80-dimensional feature vector.

Now, we still have the question why the Ri-HOG feature is rotation-invariant. As shown in Fig. 2 (b), assuming the local patch has been rotated by an angle ($\forall\ \theta$). Rotate point $p \to$ point p', which generates a new gradient system $R_\theta p = p'$; $R_\theta r = r'$; $R_\theta t = t'$; $R_\theta g = g'$. We can verify the coordinates of the gradient in point p' can be expressed by $(g^T r, g^T t)$:

$$\begin{aligned}(g'^T r', g'^T t') &= ((R_\theta g)^T R_\theta r, (R_\theta g)^T R_\theta t) \\ &= (g^T R_\theta^T R_\theta r, g^T R_\theta^T R_\theta t) \\ &= (g^T r, g^T t).\end{aligned} \quad (2)$$

All rotated points in the local patch also can obtain their coordinates of the gradient from the corresponding original points, because all gradients are rotated by the same angle θ, they are one-to-one mapping. Thus, the set of gradients on any given circle or annular spatial bin centered around the patch is invariant.

3. EXPERIMENTS

In this section we will show the details of dataset, distance metric for retrieval, and evaluation results.

3.1 Experimental Dataset

The proposed method is evaluated on the Corel-5K and Corel-10K datasets [2, 3]. In the Corel-5K dataset, there are 50 categories including 5000 images, which cover diverse contents such as fireworks, bark, microscopy images, tiles, food textures, trees, waves, pills and stained glass *etc.* The Corel-10K dataset has 10,000 images covering 100 categories, such as sunsets, beaches, flowers, buildings, cars, horses, mountains, fish, food, and doors *etc.* Each category in the Corel-5K and Corel-10K datasets contains 100 JPEG images with the size of 192×128 or 128×192.

3.2 Distance Metric and Performance Metric

In this paper, the measurement of image content similarity is evaluated by distance metric. Namely, the distance between the query image and the template image in the dataset is calculated on correlation distance. The distance metric is one of the simplest approaches, therefore, it can

Figure 3: An example of image retrieval result using the proposed method on Corel-10K (The top 12 similar template images to the query image in the dataset: the top-left image is the query image, and the images of red dashed box are the correct retrieval results).

prove the validity of descriptors most directly. Assuming the N-dimensional feature vector $T = (T_1, T_2, \cdots, T_N)$ of each template image in the dataset is extracted and stored; The feature vector of the query image is $R = (R_1, R_2, \cdots, R_N)$. Then, the correlation distance metric can be calculated as:

$$D(T, R) = \frac{\sum_{i=1}^{N} T_i R_i}{\sqrt{\sum_{i=1}^{N}(T_i)^2}\sqrt{\sum_{i=1}^{N}(R_i)^2}}. \quad (3)$$

In the experiments, N is set as 80. We use the *Precision* and *Recall* to evaluate the performance of the proposed method. These two indices are the most commonly used for evaluating image retrieval performance. Precision is the ratio of the number of retrieved similar images to the number of retrieved images; Recall is the ratio of the number of retrieved similar images to the total number of similar images. They are defined as follows:

$$\begin{aligned}P(K) &= I_K / K, \\ R(K) &= I_K / L,\end{aligned} \quad (4)$$

where L is the upper bound number of images, which are indexed from the dataset on the proposed method; K denotes the retrieval results, whose distance metrics can keep ranking in top K positions among the L similar results; I_K is the number of indexed images, whose contents are truly similar to the query image's (see the example in Fig. 3). In order to evaluate the results easily, we set $K = 12$, $L = 100$ in the same way as the setting of Liu *et al.* [2, 3]. An example of image retrieval result using the proposed method on Corel-10K is shown in Fig. 3.

Table 2: Average retrieval precision and recall on Corel datasets.

Dataset	Performance	Ri-HOG	HOG [1]	Gabor [4]	EHD [5]	MSD [2]	MTH [3]
Corel-5K	Precision (%)	**56.71**	41.16	36.22	39.46	55.92	49.84
	Recall (%)	**6.80**	4.91	4.35	4.74	6.71	5.98
Corel-10K	Precision (%)	**52.13**	33.29	29.15	32.31	45.62	41.44
	Recall (%)	**6.25**	3.94	3.50	3.88	5.48	4.97

3.3 Performance Evaluation

The retrieval accuracy of the proposed method not only depends on its rotation-invariant ability, but also on the number of bins in each annuli spatial cell. Generally, more spatial bins increase distinctiveness, but it will lead to the narrower annuli which decreases robustness. Therefore, there is a trade-off in performance between the number of annuli and their width, and we have to balance them. Table 1 shows the retrieval accuracies of the proposed method adopting the annulis spatial cell on different bins. We have observed that when the number of bins ≥ 7 on Corel-5K dataset and the number of bins ≥ 8 on Corel-10K dataset, the accuracy was not or seldom improved any more. But with the growth of bin number, the dimensionality of the feature also raises. Naturally, it is not beneficial to control the time complexity of feature extraction. Balancing the accuracy and time complexity for both of the database, we set the number of bins as 8. Hence, we set $N = 80$ in Subsection 3.2 and the dimensionality of the proposed method is 80.

Table 2 compares our method (Ri-HOG) with the existing image feature descriptors that were originally developed for content-based image retrieval, including Gabor features [4], the edge histogram descriptor (EHD) [5], the micro-structure descriptor (MSD) [2], and the multi-texton histogram (MTH) [3]. The Gabor features and the EHD are well-known feature representation methods for image retrieval, and the MTH and the MSD are the latest methods developed for image retrieval. These methods were conducted using their released codes. Besides, in order to evaluate the proposed method better, we also tried the conventional HOG [1] for image retrieval. Gabor features and EHD are texture descriptors, which can obtain good performance only in regular texture images. But images of real-world usually do not contain homogenous textures or regular textures, thus Gabor filter cannot represent the real-world images well. MTH and MSD combine color and texture, thus the describing ability of them is powerful. But they have ignored the local outline representation, this limits the discrimination power of them. The proposed method is a local feature, which is derived from HOG and good at describing the outline detailed information, furthermore, it has significantly enhanced the representation ability and rational robustness of HOG features. Therefore, its performance outperforms the other methods.

In addition, the average time usage of the Ri-HOG, HOG, Gabor filter, EHD, MSD and MTH are 167 ms, 183 ms, 1626 ms, 836 ms, 142 ms and 252 ms respectively (Windows 7.0 OS with Core i5 2.40 GHz CPU and 8 GB RAM).

4. CONCLUSION

In this paper, we have proposed a novel feature representation method for content-based image retrieval, *i.e.*, rotation-invariant histograms of oriented gradients (Ri-HOG). It is derived from Dalal *et al.*'s HOG yet ameliorated by the theory of polar coordinate. This histogram entirely differs from existing ones based on histograms. Furthermore it outperforms the conventional methods. This is important to those with closely related research interests. The vector dimension of the proposed feature is only 80. Therefore, it is a simple but efficient image retrieval approach. These also have been confirmed by the experiments.

About the further plan, we will try to adopt Ri-HOG as the feature representation for object recognition based on the cascade learning model.

5. REFERENCES

[1] N. Dalal and B. Triggs. Histograms of oriented gradients for human detection. In *Proc. IEEE Conf. Comput. Vis. Pattern Recognit. (CVPR)*, pages 886–893, Jun. 2005.

[2] G.-H. Liu, Z.-Y. Li, L. Zhang, and Y. Xu. Image retrieval based on micro-structure descriptor. *Pattern Recognition*, 44(9):2123 – 2133, 2011.

[3] G.-H. Liu, L. Zhang, Y.-K. Hou, Z.-Y. Li, and J.-Y. Yang. Image retrieval based on multi-texton histogram. *Pattern Recognition*, 43(7):2380 – 2389, 2010.

[4] B. Manjunath and W. Ma. Texture features for browsing and retrieval of image data. *IEEE Trans. PAMI*, 18(8):837–842, Aug. 1996.

[5] B. Manjunath, J.-R. Ohm, V. Vasudevan, and A. Yamada. Color and texture descriptors. *IEEE Trans. Circ. Syst . Video Tech.*, 11(6):703–715, Jun. 2001.

[6] B. S. Manjunath, P. Salembier, and T. Sikora. *Introduction to MPEG-7: multimedia content description interface.* John Wiley & Sons, 2002.

[7] T. Ojala, M. Pietikainen, and T. Maenpaa. Multiresolution gray-scale and rotation invariant texture classification with local binary patterns. *IEEE Trans. PAMI*, 24(7):971–987, Jul. 2002.

[8] G. Papari and N. Petkov. An improved model for surround suppression by steerable filters and multilevel inhibition with application to contour detection. *Pattern Recognition*, 44(9):1999 – 2007, 2011.

[9] G. Takacs, V. Chandrasekhar, S. Tsai, D. Chen, R. Grzeszczuk, and B. Girod. Fast computation of rotation-invariant image features by an approximate radial gradient transform. *IEEE Trans. Image Proc.*, 22(8):2970–2982, Aug. 2013.

[10] Q. Zhu, M.-C. Yeh, K.-T. Cheng, and S. Avidan. Fast Human Detection Using a Cascade of Histograms of Oriented Gradients. In *Proc. IEEE Conf. Comput. Vis. Pattern Recognit. (CVPR)*, pages 1491–1498, 2006.

Augmented Feature Fusion for Image Retrieval System

Yang Zhou[1], Dan Zeng[2], Shiliang Zhang[1], and Qi Tian[1]
[1]University of Texas at San Antonio, US
[2]Shanghai University, CHINA
myh511@my.utsa.edu dzeng@shu.edu.cn slzhang.jdl@gmail.com qi.tian@utsa.edu

ABSTRACT

The performance of current image retrieval system is largely determined by the quality and discriminative capability of features. Therefore, using what features and how to effectively combine the power of appropriate features are important in the system. We adopt the reciprocal neighbor based graph fusion approach for feature fusion. More importantly, we explicitly augment the original approach with the following two strategies: 1) we investigate the most suitable feature combinations on various datasets, including the deep learning feature, which has been popular for image retrieval recently; 2) we further improve the robustness of original graph fusion approach by the SVM prediction strategy.

Extensive experiments are performed on three benchmark datasets including *UKbench*, *Holidays* and *Corel-5K*, to validate the impressive performance of the augmented feature fusion. On the three datasets, our retrieval system significantly outperforms several existing algorithms. For example on *UKbench*, the N-S score of our approach achieves 3.88, which is one of the highest accuracies to the best of our knowledge.

Categories and Subject Descriptors

H.3.3 [**Information Search and Retrieval**]: Retrieval Models

General Terms

Algorithms, Experimentation, Verification.

Keywords

Feature fusion, Image retrieval, SVM prediction.

1. INTRODUCTION

With the fast development in digital techniques, the amount of digital images is increasing explosively. This trend makes image search an important and challenging research topic [19, 20]. According to the adopted image representations and the corresponding indexing strategies, we can summarize current image retrieval works into two categories: 1) global features [1, 14] indexed with hashing strategies [21, 23], and 2) local scale invariant features [12] indexed by a vocabulary tree [13] or a k-d tree [16]. Global features are effective in capturing global views and high level semantics of the images, but are sensitive to variations of illumination, scale, occlusion, *etc*. Local features describe the local details and are invariant to scale, rotation changes and occlusions. Hence, local features are effective in partial-duplicate image search, but are limited in capturing the high-level semantics. Therefore, the local and global features are complementary to each other.

To improve the image retrieval system, an effective strategy is to fuse different types of features. Generally the feature fusion can be carried out on the feature level, index level, and rank level. For the feature level fusion, in [3, 24], the authors combine different types of features in a histogram utilizing the Bag-of-Words (BoW) representation. However, it is difficult to preserve the scalability and efficiency induced by the vocabulary tree and compact hashing codes. For the index level fusion, Zhang *et al.* [26] co-indexes local feature and semantic attributes in the inverted indexes. But the framework is closely bound to the two types of features, thus it's not flexible for extension. For the rank level fusion, the works in [8, 2] combine the ranked lists from different retrieval methods with rank aggregation. However, it requires intersection among the top candidates retrieved by multiple features. We choose to fuse features on the rank level, and we adopt the reciprocal neighbor based graph fusion [25] for the feature fusion because of the following known facts: 1) it achieves better performance than the other fusion methods, this has already been validated over various datasets in [25]; 2) the framework is flexible for extension, so that it is capable to easily fuse multiple features without considering strict assumptions (e.g., requires intersection among retrievals in rank aggregation); and 3) the fusion procedure is fast.

To consider augmentations for feature fusion, firstly, we improve the fusion by utilizing appropriate feature combinations, because the complementarity of different features largely determines the performance of feature fusion. Through the extensive experimental studies, we want to expose the best feature combination over some popular benchmarks. More importantly, we also involve the deep learning feature in fusion. The deep learning feature [11, 5, 10] based on Conventional Neural Network (CNN) can be learned automatically from large-scale images without many supervisions. Hence, it is largely different from the existing hand-crafted features, and it is expected to show better generalization and discriminative abilities across datasets.

Secondly, we augment the reciprocal neighbor based graph fusion with the SVM prediction. We observe that the original approach [25] shows limited robustness, when the fused graphs are too sparse to include enough relevant images (*i.e.*, non-adequate retrievals), however, the approach in [25] arbitrarily picks up results

ICMR'15, June 23–26, 2015, Shanghai, China.

http://dx.doi.org/10.1145/2671188.2749288.

as the complement. Instead, we train the SVM classifier based on the similarity scores among top candidates, then we use the classifier to predict the list of results (*e.g.*, retrieved by local or global feature) that may achieve a higher precision. The results are used to complement the non-adequate results.

We evaluate our approach on three benchmark datasets: *UKbench*, *Holidays*, and *Corel-5K*. On these datasets, we conduct extensive experiments to test the performance of different feature combinations and the validity of the proposed SVM prediction strategy. The experimental results show that by employing the proposed augmentations, our feature fusion method outperforms several existing methods. Especially on *UKbench* dataset, the N-S score of our approach achieves 3.88, which is the best among the reported results in recent years.

We conclude our contributions as two-fold: 1) we study different feature combinations on some popular benchmark datasets of image retrieval. Especially, we include the deep learning feature in the feature fusion approach, and achieve impressive accuracy across datasets; 2) we propose the SVM prediction, which significantly improves the robustness of the original graph fusion approach [25].

2. METHODS

We firstly employ different features, *i.e.*, deep learning feature, semantic attributes, local feature, HSV color histogram, and GIST to retrieve results for query q. Then the individual retrieval results are used to build the reciprocal neighbor based graphs. Finally, the graphs are fused for retrieval re-ranking. In the following, we firstly introduce the employed features, then state the Graph fusion with SVM prediction.

2.1 Feature descriptors

Deep learning feature: We utilize the deep learning framework CAFFE [9] as the feature extractor for image retrieval, which is based on the deep Convolutional Neural Network (CNN) architecture by Krizhevsky *et al.* (2012) [10]. In fact, our testing query and database images are independent from the ImageNet dataset, so we utilize the pre-trained model on ImageNet. Because the training data of CAFFE contains millions of images and thousands of objects, it is expected to show good generalization ability and strong discriminative power across the other independent datasets.

In the CNN model, the activations of the neurons in the different layers could be used as features. In our implementation, we test the outputs of the last three hidden layers in CAFFE as the features for image retrieval. Specifically, the three layers are: 1) CAFFE_5, the output of the 5-th layer; 2) CAFFE_7, the output of the final hidden layer, *i.e.*, the 7-th layer; and 3) CAFFE_6, the layer between CAFFE_5 and CAFFE_7. The dimensionalities of CAFFE_5, CAFFE_6, and CAFFE_7 are 4096, 4096, and 1000, respectively.

To extract the deep learning feature, we firstly feed the mean centered 256×256 sized RGB images to the CAFFE model, then the values are forward propagated through 5 convolutional layers and 3 fully-connected layers. Finally we keep the outputs of the last three hidden layers as CAFFE_5, CAFFE_6, and CAFFE_7, respectively. We normalize the vectors by their l_1 norms, and then apply the square root scaling. Note that the outputs of hidden layers in CAFFE are very sparse, we hence store them with sparse matrix. During online retrieval, for each query we apply exhaustive search and measure the vector similarity with Euclidean distance.

Semantic attribute: We utilize the classification scores of 1000 SVM classifiers trained on the LSVRC10 dataset as semantic attributes. Following the work in [26], we convert the classification score to the probabilistic representation $\{p_t\}_{t=1}^{T}$ by fitting a sigmoid function, where $T = 1000$ is the number of SVM classifiers. Given a query q and database images $\{d\}$, we retrieve by exhaustive search based on the Total Variance Distance (TVD), *i.e.*, $\text{TVD}(q, d) = \sum_{t=1}^{T} |p_t(q) - p_t(d)|$.

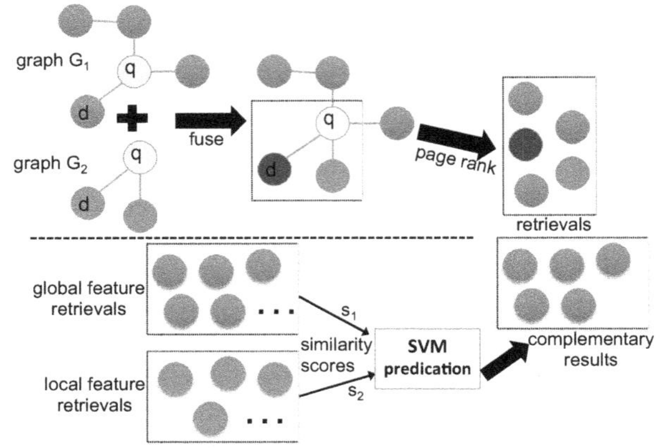

Figure 1: q is query image, d is top-k nearest reciprocal neighbor of q. The reciprocal neighbor graphs G_1 and G_2 are constructed for global feature retrievals and local feature retrievals, respectively. The two graphs are fused and page ranked for retrievals. However, the graph is sparse and results are non-adequate. We complement the retrievals by SVM prediction based on the top similarity score vectors s_1 and s_2.

Local feature: We employ the contextual weighting vocabulary tree to conduct the local feature based retrieval [22]. We extract about 2,500 SIFT descriptors from each image. For feature quantization, we train a vocabulary tree with 7 layers and 10 branches on the validation set (*i.e.*, 50K images) of the ImageNet Challenge. Then, inverted file index based strategy is leveraged for image indexing and retrieval.

Global feature: We extract the GIST feature (960-d) and HSV color histogram ($20 \times 10 \times 10$ bins for H,S,V components, which amounts to 2000-d) as the global features. To improve the retrieval efficiency and save memory, the high dimensional global feature vectors are compressed to 256-bit compact code using PCA hashing [4]. Finally, we apply retrieval by exhaustive search with Hamming distance.

2.2 Graph fusion with SVM prediction

We follow the procedure in [25] and employ the reciprocal neighbor based graph for feature fusion. The Graph fusion with SVM prediction is also illustrated in Fig. 1. For two images i and i', they are top-k nearest reciprocal neighbors if:

$$i \in N_k(i') \wedge i' \in N_k(i), \tag{1}$$

where $N_k(i)$ is the neighborhood of image i, *i.e.*, the top-k retrieved images by querying image i. According to the above definition, the top-k nearest reciprocal neighbor relationship reliably indicates that two images are visually similar.

From the retrieval results by feature f for query q, we construct an undirected weighted graph $G = (V, E, W)$ centered at query q with multiple layers. Each node $i \in V$ is the image and two images are connected by the edge $(i, i') \in E$ if they are the top-k nearest reciprocal neighbors of each other. The weight $w \in W$ of edge (i, i') is defined as the weighted Jaccard similarity between $N_k(i)$ and $N_k(i')$:

$$w(i, i') = {\alpha_0}^{l(q,i,i')} \frac{|N_k(i) \cap N_k(i')|}{|N_k(i) \cup N_k(i')|}, \tag{2}$$

where $\alpha_0 < 1$ is the decay coefficient of edge weight, $l(q,i,i') = \max(dist(q,i), dist(q,i'))$ measures the distance from (i,i') to q. As shown in Fig. 1, the first layer connected to the query image q is formed by its top-k nearest reciprocal neighbors, then each node of the first layer, *e.g.* image d, is propagated to deeper layers to expand the graph and include more relevant images. ${\alpha_0}^{l(q,i,i')}$ is designed to decrease when G expands to deeper layer $l(q,i,i')$ from query. We hence use it to reflect the relevance between images in G and the query.

For the query q, we retrieve n list of images by n features respectively, thus we build totally n graphs *i.e.*, one graph from one feature. We then fuse the n graphs to get the final graph $G' = (V', E', W')$. The graph G' is built with $V' = \cup_n V^n$, $E' = \cup_n E^n$, and $w'(i,i') = \sum_n w^n(i,i')$ $(w'(i,i') \in W')$. After obtaining the fused graph G', the final retrieval result is computed by re-ranking with PageRank [15] or Maximizing Weighted Density on the final graph. PageRank depresses the images with sparse connectivities. Maximizing Weighted Density finds the weighted maximum density subgraph centered at the query image.

We find that the top-k nearest reciprocal neighbor relationship is too strict for some queries, resulting in too sparse graphs G' in graph fusion to ensure robust recall rate during re-ranking. In such scenario, the original approach in [25] arbitrarily picks up the image list retrieved with one of the features to enrich the final result. However, this arbitrary strategy makes the retrieval quality quite unstable.

SVM prediction: We are motivated by the observation [17] that the top-N similarity scores of retrieval results could reveal the retrieval quality. For example, a sharp degradation of the similarity scores may imply a confident retrieval, and a long tail distribution in similarity scores may imply a less confident one. According to this observation, we use the distribution of similarity score as feature and build a linear SVM classifier to predict the retrieval quality of each individual feature. Specifically, we normalize similarity scores among the top $N+1$ ($N = 10$ in our work) retrieved images as the N-dim feature vector. The groundtruth of retrieval quality can be obtained according to the annotated labels of our dataset, and we annotate each query by comparing the quality of the top retrievals from different features. We then fix the regularization parameter $C = 50$ and apply a 5-fold cross-validation to train the SVM model. During online retrieval, the prediction of SVM determines the list of results that should be used to enrich the initial result produced by the graph fusion. Note that, we only employ this strategy when the fused graph G' is sparse. This largely improves the recall rate and is quite different from arbitrary selection strategy in [25]. Therefore, our approach can benefit from both graph fusion and SVM prediction.

3. EXPERIMENTS

3.1 Datasets

We use three datasets, *i.e.*, *UKbench*, *Holidays*, and *Corel-5K* as our testsets because they correspond to different image retrieval tasks. *UKbench* contains 10200 images belonging to 2550 groups. Each group contains 4 images of the same object, taken under different illumination conditions, orientations, *etc*. Hence, *UKbench* is an appropriate testset for object search. We report the N-S score, *i.e.*, the number of correct images in the first 4 returned results, to evaluate the retrieval performance. *Holidays* contains 1491 images and 500 queries. The task is to retrieve the partial-duplicate versions of queries from the 1491 images. We report the mAP (mean Average Precision) to evaluate the retrieval accuracy. *Corel-5K* contains 5000 images belonging to 50 categories. Each category contains 100 visually similar images describing the same object or scene, *e.g.*, building, balloon, bird, *etc*. Hence, *Corel-5K* is commonly used as a testset for similar image search. Following the settings in [25], we report the leave-one-out r-precision (*i.e.*, the precision for the top-r candidates averaged over the 5,000 queries).

3.2 Experimental results

In this section, we evaluate our approach in terms of the following aspects: 1) the performance of the deep learning feature for image retrieval; 2) the complementary capability of the deep learning feature for the other features in feature fusion; 3) effectiveness of the SVM prediction; 4) comparison with existing works; 5) computational efficiency. For experimental settings, we set the parameter k (*i.e.*, top-k nearest reciprocal neighbors) to 5 for *UKbench* and *Holidays*, 15 for *Corel-5K*, and we apply the Maximizing Weighted Density ranking algorithm in the graph fusion approach.

First of all, we comprehensively compare the retrieval performance among different features including CAFFE (*i.e.*, deep learning feature of three layers), VOC (*i.e.*, local feature), HSV (*i.e.*, global feature), GIST (*i.e.*, global feature), Semantic (*i.e.*, semantic attributes). The results are given in Table 1.

Table 1: Performance comparison among different features.

	UKbench	*Holidays(%)*	*Corel-5K(%)*
$CAFFE_5$	3.41	66.73	88.2
$CAFFE_6$	**3.44**	**67.67**	**89.4**
$CAFFE_7$	3.20	60.28	85.6
VOC	3.49	77.10	46.36
HSV	3.17	62.60	39.7
GIST	2.21	36.9	46.16
Semantic	3.15	70.54	79.28

Shown in Table 1, the performance of the CAFFE feature can generalize well on three datasets. $CAFFE_6$ performs better than $CAFFE_5$ and $CAFFE_7$. The deep learning feature is less competitive than local feature on *UKbench* and *Holidays* because it is a global feature in nature and is not optimal to retrieve partial-duplicate images. However, its performance is still better than the conventional global features. Moreover, the performance of CAFFE feature is dramatically better than the other features on *Corel-5K*.

We evaluate the complementary capability of different features for feature fusion. We complement the VOC with different features, the results are shown in Table 2. We also give out the best feature combination in Table 3. In Table 2, the CAFFE feature shows to be the best feature to complement the VOC feature on all three datasets. In Table 3, the best feature combinations on three datasets all involve the contribution from the CAFFE feature. However, the feature fusion does not always produce good performance. We observe that the performance of the best combination on *Corel-5K* is even worse than using the CAFFE feature alone. Low level features like VOC, HSV and GIST hence are not optimal for searching category relevant images on *Corel-5K*. The semantic attributes perform better, but is still not comparable to CAFFE due to the large noise.

Table 2: Complimentary capability of different features.

	UKbench	*Holidays(%)*	*Corel-5K(%)*
VOC+$CAFFE_6$	**3.85**	**84.96**	**83.7**
VOC+HSV	3.77	84.64	46.7
VOC+GIST	3.44	52.14	54.62
VOC+Semantic	3.76	83.85	73.7

To demonstrate the effectiveness of SVM prediction, we compare the graph fusion (with SVM prediction) with the graph fusion

Table 3: Best feature combinations on three datasets.

	combination	score
UKbench	VOC+HSV+CAFFE$_6$	3.88
Holidays(%)	VOC+HSV+CAFFE$_6$	85.52
Corel-5K(%)	Semantic+CAFFE$_6$	84.8

(without SVM prediction). Shown in Table 4, we apply SVM prediction on two feature fusions, *i.e.*, VOC+HSV and VOC+CAFFE$_6$, respectively. The feature fusions marked with * are improved by the SVM prediction. As shown in Table 4, after applying SVM prediction, the performance is improved over the original graph fusion approach, especially on *Corel-5K*.

Table 4: Effectiveness of SVM prediction, feature fusions marked with * are improved by the SVM prediction.

	UKbench	*Holidays*(%)	*Corel-5K*(%)
VOC+HSV	3.77	84.64	46.7
(VOC+HSV)*	**3.86**	**84.88**	**49.43**
VOC+CAFFE$_6$	3.85	84.96	83.7
(VOC+CAFFE$_6$)*	**3.87**	**85.37**	**88.9**

We compare our approach with the existing works in Table 5. 3.88 on *UKbench* and 85.52% on *Holidays* are achieved by fusing HSV, VOC and CAFFE$_6$. CAFFE$_6$ achieves 89.4% on *Corel-5K*.

Table 5: Comparison with existing methods.

	Ours	[25]	[26]	[8]	[7]	[18]	[6]
UKbench	**3.88**	3.77	3.60	3.68	3.55	-	3.64
Holidays(%)	**85.52**	84.6	80.86	-	84.8	80.1	84.8
Corel-5K(%)	**89.4**	54.62	-	-	-	-	-

We show the divided time periods in Table 6. The computational efficiency of the CAFFE feature is guaranteed by the vector sparsity. The online query time is even comparable to the VOC feature. The feature extraction time is about 200 ms/image on CPU including image loading, cropping, and python interfacing time. We achieve the performance on a Quad-core PC with 8 GB memory.

From the above experiments, some advantages of the CAFFE feature are shown as: 1) it shows competitive performance and satisfying generalization ability across the three datasets; 2) it is complementary to the local feature in describing the image content; 3) it is computationally efficient with the sparse representation. Finally, we show some retrieval examples in Fig. 2.

4. CONCLUSION

We combine the power of different features for image retrieval. By fusing the deep learning feature, our retrieval system significantly outperforms several existing algorithms. Also, by improving the reciprocal neighbor based graph fusion with SVM prediction, our feature fusion achieves better robustness.

Acknowledgment.
The study is supported by Natural Science Foundation of China (NSFC) 61301221, 61429201, ARO grant W911NF-12-1-0057, Faculty Research Awards by NEC Laboratories of America.

5. REFERENCES

[1] D. Cai, X. He, and J. Han. Spectral regression: a unified subspace learning framework for content-based image retrieval. In *MM*, pages 403–412, 2007.

[2] R. Fagin, R. Kumar, and D. Sivakumar. Efficient similarity search and classification via rank aggregation. In *SIGMOD*, pages 301–312, 2003.

[3] P. Gehler and S. Nowozin. On feature combination for multiclass object classification. In *ICCV*, pages 221–228, 2009.

[4] Y. Gong and S. Lazebnik. Iterative quantization: A procrustean approach to learning binary codes. In *CVPR*, pages 817–824, 2011.

[5] G. Hinton, L. Deng, D. Yu, G. E. Dahl, A.-r. Mohamed, N. Jaitly, A. Senior, V. Vanhoucke, P. Nguyen, T. N. Sainath, et al. Deep neural networks for acoustic modeling in speech recognition: The shared views of four research groups. *SPM*, 29(6):82–97, 2012.

Table 6: Divided time periods of the graph fusion approach, time is measured in ms.

	Image #	VOC	CAFFE	Feature fusion	Total
UKbench	10200	85	100	< 1	186
Holidays	1490	72	80	< 1	152
Corel-5K	5000	76	88	< 1	165

[6] H. Jégou, M. Douze, and C. Schmid. On the burstiness of visual elements. In *CVPR*, pages 1169–1176, 2009.

[7] H. Jégou, M. Douze, and C. Schmid. Improving bag-of-features for large scale image search. *IJCV*, 87(3):316–336, 2010.

[8] H. Jegou, C. Schmid, H. Harzallah, and J. Verbeek. Accurate image search using the contextual dissimilarity measure. *T-PAMI*, 32(1):2–11, 2010.

[9] Y. Jia. Caffe: An open source convolutional architecture for fast feature embedding. http://caffe.berkeleyvision.org/, 2013.

[10] A. Krizhevsky, I. Sutskever, and G. E. Hinton. Imagenet classification with deep convolutional neural networks. In *NIPS*, volume 1, page 4, 2012.

[11] Y. LeCun, K. Kavukcuoglu, and C. Farabet. Convolutional networks and applications in vision. In *ISCAS*, pages 253–256, 2010.

[12] D. G. Lowe. Distinctive image features from scale-invariant keypoints. *IJCV*, 60(2):91–110, 2004.

[13] D. Nister and H. Stewenius. Scalable recognition with a vocabulary tree. In *CVPR*, pages 2161–2168, 2006.

[14] A. Oliva and A. Torralba. Modeling the shape of the scene: A holistic representation of the spatial envelope. *IJCV*, 42(3):145–175, 2001.

[15] L. Page, S. Brin, R. Motwani, and T. Winograd. The pagerank citation ranking: Bringing order to the web. Technical report, Stanford InfoLab, 1999.

[16] J. Philbin, O. Chum, M. Isard, J. Sivic, and A. Zisserman. Object retrieval with large vocabularies and fast spatial matching. In *CVPR*, pages 1–8, 2007.

[17] D. Qin, S. Gammeter, L. Bossard, T. Quack, and L. Van Gool. Hello neighbor: Accurate object retrieval with k-reciprocal nearest neighbors. In *CVPR*, pages 777–784. IEEE, 2011.

[18] D. Qin, C. Wengert, and L. Van Gool. Query adaptive similarity for large scale object retrieval. In *CVPR*, pages 1610–1617, 2013.

[19] Q. Tian, N. Sebe, M. S. Lew, E. Loupias, and T. S. Huang. Content-based image retrieval using wavelet-based salient points. In *Photonics West 2001-Electronic Imaging*, 2001.

[20] Q. Tian, J. Yu, Q. Xue, and N. Sebe. A new analysis of the value of unlabeled data in semi-supervised learning for image retrieval. In *ICME*, 2004.

[21] A. Torralba, R. Fergus, and Y. Weiss. Small codes and large image databases for recognition. In *CVPR*, pages 1–8, 2008.

[22] X. Wang, M. Yang, T. Cour, S. Zhu, K. Yu, and T. X. Han. Contextual weighting for vocabulary tree based image retrieval. In *ICCV*, pages 209–216, 2011.

[23] Y. Weiss, A. Torralba, and R. Fergus. Spectral hashing. In *NIPS*, volume 9, page 6, 2008.

[24] S. Zhang, J. Huang, Y. Huang, Y. Yu, H. Li, and D. N. Metaxas. Automatic image annotation using group sparsity. In *CVPR*, pages 3312–3319, 2010.

[25] S. Zhang, M. Yang, T. Cour, K. Yu, and D. N. Metaxas. Query specific fusion for image retrieval. In *ECCV*, pages 660–673. 2012.

[26] S. Zhang, M. Yang, X. Wang, Y. Lin, and Q. Tian. Semantic-aware co-indexing for image retrieval. In *ICCV*, 2013.

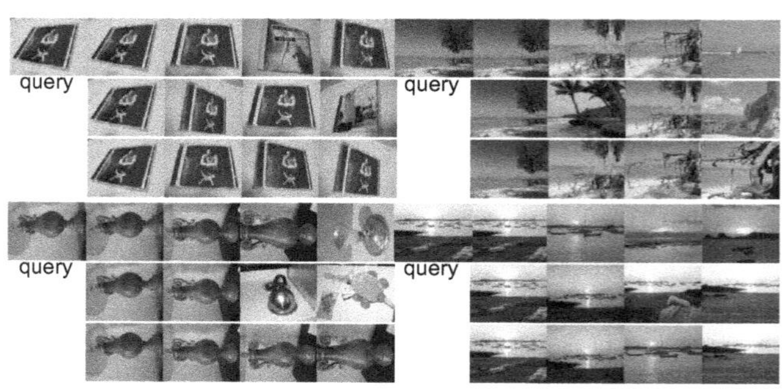

Figure 2: 4 examples of retrieval results on two datasets. The first column denotes the query image. The first, second, and third rows are retrieval results by CAFFE, VOC, and our approach, respectively. The images retrieved by CAFFE and VOC are complementary to each other and the fused results are better than merely using the individual feature.

Parallel AP Clustering and Re-ranking for Automatic Image-Text Alignment and Large-Scale Web Image Search *

Yanyun Qu
Dept of Computer Science
Xiamen University
Fujian, 361005, P.R.China
yyqu@xmu.edu

Baopeng Zhang
School of Computer and
Information Technology
Beijing Jiaotong University
Beijing, P.R.China
bpzhang@bjtu.edu.cn

Jianping Fan
Dept of Computer Science
UNC-Charlotte
Charlotte, NC 28223, USA
jfan@uncc.edu

ABSTRACT

In this paper, an automatic image-text alignment algorithm is developed for achieving more accurate indexing and retrieval of large-scale web images. First, large-scale web pages are crawled, where the informative images and their most relevant auxiliary text blocks are extracted. Second, parallel image clustering is performed to partition large-scale informative web images into a large number of clusters. By grouping the visually-similar (near-duplicate) web images into the same cluster, our parallel image clustering algorithm can significantly reduce the huge uncertainty on the relatedness between the web images and their auxiliary text terms, which can provide a good starting point for supporting automatic image-text alignment. Finally, a relevance re-ranking algorithm is developed to identify the most relevant visual text terms for the visually-similar web images in the same cluster. Our experiments on large-scale web images have obtained very positive results.

Categories and Subject escriptors
I.4.8 [**Information Storage and etrieval** : Content analysis and indexing.

General Terms
Algorithms, Performance, Experimentation

eywords
Parallel image clustering, automatic image-text alignment, relevance re-ranking, uncertainty reduction.

1. INTRODUCTION

As digital images are growing exponentially on the Internet, there is an urgent need to develop new algorithms for achieving more accurate indexing and retrieval of large-scale web images by automatically aligning the web images with their most relevant auxiliary text terms (which are extracted from the associated text documents). Achieving more accurate alignment between the web images and their auxiliary text terms can have many potential applications, such as improving Google Image and generating large-scale training images for machine learning and computer vision tasks.

Recently, great progresses were witnessed in this field. When the relatedness between the images and their associated text terms are well-defined, some pioneering work have been done to enable automatic image annotation by exploiting the image-text co-occurrences [1-3, 8-9]. However, for a web page, most of its auxiliary text terms have nothing to do with the visual content of the web images. Thus it is somewhat too idealized to assume that there is a good correspondence between the semantics of the web images and their auxiliary text terms.

Because Google Images has achieved big success on supporting keyword-based web image indexing and retrieval, some pioneering work have been done recently by performing a post-process to filter out the junk images from Google Images [4-7]. Some pioneering work have been done for achieving better associations between different medias [11-12, 15-18]. These cross-media alignment techniques have achieved better performance by coupling different information sources together, but they focus on one specific type of the image-text associations, e.g., association between human faces and names. Because of huge diversity of web images and their auxiliary text terms, these approaches for face-name alignment cannot directly applied for indexing and retrieval of large-scale web images.

Many researchers also have studied on how to better fuse multiple modalities of the web images/videos to improve image/video search results via relevance re-ranking [11-12, 15-18], where the goal for relevance re-ranking is well-defined, e.g., identifying the relatedness between the returned images/videos and the text terms for query specification.

As we know, each web page consists of web images and auxiliary text documents, which provides rich information. We focuses on finding more suitable visual text terms to improve web image indexing, where the auxiliary text documents may contain a rich vocabulary of the text terms for web content description and the relatedness between the web images and their auxiliary text terms are highly uncertain. In details, we extract the informative images and their most

*Supported by the NS of China (No. 61373077) and the NS of ujian Province (No. 2013 01257).

ICMR'15, June 23–26, 2015, Shanghai, China.
Copyright © 2015 ACM 978-1-4503-3274-3/15/06 ...$15.00.
http://dx.doi.org/10.1145/2671188.2749294.

relevant auxiliary text blocks, and then we design the parallel AP algorithm to group the informative images. After that, we develop a relevance re-ranking algorithm based on random walk scheme to identify the most relevant visual text terms for web images. Our proposed approach significantly differs from these existing work in two important respects: 1) rather than dealing with the re-ranking issue at the search time, we focus on supporting more accurate indexing of large-scale web images by achieving more precise alignment between the web images and the visual text terms, which can further result in higher accuracy rates for web image retrieval. 2) our automatic image-text alignment model is unsupervised rather than supervised,which makes it suitable to deal with large-scale web images.

This paper is organized as follows. Section 2 presents our work on extraction of informative images and their most relevant text term; Section 3 introduces our parallel clustering algorithm. Section 4 presents our relevance re-ranking algorithm based on random walk scheme; Section 5 describes our work on algorithm evaluation; We conclude in Section 6.

2. INFORMATIVE IMAGE EXTRACTION

We have crawled around $500,000$ web pages. Modern web pages may contain rich cross-medias. It is a challenging task to identify the relatedness between web images and visual text terms, because of the high diversity of web contents.

Our algorithm for informative image extraction consist of the following key components: (a) IMG tags are used to extract the web images from a web page document; (b) two filters are designed for discarding the non-informative web images.

In order to filter out the non-informative web images, both aspect ratios and image sizes are used to remove some non-informative web images. By filtering out the non-informative web images, we have extracted more than $5,000,000$ informative web images from $500,000$ web pages.

A document object model(DOM)-based method is used to extract the most relevant text blocks for each informative image. Our DOM-based method can achieve a good trade-off between the computational cost and the accuracy rate. Each informative web image is then associated with one or multiple surrounding text blocks.

3. PARALLEL IMAGE CLUSTERING

Image-text pairs can significantly narrow down the search space for extracting the relevant visual text terms for image semantics description, but the relatedness between the informative web images and the visual text terms are still uncertain. In general, the visually-similar web images may share similar semantics which can be described more effectively by using the same set of the visual text terms. Thus image clustering can be used for reducing the uncertainty on the relatedness between the informative web images and the visual text terms.

However, the computational complexity of the traditional AP clustering algorithm [10] is $O(tn^2)$, where t is the number of iterations and n is the number of images. The space complexity is $O(n^2)$. Thus, the AP clustering algorithm is prohibited for the large scale web images.

We propose the parallel AP clustering algorithm, which uses a top-down scheme for work set selection and can ensure the number of web images on each layer to be small enough for one single processor to handle. Performing a k-nearest-neighbor search is a good solution for partitioning the work set in large size into a set of sub-work-sets with smaller size. Here, we use a simple but efficient way for work set partition. We randomly start from a web image i and find its k-nearest neighbors, all these $k+1$ web images form a sub-work-set with smaller size. To ensure that all the web images are chosen by at least one sub-work-set, we maintain a frequency list $\{d(i)\}$, where $d(i)$ is used to record the chosen times of a web image i. We randomly pick a web image with the smallest value of $d(i)$ as the starting image to generate a sub-work-set, until all the web images are assigned into at least one sub-work-set and the number of sub-work-sets reaches p . The complexity of our sub-work-set selection method is $O(pn)$.

We also design the message propagation scheme. Similar to the work [13-14], we denote the forward message of exemplar k from the layer $l-1$ to l, by $\tau^{l-1}(k)$, and the feedback message of exemplar k from the layer $l+1$ to l by $\phi^{l+1}(k)$. We denote the exemplar preference k at the layer l by $c^l(k)$. We denote the responsibility by $r^l(,)$, the availability by $a^l(,)$, and the similarity by $s^l(,)$ between two exemplars at the layer l. $\tau^{l-1}(k)$ and $\phi^{l+1}(k)$ are calculated as:

$$\tau^{l-1}(k) = c^l(k) + r^l(k,k) + \sum_{k' \neq k} \max\{0, r^l(k',k)\}, \quad (1)$$

$$\phi^{l+1}(k) = \max_{k'} \left\{a^l(k,k') + s(k,k')\right\}. \quad (2)$$

Correspondingly, the responsibility updating formula is changed to:

$$r^l(i,k) = s^l(i,k) + \min\left\{\tau_i^l, -\max_{k' \neq k}(a^l(k,k') + s^l(k,k'))\right\} \quad (3)$$

The preference $\hat{c}^l(k)$ of the examplar k at the layer l is updated by: $\hat{c}^l(k) = c^l(k) + \phi^l(k)$.

By sparsifying the visual similarity matrix S, it is not necessary to pass the messages among the visually-dissimilar web images, which can dramatically reduce the communication cost for large-scale web image clustering. By performing top-down work set partition, our top-down parallel AP clustering can significantly reduce the computational cost significantly.

4. IMAGE-TEXT AUTO-ALIGNMENT

Our automatic image-text alignment algorithm takes the following major steps: (1) For the visually-similar (near-duplicate) web images in the same cluster, we first merge their associated text blocks to identify their common visual text terms and initialize their relevance scores; (2) Such relevance scores are further refined by performing random walk over a term correlation network.

Initiali ation of Term-Image elevance Score: A probabilistic approach is developed to estimate the initial relevance scores for the visual text terms. Given a visual text term t for an image cluster C, its relevance score $\rho(C,t)$ with the image cluster C is defined as:

$$\rho(C,t) = \frac{\sum_{x \in \Theta(t)} P(x,t)}{\sum_{y \in W} \sum_{r \in \Theta} P(y,r)} \quad (4)$$

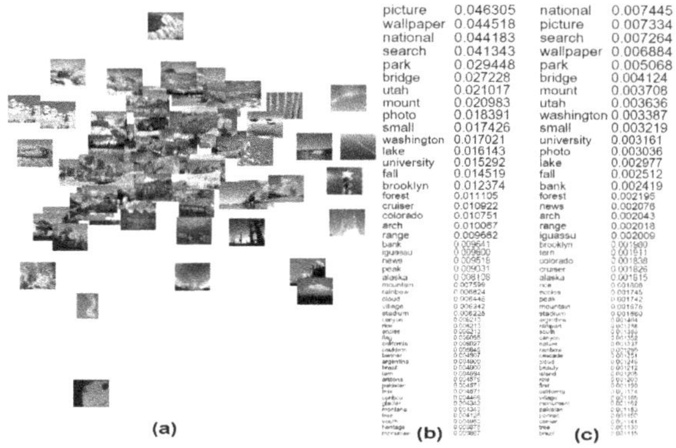

Figure 1: Image-text alignment: (a) image cluster; (b) ranked visual text terms before performing random walk; (c) re-ranked visual text terms after random walk.

where x is a web image in the cluster C, $P(x,t)$ is used to indicate the co-occurrence probability for the given visual text term $t \in W$ with the web image $x \in C$, W is the whole set of the visual text terms for the image cluster C, $\Theta(t) \subseteq \Theta$ is used to indicate a subset of the web images in the cluster C which co-occur with the given visual text term t, Θ is used to indicate the whole set of the visually-similar web images in the same cluster C.

Term Correlation Network Construction: The visual text terms in a web page are strongly inter-related and such inter-related text terms and their relevance scores should be considered jointly. Thus, a term correlation network is generated automatically for characterizing such inter-term similarities more precisely and refining the relevance scores for the inter-related visual text terms automatically. Our term correlation network $\{(V,e)\}$ contains the vertexes and the edges, and 5000 visual text terms are treated as the vertexs, and the edge weight between vertexes is their inter-term correlations which is the combination of inter-term co-occurrence correlations and inter-term visual similarities between their relevant images.

For two given visual text terms t_i and t_j, we denote their visual similarity by $\gamma(t_i,t_j)$. The co-occurrence correlation $\beta(t_i,t_j)$ between two visual text terms t_i and t_j is defined as:

$$\beta(t_i,t_j) = -P(t_i,t_j)log\frac{P(t_i,t_j)}{P(t_i)+P(t_j)} \tag{5}$$

where $P(t_i,t_j)$ is the co-occurrence probability for two visual text terms t_i and t_j, $P(t_i)$ and $P(t_j)$ are the occurrence probabilities for the visual text terms t_i and t_j.

The cross-modal inter-term correlation between t_i and t_j is finally defined as:

$$\phi(t_i,t_j) = \alpha \cdot \gamma(t_i,t_j) + (1-\alpha) \cdot \beta(t_i,t_j) \tag{6}$$

where α is the weighting factor and it is determined through cross-validation.

The combination of such cross-modal inter-term correlation can provide a powerful framework for re-ranking the relevance scores between the informative web images and the visual text terms. Our term correlation network can provide a good environment for addressing the issues of polysemy and synonyms more effectively and disambiguating the image senses precisely.

andom alk for elevance efinement: Given our term correlation network with n most significant visual text terms, we use $\rho_k(t)$ to denote the relevance score for the visual text term t at the kth iteration. The relevance scores for all these visual text terms in our term correlation network at the kth iteration can form a column vector $\overrightarrow{\rho(t)} \equiv [\rho_k(t)]_{n\times 1}$. We further define Φ as an $n \times n$ transition matrix, its element ϕ_{ij} is used to define the probability of the transition from the visual text term i to its inter-related visual text term j. ϕ_{ij} is defined as:

$$\phi_{ij} = \frac{\phi(i,j)}{\sum_k \phi(i,k)} \tag{7}$$

where $\phi(i,j)$ is the pairwise inter-term cross-modal similarity context between i and j as defined in Eq.(6).

The random walk process is thus formulated as:

$$\rho_k(t) = \theta \sum_{j\in\Omega_j} \rho_{k-1}(j)\phi_{tj} + (1-\theta)\rho(C,t) \tag{8}$$

where Ω_j is the first-order nearest neighbors of the visual text term j on the term correlation network, $\rho(C,t)$ is the initial relevance score for the given visual text term t and θ is a weight parameter. This random walk process is terminated when the relevance scores converge.

For a given image cluster C, all its visual text terms are re-ranked according to their relevance scores. The top-k visual text terms, which have higher relevance scores with the image semantics, are selected for indexing the visually-similar web images in the given image cluster C. The experimental results for re-ranking the visual text terms are given in Fig. 1. From these experimental results, one can observe that our image-text alignment algorithm can effectively identify the most relevant visual text terms for web image indexing.

5. ALGORITHM & SYSTEM EVALUATION

All our experiments are conducted on an image-text parallel set comprising around 500,000 web pages and 5,000,000 informative images. To assess the effectiveness of our proposed algorithms, our algorithm evaluation work focuses on: (a) comparing the performance differences between our image-text alignment algorithm and other well-accepted approaches; (b) assessing the effectiveness of image clustering and random walk on our algorithm for text-image alignment.

The accuracy rate ϱ is used to assess the effectiveness of the algorithms for image-text alignment, which is the ratio between the number of correct alignment images by the algorithm and the total number of web images. It is hard to manually label large-scale benchmark image set for our algorithm evaluation task. To avoid this problem, an image navigation system is designed to allow users to interactively provide their assessments of the relevances between the web images and the re-ranked visual text terms.

To assess the effectiveness of image clustering and random walk on the accuracy rate for text-image alignment, we have compared the accuracy rates for our text-image alignment algorithm under three different scenarios: (a) our algorithm without parallel image clustering; (b) our algorithm without random walk; (c) our algorithm with both parallel image clustering and random walk. As shown in Fig. 2, one can observe that incorporating parallel image clustering for uncertainty reduction and performing random walk for

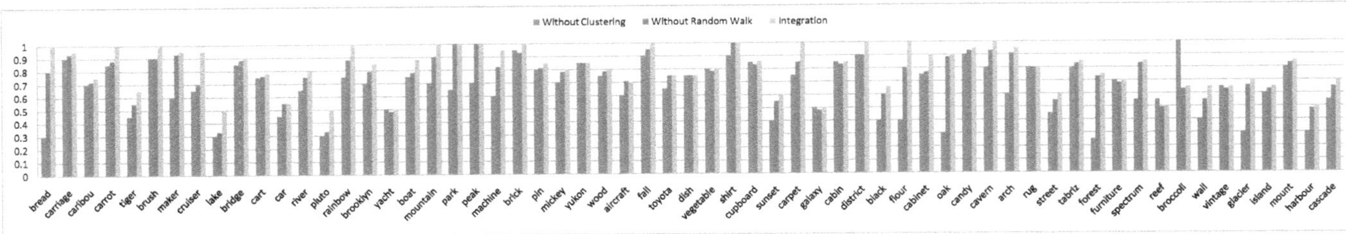

Figure 2: Text-image alignment accuracy rate, where only top 20 images are evaluated interactively.

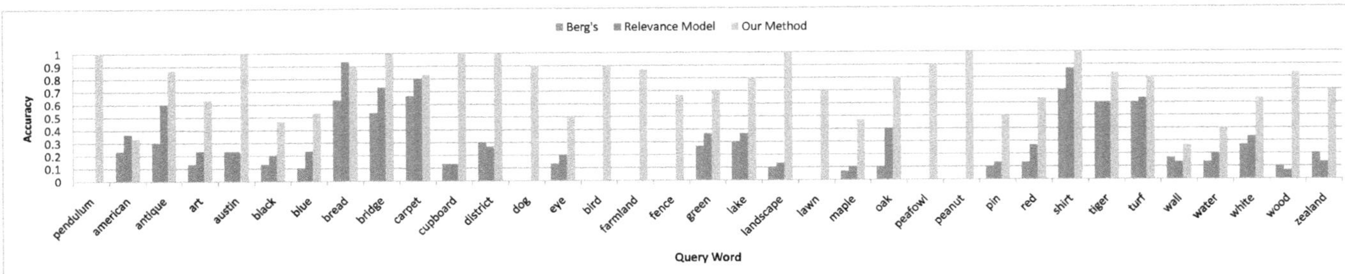

Figure 3: Comparison on the text-image alignment accuracy rates: (a) Berg's method; (b) relevance model; and (c) our method, where only top 30 images are evaluated interactively.

relevance re-ranking can significantly improve the accuracy rates for text-image alignment.

Furthermore, we have compared three approaches for image-text alignment: our approach *versus* Berg's approach [2] and cross-media relevance model [1,9]. As shown in Fig. 3, one can observe that our image-text alignment approach can significantly improve the accuracy rates on identifying the most relevant visual text terms for image semantics description and web image indexing. On the other hand, both the Berg's approach and the cross-media relevance modeling approach may not be able to find the most relevant visual text terms for web image indexing. It demonstrates that such loose image-text pairs cannot be treated as the reliable training set for learning the joint image-word relevance model accurately.

6. CONCLUSIONS

By identifying the most relevant visual text terms for indexing and retrieval of large-scale web images, our automatic image-text alignment algorithm can achieve more accurate indexing of large-scale web images, which may further provide many potential applications, such as enabling more effective keyword-based web image retrieval, harvesting large-scale web images for classifier training, and achieving cross-media alignment.

7. REFERENCES

[1] S. eng, . avrenko, . anmatha, " ultiple ernoulli relevance models for image and video annotation", AC S , 2004.

[2] T. . erg, A.C. erg, . Edwards, D.A. orsyth, "Who's in the picture", N PS, 2004.

[3] N. hou, . an, "Automatic image-text alignment for large-scale web image indexing and retrieval", *Pattern Recognition*, vol. 48, no.1, pp.205-219, 2015.

[4] . ergus, . ei- ei, P. Perona, A. isserman, " earning object categories from oogle's image search", EEE C P , 2006.

[5] D. Cai, . e, . i, W.-Y. a, .- . Wen, " ierarchical clustering of WWW image search results using visual, textual, and link information", AC ultimedia, 2004.

[6] .- . Wang, W.-Y. a, .- . ue, . i, " ulti-modal similarity propagation and its application for web image retrieval", AC ultimedia, 2004.

[7] Y. ao, . Peng, . uo, D.A. eim, . an, "An interactive approach for filtering out junk images from keyword-based oogle search results", *IEEE Trans. Circuits Syst. Video Techn.*, vol. 19, no.12, pp. 1851-1865, 2009.

[8] . an, Y. Shen, N. hou, Y. ao, " arvesting large-scale weakly-tagged image databases from the web", EEE C P , pp. 802-809, 2010.

[9] P. Pham, . oens, T. Tuytelaars, "Cross-media alignment of names and faces", *IEEE Trans. on Multimedia*, vol.12, no.1, 2010.

[10] . rey, D. Dueck, "Clustering by passing messages between data points", *Science*, vol.315, pp.972-976, 2007.

[11] D. iu, .-S, ua, . Yang, . Wang, .- . hang, "Tag ranking", WWW, 2009.

[12] Y. Shen, . an, " everaging loosely-tagged images and inter-object correlations for tag recommendation.", AC ultimedia, pp.5-14, 2010.

[13] . ivoni, C. Chung, . . rey, " ierarchical affinity propagation", UA , 2011.

[14] Y. ia, . Wang, C. hang, .S. ua, " inding image exemplars using fast sparse affinity propagation", AC ultimedia, 2008.

[15] W. su, . ennedy, S. . Chang, " ideo search reranking via information bottleneck principle", AC ultimedia, 2006.

[16] N. hou, Y. Shen, . Peng, . eng, . an, " everaging auxiliary text terms for automatic image annotation", WWW, 2011.

[17] . iu, W. ai, .-S. ua, Y. uang, S. i, " ideo search re-ranking via multi-graph propagation", AC ultimedia, 2007.

[18] C. Wang, . ing, . hang, . . hang, " mage annotation refinement using random walk with restarts", AC ultimedia, 2006.

Accio: A Data Set for Face Track Retrieval in Movies Across Age

Esam Ghaleb[1], Makarand Tapaswi[2], Ziad Al-Halah[2]
Hazım Kemal Ekenel[1], Rainer Stiefelhagen[2]
[1]Istanbul Technical University, Istanbul, Turkey
[2]Karlsruhe Institute of Technology, Karlsruhe, Germany
{ghalebe, ekenel}@itu.edu.tr, {tapaswi, ziad.al-halah, rainer.stiefelhagen}@kit.edu

ABSTRACT

Video face recognition is a very popular task and has come a long way. The primary challenges such as illumination, resolution and pose are well studied through multiple data sets. However there are no video-based data sets dedicated to study the effects of aging on facial appearance. We present a challenging face track data set, Harry Potter Movies Aging Data set (Accio[1]), to study and develop age invariant face recognition methods for videos. Our data set not only has strong challenges of pose, illumination and distractors, but also spans a period of ten years providing substantial variation in facial appearance. We propose two primary tasks: within and across movie face track retrieval; and two protocols which differ in their freedom to use external data. We present baseline results for the retrieval performance using a state-of-the-art face track descriptor. Our experiments show clear trends of reduction in performance as the age gap between the query and database increases. We will make the data set publicly available for further exploration in age-invariant video face recognition.

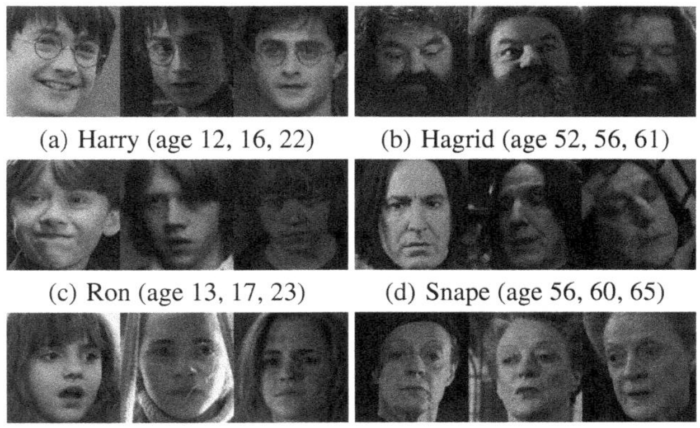

(a) Harry (age 12, 16, 22) (b) Hagrid (age 52, 56, 61)

(c) Ron (age 13, 17, 23) (d) Snape (age 56, 60, 65)

(e) Hermione (age 11, 15, 21) (f) McGonagall (age 67, 71, 76)

Figure 1: Change in character appearance across the movies

1. INTRODUCTION

Face recognition in videos has received lots of attention in recent years, and is a challenging topic in computer vision [2, 5, 18]. It has many practical applications: ranging from identifying suspects in surveillance footage [6] to identifying TV characters [5]. There have been significant developments to tackle problems of illumination, resolution, pose and expression [4, 16, 18].

In this paper, we focus our attention to another challenge which is often ignored – changes in face appearance due to aging. While there are multiple still image data sets which analyze age variation (FGNET [1], MORPH [20], CACD [3]), to the best of our knowledge, there is no video face recognition data set with age variation. Often, face track recognition proves to be harder than still image face recognition due to effects of tracking, motion blur and drastic pose variation. Such a data set will help untangle the challenge of age variation catering specially to the broadcast video domain.

We introduce and make available a large, and challenging face track dataset (see Sec. 3) to further evaluate and develop age invariant face recognition systems, specifically for videos. The data set is gathered from the eight movies of the Harry Potter series. The movies span a period of ten years and present a strong setting to study the effects of age variation along with all other challenges of video face recognition. Furthermore, the data set features a large number of face tracks with young faces (age < 20) where the effects of aging are most prominent. Along with a large number of named characters with varying age groups, the data set also contains many unknown tracks which act as distractors.

Fig. 1 shows the changes in facial appearance for six characters taken from movies 1, 4 and 8. Note that these images are deliberately chosen to have frontal pose and decent illumination to highlight the variation in their age.

As a benchmark for the face track recognition, we present two primary scenarios: (i) face track retrieval within movies; and (ii) face track retrieval across movies. Similar to LFW [10] or YouTube Faces [23] we also propose to divide the usage of data in a restricted and unrestricted setting. Sec. 4 presents more details about the challenges, and some baseline results.

2. RELATED WORK

In the following, we first discuss publicly available data sets for improving face recognition across ages. We examine the area related to face track retrieval in multimedia data, and finally discuss some prominent works in age-invariant face recognition.

2.1 Data sets

Previous face recognition data sets which focus explicitly on the problem of aging are all on still images [1, 3, 20, 21]. Data sets

[1]The Summoning Charm *Accio* in the Harry Potter series retrieves an object at a distance, here used to signify face track retrieval.

ICMR '15, June 23 - 26, 2015, Shanghai, China

ACM 978-1-4503-3274-3/15/06 $15.00.
http://dx.doi.org/10.1145/2671188.2749296

for video face track recognition are often obtained from one movie or one TV series season [2, 5] and thus do not present challenges of age variation. Popular face (track) verification data sets such as LFW [10] or YouTube Faces [23] do not discuss the problem of matching faces across age. To the best of our knowledge this is the first video face recognition data set which is obtained from challenging settings and shows clear trends of the effects of aging.

2.2 Face track retrieval in videos

Among the first popular works in face track retrieval is [22]. They detect frontal faces, track them using a region-tracking method, and use the SIFT descriptor around 4 facial landmarks for matching. This enables to search a query face track in the entire video and find corresponding shots in which the person appears. In a similar retrieval scenario, [7] includes non-frontal faces, and [13] presents a compact descriptor to match face tracks. However, after the seminal paper by Everingham *et al.* [5], most works focus on assigning a name to all face tracks (*e.g.* [2]).

2.3 Age invariant face recognition

There are multiple studies which consider the problem of aging in face recognition. Most systems can be divided in two categories:

(i) *Generative* approaches [8, 12, 17, 19] simulate the face image at the target age and then perform face recognition. Typically they build 2-D or 3-D generative models to synthesize face aging. For example, [19] uses face landmarks to estimate facial growth parameters and predicts the appearance at a certain age.,

(ii) *Discriminative* approaches such as [3, 11, 14, 15] use learning methods to build age invariant face recognition systems. For example, recently, Chen *et al.* [3] use a reference set representation for each person, his/her age, and the face landmark. To achieve an age-invariant representation, they model the problem as least squares and pool across the age space.

Apart from previous methods, there are examples of modeling the appearance through latent spaces. For example, Gong *et al.* [9] propose to use two latent factors: an age-invariant identity factor, and an age factor affected by aging. The observed face appearance is modeled as a combination of the two, and separating the observation allows to perform recognition using the identity part.

3. DATA SET

We present the Harry Potter Movies Aging Data *Accio* to study and develop age invariant face recognition and retrieval methods.

3.1 Data source

This data set is collected and organized using the eight Harry Potter movies that were released in a period of ten years – 2001 to 2011. Each movie in itself contains multiple interesting challenges (i) *illumination* - large number of bright and dark scenes; (ii) *pose* - many non-frontal tracks, actors typically do not look at cameras; (iii) *resolution* - tracks from 25 to 500 pixels; and (iv) *distractors* - roughly 40% of all face tracks are *unknown* characters which appear in the background making the problem an open set task. Finally, the use of all eight movies acts as a good source of variation in the facial appearance due to *aging*.

To obtain the face tracks, we first detect video shot boundaries. Within each shot, following [2] we perform tracking-by-detection using a particle filter. We use multi-pose detectors which cover the entire range of *pan* and *roll* face angles.

The data set contains a large number of tracks of young actors (age < 20). We believe that this is an important aspect since most of the changes in facial appearance occur early in life. Fig. 2 presents the age variation for multiple actors. Please note that the figure plots only those actors which appear in at least 2 movies.

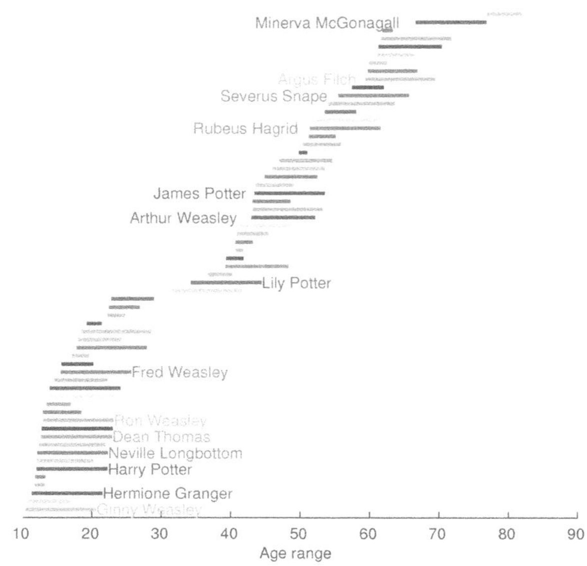

Figure 2: Actors age progression. Each line represents the age span for that actor appearing in the movies.

Table 1: Number of tracks and characters across the movies

	HP-1	HP-2	HP-3	HP-4	HP-5	HP-6	HP-7	HP-8
# characters	36	42	34	44	47	41	56	54
# face tracks	5249	5335	3919	7616	5850	3354	2910	4231
# unknown tracks	2006	1874	1437	4237	2316	1116	623	2025
# named tracks	3243	3461	2482	3379	3534	2238	2287	2206

3.2 Face track descriptors

Face tracks of the data set are encoded using state-of-the-art Video Fisher Vector Faces (VF^2) descriptor [18]. VF^2 is a face track representation that aggregates a large set of dense SIFT features which are extracted from all the face images of the track. We follow the steps and parameters from [18] and use Root-SIFT with a stride of 1 pixel. The resulting 128 dimensional feature is down-projected via PCA to 64 dimensions and augmented with the spatial location (x, y). A Gaussian Mixture Model (GMM) of 512 Gaussians is trained on all the face tracks and Fisher encoding is performed. This yields a $2 \times 512 \times 66 = 67584$ dimensional descriptor for each track. To compare two tracks we use the standard Euclidean distance between two Fisher vector descriptors for our baseline experiments.

3.3 Statistics

Table 1 presents the number of characters, the number of tracks in each movie and a split betweeen *named* and *unknown* (distractor) tracks. The dataset contains in total of 38,464 face tracks. 22,830 (59.4%) of these face tracks are labeled with one of 121 character identities as they appear in the film series. The rest of the face tracks (40.6%) belong to un-named cast and are treated as distractors for the retrieval evaluation.

Each movie in the Harry Potter film series has varying number of characters and number of tracks. The three main characters (*Harry Potter*, *Hermione Granger*, and *Ron Weasley*) encompass roughly 40-60% of all face tracks in each movie.

The actors span a range of age from 10 to 88 years. Note that we compute the age based on the movie release date and the birth

Table 2: Actors age distribution

	10-19	20-39	40-49	50+	Young	Adults
# characters	33	34	26	44	33	92
# labeled tracks	12,598	4,303	1,728	3,636	12,598	9,667

Table 3: Comparison of age-invariant face recognition data sets

	video?	#images	#people	Age span
FGNET [1]	No	1,002	82	0-45
MORPH [20]	No	55,134	13,618	0-5
CACD [3]	No	163,446	2,000	0-10
Accio (Ours)	Yes	38,464 tracks	121	0-10

year, which can add a slight discrepancy up to a couple years. The largest age difference between face tracks for the same actor is 10 years for actors which appear in both the first and last movie.

Table 2 shows the distribution of tracks and number of characters across various age spans. We see an equitable distribution of characters among the various age groups. However, most of the tracks belong to the first 10-19 (*Young*) age range.

Finally, we present in Table 3 a comparison between existing data sets. Note that unlike other data sets, ours works with face tracks, which on average are 50 frames (2 seconds) long thus yielding over 1.9 million face images.

4. EXPERIMENTS

We first define the evaluation protocol, followed by baseline experiments for face track retrieval. The retrieval experiments are evaluated using two popular measures: (i) mean average precision (MAP), and (ii) precision @ k (number of correct results in top k).

4.1 Evaluation protocol

Tasks The face track retrieval is performed as two tasks.

1. *Within* movies: In this setting, we look at individual movies one at a time. Each named track in the movie is used as a query, while the remainder (other named tracks + unknown tracks) from the same movie form the database. This setting evaluates the retrieval performance subject to typical face recognition challenges such as pose and illumination.

2. *Across* movies: In this setting we analyze the effect of age variation among the actors by evaluating face track retrieval across movies. We consider each named track within one movie (*e.g.* HP-1) as a query, while all tracks of a different movie (*e.g.* HP-2) form the database.

Benchmarks We suggest two protocols which involve both the above tasks, however vary in the extent to which data can be used to learn supervised or unsupervised models.

(i) *Restricted*: In this protocol the experiments should not use any external data. That is, only the query track is available as a positive training sample and retrieval models should not be trained using other *Accio* face tracks, or any external face images/tracks. This can be used for example to compare different face track descriptors, or perform automatic and unsupervised methods such as query expansion and domain adaptation.

(ii) *Unrestricted*: In this protocol the researchers are allowed to use *external* data for training models, for example to model the changes in facial appearance through aging. However, no other tracks from the *Accio* data set (except the query track) are to be used for training actor models.

Table 4: Within movies evaluation

	HP-1	HP-2	HP-3	HP-4	HP-5	HP-6	HP-7	HP-8
p @ 1	90.8	89.3	90.9	85.1	89.4	91.1	91.3	89.4
p @ 5	81.5	79.0	79.1	72.3	79.3	80.4	82.1	78.6
p @ 10	75.9	71.6	70.2	64.5	72.0	72.2	75.3	69.7
p @ 20	71.9	64.0	61.5	57.3	63.7	64.3	70.7	63.0
p @ 50	67.9	57.6	53.0	54.7	59.4	55.8	68.0	57.2
p @ 100	70.9	54.8	53.1	58.5	55.5	51.1	62.8	53.0
MAP	42.40	31.73	31.19	28.36	32.09	30.38	38.55	33.21

Table 5: Across movies face track retrieval performance (MAP)

	HP-1	HP-2	HP-3	HP-4	HP-5	HP-6	HP-7	HP-8
HP-1	42.4	33.1	26.8	24.5	21.5	22.2	27.4	20.0
HP-2	32.1	31.7	22.9	20.1	18.6	19.8	23.2	17.9
HP-3	23.0	20.8	31.2	19.9	18.1	21.0	23.4	16.2
HP-4	27.2	23.3	27.1	28.4	20.9	23.0	24.4	20.5
HP-5	20.3	18.5	22.0	17.4	32.1	22.5	25.7	20.8
HP-6	21.4	18.3	24.3	19.8	23.7	30.4	24.5	17.9
HP-7	24.3	20.8	24.7	19.6	26.4	24.8	38.5	25.5
HP-8	19.9	18.8	20.2	18.1	21.7	20.8	28.4	33.2

Finally, if the data is used in a different manner that does not comply with either of the two previous protocols, for example the face tracks can be used for a classification task [5], the researchers can refer to this as a *free-for-all* scheme.

4.2 Within movies face track retrieval

We now present the results of within movie face track retrieval (Task 1) under the restricted protocol. In each movie, the labeled tracks are used as a query, while all tracks from the same movie form the database. For example, in HP-1, we have 3243 tracks (taken one at a time) as query and 5248 tracks (the number of tracks minus the query) as part of the database.

Table 4 presents the performance of retrieval on the eight movies. Precision @ k (p @ k) values are presented in multiple steps [1, 5, 10, 20, 50, 100], while the MAP is used as the overall performance indicator. As expected the performance for small values of k is much higher and this can be used to perform query expansion.

4.3 Across movies face track retrieval

While the previous section evaluated performance through challenges of pose and illumination, we now look primarily at the problem of aging (Task 2). We expect that the retrieval performance is good to fair when the age difference is small (within same movie, or $\pm$ 1 movie), while it deteriorates as we compare across a large time gap (*e.g.* HP-1 vs. HP-8).

Table 5 presents overall retrieval performance in MAP comparing all eight movies. Rows represent the movie from which query tracks are obtained, while the tracks of the movie in columns serves as the database (*e.g.* query from HP-1 and database from HP-7 shows a MAP of 27.4). As can be seen in the table, the larger the age gap between the query and database the MAP performance reduces. HP-7 appears to be an exception and this could be attributed to the fact that this movie has the least number of tracks, many ($\sim$60%) of which belong to the three primary characters. The diagonal represents within movie performance and is the same as the last row of Table 4.

In Table 6, we consider all queries from the first movie HP-1 and split them into two based on age. Tracks of young actors (age < 20) when used as queries tend to perform worse in the retrieval across

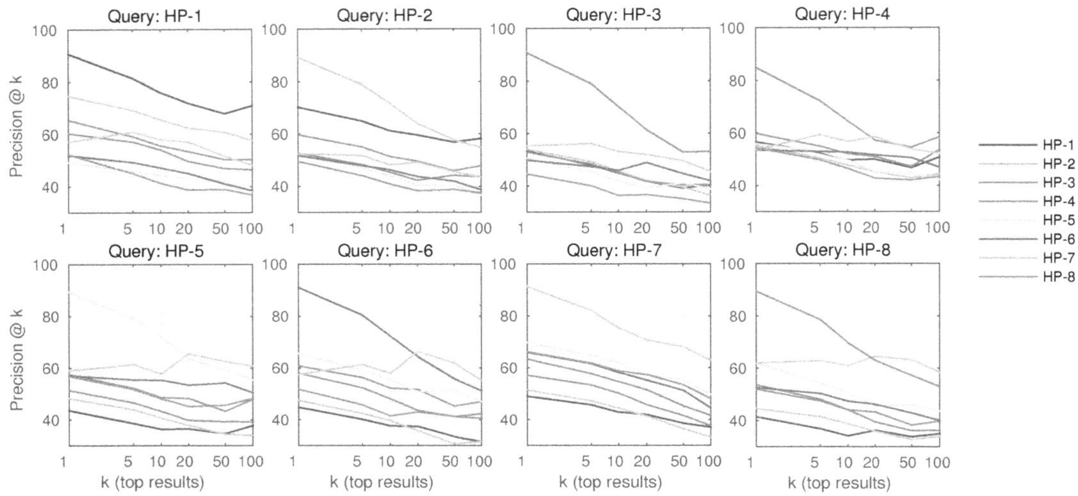

Figure 3: Precision @ k results for across movies retrieval. This figure is best viewed in color.

Table 6: Comparison of MAP scores for adult vs. young actors. The queries are taken here from HP-1 movie.

	HP-1	HP-2	HP-3	HP-4	HP-5	HP-6	HP-7	HP-8
Adult	47.5	40.9	33.6	32.5	30.5	29.8	23.0	21.8
Young	40.9	31.2	25.2	22.9	19.3	20.8	28.4	19.6

movies as compared to tracks of adults. Empirically we see that the face appearance changes more during the youth years and thus has a stronger influence (more errors) on the retrieval performance.

Finally, we present the precision @ k scores for each movie in Fig. 3. Each subplot represents queries from a single movie (mentioned in the title) and the databases are all movies (plotted as separate lines). For any subplot, note how the precision is higher for movies around the movie from which the query tracks are selected. For example, choosing queries from HP-1, the best performance is seen when comparing against tracks from HP-2, HP-3, HP-4. Similarly, for queries from HP-2, the performance against tracks from HP-1 and HP-3 is better than other movies. There are some exceptions, specially at smaller values of k, however the general trend is fairly clear. Together with Table 5, the analysis is a clear indication that age variation is a strongly felt effect in the data set.

5. CONCLUSION

We introduce the *Accio* data set for analyzing the effect of aging in video face recognition methods. *Accio* features 121 characters spread over multiple age groups, and has more than 38,000 face tracks of which a large pool (40%) are distractor tracks. We present two primary tasks for evaluation: within and across movie face track retrieval. Depending on whether the external data is used or not, we present two protocols: unrestricted and restricted. We see a steady decline in the retrieval performance as the age gap between the query and database increases. The data can be downloaded at cvhci.anthropomatik.kit.edu/projects/mma.

Acknowledgments This work was funded by the German Research Foundation under contract no. STI-598/2-1; TUBITAK within the CHIST-ERA project titled CAMOMILE, project no. 112E176; and a Marie Curie FP7 Integration Grant in the 7th EU Framework.

6. REFERENCES

[1] FG-NET Aging Database.

[2] M. Bäuml, M. Tapaswi, and R. Stiefelhagen. Semi-supervised Learning with Constraints for Person Identification in Multimedia Data. In *CVPR*, 2013.

[3] B.-C. Chen, C.-S. Chen, and W. H. Hsu. Cross-Age Reference Coding for Age-Invariant Face Recognition and Retrieval. In *ECCV*, 2014.

[4] D. Chen, X. Cao, F. Wen, and J. Sun. Blessing of Dimensionality: High-Dimensional Feature and Its Efficient Compression for Face Verification. In *CVPR*, 2013.

[5] M. Everingham, J. Sivic, and A. Zisserman. "Hello ! My name is ... Buffy" – Automatic Naming of Characters in TV Video. In *BMVC*, 2006.

[6] R. Feris, R. Bobbitt, L. Brown, and S. Pankati. Attribute-based People Search: Lessons Learnt from a Practical Surveillance System. In *ICMR*, 2014.

[7] M. Fischer, H. K. Ekenel, and R. Stiefelhagen. Person re-identification in TV series using robust face recognition and user feedback. *Multimedia Tools and Applications*, 2010.

[8] X. Geng, Z.-H. Zhou, and K. Smith-Miles. Automatic Age Estimation Based on Facial Aging Patterns. *T-PAMI*, 29(12):2234–2240, 2007.

[9] D. Gong, Z. Li, D. Lin, J. Liu, and X. Tang. Hidden Factor Analysis for Age Invariant Face Recognition. In *ICCV*, 2013.

[10] G. B. Huang, M. Ramesh, T. Berg, and E. Learned-Miller. Labeled Faces in the Wild: A Database for Studying Face Recognition in Unconstrained Environments. Technical Report 07-49, Univ. of Massachusetts, Amherst, 2007.

[11] B. Klare and A. K. Jain. Face recognition across time lapse: On learning feature subspaces. In *Intl. Joint Conf. on Biometrics*, 2011.

[12] A. Lanitis, C. Draganova, and C. Christodoulou. Comparing different classifiers for automatic age estimation. *IEEE Trans Syst Man Cybern: B Cybern*, 34(1):621–628, Feb 2004.

[13] Y. Li, R. Wang, Z. Cui, S. Shan, and X. Chen. Compact Video Code and Its Application to Robust Face Retrieval in TV-Series. In *BMVC*, 2014.

[14] Z. Li, U. Park, and A. K. Jain. A Discriminative Model for Age Invariant Face Recognition. *IEEE Trans on Inf. Forensics Security*, 6(3), 2011.

[15] H. Ling, S. Soatto, N. Ramanathan, and D. Jacobs. Face Verification Across Age Progression Using Discriminative Methods. *IEEE Trans on Inf. Forensics Security*, 5(1):82–91, 2010.

[16] E. G. Ortiz, A. Wright, and M. Shah. Face Recognition in Movie Trailers via Mean Sequence Sparse Representation-based Classification. In *CVPR*, 2013.

[17] U. Park, Y. Tong, and A. Jain. Age-Invariant Face Recognition. *T-PAMI*, 32(5):947–954, May 2010.

[18] O. M. Parkhi, K. Simonyan, A. Vedaldi, and A. Zisserman. A Compact and Discriminative Face Track Descriptor. In *CVPR*, 2014.

[19] N. Ramanathan and R. Chellappa. Modeling Age Progression in Young Faces. In *CVPR*, 2006.

[20] K. Ricanek and T. Tesafaye. Morph: A longitudinal image database of normal adult age-progression. In *IEEE FG*, 2006.

[21] S. Setty and et al. Indian Movie Face Database: A Benchmark for Face Recognition Under Wide Variations. In *NCVPRIPG*, 2013.

[22] J. Sivic, M. Everingham, and A. Zisserman. Person spotting: video shot retrieval for face sets. In *CIVR*, 2005.

[23] L. Wolf, T. Hassner, and I. Maoz. Face Recognition in Unconstrained Videos with Matched Background Similarity. In *CVPR*, 2011.

A Two-step Approach to Cross-modal Hashing

Kaiye Wang, Wei Wang, Liang Wang*, Ran He
Center for Research on Intelligent Perception and Computing
National Lab of Pattern Recognition
Institute of Automation, Chinese Academy of Sciences, Beijing 100190, China
{kaiye.wang,wangwei,wangliang,rhe}@nlpr.ia.ac.cn *

ABSTRACT

With the rapid growth of multimedia data, it is very desirable to effectively and efficiently search objects of interest across different modalities from large scale databases. Cross-modal hashing provides a very promising way to address such problem. In this paper, we propose a two-step cross-modal hashing approach to obtain compact hash codes and learn hash functions from multimodal data. Our approach decomposes the cross-modal hashing problem into two steps: generating hash code and learning hash function. In the first step, we obtain the hash codes for all modalities of data via a joint multi-modal graph, which takes into consideration both the intra-modality and inter-modality similarity. In the second step, learning hashing function is formulated as a binary classification problem. We train binary classifiers to predict the hash code for any data object unseen before. Experimental results on two cross-modal datasets show the effectiveness of our proposed approach.

Categories and Subject Descriptors

H.3.3 [**Information Storage and Retrieval**]: Information Search and Retrieval

Keywords

Similarity Search, Cross-modal Hashing, Joint Multimodal Graph, Support Vector Machine

1. INTRODUCTION

In recent years, there has been a massive explosion of multimedia data on the web, particularly on social websites. It is common that data related to the same content or object exist in different modalities (e.g., text, image, audio). When users search information by submitting a query of any media type, they may expect to receive results across various modalities, which is more comprehensive given that different modalities of data can provide complementary information to each other. However, traditional retrieval methods only perform the similarity search of the same media type. Hence, a demanding requirement for promoting information retrieval is to develop a new retrieval model that can support the similarity search for multimodal data. Recently, several approaches [8, 6] have been proposed to perform the cross-modal retrieval task. However, most of the existing cross-modal retrieval techniques are based on the brute-force linear search, which is time-consuming for large scale datasets.

A practical way to speed up the similarity search is hashing. Existing hashing methods can be categorized into uni-modal hashing, multi-view hashing and cross-modal hashing. Representative hashing methods on single modal data include spectral hashing (SH) [11], self-taught hashing [13], iterative quantization hashing (ITQ) [4], and so on. The approaches mentioned above focus on learning hash functions for data objects with homogeneous features. However, in real world applications, we often extract multiple types of features with different properties from data objects. Accordingly, multi-view hashing methods (e.g., CHMIS [12] and MFH [10]) leverage information contained in different features to learn more accurate hash codes.

Cross-modal hashing methods aim to discover correlations among different modalities of data to enable cross-modal similarity search [1, 5, 14, 9]. To the best of our knowledge, Bronstein et al. [1] propose the first cross-modal hashing method, called cross-modal similarity sensitive hashing (CMSSH). CMSSH learns hash functions for the bimodal case in a standard boosting manner. In [5], Kumar et al. propose a cross-view hashing (CVH), which performs cross-modal hashing via canonical correlation analysis. Recently, Rastegari et al. [9] propose a predictable dual-view hashing (PDH) algorithm, which maps the data from each modality to a common Hamming space, while maintaining the predictability of binary codes. However, the three methods mentioned above only consider the inter-modality similarity but ignore the intra-modality similarity. Although multimodal latent binary embedding (MLBE) [14] considers both the intra-modality and inter-modality similarity, it is easy to get trapped in local minima during learning process, which naturally results in bad performance.

In this paper, we propose a novel Two-Step Cross-Modal Hashing (TSCMH) approach, which can effectively exploit both the intra-modality and inter-modality similarity. In the first step, we feed different modalities of data into a joint multimodal graph, in which the homogeneous and heterogeneous edges are constructed according to the intra-modality

*The corresponding author.

ICMR'15, June 23–26, 2015, Shanghai, China.

http://dx.doi.org/10.1145/2671188.2749297.

similarity relationship and inter-modality similarity relationship respectively. Then, we obtain the hash codes for all modalities of data via the multimodal graph. In the second step, we learn hash functions in a standard binary classification manner, based on the hash codes obtained in the first step. Experimental results on two publicly available cross-modal datasets show the promise of our proposed approach.

2. TWO-STEP CROSS-MODAL HASHING

In this section, we describe the details of the proposed Two-Step Cross-Modal Hashing (TSCMH) approach. The main idea of TSCMH goes as follows. Different modalities of data are firstly converted into their new representations in a common Hamming space, while preserving the intra-modality similarity and the inter-modality similarity. Then, we utilize linear Support Vector Machine to learn hash functions in a binary classification manner for any data object unseen before. Consequently, we can perform fast cross-modal similarity search by efficient binary code matching in the common Hamming space.

Suppose that we have a collection of data from M different modalities, i.e., $X^p = [\mathbf{x}_1^p, \mathbf{x}_2^p, ..., \mathbf{x}_{N_p}^p] \in \mathbb{R}^{d_p \times N_p}, p = 1, 2, ..., M$, where N_p is the number of the data objects from the p-th modality, and d_p is the number of the feature dimension. $Y^p = [\mathbf{y}_1^p, \mathbf{y}_2^p, ..., \mathbf{y}_{N_p}^p] \in \{-1, 1\}^{l \times N_p}$ denotes the corresponding hash code matrix of X^p, with $\mathbf{y}_i^p$ being the hash code for $\mathbf{x}_i^p$. l is the bit number of the hash code.

2.1 Generating hash code

To well model the structure of the multimodal data, we feed different modalities of data into a joint multimodal graph according to two kinds of similarity relationships among the multimodal data. The key problem in generating hash code is similarity preserving.

1) Intra-modality similarity relationship: we hope to preserve the intra-modality similarity relationship among data points within each single modality, i.e., the hash codes of data points with the neighborhood relationship should be similar to each other. To preserve the local structural information within each single modality, a kNN similarity graph is constructed here. The similarity matrix W^p within the p-th modality is defined as below:

$$W_{ij}^p = \begin{cases} \exp(-z_{ij}^p/2\sigma^2), & \text{if } \mathbf{x}_i^p \in N_k(\mathbf{x}_j^p) \text{ or } \mathbf{x}_j^p \in N_k(\mathbf{x}_i^p) \\ 0, & \text{otherwise} \end{cases} \tag{1}$$

where z_{ij}^p is the Euclidean distance between $\mathbf{x}_i^p$ and $\mathbf{x}_j^p$, i.e., $z_{ij}^p = \left\|\mathbf{x}_i^p - \mathbf{x}_j^p\right\|^2$, and $N_k(\mathbf{x}_i^p)$ denotes the set of k nearest neighbors of $\mathbf{x}_i^p$.

2) Inter-modality similarity relationship: it is well known that although different modalities of data have different representations and are in different feature spaces, they share similar semantics if they are related to the same content or object, which can be understood as the inter-modality similarity relationship. To measure the similarity between different modalities of data, we intend to learn a common Hamming space, in which different modalities of data having similar semantics should have similar hash codes. To achieve this goal, we propose to preserve the inter-modality similarity relationship when learning the common Hamming space. According to the inter-modality similarity relationship, we define the similarity matrix W^{pq} between the p-th modality and the q-th modality as follows:

$$W_{ij}^{pq} = \begin{cases} 1, & \text{if } \mathbf{x}_i^p \text{ has similar semantics to } \mathbf{x}_j^q \\ 0, & \text{otherwise} \end{cases} \tag{2}$$

According to the two kinds of similarity relationships, we feed all different modalities of data into a joint multimodal graph. The overall similarity matrix W is defined as follows:

$$W = \begin{bmatrix} W^1 & \alpha W^{12} & \dots & \alpha W^{1M} \\ \alpha W^{21} & W^2 & \dots & \alpha W^{2M} \\ \vdots & \vdots & \ddots & \vdots \\ \alpha W^{M1} & \alpha W^{M2} & \dots & W^M \end{bmatrix} \tag{3}$$

where α is a parameter which balances the effect of the intra-modality similarity and the inter-modality similarity. Here we treat the inter-modality similarity matrices equally.

With the constructed multimodal graph, we intend to exploit the intra-modality similarity relationships and the inter-modality similarity relationships in the graph to learn the hash codes for different modalities of data. The criterion is that data points with similarity relationship should have similar hash codes, so the objective function for generating the hash codes is defined as follows:

$$\begin{aligned} \min_{Y^p, p=1,...M} \ & \frac{1}{2} \sum_{p=1}^{M} \sum_{i,j=1}^{N_p} W_{ij}^p ||\mathbf{y}_i^p - \mathbf{y}_j^p||^2 \\ & + \frac{\alpha}{2} \sum_{p=1}^{M} \sum_{q \neq p}^{M} \sum_{i=1}^{N_p} \sum_{j=1}^{N_q} W_{ij}^{pq} ||\mathbf{y}_i^p - \mathbf{y}_j^q||^2 \end{aligned} \tag{4}$$

which can be reformulated as:

$$\begin{aligned} \min_{Y} \ & \frac{1}{2} \sum_{i=1}^{N} \sum_{j=1}^{N} W_{ij} ||\mathbf{y}_i - \mathbf{y}_j||^2 \\ s.t. \ & Y \in \{-1, 1\}^{l \times N}, \ YY^T = I_l \end{aligned} \tag{5}$$

where Y denotes the hash code matrix for all modalities of data, i.e., $Y = [Y^1, Y^2, ..., Y^M]$, and N is the total number of all modalities of data, i.e., $N = \sum_{p=1}^{M} N_p$. The constraint $Y \in \{-1, 1\}^{l \times N}$ enforces the hash codes of data to be binary. $YY^T = I_l$ is imposed to avoid the trivial solution.

The optimization problem in Eq.(5) is equivalent to the issue of balanced graph partitioning and it is NP-hard. Following the literature [11], we make the problem computationally tractable by relaxing the binary constraint $Y \in \{-1, 1\}^{l \times N}$. After relaxing the binary constraint, we can rewrite the problem as follows:

$$\min_{Y} \ Tr(YLY^T) \quad s.t. \ YY^T = I_l \tag{6}$$

where $L = D - W$ is the Laplacian matrix. D is a diagonal matrix, and its entries are column sum of W, $D_{ii} = \sum_j W_{ij}$. It is known that the solution of the above optimization problem is given by the l eigenvectors of L corresponding to the l smallest eigenvalues. Then, we binarize the the real-valued eigenvectors via thresholding, in which the median value of each dimension is set as the threshold for binarization according to the maximum entropy principle.

By solving the objective function in Eq.(6), we can generate the hash codes for all modalities of data, which takes both the intra-modality and inter-modality similarity into consideration. In the next subsection, we will discuss how to learn the hash functions for the new data that are unseen before.

2.2 Learning hash function

In the previous subsection, there are no explicit hash functions derived in the hash codes generation process. In order to overcome this drawback, we aim to learn a set of hash functions for each modality to map new data into the common Hamming space. In this paper, we learn a hash function for each bit of the hash code by considering it as a binary classification problem. We take each bit $y_{ij}^p \in \{-1, 1\}$ in the learned hash code $\mathbf{y}_i^p$ for the data point $\mathbf{x}_i^p$ as a binary class label. To learn the j-th hash function $h_j^p(\cdot)$ for the p-th modality of data, we minimize the following objective function:

$$\min_{h_j^p(\cdot)} \sum_{i=1}^{N_p} J(h_j^p(\mathbf{x}_i^p),\ y_{ij}^p) \tag{7}$$

where $J(\cdot,\cdot)$ is a loss function defined on the hash code $h_j^p(\mathbf{x}_i^p)$ and the learned hash code y_{ij}^p. The loss function can be zero-one loss function, which returns 0 if two codes have the same value, and 1 otherwise. Some typical loss functions can also be used here, such as hinge loss, logistic loss, etc.

The optimization of Eq.(7) can be regarded as minimizing a certain kind of loss function given the binary class label. Clearly, it is a binary classification problem. The classifiers are the hash functions that we aim to learn. There are various methods suitable for learning such binary classifiers, including decision trees, support vector machines, neural networks, logistic regression, and so on. In this paper, we choose to use linear Support Vector Machine (SVM) [3] to learn linear hash functions. The linear hash function has the form:

$$h_j^p(\mathbf{x}_i^p) = \mathrm{sign}((\mathbf{w}_j^p)^T \mathbf{x}_i^p + b) \tag{8}$$

If necessary, we can easily obtain non-linear hash functions by using a kernel method.

2.3 Complexity analysis

The offline training process of the proposed TSCMH method consists of two steps. In the first step, constructing the intra-modality similarity matrix takes $O(\sum_{p=1}^{M}(d_p + k)N_p^2)$ time, constructing the inter-modality similarity matrix takes $O(\frac{1}{2}\sum_{p=1}^{M}\sum_{q=1}^{M} N_p N_q)$ time, and solving Eq.(6) takes $O(tlkN)$ time using the Lanczos algorithm (t is the number of iterations and it is usually quite small). In the second step, training these linear SVM classifiers takes $O(\sum_{p=1}^{M} l\bar{d}_p N_p)$ time ($\bar{d}_p$ is the average number of non-zero elements per instance). The values of M, l, and k are usually small constants. Therefore the overall time the training process takes is approximately $O(d_m N_m^2 + N)$, where $d_m N_m^2$ is the largest one among all modalities. For a new data point, the complexity time of the online code prediction is linear to the size of its dimensionality.

3. EXPERIMENTAL RESULTS

3.1 Datasets

The *Wiki image-text* dataset [8], generated from Wikipedia's "featured article", consists of 2866 image-text pairs. In each pair, the image is related to a complete text article. Each pair is annotated with a label from the vocabulary of 10 semantic classes. The representation of the text with 10 dimensions is derived from a latent Dirichlet allocation model. And each image is represented by a 128-dimensional SIFT descriptor. Following the setting in the literature [8], we take 2173 image-text pairs as the database set and the remaining 693 image-text pairs as the query set.

Another dataset used here is *NUS-WIDE-10K*: a subset selected from the NUS-WIDE dataset [2]. Images are downloaded from Flickr and each image is associated with user tags. We choose 10 classes with total 10000 images (1000 images for each class). The images are represented with 500-dimensional SIFT feature vectors, and the text tags are represented with 1000-dimensional tag occurrence feature vectors. We take 90% of the data as the database set and the remaining 10% as the query set.

3.2 Experimental settings

Experiments are conducted on two cross-modal retrieval tasks: (1) Image query vs. Text database, (2) Text query vs. Image database. Specifically, the first task is to use an image as a query to retrieve relevant texts from the text database, and the second task is to use a text as a query to retrieve relevant images from the image database. We compare the proposed TSCMH approach with three state-of-the-art methods: CVH [5], MLBE [14] and PDH [9]. For TSCMH, the parameter α is empirically set to 10. The inter-modality similarity matrices are simply determined by the class label.

We use the *Mean Average Precision (MAP)* as the evaluation metric. Given a query and a list of R retrieved results, the average precision is defined as AP $= \frac{1}{L}\sum_{r=1}^{R} P(r)\cdot rel(r)$, where L is the number of relevant documents in the retrieved set, $P(r)$ denotes the precision of the top r retrieved documents, and $rel(r) = 1$ if the rth retrieved document is relevant (where 'relevant' means belonging to the class of the query) and $rel(r) = 0$ otherwise. The MAP is the mean of the AP values over all queries. The larger the MAP, the better the performance. In our experiments, we set R=50. Besides, we also report the *precision-scope curve* [7] by varying the scope from 50 to 1000.

3.3 Results and discussion

The MAP values of all algorithms on Wiki and NUS-WIDE datasets for different code lengths {K=16, 24, 32 bit} are reported in Table 1. The precision-scope curves for two forms of tasks are plotted in Figure 1[1]. We observe that the MAP of text query is generally higher than that of image query. The reason is that the text can better describe the semantic meaning of the image-text pairs than the image. When an image query comes, since it cannot describe the high-level semantics accurately, it is difficult to find semantically similar texts for it. Even so, our method achieves competitive performance.

We also observe that the proposed TSCMH achieves the overall best performance. Particularly, TSCMH performs significantly better than the compared methods for the Text query vs. Image database task. This may be because the joint multimodal graph correctly models the structure of the multimodal data, and the generated hash codes in the first step effectively preserve the intra-modality similarity

[1]Due to space limitation, only K=24 is shown in Figure 1.

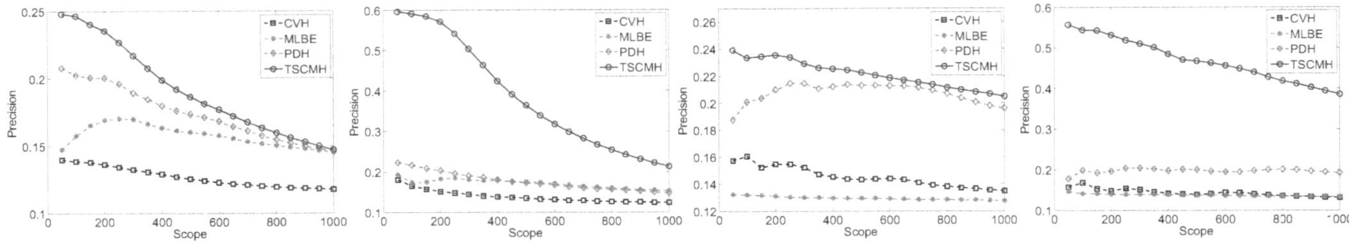

(a) Image query (b) Text query (c) Image query (d) Text query

Figure 1: Precision-scope curves on Wiki dataset (a-b) and NUS-WIDE dataset (c-d) when K=24 bit.

Table 1: MAP comparison on the Wiki and NUS-WIDE datasets.

Tasks	Methods	Wiki			NUS-WIDE		
		K=16 bit	K=24 bit	K=32 bit	K=16 bit	K=24 bit	K=32 bit
Image query vs. Text database	CVH	0.2183	0.1892	0.1814	0.2497	0.2414	0.2321
	MLBE	**0.2699**	0.1785	0.2240	0.2683	0.1584	0.2332
	PDH	0.231	0.2478	0.2290	0.1833	0.2396	0.2533
	TSCMH	**0.2649**	**0.2625**	**0.2450**	**0.2919**	**0.2764**	**0.2636**
Text query vs. Image database	CVH	0.3137	0.2674	0.2442	0.2713	0.2424	0.2478
	MLBE	0.4821	0.2350	0.2209	0.2794	0.1900	0.2864
	PDH	0.2535	0.2917	0.2826	0.2106	0.2705	0.2780
	TSCMH	**0.6275**	**0.6164**	**0.6531**	**0.5741**	**0.5707**	**0.5575**

and the inter-modality similarity. Besides that, the max-margin hyperplane produced by linear SVM ensures good generalization. The weakness of CVH and PDH is that they ignore the intra-modality similarity relationship. Although MLBE also considers both forms of similarity relationships, it is easy to get trapped in local minima during the learning process, especially when the code length is large.

4. CONCLUSION

In this paper, we have proposed a Two-Step Cross-Modal Hashing (TSCMH) approach to learn a common Hamming space, in which we can perform cross-modal similarity search between heterogeneous data. We first exploit the intra-modality and inter-modality similarity through a joint multimodal graph to learn the hash codes for all modalities of data. Then, we learn the hash functions in a binary classification manner for any data object that is unseen before. Experimental results on two benchmark datasets have shown that the proposed method outperforms several state-of-the-art methods.

5. ACKNOWLEDGMENTS

This work is jointly supported by National Basic Research Program of China (2012CB316300), and National Natural Science Foundation of China (61175003, 61135002, 61202328, 61473289).

6. REFERENCES

[1] M. M. Bronstein, A. M. Bronstein, F. Michel, and N. Paragios. Data fusion through cross-modality metric learning using similarity-sensitive hashing. In *CVPR*, pages 3594–3601, 2010.

[2] T.-S. Chua, J. Tang, R. Hong, H. Li, Z. Luo, , and Y.-T. Zheng. NUS-WIDE: A real-world web image database from national university of singapore. In *ACM International Conference on Image and Video Retrieval*, 2009.

[3] R.-E. Fan, K.-W. Chang, C.-J. Hsieh, X.-R. Wang, and C.-J. Lin. LIBLINEAR: A library for large linear classification. *JMLR*, 9:1871–1874, 2008.

[4] Y. Gong and S. Lazebnik. Iterative quantization: A procrustean approach to learning binary codes. In *CVPR*, pages 817–824, 2011.

[5] S. Kumar and R. Udupa. Learning hash functions for cross-view similarity search. In *IJCAI*, pages 1360–1365, 2011.

[6] N. Quadrianto and C. H. Lampert. Learning multi-view neighborhood preserving projections. In *ICML*, pages 425–432, 2011.

[7] N. Rasiwasia, P. J. Moreno, and N. Vasconcelos. Bridging the gap: query by semantic example. *IEEE TMM*, 9(5):923–938, 2007.

[8] N. Rasiwasia, J. C. Pereira, E. Coviello, G. Doyle, G. Lanckriet, R. Levy, and N. Vasconcelos. A new approach to cross-modal multimedia retrieval. In *ACM MM*, pages 251–260, 2010.

[9] M. Rastegari, J. Choi, S. Fakhraei, H. D. III, and L. S. Davis. Predictable dual-view hashing. In *ICML*, 2013.

[10] J. Song, Y. Yang, Z. Huang, H. Shen, and R. Hong. Multiple feature hashing for real-time large scale near-duplicate video retrieval. In *ACM MM*, pages 423–432, 2011.

[11] Y. Weiss, A. Torralba, and R. Fergus. Spectral hashing. In *NIPS*, pages 1753–1760, 2008.

[12] D. Zhang, F. Wang, and L. Si. Composite hashing with multiple information sources. In *ACM SIGIR*, pages 225–234, 2011.

[13] D. Zhang, J. Wang, D. Cai, and J. S. Liu. Self-taught hashing for fast similarity search. In *SIGIR*, pages 18–25, 2010.

[14] Y. Zhen and D.-Y. Yeung. A probabilistic model for multimodal hash function learning. In *SIGKDD*, pages 940–948, 2012.

Cross-Scenario Eyeglasses Retrieval via EGYPT Model

Xiaoling Gu Pai Peng Mengwen Li Sai Wu Lidan Shou Gang Chen
College of Computer Science and Technology, Zhejiang University, China
{belizabeth, pengpai_sh, fantasylmw, wusai, should, cg}@zju.edu.cn

ABSTRACT

In this paper, we present FGSS (Fashion Glasses Search System), an innovative cross-scenario eyeglasses retrieval system which automatically recognizes eyeglasses in real-world photos, e.g. the photo of a fashion girl with a stylish pair of eyeglasses, and retrieves a ranking list of visually similar product instances from the database. We propose a novel segmentation-free framework for FGSS to bridge two search gaps, semantic gap and feature gap, where a new type of keypoint-based scheme called EGYPT is tailored for eyeglasses to facilitate the search. In the EGYPT, we use the hybrid descriptors which combine the shape, color and texture features as a feature representation for eyeglasses. The experimental study on the real-world photo dataset and eyeglasses product dataset demonstrates the effectiveness of EGYPT model.

Categories and Subject Descriptors

H.3.3 [**Information Storage and Retrieval**]: Information Search and Retrieval

Keywords

Eyeglasses retrieval; cross-scenario; keypoint-based scheme

1. INTRODUCTION

One challenging problem posed by the online fashion shopping is that it is difficult for the users to decide whether a clothe or eyeglasses are the perfect fit for them. Recently, to address the problem, the virtual try-on systems[1,2] are developed which allow the users to see how clothes/glasses look on their bodies/faces, convincing them to make up their minds for their online purchases.

In this paper, we present an innovative eyeglasses retrieval system, *Fashion Glasses Search System* (FGSS), to support a new online eyeglasses shopping experience. Imagine that a woman is randomly browsing photo-sharing sites (e.g. Flickr, Pinterest) or hot online fashion magazines, and suddenly attracted by a model who wears an extraordinary pair of eyeglasses that suit her taste, stimulating her to purchase a similar product. In this situation, she could search with FGSS, which automatically recognizes targeted eyeglasses from noisy photos and retrieves a ranking list of visually similar product images from the database. We formulate such automatic eyeglasses retrieval as *cross-scenario eyeglasses retrieval* problem, since the query is a real-world image captured with an arbitrary background, while the eyeglasses product images are well aligned and captured in a clean background as shown in Figure 1.

(a) Example of query images with different background

(b) Example of eyeglasses images with clean background

Figure 1: Examples of query images and eyeglasses product images in cross-scenario eyeglasses retrieval

Generally, the intuition of FGSS is to bridge two gaps when searching for glasses using ordinary image search engines, namely *semantic gap* and *feature gap*.

Semantic Gap A common way to find similar eyeglasses on online shopping websites (e.g. Amazon.com) is to submit some keyword queries, such as "black square eyeglasses". However, such old-school retrieval techniques cannot support our new search interface since users find it difficult to figure out the accurate descriptive keywords. Such gap between query keywords and database images are called semantic gap. While in FGSS, we allow users to issue a query by an image, e.g. a photo of a fashion girl from online site or shot by the mobile phone.

Feature Gap As mentioned before, our query images containing noises (e.g., hair, face and background) are quite different from the eyeglasses images in our database. Even image search is supported, it is meaningless to compare the two types of images directly, as no matching result will be returned. The gap between the query images and eyeglasses images is called feature gap, because different types of images show different features. A conventional way to deal with such gap is to segment eyeglasses from query image via manual labeling or segmentation algorithms. However, man-

[1]http://fits.me/try-it-now/tryitnowvfr
[2]http://www.ray-ban.com/usa/virtual-mirror

ICMR'15, June 23–26, 2015, Shanghai, China.

http://dx.doi.org/10.1145/2671188.2749298.

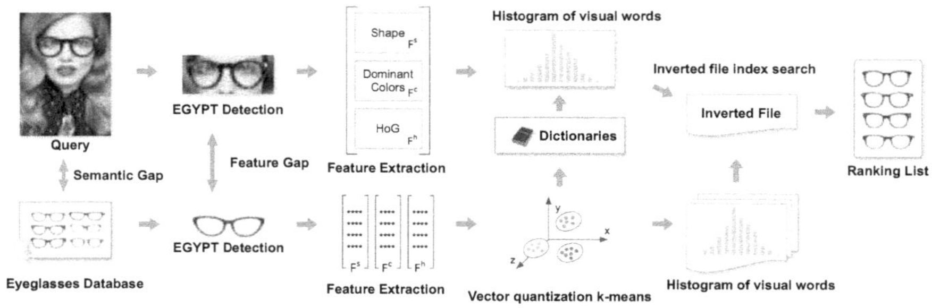

Figure 2: The framework for cross-scenario eyeglasses retrieval

ual labeling is not a trivial task and what's more, it does not necessarily guarantee accurate segmentation results either.

To narrow the gaps, we propose a segmentation-free framework for cross-scenario eyeglasses retrieval which effectively reduces the search noises. In this framework, we define a new keypoint-based scheme specially designed for eyeglasses called *EyeGlass keYPoinT* (EGYPT). Some keypoints along the glass frame are retrieved as the features. Such keypoints are robust to noisy background and are efficiently to be detected. Once keypoints have been successfully detected, we extract hybrid visual features as feature descriptors. As a result, query image and glass images are mapped into the same feature space so that they can be compared for ranking.

The main contributions of this paper can be summarized as follows:

1. To the best of our knowledge, this work is the first one which explores the eyeglasses retrieval problem in the multimedia area and has potential commercial applications.
2. We propose a novel framework for cross-scenario eyeglasses retrieval which does not require segmentation in prior.
3. We define a new type of keypoint-based scheme for eyeglasses (EGYPT) which is robust to noisy background and can be identified efficiently.
4. Based on the definition and detection of EGYPT, we also present feature descriptors as a representation for eyeglasses.

2. RELATED WORK

Object retrieval Object retrieval is an old topic and most existing work are based on the bag-of-visual-words (BOW) model [5] and its variations. A general search strategy is firstly segmenting target object out of the whole query image [4] and then feeding it into the retrieval system in the form of a BOW feature vector. However, the accuracy of such a method largely depends on the performance of segmentation on that object. Unfortunately, this still remains as a tough and hot research issue. By contrast, our proposed method does not require segmentation in advance.

Cross-scenario retrieval Cross-scenario retrieval problem is initially explored in clothing retrieval problem. Liu et al. [3] first introduced the notion of cross-scenario clothing retrieval, namely finding similar clothing photos across different photo capturing scenario. Kalantidis et al. [2] presented a scalable approach to automatically suggest relevant clothing products that can trivially scale to hundreds of product classes and millions of product images. However, these methods are not applicable in our problem since glasses consist of frames and transparent lens, showing completely different features from clothes.

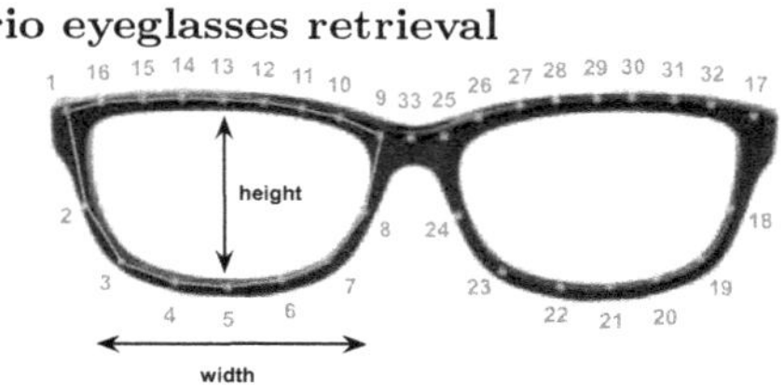

Figure 3: EGYPT scheme for describing eyeglasses

3. THE RETRIEVAL FRAMEWORK

Our framework is illustrated in Figure 2 which consists of an offline product images processing phase and an online query image processing phase.

Offline Phase In the offline phase, we retrieve keypoints for each product image in the database and combine hybrid visual features (i.e. shape, color, HoG.) as its unique descriptor. Following the procedure of bag-of-visual-words (BOW) [5] , we organize all descriptors as a unified dictionary. To efficiently retrieve the corresponding images, an inverted index is built during the offline phase.

Online Phase When we submit an image as the online query, its feature vector is constructed in an adhoc way similar to the offline phase. With the help of inverted index, we can efficiently retrieve a ranking list of images with small Manhattan distances. Top candidates are returned to users as the search results.

3.1 EGYPT Model

The EGYPT model plays a decisive role in the FGSS which affects the quality of our search results. We start our discussion with the basic design of EGYPT scheme, followed by the implementation details.

3.1.1 EGYPT Scheme

Since the appearances of glasses vary in shape and texture, we can employ the deformable models to precisely describe their characteristics. We use state-of-the-art regression-based deformable model [6], extensively used in the facial landmark localization, to find the optimal position of the set of keypoints in a glass image. Inspired by the landmarking scheme for human faces, we design the EGYPT scheme tailored for eyeglasses illustrated in Figure 3. We choose 33 keypoints to form general glasses shape as a tradeoff between accuracy and efficiency. Except for the point No.33 located in the midpoint, the remaining 32 keypoints are aligned symmetrically. Namely, for each side of the glasses, we uniformly select 7 points on the upper and lower edge respectively. Each specific structure of eyeglasses can be uniquely identified by such a scheme.

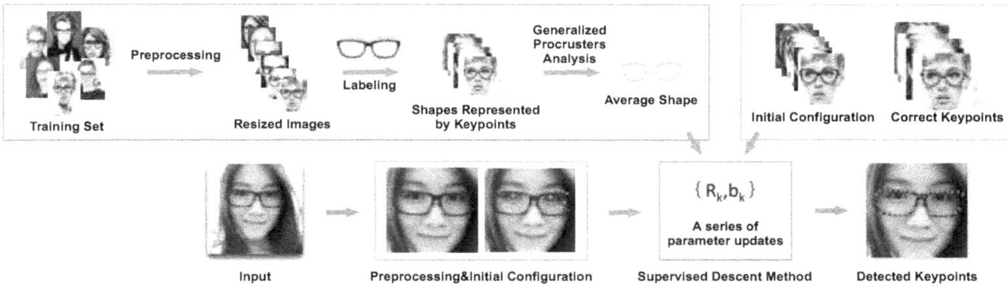

Figure 4: EGYPT detection in real-world images

3.1.2 *EGYPT Detection*

The Supervised Descent Method (SDM) [6] is a recently proposed techniques for solving general nonlinear optimization problems in computer vision. This technique can be used to solve the deformable model fitting problem by defining a local appearance model around each keypoint and an implicit non-parametric shape model. In EGYPT, we formalize the keypoints localization as an optimization problem, minimizing the following cost function over keypoint coordinate x:

Given an image $d \in \mathcal{R}^m$ of m pixels, $d(\mathbf{x}) \in \mathcal{R}^N$ represents the vector of keypoint coordinates, where N is the number of keypoints. Let h be the feature extraction function. The objective function for EGYPT detection is:

$$f(\mathbf{x}) = ||h(d(\mathbf{x})) - \phi_*||_2^2 \tag{1}$$

where $\phi_* = h(d(\mathbf{x}_*))$ represents the feature values in the manually labeled keypoints, and $\mathbf{x}_*$ is the correct N keypoints. We use almost the same approach to detect the keypoints of eyeglasses in real-world images and product images. In the following discussion, we use the example illustrated in Figure 4 to illustrate our idea.

Training Stage At the training stage, the first step is running the Viola Jones face detector to crop the face images in training set. All images are scaled to a fixed width $w = 200$ pixels. After preprocessing, every image is manually annotated with keypoints and the coordinates of all keypoints are stored as a vector in the form of $\mathbf{x} = [x_1, y_1, ..., x_N, y_N]^T$, where x_i and y_i are x and y coordinates of the i-th keypoint and N (in our case 33) is the number of keypoints used. Then the shapes in the training set are aligned with each other by Generalized Procrustes Analysis (GPA). The average shape $\overline{\mathbf{x}}$ is the mean vector shape of these aligned shapes. The initial keypoints in training stage is obtained by aligning the average shape to a predefined initial position and retrieving the points in corresponding positions.

Histogram of oriented gradients (HoG) features are extracted from patches around the keypoints to achieve a representation robust to illustrate changes. The goal of SDM is to learn a series of parameter updates, generic descent direction R_k and bias terms b_k, to produce a sequence of updates:

$$\mathbf{x}_k = \mathbf{x}_{k-1} + R_{k-1}\phi_{k-1} + b_{k-1}; \tag{2}$$

and the parameter updates R_k and b_k can be learned from a new linear regressor by minimizing

$$arg \min_{R_k, b_k} \sum_{d^i} \sum_{\mathbf{x}_k^i} ||\mathbf{x}_*^i - \mathbf{x}_k^i - R_k\phi_k^i - b_k||^2 \tag{3}$$

where i is used to index images in training data.

Testing Stage At the testing stage, we first preprocess the images and align the average shape to the initial position. Then the coordinates of keypoints are updated by the learned parameters R_k and b_k.

3.2 Eyeglasses Descriptors

After detecting EGYPT for glasses, we attempt to extract visual features for these keypoints in order to form an representative feature vector. Specifically, hybrid feature descriptors are exploited by leveraging the shape, color and texture features.

Shape Shape context [1] is widely used for measuring shape similarities or finding correspondences between point sets. However, conventional shape context failed to be a robust feature for glasses since it can not distinguish rectangular eyeglasses from square ones. Therefore, we design two simple yet effective shape related features specially for glasses:

(1)*aspect ratio*= $dist(\mathbf{x}_1 - \mathbf{x}_9)/dist(\mathbf{x}_5 - \mathbf{x}_{13})$, where $\mathbf{x}_i = [x_i, y_i]$ presented in Section 3.1, *dist* is the Euclidean distance function between two points.

(2)*slope vector*= $(slope(\mathbf{x}_1, \mathbf{x}_2), slope(\mathbf{x}_2, \mathbf{x}_3), ..., slope(\mathbf{x}_{15}, \mathbf{x}_{16}), slope(\mathbf{x}_{16}, \mathbf{x}_1))$, is $16D$ vector, *slope* is slope function between two points.

Color Considering the color of eyeglasses is relatively uniform, we sample the pixel values within 8 nearest neighborhoods of keypoint coordinations. These pixels values are clustered by Gaussian mixture models (GMM) in RGB color space. The centers of two largest GMM components are used as the representative color feature F^c.

Texture Texture features based on HoG are computed around specified keypoint locations. In practice, each keypoint generates a block, which is divided up into a regular grid of 2×2 cells. For each block accumulating a local histogram of 8 gradient directions over the pixels, thus yielding a $32D$ feature vector. The local histograms of all 33 blocks are then concatenated together to form the $33 \times 32 = 1056D$ HoG feature F^h.

4. EXPERIMENTAL RESULTS

4.1 Dataset

We collected two datasets to investigate cross-scenario eyeglasses retrieval problem: a Real-world Photo dataset (RP) and an Eyeglasses Product dataset (EP).

- *RP Dataset*: The images are collected from search engines and photo sharing web sites by using queries such as "women with eyeglasses". In total, 1250 images are collected and manually labeled with EGYPT scheme.

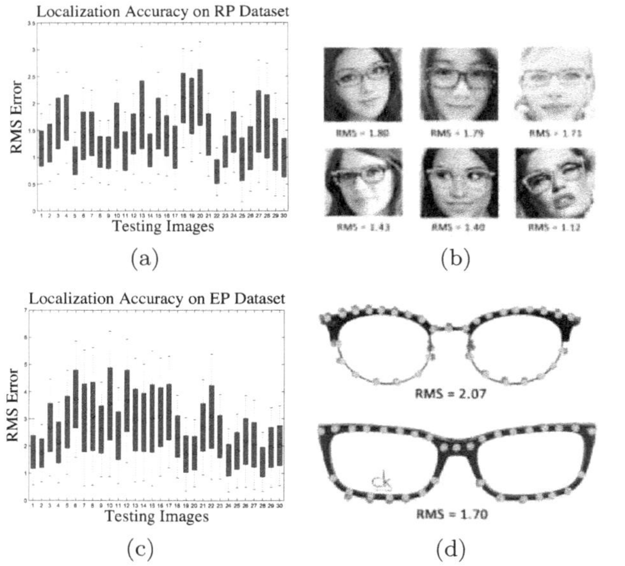

Figure 5: a) Average RMS errors and standard deviations on 30 testing images in RP dataset. b) RMS error between the SDM detection (red) and ground truth (green) in RP dataset. (c) Average RMS errors and standard deviations on 30 testing images in EP dataset. (d) RMS error between the SDM detection (red) and ground truth (green) in EP dataset.

It is worth noting that these photos are background cluttered. We leave 50 images out as query set for evaluation.

- *EP Dataset*: The images are collected from some popular online eyeglasses stores (e.g. Warby Parker, Coastal, LensCrafters). Thus, 2035 images (pure glasses) are collected and also labeled following EGYPT scheme.

4.2 Evaluation of EGYPT

To illustrate the result of detection method for eyeglasses, we show the accuracy of EGYPT model where the automatically locating keypoints are compared to the manually labeled keypoints. Due to limited space, only a few examples are shown in Figure 5. It can be seen that the detected keypoints match with eyeglasses perfectly and are close to manually labeled locations. Figure 5(a) and 5(c) plot the average RMS (Root Mean Square) errors and standard deviation on 30 testing images in RP dataset and EP dataset respectively.

4.3 Evaluation of Eyeglasses Retrieval

To qualitatively evaluate our retrieval system, we conduct a user study which 20 participants are involved in. Given each visual query and the result of ranking list images returned by our FGSS, the participants are asked to score the relevance of each product image to the visual query.

To evaluate the effectiveness of extracted hybrid visual features and the role of each single feature it plays in our retrieval system, we compare the retrieval performance by employing different visual features. The performance of our FGSS system is measured by Normalized Discounted Cumulative Gain (NDCG), which is a widely used metric in ranking systems. Figure 6 reports the NDCG values of top

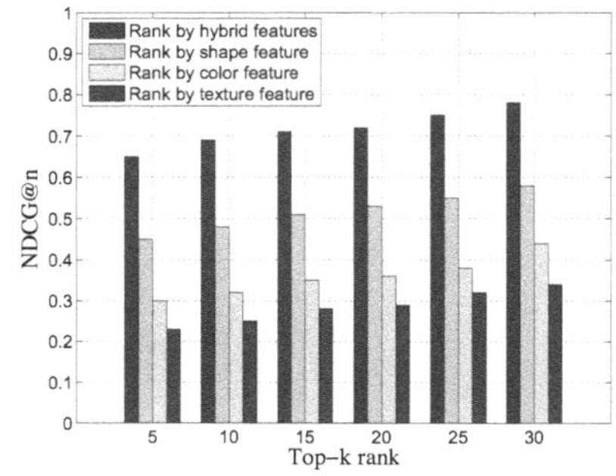

Figure 6: Ranking accuracy in NDCG@n on EP dataset

30 ranked product images on EP dataset. From the experimental results, we can find that (1) The hybrid visual features are relatively effective to retrieve glasses and outperform any single visual feature. (2) The shape descriptor is more significant than color and texture descriptors in our retrieval system. This also validates the fact that shape attribute is one of the most distinguishing visual features for glasses.

5. CONCLUSIONS

We are the first to explore the eyeglasses retrieval problem in the multimedia area and address cross-scenario eyeglasses retrieval problem. We presented an innovative cross-scenario eyeglasses retrieval system and proposed a novel segmentation-free framework. In the proposed framework, a new type of keypoint-based scheme and hybrid visual descriptors for eyeglasses are designed specifically. Promising results are achieved on our collected real-world photo dataset and eyeglasses product dataset.

6. ACKNOWLEDGMENTS

The work of Sai Wu and Xiaoling Gu was carried out at the SeSaMe Centre. It is supported by the Singapore NRF under its IRC@SG Funding Initiative and administered by the IDMPO.

7. REFERENCES

[1] S. Belongie, J. Malik, and J. Puzicha. Shape context: A new descriptor for shape matching and object recognition. In *NIPS*, 2000.

[2] Y. Kalantidis, L. Kennedy, and L.-J. Li. Getting the look: clothing recognition and segmentation for automatic product suggestions in everyday photos. In *ICMR*, 2013.

[3] S. Liu, Z. Song, G. Liu, C. Xu, H. Lu, and S. Yan. Street-to-shop: Cross-scenario clothing retrieval via parts alignment and auxiliary set. In *CVPR*, 2012.

[4] C. Rother, V. Kolmogorov, and A. Blake. "grabcut": interactive foreground extraction using iterated graph cuts. *ACM Trans. Graph.*, 23(3), 2004.

[5] J. Sivic and A. Zisserman. Video google: A text retrieval approach to object matching in videos. In *ICCV*, 2003.

[6] X. Xiong and F. D. la Torre. Supervised descent method and its applications to face alignment. In *CVPR*, 2013.

People News Search via Name-Face Association Analysis

Yong Cheng, Zhixin Liu, Yun Zhao,
Cheng Jin, Yuejie Zhang
School of Computer Science
Shanghai Key Laboratory
of Intelligent Information Processing
Fudan University, Shanghai 200433, China
{13110240027, 14210240048, 12210240077,
jc, yjzhang }@fudan.edu.cn

Tao Zhang
School of Information Management and Engineering,
Shanghai University of Finance and Economics,
Shanghai 200433, China
taozhang@mail.shufe.edu.cn

ABSTRACT
By integrating multimodal information in multimodal news, a novel scheme is developed in this paper for facilitating more effective people news search via name-face association analysis. It is treated as a problem of bi-media multimodal semantic mapping on multimodal news, and modeled as an inter-related correlation distribution over multimodal semantic representations of name-face associations. Very positive results have been obtained in our experiments using a large quantity of public multimodal news data.

Categories and Subject Descriptors
H.3.3 [**Information Storage and Retrieval**]: Information Search and Retrieval – *Search Process*

Keywords
People news search; multimodal news, multimodal pre-analysis; name-face association analysis; multimodal information discovery

1. INTRODUCTION
Over the last decade, there has been an explosive growth of multimodal news available both online and offline. Multimodal news is usually exhibited with the form of captioned news images and consists of stories about people, which makes the name queries to a specific person important [1]. Thus there is an urgent need for integrating various information sources involved in multimodal news to facilitate more accurate people news search.

Considerable research efforts have been devoted to address the semantic gap between high-level semantic concepts in news captions and low-level visual features in news images for people news search [2]. McCreadie *et al.* investigated three questions for real-time news vertical search to better serve the user's news need [3]. Mensink *et al.* focused on finding images of people within large databases of captioned news images by exploiting faces of other people that co-occur frequently with the queried person [4]. Messina *et al.* described a framework for content-based, cross-media information aggregation to multimedia news retrieval [5]. Li *et al.* proposed a framework of multimodal multi-correlation person-centric news retrieval by exploring both text and image information [6]. To achieve more effective and accurate people news search, three inter-related issues should be addressed simultaneously: 1) in-depth multimodal analysis of multimodal news to characterize semantic caption texts and visual news images more reasonably; 2) multimodal optimization to identify more precise associations between names in news captions and faces in news images; and 3) discovery of the missing important multimodal information for rare people news search.

Based on these observations above, by integrating multimodal information involved in multimodal news, a novel scheme is developed in this paper for facilitating more effective people news search via name-face association analysis. Our proposed scheme significantly differs from other earlier work in multiple respects: a) Salient names are extracted from the textual captions of multimodal news. The salient names are defined as the names that might have higher correspondence possibility with the faces in news images. Valid faces are extracted from the visual images of multimodal news. The valid faces are defined as the human faces in news images that might have higher coherence with the salient names. b) An efficient optimization algorithm based on the Fuzzy C-Means (FCM) clustering is particularly established to verify the feasibility of our automatic name-face association analysis algorithm. c) Large-scale Web news and some specific statistical information are particularly explored and integrated for discovering missing important multimodal information for rare people news search. d) By fusing the related techniques proposed in this paper, a new people news search mechanism is established to achieve more precise characterization of the correlations between name queries and multimodal news. Our experiments on a large number of public data have obtained very positive results.

2. MULTIMODAL PRE-ANALYSIS
Given a piece of multimodal news, there may appear multiple faces in the image that correspond to different names in the caption. The common fact is that the face of one person usually co-occurs with his/her name in different expression forms. The importance for each name could be different, and the potentially associated faces for each name should be detected. Thus it's necessary to evaluate the importance degree for each name in the same caption and detect the valid faces in the same image.

Since the syntactic structure is indicative of various information distributions in a text, the salient names in a news caption can be confirmed by the roles of names and the relations among names as depicted in the syntactic parse tree. Given N different names in a caption in which each name corresponds to a name cluster NC_i, i=1, ..., N, the initial rank *Relative Salience* (*RS*) for each name/name cluster is defined as:

ICMR '15, June 23-26, 2015, Shanghai, China.

DOI: http://dx.doi.org/10.1145/2671188.2749301

$$RS(NC_i) = \alpha * \frac{SNC(NC_i)}{\sum_{j=1}^{N} SNC(NC_j)} + \beta * \frac{\sum_{j=1}^{N} SPTD(NC_j) - SPTD(NC_i)}{(N-1) * \sum_{j=1}^{N} SPTD(NC_j)} + \gamma * \frac{\sum_{j=1}^{N} SPTTO(NC_j) - SPTTO(NC_i)}{(N-1) * \sum_{j=1}^{N} SPTTO(NC_j)} \quad (1)$$

$$SPTD(NC_i) = \min_{j=1}^{SNC(NC_i)} \{SPT\_Depth(NC_{ij})\}$$

$$SPTTO(NC_i) = \min_{j=1}^{SNC(NC_i)} \{SPT\_BFT-Order(NC_{ij})\}$$

$$\sum_{i=1}^{N} RS(NC_i) = 1$$

where $SNC(NC_i)$ denotes the size of NC_i, i.e., the number of names with the co-reference relation in NC_i, which can be understood as the occurrence frequency of the same names with different forms in the news caption; $SPT\_Depth(NC_{ij})$ is the depth of NC_{ij} in the syntactic parse tree; $SPT\_BFT\text{-}Order(NC_{ij})$ is the breadth-first traversal order of NC_{ij} in the syntactic parse tree, and α, β and γ are the relative importance coefficients, $\alpha+\beta+\gamma=1$.

A classic face detector, *Viola-Jones* Detector, is utilized to implement our face detection, in which the bounding boxes of the detector are treated as the outputs of the faces in images. To obtain more ideal face dataset, the faces with the undersize scale and those in the images of multimodal news which has no reasonable names in the news caption can be identified are both removed. For face normalization, Difference of Gaussians Filter is adopted to remedy the variation of illumination and restrain various noises. Each normalized face can be represented with the facial feature points by using the SIFT descriptor. The localization method is utilized to locate 9 facial feature points and the other additional 4 points (i.e., the central position of each eye, the central position of mouth and the midpoint between two eyes). For each pair of faces, the average Euclidean distance between 13 feature points on one face and those on another face is considered as the distance estimation manner under such a feature space.

3. NAME-FACE ASSOCIATION ANALYSIS

Our name-face association analysis aims at finding the optimal one-to-one name-face matching in each piece of multimodal news. Although some probability-statistical models like EM have been used to solve this task, such strategies still need to confront the serious problems such as more easily trapping into the local optimum and lacking the global information, etc. Thus an improved Fuzzy C-Means (FCM) clustering algorithm, which introduces the consideration of salient name information and integrates the limitation of name-face co-occurrence, is established to make a better solution for association analysis. The combination of salient name, face feature and name-face co-occurrence information can be regarded as a good fusion of high-level semantic features in news captions and the low-level visual features in news images under an identical clustering framework. Compared with the general FCM clustering, the improved one can better describe the multimodal features of multimodal news, and make more reasonable solution for this specific clustering issue.

Our improved FCM clustering algorithm mainly aims at optimizing the following objective function J_m.

$$J_m = \sum_{i=1}^{FN} \sum_{P_{ij}=1} U_{ij}^m * Dist(Face_i, NC\_Center_j) \quad (2)$$

where FN denotes the number of faces/face feature vectors in the face set FS for the given news set; NCN denotes the number of name clusters (NCs)/persons in the name set NS for the given news set; $Face_i$ denotes the face feature vector for the ith face in FS, $1 \le i \le FN$; NC_Center_j denotes the prototype of the center of face cluster for the jth NC in NS, $1 \le j \le NCN$; U_{ij} denotes the membership degree of $Face_i$ in NC_Center_j; m is the weighting exponent on each fuzzy membership degree and usually set empirically; $Dist(Face_i, NC\_Center_j)$ is an Euclidean distance measure between $Face_i$ and NC_Center_j; and P_{ij} denotes that if the ith face and the jth name co-occur in the same multimodal news, then P_{ij} is set as 1, otherwise as 0. This function focuses on making the optimization for the distance among the face clusters associated with different NCs, so that each cluster has both the higher intra-cluster cohesion and the farther inter-cluster distance.

a. Initialization – Different from the general FCM clustering algorithm, the improved one does not utilize the random number in [0, 1] to initialize the fuzzy partition matrix U. Considering the particularity of name-face association analysis for multimodal news, the name salience is a very important factor for representing the association strength between name and face, that is, the more salient name in the caption will have the higher possibility to associate with the face in the corresponding image. Thus the initialization for U by using the name salience can be defined as:

$$U_{ij} = \begin{cases} 0, & P_{ij} = 0 \\ RS(Name_j), & P_{ij} \neq 0 \end{cases} \quad (3)$$

where $RS(Name_j)$ denotes the important degree of $Name_j$ that co-occurs with $Face_i$ in the same multimodal news; and because $P_{ij} \neq 0$, it can be sure that $Face_i$ and $Name_j$ exactly co-occur in the same news. Meanwhile, for the different names in a news caption, the sum of all their salience values is 1, thus $\sum_{j=1}^{NCN} U_{ij} = 1$ can be guaranteed. The center of face cluster for each NC in NS is initialized according to Formula (4) with the parameter P_{ij}.

$$NC\_Center_j = \frac{\sum_{i=1}^{FN} \sum_{P_{ij}=1} U_{ij}^m * Face_i}{\sum_{i=1}^{FN} \sum_{P_{ij}=1} U_{ij}^m} \quad (4)$$

b. Iteration – This process aims at constantly amending the center of face cluster for each NC in NS according to Formulae (4) and (5), and also introduces the parameter P_{ij} that plays an important role for controlling the iteration.

$$U_{ij} = \begin{cases} 0, & P_{ij} = 0 \\ \dfrac{1}{\sum_{P_{ik}=1} \left(\dfrac{Dist(Face_i, NC\_Center_j)}{Dist(Face_i, NC\_Center_k)} \right)^{\frac{2}{m-1}}}, & P_{ij} \neq 0 \end{cases} \quad (5)$$

$$1 \le k \le NCN$$

In every iteration process, the center of face cluster for each NC in NS and the membership degree of each face in the face cluster for each NC are both recalculated and updated. After such a process, the center of each face cluster and the membership degree of each face will become more precise.

c. Output – The above iteration process will stop until the center of face cluster for each NC in NS no longer has offsets, or the number of iteration times reaches the preset maximal value. With the iteration to a convergence state, the fuzzy partition matrix (i.e., the membership degree matrix) U and each center of face cluster are both output and taken as the final name-face association analysis results, as shown in Formula (6).

$$Name-Face\_Association(Face_i) = \arg\max_{NC_j} (U_{ij}) \quad (6)$$

4. MULTIMODAL INFORMATION DISCOVERY

There still exist some extreme rare names for which the useful supplementary multimodal information cannot be acquired just through Web mining. The "*extreme rare name*" refers to the rare person that may occur only one or even zero times in the whole database, i.e., without any popularity to the public. For such rare names, the serious lack of related multimodal information will lead to the fatal deficiency of poor search performance, that is, a few or no relevant results can be returned. Thus a person-association-based mining mechanism is established for making the additional multimodal news information supplement.

a. The measurement of Event-Association Degree (EAD) – The *tf-idf* model is utilized, in which all the news captions in the multimodal news database *MND* are used to construct a dictionary with the scale of *D* and then each caption can be represented as a *D*-dimensional vector $D_{NewsCap_i}$ ($1 \le i \le |MND|$). A people news event PNE_i is defined as the caption set with the appearance of a news person $Person_i$, and $Person_i$ can be represented as the sum of all the related caption vectors. Thus the event-association degree between $Person_i$ and $Person_j$ can be measured as:

$$EAD(Person_i, Person_j) = Cos(D_{Person_i}, D_{Person_j}), 1 \le i, j \le |MND|$$

$$D_{Person_i} = \sum_{NewsCap_i \in PNE_i} D_{NewsCap_i}$$

$$PNE_i = \{News\ Caption \mid Person_i\ in\ News\ Caption\} \quad (7)$$

where *Cos*(,) denotes the Cosine similarity function.

b. The measurement of Co-Occurrence-Association Degree (COAD) – We utilize both the occurrence frequency of each news person and the co-occurrence frequency of two different persons to compute the *COAD* value between two persons of $Person_i$ and $Person_j$, as shown in Formula (8).

$$COAD(Person_i, Person_j) = \frac{CoFreq(Person_i, Person_j)}{Freq(Person_i) + Freq(Person_j)} \quad (8)$$

where *CoFreq*(,) denotes the co-occurrence frequency of two persons; and *Freq*( ) denotes the occurrence frequency of a person.

c. The measurement of Person-Association Degree (PAD) – The event-association and the co-occurrence-association are integrated to acquire the *PAD* value between two different persons of $Person_i$ and $Person_j$, as shown in Formula (9).

$$PAD(Person_i, Person_j) = \alpha * EAD(Person_i, Person_j) + (1-\alpha) * COAD(Person_i, Person_j) \quad (9)$$

where α is the relative importance factor; and *EAD*(,), *COAD*(,) and *PAD*(,) are three real numbers in [0, 1].

This manner is not only beneficial to acquire the meaningful people news search results for extreme rare name/person, but also can provide much more related "*friend*" (i.e., associated name/person) information to satisfy the understanding and information need about such extreme rare name/person.

5. EXPERIMENT AND ANALYSIS

Our dataset is established based on *Labeled Yahoo! News Data* constructed by Berg *et al.* [8] and further developed by Guillaumin *et al.* [9], in which there are 19,798 pieces of multimodal news with 52,597 names and 28,616 faces. To evaluate the effectiveness of our algorithm, Correct Association Rate (CAR) is defined as the percentage of correct associations generated in the ground truth. We have incorporated the official criteria on *Precision* (*P*), *Recall* (*R*) and *F*-measure rates for information retrieval, which aim at evaluating how well our name-face association analysis assists users on people news search.

Our name-face association analysis model is created by integrating Salient Name Identification (SNI), Valid Face Identification (VFI), Improved FCM Clustering Algorithm (IFCMA) and Multimodal Information Discovery (MID). To investigate the effect of each part, we introduce three evaluation patterns: 1) *Baseline* (*VFI*) – based on the basic pre-analysis with *VFI* for images, the baseline performance can be obtained; 2) *Baseline* (*VFI*)+*SNI* – based on the baseline model with *VFI*, *SNI* is integrated; and 3) *Baseline* (*VFI*)+*SNI*+*MID* – by fusing the baseline model with *VFI* and *SNI*, *MID* is combined together. Meanwhile, to give full exhibition to the superiority of our association analysis model, we have also performed a comparison between our method and the other existing classical approaches in recent years. Three approaches developed by Berg *et al.* [8], Guillaumin *et al.* [9] and Pham *et al.* [7] are analogous with ours to some extent, and then we accomplished them on the same dataset. The experimental results are presented in Table 1.

Table 1. The comparison results between our association analysis method and the other existing classic approaches.

Approach	Evaluation Pattern	*CAR*
Berg *et al.*'s (*Berg*) (2005)	*Berg*	**52.71%**
	Berg+SNI	56.45%
	Berg+SNI+MID	**59.93%**
Guillaumin *et al.*'s (*Guill*) (2008)	*Guill*	**54.41%**
	Guill+SNI	59.95%
	Guill+SNI+MID	**62.43%**
Pham *et al.*'s (*Pham*) (2010)	*Pham*	**55.61%**
	Pham+SNI	58.98%
	Pham+SNI+MID	**62.73%**
Our Approach (*IFCMA*-based)	*Baseline (VFI)*	**66.10%**
	Baseline (VFI)+SNI	70.40%
	Baseline (VFI)+SNI+MID	**78.80%**

It can be found from Table 1 that for the name-face association analysis by Berg/Guiilaumin/Pham *et al.*'s approaches, we can obtain the best *CAR* values of 52.71%, 54.41% and 55.61% in the evaluation patterns of *Berg*/*Guill*/*Pham* respectively. The main reason is that when considering the associations between names and faces in the same multimodal news, all these three approaches can reduce the combination ambiguities between names and faces to a certain degree and then the relatively better *CAR* values can be obtained. Compared the results of *Berg*/*Guill*/*Pham* and our baseline model with *VFI*, we can find the best *CAR* value of 66.10% appears in the results of our model, which is obviously higher than those *CAR* values for *Berg*/*Guill*/*Pham*. This implies that both of our valid face identification mechanism *VFI* and *IFCMA* are feasible for facilitating more effective name-face association evaluation. Furthermore, through fusing our *SNI* and *MID* with Berg/Guillaumin/Pham *et al.*'s approaches in turn, the better performance can be acquired, in which the best *CAR* values are considerably improved to 59.93%, 62.43% and 62.73% respectively. This confirms the prominent roles of our *SNI* and *MID* in name-face association analysis once again. Compared with the improved Berg/Guillaumin/Pham *et al.*'s approaches with *SNI* and *MID*, our association analysis model with *VFI*, *SNI*, *MID* and *IFCMA* can still present the better performance and the best *CAR* value of 78.80% differs greatly from those of Berg/Guillaumin/Pham *et al.*'s. This indicates that our approach is really superior to Berg/Guillaumin /Pham *et al.*'s, and also further confirm that our association analysis model is exactly a better way to determine name-face associations and support such a special association analysis and optimization problem more effectively.

To further explore the applicability and usefulness of our People News Search (PNS) via Name-Face Association Analysis (NFAA) on large-scale multimodal news, we particularly select 21 person names with different numbers of faces in the whole database as the query topics and carry out the search runs based on the original dataset and the dataset with association analysis. We carry out three search runs to make the evaluation for the search performance on our original dataset, that is, *TS_[No NFAA]* (Text-based search without Name-Face Association Analysis, that is, directly searching name queries in news captions), *PNS_[NFAA]* (People News Search via Name-Face Association Analysis), and *PFS_[NFAA]* (People Face Search via Name-Face Association Analysis). The *Precision* (*P*) values for each name query under such three runs are listed in Table 2, and the *Recall* (*R*) and *F*-measure (*F*) values for *PNS_[NFAA]* are also especially presented. It can be observed from Table 2 that the search performance of *PNS_[NFAA]* is much better than that of *TS_[No NFAA]* without any association analysis, and *PFS_[NFAA]* also gives the superior performance. We can find that due to the important filtering and optimizing effect of our association analysis for multimodal news, the precision values increase significantly under *PNS_[NFAA]* with *NFAA*, and the corresponding recall values for *PNS_[NFAA]* have only a slightly decline. It also confirms that our association analysis pattern can certainly beneficial to make better filtration for the meaningless name-face association information involved in multimodal news and further more effectively facilitate both the people news search and people face search performance.

Table 2. The experimental results for different search patterns.

Name Query	*TS_[No NFAA]*	*PNS_[NFAA]*			*PFS_[NFAA]*
	P	*P*	*R*	*F*	*P*
George w. Bush	59.00%	**84.00%**	**82.40%**	**83.19%**	77.00%
Colin Powell	72.80%	**94.20%**	**100.00%**	**97.01%**	87.00%
Tony Blair	59.30%	**82.20%**	**98.40%**	**89.57%**	78.80%
Donald Rumsfeld	78.70%	**96.20%**	**94.10%**	**95.14%**	91.80%
Gerhard Schroeder	66.30%	**90.50%**	**92.80%**	**91.64%**	86.50%
Ariel Sharon	58.70%	**94.00%**	**97.90%**	**95.91%**	94.00%
Hugo Chavez	59.60%	**88.60%**	**97.30%**	**92.75%**	86.20%
Junichiro Koizumi	64.70%	**88.90%**	**100.00%**	**94.12%**	80.30%
John Ashcroft	44.20%	**63.10%**	**94.20%**	**75.58%**	55.30%
Jean Chretien	62.90%	**91.30%**	**93.30%**	**92.29%**	85.90%
Vladimir Putin	48.00%	**87.90%**	**100.00%**	**93.56%**	78.20%
Silvio Berlusconi	65.70%	**93.10%**	**97.10%**	**95.06%**	90.30%
Jacques Chirac	45.80%	**75.30%**	**98.50%**	**85.35%**	69.40%
Hans Blix	42.20%	**93.70%**	**95.20%**	**94.44%**	92.10%
Arnold Schwarzenegger	67.80%	**98.20%**	**91.80%**	**94.89%**	91.20%
Andre Agassi	56.30%	**79.00%**	**90.70%**	**84.45%**	75.80%
John Negroponte	95.10%	**100.00%**	**100.00%**	**100.00%**	95.00%
David Beckham	62.10%	**89.20%**	**100.00%**	**94.29%**	73.80%
Serena Williams	40.70%	**70.50%**	**86.00%**	**77.48%**	70.50%
Gray Davis	40.90%	**73.90%**	**100.00%**	**84.99%**	66.70%
Kofi Annan	72.30%	**74.50%**	**97.20%**	**84.35%**	72.30%

We have also accomplished a comparison between our most important run for people news search via name-face association analysis and the other three classical approaches developed by Mensink *et al.* [4], Guillaumin *et al.* [9] and Li *et al.* [6] for people news search in recent years. The *P-R* curves for the name query set are shown in Figure 1. It can be seen from Figure 1 that on the original dataset the best run is based on our search model, and its results exceed those by the other three runs dramatically. For the whole name query set, the *P* values under the run of our search model are obviously higher than those under the other three runs, and the highest increase can reach to about 33%. Through comparing the results of all these four runs, it can also be further confirmed that by adopting our association analysis model, the people news search for the name query set has gained the significant improvement on the whole search performance.

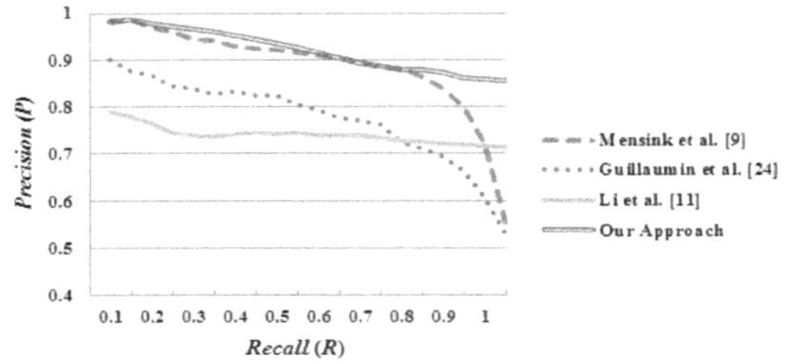

Figure 1. The comparison results between our people news search and the other existing classic search approaches.

6. CONCLUSIONS

In this paper, a new framework is introduced to support more precise people news search via name-face association analysis for large-scale multimodal news. A novel algorithm is developed by integrating salient name identification, valid face identification, improved FCM clustering algorithm, and person-association-based discovery to efficiently exploit the correlations between names and faces involved in multimodal news. Our future work will focus on making our people news search system available online, so that more Internet users can benefit from our research.

7. ACKNOWLEDGMENTS

This work is supported by National Science & Technology Pillar Program of China (2012BAH59F04), National Natural Science Fund of China (61170095; 71171126), Shanghai Philosophy Social Sciences Planning Project of China (2014BYY009), and Zhuoxue Program of Fudan University. Yuejie Zhang is the corresponding author.

8. REFERENCES

[1] Liu, C., Jiang, S., and Huang, Q. 2008. Naming Faces in Broadcast News Video by Image Google. In Proceedings of MM 2008, 717-720.

[2] Fan, J. P., He, X. F., Zhou, N., Peng, J. Y., and Jain, R. 2012. Quantitative Characterization of Semantic Gaps for Learning Complexity Estimation and Inference Model Selection. *IEEE Transactions on Multimedia*, 14(5):1414-1428.

[3] McCreadie, R., Macdonald, C., and Ounis, I. 2013. News Vertical Search: When and What to Display to Users. In *Proceedings of SIGIR 2013*, 253-262.

[4] Mensink, T., and Verbeek, J. 2008. Improving People Search Using Query Expansions How Friends Help To Find People. In *Proceedings of ECCV 2008*, 86-99.

[5] Messina, A., and Montagnuolo, M. 2009. A Generalised Cross-Modal Clustering Method Applied to Multimedia News Semantic Indexing and Retrieval. In *Proceedings of WWW 2009*, 321-330.

[6] Li, Z. C., Liu, J., Zhu, X. B., and Lu, H. Q. 2010. Multi-Modal Multi-Correlation Person-Centric News Retrieval. In *Proceedings of CIKM 2010*, 179-188.

[7] Pham, P. T., Moens, M. F., and Tuytelaars, T. 2010. Cross-Media Alignment of Names and Faces. *IEEE Transactions on Multimedia*, 12(1):13-27.

[8] Berg, T. L., Berg, A. C., Edwards, J., and Forsyth, D. A. 2005. Who's in the Picture. *Advances in Neural Information Processing Systems 17*, 37-144.

[9] Guillaumin, M., and Mensink, T., Verbeek, J. and Schmid, C. 2008. Automatic Face Naming with Caption-based Supervision. In *Proceedings of CVPR 2008*, 1-8.

Discovering the Latent Similarities of the KNN Graph by Metric Transformation

Zhenzhong Kuang
School of Geosciences, China University of Petroleum (Huadong), Qingdao, China
zzkuang@foxmail.com

Zongmin Li*
School of Geosciences, China University of Petroleum (Huadong), Qingdao, China
lizongmin@upc.edu.cn

Jianping Fan
Department of Computer Science, University of North Carolina at Charlotte, USA
jfan@uncc.edu

ABSTRACT

The manifold of the dataset turns out to be quite useful in refining the retrieval results, and the diffusion process provides an efficient solution by careful selection of the similarity neighborhood which is usually modeled as the K-nearest neighborhood (KNN) graph. However, existing works are sensitive to the topology noises induced by the first K neighbors. In this paper, we tackle the problem by studying metric transformation which aims at finding new functional relationship to dig the latent similarity. The advantage of the approach lies in its robustness towards the varying K values; that is to say, it could preserve high similarity performances even if K is very large. Except for discussing only the global KNN (i.e. the same K for all neighborhoods) graph, we also investigate to specify a different K for each neighborhood by incorporating the new penalized consensus information (PCI). We show that PCI works superior compared with the original consensus information for denoising. Experiments on multiple affinity matrices have corroborated the superiority of our method with surprising good results.

Categories and Subject Descriptors

H.3.3 [**Information Search and Retrieval**]: Retrieval models

General Terms

Theory

Keywords

Similarity discovery, Metric transformation, KNN graph, Retrieval

1. INTRODUCTION

Large amounts of multimedia data currently available has posed interesting challenges for retrieval systems. With the development of object descriptors, the retrieval performance has improved a lot both in 2D and 3D fields [15, 6, 4]. But, most of the current results are still unsatisfactory and how to improve them is a hot topic.

*Corresponding author at: 66 Changjiang West Road, Huangdao, Qingdao, Shandong 266580, China.

ICMR'15, June 23–26, 2015, Shanghai, China.

http://dx.doi.org/10.1145/2671188.2749303.

In the recent years, lots of investigations have been paid to improve the retrieval by considering the latent structure of the dataset [14, 3, 13]. The basic idea of this technology is to provide an ideal environment (i.e. the database) to perform retrieval for a given query input. As a matter of fact, the objects (images/3D shapes) in database are usually represented as features and their similarities are usually measured by some metrics, such as Euclidean distance. However, many of the similarity relationships between database objects are incorrect due to the error features or the inappropriate metrics. Now, it is still quite difficult to solve the problem by changing features and trying different metrics.

Recently, the affinity learning by diffusion has been proved quite efficient [14] in improving the affinity between database objects, among which the iterative random walks method has been widely researched by using the K-nearest neighborhood (KNN) graph. Yang et al. [13] proposed to use the constrained graph to spread the similarity. The authors of [3] introduced a self-smoothing (SSO) operator to improve a given similarity result, and Wang et al. [11] extended the approach by self-diffusion (SD) for image segmentation and clustering. To obtain a good neighborhood for affinity diffusion, Yang et al. [14] utilized the tensor product graph to incorporate high order relations. An up-to-date work [2] provided a detailed introduction of the iterative diffusion process for retrieval revisit. However, the approach suffers from the topology changes controlled by the global KNN (GKNN), which has constrained its real application. At the same time, Premachandran et al. [8] proposed to specify different K for each neighborhood by introducing a consensus information (CI) [13, 14], where we call this kind of neighborhood as 'local KNN' denoted as LKNN.

The main goal of this paper is to perform metric transformation on the KNN graph to achieve the same intention of the diffusion process for affinity learning. The advances of the shape analysis in spectral space give us lots of inspiration [5]. We know that both the diffusion process and the spectral methods operate on the affinity matrix. The former is used to improve the similarity results, while the latter has been widely studied for some other applications, like dimensionality reduction and clustering [12]. Distinctively, we regard the diffusion problem as the understanding the connectivity between graph nodes in the dimension reduced spectral space which contains much less noise while preserves the major information of the original manifold. Therefore, the original metric can be transformed to a new version by formulating new pairwise relationships, which leads to the development of new metric functions. Then, we study two distinct ways of constructing the KNN graph. On the one hand, we create a GKNN graph and verify its robustness for affinity learning. On the other, we study the LKNN graph and present an extension method of [8] to find robust neighbors, because the approach provided in [8] still suffers from lots of noise even if adopting the consensus information.

The rest of this paper is organized as follows. In Section 2, we discuss the proposed method for discovering the latent similarities of the KNN graph. In Section 3, we evaluate the proposed method by experiment. Finally, we conclude the paper in Section 4.

2. THE PROPOSED APPROACH

The aim of this section is to perform metric transformation by a new mapping $M : d \rightarrow f$ regardless of the original metric d of any forms. Next, we discuss the proposed model and the implementation details in several subsections.

2.1 Spectral Space of the KNN graph

Given a dataset $O = \{o_i\}_{i=1}^{n}$ containing n objects, we generate a distance matrix $DM = [d(i,j) = \|\zeta(o_i) - \zeta(o_j)\|_m]_{n\times n}$ by comparing pairwise features $\zeta(\cdot)$. In ideal situation, the distance $d(i,j)$ is large for inter-class objects, while it is small for intra-class objects. But, this is not always true in real cases due to errors and noises. Suppose the dataset objects exhibit clustering properties in the feature space, the contextual information becomes quite useful in alleviating the above deficiency. Take two inter-class objects o_i and o_j for example. If $d(i,j)$ is smaller than some of the intra-class distances of o_i and the distances between o_i and all the neighbors of o_j are much larger than $d(i,j)$ (i.e. far away from o_i), then we have a high probability to say that o_j is an error matching of o_i. Numerically, it is hard to judge the real errors, and a common solution is to adjust the distance values which are usually converted to the affinity values: $A(i,j) = exp(d^2(i,j)/\sigma_{ij}^2)$, where σ_{ij}^2 is a parameter used for normalization.

To describe the contextual information, a graph $G = (V, E)$ is constructed, where $V = \{v_i = o_i \in O\}$ represents the node set and $E = \{A(i,j)\}$ is the edge set. Because the edge sparsification [8] is extremely important in reducing the amount of noise, we redefine the graph by pruning the edges out of the KNN scope

$$W(i,j) = \begin{cases} A(i,j) & \text{if } v_j \in KNN(v_i) \\ 0 & \text{otherwise} \end{cases}. \quad (1)$$

Instead of using the iterative random walks [2], we prefer to discuss the problem in the spectral space by using the Laplacian matrix $L = D^{-1}(D - W)$, where the degree matrix is defined as $D(i,i) = \Sigma_{v_j \in V} W(i,j)$. Then, we derive the spectral space $S = (\Phi, \Lambda)$ based on the eigensystem $L\Phi = \Lambda\Phi$, where $\Lambda = diag(\lambda_i)_{i=1}^{\theta}, \Phi = [\phi_i]_{i=1}^{\theta}$. To get a real solution, we enforce the affinity matrix W to be symmetric by setting $W = (W + W^T)/2$.

2.2 Metric Transformation

In the spectral space $S = (\Phi, \Lambda)$, we define a normalized coordinate for the graph node based on the eigenpairs λ_l and ϕ_l

$$p_i = (g_l^i - \psi_l)_{l=1}^{\theta} \quad (2)$$

where $g_l^i = k(\lambda_l)\phi_l^i$, $\psi_l = \sum_{i=1}^{n} g_l^i/n$, $k(\lambda_l)$ is the kernel function to adjust the influence of eigenvalues, and the smallest θ eigenpairs are used to remove the noise.

On this basis, we propose to find new similarity measures by characterizing the pairwise relations. Mathematically, the distance metric function $\hat{d}(p_i, p_j) = \|p_i - p_j\|_2$ and inner product function $h(p_i, p_j) =< p_i, p_j >= h(g^i, g^j) - h(g^i, \psi) - h(g^j, \psi)$ provide the most typical solutions. The former could characterize the similarity directly, while the latter describes the similarity in a sense of togetherness regardless of their relative positions. By experiment, we find that the inner product function is not stable to describe the similarity compared with the distance metric which has exhibited interesting properties in describing the connectivity of pairwise nodes by averaging all the possible paths [9, 7]. Thus, the distance metric is more preferable. Besides, different forms of the kernel function would also affect the expression of similarity a lot, and, here, we present two of the studied kernels: $k_1(\lambda_l) = e^{-\lambda_l t}$ and $k_2(\lambda_l) = 1/\sqrt{\lambda_l}$. Because $k_2(\cdot)$ is apt to be influenced by noise [1], the exponential kernel $k_1(\cdot)$ performs superior.

To describe the latent connectivity of the KNN graph nodes, we propose to use a parameter-free kernel $k(\lambda_l) = e^{-\lambda_l}$ instead of $k_1(\lambda_l)$ because the tune of scale parameter is complicated and non-universal without intuitive criteria. Although $k(\lambda_l)$ is robust to noise, it would decrease the discriminative ability. To handle the problem, we devise a new function to unfold the latent similarity

$$f(p_i, p_j) = log(\hat{d}(p_i, p_j)/\delta + 1), \delta = \max_{1\le i,j\le n} \hat{d}(p_i, p_j) \quad (3)$$

As a result, we rank the dataset objects by $f(\cdot,\cdot)$ which is advantageous in denoising and summarizing the contextual information. Next, we present two different ways of constructing the KNN graph for metric transformation (MT) and we denote the proposed approach as MT for short.

2.3 GKNN Graph

As with prior works [2], we study the performance of the proposed method by setting a uniform K for the KNN graph of each object. Then, we set the normalization parameter for the affinity measure $A(i,j)$ as the Kth smallest distance in the KNN neighborhood of each object. In most cases, K is determined heuristically by experiment, but, for state-of-the-art [2], the available scope of K is quite small to achieve good performances (see Section 3.1). In fact, some other techniques (e.g. clustering) can be used to determine K automatically. We leave this for the future work.

2.4 LKNN Graph

In real applications, the class distribution of the dataset is unknown (maybe unevenly), which makes the global prediction of K even harder and would result in more errors. Therefore, the local KNN is more preferable. Based on the recent work [8] that the consensus information (CI) was employed to find the robust local neighbors, we extend the method by considering to penalize the farthest neighbors to purify the resulting KNN graph, because there still exist lots of noise in the KNN graph by using only CI.

Algorithm 1 : Penalized Consensus Information

Input: $PCI = [0], d(\cdot,\cdot), n$
Output: PCI
for $i = 1 \rightarrow n$ **do**
  $P = KNN(v_i), F = KFN(v_i), k = length(P)$
  for $j = 1 \rightarrow k$ **do**
    for $l = j + 1 \rightarrow k$ **do**
      $PCI(P(j), P(l)) = PCI(P(j), P(l)) + 1$
      $PCI(P(l), P(j)) = PCI(P(l), P(j)) + 1$
    end for
  end for
  for $j = 1 \rightarrow k$ **do**
    for $l = 1 \rightarrow k$ **do**
      $PCI(P(j), F(l)) = PCI(P(j), F(l)) - 1$
      $PCI(F(l), P(j)) = PCI(F(l), P(j)) - 1$
    end for
  end for
end for

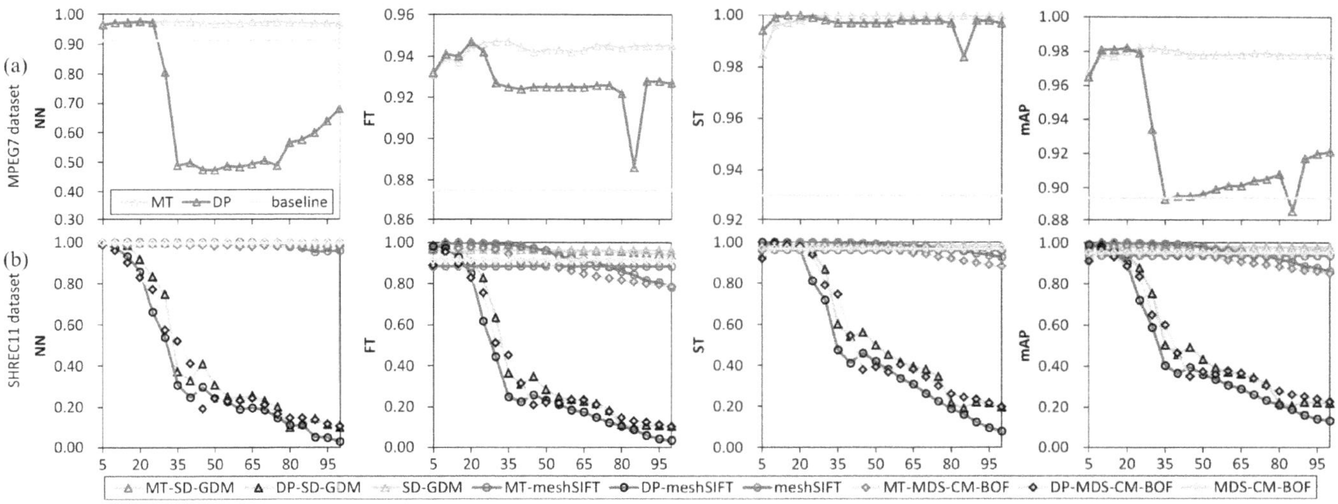

Figure 1: Comparison of the similarity propagation results of MT and DP [2] by increasing the global K value (the horizontal axis).

Table 1: Comparison of the best similarity propagation results by using the GKNN based MT and DP.

(a) MPEG7 dataset	NN	FT	ST	mAP
MT	**97.6**	**94.7**	**100**	**98.2**
DP	97.6	94.7	100	98.2
baseline	91.1	87.5	93.0	89.4
(b) SHREC11 dataset	NN	FT	ST	mAP
MT-SD-GDM	**100**	**100**	**100**	**100**
DP-SD-GDM	99.7	99.6	100	99.8
SD-GDM	100	96.2	98.4	98.0
MT-meshSIFT	**100**	**99.9**	**100**	**100**
DP-meshSIFT	99.2	98.2	99.9	99.0
meshSIFT	99.5	88.4	96.2	93.8
MT-MDS-CM-BOF	**99.0**	**97.6**	**99.4**	**98.5**
DP-MDS-CM-BOF	95.8	95.4	99.6	97.0
MDS-CM-BOF	99.5	91.3	96.9	95.0

In addition to the CI for constructing the KNN graph as with in [8], we propose to penalize the K-farthest neighbors (KFN) because they may appear as noise in the neighborhood of the other KNN procedures. With a high probability, the judgement of the dissimilarity between KNN and KFN nodes are more confidential. Thus, we suggest to obtain the node pairs by picking one node from KNN and KFN, respectively. And then, we penalize the consensus information by recording the co-occurrence times of them. We call the resulting knowledge as penalized consensus information (PCI). The procedure of collecting PCI is presented in Algorithm 1.

The noise edges can be easily removed for small PCI items. The normalization parameter for $A(i, j)$ is set as the largest distance in the neighborhood of each object. In Figure 2, we show the PCI matrix intuitively from one of our experiment. After pruning with a threshold, the obtained LKNN graph would become more preferable for affinity discovering, where the intra-class objects have a higher probability to appear in the KNN domain of each other.

3. EXPERIMENTS

We compare our method with state-of-the-art method in [2] (denoted as DP) by using both the GKNN graph and the LKNN graph [8] on two public datasets: MPEG7 dataset [2] and SHREC11 dataset [6]. The MPEG7 dataset contains 1400 images evenly divided into 70 classes, while the SHREC11 dataset contains 600 3D shapes evenly divided into 30 classes. To perform similarity propagation, four distance matrices are adopted: MPEG7 from [2]; SD-GDM, meshSIFT and MDS-CM-BOF from [6]. For convenience, we use 'MT-baseline' and 'DP-baseline' to represent the refined baseline results (e.g. MT-SD-GDM and DP-SD-GDM), and, on the MPEG7 dataset, 'MT' and 'DP' are used to represent the improved results of the baseline.

For systematic evaluation, we employ the statical tools provided in [10] and [6]: Nearest Neighbor (NN), First Tier (FT), Second Tier (ST) and Precision-Recall (PR) curve. We also report the score of mean average precision (mAP) that is approximated as the area under the PR curve. The range of these items is [0,100] in percentage and the higher the better.

3.1 Results by using the GKNN graph

On this dataset, we first evaluate the performance of our method for varying K of the GKNN graph. In Figure 1, we plot the NN, FT, ST and mAP curves on the MPEG7 and SHREC11 datasets for similarity learning by using our MT method and the DP method. According to the results on both datasets, we see that both MT and DP have improved the baseline results for small K (e.g. $K \in [5, 10]$). However, after some specific scopes of K, the performance of DP decreases quickly (e.g. Figure 1 (a) NN and mAP). On the SHREC11 dataset, we find obvious performance decrease of the results produced by the DP method (e.g. Figure 1 (b) DP-SD-GDM). Fortunately, the similarity propagation results of our method are much more robust (e.g. Figure 1 (b) MT-SD-GDM) with respect to the varying neighborhood size K, and our MT method has improved the baseline performance a lot (see Figure 1 (a) MT).

Then, in Table 1, we present the best retrieval scores. We see that, for both MT and DP, they work positively and efficiently in improving the baseline results. The major difference between them lies in the robustness to the selection of their GKNN neighborhood (despite that the accuracy of MT is better). Particularly, we see that, after performing metric transformation, MT-meshSIFT outperforms the best method SD-GDM in [6], and MT-SD-GDM has achieved 100% accuracy on all the scores. We also see that MT-meshSIFT becomes better than MT-MDS-CM-BOF, which benefits from the superior clustering performance of meshSIFT.

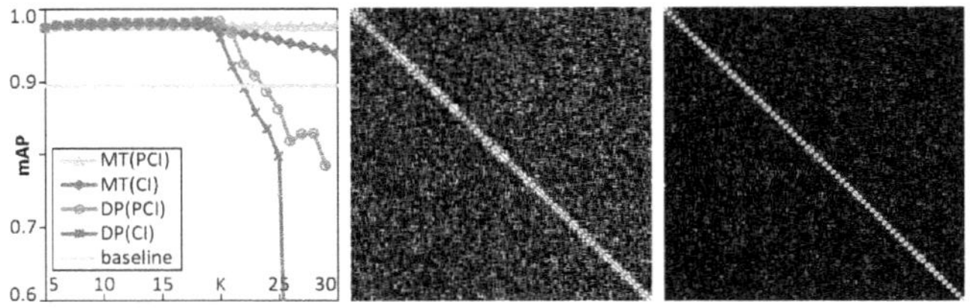

Figure 2: Experiment results on MPEG7 dataset by using the LKNN graph. From left to right, the subfigures are: the mAP curves, the CI matrix and the PCI matrix.

Table 2: Comparison of the best similarity propagation results by using the LKNN based MT and DP.

MPEG7 dataset	NN	FT	ST	mAP
MT	97.9	94.5	99.7	97.8
SHREC11 dataset	NN	FT	ST	mAP
MT-SD-GDM	99.8	99.8	99.9	99.9
MT-meshSIFT	99.8	99.5	99.9	99.7
MT-MDS-CM-BOF	99.3	96.0	99.1	97.4

3.2 Results by using the LKNN graph

Based on the PCI and CI matrices in Figure 2, it is clear that the PCI matrix contains much less noise than the CI matrix. According to the mAP curves, the advantages of the our MT method against existing works lie in two folds: (1) PCI outperforms CI (MT(PCI) versus MT(CI), DP(PCI) versus DP(CI)) for increasing K (the horizontal axis) of the LKNN graph; (2) the curves also show that the MT curves (e.g. MT(PCI)) stay above the corresponding DP curves (e.g. DP(PCI)), which again indicates that the proposed MT method is superior to the DP method [2].

Then, in Table 2, we list the retrieval results of our MT method by using the LKNN graph on the adopted datasets. We see that our method has achieved much higher accuracy than the baseline results in Table 1 (e.g. MT-SD-GDM versus SD-GDM), which indicates the efficiency of the proposed method.

Finally, we plot the PR curves for the proposed MT method by using different KNN graphs in Figure 3. We are delighted to find that the PR curves produced by our method (i.e. MT(MPEG7), MT-SD-GDM, MT-meshSIFT and MT-MDS-CM-BOF) stay above all the corresponding baseline curves.

4. CONCLUSION

We have introduced a different method to perform similarity propagation by metric transformation. We have discussed the common problem of using the GKNN graph to unfold the latent similarity information hidden in the database. To deal with the problem in depth, the penalized consensus information is further incorporated to construct the LKNN graph. Experiment results on a couple of datasets have evidently verified the robustness of the proposed method in spite of its high performance. The results have also proved the advantages of the PCI information. In all, the proposed method has achieved state-of-the-art performance for discovering the latent affinity relationships between the database objects.

5. ACKNOWLEDGMENTS

This work is partly supported by National Natural Science Foundation of China (61379106), the Shandong Provincial Natural Science Foundation (ZR2013FM036), the Fundamental Research Funds for the Central Universities (15CX06017A).

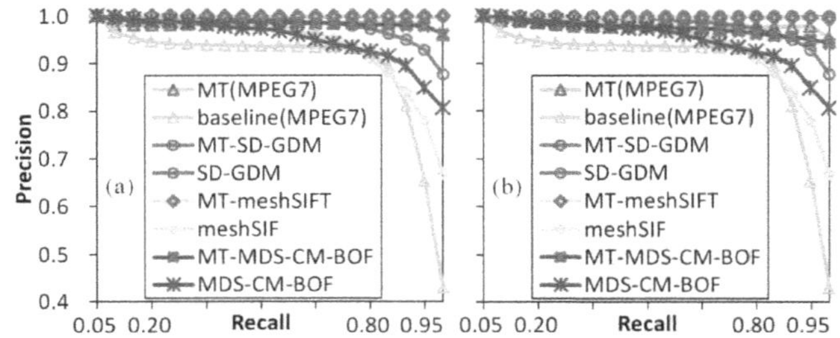

Figure 3: Comparison of the PR curves on MPEG7 dataset and SHREC11 dataset for (a) GKNN graph and (b) LKNN graph.

6. REFERENCES

[1] A. M. Bronstein, M. M. Bronstein, L. J. Guibas, and M. Ovsjanikov. Shape google: Geometric words and expressions for invariant shape retrieval. *ToG*, 30(1):1, 2011.

[2] M. Donoser and H. Bischof. Diffusion processes for retrieval revisited. In *CVPR*, pages 1320–1327, 2013.

[3] J. Jiang, B. Wang, and Z. Tu. Unsupervised metric learning by self-smoothing operator. In *ICCV*, pages 794–801, 2011.

[4] Z. Kuang, Z. Li, Q. Lv, W. Tian, and Y. Liu. Modal function transformation for isometric 3d shape representation. *Computers & Graphics*, 46:209–220, 2015.

[5] B. Lévy. Laplace-beltrami eigenfunctions towards an algorithm that understands geometry. In *SMI*, page 13, 2006.

[6] Z. Lian, A. Godil, B. Bustos, M. Daoudi, J. Hermans, S. Kawamura, Y. Kurita, G. Lavoué, H. Van Nguyen, R. Ohbuchi, et al. A comparison of methods for non-rigid 3d shape retrieval. *Pattern Recognition*, 46(1):449–461, 2013.

[7] B. Nadler, S. Lafon, R. R. Coifman, and I. G. Kevrekidis. Diffusion maps, spectral clustering and reaction coordinates of dynamical systems. *Applied and Computational Harmonic Analysis*, 21(1):113–127, 2006.

[8] V. Premachandran and R. Kakarala. Consensus of k-nns for robust neighborhood selection on graph-based manifolds. In *CVPR*, pages 1594–1601, 2013.

[9] H. Qiu and E. R. Hancock. Clustering and embedding using commute times. *PAMI*, 29(11):1873–1890, 2007.

[10] P. Shilane, P. Min, M. Kazhdan, and T. Funkhouser. The princeton shape benchmark. In *SMI*, pages 167–178, 2004.

[11] B. Wang and Z. Tu. Affinity learning via self-diffusion for image segmentation and clustering. In *CVPR*, pages 2312–2319, 2012.

[12] S. Yan, D. Xu, B. Zhang, H.-J. Zhang, Q. Yang, and S. Lin. Graph embedding and extensions: a general framework for dimensionality reduction. *PAMI*, 29(1):40–51, 2007.

[13] X. Yang, S. Koknar-Tezel, and L. J. Latecki. Locally constrained diffusion process on locally densified distance spaces with applications to shape retrieval. In *CVPR*, pages 357–364, 2009.

[14] X. Yang, L. Prasad, and L. J. Latecki. Affinity learning with diffusion on tensor product graph. *PAMI*, 35(1):28–38, 2013.

[15] L. Zheng, S. Wang, Z. Liu, and Q. Tian. Packing and padding: Coupled multi-index for accurate image retrieval. In *CVPR*, pages 4321–4328, 2014.

Formation Period Matters: Towards Socially Consistent Group Detection via Dense Subgraph Seeking

Yanhao Zhang[1], Lei Qin[3], Shengping Zhang[1], Hongxun Yao[1], Qingming Huang[1,2]
[1]Harbin Institute of Technology, Harbin, 150001, China
[2]University of Chinese Academy of Sciences, Beijing, 100049, China
[3]Inst. of Comput. Tech., Chinese Academy of Sciences, Beijing, 100190, China
{yhzhang, s.zhang, h.yao}@hit.edu.cn qinlei@ict.ac.cn qmhuang@ucas.ac.cn

ABSTRACT

Group detection becomes an important task in crowd behavior surveillance. However, most existing methods ignore the formation persistency characteristics, which predict unreliable interactions when the crowd is realistic and complex. To address this issue, we propose a novel graph-based method to declare that the formation period really matters for detecting social groups in crowd. First, we develop a socially motivated representation by modeling the formation period probability in a Bayesian manner, which results in social and temporal consistency for group member interactions. A graph is then established using individuals as nodes and formation periods as edge weights to reflect pedestrian relationships. In this way, seeking of socially consistent groups is converted into an optimization problem which seeks dense subgraphs with maximum formation likelihood within the graph structure. We employ graph shift optimization to detect groups by finding all the dense subgraphs due to its robust performance. In the experimental results on public datasets, our proposed method clearly outperforms other related state-of-the-art methods.

Categories and Subject Descriptors

H.3.1 [**Information Systems Applications**]: Content Analysis and Indexing methods

General Terms

Algorithms; Social factors; Experimentation.

Keywords

Social group; Formation period; Dense subgraph seeking

1. INTRODUCTION

Crowd activity analysis plays a significant role in video surveillance fields with diverse applications including public safety management and activity understanding for predicting crimes. Understanding complex interactions in crowded scenes just by treating each pedestrian individually is unrealistic, due to the inherent social characteristics of human behavior. Typically, interactions involve in small subsets of a crowd, at neither an individual level nor in a holistic level. Many existing works on detecting groups tend to find people getting together based on the persistence of their proximity and direction of motion [8, 3, 7, 10, 2, 1, 12, 11], which are measurable from the extracted trajectories. Pellegrini et al. [8] jointly predict trajectories and estimate group memberships by employing a Conditional Random Field (CRF), which is modeled as latent variables over a short time window. Yamaguchi et al. [10] formulate the problem of predicting groups as minimization of an energy function which encodes physical condition, personal motivation and pairwise interactions features. Ge et al. [3] present an agglomerative approach to associate trajectories, which hierarchically merges clusters by evaluating an inter-group closeness measure. Chang et al. [1] propose a soft segmentation process to partition the crowd by constructing a weighted graph.

However, existing works are lack of sociological motivation in the choice of features. Furthermore, they tend to understand the groups without considering the social consistency of formation behavior. To give an intuitive interpretation, social formation among small gathering of people sharing a common goal would indicate interaction behavior at group level. It is preserved by a dynamic process of trajectories, which can be inferred more from the group formation and the temporal evolution among their relationships. To address these issues, we underline formation characteristics inspired by social studies to declare that formation period really matters for detecting the social groups. We summarize our contributions as:

1) We present a socially consistent group detection method by exploiting the temporal formation representation for the social interactions. To our best knowledge, this is the first effort towards improving social consistency by formation period modeling.

2) Considering social cues of the groups, our proposed formation period is capable of capturing group structures and compositions of social interactions, which makes it robust and greatly invariant to represent the group behaviors.

3) We propose to construct a graph between the individuals by using formation period probability. We seek the dense subgraphs as the desired social groups within the graph structure that reflects socially consistent formation period in the crowd.

ICMR'15, June 23–26, 2015, Shanghai, China.

DOI: http://dx.doi.org/10.1145/2671188.2749305.

2. SOCIAL GROUP ANALYSIS

In this section, we analyze the social features by exploring the social formation priors in Bayesian formulation. We present a formation period representation which is competent for social group detection, especially when the distance and angle cues show inadequate capabilities for indicating social interactions.

2.1 Formation probability modeling

Given a frame $t \in \{1, \cdots, T\}$ from a crowd sequence, each tracked subject $i \in \{1, \cdots, N\}$ corresponds to one local trajectory $H_i \in \mathcal{H}$ of a person. H_i consists of T tuples $h_i^t = \{s_i^t, v_i^t, \alpha_i^t\}^{t=1...T}$, where s_i and v_i denote the position and velocity vectors of the subject i with the estimated orientation α_i at time t. Let $\mathcal{F}$ denote the set of formation within the interacting individuals, $\mathcal{G}$ be the set of all possible social groups along the interacting time $\mathcal{T}$, where each element $g \in \mathcal{G}$ is a binary vector indicating the group relationship among the subjects i and j. Our goal is to find an optimal group clusters $\mathcal{G}^*$ from $\mathcal{G}$ which best fits a given interaction time and formation set $\mathcal{T}$ and $\mathcal{F}$. To this end, we model the probability of the group indicator $\mathcal{G}$ based on $\mathcal{F}$ and $\mathcal{T}$ by considering both the spatial formation of interaction and the temporal overlap of period in a Bayesian manner as

$$p(\mathcal{G}|\mathcal{F},\mathcal{T}) \propto \underbrace{p_s(\mathcal{F}|\mathcal{G})}_{Formation}\ \underbrace{p_t(\mathcal{F}|\mathcal{G},\mathcal{T})}_{Period}\ \underbrace{p(\mathcal{G}|\mathcal{F})}_{Prior} \quad (1)$$

where $p_s(\mathcal{F}|\mathcal{G})$ measures the spatial consistency between the assignment of group $\mathcal{G}$ and the given formation set $\mathcal{F}$. $p_t(\mathcal{F}|\mathcal{G},\mathcal{T})$ measures the "period" properties of $\mathcal{G}$, which indicates the temporally pairwise interactions. Traditionally, this item can be presented as $p_t(\mathcal{T}|\mathcal{G})$, giving the likelihood that the happening of social group is based on the time of getting together. Now, the interacting time $\mathcal{T}$ is not treated equally and is instead valued by the social formation set $\mathcal{F}$. Therefore, the new likelihood $p_t(\mathcal{F}|\mathcal{G},\mathcal{T})$ can be interpreted as the probability of social formation along the interacting time $\mathcal{T}$. The last term $p(\mathcal{G}|\mathcal{F})$ is the prior probability of the formation for the groups that we regard equally for all candidates. When we maximize the probability of Eqn. 1, obviously, we expect to obtain the social groups which have the spatially consistent formation with the social formation encoded in the formation set $\mathcal{F}$ and simultaneously satisfy the pairwise interacting period.

2.2 Socially consistent feature

Formally, social aggregation theories [4] project the pedestrian trajectories onto the space which provides us useful group concepts of sustaining mutual activities. The non-linearity of the social interaction is correlated with a quantization of their mutual distance into personal, social and public space as F-formation. It is considered as a specific instance of a focused encounter as all the participants co-operate to sustain a continued period of information exchange. The idea behind this is that spatial and orientational behaviors are created by people who sustain the shared interaction space between them. To this aim, we define the proximity based probability $\phi_{ij}^{prox}(h_i, h_j|g)$ and orientation based probability $\psi_{ij}^{ori}(h_i, h_j|g)$ to give the detailed semantics of the formation. An illustration of formation period is shown in Fig. 1. The spatial formation can be measured

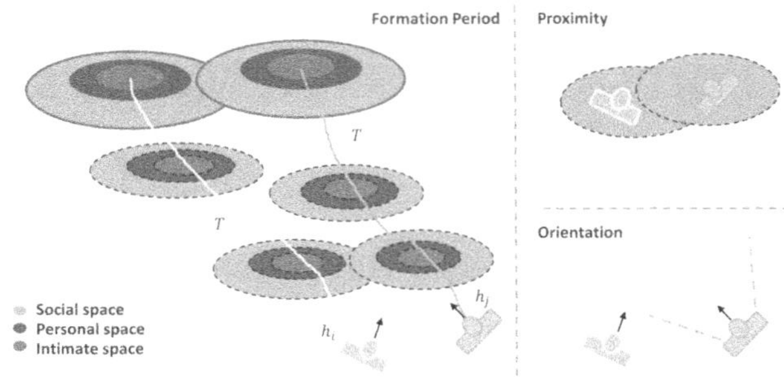

Figure 1: Formation period considers the formation of interaction in terms of both proximity and orientation on the temporal correlation.

by computing the position and angle with respect to local trajectories set $\mathcal{H}$, which is similar as the trajectories and grouping associating process [8] as a log likelihood,

$$log(p_s(\mathcal{F}|\mathcal{G})) = \sum \phi_{ij}^{prox}(h_i, h_j|g) + \sum \psi_{ij}^{ori}(h_i, h_j|g) \quad (2)$$

The proximity probability is defined as

$$\sum \phi_{ij}^{prox}(h_i, h_j|g) = \sum \log[p_{mov}(s_i|s_j\alpha_j, g_{ij} = 1)$$

$$+p_{stop}(d(s_i, s_j)|g_{ij} = 1)] - \sum \log(p(d(s_i, s_j)|g_{ij} = 0) \quad (3)$$

where $d(s_i, s_j)$ is the Euclidean distance between two positions. Corresponding to moving and stopping people in the same group, two modes of probabilities p_{mov} and p_{stop} are estimated by building a normalized histogram of the angles and speeds in the training set [8]. From the statistics, it is easy to distinguish two modes. For pedestrians in different groups, position is enough to tell apart the interaction in the public space. In terms of orientation probability, it is defined as

$$\sum \psi_{ij}^{ori}(h_i, h_j|g) = \sum p(\alpha_i, \alpha_j|g_{ij}=1) - \sum p(\alpha_i, \alpha_j|g_{ij}=0) \quad (4)$$

where the probabilities are based on whether the pedestrians have the same orientational range or not. The focused orientation can help to identify the shared space between all the formation members. This is relevant that pedestrian should be oriented towards an F-formation [2]. As before, all the estimated terms are computed with a smoothed histogram approach overall a temporal window.

Under the objective of obtaining the interaction period, we measure the temporal overlap of the trajectories between the person i and j within a temporal interaction $\mathcal{T}$. We denote the distance measurement of the social formation for each pair h_i and h_j directly as the likelihood

$$log(p_t(\mathcal{F}|\mathcal{G},\mathcal{T})) = \sum_t p_t(\mathcal{F}|g,\mathcal{T}) \propto \sum_t \delta_t(i,j) \quad (5)$$

where $\delta_t(i,j) = 1$ indicates $h_{i,j}$ are in the same group if $\|s_i^t - s_j^t\| \le r_s$ and $\|v_i^t - v_j^t\| \le r_v$, otherwise $\delta_t(i,j) = 0$. This period probability $p_t(\mathcal{F}|\mathcal{G},\mathcal{T})$ is the occurrences between person i and j within $\mathcal{T}$ that the spatial and velocity differences are below the thresholds r_s and r_v. This strategy makes grouping people walking close to each other with similar velocities capable of interacting for a long period of time.

which leads to temporal consistency to get stable groups over time and meanwhile guarantees its social formation.

3. FORMATION PERIOD SUBGRAPHS

In this section, we formulate the formation probability modeled in Sec. 2.1 into the graph shift framework, where the problem of maximizing the probability of Eqn. 1 over the possible groups $\mathcal{G}$ is converted to the form of maximizing the density of subgraphs problem. We extend the idea of finding dense subgraph in the social formation period domain to detect local social groups.

3.1 Consistency Graph Construction

A dense subgraph is a strongly connected subset of vertexes in a weighted undirected complete graph. The undirected graph is constructed by using the individuals as the graph nodes and the formation period probabilities as the edge weights. In this way, the valid formation period that is socially consistent would form a dense subgraph and could be robustly detected by the method of graph shift. Given all the trajectories extracted from the individuals, $H(h_1, ..., h_n)$ with the individual number n, we conduct formation period correlation in the product space $Q = |H| \times |H|$ and obtain $n \times n$ pairs. In order to obtain a continuous and more general measure, we substitute the original quantization with an exponential function and the proximal similarity of any trajectory pair h_i and h_j is computed as follows,

$$f_1(h_i, h_j) = \frac{1}{T}\sum_t \delta_t(i,j) \times e^{p_s(\mathcal{F}|\mathcal{G})} \qquad (6)$$

Thus, a T-frame video sequence can be represented by a trajectory graph with 3-tuple $G = (V, E, w)$, in which V is a set of vertices, $E \subseteq V \times V$ is a set of edges, w is the edge weights assigning to E. We next try to specify the detailed description based on the basic graphs. The adjacency matrix representation $A(i,j)$ for the graph G is as follows:

$$A(i,j) = \begin{cases} 0 & i = j \\ f_1(h_i, h_j) & i \neq j \end{cases} \qquad (7)$$

We can calculate the formation period similarity by Eqn. 7. The function of the similarity value can be denoted as Eqn. 6 which encodes the evaluation of temporal consistence and social formation correlation.

3.2 Detection by dense subgraph seeking

Obviously, the graph G is symmetric and nonnegative. Suppose a social group has r trajectory-pairs. It corresponds to a dense subgraph D of G with r vertices, which is a weighted counterpart of maximal clique. If we represent a subgraph by a vector x, $x \in \Delta^n$, where $\Delta^n = \{x \in R^n : x \geq 0 \,\&\, |x|_1 = 1\}$. x_i, the ith component of x, denotes the probability of this subgraph containing the vertex i. The modes of a graph G are approximately local maximizers of the graph density $g(x) = x^T Ax$. We can derive that $g(x) = \sum_i x_i(Ax)_i$. Given a vector x, the corresponding subgraph is $G(x)$. If x^* is a local maximizer of $g(x)$, the $G(x^*)$ is a dense subgraph which represents the social group. Therefore we need to calculate all local maximizers of this standard quadratic optimization function:

$$\begin{cases} maximize & g(x) = x^T Ax \\ subject\,to & x \in \Delta^n \end{cases} \qquad (8)$$

Table 1: Datasets descriptions.

Dataset	Length	Individuals	Groups	Density	Type
eth	8m 40s	386	81	low	few interactions
hotel	7m 23s	287	55	low	complex interactions
stu003	3m 40s	417	112	high	more complex behaviours

It can be solved by the replicator dynamics with neighborhood expansion in graph shift optimization [6],

$$x_i(t+1) = x_i(t)\frac{(Ax(t))_i}{x(t)^T Ax(t)}, i = 1, \ldots, n \qquad (9)$$

where $x_i(t)$ is a mode of subgraph obtained at the ith iteration. Note that the vertexes (which correspond to the candidate formation period of individuals) contained in the dense subgraph x^* are the most likely to be the valid social groups, and the value of the non-zero bin x^* now indicates the probability that a candidate formation period belongs to the socially consistent group. We conclude the merits of detecting the groups in the crowd via the consistency graph model as follows: 1) Formation periods naturally capture the social inspired knowledge, which robustly reject most of the invalid trajectory interactions, hence are effective in leveraging the influence of formation periods. Meanwhile, the formation period probability enables us to measure the group formation in a more robust and accurate way than traditional similarity of trajectories. 2) The group detection is converted to dense subgraph seeking, which is reasonable because the dense subgraph is a strongly connected subset of vertexes in a graph. According to the definition of the weights on graph edges, the correspondence between the clusters from the same similar connection has the most graph density than that from different connections or noises. 3) Our approach could handle the complex group formation situation during a temporal overlap. When a group is forming social interaction, there exist dense subgraphs corresponding to these candidate formation periods. The problem of finding dense subgraphs is easy to be solved by the graph shift algorithm. So we can obtain high robustness and accuracy of validly social formation group.

4. EXPERIMENTAL RESULTS

To demonstrate the effectiveness of our method, we conduct group detection experiments on three public datasets including the eth and hotel sequences from the BIWI Walking Pedestrians dataset [7] as well as the stu003 sequence from Crowds-By-Examples (CBE) dataset [5].

Datasets. BIWI dataset records two low crowded scenes outside a university and a bus station, while the CBE dataset records a high density crowd outside a university. Table 1 shows the detailed information of these datasets. All sequences come with a group annotation and the trajectory annotations are completed by marking the position of each individual every a few frames. These sequences are particularly challenging ranging from low to high density and various level interactions with complex condition due to low image resolution, perspective changes and cast shadows. We split the eth and hotel sequences as training set (about 2000 frames) to train the statistics features and parameters for formation period and the rest frames for testing set.

Evaluation Protocol and Analysis. To evaluate the performance of the socially consistent formation period, we compare our method with the state-of-the-art methods. We provide two evaluation approaches to justify the performance of the compared methods:

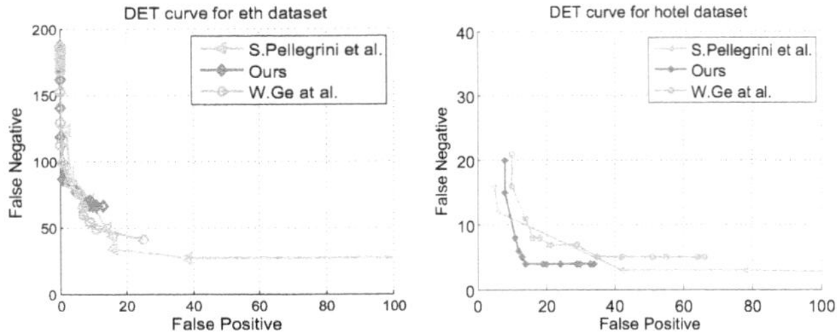

(a) (b)

Figure 2: DET curves for eth (a) and hotel (b) datasets compared with others.

(1) DET curves for pairwise links. We compare with the interaction time based approaches [8, 3] on the relatively sparse and simple BIWI eth and hotel dataset. All three methods produce similarly good results as groups are isolated and easy to tell as shown in Fig. 2. In each approach, the detected groups are compared with the ground truth. The DET curves are generated by varying the parameters of length of interaction to report false positive (when the pair is assigned to the same group which is not in the same group in the ground truth) and false negative (when the method fails to predict the pair as the same group). This clearly demonstrates the effectiveness of exploiting socially consistent interaction in the task of pairwise group relation prediction. Note that the distance and velocity based measure (Pellegrini et al. [8]) is not strong enough to distinguish group relations and produces many false links. Ge et al. [3] performs as well as ours except false positives increase when using longer trajectories. Our proposed formation period achieves the best in this less complex scene. This can be attributed to the fact that we not only measure proximity but also consider the orientational formation of the pedestrians.

(2) The precision and recall of the social group detection. The stu003 sequence is much more crowded and complex, which can be used to test the robustness for complex social interaction. To gain intuition into robustness and effectiveness of our method, we compare our results with the state-of-the-art methods [8, 3, 10, 9]. We run every model on the dataset for evaluating the impact on performances in terms of precision, recall and F-measure as shown in Table 2. Notice that the social interaction based approaches [10, 9] bridge the gaps between the social interaction and the pairwise link in finding groups, among which our method gets a significant improvement than others. This is due to sociological aspect from formation period, which is able to better generalize to describe social interaction and group relations. In addition, the subgraph seeking process enables us to measure the formation period probability in a more robust and accurate way.

Parameter tuning and Complexity. The experiments are conducted by varying the respective formation period threshold r_s and r_v, which indicate the difference between the position and velocity. These thresholds justified by the precision and recall comparison for stu003 are shown in Fig. 3, where r_s and r_v are ranging from (1,3) and (0.1,0.9), respectively. Low values bring noisy formation time which leads to large false negative detection. In general, when the value of r_s is higher than 2.5, or the r_v is smaller than 0.5, the performance will be affected. From the parameter analysis, we choose $r_s = 2$ and $r_v = 0.5$ as reasonable compromise between precision and responsiveness. Our formation period

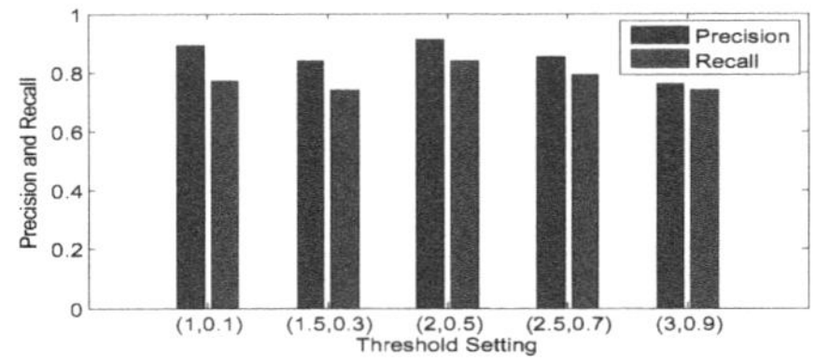

Figure 3: Precision and Recall for stu003 by varying formation period threshold r_s and r_v.

Table 2: Social group detection on stu003 dataset.

stu003 dataset	Precision	Recall	F-measure
Ours	**91.4%**	**83.4%**	**87.2%**
S.Pellegrini et al. [8]	46.0%	82.0%	58.9%
K.Yamaguchi et al. [10]	80.5%	77.0%	80.8%
W.Ge et al. [3]	51.8%	81.7%	63.4%
J.Sochman et al. [9]	85.4%	61.4%	71.3%

can not only obtain outstanding performances when used as the feature representation but also show to be more robust and turned out to be fast with the computational complexity being $O(n \times m)$ and $O(n)$ for computing $A(i, j)$.

5. CONCLUSION

In this paper, we have presented a socially consistent group detection method that represents formation period of group members in terms of social consistency. The formation and temporal information are integrated and encoded into the established graph in a Bayesian manner. Based on a graph relationship constructed with formation period probability features, the seeking of socially consistent group is casted as a dense subgraph seeking problem over the graph structure. Experimental results on three public datasets have confirmed the effectiveness and robustness of the proposed method. For future work, we will explore more promising descriptors for crowds in terms of social consistency.

6. ACKNOWLEDGMENTS

This work was supported in part by National Basic Research Program of China(973 Program): 2012CB316400 and 2015CB351802, in part by National Natural Science Foundation of China: 61133003, 61332016, 61300111, 61390510.

7. REFERENCES

[1] M.-C. Chang et al. Probabilistic group-level motion analysis and scenario recognition. In *IEEE ICCV*, 2011.

[2] M. Cristani and Bazzani. Social interaction discovery by statistical analysis of f-formations. In *BMVC*, 2011.

[3] W. Ge, R. Collins, and B. Ruback. Automatically detecting the small group structure of a crowd. In *IEEE WACV*, 2009.

[4] E. T. Hall. *The hidden dimension.* Anchor Books New York, 1969.

[5] A. Lerner, Y. Chrysanthou, and D. Lischinski. Crowds by example. In *EUROGRAPHICS*, 2007.

[6] H. Liu and S. Yan. Robust graph mode seeking by graph shift. In *IEEE ICML*, 2010.

[7] S. Pellegrini et al. You'll never walk alone: Modeling social behavior for multi-target tracking. *IEEE ICCV*, 2009.

[8] S. Pellegrini et al. Improving data association by joint modeling of pedestrian trajectories and groupings. In *ECCV*. 2010.

[9] J. Sochman et al. Who knows who-inverting the social force model for finding groups. In *IEEE ICCV Workshops*, 2011.

[10] K. Yamaguchi, A. C. Berg, L. E. Ortiz, and T. L. Berg. Who are you with and where are you going? In *IEEE CVPR*, 2011.

[11] Y. Zhang et al. Social attribute-aware force model: Exploiting richness of interaction for abnormal crowd detection. *IEEE TCSVT*, 2014.

[12] Y. Zhang et al. Beyond particle flow: Bag of trajectory graphs for dense crowd event recognition. In *IEEE ICIP*, 2013.

Memory Vectors for Particular Object Retrieval with Multiple Queries

Ronan Sicre
Inria
ronan.sicre@inria.fr

Hervé Jégou
Inria
herve.jegou@inria.fr

ABSTRACT

We address the problem of retrieving all the images containing a specific object in a large image collection, where the input query is given as a set of representative images of the object. This problem is referred to as multiple queries in the literature. For images described with bag-of-visual-words (BOW), one of the best performing approach amounts to simply averaging the query descriptors.

This paper [1] introduces an improved fusion of the object description based on the recent concept of generalized max-pooling and memory vectors, which summarizes a set of vectors by a single representative vector. They have the property of reducing the influence of frequent features. Therefore, we propose to build a memory vector for each set of queries and the membership test is performed with each image descriptor from the database, to determine its similarity with the query representative. This new strategy for multiple queries brings a significant improvement for most of the image descriptors we have considered, in particular with Convolutional Neural Networks (CNN) features.

Categories and Subject Descriptors

H.3.3 [**INFORMATION STORAGE AND RETRIEVAL**]: Information Search and Retrieval

Keywords

image retrieval; multiple queries; memory vectors

1. INTRODUCTION

The last decade has witnessed the rapid increase of multimedia data, which has raised numerous challenges regarding the management of large collections. Multimedia search in large collection, such as Content Based Image Retrieval (CBIR) has received a lot of attention. In this work, we are interested in multiple queries image retrieval, where the CBIR system has a set of representative images of an object as input. Arandjelovic *et al.* [1] show that simply averaging the scores offers a competitive performance, at least as good as taking the best scores across all queries. Another advantage is that, if the image is a vector representation (e.g., bag-of-words or the Fisher vector), one can equivalently (thanks to linearity of average) average the vector representations of the multiple queries. In this case, only the average vector has to be compared against the databases vectors describing the image collection.

In this paper, we are interested in improving this fusion strategy. Our motivation is that, when multiple queries are given as input, some of the images of the query object are very similar, see Figure 1. The redundant information dominates the representation, while rare discriminative features are comparatively overlooked.

Our solution is inspired by recent papers on image representations, namely generalized max-pooling [13] (GMP) and democratic aggregation [12], which improve the aggregation stage of coded local descriptors (such as Fisher) by reducing the influence of frequent, often uninformative, descriptors. Conversely, it gives more importance to rare and potentially highly discriminative patterns. Interestingly, GMP [13] was recently shown to be an effective way to construct a *memory vector* [8] summarizing, in a continuous manner, a vector set by a single vector. This method was introduced to perform approximate nearest neighbor queries in high-dimensional spaces. The memory vector is a compressed representation of the set used to perform a membership test.

In this paper, we model the multiple-queries set with a representative memory vector summarizing all the images. Then, for each database vector we estimate a membership score and use it to rank the images, which amounts to performing a weighted summation of the input vectors. By exploiting this dual interpretation first proposed for generalized max-pooling [13], we extend our method to other matching methods like the selective match kernel [20].

The paper is organized as follows. After a review of related works in Section 2, Section 3 presents our strategy and explains how we use it in the context of multiple-queries. Section 4 presents our experiments. Our results demonstrate the interest of our work for several image representations. Importantly, our method is especially effective with features extracted from a convolution network, outperforming the state-of-the-art of multiple-queries with short vectors.

2. RELATED WORK

Image descriptors. Our method uses on input off-the-shelf vector image representations, such as Bag-of-visual-words (BOW) [18], VLAD [11] or improved Fisher vectors [14].

[1] This work was achieved in the context of the FIRE-ID ANR Project (ANR-12-CORD-016).

ICMR'15, June 23–26, 2015, Shanghai, China.

http://dx.doi.org/10.1145/2671188.2749306 .

We are especially interested in using state-of-the-art short representations, for instance based on democratic aggregation [12]. We also consider descriptors based on Convolutional Neural Networks (CNN), which were recently shown [3] to be very successful on large scale image retrieval tasks, even when reducing the image description to a few hundreds dimensions. These vector representations can be further reduced with binarization [4] or product quantization [10].

Strategies for Multiple-queries. The last few years have witnessed massive progress on the task of finding images depicted a given object in a large database, yet this task still remains challenging when only one image is provided to the system without any annotation. However, in many applications like brand or logo detection, or on output of a text-based search system, several representative images of the objects may be available. This scenario is similar to the instance search task of Trecvid [19] evaluation campaigns.

Multiple image gives a better description of an object to handle problems such as view-point changes, viewing conditions, occlusions, background clutter, shape variation, etc. Arandjelovic & al. [1] presents this problem as well as several possible strategies to exploit these images: average query, SVM on all queries, maximum of multiple queries, average of multiple queries, and exemplar SVM on each query. Their study concludes while averaging the scores, or equivalently averaging the vector representations of the query set, is competitive while reducing the complexity because only one query is submitted. Other works in this setting have been proposed. Chen & al. [6] enrich queries with multiple views in a boosted framework. Fernando & al. [7] use pattern mining to build object specific mid-level image representation. These two strategies aim at explicitly model the query object and are relatively costly. Wu & al. [21] reduces background influence by selecting region of interest appearing in multiple queries.

GMP and memory vectors. Memory vectors [8] build a vector $\mathbf{m}(\mathcal{X})$ summarizing a set $\mathcal{X} = \{\mathbf{x_1}, ..., \mathbf{x_n}\}$ of d-dimensional vectors. This vector optimizes the *membership test*: given a query vector $\mathbf{y}$, it computes the dot product $y^\top \mathbf{m}(\mathcal{X})$ to evaluate whether $\mathbf{y} \in \mathcal{X}$, or close enough to at least one vector in $\mathcal{X}$. The vector are assumed ℓ_2-normalized and uniformly distributed on the unit-hypersphere. In practice, these assumptions do not have necessarily to hold for the method to work well. The test is formalized as the following detection problem:

- Hypothesis H1: $\mathbf{y}$ is not related to $\mathcal{X}$.
- Hypothesis H2: $\mathbf{y}$ is related to $\mathcal{X}$. For example, $\mathbf{y}$ is related to $\mathbf{x_j}$ and we write $\mathbf{y} = \alpha\mathbf{x_j} + \beta\mathbf{z}$, where $\mathbf{z}$ is a random vector orthogonal to $\mathbf{x_j}$ and $||\mathbf{z}|| = 1$. Thus, we have $\alpha^2 + \beta^2 = 1$, because $||\mathbf{y}|| = 1$.

We refer to the dot product $\mathbf{m}^\top\mathbf{y}$ as the membership score. The quality of this score obviously depends on how the vector $\mathbf{m}$ is constructed, for instance simply with the sum vector:

$$m(\mathcal{X}) = \sum_{x \in \mathcal{X}} \mathbf{x}. \quad (1)$$

In that case [8], for a large dimensionality d, the membership score the following distributions:

$$\text{H1: } \langle \mathbf{m}|\mathbf{y} \rangle \sim \mathcal{N}(0, n/d) \quad (2)$$

$$\text{H2: } \langle \mathbf{m}|\mathbf{y} \rangle \sim \mathcal{N}(\alpha, (n-1)/d) \quad (3)$$

However, it is possible to obtain a better hypothesis test. This is achieved by imposing that for any of the vector $\mathbf{x_i}$ in $\mathcal{X}$, $\mathbf{x_i}^\top\mathbf{m}(\mathcal{X}) = 1$, or simply $\mathbf{X}^\top\mathbf{m} = \mathbf{1_n}$ in matrix form, where $\mathbf{1_n}$ is a n-dimensional vector with all values set to 1. This constraint ensures that the interference with remaining vectors of $\mathcal{X}$ are eliminated when the exact same vector is submitted to the system. There are many (a subspace) solutions $\mathbf{m}(\mathcal{X})$ satisfying these constraints.

However, the false positive probability directly depends on the norm of the memory vector and therefore a good way to single a solution is to minimize its norm. In other terms, we want to minimize $||\mathbf{m}||^2$ under the constraint $\mathbf{X}^\top\mathbf{m} = \mathbf{1_n}$. The solution is given by the Moore-Penrose pseudo-inverse:

$$\mathbf{m} = (\mathbf{X}^+)^\top\mathbf{1_n} \quad (4)$$

Since $n < d$, $\mathbf{m} = \mathbf{X}(\mathbf{X}^\top\mathbf{X})^{-1}\mathbf{1_n}$. We note that if no solution exists, $\mathbf{m}^*$ minimizes $||\mathbf{X}^\top\mathbf{m} - \mathbf{1_n}||$. For large d, this construction leads to the following distributions:

$$\text{H1: } \mathbf{m}^\top Y \sim \mathcal{N}(0, ||\mathbf{m}||^2/d) \quad (5)$$

$$\text{H2: } \mathbf{m}^\top Y \sim \mathcal{N}(\alpha, \beta^2||\mathbf{m}||^2/d) \quad (6)$$

Compared to Equation 1, the improvement comes from the decrease of the variance of the scores under H2 at the cost of increasing the variance under H1. This increase under H1 is small for small n/d, meaning that using this optimized construction is comparatively better for short vectors. For a very large dimensionality, the construction of Equation 4 is asymptotically equivalent to the sum construction.

3. MULTIPLE QUERIES: OUR PROPOSAL

3.1 Memory vectors for multiple queries

Our main idea is to inverse the formulation proposed of memory vectors by summarizing the multiple representations of the object by a single vector. The memory vectors were proposed for test membership and approximate search [8], with one query being tested against a set of vectors based on a membership test. In contrast, we aggregate the queries instead of aggregating the database vectors. The query memory vector is compared to all the database vectors and the membership score is used to order them. Note, if the vector is constructed as the average of the input vectors as in Equation 1, this strategy is equivalent to the well-performing method of averaging the vectors [1]. In contrast, we optimize it by using the construction of Equation 4.

Assumptions. All the image descriptors are ℓ_2-normalized, therefore satisfying the assumption mentioned in Section 2. Additionally, the number n of vectors in the query set is significantly smaller than d. Indeed, there is typically no more than 10 images per query. More precisely, $n = 5$ images per query for Oxford5k and Paris6k used as a multiple-query, see Section 4.1. As a result, n/d is small and the membership test is likely to be effective, which fits well our objective of using short representations ranging from d=128 to 512.

Discussion. With the pseudo-inverse construction, the common parts of the combined descriptors are down-weighted and the norm of the memory vector $||\mathbf{m}||^2$ is minimized. This method has a similar effect as the democratization [12] or the GMP [13] and equalizes the influence of frequent and rare features. The main difference is that this effect is obtained across images, while previous strategies were proposed to address this problem within a given query image.

w_i	Gram matrix				
	CNN 512				
0.31	1.00	0.06	0.58	0.02	0.40
0.89	0.06	1.00	0.07	0.08	-0.03
0.55	0.58	0.07	1.00	-0.01	0.29
0.93	0.02	0.08	-0.01	1.00	-0.01
0.75	0.40	-0.03	0.29	-0.01	1.00
	triD 512				
0.68	1.00	0.01	0.43	-0.04	0.28
0.69	0.01	1.00	0.19	0.21	0.06
0.42	0.43	0.19	1.00	-0.04	0.31
0.88	-0.04	0.21	-0.04	1.00	0.03
0.61	0.28	0.06	0.31	0.03	1.00

Figure 1: Visualization of five query images from Oxford5k, and the weights and the Gram matrix for two different types of descriptors.

3.2 Retrieval pipeline

Image representations are computed with VLAD and CNN and other recent single-vector image representations. Since we are mostly interested to improve the initial ranking, we do not use any spatial verification or query expansion techniques, unlike some mentioned previous work [7].

Multi-VLAD – Vlad3c. Features are first extracted using the Hessian-Affine detector and described by RootSIFT [2], and finally rotated with PCA. VLAD are computed using 16, 64, and 256 clusters and compact representations are built by concatenating these three descriptors, power normalization, centering, and PCA to obtain 128, 256, and 512 dimensional "Vlad-3c" descriptors respectively [9, 17].

triD. We use off-the-shelf the descriptors of the recent triangulation embedding and democratization [12].

CNN features. We extract CNN descriptors pre-trained on the Imagenet dataset with the Fast CNN architecture [5]. We follow the recommendation of Babenko *et al.* [3] and use the output of the 6th layer before applying the ReLU. The descriptors are post-processed as Vlad3c and tridD: power normalized, centered, and PCA is applied.

3.3 Dual representation

To evaluate how much an image contributes to the produced memory vector, we employ the dual interpretation proposed by Murray *et al.* [13], which shows that the memory vector of the set $\mathcal{X}$ can be written as a weighted sum:

$$\mathbf{m}(\mathcal{X}) = \sum_{x_i \in \mathcal{X}} w_i \mathbf{x}_i, \qquad (7)$$

where w_i is the weight for a given vector of the query set. Denoting $\mathbf{w} = [w_1, \ldots, w_n]^\top$, the weight vector obtained is

$$\mathbf{w} = (\mathbf{X}^\top \mathbf{X})^{-1} \mathbf{1}_n. \qquad (8)$$

This formulation computes weights that can be interpreted as quantitative measures of the rarity of the different query

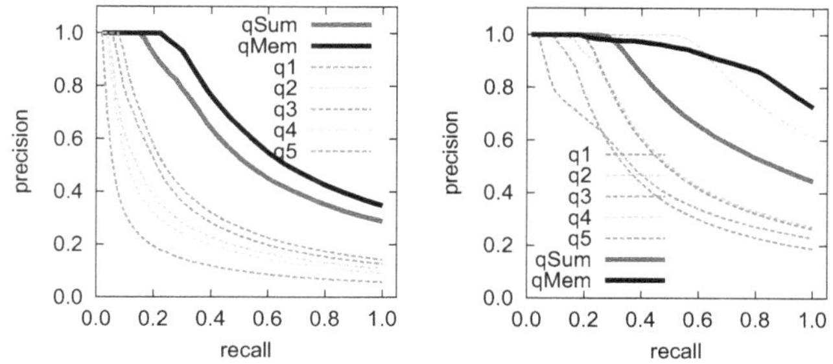

Figure 2: Precision recall curves for two different objects from Oxford5k with five query images, the sum, and the memory vector.

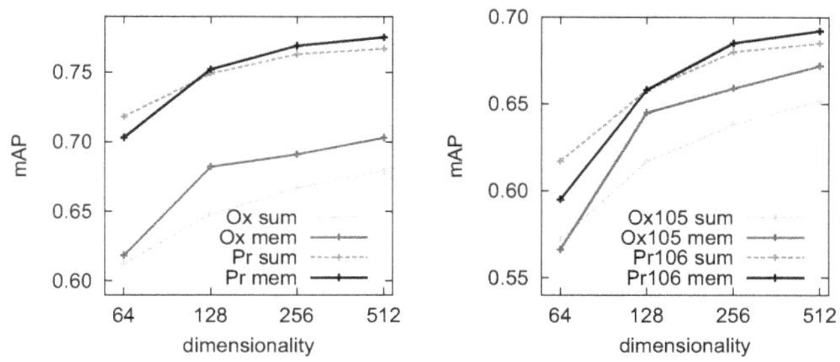

Figure 3: Comparison between sum and memory vectors for the CNN descriptors reduced to [64,128,256,512] dimensions on several datasets.

images (smaller is more frequent). We can therefore visualize the contribution of each image descriptors to the query object fused descriptor.

Figure 1 gives the weights used to build the memory vectors. Five query images of the same object are shown, as well as the Gram matrix ($\mathbf{X}^\top \mathbf{X}$) and the resulting weights for two different descriptors: CNN and tridD reduced to 512 dimensions. It is interesting to note that the first, third and fifth images are visually similar and have high similarity scores in the Gram matrix. The second and fourth images are relatively different from the other queries and have larger contributions (highest weights) in the fused descriptor.

4. EXPERIMENTS

4.1 Datasets

Oxford5k Buildings [15] is a dataset that consists of 5,062 high-resolution images. There are 55 query images, 5 for each of the 11 chosen Oxford buildings. For each query image, a bounding box on the region of interest is available. The dataset Oxford5k can be further combined with an extra 100k images from Flickr forming Oxford105k dataset.

Paris6k [16] contains 6,412 high-resolution images. The dataset has also 55 query images, with bounding boxes, from 11 landmarks in Paris. This dataset is further combined with the extra 100k images in Paris106k.

To perform multiple queries retrieval, the 5 query image descriptors of a specific landmark are combined into a single representation. These representations are used as query for each specific landmark. Performances are measured in terms of mean average precision (mAP).

Table 1: **Averaging vs our method for standard VLAD with 256 clusters, tridD, and CNN on Oxford5k and Oxford105k.**

	Oxford5k		Oxford105k	
Representations	Avg [1]	Ours	Avg [1]	Ours
Vlad 256c	0.721	**0.727**	0.685	**0.691**
tridD full	**0.792**	**0.792**	0.768	**0.769**
CNN full	0.603	**0.619**	0.581	**0.589**

Table 2: **Averaging vs our method for various reduced representations on Oxford5k and Oxford105k.**

	Oxford5k		Oxford105k	
Representations	Avg [1]	Ours	Avg [1]	Ours
Vlad-3c 128	0.557	**0.562**	0.485	**0.496**
Vlad-3c 256	0.620	**0.628**	0.545	**0.556**
Vlad-3c 512	**0.695**	**0.695**	**0.630**	0.627
tridD 128	0.653	**0.660**	0.627	**0.630**
tridD 256	0.710	**0.724**	0.685	**0.696**
tridD 512	0.750	**0.756**	0.725	**0.731**
CNN 128	0.648	**0.682**	0.617	**0.645**
CNN 256	0.667	**0.691**	0.638	**0.659**
CNN 512	0.679	**0.703**	0.652	**0.672**

4.2 Results

Precision-recall. Figure 2 shows precision recall curves for two query objects from Oxford5k. Each query image is evaluated, as well as the fused vector either with sum (equivalent to the averaging [1]) and the optimized memory vector of Equation 4. Observe the benefit of combining multiple queries with our construction compared to sum.

Full descriptors. Table 1 compares the mAP scores for the full representations on Oxford datasets, before any dimensionality reduction. We observe an increase of performance with our strategy for all representations (Vlad, tridD, CNN). It is comparatively smaller for tridD. This can be explained by the fact that the democratization method used in this method already reduces the contribution of frequent features within the image. The CNN features receive the largest improvement, which is appealing because they are the best performing descriptors.

Short vectors. Table 2 presents the results for the reduced representations with PCA to 128, 256, and 512 dimensions. We observe a larger improvement in this setup than for the full representations, especially with CNN descriptors. This is expected because high-dimensional descriptors have more chances to be orthogonal to one to another, in which case sum and optimized memory vectors are identical.

Figure 3 displays the MAP scores against the dimensionality of the CNN descriptors. For the most compact 64-dimensional descriptor, the ratio n/d is not small enough to maintain a low false positive probability and therefore the strategy is not effective. Table 3 shows some supplementary results on Paris datasets, which concur with the ones observed on Oxford buildings.

Finally, we note that centering then applying PCA on CNN descriptors offers a large performance increase in terms of MAP on our various retrieval datasets. For example, reducing the dimensionality to 512 gives an increase of 7% to 9% MAP. Furthermore, we experimentally observed that applying PCA offers better results than PCA with whitening.

Table 3: **Experiments on Paris6k and Paris106k.**

	Paris6k		Paris106k	
Representations	Avg [1]	Ours	Avg [1]	Ours
Vlad 256	0.654	**0.661**	0.521	**0.529**
Vlad-3c 128	0.565	**0.569**	**0.544**	0.543
Vlad-3c 256	0.598	**0.607**	0.574	**0.577**
Vlad-3c 512	0.629	**0.640**	0.606	**0.615**
CNN full	**0.689**	**0.689**	**0.608**	0.605
CNN 128	0.749	**0.752**	**0.658**	**0.658**
CNN 256	0.763	**0.769**	0.680	**0.685**
CNN 512	0.767	**0.775**	0.685	**0.692**

5. CONCLUSION

We have shown that it is possible to improve the fusion of multiple query descriptors. Our method is based on the recent concept of memory vectors, which summarizes a set of vectors by a single representative vector. The proposed retrieval system offers a consistent increase in performance compared to the average query on several description methods and datasets.

6. REFERENCES

[1] R. Arandjelovic and A. Zisserman. Multiple queries for large scale specific object retrieval. In *BMVC*, 2012.

[2] R. Arandjelovic and A. Zisserman. Three things everyone should know to improve object retrieval. In *CVPR*, June 2012.

[3] A. Babenko, A. Slesarev, A. Chigorin, and V. Lempitsky. Neural codes for image retrieval. *ECCV*, 2014.

[4] M. S. Charikar. Similarity estimation techniques from rounding algorithms. In *STOC*, pages 380–388, May 2002.

[5] K. Chatfield, K. Simonyan, A. Vedaldi, and A. Zisserman. Return of the devil in the details: Delving deep into convolutional nets. *BMVC*, 2014.

[6] Y. Chen, X. Li, A. Dick, and A. van den Hengel. Boosting object retrieval with group queries. *SP Letters*, 2012.

[7] B. Fernando and T. Tuytelaars. Mining multiple queries for image retrieval: On-the-fly learning of an object-specific mid-level representation. In *ICCV*, 2013.

[8] A. Iscen, T. Furon, V. Gripon, M. G. Rabbat, and H. Jégou. Memory vectors for similarity search in high-dimensional spaces. *CoRR*, 2014.

[9] H. Jégou and O. Chum. Negative evidences and co-occurences in image retrieval: The benefit of pca and whitening. In *ECCV*. 2012.

[10] H. Jegou, M. Douze, and C. Schmid. Product quantization for nearest neighbor search. *Trans. PAMI*, 2011.

[11] H. Jégou, F. Perronnin, M. Douze, J. Sánchez, P. Pérez, and C. Schmid. Aggregating local image descriptors into compact codes. *Trans. PAMI*, 2012.

[12] H. Jégou, A. Zisserman, et al. Triangulation embedding and democratic aggregation for image search. In *CVPR*, 2014.

[13] N. Murray and F. Perronnin. Generalized max pooling. *CVPR*, 2014.

[14] F. Perronnin, J. Sánchez, and T. Mensink. Improving the fisher kernel for large-scale image classification. In *ECCV*. 2010.

[15] J. Philbin, O. Chum, M. Isard, J. Sivic, and A. Zisserman. Object retrieval with large vocabularies and fast spatial matching. In *CVPR*, 2007.

[16] J. Philbin, O. Chum, M. Isard, J. Sivic, and A. Zisserman. Lost in quantization: Improving particular object retrieval in large scale image databases. In *CVPR*, 2008.

[17] B. Safadi and G. Quénot. Descriptor optimization for multimedia indexing and retrieval. In *CBMI*, 2013.

[18] J. Sivic and A. Zisserman. Video Google: A text retrieval approach to object matching in videos. In *ICCV*, 2003.

[19] A. F. Smeaton, P. Over, and W. Kraaij. Evaluation campaigns and TRECVid. In *MIR*, 2006.

[20] G. Tolias, Y. Avrithis, and H. Jégou. To aggregate or not to aggregate: Selective match kernels for image search. In *ICCV*, 2013.

[21] X. Wu and K. Kashino. Interest point selection by topology coherence for multi-query image retrieval. *MTAP*, 2014.

Semantic-aware Hashing for Social Image Retrieval

Jinhui Tang†, Zechao Li†, Liyan Zhang‡, Qingming Huang♯
†Nanjing University of Science and Technology
‡Nanjing University of Aeronautics and Astronautics
♯University of Chinese Academy of Sciences
{jinhuitang, zechao.li}@njust.edu.cn

ABSTRACT

With the proliferation of large-scale social images, recent years have witnessed the increasing amount of images with user-provided tags, which leads to considerable effort made on hashing based approximate nearest neighbor (ANN) search in huge databases. In this work, we propose a novel Semantic-aware Hashing method (SaH) by discovering knowledge from these social media resources to implement approximate similarity search. Different from the previous work, the proposed method learns semantic hashing codes by exploiting heterogeneous information from the textual and visual domains. The semantic structure in the textual domain is well preserved to learn the binary codes. To handle the noisy, incomplete, or subjective user-provided tags, the visual structure is also leveraged. On the other hand, an information theoretic regularization is exploited by using maximum entropy principle and a row-wise sparse model with $\ell_{2,p}$ $(0 < p \leq 1)$ mixed norm is introduced to filter certain noisy or redundant visual features. Experiments are conducted on a widely-used social image dataset and the comparison results demonstrate the outperforming performance of the proposed SaH method over state-of-the-art hashing techniques.

Categories and Subject Descriptors

H.3.3 [**Information Search and Retrieval**]: Retrieval models

General Terms

Algorithms, Experimentation, Theory

Keywords

Hashing; Semantic Similarity; Visual Similarity

1. INTRODUCTION

Due to the advent of digital cameras and intelligent mobile devices, many community-contributed image websites, such as Flickr[1], Zooomr[2] and Picasa[3], are becoming popular, which can facilitate millions of users to upload and share their images. We have witnessed the explosive increase in the amount of massive social images with rich user-provided metadata. Consequently, similarity (or nearest neighbor) search in large-scale datesets has attracted considerable attentions from multiple research communities, such as multimedia retrieval, and is increasingly becoming a challenging but urgent research issue.

The image similarity search problem is to find similar images (if one exists) from an image database for a query image. Many algorithms have been developed to identify similar images. As one widely-used method, hashing-based ANN learns hashing functions to encode visual features to compact binary codes, which makes significantly efficient similarity search in large scale databases possible. Recently, many hashing algorithms have been proposed, mainly on the assumption that similar images should have close binary codes, such as [1, 2, 3, 4, 5, 6]. These methods can be roughly grouped into two categories: data-independent and data-dependent. For data-independent ones, binary codes are obtained using random projections without taking the data distribution into consideration, such as the well-known Locality-Sensitive Hashing (LSH) [1]. However, the performance is degraded with short binary codes. That is, to achieve higher precision, longer length of binary codes is usually designed, which degrades the corresponding recall and results in larger space and more memory. To deal with this problem, data-dependent hashing approaches are developed to learn hashing functions from data, such as Spectral Hashing (SH) [2], Iterative Quantization (ITQ) [7], Semi-Supervised Hashing (SSH) [3], Isotropic Hashing (IsoH) [4] and Spherical Hahsing (SpH) [5]. These algorithms learn hashing functions by exploiting some structure of data, such as local smoothness.

However, it is unsuitable to apply the above methods to handle the problem of social image retrieval. Social images are associated with rich user-provided metadata, such as user-supplied tags. These tags somewhat describe the content of images, which can benefit the learning of hashing codes [8]. On the other hand, user-provided tags are actually unsatisfied since they are freely generated by amateur Web users. It leads to that the associated tags are often imprecise, biased and incomplete for describing the content of

ICMR'15, June 23–26, 2015, Shanghai, China.
Copyright © 2015 ACM 978-1-4503-3274-3/15/06 ...$15.00.
http://dx.doi.org/10.1145/2671188.2749307 .

[1]http://www.flickr.com
[2]http://www.zooomr.com
[3]http://picasa.google.com

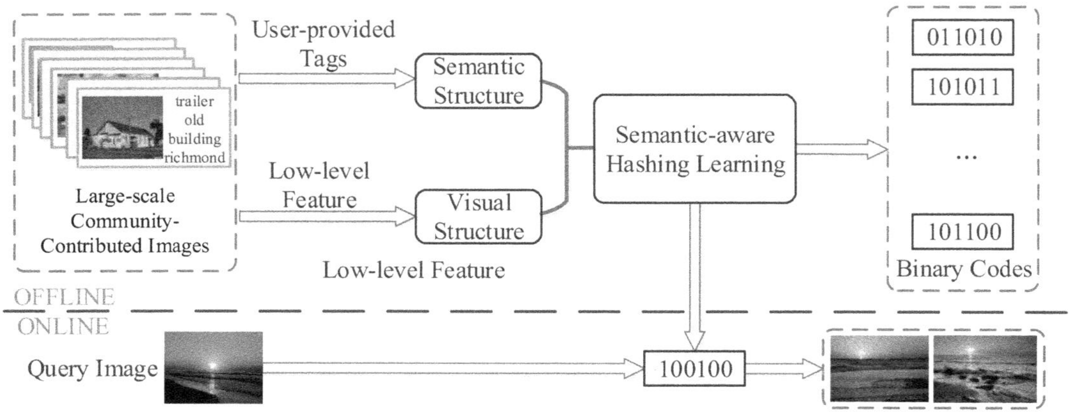

Figure 1: The illustration of the proposed semantic-aware hashing method for social image retrieval.

the images. Therefore, it is necessary to exploit these social media resources for learning hashing codes.

Towards this end, we propose a novel data-dependent hashing method, namely Semantic-aware Hashing (SaH), by discovering knowledge from the heterogeneous social media resources. To obtain an efficient hashing function, the semantic structure in the textual domain and the visual structure in the visual domain are jointly exploited, as illustrated in Fig. 1. To reduce the semantic gap, the learned hashing codes are expected to preserve the semantic structure by imposing the consistency between the pairwise similarities based on the binary codes and the tagging information. To prevent overfitting the noisy, incomplete, or subjective tagging information, the visual structure is also leveraged. On the other hand, to make the binary codes compact, the information provided by each hashing bit is expected to be maximized, which is guaranteed by an information theoretic regularization. Besides, a row-wise sparse model with $\ell_{2,p}$ $(0 < p \leq 1)$ mixed norm is attached to remove the noisy features and suppress the redundant features. The above principles are jointly exploited and rigorously formulated into an optimization problem with a well-defined objective function. And the stochastic gradient descent algorithm is used to solve the proposed optimization problem. Extensive experiments are conducted on one real-world social image dataset (i.e., NUS-WIDE dataset [9]). The effectiveness of the proposed SaH method is verified by the superior performance over state-of-the-art hashing techniques.

The main contributions are summarized as follows.

- We propose to exploit the heterogeneous data structure of community-contributed images to learn hashing functions. To our best knowledge, it is the first attempt to learn hashing functions by explicitly uncovering knowledge from the textual and visual domains simultaneously.
- Semantic-aware hashing functions can be learned by jointly maintaining the semantic and visual structures.
- From the information theoretic point of view, the information provided by each hashing bit are maximized. And a general row-wise sparse model with $\ell_{2,p}$ $(0 < p \leq 1)$ mixed norm makes the proposed method robust to noisy visual features.

2. SEMANTIC-AWARE HASHING

2.1 Preliminary

Consider a dataset consisting of n images $\{\mathbf{x}_i\}_{i=1}^n$. Let $\mathbf{X} = [\mathbf{x}_1, \cdots, \mathbf{x}_n]$ denote the data matrix, in which $\mathbf{x}_i \in \mathbb{R}^d$ is the d-dimensional feature descriptor of the i-th image. Without loss of generality, $\mathbf{X}$ is normalized to have zero mean. Suppose L hashing functions are learned to project $\mathbf{X}$ into L-bit binary representations $\mathbf{Y} \in \mathbb{B}^{L\times n}$. Given an image $\mathbf{x}_i$, a hashing function $h(\cdot)$ is used to generate a binary code $h : \mathbb{R} \mapsto \{-1, 1\}$. In this work, we utilize linear function with mean thresholding as hashing function.

$$h_l(\mathbf{x}_i) = \mathrm{sgn}(\mathbf{w}_l^T \mathbf{x}_i + b_l) \tag{1}$$

where $\mathbf{w}_l \in \mathbb{R}^d$ is a linear function to project $\mathbf{x}_i$ to a one-dimensional binary space, and b_l is the mean of the projected data. $\mathrm{sgn}(\cdot)$ is the signum function. Let $\mathbf{H} = [h_1, \cdots, h_L]$ be the sequence of L hashing functions. We can have

$$\mathbf{H}(\mathbf{x}_i) = [h_1(\mathbf{x}_i), \cdots, h_L(\mathbf{x}_i)] = \mathrm{sgn}(\mathbf{W}^T \mathbf{x}_i + \mathbf{b}) \tag{2}$$

where $\mathbf{W} = [\mathbf{w}_1, \cdots, \mathbf{w}_L] \in \mathbb{R}^{d\times L}$ is the linear transformation matrix and $\mathbf{b} = [b_1, b_2, \cdots, b_L]^T \in \mathbb{R}^L$. The corresponding binary bit can be obtained as

$$Y_{li} = \frac{1}{2}(1 + h_l(\mathbf{x}_i)). \tag{3}$$

The elements of $\mathbf{H}(\mathbf{X})$ are required to be discrete values, which leads to a NP-hard problem. The widely used solution is to relax it from discrete values to continuous values [2], i.e., the constraint that $h_l(\mathbf{x}_i) \in \{-1, 1\}$ is relaxed to that $h_l(\mathbf{x}_i) = \mathbf{w}_l^T \mathbf{x}_i \in \mathbb{R}$.

2.2 Formulation

To learn semantic hashing functions, the semantic and visual structures are jointly exploited. For simplicity, in this work the structure is mined by preserving the pairwise similarity. That is, the similarity $\mathbf{S}_H$ in the Hamming space is expected to be consistent with the semantic similarity $\mathbf{S}_T$ in the textual domain. Besides, to handle the noisy, incomplete, or subjective tagging information, $\mathbf{S}_H$ should not deviate from the visual similarity $\mathbf{S}_V$ in the visual domain.

The Hamming distance between $\mathbf{x}_i$ and $\mathbf{x}_j$ is defined as

$$d_h(i,j) = |\{l | h_l(\mathbf{x}_i) \neq \mathbf{x}_j, 1 \leq l \leq L\}| \in \{0, 1, \cdots, L\}, \tag{4}$$

where $|\Phi|$ is the number of elements in the set Φ. The binary code inner product is

$$\mathbf{y}_i^T\mathbf{y}_j = |\{l|h_l(\mathbf{x}_i) = \mathbf{x}_j, 1 \leq l \leq L\}| = L - d_h(\mathbf{x}_i, \mathbf{x}_j). \quad (5)$$

Therefore, the corresponding similarity $\mathbf{S}_H$ based on the binary representation $\mathbf{Y}$ is defined as

$$S_H(i,j) = \frac{1}{L}\mathbf{y}_i^T\mathbf{y}_j = 1 - \frac{1}{L}d_h(i,j). \quad (6)$$

We can see that $S_H(i,j) = 1$ if $d_h(i,j) = 0$ and $S_H(i,j) = 0$ if $d_h(i,j) = L$.

To eliminate the semantic gap, the consistency preservation between the pairwise similarities in the Hamming space and the textual space is encouraged. In a natural means, a least-squares cost function is used to measure the disagreement between the heterogeneous space.

$$\mathcal{O}_T = \sum_{i=1}^{n}\sum_{j=1}^{n}(S_H(i,j) - S_T(i,j))^2 = \|\mathbf{S}_H - \mathbf{S}_T\|_F^2 \quad (7)$$

By minimizing the above cost function, the learned hashing functions can well preserved the semantic structure. Unfortunately, the tagging information in the textual space is somewhat unreliable due to the noisy, incomplete or subjective tags. Thus, it is necessary to alleviate the affects of these tags and prevent overfitting the noisy semantic similarities. For this purpose, the visual structure is leveraged by maintaining the original visual similarity and the least-squares cost function is also introduced. As a consequence, we obtain the following optimization problem to preserve the semantic and visual structures.

$$\min_{\mathbf{H}} \|\mathbf{S}_H - \mathbf{S}_T\|_F^2 + \alpha\|\mathbf{S}_H - \mathbf{S}_V\|_F^2, \quad (8)$$

in which α is a nonnegative trade-off parameter to balance the importance of the semantic and visual structures.

On the other hand, the learned binary codes are expected to be compact by maximizing the information provided by each hashing bit. According to maximum entropy principle as in [2], each bit is expected to balancedly partition $\mathbf{X}$, i.e.,

$$\sum_{i=1}^{n} h_l(\mathbf{x}_i) = 0 \Leftrightarrow b_l = -\frac{1}{n}\sum_{i=1}^{n}\mathbf{w}_l^T\mathbf{x}_i = 0, \quad (9)$$

due to that $\mathbf{X}$ is normalized to be zero mean. Accordingly,

$$\mathbf{H}(\mathbf{x}_i) = \mathrm{sgn}(\mathbf{W}^T\mathbf{x}_i) \quad (10)$$

$$\mathbf{Y} = \frac{1}{2}(1 + \mathbf{H}(\mathbf{X})) = \frac{1}{2}(1 + \mathrm{sgn}(\mathbf{W}^T\mathbf{X})) \quad (11)$$

It is hard to find hashing function to meet the above balancing requirement. Fortunately, it has been proved in [3] that the maximum entropy partitioning is equivalent to maximizing the variance of a bit. Consequently, we have

$$\max \sum_{l=1}^{L} \mathrm{var}[h_l(\mathbf{X})] = \sum_{l=1}^{L} \mathrm{var}[\mathrm{sgn}(\mathbf{w}_l^T\mathbf{X})]. \quad (12)$$

Besides, the maximum variance of a hashing function is lower bounded by the scaled variance of the projected data with a positive constant ρ [3]:

$$\max \sum_{l=1}^{L} \mathrm{var}[\mathrm{sgn}(\mathbf{w}_l^T\mathbf{X})] \geq \rho\sum_{l=1}^{L} \mathrm{var}[\mathbf{w}_l^T\mathbf{X}] \quad (13)$$

The visual features are not always equally important for the task, and there are some noisy or redundant features. To deal with this problem, a row sparse model with $\ell_{2,p}$ $(0 < p \leq 1)$ mixed norm is utilized.

$$\|\mathbf{W}\|_{2,p}^p = \sum_{i=1}^{d} \|\mathbf{w}^i\|_2^p \quad (14)$$

Here $\mathbf{w}^i$ is the i-th row of $\mathbf{W}$. The i-th row of $\mathbf{W}$ shrinks to zero if the i-th feature is less discriminative or noisy.

By jointly exploiting all the above issues, we incorporate them into a unified formulation:

$$\begin{aligned}\min_{\mathbf{W}} \mathcal{O} =& \|\mathbf{S}_H - \mathbf{S}_T\|_F^2 + \alpha\|\mathbf{S}_H - \mathbf{S}_V\|_F^2 \\ & -\beta\sum_{l=1}^{L} \mathrm{var}[\mathbf{w}_l^T\mathbf{X}] + \gamma\|\mathbf{W}\|_{2,p}^p \quad (15)\\ \Leftrightarrow \min_{\mathbf{W}} \mathcal{O} =& \|\mathbf{S}_H - \mathbf{S}_T\|_F^2 + \alpha\|\mathbf{S}_H - \mathbf{S}_V\|_F^2 \\ & -\beta\mathrm{Tr}[\mathbf{W}^T\mathbf{X}\mathbf{X}^T\mathbf{W}] + \gamma\|\mathbf{W}\|_{2,p}^p \quad (16)\end{aligned}$$

where β and γ are two regularization parameters. The proposed formulation in (16) involves the $\ell_{2,p}$-norm which is non-smooth and cannot be solved in a closed form. To solve it, we develop an iterative algorithm based on the stochastic gradient descent algorithm with the learning rate η.

$$\begin{aligned}\frac{\partial\mathcal{O}}{\partial\mathbf{W}} =& \frac{1}{L}\mathbf{X}((1+\alpha)\mathbf{S}_H - \mathbf{S}_T - \alpha\mathbf{S}_V)\mathbf{Y}^T \\ & - 2\beta\mathbf{X}\mathbf{X}^T\mathbf{W} + 2\gamma\mathbf{D}\mathbf{W} \quad (17)\\ \mathbf{W} \leftarrow& \mathbf{W} - \eta\frac{\partial\mathcal{O}}{\partial\mathbf{W}} \quad (18)\\ \mathbf{D} =& \, diag\{\frac{p}{\|\mathbf{w}^1\|_2^{2-p}}, \cdots, \frac{p}{\|\mathbf{w}^d\|_2^{2-p}}\} \quad (19)\end{aligned}$$

3. EXPERIMENTS

3.1 Experimental Setting

Experiments are conducted on the NUS-WIDE dataset [9], which is a good large-scale benchmark for evaluating multimedia search techniques. There are about 270,000 images associated with 5,018 user-provided tags. To reduce too noisy tags, we removed those tags whose occurrence numbers are below 125. This dataset also provides ground-truth annotations over 81 concepts. Images associated with no tag or concept are removed. Consequently, 207,697 images and 3,137 unique tags were obtained. For visual representation, we use 1,134-D features provided by the dataset. The linear kernel is used to measure the textual similarity and the Gaussian kernel is adopted to measure the visual similarity.

For evaluation, this set is randomly divided into three parts: 1,000 images as the validation set, 1,000 images as queries, and the rest images as retrieval database and the learning data. To show the performance of SaH, we compare it with LSH [1], SH [2], USPLH [3], IsoH [4], SpH [5] and ITQ [7]. Parameters are all tuned with cross-validation among $\{10^{-4}, 10^{-3}, \cdots, 10^4\}$. For SaH, p is empirically set to 0.5 and the learning rate is initialized to 0.001. The search results are evaluated based on whether the returned images and the query sample share the same semantic labels. For Hamming ranking-based evaluation, we compute Precision and Recall among the top M returned images. For hash lookup-based evaluation, a Hamming radius of 2 is used.

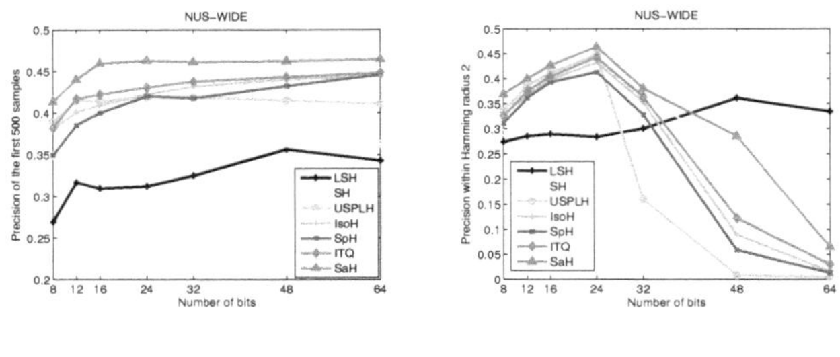

(a) (b)

Figure 2: Results on the NUS-WIDE dataset. (a) Precision of the top 500 returned images with Hamming ranking. (b) Precision within Hamming radius 2 using hash lookup.

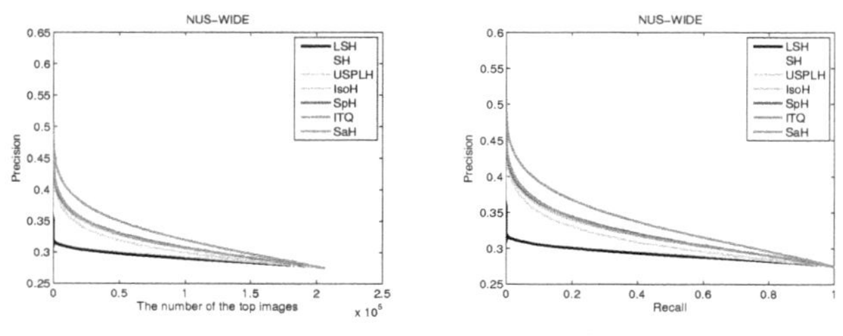

(a) (b)

Figure 3: The Precision curves and Precision-Recall curves with 24 bits on the NUS-WIDE dataset. (a) Precision curves with 24 bits. (b) Precision-Recall curves with 24 bits.

3.2 Experimental Results

In this subsection, we present the quantitative evaluation with different hashing bits varying from 8 to 48. The precision values of the top 500 returned images of Hamming ranking and Hash lookup (within Hamming radius $r = 2$) are shown in Fig. 2a and Fig. 2b, respectively. The precision curves and the precision-recall cures are shown in Fig. 3 as a complementary evaluation.

From these results, it can be observed that SaH always achieves the best performance, which can demonstrate the effectiveness of the proposed method to learn semantic binary codes. It is reasonable because the proposed method can put the semantic similar images in the same binary buckets. Besides, in most cases, SaH with less hashing bits can achieve better or competitive results to other methods with longer bits, especially in terms of precision of the first 500 returned images. It can also be seen that the worst results are often obtained by LSH, which does not consider the data distribution. It is consistent with the observations in [3]. Finally, the precision values of Hash lookup (within Hamming radius $r = 2$) for most of the compared algorithms decrease significantly with longer binary bits. It is because that the codes of images with longer bits are increasingly sparse and the number of images falling within a bucket decreases exponentially. Despite this, SaH achieves the best results among the data-dependent methods.

Finally, the qualitative performance achieved by different methods are evaluated by randomly selecting several test images. we present some examples of image retrieval results in Fig. 4. The irrelevant results are denoted with red rectangle. It can be seen that the images returned by the proposed SaH method are more relevant to the queries.

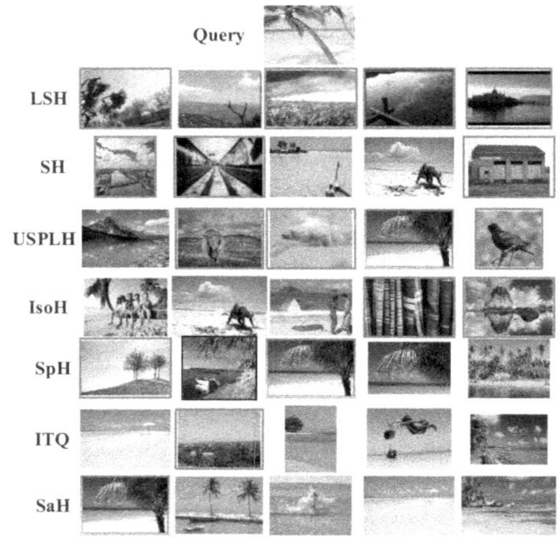

Figure 4: Some examples of social image retrieval results. Red rectangle denotes irrelevant images without any common concept with the query. Best viewed in color.

4. CONCLUSIONS

In this paper, we propose a novel hashing method by exploiting the heterogeneous structures from the textual and visual domains. It can learn semantic-aware binary codes while overcome the problem of the noisy, incomplete, or subjective user-provided tags. Meanwhile, the information provided by each bit is maximized and the noisy or redundant visual features are controlled. Extensive experiments are conducted on the widely-used NUS-WIDE dataset. The encouraging results compared with many other methods demonstrate the effectiveness of the proposed SaH method.

5. ACKNOWLEDGE

This work was partially supported by the 973 Program (No. 2014CB347600), the National Natural Science Foundation of China (Grant No. 61402228), Natural Science Fund iangsu Province (BK2012033 and BK20140058), the Program for New Century Excellent Talents in University under Grant NCET-12-0632 and the Open Projects Program of National Laboratory of Pattern Recognition.

6. REFERENCES

[1] A. Gionis, P. Indyk, and R. Motwani. Similarity search in high dimensions via hashing. In *Proc. VLDB*, 1999.

[2] Y. Weiss, A. Torralba, and R. Fergus. Spectral hashing. In *Proc. NIPS*, 2008.

[3] J. Wang, S. Kumar, and S.-F. Chang. Semi-supervised hashing for large scale search. *IEEE TPAMI*, 34(12):2393–2406, 2012.

[4] W. Kong and W.-J. Li. Isotropic hashing. In *Proc. NIPS*, 2012.

[5] J.-P. Heo, Y. Lee, J. He, S.-F. Chang, and S. Yoon. Spherical hashing. In *Proc. CVPR*, 2012.

[6] J. Tang, Z. Li, M. Wang, and R. Zhao. Neighborhood discriminant hashing for large-scale image retrieval. *IEEE TIP*, 2015. Online Publication.

[7] Y. Gong, S. Lazebnik, A. Gordo, and F. Perronnin. Iterative quantization: A procrustean approach to learning binary codes for large-scale image retrieval. *IEEE TPAMI*, 35(12):2916–2929, 2013.

[8] Z. Li, J. Liu, J. Tang, and H. Lu. Robust structured subspace learning for data representation. *IEEE TPAMI*, 2015. Online Publication.

[9] T. Chua, J. Tang, R.Hong, H. Li, Z. Luo, and Y. Zheng. NUS-WIDE: A real world web image database from national university of singapore. In *Proc. CIVR*, 2009.

Zero-shot Image Categorization by Image Correlation Exploration

LianLi Gao,
University of Electronic Science and Technology of China. Chengdu, China
lianli.gao@uestc.edu.cn

Jingkuan Song
University of Trento. Trento, Italy
jingkuan.song@unitn.it

Junming Shao
University of Electronic Science and Technology of China. Chengdu, China
junmshao@uestc.edu.cn

Xiaofeng Zhu
Guangxi Normal University. Guangxi, China
seanzhuxf@gmail.com

Heng Tao Shen
The University of Queensland. Queensland, Australia.
shenht@itee.uq.edu.au

ABSTRACT

The problem of image categorization from zero or only a few training examples, called zero-shot learning, occurs frequently, but it has hardly been studied in computer vision research. To tackle this problem, mid-level semantic attributes are introduced to identify image categories. For example, one can construct a classifier for the giant panda category by enumerating its attributes (e.g., black, white and four-footed) even without providing giant panda training images. Recently, several studies have investigated to learn attribute classifiers, based on which new classes can be detected. However, an often-encountered problem is the limited number of training data due to the time-consuming manual annotation of the attributes. Also, using single feature is hard to detect some attributes, e.g., the HSV feature is not robust enough to predict 'tusk' or 'flies' attributes. In this paper, we propose a unified semi-supervised learning (SSL) framework that learns the attribute classifiers by utilizing multiple feature and exploring the correlations between images. Specifically, we learn an optimal graph which embeds the relationships among the data points more accurately. Then, this graph is used to generate a geometrical regularizers for a semi-supervised learning model to learn the attribute classifier by utilizing both labeled and unlabeled images. Afterward, new classes can be detected based on their attribute representation. The use of SSL can boost the performances of attribute classifiers with very few training examples, and the adoption of multiple features makes the attribute prediction more robust. Experimental results on a series of real benchmark data sets suggest that semi-supervised learning do enhance the performances of attribute prediction and zero-shot categorization, compared with state-of-the-art methods.

ICMR'15, June 23–26, 2015, Shanghai, China.

http://dx.doi.org/10.1145/2671188.2749309.

Categories and Subject Descriptors

I.4.8 [**Image Processing And Computer Vision**]: Scene Analysis—*object recognition*

Keywords

attributes; image categorization; zero-shot learning

1. INTRODUCTION

In recent years, visual recognition research has achieved major successes using large datasets, robust features and modern learning algorithms. The typical scenario assumes a multi-class task where one has plenty labeled training images for each class of interest. While building recognition systems this way is feasible for categories of large common or commercial interest, one cannot expect it to solve object recognition for all natural categories [7]. Rather than constrain the system to a closed set of pre-trained object detectors, one would like to acquire models for new categories with minimal effort and training examples. Doing so is essential for lots of real applications where new categories emerge dynamically. For example, when an user defines a new class of interest to be detected in his visual data.

Zero-shot learning offers a promising solution. In zero-shot learning, a novel class is trained via description instead of labeled training examples [8]. In general, this requires the learner to have access to some mid-level semantic representation, such that an expert can define a novel unseen class by specifying a configuration of those semantic properties. In visual recognition, the semantic properties are attributes shared among categories, like black, white, or four-footed. Supposing the system can predict the presence of any such attribute in new images, then adding a new category model amounts to defining its attribute 'signature' [5]. For example, even without labeling any images of giant panda, one could build a giant panda classifier by teaching the system that giant pandas are black, white and four-footed, etc.

Therefore, if we could perfectly predict attribute presence, zero-shot learning would offer an elegant solution to generating novel classifiers on the fly [4]. However, the problem is that we cannot assume perfect attribute predictions. Visual attributes are in practice quite difficult to learn accurately.

One of the reasons is the insufficient number of training data due to the time-consuming manual annotation of the attributes. Also, most of the existing attributes learning methods are based on a single feature. Some attributes are hard to be detected from a single visual feature, e.g., it is less effective to predict 'tusk' or 'flies' using HSV feature. Hence, it is necessary to utilize multiple features to improve the attribute prediction performance.

To address the above issues, in this work, we propose learning an optimal graph from multi-cues (i.e., attributes and visual features), which can more accurately encode the relationships between data points. Then, we incorporate the learned graph with SSL model, and we further extend this model to address out-of-sample extension. It is worthwhile to highlight three aspects of the proposed approach here:

- We simultaneously learn an optimal graph to encode the similarity between images and the importance value of different features. We propose an efficient way to solve the optimization problem. The learned optimal graph can make use of different information cues to more precisely reflect the relationships among data points.
- We integrate the learned optimal graph with the SSL method, and evaluate our method for image attribute learning. In this way, a small percentage of labeled training data can achieve a satisfactory performance.
- Experiments for image categorization on real world datasets demonstrate the superiority of our method over existing methods.

2. OUR APPROACH

Zero-shot image categorization consists of two stages: attribute prediction from images and categorization on attributes. In this section, we introduce attribute prediction. More specifically, we first propose the learning of optimal graph and integrate the graph with SSL model for the task of predicting image attributes. After the attributes are predicted, we adopt DAP model in [7] to classify images from attributes, which is introduced in the next section.

2.1 Terms and Notations

$X = \{x_1, x_2, ..., x_N\}$ represents a set of N images, and $y_i = \{0,1\}^M$ is the attribute for the i-th image ($1 \leq i \leq N$), and M is the number of attributes. The first L points x_i ($i \leq L$) are with attributes Y_L, and the remaining U points x_i ($L+1 \leq i \leq N$) are without attributes. The goal is to predict the attributes F_U of the unlabeled data points, based on which the classes can be determined. Define a $N \times C$ matrix $F = \begin{bmatrix} F_L \\ F_U \end{bmatrix}$ with $F_L = Y_L$ and $F_U = \{0\}^{U*M}$.

Suppose that for each image, we have features from v cues (i.e., different features) and thus each image has v features. Let $X^t = \{x_i^t\}_{i=1}^n$ denotes the feature matrix of the t-th view of training images, where $t \in \{1, ..., v\}$.

2.2 Attribute learning

The traditional graph based semi-supervised learning usually solves the following problem:

$$\min_{F, F_l = Y_l} \sum_{ij} \|f_i - f_j\|_2^2 s_{ij} \tag{1}$$

where f_i and f_j are the attributes for the i-th and j-th images, and S is the affinity graph with each entry s_{ij} representing the similarity between two images. The affinity graph $S \in \mathbb{R}^{n \times n}$ is usually defined as follows:

$$s_{ij} = \begin{cases} e^{-\|x_i - x_j\|_2^2 / 2\sigma^2}, & \text{if } x_i \in \mathcal{N}_K(x_j) \text{ or } x_j \in \mathcal{N}_K(x_i) \\ 0, \text{else} \end{cases} \tag{2}$$

where $\mathcal{N}_K(\cdot)$ is the K-nearest-neighbor set and $1 \leq (i,j) \leq n$. The variance σ will affect the performance significantly, and it is usually empirically tuned. Also, it is derived from single information cue [10, 9]. To address these issues, we propose to learn an optimal graph S from multiple cues.

Without loss of generality, we suppose the multiple cues include given attribute information F and multiple features information $X^t = \{x_i^t\}_{i=1}^n$. An optimal graph S should be smooth on all these information cues, which can be formulated as:

$$\min_{S, \alpha} g(F, S) + \mu \sum_{t=1}^{v} \alpha^t h\left(X^t, S\right) + \beta r(S, \alpha) \tag{3}$$

where $g(F, S)$ is the penalty function to measure the smoothness of S on the label information F and $h\left(X^t, S\right)$ is the loss function to measure the smoothness of S on the feature X^t. $r(S, \alpha)$ are regularizers defined on the target S and α. μ and β are balancing parameters, and α^t determines the importance of each feature.

The penalty function $g(F, S)$ and $h\left(X^t, S\right)$ should be defined in the way such that close labels (data points) have high similarity and vice versa. In this paper, we define it as follows:

$$\begin{cases} g(F, S) = \sum_{ij} \|f_i - f_j\|_2^2 s_{ij} \\ h\left(X^t, S\right) = \sum_{ij} \left\|x_i^t - x_j^t\right\|_2^2 s_{ij} \end{cases} \tag{4}$$

where f_i and f_j are the labels of data point x_i and x_j. The regularizer term $r(S, \alpha)$ is defined as:

$$\beta r(S, \alpha) = \mu\gamma \|S\|_F^2 + \beta \|\alpha\|_2^2 \tag{5}$$

We further constraint that $S \geq 0$,$S1 = 1$,$\alpha \geq 0$ and $\alpha^T 1 = 1$. Then we can obtain the objective function for learning optimal graph by replacing $g(F, S)$, $h\left(X^t, S\right)$ and $r(S, \alpha)$ in Eq.3 using Eq.4 and Eq.5. And by combining Eq.1 with Eq.3, we can obtain the objective function for optimal-graph based SSL, as follows:

$$\begin{array}{l} \min_{S,F,\alpha} \sum_{ij} \|f_i - f_j\|_2^2 s_{ij} + \mu \sum_{tij} \left(\alpha_t \left\|x_i^t - x_j^t\right\|_2^2 s_{ij}\right) \\ +\mu\gamma \|S\|_F^2 + \beta \|\alpha\|_2^2 \\ s.t. \left\{ S \geq 0, S1 = 1, \; F_l = Y_l, \; \alpha \geq 0, \; \alpha^T 1 = 1 \right. \end{array} \tag{6}$$

2.3 Iterative optimization

We propose an iterative method to minimize the above objective function 6. Firstly, we initialize $S = \sum_t S^t / v$ with each S^t being calculated using Eq.2, and we initialize $\alpha^t = 1/v$. We further normalize S as $S = (D^{1/2})^T S D^{1/2}$. Once these initial values are given, in each iteration, we first update F given S and α, and then update S and α by fixing the other parameters. These steps are describe as below:

2.3.1 Update F

By fixing S and α, we can obtain F by optimizing (6). It is equivalent to optimize the following objective function:

$$\min_{F,F_l=Y_l}\sum_{ij}\|f_i-f_j\|_2^2 s_{ij}=\min_{F,F_l=Y_l}\left\|F(I-S)F^T\right\|_F^2 \quad (7)$$

where I is an identity matrix. Let $L=I-S$, and differentiate the objective function (7) with respect to F, we obtain:

$$\begin{aligned}&LF=0\Rightarrow\begin{bmatrix}L_{ll} & L_{lu}\\ L_{ul} & L_{uu}\end{bmatrix}\begin{bmatrix}F_l\\ F_u\end{bmatrix}=0\\ &\Rightarrow\begin{cases}L_{ll}F_l+L_{lu}F_u=0\\ L_{ul}F_l+L_{uu}F_u=0\end{cases}\end{aligned} \quad (8)$$

Then we can obtain:

$$F_u^*=-{L_{uu}}^{-1}L_{ul}F_l \quad (9)$$

2.3.2 Update S

By fixing F and α, we can obtain S by optimizing (6). It is equivalent to optimize the following objective function:

$$\sum_{ij}\|f_i-f_j\|_2^2 s_{ij}+\mu\sum_{tij}\left(\alpha_t\left\|x_i^t-x_j^t\right\|_2^2 s_{ij}\right) \quad (10)$$
$$+\mu\gamma\|S\|_F^2$$

It can be reformulated as:

$$\begin{aligned}&=\min_{S,S\geq 0,S1=1}\sum_i tr\left(\mu\gamma s_i{s_i}^T+(a_i+\mu b_i)\,{s_i}^T\right)\\ &\Rightarrow\min_{S,S\geq 0,S1=1}\sum_i tr\left(s_i{s_i}^T-\tfrac{a_i+\mu b_i}{\mu\gamma}{s_i}^T\right)\end{aligned} \quad (11)$$

and it is equivalent to:

$$\min_{S,S\geq 0,S1=1}\sum_i\left\|s_i+\frac{a_i+\mu b_i}{2\mu\gamma}\right\|_2^2 \quad (12)$$

where $b_i=\{b_{ij},1\leq j\leq n\}$ with $b_{ij}=\sum_t\alpha_t\left\|x_i^t-x_j^t\right\|_2^2$ and $a_i=\{a_{ij},1\leq j\leq n\}\in R^{1\times n}$ with $a_{ij}=\|y_i-y_j\|_2^2$.

The constraints in problem (12) is simplex [3]. We use the accelerated projected gradient method to linearly solve this problem. Then each s_i can be efficiently solved, and we will get the updated graph S.

2.3.3 Update α

By fixing F and S, we can obtain α by optimizing (6). It is equivalent to optimize the following objective function:

$$\begin{aligned}&\min_{\alpha\geq 0,\alpha^T 1=1}\mu\sum_t\alpha_t\left(\sum_{ij}\left\|x_i^t-x_j^t\right\|_2^2 s_{ij}\right)+\beta\|\alpha\|_2^2\\ &\Rightarrow\min_{\alpha\geq 0,\alpha^T 1=1}\mu d\alpha+\beta\|\alpha\|_2^2\end{aligned} \quad (13)$$

where $d=\{d_t,1\leq t\leq v\}$ with $d_t=\sum_{ij}\left\|x_i^t-x_j^t\right\|_2^2 s_{ij}$. It can be solved to obtain α similarly to (12).

We update F, S and α iteratively until the objective function (6) converges. Then we obtain the attributes F_U for the unlabeled data points.

2.4 Out-of-sample extension

Out-of-sample refers to learning an annotation function that is able to label new data points. This can be achieved by adding a fitting model and a regularizer to the objective function (6), e.g., $\|XW+\mathbf{1}b-F\|_F^2+\eta\|W\|_F^2$, where $W\in\mathbb{R}^{m\times c}$, $b\in\mathbb{R}^{1\times c}$ and $\mathbf{1}$ is a vector of all ones. To obtain the optimal solution W^*, b^* and F^* by:

$$\begin{cases}b^*=\frac{1}{n}\left(\mathbf{1}^T F-\mathbf{1}^T XW\right)\\ W^*=\left(X^T L_c X+\eta I\right)^{-1}X^T L_c F\\ F^*=(I+U-S+\omega B)^{-1}UY\\ B=L_c-L_c X\left(X^T L_c X+\eta I\right)^{-1}X^T L_c\end{cases} \quad (14)$$

where ω is the parameter for the fitting model. Due to the space limit, we omit the solution here. Then we can obtain the annotation function W and b. Note that other fitting models can also be applied here, e.g., SVM, fast image tagging [1].

3. ZERO-SHOT LEARNING

We utilize the existing DAP model in [7] for zero-shot learning. The obtained attributes F_U provide us with estimates of $p(f_m|x_i)$, referred to as an *image-attribute* layer. When the attributes f of the images are predicted, following [7], we assume that every class z induces its attribute vector f in a deterministic way, i.e., $p(f|z)=[[f=f^z]]$. By applying Bayes' rule, we obtain $p(z|f)=\frac{p(z)}{p(f^z)}[[f=f^z]]$ as the representation of the *attribute-class* layer. Combining both layers, we can calculate the posterior of a test class given an image:

$$p(z|x_i)=\sum_{f\in\{0,1\}^M}p(z|f)\,p(f|x_i)=\frac{p(z)}{p(f^z)}\prod_{m=1}^{M}(f_m^z|x_i) \quad (15)$$

As decision rule, we assigns the best output class from all test classes $z_1;\ldots;z_K$ to a test sample x_i.

4. EXPERIMENTS

To evaluate the performance of our method, we compare with other zero-shot categorization methods.

4.1 Experimental settings

We consider three publicly available datasets that have been widely used in previous work. (1) Animals with Attributes (AwA) [7] (M = 85 attributes,K = 10 unseen classes, 30,475 total images), (2) aPascal/aYahoo objects (aPY) [2] (M = 65, K = 12, 15,339 images) (3) SUN scene attributes (SUN) (M = 102, K = 10, 14,340 images). These datasets capture a wide array of categories and attributes. We use the unseen class splits specified in [9] for AwA and aPY, and randomly select the 10 unseen classes for SUN. For all three, we use the features provided with the datasets, which include color histograms, SIFT, PHOG, etc. The attribute-labeled images originate from "seen" classes in each dataset. Instead of using all the labeled images, we use 10%, 20%, ..., 100% of them in our SSL model. By default, we use 70% of the labeled images.

4.1.1 Baseline methods and evaluation metrics

To evaluate the performance of the optimal graph, we compare with different zero-shot image categorization methods, e.g., [6], [7] and [11].

Table 1: Results on three datasets

Methods	aPY		
	Accuracy	classAUC	attrAUC
Lampert et al. [7]	18.1	76.9	70.6
Yu et al. [11]	20.1	77.3	71.5
Kankuekul et al. [6]	15.8	75.5	68.8
Ours	**21.3**	**79.1**	**72.3**
Methods	AwA		
	Accuracy	classAUC	attrAUC
Lampert et al. [7]	40.5	81.4	72.8
Yu et al. [11]	**48.3**	**82.9**	**73.7**
Kankuekul et al. [6]	32.7	80.5	71.8
Ours	47.1	82.2	73.3
Methods	SUN		
	Accuracy	classAUC	attrAUC
Lampert et al. [7]	52.5	90.1	81.7
Yu et al. [11]	49.1	88.6	81.1
Kankuekul et al. [6]	42.8	87.5	79.8
Ours	**54.3**	**91.0**	**82.3**

Table 2: Results with different percentage of labeled training data on AwA dataset

Percentage	10%	20%	30%	40%	50%
Accuracy	28.6	37.1	42.6	45.9	47.1
Percentage	60%	70%	80%	90%	100%
Accuracy	47.5	47.8	48.0	47.9	47.9

We measure the quality of the categorization steps in terms of normalized multi-class accuracy (Accuracy) on the test set. For each attribute, we compute the receiver operating characteristic (ROC) curve of each predictor and averaging the areas under the curves (AUCs) over the attributes to obtain attrAUC score. And we also use the mean area under the ROC curve of class predictions (classAUC).

4.2 Results of attribute prediction

In a first set of experiments we compare our method to the other methods on the three datasets and we report Accuracy, attrAUC and classAUC in Table 1. We then evaluate the performance variance with different percent of labeled image, and illustrate the results in Table 2. From these results, we can make several observations.

- In terms of accuracy, our method outperforms other state-of-the-art zero-shot methods on aPY and SUN dataset. This indicates that the learned optimal graph can improve the performance of zero-shot image categorization even with less labeled images. Among these methods, the method proposed by Yu et al. [11] is a good competitor, and it outperforms our method in AwA dataset, even though the performance gap is marginal. On the other hand, Kankuekul et al.[6] achieve the worst performance in all datasets.

- By learning an optimal graph from multiple cues, the performance for attribute prediction and class prediction is improved compared with other zero-shot learning methods, which is reflected in the results of attrAUC and classAUC. This is due to that in our SSL model, the learned graph can more accurately encode the relationships between data points. Instead of concatenating different visual features into a long vector, we treat each feature separately and assign different importance value to each of them to learn a optimal graph.

- From Table 2, we can see that with the increase of the percentage of labeled images used, the accuracy goes up as well. However, when 70% of the labeled images are used, further increasing the labeled images can not improve the performance image categorization. This indicates that in our SSL model, a reasonable percentage of labeled images can a achieve satisfactory performance. In this way, the workload of labor-consuming human annotation can be reduced largely.

5. CONCLUSIONS

In this paper, we propose using semi-supervised learning framework to tackle the attribute prediction problem in the zero-shot image categorization problem. We utilize multiple features and attribute label information to learn an optimal graph which embeds the relationships among the data points more accurately. Then, this graph is used to generate a geometrical regularizers for a semi-supervised learning model to learn the attribute classifier. An efficient solution is proposed. Experiments on three public datasets show the superiority of our algorithm.

6. REFERENCES

[1] M. Chen, A. Zheng, and K. Q. Weinberger. Fast image tagging. In *ICML*, 2013.

[2] A. Farhadi, I. Endres, D. Hoiem, and D. A. Forsyth. Describing objects by their attributes. In *CVPR*, 2009.

[3] L. Gao, J. Song, F. Nie, Y. Yan, N. Sebe, and H. T. Shen. Optimal graph leaning with partial tags and multiple features for image and video annotation. In *CVPR*, 2015.

[4] D. Jayaraman and K. Grauman. Zero-shot recognition with unreliable attributes. In *NIPS*, 2014.

[5] D. Jayaraman, F. Sha, and K. Grauman. Decorrelating semantic visual attributes by resisting the urge to share. In *CVPR*, 2014.

[6] P. Kankuekul, A. Kawewong, S. Tangruamsub, and O. Hasegawa. Online incremental attribute-based zero-shot learning. In *CVPR*, 2012.

[7] C. H. Lampert, H. Nickisch, and S. Harmeling. Attribute-based classification for zero-shot visual object categorization. *IEEE Trans. Pattern Anal. Mach. Intell.*, 36(3):453–465, 2014.

[8] M. Palatucci, D. Pomerleau, G. E. Hinton, and T. M. Mitchell. Zero-shot learning with semantic output codes. In *NIPS*, 2009.

[9] J. Song, Y. Yang, Z. Huang, H. T. Shen, and R. Hong. Multiple feature hashing for real-time large scale near-duplicate video retrieval. In *ACM Multimedia*, pages 423–432, 2011.

[10] J. Song, Y. Yang, X. Li, Z. Huang, and Y. Yang. Robust hashing with local models for approximate similarity search. *IEEE T. Cybernetics*, 44(7):1225–1236, 2014.

[11] F. X. Yu, L. Cao, R. S. Feris, J. R. Smith, and S. Chang. Designing category-level attributes for discriminative visual recognition. In *CVPR*, 2013.

Deep Bottleneck Feature for Image Classification

Yan Song
National Engineering Laboratory of Speech and Language Information Processing
Univ. of Sci.& Tech of China
Hefei, China
songy@ustc.edu.cn

Ian McloughLin
National Engineering Laboratory of Speech and Language Information Processing
Univ. of Sci.& Tech of China
Hefei, China
ivm@ustc.edu.cn

Lirong Dai
National Engineering Laboratory of Speech and Language Information Processing, USTC
P.O.Box 4
Hefei, China
lrdai@ustc.edu.cn

ABSTRACT

Effective image representation plays an important role for image classification and retrieval. Bag-of-Features (BoF) is well known as an effective and robust visual representation. However, on large datasets, convolutional neural networks (CNN) tend to perform much better, aided by the availability of large amounts of training data. In this paper, we propose a bag of Deep Bottleneck Features (DBF) for image classification, effectively combining the strengths of a CNN within a BoF framework. The DBF features, obtained from a previously well-trained CNN, form a compact and low-dimensional representation of the original inputs, effective for even small datasets. We will demonstrate that the resulting BoDBF method has a very powerful and discriminative capability that is generalisable to other image classification tasks.

General Terms

Theory, Machine Learning

Keywords

Image Classification, Transfer Learning, BoF, CNN

1. INTRODUCTION

Effective image representation plays an important role in content based recognition and retrieval applications. Over the past decade, representations based on local features, known as bag-of-features (BoF) methods, were considered to be state-of-the-art, especially for SIFT [11] descriptors extracted from small patches. It has been shown that BoF methods may provide a degree of robustness to the changes caused by image scaling, translation and occlusion.

Recently, deep convolutional neural networks(CNN)[9] have achieved outstanding performance in large scale visual recognition competitions. This may be attributed to the high-capacity of CNN structures, with millions of parameters tuned from large scale dataset like Imagenet [4]. However, for some benchmark image recognition tasks, such as PASCAL VOC [6] and MIT Scenes [14], the performance of CNN is limited due to relative lack of training data. In such cases, a number of recent works [5, 7, 12, 15, 3] have indicated that it is preferable to transfer a previously well-trained CNN rather than to learn one directly using limited training data. For example, Razavian *et.al.* conducted a series of experiments for different recognition tasks, and demonstrated the superiority of the features extracted from a pre-trained CNN [15]. At the same time, Chatfield *et.al.* [3] report comprehensive comparisons between CNN and Improved Fisher Vector (IFV) leading to similar conclusions as [15].

Despite the proven superiority of CNN based features, they have been empirically shown to still be fairly sensitive to global translation, rotation and scaling in terms of classification accuracy [8]. Furthermore, it is argued that the images in various benchmark datasets may have significant different statistics [17]. The transferability of CNN activations decreases as the distance between source dataset and the target one increases [19]. It may therefore be interesting to use a pre-trained CNN for front-end feature extraction (to yield good features), while still exploiting a BoF framework to enjoy more robust image representation. The issue is on how to effectively encode and aggregate the higher dimensional CNN features for diverse tasks which contain limited training data.

In this paper, we thus propose using a structured CNN containing a bottleneck layer as the front-end feature extractor. As shown in Fig. 1, the number of hidden nodes in the bottleneck layer (*i.e.* FC7) is much smaller than other fully-connected layers. The CNN training will then force the activations in the bottleneck layer to form a low-dimensional compact representation of the original input. We denote the output vector of that constricted internal layer as the Deep Bottleneck Feature (DBF). Then, a bag-of-DBFs (BoDBF) method is proposed in which a second-order pooling scheme is applied on top of the DBFs. To evaluate the effectiveness of the proposed BoDBF method, we conduct extensive experiments on PASCAL VOC [6] and MIT Scenes [14]. It is shown that the proposed BoDBF can achieve state-of-the-art performance on these image classification problems, especially for the MIT Scenes dataset.

Section 2 will introduce a BoDBF framework for image classification. A general BoF pipeline is first briefly reviewed, and then a CNN with a bottleneck layer is detailed

ICMR'15, June 23–26, 2015, Shanghai, China.

DOI: http://dx.doi.org/10.1145/2671188.2749314.

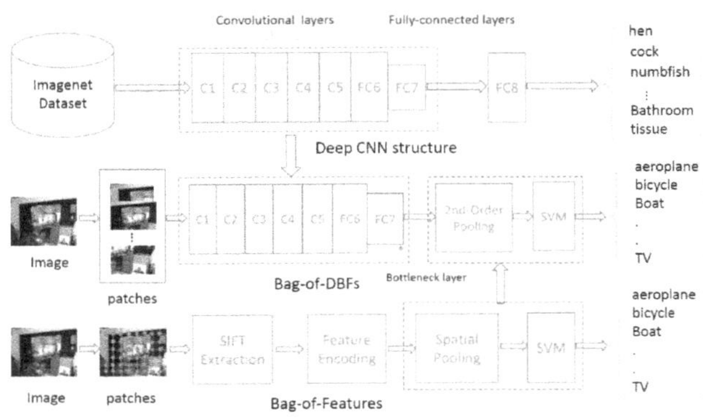

Figure 1: The BoDBF classification framework.

as the front-end feature extractor. After that, a second-order pooling scheme [2] is introduced for constructing robust image representation. Section 3 will evaluate the technique by reporting experimental classification results for PASCAL VOC 2007 and MIT Scene datasets. Section 4 presents conclusions and discusses the potential for future extension of this research.

2. DBF BASED CLASSIFICATION

The DBF based image classification framework is shown in the middle of Fig 1, which follows the traditional BoF pipeline. Generally speaking, BoF methods map the local features (*i.e.* SIFT) into a fixed-length histogram. The process mainly consists of two main phases: (i) *Feature Encoding* assigns every local feature to the nearest visual words in a dictionary. The dictionary would generally have been obtained off-line through a clustering process on a large local feature set. (ii) *Spatial pooling* counts occurrences of visual words in the image (or in spatial regions) to form a histogram representation.

From the perspective of convolution, there exists an intrinsic link between SIFT features and CNN activations. SIFT may be described as forming histograms (pooling results) of oriented edge filter responses, arranged in spatial blocks. Meanwhile, CNN activations are obtained by passing a raw image through multiple layers, each of which contain convolution and pooling operations, outputting a single high-dimensional (*i.e.* 4096) vector from subsequent fully-connected layers. In each layer, the input data is convolved with learned filters and then non-linearly transformed to output activations, and often a spatial pooling operation is applied before output. Some major differences between CNN activations and traditional SIFT features are:

large/small: SIFT features are extracted from either dense grids or detected Regions of Interest (ROIs), whereas CNN activations can preserve more spatial information over a larger patch size.

deep/shallow: From the perspective of CNN, SIFT features are the output of a shallow structure, whereas CNN activations can be derived from deeper layers, providing a compact mid-level representation of the original image. Zeiler *et.al.* showed that the reconstruction of the activations from deeper convolutional layers resembles the original image [20].

learned/fixed: The edge filters used for extracting SIFT features are generally hand-crafted, while in CNN, the filters are discriminatively learned from training data.

Due to the superior performance of CNN on large-scale visual recognition, we are interested in using the activations from deep CNN structure instead of SIFT features for effective image representation. However, these activations are generally with higher dimension, which is difficult to be modeled using traditional unsupervised learning methods. We thus introduce a special CNN structure with bottleneck layer as a front-end feature extractor.

2.1 CNN structure with Bottleneck Layer

The structure of CNN with bottleneck layer is shown on the top of Fig. 1. This is an 8-layer Zeiler and Fergus's (ZF) style CNN [20], consisting of five convolutional layers (C1-C5) and three fully-connected layers (FC6-FC8). The input image size is 224×224. The filter numbers (sizes) of the five convolutional layers are: $96(7 \times 7)$, $256(5 \times 5)$, $512(3 \times 3)$, $512(3 \times 3)$ and $512(3 \times 3)$ respectively. The first two convolutional layers have a stride of 2 pixels, and the rest have a stride of 1 pixel.

In our current implementation, the fully-connected layer FC7 is chosen as the bottleneck layer. This deep CNN is trained on the Imagenet dataset and has performance comparable to AlexNet [9] on the validation set with moderate training time.

In the BoDBF framework, we use this deep CNN structure following the BoF pipeline: the output of convolutional layers can be considered as the patch descriptor, and the bottleneck layer functions likes an encoder to produce compact codes. These codes are further pooled together to produce a global description of the image which is robust to slight transformations.

2.2 Second-order pooling of DBFs

Given a collection of m patch codes $D = (\mathbf{X}, \mathbf{F})$, where $\mathbf{X} = (\mathbf{x}_1, \ldots, \mathbf{x}_m), \mathbf{x}_i \in \mathbb{R}^n$ are the DBFs extracted from patches centered at positions $\mathbf{F} = (\mathbf{f}_1, \mathbf{f}_2, \ldots, \mathbf{f}_m), \mathbf{f}_i \in \mathbb{R}^2$.

The simplest pooling method consists in averaging the feature vectors within a spatial neighborhood, which we term first-order pooling (O1P): $\mathbf{P}_1 = \frac{1}{m}\sum_{i=1}^{m} |\mathbf{x}_i|$

In this paper, we introduce a more effective second-order method that can capture the pairwise correlations between DBFs extracted from an image. These correlations can be defined using an outer product of DBFs, which is symmetric positive definite (SPD). The second-order pooling (O2P) is

$$\mathbf{P}_2 = \frac{1}{m}\sum_{i=1}^{m} \mathbf{x}_i \cdot \mathbf{x}_i^\top \quad (1)$$

From the perspective of computational differential geometry [1], the set of symmetric positive definite matrices forms a Riemannian manifold, a non-Euclidean space. Note that linear SVM generally follows pooling, for reasons of efficiency. However in this case it is not optimal for a linear SVM to be trained from second-order pooling outputs. To address this issue, a log-Euclidean metric is proposed to map the SPD matrix $\mathbf{P}_2$ to a tangent space, $\mathbf{P}_2 = log(\mathbf{P}_2)$. It is proven with strong theoretic guarantees that this type of map can preserve the intrinsic geometric relationships as defined in the original Riemannian manifold [1]. Furthermore, the signed-square-root and l_2-normalization, corresponding

Table 1: Comparison of results on Pascal VOC 2007 dataset of each 20 classes in terms of mAP(%)

method/object class	aero	bicyc	bird	boat	bott	bus	car	cat	chair	cow
CNN-SVM [15]	89.7	81.4	86.0	85.3	45.7	76.2	84.6	84.9	64.5	62.5
SCFVC [10]	89.5	84.1	83.7	83.7	43.9	76.7	**87.8**	82.5	60.6	69.6
DBF-O2P	**91.7**	**86.0**	**88.8**	**88.0**	**55.0**	**80.5**	86.4	**88.4**	**65.3**	**73.2**
method/object class	table	dog	horse	m-bike	person	plant	sheep	sofa	train	tv
CNN-SVM [15]	70.0	80.3	83.0	78.0	87.7	50.1	75.8	59.8	88.8	72.5
SCFVC [10]	72.0	77.1	**88.7**	82.1	**94.4**	56.8	71.4	**67.7**	90.9	75.0
BoDBF-O2P	**74.7**	**85.4**	88.4	**83.7**	91.4	**60.5**	**81.2**	67.4	**91.4**	**78.5**

Table 2: Comparison of results on Pascal VOC 2007. The mean average precision over 20 classes in terms of mAP(%)

Method	MAP	Comment
SCFVC [10]	76.9	with single scale
CNN-SVM [15]	73.9	on whole image
CNNaug-SVM [15]	77.2	with augmented data
CNN-SVM [3]	78.6	with augmented data
BoDBF-O1P	75.4	single scale patches
BoDBF-IFV	76.1	CNN for single scale patches
BoDBF-O2P	**80.6**	CNN for single scale patches

to the Hellinger kernel map [18] is also applied before classification.

3. EXPERIMENT AND ANALYSIS

To evaluate the effectiveness of the proposed bag-of-DBFs method, we conduct extensive experiments on PASCAL VOC 2007 and MIT Scenes datasets.

3.1 Experimental Setting

The DBFs are extracted as follows: firstly the input images are resized so that their maximize dimension is 512 and their minimum dimension is at least 224. Next, patches of size 224×224 pixels are cropped from each image with a stride of 8 pixels. The patches are then fed into a pre-trained deep CNN, and the activations from the bottleneck layer (*i.e.* FC7) are used as DBFs. In our implementation, we exploit several deep CNN structures trained by [3] with FC7 dimensions of 128, 1024 and 2048. Use of these publicly available pre-trained structures is important in ensuring that our approach can be compared fairly with other methods. We implement the following alternative systems for comparison: 1. BoDBF-IFV: using the IFV method based on DBFs [16, 13]. 2. BoDBF-O1P: using first-order pooling, *i.e.* average pooling based on DBFs. 3. BoDBF-O2P: using second-order pooling based on DBFs. In addition, we also compare with several reported state-of-the-art methods with similar settings [8, 10].

3.2 Experiments on PASCAL VOC 2007

The PASCAL-VOC 2007 dataset [6] consists of 9963 images from 20 classes. These images include indoor and outdoor scenes, close-ups and landscapes, and strange viewpoints. The dataset is divided into three parts: (i) a training set of 2501 images, (ii) a validation set of 2510 images and (iii) a test set comprising 4952 images. Results are shown in Table 2. It is clear that the proposed BoDBF-O2P method outperforms our own BoDBF-01P and BoDBF-IFV by $5\% - 6\%$. Furthermore, we compare the results with other state-of-the-art CNN systems, CNN-SVM1 [15], SCFVC [10] and CNN-SVM2 [9]. CNN-SVMs using the same CNN structure can achieve 78.6%, which is the closest to the performance of our BoDBF-O2P system. SCFVC [10] uses sparse coding techniques for Fisher vector encoding, outperforming the BoDBF-O1P and BoDBF-IFV. However, the computational complexity of SCFVC may become expensive with high dimensional CNN features. Table.1 shows the detailed comparisons for the 20 categories, demonstrating that BoDBF-O2P achieves best performance in 16 categories, as well as being competitive in the remaining 4 categories.

3.3 Experiments on MIT Scenes dataset

The MIT scenes dataset contains 6700 images over 67 indoor scene categories. For each category, the standard training/test split consists of 80 training and 20 test images. This dataset is quite challenging due to the subtle cross-category difference. Moreover, the contents of this dataset are more different from Imagenet than PASCAL VOC 2007 is, which may help to evaluate the generalization capability of our proposed BoDBF.

Classification results are compared in Table 3. Again, the proposed BoDBF-O2P method significantly outperforms BoDBF-IFV and BoDBF-O1P. We notice that the CNN-SVM method [15, 3] perform quite well, and are closer to BoDBF on the PASCAL VOC dataset than they are on MIT Scenes. To the best our knowledge, the state-of-art performance on the MIT Scenes dataset is achieved by MOP-CNN [8], which concatenates the CNN activations using three different scales. SCFVC [10] can achieve similar performance. Compared to them, the performance of the proposed BoDBF-O2P is as high as 72.8%, which is by far the best on this dataset.

3.4 Discussion

We have evaluated the performance of the proposed BoDBF-O2P on two benchmark object datasets, i.e. PASCAL VOC and MIT Scenes. Results clearly show that the BoDBF framework can take advantage of both the robustness of BoF and the improved representation power of a deep CNN. Unlike existing methods including [8, 10], we use a fully-connected bottleneck layer as the feature encoder. Second-order pooling capture the fact that activations from the deep CNN layer are not Euclidean distributed.

Furthermore, we evaluated the performances BoDBF-O2P using activations from CNN structures with different bottleneck sizes of 128, 1024 and 2048. For 1024 and 2048 dimension DBFs, principal component analysis (PCA) was applied to reduce them to the same 128 dimensions. All

Table 3: MIT Scenes performance reporting precision averaged over all 67 classes in terms of mAP(%)

Method	MAP	Comments
SCFVC [10]	68.2	with single scale
CNN-SVM [15]	58.4	CNN feature for whole image
MOP-CNN [8]	68.9	for patches with three scales
BoDBF-O1P	59.8	for patches with single scale
BoDBF-IFV	66.2	for single scale patches
BoDBF-O2P	**72.8**	for single scale patches

results reported above used 1024 dimension DBFs reduced to 128 dimension using PCA. Thus the final dimension of BoDBF-O2P was $128 \times 129/2 = 8256$, which is less than MOP-CNN ($4096 \times 3 = 12288$) and SCFVC ($100 \times 1000 = 100,000$). Detailed comparisons for all dimension DBFs are shown in Table. 4, which indicates that all yield competitive performance and larger sizes may be unnecessary.

Table 4: The effect of different layer size in terms of mAP (%)

Dataset/Dimension	128	1024	2048
PASCAL VOC	80.3	80.6	79.1
MIT 67 Scenes	69.9	72.8	70.0

4. CONCLUSION AND FUTURE WORK

This paper has presented a novel image classification framework (*i.e.* BoDBF) based on a carefully designed CNN structure that contains a narrow bottleneck layer. The CNN, having been trained on a large image dataset, is used as the front-end feature extractor for other visual recognition tasks. In the proposed BoDBF framework, the output of convolutional layers are considered as the patch descriptors, and the bottleneck layer functions as an encoder to produce compact codes, *i.e.* DBFs. Second-order pooling scheme is further introduced to explore the correlations between DBFs. The BoDBF can take advantage of both the robustness of BoF and the improved representation power of a deep CNN, performance is excellent. In fact the experimental results, on benchmark datasets such as Pascal VOC 2007 and the MIT 67 Scenes dataset, reveal that performance exceeds that of current state-of-the-art approaches. The current results are for a relatively untuned network. In future, we would like to experiment with different CNN structures, including assessing the effects of the dimension and location of the bottleneck layer (e.g. moving it to FC6 or FC8).

5. REFERENCES

[1] V. Arsigny, P. Fillard, X. Pennec, and N. Ayache. Geometric means in a novel vector space structure on symmetric positive-definite matrices. *SIAM J. Matrix Analysis Applications*, 29(1):328–347, 2006.

[2] J. Carreira, R. Caseiro, J. Batista, and C. Sminchisescu. Semantic segmentation with second-order pooling. In *Proc. of ECCV 2012*, pages 430–443, 2012.

[3] K. Chatfield, K. Simonyan, A. Vedaldi, and A. Zisserman. Return of the devil in the details: Delving deep into convolutional nets. *Proc. of ECCV*, 2014.

[4] J. Deng, W. Dong, R. Socher, L. Li, K. Li, and F. Li. Imagenet: A large-scale hierarchical image database. In *Proc. of CVPR*, pages 248–255, 2009.

[5] J. Donahue, Y. Jia, and O. Vinyals. Decaf: A deep convolutional activation feature for generic visual recognition. In *Proc. of ICML*, pages 647–655, 2014.

[6] M. Everingham, L. Van Gool, C. K. I. Williams, J. Winn, and A. Zisserman. The pascal visual object classes (voc) challenge. *International Journal of Computer Vision*, 88(2):303–338, June 2010.

[7] R. B. Girshick and J. Donahue. Rich feature hierarchies for accurate object detection and semantic segmentation. In *Proc. of CVPR*, pages 580–587, 2014.

[8] Y. Gong, L. Wang, and R. Guo. Multi-scale orderless pooling of deep convolutional activation features. In *Proc. of ECCV*, pages 392–407, 2014.

[9] A. Krizhevsky, I. Sutskever, and G. E. Hinton. Imagenet classification with deep convolutional neural networks. In *Proc. of NIPs*, pages 1106–1114, 2012.

[10] L. Liu, C. Shen, L. Wang, A. van den Hengel, and C. Wang. Encoding high dimensional local features by sparse coding based fisher vectors. In *Advances in Neural Information Processing Systems 27, 2014, December 8-13 2014, Montreal, Quebec, Canada*, pages 1143–1151, 2014.

[11] D. G. Lowe. Distinctive image features from scale-invariant keypoints. *International Journal of Computer Vision*, 60(2):91–110, 2004.

[12] M. Oquab, L. Bottou, I. Laptev, and J. Sivic. Learning and transferring mid-level image representations using convolutional neural networks. In *Proc. of CVPR*, pages 1717–1724, 2014.

[13] F. Perronnin, J. Sánchez, and T. Mensink. Improving the fisher kernel for large-scale image classification. In *Proc. of ECCV*, pages 143–156, 2010.

[14] A. Quattoni and A. Torralba. Recognizing indoor scenes. In *Proc. of CVPR*, pages 413–420, 2009.

[15] A. S. Razavian, H. Azizpour, J. Sullivan, and S. Carlsson. CNN features off-the-shelf: an astounding baseline for recognition. *CoRR*, abs/1403.6382, 2014.

[16] J. Sanchez, F. Perronnin, T. Mensink, and J. J. Verbeek. Image classification with the fisher vector: Theory and practice. *International Journal of Computer Vision*, 105(3):222–245, 2013.

[17] A. Torralba and A. A. Efros. Unbiased look at dataset bias. In *Proc. of CVPR*, pages 1521–1528, 2011.

[18] A. Vedaldi and A. Zisserman. Efficient additive kernels via explicit feature maps. *IEEE Trans. Pattern Anal. Mach. Intell.*, 34(3):480–492, 2012.

[19] J. Yosinski, J. Clune, Y. Bengio, and H. Lipson. How transferable are features in deep neural networks? In *Proc. of NIPs*, pages 3320–3328, 2014.

[20] M. D. Zeiler and R. Fergus. Visualizing and understanding convolutional networks. In *Proc. of ECCV*, pages 818–833, 2014.

Maximally Visual-Homogeneous Region Detector for Large Scale Image Retrieval

Gang Wang, Ke Gao, Jintao Li
Key Lab of Intelligent Information Processing of Chinese Academy of Sciences (CAS)
Institute of Computing Technology, CAS, Beijing 100190, China
{wanggang01, kegao, jtli}@ict.ac.cn

ABSTRACT

Conventional local detectors often extract numerous small repeated regions in textured areas, which easily results in false matching. In order to find representative and distinctive local invariant regions, this paper proposes a Maximally Visual-Homogeneous Region (MVHR) detector. The main contributions can be summarized as 2 parts: (1) Being different from original MSER which employs single pixel intensity as ranking unit, we propose a novel sorting method based on visual homogeneity analysis on a local patch. (2) Identifying the observation scale has a close relationship with visual homogeneity analysis, a heuristic scale selection algorithm is developed to choose a proper scale according to the changes of visual homogeneity evaluation over a range of scales. Experiments demonstrate our detector can find less but representative regions with high repeatability, while still perserving competitive precision compared to the state-of-art detectors for large scale image retrieval.

Categories and Subject Descriptors

H.5.1 [**Multimedia Information Systems**]: Methodology

General Terms

Algorithms, Design, Performance, Theory.

Keywords

local feature detector, visual homogeneity, scale selection

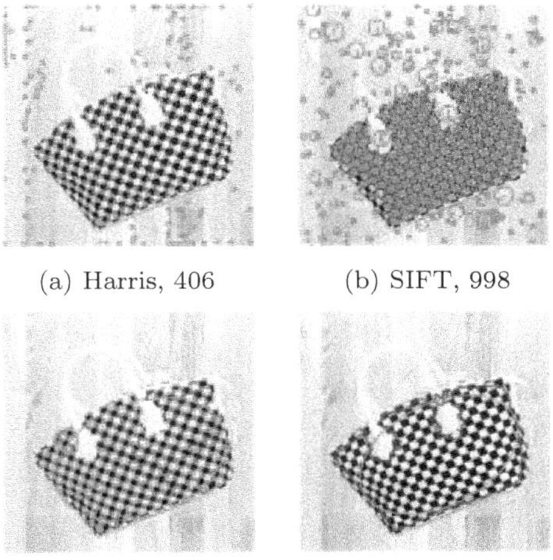

(a) Harris, 406 (b) SIFT, 998

(c) MSER, 260 (d) Ours, 1

Figure 1: Output regions detected by local feature detectors and their corresponding numbers. The red contours denote regions of interest detected by four methods. Intensity-based methods (Harris, SIFT, MSER) often split the integral object into "pieces", while the proposed detector can find few but representative visual-homogeneous regions. The blue contour shows the exact boundary detected by our method.

1. INTRODUCTION

Using local detector to extract regions of interest is an important statistic method to represent a picture [10]. For robust image matching, a "qualified" local feature detector is desired to be distinctive and repeatable under various image transformations.

MSER [6] is one of the most popular local feature detectors with good performance [7]. In principle, the method searches for closed regions which achieve local maximal stability over a range of gray value, however when coming to the textured areas, it always extracts a lot of small and redundant patches. Figure 1 (c) shows an example detection result on a handbag which is covered by many black and yellow blobs. Similar phenomenon also exists in Harris and SIFT like Figure 1 (a) and (b). These regions have similar appearances after normalization.

In order to deal with this problem, our major contribution extends MSER to perceptual consistency awareness. Visual homogeneity is defined on a certain size of window according to the space distribution of color classes. It serves as the basic visual unit instead of gray value in MSER. As is shown in Figure 1 (d), the proposed MVHR can find less but representative regions and well solves the problem as mentioned above.

Noticing that observation scale has a great influence on visual homogeneity evaluation, therefore our another

ICMR'15, June 23–26, 2015, Shanghai, China.

http://dx.doi.org/10.1145/2671188.2749315.

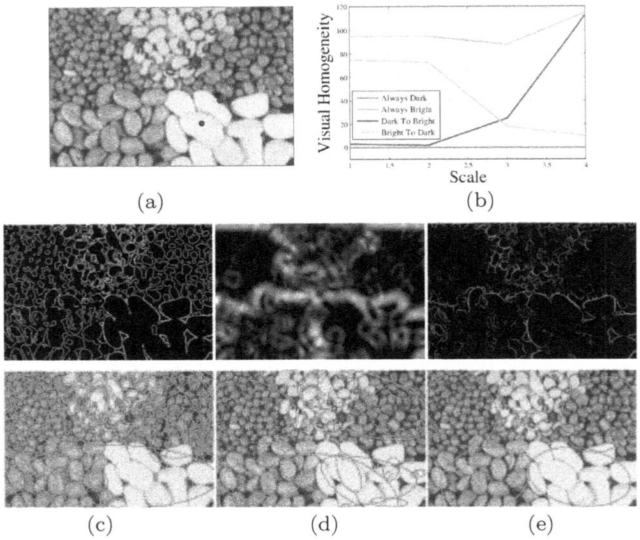

Figure 2: Scale influence on visual homogeneity evaluation and output results. (a) Origin image. (b) Three types of visual homogeneity lines as a function of scale. (c), (d), (e) Visual homogeneity maps and their corresponding output regions at min, max and proper scales respectively.

contribution focuses on a heuristic scale selection algorithm. The variation of visual homogeneity can reflect content change of a local patch over scales, which helps us to select a proper one for each pixel.

2. RELATED WORK

MSER like detectors: MSER [6] was first proposed by Matas in 2004. This method tries to find gray stable regions from the region growing process given a small global threshold δ. In order to use the more distinctive information of color, Forssen [9] adapted the MSER to color images by replacing the gray value with the color gradients. Experiments showed his work had better repeatability performance than MSER under viewpoint change and blur. Being different from the former methods, visual homogeneity is defined by analyzing of space distribution of color classes on a certain size of patch. It is used as the ranking unit instead of gray or color value of a single pixel, and therefore our method can exact more reasonable and distinctive regions.

Scale selection for texture: The definition of visual homogeneity has a close relationship with scale. Many work have been proposed to find an "optimum". Dai [3] defines texture synthesizability by considering homogeneity, repetitiveness and irregularity. Different size of sliding windows are used to scan the image. The optimal scale is chosen where the max response is achieved. Boltz in his work [2] assumes that regular texture has two types of important scale regimes. The two scales are easily decided according to the inflexion point of entropy curve as a function of scale. We evaluate the visual homogeneity at different scales and select a proper one according to the differences between each two scales.

3. THE METHOD

3.1 Evaluation of Visual Homogeneity

In our work, visual homogeneity is defined as an indicator to measure how a small area of the image shares the consistent color-class distribution. The detailed steps are stated as follows:

At first all colors $P(\vec{x})$ in the image I are classified into n color classes, $C_i, i = 1, 2, \ldots, n$ and each pixel is replaced by their corresponding representative color. During our experiments, we find the evaluation of visual homogeneity is sensitive to the color quantization. In order to overcome this drawback, we adopt the latest work of color quantization DD-11 [4], which learns color descriptors from nature pictures considering not only the differences in color space, but also the continuity in planar space.

Next, we evaluate visual homogeneity $H(\vec{x}, s)$ in the same way as J-value [1] where $\vec{x}$ is the position of pixel in the image I and s denotes the size of window Ω centered at $\vec{x}$. Let m and m_i be the mean position of total and class C_i points respectively. Then the variance of position of total and Class C_i points V and V_i can be calculated as:

$$V = \sum_{\vec{x} \in \Omega} \|\vec{x} - m\| \qquad V_i = \sum_{\vec{x}_i \in \Omega} \|\vec{x}_i - m_i\| \tag{1}$$

Finally, the visual homogeneity $H(\vec{x}, s)$ is defined as

$$H(\vec{x}, s) = \frac{V - V_T}{V_T} \qquad V_T = \sum_{i=1}^{C} V_i \tag{2}$$

where V_T is sum of variance of all classes C_i.

3.2 Heuristic Scale Selection

Unfortunately contents may have different scales in a single image like Figure 2 (a). A global scale is not appropriate for the image containing objects of different scales, but we still can get hints to select a suitable one for each pixel according to the variation of visual homogeneity over scales. Three types of cases are mainly considered:

(1) **Always dark or bright** (red and green lines in Figure 2 (b)): It denotes the value stays almost the same no matter which scale it takes. In this case, no actions need to be taken. (2) **Dark to bright** (blue line in Figure 2 (b)): Such case means the pixel is closed to the boundary. At this condition, the smaller scale is selected. (3) **Bright to dark** (cyan line in Figure 2 (b)): This always happens within a texture region. In this case, the bigger scale is preferred. The pixels centered at different color circles in Figure 2 (a) show examples of their corresponding color lines. The observations above motivate us to propose a heuristic method to automatically select a suitable value $H_F(\vec{x})$ in Algorithm 1.

The parameter T_m in Algorithm 1 is estimated as $T_m = t \times max(H(\vec{x}, s))$, which controls whether the scale of a pixel needs to be adjusted. Figure 2 (e) shows though scale selection, the high values inside of textured regions are impressed, while the high values on the boundaries and low values inside of textured areas are kept unchanged.

3.3 Discriminant Regions Detection

After evaluation of visual homogeneity, the next question is how to use the visual homogeneity map to get the desired regions. MSER provides an efficient data structure

Algorithm 1 Scale selection for $H_F(\vec{x})$

Input: $H(\vec{x}, s)_{s=1}^{s_{max}}$
Output: $H_F(\vec{x})$
Initialize: $H_F(\vec{x}) = H(\vec{x}, s_1)$
for i = 1 to $s_{max} - 1$
  for j = i + 1 to s_{max}
    for $\forall \vec{x} \in I$
      $DH = H(\vec{x}, i) - H(\vec{x}, j)$
      if $DH < -T_m$
        $H_F(\vec{x}) = min(H_F(\vec{x}), H(\vec{x}, i))$
      else if $DH > T_m$
        $H_F(\vec{x}) = min(H_F(\vec{x}), H(\vec{x}, j))$

to find 8-connected extreme regions with good repeatability, and thus is applied to our work. However, MSER often finds gray consistent regions, which leads to indistinctive descriptors. Here we filter non-discriminative regions by entropy, which provides a quantitative evaluation about the composition complexity of a given region. Detailed operations are presented as follows:

At first each value in $H_F(\vec{x})$ map is normalized into an integer ranging from 0 to 255, and then we use the standard MSER to detect maximally visual-homogeneous regions. Finally regions with entropy under a given threshold H_t are discarded. Let $P_j(\Gamma_i)$ be the occurrence probability of color class C_j in the region Γ_i, so the entropy $H(\Gamma_i)$ can be calculated as :

$$H(\Gamma_i) = -\sum_{j=1}^{11} P_j(\Gamma_i) \cdot \log P_j(\Gamma_i) \quad (3)$$

4. EXPERIMENT RESULTS

4.1 Detection Results

Aiming at solving the "over segmentation" problems of existing detectors when dealing with textured images, this paper proposes a novel local feature detector to find visual homogeneous regions. In this experiment, we set $A_{min} = 0.01$ to filter to too small regions and $H_t = 0.75$ to filter the indistinctive regions. Figure 3 shows part of the results on Corel image gallery.

In terms of quantity of detection results, Harris and SIFT find significantly more regions than MSER and ours, while most of them are repeated. The differences between MSER and ours is MSER tends to find local consistent gray regions, while ours finds visual homogeneous ones as shown in each group (d) and (e) of Figure 3.

4.2 Repeatability Test

In order to test the robustness of the newly proposed method, we use the same evaluation methodology, software and dataset in [7]. Results are presented in terms of overlap error ϵ. Region R_{μ_m} and region R_{μ_n} are considered as corresponding if $\epsilon \leq 40\%$. We compare our method with other 4 popular affine invariant detectors, namely Harris-Affine [5], MSER, IBR [11], EBR [11].

Figure 4 shows the results of repeatability test. The performance of each algorithm goes down with the transformations being severer, however our proposed

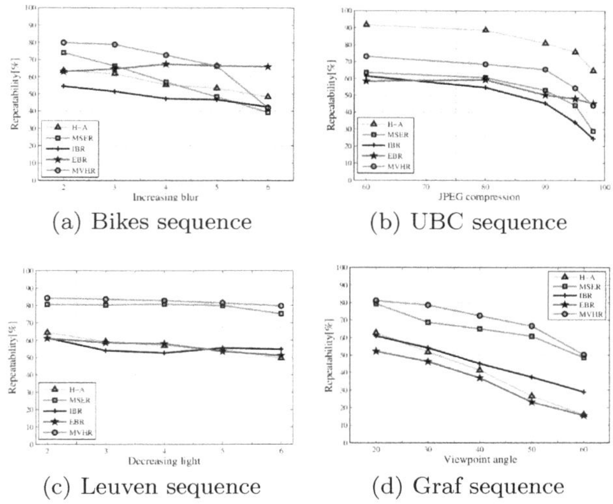

(a) Bikes sequence (b) UBC sequence

(c) Leuven sequence (d) Graf sequence

Figure 3: Repeatability under different transforms

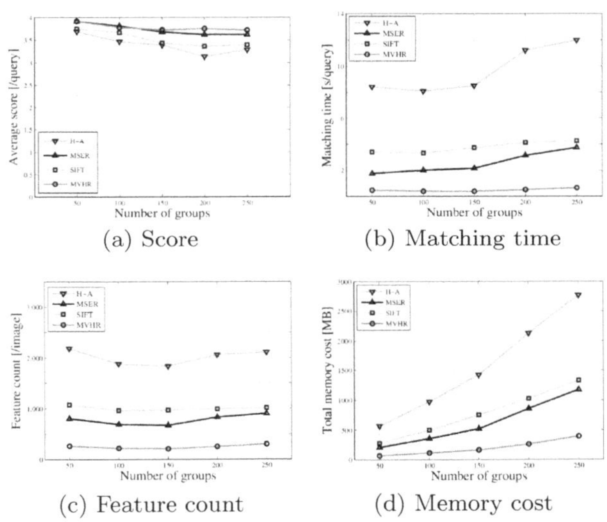

(a) Score (b) Matching time

(c) Feature count (d) Memory cost

Figure 4: Image retrieval performance

detector MVHR exhibits relatively stable and high repeatability before the transformations applied are too large. Compared to the original MSER, our detector MVHR exhibits obvious improvement in terms of blur and JPEG compression. This is because the ranking unit of MVHR is computed though sophisticated color quantization and visual homogeneity evaluation on a local patch, so it is more robust than the simple gray value of a single pixel.

4.3 Performance of Image Retrieval

Since the MVHR detector is designed for image retrieval, in this experiment, we test the performance on the popular University of Kentucky Recognition Benchmark dataset (ukbench) [8], which contains 2550 groups of objects and scenes. For the sake of fairness, 128 dimension SIFT descriptors are extracted from normalized patches for all detectors. Instead of using brutal search, k-d tree is

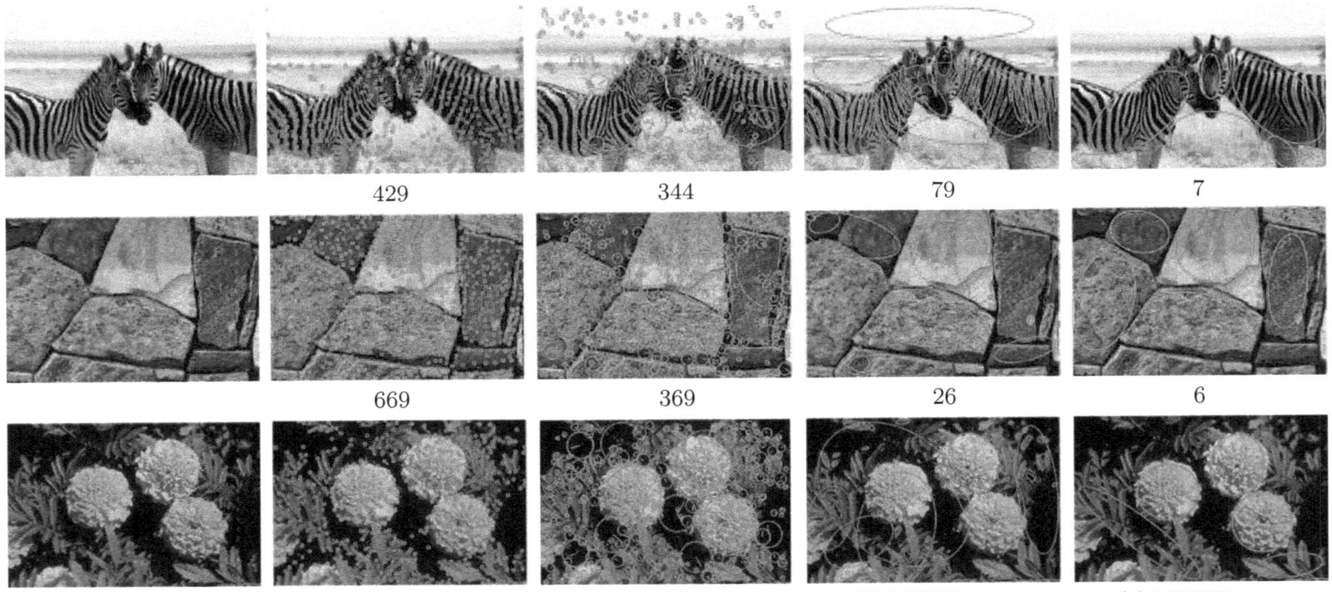

(a) Origin image (b) Harris 544 (c) SIFT 570 (d) MSER 44 (e) MVHR 5

Figure 5: Examples of output regions generated by different detectors and their corresponding numbers.

adopted in this experiment to accelerate the speed of matching. We compare our method with SIFT, MSER and Harris-affine in respect of precision score, matching time, feature number and memory cost as a function of number of groups. Matching score is calculated as the count of related pictures among the top 4 returned images. The max number of regions is more than 2 million.

Figure 5 (a) shows the extended detector MVHR exhibits improved results compared to original MSER and better performance than Harris-Affine and SIFT. This is probably because the regions found by our method have better quality than those of other three methods. Figure (c) shows that our detector produces least number of local image features, about 12.5 percentage of Harris-Affine and 30 percentage of MSER, so it naturally has the advantages with regard to the cost of memory and matching time as shown in figure (b) and (d). This is extremely important to real time applications and smart phone platform.

5. CONCLUSIONS

We have presented a novel method named MVHR to deal with the classic problem of content-based image retrieval: local feature detection. In contrast to well established intensity-based methods, the visual unit used in MVHR is measured by the evaluation of visual homogeneity on local patch, so regions produced by our method are more representative. It can be useful in not only image retrieval, but also object tracking and scene recognition.

6. ACKNOWLEDGMENTS

This work was supported by National High Technology and Research Development Program of China (863 Program, 2014AA015202); the National Nature Science Foundation of China (61271428, 61273247, 61173054); National Key Technology Research and Development Program of China (2012BAH39B02)

References

[1] Y. Deng and B. Manjunath. Unsupervised segmentation of color-texture regions in images and video. *PAMI*, 23(8):800–810, 2001.

[2] B. et al. Texture regimes for entropy-based multiscale image analysis. In *ECCV*, pages 692–705. Springer, 2010.

[3] D. D. et al. The synthesizability of texture examples. In *CVPR*, 2014.

[4] K. et al. Discriminative color descriptors. In *CVPR*, pages 2866–2873, 2013.

[5] M. et al. An affine invariant interest point detector. In *ECCV*, pages 128–142. Springer, 2002.

[6] M. et al. Robust wide-baseline stereo from maximally stable extremal regions. *Image and vision computing*, 22(10):761–767, 2004.

[7] M. et al. A comparison of affine region detectors. *IJCV*, 65(1-2):43–72, 2005.

[8] N. et al. Scalable recognition with a vocabulary tree. In *CVPR*, volume 2, pages 2161–2168. IEEE, 2006.

[9] P.-E. Forssén. Maximally stable colour regions for recognition and matching. In *CVPR*, pages 1–8, 2007.

[10] Y.-G. Jiang et al. Query-adaptive image search with hash codes. *TMM*, 15(2):442–453, 2013.

[11] T. Tuytelaars and L. Van Gool. Matching widely separated views based on affine invariant regions. *IJCV*, 59(1):61–85, 2004.

Rapid Clothing Retrieval via Deep Learning of Binary Codes and Hierarchical Search

Kevin Lin
Academia Sinica, Taiwan
kevinlin311.tw@iis.sinica.edu.tw

Huei-Fang Yang
Academia Sinica, Taiwan
hfyang@citi.sinica.edu.tw

Kuan-Hsien Liu
Academia Sinica, Taiwan
liukh@citi.sinica.edu.tw

Jen-Hao Hsiao
Yahoo! Taiwan
jenhaoh@yahoo-inc.com

Chu-Song Chen
Academia Sinica, Taiwan
song@iis.sinica.edu.tw

ABSTRACT

This paper deals with the problem of clothing retrieval in a recommendation system. We develop a hierarchical deep search framework to tackle this problem. We use a pre-trained network model that has learned rich mid-level visual representations in module 1. Then, in module 2, we add a latent layer to the network and have neurons in this layer to learn hashes-like representations while fine-tuning it on the clothing dataset. Finally, module 3 achieves fast clothing retrieval using the learned hash codes and representations via a coarse-to-fine strategy. We use a large clothing dataset where 161,234 clothes images are collected and labeled. Experiments demonstrate the potential of our proposed framework for clothing retrieval in a large corpus.

Categories and Subject Descriptors

H.3.3 [**Information Storage and Retrieval**]: Information Search and Retrieval

Keywords

Deep learning, convolutional neural networks, image retrieval.

1. INTRODUCTION

Online recommendation has become a common way of satisfying our needs on clothes. Image-based clothing retrieval plays an important role for building an online recommendation system and offers a more convenient way for customers to identify their favorite items. For example, when people saw certain clothes they like on a website, the system is expected to recommend other websites containing visually similar clothing items to him/her for price or brand comparisons.

We introduce a deep learning approach for clothes image retrieval in a recommendation system. When a clothes image selected from a large corpus is presented as a query, the system can find similar clothes efficiently in the corpus based on visual appearance. The system architecture is shown in Figure 1. Recent progresses reveal that a deep convolutional network trained on the ImageNet dataset provides rich image representations [12]. Module 1 of our system takes advantage of this representation and uses it as initial weights for further refinement. In module 2, we adapt the image representations by fine-tuning the network on the new domain of a large corpus of clothes images. To facilitate quick search, we enhance the architecture of [12] to learn the binary (hash) codes directly by adding a latent attribute layer with sigmoid outputs in this module. Finally, module 3 is for online search. Fast clothing image retrieval can be obtained through the learned hash codes and representations via a coarse-to-fine strategy.

ICMR'15, June 23–26, 2015, Shanghai, China.
Copyright © 2015 ACM 978-1-4503-3274-3/15/06 ...$15.00.
http://dx.doi.org/10.1145/2671188.2749318.

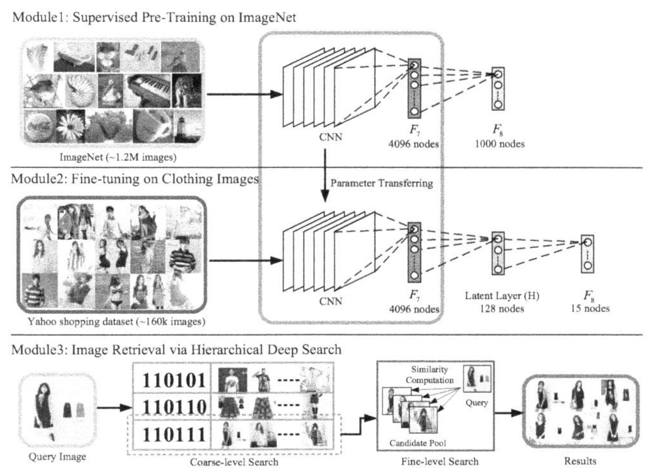

Figure 1: Our framework for rapid clothing retrieval via hierarchical deep search. We use the AlexNet [12] that is pre-trained on ImageNet for learning rich mid-level visual representations (module 1). To facilitate rapid retrieval, we add a latent layer to the network and have neurons in this layer learn hashes-like representations while fine-tuning it on the clothing dataset (module 2). Similar images are retrieved through a hierarchical search that utilizes the hashes-like and F_7 features (module 3).

To properly examine our system in this problem, a large clothing image dataset is needed. We employ a dataset from Yahoo Shopping that contains more than 160,000 clothes images to validate our approach. The dataset has several categories, which can show a great diversity of the images. The remainder of the paper is organized as follows. In Section 2, we review the related work. In Section 3, our proposed hierarchical deep search method is addressed. We conduct extensive experiments and provide discussion in Section 4. Finally, the concluding remarks are given in Section 5.

2. RELATED WORK

Liu et al. [14] targeted a system on occasion-oriented clothing recommendation. When a user inputs some occasion, e.g., sports, wedding or conference, their system can recommend appropriate clothing from the user's own photo album, or pair the user-specified reference clothing (upper or lower body) with the most suitable one from online shops.

Recently, clothing retrieval has drawn more attention due to the huge fashion market. The system proposed by Chen et al. [2] describes clothing by semantic attributes, where a list of nameable clothing attributes are generated. They extract low-level features in a pose-adaptive way and associate with complementary features for learning attribute classifiers. Then, mutual connections between attributes are used to improve the performance from independent classifiers. Their system is evaluated on a clothing attribute dataset including 1,856 images with clothed people.

Liu et al. [15] consider cross-scenario clothing retrieval. They first locate a lot of human parts by a trained human detector. Then, from the part features, they get more reliable one-to-many similarities between the query daily photo and online shopping photos. They collect a daily photo dataset containing 4,321 upper and 4,068 lower body images and an online shopping dataset consisting of 8,293 upper and 8,343 lower body images for performance evaluation. Di et al. [6] consider stylistic visual elements in clothing retrieval. An attribute vocabulary is constructed on a fine-grained clothing dataset by human annotations. The vocabulary is used to train a fine-grained visual recognition system for clothing styles. They then use a Women's Fashion Coat dataset containing 2,092 images in the experiments. Liu et al. [13] introduce the problem of parsing fashion images from color-category tags, such as red-pants and yellow-shirt. They combine the human pose estimation, MRF-based color-category inference, and super pixel-level category classifier to achieve the purpose. Their method is validated on a colorful-fashion dataset containing 2,682 images labeled with pixel-level color-category. Though various researches have been done for clothing matching and retrieval, reliable features for clothes image representation is still demanding. Besides, most approaches are validated on relatively small datasets.

Deep learning has shown its powerfulness in learning good representations from a large corpus. With the introduction of large-scale image datasets and the advances in GPU computing, convolutional neural networks (CNNs) have received great attention recently. Krizhevsky et al. [12] demonstrate that a deep CNN trained on the ImageNet containing more than one million images achieves superior performance on a 1000-class recognition problem. Besides the success on image classification, CNN-based visual representation has also shown improved performance over handcrafted features on digit recognition [3] and pedestrian detection [19].

In addition to visual recognition tasks, deep learning has recently been applied to image retrieval. The work most relevant to ours is the *Deep Search* proposed by Huang et al. [10]. They train a deep CNN that incorporates a tree-structured clothes attributes for feature learning. To deal with cluttered background, they use a human detector to locate the upper body that is fed to the network. The learned features are used for clothing retrieval. Though both our and their work take advantage of deep learning, ours differs from theirs in two aspects: (1) our method does not rely on human detection; and (2) our network learns binary codes, in addition to visual features, to facilitate quick retrieval.

In this paper, we use deep CNN for learning discriminating feature representations capable of identifying different clothes images. Unlike previous approaches using only a small set (such as several thousand) of images for training and evaluation, this work focuses on the circumstance where a large corpus containing more than 160 thousands images for performance comparison. The corpus contains clothes images of heterogeneous types collected from different online shopping stores, including those that are backgroundless or of cluttered backgrounds, with or without human. Nevertheless, we find that favorable performance can still be achieved for such heterogeneous images with the powerful deep learning framework we used, where no pre-segmentation or human detection are performed. Details of our method are described in Section 3.

3. FRAMEWORK

Figure 1 shows our framework for rapid clothing retrieval. It contains (1) supervised pre-training on ImageNet for getting rich image representations, (2) fine-tuning the network on the clothing dataset to learn domain-specific features, and (3) rapid image retrieval through learned binary codes and mid-level representations.

3.1 Supervised Pre-training on ImageNet

We use the AlexNet [12] model from CAFFE [11]. It is pre-trained on more than 1.2 million images in the ImageNet dataset on the 1000-category image classification task. The network contains 8 layers: 5 convolutional layers followed by 3 fully connected layers (F_{6-8}), together with ReLU activations and max-pooling operations. Layers F_6 and F_7 are of 4,096 nodes. Outputs of layer F_7 is fed to a 1,000-way softmax in layer F_8 to produce a probability distribution over the object classes. It has been shown that the 4096-dimensional feature vector extracted from layer F_7 performs favorably against many other handcraft features [12, 18].

3.2 Learning Domain-specific Visual Features

Though the pre-trained CNN has learned rich mid-level image representations, it is non-optimal for a particular domain. Recent studies show that domain adaptations from the AlexNet are effective on transfer-learning tasks [7, 9]. To learn visual descriptors on clothing recognition, we follow this idea to fine-tune the network on the clothing dataset via back-propagation, and thus transfer the learned features to the clothing domain. The learned descriptors will serve as visual signatures for relevant image retrieval.

However, using the fine-tuned F_7 features alone for image retrieval is computationally intensive because it requires an exhaustive search that examines the similarities (based on L_2 norm) between a query and all images in a huge dataset. To facilitate the search critical to real-world retrieval applications, a practical way is to convert the features to binary-valued codes. Such binary strings can be fast compared via Hamming distance or hashing. The binary codes could be generated by random projection (such as locality sensitivity hashing (LSH) [5]) or learning-based techniques (such as [16, 17]). However, they need a second-stage learning or processing via the features constructed for the training data and could result in searching accuracy degradation. In this paper, we enhance the AlexNet structure so that the binary codes can be learned directly from the network and avoid a second-stage learning.

We assume that the final classification results are dependent to a number of h hidden concepts (or hidden attributes) with each attribute *on* or *off*. That is, we associate the input image to a binary-valued outputs (in $\{0, 1\}^h$), and the classification depends on these hidden attributes instead of the feature vectors in $\mathbb{R}^{+4096}$ directly. To this end, we add a new layer between F_7 and F_8 as illustrated in the middle row of Figure 1. The role of this fully-connected layer (termed as *latent layer*, H) is to provide an abstraction of the F_7 and serves as a latent proxy that bridges mid-level features and semantics. H is then regulated by its succeeding classification layer F_8 that explicitly encodes semantic information of training samples. That is, images exhibiting similar activation patterns in the latent would have the same label. In our current setting, $h = 128$ and the neurons in H are activated by sigmoid functions so that

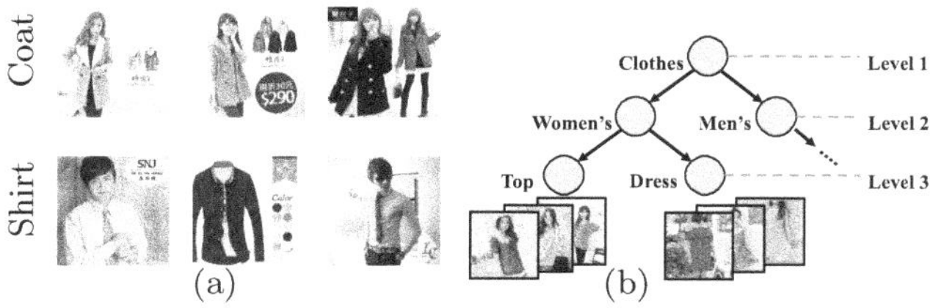

Figure 2: (a) Sample images from the Yahoo shopping dataset. The top row shows the coats images, and the bottom the shirts images from the constructed dataset. (b) Hierarchical labels of Yahoo shopping dataset. The category tree has three levels defined by Yahoo shopping sites.

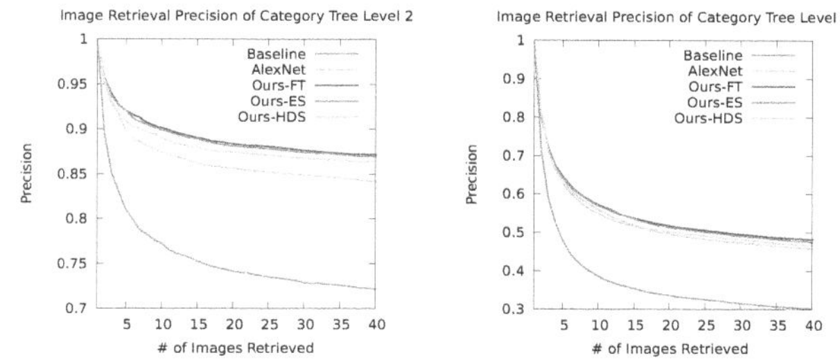

(a) Category labels at level 2 (b) Category labels at level 3

Figure 3: Image retrieval precision of the Yahoo shopping sites. (a) and (b) compare the retrieval performance on different features. The fine-tuned networks perform favorably against the AlexNet and handcrafted features in spite of k and semantic labels. Ours-HDS that utilizes both latent and F_7 descriptors achieves comparable performance to others that consider F_7 features alone.

the activations are approximated to $\{0, 1\}$. Hence, we can obtain binary codes for retrieval when the activations are binarized.

To fine-tune the network, the initial weights of the original layer are set as the pre-trained weights and the latent layer weights are randomly initialized. Stochastic gradient descent (SGD) are performed to refine the weights by maximizing the multinomial logistic regression objective. Through learning, the pre-trained weights evolve to a multi-layer function more suitable for the clothes domain. The latent layer weights can be viewed as evolved from the LSH approach (that uses random projection for binary coding) to a more favorable projection via supervision. With small modifications to a network model, our deep CNN simultaneously learns domain specific image representations and a set of hashing-like (binary coded) functions for rapid image retrieval, while it does not require constructing the hash codes in a separate stage nor dramatically altering the network model with different objective settings.

3.3 Retrieval via Hierarchical Deep Search

We deploy a coarse-to-fine, hierarchical search strategy for image retrieval. The coarse-level aims to quickly identify a small set of candidates sufficiently similar in terms of the binary-code representation. The rank of each candidate is determined through another search performed based on finer-level image representations.

Coarse-level Search. For an image, we extract the output of latent layer as its signature and obtain the binary code H^j ($j = 1 \cdots h$) by a threshold 0.5. Let $\Pi = \{I_1, I_2, \ldots, I_n\}$ denote a set of n training images and $\Pi_H = \{H_1, H_2, \ldots, H_n\}$ be the set of their corresponding binary codes. Given a query image q, the training samples with the Hamming distances to H_q less than a threshold form the pool of m image candidates, $P = \{I_1^c, I_2^c, \ldots, I_m^c\}$, which are further compared at the fine level.

Fine-level Search. We use the features of layer F_7 to identify the top k ranked images from the candidate pool P. Let V_q and V_i^P denote the feature vectors of the query image q and of the image I_i^c from the pool, respectively. We use the Euclidean distance between two feature vectors as a similarity measure. The similarity s_q^i between the query image q and the ith candidate image is defined as $s_q^i = \|V_q - V_i^P\|$. Each candidate I_i^c is ranked in ascending order by the similarity; hence, top k ranked images are identified.

4. EXPERIMENTS

We use a dataset consisting of plentiful clothing product images with a complete hierarchical category tree. It contains 161,234 clothes images collected by crawling the images from the Yahoo shopping sites. Figure 2(a) shows some samples images from our dataset. The images in each category demonstrate high levels of variation in human poses and appearances and are of noisy backgrounds or backgroundless. Some photos contain customer logos and advertisements, which are challenging to image classification and retrieval. The clothes-specific category tree is defined according to the product database from the Yahoo shopping sites. Each node in the tree represents different type of clothing, such as Men's, Women's, and so on. Figure 2(b) shows some examples of the image and with its hierarchical labels. The root of the tree represents the category Clothes. The second level consists of nodes Women's and Men's, while the third level contains a total of 15 leaf nodes representing 15 categories of clothing, such as Top, Dress, Coat, and so on. Table 1 exhibits the details of the 15 clothing categories and the number of images for each category.

Evaluation Metrics. Our framework is designed to recommend clothes items similar to the one(s) customers like on a website by searching the entire dataset. Because of this inherent characteristic in the online recommendation system, we do not divide the data into training and test sets. We randomly select 1,000 query images from the dataset for the system to retrieve visually similar ones also from the dataset. We use a ranking based criterion [15] for evaluation. Given a query image q and a similarity measure, a ranking of n images in the dataset can be assigned. We evaluate a ranking of top k images with respect to a query image q by a precision:

$$Precision@k = \frac{\sum_{i=1}^{k} Rel(i)}{k}, \quad (1)$$

where $Rel(i)$ denotes the ground truth relevance between a query q and the i-th ranked image. Here, we consider only the category label in measuring the relevance so $Rel(i) \in \{0, 1\}$ with 1 for the query and the ith image with the same label and 0 otherwise.

Performance Comparison on Different Features. The visual features play an important role in retrieving relevant images. To investigate how features affect the performance, we compare the features learned in our model with others learned by different networks. We consider the following scenarios: (1) Baseline: DPM [8] is used for human detection and the one with the highest confidence score is selected as the representative. We extract handcrafted features including HOG [4], LBP [1], and color features. Concatenating them leads to a 22,459-dimensional feature vector. (2) AlexNet: F_7 features from the pre-trained network on ImageNet. (3) Ours-FT: F_7 features from the fine-tuned AlexNet on the clothing data with only the classification layer being replaced. (4) Ours-ES: F_7 from our network, fine-tuned on the clothing data with a new latent layer, and (5) Ours-HDS: F_7 and latent features from our network. Note that we conduct an exhaustive search based on L_2-norm when either basline or F_7 features alone are used in retrieval; a hierarchical search is performed when F_7 and latent features are considered.

Table 1: 15 clothing categories and the number of images for each category in the Yahoo shopping dataset.

Top	Camis	Dress	Formal Dress	Pant Suit	Coat	Skirt	T-shirt	Polo	Shirt	Vest	Jacket	Trendy Man	Suit	Sweater	**Total**
61052	6608	27826	3719	5523	12099	420	22273	3187	6361	2119	7395	686	1000	964	161234

Figure 4: Top 5 retrieved images by different features. The red bounding boxes show the representative objects by the DPM. The blue check marks indicate the query and retrieved images share the same label; the black crosses indicate otherwise.

Besides, to better understand the relationship between the learned representations and semantics, we vary the number of class labels while fine-tuning the network and evaluate retrieval performance on the learned features. We use the 2 labels from level 2 and 15 from level 3 for investigation.

Figure 3 shows the precision at k of the Yahoo shopping sites on handcrafted features and different CNN features learned with variable semantic labels. Generally, the CNN features either from AlexNet or fine-tuned models attain improved performance over the handcrafted ones regardless of how k and the number of semantic labels differ. All the fine-tuned models perform favorably against the AlexNet. This is because the fine-tuned ones are well-adapted to the new domain and learn domain-specific image representations. Among all the fine-tuned models, Ours-FT achieves the best performance. With a latent layer added to the network, Ours-ES achieves comparable performance to Ours-FT. Ours-HDS gives similar performance to Our-FT and Ours-ES (less than 1% drop in accuracy), but taking the least search time (more details in the computational time analysis).

Exemplar Retrieval Results. The top 5 images retrieved by different features are shown in Figure 4. Clearly, the baseline method retrieve images of great diversity. On the other hand, visually similar images can be retrieved by the deep features. The fine-tuned models retrieve more images with the same label as the query than AlexNet and the baseline. Notably, Ours-HDS's results are close (or identical) to Ours-ES's. This indicates the learned binary codes are informative and of discriminative power.

Computational Time. For an image with a size of 500×500 pixels, extracting CNN features takes about 0.06 seconds on a machine with Geforce GTX 780 GPU and 3 GB memory. The search is carried out on the CPU mode with a MATLAB implementation. Performing an exhaustive search using the handcrafted features for a query takes about 30 seconds; CNN features takes 5-6 seconds. In contrast, our hierarchical search takes 0.6 seconds. In sum, benefiting from the binary codes, our proposed hierarchical deep search is 10x and 50x faster than an exhaustive search using the F_7 and handcrafted features, respectively.

5. CONCLUSIONS

We have presented a deep CNN framework for rapid clothing retrieval in a recommendation system. To facilitate search, we add a latent layer to the network for learning binary codes that can be used to quickly identify a pool of image candidates for later refinement. Experimental results on a large clothing dataset demonstrate that our hierarchical, coarse-to-fine search attains a 10x and 50x speed-up in retrieval compared to an exhaustive search using CNN and handcrafted baseline features, respectively. In the future, we plan to embrace attributes, apart from category labels, to provide the collected clothes images with more comprehensive description and to test our method on the images with attribute annotations.

6. REFERENCES

[1] T. Ahonen, A. Hadid, and M. Pietikainen. Face description with local binary patterns: Application to face recognition. *IEEE Trans. PAMI*, 28(12):2037–2041, 2006.

[2] H. Chen, A. Gallagher, and B. Girod. Describing clothing by semantic attributes. In *Proc. ECCV*, 2012.

[3] D. C. Ciresan, U. Meier, and J. Schmidhuber. Multi-column deep neural networks for image classification. In *Proc. CVPR*, 2012.

[4] N. Dalal and B. Triggs. Histograms of oriented gradients for human detection. In *Proc. CVPR*, 2005.

[5] M. Datar, N. Immorlica, P. Indyk, and V. Mirrokni. Locality-sensitive hashing scheme based on p-stable distributions. In *Proc. SCG*, 2004.

[6] W. Di, C. Wah, A. Bhardwaj, R. Piramuthu, and N. Sundaresan. Style finder: Fine-grained clothing style detection and retrieval. In *Proc. CVPR Workshops*, 2013.

[7] J. Donahue, Y. Jia, O. Vinyals, J. Hoffman, N. Zhang, E. Tzeng, and T. Darrell. DeCAF: A deep convolutional activation feature for generic visual recognition. In *Proc. ICML*, 2014.

[8] P. F. Felzenszwalb, R. B. Girshick, D. McAllester, and D. Ramanan. Object detection with discriminatively trained part based models. *IEEE Trans. PAMI*, 32(9):1627–1645, 2010.

[9] R. Girshick, J. Donahue, T. Darrell, and J. Malik. Rich feature hierarchies for accurate object detection and semantic segmentation. In *Proc. CVPR*, 2014.

[10] J. Huang, W. Xia, and S. Yan. Deep search with attribute-aware deep network. In *Proc. ACM MM*, 2014.

[11] Y. Jia, E. Shelhamer, J. Donahue, S. Karayev, J. Long, R. Girshick, S. Guadarrama, and T. Darrell. Caffe: Convolutional architecture for fast feature embedding. *arXiv preprint arXiv:1408.5093*, 2014.

[12] A. Krizhevsky, I. Sutskever, and G. E. Hinton. ImageNet classification with deep convolutional neural networks. In *Proc. NIPS*, 2012.

[13] S. Liu, J. Feng, C. Domokos, H. Xu, J. Huang, Z. Hu, and S. Yan. Fashion parsing with weak color-category labels. *IEEE Trans. Multimedia*, 16(1):253–265, 2014.

[14] S. Liu, J. Feng, Z. Song, T. Zhang, H. Lu, C. Xu, and S. Yan. Hi, magic closet, tell me what to wear! In *Proc. ACM MM*, 2012.

[15] S. Liu, Z. Song, G. Liu, C. Xu, H. Lu, and S. Yan. Street-to-shop: Cross-scenario clothing retrieval via parts alignment and auxiliary set. In *Proc. CVPR*, 2012.

[16] W. Liu, C. Mu, S. Kumar, and S.-F. Chang. Discrete graph hashing. In *Proc. NIPS*, 2014.

[17] M. Norouzi, D. J. Fleet, and R. Salakhutdinov. Hamming distance metric learning. In *Proc. NIPS*, 2012.

[18] M. Oquab, L. Bottou, I. Laptev, and J. Sivic. Learning and transferring mid-level image representations using convolutional neural networks. In *Proc. CVPR*, 2014.

[19] P. Sermanet, D. Eigen, X. Zhang, M. Mathieu, R. Fergus, and Y. LeCun. Overfeat: Integrated recognition, localization and detection using convolutional networks. In *Proc. ICLR*, 2014.

Information Gain Study for Visual Vocabulary Construction

Huu Ton Le
XLIM Laboratory
UMR CNRS 7252
University of Poitiers
France
huu.ton.le@xlim.fr

Syntyche Gbèhounou
XLIM Laboratory
UMR CNRS 7252
University of Poitiers
France
syntyche.gbehounou@xlim.fr

Thierry Urruty
XLIM Laboratory
UMR CNRS 7252
University of Poitiers
France
thierry.urruty@xlim.fr

François Lecellier
XLIM Laboratory
UMR CNRS 7252
University of Poitiers
France
francois.lecellier@xlim.fr

Christine Fernandez
XLIM Laboratory
UMR CNRS 7252
University of Poitiers
France
christine.fernandez@xlim.fr

ABSTRACT

Content Based Image Retrieval (CBIR) systems retrieve the most similar images to a query image in a collection. One of the most popular models and widely applied in this task is the Bag of Visual Words model (BoVW). In this paper, we introduce an evaluation study of different information gain models used for the construction of a visual word vocabulary. In the proposed framework, the information gain is used as discriminative information to index image features and select the ones that have the highest values of information gain. The empirical experiments made for this study evaluate the effect of four different information gain models: tf-idf, entropy, bm25, tfc with respect to different descriptors and image databases. The results show that selecting the image features based on at least one of the studied information gain model allows the retrieval process to be more accurate than the classical Bag of Visual Words model.

Categories and Subject Descriptors

H.2 [**Database Management**]: Database Applications; H.3 [**Information Storage and Retrieval**]: Content Analysis and Indexing, Information Search and Retrieval; I.4 [**Image Processing and Computer Vision**]: Scene Analysis, Image Representation, Quantization

General Terms

Algorithm, Performance, Measurement

Keywords

Bag of Visual Words model, Information gain, Vocabulary construction, Image Retrieval

ICMR'15, June 23–26, 2015, Shanghai, China.

DOI: http://dx.doi.org/10.1145/2671188.2749319.

1. INTRODUCTION

Nowadays, along with the development of technology, it has become really easy to create and to share pictures online. This phenomenon leads to an exponential growth of image databases linked to a need for new methodologies to manage such very large number of images, not only effectively but also efficiently.

One of the most popular methods for CBIR is the Bag of Visual Words model. In the BoVW model [2], images are represented by histograms of visual words and those histograms are used to index all images in the database. Many researches have been done to enhance the performance of BoVW model. In [16], we proposed a new method to construct a visual vocabulary based on information gain that combine saliency map and the well-known tf-idf scheme also included in our study.

The purpose of this paper is to evaluate the effect of different information gain models using the iterative visual words selection algorithm given in [16]. Thus, we study four different information gain models: tf-idf [14], tfc [14], bm25 [4] and entropy [8]. We exploit those models to select the best visual words in each iterative step. Exhaustive experiments on well-known datasets with several descriptors are implemented to highlight the difference between models. We also proposed to combine the visual vocabularies obtained from the four information gain models to achieve better results.

The rest of this paper is constructed as follow: Section 2 gives a brief overview of related works. The iterative visual words selection algorithm using different information gain models is presented in Section 3. Experiment results are detailed in Section 4 and Section 5 concludes our study.

2. STATE OF THE ART

The Bag of visual words model proposed by Csurka et al. [2] was inspired by the Bag of words model [5, 15] of the Information Retrieval domain. The BoVW model is made of three main stages: feature detection, feature description and vocabulary construction. The purpose of the BoVW model is to represent images by histograms of a set of local features that are defined as the visual vocabulary. Feature detection finds out a set of interesting points which contain rich local information about the image and uses the local patches around these interest points to describe the image. Feature descriptor converts each local patch of the image into a numerical vector. Finally, the vocabulary construction defines a set of visual words as a base and uses that base to affect all other features in the image. Each local feature in the images will be assigned to a visual word. Finally, this histogram of visual words is the image signature which is used for indexing all the images of a database.

Improving the BoVW model has been an active research topic recently; lots of methodologies have been introduced to enhance the performance of this model. [7, 13] make use of Fisher kernel to have a more compact representation of images. Perronnin et al. [13] use a Gaussian Mixture Model for the generative process of low level feature vector extract from the images. Jegou et al. [7] proposed a new images representation named VLAD (Vector of Locally Aggregated Descriptors) which can be considered as a simplification of the Fisher kernel. Due to the compact representations, experiments show a considerable increase in efficiency in comparison with BoVW model when using VLAD and Fisher Kernel

Feature descriptor plays an importance role in the BoVW model. Many have been created, among them the Scale Invariant Feature Transform (SIFT) proposed by Lowe [9] became one of the most popular descriptors. SIFT converts an image local feature into a vector of 128 dimensions. Other than SIFT, we can name here other popular descriptors such as: OpponentSIFT (OppSIFT) [17], SURF (Speeded Up Robust Features) [1], Color Moment Invariant (CMI) and Color moment (CM) [10].

3. ITERATIVE VISUAL WORDS SELECTION WITH DIFFERENT INFORMATION GAIN MODELS

The selection of image features to build the vocabulary of visual words plays an important role in BoVW model; a good vocabulary leads to good image representation and thus to a good retrieval accuracy. However, it is very difficult to identify what is the characteristic of a good vocabulary. Original BoVW model employs a clustering algorithm such as k-means algorithm to group similar features in the same group and uses the centroids of each group as visual vocabulary. However, Parsons et al. [12] show that those clustering algorithms do not have great performance in a high dimensional feature space. Thus, using a clustering algorithm is not always a proper choice to construct a visual vocabulary. In [16], we proposed a method to construct the vocabulary of visual words using tf-idf combined to the saliency information as information gain model. This method has proved to be more effective but also more efficient in comparison to the classical BoVW model. In this paper, we extend this model by using three other information gain models other than tf-idf model, however we do not use the saliency information in order to have a fair study on the selected information gain. Our purpose is to evaluate the effect of those models to the vocabulary construction step. We explain in this part the iterative visual words selection algorithm using different information gain models.

The first step of the algorithm is to pick up some random image features as the initial set of visual words. Our experiments have also confirmed that even the initial sets are randomly pick up, the final result is quite stable as we have run several experiments with different random initial sets and the obtained retrieval results have varied in a very narrow range.

In the second step, we use this initial vocabulary to index all the image features of the database: for all images, each feature is assigned to the closest feature in the vocabulary. Then, the information given by this distribution is used to calculate the information gain of each initial word in the vocabulary. The words are then ranked with respect to their information gain value. The words with the less information are deleted from the visual vocabulary. The algorithm loops to the second step with a subset of the initial vocabulary. In each iterative loop, we choose to delete 10% of the words until the vocabulary size decreases to an expected threshold. We use 4 different information gain formulations for our study: bm25, tfc, tf-idf and entropy. The information gain of image feature w is calculated as follow:

$$tf-idf_w = \sum_{j=0}^{N-1} \frac{n_{wj}}{C_j}.log\frac{N}{n_w}$$

$$bm25_w = \sum_{j=0}^{N-1} \frac{n_{wj}(k_1+1)}{n_{wj}+k_1.(1-b+b.\frac{C_j}{avgdl})}.\log\frac{N-n_w+0.5}{n_w+0.5}$$

$$entropy_w = -\sum_{j=0}^{N-1} n_{wj}.\log(n_{wj})$$

$$tfc_w = \sum_{j=0}^{N-1} \frac{\frac{n_{wj}}{C_j}.log\frac{N}{n_w}}{\sqrt{\sum_{k=0}^{D-1}(\frac{n_{kj}}{C_j}.log\frac{N}{n_k})^2}}$$

where N is the total number of images in the whole database, n_wj is the number of appearances of feature w in image j, C_j is the total number of image features in image j and n_w is the number of images that contain w, D is the number of image features that is used to represent image j, k_1 and b are 2 constant parameters and in our experiment, we choose k_1 equal to 1.2 and b equal to 0.75 as suggested in [4]

Note that in the bm25 formulation, if a visual word appears more than half of the database documents, its bm25 score becomes negative. To avoid negative information gain, we decided to set the bm25 score for those visual words to zero.

4. EXPERIMENTS

4.1 Experimental setup

Three image datasets were considered in our experiment:

- ***University of Kentucky Benchmark*** [11], reffered as UKB to simplify the reading. UKB contains of 10200 images divided into 2550 groups of 4 images of the same object under different conditions (rotated, blurred...). UKB score is the average number of relevant images querying all 10200 images.

- ***INRIA Holidays*** [6] is a collection of 1491 images, 500 of them are query images, and the remaining 991 images are the corresponding relevant images. The evaluation on Holidays is based on mean Average Precision score (mAP).

- ***PASCAL Visual Object Classes challenge 2012*** [3] called PASCAL VOC2012. There are 17225 images, 11530 classified. Images in PASCAL VOC2012 are categorised into 20 object classes. The score on Pascal is the number of correct matches out of 100 retrieval images.

PASCAL VOC2012 database has been used to construct the vocabulary. For each descriptor, we randomly select 4096 features as the initial visual vocabulary. For a fair evaluation, each time a random visual vocabulary is created, it is used for all information gain models: tf-idf, tfc, bm25 and entropy. Each iteration, we delete 10% of features that have smallest information gain values to obtain a new vocabulary, input of the next iteration. Thus, we have the same initial input for all information gain models but the final visual vocabularies used for retrieval are different. To study the behavior of the four selected information gain models, we calculate the retrieval score for these vocabularies with respect to the number of words (varying from 80 to 1000).

Feature extraction: we use the feature extraction tool provided by Van de Sande et al. [17] to extract four well-known descriptors: SIFT, Color Moment, Color Moment Invariant and OpponentSIFT. We do not apply any pre-filtering or keypoint selection. We are fully aware that the results we present in this paper are not at their best. The purpose of our experiment is to have the same framework for different information gain models as well as classical BoVW, so a fair comparison can be made and the results can be easily verified.

4.2 Experiment results

Figure 1 presents the result of CM descriptor on Holidays database as an example of our experiments. We can see that tf-idf, tfc and entropy models give approximatively similar retrieval results with respect to the number of words in the visual vocabulary: from 80 to 1000. However the performance of the bm25 model is not as good with this setup. We have similar observations on other experiments. There is an explanation for this phenomenon: as mentioned before, in the formulation of bm25, if a visual word appears in more than half database documents, the bm25 score for this word becomes negative and we set it to zero for our experiments. As the sizes of the vocabularies constructed for our experiments are quite small (from 80 to 1000) and also the fact that the Holidays dataset is not very big, the appearance frequency of each visual word is very high, the bm25 score of many words is assigned to zero. Thus, it seems that bm25 model is not suitable for small size of vocabularies and small image datasets. The performance of bm25 will surely increase along with the number of visual words in the vocabulary, but it is out of scope of this paper as we also aim for efficient retrieval with small vocabularies.

The global comparison between visual words selection using one of the four information gain models and the classic k-means BoVW model is presented in Table 1. All experiments have been executed with a number of visual words in the vocabulary equal to 256. Due to space limitation, we do not show all the detailed results of each descriptors on each dataset, however some remarkable results can be list such as: using tfc model, the retrieval score in comparision increase by 10.4% with SIFT descriptor on Holiday dataset, 3.4% with CMI descriptor on Nister dataset.

It is noticeable that except bm25, using the vocabulary obtained by information gain selection gives us better results than the classical k-means algorithm. The bottom row of the table shows the average difference in score of each

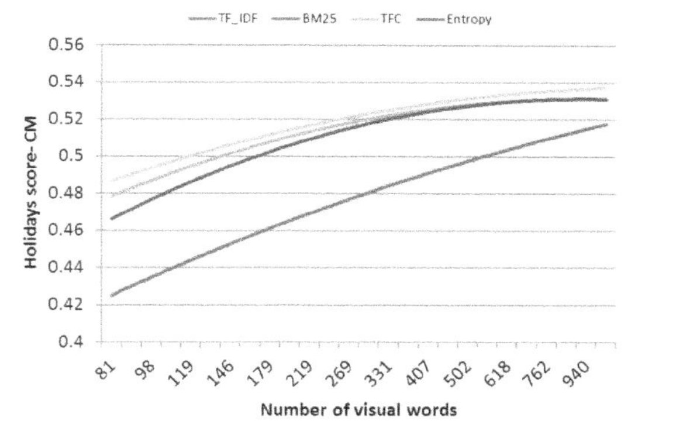

Figure 1: Score on Holidays with CM descriptor wrt number of visual words in vocabulary

information gain model against k-means algorithm. We can see that the results increase by 1.63 % with tfidf, 1.98 % with tfc and 2.28 % with entropy.

Database	tf-idf	bm25	tfc	entropy
UKB	+2.1%	-1.35%	+2.63%	+2.38%
Pascal	-0.75%	-1.5%	-0.68%	+0.4%
Holidays	+3.53%	-2.43%	4.23%	+4.05%
Mean Difference	+1.63%	-1.76%	1.98%	2.28%

Table 1: Mean differences wrt the datasets

Table 1 highlights another observation: the information gain model has different effects with respect to the datasets. This table presents the average difference score of each information gain model with respect to each dataset. We can see that information gain models have a great performance over UKB and Holidays databases, e.g. it increases the average results by 4.23% on Holidays and 2.63% on UKB with tfc model. However, using information models do not seem to work very well on Pascal, the score differences are very close to the classical BoVW.

4.3 Mixing vocabularies

Database	rr1	rr2	rank1	rank2
UKB	+2.6%	+3.3%	+2.6%	+2.8%
Pascal	-0.7%	+0.1%	-0.7%	-0.5%
Holidays	+3.3%	+4.3%	+2.5%	+3.9%
Mean Difference	+1.73%	+2.57%	+1.47%	+2.07%

Table 2: Mixing vocabulary scores

In this section, we propose to mix the vocabularies obtained by iterative visual word selection based on all different information gain models. Starting from 4 vocabularies of 256 visual words, we use two methods to select the best visual words in each vocabulary to build the final one.

Round Robin: the idea of this method is to pick the best visual words in term of information gain in each vocabulary one by one.

Minimum ranking: the idea is to rank in first positions the visual words ranked also in first positions over all the 4 vocabularies. Each visual word rank is computed as follow:

$$r(w) = r(w)_{tf-idf} + r(w)_{tfc} + r(w)_{entropy} + r(w)_{bm25} \quad (1)$$

where $r(w)$ is the rank of visual word w, $r(w)_{tf-idf}$, $r(w)_{tfc}$, $r(w)_{entropy}$ and $r(w)_{bm25}$ are the 4 ranks for the word w with respect to the information gain model used.

Note that if a visual word does not appear in one vocabulary, it will receive the highest possible rank, which is 256. After computing the new rank of all visual words belonging to the 4 vocabularies, we pick up the 256 visual words that have the minimum rank to build the final visual vocabulary.

Table 2 summarizes all the experiment results of mixing vocabularies. We still compare to the classical BoVW model; the column marked as rr1 shows the results of round robin method using all 4 information gain model, rr2 shows the result of round robin method without the vocabulary from bm25 model (poor performance on small vocabularies). Similarly, column rank1 shows the result of minimum ranking method with all 4 vocabulary and column rank2 with only 3 vocabularies.

Our first observation is that, as predicted, eliminating the vocabulary from bm25 model gives better average results. Mixing the vocabulary from tf-idf, entropy and tfc always yields the retrieval score close to the best one obtained with a single vocabulary. rr2 even gives better results with CMI on UKB database and with CM descriptor on Holidays database if we compare to any of the results obtained by a single vocabulary. rr2 is also the best mixing method as it increases 2.57% the retrieval results compared to classical k-means BoVW model, in comparison with 1.73% of rr1, 1.47 % of rank1 and 2.07% of rank2. Globally, we can conclude from this table that mixing vocabularies is a right choice when there is a lack of knowledge on the nature of database as well as when several features are used.

5. CONCLUSION

In this paper, we have introduced an evaluation study of different information gain models for the construction of a visual word vocabulary. Four information gain models are compared in this study: tf-idf, tfc, bm25 and entropy. Those models are used to calculate the information gain score of each single visual word with respect to the database. Then an iterative process is implemented to delete some visual words that have the minimum information gain value. Starting with an initial vocabulary constructed by a large number of random visual words, we step by step reduce the number of visual words in the vocabulary until we obtain the final vocabulary with an expected size. The final vocabulary can be considered as a set of the best visual words in term of information gain for one specific model. To enhance the performance of our method, we propose a framework to mix the vocabularies obtained by the different information gain models in order to get a better one.

Experiments on different image datasets with several well-known descriptors demonstrate that except the bm25 model, all other information gain models return better results than classical BoVW model. Entropy shows a little higher performance than other information gain models and improves 2.28% in comparison with k-means clustering based BoVW model. Mixing vocabularies from different information gain models even gives better results. Round robin methodology combined with the vocabularies from tfc, tf-idf and entropy enhances the results up to 2.56%.

6. REFERENCES

[1] H. Bay, T. Tuytelaars, and L. Gool. Surf: Speeded up robust features. In A. Leonardis, H. Bischof, and A. Pinz, editors, *Computer Vision – ECCV 2006*, volume 3951 of *Lecture Notes in Computer Science*, pages 404–417. Springer Berlin Heidelberg, 2006.

[2] G. Csurka, C. Bray, C. Dance, and L. Fan. Visual categorization with bags of keypoints. *Workshop on Statistical Learning in Computer Vision, ECCV*, pages 1–22, 2004.

[3] M. Everingham, L. Van Gool, C. K. I. Williams, J. Winn, and A. Zisserman. The PASCAL Visual Object Classes Challenge 2012 (VOC2012) Results. http://www.pascal-network.org/challenges/-VOC/voc2012/workshop/index.html.

[4] M. Hancock-Beaulieu, M. Gatford, X. Huang, S. E. Robertson, S. Walker, and P. W. Williams. Okapi at TREC-5. In E. M. Voorhees and D. K. Harman, editors, *Proceedings of The Fifth Text REtrieval Conference, TREC 1996, Gaithersburg, Maryland, USA, November 20-22, 1996*, volume Special Publication 500-238. National Institute of Standards and Technology (NIST), 1996.

[5] Z. Harris. Distributional structure. *Word*, 10(23):146–162, 1954.

[6] H. Jégou, M. Douze, and C. Schmid. Hamming embedding and weak geometric consistency for large scale image search. In A. Z. David Forsyth, Philip Torr, editor, *European Conference on Computer Vision*, volume I of *LNCS*, pages 304–317. Springer, oct 2008.

[7] H. Jégou, M. Douze, C. Schmid, and P. Pérez. Aggregating local descriptors into a compact image representation. In *23rd IEEE Conference on Computer Vision & Pattern Recognition (CVPR '10)*, pages 3304–3311, San Francisco, United States, 2010. IEEE Computer Society.

[8] F. R. López, H. Jiménez-Salazar, and D. Pinto. A competitive term selection method for information retrieval. In A. F. Gelbukh, editor, *CICLing*, volume 4394 of *Lecture Notes in Computer Science*, pages 468–475. Springer, 2007.

[9] D. G. Lowe. Object recognition from local scale-invariant features. *International Conference on Computer Vision*, 2:1150–1157, 1999.

[10] F. Mindru, T. Tuytelaars, L. J. V. Gool, and T. Moons. Moment invariants for recognition under changing viewpoint and illumination. *Computer Vision and Image Understanding*, 94(1-3):3–27, 2004.

[11] D. Nistér and H. Stewénius. Scalable recognition with a vocabulary tree. In *IEEE Conference on Computer Vision and Pattern Recognition (CVPR)*, volume 2, pages 2161–2168, June 2006.

[12] L. Parsons, E. Haque, and H. Liu. Subspace clustering for high dimensional data: a review. In *ACM SIGKDD*, volume 6, pages 90–105. Explorations Newsletter, 2004.

[13] F. Perronnin and C. R. Dance. Fisher kernels on visual vocabularies for image categorization. In *Conference on Computer Vision and Pattern Recognition (CVPR 2007), 18-23 June 2007, Minneapolis, Minnesota, USA*. IEEE Computer Society, 2007.

[14] G. Salton and C. Buckley. Term-weighting approaches in automatic text retrieval. *Inf. Process. Manage.*, 24(5):513–523, Aug. 1988.

[15] J. Sivic and A. Zisserman. Video Google: A text retrieval approach to object matching in videos. In *Proceedings of the International Conference on Computer Vision*, pages 1470–1477, Oct. 2003.

[16] T. Urruty, S. Gbèhounou, H. T. Le, J. Martinet, and C. Fernandez-Maloigne. Iterative random visual word selection. In *International Conference on Multimedia Retrieval, Glasgow, United Kingdom*, page 249, 2014.

[17] K. E. A. van de Sande, T. Gevers, and C. G. M. Snoek. Evaluating color descriptors for object and scene recognition. *IEEE Transactions on Pattern Analysis and Machine Intelligence*, 32(9):1582–1596, 2010.

Discriminative Latent Feature Space Learning for Cross-Modal Retrieval

Xu Tang
School of Electronic Engineering
Xidian University
Xi'an 710071, China
tangxu@stu.xidian.edu.cn

Cheng Deng
School of Electronic Engineering
Xidian University
Xi'an 710071, China
chdeng.xd@gmail.com

Xinbo Gao
School of Electronic Engineering
Xidian University
Xi'an 710071, China
xbgao@mail.xidian.edu.cn

ABSTRACT

Cross-modal retrieval has drawn much attention in recent years due to its wide applications. Most of existing methods only focus on relevance but overlook heterogeneity and discrimination of features from different modalities, and how to capture and correlate these heterogeneous features is still challenging in this field. Therefore, we propose a general model which jointly learns a discriminative latent feature space for effective cross-modal retrieval. Concretely, a class-specific dictionary is learned to account for each modality, and all resulting sparse codes are simultaneously mapped into a common feature space that describes and associates the cross-modal data. Moreover, label information is leveraged to discriminate different classes inside the intra-modality data and also merge the same class inside the inter-modality data. Cross-modal retrieval is finally performed over the learned common feature space. The experimental results confirmed that our cross-modal method outperforms several competing methods on two public datasets.

Categories and Subject Descriptors

H.3.3 [**Information Search and Retrieval**]: Retrieval models

General Terms

Algorithm

Keywords

Discriminative dictionary learning; latent space; cross-modal retrieval

1. INTRODUCTION

Due to the explosive growth of data on the Internet, there have been increasing interests in similarity search with large-scale datasets such as text, audio, images, and videos. However, most existing similarity search methods only apply to the *uni-modal* data setting, which refers to retrieve similar data items with a single modality to a query item. Nowadays, a more appealing scenario frequently arises in similarity search applications, which involves data with multiple modalities and is thus regarded as *cross-modal* problems. Taking multimedia retrieval as an example, one would like to find some textual information that can well describe an image or video [12]. Since data with different modalities reside in different feature spaces, the main challenging factor pertaining to cross-modal problems is how to capture and correlate heterogeneous features from different modalities.

Several promising approaches have been proposed to deal with cross-modal retrieval. Canonical Correlation Analysis (CCA) and its variants may be the most popular techniques that are widely used in cross-modal retrieval. Specifically, given visual and textual features, CCA maps the two modalities into a common latent space where the feature correlation between the two modalities is maximized [9]. As a supervised extension of CCA, Generalized Multiview Analysis (GMA) [10] is proposed for cross-modal retrieval.

Another kind of methods are based on Latent Dirichlet Allocation (LDA). Following the seminal work of Blei *et al.* [2], two association models, *i.e.*, correspondence LDA (corr-LDA) [1] and Topic-regression multi-modal LDA (tr-mmLDA) [8] extended from the basic LDA model, have been built to learn joint distributions of multi-modal data collections. In addition, the Hierarchical Dirichlet Process (HDP) model automatically learns some interpretable topics describing shared and private structure [11].

Although there exist some methods for solving the cross-modal retrieval problem, most of them focus on learning relevant features from two distinct feature spaces, and ignore the heterogeneous feature representation. Considering the fact that dictionary learning (DL) methods have the intrinsic power of dealing with heterogeneous features through generating particular dictionaries for different data modalities, Zhuang *et al.* propose supervised coupled dictionary learning with group structures for multi-modal retrieval (SLiM^2) [14], which jointly learns a group of mapping functions across different modalities. And a unified model is proposed for cross-domain image synthesis and recognition [4], in which a pair of dictionaries for two domains are learned, and multi-modal data is then mapped to a common feature space that captures and correlates heterogeneous data. Nevertheless, these methods overlook exploring the discrimination of multi-modal data from different classes.

ICMR'15, June 23–26, 2015, Shanghai, China.

http://dx.doi.org/10.1145/2671188.2749322.

To solve the challenges above, we propose a discriminative latent feature space learning model for cross-modal retrieval, where discriminative dictionaries and a group of mapping functions across different modalities are jointly learned to produce a common feature space. Concretely, we first learn a class-specific discriminative dictionary for each modality, and discover the discrimination of the intra-modality data in different classes when incorporating class label information. Afterwards, we map a pair of sparse codes, obtained over the learned dictionaries, to the common feature space where the relevance property of the inter-modality data in the same class can also be discovered. Experimental results on two public cross-modal datasets show that the proposed method outperforms several state-of-the-art methods.

2. THE PROPOSED METHOD

2.1 Discriminative Dictionary Learning

The classical DL method minimizes the reconstruction error of the given set of data subject to a sparsity constraint. For multi-modal data, however, the class label information is available and important usually, and the dictionary learned in classical methods cannot reflect the intrinsic structure and shared structure among the data from different classes. Therefore, discriminative DL [6] [7] is proposed to deal with this problem, which not only discover the dictionary atoms associated with each class, but also exploit the discriminative ability hidden in the sparse coefficients.

Given the data $\mathbf{X}$, each data object $\mathbf{x}_i$ has only one of C class labels. We denote the discriminative dictionary $\mathbf{D}$ and the dictionary atom $\mathbf{d}_i$ is in correspondence with only one class label. The discriminative DL is formulated as:

$$\begin{aligned}\min_{\mathbf{D},\mathbf{A}} &\|\mathbf{X}-\mathbf{D}\mathbf{A}\|_F^2+\lambda\|\mathbf{A}\|_1\\ &+\|\mathbf{X}-\mathbf{D}\mathbf{A}_{in}\|_F^2+\|\mathbf{D}\mathbf{A}_{out}\|_F^2\end{aligned} \tag{1}$$

where matrices $\mathbf{A}_{in}$ and $\mathbf{A}_{out}$ are given as:

$$\mathbf{A}_{in}(i,j)=\begin{cases}\mathbf{A}(i,j), & \mathbf{d}_i,\mathbf{x}_j\in\text{same class}\\ 0, & \text{otherwise},\end{cases}$$

$$\mathbf{A}_{out}(i,j)=\begin{cases}\mathbf{A}(i,j), & \mathbf{d}_i,\mathbf{x}_j\in\text{different class}\\ 0, & \text{otherwise}.\end{cases}$$

2.2 Problem Formulation

Suppose that there are s modalities $\mathcal{M}=\{m_1,m_2,...m_s\}$, e.g. *text* and *image*, etc. Let $\mathbf{X}_m=[\mathbf{x}_{m,1},\mathbf{x}_{m,2},\ldots,\mathbf{x}_{m,N}]\in\mathbb{R}^{p_m\times N}$ be the data matrices from $m\in\mathcal{M}$ modality. Each data object pair $\{\mathbf{x}_{m_1,i},\mathbf{x}_{m_2,i},\ldots,\mathbf{x}_{m_s,i}\}$ belongs only one of C classes and describe the same semantic content. N denotes the number of data object pairs, and p_m denotes the dimensionality of m modality.

Our model aim to obtain the sparse coefficients of data from different modalities, and to map them to a discriminative common feature space, where the data share common representation. The modal-specific dictionaries and mapping matrices are learned and coupled, which can bridge across different modalities by the latent common space. Moreover, the discriminative dictionary ensure the ability of separating different classes.

Assume that $\mathbf{D}_m=[\mathbf{D}_{m(1)},\mathbf{D}_{m(2)},\ldots,\mathbf{D}_{m(C)}]\in\mathbb{R}^{p_m\times K}$ is the discriminative dictionary from $\mathbf{X}_m$ and $\mathbf{A}_m\in\mathbb{R}^{K\times N}$ is its corresponding sparse coefficients, where K is the size of the dictionary. $\mathbf{X}_{m(c)}$ is denoted as the data $\mathbf{X}_m$ with c-th label and $\mathbf{A}_{m(c)}$ is the sparse coefficient corresponding to $\mathbf{X}_{m(c)}$ and $\mathbf{D}_{m(c)}$. The learning cross-modal discriminative DL is formulated as follows:

$$\begin{aligned}\min_{\mathbf{D}_m,\mathbf{A}_m,\mathbf{U}_m} &\sum_{m\in\mathcal{M}}\sum_{c=1}^{C}\left\|\mathbf{X}_{m(c)}-\mathbf{D}_{m(c)}\mathbf{A}_{m(c)}\right\|_F^2\\ &+\gamma\sum_{m\in\mathcal{M}}\sum_{n\neq m}\|\mathbf{U}_m\mathbf{A}_m-\mathbf{U}_n\mathbf{A}_n\|_F^2\\ &+\sum_{m\in\mathcal{M}}\lambda_m\|\mathbf{A}_m\|_1+\mu\sum_{m\in\mathcal{M}}\|\mathbf{U}_m\|_F\\ s.t.\quad &\|\mathbf{d}_{m,i}\|_2\leq 1,\quad\forall m,i.\end{aligned} \tag{2}$$

In Eq. 2, γ, λ_m and μ are regularization parameters. $\mathbf{U}_m\in\mathbb{R}^{K\times K}$ is the mapping matrix for $\mathbf{A}_m$ and $\mathbf{U}_m\mathbf{A}_m\in\mathbb{R}^{K\times N_m}$ is the mapped data of $\mathbf{X}_m$ in the K dimensional discriminative common feature space.

2.3 Optimization

Although it is difficult to optimize all the variables simultaneously, the objective function in Eq. 2 is convex to each of variables when others are fixed. Thus we conduct a iterative algorithm to optimize the variables, respectively.

Firstly, we update $\mathbf{D}_m$. By applying joint dictionary learning, $\mathbf{D}_m$ is calculated for initializing the optimization procedure. Here, the Fisher Discrimination Dictionary Learning (FDDL) scheme [13] is applied for the initialization. We consider $\mathbf{A}_m$ and $\mathbf{U}_m$ as constants when updating the dictionaries during each iteration. Therefore, the dictionary $\mathbf{D}_m$ can be updated as follows:

$$\begin{aligned}\min_{\mathbf{D}_m} &\sum_{m\in\mathcal{M}}\sum_{c=1}^{C}\left\|\mathbf{X}_{m(c)}-\mathbf{D}_{m(c)}\mathbf{A}_{m(c)}\right\|_F^2\\ &s.t.\|\mathbf{d}_{m,i}\|_2\leq 1,\quad\forall i,\end{aligned} \tag{3}$$

which is a quadratically constrained quadratic program (QC-QP) problem with respect to $\mathbf{D}_{m(c)}$ which can be updated respectively.

Next, the sparse coefficients $\mathbf{A}_m$ are we calculated when the mapping matrices $\mathbf{U}_m$ and dictionaries $\mathbf{D}_m$ are fixed. As a result, the Eq. 2 is converted into the following formula:

$$\begin{aligned}\min_{\mathbf{A}_m} &\sum_{m\in\mathcal{M}}\|\mathbf{X}_m-\mathbf{D}_m\mathbf{A}_m\|_F^2\\ &+\gamma\sum_{m\in\mathcal{M}}\sum_{n\neq m}\|\mathbf{U}_m\mathbf{A}_m-\mathbf{U}_n\mathbf{A}_n\|_F^2+\sum_{m\in\mathcal{M}}\lambda_m\|\mathbf{A}_m\|_1\end{aligned} \tag{4}$$

For the Eq. 4, the first two terms can be combined as one term:

$$\min_{\mathbf{A}_m}\sum_{m\in\mathcal{M}}\left\|\hat{\mathbf{X}}_m-\hat{\mathbf{D}}_m\mathbf{A}_m\right\|_F^2+\sum_{m\in\mathcal{M}}\lambda_m\|\mathbf{A}_m\|_1 \tag{5}$$

where $\hat{\mathbf{X}}_m=\begin{bmatrix}\mathbf{X}_m\\ \sqrt{\gamma}\mathbf{U}_n\mathbf{A}_n\end{bmatrix}$ and $\hat{\mathbf{D}}_m=\begin{bmatrix}\mathbf{D}_m\\ \sqrt{\gamma}\mathbf{U}_m\end{bmatrix}$. Then the Eq. 4 is converted into standard sparse coding problem for each modal, which can be solved by SPAMS Toolbox [5].

Finally, we update the mapping matrices $\mathbf{U}_m$. When $\mathbf{D}_m$ and $\mathbf{A}_m$ are fixed, Eq. 2 becomes a ridge regression problem and we can solve it as below:

$$\min_{\mathbf{U}_m}\gamma\sum_{m\in\mathcal{M}}\sum_{n\neq m}\|\mathbf{U}_m\mathbf{A}_m-\mathbf{U}_n\mathbf{A}_n\|_F^2+\mu\|\mathbf{U}_m\|_F^2. \tag{6}$$

Methods	mAP		
	Image query	Text query	Average
CCA	0.4345	0.3131	0.3738
GMLDA	0.4396	0.3166	0.3781
GMMFA	0.4416	0.3169	0.3792
SLIM^2	0.4271	0.4162	0.4216
Proposed	**0.4640**	**0.4344**	**0.4492**

Table 2: Comparison of mAP performance of different methods on the NUS-WIDE dataset, with the best results marked by bold font.

We can obtain the analytical solutions of $\mathbf{U}_m$ in Eq. 6 by:

$$\mathbf{U}_m = \mathbf{U}_n \mathbf{A}_n \mathbf{A}_m^T (\mathbf{A}_m \mathbf{A}_m^T + (\mu/\gamma)\mathbf{I})^{-1} \quad (7)$$

After the optimization is completed, we can apply our derived model for cross-domain retrieval task.

2.4 Cross-modal Retrieval

After the dictionary $\mathbf{D}_m$ and the mapping matrix $\mathbf{U}_m$ are learned, we can map all data of modality $m \in \mathbb{M}$ into the common space. Given a data object q_m from modality m, its sparse coefficients a_m can be achieved by:

$$\min_{a_m} \|q_m - \mathbf{D}_m a_m\|_F^2 + \lambda_m \|a_m\|_1 \quad (8)$$

Thus, the representation of p_m in the common space is generated by:

$$p_m = \mathbf{U}_m a_m \quad (9)$$

Finally, all data objects of modality are mapped in into the common space and the top N nearest neighbours of p_m are returned as results.

3. EXPERIMENTS

3.1 Datasets

Wiki Text-Image. The Wiki Text-Image dataset consists of 2,173/693(training/testing) image-text pairs which are from Wikipedia. All pairs are labeled by 10 classes. We extract SIFT descriptors for images and quantize them into Bag-of-Visual-Words (BoVW). For texts, we represent them with Bag-of-Words (BoW) by counting the word frequency. Finally we obtain two datasets: one with 500 dimensions BoVW and 1,000 dimensions BoW, and the other with 1,000 dimensions BoVW and 5,000 dimensions BoW.

NUS-WIDE. The NUS-WIDE dataset is a web image dataset which contains images and the associated tags. We select image-tags pairs with only one class and pick up the top 10 classes. We use the 500 dimensions BoVW and 1000 dimension tags feature and random take 3% and 1% each class for training set and testing set, respectively.

3.2 Experimental Settings

The retrieval performance is evaluated by mean Average Precision (mAP). The Average Precision (AP) of a set of N returned data is defined by $AP = \frac{1}{T}\sum_{r=1}^{N} P(r)\delta(r)$, where T is the number of relevant data (*i.e.*, data with the same labels) in the retrieved set, $P(r)$ denotes the precision of the top r retrieved data, and $\delta(r) = 1$ if the rth retrieved data is relevant and $\delta(r) = 0$ otherwise. We then average the AP values over all the queries in the query set to obtain the mAP measure. Here we set $N = 50$ as [14].

For a cross-modal retrieval problem, empirical studies are conducted for image-query-text task and text-query-image task. And we also calculate the average of two tasks for general evaluation. The parameters γ, λ_{text}, λ_{image} and μ are set to 1, 0.01, 0.1, 0.1 on Wiki dataset and 0.01, 0.01, 0.01, 1 on NUS-WIDE dataset, respectively. Beside, we set the size of the dictionary $K = 200$ empirically.

3.3 Performance Comparisons

We evaluate the performance of our proposed method, and compare it with several related methods: (1) CCA [3], (2) GMMFA [10], (3) GMLDA [10], and (4) SLiM^2 [14] on Wiki Text-Image dataset and NUS-WIDE dataset. All mAP results on two datasets in our experiment are shown in Table 1 and Table 2, respectively. As we see, the proposed method achieves the almost overall best performance over the datasets.

For Wiki dataset, Table 1 shows the mAP scores of different methods on the two kinds of Wiki datasets. In terms of the average score of two task, our method achieves best mAP scores of 0.2334 and 0.2444 for the two different dimensions of datesets, respectively.

The comparison of mAP results on NUS-WIDE dataset are shown in Table 2. As shown in Table 2, We see that our method outperforms other methods, which proves that our proposed method is effective.

Figure 1 shows an example of image-query-text task and text-query-image task on Wiki dataset, respectively. In order to visualize the results, we show the corresponding images to the top texts retrieved image-query-text task. Note that the results returned by our method are semantically related.

4. CONCLUSIONS

In this paper, we proposed a general cross-modal retrieval framework, where discriminative dictionaries and a common feature space incorporating label information are learned jointly. The learned common space yields not only discriminative features for different classes inside the intra-modality data, but also similar features for the same class inside the inter-modality data. Therefore, the common feature space can capture and correlate cross-modal data, where cross-modal retrieval is conducted. Experiments conducted on two public cross-modal datasets show that the proposed model works better than competing methods.

5. ACKNOWLEDGMENTS

This work is supported by the National High Technology Research and Development Program of China (2013AA01A 602), the Program for New Century Excellent Talents in University (NCET-12-0917), the Fundamental Research Funds forthe Central Universities (No. K5051302019), the Key Science and Technology Program of Shaanxi Province, China (2014K05-16).

6. REFERENCES

[1] D. M. Blei and M. I. Jordan. Modeling annotated data. In *Proceedings of the 26th Annual International ACM SIGIR Conference on Research and Development in Information Retrieval*, pages 127–134, 2003.

Methods	500-D BoVW & 1000-D BoW			1000-D BoVW & 5000-D BoW		
	mAP			mAP		
	Image query	Text query	Average	Image query	Text query	Average
CCA	0.1650	0.1883	0.1766	0.1733	0.1822	0.1777
GMLDA	0.1701	0.2161	0.1931	0.1641	0.2550	0.2096
GMMFA	0.1721	0.2180	0.1951	0.1641	**0.2761**	0.2201
SLIM^2	0.1795	0.2123	0.1959	0.2169	0.2365	0.2267
Proposed	**0.2174**	**0.2494**	**0.2334**	**0.2282**	0.2606	**0.2444**

Table 1: Comparison of mAP performance of different methods on the Wiki dataset, with the best results marked by bold font.

Figure 1: A cross-modal retrieval example by our method. The top row is image-query-text task and the bottom row is text-query-image task.

[2] D. M. Blei, A. Y. Ng, and M. I. Jordan. Latent dirichlet allocation. *The Journal of Machine Learning Research*, 3:993–1022, 2003.

[3] D. Hardoon, S. Szedmak, and J. Shawe-Taylor. Canonical correlation analysis: An overview with application to learning methods. *Neural Computation*, 16(12):2639–2664, 2004.

[4] D.-A. Huang and Y.-C. F. Wang. Coupled dictionary and feature space learning with applications to cross-domain image synthesis and recognition. In *Proceedings of IEEE International Conference on Computer Vision*, pages 2496–2503, 2013.

[5] J. Mairal, F. Bach, J. Ponce, and G. Sapiro. Online dictionary learning for sparse coding. In *Proceedings of the 26th International Conference on Machine Learning*, pages 689–696, 2009.

[6] J. Mairal, F. Bach, J. Ponce, G. Sapiro, and A. Zisserman. Discriminative learned dictionaries for local image analysis. In *Proceedings of IEEE Conference on Computer Vision and Pattern Recognition*, pages 1–8. IEEE, 2008.

[7] J. Mairal, J. Ponce, G. Sapiro, A. Zisserman, and F. R. Bach. Supervised dictionary learning. In *Advances in neural information processing systems*, pages 1033–1040, 2009.

[8] D. Putthividhy, H. T. Attias, and S. S. Nagarajan. Topic regression multi-modal latent dirichlet allocation for image annotation. In *Proceedings of IEEE Conference on Computer Vision and Pattern Recognition*, pages 3408–3415, 2010.

[9] N. Rasiwasia, J. Costa Pereira, E. Coviello, G. Doyle, G. R. Lanckriet, R. Levy, and N. Vasconcelos. A new approach to cross-modal multimedia retrieval. In *Proceedings of the ACM International Conference on Multimedia*, pages 251–260, 2010.

[10] A. Sharma, A. Kumar, H. Daume, and D. W. Jacobs. Generalized multiview analysis: A discriminative latent space. In *Proceedings of IEEE Conference on Computer Vision and Pattern Recognition*, pages 2160–2167, 2012.

[11] S. Virtanen, Y. Jia, A. Klami, and D. Trevor. Factorized multi-modal topic model. *arXiv preprint arXiv: 1210.4920*, 2012.

[12] F. Wu, Y. Han, X. Liu, J. Shao, Y. Zhuang, and Z. Zhang. The heterogeneous feature selection with structural sparsity for multimedia annotation and hashing: a survey. *International Journal of Multimedia Information Retrieval*, 1(1):3–15, 2012.

[13] M. Yang, D. Zhang, and X. Feng. Fisher discrimination dictionary learning for sparse representation. In *Proceedings of IEEE International Conference on Computer Vision*, pages 543–550, 2011.

[14] Y. Zhuang, Y. F. Wang, F. Wu, Y. Zhang, and W. Lu. Supervised coupled dictionary learning with group structures for multi-modal retrieval. In *Proceedings of the Twenty-seventh AAAI Conference on Artificial Intelligence*, pages 1070–1076, 2013.

Image Retrieval by User-oriented Ranking

Xueming Qian
Xi'anJiaotong University,China
qianxm@mail.xjtu.edu.cn

Dan Lu
Xi'anJiaotong University,China
ludandan@stu.xjtu.edu.cn

Xiaoxiao Liu
Xi'anJiaotong University,China
xiaoxiaoliu@stu.xjtu.edu.cn

ABSTRACT
Tag-based image search is an important method to process images contributed by social users in social media sharing websites like Flickr. However, existing ranking methods for tag-based image search frequently return results that are irrelevant, low-diversity or time-consuming. In this paper, we propose a user-oriented image ranking system with the consideration of image relevance, diversity and computation complexity, aiming to automatically rank images according to their visual information, semantic information and social clues. When you input a query in the user-oriented image search engine, images tagged with query are obtained as the initial results. The initial results include images contributed by different social users. Usually each user contributes several images. First we sort these users by inter-user ranking. Users that have a higher contribution to the given query rank higher. Then we sequentially implement intra-user ranking on the ranked user's image set, and only the most relevant image in each user's image set is selected. These selected images compose the final retrieval results. Experimental results on Flickr dataset show that our user-oriented ranking method is effective and efficient.

Categories and Subject Descriptors
H.3.3 **[information system]:** information search and retrieval – *Retrieval models*

General Terms
Algorithms, Measurement, Experimentation.

Keywords
Social Media; Tag-based Image Retrieval; Social Clues; Co-occurrence word.

1. INTRODUCTION
With the development of social media and web 2.0, massive amounts of images and videos spring up everywhere on the Internet. This phenomenon has brought enormous challenges to multimedia storage, indexing and retrieval. Generally speaking, tag-based image search is the most commonly used image retrieval method in social media, which enables users to formulate their queries using tags.

Nonetheless, users cannot precisely describe their request with single tags. Therefore, the query ambiguity problem comes into play.Thus, a fundamental problem in social image retrieval is how to reliably solve "query ambiguity" problems. To solve the "query ambiguity" problem, an effective approach is to provide diverse retrieval results that cover multiple topics underlying a query.

ICMR'15, June 23–26, 2015, Shanghai, China.
@ 2015 ACM. ISBN 978-1-4503-3274-3/15/06 ...$15.00.
DOI:http://dx.doi.org/10.1145/2671188.2749326

Currently, image clustering [1, 3] and duplicate removal [5,6,8,9] are the major approaches in settling the diversity problem. In [1], Cai et al. proposed a hierarchical clustering method to cluster the search results into different semantic clusters by a multimodal fusion method, which fuses visual, textual and link analysis. Similarly, In [4], Leuken et al. studied three visually diverse ranking methods to re-rank the image retrieval results, through clustering the visual features of the images. Different from clustering, Ksibi et al. [9] proposed an adaptive diverse relevance ranking algorithm to diversify the relevant search results for ambiguous queries in tag-based social image retrieval using an adaptive diversification trade-off. Yang and Wang et al. [5-6] proposed a diverse relevance ranking algorithm to maximize average diverse precision in the optimization framework by mining the semantic similarities of social images based on their visual features and tags. Sun et al. [8] proposed a DTRR method to promote the diversity performance of retrieval results by fusing both semantic and visual information of images on the basis of [6]. Despite satisfactory results have been obtained, most of them highly rely on the visual and semantic information, and ignore the essence of social images. Social images uploaded and tagged by users are user-oriented. These images are taken in user favorite angle at user available time. For the same scenic spots, various users show us diverse visual effects. Thus, user information cannot be neglected in enhancing the diversity of the retrieval results. Motivated by this intuition and above analysis, we propose a user-oriented image ranking algorithm which introduces the user information into the traditional ranking method. The contributions of this paper can be described as follows: 1)We propose a user-oriented ranking method to enhance the diversity performance, which is complementary to the existing ranking methods.2)We propose a novel algorithm to obtain the co-occurrence word set of the given query which can be utilized to boost the relevance level of the tag-based image retrieval and reduce the computational cost of our user-oriented image ranking algorithm.3)We introduce a regularization framework to evaluate the relevance scores of images with respect to the given query. Visual feature and semantic feature are merged into this framework.

The remainder of the paper is organized as follows. The system overview is illustrated in section 2. Section 3 demonstrates the offline system. The online system is depicted in section 4. Experiments on Flickr dataset are setup and shown in section 5. Finally, the conclusion and future work are given in section 6.

2. SYSTEM OVERVIEW
Our user-oriented image ranking system includes two main sections: Online and Offline. The whole system is shown in Figure 1. The offline section is the feature extraction section. In this paper, we extract the visual feature and semantic features of our image dataset. Semantic features refers to the co-occurrence word set of the given query, and tags of the images. Our online section consists of the following 2 steps: 1) Inter-user ranking. The inter-user ranking is applied to rank the corresponding users with the consideration of their contribution to the given query. 2) Intra-user ranking. A regularization framework is included in this process to attach a relevance score to each image of each user which measures their relevance level of the given query. Then, the most relevant image

is sequentially selected on the image dataset of each ranked user, which consists of our retrieval results. Hereinafter the details are displayed.

3. THE OFFLINE SYSTEM

In our offline system, the feature extraction of the image database is implemented. In this paper, we use the visual features and semantic features to represent our image dataset. The details are as follows.

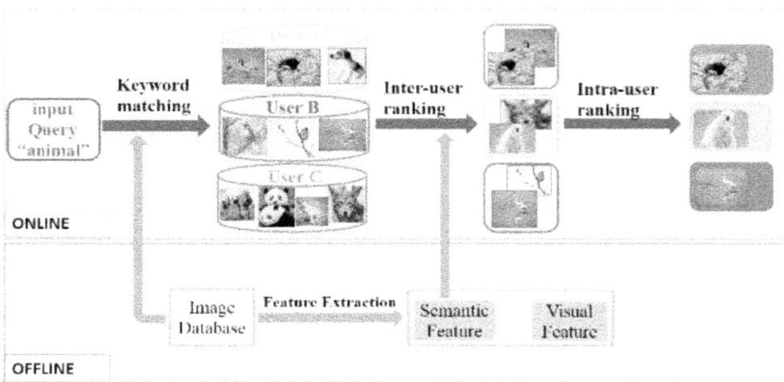

Figure 1. User-oriented image ranking system.

3.1 Visual Features

In this paper, a 215-dimensional visual vector is utilized, including a 45-dimensional color moment feature, and a 170-dimensional texture feature vector [2], [7].

A similarity matrix W whose element w_{ij} is introduced to measure the visual distance between the two images i and j, with their visual features v_i and v_j. Here w_{ij} can be directly calculated using the Gaussian kernel function with a radius parameter σ [3].

$$w_{ij} = exp\,(-\frac{\|v_i - v_j\|}{2\sigma^2}) \tag{1}$$

where $\|.\|^2$ stands for the l_2-norm of the vector. Furthermore, σ represents the radius parameter set to be the mean value of all pairwise Euclidean distance between images.

3.2 Semantic Features

In this paper, the semantic features of image is its associated tags; the semantic features of the given query is its co-occurrence word set. Co-occurrence means two words which often appeared in the text corpus in a certain order. It can also be interpreted as an indicator of semantic proximity or an idiomatic expression. Suppose that $E(q)=\{e_1,e_2,\ldots,e_l\}$ denote the co-occurrence word set about query q, l is the number of co-occurrence word with respect to the query q. Then, the image which tagged with $e_i \in E(q)$ and q is much more relevant with query q than the image which is not. Thus, we can obtain the co-occurrence word set $E(q)=\{e_1,e_2,\ldots,e_l\}$ as follows:

1) For the tag q, we get its top P tags according to their frequencies in the search results which were issued by query q in our image dataset. In this paper, we set P=100 (q is not included in the top P tags).
2) We select the tags which satisfy the following rules in the tag set selected by step 1). If $\frac{R(q,a)}{R(q)} > d*R(a)/N$, where R(q, a) is the number of images which tagged with tag q and tag a in Flicker. R(q) is the number of images which tagged with tag q in Flicker; N demonstrates the total number of images in Flickr. Then the tag a is selected, and we arranged these selected tags by R(q, a) in a descending order, which denotes S. The parameter d set to be 150 in our paper.
3) We choose the top v tags in the selected tag set S as the co-occurrence word set, where v satisfies the rule: the difference between the v-th tag frequency given the query and the (v+1)-th tag frequency given the query is maximum in tag set S.

The co-occurrence words we obtained are: sky, sun and cloud; coast, sand, ocean, and sea; band and concert; airplane, airport and aircraft; and so on. However, each element in E(q) has a different degree of importance in boosting the relevance score of the retrieval results. For example, cloud and blue are the two co-occurrence words of sky. While cloud is more important than blue with respect to the query "sky", since it plays a bigger role in identifying the sky. After obtaining the co-occurrence word set E(q) for each query q, we assign them weights which are denoted by $M(E(q))=\{M_1,M_2,\ldots,M_l\}$ based on their co-occurrence similarity, which is determined as follows:

$$M_i = exp\left\{-\frac{\max\{\log R(q),\log R(e_i)\} - log\ R(q,e_i)}{log\ N - \min\{\log R(q),\log R(e_i)\}}\right\} \tag{2}$$

Where $R(q)$, $R(q,e_i)$, N have already been defined above.

It's acknowledged that the tags associated with an image are arranged in a random order without any important or relevant information, which limits the effectiveness of tag-based image retrieval. So, we need to measure the semantic relevance level between the tag and image. Thus, a semantic relevance matrix C is put forward to measure the semantic relevance between query tagged image and the query tag. We define the average co-occurrence similarity between the query and the tag set of image i as C_i ,which is calculated as follows:

$$C_i = \frac{1}{\sum_{e_m \in E(q)} 1(e_m)} \sum_{e_m \in E(q)} M_m * 1(e_m) \tag{3}$$

where $1(e_m)$ denotes whether the image *i* containing tag e_m or not, i.e.

$$1(e_m) = \begin{cases} 1; & \text{if image i is tagged with } e_m \\ 0; & otherwise \end{cases} \tag{4}$$

4. THE ONLINE SYSTEM

Our online system carries out the following two main steps to obtain the ranked images for the query tag q: 1) inter-user ranking. 2) intra-user ranking. The details of the two main parts in the online system will be described as follows:

For the query q, we can obtain the corresponding images that all tagged with query q in our dataset, which is denoted by X. The following steps are all carried out in dataset X. X also can be further described as the follows by taking the social user's information into account, i.e.

$$X = \{X(u_1),\ldots,X(u_Z)\} = \{X_1,\ldots,X_Z\} = \\ \{\{x_{11},x_{12},\ldots,x_{1N_1}\},\{x_{21},x_{22},\ldots,x_{2N_2}\},\ldots,\{x_{Z1},x_{Z2},\ldots,x_{ZN_Z}\}\} \tag{5}$$

where $U=\{u_1,u_2,\ldots,u_Z\}$ is the user set in the image dataset X, Z is the total number of users in X; X_i or $X(u_i)$ represents the images in X uploaded by i-th user u_i ; x_{ij} is the j-th image in image dataset X_i ; N_i denotes the number of images in X_i .

4.1 Inter-user Ranking

Inter-user ranking ranks the users who uploaded images in X according to their contribution to the query q. Larger contribution users probably show viewers more professional images. And this contribution is measured upon the number of its images in X which are tagged with words in E(q).

For each user U_h, $h \in (1,2,\ldots,Z)$, we calculate its contribution to the query (denoted by UW_h) as follows:

$$UW_h = \sum_{j=1}^{k} 1(x_{hj}) \tag{6}$$

where k is the total number of images in X_h, $1(x_{hj}) = 1$ means that the image x_{hj} is tagged with word in $E(q)$, while $1(x_{hj}) = 0$ means the image is not.

$$1(x_{hj}) = \begin{cases} 1; & t_{hj} \cap E(q) \neq \varnothing \\ 0; & otherwise \end{cases} \tag{7}$$

In the above Equation, t_{hj} is the tag set of image x_{hj}.

We rank $UW_h, h \in (1,2,\ldots,Z)$ in a descending order. The larger UW_h, corresponding user ranks higher.

4.2 Intra-user Ranking

After inter-user ranking, the largest contribution user ranks highest. Then we implement intra-user ranking to select the most relevant image among each user's image set. We take the image set $X_h, h \in (1,2,3,\ldots,Z)$ as an example to demonstrate our intra-user ranking process.

For each image in $X_h = \{x_{h1}, x_{h2}, \ldots, x_{hk}\}$, its relevance score is $r = [r_1, r_2, \ldots, r_k]$. We introduced a regularization framework to obtain r, which takes the visual and semantic information into account. The regularization framework [3] is defined as follows:

$$Q(r) = \sum_{i=1}^{k}\sum_{j=1}^{k} w_{ij}\left\{r_i / \sqrt{D_{ii}} - r_j / \sqrt{D_{jj}}\right\}^2 + \lambda \sum_{i=1}^{k}(r_i - C_i)^2 ? \tag{8}$$

where Q(r) is the cost function; r_i is the relevance score of image i, $D_{ii} = \sum_{j=1}^{k} w_{ij}$, w_{ij} is the visual distance of image i and j. C_i is the semantic relevance score of image i with respect to the query q. The first term in the right-hand side of the cost function means that the relevance scores of visually similar images should be close, and the second term is a fitting constraint, which means that the relevance scores are biased with preference to the semantic relevance measurement, $\lambda > 0$ is the regularization parameter, which denotes the trade-off between these two competing items.

We aim to solve the optimization problem to get the relevance score of each image in X_h as follows:

$$r^* = argmin(Q(r)) \tag{9}$$

To address the optimization problem (9), Equation (8) can be rewrite as the matrix form as:

$$Q(r) = r^T\left(I - D^{-\frac{1}{2}} W D^{-\frac{1}{2}}\right) r + \lambda \|r - C\|^2 \tag{10}$$

where $D = Diag(D_{11}, D_{22}, \ldots, D_{kk})$, $C = [C_1, C_2, \ldots, C_k]$.

Alternatively, we can use iterative optimization algorithm to solve this problem, which avoids the intensive computation brought by the direct matrix inversion in Equation (10). The detailed steps are as follows: (1) utilize the image affinity matrix W determined by Eq.1, if $i \neq j$ and otherwise $w_{ii} = 0$. (2) compute the semantic relevance matrix C, which is illustrated in section 3.2. (3)iterate $r(t+1) = \frac{1}{1+\lambda} D^{-\frac{1}{2}} W D^{-\frac{1}{2}} r(t) + \frac{\lambda}{1+\lambda} C$ until convergence, then the optimization relevance score r of each image in X_h can be achieved.

After obtaining the relevance score r of each image in X_h, $h = \{1,2,\ldots,Z\}$, we select the image with the highest score, which is denoted by x_{fh}, $h = \{1,2,\ldots,Z\}$. Finally, we arrange the image set by $\{x_{f1}, x_{f2}, \ldots, x_{fZ}\}$ the order of their users which was arranged by their contributions. These ranked images constitute our retrieval results.

5. EXPERIMENTS

In order to demonstrate the effectiveness of the user-oriented ranking approach, we conduct an experimental comparison between the following 4 methods on 20 popular tags: airplane, beach, Beijing, bird, blue, buildings, Christmas, cityscape, forest, reflection, garden, girls, honeybee, insect, lotus, ocean, orange, sea, sky, Zebra. Our initial Flickr dataset includes 6600034 images uploaded by 7249 users and their related files recoding the information of tags and users. We remove the images that have no tag information, then 5325265 images and 7090 users left.

- Relevance ranking [3], an optimization framework is applied to automatically rank images based on visual and semantic information of images. For simplicity, we use the RR instead.
- Co-occurrence relevance ranking: an algorithm which is the same with RR except that the semantic relevance score in RR is replaced by the semantic relevance score of our proposed approach. For simplicity, we use the CRR instead.
- Diverse relevance ranking [6], which optimizes an ADP measure with the consideration of the semantic and visual information of images. We use DRR for simplicity.
- User-oriented ranking. The proposed method which fuses the user information into CRR method. We use the UOR for simplicity.

5.1 Performance Evaluation

In this part, our experiments are performed to demonstrate whether we have selected a better method for tag-based image retrieval. And the parameter λ in (10) is empirically set to be 0.1 for all queries.

The performance evaluation of our method is voted by three volunteers and this evaluation contains two parts: relevance score and diversity score. The relevance score is used to evaluate the correlation between the query and the retrieval results. And the diversity score shows the diversity performance of the retrieval results.We voted on the relevance and diversity score of the top-n results obtained through four different methods. The relevance score of the i-th image is $rel_i, i = 1,2,\ldots,n$, Each image is labeled as one of four levels: excellent(score:3), good(score:2), so-so(score:1), irrelevant (score:0). Their overall diversity score is div@n, which is labeled as one of four levels: excellent(score:3),good(score:2),soso(score:1),similar(score:0).

Once we get the value of rel_i and div@n, the ADP of the top-n image can be obtained from equation (11), (12) and (13).

$$AP@n = \frac{1}{n}\sum_{i=1}^{n}\left(\sum_{j=1}^{i}\frac{rel_j}{i}\right) \tag{11}$$

$$ADP@n = AP@n * norm\_div@n \tag{12}$$

$$norm\_div@n = \frac{div@n}{3} \tag{13}$$

5.2 Experimental Results

The top-5 results of exemplar query "honeybee" on Flickr database under the four different ranking algorithms are illustrated in Figure

2, from which we can see that the results of UOR are both relevant and diverse, whereas the others suffer from the lack of diversity. And most of the similar images in the top-5 results of RR, CRR ,DRR are comes from the same user. From this, the effectiveness of our user-oriented idea has been proven.

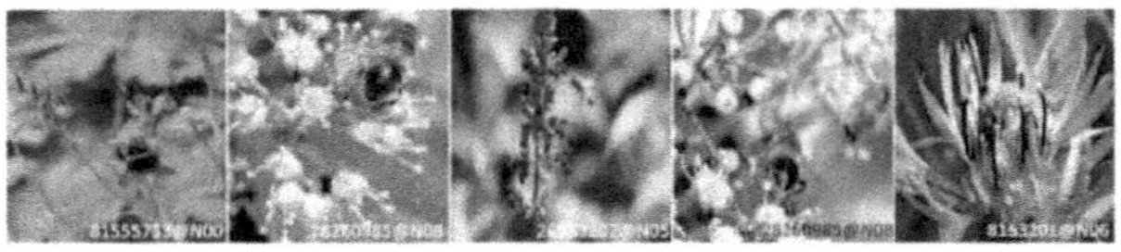

(a) Search results using RR

(b) Search results using CRR

(c) Search results using DRR

(d) Search results using UOR

Figure.2. Top 5 ranking results of an exemplar query "honeybee".

5.3 Performance Analysis

In this section, we compute ADP@20 values of all the 20 tags based on the voting. Table1 shows the mean ADP@20 and mean div@20 values of all 20 queries under the four different methods. The MAP@n values of all these four models are shown in Figure 3 to evaluate their relevance performance, where 6 different depths n are displayed for a clear see.

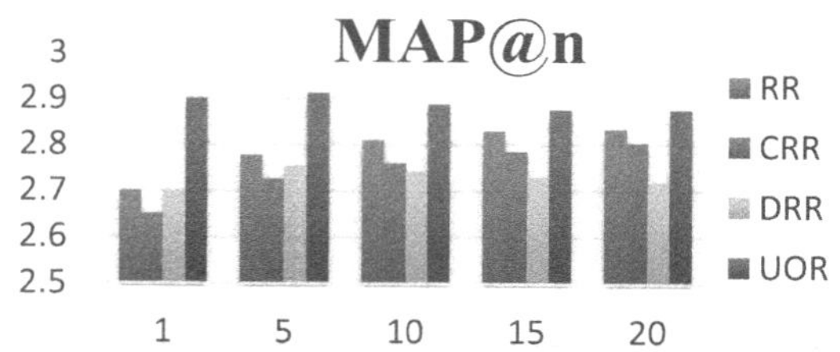

Figure.3 The Mean AP@n of all 4 ranking methods under different depths.

Table 1. The overall performance of each 4 ranking results

METHOD	RR	CRR	DRR	UOR
MADP@20	1.065	1.283	1.952	2.309
Mdiv@20	1.165	1.365	2.17	2.4

From the above charts, we can discover UOR achieves the highest scores on MAP, Mdiv@20 and mean MADP@20, which demonstrate UOR outperforms other methods. The RR has a slighter bigger MAP value and a much lower MADP@20 than the CRR method. Besides, using RR is relatively time consuming. For the RR method takes the all tags of images into consideration, CRR only considers the co-occurrence tags. When we fuse the user information into the CRR method, its MADP@20 is larger than the DRR method, diversity performance is bigger than DRR. For the semantic similarity constrain which the DRR proposed degrades the relevance degree of the results. While UOR is able to achieve a good trade-off between the relevance and diversity performance of the retrieval results. Furthermore, introducing user information adds little computation complexity to UOR. This proves the UOR is appropriate for conducting the retrieval of the large image database.

In summary, the comparison experiment results confirm the proposed method from the following three aspects: (1) The MADP@20 of the retrieval results can be promoted significantly through UOR, which can provide a rich related information to the user. (2) The semantic relevance estimation method which UOR proposed by using co-occurrence word set is not only timesaving, but also effective in measuring the semantic relevance of images with respect to the given query. (3) The computational cost of UOR method is low.

6. CONCLUSIONS

In this paper, we propose a user-oriented image ranking method for tag-based image retrieval. It leverages the visual, semantic information and social clues of images. In order to accomplish the ranking, inter-user ranking and intra-user ranking are carried out to obtain the search results. The experimental results demonstrate that our user-oriented image ranking is effective.

Acknowledgments: This work is supported in part by the Program 973 No. 2012CB316400, by NSFC No.60903121, 61173109, 61202180, 61332018, Microsoft Research Asia, and Fundamental Research Funds for the Central Universities.

7. REFERENCES

[1] D. Cai, X. He, Z. Li, WY. Ma, JR. Wen. "Hierarchical clustering of WWW image search results using visual. textual and link information," In Proceedings of the 12th annual ACM international conference on Multimedia, pp. 952-959, 2004.

[2] X. Qian, G. Liu, D. Guo. Object categorization using hierarchical wavelet packet texture descriptors. in Proc. ISM 2009, pp.44-51.

[3] D. Liu, XS. Hua, M. Wang. "Boost search relevance for tag-based social image retrieval," In *IEEE* International Conference, pp. 1636-1639, 2009.

[4] .RH. van Leuken, L. Garcia, X. Olivares. "Visual diversification of image search results." In Proceedings of the 18th international conference, pp. 341-350, ACM, 2009.

[5] K. Yang, M. Wang, XS. Hua. "Social image search with diverse relevance ranking." In Multimedia Modeling, pp. 174-184, 2010.

[6] M. Wang, K. Yang, XS. Hua. "Towards a relevant and diverse search of social images." Multimedia, IEEE Transactions on,12(8), 829-842, 2010.

[7] X. Qian, H. Wang, G. Liu, X. Hou, "HWVP: Hierarchical Wavelet Packet Texture Descriptors and Their Applications in Scene Categorization and Semantic Concept Retrieval", Multimedia Tools and Applications, May 2012.

[8] F. Sun, M. Wang, D. Wang. "Optimizing social image search with multiple criteria: Relevance, diversity, and typicality." Neurocomputing,95, 40-47, 2012.

[9] A. Ksibi, AB. Ammar. "Adaptive diversification for tag-based social image retrieval." International Journal of Multimedia Information Retrieval, 3(1), 29-39, 2014.

Spatial Constraint for Image Location Estimation

Yisi Zhao
SMILES LAB, Xi'an Jiaotong University
Xianning West Road, Xi'an, China
zyswhy0203@stu.xjtu.edu.cn

Xueming Qian
SMILES LAB, Xi'an Jiaotong University
Xianning West Road, Xi'an, China
qianxm@mail.xjtu.edu.cn

ABSTRACT
Nowadays, image location has been widely used in many application scenarios for large geo-tagged image corpora. As to images which are not geographically tagged, we can estimate their locations with the help of the large geo-tagged image set by content based image retrieval. In this paper, we propose a global feature clustering and local feature refinement based image location estimation approach. We exploit spatial information by processing useful visual words. In this process, visual word groups are generated. Moreover to improve the retrieval performance, spatial constraint is utilized to code the relative position of visual words. Here we generate a position descriptor for each visual word. Experiments show the effectiveness of our proposed approach.

Categories and Subject Descriptors
H.3.1 [**Information Systems**]: Information storage and retrieval-*content analysis and indexing.*

General Terms
Algorithms, Measurement, Performance, Experimentation

Keywords
Location estimation; Bag-of-words; Visual word group; Position descriptor

1. INTRODUCTION
In recent years, large quantities of images taken by the users are shared in social media websites such as Facebook, and Flickr every day. Many of the images are associated with the locations they were taken. As to images without geo-tags, automatic location estimation for them is possible with the help of the large scale geo-tagged photos. In this paper, our task is to estimate the location of an input image by content based image retrieval approach. State-of-the-art large scale image retrieval systems have relied on the bag-of-words (BoW) model and local descriptors, such as SIFT, SURF. Li et al. utilize multi-class SVM classifiers using bag-of-words for large scale image location estimation [3]. However, there still exist deficiencies in BoW model. Many improved approaches are proposed to enhance the discrimination, e.g. visual synonyms, embed geometry constraint [2]. Moreover, the database can be constructed with a 3D model. Liu et al. proposed an approach to estimate accurate parameters about the scene geo-information [5]. Park el al. proposed a method of viewing direction determination by utilizing Google Street View and Google Earth satellite [7]. In this paper, we further explore global feature clustering and local feature refinement based approach to complete image location estimation.

Experimental results of existing work show that the commonly generated visual words are still not as expressive as the text words. Wu et al. [1] employ Maximally Stable Extremal Regions (MSER) to bundle SIFT features into groups instead of taking all of them individually. Moreover, spatial verification enforces geometric consistent constraint on visual words that query and dataset image share, such as RANSAC and spatial coding [2]. Spatial information of visual words should be exploited for better image retrieval performance. In our work, visual words mining and spatial constraint based image location estimation approach is exploited. Firstly, we determine the refined locations of an input image using global features clustering. This step can speed up the image location estimation process by selecting candidate locations. Considering that the distribution of an image's visual words directly reflects the distribution of the image's main content, secondly, we mine the salient features and exploit spatial information to improve the image location estimation performance. In this process, (1) we utilize term frequency-inverse document frequency (tf-idf) to select visual words with higher weight. (2) we divide an image's useful visual words into multiple groups by Mean-shift clustering. A visual word group is composed of visual words in the corresponding cluster. (3) group based spatial coding is conducted. We generate a position descriptor for visual word.

The main contributions of this paper are summarized as following: 1) useful feature selection is utilized, which eliminates the effect of noisy, unstable and irrelevant features; 2) we bundle useful visual words to generate multi-group, and a group based image retrieval method is proposed; 3) spatial information of visual word group is mined. We describe each visual word's distribution in the group it belongs. The rest of the paper is organized as follows: Firstly, we provide the system overview. Secondly, we give a description on our approach in section3-5. Finally, experiments containing the comparison with the recently popular method and discussions are shown in Section6. In Section7, the conclusion is drawn.

2. SYSTEM OVERVIEW
The system of our proposed approach is shown in **Fig.1**. It consists of offline part and online part. In the offline part, we build a hierarchical index for the dataset images [4]. And we build visual word group (VWG) by Mean-shift clustering. Then each visual word's position descriptor is generated for dataset images. In the online part, (1) refined locations of an input image are pre-selected by cluster selection online. In this process, global feature clustering is utilized [4]. (2) local feature of the input image is in

ICMR'15, June 23–26, 2015, Shanghai, China.

ACM 978-1-4503-3274-3/15/06…$15.00
DOI: http://dx.doi.org/10.1145/2671188.2749327

full use. The VWG building and spatial constraint are conducted. (3) we estimate the location of the input image by VWG based image search.

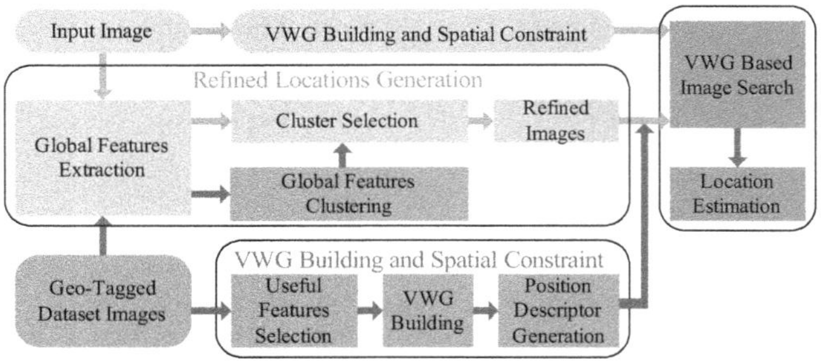

Figure1. Block diagram of the location estimation system.

3. REFINED LOCATIONS GENERATION

In the part, we introduce how to select the refined locations.

We cluster the dataset images using global features. In order to show the effectiveness of our proposed image location estimation approach, we utilize the same visual features and the suggested parameters for global features clustering in [4]. Through global feature clustering, the whole dataset can be divided into several small scale groups. K-means clustering is utilized to divide the dataset into M small clusters, denoted as $C_n(n = 1,2,\ldots,M)$. Then, we select candidate clusters according to the distance between the input image and M centers as that in [4]. The top ranked $S(S < M)$ clusters are selected. In this paper, we set S 15. We further obtain occurred locations of images in the selected clusters. The occurred locations are served as the refined locations of the input image.

4. VISUAL WORD GROUP BUILDING AND SPATIAL CONSTRAINT

In this part, we mine visual word groups for each refined image and the input image, and enforce spatial constraint to improve image location estimation performance. The detailed process includes three steps: (1) useful feature selection, (2) visual word group building, (3) position descriptor generation.

4.1 Useful Feature Selection

For an image as shown in **Fig.2 (a)**, there are 4002 SIFT points detected which are shown in **Fig.2 (b)**. However, different visual words have different weights of importance for identifying the query scene. Some visual words are non-distributive. As shown in **Fig.2 (b)**, many visual words often appear in the part of grass and trees, which are confusing for accurate location estimation. To mine useful features, we compute the score of each word by employing a tf-idf weighting scheme as follows:

$$S_w = \frac{f_w}{\sum_w f_w} \times \log \frac{N}{n_w} \quad (1)$$

where f_w is the frequency of w-th BoW in the image, n_w is the number of images containing the w-th BoW.

We keep the visual words whose scores are larger than thr. As shown in **Fig.2(c)**, there are only 169 visual words left, which is far less than the raw SIFT features. In this paper, we set $thr=0.001$. The choice of thr does influence the performance, but the impact is small in comparison with its computational cost as shown in our discussion.

(a) original image (b) all features

(c) useful features (d) VWGs

Figure2. For an input image (a), we extract 4002 raw SIFT points which are shown in (b). (c) shows the selected 169 useful visual words. In (d), we generate 24 visual word groups.

4.2 Visual Word Group Building

In this section, we build visual word group (VWG) for each image. We aim at increasing the precision of the traditional bag-of-words representation, because the VWG based methods employ group feature matching instead of single feature matching. For an image, we cluster the coordinates of its useful words by Mean-shift clustering [8]. Usually, each SIFT point has a 128-D descriptor vector and a 4-dimensional DoG key-point detector vector (x, y, scale, and orientation). Here the coordinates (x,y) of visual words are utilized. Let $v = \{(x_i, y_i)\}_{i=1}^{h}$ denote the locations of the h SIFT points after useful feature selection. To $\forall v$, Mean-shift is defined as follows:

$$\begin{cases} M_b(v) = \dfrac{1}{N_o} \sum\limits_{v_i \in S_b(v)} v_i - v \\ S_b(v) = \left\{ z : (z-v)^T (z-v) \le b^2 \right\} \end{cases} \quad (2)$$

where N_o is the number of observations falling within $S_b(v)$ region. z is the visual words falling within $S_b(v)$ region. b is the bandwidth parameter [8].

After clustering, we obtain several clusters and their corresponding centers. A cluster is considered as a VWG, which is composed of all visual words in the cluster. Until now, we represent an image with multiple VWGs. Assuming that there are L VWGs generated, we denote them as $G_l, l = 1,2,\ldots,L$. For the useful words shown in **Fig.2 (c)**, the corresponding VWGs are shown in **Fig.2 (d)**. Totally there are 24 VWGs. In order to visually display the VWGs, we mark a unique color for each VWG.

4.3 Position Descriptor Generation

This section presents our approach to represent the spatial information of visual words. We generate a position descriptor (PD) for each visual word to describe the distribution of a visual word in its corresponding VWG. Assuming that a VWG G_l has

n visual words which are denoted by $\{w_1, w_2, \ldots, w_n\}$), our representation of PD includes the following two aspects.

4.3.1 RA constraint

We set the center of a cluster as the center of the corresponding VWG. We divide the VWG space into quadrants using its center as the origin of the quadrants. For each word w_i in the G_l , we record its spatial position in relation to the origin. It reveals, for example, that a visual word tends to be below, at right relative to the center. For a VWG's word, its position matrix is defined as follows.

$$RA_i = \begin{cases} [1\ 0\ 0\ 0], \text{if } x_i > a_0, y_i > b_0 \\ [0\ 1\ 0\ 0], \text{if } x_i < a_0, y_i > b_0 \\ [0\ 0\ 1\ 0], \text{if } x_i < a_0, y_i < b_0 \\ [0\ 0\ 0\ 1], \text{if } x_i > a_0, y_i < b_0 \end{cases} \tag{3}$$

where (x_i, y_i) is the coordinates of word w_i . (a_0, b_0) are the coordinates of the center of the VWG. Thus the RA of a visual word is a 4 bit vector, which shows its relative spatial area.

4.3.2 RD constraint

We calculate the relative distance (RD) between the visual word and the center of the VWG. We calculate the distance of each visual word w_i and the center by Euclidean distance. We denote d_i as the distance of visual word w_i and the center. The relative distance of word w_i is calculated like this:

$$RD_i = \frac{d_i}{\frac{1}{n}\sum_{i=1}^{n} d_i} \tag{4}$$

We further make the normalization on the value of RD. If a word's RD is less than or equal to one, we think that the word is near to the center. The normalization is modeled as follows. Until now, we obtain each word's RA and RD relative to the VWG's center. We put them together, obtaining a five dimensional vector. The five dimensional vector is the position descriptor of visual word w_i in the VWG, denoted as PD_i .

$$RD_i = \begin{cases} 0, if\ RD_i \le 1 \\ 1, if\ RD_i \ge 1 \end{cases} \tag{5}$$

5. VWG BASED IMAGE SEARCH

An image retrieval method based on the VWG and the spatial geometric consistency is presented in this section. In the online system, the VWGs and the PD vectors of input image are generated. Then we introduce how to calculate the similarity between the input image $\#q$ and the refined image $\#r$. The process includes the following two steps.

The first step is matched group pair (MGP) detection. Let G_i^q denotes the i-th VWG from image $\#q$. And G_i^r is denoted as the j-th VWG from image $\#r$. We call the two VWGs as a MGP if they contain common visual words. The matching score of each MGP is calculated from their common visual words and their corresponding PDs. Assuming that G_i^q and G_i^r share a visual words, their corresponding PDs are denoted as $PD_q^k, (k = 1, 2 \ldots, a)$ and $PD_r^k, (k = 1, 2 \ldots, a)$ separately. By comparing PD_q^k and PD_r^k , we calculate the MGP's matching score (MS_{MGP}) as the following:

$$MS_{MGP} = \frac{1}{a}\sum_{k=1}^{a} PD_q^k \oplus PD_r^k \tag{6}$$

where $\oplus$ is Logical Exclusive OR (XOR) operation. The smaller MS_{MGP} means that spatial consistent score of the MGP is higher. Thus the two images are more similar. If some parts of two images match well, we can get images we want. It has better performance than that way of considering the entire content of an image. Moreover, our VWG is unbounded with its position and shape.

The second step is MS_{MGP} selection. Assuming that the input image $\#q$ and the refined image $\#r$ have m MGPs, we can obtain m values about MS_{MGP} . In this paper, the minimum value is selected as the score of the refined image to the input image. Then we rank the refined images based on their scores. Moreover, we take the number of MGPs into consideration. The initial results are re-ranked according to the number of MGPs. At last, the top ranked k images are selected. We count the number of images for each occurred location. The majority location in the k images is assigned for the input image.

6. EXPERIMENTATION

In order to test the performance of the proposed location estimation approach, comparisons are made with IM2GPS [9], CS [4], spatial coding based approach [2] (denoted as SC), method of salient region mining using maximally stable extremal region [1] (denoted as MSER), method of adopting word spatial arrangement [6] (denoted as WSA) and ours (denoted as VWG). Here, the method MSER is that we utilize maximally stable extremal region [1] instead of our VWG to bundle visual words into groups. Other parts of method MSER is the same as our method. We do this is to show the effectiveness of our mean-shift based salient group detection. Similarly, the method WSA is that we adopt word spatial arrangement (WSA) [6] instead of position descriptor generation in our method.

6.1 Datasets

Experiments are done on two datasets: OxBuild, GOLD. OxBuild is used for preliminary tests. The GPS numbers of OxBuild5000 is 11. 100 images are selected randomly from the whole dataset as the test set, while the rest is served as training set in the offline system. GOLD contains more than 3.3 million images together with their Geo-tags [4]. And 80 travel spots are selected, i.e. the number of locations is 80. The test dataset for the 80 sites contains 5000 images.

6.2 Performance Evaluation

For an input image, if the estimated location is exact with ground-truth, it is correctly estimated. Assuming that the recognition rate of the i-th spot (RR_i) is the correct, then average recognition rate (AR) is utilized to evaluate the performance.

$$AR = \frac{1}{G}\sum_{i=1}^{G} RR_i \tag{7}$$

$$RR_i = \frac{NC_i}{NI_i} \times 100\%, i \in \{1, 2, \ldots, G\} \tag{8}$$

where NC_i is the correct estimated image number, NI_i is the test image number. G is the number of dataset locations.

6.3 Performance Comparison

The location estimation performance of IM2GPS, SC, CS, MSER, WSA and VWG are shown in **Fig.3**. It is clear from **Fig.3** that our method can outperform the other methods in OxBuild and GOLD. The average recognition rates of spatial coding (SC) in the two test dataset are 70.39% and 59.48% while the results of Cosine Similarity (CS) are 89.27% and 84.86%. The performances of MSER in the two test dataset are 91.12% and 85.47%. The performances of our VWG in the two test dataset are 93.85% and 88.16% which get performance improvements.

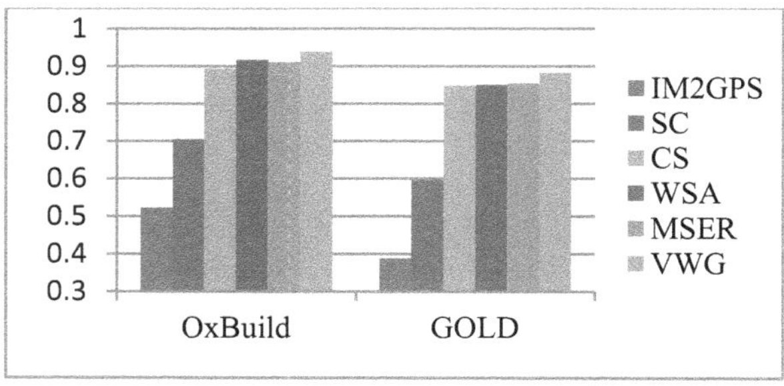

Figure3. ARs of IM2GPS, SC, CS, WSA and MSER, VWG.

6.4 Discussion

The performance of our approach is influenced by several factors. Hereinafter, we carry out the discussion.

6.4.1 The impact of using useful features or not

For images, some visual words may be semantically closer to a certain scene. We carry out the useful feature selection. The situation that all features are used for image retrieval is discussed here. It can be seen from **Table1** that the performance of using useful features is larger on the contrary. **Table2** shows the average time cost of using useful features is lower. Selecting salient words is of significance for image retrieval.

Table1. Average recognition rates (%) of using all features and useful features of images

Dataset	All features	Useful features
OxBuild	92.54	93.85
GOLD	86.97	88.16

Table2. The comparison of average computational costs (ms)

Dataset	All features	Useful features
OxBuild	795.201	380.618
GOLD	1017.937	623.143

Table3. Average recognition rates (%) of using RA or RD

Dataset	RA	RD	PD
OxBuild	91.52	90.65	93.85
GOLD	84.70	85.17	88.16

6.4.2 The impact of different spatial contraints

In our experiments, we generate a position descriptor PD for each visual word, which includes two aspects: the relative area RA and the relative distance RD. Here we discuss the impact of using RA or RD respectively to image location estimation performance. The corresponding results are shown in **Table3** respectively. We find that combining both RA and RD better performances are achieved.

6.4.3 The impact of bandwidth b

In the section of VWGs generation, we cluster the useful words by Mean-shift cluster. So, the multi-VWG generation is closely connected with the bandwidth b. Here, we discuss the impact of bandwidth b. **Fig.4** shows that with the increase of b, the AR is first increasing and then into decline. b is set 70 in the baseline.

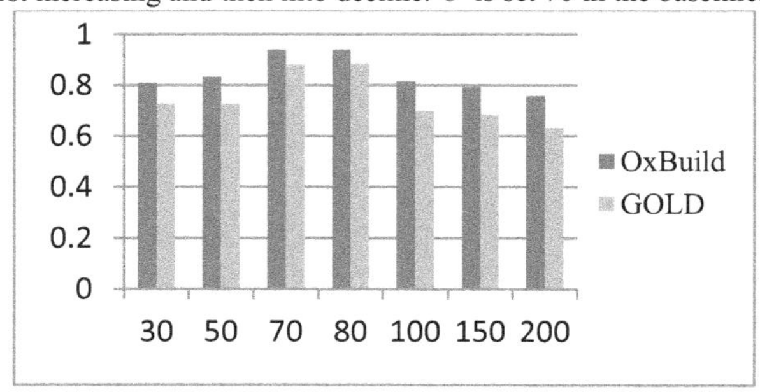

Figure4. Impact of bandwidth b to image location estimation performance.

7. CONCLUSION

In this paper, we present a method of image location estimation, which is based on global feature clustering and local feature refinement. Firstly, refined locations of an input image are pre-selected. Secondly, we localize the image by local feature refinement. In this process, visual word groups are generated and spatial information for words in VWG are coded. At last, group based image search is conducted. Experiments show the effectiveness of our proposed approach.

Acknowledgments. This work is supported partly by the Program 973 No. 2012CB316400, by NSFC No.60903121, 61 173109, 61202180, 61332018, Microsoft Research Asia, and Fundamental Research Funds for the Central Universities.

8. REFERENCES

[1] Z. Wu, Q. Ke, M. Isard, and J. Sun, "Bundling features for large scale partial-duplicate web image search," IEEE Conference on CVPR, pp. 25-32, 2009.

[2] W. Zhou, Y. Lu, H. Li, Y. Song, Q. Tian, "Spatial Coding for Large Scale Partial-Duplicate Web Image Search," MM'10, Firenze, Italy. Copyright 2010 ACM.

[3] Y. Li, D.J. Crandall, D.P. Huttenlocher, "Landmark Classification in Large-scale Image Collections," ICCV'09.

[4] Jing Li, Xueming Qian, Yuan Yan Tang, Linjun Yang, and Tao Mei, "GPS estimation for places of interest from social users' uploaded photos", IEEE Trans. Multimedia 2013.

[5] H. Liu, T. Mei, J. Luo, H. Li, and S. Li, "Finding perfect rendezvous on the go: accurate mobile visual localization and its applications to routing," ACM Multimedia, 2012.

[6] Otávio A.B. Penatti, Fernanda B.Silva, Eduardo Valle, "Visual word spatial arrangement for image retrieval and classification," Pattern Recognition 47(2), 2014.

[7] M. Park, J. Luo, R. T. Collins, Y. Liu, "Beyond GPS: Determining the Camera Viewing Direction of A Geo-tagged Image," MM'10, October 25–29, 2010.

[8] K. Fukunaga, L.Hostetler, "The estimation of the gradient of a density function, with applications in pattern recognition," IEEE Transactions on Information Theory, vol.21, 1975.

[9] J. Hays and A. A. Efros, "IM2GPS: estimating geographic information from a single image," In CVPR, 2008.

Shape-based Object Matching Using Point Context

Cong Yang, Christian Feinen, Oliver Tiebe, Kimiaki Shirahama and Marcin Grzegorzek
Research Group for Pattern Recognition
University of Siegen, Germany
Hoelderlinstr. 3, D-57076 Siegen
{cong.yang,marcin.grzegorzek}@uni-siegen.de

ABSTRACT

This paper proposes a novel object matching algorithm based on shape contours. In order to ensure low computational complexity in shape representation, our descriptor is composed by a small number of interest points which are generated by considering both curvatures and the overall shape trend. To effectively describe each point of interest, we introduce a simple and highly discriminative point descriptor, namely Point Context, which represents its geometrical and topological location. For shape matching, we observed that the correspondences are not only dependent on the similarities between these single points in different objects, but they are also related to the geometric relations between multiple points of interest in the same object. Therefore, a high-order graph matching formulation is introduced to merge the single point similarities and the similarities between point triangles. The main contributions of this paper include (i) the introduction of a novel shape descriptor with robust shape points and their descriptors and (ii) the implementation of a high-order graph matching algorithm that solves the shape matching problem. Our method is validated through a series of object retrieval experiments on four datasets demonstrating its robustness and accuracy.

Categories and Subject Descriptors

I.4.8 [**Image Processing and Computer Vision**]: Scene Analysis; I.5.4 [**Pattern Recognition**]: Computer Vision; I.5.3 [**Pattern Recognition**]: Similarity Measures; F.2.2 [**Analysis of Algorithms and Problem Complexity**]: Pattern Matching

General Terms

Experimentation, Performance

Keywords

Shape matching; Interest point detection; Point context; High-order graph matching

ICMR '15, June 23 - 26, 2015, Shanghai, China

http://dx.doi.org/10.1145/2671188.2749329

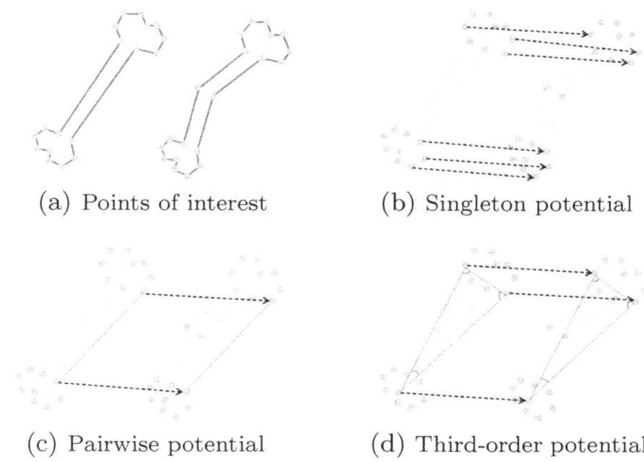

(a) Points of interest (b) Singleton potential

(c) Pairwise potential (d) Third-order potential

Figure 1: Different potentials for object matching.

1. INTRODUCTION

Object recognition is a process for identifying a specific object in a digital image or video, useful for a number of applications. Shape analysis plays a key role in understanding or identifying objects in images [11, 13]. Contour-based shape matching generally consists of two main processes, shape representation and matching.

For the shape representation process, there are three main challenges. The first challenge is how to extract efficient descriptors that are invariant to shape rotation, translation and scaling. The second one is how to extract appropriate shape descriptors in images that are often noisy and/or distorted. The third challenge is how to generate shape descriptors with low computation complexity. In order to solve these problems we represent the shape only with a small number of interest points. We detect these points by considering both curvatures and the overall shape trend. Secondly, there is only a limited number of these points in each object, which can reduce the computational complexity for searching correspondences dramatically.

For the shape matching process, even using only the proposed points of interest, several points are inevitably extracted regardless of their irrelevance to the matching process (the right bone in Figure 1(a)). Moreover, some extracted points in the same object may have very similar geometrical locations because of their small distances or symmetry. However, most existing methods [10, 1, 6] only consider the relationship between single points in different objects. This could lead to ambiguous matching because many different points may have similar descriptors [5, 13]. It has been shown that high-order graph matching is a powerful framework to establish feature correspondences, combining both appearance similarity and geometric compatibility [12]. As shown in Figure 1(b), singleton point matching is a well-know assignment problem. For the pairwise matching (Figure 1(c)), it finds consistent correspondences between two sets of points, by taking in consideration both how well the features' descriptor match and how well their pairwise geometric constraints are satisfied. For the high-order matching (mostly third-order, see Figure 1(d)), it considers the cost of matching three correspondences. With this observation, we present a high-order graph matching strategy for improving correspondences between our points of interest.

2. SHAPE DESCRIPTOR

In this section, we first describe the method that generates robust points of interest along the shape boundary. After that, the point descriptor, namely point context, is introduced and analysed. Finally, we construct the shape descriptor with the interest points and their associated point context features.

2.1 Points of Interest

In this section an approach [5] is employed on an arbitrary given shape Ω to select boundary points $\boldsymbol{p}_i$ which are significant for the perceptual appearance. The general idea is to detect contour regions like the legs or the tail of an elephant characterised by a higher curvature toward the overall shape trend. Therefore, either a single or multiple *reference points* $(\boldsymbol{x}_i)$ inside the shape are determined to compute the distance between each single contour point and its closest reference. By arranging these values sequentially, a signal $\boldsymbol{s}$ is generated that can be used to detect peaks. The desired subset of contour points is then obtained by assigning the corresponding contour point to each peak.

2.2 Point Context

Inspired by [9, 8], for points of interest $\boldsymbol{p}_i, (i = 1, \ldots, m)$, we propose a point descriptor, Point Context, which can intuitively capture its geometrical and topological locations. We consider the set of vectors originating from p_i to all other sample points on a shape contour. These vectors express the configuration of the entire shape relative to the reference point. More specifically, let P denote a sequence of interest points $P = \{\boldsymbol{p}_1, \cdots \boldsymbol{p}_m\}$ and Q denote a finite number of contour sample points $Q = \{\boldsymbol{q}_1, \cdots, \boldsymbol{q}_n\}$, $P \notin Q$. All points in P and Q are represented by their coordinate locations. Points in Q are ordered clockwise along the shape contour. For each single point of interest $\boldsymbol{p}_i$, we compute two vectors, one presenting all distances and the second representing all pairwise orientations of vectors from $\boldsymbol{p}_i$ to each sample point $\boldsymbol{q}_k \in Q$, $(k = 1, \cdots, n)$. A distance $D^{\boldsymbol{p}_i}(k)$ from $\boldsymbol{p}_i$ to $\boldsymbol{q}_k$ is defined as Euclidean distance in the log space

$$D^{\boldsymbol{p}_i}(k) = \log(1 + \|\overrightarrow{\boldsymbol{p}_i} - \overrightarrow{\boldsymbol{q}_k}\|^2) \quad . \tag{1}$$

In order to avoid the situation where the input of log is zero, we add one to Euclidean distance. An orientation $\Theta^{\boldsymbol{p}_i}(k)$ from $\boldsymbol{p}_i$ to $\boldsymbol{q}_k$ is defined as the orientation of vector $\overrightarrow{\boldsymbol{p}_i} - \overrightarrow{\boldsymbol{q}_k}$:

$$\Theta^{\boldsymbol{p}_i}(k) = \operatorname{atan2}(\overrightarrow{\boldsymbol{p}_i} - \overrightarrow{\boldsymbol{q}_k}) \quad . \tag{2}$$

where atan2 stands for the four quadrant inverse tangent which can ensure $\Theta^{\boldsymbol{p}_i}(k) \in [-\pi, \pi]$. Together with the distances, a single point of interest $\boldsymbol{p}_i$ is encoded in two n-dimensional vectors $D^{\boldsymbol{p}_i}$ and $\Theta^{\boldsymbol{p}_i}$.

Our proposed point descriptor differs from the methods [5] and [3] in the following aspects. Firstly, we only consider the feature vectors from points of interest instead of roughly uniform spacing or randomly picking for selecting sample points. This strategy can reduce the mismatches and computational complexity conspicuously. Secondly, the proposed point descriptor is naturally translation and rotation invariant [1]. However, approaches in [5, 3] are not intrinsically rotation invariant. In order to solve this problem, they use the tangent angle on each point to turn the shape. This is not robust enough for some points which have no reliable tangents. Moreover, some local appearance features could lose their discriminative power if the shape is rotated.

Eventually, based on our method, for a given arbitrary shape Ω, its contour $\partial\Omega$ can be represented with the locations as well as the distance and orientation vectors of all points of interest from the contour:

$$\partial\Omega = \{\boldsymbol{p}_i, D^{\boldsymbol{p}_i}, \Theta^{\boldsymbol{p}_i}\} \quad . \tag{3}$$

3. SHAPE MATCHING

In this section, we first formulate our shape matching based on the properties of interest points and point context features. The formulation is composed by potential functions with different orders. After that, we introduce the definitions of potential functions.

3.1 Formulation of Shape Matching

Let P_1 and P_2 denote the set of interest points from two shapes S_1 and S_2 respectively. $\boldsymbol{p}_i$ and $\boldsymbol{p}'_j$ denote a single point of interest in P_1 and P_2 respectively. $P \triangleq P_1 \times P_2$ denotes the set of possible correspondences. We define the Boolean indicator variable

$$x_a = \begin{cases} 1 & \text{if } a = (\boldsymbol{p}_i, \boldsymbol{p}'_j) \in P \text{ is a correspondence} \\ 0 & \text{otherwise} \end{cases} \quad . \tag{4}$$

In our definition, a basic constraint is that each point $\boldsymbol{p}_i$ in P_1 is mapped to at most one point $\boldsymbol{p}'_j$ in P_2, while for each point $\boldsymbol{p}'_j$ in P_2 there is at most one point $\boldsymbol{p}_i$ in P_1 mapping to it. Therefore, we have the set of feasible solutions:

$$\begin{aligned} \zeta = \{\mathbf{x} \in \{0,1\}^{P_1 \times P_2} \mid \sum_{\boldsymbol{p}_i \in P_1} x_{\boldsymbol{p}_i, \boldsymbol{p}'_j} \leqslant 1, \sum_{\boldsymbol{p}'_j \in P_2} x_{\boldsymbol{p}_i, \boldsymbol{p}'_j} \leqslant 1, \\ \forall \boldsymbol{p}_i \in P_1 \text{ and } \forall \boldsymbol{p}'_j \in P_2\} \end{aligned} \quad . \tag{5}$$

Inspired by [4, 14], our high-order (degree 3) matching formulation is required to be as follows:

$$\begin{aligned} \min_{\mathbf{x} \in \zeta} \{E(\mathbf{x}|\theta) = \sum_{a \in P} \theta_a x_a + \sum_{(a,b) \in P \times P} \theta_{ab} x_a x_b + \\ \sum_{(a,b,c) \in P \times P \times P} \theta_{abc} x_a x_b x_c\} \end{aligned} \quad . \tag{6}$$

where θ_a is the matching cost for each correspondence $a \in P$ (Figure 1(b)), θ_{ab} for a pair of correspondences $(a, b) \in P \times P$ (Figure 1(c)), and θ_{abc} for a triplet of correspondences $(a, b, c) \in P \times P \times P$ (Figure 1(d)). Since the matching constraint in Eq. 5 makes the optimisation problem in Eq. 6 difficult to solve, we employ the dual-decomposition method [14] to re-formulate the original problem as the union of several sub-problems that are easier to solve.

[1]Cooperating with Eq. 7, our descriptor is also scale invariant.

3.2 Potential Functions

In this paper, we only consider the first and third order terms since a triplet (Figure 1(d)) in one shape would have fewer similar triplets in the other. Moreover, this strategy can be used to avoid the over-fitting problem as the singleton potentials still offer the major contribution for the shape similarity with our proposed point context descriptors.

3.2.1 The Singleton Potential

In order to define the singleton potential θ_a, for each correspondence $(\boldsymbol{p}_i, \boldsymbol{p}'_j)$ we fully use the properties of its point context features. Given two points of interest $\boldsymbol{p}_i$ and $\boldsymbol{p}'_j$ from two shapes S_1 and S_2, respectively, we first compute the affinity vectors between the corresponding elements in their distance and orientation vectors:

$$A_D(\boldsymbol{p}_i, \boldsymbol{p}'_j) = \exp(-\frac{(D^{\boldsymbol{p}_i}(k) - D^{\boldsymbol{p}'_j}(k))^2}{(\max(D^{\boldsymbol{p}_i})\sigma)^2}) \quad . \tag{7}$$

$$A_\Theta(\boldsymbol{p}_i, \boldsymbol{p}'_j) = \exp(-\frac{(\Theta^{\boldsymbol{p}_i}(k) - \Theta^{\boldsymbol{p}'_j}(k))^2}{\delta^2}) \quad . \tag{8}$$

where σ and δ represent the tolerance of distance and orientation differences, respectively. We set $\sigma = 0.2$ and $\delta = \pi/4$ in all experiments. Like in Eq. 1, $k = 1, \cdots, n$. To get a scale invariant value of $A_D(\boldsymbol{p}_i, \boldsymbol{p}'_j)$, we divide each distance difference by the maximum of the first distance vector.

Since both A_D and A_Θ are normalised, we can simply add them to obtain the affinity vector:

$$A(\boldsymbol{p}_i, \boldsymbol{p}'_j) = A_D(\boldsymbol{p}_i, \boldsymbol{p}'_j) + A_\Theta(\boldsymbol{p}_i, \boldsymbol{p}'_j) \quad . \tag{9}$$

Observing that A is a $n-$dimensional vector representing the similarities of corresponding pairs from $\boldsymbol{p}_i$ and $\boldsymbol{p}'_j$. The similarity between $\boldsymbol{p}_i$ and $\boldsymbol{p}'_j$ can be calculated by the mean value of $A(\boldsymbol{p}_i, \boldsymbol{p}'_j)$. Consequently, the singleton potential for a correspondence $(\boldsymbol{p}_i, \boldsymbol{p}'_j)$ is defined as

$$\theta_a = \theta_{\boldsymbol{p}_i, \boldsymbol{p}'_j} = \frac{1}{n}\sum_{k=1}^{n} A(k) \quad . \tag{10}$$

3.2.2 The High-Order Potential

In this paper, we treat the third-order (triangle in Figure 1(d)) as the high-order potentials. The angles of a triangle are scale and rotation invariant. Thus we can describe each triangle by its three angles. In practice, we describe each triangle by the sine of its three angles to speed-up the computation. Suppose that P_1 and P_2 are the set of interest points for two shapes S_1 and S_2, respectively. For any two triplets, $(\boldsymbol{p}^1_i, \boldsymbol{p}^1_j, \boldsymbol{p}^1_k) \in S_1$ and $(\boldsymbol{p}^2_i, \boldsymbol{p}^2_j, \boldsymbol{p}^2_k) \in S_2$, the triple potential for each possible triple matching $(\boldsymbol{p}^1_i, \boldsymbol{p}^1_j, \boldsymbol{p}^1_k) \rightarrow (\boldsymbol{p}^2_i, \boldsymbol{p}^2_j, \boldsymbol{p}^2_k)$ is defined with a truncated Gaussian kernel:

$$\theta_{abc} = \theta_{\boldsymbol{p}^1_i, \boldsymbol{p}^1_j, \boldsymbol{p}^1_k, \boldsymbol{p}^2_i, \boldsymbol{p}^2_j, \boldsymbol{p}^2_k} = \begin{cases} \exp(-\gamma \| f_{i_1,j_1,k_1} - f_{i_2,j_2,k_2} \|^2) & \text{if } \| f_{i_1,j_1,k_1} - f_{i_2,j_2,k_2} \| \leqslant \vartheta \\ 0 & \text{otherwise} \end{cases} \tag{11}$$

where f_{i_1,j_1,k_1} and f_{i_2,j_2,k_2} are the feature vectors (sine) describing the triplets $(\boldsymbol{p}^1_i, \boldsymbol{p}^1_j, \boldsymbol{p}^1_k)$ and $(\boldsymbol{p}^2_i, \boldsymbol{p}^2_j, \boldsymbol{p}^2_k)$, respectively. Points in both triplets are ordered in a clockwise fashion with the singleton potential pair as its starting point $\boldsymbol{p}^1_i$ and $\boldsymbol{p}^2_i$. We use the truncated Gaussian kernel to scatter and reduce matching times since the number of possible triple matching is huge and it is not necessary to compute them completely. In this paper, we take $\gamma = 2$ in our experiment. With Eq. 11, for each tuple i of P_1, we find the features of P_2 in a neighbourhood of size ϑ ($\vartheta = 350$ in our experiment). Based on [4] we only sample 20 triangles per points in P_1 since this number of triangles is more than enough to obtain a robust matching. Then, we sample all the possible triangles of P_2, and compute their descriptors. We employ a kd-tree to store them efficiently.

4. EXPERIMENTAL RESULTS

In this section we first evaluate the proposed interest point detector and point context feature independently in several shape retrieval experiments. After that, we evaluate and compare the performance of the proposed matching method with some traditional point matching methods to illustrate our advantages. In the object retrieval experiments, for each of the shapes used as a query, we have checked whether the retrieved results are correct, i.e., belong to the same class as the query. For quantitative comparison, we kept the experimental convention proposed in [1] and considered the 10 best matches for each query.

4.1 Evaluation of Interest Point Detection

In this subsection, we compare the retrieval performances on Kimia216 [1] dataset using interest points detected by the proposed method and the most related DCE [7] method. Based on the generated interesting points, we compare their retrieval performances using both shape context method [3] and our proposed matching method. Both methods use the same point descriptor and the match algorithm, except the interest point detector. As shown in Table 1, retrieval results based on the proposed interesting point detector perform better in both methods. The main reason is the property of interesting points generated by DCE method is highly related to the stop parameter k (DCE results are collected with $k = 10$ which got the best retrieval result for comparison). Obviously, it is impractical to set appropriate k manually on each object. On the contrary, our method can generate stable interesting points without degree parameters.

SC [3]	1st	2nd	3rd	4th	5th	6th	7th	8th	9th	10th
IP1 [7]	216	210	195	184	181	172	161	146	148	128
IP2	**216**	**212**	**206**	**197**	**191**	**190**	**186**	**186**	**183**	**171**

PC	1st	2nd	3rd	4th	5th	6th	7th	8th	9th	10th
IP1 [7]	216	211	205	196	192	191	186	178	177	175
IP2	**216**	**212**	**211**	**211**	**205**	**200**	**201**	**195**	**193**	**195**

Table 1: Experimental comparison on Kimia216 dataset. Interesting points are detected separately using the proposed method (IP2) and the DCE [7] method (IP1). IP1 and IP2 are then compared using Shape Context (SC) [3] and the proposed Point Context (PC) matching methods.

4.2 Evaluation of Point Context

In order to evaluate the performance of point context descriptor, we compare the retrieval performance using Point Context to other most related descriptors in [3, 5] on MPEG400 dataset. The shapes in this dataset have much larger intra-class variations and inter-class similarities than the MPEG7. Except descriptors, all performances are obtained using the same interest points based on our proposed method and matched by the Hungarian algorithm. As illustrated in Table 2, the point context feature achieves the best performance among three descriptors.

	1st	2nd	3rd	4th	5th	6th	7th	8th	9th	10th
SC [3]	370	343	310	302	277	272	265	264	239	240
PCCS [5]	377	351	336	331	317	302	287	282	273	262
Our	**391**	**377**	**372**	**364**	**356**	**343**	**338**	**319**	**304**	**276**

Table 2: Experimental comparison of our point context descriptor to the Shape Context (SC) [3] and partition points-based descriptors (PCCS) [5] using the interesting points generated by our proposed method on MPEG400 dataset. The matching algorithm on all the three methods are Hungarian algorithm.

4.3 Evaluation of High-Order Matching

In this part, with some objects from Kimia99 [2] dataset, we first evaluate the matching performance of the proposed high-order graph matching to the traditional Hungarian matching method. The interesting points in both matching methods are generated and represented by the proposed method. After that, we compare the proposed matching method against the state-of-art method in [5] with the same objects. In Figure 2, we match two hands with some deformations among their fingers. Since there are more interesting points in the left hand than the right one, with our basic constraint in Section 3.1, some points in the left hand will be jumped.

As shown in Figure 2(a), there are some mismatched interesting points because of the similar points in both shapes. Moreover, the geometrical relations among the interesting points are not considered. Figure 2(b) shows that the proposed high-order potentials yield apparently better matching. In Figure 2(c), based on human perception there are several mismatched points. Similar to hands, this is due to their symmetric silhouette and there are also many similar points in one object which could affect the matching performance. In contrast, as shown in Figure 2(d), with the point context feature and our proposed potentials, all points in the left tool can find its correspondences correctly.

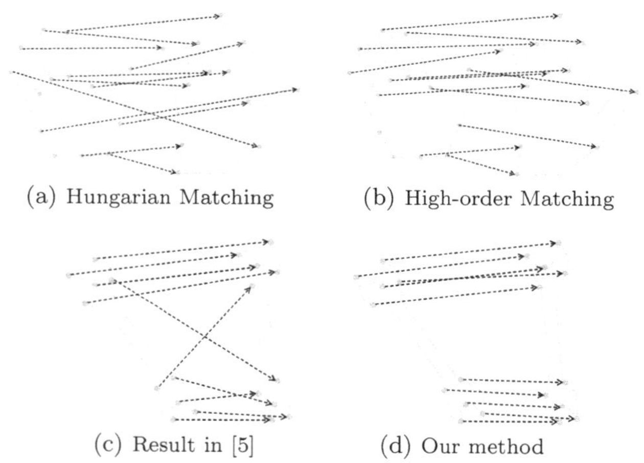

(a) Hungarian Matching (b) High-order Matching (c) Result in [5] (d) Our method

Figure 2: Object matching with different potentials and comparing the matching result of the proposed method to [5].

5. CONCLUSION

In this paper, a novel shape matching method based on the point context descriptors and high-order graph matching is presented. The main idea is to generate some interesting points on each shape contour for correspondence matching. The generated interesting points are robust for shape deformation. For each interesting point, we propose a point descriptor, point context, to capture its geometrical locations. In order to involve not only the singleton assignments, but also the geometrical relations of tribes with different interesting points for shape matching, we propose potentials for the singleton and triplet terms.

Acknowledgement. Research activities leading to this work have been supported by the China Scholarship Council (CSC) and the German Research Foundation (DFG) within the Research Training Group 1564 (GRK 1564).

6. REFERENCES

[1] X. Bai and L. Latecki. Path similarity skeleton graph matching. *PAMI*, 30(7):1282–1292, 2008.

[2] X. Bai, L. Latecki, and W. yu Liu. Skeleton pruning by contour partitioning with discrete curve evolution. *PAMI*, 29(3):449–462, 2007.

[3] S. Belongie, J. Malik, and J. Puzicha. Shape matching and object recognition using shape contexts. *PAMI*, 24(4):509–522, 2002.

[4] O. Duchenne, F. Bach, I.-S. Kweon, and J. Ponce. A tensor-based algorithm for high-order graph matching. *PAMI*, 33(12):2383–2395, Dec 2011.

[5] C. Feinen, C. Yang, O. Tiebe, and M. Grzegorzek. Shape matching using point context and contour segments. In *ACCV*. Springer LNCS, November 2014.

[6] L. Latecki, Q. Wang, S. Koknar-Tezel, and V. Megalooikonomou. Optimal subsequence bijection. In *ICMD*, pages 565–570, Oct 2007.

[7] L. J. Latecki and R. LakÃd'mper. Convexity rule for shape decomposition based on discrete contour evolution. *CVIU*, 73:441–454, 1999.

[8] C. Lu, L. Latecki, N. Adluru, X. Yang, and H. Ling. Shape guided contour grouping with particle filters. In *ICCV*, pages 2288–2295, September 2009.

[9] T. Ma and L. Latecki. From partial shape matching through local deformation to robust global shape similarity for object detection. In *CVPR*, pages 1441–1448, June 2011.

[10] Y. Rubner, C. Tomasi, and L. J. Guibas. The earth mover's distance as a metric for image retrieval. *Int. J. Comput. Vision*, 40(2):99–121, November 2000.

[11] S. P. Tadeusiewicz R., Ogiela M.R. Notes on a linguistic description as the basis for automatic image understanding. *Int. Journal of Applied Mathematics and Computer Science*, 19(1):143–150, 2009.

[12] L. Torresani, V. Kolmogorov, and C. Rother. Feature correspondence via graph matching: Models and global optimization. In *ECCV*, volume 5303, pages 596–609. Springer Berlin Heidelberg, 2008.

[13] O. van Kaick, H. Zhang, G. Hamarneh, and D. Cohen-Or. A survey on shape correspondence. *Computer Graphics Forum*, 30(6):1681–1707, 2011.

[14] Y. Zeng, C. Wang, Y. Wang, X. Gu, D. Samaras, and N. Paragios. Dense non-rigid surface registration using high-order graph matching. In *CVPR*, pages 382–389, June 2010.

Large Scale Image Annotation via Deep Representation Learning and Tag Embedding Learning

Yonghao He, Jian Wang, Cuicui Kang, Shiming Xiang, Chunhong Pan
{yhhe, jian.wang, cckang, smxiang, chpan}@nlpr.ia.ac.cn

ABSTRACT

In this paper, we focus on the issue of large scale image annotation, whereas most existing methods are devised for small datasets. A novel model based on deep representation learning and tag embedding learning is proposed. Specifically, the proposed model learns an unified latent space for image visual features and tag embeddings simultaneously. Furthermore, a metric matrix is introduced to estimate the relevance scores between images and tags. Finally, an objective function modeling triplet relationships (irrelevant tag, image, relevant tag) is proposed with maximum margin pursuit. The proposed model is easy to tackle new images and tags via online learning and has a relatively low test computation complexity. Experimental results on NUS-WIDE dataset demonstrate the effectiveness of the proposed model.

Keywords

Large Scale Image Annotation; Deep Representation Learning; Tag Embedding Learning

1. INTRODUCTION

In the era of big data, there are many image related applications, such as keyword based image search and picture recommendation, in need of image annotation. Plentiful tags, as high level semantic features, are assigned to images to definitely improve the quality of these applications. In this paper, we address the issue of large scale image annotation, namely a large number of images with tags engaged. Many existing methods [2, 19, 14, 10, 3, 15, 1] for image annotation are established on small datasets, such as Corel5K [6], IAPRTC-12 [9] and ESP-game [18]. These datasets have only around 5000 to 20000 images, and these methods are difficult to be applied to large datasets. By contrast, we focus on designing an algorithm that can handle a large number of images.

There exist some methods [20, 8] for large scale image annotation (we omit the review of those methods for small scale datasets). Weston *et al.* [20] proposed a method (called WSABIE) to optimize top k tag lists for images. In this method, tag embeddings are initialized with random variables in a low-dimensional space. Then a projection matrix is used to transform the image features into the tag embedding space. In such space, the relevance scores between images and tags are measured by inner product. Finally, the objective is to minimize weighted approximate-rank pairwise (WARP) loss. The model parameters are tag embeddings and projection matrix that can be learned recursively via online updating. Recently, in [8], Gong *et al.* used convolutional neural network (CNN) [12] to map raw image data to tag indicator space. Three categories of loss functions for CNN are studied, namely cross-entropy loss with softmax, pairwise hinge loss and WARP. The results show that ranking based CNN (pairwise hinge loss and WARP) is better than classification based CNN (cross-entropy loss with softmax). One of the advantages of ranking based CNN is that the test computation complexity is a constant. However, when new tags appear, the number of output layer nodes has to be increased and the network needs to be retrained. Besides these two methods, kNN and probability SVM [8] are feasible to solve this problem. In kNN based method, tag votes are collected through top k nearest neighbors. This straightforward method can achieve state-of-the-art performance, which will be presented in experiment section. Whereas, it is time-consuming to find nearest neighbors in large datasets. The probability SVM based method is to train many one-vs-all classifiers for each tag. The drawbacks of this method is that tags have no mutual interactions and the classifiers may not be sufficiently trained due to sample imbalance.

In this paper, we propose a novel model based on **D**eep **R**epresentation learning and tag **E**mbedding **L**earning (**DR EL**). First, images and tags are represented as visual features and embedding vectors, respectively. Tag embedding vectors are created for each tag and randomly initialized. They will be updated in the learning process. The merit of tag embeddings is to make the direct interactions between tags and images possible in the unified latent space. Then, two deep neural networks (DNN) are used to do feature learning while mapping image features and tag embeddings from their original spaces to an unified latent space. In the latent space, the relevance scores between images and tags are estimated by a metric matrix. Finally, a pairwise hinge loss for triplets (irrelevant tag, image, relevant tag) are adopted with maximum margin pursuit. The model parameters, including weights of two DNNs, the metric matrix and tag embeddings, are learned through stochastic gradient

ICMR '15, June 23 - 26, 2015, Shanghai, China

http://dx.doi.org/10.1145/2671188.2749330.

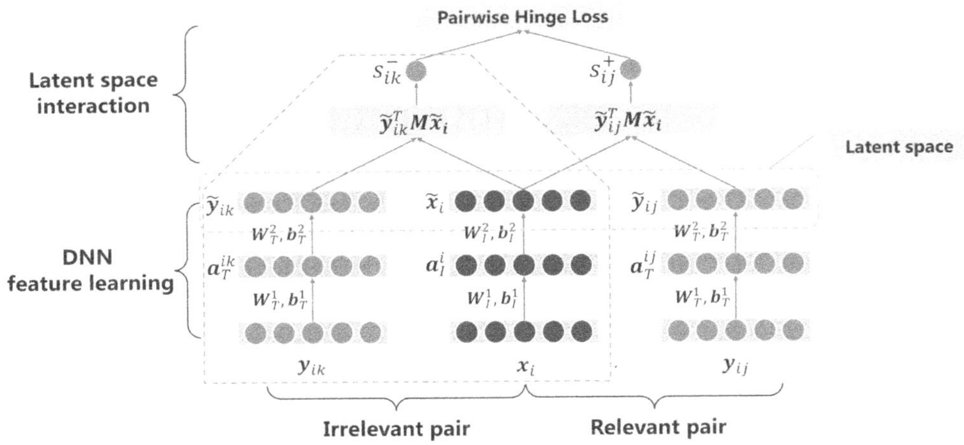

Figure 1: Architecture of the proposed model. The input is a triplet (irrelevant tag, image, relevant tag). Through two specific DNNs, the image features and tag embeddings are nonlinearly mapped to the latent space. In the latent space, we use a metric matrix to calculate the relevance scores between images and tags. The irrelevant and relevant image-tag pairs are put to the pairwise hinge loss based objective function to optimize the model parameter. The process of test phase is highlighted in the red dashed box.

descent and backpropagation. The proposed model is easy to handle new images and tags via online learning. Actually, the model in [20] can be viewed as a "shallow" type of ours. Both methods have a relatively low test computation complexity of $O(T)$ (T is the number of tags). The experimental results demonstrate the effectiveness of the proposed model compared to state-of-the-art methods.

2. THE PROPOSED MODEL

We first introduce some notations: the training set contains N images $\{\mathbf{x}_i\}_{i=1}^N$ ($\mathbf{x}_i$ are visual feature vectors) and T tags $\{\mathbf{y}_i\}_{i=1}^T$ ($\mathbf{y}_i$ are randomly initialized embedding vectors). For each image $\mathbf{x}_i$, its associated relevant tag set is $\mathcal{T}_{i+} = \{\mathbf{y}_{ij}\}_{j=1}^{j=n_i}$ and irrelevant tag set is $\mathcal{T}_{i-} = \{\mathbf{y}_{ik}\}_{k=1}^{k=T-n_i}$, n_i is the number of relevant tags.

The architecture of the proposed model is illustrated in Fig. 1. Generally, the model consists of two parts: the DNN feature learning and latent space interaction. In the DNN feature learning, image features and tag embeddings are mapped from the original spaces to the latent space. For image features, the transformation is formulated as:

$$\mathbf{a}_I^i = f(\mathbf{W}_I^1\mathbf{x}_i + \mathbf{b}_I^1), \tag{1}$$

$$\tilde{\mathbf{x}}_i = f(\mathbf{W}_I^2\mathbf{a}_I^i + \mathbf{b}_I^2), \tag{2}$$

where $\mathbf{W}_I^1, \mathbf{W}_I^2$ and $\mathbf{b}_I^1, \mathbf{b}_I^2$ are weights and bias respectively, $f(\cdot)$ is sigmoid function and $\tilde{\mathbf{x}}_i$ are representations of images in the latent space (the dimensions of these variables are presented in Section 3.2&3.5). Similarly, $\tilde{\mathbf{y}}_i$ are representations of tags in the latent space. There are two hidden layers for both DNNs, and the second hidden layer is for the latent space (highlighted in blue dashed box in Fig. 1). The reasons of this nonlinear transformation process is two-fold: 1) the resulting latent space makes images and tags interact easily for relevance score estimation; 2) this process is the feature learning directly driven by the model objective.

In Fig. 1, images and tags are organized into irrelevant pairs (the left part of Fig. 1) and relevant pairs (the right part of Fig. 1). A metric matrix $\mathbf{M}$ is employed to compute the relevance scores of these pairs:

$$s_{ik}^- = \tilde{\mathbf{y}}_{ik}^T\mathbf{M}\tilde{\mathbf{x}}_i, \tag{3}$$

$$s_{ij}^+ = \tilde{\mathbf{y}}_{ij}^T\mathbf{M}\tilde{\mathbf{x}}_i, \tag{4}$$

where s_{ik}^- and s_{ij}^+ are relevance scores for irrelevant and relevant pairs (the larger, the more relevant). The matrix $\mathbf{M}$ can capture more complex relationships than just inner product used in [20], that is, the interactions of each dimension between $\tilde{\mathbf{y}}_{ij}$ ($\tilde{\mathbf{y}}_{ik}$) and $\tilde{\mathbf{x}}_i$ can be adjusted by matrix $\mathbf{M}$.

The objective of the our model is to increase relevance scores of relevant pairs, while decreasing relevance scores of irrelevant pairs. Here, we adopt pairwise hinge loss:

$$\max(0, m + s_{ik}^- - s_{ij}^+), \tag{5}$$

where m is used to control margin size (m is set to 1 in experiments). Hinge loss is used in a ranking objective with the notion of large margin. In this case, it makes relevant pairs rank ahead of irrelevant pairs. The final objective function is formulated as:

$$\min_{\boldsymbol{\theta}} \frac{1}{T_N}\sum_{i=1}^{N}\sum_{\mathbf{y}_{ij}\in\mathcal{T}_{i+}}\sum_{\mathbf{y}_{ik}\in\mathcal{T}_{i-}} \max(0, m + s_{ik}^- - s_{ij}^+), \tag{6}$$

where $\boldsymbol{\theta}$ is the model parameter and T_N is the number of triplets generated according to N training images with their tags. Since the deep model has many parameters to be learned, a large number of samples need to be trained to prevent overfitting. The form of triplets can expand N training images to much more training triplets[1]. Parameters involved in the proposed model are DNN weights $(\mathbf{W}_I^1, \mathbf{b}_I^1, \mathbf{W}_I^2, \mathbf{b}_I^2, \mathbf{W}_T^1, \mathbf{b}_T^1, \mathbf{W}_T^2, \mathbf{b}_T^2)$, the metric matrix $\mathbf{M}$ and tag embeddings $(\mathbf{y}_i)$. Error backpropagation and stochastic gradient descent are used to optimize the proposed model.

[1]For example, there are 100 images and 10 tags. Each image has 2 tags on average. The number of triplets is 1600 ($C_{100}^1 \times C_2^1 \times C_8^1$).

In the test phase, relevance scores between the test image and all tags are calculated through the forward pass of the structure (highlighted in red dashed box in Fig. 1), and tags with highest scores are taken as the final annotations.

Furthermore, the proposed model can handle new training images with new tags. The new data can be processed by the same way in which the original training data is processed. This online updating only fine-tunes the model parameters without changing the model structure, which is not feasible for method in [8].

Test computation complexity. According to the description of the proposed model, the final annotations are determined by the relevance scores between the test image and all tags. Therefore, test computation complexity of the proposed model is $O(T)$. Similarly, the text complexity of method in [20] and probability SVM [17] based method is also $O(T)$. For kNN based method, the test complexity will increase to $O(N)$ because the distances between the test image and all training images need to be calculated (in practice, $N \gg T$). The method in [8] only requires a single forward pass of CNN for testing, resulting in a computation complexity $O(C)$, C is a constant.

3. EXPERIMENTS

3.1 Dataset

The dataset used in the experiment is NUS-WIDE [4], which is the largest publicly released multilabel dataset. In this dataset, 269,648 images with 81 different concepts[2] are collected from Flickr. Since the compared method [8] uses CNN, it needs raw images as inputs that are not provided instead of source URLs. However, some URLs are no longer valid and some images have no tags, the final set contains 113,290 images. We randomly divide it into the training set (103,290 images) and the test set (10,000 images).

3.2 Features

We conduct two groups of experiments with low level visual features and off-the-shelf CNN features (it is widely accepted to use learned CNN models as feature extractors [16, 7]), respectively. The low level features include 64-dimensional color histogram, 144-dimensional color correlogram, 73-dimensional edge direction histogram, 128-dimensional wavelet texture, 255-dimensional block-wise color moments and 500-dimensional bag of words based on SIFT descriptor [13]. As for CNN features, we use the model trained on Imagenet [5], provided by Caffe[3] [11]. The dimension of CNN feature is 4096. Additionally, the method in [8] with raw images as inputs is compared with other methods using off-the-shelf CNN features

3.3 Compared Methods

The methods listed below are taken for comparison:

- **WSABIE** [20]. This method projects images features to tag embedding space, and then relevance scores are calculated using inner product.
- **CNN**$_{softmax}$, **CNN**$_{hingeloss}$, **CNN**$_{WARP}$ [8]. CNN based methods must take raw images as inputs, and we implement them using toolkit MatConvNet[4]. Furthermore, the parameters of these CNN models are initialized with the same model that is used to extract off-the-shelf CNN features.
- **SVM**. For each tag, a probabilistic SVM [17] is trained. The tags with highest probabilities are determined as the final annotations.
- ***k*NN**. The kNN based method follows the same manner as in [8]. The k is set to 100 for both experiments.

[2]Following [8], we directly regard concepts as tags.

[3]http://caffe.berkeleyvision.org/

[4]http://www.vlfeat.org/matconvnet/

Table 1: Annotation results with low level features.

Method	mP	mR	F1	N_+
***k*NN**	0.1896	0.2216	0.2043	74
SVM	0.0878	0.2358	0.1279	78
WASBIE	0.1083	0.3025	0.1595	81
DREL	0.1614	0.3193	0.2144	81

Table 2: Annotation results with CNN features.

Method	mP	mR	F1	N_+
***k*NN**	0.2566	0.3826	0.3072	81
SVM	0.1147	0.4192	0.1801	81
WASBIE	0.1667	0.4677	0.2458	81
CNN$_{softmax}$	0.1903	0.4896	0.2741	81
CNN$_{hingeloss}$	0.2063	0.4718	0.2871	81
CNN$_{WARP}$	0.1996	0.4637	0.2790	78
DREL	0.2295	0.4223	0.2973	81

3.4 Evaluation Protocol

We follow the conventional protocol in [14] to evaluate all methods, namely mean recall (mR) over all tags, mean precision (mP) over all tags, F1 ($F1 = \frac{2*mP*mR}{mP+mR}$) score and N_+ (the number of tags that have non-zero recall). The top 5 tags are regarded as the final annotations for each image.

3.5 Setting of the Proposed Structure

Since we take two groups of experiments using low level features and CNN features respectively, two different groups of DNNs are used. Specifically, for low level features, the number of nodes for each layer in image DNN and tag DNN are 1164-1024-1024 and 256-512-1024. For CNN features, the structure is changed to 4096-2048-1024 for image DNN and 256-512-1024 for tag DNN.

3.6 Experimental Results

The results of two groups of experiments are presented in Table 1 and Table 2, respectively.

From Table 1 and Table 2, we can make some observations. In low level feature based results, our method and kNN can achieve state-of-the-art performances with high F1 scores. kNN trends toward a higher mean precision but relatively a lower mean recall and N_+. WASBIE and our method can obtain higher mean recall and full N_+, but mean precision of WASBIE is lower than ours partially due to its "shallow" structure. SVM performs poor because it isolates all tags from each other.

In Table 2, CNN feature based results are shown. It can be observed that the overall performances are much higher than those using low level features. Actually, off-the-shelf CNN features always result in high performance [16]. kNN, three

CNN based methods and our method can achieve state-of-the-art performances. All methods obtain full N_+ except for CNN_{WARP}. kNN still shows the same trend of higher mean precision and lower mean recall, but the highest F1 score. Three CNN based methods have higher mean recall, in particular, $CNN_{softmax}$ gain additional 10% mean recall compared to kNN. Our method outperforms WASBIE in mean precision and F1, again demonstrating the superiority of the deep structure.

In summary, first, CNN features are much better than low level features for the task of image annotation. Second, our method and kNN can achieve state-of-the-art performances, whereas the proposed method has much lower test computation complexity. Third, the proposed method can significantly outperform WASBIE, which demonstrates the effectiveness of deep representation learning. Finally, CNN based methods are effective. However, they have to be retrained with new images and tags, which is not necessary in our method.

4. CONCLUSIONS

In this paper, a novel model is proposed for large scale image annotation via deep representation learning and tag embedding learning. Image features and randomly initialized tag embeddings are refined and mapped to the latent space through two deep neural networks. In such latent space, relevance scores between images and tags are calculated through a metric matrix. Finally, a pairwise hinge loss based objective function is adopted to optimize the model parameters with notion of large margin. The proposed model can accept new images and tags for training via online learning without modifying the structure. Furthermore, the proposed method has low test computation complexity of $O(T)$. The comparative results with state-of-the-art methods on NUS-WIDE dataset demonstrate the effectiveness of our method.

5. ACKNOWLEDGMENTS

This work was supported in part by the National Basic Research Program of China under Grant 2012CB316304, the National Natural Science Foundation of China under Grants 61331018, and the Beijing Nature Science Foundation under Grant 4142057.

6. REFERENCES

[1] L. Ballan, T. Uricchio, L. Seidenari, and A. Del Bimbo. A cross-media model for automatic image annotation. In *ACM International Conference on Multimedia Retrieval*, pages 73–80, 2014.

[2] G. Carneiro, A. Chan, P. Moreno, and N. Vasconcelos. Supervised learning of semantic classes for image annotation and retrieval. *IEEE Transactions on Pattern Analysis and Machine Intelligence*, 29(3):394–410, 2007.

[3] M. Chen, A. Zheng, and K. Weinberger. Fast image tagging. In *International Conference on Machine Learning*, pages 1274–1282, 2013.

[4] T. Chua, J. Tang, R. Hong, H. Li, Z. Luo, and Y. Zheng. Nus-wide: a real-world web image database from national university of singapore. In *ACM International Conference on Image and Video Retrieval*, page 48, 2009.

[5] J. Deng, W. Dong, R. Socher, L. Li, K. Li, and L. Fei-Fei. Imagenet: a large-scale hierarchical image database. In *IEEE International Conference on Computer Vision and Pattern Recognition*, pages 248–255, 2009.

[6] P. Duygulu, K. Barnard, J. de Freitas, and D. Forsyth. Object recognition as machine translation: Learning a lexicon for a fixed image vocabulary. In *European Conference on Computer Vision*, pages 97–112. 2006.

[7] R. Girshick, J. Donahue, T. Darrell, and J. Malik. Rich feature hierarchies for accurate object detection and semantic segmentation. *arXiv preprint arXiv:1311.2524*, 2013.

[8] Y. Gong, Y. Jia, T. Leung, A. Toshev, and S. Ioffe. Deep convolutional ranking for multilabel image annotation. 2014.

[9] M. Grubinger, P. Clough, H. Muller, and T. Deselaers. The iapr tc-12 benchmark: A new evaluation resource for visual information systems. In *International Workshop OntoImage*, pages 13–23, 2006.

[10] M. Guillaumin, T. Mensink, J. Verbeek, and C. Schmid. Tagprop: discriminative metric learning in nearest neighbor models for image auto-annotation. In *IEEE International Conference on Computer Vision*, pages 309–316, 2009.

[11] Y. Jia, E. Shelhamer, J. Donahue, S. Karayev, J. Long, R. Girshick, S. Guadarrama, and T. Darrell. Caffe: convolutional architecture for fast feature embedding. In *ACM International Conference on Multimedia*, pages 675–678, 2014.

[12] Y. LeCun, L. Bottou, Y. Bengio, and P. Haffner. Gradient-based learning applied to document recognition. *Proceedings of the IEEE*, 86(11):2278–2324, 1998.

[13] D. Lowe. Distinctive image features from scale-invariant keypoints. *International Journal of Computer Vision*, 60(2):91–110, 2004.

[14] A. Makadia, V. Pavlovic, and S. Kumar. A new baseline for image annotation. In *European Conference on Computer Vision*, pages 316–329. 2008.

[15] V. Murthy, E. Can, and R. Manmatha. A hybrid model for automatic image annotation. In *ACM International Conference on Multimedia Retrieval*, pages 369–376, 2014.

[16] A. Razavian, H. Azizpour, J. Sullivan, and S. Carlsson. Cnn features off-the-shelf: an astounding baseline for recognition. *arXiv preprint arXiv:1403.6382*, 2014.

[17] V. Vapnik and V. Vapnik. *Statistical learning theory*, volume 2. Wiley New York, 1998.

[18] L. Von Ahn and L. Dabbish. Labeling images with a computer game. In *ACM SIGCHI Conference on Human Factors in Computing Systems*, pages 319–326, 2004.

[19] C. Wang, S. Yan, L. Zhang, and H. Zhang. Multi-label sparse coding for automatic image annotation. In *IEEE International Conference on Computer Vision and Pattern Recognition*, pages 1643–1650, 2009.

[20] J. Weston, S. Bengio, and N. Usunier. Large scale image annotation: learning to rank with joint word-image embeddings. *Machine Learning*, 81(1):21–35, 2010.

Probabilistic Matrix Factorization With Semantic And Visual Neighborhoods For Image Tag Completion

Dimitrios Rafailidis
Department of Informatics
Aristotle University, Thessaloniki, Greece
draf@csd.auth.gr

ABSTRACT

We present an image tag completion method, namely PMF-SVN, where the key idea is to exploit images' Semantically and Visually similar Neighborhoods (SVNs) in the learning process of a Probabilistic Matrix Factorization (PMF) framework. We propose a two-step SVN formation algorithm that can generate an image set with the images being both visually and semantically similar. Furthermore, we introduce an efficient way to incorporate the formed SVNs into the learning process of PMF, under the constraint that the latent features of each image are averaged by the features of the images that belong to its SVN. In our experiments with benchmark datasets, we show that the proposed PMF-SVN method outperforms competitive baselines, in terms of completion accuracy, by efficiently capturing the semantical and visual associations between images and tags in SVNs.

Categories and Subject Descriptors

H.3.3 [**Information Storage and Retrieval**]: Information Search and Retrieval

General Terms

Algorithms, Measurement, Experimentation

Keywords

Tag Completion; Image Annotation; Matrix Factorization

1. INTRODUCTION

With the advent of social media platforms in the past decade, image tagging has gained a lot of attraction by researchers. Tags are provided by users in the form of free text and they are usually imprecise, containing noise to efficiently describe the visual content of images [2, 7]. Meanwhile, users often avoid assigning tags to images, making image tags incomplete. To deal with noisy and incomplete tags, several completion methods [2, 3, 7] have been recently proposed, to capture relevant tag-image associations and consequently to add the missing tags.

ICMR'15, June 23–26, 2015, Shanghai, China.

http://dx.doi.org/10.1145/2671188.2749333.

Although tag completion methods have several applications such as image retrieval [7], event detection [1], etc., several real world problems limit their performance. The different tag choices introduce several problems; for example, a tag with multiple meanings (polysemy), different tags with similar meanings (synonymy), as well as using general versus specialized tags to refer to the same concept, just to name a few. Matrix factorization techniques are suitable for facing the aforementioned problems, since such techniques can reveal the latent tag-image associations and complete the missing tags, accordingly. However, in many cases their performance is negatively affected by the very sparse annotations of images, since in this case there are only few annotations on which to base the generation of the latent tag-image associations and consequently the completion of relevant tags is limited. To solve the problem of images' sparse annotations, several tag completion methods [2, 3, 7] exploit the visual features to construct relevant image-tag associations by forming representations of the missing tags of an image using the tags of its visually similar images. However, this may also limit the performance of tag completion, since images that are visually similar are not necessarily semantically similar. What is therefore required is an efficient way to capture the associations between visually and semantically similar images.

Our contribution is summarized as follows, **(C1:)** we propose an efficient algorithm to generate for each image a set of semantically and visually similar images based on the textual information of tags and the visual features of images, forming thus a Semantically and Visually similar Neighborhood (SVN) for each image; **(C2:)** we introduce an efficient way to incorporate the formed SVNs into the learning process of PMF to solve the image tag completion problem.

2. RELATED WORK

Image auto-annotation methods [5] are related to the image tag completion problem; however, these methods differ, since the majority of existing auto-annotation methods assume that images in training set are completely annotated with appropriate tags [2, 3], whereas tag completion methods add missing relevant tags, given a dataset made up of partially annotated images. Also, several tag refinement methods have been proposed, such as the work of [8], focused more on removing noisy tags but less on completion.

More relevant to our work, Wu et al. [7] proposed to address the tag completion problem by searching for the optimal tagging matrix consistent with both tags and visual similarities. Recently, Lin et al. [3] introduced an image tag completion method via image-specific and tag-specific Linear Sparse Reconstruction (LSR), which reconstructs each image and each tag with the remaining ones using a sparse coding technique. Then, both image-specific and tag-specific reconstructions are merged, in order to complete missing relevant tags. Feng et al. [2] proposed a tag completion algorithm (TCMR) which aims to simultaneously enrich the missing tags and remove noisy ones, by exploiting the statistical dependence between image features and tags via a graph Laplacian. The impact of incomplete and noisy tags was reduced by assigning high weights to tags that are consistent with image features, and low weights otherwise.

3. PROPOSED PMF-SVN

3.1 Problem Definition & PMF

Problem Definition: Given N tags and M images, initially we calculate a matrix $R = [R_{t,i}] \in \mathbb{R}^{N\times M}$, where each element $R_{t,i}$=1 denotes the degree of relevance between tag t and image i, and $R_{t,i}$=0 otherwise. Matrix R is usually very sparse, since most of its elements are expected to be missing in the tag completion problem. Also, we compute a similarity matrix $S = [S_{i,j}] \in \mathbb{R}^{M\times M}$ based on a visual similarity function $f_V(\cdot)$, with $S_{i,j}$=$f_V(i,j)$ (Section 3.2). The image tag completion problem is defined as follows: given matrix R with the existing tag assignments between N tags and M images, as well as the visual similarities of the M images in S, the goal is to complete the relevant missing tag-image associations in R.

Probabilistic Matrix Factorization (PMF): matrix factorization methods, such as the PMF model [6], construct a latent-feature D-dimensional space in which they represent each tag and image. Let $U \in \mathbb{R}^{D\times N}$ be a matrix whose t-th column vector, denoted as U_t, represents the t-th tag in the D-dimensional space. Similarly, let $V \in \mathbb{R}^{D\times M}$ matrix whose i-th column vector, denoted as V_i, represents the i-th image in the same D-dimensional space. Using the initial matrix $R \in \mathbb{R}^{N\times M}$ as training data, matrix factorization techniques learn, i.e. compute the elements of matrices U and V, so that they can approximate matrix R with matrix $\widehat{R}$, such that $R \approx \widehat{R} = U^T V$. The process of learning matrices U and V can be expressed in the probabilistic framework of PMF, where the likelihood of observing a specific tag-image association in R can be expressed as:

$$p(R|U,V;\sigma_R^2) = \prod_{t=1}^{N}\prod_{i=1}^{M} \left[\mathfrak{N}(R_{t,i}|U_t^T V_i;\sigma_R^2)\right]^{\mathbf{1}_R(t,i)} \quad (1)$$

where $\mathfrak{N}(\mu,\sigma^2)$ denotes the normal distribution with mean μ and variance σ^2; and $\mathbf{1}_R(t,i)$ denotes the indicator function with 1 if $R_{t,i}$ is known, i.e. not null, or 0 otherwise. Eq. (1) makes the premise that each known relation, represented with the element $R_{t,i}$ is an independent and identically distributed *(iid)* random variable that follows a normal distribution whose mean values is equal to $\widehat{R}_{t,i} = U_t^T V_i$ and whose variance σ^2 is treatment as hyperparameter. Based on the Bayes theorem and the likelihood function of Eq. (1), we can obtain the posterior probability of U and V:

$$p(U,V|R;\sigma_R^2,\sigma_U^2,\sigma_V^2) \propto \prod_{t=1}^{N}\prod_{i=1}^{M} \left[\mathfrak{N}(R_{t,i}V_i;\sigma_R^2)\right]^{\mathbf{1}_R(t,i)} \times \quad (2)$$

$$\ldots \times \prod_{t=1}^{N}\left[\mathfrak{N}(U_t|0;\sigma_U^2)\right] \times \prod_{i=1}^{M}\left[\mathfrak{N}(V_i|0;\sigma_V^2)\right]$$

where Eq. (2) makes the premise that the features U_t of each tag t, as well as the features V_i of each image i in the D-dimensional space, are also *iid* random variables following normal distribution with zero mean and variances σ_U^2 and σ_V^2, respectively. To compute the low rank D approximation $\widehat{R}$, we have to calculate U and V, so as to maximize the probability of observing the given tag-image associations in R. We pose the image tag completion problem as a problem of maximizing the posterior probability in Eq. (2). The proposed PMF-SVN method consists of the following two steps, (i) for the M images, M respective SVNs are constructed based on the SVN formation algorithm of Section 3.2; (ii) the M constructed SVNs are incorporated into the learning process of PMF, by transforming the maximization problem of Eq. (2) into a minimization problem, which is furthermore solved using the optimization algorithm of gradient descent.

3.2 SVN Formation Algorithm

The inputs of the SVN formation algorithm are: (i) an image q; (ii) the tag set $\mathcal{T}_q$, i.e. the set of tags assigned to q based on R; (iii) a visual threshold ϵ. The algorithm returns the semantically and visually similar neighborhood (SVN) of image q as set $\mathcal{N}^+(q)$. In the SVN formation algorithm the following functions are defined:

(i) *Visual similarity function* $f_V(\cdot)$*:* a bag-of-words model based on densely sampled SIFT descriptors is used to represent the visual content, and $f_V(\cdot)$ is generated by normalizing the $L2$-norm of image features in [0 1], transformed to similarity with $S_{i,j} = f_V(i,j)$.

(ii) *Aggregated visual similarity function* $f_A(\cdot)$*:* is computed between an image set $\mathcal{I}$ and an image x as follows:

$$f_A(\mathcal{I},x) = \sum_{i\in\mathcal{I}} f_V(i,x) \quad (3)$$

(iii) *Tag similarity function* $f_T(\cdot)$*:* is calculated according to the Dice similarity [4], ranging in [0 1]:

$$f_T(t_x,t_k) = \frac{2\cdot|\mathcal{I}_{t_x}\cap\mathcal{I}_{t_k}|}{|\mathcal{I}_{t_x}|+|\mathcal{I}_{t_k}|} \quad (4)$$

where $\mathcal{I}_{t_x}$ and $\mathcal{I}_{t_k}$ denote the sets of images that have been annotated with tags t_x and t_k, respectively.

(iv) *Sum-of-Squared Error function* $SSE(\cdot)$: is calculated between a tag t_x and a tag set $\mathcal{T}$, also in the range of [0 1]:

$$SSE(t_x,\mathcal{T}) = \frac{1}{|\mathcal{T}|}\cdot\sum_{t_k\in\mathcal{T}}\Big(1 - f_T(t_x,t_k)\Big)^2 \quad (5)$$

Initialization step: In line 4 of Algorithm 1, image q is posed as query to generate the set $\mathcal{N}(q)$ with the visual neighbors r based on the visual similarity function $f_V(\cdot)$, with $f_V(q,r) \geq \epsilon$, $\forall\ r \in \mathcal{N}(q)$. In line 5, $\forall$ tag $t_x \in \mathcal{T}_q$ the SSE function $SSE(t_x,\mathcal{T}_q)$ is calculated to identify the tag t_m of image query q that generates the minimum SSE:

$$t_m = \arg\min_{t_x \in \mathcal{T}_q} SSE(t_x, \mathcal{T}_q) \quad (6)$$

In line 6, we set a a threshold SSE_{thres} equal to the minimum SSE of the identified tag $t_m \in \mathcal{T}_q$. Next, in lines 7-13 each image $r \in \mathcal{N}(q)$ is inserted to the set $\mathcal{N}^+(q)$, if the following condition is satisfied:

$$SSE(t_m, \mathcal{T}_{r_j}) \leq SSE_{thres} \quad (7)$$

where $\mathcal{T}_{r_j}$ is the tag set of the visual neighbor r_j. Initialization finishes with the update of SSE_{thres}, in line 14.

Iterative step: In line 18, the previously identified set $N^+(q)$ is considered as a new query set $\mathcal{Q} \leftarrow \mathcal{N}^+(q)$. According to the aggregated visual similarity function $f_A(\mathcal{Q}, r)$ of Eq.(3), a new set $\mathcal{N}(Q)$ of visual neighbors is generated in line 19. Next, similar to the initialization step, the visual neighbors $r \in \mathcal{N}(Q)$ are examined on the condition of the SSE_{thres} in line 22, where each r is inserted into $\mathcal{N}^+(q)$, accordingly. In line 27, threshold SSE_{thres} is updated and the iterative step terminates if $\mathcal{N}^+(q)$ is preserved.

ALGORITHM 1: SVN formation algorithm

Input: (1) image q; (2) tag set $\mathcal{T}_q$; (3) visual threshold ϵ
Output: SVN set $\mathcal{N}^+(q)$.

1
2 **Initialization step**
3 $\mathcal{N}^+(q) \leftarrow \varnothing$;
4 Calculate $\mathcal{N}(q) = \{r_1, r_2, \ldots, r_{|\mathcal{N}(q)|}\}$, with $f_V(q, r_j) \geq \epsilon$;
5 Identify tag t_m with the minimum SSE based on (6);
6 Set SSE_{thres}=$SSE(t_m, \mathcal{T}_q)$;
7 **for** $(j = 1 : |\mathcal{N}(q)|)$;
8 **do**
9   **if** $(SSE(t_m, \mathcal{T}_{r_j}) \leq SSE_{thres})$;
10   **then**
11   Update $\mathcal{N}^+(q) \leftarrow \{\mathcal{N}^+(q), r_j\}$;
12   **end**
13 **end**
14 Update $SSE_{thres} = \min_{\forall r_j \in \mathcal{N}^+(q)} \left(SSE(t_m, \mathcal{T}_{r_j})\right)$;
15
16 **Iterative step**
17 **repeat**
18   Set $\mathcal{Q} \leftarrow \mathcal{N}^+(q)$;
19   Calculate $\mathcal{N}(\mathcal{Q})$ based on $f_A(\mathcal{Q}, r) \geq \epsilon$ and (3);
20   **for** $(j = 1 : |\mathcal{N}(\mathcal{Q})|)$;
21   **do**
22   **if** $(SSE(t_m, \mathcal{T}_{r_j}) \leq SSE_{thres})$;
23   **then**
24   Update $\mathcal{N}^+(q) \leftarrow \{\mathcal{N}^+(q), r_j\}$;
25   **end**
26   **end**
27   Update $SSE_{thres} = \min_{\forall r_j \in \mathcal{N}^+(q)} \left(SSE(t_m, \mathcal{T}_{r_j})\right)$;
28 **until** $(|\mathcal{N}^+(Q)| = |\mathcal{N}^+(q)|$;
29 **return** $\mathcal{N}^+(q)$;

3.3 Learning PMF With SVNs

Incorporation of SVNs into PMF: Let V_i and V_j denote the feature vectors of the i-th and j-th image in the D-dimensional latent-feature space. If image j is in the i-th SVN $\mathcal{N}^+(i)$ of image i, then the learning process of PMF should compute V_i by taken into account V_j. This means that the learning process should consider the semantical and visual information in $\mathcal{N}^+(i)$. This is achieved by firstly expressing the dependency of matrix V on S as:

$$p(V|T; \sigma_V^2, \sigma_S^2) \propto p(V|T; \sigma_S^2) \times p(V|\sigma_V^2) \quad (8)$$

where the first factor $p(V|T; \sigma_S^2)$ expresses the dependence of V on S and the second factor $p(V|\sigma_V^2)$ is the prior probability of V. Given the i-th SVN $\mathcal{N}^+(i)$ of image i, we have:

$$p(V|T; \sigma_S^2) = \prod_{i=1}^{M} \left[\mathfrak{N}\Big(V_i | \sum_{j \in \mathcal{N}^+(i)} S_{i,j}; \sigma_S^2\Big)\right] \quad (9)$$

Eq. (9) considers that the D-dimensional feature vector V_i follows normal distribution with mean equal to the average of the features of the images that belong to its SVN $\mathcal{N}^+(i)$. Based on Eq. (9) we reformulate the posterior probability of U and V in Eq. (2):

$$p(U, V|R; \sigma_R^2, \sigma_U^2, \sigma_V^2, \sigma_S^2) \propto \prod_{t=1}^{N}\prod_{i=1}^{M} \left[\mathfrak{N}(R_{t,i}|U_t^T V_i; \sigma_R^2)\right]^{\mathbf{1}_R(t,i)} \times \quad (10)$$

$$\ldots \times \prod_{t=1}^{N} \left[\mathfrak{N}(U_t|0; \sigma_U^2)\right] \times \prod_{i=1}^{M} \left[\mathfrak{N}(V_i| \sum_{j \in \mathcal{N}^+(i)} S_{i,j} V_j; \sigma_S^2)\right] \times$$

$$\ldots \times \prod_{i=1}^{M} \left[\mathfrak{N}(V_i|0; \sigma_V^2)\right]$$

Objective Function: Eq. (10) provides the basis for learning U and V by exploiting the semantically and visually information of the SVNs. The learning process is performed by calculating those U and V variables that maximize the posterior probability of Eq. (10). Since the natural logarithm function $\ln(p(U, V|R; \sigma_R^2, \sigma_U^2), \sigma_V^2, \sigma_S^2)$ is monotonically increasing, we proceed by minimizing its arithmetic-negation function $L(U, V) = -\ln(p(U, V|R; \sigma_R^2, \sigma_U^2), \sigma_V^2, \sigma_S^2)$. Thus, the maximization problem of Eq. (10) is transformed to the following minimization problem:

$$L(U, V) = \frac{1}{2}\sum_{t=1}^{N}\sum_{i=1}^{M} \mathbf{1}_R(t, i)(R_{t,i} - U_t^T V_i)^2 + \frac{\lambda_U}{2}\sum_{t=1}^{N} U_t^T U_t + \quad (11)$$

$$\frac{\lambda_V}{2}\sum_{i=1}^{M} V_i^T V_i + \frac{\lambda_S}{2}\sum_{i=1}^{M}\Big((V_i - \sum_{j \in \mathcal{N}^+(i)} S_{i,j} V_j)^T (V_i - \sum_{j \in \mathcal{N}^+(i)} S_{i,j} V_j)\Big)$$

where $\lambda_U = \sigma_R^2/\sigma_U^2$, $\lambda_V = \sigma_R^2/\sigma_V^2$ and $\lambda_S = \sigma_R^2/\sigma_S^2$ are the regularization parameters to avoid model overfitting. For reasons of simplicity we set $\lambda_U = \lambda_V = 10^{-3}$ and λ_S=1. To minimize the objective function $L(U, V)$ in Eq. (11), which is a convex function, we use the gradient descent on $\partial L/\partial U_t$ and $\partial L/\partial V_i$ for each pair U_t and V_i, and iteratively update their values. Given a learning rate η, in each iteration (a.k.a. epoch), updating is performed as follows:

$$U_t \leftarrow U_t - \eta\frac{\partial L}{\partial U_t}\ ,\ V_i \leftarrow V_i - \eta\frac{\partial L}{\partial V_i} \quad (12)$$

4. EXPERIMENTS

Datasets: In our experiments, we used the benchmark datasets (i) IAPR TC12 from ImageCLEF and (ii) ESP Game, with their features publicly available at [9]. Each

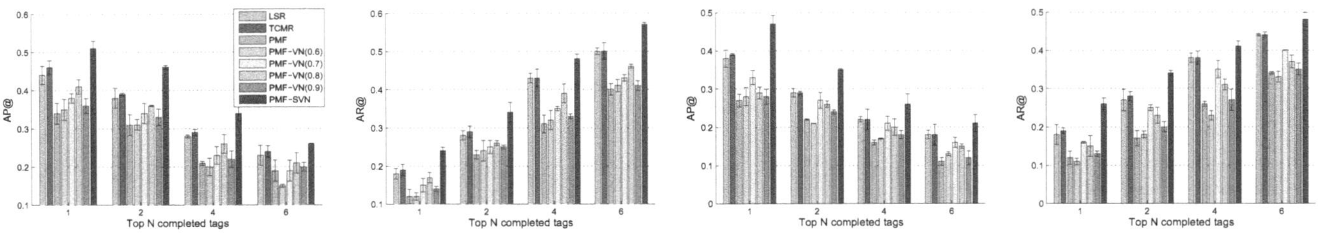

(a) IAPR TC12 (@AP) IAPR TC12 (@AR) (c) ESP game (@AP) (d) ESP game (@AR)

Figure 1: Comparison of PMF-SVN against LSR, TCMR, PMF and PMF-VN(ϵ).

dataset was split into training and test set. Following the evaluation protocol of [2], each image in the training set has 4 tags. The rest tags of each image were deleted from the training set and used as ground-truth tags in the test set. According to [2, 3], we evaluated the tag completion accuracy by Average Precision ($AP@N$), Average Recall ($AR@N$) and Coverage ($C@N$).

Methods: Regarding the proposed PMF-SVN, the learning rate η in Eq. (11) was varied in $[10^{-3}10^{3}]$ with a step of 10, where the concluded η were 10^{-1} and 10^{-2} for IAPR TC12 and ESP game, respectively, denoting that dataset ESP game required a more conservative learning strategy than IAPR TC12. According to Algorithm 1 the proposed PMF-SVN generated SVNs with 7.23 and 11.46 images on average for IAPR TC12 and ESP game. LSR [3] and TCMR [2] were considered as current baselines (Section 2). The parameter values in the baselines were determined by cross-validation, using the publicly available implementations of LSR and TCMR at [10] and [11], respectively. Also, we compared the proposed PMF-SVN against the baseline PMF model [6] which does not exploit any additional information in the learning process by trying to maximize the posterior probability in Eq. (2). Finally, to evaluate the SVN formation Algorithm 1, we also considered as baseline the PMF-VN(ϵ) method, which in contrast to PMF-SVN, uses solely the Visual Neighborhood (VN) $\mathcal{N}(i)$ for each image i, with $f_V(i,r) \geq \epsilon \ \forall r \in \mathcal{N}(i)$, by replacing $\mathcal{N}^{+}(i)$ with $\mathcal{N}(i)$ in the learning process of Section 3.3.

Results: In Figure 1, the experimental results are presented. In the baseline PMF-VN(ϵ) method, we varied the visual threshold in [0.6 0.7 0.8 0.9]. For PMF-VN(ϵ) the optimal values of the visual threshold ϵ are 0.8, i.e. PMF-VN(0.8) and 0.7, i.e. PMF-VN(0.7) for IAPR TC12 and ESP Game, respectively. The highest visual threshold ϵ=0.9, i.e. PMF-VN(0.9), does not improve the completion accuracy of PMF by limiting the size of the Visual Neighborhood (VN) and consequently having limited impact on PMF; meanwhile the lowest visual threshold ϵ=0.6, i.e. PMF-VN(0.6), generates large visual neighborhoods with less visually similar images, introducing thus noise in PMF. Hence, by solely considering visual neighbors in PMF, there is a glass ceiling in terms of completion accuracy, since baseline PMF-VN(ϵ) does not reach the completion accuracy of LSR and TCMR for any ϵ variation. For the proposed PMF-SVN we consider the same optimal ϵ thresholds, i.e. 0.8 and 0.7 for TAPR TC12 and ESP game. PMF-SVN outperforms PMF and PMF-VN(ϵ), since PMF-SVN based on Algorithm 1 forms SVNs with images that are both semantically and visually similar. Moreover, the proposed PMF-SVN method completes tags more accurate than TCMR and LSR. As also presented in [2], TCMR and LSR have comparable performance in terms of $AP@N$ and $AR@N$ on IAPR TC12 and EPS game; however TCMR achieves higher coverage $C@N$ than LSR. Hence, except the experiments of Fig. 1, we measured the coverage $C@N$, where we observed that PMF-SVN achieves also higher coverage than TCMR; for instance, PMF-SVN achieves $C@2$=[0.7 0.57] in IAPR TC12 and ESP game, whereas TCMR is limited to $C@2$=[0.61 0.51], indicating that PMF-SVN can complete relevant tags for more images than TCMR.

5. CONCLUSIONS

In this paper we propose PMF-SVN, an efficient method to solve the tag completion problem. The key idea is to capture the semantical and visual correlations of images and to form SVNs, incorporating thus SVNs into the learning process of a probabilistic matrix factorization framework. Our experimental evaluation on benchmark datasets demonstrates the superiority of PMF-SVN over baselines. Our future work includes an adaptive strategy for both the SVN formation algorithm and the learning process of PMF to evaluate PMF-SVN on the evolving data of social media.

6. REFERENCES

[1] J. Chen, Y. Cui, G. Ye, D. Liu, and S. Chang. Event-driven semantic concept discovery by exploiting weakly tagged internet images. In *ICMR*, page 1, 2014.

[2] Z. Feng, S. Feng, R. Jin, and A. K. Jain. Image tag completion by noisy matrix recovery. In *ECCV*, pages 424–438, 2014.

[3] Z. Lin, G. Ding, M. Hu, J. Wang, and X. Ye. Image tag completion via image-specific and tag-specific linear sparse reconstructions. In *CVPR*, pages 1618–1625, 2013.

[4] B. Markines, C. Cattuto, F. Menczer, D. Benz, A. Hotho, and G. Stumme. Evaluating similarity measures for emergent semantics of social tagging. In *WWW*, pages 641–650, 2009.

[5] S. Moran and V. Lavrenko. Sparse kernel learning for image annotation. In *ICMR*, page 113, 2014.

[6] R. Salakhutdinov and A. Mnih. Probabilistic matrix factorization. In *NIPS*, pages 1257–1264, 2008.

[7] L. Wu, R. Jin, and A. K. Jain. Tag completion for image retrieval. *IEEE Trans. Pattern Anal. Mach. Intell.*, 35(3):716–727, 2013.

[8] G. Zhu, S. Yan, and Y. Ma. Image tag refinement towards low-rank, content-tag prior and error sparsity. In *ACM Multimedia*, pages 461–470, 2010.

[9] `http://lear.inrialpes.fr/people/guillaumin/data.php`.

[10] `https://sites.google.com/site/linzijia72/`.

[11] `http://www.cse.msu.edu/~fengzhey/downloads/src/`.

Exploiting Multiple Web Resources towards Collecting Positive Training Samples for Visual Concept Learning

Olga Papadopoulou
Information Technologies Institute / CERTH
Thermi 57001, Greece
olgapapa@iti.gr

Vasileios Mezaris
Information Technologies Institute / CERTH
Thermi 57001, Greece
bmezaris@iti.gr

ABSTRACT

The number of images uploaded to the web is enormous and is rapidly increasing. The purpose of our work is to use these for acquiring positive training data for visual concept learning. Manually creating training data for visual concept classifiers is an expensive and time consuming task. We propose an approach which automatically collects positive training samples from the Web by constructing a multitude of text queries and retaining for each query only very few top-ranked images returned by each one of the different web image search engines (Google, Flickr and Bing). In this way, we sift the burden of false positive rejection to the Web search engines and directly assemble a rich set of high-quality positive training samples. Experiments on forty concepts, evaluated on the ImageNet dataset, show the merit of the proposed approach.

Keywords

Visual concept detection, Learning from Web data, Multiple text queries, Automatic training set construction

1. INTRODUCTION

Concept detection in images and video is a topic that has received significant attention. Most concept detection approaches proposed in the literature use manually-annotated data samples as training data for a machine learning method. The use of such manually-generated training data is also predominant in competitions such as TRECVID [1], which is organized annually for video annotation. However, manual image or video annotation with concept labels is a costly task, and its cost increases while the need of new concepts arises. This has inspired several recent works to investigate new techniques of collecting annotated image or video samples from the web, to use them as training data. Web images are often annotated with tags; however, these in many cases do not describe the visual content of the image [2, 3]. This happens due to different annotation criteria of the human Web users who annotate their images subjectively and with tags that are often meaningless when seen outside of personal context, or irrelevant to the target concepts of a visual classifier.

While most literature works try to overcome the above problem by downloading a large pool of Web images and subsequently applying to them some proprietary filtering or ranking algorithm, aiming to single-out those which truly contain the target concept, we are proposing a new approach which shifts the burden of the latter process to the Web. Our approach is motivated by the shape of the precision curve of Web image search results. Specifically, the precision of the search results for the first few top-ranked images (e.g., the first 50) is typically very high (above 90%), and decreases while the number of returned images (i.e. recall) increases. This means that by limiting ourselves to collecting just these few top results of a Web search engine, which were ranked as top results by considering a vast amount of Web resources that we could not possible take advantage of in a proprietary post-query selection process, we can render obsolete the latter process and still obtain high-quality training data. The above process could have the downside, though, that the size of the collected training corpus would be very small. To alleviate this, we propose a multi-query approach that automatically formulates multiple queries that are related to a single visual concept and returns the top-ranked images for each of them.

The rest of the paper is organized as follows. Section 2 reviews the related literature. In Section 3 the proposed framework is presented. A detailed description of the proposed approach is given in Section 4, and the experimental results are presented in Section 5. Finally, conclusions are drawn in Section 6.

2. RELATED WORK

The acquisition of positive and negative training examples is a vital step towards training a visual concept detector. Two main directions are followed for collecting the required training data: i) manual labeling of training data and ii) automatic collection of training samples from the Web. The first direction is extensively used in the literature and in benchmarking activities related to concept detection, such as TRECVID [1] and ImageNet [4]. However, the significant effort and scalability limitations arising from the need to manually annotate a high number of images or videos for every different concept that one needs to train a detector for, have motivated several recent works to explore the possibility of collecting training data automatically from the Web. The procedure that most of the related methods follow in

ICMR'15, June 23–26, 2015, Shanghai, China.

http://dx.doi.org/10.1145/2671188.2749338.

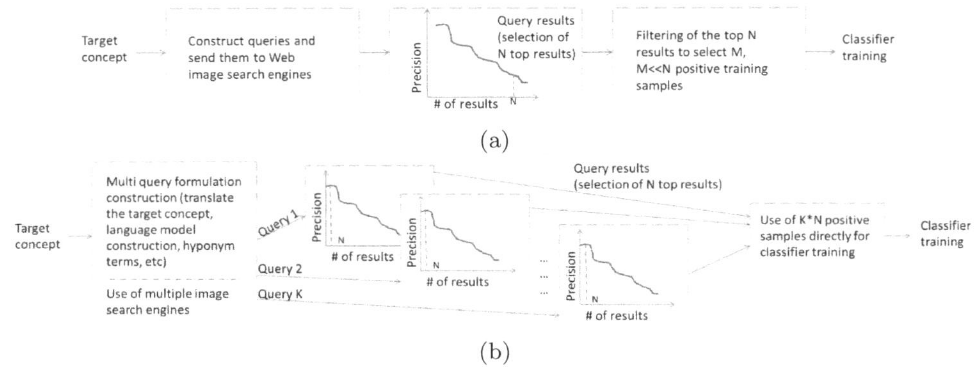

Figure 1: (a) Typical approach for collecting positive training samples from the Web, for visual concept detector training. (b) Proposed approach.

this direction is illustrated in Fig. 1(a): i) they construct one or a few queries that relate to the target concept, and they query the Web using one of the available image search engines, ii) they download a large number N of images that are returned for each query, iii) they apply a filtering or ranking algorithm on these collected images so as to discard the ones that, based on various criteria, are believed to be false positives. Specifically, in [5], given a concept, the WordNet ontology is used for producing a concept hierarchy, with the target concept as root node. Each node (concept) in the hierarchy is used for querying a search engine (Flickr) and download the top-ranked images. After that, the downloaded images of each node are pruned using a method called Semantic Field (SF). The final set of positive training samples for the target concept is constructed by pooling examples from all the nodes in the hierarchy. Similarly, in [6] a large amount of training examples are initially downloaded for each formulated query and are then pruned, with the difference that a text-based Web search engine is used for querying. Other works rely on a small, highly accurate set of positive training samples to start with and an incremental approach for obtaining the final training corpus, e.g., Li et al. [7].

Apart from collecting positive training examples from the Web, some works deal with the selection of negative examples. For this, random sampling is the most commonly used approach [8].

3. PROPOSED FRAMEWORK

An overview of the proposed approach is given in Fig. 1(b). In contrast to the typical approach of the literature (Fig. 1(a)), we shift the burden of selecting a high-quality set of positive samples to the Web image search engines, by exploiting the fact that when N receives a sufficiently low value, the N top results of a web query are almost always correct. Doing this when using a single query, however, significantly limits the number of positive samples that we would collect; to alleviate this, we adopt instead a multi-query approach which formulates K queries, i) by translating the target concept to different languages, ii) combining the target concept term with related WordNET terms, and iii) similarly combining the original target concept with terms extracted by Web text search. In this way we get only N images per query but overall several hundreds or even thousands of images per concept.

Performing some tests on the results of Web image search engines, we confirmed that for low values of N, the top$-N$ results are almost always correct. For instance, we queried the Google image search engine for concept *bird* and the Flickr image search engine for concept *animal*, and manually evaluated the top 1000 returned results. Going at a depth of $\simeq 600-900$ images (as in, for instance [5, 6]), the average precision is between $\simeq 55\% - 80\%$ in our example queries. On the contrary, at a depth of only e.g., 50 images, a very clean set of training samples (average precision $> \simeq 95\%$) can be directly retrieved.

The advantages of the proposed approach are reduced computational complexity, since no post-processing (i.e. pruning) is applied to the Web search results, and accuracy of resulting concept detectors, which is due to having a set of well-annotated positive training samples.

4. FORMULATING MULTIPLE CONCEPT-RELATED QUERIES

Given a target concept, three sets of queries are formulated in order to query Google, Bing and Flickr image search engines and select positive training examples. In Fig. 2, the proposed method's steps are shown, and a detailed description of each query set is presented below.

"Translation" set of queries

The target concept is first automatically translated into fifteen languages[1] and the translated terms are used to query the Google and Bing image search engines. In each case the Google or Bing domain of the specific country is called, in order to avoid receiving duplicate results; for example, for German: google.de and de.bing.com. Flickr image search does not provide such functionality, thus it is not used in this query set.

The maximum number of images that we can collect by applying the *Translation set* of queries for a target concept is calculated by $T_{tr} = E * N * L$, where E is the number of different image search engines that we use ($E = 2$), N is the number of top-ranked images that we retain and L is the number of different languages ($L = 15$). In practice, despite the translation and the use of different country

[1]German, French, Greek, Italian, Spanish, Chinese, Indonesian, Russian, Romanian, Bulgarian, Danish, Dutch, Finish, Hungarian, Portuguese; using Google translate

domains during Web search, we will still receive some duplicate images. In tests with a few example concepts and for $N = 24$ (720 images downloaded in total per concept) we saw that the amount of duplicate images per target concept varied between 5% and 45% of T_{tr}.

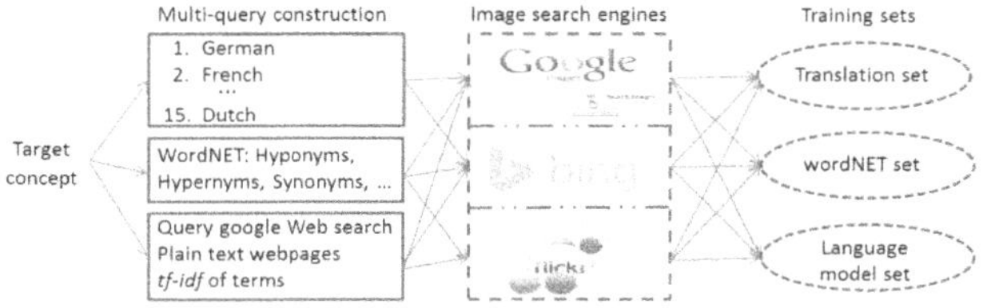

Figure 2: Training data collection for a target concept

"wordNET" set of queries

The second set of queries is built using the WordNET [9] lexical database. WordNET groups English words into sets, such as synonyms, hyponyms, hypernyms, which are called *synsets*. For each target concept, we get from WordNET a list of such related terms. Our queries to the Web image search engines are then formed by combining each of the returned terms with the target concept using AND (&) (i.e. target_concept & wordNET_term).

Although the extracted terms should be semantically related to the target concept, this is not always the case. In such a case the images that will be returned by this term combination will not visually depict the target concept. For example, a *synset* term returned for target concept "dog" is "hot dog". Images returned by the "dog & hot dog" term combination will often not depict the animal dog. Such noisy results should not be included in our training corpus, thus should not be retrieved at all. In order to achieve this, we calculate the similarity of each wordNET-extracted term with the target concept by applying: i) the *umbc* similarity measure [10], which combines the use of thesaurus (e.g., WordNET) and statistics from a large corpus for computing word similarity and ii) the *easyesa* similarity measure, [11], which uses the Wikipedia commonsense knowledge base for a statistical analysis of the co-occurrence of words in the text. Based on experiments on five concepts and their related terms extracted by WordNET, we heuristically chose the value of thresholds $t_u = 0.5$ and $t_e = 0.05$, for the above similarity measures, and we perform the term combination queries described above only when the *umbc* and *easyesa* similarity scores of the two terms being combined are above the corresponding threshold. We assume that these threshold values are suitable for all concepts and we use them throughout our experiments with forty concepts in Section 5.

"Language model" set of queries

The third set of queries is based on text Web search results. The web is flooded with text, and we use it to retrieve more terms related to the target concept and build some sort of a language model for the latter. These terms are combined with the target concept, similarly to what was done in the previous subsection, to construct more text-queries. The steps that we follow are: Given a target concept i) a query of the target concept term is sent to the Google text search engine, ii) the W first Web pages are retrieved, iii) the text of the retrieved Web pages is extracted, iv) term frequency inverse - document frequency (td-idf) [12], which reflects how important a word is to a document in a collection or corpus, is applied on the extracted plain text, resulting in a vector of related or not-related terms. Terms with td-idf higher than t_τ are considered related to the target concept. We set $t_\tau = 0.01$ by conducting similar experiments to those described above for t_u and t_e.

However, there are cases where a term appears frequently in the text of a Web page returned by querying the target concept but is not visually related with it. For example, the returned terms with highest tf-idf for target concept *airplane* are: airplane, plane, aircraft, jet, paper airplane, rc airplane, flight, cockpit, flying, **passenger**, **pilot**, **passenger cabin**,... Several terms, such as the ones in bold, are related to the target concept but do not visually describe it. To reject these terms, we again further assess the suitability of each term combination using measures *umbc* and *easyesa*, together with their previously set thresholds (t_u, t_e). The retained terms are combined (AND (&)) with the target concept to generate additional queries.

5. EXPERIMENTAL RESULTS

We experimented with a pool of forty concepts and an evaluation set of 17881 images from ImageNet dataset [4]. The positive training samples for training our concept detectors are collected from the Web using three image search engines and the multi-query formulation approach, as described in Section 4. Negative sample selection is out of the scope of our study; thus, the commonly-used solution of random selection is adopted and approximately 5000 images are used as the negative training samples. The same negative samples are used throughout the experiments.

For training concept detectors, we used the SIFT, RGB-SIFT and opponentSIFT local descriptors and the methodology of [13]. The trained concept detectors output, when assessing a new image, is a score in the range [0,1], where higher values indicate higher confidence that the image in question depicts the concept.

For evaluating a trained concept detector, this detector is applied to the entire evaluation set, the set's images are ordered according to the detector's output score (in descending order) and Average Precision (AP) [14] is calculated; Mean Average Precision (MAP) is also calculated as the mean AP value across all concepts.

Use of the different training sets

The proposed multi-query approach collects positive training samples using three sets of queries, as detailed in Section 4. We evaluate the use of the collected positive examples in two ways:

Early fusion (union of the training sets): We consider the images returned by all constructed queries for a given concept as a single training set, on which the detector is trained.

Late fusion (individual training sets): We consider the images returned by each of the three query sets as a separate training set; for the given concept, a different detector is trained on each and the three detectors are combined by late fusion (averaging of output scores).

In Table 1, the concept detection results are presented for the two above cases. These results show that *Late fusion* consistently produces better results than *Early fusion*, and also better than using alone any one of the training sets assembled using a single set of queries. Therefore, the *Late fusion* approach is adopted in the rest of the experiments.

Optimal number of top-ranked images to download

The above experiment was run for different values of N, in order to also examine the optimal number of top-ranked images to download per query and target concept. From the results of Table 1 we can see that the optimal is $N = 24$. The MAP increases while the value of N increases from 8 to 24, because more positive examples are included in the training corpus without introducing significant noise, but then starts to decrease, as a result of the set of positive training samples becoming more noisy.

Table 1: MAP for different training sets and the number of retained top-ranked images $N = 8, 16, 24$ and 32

Training set\ N value	Top8	Top16	Top24	Top32
Translation set	0.347	0.363	0.37	0.316
wordNET set	0.308	0.331	0.35	0.34
Language model set	0.281	0.305	0.33	0.32
Early fusion	0.35	0.36	0.37	0.35
Late fusion	0.387	0.399	**0.41**	0.4

Comparisons

We compared the proposed approach with the following:

Baseline: a query of the target concept term is sent to the Flickr image search engine and a fixed number X of examples is returned. We empirically set $X = 600$, as is often the case in the literature. All images returned are considered positive training examples, and no further pruning is applied on the images.

ImageNet examples: We downloaded the manually annotated images of the target concepts and trained the classifiers.

Zhu et al. [5]: We implemented the sampling approach introduced in [5] and trained SVM-based classifiers (following the methodology of [13]) with the selected examples.

Table 2: Comparison with baselines and SoA

Approach	MAP
Baseline	0.252
Zhu et al. [5]	0.3

Approach	MAP
ImageNet examples	0.46
Proposed approach	0.41

Table 3: Relevance fraction for a few concepts

Approach\Concepts	animal	bear	beach	boat	book
Baseline	0.79	0.57	0.69	0.62	0.47
Zhu et al. [5]	0.79	0.75	0.81	0.64	0.53
Translation set	0.91	0.87	0.96	0.77	0.87
wordNET set	0.82	0.6	0.96	0.91	0.85
Lang. model set	0.7	0.55	0.75	0.72	0.86
Proposed approach	0.86	0.8	0.84	0.82	0.87

In Table 2, the results of all conducted experiments, in terms of MAP, are presented. As expected, the Baseline approach is the one that performed the worst, with MAP equal to 0.252, since its training set contained many noisy samples. The ImageNet manually-generated training set resulted in the best trained concept detectors, with MAP equal to 0.46. The implemented state-of-the-art approach, Zhu et al. [5], performed better than the Baseline, achieving a MAP of 0.3. Our proposed approach with a MAP of 0.41 significantly outperforms the baseline and [5].

To explicitly assess whether false positives are included in the positive training samples that we collect with the proposed approach, we manually checked this for a small number of concepts. We quantify the results of this manual assessment by calculating the *fraction of relevance*, which is defined as the fraction of true positives in the collected image set. As shown in Table 3 the proposed approach collects fewer false positives than the compared approaches.

6. CONCLUSIONS

Web images are suitable candidates to serve as training examples for visual concept learning. We have presented an approach of multi-query formulation for collecting positive training examples from the Web. Top-ranked images that are returned by image search engines, as a result of automatically formulating and submitting a large number of queries, allow us to directly collect high-quality sets of positive training samples.

7. ACKNOWLEDGMENTS

This work was supported by the EC under contracts FP7-600826 ForgetIT and FP7-287911 LinkedTV.

8. REFERENCES

[1] P. Over, G. Awad, et al., "Trecvid 2014 – an overview of the goals, tasks, data, evaluation mechanisms and metrics," in *Proc. TRECVID 2014*. NIST, USA, 2014.

[2] X. Li, C. G. Snoek, et al., "Harvesting social images for bi-concept search," *IEEE Trans. on Multimedia*, vol. 14, no. 4, pp. 1091–1104, 2012.

[3] X. Li, C. G. Snoek, and M. Worring, "Unsupervised multi-feature tag relevance learning for social image retrieval," in *Proc. Int. Conf. on Image and Video Retrieval*. ACM, 2010, pp. 10–17.

[4] J. Deng, W. Dong, et al., "Imagenet: A large-scale hierarchical image database," in *Proc. Int. Conf. on Computer Vision and Pattern Recognition*. IEEE, 2009, pp. 248–255.

[5] S. Zhu, C.-W. Ngo, and Y.-G. Jiang, "Sampling and ontologically pooling web images for visual concept learning," *IEEE Trans. on Multimedia*, vol. 14, no. 4, pp. 1068–1078, 2012.

[6] F. Schroff, A. Criminisi, and A. Zisserman, "Harvesting image databases from the web," *IEEE Trans. on Pattern Analysis and Machine Intelligence*, vol. 33, no. 4, pp. 754–766, 2011.

[7] L.-J. Li and L. Fei-Fei, "Optimol: automatic online picture collection via incremental model learning," *Int. Journal of Computer Vision*, vol. 88, no. 2, pp. 147–168, 2010.

[8] X. Li and C. G. Snoek, "Visual categorization with negative examples for free," in *Proc. 17th ACM Int. Conf. on Multimedia*, 2009, pp. 661–664.

[9] C. Fellbaum, *WordNet: An Electronic Lexical Database*, Bradford Books, 1998.

[10] L. Han, A. Kashyap, et al., "Umbc ebiquity-core: Semantic textual similarity systems," in *Proc. 2nd Joint Conf. on Lexical and Computational Semantics*, 2013, vol. 1, pp. 44–52.

[11] D. Carvalho, C. Calli, et al., "Easyesa: A low-effort infrastructure for explicit semantic analysis," in *Proc. 13th Int. Semantic Web Conference (ISWC)*, 2014.

[12] J. Ramos, "Using tf-idf to determine word relevance in document queries," in *Proc. 1st Instructional Conf. on Machine Learning*, 2003.

[13] F. Markatopoulou, N. Pittaras, et al., "A study on the use of a binary local descriptor and color extensions of local descriptors for video concept detection," in *Proc. MultiMedia Modeling, Springer*, 2015, pp. 282–293.

[14] A. F. Smeaton, P. Over, and W. Kraaij, "Evaluation campaigns and trecvid," in *Proc. 8th ACM Int. Workshop on Multimedia Information Retrieval*, 2006, pp. 321–330.

CRMActive: An Active Learning Based Approach for Effective Video Annotation and Retrieval

Moitreya Chatterjee
USC Institute for Creative Technologies
Playa Vista, CA, USA
metro.smiles@gmail.com

Anton Leuski
USC Institute for Creative Technologies
Playa Vista, CA, USA
leuski@ict.usc.edu

ABSTRACT

Conventional multimedia annotation/retrieval systems such as Normalized Continuous Relevance Model (NormCRM) [7] require a fully labeled training data for a good performance. Active Learning, by determining an order for labeling the training data, allows for a good performance even before the training data is fully annotated. In this work we propose an active learning algorithm, which combines a novel measure of sample uncertainty with a novel clustering-based approach for determining sample density and diversity and integrate it with NormCRM. The clusters are also iteratively refined to ensure both feature and label-level agreement among samples. We show that our approach outperforms multiple baselines both on a new, open dataset and on the popular TRECVID corpus at both the tasks of annotation and text-based retrieval of videos.

Categories and Subject Descriptors

H.3.3 [**Information Search and Retrieval**]: Clustering, Retrieval Models; H.5.1 [**Multimedia Information Systems**]: Video (e.g., tape, disk, DVI)

Keywords

Active Learning; Clustering; Uncertainty; Informativeness

1. INTRODUCTION

The ubiquity of multimedia content in our daily lives requires effective tools for multimedia annotation and retrieval. Multimedia annotation tools automatically annotate image or video content (samples) with text labels specifying different objects, events, etc. called *concepts*. A typical multimedia retrieval system, on the other hand, ranks the multimedia samples based on their relevance to the user's text query. Generally, the retrieval is done by comparing the query to the sample concept labels. Thus an exhaustive annotation of the sample is often a pre-requisite for such retrieval systems.

ICMR'15, June 23–26, 2015, Shanghai, China.

http://dx.doi.org/10.1145/2671188.2749342.

Normalized Continuous Relevance Model (NormCRM) [7] is an example of a technique that allows for a direct retrieval of samples without having to annotate them. However training this model (like many others), requires fully annotated data. The human-effort costs of concept annotation is significant and this raises an interesting research question: is there a way to achieve a decent annotation/retrieval performance without requiring a fully annotated training dataset?

The community has taken to *Active Learning* to address this issue [5]. Active Learning, is a machine learning technique that interactively selects unlabeled samples and queries an oracle to provide labels for the samples. Such a system outputs an order of labeling the samples such that a decent annotation/retrieval performance is achieved before all unlabeled data is queried. A typical active learning system consists of a learning engine, which does the annotation/retrieval and a sample selection engine, responsible for determining the labeling order of the unlabeled samples.

In this work, we use NormCRM as the learning engine and propose a novel sample selection algorithm. We call the system CRMActive and apply it for video annotation and retrieval tasks. The algorithm uses a measure of *informativeness* for ranking unlabeled samples during active learning. The informativeness combines a new measure of sample uncertainty with a novel cluster-refinement approach for determining sample density and diversity. Our experiments show CRMActive outperforms a state-of-the-art baseline.

2. PROPOSED APPROACH

Normalized Continuous Relevance Model (NormCRM) is a generative annotation/retrieval technique [7]. Let's consider a video sample I defined by a M-dimensional feature vector $\mathbf{r}$ and $\mathcal{V}$ be the vocabulary of all concept labels (each concept 1 word long). NormCRM defines conditional probability for using a label word $w \in \mathcal{V}$ to annotate the video I, as $P(w|\mathbf{r}) = P(w, \mathbf{r})/P(\mathbf{r})$. Lavrenko et al. [7] suggest that for annotation we pick the top-k words with highest $P(w_i|\mathbf{r})$, $i = 1, 2, ..., k$. For the task of retrieval using a query word w, we pick the top-t videos with highest $P(w|\mathbf{r}_i)$, $i = 1, 2, ..., t$. In both cases, the joint-distribution of words and features $P(\mathbf{w}, \mathbf{r})$ is estimated from the training data by

$$P(\mathbf{w}, \mathbf{r}) = \sum_{J \in T} (P(J) \prod_{w \in \mathbf{w}} P(w|J) \prod_{r_i \in \mathbf{r}, i=1}^{M} P(r_i|J)),$$

where T is the set of training video samples and $\mathbf{w}$ is the set of words in question.

However, NormCRM requires a fully annotated data for training. To address this, we propose an Active Learning approach that combines NormCRM with a sample selection engine. The engine selects samples for annotation based on their *informativeness*, which we calculate by combining measures of sample *uncertainty*, *density* and *diversity*.

Sample Uncertainty is a measure of how uncertain the learning engine is about the sample labels. Entropy and distance of the sample from the decision boundary have been explored as sample uncertainty measures [9, 12]. However, these techniques do not capture the ambiguity between the relevant labels and the irrelevant ones for NormCRM-based models. Hence, we define a novel measure of uncertainty of an unlabeled sample (a M-dimensional vector $\mathbf{x}$) as:

$$unct(\mathbf{x}) = \frac{1}{P(w_1|\mathbf{x}) - P(w_{k+1}|\mathbf{x})}, \quad (1)$$

where $w_1, ..., w_k$ (in decreasing order of relevance) are the top-k most relevant labels assigned to $\mathbf{x}$. The denominator in Eq. 1 gives a measure of the gap (distance) between the posterior probabilities of the most relevant label and the first irrelevant one and can thus be used to obtain uncertainty.

Sample Density is a measure of how likely a certain sample is to occur given the underlying distribution that generated the data while a high *Sample Diversity* score ensures that the samples chosen for labeling aren't too similar to each other. To compute sample density and diversity, we start by clustering all samples in the training data $\mathcal{X} = \{\mathbf{x}_1, \mathbf{x}_2, ..., \mathbf{x}_N\}$, consisting of the initial labeled training data $\mathcal{L}$ and the unlabeled training data $\mathcal{U}$ ($\mathcal{X} = \mathcal{L} \cup \mathcal{U}$). We first represent every sample in the visual feature space and perform X-Means clustering. X-Means is a variant of K-Means, which automatically picks the parameter K by comparing the Bayesian Information Criterion (BIC) scores of the clustering system for a range of values of K and picking the one with an optimal score [8]. We then check if every labeled sample shares a concept with at least one other labeled sample in the same cluster. If we find a sample that shares no labels, we create a new cluster for it and redistribute unlabeled samples from the original cluster between the old and the new clusters using 2-Means.

In order to measure the extent of agreement among the labeled samples in a cluster, both in terms of their visual features and their labels, we use *Empirical Entropy* [3]. For a cluster C, it is defined as:

$$h^C = -\frac{1}{n}\sum_{i=1}^{n} \log(\frac{1}{n}\sum_{j=1}^{n} K(\mathbf{x}_i, \mathbf{x}_j)), \quad (2)$$

where there are $n > 1$ labeled samples in the cluster and $K(.,.)$ is a kernel function. A kernel is a mapping : $\chi \times \chi \rightarrow \mathbb{R}$, where χ is the input space. A kernel may be considered as a measure of similarity. For continuous input spaces, such as video features, a Gaussian kernel is often used [13]:

$$K_{Gauss}(\mathbf{x}, \mathbf{x}') = \exp(-||\mathbf{x} - \mathbf{x}'||^2/2\sigma^2),$$

where $\mathbf{x}, \mathbf{x}' \in \mathcal{X}$. For discrete input spaces, such as the space of labels, a Bernoulli product kernel may be used [6]:

$$K_{Bern}(\mathbf{x}, \mathbf{x}') = \prod_{d=1}^{D}[(\gamma_d^{x_d} \times \gamma_d^{x'_d}) \times (1-\gamma_d)^{(1-x_d)} \times (1-\gamma_d)^{(1-x'_d)}],$$

where $\mathbf{x}, \mathbf{x}' \in \{0,1\}^D$, x_d, x'_d shows the presence (1) or absence (0) of the dth concept and γ_d is the probability of the dth concept occurring. In order to capture the notion of sample similarity both from the visual and label perspectives, we define a new kernel as a combination of the two [4]:

$$K(\mathbf{x}, \mathbf{x}') = K_{Bern}(\mathbf{x}, \mathbf{x}') \times K_{Gauss}(\mathbf{x}, \mathbf{x}')$$

Once we clustered the sample videos, we compute the sample density of an unlabeled sample $\mathbf{x}$ in cluster C as

$$den(\mathbf{x}) = \frac{p(\mathbf{x})}{\max_{\mathbf{x}_i \in \mathcal{X}} p(\mathbf{x}_i)},$$

where $p(\mathbf{x})$ is the kernel density estimate:

$$p(\mathbf{x}) = \frac{1}{|C|}\sum_{\mathbf{x}_i \in C} K_{Gauss}(\mathbf{x}, \mathbf{x}_i)$$

and $|C|$ is the total number of samples in cluster C.

Algorithm 1 CRMActive

Input: The set $\mathcal{L} = \{\mathbf{l}_1, \mathbf{l}_2, ..., \mathbf{l}_P\}$, their labels $\mathcal{Y} = \{\mathbf{y}_1, \mathbf{y}_2, ..., \mathbf{y}_P\}$ where $\mathbf{y}_i \in \{0,1\}^D$, the set $\mathcal{U} = \{\mathbf{u}_1, \mathbf{u}_2, ..., \mathbf{u}_Q\}$ and K :- nos. of samples to pick in a batch.
Output: The set $\mathcal{L}$, containing the order in which the unlabeled samples are labeled.
Algorithm:
Perform X-Means, using the visual features, on the set of $\mathcal{L} \cup \mathcal{U}$ samples. Say, T be the optimal number of clusters and let $rep(C_i)$ denote the representative sample of cluster C_i.
Check if $\forall \mathbf{l}_j, \mathbf{l}_j \in \mathcal{L}, \mathbf{l}_j \in C_k, \mathbf{l}_j$ shares ≥ 1 concept with at least 1 labeled sample in C_k, otherwise call Redistribute($C_k, \mathbf{l}_j$).
h_{worst} := NIL // Initialize h_{worst}
while $\mathcal{U} \neq \phi$ **do**
  Train NormCRM using $\mathcal{L}$, evaluate model on test set.
  Update h_{worst} to max. entropy value among all clusters with at least 2 labeled samples
  Compute $Info(\mathbf{x}_i), \forall \mathbf{x}_i \in \mathcal{U}$
  Pick top-K samples, **Lab** $= \{\mathbf{a}_1, \mathbf{a}_2, ..., \mathbf{a}_K\}$ for labeling.
  $\mathcal{L} := \mathcal{L} \cup$ **Lab**, $\mathcal{U} := \mathcal{U} -$ **Lab** // Update the lists
  // Now refine the clusters based on newly labeled samples
  for $j = 1, 2, ...,$ K **do**
    if h_{worst} = NIL **then** // If h_{worst} is not set
      Check if sample $\mathbf{a}_j, \mathbf{a}_j \in C_k$ shares ≥ 1 concept with at least 1 labeled sample in C_k, otherwise call Redistribute($C_k, \mathbf{a}_j$).
    else// Determine which sample in C_k to knock out
      Compute h^{C_k}, where $\mathbf{a}_j \in C_k$ //$C_k > 1$ labeled sample
      if $h^{C_k} > h_{worst}$ **then** // Exceeds threshold
        for $r = 1, 2, ...,$ # labeled samples in C_k **do**
          $C'_k := C_k - r^{th}$ labeled sample in C_k
          if $h^{C'_k} \leq h_{worst}$ **then** // Meets threshold
            W $:= r^{th}$ labeled sample
            Redistribute(C_k, **W**) // Split cluster
            break

Our definition of the sample density, though similar to Zha et al. [13], differs by using clusters, which are refined (see later in this section), to determine the neighboring samples of $\mathbf{x}$ rather than a static set of its k-nearest neighbors.

procedure REDISTRIBUTE(Samples in C_k, **a**)
  Input: Set of all samples in cluster C_k & the seed sample **a**
  Output: Updated set of clusters
  Algorithm:
  Create a new cluster, C'_k, with **a** as the centroid.
  Perform **2-Means** on the unlabeled samples of cluster C_k with $rep(C_k)$ and **a** as the two initial cluster centroids.
  Update $rep(C'_k)$ as the representative sample of cluster C'_k.
  Determine the centroid of the labeled and the remaining unlabeled samples in C_k and similarly update $rep(C_k)$.

To compute the sample diversity, we use the angular distance between features similar to Brinker's technique [2]. However we choose only the representative samples of every cluster (i.e. the sample closest to the cluster centroid),

$rep(C)$, rather than all the samples in $\mathcal{X}$, to gain speed. Diversity of the unlabeled samples is thus, defined as:

$$div(\mathbf{x}) = 1 - \max_{\mathbf{x}_i \in \mathcal{S}} \frac{K_{Gauss}(\mathbf{x}, \mathbf{x}_i)}{\sqrt{K_{Gauss}(\mathbf{x}, \mathbf{x}) \times K_{Gauss}(\mathbf{x}_i, \mathbf{x}_i)}},$$

where $\mathcal{S}$ is the set of all T cluster representatives $\mathcal{S} = \{rep(C_1), rep(C_2), ..., rep(C_T)\}$. We combine these measures to define the *informativeness* of an unlabeled sample $\mathbf{x}$:

$$Info(\mathbf{x}) = \lambda_1 \times unct(\mathbf{x}) + \lambda_2 \times den(\mathbf{x}) + \lambda_3 \times div(\mathbf{x}).$$

We rank the unlabeled samples in the order of decreasing $Info(\mathbf{x})$ score to select a batch of top-K samples for labeling. While Zha et al. use a combination of sample local structure, density, diversity, and relevance to score the samples [13], our approach differs, most notably, in the use of clustering and the novel uncertainty measure.

Equation 2 shows that a cluster with low inter-sample disagreement has a low entropy. As more samples in a cluster C are labeled, the disagreement among its labeled samples increases. This changes the empirical entropy h^C in a monotonically non-decreasing fashion. We refine the clusters by doing the following: After each labeling batch the algorithm finds the cluster with the worst entropy and uses its h^C as the threshold to decide whether to keep or split a cluster during the next batch. This is repeated for successive iterations. If a newly labeled sample increases the cluster entropy beyond the batch threshold, then we use grid search to find the first sample without which the cluster meets the entropy threshold. We create a new cluster for the sample and rearrange the unlabeled samples via 2-Means (see Algorithm. 1).

3. EXPERIMENTS

We conduct two sets of experiments. In each set, the dataset is divided into training and test subsets. For the first set of experiments, the task of an algorithm is to annotate a test video with a subset of concepts from the vocabulary. The algorithm starts with the training data set divided into labeled ($\mathcal{L}$) and unlabeled ($\mathcal{U}$) parts. Initially only a small subset of the training set is considered to be labeled. The algorithm uses this information to annotate the test set with concept labels. For the next step, the algorithm selects a batch of K unlabeled training samples, we reveal the labels for the selected samples, and the algorithm repeats the annotation task. For every iteration, we report the average precision (AP) scores on the test-set for each concept.

In the second set of experiments, an algorithm ranks the test samples by their similarity to a single word query without annotating the test samples. Again, the algorithm starts with the training dataset divided into labeled and unlabeled parts. For each concept label in the vocabulary, the algorithm ranks the test samples by their similarity to the concept. It then selects a batch of K unlabeled training samples, we reveal the labels for the selected samples, and the algorithm repeats the ranking task. For each round, we report the AP scores for the top 5 images/videos.

3.1 Datasets

TRECVID 2007: The TRECVID 2007 video corpus has 110 short video clips [1] . Each frame in every video is annotated with at most 16 concept labels selected from a set of 36 concepts such as "crowd", "building", "airplane", etc. This corpus has been used extensively in video annotation experiments [13]. For every frame we compute a 225-dimensional feature vector (color moment, edge orientation histogram, wavelet PWTTWT texture) as described in the work of Zha et al. [13]. We test our model on the frames from 13 randomly selected videos and we use the rest of the data (frames from 97 videos) for training. We selected 4000 frames from the training data as the initial set of labeled samples $\mathcal{L}$, containing at least 1 positive example of every concept. We set, batch size, K to 2400.

USC SmartBody: SmartBody is an open virtual character animation platform. It ships with a library of 274 animations such as walking, pointing, eye-brow raising, lip corner stretching, etc. [11]. The animations are defined on a 3D skeleton of 119 individual joints and the joints 3D coordinates are available from the SmartBody API. We annotated each animation using at most 6 concept labels from a set of 30 labels such as "Legs", "Arms", "Face", "Left", "Right", etc. The X-axis of Figure 1 gives an exhaustive list of all the concepts. We annotated the animations at the video clip level (i.e. the individual frames are not annotated). We handpicked 9 out of 119 joints (neck, left(L)/right(R) shoulders, L/R elbows, L/R hip joints, and L/R knees). For each frame in an animation we calculated the skeleton angles at these joints [10] and encoded the differences between the minimum and the maximum values for the angles during the whole animation sequence as a 9-dimensional feature vector. The dataset will be available at our web site[1]. We randomly selected 24 animations for testing and we use the rest of the data (250 animations) for training. We selected 40 animations from the training data as the initial set of labeled samples $\mathcal{L}$, containing at least one positive example of each concept. We now set, batch size, K to 23.

3.2 Baseline Systems

For the annotation task we compare CRMActive with two methods. The first one is an active learning system that uses NormCRM as the learning engine while the samples are selected randomly. The results are averaged over 3 runs with different random seeds. The second baseline is the method proposed by Zha et al. (state-of-the-art) [13]. We determine the two NormCRM smoothing parameters λ and β [7] and the validated parameters of the second baseline using 10-fold cross-validation on the first annotation batch. These values are then fixed for successive rounds. The values of the fixed parameters for the second baseline are reused from the paper [13]. For CRMActive, probability γ_d, is re-estimated from the labeled training data on each annotation batch and the weighting parameters $\lambda_i = \frac{1}{3}, i = 1..3$. Finally, both NormCRM and CRMActive work by ranking annotation concepts, so we assign the top 16 concepts for TRECVID 2007 and the top 6 for SmartBody as relevant. For direct retrieval, CRMActive is compared only with the first baseline discussed above, since no prior work is known.

3.3 Results and Discussion

The results in Table 1 show that the NormCRM-based models, i.e. the first baseline (NormCRM) and CRMActive, generally perform better than the Zha et al. approach for annotation. We believe that this is because NormCRM captures the inter-label correlation, while Zha et al. trains individual classifiers for every concept. Also, the NormCRM-based systems jointly model the labels and features and it

[1]http://nld.ict.usc.edu/group/corpora/smartbody-annot

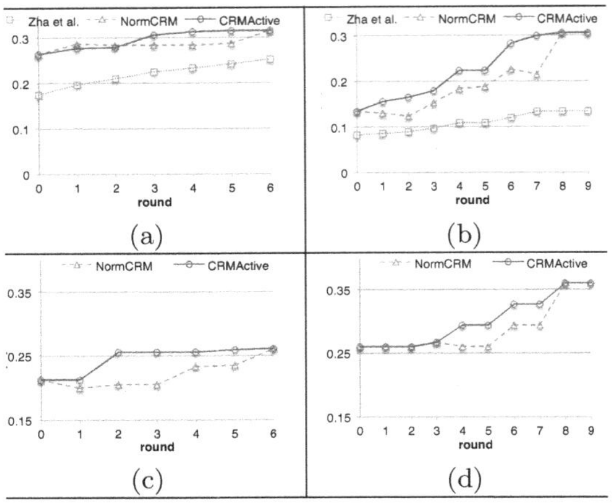

Table 1: AP scores (on Y-axis) for annotation on TRECVID (a), SmartBody (b) and AP scores (on Y-axis) for retrieval of top-5 videos on TRECVID (c), SmartBody (d).

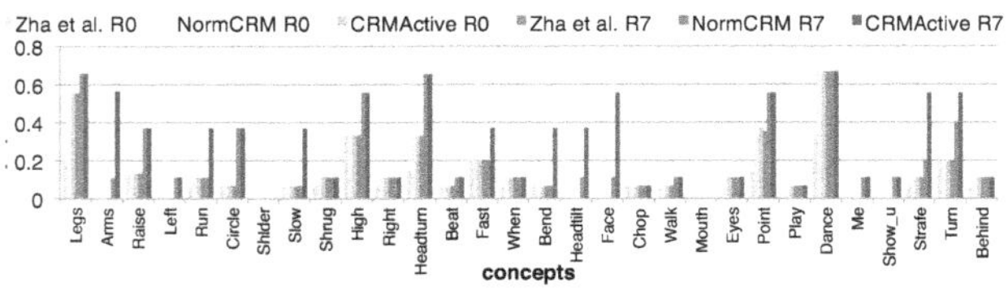

Figure 1: Precision scores for annotation of individual concepts of SmartBody for Round 0 (R0) and Round 7 (R7) of active learning.

allows them to capture the patterns from both these perspectives. CRMActive trains a more robust model early on by selecting the more informative samples; it results in its monotonic non-decreasing AP score for annotation/retrieval. This is in contrast with the occasional dips in the AP scores of the random baseline, which might potentially select some of the relatively noisy training samples early on. Figure 2 shows a sample annotation result on the SmartBody dataset using CRMActive. We see that the model gets all top 3 labels correct at Round 7, before the data is fully annotated.

Figure 1 shows the annotation performance of all the models for the individual concepts of the SmartBody dataset over two rounds (initial and towards the end). The concept scores for the NormCRM are obtained by averaging over the results of 3 runs. We notice a performance gain for all the models across most concepts over the two rounds, indicating that more training data helps. We also notice that CRMActive performs best on all concepts. All models do well on concepts with many positive examples (e.g., Legs) or complex concepts (e.g., Dance).

4. CONCLUSIONS

In this work, we proposed a sample selection algorithm based on active learning by combining a novel measure of sample uncertainty and a novel cluster-refinement approach for determining sample density and diversity. This approach is shown to outperform multiple baselines at both annotation and retrieval tasks. Our experiments also reveal the pros of using a generative approach of jointly modeling both the features and labels. CRMActive is thus shown to be a promising active learning approach to explore.

Acknowledgements

This material is based on work supported in part by the DreamWorks Animation SKG. Any opinions, findings, conclusions or recommendations expressed in this material are the authors' and do not reflect those of the sponsors.

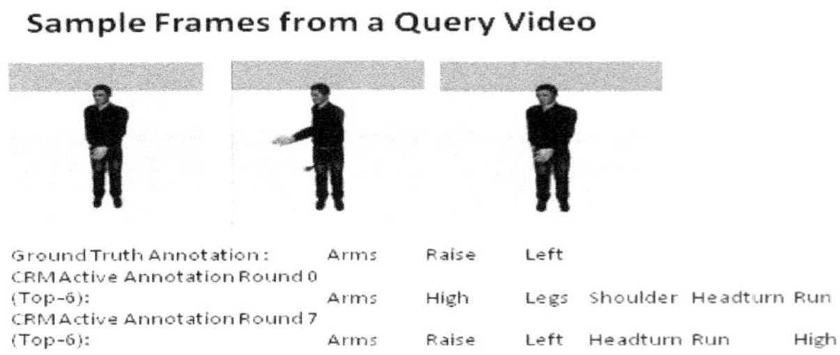

Figure 2: A sample annotation result on SmartBody dataset, showing the top-6 annotated labels by CRMActive after Round 0 and Round 7.

5. REFERENCES

[1] Trecvid 2007: Trec video retrieval evaluation. link: http://www-nlpir.nist.gov/projects/tv2007/tv2007.html.

[2] K. Brinker. Incorporating diversity in active learning with support vector machines. In *Proceedings of ICML*, volume 3, pages 59–66, 2003.

[3] C. K. Dagli et al. Leveraging active learning for relevance feedback using an information theoretic diversity measure. In *Image and Video Retrieval*. 2006.

[4] M. G. Genton. Classes of kernels for machine learning: a statistics perspective. *The Journal of Machine Learning Research*, 2:299–312, 2002.

[5] T. S. Huang et al. Active learning for interactive multimedia retrieval. *Proceedings of the IEEE*, 2008.

[6] T. Jebara, R. Kondor, and A. Howard. Probability product kernels. *The Journal of Machine Learning Research*, 5:819–844, 2004.

[7] V. Lavrenko, S. Feng, and R. Manmatha. Statistical models for automatic video annotation and retrieval. In *Proceedings of ICASSP*, volume 3, 2004.

[8] D. Pelleg, A. W. Moore, et al. X-means: Extending k-means with efficient estimation of the number of clusters. In *Proceedings of ICML*, pages 727–734, 2000.

[9] G.-J. Qi et al. Video annotation by active learning and cluster tuning. In *CVPR Workshops*, 2006.

[10] J. Sedmidubsky and J. Valcik. Retrieving similar movements in motion capture data. In *Similarity Search and Applications*, pages 325–330. 2013.

[11] M. Thiebaux, S. Marsella, A. N. Marshall, and M. Kallmann. Smartbody: Behavior realization for embodied conversational agents. In *AAMAS*, 2008.

[12] S. Tong and E. Chang. Support vector machine active learning for image retrieval. In *Ninth ACM MM*, 2001.

[13] Z.-J. Zha et al. Interactive video indexing with statistical active learning. *Multimedia, IEEE Transactions on*, 14(1), 2012.

Personalized Egocentric Video Summarization for Cultural Experience

Patrizia Varini, Giuseppe Serra and Rita Cucchiara
Dipartimento di Ingegneria "Enzo Ferrari", Università degli Studi di Modena e Reggio Emilia
Via Vignolese, 905/b, Modena MO 41125, Italy
name.surname@unimore.it

ABSTRACT

Recent egocentric video summarization approaches have dealt with motion analysis and social interaction without considering that user can be interested in preserving only part of the video related to his interests. In this paper we propose a new method for personalized video summarization of cultural experiences with the goal of extracting from the streams only the scenes corresponding to a user's specific topics request, chosen among the shots in which it's possible to deduce that the visitor was focusing on a point of interest. Preliminary experiments show that our approach is promising and allows visitor to better customize the summary of his experience.

Categories and Subject Descriptors

I.4 [**Image processing and computer vision**]: Applications

General Terms

Algorithms, Design, Experimentation

Keywords

Video summarization, egocentric vision, wearable devices

1. INTRODUCTION

Video summarization is gaining an increasing attention in multimedia and vision research community as humans need a fast growing support to analyze, crawl and search specific contents in the large and continuously swelling amount of digital video streams available on the internet.

In current literature, most methods for video summarization are based on visual features analysis, visual saliency or video quality assessment. Potapov *et al.* [6] achieve category specific video summarization, first obtaining temporal segmentation into semantically-consistent segments, delimited not only by shot boundaries but also general change points, then apply a SVM classifier to each segment to assigns category relevance score to each segment. Jain *et al.* [1] recognize shared content in videos and joint attention by finding the number of overlapping 3D static points.

ICMR '15, June 23 - 26, 2015, Shanghai, China
Copyright 2015 ACM 978-1-4503-3274-3/15/06...$15.00.
http://dx.doi.org/10.1145/2671188.2749343.

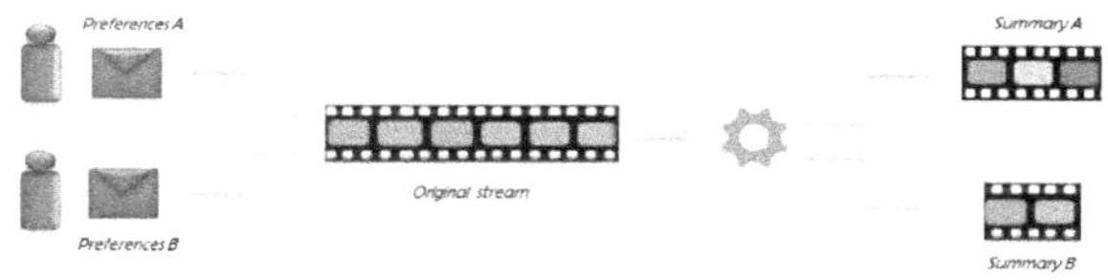

Figure 1: User requests personalized summarization

Recently the wide spreading use of head-mounted cameras has made popular life-logging video. Typically this egocentric videos consist of very long streams of data with a ceaseless jumping appearance, very frequent changes of observer's focus and lack of hard cuts between scenes, thus requiring new methodologies.

Lee *et al.* [4] proposed a egocentric video summarization method that focuses on learning importance cues for each frame, such as objects and people the camera wearer interacts with. In particular, they measure importance on a combination of interaction distance, gaze, object-like appearance and motion and likelihood of a person's face within a region.

Lu and Grauman [5] handle egocentric video summarization partitioning videos into sub-shots on the basis of motion features analysis, smooth the classification with a MRF and then select a chain of sub-shots choosing the ones in which they can detect the reciprocal influence propagation between important objects and characters. Yeung *et al.* [7] present techniques to evaluate video summarization through text, by measuring how well a video summary is able to retain the semantic information contained in its original stream making use of textual summarization benchmarking tools.

Although these summarization techniques deal with egocentric characteristics, they do not take into account the particular user's preferences. In fact, a user can prefer to remember some events rather than others (see Fig. 1). For example, some users might be concerned only with romanesque and baroque art, and might not be interested in preserve shots related with modern art or other kinds of experiences (food, shopping etc.), viceversa users which might be interested only in contemporary architecture might like to discard shots related to ancient art.

In this paper we present a method of user personalized egocentric video summarization in a cultural experience sce-

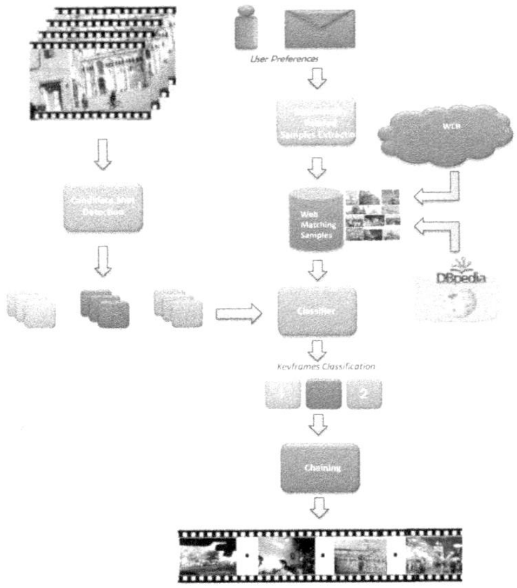

Figure 2: Schematization of the proposed method

nario. The approach relies on extracting from the stream only the scenes, chosen among specific shots assembled with groups of frames that can be put in relation with an observer's attention behaviour, matching some questioner user's declared topics of interest, so that different users typically obtain different summaries from the same stream. User's preferences are represented by different groups of keywords. Since user's declared topics of interest can not be constrained, we propose a data-driven approach that extracts positive and negative training samples from the web. Our preliminary experimental results show that this approach is able to exploit user's preference to obtain a personalized summarization of a cultural visit video.

2. PERSONALIZED SUMMARIZATION

Our approach can be roughly described as the set of two main tasks (see Fig. 2). The first aims to identify the candidates of the relevant scenes, discarding all the groups of frames related to irrelevant experiences or in which the observer is changing his focus of attention, and ends with the candidate shots detection and keyframes extraction. Discarding the non relevant shots and limiting the analysis to keyframes, aims to reduce the computational overhead and to focus on the research of presumably relevant features. Our hypothesis relies on the assumption, tailored on a typical cultural experience scenario, that the relevant scenes are associated to a camera's viewer behavior due to the presence of attention patterns. The second task aims to extract from the candidate shots only the ones that maximize the score of semantic relatedness to the preferences requested by the user and the visual diversity. To achieve this goal we build specific classifiers of the topics of interest and find out the scenes that achieve the highest score. In order to identify reliable image training samples from the web, we evaluate importance on semantic relatedness with user input using DBpedia and visual difference.

2.1 Candidate shot detection

We are interested in identifying and extracting from the original stream shots that can be put in relation with the due of camera wearer "paying attention" pattern. In general, in a cultural experience scenario visitor can have different behaviours, but we focus on four attitude patterns: transit from one point of interest to another, changing the focus of attention, paying attention to something which is relevant, or wandering around without showing signs of interest. Of course behaviours are not directly detectable but we put them in relation with detectable motion patterns from video analysis.

Thus, we define the following observable motion classes: "Static", "Walking", "Higher speed" (running, jumping, falling, etc), "On wheels" (driving, on bus, etc.), "Head Rolling" and "Head Pitching".

Therefore we model camera's wearer pattern behaviours as a Hidden Markov Models with the four behaviour states and the six directly observables defined upper.

In a general Hidden Markov Model with N hidden states and M observables, the model is completely described by the initial state probability, the transition $N \times N$ matrix with elements $a_{ij} = p(q_{t+1} = j | q_t = i), 1 \leq i, j \leq N$ and emission probabilities $N \times M$ matrix with elements $b_{jk} = p(o_t = \theta_k | q_t = j), 1 \leq j \leq N, 1 \leq k \leq M$.

The transition matrix pdf was initialized assumimg that the "transit" and "wandering around" states were the most frequent, the emission matrix was initialized evaluating the probability to observe the emission o_t in the q_t state.

Once defined the model, we have used Baum-Welch algorithm for training to obtain a better detection of the interest sequences of events. The models were fed with observables vector and probability of precedent state and Viterbi algorithm was iterated to specialize the parameters.

To classify the observable primitive classes, we analyze frame quality assessment features and motion pattern by partitioning frame using a 3×3 grid. In particular blurriness is used to assess quality frame. We compute this feature by using the method proposed by Roffet *et al.* [2]. They assume that the sharpness of an image is contained in its gray component and estimate the blur annoyance only on the luminance component, computing and evaluating the line and row difference between the original image and the image obtained applying to it a horizontal and a vertical strong low-pass filter. The blurriness descriptor is obtained by concatenating sector features.

Motion feature is based on optic flow and its gradient histograms estimated using the Farneback algorithm. Considering the optic flow computed for each couple of consecutive frames, the relative apparent velocity and acceleration gradient of each pixel is V_x, V_y, A_x and A_y. These values are expressed in polar coordinates as in the following:

$$M_V = \sqrt{V_x^2 + V_y^2} \qquad \theta_V = \arctan(V_y/V_x) \qquad (1)$$

$$M_A = \sqrt{A_x^2 + A_y^2} \qquad \theta_A = \arctan(A_y/A_x) \qquad (2)$$

We compute a histogram by concatenating the magnitudes M_V and M_A (quantized in eight bins), with the orientations θ_V and θ_A, (quantized in eight bins) weighting them by their magnitude respectively.

In order to reduce the jumpy values of motion measures due to meaningless head motion, the feature vector descriptors have been averaged over a window of about 20 frames (when acquiring at 29 FPs). This window corresponds to a duration of less than a second and it has been considered to be a reasonable compromise to reduce randomness without information loss. In fact, the typical interval duration of head movement in the "paying attention" pattern has been put in relation to visual fixation, studied using gaze analysis, that is about 330 ms [3] but has a wide range of variation. To speed up classification task, a linear multiclass SVM has been trained over the six identified classes.

2.2 Semantic classification and Shot chain

To identify the set of candidate shots that maximize the relatedness to the user's preferences we build a visual recognition system based on discrete classifiers. Since topics of interest requested by the user can be infinite, visual classification based on a number of rigidly defined classes is not feasible. To deal with this problem we proposed a data-driven approach that gathers positive and negative training samples from the web. To obtain a reliable training set, we analyze importance on semantic relatedness with user's preference and we expand semantically them using DBpedia.

In fact, DBpedia semantic network has become a new enabling resource for semantic processing and natural language processing, with its wide spread semantic coverage, its constant updates and its semantic support structure, taxonomies (hyponyms, hyperonyms, synonyms, antonyms), translations for each lexical word, cross references between related topics, disambiguation pages, ontology management and topic inference.

We regard Dbpedia as a undirected weighted graph $G = \{V, E\}$ where $V = \{1, ...n\}$ are the nodes representig concepts and $E \subset V \times V$ are the edges representing the links among nodes. To detect semantic community in DBpedia we use the recursive Girvan-Newman algorithm. The algorithm starts with computing the "betweenness" score for each of the edges ("betweenness" of an edge is the number of shortest paths between pairs of nodes that run along it). Remove the edge with the highest score. Compute the betweenness of all edges affected by the removal. The last two steps are repeated until no edges remain.

At last for each detected semantic community including the user keywords and at most other K terms (in our experiments we fixed K=3), we evaluate average of the shortest paths between communities members and the geolocalized place where the video has been captured using Dijkstra algorithm. The basic intuition is that semantic concepts that are strictly related with user's preferences and visit location can improve the search terms for collecting training images.

Let's suppose a user's preference is "Reinessance" and the video is captured in Ferrara city. Fig 3 shows the positive examples, selecting images with high relevance score from a google image search engine, and negative samples randomly taken. With our approach (see Fig. 4) this user's preference is expanded in the semantic community "Reinessance Ferrara Diamond-palace". Therefore positive samples are extracted from a image search on this set of terms, explicitly excluding all images labeled with semantic concepts or tags that have a shortest path distance from the expanded preference over a threshold. Negative samples are gathered using a search of semantic concepts reached moving on the graph from the expanded preference of N steps (we empirically fix it to ten). Finally, starting from the positive and negative samples extracted we build semantic classifiers using the Bag of Words approach (BOW).

Figure 3: Example of positive and negative samples without geolocalization and semantic expansion (keyword: Reinessance. Location: Ferrara)

Figure 4: Example of positive and negative samples with the proposed geolocalization and semantic expansion. (keyword: Reinessance. Location: Ferrara)

Relevance of each shots is computed taking into account classification scores (S) and visual diversity (D):

$$R(s) = w_1 S + w_2 D \quad (3)$$

For each shot, S is computed as the sum of the scores obtained on each keyframe by all classifiers learned form the expanded preference communities and normalized by shot length. To measure visual diversity D, we represent a shot as a phrase (string) formed by the concatenation of the bag-of-words representations of consecutive characters (keyframes). To compare these phrases (or shots) we use the Needleman-Wunsch distance defined as the number of operations required to transform one string into the other. In particular, D is the normalized sum of the distances of the shot with respect to the adjacent ones. Based on preliminary experiments, we empirically fix the weighting coefficients w_1 and w_2.

3. EXPERIMENTAL RESULTS

To evaluate the performance of our approach we collected ten videos captured by tourists that spend some time to visit cultural cities. Each video is about one hour long and taken in a uncontrolled setting. They show the experience visitors such as a visit of cultural interest point (church, monument etc), shopping or walking. The camera is placed on the tourist's head and captures a 720 × 576, 29 frames per second RGB image sequence.

A subset of 7200 annotated frames is used in order to test our methodology to recognize the motion classes: "Static", "Walking", "High speed", "On wheels", "Head Roll" and "Head Pitch". First, we examine the effectiveness of our feature vector representing frame quality assessment features and motion pattern.

In Table 1 we compare average class accuracy of our results to the features proposed by Lu *et al.* [5] (based on blurriness, optical flow orientations weighted over magnitudes and magnitudes). The Figure 5 shows the performance of the two feature descriptors per class.

As can be see our descriptor achieves a better performance. In fact, adding descriptors related to apparent ac-

	Lu *et al.* [5]	**Our approach**
Accuracy	62.92	**72.48**

Table 1: Comparision of classification accuracy.

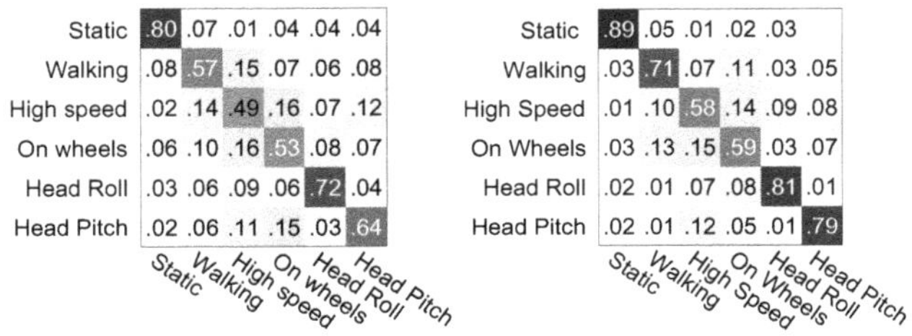

(a) (b)

Figure 5: Classification accuracy using different descriptors: a) feature vector proposed by Lu *et al.* [5]; b) our feature vector.

celeration can help to distinguish abrupt and random movements of the head from other kinds of motion within the frame since these features are more sensible with respect to the apparent velocity.

In addition, we evaluate the ability of our approach to collect reliable training set analyzing the semantic relatedness of user's preference with DBpedia knowledge structure. We show the results of two experiments where the user's preferences are expressed by keywords "Romanesque" and "Baroque" for the first one and by "Picture cards" and "Clothes Shopping"' for second. To analyze our results we compare the performance obtained by classifiers trained with web images extracted using the proposed geolocalization and semantic expansion with classifiers learned using only the user keywords. In particular, for each image we extract SIFT descriptors computed at four scales (4, 6, 8, and 10), over a dense regular grid with a spacing of 6 pixels. The codebook size is set to 2000. Images are hierarchically partitioned into 1×1, 2×2 and 4×4 blocks on 3 levels respectively. SVM classifiers have been trained on the collected images (60% for training and 40% validation and testing) and performance was evaluated using 10-fold crossvalidation. Fig. 6 shows the classification comparison between our approach and the baseline in term the F1-score. Notice that in all cases classification performances outperform the baseline. In particular, we observe that the information about visit location can better restrict the visual appearances of the topics of interest requested by the user.

Finally, we perform a "blind taste test" in which, for each video of the dataset, the summarization based on our approach and a baseline are shown to eight students, that have to report which summary best meets the user's preferences related to video. We first show to the students a browsable sped-up version of the entire original videos, and ask them to write down the shots in which they think the users's preferences given as sample input are fit. Afterward, for each original video, we show them two summaries: one is obtained with the proposed method, the other is from a baseline method in which all candidate shots are chained. We do not reveal the order as it is randomly obtained. After viewing both, the subject is asked, "Which summary better shows the relevant events taking into account the user's

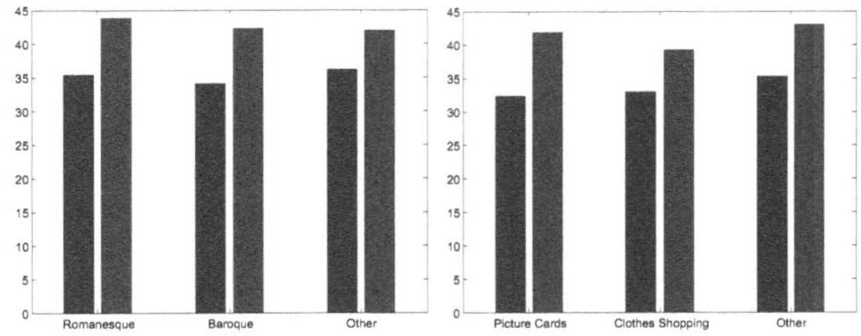

(a) (b)

Figure 6: Classification comparison between classifiers trained with only the user's preference (blue hist.) and with proposed geolocalization and semantic expansion (red hist.).

preferences?". We used a Likert scale with a score between 1 and 5, where 1 was "no good summarization" and 5 "perfect summarization". This test shows that 84% of the comparisons assigns a higher score to summaries obtained with our approach with respect to the baseline.

4. CONCLUSIONS

In this paper we have introduced a novel approach to user personalized egocentric video summarization in a cultural experience scenario. The approach focused on extracting from the original video the relevant shots with a "paying attention" pattern. These candidate shots are further filtered in order to obtain a summary matching the requested user preferences. Our preliminary results show that the proposed approach is able to take into account user's preference in order to obtain a personalized summarization.

Acknowledgments

This work was partially supported by the Fondazione Cassa di Risparmio di Modena project "Vision for Augmented Experiences" and the PON R&C project DICET-INMOTO (Cod. PON04a2_D).

5. REFERENCES

[1] S. Antani, R. Kasturi, and R. Jain. A survey on the use of pattern recognition methods for abstraction, indexing and retrieval of images and video. *Pattern Recognition*, 35(4):945 – 965, 2002.

[2] F. Crété-Roffet, T. Dolmiere, P. Ladret, M. Nicolas, et al. The blur effect: Perception and estimation with a new no-reference perceptual blur metric. In *Proc. of SPIE*, 2007.

[3] J. M. Henderson. Regarding scenes. *Current Directions in Psychological Science*, 16(4):219–222, 2007.

[4] Y. J. Lee, J. Ghosh, and K. Grauman. Discovering important people and objects for egocentric video summarization. In *Proc. of CVPR*, 2012.

[5] Z. Lu and K. Grauman. Story-driven summarization for egocentric video. In *Proc. of CVPR*, 2013.

[6] D. Potapov, M. Douze, Z. Harchaoui, and C. Schmid. Category-specific video summarization. In *Proc. of ECCV*, 2014.

[7] S. Yeung, A. Fathi, and L. Fei-Fei. Videoset: Video summary evaluation through text. *CoRR*, abs/1406.5824, 2014.

EMIF: Towards a Scalable and Effective Indexing Framework for Large Scale Music Retrieval

Jialie Shen†, Tao Mei§, Dacheng Tao★, Xuelong Li‡, and Yong Rui§
†Singapore Management University, Singapore
§Microsoft Research Asia, Beijing, China
★University of Technology, Sydney, Australia
‡Xi'an Institute of Optics and Precision Mechanics, Chinese Academy of Sciences, Xi'an, China
jlshen@smu.edu.sg; {tmei, yongrui}@microsoft.com; dacheng.tao@gmail.com; xuelongli@ieee.org

ABSTRACT

This article presents a novel indexing framework called EMIF (Effective Music Indexing Framework) to facilitate scalable and accurate content based music retrieval. EMIF system architecture is designed based on a "classification-and-indexing" principle and consists of two main functionality layers: 1) a novel semantic-sensitive classification to identify input music's category and 2) multiple indexing structures - one local indexing structure corresponds to one semantic category. EMIF's layered architecture not only enables superior search accuracy but also reduces query response time significantly. To evaluate the system, a set of comprehensive experimental studies have been carried out using large test collection and EMIF demonstrates promising performance over state-of-the-art approaches.

Categories and Subject Descriptors

H.3.3 [**Information Search and Retrieval**]; H.5.5 [**Sound and Music Computing**]: Systems

Keywords

Content based Music Retrieval; Indexing Structure; Retrieval

1. INTRODUCTION

The last decade has witnessed a fast growth in digital music from various application domains [9]. To support effective management of such a large volume of music data, how to improve search efficiency becomes very important issue [3]. Particularly, there has been growing interest in studying indexing techniques for content based music retrieval (CBMR). The typical examples include the M-tree [15], LSH [16, 17], CM*F [11], QUC-Tree [12] and so on. Although the approaches have demonstrated promising performance in certain applications, there are still many open questions and unsolved research issues. First, we believe that while main research focus for developing multi-dimensional indexing scheme is effeciency improvement, how to enhance search accuracy has been becoming more and more important. Unfortunately, much less attention has been paid on it in the previous work. Further, most of existing indexing schemes for CBMR is developed based on "feature transformation" paradigm. In general, it has two nested issues: (1) how to compute small but effective signature to represent complex music contents based on low level acoustic features, and (2) how to design advanced architecture to facilitate fast and accurate search.

Motivated by the analysis given above, this paper presents a novel indexing framework called EMIF [1] to facilitate effective and efficient music information retrieval. Distinguished from previous approaches, architecture of our technique is designed based on a "Classify-and-Indexing" principle and uses a layered structure including two basic components - Classification Module and Indexing Module. This innovation enables superior search efficiency and effectiveness. To achieve good music classification accuracy, multiple acoustic feature based music class profiling model is proposed to characterize different music categories. Together with Logistic regression based likelihood value estimation and combination scheme, it can enhance categorization effectiveness and thus improve the overall retrieval accuracy greatly. Meanwhile, a novel deep learning based music signature generation scheme is proposed to compute compact and comprehensive music descriptor. It can effectively fuse various kinds of acoustic features for the purpose of indexing and search by leveraging a wide range of mature multidimensional indexing techniques.

2. SYSTEM ARCHITECTURE OF EMIF

EMIF has two main components: classification module and indexing module. When it receives input music, classification module will identify music category. Then top k query processing is carried out using the corresponding local indexing tree in the indexing module. In following, we give a detailed introduction on system architecture of EMIF.

2.1 Classification Module

2.1.1 Multifeature based Statistical Class Modelling

To characterize each high level semantic category (or class), we develop a Music Category Modelling Module (MCMM) to construct a multiple feature based statistical scheme. Each MCMM in EMIF corresponds to one music category in the database. Each MCMM is made up of two parts: 1) feature extraction, and 2) a set of LDMMs (Linear Discriminative Mixture Model) built for statistical modelling of music class based on various kinds of acoustic features. A LDMM is a stochastic model combining the advantages of LDA and Gaussian Mixture Model (GMM). The novelty

[1] **EMIF** stands for **E**ffective **M**usic **I**ndexing **F**ramework

ICMR'15, June 23–26, 2015, Shanghai, China.

http://dx.doi.org/10.1145/2671188.2749346.

of LDMM is its great capability and flexibility for effective feature modelling. In MCMM, each LDMM corresponds to one acoustic feature type.

Feature extraction aims to calculate a numerical summarisation of music documents. EMIF applies the partition-based approach to extract multiple local features. When receiving input music, EMIF firstly segments it into small blocks and then different kinds of acoustic features are extracted from each block as basic content representation. Specifically, the features considered in this study include timbre, rhythm and pitch. The extraction process can be denoted as $\boldsymbol{V}_f = Extract_f(mo) = [\boldsymbol{v}_{1f}, \boldsymbol{v}_{2f}, ..., \boldsymbol{v}_{Bf}]$, where $\boldsymbol{V}_f$ is the set of vectors for a feature f extracted from the B blocks of the input music object mo. For our system, GMM is used as a statistical processor to model feature distributions for the particular semantic concepts. Based on each kind of feature, a GMM based category model can be trained separately for the task of class identification. In this study, we consider three different acoustic features including timbre feature, rhythm feature [14] and pitch feature [13].

In order to gain effective music category identification, EMIF constructs a statistical model for each class using multiple features. To achieve this, the individual feature of the music is extracted, and then, individual profiling model for one class is constructed using each feature. In EMIF, category profiling captures statistical properties of different features using Linear Discriminative Mixture Model (LDMM), which is a novel classification scheme combining the advantages of both LDA and GMMs. The main advantage of LDA over other linear subspace methods is to generate a discriminative feature space to maximize the ratio of between-class scatter against within-class scatter (Fisher's criterion) [2, 5]. In the LDMM for each acoustic feature, LDA is used as feature extraction that provides a linear transformation of raw features (n dimension) to m dimensional subspace (m dimension, $m < n$). Consequently, the samples belonging to the same category are closer and the samples from different categories are far apart. At the same time, since LDA can significantly reduce the dimensionality of raw feature, LDMM's training and classification will be much faster. With GMM, the probability of class c can be modeled as a random variable drawn from a probability distribution for a particular feature f after LDA transformation. Given a parameter set Θ_f^s based on feature f, the probability distribution is present as a mixture of multivariate component densities: $P_f^c(\boldsymbol{V}_f|\Theta_f^s) = \prod_{b=1}^{B}\{\sum_{j=1}^{J} w_{fj}^c p_f^c(\boldsymbol{v}_{bf}|\,\boldsymbol{\mu}_{fj}^c, \boldsymbol{\Sigma}_{fj}^c)\}$. The Gaussian density is used as the multivariate component in this study, according to GMM $\Theta_f^s = \{w_{fj}^c, \boldsymbol{\mu}_{fj}^c, \boldsymbol{\Sigma}_{fj}^c|\ where\ 1 < j < J\}$, where w_{fj}^c, $\boldsymbol{\mu}_{fj}^c$ and $\boldsymbol{\Sigma}_{fj}^c$ denote, respectively, mixture weights, mean vectors and covariance matrices. Also, $p_f^c(\boldsymbol{v}_{bf}|\,\boldsymbol{\mu}_{fj}^c, \boldsymbol{\Sigma}_{fj}^c)$ is the probability of a class label c based on feature f extracted from segment b. Given feature vector $\boldsymbol{v}_{bf}$, it can be easily calculated using the Gaussian density function and associated parameters $\{\boldsymbol{\mu}_{fj}^c, \boldsymbol{\Sigma}_{fj}^c\}$.

To effectively estimate model parameters, EMIF applies EM algorithm [1]. The EM is an iterative method to estimate and optimize some unknown parameters based on given data set. Since EMIF considers multiple features, the overall training procedure will be repeated multiple times, once for each feature. After the training process of system is completed, the likelihood value generated based on feature f for input feature vector $\boldsymbol{V}_f$ can be given as below,

$$\begin{aligned} l_f^c &= log(P_f^c(\boldsymbol{V}_f|\Theta_f^s)) \\ &= \sum_{b=1}^{B} log(\{\sum_{j=1}^{J} w_{fj}^c p_f^c(\boldsymbol{v}_{bf}|\,\boldsymbol{\mu}_{fj}^c, \boldsymbol{\Sigma}_{fj}^c)\}) \end{aligned} \tag{1}$$

An overall likelihood value can be derived based on various features for category c, denoted as $L^c = C^c(\vec{l^c}, \vec{W^c})$, where $\vec{l^c} = \{l_1^c, l_2^c, ..., l_F^c\}$ and $\vec{W^c} = \{W_1^c, W_2^c, ..., W_F^c\}$ include all the combination weights and scores from the category profiling model for class c. C^c is likelihood value combination function. When classifying input music, L^c can be used to measure the universal similarity distance between and input music and a class label c. Thus, how to compute combination weights is very important and in fact, the simplest way to determine combination weights would be to assign all combination weights same value regardless of their scores. However, the key disadvantage of the approach is the inability to take into account different features' effects on music classification.

2.1.2 *Fusion Weight Estimation*

How to fuse likelihood value generated based on different features is important to music classification performance in classification module of EMIF. To gain a comprehensive statistical model for each music category, EMIF applies the Logistic function as a combination scheme C^c to estimate an overall likelihood score between input song and class c [6, 7]. Basic idea of the approach is same to the one applied in HSI singer identification system [10]. By using Logistic function, overall likelihood value L^c can be scaled to [0,1] and formulated as below,

$$L^c = C^c(\vec{l^c}, \vec{W^c}) = \frac{1}{1 + exp(-y_c \sum_{f=1}^{F} W_f^c\, l_f^c)} \tag{2}$$

where $y_c = 1$ when c is input music's category, $y_c = -1$ otherwise, W_f^c denotes the fusion weight to compute the overall likelihood value generated based on feature f for class c. By using Equation 3, we can compute the likelihood value for the learning samples

$$\prod_{m=1}^{M} \frac{1}{1 + exp(-y_c \sum_{f=1}^{F} W_f^c\, l_f^c)}, \tag{3}$$

where M is the total number of learning examples. To train the model, we apply the learning algorithm introduced in [10], whose goal is to gain the overall likelihood value maximization.

2.2 Indexing Module

Indexing module contains multiple local indexing structures, one per music class. Each local indexing structures has two major components: music signature generation scheme based deep learning and multidimensional indexing scheme.

2.2.1 *Deep Music Signature Generation*

In EMIF, a deep learning based music signature generation scheme (DMSG) is developed to combine various low level acoustic features extracted from different segments into Deep Music Signature (DMS) - a set of linear vectors. Its physical representation can be $DMS = \{dms_1, dms_2, ..., dms_B\}$, where B is number of blocks in the music. Then, linear similarity functions (e.g., Euclidean distance) can be applied to calculate the similarity between two music documents based on their DMSs. DMSC is deep neural network architecture based on Stacked Denoising Autoencoder (SDA) and principal components analysis (PCA).

- PCA is used to preprocess raw input features from different blocks via linear transformation and speed up learning of SDA.
- SDA is adopted to pretrain neural networks for each block with unlabelled data.

- For each block of input music documents, the parameters of SDA are optimized via stochastic gradient descent.

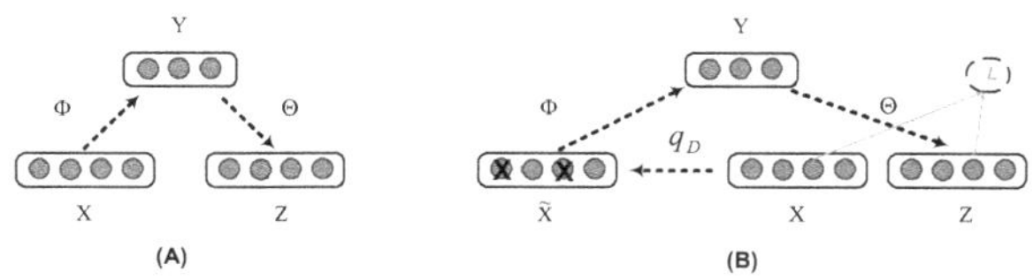

Figure 1: (A) Autoencoder (B) Denoising Autoencoder

Both Denoising Autoencoder (DAE) and Stacked Denoising Autoencoder (SDA) are developed based on Autoencoder (AE). They consists of two key components - encoder and decoder. Encoder transforms an input X into hidden representation y and decoder maps it back to a reconstructed d dimensional vector z. Figure 1 (A) illustrates basic idea of AE. In EMIF, the hidden layer is encoded by a nonlinear one-layer neural network and the mapping can be $Y = \Phi(X)$. The reconstruction from hidden representation Y can be computed using $Z = \Theta(Y)$. Various kinds of distributional assumptions can be applied on the input given the code. Also, different loss functions can be used to measure reconstruction errors on the output side. In EMIF, since we assume the distribution $dist(X|Z)$ is Gaussian, squared error loss can be $L_{sqe}(X, Z) = ||X - Z||^2$. In real world, the reconstruction criterion alone may not be always able to guarantee the generation of effective raw data representation. It might easily lead to the undesirable result - "simply copy the input". Thus, DAE is proposed to avoid this phenomenon by taking different strategy - training neural network locally to denoise noisy versions of initial inputs. The part (B) of Figure 1 visualizes the basic idea of DAE. It is done by firstly constructing X's corrupted version $\widetilde{X}$ via a stochastic mapping $\widetilde{X} - q_D(\widetilde{X}|X)$. q_D is a function to corrupt X and the corrupted input $\widetilde{X}$ is then mapped to a hidden representation $Y = \Phi_1(X)$, where Y is then used to reconstruct the initial version of X by $Z = \Theta(Y)$. The reconstruction error $L(X, Z)$ in stead of $L(\widetilde{X}, Z)$ is minimized in DAE. During the training, each round one training example X is given, a different version of corrupted X is generated based on function q_D.

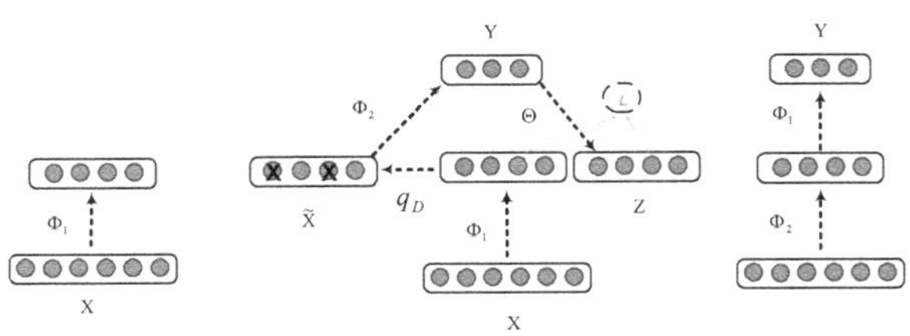

Figure 2: Stacking Denoising Autoencoder

In EMIF, SDA is applied to build deep learning architecture for computing DMS as basic component, one for each music block. We initialize the deep neural network using the same strategy which stacking RBMs in deep belief networks apply. Figure 2 illustrates the procedure to gain multilayer DAE. Firstly, the corrupted input is only used for training each layer at very beginning. This is very important to learn effective features. Right after the mapping function Φ has been learnt successfully, it can be applied to process uncorrupted inputs. Then, to train the neurons in the next layer, corrupted training examples will be used as inputs. After a set of encoders are trained and stacked as SDAs, outputs from top layer will serve as music content representation - DMS and inputs to existing multidimensional indexing structure (e.g., R-Tree or Hybrid Tree) for effective and efficient music search.

2.3 Music Query Processing

EMIF system construction includes two key steps. At the initial step, various kinds of acoustic features are extracted from input music. Then the parameters of the multiple feature based statistical modelling module for each category can be estimated using EM procedure. After classification module is trained, we will construct C indexing structures based on DMSG in conjuncture with indexing method, one per music category. In this study, we apply Hybrid tree due to its efficiency[4].

After system training and configuration, EMIF firstly identifies the category of input music using classification module. Once that class label has been determined, the top k query process can be carried out based on the corresponding local indexing structure.

3. EMPIRICAL STUDY

This section presents an experimental study to evaluate the proposed method and its competitive schemes. The dataset (Dataset I) used for the empirical study contains 5000 music items covering ten genres with 500 songs each genre. This dataset is very similar to the test collection used in [8, 14]. The test query we consider is to find music that has similar genre from database constructed using Dataset I. We compare EMIF with three different approaches including CM*F+Hybrid Tree (CM*F+HT), DWCH+Hybrid tree (DWCH+HT) and MARSYAS+Hybrid tree (MARS+HT). Our results demonstrate the superiority of EMIF over different approaches, including improvements on retrieval accuracy and efficiency in terms of the query response time.

3.1 Effectiveness Comparison

In the first experiment, we report a comparative study on the retrieval effectiveness of the CM*F+HT, DWCH+HT, MARS+HT, and EMIF. Tables 1 illustrates the query precision in terms of two different measurements: P@10 and MAP. Specifically, in each test, we randomly select query examples from the database and there is no overlap between query sets and training sets. It can be clearly seen that EMIF achieves significant improvement on query accuracies for all cases. In particular, the EMIF method improves the query effectiveness, on average, 10.2% for P@10 and by 12.2% for MAP. These results indicate that EMIF, whose structure integrates classification scheme and multiple indexing structures into single framework, is more effective than other approaches for CBMR task. This superior effectiveness is due to the multiple layer structure combining classification model and a Logistic regression based likelihood score fusion scheme. Furthermore, the indexing structure supporting query process on the music from individual category lead to a much smaller searching space and faster retrieval.

Query Methods	Query Accuracy	
	P@10	MAP
EMIF	0.617	0.511
CM*F+HT	0.438	0.385
DWCH+HT	0.372	0.302
MARS+HT	0.297	0.275

Table 1: Query accuracy comparison of EMIF and other approaches for music retrieval

Size of Result Set	Query Response Time(Sec)			
	EMIF	CM*F+HT	DWCH+HT	MARS+HT
5	**0.065**	0.073	0.086	0.095
10	**0.089**	0.109	0.172	0.209
15	**0.097**	0.205	0.259	0.287
20	**0.132**	0.258	0.332	0.385

Table 2: Query response time comparison of EMIF and other approaches

3.2 Efficiency Comparison

Query response time is another important aspect for system performance evaluation, especially when scale of the music dataset becomes large. Comparing to traditional indexing structure, although the statistical concept model in EMIF lifts the accuracy significantly, they might introduce query cost overhead. Thus, the second set of experiments evaluate and compare query efficiency of the EMIF and other competitors. The test was run with 1000 query examples randomly selected from the music dataset. Table 2 shows the query response time of different methods with various size of the result sets. From the experimental results summarised in the table, we can see that EMIF achieves great saving in terms of query speed against the other approaches for all sizes of result sets. MARS+HT performs worst among six different approaches tests. EMIF achieves the fastest response time and compared to other approaches, performance gain is very significant. We believe that the main reason behind efficiency enhancement is EMIF's layered structure facilitating retrieval processing based on index structure built for single music class. It suggests a more compact searching space (smaller indexing structure). Consequently we can observe significant reduction in query response time.

4. CONCLUSION

In this research, we propose and evaluate an intelligent indexing framework called EMIF based on the "classify-and-indexing" design principle. To achieve accurate music classification, an independent LDMM-based profiling model for individual music category is constructed using multiple features to generate likelihood score. Moreover, EMIF's layered architecture enables more compact indexing structure for each music category and consequently achieve a significant reduction on query execution time. To validate our approach, a series of comprehensive experimental studies have been carried out over large scale test collection and the results reveal the various advantages of EMIF over the existing state-of-the-art indexing methods.

Acknowledgement

Jialie Shen is supported by Microsoft Research Asia Grant (FY14-RES-OPP-048) - "My Mobile Music: Towards Cloud based Intelligent Music Recommendation on the Move".

5. REFERENCES

[1] N. L. A. Dempster and D. Rubin. Maximum likelihood from incomplete data via the em algorithm. *Journal of the Royal Statistical Society, Series B*, 39(1), 1977.

[2] C. M. Bishop. *Neural Network for Pattern Recognition.* Oxford University Press, 2000.

[3] C. Böhm, S. Berchtold, and D. A. Keim. Searching in high-dimensional spaces: Index structures for improving the performance of multimedia databases. *ACM Computing Surveys*, 33(3), 2001.

[4] K. Chakrabarti and S. Mehrotra. The hybrid tree: An index structure for high dimensional feature spaces. In *Proc. of ICDE Conference (ICDE'99)*, 1999.

[5] R. O. Duda, P. E. Hart, and D. G. Stork. *Pattern Classification.* John Wiley & Sons, 2000.

[6] T. Hastie, R. Tibshirani, and J. Friedman. *The Elements of Statistical Learning: Data Mining, Inference, and Prediction.* Springer Verlag, 2001.

[7] M. I. Jordan. Why the logistic function? a tutorial discussion on probabilities and neural networks. Technical Report 9503, Massachusetts Institute of Technology, 1995.

[8] T. Li, M. Ogihara, and Q. Li. A comparative study on content-based music genre classification. In *Proc. of ACM SIGIR Conference (SIGIR'03)*, 2003.

[9] F. Pachet. Content management for electronic music distribution. *Communications of the ACM*, 46(4), 2003.

[10] J. Shen, J. Shepherd, B. Cui, and K. Tan. A novel framework for efficient automated singer identification in large music databases. *ACM Trans. Inf. Syst.*, 27(3), 2009.

[11] J. Shen, J. Shepherd, and A. Ngu. Towards effective content-based music retrieval with multiple acoustic feature combination. *IEEE Transactions on Multimedia*, 8(6), 2006.

[12] J. Shen, D. Tao, and X. Li. Quc-tree: Integrating query context information for efficient music retrieval. *IEEE Transactions on Multimedia*, 11(2):313–323, 2009.

[13] T. Tolonen and M. Karjalainen. A computationally efficient multipitch analysis model. *IEEE Transactions on Speech and Audio Processing*, 8(6):708–716, November 2000.

[14] G. Tzanetakis and P. R. Cook. Musical genre classification of audio signals. *IEEE Transactions on Speech and Audio Processing*, 10(5), 2002.

[15] G. Xia, T. Huang, Y. Ma, R. Dannenberg, and C. Faloutsos. Midifind: Similarity search and popularity mining in large midi databases. In M. Aramaki, O. Derrien, R. Kronland-Martinet, and S. Ystad, editors, *Sound, Music, and Motion*, volume 8905 of *Lecture Notes in Computer Science*, pages 259–276. Springer International Publishing, 2014.

[16] C. Yang. Efficient acoustic index for music retrieval with various degrees of similarity. In *ACM MM*, 2002.

[17] Y. Yu, M. Crucianu, V. Oria, and E. Damiani. Combining multi-probe histogram and order-statistics based lsh for scalable audio content retrieval. In *ACM MM*, 2010.

Specific Person Retrieval via Incomplete Text Description

Mang Ye[1,2], Chao Liang[1,2,*], Zheng Wang[1,2], Qingming Leng[3], Jun Chen[1,2], Jun Liu[1,2]

[1]National Engineering Research Center for Multimedia Software,
School of Computer, Wuhan University, Wuhan, 430072, China
{yemang,cliang,wangzwhu,chenj,jliu_newbee}@whu.edu.cn
[2]Research Institute of Wuhan University in Shenzhen, China
[3]School of Information Science & Technology, Jiujiang University, China
lengqingming@126.com

ABSTRACT

Searching for specific persons from surveillance videos captured by different cameras, is a key yet under-addressed challenge in multimedia system. Related person retrieval works mainly focus on searching person by visual appearance, known as person re-identification. However, the initial visual image may not be available in some practical applications. For example, the criminal is described by a text description indirectly, "*A young woman wearing a red casual with a backpack*", the traditional methods can not conquer this issue. Based on a set of pre-defined attributes that the text description query can be transformed to an attribute vector, thus can be used to retrieval in the gallery set. And yet, the user-provided attributes are sometimes incomplete. This new issue is defined as Specific Person Retrieval via Incomplete Text Description. In this paper, we conduct a specific attribute completion to enrich the original text query and generate a more expressive attribute vector. Then, a pairwise-based metric learning is introduced for completed attribute vectors. Extensive experiments conducted on two benchmark datasets have shown our superior performance.

Categories and Subject Descriptors

J.m [**Computer Applications**]: Miscellaneous;
H.3.3 [**Information Systems**]: INFORMATION STORAGE AND RETRIEVAL— *Retrieval models*

General Terms

Theory

Keywords

Person Retrieval, Attribute, Attribute Completion

1. INTRODUCTION

Specific person retrieval for video surveillance attracts a lot of attention in multimedia retrieval system [4]. Most of the existing approaches exploit person's visual appearance (single or multiple images of the query person) to search across different non-overlapping cameras, known as person re-identification [7,16,17]. However, in some practical surveillance application, merely text descriptions rather than visual appearances are available. For example, the witness told the police that the appearance of the criminal by oral text description, "*A young woman wearing a red casual with a backpack*", as shown in Fig. 1. Traditional person re-identification methods can't handle this issue, where the visual appearance of the query person is not obtainable. We named this novel issue as *specific person retrieval via text description*.

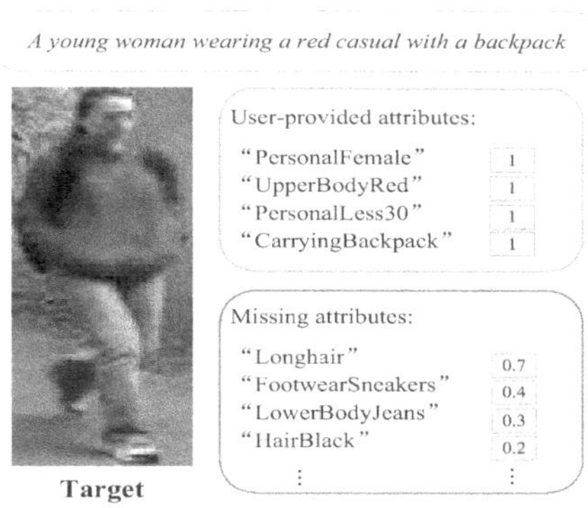

Figure 1: An illustration example of user-provided attributes. It can be seen that the user-provided attributes are incomplete. The attributes are derived from [3]. And the missing attributes are partly completed, where the value of each attribute denotes the owning probability..

In this condition, it is critical to solve this specific person retrieval problem merely by given specific attributes, which can be abstracted from the oral text description [10]. Related person re-identification have addressed some attribute-based methods. Layne *et al.* [8] learned a selection and weighting of mid-level semantic attributes to describe people. Liu *et al.* [10] propose a novel Attribute Restricted Latent Topic Model (ARLTM) to encode targets into semantic topics. Nguyen *et al.* [1] proposed an approach to exploit relationships between attributes for refining attribute detection results. Nevertheless, the above approaches are not proper for current issue for the reason that their attributes are originated from the person appearance, where the probe image is unavailable.

*indicates corresponding author

ICMR'15, June 23–26, 2015, Shanghai, China.

http://dx.doi.org/10.1145/2671188.2749347.

Furthermore, the user-provided attributes are usually incomplete, as revealed in [15]. Specially, 61 attributes are pre-defined for person description in [3], while the user-provided text description can not cover all the pre-defined attributes, as illustrated in Fig.1. The incompleteness of user-provided attributes probably leads to performance degradations for person retrieval [10]. In a wider range level, attribute completion is widely conducted in traditional TBIR (tag-based image retrieval) [2,15]. Motivated by [9], we conduct a linear sparse reconstruction to complete the incomplete attributes. Specially, the original user-provided attribute vector is reconstructed with the training ones under constrains of sparsity. To better measuring the attribute vector similarity, a pairwise-based metric learning framework is firstly conducted for attributes.

In this paper, we present a novel method to solve the above new problem, *i.e.* person retrieval via incomplete text description in surveillance camera network. It can be divided into two procedures: off-line and on-line processing. For the off-line processing, several attribute classifiers are trained to detect the attributes of the gallery images and a distance metric based on attribute vectors is learned for the distance measure. For the on-line processing, a linear sparse reconstruction is conducted to complete the user-provided attributes. And then, the learnt distance metric is adopted for the completed attribute vectors.

The main contribution of this paper can be summarized as follows:

- A new issue which is very important for practical surveillance application is addressed, while the specific person retrieval via incomplete text description in camera network is seldom investigated.
- A linear sparse reconstruction [9] is introduced for incomplete user-provided attributes while the attribute incompleteness is seldom investigated in person retrieval. Metric learning is firstly conducted for attribute distance measure, while metric learning is usually utilized for visual descriptions.
- Extensive experiments conducted on two representative datasets, the VIPeR [5] and PRID2011 [6], have shown our superior performance.

2. THE APPROACH

The framework of our approach is shown in Fig.2. It can be divided into two main parts: *Off-line Processing* and *On-line Processing*. While the off-line processing mainly focus on training attribute classifiers and training distance metric, and the on-line processing introduces a linear sparse reconstruction to complete the original attribute vector, and then distance measure is conducted with the learned metric M to rank the results. The detail is discussed in the following.

2.1 Off-line Processing

The off-line processing pre-computes non-query images visual feature vectors and attribute vectors in order for the run-time query specific operations to be fast. Furthermore, to better computing their similarity, a pairwise-based metric learning framework is introduced to learn a distance metric.

Attribute SVM Training. A linear SVM is adopted to train the attributes classifiers for the reason that it is both fast to train and fast to test. The training data consists of the visual feature vectors extracted on the the training images, together with the pre-labeled attributes contributed by [3]. For each kind of attribute, a linear classifier is

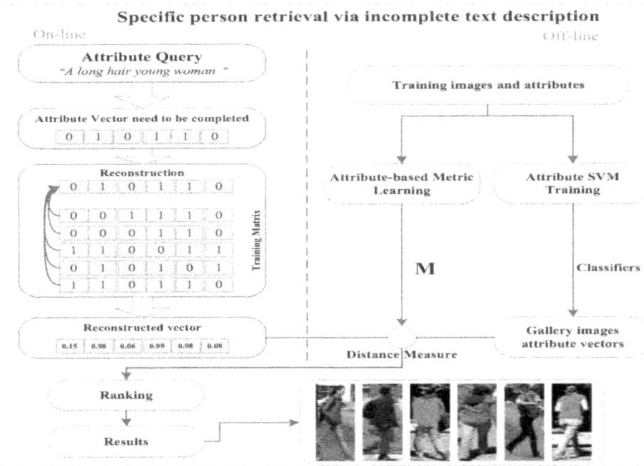

Figure 2: The framework of our retrieval system.

trained. We treat the ones contain the attribute as positive samples while the others as negative. The classifier is trained using the software package Vlfeat[1], which is optimized for linear classifiers and has complexity linear in the number of training samples. And the experiments have shown the superior classifying performance comparing with results reported in other papers.

Gallery image attribute vectors. Based on the training classifiers, attribute vectors can be extracted for the gallery images. Note that the output value of the classifiers for each attribute is from minus infinity to plus infinity. But for better distance measure, we transform the original value to (0,1) by a logistic function as shown in

$$a = \frac{1}{1+e^{-a_0}} \tag{1}$$

where the a_0 denotes the original output of the classifier, a is the transformed value that indicates the probability of owing this attribute. Specially, x is more closer to 1 indicates that it will more probably to own this attribute. "$a = 0$" expresses that the image do not have this attribute.

Attribute-based metric learning. For better measuring the attribute vector similarity, metric learning is conducted. Given a pair of samples x_i and x_j (x_i , $x_j \in R_d$), the Mahalanobis distance between them is:

$$d_M^2(x_i, x_j) = (x_i - x_j)^T M (x_i - x_j) \tag{2}$$

where $M \geq 0$ is a positive semi-definite matrix. Based on a statistical inference point of view, KISSME defines the Mahalanobis distance matrix M by

$$M = \Sigma_{y_{ij}=1}^{-1} - \Sigma_{y_{ij}=0}^{-1} \tag{3}$$

where

$$\Sigma_{y_{ij}=1} = \sum_{y_{ij}=1} (x_i - x_j)(x_i - x_j)^T \tag{4}$$

$$\Sigma_{y_{ij}=0} = \sum_{y_{ij}=0} (x_i - x_j)(x_i - x_j)^T \tag{5}$$

denote the covariance matrices for similar pairs $y_{ij} = 1$ and dissimilar pairs $y_{ij} = 0$ respectively. Then, M can be learned easily from the training samples. More details can be found in KISSME [7]. The learned matrix M is used for computing the distance between the attribute vectors.

[1]It is available in http://www.vlfeat.org/

2.2 On-line Processing

The on-line processing firstly formulate an original attribute vector by the text description, and then a linear sparse reconstruction is introduced to construct a completed vector. After that, with the per-trained distance matrix M in Section 2.1, the reconstructed attribute vector is adopted to query in the original gallery image set. And then, the final ranking results are achieved.

Attribute vector need to be completed. According to the user-provided text query, we formulate an original attribute vector $t_{1\times n}$, where n denotes the number of pre-defined attributes. Specially, the ones user provided is labeled as 1, the unlabeled ones is 0.

Reconstruction. Given a to-be-reconstructed vector $t_{1\times n}$, and the training attribute matrix $\widehat{T}_{m\times n}$, where m is the number of training images. Linear sparse reconstruction aims to reconstructing an attribute vector with the other images' attribute vectors $\widehat{T}$. Furthermore, based on the observation that images associated with an identical attribute tends to share more common semantic content and thus form a group [12]. For example, *"hair-long"* are more likely to be a *"female"*, we name it as *occurrence*. Moreover, another observation about *exclusiveness* is considered, for instance, *"male"* and *"female"*, which illustrates that the two attributes are unlikely to appeared at the same time. Therefore, a group sparse structure is introduced for the reconstruction weight. Here, we denote the reconstruction weighting vector as w, the ith group of reconstruction weight is defined as $g_i = \{w_{(i,1)}, w_{(i,2)}, \cdots, w_{(i,|g_i|)}\}$, where (i,j) is the index of the jth weight of the ith group in the weighting vector w. As can be seen that each attribute corresponds to a group of reconstruction weights, *i.e.*, the weights of images containing this attribute. Specially, higher weights for the *occurrence* and lower weights for *exclusiveness*. Since the images would be labeled with several attributes and thus the groups may be overlapped. And the reconstruction problem is formulated as:

$$J(w) = \min_{w} \left\| W(t - \widehat{T}w) \right\|_2^2 + \lambda \sum_{i=1}^{n} \|g_i\|_2 \qquad (6)$$

where $t_{1\times n}$ is the user-provided attribute vector, $\widehat{T}_{m\times n}$ is the dictionary matrix containing attribute vectors of the training images, $w_{m\times 1}$ is the objective reconstructing weighting vector, λ is a tuning factor for balancing the group sparsity. Specially, the group sparsity $\Sigma_{i=1}^{n}\|g_i\|_2$ is the combination of both $L1$ and $L2$ norms [12]. The $L1$ norm is used for emphasizing inter-group sparsity since only a few tags are associated with the target query image (*i.e.* inter-group sparsity). As for the reason that images in the same group are all supposed to contribute to the reconstruction if the corresponding attribute would be associated (*i.e.* intra-group smoothing), the $L2$ norm is adopted for the smoothing intra-group weights. Additionally, it is reasonable that the labelled attributes (*i.e.* non-zero entries) should be assigned higher weights. Therefore, a diagonal matrix for weighting the reconstruction residual of each entry in t is introduced, defined as $W_{i,i} = exp(t_i)$. It can be seen that the unlabelled ones (*i.e.* zero entries) are assigned with lower values.

With the linear sparse reconstruction, an optimal weighting vector w is obtained. Then the reconstructed vector $\widehat{t}$ is achieved by $\widehat{t} = \widehat{T}w$. Specifically, in our experiments the maximal value of $\widehat{t}$ is normalized as 1.

Table 1: Attribute detection accuracy on VIPeR.

Attributes	[8]	[3]	Ours	Attributes	[8]	[3]	Ours
shorts	0.74	0.56	**0.89**	male	0.68	**0.81**	0.66
jeans	0.73	**0.76**	0.73	backpack	0.52	0.67	**0.68**
vnecks	0.53	0.51	**0.81**	logo	0.58	0.51	**0.84**
sunglasses	0.60	0.52	**0.70**	stripes	0.47	0.52	**0.87**
longhair	0.55	**0.73**	0.63	skirt	0.76	0.64	**0.92**
sandals	0.58	0.50	**0.82**	**Average**	0.59	0.71	**0.76**

Ranking. By the reconstructed vector $\widehat{t}$ and the pre-processed gallery images attribute vectors, together with the learned distance matrix M, the distances between the query and the gallery images are obtained. According to the computed distances, the retrieval results are ranked.

3. EXPERIMENTS

3.1 Datasets and evaluation protocol

Datasets. Two publicly representative datasets, the VIPeR dataset [5] and the PRID2011 [6] dataset are adopted to verify our approach. We chose these datasets as they provide many challenges faced in practical surveillance, *i.e.*, viewpoint, pose and illumination changes, different backgrounds, occlusions, etc. The VIPeR dataset contains 632 persons , each of which has two images with drastic appearance difference between most of the matched image pairs, and the images are normalized to 128×48 pixels. PRID dataset is a challenge dataset for person re-identification with more camera characteristics variation than VIPeR. Particularly, 400 shots of the first 200 person from each view of the single-shot version are adopted to carry out the experiments. The images are scaled to 128×64 pixels.

Features. The visual features are extracted for training the SVM classifiers and generate the attribute vector of the gallery images. Similar to [5], a combination feature descriptor consisting of color and texture features is conducted. Specifically, for each image, the RGB and HSV color histograms and LBP descriptor are extracted from overlapping blocks of size 16×16 and stride of 8×8.

Attributes. The attributes we adopted are derived from [3], *i.e.* PETA dataset. The dataset contains 61 kinds of attributes. Since some of the attributes are rarely appeared, we delete some of the attributes as done in [3], with only 35 pre-defined attributes are remained, such as *"personalFemale"*, *"personLess30"*, *"carryingbackpack"*.

Evaluation protocol. For each dataset, we select half for training, while the retrieval performance is reported on the held out test portion. Firstly, we evaluate the performance of SVM classifiers based on the attribute detection accuracy. Moreover, we evaluate the retreival performance with the averaged cumulative match characteristic (CMC) curve [14] over 10 trials. Specially, we randomly select $5-8$ attributes of each query as the original text query. As recommended in [9], the tuning factor λ is set as $\lambda = 2$.

3.2 Attributes Detection

The attribute detection performance is reported with accuracy, some results on VIPeR dataset are shown in Table 1. With the SVM package based on [13], the average detection accuracy is about 76%, and more than a half attribute

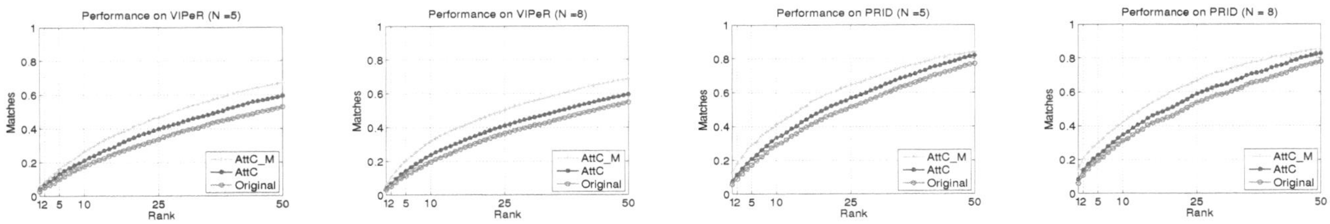

(a) On VIPeR (N = 5) (b) On VIPeR (N = 8) (c) On PRID2011 (N = 5) (d) On PRID2011 (N = 8)

Figure 3: Retrieval results on VIPeR and PRID2011 dataset. N denotes the number of attributes of the original query. While "*Original* " is the original retrieval result. "*AttC* " indicates the attribute completion result and "*AttC_M* " represent the metric learning result after the attribute completion, respectively.

Table 2: Comparable results on VIPeR dataset.

Method	rank@1	5	10	25	50
W.AIR [8]	4.84	17.44	29.24	**50.60**	68.64
MLA [11]	5.06	19.24	29.06	48.06	68.00
AttRel [1]	*	12.51	23.34	40.70	*
AttC(N=8)	3.91	12.76	23.61	41.13	59.49
AttC_M(N=8)	**5.77**	**20.13**	**31.84**	50.29	**68.72**

detectors can achieve an accuracy above 70%, which is a little higher than the results reported in [1, 3, 8]. The attribute detection accuracy is on PRID2011 dataset is about 73%, while most of the attribute classifiers can achieve an accuracy over 65%.

3.3 Retrieval performance

The retrieval results are reported with CMC curves. Specially, to evaluate the attribute completion performance, we randomly select N attributes for each text query. The results are shown in Fig.3 and several conclusions can be drawn as follows. (1) Attribute completion is effective. The retrieval results are significantly improved with the attribute completion. Specially, the average improvement at rank@10 is about 17.2% and 15.7% for rank@25, respectively. (2) Metric learning for attribute vectors are still satisfying. While the metric learning is usually adopted for visual features and seldom conducted for attribute distance measure. As illustrated in our experiments shown in the figures, the improvements are noteworthy. (3) Query with more attributes is better. Based on the comparison that the retrieval results of $N = 8$ are better than $N = 5$, thus can be seen that with more attributes provided, the results is better.

Furthermore, the results compare favorably with the related attribute-based person re-identification works as shown in Table.2. Note that the related works are conducted based on the visual information of the query person while it is unused in our experiments.

Acknowledgement. The research was supported by National Nature Science Foundation of China (61303114, 61231015, 61170023), the Specialized Research Fund for the Doctoral Program of Higher Education (20130141120024), the Technology Research Project of Ministry of Public Security (2014JSYJA016), the China Postdoctoral Science Foundation funded project (2013M530350), the major Science and Technology Innovation Plan of Hubei Province (2013AAA020), the Key Technology R&D Program of Wuhan (2013030409020109), the Guangdong-Hongkong Key Domain Breakthrough Project of China (2012A090200007), and the Special Project on the Integration of Industry, Education and Research of Guangdong Province (2011B090400601).Nature Science Foundation of Hubei Province (2014CFB712).

4. CONCLUSION

In this paper, a new issue for specific person retrieval task in camera network is addressed. And a general framework to solve this issue is proposed. The original text query is transformed to an incomplete attribute vector and completed by a linear sparse reconstruction, and then a pairwise-based metric learning is adopted to refine the results. Extensive experiments show the superiority of our proposed approach. In the future work, better combination of visual information and attributes needs to be further investigated.

5. REFERENCES

[1] N. N. B, N. V. H, D. T. N, and et al. Attrel: An approach to person re-identification by exploiting attribute relationships. In *Multimedia Modeling (MMM)*, 2015.

[2] X. Cao, H. Zhang, X. Guo, S. Liu, and X. Chen. Image retrieval and ranking via consistently reconstructing multi-attribute queries. In *ECCV*, 2014.

[3] Y. Deng, P. Luo, C. C. Loy, and X. Tang. Pedestrian attribute recognition at far distance. In *ACM MM*, 2014.

[4] N. Gheissari, T. B. Sebastian, and R. Hartley. Person reidentification using spatiotemporal appearance. In *CVPR*, 2006.

[5] D. Gray, S. Brennan, and H. Tao. Evaluating appearance models for recognition, reacquisition, and tracking. In *PETS workshop*, 2007.

[6] M. Hirzer, C. Beleznai, P. M. Roth, and H. Bischof. Person re-identification by descriptive and discriminative classification. In *Image Analysis*. 2011.

[7] M. Kostinger, M. Hirzer, P. Wohlhart, and et al. Large scale metric learning from equivalence constraints. In *CVPR*, 2012.

[8] R. Layne, T. M. Hospedales, S. Gong, and Q. Mary. Person re-identification by attributes. In *BMVC*, 2012.

[9] Z. Lin, G. Ding, M. Hu, J. Wang, and et al. Image tag completion via image-specific and tag-specific linear sparse reconstructions. In *CVPR*, 2013.

[10] X. Liu, M. Song, Q. Zhao, D. Tao, and et al. Attribute-restricted latent topic model for person re-identification. In *PR*, 2012.

[11] L. R, H. T. M, and G. S. Towards person identification and re-identification with attributes. In *ECCV workshop*, 2012.

[12] Z. S, H. J, H. Y, and et al. Automatic image annotation using group sparsity. In *CVPR*, 2010.

[13] S. Shalev-Shwartz and T. Zhang. Stochastic dual coordinate ascent methods for regularized loss. In *JMLR*, 2013.

[14] X. Wang, G. Doretto, T. Sebastian, J. Rittscher, and P. Tu. Shape and appearance context modeling. In *ICCV*, 2007.

[15] L. Wu, R. Jin, and A. Jain. Tag completion for image retrieval. In *PAMI*, 2013.

[16] M. Ye, J. Chen, Q. Leng, and et al. Copuled-view based ranking optimization for person re-identification. In *Multimedia Modeling (MMM)*, 2015.

[17] R. Zhao, W. Ouyang, and X. Wang. Unsupervised salience learning for person re-identification. In *CVPR*, 2013.

Combining Generic and Specific Information for Cross-modal Retrieval

Thi Quynh Nhi Tran
CEA-LIST,
Vision & Content Engineering Laboratory
Gif-sur-Yvette, France
thiquynhnhi.tran@cea.fr

Hervé Le Borgne
CEA-LIST,
Vision & Content Engineering Laboratory
Gif-sur-Yvette, France
herve.le-borgne@cea.fr

Michel Crucianu
CEDRIC-CNAM
Paris, France
michel.crucianu@cnam.fr

ABSTRACT

Cross-modal retrieval increasingly relies on joint statistical models built from large amounts of data represented according to several modalities. However, some information that is poorly represented by these models can be very significant for a retrieval task. We show that, by appropriately identifying and taking such information into account, the results of cross-modal retrieval can be strongly improved. We apply our model to three benchmarks for the text illustration task and find that the more data has misrepresented information, the more our model is comparatively effective.

Categories and Subject Descriptors

H.3.3 [**Information Storage and Retrieval**]: Information Search and Retrieval—*Retrieval Models*

General Terms

Algorithms, Experimentation

Keywords

Cross-modal retrieval; text illustration; canonical correlation analysis

1. INTRODUCTION

This paper focuses on cross-modal retrieval, where queries from one (or several) modalities can be matched to entries from one (or several) others. Recent work addressed this issue by attempting to develop models where all the involved modalities are mapped to a latent space that can be directly employed in several retrieval scenarios including text illustration or image annotation. Canonical correlation analysis (CCA), introduced by [6], allows to find such a latent space and was successfully employed or extended in many recent proposals. Let us consider a sample, e.g. a set of images, represented by two sets of variables (or two "views"), e.g. the visual features and the associated keywords. CCA will find linear combinations of variables from each set that are maximally correlated to each other. These linear combinations form a latent space where data issued from any of the two sets of variables (views) can be represented.

CCA was first applied to cross-modal retrieval in [5], where a kernel extension (Kernel CCA, KCCA) was also introduced in order to allow for more general, nonlinear latent spaces. Since not all the words (or tags) annotating an image have equal importance, [7] proposed a method taking advantage of their importance when building the KCCA representation. The importance of words for an image is obtained from the order of words in the annotations provided by users for that image. Gong et al. [4] put forward a multi-view (K)CCA method: a third view, explicitly representing image's high-level semantics, is taken into account when searching for the latent space. This "semantic" view corresponds to ground-truth labels, search keywords or semantic topics obtained by clustering tags. In [1], Costa Pereira et al. proposed semantic correlation matching (SCM), where the mappings of images and text by CCA are transformed into semantic vectors produced by supervised classifiers with respect to predefined semantic classes. As an alternative to CCA-based approaches to cross-modal retrieval, [8] introduced a regularized manifold alignment method. Recently, a deep architecture combining representation learning and correlation learning supporting cross-modal retrieval was proposed in [2].

The development of a latent joint representation for two or more views relies on extracting statistical regularities from a preferably large amount of data. Any piece of data having very few occurrences in the training set or very weak relations with other data is ignored in the resulting joint model. However, in a *retrieval* context, pieces of data that are rare in the training set or even new in the test set, such as names or trademarks, can be very significant in selecting the relevant results. It is then necessary to extend the retrieval framework beyond the joint model in order to be able to include "non regular but likely to be relevant" information. One should be able to identify such information (distinguish it from noise) and find ways to combine it with the evidence provided by the joint model. We consider these issues in the specific application context of text illustration tasks.

The proposed approach is described in Section 2. Section 3 presents the experimental results, followed by a discussion. One of the experiments considers domain transfer,

ICMR'15, June 23–26, 2015, Shanghai, China.

http://dx.doi.org/10.1145/2671188.2749348 .

emphasizing the need to make use of information that may be absent from the training data.

2. PROPOSED APPROACH

2.1 Canonical Correlation Analysis

For data simultaneously represented in two different vector spaces, CCA [6, 5] finds maximally correlated linear subspaces of the initial spaces. Consider two random variables, X and Y, taking values in $\mathbb{R}^{d_X}$ and respectively $\mathbb{R}^{d_Y}$. Consider n samples $\{(x_i, y_i)\}_{i=1}^{n} \subset \mathbb{R}^{d_X} \times \mathbb{R}^{d_Y}$. CCA simultaneously seeks directions $w_x \in \mathbb{R}^{d_X}$ and $w_y \in \mathbb{R}^{d_Y}$ that maximize the correlation between the projections of x onto w_x and y onto w_y,

$$w_x^*, w_y^* = \underset{w_x, w_y}{argmax} \frac{{w_x}^T C_{XY} w_y}{\sqrt{{w_x}^T C_{XX} w_x {w_y}^T C_{YY} w_y}} \quad (1)$$

where C_{XX}, C_{YY} denote the autocovariance matrices of X and Y respectively, while C_{XY} is the cross-covariance matrix. The solutions w_x^* and w_y^* are eigenvectors of $C_{XX}^{-1} C_{XY} C_{YY}^{-1} C_{YX}$ and respectively $C_{YY}^{-1} C_{YX} C_{XX}^{-1} C_{XY}$. The eigenvectors corresponding to the d largest eigenvalues yield basis $W_x = [w_x^1, w_x^2, .., w_x^d]$ in $\mathbb{R}^{d \times d_X}$ and $W_y = [w_y^1, w_y^2, .., w_y^d]$ in $\mathbb{R}^{d \times d_Y}$ that define projections onto the desired "common" space.

2.2 Specific information and cross-modal retrieval

Consider a reference base of multi-modal documents $\{(x_j, y_j)\}_{j=1}^{p}$ that is *a priori* different from the learning base used to compute the CCA model. Cross-modal retrieval essentially consists in estimating the similarity between a query q and all the documents of this reference database. The query can be represented by one modality only (x_q or y_q). In CCA-based cross-modal retrieval, the similarity is computed after projection onto the "common" subspace.

Let us now investigate the consequence of poorly represented data is such a scheme. For instance, consider that the modality $Y = (V, S)$ is a textual feature vector that is composed of subspace V of the vocabulary well represented by the training data and a subspace S of *specific* vocabulary that is *infrequent* in training data, thus poorly represented by the CCA model. Since data in S is infrequent, we assume the cross-covariance matrix is null ($C_{VS} = C_{XS} \approx 0$) and the autocovariance of S is the identity ($C_{SS} = I_S$). With such approximations, the projection matrix becomes

$$W_y = \begin{bmatrix} W_v & 0 \\ 0 & I_s \end{bmatrix} \quad (2)$$

where W_v is the projection matrix obtained by CCA on (X, V) and I_S the identity matrix on S. Hence, the retrieval process within the CCA subspace relies on the (cosine) similarity between a query $y_q = \binom{v_q}{s_q}$ and a document described by $y_d = \binom{v_d}{s_d}$:

$$\underset{CCA(X,Y)}{Sim}(y_q, y_d) = \frac{< W_y^T y_q, W_y^T y_d >}{||W_y^T y_q|| \, ||W_y^T y_d||} = \frac{y_q^T W_y W_y^T y_d}{||W_y^T y_q|| \, ||W_y^T y_d||} \quad (3)$$

Combining (2) and (3) results into:

$$\underset{CCA(X,Y)}{Sim}(y_q, y_d) = \underset{CCA(X,V)}{Sim}(v_q, v_d) + \frac{s_q^T \cdot s_d}{||W_v^T v_q|| \, ||W_v^T v_d||} \quad (4)$$

On the right hand side, the first term is the similarity according to a CCA model computed on well-represented data. In the second term, the impact of S data is biased by the CCA-based denominator. To fix this, we propose to remove the CCA-based weighting from the second term and use a boolean model for this specific information. In other words, we keep only $s_q^T \cdot s_d$ with s_i a binary vector. So the second term simply reflects the number of common specific dimensions (corresponding to infrequent words). However, with such a model, when two documents share the same number of specific dimensions ($s_q^T \cdot s_{d1} = s_q^T \cdot s_{d2}$) their relative similarity to the query only depends on the first term (CCA similarity), that may be inaccurate in this case since the documents have specific dimensions. Hence, we propose to weight the second term by a better adapted measure of similarity, given by the well-known TF-IDF model. Finally, the model we propose (denoted by CCA*) can be written:

$$\underset{CCA^*}{Sim}(y_q, y_d) = \underset{CCA(X,V)}{Sim}(v_q, v_d) + s_q^T \cdot s_d \cdot \underset{TF-IDF}{Sim}(v_q, v_d) \quad (5)$$

When $y = \binom{v}{s}$ does not contain any specific dimension ($s = 0$) our model is equivalent to the classic CCA-based retrieval model. On the contrary, when $s \neq 0$ the second term may become dominant in the similarity estimation. Note that our model supports cross-modal retrieval since the similarity in the CCA space can be estimated from the projection of any feature (x or y). For instance:

$$\underset{CCA^*}{Sim}(y_q, x_d) = \underset{CCA(X,V)}{Sim}(v_q, x_d) + s_q^T \cdot s_d \cdot \underset{TF-IDF}{Sim}(v_q, v_d) \quad (6)$$

3. EXPERIMENTAL EVALUATION

The proposed method for automatic text illustration is evaluated on the BBC News dataset [3] and on a larger Wikipedia collection. We start by comparing our method with several baselines on the BBC News illustration task. Then, we specifically study the impact of information that is absent from the training data by considering a *domain transfer* context: training is performed on an independent dataset and testing on the BBC news dataset. We end up by a comparison on the Wikipedia collection, where the proposed method makes use of a large amount of specific information in comparison with the first two experiments.

3.1 Experimental Setting

BBC News dataset was introduced in [3] for image annotation and text illustration. It consists of 3121 articles for training and 240 for testing, downloaded from the BBC News website. Each article is accompanied by an image and associated caption. This dataset is especially challenging for text illustration because of its small size and the quite indirect relation between textual and visual content in most news articles. For many articles, other images in the collection can be objectively considered more relevant to the article's content than the image selected by the author.

Wikipedia 2010. We use the set of 106,822 articles in English from the ImageCLEF2010 Wikipedia dataset[1]. Each article is accompanied by an image and associated caption. We take 106,582 samples for training and 240 for testing to be consistent with the former benchmark.

Evaluation method. We employ the evaluation methodology based on top-1 accuracy proposed in [3]. For a query

[1]http://imageclef.org/2010/wiki

article, the system is expected to rank first the image that was selected by the author of the article. The reported accuracy is thus the percentage of successfully matched image-article pairs in the test set. We discuss the strictness of this evaluation in Section 3.5.

Content representation. To represent visual content we use OverFeat [9], widely known to provide powerful features for several classification tasks. More precisely, we employ 3072-dimensional vectors which are the layer-18 outputs at the stage 6 of the fast OverFeat network and further L2-normalize them. To represent texts, we construct the dictionary by removing stop words, stemming the remaining words and filtering the stems by their frequency. The BBC News vocabulary $\mathcal{V}_{bbc}$ has 23,617 words that are either stems appearing at least twice in the training set or proper nouns from this set. The Wikipedia vocabulary $\mathcal{V}_{wp}$ has 19,653 words, each appearing at least 5 and at most 1500 times. Texts have a TF-IDF representation, L2-normalized.

Baselines. The proposed method is compared with three text illustration methods presented in [3]. The first two baselines disregard visual content. *Overlap* selects the image whose caption has the largest number of words in common with the test document. In *Vector Space Model (VSM)*, articles and captions are represented by TF-IDF vectors and the cosine similarity measure is used to find the image whose caption is most similar to the test article. A vocabulary of about 6,300 words (as in [3]) or larger is used for texts. *mixLDA*[3] considers both visual and textual content in defining a latent space. The method consists in computing the probability of each visual term in the visual vocabulary to a given text query through hidden topics and delivering a ranked list of relevant visual terms for the query. The image having the highest overlap with the top 30 visual terms in the list is considered as the best image to illustrate the text.

Notations. We denote by CCA_{cap} (CCA_{img}) the basic CCA illustration model in which document-to-caption (document-to-image) nearest neighbor search with cosine similarity measure is applied on document and caption (image) projections. The models in Eq.(5) and Eq.(6) are denoted by CCA^*_{cap} and CCA^*_{img} respectively. In our experiments, CCA spaces are constructed from images and text that cumulates documents (articles) and captions.

3.2 Results on BBC News

We first compare the basic CCA model to the three baselines. CCA dimension selection is performed via 10-fold cross-validation on the 3121-articles *training* set of BBC News. We retain 2500 as the projection dimension since it corresponds to the highest score, see Fig. 1. As shown in Table 1, the corresponding accuracy of CCA_{cap} on the test set is 76.7%, higher than the accuracy of all the baselines including ones presented in [3] as well as the Vector Space $\text{VSM}_{\mathcal{V}_{bbc}}$ model with the larger $\mathcal{V}_{bbc}$ vocabulary. The large improvement of $\text{VSM}_{\mathcal{V}_{bbc}}$ (73.8%) over $\text{VSM}_{\mathcal{V}_{[3]}}$ (38.7%) highlights the importance of an appropriate text representation for this task. The fact that the textual baseline $\text{VSM}_{\mathcal{V}_{bbc}}$ yields a high illustration performance, together with the weak score of CCA_{img} (5.4%), are indications that in the BBC News dataset the visual and textual contents are rather poorly related, so the latent representation learned by CCA is not so reliable. Meanwhile, the VSM model can easily take advantage of the connection between documents and captions, that appears to be strong.

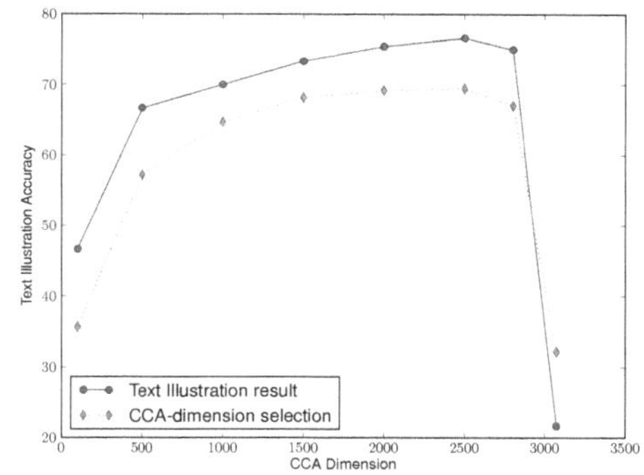

Figure 1: CCA_{cap} result and dimension selection

Table 1: Results on BBC News

Model	Accuracy(%)	10-fold CV Accuracy(%)
Overlap [3]	31.3	-
$\text{VSM}_{\mathcal{V}_{[3]}}$ [3]	38.7	-
mixLDA [3]	57.3	-
$\text{VSM}_{\mathcal{V}_{bbc}}$	73.8	72.8 ± 2.1
CCA_{img}	5.4	8.9 ± 1.7
CCA_{cap}	76.7	74.7 ± 2.5
CCA^*_{img}	15.8	19.0 ± 2.0
CCA^*_{cap}	80.8	78.9 ± 2.4

To apply the CCA^* model we proposed in Section 2, we identify the vocabulary $\mathcal{S}_{bbc}$ of 41 specific words that are present in 240 testing captions but not in the initial vocabulary $\mathcal{V}_{bbc}$. As shown in Table 1, our CCA^*_{cap} model achieves the best score with 80.8% accuracy. The third column in Table 1 reports the results of proposed models using a 10-fold cross-validation on 3,361 BBC News data. The results show that the CCA^*_{cap} model outperforms the others.

3.3 Results in a domain transfer context

For the second experiment we develop the latent CCA space using the large ImageCLEF 2013 Photo Annotation and Retrieval dataset[2] and we evaluate text illustration on the same BBC News test set of 240 documents. Our aim is to study the impact of having a larger difference between the vocabularies of the test set and of the training set, which is an important issue in practical applications. The ImageCLEF 2013 collection includes 250,000 images downloaded from the Internet. Each image has at most 100 tags (words) extracted from the content of the web page where the image appears. The textual vocabulary $\mathcal{V}_{ic}$ for the ImageCLEF 2013 training dataset contains 18,003 words occurring each between 5 and 1500 times. The CCA space has 3072 dimensions here and is learned from images and tags using OverFeat features of size 3072 and TF-IDF textual representations. In this domain transfer context, there are 208 specific words $\mathcal{S}_{ic}$ present in the BBC News test set captions but not in $\mathcal{V}_{ic}$. Table 2 reports the performance of three models in this context: $\text{VSM}_{\mathcal{V}_{ic}}$, CCA_{cap} and CCA^*_{cap}. By taking the specific information into account, our model significantly improves the result of basic CCA, showing that it can be quite effective in a domain transfer context. However, while CCA^*_{cap} with the latent space obtained on Image-

[2]http://www.imageclef.org/2013/photo/annotation

Table 2: Results on BBC News with domain transfer

Model	Accuracy(%)
$\text{VSM}_{\mathcal{V}_{ic}}$	53.8
CCA_{cap}	43.3
CCA^*_{cap}	61.3

Table 3: Results on Wikipedia 2010

Model	Accuracy(%)
$\text{VSM}_{\mathcal{V}_{wp}}$	20.8
CCA_{img}	9.2
CCA_{cap}	16.3
CCA^*_{img}	58.3
CCA^*_{cap}	55.4

CLEF 2013 works better than the state-of-the-art mixLDA on BBC News (57.3%, see Table 1), it is weaker than the CCA^*_{cap} with the model learned on the proper BBC News training corpus (80.8%). This reveals that the two datasets, ImageCLEF 2013 and BBC News, present rather different relations between images and words.

3.4 Results on Wikipedia 2010

For the third experiment we consider the Wikipedia 2010 collection that can be directly employed for text illustration while being larger than the BBC News dataset. The results of the Vector Space model baseline, of the basic CCA model and of the proposed CCA* model are shown in Table 3. As for the first experiment, the CCA space is obtained from images and texts that cumulate documents and captions, using the features described in Section 3.1. From the testing set captions, we determined 2868 specific words out of the training vocabulary $\mathcal{V}_{wp}$. Our approach CCA^*_{cap} improves the text illustration accuracy over basic CCA from 16.25% to 55.4% and significantly outperforms the Vector Space model (20.8%). The cross-modal model CCA^*_{img} of Eq. (6) with visual features obtains even better results (58.3%).

3.5 Discussion

The method we proposed aims to make better use of specific information that is poorly represented by a learned cross-modal model but nevertheless likely to be relevant for retrieval. In the text illustration experiments presented above, this information corresponds to words that are present in the test data but absent from the training data (or below the filtering threshold). This selection condition may appear weak, but for large datasets the training vocabulary covers most of the common words, so the words that are new in the test set are mostly names, trademarks or other very informative tags.

An evaluation based on the top-1 result alone is quite strict for text illustration. The system must return as first relevant result the very image chosen by the author, but it may not be the best one to illustrate the document. Actually, in many cases, for both BBC News and Wikipedia 2010, other images in the collection are at least as relevant for the document. It is then important to also evaluate the methods based on the accuracy of top-k results, with $k > 1$. As shown in Table 4 for $k = 10$, the proposed method compares well with the Vector Space model on both datasets.

Table 4: Results with top-10 evaluation

Model	BBC News	Wikipedia
VSM	94.2	27.1
CCA^*_{cap}	95.0	70.8

4. CONCLUSION

We proposed a new approach for CCA-based cross-modal retrieval that takes advantage of information that is poorly represented in the training data but likely to be relevant for the task. We have shown its interest in the context of a challenging text illustration task formulated as top-1 cross-modal retrieval. The new approach was compared to others on a previously published benchmark and shown to produce better results. We also proposed two new benchmarks that are more realistic in the sense that they contain more data that is new in the test set with respect to the training set. The results show that the proposed method improves even more effectively over the performance of CCA in these cases.

5. AKNOWLEDGEMENT

This work is partially supported by the Datascale project, funded by the French Ministère de l'economie, des finances et de l'industrie and the USEMP FP7 project, funded by the EC under contract number 611596.

6. REFERENCES

[1] J. Costa Pereira, E. Coviello, G. Doyle, N. Rasiwasia, G. Lanckriet, R. Levy, and N. Vasconcelos. On the role of correlation and abstraction in cross-modal multimedia retrieval. *TPAMI*, 36(3):521–535, 2014.

[2] F. Feng, X. Wang, and R. Li. Cross-modal retrieval with correspondence autoencoder. In *Proc. of ACM Intl. Conf. on Multimedia*, MM '14, 2014.

[3] Y. Feng and M. Lapata. Topic models for image annotation and text illustration. In *Human Language Technologies: 2010 Annual Conf. of the North American Chapter of the Association for Computational Linguistics*, HLT '10, pages 831–839, 2010.

[4] Y. Gong, Q. Ke, M. Isard, and S. Lazebnik. A multi-view embedding space for modeling internet images, tags, and their semantics. *IJCV*, 106(2):210–233, Jan. 2014.

[5] D. R. Hardoon, S. R. Szedmak, and J. R. Shawe-Taylor. Canonical correlation analysis: An overview with application to learning methods. *Neural Comput.*, 16(12):2639–2664, Dec. 2004.

[6] H. Hotelling. Relations between two sets of variables. *Biometrika*, 28:312–377, 1936.

[7] S. J. Hwang and K. Grauman. Learning the relative importance of objects from tagged images for retrieval and cross-modal search. *IJCV*, 100(2):134–153, Nov. 2012.

[8] X. Mao, B. Lin, D. Cai, X. He, and J. Pei. Parallel field alignment for cross media retrieval. In *Proc. of ACM Intl. Conf. on Multimedia*, MM '13, 2013.

[9] P. Sermanet, D. Eigen, X. Zhang, M. Mathieu, R. Fergus, and Y. LeCun. Overfeat: Integrated recognition, localization and detection using convolutional networks. *CoRR*, abs/1312.6229, 2013.

3D Sketch-Based 3D Model Retrieval

Bo Li, Yijuan Lu, Azeem Ghumman, Bradley Strylowski, Mario Gutierrez,
Safiyah Sadiq, Scott Forster, Natacha Feola, Travis Bugerin
Department of Computer Science, Texas State University
San Marcos, Texas, USA
{b_l58, lu, a_z65, b_s211, mag262, s_s451, smf85, n_f27, tlb165}@txstate.edu

ABSTRACT

How to draw 3D sketches in a three-dimensional space and how to use a hand-drawn 3D sketch to search similar 3D models are brand new and challenging research topics. In this paper, we make an initial study on 3D sketching and propose a novel 3D sketch-based 3D model retrieval system. Our system allows users to freely draw 3D sketches in the air as well as to find similar 3D models given human-drawn 3D sketches. Promising retrieval performance has been achieved in experiments based on 300 collected 3D sketches and a recent large scale sketch-based 3D shape retrieval benchmark.

Categories and Subject Descriptors

H.3.3 [**Information Storage and Retrieval**]: Information Search and Retrieval

Keywords

Sketch-based 3D model retrieval; 3D sketch; Kinect

1. MOTIVATION

Since prehistoric times, sketching has been a universal form of communication used by humans to depict the visual world. Today, sketching has become one of the most natural ways to provide a visual search query for search, e.g., one can search images, videos, and 3D models on the Internet by sketching an object or scene on a touch phone/tablet.

Currently, all existing sketch-based 3D model retrieval systems rely on 2D sketching technology, which requires users to draw a sketch on a two-dimensional plane (paper, touch screen). Constraining a sketch to two dimensions limits the 3D information that the shape can communicate, creating a huge semantic gap between the iconic representation of a 2D sketch and the accurate 3D coordinate representation of a 3D model. This gap makes 2D sketch-based 3D model retrieval very challenging [3].

Bothered by this gap, an interesting question is raised: "Can we do 3D sketching such that we can perform 3D sketch-based 3D model retrieval?" If it were possible for users to sketch an object in all three dimensions in a 3D space (for example, in the air) by utilizing hand gestures, the 3D sketch should provide a better description of the object than a 2D sketch. The 3D sketch not only encodes 3D information, such as depth and features of more facets of the object, but also includes the salient 3D feature lines of its counterpart of 3D models. However, there is a scarcity of comprehensive research supporting methods that allow users to sketch 3D objects in a 3D space. In addition, how to understand (translate) 3D sketches drawn by human hands and how to match 3D sketches with 3D models become new research problems.

In this paper, we perform an initial study of 3D sketching technology and develop a 3D sketching virtual drawing "board". We investigate 3D sketch and model matching problems and build a novel 3D sketch-based 3D model retrieval system, whose performance is tested on a large scale sketch-based 3D shape retrieval benchmark dataset and a collected human 3D sketch dataset.

To our best knowledge, this work is the first attempt to explore 3D sketching in a 3D space and to develop an innovative retrieval system that enables users to search 3D models based on hand-drawn 3D sketches. The implications of this work could be tremendous, as 3D sketching allows for more direct communication in a user's drawing, which could not only enhance 3D model retrieval accuracy, but also provide a possibility for other human sketch related applications, such as virtual try-on systems for clothes, glasses and watches. The main contributions introduced in this paper are highlighted as follows:

- A novel 3D sketching virtual drawing "board" (software) is proposed and implemented, which allows users to freely draw 3D sketches in the air (a real 3D space). Based on this developed 3D sketching virtual drawing board, the first human 3D sketch dataset is collected.
- A 3D sketch-based 3D model retrieval system is introduced for the first time to solve the matching problem between 3D sketches and models.
- Our proposed approach shows promising application potential for 3D sketch understanding or recognition, large scale 3D model search, and on-line 3D model shopping, etc.
- Our work will explicitly guide the research in 3D sketching and provide a path for large scale sketch-based image, video, and object retrieval.

ICMR'15, June 23–26, 2015, Shanghai, China.

http://dx.doi.org/10.1145/2671188.2749349.

2. BACKGROUND

Sketch-based 3D model retrieval targets on retrieving 3D models given a hand-drawn query sketch. Recently, sketch-based 3D model retrieval has attracted much attention since it can be widely used in sketch-based rapid prototyping, recognition, mobile 3D search, 3D printing, 3D animation production and etc. Many related algorithms have been proposed [3] which use a 2D hand-drawn sketch as a query. A series of Shape Retrieval Contest (SHREC) tracks on this topic have been held in conjunction with the Eurographics Workshops on 3D Object Retrieval (3DOR) over the past three years. Some new benchmark datasets, such as the large scale SHREC'13 Sketch Track Benchmark (SHREC13STB) [2] which contains 7,200 2D sketches and 1,258 3D models of 90 classes, have been built and released to the public. Due to the semantic gap between the two different representations of rough sketches and accurate 3D models, sketch-based 3D model retrieval remains one of most challenging research topics in the field of 3D model retrieval. In order to bridge the gap, we propose a 3D sketching solution and develop a sketch-based 3D model retrieval system that uses human 3D sketches, which is described in detail in the following sections.

3. OUR APPROACH

3.1 3D Sketching

How to design a smart, user friendly, and inexpensive 3D sketching virtual drawing "board", which allows users to easily create 3D sketches, is one of crucial problems of this project. We propose to implement this virtual "board" with the Microsoft Kinect, considering it is a popular and low cost motion sensing input device and offers a built-in color VGA video camera, depth sensor, and multi-array microphone.

We utilize the RGB video camera on the Kinect to allow the user to see exactly what they are drawing in the surrounding 3D space (in the air), and make use of the depth sensor to capture the depth information communicated in the 3D sketches. The video and depth sensors have a pixel resolution of 640x480 and run at 30 frames per second. With this capability, users are able to engage the tracking function of Kinect to monitor the 3D locations of their hands in a 3D space while drawing. To facilitate sketching and retrieval, we also develop a voice-activated Kinect-based 3D sketching Graphical User Interface (GUI) (shown in Fig. 1) that supports the tracking function. The proposed interface can not only track the movement of a user's hand, but also support voice commands (e.g. start, left, right, pause, resume, search, and reset) allowing a user to pause in the middle of a drawing or completely restart a sketch as well as to switch between left and right hands while drawing. Users can also select front or side view display and point or line mode for sketch viewing. All the above operations can be performed in real-time. In experiments, we have observed that the interactive feedback greatly helps the user in drawing a 3D sketch and improves users' drawing experience.

Although the Microsoft Kinect is able to detect and track 48 individual points on the user's body, the captured hand motion data contains a lot of noise, mostly due to the fact that when users perform sketching in the air they could shake and rarely have perfectly steady hands while drawing. The introduced noise can significantly affect the 3D model retrieval performance. To combat this, a Kalman filter is applied, which is an optimal estimator that infers parameters of interest from inaccurate and uncertain observations. In our experiments, we find the Kalman filter successfully filters partial noise and predicts smoother sketch curves.

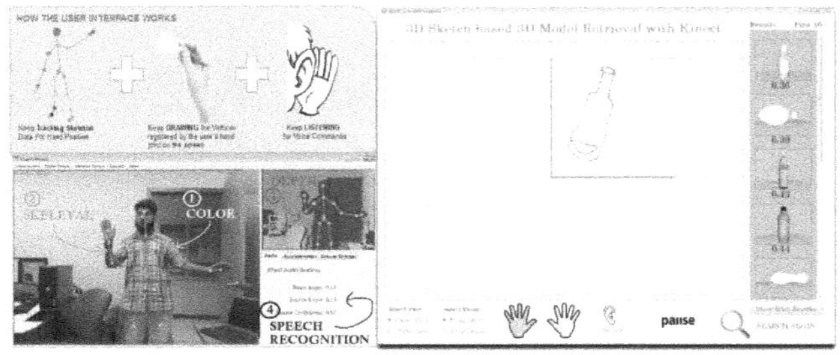

Figure 1: System Graphical User Interface (GUI).

3.2 3D Sketch-Based 3D Model Retrieval System

Based on the above 3D sketching platform, we build an efficient 3D sketch-based 3D model retrieval system. Figure 2 shows the framework of our retrieval system, which contains both online and offline processes and consists of three major components: data processing, feature extraction, and matching.

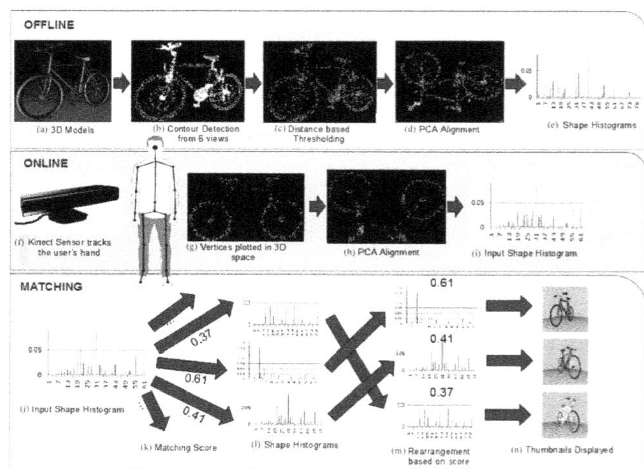

Figure 2: System framework.

(1) Data processing. The major task of the data processing component is to generate 3D outlines of 3D models. First, 3D normalization is performed for each 3D model: 3D alignment based on Principle Component Analysis (PCA) is first performed, and then translate the origin to the center of the model's bounding sphere, and finally scale the model such that the radius of the bounding sphere is 1. Second, the 3D outline for the model is generated by integrating the 3D contour points of its six principle views (front, back, left, right, top, and bottom views). One sample result is demonstrated in Fig. 2 (b). Third, an approximately uniform point sampling is performed by setting a 3D distance threshold between the 3D points. This step is to improve the robustness of our algorithm w.r.t the different resolutions of 3D outlines and sketches. Fig. 2 (c) shows the final 3D outline of the bicycle model after performing the sampling. Finally, a PCA alignment is executed (Fig. 2 (d)) on the 3D outline. The same normalization process will be applied on an online hand-drawn 3D sketch.

(2) Feature extraction. Descriptive visual features need to be extracted from both 3D models and 3D sketches in order to perform effective and efficient sketch-model matching and retrieval. Extensive research has been conducted to generate a number of 3D shape descriptors in characterizing complete and perfect 3D models. However, many of them require a 3D mesh model as input and only a few of them are applicable to represent a 3D sketch which is essentially a sparse point cloud (a very abstract and inaccurate representation of a 3D object). Therefore, a large research space remains unexplored in terms of comparing an inaccurate point cloud of a 3D sketch with an accurate 3D model.

In this paper, we investigate using the 3D shape histogram [1] as a representative feature for both 3D models and 3D sketches considering its descriptiveness, high efficiency, and simplicity. The 3D shape histogram divides the 3D space occupied by a 3D model/sketch into a set of shell, sector or spiderweb bins and counts the percentage of the vertices falling in each bin to form a histogram as the 3D shape histogram descriptor. One visualization example of the process is shown in Fig. 3. Considering the inherent nature of the representations for a 3D sketch and a 3D outline, as well as the efficiency issue, for each 3D sketch or outline, its 3D shape histogram [1] descriptor is extracted based on the spiderweb model (20 shells, 6 sectors, 120 bins in total) (Fig. 2 (e)).

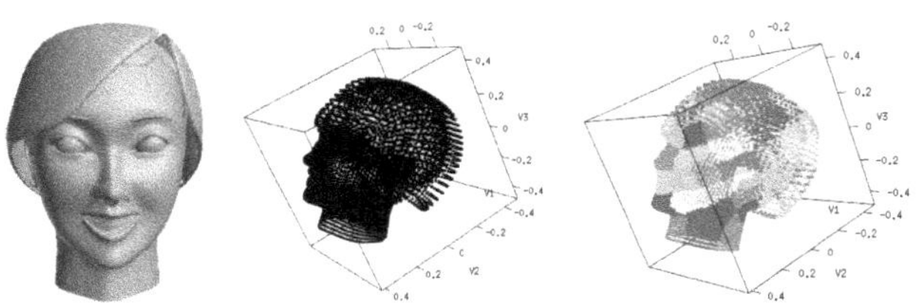

(a) 3D model (b) point mode (c) feature visualization

Figure 3: An example to visualize the 3D shape histogram feature (different bins) of the m349 model in the Princeton Shape Benchmark (PSB) [4] dataset.

(3) 3D sketch-3D model matching. The histogram of the 3D sketch is compared with the histograms of all the 3D outlines generated from the 3D models based on the Euclidean distance (Fig. 2 (k)). Then, the distances are sorted in ascending order (Fig. 2 (m)), and finally the thumbnails of the top ten 3D models are listed accordingly in real-time on the right side of the GUI, as shown in Fig. 2 (n). Users can also browse the next 10 results by saying the voice command "Show more results".

4. EXPERIMENTS AND DISCUSSIONS

4.1 Kinect300 Dataset Collection

Based on the developed 3D sketching virtual drawing "board", we have collected a 3D sketch dataset named Kinect300 which comprises 300 sketches in 30 object categories (see Fig. 4), each with 10 sketches. Seventeen users (4 females and 13 males) with an average age of 21 years participated in the 3D sketch data collection, where each user drew sketches of several categories. Among 17 users, only two of the males have a background in art.

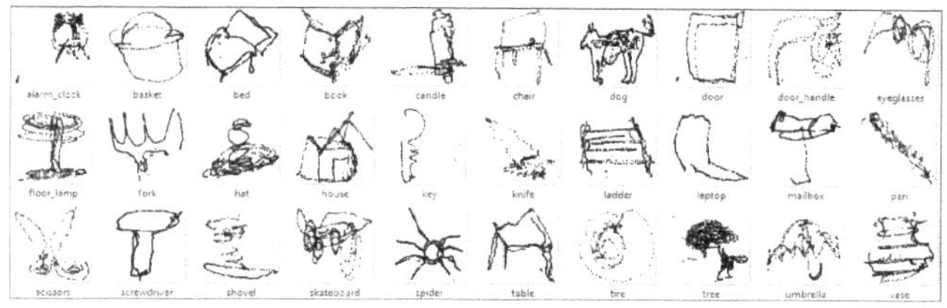

Figure 4: Example 3D sketches (one example per class, shown in one view) of our Kinect300 dataset.

4.2 Retrieval Experiments

To comprehensively evaluate the performance of our retrieval system presented in Section 3.2, we performed the following three types of experiments based on six commonly used evaluation metrics [4]: Nearest Neighbor (NN), First Tier (FT), Second Tier (ST), E-Measure (E), Discounted Cumulative Gain (DCG) and Precision-Recall (PR).

- **outline-model retrieval:** query is a 3D outline generated from a 3D model; targets are 3D models from the *same* dataset. This experiment tests the retrieval performance of searching a similar 3D model given a perfect 3D outline (not a rough human 3D sketch). Here, the SHREC13STB benchmark (target dataset only) is chosen as the target dataset, which contains 1,258 target 3D models of 90 classes.

- **sketch-sketch retrieval:** query is a 3D sketch; targets are 3D sketches from the same dataset. This experiment tests the performance of similar 3D model retrieval given a hand-drawn 3D sketch. Since users sketch objects differently, the variety of human sketches even within categories can be extremely high. We want to test whether sketches within the same category drawn by various users can be retrieved given a single user sketch. Kinect300 is used as the target dataset in this experiment.

- **sketch-model retrieval:** query is a hand-drawn 3D sketch; targets are 3D models of real objects. This experiment tests the performance of similar 3D model retrieval given a human 3D sketch. The Kinect300 3D sketch dataset is used as the query set and the SHREC13STB benchmark (target dataset only) is used as the target dataset. Please note that only 21 of the 30 classes in Kinect300 have relevant 3D models in the SHREC13STB target dataset, thus when computing the retrieval performance we only consider the results of these 21 classes. The 9 classes that have no relevant 3D models are: alarm clock, basket, candle, door handle, eyeglasses, fork, key, pen, and scissors.

Thanks to the high efficiency of the 3D shape histogram and the Kalman Filter, all the above retrieval experiments are performed in real-time. For example, it takes only 1.22 sec to perform a 3D model retrieval given a hand-drawn 3D sketch (type 3) on a modern computer (CPU: Intel Xeon X5675 @3.07 GHz). The experimental results are listed in Fig. 5 and Table 1. As expected, the performance of outline-model retrieval is better than the performance of sketch-sketch retrieval, which outperforms the sketch-model retrieval. We can observe that the 3D shape histogram has good descriptive ability in capturing the vertex distribution pattern of a 3D model and a perfect 3D outline. But it doesn't have strong discrimination power in differentiating all 3D models coming from different categories. Thus, given a 3D outline, 3D models from irrelevant categories may be returned. We also find that the 3D shape histogram is sensitive to noise. All the 3D sketches we currently collect are quite abstract and noisy since most users have little drawing experience. When users are sketching, they often pause their hands or move their hands back and forth in the air. The sketch lines they draw are rarely smooth and continuous. The paused areas contain a large amount of dense points. Although the Kalman filter can help remove outliers and smooth the tracked sketching 3D points, the noise can still propagate into the query sketch. This partially explains why the performance of sketch-sketch retrieval is even worse.

Among these three experiments, the most challenging is sketch-model retrieval, which attempts to retrieve similar 3D models from the SHREC13STB benchmark given a 3D sketch in the Kinect300 dataset. The query dataset and target dataset are different. The query sketch and the target 3D models are not even one to one correspondent since we don't ask users to sketch existing 3D models in the 3D benchmark dataset. Additionally, our collected Kinect300 dataset is a diverse dataset, which contains many challenging categories such as dog, human, face, house.... For these categories, drawing a simple and compact sketch can be a challenging task. Therefore, it is not surprising to see that the performance of the third experiment is far below the performance of other two. It also raises a challenging but interesting problem specific to this type of 3D model retrieval: how to effectively compare an inaccurate hand-drawn 3D sketch with an accurate 3D model? However, many simple categories, including wineglass, sword, airplanes, and balloons, display good retrieval results that suggest further research could significantly improve the retrieval performance. Figure 6 shows two examples using sketches with different complexity.

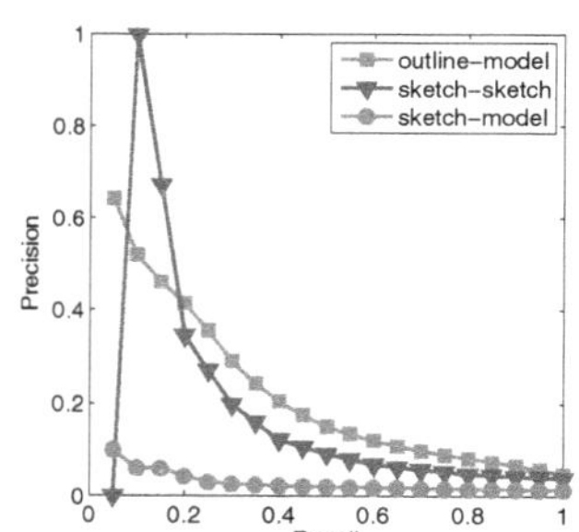

Figure 5: Precision-Recall performance.

There is still much room left for further improvement in this challenging task of 3D sketch-based 3D model retrieval. More descriptive shape descriptors are deserved for our further exploration for this specific type of retrieval. In addition, the 3D sketches we currently collect are quite abstract and noisy. Better denoising and smoothing algorithms will

Table 1: Other performance metrics.

Benchmark	NN	FT	ST	E	DCG
outline-model	0.391	0.156	0.238	0.121	0.486
sketch-sketch	0.167	0.087	0.139	0.092	0.360
sketch-model	0.029	0.021	0.038	0.021	0.254

be investigated to further remove noisy points (e.g. the dot in the alarm clock example in Fig. 4) created during 3D sketching. To further improve the performance of our retrieval system, supervised learning could be applied to help better understand 3D sketch structure before performing matching and retrieval.

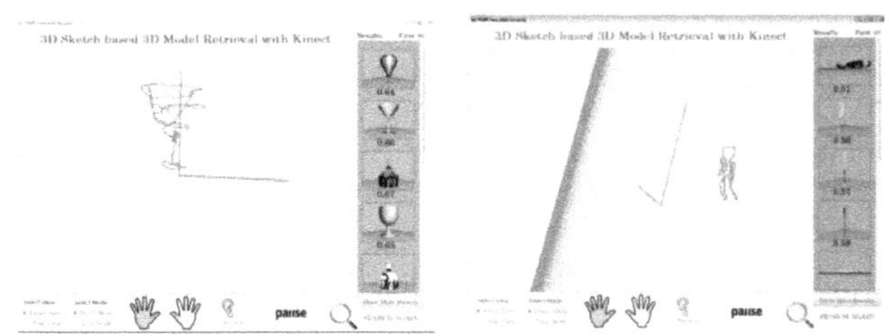

(a) Simple (b) Complicated

Figure 6: Two example retrieval results using sketches with different complexity.

5. CONCLUSIONS AND FUTURE WORK

3D sketching in 3D space and 3D sketch-based 3D model retrieval are brand new research topics. Currently, software does not exist that allows users to include depth information in their sketches. Very little preliminary work exists in this field, allowing for exciting and interesting research results. In this paper, a novel 3D sketching virtual drawing "board" is proposed and a 3D sketch-based 3D model retrieval system is developed. Future goals include developing descriptive and discriminant 3D shape descriptors to represent 3D sketches and 3D models, collecting a larger number of 3D sketches from more diverse users, and training our system for better 3D sketch and 3D model matching.

Acknowledgments

This work is supported by Army Research Office grant W911NF-12-1-0057, NSF CRI-1305302, NSF CNS-1358939 and NSF OCI-1062439.

6. REFERENCES

[1] M. Ankerst, G. Kastenmüller, and et al. 3D shape histograms for similarity search and classification in spatial databases. In *SSD*, pages 207–226, 1999.
[2] B. Li, Y. Lu, and et al. SHREC'13 track: Large scale sketch-based 3D shape retrieval. In *3DOR*, pages 89–96, 2013.
[3] B. Li, Y. Lu, and et al. A comparison of 3D shape retrieval methods based on a large-scale benchmark supporting multimodal queries. *CVIU*, 131:1–27, 2015.
[4] P. Shilane, P. Min, and et al. The Princeton shape benchmark. In *SMI*, pages 167–178, 2004.

Boosting Prediction of Geo-location for Web Images Through Integrating Multiple Knowledge Sources

Hao Kuang, Shiai Zhu, Abdulmotaleb El Saddik
Multimedia Computing Research Laboratories, University of Ottawa, Canada
hkuan041@uottawa.ca, zshiai@gmail.com, elsaddik@uottawa.ca

ABSTRACT

Estimating geographical information of a given photo is a challenging task due to the massive spread of candidate locations on the earth. With the help of freely available geo-tagged Web images, the problem can be addressed by propagating geo-coordinates (latitude and longitude) of geo-related training data, which is obtained using document retrieval techniques. The state-of-the-art approach adopts language modeling technique to estimate the probability distribution of image associated tags in a local region. Under this framework, we propose to differentiate the tags based on the knowledge explored from multiple sources. Finally, a set of geo-informative tags are identified and further emphasized during the model learning and geo-location prediction. In addition, accurate geo-coordinates are estimated by incorporating the image visual information. Experiments on a large-scale geo-tagged Flickr image dataset demonstrate the effectiveness of proposed method at different levels of evaluation granularity.

Categories and Subject Descriptors

H.3.1 [**Information Storage and Retrieval**]: Content Analysis and Indexing

Keywords

Image geo-location, Language model, Geo-aware tags

1. INTRODUCTION

With the emergence of different sensors integrated with portable devices (e.g., smartphone and tablet), traditional media data (e.g., image and video) are enriched with some additional information (meta-data), such as geo-location generated by built-in or external GPS devices. This new feature provides an open opportunity for the location needed services, such as travel recommendation [15], image browsing by location [2] and landmark image search [10]. Besides these applications, geo-coordinates associated with images are helpful in many other ways. In [13], Liao et al. propose a geo-aware textual feature for geo-aware image classification by propagating tags from visual and geographic neighbors. City specified visual attributes are identified through analyzing geo-tagged images in [17]. In [1], geographic information is leveraged to obtain priors about a target object and facilitate the localization of the object in a coming new image.

ICMR'15, June 23–26, 2015, Shanghai, China.

http://dx.doi.org/10.1145/2671188.2749351.

Figure 1: Example images from Flickr.

Many tasks benefit from the dramatically growing geographic data, nevertheless, the portion of images with accurate geo-coordinates is still relatively small (5% as reported in [5]). Thus automatic prediction of image geo-location is in high demand, and has attracted widespread interest recently. While intensive research efforts have been devoted on this direction, estimating the target location from a wide spread of candidates on the earth is not trivial. With a sheer amount of user-generated images on the Web, a straightforward way is to convert the problem to searching geo-tagged reference images. The geo-coordinates of returned results are further propagated to the query images. Both textual and visual information are explored in the literature. Visual based approaches [8, 12] model each candidate location with a set of representative images. The relevance between query images and locations is estimated by employing visual matching techniques. In [3], location-discriminative image regions are discovered using latent SVM learned on the images of each location. In [16], geo-coordinates are refined using random walk on an image graph, where edge is determined by matching the visual content. While visual feature may perform well on locations with landmarks or discriminative scenes, it cannot provide sufficient clues for localizing more general images. For example, compared to Figure 1(a), where the visual content clearly indicates the image location, Figure 1(b) is easily assigned to other locations with fountain using image matching.

In contrast to visual information, user contributed text annotations usually convey strong clues of the location where this photo was taken, such as "Washington DC", "Capitol Hill" in Figure 1. Thus utilizing image tags is a plausible way. In [14], a probability language model is proposed, on which many successful systems [11, 9, 6] are built. In this model, each location is represented as a tag distribution estimated from the images taken around this location. Given a query image, the associated tags are used to estimate the relevance between the query and each candidate location. As some tags such as "Capitol Hill" are more informative than tags like "lake", the tag distribution is further modified by boosting location names presented in external manually constructed sources such as GeoNames. However, geographical names may indicate different ranges of area on the earth. For example, "Capitol Hill" is more indicative than "Washington DC" for localizing images, nevertheless, they are treated equally in [14]. Besides, user generated geo-aware tags may be not included in the database. In this paper, we propose to identify and boost the geo-aware and informative tags based on knowledge learned from multiple sources. In specific, we jointly consider GeoNames database, tag distribution among candidate regions and geographic spread of tags. In addition, the importance of tags is not only utilized in learning language model, but also in the prediction process. Finally, visual information is incorporated in the fine-grained geo-coordinates estimation. Instead of fusing the results from two modalities as in [9, 4], which is risky since visual clues are much weaker and may hurt the results, we use visual feature to search similar images only within a small local region estimated by language model. In this way, the performance at fine granularity can be improved, and meanwhile the overall performance at coarse granularity will be not degraded.

2. TAG-BOOSTED LANGUAGE MODEL

Figure 2 shows the overall framework of our approach. The world map is split into $m \times n$ grids based on the longitude/latitude coordinate. We set the interval of both longitude and latitude as one degree. A collection of geo-tagged training images is assigned to the corresponding grids based on their geo-coordinates. Then a set of geo-aware tags are identified using knowledge from multiple sources. These tags are further emphasized in modeling the tag distribution of each grid using language model. Given a query image, the most likely grid is estimated using the learned language model and geo-informative tags. Finally, the accurate geo-location is predicted by propagating the geo-coordinates of similar training images within the selected grid.

2.1 Probability Language Model

A grid $l \in \mathcal{L}$ is represented as a bag of tags associated with the images assigned to l. Given a query image x with a tag list $\mathcal{T}$, the grid l_x where x is most likely taken is determined by

$$l_x = \arg\max_{l \in \mathcal{L}} P(l|\mathcal{T}). \tag{1}$$

Assuming the tags in $\mathcal{T}$ are generated independently, we can use Bayes' rule and get

$$P(l|\mathcal{T}) \propto P(l) \times \prod_{t \in \mathcal{T}} P(t|l). \tag{2}$$

Then the $P(t|l)$ is estimated by representing each grid as a multinomial distribution over tags. Given a tag vocabulary

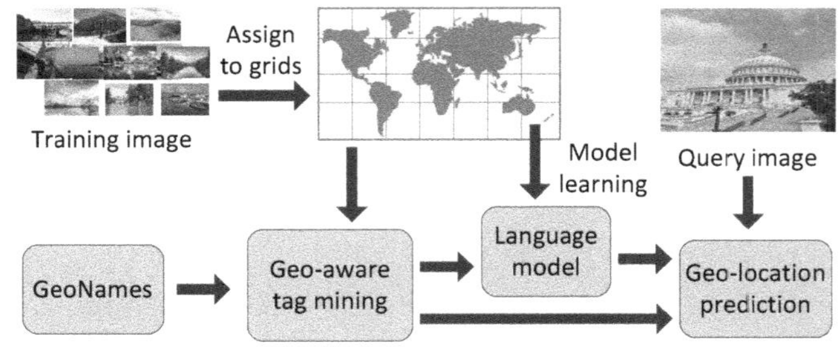

Figure 2: Overall framework of the proposed approach.

V, $P(t|l)$ is computed by counting its frequency in l:

$$P(t|l) = \frac{\#(t,l) + 1}{\sum_{t_i \in V}(\#(t_i,l) + 1)}, \tag{3}$$

where plus-one smoothing is used to avoid zero probability when t does not appear in l. Intuitively, $P(l|\mathcal{T})$ can be considered as relevance score between the query image x and a candidate grid l. The prior distribution of grids $P(l)$ can be considered to be uniform and eliminated from Equation 2. By using logarithms on Equation 2, the relevance can be estimated by

$$\log(P(l|\mathcal{T})) \propto \sum_{t \in \mathcal{T}} \log(P(t|l)). \tag{4}$$

2.2 Geo-aware Tag Mining

As discussed in section 1, the location specified tags such as city names or landmark building names can be integrated in the language model by boosting the probability $P(t|l)$ of these tags. To identify the geo-aware tags, we define following four measurements to determine the tag informativeness.

GeoNames. Geonames database consists of location names contributed by Web users. Similar to [14], we define weights $w_t^g = 1$ for tags listed in the database, and $w_t^g = o$ otherwise.

IDF. In addition to the knowledge source i.e. GeoNames, tag distribution among grids is also important. One well-known weighting method is inverse document frequency (IDF), which will assign higher weights to tags appeared in less grids and penalize frequent tags. Formally, it is defined as $w_t^{idf} = log(N/|\{l : t \in l\}|)$, where N is the total number of grids, and $|\{l : t \in l\}|$ is the number of grids including t.

KL-divergence. IDF is based on the statistic of absence or presence of tags in grids, nevertheless, the distribution of tags within the grids is neglected. For instance, tags appearing in same number of grids will have same IDF values. However, the tag frequently observed in a specific grid would be more representative for that grid than others. To reflect this property, we define a measurement derived from the tag frequency $\#(t,l)$ in grids. In specific, a tag t is more informative if there is more change of grid distribution from prior $P(\mathcal{L})$ to the conditional distribution $P(\mathcal{L}|t)$ given tag t. This can be measured using KL-divergence between the prior and conditional distributions.

$$w_t^{kl} = KL[P(\mathcal{L})\|P(\mathcal{L}|t)] = \sum_{l \in \mathcal{L}} P(l) \log[\frac{P(l)}{P(l|t)}], \tag{5}$$

where $P(l)$ is computed as the number of tags in l divided by the number of tags in the corpus, and $P(l|t)$ is estimated by

$\#(l,t)/\sum_{l' \in \mathcal{L}} \#(l',t)$. For some common tags (e.g., "hospital"), the conditional probability would be flat as they frequently appear in many grids. On the other hand, conditional probabilities of informative tags such as "NewYork", which may be randomly distributed in many grids, will peak in the grid around NewYork City. KL-divergence would be better to differentiate the two cases than IDF.

Spatial Variance. Both IDF and KL-divergence are defined according to the tag distribution among grids without explicitly considering geo-information. They are discriminative for grids with unique tags. We further consider the geographical spread of a tag to estimate its importance for localizing query images. The motivation is that the one appeared in geographical closer grids are more indicative than the one spread widely on the map. For example, supposing both "London" and "Ottawa" appear in two grids respectively, the two grids having "Ottawa" are around the Ottawa City, while "London" may appear in Canada or England. As the two tags have same document frequency, both IDF and KL-divergence fail to differentiate them. In this paper, we first compute the spatial variance σ_t of images with tag t. Then the weight is defined as $w_t^s = exp(-\beta\sigma_t)$, where β is a decay factor.

After normalizing the above four measurements into range [0,1], we assign a joint weight w_t for each tag through linear fusion. Our proposed boosted language model is defined by simply replacing $\#(t,l)$ in Equation 3 with $(1+\beta_1) \times \#(t,l)$, where β_1 is a weighting factor. In this way, the tag distribution within a grid is modified to emphasize the geo-informative tags. In addition, the influence of these tags is further enhanced during prediction by replacing $\log(P(t|l))$ in Equation 4 with $(1+\beta_2) \times \log(P(t|l))$, where β_2 is also a weighting factor. Note that the estimated tag weights are assigned to both present tags and absent tags (with plus-one smoothing) in the detection process using Equation 4.

2.3 Accurate Geo-coordinates Prediction

With language models, the most likely grid can be estimated according to Equation 1. Since each grid covers several hundred kilometers on the map, an accurate geo-coordinates is necessary. A straightforward way is to propagate the geo-coordinates of similar images within the selected grid to the query image. While the effectiveness of visual feature is limited in the global search, it is expected to be helpful when search is performed within a local region, where much less training images are considered. In other words, if there is a training image taken at a same place with the query image, the chance of finding it using visual feature becomes high after the search area is localized. In this paper, we use Jaccard coefficient to compute the textual similarity between two tag lists, and Cosine similarity on the visual features. The most similar image is identified using the linearly fused textual and visual similarities.

3. EXPERIMENTS

3.1 Settings and Evaluation Criteria

Our experiments are conducted on the dataset used in MediaEval placing task 2013 [7], which includes more than 8.5 million images with geo-coordinates, and several sets of testing data. After stop-words removal and stemming, we get 6.6 million images with tags. These images are assigned to the split grids according to their geo-coordinates, and

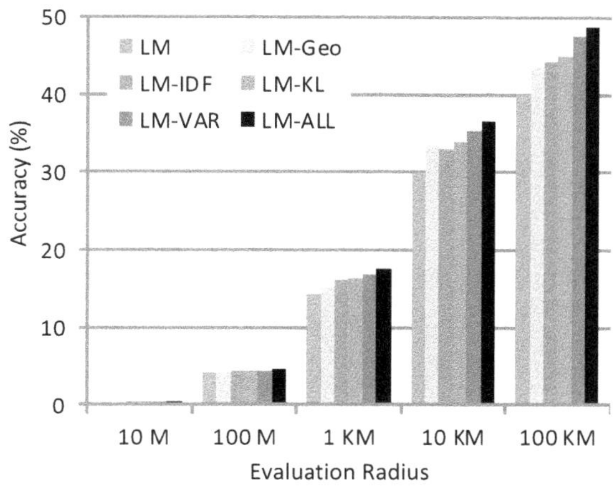

Figure 3: Accuracy performance of different language model based approaches with respect to different evaluation granularities.

finally we have 8,097 non-empty grids. Visual feature used in the accurate geo-coordinates prediction is 144 dimensional CEDD provided by MediaEval, which performs well in this task. The experiments are conducted on the first testing set including 5,300 images. To evaluate the approaches, we adopt the two standard criteria used in MediaEval. The first one is hitting rate or accuracy of predictions within a given circle radius (10 M, 100 M, 1 KM, 10 KM and 100 KM). The second one is the absolute error distance in kilometers between estimated and ground-truth coordinates.

3.2 Results and Discussions

3.2.1 Effectiveness of Identified Tags

The baseline method is the primary language model (LM) proposed in [14]. Our proposed tag-boosted approach is LM-ALL, where four measurements are jointly considered. In addition, LM-Geo, LM-IDF, LM-KL and LM-VAR are four simplified boosted language models using one of the four measurements respectively. Note that visual information is not used in this experiment. The prediction results at several evaluation radiuses are showed in Figure 3. By incorporating estimated importance of user tags, all the five boosted language modeling approaches improve the baseline significantly. Meanwhile, the improvements are consistently observed for different evaluation radiuses. LM-ALL using all the information achieves best results with 22% improvement of accuracy (radius = 1 KM) over baseline. Among the four measurements, LM-VAR using spatial variance of tags performs better than others. This is because that statistic based on geographical spread of tags is the most informative clue for localizing the query tags. The two methods LM-IDF and LM-KL using tag distribution among grids generate similar improvements over baseline, which indicates that informative tags are helpful to distinguish candidate grids. Although LM-Geo performs worse than other measurements as equal weights are assigned to the location names, it still improves the accuracy at 1 KM radius by 7% over LM. Another reason may be that statistics from user generated tags can be better to capture user tagging behaviors. Similar conclusions can be made from the average distance errors

Table 1: **Average error distance in kilometers over all testing images.**

	LM	LM -Geo	LM -IDF	LM -KL	LM -VAR	LM -ALL
Error (KM)	506	331	261	260	142	**129**

Table 2: Identified geo-aware tags using four measurements.

GeoNames	churchhill, shanghai, ottawa, chimay, cheste, baras, bannu, paris, sedan, tabaco.
IDF	soestdijk, luanco, amboyrd, westmalvern bike parking corral, porter school, audimax.
KL	germany, newyork, turkey, canada, paris, raleigh, australia, cambridgeshire, disney.
Variance	soestdijk, bike parking corral, baselstadt, CEU San Pablo, porter school, luanco.

of estimation showed in Table 1. LM-ALL significantly reduces the error from 506 KM of baseline to 129 KM. Table 2 further shows some identified tags using presented four measurements respectively. For GeoNames, we randomly select some city names from the database. Since all the training images are grouped according to their geo-coordinates, informative tags identified by KL and IDF include many location names but with different weights. In addition, spatial variance tends to select the tags (e.g., "baselstadt") used only in a local area. These tags appearing in a query image strongly support its geo-location. Thus LM-VAR performs better than other three measurements. Best result is achieved by LM-ALL which combines the tags representing different location granularities.

3.2.2 Visual Feature Evaluation

To evaluate the usefulness of visual feature, we first show the result of 1NN visual matching (V-1NN) approach which is purely based on visual information of query images. As showed in Table 3, as to be expected, the estimation is extremely imprecise. This is consistent to the observations in [4, 9]. The reason is that both training and testing images are all general images rather than landmarks with strong clues indicating the location information. In addition, different from other retrieval problems, a small difference between two image matching results may result in large errors of geo-location estimation. In our method, the visual feature is leveraged in accurate geo-coordinates estimation within a local area selected by language models. We show the results of LM-V and LM-ALL-V, which respectively utilize LM and LM-ALL methods for localizing the most likely grid. For LM-V and LM-ALL-V, accurate geo-coordinate is predicted using both textual and visual features described in section 2.3. From Table 3, we can see that LM-V and LM-ALL-V incorporating visual feature improve LM and LM-ALL respectively when evaluation radius is 10 M or 100 M. Since the LM-V and LM-ALL-V are based on the initial grid localization results, the improvements at coarse evaluation granularities (larger radius) are marginal. In other words, utilizing visual feature at localized regions can improve the fine-grained prediction results without hurting the overall performance.

Table 3: Performance comparison of different methods with or without using visual features.

	Accuracy (%)					Error
	10 M	100 M	1 KM	10 KM	100 KM	(KM)
V-1NN	0.0	0.05	0.12	0.40	1.02	6876
LM	0.22	4.13	14.28	29.94	39.96	506
LM-V	**0.42**	**4.68**	14.53	30.06	39.99	505
LM-ALL	0.32	4.48	17.47	36.44	48.76	129
LM-ALL-V	**0.49**	**4.96**	17.62	36.47	48.89	125

4. CONCLUSIONS

We have presented a tag-boosted language model for image geo-location prediction based on a set of geo-aware tags, which are identified from GeoNames database, statistics of tag distribution among geo-grids and the tag spatial variance. Incorporating the importance of these tags into model learning and prediction, the performance is improved significantly at different levels of evaluation granularity. In addition, visual information has been proved to be helpful in fine-grained location estimation. As image matching is helpful to the global search of certain kinds of images (e.g., landmark), we will leverage the visual information in a query-adaptive way in the future work.

5. REFERENCES

[1] S. Ardeshir, A. R. Zamir, A. Torroella, and M. Shah. Gis-assisted object detection and geospatial localization. In *ECCV*, 2014.

[2] D. J. Crandall, L. Backstrom, D. P. Huttenlocher, and J. M. Kleinberg. Mapping the world's photos. In *WWW*, 2009.

[3] Q. Fang, J. Sang, and C. Xu. Giant: geo-informative attributes for location recognition and exploration. In *ACM Multimedia*, 2013.

[4] G. Friedland, J. Choi, and A. Janin. Video2gps: a demo of multimodal location estimation on flickr videos. In *ACM Multimedia*, 2011.

[5] G. Friedland, O. Vinyals, and T. Darrell. Multimodal location estimation. In *ACM Multimedia*, 2010.

[6] C. Hauff and G.-J. Houben. Placing images on the world map: a microblog-based enrichment approach. In *SIGIR*, 2012.

[7] C. Hauff, B. Thomee, and M. Trevisiol. Working notes for the placing task at mediaeval 2013. In *MediaEval*, 2013.

[8] J. Hays and A. A. Efros. IM2GPS: estimating geographic information from a single image. In *CVPR*, 2008.

[9] P. Kelm, S. Schmiedeke, J. Choi, G. Friedland, V. N. Ekambaram, K. Ramchandran, and T. Sikora. A novel fusion method for integrating multiple modalities and knowledge for multimodal location estimation. In *GeoMM '13*, 2013.

[10] L. S. Kennedy and M. Naaman. Generating diverse and representative image search results for landmarks. In *WWW*, 2008.

[11] O. V. Laere, S. Schockaert, and B. Dhoedt. Finding locations of flickr resources using language models and similarity search. In *ICMR*, 2011.

[12] X. Li, M. Larson, and A. Hanjalic. Geo-visual ranking for location prediction of social images. In *ICMR*, 2013.

[13] S. Liao, X. Li, X. Wang, and X. Du. Building geo-aware tag features for image classification. In *ICME*, 2014.

[14] P. Serdyukov, V. Murdock, and R. van Zwol. Placing flickr photos on a map. In *SIGIR*, 2009.

[15] T. Yamasaki, A. Gallagher, and T. Chen. Personalized intra- and inter-city travel recommendation using large-scale geotags. In *GeoMM '13*, 2013.

[16] A. R. Zamir, S. Ardeshir, and M. Shah. Gps-tag refinement using random walks with an adaptive damping factor. In *CVPR*, 2014.

[17] B. Zhou, L. Liu, A. Oliva, and A. Torralba. Recognizing city identity via attribute analysis of geo-tagged images. In *ECCV*, 2014.

Expression Recognition from Visible Images with the Help of Thermal Images

Xiaoxiao Shi, Shangfei Wang, Yachen Zhu
University of Science and Technology of China
Hefei, Anhui, P.R.China, 230027
bianhua@mail.ustc.edu.cn
sfwang@ustc.edu.cn
zhuyc@mail.ustc.edu.cn

ABSTRACT

Most facial expression recognition research focused on visible spectrum, which is sensitive to illumination changes. While thermal images, recording facial temperature distribution, are robust to light conditions. Therefore, expression recognition by visible and thermal image fusion is promising. However, in most cases, only visible images are available, since thermal cameras are much more expensive than visible cameras, which are popular in our daily life. Thus, in this paper, we propose a novel visible expression recognition approach by using thermal infrared data as privileged information, which is only available during training. First, active appearance model parameters and three defined head motion features are extracted from visible spectrum images, and several thermal statistical features are extracted from thermal infrared images. Second, feature selection is performed using the F-test statistic. Third, a new visible feature space is constructed using canonical correlation analysis under the help of thermal infrared images. After that, a support vector machine is adopted as the classifier on the constructed visible feature space. Experiments on the NVIE and Equinox database show the effectiveness of the proposed methods, and demonstrate that thermal infrared images' supplementary role for visible facial expression recognition.

Keywords

thermal images; privileged information; support vector machine; canonical correlation analysis

1. INTRODUCTION

Facial expression, as one major method of human to display their emotions, has attracted increased attention in many areas of human-computer interaction. Considerable progress has been achieved in the field of facial expression using visible images and videos recently [1]. Most of existing methods, however, are not robust to illumination changes. While, thermal infrared (IR) images, which record temperature distribution, are not sensitive to illumination conditions. Hence, facial expression recognition with the help of IR can improve recognition performance in uncontrolled environments.

To the best of our knowledge, little attention has been paid to facial expression recognition by combining visible and IR images. Only two reported efforts could be found [2][3]. Yoshitomi et al. proposed to recognize affective states using decision-level fusion of voices, visual and infrared facial images. First, visible and IR features were extracted by Discrete Cosine Transformation (DCT). Then, two neural network (NN) classifiers are trained for visual and IR features respectively. In addition, Hidden Markov Models (HMMs) were adopted for emotion detection from voices. Finally, the recognition results of the three classifiers were integrated by a simple weighted voting. Experiments were conducted on a posed expression database. Wang et al. [4] proposed to fuse visible features and IR features for facial expression recognition from both decision-level and feature-level. Specifically, two Bayesian Networks (BN) and two Support Vector Machines (SVM) are proposed to perform decision-level fusion and feature-level fusion. The experiments on the NVIE spontaneous database show that all methods yield improvements on the performance of facial expression recognition compared with only using visible features. These two works prove that it is promising to recognize expression by fusing visible and thermal images, when two modalities are available during both training and testing.

In many supervised learning applications, additional information, besides the labels, is often available during training, but is not available during testing. Such additional information is called privileged or hidden information. Recently, Vapnik et al. [illegible] introduced a new learning model, called Learning Using Privileged Information (LUPI), and proposed a discriminative model called SVM+ [5]. The basic idea of SVM+ is to use privileged information to predict the slack variables in the SVM. Their experimental results of digit recognition [illegible] demonstrate that SVM+ classifier trained on low-resolution digit images with the help of privileged information (poetic descriptor) reaches similar accuracies compared with the results trained on high-resolution images with SVM.

Similar for expression recognition in practice, in most cases, only one camera modality, i.e. visible, is available, since visible cameras are much cheaper than thermal infrared cameras, and widely used in our daily life. Therefore, only

ICMR'15, June 23–26, 2015, Shanghai, China.

DOI: http://dx.doi.org/10.1145/2671188.2749355.

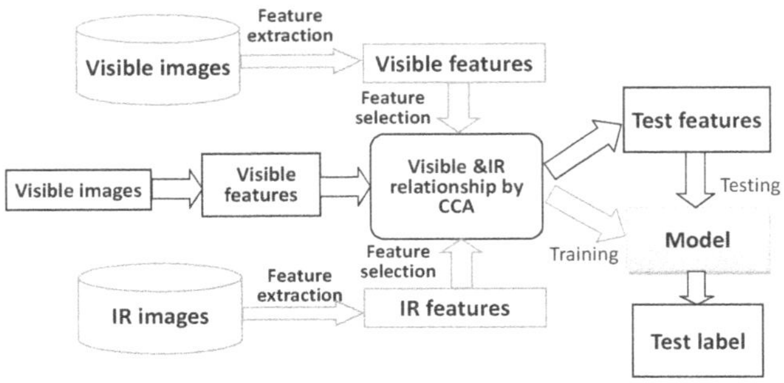

Figure 1: Framework of the proposed method

visible images are available during testing even images of two modalities are available during training. Using thermal infrared images as privileged information may construct a better classifier than using the available modality alone.

Thus, in this paper, we recognize expression from visible spectrum images, while IR images are regarded as privileged information. First, features are extracted from both visible spectrum and infrared images. For visible images, the active appearance model (AAM) [6] parameters, capturing both appearance and shape information, are extracted from apex expression images. In addition, three head motion features are extracted. For IR images, the relative temperature, the difference between temperature matrices of the apex and onset images, is adopted instead of the absolute temperature. Several statistical features are extracted from temperature matrices. Second, we perform feature selection using the F-test statistic. Third, a new visible spectrum feature space is constructed with the help of infrared features using Canonical Correlation Analysis (CCA). After that, a SVM is trained on the new visible spectrum feature space. Experiments are conducted on the Natural Visible and Infrared facial Expression (NVIE) spontaneous database [7] and the Equinox posed database to evaluate the effectiveness of our proposed approach.

2. PROPOSED METHOD

Our proposed method is shown in Fig. 1. First, features of visible image and IR image are extracted. Second, feature selection is performed to select distinctive features by using F-selection. After that, relations between visible feature and IR feature are built using CCA. Third, visible features are transformed according to this relationship and used for training classifiers. The thermal features, as privileged information, are used to optimize the visible features during training. During testing, the privileged information, IR images, is not available. Only visible features are available, and transformed to the new feature space, and used to recognize expressions.

2.1 Visible feature extraction

Visible feature extraction is similar to the method proposed by Wang et al. [1]. First, eyes are located using an AdaBoost and Haar feature eye location method [8]. Then, three head motion features, i.e. the velocities of head motion in horizontal and vertical direction, and the head's rotational speed, are extracted according to Eq. 1-3.

$$Velocity_x = \frac{C_x^{apex} - C_x^{onset}}{frame^{apex} - frame^{onset}} \tag{1}$$

$$Velocity_y = \frac{C_y^{apex} - C_y^{onset}}{frame^{apex} - frame^{onset}} \tag{2}$$

$$Velocity_r = \frac{\left| \arctan \frac{R_y^{apex} - L_y^{apex}}{R_x^{apex} - L_x^{apex}} - \arctan \frac{R_y^{onset} - L_y^{onset}}{R_x^{onset} - L_x^{onset}} \right|}{frame^{apex} - frame^{onset}} \tag{3}$$

where the coordinates of the left pupil's location are expressed as (L_x, L_y), (R_x, R_y), which represent the right pupil's location, and (C_x, C_y) is the coordinate of the center of two pupils's location. Frame difference between the apex and onset image represents the duration of each expression. In addition, we use AAM to extract visible features from the apex expressional images, since the AAM captures information about both appearance and shape.

2.2 IR feature extraction

IR features are extracted from the differential temperature matrix between apex and onset IR images. In this way, the influence of ambient temperature and the temperature drift of IR cameras are eliminated. First, using the method devised by Tong et al. [9], four points (centers of the eyes, the tip of the nose, and tip of the jaw) are automatically located on the apex and onset IR images. By exploiting these points, the apex and onset IR images are rotated, then resized, and cropped into images with size of $H \times W$ $(H, W \in \mathbb{N}^+)$. Later, temperature matrix corresponds to normalized onset IR image is subtracted from that of normalized apex IR image to obtain the differential temperature.

Subarea of eyes is not taken into consideration here (since the target may be wearing glasses) because IR light is opaque to glasses. We divide facial region into one hundred grids with the same size of $w \times w (w \in \mathbb{N}^+)$. For each grid, four statistical parameters, including mean, standard deviation, maximum, and minimum, are calculated as IR features.

2.3 Feature selection

In order to select distinctive features for classification, the F-test statistic [10] is used according to Eq. 4.

$$\begin{aligned} F - statistic &= \frac{between - group\ variability}{within - group\ variability} \\ &= \frac{\sum_{c=1}^{N} n_c(\bar{x_c} - \bar{x})^2}{\sum_{c=1}^{N}(n_c - 1)\sigma_c^2}\left(\frac{n-N}{N-1}\right) \end{aligned} \tag{4}$$

where N represents the size of classes, n_c is the number of samples of class c, and σ_c^2 is the variance within class c, n is total number of samples, $\bar{x_c}$ is the average of feature x within class c, $\bar{x}$ is the global mean of feature x. Features are selected from high to low according to the calculated F-statistics of all features.

2.4 Constructing a new visible feature space

After feature selection, we construct a new visible feature space with the help of thermal infrared features using CCA. The main idea of CCA is to assess the relationship between metric independent variables and multiple dependent measures. In our approach, denote the original training features of visible and thermal infrared images by $\mathbf{V}$ and $\mathbf{I}$. The goal of CCA is to find $\mathbf{a}$ and $\mathbf{b}$, and use them to construct canonical components $\mathbf{F}$ and $\mathbf{G}$

$$\mathbf{F} = \mathbf{V}\mathbf{a}, \tag{5}$$

$$\mathbf{G} = \mathbf{I}\mathbf{b}, \tag{6}$$

where $\mathbf{F}$ and $\mathbf{G}$ are corresponding canonical components which have the highest Pearson Correlation Coefficients, and the objective function is:

$$\max_{\mathbf{a},\mathbf{b}} \frac{\hat{E}\langle \mathbf{V}, \mathbf{a}\rangle \langle \mathbf{I}, \mathbf{b}\rangle}{\sqrt{\hat{E}\langle \mathbf{V}, \mathbf{a}\rangle^2 \hat{E}\langle \mathbf{I}, \mathbf{b}\rangle^2}} \tag{7}$$

where $\hat{E}$ is the empirical expectation. Here we use the approach described in [illegible] to solve this problem.

Thus, $\mathbf{a}$ is the eigenvector of $(\mathbf{V}^T\mathbf{V})^{-1}\mathbf{V}^T\mathbf{I}(\mathbf{I}^T\mathbf{I})^{-1}\mathbf{I}^T\mathbf{V}$, and $\mathbf{b}$ is the eigenvector of $(\mathbf{I}^T\mathbf{I})^{-1}\mathbf{I}^T\mathbf{V}(\mathbf{V}^T\mathbf{V})^{-1}\mathbf{V}^T\mathbf{I}$.

Then, the relations between these two spaces can be described as follows:

$$\mathbf{F} = \frac{1}{\beta}\mathbf{V}(\mathbf{V}^T\mathbf{V})^{-1}\mathbf{V}^T\mathbf{G}, \tag{8}$$

$$\mathbf{G} = \frac{1}{\beta}\mathbf{I}(\mathbf{I}^T\mathbf{I})^{-1}\mathbf{I}^T\mathbf{F}, \tag{9}$$

where $\beta = \mathbf{a}^T\mathbf{V}^T\mathbf{I}\mathbf{b}$. After exploiting this relation, we adopt it in training and testing phases.

For visible expression recognition, which means thermal infrared features are used as privileged information during training, $\mathbf{F}$ is employed for training the model. During testing, let $\mathbf{V}_t$ be the testing visible features, transfer $\mathbf{V}_t$ into the thermal-related space $\mathbf{V}'_t$ by

$$\mathbf{V}'_t = \mathbf{V}_t\mathbf{a}. \tag{10}$$

2.5 Expression recognition

A SVM classifier is employed to recognize expressions from visible images. During training, both visible features and IR features are available. Therefore, we obtain the visible feature space using F of Eq. 5 and IR feature space using Eq. 6. Then, they are used for training classifiers. During testing, without IR images, the visible features are transformed into visible space using $\mathbf{V}'_t$ in Eq. 10.

3. EXPERIMENTAL RESULTS AND ANALYSES

3.1 Experimental conditions

Currently, there are only two reported studies of facial expression recognition based on fusion of IR and visible images [illegible][illegible], as mentioned in the introduction section. The database used in [illegible] is not publicly available. Another study [illegible] also adopted the NVIE database. Thus, we conduct experiments on the NVIE database. The NVIE spontaneous database contains both visible and IR images of 123 subjects. The same samples adopted in [illegible] are used in our experiments. A 10-fold cross validation is adopted.

All visible expression sequences have been labeled by five students on the intensity of six basic facial expressions (happiness, sadness, surprise, fear, anger, and disgust) with a three point scales (0, 1 and 2). The expression with the highest average intensity is used as the expression label for the visible and IR image sequences. In this paper, we choose experimental samples under the following criteria. First, the average intensity associated with a sample label must be larger than 1. Second, as three expressions (happiness, fear and disgust) were successfully induced in most cases when the NVIE spontaneous database was constructed, a sample label has to be one of happiness, fear and disgust. Third, the sample should consist of both visible and IR image sequences. Following these criteria, we obtain a total of 535 samples from 123 subjects under different illuminations.

Table 1: Expression recognition results on NVIE Visible images

	SVM			SVM+			our method		
	disgust	fear	happiness	disgust	fear	happiness	disgust	fear	happiness
disgust	**118**	6	43	**107**	17	43	**126**	15	26
fear	35	**89**	16	25	**100**	15	39	**90**	11
happiness	30	2	**196**	19	10	**199**	29	6	**193**
F1-score	0.746			0.748			0.753		
Accuracy	75.33%			75.89%			76.45%		
Kappa	0.616			0.626			0.637		

Our experimental results are obtained by applying a 10-fold cross validation method on all samples according to the subjects. Owing to the high dimension of IR features, we perform IR feature selection. Another 10-fold cross validation is applied on the training set to choose a dimension combination of visible features that achieves the highest accuracy rate on the validated set. We compare the proposed methods with that of using visible alone and SVM+.

To further validate the effect of our method, we also conduct an experiment on Equinox database.

The Equinox face database [illegible] is simultaneously collected under visible, mid-wave infrared, and long-wave infrared spectrum. It contains frontal faces with three different light directions (frontal, right and left) and three facial expressions (frown, surprise and smile). The long-wave infrared and the corresponding visible images are used in this paper. A total of 1269 image pairs from 91 subjects are obtained, including 321 image pairs of 26 female subjects and 948 image pairs of 65 male subjects.

3.2 Experimental results on NVIE database

Table 1 compares the expression recognition results using our proposed approach with using SVM and SVM+ on visible features. The accuracy using visible features is 75.33%, and increases to 76.45% when IR features are used as privileged information through CCA. In addition, Kappa value and F1-score also increase from 0.616/0.746 to 0.637/0.753. Besides, fear and happiness expression recognition is improved. Specifically, when merely using visible images, 118 disgust, 89 fear together with 196 happiness faces are correctly identified. While with the help of IR features, correctly identified numbers rise to 126 and 90 for disgust and fear expressions respectively. Although correctly identified happiness number slightly decrease from 196 to 193, the number of false positive of happiness also decrease from 59 to 37. Hence, the recognition performance for all expressions is improved by using thermal images as privileged information.

The performance of our method is also better than the results on SVM+, since accuracy and Kappa values are higher. Accuracy, Kappa value and F1-score increase from 75.89%/0.626/0.748 to 76.45%/0.637/0.753. Correctly iden-

Table 2: Expression recognition results on Equinox Visible images

	SVM			SVM+			our method		
	smile	surprise	frown	smile	surprise	frown	smile	surprise	frown
smile	**332**	33	65	**327**	42	61	**350**	28	52
surprise	77	**263**	74	61	**304**	49	59	**287**	68
frown	48	27	**345**	41	38	**341**	41	30	**349**
F1-score	0.742			0.769			0.779		
Accuracy	74.37%			76.90%			78.01%		
Kappa	0.615			0.653			0.670		

tified fear and happiness face number rise by 2.34% and 6.48% especially. The improvement of using IR features as privileged information indicates the IR features can benefit recognizing visible facial expressions.

3.3 Experimental results on Equinox database

Table 2 compares the experimental results on Equinox database using our proposed approach with that of SVM and SVM+. Using SVM on visible features, the accuracy is 74.37% , Kappa value and F1-score are 0.615/0.742. When IR features are used as privileged information through CCA, the accuracy increases by 3.64% which is up to 78.01%, Kappa value and F1-score also increase to 0.670/0.779. In this experiment, performance on each expression is improved. When merely using visible images, 332 smile, 263 surprise together with 345 frown faces are correctly identified. Respectively, the accuracies are 72.65%, 81.42% and 71.28%. With the help of IR features, however, correctly identified numbers increase. The accuracies change to 77.78, 83.19 and 74.41 percent.

Comparing with SVM+, accuracy, Kappa value and F1-score are rise by 1.11%, 0.017 and 0.010. Correctly identified smile and surprise face number rise by 1.56% and 4.02%. Hence, the recognition performance for all expressions is improved by using privileged information. IR features' robustness to illumination may improve visible features by transferring feature space by CCA. Experiments on NVIE and Equinox databases demonstrate that thermal images, which are obtained as privileged information, can help visible images to construct a better classier during testing.

3.4 Comparison with related works

In this section we compare the performance of our proposed method with related works. As mentioned above, there are two reported studies on facial expression recognition using both IR and visible images [2][4]. The database in [2] is not publicly available. Furthermore, the method in [2] also uses audio signal alongside IR and visible. Therefore, it is difficult to perform a fair comparison with the method in [2] since our method uses only IR and visible images. The other study [4] conducted experiments on the NVIE database. Thus, we compare our expression recognition results with theirs directly, as shown in Table 3.

Comparing our results with those in [4], we can find that the performance of our method is similar to that of decision-level fusion and feature-level fusion in both accuracy and kappa coefficient. Decision-level fusion and feature-level fusion require thermal images for both train and testing process, while our proposed approach only needs thermal images during training, and can achieve comparable performance.Since thermal images may not be obtained conveniently, our approach is more practical than fusing IR and visible features, which further demonstrates the effectiveness of our approach.

Table 3: Compared with other fusion methods

Methods	Accuracy	Kappa
SVM with privileged information	76.45%	0.637
SVM Decision-level fusion [4]	76.45%	0.636
SVM Feature-level fusion [4]	76.82%	0.639

4. CONCLUSION

In this paper, we propose a novel expression recognition approach with privileged information by exploiting relations between visible and IR images. CCA is used to construct the relationship between visible and IR features, which could help to calibrate visible features. This model effectively solves the light-sensitive problem of visible images with the help of infrared images, which greatly improves the robustness of the recognition system. The experimental results verify the effectiveness of our approach.

5. ACKNOWLEDGMENTS

This paper is supported by the NSFC (61175037, 61473270).

6. REFERENCES

[1] Vinay Bettadapura. Face expression recognition and analysis: the state of the art. *arXiv preprint arXiv:1203.6722*, 2012.

[2] Yasunari Yoshitomi, Sung-Ill Kim, Takako Kawano, and T Kilazoe. Effect of sensor fusion for recognition of emotional states using voice, face image and thermal image of face. In *Robot and Human Interactive Communication, 2000. RO-MAN 2000. Proceedings. 9th IEEE International Workshop on*, pages 178–183. IEEE, 2000.

[3] Zhaoyu Wang and Shangfei Wang. Spontaneous facial expression recognition by using feature-level fusion of visible and thermal infrared images. In *Machine Learning for Signal Processing (MLSP), 2011 IEEE International Workshop on*, pages 1–6. IEEE, 2011.

[4] Shangfei Wang, Shan He, Yue Wu, Menghua He, and Qiang Ji. Fusion of visible and thermal images for facial expression recognition. *Frontiers of Computer Science*, 8(2):232–242, 2014.

[5] Vladimir Vapnik and Akshay Vashist. A new learning paradigm: Learning using privileged information. *Neural Networks*, 22(5):544–557, 2009.

[6] Timothy F Cootes, Gareth J Edwards, and Christopher J Taylor. Active appearance models. *IEEE Transactions on pattern analysis and machine intelligence*, 23(6):681–685, 2001.

[7] Shangfei Wang, Zhilei Liu, Siliang Lv, Yanpeng Lv, Guobing Wu, Peng Peng, Fei Chen, and Xufa Wang. A natural visible and infrared facial expression database for expression recognition and emotion inference. *Multimedia, IEEE Transactions on*, 12(7):682–691, 2010.

[8] Yanpeng Lv and Shangfei Wang. A spontaneous facial expression recognition method using head motion and aam features. In *Nature and Biologically Inspired Computing (NaBIC), 2010 Second World Congress on*, pages 334–339. IEEE, 2010.

[9] Yan Tong, Yang Wang, Zhiwei Zhu, and Qiang Ji. Robust facial feature tracking under varying face pose and facial expression. *Pattern Recognition*, 40(11):3195–3208, 2007.

[10] Chris HQ Ding. Analysis of gene expression profiles: class discovery and leaf ordering. In *Proceedings of the sixth annual international conference on Computational biology*, pages 127–136. ACM, 2002.

[11] David Weenink. Canonical correlation analysis. In *Proceedings of the Institute of Phonetic Sciences of the University of Amsterdam*, volume 25, pages 81–99, 2003.

[12] Equinox. Multimodal face database. http://www.equinoxsensors.com/products/HID.html. (last accessed 2012).

Multi-facet Learning using Deep Convolutional Neural Network for Person-Related Categories in Photos

Liangliang Cao
IBM Research, U.S.
liangliang.cao@us.ibm.com

Zhicheng Yan
University of Illinois at Urbana-Champaign
zyan3@illinois.edu

John R. Smith
IBM Research, U.S.
jsmith@us.ibm.com

ABSTRACT

This paper proposes to leverage multiple facets of person photos to improve the training of deep neural networks. Existing studies usually require a lot of labeled images to train deep convolutional networks. Our study suggests exploring multiple datasets and learning effective representation to learn related visual concepts. The practice of learning from multiple facets implicitly enforces to share features for image recognition. We show deep neural network benefits from the learning of multiple person-related categories in photos. Faceted classification systems learn from multiple resources, and alleviate the overfitting problems in deep learning. Moreover, by exploring multiple taxonomies of an object, it provides a finer annotation for the query images.

Categories and Subject Descriptors

I.5.4 [**Applications**]: Computer Vision; H.3.3 [**Information Search and Retrieval**]: Retrieval models

General Terms

Experimentation

Keywords

facet learning, deep convolutional neural network

1. INTRODUCTION

In the past few years, we have seen quite a number of successes of deep neural networks in different domains. The success of deep learning is blessed by the dramatic number of parameters. For example, the recent seminal work [10] built deep convolutional neural network (CNN) models with more than 60 million parameters, which is about 1000 times more than that in the tradition bag-of-words models. However, the challenge of training a deep neural network lies in the requirement of large amount of training data, which helps not only to learn a robust representation but also to reduce the risk of overfitting. Especially, when there are limited training samples, a flexible model with huge amount of parameters may lead to a high accuracy in the training set, but poor performance in the testing set.

ICMR'15, June 23–26, 2015, Shanghai, China.

http://dx.doi.org/10.1145/2671188.2749356.

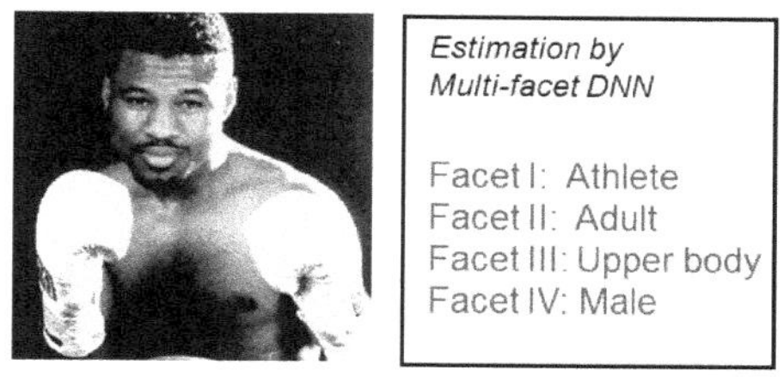

Figure 1: Annotation results by our multi-facet network.

In contrast, in some scenarios, it is not an easy task to get massive amount of labeled data. Researchers have spent a lot of efforts in building impressive large scale visual datasets including NUS-WIDE [2] and ImageNet [5]. However, for a new application, we probably cannot afford a long time to wait for the training data and to clean the labels. The labeling task becomes more difficult if the categories are not mutually exclusive and the users have to make a decision for every possible label, which will inevitably bring label noise and inconsistency.

One possible way to alleviate the lack of training samples is to leverage multiple datasets. Since many computer vision researchers have collected substantially many datasets in different applications, it is attractive to combine them and to build a big training set. However, the existing labels may not be consistent from one dataset to another, and it is often not possible in practice to process a dataset labeled for several tasks. If we limit ourselves to jointly annotations for visual concepts, it will prevent the use of deep learning in many applications.

In this paper, we proposed to conduct multiple facet learning with deep neural networks. Here a facet comprises clearly defined, mutually exclusive, and collectively exhaustive aspects, properties or characteristics of a class or specific subject. The idea of facet learning comes from S. R. Ranganathan [14], who proposed to organize library catalogs in multiple ways, rather than in a single, predetermined, taxonomic order. For example, a collection of books might be classified including an author facet, a subject facet, a date facet, etc. As suggested by [16], the visual world requires multiple dimensions to be modeled simultaneously, and a faceted classification scheme can represent these multiple, visual perspectives. Facet has been successfully applied to the image search problem in the Flammento system[1].

The idea of combining facet learning and deep neural network provides a way of leveraging and extending existing datasets in a practical and disciplined manner. Since it is impractical to label an image with all possible concepts, we encourage the users to choose different images to label. However, we force every labeling effort follows a fact participation, which is an exhaustive separation in some semantic space. In other words, each dataset should be associated with a facet, and different facets can be correlated or independent with each other. Figure **??** demonstrates an example of improving the annotation from deep convolutional network trained from ImageNet. The details of our method will be explained in the following sections.

2. RELATED WORK

Multiple facet learning can be viewed as an extension of multi-task learning, since it borrows more images from different resources to train big models. We can gain insights from the previous works in SVMs and Adaboost learning. Below we review related works in both SVM and deep learning society, and we hope to provide a big picture on why we think multiple facet learning is helpful in deep learning.

Multi-class and multi-task learning. A classical work in multi-class learning is multiple-class classifiers using error-correcting output codes (ECOC) [6], which classifies an example by running each set of classifiers, and looks for the closest matching row in the code matrix. [21] proposes to share features across multiple object classes. [1] develops a learning-by-focusing framework to distinguish ambiguous concept pairs. There are also many other works to explore multi-task learning algorithms for various applications [23] [22] [13].

Transfer learning and domain adaptation. The idea of leveraging knowledge from different resource has motivated the studies of transfer learning and cross domain learning. Multimedia and computer vision researchers have developed a number of algorithms for domain adaptation [24] [8]. Note that the goal of cross domain learning is different from the problem discussed in this paper. In cross domain learning or transfer learning, the purpose is to adapt classifiers to the target domain where no labeled examples are available. In contrast, the multiple facet learning aims to explore multiple resources to improve the performance in all the facets.

The idea of multi-task learning and transfer learning is inspiring to our work. However, the studies reviewed above are based on SVMs and Adaboost instead of deep neural networks. SVM is built on the concept of "max margin classifier" which provides an effective way of regularizing overfitting. In contrast, deep neural network employs numerous parameters to learn complicate phenomenon in a multiple layer structure. These differences imply that the multi-facet learning with deep neural network is significantly different with those using SVM models. SVM optimizes a convex cost function and find its global minimum, while the cost function of deep neural network is non-convex and we can only find its local minimum. We will see later that the multi-facet learning in this paper will choose a optimization strategy different from traditional SVM learning.

[1]http://orange.sims.berkeley.edu/cgi-bin/flamenco.cgi/famuseum/Flamenco

Related work in deep learning. Deep neural network has shown great success [12] [10] [19] with the ability to learn abstract representations that support transfer to novel but related tasks. Recently introduced deep learning models, including deep Boltzmann machines, deep convolutional networks, deep belief networks, deep autoencoders, and many others have been shown to learn useful feature representations for many high-dimensional data. Some recent studies [15] [7] show that it is attractive to use the off-the-shelf deep convolutional neural network trained from ImageNet as a feature representation. [4] built multiple task neural networks in NLP applications. In their work, the entire network is trained on different tasks, including part-of-speech tags, chunks, named entity tags, semantic roles, semantically similar words and the language model. Different from our work, [4] is for documents and sentences with a shared vocabulary, instead of visual signals with varying filters and more parameters. In visual recognition domain, [3] proposed a multi-column deep neural network structure where each input image can be preprocessed as blocks. An arbitrary number of columns can be trained on inputs preprocessed in different ways. [9] generalizes one classification task of traditional DNN into multiple binary classification tasks through defining the output layer with a negative class node and a positive class node for each label. [11] shows that it is promising to build high-level features using large scale unsupervised learning. However, the cost of such learning is very high and the performance may be inferior compared with supervised learning. [17] learns a joint representation of multimodal data, i.e., images and tags. Although these works shed light on the emerging interests in deep learning, the problems discussed in the above paper are not multi-facet recognition and hence different from our work.

3. MULTI-FACET CONVOLUTIONAL NETWORK

This paper considers employing multiple facets to help the training of deep convolutional neural networks. We consider four datasets for different facets:

1. **Affiliation facet**: includes athlete, automobile-driver, carpenter, electrician, fire fighter, lama, mechanic, military people, motorcycle cop, news presenter, prisoner, priest, veterinarian, unknown affiliation, and non-human. There are 7424 images in this facet.
2. **Age facet**: includes baby, child, adult, elderly person, and non-human. There are 10752 images in this facet.
3. **Bodyview facet**: includes face, upper body, full body, and non-human. There are 4352 images in this facet.
4. **Gender facet**: includes female, male, and non-human. There are 11008 images in this facet.

Note that new facets may be created at any time without disruption of a single hierarchy or reorganizing other facets. Existing facets may be used as a first step in a search process. We may add more facets in the future like races, hair styles, seasonal dress fashions, and etc. Facet based learning acknowledges that world of knowledge is growing, and a system needs to be developed that could grow with the knowledge.

We should emphasize the "non-human" concept is introduced in every facet which is very heterogeneous in appearance. Such a category makes the recognition much harder, however, it reflects the requirements in real applications. Since we want to apply multiple facet models for annotation, we hope every facet provides a complete coverage of the semantic space. In any facet, the distribution of images is roughly even in every category. We randomly select 1000 image as the testing set for every facet and the other images as the training set.

For every facet, we employ the seven-layer deep neural network structure following Krizhevsky et al's seminal work [10]. The deep neural network composed of five convolutional layers and two fully connected layers. The first, second, and the last convolutional layers are followed by a 2×2 maximum pooling operation. Figure 2 illustrates the structure of our joint facet learning model. In our experiment, the learning rate α is chosen as $\alpha = 0.005$. We tried to decease the learning rate during our training, however, found no obvious improvement, which is probably due to the fact of limited training samples. We also use $momentum = 0.9$ as suggested in [18]. The difference between this work and [10] is two fold: First, the number of concept in each facet is different, so that the number of output neuron in the last layer is different. Moreover, we hope the neural networks in the four facets share similar elements, i.e., filters and neurons, so that learning from different facets can benefit each other.

Although the naive SGD can optimize the neural network pretty efficiently, it will very likely fail into a non-perfect local minimum, especially when the number of training samples is limited. To solve this problem, we still employ the framework of stochastic learning and develop a facet based learning approach. Since facet labels are annotated on different images, we can apply the stochastic gradient descent to learn jointly the parameters and representations. In traditional neural network training, we randomly select samples and compute the gradient descent. In contrast, in multiple facet learning, we first select a facet, and then choose random samples and compute the gradient of the model in that facet. During the training stage, by learning from multiple facets, the deep neural network is exposed to more images, which alleviates the high requirement of more training samples. The multi-facet learning framework contributes to build a more reliable model by learning more accurate features and regularizing classification models. Algorithm 1 shows our joint learning algorithm of multiple facets.

A very important practical issue in deep learning is how to initialize the network [18]. In this work, we first train a network using 1.2 million ImageNet images [5], and then borrow the constitutional layers and the first fully connected layer as the initialization of our facet learning. The benefit of this initialization is to borrow the filters and patterns learned from a bigger dataset, so that the fine tuning step will have higher chance to find a good minimum. We find this initialization works better than the random initialization. We will report our results in the next section.

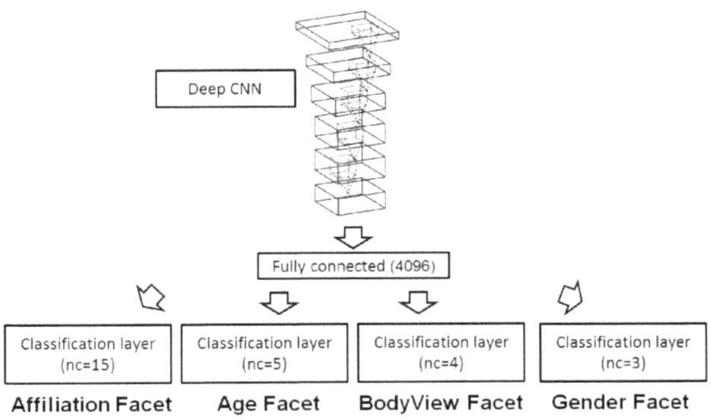

Figure 2: Structure of multi-facet deep CNN.

Algorithm 1 Multi-Facet Deep Neural Network Learning Algorithm.

Input: Training data $\{\mathbf{x}_i^f, y_i^f\}$ from facets $1 \leq f \leq 4$.
Learning:

1. Initialize the deep neural network C^f for every facet f.
2. For every facet f
   2.1 Randomly choose another facet m, and copy the filters and neurons in C^m to C^f
   2.2 Update C^f by learning from $\{\mathbf{x}_i^f, y_i^f\}$ until the validation error does not decrease.
   2.3 Compare the performance of C^f with that in the last iteration, and keep the one with better performance.
3. Go back to step 2 until the model does not improve.

Output: Neural network C^f for every facet f.

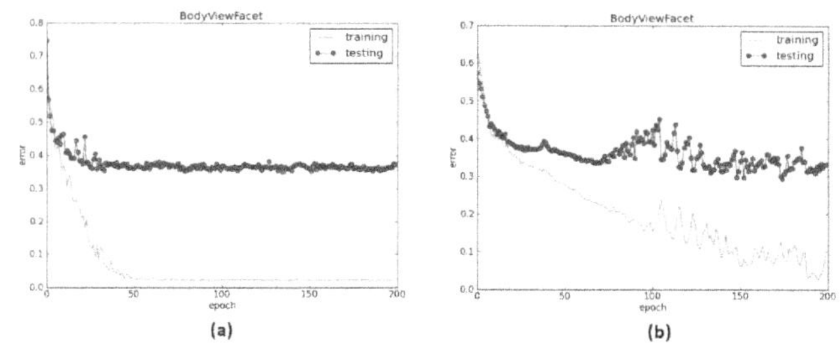

Figure 3: (a) Overfitting problem in single facet learning.(b) Jointly learning with multiple facets.

4. EXPERIMENTAL RESULTS

This section compares the performance of our multi-facet deep learning on the person-related dataset described in the previous section. Note that every facet includes a "non-human" category to match the real world scenarios but also significantly increase the difficulty of recognition. However, we can compare the performance of multiple baselines and the relative improvement can validate the contribution of multiple facet learning.

The first baseline is to use existing deep neural network as a off-the-shelf feature extractor. Some recent studies [15] [7] suggest using the off-the-shelf deep convolutional neural network for general visual recognitions. Following their approach, we apply the neural network trained on ImageNet data to every photo in the human facets. After the features are extracted, we apply a linear SVM to recognize categories in different facets.

We also compare the SVM with a traditional feature, i.e., tiny image [20]. Our results show that the SVM with CNN feature significantly outperforms SVM with tiny image feature in all the four facets. However, we should realize that the concepts in ImageNet LSVRC do not include human face, so the features from existing deep CNN model are not ideal for our problems.

Table 1: Recognition error of multi-facet CNN and baseline algorithms.

Facets	Affiliation	Age	Bodyview	Gender
SVM+tinyimage	0.732	0.677	0.563	0.592
SVM+CNN feature	0.636	0.467	0.444	0.438
CNN	**0.451**	0.401	0.370	0.360
Multi-facet CNN	**0.451**	**0.373**	**0.320**	**0.332**

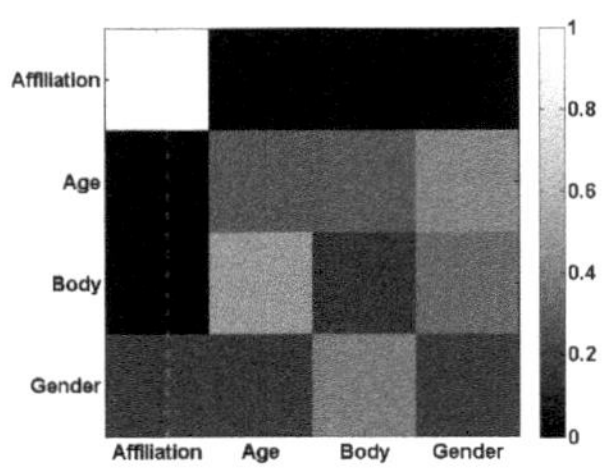

Figure 4: Contribution from different facets

Another baseline is to train convolutional neural network on our human facet data directly. We follow the model in [10] and only change the number of neurons in the last layer as the number of concepts in different facet. The resulted CNN outperforms the SVM with off-the-shelf features. However, if we take a closer look at the training procedure of CNN, we find that the resulted CNN suffers significantly from the overfitting problem. Since there are more parameters in the models than the number of training samples, we can expect the model can fit almost perfectly the training set well but may not generalize well to the testing set. As Figure 3 shows, we can see that the training error decreases dramatically while the testing error remains high. Since the model learns the classifier from different facets simultaneously, it can borrow the trained filters and structures from other facets. As a result shown in Figure 3, it has more chance to escape from the local minimum and hence a lower testing error.

Table 1 compares the performance of multi-facet learning and other methods. It shows that multi-facet CNN is a better choice than the baselines.

To explore the interaction among different facets, Figure 4 shows the percentage of benefits from other facets during the jointly training. It can be seen that learning neural network in the affiliation facet does not benefit from the learning in other facets. This is probably because the affiliation facet is different from other human face images. However, the network of affiliation helps the procedure of training other facets. The experimental results suggest that it will be beneficial to combine more data into training, even they are from different facet and do not follow the same labeling strategy.

5. DISCUSSION AND FUTURE WORK

This paper aims to enrich the semantic space with human specific concepts. Since the ImageNet LSVRC missed certain categories including human face and human portrait, we extend our semantic space with multiple facets, e.g., age, gender, body part, and uniform of different affiliations. Our experimental results show that the multi-facet convolutional neural network outperforms single facet learning.

6. REFERENCES

[1] L. Cao, L. Gong, J. R. Kender, N. C. Codella, and J. R. Smith. Learning by focusing: A new framework for concept recognition and feature selection. In *ICME*, 2013.

[2] T.-S. Chua, J. Tang, R. Hong, and et al. NUS-WIDE: A real-world web image database from national university of singapore. In *CIVR*, 2009.

[3] D. C. Ciresan, U. Meier, and J. Schmidhuber. Multi-column deep neural networks for image classification. In *CVPR*, pages 3642–3649, 2012.

[4] R. Collobert and J. Weston. A unified architecture for natural language processing: deep neural networks with multitask learning. In *ICML*, pages 160–167, 2008.

[5] J. Deng, W. Dong, and et al. ImageNet: A Large-Scale Hierarchical Image Database. In *CVPR*, 2009.

[6] T. G. Dietterich and G. Bakiri. Solving multiclass learning problems via error-correcting output codes. *J. Artif. Intell. Res.*, 2:263–286, 1995.

[7] J. Donahue, Y. Jia, O. Vinyals, and et al. Decaf: A deep convolutional activation feature for generic visual recognition. *CoRR*, abs/1310.1531, 2013.

[8] B. Gong, Y. Shi, F. Sha, and K. Grauman. Geodesic flow kernel for unsupervised domain adaptation. In *CVPR*, pages 2066–2073, 2012.

[9] Y. Huang, W. Wang, L. Wang, and T. Tan. Multi-task deep neural network for multi-label learning. In *ICIP*, 2013.

[10] A. Krizhevsky, I. Sutskever, and G. E. Hinton. Imagenet classification with deep convolutional neural networks. In *NIPS*, pages 1106–1114, 2012.

[11] Q. Le, M. Ranzato, R. Monga, and et al. Building high-level features using large scale unsupervised learning. In *ICML*, 2012.

[12] Y. LeCun, L. Bottou, Y. Bengio, and P. Haffner. Gradient based learning applied to document recognition. *Proceedings of the IEEE*, 86(11):2278–2324, 1998.

[13] Y. Liu, D. Xu, I. W. Tsang, and J. Luo. Textual query of personal photos facilitated by large-scale web data. *PAMI*, 33(5):1022–1036, 2011.

[14] S. Ranganathan. *Colon Classification*. Ess Publications, Delhi, India.

[15] A. S. Razavian, H. Azizpour, J. Sullivan, and S. Carlsson. Cnn features off-the-shelf: an astounding baseline for recognition. *CoRR*, abs/1403.6382, 2014.

[16] J. R. Smith. Just the facets. *IEEE MultiMedia*, 20(1):92, 2013.

[17] N. Srivastava and R. Salakhutdinov. Learning representations for multimodal data with deep belief nets. In *ICML Workshop*, 2012.

[18] I. Sutskever, J. Martens, G. Dahl, and G. Hinton. On the importance of initialization and momentum in deep learning. In *ICML*, pages 1139–1147, 2013.

[19] Y. Taigman, M. Yang, M. Ranzato, and L. Wolf. Deepface: Closing the gap to human-level performance in face verification. In *CVPR*, 2014.

[20] A. Torralba, R. Fergus, and W. T. Freeman. 80 million tiny images: A large data set for nonparametric object and scene recognition. *PAMI*, 30(11):1958–1970, 2008.

[21] A. Torralba, K. P. Murphy, and W. T. Freeman. Sharing features: Efficient boosting procedures for multiclass object detection. In *CVPR*, pages 762–769, 2004.

[22] A. Vezhnevets and J. M. Buhmann. Towards weakly supervised semantic segmentation by means of multiple instance and multitask learning. In *CVPR*, pages 3249–3256, 2010.

[23] X. Wang, C. Zhang, and Z. Zhang. Boosted multi-task learning for face verification with applications to web image and video search. In *CVPR*, pages 142–149, 2009.

[24] J. Yang, R. Yan, and A. G. Hauptmann. Cross-domain video concept detection using adaptive svms. In *ACM Multimedia*, pages 188–197, 2007.

Sketch-based Image Retrieval via Shape Words

Changcheng Xiao[1]* Changhu Wang[2]† Liqing Zhang[1], Lei Zhang[3]
[1]Shanghai Jiao Tong University, Shanghai, China
[2]Microsoft Research, Beijing, China
[3]Microsoft Corporation, Redmond, USA
xchangcheng@gmail.com, chw@microsoft.com,
zhang-lq@cs.sjtu.edu.cn, leizhang@microsoft.com

ABSTRACT

The explosive growth of touch screens has provided a good platform for sketch-based image retrieval. However, most previous works focused on low level descriptors of shapes and sketches. In this paper, we try to step forward and propose to leverage *shape words* descriptor for sketch-based image retrieval. First, the *shape words* are defined and an efficient algorithm is designed for *shape words* extraction. Then we generalize the classic Chamfer Matching algorithm to address the *shape words* matching problem. Finally, a novel inverted index structure is proposed to make *shape words* representation scalable to large scale image databases. Experimental results show that our method achieves competitive accuracy but requires much less memory, e.g., less than 3% of memory storage of MindFinder. Due to its competitive accuracy and low memory cost, our method can scale up to much larger database.

Categories and Subject Descriptors

H.3.3 [**Information Retrieval**]: Search Process, Query formulation

Keywords

Sketch-based Image Retrieval; Shape Words

1. INTRODUCTION

Owing to the popularity of digital cameras, millions of new digital images are freely accessible online every day, which brings a great opportunity for image retrieval. Usually, users search images with text queries. But the shape and location of the object are hard to be formulated with a few keywords. Thus, query-by-example (QBE) was proposed. However, in QBE, the query has to be an example image, which is usually the reason of searching. As the popularity of touch-screen devices, searching images by drawing has become a highly desired feature for users, which is complementary and thus can be combined with query-by-keyword and query-by-example modalities.

Figure 1: Example results of our system. Suppose we want to search for a bike. We may draw two circles as its wheels and draw some line segments as its frame. When we draw these sketches the system will extract shape words (line segments and circular arcs) and search similar images with these shape words.

Sketch based image retrieval (SBIR) has been extensively studied since 1990s, and stepped into large-scale scenarios in recent years. In 2010, Eitz et al. [5] built an SBIR system based on Tensor descriptors by linearly scanning the whole database for each query, which greatly limits its scalability. In 2011, Cao et al. [3] built the MindFinder system based on indexable Oriented Chamfer Matching (OCM) to solve the indexing problem of SBIR. In 2012, Zhou et al. [8] proposed a convolution based descriptor, and Kai-Yu Tseng [7] proposed to use 'HashBits' to compress the Distance Transform descriptor. In 2013, Sun et al. [6] built a billion scale SBIR system with vector-like Chamfer feature pairs.

However, most of these methods [3, 5, 6, 7, 8] focus on low level descriptors of sketches like local patches or edge pixels, which require huge amount of memory storage. In this work, we try to go one step forward and see the shapes/sketches in a higher view. Different from MindFinder [4] which indexes and matches with (sampled) edge pixels, we propose to use *shape words* to represent both the query sketch and database images. As shown in Fig. 1, when asked to draw a

*Changcheng Xiao performed this work while being an intern at Microsoft Research Asia.
†Corresponding author.

ICMR'15, June 23–26, 2015, Shanghai, China.

ACM 978-1-4503-3274-3/15/06 ...$15.00.
http://dx.doi.org/10.1145/2671188.2749360.

bike, most users will probably draw two circles as its wheels and draw a triangle as its frame. Ideally, it will be quite powerful if we can successfully extract the triangles and circles from images, and match them with the shapes of the query sketch. However, it's still a very challenging task to extract such shapes from natural images with high precision/recall. To balance the robustness and computational complexity, we leverage a middle level descriptor between edge pixels and shapes, i.e., line segments and circular arcs, as *shape words*. We propose an efficient algorithm for *shape words* extraction, followed by a generalization of the classic Chamfer Matching algorithm [1] for *shape words*' matching. Finally, a novel inverted index structure is proposed to make *shape words* representation scalable to large scale image databases. The experimental results demonstrate the high memory efficiency and retrieval accuracy of the proposed method.

2. SHAPE WORDS REPRESENTATION

In this section, we introduce the *shape words* representation followed by its extraction algorithm. First, we convert the natural image to a stroke-like representation by salient boundary extraction and stroke decomposition. Then we extract *shape words* from these strokes. The framework of *shape words* extraction is illustrated in Fig. 2.

2.1 Shape Words Design Strategy

Our goal is to define a robust while compact descriptor to encode the precise structure information of shapes and sketches. Edge pixels are the smallest components of sketches and they are robust to local distortions[3]. However, single edge pixel only carries limited information (e.g., gradient) of sketches. What's worse, there are thousands of edge pixels in a single image, which require a large amount of memory to index. Shapes like circles and triangles are informative and compact but they are not robust in extraction and matching. Thus, we compromise between the edge pixels and real shapes, and propose *shape words*.

Definition 1. A *shape word* is a small segment constructed by a group of connected edge pixels. Different *shape words* have different properties like location, direction and size.

In this paper, we choose line segments and circular arcs as *shape words*. The *shape words* based representation is robust to represent any sketch and very compact at the same time. A line segment can be represented by a tuple $L = (x, y, l, \theta)$, in which (x, y), l, θ represent the center location, length, and direction of the line segment. A circular arc is represented by a tuple $C = (x, y, r, \theta_1, \theta_2)$, in which (x, y), r, θ_1, θ_2 are the center location, radius, and angle range of the circular arc. Based on these representations, a natural image or a user sketch can be represented by a bag of *shape words* as:

$$\overline{\mathcal{F}} = \{L_1, L_2, \ldots C_1, C_2, \ldots\}. \quad (1)$$

In our Flickr1M dataset, the number of *shape words* is just about 3% of the number of edge pixels.

2.2 Stroke-like Representation

Given a natural image, we first resize it to make sure that its longer side contains 200 pixels. Then we apply Canny Edge Detector [2] to extract the salient edges of the image, in which we choose proper thresholds to remove the clutter details while keep the salient edges at the same time.

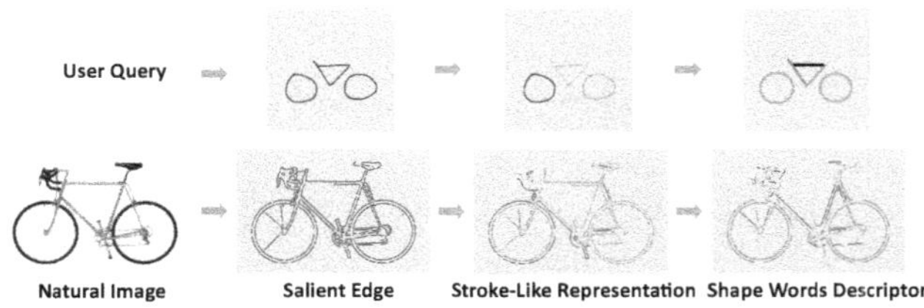

Figure 2: Framework of shape words extraction.

In order to extract the *shape words* from user sketches and natural edge images, we have to convert them to stroke-like representations. Although we can decompose user sketches to strokes easily, it isn't a trivial task to extract strokes from edge images. However, as different stroke decomposition results will not affect the *shape words* representation too much, we extract strokes by simply considering the connectivity of edge pixels. At the end of this step, we can represent the user sketch or a natural image by a stroke set $\overline{S}$.

2.3 Shape Words Extraction

First, we extract the interest point set *IP(S)* of a stroke S by calculating its polygonal approximation end points. Then we extract *shape words* set *SW(S)* by searching maximum successive interest points with least square fitting error *(LSFE)* smaller than a predefined threshold. The detail of *shape words* extraction algorithm is as follows:

Algorithm 1 Shape Words Extraction

Define:
$\overline{FL}$ is the line defined by the point F and L
$S_{A\to B}$ is a sub stroke of S from point/index A to B
$LSF, LSFE$ are the least square fitting and fitting error
$T_{split}, T_{line}, T_{arc}$ are predefined thresholds
for *Stroke* $S \in \overline{S}$ **do**
  Stage 1: Extract interest points set $IP(S)$
  Add its first and last point F, L to $IP(S)$
  $[P_{max}, Dist_{max}] = Argmax_P(EuclidDist_{P\to\overline{FL}}), P \epsilon S$
  if $Dist_{max} \geq T_{split}$ **then**
    Calculate $IP(S_{F\to P_{max}}), IP(S_{P_{max}\to L})$ recursively
    $IP(S) = IP(S_{F\to P_{max}}) \cup IP(S_{P_{max}\to L})$
  end if
  Stage 2: Extract shape words set $SW(S)$
  for $j = 1 \to size(IP(S)) - 1$ **do**
    $k \in [j+1, size(IP(S))]$
    $Line_k = Argmax_k(LSFE_{line}(S_{i\to k}) \leq T_{line})$
    $Arc_k = Argmax_k(LSFE_{arc}(S_{i\to k}) \leq T_{arc})$
    $[L, Err_l] = LSF_{line}(S_{i\to Line_k})$
    $[C, Err_a] = LSF_{arc}(S_{i\to Arc_k})$
    if $Line_k > Arc_k | (Line_k == Arc_k \& Err_l \leq Err_a)$ **then**
      Add line segment L to $SW(S)$
    else
      Add circular arc C to $SW(S)$
    end if
    $j = Max(Line_k, Arc_k)$
  end for
end for

After all the *shape words* are extracted, the sketch query or the natural image can be represented by a bag of *shape words* as in Equation 1.

3. MATCHING AND INDEXING

In this section, we generalize the classic Chamfer Matching [1] to address the *shape words* matching problem. Then, we propose an efficient index structure for fast matching.

3.1 Shape Words Matching

Given a query sketch $\mathcal{Q}$, we want to find the best matched image(s) $\mathcal{D}$ in the database, both of which are represented by a bag of *shape words*. Thus we need to measure the similarity of $\mathcal{Q}$ and $\mathcal{D}$, denoted by $Sim_{Q,D}$.

First, we introduce the classic Chamfer Matching [1] for raw curve matching. Then we generalize the classic Chamfer Matching for *shape words* matching.

3.1.1 Classic Chamfer Matching

The classic Chamfer Matching similarity from a database image $\mathcal{D}$ to the query sketch $\mathcal{Q}$ is defined as:

$$Sim_{D\to Q} = \frac{1}{|D|}\sum_{p\epsilon D}\max_{q\epsilon Q} sim(p,q). \tag{2}$$

Chamfer Matching algorithm seeks to find the nearest pixel on the query sketch $\mathcal{Q}$ for each pixel of the database image $\mathcal{D}$. So we can define $sim(p,q)$ above as $\frac{1}{Dist(p,q)}$. Here, $|D|$ is the total number of edge pixels of $\mathcal{D}$. Similarly, we can define the similarity from $\mathcal{Q}$ to $\mathcal{D}$ as:

$$Sim_{Q\to D} = \frac{1}{|Q|}\sum_{q\epsilon Q}\max_{p\epsilon D} sim(q,p). \tag{3}$$

The symmetric Chamfer Matching similarity is given by:

$$Sim_{D,Q} = (Sim_{D\to Q}\cdot Sim_{Q\to D})^{\frac{1}{2}}. \tag{4}$$

3.1.2 Chamfer Matching for Shape Words

Chamfer Matching algorithm was actually designed for pixel-based raw curve matching. So in order to apply it to *shape words* matching, we have to generalize its matching units from pixels to *shape words* and define the similarity of *shape words*.

In the raw curve case, the Euclidean distance is applied to define the similarity of pixels. For two *shape words* p and q, we consider their type similarity $sim^t(p,q)$, location similarity $sim^l(p,q)$ and size similarity $sim^s(p,q)$. So the similarity of p and q can be defined as:

$$sim(p,q) = sim^t(p,q)\cdot sim^l(p,q)\cdot sim^s(p,q), \tag{5}$$

where each term is defined as:

$$sim^t(p,q) = \begin{cases} 1 & \text{the same type of } \textit{shape words}, \\ 0 & \text{otherwise.}\end{cases} \tag{6}$$

$$sim^l(p,q) = \begin{cases} 1 & Dist(p,q)\le R, \\ 0 & \text{otherwise.}\end{cases} \tag{7}$$

$$sim^s(p,q) = Overlap(p,q). \tag{8}$$

In Equation 7, $Dist(p,q)$ is the center distance of two *shape words* and R is the tolerance radius for $Dist(p,q)$ ($R = 15$ in our experiments). We define $Overlap(p,q)$ by considering the index structure, in which we quantize the length of *shape words* to a limited number of bins. For the same type of *shape words*, their $Overlap$ is just the maximal length they share if they are close enough.

After defining the similarity of *shape words*, we can use Equation 4 to compute the similarity score of $\mathcal{Q}$ and $\mathcal{D}$. $|D|$ and $|Q|$ are the total length of *shape words*.

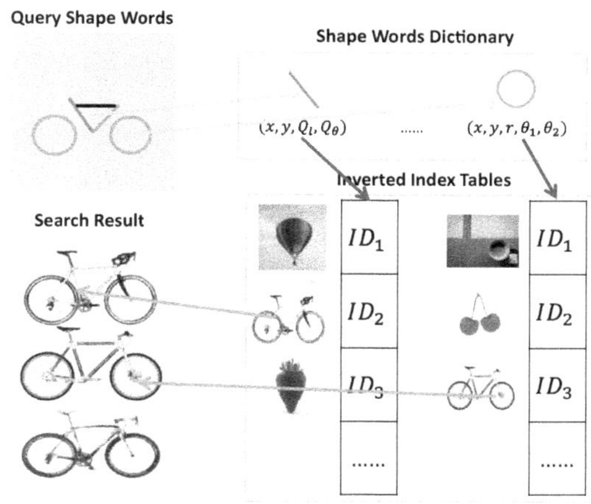

Figure 3: Shape words index structure.

3.2 Shape Words Index Structure

One of the most important design strategies for *shape words* representation and their matching algorithm is to make them indexable and thus scalable to large scale databases.

As there are two kinds of *shape words*, we build one inverted table for each of them. In order to build the inverted index tables, we need to quantize the two kinds of *shape words* first. For a line segment $L = (x,y,l,\theta)$, we quantize its directions θ to Q_θ (6 bins), i.e., $-15^\circ \sim 15^\circ$,$15^\circ \sim 45^\circ$,...,$135^\circ \sim 165^\circ$, and its length l to Q_l (20 bins). For a circular arc $C = (x,y,r,\theta_1,\theta_2)$, we quantize its radius r to Q_r (10 bins). We treat each line segment and circular arc as a *shape word* in the dictionary. As all the database images have been resized to 200×200, the dictionary size for the line segments is $200\times 200\times 20\times 6 = 4.8M$, and the dictionary size for the circular arcs is $200\times 200\times 10 = 0.4M$.

If an image ID contains a line segment $L = (x,y,l,\theta)$, a item ID will be inserted to the list at (x,y,Q_l,Q_θ). As there are much less circular arcs, we choose to store their angle range information in the inverted table. Thus if an image ID contains a circular arc $C = (x,y,r,\theta_1,\theta_2)$, an item (ID,θ_1,θ_2) will be inserted to the list at (x,y,Q_r).

For a sketch query $\mathcal{Q}$ in Fig. 3, we first extract its *shape words* and quantize them as above. Next, we propagate each *shape word* to its neighbors with distance smaller than R. Then we retrieve the inverted list of the *shape word* in these neighbors and compute their similarity score using Equation 5. Finally, we compute the two-way similarity score $Sim_{D,Q}$ with Equation 2 $\sim$ 4 and rank all the database images with their similarity scores.

4. EXPERIMENTS

To evaluate the performance of the proposed method on a large scale dataset, we built a new image dataset called Flickr1M. (1) We defined 500 object categories and used their keywords to search on Flickr and Google. Each category contains about 2K images. (2) We chose 100 meaningful categories for SBIR. Then we invited five subjects to skim through the object images and draw a sketch for each of the 100 object categories. Hence, we have $100\times 5 = 500$ sketches in total. (3) The images of other 400 categories are

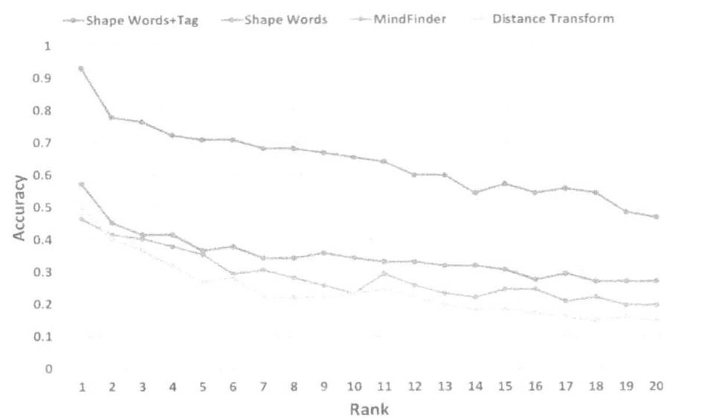

Figure 4: Retrieval accuracy on sketch-based image retrieval.

treated as the distracting images. Overall we collected 1.3M images and 500 sketches.

Then we built an SBIR system with the proposed method on this new dataset and compared its memory cost and retrieval accuracy with the MindFinder approach [3], which is one of the state-of-the-art SBIR approaches. Different from our method, MindFinder uses edge pixels for indexing and matching. We also compared with the HashBits approach [7]. As hashing and binarization will sacrifice some accuracy for efficiency, which makes Distance Transform hold the upper bound accuracy of this method. Thus, we chose to compare with Distance Transform directly.

All the experiments were conducted on a server with 2 Intel Xeon 2.66GHz Six-Core processors and 64GB memory. The average retrieval time of our system is about 1 second.

4.1 Memory Cost Saving

In Flickr1M, an image has 1361 edge pixels in average. For MindFinder approach, it needs to index about $1361 \times 1.3M = 1769.3M$ items, which costs $1769.3M \times 4Bytes \approx 6.91GB$ memory. Proper pixel sampling can reduce memory cost but may lose some accuracy. For comparison, an image has only 46.07 *shape words* in average. Thus for *shape words* method, we only need to index about $46.07 \times 1.3M \approx 59.89M$ items. As we have to encode a little more information, our system needs $240M$ memory[1] for the index structure, which is only 3.4% of MindFinder approach without sampling. MindFinder needs another 1.5G memory to store the raw curve features for two-way Chamfer Matching. So the memory cost of our system is actually less than 3% of MindFinder, which is as good as HashBits method [7].

4.2 Retrieval Accuracy

In this task, we evaluate the effectiveness of our system. We invited those 5 subjects to search their 100 sketches in the three systems: *Shape Words*, *MindFinder* and *Distance Transform*. Besides, subjects were asked to add proper tags for every sketch query to facilitate their searches. This approach is denoted by *Shape Words + Tag*. The measurement is defined as the proportion of all the 500 search tasks that could rank a similar image at rank position k.

The results are shown in Fig. 4. We can see that, *Shape Words* performs a little better than *MindFinder* and *Distance Transform*. By checking the results of each query, we found that our system performed better for those queries with obvious structures. As a negative example, a query of a bird doesn't have obvious shape structure. There will be more distortions when users draw such objects. Edge pixel-based method like *MindFinder* has better tolerance for this. Fig. 5 shows several sketch queries and the corresponding top search results.

[1] $(46.07 + 0.02 \times 3) \times 1.3M \times 4Bytes \approx 240MB$

Figure 5: Example queries and corresponding results. Images marked by red cross indicate that they are irrelevant with the query.

5. CONCLUSIONS

In this paper, we proposed to use *shape words* to balance the robustness and compactness of large scale SBIR. We also designed efficient extraction, matching and indexing algorithms for the *shape words* representation. Experimental results show that our method achieves competitive accuracy but requires much less memory.

6. ACKNOWLEDGMENTS

The work of first and third authors was supported by the National Natural Science Foundation of China (Grant No. 61272251) and National Key Basic Research Program of China (Grant No. 2015CB856004).

7. REFERENCES

[1] G. Borgefors. Hierarchical chamfer matching: A parametric edge matching algorithm. *IEEE PAMI*, 1988.

[2] J. Canny. A computational approach to edge detection. *IEEE PAMI*, 1986.

[3] Y. Cao, C. Wang, L. Zhang, and L. Zhang. Edgel index for large-scale sketch-based image search. CVPR, 2011.

[4] Y. Cao, H. Wang, C. Wang, Z. Li, L. Zhang, and L. Zhang. Mindfinder: Interactive sketch-based image search on millions of images. MM, 2010.

[5] M. Eitz, K. Hildebrand, T. Boubekeur, and M. Alexa. A descriptor for large scale image retrieval based on sketched feature lines. SBIM, 2009.

[6] X. Sun, C. Wang, C. Xu, and L. Zhang. Indexing billions of images for sketch-based retrieval. MM, 2013.

[7] K.-Y. Tseng, Y.-L. Lin, Y.-H. Chen, and W. H. Hsu. Sketch-based image retrieval on mobile devices using compact hash bits. MM, 2012.

[8] R. Zhou, L. Chen, and L. Zhang. Sketch-based image retrieval on a large scale database. MM, 2012.

Multiple Aesthetic Attribute Assessment by Exploiting Relations Among Aesthetic Attributes

Zhen Gao, Shangfei Wang*
University of Science and Technology of China
Hefei, Anhui, P.R.China, 230027
gzgqllxh@mail.ustc.edu.cn,
sfwang@ustc.edu.cn

Qiang Ji
Rensselaer Polytechnic Institute
Troy, NY, USA, 12180
qji@ecse.rpi.edu

ABSTRACT

Current research of aesthetic assessment for images assumes one aesthetic score or one aesthetic label for an image, ignoring the relations of multiple aesthetic-related attributes. However, most images can be described by multiple aesthetic attributes simultaneously. Therefore, in this paper, we propose multiple aesthetic attribute prediction and classification by modeling relations among aesthetic attributes through Bayesian Networks (BN). In order to realize continuous aesthetic attribute prediction, each aesthetic attribute is represented by a three-node BN, including the discretized aesthetic attribute label, the predicted aesthetic attribute score, and the measurement of the aesthetic attribute score. In addition, the relations among multiple aesthetic attributes are modeled by another discrete BN, whose structure and conditional probabilities are learned from the training data. The attribute measurements are obtained by an existing image-driven regression method. With the learned BN, we infer the true discrete label and continuous score for each attribute by combining the relations among attributes with the previously obtained measurements. Experiments on the Memorability dataset show the superiority of our proposed approach to current image-driven methods for both multiple continuous aesthetic attribute score prediction and multiple discrete aesthetic attribute label classification, indicating the effectiveness of the captured relations for aesthetic quality assessment.

Categories and Subject Descriptors

I.5.1 [**Pattern Recognition**]: model—*Statistical*

Keywords

Aesthetic assessment; Bayesian Network; Multi-label tasks

*This is the corresponding author (Telephone: +86-551-3602824).

ICMR'15, June 23–26, 2015, Shanghai, China.

DOI: http://dx.doi.org/10.1145/2671188.2749363.

1. INTRODUCTION

Aesthetic quality assessment for images has attracted increasing attention due to its wide application in recent years. For example, users could obtain realtime advices for a better photo by using aesthetic quality assessment in a camera. Advertisers could select images to make advertisements more attractive with the help of aesthetic quality assessment.

Current work of aesthetic quality assessment can be classified into two groups, aesthetic classification and aesthetic prediction. The first group regards aesthetic quality assessment as a binary classification, i.e. aesthetic and unaesthetic. For example, Datta et al. [1] designed special aesthetic features, and used the Support Vector Machine (SVM) and Decision Tree (DT) to recognize aesthetic and unaesthetic images. Mark and David [2] adopted the AdaBoost method to select features and classify aesthetic quality. Dhar et al. [3] proposed to estimate several types of high-level attributes (i.e. compositional attributes, content attributes, and sky-illumination attributes) first, and then used the predicted attributes as the middle-level features to recognize the aesthetic label by SVM. Su et al. [4] proposed to represent images with bag-of-aesthetics-preserving features, and use Adaboost for aesthetic modeling. Luo and Tang [5] formulated a number of high-level semantic features from the extracted subject and background region, and then use Bayes classifier, SVM and Gentle AdaBoost for aesthetic quality evaluation. Lo et al. [6] designed aesthetic features with high efficiency to compute and these features have good performance compared with other kinds fo features. Lu et al. [7] proposed a double-column deep convolutional neural network approach for aesthetic quality categorization. The second group considers aesthetic quality assessment as a regression problem, i.e. continuous aesthetic score prediction. Datta et al. [1] proposed to use the Linear Regression (LR) with polynomial terms of the features to predict the aesthetic rating. Bhattacharya et al. [8] proposed to capture image aesthetics using a support vector regression(SVR). Obrador et al. [9] designed a category-based method with SVR to assess the aesthetic appeal of photographs.

Current studies assume that there is only one aesthetic label or score for an image. However, users often assess the aesthetic quality of an image from different aspects. For example, an image, as shown in Fig. 1, can be described by different aesthetic attributes, such as aesthetic, attractive, memorable etc, simultaneously. There exist certain semantic relations among these high-level aesthetic attributes. Therefore, in this paper, we formulate the aesthetic assess-

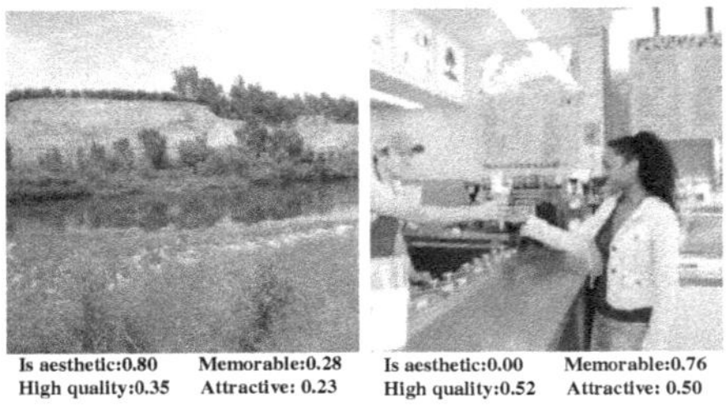

Figure 1: images with aesthetic attributes

ment as a multi-label task, which predicts multiple aesthetic attributes together by exploring the relations among them.

Specifically, we propose to use Bayesian Networks (BN) to capture the relations among aesthetic attributes to help both aesthetic classification and prediction. First, each aesthetic attribute is represented by a three-node BN as shown in Fig. 3(b), consisting of the discretized label, the ground-truth score, and the corresponding measurement. Second, another BN, whose structure and parameters are learned from the ground-truth labels, is constructed to model the relations among multiple discretized aesthetic attributes as shown in Fig. 3(a). Third, the above two BNs are merged as shown in the dashed circle in Fig. 3(a) as one BN. Support Vector Regression (SVR) is adopted to obtain the measurements for the continuous aesthetic scores. Finally, the constructed BN is used to infer both multiple continuous aesthetic attribute scores and multiple discrete aesthetic attribute tags by combining the measurements obtained from the image-driven methods with the dependencies among aesthetic attributes. Experiments on the Memorability dataset show that for the continuous aesthetic-related attribute prediction, our BN model outperforms the support vector regression; For the discrete aesthetic-related attribute classification, our BN model outperforms the support vector machine, demonstrating that the relations captured by our BN model contribute to both aesthetic attribute prediction and classification.

2. THE FRAMEWORK OF OUR METHOD

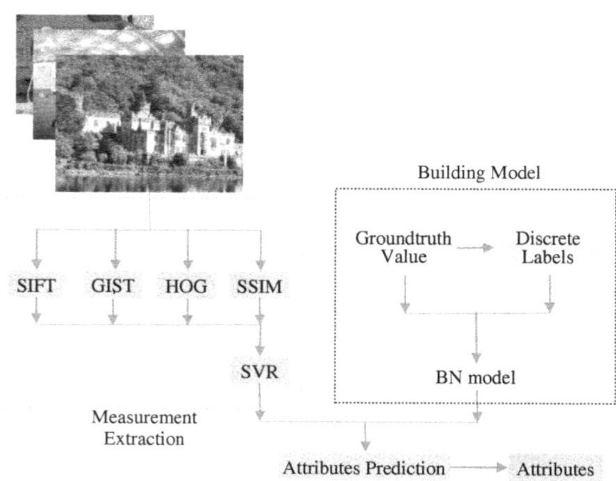

Figure 2: The framework of our method

As shown in Fig 2, the framework of our approach consists of two modules, measurement acquisition and multi-attribute relation modeling. In the training phase, we first train SVRs individually to predict the rating for each aesthetic attribute as the measurement. Then we discretize the ground-truth value into two classes based on the mean value and train the BN to capture the semantic relationships among these attributes. In the test phase, we infer the continuous ratings and discrete labels for the aesthetic attributes given the measurements of test samples.

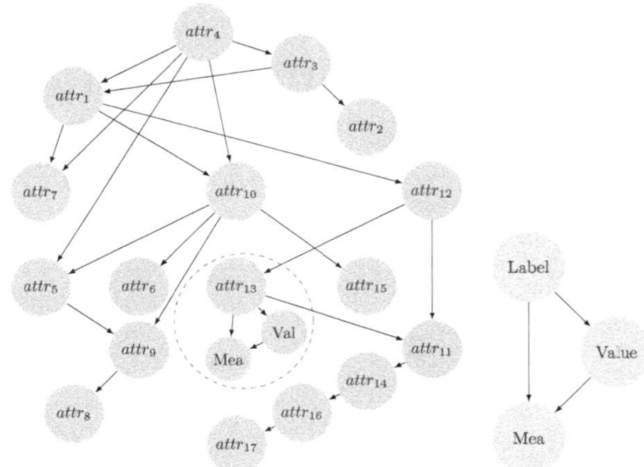

(a) the structure of our BN (b) each node

Figure 3: Our BN model

2.1 Measurement Acquisition

We use the multi-kernel method like Isola [10] to extract the measurements. For each image, we first extract global image descriptors, including scale-invariant feature transform (SIFT) [11], gist [12], histogram of oriented gradient (HOG) [13], and self-similarities (SSIM) [14]. Then, we use an RBF kernel for the gist features, and histogram intersection kernels for the other features. We combine all feature kernels to form the total feature kernel. We train SVRs individually for each aesthetic attribute with the same feature kernel. The outputs of each SVR are used as the measurements of the BN model in the following steps.

2.2 Modeling the Relations among Multiple Aesthetic Attributes

The key of our method is modeling the relations among the aesthetic attributes by a Bayesian network, as shown in 2.2. Since we want to assess aesthetic quality both continuously and discretely, a hybrid BN consists of both continuous and discrete variables should be learned from ground-truth data. However, the structure learning for a hybrid BN is still a challenge. Therefore, in this paper, we propose a method to simplify the BN structure learning with both continuous and discrete nodes.

We first discretize each continuous attribute into the label with two classes based on the mean value of the ground-truth value. We use the discrete labels to learn the BN structure to model the relationships among aesthetic attributes. Then, we link the discrete nodes with corresponding continuous nodes.

2.2.1 *BN Structure Learning*

The BN structure learning is to find a BN structure G

which maximizes the objective function given the data set of multiple target labels. In this work, the data set is the multiple discretized attribute labels $DL = (x_i)_{i=1}^n$ where $x_i = (Attr_1^{(i)}, Attr_2^{(i)}, ..., Attr_m^{(i)})$, n is the number of the samples and m is the number of the attributes. We employ the Bayesian Information Criterion (BIC) score function as the objective function which is defined as follows:

$$Score(G) = max_\theta log(p(DL|G, \theta)) - \frac{Dim_G}{2} logn \quad (1)$$

where the first term is the log-likelihood function of parameters θ with respect to the data set DL given the structure G, representing the fitness of the structure G to the data; the second term is to control the complexity of the structure and Dim_G indicates the number of independent parameters. The BN structure learning algorithm proposed by Campos et al [15] is adopted here.

After learning the BN structure among multiple discrete aesthetic attributes, we link each discrete label to two continuous nodes, representing the predicted aesthetic attribute score and its corresponding measurement, as shown in Fig. 3(b). These two BN structures together constitute our BN structure.

2.2.2 *BN Parameters Learning*

During the training, the parameters of our BN network are estimated using the maximum-likelihood estimation (MLE), as shown in Equ. 2:

$$\theta_{MLE} = argmax_{\theta \in \Theta}(\frac{1}{n}\sum_{i=1}^{n}\sum_{j=1}^{m} lnP(x_{ij}|pa(x_{ij}); \theta)) \quad (2)$$

where θ is the parameter, $x_1, x_2, ..., x_n$ are n independent samples, x_{ij} is the value of the jth node of the ith sample, $Pa(x_{ij})$ is the value of the jth node's parents of the ith sample.

2.3 BN Inferring

During testing, our BN infers the posterior probability of the unobserved nodes by combining the likelihood from the given measurements of test samples with the prior model. Let L_i, V_i and M_i, $i \in \{1, 2, ..., m\}$, denote the discrete labels, the corresponding continuous values and the corresponding measurements respectively. Then,

$$\begin{aligned} &P(L_1, ..., L_m, V_1, ..., V_m | M_1, ..., M_m) \\ &\propto \Pi_{i=1}^m P(M_i|L_i, V_i) \Pi_{i=1}^m P(V_i|L_i) \Pi_{i=1}^m P(L_i|pa(L_i)) \end{aligned} \quad (3)$$

The condition probability in the equation is learned in the training phase. The inferred results are $(L_1, ..., L_m, V_1, ..., V_m)$ with the highest probability given $M_1, \cdots, M_m$. In practice, we use the junction tree algorithm [16] to estimate the posterior probability effectively.

3. EXPERIMENTS

3.1 Experimental Conditions

To the best of our knowledge, there are seven databases containing the label of aesthetics, i.e. the Flickr dataset [17], the Photo.Net dataset [18], the DPChallenge dataset [19], the Terragalleria dataset [20], AVA [21], CUHK [22] and the Memorability dataset [23]. The former six datasets provide only one aesthetic label, and the seventh databases have 17 aesthetic attributes. Therefore, we adopt the last database, Memorability dataset, for our experiment. This dataset consists of 2222 images selected from the SUN database with 923 attributes. Among them, 17 attributes are related to aesthetics, as shown in Table 1 [23], where, the attributes with a "?" are binary attributes, those with a ';' are on a scale of 1-5. Every image was annotated by 10 subjects. The average score (which is normalized) is recorded as the rating of each attribute.

Table 1: The 17 aesthetics attributes

ID	Attributes	ID	Attributes
1	Post-card like?	10	Memorable vs. Not memorable;
2	Buy this painting?	11	Sky present?
3	Hang-on wall?	12	Clear vs. Cloudy sky;
4	Is aesthetic?	13	Blue vs. Sunset sky;
5	Pleasant vs. Unpleasant;	14	Zoomed in vs. out;
6	Unusual vs. Routine;	15	Top down vs. Side view;
7	Striking vs. Boring colors;	16	Picture of mainly one object vs. Whole scene;
8	High(expert) vs. Poor quality;	17	Single focus vs. Many foci;
9	Attractive vs. Dull photo;		

To validate our proposed aesthetic attribute prediction and classification, two experiments are conducted: the image-driven aesthetic attribute prediction and classification, and our proposed method. The image-driven aesthetic attribute prediction are the same as the initial measurement estimation discussed in section 2.1, and the image-driven aesthetic attribute classification is similar to prediction, by using support vector machine as a classifier. Ten-fold cross-validation is adopted in our experiment to validate the effectiveness of our model. For the continuous value, we use the Pearson product-moment correlation coefficient (PMCC) to evaluate the performance, since the ratings of the aesthetic attributes in this databases have been normalized. For the discrete labels, we adopt three commonly used metrics, i.e, F1-score, Kappa and Accuracy.

3.2 Results and Analysis

Table 2: Results of aesthetic attribute prediction

	SVR	our BN		SVR	our BN
Attr1	0.617	**0.632**	Attr10	0.570	0.566
Attr2	0.601	**0.616**	Attr11	0.798	**0.817**
Attr3	0.616	**0.625**	Attr12	0.732	**0.745**
Attr4	0.565	**0.579**	Attr13	0.660	**0.690**
Attr5	0.543	**0.567**	Attr14	0.399	**0.405**
Attr6	0.487	**0.492**	Attr15	0.212	**0.219**
Attr7	0.429	**0.455**	Attr16	0.410	**0.416**
Attr8	0.380	**0.395**	Attr17	0.362	**0.384**
Attr9	0.528	**0.541**	average	0.524	**0.538**

The learned Bayesian network, as shown in Fig. 3(a), captures the dependencies among multiple aesthetic attributes. Furthermore, we quantify such relations using a conditional probability of $P(Attr_i|Attr_j)$, measuring the probability of $Attr_i$ happens given $Attr_j$. We find that $Attr_4$ (aesthetic) is often accompanied by $Attr_1$ (post-card like) , $Attr_3$ (Hang-on wall?) with high probability (0.93, and 0.92). It makes sense that people always hang the paintings or photos which are aesthetic on the wall, and these images are post-card like. Meanwhile, P($Attr_{10}$ (memorable) | $Attr_4$) is 0.26. It indicates that to be aesthetic is not the pre-condition of to be memorable. Current research [23] find that images of enclosed spaces containing people with visible faces are memorable, while images of vistas and peaceful scenes are not. For example, the right images of Fig. 1 is more memorable than the left one, since the right image contains a smiling woman and a smiling man, even though the left nature image is more aesthetic. All these probabilistic dependencies are effectively modeled by the BN in Fig. 3(a). Thus, it help aesthetic attribute prediction and classification.

Table 2 and Table 3 show the experimental results of aesthetic attribute prediction and classification respectively. From Table 2, we can find that our proposed method outperforms the image-driven method for almost every attribute except $Attr_{10}$. As shown in Table 3, compared with image-driven method, our method improves the classification performance for all attributes for at least one evaluation metric, except for $Attr_{14}$. These results demonstrate the embedded relations among aesthetic attributes can improve the performance of both prediction and classification.

Table 3: Results of aesthetic attribute classification

	F1 Score		Accuracy		Kappa	
	SVM	BN	SVM	BN	SVM	BN
Attr1	0.660	**0.711**	77.0%	**77.6%**	0.487	**0.531**
Attr2	0.627	**0.686**	75.2%	**77.0%**	0.442	**0.506**
Attr3	0.656	**0.684**	76.6%	**76.9%**	0.480	**0.502**
Attr4	0.696	0.676	72.1%	**72.5%**	0.440	**0.445**
Attr5	0.687	**0.695**	71.1%	**72.4%**	0.420	**0.446**
Attr6	0.618	**0.653**	68.6%	**69.5%**	0.353	**0.381**
Attr7	0.538	**0.611**	70.0%	**70.8%**	0.326	**0.378**
Attr8	0.553	**0.602**	64.6%	**65.8%**	0.271	**0.303**
Attr9	0.692	**0.723**	68.8%	**69.6%**	0.376	**0.396**
Attr10	0.692	0.686	71.2%	**72.1%**	0.421	**0.439**
Attr11	0.866	**0.868**	87.8%	**88.2%**	0.754	**0.762**
Attr12	0.815	**0.817**	85.2%	**85.5%**	0.691	**0.697**
Attr13	0.821	**0.832**	84.5%	**85.4%**	0.685	**0.703**
Attr14	0.629	0.625	64.1%	64.0%	0.282	0.280
Attr15	0.343	**0.454**	58.4%	**59.0%**	0.100	**0.140**
Attr16	0.623	**0.624**	65.3%	64.8%	0.305	0.292
Attr17	0.627	**0.650**	64.0%	64.0%	0.280	0.280
avg	0.655	**0.682**	72.0%	**72.7%**	0.418	**0.440**

3.3 Comparison With Related Works

To the best of our knowledge, the Memorability dataset is the only database which contains more than one aesthetic attributes. However, few work uses this dataset for aesthetic quality assessment. Therefore, we list several aesthetic quality assessment works on other databases as a reference in Table 4. From Table 4, we can find that the performance of aesthetic attribute classification ranges from 61.18% to 86%. Thus, our method is comparable with current work for aesthetic classification. For continuous aesthetic rating, Datta et al. [1] use the residual sum-of-squares to evaluate their results. Because their aesthetic rating lies in $[1, 7]$, while our rating is in $[0, 1]$, our R^2_{res} is 0.0342, which is much smaller than theirs.

Furthermore, we compare our aesthetic attribute classification method with Lo et al.'s [6] on the Memorability dataset, since their code is publicly available. From the last line of Table 4, we can find that our method outperforms theirs. It further demonstrates the superiority of our proposed method.

Table 4: Related works

Method	labels type	dataset	results
SVM [1]	2-class	Photo.net	Accuracy:70.12%
DT [1]	2-class	Photo.net	Accuracy:62.30%
LR [1]	continuous	Photo.net	R^2_{res}:0.5020
AdaBoost [2]	2-class	DPChallenge	Accuracy:61.18%
AdaBoost [2]	2-class	Apollo	Accuracy:81.9%
SVM [6]	2-class	CUHK	Accuracy:86%
RDCNN [7]	2-class	Ava	Accuracy:74.46%
SVM[1]	2-class	Memorability	Accuracy:61.48%

[1] We conduct this experiment using the same method as Lo et al. [6] to compare with our work.

4. CONCLUSIONS

In this paper, we consider the aesthetic attribute prediction and classification problem as a multi-label task. We use the BN to capture the relationships among aesthetic attributes to help both attribute prediction and classification. We design a hybrid BN model, which can infer both continuous aesthetic attribute scores and discrete aesthetic attribute labels. Experimental results on the the Memorability dataset show that our approach can effectively capture the probabilistic dependencies among multiple aesthetic attributes. Thus, our approach outperforms image-driven methods.

5. ACKNOWLEDGEMENTS

This paper is supported by the NSFC (61175037, 61228304, 61473270).

6. REFERENCES

[1] Ritendra Datta, Dhiraj Joshi, Jia Li, and James Z Wang, "Studying aesthetics in photographic images using a computational approach," in *ECCV 2006*, pp. 288–301. Springer, 2006.

[2] Mark Desnoyer and David Wettergreen, "Aesthetic image classification for autonomous agents," in *ICPR 2010*. IEEE, 2010, pp. 3452–3455.

[3] S. Dhar, V. Ordonez, and T.L. Berg, "High level describable attributes for predicting aesthetics and interestingness," in *CVPR 2011*, June 2011, pp. 1657–1664.

[4] Hsiao-Hang Su, Tse-Wei Chen, Chieh-Chi Kao, Winston H. Hsu, and Shao-Yi Chien, "Scenic photo quality assessment with bag of aesthetics-preserving features," in *ACM MM'11*. 2011, pp. 1213–1216, ACM.

[5] Yiwen Luo and Xiaoou Tang, "Photo and video quality evaluation: Focusing on the subject," in *ECCV 2008*, pp. 386–399. Springer, 2008.

[6] Kuo-Yen Lo, Keng-Hao Liu, and Chu-Song Chen, "Assessment of photo aesthetics with efficiency," in *ICPR 2012*. IEEE, 2012, pp. 2186–2189.

[7] Xin Lu, Zhe Lin, Hailin Jin, Jianchao Yang, and James Z. Wang, "Rapid: Rating pictorial aesthetics using deep learning," in *ACM MM'14*. 2014, pp. 457–466, ACM.

[8] Subhabrata Bhattacharya, Rahul Sukthankar, and Mubarak Shah, "A framework for photo-quality assessment and enhancement based on visual aesthetics," in *ACM MM'10*. 2010, pp. 271–280, ACM.

[9] Pere Obrador, Michele Saad, Poonam Suryanarayan, and Nuria Oliver, "Towards Category-Based Aesthetic Models of Photographs," in *Proceedings of the 18th International Conference on Advances in Multimedia Modeling – Volume Part I (MMM 2012)*, 2012, pp. 63–76.

[10] Phillip Isola, Jianxiong Xiao, Antonio Torralba, and Aude Oliva, "What makes an image memorable?," in *CVPR 2011*, 2011, pp. 145–152.

[11] Svetlana Lazebnik, Cordelia Schmid, and Jean Ponce, "Beyond bags of features: Spatial pyramid matching for recognizing natural scene categories," in *CVPR 2006*. IEEE, 2006, vol. 2, pp. 2169–2178.

[12] Aude Oliva and Antonio Torralba, "Modeling the shape of the scene: A holistic representation of the spatial envelope," *IJCV*, vol. 42, no. 3, pp. 145–175, 2001.

[13] Pedro F Felzenszwalb, Ross B Girshick, David McAllester, and Deva Ramanan, "Object detection with discriminatively trained part-based models," *TPAMI*, vol. 32, no. 9, pp. 1627–1645, 2010.

[14] Eli Shechtman and Michal Irani, "Matching local self-similarities across images and videos," in *CVPR 2007*. IEEE, 2007, pp. 1–8.

[15] Cassio P De Campos and Qiang Ji, "Efficient structure learning of bayesian networks using constraints," *JMLR*, vol. 12, pp. 663–689, 2011.

[16] David Kahle, Terrance Savitsky, Stephen Schnelle, and Volkan Cevher, "Junction tree algorithm," *STAT*, vol. 631, 2008.

[17] "Flickr [online]," `http://www.flickr.com`.

[18] "Photo.net [online]," `http://photo.net`.

[19] "Dpchallenge [online]," `http://www.dpchallenge.com`.

[20] "Terragalleria [online]," `http://www.terragalleria.com`.

[21] Naila Murray, Luca Marchesotti, and Florent Perronnin, "Ava: A large-scale database for aesthetic visual analysis," in *CVPR 2012*. IEEE, 2012, pp. 2408–2415.

[22] Wei Luo, Xiaogang Wang, and Xiaoou Tang, "Content-based photo quality assessment," in *ICCV 2011*. IEEE, 2011, pp. 2206–2213.

[23] Phillip Isola, Devi Parikh, Antonio Torralba, and Aude Oliva, "Understanding the intrinsic memorability of images," in *NIPS*, 2011, pp. 2429–2437.

Emotion Recognition from EEG Signals using Hierarchical Bayesian Network with Privileged Information

Zhen Gao, Shangfei Wang*
University of Science and Technology of China
Hefei, Anhui, P.R.China, 230027
gzgqllxh@mail.ustc.edu.cn, sfwang@ustc.edu.cn

ABSTRACT

Current work of emotion recognition from electroencephalogram (EEG) signals mainly focuses on the generality among users, ignoring users' specificity. However, users' emotion is a subjective phenomenon with both common and specific characteristics. Therefore, we propose a novel emotion recognition method using hierarchical Bayesian network to handle generality and specificity of emotions simultaneously. Specifically, by modeling the prior distributions of parameters for each subject, the classifier for a subject is learned together with those of others, with a shared representation. In addition, by marginalizing over the node of subjects, the subject information is used as privileged information, which is only required during training to build a better classifier. Experimental results on the MAHNOB-HCI and DEAP databases demonstrate that our model with the subject id as privileged information can improve the emotion recognition performance.

Categories and Subject Descriptors

I.5.1 [**Pattern Recognition**]: model—*Statistical*

Keywords

Emotion Recognition; EEG; Hierarchical Bayesian Network; Privileged Information

1. INTRODUCTION

Emotion recognition has attracted increased attention in recent years. Current research detects users' emotions from facial expression, speech, and physiological signals. Although facial expressions and speech are important methods of human to display their emotions, they are the outer representation of emotions, and not always the same as the inner emotions, since people can conceal their emotions in facial expressions and speeches. While, physiological signals reflect unconscious changes in bodily functions, which are controlled by the Sympathetic Nervous System (SNS). They are infeasible to be changed consciously. Therefore, the emotion related information embedded in physiological signals are much more reliable compared with that in facial expressions and speeches. Furthermore, with the development of wearable computing techniques, it become more and more easy to collect users' physiological signals. Thus, considerable progresses have been made on emotion recognition from philological signals, especially from EEG signals, due to its various real-world applications of brain-computer interface for normal people. EEG signals can reflect the person's feelings which can be used in multimedia retrieval.

Current emotion recognition from EEG signals consists of two steps: feature extraction and emotion classification. The goal of feature extraction is to draw the discriminating features to map the EEG features to the corresponding emotion states. For example, Lin et al [1] extracted the power spectrum features which characterize the EEG dynamics during music listening. EEG signals were decomposed into different frequency sub-bands and Daubechies wavelet function was chosen in [2]. Aftanas et al [3] used two non-linear measures, Kolmogorov entropy and the principal Lyapunov exponent, calculated from EEG segments to characterize the complex dynamics. After feature extraction, various classifiers have been adopted for emotion recognition. Petrantonakis and Hadjileontiadis [4] applied genetic algorithms to accomplish a robust emotion recognition model based on EEG features. Back-propagation neural network is adopted by Yuen et al [5] to map the statical EEG features to five types of emotions.

Although various approaches have been developed for emotion recognition from EEG signals, there still exist some limitations on traditional EEG-based emotion recognition framework. One of the major limitations is that almost all existing approaches focus on the generality characteristics of emotions among users, without considering the users' specificity of emotions. In fact, EEG signals for the same emotion from different subjects may vary a lot. Training a classifier for each subject may be a potential solution. However, it requires a big amount of data for every subject. In addition, classifiers for different subjects are not totally independent, and there is generality among subjects.

In this paper, we propose a hierarchical Bayesian network(HBN) to handle generality and specificity of emotions simultaneously. Specifically, we use the hyper-parameters to define the prior distributions of parameters for different

*This is the corresponding author (Telephone: +86-551-3602824).

ICMR'15, June 23–26, 2015, Shanghai, China.

DOI: http://dx.doi.org/10.1145/2671188.2749364.

subjects and each subject can benefit from others via the hyper-parameters. The information of subject is available during training to build a better classifier. During testing, through marginalizing over the node of subject, the subject information is not required. Such information, which is only required during training, is referred as privileged information. Experimental results on the MAHNOB-HCI and Deap databases demonstrate that the subject information and HBN make contributions to the improvement of emotion recognition.

Our paper is organized as follows. In Section 1, we illustrate the framework of our method and explain our method in details. We present the experimental results on two databases and analyse the results in Section 3. In Section 4, we briefly conclude our work.

2. THE FRAMEWORK OF OUR METHOD

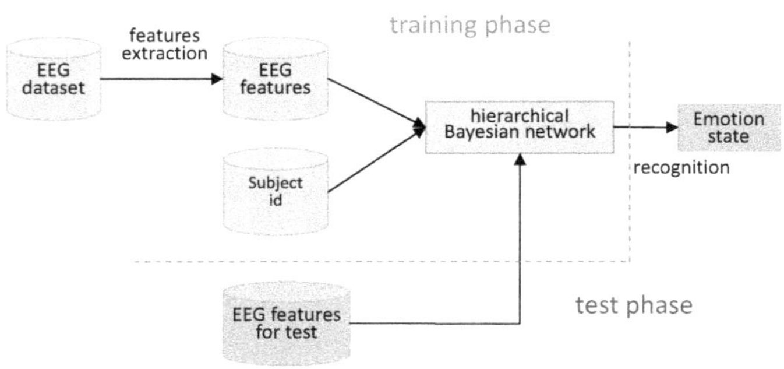

Figure 1: The framework of our method

The framework of our method is shown in Fig. 1. We first extract five frequency features from each channel of EEG signals. The EEG features and the subject id of each training sample are provided to train our HBN. With hyper-parameters and the subject id as privileged information, our model can capture the specificity of each subject and generality among different subjects. The subject id is the only extra information which is only available during training. In the test phase, we infer the emotion state with only the EEG features by marginalizing over the variable of subjects.

2.1 EEG Feature Extraction

We first carried out the noise mitigation. We removed the HEGO and VEOG and a bandpass filter was adopted with a lower cutoff frequency of 0.3 Hz and a higher cutoff frequency of 45 Hz to remove DC drifts and suppress the 50 Hz power line interference [6, 7]. We calculated the power spectrum (PS) from delta(0-4 Hz), theta(4-8 Hz), alpha(8-13 Hz), beta(13-30 Hz) and gamma(30-45 Hz), five frequency sub-bands for 32 electrodes and the PS asymmetry between 14 pairs of electrodes from alpha, beta, theta and gamma, four sub-bands [8]. We use the ratio of the power in each frequency band to the overall power as features. Totally, there are 216 EEG features extracted.

2.2 The Hierarchical Bayesian Network

Fig. 2 shows our HBN. The node S represents the subject id, the node X is on behalf of the features and the node Y indicates the emotion labels. The nodes μ, σ, μ_s and σ_s represent the coefficients to model the distributions. In

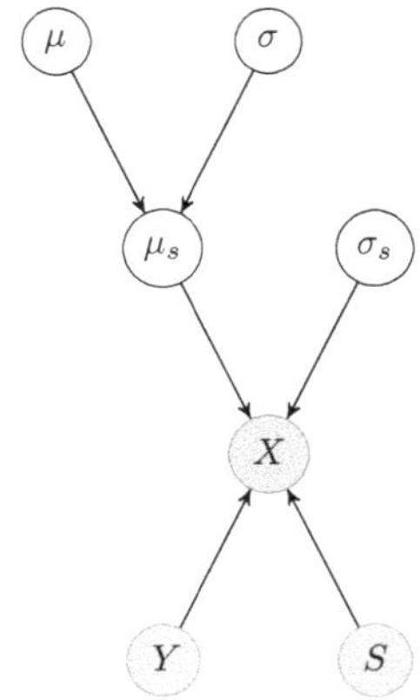

Figure 2: Our hierarchical Bayesian network

the training phase, variables X, Y and S are observed. We assume that they obey the Gaussian distribution as follows:

$$p(X|Y,S) = \prod_{i=1}^{m} p(X_i|Y,S) \quad (1)$$

$$= \prod_{i=1}^{m} \mathcal{N}(X_i|\mu_{syi}, \sigma_{syi}) \quad (2)$$

where m is the number of features, the subscript i indicates the ith features, the subscript s indicates the subject id and the subscript y indicates the emotion label.

As shown in Eq. 1, we assume that different kinds of features are independent of each other and each of them obeys the Gaussian distribution with the mean value μ_{syi} and the variance σ_{syi}. It is similar with the naive bayes model. The subject id is used in this part of our model to capture the specificity of each subject.

To obtain generality among different subjects, we use a prior distribution on the subject-specific parameters μ_s and σ_s with hyper-parameters μ and σ. The prior distribution is defined as follows:

$$p(\mu_{syi}|\mu_{yi}, \sigma_{yi}) = \mathcal{N}(\mu_{syi}|\mu_{yi}, \sigma_{yi}) \quad (3)$$

This prior encourages distributions for different subjects to have similar parameters, unless there is good evidence to make the parameters specifical.

Totally, combining the above two parts, the probability of variables X, Y and S can be defined as follows:

$$p(X|Y,S) = \prod_{i=1}^{m} \mathcal{N}(X_i|\mu_{syi}, \sigma_{syi}) \mathcal{N}(\mu_{syi}|\mu_{yi}, \sigma_{yi}) \quad (4)$$

Our HBN handles generality and specificity of emotions simultaneously with only extra information of the subject id, which is only available during training.

2.3 Estimating Parameters

Given the training dataset $DL = \{D^1, D^2, \cdots, D^n\}$, we try to estimate the parameters θ which include μ_s,σ_s,μ and σ, where n is the number of training samples and $D^i =$

$\{X^i, S^i, Y^i\}$. The posterior probability is shown as Eq. 5.

$$p(\theta|DL) \propto \prod_{i=1}^{n} p(D^i|\theta) \propto \prod_{i=1}^{n}\prod_{j=1}^{m} \mathcal{N}(X_j^i|\mu_{syj}, \sigma_{syj})\mathcal{N}(\mu_{syj}|\mu_{yj}, \sigma_{yj}) \quad (5)$$

We use the Gibbs sampling method to draw samples $\{\theta^1, \theta^2, \cdots\}$ from the posterior probability distribution. We adopt the samples when sampling process converges and use the mean value of these samples as the estimated value of each parameter. For details, please refer to [9].

2.4 Inferring Emotion States

In the test phase, we just use the EEG features of each test sample to infer the emotion state. Eq. 6 shows the posterior probability of each emotion state, marginalizing over subjects.

$$p(y|x) \propto p(x, y) = p(y) \cdot p(x|y) = p(y) \cdot \sum_{s}(p(x|y, s) \cdot p(s)) \quad (6)$$

where x represents eeg features, y is the emotion label, s is the subject id, $p(y)$ means the prior probability of each label, $p(s)$ means the prior probability of each subject, $p(x|y, s)$ is defined as Eq. 5.

The classification result is determined by the emotion state with the highest posterior probability shown as follows:

$$Y = \underset{y}{\operatorname{argmax}}\, p(y|x) \quad (7)$$

3. EXPERIMENTS

3.1 Experimental Conditions

To evaluate the effectiveness of our method, we conduct experiments on two databases, the MAHNOB-HCI [10] and Deap databases [11].

The MAHNOB-HCI database is a multi-modal database for affect recognition and implicit tagging. 27 participants watched 20 emotional videos and self-reported their felt emotions using 9-scale ratings (1-9). Total 533 EEG segments are collected. We divide them into positive (rating 6-9) and negative (rating 1-5). Totally, in valence space, there are 289 positive and 244 negative samples. In arousal space, there are 268 positive and 265 negative samples.

The Deap database is a database for emotion analysis using physiological signals. We use 1216 EEG segments which are collected from 32 participants watching 38 one-minute long excerpts of music videos. Participants rated each video of 9 levels of arousal and valence. In our work, we defined the samples as positive if their ratings are larger than 5. Otherwise, we define them as negative. For valence, 672 EEG recordings are positive and 544 are negative. For arousal, 726 EEG recordings are positive, and 490 are negative samples.

We conduct two experiments on each database: emotion recognition with the naive bayes model merely using EEG features and our HBN with the subject id as privileged information. Leave-one-video out cross-validations are adopted in our experiment. We use the Principle Component Analysis (PCA) to reduce the dimension of EEG features using 85% principal components. Three commonly-used metrics Accuracy, F1 score and Kappa are adopted to evaluate the performance.

3.2 Experimental Results and Analyses

Table 1: Emotion recognition results on the MAHNOB-HCI database in valence space

	Naive Bayes		Our method	
	Positive	Negative	Positive	Negative
Positive	138	151	164	125
Negative	90	154	105	139
Accuracy	56.1%		56.9%	
F1 score	0.548		0.547	
Kappa	0.107		0.136	

Table 2: Emotion recognition results on the Deap database in valence space

	Naive Bayes		Our method	
	Positive	Negative	Positive	Negative
Positive	326	346	390	282
Negative	223	321	229	315
Accuracy	53.2%		58.0%	
F1 score	0.530		0.552	
Kappa	0.074		0.158	

3.2.1 Valance Recognition

The emotional valence recognition results on the two databases are shown in Tab. 1 and Tab. 2. From these two tables, we can find that our model outperforms the naive bayes classifier merely using EEG features and from the confusion matrix, we see that the naive bayes classifier is biased into classifying the samples to the negative class. However, our method corrected this bias.

Tab. 1 shows the recognition results in valence space on the MAHNOB-HCI database. Our method increases the performance of Accuracy and Kappa by 0.8% and 0.029 but slightly decreases the F1 score by 0.001. From the confusion matrix, the naive bayes model is biased to the negative class and the F1 score depends on the minority class. Hence, it is slightly better. However, our method corrects the bias. Tab. 2 shows recognition results in the Deap database. Our method increases the three metrics by 4.7%, 0.022 and 0.084. The improvement shows the subject information and HBN capture the specificity of each subject and generality of different subjects to improve the recognition performance in valence space.

3.2.2 Arousal Recognition

Table 3: Emotion recognition results on the MAHNOB-HCI database in arousal space

	Naive Bayes		Our method	
	Positive	Negative	Positive	Negative
Positive	117	151	170	98
Negative	72	193	99	166
Accuracy	58.2%		63.0%	
F1 score	0.634		0.628	
Kappa	0.165		0.261	

Tab. 3 and Tab. 4 shows emotional recognition results in arousal space on the two databases. The results show that our model improves the performance of the naive bayes model. Meanwhile, our method corrects the bias.

From Tab. 1, we can find our method increases the performance of Accuracy and Kappa by 4.8% and 0.096 but

Table 4: Emotion recognition results on the Deap database in arousal space

	Naive Bayes		Our method	
	Positive	Negative	Positive	Negative
Positive	428	298	469	257
Negative	227	263	249	241
Accuracy	56.8%		58.4%	
F1 score	0.501		0.488	
Kappa	0.123		0.138	

slightly decreases the F1 score by 0.006. From the confusion matrix, we find that our method has no bias but the naive bayes is biased. In this respect, our method outperforms the naive bayes. The arousal recognition results in the Deap database can be found in Tab. 4. The accuracy and Kappa are improved by 1.6% and 0.015 from our model compared with the naive bayes. The F1 score is slight decreased by 0.013. We can find that these two classes are quite unbalanced, which makes the task more challenging.

From the recognition results in both valence and arousal space, it is obviously that our model outperforms the naive bayes. Cooperating with the subject id during training, we train a superior model capturing the specificity of each subject. The user-specific parameters benefit from each other via the hyper-parameters in the HBN. In the test phase, which only the EEG features, we infer the emotion states and achieve better results.

3.3 Comparison with Related Works

Table 5: Related Works [12] on the MAHNOB-HCI database

	Valance		Arousal	
	Positive	Negative	Positive	Negative
Positive	172	117	176	92
Negative	119	125	120	145
Accuracy	55.7%		60.2%	
F1 score	0.514		0.578	
Kappa	0.108		0.204	

Soleymani et al. [10] collected the MAHNOB-HCI database. Sine their work divided the emotion space into 3 kinds (positive, negative, neutral), we can't compare with their work directly. Zhu et al. [12] conducted similar experiments merely using EEG features on the MANNOB-HCI database. We compare with theirs. SVM is adopted by them and the results are shown in Tab. 5. In valence space, their work is similar to the naive bayes and our method is better than theirs. In arousal space, their work is better than the naive bayes model but still worse than our method. The results demonstrate the effectiveness of our HBN with the help of subject information.

Table 6: Related Works on the Deap database

Method	Valance		Arousal	
	Accuracy	F1 score*	Accuracy	F1 score*
Deap [11]	0.576	0.563	0.620	0.583
Our Method	0.580	0.578	0.584	0.569

The Deap database is collected by Koelstra et al. [11]. They designed a user-specific method which means they trained different classifiers for each subject to recognize users' emotions. We use the same cross-validation as theirs. We listed their results and ours in Tab. 6, where F1 score* means average F1 score for both classes as in [11]. For valence, our method is better than theirs. For arousal, ours is slightly worse than theirs However, their method is a user-specific method, while we only required the subject id during training. The results show that our method is comparable with theirs.

4. CONCLUSION

In this paper, we propose a novel emotion recognition method using the HBN with the subject id as the privileged information. The subject information help our model capture the specificity of each subject and the HBN prior captures generality among different subjects. The results on the MAHNOB-HCI and Deap databases demonstrate that our model effectively improves the performance compared to the methods using merely EEG features.

5. ACKNOWLEDGEMENTS

This paper is supported by the NSFC (61175037, 61473270).

6. REFERENCES

[1] Yuan-Pin Lin, Chi-Hong Wang, Tzyy-Ping Jung, Tien-Lin Wu, Shyh-Kang Jeng, Jeng-Ren Duann, and Jyh-Horng Chen, "Eeg-based emotion recognition in music listening," *Biomedical Engineering, IEEE Transactions on*, vol. 57, no. 7, pp. 1798–1806, 2010.

[2] Abdulhamit Subasi, "Eeg signal classification using wavelet feature extraction and a mixture of expert model," *Expert Systems with Applications*, vol. 32, no. 4, pp. 1084–1093, 2007.

[3] Ljubomir I Aftanas, Natalia V Lotova, Vladimir I Koshkarov, Vera L Pokrovskaja, Serguei A Popov, and Victor P Makhnev, "Non-linear analysis of emotion eeg: calculation of kolmogorov entropy and the principal lyapunov exponent," *Neuroscience letters*, vol. 226, no. 1, pp. 13–16, 1997.

[4] Panagiotis C Petrantonakis and Leontios J Hadjileontiadis, "Emotion recognition from brain signals using hybrid adaptive filtering and higher order crossings analysis," *Affective Computing, IEEE Transactions on*, vol. 1, no. 2, pp. 81–97, 2010.

[5] Chai Tong Yuen, Woo San San, Tan Ching Seong, and Mohamed Rizon, "Classification of human emotions from eeg signals using statistical features and neural network," *International Journal of Integrated Engineering*, vol. 1, no. 3, 2011.

[6] Sander Koelstra, Ashkan Yazdani, Mohammad Soleymani, Christian Muhl, Jong-Seok Lee, Anton Nijholt, Thierry Pun, Touradj Ebrahimi, and Ioannis Patras, "Single trial classification of eeg and peripheral physiological signals for recognition of emotions induced by music videos," *Lecture Notes in Computer Science*, vol. 6334 LNAI, pp. 89 – 100, 2010.

[7] Sander Koelstra, Christian Muhl, and Ioannis Patras, "Eeg analysis for implicit tagging of video data," Amsterdam, Netherlands, 2009, pp. 1 – 6, IEEE.

[8] Zhong Ji and Shuren Qin, "Detection of eeg basic rhythm feature by using band relative intensity ratio(brir)," Hong Kong, 2003, vol. 6, pp. 429 – 432.

[9] David Lunn, David Spiegelhalter, Andrew Thomas, and Nicky Best, "The bugs project: Evolution, critique and future directions," *Statistics in medicine*, vol. 28, no. 25, pp. 3049–3067, 2009.

[10] Mohammad Soleymani, Jeroen Lichtenauer, Thierry Pun, and Maja Pantic, "A multimodal database for affect recognition and implicit tagging," *Affective Computing, IEEE Transactions on*, vol. 3, no. 1, pp. 42–55, 2012.

[11] Sander Koelstra, Christian Muhl, Mohammad Soleymani, Jong-Seok Lee, Ashkan Yazdani, Touradj Ebrahimi, Thierry Pun, Anton Nijholt, and Ioannis Patras, "Deap: A database for emotion analysis; using physiological signals," *Affective Computing, IEEE Transactions on*, vol. 3, no. 1, pp. 18–31, 2012.

[12] Yachen Zhu, Shangfei Wang, and Qiang Ji, "Emotion recognition from users' eeg signals with the help of stimulus videos," in *Multimedia and Expo (ICME), 2014 IEEE International Conference on*. IEEE, 2014, pp. 1–6.

Multi-Label Active Learning with Chi-Square Statistics for Image Classification

Chen Ye
The Institute of Intelligent Information Processing and Application,
Soochow University
Suzhou 215006, China

Jian Wu*
The Institute of Intelligent Information Processing and Application,
Soochow University
Suzhou 215006, China
jianwu@suda.edu.cn

Victor S. Sheng
Department of Computer Science,
University of Central Arkansas
Conway 72035, USA

Shiquan Zhao
The Institute of Intelligent Information Processing and Application,
Soochow University
Suzhou 215006, China

Pengpeng Zhao
The Institute of Intelligent Information Processing and Application,
Soochow University
Suzhou 215006, China

Zhiming Cui
The Institute of Intelligent Information Processing and Application,
Soochow University
Suzhou 215006, China

ABSTRACT

Active learning is to select the most informative examples to request their labels. Most previous studies in active learning for multi-label classification didn't pay enough attention on label correlations. This leads to a bad performance for classification. In this paper, we proposed a chi-square statistics multi-label active learning (CSMAL) algorithm, which uses chi-square statistics to accurately evaluate correlations between labels. CSMAL considers not only positive relationships but also negative ones. It uses the average correlation between a potential label and its rest unlabeled labels as the label information for each sample-label pair. CSMAL further integrates uncertainty and label information to select example-label pairs to request labels. Our empirical results demonstrate that our proposed method CSMAL outperforms the state-of-the-art active learning methods for multi-label classification. It significantly reduces the labeling workloads and improves the performance of a classifier built.

Categories and Subject Descriptors

I.5.2 [**Design Methodology**]: Classifier design and evaluation

General Terms

Algorithms, Measurement.

Keywords

Active learning, multi-label image classification, chi-square statistics, label correlation

ICMR '15, June 23 - 26, 2015, Shanghai, China
Copyright 2015 ACM 978-1-4503-3274-3/15/06...$15.00
http://dx.doi.org/10.1145/2671188.2749365

1. INTRODUCTION

In real-world applications, each image usually has multiple labels. This leads to multi-label classification. Multi-label classification has received broad attentions in recent years [1].

Active learning [2] is one of the most effectively approaches used in image classification to build an effective classifier with limited resources. The core of active learning is sampling. In previous years, the most studies of active learning on image classification focus on single-label [3-4]. The research on multi-label active learning (MLAL) for image classification is very rare.

The studies on MLAL can be divided into two categories: example-based and example-label MLAL. The example-based MLAL selects examples to query all of their labels simultaneously [5-8]. When the number of labels for each image is large, labeling all labels of each image is expensive or time consuming. There are a few studies on example-label MLAL [9-10], which select examples to query its partial labels.

Example-based MLAL methods have to require all labels of a selected unlabeled example from human experts. Li et al. [5] is the first research using active learning for multi-label classification. They calculate the loss only on the most certainly predicted class of this image, which called Max Loss (ML). Li and Guo [8] combined a max-margin prediction uncertainty selection strategy with a label cardinality inconsistency strategy together for multi-label active learning. This strategy chooses an unlabeled example that would lead to the greatest reduction in the future prediction error from a pre-selected small subset. However, its computation cost is so high that it has no real-world applications.

Unlike example-based methods, example-label MLAL methods only require partial labels of a selected unlabeled example from human experts. Qi et al. [9] proposed a two-dimensional active learning method (2DAL), which not only considers the example dimension but also the label dimension and conducts example selection over example-label pairs instead of solely examples. Wu et al. [10] proposed a method to select the most uncertain example-label pair to decrease the labeling cost.

In this paper, we will use chi-square statistics to evaluate the correlations between all labels. Specifically, we will evaluate the correlation between a potential label and its rest labels of an example, and use the correlation as the label relationship of an example-label pair. Our experimental results reveal that our proposed active learning strategy consistently outperforms the state-of-the-art approaches.

The rest of this paper is organized as follows. In the next section, we discuss the label correlation strategies. Section 3 introduces our entire sampling strategy. Section 4 shows our experimental results on several data sets, compared with other methods. Section 5 concludes this paper and presents some future work.

2. LABEL CORRELATION EXPLORING

Some earlier studies on multi-label classification even do not take label correlations into consideration, and fail to accurately predict the label combination for a new example. For a multi-label dataset, its labels have high correlations. A traditional method for estimating the label correlation calculates the number of examples that have the same label pairs. Figure 1 shows the percentage of the number of examples that simultaneously have the corresponding label pairs. From this figure we can see that most label pairs are correlated to each other.

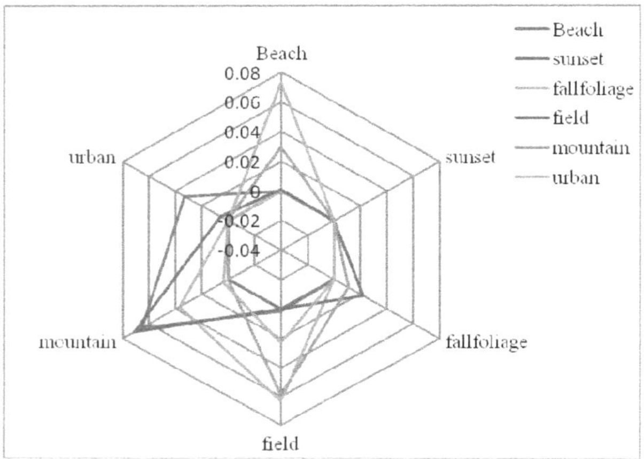

Figure 1. The mutual relationships among all labels on the dataset Scene.

The traditional ways to measure the correlation among all labels are just taking positive correlation into consideration. A complete estimation should also include the negative correlation of a label pair. In the paper, we will develop a complete correlation estimation of each label pair.

To achieve our goal, we utilize the chi-square statistics [11] to estimate the correlations between all label pairs. A chi-square test is a very widely used hypothesis testing method. The chi-square statistics is defined as follows:

$$M_{ij} = \frac{AD - BC}{\sqrt{(A+B)(A+C)(C+D)(B+D)}} \tag{1}$$

Table 1. The statistical table of the label pair y_i and y_j

	y_j	$\neg y_j$
y_i	A	B
$\neg y_i$	C	D

Note that the chi-square statistics value is symmetric, i.e. $M_{ij} = M_{ji}$. When $M_{ij} < 0$ indicates the relationship is negative. Otherwise, it indicates that the relationship is positive, and the higher the value the greater the correlation is.

From Figure 2, we can see that the correlations of all label pairs on the dataset Scene are negative, which is totally different from the correlations shown in Figure 1. Specifically, the label beach has much higher negative correlations with the label sunset and fallfoliage than with other labels that are no correlated in Figure 1. The label mountain also has the smallest negative correlation with the label field. However, the degree of the negative correlation between mountain and urban is much greater than that between mountain and sunset.

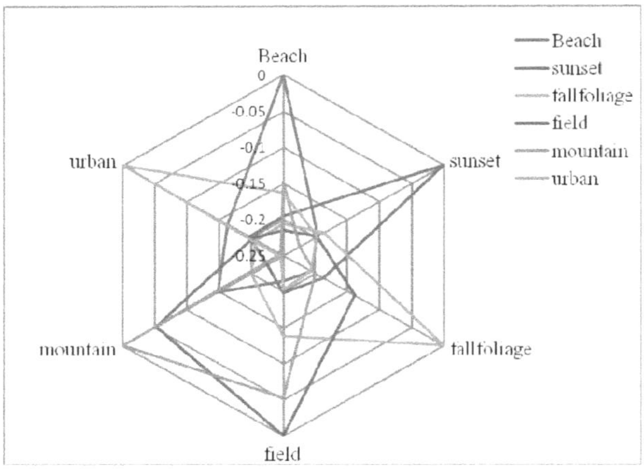

Figure 2. The chi-square statistics correlations of all the labels on the dataset Scene.

To summarize, from the above analysis, we can conclude that the chi-square statistics is able to capture both positive and negative correlations between labels. This method can not only can correct some correlations found using traditional methods, but also find new correlations between all labels.

3. CHI-SQUARE STATISTICS BASED MULTI-LABEL ACTIVE LEARNING

We propose a chi-square statistics based multi-label active learning strategy, called CSMAL. It utilizes the information of an unlabeled label of an example and the correlations of its example-label pairs to select example-label pairs to request labels How do we evaluate the informativeness of an unlabeled label of an example and the correlations of its example-label pairs is the core of our CSMAL.

We use the uncertainty measurement in CSMAL to evaluate the informativeness of an unlabelled label of an example, which is defined as follows:

$$E_{ij} = \left|\frac{1}{2} - p(s_j = 1 \mid x_i)\right| \tag{2}$$

where $p(s_j = 1 \mid x_i)$ denotes the probability of the label s_j of example x_i belonging to positive class.

It is obvious that the unlabeled labels of an example impact whether an example-label pair would be selected or not. We use the average value of unlabeled labels for one example-label pair to evaluate the degree of relationship of this example-label pair on the entire labels. Therefore, the informativeness of the j -th label of the example x_i, denoted as MU_{ij}, is defined as follows.

$$MU_{ij} = \begin{cases} \frac{1}{l_u} \sum_{y_k \in UL(x_i)} |M_{jk}| & l_u > 1 \\ 0 & l_u = 1 \end{cases} \tag{3}$$

where l_u is the number of unlabeled labels of x_i, and $UL(x_i)$ is the unlabeled labels of x_i, M_{jk} is the correlation value between label y_j and y_k.

CSMAL integrates uncertainty and correlation together using the following equation.

$$U_{ij} = E_{ij} * \alpha - MU_{ij} * (1-\alpha) \tag{4}$$

where α is a coefficient used to leverage the importance between the uncertainty of an unlabeled label and its label correlation. The whole query strategy is defined as follows.

$$(x^*, y^*) = \underset{x_i \in U, j \in \{1,\dots,l\}}{\arg\min}\ U_{ij} \tag{5}$$

4. EXPERIMENTS

In this section, we investigate the effectiveness of our proposed multi-label active learning method CSMAL by comparing with another proposed method with traditional correlation estimation (TMAL) and other three methods, i.e., multi-label SVM active learning for image classification (MML) [5], active learning with multi-label SVM classification (Adaptive) [8], and multi-label Active Learning for Image Classification (MLAL) [10]. Note that the procedure of TMAL is the same as CSMAL, except that TMAL uses a traditional way to estimate the correlations.

For each dataset, it uses 70% as a training set and 30% as a test set. Three different evaluation metrics are used, accuracy, macro F1 and micro F1. We repeat each experiment 10 times and report the average results. We evaluate the performance of our proposed approaches on six image datasets from MULAN [1]. **Scene** is an image collection for outdoor scene recognition with six scenes. **Corel5k** is a typical image dataset with 374 labels. **NUS-WIDE1** is a subset of the image dataset NUS-WIDE with 81 labels. **Corel16k001** is the subset of the image dataset Corel16k with 153 labels.

Figures 3~6 show our experimental results on these datasets. Figure 3 shows that our method converges faster, and the converge results on this dataset indicate that our proposed method CSMAL performs much better than other methods, especially using macro F1 and micro F1 as the evaluation measures. The Adaptive method is the second best. This is because it utilizes the label cardinality and it is useful. TMAL is the second worst method. This is because the correlation it mined is not right as we mentioned in Section 2. The correlation between all labels should be negative not positive.

From these figures, we can make the following conclusions. Our proposed algorithm CSMAL always performs the best on these datasets, based on the three measurements. This indicates the chi-square statistics are useful for accurately estimating the correlations among labels in multi-label classification. CSMAL makes use of these correlations to sample the most informative sample-label pairs, which are the most representative. Among the other comparison methods, it is difficult to make a general conclusion, which one performs better. The ranks among these comparison methods vary. Adaptive performs the second on the dataset Scene, but the worse on the Corel16k001. From these figures, we also found that the three measurements support each other. The algorithm ranks based on accuracy keep the same if macro F1 or micro F1 is used. Only one exception appears on the subset NUS-WIDE1, where the ranks change with different measurements.

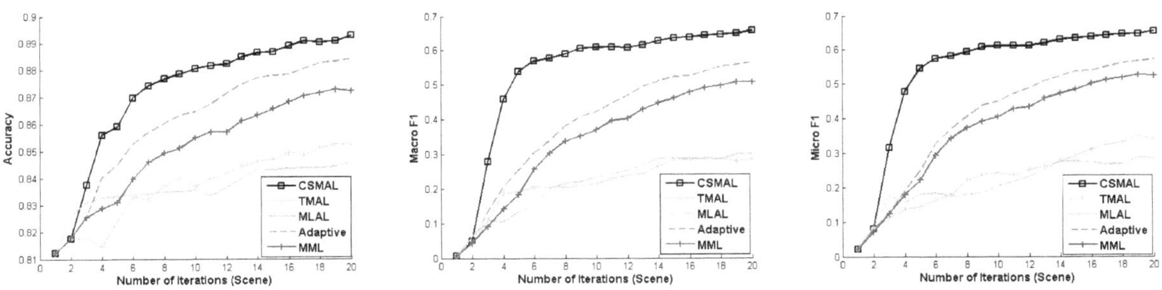

(a) Accuracy **(b) Macro F1** **(c) Micro F1**

Figure 3. Results over 10 runs on the dataset Scene.

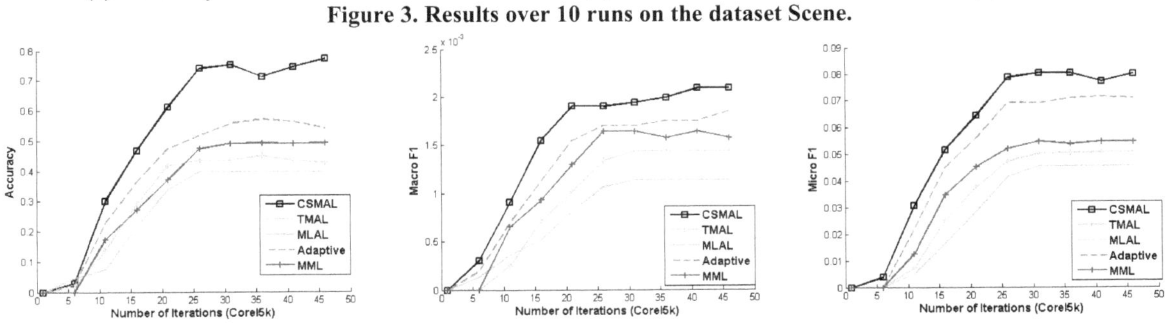

(a) Accuracy **(b) Macro F1** **(c) Micro F1**

Figure 4. Results over 10 runs on the dataset Corel5k.

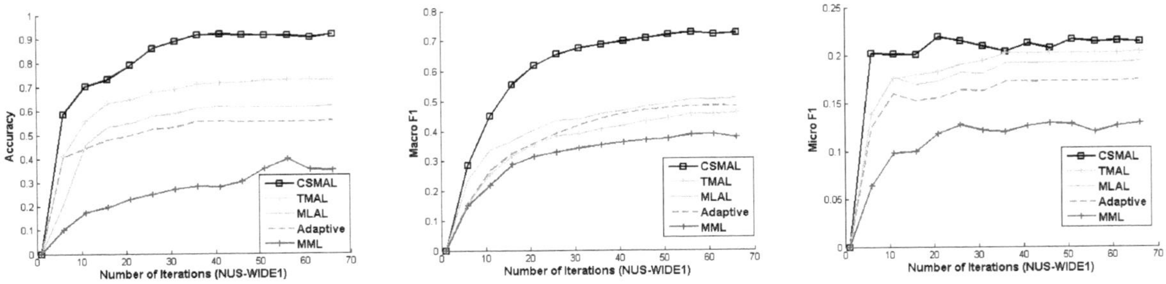

(a) Accuracy **(b) Macro F1** **(c) Micro F1**

Figure 5. Results over 10 runs on the dataset NUS-WIDE1.

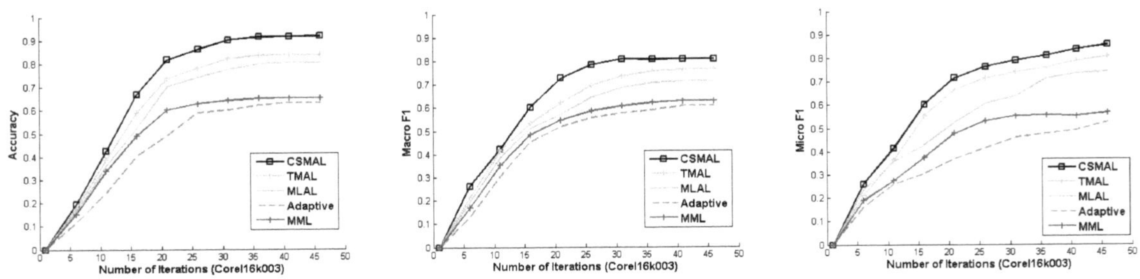

(a) Accuracy **(b) Macro F1** **(c) Micro F1**

Figure 6. Results over 10 runs on the dataset Corel16k001.

5. CONCLUSION AND FUTURE WORK

In this paper we proposed a novel chi-square statistics multi-label active learning method (CSMAL) to find unlabeled example-label pairs that are uncertain and informative. The optimization goal is to select data to be labeled that can minimize the uncertainty and maximize the coefficient relationship of each example-label pair. Our experimental results show that our proposed method CSMAL outperforms the state-of-the-art active learning techniques on multi-label classification and can significantly reduce the labeling cost. In the future, our study will focus on how to annotate the selected example-label pairs.

6. ACKNOWLEDGMENTS

This research was partially supported by the Natural Science Foundation of China under grant No.61170020, 61402311 and 61440053, Jiangsu Province Colleges and Universities Natural Science Research Project under grant No.13KJB520021, Jiangsu Province Technology Innovation Fund Project for Science and Technology Enterprises under grant No.BC2013124, 2013 Suzhou Municipal Fund Project for Speeding up the Information Construction, and the U.S. National Science Foundation (IIS-1115417).

7. REFERENCES

[1] Tsoumakas G, Spyromitros-Xioufis E, Vilcek J, et al. (2011). "Mulan: A java library for multi-label learning," *The Journal of Machine Learning Research,* 12, pp.2411-2414.

[2] B. Settles. "Active Learning Literature Survey," Computer Science Technical Report 1648, University of Wisconsin-Madison, USA, 2010.

[3] A. Holub, P. Perona, and M. C. Burl. "Entropy-based Active Learning for Object Recognition," In *Proceedings of the IEEE Conference on Computer Vision and Pattern Recognition (CVPR),* 2008, pp.1-8.

[4] A. J. Joshi, F. Porikli, and N. Papanikolopoulos, "Multi-class Active Learning for Image Classification," In *Proceedings of the IEEE Conference on Computer Vision and Pattern Recognition (CVPR),* 2009, pp.2372-2379.

[5] X. Li, L. Wang, and E. Sung, "Multilabel SVM Active Learning for Image Classification," In *Proceedings of the International Conference on Image Processing (ICIP),* 2004, vol.4, pp.2207-2210.

[6] Brinker K. "On Active Learning in Multi-label Classification," *From Data and Information Analysis to Knowledge Engineering,* Springer Berlin Heidelberg, 2006, pp.206-213.

[7] M. Singh, E. Curran, and P. Cunningham, "Active Learning for Multi-label Image Annotation," In *Proceedings of the Irish Conference on Artificial Intelligence and Cognitive Science (AICS),* 2008.

[8] X. Li and Y. Guo, "Active Learning with Multi-label SVM Classification," In *Proceedings of the International Joint Conference on Artificial Intelligence (IJCAI),* 2013, pp. 1479-1485.

[9] Guo-Jun Qi, Xian-Sheng Hua, Yong Rui, Jinhui Tang, and Hong-Jiang Zhang, "Two-dimensional Active Learning for Image Classification," In *Proceedings of the IEEE International Conference on Computer Vision (CVPR),* 2008, pp.1-8.

[10] Jian Wu, Victor S. Sheng, Jing Zhang, Pengpeng Zhao, Zhiming Cui. "Multi-label Active Learning for Image Classification," In *Proceedings of the 21st International Conference on Image Processing (ICIP),* 2014, pp.5227-5231.

[11] Jacob Cohen, Patricia Cohen, Stephen G. West, and Leona S. Aiken. "Applied Multiple Regression/Correlation Analysis for the Behavioral Sciences," Psychology Press, 2002.

Multiple Measurements and Joint Dimensionality Reduction for Large Scale Image Search with Short Vectors

Filip Radenović
CMP, Faculty of EE
CTU in Prague
radenfil@cmp.felk.cvut.cz

Hervé Jégou
INRIA, Rennes
herve.jegou@inria.fr

Ondřej Chum
CMP, Faculty of EE
CTU in Prague
chum@cmp.felk.cvut.cz

ABSTRACT

This paper addresses the construction of a short-vector (128D) image representation for large-scale image and particular object retrieval. In particular, the method of joint dimensionality reduction of multiple vocabularies is considered. We study a variety of vocabulary generation techniques: different k-means initializations, different descriptor transformations, different measurement regions for descriptor extraction. Our extensive evaluation shows that different combinations of vocabularies, each partitioning the descriptor space in a different yet complementary manner, results in a significant performance improvement, which exceeds the state-of-the-art.

Categories and Subject Descriptors

H.3.3 [**Information Storage and Retrieval**]: Information Search and Retrieval

Keywords

image retrieval; multiple vocabularies; short codes

1. INTRODUCTION

LARGE-SCALE image retrieval techniques have been developing and improving greatly for more than a decade. Many of the current state-of-the-art approaches [16, 4, 8] are based on the bag-of-words (BOW) approach originally proposed by Sivic and Zisserman [23]. Another popular image representation arises from aggregating local descriptors like Fisher kernel [19] and Vector of Locally Aggregated Descriptors (VLAD) [10].

The BOW vectors are high dimensional (up to 64 million dimensions in [15]), so, due to the high memory and computational requirements, search is limited to a several million images on a single machine. There are more scalable approaches that tackle this problem by generating compact image representations [24, 19, 10], where the image is described by a short vector that can be additionally compressed into compact codes using binarization [24, 26], product quantization [9]. In this paper we propose and experimentally evaluate simple techniques that additionally boost retrieval performance, but at the same time preserve low memory and computational costs.

Short vector image representations are often generated using the principal component analysis (PCA) technique to perform the dimensionality reduction over high-dimensional vectors. Jegou and Chum [6] study the effects of PCA on BOW representations. They show that both steps of PCA procedure, i.e., centering and selection of de-correlated (orthogonal) basis minimizing the dimensionality reduction error, improve retieval performance. Centering (mean subtraction) of BOW vectors provides a boost in performance by adding a higher value to the negative evidence: given two BOW vectors, a visual word jointly missing in both vectors provides useful information for the similarity measure [6]. Additionnaly, they advocate the joint dimensionality reduction with multiple vocabularies to reduce the quantization artifacts underlying BOW and VLAD. These vocabularies are created by using different initializations for the k-means algorithm, which may produce relatively highly correlated vocabularies.

In this paper, we propose to reduce the redundancy of the joint vocabulary representation (before the joint dimensionality reduction) by varying parameters of the local feature descriptors prior to the k-means quantization. In particular, we propose: (i) different sizes of measurement regions for local description, and (ii) different power-law normalizations of local feature descriptors. In this way, created vocabularies will be more complementary and joint dimensionality reduction of concatenated BOW vectors originating from several vocabularies will carry more information. Even though the proposed approaches are simple, we show that they provide significant boosts to retrieval performance with no memory or computational overhead at the query time.

Related work. This paper can be seen as an extension of [6], details of which are given later in Section 2.3. A number of papers report results with short descriptors obtained by PCA dimensionality reduction. In [10] and [19], aggregated descriptors (VLAD and Fisher vector respectively) are used followed by PCA to produce low dimensional image descriptors. In a paper about VLAD [2], authors propose a method for adaptation of the vocabulary built on an independent dataset (adapt) and intra-normalization (innorm) method that L_2 normalizes all VLAD components independently, which suppresses the burstiness effect [7]. In [11], a 'democratic' weighted aggregation method for burstiness

ICMR'15, June 23–26, 2015, Shanghai, China.

http://dx.doi.org/10.1145/2671188.2749366.

supression is introduced. In this paper, we compare results of all the aforementioned methods using low dimensional descriptors $D' = 128$.

The rest of the paper is organized as follows: Section 2 gives a brief overview of several methods: bag-of-words (BOW), efficient PCA dimensionality reduction of high dimensional vectors, and baseline retrieval with multiple vocabularies. Section 3 introduces novel methods for joint dimensionality reduction of multiple vocabularies and presents extensive experimental evaluations. Main conclusions are given in Section 4.

2. BACKGROUND AND BASELINE

This section gives a short overview of the background of bag-of-words based image retrieval and the method used in [6]. Key steps and ideas are discussed in higher detail to help understanding of the paper.

2.1 Bag-of-words (BOW) image representation

First efficient image retrieval based on BOW image representation was proposed by Sivic and Zisserman [23]. They use local descriptors extracted in an image in order to construct a high-dimensional global descriptor. This procedure follows four basic steps:

1. For each image in the dataset, regions of interest are detected [14, 13] and described by an invariant descriptor which is d-dimensional. In this work we use the multi-scale Hessian-Affine [18] and MSER [13] detectors, followed by SIFT [12] or RootSIFT [1] descriptors. The rotation of the descriptor is either determined by the detected dominant orientation [12], or by the gravity vector assumption [18]. The descriptors are extracted from different sizes of measurement regions [13], as described in detail in Section 3.

2. Descriptors extracted from the training (independent) dataset are clustered into k clusters using the k-means algorithm, which creates a visual vocabulary.

3. For each image in the dataset, a histogram of occurrences of visual words is computed. Different weighting schemes can be used, the most popular is inverse document frequency (*idf*), which generates a D dimensional BOW vector (D=k).

4. All resulting vectors are L_2 normalized, as suggested in [23], producing final global image representations used for searching.

2.2 Efficient PCA of high dimensional vectors

In most of the cases BOW image representations have very high number of dimensions (D can take values up to 64 million [15]). In these cases the standard PCA method (reducing D to D') computing the full covariance matrix is not efficient. The dual gram method can be used to learn the first D' eigenvectors and eigenvalues. Instead of computing the $D \times D$ covariance matrix $\boldsymbol{C}$, the dual gram method computes the $n \times n$ matrix $\boldsymbol{Y}^T\boldsymbol{Y}$, where $\boldsymbol{Y}$ is a set of vectors used for learning, and n is the number of vectors in the set $\boldsymbol{Y}$. Eigenvalue decomposition is performed using the Arnoldi algorithm, which iteratively computes the D' desired eigenvectors corresponding to the largest eigenvalues. This method is more efficient than the standard covariance matrix method if the number of vectors n of the training set is smaller than the number of vector dimensions D, which is usually the case in the BOW approach.

Jegou and Chum [6] analyze the effects of PCA dimensionality reduction on the BOW and VLAD vectors. They show that even though PCA successfully deals with the problem of negative evidence (higher importance of jointly missing visual words in compared BOW vectors), it ignores the problem of co-occurrences (co-occurences lead to over-count some visual patterns when comparing two image vector representation, see [3]). In order to tackle the aforementioned problem, they propose performing a whitening operation, similar to the one done in independent component analysis [5] (implicitly performed by the Mahalanobis distance), jointly with the PCA. In our experiments we will use dimensionality reduction from D to D' components, as done in [6]:

1. Every image vector $v = (v_1, \ldots, v_D)$ is post-processed using power-law normalization [19]: $v_i := |v_i|^\beta \times sign(v_i)$, with $0 \leq \beta < 1$ as a fixed constant. Vector v is L_2 normalized after processing. It has been shown [10] that this simple procedure reduces the impact of multiple matches and visual bursts [7]. In all our experiments $\beta = 0.5$, denoted as signed square rooting (SSR).

2. First D' eigenvectors of matrix $\boldsymbol{C}$ are learned using power-law normalized training vectors $\boldsymbol{Y} = [Y_1|\ldots|Y_n]$, corresponding to the largest D' eigenvalues $\lambda_1, \ldots, \lambda_{D'}$.

3. Every power-law normalized image descriptor used for searching X is PCA-projected and truncated, and at the same time whitened and re-normalized to a new vector $\hat{X}$, as in [6].

In order to compare results in a fair manner, we will use $D' = 128$ dimensions for all our experiments following the trend of previous research in short image representations.

2.3 The baseline method

This paper builds upon the work [6], which is briefly reviewed in this section. In [6], a joint dimensionality reduction of multiple vocabularies is proposed. Image representation vectors are separately SSR normalized for each vocabulary, concatenated and then jointly PCA-reduced and whitened as explained in the Section 2.2. The *idf* term is ignored, and it is noted that the influence is limited when used with multiple vocabularies. Comparing to the straightforward concatenation, where the results do not noticeably improve after adding multiple vocabularies, it can be noticed that an improvement in performance is achieved even when keeping low memory requirements by using PCA dimensionality reduction. However, for some vocabularies (i.e. $k = 2$k), performance is dropping after only few vocabularies used.

Datasets and evaluation. Results of all methods are evaluated on **Oxford5k, Oxford105k** [20] and **Holidays** [8] datasets that are widely used in the image retrieval area. The performance is reported as mean average precision (mAP). As a training dataset for vocabulary construction and image representation level PCA learning in both cases we use **Paris6k** [21]. Also, we compare our results with other approaches evaluated on the same datasets.

3. SOURCES OF MULTIPLE CODEBOOKS

We propose combining multiple vocabularies that are differing not just in random initialization of clustering procedure, but also in the data used for clustering. The feature data are alternated in the process of local features description. This process is not trying to synthesize appearance deformations, but rather varying certain design choices in the pipeline of feature description, such as the relative size of the measurement region. Vocabularies created in this manner will contain less redundancy. This is combined with joint PCA dimensionality reduction (as described in Sections 2.2 and 2.3) in order to produce short-vector image representations that are used for searching the most similar images in the dataset.

Multiple measurement regions. An affine invariant descriptor of an affine covariant region can be extracted from any affine covariant constructed measurement region [13]. As an example of a measurement region that is, in general, of a different shape than the detected region, is an ellipse fitted to the regions, as proposed by [25] and also used for MSERs [13]. An important parameter is the relative scale of the measurement region with respect to the scale of the detected region. Since the output of the detector is designed to be repeatable, it is usually not discriminative. To increase the disriminability of the descriptor, it is commonly extracted from area larger than the detected region. In case of [18], the relative change in the radius is $r = 3\sqrt{3}$. The larger the region, the higher discriminability of the descriptor, as long as the measurement region covers a close-to-planar surface. On the other hand, larger image patches have higher chance of hitting depth discontinuities and thus being corrupted. To take the best of this trade off, we propose to construct multiple vocabularies over descriptors extracted at multiple relative scales of the measurement regions. Including lower scales leverages the disadvantages of large measurement regions, while joint dimensionality reduction eliminates the dependencies between the representations.

We consider using different sizes of measurement regions: $0.5 \times r$, $0.75 \times r$, $1 \times r$, $1.25 \times r$, $1.5 \times r$; creating slightly different SIFT descriptors used to learn every vocabulary. Implementation is very simple and during online stage the computation has to be done only for the features from query image region. Though simple, this method provides significant improvement even when concatenating vocabularies of small sizes (i.e. k = 2k and k = 1k). We also explore the use of vocabularies with different sizes. All BOW vectors in this case are weighted proportionally to the logarithm of their vocabulary size [6]. In each step we concatenate a new bundle of vocabularies with multiple sizes, calculated with a different measurement region. We notice improvement when using multiple vocabulary sizes as well. This approach is denoted as mMeasReg.

Multiple power-law normalized SIFT descriptors. SIFT descriptors [12] were the popular choice in most of the image retrieval systems for a long time. Arandjelovic *et al.* [1] show that using a Hellinger kernel instead of standard Euclidian distance to measure the similarity between SIFT descriptors leads to a noticeable performance boost in retrieval system. The kernel is implemented by simply square rooting every component of SIFT descriptor. Using Euclidian distance on these new RootSIFT descriptors will give the same result as using Hellinger kernel on the original SIFT descriptors. In general, a power-law normalization [19] with any power $0 \leq \beta \leq 1$ can be applied to the descriptors ($\beta = 0.5$ resulting in RootSIFT [1]). Voronoi cells constructed in power-law normalized descriptor spaces can be seen as non-linear hyper-surfaces separating the features in the original (SIFT) descriptor space. Concatenation of such feature space partitionings reduces the redundant information.

There is no additional memory required and the change can be done on-the-fly with virtually no additional computational cost using simple power operation. We consider building four different vocabularies using: SIFT and SIFT with every component to the power of 0.4, 0.5, 0.6 (denoted as $\text{SIFT}^{0.4}$, $\text{SIFT}^{0.5}$, $\text{SIFT}^{0.6}$ respectively). Concatenation is done on single vocabularies and on a bundle of vocabularies with different sizes. Adding all mentioned SIFT modifications to the process of vocabulary creation achieves noticeable improvement of retrieval performance in the case of all vocabulary sizes. We denote this method as mRootSIFT.

Combining vocabularies of different SIFT exponents improves over combining different vocabularies of a single SIFT exponent. For example, for 4×2k vocabularies, the mAP on Oxford5k is 46.5 for $4 \times \text{SIFT}^{0.5}$, and 47.7 for exponent combination.

Multiple feature detectors. In the Video Google approach [23] the authors combine vocabularies created from two different feature types. In this paper we attempt to combine Hessian-Affine [18] and MSER [13] detectors. Surprisingly, we notice that after the joint PCA reduction there is a decrease in performance.

3.1 Comparison with the state-of-the-art

Comparison with the current methods dealing with short vector image representation is given in Table 1. Authors of the baseline approach on multiple vocabularies (mVocab) did not provide results for Oxford5k and Oxford105k datasets using all of their proposed methods, so we reimplemented and presented the corresponding results. Compared to their best method on Oxford5k that achieves 42.9 mAP, our best method (48.8 mAP) obtains significant relative improvement of 13.8%. In fact, all our methods outperform mVocab baseline methods on Oxford5k by a noticeable margin, with an improvement of 9.3% in the case of our worst performing method. When evaluating large-scale retrieval on Oxford105k dataset our methods again outperform the baseline method, relative improvement is 17.9% for our best performing method, and 10.8% for the worst performing one. In order to make a fair comparison when evaluating on Holidays dataset we again reimplemented the baseline approach, using Paris6k for learning the vocabularies and PCA projections (as we did in all our methods). In this case, the relative improvement is 4.3% with our best method (from 64.5 mAP to 67.3 mAP). We also compare our methods to two recent state-of-the-art approaches on short representations [2, 11]. On Oxford5k and Oxford105k we improve as much as 8.9% and 10.7%, respectively, compared to VLAD based approach [2], and 12.7% and 17.3%, respectively, compared to T-embedding based approach [11]. On Holidays dataset relative improvement is 7.7% compared to the former and 9.1% compared to the latter. Note that the dataset used for learning of the meta-data for Holidays is different: we use Paris6k, while both [2] and [11] are using an independent dataset comprising of 60k images downloaded from Flickr.

4. CONCLUSIONS

Methods for multiple vocabulary construction were studied and evaluated in this paper. Following [6], the concate-

Table 1: **Comparison with the state-of-the-art on short vector image representation ($D' = 128$): Results marked with * are obtained after our reimplementation of the methods using feature detector and descriptor as described in Section 2.1 and Paris6k as a learning dataset.**

Method	Vocabulary	Oxford5k	Oxford105k	Holidays
GIST [17]	N/A	–	–	36.5
BOW [23]	k=20k	19.4	–	45.2
Improved Fisher [19]	k=64	30.1	–	56.5
VLAD [10]	k=64	–	–	51.0
VLAD+SSR [10]	k=64	28.7	–	55.7
$\phi_\Delta+\psi_d$+RN [11]	k=16	43.3	35.3	61.7
mVocab/BOW [6]	k=4×8k	41.3/41.4*	–/33.2*	56.7/63.0*
mVocab/BOW [6]	k=2×(32k+...+128)	–/42.9*	–/35.1*	60.0/64.5*
mVocab/VLAD [6]	k=4×256	–	–	61.4
mVocab/VLAD+adapt+innorm [2]	k=4×256	44.8	37.4	62.5
mMeasReg/mVocab/BOW	k=5×2k	46.9	38.9	66.9
mMeasReg/mVocab/BOW	k=4×(4k+...+128)	47.7	39.2	67.3
mRootSIFT/mVocab/BOW	k=4×2k	47.7	39.8	64.3
mRootSIFT/mVocab/BOW	k=4×(2k+...+128)	48.8	41.4	65.6

nated BOW image representations from multiple vocabularies were subject to joint dimensionality reduction to 128D descriptors. We have experimentally shown that generating diverse multiple vocabularies has crucial impact on search performance. Each of the multiple vocabularies was learned on local feature descriptors obtained with varying parameter settings. That includes feature descriptors extracted from measurement regions of different scales, and different power-law normalizations of the SIFT descriptors prior to k-means quantization. The proposed vocabulary constructions improve performance over the baseline method [6], where only different initializations were used to produce multiple vocabularies. More importantly, the *all* proposed methods exceed the state-of-the-art results [2, 11] by a large margin. The choice of the optimal combination of vocabularies to combine still remains an open problem.

Extended version of this paper with more experiments is available on arXiv, see [22].

Acknowledgements. The authors were supported by MSMT LL1303 ERC-CZ and ERC VIAMASS no. 336054 grants.

5. REFERENCES

[1] R. Arandjelovic and A. Zisserman. Three things everyone should know to improve object retrieval. In *Proc. CVPR*, pages 2911–2918, 2012.

[2] R. Arandjelović and A. Zisserman. All about VLAD. In *Proc. CVPR*, 2013.

[3] O. Chum and J. Matas. Unsupervised discovery of co-occurrence in sparse high dimensional data. In *Proc. CVPR*, 2010.

[4] O. Chum, J. Philbin, J. Sivic, M. Isard, and A. Zisserman. Total recall: Automatic query expansion with a generative feature model for object retrieval. In *Proc. ICCV*, 2007.

[5] P. Comon. Independent component analysis, a new concept? *Signal processing*, 36(3):287–314, 1994.

[6] H. Jégou and O. Chum. Negative evidences and co-occurrences in image retrieval: the benefit of PCA and whitening. In *Proc. ECCV*, Firenze, Italy, Oct. 2012.

[7] H. Jégou, M. Douze, and C. Schmid. On the burstiness of visual elements. In *Proc. CVPR*, 2009.

[8] H. Jégou, M. Douze, and C. Schmid. Improving bag-of-features for large scale image search. *IJCV*, 87(3):316–336, 2010.

[9] H. Jégou, M. Douze, and C. Schmid. Product quantization for nearest neighbor search. *IEEE PAMI*, 33(1):117–128, 2011.

[10] H. Jégou, F. Perronnin, M. Douze, J. Sánchez, P. Pérez, and C. Schmid. Aggregating local image descriptors into compact codes. *IEEE PAMI*, 34(9):1704–1716, 2012.

[11] H. Jégou, A. Zisserman, et al. Triangulation embedding and democratic aggregation for image search. In *Proc. CVPR*, 2014.

[12] D. G. Lowe. Distinctive image features from scale-invariant keypoints. *Proc. ICCV*, 60(2):91–110, 2004.

[13] J. Matas, O. Chum, M. Urban, and T. Pajdla. Robust wide baseline stereo from maximally stable extremal regions. In *Proc. BMVC*, volume 1, pages 384–393, 2002.

[14] K. Mikolajczyk and C. Schmid. Scale & affine invariant interest point detectors. *IJCV*, 1(60):63–86, 2004.

[15] A. Mikulik, M. Perd'och, O. Chum, and J. Matas. Learning vocabularies over a fine quantization. *IJCV*, pages 1–13, 2012.

[16] D. Nister and H. Stewenius. Scalable recognition with a vocabulary tree. In *Proc. CVPR*, 2006.

[17] A. Oliva and A. Torralba. Modeling the shape of the scene: A holistic representation of the spatial envelope. *IJCV*, 42(3):145–175, 2001.

[18] M. Perdoch, O. Chum, and J. Matas. Efficient representation of local geometry for large scale object retrieval. In *Proc. CVPR*, 2009.

[19] F. Perronnin, Y. Liu, J. Sanchez, and H. Poirier. Large-scale image retrieval with compressed fisher vectors. In *Proc. CVPR*, 2010.

[20] J. Philbin, O. Chum, M. Isard, J. Sivic, and A. Zisserman. Object retrieval with large vocabularies and fast spatial matching. In *Proc. CVPR*, 2007.

[21] J. Philbin, O. Chum, M. Isard, J. Sivic, and A. Zisserman. Lost in quantization: Improving particular object retrieval in largescale image databases. In *Proc. CVPR*, 2008.

[22] F. Radenovic, H. Jegou, and O. Chum. Multiple Measurements and Joint Dimensionality Reduction for Large Scale Image Search with Short Vectors - Extended Version. *ArXiv e-prints*, Apr. 2015.

[23] J. Sivic and A. Zisserman. Video google: A text retrieval approach to object matching in videos. In *Proc. ICCV*, pages 1470–1477, 2003.

[24] A. Torralba, R. Fergus, and Y. Weiss. Small codes and large image databases for recognition. In *Proc. CVPR*, pages 1–8. IEEE, 2008.

[25] T. Tuytelaars and L. Van Gool. Wide baseline stereo matching based on local, affinely invariant regions. In *Proc. BMVC*, 2000.

[26] Y. Weiss, A. Torralba, and R. Fergus. Spectral hashing. In *Proc. NIPS*, pages 1753–1760, 2009.

Exploring EEG for Object Detection and Retrieval

Eva Mohedano, Kevin McGuinness, Graham Healy, Noel E. O'Connor and Alan F. Smeaton
Insight Center for Data Analytics
Dublin City University
Dublin, Ireland
eva.mohedano@insight-centre.org

Amaia Salvador, Sergi Porta, and Xavier Giró-i-Nieto
Image Processing Group
Universitat Politècnica de Catalunya
Barcelona, Catalonia/Spain
{amaia.salvador, xavier.giro}@upc.edu

ABSTRACT

This paper explores the potential for using Brain Computer Interfaces (BCI) as a relevance feedback mechanism in content-based image retrieval. Several experiments are performed using a rapid serial visual presentation (RSVP) of images at different rates (5Hz and 10Hz) on 8 users with different degrees of familiarization with BCI and the dataset. We compare the feedback from the BCI and mouse-based interfaces in a subset of TRECVid images, finding that, when users have limited time to annotate the images, both interfaces are comparable in performance. Comparing our best users in a retrieval task, we found that EEG-based relevance feedback can outperform mouse-based feedback.

Categories and Subject Descriptors

H.3.3 [**Information Search and Retrieval**]: Relevance feedback; H.5.2 [**User Interfaces**]: Input devices and strategies

General Terms

Experimentation, Design

Keywords

Brain-computer interfaces, Electroencephalography, Rapid Serial Visual Presentation, Classification, Instance Retrieval

1. MOTIVATION

The exponential growth of visual content and its huge diversity has motivated considerable research on how documents can be retrieved according to user intentions when formulating a query. Advances in image processing and computer vision have provided tools for a perceptual and semantic interpretation of both the query and the indexed content. This has allowed the development of retrieval systems capable of processing queries by example and concepts.

ICMR'15, June 23–26, 2015, Shanghai, China.

DOI: http://dx.doi.org/10.1145/2671188.2749368.

The role of a human user during visual retrieval is critical, and his judgment about the correctness of the retrieved results can greatly speed up the search processes. This kind of relevance feedback has been demonstrated to significantly improve retrieval performance in image [10] and video [1] retrieval. Manually annotating images using a mouse, especially in a visual retrieval context can be tedious and mentally exhausting. In that such a scenario, EEG-based brain computer interfaces offer a potential solution as a mechanism to quickly annotate images.

2. RELATED WORK

EEG signals have been used for object detection in [2], where authors aim to detect airplanes in a dataset of satellite images from the city of London. The work in [3] expands the catalog of objects in very simple images, where the object on a black background occupies the whole image.

EEG signals have been also used for image retrieval in [9], where authors used EEG relevance annotations to retrieve specific concepts in a complex dataset of keyframes from TRECVid 2005. However, while that work aimed at detecting concepts depicted by the whole image, we focus on the more challenging task of detecting a local object in a complex scenario. Another similar work [8], addresses the usage of EEG for image retrieval by formulating the problem as a semi-supervised learning problem. The noisy relevance labels generated by EEG classifiers on a small subset of a large database are expanded through a visual similarity graph. In our experiments, the highest and lowest EEG relevance scores are used to train a binary classifier, instead of feeding a semi-supervised algorithm. This way results are more comparable to the binary relevance labels collected with the mouse interface.

3. EXPERIMENTAL SET-UP

Following previous work on EEG-based image retrieval [3, 4, 8], the experimental design was based in the 'oddball paradigm,' in which two different stimuli are presented to the user in random order and with different probabilities. One stimulus (the 'target') appears with low probability during the visual presentation and the other (the 'distractor') appears frequently. Users are asked to focus on detecting the target and to express their reaction by either counting or pressing a button.

In this context, it has been found that when a user reacts to a target stimulus, a P300 wave appears in the captured brain signals. This wave is a kind of Event Related Potential (ERP) and it consists in a positive peak in the EEG activity around the 250ms-500ms range after the stimulus presentation.

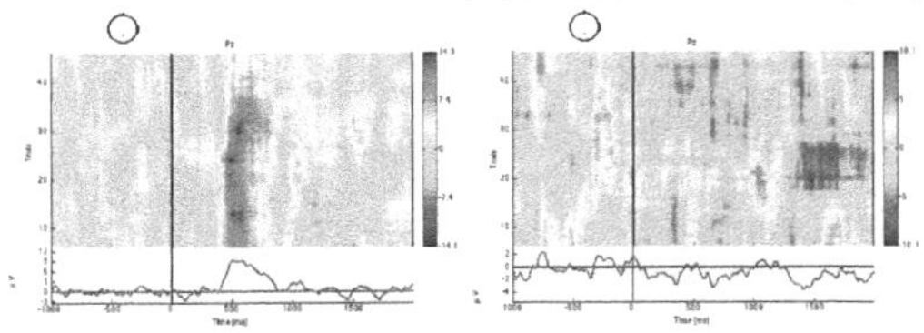

Figure 1: Visual evidence of discriminative P300 response on averaged epochs for 1000 images (5 blocks of 200) captured at 5Hz for the Pz channel. On the left, the response on target images. On the right, the response for 50 distractors.

For our experiments, we selected a 'real world' set of images from a subset of the TRECVid 2013 instance search dataset. Three queries were selected, each one containing 4 visual examples. Figure 2 shows one visual example of each of the three selected queries. Using the ground truth labels provided by TRECVid, 1000 images were selected for each query. To adapt the data to the oddball paradigm, the 'target' ratio of the dataset has been set to 5% (i.e. for each query, 50 relevant images and 950 non-relevant images are used).

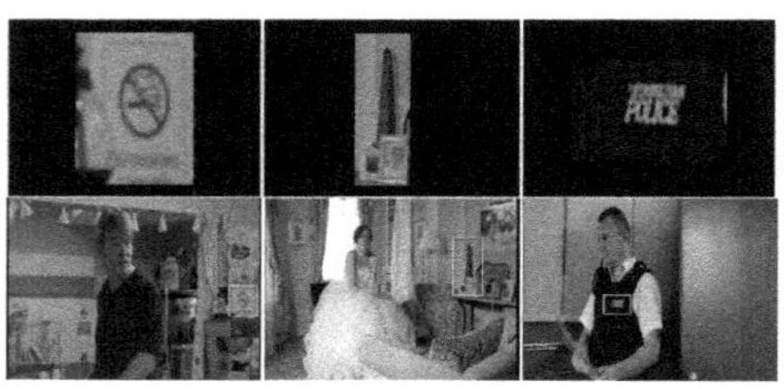

Figure 2: Visual examples of the three query objects (top) and the actual images where they appear (bottom). From left to right: 1. A circular 'no smoking' logo, 2. A small red obelisk, 3. A Metropolitan Police logo.

The selected images are presented in a Rapid Serial Visual Presentation (RSVP). For each query, the 1000 images are divided in 5 blocks of 200 images keeping a 5% target ratio within each block (i.e. 10 'target' images and 190 'distractors'). Once this division is done, the images are randomly sorted within the block. These blocks are presented to the user one after the other, allowing him/her to rest for a few seconds between blocks. The user's task consisted in counting/pressing a button every time that they detected a target image during the RSVP. The visualization rates that have been tested in our experiments are 5Hz and 10Hz, therefore the duration of the experiment for a single query is 200 and 100 seconds.

Eight volunteers between the ages of 19 and 33 participated in the experiments: six women and two men. Of the eight users that participated in the task, two completed the experiment with a RSVP at 10Hz and four at 5Hz. The last two users completed the task twice, once at 10Hz and once at 5Hz.

The BCI device used was a 32 channel actiCHamp amplifier, which was connected to the user locating the electrodes according to the 10-20 system.

4. EEG SIGNAL PROCESSING

The signals captured by each one of the 32 sensors were re-referenced to the average of all the channels. Then, the sample rate was reduced from the original 1000Hz to 250Hz and the signals were band-pass filtered from 0.1Hz to 20Hz. The epochs related to each visual stimulus were extracted, obtaining 1000 epochs with EEG activity from 1 second before to 2 seconds after each image. Then, for each of the 32 signals, the period from 200ms to 1s was taken as the discriminant time region to discern between EEG responses of targets and distractors (see Figure 1) and with the sample rate reduced to 20Hz, generating a 16 sample vector per channel. Each of the 16 samples per channel was the result of computing the average of 24 samples windows with 50% of overlap between each other, which we found was a better strategy than to just decimate the signal. Finally, we build a single feature vector for the image as the concatenation of the 32 channels, generating a 512-dimension vector per image.

We used a linear SVM model with default parameters to classify the EEG signals. Every user had his/her own models, i.e. for each user, the data associated to the presentation of 2 queries (2000 EEG epochs) was used as training examples, and the remaining query was used for testing. This procedure was repeated 3 times to obtain a classification prediction for the images of the three queries.

We used the Area Under the Curve (AUC) of the Receiver Operating Characteristic space (ROC) to evaluate the performance of the models.

5. OBJECT DETECTION

After generating a relevance score by using the SVM models, the images were ranked from higher to lower relevance score. The top row of figure 3 shows a few examples of some of the correctly classified images for query. In these examples we can see images that have been correctly detected as relevant despite of the fact that, in most of them, the object appears to be very small (sometimes even incomplete). Such behavior suggests that users do not only recognize the object itself, but also its context.

The bottom row of figure 3 shows some sample images that obtained high SVM scores for target object, despite not being relevant to the query. It is interesting to see that all these images contain objects that are similar to the queried object. This also suggests that users respond not only to the general appearance of the image but also to the object they are looking for.

5.1 User diversity

Figure 4 shows the ROC curves for all the users who participated in the experiment. Due to the the huge diversity in user's performance, we define two user profiles:

- The *expert* user, who is familiar with the presented images (they have seen the images in advance) and with the purposes of the experiment.
- The *novice* user, who has had no previous exposure to the images.

Figure 3: Images with high SVM classifier scores for user A and and query 2 (top) and images with high SVM classifier scores (yet not relevant) for user D and query 1 (bottom).

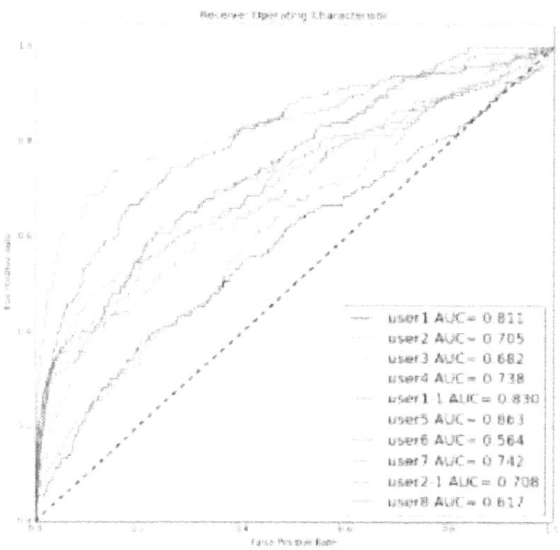

Figure 4: ROC curves for the 8 users. Users have as many curves as the number of experiments they performed.

Following the criteria stated above, 3 of our users were selected as experts and 5 of them as novice users. We then average the AUC values of the three queries for expert and novice users separately, reaching values of 0.758 and 0.642, respectively. The average AUC achieved by expert users is significantly higher than the one for novice users (t-test, p=0.005317, sample size = 9). This is a reasonable result, since expert users are already familiar with the images look like prior to the experiment, which gives them an advantage.

5.2 Visualization rates: 5Hz vs 10Hz

The second experiment explores the impact of different visualization rates in users' performance. We compare the performance achieved by those users who did the experiment at 10Hz with those who did it at 5Hz. We average the AUC values of the three queries for 5 and 10 Hz experiments separately, obtaining values of 0.775 and 0.734, respectively. This difference between the two is, however, not significant (t-test, p = 0.1397, sample size = 12), which leads us to conclude that 10Hz is a reasonable visualization rate for users to be able to identify objects in complex images and, more importantly, reduces the length of the experiment by half.

6. EEG VS. MOUSE FOR RETRIEVAL

In order to compare EEG- with mouse-based annotations, we use the interface from [6] on the same set of images described in Section 3. This interface displays the images in a thumbnail grid in the same order as in the EEG experiment. The time given to the users to annotate the images with the mouse interface is the same time spend visualizing images in the EEG setup, i.e. 200 seconds for the 5Hz configuration and 100 seconds for the 10 Hz one.

6.1 Retrieval within our dataset

The annotations obtained with both EEG and mouse-based mechanisms were used to sort the 1000 images for each query and produce a ranking.

The ranking for the mouse setup is constructed as follows: Given a set of positive annotations and their time stamps, we define two sets of images p_a and n_a, where p_a are the positive annotations themselves and n_a contains all those unmarked images presented before the last positive annotation (i.e. we assume that all the observed images that have not been clicked are negative). Then, the ranking is built to ensure that the images in p_a are always on top and the images in n_a are always at the bottom. The remaining set of images are placed in between in the same order in which they were displayed in the mouse interface.

The ranking for EEG is constructed by just sorting all the images by their SVM score in descending order.

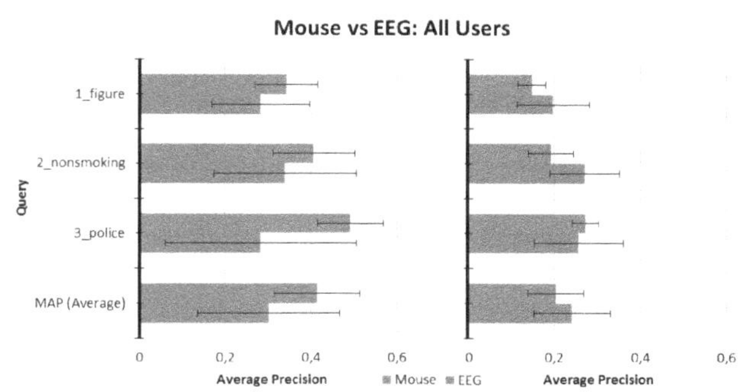

Figure 5: Mouse vs EEG. On the left, averaged values for all Users at 5Hz / 200 seconds. On the right, for 10Hz / 100 seconds.

Figure 5 shows an accuracy drop in both Mouse and EEG when time is reduced from 200 to 100. Interestingly, this drop in performance is a lot higher for the Mouse-based mechanism. The same time limitation on the EEG approach does not seem to significantly affect the final accuracy, which points out the potential of EEG signals, specially when the images are displayed at high frequency rates.

6.2 Retrieval in a larger dataset

This last experiment consists of combining the collected annotations with visual descriptors to retrieve images from a bigger dataset. The chosen dataset consists of 23,614 frames selected from the TRECVid Instance Search dataset from 2013. We extract visual descriptors for all our images from a Convolutional Neural Network (CNN) pre-trained with ImageNet [7] using the *Caffe* software [5]. The selected feature vector is the output of Layer 7 (the second top fully connected layer), which has 4,096 dimensions.

We then train a linear SVM model with default parameters for each query from the obtained annotations. This model is used to score to all images in the larger dataset and then sorted in descending order.

In order to train the model it is necessary to select positive and negative examples. For the mouse-based interface, we consider as positive examples all the images clicked by the users. Negative examples are those observed images that the user saw but did not click during the annotation time. In the EEG case, the annotations are selected according to the confidence scores given by the EEG models. We sort the images in descending order and take the top 10 and bottom 100 images as positive and negative examples, respectively.

The mean average precision values considering three queries and users for the mouse and EEG systems are 0.27 and 0.21 respectively. Results for the mouse configuration are significantly higher, but these results are averaged across all the users, and we know that there is a high variability among them (Section 5.1) and that this variability is especially present in the EEG case.

To make a comparison that is not subject to user diversity, Figure 6 shows the performance of the best user for both interfaces, in the two time configurations. As expected, when the user interaction time is set to 200s (5Hz RSVP), the mouse-based annotations are more effective than the EEG ones, obtaining mean AP of 0.49 vs 0.27, respectively. Nevertheless, when we consider the best users for the the 100s configuration (10Hz RSVP), we obtain a similar performance for the two, with EEG a slightly better on average with a mAP value of 0.37 against a 0.32 for mouse-based feedback.

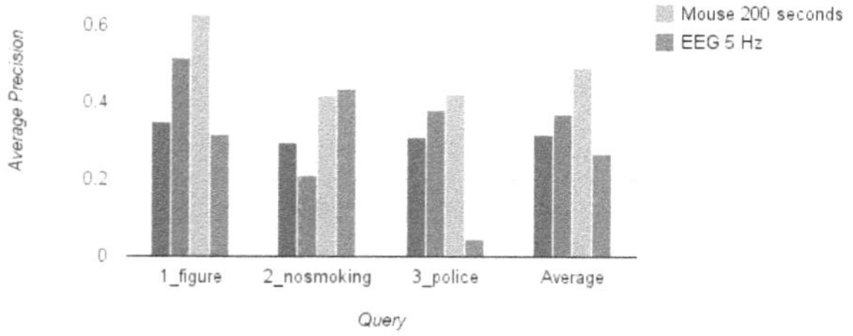

Figure 6: Average Precision comparison between mouse and EEG annotations for the best user

7. CONCLUSION

In this paper, we have presented and studied the potential application of EEG as a mechanism towards relevance feedback and compared it to the traditional "click-based" one for an object retrieval task. We have compared the EEG-based relevance feedback signal with standard "click-based" relevance feedback from a mouse and find that comparable accuracy can be achieved with the EEG-based approach, especially for those users who are familiar with both the brain computer interface and the image dataset. We have seen that there is potential for EEG specially when using higher RSVP rates, which allow for faster annotation with little drop in performance.

Acknowledgements

This publication has emanated from research conducted with the financial support of Science Foundation Ireland (SFI) under grant number SFI/12/RC/2289, project BigGraph TEC2013-43935-R, funded by the Spanish Ministerio de Economía y Competitividad and the European Regional Development Fund (ERDF), as well as the donation of a GeoForce GTX Titan Z from NVIDIA Corporation.

8. REFERENCES

[1] A. Amir, M. Berg, and H. Permuter. Mutual relevance feedback for multimodal query formulation in video retrieval. In *Proceedings of the 7th ACM SIGMM International Workshop on Multimedia Information Retrieval*, MIR '05, pages 17–24, 2005.

[2] N. Bigdely-Shamlo, A. Vankov, R. R. Ramirez, and S. Makeig. Brain activity-based image classification from rapid serial visual presentation. *Neural Systems and Rehabilitation Engineering, IEEE Transactions on*, 16(5):432–441, 2008.

[3] G. Healy and A. F. Smeaton. Optimising the number of channels in eeg-augmented image search. In *Proceedings of the 25th BCS Conference on Human-Computer Interaction*, pages 157–162. British Computer Society, 2011.

[4] Y. Huang, D. Erdogmus, M. Pavel, S. Mathan, and K. E. Hild II. A framework for rapid visual image search using single-trial brain evoked responses. *Neurocomputing*, 74(12):2041–2051, 2011.

[5] Y. Jia, E. Shelhamer, J. Donahue, S. Karayev, J. Long, R. Girshick, S. Guadarrama, and T. Darrell. Caffe: Convolutional architecture for fast feature embedding. In *Proceedings of the ACM International Conference on Multimedia*, pages 675–678, 2014.

[6] K. McGuinness, E. Mohedano, Z. Zhang, F. Hu, R. Abatal, C. Gurrin, N. O'Connor, A. F. Smeaton, A. Salvador Aguilera, X. Giró Nieto, et al. Insight centre for data analytics (dcu) at trecvid 2014: instance search and semantic indexing tasks. 2014.

[7] O. Russakovsky, J. Deng, H. Su, J. Krause, S. Satheesh, S. Ma, Z. Huang, A. Karpathy, A. Khosla, M. Bernstein, A. C. Berg, and L. Fei-Fei. ImageNet Large Scale Visual Recognition Challenge, 2014.

[8] J. Wang, E. Pohlmeyer, B. Hanna, Y.-G. Jiang, P. Sajda, and S.-F. Chang. Brain state decoding for rapid image retrieval. In *Proceedings of the 17th ACM international conference on Multimedia*, pages 945–954. ACM, 2009.

[9] J. Yang. *A general framework for classifier adaptation and its applications in multimedia*. PhD thesis, Carnegie Mellon University, 2009.

[10] X. S. Zhou and T. S. Huang. Relevance feedback in image retrieval: A comprehensive review. *Multimedia systems*, 8(6):536–544, 2003.

Kernel Local Descriptors with Implicit Rotation Matching

Andrei Bursuc, Giorgos Tolias, and Hervé Jégou
Inria
{firstname.lastname}@inria.fr

ABSTRACT

In this work we design a kernelized local feature descriptor and propose a matching scheme for aligning patches quickly and automatically. We analyze the SIFT descriptor from a kernel view and identify and reproduce some of its underlying benefits. We overcome the quantization artifacts of SIFT by encoding pixel attributes in a continuous manner via explicit feature maps. Experiments performed on the patch dataset of Brown *et al.* [3] show the superiority of our descriptor over methods based on supervised learning.

Categories and Subject Descriptors

I.4.10 [**Image Processing and Computer Vision**]: Image Representation

General Terms

Algorithms and Experimentation

Keywords

local descriptor; kernel descriptor; rotation invariance

1. INTRODUCTION

In this paper we deal with the design of a local descriptor, which is one of the fundamental problems in computer vision. A variety of tasks, such as image classification, retrieval, detection, and registration, rely on descriptors derived from local patches. The local patches can be originated from dense sampling [ ] or from a sparse feature detector [ ] which is co-variant to certain image transformations.

A variety of local descriptors builds upon image gradients. A standard choice is to build a histogram of gradient orientations, as in SIFT [7]. Another example concerns methods that rely on pixel intensities, *e.g.* by pairwise comparisons [ ]. Learning [3] based on pairs of similar and non-similar patches is employed to select the spatial pooling regions and for dimensionality reduction [10].

In this work, we focus on a kernelized view of patch descriptors. In particular, we are motivated by the kernel descriptor of Bo *et al.* [2]. However, in our method we encode pixels in polar coordinates and rely on explicit feature maps [12], which provide a better approximation by Fourier series. We present a kernelized framework for local descriptors, out of which, known descriptors such as SIFT and our proposed descriptor are derived. This viewpoint of SIFT highlights some of its advantages and drawbacks: namely the encoding of the pixel position and the hard assignment which inevitably inserts some artifacts. We rather offer continuous encoding of pixel position and gradient orientations.

There are local descriptors that are rotation invariant by construction [8]. An alternative approach is to rely on the dominant orientation [7] of the patch in order to provide rotation invariance. The patches are rotated with respect to this dominant angle and transformed to up-right. Therefore, such descriptors are sensitive to this angle. In addition, in several tasks it is necessary to detect several multiple angles per patch, which further increases the computational cost of the procedures that follow. We adapt the latter choice of up-right patches and develop a fast patch alignment method with respect to rotation. Patch similarity is computed for multiple rotations at a slight increase of the computational cost. It allows us to handle the sensitivity to dominant orientation estimation and to dispense with the need for multiple dominant angles. This procedure is similar to the trigonometric polynomial of Tolias *et al.* [11], but at a patch level. It further resembles the way that Henriques *et al.* [6] speed-up learning with multiple shifted versions of negative samples, instead of performing costly sliding window based mining.

Our contribution includes a novel kernel local descriptor that encodes pixel position and gradient orientation in a continuous manner. It is also accompanied by an efficient way to compute patch similarity for multiple rotations, which constitutes our second contribution.

2. LOCAL DESCRIPTORS: KERNEL VIEW

Match kernels have gained an increasing interest after it was shown that it is possible to approximate non-linear kernels with linear ones by using an appropriate feature map [9, 12]. Similarity of sets can be efficiently computed with match kernels just by embedding the features in a suitable feature space in advance. Match kernels provide new grounds for designing better similarity functions.

Here, we define kernel descriptors over sets of pixels belonging to the same patch. An image patch can be considered as a set of pixels $\mathcal{X} = \{\mathbf{x}\}$. Without loss of generality we assume that we are dealing with grayscale patches. The relative position of a pixel $\mathbf{x}$ with respect to the patch center

ICMR'15, June 23–26, 2015, Shanghai, China.

http://dx.doi.org/10.1145/2671188.2749379.

is expressed in polar coordinates and denoted by $(\varphi_{\mathbf{x}}, \rho_{\mathbf{x}})$. We employ gradient information, thus each pixel is described by the gradient magnitude $m_{\mathbf{x}}$ and the gradient orientation $\theta_{\mathbf{x}}$. The latter is expressed relatively to the angle $\varphi_{\mathbf{x}}$ (Figure 3). The pixel position and its gradient information are referred as *pixel attributes* in the following. Two patches $\mathcal{X}$ and $\mathcal{Y}$ can be now compared via a match kernel of the form

$$\mathcal{K}(\mathcal{X}, \mathcal{Y}) = \gamma(\mathcal{X})\gamma(\mathcal{Y}) \sum_{\mathbf{x} \in \mathcal{X}} \sum_{\mathbf{y} \in \mathcal{Y}} k(\mathbf{x}, \mathbf{y}), \quad (1)$$

where k is the local kernel and γ is the normalization factor ensuring that self-similarity $\mathcal{K}(\mathcal{X}, \mathcal{X}) = 1$. The local kernel computes the similarity between two pixels $\mathbf{x}$ and $\mathbf{y}$, while the global kernel $\mathcal{K}$ accumulates similarities of all pairs of pixels. An interesting option is to obtain such a kernel by mapping pixels attributes to a higher-dimensional space with a feature map $\psi : \mathbf{x} \rightarrow \psi(\mathbf{x})$, such that the inner product evaluates the local kernel $k(\mathbf{x}, \mathbf{y}) = \langle \psi(\mathbf{x}) | \psi(\mathbf{y}) \rangle$. The match kernel can be now expressed as:

$$\mathcal{K}(\mathcal{X}, \mathcal{Y}) = \gamma(\mathcal{X})\gamma(\mathcal{Y}) \sum_{\mathbf{x} \in \mathcal{X}} \sum_{\mathbf{y} \in \mathcal{Y}} \langle \psi(\mathbf{x}) | \psi(\mathbf{y}) \rangle = \langle \mathbf{X} | \mathbf{Y} \rangle, \quad (2)$$

where $\mathbf{X} = \gamma(\mathcal{X}) \sum_{\mathbf{x} \in \mathcal{X}} \psi(\mathbf{x})$ and $\mathbf{Y} = \gamma(\mathcal{Y}) \sum_{\mathbf{y} \in \mathcal{Y}} \psi(\mathbf{y})$ are the local descriptors of patches $\mathcal{X}$ and $\mathcal{Y}$, respectively. Note that all the pairwise similarities are never explicitly enumerated; the linearity of the inner-product allows us to aggregate in advance the pixel feature vectors per patch.

Several popular methods for patch and image description can be actually described by this framework, among which SIFT. The SIFT descriptor is arguably one of the most popular and effective local feature descriptors in various computer vision applications. Some of the underlying advantages of SIFT can be emphasized better from a kernel perspective.

In the case of SIFT, consider that each pixel $\mathbf{x}$ is mapped to $\psi(\mathbf{x}) \in \mathbb{R}^{128}$, which is a sparse feature map due to the quantization of gradient orientation and spatial location. The aggregation of all pixel feature maps $\psi(\mathbf{x})$ results to the SIFT descriptor. The similarity of two SIFT descriptors can be then computed via inner product. The quantization to the spatial grid and to the orientation bins enforces to take into account only pixels with similar gradient orientations and spatial positions. The hard assignment in the quantization process inevitably inserts some artifacts and leads to a loss in the selectivity of the similarity function.

In the following, we design a kernelized local descriptor that imitates some of the advantages of the SIFT descriptor. At the same time, we alleviate some of drawbacks related to the quantization artifacts by encoding pixel position and gradient orientation in a continuous manner.

3. METHOD

We want to exploit jointly the photometric and position information of all patch elements (pixels). We target a kernel function for patch elements that reflects their resemblance in terms of gradients and their proximity in terms of their spatial position. To this effect, the local kernel $k(\mathbf{x}, \mathbf{y})$ can be decomposed into $k_\theta(\theta_{\mathbf{x}}, \theta_{\mathbf{y}})\, k_\varphi(\varphi_{\mathbf{x}}, \varphi_{\mathbf{y}})\, k_\rho(\rho_{\mathbf{x}}, \rho_{\mathbf{y}})$. It captures the similarity of the gradients with k_θ, and the spatial proximity on each coordinate separately with k_φ and k_ρ. Our match kernel now becomes

$$\mathcal{K}(\mathcal{X}, \mathcal{Y}) \propto \sum_{\mathbf{x} \in \mathcal{X}} \sum_{\mathbf{y} \in \mathcal{Y}} \tilde{m}_{\mathbf{x}}\, \tilde{m}_{\mathbf{y}}\, k_\theta(\theta_{\mathbf{x}}, \theta_{\mathbf{y}})\, k_\varphi(\varphi_{\mathbf{x}}, \varphi_{\mathbf{y}})\, k_\rho(\rho_{\mathbf{x}}, \rho_{\mathbf{y}}),$$

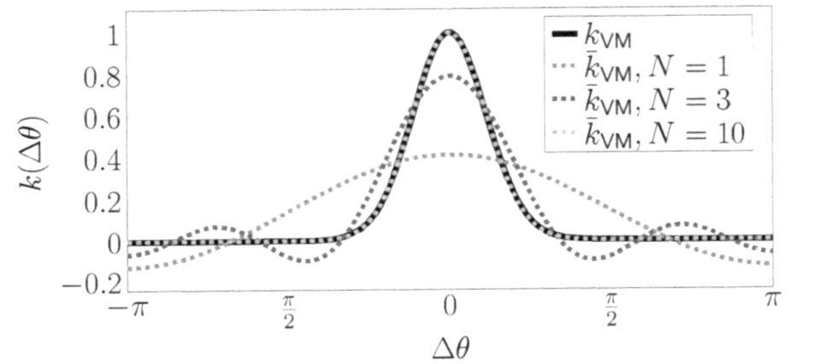

Figure 1: Target weighting function (Von Mises) and the corresponding approximations with 1, 3 and 10 frequencies.

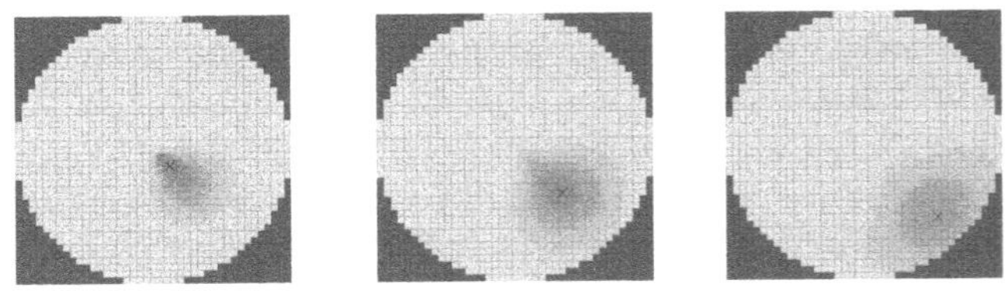

Figure 2: Visualization of the 2D weighting function for 3 sample pixels (shown by a cross). Colors reflect the spatial similarity to other pixels. Red (yellow) color corresponds to maximum (minimum) similarity. Blue color corresponds to the area that is neglected by our descriptor.

where the magnitude $\tilde{m}_{\mathbf{x}} = G(\rho_x, \sigma) * \sqrt{m_{\mathbf{x}}}$ is weighted by a Gaussian window in order to give higher importance to the patch center. In this fashion, our match kernel turns into scalar value comparison, such as angles and radii. Typically, non-linear functions are employed for such a comparison.

3.1 Feature maps for pixel attributes

We employ a normalized version of the Von Mises distribution [11] (normal distribution for angles) in order to compare two angles:

$$k_{VM}(\theta_1, \theta_2) = k_{VM}(\Delta\theta) = \frac{\exp(\kappa \cos(\Delta\theta)) - \exp(-\kappa)}{2\sinh(\kappa)}. \quad (3)$$

This is a stationary kernel that depends only on the difference of the two angles $\Delta\theta = \theta_1 - \theta_2$. The selectivity of the function is controlled by parameter κ.

We define a mapping $\phi : [-\pi, \pi] \rightarrow \mathbb{R}^M$ of an angle θ to a vector $\phi(\theta)$ such that the inner product of two such vectors approximates the target function, that is $\phi(\theta_1)^\top \phi(\theta_2) = \bar{k}_{VM}(\theta_1, \theta_2) \approx k_{VM}(\theta_1, \theta_2)$. For this purpose we make use of explicit feature maps [12] and follow the methodology of Tolias *et al.* [11]. The desired mapping is

$$\phi(\theta) = (\sqrt{\gamma_0}, \sqrt{\gamma_1}\cos(\theta), \sqrt{\gamma_1}\sin(\theta), \ldots, \sqrt{\gamma_N}\cos(N\theta), \sqrt{\gamma_N}\sin(N\theta))^\top, \quad (4)$$

where γ_i is the i-th Fourier coefficient of Von Mises (3). The approximation by N Fourier coefficients (coresponding to N frequencies) produces a vector of $M = 2N + 1$ dimensions. The number of frequencies influences the accuracy of the approximation. Figure 1 illustrates the target function and its approximation for different values of N.

We choose the Von Mises to implement all 3 local kernels k_θ, k_φ and k_ρ. The mapping of Equation (4) is trivially used on local kernels k_θ and k_φ, since they deal with angles. We further map the radius of pixel $\mathbf{x}$ to an angle by $\tilde{\rho}_{\mathbf{x}} = \rho_{\mathbf{x}}\pi$, with $\rho_{\mathbf{x}} \in [0, 1]$. In this way, we are now able to use the same

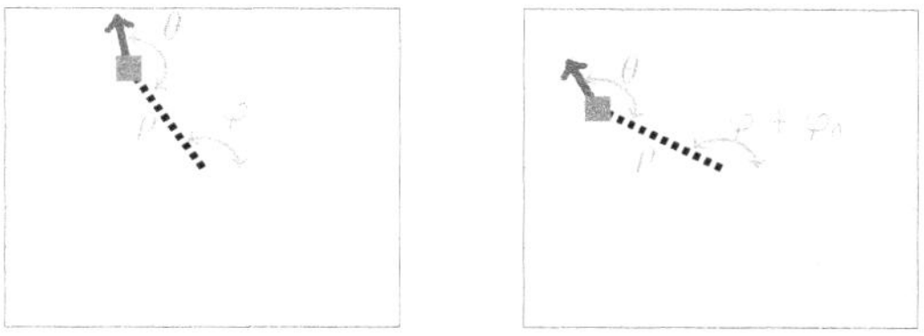

Figure 3: A sample patch and a corresponding pixel denoted by red rectangle. The gradient vector is shown by a blue arrow. The initial patch (left), is rotated by angle φ_δ (right). Both radius ρ and angle θ remain unchanged, while only angle φ changes.

mapping of scalar to vectors for the radius also. In Figure 2 we visualize the combination of the two local kernels k_ρ and k_φ (by their product) that evaluate the spatial proximity.

3.2 Wrapping up the descriptor

Each patch element $\mathbf{x}$ is now associated to three vectors describing its attributes, namely $\phi(\theta_\mathbf{x})$, $\phi(\varphi_\mathbf{x})$ and $\phi(\tilde{\rho}_\mathbf{x})$. In order to obtain a single descriptor we propose to describe $\mathbf{x}$ by the Kronecker product of these vectors, defined by $\psi(\mathbf{x}) = \tilde{m}_\mathbf{x}\phi(\theta_\mathbf{x}) \otimes \phi(\varphi_\mathbf{x}) \otimes \phi(\tilde{\rho}_\mathbf{x})$. By aggregating such vectors for all patch elements, the patch descriptor is now formed by $\mathbf{X} \propto \sum_{\mathbf{x}\in\mathcal{X}} \psi(\mathbf{x})$.

By using the Kronecker product properties we can show that comparing two such local descriptors via inner product is equivalent to the approximation of our match kernel:

$$\begin{aligned}\langle \mathbf{X}|\mathbf{Y}\rangle &\propto \sum_{\mathbf{x}\in\mathcal{X}} \psi(\mathbf{x})^\top \sum_{\mathbf{y}\in\mathcal{Y}} \psi(\mathbf{y}) = \sum_{\mathbf{x}\in\mathcal{X}} \sum_{\mathbf{y}\in\mathcal{Y}} \psi(\mathbf{x})^\top \psi(\mathbf{y}) \\ &\approx \sum_{\mathbf{x}\in\mathcal{X}} \sum_{\mathbf{y}\in\mathcal{Y}} \tilde{m}_\mathbf{x}\, \tilde{m}_\mathbf{y}\, k_\theta(\theta_\mathbf{x}, \theta_\mathbf{y})\, k_\varphi(\varphi_\mathbf{x}, \varphi_\mathbf{y})\, k_\rho(\tilde{\rho}_\mathbf{x}, \tilde{\rho}_\mathbf{y}) \\ &= \mathcal{K}(\mathcal{X}, \mathcal{Y}). \end{aligned} \tag{5}$$

The desired property of our mapping is the linearity of the inner product used to compare two vectors, which approximates a non-linear function comparing two angles. The pixel representation can be then aggregated in advance for each patch. The dimensionality of the local descriptor is equal to $(2N_\theta + 1)(2N_\varphi + 1)(2N_\rho + 1)$, where different number of frequencies can be used for each pixel attribute (N_θ, N_φ and N_ρ) depending on the use-case. The descriptor is subsequently square-rooted and L_2-normalized.

3.3 Fast rotation alignment

At this stage, our match kernel and, equivalently, the kernel descriptor assume that all patches have the same global orientation. Patches are typically orientated to up-right position according to their dominant orientation. We adopt the same choice. However, this type of alignment can be quite noisy. We propose a method for identifying the rotation that maximizes the patch similarity and aligns them in an optimal way. We achieve this without explicitly computing the descriptors for all possible rotations.

Imagine that a patch $\mathcal{X}$ is rotated by an angle φ_δ into patch $\mathcal{X}_\delta$, and denote the descriptor of the rotated patch by $\mathbf{X}_\delta$. The only pixel attribute that changes is the angle φ, shifted by φ_δ, as illustrated in the toy example of Figure 3. Under this point of view and with respect to variable φ, it can be seen that local descriptor $\mathbf{X}$ is decomposed into the following sub-vectors $[\mathbf{X}_0{}^\top, \mathbf{X}_{1,c}{}^\top, \mathbf{X}_{1,s}{}^\top, \ldots, \mathbf{X}_{N,c}{}^\top, \mathbf{X}_{N,s}{}^\top]^\top$.

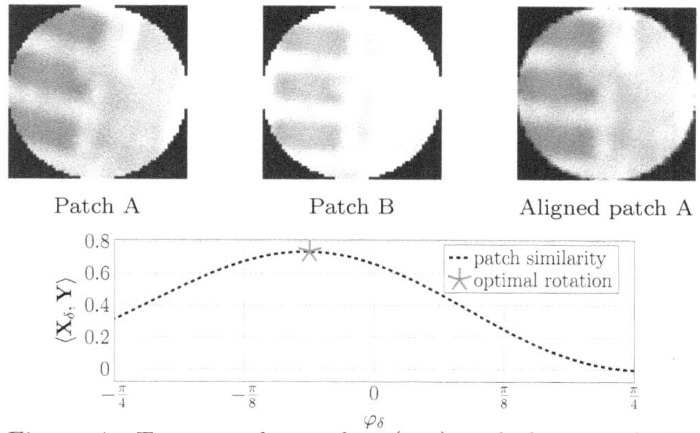

Figure 4: Two sample patches (top) and their similarity (bottom) for multiple rotations of patch A. At the (top) right, patch A is rotated by the optimal orientation.

$\mathbf{X}_0$ is constant for any patch rotation. The sub-vectors $\mathbf{X}_{i,c}$ and $\mathbf{X}_{i,s}$ are related to components of the form $cos(i\varphi_\mathbf{x})$ and $sin(i\varphi_\mathbf{x})$, respectively, for frequency i.

Interestingly, by using simple trigonometric identities, it turns out [11] that the similarity of two patches, when one of them undergoes rotation, forms a trigonometric polynomial:

$$\begin{aligned}\langle \mathbf{X}_\delta|\mathbf{Y}\rangle =& \langle \mathbf{X}_0|\mathbf{Y}_0\rangle + \sum_{n=1}^{N_\varphi} \cos(n\varphi_\delta)\ \left(\langle \mathbf{X}_{n,c}|\mathbf{Y}_{n,c}\rangle + \langle \mathbf{X}_{n,s}|\mathbf{Y}_{n,s}\rangle\right) \\ &+ \sum_{n=1}^{N_\varphi} \sin(n\varphi_\delta)\ \left(-\langle \mathbf{X}_{n,c}|\mathbf{Y}_{n,s}\rangle + \langle \mathbf{X}_{n,s}|\mathbf{Y}_{n,c}\rangle\right). \end{aligned} \tag{6}$$

The complexity of computation of the polynomial coefficients in Equation (6) is less than twice the cost to compute the standard similarity between two kernel descriptors, while the cost to evaluate similarity for multiple angles φ_δ is negligible. In Figure 4 we present an example of the similarity of two patches under multiple rotations. The rotation of maximum similarity is used to align the patches.

4. EXPERIMENTS

We compare our descriptor against the state-of-the-art RootSIFT [1], and its counterpart rotated by PCA, noted as RootSIFT-PCA in the following. We further compare with the learned descriptors of Simonyan *et al.* [10] and the ones of Brown *et al.* [3] that rely on pairs of known related and non-related patches. We do not consider in our evaluation the descriptor of Bo *et al.* [2] as it is optimized to be used in image level aggregated manner for image classification, whereas we test patch similarities. We use a patch dataset [3] comprising three subsets, Notre Dame, Liberty and Yosemite, corresponding to different landmarks on which 3D reconstruction was performed. Each subset consists of 450k image patches of size 64 × 64 which are derived from keypoints detected with Difference-of-Gaussians. They are normalized with respect to scale and rotation. The ground-truth denotes the groups of similar patches, and two patches are considered similar if they are projections of the same 3D point.

4.1 Implementation details

We refer to our kernel descriptor as $KD_{N_\theta,N_\varphi,N_\rho}$ and evaluate for different number of frequencies. Parameter κ is always fixed and equal to 8, except for the case of $N_\rho = 1$

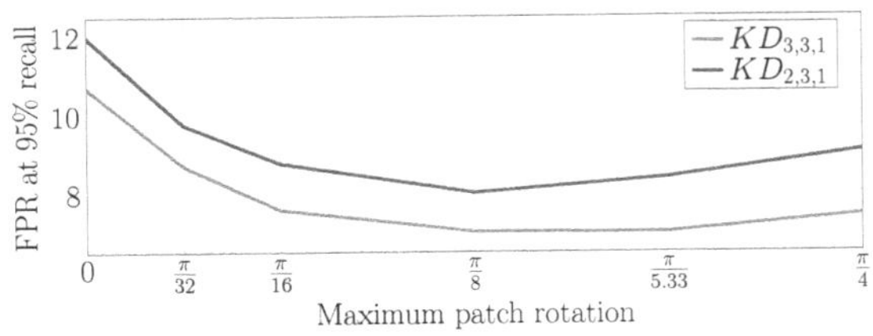

Figure 5: Impact of the rotation alignment on the performance. We evaluate patch similarity for 0, 4, 8, 16, 24 and 32 fixed rotations at each direction (clockwise and counter-clockwise). Results reported on Notre Dame dataset.

when κ is 2. In order to avoid artifacts for the computation of the rotated patches, we keep only the pixels inside the circle inscribed in the patch, as shown in Fig. 4.

Post-processing. The patch descriptor is power-law normalized with the power-law exponent α set to 0.5. For the PCA rotated variant, we obtain better results for $\alpha = 1$. For this case, we apply powerlaw normalization with $\alpha = 0.5$ after the projection. We proceed similarly for RootSIFT-PCA.

Orientation alignment. In order to align two patches we test up to 64 fixed rotations on each direction with a step of $\pi/128$. We find a good trade-off for rotations in the interval $[-\pi/8, \pi/8]$. Since the patches are already up-right, our algorithm reduces the quantization errors in the computation of the dominant orientations.

4.2 Hypothesis test

We evaluate our kernel descriptors following the standard protocol, generate the ROC curves and report false positive rate (FPR) at 95% recall. In Figure 5 we illustrate how performance improves by evaluating similarities for multiple patch rotations. After some extent performance decreases, since patches are already up-right by the rough dominant orientation and we are only introducing noisy matches.

We now consider each of the six possible combinations of training and test sets and we test 100k pairs for each run. Table 1 compares the error rates of our kernel descriptor against other local descriptors. Our descriptor is better than RootSIFT and RootSIFT-PCA and its performance is reaching that of learned descriptors [10]. While our kernel descriptor is higher dimensional, it doesn't require any training. We further evaluate it with PCA learned on a different dataset in order to obtain more compact descriptors. Although we cannot test multiple rotations anymore, the performance improves significantly outperforming more sophisticated methods trained over annotated pairs of similar and non-similar patches.

4.3 Nearest neighbors

We further evaluate our descriptor on a nearest neighbor search task using the patch dataset. We randomly select 1,000 query patches and report recall at the top R retrieved patches. This task is performed on a single subset at a time. Results for using Notre Dame as test set and Yosemite as learning set are reported in Table 2. Our kernel descriptors appear to perform the best, while the rotation alignment improves once more.

5. CONCLUSIONS

We proposed a kernel descriptor equipped with continuous encoding and a fast rotation alignment process. Interestingly, it achieves superior performance even compared to methods that employ supervised learning.[1]

Train	Test	RootSIFT	RootSIFT-PCA	Simonyan [10]	Brown[3]	$KD_{2,3,1}$	$KD_{3,3,1}$	$KD_{3,2,2}$-PCA
ND	Lib	29.64	19.34	**12.42**	16.85	21.58	20.06	13.17
Yos	Lib		19.95	14.58	18.27			**14.53**
ND	Yos	26.69	18.37	10.08	13.55	11.07	9.66	**8.31**
Lib	Yos		19.52	11.18	N/A			**9.65**
Lib	ND	22.06	13.90	7.22	N/A	7.99	7.00	**6.36**
Yos	ND		13.98	6.82	11.98			**6.50**
Mean		26.14	17.51	10.38	15.16	13.55	12.24	**9.75**
Dimensions		128	80	73-77	29-36	105	147	80
Learning		N	US	S	S	N	N	US

Table 1: False positive rate (%) at 95% recall. Learning type: N-none, US-unsupervised, S-supervised.

R	1	5	10	100	1000	10000
RootSIFT	8.5	24.4	33.0	62.9	79.7	90.6
RootSIFT-PCA	8.8	23.9	32.7	61.4	78.4	90.4
$KD_{3,3,1}$ (No rotations)	9.1	24.7	34.6	64.9	80.8	91.3
$KD_{3,3,1}$ (16 rotations)	**8.8**	**26.2**	**37.3**	**68.3**	**84.4**	**93.1**
$KD_{3,3,1} - PCA$	9.4	24.9	35.2	66.4	82.9	92.4

Table 2: Recall computed at R top ranked patches for 1000 randomly selected patch queries on Notredame dataset. Learning for PCA is performed on Yosemite dataset, and the dimensionality is reduced to 80 components.

6. REFERENCES

[1] R. Arandjelovic and A. Zisserman. Three things everyone should know to improve object retrieval. In *CVPR*, 2012.

[2] L. Bo, X. Ren, and D. Fox. Kernel descriptors for visual recognition. In *NIPS*, Dec. 2010.

[3] M. Brown, G. Hua, and S. Winder. Discriminative learning of local image descriptors. *Trans. PAMI*, 33(1):43–57, 2011.

[4] M. Calonder, V. Lepetit, C. Strecha, and P. Fua. Brief: Binary robust independent elementary features. In *ECCV*, Oct. 2010.

[5] L. Fei-Fei and P. Perona. A bayesian hierarchical model for learning natural scene categories. In *CVPR*, 2005.

[6] J. F. Henriques, J. Carreira, R. Caseiro, and J. Batista. Beyond hard negative mining: Efficient detector learning via block-circulant decomposition. In *ICCV*, 2013.

[7] D. Lowe. Distinctive image features from scale-invariant keypoints. *IJCV*, 60(2):91–110, Nov. 2004.

[8] T. Ojala, M. Pietikainen, and T. Maenpaa. Multiresolution gray-scale and rotation invariant texture classification with local binary patterns. *Trans. PAMI*, 24(7):971–987, 2002.

[9] A. Rahimi and B. Recht. Random features for large-scale kernel machines. In *NIPS*, 2007.

[10] K. Simonyan, A. Vedaldi, and A. Zisserman. Learning local feature descriptors using convex optimisation. *Trans. PAMI*, 2014.

[11] G. Tolias, T. Furon, and H. Jégou. Orientation covariant aggregation of local descriptors with embeddings. In *ECCV*, Sep. 2014.

[12] A. Vedaldi and A. Zisserman. Efficient additive kernels via explicit feature maps. *Trans. PAMI*, 34(3):480–492, Mar. 2012.

[1] This work was supported by ERC grant VIAMASS no. 336054 and ANR project Fire-ID.

Semantic Concept Annotation for User Generated Videos Using Soundtracks

Qin Jin[1,2], Junwei Liang[1], Xixi He[1], Gang Yang[1], Jieping Xu[1], Xirong Li[1,2]
[1]Multimedia Computing Lab, School of Information, Renmin University of China, 100872, China
[2]Key Lab of Data Engineering and Knowledge Engineering, Renmin University of China, 100872, China
{qjin,chunwei,xixilanmi,yanggang,xjieping,xirong}@ruc.edu.cn

ABSTRACT

With the increasing use of audio sensors in user generated content (UGC) collections, semantic concept annotation from video soundtracks has become an important research problem. In this paper, we investigate reducing the semantic gap of the traditional data-driven bag-of-audio-words based audio annotation approach by utilizing the large-amount of wild audio data and their rich user tags, from which we propose a new feature representation based on semantic class model distance. We conduct experiments on the data collection from HUAWEI Accurate and Fast Mobile Video Annotation Grand Challenge 2014. We also fuse the audio-only annotation system with a visual-only system. The experimental results show that our audio-only concept annotation system can detect semantic concepts significantly better than does random guessing. The new feature representation achieves comparable annotation performance with the bag-of-audio-words feature. In addition, it can provide more semantic interpretation in the output. The experimental results also prove that the audio-only system can provide significant complementary information to the visual-only concept annotation system for performance boost and for better interpretation of semantic concepts both visually and acoustically.

Categories and Subject Descriptors

H.5.5 [**Information Interfaces and Presentation**]: Sound and Music Computing –*Signal analysis, synthesis, and processing.*

General Terms

Algorithms; Experimentation; Measurement.

Keywords

Semantic Concept Annotation; Audio Analysis; Consumer Videos.

1. INTRODUCTION

With the rapid introduction of mobile devices in our everyday life, there appears explosively growing amount of user generated content (UGC) videos on social networking services, such as YouTube, Dailymotion, Youku and Tudou in China. Such rich data resources have attracted tremendous research interest in developing automatic technologies for organizing and indexing multimedia content [1]. Automatic semantic concept annotation for UGC videos has been one of the hot research topics. Although the visual information in a video is clearly very important for semantic concept annotation, we believe that the soundtrack may offer a useful and complementary source of information, especially when the visual part fails (occlusion or absence). In this paper we address this challenge by exploiting acoustic information – the soundtrack of a video – to see what useful descriptors can be reliably extracted from this modality.

We summarize the previous related research work in soundtrack analysis and audio concept or event detection from the following three areas of focus: Number of sound classes; Quality of the audio data; Granularity of the audio processing. Much early works focused on a small number of sound classes such as speech, music, silence, noise, or applause. Various acoustic features (such as Mel-Frequency Cepstral Coefficients (MFCCs), zero-crossing rate, short-time energy, pitch, and spectral peak tracks [3-5] etc.) and their derivative features such as posterior probability features [4] plus various classifiers including Gaussian Mixture Models [3], Hidden Markov Models [6], Support Vector Machines [7] and so on have been explored. Early works focused on relatively carefully produced audios, such as broadcast audio or movie soundtracks [3-7]. There is also a lot of research on classifying less constrained environmental sounds [8-11], such as in surveillance applications or context-awareness in mobile devices. In recent years, the growing popularity of video sharing services, such as YouTube, Dailymotion, and Youku, enables the use of a quickly increase amount of user-generated videos. The soundtracks in UGC videos are typically of poor quality and often contain only sparse instances of class-relevant sounds. Thus, working on this data becomes a more challenging task. The soundtrack analysis of consumer videos [12-15] is less researched, particularly when considering the analysis at a finer video resolution, at the frame level. Even though the semantic indexing (SIN) task in TRECVID [16] has been a subtask of localizing concepts at the frame-level since 2013, few studies have utilized a purely auditory method to help to achieve the goal. The bag-of-audio-word [13,15] along with other approaches like pLSA-of-GMM [12] suffer from the drawback that the results are unable to provide semantic interpretation. Rather than specifying and labeling the sub-concepts, we add the semantic interpretation by using "data in the wild" according to particular rules.

The study in this paper is conducted on the data from the grand challenge in the International Conference on Multimedia & Expo (ICME) 2014: HUAWEI Accurate and Fast Mobile Video Annotation Challenge [16]. The goal of this task is to analyze UGC videos and annotate their contents automatically at the frame level: any of the target concepts appear in this frame or not. Comparing to the semantic concept annotation task at the entire-video level or at the supra-segmental level in previous research, this task requires annotation with finer resolution, and it certainly is a more challenging task. In this paper, we focus on six semantic

ICMR'15, June 23–26, 2015, Shanghai, China.
COPYRIGHT © 2015 ACM 978-1-4503-3274-3/15/06…$15.00.
http://dx.doi.org/10.1145/2671188.2749388

concept classes, which cover objects (e.g. "car", "dog", and "kids"), scenes (e.g. "beach"), and events ("football" and "party"). This paper provides a semantically enhanced approach to extract low-level audio features using the traditional bag-of-audio-word method while at the same time maintaining the readability of the results, which we learn from freely available audio data from the Internet, and their descriptions.

2. AUDIO-ONLY ANNOTATION SYSTEM

Our semantic concept annotation system using soundtrack/audio information [19] contains two major components: audio features extraction and concept annotation model training

2.1 Feature Extraction

We first extract the mono soundtrack from a video and re-sampled it to 8kHz. In order to detect concepts at the frame level, we chunk the audio stream into a sequence of 3-sec snippets with 1-sec shift. We then extract audio features and apply concept detection to the snippets. Our frame-based low-level feature is the Mel-frequency Cepstral Coefficients (MFCCs) over short-time window of 25ms with a 10ms shift as our fundamental frame-level feature. Each 25ms frame of a video soundtrack is then represented as a 39-dim MFCC feature vector (13-dim MFCC + delta + delta delta). Each snippet is then represented by a set of MFCC feature vectors. Based on the love-level MFCC features, we derive following other higher-level feature representations.

2.1.1 Bag-of-Audio-Words (BoAW) Feature

The audio words (or acoustic codebook) are generated in a data-driven fashion. To be specific, the codebook is learned by applying the Kmeans clustering algorithm to the 39-dimensional MFCC features from the whole training dataset. Each of the learned K means is considered as one audio word. Each soundtrack snippet is then represented as a distribution over these K codewords by using a soft-assignment (by adding the closest 5 codewords' counts) of MFCC features to these codewords. This is the feature we use in our baseline system.

2.1.2 Semantics-Derived (SD) Feature

In order to maintain the good performance of the representation while improving the semantic interpretability of the results, we propose the semantics-derived (SD) Feature. This feature generation consists of four steps: 1) downloading wild data (in this experiment we use data from *freesound*); 2) selecting sound classes via tag selection from the wild data; 3) building SVM classifiers for sound classes; 4) generating feature representations for a snippet by scoring it against the sound class models.

2.1.2.1 Wild Data Downloading

We find that freesound.org [20] is a good repository covering a wide range of user-collected recordings. We first search audios for the six target concepts (car, dog, kids, beach, football, and party) by using the concept name as a textual query in the freesound search engine. This returns audio segments, which contain similar tags or description to the query text. Next we use each of the returned audio segments as a query to search for acoustically similar audio segments in the freesound similarity search engine, which returns audio segments that have similar statistics over audio features, such as the zero-crossing rate. We keep all the text similarity results and the top 20 acoustic similarity results for each search. Finally, we filter out the audios with bad quality, or those with abnormal coding. Eventually, we collect 35681 audio files. The resulting wild audio dataset has a total duration of about 763 hours, and the median of a file's duration is 20 seconds. We split the freesound dataset into a training set of 28544 files and a testing set using the remainder of the files.

2.1.2.2 Sound Class/Tag Selection

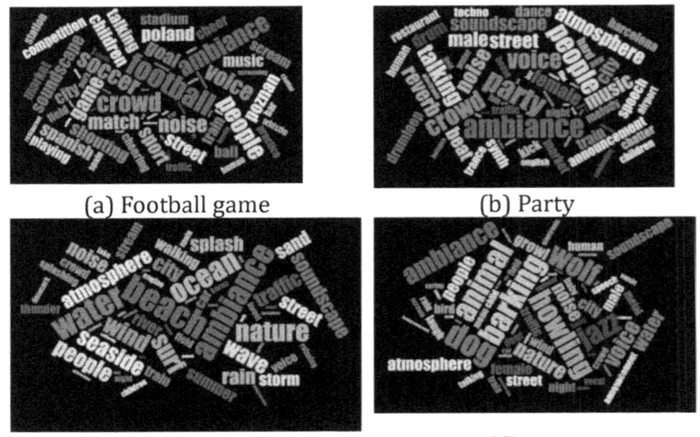

(a) Football game (b) Party

(c) Beach (d) Dog

Figure 1. Tag Selection Examples for some Concepts

Each wild audio file contains tags created by the uploader. In order to select semantic classes with sufficient samples to train reliable classifiers, we select the top n most frequent tags that appeared in each concept's search results. We choose 150 most frequent tags from each concept's text similarity search results and 300 most frequent tags from their acoustic similarity search results. Some concepts share tags, for example, "football game" and "party" share tags like 'noise' and 'crowd', which indicates their acoustic similarity. At the same time, "football game" also contains tags that "dog" doesn't, such as 'shout' or 'cheer', which indicates acoustic differences. In this way, we obtain 579 tags. Examples of tags selected for the concepts "football game", "party", "beach", "dog" are shown as a word cloud according to their occurrence frequencies in Figure 1.

2.1.2.3 Sound Class Model Training

We train SVM classifiers for each of the 579 semantic classes. We chunk each audio file into 3-sec snippets with 1-sec overlap. We extract BoAW features for each snippet using a codebook clustered on the whole wild data training set by the Kmeans algorithm. For each semantic class, we use audio files that contain a particular tag as positive samples, and keep the rest as negative samples to train a classifier for each of the 579 semantic classes.

2.1.2.4 Sound Class Scoring

We use the sound-class classifiers trained from the freesound data to derive a new feature representation. A soundtrack snippet is compared to the sound-class classifiers, and the SVM scores from the 579 classifiers are concatenated to form a 579-dimensional new feature vector for each snippet. Considering it to be straight-forward to generate the BoAW features using freesound data as well, we generate the 4096 audio words using the freesound data via Kmeans clustering, and create the BoAW features accordingly. Since here the audio words are learned from freesound data, we name this bag-of-word feature as FS-BoAW. We also combine the 579-dimensional feature with the 4096-dimensional FS-BoAW feature to form a new feature representation (concatenated after scaling the 579-dimensional feature into the same range of the FS-BoAW feature). We call these features 'stand-alone SD features' and 'combined SD features', respectively.

2.2 Concept Annotation Models

After we extract the features, we train a binary SVM classifier for each of the six concepts. Because the training data is overwhelmed by negative examples, we train classifiers using the Negative Bootstrap algorithm [21]. The algorithm takes a fixed number (N) of positive examples and iteratively selects those negative examples, which are misclassified the most by the current classifiers. The algorithm randomly samples $10xN$ number of negative examples from the remaining negative examples as candidates at each iteration. An ensemble of classifiers trained in the previous iterations is used to classify each of the negative candidate examples. The top N most misclassified candidates are selected and used together with the N positive examples to train a new classifier. The algorithm takes several bags of positive examples and performs the training independently on each of the positive bags, and the classifiers are compressed at the end. In order to improve the efficiency of the training process, we use the Fast intersection kernel SVM (FikSVM) as reported in [22].

3. EXPERIMENTS

3.1 Data Description

The HUAWEI grand challenge dataset contains of 2,666 UGC videos. Originally, the concepts to be annotated are 10 semantic concept classes, covering objects (e.g. “car”, “dog”, “flower”, “food” and “kids”), scenes (e.g. “beach”, “city view” and “Chinese antique building”) and events (“football” and “party”). We discovered that the soundtracks of videos samples for “flower”, “food”, “city view” and “Chinese antique building” contain mostly post-edited pure music. We therefore exclude these four concepts in our study on this dataset, only focusing the remaining six concepts. The data set contains a total duration of about 70 hours of videos excluding those videos with pure music. We divide the dataset into a training set (1014 videos), a development set for tuning model parameters and fusions weights (362 videos), and a test set (656 videos). The amount of negative examples is 10 times larger than the amount of positive examples. The entire dataset has manual labels at the frame level.

As we looked more closely into the provided ground truth files, we came to believe that the provided manual labels are based on visual content. For example, the videos with image of dogs in the foreground and with children talking from behind the camera are only labeled with “dog” but not with “kids”. The videos where a dog’s barking can be heard in the soundtrack but no dog to be seen in the video do not have a “dog” label. In order to further investigate the semantic concept annotation from both an audio and a visual point of view, we need consistent ground truth with both audio and visual evidences. Therefore, we hand-labeled the entire dataset by only listening to the soundtracks without looking at the videos to generate the new audio-driven ground truth for the six target concepts.

We build an audio/soundtrack annotation system trained using the audio-driven ground truth. We also build a visual annotation system trained using the visual-driven ground truth. In following experiments, we use the audio-driven ground truth to evaluate the soundtrack annotation system and the intersection ground truth for comparing the audio-only, visual-only and fusion systems.

3.2 Baseline Results

We use the average precision to evaluate the concept annotation performance for each concept class. The detailed baseline results are shown in Table 1. The baseline system with HW-BoAW features of 4096 dimensions (which means the 4096 audio words were learnt from the target HUAWEI dataset) yields a mean AP (mAP) of over 0.497 on all six concepts. We randomly generate a ranked result for several times to get the mean random guess results of mAP 0.106, which is close to the percentage of positive examples in the testing set. From these results, we can see that the concept annotation based on the soundtrack only achieves significantly better performance than random guessing does. We can also see that some concept classes, which are acoustically easy to distinguish such as “football game”, “kids”, clearly yield much better performance than others (with APs of 0.793 and 0.575, respectively). We also generate the 4096 audio words via clustering the freesound data for the BoAW features (FS-BoAW). The FS-BoAW achieves a comparable performance to the HW-BoAW. This implies some potential benefit for the FS-BoAW features: when the labeled target training data is limited or unavailable, we can still generate a similar feature representation using audio words learned from wild data.

Table 1: *Baseline annotation performance comparison*

	beach	car	dog	fb-game	kids	party	mAP
HW-BoAW	0.161	0.489	0.476	0.793	0.575	0.490	**0.497**
FS-BoAW	0.162	0.480	0.461	0.797	0.571	0.476	**0.491**
Random guess	*0.055*	*0.165*	*0.018*	*0.153*	*0.106*	*0.139*	***0.106***

(c) Test Example for Kids

Figure 2. Semantic Interpretation from SD Features

3.3 Semantics-Derived Features Results

As described in section 2.1.2, we build 579 semantic concept classifiers from the freesound data and use them to generate the SD feature representation. Concept classifiers for the six target concepts are then trained using the SD features, and annotation of the testing data follows. The stand-alone SD features yield a mAP of 0.443, and the combined SD features yield a mAP of 0.499 over the six concepts. Although the combined SD features only slightly outperform the baseline system, it provides a lot of additional semantic information in the output, as shown in Figure 6. The word clouds are generated according to the value of each dimension in the SD features. In Figure 2, we see for the test video example of “kids”, the top ranked SD feature dimensions correspond to “street”, “city”, “subway”. We can infer that the video is recorded near streets in the city rather than on the country side, which we cannot determine by just using the BoAW features or even the visual cues.

4. FUSION OF AUDIO AND VISUAL

In the following experiments, we evaluate the fusion performance on the contents that are both visually and acoustically identifiable. Please note that the intersection of the audio-driven and visual-driven ground truth is used to evaluate the fusion system. The fusion weights are learned following the approach in [23].

The experimental results in Table 2 show that the audio and visual streams contain complementary information for interpreting a semantic concept. A relative improvement of 30% is achieved when combining both modalities. Figure 3 shows the confusion matrices for the three systems. Each matrix in Figure 10 is normalized to the same scale so that they can be compared to one another. In Figure 3(a) and 3(b) we see that although the audio-only system makes more mistakes overall, it makes fewer mistakes distinguishing "kids" from "football game" and "kids" from "party". After fusion, the visual system's weakness has been reduced, as we show in Figure 3(c).

Table 2: *Annotation performance comparison among the audio-only, visual-only and fusion systems*

Concept	Audio-only	Visual-only	Fusion	Audio Weights
Beach	0.133	0.447	0.542	0.42
Car	0.212	0.374	0.448	0.38
Dog	0.476	0.133	0.497	0.95
Fb-game	0.798	0.945	0.969	0.41
Kids	0.529	0.265	0.578	0.82
Party	0.401	0.808	0.839	0.30
mAP	**0.425**	**0.495**	**0.645**	-

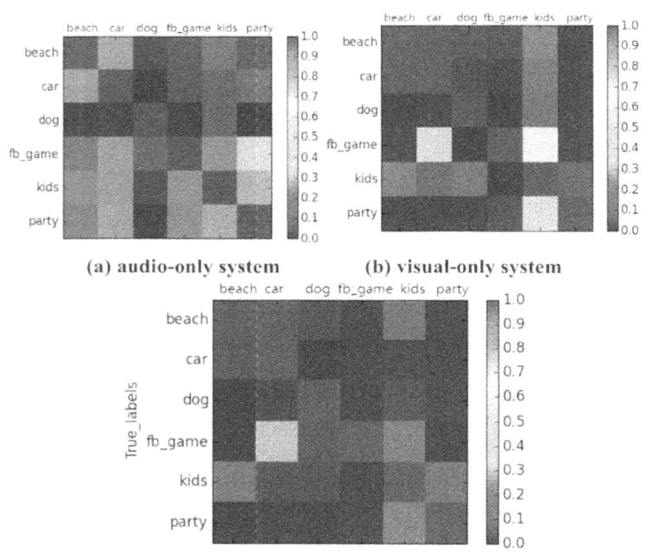

(a) audio-only system **(b) visual-only system**

(c) fusion system

Figure 3. Confusion matrices for different systems.

5. CONCLUSIONS

In this study, we illustrate the viability of classifying concepts of consumer videos based only on soundtrack data. The audio only system achieves a significantly better performance than just random guessing. We show how to make use of freely available wild data, and how to bridge the semantic gap using the bag-of-audio-word method. We explore explicitly adding semantic detail to the feature representation. We propose a semantics-derived feature representation by using a large-scale dataset which we downloaded from freesound, and which we combine with a bag-of-word feature representation. The combined semantics-derived feature not only provides semantic information in the output but also outperforms the baseline features. Finally, we fuse the audio-only system with the visual-only system, and such achieves a relative improvement of 30%. Our simple strategy to enhance the semantic interpretation using wild data shows promising results. In future work, we plan to explore latent and embedding approaches for the semantic enhancement.

6. ACKNOWLEDGEMENT

This work is supported by the Fundamental Research Funds for the Central Universities and the Research Funds of Renmin University of China (No. 14XNLQ01), the Beijing Natural Science Foundation (No. 4142029), NSFC (No. 61303184), SRFDP (No. 20130004120006).

7. REFERENCES

[1] C. Snoek, and M. Worring: Concept-based Video Retrieval. Foundations and Trends in Information Retrieval, 2009.

[2] P. Over, et al.: TRECVID 2013 -- An Overview of the Goals, Tasks, Data, Evaluation Mechanisms and Metrics. TRECVID 2013, USA.

[3] J. Saunders: Real-time discrimination of broadcast speech/music. ICASSP, 1996.

[4] G. Williams and D. P. W. Ellis: Speech/music discrimination based on posterior probability features. Eurospeech, Budapest, 1999.

[5] T. Zhang and C.-C. J. Kuo: Audio content analysis for online audiovisual data segmentation and classification. IEEE Tr. Speech and Audio Proc., vol. 9, no. 4, pp. 441–457, 2001.

[6] J. Ajmera, I. McCowan, H. Bourlard: Speech/music segmentation using entropy and dynamism features in a hmm classification framework. Speech Communication, (40), 351–363, 2003.

[7] K. Lee and D. P. W. Ellis: Detecting music in ambient audio by long window autocorrelation. ICASSP, 2008.

[8] D. P. W. Ellis and K. Lee: Minimal-impact audio-based personal archives. ACM Workshop on Continuous Archival and Retrieval of Personal Experiences, New York, NY, October 2004.

[9] S. Chu, S. Narayanan, and C.-C. J. Kuo: Content analysis for acoustic environment classification in mobile robots. AAAI Fall Symposium, Aurally Informed Performance: Integrating Machine Listening and Auditory Presentation in Robotic Systems, 2006.

[10] A. Eronen, et al.: Audio-based context recognition. IEEE TASLP, (14), no. 1, pp. 321–329, Jan. 2006.

[11] E. Wold, et al.: Content-based Classification, Search, and Retrieval of Audio," IEEE Multimedia, 3(3), 1996.

[12] K. Lee and D.P.W. Ellis: Audio-Based Semantic Concept Classification for Consumer Video, IEEE TASLP, 18(6), 2010.

[13] Q. Jin, P. Schulam, S. Rawat, S. Burger, D. Ding, F. Metze. "Categorizing Consumer Videos Using Audio," Interspeech, 2012.

[14] L. Ma, B. Milner, and D. Smith: Acoustic Environment Classification. ACM Trans. on Speech and Language Processing, 3(2), 2006.

[15] L. Brown, et al.: IBM Research and Columbia University TRECVID-2013. In: TRECVID Workshop, 2013.

[16] ICME 2014 Huawei Accurate and Fast Mobile Video Annotation Challenge http://www.icme2014.org/huawei-accurate-and-fast-mobile-video-annotation-challenge.

[17] X.B. Xue, Z.H. Zhou: Distributional Features for Text Categorization. IEEE Transactions on Knowledge and Data Engineering, 21(3), 2008.

[18] J. Philbin, et al.: Object retrieval with large vocabularies and fast spatial matching. CVPR 2007.

[19] J. Liang, et al.: Semantic Concept Annotation of Consumer Videos at Frame-level Using Audio. Pacific-Rim Conference on Multimedia (PCM), 2014.

[20] Freesound data repository: http://www.freesound.org

[21] X. Li, C. Snoek, M. Worring, D. Koelma, A. Smeulders: Bootstrapping Visual Categorization With Relevant Negatives. IEEE Transactions on Multimedia, 15(4), 2013.

[22] S. Maji, A. Berg, J. Malik: Classification using international kernel support vector machines is efficient. In: CVPR 2008.

[23] X. Li, C. Snoek, M. Worring, A. Smeulders, "Fusing concept detection and geo context for visual search", ICMR 2012.

Automatic Image Annotation using Deep Learning Representations

Venkatesh N. Murthy, Subhransu Maji, R. Manmatha
School of Computer Science
University of Massachusetts, Amherst, MA, USA.
{venk, smaji, manmatha}@cs.umass.edu

ABSTRACT

We propose simple and effective models for the image annotation that make use of Convolutional Neural Network (CNN) features extracted from an image and word embedding vectors to represent their associated tags. Our first set of models is based on the Canonical Correlation Analysis (CCA) framework that helps in modeling both views – visual features (CNN feature) and textual features (word embedding vectors) of the data. Results on all three variants of the CCA models, namely linear CCA, kernel CCA and CCA with k-nearest neighbor (CCA-KNN) clustering, are reported. The best results are obtained using CCA-KNN which outperforms previous results on the Corel-5k and the ESP-Game datasets and achieves comparable results on the IAPRTC-12 dataset. In our experiments we evaluate CNN features in the existing models which bring out the advantages of it over dozens of handcrafted features. We also demonstrate that word embedding vectors perform better than binary vectors as a representation of the tags associated with an image. In addition we compare the CCA model to a simple CNN based linear regression model, which allows the CNN layers to be trained using back-propagation.

Categories and Subject Descriptors

H.3.1 [**Information Storage and Retrieval**]: Content Analysis and indexing; I.2.10 [**Artificial Intelligence**]: Visual and Scene Understanding

Keywords

Image annotation, deep learning, word embeddings, CCA

1. INTRODUCTION

The metadata tags associated with images/videos are often used to search them. It is desirable to generate such tags automatically. Automatic image annotation is a labelling problem wherein the task is to predict multiple textual labels for an unseen image describing its contents or visual appearance [10, 2, 4, 13]. In these papers the goal is to predict a fixed number of tags for a given test image that accurately describe the visual content. Multiple features with the right type of model are shown to improve the annotation performance significantly in the current state of the art system [15, 4]. Yet, the dozens of handcrafted features serve as a bottleneck in designing scalable realtime systems. Hence, we use a feature (representing an image) from a Convolutional Neural Network (CNN) along with the word embedding vectors (representing the tags associated with it) in our proposed models. Here CNN features are extracted for images using a pre-trained VGG-16 [14] network, and the word embedding vector for a tag is extracted using a pre-trained skip-gram architecture (word2vec of [11]); both these networks are publicly available. This work, to the best of our knowledge, is the first attempt to use CNN features and word embedding vectors to solve the image annotation task and report results on all three standard datasets.

Our proposed models incorporate both CNN features and text features (word embedding vector), one set of models is based on the CCA and its variants and the other model is based on CNN regression. One variant, CCA-KNN significantly outperforms all the previously published results. We are able to achieve this without requiring any computationally expensive metric learning approaches as used by almost all successful models [13, 1, 12, 15]. Some papers using CCA for combing image and text have been previously proposed [3, 1], but the key differences are, we use CNN features as opposed to multiple handcrafted features (representing images) and we use word embedding vectors instead of binary vectors (representing tags). We show that the CNN feature outperforms multiple handcrafted features in [1].

In the CNN based model, the last layer of CaffeNet is replaced with a projection layer (to perform regression) and the resulting network is trained to map images to semantically meaningful word embedding vectors. This type of modeling has two advantages: firstly, it does not require dozens of handcrafted features; there is no need for metric learning or ways to combine those features efficiently. Secondly, the approach is substantially simpler to formulate than any other generative or discriminative models. In addition, we also provide the effectiveness of CNN features when used in other previously existing models.

2. PREVIOUS WORK

A large number of models have been proposed for automatic image annotation and retrieval. We discuss a few of the most successful ones. The models may be broadly

ICMR'15, June 23–26, 2015, Shanghai, China.

http://dx.doi.org/10.1145/2671188.2749391.

grouped into three groups - generative models, discriminative models and nearest neighbor based models. Examples of generative models are Cross Media Relevance Model (CMRM) [6], Continuous Relevance Model (CRM) and Multiple Bernoulli Relevance Model (MBRM) [2] . These may be viewed as mixture models or as nearest neighbor based approaches. They work by computing the joint probability of words and visual features. Given a test image, the model is used to compute conditional probability scores for words. Visual features are represented either by discretizing and clustering them or by using a kernel density estimate. The visual features are modeled using a multinomial distribution and the best results are obtained by modeling the words using a multiple Bernoulli distribution. Several successful nearest neighbor based models have been inspired by MBRM including Joint Equal Contribution (JEC) model [10], TagProp [4] and the 2PKNN model[15]. TagProp uses metric learning over a large number of features. The 2PKNN (two-pass KNN) technique finds semantic neighbors for each test image and the tags are predicted based on the weighted combination of distances. The optimal weights to combine base distances and features was determined via metric learning. Recently an attempt was made to improve the performance of CRM using Sparse Kernel Learning (SKL-CRM) [12] , in which they try to learn the optimal combination of kernels for the features.

3. FEATURE EXTRACTION

Here, we provide details about how the CNN features are extracted for images, followed by details about how to use word embedding vectors to represent the tags.

3.1 CNN features

Given an image, we extract a 4096-dimensional feature vector (X) using a pre-trained CNN on the ILSVRC-2012 dataset as described in Simonyan et al. [14]. We explored both VGG-16 and VGG-19 layered architecture features. Since both of them gave similar results, we used VGG-16. Features extracted from Caffe-Net provided by Caffe [7] (similar to AlexNet [9]) did not work as well as VGG-16, hence we used VGG-16 features for all our experiments. The features are computed by forward propagating a mean-subtracted 224x224 RGB image through eight convolutional layers and three fully connected layers. In our case, we resize all the images irrespective of their aspect ratio to 224x224 to make it compatible with the CNN.

3.2 Word embeddings

For each tag associated with an image, we represent the tag (word) by a 300 dimensional real valued feature vector using a Word2Vec tool and we call it as a word embedding vector ($E \in R^{l \times q}$), where l is the number of labels and $q = 300$ dimensions. These word vectors are obtained from a pre-trained skip-gram text modeling architecture introduced by Mikolov et al. [11]. It was shown that the model learns similar embedding vectors for semantically related words. Therefore, we use it to represent the annotations. We take the average of all the word embedding vectors (Y) associated with multiple tags representing an image. Formally, if there are k tags associated with an image I then $Y = \frac{1}{k}\sum_{i=1}^{k} E_i$ and their association is represented as $\{I, Y\}$. While reporting the result we refer to word embedding vectors as W2V.

3.3 Canonical Correlation Analysis (CCA)

Given a pair of views for an image – a visual feature (X, i.e., CNN feature) and the other the (Y, i.e., word embedding vector), CCA computes projections w_x and w_y for X and Y respectively to maximize their correlation. Concretely, for M samples, let $X \in R^{m \times p}$ and $Y \in R^{m \times q}$ be the two views of the data, then the projection vectors w_x *and* w_y are computed by maximizing the correlation coefficient ρ

$$\rho = \underset{w_x, w_y}{\arg\max} \frac{w_x^T X Y^T w_y}{\sqrt{(w_x^T X X^T w_x)(w_y^T Y Y^T w_y)}} \quad (1)$$

The dimensionality of these new basis vectors is less than or equal to the smallest dimensionality of the two variables. The canonical correlations are invariant to affine transformations of the variables. The solution is found by formulating it as a generalized eigenvalue problem [5]:

$$XY^T(YY^T)^{-1}YX^T w_x = \eta XX^T w_x, \quad (2)$$

where η is the eigenvalue corresponding to the eigenvector w_x. Multiple projectors can also be found which form a projection matrix $W_x \in R^{p \times l} \in$ and similarly $W_y \in R^{q \times l}$. In the case of regularized CCA, a term λI with $\lambda > 0$ is used to avoid overfitting.

3.4 Kernel CCA (KCCA)

Since CCA can only capture linear relationships, we propose to use a χ^2 kernel for exploiting the non linear relationships. The χ^2 kernel was found to be well suited in our experiments. The visual feature X is mapped to a high dimensional feature space $\mathcal{H}_x$ using a function ϕ_x. The ϕ_x mapping is achieved using a positive definite kernel function $K_x = \langle \phi_x, \phi_x \rangle \in R^{m \times m}$, where $\langle :, : \rangle$ is an inner product in $\mathcal{H}_x$. Similarly, the word embedding vector Y is mapped to $\mathcal{H}_y$ using the kernel function $K_y = \langle \phi_y, \phi_y \rangle \in R^{mxm}$. Kernel CCA finds the solution of w_x and w_y as a linear combination of the training data:
$w_x = \sum_{i=1}^{m} \alpha_i \phi_x(x_i)$ and $w_y = \sum_{i=1}^{m} \beta_i \phi_y(y_i)$. Since feature vector dimensions were high overfitting is an issue. To avoid this we used a regularized kernel CCA which finds $\hat{\boldsymbol{\alpha}}, \hat{\boldsymbol{\beta}}$ by maximizing the following objective function:

$$\underset{\boldsymbol{\alpha}, \boldsymbol{\beta}}{\arg\max} \frac{\boldsymbol{\alpha}^T K_x K_y \boldsymbol{\beta}}{\sqrt{(\boldsymbol{\alpha}^T K_x^2 \boldsymbol{\alpha} + r_x \boldsymbol{\alpha}^T K_x \boldsymbol{\alpha})(\boldsymbol{\beta}^T K_y^2 \boldsymbol{\beta} + r_y \boldsymbol{\beta}^T K_y \boldsymbol{\beta})}} \quad (3)$$

The solution yields top l eigenvectors $\mathcal{W}_x = [\boldsymbol{\alpha}^1 \ldots \boldsymbol{\alpha}^l]$ and $\mathcal{W}_y = [\boldsymbol{\beta}^1 \ldots \boldsymbol{\beta}^l]$ which form the projection matrix.

3.4.1 Implementation details

CCA and KCCA with regularization was implemented as explained in [5]. Regularization was found to be important to avoid overfitting resulting in better performance. In the case of linear CCA, we project X onto W_x, project Y onto W_y and project E onto W_y:

$$U = (X - \mu_X)W_x \,,\; V = (Y - \mu_Y)W_y \text{ and } Z = EW_y \quad (4)$$

Given a test image I_t, we extract deep learning visual features V_t and project it using w_x as $T = (V_t - \mu_X)W_x$ and compute the correlation distance to V. The corresponding tags associated with the closest matching V_i are assigned to the test image (tags are also ranked according to their frequency in the training dataset). If the tags are less than the fixed annotation length then we pick the next closest match and transfer the tags, we repeat this until we obtain the required set of tags, in our case its five (to compare with previous work).

Similarly, in the case of KCCA, we kernelize X, Y and Z and later project onto $\mathcal{W}_x, \mathcal{W}_y, \mathcal{W}_x$ respectively. For a test image, we kernelize the visual features and follow the same procedure as above.

In CCA with KNN clustering (CCA-KNN) setup, after finding the correlation distance of T with V, we choose K semantic neighbor samples from each cluster (grouped according to its labels) for that particular test image and now their associated tags form a subset of tags Z_k (potential candidates for a test image). Later, we rank the words w for a test image I_t according to its probability score of:

$$P(I_t|w) = \sum_k \exp(-D(T, Z_k))1_k(w) \tag{5}$$

where, $D(T, Z_k)$ is the correlation distance between T and Z_k and $1_k(w)$ is an indicator function which takes a value 1 if the tag is present among neighbors and 0 otherwise.

3.5 CNN-based regression model

Inspired by the success of deep CNN architectures [9, 14]on the large scale image classification task, we use it to solve the task of automatic image annotation. To the best of our knowledge, this is the first attempt to formulate this problem based on a CNN The idea is to formulate the problem as a linear regression. We achieve this by replacing the last layer of Caffe-Net with a projection layer (fully connected layer) and we call it as a CNN regressor (CNN-R). CNN provides the mapping function which regresses the fixed size of the input image to a word embedding vector. For further architecture details, please refer to [9]. In this setup, we increased the learning rate for the newly introduced layer while reducing it for all the other previous layers and the reason being that we are trying to fine-tune the network previously trained on 1.2 million images. The input image size was fixed to be 227x227 and the final regressed output was a 300 dimensional vector. Since we have chosen to do linear regression, we use Euclidean loss (L2) instead of Softmax loss during the training phase. The prediction layer tries to predict the word embedding vector by minimizing the L2 loss depending on which, the model parameters are updated using Back propagation algorithm.

4. EXPERIMENTS

We evaluate on three standard publicly available image annotation datasets - Corel-5k [2], ESP-Game and IAPRC-12 [10]. These datasets contain a variety of images like natural scene, game, sketches, transportation vehicles, personal photos and so on, thus making it a challenging task.

Most papers use one type of metric, but there is a small number of papers which use other metrics (For instance, In [8] the precision and recall are computed **per word** but they are computed only for **non-zero recall** words and their average over all non-zero recall words are reported). We use the standard (most widely reported type of evaluation where the recall and precision are computed **per word** and their average over all the words are reported [13, 1, 12, 15, 10, 2]. We strictly adhere to computing the recall and precision **per word** (for all the words) and reporting their means over all the words, thus making it a fair comparison to the majority of the works in this area. Along with that, we also report **N+** denoting the number of words with non-zero recall value.

4.1 Experimental results and discussion

In order to have a fair comparison with the previously reported results, we follow the same train and test split as reported in [4] and also fix the length of the annotations (five tags) for a test image. In the first subsection, we evaluate the CNN features with our proposed model and compare its performance with all other previous work. We also provide the results of using some existing models, 2PKNN, JEC and SVM-DMBRM, with the new set of CNN features. This helps in understanding how well the CNN features perform against 15 handcrafted features (local + global).

In the second subsection, we evaluate the importance of the word embedding vectors. We do this by picking the best performing model in Table 1 and use word embedding vectors instead of frequency counts to represent the tags. Since each image is annotated with a unique set of tags in all three datasets, the frequency vector representing the tags of an image just turns out be a simple binary vector (BV).

4.1.1 Evaluation of CNN features

Results are presented in the Table 1. We see that our proposed CCA-KNN[1] model outperforms all other previous work on Corel-5k and ESP-Game datasets. More precisely, our method provides 2.6% and 13.5% increase in F1 measure on Corel-5k and ESP-Game datasets respectively over the next best method. Also we are better in terms of N+ (# non-zero recall) measure, which is a clear indication that our method generalizes well to unseen test images. In the case of IAPRTC-12 dataset, our model yields comparable results to the state-of-the-art.

We ran CNN features with some of the other models in the literature (JEC, 2PKNN and SVM-DBRM). In the case of 2PKNN the results were worse than using all 15 feature vectors while for the other two models the results were better or comparable to using their original set of features. This indicates that CNN features are powerful and are a good candidate for replacing a large set of features.

4.1.2 Importance of word embeddings

Table 1 also shows that word embedding vectors (W2V) work better than binary vectors (BV) with our best performing model CCA-KNN. This suggests that word embedding vectors provide a better representation for words than their binary form – presumably because semantically related words tend to have similar word embedding vectors.

4.1.3 Evaluation of CNN-R model

Experimental evaluation results of our CNN-R models on all three datasets are provided in Table 1 with comparison to some of the best performing models in the literature. From Table 1, we see that CNN-R outperforms many previous models but not the CCA models with CNN features and is competitive with the the 2PKNN model and Tagprop. CNN-R has a clear advantage over all the existing methods for the following reasons: no need to extract multiple low level features and to incorporate high level semantics; no metric learning; we can fine-tune the deep architecture even

[1]Qualitative result analysis at `http://goo.gl/wS4jSl`

	Feature		Corel-5K				ESP Game				IAPRTC-12			
Method	Visual	text	P	R	F	N+	P	R	F	N+	P	R	F	N+
JEC [10]	HC	-	27	32	29	139	22	25	23	224	28	29	29	250
MBRM [2]	HC	-	24	25	25	122	18	19	19	209	24	23	24	223
TagProp(σML) [4]	HC	-	33	42	37	160	39	27	32	239	46	35	40	266
2PKNN [15]	HC	-	39	40	39.5	177	51	23	31.7	245	49	32	38.7	274
2PKNN+ML [15]	HC	-	44	46	45	191	53	27	36	252	54	37	**44**	278
SVM-DMBRM [13]	HC	-	36	48	41	197	**55**	25	34	259	56	29	38	**283**
KCCA-2PKNN [1]	HC	-	42	46	44	179	-	-	-	-	**59**	30	40	259
SKL-CRM [12]	HC	-	39	46	42	184	41	26	32	248	47	32	38	274
JEC	VGG-16	-	31	32	32	141	26	22	24	234	28	21	24	237
2PKNN	VGG-16	-	33	30	32	160	40	23	29	250	38	23	29	261
SVM-DMBRM	VGG-16	-	42	45	43	186	51	26	35	251	58	27	37	268
CCA	VGG-16	W2V	35	46	40	172	29	32	30	250	33	32	33	268
KCCA	VGG-16	W2V	39	**53**	45	184	30	36	33	252	38	**39**	38	273
CCA-KNN	VGG-16	BV	39	51	44	192	44	32	37	254	41	34	37	273
CCA-KNN	VGG-16	W2V	**42**	52	**46**	**201**	46	**36**	**41**	**260**	45	38	41	278
CNN-R	Caffe-Net	W2V	32	41.3	37.2	166	44.5	28.5	34.7	248	49	31	37.9	272

Table 1: Experimental results of our proposed models with previously reported best scores on all three datasets. P: Average Precision, R: Average Recall, N+: Number of distinct words that are correctly assigned to at least one test image.

for a small dataset and this type of model is also capable of predicting new set of previously unseen classes with the help of word embeddings vectors. We believe that the performance can be improved further with some regularization.

5. CONCLUSION

We have explored CNN features and word embedding vectors for image annotation task and have introduced some new models to take advantage of both these features. Empirically, one of our proposed model CCA-KNN yields better results when compared to previous work. We also validated the advantage of using CNN features over 15 handcrafted features for some existing models and showed that performance is often comparable to their previously reported results. CNN features avoids the use of computing multiple engineered features and also the computationally expensive process of metric learning (a trend in most recent papers). We also introduce a simple and efficient way of formulating the image annotation problem as a CNN based regressor which may be very useful in the real world applications.

6. ACKNOWLEDGMENTS

This work was supported in part by the Center for Intelligent Information Retrieval and in part by NSF grant #IIS-0910884. Any opinions, findings and conclusions or recommendations expressed in this material are those of the authors and do not necessarily reflect those of the sponsor.

7. REFERENCES

[1] L. Ballan, T. Uricchio, L. Seidenari, and A. Del Bimbo. A cross-media model for automatic image annotation. In *ICMR*, page 73, 2014.

[2] S. L. Feng, R. Manmatha, and V. Lavrenko. Multiple bernoulli relevance models for image and video annotation. In *CVPR'04*, pages 1002–1009, 2004.

[3] Y. Gong, Q. Ke, M. Isard, and S. Lazebnik. A multi-view embedding space for modeling internet images, tags, and their semantics. *IJCV*, 106(2):210–233, 2014.

[4] M. Guillaumin, T. Mensink, J. Verbeek, and C. Schmid. Tagprop: Discriminative metric learning in nearest neighbor models for image auto-annotation. In *In ICCV*, 2009.

[5] D. Hardoon, S. Szedmak, and J. Shawe-Taylor. Canonical correlation analysis: An overview with application to learning methods. *Neural computation*, 16(12):2639–2664, 2004.

[6] J. Jeon, V. Lavrenko, and R. Manmatha. Automatic image annotation and retrieval using cross-media relevance models. In *SIGIR '03*, pages 119–126, 2003.

[7] Y. Jia, E. Shelhamer, J. Donahue, S. Karayev, J. Long, R. Girshick, S. Guadarrama, and T. Darrell. Caffe: Convolutional architecture for fast feature embedding. In *ACM MM*, pages 675–678, 2014.

[8] M. M. Kalayeh, H. Idrees, and M. Shah. Nmf-knn: Image annotation using weighted multi-view non-negative matrix factorization. In *CVPR'14*, 2014.

[9] A. Krizhevsky, I. Sutskever, and G. E. Hinton. Imagenet classification with deep convolutional neural networks. In *NIPS*, pages 1097–1105, 2012.

[10] A. Makadia, V. Pavlovic, and S. Kumar. A new baseline for image annotation. In *ECCV '08*, pages 316–329, 2008.

[11] T. Mikolov, K. Chen, G. Corrado, and J. Dean. Efficient estimation of word representations in vector space. *arXiv preprint arXiv:1301.3781*, 2013.

[12] S. Moran and V. Lavrenko. A sparse kernel relevance model for automatic image annotation. *ntl. Journal of Multimedia Information Retrieval*, 3(4):209–229, 2014.

[13] V. N. Murthy, E. F. Can, and R. Manmatha. A hybrid model for automatic image annotation. In *ICMR'14*, pages 369:369–369:376, 2014.

[14] K. Simonyan and A. Zisserman. Very deep convolutional networks for large-scale image recognition. *arXiv preprint arXiv:1409.1556*, 2014.

[15] Y. Verma and C. V. Jawahar. Image annotation using metric learning in semantic neighborhoods. In *ECCV'12*, pages 836–849, 2012.

My Day in Review
Visually Summarising Noisy Lifelog Data

Soumyadeb Chowdhury[1], Philip J. McParlane[2], Md. Sadek Ferdous[3], Joemon Jose[4]
School of Computing Science, University of Glasgow
{Soumyadeb.Chowdhury[1], Sadek. Ferdous[3], Joemon.Jose[4]}@glasgow.ac.uk, p.mcparlane.1@research.gla.ac.uk[2]

ABSTRACT
Lifelogging devices, which seamlessly gather various data about a user as they go about their daily life, have resulted in users amassing large collections of noisy photographs (e.g. visual duplicates, image blur), which are difficult to navigate, especially if they want to review their day in photographs. Social media websites, such as Facebook, have faced a similar information overload problem for which a number of summarization methods have been proposed (e.g. news story clustering, comment ranking *etc.*). In particular, Facebook's '*Year in Review*' received much user interest where the objective for the model was to identify key moments in a user's year, offering an automatic visual summary based on their uploaded content. In this paper, we follow this notion by automatically creating a review of a user's day using lifelogging images. Specifically, we address the quality issues faced by the photographs taken on lifelogging devices and attempt to create visual summaries by promoting visual and temporal-spatial diversity in the top ranks. Conducting two crowdsourced evaluations based on 9k images, we show the merits of combining time, location and visual appearance for summarization purposes.

Categories and Subject Descriptors
H.3.1 [Information Storage and Retrieval]: Content Analysis and Indexing.

Keywords
Wearable camera; Autographer; lifelog images; GPS; temporal; spatial; clustering; GIST features; key moments; crowdsourcing.

1. INTRODUCTION
Lifelogging represents a way of digitally recording data (referred to as *lifelogs*) which capture a *lifelogger's* experiences, in varying amount of detail, for a variety of purposes, using a *lifelogging* device. These devices capture experiences in our daily routine without the need of explicit interaction due to their hands-free nature. Most prior works [for example, 1 and 2] have segmented unprocessed lifelog data into meaningful units called events, which are a collection of temporally related sequence of lifelog data, over a period of time, with a defined beginning and end. To our knowledge, no previous study has extended the notion of temporal-spatial clustering to consider the visual aspects for lifelogging data abstraction. In this paper, we combine visual scene evidences with the time and location information in order to identify the most representative lifelog images as *key moments* in order to summarise a user's day. This feature is similar to Facebook's '*Year in Review*'[1], which automatically compiles some of most liked images in the user's feed and presents them in to a neat timeline. The feature deployed by Facebook relied upon the number of likes (a user input) and did not consider if the images, either belong to the user or they were publicly available content over the web (e.g. quotes, cartoons etc.). In the context of the relevant use-cases, the automatic generation of *key moments* would be useful to an array of actors, but not limited to: lifeloggers, researchers interested in lifelogger's daily life experience, community councils interested in community biographies of a sample population. The research presented in this paper attempts to address the following research questions:

RQ1: How can we effectively structure lifelog images to generate *key moments*, i.e. a review of a lifelogger's day?

The above research question is further partitioned into:

RQ1.1: How do we reduce the amount of noise in lifelogging collection (i.e. low quality, blurry and repetitive images)?

RQ1.2: Can we effectively exploit temporal-spatial information obtained from the lifelogs to generate a summary of the daily moments of one's life?

RQ1.3: Can we combine visual scene features in addition to the temporal-spatial information to improve the summarisation of daily moments?

2. RELATED LITERATURE
In most of the existing research with lifelogging devices, the lifelogs are structured into activities or events [1, 2]. These events merge various sources of sensed data together into a meaningful and logical unit. Anguera et al. [3] and many other lifelogging researchers have shown the potential of using meta information obtained from the lifelogs to automatically generate annotations. Prior work reported by Wang and Smeaton [4] categorised daily activities, which were used to define events. Lazer et al. [5] have used GPS sensors in cell phones to annotate the lifelogs using their respective location. Gurrin et al. [6] have used WiFi sensors to identify fine-grained locations of events. A recent study reported in Kikhia et al. [7] has presented an approach to present lifelogs based on places and activities obtained from the GPS data. However, this work does not report eliminating noisy and duplicate images, before clustering the lifelogs using GPS locations. One of the earliest works presented by Doherty and Smeaton [8] used lifelog images with geographic data, to examine how the visual and location information might be useful to recall events from the past. It was concluded that lifelog images helped in recalling past activities, whereas location data supports inferential processes.

3. Proposed Approach
In this section we will give a brief overview of the devices used to capture the lifelogs, followed by the techniques used to eliminate

[1] http://yearinreview.fb.com/

ICMR '15, June 23 - 26, 2015, Shanghai, China
Copyright 2015 ACM 978-1-4503-3274-3/15/06…$15.00
http://dx.doi.org/10.1145/2671188.2749393

noisy (blurred, duplicate) lifelog images, and finally the clustering techniques employed to generate key moments.

3.1 Lifelog Capturing Phase

For the research reported in this paper, we have used two devices to collect the lifelogs: (i) Autographer – a wearable camera, which can record more than 100 images per hour [9]; (ii) GPS device – recording location logs every 5 seconds. In the current scenario, location sensors in the Autographer takes almost 5 to 6 minutes to capture a GPS fix, as opposed to 1 to 2 minutes claimed by the manufacturers. The lifelogs were collected by one of the authors.

3.2 Image Selection

One of the main problems in the automatic organization of the lifelogs obtained from the wearable camera is managing noisy photographs, most predominantly: (i) blurry images and (ii) visual duplicates. In the following subsections, we discuss the techniques employed to address *RQ1.1*.

3.2.1 Blurry Images

As the images are shot hands free and often whilst on the move, the image quality, in particular image sharpness, is often very low. In order to automatically identify blurry images, we adopt the technique proposed by Tong et al. [10], which employs edge type and sharpness analysis using a *Haar wavelet transform*. This technique computes a blur score B (where $0 \leq B \leq 1$) for a given image. Figure 1, highlights the blur distribution for all the images in our collection, where a lower score (Blur %) implies a sharper image. In this work, we have selected only those images, where $B < 0.38$. This parameter is selected empirically, in order to remove the long tail of the distribution, which contains images which are blurrier than 80% of the overall population. We believe that blurred images will not be useful in the sense of not providing enough information. However, such images (low quality) can be used for tasks like, elicitation based-surveys, where a social scientist may require all the images, irrespective of their quality.

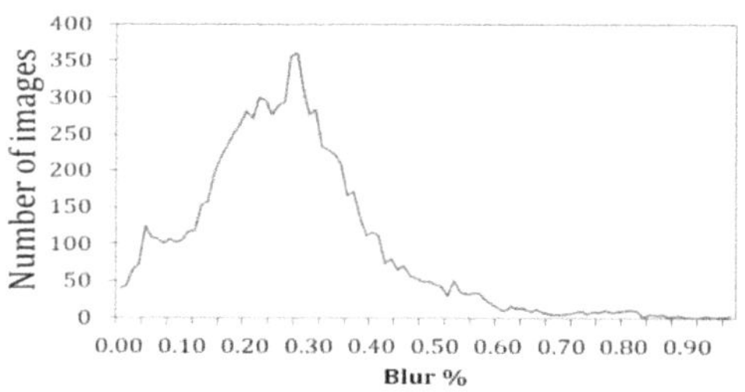

Figure 1. Blur score distribution of the lifelog collection

3.2.2 Duplicate Images

As the lifeloggers may be stationary for longer periods of time (i.e. sitting at the office desk, travelling in a car/bus etc.) and have limited control over as to when an image is captured, multiple image duplicates tend to exist within the lifelogs. These visual duplicates must be identified in order to avoid selecting duplicate images as *key moments* in a user's day, which would further alleviate the information overload problem for our scenario

In this work we have detected the duplicate and near-duplicate images using a popular hashing function technique presented in Tang et al. [11]. Hashing functions are used to generate fixed-length output strings, which act as a shortened reference to the initial data. In this work, we have used a hashing method, called the Perceptual Hash (pHash), which has been shown to give high detection performance for resized, cropped and exposure compensated images [11]. We hypothesise that detecting images which have these alterations will capture many of the duplicates taken by lifelogging devices. We chose a hashing function to detect duplicate images in the lifelog collection due to its high performance, while maintaining low computational expense in extraction and matching between the images. By adopting the aforementioned method, we also ensure its scalability in large lifelogging collections. To detect the visual duplicates in our lifelog collection, we adopt the following procedure:

Step 1: We first compute the pHash string (using the tools available at http://www.phash.org/) for each image.

Step 2: Single pass clustering is then employed on all the images in our collection, using the hamming distance as a measure to compare between two pHash strings for a given pair of images.

Step 3: Specifically, an image is added to an existing cluster if its hamming distance is small enough (T<8 as suggested in the existing work [12]), otherwise the image is added to a new cluster. For clusters containing multiple images (i.e. duplicates), we select only the sharpest image (i.e. lowest B).

3.3 Image Ranking

Once the blurred and duplicate images are removed, a second stage of ranking is carried out, in order to generate the *key moments*. The goal of image ranking in web search is to maximize the relevance of images in the top ranks with respect to a textual query. This differs from ranking lifelog images to generate automatic *key moments*, due to the absence of any query or similar user involvement, as well as textual annotations, which makes the ranking a non-trivial and ambiguous problem. We achieve the automatic generation of key moments by clustering images based on a number of visual and geospatial features, as follows.

3.3.1 Visual Clustering

Our first approach attempts to cluster images based on their *visual scene,* i.e. group images which have a similar "visual landscape" (e.g. images taken in a single room or place). In order to achieve our goal, we extract the GIST visual features [13]. This feature has been adopted by many works in the past to achieve state-of-the-art scene classification accuracy, and is most suitable for our purpose. For each day's lifelog images obtained from the lifelogger, we execute the following approach:

Step 1: We consider the images which have passed our selection process, i.e. all blurred and duplicate images are removed.

Step 2: The normalised 512-D GIST features for each of the images obtained in step 1 are extracted,

Step 3: Clustering is employed using the Expectation-maximization (EM) algorithm. We employ this method over other popular clustering techniques (such as K-means), as the EM approach does not require an initial number of clusters to be set (i.e. K). This is important as we do not know the prior number of clusters or 'moments' for any given day.

3.3.2 Temporal-spatial Clustering

Time and location are crucial evidences for the purposes of segmenting images into various clusters or *moments*. Therefore, we consider these features in our work. Firstly, we model an image's time as the minute of the day in which it was captured normalised by the number of minutes in a day (e.g. 2:40pm is modeled as 880/1440 = 0.58), referred to as t (where $0<=t<=1$). Specifically, we model an image's location using its GPS co-ordinates. We normalise the longitude (l_1) and latitude (l_2) values for each image based on the maximum value recorded for each day. As the GPS equipment does not function well indoors, there are many images which do not contain GPS co-ordinates. In this case, we set the longitude and latitude as the mean value for a given day. This approach is employed, opposed to setting these values to 0, in order to avoid skewing the dataset when an image lacks GPS information. We therefore model an image as a 3-D vector (i.e.[t, l_1, l_2]) of its time and location. This relates to *RQ 1.2*, which was presented in Section 1.

3.3.3 Combining Visual and Temporal-spatial Clustering

Finally, we combine the visual and temporal-spatial aspects by concatenating the two feature vectors, resulting in a 515-D vector, before clustering using the EM approach. We hypothesise that visual appearance, time and location are all essential in the clustering process and will complement each other to summarise large collections of lifelog images, by automatically generating key moments within a user's day. Such a combined clustering approach has not yet been studied in previous works and is beneficial in scenarios where location information is unavailable, either due to device constraints or other factors. This relates to *RQ1.3*, which was presented in Section 1.

4. Experiments

In this section, we discuss a number of statistics and limitations of the lifelogs collected, followed by the various systems used for the crowdsourced evaluation and the experimental procedure.

4.1 Data Collection

Table 1 shows the statistics related to the lifelogs captured by one of the authors over a period of 13 days. The lifelogging devices (Autographer and GPS) were used from 8:30am to 6pm. However, the image capturing was stopped on a number of occasions, as required by the lifelogger, which is not discussed further in this paper. According to the statistics reported in Table 1, the number of images containing locations is only 14% because the GPS device did not log the locations while the lifelogger was indoors, i.e. inside buildings. The lifelogs collected for the research presented in this paper is ethically approved through the lifelogger's informed consent.

Table 1. Lifelog Image Collection Statistics

Total Images	9,080
# of days	13
Average # Images captured per day	698
% of blurred images	16.6%
% of images containing location information	14%

4.2 Experimental Systems

Random (S_{random}): Due to the lack of benchmarks, especially in the context of generating the key moments of a user's day, we firstly propose ranking images randomly for each day, as a weak baseline. In this system, 5 random images are selected.

Removing blurred images and duplicates (S_{select}): The noisy images, i.e. blurred and visual duplicates are removed using the selection approaches presented in Sections 3.2.1 and 3.2.2 respectively, before 5 images are selected randomly. This system will be considered a stronger baseline compared to S_{random}.

Visual Clustering (S_{visual}): This approach has been presented in Section 3.3.1 to visually cluster all images gathered after the selection process. In this approach, we select the sharpest image (i.e. lowest *B*) from the 5 largest clusters. In the case where less than 5 clusters exist, we select the 2nd sharpest image from each cluster and so on.

Temporal-spatial clustering ($S_{temp\text{-}spatial}$): This approach has been detailed in Section 3.3.2, to cluster images obtained after the selection process, based upon their spatial and temporal information. We use the same image selection process as in S_{visual} by selecting the sharpest images from the largest clusters.

Combined clustering ($S_{combined}$): Our final approach combines S_{visual} and $S_{temp\text{-}spatial}$ to rank the images obtained after the selection process. We select the sharpest images from the largest clusters.

4.3 Crowdsourcing Evaluation

As we are not evaluating events, activities or similar segmentation units, which can be *only* identified by the lifelogger, we instead employ a taskforce of crowdsourced evaluators in order to judge the *quality* and *diversity* of the top tanked images for each experimental system, thus increasing the speed and broadening the opinion of our evaluation. Moreover a crowdsourced evaluation will benefit use cases like generating community biographies for city councils and policy makers, where the lifelog images are not necessarily used by the lifeloggers, but sourced to external sources for a specific purpose, where quality and diversity are essential dimensions. Two separate crowdsourced evaluations were taken out on a popular crowdsourcing platform *CrowdFlower* (CF) [14].

4.3.1 Evaluating Image Quality

Our first evaluation attempts to judge the *quality* of five top ranked images for each system. The evaluators are asked the following questions with regards to a presented image: (1) How clear is the photograph? *Each evaluator is asked to rate on a Likert scale ranging from 0 (very blurry) to 5 (very sharp).* (2) How "interesting" is the photograph? Consider the scene and the objects, for example an image of a door or wall would be considered *'uninteresting'*. An image of a street or depicting an activity (using a computer, eating etc.), would be considered 'interesting'. *Each evaluator is asked to rate on a Likert scale from 0 (very boring) to 5 (very interesting).* The first question aims to validate the blur detection part of our image selection process with the second attempting to gauge the noise reduction from an image interestingness perspective. Although image interestingness is ill-defined and "in the eye of the beholder", we believe that by measuring perceived interest from a wide spectrum of crowdsourced evaluators, we will gain some insight into the user's engagement.

Each evaluator was presented with 5 images from those selected by various systems detailed in Section 4.2. Each image was evaluated by 3 separate evaluators with the survey scores averaged. Each evaluator was paid $0.03 on completion of this task. For our two questions (both with 6 different options), evaluator agreement of 66% and 56% was achieved. Evaluator agreement, computed by *CrowdFlower*, describes the level of agreement between multiple contributors (weighted by the contributors' trust scores). The fairly low agreement level achieved is mainly due to the high number of options available for each question (i.e. 6) and the difficultly in gauging how relevant an image is for summarization purposes in the context of lifelogging. Hence, we take the average scores for 3 different users for each question to reduce the diversity in opinion.

4.3.2 Evaluating Image Diversity

In order to evaluate the visual diversity of the top ranked images, a second crowdsourced evaluation is conducted. The evaluators are asked to judge the "visual similarity" of the image pairs. *Each evaluator is asked to rate the visual similarity on a Likert scale ranging from 0 (completely different) to 5 (Identical).* For our question judging the visual similarity (having 6 different options), the users achieved a 70.4% agreement level.

5. Results

Based on the judgements made in the two evaluations, we are able to quantify the sharpness, interestingness and visual similarity in the top 5 ranked images for each system. Table 2 shows the average statistics obtained from both the evaluations, and clearly demonstrates the effectiveness of $S_{combined}$ system. Statistical significance results against our S_{random} baseline are denoted as * being $p < 0.05$, ** being $p < 0.01$ and *** being $p<0.001$.

Table 2. Results from Evaluation ('v' denotes very).

System	Sharpness (0=v blurry, 5 = v sharp)	Interestingness (0= v boring, 5= v interesting)	Visual similarity (0= v different, 5= v similar)
S_{random}	3.07	2.22	2.01
S_{select}	3.28	2.35	1.38*
S_{visual}	3.45**	2.37	1.54
$S_{temp\text{-}spatial}$	3.45***	2.47*	1.32*
$S_{combined}$	**3.45*** **	**2.51***	**1.21***

In relation to RQ1.1, considering the effectiveness of the selection methods, i.e. achieved by S_{select}, we observe that the two major problems faced by lifelogging devices (i.e. blurred and duplicate images) can be automatically alleviated resulting in a 7% increase to image sharpness and 31% decrease to visual duplicates in the top 5 ranks, compared to our S_{random} baseline.

In relation to RQ1.2 and RQ1.3, i.e. effectiveness of the ranking/clustering methods, the evaluation demonstrates that the images which are clustered based upon the combination of all three aspects proposed within this paper (i.e. $S_{combined}$) received the highest average score (Table 2, last row) for each of the three aforementioned features. The $S_{combined}$ also achieved a 21% increase (on average) over the S_{random} baseline for all the three features. The reduction of noise, i.e. eliminating blurry images and visual duplicates significantly improves image *interestingness* implying a positive correlation.

By improving the quality (i.e. sharpness and interestingness) and visual diversity of the images taken by lifeloggers, we would expect to improve the user's search and retrieval experience when reviewing their images for a day. Firstly, we would expect our filtering approach to significantly reduce browsing time as almost 60% of images in our collection were either too blurry or a visual duplicate. Secondly, by promoting visual diversity using our proposed clustering techniques, we would expect a user to more effectively review their lifelogging visual data by presenting them with 5 visually diverse images (out of thousands of images).

6. Conclusion

This paper extends the notion of structuring lifelog data by evaluating a number of techniques to automatically generate good quality and visually diverse images in order to form key moments, summarising a lifelogger's daily life. Two crowdsourced evaluations demonstrated that the most effective technique to generate such key moments would rely upon eliminating blurred and visually duplicate images, followed by temporal, spatial and visual scene (using GIST) clustering. The techniques reported in this paper also contribute to decreasing the information overload problem posed by lifelogging devices. The techniques presented in this paper will be applied to a project, where we are piloting with 100 lifeloggers for ~12 months to capture user experiences in a modern city on a daily basis. The objective is to archive data to facilitate researchers from various disciplines to conduct human computational tasks. We firmly believe that it is also crucial to consider how to present the lifelog data, which conforms to the needs of all the possible actors using it, for example, urban science researchers could explore traits in transportation usage behavior, policy makers and city councils can explore traits using community biographies to better understand needs of a community and improve their lifestyle.

ACKNOWLEDGMENT

The authors acknowledge support from Integrated Multimedia City Data (iMCD), a project within the ESRC-funded Urban Big Data Centre (ES/L011921/1).

REFERENCES

[1] Doherty, A., Kelly, P., & Foster, C. "Wearable Cameras: Identifying Healthy Transportation Choices." *IEEE Pervasive Computing* 12.1 (2013): 44-47.

[2] Doherty, Aiden R., et al. "Experiences of aiding autobiographical memory using the SenseCam." *Human–Computer Interaction* 27. 1-2 (2012): 151-174.

[3] Anguera, X., Xu, J., & Oliver, N. "Multimodal photo annotation and retrieval on a mobile phone." ACM MIR, 2008.

[4] Wang, P., & Smeaton, A. F. "Semantics-based selection of everyday concepts in visual lifelogging." *International Journal of Multimedia Information Retrieval* 1.2 (2012): 87-101

[5] Lazer, D, et al. "Life in the network: the coming age of computational social science." *Science (NY)* 323.5915 (2009): 721.

[6] Gurrin, C, et al. "The smartphone as a platform for wearable cameras in health research." *American journal of preventive medicine* 44.3 (2013): 308-313.

[7] Kikhia, B, et al. "Structuring and Presenting Lifelogs Based on Location Data." *Pervasive Computing Paradigms for Mental Health*. Springer International Publishing, 2014. 133-144.

[8] Doherty, A. R., & Smeaton, A. F."Automatically augmenting lifelog events using pervasively generated content from millions of people." *Sensors* 10.3 (2010): 1423-1446.

[9] http://www.autographer.com, last accessed: 1 April, 2015.

[10] Tong, H, et al. "Blur detection for digital images using wavelet transform." *Multimedia and Expo, 2004. ICME'04.*

[11] Tang, Z., Dai, Y., & Zhang, X. "Perceptual hashing for color images using invariant moments." *Appl. Math* 6.2S (2012): 643S-650S.

[12] Chum, O., Philbin, J., & Zisserman, A. "Near Duplicate Image Detection: min-Hash and tf-idf Weighting." *BMVC*. Vol. 810. 2008.

[13] Oliva, A., & Torralba, A.. "Building the gist of a scene: The role of global image features in recognition." *Progress in brain research* 155 (2006): 23-36.

[14] http://www.crowdflower.com, last accessed: 1 April, 2015.

Audio-Based Multimedia Event Detection with DNNs and Sparse Sampling

Khalid Ashraf[1], Benjamin Elizalde[2], Forrest Iandola[1], Matthew Moskewicz[1],
Julia Bernd[2], Gerald Friedland[2], Kurt Keutzer[1]
[1]EECS Department, University of California, Berkeley, CA
[2]International Computer Science Institute, Berkeley, CA
{ashrafkhalid,forresti,moskewcz,keutzer}@berkeley.edu
{benmael,jbernd,fractor}@icsi.berkeley.edu

ABSTRACT

This paper presents advances in analyzing audio content information to detect events in videos, such as a parade or a birthday party. We developed a set of tools for audio processing within the predominantly vision-focused deep neural network (DNN) framework Caffe. Using these tools, we show, for the first time, the potential of using only a DNN for audio-based multimedia event detection. Training DNNs for event detection using the entire audio track from each video causes a computational bottleneck. Here, we address this problem by developing a sparse audio frame-sampling method that improves event-detection speed and accuracy. We achieved a 10 percentage-point improvement in event-classification accuracy, with a 200x reduction in the number of training input examples as compared to using the entire track. This reduction in input feature volume led to a 16x reduction in the size of the DNN architecture and a 300x reduction in training time. We applied our method using the recently released YLI-MED dataset and compared our results with a state-of-the-art system and with results reported in the literature for TRECVID MED. Our results show much higher MAP scores compared to a baseline i-vector system—at a significantly reduced computational cost. The speed improvement is relevant for processing videos on a large scale, and could enable more effective deployment in mobile systems.

Categories and Subject Descriptors

G.3 [**PROBABILITY AND STATISTICS**]: Statistical software; Time series analysis

Keywords

Multimedia Event Detection; Audio; Video; Deep Neural Networks; Caffe

ICMR '15 June 23 - 26, 2015, Shanghai, China
© 2015 ACM ISBN 978-1-4503-3274-3/15/06 ...$15.00
DOI: http://dx.doi.org/10.1145/2671188.2749396.

1. INTRODUCTION

Web videos have significant visual and audio content that is not fully described in their textual metadata. It is therefore necessary to develop tools that can automatically analyze that content. Multimedia event detection (MED) aims to identify the event(s) depicted in a user-generated video, such as a flash mob or someone making a sandwich, by using the content characteristics of the video. Much recent work in this area is related to NIST's annual TRECVID Multimedia Event Detection evaluation, and results in that benchmark define the state of the art.

Multimedia event detection based on audio has been approached in a variety of ways. Many of the most successful recent approaches [6, 8, 2] rely mainly on a combination of low-level features, especially Mel Frequency Cepstral Coefficients (MFCCs), followed by a Bag of Words. The final detection in these approaches is computed using Support Vector Machines (SVMs). Additionally, recent MED research has increasingly revolved around semantic or humanly explainable approaches. As a result, the focus in audio has shifted toward detecting identifiable audio concepts such as laughter or clapping. For example, a TNET-based [10] deep neural network (DNN) has been employed for an audio concept–classification step and complemented with Hidden Markov Models (HMMs) for audio-based event detection [4]. However, a review of recent work shows that DNNs have been explored largely for the computer vision aspect of MED and for fusion steps. Despite their high accuracy in other domains, DNNs alone have not yet been used for audio-based video-event detection.

Last year, the computer-vision DNN framework Caffe won the ACM Multimedia 2014 Open Source Software competition. It is a clean and modifiable framework for state-of-the-art deep learning [5], so we decided to leverage this efficient, well-known tool for our task. In this work, we developed tools based on Caffe that can be used for audio processing. Then we showed, for the first time, the potential of using only DNNs (without HMMs) for the audio-based video-event detection task. Training DNNs for event detection using the entire audio track from each video is computationally expensive. We addressed this problem by developing a sparse audio frame–sampling method that optimizes the representation of the audio file for event-detection performance. We achieved a notable event-classification accuracy improvement (10 percentage points), with a 200x reduction in the number of training input examples required as compared to dense sampling. This reduction in input feature volume en-

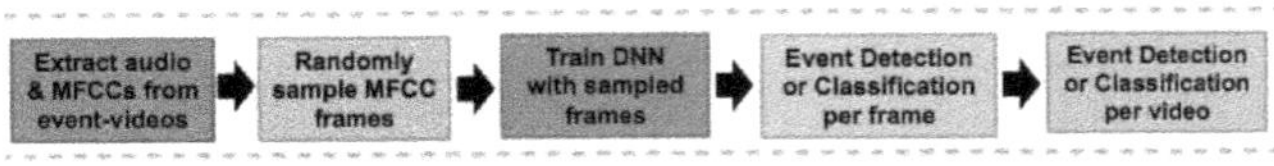

Figure 1: Pipeline for audio-based multimedia event detection or classification using a DNN.

abled a 16x reduction in the size of the DNN architecture and a 300x reduction in training time. We applied our methods to the recently released open-source YLI-MED dataset, and compared our results with a state-of-the-art system and with results reported in the literature for TRECVID MED 2013. We achieve higher MAP scores than a baseline i-vector system for audio-based video-event detection.

Our methodology and tools are described in Sec. 2, along with the comparison system. The datasets are described in Sec. 3. In Sec. 4, we present our experiments and highlight the most relevant results. Sec. 5 summarizes our conclusions.

2. DESCRIPTION OF SYSTEMS

In Sec. 2.1, we describe the feature extraction step that begins the pipeline for both systems we tested in this work. In Sec. 2.2, we describe how we used the deep neural network framework Caffe for audio-based video event detection and classification. In Sec. 2.3, we describe the i-vector detection system, which we used as a baseline for comparison.

2.1 Audio Preprocessing

In both tasks, the first step was to extract MFCC features from the audio track. We decided to use this standard preprocessing feature in these initial experiments for the sake of comparability. For the DNN, we used a total of 14 feature dimensions, including energy, while for the i-vector, we used 20, with delta and double delta for a total of 60 dimensions. Each feature frame was computed using a 25 ms Hamming window with a stride size of 10ms per frame shift. After a mean and variance normalization step, we applied a context window of 49 consecutive frames (centered at the 25th frame). We next performed a feature size reduction step in which the Discrete Cosine Transform (DCT) was applied to decorrelate the information in time. The total NN input feature consists of 462 frames.

2.2 Audio Processing Using Caffe

Our full pipeline for event detection and classification using a DNN is depicted in Figure 1. In sum, the MFCC features are sparsely sampled and fed into the neural net (more details on sampling are given in Sec. 4.1). Each sample training frame is labeled with an event name. The DNN performs classification or detection on the test MFCC frames, to identify the video as belonging to a particular event. For classification, the DNN is trained on all the events and performs multi-class classification to identify videos as depicting one of the events. In detection, the DNN performs binary classification between a given event and the negative event. There is thus one binary detector for each event category.

Caffe [5] is essentially oriented toward vision applications. Our first step in using Caffe as the basis for a video-analysis framework was to develop or incorporate tools specifically for analyzing audio signals; these tools are open-source and publicly available.[1] We incorporated a context window for capturing correlation in the temporal dimension, a Discrete Cosine Transform to decorrelate the data, and a Restricted Boltzmann Machine (RBM) for pre-training the DNN.

2.3 The i-Vector System

I-vector-based systems have been previously used for audio-based event detection in the TRECVID MED evaluations [11, 3], and thus provide a helpful baseline for comparison. The i-vector can be thought of as a low-dimensional representation of the identity of each event class. A log-likelihood ratio for similarity between test data and event classes is computed using a generative Probabilistic Linear Discriminant Analysis (pLDA). The Within-Class Covariance Normalization (WCCN) and pLDA system components normalize for the within- and between-class i-vector scatter of the events. This accounts for cases where examples of the same event have distinctive audio profiles, and where different events have similar audio elements. Details on the system used for these experiments are in Elizalde et al. 2013 [3].

3. CORPORA USED

The TRECVID MED dataset [9] used in much previous MED work is comprised of web videos labeled for the events depicted; however, use is restricted to evaluation-related research. Therefore, for these experiments we used YLI-MED, which is inspired by TRECVID MED and is annotated for some of the same events [1]. YLI-MED is drawn from the Yahoo Flickr Creative Commons 100 Million (YFCC100M) dataset.YLI-MED Version 1 contains 10 events as well as non-event videos. For training, there are 1000 event videos (100 per) and 5,000 non-event videos. For testing, there are 823 event videos and 43,638 non-event videos.

4. EXPERIMENTS & RESULTS

In this section, we present multimedia event detection and classification results obtained using our adapted Caffe framework vs. a baseline system. First, using the YLI-MED dataset, we studied event *classification*, tuning our audio–frame sampling method (Sec. 4.1) and neural net architecture (Sec. 4.2) for classification speed and accuracy. In Sec. 4.3, we describe how we included YLI-MED non-event background samples in the training and testing sets to study event *detection*. We compared our event-detection results with other results in the literature; we also used an i-vector system trained on TRECVID MED and tested on YLI-MED to show the comparability between the two datasets (Sec. 4.3).

4.1 Sparse Audio Sampling for Speed and Accuracy

The main bottleneck in performing DNN-based video event detection is at the input stage. The extracted audio features are represented as frames.Web videos are usually between 2 and 3 minutes long, and thus processing thousands of videos—each including thousands of frames—is slow. Moreover, global optimization of a DNN with a stochastic gradient descent method is difficult with such a high number of example frames.

Answering the question "What is this video about?" requires listening to multiple segments of the video. We were interested in seeing if we could achieve a comparable result by using arbitrary segments of the video rather than the

[1] https://github.com/ashrafk/audioCaffeInitial

Method	Per-Frame Accuracy(%)	Video-Level Accuracy(%)
DNN(2000:2000:2000:10), All Frames Input	18.3	27.4
DNN(2000:2000:2000:10), 100 Frames Input	28.6	36.8
DNN(600:600:10), 100 Frames Input	29.3	37.4

Table 1: Accuracy of selected DNN-based event-classification configurations tested in this work.

whole. It turns out that it is possible to achieve not only improved efficiency but also improved accuracy. The DNN can find correlations among these arbitrarily sampled points, and from that, represent the entire event.

For each training and test video in the YLI-MED dataset, we sampled a fixed number of frames in each trial, varying the frame separation based on the video length. In our experiments, we varied the number of sampled frames per video from 20 to 150. We found that 100 frames per video gave the highest neural net per-frame accuracy, at 28.6%, with a video-level event classification accuracy of 36.8%. In contrast, when densely feeding the entire audio track into the DNN, the per-frame accuracy was only 18.3%, which translated to a video-level classification accuracy of 27.4%.

4.2 Optimizing the Neural Net Architecture

Having selected an efficient and accurate frame sampling method, we moved on to exploring neural network architectures. Starting with a 400:400:10 network (where 400:400:10 means 400d inner product $\rightarrow$ sigmoid $\rightarrow$ 400d inner product $\rightarrow$ sigmoid $\rightarrow$ 10d softmax), we initially increased the number of hidden units by increments of 100 in the layers up to 800. We found that a 600:600:10 neural net gave the highest per-frame accuracy, at 29.3%, which resulted in 37.4% accuracy on video-level event classification. These results are summarized in Table 1. We also varied the depth of the neural net. However, adding another layer did not improve the accuracy significantly.

4.3 Comparing Methods for Event Detection

We used the sparse 100-frame audio sampling and the DNN architecture described in Secs. 4.1 and 4.2 to perform event detection. For binary detection, we replaced the 10d softmax layer with a 2d softmax layer (600:600:2). In this section, we describe the detection methods and results, and compare them with those described in previous literature.

4.3.1 MAP scores

For detection, the DNN was trained on the individual YLI-MED event videos (100 per) and a similar number of negatives. Once the DNN was trained to achieve the highest cross-validation accuracy, posterior probabilities were calculated for the test positive examples for each event and for the full set of ~43,600 test negative examples. Cumulative probability was used to determine whether each test file belonged to each target event. Average precision (AP) for each event was calculated from the true positives (TP) and false positives (FP) among the full 44K test set. The mean average precision (MAP) is calculated by averaging the AP scores for individual events over all the 10 YLI-MED events. The resulting MAP scores are shown in Table 2.

Event Category	i-vector TV/YL	i-vector YL/YL	Caffe YL/YL
Birthday Party	0.31	0.37	1.10
Flash Mob	0.22	0.12	0.89
Getting a Vehicle Unstuck	0.07	0.12	0.61
Parade	0.21	0.32	1.62
Person Attempting a Board Trick	0.20	0.23	1.34
Pers. Grooming an Animal	0.09	0.11	1.12
Person Hand-Feeding an Animal	0.22	0.28	1.71
Person Landing a Fish	0.05	0.10	0.67
Wedding Ceremony	0.25	0.32	0.92
Working on a Woodworking Project	0.11	0.19	1.81
Overall MAP	0.17	0.22	1.18

Table 2: Event-detection MAP percentage scores for: the i-vector system trained on TRECVID MED (col1), and trained on YLI-MED (col2), both tested on YLI-MED; Caffe-based DNN system (col3) trained and tested on YLI-MED.

Most previous work on audio-based multimedia event detection has used the TRECVID MED dataset. The highest reported audio-based MAP score for the TRECVID MED 2013 dataset is 14.6% [7]. TRECVID MED data is not publicly available, so we were unable to make a direct comparison with the state of the art. However, we had previously trained an i-vector system on the TRECVID MED 2013 data (see Sec. 2.3), achieving a MAP of 7% testing it on that data [3]. For the current project, we used this TRECVID MED-trained system and tested it on YLI-MED, to assess the comparability of the two datasets, before using YLI-MED to compare the i-vector and DNN detection approaches. Under these conditions, i-vector achieved a MAP score of 0.17%.[2] Then we both trained and tested the i-vector system on the YLI-MED dataset. The MAP score in this case improved to 0.22%.

In comparison, the DNN event-detection system with sampled-MFCC input achieved a MAP of 1.1% on the YLI-MED, at a much lower computation cost (see Sec. 4.3.2). It is exciting to observe such improvement in MAP scores compared to the i-vector system on the same dataset, at a significantly lower computational cost. Also, it should be noted that the DNN-based detection was performed on a raw input signal, without segmentation. In contrast, the state-of-the-art result [7] was obtained after performing unsupervised clustering on the input audio, and also with many fewer negative examples (25k in TRECVID 2013 compared to 43K in YLI-MED). Our sparsely sampled DNN method has proven its potential by showing improved accuracy results compared to full audio samples, and we anticipate that fine-tuning the accuracy by segmenting the input audio will be a very promising area for future research.

4.3.2 Speed and memory

Irrespective of dataset, the Caffe framework consistently gave a ~1.5x speedup on a Tesla K40 GPU, compared to a TNET-based DNN [10]. The next level of speedup came

[2]It is not known how much overlap there may be between the training and test sets across the two datasets.

Method	Train Time (hr)	Test Time (hr)	Training Speedup	Model Size (MB)
i-Vector	2.71	7.8	1x	5100
DNN: Full	10.33	NA	0.26x	48
DNN: Sparse Sampled	0.034	0.748	78.4x	3

Table 3: Speed and memory required for the event-detection methods compared in this work.

from representing the input video events with sparsely sampled frames of the MFCC features. Sparse frame sampling reduces the training- and test- data volume significantly. A typical video in the YLI-MED dataset is around 3 minutes long, so there are about 18,000 MFCC frames per video. Sampling only 100 audio frames per video resulted in about a 200x reduction in input frame numbers, while still achieving high classification accuracy results.

Reducing the number of input frames in turn reduces the size of the DNN required to obtain high accuracy. For example, as shown in Table 3, with the full-length audio track, the best DNN architecture is 2000:2000:2000:10 (to achieve 18.3% per-frame classification accuracy), while sparse sampling of the input frames gave an optimum per-frame accuracy with a 600:600:10 DNN. The DNN with dense audio sampling takes up about 48MB of storage, whereas the DNN with sparse frame input takes only about 3MB. In contrast, the baseline i-vector system takes 5.1GB—that is, 1700x more than the sampled DNN system. The smaller DNN facilitated a 300x and 78.4x training-time speedup compared to the full-input DNN and the i-vector system, respectively. We could not perform a complete test of the full-input DNN due to the prohibitively long run time, but an overall 10x testing speedup was observed for the sampled DNN compared to the i-vector system.

5. CONCLUSIONS

In summary, we have built several tools for audio analysis within the DNN framework Caffe, which we have made publicly available. We explored, for the first time, the potential of using DNNs without HMMs for audio-based video-event detection. We achieved a 10 percentage-point improvement in event-classification accuracy by optimizing sampling and DNN topology, with a 200x reduction in the number of input frames as compared with using all of the frames. This reduction in input frame numbers resulted in a 16x reduction in the size of the DNN required for maximum accuracy. The combination of input-data volume and DNN size reduction gave an overall 300x and 78.4x speedup in training time compared to the full-audio DNN and i-vector systems respectively. When evaluated on the newly released YLI-MED dataset, our DNN system with sparse frame sampling showed higher accuracy than the baseline i-vector results, at a significantly lower computation cost. These improvements in speed and accuracy are relevant for processing videos at a larger scale, as well as for potential deployment of video analysis on mobile platforms.

6. ACKNOWLEDGMENTS

This work was supported in part by the National Science Foundation under Award #1251276, SMASH (Scalable Multimedia content AnalysiS in a High-level language). It was also supported by Lawrence Livermore National Laboratory, operated by Lawrence Livermore National Security, LLC, for the U.S. Department of Energy, National Nuclear Security Administration, under Contract DE-AC52-07NA27344.

7. REFERENCES

[1] J. Bernd, D. Borth, B. Elizalde, G. Friedland, H. Gallagher, L. Gottlieb, A. Janin, S. Karabashlieva, J. Takahashi, and J. Won. The YLI-MED corpus: Characteristics, procedures, and plans (ICSI Technical Report TR-15-001). *arXiv:1503.04250*, 2015.

[2] H. Cheng, J. Liu, S. Ali, O. Javed, Q. Yu, A. Tamrakar, A. Divakaran, H. S. Sawhney, R. Manmatha, J. Allan, A. Hauptmann, M. Shah, S. Bhattacharya, A. Dehghan, G. Friedland, et al. SRI-Sarnoff AURORA system at TRECVID 2012: Multimedia event detection and recounting. In *Proceedings of TRECVID 2012*. NIST, USA, 2012.

[3] B. Elizalde, H. Lei, and G. Friedland. An i-vector representation of acoustic environments for audio-based video event detection on user generated content. In *ISM*, 2013.

[4] B. Elizalde, M. Ravanelli, and G. Friedland. Audio-concept features and hidden Markov models for multimedia event detection. In *SLAM@INTERSPEECH*, 2014.

[5] Y. Jia, E. Shelhamer, J. Donahue, S. Karayev, J. Long, R. Girshick, S. Guadarrama, and T. Darrell. Caffe: Convolutional architecture for fast feature embedding. *arXiv preprint arXiv:1408.5093*, 2014.

[6] Z. Lan, L. Jiang, S.-I. Yu, C. Gao, S. Rawat, Y. Cai, S. Xu, H. Shen, X. Li, Y. Wang, W. Sze, Y. Yan, Z. Ma, N. Ballas, D. Meng, W. Tong, Y. Yang, S. Burger, F. Metze, et al. Informedia @ TRECVID 2013. In *Proceedings of TRECVID 2013*. NIST, USA, 2013.

[7] F. Metze, S. Rawat, and Y. Wang. Improved audio features for large-scale multimedia event detection. *ICME*, 2014.

[8] P. Natarajan, P. Natarajan, S. Wu, X. Zhuang, A. Vazquez Reina, S. N. Vitaladevuni, K. Tsourides, C. Andersen, R. Prasad, G. Ye, D. Liu, S.-F. Chang, I. Saleemi, M. Shahand, Y. Ng, et al. BBN VISER TRECVID 2012 multimedia event detection and multimedia event recounting systems. In *Proceedings of TRECVID 2012*. NIST, USA, 2012.

[9] P. Over, G. Awad, M. Michel, J. Fiscus, G. Sanders, W. Kraaij, A. F. Smeaton, and G. Quénot. TRECVID 2013 – an overview of the goals, tasks, data, evaluation mechanisms and metrics. In *Proceedings of TRECVID 2013*. NIST, USA, 2013.

[10] K. Vesely, L. Burget, and F. Grezl. Parallel training of neural networks for speech recognition. In *Proceedings of INTERSPEECH*, 2010.

[11] X. Zhuang, S. Tsakalidis, S. Wu, P. Natarajan, R. Prasad, and P. Natarajan. Compact audio representation for event detection in consumer media. In *INTERSPEECH*, 2012.

Learning Binary Codes for Hashing via Feature Decomposition

Xiao-Jiao Mao Zhen-Fei Ju Rui Xu Yu-Bin Yang
State Key Laboratory for Novel Software Technology,
Nanjing University, 210093, China
yangyubin@nju.edu.cn

ABSTRACT

Binary code learning techniques have been actively studied for hashing based nearest neighbor search in recent years. However, most existing techniques directly map the data into a Hamming space, which ignores the inherent property that original features may lie in different subspaces. To address this issue, this paper proposes a novel method by learning binary codes on the latent components decomposed from the original features of the data. We assume that each latent component represents an underlying feature subspace and similar/dissimilar data may contain the same/different latent components. As a result, the decomposition step distinguishes the original data better and consequently improves the discriminative power of binary codes. The experimental results of image retrieval tasks carried out on the commonly used benchmark datasets show that the proposed method outperforms other state-of-the-art methods on generating similarity-preserving binary codes.

Categories and Subject Descriptors

H.3 [**INFORMATION STORAGE AND RETRIEVAL**]: Content Analysis and Indexing

Keywords

Hashing; binary code; feature decomposition; latent component

1. INTRODUCTION

With the rapid development of the Internet, a huge number of visual data are available online and thus urges the demand for corresponding applications such as image retrieval and image recognition. Nearest neighbor search (NNS), as a fundamental technique in such applications, has become a significant challenge due to the pursuit of searching efficiency in large databases. Hashing techniques[1, 4, 13, 7, 10, 5, 8] have been proposed and widely studied for NNS in recent years. Generally, these methods project original features into compact binary codes, which are then used as indexes for NNS, and preserve similarity among them in the meantime. Nevertheless, most existing methods usually directly project features with a set of hash functions, thus ignore the inherent property that original features may lie in different subspaces.

In this paper, we propose a novel hashing method based on decomposing the features into latent components, each of which represents an underlying feature subspace. A feature is firstly decomposed into latent components with several pre-learned filters to obtain a component matrix, from which the binary codes are learned. The decomposition step has the following benefits. First of all, the two-dimension data structure, i.e. matrix, can carry more information than the original one-dimension feature vector. Secondly, the discriminative power between different features can be enhanced because if two features are similar, they may potentially contain the same component and consequently have strong activations to the corresponding filter.

The rest of this paper is organized as follows. Section 2 provides a brief review of the related work. Section 3 describes the details of the proposed binary code learning method. Experimental results are provided in Section 4. Finally, Section 5 makes the concluding remarks.

ICMR'15, June 23–26, 2015, Shanghai, China.

http://dx.doi.org/10.1145/2671188.2749397 .

2. RELATED WORK

Tree-based methods, such as KD-tree [2], have been widely studied for NNS. However, they may degrade into linear search in the worst case [6]. Recently, hashing techniques, which normally map high dimensional data to compact binary codes, have been actively studied. Since the Hamming distance between two binary codes can be efficiently computed via exclusive "OR" operation, adopting compact binary codes for NNS is becoming a common practice which provides constant or sub-linear time complexity.

Locality Sensitive Hashing (LSH) [3] [1], in which the projections are randomly generated independent of the data, is a widely used hashing technique. However, due to the data-blindness, LSH requires more hash tables and longer codes to achieve satisfied precision and recall [11]. Motivated by the idea of data rotation, Iterative Quantization (ITQ) [4] performs Principle Component Analysis (PCA) to reduce the dimensionality of data and then minimizes the quantization loss, i.e. mapping data to vertices of the binary hypercube, by learning an optimal rotation matrix. Graph-based methods, such as Spectral Hashing (SH) [13] and Anchor Graph Hashing (AGH) [7], automatically discover the neighborhood structure inherent in data to learn compact binary codes for hashing. Recent studies [10, 5, 8] show that incorporating label information improves the semantic search performance. Semantic Hashing (RBM) [10] leverages Restricted Boltzmann Machines to construct a multi-layer auto-encoder to encode low dimensional binary codes. Binary reconstructive embedding (BRE) [5] makes a loss function that penalizes the squared error between the original distances and the reconstructed distances. Although utilizing labels achieves better accuracy in semantic NNS, supervised methods are normally more difficult to be optimized and slower to be trained.

Different from these methods which generate binary codes directly from the original feature, we propose a feature decomposition step to better represent the data by the latent components. Firstly, a de-convolution operation [15] is adopted to decompose the original features with several pre-learned filters to obtain the component matrix. Afterwards, 2-dimension Principle Component Analysis (2DPCA) [14] is taken as the regularization term of the overall cost function in order to reduce the dimensionality of the component matrix. Linear projections are then learned for each component to generate the binary codes.

3. LEARNING BINARY CODES VIA FEATURE DECOMPOSITION

3.1 Feature Decomposition

Given the features of n points denoted as $X = [x_1, x_2, \ldots, x_n], x_i \in \mathbb{R}^d$, we obtain their latent components via deconvolutional reconstruction [15]. Specifically, each feature x_i is represented as a linear sum of m latent components $z_j^i \in \mathbb{R}^{k+d-1}$ convolved with filters $f_j \in \mathbb{R}^k$:

$$\sum_{j=1}^{m} z_j^i \oplus f_j = x_i \tag{1}$$

where $\oplus$ denotes convolution operation. $Z_i = [z_1^i, z_2^i, \ldots, z_m^i]^T$ is the component matrix of x_i. A latent component is assumed to represent a underlying subspace. For two arbitrary points, if they are similar, they may lie under the same subspace and thus both acquire strong activations to the same corresponding filter. What we have to do is learning proper filters. Since Eq. 1 is an under-determined system, we introduce 2DPCA as a regularization term. On the other hand, adopting 2DPCA also reduces the dimensionality of the component matrix.

Opposed to PCA, 2DPCA is based on 2D matrices rather than 1D vectors. Let H denote a q-dimension unitary column vector. The idea of 2DPCA is to project A, an $p \times q$ matrix, onto Y by using the following linear transformation:

$$Y = AH \tag{2}$$

2DPCA explains that the total scatter of the projected samples, which is characterized by the trace of the covariance matrix, can be introduced to measure the discriminative power of the projection vector H. The covariance matrix S_H is denoted by:

$$S_H = E[(A - EA)H][(A - EA)H]^T \tag{3}$$

Then we have:

$$J(H) = trace(S_H) = H^T GH \tag{4}$$

where

$$G = E[(A - EA)^T (A - EA)] \tag{5}$$

Given a component matrix Z_i, for each 2DPCA projection, we have:

$$y_k^i = Z_i h_k, k = 1, 2, \ldots, b. \tag{6}$$

The lower dimensional matrix $Z_{pri} = [y_1^i, y_2^i, ..., y_k^i]$ is called the principle component matrix of Z_i. To this end, the overall cost function of our algorithm can be denoted as:

$$J(Z, F, H) = \sum_{i=1}^{n} \|Z_i \oplus F - x_i\|^2 - \lambda \sum_{k=1}^{b} h_k^T G h_k \tag{7}$$

where $H = [h_i, h_2, ..., h_k]$, $Z_i \oplus F$ is short for the linear sum in Eq. 1 and G is evaluated by:

$$G = \frac{1}{n} \sum_{i=1}^{n} (Z_i - \overline{Z})^T (Z_i - \overline{Z}) \tag{8}$$

λ is a constant that balances the relative contributions of the reconstruction error of x_i and the sum of traces of the covariance matrix.

Since the above objective function is convex for each parameter, it is optimized by gradient descent method. We fix other variables when updating one. The updating steps are described in details as follows.

Fix F, H and update Z. Each Z_i in Eq. 7 is solved independently from the others. Taking the derivatives of $J(Z, F, H)$ with respect to Z_i, we have:

$$\frac{\partial J}{\partial Z_i} = 2(Z_i \oplus F - x_i) \oplus F^T + (\frac{2}{n} Z_i - \frac{2}{n^2} \sum_{j=1}^{n} Z_j) H H^T \tag{9}$$

Then, Z_i is updated by:

$$Z_i^{(t+1)} = Z_i^{(t)} - \gamma \frac{\partial J}{\partial Z_i} \tag{10}$$

where γ is the learning rate.

Fix Z, H and update F. Taking the derivatives of $J(Z, F, H)$ with respect to F:

$$\frac{\partial J}{\partial F} = 2 Z_i \oplus (Z_i \oplus F - x_i) \tag{11}$$

Then, F is updated by:

$$F^{(t+1)} = F^{(t)} - \gamma \frac{\partial J}{\partial F} \tag{12}$$

Fix Z, F and update H. We take h_i as the eigenvectors of G corresponding to the b largest eigenvalues.

In the training phase, Z, F and H are iteratively updated until the loss function is converged. After learning F, the component matrix is directly inferred with F in the testing phase, and then projected into principle component matrix with H. For each data point in the database, we compute:

$$y_k^i = Z_i h_k, \qquad k = 1, 2, \ldots, b \tag{13}$$

Let $Y_k = [y_k^1, y_k^2, \ldots, y_k^n]$, where n is the size of database.

3.2 Binary Quantization

Linear projection with thresholding is used to quantize the principle component matrix into binary codes. Specifically, for a given principle component matrix Y_k, the kth hash function is denoted as:

$$f_k(x_i) = sign(w_k^T y_k^i + b_k). \quad (14)$$

Prior studies [13] [12] have demonstrated that a generated bit should have an equal probability of 0 or 1 in order to achieve better coding efficiency. We follow this protocol and zero-center each Y_k to force $b = 0$.

To preserve the similarity among data, we employ the object function given in [12] to quantize the principle component matrix into binary codes:

$$J(W) = \sum_k \Big\{ \sum_{(y_k^i, y_k^j) \in \mathcal{M}} f_k(y_k^i) f_k(y_k^j) - \sum_{(y_k^i, y_k^j) \in \mathcal{C}} f_k(y_k^i) f_k(y_k^j) \Big\}, \quad (15)$$

where $\mathcal{M}$ is the set of neighboring pairs y_k^i and y_k^j. y_k^i and y_k^j either are neighbors in a metric space, or share common class labels. $\mathcal{C}$ is the set of non-neighboring pairs. We may define the label matrix $S \in \mathbb{R}^{n \times n}$ incorporating with the pairwise label information as:

$$S_{ij} = \begin{cases} 1 & : \quad (y_k^i, y_k^j) \in \mathcal{M} \\ -1 & : \quad (y_k^i, y_k^j) \in \mathcal{C} \end{cases} \quad (16)$$

Herewith, $J(W)$ can be denoted as:

$$\begin{aligned} J(W) &= \frac{1}{2} \sum_k f_k(Y_k) S f_k(Y_k)^T \\ &= \frac{1}{2} \sum_k sgn(w_k^T Y_k) S sgn(w_k^T Y_k)^T \end{aligned} \quad (17)$$

where $W = [w_1, w_2, \dots, w_b]$. We learn optimal hyperplane matrix W by maximizing objective function $J(W)$. However, the above problem is difficult to solve since $J(W)$ is non-differentiable. We adopt an intuitive relaxation to relax the binary constraint:

$$J(W) = \sum_k \Big\{ \sum_{(y_k^i, y_k^j) \in \mathcal{M}} w_k^T y_k^i {y_k^j}^T w_k - \sum_{(y_k^i, y_k^j) \in \mathcal{C}} w_k^T y_k^i {y_k^j}^T w_k \Big\}, \quad (18)$$

The above function can be represented in matrix form:

$$J(W) = \frac{1}{2} \sum_k w_k^T Y_k S Y_k^T w_k \quad (19)$$

To maximize objective function $J(W)$, we take each w_k as the eigenvectors of $Y_k S Y_k^T$ corresponding to the largest eigenvalues. Afterwards, the binary codes are obtained via the following equation:

$$B_k(x_i) = sign(w_k^T y_k^i). \quad (20)$$

4. EXPERIMENTS

4.1 Datasets and Protocols

The experiments are carried out on two image benchmark datasets: MNIST and CIFAR-10. Since MNIST and CIFAR-10 are fully labeled, we can easily define the semantic neighbors and obtain the label matrix S. 1,000 images are randomly selected as queries and the remaining images are used as the database for each dataset. For CIFAR-10, each image is represented by a 512-dimension GIST feature vector [9]. We compare our method with five state-of-the-art methods including LSH [1], SH [13], BRE [5], ITQ [4] and AGH [7]. The parameters for these methods are set as they suggested. Mean Average Precision (mAP) and Precision-Recall curve of Hamming ranking are used as the evaluation criterions. All the data points in the database are ranked according to their Hamming distances from the query, and top 50 of them are kept as the retrieval results.

4.2 Results

Fig.2 shows the Hamming ranking performance of the compared methods measured by Mean Average Precision. The number of binary bits varies from 16 to 96. We return top 50 points to obtain the Mean Average Precision of Hamming ranking. SH acquires better performance than LSH in short code length cases, as mentioned in [13], but SH loses its advantage when code length increases. BRE incorporates supervised information and improves the hashing performance over LSH and SH. Generally, our method achieves higher Mean Average Precision than BRE, SH and LSH. Our method intents to enhance the discriminative power of each bit in the binary codes, thus more discriminative binary codes are obtained. Meanwhile, the results illustrate that our method achieves better benefits over other methods as the code length increases, especially for the code length larger than 48. AGH works better than our method on MNIST with bit length smaller than 48, but we gain substantial improvements over AGH on CIFAR-10. ITQ slightly outperforms our method on CIFAR-10 with bit 16, 24 and 32, but it is inferior to our method on MNIST. The reason for acquiring lower performance in the case of short binary codes may be that a small number of components cannot provide enough discriminative information.

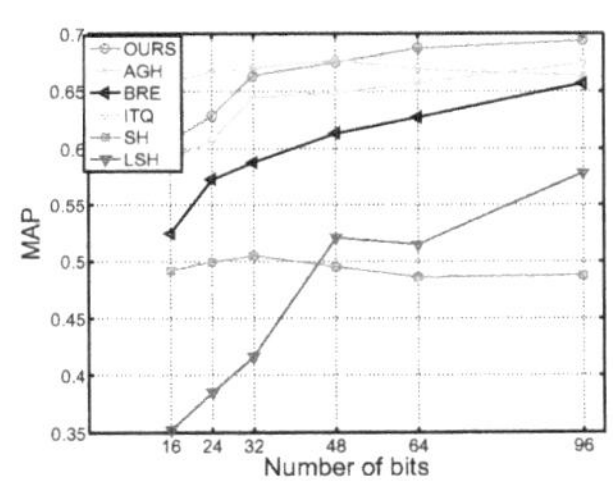

(a) mAP on MNIST

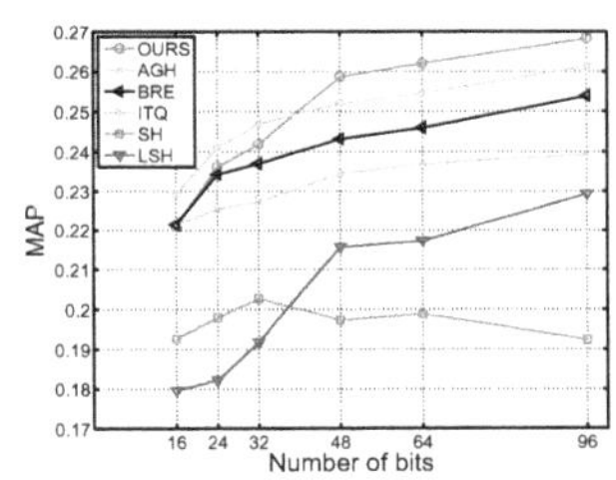

(b) mAP on CIFAR-10

Figure 2: The Mean Average Precision of top 50 on MNIST and CIFAR-10.

Fig.3 shows the Hamming ranking performance of the compared methods on MNIST and CIFAR-10 measured by Precision-Recall curve. The Precision-Recall curve is measured using 48 bit binary codes. The main observation is that our method outperforms others on MNIST. AGH ranks the second among all the methods and it comes near to our method on recall rate larger than 0.3. Both our method and AGH are far better than the other methods on Precision-Recall evaluation. On CIFAR-10, our method slightly outperforms others on recall larger than 0.2. The images in CIFAR-10 are visually much more complex than the handwritten digits and closer to real world applications, which makes the performance improvements less evident than that on MNIST. But our method still achieves the best results. To better visualize the quality of nearest neighbors search, we show top neighbors retrieved by different techniques on MNIST and CIFAR-10 dataset in Fig. 1.

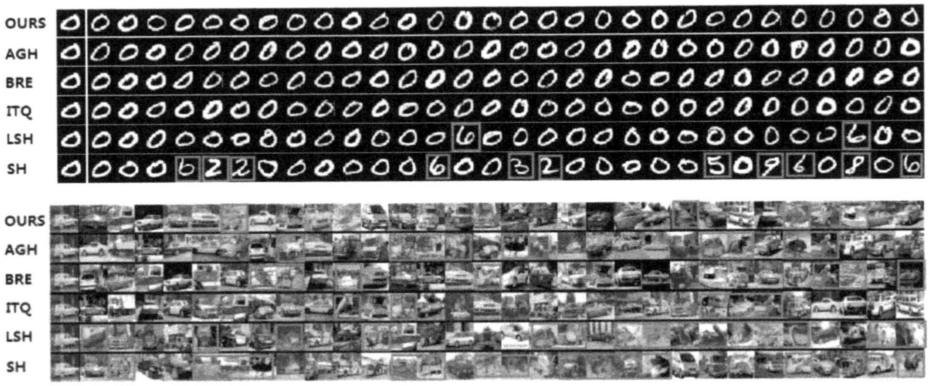

Figure 1: The 30 nearest neighbors returned by different methods on the MNIST and CIFAR-10 dataset using 48-bit code. The column on the left represents the query image. The red rectangles show the false positives.

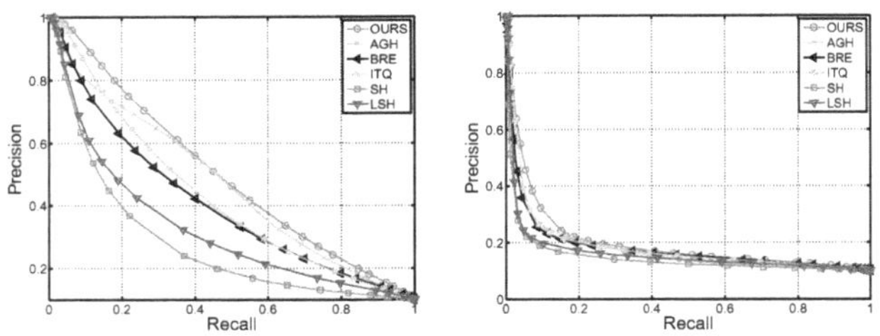

(a) PR curves on MNIST (b) PR curves on CIFAR-10

Figure 3: The Mean Precision-Recall curve with bit 48 on MNIST and CIFAR-10.

5. CONCLUSION

This paper presents a novel binary code learning method base on feature decomposition. The component decomposition procedure better represents the original data and enhances the discriminative power of the generated binary codes. Experimental results show that our method outperforms state-of-the-art hashing techniques. In the future, to make hashing performance better, we will focus on designing algorithms which can learn better representations of latent components for the original features, and developing new hash function forms as well.

6. ACKNOWLEDGMENTS

This work is supported by the Program for New Century Excellent Talents of MOE China (Grant No.NCET-11-0213), the Natural Science Foundation of China (Grant Nos. 61273257, 61321491), the Program for Distinguished Talents of Jiangsu(Grant No. 2013-XXRJ-018), and the Scientific Research Foundation of Graduate School of Nanjing University(Grant No. 2014CL03)

7. REFERENCES

[1] M. Datar, N. Immorlica, P. Indyk, and V. S. Mirrokni. Locality-sensitive hashing scheme based on p-stable distributions. In *ACM SoCG*, pages 253–262, 2004.

[2] J. H. Friedman, J. L. Bentley, and R. A. Finkel. An algorithm for finding best matches in logarithmic expected time. *ACM TOMS*, 3(3):209–226, 1977.

[3] A. Gionis, P. Indyk, and R. Motwani. Similarity search in high dimensions via hashing. In *VLDB*, pages 518–529, 1999.

[4] Y. Gong, S. Lazebnik, A. Gordo, and F. Perronnin. Iterative quantization: A procrustean approach to learning binary codes for large-scale image retrieval. *IEEE TPAMI*, 35(12):2916–2929, 2013.

[5] B. Kulis and T. Darrell. Learning to hash with binary reconstructive embeddings. In *NIPS*, pages 1042–1050, 2009.

[6] T. Liu, A. W. Moore, A. G. Gray, and K. Yang. An investigation of practical approximate nearest neighbor algorithms. In *NIPS*, pages 825–832, 2004.

[7] W. Liu, J. Wang, S. Kumar, and S. Chang. Hashing with graphs. In *ICML*, pages 1–8, 2011.

[8] M. Norouzi and D. J. Fleet. Minimal loss hashing for compact binary codes. In *ICML*, pages 353–360, 2011.

[9] A. Oliva and A. Torralba. Modeling the shape of the scene: A holistic representation of the spatial envelope. *IJCV*, 42(3):145–175, 2001.

[10] R. Salakhutdinov and G. E. Hinton. Learning a nonlinear embedding by preserving class neighbourhood structure. In *AISTATS*, pages 412–419, 2007.

[11] F. Shen, C. Shen, Q. Shi, A. van den Hengel, and Z. Tang. Inductive hashing on manifolds. In *CVPR*, pages 1562–1569, 2013.

[12] J. Wang, O. Kumar, and S. Chang. Semi-supervised hashing for scalable image retrieval. In *CVPR*, pages 3424–3431, 2010.

[13] Y. Weiss, A. Torralba, and R. Fergus. Spectral hashing. In *NIPS*, pages 1753–1760, 2008.

[14] J. Yang, D. Zhang, A. F. Frangi, and J. Yang. Two-dimensional PCA: A new approach to appearance-based face representation and recognition. *IEEE TPAMI*, 26(1):131–137, 2004.

[15] M. D. Zeiler, D. Krishnan, G. W. Taylor, and R. Fergus. Deconvolutional networks. In *CVPR*, pages 2528–2535, 2010.

Multimodal Learning with Deep Boltzmann Machine for Emotion Prediction in User Generated Videos

Lei Pang, Chong-Wah Ngo
Department of Computer Science, City University of Hong Kong, Kowloon, Hong Kong
leipang3-c@my.cityu.edu.hk, cscwngo@cityu.edu.hk

ABSTRACT

Detecting emotions from user-generated videos, such as "anger" and "sadness", has attracted widespread interest recently. The problem is challenging as effectively representing video data with multi-view information (e.g., audio, video or text) is not trivial. In contrast to the existing works that extract features from each modality (view) separately followed by early or late fusion, we propose to learn a joint density model over the space of multi-modal inputs (including visual, auditory and textual modalities) with Deep Boltzmann Machine (DBM). The model is trained directly on the user-generated Web videos without any labeling effort. More importantly, the deep architecture enlightens the possibility of discovering the highly non-linear relationships that exist between low-level features across different modalities. The experiment results show that the DBM model learns joint representation complementary to the hand-crafted visual and auditory features, leading to 7.7% performance improvement in classification accuracy on the recently released VideoEmotion dataset.

Categories and Subject Descriptors

H.4 [**Information Systems Applications**]: Miscellaneous

General Terms

Performance, Experimentation

Keywords

Emotion analysis; Multimodal learning; Deep Boltzmann Machine

1. INTRODUCTION

While intensive research efforts have been devoted to emotion analysis on documents or images, emotion prediction on user-generated videos is still a relatively new and largely untapped research area. With the popularity of social websites and mobile devices with high quality cameras, there is a large volume of unedited videos generated by users to record all kinds of activities in our life. Automatically understanding the emotions from these videos with diverse contents is in high demand for many applications [5]. For example, when searching information about a resort, the retrieved videos can be reranked based on their emotions to provide implicit comments. In addition, when asking opinion-related questions about hot events, providing emotion tags for retrieved videos helps users more quickly understand the sentiment of public's view.

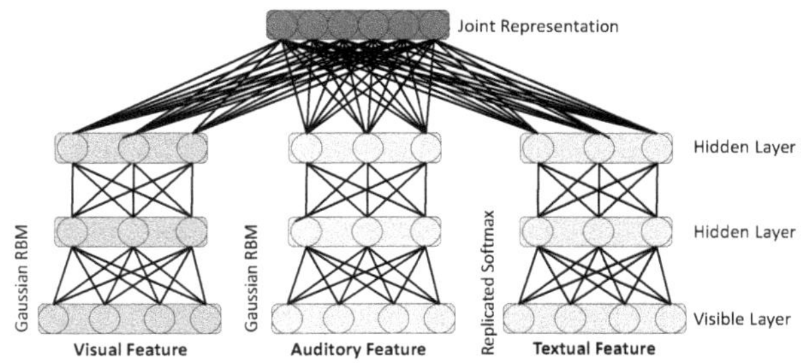

Figure 1: The multimodal DBM that models the joint distribution over visual, auditory and textual features. All layers but the first (bottom) layers use standard binary units. Gaussian RBM model is used to model the distributions over the visual and auditory features. Replicated Softmax topic model is applied for mining the textual features.

While there have been significant progresses made on the emotion prediction in images [2, 6, 15], previous efforts on video emotion analysis are mainly conducted in movie domain [1, 11, 12, 14]. In these works, a variety of visual and auditory features have been exploited, including low-level features [1, 5] such as HOG (Histogram of Gradients) from visual features and zero-crossing rate from auditory features, and semantic-level features [2, 5, 6] such as concept features from SentiBank [2]. Although jointly using visual and auditory features improves the performance and shows promising results on emotion classification of Hollywood movies [1, 11, 12, 14], little effort has been devoted to learn a joint representation over visual and auditory modalities. In [12], SVM classifiers are trained on the fused feature vectors that concatenate both visual and auditory features. The same early fusion is also adopted in [14], but with Conditional Random Field (CRF) to model the temporal information for classification. In [11], two Baysian classifiers are trained on visual and auditory features separately and the output scores are linearly fused to generate the final prediction. In [1], late fusion is adopted to linearly combine outputs of SVM classifiers. In short, these works adopt either early or

ICMR'15, June 23–26, 2015, Shanghai, China.

http://dx.doi.org/10.1145/2671188.2749400.

late fusion to combine the visual and auditory modalities. A more advanced approach is proposed in [5], where multiple kernels defined for individual features are linearly fused to learn a kernel SVM classifier. We argue that these methods may work well for combining different features in the same modality, but poorly for different modalities. The reason is that different modalities have different kinds of representations and correlational structures, making it difficult for a shallow combination to discover relationships across modalities, especially the highly non-linear relationships [10].

In this paper, we focus on how to learn a joint representation of visual and auditory modalities for emotion prediction. To learn the highly non-linear relationships among different modalities with very different statistical properties, we adopt the Multimodal Deep Boltzmann Machine (DBM) [10]. The learning of DBM is unsupervised and thus is suitable for our case as a plenty of unlabeled video data is available on the Web. Among the user-generated videos, the textual information (e.g., title and description) is somewhat invariant to large changes in the visual and auditory modalities [2]. For example, the videos expressing "joy" emotion range from showing a wedding party with romantic music to recording a single person enjoying delicious food, while the textual information always conveys similar words (i.e., happy night). As discussed in [10], this invariance provides a rich learning signal for mapping the variant visual and auditory features to the coherent concept level features. Hence, we expand the multimodal DBM in [10] from two pathways to three pathways, which includes visual, auditory and textual information as shown in Figure 1. In the model, all layers but the first (bottom) layers are binary-valued. All the modalities are first modeled with a two-layer DBM [8] separately. In this stage, the visual and auditory modalities are modeled with Gaussian Restricted Boltzmann Machines (RBMs) [4], which have been widely used for modeling real-valued inputs for speech and vision tasks, whereas the textual modality is modeled with Replicated Softmax model [9], which has been shown to be effective in modeling sparse word count vectors. An additional layer of binary hidden units is added on top of the final layer of each modality to learn the joint representation over the three modalities.

The main contribution of this work is the learning of a joint representation over multiple modalities using unlabeled user-generated videos on the Web. Basically, this work demonstrates a promising way to make use of the large amount of unlabelled user-generated videos for improving the performance of emotion prediction.

2. MULTIMODAL DEEP BOLTZMANN MACHINE

Let $\mathbf{v}^m \in \mathbb{R}^M$ and $\mathbf{v}^a \in \mathbb{R}^A$ denote the real-valued input from visual and auditory inputs. Meanwhile, $\mathbf{v}^t \in \{1, \ldots, K\}$ denotes associated metadata (i.e., title and description) containing N words, with v_k^t denoting the count for the kth word. In addition, the hidden layers of visual pathway are denoted as $\mathbf{h}^{(1m)} \in \{0,1\}^{F_1^m}$, $\mathbf{h}^{(2m)} \in \{0,1\}^{F_2^m}$. Meanwhile, $\mathbf{h}^{(1a)} \in \{0,1\}^{F_1^a}$, $\mathbf{h}^{(2a)} \in \{0,1\}^{F_2^a}$ are for auditory pathway and $\mathbf{h}^{(1t)} \in \{0,1\}^{F_1^t}$, $\mathbf{h}^{(2t)} \in \{0,1\}^{F_2^t}$ are for textual pathway.

As shown in Figure 1, each modality is first modeled with a separate two-layer DBM [8]. The probability that generates a visible vector $\mathbf{v}_m$ by the visual-pathway DBM with Gaussian RBM [4] is given by

$$P(\mathbf{v}^m;\theta^m) = \frac{1}{\mathcal{Z}(\theta^m)} \sum_{\mathbf{h}^{(1m)},\mathbf{h}^{(2m)}} exp(-E(\mathbf{v}^m, \mathbf{h}^{(1m)}, \mathbf{h}^{(2m)};\theta^m)) \tag{1}$$

where $\mathcal{Z}(\theta^m)$ is the partition function and the free energy E is given by

$$\begin{aligned} E(\mathbf{v}^m, \mathbf{h}^{(1m)}, \mathbf{h}^{(2m)};\theta^m) &= \sum_{i=1}^{M} \frac{(v_{mi} - b_{mi})^2}{2\delta_{mi}^2} \\ - \sum_{i=1}^{M}\sum_{j=1}^{F_1^m} \frac{v_{mi}}{\delta_{mi}} W_{ij}^{(1m)} h_j^{(1m)} &- \sum_{j=1}^{F_1^m}\sum_{l=1}^{F_2^m} h_j^{(1m)} W_{jl}^{(2m)} h_j^{(2m)} \end{aligned} \tag{2}$$

Note that for brevity, the bias terms on the hidden layers are omitted. The probability for an auditory vector $\mathbf{v}_a$ is similar to that of visual-pathway DBM. Here, we only give the formula of free energy E from textual-pathway with Replicated Softmax [9]

$$\begin{aligned} E(\mathbf{v}^t, \mathbf{h}^{(1t)}, \mathbf{h}^{(2t)};\theta^t) &= -\sum_{k=1}^{K} b_k^t v_k^t - \sum_{k=1}^{K}\sum_{j=1}^{F_1^t} W_{k,j}^{(1t)} h_j^{(1t)} v_k^t \\ - \sum_{j=1}^{F_1^t}\sum_{l=1}^{F_2^t} W_{jl}^{(2t)} h_j^{(1t)} h_l^{(2t)} &- N\sum_{j=1}^{F_1^t} b_j^{(1t)} h_j^{(1t)} - \sum_{l=1}^{F_2^t} b_l^{(2t)} h_l^{(2t)} \end{aligned} \tag{3}$$

The multimodal DBM is formed by adding an additional binary-valued layer $\mathbf{h}^{(3)} \in \{0,1\}^{F_3}$ on top of the second hidden layers from different pathways ($\mathbf{h}^{2m}, \mathbf{h}^{2a}, \mathbf{h}^{2t}$). Then, the joint density distribution over the multimodal inputs is given by

$$\begin{aligned} P(\mathbf{v}^m, \mathbf{v}^a, \mathbf{v}^t;\theta) &= \sum_{h^{(2m)},h^{(2a)},h^{(2t)},h^{(3)}} P(h^{(2m)}, h^{(2a)}, h^{(2t)}, h^{(3)}) \\ &(\sum_{h^{(1m)}} P(v^m, h^{(1m)}, h^{(2m)}))(\sum_{h^{(1a)}} P(v^a, h^{(1a)}, h^{(2a)})) \\ &(\sum_{h^{(1t)}} P(v^t, h^{(1t)}, h^{(2t)})) \end{aligned} \tag{4}$$

2.1 Network training

Multiple layers of hidden units and multiple modalities make the learning difficult [10]. Therefore, the learning is split into two stages. First, each RBM component of multimodal DBM is pretrained by using the greedy layerwise pretraining strategy [8]. Then, the learnt parameters are used to initialize the parameters of all layers in multimodal DBM, and the mutlimodal DBM is trained to finetune different modalities in an unified way. As discussed in [3], 1-step contrastive divergence (CD_1) is adopted for pretraining. Meanwhile, persistent contrastive divergence (PCD) is used for the whole multimodal DBM learning, which learns significantly better models than CD_1 but costs more time than CD_1.

2.2 Feature Extraction and Classification

Based on the joint distribution of multimodal DBM (Equation 4), we can easily infer the conditional distribution over the joint representation layer as the final features extracted from the model by logistic function $\sigma(x)$:

$$p(h_p^{(3)} = 1|\mathbf{h}^{(2)}) = \sigma(\sum_{l=1}^{F_2^m} W_{lp}^{(3m)} h_l^{(2m)} + \sum_{l=1}^{F_2^a} W_{lp}^{(3a)} h_l^{(2a)} + \sum_{l=1}^{F_2^t} W_{lp}^{(3t)} h_l^{(2t)} + b_p^{(3)})$$

When extracting the features, we adopt the mean-field update to approximate the true posteriors [8]. Since the multimodal DBM is a fully generative model, we can still generate the joint feature representation even when some modalities are missing by unclamping the missing inputs and updating them after each mean-field update. The inputs are updated based on the conditional distribution as follows:

$$v_i^m|\mathbf{h}^{(1m)} \sim \mathcal{N}(\delta_i \sum_{j=1}^{F_1^m} W_{ij}^{(1m)} h_j^{(1m)} + b_i^m, \delta_i^2)$$

$$v_i^a|\mathbf{h}^{(1a)} \sim \mathcal{N}(\delta_i \sum_{j=1}^{F_1^a} W_{ij}^{(1a)} h_j^{(1a)} + b_i^a, \delta_i^2)$$

$$p(v_{ik}^t = 1|\mathbf{h}^{(1t)}) = \frac{exp(\sum_{j=1}^{F_1^t} h_j^{(1t)} W_{jk}^{(1t)} + b_k^t)}{\sum_{q=1}^{K} exp(\sum_{j=1}^{F_1^t} h_j^{(1t)} * W_{jq}^{1t} + b_k^t)}$$

The multimodal DBM can effectively fill in the missing modalities. The generated modalities can serve as a plausible proxy for extracting the final output joint representation [10].

With the joint representation as feature, emotion prediction models can be easily trained with linear or non-linear classifiers. In this paper, we adopt the standard Gaussian RBF kernel SVM, which shows good classification performance on real-valued features [5]. One-against-all strategy is adopted to train a separate classifier for each emotion category, and a test sample is assigned to the category with the highest prediction score.

3. EXPERIMENTS

3.1 Dataset and Model Learning

The multimodal DBM is trained on 156,219 videos crawled from YouTube. To make sure that the dataset consists of emotion-related videos and has a balanced distribution over all kinds of emotion-related high-level concepts, the Adjective Noun Pairs (ANPs) provided by SentiBank [2] are used as searching keywords. These ANPs are all emotion-related concepts, such as "happy kids" or "creepy spider". In this work, all the 3,244 ANPs are used. For each ANP, at most 100 videos are collected and the duration of each video is limited to 2 minutes since a long video usually has multiple different concepts. We adopt the same visual and audio feature sets used in [5]. The visual features include Dense SIFT, HOG, SSIM, GIST, and LBP. The MFCC and Audio-Six are extracted as audio clues. Among these features, Dense SIFT, HOG, SSIM and MFCC are quantized into a bag-of-words representation. The visual features are extracted using the codes from the authors of [13] and the audio features are extracted using the software by [7]. Finally, the visual and auditory information are represented as 20,651-dimensional and 4,000-dimensional features respectively. By adopting the same features as [5], the effectiveness of the joint representation by multimodal DBM can be more objectively evaluated. In addition to visual and auditory information, we also make use of the textual description associated with videos. Each associated metadata is represented using a vocabulary of the 3,413 most frequent words (whose frequencies are larger than 800). The average number of words associated with a video is 7.13 with a standard deviation of 6.21.

The visual-pathway consists of a Gaussian RBM with 20,651 visible units followed by 2 standard binary-valued layers with 2048 and 1024 hidden units. The auditory-pathway has the same settings as visual-pathway except that the number of visible units is 4,000. Meanwhile, the textual-pathway consists of a Replicated Softmax Model with 3,413 visible units followed by 2 layers of 1,024 hidden units. The joint layer contains 3,072 hidden units. As mentioned in Section 2.1, each pathway is pretrained using a stack of modified RBMs by CD_1 for initializing the DBM model. During pretraining and DBM learning, each dimension of visual and auditory features is mean-centered and normalized to unit variance to avoid the instability problem [3]. In addition, to avoid running separate Markov chains for each word count to get sufficient statistics for model distribution, all word count vectors are scaled so that they sum to 5 [10]. The model is implemented upon the open source tool "deepnet"[1].

Category	$\mathbf{h}^{(1m)}$	$\mathbf{h}^{(2m)}$	$\mathbf{h}^{(3)}$	$\mathbf{h}^{(2a)}$	$\mathbf{h}^{(1a)}$
Anger	0.297	**0.364**	0.294	0.124	0.112
Anticipation	0.040	**0.080**	0.067	0.024	0.034
Disgust	0.228	**0.277**	0.267	0.311	0.145
Fear	0.415	**0.406**	0.395	0.211	0.233
Joy	0.428	0.397	**0.442**	0.291	0.385
Sadness	0.154	0.176	0.217	0.226	**0.235**
Surprise	**0.676**	0.669	0.666	0.665	0.643
Trust	0.093	0.130	**0.136**	0.117	0.077
Overall	0.350	0.360	**0.371**	0.302	0.290

Table 1: Prediction accuracies for each emotion category of VideoEmotion dataset [5] obtained by applying one-vs-all SVM to representations learned at different layers. The highest accuracy of each category is highlighted.

3.2 Classification Performance

The emotion prediction is conducted on VideoEmotion dataset [5], which consists of 1,101 videos and the videos are classified into 8 categories. To measure the effectiveness of DBM, three different combination settings are adopted. Section 3.2.1 shows the performance achieved on combining visual and auditory features. Section 3.2.2 compares the performance of using visual or auditory features to that of using SentiBank [2]. Section 3.2.3 reports the result of combining DBM with [5] by average late fusion.

3.2.1 Multimodal Inputs

Since the associated metadata of each video is not provided in VideoEmotion [5], the input to the textual-pathway in DBM is initialized to zeros. The model is allowed to update the state of the textual input layer when performing mean-field update. In this experiment, we run the mean-field update for 5 times [10]. Table 1 shows the prediction performance for each emotion category. The representations extracted at different layers are used to train the one-vs-all SVM classifiers based on the training data given in [5]. From the table, we can see that the joint representation from joint hidden layer ($\mathbf{h}^{(3)}$) achieves the best performance on the whole dataset, which improves that of the second visual hidden layer and auditory hidden layer by 3.1% and 22.8% respectively. We have also observed that the classifier trained on the representation from the second hidden layer outperforms that from the first hidden layer in both visual and auditory pathways. Although the joint representation does not always achieve the best performance, the performance on joint representation is the most consistent one, which is

[1]https://github.com/nitishsrivastava/deepnet

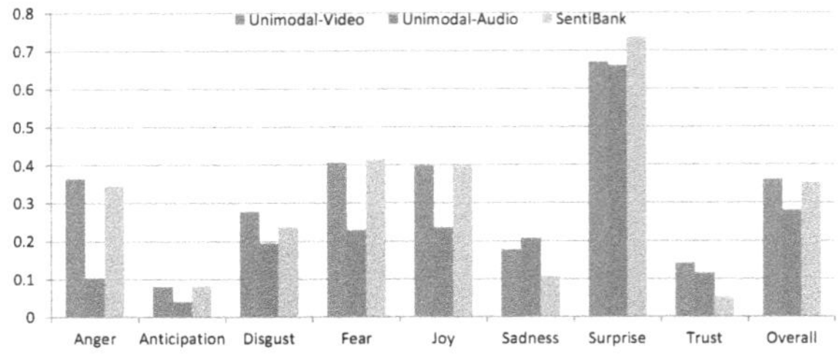

Figure 2: Prediction accuracies. Unimodal-Video and Unimodal-Audio are the classifiers trained on the joint representation generated by using only the visual or auditory information through DBM.

mostly attributed to the well balance over the visual and auditory features in the joint representation.

3.2.2 Unimodal Input

In this section, we want to verify the effectiveness of DBM when some modalities are missing. The method proposed in [2] is a good baseline, which also models the emotion prediction task in a hierarchical way by first training ANP detectors and then training SVM-based emotion classifiers on the responses from ANP detectors. In addition, only visual information is used in [2]. For comparison, we generate the joint representation from DBM by using only visual information (Unimodal-Video) or auditory information (Unimodal-Audio). In Unimodal-Video, the auditory and textual information are initialized with zeros and these information are updated when performing mean-field update. Similarly for the Unimodal-Audio, the visual and textual information are initialized with zeros and updated in the same way. As shown in Figure 2, Unimodal-Video outperforms SentiBank by 2.7%. Unimodal-Video exhibits better performance than SentiBank in 4 categories, especially in those categories where Unimodal-Audio achieves better performance. This shows that the DBM model effectively fills in the missing modalities.

3.2.3 Average Fusion

To see whether DBM model learns unique correlation between visual and auditory information, the prediction scores from DBM and [5] are averagely fused. Generally speaking, the joint representation from DBM can be treated as latent attributes. Therefore, two fusion settings are adopted. First, the DBM score is combined with the prediction score from [5] using only visual and auditory features (V.+Au.+DBM). Second, the DBM score is fused with the score from [5] using visual, auditory and attribute features (V.+Au.+At.+DBM). From the Table 2, we can see that V.+Au.+DBM achieves better performance than both V.+Au. and V.+Au.+At., which indicates that DBM mines more information than the attribute features used in [5]. In addition, we also observe that V.+Au.+At.+DBM improves the accuracy of V.+Au.+At. by 7.7%, which is so far the best reported performance on this dataset to the best of our knowledge. This result basically indicates that the joint representation is complementary to hand-crafted features, by providing additional latent attributes modeling non-linear relationships among different modalities.

4. CONCLUSION

We have presented the learning of joint representation from multiple modalities with DBM. The joint representation has demonstrated the effectiveness of learning unique correlation among different modalities, and being capable of dealing with the problem when some modalities of training or testing examples are missing. Currently, the model still needs hand-crafted features as inputs. We will leverage the strength of RBMs and Convolutional Neural Network to learn features directly from raw inputs in the future.

Category	V.+Au.	V.+Au. +DBM	V.+Au. +At.	V.+Au. +At.+DBM
Anger	**0.549**	0.527	0.527	0.509
Anticipation	0.028	**0.067**	**0.067**	0.034
Disgust	0.399	0.381	**0.438**	0.399
Fear	0.396	0.484	0.471	**0.545**
Joy	0.480	0.557	0.484	**0.590**
Sadness	**0.289**	0.274	0.208	0.217
Surprise	0.746	0.802	0.767	**0.828**
Trust	0.311	**0.327**	0.287	0.312
Overall	0.451	0.484	0.463	**0.499**

Table 2: Prediction accuracies by late fusion with the features from [5]. The notations V., Au., and At. represent visual, auditory and attribute features respectively.

5. ACKNOWLEDGMENTS

The work described in this paper was supported by a grant from the Research Grants Council of the Hong Kong Special Administrative Region, China (CityU 11210514), and a grant from the National Hi-Tech Research and Development Program (863 Program) of China under Grant 2014AA015102. The Tesla K40 used for this research was donated by the NVIDIA Corporation.

6. REFERENCES

[1] Y. Baveye, J.-N. Bettinelli, E. Dellandreá, L. Chen, and C. Chamaret. A large video database for computational models of induced emotion. In *ACII*, 2013.

[2] D. Borth, R. Ji, T. Chen, T. Breuel, and S.-F. Chang. Large-scale visual sentiment ontology and detectors using adjective noun pairs. In *ACM MM*, 2013.

[3] G. Hinton. A practical guide to training restricted boltzmann machines. Technical report, 2010.

[4] G. Hinton and R. Salakhutdinov. Reducing the dimensionality of data with neural networks. *Science*, 313:504 – 507, 2006.

[5] Y.-G. Jiang, B. Xu, and X. Xue. Predicting emotions in user-generated videos. In *AAAI*, 2014.

[6] B. Jou, S. Bhattacharya, and S.-F. Chang. Predicting viewer perceived emotions in animated gifs. In *ACM MM*, 2014.

[7] B. Mathieu, S. Essid, T. Fillon, J. Prado, and G. Richard. Yaafe, an easy to use and efficient audio feature extraction software. In *ISMIR*, 2010.

[8] R. Salakhutdinov and G. Hinton. Deep Boltzmann machines. In *AI Statistics*, 2009.

[9] R. Salakhutdinov and G. Hinton. Replicated softmax: an undirected topic model. In *NIPS*, 2010.

[10] N. Srivastava and R. Salakhutdinov. Multimodal learning with deep boltzmann machines. *JMLR*, 15:2949–2980, 2014.

[11] R. M. Teixeira, T. Yamasaki, and K. Aizawa. Determination of emotional content of video clips by low-level audiovisual features. *Multimed. tools appl.*, pages 1–29, 2011.

[12] H. L. Wang and L.-F. Cheong. Affective understanding in film. *CSVT*, 16(6):689–704, 2006.

[13] J. Xiao, J. Hays, K. A. Ehinger, A. Oliva, and A. Torralba. Sun database: Large-scale scene recognition from abbey to zoo. In *CVPR*, 2010.

[14] M. Xu, C. Xu, X. He, J. S. Jin, S. Luo, and Y. Rui. Hierarchical affective content analysis in arousal and valence dimensions. *Signal Proc.*, 93:2140–2150, 2013.

[15] Q. You, J. Luo, H. Jin, and J. Yang. Robust image sentiment analysis using progressively trained and domain transferred deep networks. In *AAAI*, 2015.

Improving Automatic Name-Face Association using Celebrity Images on the Web

Zhineng Chen[1], Bailan Feng[1], Chong-Wah Ngo[2], Caiyan Jia[3], Xiangsheng Huang[1]
{zhineng.chen, bailan.feng}@ia.ac.cn, cscwngo@cityu.edu.hk, cyjia@bjtu.edu.cn, xiangsheng.huang@ia.ac.cn
[1] Institute of Automation, Chinese Academy of Sciences, Beijing, China
[2] Department of Computer Science, City University of Hong Kong, Hong Kong, China
[3] School of Computer and Information Technology, Beijing Jiaotong University, Beijing, China

ABSTRACT
This paper investigates the task of automatically associating faces appearing in images (or videos) with their names. Our novelty lies in the use of celebrity Web images to facilitate the task. Specifically, we first propose a method named *Image Matching* (IM), which uses the faces in images returned from name queries over an image search engine as the gallery set of the names, and a probe face is classified as one of the names, or none of them, according to their matching scores and compatibility characterized by a proposed *Assigning-Thresholding* (AT) pipeline. Noting IM could provide guidance for association for the well-established *Graph-based Association* (GA), we further propose two methods that jointly utilize the two kinds of complementary cues. They are: the early fusion of IM and GA (EF-IMGA) that takes the IM score as an additional information source to help the association in GA, and the late fusion of IM and GA (LF-IMGA) that combines the scores from both IM and GA obtained individually to make the association. Evaluations on datasets of captioned news images and Web videos both show the proposed methods, especially the two fused ones, provide significant improvements over GA.

Categories and Subject Descriptors
H.3.3 [**Information Storage and Retrieval**]: Information Search and Retrieval

Keywords
name-face association, celebrity image, multimedia fusion.

1. INTRODUCTION
With the overwhelming volume of people-related images and videos available on the Web, the searching and browsing of multimedia archives by person names is becoming increasingly popular to end users. A key issue to enable such services is how to find the images (or videos) regarding to each person. A common technique toward this target is text-based name matching, which associates an image with a particular person if his/her name appears in surrounding context of the image like captions, subtitles, tags, etc.

ICMR'15, June 23 – 26, 2015, Shanghai, China.

http://dx.doi.org/10.1145/2671188.2749401

This technique is efficient as there are huge quantities of multimedia documents appearing together with names. However, this is hard to say as an effective solution, because the appearance of people and their names are not always consistent, or saying, an image with a particular name does not imply the person would appear in it. As a result, the found images could very likely contain many irrelevant results.

Visual-based refinement on the faces extracted from images returned from the name matching is shown to be a useful way to remove irrelevant results. The task is also referred to as name-face association [1-3] in the literature. Over decades many techniques have been proposed for this task in the domains of new videos [4], TV series [5], movies [6-7], news images [2, 3, 8] and Web videos [9-11]. Basically, these techniques differ in the way of how the refinement is formulated, and most of them heavily depend on characteristics of the domains and contextual cues available. Nevertheless, among them the *Graph-based Association* (GA) proposed by Guillaumin *et al.* [2] gives rise to our extra attention. In this work, with the assumption that the faces of a person should exhibit higher visual similarity, the problem of name-face association is converted to identifying densely connected sub-graphs corresponding to the names. The work is appealing for its unsupervised nature, and it is capable of scaling up to large dataset containing many people and faces. However, GA without essential knowledge about people such as how a particular person looks like is somehow difficult and is probably to generate noisy results.

On the other hand, there are studies leveraging online images to disambiguate people. In [9], celebrity face models are learnt by automatically crawling online photos. The Cast2Face approach is proposed in [6], where the movie cast is used to retrieve a set of faces for each actor using Google image search, and then face tracks in the movie are identified as the actor with the lowest reconstruction error under a multi-task joint sparse representation framework. The work by [10] also shows that celebrity faces from Google are useful for face tagging. Celebrity images available online could be seen as vivid cues in understanding people.

In this paper, we study the issue of automatic name-face association by exploiting celebrity images on the Web. To this end, we first propose a method named *Image Matching* (IM) to implement the matching between face and name, where the name is restricted to a few ones that the face is possibly assigned to and is represented by a set of images indexed by Google. To ensure the matching can compatible with common constraints made for name-face association [2-3], a pipeline named *Assigning-Thresholding* (AT) is also proposed. Observing the similarity captured by IM can be viewed as the probability of a probe face belonging to a particular person. It is different with that captured by GA. We further propose to fuse the two kinds of complementary cues to benefit the association. Specifically, we consider both the early and late fusion of IM and GA. The early fusion version, termed as EF-IMGA, takes the IM score as an additional information source, which provides weak supervision could be interpreted as who looks more like the probe face, to help the association in GA. In contrast, the late fusion version, termed as LF-IMGA, directly combines the scores from both IM and GA obtained individually to make the association. We evaluate the proposed three methods on both captioned news images and Web videos. Experimental results show that all the methods improve the performance of name-face association. Moreover, the two fused schemes can surpass the GA results by a large margin under different conditions.

2. THE APPROACH

2.1 Preliminaries

Name-face association can be seen as the following challenge: given an image (or video) dataset with faces and names, establish the latent associations between the faces and names in each image. It is generally seen as a constrained optimization problem, which should satisfies the following constraints: (a) a face can associate with at most one name appearing in its surrounding context, or null if no corresponding name is found (null assignment), and (b) a name can be assigned to at most one face in an image.

Since our work is closely related to the well-established *Graph-based Association* (GA) [2], we first give a short review of the method. Given a set of images with faces and names, GA constructs a similarity graph with all the faces as nodes and visual similarities between faces as weights of edges. The objective is to find all sub-graphs corresponding to the names. In the implementation, each sub-graph is initialized with all faces in images containing a particular name. By doing this the sub-graphs may overlapped and both constraints above are temporarily relaxed. Then, GA optimizes name-face assignments image-by-image, where the similarity between probe face f_i^p and sub-graph S_j corresponding to name n_j, denoted as SGA_{ij}, is computed by

$$SGA_{ij} = \frac{1}{T}\sum_{t=1}^{T} exp(-d^2(\boldsymbol{v}_i^p, \boldsymbol{v}_t^j)/\sigma) \quad (1)$$

where $\boldsymbol{v}_i^p$ and $\boldsymbol{v}_t^j$ are face descriptors of the probe face and the t-th face, i.e., f_t^j, in all T faces of sub-graph S_j, respectively. σ is the heat kernel parameter, $d(\cdot,\cdot)$ is the Euclidean distance.

By using Eq.1, each face is assigned only to the most similar sub-graph. After all images have been optimized, the constraints are correctly enforced. Since sub-graphs are altered in the optimization, recalculation of Eq.1 would generate different similarities thus affects the assignments previously made. This optimization process is repeated iteratively until a fixed number of times are reached or it is converged, i.e., all sub-graphs are not altered in two consecutive iterations. Based on the optimized results, name-face associations are revealed accordingly. Readers are referred to [2] for more details.

2.2 Image Matching

With the observation that face photos of celebrities can be easily searched from the Web, it becomes a feasible way of using celebrity Web faces to distinguish who is destination person from a few candidates without human intervention. Generally, for a probe face f_i^p, let $\mathcal{N} = \{n_1, n_2, \cdots, n_M\}$ be the M candidate names and $\mathcal{F}_j = \{f_1^j, f_2^j, \cdots, f_K^j\}$ be the K faces in the top ranked images returned from Google image search by using n_j as the query. The similarity between probe face f_i^p and name n_j is computed by

$$SIM_{ij} = \min_{1 \le t \le K} \left\| exp(-d^2(\boldsymbol{v}_i^p, \boldsymbol{v}_t^j)/\sigma) \right\| \quad (2)$$

where $\boldsymbol{v}_t^j$ is the face descriptor of the t-th face in $\mathcal{F}_j$, K controls the number of Web faces taken into account and whose influence will be discussed in the experiment section.

Using Eq.2, we obtain the similarity between every probe face and every name. Thus, a naive way to implement the association seems to be assigning name with the highest SIM_{ij} to each face. However, this strategy would violate the common constraints of name-face association, i.e., unable to make the null assignment and assigning a name to more than one face in an image.

To settle the two problems, we propose a 2-step pipeline named *Assigning-Thresholding* (AT). AT first seeks the optimal name-face assignments at image (or video frame) level, and then thresholds on the obtained similarities to decide null assignments. Specifically, in image-level assignment, we firstly collect the n faces and m names corresponding to an image. Secondly, similar to the idea introduced by [2], a bipartite graph with $n + m$ nodes on both sides is constructed to enable matching types of name-face, name-null and face-null. Thirdly, the problem of bipartite graph matching is efficiently solved by applying the Hungarian algorithm on a corresponding cost matrix, from which optimal assignments of the image are derived.

How to set the cost matrix is an essential step to the success of the assignment. In [2], for costs of real name-face pairs, they are set to negative similarity of the name and face, e.g., $-SGA_{ij}$. For costs of those name-null and face-null pairs, the former ones are set to 0 while the latter ones are set to a constant threshold value that serves as the sentinel to null assignments. That is, smaller costs of face-null pairs will generate more number of null assignments. However, as claimed by [3], setting threshold via this way is not intuitive thus increase the difficulty of determining null assignments. Therefore, we keep the costs for real name-face pairs intact and set the costs for name-null and face-null pairs, respectively defined as $cost\_mf$ and $cost\_nf$, to:

$$cost\_mf = -\frac{m \cdot s_{aver}}{2(n+m)} \text{ and } cost\_nf = -\frac{n \cdot s_{aver}}{2(n+m)} \quad (3)$$

where $s_{aver} = \sum_{i=1}^{n}\sum_{j=1}^{m} SIM_{ij}$ is the average IM similarity between the n faces and m names. This setting benefits the assignment from two aspects. First, it takes both the similarity and the distribution of name and face within an image into account. For example, given an image with large m and small n, Eq.3 is more likely to make name null assigned and less likely to make face null assigned, which is in accordance with common sense. Second, by allocating relatively large (negative) costs to those name-null and face-null pairs, the Hungarian algorithm is less likely to assign face and name to null unless the evident is confident enough. Thus in most cases, a face would associate with a name compatible with the constraints, and their similarity, saying SIM_{ij}, can be viewed as confidence of the assignment.

The *Assigning* step does not address the problem of null assignments. We thus further employ a *Thresholding* step to determine whether an assigned name-face pair should be confirmed as a true association or not. Null assignment is declared if the similarity of a name-face pair, i.e., SIM_{ij}, is below an empirically set threshold θ. Preliminary results show that the AT pipeline could lead to 3%-7% improvements over the raw implementation [2].

In IM, an issue worth mentioning is the correctness of the faces in top ranked images from Google. Generally, the correctness is high for well-known celebrities like those in this paper. But the assumption not always holds for less famous celebrities. Thus, we plan to apply some filtering techniques to remove the noisy faces before feeding them into IM. This will be discussed elsewhere.

2.3 EF-IMGA

The similarity captured by IM can be seen as a kind of external information source that tells us how similar a probe face looks like a particular person. In contrast, the similarity captured by GA, e.g., SGA_{ij}, is computed based upon all or a part of faces in images having the name. Compared with SIM_{ij}, SGA_{ij} is more noisy and less supervised especially those obtained from the first few iterations. Motivated by this, we propose to fuse the two kinds of similarities to benefit the association.

We first discuss the early fusion of IM and GA, i.e., EF-IMGA. EF-IMGA takes the IM similarity as an additional source in image-level optimization of GA, aiming at facilitating the name-face assignment. It fuses the two kinds of similarities using:

$$SEF_{ij} = \alpha \cdot SIM_{ij} + (1 - \alpha) \cdot SGA_{ij} \qquad (4)$$

where α is the weight to generate the fused EF score, i.e., SEF_{ij}.

Fusing the IM and GA similarities using Eq.4 would benefit the association as follows. For GA, the incorporated IM similarity would guide the EF score more targeted toward the name should be assigned, by which some assignments made by inaccurate GA scores could be rectified. For IM, taking into account the GA similarity can reduce the bias of external data, as the IM similarity is obtained independent of the images to be associated.

With the EF score obtained by Eq.4, the proposed AT pipeline is applied to produce the association results. Note that the difference of IM and EF-IMGA lies in that EF-IMGA uses SEF_{ij} in Eq.4 rather than SIM_{ij} in Eq.2 to perform the association.

2.4 LF-IMGA

We then discuss the late fusion of IM and GA, i.e., LF-IMGA. In LF-IMGA, IM and GA provide their decisions, namely s_{ij}^{IM} and s_{ij}^{GA}, on every probe face and every probable name individually in advance. The fused LF score, i.e., SLF_{ij}, is then obtained by:

$$SLF_{ij} = \beta \cdot s_{ij}^{IM} + (1 - \beta) \cdot s_{ij}^{GA} \qquad (5)$$

where β is a weight linearly fused the two kinds of scores.

In Eq.5, we set $s_{ij}^{IM} = SIM_{ij}$ as the external Web images remain intact. To set s_{ij}^{GA}, we first use SGA_{ij} derived from Eq.1 plus with our AT pipeline to perform the association. It is an iterative process that ends with partitioning the whole face graph to many sub-graphs. Based on this, s_{ij}^{GA} is obtained by calculating the similarity between probe face f_i^p and sub-graphs S_j. Note that what we interested here is the score rather than the association decision.

Table 1. FP and FA of IM for different *K* at an FR of approximately 0.5 on LYN and WC.

		K=10	*K*=20	*K*=30	*K*=all
LYN	FA	0.5937	0.6062	0.6106	0.6124
	FP	0.7579	0.8045	0.8202	0.8245
WC	FA	0.5831	0.6077	0.6095	0.6097
	FP	0.5738	0.6584	0.6659	0.6684

Note: *K*=all means all faces from the top 64 images are considered.

With the LF score obtained by Eq.5, the proposed AT pipeline is also used to produce the association results. EF-IMGA and LF-IMGA differ in the way of how the GA similarity is calculated and when the two kinds of similarities are combined.

3. EXPERIMENTS

3.1 Dataset and experimental setup

We use two datasets constructed in real life conditions to evaluate the proposed methods. The first one is the *test* set of *Labeled Yahoo! news* (LYN), which has 9,362 captioned news images of the 23 most frequently occurred people and their friends [2]. The dataset contains a total of 14,827 faces and 1,071 different people. The other one is the *core* set of *WebV-Cele* (WC), which contains 3,194 videos with 41,228 faces and 144 celebrity names [11]. The two datasets are of different media types and therefore pose different challenges. Faces in LYN, despite captured "in the wild", are official news pictures that are often sharply focused and in high resolution, which stand for a relative high quality testbed. On the other hand, faces in WC are extracted from Web videos. They are less likely to be captured well and are often with low resolution. They thus stand for a more challenging testbed.

We evaluate the methods using three metrics measured the performance of name-face association at the face level, namely Face Accuracy (FA), Face Precision (FP) and Face Recall (FR). FA is the fraction of correctly associated faces (including null assignments) over all the detected faces. FP is the same as FA, except that null assigned faces are not included for evaluation. FR calculates the fraction of correctly associated faces over all the labeled celebrity faces. In all the experiments, we omit faces that are labeled as "_notaface" (in LYN) or "hard-to-determine" (in WC). As the face descriptor, we use the 1937-dimensional feature vector extracted from 13 facial regions [5].

3.2 Evaluations

3.2.1 *Influence of K in IM*

We first evaluate the influence of *K* in IM. The parameter *K* determines how many faces in top ranked images from Google are evaluated. We set *K* to different numbers (maximal 64). The results are listed in Tab.1. To make the results comparable, we adjust thresholds such that the methods all have an FR of around 0.5.

As can be seen, the performance steadily improves with the increase of *K*, showing that more Web facial images is helpful in characterizing probe faces from both news images and Web videos. We also observe that the results for LYN are significantly better than those for WC. That is in accordance with expected, as matching between image and video face is more challenge than matching within image faces. When *K* reaches to 30, the improvements are marginal. Since the computational cost of IM grows linearly with *K*, we fix $K = 30$ in the following evaluations.

3.2.2 *Sensibility analysis of parameter α and β*

We then analyze the sensibility of parameter α in Eq.4 and β in Eq.5, which are weights in early fusion (EF) and late fusion (LF), respectively. Specifically, we range the parameters from 0 to 1.0 with an increasing step of 0.1. The results are given in Fig.1, where EF-IMGA (LF-IMGA) on both datasets is presented in the left (right) figure. Thresholds are also adjusted such that all results are w.r.t. an FR of around 0.5. It is seen that setting both parameters to 1, i.e., the IM case, perform better than setting them to 0, i.e., the GA case. The optimal performance is achieved by setting both parameters to 0.7 for LYN and 0.6 for WC. In this setting,

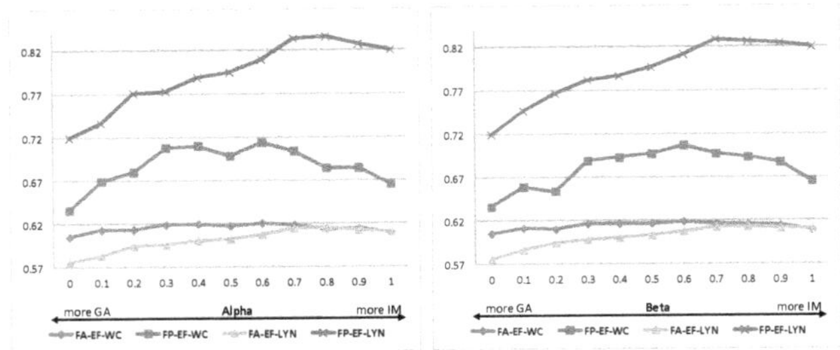

Figure 1: Performance of EF-IMGA and LF-IMGA on both LYN and WC w.r.t. parameters α (left) and β (right).

both EF-IMGA and LF-IMGA perform better than IM on both datasets especially for WC, implying that the name-face association indeed benefits from the fusion of the two kinds of information. The relatively large improvements for EF-IMGA (LF-IMGA) compared with IM on WC are likely to be interpreted as: one on hand, although IM between image and video face are not as straightforward as within image faces, it provides cues that are more different and thus strongly complementary to the cues of GA. On the other hand, the performance of IM on LYN is around 0.82, leaving only a relatively small room to be improved.

3.2.3 Name-face association results

Based on above observations, we compared the proposed IM, EF-IMGA and LF-IMGA with GA [2], to quantitatively analyze the improvements gained by using celebrity images on the Web.

Fig.2 shows FA-FR and FP-FR curves of the four methods on both datasets. The curves are obtained by calculating FA, FP and FR based on different thresholds. The performance of text-based name matching, i.e., FP-Text, is also plotted for reference using horizontal dotted lines. As anticipated, FA-FR curves consistently drop with the growth of FR. However, FP-FR curves experience a first growth and then decline process. This can be explained as the effect of null assignments. When FR is low, many celebrity faces are null assigned because of rigorous set thresholds. The errors are gradually rectified with the growth of FR. When FR becomes high, it causes a new problem of a majority of unknown faces are also assigned with names. Another interesting observation is IM along also performs better than GA even on WC, implying face appearance "in the wild" is so diverse that even IM between heterogeneous domains sounds to be a more stable choice.

We also summarize the results with FRs of around 0.2, 0.5 and 0.8 on both datasets in Tab.2. They are regarded as three typical scenarios of high, middle and low FAs corresponding to applications with different goals. Comparing the two fused methods, EF gives slightly better results in most cases, implying fusing at the feature level, i.e., combining the two kinds of similarity to iteratively guide the name-face assignment in AT, is more reasonable

Table 2. Performance of the four methods w.r.t. different levels of FRs on LYN and WC.

		FA			FP		
		FR=0.2	FR=0.5	FR=0.8	FR=0.2	FR=0.5	FR=0.8
LYN	GA	0.5133	0.5762	0.5587	0.8868	0.7197	0.5836
	IM	0.5168	0.6106	0.6091	0.9121	0.8202	0.6457
	EF	**0.5189**	**0.6151**	**0.6156**	**0.9404**	**0.8359**	**0.6568**
	LF	0.5178	0.6124	0.6123	0.9336	0.8288	0.6525
WC	GA	0.5782	0.6051	0.5446	0.8279	0.6365	0.4884
	IM	0.5781	0.6095	0.5613	0.8510	0.6659	0.5143
	EF	0.5812	**0.6205**	**0.5701**	0.9038	**0.7142**	**0.5278**
	LF	**0.5813**	0.6187	0.5650	**0.9046**	0.7070	0.5190

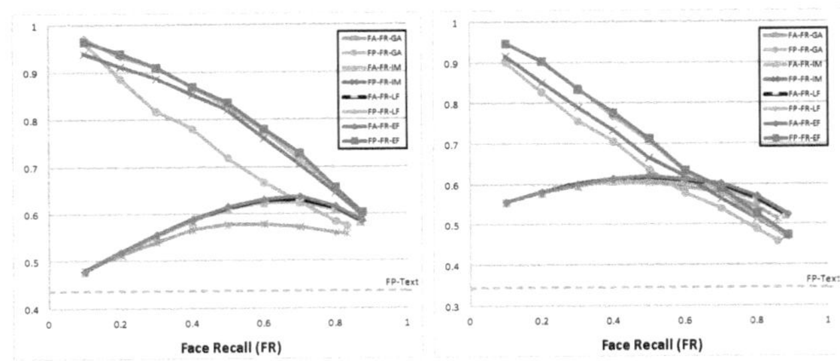

Figure 2: FA-FR and FP-FR curves of GA, IM, EF-IMGA and LF-IMGA on LYN (left) and WC (right).

than at the decision level. It is also observed that the two fused methods perform better than GA by a large margin. For example, by using EF and LF, the maximum improvements on both datasets are up to 10.2% and 9.6% in terms of FA, and 16.1% and 15.2% in terms of FP, respectively. The improvements clearly validate the effectiveness of exploiting celebrity images on the Web.

4. CONCLUSION

We have proposed the IM, EF-IMGA and LF-IMGA methods for automatically associating faces appearing in images (or videos) with their names. The experiments conducted on both LYN and WC datasets basically validate our proposal, from which significant performance improvements are observed when compared with GA. The measurement of the similarity between heterogeneous face and name, though, is limited by the fact that faces "in the wild" are of high diversity. Thus, future work includes the incorporation of more contextual cues to further strengthen the calculation of the name-face similarity. We are also interested in generalizing the methods to dealing with less famous people.

5. ACKNOWLEDGMENTS

The research is supported by the National Natural Science Foundation of China (#61303175, #61272290, #61473030).

6. REFERENCES

[1] T. L. Berg, A. C. Berg, et al, Name and face in the news, IEEE CVPR, pp. 848-854, 2004.

[2] M. Guillaumin, T. Mensink, J. Verbeek, Face recognition from caption-based supervision. Int. J. Comput. Vis., 96(1): 64-82, 2012.

[3] J. Bu, B. Xu, C. Wu, et al, Unsupervised face-name association via commute distance. ACM Multimedia, pp. 219-228, 2012.

[4] S. Satoh, Y. Nakamura, T. Kanade, Name-it: naming and detecting faces in news videos. IEEE MultiMedia, 6(1): 22-35, 1999.

[5] M. Everingham, J. Sivic, A. Zisserman, Hello! my name is ... buffy -- automatic naming of characters in TV videos, In BMVC, pp. 889-908, 2006.

[6] M. Xu, X. Yuan, J. Shen, S. Yan, Cast2Face: character identification in movie with actor-character correspondence. ACM Multimedia, pp. 831-834, 2010.

[7] Y. Zhang, C. Xu, H. Lu, Character identification in feature-length films using global face-name matching. IEEE Trans. on Multimedia, 11(7):1276-1288, 2009.

[8] D. Ozkan, P. Duygulu, Interesting faces: a graph-based approach for finding people in news. Pattern Recognition, 43(5): 1717-1735, 2010.

[9] M. Zhao, J. Yagnik et al, Large-scale learning and recognition of faces in Web videos. IEEE FGR, pp. 1-7, 2008.

[10] Z. Chen, C.W. Ngo, J. Cao, W. Zhang, Community as a connector: associating faces with celebrity names in Web videos. ACM Multimedia, pp. 809-812, 2012.

[11] Z. Chen, C.W. Ngo, W. Zhang, J. Cao, Y. G. Jiang, Name-face association in Web videos: a large-scale dataset, baselines, and open issues. J. Comput. Sci. Technol., 29(5): 785-798, 2014.

End-to-End Photo-Sketch Generation via Fully Convolutional Representation Learning

Liliang Zhang
Sun Yat-sen University
zhangll.level0@gmail.com

Liang Lin *
Sun Yat-sen University
linliang@ieee.org

Xian Wu
Sun Yat-sen University
sysuwuxian@gmail.com

Shengyong Ding
Sun Yat-sen University
marcding@163.com

Lei Zhang
The Hong Kong Polytechnic University
cslzhang@comp.polyu.edu.hk

ABSTRACT

Sketch-based face recognition is an interesting task in vision and multimedia research, yet it is quite challenging due to the great difference between face photos and sketches. In this paper, we propose a novel approach for photo-sketch generation, aiming to automatically transform face photos into detail-preserving personal sketches. Unlike the traditional models synthesizing sketches based on a dictionary of exemplars, we develop a fully convolutional network to learn the end-to-end photo-sketch mapping. Our approach takes whole face photos as inputs and directly generates the corresponding sketch images with efficient inference and learning, in which the architecture is stacked by only convolutional kernels of very small sizes. To well capture the person identity during the photo-sketch transformation, we define our optimization objective in the form of joint generative-discriminative minimization. In particular, a discriminative regularization term is incorporated into the photo-sketch generation, enhancing the discriminability of the generated person sketches against other individuals. Extensive experiments on several standard benchmarks suggest that our approach outperforms other state-of-the-arts in both photo-sketch generation and face sketch verification.

Categories and Subject Descriptors

I.2.10 [ARTIFICIAL INTELLIGENCE]: Vision and Scene Understanding

Keywords

Sketch-photo generation; face verification; neural nets

*Corresponding author is Liang Lin. This work was supported by the Hi-Tech Research and Development Program of China (no.2013AA013801), Guangdong Natural Science Foundation (no.S2013050014548), and the Hong Kong Scholar program.

ICMR'15, June 23–26, 2015, Shanghai, China.

DOI: http://dx.doi.org/10.1145/2671188.2749321.

1. INTRODUCTION

Sketch is an important artistic drawing style and may be the simplest form since it is only composed of lines. An interesting application is searching image databases using free-hand sketch queries [18, 15].

However, drawing a vivid sketch portrait is time consuming even for a skilled artist. Automatic face sketch generation has been studied for a long time and it has many useful applications for digital entertainment [11].

Another important application based on face sketch is to assist law enforcement. Assumed that we need to automatically retrieval a photo from the database for a query image, which help the police to narrow down the suspect quickly. Unfortunately, the photo of the suspect maybe unavailable in most cases. To deal with such a problem, the best substitute available is an artist drawing based on the recollection of an eyewitness.

In this situation, we only focus on sketches without exaggeration, so that the sketch can realistically reflect the real person. Figure 1 shows two samples of photo-sketch pairs in CUHK Face Sketch Database [22].

(a) (b)

Figure 1: Samples of photo-sketch pairs: (a) photos; (b) sketches drawn by artist

Figure 1 indicates the great difference between photos and sketches. Thus, photo based face verification methods cannot be directly applied in this problem. The key to sketch based face verification is to reduce the modality difference between photos and sketches.

One intuitive idea is to recover the photo image from a sketch. However, it's an ill-pose problem because a sketch may lose many informations during the drawing procedure. An alternative way is to generate a pseudo-sketch from a photo, which has been discussed in [20, 12, 22].

The original generation scheme is trying to find a transformation from photos to sketches. Intuitively, it should be a complex nonlinear mapping. Thus, former works like [20, 12, 22, 24, 25, 21, 19] simplify the generation problem to *synthesis* form. The underlying assumption is that, if two photo images (or patches) are similar, their corresponding sketch images (or patches) should also be similar. Thus, if we find out a way to use other photo images (or patches) to synthesize a photo image (or patch), then we can use the corresponding sketch images (or patches) to synthesize its pseudo-sketch.

However, this simplification may has some limitation, especially the scalability. The time cost in synthesis based method grows linearly with the amounts of training data, because it need to use the samples in training set to synthesize a new one.

On the contrary, our method try to *directly* solve the generation problem with an end-to-end model called fully convolutional network (FCN), which can be regarded as a special kind of convolutional neural networks (CNNs). More precisely, FCN is stacked by *only* convolutional layers. It can solve complex nonlinear problem while producing pixel-wise outputs, which is very suitable for the photo-sketch generation problem. Please refer to Figure 2 to get an intuitive idea.

The main contributions of this work are three-folds. First, an end-to-end photo-sketch generation model is studied with a novel architecture of fully convolutional networks, which is original to the best of our knowledge. Second, we present a joint generative-discriminative formulation driving the network optimization, such that the generated face sketches can characterize the person detail as well as the discriminability against other individuals. Third, our system demonstrates superior performances compared with other state-of-the-art approaches on several benchmarks.

Rest of the paper is organized as follows: Section 2 discusses the relative work in photo-sketch synthesis and convolutional neural networks. In Section 3, we will interpret our model and its implementation. In Section 4, extensive experiments suggest that our approach outperforms other state-of-the-art methods on several benchmarks. In Section 5, we draw the conclusion of our work and list some ideas we may adopt in the future.

2. RELATIVE WORK

2.1 Photo-Sketch Synthesis and Recognition

In recent ten years, there has been several works on the topic of photo-sketch synthesis and recognition.

Tang and Wang [20] were the first to address the problem with a significant amount of database. They proposed a synthesis method based on eigen transformation (ET). It was under the assumption that the photo-sketch mapping can be approximated as linear, yet this assumption may be too strong especially when the hair region was included. Then, it used reconstruction error based distance for recognition.

Liu et al. [12] proposed a nonlinear face sketch synthesis method called locally linear embedding (LLE), which can be considered as an improved version of [20]. Instead of modelling the whole image, it applied ET on local patches with overlapping. It adopted a kernel-based nonlinear LDA discriminative classifier for sketch recognition.

Another local-based strategy proposed by Xiao et al. [24] was based on Embedded Hidden Markov model (E-HMM). They transformed the sketches to pseudo-photos and applied eigenface algorithm for recognition.

In [22], Wang and Tang proposed a multiscale Markov Random Fields (MRF) for face photo-sketch synthesis, which can be both applied to photo-to-sketch synthesis and sketch-to-photo synthesis. They evaluated a series of classifiers on the pseudo-images. Random Sample LDA (RS-LDA) performed best among them. Zhang et al. [26] then improved the MRF framework by adding shape priors and descriptors robust to lighting variations.

Most of methods above may lose some vital details, which influenced the visual quality and face recognition performance. Thus, Zhang et al. [25] added a refinement step on existing approaches. They applied a support vector regression (SVR) based model to synthesize the high-frequency information. Similarly, Gao et al. [5] proposed a new method called SNS-SRE with two steps, *i.e.* sparse neighbor selection (SNS) to get an initial estimation and sparse-representation-based enhancement (SRE) for further improvement.

2.2 Pixel-Wise Predections via CNNs

Convolutional neural network (CNN) was widely used in computer vision. Its typical structure contains a series of convolutional and pooling layers as feature extractors, and several full connected layers as classifiers to give prediction. It has achieved great success in large scale object classification, localization and detection [9, 7, 16, 6].

One important application of CNN was to produce dense or even pixel-wise predictions. Sermanet et al. [16] developed a CNN-based framework called OverFeat, which integrated recognition, localization and detection. The key component was a pooling layer with offsets, which can imitate sliding window technique and produce dense outputs in the final layer. A similar idea called spatial pyramid pooling (SPP) was proposed by He et al. [7], which was also modified the last pooling layer. Wang et al. [23] proposed a joint architecture for generic object extraction, and Luo et al. [14] applied a deep decompositional network for pedestrian parsing. Both of them shared an idea, which is adopting a full connected layer on the top of the network to produce a dense prediction. Moreover, patch-by-patch scanning technique on the original image has been studied by Ciresan et al. [1] in neuronal membrane segmentation and Farabet et al. [4] for scene labeling.

Recently, Dong et al. [3] applied CNN for image super-resolution and it can produce a pixel-wise output. They discussed its relationship to sparse-coding-based methods, and concluded that they can use three convolutional layers to simulate the representation-mapping-reconstruction procedure in sparse coding.

Our work was mostly inspired by [3]. We conducted our early experiments via their network and then further improved it. We called it fully convolutional network (FCN, a similar idea was also proposed in [13]), for it only contains convolutional layers and the corresponding activation function, but without any other layers like pooling, full connected, local response normalization (LRN), *etc.* We would further discuss it in Section 3.2.

3. PHOTO-SKETCH GENERATION

3.1 Formulation

In our model, we use two constraints for sketch generation. The first one is the generated sketches should be as close to the ones drawn by artists as possible. This encourages the deep network to learn the sketching skills from the artists. The second one is the generated sketches should be able to facilitate the law enforcement. That is, given a sketch drawn by the artist, it should be able to identify the subject in the photo database. These two constraints are introduced as generative loss and discriminative regularizer in our objective function, which is similar to [2].

Suppose there are N subjects in the training set with each subject containing one photo P_i and one sketch S_i. We use $f(\mathbf{W}, P_i)$ to denote the sketch generated by a fully convolutional network parameterized by $\mathbf{W}$. We define our loss function as follows where L_{gen} and $L_{discrim}$ represent the generative loss and the discriminative regularizer respectively. Here we use α to control the weight of the discriminative regularizer to the overall objective.

$$L(P, S, \mathbf{W}) = L_{gen}(P, S, \mathbf{W}) + \alpha L_{discrim}(P, S, \mathbf{W}) \quad (1)$$

For the generative loss, we use a straight function which is defined as the pixel-wise difference between the ground-truth sketch and the generated one.

$$L_{gen}(P, S, \mathbf{W}) = \frac{1}{N}\sum_{i=1}^{N}(S_i - f(\mathbf{W}, P_i))^2 \quad (2)$$

For the discriminative regularizer, we encourage the drawn sketch of one particular person should be different from the generated sketch of another person as defined by the following function.

$$L_{discrim}(P, S, \mathbf{W}) = \frac{1}{N(N-1)}\sum_{i=1}^{N}\sum_{j=1, j\neq i}^{N}\log\left(1 + \mathrm{e}^{-\frac{(S_i - f(W, P_j))^2}{\lambda}}\right) \quad (3)$$

λ is a parameter used to avoid numeric overflow.

Parameter Optimization Using this model, the learning process is to minimize the loss function $L(P, S, \mathbf{W})$. This is achieved by the standard network propagation algorithm in the batch training manner. More precisely, in each iteration, we randomly select a set of photo-sketch pairs and construct the generative loss items and discriminative regularizer items respectively. In order to derive the gradient with respect to the network parameter $\mathbf{W}$, the key step is to calculate the partial derivative of the loss function with respect to the output (generated sketch) of each photo. As one photo may be involved into several cost items, we need to go through each items to accumulate the derivative with respect to the output. Algorithm 1 gives the details of the learning process.

Algorithm 1 Parameter Optimization

Require:
Training photos $\{P_i\}$ and sketches $\{S_i\}$;
Ensure:
Network Parameters $\mathbf{W}$

```
while t < T do
    t ← t + 1;
    Randomly select a subset of photos and sketches
    {P'_i}, {S'_j} from the training set;
    for all P'_i do
        Do forward propagation to get f(W, P'_i)
    end for
    ΔW = 0
    for all P'_i do
        Calculate the partial derivative with respect to the
        output: ∂L / ∂f(W, P'_i)
        Run backward propagation to obtain the gradient
        with respect to the network parameter: ΔW_i
        Accumulate the gradient: W+ = ΔW_i
    end for
    W^t = W^{t-1} − λ_t ΔW
end while
```

3.2 Fully Convolutional Representation

In this subsection, we will discuss the property of convolutional layers and how they can be cascaded as a pixel-wise fully convolutional representation of an input image.

Composition of Convolutions A typical convolutional layer has K kernels with activation function f can be formulated as

$$y_{ij}^k = f((\mathbf{W}_k * x)_{ij} + b_k) \quad (4)$$

x denotes the input feature maps. $k \in \{1, 2, ..., K\}$ denotes the index of a filter, and $\mathbf{W}_k$ and b_k are the k-th filter weights and bias. y_{ij}^k denotes the element at the coordinate (i, j) on the k-th output feature map.

Equation (4) indicates that the convolutional operation preserves the spatial relationship. What's more, composition of convolutions will not change this property, *i.e.* we can use a stack of convolutional layers to represent a complex nonliear mapping, which can be adopted on an input of arbitrary size, and then produce a corresponding spatial output.

Relationship to the Patch-Wise Representation In Equation (4), a pixel on the output feature map only will be influenced by a *patch* on the input feature map, *i.e.* its receptive field. This property is also maintained under composition of convolutions. Thus, fully convolutional representation on the whole image can be regarded as a *batch* of patch-wise representation on patches of the image. Nevertheless, fully convolutional representation is much more efficient, for the patches overlap significantly (we set stride to 1 in all layers).

Border Effect Trade-Off Convolutional operations will shrink the size of the feature map. For example, if we adopt a (3×3) convolution operator on a (3×3) input, the output size will be shrank to (1×1).

As more convolutional layers stacked up, more shrinks will be accumulated in the outputs. A possible solution is to add proper padding before the convolution operation. But it will bring on *border effects*, which has been claimed in [3].

Thus, in the trade-off, we don't use padding in the convolutional layers during both the training and testing time. Each (155×200) photo image will be shrank to (143×188) in the representation (See Figure 2).

3.3 Implementation

Pre-processing As it is described in [22], all the photos and sketches are translated, rotated, and scaled such that the two eye centers of all the face images are at fixed position in the pre-processing step. This simple geometric nor-

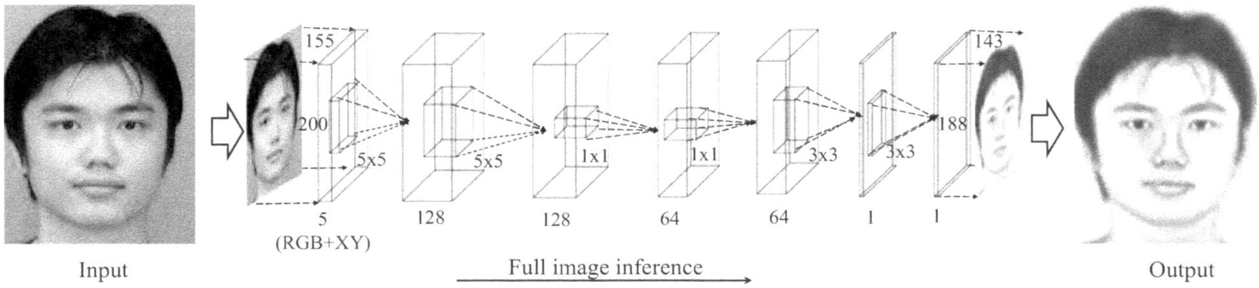

Figure 2: The overview of our model. It takes a full-size photo image as input and directly generates a full-size pseudo-sketch as output. The middle part is the architecture of our fully convolutional network. It contains six convolutional layers, with rectified linear units as activation functions (omitted in the figure).

malization step makes the same face components in different images in roughly alignment.

Another pre-processing step is inspired by the results[1] of [22]. The transformation mentioned above produces a (200×250) image, but it may have some black regions on the border areas. We crop the (155×200) center part of the image in order to exclude this negative influence.

Since we choose to avoid border effects, the sketch images need to be cropped to (143×188) to fit in the network output dimension.

Spatial Patch-wise Learning with Overlapping From the previous works on photo-sketch synthesis[12, 22], patch-wise learning with overlapping is very important to handle the non-linearity between photos and sketches. Intuitively, patches in different positions are diverse from others (*e.g.* eye patches, nose patches and mouth patches). Therefore, learning different patch representations in different spatial positions respectively is a very straightforward idea.

We handle it by adding additional XY channels in the input, *i.e.* the input image data contain five channels, three RGB channels of the photo image, and two channels of the corresponding coordinate (i, j). This tiny modification significantly improves the result, which will be discussed in Section 4.3.

Network Architecture We apply the network proposed in [3] in our early experiments, then we modify its architecture for further enhancement. We borrow the idea in [17], which has a great success in ILSVRC-2014. Their main contribution is to deeper the CNN under computational constraints via very small (3×3) convolutional filters in all layers.

Similarly, we modify the 3 layers network in [3] into a 6 layers network, which is shown in Figure 2. For the (9×9), (1×1), (5×5) convolutional layer in [3], we replace them with two (5×5), (1×1) and (3×3) convolutional layers respectively. Moveover, we double the filter amounts in every layer to improve the network's capacity.

We call it *medium network* due to its size. We have two similar architectures called small network and large network, which will be further discussed in Section 4.3.

Training Details Our results are based on our medium network (See Figure 2). As mentioned above, we first pre-process the photo images into (155×200) and the sketch images into (143×188). The optimization objective has been discussed in Section 3.1. We set λ as 10^9 and set α as 10^4.

We use Caffe [8] for implementation. The filter weights are initialized by drawing randomly from a Gaussian distribution with zero mean and standard deviation 0.01, and the bias are initialized by zero. We set the learning rate as 10^{-11}, then it takes several hours to converge on a NVIDIA Tesla K40 GPU.

4. EXPERIMENTS

We evaluate our model on CHUK student dataset [22]. It includes 188 faces. 88 faces are selected for training and remaining 100 faces are selected for testing. For each face, there is a sketch drawn by the artist and a photo taken in a frontal pose, under normal lighting condition, and with a neural expression.

We mainly do three aspects of experiments, which will be shown in the next three subsections. Section 4.1 will discuss our photo-sketch generation results and comparison with the synthesis based method in [22]. Section 4.2 will show that our generated pseudo-sketches significantly reduce the modality between photos and sketches. Thus they can be adopted to a sketch-based face verification system. Section 4.3 will involve empirical study about our model. Several factors such as network depth and filter numbers will be discussed on the evaluation protocol both qualitatively and quantitatively.

4.1 Face-Sketch Generation

In Figure 3, we show some examples of our generated results and compare them to [22]. For fair comparison, we list all 14 pseudo-sketches which can be found on their website.

Figure 3 indicates that our results contain more vital details. For example, the man in column (e) of the first row has two little locks of hair on his forehead. But this detail is missing in the pseudo-sketch in [22] (in column (g)). On the contrary, our generated result (in column(f)) retains this detail information which may be very important to distinguish this man from others. Another example is the woman in column (a) of the second row. She has a distinctive feature comparing to other persons in the database, for she has two big eyes. Our method can also capture this detail in the pseudo-sketch (in column(b)).

It suggests that synthesis based methods may fail in some cases. The main reason is that they are under an assumption that the synthesized sketch image (or patch) can be recon-

[1] http://www.ee.cuhk.edu.hk/~xgwang/sketch_multiscale.html

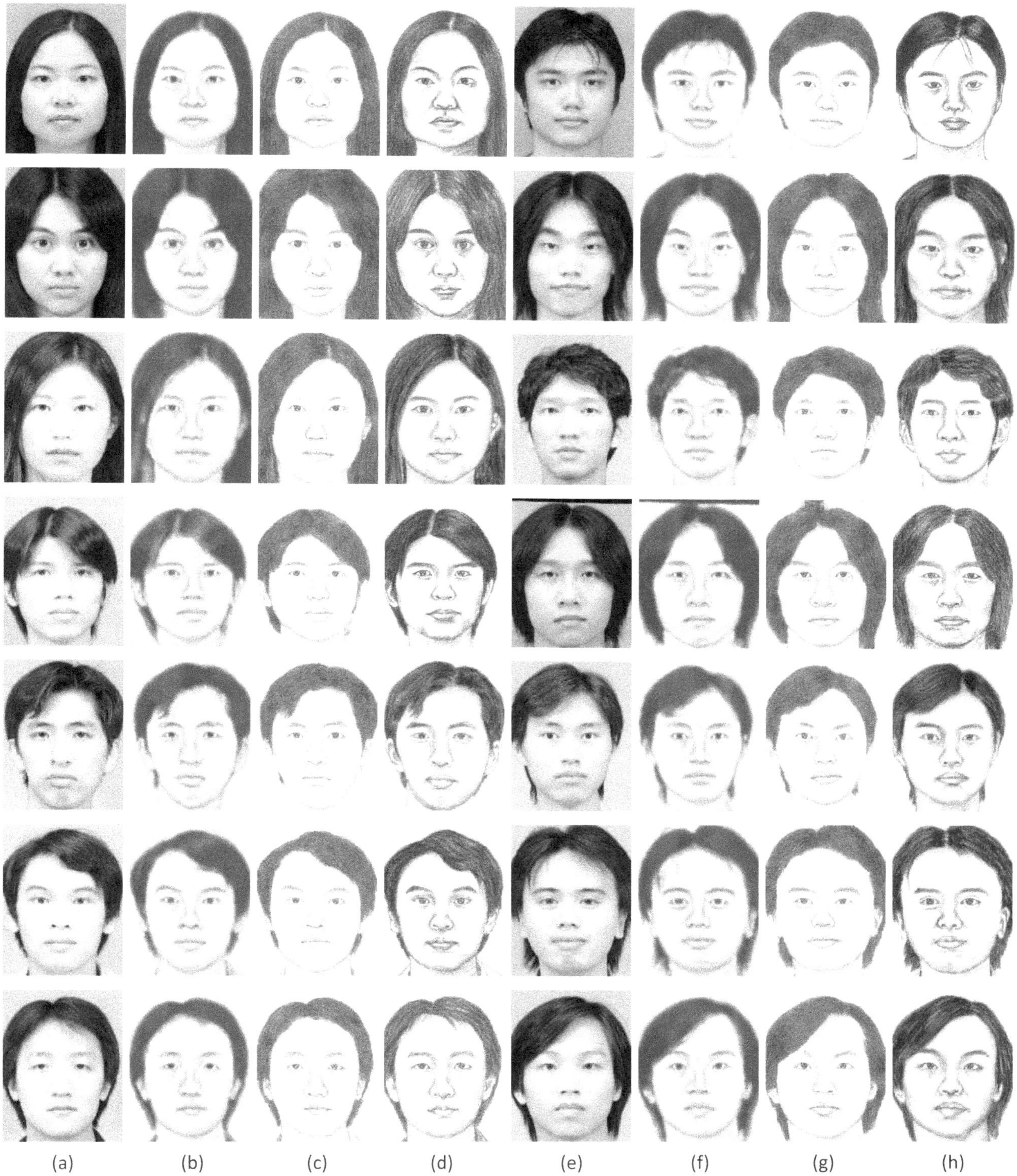

Figure 3: Compared to synthesis based method [22], our generative approach could retain more details in the original photos, *e.g.* the two locks of hair in forehead of the man in column (e) of row 1; the two big eyes of the woman in column (a) of row 2. (a)&(e) photos; (b)&(f) our generative pseudo-sketches; (c)&(g) synthesized pseudo-sketches in [22]; (d)&(h) sketches drawn by the artist.

structed by the sketch images (or patches) in the training set. However, this assumption may be too strong, for some persons have their facial distinctions in fact.

Our generative method overcomes this difficulty. We try to *directly* learn the transformation from photo space to sketch space. Even though it's a complex nonlinear mapping, FCN has the capacity to handle this challenge.

Compared to traditional synthesized method, our novel generative approach has two folds of advantages. Firstly, it could retain more detail information from the photos. Secondly, our inference time is independent on the amount of training data. The time cost in synthesis based method grows linearly with the data amounts, while the runtime of our approach is only affected by the size of the input photo.

4.2 Sketch-Based Face Verification

In this subsection, we will show that our generated pseudo-sketch significantly reduce the modality between photos and sketches. We follow the same testing procedure in [20, 12, 22], which can be concluded in two steps: (a) convert the photos in testing set into corresponding pseudo-sketches; (b) define a feature or transformation to measure the distance between the query sketch and the pseudo-sketches.

In our implementation, we use our model to generate the pseudo-sketches in procedure (a), and use our generative loss (see Equation (2)) as the distance measurement. Since the sizes of our pseudo-sketches are (188×143), we also crop the query sketch into (188×143).

Following the same protocol described in [20], we compare our approach with previous methods on cumulative match score (CMS) in Table 1. CMS measures the percentage of "the correct answer is in the top n matches", where n is called the rank.

As shown in Table 1, we form a baseline experiment, which is to convert the photo into gray scale as somehow "pseudo-sketch" to clarify the modality difference between photo space and sketch space. In this baseline, the accuracy for the first rank only equals to 41%, which is far away from satisfying. In early method like ET described in [20], has got 71% for the top one match. Latter trials in [22], [26], [25] have greatly improved the verification accuracy on top one candidate to 96%, 99% and even 100%.

From the last row in Table 1, our approach also gets 100% correct answer on its first guess. It's worth to notice that our approach is quite different from the former methods, for it applies generation instead of synthesis.

	Rank 1	Rank 3	Rank 5	Rank 10
Baseline	41	56	59	70
ET [20]	71	81	88	96
MRF [22]	96	-	-	100
MRF+ [26]	99	-	-	100
SVR [25]	100	-	-	-
Ours	**100**	**100**	**100**	**100**

Table 1: Cumulative Match Scores (CMS) comparison on full training set (88 photo-sketch pairs). Our method achieves 100% accuracy on the first guess.

Moreover, our generative method is very robust and has excellent generalization ability. In Figure 4, it suggests that our method can using a portion of training data to get a 100% accuracy for the first rank. For example, we only need 5 training samples to get to 95% accuracy, and 27 training samples is enough to get a 100% score for top one candidate.

We also design a verification on our optimization objective on Figure 4. It suggests that the model trained with the discriminative regularizer consistently outperforms the model trained without discriminative regularizer.

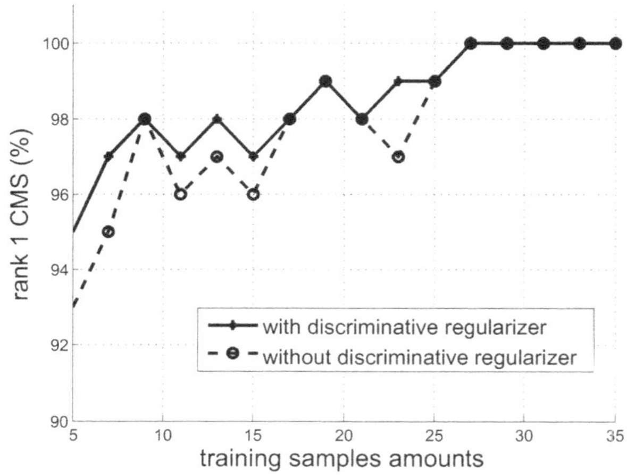

Figure 4: The model trained with discriminative regularizer consistently outperforms the model trained without discriminative regularizer. Both model gets 100% accuracy on rank 1 candidate while involves less than half training samples. *i.e.* 27 samples in 88 photo-sketch pairs.

4.3 Empirical Study

In this subsection, further analyses will be conducted on the factors which affect our photo-sketch generation performance.

Different Network Architectures Our first concern is about the depth of the network and the numbers of filters. We use the network proposed in [3] (we call it SR network) in our early experiments. However, the result is not quite satisfying, for this network seems too small to learn the complex nonlinear mapping from photos to sketches. Thus, we improve the network by: (a) adding more layers to the network; and (b) adding more numbers of filters to each layer.

We conduct our experiments on three different network architectures. Due to their scales, we call them small, medium and large network respectively.

The medium network architecture can be found in Figure 2. The difference between it and SR network please refer to Section 3.3. Moreover, the only difference between our small, medium and large network is their filter numbers. The medium network has two times of filters compared to the small one. And the large network doubles the filter numbers of the medium network.

For comparison, we define a measurement call $MPRL$, which is short for *multiscale pixel-wise reconstruction loss*. It evaluates the pixel-wise accuracy on different scales. To explain $MPRL$, we firstly introduce *pixel-wise reconstruction loss* (PRL) on one photo-sketch pair.

For a photo-sketch pair, we denote the sketch as the ground truth (GT) and generated pseudo-sketch as the prediction

Multiscale Pixel-wise Reconstruction Loss

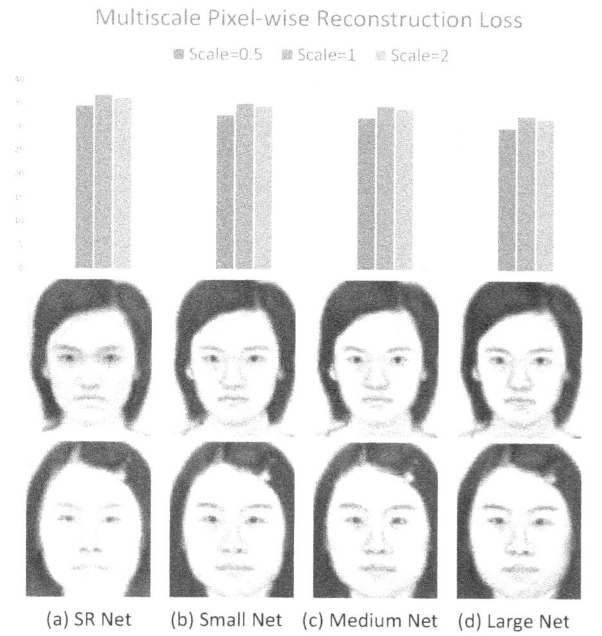

Figure 5: Comparison on the $MPRL$ measurement and generative pseudo-sketches via different network architectures. The model achieves better performance while to deeper the network or to add more filters. (a-d) pseudo-sketches generated via network in [3], our small network, our medium network and our large network.

(P). Both of their sizes are $(W \times H)$. Thus, PRL can be formulated as

$$PRL = \frac{1}{W \times H}\sqrt{\sum_{x=1}^{W}\sum_{y=1}^{H}(GT(x,y) - P(x,y))^2} \quad (5)$$

$MPRL$ is the multiscale version of PRL. In practice, for each photo-sketch pair, we rescale both the GT and the P to three scales $\{0.5, 1, 2\}$ and evaluate their PRL to form the $MPRL$. Then, for the whole test set, we evaluate all the pairs and average their $MPRL$ as the final measurement.

Figure 5 summarizes the results both in qualitative and quantitative. The $MPRL$ of SR network is $\{34.5, 36.8, 36.2\}$. Our small network reduces it to $\{32.6, 35.0, 34.4\}$. Then, our medium and large network get better performance as $\{32.1, 34.6, 34.0\}$ and $\{30.0, 32.5, 31.9\}$.

The pseudo-sketch examples generated by each network are on the bottom part of Figure 5. It suggests that the results of SR network can capture the overall structures, but they are far away from satisfying in details. Then, Our small network's generation is quite better and has clearer contours. Moreover, the pseudo-sketches generated by medium network are more vivid than the small ones. The results of large network are as good as medium ones, but the large network is much more time consuming.

Table 2 shows that our small network is almost as fast as the SR network. The medium network's cost is about 2 times of the small one, and the large network's runtime is about three times of the medium one.

To balance the effectiveness and efficiency, we prefer our medium network as the final choice.

	SR Net	Small Net	Medium Net	Large Net
Time	8.5ms	8.6ms	17.1ms	50.8ms

Table 2: Runtime of single (155×200) image on NVIDIA Tesla K40 GPU

Difference between trained with and without XY channels Now we consider another factor that influences the model's performance. As mentioned above, we add XY channels to the RGB color channels. We assume these additional spatial messages could help the network to distinguish different spatial patches and learning different representation on them.

Similarly, we use $MPRL$ for quantitative measurement and use pseudo-sketch comparison for qualitative analysis. In Figure 6, the left part is for results generated by our medium network but trained without XY channels, and the right part is for results generated by our medium network trained normally. Figure 6 suggests that latter one outperforms former one both in numbers and perception.

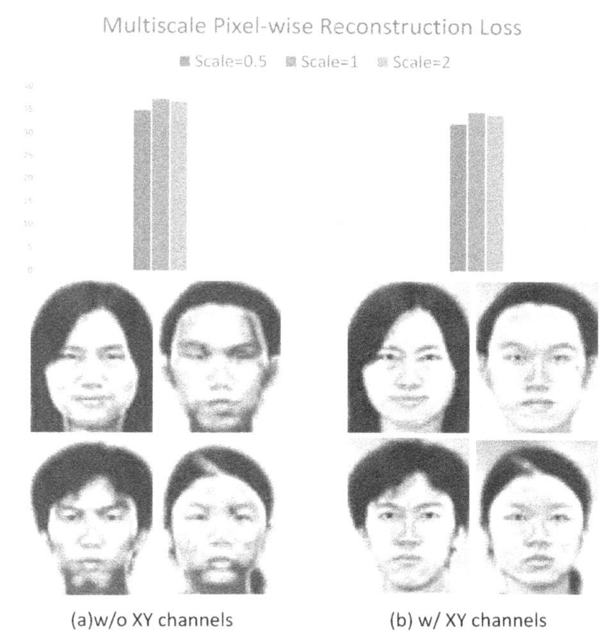

Figure 6: Comparison on the $MPRL$ measurement and generative pseudo-sketches via network trained without and with XY channels. Adding XY channels can make the model more robust. (a) pseudo-sketches generated via network trained without XY channels; (b) pseudo-sketches generated via network trained with XY channels.

5. CONCLUSION AND FUTURE WORK

In this paper, we propose an end-to-end fully convolutional network in order to directly model the complex nonlinear mapping between face photos and sketches. From the experiments, we find out that fully convolutional network is a powerful tool which can handle this difficult problem while providing a pixel-wise prediction both effectively and efficiently.

However, this solution still has some limitations. Firstly, the synthesized pseudo-sketches in [22] have shaper edges and clearer contours than our generated ones. Secondly, the database involved in our experiments only contains Asiatic face images, which may limit the generalization ability of our model to other racial groups.

In future work, we will further improve our loss function and try various databases in our experiments, and we may explore about the relation between our work and those involved with non-photorealistic rendering [10].

Acknowledgements We gratefully acknowledge NVIDIA for GPU donations.

References

[1] D. Ciresan, A. Giusti, L. M. Gambardella, and J. Schmidhuber. Deep neural networks segment neuronal membranes in electron microscopy images. In *Advances in neural information processing systems*, pages 2843–2851, 2012.

[2] S. Ding, L. Lin, G. Wang, and H. Chao. Deep Feature Learning with Relative Distance Comparison for Person Re-identification. *Pattern Recognition*, 2015. doi: 10.1016/j.patcog.2015.04.005.

[3] C. Dong, C. C. Loy, K. He, and X. Tang. Learning a deep convolutional network for image super-resolution. In *Computer Vision–ECCV 2014*, pages 184–199. Springer, 2014.

[4] C. Farabet, C. Couprie, L. Najman, and Y. LeCun. Learning hierarchical features for scene labeling. *Pattern Analysis and Machine Intelligence, IEEE Transactions on*, 35(8):1915–1929, 2013.

[5] X. Gao, N. Wang, D. Tao, and X. Li. Face sketch–photo synthesis and retrieval using sparse representation. *Circuits and Systems for Video Technology, IEEE Transactions on*, 22(8):1213–1226, 2012.

[6] R. Girshick, J. Donahue, T. Darrell, and J. Malik. Rich feature hierarchies for accurate object detection and semantic segmentation. *arXiv preprint arXiv:1311.2524*, 2013.

[7] K. He, X. Zhang, S. Ren, and J. Sun. Spatial pyramid pooling in deep convolutional networks for visual recognition. In *Computer Vision–ECCV 2014*, pages 346–361. Springer, 2014.

[8] Y. Jia, E. Shelhamer, J. Donahue, S. Karayev, J. Long, R. Girshick, S. Guadarrama, and T. Darrell. Caffe: Convolutional architecture for fast feature embedding. *arXiv preprint arXiv:1408.5093*, 2014.

[9] A. Krizhevsky, I. Sutskever, and G. E. Hinton. Imagenet classification with deep convolutional neural networks. In *Advances in neural information processing systems*, pages 1097–1105, 2012.

[10] L. Lin, K. Zeng, Y. Wang, Y.-Q. Xu, and S.-C. Zhu. Video stylization: Painterly rendering and optimization with content extraction. *Circuits and Systems for Video Technology, IEEE Transactions on*, 23(4):577–590, 2013.

[11] J. Liu, Y. Chen, and W. Gao. Mapping learning in eigenspace for harmonious caricature generation. In *Proceedings of the 14th annual ACM international conference on Multimedia*, pages 683–686. ACM, 2006.

[12] Q. Liu, X. Tang, H. Jin, H. Lu, and S. Ma. A nonlinear approach for face sketch synthesis and recognition. In *Computer Vision and Pattern Recognition, 2005. CVPR 2005. IEEE Computer Society Conference on*, volume 1, pages 1005–1010. IEEE, 2005.

[13] J. Long, E. Shelhamer, and T. Darrell. Fully convolutional networks for semantic segmentation. *CVPR (to appear)*, Nov. 2015.

[14] P. Luo, X. Wang, and X. Tang. Pedestrian parsing via deep decompositional network. In *Computer Vision (ICCV), 2013 IEEE International Conference on*, pages 2648–2655. IEEE, 2013.

[15] S. Ren, C. Jin, C. Sun, and Y. Zhang. Sketch-based image retrieval via adaptive weighting. In *Proceedings of International Conference on Multimedia Retrieval*, page 427. ACM, 2014.

[16] P. Sermanet, D. Eigen, X. Zhang, M. Mathieu, R. Fergus, and Y. LeCun. Overfeat: Integrated recognition, localization and detection using convolutional networks. In *International Conference on Learning Representations (ICLR 2014)*. CBLS, April 2014.

[17] K. Simonyan and A. Zisserman. Very deep convolutional networks for large-scale image recognition. *arXiv preprint arXiv:1409.1556*, 2014.

[18] J. R. Smith and S.-F. Chang. Visualseek: a fully automated content-based image query system. In *Proceedings of the fourth ACM international conference on Multimedia*, pages 87–98. ACM, 1997.

[19] Y. Song, L. Bao, Q. Yang, and M.-H. Yang. Real-time exemplar-based face sketch synthesis. In *Proceedings of European Conference on Computer Vision*, pages 800–813, 2014.

[20] X. Tang and X. Wang. Face sketch recognition. *Circuits and Systems for Video Technology, IEEE Transactions on*, 14(1):50–57, 2004.

[21] S. Wang, L. Zhang, L. Y., and Q. Pan. Semi-coupled dictionary learning with applications in image super-resolution and photo-sketch synthesis. In *International Conference on Computer Vision and Pattern Recognition (CVPR)*. IEEE, 2012.

[22] X. Wang and X. Tang. Face photo-sketch synthesis and recognition. *Pattern Analysis and Machine Intelligence, IEEE Transactions on*, 31(11):1955–1967, 2009.

[23] X. Wang, L. Zhang, L. Lin, Z. Liang, and W. Zuo. Deep joint task learning for generic object extraction. In *Advances in Neural Information Processing Systems*, pages 523–531, 2014.

[24] B. Xiao, X. Gao, D. Tao, and X. Li. A new approach for face recognition by sketches in photos. *Signal Processing*, 89(8):1576–1588, 2009.

[25] J. Zhang, N. Wang, X. Gao, D. Tao, and X. Li. Face sketch-photo synthesis based on support vector regression. In *Image Processing (ICIP), 2011 18th IEEE International Conference on*, pages 1125–1128, Sept 2011. doi: 10.1109/ICIP.2011.6115625.

[26] W. Zhang, X. Wang, and X. Tang. Lighting and pose robust face sketch synthesis. In *Computer Vision–ECCV 2010*, pages 420–433. Springer, 2010.

Teaching Video Analytics Based on Student Spatial and Temporal Behavior Mining

Jinxian Qin[1], Yaqian Zhou[2], Hong Lu[1], Heqing Ya[2]
[1]Shanghai Engineering Research Center for Video Technology and System
School of Computer Science, Fudan University, Shanghai, P. R. China
[2]Shanghai Key Laboratory of Intelligent Information Processing
School of Computer Science, Fudan University, Shanghai, P. R. China
{13210240059, zhouyaqian, honglu, 11300240068}@fudan.edu.cn

ABSTRACT

In this paper, we propose to mine the class videos and analyze the behaviors of students to obtain the information on the focus of the students during one class. As a methodological contribution, we investigate face detection, tracking, and verification techniques to measure student engagement from the video records. We also analyze several behaviors of a single student or groups of students, such as temporal behaviors and spatial behaviors. Furthermore, we mine the relationship between students' behaviors and grades throughout the whole semester, including 16 weeks. This work can help teachers to improve the quality of class, find students who tend to get bad grades and give these students timely help. Experimental results on the test videos of different kinds of classes demonstrate the effectiveness of the proposed method.

Figure 1: Class videos used in our research. The videos are from the classes of (a) physics, (b) computer science, (c) Chinese, and (d) morality.

Categories and Subject Descriptors

H.4 [**Information Systems Applications**]: Miscellaneous; D.2.8 [**Software Engineering**]: Metrics—*performance measures*

Keywords

Student Behavior Analysis; Face Detection; Face Tracking; Face Verification; Temporal Behavior; Spatial Behavior

1. INTRODUCTION

With the rapid growth of the online education, it is necessary to track the students' behavior for improving the education quality. Educators' awareness of how students engage in the learning process, how they perform on the assigned learning and assessment tasks, and where they experience difficulties are imperative. Contemporary learning analytics, however, provide rather basic analytics such as simple statistics on technology usage or low-level data on a student's interaction with learning content (e.g., page view).

In-classroom observation is one of the main approaches for learning analytics. Traditional human observation is tedious and incomplete. On the other hand, video based automatic student behavior analytics can overcome the shortcomings of human observation and avoid the bias. It can pay attention to each student and in each moment. In our research, we are specifically interested in investigating the use of video analysis technologies for learning analysis. As shown in Figure 1, video can record students' learning activities, their interactions with learning contents, and other participants of their learning processes. To develop such a learning analytics system, we make use of the face detection, tracking, and verification technologies.

In this paper, we analyze the behaviors of students to obtain the information of the students' focus during one class. For a single student, we detect several behaviors, such as taking notes, and focusing on teacher. For groups of students, we analyze temporal and spatial behaviors and mine the relationship between students' behaviors and the grades. The information can also be served to analyze the teaching style of the teachers and allow them to make better-informed decisions on their instructional strategies. Based on the information, teachers can constantly adapt their courses (both structure and content) to assure students' comprehensibility, high performance, and learning efficiency. On the other hand, based on the analysis of the students' behavior, teachers can classify the students, give different suggestions to students, provide them more suitable learning style and content. Furthermore, combined with the students' period scores of exams, how the learning behavior is related to the student's score can be analyzed. Based on our study, it is the first attempt on this problem.

The paper is organized as follows. Related work is reviewed in Section 2. Section 3 describes the methods used in our system, i.e. the face detection, tracking, and verification, and the behavior

ICMR'15, June 23–26, 2015, Shanghai, China.
Copyright © 2015 ACM 978-1-4503-3274-3/15/06 ...$15.00.
http://dx.doi.org/10.1145/2671188.2749357.

analysis. Section 4 illustrates the experimental results. We finally conclude the paper in Section 5.

2. RELATED WORK

2.1 Teaching Video Analytics

Based on the study, normally the lecture video analysis focuses on the lecture content, such as the teacher's presentation, the content of the teacher's talk, the blackboard content, etc. Specifically, [8] analyzes the blackboard-style lecture videos to help students quickly find a particular concept in the video. These systems are called *NoteVideo* and *NoteVideo+*. The systems first identify the conceptual 'objects' of a blackboard-based video. Then it creates a summarized image of the video and use the image as an in-scene navigation interface. The interface helps users to quickly locate the video frame where the object first appears.

Furthermore, the video content analysis can help users to better understand the teaching content and help to get the summarization information. Specifically, a volume-based interface for video summarization and navigation is presented in [10]. [4] proposes to track and group video features, and further enable interactive manipulation. The applications include film and video editing, visual tagging, and authoring rich media such as hyperlinked video.

In [16], a system which can automatically recognize the positions and identities of the students in classroom is proposed. Specifically, the system recognizes each student, builds the social networks for students, and analyzes the relationship between the students' grades and positions. But no more work has been done for students' behavior analysis.

2.2 Human Behavior Analytics

[11] addresses the problem of automatically detecting participants' influence levels in meetings. It uses camera to record the meeting and machine learning techniques to detect the influence between participants automatically.

Normally high-level activity summarization and context-dependent inactivity detection are important in many applications. [9] introduces a vision system which can automatically give semantic summarization of human activity in home environment. The learned models of spatial context are used in conjunction with a tracker to achieve this goal.

Crowd behavior analysis is a new area of interest in the computer vision research community. [7] proposes a novel method to detect and localize abnormal behaviors in crowd videos using Social Force model. This method can be used in the field of transportation and public safety.

On the other hand, we focus on analyzing the students' behaviors to obtain the class information. Based on our study, it is the first attempt on this problem. We use the techniques related to face detection, tracking, and verification, and we build models of students' behaviors.

2.3 Face Detection, Tracking, and Verification

[5] presents a framework to evaluate object (such as face, text, and vihicle) detection and tracking in a video. In the evaluation of face detection, the baseline methods are the Viola-Jones face detector [15] and the extension by Lienhart and Maydt [6]. Viola's method uses the "integral image" and extracts the Haar-like binary wavelet features to train a cascade of classifiers. The method is one of the milestones in the area of real-time face processing in video. Although the method is effective in detecting frontal-view faces, the tilted or occluded faces are hard to detect. Other detection difficulties include head pose variation, light variation, etc. [13] proposes to use the skin-color probability to model the face color. Then heuristic rule is proposed for face-ratio analysis. Bayesian cost analysis is used for classification. And the classification result is used for face detection and tracking.

Face tracking is important for different applications. Some applications need to track the face location information. Others need to track the facial muscle movements. [17] surveys the object tracking methods. Based on the description models, the tracking methods can be grouped into point tracking, kernel tracking, and silhouette tracking methods. And based on properties, the tracking methods can be grouped into feature-based, template-based, and optical-flow methods. The commonly used methods include CamShift [2], optical-flow, and particle filter.

Face verification aims to determine whether two given faces refer to the same person. We use face verification method to recognize students in different classes. Thus we can analyze their behaviors, and further analyze the relationship between their behaviors with the grades. [18] proposes a collaborative approach to improve the performance of face verification and human attribute learning. [12] proposes a novel Expanded Parts based Metric Learning (EPML) model for face verification. The model is able to mine the discriminative regions at the right locations and scales. Thus this method performs well in the presence of occlusions.

3. METHOD

Our goal is to track and analyze the students' behavior. One possible solution is to use the camera and detect students from the video to analyze their behavior patterns. Though numerous methods have been proposed for human detection, face detection, and face verification, using these methods in class analysis has not been investigated systematically and remains a relatively unknown area.

In the remainder of this section, we first define the students' behaviors, then describe the methods for face detection, tracking and verification, and show the method to analyze the students' behaviors from class videos. Figure 2 shows overview of the method in this paper.

3.1 Single Student's Behaviors

It is meaningful to analyze the behaviors of a single student. The analysis result can be used to rate this student's performance in class, and make teacher's management more efficient.

For one student, we can define the student's behaviors as follows.

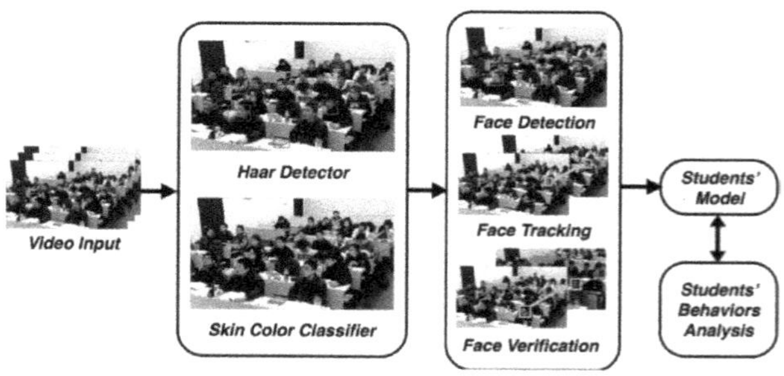

Figure 2: Method overview. The input of the system is the class video. We propose a detection method which combines haar detector and skin color classifier. With the help of face tracking and verification method, we can obtain each student's location and states. We use these information to analyze several behaviors of students.

3.1.1 *Focusing on the blackboard or teacher*

Normally, students spend most of the class time looking at blackboard or teacher. The most significant characteristic is that students raise their heads for a long time, with little pose change.

3.1.2 *Taking notes*

Some students have the habit of taking notes. This behavior can be detected by the frequency of raising head. A student is busy taking notes shows a high frequency of raising head in a short period of time.

3.1.3 *Others*

Students also have other behaviors, such as reading books, using computers, chatting with others, etc. These behaviors can be grouped into one class since it indicates that the student is not concentrated on the class content. Moreover, these behaviors show the same property that we can not detect the student's frontal face. Furthermore, we use more complicated methods to identify whether a student is studying or not, and mine the student's learning patterns.

3.2 Groups of Students' Behaviors

Besides analysis on one student, it is also important to define behaviors of a group of student. These behaviors are valuable since it can demonstrate the teaching style. We define the behaviors of a group of students as below.

3.2.1 *Groups of Students in Different Times*

Students' behaviors in 5-minute at the beginning of class may be totally different from the behaviors at the end of class. To analyze this temporal information of group of students' behaviors is crucial. This information can let teachers know when students are less concentrated, and help teachers to find ways to attract students' attention.

3.2.2 *Groups of Students at Different Spaces*

Except the temporal information, we also mine the spatial information of groups of students. For instance, students sitting in the front rows may show different behaviors with students in the back rows of the classroom. Normally students sitting in the front rows are more concentrated on the class.

3.3 Face Detection

In order to analyze students' behaviors, we need first detect students. Since in most classes all students are seated, methods such as human detection using the whole body information do not work effectively. With an appropriate position of camera, we can see all students' faces. Thus we use face detection method to detect students.

If a student's face can be detected, the system will consider this student raises his/her head. Otherwise, this student lowers his/her head. Figure 3 presents the proposed face detection method and the result.

3.3.1 *The Viola-Jones Face Detector*

As we can see in Figure 3(a), over 80 students are in the camera view. Subject to camera's resolution, each student only shows a very small view, especially for those students sitting in the back rows of the classroom. In this situation, we perform the basic and effective method proposed by Viola and Jones [15] and the extension of Lienhart and Maydt [6] for face detection.

Figure 3(c) shows the result of Viola's face detection method. We can figure out that Viola's method can not take full advantage of the temporal information of the video. Further results show that

Figure 3: Face detection method. (a) The source input frame. (b) Hand-labeled ground truth, green rectangles indicate the raised heads. (c) The result of Viola's method. (d) The result of proposed skin color classifier, skin color pixels are painted with red color. (e) Using color classifier to verify the detected face areas by Viola's method. (f) Using color classifier to verify the unfound face areas in model, green rectangles with blue pixels are those areas not found by Viola's method, but treat as face areas by proposed method, which use temporal information to enhance the performance.

it can obtain satisfactory detection performance with frontal faces, and some side-view faces can not be detected. This drawback will have impact on the analysis result of student's behaviors.

3.3.2 *Skin Color Based Classifier*

From Figure 3(c) and Figure 5, we can find that though Viola's method is failed to detect some faces, there are a lot of pixels having the skin color. Then we can build a classifier based on skin color for each pixel, and use the model to identify whether this area is a face area or not. In the training phase, some skin pixels and non-skin pixels are used as training data. RGB values of these pixels' are used as color feature. Support Vector Machine (SVM) [14] is used as classifier due to its efficacy.

Figure 3(d) shows the detection result by using skin color. In the figure, Red represents that the pixel is classified as skin. We can see that though most face areas are detected, the false alarm rate is still high. It is because that the colors of other body parts such as the neck and arms are similar to the color of the face.

3.3.3 *Proposed Detection Method*

From what has been discussed above, we can see that Viola's method is effective, but it can not handle video very well. Skin color based method can detect almost all face areas in video but the false alarm rate is high.

In our system, to take advantage of temporal information, we propose a detection method which combines Viola's method and skin color based classifier. The details are described as below.

For each video, our system builds a face detection model M. The possible positions and stages of each student's face are stored in M. At the beginning of the video, M is initialized as an empty set. Suppose at a certain frame, we have n students detected and saved in model M, i.e.

$$M = \{f_{M1}, f_{M2}, \ldots, f_{Mn}\} \quad (1)$$

where, f_{Mk} means the face of kth student in model M. For each input frame in the video, we first reset all face areas' states as not found in M. Then we use Viola's method to detect faces and skin color based method to classify each pixel. The result of Viola's method is the set of detected face areas, denoted as F_V, and the result of skin color based method is the set of all face color pixels, denoted as P_C.

For each detected face area $f_V \in F_V$, we use the skin color classification result to verify whether it contains a face or not.

$$\begin{cases} \text{face area}, & R(f_V) \geq T_L \\ \text{non-face area}, & R(f_V) < T_L \end{cases} \quad (2)$$

where,

$$R(f_V) = \frac{\sharp\{p|p \in f_V \cap P_C\}}{\sharp\{p|p \in f_V\}} \quad (3)$$

is the ratio of number of pixels verified by the color classifier in detected face area f_V and the number of pixels of f_V. p is the pixels in the face area, and T_L the threshold to determine whether this area contains a face or not.

The face areas are used to update the model M's corresponding face areas. The update strategy is as below:

- If there is no corresponding face area in M, add f_V to M as a new face area.
- If there is a corresponding face area $f_M \in M$, replace f_M with f_V, and mark its state as found.

The detection result is shown in Figure 3(e). Compared with the ground truth in Figure 3(b), we can see that there are some face areas not found. Two possible reasons can cause these areas not found: one is these student lower their head, the other is Viola's method failed to detect these faces. So we need to verify the not found face areas in model M, denoted as M^*. For each not found face area $f_{M^*} \in M^*$, but it appears in the previous frames, we use the classification result again to verify it, and mark those face areas as found.

$$\begin{cases} \text{face area}, & R(f_{M^*}) \geq T_H \\ \text{non-face area}, & R(f_{M^*}) < T_H \end{cases} \quad (4)$$

where the threshold T_H is different from Equation (2). If the skin color based classifier is of high accuracy, this threshold can be set to 0.8 or higher. In our experiments, we set T_L to 0.4 and T_H to 0.7 based on our empirical study.

3.4 Face Tracking

To detect each student and analyze one's behaviors, tracking methods are used in the system. We need to find out the correspondence between the detected face areas in current frame and face areas in previous frames. In our system, previous frames' face areas are saved in face detection model M.

For each input frame, F_N is the set of all detected face areas in current frame, and F_M is the set of all face areas exist in the model M. Each face area $f_{N_i} \in F_N$ gives each face area $f_{M_j} \in F_M$ a vote v_{ij}:

$$v_{ij} = \frac{I_{ij}^2}{S_i S_j} \quad (5)$$

where I_{ij} is the intersection area of S_i and S_j, S_i and S_j are the areas of f_{N_i} and f_{M_j}, respectively.

Then, for each face area $f_{M_j} \in F_M$, we find the best matching face area $f_{N_{best}} \in F_N$ to update f_{M_j}:

$$f_{N_{best}} = \arg\max_{f_{N_i} \in F_N} \{w_{ij}v_{ij} | w_{ij}v_{ij} \geq T\} \quad (6)$$

where w_{ij} is the weight for vote v_{ij}, T the threshold to exclude the weighted votes which are too small.

Weight w_{ij} is introduced to make sure closed face areas do not disturb each other. It can be set on the similarity of visual features of face areas. In our experiments, we first resize the face areas of f_{M_j} and f_{N_i} into the same scale of 40×40 and then compute the summation of similarity of pixel's RGB value as the weight. Threshold T is used to exclude the impossible weighted votes. If f_{M_j} does not get any possible weighted vote, it means f_{M_j} disappears in the current frame.

Finally, if f_{M_j} does not match any face area in model M, it means this area is detected for the first time. We need to add it to model M as a new face area.

3.5 Face Verification

It is challenging to identify each student in the class videos, since the students in back rows show small face areas. With the help of the tracking method, we can have many face images during the entire class. It can resolve the problems of lowing face. We select the raised front faces of one person for face verification. Low level features such as histogram of gradient (HOG) [3], local binary pattern (LBP) [1], and color histogram in HSV color space are used to represent face areas. Principal component analysis (PCA) is used to reduce the dimension of the features. SVM is used as the classifier to compare the two face area sets for face verification.

3.6 Behavior Analysis

In previous sections, we define the behaviors of students and the methods to detect, track and recognize faces. In this section, we present how to use the proposed method to analyze students' behaviors.

For single student's behaviors, our system has saved each student's state (head raised or not) in model M for each frame. If one student is kept looking at blackboard or teacher, the method will detect his/her face in continuous frames for a long time. If this student is taking notes, the frequency of raising head is high in a short time. Otherwise the system can not detect this student's face for a long time. Then we can believe this student is not concentrated on the class content.

For groups of students, our system collects the behaviors of every student in the group, obtain the statistics information, and compare the differences between different groups. To analyze the groups' behaviors at different times, we divide the model into several segments based on class time (for example, 0-5 minutes, ..., 40-45 minutes). To analyze the groups' behaviors at different spaces, we divide the students into several groups based on their locations (for example, the front three rows, the back five rows, etc). In different segments, we calculate the number of students whose head is raised in each frame x, denoted as $N(x)$, then analyze some statistics of $N(x)$, such as mean, variance, sharp change positions, etc. We use this information to compare with other groups' behaviors information.

4. EXPERIMENT

In this section, we describe the experiments performed. First, the experimental datasets is described. Then the face detection, tracking, and verification methods are evaluated. Finally, the student behavior analysis results are presented.

Figure 4: Physics class videos cover the whole semester. (a) is captured in week 4 (18 Mar., 2014), (b) in week 9, (c) in week 12, and (d) in week 16.

Class	# of videos	Resolution	Length (min)	# of students
Physics	16	1024*576	46	28
Computer Science	1	720*576	45	16
Chinese	1	1024*576	93	49
Morality	1	1920*1080	102	83

Table 1: Class videos used in the experiment.

4.1 Datasets

In our experiment, we use 19 videos from 4 different classes to evaluate the proposed method. Among them, 16 videos are from physics class. These videos cover the whole semester. Some sample images of the physics class are shown in Figure 4. As shown in Figure 1, the other videos are from classes of computer science, Chinese, and morality. The statistics information of the videos are given in Table 1. It can be observed that there are a large number of students in the videos. Specifically, in morality class video, there are 83 students. It makes the analysis challenging since some faces appearing in the back rows of the classroom are small.

4.2 Face Detection, Tracking, and Verification Experiment

The experimental results of face detection and tracking method are shown in Figure 5. Since our aim is to study the students' behaviors, and limited to the amount of the dataset, we use first 5-minute video to train the optimal parameters of our system for each class. This is also a more efficient way to annotate all the video material.

Figure 5(b) shows that Viola-Jones face detector can detect 6 face areas, and the ground truth of faces is 10 face areas. Our proposed method can detect 9 face areas, as shown in Figure 5(d). Three new green rectangles with blue pixels are not detected by Viola's method since they are tilted or occluded. These faces are further detected by incorporating temporal information. The remaining one undetected face area is due to that it has not been detected by Viola's method and not stored in our model. Once it is detected, the model can store this area and detect it using skin color classifier in the following frames.

Another drawback of Viola's method is that it is also has some false alarms of non-face areas. These areas are corrected by using the skin color based classifier as shown in Figure 5(c).

Figure 5: Experimental result of face detection and tracking methods. (a) The source input frame, the ground truth of the face is labeled by green rectangle. (b) The result of Viola's method. (c) Using color-based classification to verify the face areas detected by Viola's method. (d) Using color-based classifier to track the missed face areas. The green rectangle pointed by red arrow in (b) shows that Viola's method detects a non-face area as a face area.

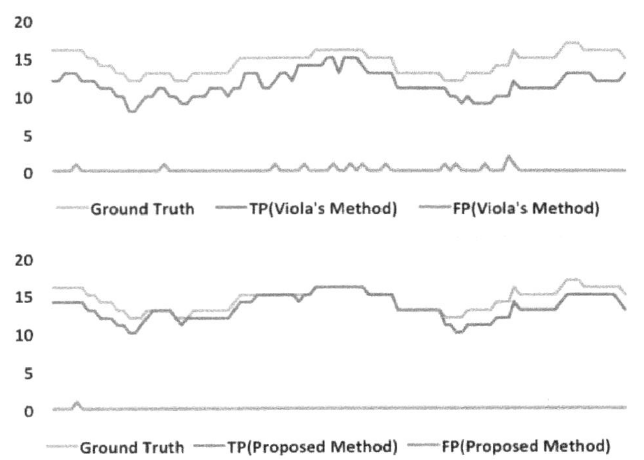

Figure 6: Experimental results of Viola's method and the proposed method on 100 frames. Hand-labeled ground truth is illustrated by green line. Blue line is the TP result. Red line is the FP result.

A more detail performance comparison is shown in Figure 6. The metrics used are true positive (TP), which estimates the number of correct detections, and false positive (FP), which estimates the number of false alarms. We can observe that the proposed method can obtain better performance.

The experimental results of face verification are shown in Figure 7. It can be observed that face verification can help us to recognize students in different videos.

4.3 Behavior Analysis Experiment

Based on face detection, tracking, and verification, we can obtain each student's behaviors throughout the semester, and further mine the relationship between behaviors and grades.

Figure 7: Experimental result of face verification method. Left image and Right image are captured in different weeks of physics class. The corresponding faces in different videos are connected by green arrows.

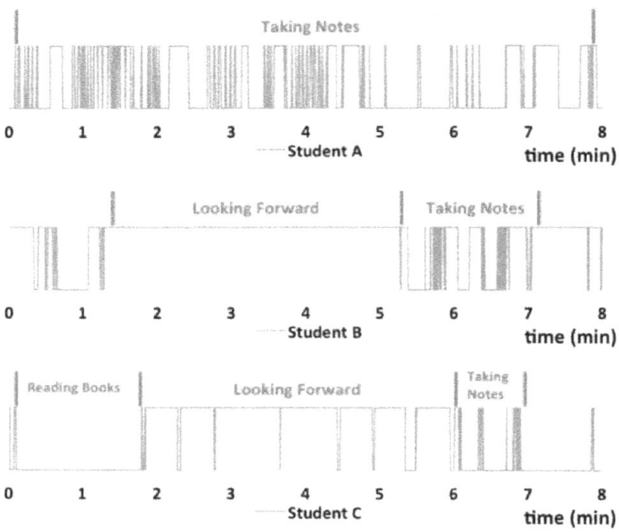

Figure 8: Line chart for three students' behavior analysis on 8-minute period. Time is on the horizontal axis and the head's state on the vertical one. The blue line on the bottom means the student lower his/her head. Otherwise, the student keeps raising the head. The text indicates the behavior analysis result. The red lines indicate the beginning time and end time of different behaviors.

4.3.1 *Experiment on Single Student's Behavior*

Figure 8 shows the analysis result for three students' behavior in an 8 minutes period of physics class. From the result we can find that different students show different behavior patterns. Student 1 is taking notes, and the result shows a very high frequency of raising head. But the total time of raising head of Student 1 is relatively low, i.e. less than 3 minutes. At the same time, student 2 looks forward for a long time. For time periods of minute 5 to minute 7, he starts to take notes. Student 3 lowers his head from about minute 0 to minute 2, looks at blackboard from minute 2 to minute 6, and takes notes from minute 6 to minute 7.

4.3.2 *Experiment on Groups of Students' Temporal Behaviors*

Besides research on a single student, we explore the temporal and spatial behaviors of groups of students in morality class. Figure 9 shows the behaviors of all students in different times of classes. We select three typical periods, the beginning of class, the middle of class, and the end of class. Each period contains 5 minutes.

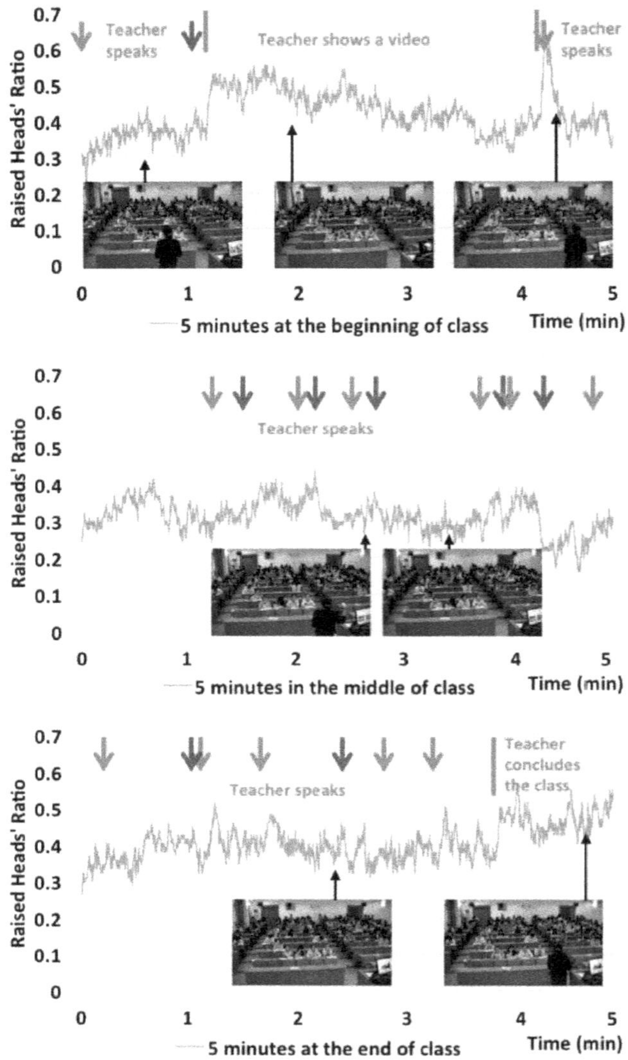

Figure 9: Line chart for three groups of students' temporal behavior analysis on 5-minute video of morality class. Time on the horizontal axis. The ratio between the number of raising heads and the number of students is on the vertical axis. The red arrow indicates the time slot when the teacher walks towards the student. The blue arrow indicates the time slot when the teacher steps back. The teacher's behaviors are labeled according to the video content.

From the result we can observe that most students are normally concentrated on the class content at the beginning of class. Teacher's showing videos and walking forward can attract the students' attention significantly. In the middle of class, lots of students lose their attention to class content and lower their heads to do other things. It can be suggested it is a good time to do something to draw students' attention, such as showing videos, playing jokes, etc.

4.3.3 *Experiment on Groups of Students' Spatial Behaviors*

To analyze students' spatial behaviors, we divide all the students in morality class into three groups based on their locations, i.e. in

Group	# of students	# of detected students	Rows
Group 1	12	12	1-3
Group 2	25	24	4-6
Group 3	46	42	7-10

Table 2: Statistics information of three groups of students.

front, middle, and back of the classroom. The statistics information of the three groups of students is given in Table 2.

We use a 5-minute video to analyze each group's behaviors. The analysis result is shown in Figure 10.

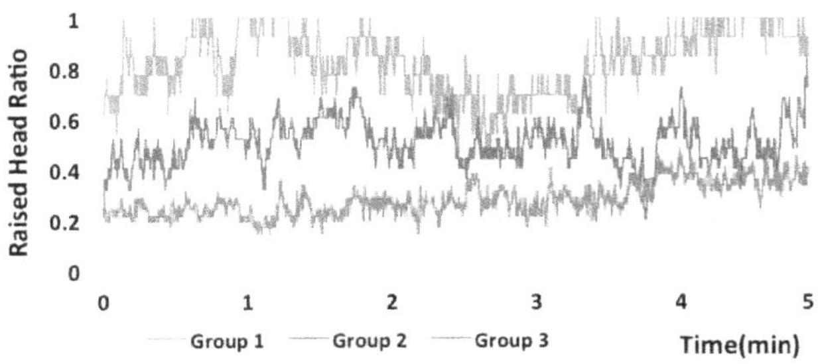

Figure 10: Line chart for groups' spatial behaviors. Time is on the horizontal axis and head's state on the vertical one.

From the result we can figure out that:

- Students sitting in the front rows are more concentrated on the class content. Almost all students in this group keep raising their heads.
- Most students sitting in the back rows do their own jobs. Near 20% students raise their heads.
- Students sitting in the front rows show more attention than others. It can be observed that the green line fluctuates much and the red line only changes in a small range.

4.3.4 *Experiment on the Relationship between Positions and Grades*

We also analyze the relationship between students' positions and their grades in physics class throughout the whole semester. We select 14 students to track, recognize, and analyze. Figure 11 is the scatter plot of the students' grade points with their seat rows. The Pearson Correlation Coefficient is -0.6. It shows a strong correlation between positions of the students' with their scores. Specifically, students sitting in the front rows generally obtain a good score.

4.3.5 *Experiment on the Relationship between Raising Heads and Grades*

We analyze the relationship between students' behaviors and their grades in physics class throughout the whole semester. In this analysis, we focus on three aspects of students' behaviors: the total time of raising head, the frequency of raising head, and the interval between two raising head events. The analysis result is shown in Figure 12. It can be observed from Figure 12 that:

- Best students (grade A) are more concentrated on the class. Their total time of raising head is rather high. At the same time, their frequency of raising head is relatively low. We can draw the conclusion that they spend more time on looking at blackboard, listening to teacher, and thinking. From the long average length of raising head intervals, we can infer that they only write necessary notes.
- Underachievers (grade D/F) raise their head frequently. If students can not get the teacher's point, they will be more and more anxious. Therefore, they will blindly take notes but spend little time thinking, leading to more confusion, which is a vicious circle.

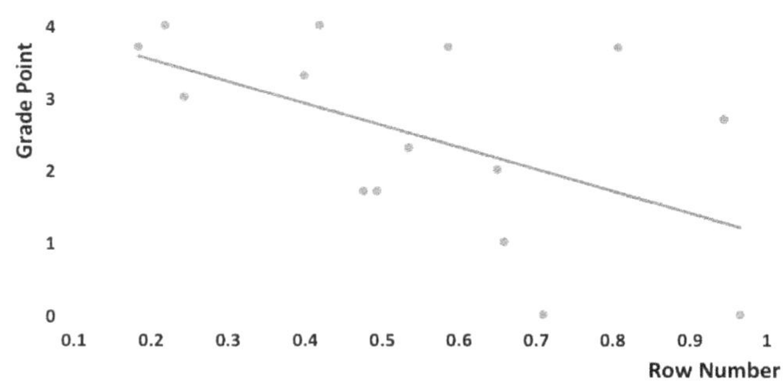

Figure 11: The relationship between students' positions and their grades. The row number is on the horizontal axis. It is normalized and row 0 is the front row. The grade point is on the vertical axis. The best grade point is 4. The line shows the fitting result.

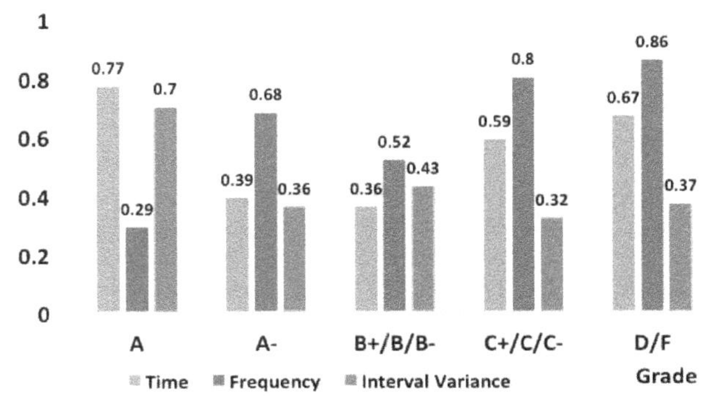

Figure 12: The relationship between students' behaviors and their grades. Final grade is on the horizontal axis. The normalized raising head time (Time), frequency of raising heads (Frequency), and the variance of time between two raising head events (Interval Variance) are on the vertical axis.

4.3.6 *Experiment on Student Clusters and Grades*

To analyze whether students with the same grade tends to sit together, we use the position of face areas to find the closest students and compare their grades. The average of the differences in grade point and the percentage of students whose spatially near neighbors' grade is only one level above or below (i.e. difference of grade point is less than or equal to 0.4) are compared with the case of randomly generated seating chart. Table 3 shows the value of the average difference in grade point and the percentage of students having small difference in score with their neighbors. It can be observed that the average difference of Grade Point is lower than the

	Average difference of grade point	Student's percentage
Actual value	1.22	0.38
Random value	1.31	0.30

Table 3: Statistics information of students' spatial cluster and their grades.

random situation. And the percentage is higher. It means that the students sitting together are likely to obtain similar grade points.

5. CONCLUSIONS

In this paper, we propose to mine the class video and analyze the behaviors of students during the class. This information is useful since it can serve to analyze the teaching styles of the teachers' and the learning styles of students'. We can further use it to allow educators to make better-informed decisions on their instructional strategies. Teachers can constantly adapt their courses (both structure and content) to assure comprehensibility, high performance, and learning efficiency of their students.

Our method is based on face detection, tracking, and verification. Experimental results show that by incorporating temporal information, the problem of face occlusion can be resolved. Also, face verification enables us to recognize students in different videos.

In the experiment, we use videos recorded from four different classes. Among them, 16 videos are from physics class throughout the whole semester. We have analyzed the behaviors of single student, temporal and spatial behaviors of student groups, etc. Furthermore, we mine the relationship between students' class behaviors and their grades. The behavior information can be used in the teacher's class management. It can also give students some guidelines on how to improve the attention, grasp the content of the class.

As for future work, we plan to guide teachers in improving teaching style to make the class interesting and help students to improve grades. Head pose estimation and facial expression analysis are expected to be added. Due to the face areas in the video are small, the tasks are challenging.

6. ACKNOWLEDGEMENTS

The authors would like to thank Dr. Yan Ding for her valued discussion, Professor Fang Lu for providing the comprehensive teaching material, and thank the anonymous reviewers for their helpful comments.

This work was supported in part by the National Natural Science Foundation of China (No. 61170094), 863 Program 2014AA015101, Shanghai Committee of Science and Technology (14JC1402202), and Shanghai Leading Academic Discipline Project (B114).

7. REFERENCES

[1] T. Ahonen, A. Hadid, and M. Pietikainen. Face description with local binary patterns: Application to face recognition. *IEEE Transactions on Pattern Analysis and Machine Intelligence*, 28:2037 – 2041, 2006.

[2] G. R. Bradski. Computer vision face tracking for use in a perceptual user interface. *Intel Technology Journal, 2nd Quarter*, 1998.

[3] N. Dalal and B. Triggs. Histograms of oriented gradients for human detection. *IEEE International Conference on Computer Vision and Pattern Recognition*, 1:886–893, 2005.

[4] D. B. Goldman, C. Gonterman, B. Curless, D. Salesin, and S. M. Seitz. Video object annotation, navigation, and composition. *ACM Symposium on User Interface Software and Technology*, pages 3–12, 2008.

[5] R. Kasturi, D. Goldgof, P. Soundararajan, V. Manohar, J. Garofolo, R. Bowers, M. Boonstra, V. Korzhova, and J. Zhang. Framework for performance evaluation of face, text, and vehicle detection and tracking in video: Data, metrics, and protocol. *IEEE Transactions on Pattern Analysis and Machine Intelligence*, 31(2):319–336, February 2009.

[6] R. Lienhart and J. Maydt. An extended set of harr-like features for rapid object detection. *IEEE International Conference on Image Processing*, pages 900–903, 2002.

[7] R. Mehran, A. Oyama, and M. Shah. Abnormal crowd behavior detection using social force model. *IEEE International Conference on Computer Vision and Pattern Recognition*, pages 935 – 942, 2009.

[8] T.-J. K. Monserrat, S. Zhao, K. McGee, and A. V. Pandey. Notevideo: facilitating navigation of blackboard-style lecture videos. *ACM SIGCHI Conference on Human Factors in Computing Systems*, pages 1139–1148, 2013.

[9] H. Nait-Charif and S. J. McKenna. Activity summarisation and fall detection in a supportive home environmen. *Proceedings of the 17th International Conference on Pattern Recognition*, 4:323 – 326, 2004.

[10] C. Nguyen, Y. Niu, and F. Liu. Video summagator: An interface for video summarization and navigation. *ACM SIGCHI Conference on Human Factors in Computing Systems*, pages 647–650, 2012.

[11] R. Rienks, D. Zhang, D. Gatica-Perez, and W. Post. Detection and application of influence rankings in small group meetings. *Proceedings of the 8th International Conference on Multimodal Interfaces*, pages 257–264, 2006.

[12] G. Sharma, F. Jurie, and P. Pérez. Epml: Expanded parts based metric learning for occlusion robust face verification. *Asian Conference on Computer Vision*, pages 1–15, 2014.

[13] P. Vadakkepat, P. Lim, L. C. D. Silva, L. Jing, and L. L. Ling. Multimodal approach to human-face detection and tracking. *IEEE Transactions on Industrial Electronics*, 55(3):1385–1393, March 2008.

[14] V. Vapnik. *The Nature of Statistical Learning Theory*. New York: Springer-Verlag, 1995.

[15] P. Viola and M. Jones. Robust real-time object detection. *IEEE Journal of Computer Vision*, 4:34–47, 2002.

[16] X.-Y. Wei and Z.-Q. Yang. Mining in-class social networks for large-scale pedagogical analysis. *Proceedings of the 20th ACM International Conference on Multimedia*, pages 639–648, 2012.

[17] A. Yilmaz, O. Javed, and M. Shah. Object tracking: A survey. *ACM Computing Surveys*, 38(4):1–45, 2006.

[18] L. Zhang, B. Denney, and J. Lu. A collaborative approach for face verification and attributes refinement. *Multimedia Modeling*, 281:620–634, 2014.

Multi-view Face Detection Using Deep Convolutional Neural Networks

Sachin Sudhakar Farfade
Yahoo
fsachin@yahoo-inc.com

Mohammad Saberian
Yahoo
saberian@yahoo-inc.com

Li-Jia Li
Yahoo
lijiali.vision@gmail.com

ABSTRACT

In this paper we consider the problem of multi-view face detection. While there has been significant research on this problem, current state-of-the-art approaches for this task require annotation of facial landmarks, e.g. TSM [25], or annotation of face poses [28, 22]. They also require training dozens of models to fully capture faces in all orientations, e.g. 22 models in HeadHunter method [22]. In this paper we propose Deep Dense Face Detector (DDFD), a method that does not require pose/landmark annotation and is able to detect faces in a wide range of orientations using a *single* model based on deep convolutional neural networks. The proposed method has minimal complexity; unlike other recent deep learning object detection methods [9], it does not require additional components such as segmentation, bounding-box regression, or SVM classifiers. Furthermore, we analyzed scores of the proposed face detector for faces in different orientations and found that 1) the proposed method is able to detect faces from different angles and can handle occlusion to some extent, 2) there seems to be a correlation between distribution of positive examples in the training set and scores of the proposed face detector. The latter suggests that the proposed method's performance can be further improved by using better sampling strategies and more sophisticated data augmentation techniques. Evaluations on popular face detection benchmark datasets show that our single-model face detector algorithm has similar or better performance compared to the previous methods, which are more complex and require annotations of either different poses or facial landmarks.

Categories and Subject Descriptors

I.4 [**IMAGE PROCESSING AND COMPUTER VISION**]: Applications

General Terms

Application

ICMR'15, June 23–26, 2015, Shanghai, China.

ACM 978-1-4503-3274-3/15/06 ...$15.00.
DOI: http://dx.doi.org/10.1145/2671188.2749408 .

Figure 1: An example of user generated photos on social networks that contains faces in various poses, illuminations and occlusions. The bounding-boxes and corresponding scores show output of our proposed face detector.

Keywords

Face Detection, Convolutional Neural Network, Deep Learning

1. INTRODUCTION

With the wide spread use of smartphones and fast mobile networks, millions of photos are uploaded everyday to the cloud storages such as Dropbox or social networks such as Facebook, Twitter, Instagram, Google+, and Flicker. Organizing and retrieving relevant information from these photos is very challenging and directly impact user experience on those platforms. For example, users commonly look for photos that were taken at a particular location, at a particular time, or with a particular friend. The former two queries are fairly straightforward, as almost all of today's cameras embed time and GPS location into photos. The last query, i.e. contextual query, is more challenging as there is no explicit signal about the identities of people in the photos. The key for this identification is the detection of human faces. This has made low complexity, rapid and accurate face detection an essential component for cloud based photo sharing/storage platforms.

For the past two decades, face detection has always been an active research area in the vision community. The seminal work of Viola and Jones [40] made it possible to rapidly detect up-right faces in real-time with very low computational complexity. Their detector, called detector cascade, consists of a sequence of simple-to-complex face classifiers and has attracted extensive research efforts. Moreover, detector cascade has been deployed in many commercial products such as smartphones and digital cameras. While cascade detectors can accurately find visible up-right faces, they often fail to detect faces from different angles, e.g. side view or partially occluded faces. This failure can significantly impact the performance of photo organizing software/applications since user generated content often contains faces from different angles or faces that are not fully visible; see for example Figure 1. This has motivated many works on the problem of multi-view face detection over the past two decades. Current solutions can be summarized into three categories:

- Cascade-based: These methods extend the Viola and Jones detector cascade. For example, [41] proposed to train a detector cascade for each view of the face and combined their results at the test time. Recently, [22] combined this method with integral channel features [3] and soft-cascade [1], and showed that by using 22 cascades, it is possible to obtain state-of-the-art performance for multi-view face detection. This approach, however, requires face orientation annotations. Moreover its complexity in training and testing increases linearly with the number of models. To address the computational complexity issue, Viola and Jones [39] proposed to first estimate the face pose using a tree classifier and then run the cascade of corresponding face pose to verify the detection. While improving the detection speed, this method degrades the accuracy because mistakes of the initial tree classifier are irreversible. This method is further improved by [13, 12] where, instead of one detector cascade, several detectors are used after the initial classifier. Finally, [35] and [28] combined detector cascade with multiclass boosting and proposed a method for multiclass/multi-view object detection.

- DPM-based: These methods are based on the deformable part models technique [5] where a face is defined as a collection of its parts. The parts are defined via unsupervised or supervised training, and a classifier, latent SVM, is trained to find those parts and their geometric relationship. These detectors are robust to partial occlusion because they can detect faces even when some of the parts are not present. These methods are, however, computationally intensive because 1) they require solving a latent SVM for each candidate location and 2) multiple DPMs have to be trained and combined to achieve the state-of-the-art performance [22, 25]. Moreover, in some cases DPM-based models require annotation of facial landmarks for training, e.g [25].

- Neural-Network-based: There is a long history of using neural networks for the task of face detection [38, 37, 27, 8, 7, 6, 26, 11, 24, 23]. In particular, [38] trained a two-stage system based on convolutional neural networks. The first network locates rough positions of faces and the second network verifies the detection and makes more accurate localization. In [27], the authors trained multiple face detection networks and combined their output to improve the performance. [8] trained a single multi-layer network for face detection. The trained network is able to partially handle different poses and rotation angles. More recently, [23] proposed to train a neural network jointly for face detection and pose estimation. They showed that this joint learning scheme can significantly improve performance of both detection and pose estimation. Our method follows the works in [8, 23] but constructs a deeper CNN for face detection.

The key challenge in multi-view face detection, as pointed out by Viola and Jones [39], is that learning algorithms such as Boosting or SVM and image features such as HOG or Haar wavelets are not strong enough to capture faces of different poses and thus the resulted classifiers are *hopelessly inaccurate*. However, with recent advances in deep learning and GPU computation, it is possible to utilize the high capacity of deep convolutional neural networks for feature extraction/classification, and train a *single* model for the task of multi-view face detection.

Deep convolutional neural network has recently demonstrated outstanding performance in a variety of vision tasks such as face recognition [34, 30], object classification [19, 31], and object detection [9, 29, 18, 32]. In particular [19] trained an 8-layered network, called AlexNet, and showed that deep convolutional neural networks can significantly outperform other methods for the task of large scale image classification. For the task of object detection, [9] proposed R-CNN method that uses an image segmentation technique, selective search [36], to find candidate image regions and classify those candidates using a version of AlexNet that is fine-tuned for objects in the PASCAL VOC dataset. More recently, [33] improved R-CNN by 1) augmenting the selective search proposals with candidate regions from multibox approach [4], and 2) replacing 8-layered AlexNet with a much deeper CNN model of GoogLeNet [31]. Despite state-of-the-art performance, these methods are computationally suboptimal because they require evaluating a CNN over more than 2,000 overlapping candidate regions independently. To address this issue, [18] recently proposed to run the CNN model on the full image once and create a feature pyramid. The candidate regions, obtained by selective search, are then mapped into this feature pyramid space. [18] then uses spatial pyramid pooling [20] and SVM on the mapped regions to classify candidate proposals. Beyond region-based methods, deep convolutional neural networks have also been used with sliding window approach, e.g. OverFeat [29] and deformable part models [10] for object detection and [17] for human pose estimation. In general, for object detection these methods still have an inferior performance compared to region-based methods such as R-CNN [9] and [33]. However, in our face detection experiments we found that the region-based methods are often very slow and result in relatively weak performance.

In this paper, we propose a method based on deep learning, called Deep Dense Face Detector (DDFD), that does not require pose/landmark annotation and is able to detect faces in a wide range of orientations using a *single* model. The proposed method has minimal complexity because unlike recent deep learning object detection methods such as [9], it does not require additional components for segmentation, bounding-box regression, or SVM classifiers. Compared to previous convolutional neural-network-based face detectors such as [8], our network is deeper and is trained on a significantly larger training set. In addition, by analyzing detection confidence scores, we show that there seems to be a correlation between the distribution of positive examples in the training set and the confidence scores of the proposed detector. This suggests that the performance of our method can be further improved by using better sampling strategies and more sophisticated data augmentation techniques. In our experiments, we compare the proposed method to a deep learning based method, R-CNN, and several cascade and DPM-based methods. We show that DDFD can achieve similar or better performance even without using pose annotation or information about facial landmarks.

2. PROPOSED METHOD

In this section, we provide details of the algorithm and training process of our proposed face detector, called Deep Dense Face Detector (DDFD). The key ideas are 1) leverage the high capacity of deep convolutional networks for classification and feature extraction to learn a single classifier for detecting faces from multiple views and 2) minimize the computational complexity by simplifying the architecture of the detector.

We start by fine-tuning AlexNet [19] for face detection. For this we extracted training examples from the AFLW dataset [21], which consists of 21K images with 24K face annotations. To increase the number of positive examples, we randomly sampled sub-windows of the images and used them as positive examples if they had more than a 50% IOU (intersection over union) with the ground truth. For further data augmentation, we also randomly flipped these training examples. This resulted in a total number of 200K positive and and 20 millions negative training examples. These examples were then resized to 227×227 and used to fine-tune a pre-trained AlexNet model [19]. For fine-tuning, we used 50K iterations and batch size of 128 images, where each batch contained 32 positive and 96 negative examples.

Using this fine-tuned deep network, it is possible to take either region-based or sliding window approaches to obtain the final face detector. In this work we selected a sliding window approach because it has less complexity and is independent of extra modules such as selective search. Also, as discussed in the experiment section, this approach leads to better results as compared to R-CNN.

Our face classifier, similar to AlexNet [19], consists of 8 layers where the first 5 layers are convolutional and the last 3 layers are fully-connected. We first converted the fully-connected layers into convolutional layers by reshaping layer parameters [14]. This made it possible to efficiently run the CNN on images of any size and obtain a heat-map of the face classifier. An example of a heat-map is shown in Figure 2-right. Each point in the heat-map shows the CNN response, the probability of having a face, for its corresponding 227×227 region in the original image. The detected regions were then processed by non-maximal suppression to accurately localize the faces. Finally, to detect faces of different sizes, we scaled the images up/down and obtained new heat-maps. We tried different scaling schemes and found that rescaling image 3 times per octave gives reasonably good performance. This is interesting as many of the other methods such as [22, 2] requires a significantly larger number of resizing per octave, e.g. 8. Note that, unlike R-CNN [9], which uses SVM classifier to obtain the final score, we removed the SVM module and found that the network output are informative enough for the task of face detection.

Face localization can be further improved by using a bounding-box regression module similar to [29, 9]. In our experiment, however, adding this module degraded the performance. Therefore, compared to the other methods such as R-CNN [9], which uses selective search, SVM and bounding-box regression, or DenseNet [10], which is based on the deformable part models, our proposed method (DDFD) is fairly simple. Despite its simplicity, as shown in the experiments section, DDFD can achieve state-of-the-art performance for face detection.

2.1 Detector Analysis

In this section, we look into the scores of the proposed face detector and observe that there seems to be a correlation between those scores and the distribution of positive examples in the training set. We can later use this hypothesis to obtain better training set or to design better data augmentation procedures and improve performance of DDFD.

We begin by running our detector on a variety of faces with different in-plane and out-of-plane rotations, occlusions and lighting conditions (see for example Figure 1, Figure 2-left and Figure 3). First, note that in all cases our detector is able to detect the faces except for the two highly occluded ones in Figure 1. Second, for almost all of the detected faces, the detector's confidence score is pretty high, close to 1. Also as shown in the heat-map of Figure 2-right, the scores are close to zero for all other regions. This shows that DDFD has very strong discriminative power, and its output can be used directly without any post-processing steps such as SVM, which is used in R-CNN [9]. Third, if we compare the detector scores for faces in Figure 2-left, it is clear that the up-right frontal face in the bottom has a very high score of 0.999 while faces with more in-plane rotation have less score. Note that these scores are output of a sigmoid function, i.e. probability (soft-max) layer in the CNN, and thus small changes in them reflects much larger changes in the output of the previous layer. It is interesting to see that the scores decrease as the in-plane rotation increases. We can see the same trend for out-of-plane rotated faces and occluded faces in Figures 1 and 3. We hypothesize that this trend in the scores is not because detecting rotated face are more difficult but it is because of lack of good training examples to represent such faces in the training process.

To examine this hypothesis, we looked into the face annotations for AFLW dataset [21]. Figure 4 shows the distribution of the annotated faces with regards to their in-plane, pitch (up and down) and yaw (left to right) rotations. As shown in this figure, the number of faces with more than 30 degrees out-of-plane rotation is significantly lower than the faces with less than 30 degree rotation. Similarly, the number of faces with yaw or pitch less than 50 degree is significantly larger than the other ones. Given this skewed training set, it not surprising that the fine-tuned CNN is more confident about up-right faces. This is because the CNN is trained to minimize the risk of the soft-max loss function

$$\mathcal{R} = \sum_{x_i \in \mathcal{B}} \log \left[prob(y_i|x_i)\right], \quad (1)$$

where $\mathcal{B}$ is the example batch that is used in an iteration of stochastic gradient descent and y_i is the label of example x_i. The sampling method for selecting examples in $\mathcal{B}$ can

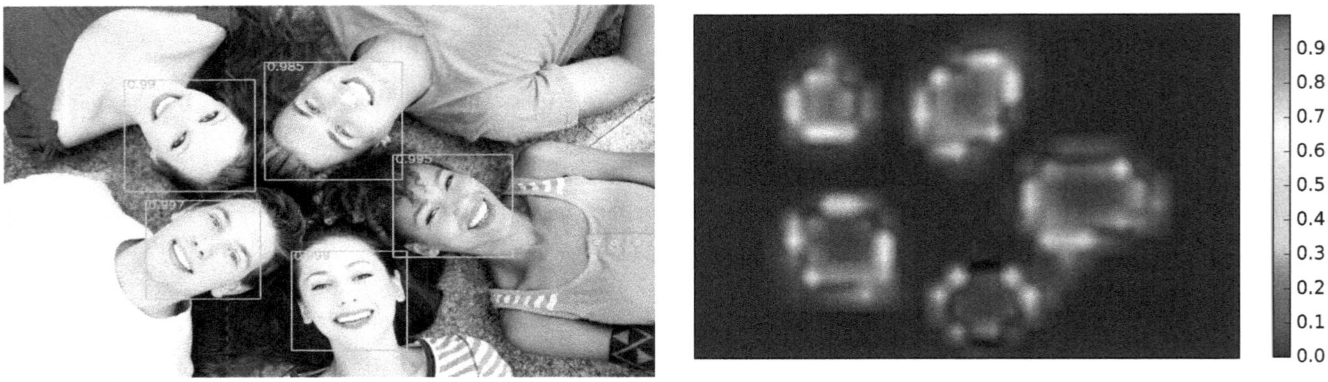

Figure 2: left) an example image with faces in different in-plane rotations. It also shows output of our proposed face detector after NMS along with corresponding confidence score for each detection. right) heat-map for the response of DDFD scores over the image.

significantly hurt performance of the final detector. In an extreme case if $\mathcal{B}$ never contains any example of a certain class, the CNN classifier will never learn the attributes of that class.

In our implementation $|\mathcal{B}| = 128$ and it is collected by randomly sampling the training set. However, since the number of negative examples are 100 times more than the number of positive examples, a uniform sampling will result in only about 2 positive examples per batch. This significantly degrades the chance of the CNN to distinguish faces from non-faces. To address this issue, we enforced one quarter of each batch to be positive examples, where the positive examples are uniformly sampled from the pool of positive training samples. But, as illustrated in Figure 4, this pool is highly skewed in different aspects, e.g. in-plane and out-of-plane rotations. The CNN is therefore getting exposed with more up-right faces; it is thus not surprising that the fine-tuned CNN is more confident about the up-right faces than the rotated ones. This analysis suggests that the key for improving performance of DDFD is to ensure that all categories of the training examples have similar chances to contribute in optimizing the CNN. This can be accomplished by enforcing population-based sampling strategies such as increasing selection probability for categories with low population.

Similarly, as shown in Figure 1, the current face detector still fails to detect faces with heavy occlusions. Similar to the issue with rotated faces, we believe that this problem can also be addressed through modification of the training set. In fact, most of the face images in the AFLW dataset [21] are not occluded, which makes it difficult for a CNN to learn that faces can be occluded. This issue can be addressed by using more sophisticated data augmentation techniques such as occluding parts of positive examples. Note that simply covering parts of positive examples with black/white or noise blocks is not useful as the CNN may learn those artificial patterns.

To summarize, the proposed face detector based on deep CNN is able to detect faces from different angles and handle occlusion to some extent. However, since the training set is skewed, the network is more confident about up-right faces and better results can be achieved by using better sampling strategies and more sophisticated data augmentation techniques.

3. EXPERIMENTS

We implemented the proposed face detector using the Caffe library [16] and used its pre-trained Alexnet [19] model for fine-tuning. For further details on the training process of our proposed face detector please see section 2. After converting fully-connected layers to convolutional layers [14], it is possible to get the network response (heat-map) for the whole input image in one call to Caffe code. The heat-map shows the scores of the CNN for every 227×227 window with a stride of 32 pixels in the original image. We directly used this response for classifying a window as face or background. To detect faces of smaller or larger than 227×227, we scaled the image up or down respectively.

We tested our face detection approach on PASCAL Face [42], AFW [25] and FDDB [15] datasets. For selecting and tuning parameters of the proposed face detector we used the PASCAL Face dataset. PASCAL Face dataset consists of 851 images and 1341 annotated faces, where annotated faces can be as small as 35 pixels. AFW dataset is built using Flickr images. It has 205 images with 473 annotated faces, and its images tend to contain cluttered background with large variations in both face viewpoint and appearance (aging, sunglasses, make-ups, skin color, expression etc.). Similarly, FDDB dataset [15] consists of 5171 annotated faces with 2846 images and contains occluded, out-of-focus, and low resolution faces. For evaluation, we used the toolbox provide by [22] with corrected annotations for PASCAL Face and AFW datasets and the original annotations of FDDB dataset.

We started by finding the optimal number of scales for the proposed detector using PASCAL dataset. We upscaled images by factor of 5 to detect faces as small as $227/5 = 45$ pixels. We then down scaled the image with by a factor, f_s, and repeated the process until the minimum image dimension is less than 227 pixels. For the choice of f_s, we chose $f_s \in \{\sqrt{0.5} = 0.7071, \sqrt[3]{0.5} = 0.7937, \sqrt[5]{0.5} = 0.8706, \sqrt[7]{0.5} = 0.9056\}$; Figure 5 shows the effect of this parameter on the precision and recall of our face detector (DDFD). Decreasing f_s allows the detector to scan the image finer and increases the computational time. According to Figure 5, it seems that these choices of f_s has little impact on the performance of the detector. Surprisingly, $f_s = \sqrt[3]{0.5}$ seems to have slightly better performance although it does

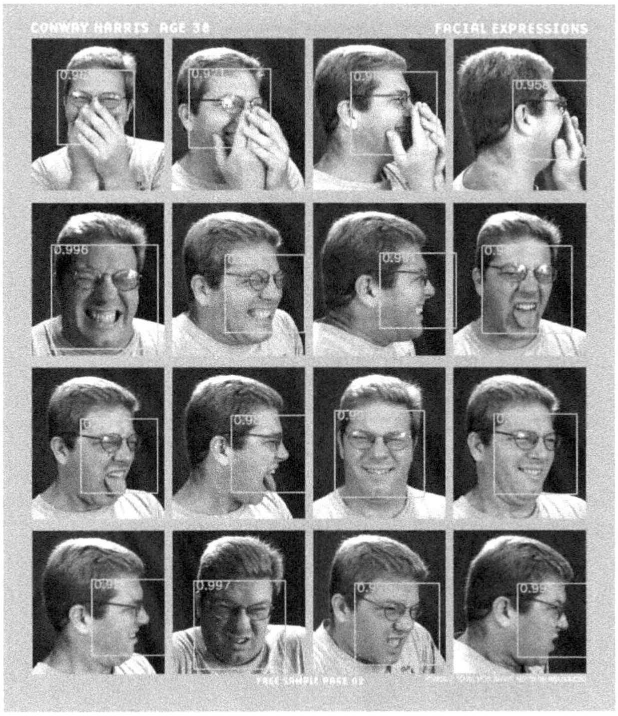

Figure 3: A set of faces with different out-of-plane rotations and occlusions. The figure also shows output of our proposed face detector after NMS along with the corresponding confidence score for each detection.

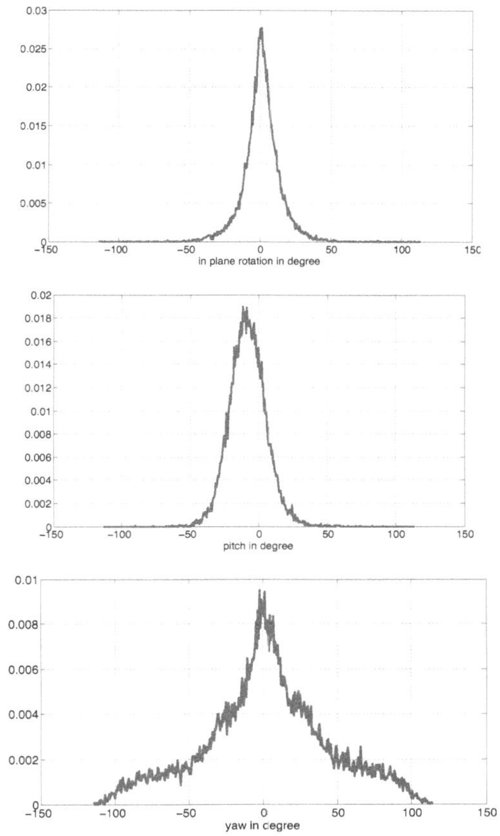

Figure 4: Histogram of faces in AFLW dataset based on their top) in-plane, middle) pitch (up and down) and bottom) yaw(left to right) rotations.

not scan the image as thorough as $f_s = \sqrt[5]{0.5}$ or $f_s = \sqrt[7]{0.5}$. Based on this experiment we use $f_s = \sqrt[3]{0.5}$ for the rest of this paper.

Another component of our system is the non-maximum suppression module (NMS). For this we evaluated two different strategies:

- **NMS-max**: we find the window of the maximum score and remove all of the bounding-boxes with an IOU (intersection over union) larger than an overlap threshold.
- **NMS-avg**: we first filter out windows with confidence lower than 0.2. We then use groupRectangles function of OpenCV to cluster the detected windows according to an overlap threshold. Within each cluster, we then removed all windows with score less than 90% of the maximum score of that cluster. Next we averaged the locations of the remaining bounding-boxes to get the detection window. Finally, we used the maximum score of the cluster as the score of the proposed detection.

We tested both strategies and Figure 6 shows the performance of each strategy for different overlap thresholds. As shown in this figure, performance of both methods vary significantly with the overlap threshold. An overlap threshold of 0.3 gives the best performance for NMS-max while, for NMS-avg 0.2 performs the best. According to this figure, NMS-avg has better performance compared to NMS-max in terms of average precision.

Finally, we examined the effect of a bounding-box regression module for improving detector localization. The idea is to train regressors to predict the difference between the locations of the predicted bounding-box and the ground truth. At the test time these regressors can be used to estimate the location difference and adjust the predicted bounding-boxes accordingly. This idea has been shown to improve localization performance in several methods including [5, 29, 4]. To train our bounding-box regressors, we followed the algorithm of [9] and Figure 7 shows the performance of our detector with and without this module. As shown in this figure, surprisingly, adding a bounding-box regressors degrades the performance for both NMS strategies. Our analysis revealed that this is due to the mismatch between the annotations of the training set and the test set. This mismatch is mostly for side-view faces and is illustrated in Figure 8. In addition to degrading performance of bounding-box regression module, this mismatch also leads to false miss-detections in the evaluation process.

3.1 Comparison with R-CNN

R-CNN [9] is one of the current state-of-the-art methods for object detection. In this section we compare our proposed detector with R-CNN and its variants.

We started by fine-tuning AlexNet for face detection using the process described in section 2. We then trained a SVM

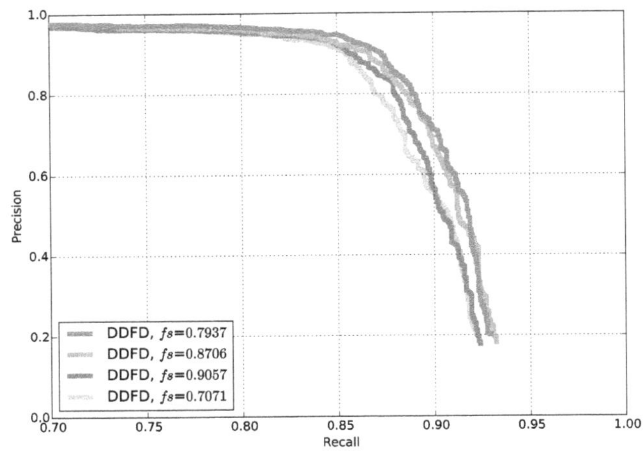

Figure 5: Effect of scaling factor on precision and recall of the detector.

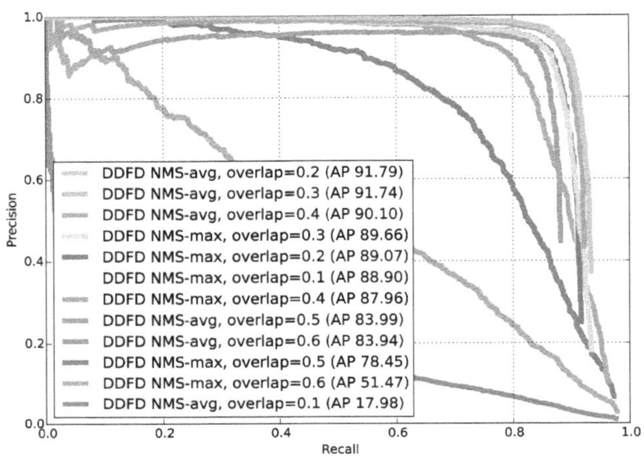

Figure 6: Effect of different NMS strategies and their overlap thresholds.

classifier for face classification using output of the seventh layer ($fc7$ features). We also trained a bounding-box regression unit to further improve the results and used NMS-max for final localization. We repeated this experiment on a version of AlexNet that is fine-tuned for PASCAL VOC 2012 dataset and is provided with R-CNN code. Figure 9 compares the performance of our detector with different NMS strategies along with the performance of R-CNN methods with and without bounding-box regression. As shown in this figure, it is not surprising that performance of the detectors with AlexNet fine-tuned for faces (Face-FT) are better than the ones that are fine-tuned with PASCAL-VOC objects (VOC-FT). In addition, it seems that bounding-box regression can significantly improve R-CNN performance. However, even the best R-CNN classifier has significantly inferior performance compared to our proposed face detector independent of the NMS strategy. We believe the inferior performance of R-CNN are due to 1) the loss of recall since selective search may miss some of face regions and 2) loss in localization since bounding-box regression is not perfect and may not be able to fully align the segmentation bounding-

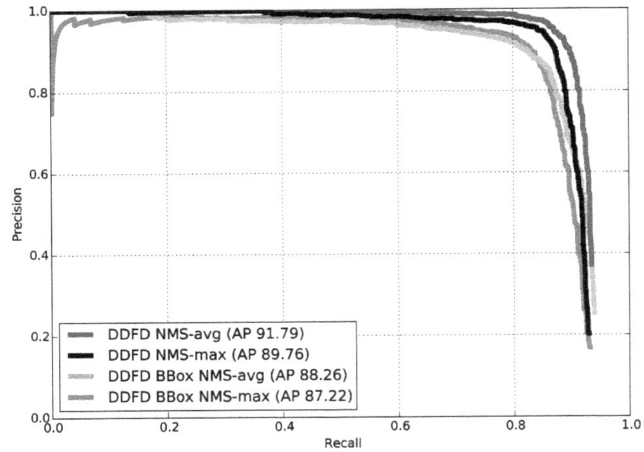

Figure 7: Performance of the proposed face detector with and without bounding-box regression.

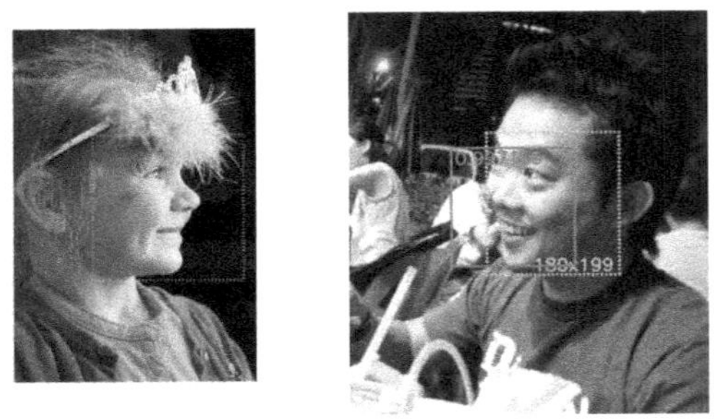

Figure 8: Annotation of a side face in left) training set and right) test set. The red bounding-box is the predicted bounding-box by our proposed detector. This detection is counted as a false positive as its IOU with ground truth is less than 50%.

boxes, provided by selective search [36], with the ground truth.

3.2 Comparisons with state-of-the-art

In this section we compare the performance of our proposed detector with other state-of-the-art face detectors using publicly available datasets of PASCAL faces [42], AFW [25] and FDDB [15]. In particular, we compare our method with 1) DPM-based methods such as structural model [42] and TSM [25] and 2) cascade-based method such as head hunter [22]. Figures 10 and 11 illustrate this comparison. Note that these comparison are not completely fair as most of the other methods such as DPM or HeadHunter use extra information of view point annotation during the training. As shown in these figures our single model face detector was able to achieve similar or better results compared to the other state-of-the-art methods, without using pose annotation or information about facial landmarks.

4. CONCLUSIONS AND FUTURE WORK

In this paper, we proposed a face detection method based on deep learning, called Deep Dense Face Detector (DDFD). The proposed method does not require pose/landmark annotation and is able to detect faces in a wide range of ori-

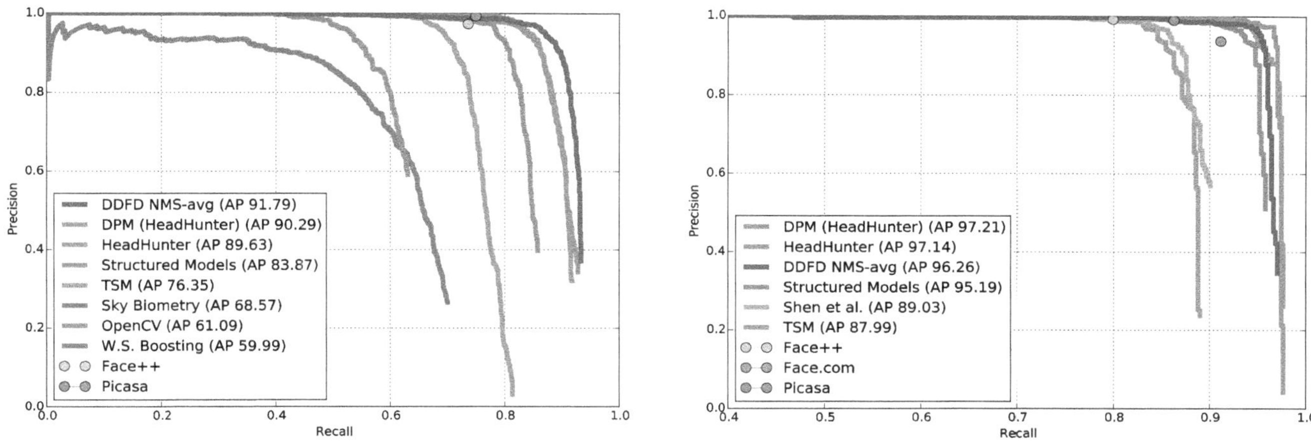

Figure 10: Comparison of different face detectors on left) PASCAL faces and right) AFW dataset.

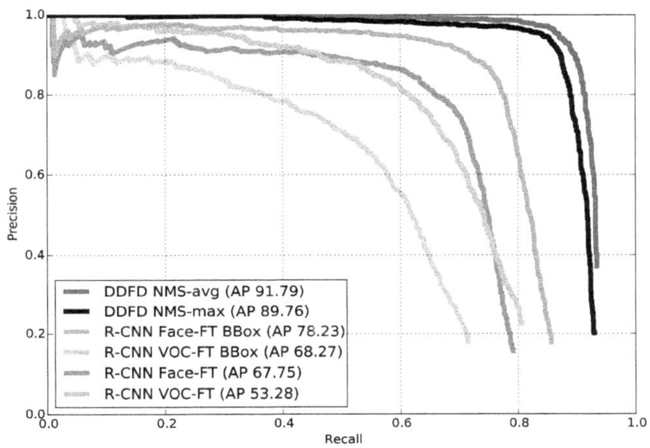

Figure 9: Comparison of our face detector, DDFD, with different R-CNN face detectors.

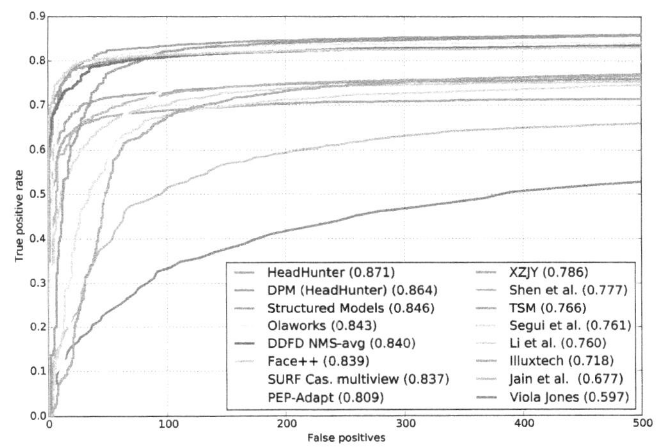

Figure 11: Comparison of different face detectors on FDDB dataset.

entations using a *single* model. In addition, DDFD is independent of common modules in recent deep learning object detection methods such as bounding-box regression, SVM, or image segmentation. We compared the proposed method with R-CNN and other face detection methods that are developed specifically for multi-view face detection e.g. cascade-based and DPM-based. We showed that our detector is able to achieve similar or better results even without using pose annotation or information about facial landmarks. Finally, we analyzed performance of our proposed face detector on a variety of face images and found that there seems to be a correlation between distribution of positive examples in the training set and scores of the proposed detector. In future we are planning to use better sampling strategies and more sophisticated data augmentation techniques to further improve performance of the proposed method for detecting occluded and rotated faces.

5. REFERENCES

[1] L. Bourdev and J. Brandt. Robust object detection via soft cascade. In *Proceedings of CVPR*, 2005.

[2] P. Dollár, R. Appel, S. Belongie, and P. Perona. Fast feature pyramids for object detection. *IEEE Transactions on Pattern Analysis and Machine Intelligence*, 2014.

[3] P. Dollar, Z. Tu, P. Perona, and S. Belongie. Integral channel features. In *Proceedings of the British Machine Vision Conference*, 2009.

[4] D. Erhan, C. Szegedy, A. Toshev, and D. Anguelov. Scalable object detection using deep neural networks. 2014.

[5] P. Felzenszwalb, D. McAllester, and D. Ramanan. A discriminatively trained, multiscale, deformable part model. In *Proceedings of CVPR*, 2008.

[6] C. Garcia and M. Delakis. A Neural Architecture for Fast and Robust Face Detection. In *Proceedings of IEEE-IAPR International Conference on Pattern Recognition*, Aug. 2002.

[7] C. Garcia and M. Delakis. Training Convolutional Filters for Robust Face Detection. In *Proceedings of IEEE International Workshop of Neural Networks for Signal Processing*, Sept. 2003.

[8] C. Garcia and M. Delakis. Convolutional face finder: a neural architecture for fast and robust face detection.

IEEE Transactions on Pattern Analysis and Machine Intelligence, 2004.

[9] R. Girshick, J. Donahue, T. Darrell, and J. Malik. Rich feature hierarchies for accurate object detection and semantic segmentation. In *Proceedings of CVPR*, 2014.

[10] R. B. Girshick, F. N. Iandola, T. Darrell, and J. Malik. Deformable part models are convolutional neural networks. *CoRR*, 2014.

[11] P. E. Hadjidoukas, V. V. Dimakopoulos, M. Delakis, and C. Garcia. A high-performance face detection system using openmp. *Concurrency and Computation: Practice and Experience*, 2009.

[12] C. Huang, H. Ai, Y. Li, and S. Lao. Vector boosting for rotation invariant multi-view face detection. In *Proceedings of ICCV*, 2005.

[13] C. Huang, H. Ai, Y. Li, and S. Lao. High-performance rotation invariant multiview face detection. *IEEE Transactions on Pattern Analysis and Machine Intelligence*, 2007.

[14] F. Iandola, M. Moskewicz, S. Karayev, R. Girshick, T. Darrell, and K. Keutzer. Densenet: Implementing efficient convnet descriptor pyramids. *arXiv preprint arXiv:1404.1869*, 2014.

[15] V. Jain and E. Learned-Miller. Fddb: A benchmark for face detection in unconstrained settings. Technical Report UM-CS-2010-009, University of Massachusetts, Amherst, 2010.

[16] Y. Jia, E. Shelhamer, J. Donahue, S. Karayev, J. Long, R. Girshick, S. Guadarrama, and T. Darrell. Caffe: Convolutional architecture for fast feature embedding. *arXiv preprint arXiv:1408.5093*, 2014.

[17] Y. L. Jonathan J. Tompson, Arjun Jain and C. Bregler. Joint training of a convolutional network and a graphical model for human pose estimation. In *Proceedings of NIPS*, 2014.

[18] S. R. Kaiming He, Xiangyu Zhang and J. Sun. Spatial pyramid pooling in deep convolutional networks for visual recognition. In *Proceedings of ECCV*, 2014.

[19] A. Krizhevsky, I. Sutskever, and G. E. Hinton. Imagenet classification with deep convolutional neural networks. In *Proceedings of NIPS*, 2012.

[20] S. Lazebnik, C. Schmid, and J. Ponce. Beyond bags of features: Spatial pyramid matching for recognizing natural scene categories. In *Proceedings of CVPR*, 2006.

[21] P. M. R. Martin Koestinger, Paul Wohlhart and H. Bischof. Annotated facial landmarks in the wild: A large-scale, real-world database for facial landmark localization. In *Proceedings of IEEE International Workshop on Benchmarking Facial Image Analysis Technologies*, 2011.

[22] M. Mathias, R. Benenson, M. Pedersoli, and L. Van Gool. Face detection without bells and whistles. In *Proceedings of ECCV*, 2014.

[23] M. Osadchy, Y. L. Cun, and M. L. Miller. Synergistic face detection and pose estimation with energy-based model. In *Proceedings of NIPS*, 2005.

[24] R. Osadchy, M. Miller, and Y. LeCun. Synergistic face detection and pose estimation with energy-based model. In *Proceedings of NIPS*, 2004.

[25] D. Ramanan. Face detection, pose estimation, and landmark localization in the wild. In *Proceedings of CVPR*, 2012.

[26] S. Roux, F. Mamalet, and C. Garcia. Embedded convolutional face finder. In *Proceedings of IEEE International Conference on Multimedia and Expo*, 2006.

[27] H. Rowley, S. Baluja, and T. Kanade. Neural network-based face detection. In *Proceedings of CVPR*, 1996.

[28] M. Saberian and N. Vasconcelos. Multi-resolution cascades for multiclass object detection. In *Proceedings of NIPS*. 2014.

[29] P. Sermanet, D. Eigen, X. Zhang, M. Mathieu, R. Fergus, and Y. LeCun. Overfeat: Integrated recognition, localization and detection using convolutional networks. In *Proceedings of International Conference on Learning Representations*, 2014.

[30] Y. Sun, Y. Chen, X. Wang, and X. Tang. Deep learning face representation by joint identification-verification. In *Proceedings of NIPS*. 2014.

[31] C. Szegedy, W. Liu, Y. Jia, P. Sermanet, S. Reed, D. Anguelov, D. Erhan, V. Vanhoucke, and A. Rabinovich. Going deeper with convolutions. *CoRR*, 2014.

[32] C. Szegedy, S. Reed, D. Erhan, and D. Anguelov. Scalable, high-quality object detection. *CoRR*, 2014.

[33] C. Szegedy, S. Reed, D. Erhan, and D. Anguelov. Scalable, high-quality object detection. *CoRR*, 2014.

[34] Y. Taigman, M. Yang, M. Ranzato, and L. Wolf. Deepface: Closing the gap to human-level performance in face verification. In *Proceedings of CVPR*, 2014.

[35] A. Torralba, K. Murphy, and W. Freeman. Sharing visual features for multiclass and multiview object detection. *IEEE Transactions on Pattern Analysis and Machine Intelligence*, 2007.

[36] J. Uijlings, K. van de Sande, T. Gevers, and A. Smeulders. Selective search for object recognition. *International Journal of Computer Vision*, 2013.

[37] R. Vaillant, C. Monrocq, and Y. LeCun. An original approach for the localisation of objects in images. In *Proceedings of International Conference on Artificial Neural Networks*, 1993.

[38] R. Vaillant, C. Monrocq, and Y. LeCun. Original approach for the localisation of objects in images. *IEE Proc on Vision, Image, and Signal Processing*, 1994.

[39] M. Viola and P. Viola. Fast multi-view face detection. In *Proceedings of CVPR*, 2003.

[40] P. Viola and M. J. Jones. Robust real-time face detection. *International Journal of Computer Vision*, 2004.

[41] B. Wu, H. Ai, C. Huang, and S. Lao. Fast rotation invariant multi-view face detection based on real adaboost. In *IEEE International Conference on Automatic Face and Gesture Recognition*, 2004.

[42] J. Yan, X. Zhang, Z. Lei, and S. Li. Face detection by structural models.

Music Positioning and Annotation For Television Videos

Gang Yang[1,2] Jieping Xu[1,2*] Xirong Li[1,2,3]
[1]School of Information, Renmin University of China, 100872, China
[2]Key Lab of Data Engineering and Knowledge Engineering, Renmin University of China, 100872, China
[3]Shanghai Key Laboratory of Intelligent Information Processing, 200443 China
yanggang@ruc.edu.com, xjieping@ruc.edu.cn, xirong@ruc.edu.cn

ABSTRACT

This paper proposed a framework to assist highlighting and annotating music utilization situation automatically within videos, further to supervise and protect music copyrights. Nowadays, music copyrighters pay attention to their rights increasingly, thus music embedded in TV channel videos should be validated to avoid infringing. Our framework supports Music Copyrighter Society of China(MCSC) to do statistic works to protect the copyright owners. In our framework, through AV separation, feature extractor, classification and assemblage functions, music positioning could be confirmed effectively. Then applying music fingerprint retrieving, music could be annotated automatically with high accuracy. Moreover, our framework is a closed loop self-adaptation system as it can be re-trained regularly to expand annotation database and enhance classifier's efficiency. The system based on our framework has been implemented in MCSC and its effectiveness has been evaluated in a real-life scenario. The results, on experiments of the real-life TV stations and comparisons of former works, show that the music positioning and annotation completed automatically by our system have significant improvement about over 30 times enhancement on the working efficiency.

Categories and Subject Descriptors

D.2.8 [**Software Engineering**]: Metrics—*complexity measures, performance measures*

Keywords

Music retrieving, automatic annotation, classification

*Corresponding author. This research was partially supported by the Fundamental Research Funds for the Central Universities, and the Research Funds of Renmin University of China (No. 14XNLQ01), the grants from the Natural Science Foundation of China (No. 61402032), NSFC (No. 61303184), SRFDP (No. 20130004120006) and Shanghai Key Laboratory of Intelligent Information Processing, China (Grant No. IIPL-2014-002).

ICMR'15, June 23–26, 2015, Shanghai, China.

http://dx.doi.org/10.1145/2671188.2749324.

1. INTRODUCTION

"If you are a musician and published a new song, how can you track TV stations which use the song but without paying it?" This question reveals a music copyright protection problem. Music Copyrighter Society of China(MCSC) cares for the different music used in television videos for protecting the interests of musicians. MCSC collects a large number of TV shows with music programs from different TV stations every day, and wishes to find out the music positions in complex audio signals of TV channels, and further recognize the music information including music author, title, singer, TV channel, music length, etc. Manual music positioning and annotation are adopted widely in the past. However, this way gradually suffers from information explosion. The automatic music processing system to realize automatic music positioning within audio stream and music annotation based on annotation database is becoming necessary.

For music positioning, classification on audio signals is useful to identify where a music is, and further locates the music. There have been many papers discussing the classification about audio signals[2][5]. The classification of audio data including music, speech and noise achieved good results. But few have mentioned the different music classification including music, speech with music and singing with music, etc. Aimed this point, classification methods, such as Bayes classifier[1], back-propagation network[4] and support vector machine (SVM)[2], could be wildly used to determine the various patterns classes. Furthermore, music information automatic annotation is another problem. Music fingerprint which is a condensed digital summary to music contents, can be used to identify a music[6]. By content-based music similarity computation, music is retrieved to obtain its annotated information automatically.

In the paper, the practical application in MCSC is to study the music position required annotation in real audio streams. The main challenge of the application is the music analysis under complex sound environments, especially embedded advertisements and signal noise, which exist in the videos of different TV channels. We proposed a framework and constructed our system on automatic music positioning and annotation for television videos. To the best of our knowledge, the constructed system is the first commercial music positioning and annotating system to support the protection of music copyright in China.

2. MUSIC POSITIONING AND ANNOTATION

The music positioning and annotation framework is proposed in Fig. 1 to search music specific positions and annotate music information automatically. The framework is constructed by Browser/Server architecture, which potentially supports mobile applications. And modular design is adopted to adapt to the modification of music processing requirement. The framework mainly includes two parts. The part of data analysis and decision, which is deployed in server, implements the functions of audio and video separation, music positioning and music automatic annotation. The part of interface which can be embedded in web browsers illustrates the analysis results and receives operators' feedback. Based on our framework, we have realized a system named MPAS.

When a video file is imported into the framework, AV separation model would extract sounds and images to form independent audio files and image files. Then audio features, like Mel-frequency cepstrum coefficients(MFCC), are extracted to form amount of sound clips features to describe the sound stream. Here, every clip, restricted to be a sound segment with only one second length, is provided to the music classifier to determine what sound category it belongs to. The clip classification results are useful to assemble a continuous sound stream to validate music. Through music starting points component, precise music starting points are determined, and further locate music positions. Subsequently, from the beginning position of the found music, our framework searches key clips in the music annotation database through extracting music fingerprints. The music annotation database previously stores a large number of music annotated information and fingerprints, so the database can use music similarity matching algorithm to return the most similar music and its relative annotations. The music information automatically fills the music properties in the music annotation model and exhibits in the client browser. Specially, if operators find the music annotation existing errors, they could correct these annotation information and update annotation database. At the same time, the updated music information is able to further enhance the accuracy of music classifier. The whole procedure constitutes a closed loop self-adaptation strategy that can gradually optimize its music positioning module and music annotation module. This characteristic is well suit for the practical applications in real-life scenario.

2.1 Definitions of Music Positioning

Videos gathered from TV channels are separated to be audio stream and video stream. In audio stream, audio clip is an audio segment with time length t. In MPAS, an audio stream is split to many audio clips denoted by $(x_1, x_2, ...x_n)$, where n is the number of clips in the audio stream. In order to find music positions, every audio clip should be validated what kind of segment it belongs to. By analyzing different types TV videos, we found that sounds in TV videos could be classified into six categories for identifying music. They include instrument music, speech with music, singing with music, noise, speech and silence. In MPAS, according to audio reality of TV channels, we partitioned audio clips to be three classes. The three classes are shown in Table 1. In audio stream, it is difficult to confirm where is the music starting position due to the complex music environments, especially the situations confusing singing, speech with background music and advertisements. Thus the definitions of music starting point and music length are necessary to be presented as follows:

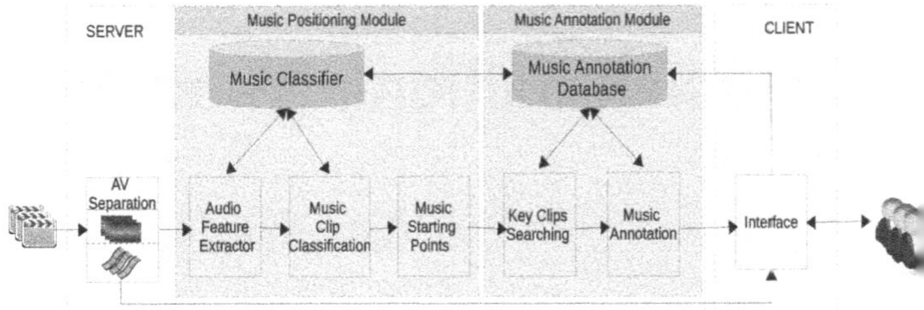

Figure 1: The framework flowchart and functional structure.

Definition 1. Music starting point, denoted as x_s, is positioned in a specific clip x_i which satisfies the following limitations respectively: *Hard limitation*: $x_{i-1} = 0$ and $(x_{i+j} = 2$ or $x_{i+j} = 1)$; $j = 0, 1, ..., M$. *Soft limitation*: $x_{i-1} = 1$ and $x_{i+j} = 2$, $j = 0, 1, ..., M$; or x_i conforms to hard limitation. M gives the limitation of music granularity. When checking fine-granularity music, M could be set to be a small value ($M \geq 3$) that is able to find short music.

Definition 2. Music length is the size of continuous music clips, which can also be defined as two types: *Hard length*: $\mathrm{HL}_{len}=I_{x_e} - I_{x_s}$ where x_e=0 and there is no clip who satisfies $x_i = 0$ existing between x_e and x_s. *Soft length*: $\mathrm{SL}_{len}=I_{x_e} - I_{x_s}$ where x_e=0 when x_s satisfies hard limitation of music starting point, moreover there is no clip who satisfies $x_i = 0$ existing between x_e and x_s. Here, x_e, the last music clip of current music, is located behind x_s, and I is the continuous clip index.

Table 1: Classes of audio clips

Class Name	Class Notation	The Categories in the Class
Non-Music	x_i=0	noise, speech, silence
Mix-Music	x_i=1	speech with music, singing with music
Pure-Music	x_i=2	instrument music

2.2 Music Positioning Module

The music positioning module includes four components cooperated mutually to realize the function of finding music in videos and positioning the music. The audio feature extractor extracts sufficient features to express the audio characteristics. Here, to balance the complexity and efficiency of MPAS, MFCC features are applied. MFCC features provide a compact representation of the signal's spectral envelopes, which are good correlations of the timbre. It's powerful enough to distinguish audio clips. Moreover, it should be emphasized that the music classifier is trained by the same MFCC features extracted by the music feature extractor offline. In MPAS, the music classifier is a one layer support vector machine(SVM) with RBF kernel.

The tagged video data classified three classes are used to train the classifier. After the audio clips are classified into three classes, assembling procedure finds the music starting points and makes certain of the music length. As in TV channels advertisements regularly use short music to decorate their contents, we initialized M=5 to find short music and filter noise in videos. The hard limitation of music starting point can render pure music such as concert music and movie songs. The soft limitation of music starting point can almost find all of different music in videos. Music starting points effectively help participants to recognize music to annotate music information, because music menu is usually displayed at the beginning of the music in videos.

2.3 Music Annotation Module

The music annotation module is based on a music fingerprint and annotation database, which contains the fingerprints and annotations of the large library of songs from television video streams. "Fingerprinting" techniques focus on finding almost-identical music recordings while tolerating small amount of noise distortions[6]. A song can be represented by a unique music fingerprint. The music clips are computed their fingerprints based on music frequency domain whose log sub-band energy is quantized into (0,1), which saves the storage space. And some 32-bit sub-band (0,1) build fingerprinting database.

New audio clips' fingerprints are searched in the fingerprinting database and retrieved a music annotation associated with the audio fingerprint through inverted index. Each music extracts two music pieces' fingerprints and matches in two stages: *lookup and minimum-distance matching.* The music annotation database contains a lookup table(LUT) with all possible 32 bit sub-fingerprints as an entry[3]. All the same 32-bit sub-fingerprints are indexed and pruning. Feature-based similarity is trivially obtained by defining similarity measures from the fingerprints. The adopted way of similarity measures in the module is computing the hamming distance that is computed of the music pieces' fingerprints and the stored fingerprints. Two music pieces retrieved in database could improve the system accuracy. Finally, a music with the minimum-distance sub-fingerprint and all the annotations is located.

2.4 Closed Loop Self-adaptive Strategy

A specific characteristic of our framework is its closed loop self-adaptive strategy, which could enhance the system performance gradually. The strategy produces a data flowing by the mutual effects of three functional parts divided from different angles. The classifier module could assist to classify and annotate music with few interferences. The automatic annotation database could help participants to increase music recognizing efficiency, further enhance recognition accuracy. Moreover, the new tagged music updated by participants could export the positive training samples to expand the scale of annotation data set. Then, the annotation data set can provide larger training data set which has been labeled carefully and correctly to re-train the classifier. Therefore, the classifier would get higher accuracy to position music automatically, and further decreases user interactions to produce annotated music. Moreover, the annotation database could extend its data scale by grasping music information from Internet. Through grabbing reliable music information from authoritative music sites, not only the scale of annotation database but also the accuracy of music information could be enhanced. Totally, the closed loop self-adaptive strategy can upgrade the framework modules to fit for different types of TV channels and programs.

3. APPLICATION AND EVALUATION

We deployed MPAS on a platform of IBM weblogic with Oracle database, realized with SSH (Struts+Spring+Hibernate) web architecture. Fig.2 shows a screen shot of MPAS where a Chinese video was analyzed. It illustrates several important functional interfaces including music positioning, music annotation, music fingerprint extracting, video batch importing, statistics analysis, etc. Specifically, the arrows below the video timeline are the found music starting points.

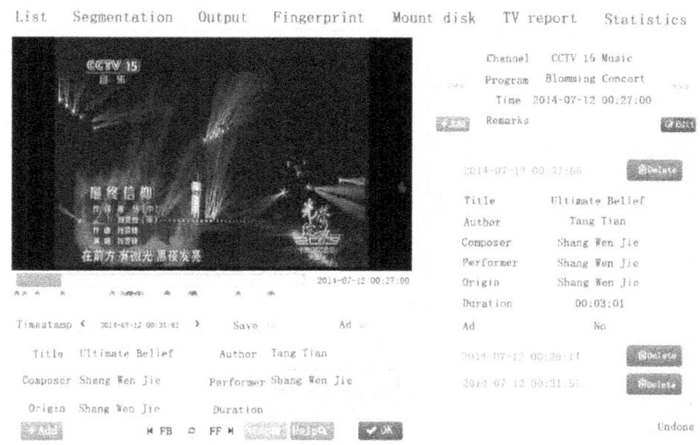

Figure 2: MPAS interface.

Table 2: The tagged data in data set $DS1$.

Type	pure music	speech with music	singing with music	speech	noise	silence
Tagged Number	3642	3366	1735	2004	1128	292
Length of Time(s)	48597	133189	71996	86391	7200	3829

3.1 Data set

As MPAS orients to deal with practical television videos in real company environments, the training data set was built on lots of videos(46.5GB) recorded from most of TV channels in China. Via watching and listening those TV videos, participants have carefully annotated six categories of video clips to construct the tagged data. The tagged data set $DS1$ is summarized in Table. 2. Due to the limitation of video species, the category of speech with music has the most training clips, and silence has the lest. We randomly selected 80% tagged data to train our system, and the remained data were used to test.

To evaluate the performance fairly, a second data set $DS2$ was tested, which includes two subsets $G1$ and $G2$ produced separately from the similar and different TV channels. Subset $G1$ has 50 videos(25GB), and subset $G2$ has 40 videos(21GB). The same participants who tagged data set $DS1$ have also annotated the subset $G1$. And the subset $G2$ was tagged by other participants. Moreover, data of real-life scenarios in MCSC were also used to evaluate MPAS performance. That will reveal the real performance and application worth of MPAS.

3.2 Experiment Evaluation

For music positioning in TV channel videos, we focus on whether our music positioning module can find the right music locations, and whether the classified method is competent enough to complete the task. We tested back-propagation neural network(BP) to exchange the SVM algorithm of MPAS to compare our classifier performance[4]. As BP neural network is a general classified algorithm widely used, the

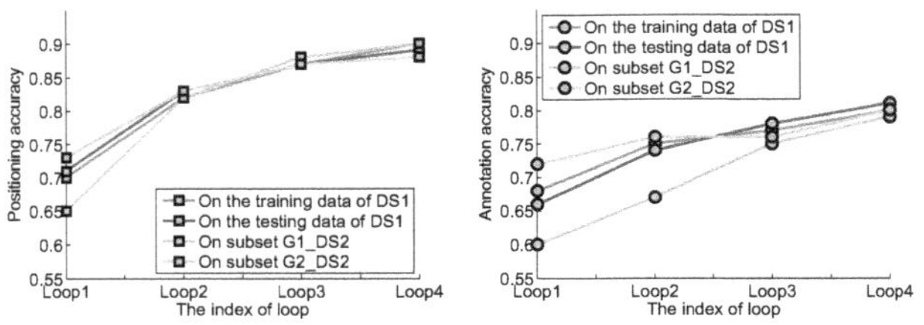

Figure 3: The optimization procedure of positioning and annotation accuracy with the utilization of closed loop self-adaptive strategy.

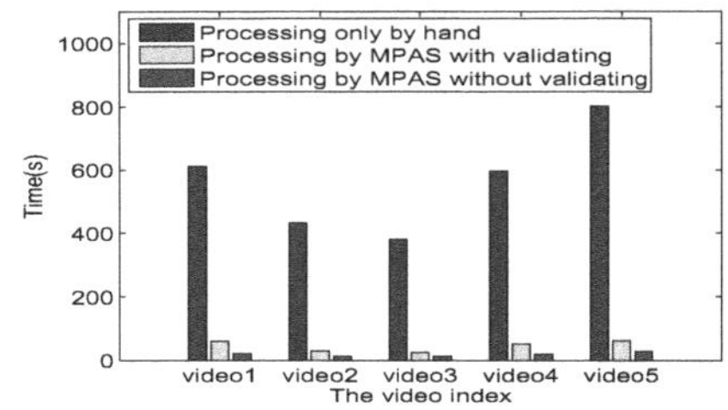

Figure 4: The comparisons among system annotation and manual annotation by one person.

comparisons, shown in Table 3, demonstrate great significance to highlight the performance of our music classifier. In Table 3, the accuracy reflects the ratio between the number of right predicted clips and total clips. It is obvious that SVM is more suitable for classifying audio clips.

Table 3: The accuracy of audio clips classification.

	Training Data in *DS1*	Testing Data in *DS1*	*G1_DS2*	*G2_DS2*
SVM	88%	80%	75%	76%
BP	74%	72%	71%	68%

The closed loop self-adaptive strategy aims to gradually improve system performance. In our test, MPAS was employed to positioning and annotating music on four data sets with four sequential loops. For better comparison quantified reasonably, the interval of one working hour is regarded as a loop. The comparison results are illustrated in Fig. 3. It's shown that the positioning accuracy and annotation accuracy both are increased step by step. Moreover, the improvement in former loops is greater than later. As the music annotation database and music classifier are continuous to infuse new music features and annotations, MPAS could obtain higher accuracy in later loop. This characteristic also conforms to the reality of working situation that popular music are tagged easily and early. Moreover, the positioning accuracy on data set *G*2 is poor relatively because those data were gathered from different TV channels and tagged by different participants.

3.3 User Evaluation

We compared the real-life business processing situations with or without MPAS. Without MPAS, MCSC employed 10 taggers to handle videos. Generally, 10 taggers annotating 60 videos needed one hour. Moreover, participants were easy to lose short music. On the other hand, with the help of MPAS, videos can be analyzed in nights. And in working time, the system just need one participant to validate the analysis results. A participant could validate 60 videos in one hour nearly without missing any music. Similarly, 5 random videos totally about 10 hours, which simultaneously contain 80 music required annotation and many unnecessary music, were annotated separately by hand and by MPAS. The music annotated information contained the music title, librettist, composer, etc. When tagged by MPAS, we investigated two situations, in which videos were processed by MPAS with manual validating or without validating.

Fig. 4 shows the efficiency comparison between hand-annotation and automatic annotation of MPAS. The music starting point positioning and annotation averagely spend 10 minutes to deal with a video by hand. Usually the video contains many short advertisements and noises that hamper the process of positioning and annotating. It's also a time-consuming process that the participants try to annotate all music without missing. On the other hand, MPAS is efficient. If just using MPAS to position and annotate music in videos, the efficiency is almost increased more than 30 times. If manually validating the results of automatic annotation, the processing efficiency is also about over 10 times of hand-annotation. MPAS contains the capability of multiple threads and off-line process, thus the application of MPAS has greatly enhanced the working efficiency of MCSC.

4. CONCLUSIONS

For music copyright protection, this paper proposed a framework to realize automatic music positioning and annotation in videos of TV channels. By comparison of large number of experiments, the audio clips should classify three classes including non-music, mix-music and pure-music to fit for different music applications in real-life scenario. The system based on our framework has been constructed and deployed in Music Copyrighter Society of China. Experiments and actual applications reveal our framework and system are powerful to automatically process large-scale TV channel videos, further protect music copyrights effectively.

5. REFERENCES

[1] W. Dai. Transferring Naive Bayes Classifiers for Text Classification. In *AAAI*, pages 540–545, 2007.

[2] Z. Fu, A. Robles-Kelly, and J. Zhou. Mixing Linear SVMs for Nonlinear Classification. *IEEE Transactions on Neural Networks*, 21:1963–1975, 2010.

[3] M. Haro, J. Serra, P. Herrera, and A. Corral. Zipf's Law in Short-Time Timbral Codings of Speech, Music, and Environmental Sound Signals. *PLOS One*, 7, 2012.

[4] H. H. Orkcu and H. Bal. Comparing performances of backpropagation and genetic algorithms in the data classification. *Expert Systems With Applications*, 38:3703–3709, 2011.

[5] E. Pampalk and M. Goto. MusicSun: A New Approach to Artist Recommendation. In *International Society for Music Information Retrieval Conference*, 2007.

[6] Y. Yu, M. Crucianu, V. Oria, and E. Damiani. Combining multi-probe histogram and order-statistics based LSH for scalable audio content retrieval. In *ACM Multimedia Conference*, pages 381–390, 2010.

KinectSBR: A Kinect-Assisted 3D Sketch-Based 3D Model Retrieval System

Bo Li, Yijuan Lu, Azeem Ghumman, Bradley Strylowski, Mario Gutierrez, Safiyah Sadiq, Scott Forster, Natacha Feola, Travis Bugerin
Department of Computer Science, Texas State University
San Marcos, Texas, USA
{b_l58, lu, a_z65, b_s211, mag262, s_s451, smf85, n_f27, tlb165}@txstate.edu

ABSTRACT

How to draw 3D sketches and how to search 3D models based on a hand-drawn 3D sketch are interesting but challenging questions. In this demonstration, we try to answer them by developing a novel Kinect-assisted 3D sketch-based 3D model retrieval system which also allows users to freely draw 3D sketches in a 3D space. We demonstrate its promising potentials in both collecting 3D sketch data and conducting 3D sketch-based 3D model retrieval.

Categories and Subject Descriptors

H.3.3 [**Information Storage and Retrieval**]: Information Search and Retrieval; I.3.8 [**Computer Graphics**]: Applications

Keywords

Sketch-based 3D model retrieval; 3D sketch; Kinect

1. INTRODUCTION

A 2D sketch lacks the 3D shape information of the object it represents, which generates a large semantic gap between the iconic representation of the 2D sketch and the accurate representation of the 3D model behind. It is this gap that makes 2D sketch-based 3D modeling retrieval a very challenging task [3]. Motivated by this, we consider whether using 3D sketches for 3D model retrieval poses a viable alternative, one that would completely bypass the formidable semantic gap. If an interface is available to allow users to draw a 3D sketch of an object in free space (e.g., in the air), users would have the ability to encode the object's 3D information while expressing its features with salient 3D lines, just as the information stored in the counterpart 3D model.

In this demonstration, a virtual 3D sketching drawing "board" is first developed and then a novel 3D sketch-based 3D model retrieval system is created based on the board. By retrieving 3D models from a large scale sketch-based 3D shape retrieval benchmark (target dataset only) for 300 human sketches collected from seventeen users by utilizing the 3D sketching board, we demonstrate the promising retrieval performance of the system. According to our knowledge, we are the first that explores 3D sketching in a 3D space and develops an innovative retrieval system that enables users to search 3D models using hand-drawn 3D sketches.

ICMR'15, June 23ˇ26, 2015, Shanghai, China.

http://dx.doi.org/10.1145/2671188.2749350.

2. SYSTEM OVERVIEW

2.1 3D Sketching

We begin by developing a virtual 3D sketching "board" (see Fig. 1 (a)) with the Microsoft Kinect, which we designed to track the location of a user's hand in a 3D space. To enable a mode of hands-free interaction with the GUI, we implement a voice-activated interface that supports a list of voice commands (e.g. start, left, right, pause, resume, search, and reset). We also integrate a Kalman filter, which reduces background noise and predicts smoother sketches.

2.2 Retrieval System

An efficient **K**inect-assisted 3D **S**ketch-**B**ased 3D model **R**etrieval system (**KinectSBR**, see Fig. 1 (b)) is built based on the above 3D sketching platform. It has both online and offline processes and consists of three major components.

(1) Data processing. The process targets generating a normalized 3D outline for a 3D model. A Principle Component Analysis (PCA)-based 3D normalization process is first applied on the 3D model, followed by integrating the 3D contour points of its six standard views (Fig. 1 (b): (b)) to generate the complete 3D outline. Next, we perform an approximately uniform point sampling on the 3D outline based on a distance threshold between the 3D points (Fig. 1 (b): (c)). Finally, a PCA alignment is performed (Fig. 1 (b): (d)) on the 3D outline. The same normalization process is applied to hand-drawn 3D sketch queries.

(2) Feature extraction. Motivated by the inherent nature (point cloud) of 3D sketches and 3D outlines, we represent both with efficiently-extracted 3D shape histograms [1] (20 shells, 6 sectors, 120 bins in total) (see Fig. 1 (b): (e)).

(3) 3D sketch-3D model matching. Euclidean distances between the 3D shape histograms of the 3D sketch query and all the target 3D models are first computed (Fig. 1 (b): (k)) and then sorted ascendingly (Fig. 1 (b): (m)). Finally, we display the thumbnails of the top ten 3D models accordingly on the right of the GUI (Fig. 1 (b): (n)). Users have the option to access more results with the appropriate voice command (e.g. "more results").

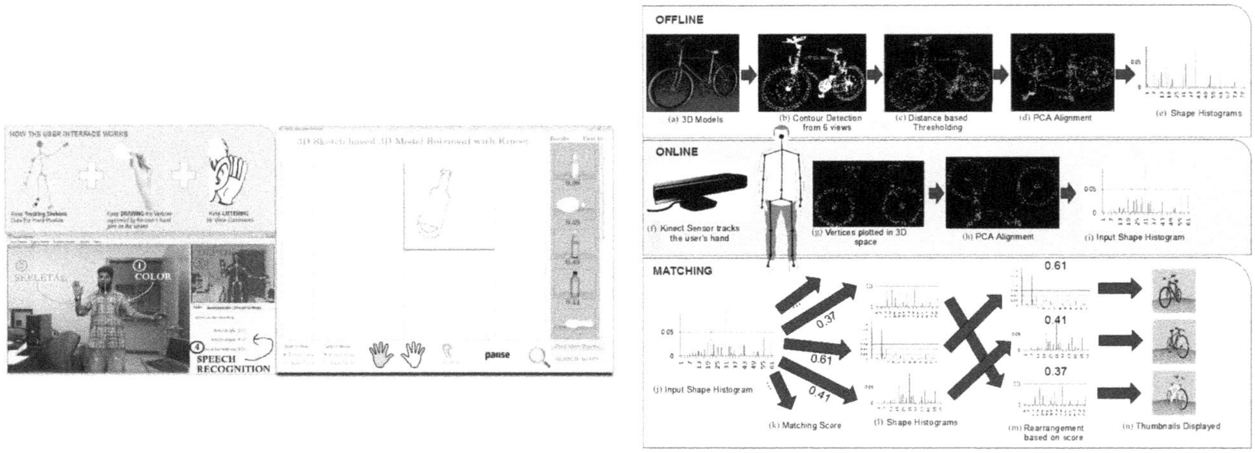

(a) GUI (b) Framework

Figure 1: System Graphical User Interface (GUI) and framework.

3. DEMONSTRATIONS

We will demonstrate that our KinectSBR system enables users to perform: **(1) 3D sketching:** use one hand to sketch a 3D sketch in the air when standing within 5 meters in front of a Kinect; **(2) 3D sketch-based 3D model retrieval:** continue to conduct a search of 3D models based on the drawn 3D sketch from a large scale 3D model dataset. We demonstrate these via the two following experiments.

3.1 Kinect300 3D Sketch Dataset Collection

Considering objects' diversity, complexity and popularity, we construct the first 3D sketch dataset, the Kinect300, using our virtual 3D sketching "board" (Section 2.1). The Kinect300 consists of 300 sketches, uniformly divided into 30 categories. Seventeen users contributed to the 3D sketch data collection; each user was asked to draw a 3D sketch for several preselected categories.

Before the start of each user's data collection session, the user was allowed to sketch several unrecorded drawings to accustom themselves with the drawing rules of the application and with the practice of drawing in a three-dimensional space. After this brief training, the user was asked to sketch for each of a number of predefined categories.

3.2 3D Sketch-Based 3D Model Retrieval

Based on the retrieval system presented in Section 2.2 and the Kinect300 dataset collected above, we perform a 3D sketch-based 3D model retrieval experiment. The Kinect300 is used as the 3D query set, while the 3D target dataset is that of the SHREC'13 Sketch Track Benchmark [2], which contains 1258 3D models of 90 classes. Based on the five commonly-used evaluation metrics defined in [4], we achieved the following performance: Nearest Neighbor: 0.029, First Tier: 0.021, Second Tier: 0.038, E-Measure: 0.021, Discounted Cumulative Gain: 0.254. The retrieval performance reveals a nontrivial challenge existing in this type of 3D model retrieval: effectively matching an inaccurate hand-drawn 3D sketch with accurate 3D models. However, the good results we obtained with simple sketches demonstrates the potential of our approach. For example, good performance has been obtained in categories such as airplane, balloon, sword, and wineglass, though more complicated classes such as human, face and house produce inferior results. Figure 2 shows two example searches with sketches of different complexity. Finally, with the high efficiency of the 3D shape histogram and the Kalman filter, the above retrieval can be conducted in real-time: our algorithm completes a query in only 1.22 sec on a modern computer (Intel CPU @3.07 GHz).

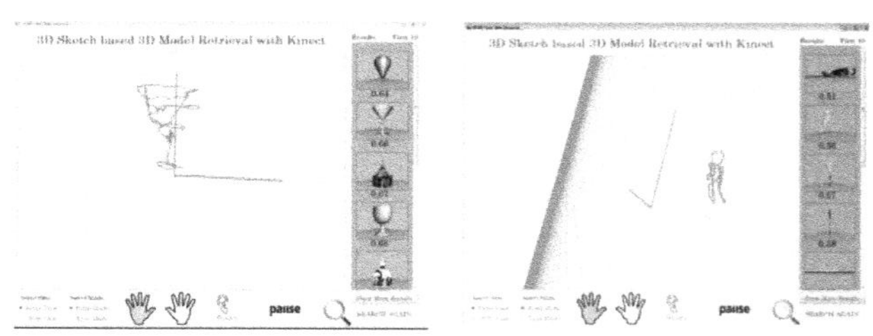

(a) Simple (b) Complicated

Figure 2: Two example retrieval results for sketches of different complexity.

Acknowledgments

This work is supported by Army Research Office grant W911NF-12-1-0057, NSF CRI-1305302, NSF CNS-1358939 and NSF OCI-1062439.

4. REFERENCES

[1] M. Ankerst, G. Kastenmüller, and et al. 3D shape histograms for similarity search and classification in spatial databases. In *SSD*, pages 207–226, 1999.

[2] B. Li, Y. Lu, and et al. SHREC'13 track: Large scale sketch-based 3D shape retrieval. In *3DOR*, pages 89–96, 2013.

[3] B. Li, Y. Lu, and et al. A comparison of 3D shape retrieval methods based on a large-scale benchmark supporting multimodal queries. *CVIU*, 131:1–27, 2015.

[4] P. Shilane, P. Min, and et al. The Princeton shape benchmark. In *SMI*, pages 167–178, 2004.

An Improved System For Real-Time Scene Text Recognition

Haojin Yang, Cheng Wang, Xiaoyin Che, Sheng Luo, Christoph Meinel
Hasso Plattner Institute (HPI), University of Potsdam, Germany
P.O. Box 900460,
D-14440 Potsdam
{haojin.yang, cheng.wang, xiaoyin.che, sheng.luo, meinel}@hpi.de

ABSTRACT

In this paper we showcase a system for real-time text detection and recognition. We apply deep features created by Convolutional Neural Networks (*CNNs*) for both *text detection* and *word recognition* task. For text detection we follow the common localization-verification scheme which already shown its excellent ability in numerous previous work. In text localization stage, textual regions are roughly detected by using a MSERs (*Maximally Stable Extremal Regions*) detector with high recall rate. False alarms are then eliminated by using a CNNs classifier, and remaining text regions are further grouped into words. In the word recognition stage, we developed an skeleton-based text binarization method for segmenting text from its background. A CNNs based recognizer is then applied for recognizing character. The initial experiments show the powerful ability of deep features for text classification comparing with commonly used visual features. Our current implementation demonstrates real-time performance for recognizing scene text by using a standard PC with webcam.

Categories and Subject Descriptors

H.3.1 [**Information Storage and Retrieval**]: Content Analysis and Indexing—*Indexing methods*; H.5.1 [**Information Interfaces and Presentation**]: Multimedia Information Systems—*Video*

General Terms

Algorithms, Demonstration, Experimentation

Keywords

Video OCR; Scene Text Recognition; Multimedia Indexing

ICMR'15, June 23–26, 2015, Shanghai, China.
Copyright © 2015 ACM 978-1-4503-3274-3/15/06 ...$15.00.
http://dx.doi.org/10.1145/2671188.2749352.

1. INTRODUCTION

In the last decade digital libraries and web video portals have become more and more popular. The amount of video data available on the World Wide Web (*WWW*) is growing rapidly. According to the official statistic-report of the popular video portal YouTube[1], 100 hours of video are uploaded every minute. Therefore, how to efficiently retrieve video data on the WWW or within large video archives has become a very important and challenging task.

On the other hand, due to the rapid popularization of smart mobile and wearable devices, large amounts of self-recorded "lifelogging" videos are created on the web. Generally, it lacks metadata for indexing such kind of videos, since the only searchable textual content is often the title given by the video uploader, which is typically brief and subjective. A more general solution is highly desired for gathering video metadata automatically.

Text in video is one of the most important high-level semantic features, which directly depicts the video content. In general text displayed in a video can be categorized into scene text and overlay text [9]. In contrast to overlay text, to detect and recognize scene text is often more challenging. There are numerous problems affecting the recognition results, as e.g., texts appeared in a nature scene image can be in a very small size with high variety of contrast; motion changes of the camera may affect the size, shape and brightness of text content, and may lead to geometrical distortion. All of those factors have to be considered in order to obtain a correct OCR (*Optical Character Recognition*) result.

In this work, we address both text detection and recognition issues for video images. In the text detection, we follow the commonly used localization-verification scheme, in which a MSERs (*Maximally Stable Extremal Regions*) [11] detector is applied intended to identify text candidate regions with high recall rate. Then candidate regions are verified by a text/non-text classifier which is trained based on Convolutional Neural Networks (*CNNs*). Finally, remaining text regions are grouped into words relying on their position and size information. For text recognition we have developed a novel skeleton-based binarization algorithm in order to separate text from complex background to make it processible for OCR engines. We further developed a CNN-based word recognizer for processing scene text content. Our initial experimental results demonstrate the superiors ability of CNN features for text classification comparing to other commonly used visual features such as Scale-Invariant Fea-

[1] https://www.youtube.com/yt/press/statistics.html

ture Transform (*SIFT*) [10] and Histogram of Oriented Gradients (*HOG*) [12] etc. The demonstrated system achieved real-time performance[2] on a standard PC platform (3.2 GHz CPU×4, 4G RAM) with webcam.

The rest of the paper is organized as follows: section 2 reviews previous work, whereas the section 3 describes the system architecture and involved techniques. Section 4 provides initial experimental results and demonstrates exemplary real-time recognition results. Section 5 concludes the paper with an outlook on future work.

2. RELATED WORK

Most of proposed scene-text detection methods can be briefly divided into two categories, either based on connected components (*CCs*) or sliding windows. The CCs based approaches include Stroke Width Transform (*SWT*) [5], MSERs [13], Oriented Stroke [14] etc. One of the significant benefits of CCs based method is its computational efficiency since the detection is often an one pass process across image pixels. The sliding window based methods as e.g., [17, 3, 16, 7] usually apply representative visual features to train a machine learning classifier for text detection. Here hand-crafted features [16, 10, 2] as well as deep features [17, 3, 7] can be applied, and text regions will be detected by scanning the whole image with a sub-window in multiple scales with a potential overlapping. In [17, 3, 7], sliding window based methods with deep features achieved promising accuracy for end-to-end text recognition. However, their proposed approaches may hard to achieve sufficient performance for real-world application due to the expensive computation time.

In our approach, we intended to take advantages from both categories, i.e. the computation benefit of CCs based algorithm and the powerful text-classification ability of deep features.

3. SYSTEM DEMONSTRATION

In [17, 7], the authors were intended to achieve the best end-to-end text recognition accuracy. Therefore in the text detection step, their systems have been tuned to produce text candidates with high recall, and the subsequent recognition engines will further eliminate the false alarms. At this point, we argue that this kind of design may lower the overall system efficiency. From our experiences we learned that the OCR engine is normally less efficient than the text detector for processing same amount of image pixels concerning running time. Since we want to design a system with real-time capability, we thus keep the text detection process as accurate as possible, and only pass the text candidates with high confidence to the recognition stage.

3.1 Text Localization

In this step we apply a MESRs based detector to roughly detect text regions from the input video frame with high recall rate. MSERs define an Extremal Region (*ER*) as a connected component of image pixels having intensity contrast against its boundary pixels [11]. Those ERs can be controlled by tuning the intensity thresholds. A low threshold would result in a large number of low-level ERs which are separated by small contrast differences amount pixels. While increasing the threshold the low-level ERs will be merged to construct a higher level one. In our current implementation we adapted the detector to ensure that 95% of text regions will be remained as candidates from the input images. All candidate regions will be further verified by using a grouping method and CNN classifier.

[2]Similar to [13], we consider the real-time ability of a video text recognition system if its response time is comparable to a human.

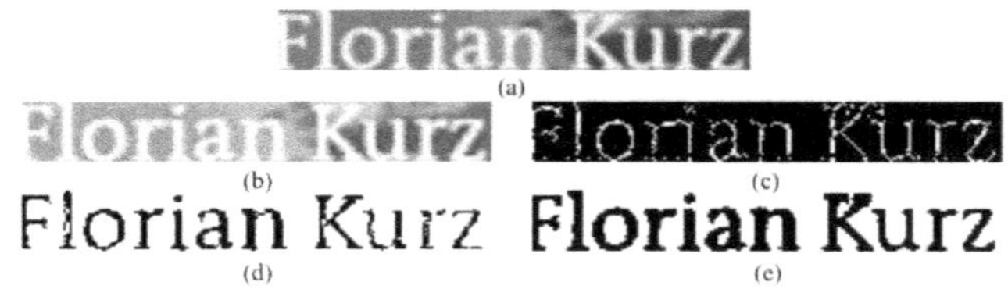

Figure 1: Seed selection and region growing results: (a) original text line image, (b) grayscale image, (c) skeleton image, (d) seed-selection result, (e) region growing result

3.2 Text Verification

In the verification stage, we first roughly generate the text-region-pairs from ERs according to their positions. Then each region-pair will be verified by using several heuristics including normalized color distance, object-center distance, minimal height ratio, maximal intensity distance. This procedure can help to filter out many simple false alarms. The remaining difficult non-text patterns as e.g., windows, blocks, trees, garden fens will be handled by CNN classifier.

To verify the text regions, we trained a text/non-text classifier based on CNNs. Our networks have two convolutional layers with 20, 50 filters respectively. We apply *Maxout* pooling layer [6] after each convolution with group size 2. The input image size is 24×24 and the convolutional kernel size is 5×5. The sequence continues by a inner-product layer (500 filters), ReLU layer and another inner-product layer (2 filters). Inspired by [6] and [7] we also utilized dropout (0.5) combined with maxout layers. The output of the last layer is fed into a SVM [4] classifier to obtain a binary decision. We gathered about 180k positive and 360k negative character samples from various datasets to build the training and test dataset. The verification process follows the sliding-window metrics, and we use majority voting to distinguish text objects and false alarms.

3.3 Text Segmentation

Text pixels from the detected text lines need to be separated from background by applying appropriate segmentation/binarization techniques for further OCR processing. We developed a novel skeleton-based approach for video text binarization, which consists of three steps: First, we determine the text gradient direction for each text line object by analyzing the content distribution of their skeleton maps. We then calculate the threshold value for seed-selection by using the skeleton map which has been created with the correct gradient direction. Subsequently, a seed-region growing procedure starts from each seed pixel and extends the seed-region in its north, south, east, and west orientations. The region grows iteratively until it reaches the character boundary. Figure 1 shows the workflow of the algorithm. Our skeleton based binarization methods achieved the first and second place in ICDAR 2011 text segmentation challenge for born digital images. More details of this method can be found in [18].

3.4 Word Recognition

In this step verified text objects are first separated into words. Then we also apply sliding-window metrics to recognize characters within each word. We use a similar setup for training the character recognizer as the text/non-text classifier. The only difference is that the output of the second inner-product layer is 62, and the final output is fed into softmax-classifier for creating 62-way classification result. Unlike the recognition procedure in [17, 7], before character recognition we try to find the character positions and boundaries by using contour detection method. Subsequently, for each character candidate we produce a set of recognition responses by adjusting the sliding-window positions, e.g. shift the boundary position to left or to right with certain percentages. The word response is created based on character candidates with best response-scores. Here several post-processing techniques could be applied to further improve the recognition result. As e.g., by using non-maximal suppression we could remove the duplicated words from the result. We could also use spell-checking tool to create suggested word lexicon for each word response, and apply beam search algorithm to find the final result. The post-processing procedures will be studied and implemented as the next step of our work.

4. INITIAL EXPERIMENTAL RESULTS

Most of machine learning based text detection and recognition methods take use of representative features to discriminate text from other objects. The ability of applied visual features directly affect the system accuracy and efficiency. Deep learning techniques have been applied to numerous challenging research problems, and created break-record improvements in recent several years. In this work, we conducted experiments to investigate the accuracy of CNNs deep features comparing to several commonly used visual features for text classification. The selected hand-crafted visual features include SIFT [10], SURF [2], HOG [12] and eLBP (*Edge-based Local Binary Pattern*) [1]. The parameters of each hand-crafted feature have been optimized by using exhaustive-search metrics. Our CNNs classifier is trained based on *Caffe* framework [8].

We utilized the commonly used evaluation methodology: classification accuracy and F-measure scores in the experiment. The evaluation dataset was created by Wang et al.[17], which consists of 15000 (text: 5000, non-text: 10000) cropped character image samples for training and another 7500 (text: 2500, non-text: 5000) samples for testing. All samples were extracted from ICDAR 2003 dataset. SVM classifier with RBF-kernel has been used for all test runs. The parameter optimization of SVM has been executed by cross-validation.

Table 1 shows the classification results, from which it is easy to realize that the CNNs deep features significantly outperformed the other visual features for scene text classification. It once again proved the strong ability of deep features for solving computer vision problem. CNNs feature improves on the second best one (eLBP) by **14%** of classification accuracy.

Figure 2 demonstrates an exemplary end-to-end text recognition result of our system by using a webcam in real-time.

Feature	Accuracy	F_1 Measure	Recall	Precision
HOG	0.58	0.27	0.32	0.23
SURF	0.78	0.58	0.46	0.81
SIFT	0.78	0.65	0.69	0.61
eLBP	0.83	0.73	0.76	0.69
CNNs	**0.97**	**0.95**	**0.93**	**0.97**

Table 1: Text classification results by using hand crafted visual features and CNNs deep features

Figure 2: Exemplary recognition result of our system by using a webcam in real-time

The detailed evaluation of our skeleton-based text segmentation method can be found in [18].

5. CONCLUSION AND FUTURE WORK

In this paper, we showcased a system for text detection and recognition in nature scene videos. This system achieved real-time recognition performance by using a standard computer with webcam. The proposed system consist of text detection, text verification, text segmentation and word recognition processes. We use a MESRs detector to rapidly create text candidate regions, and verify them by applying a CNNs based text classifier. The text contents are extracted by using a novel skeleton-based binarization method, which is followed by a CNNs based word recognizer for obtaining end-to-end recognition result.

In the future work, as inspired by [15], we plan to investigate various filter-operations in CNNs, intended to further improve system efficiency. In this paper, so far, we only reported our initial experimental results. The detailed evaluation for text detection, word recognition and end-to-end text recognition will be performed by using appropriate ICDAR benchmarks.

6. REFERENCES

[1] M. Anthimopoulos, B. Gatos, and I. Pratikakis. A two-stage scheme for text detection in video images. *Journal of Image and Vision Computing*, 28:1413–1426, 2010.

[2] H. Bay, A. Ess, T. Tuytelaars, and L. Van Gool. Speeded-up robust features (surf). *Comput. Vis. Image Underst.*, 110(3):346–359, June 2008.

[3] A. Coates, B. Carpenter, C. Case, S. Satheesh, B. Suresh, T. Wang, D. J. Wu, and A. Y. Ng. Text detection and character recognition in scene images with unsupervised feature learning. In *Proc. of International Conference on Document Analysis and Recognition*, ICDAR '11, pages 440–445, Washington, DC, USA, 2011. IEEE Computer Society.

[4] C. Cortes and V. Vapnik. Support-vector networks. *Machine Learning*, 20:273–297, 1995.

[5] B. Epshtein, E. Ofek, and Y. Wexler. Detecting text in natural scenes with stroke width transform. In *Proc. of International Conference on Computer Vision and Pattern Recognition*, pages 2963–2970, 2010.

[6] I. J. Goodfellow, D. Warde-Farley, M. Mirza, A. C. Courville, and Y. Bengio. Maxout networks. In *Proceedings of the 30th International Conference on Machine Learning, ICML 2013, Atlanta, GA, USA, 16-21 June 2013*, pages 1319–1327, 2013.

[7] M. Jaderberg, A. Vedaldi, and A. Zisserman. Deep features for text spotting. In *Proc. of European Conference on Computer Vision (ECCV)*. Springer, 2014.

[8] Y. Jia, E. Shelhamer, J. Donahue, S. Karayev, J. Long, R. Girshick, S. Guadarrama, and T. Darrell. Caffe: Convolutional architecture for fast feature embedding. *arXiv preprint arXiv:1408.5093*, 2014.

[9] K. Jung, K. I. Kim, and A. K. Jain. Text information extraction in images and video: a survey. *Pattern Recognition*, 37(5):977–997, 2004.

[10] D. G. Lowe. Distinctive image features from scale-invariant keypoints. *Int. J. Comput. Vision*, 60(2):91–110, Nov. 2004.

[11] J. Matas, O. Chum, M. Urban, and T. Pajdla. Robust wide-baseline stereo from maximally stable extremal regions. *Image and Vision Computing*, 22(10):761 – 767, 2004. British Machine Vision Computing 2002.

[12] B. T. N. Dala. Histograms of oriented gradients for human detection. In *Proc. IEEE Conference on Computer Vision and Pattern Recognition*, volume 1, pages 886–893, 2005.

[13] L. Neumann and J. Matas. Real-time scene text localization and recognition. In *Computer Vision and Pattern Recognition (CVPR), 2012 IEEE Conference on*, pages 3538–3545, June 2012.

[14] L. Neumann and J. Matas. Scene text localization and recognition with oriented stroke detection. In *Computer Vision (ICCV), 2013 IEEE International Conference on*, pages 97–104, Dec 2013.

[15] A. Sironi, B. Tekin, R. Rigamonti, V. Lepetit, and P. Fua. Learning separable filters. *IEEE Transactions on Pattern Analysis and Machine Intelligence*, 99(PrePrints):1, 2014.

[16] K. Wang, B. Babenko, and S. Belongie. End-to-end scene text recognition. In *Computer Vision (ICCV), 2011 IEEE International Conference on*, pages 1457–1464, Nov 2011.

[17] T. Wang, D. Wu, A. Coates, and A. Ng. End-to-end text recognition with convolutional neural networks. In *Pattern Recognition (ICPR), 2012 21st International Conference on*, pages 3304–3308, Nov 2012.

[18] H. Yang, B. Quehl, and H. Sack. A framework for improved video text detection and recognition. *Multimedia Tools and Applications*, pages 1–29, 2012. 10.1007/s11042-012-1250-6.

DigInPix: Visual Named-Entities Identification in Images and Videos

Pierre Letessier
Ina, France
pierre.letessier@ina.fr

Nicolas Hervé
Ina, France
nicolas.herve@ina.fr

Alexis Joly
INRIA Zenith, LIRMM, France
alexis.joly@inria.fr

Hakim Nabi, Mathieu Derval, Olivier Buisson
Ina, France
firstname.lastname@ina.fr

ABSTRACT

This paper presents an automatic system able to identify visual named-entities appearing in images and videos, among a list of 25,000 entities, aggregated from Wikipedia lists, and more specific websites. DigInPix is a generic application designed to identify different kinds of entities. In this first attempt, we only focus on logo identification (more generally on legal persons). The identification process mainly relies on an efficient CBIR system, searching in an indexed image database composed of 600,000 weak-labelled images crawled from Google Images. DigInPix proposes a responsive-design html5 interface[1] for testing purposes.

Categories and Subject Descriptors

H.3.1 [**Information Storage and Retrieval**]: Content Analysis and Indexing—*Dictionaries*

Keywords

Named-entities identification; CBIR; logos; images; videos

1. INTRODUCTION

Named-entities recognition and disambiguation in text documents is a well-known problem of the Natural Language Processing community, and there now exists some pretty good solutions, such as those submitted to the Microsoft Entity Recognition and Disambiguation Challenge [2]. In the same time, a lot of progresses have been made on image (instance) retrieval (logos, buildings, etc.) [1, 6, 10], and image classification, as demonstrated by recent results on the popular ImageNet dataset [9, 11, 12], or on fine-grained and instance classification tasks [3, 5]. Very few works did however specifically address the problem of recognizing very large numbers of named-entities (such as firms, government bodies, political parties, societies, associations, etc.) in images and videos. It can actually be very tricky to visually identify a named-entity based on global representations, especially when its visual representation is very small (tens of pixels). Furthermore, while a named-entity can be textually represented by a small synset, a visual synset has to deal with many variations (definition, encoding, scale, rotation, illumination, etc.).

Most existing related works were limited to the recognition of few tens of classes (37 logos in BelgaLogos dataset [6], 32 logos in FlickrLogos dataset [10]), each targeted entity being modeled by a single logotype. The only achievement dealing with more realistic numbers of entities and richer visual identities is the recent work of Leveau et al. [7]. The authors actually reported in that paper an experiment with more than 5,000 entities represented by a (noisy) training set of 370K images automatically crawled through a web search engine. The key point of their method it to rely on an efficient instance-based classification scheme (with fine-grained geometric constraints) rather than on the offline training of a supervised classifier on common aggregated image representations (such as Bag-of-words, VLAD or Fisher Vectors features [9]). They did show that such scheme outperforms state-of-the-art classification techniques on several challenging datasets while being much more scalable.

This paper describes an operational and interactive web application following a similar approach but at a larger scale (i.e. 25,000 entities and 600,000 images) and with additional

[1] http://diginpix.ina.fr

ICMR'15, June 23–26, 2015, Shanghai, China.

ACM 978-1-4503-3274-3/15/06 ...$15.00.
http://dx.doi.org/10.1145/2671188.2749369.

features such as browsing functionalities and the possibility to process video contents. The core engine makes use of local descriptors hashing techniques and a scalable indexing and search structure based on hash tables. This allows matching all local descriptors one by one in the full index and favors a more precise matching of small objects in highly cluttered pictures. Using geometry in addition to this raw scheme further improves the search performances (thanks to a RANSAC-like spatial reranking algorithm) and the instance-based classifier is shown to provide very promising automatic annotation performances.

2. PROPOSED APPROACH

2.1 Creation of the dictionaries

We call "dictionary" a list of named-entities, grouped together because they belong to a high level concept (e.g. legal persons, physical persons, paintings, buildings, etc.). With each entity, we associate a set of images trying to represent its whole visual diversity. The easiest way to create a dictionary is to import an existing database, but such databases are quite infrequent and incomplete (especially when collaborative).

So the most common way to create this kind of dictionary is to crawl the web and download images. To build our legal persons dictionary, we first collected a list of 25,000 entities found on Wikipedia lists, Top-N company rankings, and specific websites talking about sport clubs, cars, political parties, etc.

For all entities, we then used a popular image search engine, querying the named-entities textual representations associated with disambiguation keywords like "logo", or the entity categories, in order to obtain their visual representation. It is important to notice that the results are often very noisy, except for the most common entities, and we can only consider the downloaded images as weak-labelled, which is the cause of most of the identification mistakes.

2.2 Video vs. image pipeline

Both video and image contents can be uploaded and processed by the application (only images for public users). When dealing with videos, keyframes are first extracted whenever the content changes significantly, i.e. new shot, moving camera, new objects appearing, etc., thanks to a keyframe detector using grid-based histograms of LBP features. The time between two keyframes typically varies from 100ms to 30s. All the detected keyframes are then processed one by one in the same way than single images. They are first issued as queries to the visual search engine described within subsection 2.2.1. In a second step, the returned matched images are passed to the instance-based classifier described in section 2.2.2). It returns a list of the most probable named-entities visible in each query image (the automatic annotations). In the case of videos, a last step is finally completed to merge the automatic annotations of all keyframes (see section 2.2.2). It returns a ranked list of all the entities detected in the video according to their number of occurrences.

2.2.1 Visual Search Engine

All images are described with SIFT features [8], which are then compressed to 128-bit binary hash codes. This is done by first computing a principal component analysis in the original feature space followed by a binary quantization. The binary quantization of each component of a hash code $\mathbf{h}(\mathbf{x})$ is computed as:

$$h_j = sgn(\mathbf{a_j}^T\mathbf{x} - \mu_\mathbf{j})$$

where $\mathbf{a_j}$ is the j-th eigenvector resulting from the principal component analysis and

$$\mu_\mathbf{j} = \frac{1}{N}\sum_{\mathbf{x}} \mathbf{a_j}^T\mathbf{x}$$

is the mean of all the projected values. The distance between any two features $\mathbf{x}$ and $\mathbf{z}$ can then be efficiently approximated by the Hamming distance between $\mathbf{h}(\mathbf{z})$ and $\mathbf{h}(\mathbf{x})$. To avoid scanning the whole dataset, the hash codes $\mathbf{h}(\mathbf{x})$ derived from the local features of the training set are then indexed in a hash table whose keys are the t-length prefix of the hash codes $\mathbf{h}(\mathbf{x})$. At search time, the hash code $\mathbf{h}(\mathbf{q})$ of a query feature $\mathbf{q}$ is computed as well as its t-length prefix. We then use a probabilistic multi-probe search algorithm inspired by the one of [4] and allowing to efficiently return the approximate K-Nearest Neighbors (K-NN) of each query feature. We however use a simpler search model than the one of [4], based on a normal distribution with independent components parameterized by a single vector σ that is trained over the exact nearest neighbors of the training samples. The raw visual matches returned by the approximate K-NN search are finally filtered by a spatial consistency checking. We therefore estimate an affine transformation (by a RANSAC algorithm) between the query image and each matched image in the training set (i.e. the ones having at least two matches in the set of the returned approximate K-NN's). At the end of this step, we have a set of M^Q images similar to the query image Q, each associated with a similarity score S_i^Q.

2.2.2 Instance-based classifier

We compute the reliability scores of the eth entity for a query image Q by the following equation:

$$R_e^Q = \sum_{i=1}^{M_e^Q} S_i^Q$$

where M_e^Q is the size of the subset of images associated in the dictionary with the eth name-entity, and retrieved by the previously described CBIR system.

This score has to be normalised between 0 and 100%, in order to be displayed and understood by the users. It is done with:

$$\hat{R}_e^Q = \tanh\left(\max\left(\left\{\frac{R_e^Q - \alpha}{\beta}, 0\right\}\right)\right)$$

where $\alpha = 2$ and $\beta = 80$, both empirically set, after testing with a pool of users.

In the Graphical User Interface (GUI), we only display the entities with a score $\hat{R}_e^Q$ greater than 3%. This threshold has been chosen very low to favor a high recall (preferred by expert users), rather than a high precision (more adapted to non expert users).

When dealing with a video, we display the detected entities in each keyframe following the same paradigm but we also display a global score for every entities detected in the vth video. This global score is computed as the maximum score across all the keyframes:

$$\hat{G}_e^V = \max_{Q \in V} \hat{R}_e^Q$$

Considering that global score, we again filter the displayed entities by keeping only those in the top 25 reliability scores $\hat{G}_e^V$, and also those having a score higher than 50%, even if they are not in the top 25.

2.2.3 Results

In order to evaluate our system, we built a test dataset of 2,000 images from Flickr, containing 285 different named-entities. It was built by querying the Flickr text search engine with the name of 100 popular entities appearing in French sport events (Tour de France, Roland Garros, 24h du Mans, etc.). As many other entities also appeared in these images, we had to manually annotate them and finally obtained a groundtruth on 285 entities. The graph in the figure 1 shows the precision/recall curve achieved by our named-entity detection scheme on these 2,000 images (using the web crawl of 25,000 entities and 600,000 images as training set). The curves were obtained by varying the threshold on the reliability score $\hat{R}_e^Q$. We can see that with this quite realistic test dataset we achieve a precision of 80% for a recall of 30%. We can also note that we cannot perform more than 40% of recall, probably due to the amount of bad-labelled images in the dictionary, and to the very small entities we have in the test images. These images are not very big either: their average-size is 214 Kpx.

In the case of a constant load (analysing the 2,000 test images as soon as possible), DiglnPix can process an image in less than 2 seconds. In real conditions, it can be slightly longer, due to the server load. Processing time can even be as much as tens of seconds for large images, since the algorithm complexity is almost linear in the number of visual features (i.e. the image size).

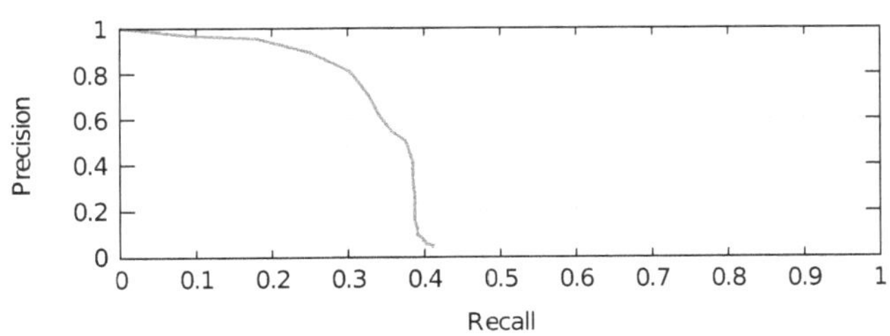

Figure 1: Evaluation

each of them. Figure 2 presents an example of an analysed image, where DiglnPix identified six named-entities, sorted by reliability. The user then has the possibility to click on any of them to access to all their informations (see section 3.2), and can jump to the other documents in which it has been identified.

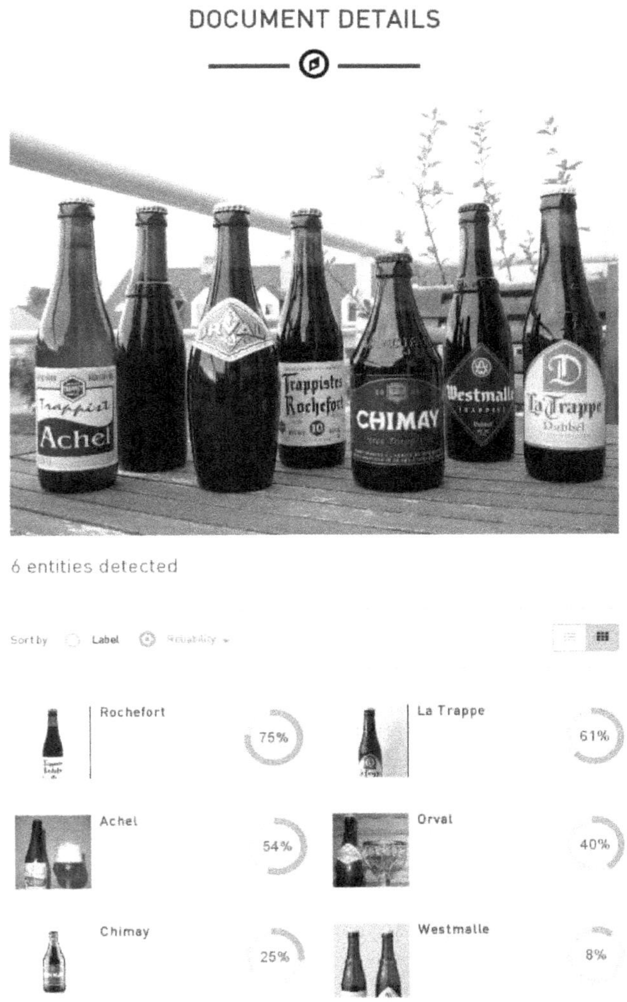

Figure 2: An analysed image with 6 detected entities

3. DEMONSTRATOR

The DiglnPix's GUI is a responsive and flat design web-application. All actions are accessible on the same single page. There are two main actions to do with DiglnPix: the first one is to analyse one's own photo, and the second is to browse the dictionaries as well as the videos of the sport collection taken from Ina's archives (automatically annotated by our named-entity detection scheme).

3.1 Analysing one's own image

Users can upload their own image (or video) from a local drive or from an image url. After the named-entity identification process, the GUI displays the analysed image, with the list of detected entities, and the reliability score $\hat{R}_e^Q$ for

3.2 Browsing data

There are two categories of browsable datas in DiglnPix: the dictionaries data and the analysed documents.

Users can browse the named-entities in each dictionary, sort them by label, or by their number of detections in the whole set of analysed documents, and filter them by their first character. For each entity, DiglnPix display the list of representative images crawled from the web, and used by the algorithm to recognize this entity.

The analysed documents (images or videos) are distributed in coherent collections. Initially, only one demo collection of sports videos is proposed. The user can click any of them to see the list of detected named-entities. If the document is a video, DigInPix displays it in an open-source video player[2] enriched with timelines showing the time stamps at which each entity was detected. These time stamps are symbolised by clickable points on the line, as shown in the figure 3. Many buttons are available to handle the player, and the little gear in the bottom-right corner enables or disables the tooltips explaining their use.

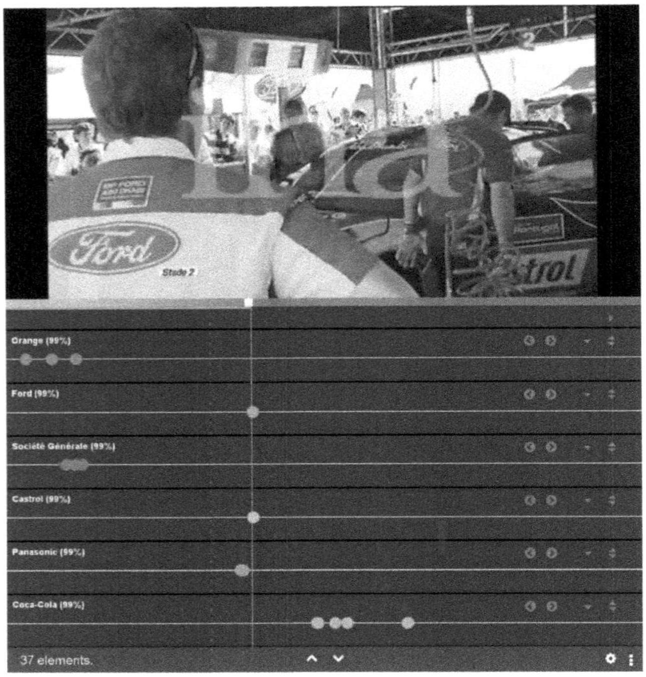

Figure 3: The video player with timelines

4. CONCLUSIONS

DigInPix is a first attempt to provide public access to our large-scale named-entities identification algorithm, and we think that there is room for further improvements. The first one could be to add new dictionaries, in particular buildings, places, paintings and faces, among many others. Another great improvement would be to interactively clean or revise the bad-labelled images which cause most of the identification errors. For this, we intend to develop new interfaces to provide users an easy way to participate, and give feedback. Finally, we could improve the user experience by drawing the precise location of the detected named-entities in the images and videos, as allowed by our video player, and also track the entities between the keyframes.

[2]http://ina-foss.github.io/amalia.js

5. ACKNOWLEDGEMENT

We wish to thank the developers who participated in this project.

6. REFERENCES

[1] R. Arandjelovic and A. Zisserman. Three things everyone should know to improve object retrieval. In *CVPR*, 2012.

[2] D. Carmel, M.-W. Chang, E. Gabrilovich, B.-J. P. Hsu, and K. Wang. ERD 2014: Entity recognition and disambiguation challenge. *SIGIR Forum*, 2014.

[3] P.-H. Gosselin, N. Murray, H. Jégou, and F. Perronnin. Revisiting the fisher vector for fine-grained classification. *Pattern Recognition Letters*, 2014.

[4] A. Joly and O. Buisson. A posteriori multi-probe locality sensitive hashing. In *ACM MM*, 2008.

[5] J. Krapac, F. Perronnin, T. Furon, and H. Jégou. Instance classification with prototype selection. In *Proceedings of International Conference on Multimedia Retrieval*, page 431. ACM, 2014.

[6] P. Letessier, O. Buisson, and A. Joly. Consistent visual words mining with adaptive sampling. In *ICMR*, 2011.

[7] V. Leveau, A. Joly, O. Buisson, P. Letessier, and P. Valduriez. Recognizing thousands of legal entities through instance-based visual classification. In *Proceedings of the ACM International Conference on Multimedia*, pages 1029–1032. ACM, 2014.

[8] D. G. Lowe. Object recognition from local scale-invariant features. In *ICCV*, 1999.

[9] F. Perronnin, J. Sánchez, and T. Mensik. Improving the fisher kernel for large-scale image classification. In *ECCV*, 2010.

[10] S. Romberg, L. G. Pueyo, R. Lienhart, and R. Van Zwol. Scalable logo recognition in real-world images. In *ICMR*, 2011.

[11] K. Simonyan and A. Zisserman. Very deep convolutional networks for large-scale image recognition. *arXiv preprint:1409.1556*, 2014.

[12] C. Szegedy, W. Liu, Y. Jia, P. Sermanet, S. Reed, D. Anguelov, D. Erhan, V. Vanhoucke, and A. Rabinovich. Going deeper with convolutions. *CoRR*, abs/1409.4842, 2014.

Mobile Media Thumbnailing

Yingying Chen, Jinqiao Wang, Jing Liu and Hanqing Lu
National Lab of Pattern Recognition, Institute of Automation
Chinese Academy of Sciences, Beijing 100190, China
{yingying.chen, jqwang, jliu, luhq}@nprl.ia.ac.cn

ABSTRACT

With the development of Multimedia and Internet techniques, massively increasing visual data, such as image and video, need to be shown and browsed as thumbnails in various digital display platforms, like PC, cell phone, etc. This demonstration presents a grid based adaptive media thumbnailing approach to maximize user experience in mobile image and video browsing. After representative frame extraction by spectral clustering and salient region detection, we obtain thumbnails with three resizing operators: cropping, warping and scaling, and adaptively fuse them into a unified grid based convex programming problem which could be solved simultaneously and efficiently through numerical optimization. Extensive experiments and comparisons on HUAWEI Honor 6 and Samsung S5 demonstrate that the proposed method achieves an excellent information preservation for thumbnails in mobile devices.

Categories and Subject Descriptors

I.2.10 [**Vision and Scene Understanding**]: Video analysis

General Terms

Algorithms, experimentation

Keywords

Video thumbnail, media retargeting

1. INTRODUCTION

Due to the proliferation of image data presented on various devices with different sizes, from TV screens to cell phones, how to present and browse image and video data efficiently becomes an important issue and thumbnail has been used broadly. Most existing image tools generate thumbnails through scaling the source image uniformly to adapt to various digital display platforms. However, this intuitive strategy inevitably causes noticeable distortion and shrinkage on the image content, which affects users' browsing experience and limits the accuracy of searching or recognizing images based on thumbnails. As a technique focuses on preserving visual information of important image content, image retargeting is considered as an alternative solution for thumbnail generation. However, when the target size is very small, especially 120×120 or even smaller, existing retargeting approaches with single strategy can hardly guarantee that important content within the thumbnail is clear or big enough to be viewed.

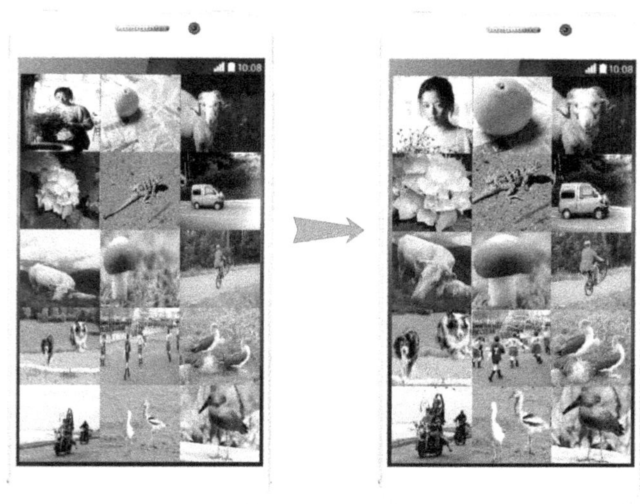

Tradition thumbnails — Our thumbnails

Figure 1: Comparison between traditional thumbnails and the proposed thumbnails.

To develop an ideal thumbnail generator, we combine multiple operators like cropping, warping and scaling into a grid based convex programming framework for thumbnail generation to integrate the advantages and compensate the defect of each operator. Some examples of traditional approaches and the proposed approach are shown in Fig. 1, which shows our approach achieves a better visual effect by rearranging important objects more compactly.

2. SYSTEM OVERVIEW

As shown in Fig. 2, for an input video we firstly extract representative frames by spectral clustering [3] and detect salient regions. Then we fuse three retargeting strategies

ICMR'15, June 23–26, 2015, Shanghai, China.

http://dx.doi.org/10.1145/2671188.2749409.

Figure 2: Pipeline of mobile media thumbnailing.

including cropping, warping and scaling, and simultaneously optimize them to generate thumbnails.

3. IMPLEMENTATION DETAILS

3.1 Representative frame selection

The selection of representative images for input videos involves scene change detection and keyframe clustering. The scene similarity takes into account color and temporal similarities between the sets of keyframes. A weighted graph is constructed for the scenes of an input video. After spectral clustering, one keyframe is selected from each cluster as the representative image. We apply a simple ranking criterion to select the keyframe of a longer scene as the thumbnail.

3.2 Warping, cropping and scaling

We adaptively fuse three resizing operators based on grid optimization for mobile thumbnailing. Grid based warping is employed to preserve the spatially important content from obvious shape distortion. Additionally, we incorporate a cropping energy term, which provides system with more space for completely presenting the important content through cropping some regions out selectively. The cropping term should satisfy requirements that the most important information is preserved preferentially and smooth geometric structure is not influenced. With warping and cropping, we free up more space to display the important content, rearrange the salient objects compactly and preserve the geometric structure of objects smoothly. To address the information loss due to scale changes, we further incorporate a scaling term for each grid to guarantee foreground objects at a proper size. The minimizing of the three energies can be solved as a convex programming problem, which can be resorted to the numerical optimization efficiently.

4. EXPERIMENT

To test the effectiveness and efficiency of our approach, we run experiments on mobile phones (HUAWEI Honor 6 and Samsung S5). For an image in the size of 700×500, the time cost is about 20ms for a thumbnail 120×120. The comparison results with ISC [1], SPW [4], SOAR_{tp} [2], SOAR_{cr} [2] are shown in Fig. 3. Since we jointly optimize the warping, cropping and scaling functions together, the scale of important objects looks more appropriate and some background information is effectively condensed. In this way, the image structure has less deformation and looks more natural.

Figure 3: Comparison with state-of-the-art approaches.

5. CONCLUSIONS

In this paper, we present a technical implementation of mobile image thumbnailing. We select representative frame by spectral clustering and combine multiple resizing operators for thumbnail generation. Numerical optimization is utilized to efficiently solve the problem of grid based convex programming. Extensive experiments on mobile phones show the promise of the proposed solution.

6. ACKNOWLEDGMENT

This work was supported by 863 Program 2014AA015104, and National Natural Science Foundation of China 61273034, and 61332016.

7. REFERENCES

[1] M. Rubinstein, A. Shamir, and S. Avidan. Improved seam carving for video retargeting. In *ACM Transactions on Graphics (TOG)*, volume 27, page No.16. ACM, 2008.

[2] J. Sun and H. Ling. Scale and object aware image thumbnailing. *International journal of computer vision*, 104(2):135–153, 2013.

[3] J. Wang, L.-Y. Duan, Q. Liu, H. Lu, and J. S. Jin. A multimodal scheme for program segmentation and representation in broadcast video streams. *IEEE Transactions on Multimedia*, 10(3):393–408, 2008.

[4] G.-X. Zhang, M.-M. Cheng, S.-M. Hu, and R. R. Martin. A shape-preserving approach to image resizing. In *Computer Graphics Forum*, volume 28, pages 1897–1906. Wiley Online Library, 2009.

IdeaPanel: A Large Scale Interactive Sketch-based Image Search System

Changcheng Xiao[1]* Changhu Wang[2]† Liqing Zhang[1], Lei Zhang[3]
[1]Shanghai Jiao Tong University, Shanghai, China
[2]Microsoft Research, Beijing, China
[3]Microsoft Corporation, Redmond, USA
xchangcheng@gmail.com, chw@microsoft.com,
zhang-lq@cs.sjtu.edu.cn, leizhang@microsoft.com

ABSTRACT

In this work, we introduce the IdeaPanel system, an interactive sketch-based image search engine with millions of images. IdeaPanel enables users to sketch the target image in their minds and also supports tagging to describe their intentions. After a search is triggered, similar images will be returned in real time, based on which users can interactively refine their query sketches until ideal images are returned. Different from existing work, most of which requires a huge amount of memory for indexing and matching, IdeaPanel can achieve very competitive performance but requires much less memory storage. IdeaPanel needs only about $240MB$ memory to index $1.3M$ images (less than 3% of previous MindFinder system). Due to its high accuracy and low memory cost, IdealPanel can scale up to much larger database and thus has larger potential to return the most desired images for users.

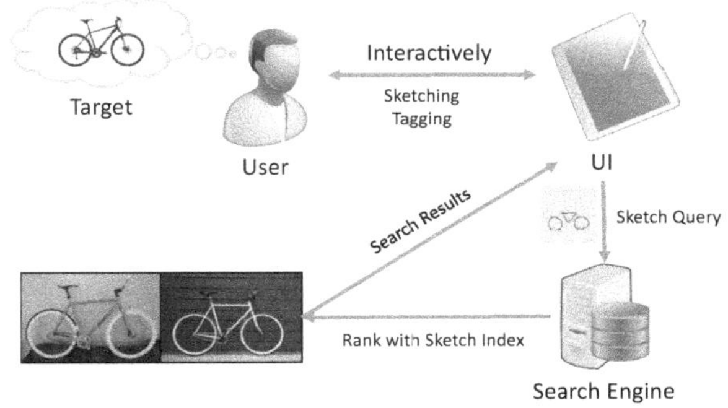

Figure 1: Illustration of the IdeaPanel system. Users can draw the major curves of the target image on the canvas panel. Then natural images with similar contours will be returned in real time.

Categories and Subject Descriptors

H.3.3 [**Information Search and Retrieval**]: Search Process, Query formulation; H.5.2 [**User Interfaces**]: User-centered Design

Keywords

Sketch-based Image Retrieval; Shape Words

1. INTRODUCTION

Owing to the prevalence of Internet and mobile phones, billions of digital images are now freely accessible online, which bring a great opportunity for large scale image search. Usually, users search images with text queries. However, the shape and location of the object cannot be easily formulated as a few keywords. Thus, query-by-example (QBE) was proposed. However, in QBE, a typical query is an example image, which is usually the reason of searching.

To overcome existing problems of current image search engines. A natural solution is to enable users to flexibly express their intentions by providing them a pen and a drawing panel. With the popularity of touch-screen devices, all necessary prerequisites to sketch-based image retrieval (SBIR) are ready. As illustrated in Fig. 1 & 2, users can detail their ideas by interactively drawing sketches, which will be the queries to our system. Natural images with similar contours will be returned in real time, and users can interactively refine their sketches or add some tags until ideal images are returned. SBIR is complementary and thus can be combined with query-by-keyword and query-by-example modalities.

Sketch based image retrieval has been extensively studied since 1990s [3], and stepped into large-scale scenarios in recent years [4, 2, 6, 5]. However, most of these methods focus on low level descriptors of sketches like local patches [4] or edge pixels [2], which requires huge amount of memory (e.g. MindFinder [2] requires $8GB$ memory for $2.1M$ images). Some hash-based methods [6, 5] have been proposed to save the memory cost of SBIR system while sacrificing some accuracy at the same time.

In this work, we systematically solve the representation, matching and indexing problems of large scale sketch-based image retrieval. We try to step forward and see the sketches in a higher view. Different from MindFinder [2] which in-

*Changcheng Xiao performed this work while being an intern at Microsoft Research Asia.
†Corresponding author.

ICMR'15, June 23–26, 2015, Shanghai, China.

ACM 978-1-4503-3274-3/15/06 ...$15.00.
http://dx.doi.org/10.1145/2671188.2749410.

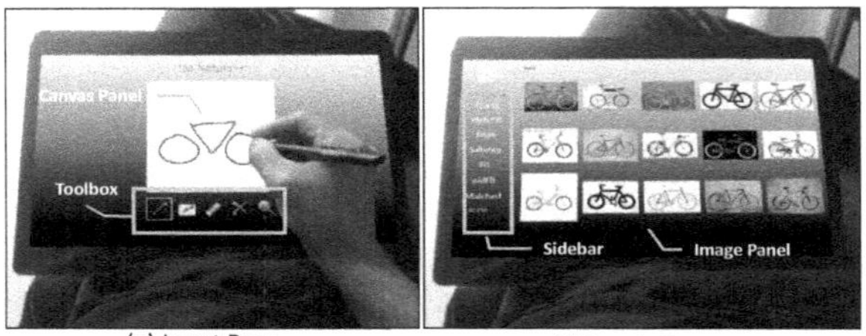

(a) Input Page (b) Result Page

Figure 2: The Windows 8 Metro UI of IdeaPanel.

dexes and matches with (sampled) edge pixels, we propose to represent both the query sketch and the natural image in the database as a bag of *shape words*. As shown in Fig. 2, when drawing a bike, most users will probably draw two circles as its wheels followed by a triangle as its frame. Ideally, it will be quite powerful if we can successfully extract the triangles and circles from database images, and match them with the shapes of the query sketch. However, it's still a very challenging task to extract such shapes from natural images with high precision and recall. To balance the robustness and computational complexity, we leverage a middle level descriptor between edge pixels and shapes, i.e., line segments and circular arcs, as *shape words*. We propose an efficient algorithm for *shape words* extraction, followed by a generalization of the classical Chamfer Matching algorithm [1] for *shape words*' matching. Finally, a novel inverted index structure is proposed to make *shape words* representation scalable to large scale image databases.

Based on the *shape words* representation, we build the IdeaPanel system on two image databases, with $1.3M$ and $4.5M$ natural images respectively. Owing to the compact representation, novel matching and indexing strategies, IdeaPanel only requires 3% memory storage of the MindFinder system while holds very competitive accuracy at the same time.

2. SYSTEM OVERVIEW

In this section, we introduce the major functions of the IdeaPanel system. As shown in Fig. 2, the UI of IdeaPanel contains two pages: the input page and the result page. The input page provides a canvas panel to help users flexibly express their search intentions. Below the canvas panel is the toolbox, which enables users to quickly edit their sketches or add some tags. When a search is finished, the returned images will be shown in the image panel of the result page.

The major querying operation of IdeaPanel is sketching, which describes the main curves of the image in the user's mind. As some complex objects are not easy to draw by normal users, our system also enables users to add some tags to constrain the semantic subject of the returned images. So our system support the following two query modes:

Query by Sketch
: Draw the major curves of the target image within the canvas panel (Fig. 2 (a)). When finished, click the search button to start the search. Fig. 3 shows some example hand-drawn sketches.

Query by Sketch + Tag
: Click the text box button in the toolbox, type in some keywords, and click the search button to start a new search. Users are also allowed to directly filter the returned images by choosing a proper tag in the slide bar of the result page.

Figure 3: Examples of hand-drawn sketches.

Figure 4: Example queries and corresponding results. Images marked by red cross indicate that they are irrelevant with the query.

Fig. 4 shows several example sketch queries and corresponding top results, which are precise and structure sensitive.

3. ACKNOWLEDGMENTS

The work of first and third authors was supported by the National Natural Science Foundation of China (Grant No. 61272251) and National Key Basic Research Program of China (Grant No. 2015CB856004).

4. REFERENCES

[1] G. Borgefors. Hierarchical chamfer matching: A parametric edge matching algorithm. *IEEE PAMI*, 1988.

[2] Y. Cao, H. Wang, C. Wang, Z. Li, L. Zhang, and L. Zhang. Mindfinder: Interactive sketch-based image search on millions of images. ACM MM, 2010.

[3] R. Datta, D. Joshi, J. Li, and J. Z. Wang. Image retrieval: Ideas, influences, and trends of the new age. *ACM Comput. Surv.*, 40:5:1–5:60, 2008.

[4] M. Eitz, K. Hildebrand, T. Boubekeur, and M. Alexa. A descriptor for large scale image retrieval based on sketched feature lines. SBIM, 2009.

[5] X. Sun, C. Wang, C. Xu, and L. Zhang. Indexing billions of images for sketch-based retrieval. ACM MM, 2013.

[6] K.-Y. Tseng, Y.-L. Lin, Y.-H. Chen, and W. H. Hsu. Sketch-based image retrieval on mobile devices using compact hash bits. ACM MM, 2012.

A Sparse Ensemble Learning System For Efficient Semantic Indexing *

Sheng Tang, Hui Chen, Yu Li, Jun-Bin Xiao, Jin-Tao Li
Institute of Computing Technology, Chinese Academy of Sciences, Beijing, China
{ts, chenhui, liyu, xiaojunbin, jtli}@ict.ac.cn

ABSTRACT

This demo presents an extremely efficient concept detection system based on a novel bag of words extraction method and sparse ensemble learning. We will show that the presented system can efficiently build the concept detectors upon millions of images, and achieve real-time concept detection on unseen images with the state-of-the-arts accuracy. To do so, we first develop an efficient bag of visual words (BoW) construction method based on sparse non-negative matrix factorization (NMF) and GPU enabled SIFT feature extraction. We then develop a sparse ensemble learning method to build the detection model, which drastically reduces learning time in order of magnitude over traditional methods like Support Vector Machine. The demo video of the system is available at YouTube: http://youtu.be/57obnlCxqAs

Categories and Subject Descriptors

I.2.10 [**Vision and Scene Understanding**]: Visions

General Terms

Algorithms, Experimentation, Performance

Keywords

Ensemble learning, Sparse coding, Semantic indexing

1. INTRODUCTION

Semantic indexing or visual concept detection is to predict the presence of certain concepts, such as building and flower, etc, in images and video shots [1]. It is essentially a classification task, in which a classifier is usually learned based on a set of training images or video keyframes. Visual concept detection on real life data, like web images and videos, is computationally expensive. Learning detectors usually involves huge volume of training data. Realtime feature extraction and classification are challenging too. The efficiency challenges become especially prominent when building a realtime concept detector on millions of samples.

In this demonstration, we present an extremely efficient concept detection system. The presented system can efficiently build the concept detection model upon millions of images, and meanwhile, perform realtime concept detection with the state-of-the-arts accuracy. To do so, we first develop an efficient bag of visual words (BoW) construction method based on sparse non-negative matrix factorization (NMF) and GPU enabled SIFT feature extraction [2]. We then build the detection model based on our work of sparse ensemble learning [1]. The sparse ensemble learning brings order of magnitude more efficient model learning than traditional methods like Support Vector Machine (SVM). The model sparsity also leads to both low memory space and high classification speed. We also construct a large training set with both pseudo relevance feedback of negative samples and interactive feedback of positive samples. The dataset including images, annotation, ground truth and our results are available at [3].

2. SPARSE BOW

We utilize the bag-of-visual words (BoW) as image feature. To achieve high efficiency for realtime applications, we use the GPU-enabled SiftGPU [2] for fast SIFT extraction. Rather than traditional vector quantization (VQ), we propose SparseBoW by using sparse coding to generate BoW. Sparse coding can achieve lower reconstruction error, thus lower information loss in quantization, resulting from less restrictive constraint [4]. Specifically, we use sparse NMF due to its use of non-negativity constraints that allow only additive instead of subtractive combinations which exhibits its advantages in learning parts-based representations [1].

Instead of using the max pooling function on the sparse codes as in [4], we propose to compute the BoW through a soft-weighting scheme. Suppose $x_i \in \mathbf{R}^l$ is the i-th local descriptor from the observed feature matrix $\mathbf{X} = [x_1, \ldots, x_N] \in \mathbf{R}^{l\times N}$, and d_j is the atom from a learned dictionary $\mathbf{D} = [d_1, \ldots, d_k] \in \mathbf{R}^{l\times k}$, and the SIFT dimensionality $l = 128$, we compute the BoW histogram $\{z_j\}_{j=1}^{k}$through weighted sum of similarities between descriptors and dictionary atoms with ℓ_1-normalized sparse code as:

$$z_j = \sum_{i=1}^{N} \left(\frac{\alpha_{ij}}{\sum_{j=1}^{M} \alpha_{ij}} sim(x_i, d_j) \right) \quad (1)$$

where the sparse code α_{ij} denotes the non-zero responses of local descriptor x_i to the corresponding atom d_j. The measure $sim(x_i, d_j)$ represents the similarity between x_i and d_j.

*This work was supported by National Nature Science Foundation of China (61173054), Beijing Natural Science Foundation (4152050), and 863 Project (2014AA015202).

ICMR'15, June 23–26, 2015, Shanghai, China.

DOI: http://dx.doi.org/10.1145/2671188.2749411.

Table 1: Time Comparison (ms)

Method	SIFT	BoW	Total
BoW(SIFT+K-means VQ)	912	828	1740
SparseBoW(SiftGPU+Sparse NMF)	34	108	142

In this demonstration, we use the cosine similarity and restrict the maximum number of non-zero responses (sparsity) $M = 4$ during sparse coding. Since M is far less than the vocabulary size k(=512 in our system), the extraction of BoW takes only 142 ms, about 12 times faster than traditional BoW extraction through K-means VQ as shown in Table 1.

3. SPARSE ENSEMBLE LEARNING

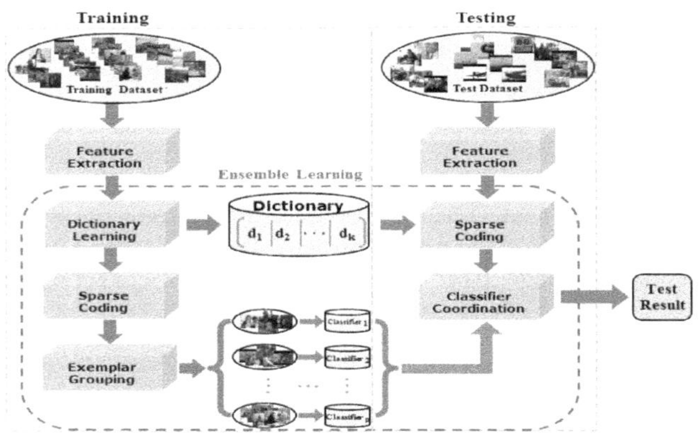

Figure 1: System Framework of SEL

Large scale training dataset imposes a great challenge for efficiency of both training and testing. To overcome the low efficiency and unscalability of the classical methods based on global classification, we proposed sparse ensemble learning (SEL) for visual concept detection in [1]. As shown in Figure 1, it leverages sparse code of image features for both partition of large scale training set into small localities for efficient training and coordination of the individual classifiers in each locality for final classification. The sparsity ensures that only a small number of classifiers in the ensemble will fire on a testing sample, which not only gives better AP than other fusion methods like average fusion and Adaboost, but also allows the high efficiency of online detection.

4. TRAINING DATA COLLECTION

Although the explosion of Internet images makes it much easier to collect the training data, how to annotate such large scale data becomes a challenge. Here, we adopt a feedback annotation mechanism to alleviate the human labeling efforts. First, we select 110K images from MIRFlickr dataset [5], 17K newly downloaded images from Flickr and 113K images from ImageNet on 8 concepts from TRECVID: cityscape, building, plant, waterscape, landscape, car, animal and flower. We then take these images as seed to learn concept detectors, and apply them on the rest of images in MIRFlickr dataset. Through the interactive interface in our demo, 8 annotators are asked to check the samples with high scores for each concept. After manual checking, we add both false positive and true positive samples into our final training set. For images with very low score, we treat them as negative training data. The rational is that samples with very low scores are often true negative samples with very high probability (above 99% in our experiments due to the high recall rate of our system). Totally, we collect over 540K training images with minimal human labeling since the proportion of high score samples to be checked is very small.

5. DEMONSTRATION

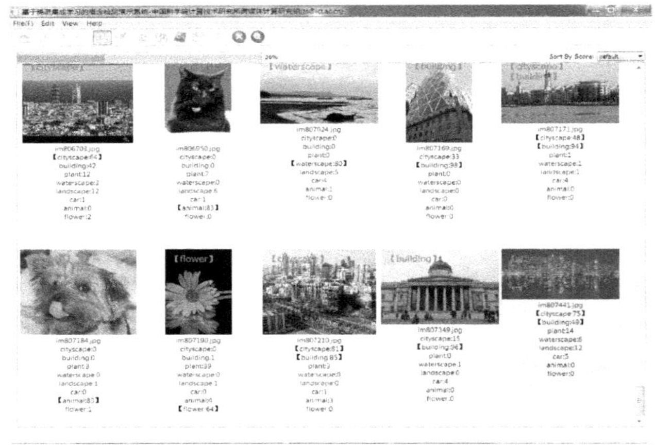

Figure 2: System Interface

In this demonstration, we will show that the system can build detection models on millions of training images very efficiently. Figure 2 shows the interface of the concept detection system. The system is an integration of our efficient SparseBoW feature(prior fusion with edge histogram and color moments) and the SEL framework (the number of localities is 1024, and the replication parameter $L = 3$). The training of a concept detector (not including feature extraction) takes around 2 hours on 0.54 million of images (actually 1.6M samples after assigning a sample to multiple L localities in the SEL framework). To the best of our knowledge, this efficiency outperforms all existing systems.

The demo will also show that concept detection on unseen images achieves realtime efficiency with the state-of-the-arts accuracy. It takes about 320 ms for all of 8 concepts detectors to examine one image. Specifically, the feature extraction for BoW takes 142 ms, edge histogram 20 ms and color moments 70 ms. The classification process only costs about 11 ms per concept. As shown in our web [3], the mean average precision (MAP) over the 8 concepts is 0.603. Over 90% of the top 100 among result lists are correct for the 6 concepts: building, cityscape, flower, plant, landscape, waterscape, which shows the effectiveness of our SEL method.

To further improve the precision, we will replace the current features in our SEL framework with the more effective features learned from deep Convolutional Neural Networks.

6. REFERENCES

[1] Sheng Tang, Yan-Tao Zheng, Yu Wang, and Tat-Seng Chua. Sparse ensemble learning for concept detection. *IEEE Transactions on Multimedia*, 14(1):43–54, Feb. 2012.

[2] Changchang Wu. SiftGPU: A GPU implementation of scale invariant feature transform (SIFT). http://cs.unc.edu/~ccwu/siftgpu, 2007.

[3] Sheng Tang. MCG-LSDVCD: A large scale dataset for visual concept detection. http://mcg.ict.ac.cn/mcg-sel.html, 2013.

[4] Jianchao Yang, Kai Yu, Yihong Gong, and Thomas Huang. Linear spatial pyramid matching using sparse coding for image classification. In *CVPR '09*, 2009.

[5] Mark J. Huiskes, Bart Thomee, and Michael S. Lew. New trends and ideas in visual concept detection: the MIR flickr retrieval evaluation initiative. In *MIR '10*, 2010.

A Multi-Sensory Gesture-Based Occupational Therapy Environment for Controlling Home Appliances

Ahmad M Qamar[1,3], Ahmed Riaz Khan[2], Syed Osama Husain[2], Md. Abdur Rahman[1], Saleh Basalamah[1,2]

[1]College of Computer and Information Systems, Umm Al-Qura University, Makkah, KSA

[2]KACST GIS Technology Innovation Center, Umm Al-Qura University, Makkah, KSA

[3]School of Computer Science, Universiti Sains Malaysia, Penang, Malaysia

{amqamar, marahman, smbasalamah}@uqu.edu.sa, {akhan, shussain}@gistic.org

ABSTRACT

The proliferation of networked home appliances, coupled with the popularity of low cost gesture detection sensors has made it possible to create smart home environments where users can manipulate devices of daily use through gestures. In this paper, we present a multi-sensory environment that allows a disabled person to control actual devices around the house that are presented to her in a mixed reality environment, as part of occupational therapy exercises. An analytical engine processes the motion data collected by gesture recognition sensors, measures recovery metrics, such as joint range of motion and speed of movement, etc. and presents the results to the therapist or the patient in the form of graphs and exercise statistics. We have incorporated intuitive 2D and 3D user interfaces into the environment to make the therapy experience more engaging and immersive for the disabled people. From the multimedia occupational therapy exercise data analysis, a therapist can get determine the ability of a patient to perform daily life activities without the help of others.

Categories and Subject Descriptors

Computing Methodologies – Artificial Intelligence - Computer vision- Computer vision tasks- Biometrics

General Terms

Human Factors.

Keywords

Kinect; Leap; Myo; Smart Homes; Therapy; Serious Games.

1. INTRODUCTION

Exponential growth of the world population and rapid increase in knowledge have resulted in an increase in the average life expectancy of human beings. People now have access to better medical facilities and hence, have better prospects when it comes to treating fatal diseases. As a result, a significant population of modern societies is composed of the elderly who become victims of various physical disabilities due to older age. Moreover, thousands of normal, healthy individuals become victims of accidents or other diseases every year, which leaves them in a condition that inhibits free physical movement. There are various methods of physical therapy available that require the patient to perform a number of exercises throughout a certain time period consistently, in the presence of an actual or virtual therapist. These exercises serve as means of rehabilitation for the person but can drag out over long and tedious stretches of time, becoming difficult to manage.

In this paper, we present a gesture based smart home appliance management system that also acts as an occupational therapy platform for a disabled individual. All the appliances in the house are interconnected through a smart system, which is modeled as a state machine. Gestures from different multimedia devices are combined into a universal gesture library where each gesture is interpreted as a specific action that results when that gesture is performed. Each action has a state assigned to it, and the gestures corresponding to these actions can be changed to perform other actions. When a disabled person makes certain gestures in the automated environment (e.g., switching a light bulb off), specific physical/therapeutic data is collected by the device used to perform the gesture. The data is collected without interfering with the daily regimen of the patient, which allows her to continue her routine and examine her health and performance at the same time.

With the proliferation of economically priced sensor devices like the Microsoft Kinect, the Leap Motion controller and the Myo EMG device from Thalmic labs, hardware and software based frameworks that support online remote therapy monitoring for physically disabled patients have become an interesting area of research. In [1], the authors have devised a framework for remotely monitoring Hemiplegic patients using Kinect. Frameworks such as Mira Rehab[1], Jintronix[2], 5plustherapy[3], Motioncare360[4], Doctor Kinetic[5], KinectoTherapy[6], Heremo[7], Remotion360[8], and Welfare Denmark[9] also provide a therapist the facility to remotely track improvement metrics of physically disabled patients. In [2,3] the authors present serious games-based environments using Kinect to provide therapy to physically disabled patients. Other systems have been developed to provide occupational therapy to disabled individuals. In [4], the authors have designed a virtual reality based environment to provide occupational therapy to disabled individuals. In [5], the authors

ICMR '15, June 23–26, 2015, Shanghai, China

DOI: http://dx.doi.org/10.1145/2671188.2749412

[1] http://www.mirarehab.com
[2] http://www.jintronix.com
[3] http://www.5plustherapy.com
[4] http://www.motioncare360.com
[5] http://doctorkinetic.nl/
[6] http://www.kinectotherapy.in/
[7] http://heremo.com/
[8] http://www.infostrat.com/solutions/Remotion360
[9] http://www.welfaredenmark.dk/uk/solutions/

present a wireless glove based network of sensors connected to a smart phone through bluetooth to control a 3D game environment. A disabled person often faces difficulty in moving around the house even for small chores such as turning the light off or controlling home appliances. A smart home environment can be of great help to such an individual. In [6] the authors have developed a 3D GUI to control a smart home household. In [7], the authors have used 3D tools to design and develop mixed reality based smart home environments. However, none of the above works has tried to combine smart home control with occupational therapy in a mixed reality environment using natural user gestures.

We combine three different gesture recognition devices namely Myo, Leap Motion and Kinect2 within our framework. The Myo uses brain signal intercepted as electrical voltage passing through the hand muscles. Since MYO uses Bluetooth Low Energy (BLE), it does not require line of sight and can control appliance within a home area. This helps a disabled person control appliances from anywhere in the house. However, Myo supports only a subset of gestures as compared to Leap Motion and Kinect2. We resort to Leap Motion and Kinect2 to support a wide range of occupational therapy gestures. We have incorporated two state of the art home appliances for the proof of concept demo. However, we have developed a generic state machine diagram for controlling appliances in a smart home, where the gestures can be customized to support occupational therapy.

2. SYSTEM ARCHITECTURE

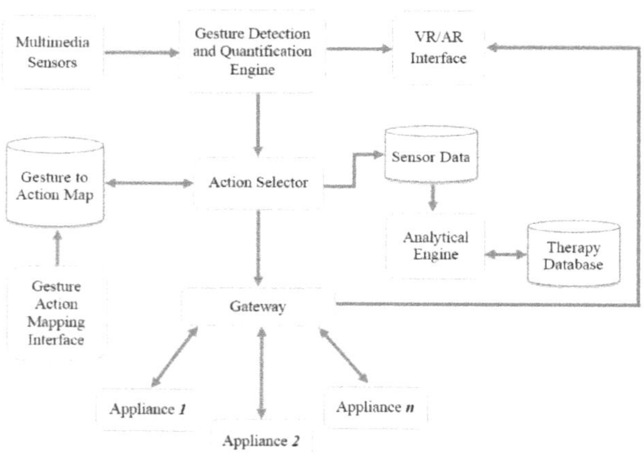

Figure 1: System Architecture

Figure 1 depicts the architecture of the presented system. Gesture data from various ***Multimedia Sensors*** connected to the system is received by a ***Gesture Detection and Quantification Engine***, which interprets meaningful occupational therapeutic gestures from raw multimedia sensor data. The ***Gesture to Action Map*** contains all the gestures that are interpreted by the system and are stored corresponding to the current action assigned to these gestures. A ***Gesture Action Mapping Interface*** provides a configurable environment to the user for selecting the desired action corresponding to all the available gestures from the connected devices. This information is sent to the ***Gesture to Action Map*** with the updated actions of the gestures. The ***Gesture Detection and Quantification Engine*** provides the gesture being performed to the ***Action Selector***, which fetches the corresponding action from the ***Gesture to Action Mapping*** component and passes that action to the appliance ***Gateway*** providing a way to select, control and monitor the state of the various appliances connected to the system. The ***Action Selector*** passes the selected action and the ***Gesture Detection and Quantification Engine*** provides the ***Virtual Reality / Augmented Reality (VR/AR) Interface*** with the detected gesture to be displayed to the user. This detected gesture is also stored in a ***Sensor Data*** repository connected to an ***Analytical Engine***, which queries a ***Therapy Database*** to confirm the therapy being performed based on the detected gesture. Using data aggregated over multiple sessions, this engine then displays the various analytics drawn from this information in the form of graphs and charts on the ***VR/AR Interface***. The Gateway is used to control different appliances in a house.

3. IMPLEMENTATION

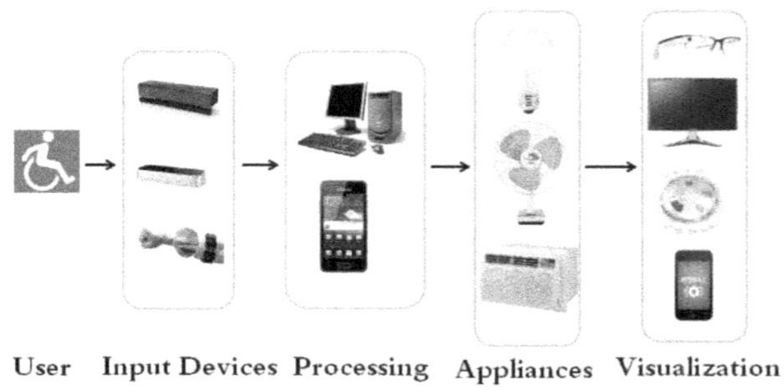

Figure 2: System Control Flow

Figure 2 shows our proposed system, which employs various off the shelf multimedia devices to accomplish its goals. The ***Gesture Input Devices*** used to gather occupational therapeutic data from a ***User*** and to perform control gestures are the Microsoft Kinect V2 sensor, Leap Motion and Myo armband. The comprehensive user interface (with live feedback) allows users to control different home appliances using gestures and also to configure gestures from these three devices according to their needs, e.g., if by default making a fist with the Myo armband on turns a light on or off, a user can configure the gesture (fist) to change the action performed by it as suited to her desires. Any gesture performed by the user is automatically detected by the appropriate device.

This occupational therapeutic gesture data is captured by a ***Gesture Processing & Recognition*** device, which is either a smartphone or a PC paired with the ***Input Device***. At this stage, the state of body joints is interpreted by software to interpret the gesture. The mapped action is then looked up and activated by sending a signal to the appropriate ***Smart home Appliance.*** At the same time, a constant visual feed is streamed to a set of available virtual reality/augmented reality based ***Visualization Interfaces***. In our current application, we have implemented a PC based 2D/3D interface and a smartphone based user interface. We are planning to incorporate Google Glass or a smart lens as a visual interface in the near future. Figure 3 shows the detailed state machine diagram.

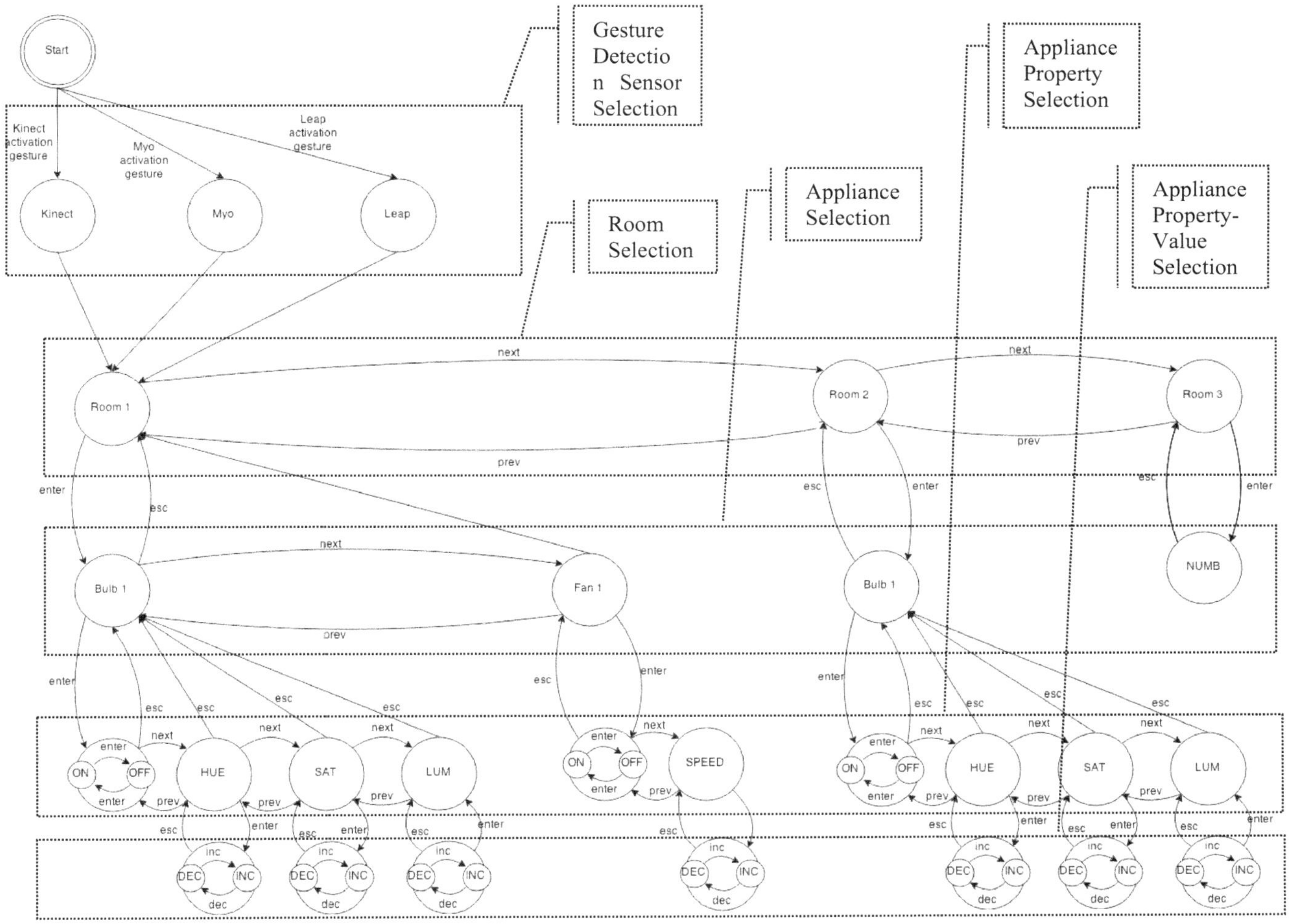

Figure 3: Generic state machine diagram of controlling smart home appliances through multi-modal gestures recognition devices

As shown in Figure 3, from the start state, a user has to first choose the type of gesture control device by entering the *gesture device selection state*. In this state, a user can browse between different available options and then select one of them using a pre-defined gesture that is common to all the devices. Once a device is selected, a user can go to the *room selection state* where he can browse among different rooms using certain gestures. Once a certain room is focused, a specific gesture will help the user select any room. Once a room is selected, he can now browse different appliances in that room. Similarly, once an appliance is selected, he can enter into the property selection state. From the available properties, he can choose one of the states. For example, in the demo, we have a light bulb that has 4 different states: on/off, hue, saturation and brightness. A user can choose any of the properties using a gesture. Once a property is selected, a user can define values of that property using certain gestures. For example, for the on/off property, wave left turns the light off and wave right turns it on. For hue, saturation and brightness, clockwise hand rotation increases the value and counterclockwise rotation decreases the value. In summary, using only 6 gestures a user can do all the operations shown in Figure 3. These 6 gestures are as follows: enter (select), esc (deselect), next, prev (previous), inc (increase), dec (decrease).

In our demo scenario, gesture input devices namely Kinect2, Myo and Leap Motion send signals over BLE and USB 3.0 to a PC and an Android smartphone. The signals from these devices are wrapped to enable use with web technologies and protocols by means of our developed middleware. The middleware for Kinect2 uses the enhanced v2 SDK from where the joint direction quaternions are converted to Euler angles relevant to physiotherapists; for Leap Motion, the vendor supplied JavaScript v2 API is used and for Myo the native v3 API is wrapped with NodeJS. The gestures received from these devices, after being mapped and processed are translated to commands sent to smart appliances; in our case the aplliances are the LiFX and Phillips Hue smart bulbs. The LiFX bulb is controlled via TCP/IP by means of socket programming on NodeJS, whereas the Phillips Hue is controlled by issuing commands and getting the current status from the vendor hub via the ZigBee IEEE 802.15.4 standard. The Phillips Hub is issued commands over its HTTP API using a JavaScript HTTP client. Figure 4 shows different user interfaces that help in achieving different states shown in Figure 3. We have created a 3D serious game environment that a user can navigate using gestures, thereby entering different rooms and controlling appliances in the virtual world (see Figure 4 (a)), which represent their counterparts in the physical world. This is done through a smartphone application using Android OS (see Figure 4 (b)). Also, for lightweight browsers, we have developed

2D user interfaces as shown in Figure 4 (c-f). In each interface, the states of the objects are mapped to the physical appliances. Figure 5 shows the setup of our proposed demo environment.

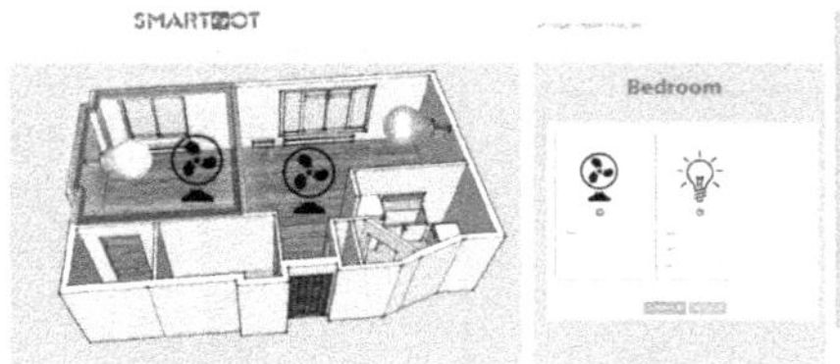

(a)

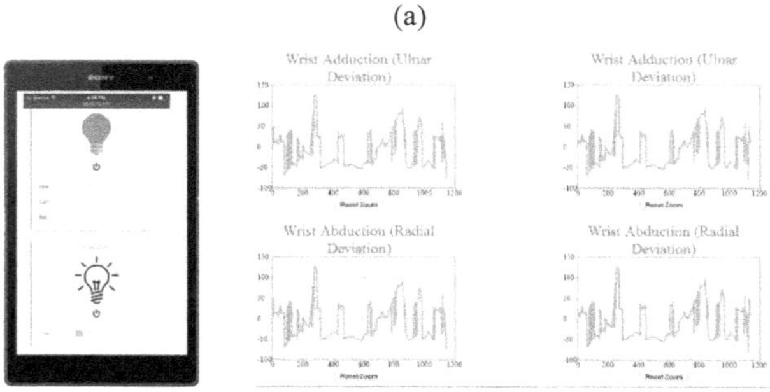

(b)

(c)

(d)

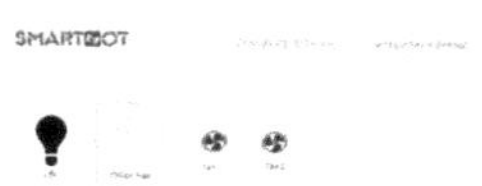

(e)

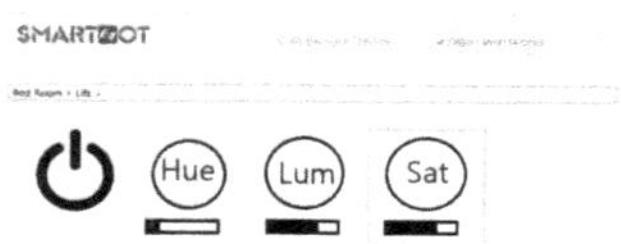

(f)

Figure 4: (a) a sample of 2D/3D Web-based room interface (b-left) Smart phone based interface to control appliances (b-right) Graph plot of improvement metrics (c) User chooses an input device (d) User selects from existing rooms (e) User selects a smart device (f) User changes property of smart bulb

CONCLUSION

This paper presents an innovative and non-invasive method of smart home automation based assisted therapy. The patient is facilitated in the sense that she is able to carry out with her routine in a convenient fashion. Moreover, the gestures are designed in a way so as to monitor the therapeutic progress of the patient and, if required, be modified to suit her disabilities in a better way. Data

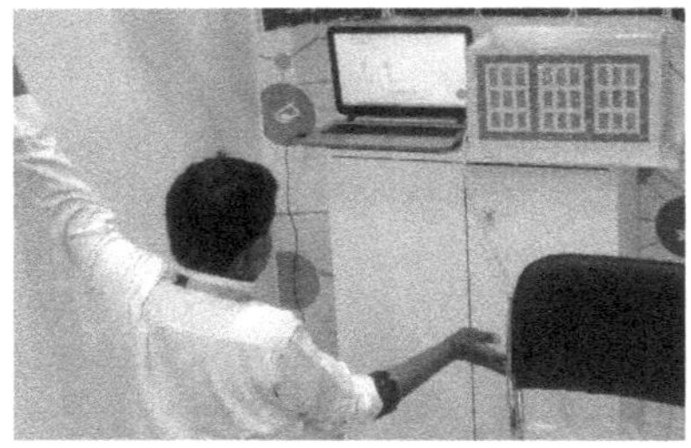

Figure 5: A user wearing Myo in his hand controls lights with different appliances in each room of a house prototype.

gathered from our experiments suggests that the patient can easily be motivated to overcome specific disabilities without the need for long trips to the hospital for the sake of rehabilitation, thus having minimal impact on her daily life.

4. ACKNOWLEDGMENTS

This project was supported by the NSTIP strategic technologies program (11-INF1700-10) and (11-INF1703-10) of the Kingdom of Saudi Arabia.

5. REFERENCES

[1] Rahman, M. A., Hossain, D., Qamar, A., M., Rehman, F. U., Toonsi, A. H., Ahmed, M., El Saddik, A., and Basalamah, S. 2014. A Low-cost Serious Game Therapy Environment with Inverse Kinematic Feedback for Children Having Physical Disability. In *Proceedings of International Conference on Multimedia Retrieval* (Glasgow, UK, April 2014). ICMR '14. ACM, 529-531.

[2]Madeira, R. N., Costa, L., and Postolache, O. 2014. PhysioMate - Pervasive physical rehabilitation based on NUI and gamification. In *Proc. of Int. Conf. and Expo. on Electrical and Power Engineering* (Oct. 2014). IEEE, 612-616.

[3]Duarte, N., Postolache, O., and Scharcanski, J. 2014. KSGphysio - Kinect serious game for physiotherapy. In *Proceedings of International Conference and Exposition on Electrical and Power Engineering* (Oct. 2014). IEEE, 606-611.

[4] Alamri, A., Cha, J., and El Saddik, A. 2010. AR-REHAB: An Augmented Reality Framework for Poststroke-Patient Rehabilitation. *IEEE Trans. Instr. and Meas.*, 59, 10 (Oct. 2010), 2554-2563.

[5] Halic, T., Kockara, S., Demirel, D., Willey, M., and Eichelberger, K. 2014. MoMiReS: Mobile mixed reality system for physical & occupational therapies for hand and wrist ailments. In *Proceedings of Innovations in Technology Conference* (May 16, 2014). InnoTek '14. IEEE, 1-6.

[6] Borodulkin, L., Ruser, H., and Trankler, H.-R. 2002. 3D virtual "smart home" user interface. In *Proceedings of International Symposium on Virtual and Intelligent Measurement Systems* (May 2002). VIMS' 02. IEEE, 111-115.

[7] Lee, J. Y., Seo, D., Rhee, G. W., Hong, S. H., and Nam, J. –S. 2008. Virtual and Pervasive Smart Home Services Using Tangible Mixed Reality. In *Proceedings of International Symposium on Parallel and Distributed Processing with Applications* (Dec. 2008). ISPA '08. IEEE, 403-408.

Incremental Multimodal Query Construction for Video Search

Shicheng Xu[1], Huan Li[1], Xiaojun Chang[2], Shoou-I Yu[1], Xingzhong Du[2], Xuanchong Li[1], Lu Jiang[1], Zexi Mao[1], Zhenzhong Lan[1], Susanne Burger[1], and Alexander Hauptmann[1]
[1]School of Computer Science, Carnegie Mellon University, Pittsburgh, PA, 15213, USA
[2]ITEE, The University of Queensland, Brisbane St Lucia, QLD 4072, Australia
{shicheng, iyu, xcli, lujiang, zexim, lanzhzh, sburger, alex}@cs.cmu.edu
lihuan.0611@outlook.com, cxj273@gmail.com, x.du@uq.edu.au

ABSTRACT

Recent improvements in content-based video search have led to systems with promising accuracy, thus opening up the possibility for interactive content-based video search to the general public. We present an interactive system based on a state-of-the-art content-based video search pipeline which enables users to do multimodal text-to-video and video-to-video search in large video collections, and to incrementally refine queries through relevance feedback and model visualization. Also, the comprehensive functionalities enhance a flexible formulation of multimodal queries with different characteristics. Quantitative and qualitative analysis shows that our system is capable of assisting users to incrementally build effective queries over complex event topics.

Categories and Subject Descriptors

H.3.1 [**Information Storage and Retrieval**]: Content Analysis and Indexing; H.3.3 [**Information Storage and Retrieval**]: Information Search and Retrieval

General Terms

Design, Experimentation

Keywords

Content-Based Video Search, Multimodal Query Generation, Multimedia Event Detection

1. INTRODUCTION

The unprecedented growth of user-generated videos has led to the development of large-scale video search systems. Existing commercial systems mainly rely on text metadata to search for relevant videos. However, metadata provide only a very limited description of a video, and many videos do not contain any metadata at all. To overcome this constraint, much research [1, 2, 3] has been dedicated to design effective content-based video search systems. These system analyze the visual and audio signals to harvest discriminative information from the video directly. The research of the past few years helped content-based search systems to achieve a very promising accuracy which now opens up the possibility to be used by the general public.

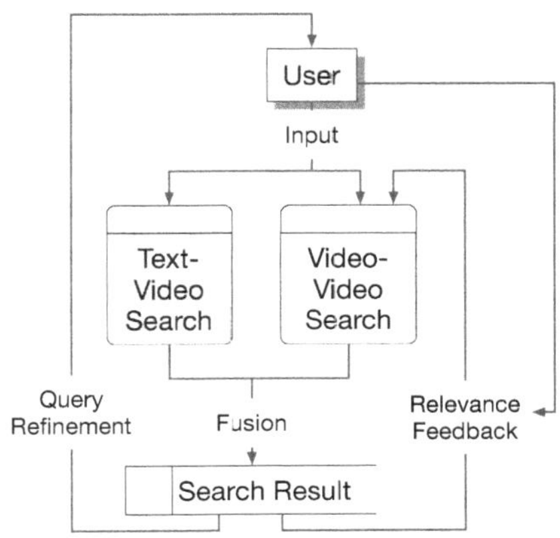

Figure 1: Overview of the query construction process.

A crucial element of video retrieval is building a well formulated query. This is challenging because a user searching for information in videos needs to address multiple modalities to build an executable and effective query. The key contribution of our system is that it provides an interface to seamlessly combine two different search modes: text-to-video search and video-to-video search. This enhances the quality of content-based video search, thus allowing a query to evolve from scratch supported by relevance feedback and query model visualization. In summary, the contributions of our demo system are as follows:

1. We present a live system which integrates text-to-video, video-to-video, and query refinement abilities for the incremental multimodal construction of a query. Quantitative and qualitative analysis shows that our system is able to help users to formulate effective queries.
2. Our system supports content-based video search with over 2500 high-quality pretrained semantic concept detectors. To the best of our knowledge, we are one of the first systems to have this capability.

ICMR'15, June 23–26, 2015, Shanghai, China.

DOI: http://dx.doi.org/10.1145/2671188.2749413.

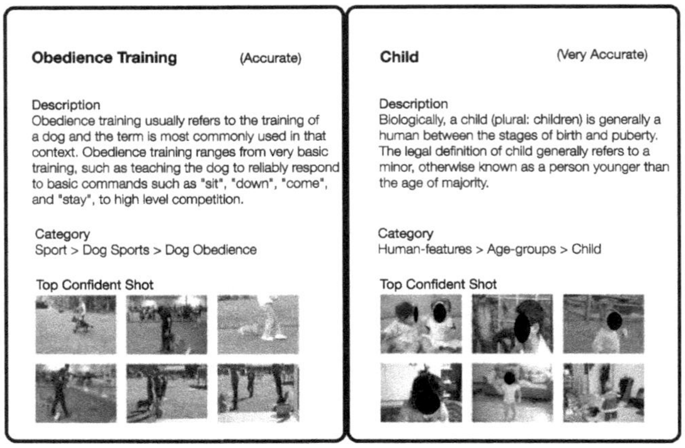

Figure 2: Concept profiles for "obedience training" and "child", including name, accuracy level classified by precision, description from Wikipedia, manually created content taxonomy, and top confident video shots. Here "obedience training" also detects "walking with dog", and "child" shows mainly images of babies rather than teenagers.

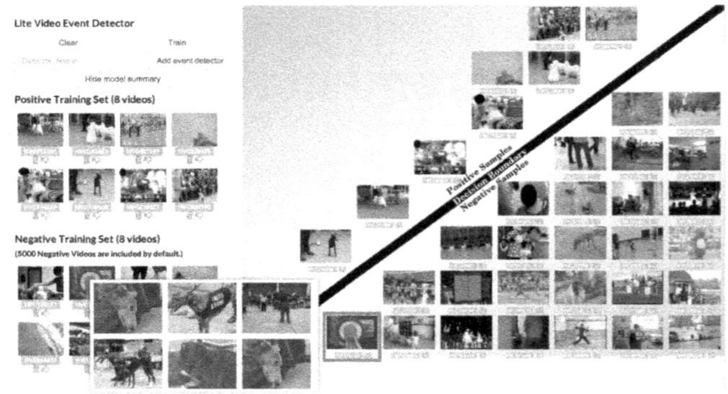

Figure 3: Training panel of a dog show video detector. The left side shows positive and negative training sets (5K background videos are included by default as negative). The right side shows the model visualization of the trained model. The closer the thumbnails are to the decision boundary, the more confusable are the video examples. The bottom left negative video was mislabeled, and can be inspected by more frames in a tooltip.

2. SYSTEM OVERVIEW

Consider the following scenario for using our system. A user searches for a particular information in a video database. He begins the query process by first utilizing the text-to-video search module to find an initial set of relevant videos. However, bridging the semantic gap between text and video is very challenging, therefore only a small number of relevant videos appears. The user can now either reformulate the text query, or select and send the resulting relevant videos to our video-to-video search module, which has shown to outperform text-to-video search. Additional relevant videos found in the second iteration can then again be utilized to further improve the query. The user can iteratively continue this incremental relevance feedback process until he is satisfied with the result. Figure 1 shows an overview of the system. The following sections describe each component in detail.

3. TEXT-TO-VIDEO SEARCH

In a real-world scenario of a video search, users typically start their search using query words rather than providing video examples. The task is called Zero-Example search [6]. For example, if a user wants to find dog show videos, he may use "dog" and "obedience" as query. Similarly to text-to-text search, a video can be treated as a document, too, based on the results of ASR (Audio Speech Recognition), OCR (Optical Character Recognition), and intermediate concept detection [5]. In our sytem, we use a standard text-retrieval model for ASR and OCR. Unlike searching user-generated metadata, our content-based retrieval system requires no metadata and can directly search for semantic concepts in videos. Our concept dictionary is of limited size. To avoid mismatches between the words in a query and the concept names in our list, we perform semantic matching by computing the word similarity using word2vec [9] so that e.g. for a given concept "obedience", the system would find concepts such as "conformation show" and "dog agility".

Sometimes a concept name represents sub concepts. For example, "child" can include everything from baby to grade school age. It is therefore helpful to not just refer to the name of a concept, but also provide a description, a taxonomy of categories, and top confident video shot examples. We show the top six confident shots of each concept in our system to assist the user to select related concepts. The top shots not only demonstrate the preference of that concept detector, but also help the user to better understand the concept name and what content it represents, see Figure 2.

4. VIDEO-TO-VIDEO SEARCH

For a modern machine learning algorithm like a support vector machine (SVM [14]), a handful of video query examples is already enough to train a video detector. These initial videos can be either uploaded by the user or the user performs a text-to-video search. The search results are collected in a list of potential positive examples. The user can skim though these videos and add them into the positive or negative training sets for the model training.

If a user mislabels training videos, the performance of the detector will drop. An effective way to avoid for mislabeled videos going into the training is to examine the support vectors of the SVM model. During training, the model finds a hyperplane that separates positives and negatives, support vectors are the samples on the margin. As shown in Figure 3, we rank these support vectors by how much the decision boundary is violated. That is, those videos that are not clear negative or positive examples and have a higher potential to be false positives or negatives will be shown closer to the boundary than the unambiguous cases. This allows a user to easily detect mislabeled videos, correct their labels, and eventually retrain a better model.

Since increasing number of positive videos in the training can boost the accuracy [4], we want to encourage the user to aggregate more positive samples. We therefore allow loading back previous training models, and adding new video examples from search result incrementally. This relevance feedback process can be repeated until no more positives

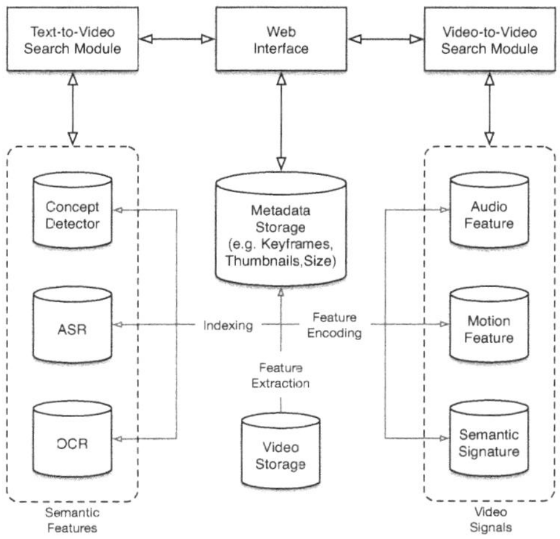

Figure 4: Relationship between modules and databases.

are found, or it meets the user satisfaction. During this query refinement stage, we use single features to let the user quickly refine queries. After the training set is converged, the system will retrain a model with multiple features for a better performance.

5. QUANTITATIVE ANALYSIS

The system consists of three modules, the web interface, the text-to-video, and the video-to-video search modules. A user interacts with the web interface to formulate a query, which will be sent to search modules to retrieve a video rank list. We use the challenging TRECVID Multimedia Event Detection 2014 corpus, which is the state-of-the-art largest corpus of Internet multimedia files for event detection [11, 10]. We rely on three video partitions defined by NIST: MEDTest, Event kits and Background, including 23K, 2K and 5K videos, respectively. MEDTest and Event kits come with a ground truth annotation at the video level for 20 event categories, for example *Attempting a bike trick*, *Dog show*, or *Making a sandwich*. A subset of 10 events is included in our system. Event kits and MEDTest are utilized for the video detector training and testing, respectively. Random videos are selected from the Background set as default negatives. We preprocessed these videos by feature extraction, feature encoding, and indexing, see Figure 4.

Semantic Features: To obtain a better concept coverage and user experience, we utilize a pool of more than 2500 shot-based concept detectors which are trained by a self-paced learning pipeline [7] using improved dense trajectory features [13]. We manually renamed these concept names into readable terms, and classified them in a concept hierarchy tree. The concept detection score is fused with ASR [12] and OCR detection scores by weighted fusion, and then is fed into a reranking model [6]. Users can adjust the weight of each query to specify the relevance.

Video Features: We provide the improved dense trajectory features [13], and a 824-dimension semantic signature at the query refinement stage to let users tradeoff between efficiency and accuracy. The semantic signature consists of concept detectors trained upon the TRECVID SIN task and the Sports-1M dataset [8] with 346 and 478 concepts, respectively. When a user saves the final video detector query, the system will retrain the model with multiple features. We choose 19 low level features from [3], including one ASR [12], three Mel Frequency Cepstral Coefficients (MFCC) variants, three dense trajectory variants, and 12 Deep Convolutional Neural Network (DCNN) variants. A linear kernel is precomputed for each low-level feature, and stored as a binary file. We use linear SVM from LIBSVM [14] for the model training. Both model parameter **w** and test features are compressed by product quantization [15].

	Time(ms)		**Size(GB)**	**mAP**
	Train	Test		
Text-to-video [1]	30		1.10	0.181
Semantic	364		0.31	0.123
Dense Trajectory	24759	473	0.64	0.117
19 Features	74179	10140	9.88	0.180

Table 1: Comparison of efficiency and accuracy

Efficiency and Accuracy: We compare the training and testing time, feature storage size, and performance of two search modules in Table 1. For text-to-video search, there is no separate training and testing. For video-to-video search, we compare three feature settings: improved dense trajectories [13], semantic signature, and 19 features. We randomly select 10 positives and use default negatives from the Background partition for training, then test the model on the MEDTest partition. We perform the experiment on a workstation with two Intel Xeon processors E5649@2.53GHZ and 64GB of memory. The mAP(mean Average Precision) is computed with PS12 event sets [10] of 10 event categories. With a fine-grained query, text-to-video search can achieve a comparable accuracy to 19 features.

6. QUALITATIVE ANALYSIS

To investigate how our query interface can help a novice user to create a good query, we invited 10 users between the age of 20 and 30 to compose queries for 10 event categories. Each user was asked to read two event definitions, and then create a text-to-video query for each event, see Iteration 1 and Iteration 2. Then the query was refined by using the search result to create a video detector, which would be retrained iteratively, see Iteration 3-5.

Iteration 1: Input 3-10 keywords and add related concepts by concept names.

Iteration 2: Refine Iteration 1 by adjusting the weight of the concept with the top confident shots.

Iteration 3-5: Apply previous query, create or refine the video detector query by adding more positives or negatives with relevance feedback and model visualization.

As a comparison, expert users created text-to-video queries following the same strategy. The novice user queries are refined over five iterations, while the expert user queries are refined over three iterations. Each iteration of Iteration 3-5 can be broken down to two stages, the relevance feedback and the model refinement. We record the number of positives added from the previous search result by relevance feedback, and from the false positives by model refinement. The top 500 retrieved videos are evaluated for mAP.

[1]Reranking [6] is not applied in text-to-video experiment.

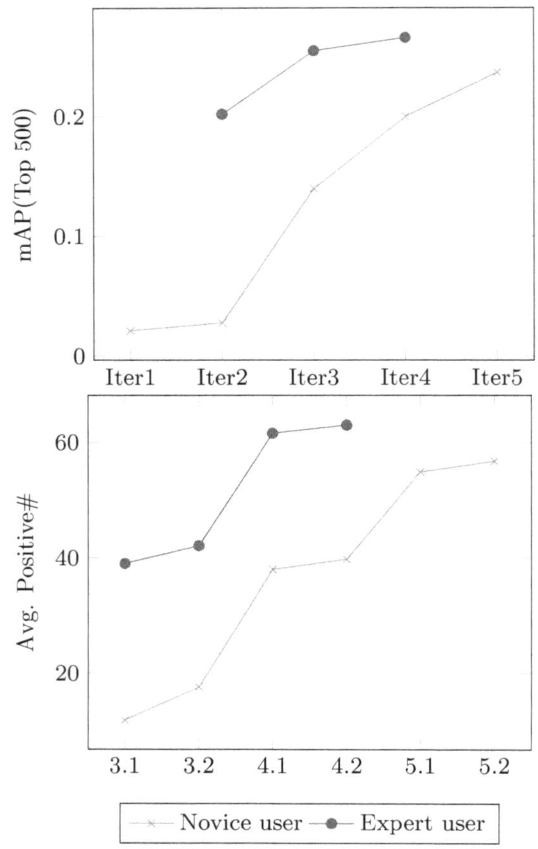

Figure 5: Qualitative Analysis Result

Figure 5 shows that our system can effectively improve a user-defined query and find more positives, even when the quality of the initial result returned by the text-to-video search is very poor. Comparing the text-to-video queries created by novice users and experts shows that it is tricky for novice users to search for videos based on their own understanding of an event description. They do not distinguish between speech/audio oriented events and visual oriented events, and they tend to select more weakly-related concepts, which hurts the search performance.

7. DEMONSTRATION

We will demonstrate how to incrementally build multimodal queries with our user interface, as shown in Figure 6. Users start with a text-to-video search by typing keywords in the top-left search box. The search result is shown in the right panel. Then users click on thumbs-up and thumbs-down buttons to select positive and negative examples for the video-to-video search. Different types of queries can be combined to a final multimodal query. In summary, the system introduces different effective ways to build a query for video search to maximize the search performance on complex event detection.

Acknowledgements This work has been supported in part by Intelligence Advanced Research Projects Activity (IARPA) via Department of Interior National Business Center contract number D11PC20068 and by the Department of Defense, U. S. Army Research Office (W911NF-13-1-0277). The U.S. government is authorized to reproduce and distribute reprints for Governmental purposes notwithstanding any copyright annotation thereon. Disclaimer: The views and conclusions contained herein are those of the authors and should not be interpreted as necessarily representing the official policies or endorsements, either expressed or implied, of NSF, ARO, IARPA, DoI/NBC or the U.S. Government.

Figure 6: Final screenshot after three iterations. The left query bucket summarizes the user-created multi-modal query. The right panel presents a compact view of the search result, thumbnails surrounded by blue box are the positives used in the video detector.

8. REFERENCES

[1] P. Natarajan, S. Wu, S. Vitaladevuni, X. Zhuang, S. Tsakalidis, U. Park, and R. Prasad. Multimodal feature fusion for robust event detection in web videos. In *CVPR*, 2012.

[2] A. Tamrakar, S. Ali, Q. Yu, J. Liu, O. Javed, A. Divakaran, H. Cheng, and H. Sawhney. Evaluation of low-level features and their combinations for complex event detection in open source videos. In *CVPR*, 2012.

[3] S.-I. Yu, L. Jiang, Z. Mao, et al. Cmu-informedia @ trecvid. In *TRECVID Video Retrieval Evaluation Workshop*, 2014.

[4] A. Habibian, M. Mazloom, and C. G. Snoek. On-the-fly video event search by semantic signatures. In *Proceedings of International Conference on Multimedia Retrieval*. ACM, 2014.

[5] A. G. Hauptmann, M. G. Christel, and R. Yan. Video retrieval based on semantic concepts. *Proceedings of the IEEE*, 2008.

[6] L. Jiang, D. Meng, T. Mitamura, and A. G. Hauptmann. Easy samples first: self-paced reranking for zero-example multimedia search. In *Proceedings of the ACM International Conference on Multimedia*, pages 547–556. ACM, 2014.

[7] L. Jiang, D. Meng, S.-I. Yu, Z. Lan, S. Shan, and A. Hauptmann. Self-paced learning with diversity. In *Advances in Neural Information Processing Systems 27*. 2014.

[8] A. Karpathy, G. Toderici, S. Shetty, T. Leung, R. Sukthankar, and L. Fei-Fei. Large-scale video classification with convolutional neural networks. In *CVPR*, 2014.

[9] T. Mikolov, I. Sutskever, K. Chen, G. S. Corrado, and J. Dean. Distributed representations of words and phrases and their compositionality. In *Advances in Neural Information Processing Systems*, 2013.

[10] P. Over, G. Awad, J. Fiscus, and G. Sanders. Trecvid 2013–an introduction to the goals, tasks, data, evaluation mechanisms, and metrics. *TRECVID Workshop*, 2013.

[11] S. Strassel, A. Morris, J. G. Fiscus, C. Caruso, H. Lee, P. Over, J. Fiumara, B. Shaw, B. Antonishek, and M. Michel. Creating havic: Heterogeneous audio visual internet collection. In *LREC*. Citeseer, 2012.

[12] Y. Miao, F. Metze, and S. Rawat. Deep maxout networks for low-resource speech recognition. In *ASRU*, 2013.

[13] H. Wang and C. Schmid. Action recognition with improved trajectories. In *IEEE International Conference on Computer Vision*, Sydney, Australia, 2013.

[14] C.-C. Chang and C.-J. Lin. LIBSVM: A library for support vector machines. *ACM Transactions on Intelligent Systems and Technology*, 2011.

[15] H. Jegou, M. Douze, and C. Schmid. Product quantization for nearest neighbor search. *Pattern Analysis and Machine Intelligence, IEEE Transactions on*, 2011.

Author Index

www.ingramcontent.com/pod-product-compliance
Ingram Content Group UK Ltd.
Pitfield, Milton Keynes, MK11 3LW, UK
UKHW051419290926
15471UKWH00009B/1683

9 781450 338790